THE EXPOSITOR'S BIBLE

A COMPLETE EXPOSITION OF THE BIBLE,
IN SIX VOLUMES, WITH INDEX

EDITED BY
W. ROBERTSON NICOLL
C.H., D.D., LL.D.

WITH A GENERAL INTRODUCTION AND A BRIEF
BIOGRAPHICAL AND LITERARY INTRODUCTION TO
EACH BOOK OF THE BIBLE

BY
THE REVEREND OSCAR L. JOSEPH, Litt.D.
AUTHOR OF "THE HISTORICAL DEVELOPMENT OF CHRISTIANITY,"
"THE DYNAMIC MINISTRY," ETC.

Vol. I

GENESIS—RUTH

Baker Book House
Grand Rapids, Michigan 49506

Reprinted 1982 by
Baker Book House Company

Six-Volume Set

ISBN: 0-8010-6685-9

Printed in the United States of America

The first American edition
of this set was published in 1903 as
An Exposition of the Bible

THE EXPOSITOR'S BIBLE

CONTENTS OF VOLUME ONE

	PAGE
THE BOOK OF GENESIS .... MARCUS DODS, D.D.	1
THE BOOK OF EXODUS .... G. A. CHADWICK, D.D.	117
THE BOOK OF LEVITICUS .... S. H. KELLOG, D.D.	233
THE BOOK OF NUMBERS .... ROBERT A. WATSON, M.A.	381
THE BOOK OF DEUTERONOMY .... ANDREW HARPER, B.D.	487
THE BOOK OF JOSHUA .... WILLIAM GARDEN BLAIKIE, D.D.	629
THE BOOK OF JUDGES .... ROBERT A. WATSON, D.D.	739
THE BOOK OF RUTH .... ROBERT A. WATSON, D.D.	835

GENERAL INTRODUCTION

By The Reverend Oscar L. Joseph, Litt.D.

The Expositor's Bible is the recognized standard of expository commentaries. It was written by twenty-nine eminent scholars who were also preachers. Although some of them later occupied professorial positions they had all been preachers whose ministrations were of a high order of excellence. They retained their preaching instinct and insight even after they had vacated the pulpit for the chair.

These writers also represent every important branch of Protestantism. The Expositor's Bible may thus be regarded as an interdenominational exposition. It declares the catholicity of Christian experience, scholarship and churchmanship. It conclusively demonstrates the hearty agreement of all thoughtful persons on the profound realities and essentials of the Christian Faith. It shows how this Faith is to be preached with the conviction and persuasiveness which its opulent gospel justly merits.

This notable work was conceived and carried out by that genius among editors, Sir William Robertson Nicoll, C.H., D.D., LL.D. He had an exceptional knowledge of religious and literary, of theological and philosophical, thought. He understood what were the most urgent needs of the church as to spiritual enlightenment, for the better exercise of the Church's mission in advancing the Kingdom of Christ to earth's remotest bounds.

Sir William was born in the Free Church Manse, Lumsden, Aberdeenshire, on October 10, 1851. He was the son of the Rev. Harry Nicoll, a bookman of rare accomplishments, concerning whose obscure but faithful ministry in a rural parish he wrote a charming volume, entitled "My Father." He graduated from Aberdeen University with the degree of M.A. in 1870. After completing his theological course at the Free Church Divinity Hall, Aberdeen, in 1874, he was ordained minister of the Free Church, Dufftown, the same year. He was called to the Free Church, Kelso, in 1877, from which he resigned in 1886 owing to ill health.

During his pastorate at Kelso he accepted the Editorship of *The Expositor* in 1885, as the successor of Dr. Samuel Cox, the leading expositor of the Bible in his day. This position was held by Sir William until his death on May 4, 1923. Under his leadership this monthly journal attained a prominent place among theological periodicals. He wrote very little for it, but he secured some of the leading British, American and Continental scholars and preachers to contribute to its pages. Herein he excelled as an editor, whose chief business is to understand the needs of the day and to select writers competent to meet those needs. His success in this respect might be indicated by the fact that some first-class volumes originally appeared in *The Expositor*. Among these were Professor A. B. Bruce's "St. Paul's Conception of Christianity," Principal A. M. Fairbairn's "Studies in the Life of Christ," Dr. Alexander Maclaren's "Colossians," Bishop Westcott's "Christus Consummator," Principal A. E. Garvie's "Studies in the Inner Life of Jesus," Sir George Adam Smith's "Historical Geography of the Holy Land." Indeed, there was no periodical which contained so little ephemeral matter. Its bound volumes are a permanent contribution to theological and expository literature.

A gratifying testimonial to Sir William's services as editor of *The Expositor* was presented to him on his seventieth birthday in 1921. This address of appreciation was signed by seven distinguished scholars of Oxford University, who voiced the sentiments of all contributors to this magazine. A few sentences from this document are worth quoting: "While seeing to the maintenance of the reverential attitude which the subjects demand and the standard of scholarship which our time has set up, you have accepted contributions from all schools of thought, and in the belief that the attainment of truth should be the goal of research have enabled seekers after truth to communicate their results to the public, regardless of the favor with which they are likely to be received by any of the circles whom your magazine reaches. You have frequently helped to popularise the discoveries of archæology and criticism, and familiarised your readers with eminent theologians by the biographical essays which you have inserted."

GENERAL INTRODUCTION

This extended reference to Sir William's association with *The Expositor* is made so as to be able to appreciate the fine quality of his other undertakings. He founded *The British Weekly* in 1886, "for the advocacy of social and Christian progress," and edited it till his death. The stamp of his personality and versatility was seen in every issue of this journal, which had an extensive circulation in all English-speaking lands. Its first page was once characterised by Professor Rendel Harris as "the gold mine of *The British Weekly*." With few exceptions the editorials on this page were written by Sir William. Their unusual value, from the standpoint of religion and literature, fully justified their republication in book form. Among these volumes were "The Return of the Cross," "The Church's One Foundation," "The Garden of Nuts," "Reunion in Eternity," "Princes of the Church."

He was constantly inaugurating new ventures with an amazing fertility of resourcefulness. In 1891 he began *The Bookman* and rallied to its support several of the leading lights in literature. Apart from its valued articles and book reviews, the rare discernment of the editor led to his discovery of many writers, whose volumes of fiction and belles-lettres have greatly enriched modern literature. He was always on the alert for promising authors. It was thus through his impetus that the world heard of Sir James Barrie, Ian Maclaren, Ellen Thorneycroft Fowler, John Buchan, S. R. Crockett, David Smith, James Moffatt and other well-known writers. Professor Marcus Dods well expressed the thoughts of this company in one of his last letters to Sir William: "On looking back over the last twenty-five years, I see how very much I am indebted to you for giving me opportunities and encouragement, without which I should have addressed a very much smaller audience."

It is however in the realm of theological and Biblical thought that Sir William's work is of special interest to us. He edited several series such as "The Household Library of Exposition," "The Foreign Biblical Library," "The Theological Educator," "The Clerical Library," "The Expositor's Greek Testament" and THE EXPOSITOR'S BIBLE. It might appear too much like a catalogue of titles to list the several biographies and over twenty other volumes which he wrote in addition to hundreds of articles in his own and in other papers. His prodigious output was all the more amazing in view of the fact that his indomitable energy overcame the handicap of chronic ill health. It was a common occurrence for him to dictate thirty thousand words a week, while remaining in bed for two or three days of this period. And yet with calm courage he took up one task after another and performed it with intrepid determination, undeviating fidelity and unsurpassed *finesse*.

T. H. Darlow has written a judicious biography of this extraordinary man. "William Robertson Nicoll, Life and Letters," introduces us to one who was a mystic and humanist, a theologian and a politician, an author and editor, who combined sagacity with spirituality and worldliness with other-worldliness. This biography is a balanced appraisal of Sir William's complex character and diversified achievements.

It is no reflection on his other undertakings to say that THE EXPOSITOR'S BIBLE is his greatest editorial contribution. The inception of this work took place at a time when critical and historical scholarship had arrived at mature and reliable conclusions concerning the text and truth of the Bible. What had been regarded as subversive of the Christian Faith was now accepted without question. To be sure, there have been changes and even modifications in the attitude toward certain subjects, but the general consensus of Biblical scholarship has not been thereby affected. None of the results has in the least undermined the accepted view of the Church that the Bible is the Revelation of the spiritual life, imparted "by divers portions and in divers manners," and marked by energy, variety and adaptability. The Bible continues to occupy its place of finality as the supreme Authority on Religion and Morals. This is the basis on which THE EXPOSITOR'S BIBLE was written.

Indeed, there is no book like the Bible, which has yielded its treasures, new and old, to the searching light of the most exacting investigations. The scientific analysis of the text; the historical study of the documents as to date, authorship and composition; the work of archæologists in the departments of Egyptology, Assyriology and Paleography; the discoveries of the Tel-el-Amarna Tablets in the Nile Valley throwing light on the

GENERAL INTRODUCTION

Old Testament, of the Oxyrhynchus Papyri in Central Egypt and numerous inscriptions and papyri in Greece, Egypt and Asia Minor which have revolutionised the understanding of New Testament Greek as the language of the common people and not of the classicists; the study of Aramaic for a better interpretation of the New Testament; the study of Comparative Religion and of the Mystery Religions in giving the religion of the Old and the New Testaments a larger setting and in demonstrating the unique superiority and supremacy of the Divine Revelation—all these results of scholarship had given a challenging importance to the Bible.

The time was therefore most auspicious for an undertaking that would make use of these results for a fuller and more adequate exposition of the Scriptures. It had to be a positive and constructive exposition. Unlike other commentaries which were grammatical and critical, it must be historical and religious, and deal with the Books of the Bible, not in isolated sentences or passages, but in connection with the entire context of each Book taken as a whole. Each Book moreover had to be related to the main river of the historical revelation, so that its general and specific teaching might be made more vividly impressive. In this way the Bible would speak for itself. But above all, the work had to be done with special emphasis upon the preaching values of the whole Bible.

This was also the day when preaching had reached the high-water mark of excellence. The pulpits in Great Britain were occupied by such distinguished men as C. H. Spurgeon, R. W. Dale, Alexander Maclaren, Joseph Parker, Canon Liddon, Archbishop Magee, John Caird, Alexander Whyte, Canon Scott-Holland, Dean Farrar, James Stalker, Hugh Price Hughes, George Matheson. The American pulpit was honored by equally great preachers, such as Henry Ward Beecher, Phillips Brooks, John Hall, Matthew Simpson, W. M. Taylor, R. S. Storrs, Reuen Thomas. Any volumes of Scripture exposition that claimed to be worthy of the name had to come up to the standards of magnificent preaching of these leaders of the pulpit.

It was doubtless a difficult task to select writers whose undoubted gifts of scholarship would be combined with expository talents. Such men were to have a clear grasp of the many-sided message of Christianity, illuminated by literature, philosophy and science. But more than this, they should have the skill to express their convictions in choice language, understood by the people, so as to give them a clear understanding of the mind of the prophets and the apostles and especially of Jesus Christ, for the practical guidance of life. THE EXPOSITOR'S BIBLE has met all these requirements, and it conclusively demonstrates how the Scriptures are to be expounded with integrity, with clarity and with compelling conviction.

There are some who lament the decay of the modern pulpit. These are surely difficult times. The voice of authority is dimly heard and there is a determined revolt against *ex cathedra* utterances. The movement of democracy has discarded many traditions. The advance of science has compelled the revision of many cherished ideas. The new psychology and the new philosophy claim to offer a new religion which dazzles the few and embarrasses the many with its dilettante promises and postponed fulfilments. The social implications of Christianity are tending to obscure its spiritual affirmations. Humanism magnifies the supreme worth of human life, but it ignores the perversions and desecrations due to sin; it virtually teaches that man can lift himself with his boot straps and discard as superfluous the intervention of the Redeemer Christ. The so-called liberal theology is frantically endeavoring to hold up a Christ without the Cross and to preach ethical perfection without the spiritual dynamic. The so-called conservative theology is busy bolstering up discredited positions, unmindful of the wide difference between theological dogma and religious truth. Many preachers are defending the gospel and have apparently forgotten that their mission is to declare the gospel with the conviction of evangelical experience and with the constraint of evangelistic zeal.

The times clamorously demand the return to Bible preaching, fortified by scholarly ability and distinguished by fidelity to the entire range of the Biblical Revelation. Such preaching must recognize the organic synthesis of the whole Bible. It must understand that the progressive and peerless revelation of the Will of God, from less to more, was imparted by the processes of history, through the experience of many individuals and under various circumstances.

GENERAL INTRODUCTION

The mistaken idea that the Old Testament has become antiquated needs to be corrected. Indeed, nowhere in all literature, outside the New Testament, are there such calls to worship, such notes of reverence, such aspirations for communion with God, such proofs of the Divine Providence, such a passion for individual, social and national righteousness, such a certainty of the final establishment of the Kingdom of God in the world.

Principal George Adam Smith once gave convincing utterance to this fact: "From the time of the author of the Epistle to the Hebrews onwards to the generation before our own, it has been among the personal characters of Israel's history that the greatest preachers in the English language have found much of their richest material and strongest inspiration. It was not the miracles of Old Testament history nor the national events, upon which the preaching of our fathers fed and grew strong, but the personal elements; the development of character, the moral struggles, checks, catastrophes and recoveries, in which so many Books of the Old Testament are so very rich." [1]

Principal Smith is one of the most brilliant illustrations among modern preachers of how the Old Testament should be used in the pulpit. His two volumes on "Isaiah" in THE EXPOSITOR'S BIBLE impress us by his mastery of the extensive scholarship of his subject. But more even than this is his unsurpassed passion and eloquence in expounding the ancient prophets in terms of modern life. Any one who studies these two volumes as well as the two on "The Book of the Twelve Prophets" and the Yale Lectures on "Modern Criticism and the Preaching of the Old Testament," will readily see what a wealth of preaching material is contained within the pages of the Old Testament. This fact is also shown by the writers of the other volumes on the Old Testament in THE EXPOSITOR'S BIBLE.

What can be said for the New Testament? It is the only reliable record of the life and teaching of Jesus Christ, who is the watershed of the Divine Revelation. In Him we have everything we need to know and to experience of God and of fellowship with Him in the distracting passages of life's journey. Professor Adolf Deissmann refers to the New Testament as "the book for humanity, ancient but eternal, not one of the paralysing forces of the past, but full of eternal strength to make strong and to make free." He adds these significant words: "And because of the figure that emerges from the book—the Redeemer accompanied by the multitude of the redeemed, blessing and consoling, exhorting and renewing, revealing Himself anew to every generation of the weary and heavy-laden, and growing from century to century more great—the New Testament is the Book of Life." [2]

How the New Testament is to be expounded by the pulpit is well illustrated by the volumes of Principal Marcus Dods on "The Gospel of St. John," of Professor Findlay on "The Epistle to the Ephesians," of Principal Denney on "The Epistle to the Thessalonians." These three volumes are selected because they represent some of the different ways in which expository preaching might be made effective. But the same purpose might be served by referring to the other volumes on the New Testament in THE EXPOSITOR'S BIBLE.

There are various types of preaching. In his recent volume, "What to Preach," President Henry Sloane Coffin discussed some of these types. They all center on the Bible. In support of his thesis that the Bible is prolific in preaching material, Dr. Coffin has submitted subjects, Scriptures passages and methods of treatment, which are a veritable revelation to the preacher of the inexhaustible riches of the Book of books. Expository preaching is made dull and diffuse only by the man who does not know the wide expanses of the Bible. It is made interesting and profitable by the preacher who has the poetic sense, the vivid imagination, the knowledge of literature and history, the experience of spiritual realities.

Professor George Jackson recently declared that "one of the most disquieting facts about the average present-day candidate is his lamentable ignorance of the English Bible." This reference to men entering the ministry of the British Churches is equally applicable to the United States. Professor Peake on another recent occasion spoke

---

[1] "Modern Criticism and the Preaching of the Old Testament," p. 74 f.
[2] "Light from the Ancient East," pp. 400, 419. A revised edition of this great work, long out of print, has just been published by George H. Doran Company.

GENERAL INTRODUCTION

gravely of the appalling ignorance of the Bible of young people and congregations. These are not alarmist utterances. The solution is obvious. It lies with preachers who are to become better acquainted with the Bible and concentrate their attention in expounding it with all the ability and energy that might be commanded.

The preacher who crowds out the Bible in favor of literary, scientific and social topics, colored by a "pious secularity," will find that his function as a preacher has got crowded out. No essays, miscalled sermons, upon ethical and social themes, treated independently of the Bible, can give the positive belief in God, the vivid assurance of Christ's pardoning grace, the quickening power of the Holy Spirit, such as can be conveyed by the comprehensive and considerate exposition of the Bible in all the spacious realms of its sublimely melioristic utterances.

Right here we are met with the welcome aid of THE EXPOSITOR'S BIBLE. It must be acknowledged that a company of writers of the same caliber and qualifications could hardly be brought together at the present day. Such a confession should not in the least be regarded as reflecting unfavorably upon the men who preach the best sermons. It is simply a recognition of sheer inability, in view of what has already been said about modern preaching in these transition times. A more favorable time for a similar undertaking may yet come. But the forecast is not encouraging that it will be in the near future.

Meanwhile, THE EXPOSITOR'S BIBLE adequately meets our needs. Turn to any of these volumes and there is always a sense of satisfaction that the authors are dealing squarely with their subjects, without any attempt to sidestep difficulties by explaining them away, or to camouflage ignorance with wordy generalisations and pious phrases. All the writers are not equally progressive in matters of scholarship. Nor is this to be desired, for no party has a monopoly of truth, and scholarship has not said its last word. Indeed, the glory of the Gospel is that it is held by men who practice the noble principle of "malice toward none and charity for all," in the name of the Comprehensive Christ of our redemption.

I do not mean to say that every volume in THE EXPOSITOR'S BIBLE has equal excellence. Not every author is a George Adam Smith or an Alexander Maclaren. But I do affirm that every volume has distinctive merit and that it expounds the particular Book of the Bible with the sympathy of insight and with an appreciation of its special values for us. Not one falls below the exacting standard set by Sir W. Robertson Nicoll, the editor. He undertook to produce an exposition of the Bible adapted to the needs of the average pastor and Bible student. And he has succeeded. Both clergy and laity are here helped to understand the Scriptures as "profitable for teaching, for reproof, for correction, for instruction which is in righteousness."

Such an achievement on the high scale of consistent superiority and practical usefulness is cause for gratulation. THE EXPOSITOR'S BIBLE is at once a commentary and an exposition. Minor details, technical questions, critical issues, do not distract the student by their obtrusive insistence. They are relegated to footnotes which might be taken or left at the reader's discretion, although the wise reader will not readily overlook them. All who have used THE EXPOSITOR'S BIBLE are unanimous in hearty commendation of its genuine worth.

The revival of religion about which so much is heard at conferences and conventions is assuredly of the greatest moment. It will come when there is a renaissance of Bible preaching of the kind found in THE EXPOSITOR'S BIBLE. Here are the ways and means awaiting every preacher who desires to bring it about. Let him study these volumes with interest and also encourage his Church School teachers and other Bible students to use them. He will then create the desirable atmosphere in which Bible preaching shall flourish, so that the Church may be awakened to a sense of privilege and responsibility to make Christ Lord of all.

The Book of Genesis
By Principal Marcus Dods, D.D.

DOCTOR DODS was pastor of Renfield Free Church, Glasgow, for twenty-five years. In 1889 he was elected Professor of New Testament Exegesis, New College, Edinburgh, and in 1907 he succeeded Principal Rainy but retained his own chair in the College. His numerous writings include "The Parables of Our Lord," "The Bible, Its Origin and Nature," "Erasmus and Other Essays," "Israel's Iron Age," "Christ and Man," the volumes in The Expositor's Bible on the Gospel of St. John and the First Epistle to the Corinthians.

His unique qualifications as a preacher are well shown in this volume on the Book of Genesis. The discerning analyses of motives and character and the vivid portrayal of life give a pungent reality to that early day. The deep religious interest of this first book of the Bible and its high moral level are expounded by Principal Dods with a keen appreciation of its timely values for us.

CONTENTS

	PAGE
CHAPTER I.	
The Creation, ...	5
CHAPTER II.	
The Fall, ...	8
CHAPTER III.	
Cain and Abel, ...	11
CHAPTER IV.	
Cain's Line, and Enoch, ...	15
CHAPTER V.	
The Flood, ...	18
CHAPTER VI.	
Noah's Fall, ...	21
CHAPTER VII.	
The Call of Abraham, ...	24
CHAPTER VIII.	
Abram in Egypt, ...	28
CHAPTER IX.	
Lot's Separation from Abram, . . .	31
CHAPTER X.	
Abram's Rescue of Lot, ...	34
CHAPTER XI.	
Covenant with Abram, ...	38
CHAPTER XII.	
Birth of Ishmael, ...	41
CHAPTER XIII.	
The Covenant Sealed, ...	44
CHAPTER XIV.	
Abraham's Intercession for Sodom, . .	47
CHAPTER XV.	
Destruction of the Cities of the Plain, .	51

	PAGE
CHAPTER XVI.	
Sacrifice of Isaac, ...	54
CHAPTER XVII.	
Ishmael and Isaac, ...	57
CHAPTER XVIII.	
Purchase of Machpelah, . . .	61
CHAPTER XIX.	
Isaac's Marriage, ...	64
CHAPTER XX.	
Esau and Jacob, ...	68
CHAPTER XXI.	
Jacob's Fraud, ...	71
CHAPTER XXII.	
Jacob's Flight and Dream, . . .	74
CHAPTER XXIII.	
Jacob at Peniel, ...	77
CHAPTER XXIV.	
Jacob's Return, ...	81
CHAPTER XXV.	
Joseph's Dreams, ...	84
CHAPTER XXVI.	
Joseph in Prison, ...	89
CHAPTER XXVII.	
Pharaoh's Dreams, ...	93
CHAPTER XXVIII.	
Joseph's Administration, ...	97
CHAPTER XXIX.	
Visits of Joseph's Brethren, . . .	100
CHAPTER XXX.	
The Reconciliation, ...	104
CHAPTER XXXI.	
The Blessings of the Tribes, . . .	108

THE BOOK OF GENESIS

BY MARCUS DODS, D. D.

CHAPTER I.

THE CREATION.

Genesis i. and ii.

If any one is in search of accurate information regarding the age of this earth, or its relation to the sun, moon, and stars, or regarding the order in which plants and animals have appeared upon it, he is referred to recent text-books in astronomy, geology, and palæontology. No one for a moment dreams of referring a serious student of these subjects to the Bible as a source of information. It is not the object of the writers of Scripture to impart physical instruction or to enlarge the bounds of scientific knowledge. But if any one wishes to know what connection the world has with God, if he seeks to trace back all that now is to the very fountain-head of life, if he desires to discover some unifying principle, some illuminating purpose in the history of this earth, then we confidently refer him to these and the subsequent chapters of Scripture as his safest, and indeed his only, guide to the information he seeks. Every writing must be judged by the object the writer has in view. If the object of the writer of these chapters was to convey physical information, then certainly it is imperfectly fulfilled. But if his object was to give an intelligible account of God's relation to the world and to man, then it must be owned that he has been successful in the highest degree.

It is therefore unreasonable to allow our reverence for this writing to be lessened because it does not anticipate the discoveries of physical science; or to repudiate its authority in its own department of truth because it does not give us information which it formed no part of the writer's object to give. As well might we deny to Shakespeare a masterly knowledge of human life, because his dramas are blotted by historical anachronisms. That the compiler of this book of Genesis did not aim at scientific accuracy in speaking of physical details is obvious, not merely from the general scope and purpose of the Biblical writers, but especially from this, that in these first two chapters of his book he lays side by side two accounts of man's creation which no ingenuity can reconcile. These two accounts, glaringly incompatible in details, but absolutely harmonious in their leading ideas, at once warn the reader that the writer's aim is rather to convey certain ideas regarding man's spiritual history and his connection with God, than to describe the process of creation. He does describe the process of creation, but he describes it only for the sake of the ideas regarding man's relation to God and God's relation to the world which he can thereby convey. Indeed what we mean by scientific knowledge was not in all the thoughts of the people for whom this book was written. The subject of creation, of the beginning of man upon earth, was not approached from that side at all; and if we are to understand what is here written we must burst the trammels of our own modes of thought and read these chapters not as a chronological, astronomical, geological, biological statement, but as a moral or spiritual conception.

It will, however, be said, and with much appearance of justice, that although the first object of the writer was not to convey scientific information, yet he might have been expected to be accurate in the information he did advance regarding the physical universe. This is an enormous assumption to make on *à priori* grounds, but it is an assumption worth seriously considering because it brings into view a real and important difficulty which every reader of Genesis must face. It brings into view the twofold character of this account of creation. On the one hand it is irreconcilable with the teachings of science. On the other hand it is in striking contrast to the other cosmogonies which have been handed down from prescientific ages. These are the two patent features of this record of creation and both require to be accounted for. Either feature alone would be easily accounted for; but the two co-existing in the same document are more baffling. We have to account at once for a want of perfect coincidence with the teachings of science, and for a singular freedom from those errors which disfigure all other primitive accounts of the creation of the world. The one feature of the document is as patent as the other and presses equally for explanation.

Now many persons cut the knot by simply denying that both these features exist. There is no disagreement with science, they say. I speak for many careful enquirers when I say that this cannot serve as a solution of the difficulty. I think it is to be freely admitted that, from whatever cause and however justifiably, the account of creation here given is not in strict and detailed accordance with the teaching of science. All attempts to force its statements into such accord are futile and mischievous. They are futile because they do not convince independent enquirers, but only those who are unduly anxious to be convinced. And they are mischievous because they unduly prolong the strife between Scripture and science, putting the question on a false issue. And above all, they are to be condemned because they do violence to Scripture, foster a style of interpretation by which the text is forced to say whatever the interpreter desires, and prevent us from recognising the real nature of these sacred writings. The Bible needs no defence such as false constructions of its language bring to its aid. They are its worst friends who distort its words that they may yield a meaning more in accordance with scientific truth. If, for example, the word "day" in these chapters, does not mean a period of twenty-four hours, the interpretation of Scripture is hopeless. Indeed if we are to bring these chapters into any comparison at all with science, we find at once various discrepancies. Of a creation of sun, moon, and stars, subsequent to the creation of this earth, science can have but one thing to say. Of the existence of fruit trees prior to the existence of the sun, science knows nothing. But for a candid and unsophisticated reader without a special theory to maintain, details are needless.

Accepting this chapter then as it stands, and believing that only by looking at the Bible as it actually is can we hope to understand God's method of revealing Himself, we at once perceive that ignorance of some departments of truth does not disqualify a man for knowing and imparting truth about God. In order to be a medium of revelation a man does not need to be in advance of his age in secular learning. Intimate communion with God, a spirit trained to discern spiritual things, a perfect understanding of and zeal for God's purpose, these are qualities quite independent of a knowledge of the discoveries of science. The enlightenment which enables men to apprehend God and spiritual truth has no necessary connection with scientific attainments. David's confidence in God and his declarations of His faithfulness are none the less valuable, because he was ignorant of a very great deal which every schoolboy now knows. Had inspired men introduced into their writings information which anticipated the discoveries of science, their state of mind would be inconceivable, and revelation would be a source of confusion. God's methods are harmonious with one another, and as He has given men natural faculties to acquire scientific knowledge and historical information, He did not stultify this gift by imparting such knowledge in a miraculous and unintelligible manner. There is no evidence that inspired men were in advance of their age in the knowledge of physical facts and laws. And plainly, had they been supernaturally instructed in physical knowledge they would so far have been unintelligible to those to whom they spoke. Had the writer of this book mingled with his teaching regarding God, an explicit and exact account of how this world came into existence—had he spoken of millions of years instead of speaking of days—in all probability he would have been discredited, and what he had to say about God would have been rejected along with his premature science. But speaking from the point of view of his contemporaries, and accepting the current ideas regarding the formation of the world, he attached to these the views regarding God's connection with the world which are most necessary to be believed. What he had learned of God's unity and creative power and connection with man, by the inspiration of the Holy Ghost, he imparts to his contemporaries through the vehicle of an account of creation they could all understand. It is not in his knowledge of physical facts that he is elevated above his contemporaries, but in his knowledge of God's connection with all physical facts. No doubt, on the other hand, his knowledge of God reacts upon the entire contents of his mind and saves him from presenting such accounts of creation as have been common among polytheists. He presents an account purified by his conception of what was worthy of the supreme God he worshipped. His idea of God has given dignity and simplicity to all he says about creation, and there is an elevation and majesty about the whole conception, which we recognise as the reflex of his conception of God.

Here then instead of anything to discompose us or to excite unbelief, we recognise one great law or principle on which God proceeds in making Himself known to men. This has been called the Law of Accommodation. It is the law which requires that the condition and capacity of those to whom the revelation is made must be considered. If you wish to instruct a child, you must speak in language the child can understand. If you wish to elevate a savage, you must do it by degrees, accommodating yourself to his condition, and winking at much ignorance while you instil elementary knowledge. You must found all you teach on what is already understood by your pupil, and through that you must convey further knowledge and train his faculties to higher capacity. So was it with God's revelation. The Jews were children who had to be trained with what Paul somewhat contemptuously calls "weak and beggarly elements," the A B C of morals and religion. Not even in morals could the absolute truth be enforced. Accommodation had to be practised even here. Polygamy was allowed as a concession to their immature stage of development: and practices in war and in domestic law were permitted or enjoined which were inconsistent with absolute morality. Indeed the whole Jewish system was an adaptation to an immature state. The dwelling of God in the Temple as a man in his house, the propitiating of God with sacrifice as of an Eastern king with gifts; this was a teaching by picture, a teaching which had as much resemblance to the truth and as much mixture of truth as they were able then to receive. No doubt this teaching did actually mislead them in some of their ideas; but it kept them on the whole in a right attitude toward God, and prepared them for growing up to a fuller discernment of the truth.

Much more was this law observed in regard to such matters as are dealt with in these chapters. It was impossible that in their ignorance of the rudiments of scientific knowledge, the early Hebrews should understand an absolutely accurate account of how the world came into being; and if they could have understood it, it would have been useless, dissevered as it must have been from the steps of knowledge by which men have since arrived at it. Children ask us questions in answer to which we do not tell them the exact full truth, because we know they cannot possibly understand it. All that we can do is to give them some provisional answer which conveys to them some information they can understand, and which keeps them in a right state of mind, although this information often seems absurd enough when compared with the actual facts and truth of the matter. And if some solemn pedant accused us of supplying the child with false information, we would simply tell him he knew nothing about children. Accurate information on these matters will infallibly come to the child when he grows up; what is wanted meanwhile is to give him information which will help to form his conduct without gravely misleading him as to facts. Similarly, if any one tells me he cannot accept these chapters as inspired by God, because they do not convey scientifically accurate information regarding this earth, I can only say that he has yet to learn the first principles of revelation, and that he misunderstands the conditions on which all instruction must be given.

My belief then is, that in these chapters we have the ideas regarding the origin of the world and of man which were naturally attainable in the country where they were first composed, but with those important modifications which a monotheistic belief necessarily suggested. So far as merely physical knowledge went, there is probably little here that was new to the contemporaries of the writer; but this already familiar knowledge was used by him as the vehicle for conveying his faith in the unity, love, and wisdom of God the creator. He laid a firm foundation for the history of God's relation to man. This was his object, and this he accomplished. The Bible is the book to which we turn for information regarding the history of God's revelation of Himself, and of His will towards men; and in these chapters we have the suitable introduction to this history. No changes in our knowledge of physical truth can at all affect the teaching of these chapters. What they teach regarding the relation of man to God is independent of the physical details in which this teaching is embodied, and can as easily be attached to the most modern statement of the physical origin of the world and of man.

What then are the truths taught us in these chapters? The first is that there has been a creation, that things now existing have not just grown of themselves, but have been called into being by a presiding intelligence and an originating will. No attempt to account for the existence of the world in any other way has been successful. A great deal has in this generation been added to our knowledge of the efficiency of material causes to produce what we see around us; but when we ask what gives harmony to these material causes, and what guides them to the production of certain ends, and what originally produced them, the answer must still be, not matter but intelligence and purpose. The best informed and most penetrating minds of our time affirm this. John Stuart Mill says: "It must be allowed that in the present state of our knowledge the adaptations in nature afford a large balance of probability in favor of creation by intelligence." Professor Tyndall adds his testimony and says: "I have noticed during years of self-observation that it is not in hours of clearness and vigor that [the doctrine of material atheism] commends itself to my mind—that in the hours of stronger and healthier thought it ever dissolves and disappears, as offering no solution of the mystery in which we dwell and of which we form a part."

There is indeed a prevalent suspicion, that in presence of the discoveries made by evolutionists the argument from design is no longer tenable. Evolution shows us that the correspondence of the structure of animals, with their modes of life, has been generated by the nature of the case; and it is concluded that a blind mechanical necessity and not an intelligent design rules all. But the discovery of the process by which the presently existing living forms have been evolved, and the perception that this process is governed by laws which have always been operating, do not make intelligence and design at all less necessary, but rather more so. As Professor Huxley himself says: "The teleological and mechanical views of nature are not necessarily exclusive. The teleologist can always defy the evolutionist to disprove that the primordial molecular arrangement was not intended to evolve the phenomena of the universe." Evolution, in short, by disclosing to us the marvellous power and accuracy of natural law, compels us more emphatically than ever to refer all law to a supreme, originating intelligence.

This then is the first lesson of the Bible; that at the root and origin of all this vast material universe, before whose laws we are crushed as the moth, there abides a living conscious Spirit, who wills and knows and fashions all things. The belief of this changes for us the whole face of nature, and instead of a chill, impersonal world of forces to which no appeal can be made, and in which matter is supreme, gives us the home of a Father. If you are yourself but a particle of a huge and unconscious universe—a particle which, like a flake of foam, or a drop of rain, or a gnat, or a beetle, lasts its brief space and then yields up its substance to be moulded into some new creature; if there is no power that understands you and sympathises with you and makes provision for your instincts, your aspirations, your capabilities; if man is himself the highest intelligence, and if all things are the purposeless result of physical forces; if, in short, there is no God, no consciousness at the beginning as at the end of all things, then nothing can be more melancholy than our position. Our higher desires which seem to separate us so immeasurably from the brutes, we have, only that they may be cut down by the keen edge of time, and wither in barren disappointment; our reason we have, only to enable us to see and measure the brevity of our span, and so live our little day, not joyously as the unforeseeing beasts, but shadowed by the hastening gloom of anticipated, inevitable, and everlasting night; our faculty for worshipping and for striving to serve and to resemble the perfect living One, that faculty which seems to be the thing of greatest promise and of finest quality in us, and to which is certainly due the largest part of what is admirable and profitable in human history, is the most mocking and foolishest of all our parts. But, God be thanked, He has revealed himself to us; has given us in the harmonious and progressive movement of all around us, sufficient indication that, even in the material world, intelligence and purpose reign; an indication which becomes immensely clearer as we pass into the world of man; and which, in presence of the person and life of Christ, attains the brightness of a conviction which illuminates all besides.

The other great truth which this writer teaches is, that man was the chief work of God, for whose sake all else was brought into being. The work of creation was not finished till he appeared: all else was preparatory to this final product. That man is the crown and lord of this earth is obvious. Man instinctively assumes that all els has been made for him, and freely acts upon this assumption. But when our eyes are lifted from this little ball on which we are set and to which we are confined, and when we scan such other parts of the universe as are within our ken, a keen sense of littleness oppresses us; our earth is after all so minute and apparently inconsiderable a point, when compared with the vast suns and planets that stretch system on system into illimitable space. When we read even the rudiments of what astronomers have discovered regarding the inconceivable vastness of the universe, the huge dimensions of the heavenly bodies, and the grand scale on which everything is framed, we find rising to our lips, and with tenfold reason, the words of David: "When I consider Thy heavens, the work of Thy fingers; the moon and the stars which Thou hast ordained; what is man that

Thou art mindful of him, or the son of man that Thou visitest him?" Is it conceivable that on this scarcely discernible speck in the vastness of the universe, should be played out the chiefest act in the history of God? Is it credible that He whose care it is to uphold this illimitable universe, should be free to think of the wants and woes of the insignificant creatures who quickly spend their little lives in this inconsiderable earth?

But reason seems all on the side of Genesis. God must not be considered as sitting apart in a remote position of general superintendence, but as present with all that is. And to Him who maintains these systems in their respective relations and orbits, it can be no burden to relieve the needs of individuals. To think of ourselves as too insignificant to be attended to is to derogate from God's true majesty and to misunderstand His relation to the world. But it is also to misapprehend the real value of spirit as compared with matter. Man is dear to God because he is like Him. Vast and glorious as it is, the sun cannot think God's thoughts; can fulfil but cannot intelligently sympathise with God's purpose. Man, alone among God's works, can enter into and approve of God's purpose in the world and can intelligently fulfil it. Without man the whole material universe would have been dark and unintelligible, mechanical and apparently without any sufficient purpose. Matter, however fearfully and wonderfully wrought, is but the platform and material in which spirit, intelligence, and will may fulfil themselves and find development. Man is incommensurable with the rest of the universe. He is of a different kind and by his moral nature is more akin to God than to His works.

Here the beginning and the end of God's revelation join hands and throw light on one another. The nature of man was that in which God was at last to give His crowning revelation, and for that no preparation could seem extravagant. Fascinating and full of marvel as is the history of the past which science discloses to us; full as these slow-moving millions of years are in evidences of the exhaustless wealth of nature, and mysterious as the delay appears, all that expenditure of resources is eclipsed and all the delay justified when the whole work is crowned by the Incarnation, for in it we see that all that slow process was the preparation of a nature in which God could manifest Himself as a Person to persons. This is seen to be an end worthy of all that is contained in the physical history of the world: this gives completeness to the whole and makes it a unity. No higher, other end need be sought, none could be conceived. It is this which seems worthy of those tremendous and subtle forces which have been set at work in the physical world, this which justifies the long lapse of ages filled with wonders unobserved, and teeming with ever new life, this above all which justifies these latter ages in which all physical marvels have been outdone by the tragical history of man upon earth. Remove the Incarnation and all remains dark, purposeless, unintelligible: grant the Incarnation, believe that in Jesus Christ the Supreme manifested Himself personally, and light is shed upon all that has been and is.

Light is shed on the individual life. Are you living as if you were the product of blind mechanical laws, and as if there were no object worthy of your life and of all the force you can throw into your life? Consider the Incarnation of the Creator, and ask yourself if sufficient object is not given to you in His call that you be conformed to His image and become the intelligent executor of His purposes? Is life not worth having even on these terms? The man that can still sit down and bemoan himself as if there were no meaning in existence, or lounge languidly through life as if there were no zest or urgency in living, or try to satisfy himself with fleshly comforts, has surely need to turn to the opening page of Revelation and learn that God saw sufficient object in the life of man, enough to compensate for millions of ages of preparation. If it is possible that you should share in the character and destiny of Christ, can a healthy ambition crave anything more or higher? If the future is to be as momentous in results as the past has certainly been filled with preparation, have you no caring to share in these results? Believe that there is a purpose in things; that in Christ, the revelation of God, you can see what that purpose is, and that by wholly uniting yourself to Him and allowing yourself to be penetrated by His Spirit you can participate with Him in the working out of that purpose.

CHAPTER II.

THE FALL.

Genesis iii.

PROFOUND as the teaching of this narrative is, its meaning does not lie on the surface. Literal interpretation will reach a measure of its significance, but plainly there is more here than appears in the letter. When we read that the serpent was more subtile than any beast of the field which the Lord God had made, and that he tempted the woman, we at once perceive that it is not with the outer husk of the story we are to concern ourselves, but with the kernel. The narrative throughout speaks of nothing but the brute serpent; not a word is said of the devil, not the slightest hint is given that the machinations of a fallen angel are signified. The serpent is compared to the other beasts of the field, showing that it is the brute serpent that is spoken of. The curse is pronounced on the beast, not on a fallen spirit summoned for the purpose before the Supreme; and not in terms which could apply to a fallen spirit, but in terms that are applicable only to the serpent that crawls. Yet every reader feels that this is not the whole mystery of the fall of man: moral evil cannot be accounted for by referring it to a brute source. No one, I suppose, believes that the whole tribe of serpents crawl as a punishment of an offence committed by one of their number, or that the whole iniquity and sorrow of the world are due to an actual serpent. Plainly this is merely a pictorial representation intended to convey some general impressions and ideas. Vitally important truths underlie the narrative and are bodied forth by it; but the way to reach these truths is not to adhere too rigidly to the literal meaning, but to catch the general impression which it seems fitted to make.

No doubt this opens the door to a great variety of interpretation. No two men will attach to it precisely the same meaning. One says, the serpent is a symbol for Satan, but Adam and Eve are historical persons. Another says, the tree of the knowledge of good and evil is a figure, but the driving out from the garden is real. Another maintains that the whole is a picture, putting in a visible, intelligible shape certain vitally important truths regarding the history of our race. So that every man is left very much to his own judgment, to read the narrative candidly and in such light from other sources as he has, and let it make its own impression upon him. This would be a sad result if the object of the Bible were to bring us all to a rigid uniformity of belief in all matters; but the object of the Bible is not that, but the far higher object of furnishing all varieties of men with sufficient light to lead them to God. And this being so, variety of interpretation in details is not to be lamented. The very purpose of such representations as are here given is to suit all stages of mental and spiritual advancement. Let the child read it and he will learn what will live in his mind and influence him all his life. Let the devout man who has ranged through all science and history and philosophy come back to this narrative, and he feels that he has here the essential truth regarding the beginnings of man's tragical career upon earth.

We should, in my opinion, be labouring under a misapprehension if we supposed that none even of the earliest readers of this account saw the deeper meaning of it. When men who felt the misery of sin and lifted up their hearts to God for deliverance, read the words addressed to the serpent, "I will put enmity between thee and the woman, and between thy seed and her seed; it shall bruise thy head, and thou shalt bruise his heel"—is it reasonable to suppose that such men would take these words in their literal sense, and satisfy themselves with the assurance that serpents, though dangerous, would be kept under, and would find in the words no assurance of that very thing they themselves were all their lifetime striving after, deliverance from the evil thing which lay at the root of all sin? No doubt some would accept the story in its literal meaning,—shallow and careless men, whose own spiritual experience never urged them to see any spiritual significance in the words, would do so; but even those who saw least in the story, and put a very shallow interpretation on its details, could scarcely fail to see its main teaching.

The reader of this perennially fresh story is first of all struck with the account given of man's primitive condition. Coming to this narrative with our minds coloured by the fancies of poets and philosophers, we are almost startled by the check which the plain and sober statements of this account give to an unpruned fancy. We have to read the words again and again to make sure we have not omitted something which gives support to those glowing descriptions of man's primitive condition. Certainly he is described as innocent and at peace with God, and in this respect no terms can exaggerate his happiness. But in other respects the language of the Bible is surprisingly moderate. Man is represented as living on fruit, and as going unclothed, and, so far as appears, without any artificial shelter either from the heat of the sun or the cold of night. None of the arts were as yet known. All working of metals had yet to be discovered, so that his tools must have been of the rudest possible description; and the arts, such as music, which adorn life and make leisure enjoyable, were also still in the future.

But the most significant elements in man's primitive condition are represented by the two trees of the garden; by trees, because with plants alone he had to do. In the centre of the garden stood the tree of life, the fruit of which bestowed immortality. Man was therefore naturally mortal, though apparently with a capacity for immortality. How this capacity would have actually carried man on to immortality had he not sinned, it is vain to conjecture. The mystical nature of the tree of life is fully recognised in the New Testament, by our Lord, when He says: "To him that overcometh will I give to eat of the tree of life, which is in the midst of the Paradise of God;" and by John, when he describes the new Jerusalem: "In the midst of the street of it, and on either side of the river, was there the tree of life, which bare twelve manner of fruits, and yielded her fruit every month: and the leaves of the tree were for the healing of the nations." Both these representations are intended to convey, in a striking and pictorial form, the promise of life everlasting.

And as of the tree of life which stands in the Paradise of the future it is said "Blessed are they that do His commandments, that they may have right to the tree of life;" so in Eden man's immortality was suspended on the condition of obedience. And the trial of man's obedience is imaged in the other tree, the tree of the knowledge of good and evil. From the child-like innocence in which man originally was, he was to pass forward into the condition of moral manhood, which consists not in mere innocence, but in innocence maintained in presence of temptation. The savage is innocent of many of the crimes of civilised men because he has no opportunity to commit them; the child is innocent of some of the vices of manhood because he has no temptation to them. But this innocence is the result of circumstance, not of character; and if savage or child is to become a mature moral being he must be tried by altered circumstances, by temptation and opportunity. To carry man forward to this higher stage trial is necessary, and this trial is indicated by the tree of knowledge. The fruit of this tree is prohibited, to indicate that it is only in presence of what is forbidden man can be morally tested, and that it is only by self-command and obedience to law, and not by the mere following of instincts, that man can attain to moral maturity. The prohibition is that which makes him recognise a distinction between good and evil. He is put in a position in which good is not the only thing he can do; an alternative is present to his mind, and the choice of good in preference to evil is made possible to him. In presence of this tree childlike innocence was no longer possible. The self-determination of manhood was constantly required. Conscience, hitherto latent, was now evoked and took its place as man's supreme faculty.

It is in vain to think of exhausting this narrative. We can, at the most, only remark upon some of the most salient points.

(1) Temptation comes like a serpent; like the most subtle beast of the field; like that one creature which is said to exert a fascinating influence on its victims, fastening them with its glittering eye, stealing upon them by its noise-

less, low, and unseen approach, perplexing them by its wide circling folds, seeming to come upon them from all sides at once, and armed not like the other beasts with one weapon of offence—horn, or hoof, or teeth—but capable of crushing its victim with every part of its sinuous length. It lies apparently dead for months together, but when roused it can, as the naturalist tells us, "outclimb the monkey, outswim the fish, outleap the zebra, outwrestle the athlete, and crush the tiger." How naturally in describing temptation do we borrow language from the aspect and movements of this creature. It does not need to hunt down its victims by long-continued pursuit, its victims come and put themselves within its reach. Unseen, temptation lies by our path, and before we have time to think we are fascinated and bewildered, its coils rapidly gather round us and its stroke flashes poison through our blood. Against sin, when once it has wreathed itself around us, we seem helpless to contend; the very powers with which we could resist are benumbed or pinned useless to our side—our foe seems all round us, and to extricate one part is but to become entangled in another. As the serpent finds its way everywhere, over every fence or barrier, into every corner and recess, so it is impossible to keep temptation out of the life; it appears where least we expect it and when we think ourselves secure.

(2) Temptation succeeds at first by exciting our curiosity. It is a wise saying that "our great security against sin lies in being shocked at it. Eve gazed and reflected when she should have fled." The serpent created an interest, excited her curiosity about this forbidden fruit. And as this excited curiosity lies near the beginning of sin in the race, so does it in the individual. I suppose if you trace back the mystery of iniquity in your own life and seek to track it to its source, you will find it to have originated in this craving to taste evil. No man originally meant to become the sinner he has become. He only intended, like Eve, to taste. It was a voyage of discovery he meant to make; he did not think to get nipped and frozen up and never more return from the outer cold and darkness. He wished before finally giving himself to virtue, to see the real value of the other alternative.

This dangerous craving has many elements in it. There is in it the instinctive drawing towards what is mysterious. One veiled figure in an assembly will attract more scrutiny than the most admired beauty. An appearance in the heavens that no one can account for will nightly draw more eyes than the most wonderful sunset. To lift veils, to penetrate disguises, to unravel complicated plots, to solve mysteries, this is always inviting to the human mind. The tale which used to thrill us in childhood, of the one locked room, the one forbidden key, bears in it a truth for men as well as for children. What is hidden must, we conclude, have some interest for us—else why hide it from us? What is forbidden must have some important bearing upon us. Else why forbid it? Things which are indifferent to us are left in our way, obvious, and without concealment. But as action has been taken regarding the things that are forbidden, action in view of our relation to them, it is natural to us to desire to know what these things are and how they affect us.

There is added to this in young persons, a sense of incompleteness. They wish to be grown up. Few boys wish to be always boys. They long for the signs of manhood, and seek to possess that knowledge of life and its ways which they very much identify with manhood. But too commonly they mistake the path to manhood. They feel as if they had a wider range of liberty and were more thoroughly men when they transgress the limits assigned by conscience. They feel as if there were a new and brighter world outside that which is fenced round by strict morality, and they tremble with excitement on its borders. It is a fatal delusion. Only by choosing the good in presence of the evil are true manhood and real maturity gained. True manliness consists mainly in self-control, in a patient waiting upon nature and God's law, and when youth impatiently breaks through the protecting fence of God's law, and seeks growth by knowing evil, it misses that very advancement it seeks, and cheats itself out of the manhood it apes.

(3) Through this craving for an enlarged experience unbelief in God's goodness finds entrance. In the presence of forbidden pleasure we are tempted to feel as if God were grudging us enjoyment. The very arguments of the serpent occur to our mind. No harm will come of our indulging; the prohibition is needless, unreasonable, and unkind; it is not based on any genuine desire for our welfare. This fence that shuts us out from knowing good and evil is erected by a timorous asceticism, by a ridiculous misconception of what truly enlarges human nature; it shuts us into a poor narrow life. And thus suspicions of God's perfect wisdom and goodness find entrance; we begin to think we know better than He what is good for us, and can contrive a richer, happier life than He has provided for us. Our loyalty to Him is loosened, and already we have lost hold of His strength and are launched on the current that leads to sin, misery, and shame. When we find ourselves saying Yes, where God has said No; when we see desirable things where God has said there is death; when we allow distrust of Him to rankle in our mind, when we chafe against the restrictions under which we live and seek liberty by breaking down the fence instead of by delighting in God, we are on the highway to all evil.

(4) If we know our own history we cannot be surprised to read that one taste of evil ruined our first parents. It is so always. The one taste alters our attitude towards God and conscience and life. It is a veritable Circe's cup. The actual experience of sin is like the one taste of alcohol to a reclaimed drunkard, like the first taste of blood to a young tiger, it calls out the latent devil and creates a new nature within us. At one brush it wipes out all the peace, and joy, and self-respect, and boldness of innocence, and numbers us among the transgressors, among the shame-faced, and self-despising, and hopeless. It leaves us possessed with unhappy thoughts which lead us away from what is bright, and honourable, and good, and like the letting out of water it seems to have tapped a spring of evil within us. It is but one step, but it is like the step over a precipice or down the shaft of a mine; it cannot be taken back, it commits to an altogether different state of things.

(5) The first result of sin is shame. The form in which the knowledge of good and evil comes

to us is the knowing we are naked, the consciousness that we are stripped of all that made us walk unabashed before God and men. The promise of the serpent while broken in the sense is fulfilled to the ear; the eyes of Adam and Eve were opened and they knew that they were naked. Self-reflection begins, and the first movement of conscience produces shame. Had they resisted temptation, conscience would have been born, but not in self-condemnation. Like children they had hitherto been conscious only of what was external to themselves, but now their consciousness of a power to choose good and evil is awakened and its first exercise is accompanied with shame. They feel that in themselves they are faulty, that they are not in themselves complete; that though created by God, they are not fit for His eye. The lower animals wear no clothes because they have no knowledge of good and evil; children feel no need of covering because as yet self-consciousness is latent, and their conduct is determined for them; those who are re-made in the image of God and glorified as Christ is, cannot be thought of as clothed, for in them there is no sense of sin. But Adam's clothing himself and hiding himself were the helpless attempts of a guilty conscience to evade the judgment of truth.

(6) But when Adam found he was no longer fit for God's eye, God provided a covering which might enable him again to live in His presence without dismay. Man had exhausted his own ingenuity and resources, and exhausted them without finding relief to his shame. If his shame was to be effectually removed, God must do it. And the clothing in coats of skins indicates the restoration of man, not indeed to pristine innocence, but to peace with God. Adam felt that God did not wish to banish him lastingly from His presence, nor to see him always a trembling and confused penitent. The self-respect and progressiveness, the reverence for law and order and God, which came in with clothes, and which we associate with the civilised races, were accepted as tokens that God was desirous to co-operate with man, to forward and further him in all good.

It is also to be remarked that the clothing which God provided was in itself different from what man had thought of. Adam took leaves from an inanimate, unfeeling tree; God deprived an animal of life, that the shame of His creature might be relieved. This was the last thing Adam would have thought of doing. To us life is cheap and death familiar, but Adam recognised death as the punishment of sin. Death was to early man a sign of God's anger. And he had to learn that sin could be covered not by a bunch of leaves snatched from a bush as he passed by and that would grow again next year, but only by pain and blood. Sin cannot be atoned for by any mechanical action nor without expenditure of feeling. Suffering must ever follow wrongdoing. From the first sin to the last, the track of the sinner is marked with blood. Once we have sinned we cannot regain permanent peace of conscience save through pain, and this not only pain of our own. The first hint of this was given as soon as conscience was aroused in man. It was made apparent that sin was a real and deep evil, and that by no easy and cheap process could the sinner be restored. The same lesson has been written on millions of consciences since. Men have found that their sin reaches beyond their own life and person, that it inflicts injury and involves disturbance and distress, that it changes utterly our relation to life and to God, and that we cannot rise above its consequences save by the intervention of God Himself, by an intervention which tells us of the sorrow He suffers on our account.

For the chief point is that it is God who relieves man's shame. Until we are certified that God desires our peace of mind we cannot be at peace. The cross of Christ is the permanent witness to this desire on God's part. No one can read what Christ has done for us without feeling sure that for himself there is a way back to God from all sin—that it is God's desire that his sin should be covered, his iniquity forgiven. Too often that which seems of prime importance to God seems of very slight importance to us. To have our life founded solidly in harmony with the Supreme seems often to excite no desire within us. It is about sin we find man first dealing with God, and until you have satisfied God and yourself regarding this prime and fundamental matter of your own transgression and wrong-doing you look in vain for any deep and lasting growth and satisfaction. Have you no reason to be ashamed before God? Have you loved Him in any proportion to His worthiness to be loved? Have you cordially and habitually fallen in with His will? Have you zealously done His work in the world? Have you fallen short of no good He intended you should do and gave you opportunity to do? Is there no reason for shame on your part before God? Has His desire to cover sin no application to you? Can you not understand His meaning when He comes to you with offers of pardon and acts of oblivion? Surely the candid mind, the clear-judging conscience can be at no loss to explain God's solicitous concern for the sinner; and must humbly own that even that unfathomable Divine emotion which is exhibited in the cross of Christ, is no exaggerated and theatrical demonstration, but the actual carrying through of what was really needed for the restoration of the sinner. Do not live as if the cross of Christ had never been, or as if you had never sinned and had no connection with it. Strive to learn what it means; strive to deal fairly with it and fairly with your own transgressions and with your present actual relation to God and His will.

CHAPTER III.

CAIN AND ABEL.

GENESIS iv.

It is not the purpose of this narrator to write the history of the world. It is not his purpose to write even the history of mankind. His object is to write the history of redemption. Starting from the broad fact of man's alienation from God, he means to trace that element in human history which results in the perfect re-union of God and man. The keynote has been struck in the promise already given that the seed of the woman should prevail over the seed of the serpent, that the effects of man's voluntary dissociation from God should be removed. It is the fulfilment of this promise which is traced by this writer. He steadily pursues that one line of history which runs directly towards this fulfilment; turning aside now and again to pursue, to a greater or less distance, diverging lines, but always returning to the grand highway on which the promise travels. His method is first to dispose of collateral matter and then to proceed with his main theme. As here, he first disposes of the line of Cain and then returns to Seth through whom the line of promise is maintained.

The first thing we have to do with outside the garden is death—the curse of sin speedily manifests itself in its most terrible form. But the sinner executes it himself. The first death is a murder. As if to show that all death is a wrong inflicted on us and proceeds not from God but from sin, it is inflicted by sin and by the hand of man. Man becomes his own executioner, and takes part with Satan, the murderer from the beginning. But certainly the first feeling produced by these events must have been one of bitter disappointment, as if the promise were to be lost in the curse.

The story of Cain and Abel was to all appearance told in order to point out that from the very first men have been divided into two great classes, viewed in connection with God's promise and presence in the world. Always there have been those who believed in God's love and waited for it, and those who believed more in their own force and energy. Always there have been the humble and self-diffident who hoped in God, and the proud and self-reliant who felt themselves equal to all the occasions of life. And this story of Cain and Abel and the succeeding generations does not conceal the fact, that for the purposes of this world there has been visible an element of weakness in the godly line, and that it is to the self-reliant and God-defying energy of the descendants of Cain that we owe much of the external civilisation of the world. While the descendants of Seth pass away and leave only this record, that they "walked with God," there are found among Cain's descendants, builders of cities, inventors of tools and weapons, music and poetry and the beginnings of culture.

These two opposed lines are in the first instance represented by Cain and Abel. With each child that comes into the world some fresh hope is brought; and the name of Cain points to the expectation of his parents that in him a fresh start would be made. Alas! as the boy grew they saw how vain such expectation was and how truly their nature had passed into his, and how no imparted experience of theirs, taught him from without, could countervail the strong propensities to evil which impelled him from within. They experienced that bitterest punishment which parents undergo, when they see their own defects and infirmities and evil passions repeated in their children and leading them astray as they once led themselves; when in those who are to perpetuate their name and remembrance on earth they see evidence that their faults also will be perpetuated; when in those whom they chiefly love they have a mirror ceaselessly held up to them forcing them to remember the follies and sins of their own youth. Certainly in the proud, self-willed, sullen Cain no redemption was to be found.

Both sons own the necessity of labour. Man is no longer in the primitive condition, in which he had only to stretch out his hand when hungry, and satisfy his appetite. There are still some regions of the earth in which the trees shower fruit, nutritious and easily preserved, on men who shun labour. Were this the case throughout the world, the whole of life would be changed. Had we been created self-sufficing or in such conditions as involved no necessity of toil, nothing would be as it now is. It is the need of labour that implies occasional starvation and frequent poverty, and gives occasion to charity. It is the need of labour which involves commerce and thereby sows the seed of greed, worldliness, ambition, drudgery. The ultimate physical wants of men, food and clothes, are the motive of the greater part of all human activity. Trace to their causes the various industries of men, the wars, the great social movements, all that constitutes history, and you find that the bulk of all that is done upon earth is done because men must have food and wish to have it as good and with as little labour as possible. The broad facts of human life are in many respects humiliating.

The disposition of men is consequently shown in the occupations they choose and the idea of life they carry into them. Some, like Abel, choose peaceful callings that draw out feeling and sympathy; others prefer pursuits which are stirring and active. Cain chose the tillage of the ground, partly no doubt from the necessity of the case, but probably also with the feeling that he could subdue nature to his own purposes notwithstanding the curse that lay upon it. Do we not all sometimes feel a desire to take the world as it is, curse and all, and make the most of it; to face its disease with human skill, its disturbing and destructive elements with human forethought and courage, its sterility and stubbornness with human energy and patience? What is stimulating men still to all discovery and invention, to forewarn seamen of coming storms, to break a precarious passage for commerce through eternal ice or through malarious swamps, to make life at all points easier and more secure? Is it not the energy which opposition excites? We know that it will be hard work; we expect to have thorns and thistles everywhere, but let us see whether this may not after all be a thoroughly happy world, whether we cannot cultivate the curse altogether out of it. This is indeed the very work God has given man to do—to subdue the earth and make the desert blossom as the rose. God is with us in this work, and he who believes in God's purpose and strives to reclaim nature and compel it to some better products than it naturally yields, is doing God's work in the world. The misery is that so many do it in the spirit of Cain, in a spirit of self-confident or sullen alienation from God, willing to endure all hardship but unable to lay themselves at God's feet with every capacity for work and every field He has given them to till for Him and in a spirit of humble love to co-operate with Him. To this spirit of godless energy, of merely selfish or worldly ambition and enterprise, the world owes not only much of its poverty and many of its greatest disasters, but also the greater part of its present advantages in external civilisation. But from this spirit can never arise the meekness, the patience, the tenderness, the charity which sweeten the life of society and are more to be desired than gold; from this spirit and all its achievements the natural outcome is the proud, vindictive, self-glorifying war-song of a Lamech.

The incompatibility of the two lines and the

persecuting spirit of the godless are set forth by the after history of Cain and Abel. The one line is represented in Cain, who with all his energy and indomitable courage, is depicted as of a dark, morose, suspicious, jealous, violent temper; a man born under the shadow of the fall. Abel is described in contrast as guileless and sunny, free from harshness and resentment. What was in Cain was shown by what came out of him, murder. The reason of the rejection of his offering was his own evil condition of heart. "If thou doest well, shalt not thou also be accepted;" implying that he was not accepted because he was not doing well. His offering was a mere form; he complied with the fashion of the family; but in spirit he was alienated from God, cherishing thoughts which the rejection of his offering brings to a head. He may have seen that the younger son won more of the parents' affection, that his company was more welcome. Jealousy had been produced, that deep jealousy of the humble and godly which proud men of the world cannot help betraying and which has so very often in the world's history produced persecution.

This cannot be considered too weak a motive to carry so enormous a crime. Even in a highly civilised age we find an English statesman saying: "Pique is one of the strongest motives in the human mind. Fear is strong, but transient. Interest is more lasting, perhaps, and steady, but weaker; I will ever back pique against them both. It is the spur the devil rides the noblest tempers with, and will do more work with them in a week, than with other poor jades in a twelvemonth." And the age of Cain and Abel was an age in which impulse and action lay close together, and in which jealousy is notoriously strong. To this motive John ascribes the act: "Wherefore slew he him? Because his own works were evil, and his brother's righteous."

We have now learned better how to disguise our feelings; and we are compelled to control them better; but now and again we meet with a deep-seated hatred of goodness which might give rise to almost any crime. Few of us can say that for our own part we have extinguished within us the spirit that disparages and depreciates and fixes the charge of hypocrisy or refers good actions to interested motives, searches out failings and watches for haltings and is glad when a blot is found. Few are filled with unalloyed grief when the man who has borne an extraordinary reputation turns out to be just like the rest of us. Many of us have a true delight in goodness and humble ourselves before it when we see it, and yet we know also what it is to be exasperated by the presence of superiority. I have seen a schoolboy interrupt his brother's prayers, and gird at him for his piety, and strive to draw him into sin, and do the devil's work with zest and diligence. And where goodness is manifestly in the minority how constantly does it excite hatred that pours itself out in sneers and ridicule and ignorant calumny.

But this narrative significantly refers this early quarrel to religion. There is no bitterness to compare with that which worldly men who profess religion feel towards those who cultivate a spiritual religion. They can never really grasp the distinction between external worship and real godliness. They make their offerings, they attend to the rites of the religion to which they belong, and are beside themselves with indignation if any person or event suggests to them that they might have saved themselves all their trouble, because these do not at all constitute religion. They uphold the Church, they admire and praise her beautiful services, they use strong but meaningless language about infidelity, and yet when brought in contact with spirituality and assured that regeneration and penitent humility are required above all else in the kingdom of God, they betray an utter inability to comprehend the very rudiments of the Christian religion. Abel has always to go to the wall because he is always the weaker party, always in the minority. Spiritual religion, from the very nature of the case, must always be in the minority; and must be prepared to suffer loss, calumny, and violence, at the hands of the worldly religious, who have contrived for themselves a worship that calls for no humiliation before God and no complete surrender of heart and will to Him. Cain is the type of the ignorant religious, of the unregenerate man who thinks he merits God's favour as much as any one else; and Cain's conduct is the type of the treatment which the Christ-like and intelligent godly are always likely to receive at such hands.

We never know where we may be led by jealousy and malice. One of the striking features of this incident is the rapidity with which small sins generate great ones. When Cain went in the joy of harvest and offered his first fruits no thought could be further from his mind than murder. It may have come as suddenly on himself as on the unsuspecting Abel, but the germ was in him. Great sins are not so sudden as they seem. Familiarity with evil thought ripens us for evil action; and a moment of passion, an hour's loss of self-control, a tempting occasion, may hurry us into irremediable evil. And even though this does not happen, envious, uncharitable, and malicious thoughts make our offerings as distasteful as Cain's. He that loveth not his brother knoweth not God. First be reconciled to thy brother, says our Lord, and then come and offer thy gift.

Other truths are incidentally taught in this narrative.

(1) The acceptance of the offering depends on the acceptance of the offerer. God had respect to Abel and his offering—the man first and then the offering. God looks through the offering to the state of soul from which it proceeds; or even, as the words would indicate, sees the soul first and judges and treats the offering according to the inward disposition. God does not judge of what you are by what you say to Him or do for Him, but He judges what you say to Him and do for Him by what you are. "By *faith*," says a New Testament writer, "Abel offered a more acceptable sacrifice than Cain." He had the faith which enabled him to believe that God is, and that He is a rewarder of them that diligently seek Him. His attitude towards God was sound; his life was a diligent seeking to please God; and from all such persons God gladly receives acknowledgment. When the offering is the true expression of the soul's gratitude, love, devotedness, then it is acceptable. When it is a merely external offering, that rather veils than expresses the real feeling; when it is not vivified and rendered significant by any spiritual act on the part of the worshipper, it is plainly of no effect.

What is true of all sacrifices is true of the

sacrifice of Christ. It remains invalid and of none effect to those who do not through it yield themselves to God. Sacrifices were intended to be the embodiment and expression of a state of feeling towards God, of a submission or offering of men's selves to God; of a return to that right relation which ought ever to subsist between creature and Creator. Christ's sacrifice is valid for us when it is that outward thing which best expresses our feeling towards God and through which we offer or yield ourselves to God. His sacrifice is the open door through which God freely admits all who aim at a consecration and obedience like to His. It is valid for us when through it we sacrifice ourselves. Whatever His sacrifice expresses we desire to take and use as the only satisfactory expression of our own aims and desires. Did Christ perfectly submit to and fulfil the will of God? So would we. Did He acknowledge the infinite evil of sin and patiently bear its penalties, still loving the Holy and Righteous God? So would we endure all chastening, and still resist unto blood striving against sin.

(2) Again, we here find a very sharp and clear statement of the welcome truth, that continuance in sin is never a necessity, that God points the way out of sin, and that from the first He has been on man's side and has done all that could be done to keep men from sinning. Observe how He expostulates with Cain. Take note of the plain, explicit fairness of the words in which He expostulates with him—instance, as it is, of how absolutely in the right God always is, and how abundantly He can justify all His dealings with us. God says as it were to Cain; Come now: and let us reason together. All God wants of any man is to be reasonable; to look at the facts of the case. "If thou doest well, shalt thou not (as well as Abel) be accepted? and if thou doest not well, sin lieth at the door," that is, if thou doest not well, the sin is not Abel's nor any one's but thine own, and therefore anger at another is not the proper remedy, but anger at yourself, and repentance.

No language could more forcibly exhibit the unreasonableness of not meeting God with penitent and humble acknowledgment. God has fully met our case, and has satisfied all its demands, has set Himself to serve us and laid Himself out to save us pain and misery, and has so entirely succeeded in making salvation and blessedness possible to us, that if we continue in sin we must trample not only upon God's love and our own reason, but on the very means of salvation. State your case at the worst, bring forward every reason why your countenance should be fallen as Cain's and why your face should lower with the gloom of eternal despair—say that you have as clear evidence as Cain had that your offerings are displeasing to God, and that while others are accepted you receive no token from Him,—in answer to all your arguments, these words addressed to Cain rise up. If not accepted already you have the means of being so. If you do well to be hardened in sin it is not because it is necessary, nor because God desires it. If you are to continue in sin you must put aside His hand. It can only be *sin* which causes you either to despair of salvation or keeps you any way separate from God—there is no other thing worse than sin, and for sin there is an offering provided. You have not fallen into some lower grade of beings than that which is designated sinners, and it is sinners that God in His mercy hems in with this inevitable dilemma He presented to Cain.

If, therefore, you continue at war with God it is not because you must not do otherwise: if you go forward to any new thought, plan, or action unpardoned; if acceptance of God's forgiveness and entrance into a state of reconciliation with Him be not your first action, then you must thrust aside His counsel, backed though it is with every utterance of your own reason. Some of us may be this day or this week in as critical a position as Cain, having as truly as he the making or marring of our future in our hands, seeing clearly the right course, and all that is good, humble, penitent, and wise in us urging us to follow that course, but our pride and self-will holding us back. How often do men thus barter a future of blessing for some mean gratification of temper or lust or pride; how often by a reckless, almost listless and indifferent continuance in sin do they let themselves be carried on to a future as woful as Cain's; how often when God expostulates with them do they make no answer and take no action, as if there were nothing to be gained by listening to God—as if it were a matter of no importance what future I go to—as if in the whole eternity that lies in reserve there were nothing worth making a choice about—nothing about which it is worth my while to rouse the whole energy of which I am capable, and to make, by God's grace, the determination which shall alter my whole future —to choose for myself and assert myself.

(3) The writer to the Hebrews makes a very striking use of this event. He borrows from it language in which to magnify the efficacy of Christ's sacrifice, and affirms that the blood of Christ speaketh better things, or, as it must rather be rendered, crieth louder than the blood of Abel. Abel's blood, we see, cried for vengeance, for evil things for Cain, called God to make inquisition for blood, and so pled as to secure the banishment of the murderer. The Arabs have a belief that over the grave of a murdered man his spirit hovers in the form of a bird that cries "Give me drink, give me drink," and only ceases when the blood of the murderer is shed. Cain's conscience told him the same thing; there was no criminal law threatening death to the murderer, but he felt that men would kill him if they could. He heard the blood of Abel crying from the earth. The blood of Christ also cries to God, but cries not for vengeance but for pardon. And as surely as the one cry was heard and answered in very substantial results; so surely does the other cry call down from heaven its proper and beneficent effects. It is as if the earth would not receive and cover the blood of Christ, but ever exposes it before God and cries to Him to be faithful and just to forgive us our sins. This blood cries louder than the other. If God could not overlook the blood of one of His servants, but adjudged it to its proper consequences, neither is it possible that He should overlook the blood of His Son and not give to it its proper result.

If then you feel in your conscience that you are as guilty as Cain, and if sins clamour around you which are as dangerous as his, and which cry out for judgment upon you, accept the assurance that the blood of Christ has a yet louder cry for mercy. If you had been Abel's murderer, would you have been justly afraid of God's anger? Be as sure of God's mercy now. If you had stood over his lifeless body and seen the earth refusing to cover his blood, if you felt the stain of it crimson on your conscience and if by night you started from your sleep striving vainly to wash it from your hands, if by every token you felt yourself exposed to a just punishment, your fear would be just and reasonable were nothing else revealed to you. But there is another blood equally indelible, equally clamorous. In it you have in reality what is elsewhere pretended in fable, that the blood of the murdered man will not wash out, but through every cleansing oozes up again a dark stain on the oaken floor. This blood can really not be washed out, it cannot be covered up and hid from God's eye, its voice cannot be stifled, and its cry is all for mercy.

With how different a meaning then comes now to us this question of God's: "Where is thy brother?" Our Brother also is slain. Him Whom God sent among us to reverse the curse, to lighten the burden of this life, to be the loving member of the family on Whom each leans for help and looks to for counsel and comfort—Him Who was by His goodness to be as the dayspring from on high in our darkness, we found *too* good for our endurance and dealt with as Cain dealt with his more righteous brother. But He Whom we slew God has raised again to give repentance and remission of sins, and assures us that His blood cleanseth from all sin. To every one therefore He repeats this question, "Where is thy brother?" He repeats it to every one who is living with a conscience stained with sin; to every one that knows remorse and walks with the hanging head of shame; to every one whose whole life is saddened by the consciousness that all is not settled between God and himself; to every one who is sinning recklessly as if Christ's blood had never been shed for sin; and to every one who, though seeking to be at peace with God, is troubled and downcast—to all God says, "Where is thy brother?" tenderly reminding us of the absolute satisfaction for sin that has been made, and of the hope towards God we have through the blood of His Son.

CHAPTER IV.

CAIN'S LINE, AND ENOCH.

Genesis iv. 12-24.

"My punishment is greater than I can bear," so felt Cain as soon as his passion had spent itself and the consequences of his wickedness became apparent—and so feels every one who finds he has now to live in the presence of the irrevocable deed he has done. It seems too heavy a penalty to endure for the one hour of passion; and yet as little as Cain could rouse the dead Abel so little can we revive the past we have destroyed. Thoughtlessness has set in motion agencies we are powerless to control; the whole world is changed to us. One can fancy Cain turning to see if his victim gave no sign of life, striving to reanimate the dead body, calling the familiar name, but only to see with growing dismay that the one blow had finished all with which that name was associated, and that he had made himself a new world. So are we drawn back and back in thought to that which has for ever changed life to us, striving to see if there is no possibility of altering the past, but only to find we might quite as well try to raise the dead. No voice responds to our cries of grief and dismay and too late repentance. All life now seems but a reaping of the consequences of the past. We have put ourselves in every respect at a disadvantage. The earth seems cursed so that we are hampered in our employments and cannot make as much of them as we would had we been innocent. We have got out of right relations to our fellow-men and cannot feel the same to them as we ought to feel; and the face of God is hid from us, so that now and again as time after time our hopes are blighted, our life darkened and disturbed by the obvious results of our own past deeds, we are tempted to cry out with Cain: "My punishment is greater than I can bear."

Yet Cain's punishment was less than he expected. He was not put to death as he would have been at any later period of the world's history, but was banished. And even this punishment was lightened by his having a token from God, that he would not be put to death by any zealous avenger of Abel. He would experience the hardships of a man entering unexplored territory, but to an enterprising spirit this would not be without its charms. As the fresh beauties of the world's youth were disclosed to him and by their bright and peaceful friendliness allayed the bitterness of his spirit, and as the mysteries and dangers of the new regions excited him and called his thoughts from the past, some of the old delight in life may have been recovered by him. Probably in many a lonely hour the recollection of his crime would return and with it all the horrors of a remorse which would drive rest and peace from his soul, and render him the most wretched of men. But busied as he was with his new enterprises, there is little doubt that he would find it, as it is still found, not impossible to banish such dreary thoughts and live in the measure of contentment which many enjoy who are as far from God as Cain.

It is not difficult to detect the spirit he carried with him, and the tone he gave to his line of the race. The facts recorded are few but significant. He begat a son, he built a city; and he gave to both the name Enoch, that is "initiation," or "beginning," as if he were saying in his heart. "What so great harm after all in cutting short one line in Abel? I can begin another and find a new starting point for the race. I am driven forth cursed as a vagabond, but a vagabond I will not be; I will make for myself a settled abode, and I will fence it round with knife-blade thorns so that no man will be able to assault me."

In this settling of Cain, however, we see not any symptom of his ceasing to be a vagabond, but the surest evidence that now he was content to be a fugitive from God and had cut himself off from hope. His heart had found rest and had found it apart from God. *Here*, in this city he would make a fresh beginning for himself and for men. Here he abandoned all clinging memories of former things, of his old home, and of the God there worshipped. He had wisdom enough not to call his city by his own name, and so invite men to consider his former career or trace back anything to his old life. He cut it all off from him; his crime, his God also, all that was in it was to be no more to him and his comrades. He would make a clean start, and that men might be led to expect a great future he called his city, Enoch, a Beginning.

But it is one thing to forgive ourselves, another thing to have God's forgiveness. It is one thing to reconcile ourselves to the curse that runs through our life, another thing to be reconciled to God and so defeat the curse. It is sometimes, though by no means always, possible to escape some of the consequences of sin: we can change our front so as to lessen the breadth of life that is exposed to them, or we can accustom and harden ourselves to a very second-rate kind of life. We can teach ourselves to live without much love in our homes or in our connections with those outside; we can learn to be satisfied if we can pay our way and make the time pass and be outwardly like other people; we can build a little city, and be content to be on no very friendly terms with any but the select few inside the trench, and actually be quite satisfied if we can *defend ourselves against* the rest of men; we can forget the one commandment, that we should love one another. We can all find much in the world to comfort, to lull, to soothe sorrowful but wholesome remembrances; much to aid us in an easy treatment of the curse; much to shed superficial brightness on a life darkened and debased by sin, much to hush up the sad echoes that mutter from the dark mountains of vanity we have left behind us, much that assures us we have nothing to do but forget our old sins and busily occupy ourselves with new duties. But no David will say, nor will any man of true spiritual discernment say, "Blessed is the man whose transgression is *forgotten;*" but only, "Blessed is the man whose transgression is forgiven." By all means make a fresh start, a new beginning, but let it be in your own broken heart, in a spirit humble and contrite, frankly acknowledging your guilt and finding rest and settlement for your soul in reconciliation with God.

It is in the family of Lamech the characteristics of Cain's line are most distinctly seen, and the significance of their tendencies becomes apparent. As Cain had set himself to cultivate the curse out of the world, so have his children derived from him the self-reliant hardiness and hardihood which are resolute to make of this world as bright and happy a home as may be. They make it their task to subdue the world and compel it to yield them a life in which they can delight. They are so far successful that in a few generations they have formed a home in which all the essentials of civilised life are found—the arts are cultivated and female society is appreciated.

Of his three sons, Jabal—or "Increase"—was "the father of such as dwell in tents and of such as have cattle." He had originality enough to step beyond all traditional habits and to invent a new mode of life. Hitherto men had been tied to one spot by their fixed habitations, or found shelter when overtaken by storm in caves or trees. To Jabal the idea first occurs, I can carry my house about with me and regulate its movements and not it mine. I need not return every night this long weary way from the pastures, but may go wherever grass is green and streams run cool. He and his comrades would thus become aware of the vast resources of other lands, and would unconsciously lay the foundations both of commerce and of wars of conquest. For both in ancient and more modern times the most formidable armies have been those vast moving shepherd races bred outside the borders of civilisation and flooding as with an irresistible tide the territories of more settled and less hardy tribes.

Jubal again was, as his name denotes, the reputed father of all such as handle the harp and the organ, stringed and wind instruments. The stops of the reed or flute and the divisions of the string being once discovered, all else necessarily followed. The twanging of a bow-string in a musical ear was enough to give the suggestion to an observant mind; the varying notes of the birds; the winds, expressing at one time unbridled fury and at another a breathing benediction, could not fail to move and stir the susceptible spirit. The spontaneous though untuned singing of children, that follows no mere melody made by another to express *his* joy, but is the instinctive expression of their own joy, could not but give however meagrely the first rudiments of music. But here was the man who first made a piece of wood help him; who out of the commonest material of the physical world found for himself a means of expressing the most impalpable moods of his spirit. Once the idea was caught that matter inanimate as well as animate was man's servant and could do his finest work for him, Jabal and his brother Jubal would make rapid work between them. If the rude matter of the world could *sing* for them, what might it not do for them? They would see that there was a precision in machine-work which man's hand could not rival—a regularity which no nervous throb could throw out and no feeling interrupt, and yet at the same time, when they found how these rude instruments responded to every finest shade of feeling, and how all external nature seemed able to express what was in man, must it not have been the birth of poetry as well as of music? Jubal in short originates what we now compendiously describe as the Fine Arts.

The third brother again may be taken as the originator of the Useful Arts—though not exclusively—for being the instructor of every artificer in brass and iron, having something of his brother's genius for invention and more than his brother's handiness and practical faculty for embodying his ideas in material forms, he must have promoted all arts which require tools for their culture.

Thus among these three brothers we find distributed the various kinds of genius and faculty which ever since have enriched the world. Here in germ was really all that the world can do. The great lines in which individual and social activity have since run were then laid down.

This notable family circle was completed by Naamah, the sister of Tubal-Cain. The strength of female influence began to be felt contemporaneously with the cultivation of the arts. Very early in the world's history it was perceived that although debarred from the rougher activities of life, women have an empire of their own. Men have the making of civilisation, but women have the making of men. It is they who form the character of the individual and give its tone to the society in which they live. It is natural to men to consider the feelings and tastes of women and to adapt their manners and conversation to them; and it is for women to exercise worthily the sway they thus possess. Practically and to a large extent women settle what subjects shall be spoken of, and in what tone, trifling or serious; and each ought therefore to recognise her own burden of responsibility, and see to it that the deference paid to her shall not lower him who pays it, and that the respect shown to her shall help him who shows it to respect what is pure and true, charitable, just, and worthy. Let women show that it is worldly trifling or slanderous malignity or empty tittle-tattle that delights them, then they act the part of Eve and tempt to sin; let them show that they prize most highly the mirth that is innocent and the conversation that is elevating and helpful, and while they win admiration for themselves they win it also for what is healthy and purifying. No woman can renounce her influence; helpful or hurtful she certainly is and must be, in proportion as she is pleasing and attractive.

Thus early did it appear how much of what is admirable and serviceable clung to human nature apart from any recognition of God. The worldly life was then what it is now, a life not wholly and obviously polluted by excess, nor destroyed by violence, but displaying features which appeal to our sensibilities and provoke applause; a life of manifold beauty, of great power and resource, of abundant promise. There is abundant material in the world for beautifying and elevating human life, and this material may be used and is used by men who acknowledge neither its origin in God nor the ends He would serve by it. The interests of men may be advanced and the best work of the world done by three distinct classes of men—by those who work as God's children in thorough sympathy with His purposes; by those who do not know God but who are humble in heart and would sympathise with God's purposes, did they become acquainted with them; and by those who are proud and self-willed, positively alienated from God, and who do the world's work for their own ends. And so far as the external work goes the last-named class of men may be most efficient. In mental endowment, social and political wisdom, scientific aptitude, and all that tends to substantial utility, it is quite possible they may excel the godly, for "not many noble, not many wise are called." But we have nothing to measure permanent success by, save conformity with God's will; and we have nothing by which we can estimate how character will endure and how deeply it is rooted save conformity with the nature of God. If a man believes in God, in one Supreme Who rules and orders all things for just, holy, and wise ends; if he is in sympathy with the nature and will of God and finds his truest satisfaction in forwarding the purposes of God, then you have a guarantee for this man's continuance in good and for his ultimate success.

The precarious nature of all godless civilisation and the real tendency of self-sufficing pride are shown in Lamech.

It is in Lamech the tendency culminates and in him the issue of all this brilliant but godless life is seen. Therefore though he is the father, the historian speaks of him *after* his children. In his one recorded utterance his character leaps to view definite and complete—a character of boundless force, self-reliance, and godlessness. It is a little uncertain whether he means that he has actually slain a man, or whether he is putting a hypothetical case—the character of his speech is the same whichever view is taken.

"I have slain," he says, or suppose I slay, "a man for wounding me,
A young man for hurting me:
But if Cain shall be avenged seven-fold—then Lamech seventy and seven-fold."

That is, I take vengeance for myself with those good weapons my son has forged for me. He has furnished me with a means of defence many times more effectual than God's avenging of Cain. This is the climax of the self-sufficiency to which the line of Cain has been tending. Cain besought God's protection; he needed God for at least one purpose, this one thread bound him yet to God. Lamech has no need of God for any purpose; what his sons can make and his own right hand do is enough for him. This is what comes of finding enough in the world without God—a boastful, self-sufficient man, dangerous to society, the incarnation of the pride of life. In the long run separation from God becomes isolation from man and cruel self-sufficiency.

The line of Seth is followed from father to son, for the sake of showing that the promise of a seed which should be victorious over evil was being fulfilled. Apparently it is also meant that during this uneventful period long ages elapsed. Nothing can be told of these old-world people but that they lived and died, leaving behind them heirs to transmit the promise.

Only once is the monotony broken; but this in so striking a manner as to rescue us from the idea that the historian is mechanically copying a barren list of names. For in the seventh generation, contemporaneous with the culmination of Cain's line in the family of Lamech, we come upon the simple but anything but mechanical statement: "Enoch walked with God and he was not; for God took him." The phrase is full of meaning. Enoch walked with God because he was His friend and liked His company, because he was going in the same direction as God, and had no desire for anything but what lay in God's path. We walk with God when He is in all our thoughts; not because we consciously think of Him at all times, but because He is naturally suggested to us by all we think of; as when any person or plan or idea has become important to us, no matter what we think of, our thought is always found recurring to this favourite object, so with the godly man everything has a connection with God and must be ruled by that connection. When some change in his circumstances is thought of, he has first of all to determine how the proposed change will affect his connection with God—will his conscience be equally clear, will he be able to live on the same friendly terms with God, and so forth. When he falls into sin he cannot rest till he has resumed his place at God's side and walks again with Him. This is the general nature of walking with God; it is a persistent endeavour to hold all our life open to God's inspection and in conformity to His will; a readiness to give up what we find does cause any misunderstanding between us and God; a feeling of loneliness if we have not some satisfaction in our efforts at holding fellowship with God, a cold and desolate feeling when we are conscious of doing something that displeases Him. This walking with God necessarily tells on the whole life and character. As you instinctively avoid subjects which you know will jar upon the feelings of your friend, as you naturally endeavour to suit yourself to your company, so when the consciousness of God's presence begins to have some weight with you, you are found instinctively endeavouring to please Him, repressing the thoughts you know He disapproves, and endeavouring to educate such dispositions as reflect His own nature.

It is easy then to understand how we may practically walk with God—it is to open to Him all our purposes and hopes, to seek His judgment on our scheme of life and idea of happiness—it is to be on thoroughly friendly terms with God. Why then do any not walk with God? Because they seek what is wrong. You would walk with Him if the same idea of good possessed you as possesses Him; if you were as ready as He to make no deflexion from the straight path. Is not the very crown of life depicted in the testimony given to Enoch, that " he pleased God"? Cannot you take your way through life with a resolute and joyous spirit if you are conscious that you please Him Who judges not by appearances, not by your manners, but by your real state, by your actual character and the eternal promise it bears? Things were not made easy to Enoch. In evil days, with much to mislead him, with everything to oppose him, he had by faith and diligent seeking, as the Epistle to the Hebrews says, to cleave to the path on which God walked, often left in darkness, often thrown off the track, often listening but unable to hear the footfall of God or to hear his own name called upon, receiving no sign but still diligently seeking the God he knew would lead him only to good. Be it yours to give such diligence. Do not accept it as a thing fixed that you are to be one of the graceless and ungodly, always feeble, always vacillating, always without a character, always in doubt about your state, and whether life might not be some other and better thing to you.

"Enoch was not, for God took him." Suddenly his place on earth was empty and men drew their own conclusions. He had been known as the Friend of God, where could he be but in God's dwelling-place? No sickness had slowly worn him to the grave, no mark of decay had been visible in his unabated vigour. His departure was a favour conferred and as such men recognised it. "God has taken him," they said, and their thoughts followed upward, and essayed to conceive the finished bliss of the man whom God has taken away where blessing may be more fully conferred. His age corresponded to our thirty-three, the age when the world has usually got fair hold of a man, when a man has found his place in life and means to live and see good days. The awkward, unfamiliar ways of youth that keep him outside of much of life are past, and the satiety of age is not yet reached; a man has begun to learn there is something he can do, and has not yet learned how little. It is an age at which it is most painful to relinquish life, but it was at this age God took him away, and men knew it was in kindness. Others had begun to gather round him, and depend upon him, hopes were resting in him, great things were expected of him, life was strong in him. But let life dress itself in its most attractive guise, let it shine on a man with its most fascinating smile, let him be happy at home and the pleasing centre of a pleasing circle of friends, let him be in that bright summer of life when a man begins to fear he is too prosperous and happy, and yet there is for man a better thing than all this, a thing so immeasurably and independently superior to it that all this may be taken away and yet the man be far more blessed. If God would confer His highest favours, He must take a man out of all this and bring him closer to Himself.

CHAPTER V.

THE FLOOD.

Genesis v.-ix.

The first great event which indelibly impressed itself on the memory of the primeval world was the Flood. There is every reason to believe that this catastrophe was co-extensive with the human population of the world. In every branch of the human family traditions of the event are found. These traditions need not be recited, though some of them bear a remarkable likeness to the Biblical story, while others are very beautiful in their construction, and significant in individual points. Local floods happening at various times in different countries could not have given birth to the minute coincidences found in these traditions, such as the sending out of the birds, and the number of persons saved. But we have as yet no material for calculating how far human population had spread from the original centre. It might apparently be argued that it could not have spread to the sea-coast, or that at any rate no ships had as yet been built large enough to weather a severe storm; for a thoroughly nautical population could have had little difficulty in surviving such a catastrophe as is here described. But all that can be affirmed is that there is no evidence that the waters extended beyond the inhabited part of the earth; and from certain details of the narrative, this part of the earth may be identified as the great plain of the Euphrates and Tigris.

Some of the expressions used in the narrative might indeed lead us to suppose that the writer understood the catastrophe to have extended over the whole globe; but expressions of similar largeness elsewhere occur in passages where their meaning must be restricted. Probably the most convincing evidence of the limited extent of the Flood is furnished by the animals of Australia. The animals that abound in that island are different from those found in other parts of the world, but are similar to the species which are found fossilised in the island itself, and which therefore must have inhabited these same regions long anterior to the Flood. If then the Flood extended to Australia and destroyed all animal life there, what are we compelled to suppose as the order of events? We must suppose that the creatures, visited by some presentiment of what was to happen many months after, selected specimens of their number, and that these specimens by some unknown and quite inconceivable means crossed thousands of miles of sea, found their way through all kinds of perils from unaccustomed climate, food, and beasts of prey; singled out Noah by some inscrutable instinct, and surrendered themselves to his keeping. And after the year in the ark expired, they turned their faces homewards, leaving behind them no progeny, again preserving themselves intact, and transporting themselves by some unknown means to their island home. This, if the

Deluge was universal, must have been going on with thousands of animals from all parts of the globe; and not only were these animals a stupendous miracle in themselves, but wherever they went they were the occasion of miracle in others, all the beasts of prey refraining from their natural food. The fact is, the thing will not bear stating.

But it is not the physical but the moral aspects of the Flood with which we have here to do. And, first, this narrator explains its cause. He ascribes it to the abnormal wickedness of the antediluvians. To describe the demoralised condition of society before the Flood, the strongest language is used. "God saw that the wickedness of man was great," monstrous in acts of violence, and in habitual courses and established usages. "Every imagination of the thoughts of his heart was only evil continually,"—there was no mixture of good, no relentings, no repentances, no visitings of compunction, no hesitations and debatings. It was a world of men fierce and energetic, violent and lawless, in perpetual war and turmoil; in which if a man sought to live a righteous life, he had to conceive it of his own mind and to follow it out unaided and without the countenance of any.

This abnormal wickedness again is accounted for by the abnormal marriages from which the leaders of these ages sprang. Everything seemed abnormal, huge, inhuman. As there are laid bare to the eye of the geologist in those archaic times vast forms bearing a likeness to forms we are now familiar with, but of gigantic proportions and wallowing in dim, mist-covered regions; so to the eye of the historian there loom through the obscurity colossal forms perpetrating deeds of more than human savagery, and strength, and daring; heroes that seem formed in a different mould from common men.

However we interpret the narrative, its significance for us is plain. There is nothing prudish in the Bible. It speaks with a manly frankness of the beauty of women and its ensnaring power. The Mosaic law was stringent against intermarriage with idolatresses, and still in the New Testament something more than an echo of the old denunciation of such marriages is heard. Those who were most concerned about preserving a pure morality and a high tone in society were keenly alive to the dangers that threatened from this quarter. It is a permanent danger to character because it is to a permanent element in human nature that the temptation appeals. To many in every generation, perhaps to the majority, this is the most dangerous form in which worldliness presents itself; and to resist this the most painful test of principle. With natures keenly sensitive to beauty and superficial attractiveness, some are called upon to make their choice between a conscientious cleaving to God and an attachment to that which in the form is perfect but at heart is defective, depraved, godless. Where there is great outward attraction a man fights against the growing sense of inward uncongeniality, and persuades himself he is too scrupulous and uncharitable, or that he is a bad reader of character. There may be an undercurrent of warning; he may be sensible that his whole nature is not satisfied, and it may seem to him ominous that what is best within him does not flourish in his new attachment, but rather what is inferior, if not what is worst. But all such omens and warnings are disregarded and stifled by some such silly thought as that consideration and calculation are out of place in such matters. And what is the result? The result is the same as it ever was. Instead of the ungodly rising to the level of the godly, he sinks to hers. The worldly style, the amusements, the fashions once distasteful to him, but allowed for her sake, become familiar, and at last wholly displace the old and godly ways, the arrangements that left room for acknowledging God in the family; and there is one household less as a point of resistance to the incursion of an ungodly tone in society, one deserter more added to the already too crowded ranks of the ungodly, and the life-time if not the eternity of one soul embittered. Not without a consideration of the temptations that do actually lead men astray did the law enjoin: "Thou shalt not make a covenant with the inhabitants of the land, nor take of their daughters unto thy sons."

It seems like a truism to say that a greater amount of unhappiness has been produced by mismanagement, folly, and wickedness in the relation subsisting between men and women than by any other cause. God has given us the capacity of love to regulate this relation and be our safe guide in all matters connected with it. But frequently, from one cause or another, the government and direction of this relation are taken out of the hands of love and put into the thoroughly incompetent hands of convenience, or fancy, or selfish lust. A marriage contracted from any such motive is sure to bring unhappiness of a long-continued, wearing, and often heart-breaking kind. Such a marriage is often the form in which retribution comes for youthful selfishness and youthful licentiousness. You cannot cheat nature. Just in so far as you allow yourself to be ruled in youth by a selfish love of pleasure, in so far do you incapacitate yourself for love. You sacrifice what is genuine and satisfying, because provided by nature, to what is spurious, unsatisfying, and shameful. You cannot afterwards, unless by a long and bitter discipline, restore the capacity of warm and pure love in your heart. Every indulgence in which true love is absent is another blow given to the faculty of love within you—you make yourself in that capacity decrepit, paralyzed, dead. You have lost, you have killed the faculty that should be your guide in all these matters, and so you are at last precipitated without this guidance into a marriage formed from some other motive, formed therefore against nature, and in which you are the everlasting victim of nature's relentless justice. Remember that you cannot have both things, a youth of loveless pleasure and a loving marriage—you must make your choice. For as surely as genuine love kills all evil desire; so surely does evil desire kill the very capacity of love, and blind utterly its wretched victim to the qualities that ought to excite love.

The language used of God in relation to this universal corruption strikes every one as remarkable. "It repented the Lord that He had made man on the earth, and it grieved Him at His heart." This is what is usually termed anthropomorphism, $i.\,e.$, the presenting of God in terms applicable only to man; it is an instance of the same mode of speaking as is used when we speak of God's hand or eye or heart. These expressions are not absolutely true, but they are useful and convey to us a meaning which could scarcely otherwise be expressed. Some persons think that the use of these expressions proves that in early times God was thought of as wearing a body and as being very like ourselves in His inward nature. And even in our day we have been ridiculed for speaking of God as a magnified man. Now in the first place the use of such expressions does not prove that even the earliest worshippers of God believed Him to have eyes and hands and a body. *We* freely use the same expressions though we have no such belief. We use them because our language is formed for human uses and on a human level, and we have no capacity to frame a better. And in the second place, though not absolutely true they do help us towards the truth. We are told that it degrades God to think of Him as hearing prayer and accepting praise; nay, that to think of Him as a Person at all, is to degrade Him. We ought to think of Him as the Absolutely Unknowable. But which degrades God most, and which exalts Him most? If we find that it is impossible to worship an absolutely unknowable, if we find that practically such an idea is a mere nonentity to us, and that we cannot in point of fact pay any homage or show any consideration to such an empty abstraction, is not this really to lower God? And if we find that when we think of Him as a Person, and ascribe to Him all human virtue in an infinite degree, we can rejoice in Him and worship Him with true adoration, is not this to exalt Him? While we call Him our Father we know that this title is inadequate; while we speak of God as planning and decreeing we know that we are merely making shift to express what is inexpressible by us—we know that our thoughts of Him are never adequate and that to think of Him at all is to lower Him, is to think of Him inadequately; but when the practical alternative is such as it is, we find we do well to think of Him with the highest personal attributes we can conceive. For to refuse to ascribe such attributes to Him because this is degrading Him, is to empty our minds of any idea of Him which can stimulate either to worship or to duty. If by ridding our minds of all anthropomorphic ideas and refusing to think of God as feeling, thinking, acting as men do, we could thereby get to a really higher conception of Him, a conception which would practically make us worship Him more devotedly and serve Him more faithfully, then by all means let us do so. But if the result of refusing to think of Him as in many ways like ourselves, is that we cease to think of Him at all or only as a dead impersonal force, then this certainly is not to reach a higher but a lower conception of Him. And until we see our way to some truly higher conception than that which we have of a Personal God, we had better be content with it.

In short, we do well to be humble, and considering that we know very little about existence of any kind, and least of all about God's, and that our God has been presented to us in human form, we do well to accept Christ as our God, to worship, love, and serve Him, finding Him sufficient for all our wants of this life, and leaving it to other times to get the solution of anything that is not made plain to us in Him. This is one boon that the science and philosophy of our day have unintentionally conferred upon us. They have laboured to make us feel how remote and inaccessible God is, how little we can know Him, how truly He is past finding out; they have laboured to make us feel how intangible and invisible and incomprehensible God is, but the result of this is that we turn with all the stronger longing to Him who is the Image of the Invisible God, and on whom a voice has fallen from the excellent glory, "This is My beloved Son, hear Him."

The Flood itself we need not attempt to describe. It has been remarked that though the narrative is vivid and forcible, it is entirely wanting in that sort of description which in a modern historian or poet would have occupied the largest space. "We see nothing of the death-struggle; we hear not the cry of despair; we are not called upon to witness the frantic agony of husband and wife, and parent and child, as they fled in terror before the rising waters. Nor is a word said of the sadness of the one righteous man, who, safe himself, looked upon the destruction which he could not avert." The Chaldean tradition which is the most closely allied to the Biblical account is not so reticent. Tears are shed in heaven over the catastrophe, and even consternation affected its inhabitants, while within the ark itself the Chaldean Noah says, "When the storm came to an end and the terrible water-spout ceased, I opened the window and the light smote upon my face. I looked at the sea attentively observing, and the whole of humanity had returned to mud, like seaweed the corpses floated. I was seized with sadness; I sat down and wept and my tears fell upon my face."

There can be little question that this is a true description of Noah's feeling. And the sense of desolation and constraint would rather increase in Noah's mind than diminish. Month after month elapsed; he was coming daily nearer the end of his food, and yet the waters were unabated. He did not know how long he was to be kept in this dark, disagreeable place. He was left to do his daily work without any supernatural signs to help him against his natural anxieties. The floating of the ark and all that went on in it had no mark of God's hand upon it. He was indeed *safe* while others had been destroyed. But of what good was this safety to be? Was he ever to get out of this prison-house? To what straits was he to be first reduced? So it is often with ourselves. We are left to fulfil God's will without any sensible tokens to set over against natural difficulties, painful and pinching circumstances, ill health, low spirits, failure of favourite projects and old hopes—so that at last we come to think that perhaps safety is all we are to have in Christ, a mere exemption from suffering of one kind purchased by the endurance of much suffering of another kind; that we are to be thankful for pardon on any terms; and escaping with our *life*, must be content though it be bare. Why, how often does a Christian wonder whether, after all, he has chosen a life that he can endure, whether the monotony and the restraints of the Christian life are not inconsistent with true enjoyment?

This strife between the felt restriction of the Christian life and the natural craving for abundant life, for entrance into all that the world can show us, and experience of all forms of enjoyment—this strife goes on unceasingly in the heart of many of us as it goes on from age to age in the world. Which is the true view of life, which is the view to guide *us* in choosing and refusing the enjoyments and pursuits that are presented to us? Are we to believe that the ideal man for this life is he who has tasted all culture and delight, who believes in nature, recognising no fall and seeking for no redemption, and makes enjoyment his end; or he who sees that all enjoyment is deceptive till man is set right morally, and who spends himself on this, knowing that blood and misery must come before peace and rest, and crowned as our King and Leader, not with a garland of roses, but with the crown of Him Who is greatest of all, because servant of all—to Whom the most sunken is not repulsive, and Who will not abandon the most hopeless? This comes to be very much the question, whether this life is final or preparatory?—whether, therefore, our work in it should be to check lower propensities and develop and train all that is best in character, so as to be fit for highest life and enjoyment in a world to come—or should take ourselves as we find ourselves, and delight in this present world? whether this is a placid eternal state, in which things are very much as they should be, and in which therefore we can live freely and enjoy freely; or whether it is a disordered, initial condition in which our main task should be to do a little towards putting things on a better rail and getting at least the germ and small beginnings of future good planted in one another? So that in the midst of all felt restriction, there is the highest hope, that one day we shall go forth from the narrow precincts of our ark, and step out into the free bright sunshine, in a world where there is nothing to offend, and that the time of our deprivation will seem to have been well spent indeed, if it has left within us a capacity permanently to enjoy love, holiness, justice, and all that is delighted in by God Himself.

The use made of this event in the New Testament is remarkable. It is compared by Peter to baptism, and both are viewed as illustrations of salvation by destruction. The eight souls, he says, who were in the ark, "were saved by water." The water which destroyed the rest saved them. When there seemed little hope of the godly line being able to withstand the influence of the ungodly, the Flood came and left Noah's family in a new world, with freedom to order all things according to their own ideas. In this Peter sees some analogy to baptism. In baptism, the penitent who believes in the efficacy of Christ's blood to purge away sin, lets his defilement be washed away and rises new and clean to the life Christ gives. In Christ the sinner finds shelter for himself and destruction for his sins. It is God's wrath against sin that saves us by destroying our sins; just as it was the Flood which devastated the world, that at the same time, and thereby, saved Noah and his family.

In this event, too, we see the completeness of God's work. Often we feel reluctant to surrender our sinful habits to so final a destruction as is implied in being one with Christ. The expense at which holiness is to be bought seems almost too great. So much that has given us pleasure must be parted with; so many old ties sundered, a condition of holiness presents an aspect of dreariness and hopelessness; like the world after the flood, not a moving thing on the surface of the earth, everything levelled, prostrate, and washed even with the ground; here the corpse of a man, there the carcase of a beast; here mighty forest timber swept prone like the rushes on the banks of a flooded stream, and there a city without inhabitants, everything dank, dismal, and repellent. But this is only one aspect of the work; the beginning, necessary if the work is to be thorough. If any part of the sinful life remain it will spring up to mar what God means to introduce us to. Only that is to be preserved which we can take with us into our ark. Only that is to pass on into our life which we can retain while we are in true connection with Christ, and which we think can help us to live as His friends, and to serve Him zealously.

This event then gives us some measure by which we can know how much God will do to maintain holiness upon earth. In this catastrophe every one who strives after godliness may find encouragement, seeing in it the Divine earnestness of God for good and against evil. There is only one other event in history that so conspicuously shows that holiness among men is the object for which God will sacrifice everything else. There is no need now of any further demonstration of God's purpose in this world and His zeal for carrying it out. And may it not be expected of us His children, that we stand in presence of the cross until our cold and frivolous hearts catch something of the earnestness, the "resisting unto blood striving against sin," which is exhibited there? The Flood has not been forgotten by almost any people under heaven, but its moral result is *nil*. But he whose memory is haunted by a dying Redeemer, by the thought of One Whose love found its most appropriate and practical result in dying for him, *is* prevented from much sin, and finds in that love the spring of eternal hope, that which his soul in the deep privacy of his most sacred thoughts can feed upon with joy, that which he builds himself round and broods over as his inalienable possession.

CHAPTER VI.

NOAH'S FALL.

GENESIS ix. 20-27.

NOAH in the ark was in a position of present safety but of much anxiety. No sign of any special protection on God's part was given. The waters seemed to stand at their highest level still; and probably the risk of the ark's grounding on some impracticable peak, or precipitous hill-side, would seem as great a danger as the water itself. Five months had elapsed, and though the rain had ceased the sky was heavy and threatening, and every day now was worth many measures of corn in the coming harvest. A reflection of the anxiety within the ark is seen in the expression, "And God remembered Noah." It was needful to say so, for there was as yet no outward sign of this.

To such anxieties all are subject who have availed themselves of the salvation God provides. At the first there is an easy faith in God's aid; there are many signs of His presence; the subjects in whom salvation operates have no disposition or temptation to doubt that God is with them and is working for them. But this initial stage is succeeded by a very different state of things. We seem to be left to ourselves to cope with the world and all its difficulties and temptations in our own strength. Much as we crave some sign that God remembers us, no sign is given. We no longer receive the same urgent impulses to holiness of life; we have no longer the same freshness in devotion as if speaking to a God at hand. There is nothing which of itself and without reasoning about it says to us, Here is God's hand upon me.

In fact, the great part of our life has to be spent under these conditions, and we need to hold some well-ascertained principle regarding God's dealings, if our faith is to survive. And here in God's treatment of Noah we see that God may as certainly be working for us when not working directly upon us, as when His presence is palpable. His absence from us is as needful as His presence. The clouds are as requisite for our salvation as the sunny sky. When therefore we find that salvation from sin is a much slower and more anxious matter than we once expected it to be, we are not to suppose that God is not hearing our prayers. When Noah day by day cried to God for relief, and yet night after night found himself "cribb'd, cabin'd, and confined," with no sign from God but such as faith could apprehend, depend upon it he had very different feelings from those with which he first stepped into the ark. And when we are left to one monotonous rut of duty and to an unchanging and dry form of devotion, when we are called to learn to live by faith, not by sight, to learn that God's purposes with us are spiritual, and that slow and difficult growth in self-command and holiness is the best proof that He hears our prayers, we must strive to believe that this also, is a needful part of our salvation; and we must especially be on our guard against supposing that as God has ceased to disclose Himself to us, and so to make faith easy, we may cease to disclose ourselves to Him.

For this is the natural and very frequent result of such an experience. Discouraged by the obscurity of God's ways and the difficulty of believing when the mind is not sustained by success or by new thoughts or manifest tokens of God's presence, we naturally cease to look for any clear signs of God's concernment about our state, and rest from all anxious craving to know God's will about us. To this temptation the majority of Christian people yield, and allow themselves to become indifferent to spiritual truth and increasingly interested in the non-mysterious facts of the present world, attending to present duties in a mechanical way, seeing that their families have enough to eat and that all in their little ark are provided for. But to this temptation Noah did not yield. Though to all appearance abandoned by God, he did what he could to ascertain what was beyond his immediate sight and present experience. He sent out his raven and his dove. Not satisfied with his first enquiry by the raven, which could flit from one piece of floating garbage to another, he sent out the dove, and continued to do so at intervals of seven days.

Noah sent out the raven first, probably because it had been the most companionable bird and seemed the wisest, preferable to "the silly dove;" but it never came back with God's message. And so has one often found that an enquiry into God's will, the examination, for example, of some portion of Scripture, undertaken with a prospect of success and with good human helps, has failed, and has failed in this peculiar ravenlike way; the enquiry has settled down on some worthless point, on some rotting carcase, on some subject of passing interest or worldly learning, and brings back no message of God to us. On the other hand, the continued use, Sabbath after Sabbath, of God's appointed means, and the patient waiting for some message of God to come to us through what seems a most unlikely messenger, will often be rewarded. It may be but a single leaf plucked off that we get, but enough to convince us that God has been mindful of our need, and is preparing for us a habitable world.

Many a man is like the raven, feeding himself on the destruction of others, satisfied with knowing how God has dealt with others. He thinks he has done his part when he has found out who has been sinning and what has been the result. But the dove will not settle on any such resting-place, and is dissatisfied until for herself she can pluck off some token that God's anger is turned away and that now there is peace on earth. And if only you wait God's time and renew your endeavours to find such tokens, some assurance will be given you, some green and growing thing, some living part, however small, of the new creation which will certify you of your hope.

On the first day of the first month, New Year's day, Noah removed the covering of the ark, which seems to have stranded on the Armenian tableland, and looked out upon the new world. He cannot but have felt his responsibility, as a kind of second Adam. And many questionings must have arisen in his mind regarding the relation of the new to the old. Was there to be any connection with the old world at all, or was all to begin afresh? Were the promises, the traditions, the events, the genealogies of the old world of any significance now? The Flood distinctly marked the going out of one order of things and the establishment of another. Man's career and development, or what we call history, had not before the Flood attained its goal. If this development was not to be broken short off, and if God's purpose in creation was to be fulfilled, then the world must still go on. Some worlds may perhaps die young, as individuals die young. Others endure through hair-breadth escapes and constant dangers, find their way like our planet through showers of fire, and pass without collision the orbits of huge bodies, carrying with them always, as our world does, the materials of their destruction within themselves. But catastrophes do not cut short, but evolve God's purposes. The Flood came that God's purpose might be fulfilled. The course of nature was interrupted, the arrangements of social and domestic life were overturned, all the works of men were swept away that this purpose might be fulfilled. It was expedient that one generation should die for all generations; and this generation having been taken out of the way, fresh provision is made for the co-operation of man with God. On man's part there is an emphatic acknowledgment of God by sacrifice; on God's part there is a renewed grant to man of the world and its fulness, a renewed assurance of His favour.

This covenant with Noah was on the plane of nature. It is man's natural life in the world which is the subject of it. The sacredness of life is its great lesson. Men might well wonder whether God did not hold life cheap. In the old world violence had prevailed. But while Lamech's sword may have slain its thousands, God had in the Flood slain tens of thousands. The covenant, therefore, directs that human life must be reverenced. The primal blessing is renewed. Men are to multiply and replenish the earth; and the slaughter of a man was to be reckoned a capital crime; and the maintenance of life was guaranteed by a special clause, securing the regularity of the seasons. If, then, you ask, Was this just a beginning again where Adam began? Did God just wipe out man as a boy wipes his slate clean, when he finds his calculation is turning out wrong? Had all these generations learned nothing; had the world not grown at all since its birth?—the answer is, it had grown, and in two most important respects, —it had come to the knowledge of the uniformity of nature and the necessity of human law. This great departure from the uniformity of nature brought into strong relief its normal uniformity, and gave men their first lesson in the recognition of a God who governs by fixed laws. And they learned also from the Flood that wickedness must not be allowed to grow unchecked and attain dimensions which nothing short of a flood can cope with.

Fit symbol of this covenant was the rainbow. Seeming to unite heaven and earth, it pictured to those primitive people the friendliness existing between God and man. Many nations have looked upon it as not merely one of the most beautiful and striking objects in nature, but as the messenger of heaven to men. And arching over the whole horizon, it exhibits the all-embracing universality of the promise. They accepted it as a sign that God has no pleasure in destruction, that He does not give way to moods, that He does not always chide, that if weeping may endure for a night joy is sure to follow. If any one is under a cloud, leading a joyless, hopeless, heartless life, if any one has much apparent reason to suppose that God has given him up to catastrophe, and lets things run as they may, there is some satisfaction in reading this natural emblem and recognising that without the cloud, nay, without the cloud breaking into heavy sweeping rains, there cannot be the bow, and that no cloud of God's sending is permanent, but will one day give place to unclouded joy. Let the prayer of David be yours, "I know, O Lord, that Thy judgments are right, and that Thou in faithfulness hast afflicted me. Let, I pray Thee, Thy merciful kindness be for my comfort according to Thy word unto Thy servant."

It may be felt that the matters about which God spoke to Noah were barely religious, certainly not spiritual. But to take God as our God in any one particular is to take Him as our God for all. If we can eat our daily bread as given to us by our Father in heaven, then we are heirs of the righteousness which is by faith. It is because we wait for some wonderful and out-of-the-way proofs that God is keeping faith with us that we so much lack a real and living faith. If you think of God only in connection with some spiritual difficulty, or if you are waiting for some critical spiritual experience about which you may deal with God,—if you are not transacting with Him about your daily work, about your temporal wants and difficulties, about your friendships and your tastes, about that which makes up the bulk of your thought, feeling, and action,—then you have yet to learn what living with God means. You have yet to learn that God the Infinite Creator of all is present in all your life. We are not in advance of Noah, but behind him, if we cannot speak to God about common things.

Besides, the relation of man to God was sufficiently determined by this covenant. When any man in that age began to ask himself the question which all men in all ages ask, How shall I win the favour of God? it must, or it might, at once have struck him, Why, God has already favoured me and has bound Himself to me by express and solemn pledges. And radically this is all that any one needs to know. It is not a change in God's attitude towards you that is required. What is required is that you believe what is actually the case, that the Holy God loves you already and is already seeking to bless you by making you like Himself. Believe that, and let the faith of it sink more and more deeply into your spirit, and you will find that you are saved from your sin.

What remains to be told of Noah is full of moral significance. Rare indeed is a *wholly* good man; and happy indeed is he who throughout his youth, his manhood, and his age lets principle govern all his actions. The righteous and rescued Noah lying drunk on his tent-floor is a sorrowful spectacle. God had given him the earth, and this was the use he made of the gift; melancholy presage of the fashion of his posterity. He had God to help him to bear his responsibilities, to refresh and gladden him; but he preferred the fruit of his vineyard. Can the most sacred or impressive memories secure a man against sin? Noah had the memory of a race drowned for sin and of a year in solitude with God. Can the dignity and weight of responsibility steady a man? This man knew that to him God had declared His purpose and that he only could carry it forward to fulfilment. In that heavy, helpless figure, fallen insensible in his tent, is as significant a warning as in the Flood.

Noah's sin brings before us two facts about sin. First, that the smaller temptations are often the most effectual. The man who is invulnerable on the field of battle amidst declared and strong enemies falls an easy prey to the assassin in his own home. When all the world was against him, Noah was able to face single-handed both scorn and violence, but in the midst of his vineyard, among his own people who understood him and needed no preaching or proof of his virtue, he relaxed.

He was no longer in circumstances so difficult as to force him to watch and pray, as to drive him to God's side. The temptations Noah had before known were mainly from without; he now learnt that those from within are more serious. Many of us find it comparatively easy to carry clean hands before the public, or to demean ourselves with tolerable seemliness in circumstances where the temptation may be very strong but is also very patent; but how careless are we often in our domestic life, and how little strain do we put upon ourselves in the company of those whom we can trust. What petulance and irritability, what angry and slanderous words, what sensuality and indolence could our own homes witness to! Noah is not the only man who has walked uprightly and kept his garment unspotted from the world so long as the eye of man was on him, but who has lain uncovered on his own tent-floor.

Secondly, we see here how a man may fall into new forms of sin, and are reminded especially of one of the most distressing facts to be observed in the world, viz., that men in their prime and even in their old age are sometimes overtaken in sins of sensuality from which hitherto they have kept themselves pure. We are very ready to think we know the full extent of wickedness to which we may go; that by certain sins *we* shall never be much tempted. And in some of our predictions we may be correct; our temperament or our circumstances may absolutely preclude some sins from mastering us. Yet who has made but a slight alteration in his circumstances, added a little to his business, made some new family arrangements, or changed his residence, without being astonished to find how many new sources of evil seem to have been opened within him? While therefore you rejoice over sins defeated, beware of thinking your work is nearly done. Especially let those of us who have for years been fighting mainly against one sin beware of thinking that if only *that* were defeated we should be free from sin. As a man who has long suffered from one bodily disease congratulates himself that at least he knows what he may expect in the way of pain, and will not suffer as some other man he has heard of does suffer; whereas though one disease may kill others, yet some diseases only prepare the body for the assault of worse ailments than themselves, and the constitution at last breaks up under a combination of ills that make the sufferer a pity to his friends and a perplexity to his physicians. And so is it in the spirit; you cannot say that because you are so consumed by one infirmity, others can find no room in you. In short, there is nothing that can secure us against the unspeakable calamity of falling into new sins, except the direction given by our Lord, "Watch and pray, lest ye enter into temptation." There *is need* of watching, else this precept had never been uttered; too many things absolutely needful for us to do have to be enjoined upon us to leave any room for the injunction of precepts that are unnecessary, and he who is not watching has no security that he shall not sin so as to be a scandal to his friends and a shame to himself.

Noah's sin brought to light the character of his three sons—the coarse irreverence of Ham, the dignified delicacy and honour of Shem and Japheth. The bearing of men towards the sins of others is always a touch-stone of character. The full exposure of sin where good is expected to come of the exposure and when it is done with sorrow and with shame is one thing, and the exposure of sin to create a laugh and merely to amuse is another. They are the true descendants of Ham, whether their faces be black or white, and whether they go with no clothes or with clothes that are the product of much thought and anxiety, who find pleasure in the mere contemplation of deeds of shame, in real life, on the boards of the theatre, in daily journals, or in works of fiction. Extremes meet, and the savage grossness of Ham is found in many who count themselves the last and finest product of culture. It is found also in the harder and narrower set of modern investigators, who glory in exposing the scientific weakness of our forefathers, and make a jest of the mistakes of men to whom they owe much of their freedom, and whose shoe latchet they are not worthy to tie, so far as the deeper moral qualities go.

But neither is religious society free from this same sin. The faults and mistakes and sins of others are talked over, possibly with some show of regret, but with, as we know, very little real shame and sadness, for these feelings prompt us, not to talk them over in companies where no good can be done in the way of remedy, but to cover them as these sorrowing sons of Noah, with averted eye and humbled head. Charity is the prime grace enjoined upon us and charity *covers* a multitude of sins. And whatever excuses for exposing others we may make, however we may say it is only a love of truth and fair play that makes us drag to light the infirmities of a man whom others are praising, we may be very sure that if all *evil* motives were absent this kind of evil speaking would cease among us. But there is a malignity in sin that leaves its bitter root in us all, and causes us to be glad when those whom we have been regarding as our superiors are reduced to our poor level. And there is a cowardliness in sin which cannot bear to be alone, and eagerly hails every symptom of others being in the same condemnation.

Before exposing another, think first whether your own conduct could bear a similar treatment, whether you have never done the thing you desire to conceal, said the thing you would blush to hear repeated, or thought the thought you could not bear another to read. And if you be a Christian, does it not become you to remember what you yourself have learnt of the slipperiness of this world's ways, of your liability to fall, of your sudden exposure to sin from some physical disorder, or some slight mistake which greatly extenuates your sin, but which you could not plead before another? And do you know nothing of the difficulty of conquering one sin that is rooted in your constitution, and the strife that goes on in a man's own soul and in secret though he show little immediate fruit of it in his life before men? Surely it becomes us to give a man credit for much good resolution and much sore self-denial and endeavour, even when he fails and sins still, because such we know to be our own case, and if we disbelieve in others until they can walk with perfect rectitude, if we condemn them for one or two flaws and blemishes, we shall be tempted to show the same want of charity towards ourselves, and fall at length into that miserable and hopeless condition that believes in no regenerating spirit nor in any holiness attainable by us.

CHAPTER VII.

THE CALL OF ABRAHAM.

Genesis xi. 27-xii. 5.

With Abraham there opens a new chapter in the history of the race; a chapter of the profoundest significance. The consequences of Abraham's movements and beliefs have been limitless and enduring. All succeeding time has been influenced by him. And yet there is in his life a remarkable simplicity, and an entire absence of such events as impress contemporaries. Among all the forgotten millions of his own time he stands alone a recognisable and memorable figure. But around his figure there gathers no throng of armed followers; with his name, no vast territorial dominion, no new legislation, not even any work of literature or art is associated. The significance of his life was not military, nor legislative, nor literary, but religious. To him must be carried back the belief in one God. We find him born and brought up among idolaters; and although it is certain there were others besides himself who here and there upon earth had dimly arrived at the same belief as he, yet it is certainly from him the Monotheistic belief has been diffused. Since his day the world has never been without its explicit advocacy. It is his belief in the true God, in a God who manifested His existence and His nature by responding to this belief, it is this belief and the place he gave it as the regulating principle of all his movements and thoughts, that have given him his everlasting influence.

With Abraham there is also introduced the first step in a new method adopted by God in the training of men. The dispersion of men and the divergence of their languages are now seen to have been the necessary preliminary to this new step in the education of the world—the fencing round of one people till they should learn to know God and understand and exemplify His government. It is true, God reveals Himself to all men and governs all; but by selecting one race with special adaptations, and by giving to it a special training, God might more securely and more rapidly reveal Himself to all. Each nation has certain characteristics, a national character which grows by seclusion from the influences which are forming other races. There is a certain mental and moral individuality stamped upon every separate people. Nothing is more certainly retained; nothing more certainly handed down from generation to generation. It would therefore be a good practical means of conserving and deepening the knowledge of God, if it were made the national interest of a people to preserve it, and if it were closely identified with the national characteristics. This was the method adopted by God. He meant to combine allegiance to Himself with national advantages, and spiritual with national character, and separation in belief with a distinctly outlined and defensible territory.

This method, in common with all Divine methods, was in strict keeping with the natural evolution of history. The migration of Abraham occurred in the epoch of migrations. But although for centuries before Abraham new nations had been forming, none of them had belief in God as its formative principle. Wave upon wave of warriors, shepherds, colonists have left the prolific plains of Mesopotamia. Swarm after swarm has left that busy hive, pushing one another further and further west and east, but all have been urged by natural impulses, by hunger, commerce, love of adventure and conquest. By natural likings and dislikings, by policy, and by dint of force the multitudinous tribes of men were finding their places in the world, the weaker being driven to the hills, and being schooled there by hard living till their descendants came down and conquered their conquerors. All this went on without regard to any very high motives. As it was with the Goths who invaded Italy for her wealth, as it is now with those who people America and Africa because there is land or room enough, so it was then. But at last God selects one man and says, "*I* will make of thee a great nation." The origin of this nation is not facile love of change nor lust of territory, but belief in God. Without this belief this people had not been. No other account can be given of its origin. Abraham is himself already the member of a tribe, well-off and likely to be well-off; he has no large family to provide for, but he is separated from his kindred and country, and led out to be himself a new beginning, and this because, as he himself throughout his life said, he heard God's call and responded to it.

The city which claims the distinction of being Abraham's birthplace, or at least of giving its name to the district where he was born, is now represented by a few mounds of ruins rising out of the flat marshy ground on the western bank of the Euphrates, not far above the point where it joins its waters to those of the Tigris and glides on to the Persian gulf. In the time of Abraham, Ur was the capital city which gave its name to one of the most populous and fertile regions of the earth. The whole land of Accad, which ran up from the sea-coast to Upper Mesopotamia (or Shinar), seems to have been known as Ur-ma, the land of Ur. This land was of no great extent, being little if at all larger than Scotland, but it was the richest of Asia. The high civilisation which this land enjoyed even in the time of Abraham has been disclosed in the abundant and multifarious Babylonian remains which have recently been brought to light.

What induced Terah to abandon so prosperous a land can only be conjectured. It is possible that the idolatrous customs of the inhabitants may have had something to do with his movements. For while the ancient Babylonian records reveal a civilisation surprisingly advanced, and a social order in some respects admirable, they also make disclosures regarding the worship of the gods which must shock even those who are familiar with the immoralities frequently fostered by heathen religions. The city of Ur was not only the capital, it was the holy city of the Chaldeans. In its northern quarter rose high above the surrounding buildings the successive stages of the temple of the moon-god, culminating in a platform on which the priests could both accurately observe the motions of the stars and hold their night-watches in honour of their god. In the courts of this temple might be heard breaking the silence of midnight one of those magnificent hymns, still preserved, in which idolatry is seen in its most attractive dress, and in which the Lord of Ur is invoked in terms not unworthy of the living God. But in these same temple-courts Abraham may have seen the firstborn led to the altar, the fruit of the body sacrificed to atone for the sin of the soul; and here too he must have seen other sights even more shocking and repulsive. Here he was no doubt taught that strangely mixed religion which clung for generations to some members of his family. Certainly he was taught in common with the whole community to rest on the seventh day; as he was trained to look to the stars with reverence and to the moon as something more than the light which was set to rule the night.

Possibly then Terah may have been induced to move northwards by a desire to shake himself free from customs he disapproved. The Hebrews themselves seem always to have considered that his migration had a religious motive. "This people," says one of their old writings, "is descended from the Chaldeans, and they sojourned heretofore in Mesopotamia because they would not follow the gods of their fathers which were in the land of Chaldea. For they left the way of their ancestors and worshipped the God of heaven, the God whom they knew; so they cast them out from the face of their gods, and they fled into Mesopotamia and sojourned there many days. Then their God commanded them to depart from the place where they sojourned and to go into the land of Canaan." But if this is a true account of the origin of the movement northwards, it must have been Abraham rather than his father who was the moving spirit of it; for it is certainly Abraham and not Terah who stands as the significant figure inaugurating the new era.

If doubt rests on the moving cause of the migration from Ur, none rests on that which prompted Abraham to leave Charran and journey towards Canaan. He did so in obedience to what he believed to be a Divine command, and in faith on what he understood to be a Divine promise. How he became aware that a Divine command thus lay upon him we do not know. Nothing could persuade him that he was not commanded. Day by day he heard in his soul what he recognised as a Divine voice, saying: "Get thee out of thy country and from thy kindred and from thy father's house, unto a land that I will show thee!" This was God's first revelation of Himself to Abraham. Up to this time Abraham to all appearance had no knowledge of any God but the deities worshipped by his fathers in Chaldea. Now, he finds within himself impulses which he cannot resist and which he is conscious he ought not to resist. He believes it to be his duty to adopt a course which may look foolish and which he can justify only by saying that his conscience bids him. He recognises, apparently for the first time, that through his conscience there speaks to him a God Who is supreme. In dependence on this God he gathered his possessions together and departed.

So far, one may be tempted to say, no very unusual faith was required. Many a poor girl has followed a weakly brother or a dissipated father to Australia or the wild west of America; many a lad has gone to the deadly west coast of Africa with no such prospects as Abraham. For Abraham had the double prospect which makes migration desirable. Assure the colonist that he will find land and have strong sons to till and hold and leave it to, and you give him all the motive he requires. These were the promises made to Abraham—a land and a seed. Neither was there at this period much difficulty in believing that both promises would be fulfilled. The land he no doubt expected to find in some unoccupied territory. And as regards the children, he had not yet faced the condition that only through Sarah was this part of the promise to be fulfilled.

But the peculiarity in Abraham's abandonment of present certainties for the sake of a future and unseen good is, that it was prompted not by family affection or greed or an adventurous disposition, but by faith in a God Whom no one but himself recognised. It was the first step in a life-long adherence to an Invisible, Spiritual Supreme. It was that first step which committed him to life-long dependence upon and intercourse with One Who had authority to regulate his movements and power to bless him. From this time forth all that he sought in life was the fulfilment of God's promise. He staked his future upon God's existence and faithfulness. Had Abraham abandoned Charran at the command of a widely ruling monarch who promised him ample compensation, no record would have been made of so ordinary a transaction. But this was an entirely new thing and well worth recording, that a man should leave country and kindred and seek an unknown land under the impression that thus he was obeying the command of the unseen God. While others worshipped sun, moon, and stars, and recognised the Divine in their brilliance and power, in their exaltation above earth and control of earth and its life, Abraham saw that there was something greater than the order of nature and more worthy of worship, even the still small voice that spoke within his own conscience of right and wrong in human conduct, and that told him how his own life must be ordered. While all around him were bowing down to the heavenly host and sacrificing to them the highest things in human nature, he heard a voice falling from these shining ministers of God's will, which said to him, "See thou do it not, for we are thy fellow-servants; worship thou God!" This was the triumph of the spiritual over the material; the acknowledgment that in God there is something greater than can be found in nature; that man finds his true affinity not in the things that are seen but in the unseen Spirit that is over all. It is this that gives to the figure of Abraham its simple grandeur and its permanent significance.

Under the simple statement "The Lord said unto Abram, Get thee out of thy country," there are probably hidden years of questioning and meditation. God's revelation of Himself to Abram in all probability did not take the determinate form of articulate command without having passed through many preliminary stages of surmise and doubt and mental conflict. But once assured that God is calling him, Abraham responds quickly and resolutely. The revelation has come to a mind in which it will not be lost. As one of the few theologians who have paid attention to the method of revelation has said: "A Divine revelation does not dispense with a certain character and certain qualities of mind in the person who is the instrument of it. A man who throws off the chains of authority and association must be a man of extraordinary independence and strength of mind, although he does so in obedience to a Divine revelation; because no miracle, no sign or wonder which accompanies a revelation can by its simple stroke force human nature from the innate hold of custom and the adhesion to and fear of established opinion; can enable it to confront the frowns of men, and take up truth opposed to general prejudice, except there is in the man himself, who is the recipient of the revelation, a certain strength of mind and independence which concurs with the Divine intention."

That Abraham's faith triumphed over exceptional difficulties and enabled him to do what no other motive would have been strong enough to accomplish, there is therefore no call to assert. During his after-life his faith was severely tried, but the mere abandonment of his country in the hope of gaining a better was the ordinary motive of his day. It was the *ground* of this hope, the belief in God, which made Abraham's conduct original and fruitful. That sufficient inducement was presented to him is only to say that God is reasonable. There is always sufficient inducement to obey God; because life is reasonable. No man was ever commanded or required to do anything which it was not for his advantage to do. Sin is a mistake. But so weak are we, so liable to be moved by the things present to us and by the desire for immediate gratification, that it never ceases to be wonderful and admirable when a sense of duty enables a man to forego present advantage and to believe that present loss is the needful preliminary of eternal gain.

Abraham's faith is chosen by the author of the Epistle to the Hebrews as an apt illustration of his definition of Faith, that it is "the substance of things hoped for, the evidence of things not seen." One property of faith is that it gives to things future, and which are as yet only hoped for, all the reality of actual present existence. Future things may be said to have no existence for those who do not believe in them. They are not taken into account. Men do not shape their conduct with any reference to them. But when a man believes in certain events that are to be, this faith of his lends to these future things the reality, the "substance" which things actually existing in the present have. They have the same weight with him, the same influence upon his conduct.

Without some power to realise the future and to take account of what is to be as well as of what already is, we could not carry on the common affairs of life. And success in life very greatly depends on foresight, or the power to see clearly what is to be and give it due weight. The man who has no foresight makes his plans, but being unable to apprehend the future his plans are disconcerted. Indeed it is one of the most valuable gifts a man can have, to be able to say with tolerable accuracy what is to happen and what is not; to be able to sift rumours, common talk, popular impressions, probabilities, chances, and to be able to feel sure what the future will really be; to be able to weigh the character and commercial prospects of the men he deals with, so as to see what must be the issue of their operations and whom he may trust. Many of our most serious mistakes in life arise from our inability to imagine the consequences of our actions and to forefeel how these consequences will affect us.

Now faith largely supplies the want of this imaginative foresight. It lends substance to things future. It believes the account given of the future by a trustworthy authority. In many ordinary matters all men are dependent on the testimony of others for their knowledge of the result of certain operations. The astronomer, the physiologist, the navigator, each has his department within which his predictions are accepted as authoritative. But for what is beyond the ken of science no faith in our fellow-men avails. Feeling that if there is a life beyond the grave, it must have important bearings on the present, we have yet no data by which to calculate what will then be, or only data so difficult to use that our calculations are but guesswork. But faith accepts the testimony of God as unhesitatingly as that of man and gives reality to the future He describes and promises. It believes that the life God calls us to is a better life, and it enters upon it. It believes that there is a world to come in which all things are new and all things eternal; and, so believing, it cannot but feel less anxious to cling to this world's goods. That which embitters all loss and deepens sorrow is the feeling that this world is all; but faith makes eternity as real as time and gives substantial existence to that new and limitless future in which we shall have time to forget the sorrows and live past the losses of this present world.

The radical elements of greatness are identical from age to age, and the primal duties which no good man can evade do not vary as the world grows older. What we admire in Abraham we feel to be incumbent on ourselves. Indeed the uniform call of Christ to all His followers is even in form almost identical with that which stirred Abraham, and made him the father of the faithful. "Follow Me," says our Lord, "and every one that forsaketh houses, or brethren, or sisters, or father, or mother, or wife, or children, or lands, for My name's sake, shall receive an hundredfold, and shall inherit everlasting life." And there is something perennially edifying in the spectacle of a man who believes that God has a place and a use for him in the world, and who puts himself at God's disposal; who enters upon life refusing to be bound by the circumstances of his upbringing, by the expectations of his friends, by prevailing customs, by prospect of gain and advancement among men; and resolved to listen to the highest voice of all, to discover what God has for him to do upon earth and where he is likely to find most of God; who virtually and with deepest sincerity says, Let God choose my destination: I have good land here, but if God wishes me elsewhere, elsewhere I go: who, in one word, believes in the call of God to himself, who admits it into the springs of his conduct, and recognises that for him also the highest life his conscience can suggest is the only life he can live, no matter how cumbrous and troublesome and expensive be the changes involved in entering it. Let the spectacle take hold of your imagination—the spectacle of a man believing that there is something more akin to himself and higher than the material life and the great laws that govern it, and going calmly and hopefully forward into the unknown, because he knows that God is with him, that in God is our true life, that man liveth not by bread only, but by every word that cometh out of the mouth of God.

Even thus then may we bring our faith to a true and reliable test. All men who have a confident expectation of future good make sacrifices or run risks to obtain it. Mercantile life proceeds on the understanding that such ventures are reasonable and will always be made. Men might if they liked spend their money on present pleasure, but they rarely do so. They prefer to put it into concerns or transactions from which they expect to reap large returns. They have faith, and as a necessary consequence they make ventures. So did these Hebrews—they ran a great risk, they gave up the sole means of livelihood they had any experience of and entered what they knew to be a bare desert, because they believed in the land that lay beyond and in God's promise. What then has your faith done? What have you ventured that you would not have ventured but for God's promise. Suppose Christ's promise failed, in what would you be the losers? Of course you would lose what you call your hope of heaven—but what would you find you had lost in this world? When a merchant's ships are wrecked or when his investment turns out bad, he loses not only the gain he hoped for, but the means he risked. Suppose then Christ were declared bankrupt, unable to fulfil your expectations, would you really find that you had ventured so much upon His promise that you are deeply involved in His bankruptcy, and are much worse off in this world and now than you would otherwise have been? Or may I not use the words of one of the most cautious and charitable of men, and say, " I really fear, when we come to examine, it will be found that there is nothing we resolve, nothing we do, nothing we do not do, nothing we avoid, nothing we choose, nothing we give up, nothing we pursue, which we should not resolve, and do, and not do, and avoid, and choose, and give up, and pursue, if Christ had not died and heaven were not promised us." If this be the case—if you would be neither much better nor much worse though Christianity were a fable—if you have in nothing become poorer in this world that your reward in heaven may be greater, if you have made no investments and run no risks, then really the natural inference is that your faith in the future inheritance is small. Barnabas sold his Cyprus property because he believed heaven was his, and his bit of land suddenly became a small consideration; useful only in so far as he could with the mammon of unrighteousness make himself a mansion in heaven. Paul gave up his prospects of advancement in the nation, of which he would of course as certainly have become the leader and first man as he took that position in the Church, and plainly tells us that having made so large a venture on Christ's word, he would if his word failed be a great loser, of all men most miserable because he had risked his all *in this life* on it. People sometimes take offence at Paul's plain way of speaking of the sacrifices he had made, and of Peter's plain way of saying " we have left all and followed Thee, what shall we have therefore?" but when people have made sacrifices they know it and can specify them, and a faith that makes no sacrifices is no good either in this world's affairs or in religion. Self-consciousness may not be a very good thing: but self-deception is a worse.

Here as elsewhere a clear hope sprang from faith. Recognising God, Abraham knew that there was for men a great future. He looked forward to a time when all men should believe as he did, and in him all families of the earth be blessed. No doubt in these early days, when all men were on the move and striving to make a name and a place for themselves, an onward look might be common. But the far-reaching extent, the certainty, and the definiteness of Abraham's view of the future were unexampled. There far back in the hazy dawn he stood while the morning mists hid the horizon from every other eye, and he alone discerns what is to be. One clear voice and one only rings out in unfaltering tones and from amidst the babel of voices that utter either amazing follies or misdirected yearnings, gives the one true forecast and direction—the one living word which has separated itself from and survived all the prognostications of Chaldean soothsayers and priests of Ur, because it has never ceased to give life to men. It has created for itself a channel and you can trace it through the centuries by the living green of its banks and the life it gives as it goes. For this hope of Abraham has been fulfilled; the creed and its accompanying blessing which that day lived in the heart of one man only has brought blessing to all the families of the earth.

CHAPTER VIII.

ABRAM IN EGYPT.

GENESIS xii. 6-20.

ABRAM still journeying southward, and not as yet knowing where his shifting camp was finally to be pitched, came at last to what may be called the heart of Palestine, the rich district of Shechem. Here stood the oak of Moreh, a well-known landmark and favourite meeting-place. In after years every meadow in this plain was owned and occupied, every vineyard on the slopes of Ebal fenced off, every square yard specified in some title-deed. But as yet the country seems not to have been densely populated. There was room for a caravan like Abraham's to move freely through the country, liberty for a far-stretching encampment such as his to occupy the lovely vale that lies between Ebal and Gerizim. As he rested here and enjoyed the abundant pasture, or as he viewed the land from one of the neighbouring hills, the Lord appeared to him and made him aware that this was the land designed for him. Here accordingly, under the spreading oak round whose boughs had often clung the smoke of idolatrous sacrifice, Abram erects an altar to the living God in devout acceptance of the gift, taking possession as it were of the land jointly for God and for himself. Little harm will come of worldly possessions so taken and so held.

As Abram traversed the land, wondering what were the limits of his inheritance, it may have seemed far too large for his household. Soon he experiences a difficulty of quite the opposite kind; he is unable to find in it sustenance for his followers. Any notion that God's friendship would raise him above the touch of such troubles as were incident to the times, places, and circumstances in which his life was to be spent, is quickly dispelled. The children of God are not exempt from any of the common calamities; they are only expected and aided to be calmer and wiser in their endurance and use of them. That we suffer the same hardships as all other men is no proof that we are not eternally associated with God, and ought never to persuade us our faith has been in vain.

Abram, as he looked at the bare, brown, cracked pastures and at the dry watercourses filled only with stones, thought of the ever-fresh plains of Mesopotamia, the lovely gardens of Damascus, the rich pasturage of the northern borders of Canaan; but he knew enough of his own heart to make him very careful lest these remembrances should make him turn back. No doubt he had come to the promised land expecting it to be the real Utopia, the Paradise which had haunted his thoughts as he lay among the hills of Ur watching his flocks under the brilliant midnight sky. No doubt he expected that here all would be easy and bright, peaceful and luxurious. His first experience is of famine. He has to look on his herd melting away, his favourite cattle losing their appearance, his servants murmuring and obliged to scatter. In his dreams he must have night after night seen the old country, the green breadth of the land that Euphrates watered, the heavy-headed corn bending before the warm airs of his native land; but morning by morning he wakes to the same anxieties, to the sad reality of parched and burnt-up pastures, shepherds hanging about with gloomy looks, his own heart distressed and failing. He was also a stranger here who could not look for the help an old resident might have counted on. It was probably years since God had made any sign to him. Was the promised land worth having, after all? Might he not be better off among his old friends in Charran? Should he not brave their ridicule and return? He will not so much as make it possible to return. He will not even for temporary relief go north towards his old country, but will go to Egypt, where he cannot stay, and from which he must return to Canaan.

Here, then, is a man who plainly believes that God's promise cannot fail; that God will magnify His promise, and that it above all else is worth waiting for. He believes that the man who seeks without flinching, and through all disappointment and bareness, to do God's will, shall one day have an abundantly satisfying reward, and that meanwhile association with God in carrying forward His abiding purposes with men is more for a man to live upon than the cattle upon a thousand hills. And thus famine rendered to Abram no small service if it quickened within him the consciousness that the call of God was not to ease and prosperity, to land-owning and cattle-breeding, but to be God's agent on earth for the fulfilment of remote but magnificent purposes. His life might seem to be down among the commonplace vicissitudes, pasture might fail, and his well-stocked camp melt away, but out of his mind there could not fade the future God had revealed to him. If it had been his ambition to give his name to a tribe and be known as a wide-ruling chief, that ambition is now eclipsed by his desire to be a step towards the fulfilment of that real end for which the whole world is. The belief that God has called him to do His work has lifted him above concern about personal matters; life has taken a new meaning in his eyes by its connection with the Eternal.

The extraordinary country to which Abram betook himself, and which was destined to exercise so profound an influence on his descendants, had even at this early date attained a high degree of civilisation. The origin of this civilisation is shrouded in obscurity, as the source of the great river to which the country owes its prosperity for many centuries kept the secret of its birth. As yet scholars are unable to tell us with certainty what Pharaoh was on the throne when Abram went down into Egypt. The monuments have preserved the effigies of two distinct types of rulers; the one simple, kindly, sensible, stately, handsome, fearless, as of men long accustomed to the throne. These are the faces of the native Egyptian rulers. The other type of face is heavy and massive, proud and strong but full of care, with neither the handsome features nor the look of kindliness and culture which belong to the other. These are the faces of the famous Shepherd kings who held Egypt in subjection, probably at the very time when Abram was in the land.

For our purposes it matters little whether Abram's visit occurred while the country was under native or under foreign rule, for long before the Shepherd kings entered Egypt it enjoyed a complete and stable civilisation. Whatever dynasty Abram found on the throne, he certainly found among the people a more refined social life than he had seen in his native city, a much purer religion, and a much more highly developed moral code. He must have kept himself entirely aloof from Egyptian society if he failed to discover that they believed in a judgment after death, and that this judgment proceeded upon a severe moral code. Before admission into the Egyptian heaven the deceased must swear that "he has not stolen nor slain any one intentionally; that he has not allowed his devotions to be seen; that he has not been guilty of hypocrisy or lying; that he has not calumniated any one nor fallen into drunkenness or adultery; that he has not turned away his ear from the words of truth; that he has been no idle talker; that he has not slighted the king or his father." To a man in Abram's state of mind the Egyptian creed and customs must have conveyed many valuable suggestions.

But virtuous as in many respects the Egyptians were, Abram's fears as he approached their country were by no means groundless. The event proved that whatever Sarah's age and appearance at this time were, his fears were something more than the fruit of a husband's partiality. Possibly he may have heard the ugly story which has recently been deciphered from an old papyrus, and which tells how one of the Pharaohs, acting on the advice of his princes, sent armed men to fetch a beautiful woman and make away with her husband. But knowing the risk he ran, why did he go? He contemplated the possibility of Sarah's being taken from him; but, if this should happen, what became of the promised seed? We cannot suppose that, driven by famine from the promised land, he had lost all hope regarding the fulfilment of the other part of the promise. Probably his idea was that some of the great men might take a fancy to Sarah, and that he would so temporise with them and ask for her such large gifts as would hold them off for a while until he could provide for his people and get clear out of the land. It had not occurred to him that she might be taken to the palace. Whatever his idea of the probable course of events was, his proposal to guide them by disguising his true relationship to Sarah was unjustifiable. And his feelings during these weeks in Egypt must have been far from enviable as he learned that of all virtues the Egyptians set greatest store by truth, and that lying was the vice they held in greatest abhorrence.

Here then was the whole promise and purpose of God in a most precarious position; the land abandoned, the mother of the promised seed in a harem through whose guards no force on earth could penetrate. Abram could do nothing but go helplessly about, thinking what a fool he had been, and wishing himself well back among the parched hills of Bethel. Suddenly there is a panic in the royal household; and Pharaoh is made aware that he was on the brink of what he himself considered a great sin. Besides effecting its immediate purpose, this visitation might have taught Pharaoh that a man cannot safely sin within limits prescribed by himself. He had not intended such evil as he found himself just saved from committing. But had he lived with perfect purity, this liability to fall into transgression, shocking to himself, could not have existed. Many sins of most painful consequence we commit, not of deliberate purpose, but because our previous life has been careless and lacking in moral tone. We are mistaken if we suppose that we can sin within a certain safe circle and never go beyond it.

By this intervention on God's part Abram was saved from the consequences of his own scheme, but he was not saved from the indignant rebuke of the Egyptian monarch. This rebuke indeed did not prevent him from a repetition of the same conduct in another country, conduct which was met with similar indignation: "What have I offended thee, that thou hast brought on me and on my kingdom this great sin? Thou hast done deeds unto me that ought not to be done. What sawest thou that thou hast done this thing?" This rebuke did not seem to sink deeply into the conscience of Abram's descendants, for the Jewish history is full of instances in which leading men do not shrink from manœuvre, deceit, and lying. Yet it is impossible to suppose that Abram's conception of God was not vastly enlarged by this incident, and this especially in two particulars.

(1) Abram must have received a new impression regarding God's truth. It would seem that as yet he had no very clear idea of God's holiness. He had the idea of God which Mohammedans entertain, and past which they seem unable to get. He conceived of God as the Supreme Ruler; he had a firm belief in the unity of God and probably a hatred of idolatry and a profound contempt for idolaters. He believed that this Supreme God could always and easily accomplish His will, and that the voice that inwardly guided him was the voice of God. His own character had not yet been deepened and dignified by prolonged intercourse with God and by close observation of His actual ways; and so as yet he knows little of what constitutes the true glory of God.

For learning that truth is an essential attribute of God he could not have gone to a better school than Egypt. His own reliance on God's promise might have been expected to produce in him a high esteem for truth and a clear recognition of its essential place in the Divine character. Apparently it had only partially had this effect. The heathen, therefore, must teach him. Had not Abram seen the look of indignation and injury on the face of Pharaoh, he might have left the land feeling that his scheme had succeeded admirably. But as he went at the head of his vastly increased household, the envy of many who saw his long train of camels and cattle, he would have given up all could he have blotted from his mind's eye the reproachful face of Pharaoh and nipped out this entire episode from his life. He was humbled both by his falseness and his foolishness. He had told a lie, and told it when truth would have served him better. For the very precaution he took in passing off Sarai as his sister was precisely what encouraged Pharaoh to take her, and produced the whole misadventure. It was the heathen monarch who taught the father of the faithful his first lesson in God's holiness.

What he so painfully learned we must all learn, that God does not need lying for the attainment of His ends, and that double-dealing is always short-sighted and the proper precursor of shame. Frequently men are tempted like Abram to seek a God-protected and God-prospered life by conduct that is not thoroughly straightforward. Some of us who statedly ask God to bless our endeavours, and who have no doubt that God approves the ends we seek to accomplish, do yet adopt such means of attaining our ends as not even men with any high sense of honour would countenance. To save ourselves from trouble, inconvenience, or danger, we are tempted to evasions and shifts which are not free from guilt. The more one sees of life, the higher value does he set on truth. Let lying be called by whatever flattering title men please—let it pass for diplomacy, smartness, self-defence, policy, or civility—it remains the device of the coward, the absolute bar to free and healthy intercourse, a vice which diffuses itself through the whole character and makes growth impossible. Trade and commerce are always hampered and retarded, and often overwhelmed in disaster, by the determined and deliberate doubleness of those who engage in them; charity is minimised and withheld from its proper objects by the suspiciousness engendered in us by the almost universal falseness of men; and the habit of making things seem to others what they are not, reacts upon the man himself and makes it difficult for him to feel the abiding effective reality of anything he has to do with or even of his own soul. If then we are to know the living and true God we must ourselves be true, transparent, and living in the light as He is the Light. If we are to reach His ends we must adopt His means and abjure all crafty contrivances of our own. If we are to be His heirs and partners in the work of the world, we must first be His children, and show that we have attained our majority by manifesting an indubitable resemblance to His own clear truth.

(2) But whether Abram fully learned this lesson or not, there can be little doubt that at this time he did receive fresh and abiding impressions of God's faithfulness and sufficiency. In Abram's first response to God's call he exhibited a remarkable independence and strength of character. His abandonment of home and kindred, on account of a religious faith which he alone possessed, was the act of a man who relied much more on himself than on others, and who had the courage of his convictions. This qualification for playing a great part in human affairs he undoubtedly had. But he had also the defects of his qualities. A weaker man would have shrunk from going into Egypt and would have preferred to see his flocks dwindle rather than take so venturesome a step. No such hesitations could trammel Abram's movements. He felt himself equal to all occasions. That part of his character which was reproduced in his grandson Jacob, a readiness to rise to every emergency that called for management and diplomacy, an aptitude for dealing with men and using them for his purposes—this came to the front now! To all the timorous suggestions of his household he had one reply: Leave it all to me; I will bring you through. So he entered Egypt confident that, single-handed, he could cope with their Pharaohs, priests, magicians, guards, judges, warriors; and find his way

through the finely-meshed net that held and examined every person and action in the land.

He left Egypt in a much more healthy state of mind, practically convinced of his own inability to work his way to the happiness God had promised him, and equally convinced of God's faithfulness and power to bring him through all the embarrassments and disasters into which his own folly and sin might bring him. His own confidence and management had placed God's promise in a position of extreme hazard; and without the intervention of God Abram saw that he could neither recover the mother of the promised seed nor return to the land of promise. Abram is put to shame even in the eyes of his household slaves; and with what burning shame must he have stood before Sarai and Pharaoh, and received back his wife from him whose wickedness he had feared, but who so far from meaning sin, as Abram suspected, was indignant that Abram should have made it even possible. He returned to Canaan humbled and very little disposed to feel confident in his own powers of managing in emergencies; but quite assured that God might at all times be relied on. He was convinced that God was not depending upon him, but he upon God. He saw that God did not trust to his cleverness and craft, no, nor even to his willingness to do and endure God's will, but that He was trusting in Himself, and that by His faithfulness to His own promise, by His watchfulness and providence, He would bring Abram through all the entanglements caused by his own poor ideas of the best way to work out God's ends and attain to His blessing. He saw, in a word, that the future of the world lay not with Abram but with God.

This certainly was a great and needful step in the knowledge of God. Thus early and thus unmistakably was man taught in how profound and comprehensive a sense God is his Saviour. Commonly it takes a man a long time to learn that it is God who is saving him, but one day he learns it. He learns that it is not his own faith but God's faithfulness that saves him. He perceives that he needs God throughout, from first to last; not only to make him offers, but to enable him to accept them; not only to incline him to accept them to-day, but to maintain within him at all times this same inclination. He learns that God not only makes him a promise and leaves him to find his own way to what is promised; but that He is with him always, disentangling him day by day from the results of his own folly and securing for him not only possible but actual blessedness.

Few discoveries are so welcome and gladdening to the soul. Few give us the same sense of God's nearness and sovereignty; few make us feel so deeply the dignity and importance of our own salvation and career. This is God's affair; a matter in which are involved not merely our personal interests, but God's responsibility and purposes. God calls us to be His, and He does not send us a-warring on our own charges, but throughout furnishes us with *everything* we need. When we go down to Egypt, when we quite diverge from the path that leads to the promised land and worldly straits tempt us to turn our back upon God's altar and seek relief by our own arrangements and devices, when we forget for a while how God has identified our interests with His own and tacitly abjure the vows we have silently registered before Him, even then He follows us and watches over us and lays His hand upon us and bids us back. And this only is our hope. Not in any determination of our own to cleave to Him and to live in faith on His promise can we trust. If we have this determination, let us cherish it, for this is God's present means of leading us onwards. But should this determination fail, the shame with which you recognise your want of steadfastness may prove a stronger bond to hold you to Him than the bold confidence with which to-day you view the future. The waywardness, the foolishness, the obstinate depravity that cause you to despair, God will conquer. With untiring patience, with all-foreseeing love, He stands by you and will bring you through. His gifts and calling are without repentance.

CHAPTER IX.

LOT'S SEPARATION FROM ABRAM.

GENESIS xiii.

ABRAM left Egypt thinking meanly of himself, highly of God. This humble frame of mind is disclosed in the route he chooses; he went straight back "unto the place where his tent had been at the beginning, unto the altar which he had made there at the first." With a childlike simplicity he seems to own that his visit to Egypt had been a mistake. He had gone there supposing that he was thrown upon his own resources, and that, in order to keep himself and his dependants alive, he must have recourse to craft and dishonesty. By retracing his steps and returning to the altar at Bethel, he seems to acknowledge that he should have remained there through the famine in dependence on God.

Whoever has attempted a similar practical repentance, visible to his own household and affecting their place of abode or daily occupations, will know how to estimate the candour and courage of Abram. To own that some distinctly marked portion of our life, upon which we entered with great confidence in our own wisdom and capacity, has come to nothing and has betrayed us into reprehensible conduct, is mortifying indeed. To admit that we have erred and to repair our error by returning to our old way and practice, is what few of us have the courage to do. If we have entered on some branch of business or gone into some attractive speculation, or if we have altered our demeanour towards some friend, and if we are finding that we are thereby tempted to doubleness, to equivocation, to injustice, our only hope lies in a candid and straightforward repentance, in a manly and open return to the state of things that existed in happier days and which we should never have abandoned. Sometimes we are aware that a blight began to fall on our spiritual life from a particular date, and we can easily and distinctly trace an unhealthy habit of spirit to a well-marked passage in our outward career; but we shrink from the sacrifice and shame involved in a thoroughgoing restoration of the old state of things. We are always so ready to fancy we have done enough, if we get one heartfelt word of confession uttered; so ready, if we merely turn our faces towards God, to think our restoration complete. Let us make a point of getting through mere beginnings of repentance, mere intention to recover God's favour and a sound condition of life, and let us return and return till we bow at God's very altar again, and know that His hand is laid upon us in blessing as at the first.

Out of Egypt Abram brought vastly increased wealth. Each time he encamped, quite a town of black tents quickly rose round the spot where his fixed spear gave the signal for halting. And along with him there journeyed his nephew, apparently of almost equal, or at least considerable wealth; not dependent on Abram, nor even a partner with him, for "Lot also had flocks and herds and tents." So rapidly was their substance increasing that no sooner did they become stationary than they found that the land was not able to furnish them with sufficient pasture. The Canaanite and the Perizzite would not allow them unlimited pasture in the neighbourhood of Bethel; and as the inevitable result of this the rival shepherds, eager to secure the best pasture for their own flocks and the best wells for their own cattle and camels, came to high words and probably to blows about their respective rights.

To both Abram and Lot it must have occurred that this competition between relatives was unseemly, and that some arrangement must be come to. And when at last some unusually blunt quarrel took place in presence of the chiefs, Abram divulges to Lot the scheme which had suggested itself to him. This state of things, he says, must come to an end; it is unseemly, unwise, and unrighteous. And as they walk on out of the circle of tents to discuss the matter without interruption, they come to a rising ground where the wide prospect brings them naturally to a pause. Abram looking north and south and seeing with the trained eye of a large flock-master that there was abundant pasture for both, turns to Lot with a final proposal: "Is not the whole land before thee? Separate thyself, I pray thee, from me: if thou wilt take the left hand, then I will go to the right; or if thou depart to the right hand, then I will go to the left."

Thus early did wealth produce quarrelling among relatives. The men who had shared one another's fortunes while comparatively poor, no sooner become wealthy than they have to separate. Abram prevented quarrel by separation. "Let us," he says, "come to an understanding. And rather than be separate in heart, let us be separate in habitation." It is always a sorrowful time in family history when it comes to this, that those who have had a common purse and have not been careful to know what exactly is theirs and what belongs to the other members of the family, have at last to make a division and to be as precise and documentary as if dealing with strangers. It is always painful to be compelled to own that law can be more trusted than love, and that legal forms are a surer barrier against quarrelling than brotherly kindness. It is a confession we are sometimes compelled to make, but never without a mixture of regret and shame.

As yet the character of Lot has not been exhibited, and we can only calculate from the relation he bears to Abram what his answer to the proposal will probably be. We know that Abram has been the making of his nephew, and that the land belongs to Abram; and we should expect that in common decency Lot would set aside the generous offer of his uncle and demand that he only should determine the matter. "It is not for me to make choice in a land which is wholly yours. My future does not carry in it the import of yours. It is a small matter what kind of subsistence I secure or where I find it. Choose for yourself, and allot to me what is right." We see here what a safeguard of happiness in life right feeling is. To be in right and pleasant relations with the persons around us will save us from error and sin even when conscience and judgment give no certain decision. The heart which feels gratitude is beyond the need of being schooled and compelled to do justly. To the man who is affectionately disposed it is superfluous to insist upon the rights of other persons. The instinct which tells a man what is due to others and makes him sensitive to their wrongs will preserve him from many an ignominious action which would degrade his whole life. But such instinct was a-wanting in Lot. His character, though in some respects admirable, had none of the generosity of Abram's in it. He had allowed himself on countless previous occasions to take advantage of Abram's unselfishness. Generosity is not always infectious; often it encourages selfishness in child, relative, or neighbour. And so Lot, instead of rivalling, traded on his uncle's magnanimity; and chose him all the plains of Jordan because in his eye it was the richest part of the land.

This choice of Sodom as a dwelling-place was the great mistake of Lot's life. He is the type of that very large class of men who have but one rule for determining them at the turning points of life. He was swayed solely by the consideration of worldly advantage. He has nothing deep, nothing high in him. He recognises no duty to Abram, no gratitude, no modesty; he has no perception of spiritual relations, no sense that God should have something to say in the partition of the land. Lot may be acquitted of a good deal which at first sight one is prompted to lay to his charge, but he cannot be acquitted of showing an eagerness to better himself, regardless of all considerations but the promise of wealth afforded by the fertility of the Jordan valley. He saw a quick though dangerous road to wealth. There seemed a certainty of success in his earthly calling, a risk only of moral disaster. He shut his eyes to the risk that he might grasp the wealth; and so doing, ruined both himself and his family.

The situation is one which is ceaselessly repeated. To men in business or in the cultivation of literature or art, or in one of the professions, there are presented opportunities of attaining a better position by cultivating the friendship or identifying oneself with the practice of men whose society is not in itself desirable. Society is made up of little circles, each of which has its own monopoly of some social or commercial or political advantage, and its own characteristic tone and enjoyments and customs. And if a man will not join one of these circles and accommodate himself to the mode of carrying on business and to the style of living it has identified with itself, he must forego the advantages which entrance to that circle would secure for him. As clearly as Lot saw that the well-watered plain stretching away under the sunshine was the right place to exercise his vocation as a flock-master, so do we see that associated with such and such persons and recognised as one of them, we shall be able more effectively than in any other position to use whatever natural gifts we have, and win the recognition and the profit these gifts seem to warrant. There is but one drawback. "The men of Sodom were wicked and sinners before the Lord exceedingly." There is a tone you do not like; you hesitate to identify yourself with men who live solely and with cynical frankness only for gain; whose every sentence betrays the contemptible narrowness of soul to which worldliness condemns men; who live for money and who glory in their shame.

The very nature of the world in which we live makes such temptation universal. And to yield is common and fatal. We persuade ourselves we need not enter into close relations with the persons we propose to have business connections with. Lot would have been horrified, that day he made his choice, had it been told him his daughters would marry men of Sodom. But the swimmer who ventures into the outer circle of the whirlpool finds that his own resolve not to go further presents a very weak resistance to the water's inevitable suction. We fancy perhaps that to refuse the companionship of any class of men is pharisaic; that we have no business to condemn the attitude towards the Church, or the morality, or the style of living adopted by any class of men among us. This is the mere cant of liberalism. We do not condemn persons who suffer from smallpox, but a smallpox hospital would be about the last place we should choose for a residence. Or possibly we imagine we shall be able to carry some better influences into the society we enter. A vain imagination; the motive for choosing the society has already sapped our power for good.

Many of the errors of worldly men only reveal their most disastrous consequences in the second generation. Like some virulent diseases they have a period of incubation. Lot's family grew up in a very different atmosphere from that which had nourished his own youth in Abram's tents. An adult and robust Englishman can withstand the climate of India; but his children who are born in it cannot. And the position in society which has been gained in middle life by the carefully and hardily trained child of a God-fearing household may not very visibly damage his own character, but may yet be absolutely fatal to the morality of his children. Lot may have persuaded himself he chose the dangerous prosperity of Sodom mainly for the sake of his children; but in point of fact he had better have seen them die of starvation in the most barren and parched desolation. And the parent who disregards conscience and chooses wealth or position, fancying that thus he benefits his children, will find to his life-long sorrow that he has entangled them in unimagined temptations.

But the man who makes Lot's choice not only does a great injury to his children, but cuts himself off from all that is best in life. We are safe to say that after leaving Abram's tents Lot never again enjoyed unconstrainedly happy days. The men born and brought up in Sodom were possibly happy after their kind and in their fashion; but Lot was not. His soul was daily vexed. Many a time while hearing the talk of the men his daughters had married, must Lot have gone out with a sore heart, and looked to the distant hills that hid the tents of Abram, and longed for an hour of the company he used to enjoy. And the society to which you are tempted to join yourself may not be unhappy, but you can take no surer means of beclouding, embittering, and ruining your whole life than by joining it. You cannot forget the thoughts you once had, the friendships you once delighted in, the hopes that shed brightness through all your life. You cannot blot out the ideal that once you cherished as the most animating element of your life. Every day there will be that rising in your mind which is in the sharpest contrast to the thoughts of those with whom you are associated. You will despise them for their shallow, worldly ideas and ways; but you will despise yourself still more, being conscious that what they are through ignorance and upbringing, you are in virtue of your own foolish and mean choice. There is that in you which rebels against the superficial and external measure by which they judge things, and yet you have deliberately chosen these as your associates, and can only think with heart-broken regret of the high thoughts that once visited you and the hopes you have now no means of fulfilling. Your life is taken out of your own hands; you find yourself in bondage to the circumstances you have chosen; and you are learning in bitterness, disappointment, and shame, that indeed "a man's life consisteth not in the abundance of the things which he possesseth." To determine your life solely by the prospect of worldly success is to risk the loss of the best things in life. To sacrifice friendship or conscience to success in your calling is to sacrifice what is best to what is lowest, and to bind yourself to the highest human happiness. For happily the essential elements of the highest happiness are as open to the poor as to the rich, to the unsuccessful as to the successful—love of wife and children, congenial and educating friendships, the knowledge of what the best men have done and the wisest men have said; the pleasure and impulse, the sentiments and beliefs which result from our knowledge of the heroic deeds done from year to year among men; the enlivening influence of examples that tell on all men alike, young and old, rich and poor; the insight and strength of character that are won in the hard wrestle with life; the growing consciousness that God is in human life, that He is ours and that we are His —these things and all that makes human life of value are universal as air and sunshine, but must be missed by those who make the world their object.

Though in point of fact Lot cut himself off by his choice from direct participation in the special inheritance to which Abram was called by God, it might perhaps be too much to say that his choice of the valley of Jordan was an explicit renunciation of the special blessedness of those who find their joy in responding to God's call and doing His work in the world. It might also be extravagant to say that his choice of the richest land was prompted by the feeling that he was not included in the promise to Abram, and might as well make the most of his present opportunities. But it is certain that Abram's generosity to Lot arose out of his sense that in God he himself had abundant possession. In Egypt he had learned that in order to secure all that is worth having a man need never resort to duplicity, trickery, bold lying. He now learns that in order to enter on his own God-provided lot, he need shut no other man out of his. He is taught that to acknowledge amply the rights of other men is the surest road to the enjoyment of his own rights. He is taught that there is room in God's plan for every man to follow his most generous impulses and the highest views of life that visit him.

It was Abram's simple belief that God's promise was meant and was substantial, that made him indifferent as to what Lot might choose. His faith was judged in this scene, and was proved to be sound. This man, whose very calling it was to own this land, could freely allow Lot to choose the best of it. Why? Because he has learned that it is not by any plan of his own he is to come into possession; that God Who promised is to give him the land in His own way, and that his part is to act uprightly, mercifully, like God. Wherever there is faith, the same results will appear. He who believes that God is pledged to provide for him cannot be greedy, anxious, covetous; can only be liberal, even magnanimous. Any one can thus test his own faith. If he does not find that what God promises weighs substantially when put in the scales with gold; if he does not find that the accomplishment of God's purpose with him in the world is to him the most valuable thing, and actually compels him to think lightly of worldly position and ordinary success; if he does not find that in point of fact the gains which content a man of the world shrivel and lose interest, he may feel tolerably certain he has no faith and is not counting as certain what God has promised.

It is commonly observed that wealth pursues the men who part with it most freely. Abram had this experience. No sooner had he allowed Lot to choose his portion than God gave him assurance that the whole would be his. It is "the meek" who "inherit the earth." Not only have they, in their very losses and while suffering wrong at the hands of their fellows, a purer joy than those who wrong them; but they know themselves heirs of God with the certainty of enjoying all His possessions that can avail for their advantage. Declining to devote themselves as living sacrifices to business they hold their soul at leisure for what brings truest happiness, for friendship, for knowledge, for charity. Even in this life they may be said to inherit the earth, for all its richest fruits are theirs—the ground may belong to other men, but the beauty of the landscape is theirs without burden—and ever and anon they hear such words as were now uttered to Abram. They alone are inclined or able to receive renewed assurances that God is mindful of His promise and will abundantly bless them. It is they who are in no haste to be rich, and are content to abide in the retired hill-country where they can freely assemble round God's altar; it is they who seek first the kingdom of God and make sure of that, whatever else they put in hazard, to whom God's encouragements come. You wonder at the certainty with which others speak of hearing God's voice and that so seldom you have the joy of knowing that God is directing and encouraging you. Why should you wonder, if you very well know that your attention is directed mainly to the world, that your heart trembles and thrills with all the fluctuations of your earthly hopes, that you wait for news and listen to every hint that can affect your position in life? Can you wonder that an ear trained to be so sensitive to the near earthly sounds, should quite have lost the range of heavenly voices?

Of the assurance here given him Abram was probably much in need when Lot had withdrawn with his flocks and servants. When the warmth of feeling cooled and allowed the somewhat unpleasant facts of the case to press upon his mind; and when he heard his shepherds murmuring that, after all the strife they had maintained for their master's rights, he should have weakly yielded these to Lot; and when he reflected, as now he inevitably would reflect, how selfish and ungrateful Lot had shown himself to be, he must have been tempted to think he had possibly made a mistake in dealing so generously with such a man. This reflection on himself might naturally grow into a reflection upon God, Who might have been expected so to order matters as to give the best country to the best man. All such reflections are precluded by the renewed grant he now receives of the whole land.

It is always as difficult to govern our heart wisely after as before making a sacrifice. It is as difficult to keep the will decided as to make the original decision; and it is more difficult to think affectionately of those for whom the sacrifice has been made, when the change in their condition and our own is actually accomplished. There is a natural reaction after a generous action which is not always sufficiently resisted. And when we see that those who refuse to make any sacrifices are more prosperous and less ruffled in spirit than ourselves we are tempted to take matters into our own hand, and, without waiting upon God, to use the world's quick ways. At such times we find how difficult it is to hold an advanced position, and how much unbelief mingles with the sincerest faith, and what vile dregs of selfishness sully the clearest generosity; we find our need of God and of those encouragements and assistances He can impart to the soul. Happy are we if we receive them and are enabled thereby to be constant in the good we have begun; for all sacrifice is good begun. And as Abram saw, when the cities of the plain were destroyed, how kindly God had guided him; so when our history is complete, we shall have no inclination to grumble at any passage of our life which we entered by generosity and faith in God, but shall see how tenderly God has held us back from much that our soul has been ardently desiring, and which we thought would be the making of us.

CHAPTER X.

ABRAM'S RESCUE OF LOT.

GENESIS xiv.

THIS chapter evidently incorporates a contemporary account of the events recorded. So antique a document was it even when it found its place in this book, that the editor had to modernise some of its expressions that it might be intelligible. The places mentioned were no longer known by the names here preserved—Bela, the vale of Siddim, En-mishpat, the valley of Shaveh, all these names were unknown even to the persons who dwelt in the places once so designated. It can scarcely have been Abram who wrote down the narrative, for he himself is spoken of as Abram the Hebrew, the man born beyond the Euphrates, which is a way of speaking of himself no one would naturally adopt

From the clear outline given of the route followed by the expedition of Chedorlaomer, it might be supposed that some old staff-secretary had reported on the campaign. However that may be, the discoveries of the last two or three years have shed light on the outlandish names that have stood for four thousand years in this document, and on the relations subsisting between Elam and Palestine.

On the bricks now preserved in our own British Museum the very names we read in this chapter can be traced, in the slightly altered form which is always given to a name when pronounced by different races. Chedorlaomer is the Hebrew transliteration of Kudur Lagamar; Lagamar was the name of one of the Chaldean deities, and the whole name means Lagamar's son, evidently a name of dignity adopted by the king of Elam. Elam comprehended the broad and rich plains to the east of the lower course of the Tigris, together with the mountain range (8,000 to 10,000 feet high) that bounds them. Elam was always able to maintain its own against Assyria and Babylonia, and at this time it evidently exercised some kind of supremacy not only over these neighbouring powers, but as far west as the valley of the Jordan. The importance of keeping open the valley of the Jordan is obvious to every one who has interest enough in the subject to look at a map. That valley was the main route for trading caravans and for military expeditions between the Euphrates and Egypt. Whoever held that valley might prove a most formidable annoyance and indeed an absolute interruption to commercial or political relations between Egypt and Elam, or the Eastern powers. Sometimes it might serve the purpose of East and West to have a neutral power between them, as became afterwards clear in the history of Israel, but oftener it was the ambition of either Egypt or of the East to hold Canaan in subjection. A rebellion therefore of these chiefs occupying the vale of Siddim was sufficiently important to bring the king of Elam from his distant capital, attaching to his army as he came his tributaries Amraphel king of Shinar or northern Chaldea, Arioch king of a district on the east of the Euphrates, and finally Tidal, or rather Tur-gal, *i. e.*, the great chief, who ruled over the nations or tribes to the north of Babylonia.

Susa, the capital of Elam, lies almost on the same parallel as the vale of Siddim, but between them lie many hundred miles of impracticable desert. Chedorlaomer and his army followed therefore much the same route as Terah in his emigration, first going northwest up the Euphrates and then crossing it probably at Carchemish, or above it, and coming southward towards Canaan. But the country to the east of the Jordan and the Dead Sea was occupied by warlike and marauding tribes who would have liked nothing better than to swoop down on a rich booty-laden Eastern army. With the sagacity of an old soldier therefore, Chedorlaomer makes it his first business to sweep this rough ground, and so cripple the tribes in his passage southwards, that when he swept round the lower end of the Dead Sea and up the Jordan valley he should have nothing to fear at least on his right flank. The tribe that first felt his sword was that of the Rephaim, or giants. Their stronghold was Ashteroth Karnaim, or Ashteroth of the two horns, a town dedicated to the goddess Astarte, whose symbol was the crescent or two-horned moon. The Zuzims and the Emims, " a people great and many and tall," as we read in Deuteronomy, next fell before the invading host. The Horites, *i. e.*, cave-dwellers or troglodytes, would scarcely hold Chedorlaomer long, though from their hilly fastnesses they might do him some damage. Passing through their mountains he came upon the great road between the Dead Sea and the Elanitic Gulf—but he crossed this road and still held westward till he reached the edge of what is roughly known as the Desert of Sinai. Here, says the narrative (ver. 7), they returned, that is, this was their furthest point south and west, and here they turned and made for the vale of Siddim, smiting the Amalekites and the Amorites on their route.

This is the only part of the army's route that is at all obscure. The last place they are spoken of as touching before reaching the vale of Siddim is Hazezon-Tamar, or as it was afterwards and is still called, Engedi. Now Engedi lies on the western shore of the Dead Sea about half-way up from south to north. It lies on a very steep, indeed artificially made, pass and is a place of much greater importance on that account than its size would make it. The road between Moab and Palestine runs by the western margin of the Dead Sea up to this point, but beyond this point the shore is impracticable, and the only road is through the Engedi pass on to the higher ground above. If the army chose this route then they were compelled to force this pass; if on the other hand they preferred during their whole march from Kadesh to keep away west of the Dead Sea on the higher ground, then they would only detail a company to pounce upon Engedi, as the main army passed behind and above. In either case the main body must have been if not actually within sight of, yet only a few miles from, the encampment of Abram.

At length, as they dropped down through the practicable passes into the vale of Siddim, their grand object became apparent, and the kings of the five allied towns, probably warned by the hill-tribes weeks before, drew out to meet them. But it is not easy to check an army in full career, and the wells of bitumen, which those who knew the ground might have turned to good purpose against the foreigners, actually hindered the home troops and became a trap to them. The rout was complete. No second stand or rally was attempted. The towns were sacked, the fields swept, and so swift were the movements of the invaders that although Abram was barely twenty miles off, and no doubt started for the rescue of Lot the hour he got the news, he did not overtake the army, laden as it was with spoil and retarded by prisoners and wounded, until they had reached the sources of Jordan.

But well-conceived and brilliantly executed as this campaign had been, the experienced warrior had failed to take account of the most formidable opponent he would have to reckon with. Those that escaped from the slaughter at Sodom took to the hills, and either knowing they would find shelter with Abram or more probably blindly running on, found themselves at nightfall within sight of the encampment at Hebron. There is no delay on Abram's part; he hastily calls out his men, each snatching his bow, his sword, and his spear, and slinging over his shoulders a few days' provision. The neighbouring Amorite chiefs Aner, Mamre, and Eschol join them, probably with a troop each, and before many hours are lost they are down the passes and in hot pursuit. Not however till they had traversed a hundred and twenty miles or more do they overtake the Eastern army. But at Dan, at the very springs of the Jordan, they find them, and making a night attack throw them into utter confusion and pursue them as far as Hobah, a village near Damascus, that retains to this day the same name.

One is naturally curious to see how Abram will conduct himself in circumstances so unaccustomed. From leading a quiet pastoral life he suddenly becomes the most important man in the country, a man who can make himself felt from the Nile to the Tigris. From a herd he becomes a hero. But, notoriously, power tries a man, and, as one has often seen persons make very glaring mistakes in such altered circumstances and alter their characters and beliefs to suit and take advantage of the new material and opportunities presented to them, we are interested in seeing how a man whose one rule of action has hitherto been faith in a promise given him by God, will pass through such a trial. Can a spiritual quality like faith be of much service in rough campaigning and when the man of faith is mixed up with persons of doubtful character and unscrupulous conduct, and brought into contact with considerable political powers? Can we trace to Abram's faith any part of his action at this time? No sooner is the question put than we see that his faith in God's promise was precisely that which gave him balance and dignity, courage and generosity in dealing with the three prominent persons in the narrative. He could afford to be forgiving and generous to his grand competitor Lot, precisely because he felt sure God would deal generously with himself. He could afford to acknowledge Melchizedek and any other authority that might appear, as his superior, and he would not take advantage, even when at the head of his men eager for more fighting, of the peaceful king who came out to propitiate him, because he knew that God would give him his land without wronging other people. And he scorned the wages of the king of Sodom, holding himself to be no mercenary captain, nor indebted to any one but God. In a word, you see faith producing all that is of importance in his conduct at this time.

Lot is the person who of all others might have been expected to be forward in his expressions of gratitude to Abram—not a word of his is recorded. Ashamed he cannot but have been, for if Abram said not a word of reproach, there would be plenty of Lot's old friends among Abram's men who could not lose so good an opportunity of twitting him about the good choice he had made. And considering how humiliating it would have been for him to go back with Abram and abandon the district of his adoption, we can scarcely wonder that he should have gone quietly back to Sodom, well as he must by this time have known the nature of the risks he ran there. For, after all, this warning was not very loud. The same thing, or a similar thing, might have happened had he remained with Abram. The warning was unobtrusive, as the warnings in life mostly are; audible to the ear that has been accustomed to listen to the still small voice of conscience, inaudible to the ear that is trained to hear quite other voices. God does not set angels and flaming swords in every man's path. The little whisper that no one hears but ourselves only, and that says quite quietly that we are continuing in a wrong course, is as certain an indication that we are in danger, as if God were to proclaim our case from heaven with thunder or the voice of an archangel. And when a man has persistently refused to listen to conscience it ceases to speak, and he loses the power to discern between good and evil and is left wholly without a guide. He may be running straight to destruction and he does not know it. You cannot live under two principles of action, regard to worldly interest and regard to conscience. You can train yourself to great acuteness in perceiving and following out what is for your worldly advantage, or you can train yourself to great acuteness of conscience; but you must make your choice, for in proportion as you gain sensitiveness in the one direction you lose it in the other. If your eye is *single* your whole body is full of light; but if the light that is in thee be darkness, how great is that darkness!

Melchizedek is generally recognised as the most mysterious and unaccountable of historical personages; appearing here in the King's Vale no one knows whence, and disappearing no one knows whither, but coming with his hands full of substantial gifts for the wearied household of Abram, and the captive women that were with him. Of each of the patriarchs we can tell the paternity; the date of his birth, and the date of his death; but this man stands with none to claim him, he forms no part of any series of links by which the oldest and the present times are connected. Though possessed of the knowledge of the Most High God, his name is not found in any of those genealogies which show us how that knowledge passed from father to son. Of all the other great men whose history is recorded a careful genealogy is given; but here the writer breaks his rule, and breaks it where, had there not been substantial reason, he would most certainly have adhered to it. For here is the greatest man of the time, a man before whom Abram the father of the faithful, the honoured of all nations, bowed and paid tithes; and yet he appears and passes away likest to a vision of the night. Perhaps even in his own time there was none that could point to the chamber where first he was cradled, nor show the tent round which first he played in his boyhood, nor hoard up a single relic of the early years of the man that had risen to be the first man upon earth in those days. So that the Apostle speaks of him as a very type of all that is mysterious and abrupt in appearance and disappearance, " without father, without mother, without descent, having neither beginning of days, nor end of life," and as he significantly adds, " made like unto the Son of God." For as Melchizedek stands thus on the page of history, so our Lord in reality—as the one has no recorded pedigree, and holds an office beginning and ending in his own person, so our Lord, though born of a woman, stands separate from sinners and quite out of the ordinary line of generations, and exercises an office which he received hereditarily from none, and which he could commit to no successor. As the one stands apparently disconnected from all before and after him, so the Other in point of fact did thus suddenly emerge from eternity, a problem to all who saw Him; owning the authority of earthly parents, yet claiming an antiquity greater than Abram's; appearing suddenly to the captivity led captive, with His hands full of gifts, and His lips dropping words of blessing.

Melchizedek is the one personage on earth whom Abram recognises as his spiritual superior. Abram accepts his blessing and pays him tithes; apparently as priest of the Most High God; so that in paying to him, Abram is giving the tenth of his spoils to God. This is not any mere courtesy of private persons. It was done in presence of various parties of jealously watchful retainers. Men of rank and office and position *consider* how they should act to one another and who should take precedence. And Abram did deliberately, and with a perfect perception of what he was doing, whatever he now did. Manifestly therefore God's revelation of Himself was not as yet confined to the one line running from Abram to Christ. Here was a man of whom we really do not know whether he was a Canaanite, a son of Ham or a son of Shem; yet Abram recognises him as having knowledge of the true God, and even bows to him as his spiritual superior in office, if not in experience. This shows us how little jealousy Abram had of others being favoured by God, how little he thought *his* connection with God would be less secure if other men enjoyed a similar connection, and how heartily he welcomed those who with different rites and different prospects yet worshipped the living God. It shows us also how apt we are to limit God's ways of working; and how little we understand of the connections He has with those who are not situated as we ourselves are. Here while all our attention is concentrated on Abram as carrying the whole spiritual hope of the world, there emerges from an obscure Canaanite valley a man nearer to God than Abram is. From how many unthought-of places such men may at any time come out upon us, we really can never tell.

Again Melchizedek is evidently a title, not a name—the word means King of Righteousness, or Righteous King. It may have been a title adopted by a line of kings, or it may have been peculiar to this one man. But these old Canaanites, if Canaanites they were, had got hold of a great principle when they gave this title to the king of their city of Salem or Peace. They perceived that it was the righteousness, the justice, of their king that could best uphold their peaceful city. They saw that the right king for them was a man not grinding his neighbours by war and taxes, not overriding the rights of others and seeking always enlargement of his own dominion; nor a merely merciful man, inclined to treat sin lightly and leaning always to laxity; but the man they would choose to give them peace was the righteous man who might sometimes seem overscrupulous, sometimes overstern, who would sometimes be called romantic and sometimes fanatical, but through all whose dealings it would be obvious that justice to all parties was the aim in view. Some of them might not be good enough to love a ruler who made no more of their special interest than he did of others, but all would possibly have wit enough to see that only by justice could they have peace. It is the reflex of God's government in which righteousness is the foundation of peace, a righteousness unflinching and invariable, promulgating holy laws and exacting punishment from all who break them. It is this that gives us hope of eternal peace, that we know God has not left out of account facts that must yet be reckoned with, nor merely lulled the unquiet forebodings of conscience, but has let every righteous law and principle find full scope, has done righteously in offering us pardon so that nothing can ever turn up to deprive us of our peace. And it is quite in vain that any individual holds before his mind the prospect of peace, *i. e.*, of permanent satisfaction, so long as he is not seeking it by righteousness. In so far as he is keeping his conscience from interfering, in so far is he making it impossible to himself to enter into the condition for the sake of which he is keeping conscience from regulating his conduct.

Lastly, Abram's refusal of the king of Sodom's offers is significant. Naturally enough, and probably in accordance with well-established usage, the king proposes that Abram should receive the rescued goods and the spoil of the invading army. But Abram knew men, and knew that although now Sodom was eager to show that he felt himself indebted to Abram, the time would come when he would point to this occasion as laying the foundation of Abram's fortune. When a man rises in the world every one will tell you of the share he had in raising him, and will convey the impression that but for assistance rendered by the speaker he would not have been what he now is. Abram knows that he is destined to rise, and knows also by Whose help he is to rise. He intends to receive all from God; and therefore not a thread from Sodom. He puts his refusal in the form adopted by the man whose mind is made up beyond revisal. He has "vowed" it. He had anticipated such offers and had considered their bearing on his relations to God and man; and taking advantage of the unembarrassed season in which the offer was as yet only a possibility he had resolved that when it was actually made he would refuse it, no matter what advantages it seemed to offer. So should we in our better seasons and when we know we are viewing things healthily, conscientiously, and righteously, determine what our conduct is to be, and if possible so commit ourselves to it that when the right frame is passed we cannot draw back from the right conduct. Abram had done so, and however tempting the spoils of the Eastern kings were, they did not move him. His vow had been made to the Possessor of heaven and earth, in Whose hand were riches beyond the gifts of Sodom.

Here again it is the man of faith that appears. He shows a noble jealousy of God's prerogative to bless him. He will not give men occasion to say that any earthly monarch has enriched him. It shall be made plain that it is on God he is depending. In all men of faith there will be something of this spirit. They cannot fail so to frame their life as to let it come clearly out that for happiness, for success, for comfort, for joy, they are in the main depending on God. That this cannot be done in the complex life of modern society, no one will venture to say in presence of this incident. Could we more easily have shown our reliance upon God in the hurry of a sudden foray, in the turmoil and intense action of a midnight attack and hand-to-hand conflict, in the excitement and elation of a triumphal progress, the kings of the country vying with one another to do us honour and the rescued captives lauding our valour and generosity? No one fails to see what it was that balanced Abram in this intoxicating march. No one asks what enabled him, while leading his armed followers flushed with success through a land weakened by recent dismay and disaster, to restrain them and himself from claiming the whole land as his. No one asks what gave him moral perception to see that the opportunity given him of winning the land by the sword was a temptation, not a guiding providence. To every reader it is obvious that his dependence on God was his safeguard and his light. God would bring him by fair and honourable means to his own. There was no need of violence, no need of receiving help from doubtful allies. This is true nobility; and this, faith always produces. But it must be a faith like Abram's; not a quick and superficial growth, but a deeply-rooted principle. For against all temptations this only is our sure defence, that already our hearts are so filled with God's promise that other offers find no craving in us, no empty, dissatisfied spot on which they can settle. To such faith God responds by the elevating and strengthening assurance, "I am thy shield, and thy exceeding great reward."

CHAPTER XI.

COVENANT WITH ABRAM.

Genesis xv.

Of the nine Divine manifestations made during Abram's life this is the fifth. At Ur, at Kharran, at the oak of Moreh, at the encampment between Bethel and Ai, and now at Mamre, he received guidance and encouragement from God. Different terms are used regarding these manifestations. Sometimes it is said "The Lord appeared unto him;" here for the first time in the course of God's revelation occurs that expression which afterwards became normal, "The word of the Lord came unto Abram." Throughout the subsequent history this word of the Lord continues to come, often at long intervals, but always meeting the occasion and needs of His people and joining itself on to what had already been declared, until at last the Word became flesh and dwelt among us, giving thus to all men assurance of the nearness and profound sympathy of their God. To repeat this revelation is impossible. A repetition of it would be a denial of its reality. For a second life on earth is allowed to no man; and were our Lord to live a second human life it were proof He was no true man, but an anomalous, unaccountable, uninstructive, appearance or simulacrum of a man.

But though these revelations of God are finished, though complete knowledge of God is given in Christ, God comes to the individual still through the Spirit Whose office it is to take of the things of Christ and show them to us. And in doing so the law is observed which we see illustrated here. God comes to a man with further encouragement and light for a new step when he has conscientiously used the light he already has. The temper that "seeks for a sign," and expects that some astounding providence should be sent to make us religious is by no means obsolete. Many seem to expect that before they act on the knowledge they have, they will receive more. They put off giving themselves to the service of God under some kind of impression that some striking event or much more distinct knowledge is required to give them a decided turn to a religious life. In so doing they invert God's order. It is when we have conscientiously followed such light as we have, and faithfully done all that we know to be right, that God gives us further light. It was immediately on the back of faithful action that Abram received new help to his faith.

The time was seasonable for other reasons. Never did Abram feel more in need of such assurance. He had been successful in his midnight attack and had scattered the force from beyond Euphrates, but he knew the temper of these Eastern monarchs well enough to be aware that there was nothing they hailed with greater pleasure than a pretext for extending their conquests and adding to their territory. To Abram it must have appeared certain that the next campaigning season would see his country invaded and his little encampment swept away by the Eastern host. Most appropriate, therefore, are the words: "Fear not, Abram: I am thy shield."

But another train of thoughts occupied Abram's mind perhaps even more unceasingly at this time. After busy engagement comes dulness; after triumph, flatness and sadness. I have pursued kings, got myself a great name, led captivity captive. Men are speaking of me in Sodom, and finding that in me they have a useful and important ally. But what is all this to my purpose? Am I any nearer my inheritance? I have got all that men might think I needed; they may be unable to understand why now, of all times, I should seem heartless; but, O Lord, Thou knowest how empty these things seem to me, and what wilt Thou give me? Abram could not understand why he was kept so long waiting. The child given when he was a hundred years old might equally have been given twenty-five years before, when he first came to the land of Canaan. All Abram's servants had their children, there was no lack of young men born in his encampment. He could not leave his tent without hearing the shouts of other men's children, and having them cling to his garments—but "to me Thou hast given no seed; and lo! one born in mine house, a slave, is mine heir."

Thus it often is that while a man is receiving much of what is generally valued in the world, the one thing he himself most prizes is beyond his reach. He has his hope irremovably fixed on something which he feels would complete his life and make him a thoroughly happy man; there is one thing which, above all else, would be a right and helpful blessing to him. He speaks of it to God. For years it has framed a petition for itself when no other desire could make itself heard. Back and back to this his heart comes, unable to find rest in anything so long as this is withheld. He cannot help feeling that it is God who is keeping it from him. He is tempted to say, "What is the use of all else to me, why give me things Thou knowest I care little for, and reserve the one thing on which my happiness depends?" As Abram might have said: "Why make me a great name in the land, when there is no one to keep it alive in men's memories; why increase my possessions when there is none to inherit but a stranger?"

Is there then any resulting benefit to character in this so common experience of delayed expectations? In Abram's case there certainly was.

It was in these years he was drawn close enough to God to hear Him say, "*I am thy exceeding great reward.*" He learned in the multitude of his debating about God's promise and the delay of its fulfilment, that God was more than all His gifts. He had started as a mere hopeful colonist and founder of a family; these twenty-five years of disappointment made him the friend of God and the Father of the Faithful. Slowly do we also pass from delight in God's gifts to delight in Himself, and often by a similar experience. From what have you received truest and deepest pleasure in life? Is it not from your friendships? Not from what your friends have given you or done for you; rather from what you have done for them; but chiefly from your affectionate intercourse. You, being persons, must find your truest joy in persons, in personal love, personal goodness and wisdom. But friendship has its crown in the friendship of God. The man who knows God as his friend and is more certain of God's goodness and wisdom and steadfastness than he can be of the worth of the man he has loved and trusted and delighted in from his boyhood, the man who is always accompanied by a latent sense of God's observation and love, is truly living in the peace of God that passeth understanding. This raises him above the touch of worldly losses and restores him in all distresses, even to the surprise of observers; his language is, "There may be many that will say, Who will show us any good? Lord, lift Thou up the light of Thy countenance upon us. *Thou* hast put gladness in my heart more than in the time that their corn and their wine increased."

But evidently there was still another feeling in Abram's heart at this particular point in his career. He could not bear to think he was to miss that very thing which God had promised him. The keen yearning for an heir which God's promise had stirred in him was not lost sight of in the great saying, "*I am thy exceeding great reward.*" When he was journeying back to his encampment not a shoestring richer than he left, and while he heard his men, disappointed of booty, murmuring that he should be so scrupulous, he cannot but have felt some soreness that he should be set before his little world as a man who had the enjoyment neither of this world's rewards nor of God. And here must have come the strong temptation that comes to every man: Might it not be as well to take what he could get, to enjoy what was put fairly within his reach, instead of waiting for what seemed so uncertain as God's gift? It is painful to be exposed to the observation of others or to our own observation, as persons who, on the one hand, refuse to seek happiness in the world's way, and yet are not finding it in God. You have possibly with some magnanimity rejected a tempting offer because there were conditions attached to which conscience could not reconcile itself; but you find that you are in consequence suffering greater privations than you expected and that no providential intervention seems to be made to reward your conscientiousness. Or you suddenly become aware that though you have for years refused to be mirthful or influential or successful or comfortable in the world's way and on the world's terms, you are yet getting no substitute for what you refuse. You will not join the world's mirth, but then you are morose and have no joy of any kind. You will not use means you disapprove of for influencing men, but neither have you the influence of a strong Christian character. In fact by giving up the world you seem to have contracted and weakened instead of enlarging and deepening your life.

In such a condition we can but imitate Abram and cast ourselves more resolutely on God. If you find it most weary and painful to deny yourself in these special ways which have fallen to be your experience, you can but utter your complaint to God, assured that in Him you will find consideration. He knows why He has called you, why He has given you strength to abandon worldly hopes; He appreciates your adherence to Him and He will renew your faith and hope. If day by day you are saying, "Lead Thou me on," if you say, "What wilt Thou give me?" not in complaint but in lively expectation, encouragement enough will be yours.

The means by which Abram's faith was renewed were appropriate. He has been seeing in the tumult and violence and disappointment of the world much to suggest the thought that God's promise could never work itself out in the face of the rude realities around him. So God leads him out and points him to the stars, each one called by his name, and thus reminds the Chaldæan who had so often gazed at and studied them in their silent steady courses, that his God has designs of infinite sweep and comprehension; that throughout all space His worlds obey His will and all harmoniously play their part in the execution of His vast design; that we and all our affairs are in a strong hand, but moving in orbits so immense that small portions of them do not show us their direction and may seem to be out of course. Abram is led out alone with the mighty God, and to every saved soul there comes such a crisis when before God's majesty we stand awed and humbled, all complaints hushed, and indeed our personal interests disappear or become so merged in God's purposes that we think only of Him; our mistakes and wrong-doing are seen now not so much as bringing misery upon ourselves as interrupting and perverting His purposes, and His word comes home to our hearts as stable and satisfying.

It was in this condition that Abram believed God, and He counted it to him for righteousness. Probably if we read this without Paul's commentary on it in the fourth of Romans, we should suppose it meant no more than that Abram's faith, exercised as it was in trying circumstances, met with God's cordial approval. The faith or belief here spoken of was a resolute renewal of the feeling which had brought him out of Chaldæa. He put himself fairly and finally into God's hand to be blessed in God's way and in God's time, and this act of resignation, this resolve that he would not force his own way in the world but would wait upon God, was looked upon by God as deserving the name of righteousness, just as much as honesty and integrity in his conduct with Lot or with his servants. Paul begs us to notice that an act of faith accepting God's favour is a very different thing from a work done for the sake of winning God's favour. God's favour is always a matter of grace, it is favour conferred on the undeserving; it is never a matter of debt, it is never favour conferred because it has been won. To put this beyond doubt he appeals to this righteousness of

Abram's. How, he asks, did Abram achieve righteousness? Not by observing ordinances and commandments; for there were none to observe; but by trusting God, by believing that already without any working or winning of his, God loved him and designed blessedness for him; in short by referring his prospect of happiness and usefulness wholly to God and not at all to himself. This is the essential quality of the godly; and having this, Abram had that root which produced all actual righteousness and likeness to God.

It is sufficiently obvious in such a life as Abram's why faith is the one thing needful. Faith is required because it is only when a man believes God's promise and rests in His love that he can co-operate with God in severing himself from iniquitous prospects and in so living for spiritual ends as to enter the life and the blessedness God calls him to. The boy who does not believe his father, when he comes to him in the midst of his play and tells him he has something for him which will please him still better, suffers the penalty of unbelief by losing what his father would have given him. All missing of true enjoyment and blessedness results from unbelief in God's promise. Men do not walk in God's ways because they do not believe in God's ends. They do not believe that spiritual ends are as substantial and desirable as those that are physical.

Abram's faith is easily recognised, because not only had he not wrought for the blessing God promised him, but it was impossible for him even to see how it could be achieved. That which God promised was apparently quite beyond the reach of human power. It serves then as an admirable illustration of the essence of faith; and Paul uses it as such. It is not because faith is the root of all actual righteousness that Paul describes it as "imputed for righteousness." It is because faith at once gives a man possession of what no amount of working could ever achieve. God now offers in Christ righteousness, that is to say, justification, the forgiveness of sins and acceptance with God with all the fruits of this acceptance, the indwelling Divine Spirit and life everlasting. He offers this freely as he offered to Abram what Abram could never have won for himself. And all that we are asked to do is to accept it. This is all we are asked to do in order to our becoming the forgiven and accepted children of God. After becoming so, there of course remains an infinite amount of service to be rendered, of work to be done, of self-discipline to be undergone. But in answer to the awakened sinner's enquiry, "What must I do to be saved," Paul replies, "You are to *do* nothing; nothing you can do can win God's favour, because that favour is already yours; nothing you can do can achieve the rectification of your present condition, but Christ has achieved it. Believe that God is with you and that Christ can deliver you and commit yourself cordially to the life you are called to, hopeful that what is promised will be fulfilled."

Abram's faith, cordial as it was, yet was not independent of some sensible sign to maintain it. The sign given was twofold: the smoking furnace and a prediction of the sojourn of Abram's posterity in Egypt. The symbols were similar to those by which on other occasions the presence of God was represented. Fire, cleansing, consuming, and unapproachable, seemed to be the natural emblem of God's holiness. In the present instance it was especially suitable, because the manifestation was made after sundown and when no other could have been seen. The cutting up of the carcases and passing between the pieces was one of the customary forms of contract. It was one of the many devices men have fallen upon to make sure of one another's word. That God should condescend to adopt these modes of pledging Himself to men is significant testimony to His love; a love so resolved on accomplishing the good of men that it resents no slowness of faith and accommodates itself to unworthy suspicions. It makes itself as obvious and pledges itself with as strong guarantees to men as if it were the love of a mortal whose feelings might change and who had not clearly foreseen all consequences and issues.

The prediction of the long sojourn of Abram's posterity in Egypt was not only helpful to those who had to endure the Egyptian bondage, but also to Abram himself. He no doubt felt the temptation, from which at no time the Church has been free, to consider himself the favourite of heaven before whose interests all other interests must bow. He is here taught that other men's rights must be respected as well as his, and that not one hour before absolute justice requires it, shall the land of the Amorites be given to his posterity. And that man is considerably past the rudimentary knowledge of God who understands that every act of God springs from justice and not from caprice, and that no creature upon earth is sooner or later unjustly dealt with, by the Supreme Ruler. In the life of Abram it becomes visible, how, by living with God and watching for every expression of His will, a man's knowledge of the Divine nature enlarges; and it is also interesting to observe that shortly after this he grounds all his pleading for Sodom on the truth he had learned here: "Shall not the Judge of *all the earth* do right?"

The announcement that a long interval must elapse before the promise was fulfilled must no doubt have been a shock to Abram; and yet it was sobering and educative. It is a great step we take when we come clearly to understand that God has a great deal to do with us before we can fully inherit the promise. For God's promise, so far from making everything in the future easy and bright, is that which above all else discloses how stern a reality life is; how severe and thorough that discipline must be which makes us capable of achieving God's purposes with us. A horror of great darkness may well fall upon the man who enters into covenant with God, who binds himself to that Being whom no pain nor sacrifice can turn aside from the pursuance of aims once approved. When we look forward and consider the losses, the privations, the self-denials, the delays, the pains, the keen and real discipline, the lowliness of the life to which fellowship with God leads men, darkness and gloom and smoke darken our prospect and discourage us; but the smoke is that which arises from a purifying fire that purges away all that prevents us from living spiritually; a darkness very different from that which settles over the life which amidst much present brightness carries in it the consciousness that its course is downwards, that the blows it suffers are deadening, that its sun is steadily nearing its setting and that everlasting night awaits it.

But over all other feelings this solemn transacting with God must have produced in Abram a humble ecstasy of confidence. The wonderful mercy and kindness of God in thus binding Himself to a weak and sinful man cannot but have given him new thoughts of God and new thoughts of himself. With fresh elevation of mind and superiority to ordinary difficulties and temptations would he return to his tent that night. In how different a perspective would all things stand to him now that the Infinite God had come so near to him. Things which yesterday fretted or terrified him seemed now remote: matters which had occupied his thought he did not now notice or remember. He was now the Friend of God, taken up into a new world of thoughts and hopes; hiding in his heart the treasure of God's covenant, brooding over the infinite significance and hopefulness of his position as God's ally.

For indeed this was a most extraordinary and a most encouraging event. The Infinite God drew near to Abram and made a contract with him. God as it were said to him, I wish you to count upon Me, to make sure of Me: I therefore pledge Myself by these accustomed forms to be your Friend.

But it was not as an isolated person, nor for his own private interests alone that Abram was thus dealt with by God. It was as a medium of universal blessing that he was taken into covenant with God. The kindness of God which he experienced was merely an intimation of the kindness all men would experience. The laying aside of unapproachable dignity and entrance into covenant with a man was the proclamation of His readiness to be helpful to all and to bring Himself within reach of all. That you may have a God at hand He thus brought Himself down to men and human ways, that your life may not be vain and useless, dark and misguided, and that you may find that you have a part in a well-ordered universe in which a holy God cares for all and makes His strength and wisdom available for all. Do not allow these intimations of His mercy to go for nothing, but use them as intended for your guidance and encouragement.

CHAPTER XII.

BIRTH OF ISHMAEL.

Genesis xvi.

In this unpretending chapter we have laid bare to us the origin of one of the most striking facts in the history of religion: namely, that from the one person of Abram have sprung Christianity and that religion which has been and still is its most formidable rival and enemy, Mohammedanism. To Ishmael, the son of Abram, the Arab tribes are proud to trace their pedigree. Through him they claim Abram as their father, and affirm that they are his truest representatives, the sons of his first-born. In Mohammed, the Arabian, they see the fulfilment of the blessing of Abram, and they have succeeded in persuading a large part of the world to believe along with them. Little did Sarah think when she persuaded Abram to take Hagar that she was originating a rivalry which has run with keenest animosity through all ages and which oceans of blood have not quenched. The domestic rivalry and petty womanish spites and resentments so candidly depicted in this chapter, have actually thrown on the world from that day to this one of its darkest and least hopeful shadows. The blood of our own countrymen, it may be of our own kindred, will yet flow in this unappeasable quarrel. So great a matter does a little fire kindle. So lasting and disastrous are the issues of even slight divergences from pure simplicity.

It is instructive to observe how long this matter of obtaining an heir for Abram occupies the stage of sacred history and in how many aspects it is shown. The stage is rapidly cleared of whatever else might naturally have invited attention, and interest is concentrated on the heir that is to be. The risks run by the appointed mother, the doubts of the father, the surrender now of the mother's rights,—all this is trivial if it concerned only one household, important only when you view it as significant for the race. It was thus men were taught thoughtfully to brood upon the future and to believe that, though Divine, blessing and salvation would spring from earth: man was to co-operate with God, to recognise himself as capable of uniting with God in the highest of all purposes. At the same time, this long and continually deferred expectation of Abram was the simple means adopted by God to convince men once for all that the promised seed is not of nature but of grace, that it is God who sends all effectual and determining blessing, and that we must learn to adapt ourselves to His ways and wait upon Him.

The first man, then, whose religious experience and growth are recorded for us at any length, has this one thing to learn, to trust God's word and wait for it. In this everything is included. But gradually it appears to us all that this is the great difficulty, to wait; to let God take His own time to bless us. It is hard to believe in God's perfect love and care when we are receiving no present comfort or peace; hard to believe we shall indeed be sanctified when we seem to be abandoned to sinful habit; hard to pass all through life with some pain, or some crushing trouble, or some harassing anxiety, or some unsatisfied craving. It is easy to start with faith, most trying to endure patiently to the end. It is thus God educates His children. Compelled to wait for some crowning gift, we cannot but study God's ways. It is thus we are forced to look below the surface of life to its hidden meanings and to construe God's dealings with ourselves apart from the experience of other men. It is thus we are taught actually to loosen our hold of things temporal and to lay hold on what is spiritual and real. He who leaves himself in God's hand will one day declare that the pains and sorrows he suffered were trifling in comparison with what he has won from them.

But Sarah could not wait. She seems to have fixed ten years as the period during which she would wait; but at the expiry of this term she considered herself justified in helping forward God's tardy providence by steps of her own. One cannot severely blame her. When our hearts are set upon some definite blessing things seem to move too slowly, and we can scarcely refrain from urging them on without too scrupulously enquiring into the character of our methods. We are willing to wait for a certain time, but beyond that we must take the matter into our own hand. This incident shows, what all life shows, that whatever be the boon you seek, you do yourself an injury if you cease to seek it in the best possible form and manner, and decline upon some lower thing which you can secure by some easy stratagem of your own.

The device suggested by Sarah was so common that the wonder is that it had not long before been tried. Jealousy or instinctive reluctance may have prevented her from putting it in force. She might no doubt have understood that God, always working out His purposes in consistency with all that is most honourable and pure in human conduct, requires of no one to swerve a hair's-breadth from the highest ideal of what a human life should be, and that just in proportion as we seek the best gifts and the most upright and pure path to them does God find it easy to bless us. But in her case it was difficult to continue in this belief; and at length she resolved to adopt the easy and obvious means of obtaining an heir. It was unbelieving and foolish, but not more so than our adoption of practices common in our day and in our business which we know are not the best, but which we nevertheless make use of to obtain our ends because the most righteous means possible do not seem workable in our circumstances. Are you not conscious that you have sometimes used a means of effecting your purpose, which you would shrink from using habitually, but which you do not scruple to use to tide you over a difficulty, an extraordinary device for an extraordinary emergency, a Hagar brought in for a season to serve a purpose, not a Sarah accepted from God and cherished as an eternal helpmeet. It is against this we are here warned. From a Hagar can at the best spring only an Ishmael, while in order to obtain the blessing God intends we must betake ourselves to God's barren-looking means.

The evil consequences of Sarah's scheme were apparent first of all in the tool she made use of. Agur the son of Jakeh says: "For three things the earth is disquieted, and for four which it cannot bear. For a servant when he reigneth, and a fool when he is filled with meat; for an odious woman when she is married, and an handmaid that is heir to her mistress." Naturally this half-heathen girl, when she found that her son would probably inherit all Abram's possessions, forgot herself, and looked down on her present, nominal mistress. A flood of new fancies possessed her vacant mind and her whole demeanour becomes insulting to Sarah. The slave-girl could not be expected to sympathise with the purpose which Abram and Sarah had in view when they made use of her. They had calculated on finding only the unquestioning, mechanical obedience of the slave, even while raising her practically to the dignity of a wife. They had fancied that even to the deepest feelings of her woman's heart, even in maternal hopes, she would be plastic in their hands, their mere passive instrument. But they have entirely miscalculated. The slave has feelings as quick and tender as their own, a life and a destiny as tenaciously clung to as their God-appointed destiny. Instead of simplifying their life they have merely added to it another source of complexity and annoyance. It is the common fate of all who use others to satisfy their own desires and purposes. The instruments they use are never so soulless and passive as it is wished. If persons cannot serve you without deteriorating in their own character, you have no right to ask them to serve you. To use human beings as if they were soulless machines is to neglect radical laws and to inflict the most serious injury on our fellow-men. Mistresses who do not treat their servants with consideration, recognising that they are as truly women as themselves, with all a woman's hopes and feelings, and with a life of their own to live, are committing a grievous wrong, and evil will come of it.

In such an emergency as now arose in Abram's household, character shows itself clearly. Sarah's vexation at the success of her own scheme, her recrimination and appeal for strange justice, her unjustifiable treatment of Hagar, Abram's Bedouin disregard of the jealousies of the women's tent, his Gallio-like repudiation of judgment in such quarrels, his regretful vexation and shame that through such follies, mistakes, and wranglings, God had to find a channel for His promise to flow—all this discloses the painful ferment into which Abram's household was thrown. Sarah's attempt to rid herself with a high hand of the consequences of her scheme was signally unsuccessful. In the same inconsiderate spirit in which she had put Hagar in her place, she now forces her to flee, and fancies that she has now rid herself and her household of all the disagreeable consequences of her experiment. She is grievously mistaken. The slave comes back upon her hands, and comes back with the promise of a son who should be a continual trouble to all about him. All through Ishmael's boyhood Abram and Sarah had painfully to reap the fruits of what they had sown. We only make matters worse when we endeavour by injustice and harshness to crush out the consequences of wrong-doing. The difficulties into which sin has brought us can only be effectually overcome by sincere contrition and humiliation. It is not all in a moment nor by one happy stroke you can rectify the sin or mistake of a moment. If by your wise devices you have begotten young Ishmaels, if something is every day grieving you and saying to you, "This comes of your careless inconsiderate conduct in the past," then see that in your vexation there is real penitence and not a mere indignant resentment against circumstances or against other people, and see that you are not actually continuing the fault which first gave birth to your present sorrow and entanglement.

When Hagar fled from her mistress she naturally took the way to her old country. Instinctively her feet carried her to the land of her birth. And as she crossed the desert country where Palestine, Egypt, and Arabia meet, she halted by a fountain, spent with her flight and awed by the solitude and stillness of the desert. Her proud spirit is broken and tamed, the fond memories of her adopted home and all its customs and ways and familiar faces and occupations, overtake her when she pauses and her heart reacts from the first excitement of hasty purpose and reckless execution. To whom could she go in Egypt? Was there one there who would remember the little slave girl or who would care to show her a kindness? Has she not acted madly in fleeing from her only protectors? The desolation around her depicts her own condition. No motion stirs as far as her eye can reach, no bird flies, no leaf trembles, no cloud floats over the scorching sun, no sound breaks the death-like quiet; she feels as if in a tomb, severed from all life, forgotten of all. Her spirit is breaking under this sense of desolation, when suddenly her heart stands still as she hears a voice utter her own name "Hagar, Sarai's maid." As readily as every other person when God speaks to them, does Hagar recognise Who it is who has followed her into this blank solitude. In her circumstances to hear the voice of God left no room for disobedience. The voice of God made audible through the actual circumstances of our daily life acquires a force and an authority we never attached to it otherwise.

Probably, too, Hagar would have gone back to Abram's tents at the bidding of a less authoritative voice than this. Already she was softening and repenting. She but needed some one to say, "Go back." You may often make it easier for a proud man to do a right thing by giving him a timely word. Frequently men stand in the position of Hagar, knowing the course they ought to adopt and yet hesitating to adopt it until it is made easy to them by a wise and friendly word.

In the promise of a son which was here given to Hagar and the prediction concerning his destiny, while there was enough to teach both her and Abram that he was not to be the heir of the promise, there was also much to gratify a mother's pride and be to Hagar a source of continual satisfaction. The son was to bear a name which should commemorate God's remembrance of her in her desolation. As often as she murmured it over the babe or called it to the child or uttered it in sharp remonstrance to the refractory boy, she was still reminded that she had a helper in God who had heard and would hear her. The prediction regarding the child has been strikingly fulfilled in his descendants; the three characteristics by which they are distinguished being precisely those here mentioned. "He will be a wild man," literally, "a wild ass among men," reminding us of the description of this animal in Job: "Whose house I have made the wilderness, and the barren land his dwelling. He scorneth the multitude of the city, neither regardeth he the crying of the driver. The range of the mountains is his pasture, and he searcheth after every green thing." Like the zebra that cannot be domesticated, the Arab scorns the comforts of civilised life, and adheres to the primitive dress, food, and mode of life, delighting in the sensation of freedom, scouring the deserts, sufficient with his horse and spear for every emergency. His hand also is against every man, looking on all as his natural enemies or as his natural prey; in continual feud of tribe against tribe and of the whole race against all of different blood and different customs. And yet he "dwells in the presence of his brethren;" though so warlike a temper would bode his destruction and has certainly destroyed other races, this Ishmaelite stock continues in its own lands with an uninterrupted history. In the words of an authoritative writer: "They have roved like the moving sands of their deserts; but their race has been rooted while the individual wandered. That race has neither been dissipated by conquest, nor lost by migration, nor confounded with the blood of other countries. They have continued to dwell in the presence of all their brethren, a distinct nation, wearing upon the whole the same features and aspects which prophecy first impressed upon them."

What struck Hagar most about this interview was God's presence with her in this remote solitude. She awakened to the consciousness that duty, hope, God, are ubiquitous, universal, carried in the human breast, not confined to any place. Her hopes, her haughtiness, her sorrows, her flight, were ll known. The feeling possessed her which was afterwards expressed by the Psalmist: "Thou knowest my down-sitting, and mine uprising, Thou understandest my thoughts afar off. Thou compassest my path and my lying down, and art acquainted with all my ways. Thou tellest my wanderings; put Thou my tears in Thy bottle; are they not in Thy book?" Even here where I thought to have escaped every eye, have I been following and at length found Him that seeth me. As truly and even more perceptibly than in Abram's tents, God is with her here in the desert. To evade duty, to leave responsibility behind us, is impossible. In all places we are God's children, bound to accept the responsibilities of our nature. In all places God is with us, not only to point out our duty but to give us the feeling that in adhering to duty we adhere to Him, and that it is because He values us that He presses duty upon us. With Him is no respect of persons; the servant is in his sight as vivid a personality as the mistress, and God appears not to the overbearing mistress but to the overborne servant.

Happy they who when God has thus met them and sent them back on their own footsteps, a long and weary return, have still been so filled with a sense of God's love in caring for them through all their errors, that they obey and return. All round about His people does God encamp, all round about His flock does the faithful Shepherd watch and drive back upon the fold each wanderer. Not only to those who are consciously seeking Him does God reveal Himself, but often to us at the very farthest point of our wandering, at our extremity, when another day's journey would land us in a region from which there is no return. When our regrets for the past become intolerably poignant and bitter; when we see a waste of years behind us barren as the sand of the desert, with nothing done but what should but cannot be undone; when the heart is stupefied with the sense of its madness and of the irretrievable loss it has sustained, or when we look to the future and are persuaded little can grow up in it out of such a past, when we see that all that would have prepared us for it has been lightly thrown aside or spent recklessly for nought, when our hearts fail us, this is God besetting us behind and before. And may He grant us strength to pray, "Show me Thy ways, O Lord, teach me Thy paths. Lead me in Thy truth and teach me: for Thou art the God of my salvation; on Thee do I wait all the day."

The quiet glow of hopefulness with which Hagar returned to Abram's encampment should possess the spirit of every one of us. Hagar's prospects were not in all respects inviting. She knew the kind of treatment she was likely to receive at the hands of Sarah. She was to be a bondwoman still. But God had persuaded her of His care and had given her a hope large enough to fill her heart. That hope was to be fulfilled by a return to the home she had fled from, by a humbling and painful experience. There is no person for whom God has not similar encouragement. Frequently persons forget that God is in their life, fulfilling His purposes. They flee from what is painful; they lose their bearings in life and know not which way to turn; they do not fancy there is help for them in God. Yet God is with them; by these very circumstances that reduce them to desolateness and despair He leads them to hope in Him. Each one of us has a place in His purpose; and that place we shall find not by fleeing from what is distressing but by submitting ourselves cheerfully to what He appoints. God's purpose is real, and life is real, meant to accomplish not our present passing pleasure, but lasting good in conformity with God's purpose. Be sure that when you are bidden back to duties that seem those of a slave, you are bidden to them by God, Whose purposes are worthy of Himself and Whose purposes include you and all that concerns you.

There are, I think, few truths more animating than this which is here taught us, that God has a purpose with each of us; that however insignificant we seem, however friendless, however hardly used, however ousted even from our natural place in this world's households, God has a place for us; that however we lose our way in life we are not lost from His eye; that even when we do not think of choosing Him He in His Divine, all-embracing love chooses us, and throws about us bonds from which we cannot escape. Of Hagar many were complacently thinking it was no great matter if she were lost, and some might consider themselves righteous because they said she deserved whatever mishap might befall her. But not so God. Of some of us, it may be, others may think no great blank would be made by our loss; but God's compassion and care and purpose comprehend the least worthy. The very hairs of your head are all numbered by Him. Nothing is so trivial and insignificant as to escape His attention, nothing so intractable that He cannot use it for good. Trust in Him, obey Him, and your life will yet be useful and happy.

CHAPTER XIII.

THE COVENANT SEALED.

GENESIS xvii.

ACCORDING to the dates here given fourteen years had passed since Abram had received any intimation of God's will regarding him. Since the covenant had been made some twenty years before, no direct communication had been received; and no message of any kind since Ishmael's birth. It need not, therefore, surprise us that we are often allowed to remain for years in a state of suspense, uncertain about the future, feeling that we need more light and yet unable to find it. All truth is not discovered in a day, and if that on which we are to found for eternity take us twenty years or a life's experience to settle it in its place, why should we on this account be overborne with discouragement? They who love the truth and can as little abstain from seeking it as the artist can abstain from admiring what is lovely, will assuredly have their reward. To be expectant yet not impatient, unsatisfied yet not unbelieving, to hold mind and heart open, assured that light is sown for the upright and that all that is has lessons for the teachable, this is our proper attitude.

> Think you, 'mid all this mighty sum
> Of things for ever speaking,
> That nothing of itself will come,
> But we must still be seeking?

We appreciate the significance of a revelation in proportion as we understand the state of mind to which it is made. Abram's state of mind is disclosed in the exclamation: "Oh, that Ishmael might live before Thee!" He had learned to love the bold, brilliant, domineering boy. He saw how the men liked to serve him and how proud they were of the young chief. No doubt his wild intractable ways often made his father anxious. Sarah was there to point out and exaggerate all his faults and to prognosticate mischief. But there he was, in actual flesh and blood, full of life and interest in everything, daily getting deeper into the affections of Abram, who allowed and could not but allow his own life to revolve very much around the dashing, attractive lad. So that the reminder that he was not the promised heir was not entirely welcome. When he was told that the heir of promise was to be Sarah's child, he could not repress the somewhat peevish exclamation: "Oh, that Ishmael might serve Thy turn!" Why call me off again from this actual attainment to the vague, shadowy, non-existent heir of promise, who surely can never have the brightness of eye and force of limb and lordly ways of this Ishmael? Would that what already exists in actual substance before the eye might satisfy Thee and fulfil Thine intention and supersede the necessity of further waiting! Must I again loosen my hold, and part with my chief attainment? Must I cut my moorings and launch again upon this ocean of faith with a horizon always receding and that seems absolutely boundless?

We are familiar with this state of mind. We wish God would leave us alone. We have found a very attractive substitute for what He promises, and we resent being reminded that our substitute is not, after all, the veritable, eternal, best possession. It satisfies our taste, our intellect, our ambition; it sets us on a level with other men and gives us a place in the world; but now and again we feel a void it does not fill. We have attained comfortable circumstances, success in our profession, our life has in it that which attracts applause and sheds a brilliance over it; and we do not like being told that this is not all. Our feeling is Oh, that this might do! that this might be accepted as perfect attainment! it satisfies me (all but a little bit); might it not satisfy God? Why summon me again away from domestic happiness, intellectual enjoyment, agreeable occupations, to what really seems so unattainable as perfect fellowship with God in the fulfilment of His promise? Why spend all my life in waiting and seeking for high spiritual things when I have so much with which I can be moderately satisfied? For our complaint often is not that God gives so little but that He offers too much, more than we care to have; that He never will let us be content with anything short of what perfectly fulfils His perfect love and purpose.

This being Abram's state of mind, he is aroused from it by the words: "I am the Almighty God; walk before Me and be thou perfect." I am the Almighty God, able to fulfil your highest hopes and accomplish for you the brightest ideal that ever My words set before you. There is no need of paring down the promise till it square with human probabilities, no need of relinquishing one hope it has begotten, no need of adopting some interpretation of it which may make it seem easier to fulfil, and no need of striving to fulfil it in any second-rate way. All possibility lies in this: I am the Almighty God. Walk before Me and be thou perfect, therefore. Do not train your eye to earthly distances and earthly magnitudes and limit your hope accordingly, but live in the presence of the Almighty God. Do not defer the advices of conscience and of your purest aspirations to some other possible world; do not settle down at the low level of godless nature and of the men around you; do not give way to what you yourself know to be weakness and evidence of defeat; do not let self-indulgence take the place of My commandments, indolence supplant resolution and the likelihoods of human calculation obliterate the hopes stirred by the Divine call: Be thou perfect. Is not this a summons that comes appropriately to every man? Whatever be our contentment, our attainments, our possessions, a new light is shed upon our condition when we measure it by God's idea and God's resources. Is my life God's ideal? Does that which satisfies me satisfy Him?

The purpose of God's present appearance to Abram was to renew the covenant, and this He does in terms so explicit, so pregnant, so magnificent that Abram must have seen more distinctly than ever that he was called to play a very special part in God's providence. That kings should spring from him, a mere pastoral nomad in an alien country, could not suggest itself to Abram as a likely thing to happen. Indeed, though a line of kings or two lines of kings did spring from him through Isaac, the terms of the prediction seem scarcely exhausted by that fulfilment. And accordingly Paul without hesitation or reserve transfers this prediction to a spiritual region, and is at pains to show that the many nations of whom Abram was to be the father, were not those who inherited his blood, his natural appearance, his language and earthly inheritance, but those who inherited his spiritual qualities and the heritage in God to which his faith gave him entrance. And he argues that no difference of race or disadvantages of worldly position can prevent any man from serving himself heir to Abram, because the seed, to whom as well as to Abram the promise was made, was Christ, and in Christ there is neither Jew, nor Gentile, bond nor free, but all are one.

In connection then with this covenant in which God promised that He would be a God to Abram and to his seed, two points of interest to us emerge. First that Christ is Abram's heir. In His use of God's promise we see its full significance. In His life-long appropriation of God we see what God meant when He said, "I will be a God to thee and to thy seed." We find our Lord from the first living as one who felt His life encompassed by God, embraced and comprehended in that higher life which God lives through all and in all. His life was all and whole a life in God. He recognised what it is to have a God, one Whose will is supreme and unerringly good, Whose love is constant and eternal, Who is the first and the last, beyond Whom and from under Whom we can never pass. He moved about in the world in so perfectly harmonious a correspondence with God, so merging Himself in God and His purpose and with so unhesitating a reliance upon Him, that He seemed and was but a manifestation of God, God's will embodied, God's child, God expressing Himself in human nature. He showed us once for all the blessedness of true dependence, fidelity and faith. He showed us how that simple promise "I will be a God to thee," received in faith, lifts the human life into fellowship with all that is hopeful and inspiring, with all that is purifying, with all that is real and abiding.

But a second point is, that Jesus was the heir of Abram not merely because He was his descendant, a Jew with all the advantages of the Jew, but because, like Abram, He was full of faith. God was the atmosphere of His life. But He claimed God not because He was Jewish, but because He was human. Through the Jews God had made Himself known, but it was to what was human not to what was Jewish He appealed. And it was as Son of man not as son of Israel or of Adam that Jesus responded to God and lived with Him as His God. Not by specially Jewish rites did Jesus approach and rest in God, but by what is universal and human, by prayer to the Father, by loving obedience, by faith and submission. And thus we too may be joint-heirs with Christ and possess God. And if we think of ourselves as left to struggle with natural defects amidst irreversible natural laws; if we begin to pray very heartlessly, as if He who once listened were now asleep or could do nothing; if our life seems profitless, purposeless, and all unhinged; then let us look back to this sure promise of God, that He will be our God: *our* God, for, if Christ's God, then ours, for if we be Christ's then are we Abram's seed and heirs according to the promise. How few in any given day are living on this promise: how few attach reality to God's continuous revelation of Himself, the reality in this world's transitory history: how few can believe in the nearness and observance and love of God: how few can strenuously seek to be holy or understand where abiding happiness is to be found; for all these things are here. Yet who knocks at this door? Who makes, as Christ made, his life a unity with God, undismayed, unmurmuring, unreluctant, neither fearful of God nor disobedient, but diligent, earnest, jubilant, because God has said, "I will be thy God." Do you believe these things and can you forbear to use them? Do you believe that it is open to you, whosoever you are, to have the Eternal and Supreme God for your God, that He may use all His Divine nature in your behalf; have you conceived what it is that God means when He extends to you this offer, and can you decline to accept it, can you do otherwise than cherish it and seek to find more and more in it every day you live?

Two seals were at this time affixed to the covenant: the one for Abram himself, the other for every one who shared with him in his blessings of the covenant. The first consisted in the change of his own name to Abraham, "the father of a multitude," and of his wife's to Sarah, "princess" or "queen," because she was now announced as the destined mother of kings. And however Abraham would be annoyed to see the hardly surpressed smile on the ironical faces of his men as he boldly commanded them to call him by a name whose verification seemed so grievously to lag; and however indignant and pained he may have been to hear the young Ishmael jeering Sarah with her new name, and lending to it every tone of mockery and using it with insolent frequency, yet Abraham knew that these names were not given to deceive; and probably as the name of Abraham has become one of the best known names on earth, so to himself did it quickly acquire a preciousness as God's voice abiding with him, God's promise renewed to him through every man that addressed him, until at length the child of promise lying on his knees took up its first syllable and called him "Abba."

This seal was special to Abraham and Sarah, the other was public. All who desired to partake with Abraham in the security, hope, and happiness of having God as their God, were to submit to circumcision. This sign was to determine who were included in the covenant. By this outward mark encouragement and assurance of faith were to be quickened in the heart of all Abraham's descendants.

The mark chosen was significant. It was indeed not distinctive in its outward form; so little so that at this day no fewer than one hundred and fifty millions of the race make use of the same rite for one purpose or other. All the descendants of Ishmael of course continue it, but also all who have their religion, that is, all Mohammedans; but besides these, some tribes in South America, some in Australia, some in the South Sea Islands, and a large number of Kaffir tribes. The ancient Egyptians certainly practised it, and it has been suggested that Abraham may have become acquainted with the practice during his sojourn in Egypt. It is however uncertain whether the practice in Egypt runs back to so early a time. If it were an established Egyptian usage, then of course Hagar would demand for her boy at the usual age the rite which she had always associated with entrance on a new stage of life. But even supposing this was the case, the rite was none the less available for the new use to which it was now put. The rainbow existed before the Flood; bread and wine existed before the night of the Lord's Supper; baptisms of various kinds were practised before the days of the Apostles. And for this very reason, when God desired a natural emblem of the stability of the seasons He chose a striking feature of nature on which men were already accustomed to look with pleasure and hope; when He desired symbols of the body and blood of the Redeemer He took those articles which already had a meaning as the most efficacious human nutriment: when He desired to represent to the eye the renunciation of the old life and the birth to a new life which we have by union with Christ, He took that rite which was already known as the badge of discipleship; and when He desired to impress men by symbol with the impurity of nature and with our dependence on God for the production of all acceptable life, He chose that rite which, whether used before or not, did most strikingly represent this.

With the significance of circumcision to other men who practise it, we have here nothing to do. It is as the chief sacrament of the old covenant, by which God meant to aid all succeeding generations of Hebrews in believing that God was their God. And this particular mark was given, rather than any other, that they might recognise and ever remember that human nature was unable to generate its own Saviour, that in man there is a native impurity which must be laid aside when he comes into fellowship with the Holy God. And these circumcised races, although in many respects as unspiritual as others, have yet in general perceived that God is different from nature, a Holy Being to Whom we cannot attain by any mere adherence to nature, but only by the aid He Himself extends to us in ways for which nature makes no provision. The lesson of circumcision is an old one and rudely expressed, but it is vital; and no abhorrence of the circumcised for the uncircumcised too strongly, however unjustly, emphasises the distinction that actually subsists between those who believe in nature and those who believe in God.

The lesson is old, but the circumcision of the heart to which the outward mark pointed, is ever required. That is the true seal of our fellowship with God; the earnest of the Spirit which gives promise of eternal union with the Holy One; the relentings, the shame, the softening of heart, the adoration and reverence for the holiness of God, the thirst for Him, the joy in His goodness, these are the first fruits of the Spirit, which lead on to our calling God Father, and feeling that to be alone with Him is our happiness. It is this putting aside of our natural confidence in nature and absorption in nature, and this turning to God as our confidence and our life, which constitutes the true circumcision of the heart.

Believing as Abraham was, he could not forbear smiling when God said that Sarah would be the mother of the promised seed. This incredulity of Abraham was so significant that it was commemorated in the name of Isaac, the laugher. This heir was typical of all God's best gifts, at first reckoned impossible, at last filling the heart with gladness. The smile of incredulity became the laughter of joy when the child was born and Sarah said, "God hath made me to laugh, so that all that hear will laugh with me." It is they who expect things so incongruous and so impossible to nature unaided that they smile even while they believe, who will one day find their hopes fulfilled and their hearts running over with joyful laughter. If your heart is fixed only on what you can accomplish for yourself, no great joy can ever be yours. But frame your actual hopes in accordance with the promise of God, expect holiness, fulness of joy, animating partnership with God in the highest matters, the resurrection of the dead, the life everlasting, and one day you will say, "God hath made me to laugh." But Abraham prostrating himself to hide a smile is the symbol of our common attitude. We profess to believe in a God of unspeakable power and goodness, but even while we do so we find it impossible to attach a sense of reality to His promises. They are kindly, well-intentioned words, but are apparently spoken in neglect of solid, obstinate facts. How hard is it for us to learn that God is the great reality, and that the reality of all else may be measured by its relation to Him.

Sarah's laughter had a different meaning. Indeed Sarah does not appear to have been by any means a blameless character. Her conduct towards Hagar showed us that she was a woman capable of generous impulses but not of the strain of continued magnanimous conduct. She was capable of yielding her wifely rights on the impulse of the brilliant scheme that had struck her, but like many other persons who can begin a magnanimous or generous course of conduct, she could not follow it up to the end, but failed disgracefully in her conduct towards her rival. So now again she betrays characteristic weakness. When the strangers came to Abraham's tent, and announced that she was to become a mother, she smiled in superior, self-assured, woman's wisdom. When the promise threatened no longer to hover over her household as a mere sublime and exalting idea which serves its purpose if it keep them in mind that God has spoken to them, but to take place now among the actualities of daily occurrence, she hails this announcement with a laugh of total incredulity. Whatever she had made of God's word, she had not thought it was really and veritably to come to pass; she smiled at the simplicity which could speak of such an unheard-of thing.

This is true to human nature. It reminds you how you have dealt with God's promises,—nay, with God's commandments—when they offered to make room for themselves in the everyday life of which you are masters, every detail of which you have arranged, seeming to know absolutely the laws and principles on which your particular line of life must be carried on. Have you never smiled at the simplicity which could set about making actual, about carrying out in practical life, in society, in work, in business, those thoughts, feelings, and purposes, which God's promises beget? Sarah did not laugh outright, but smiled behind the Lord; she did not mock Him to His face, but let the compassionate expression pass over her face with which we listen to the glowing hopes of the young enthusiast who does not know the world. Have we not often put aside God's voice precisely thus; saying within us, We know what kind of things can be done by us and others and what need not be attempted; we know what kind of frailties in social intercourse we must put up with, and not seek to amend; what kind of practices it is vain to think of abolishing; we know what use to make of God's promise and what use not to make of it; how far to trust it, and how far to give greater weight to our knowledge of the world and our natural prudence and sense? Does not our faith, like Sarah's, vary in proportion as the promise to be believed is unpractical? If the promise seems wholly to concern future things, we cordially and devoutly assent; but if we are asked to believe that God intends within the year to do so-and-so, if we are asked to believe that the result of God's promise will be found taking a substantial place among the results of our own efforts—then the derisive smile of Sarah forms on our face.

To look at the crowds of persons professing religion, one would suppose nothing was commoner than faith. There is nothing rarer. Devoutness is common, righteousness of life is common; a contempt for every kind of fraud and underhand practice is common; a high-minded disregard for this world's gains and glories is common; an abhorrence of sensuality and an earnest thirst for perfection are common —but faith? Will the Son of man when He comes find it on earth? May not the messengers of God yet say, Who hath believed our report? Why, the great majority of Christian people have never been near enough to spiritual things to know whether they are or are not; they have never narrowly weighed spiritual issues and trembled as they watched the uncertain balance; they say they believe God and a future of happiness because they really do not know what they are talking about—they have not measured the magnitude of these things. Faith is not a blind and careless assent to matters of indifference, faith is not a state of mental suspense with a hope that things may turn out to be as the Bible says. Faith is the firm persuasion that these things are so. And he who at once knows the magnitude of these things and believes that they are so, must be filled with a joy that makes him independent of the world, with an enthusiasm which must seem to the world like insanity. It is quite a different world in which the man of faith lives.

CHAPTER XIV.

ABRAHAM'S INTERCESSION FOR SODOM.

GENESIS xviii.

THE scene with which this chapter opens is one familiar to the observer of nomad life in the East. During the scorching heat and glaring light of noon, while the birds seek the densest foliage and the wild animals lie panting in the thicket and everything is still and silent as midnight, Abraham sits in his tent door under the spreading oak of Mamre. Listless, languid, and dreamy as he is, he is at once aroused into brightest wakefulness by the sudden apparition of three strangers. Remarkable as their appearance no doubt must have been, it would seem that Abraham did not recognise the rank of his visitors; it was, as the writer to the Hebrews says, "unawares" that he entertained angels. But when he saw them stand as if inviting invitation to rest, he treated them as hospitality required him to treat any wayfarers. He sprang to his feet, ran and bowed himself to the ground, and begged them to rest and eat with him. With the extraordinary, and as it seems to our colder nature extravagant courtesy of an Oriental, he rates at the very lowest the comforts he can supply; it is only a little water he can give to wash their feet, a morsel of bread to help them on their way, but they will do him a kindness if they accept these small attentions at his hands. He gives, however, much more than he offered, seeks out the fatted calf and serves while his guests sit and eat. The whole scene is primitive and Oriental, and "presents a perfect picture of the manner in which a modern Bedawee Sheykh receives travellers arriving at his encampment;" the hasty baking of bread, the celebration of a guest's arrival by the killing of animal food not on other occasions used even by large flock-masters; the meal spread in the open air, the black tents of the encampment stretching back among the oaks of Mamre, every available space filled with sheep, asses, camels,—the whole is one of those clear pictures which only the simplicity of primitive life can produce.

Not only, however, as a suitable and pretty introduction which may ensure our reading the subsequent narrative is it recorded how hospitably Abraham received these three. Later writers saw in it a picture of the beauty and reward of hospitality. It is very true, indeed, that the circumstances of a wandering pastoral life are peculiarly favourable to the cultivation of this grace. Travellers being the only bringers of tidings are greeted from a selfish desire to hear news as well as from better motives. Life in tents, too, of necessity makes men freer in their manners. They have no door to lock, no inner rooms to retire to, their life is spent outside, and their character naturally inclines to frankness and freedom from the suspicions, fears, and restraints of city life. Especially is hospitality accounted the indispensable virtue, and a breach of it as culpable as a breach of the sixth commandment, because to refuse hospitality is in many regions equivalent to subjecting a wayfarer to dangers and hardships under which he is almost certain to succumb.

"This tent is mine," said Yussouf. "but no more
Than it is God's ; come in, and be at peace ;
Freely shalt thou partake of all my store,
As I of His Who buildeth over these
Our tents His glorious roof of night and day,
And at Whose door none ever yet heard Nay."

Still we are of course bound to import into our life all the suggestions of kindly conduct which any other style of living gives us. And the writer to the Hebrews pointedly refers to this scene and says, "Let us not be forgetful to entertain strangers, for thereby some have entertained angels unawares." And often in quite a prosaic and unquestionable manner does it become apparent to a host, that the guest he has been entertaining has been sent by God, an angel indeed ministering to his salvation, renewing in him thoughts that had been dying out, filling his home with brightness and life like the smile of God's own face, calling out kindly feelings, provoking to love and to good works, effectually helping him onwards and making one more stage of his life endurable and even blessed. And it is not to be wondered at that our Lord Himself should have continually inculcated this same grace; for in His whole life and by His most painful experience were men being tested as to who among them would take the stranger in. He who became man for a little that He might for ever consecrate the dwelling of Abraham and leave a blessing in his household, has now become man for evermore, that we may learn to walk carefully and reverentially through a life whose circumstances and conditions, whose little socialities and duties, and whose great trials and strains He found fit for Himself for service to the Father. This tabernacle of our human body has by His presence been transformed from a tent to a temple, and this world and all its ways that He approved, admired, and walked in, is holy ground. But as He came to Abraham trusting to his hospitality, not sending before him a legion of angels to awe the patriarch but coming in the guise of an ordinary wayfarer; so did He come to His own and make His entrance among us, claiming only the consideration which He claims for the least of His people, and granting to whoever gave Him *that* the discovery of His Divine nature. Had there been ordinary hospitality in Bethlehem that night before the taxing, then a woman in Mary's condition had been cared for and not superciliously thrust among the cattle, and our race had been delivered from the everlasting reproach of refusing its God a cradle to be born and sleep His first sleep in, as it refused Him a bed to die in, and left cha ce to provide Him a grave in which to sleep His latest sleep. And still He is coming to us all requiring of us this grace of hospitality, not only in the case of every one who asks of us a cup of cold water and whom our Lord Himself will personate at the last day and say, "*I* was a stranger and ye took Me in;" but also in regard to those claims upon our heart's reception which He only in His own person makes.

But while we are no doubt justified in gathering such lessons from this scene, it can scarcely have been for the sake of inculcating hospitality that these angels visited Abraham. And if we ask, Why did God on this occasion use this exceptional form of manifesting Himself; why, instead of approaching Abraham in a vision or in word as had been found sufficient on former occasions, did He now adopt this method of becoming Abraham's guest and eating with him? —the only apparent reason is that He meant this also to be the test applied to Sodom. There too His angels were to appear as wayfarers, dependent on the hospitality of the town, and by the people's treatment of these unknown visitors their moral state was to be detected and judged. The peaceful meal under the oaks of Mamre, the quiet and confidential walk over the hills in the afternoon when Abraham in the humble simplicity of a godly soul was found to be fit company for these three—this scene where the Lord and His messengers receive a becoming welcome and where they leave only blessing behind them, is set in telling contrast to their reception in Sodom, where their coming was the signal for the outbursts of a brutality one blushes to think of, and elicited all the elements of a mere hell upon earth.

Lot would fain have been as hospitable as Abraham. Deeper in his nature than any other consideration was the traditional habit of hospitality. To this he would have sacrificed everything—the rights of strangers were to him truly inviolable. Lot was a man who could as little see strangers without inviting them to his house as Abraham could. He would have treated them handsomely as his uncle; and what he could do he did. But Lot had by his choice of a dwelling made it impossible he should afford safe and agreeable lodging to any visitor. He did his best, and it was not his reception of the angels that sealed Sodom's doom, and yet what shame he must have felt that he had put himself in circumstances in which his chief virtue could not be practised. So do men tie their own hands and cripple themselves so that even the good they would take pleasure in doing is either wholly impossible or turns to evil.

In divulging to Abraham His purpose in visiting Sodom, it is enounced here that God acted on a principle which seems afterwards to have become almost proverbial. Surely the Lord will do nothing but He revealeth His secret unto His servants the prophets. There are indeed two grounds stated for making known to Abraham this catastrophe. The reason that we should naturally expect, viz., that he might go on and warn Lot is not one of them. Why then make any announcement to Abraham if the catastrophe cannot be averted, and if Abraham is to turn back to his own encampment? The first reason is: "Shall I hide from Abraham that thing which I do? *Seeing that Abraham* shall surely become a great and mighty nation, and all the nations of the earth shall be blessed in him." In other words, Abraham has been made the depository of a blessing for all nations, and account must therefore be given to him when any people is summarily removed beyond the possibility of receiving this blessing. If a man has got a grant for the emancipation of the slaves in a certain district, and is informed on landing to put this grant in force that fifty slaves are to be executed that day, he has certainly a right to know and he will inevitably desire to know that this execution is to be, and why it is to be. When an officer goes to negotiate an exchange of prisoners, if two of the number cannot be exchanged, but are to be shot, he must be informed of this and account of the matter must be given him. Abraham often brooding on God's promise, living indeed upon it, must have felt a vague sympathy with all men, and a sympathy not at all vague, but most powerful and practical, with the men in the Jordan valley whom he had rescued from Chedorlaomer. If he was to be a blessing to any nation it must surely be to those who were within an afternoon's walk of his encampment and among whom his nephew had taken up his abode. Suppose he had not been told, but had risen next morning and seen the dense cloud of smoke overhanging the doomed cities, might he not with some justice have complained that although God had spoken to him the previous day, not one word of this great catastrophe had been breathed to him.

The second reason is expressed in the nineteenth verse; God had chosen Abraham that he might command his children and his household after him to keep the way of the Lord, to do justice and judgment that the Lord might fulfil His promise to Abraham. That is to say, as it was only by obedience and righteousness that Abraham and his seed were to continue in God's favour, it was fair that they should be encouraged to do so by seeing the fruits of unrighteousness. So that as the Dead Sea lay throughout their whole history on their borders reminding them of the wages of sin, they might never fail rightly to interpret its meaning, and in every great catastrophe read the lesson "except ye repent ye shall all likewise perish." They could never attribute to chance this predicted judgment. And in point of fact frequent and solemn reference was made to this standing monument of the fruit of sin.

As yet there was no moral law proclaimed by any external authority. Abraham had to discover what justice and goodness were from the dictates of his own conscience and from his observation upon men and things. But he was at all events persuaded that only so long as he and his sought honestly to live in what they considered to be righteousness would they enjoy God's favour. And they read in the destruction of Sodom a clear intimation that certain forms of wickedness were detestable to God.

The earnestness with which Abraham intercedes for the cities of the plain reveals a new side of his character. One could understand a strong desire on his part that Lot should be rescued, and no doubt the preservation of Lot formed one of his strongest motives to intercede, yet Lot is never named, and it is, I think, plain that he had more than the safety of Lot in view. He prayed that the city might be spared, not that the righteous might be delivered out of its ruin. Probably he had a lively interest in the people he had rescued from captivity, and felt a kind of protectorate over them as he sometimes looked down on them from the hills near his own tents. He pleads for them as he had fought for them, with generosity, boldness, and perseverance; and it was his boldness and unselfishness in fighting for them that gave him boldness in praying for them.

There has come into vogue in this country a kind of intercession which is the exact reverse of this of Abraham—an obtuse, mechanical intercession about whose efficacy one may cherish a reasonable suspicion. The Bible and common sense bid us pray with the Spirit and with the *understanding;* but at some meetings for prayer you are asked to pray for people you do not know and have no real interest in. You are not told even their names, so that if an answer is sent you could not identify the answer, nor is any clue given you by which, if God should propose to use you for their help, you could know where the help was to be applied. For all you know the slip of paper handed in among a score of others may misrepresent the circumstances; and even supposing it does not, what likeness to the effectual fervent prayer of an anxious man has the petition that is once read in your hearing and at once and for ever blotted from your mind by a dozen others of the same kind. Not so did Abraham pray; he prayed for those he knew and had fought for; and I see no warrant for expecting that our prayers will be heard for persons whose good we seek in no other way than prayer, in none of those ways which in all other matters our conduct proves we judge more effectual than prayer. When Lot was carried captive Abraham did not think it enough to put a petition for him in his evening prayer. He went and *did* the needful thing, so that now when there is nothing else he can do but pray, he intercedes, as few of us can without self-reproach or feeling that had we only done our part there might now be no need of prayer. What confidence can a parent have in praying for a son who is going to a country where vice abounds, if he has done little or nothing to infix in his boy's mind a love of virtue? In some cases the very persons who pray for others are themselves the obstacles preventing the answer. Were we to ask ourselves how much we are prepared to do for those for whom we pray, we should come to a more adequate estimate of the fervency and sincerity of our prayers.

The element in Abraham's intercession that jars on the reader is the trading temper that strives always to get the best possible terms. Abraham seems to think God can be beaten down and induced to make smaller and smaller demands. No doubt this style of prayer was suggested to Abraham by the statement on God's part that He was going to Sodom to see if its iniquity was so great as it was reported; that is, to number, as it were, the righteous men in it. Abraham seizes upon this and asks if He would not spare it if fifty were found in it. But Abraham, knowing Sodom as he did, could not have supposed this number would be found.

Finding, then, that God meets him so far, he goes on step by step getting larger in his demands, until when he comes to ten he feels that to go farther would be intolerably presumptuous. Along with this audacious beating down of God, there is a genuine and profound reverence and humility which at each renewal of the petition dictate some such expression as: " I who am but dust and ashes," " Let not my Lord be angry."

It is remarkable too that, throughout, it is for justice Abraham pleads, and for justice of a limited and imperfect kind. He proceeds on the assumption that the town will be judged as a town, and either wholly saved or wholly destroyed. He has no idea of individual discrimination being made, those only suffering who had sinned. And yet it is this principle of discrimination on which God ultimately proceeds, rescuing Lot. Yet is not this intercession the history of what every one who prays passes through, beginning with the idea that God is to be won over to more liberal views and a more munificent intention, and ending with the discovery that God gives what we should count it shameless audacity to ask? We begin to pray,

"As if ourselves were better certainly
Than what we come to—Maker and High Priest,"

and we leave off praying assured that the whole is to be managed by a righteousness and love and wisdom, which we cannot plan for, which any love or desire of ours would only limit the action of, and which must be left to work out its own purposes in its own marvellous ways. We begin, feeling that we have to beat down a reluctant God and that we can guide the mind of God to some better thing than He intends: when the answer comes we recognise that what we set as the limit of our expectation God has far overstepped, and that our prayer has done little more than show our inadequate conception of God's mercy.

Not only in this respect but throughout this chapter there is betrayed an inadequate conception of God. The language is adapted to the use of men who are as yet unable to conceive of one Infinite, Eternal Spirit. They think of Him as one who needs to come down and institute an inquiry into the state of Sodom, if He is to know with accuracy the moral condition of its inhabitants. We can freely use the same language, but we put into it a meaning that the words do not literally bear: Abraham and his contemporaries used and accepted the words in their literal sense. And yet the man who had ideas of God in some respects so rudimentary was God's Friend, received singular tokens of His favour, found His whole life illuminated with His presence, and was used as the point of contact between heaven and earth, so that if you desire the first lessons in the knowledge of God which will in time grow into full information, it is to the tent of Abraham you must go. This surely is encouraging; for who is not conscious of much difficulty in thinking rightly of God? Who does not feel that precisely here, where the light should be brightest, clouds and darkness seem to gather? It may indeed be said that what was excusable in Abraham is inexcusable in us; that we have that day, that full noon of Christ to which he could only, out of the dusky dawn, look forward. But after all may not a man with some justice say: Give me an afternoon with God, such as Abraham had; give me the opportunity of converse with a God submitting Himself to question and answer, to those means and instruments of ascertaining truth which I daily employ in other matters, and I will ask no more? Christ has given us entrance into the final stage of our knowledge of God, teaching us that God is a Spirit and that we cannot see the Father; that Christ Himself left earth and withdrew from the bodily eye that we might rely more upon spiritual modes of apprehension and think of God as a Spirit. But we are not at all times able to receive this teaching, we are children still and fall back with longing for the times when God walked and spoke with man. And this being so, we are encouraged by the experience of Abraham. We shall not be disowned by God though we do not know Him perfectly. We can but begin where we are, not pretending that that is clear and certain to us which in fact is not so, but freely dealing with God according to the light we have, hoping that we too, like Abraham, shall see the day of Christ and be glad; shall one day stand in the full light of ascertained and eternal truth, knowing as we are known.

In conclusion, we shall find when we read the following chapter, and especially the prayer of Lot that he might not be driven to the wild mountain district, but might occupy the little town of Zoar which was saved for his sake—we shall find that much light is reflected on this prayer of Abraham. Without trenching on what may be more fitly spoken of afterwards, it may now be observed that the difference between Lot and Abraham, as between man and man generally, comes out nowhere more strikingly than in their prayers. Abraham had never prayed for himself with a tithe of the persistent earnestness with which he prays for Sodom—a town which was much indebted to him, but towards which for more reasons than one a smaller man would have borne a grudge. Lot, on the other hand, much indebted to Sodom, identified indeed with it, one of its leading citizens, connected by marriage with its inhabitants, is in no agony about its destruction, and has indeed but one prayer to offer, and that is, that when all his fellow-townsmen are destroyed, he may be comfortably provided for. While the men he has bargained and feasted with, the men he has made money out of and married his daughters to, are in the agonies of an appalling catastrophe and so near that the smoke of their torment sweeps across his retreat, he is so disengaged from regrets and compassion that he can nicely weigh the comparative comfort and advantage of city and rural life. One would have thought better of the man if he had declined the angelic rescue and resolved to stand by those in death whose society he had so coveted in life. And it is significant that while the generous, large-hearted, devout pleading of Abraham is in vain, the miserable, timorous, selfish petition of Lot is heard and answered. It would seem as if sometimes God were hopeless of men, and threw to them in contempt the gifts they crave, giving them the poor stations in this life their ambition is set upon, because He sees they have made themselves incapable of enduring hardness, and so quelling their lower nature. An answered prayer is not always a blessing, sometimes it is a doom: " He sent them meat to the full: but while their meat was yet in their mouths, the wrath of God came upon them and slew the fattest of them."

Probably had Lot felt any inclination to pray for his townsmen, he would have seen that for him to do so would be unseemly. His circumstances, his long association with the Sodomites, and his accommodation of himself to their ways had both eaten the soul out of him and set him on quite a different footing towards God from that occupied by Abraham. A man cannot on a sudden emergency lift himself out of the circumstances in which he has been rooted, nor peel off his character as if it were only skin-deep. Abraham had been living an unworldly life in which intercourse with God was a familiar employment. His prayer was but the seasonable flower of his life, nourished to all its beauty by the habitual nutriment of past years. Lot in his need could only utter a peevish, pitiful, childish cry. He had aimed all his life at being comfortable, he could not now wish anything more than to be comfortable. "Stand out of my sunshine," was all he could say, when he held by the hand the plenipotentiary of heaven, and when the roar of the conflict of moral good and evil was filling his ears—a decent man, a righteous man, but the world had eaten out his heart till he had nothing to keep him in sympathy with heaven.

Such is the state to which men in our society, as in Sodom, are brought by risking their spiritual life to make the most of this world.

CHAPTER XV.

DESTRUCTION OF THE CITIES OF THE PLAIN.

Genesis xix.

While Abraham was pleading with the Lord the angels were pursuing their way to Sodom. And in doing so they apparently observed the laws of those human forms which they had assumed. They did not spread swift wings and alight early in the afternoon at the gates of the city; but taking the usual route, they descended from the hills which separated Abraham's encampment from the plain of the Jordan, and as the sun was setting reached their destination. In the deep recess which is found at either side of the gateway of an Eastern city, Lot had taken his accustomed seat. Wearied and vexed with the din of the revellers in the street, and oppressed with the sultry doom-laden atmosphere, he was looking out towards the cool and peaceful hills, purple with the sinking sun behind them, and letting his thoughts first follow and then outrun his eye; he was now picturing and longing for the unseen tents of Abraham, and almost hearing the cattle lowing round at evening and all the old sounds his youth had made familiar.

He is recalled to the actual present by the footfall of the two men, and little knowing the significance of his act, invites them to spend the night under his roof. It has been observed that the historian seems to intend to bring out the quietness and the ordinary appearance of the entire circumstances. All goes on as usual. There is nothing in the setting sun to say that for the last time it has shone on these rich meadows, or that in twelve hours its rising will be dimmed by the smoke of the burning cities. The ministers of so appalling a justice as was here displayed enter the city as ordinary travellers. When a crisis comes, men do not suddenly acquire an intelligence and insight they have not habitually cultivated. They cannot suddenly put forth an energy nor exhibit an apt helpfulness which only character can give. When the test comes, we stand or fall not according to what we would wish to be and now see the necessity of being, but according to what former self-discipline or self-indulgence has made us.

How then shall this angelic commission of enquiry proceed? Shall it call together the elders of Sodom—or shall it take Lot outside the city and cross-examine him, setting down names and dates and seeking to come to a fair judgment. Not at all—there is a much surer way of detecting character than by any process of examination by question and answer. To each of us God says:

> "Since by its *fruit* a tree is judged,
> Show me thy fruit, the *latest act* of thine!
> For in the *last* is summed the first, and all,—
> What thy life last put heart and soul into,
> There shall I taste thy product."

It is thus these angels proceed. They do not startle the inhabitants of Sodom into any abnormal virtue nor present opportunity for any unwonted iniquity. They give them opportunity to act in their usual way. Nothing could well be more ordinary than the entrance to the city of two strangers at sunset. There is nothing in this to excite, to throw men off their guard, to overbalance the daily habit, or give exaggerated expression to some special feature of character. It is thus we are all judged—by the insignificant circumstances in which we act without reflection, without conscious remembrance of an impending judgment, with heart and soul and full enjoyment.

First Lot is judged. Lot's character is a singularly mixed one. With all his selfishness, he was hospitable and public-spirited. Lover of good living, as undoubtedly he was, his courage and strength of character are yet unmistakable. His sitting at the gate in the evening to offer hospitality may fairly be taken as an indication of his desire to screen the wickedness of his townsmen, and also to shield the stranger from their brutality. From the style in which the mob addressed him, it is obvious that he had made himself offensive by interfering to prevent wrong-doing. He was nicknamed "the Censor," and his eye was felt to carry condemnation. It is true there is no evidence that his opposition had been of the slightest avail. How could it avail with men who knew perfectly well that with all his denunciation of their wicked ways, he preferred their money-making company to the desolation of the hills, where he would be vexed with no filthy conversation, but would also find no markets? Still it is to Lot's credit that in such a city, with none to observe, none to applaud, and none to second him, he should have been able to preserve his own purity of life and steadily to resist wrong-doing. It would be cynical to say that he cultivated austerity and renounced popular vices as a salve to a conscience wounded by his own greed.

That he had the courage which lies at the root of strength of character became apparent as the last dark night of Sodom wore on. To go out among a profligate, lawless mob, wild with passion and infuriated by opposition—to go out and shut the door behind him—was an act of true courage. His confidence in the influence he had gained in the town cannot have blinded him to the temper of the raging crowd at his door. To defend his unknown guests he put himself in a position in which men have frequently lost life.

In the first few hours of his last night in Sodom, there is much that is admirable and pathetic in Lot's conduct. But when we have said that he was bold and that he hated other men's sins, we have exhausted the more attractive side of his character. The inhuman collectedness of mind with which, in the midst of a tremendous public calamity, he could scheme for his own private well-being is the key to his whole character. He had no feeling. He was cold-blooded, calculating, keenly alive to his own interest, with all his wits about him to reap some gain to himself out of every disaster; the kind of man out of whom wreckers are made, who can with gusto strip gold rings off the fingers of doomed corpses; out of whom are made the villains who can rifle the pockets of their dead comrades on a battlefield, or the politicians who can still ride on the top of the wave that hurls their country on the rocks. When Abraham gave him his choice of a grazing ground, no rush of feeling, no sense of gratitude, prevented him from making the most of the opportunity. When his house was assailed, he had coolness, when he went out to the mob, to shut the door behind him that those within might not hear his bargain. When the angel, one might almost say, was flurried by the impending and terrible destruction, and was hurrying him away, he was calm enough to take in at a glance the whole situation and on the spot make provision for himself. There was no need to tell him not to look back as his wife did: no deep emotion would overmaster him, no unconquerable longing to see the last of his dear friends in Sodom would make him lose one second of his time. Even the loss of his wife was not a matter of such importance as to make him forget himself and stand to mourn. In every recorded act of his life appears this same unpleasant characteristic.

Between Lot and Judas there is an instructive similarity. Both had sufficient discernment and decision of character to commit themselves to the life of faith, abandoning their original residence and ways of life. Both came to a shameful end, because the motive even of the sacrifices they made was self-interest. Neither would have had so dark a career had he more justly estimated his own character and capabilities, and not attempted a life for which he was unfit. They both put themselves into a false position; than which nothing tends more rapidly to deteriorate character. Lot was in a doubly false position, because in Sodom, as well as in Abraham's shifting camp, he was out of place. He voluntarily bound himself to men he could not love. One side of his nature was paralysed; and that the side which in him especially required development. It is the influence of home life, of kindly surroundings, of friendships, of congenial employment, of everything which evokes the free expression of what is best in us; it is this which is a chief factor in the development of every man. But instead of the genial and fertilising influence of worthy friendships, and ennobling love, Lot had to pretend good-will where he felt none, and deceit and coldness grew upon him in place of charity. Besides, a man in a false position in life, out of which he can by any sacrifice deliver himself, is never at peace with God until he does deliver himself. And any attempt to live a righteous life with an evil conscience is foredoomed to failure.

And if it still be felt that Lot was punished with extreme severity, and that if every man who chose a good grazing ground or a position in life which was likely to advance his fortune were thereby doomed to end his days in a cave and under the darkest moral brand, society would be quite disintegrated, it must be remembered that, in order to advance his interests in life, Lot sacrificed much that a man is bound by all means to cherish; and further, it must be said that our destinies are thus determined. The whole iniquity and final consequences of our disposition are not laid before us in the mass; but to give the rein to any evil disposition is to yield control of our own life and commit ourselves to guidance which cannot result in good, and is of a nature to result in utter shame and wretchedness.

Turning from the rescued to the destroyed, we recognise how sufficient a test of their moral condition the presence of the angels was. The inhabitants of Sodom quickly afford evidence that they are ripe for judgment. They do nothing worse than their habitual conduct led them to do. It is not for this one crime they are punished; its enormity is only the legible instance which of itself convicts them. They are not aware of the frightful nature of the crime they seek to commit. They fancy it is but a renewal of their constant practice. They rush headlong on destruction and do not know it. How can it be otherwise? If a man *will not* take warning, if he will persist in sin, then the day comes when he is betrayed into iniquity the frightful nature of which he did not perceive, but which is the natural result of the life he has led. He goes on and will not give up his sin till at last the final damning act is committed which seals his doom. Character tends to express itself in one perfectly representative act. The habitual passion, whatever it is, is always alive and seeking expression. Sometimes one consideration represses it, sometimes another; but these considerations are not constant, while the passion is, and must therefore one day find its opportunity—its opportunity not for that moderate, guarded, disguised expression which passes without notice, but for the full utterance of its very essence. So it was here: the whole city, small and great, young and old, from every quarter came together unanimous and eager in prosecuting the vilest wickedness. No further investigation or proof was needed: it has indeed passed into a proverb: "they *declare* their sin as Sodom."

To punish by a special commission of enquiry is quite unusual in God's government. Nations are punished for immorality or for vicious administration of law or for neglect of sanitary principles by the operation of natural laws. That is to say, there is a distinctly traceable connection between the crime and its punishment; the one being the natural cause of the other. That nations should be weakened, depopulated, and ultimately sink into insignificance, is the natural result of a development of the military spirit of a country and the love of glory. That a population should be decimated by cholera or small-pox is the inevitable result of neglecting intelligible laws of health. It seems to me absurd to put this destruction of Sodom in the same category. The descent of meteoric stones from the sky is not the natural result of immorality. The vices of these cities have disastrous national results which are quite legibly written in some races existing in the present day. We have here to do not with what is natural but with what is miraculous. Of course it is open to any one to say, " It was merely accidental—it was a mere coincidence that a storm of lightning so violent as to set fire to the bituminous soil should rage in the valley, while on the hills a mile or two off all was serene; it was a mere coincidence that meteoric stones or some instrument of conflagration should set on fire just these cities, not only one of them but four of them, and no more." And certainly were there nothing more to go upon than the fact of their destruction, this coincidence, however extraordinary, must still be admitted as wholly natural, and having no relation to the character of the people destroyed. It might be set down as pure accident, and be classed with storms at sea, or volcanic eruptions, which are due to physical causes and have no relation to the moral character of those involved, but indiscriminately destroy all who happen to be present.

But we have to account not only for the fact of the destruction but for its prediction both to Abraham and to Lot. Surely it is only reasonable to allow that such prediction was supernatural; and the prediction being so, it is also reasonable to accept the account of the event given by the predictors of it, and understand it not as an ordinary physical catastrophe, but as an event contrived with a view to the moral character of those concerned, and intended as an infliction of punishment for moral offences. And before we object to a style of dealing with nations so different from anything we now detect, we must be sure that a quite different style of dealing was not at that time required. If there is an intelligent training of the world, it must follow the same law which requires that a parent deal in one way with his boy of ten and in another with his adult son.

Of Lot's wife the end is recorded in a curt and summary fashion. "His wife looked back from behind him, and she became a pillar of salt." The angel, knowing how closely on the heels of the fugitives the storm would press, had urgently enjoined haste, saying, " Look not behind thee, neither stay thou in all the plain." Rapid in its pursuit as a prairie fire, it was only the swift who could escape it. To pause was to be lost. The command, " Look not behind thee " was not given because the scene was too awful to behold, for what men can endure men may behold, and Abraham looked upon it from the hill above. It was given simply from the necessity of the case and from no less practical and more arbitrary reason. Accordingly, when the command was neglected, the consequence was felt. Why the infatuated woman looked back one can only conjecture. The woful sounds behind her, the roar of the flame and of Jordan driven back, the crash of falling houses and the last forlorn cry of the doomed cities, all the confused and terrific din that filled her ear, may well have paralysed her and almost compelled her to turn. But the use our Lord makes of her example shows us that He ascribed her turning to a different motive. He uses her as a warning to those who seek to save out of the destruction more than they have time to save, and so lose all. " He which shall be on the housetop, and his stuff in the house, let him not come down to take it away; and he that is in the field, let him likewise not return back. Remember Lot's wife." It would seem, then, as if our Lord ascribed her tragic fate to her reluctance to abandon her household stuff. She was a wife after Lot's own heart, who in the midst of danger and disaster had an eye to her possessions. The smell of fire, the hot blast in her hair, the choking smoke of blazing bitumen, suggested to her only the thought of her own house decorations, her hangings, and ornaments, and stores. She felt keenly the hardship of leaving so much wealth to be the mere food of fire. The thought of such intolerable waste made her more breathless with indignation than her rapid flight. Involuntarily as she looks at the bleak, stony mountains before her, she thinks of the rich plain behind; she turns for one last look, to see if it is impossible to return, impossible to save anything from the wreck. The one look transfixes her, rivets her with dismay and horror. Nothing she looked for can be seen; all is changed in wildest confusion. Unable to move, she is overtaken and involved in the sulphurous smoke, the bitter salts rise out of the earth and stifle her and encrust around her and build her tomb where she stands.

Lot's wife by her death proclaims that if we crave to make the best of both worlds, we shall probably lose both. Her disposition is not rare and exceptional as the pillar of salt which was its monument. She is not the only woman whose heart is so fixedly set upon her household possessions that she cannot listen to the angel-voices that would guide her. Are there none but Lot's wife who show that to them there is nothing so important, nothing else indeed to live for at all, but the management of a house and the accumulation of possessions? If all who are of the same mind as Lot's wife shared her fate the world would present as strange a spectacle as the Dead Sea presents at this day. For radically it was her divided mind which was her ruin. She had good impulses, she saw what she ought to do, but she did not do it with a mind made up. Other things divided her thoughts and diverted her efforts. What else is it ruins half the people who suppose themselves well on the way of life? The world is in their heart; they cannot pursue with undivided mind the promptings of a better wisdom. Their heart is with their treasure, and their treasure is really not in spiritual excellence, not in purity of character, not in the keen bracing air of the silent mountains where God is known, but in the comforts and gains of the luxurious plain behind.

We are to remember Lot's wife that we may bear in mind how possible it is that persons who promise well and make great efforts and bid fair to reach a place of safety may be overtaken by destruction. We can perhaps tell of exhausting effort, we may have outstripped many in practical repentance, but all this may only be petrified by present carelessness into a monument recording how nearly a man may be saved and yet be destroyed. " Have ye suffered all these things in vain, if it be yet in vain?" " Ye have run well, what now hinders you?" The question always is, not, what have you done, but what are you now doing? Up to the site of the pillar, Lot's wife had done as well as Lot, had kept pace with the angels; but her failure at that point destroyed her.

The same urgency may not be felt by all; but it should be felt by all to whose conscience it has been distinctly intimated that they have become involved in a state of matters which is ruinous. If you are conscious that in your life there are practices which may very well issue in moral disaster, an angel has taken you by the hand and bid you flee. For you to delay is madness. Yet this is what people will do. Sagacious men of the world, even when they see the probability of disaster, cannot bear to come out with loss. They will always wait a little longer to see if they cannot rescue something more, and so start on a fresh course with less inconvenience. They will not understand that it is better to live bare and stripped with a good conscience and high moral achievement, than in abundance with self-contempt. What they have always seems more to them than what they are.

CHAPTER XVI.

SACRIFICE OF ISAAC.

GENESIS xxii.

THE sacrifice of Isaac was the supreme act of Abraham's life. The faith which had been schooled by so singular an experience and by so many minor trials was here perfected and exhibited as perfect. The strength which he had been slowly gathering during a long and trying life was here required and used. This is the act which shines like a star out of those dark ages, and has served for many storm-tossed souls over whom God's billows have gone, as a mark by which they could still shape their course when all else was dark. The devotedness which made the sacrifice, the trust in God that endured when even such a sacrifice was demanded, the justification of this trust by the event, and the affectionate fatherly acknowledgment with which God gloried in the man's loyalty and strength of character—all so legibly written here—come home to every heart in the time of its need. Abraham has here shown the way to the highest reach of human devotedness and to the heartiest submission to the Divine will in the most heartrending circumstances. Men and women living our modern life are brought into situations which seem as torturing and overwhelming as those of Abraham, and all who are in such conditions find, in his loyal trust in God, sympathetic and effectual aid.

In order to understand God's part in this incident and to remove the suspicion that God imposed upon Abraham as a duty what was really a crime, or that He was playing with the most sacred feelings of His servant, there are one or two facts which must not be left out of consideration. In the first place, Abraham did not think it wrong to sacrifice his son. His own conscience did not clash with God's command. On the contrary, it was through his own conscience God's will impressed itself upon him. No man of Abraham's character and intelligence could suppose that any word of God could make that right which was in itself wrong, or would allow the voice of conscience to be drowned by some mysterious voice from without. If Abraham had supposed that in all circumstances it was a crime to take his son's life, he could not have listened to any voice that bade him commit this crime. The man who in our day should put his child to death and plead that he had a Divine warrant for it would either be hanged or confined as insane. No miracle would be accepted as a guarantee for the Divine dictation of such an act. No voice from heaven would be listened to for a moment, if it contradicted the voice of the universal conscience of mankind. But in Abraham's day the universal conscience had only approbation to express for such a deed as this. Not only had the father absolute power over the son, so that he might do with him what he pleased; but this particular mode of disposing of a son would be considered singular only as being beyond the reach of ordinary virtue. Abraham was familiar with the idea that the most exalted form of religious worship was the sacrifice of the first-born. He felt, in common with godly men in every age, that to offer to God cheap sacrifices while we retain for ourselves what is truly precious, is a kind of worship that betrays our low estimate of God rather than expresses true devotion. He may have been conscious that in losing Ishmael he had felt resentment against God for depriving him of so loved a possession; he may have seen Canaanite fathers offering their children to gods he knew to be utterly unworthy of any sacrifice; and this may have rankled in his mind until he felt shut up to offer his all to God in the person of his son, his only son, Isaac. At all events, however, it became his conviction that God desired him to offer his son; this was a sacrifice which was in no respect forbidden by his own conscience.

But although not wrong in Abraham's judgment, this sacrifice was wrong in the eye of God; how then can we justify God's command that He should make it? We justify it precisely on that ground which lies patent on the face of the narrative—God meant Abraham to make the sacrifice in spirit, not in the outward act. He meant to write deeply on the Jewish mind the fundamental lesson regarding sacrifice, that it is in the spirit and will all true sacrifice is made. God intended what actually happened, that Abraham's sacrifice should be complete and that human sacrifice should receive a fatal blow. So far from introducing into Abraham's mind erroneous ideas about sacrifice, this incident finally dispelled from his mind such ideas and permanently fixed in his mind the conviction that the sacrifice God seeks is the devotion of the living soul, not the consumption of a dead body. God met him on the platform of knowledge and of morality to which he had attained, and by requiring him to sacrifice his son taught him and all his descendants in what sense alone such sacrifice can be acceptable. God meant Abraham to sacrifice his son, but not in the coarse material sense. God meant him to yield the lad truly to Him; to arrive at the consciousness that Isaac more truly belonged to God than to him, his father. It was needful that Abraham and Isaac should be in perfect harmony with the Divine will. Only by being really and absolutely in God's hand could they, or can any one, reach the whole and full good designed for them by God.

How old Isaac was at the time of this sacrifice there is no means of accurately ascertaining. He was probably in the vigor of early manhood. He was able to take his share in the work of cutting wood for the burnt offering and carrying the faggots a considerable distance. It was necessary too that this sacrifice should be made on Isaac's part not with the timorous shrinking or ignorant boldness of a boy, but with the full comprehension and deliberate consent of maturer years. It is probable that Abraham was already preparing, if not to yield to Isaac the family headship, yet to introduce him to a share in the responsibilities he had so long borne alone. From the touching confidence in one another which this incident exhibits, a light is reflected on the fond intercourse of former years. Isaac was at that time of life when a son is closest to a father, mature but not independent; when all that a father can do has been done, but while as yet the son has not passed away into a life of his own.

And Isaac was no ordinary son. The man of business who has encouraged and solaced himself in his toil by the hope that his son will reap the fruit of it and make his old age easy and honoured, but who outlives his son and sees the effort of his life go for nothing, the proprietor who bears an ancient name and sees his heir die —these are familiar objects of pathetic interest, and no heart is so hard as to refuse a tear of sympathy when brought into view of such heart-withering bereavements. But in Abraham all fatherly feelings had been evoked and strengthened and deepened by a quite peculiar experience. By a special and most effectual discipline he had been separated from the objects which ordinarily divide men's attention and eke out their contentment in life, and his whole hopes had been compelled to centre in his son. It was not the perpetuation of a name nor the transmission of a well-known and valuable property; it was not even the gratification of the most justifiable and tender of human affections, that was crushed and thwarted in Abraham by this command; but it was also and especially that hope which had been aroused and fostered in him by extraordinary providences and which concerned, as he believed, not himself alone but all men.

Manifestly no harder task could have been set to Abraham than that which was imposed on him by the command, "Take now thy son, thine only son, Isaac, whom thou lovest," this son of thine in whom all the promises are yea and amen to thee, this son for whose sake thou gavest up home and kindred, and banished thy firstborn Ishmael, this son whom thou lovest, and offer him for a burnt-offering. This son, Abraham might have said, whom I have been taught to cherish, putting aside all other affections that I might love him above all, I am now with my own hand to slay, to slay with all the terrible niceties and formalities of sacrifice *and with all the love and adoration of sacrifice*. I am with my own hand to destroy all that makes life valuable to me, and as I do so I am to love and worship Him who commands this sacrifice. I am to go to Isaac, whom I have taught to look forward to the fairest happiest life, and I am to contradict all I ever told him and tell him now that he has only grown to maturity that he might be cut down in the flush and hope of opening manhood. What can Abraham have thought? Possibly the thought would occur that God was now recalling the great gift He had made. There is always enough conscience of sin in the purest human heart to engender self-reproach and fear on the faintest occasion; and when so signal a token of God's displeasure as this was sent, Abraham may well have believed himself to have been unwittingly guilty of some great crime against God, or have now thought with bitterness of the languid devotion he had been offering Him. I have in sacrificing a lamb been as if I had been cutting off a dog's neck, profane and thoughtless in my worship, and now God is solemnising me indeed. I have in thought or desire kept back the prime of my flock, and God is now teaching me that a man may not rob God. Who could have been surprised if in this horror of great darkness the mind of Abraham had become unhinged? Who could wonder if he had slain *himself* to make the loss of Isaac impossible? Who could wonder if he had sullenly ignored the command, waited for further light, or rejected an alliance with God which involved such lamentable conditions? Nothing that could befall him in consequence of disobedience, he might have supposed, could exceed in pain the agony of obedience. And it is always easier to endure the pain inflicted upon us by circumstances than to do with our own hand and free will what we know will involve us in suffering. It is not mere resignation but active obedience that was required of Abraham. His was not the passive resignation of the man out of whose reach death or disaster has swept his dearest treasures, and who is helped to resignation by the consciousness that no murmuring can bring them back—his was the far more difficult act of resignation, which has still in possession all that it prizes, and may withhold these treasures if it pleases, but is called by a higher voice than that of self-pleasing to sacrifice them all.

But though Abraham was the chief, he was not the sole actor in this trying scene. To Isaac this was the memorable day of his life, and quiescent and passive as his character seems to have been, it cannot but have been stirred and strained now in every fibre of it. Abraham could not find it in his heart to disclose to his son the object of the journey; even to the last he kept him unconscious of the part he was himself to play. Two long days' journey, days of intense inward commotion to Abraham, they went northward. On the third day the servants were left, and father and son went on alone, unaccompanied and unwitnessed. "So they went," as the narrative twice over says, "both of them together," but with minds how differently filled; the father's heart torn with anguish and distracted by a thousand thoughts, the son's mind disengaged, occupied only with the new scenes and with passing fancies. Nowhere in the narrative does the completeness of the mastery Abraham had gained over his natural feelings appear more strikingly than in the calmness with which he answers Isaac's question. As they approach the place of sacrifice Isaac observes the silent and awestruck demeanour of his father, and fears that it may have been through absence of mind he has neglected to bring the lamb. With a gentle reverence he ventures to attract Abraham's attention: "My father;" and he said, "Here am I, my son." And he said, "Behold the fire and the wood, but where is the lamb for a burnt offering?" It is one of those moments when only the strongest heart can bear up calmly and when only the humblest faith has the right word to say. "My son, the Lord will provide Himself a lamb for a burnt offering."

Not much longer could the terrible truth be hidden from Isaac. With what feelings must he have seen the agonised face of his father as he turned to bind him and as he learned that he must prepare not to sacrifice but to be sacrificed. Here then was the end of those great hopes on which his youth had been fed. What could such contradiction mean? Was he to submit even to his father in such a matter? Why should he not expostulate, resist, flee? Such ideas seem to have found short entertainment in the mind of Isaac. Trained by long experience to trust his father, he obeys without complaint or murmur. Still it cannot cease to be matter of admiration and astonishment that a young man should have been able on so brief a notice, through so shocking a way, and with so startling a reversal of his expectations, to forego all right to choose for himself, and yield himself implicitly to what he believed to be God's will. By a faith so absolute Isaac became indeed the heir of Abraham. When he laid himself on the altar, trusting his father and his God, he came of age as the true seed of Abraham and entered on the inheritance, making God his God. At that supreme moment he made himself over to God, he put himself at God's disposal; if his death was to be helpful in fulfilling God's purpose he was willing to die. It was God's will that must be done, not his. He knew that God could not err, could not harm His people; he was ignorant of the design which his death could fulfil, but he felt sure that his sacrifice was not asked in vain. He had familiarised himself with the thought that he belonged to God; that he was on earth for God's purposes, not for his own; so that now, when he was suddenly summoned to lay himself formally and finally on God's altar, he did not hesitate to do so. He had learned that there are possessions more worth preserving than life itself, that

> "Manhood is the one immortal thing
> Beneath Time's changeful sky"—

he had learned that "length of days is knowing when to die."

No one who has measured the strain that such sacrifice puts upon human nature can withhold his tribute of cordial admiration for so rare a devotedness, and no one can fail to see that by this sacrifice Isaac became truly the heir of Abraham. And not only Isaac, but every man attains his majority by sacrifice. Only by losing our life do we begin to live. Only by yielding ourselves truly and unreservedly to God's purpose do we enter the true life of men. The giving up of self, the abandonment of an isolated life, the bringing of ourselves into connection with God, with the Supreme and with the whole, this is the second birth. To reach that full stream of life which is moved by God's will and which is the true life of men, we must so give ourselves up to God that each of His commandments, each of His providences, all by which He comes into connection with us, has its due effect upon us. If we only seek from God help to carry out our own conception of life, if we only desire His power to aid us in making of this life what we have resolved it shall be, we are far indeed from Isaac's conception of God and of life. But if we desire that God fulfil in us, and through us, His own conception of what our life should be, the only means of attaining this desire is to put ourselves fairly into God's hand, unflinchingly to do what we believe to be His will irrespective of present darkness and pain and privation. He who thus bids an honest farewell to earth and lets himself be bound and laid upon God's altar, is conscious that in renouncing himself he has won God and become His heir.

Have you thus given yourselves to God? I do not ask if your sacrifice has been perfect, nor whether you do not ever seek great things still for yourselves; but do you know what it is thus to yield yourself to God, to put God first, yourself second or nowhere? Are you even occasionally quite willing to sink your own interests, your own prospects, your own native tastes, to have your own worldly hopes delayed or blighted, your future darkened? Have you even brought your intellect to bear upon this first law of human life, and determined for yourself whether it is the case or not that man's life, in order to be profitable, joyful, and abiding, must be lived in God? Do you recognise that human life is not for the individual's good, but for the common good, and that only in God can each man find his place and his work? All that we give up to Him we have in an ampler form. The very affections which we are called to sacrifice are purified and deepened rather than lost. When Abraham resigned his son to God and received him back their love took on a new delicacy and tenderness. They were more than ever to one another after this interference of God. And He meant it to be so. Where our affections are thwarted or where our hopes are blasted, it is not our injury, but our good, that is meant; a fineness and purity, an eternal significance and depth, are imparted to affections that are annealed by passing through the fire of trial.

Not till the last moment did God interpose with the gladdening words, "Lay not thine hand upon the lad, neither do thou anything unto him; for now I know that thou fearest God, seeing thou hast not withheld thy son, thine only son, from Me." The significance of this was so obvious that it passed into a proverb: "In the mount of the Lord it shall be provided." It was there, and not at any earlier point, Abraham saw the provision that had been made for an offering. Up to the moment when he lifted the knife over all he lived for, it was not seen that other provision was made. Up to the moment when it was indubitable that both he and Isaac were obedient unto death, and when in will and feeling they had sacrificed themselves, no substitute was visible, but no sooner was the sacrifice complete in spirit than God's provision was disclosed. It was the spirit of sacrifice, not the blood of Isaac, that God desired. It was the noble generosity of Abraham that God delighted in, not the fatherly grief that would have followed the actual death of Isaac. It was the heroic submission of father and son that God saw with delight, rejoicing that men were found capable of the utmost of heroism, of patient and unflinching adherence to duty. At any point short of the consummation, interposition would have come too soon, and would have prevented this educative and elevating display of the capacity of men for the utmost that life can require of them. Had the provision of God been made known one minute before the hand of Abraham was raised to strike, it would have remained doubtful whether in the critical moment one or other of the parties might not have failed. But when the sacrifice was complete, when already the bitterness of death was past, when all the agonizing conflict was over, the anguish of the father mastered, and the dismay of the son subdued to perfect conformity with the supreme will, then the full reward of victorious conflict was given, and God's meaning flashed through the darkness, and His provision was seen.

This is the universal law. We find God's provision only on the mount of sacrifice, not at any stage short of this, but only there. We must go the whole way in faith; what lies before us as duty, we must do; often in darkness and utter misery, seeing no possibility of escape or relief, we must climb the hill where we are to abandon all that has given joy and hope to our life; and not before the sacrifice has been actually made can we enter into the heaven of victory God provides. You may be called to sacrifice your youth, your hopes of a career, your affections, that you may uphold and soothe the lingering days of one to whom you are naturally bound. Or your whole life may have centred in an affection which circumstances demand you shall abandon: you may have to sacrifice your natural tastes and give up almost everything you once set your heart on; and while to others the years bring brightness and variety and scope, to you they may be bringing only monotonous fulfilment of insipid and uncongenial tasks. You may be in circumstances which tempt you to say, Does God see the inextricable difficulty I am in? Does He estimate the pain I must suffer if immediate relief do not come? Is obedience to Him only to involve me in misery from which other men are exempt? You may even say that although a substitute was found for Isaac, no substitute has been found for the sacrifice you have had to make, but you have been compelled actually to lose what was dear to you as life itself. But when the character has been fully tried, when the utmost good to character has been accomplished, and when delay of relief would only increase misery, then relief comes. Still the law holds good, that as soon as you in spirit yield to God's will, and with a quiet submissiveness consent to the loss or pain inflicted upon you, in that hour your whole attitude to your circumstances is transformed, you find rest and assured hope. Two things are certain: that, however painful your condition is, God's intention is not to injure, but to advance you, and that hopeful submission is wiser, nobler, and every way better than murmuring and resentment.

Finally, these words, "The Lord will provide," which Abraham uttered in that exalted frame of mind which is near to the prophetic ecstasy, have been the burden sung by every sincere and thoughtful worshipper as he ascended the hill of God to seek forgiveness of his sin, the burden which the Lord's worshipping congregation kept on its tongue through all the ages, till at length, as the angel of the Lord had opened the eyes of Abraham to see the ram provided, the voice of the Baptist "crying in the wilderness" to a fainting and well-nigh despairing few turned their eye to God's great provision with the final announcement, "Behold the Lamb of God." Let us accept this as a motto which we may apply, not only in all temporal straits, when we can see no escape from loss and misery, but also in all spiritual emergency, when sin seems a burden too great for us to bear, and when we seem to lie under the uplifted knife of God's judgment. Let us remember that God's desire is not that we suffer pain, but that we learn obedience, that we be brought to that true and thorough confidence in Him which may fit us to fulfil His loving purposes. Let us, above all, remember that we cannot know the grace of God, cannot experience the abundant provision He has made for weak and sinful men, until we have climbed the mount of sacrifice and are able to commit ourselves wholly to Him. Not by attacking our manifold enemies one by one, nor by attempting the great work of sanctification piecemeal, shall we ever make much growth or progress, but by giving ourselves up wholly to God and by becoming willing to live in Him and as His.

CHAPTER XVII.

ISHMAEL AND ISAAC.

GENESIS xxi., xxii.

"Abraham had two sons, the one by a bondmaid, the other by a freewoman. * * * Which things are an allegory."—GALATIANS iv. 22.

"Abraham stretched forth his hand, and took the knife to slay his son."—GENESIS xxii. 10.

IN the birth of Isaac, Abraham at length sees the long-delayed fulfilment of the promise. But his trials are by no means over. He has himself introduced into his family the seeds of discord and disturbance, and speedily the fruit is borne. Ishmael, at the birth of Isaac, was a lad of fourteen years, and, reckoning from Eastern customs, he must have been over sixteen when the feast was made in honour of the weaned child. Certainly he was quite old enough to understand the important and not very welcome alteration in his prospects which the birth of this new son effected. He had been brought up to count himself the heir of all the wealth and influence of Abraham. There was no alienation of feeling between father and son: no shadow had flitted over the bright prospect of the boy as he grew up; when suddenly and unexpectedly there was interposed between him and his expectation the effectual barrier of this child of Sarah's. The importance of this child to the family was in due course indicated in many ways offensive to Ishmael; and when the feast was made, his spleen could no longer be repressed. This weaning was the first step in the direction of an independent existence, and this would be the point of the feast in celebration. The child was no longer a mere part of the mother, but an individual, a member of the family. The hopes of the parents were carried forward to the time when he should be quite independent of them.

But in all this there was great food for the ridicule of a thoughtless lad. It was precisely the kind of thing which could easily be mocked without any great expenditure of wit by a boy of Ishmael's age. The too visible pride of the aged mother, the incongruity of maternal duties with ninety years, the concentration of attention and honours on so small an object,—all this was, doubtless, a temptation to a boy who had probably at no time too much reverence. But the words and gestures which others might have disregarded as childish frolic, or, at worst, as the unseemly and ill-natured impertinence of a boy who knew no better, stung Sarah, and left a poison in her blood that infuriated her. "Cast out that bondwoman and her son," she demanded of Abraham. Evidently she feared the rivalry of this second household of Abraham, and was resolved it should come to an end. The mocking of Ishmael is but the violent concussion that at last produces the explosion, for which material has long been laid in train. She had seen on Abraham's part a clinging to Ishmael, which she was unable to appreciate. And though her harsh decision was nothing more than the dictate of maternal jealousy, it did prevent things from running on as they were until even a more painful family quarrel must have been the issue.

The act of expulsion was itself unaccountably harsh. There was nothing to prevent Abraham sending the boy and his mother under an escort to some safe place; nothing to prevent him from giving the lad some share of his possessions sufficient to provide for him. Nothing of this kind was done. The woman and the boy were simply put to the door; and this, although Ishmael had for years been counted Abraham's heir, and though he was a member of the covenant made with Abraham. There may have been some law giving Sarah absolute power over her maid; but if any law gave her power to do what was now done, it was a thoroughly barbarous one, and she was a barbarous woman who used it.

It is one of those painful cases in which one poor creature clothed with a little brief authority stretches it to the utmost in vindictive maltreatment of another. Sarah happened to be mistress, and, instead of using her position to make those under her happy, she used it for her own convenience, for the gratification of her own spite, and to make those beneath her conscious of her power by their suffering. She happened to be a mother, and instead of bringing her into sympathy with all women and their children, this concentrated her affection with a fierce jealousy on her own child. She breathed freely when Hagar and Ishmael were fairly out of sight. A smile of satisfied malice betrayed her bitter spirit. No thought of the sufferings to which she had committed a woman who had served her well for years, who had yielded everything to her will, and who had no other natural protector but her, no glimpses of Abraham's saddened face, visited her with any relentings. It mattered not to her what came of the woman and the boy to whom she really owed a more loving and careful regard than to any except Abraham and Isaac. It is a story often repeated. One who has been a member of the household for many years is at last dismissed at the dictate of some petty pique or spite as remorselessly and inhumanly as a piece of old furniture might be parted with. Some thoroughly good servant, who has made sacrifices to forward his employer's interest, is at last, through no offence of his own, found to be in his employer's way, and at once all old services are forgotten, all old ties broken, and the authority of the employer, legal but inhuman, is exercised. It is often those who can least defend themselves who are thus treated; no resistance is possible, and also, alas! the party is too weak to face the wilderness on which she is thrown out, and if any cares to follow her history, we may find her at the last gasp under a bush.

Still, both for Abraham and for Ishmael, it was better this severance should take place. It was grievous to Abraham; and Sarah saw that for this very reason it was necessary. Ishmael was his firstborn, and for many years had received the whole of his parental affection: and, looking on the little Isaac, he might feel the desirableness of keeping another son in reserve, lest this strangely-given child might as strangely pass away. Coming to him in a way so unusual, and having perhaps in his appearance some indication of his peculiar birth, he might seem scarcely fit for the rough life Abraham himself had led. On the other hand, it was plain that in Ishmael were the very qualities which Isaac was already showing that he lacked. Already Abraham was observing that with all his insolence and turbulence there was a natural force and independence of character which might come to be most useful in the patriarchal household. The man who had pursued and routed the allied kings could not but be drawn to a youth who already gave promise of capacity for similar enterprises—and this youth his own son. But can Abraham have failed to let his fancy picture the deeds this lad might one day do at the head of his armed slaves? And may he not have dreamt of a glory in the land not altogether such as the promise of God encouraged him to look for, but such as the tribes around would acknowledge and fear? All the hopes Abraham had of Ishmael had gained firm hold of his mind before Isaac was born; and before Isaac grew up, Ishmael must have taken the most influential place in the house and plans of Abraham. His mind would thus have received a strong bias towards conquests and forcible modes of advance. He might have been led to neglect, and, perhaps, finally despise, the unostentatious blessings of heaven.

If, then, Abraham was to become the founder, not of one new warlike power in addition to the already too numerous warlike powers of the East, but of a religion which should finally develop into the most elevating and purifying influence among men, it is obvious that Ishmael was not at all a desirable heir. Whatever pain it gave to Abraham to part with him, separation in some form had become necessary. It was impossible that the father should continue to enjoy the filial affection of Ishmael, his lively talk, and warm enthusiasm, and adventurous exploits, and at the same time concentrate his hope and his care on Isaac. He had, therefore, to give up, with something of the sorrow and self-control he afterwards underwent in connection with the sacrifice of Isaac, the lad whose bright face had for so many years shone in all his paths. And in some such way are we often called to part with prospects which have wrought themselves very deep into our spirit, and which, indeed, just because they are very promising and seductive, have become dangerous to us, upsetting the balance of our life, and throwing into the shade objects and purposes which ought to be outstanding. And when we are thus required to give up what we were looking to for comfort, for applause, and for profit, the voice of God in its first admonition sometimes seems to us little better than the jealousy of a woman. Like Sarah's demand, that none should share with her son, does the requirement seem which indicates to us that we must set nothing on a level with God's direct gifts to us. We refuse to see why we may not have all the pleasures and enjoyments, all the display and brilliance that the world can give. We feel as if we were needlessly restricted. But this instance shows us that when circumstances compel us to give up something of this kind which we have been cherishing, room is given for a better thing than itself to grow.

For Ishmael himself, too, wronged as he was in the mode of his expulsion, it was yet far better that he should go. Isaac *was* the true heir. No jeering allusions to his late birth or to his appearance could alter that fact. And to a temper like Ishmael's it was impossible to occupy a subordinate, dependent position. All he required to call out his latent powers was to be thrown thus on his own resources. The daring and high spirit and quickness to take offence and use violence, which would have wrought untold mischief in a pastoral camp, were the very qualities which found fit exercise in the desert, and seemed there only in keeping with the life he had to lead. And his hard experience at first would at his age do him no harm, but good only. To be compelled to face life single-handed at the age of sixteen is by no means a fate to be pitied. It was the making of Ishmael, and is the making of many a lad in every generation.

But the two fugitives are soon reminded that, though expelled from Abraham's tents and protection, they are not expelled from his God. Ishmael finds it true that when father and mother forsake him, the Lord takes him up. At the very outset of his desert life he is made conscious that God is still his God, mindful of his wants, responsive to his cry of distress. It was not through Ishmael the promised seed was to come, but the descendants of Ishmael had every inducement to retain faith in the God of Abraham, who listened to their father's cry. The fact of being excluded from certain privileges did not involve that they were to be excluded from all privileges. God still "heard the voice of the lad, and the angel of God called to Hagar out of heaven."

It is this voice of God to Hagar that so speedily, and apparently once for all, lifts her out of despair to cheerful hope. It would appear as if her despair had been needless; at least from the words addressed to her, "What aileth thee, Hagar?" it would appear as if she might herself have found the water that was close at hand, if only she had been disposed to look for it. But she had lost heart, and perhaps with her despair was mingled some resentment, not only at Sarah, but at the whole Hebrew connection, including the God of the Hebrews, who had before encouraged her. Here was the end of the magnificent promise which that God had made her before her child was born—a helpless human form gasping its life away without a drop of water to moisten the parched tongue and bring light to the glazing eyes, and with no easier couch than the burning sand. Was it for this, the bitterest drop that, apart from sin, can be given to any parent to drink, she had been brought from Egypt and led through all her past? Had her hopes been nursed by means so extraordinary only that they might be so bitterly blighted? Thus she leapt to her conclusions, and judged that because her skin of water had failed God had failed her too. No one can blame her, with her boy dying before her, and herself helpless to relieve one pang of his suffering. Hitherto, in the well-furnished tents of Abraham, she had been able to respond to his slightest desire. Thirst he had never known, save as the relish to some boyish adventure. But now, when his eyes appeal to her in dying anguish, she can but turn away in helpless despair. She cannot relieve his simplest want. Not for her own fate has she any tears, but to see her pride, her life and joy, perishing thus miserably, is more than she can bear.

No one can blame, but every one may learn from her. When angry resentment and unbelieving despair fill the mind, we may perish of thirst in the midst of springs. When God's promises produce no faith, but seem to us so much waste paper, we are necessarily in danger of missing their fulfilment. When we ascribe to God the harshness and wickedness of those who represent Him in the world, we commit moral suicide. So far from the promises given to Hagar being now at the point of extinction, this was the first considerable step toward their fulfilment. When Ishmael turned his back on the familiar tents, and flung his last gibe at Sarah, he was really setting out to a far richer inheritance, so far as this world goes, than ever fell to Isaac and his sons.

But the chief use Paul makes of this entire episode in the history is to see in it an allegory, a kind of picture made up of real persons and events, representing the impossibility of law and gospel living harmoniously together, the incompatibility of a spirit of service with a spirit of sonship. Hagar, he says, is in this picture the likeness of the law given from Sinai, which gendereth to bondage. Hagar and her son, that is to say, stand for the law and the kind of righteousness produced by the law,—not superficially a bad kind; on the contrary, a righteousness with much dash and brilliance and strong manly force about it, but at the root defective, faulty in its origin, springing from the slavish spirit. And first Paul bids us notice how the free-born is persecuted and mocked by the slave-born, that is, how the children of God who are trying to live by love and faith in Christ are put to shame and made uneasy by the law. They believe they are God's dear children, that they are loved by Him, and may go out and in freely in His house as their own home, using all that is His with the freedom of His heirs; but the law mocks them, frightens them, tells them *it* is God's firstborn; law lying far back in the dimness of eternity, co-eval with God Himself. It tells them they are puny and weak, scarcely out of their mother's arms, tottering, lisping creatures, doing much mischief, but none of the housework, at best only getting some little thing to pretend to work at. In contrast to their feeble, soft, unskilled weakness, it sets before them a finely-moulded, athletic form, becoming disciplined to all work, and able to take a place among the serviceable and able-bodied. But with all this there is in that puny babe a life begun which will grow and make it the true heir, dwelling in the house and possessing what it has not toiled for, while the vigorous, likely-looking lad must go into the wilderness and make a possession for himself with his own bow and spear.

Now, of course, righteousness of life and character, or perfect manhood, is the end at which all that we call salvation aims, and that which can give us the purest, ripest character is salvation for us; that which can make us, for all purposes, most serviceable and strong. And when we are confronted with persons who might speak of service we cannot render, of an upright, unfaltering carriage we cannot assume, of a general human worthiness we can make no pretension to, we are justly perturbed, and should regain our equanimity only under the influence of the most undoubted truth and fact. If we can honestly say in our hearts, "Although we can show no such work done, and no such masculine growth, yet we have a life in us which is of God, and will grow;" if we are sure that we have the spirit of God's children, a spirit of love and dutifulness, we may take comfort from this incident. We may remind ourselves that it is not he who has at the present moment the best appearance who always abides in the father's home, but he who is by birth the heir. Have we or have we not the spirit of the Son? not feeling that we must every evening make good our claim to another night's lodging by showing the task we have accomplished, but being conscious that the interests in which we are called to work are our own interests, that we are heirs in the father's house, so that all we do for the house is really done for ourselves. Do we go out and in with God, feeling no need of His commands, our own eye seeing where help is required, and our own desires being wholly directed towards that which engages all His attention and work?

For Paul would have each of us apply, allegorically, the words, Cast out the bondwoman and her son, that is, cast out the legal mode of earning a standing in God's house, and with this legal mode cast out all the self-seeking, the servile fear of God, the self-righteousness, and the hard-heartedness it engenders. Cast out wholly from yourself the spirit of the slave, and cherish the spirit of the son and heir. The slave-born may seem for a while to have a firm footing in the father's house, but it cannot last. The temper and tastes of Ishmael are radically different from those of Abraham, and when the slave-born becomes mature, the wild Egyptian strain will appear in his character. Moreover, he looks upon the goods of Abraham as plunder; he cannot rid himself of the feeling of an alien, and this would, at length, show itself in a want of frankness with Abraham—slowly, but surely, the confidence between them would be worn out. Nothing but being a child of God, being born of the Spirit, can give the feeling of intimacy, confidence, unity of interest, which constitutes true religion. All we do as slaves goes for nothing; that is to say, all we do, not because we see the good of it, but because we are commanded; not because we have any liking for the thing done, but because we wish to be paid for it. The day is coming when we shall attain our majority, when it will be said to us by God, Now, do whatever you like, whatever you have a mind to; no surveillance, no commands are now needed; I put all into your own hand. What, in these circumstances, should we straightway do? Should we, for the love of the thing, carry on the same work to which God's commands had driven us; should we, if left absolutely in charge, find nothing more attractive than just to prosecute that idea of life and the world set before us by Christ? Or should we see that we had merely been keeping ourselves in check for a while, biding our time, untamed as Ishmael, craving the rewards but not the life of the children of God? The most serious of all questions these—questions that determine the issues of our whole life, that determine whether our home is to be where all the best interests of men and the highest blessings of God have their seat, or in the pathless desert where life is an aimless wandering, dissociated from all the forward movements of men.

The distinction between the servile spirit and the spirit of sonship being thus radical, it could be by no mere formality, or exhibition of his legal title, that Isaac became the heir of God's heritage. His sacrifice on Moriah was the requisite condition of his succession to Abraham's place; it was the only suitable celebration of his majority. Abraham himself had been able to enter into covenant with God only by sacrifice; and sacrifice not of a dead and external kind, but vivified by an actual surrender of himself to God, and by so true a perception of God's holiness and requirements that he was in a horror of great darkness. By no other process can any of his heirs succeed to the inheritance. A true resignation of self, in whatever outward form this resignation may appear, is required that we may become one with God in His holy purposes and in His eternal blessedness. There could be no doubt that Abraham had found a true heir, when Isaac laid himself on the altar and steadied his heart to receive the knife. Dearer to God, and of immeasurably greater value than any service, was this surrender of himself into the hand of his Father and his God. In this was promise of all service and all loving fellowship. "Precious in the sight of the Lord is the death of His saints. O Lord, truly I am Thy servant; I am Thy servant, the son of Thine handmaid: Thou hast loosed my bonds."

So incomparable with the most distinguished service did this sacrifice of Isaac's self appear, that the record of his active life seems to have had no interest to his contemporaries or successors. There was but this one thing to say of him. No more seemed needful. The sacrifice was indeed great, and worthy of commemoration. No act could so conclusively have shown that Isaac was thoroughly at one with God. He had much to live for; from his birth there hovered round him interests and hopes of the most exciting and flattering nature; a new kind of glory such as had not yet been attained on earth was to be attained, or, at any rate, approached in him. This glory was certain to be realised, being guaranteed by God's promise, so that his hopes might launch out in the boldest confidence and give him the aspect and bearing of a king; while it was uncertain in the time and manner of its realisation, so that the most attractive mystery hung around his future. Plainly his was a life worth entering on and living through; a life fit to engage and absorb a man's whole desire, interest, and effort; a life such as might well make a man gird himself and resolve to play the man throughout, that so each part of it might reveal its secret to him, and that none of its wonder might be lost. It was a life which, above all others, seemed worth protecting from all injury and risk, and for which, no doubt, not a few of the homeborn servants in the patriarchal encampment would have gladly ventured their own. There have, indeed, been few, if any, lives of which it could so truly be said, The world cannot do without this—at all hazards and costs this must be cherished. And all this must have been even more obvious to its owner than to any one else, and must have begotten in him an unquestioning assurance, that he at least had a charmed life, and would live and see good days. Yet with whatever shock the command of God came upon him, there is no word of doubt or remonstrance or rebellion. He gave his life to Him who had first given it to him. And thus yielding himself to God, he entered into the inheritance, and became worthy to stand to all time the representative heir of God, as Abraham by his faith had become the father of the faithful.

CHAPTER XVIII.

PURCHASE OF MACHPELAH.

Genesis xxiii.

It may be supposed to be a needless observation that our life is greatly influenced by the fact that it speedily and certainly ends in death. But it might be interesting, and it would certainly be surprising, to trace out the various ways in which this fact influences life. Plainly every human affair would be altered if we lived on here for ever, supposing that were possible. What the world would be had we no predecessors, no wisdom but what our own past experience and the genius of one generation of men could produce, we can scarcely imagine. We can scarcely imagine what life would be or what the world would be did not one generation succeed and oust another and were we contemporary with the whole process of history. It is the grand irreversible and universal law that we give place and make room for others. The individual passes away, but the history of the race proceeds. Here on earth in the meantime, and not elsewhere, the history of the race is being played out, and each having done his part, however small or however great, passes away. Whether an individual, even the most gifted and powerful, could continue to be helpful to the race for thousands of years, supposing his life were continued, it is needless to inquire. Perhaps as steam has force only at a certain pressure, so human force requires the condensation of a brief life to give it elastic energy. But these are idle speculations. They show us, however, that our life beyond death will be not so much a prolongation of life as we now know it as an entire change in the form of our existence; and they show us also that our little piece of the world's work must be quickly done if it is to be done at all, and that it will not be done at all unless we take our life seriously and own the responsibilities we have to ourselves, to our fellows, to our God.

Death comes sadly to the survivor, even when there is as little untimeliness as in the case of Sarah; and as Abraham moved towards the familiar tent the most intimate of his household would stand aloof and respect his grief. The stillness that struck upon him, instead of the usual greeting, as he lifted the tent-door; the dead order of all inside; the one object that lay stark before him and drew him again and again to look on what grieved him most to see; the chill which ran through him as his lips touched the cold, stony forehead and gave him sensible evidence how gone was the spirit from the clay—these are shocks to the human heart not peculiar to Abraham. But few have been so strangely bound together as these two were, or have been so manifestly given to one another by God, or have been forced to so close a mutual dependence. Not only had they grown up in the same family, and been together separated from their kindred, and passed through unusual and difficult circumstances together, but they were made co-heirs of God's promise in such a manner that neither could enjoy it without the other. They were knit together, not merely by natural liking and familiarity of intercourse, but by God's choosing them as the instrument of His work and the fountain of His salvation. So that in Sarah's death Abraham doubtless read an intimation that his own work was done, and that his generation is now out of date and ready to be supplanted.

Abraham's grief is interrupted by the sad but wholesome necessity which forces us from the blank desolation of watching by the dead to the active duties that follow. She whose beauty had captivated two princes must now be buried out of sight. So Abraham stands up from before his dead. Such a moment requires the resolute fortitude and manly self-control which that expression seems intended to suggest. There is something within us which rebels against the ordinary ongoing of the world side by side with our great woe; we feel as if either the whole world must mourn with us, or we must go aside from the world and have our grief out in private. The bustle of life seems so meaningless and incongruous to one whom grief has emptied of all relish for it. We seem to wrong the dead by every return of interest we show in the things of life which no longer interest *him*. Yet he speaks truly who says:

> "When sorrow all our heart would ask,
> We need not shun our daily task,
> And hide ourselves for calm;
> The herbs we seek to heal our woe,
> Familiar by our pathway grow,
> Our common air is balm."

We must resume our duties, not as if nothing had happened, not proudly forgetting death and putting grief aside as if this life did not need the chastening influence of such realities as we have been engaged with, or as if its business could not be pursued in an affectionate and softened spirit, but acknowledging death as real and as humbling and sobering.

Abraham then goes forth to seek a grave for Sarah, having already with a common predilection fixed on the spot where he himself would prefer to be laid. He goes accordingly to the usual meeting-place or exchange of these times, the city-gate, where bargains were made, and where witnesses for their ratification could always be had. Men who are familiar with Eastern customs rather spoil for us the scene described in this chapter by assuring us that all these courtesies and large offers are merely the ordinary forms preliminary to a bargain, and were as little meant to be literally understood as we mean to be literally understood when we sign ourselves "your most obedient servant." Abraham asks the Hittite chiefs to approach Ephron on the subject, because all bargains of the kind are negotiated through mediators. Ephron's offer of the cave and field is merely a form. Abraham quite understood that Ephron only indicated his willingness to deal, and so he urges him to state his price, which Ephron is not slow to do; and apparently his price was a handsome one, such as he could not have asked from a poorer man, for he adds, "What are four hundred shekels between wealthy men like you and me? Without more words let the bargain be closed—bury thy dead."

The first landed property, then, of the patriarchs is a grave. In this tomb were laid Abraham and Sarah, Isaac and Rebekah; here, too, Jacob buried Leah, and here Jacob himself desired to be laid after his death, his last words being, "Bury me with my fathers in the cave that is in the field of Ephron the Hittite." This grave, therefore, becomes the centre of the land. Where the dust of our fathers is, there is our country; and as you may often hear aged persons, who are content to die and have little else to pray for, still express a wish that they may rest in the old well-remembered churchyard where their kindred lie, and may thus in the weakness of death find some comfort, and in its solitariness some companionship from the presence of those who tenderly sheltered the helplessness of their childhood; so does this place of the dead become henceforth the centre of attraction for all Abraham's seed to which still from Egypt their longings and hopes turn, as to the one magnetic point which, having once been fixed there, binds them ever to the land. It is this grave which binds them to the land. This laying of Sarah in the tomb is the real occupation of the land.

During the lapse of ages, all around this spot has been changed again and again; but at some remote period, possibly as early as the time of David, the reverence of the Jews built these tombs round with masonry so substantial that it still endures. Within the space thus enclosed there stood for long a Christian church, but since the Mohammedan domination was established, a mosque has covered the spot. This mosque has been guarded against Christian intrusion with a jealousy almost as rigid as that which excludes all unbelievers from approaching Mecca. And though the Prince of Wales was a few years ago allowed to enter the mosque, he was not permitted to make any examination of the vaults beneath, where the original tomb must be.

It is evident that this narrative of the purchase of Machpelah and the burial of Sarah was preserved, not so much on account of the personal interest which Abraham had in these matters, as on account of the manifest significance they had in connection with the history of his faith. He had recently heard from his own kindred in Mesopotamia, and it might very naturally have occurred to him that the proper place to bury Sarah was in his fatherland. The desire to lie among one's people is a very strong Eastern sentiment. Even tribes which have no dislike to emigration make provision that at death their bodies shall be restored to their own country. The Chinese notoriously do so. Abraham, therefore, could hardly have expressed his faith in a stronger form than by purchasing a burying-ground for himself in Canaan. It was equivalent to saying in the most emphatic form that he believed this country would remain in perpetuity the country of his children and people. He had as yet given no such pledge as this was, that he had irrevocably abandoned his fatherland. He had bought no other landed property; he had built no house. He shifted his encampment from place to place as convenience dictated, and there was nothing to hinder him from returning at any time to his old country. But now he fixed himself down; he said, as plainly as acts can say, that his mind was made up that this was to be in all time coming his land; this was no mere right of pasture rented for the season, no mere waste land he might occupy with his tents till its owner wished to reclaim it; it was no estate he could put into the market whenever trade should become dull and he might wish to realise or to leave the country; but it was a kind of property which he could not sell and could not abandon.

Again, his determination to hold it in perpetuity is evident not only from the nature of the property, but also from the formal purchase and conveyance of it—the complete and precise terms in which the transaction is completed. The narrative is careful to remind us again and again that the whole transaction was negotiated in the audience of the people of the land, of all those who went in at the gate, that the sale was thoroughly approved and witnessed by competent authorities. The precise subjects made over to Abraham are also detailed with all the accuracy of a legal document—"the field of Ephron, which was in Machpelah, which was before Mamre, the field and the cave which was therein, and all the trees that were in the field, that were in all the borders round about, were made sure unto Abraham for a possession in the presence of the children of Heth, before all that went in at the gate of this city." Abraham had no doubt of the friendliness of such men as Aner, Eshcol, and Mamre, his ancient allies, but he was also aware that the best way to maintain friendly relations was to leave no loophole by which difference of opinion or disagreement might enter. Let the thing be in black and white, so that there may be no misunderstanding as to terms, no expectations doomed to be unfulfilled, no encroachments which must cause resentment, if not retaliation. Law probably does more to prevent quarrels than to heal them. As statesmen and historians tell us that the best way to secure peace is to be prepared for war, so legal documents seem no doubt harsh and unfriendly, but really are more effective in maintaining peace and friendliness than vague promises and benevolent intentions. In arranging affairs and engagements one is always tempted to say, Never mind about the money, see how the thing turns out and we can settle that by-and-bye; or, in looking at a will, one is tempted to ask, of what strength is Christian feeling—not to say family affection—if all these hard-and-fast lines need to be drawn round the little bit of property which each is to have? But experience shows that this is false delicacy, and that kindliness and charity may be as fully and far more safely expressed in definite and legal terms than in loose promises or mere understandings.

Again, Abraham's idea in purchasing this sepulchre is brought out by the circumstance that he would not accept the offer of the children of Heth to use one of their sepulchres. This was not pride of blood or any feeling of that sort, but the right feeling that what God had promised as His own peculiar gift must not seem to be given by men. Possibly no great harm might have come of it if Abraham had accepted the gift of a mere cave, or a shelf in some other man's burying-ground; but Abraham could not bear to think that any captious person should ever be able to say that the inheritance promised by God was really the gift of a Hittite.

Similar captiousness appears not only in the experience of the individual Christian, but also in the treatment religion gets from the world. It is quite apparent, that is to say, that the world counts itself the real proprietor here, and Christianity a stranger fortunately or unfortunately thrown upon its shores and upon *its mercy.* One cannot miss noticing the patronising way of the world towards the Church and all that is connected with it, as if it alone could give it those things needful for its prosperity—and especially willing is it to come forward in the Hittite fashion and offer to the sojourner a sepulchre where it may be decently buried, and as a dead thing lie out of the way.

But thoughts of a still wider reach were no doubt suggested to Abraham by this purchase. Often must he have brooded on the sacrifice of Isaac, seeking to exhaust its meaning. Many a talk in the dusk must his son and he have had about that most strange experience. And no doubt the one thing that seemed always certain about it was, that it is through death a man truly becomes the heir of God; and here again in this purchase of a tomb for Sarah it is the same fact that stares him in the face. He becomes a proprietor when death enters his family; he himself, he feels, is likely to have no more than this burial-acre of possession of his land; it is only by dying he enters on actual possession. Till then he is but a tenant, not a proprietor; as he says to the children of Heth, he is but a stranger and a sojourner among them, but at death he will take up his permanent dwelling in their midst. Was this not to suggest to him that there might be a deeper meaning underlying this, and that possibly it was only by death he could enter fully into all that God intended he should receive? No doubt in the first instance it was a severe trial to his faith to find that even at his wife's death he had acquired no firmer foothold in the land. No doubt it was the very triumph of his faith that though he himself had never had a settled, permanent residence in the land, but had dwelt in tents, moving about from place to place, just as he had done the first year of his entrance upon it, yet he died in the unalterable persuasion that the land was his, and that it would one day be filled with his descendants. It was the triumph of his faith that he believed in the performance of the promise as he had originally understood it; that he believed in the gift of the actual visible land. But it is difficult to believe that he did not come to the persuasion that God's friendship was more than any single thing He promised; difficult to suppose he did not feel something of what our Lord expressed in the words that God is the God of the living, not of the dead; that those who are His enter by death into some deeper and richer experience of His love.

Such is the interpretation put upon Abraham's attitude of mind by the writer, who of all others saw most deeply into the moving principles of the Old Testament dispensation and the connection between old things and new—I mean the writer of the Epistle to the Hebrews. He says that persons who act as Abraham did declare plainly that they seek a country; and if on finding they did not get the country in which they sojourned they thought the promise had failed, they might, he says, have found opportunity to return to the country whence they came at first. And why did they not do so? Because they sought a better, that is, an heavenly country. Wherefore God is not ashamed to be called their God, for He hath prepared for them a city; as if He said, God would have been ashamed of Abraham if he had been content with less, and had not aspired to something more than he received in the land of Canaan.

Now how else could Abraham's mind have been so effectually lifted to this exalted hope as by the disappointment of his original and much tamer hope? Had he gained possession of the land in the ordinary way of purchase or conquest, and had he been able to make full use of it for the purposes of life; had he acquired meadows where his cattle might graze, towns where his followers might establish themselves, would he not almost certainly have fallen into the belief that in these pastures and by his worldly wealth and quiet and prosperity he was already exhausting God's promise regarding the land? But buying the land for his dead he is forced to enter upon it from the right side, with the idea that not by present enjoyment of its fertility is God's promise to him exhausted. Both in the getting of his heir and in the acquisition of his land his mind is led to contemplate things beyond the range of earthly vision and earthly success. He is led to the thought that God having become his God, this means blessing eternal as God Himself. In short Abraham came to believe in a life beyond the grave on very much the same grounds as many people still rely on. They feel that this life has an unaccountable poverty and meagreness in it. They feel that they themselves are much larger than the life here allotted to them. They are out of proportion. It may be said that this is their own fault; they should make life a larger, richer thing. But that is only apparently true; the very brevity of life, which no skill of theirs can alter, is itself a limiting and disappointing condition. Moreover, it seems unworthy of God as well as of man. As soon as a worthy conception of God possesses the soul, the idea of immortality forthwith follows it. We instinctively feel that God can do far more for us than is done in this life. Our knowledge of Him here is most rudimentary; our connection with Him obscure and perplexed, and wanting in fulness of result; we seem scarcely to know whose we are, and scarcely to be reconciled to the essential conditions of life, or even to God;—we are, in short, in a very different kind of life from that which we can conceive and desire. Besides, a serious belief in God, in a personal Spirit, removes at a touch all difficulties arising from materialism. If God lives and yet has no senses or bodily appearance, we also may so live; and if His is the higher state and the more enjoyable state, we need not dread to experience life as disembodied spirits.

It is certainly a most acceptable lesson that is read to us here—viz., that God's promises do not shrivel but grow solid and expand as we grasp them. Abraham went out to enter on possession of a few fields a little richer than his own, and he found an eternal inheritance. Naturally we think quite the opposite of God's promises; we fancy they are grandiloquent and magnify things, and that the actual fulfilment will prove unworthy of the language describing it. But as the woman who came to touch the hem of Christ's garment, with some dubious hope that thus her body might be healed, found herself thereby linked to Christ for evermore, so always, if we meet God at any one point and honestly trust Him for even the smallest gift, He makes that the means of introducing Himself to us and getting us to understand the value of His better gifts. And indeed, if this life were all, might not God well be ashamed to call Himself our God? When He calls Himself our God He bids us expect to find in Him inexhaustible resources to protect and satisfy and enrich us. He bids us cherish boldly all innocent and natural desires, believing that we have in Him one who can gratify every such desire. But if this life be all, who can say existence has been perfectly satisfactory—if there be no reversal of what has here gone wrong, no restoration of what has here been lost, if there be no life in which conscience and ideas and hopes find their fulfilment and satisfaction, who can say he is content and could ask no more of God? Who can say he does not see what more God could do for him than has here been done? Doubtless there are many happy lives, doubtless there are lives which carry in them a worthiness and a sacredness which manifest God's presence, but even such lives only more powerfully suggest a state in which all lives shall be holy and happy, and in which, freed from inward uneasiness and shame and sorrow, we shall live unimpeded the highest life, life as we feel it ought to be. The very joys men have here experienced suggest to them the desirableness of continued life; the love they have known can only intensify their yearning for this perpetual enjoyment; their whole experience of this life has served to reveal to them the endless possibilities of growth and of activity that are bound up in human nature; and if death is to end all this, what more has life been to any of us than a seed-time without a harvest, an education without any sphere of employment, a vision of good that can never be ours, a striving after the unattainable? If this is all that God can give us we must indeed be disappointed in Him.

But He is disappointed in us if we do not aspire to more than this. In this sense also He is ashamed to be called our God. He is ashamed to be known as the God of men who never aspire to higher blessings than earthly comfort and present prosperity. He is ashamed to be known as connected with those who think so lightly of His power that they look for nothing beyond what every man calculates on getting in this world. God means all present blessings and all blessings of a lower kind to lure us on to trust Him and seek more and more from Him. In these early promises of His He says nothing expressly and distinctly of things eternal. He appeals to the immediate wants and present longings of men—just as our Lord while on earth drew men to Himself by healing their diseases. Take, then, any one promise of God, and, however small it seems at first, it will grow in your hand; you will find always that you get more than you bargained for, that you cannot take even a little without going further and receiving all.

CHAPTER XIX.

ISAAC'S MARRIAGE.

GENESIS xxiv.

"Favour is deceitful, and beauty is vain; but a woman that feareth the Lord, she shall be praised."—PROV. xxxi. 30.

"WHEN a son has attained the age of twenty years, his father, if able, should marry him, and then take his hand and say, I have disciplined thee, and taught thee, and married thee; I now seek refuge with God from thy mischief in the present world and the next." This Mohammedan tradition expresses with tolerable accuracy the idea of the Eastern world, that a father has not discharged his responsibilities towards his son until he finds a wife for him. Abraham no doubt fully recognised his duty in this respect, but he had allowed Isaac to pass the usual age. He was thirty-seven at his mother's death, forty when the events of this chapter occurred. This delay was occasioned by two causes. The bond between Isaac and his mother was an unusually strong one; and alongside of that imperious woman a young wife would have found it even more difficult than usual to take a becoming place. Besides, where was a wife to be found? No doubt some of Abraham's Hittite friends would have considered any daughter of theirs exceptionally fortunate who should secure so good an alliance. The heir of Abraham was no inconsiderable person even when measured by Hittite expectations. And it may have taxed Abraham's sagacity to find excuses for not forming an alliance which seemed so natural, and which would have secured to him and his heirs a settled place in the country. This was so obvious, common, easily accomplished a means of gaining a footing for Isaac among somewhat dangerous neighbours, that it stands to reason Abraham must often have weighed its advantages.

But as often as he weighed the advantages of this solution of his difficulty, so often did he reject them. He was resolved that the race should be of pure Hebrew blood. His own experience in connection with Hagar had given this idea a settled prominence in his mind. And, accordingly, in his instructions to the servant whom he sent to find a wife for Isaac, two things were insisted on—1st, that she should not be a Canaanite; and, 2d, that on no pretext should Isaac be allowed to leave the land of promise and visit Mesopotamia. The steward, knowing something of men and women, foresaw that it was most unlikely that a young woman would forsake her own land and preconceived hopes and go away with a stranger to a foreign country. Abraham believes she will be persuaded. But in any case, he says, one thing must be seen to; Isaac must on no account be induced to leave the promised land even to visit Mesopotamia. God will furnish Isaac with a wife without putting him into circumstances of great temptation, without requiring him to go into societies in the slightest degree injurious to his faith. In fact, Abraham refused to do what countless Christian mothers of marriageable sons and daughters do without compunction. He had an insight into the real influences that form action and determine careers which many of us sadly lack.

And his faith was rewarded. The tidings from his brother's family arrived in the nick of time. Light, he found, was sown for the upright. It happened with him as it has doubtless often happened with ourselves, that though we have been looking forward to a certain time with much anxiety, unable even to form a plan of action, yet when the time actually came, things seemed to arrange themselves, and the thing to do became quite obvious. Abraham was persuaded God would send His angel to bring the affair to a happy issue. And when we seem drifting towards some great upturning of our life, or when things seem to come all of a sudden and in crowds upon us, so that we cannot judge what we should do, it is an animating thought that another eye than ours is penetrating the darkness, finding for us a way through all entanglement and making crooked things straight for us.

But the patience of Isaac was quite as remarkable as the faith of Abraham. He was now forty years old, and if, as he had been told, the great aim of his life, the great service he was to render to the world, was bound up with the rearing of a family, he might with some reason be wondering why circumstances were so adverse to the fulfilment of this vocation. Must he not have been tempted, as his father had been, to take matters into his own hand? Fathers are perhaps too scrupulous about telling their sons instructive passages from their own experience; but when Abraham saw Isaac exercised and discomposed about this matter, he can scarcely have failed to strengthen his spirit by telling him something of his own mistakes in life. Abraham must have seen that everything depended on Isaac's conduct, and that he had a very difficult part to play. He himself had been supernaturally encouraged to leave his own land and sojourn in Canaan; on the other hand, by the time Jacob grew up, the idea of the promised land had become traditional and fixed; though even Jacob, had he found Laban a better master, might have permanently renounced his expectations in Canaan. But Isaac enjoyed the advantages neither of the first nor of the third generation. The coming into Canaan was not his doing, and he saw how little of the land Abraham had gained. He was under strong temptation to disbelieve. And when he measured his condition with that of other young men, he certainly required unusual self-control. And to every one who would urge, Youth is passing, and I am not getting what I expected at God's hand; I have not received that providential leading I was led to expect, nor do I find that my life is made simpler; it is very well to tell me to wait, but life is slipping away, and we may wait too long—to every one whose heart urges such murmurs, Abraham through Isaac would say: But if you wait for God you get something, some positive good, and not some mere appearance of good; you at last do get begun, you get into life at the right door; whereas, if you follow some other way than that which you believe God wishes to lead you in, you get nothing.

Isaac's continence had its reward. In the suitableness of Rebekah to a man of his nature, we see the suitableness of all such gifts of God as are really waited for at His hand. God may keep us longer waiting than the world does, but He gives us never the wrong thing. Isaac had no idea of Rebekah's character; he could only yield himself to God's knowledge of what he needed; and so there came to him, from a country he had never seen, a help-meet singularly adapted to his own character. One cannot read of her lively, bustling, almost forward, but obliging and generous conduct at the well, nor of her prompt, impulsive departure to an unknown land, without seeing, as no doubt Eliezer very quickly saw, that this was exactly the woman for Isaac. In this eager, ardent, active, enterprising spirit, his own retiring and contemplative, if not sombre disposition found its appropriate relief and stimulus. Hers was a spirit which might indeed, with so mild a lord, take more of the management of affairs than was befitting; and when the wear and tear of life had tamed down the girlish vivacity with which she spoke to Eliezer at the well, and leapt from the camel to meet her lord, her active-mindedness does appear in the disagreeable shape of the clever scheming of the mother of a family. In her sons you see her qualities exaggerated: from her, Esau derived his activity and open-handedness; and in Jacob, you find that her self-reliant and unscrupulous management has become a self-asserting craft which leads him into much trouble, if it also sometimes gets him out of difficulties. But such as Rebekah was, she was quite the woman to attract Isaac and supplement his character.

So in other cases where you find you must leave yourself very much in God's hand, what He sends you will be found more precisely adapted to your character than if you chose it for yourself. You find your whole nature has been considered,—your aims, your hopes, your wants, your position, whatever in you waits for something unattained. And as in giving to Isaac the intended mother of the promised seed, God gave him a woman who fitted in to all the peculiarities of his nature, and was a comfort and a joy to him in his own life; so we shall always find that God, in satisfying His own requirements, satisfies at the same time our wants—that God carries forward His work in the world by the satisfaction of the best and happiest feelings of our nature, so that it is not only the result that is blessedness, but blessing is created along its whole course.

Abraham's servant, though not very sanguine of success, does all in his power to earn it. He sets out with an equipment fitted to inspire respect and confidence. But as he draws nearer and nearer to the city of Nahor, revolving the delicate nature of his errand, and feeling that definite action must now be taken, he sees so much room for making an irreparable mistake that he resolves to share his responsibility with the God of his master. And the manner in which he avails himself of God's guidance is remarkable. He does not ask God to guide him to the house of Bethuel; indeed, there was no occasion to do so, for any child could have pointed out the house to him. But he was a cautious person, and he wished to make his own observations on the appearance and conduct of the younger women of the household, before in any way committing himself to them. He was free to make these observations at the well; while he felt it must be very awkward to enter Laban's house with the possibility of leaving it dissatisfied. At the same time, he felt it was for God rather than for him to choose a wife for Isaac. So he made an arrangement by which the interposition of God was provided for. He meant to make his own selection, guided necessarily by the comparative attractiveness of the women who came for water, possibly also by some family likeness to Sarah or Isaac he might expect to see in any women of Bethuel's house; but knowing the deceitfulness of appearances, he asked God to confirm and determine his own choice by moving the girl he should address to give him a certain answer. Having arranged this, "Behold! Rebekah came out with her pitcher upon her shoulder, and the damsel was very fair to look upon." In the Bible the beauty of women is frankly spoken of without prudery or mawkishness as an influence in human affairs. The beauty of Rebekah at once disposed Eliezer to address her, and his first impression in her favour was confirmed by the obliging, cheerful alacrity with which she did very much more than she was asked, and, indeed, took upon herself, through her kindness of disposition, a task of some trouble and fatigue.

It is important to observe then in what sense and to what extent this capable servant asked a sign. He did not ask for a bare, intrinsically insignificant sign. He might have done so. He might have proposed as a test, Let her who stumbles on the first step of the well be the designed wife of Isaac; or, Let her who comes with a certain-coloured flower in her hand—or so forth. But the sign he chose was significant, because dependent on the character of the girl herself; a sign which must reveal her good-heartedness and readiness to oblige and courteous activity in the entertainment of strangers —in fact, the outstanding Eastern virtue. So that he really acted very much as Isaac himself must have done. He would make no approach to any one whose appearance repelled him; and when satisfied in this particular, he would test her disposition. And of course it was these qualities of Rebekah which afterwards caused Isaac to feel that this was the wife God had designed for him. It was not by any arbitrary sign that he or any man could come to know who was the suitable wife for him, but only by the love she aroused within him. God has given this feeling to direct choice in marriage; and where this is wanting, nothing else whatever, no matter how astoundingly providential it seems, ought to persuade a man that such and such a person is designed to be his wife.

There are turning points in life at once so momentous in their consequence, and affording so little material for choice, that one is much tempted to ask for more than providential leading. Not only among savages and heathen have omens been sought. Among Christians there has been manifest a constant disposition to appeal to the lot, or to accept some arbitrary way of determining which course we should follow. In very many predicaments we should be greatly relieved were there some one who could at once deliver us from all hesitation and mental conflict by one authoritative word. There are, perhaps, few things more frequently and determinedly wished for, nor regarding which we are so much tempted to feel that such a thing should be, as some infallible guide before whom we could lay every difficulty; who would tell us at once what ought to be done in each case, and whether we ought to continue as we are or make some change. But only consider for a moment what would be the consequence of having such a guide. At every important step of your progress you would, of course, instantly turn to him; as soon as doubt entered your mind regarding the moral quality of an action, or the propriety of a course you think of adopting, you would be at your counsellor. And what would be the consequence? The consequence would be, that instead of the various circumstances, experiences, and temptations of this life being a training to you, your conscience would every day become less able to guide you, and your will less able to decide, until, instead of being a mature son of God, who has learned to conform his conscience and will to the will of God, you would be quite imbecile as a moral creature. What God desires by our training here is, that we become like to Him; that there be nurtured in us a power to discern between good and evil; that by giving our own voluntary consent to His appointments, and that by discovering in various and perplexing circumstances what is the right thing to do, we may have our own moral natures as enlightened, strengthened, and fully developed every way as possible. The object of God in declaring His will to us is not to point out particular steps, but to bring our wills into conformity with His, so that, whether we err in any particular step or no, we shall still be near to Him in intention. He does with us as we with children. We do not always at once relieve them from their little difficulties, but watch with interest the working of their own conscience regarding the matter, and will give them no sign till they themselves have decided.

Evidently, therefore, before we may dare to ask a sign from God, the case must be a very special one. If you are at present engaged in something that is to your own conscience doubtful, and if you are not hiding this from God, but would very willingly, so far as you know your own mind, do in the matter what He pleases— if no further light is coming to you, and you feel a growing inclination to put it to God in this way: " Grant, O Lord, that something may happen by which I may know Thy mind in this matter "—this is asking from God a kind of help which He is very ready to give, often leading men to clearer views of duty by events which happen within their knowledge, and which having no special significance to persons whose minds are differently occupied, are yet most instructive to those who are waiting for light on some particular point. The danger is not here, but in fixing God down to the special thing which shall happen as a sign between Him and you; which, when it happens, gives no fresh light on the subject, leaves your mind still *morally* undecided, but only binds you, by an arbitrary bargain of your own, to follow one course rather than another. This matter that you would so summarily dispose of may be the very thread of your life which God means to test you by; this state of indecision which you would evade, God may mean to continue until your moral character grows strong enough to rise above it to the right decision.

No one will suppose that Rebekah's readiness to leave her home was due to mere light-mindedness. Her motives were no doubt mixed. The worldly position offered to her was good, and there was an attractive spice of romance about the whole affair which would have its charm.

She may also be credited with some apprehension of the great future of Isaac's family. In after life she certainly showed a very keen sense of the value of the blessings peculiar to that household. And, probably above all, she had an irresistible feeling that this was her destiny. She saw the hand of God in her selection, and with a more or less conscious faith in God she passed to her new life.

Her first meeting with her future husband is not the least picturesque passage in this most picturesque narrative. Isaac had gone out on that side of the encampment by which he knew his father's messenger was most likely to approach. He had gone out "to meditate at eventide;" his meditation being necessarily directed and intensified by his attitude of critical expectancy.

The evening light, in our country hanging dubiously between the glare of noon and the darkness of midnight, invites to that condition of mind which lies between the intense alertness of day and the deep oblivion of sleep, and which seems the most favourable for the meditation of divine things. The dusk of evening seems interposed between day and night to invite us to that reflection which should intervene betwixt our labour and our rest from labour, that we may leave our work behind us satisfied that we have done what we could, or, seeing its faultiness, may still lay us down to sleep with God's forgiveness. It is when the bright sunlight has gone, and no more reproaches our inactivity, that friends can enjoy prolonged intercourse, and can best unbosom to one another, as if the darkness gave opportunity for a tenderness which would be ashamed to show itself during the twelve hours in which a man shall work. And all that makes this hour so beloved by the family circle, and so conducive to friendly intercourse, makes it suitable also for such intercourse with God as each human soul can attempt. Most of us suppose we have some little plot of time railed off for God morning and evening, but how often does it get trodden down by the profane multitude of this world's cares, and quite occupied by encroaching secular engagements. But evening is the time when many men are, and when all men ought to be, least hurried; when the mind is placid, but not yet prostrate; when the body requires rest from its ordinary labour, but is not yet so oppressed with fatigue as to make devotion a mockery; when the din of this world's business is silenced, and as a sleeper wakes to consciousness when some accustomed noise is checked, so the soul now wakes up to the thought of itself and of God. I know not whether those of us who have the opportunity have also the resolution to sequester ourselves evening by evening, as Isaac did; but this I do know, that he who does so will not fail of his reward, but will very speedily find that his Father who seeth in secret is manifestly rewarding him. What we all need above all things is to let the mind *dwell* on divine things—to be able to sit down knowing we have so much clear time in which we shall not be disturbed, and during which we shall think directly under God's eye—to get quite rid of the feeling of getting through with something, so that without distraction the soul may take a deliberate survey of its own matters. And so shall often God's gifts appear on our horizon when we lift up our eyes, as Isaac "lifted up his eyes and saw the camels coming" with his bride.

Twilight, "nature's vesper-bell," or the light shaded at evening by the hills of Palestine, seems, then, to have called Isaac to a familiar occupation. This long-continued mourning for his mother, and his lonely meditation in the fields, are both in harmony with what we know of his character, and of his experience on Mount Moriah. Retiring and contemplative, willing to conciliate by concession rather than to assert and maintain his rights against opposition, glad to yield his own affairs to the strong guidance of some other hand, tender and deep in his affections, to him this lonely meditation seems singularly appropriate. His dwelling, too, was remote, on the edge of the wilderness, by the well which Hagar had named Lahai-roi. Here he dwelt as one consecrated to God, feeling little desire to enter deeper into the world, and preferring the place where the presence of God was least disturbed by the society of men. But at this time he had come from the south, and was awaiting at his father's encampment the result of Eliezer's mission. And one can conceive the thrill of keen expectancy that shot through him as he saw the female figure alighting from the camel, the first eager exchange of greetings, and the gladness with which he brought Rebekah into his mother Sarah's tent and was comforted after his mother's death. The readiness with which he loved her seems to be referred in the narrative to the grief he still felt for his mother; for as a candle is never so easily lit as just after it has been put out, so the affection of Isaac, still emitting the sad memorial of a past love, more quickly caught at the new object presented. And thus was consummated a marriage which shows us how thoroughly interwrought are the plans of God and the life of man, each fulfilling the other.

For as the salvation God introduces into the world is a practical, every-day salvation to deliver us from the sins which this life tempts us to, so God introduced this salvation by means of the natural affections and ordinary arrangements of human life. God would have us recognise in our lives what He shows us in this chapter, that He has made provision for our wants, and that if we wait upon Him He will bring us into the enjoyment of all we really need. So that if we are to make any advance in appropriating to ourselves God's salvation, it can only be by submitting ourselves implicitly to His providence, and taking care that in the commonest and most secular actions of our lives we are having respect to His will with us, and that in those actions in which our own feelings and desires seem sufficient to guide us, we are having regard to His controlling wisdom and goodness. We are to find room for God everywhere in our lives, not feeling embarrassed by the thought of His claims even in our least constrained hours, but subordinating to His highest and holiest ends everything that our life contains, and acknowledging as His gift what may seem to be our own most proper conquest or earning.

CHAPTER XX.

ESAU AND JACOB.

Genesis xxv.

"He goeth as an ox goeth to the slaughter, till a dart strikes through his liver; as a bird hasteth to the snare, and knoweth not that it is for his life."—Prov. vii. 22, 23.

The character and career of Isaac would seem to tell us that it is possible to have too great a father. Isaac was dwarfed and weakened by growing up under the shadow of Abraham. Of his life there was little to record, and what was recorded was very much a reproduction of some of the least glorious passages of his father's career. The digging of wells for his flocks was among the most notable events in his commonplace life, and even in this he only re-opened the wells his father had dug.

In him we see the result of growing up under too strong and dominant an external influence. The free and healthy play of his own capacities and will was curbed. The sons of outstanding fathers are much tempted to follow in the wake of *their* success, and be too much controlled and limited by the example therein set to them. There is a great deal to induce a son to do so; this calling has been successful in his father's case, what better can he do than follow? Also he may get the use of his *wells*—those sources his father has opened for the easier or more abundant maintenance of those dependent on him, the business he has established, the practice he has made, the connections he has formed—these are useful if he follows in his father's line of life. But all this tends, as in Isaac's case, to the stunting of the man himself. Life is made too easy for him.

Isaac has been called "the Wordsworth of the Old Testament," but his meditative disposition seems to have degenerated into mere dreamy apathy, which, at last, made him the tool of the more active-minded members of his family, and was also attended by its common accompaniment of sensuality. It seems also to have brought him to a condition of almost entire bodily prostration, for a comparison of dates shows that he must have spent forty or fifty years in blindness and incapacity for all active duty. Neither can this greatly surprise us, for it is abundantly open to our own observation that men of the finest spiritual discernment, and of whose godliness in the main one cannot doubt, are also frequently the prey of the most childish tastes, and most useless even to the extent of doing harm in practical matters. They do not see the evil that is growing in their own family; or, if they see it, they cannot rouse themselves to check it.

Isaac's marriage, though so promising in the outset, brought new trial into his life. Rebekah had to repeat the experience of Sarah. The intended mother of the promised seed was left for twenty years childless—to contend with the doubts, surmises, evil proposals, proud challengings of God, and murmurings, which must undoubtedly have arisen even in so bright and spirited a heart as Rebekah's. It was thus she was taught the seriousness of the position she had chosen for herself, and gradually led to the implicit faith requisite for the discharge of its responsibilities. Many young persons have a similar experience. They seem to themselves to have chosen a wrong position, to have made a thorough mistake in life, and to have brought themselves into circumstances in which they only retard, or quite prevent, the prosperity of those with whom they are connected. In proportion as Rebekah loved Isaac, and entered into his prospects, must she have been tempted to think she had far better have remained in Padan-aram. It *is* a humbling thing to stand in some other person's way; but if it is by no fault of ours, but in obedience to affection or conscience we are in this position, we must, in humility and patience, wait upon Providence as Rebekah did, and resist all morbid despondency.

This second barrenness in the prospective mother of the promised seed was as needful to all concerned as the first was; for the people of God, no more than any others, can learn in one lesson. They must again be brought to a real dependence on God as the Giver of the heir. The prayer with which Isaac "entreated" the Lord for his wife "because she was barren" was a prayer of deeper intensity than he could have uttered had he merely remembered the story that had been told him of his own birth. God must be recognised again and again, and throughout, as the Giver of life to the promised line. We are all apt to suppose that when once we have got a thing in train and working we can get on without God. How often do we pray for the bestowal of a blessing, and forget to pray for its continuance? How often do we count it enough that God has conferred some gift, and, not inviting Him to continue His agency, but trusting to ourselves, we mar His gift in the use? Learn, therefore, that although God has given you means of working out His salvation, your Rebekah will be barren without His continued activity. On His own means you must re-invite His blessing, for without the continuance of His aid you will make nothing of the most beautiful and appropriate helps He has given you.

It was by pain, anxiety, and almost dismay, that Rebekah received intimation that her prayer was answered. In this she is the type of many whom God hears. Inward strife, miserable forebodings, deep dejection, are often the first intimations that God is listening to our prayer and is beginning to work within us. You have prayed that God would make you more a blessing to those about you, more useful in your place, more answerable to His ends: and when your prayer has risen to its highest point of confidence and expectation, you are thrown into what seems a worse state than ever, your heart is broken within you, you say, Is this the answer to my prayer, is this God's blessing; if it be so, why am I thus? For things that make a man serious happen when God takes him in hand, and they that yield themselves to His service will not find that that service is all honour and enjoyment. Its first steps will often land us in a position we can make nothing of, and our attempts to aid others will get us into difficulties with them; and especially will our desire that Christ be formed in us bring into such lively action the evil nature that is in us that we are torn by the conflict, and our heart lies like the ground of a fierce struggle, seamed and furrowed, tossed and confused: As soon as there is a movement within us in one direction, immediately there is an opposing movement: as soon as one of the natures says, Do this; the other says, Do it not. The better nature is gaining slightly the upper hand, and by a long, steady strain, seems to be wearying out the other, when suddenly there is one quick stroke and the evil nature conquers. And every movement of the parties is with pain to ourselves; either conscience is wronged, and gives out its cry of shame, or our natural desires are trodden down, and that also is pain. And so disconnected and connected are we, so entirely one with both parties, and yet so able to contemplate both, that Rebekah's distress seems aptly enough to symbolise our own. And whether the symbol be apt or no, there can be no question that he who enquires of the Lord as she did, will receive a similar assurance that there are two natures within him, and that "the elder shall serve the younger;" the nature last formed, and that seems to give least promise of life, shall master the original, eldest born child of the flesh.

The children whose birth and destinies were thus predicted, at once gave evidence of a difference even greater than that which will often strike one as existing between two brothers, though rarely between twins. The first was born, all over like a hairy garment, presenting the appearance of being rolled up in a fur cloak or the skin of an animal—an appearance which did not pass away in childhood, but so obstinately adhered to him through life that an imitation of his hands could be produced with the hairy skin of a kid. This was by his parents considered ominous. The want of the hairy covering which the lower animals have, is one of the signs marking out man as destined for a higher and more refined life than they; and when their son appeared in this guise, they could not but fear it prognosticated his sensual, animal career. So they called him Esau. And so did the younger son from the first show his nature, catching the heel of his brother, as if he were striving to be firstborn; and so they called him Jacob, the heel-catcher or supplanter—as Esau afterwards bitterly observed, a name which precisely suited his crafty, plotting nature, shown in his twice over tripping up and overthrowing his elder brother. The name which Esau handed down to his people was, however, not his original name, but one derived from the colour of that for which he sold his birthright. It was in that exclamation of his, "Feed me with that same *red*," that he disclosed his character.

So different in appearance at birth, they grew up of very different character, and as was natural, he who had the quiet nature of his father was beloved by the mother, and he who had the bold, practical skill of the mother was clung to by the father. It seems unlikely that Rebekah was influenced in her affection by anything but natural motives, though the fact that Jacob was to be the heir must have been much on her mind, and may have produced the partiality which maternal pride sometimes begets. But before we condemn Isaac, or think the historian has not given a full account of his love for Esau, let us ask what we have noticed about the growth and decay of our own affections. We are ashamed of Isaac; but have we not also been sometimes ashamed of ourselves on seeing that our affections are powerfully influenced by the gratification of tastes almost or quite as low as this of Isaac's? He who cunningly panders to our taste for applause, he who purveys for us some sweet morsel of scandal, he who flatters or amuses us, straightway takes a place in our affections which we do not accord to men of much finer parts, but who do not so minister to our sordid appetites.

The character of Jacob is easily understood. It has frequently been remarked of him that he is thoroughly a Jew, that in him you find the good and bad features of the Jewish character very prominent and conspicuous. He has that mingling of craft and endurance which has enabled his descendants to use for their own ends those who have wronged and persecuted them. The Jew has, with some justice and some injustice, been credited with an obstinate and unscrupulous resolution to forward his own interests, and there can be no question that in this respect Jacob is the typical Jew—ruthlessly taking advantage of his brother, watching and waiting till he was sure of his victim; deceiving his blind father, and robbing him of what he had intended for his favourite son; outwitting the grasping Laban, and making at least his own out of all attempts to rob him; unable to meet his brother without stratagem; not forgetting prudence even when the honour of his family is stained; and not thrown off his guard even by his true and deep affection for Joseph. Yet, while one recoils from this craftiness and management, one cannot but admire the quiet force of character, the indomitable tenacity, and, above all, the capacity for warm affection and lasting attachments, that he showed throughout.

But the quality which chiefly distinguished Jacob from his hunting and marauding brother was his desire for the friendship of God and sensibility to spiritual influences. It may have been Jacob's consciousness of his own meanness that led him to crave connection with some Being or with some prospect that might ennoble his nature and lift him above his innate disposition. It is an old, old truth that not many noble are called; and, seeing quite as plainly as others see their feebleness and meanness, the ignoble conceive a self-loathing which is sometimes the beginning of an unquenchable thirst for the high and holy God. The consciousness of your bad, poor nature may revive within you day by day, as the remembrance of physical weakness returns to the invalid with every morning's light; but to what else can God so effectively appeal when he offers you present fellowship with Himself and eventual conformity to His own nature?

It has been pointed out that the weakness in Esau's character which makes him so striking a contrast to his brother is his inconstancy.

"That one error
Fills him with faults; makes him run through all the sins."

Constancy, persistence, dogged tenacity is certainly the striking feature of Jacob's character. He could wait and bide his time; he could retain one purpose year after year till it was accomplished. The very motto of his life was, "I will not let Thee go except Thou bless me." He watched for Esau's weak moment, and took advantage of it. He served fourteen years for the woman he loved, and no hardship quenched his love. Nay, when a whole lifetime intervened, and he lay dying in Egypt, his constant heart still turned to Rachel, as if he had parted with her but yesterday. In contrast with this tenacious, constant character stands Esau, led by impulse, betrayed by appetite, everything by turns and nothing long. To-day despising his birthright, to-morrow breaking his heart for its loss;

to-day vowing he will murder his brother, to-morrow falling on his neck and kissing him; a man you cannot reckon upon, and of too shallow a nature for anything to root itself deeply in.

The event in which the contrasted characters of the twin brothers were most decisively shown, so decisively shown that their destinies were fixed by it, was an incident which, in its external circumstances, was of the most ordinary and trivial kind. Esau came in hungry from hunting: from dawn to dusk he had been taxing his strength to the utmost, too eagerly absorbed to notice either his distance from home or his hunger; it is only when he begins to return depressed by the ill-luck of the day, and with nothing now to stimulate him, that he feels faint; and when at last he reaches his father's tents, and the savoury smell of Jacob's lentiles greets him, his ravenous appetite becomes an intolerable craving, and he begs Jacob to give him some of his food. Had Jacob done so with brotherly feeling there would have been nothing to record. But Jacob had long been watching for an opportunity to win his brother's birthright, and though no one could have supposed that an heir to even a little property would sell it in order to get a meal five minutes sooner than he could otherwise get it, Jacob had taken his brother's measure to a nicety, and was confident that present appetite would in Esau completely extinguish every other thought.

It is perhaps worth noticing that the birthright in Ishmael's line, the guardianship of the temple at Mecca, passed from one branch of the family to another in a precisely similar way. We read that when the guardianship of the temple and the governorship of the town "fell into the hands of Abu Gabshan, a weak and silly man, Cosa, one of Mohammed's ancestors, circumvented him while in a drunken humour, and bought of him the keys of the temple, and with them the presidency of it, for a bottle of wine. But Abu Gabshan being gotten out of his drunken fit, sufficiently repented of his foolish bargain; from whence grew these proverbs among the Arabs: More vexed with late repentance than Abu Gabshan; and, More silly than Abu Gabshan—which are usually said of those who part with a thing of great moment for a small matter."

Which brother presents the more repulsive spectacle of the two in this selling of the birthright it is hard to say. Who does not feel contempt for the great, strong man, declaring he will die if he is required to wait five minutes till his own supper is prepared; forgetting, in the craving of his appetite, every consideration of a worthy kind; oblivious of everything but his hunger and his food; crying, like a great baby, Feed me with that *red!* So it is always with the man who has fallen under the power of sensual appetite. He is always going to die if it is not immediately gratified. He *must* have his appetite satisfied. No consideration of consequences can be listened to or thought of; the man is helpless in the hands of his appetite—it rules and drives him on, and he is utterly without self-control; nothing but physical compulsion can restrain him.

But the treacherous and self-seeking craft of the other brother is as repulsive; the cold-blooded, calculating spirit that can hold every appetite in check, that can cleave to one purpose for a life-time, and, without scruple, take advantage of a twin-brother's weakness. Jacob knows his brother thoroughly, and all his knowledge he uses to betray him. He knows he will speedily repent of his bargain, so he makes him swear he will abide by it. It is a relentless purpose he carries out—he deliberately and unhesitatingly sacrifices his brother to himself.

Still, in two respects, Jacob is the superior man. He can appreciate the birthright in his father's family, and he has constancy. Esau might be a pleasant companion, far brighter and more vivacious than Jacob on a day's hunting; free and open-handed, and not implacable; and yet such people are not satisfactory friends. Often the most attractive people have similar inconstancy; they have a superficial vivacity, and brilliance, and charm, and good-nature, which invite a friendship they do not deserve.

Parents frequently make the mistake of Isaac, and think more highly of the gay, sparkling, but shallow child, than of the child who cannot be always smiling, but broods over what he conceives to be his wrongs. Sulkiness is itself not a pleasing feature in a child's character, but it may only be the childish expression of constancy, and of a depth of character which is slow to let go any impression made upon it. On the other hand, frankness and a quick throwing aside of passion and resentment are pleasing features in a child, but often these are only the expressions of a fickle character, rapidly changing from sun to shower like an April day, and not to be trusted for retaining affection or good impressions any longer than it retains resentment.

But Esau's despising of his birthright is that which stamps the man and makes him interesting to each generation. No one can read the simple account of his reckless act without feeling how justly we are called upon to "look diligently lest there be among us any profane person as Esau, who, for one morsel of meat, sold his birthright." Had the birthright been something to eat, Esau would not have sold it. What an exhibition of human nature! What an exposure of our childish folly and the infatuation of appetite! For Esau has company in his fall. We are all stricken by his shame. We are conscious that if God had made provision for the flesh we should have listened to Him more readily. "But what will this birthright profit us?" We do not see the good it does: were it something to keep us from disease, to give us long unsated days of pleasure, to bring us the fruits of labour without the weariness of it, to make money for us, where is the man who would not value it—where is the man who would lightly give it up? But because it is only the favour of God that is offered, His endless love, His holiness made ours, this we will imperil or resign for every idle desire, for every lust that bids us serve it a little longer. Born the sons of God, made in His image, introduced to a birthright angels might covet, we yet prefer to rank with the beasts of the field, and let our souls starve if only our bodies be well tended and cared for.

There is in Esau's conduct and after-experience so much to stir serious thought, that one always feels reluctant to pass from it, and as if much more ought to be made of it. It reflects so many features of our own conduct, and so clearly shows us what we are from day to day liable to, that we would wish to take it with us through life as a perpetual admonition. Who does not know of those moments of weakness, when we are fagged with work, and with our physical energy our moral tone has become relaxed? Who does not know how, in hours of reaction from keen and exciting engagements, sensual appetite asserts itself, and with what petulance we inwardly cry, We shall die if we do not get this or that paltry gratification? We are, for the most part, inconstant as Esau, full of good resolves to-day, and to-morrow throwing them to the winds—to-day proud of the arduousness of our calling, and girding ourselves to self-control and self-denial, to-morrow sinking back to softness and self-indulgence. Not once as Esau, but again and again we barter peace of conscience and fellowship with God and the hope of holiness, for what is, in simple fact, no more than a bowl of pottage. Even after recognising our weakness and the lowness of our tastes, and after repenting with self-loathing and misery, some slight pleasure is enough to upset our steadfast mind, and make us as plastic as clay in the hand of circumstances. It is with positive dismay one considers the weakness and blindness of our hours of appetite and passion: how one goes then like an ox to the slaughter, all unconscious of the pitfalls that betray and destroy men, and how at any moment we ourselves may truly sell our birthright.

CHAPTER XXI.

JACOB'S FRAUD.

GENESIS xxvii.

"The counsel of the Lord standeth for ever."—PSALM xxxiii. 11.

THERE are some families whose miserable existence is almost entirely made up of malicious plottings and counter-plottings, little mischievous designs, and spiteful triumphs of one member or party in the family over the other. It is not pleasant to have the veil withdrawn, and to see that where love and eager self-sacrifice might be expected their places are occupied by an eager assertion of rights, and a cold, proud, and always petty and stupid, nursing of some supposed injury. In the story told us so graphically in this page, we see the family whom God has blessed sunk to this low level, and betrayed by family jealousies into unseemly strife on the most sacred ground. Each member of the family plans his own wicked device, and God by the evil of one defeats the evil of another, and saves His own purpose to bless the race from being frittered away and lost. And it is told us in order that, amidst all this mess of human craft and selfishness, the righteousness and stability of God's word of promise may be more vividly seen. Let us look at the sin of each of the parties in order, and the punishment of each.

In the Epistle to the Hebrews Isaac is commended for his faith in blessing his sons. It was commendable in him that, in great bodily weakness, he still believed himself to be the guardian of God's blessing, and recognised that he had a great inheritance to bequeath to his sons. But, in unaccountable and inconsistent contempt of God's expressed purpose, he proposes to hand over this blessing to Esau. Many things had occurred to fix his attention upon the fact that Esau was not to be his heir. Esau had sold his birthright, and had married Hittite women, and his whole conduct was, no doubt, of a piece with this, and showed that, in his hands, any spiritual inheritance would be both unsafe and unappreciated. That Isaac had some notion he was doing wrong in giving to Esau what belonged to God, and what God meant to give to Jacob, is shown from his precipitation in bestowing the blessing. He has no feeling that he is authorized by God, and therefore he cannot wait calmly till God should intimate, by unmistakable signs, that he is near his end; but, seized with a panic lest his favourite should somehow be left unblessed, he feels, in his nervous alarm, as if he were at the point of death, and, though destined to live for forty-three years longer, he calls Esau that he may hand over to him his dying testament. How different is the nerve of a man when he knows he is doing God's will, and when he is but fulfilling his own device. For the same reason, he has to stimulate his spirit by artificial means. The prophetic ecstasy is not felt by him; he must be exhilarated by venison and wine, that, strengthened and revived in body, and having his gratitude aroused afresh towards Esau, he may bless him with all the greater vigour. The final stimulus is given when he smells the garments of Esau on Jacob, and when that fresh earthy smell which so revives us in spring, as if our life were renewed with the year, and which hangs about one who has been in the open air, entered into Isaac's blood, and lent him fresh vigour.

It is a strange and, in some respects, perplexing spectacle that is here presented to us—the organ of the Divine blessing represented by a blind old man, laid on a "couch of skins," stimulated by meat and wine, and trying to cheat God by bestowing the family blessing on the son of his own choice to the exclusion of the divinely-appointed heir. Out of such beginnings had God to educate a people worthy of Himself, and through such hazards had He to guide the spiritual blessing He designed to convey to us all.

Isaac laid a net for his own feet. By his unrighteous and timorous haste he secured the defeat of his own long-cherished scheme. It was his hasting to bless Esau which drove Rebekah to checkmate him by winning the blessing for her favourite. The shock which Isaac felt when Esau came in and the fraud was discovered is easily understood. The mortification of the old man must have been extreme when he found that he had so completely taken himself in. He was reclining in the satisfied reflection that for once he had overreached his astute Rebekah and her astute son, and in the comfortable feeling that, at last, he had accomplished his one remaining desire, when he learns from the exceeding bitter cry of Esau that he has himself been duped. It was enough to rouse the anger of the mildest and godliest of men, but Isaac does not storm and protest—"he trembles exceedingly." He recognises, by a spiritual insight quite unknown to Esau, that this is God's hand, and deliberately confirms, with his eyes open, what he had done in blindness: "I have blessed him: *Yea*, and he shall be blessed." Had he wished to deny the validity of the blessing, he had ground enough for doing so. He had not really given it: it had been stolen from him. An act must be judged by its intention, and he had been far from intending to bless Jacob. Was he to consider himself bound by what he had done under a misapprehension? He had given a blessing to one person under the impression that he was a different person; must not the blessing go to him for whom it was designed? But Isaac unhesitatingly yielded.

This clear recognition of God's hand in the matter, and quick submission to Him, reveals a habit of reflection, and a spiritual thoughtfulness, which are the good qualities in Isaac's otherwise unsatisfactory character. Before he finished his answer to Esau, he felt he was a poor feeble creature in the hand of a true and just God, who had used even his infirmity and sin to forward righteous and gracious ends. It was his sudden recognition of the frightful way in which he had been tampering with God's will, and of the grace with which God had prevented him from accomplishing a wrong destination of the inheritance, that made Isaac tremble very exceedingly.

In this humble acceptance of the disappointment of his life's love and hope, Isaac shows us the manner in which we ought to bear the consequences of our wrong-doing. The punishment of our sin often comes through the persons with whom we have to do, unintentionally on their part, and yet we are tempted to hate them because they pain and punish us, father, mother, wife, child, or whoever else. Isaac and Esau were alike disappointed. Esau only saw the supplanter, and vowed to be revenged. Isaac saw God in the matter, and trembled. So when Shimei cursed David, and his loyal retainers would have cut off his head for so doing, David said, "Let him alone, and let him curse: it may be that the Lord hath bidden him." We can bear the pain inflicted on us by men when we see that they are merely the instruments of a divine chastisement. The persons who thwart us and make our life bitter, the persons who stand between us and our dearest hopes, the persons whom we are most disposed to speak angrily and bitterly to, are often thorns planted in our path by God to keep us on the right way.

Isaac's sin propagated itself with the rapid multiplication of all sin. Rebekah overheard what passed between Isaac and Esau, and although she might have been able to wait until by fair means Jacob received the blessing, yet when she sees Isaac actually preparing to pass Jacob by and bless Esau, her fears are so excited that she cannot any longer quietly leave the matter in God's hand, but must lend her own more skilful management. It may have crossed her mind that she was justified in forwarding what she knew to be God's purpose. She saw no other way of saving God's purpose and Jacob's rights than by her interference. The emergency might have unnerved many a woman, but Rebekah is equal to the occasion. She makes the threatened exclusion of Jacob the very means for at last finally settling the inheritance upon him. She braves the indignation of Isaac and the rage of Esau, and fearless herself, and confident of success, she soon quiets the timorous and cautious objections of Jacob. She knows that for straightforward lying and acting a part she was sure of good support in Jacob. Luther says, "Had it been me, I'd have dropped the dish." But Jacob had no such tremors—could submit his hands and face to the touch of Isaac, and repeat his lie as often as needful.

An old man bedridden like Isaac becomes the subject of a number of little deceptions which may seem, and which may be, very unimportant in themselves, but which are seen to wear down the reverence due to the father of a family, and which imperceptibly sap the guileless sincerity and truthfulness of those who practise them. This overreaching of Isaac by dressing Jacob in Esau's clothes, might come in naturally as one of those daily deceptions which Rebekah was accustomed to practise on the old man whom she kept quite in her own hand, giving him as much or as little insight into the doings of the family as seemed advisable to her. It would never occur to her that she was taking God in hand; it would seem only as if she were making such use of Isaac's infirmity as she was in the daily practice of doing.

But to account for an act is not to excuse it. Underlying the conduct of Rebekah and Jacob was the conviction that they would come better speed by a little deceit of their own than by suffering God to further them in His own way—that though God would certainly not practise deception Himself, He might not object to others doing so—that in this emergency holiness was a hampering thing which might just for a little be laid aside that they might be more holy afterwards—that though no doubt in ordinary circumstances, and as a normal habit, deceit is not to be commended, yet in cases of difficulty, which call for ready wit, a prompt seizure, and delicate handling, men must be allowed to secure their ends in their own way. Their unbelief thus directly produced immorality—immorality of a very revolting kind, the defrauding of their relatives, and repulsive also because practised as if on God's side, or, as we should now say, "in the interests of religion."

To this day the method of Rebekah and Jacob is largely adopted by religious persons. It is notorious that persons whose ends are good frequently become thoroughly unscrupulous about the means they use to accomplish them. They dare not say in so many words that they may do evil that good may come, nor do they think it a tenable position in morals that the end sanctifies the means; and yet their consciousness of a justifiable and desirable end undoubtedly does blunt their sensitiveness regarding the legitimacy of the means they employ. For example, Protestant controversialists, persuaded that vehement opposition to Popery is good, and filled with the idea of accomplishing its downfall, are often guilty of gross misrepresentation, because they do not sufficiently inform themselves of the actual tenets and practices of the Church of Rome. In all controversy, religious and political, it is the same. It is always dishonest to circulate reports that you have no means of authenticating: yet how freely are such reports circulated to blacken the character of an opponent, and to prove his opinions to be dangerous. It is always dishonest to condemn opinions we have not inquired into, merely because of some fancied consequence which these opinions carry in them: yet how freely are opinions condemned by men who have never been at the trouble carefully to inquire into their truth. They do not feel the dishonesty of their position, because they have a general consciousness that they are on the side of religion, and of what has generally passed for truth. All keeping back of facts which are supposed to have an unsettling effect is but a repetition of this sin.

There is no sin more hateful. Under the appearance of serving God, and maintaining His cause in the world, it insults Him by assuming that if the whole bare, undisguised truth were spoken, His cause would suffer.

The fate of all such attempts to manage God's matters by keeping things dark, and misrepresenting fact, is written for all who care to understand in the results of this scheme of Rebekah's and Jacob's. They gained nothing, and they lost a great deal, by their wicked interference. They gained nothing; for God had promised that the birthright would be Jacob's, and would have given it him in some way redounding to his credit and not to his shame. And they lost a great deal. The mother lost her son; Jacob had to flee for his life, and, for all we know, Rebekah never saw him more. And Jacob lost all the comforts of home, and all those possessions his father had accumulated. He had to flee with nothing but his staff, an outcast to begin the world for himself. From this first false step onwards to his death, he was pursued by misfortune, until his own verdict on his life was, "Few and evil have been the days of the years of my life."

Thus severely was the sin of Rebekah and Jacob punished. It coloured their whole after-life with a deep sombre hue. It was marked thus, because it was a sin by all means to be avoided. It was virtually the sin of blaming God for forgetting His promise, or of accusing Him of being unable to perform it: so that they, Rebekah and Jacob, had, forsooth, to take God's work out of His hands, and show Him how it ought to be done. The announcement of God's purpose, instead of enabling them quietly to wait for a blessing they knew to be certain, became in their unrighteous and impatient hearts actually an inducement to sin. Abraham was so bold and confident in his faith, at least latterly, that again and again he refused to take as a gift from men, and on the most honourable terms, what God had promised to give him: his grandson is so little sure of God's truth, that he will rather trust his own falsehood; and what he thinks God may forget to give him, he will steal from his own father. Some persons have especial need to consider this sin—they are tempted to play the part of Providence, to intermeddle where they ought to refrain. Sometimes just a little thing is needed to make everything go to our liking—the keeping back of one small fact, a slight variation in the way of stating the matter, is enough—things want just a little push in the right direction: it is wrong, but very slightly so. And so they are encouraged to close for a moment their eyes and put to their hand.

Of all the parties in this transaction none is more to blame than Esau. He shows now how selfish and untruthful the sensual man really is, and how worthless is the generosity which is merely of impulse and not bottomed on principle. While he so furiously and bitterly blamed Jacob for supplanting him, it might surely have occurred to him that it was really he who was supplanting Jacob. He had no right, divine or human, to the inheritance. God had never said that His possession should go to the oldest, and had in this case said the express opposite. Besides, inconstant as Esau was, he could scarcely have forgotten the bargain that so pleased him at the time, and by which he had sold to his younger brother all title to his father's blessings. Jacob was to blame for seeking to win his own by craft, but Esau was more to blame for endeavouring furtively to recover what he knew to be no longer his. His bitter cry was the cry of a disappointed and enraged child, what Hosea calls the "howl" of those who seem to seek the Lord, but are really merely crying out, like animals, for corn and wine. Many that care very little for God's love will seek His favours; and every wicked wretch who has in his prosperity spurned God's offers will, when he sees how he has cheated himself, turn to God's gifts, though not to God, with a cry. Esau would now very gladly have given a mess of pottage for the blessing that secured to its receiver "the dew of heaven, the fatness of the earth, and plenty of corn and wine." Like many another sinner, he wanted both to eat his cake and have it. He wanted to spend his youth sowing to the flesh, and have the harvest which those only can have who have sown to the spirit. He wished both of two irreconcilable things—both the red pottage and the birthright. He is a type of those who think very lightly of spiritual blessings while their appetites are strong, but afterwards bitterly complain that their whole life is filled with the results of sowing to the flesh and not to the spirit.

"We barter life for pottage; sell true bliss
 For wealth or power, for pleasure or renown;
Thus, Esau-like, our Father's blessing miss,
 Then wash with fruitless tears our faded crown."

The words of the New Testament, in which it is said that Esau "found no place for repentance, though he sought it carefully with tears," are sometimes misunderstood. They do not mean that he sought what we ordinarily call repentance, a change of mind about the value of the birthright. He *had* that; it was this that made him weep. What he sought now was some means of undoing what he had done, of cancelling the deed of which he repented. His experience does not tell us that a man once sinning as Esau sinned becomes a hardened reprobate whom no good influence can impress or bring to repentance, but it says that the sin so committed leaves irreparable consequences—that no man can live a youth of folly and yet find as much in manhood and maturer years as if he had lived a careful and God-fearing youth. Esau had irrecoverably lost that which he would now have given all he had to possess; and in this, I suppose, he represents half the men who pass through this world. He warns us that it is very possible, by careless yielding to appetite and passing whim, to entangle ourselves irrecoverably for this life, if not to weaken and maim ourselves for eternity. At the time, your act may seem a very small and secular one, a mere bargain in the ordinary course, a little transaction such as one would enter into carelessly after the day's work is over, in the quiet of a summer evening or in the midst of the family circle; or it may seem so necessary that you never think of its moral qualities, as little as you question whether you are justified in breathing; but you are warned that if there be in that act a crushing out of spiritual hopes to make way for the free enjoyment of the pleasures of sense—if there be a deliberate preference of the good things of this life to the love of God—if, knowingly, you make light of spiritual blessings, and count them unreal when weighed against obvious worldly advantages—then the consequences of that act will in this life bring to you great discomfort and uneasiness, great loss and vexation, an agony of remorse, and a life-long repentance. You are warned of this, and most touchingly, by the moving entreaties, the bitter cries and tears of Esau.

But even when our life is spoiled irreparably, a hope remains for our character and ourselves—not certainly if our misfortunes embitter us, not if resentment is the chief result of our suffering; but if, subduing resentment, and taking blame to ourselves instead of trying to fix it on others, we take revenge upon the real source of our undoing, and extirpate from our own character the root of bitterness. Painful and difficult is such schooling. It calls for simplicity, and humility, and truthfulness—qualities not of frequent occurrence. It calls for abiding patience; for he who begins thus to sow to the spirit late in life must be content with inward fruits, with peace of conscience, increase of righteousness and humility, and must learn to live without much of what all men naturally desire.

While each member of Isaac's family has thus his own plan, and is striving to fulfil his private intention, the result is, that God's purpose is fulfilled. In the human agency, such faith in God as existed was overlaid with misunderstanding and distrust of God. But notwithstanding the petty and mean devices, the short-sighted slyness, the blundering unbelief, the profane worldliness of the human parties in the transaction, the truth and mercy of God still find a way for themselves. Were matters left in our hands, we should make shipwreck even of the salvation with which we are provided. We carry into our dealings with it the same selfishness, and inconstancy, and worldliness which made it necessary: and had not God patience to bear with, as well as mercy to invite us; had He not wisdom to govern us in the use of His grace, as well as wisdom to contrive its first bestowal, we should perish with the water of life at our lips.

CHAPTER XXII.

JACOB'S FLIGHT AND DREAM.

GENESIS xxvii. 41—xxviii.

"So foolish was I, and ignorant: I was as a beast before Thee. Nevertheless I am continually with thee."—PSALM lxxiii. 22.

IT is so commonly observed as to be scarcely worth again remarking, that persons who employ a great deal of craft in the management of their affairs are invariably entrapped in their own net. Life is so complicated, and every matter of conduct has so many issues, that no human brain can possibly foresee every contingency. Rebekah was a clever woman, and quite competent to outwit men like Isaac and Esau, but she had in her scheming neglected to take account of Laban, a man true brother to herself in cunning. She had calculated on Esau's resentment, and knew it would last only a few days, and this brief period she was prepared to utilise by sending Jacob out of Esau's reach to her own kith and kin, from among whom he might get a suitable wife. But she did not reckon on Laban's making her son serve fourteen years for his wife, nor upon Jacob's falling so deeply in love with Rachel as to make him apparently forget his mother.

In the first part of her scheme she feels herself at home. She is a woman who knows exactly how much of her mind to disclose, so as effectually to lead her husband to adopt her view and plan. She did not bluntly advise Isaac to send Jacob to Padan-aram, but she sowed in his apprehensive mind fears which she knew would make him send Jacob there; she suggested the possibility of Jacob's taking a wife of the daughters of Heth. She felt sure that *Isaac* did not need to be told where to send his son to find a suitable wife. So Isaac called Jacob, and said, Go to Padan-aram, to the house of thy mother's father, and take thee a wife thence. And he gave him the family blessing—God Almighty give thee the blessing of Abraham, to thee, and to thy seed with thee—so constituting him his heir, the representative of Abraham.

The effect this had on Esau is very noticeable. He sees, as the narrative tells us, a great many things, and his dull mind tries to make some meaning out of all that is passing before him. The historian seems intentionally to satirise Esau's attempt at reasoning, and the foolish simplicity of the device he fell upon. He had an idea that Jacob's obedience in going to seek a wife of another stock than he had connected himself with would be pleasing to his parents; and perhaps he had an idea that it would be possible to steal a march upon Jacob in his absence, and by a more speedily affected obedience to his parents' desire, win their preference, and perhaps move Isaac to alter his will and reverse the blessing. Though living in the chosen family, he seems to have had not the slightest idea that there was any higher will than his father's being fulfilled in their doings. He does not yet see why he himself should not be as blessed as Jacob; he cannot grasp at all the distinction that grace makes; cannot take in the idea that God has chosen a people to Himself, and that no natural advantage or force or endowment can set a man among that people, but only God's choice. Accordingly, he does not see any difference between Ishmael's family and the chosen family; they are both sprung from Abraham, both are naturally the same, and the fact that God expressly gave His inheritance past Ishmael is nothing to Esau—an act of *God* has no meaning to him. He merely sees that he has not pleased his parents as well as he might by his marriage, and his easy and yielding disposition prompts him to remedy this.

This is a fine specimen of the hazy views men have of what will bring them to a level with God's chosen. Through their crass insensibility to the high righteousness of God, there still does penetrate a perception that if they are to please Him there are certain means to be used for doing so. There are, they see, certain occupations and ways pursued by Christians, and if by themselves adopting these they can please God, they are quite willing to humour Him in this. Like Esau, they do not see their way to drop their old connections, but if by making some little additions to their habits, or forming some new connection, they can quiet this controversy that has somehow grown up between God and His children,—though, so far as they see, it is a very unmeaning controversy,—they will very gladly enter into any little arrangement for the purpose. We will not, of course, divorce the world, will not dismiss from our homes and hearts what God hates and means to destroy, will not accept God's will as our sole and absolute law, but we will so far meet God's wishes as to add to what we have adopted something that is almost as good as what God enjoins: we will make any little alterations which will not quite upset our present ways. Much commoner than hypocrisy is this dim-sighted, blundering stupidity of the really profane worldly man, who thinks he can take rank with men whose natures God has changed, by the mere imitation of some of their ways; who thinks, that as he cannot without great labour, and without too seriously endangering his hold on the world, do precisely what God requires, God may be expected to be satisfied with a something like it. Are we not aware of endeavouring at times to cloak a sin with some easy virtue, to adopt some new and apparently good habit, instead of destroying the sin we know God hates; or to offer to God, and palm upon our own conscience, a mere imitation of what God is pleased with? Do you attend Church, do you come and decorously submit to a service? That is not at all what God enjoins, though it is like it. What He means is, that you worship Him, which is a quite different employment. Do you render to God some outward respect, have you adopted some habits in deference to Him, do you even attempt some private devotion and discipline of the spirit? Still what He requires is something that goes much deeper than all that; namely, that you love Him. To conform to one or two habits of godly people is not what is required of us; but to be at heart godly.

As Jacob journeyed northwards, he came, on the second or third evening of his flight, to the hills of Bethel. As the sun was sinking he found himself toiling up the rough path which Abraham may have described to him as looking like a great staircase of rock and crag reaching from earth to sky. Slabs of rock, piled one upon another, form the whole hillside, and to Jacob's eye, accustomed to the rolling pastures of Beer-sheba, they would appear almost like a structure built for superhuman uses, well founded in the valley below, and intended to reach to unknown heights. Overtaken by darkness on this rugged path, he readily finds as soft a bed and as good shelter as his shepherd-habits require, and with his head on a stone and a corner of his dress thrown over his face to preserve him from the moon, he is soon fast asleep. But in his dreams the massive staircase is still before his eyes, and it is no longer himself that is toiling up it as it leads to an unexplored hill-top above him, but the angels of God are ascending and descending upon it, and at its top is Jehovah Himself.

Thus simply does God meet the thoughts of Jacob, and lead him to the encouragement he needed. What was probably Jacob's state of mind when he lay down on that hill-side? In the first place, and as he would have said to any man he chanced to meet, he wondered what he would see when he got to the top of this hill; and still more, as he may have said to Rebekah, he wondered what reception he would meet with from Laban, and whether he would ever again see his father's tents. This vision shows him that his path leads to God, that it is He who occupies the future; and, in his dream, a voice comes to him: "I am with thee, and will keep thee in all places whither thou goest, and will bring thee again into this land." He had, no doubt, wondered much whether the blessing of his father was, after all, so valuable a possession, whether it might not have been wiser to take a share with Esau than to be driven out homeless thus. God has never spoken to him; he has heard his father speak of assurances coming to him from God, but as for him, through all the long years of his life he has never heard what he could speak of as a voice of God. But this night these doubts were silenced—there came to his soul an assurance that never departed from it. He could have affirmed he heard God saying to him: "I am the Lord God of thy father Abraham, and the God of Isaac: the land whereon thou liest, to thee will I give it." And lastly, all these thoughts probably centred in one deep feeling, that he was an outcast, a fugitive from justice. He was glad he was in so solitary a place, he was glad he was so far from Esau and from every human eye; and yet—what desolation of spirit accompanied this feeling: there was no one he could bid good-night to, no one he could spend the evening hour with in quiet talk; he was a banished man, whatever fine gloss Rebekah might put upon it, and deep down in his conscience there was that which told him he was not banished without cause. Might not God also forsake him—might not God banish him, and might he not find a curse pursuing him, preventing man or woman from ever again looking in his face with pleasure? Such fears are met by the vision. This desolate spot, unvisited by sheep or bird, has become busy with life, angels thronging the ample staircase. Here, where he thought himself lonely and outcast, he finds he has come to the very gate of heaven. His fond mother might at that hour, have been visiting his silent tent and shedding ineffectual tears on his abandoned bed, but he finds himself in the very house of God, cared for by angels. As the darkness had revealed to him the stars shining overhead, so, when the deceptive glare of waking life was dulled by sleep, he saw the actual realities which before were hidden.

No wonder that a vision which so graphically showed the open communication between earth and heaven should have deeply impressed itself on Jacob's descendants. What more effectual consolation could any poor outcast, who felt he had spoiled his life, require than the memory of this staircase reaching from the pillow of the lonely fugitive from justice up into the very heart of heaven? How could any most desolate soul feel quite abandoned so long as the memory retained the vision of the angels thronging up and down with swift service to the needy? How could it be even in the darkest hour believed that all hope was gone, and that men might but curse God and die, when the mind turned to this bridging of the interval between earth and heaven?

In the New Testament we meet with an instance of the familiarity with this vision which true Israelites enjoyed. Our Lord, in addressing Nathanael, makes use of it in a way that proves this familiarity. Under his fig-tree, whose broad leaves were used in every Jewish garden as a screen from observation, and whose branches were trained down so as to form an open-air oratory, where secret prayer might be indulged in undisturbed, Nathanael had been declaring to the Father his ways, his weaknesses, his hopes. And scarcely more astonished was Jacob when he found himself the object of this angelic ministry on the lonely hill-side, than was Nathanael when he found how one eye penetrated the leafy screen, and had read his thoughts and wishes. Apparently he had been encouraging himself with t is vision, for our Lord, reading his thoughts, says: "Because I said unto thee, When thou wast under the fig-tree I saw thee, believest thou? Thou shalt see greater things than these—thou shalt see heaven opened, and the angels of God ascending and descending upon the Son of man."

This, then, is a vision for us even more than for Jacob. It has its fulfilment in the times after the Incarnation more manifestly than in previous times. The true staircase by which heavenly messengers ascend and descend is the Son of man. It is He who really bridges the interval between heaven and earth, God and man. In His person these two are united. You cannot tell whether Christ is more Divine or human, more God or man—solidly based on earth, as this massive staircase, by His real humanity, by His thirty-three years' engagement in all human functions and all experiences of this life, He is yet familiar with eternity, His name is "He that came down from heaven," and if your eye follows step by step to the heights of His person, it rests at last on what you recognise as Divine. His love it is that is wide enough to embrace God on the one hand, and the lowest sinner on the other. Truly He is the way, the stair, leading from the lowest depth of earth to the highest height of heaven. In Him you find a love that embraces you as you are, in whatever condition, however cast down and defeated, however embittered and polluted—a love that stoops tenderly to you and hopefully, and gives you once more a hold upon holiness and life, and in that very love unfolds to you the highest glory of heaven and of God.

When this comes home to a man in the hour of his need, it becomes the most arousing revelation. He springs from the troubled slumber we call life, and all earth wears a new glory and awe to him. He exclaims with Jacob, "How dreadful is this place. Surely the Lord is in this place, and I knew it not." The world, that had been so bleak and empty to him, is filled with a majestic vital presence. Jacob is no longer a mere fugitive from the results of his own sin, a shepherd in search of employment, a man setting out in the world to try his fortune; he is the partner with God in the fulfilment of a Divine purpose. And such is the change that passes on every man who believes in the Incarnation, who feels himself to be connected with God by Jesus Christ; he recognises the Divine intention to uplift his life and to fill it with new hopes and purposes. He feels that humanity is consecrated by the entrance of the Son of God into it: he feels that all human life is holy ground since the Lord Himself has passed through it. Having once had this vision of God and man united in Christ, life cannot any more be to him the poor, dreary, commonplace, wretched round of secular duties and short-lived joys and terribly punished sins it was before: but it truly becomes the very gate of heaven; from each part of it he knows there is a staircase rising to the presence of God, and that out of the region of pure holiness and justice there flow to him heavenly aids, tender guidance, and encouragement.

Do you think the idea of the Incarnation too aërial and speculative to carry with you for help in rough, practical matters? The Incarnation is not a mere idea, but a fact as substantial and solidly rooted in life as anything you have to do with. Even the shadow of it Jacob saw carried in it so much of what was real that when he was broad awake he trusted it and acted on it. It was not scattered by the chill of the morning air, nor by that fixed staring reality which external nature assumes in the gray dawn as one object after another shows itself in the same spot and form in which night had fallen upon it. There were no angels visible when he opened his eyes: the staircase was there, but it was of no heavenly substance, and if it had any secret to tell, it coldly and darkly kept it. There was no retreat for the runaway from the poor common facts of yesterday. The sky seemed as far from earth as it did yesterday, his track over the hill as lonely, his brother's wrath as real;—but other things also had become real; and as he looked back from the top of the hill on the stone he had set up, he felt the words, "I am with thee in all places whither thou goest," graven on his heart, and giving him new courage; and he knew that every footfall of his was making a Bethel, and that as he went he was carrying God through the world. The bleakest rains that swept across the hills of Bethel could never wash out of his mind the vision of bright-winged angels, as little as they could wash off the oil or wear down the stone he had set up. The brightest glare of this world's heyday of real life could not outshine and cause them to disappear; and the vision on which we hope is not one that vanishes at cockcrow, nor is He who connects us with God shy of human handling, but substantial as ourselves. He offered Himself to every kind of test, so that those who knew Him for years could say, with the most absolute confidence, "That which we have heard, which we have seen with our eyes, which we have looked upon, and our hands have handled of the Word of Life . . . declare we unto you, that ye also may have fellowship with us: and truly our fellowship is with the Father, and with His Son Jesus Christ."

Jacob obeyed a good instinct when he set up as a monumental stone that which had served as his pillow while he dreamt and saw this inspiring vision. He felt that, vivid as the impression on his mind then was, it would tend to fade, and he erected this stone that in after days he might have a witness that would testify to his present assurance. One great secret in the growth of character is the art of prolonging the quickening power of right ideas, of perpetuating just and inspiring impressions. And he who despises the aid of all external helps for the accomplishment of this object is not likely to succeed. Religion, some men say, is an inward thing: it does not consist of public worship, ordinances, and so forth, but it is a state of spirit. Very true; but he knows little of human nature who fancies a state of spirit can be maintained without the aid of external reminders, presentations to eye and ear of central religious truths and facts. We have all of us had such views of truth, and such corresponding desires and purposes, as would transform us were they only permanent. But what a night has settled on our past, how little have we found skill to prolong the benefit arising from particular events or occasions. Some parts of our life, indeed, require no monument, there is nothing *there* we would ever again think of, if possible; but, alas! these, for the most part, have erected monuments of their own, to which, as with a sad fascination, our eyes are ever turning—persons we have injured, or who, somehow, so remind us of sin, that we shrink from meeting them—places to which sins of ours have attached a reproachful meaning. And these natural monuments must be imitated in the life of grace. By fixed hours of worship, by rules and habits of devotion, by public worship, and especially by the monumental ordinance of the Lord's Supper, must we cherish the memory of known truth, and deepen former impressions.

To the monument Jacob attached a vow, so that when he returned to that spot the stone might remind him of the dependence on God he now felt, of the precarious situation he was in when this vision appeared, and of all the help God had afterwards given him. He seems to have taken up the meaning of that endless chain of angels ceaselessly coming down full of blessing, and going up empty of all but desires, requests, aspirations. And if we are to live with clean conscience and with heart open to God, we must so live that the messengers who bring God's blessings to us shall not have an evil report to take back of the manner in which we have received and spent His bounty.

This whole incident makes a special appeal to those who are starting in life. Jacob was no longer a young man, but he was unmarried, and he was going to seek employment with nothing to begin the world with but his shepherd's staff, the symbol of his knowledge of a profession. Many must see in him a very exact reproduction of their own position. They have left home, and it may be they have left it not altogether with pleasant memories, and they are now launched on the world for themselves, with nothing but their staff, their knowledge of some business. The spot they have reached may seem as desolate as the rock where Jacob lay, their prospects as doubtful as his. For such an one there is absolutely no security but that which is given in the vision of Jacob—in the belief that God will be with you in all places, and that even now on that life which you are perhaps already wishing to seclude from all holy influences, the angels of God are descending to bless and restrain you from sin. Happy the man who, at the outset, can heartily welcome such a connection of his life with God; unhappy he who welcomes whatever blots out the thought of heaven, and who separates himself from all that reminds him of the good influences that throng his path. The desire of the young heart to see life and know the world is natural and innocent, but how many fancy that in seeing the lowest and poorest perversions of life they see life—how many forget that unless they keep their hearts pure they can never enter into the best and richest and most enduring of the uses and joys of human life. Even from a selfish motive and the mere desire to succeed in the world, every one starting in life would do well to consider whether he really has Jacob's blessing and is making his vow. And certainly every one who has any honour, who is governed by any of those sentiments that lead men to noble and worthy actions, will frankly meet God's offers and joyfully accept a heavenly guidance and a permanent connection with God.

Before we dismiss this vision, it may be well to look at one instance of its fulfilment, that we may understand the manner in which God fulfils His promises. Jacob's experience in Haran was not so brilliant and unexceptionable as he might perhaps expect. He did, indeed, at once find a woman he could love, but he had to purchase her with seven years' toil, which ultimately became fourteen years. He did not grudge this; because it was customary, because his affections were strong, and because he was too independent to send to his father for money to buy a wife. But the bitterest disappointment awaited him. With the burning humiliation of one who has been cheated in so cruel a way, he finds himself married to Leah. He protests, but he cannot insist on his protest, nor divorce Leah; for, in point of fact, he is conscious that he is only being paid in his own coin, foiled with his own weapons. In this veiled bride brought in to him on false pretences he sees the just retribution of his own disguise when, with the hands of Esau he went in and received his father's blessing. His mouth is shut by the remembrance of his own past. But submitting to this chastisement, and recognising in it not only the craft of his uncle, but the stroke of God, that which he at first thought of as a cruel curse became a blessing. It was Leah much more than Rachel that built up the house of Israel. To this despised wife six of the tribes traced their origin, and among these was the tribe of Judah. Thus he learned the fruitfulness of God's retribution—that to be humbled by God is really to be built up, and to be punished by Him the richest blessing. Through such an experience are many persons led: when we would embrace the fruit of years of toil God thrusts into our arms something quite different from our expectation—something that not only disappoints, but that at first repels us, reminding us of acts of our own we had striven to forget. Is it with resentment you still look back on some such experience, when the reward of years of toil evaded your grasp, and you found yourself bound to what you would not have worked a day to obtain?—do you find yourself disheartened and discouraged by the way in which you seem regularly to miss the fruit of your labour? If so, no doubt it were useless to assure you that the disappointment may be more fruitful than the hope fulfilled, but it can scarcely be useless to ask you to consider whether it is not the fact that in Jacob's case what was thrust upon him *was* more fruitful than what he strove to win.

CHAPTER XXIII.

JACOB AT PENIEL.

Genesis xxxii.

"Humble yourselves in the sight of the Lord, and he shall lift you up."—James iv. 10.

Jacob had a double reason for wishing to leave Padan-aram. He believed in the promise of God to give him Canaan: and he saw that Laban was a man with whom he could never be on a thoroughly good understanding. He saw plainly that Laban was resolved to make what he could out of his skill at as cheap a rate as possible—the characteristic of a selfish, greedy, ungrateful, and therefore, in the end, ill-served master. Laban and Esau were the two men who had hitherto chiefly influenced Jacob's life. But they were very different in character. Esau could never see that there was any important difference between himself and Jacob—except that his brother was trickier. Esau was the type of those who honestly think that there is not much in religion, and that saints are but white-washed sinners. Laban, on the contrary, is almost superstitiously impressed by the distinction between God's people and others. But the chief practical issue of this impression is, not that he seeks God's friendship for himself, but that he tries to make a profitable use of God's friends. He seeks to get God's blessing, as it were, at secondhand. If men could be related to God indirectly, as if in law and not by blood, that would suit Laban. If God would admit men to his inheritance on any other terms than being sons in the direct line, if there were some relationship once removed, a kind of sons-in-law, so that mere connection with the godly, though not with God, would win His blessing, this would suit Laban.

Laban is the man who appreciates the social value of virtue, truthfulness, fidelity, temperance, godliness, but wishes to enjoy their fruits without the pain of cultivating the qualities themselves. He is scrupulous as to the character of those he takes into his employment, and seeks to connect himself in business with good men. In his domestic life he acts on the idea which his experience has suggested to him, that persons really godly will make his home more peaceful, better regulated, safer than otherwise it might be. If he holds a position of authority, he knows how to make use, for the preservation of order and for the promotion of his own ends, of the voluntary efforts of Christian societies, of the trustworthiness of Christian officials, and of the support of the Christian community. But with all this recognition of the reality and influence of godliness, he never for one moment entertains the idea of himself becoming a godly man. In all ages there are Labans, who clearly recognise the utility and worth of a connection with God, who have been much mixed up with persons in whom that worth was very conspicuous, and who yet, at the last, "depart and return unto their place," like Jacob's father-in-law, without having themselves entered into any affectionate relations with God.

From Laban, then, Jacob was resolved to escape. And though to escape with large droves of slow-moving sheep and cattle, as well as with many women and children, seemed hopeless, the cleverness of Jacob did not fail him here. He did not get beyond reach of pursuit; he could never have expected to do so. But he stole away to such a distance from Haran as made it much easier for him to come to terms with Laban, and much more difficult for Laban to try any further device for detaining him.

But, delivered as he was from Laban, he had an even more formidable person to deal with. As soon as Laban's company disappear on the northern horizon, Jacob sends messengers south to sound Esau. His message is so contrived as to beget the idea in Esau's mind that his younger brother is a person of some importance, and yet is prepared to show greater deference to himself than formerly. But the answer brought back by the messengers is the curt and haughty despatch of the man of war to the man of peace. No notice is taken of Jacob's vaunted wealth. No proposal of terms as if Esau had an equal to deal with, is carried back. There is only the startling announcement: "Esau cometh to meet thee, and four hundred men with him." Jacob at once recognises the significance of this armed advance on Esau's part. Esau has not forgotten the wrong he suffered at Jacob's hands, and he means to show him that he is entirely in his power.

Therefore was Jacob "greatly afraid and distressed." The joy with which, a few days ago, he had greeted the host of God, was quite overcast by the tidings brought him regarding the host of Esau. Things heavenly do always look so like a mere show; visits of angels seem so delusive and fleeting; the exhibition of the powers of heaven seems so often but as a tournament painted on the sky, and so unavailable for the stern encounters that await us on earth, that one seems, even after the most impressive of such displays, to be left to fight on alone. No wonder Jacob is disturbed. His wives and dependants gather round him in dismay; the children, catching the infectious panic, cower with cries and weeping about their mothers; the whole camp is rudely shaken out of its brief truce by the news of this rough Esau, whose impetuosity and warlike ways they had all heard of and were now to experience. The accounts of the messengers would no doubt grow in alarming descriptive detail as they saw how much importance was attached to their words. Their accounts would also be exaggerated by their own unwarlike nature, and by the indistinctness with which they had made out the temper of Esau's followers, and the novelty of the equipments of war they had seen in his camp. Could we have been surprised had Jacob turned and fled when thus he was made to picture the troops of Esau sweeping from his grasp all he had so laboriously earned, and snatching the promised inheritance from him when in the very act of entering on possession? But though in fancy he already hears their rude shouts of triumph as they fall upon his defenceless band, and already sees the merciless horde dividing the spoil with shouts of derision and coarse triumph, and though all around him are clamouring to be led into a safe retreat, Jacob sees stretched before him the land that is his, and resolves that, by God's help, he shall win it. What he does is not the act of a man rendered incompetent through fear, but of one who has recovered from the first shock of alarm and has all his wits about him. He disposes his household and followers in two companies, so that each might advance with the hope that it might be the one which should not meet Esau; and having done all that his circumstances permit, he commends himself to God in prayer.

After Jacob had prayed to God, a happy thought strikes him, which he at once puts in execution. Anticipating the experience of Solomon, that "a brother offended is harder to be won than a strong city," he, in the style of a skilled tactician, lays siege to Esau's wrath, and directs against it train after train of gifts, which, like successive battalions pouring into a breach, might at length quite win his brother. This disposition of his peaceful battering trains having occupied him till sunset, he retires to the short rest of a general on the eve of battle. As soon as he judges that the weaker members of the camp are refreshed enough to begin their eventful march, he rises and goes from tent to tent awaking the sleepers, and quickly forming them into their usual line of march, sends them over the brook in the darkness, and himself is left alone, not with the depression of a man who waits for the inevitable, but with the high spirits of intense activity, and with the return of the old complacent confidence of his own superiority to his powerful but sluggish-minded brother—a confidence regained now by the certainty he felt, at least for the time, that Esau's rage could not blaze through all the relays of gifts he had sent forward. Having in this spirit seen all his camp across the brook, he himself pauses for a moment, and looks with interest at the stream before him, and at the promised land on its southern bank. This stream, too, has an interest for him as bearing a name like his own—a name that signifies the "struggler," and was given to the mountain torrent from the pain and difficulty with which it seemed to find its way through the hills. Sitting on the bank of the stream, he sees gleaming through the darkness the foam that it churned as it writhed through the obstructing rocks, or heard through the night the roar of its torrent as it leapt downwards, tortuously finding its way towards Jordan; and Jacob says, So will I, opposed though I be, win my way, by the circuitous routes of craft or by the impetuous rush of courage, into the land whither that stream is going. With compressed lips, and step as firm as when, twenty years before, he left the land, he rises to cross the brook and enter the land—he rises, and is seized in a grasp that he at once owns as formidable. But surely this silent close, as of two combatants who at once recognise one another's strength, this protracted strife, does not look like the act of a depressed man, but of one whose energies have been strung to the highest pitch, and who would have borne down the champion of Esau's host had he at that hour opposed his entrance into the land which Jacob claimed as his own, and into which, as his glove, pledging himself to follow, he had thrown all that was dear to him in the world. It was no common wrestler that would have been safe to meet him in that mood.

Why, then, was Jacob thus mysteriously held back while his household were quietly moving forward in the darkness? What is the meaning, purpose, and use of this opposition to his entrance? These are obvious from the state of mind Jacob was in. He was going forward to meet Esau under the impression that there was no other reason why he should not inherit the land but only his wrath, and pretty confident that by his superior talent, his mother-wit, he could make a tool of this stupid, generous brother of his. And the danger was, that if Jacob's device had succeeded, he would have been confirmed in these impressions, and have believed that he had won the land from Esau, with God's help certainly, but still by his own indomitable pertinacity of purpose and skill in dealing with men. Now, this was not the state of the case at all. Jacob had, by his own deceit, become an exile from the land, had been, in fact, banished for fraud; and though God had confirmed to him the covenant, and promised to him the land, yet Jacob had apparently never come to any such thorough sense of his sin and entire incompetency to win the birthright for himself, as would have made it *possible* for him to receive simply as God's gift this land which as God's gift was alone valuable. Jacob does not yet seem to have taken up the difference between inheriting a thing as God's gift, and inheriting it as the meed of his own prowess. To such a man God cannot *give* the land; Jacob cannot receive it. He is thinking only of winning it, which is not at all what God means, and which would, in fact, have annulled all the covenant, and lowered Jacob and his people to the level simply of other nations who had to win and keep their territories at their risk, and not as the blessed of God. If Jacob then is to get the land, he must take it as a gift, which he is not prepared to do. During the last twenty years he has got many a lesson which might have taught him to distrust his own management, and he had, to a certain extent, acknowledged God; but his Jacob-nature, his subtle, scheming nature, was not so easily made to stand erect, and still he is for wriggling himself into the promised land. He is coming back to the land under the impression that God needs to be managed; that even though we have His promises it requires dexterity to get them fulfilled; that a man will get into the inheritance all the readier for knowing what to veil from God and what to exhibit; when to cleave to His word with great profession of most humble and absolute reliance on Him, and when to take matters into one's own hand. Jacob, in short, was about to enter the land as Jacob, the supplanter, and that would never do; he was going to win the land from Esau by guile, or as he might; and not to receive it from God. And therefore, just as he is going to step into it, there lays hold of him, not an armed emissary of his brother, but a far more formidable antagonist—if Jacob will win the land, if it is to be a mere trial of skill, a wrestling match, it must at least be with the right person. Jacob is met with his own weapons. He has not chosen war, so no armed opposition is made; but with the naked force of his own nature, he is prepared for any man who will hold the land against him; with such tenacity, toughness, quick presence of mind, elasticity, as nature has given him, he is confident he can win and hold his own. So the real proprietor of the land strips himself for the contest, and lets him feel, by the first hold he takes of him, that if the question be one of mere strength he shall never enter the land.

This wrestling therefore was by no means actually or symbolically prayer. Jacob was not aggressive, nor did he stay behind his company to spend the night in praying for them. It was God who came and laid hold on Jacob to prevent him from entering the land in the temper he was in, and as Jacob. He was to be taught that it was not only Esau's appeased wrath, or his own skilful smoothing down of his brother's ruffled temper, that gave him entrance; but that a nameless Being, Who came out upon him from the darkness, guarded the land, and that by His passport only could he find entrance. And henceforth, as to every reader of this history so much more to Jacob's self, the meeting with Esau and the overcoming of his opposition were quite secondary to and eclipsed by his meeting and prevailing with this unknown combatant.

This struggle had, therefore, immense significance for the history of Jacob. It is, in fact, a concrete representation of the attitude he had maintained towards God throughout his previous history; and it constitutes the turning point at which he assumes a new and satisfactory attitude. Year after year Jacob had still retained confidence in himself; he had never been thoroughly humbled, but had always felt himself able to regain the land he had lost by his sin. And in this struggle he shows this same determination and self-confidence. He wrestles on indomitably. As Kurtz, whom I follow in his interpretation of this incident, says, "All along Jacob's life had been the struggle of a clever and strong, a pertinacious and enduring, a self-confident and self-sufficient person, who was sure of the result only when he helped himself—a contest with God, who wished to break his strength and wisdom, in order to bestow upon him real strength in divine weakness, and real wisdom in divine folly." All this self-confidence culminates now, and in one final and sensible struggle, his Jacob-nature, his natural propensity to wrest what he desires and win what he aims at, from the most unwilling opponent, does its very utmost and does it in vain. His steady straining, his dexterous feints, his quick gusts of vehement assault, make no impression on this combatant and move him not one foot off his ground. Time after time his crafty nature puts out all its various resources, now letting his grasp relax and feigning defeat, and then with gathered strength hurling himself on the stranger, but all in vain. What Jacob had often surmised during the last twenty years, what had flashed through him like a sudden gleam of light when he found himself married to Leah, that he was in the hands of one against whom it is quite useless to struggle. he now again begins to suspect. And as the first faint dawn appears, and he begins dimly to make out the face, the quiet breathing of which he had felt on his own during the contest, the man with whom he wrestles touches the strongest sinew in Jacob's body, and the muscle on which the wrestler most depends shrivels at the touch and reveals to the falling Jacob how utterly futile had been all his skill and obstinacy, and how quickly the stranger might have thrown and mastered him.

All in a moment, as he falls, Jacob sees how it is with him, and Who it is that has met him thus. As the hard, stiff, corded muscle shrivelled, so shrivelled his obdurate, persistent self-confidence. And as he is thrown, yet cleaves with the natural tenacity of a wrestler to his conqueror; so, utterly humbled before this Mighty One whom now he recognises and owns, he yet cleaves to Him and entreats His Blessing. It is at this touch, which discovers the Almighty power of Him with whom he has been contending, that the whole nature of Jacob goes down before God. He sees how foolish and vain has been his obstinate persistence in striving to trick God out of His blessing, or wrest it from Him, and now he owns his utter incapacity to advance one step in this way, he admits to himself that he is stopped, weakened in the way, thrown on his back, and can effect nothing, simply nothing, by what he thought would effect all; and, therefore, he passes from wrestling to praying, and with tears, as Hosea says, sobs out from the broken heart of the strong man, "I will not let thee go except thou bless me." In making this transition from the boldness and persistence of self-confidence to the boldness of faith and humility, Jacob becomes Israel—the supplanter, being baffled by his conqueror, rises a Prince. Disarmed of all other weapons, he at last finds and uses the weapons wherewith God is conquered, and with the simplicity and guilelessness now of an Israelite indeed, face to face with God, hanging helpless with his arms around Him, he supplicates the blessing he could not win.

Thus, as Abraham had to become God's heir in the simplicity of humble dependence on God; as Isaac had to lay himself on God's altar with absolute resignation, and so become the heir of God, so Jacob enters on the inheritance through the most thorough humbling. Abraham had to give up all possessions and live on God's promise; Isaac had to give up life itself; Jacob had to yield his very self, and abandon all dependence on his own ability. The new name he receives signalizes and interprets this crisis in his life. He enters his land not as Jacob, but as Israel. The man who crossed the Jabbok was not the same as he who had cheated Esau and outwitted Laban and determinedly striven this morning with the angel. He was Israel, God's prince, entering on the land freely bestowed on him by an authority none could resist; a man who had learned that in order to receive from God, one must ask.

Very significant to Jacob in his after life must have been the lameness consequent on this night's struggle. He, the wrestler, had to go halting all his days. He who had carried all his weapons in his own person, in his intelligent watchful eye and tough right arm, he who had felt sufficient for all emergencies and a match for all men, had now to limp along as one who had been worsted and baffled and could not hide his shame from men. So it sometimes happens that a man never recovers the severe handling he has received at some turning point in his life. Often there is never again the same elastic step, the same free and confident bearing, the same apparent power, the same appearance to our fellow-men of completeness in our life; but, instead of this, there is a humble decision which, if it does not walk with so free a gait, yet knows better what ground it is treading and by what right. To the end some men bear the marks of the heavy stroke by which God first humbled them. It came in a sudden shock that broke their health, or in a disappointment which nothing now given can ever quite obliterate the trace of, or in circumstances painfully and permanently altered. And the man has to say with Jacob, I shall never now be what I might have been; I was resolved to have my own way, and though God in His mercy did not suffer me to destroy myself, yet to drive me from my purpose He was forced to use a violence, under the effects of which I go halting all my days, saved and whole, yet maimed to the end of time. I am not ashamed of the mark, at least when I think of it as God's signature I am able to glory in it, but it never fails to remind me of a perverse wilfulness I am ashamed of. With many men God is forced to such treatment; if any of us are under it, God forbid we should mistake its meaning and lie prostrate and despairing in the darkness instead of clinging to Him Who has smitten and will heal us.

For the treatment which Jacob received at Peniel must not be set aside as singular or exceptional. Sometimes God interposes between us and a greatly-desired possession which we have been counting upon as our right and as the fair and natural consequence of our past efforts and ways. The expectation of this possession has indeed determined our movements and shaped our life for some time past, and it would not only be assigned to us by men as fairly ours, but God also has Himself seemed to encourage us to win it. Yet when it is now within sight, and when we are rising to pass the little stream which seems alone to separate us from it, we are arrested by a strong, an irresistible hand. The reason is, that God wishes us to be in such a state of mind that we shall receive it as His gift, so that it becomes ours by an indefeasible title.

Similarly, when advancing to a spiritual possession, such checks are not without their use. Many men look with longing to what is eternal and spiritual, and they resolve to win this inheritance. And this resolve they often make as if its accomplishment depended solely on their own endurance. They leave almost wholly out of account that the possibility of their entering the state they long for is not decided by their readiness to pass through any ordeal, spiritual or physical, which may be required of them, but by God's willingness to give it. They act as if by taking advantage of God's promises, and by passing through certain states of mind and prescribed duties, they could, irrespective of God's present attitude toward them and constant love, win eternal happiness. In the life of such persons there must therefore come a time when their own spiritual energy seems all to collapse in that painful, utter way in which, when the body is exhausted, the muscles are suddenly found to be cramped and heavy and no longer responsive to the will. They are made to feel that a spiritual dislocation has taken place, and that their eagerness to enter life everlasting no longer stirs the active energies of the soul.

In that hour the man learns the most valuable truth he can learn, that it is God Who is wishing to save him, not he who must wrest a blessing from an unwilling God. Instead of any longer looking on himself as against the world, he takes his place as one who has the whole energy of God's will at his back, to give him rightful entrance into all blessedness. So long as Jacob was in doubt whether it was not some kind of man that was opposing him, he wrestled on; and our foolish ways of dealing with God terminate, when we recognise that He is not such an one as ourselves. We naturally act as if God had some pleasure in thwarting us—as if we could, and even ought to, maintain a kind of contest with God. We deal with Him as if He were opposed to our best purposes and grudged to advance us in all good, and as if He needed to be propitiated by penitence and cajoled by forced feelings and sanctimonious demeanour. We act as if we could make more way were God not in our way, as if our best prospects began in our own conception and we had to win God over to our views. If God is unwilling, then there is an end: no device nor force will get us past Him. If He is willing, why all this unworthy dealing with Him, as if the whole idea and accomplishment of salvation did not proceed from Him?

CHAPTER XXIV.

JACOB'S RETURN.

GENESIS xxxv.

"As for me, when I came from Padan, Rachel died by me in the land of Canaan in the way."—GEN. xlviii. 7.

THE words of the Wrestler at the brook Jabbok, "Let me go, for the day breaketh," express the truth that spiritual things will not submit themselves to sensible tests. When we seek to let the full daylight, by which we discern other objects, stream upon them, they elude our grasp. When we fancy we are on the verge of having our doubts for ever scattered, and our suppositions changed into certainties, the very approach of clear knowledge and demonstration seems to drive those sensitive spiritual presences into darkness. As Pascal remarked, and remarked as the mouth-piece of all souls that have earnestly sought for God, the world only gives us indications of the presence of a God Who conceals Himself. It is, indeed, one of the most mysterious characteristics of our life in this world that the great Existence which originates and embraces all other Beings should Himself be so silent and concealed: that there should be need of subtle arguments to prove His existence, and that no argument ever conceived has been found sufficiently cogent to convince all men. One is always tempted to say, how easy to end all doubt, how easy for God so to reveal Himself as to make unbelief impossible, and give to all men the glad consciousness that they have a God.

The reason of this "reserve" of God must lie in the nature of things. The greatest forces in nature are silent and unobtrusive and incomprehensible. Without the law of gravitation the universe would rush into ruin, but who has ever seen this force? Its effects are everywhere visible, but itself is shrouded in darkness and cannot be comprehended. So much more must the Infinite Spirit remain unseen and baffling all comprehension. "No man hath seen God at any time" must ever remain true. To ask for God's name, therefore, as Jacob did, is a mistake. For almost every one supposes that when he knows the name of a thing he knows also its nature. The giving of a name, therefore, tends to discourage enquiry, and to beget an unfounded satisfaction as if, when we know what a thing is called, we know what it is. The craving, therefore, which we all feel in common with Jacob—to have all mystery swept from between us and God, and to see Him face to face, so that we may know Him as we know our friends—is a craving which cannot be satisfied. You cannot ever know God as He is. Your mind cannot comprehend a Being who is pure Spirit, inhabiting no body, present with you here but present also hundreds of millions of miles away, related to time and to space and to matter in ways utterly impossible for you to comprehend.

What is possible, God has done. He has made Himself known in Christ. We are assured, on testimony that stands every kind of test, that in Him, if nowhere else, we find God. And yet even by Christ this same law of reserve if not concealment was observed. Not only did He forbid men and devils to proclaim who He was, but when men, weary of their own doubts and debatings, impatiently challenged him, "If thou be the Christ tell us plainly," He declined to do so. For really men must grow to the knowledge of Him. Even a human face cannot be known by once or twice seeing it; the practised artist often misses the expression best loved by the intimate friend, or by the relative whose own nature interprets to him the face in which he sees himself reflected. Much more can the child of God only attain to the knowledge of his Father's face by first of all *being* a child of God, and then by gradually growing up into His likeness.

But though God's operation is in darkness the results of it are in the light. "As Jacob passed over Peniel, the *sun rose* upon him, and he halted upon his thigh." As Jacob's company halted when they missed him, and as many anxious eyes were turned back into the darkness, they were unable still to see him; and even when the darkness began to scatter, and they saw dimly and far off a human figure, the sharpest eyes among them declare it cannot be Jacob, for the gait and walk, which alone they can judge by at that distance and in that light, are not his. But when at last the first ray of sunlight streams on him from over the hills of Gilead, all doubt is at an end; it *is* Jacob, but halting on his thigh. And he himself finds it is not a strain which the walking of a few paces will ease, nor a night cramp which will pass off, nor a mere dream which would vanish in broad day, but a real permanent lameness which he must explain to his company. Has he missed a step on the bank in the darkness, or stumbled or slipped on the slippery stones of the ford? It is a far more real thing to him than any such accident. So, however others may discredit the results of a work on the soul which they have not seen—however they may say of the first and most obvious results, "This is but a sickness of soul which the rising sun will dispel; a feigned peculiarity of walk which will be forgotten in the bustle of the day's work"—it is not so, but every contact with real life makes it more obvious that when God touches a man the result is real. And as Jacob's household and children in all generations counted that sinew which shrank sacred, and would not eat of it, so surely should we be reverential towards God's work in the soul of our neighbour, and respect even those peculiarities which are often the most obvious first-fruits of conversion, and which make it difficult for us to walk in the same comfort with these persons, and keep step with them as easily as once we did. A reluctance to live like other good people, an inability to share their innocent amusements, a distaste for the very duties of this life, a harsh or reserved bearing towards unconverted persons, an awkwardness in speaking of their religious experience, as well as an awkwardness in applying it to the ordinary circumstances of their life,—these and many other of the results of God's work on the soul should not be rudely dealt with, but respected; for though not in themselves either seemly or beneficial, they are evidence of God's touch.

After this contest with the angel, the meeting of Jacob with Esau has no separate significance. Jacob succeeds with his brother because already he has prevailed with God. He is on a satisfactory footing now with the Sovereign who alone can bestow the land and judge betwixt him and his brother. Jacob can no longer suppose that the chief obstacle to his advance is the resentment of Esau. He has felt and submitted to a stronger hand than Esau's. Such schooling we all need: and get, if we will take it. Like Jacob, we have to make our way to our end through numberless human interferences and worldly obstacles. Some of these we have to flee from, as Jacob from Laban; others we must meet and overcome, as our Esaus. Our own sin or mistake has put us under the power of some whose influence is disastrous; others, though we are not under their power at all, yet, consciously or unconsciously to themselves, continually cross our path and thwart us, keep us back and prevent us from effecting what we desire, and from shaping things about us according to our own ideas. And there will, from time to time, be present to our minds obvious ways in which we could defeat the opposition of these persons, and by which we fancy we could triumph over them. And what we are here taught is, that we need look for no triumph, and it is a pity for us if we win a triumph over any human opposition, however purely secular and unchristian, without first having prevailed with God in the matter. He comes in between us and all men and things, and, laying His hand on us, arrests us from further progress till we have to the very bottom and in every part adjusted the affair with Him—and then, standing right with Him, we can very easily, or at least we *can*, get right with all things. And it should be a suggestive and fruitful thought to the most of us that, in all cases in which we sin against our brother, God presents Himself as the champion of the wronged party. One day or other we must meet not the strongest putting of all those cases in which we have erred as the offended party could himself put them, but we must meet them as put by the Eternal Advocate of justice and right, who saw our spirit, our merely selfish calculating, our base motive, our impure desire, our unrighteous deed. Gladly would Jacob have met the mightiest of Esau's host in place of this invincible opponent, and it is this same Mighty One, this same watchful guardian of right Who threw Himself in Jacob's way, Who has His eye on us, Who has tracked us through all our years, and Who will certainly one time appear in our path as the champion of every one we have wronged, of every one whose soul we have put in jeopardy, of every one to whom we have not done what God intended we should do, of every one whom we have attempted merely to make use of; and in stating their case and showing us what justice and duty would have required of us, He will make us feel, what we cannot feel till He Himself convinces us, that, in all our dealings with men, wherein we have wronged them we have wronged Him.

The narrative now prepares to leave Jacob and make room for Joseph. It brings him back to Bethel, thereby completing the history of his triumph over the difficulties with which his life had been so thickly studded. The interest and much of the significance of a man's life come to an end when position and success are achieved. The remaining notices of Jacob's experience are of a sorrowful kind; he lives under a cloud until at the close the sun shines out again. We have seen him in his youth making experiments in life; in his prime founding a family and winning his way by slow and painful steps to his own place in the world; and now he enters on the last stage of his life, a stage in which signs of breaking up appear almost as soon as he attains his aim and place in life.

After all that had happened to Jacob, we should have expected him to make for Bethel as rapidly as his unwieldy company could be moved forwards. But the pastures that had charmed the eye of his grandfather captivated Jacob as well. He bought land at Shechem, and appeared willing to settle there. The vows which he had uttered with such fervour when his future was precarious are apparently quite forgotten, or more probably neglected, now that danger seems past. To go to Bethel involved the abandonment of admirable pastures, and the introduction of new religious views and habits into his family life. A man who has large possessions, difficult and precarious relations to sustain with the world, and a household unmanageable from its size, and from the variety of dispositions included in it, requires great independence and determination to carry out domestic reform on religious grounds. Even a slight change in our habits is often delayed because we are shy of exposing to observation fresh and deep convictions on religious subjects. Besides, we forget our fears and our vows when the time of hardship passes away; and that which, as young men, we considered almost hopeless, we at length accept as our right, and omit all remembrance and gratitude. A spiritual experience that is separated from your present by twenty years of active life, by a foreign residence, by marriage, by the growing up of a family around you, by other and fresher spiritual experiences, is apt to be very indistinctly remembered. The obligations you then felt and owned have been overlaid and buried in the lapse of years. And so it comes that a low tone is introduced into your life, and your homes cease to be model homes.

Out of this condition Jacob was roughly awakened. Sinning by unfaithfulness and softness towards his family, he is, according to the usual law, punished by family disaster of the most painful kind. The conduct of Simeon and Levi was apparently due quite as much to family pride and religious fanaticism as to brotherly love or any high moral view. In them first we see how the true religion, when held by coarse and ungodly men, becomes the root of all evil. We see the first instance of that fanaticism which so often made the Jews a curse rather than a blessing to other nations. Indeed, it is but an instance of the injustice, cruelty, and violence that at all times result where men suppose that they themselves are raised to quite peculiar privileges and to a position superior to their fellows, without recognising also that this position is held by the grace of a holy God and for the good of their fellows.

Jacob is now compelled to make a virtue of necessity. He flees to Bethel to escape the vengeance of the Shechemites. To such serious calamities do men expose themselves by arguing with conscience and by refusing to live up to their engagements. How can men be saved from living merely for sheep-feeding and cattle-breeding and trade and enjoyment? how can they be saved from gradually expelling from their character all principle and all high sentiment that conflicts with immediate advantage and present pleasure, save by such irresistible blows as here compelled Jacob to shift his camp? He has spiritual perception enough left to see what is meant. The order is at once issued: "Put away the strange gods that are among you, and be clean, and change your garments: and let us arise, and go up to Bethel; and I will make there an altar unto God, who answered me in the day of my distress, and was with me in the way which I went." Thus frankly does he acknowledge his error, and repair, so far as he can, the evil he has done. Thus decidedly does he press God's command on those whom he had hitherto encouraged or connived at. Even from his favourite Rachel he takes her gods and buries them. The fierce Simeon and Levi, proud of the blood with which they had washed out their sister's stain, are ordered to cleanse their garments and show some seemly sorrow, if they can.

If years go by without any such incident occurring in our life as drives us to a recognition of our moral laxity and deterioration, and to a frank and humble return to a closer walk with God, we had need to strive to awaken ourselves and ascertain whether we are living up to old vows and are really animated by thoroughly worthy motives. It was when Jacob came back to the very spot where he had lain on the open hill-side, and pointed out to his wives and children the stone he had set up to mark the spot, that he felt humbled as he cast his eye over the flocks and tents he now owned. And if you can, like Jacob, go back to spots in your life which were very woful and perplexed, years even when all continued dreary, dark, and hopeless, when friendlessness and poverty, bereavement or disease, laid their chilling, crushing hands upon you, times when you could not see what possible good there was for you in the world; and if now all this is solved, and your condition is in the most striking contrast to what you can remember, it becomes you to make acknowledgment to God such as you may have made to your friends, such acknowledgment as makes it plain that you are touched by His kindness. The acknowledgment Jacob made was sensible and honest. He put away the gods which had divided the worship of his family. In our life there is probably that which constantly tends to usurp an undue place in our regard; something which gives us more pleasure than the thought of God, or from which we really expect a more palpable benefit than we expect from God, and which, therefore, we cultivate with far greater assiduity. How easily, if we really wish to be on a clear footing with God, can we discover what things should be cast revengefully from us, buried and stamped upon and numbered with the things of the past. Are there not in your life any objects for the sake of which you sacrifice that nearness to God, and that sure hold of Him you once enjoyed? Are you not conscious of any pursuits, or hopes, or pleasures, or employments which practically have the effect of making you indifferent to spiritual advancement, and which make you shy of Bethel—shy of all that sets clear before you your indebtedness to God, and your own past vows and resolves?

"But," continues the narrative, "*but* Deborah, Rebekah's nurse, died;" that is, although Jacob and his house were now living in the fear of God, that did not exempt them from the ordinary distresses of family life. And among these, one that falls on us with a chastening and mild sadness all its own, occurs when there passes from the family one of its oldest members, and one who has by the delicate tact of love gained influence over all, and has by the common consent become the arbiter and mediator, the confidant and counsellor of the family. They, indeed, are the true salt of the earth whose own peace is so deep and abiding, and whose purity is so thorough and energetic, that into their ear we can disburden the troubled heart or the guilty conscience, as the wildest brook disturbs not and the most polluted fouls not the settled depths of the all-cleansing ocean. Such must Deborah have been, for the oak under which she was buried was afterwards known as "the oak of weeping." Specially must Jacob himself have mourned the death of her whose face was the oldest in his remembrance, and with whom his mother and his happy early days were associated. Very dear to Jacob, as to most men, were those who had been connected with and could tell him of his parents, and remind him of his early years. Deborah, by treating him still as a little boy, perhaps the only one who now called him by the pet name of childhood, gave him the pleasantest relief from the cares of manhood and the obsequious deportment of the other members of his household towards him. So that when she went a great blank was made to him: no longer was the wise and happy old face seen in her tent door to greet him of an evening; no longer could he take refuge in the peacefulness of her old age from the troubles of his lot: she being gone, a whole generation was gone, and a new stage of life was entered on.

But a heavier blow, the heaviest that death could inflict, soon fell upon him. She who had been as God's gift and smile to him since ever he had left Bethel at the first is taken from him now that he is restored to God's house. The number of his sons is completed, and the mother is removed. Suddenly and unexpectedly the blow fell, as they were journeying and fearing no ill. Notwithstanding the confident and cheering, though ambiguous, assurances of those about her, she had that clear knowledge of her own state which, without contradicting, simply put aside such assurances, and, as her soul was departing, feebly named her son Benoni, Son of my sorrow. She felt keenly what was, to a nature like hers, the very anguish of disappointment. She was never to feel the little creature stirring in her arms with personal human life, nor see him growing up to manhood as the son of his father's right hand. It was this sad death of Rachel's which made her the typical mother in Israel. It was not an unclouded, merely prosperous life which could fitly have foreshadowed the lives of those by whom the promised seed was to come; and least of all of the virgin to whom it was said, "A sword shall pierce through thine own soul also." It was the wail of Rachel that poetical minds among the Jews heard from time to time mourning their national disasters—"Rachel weeping" for her children, when by captivity they were separated from their mother country, or when, by the sword of Herod, the mothers of Bethlehem were bereaved of their babes. But it was also observed that that which brought this anguish on the mothers of Bethlehem was the birth there of the last Son of Israel, the blossom of this long-growing plant, suddenly born after a long and barren period, the son of Israel's right hand.

Still another death is registered in this chapter. It took place twelve years after Joseph went into Egypt, but is set down here for convenience. Esau and Jacob are, for the last time, brought together over their dead father—and for the last time, as they see that family likeness which comes out so strikingly in the face of the dead. do they feel drawn with brotherly affection to greet one another as sons of one father. In the dead Isaac, too, they find an object of veneration more impressive than they had found in the living father: the infirmities of age are exchanged for the mystery and majesty of death; the man has passed out of reach of pity, of contempt: the shrill, uncontrolled treble is no longer heard, there are no weak, plaintive movements, no childishness; but a solemn, august silence, a silence that seems to bid on-lookers be still and refrain from disturbing the first communings of the departed spirit with things unseen.

The tenderness of these two brothers towards one another and towards their father was probably quickened by remorse when they met at his deathbed. They could not, perhaps, think that they had hastened his end by causing him anxieties which age has not strength to throw off; but they could not miss the reflection that the life now closed and finally sealed up might have been a much brighter life had they acted the part of dutiful, loving sons. Scarcely can one of our number pass from among us without leaving in our minds some self-reproach that we were not more kindly towards him, and that now he is beyond our kindness; that our opportunity for being brotherly towards *him* is for ever gone. And when we have very manifestly erred in this respect, perhaps there are among all the stings of a guilty conscience few more bitterly piercing than this. Many a son who has stood unmoved by the tears of a living mother—his mother by whom he lives, who has cherished him as her own soul, who has forgiven and forgiven and forgiven him, who has toiled and prayed, and watched for him—though he has hardened himself against her looks of imploring love and turned carelessly from her entreaties and burst through all the fond cords and snares by which she has sought to keep him, has yet broken down before the calm, unsolicitous, resting face of the dead. Hitherto he has not listened to her pleadings, and now she pleads no more. Hitherto she has heard no word of pure love from him, and now she hears no more. Hitherto he has done nothing for her of all that a son may do, and now there is nothing he can do. All the goodness of her life gathers up and stands out at once, and the time for gratitude is past. He sees suddenly, as by the withdrawal of a veil, all that that worn body has passed through for him, and all the goodness these features have expressed, and now they can never light up with joyful acceptance of his love and duty. Such grief as this finds its one alleviation in the knowledge that we may follow those who have gone before us; that we may yet make reparation. And when we think how many we have let pass without those frank, human, kindly offices we might have rendered, the knowledge that we also shall be gathered to our people comes in as very cheering. It is a grateful thought that there is a place where we shall be able to live rightly, where selfishness will not intrude and spoil all, but will leave us free to be to our neighbour all that we ought to be and all that we would be.

CHAPTER XXV.

JOSEPH'S DREAMS.

Genesis xxxvii.

"Surely the wrath of man shall praise thee."—Psalm lxxvi. 10.

The migration of Israel from Canaan to Egypt was a step of prime importance in the history. Great difficulties surrounded it, and very extraordinary means were used to bring it about.

The preparatory steps occupied about twenty years, and nearly a fourth of the Book of Genesis is devoted to this period. This migration was a new idea. So little was it the result of an accidental dearth, or of any of those unforeseen calamities which cause families to emigrate from our own country, that God had forewarned Abraham himself that it must be. But only when it was becoming matter of actual experience and of history did God make known the precise object to be accomplished by it. This He makes known to Jacob as he passes from Canaan; and as, in abandoning the land he had so painfully won, his heart sinks, he is sustained by the assurance, "Fear not to go down into Egypt; I will there make thee a great nation."

The meaning of the step, and the suitableness of the time and of the place to which Israel migrated, are apparent. For more than two hundred years now had Abraham and his descendants been wandering as pilgrims, and as yet there were no signs of God's promise being kept to them. That promise had been of a land and of a seed. Great fecundity had been promised to the race; but instead of that there had been a remarkable and perplexing barrenness, so that after two centuries one tent could contain the whole male population. In Jacob's time the population began to increase, but just in proportion as this part of the promise showed signs of fulfilment did the other part seem precarious. For, in proportion to their increase, the family became hostile to the Canaanites, and how should they ever get past that critical point in their history at which they would be strong enough to excite the suspicion, jealousy, and hatred of the indigenous tribes, and yet not strong enough to defend themselves against this enmity? Their presence was tolerated, just as our countrymen tolerated the presence of French refugees, on the score of their impotence to do harm. They were placed in a quite anomalous position; a single family who had continued for two hundred years in a land which they could only seem in jest to call theirs, dwelling as guests amid the natives, maintaining peculiar forms of worship and customs. Collision with the inhabitants seemed unavoidable as soon as their real character and pretensions oozed out, and as soon as it seemed at all likely that they really proposed to become owners and masters in the land. And, in case of such collision, what could be the result, but that which has ever followed where a few score men, brave enough to be cut down where they stood, have been exposed to mass after mass of fierce and bloodthirsty barbarians? A small number of men have often made good their entrance into lands where the inhabitants greatly outnumbered them, but these have commonly been highly disciplined troops, as in the case of the handful of Spaniards who seized Mexico and Peru; or they have been backed by a power which could aid with vast resources, as when the Romans held this country, or when the English lad in India left his pen on his desk and headed his few resolute countrymen, and held his own against unnumbered millions. It may be argued that if even Abraham with his own household swept Canaan clear of invaders, it might now have been possible for his grandson to do as much with increased means at his disposal. But, not to mention that every man has not the native genius for command and military enterprise which Abraham had, it must be taken into account that a force which is quite sufficient for a marauding expedition or a night attack, is inadequate for the exigencies of a campaign of several years' duration. The war which Jacob must have waged, had hostilities been opened, must have been a war of extermination, and such a war must have desolated the house of Israel if victorious, and, more probably by far, would have quite annihilated it.

It is to obviate these dangers, and to secure that Israel grow without let or hindrance, that Jacob's household is removed to a land where protection and seclusion would at once be secured to them. In the land of Goshen, secured from molestation partly by the influence of Joseph, but much more by the caste-prejudices of the Egyptians, and their hatred of all foreigners, and shepherds in particular, they enjoyed such prosperity and attained so rapidly the magnitude of a nation that some, forgetful alike of the promise of God and of the natural advantages of Israel's position, have refused to credit the accounts given us of the increase in their population. In a land so roomy, so fertile, and so secluded as that in which they were now settled, they had every advantage for making the transition from a family to a nation. Here they were preserved from all temptation to mingle with neighbours of a different race, and so lose their special place as a people called out by God to stand alone. The Egyptians would have scorned the marriages which the Canaanites passionately solicited. Here the very contempt in which they were held proved to be their most valuable bulwark. And if Christians have any of the wisdom of the serpent, they will often find in the contempt or exclusiveness of worldly men a convenient barrier, preventing them, indeed, from enjoying some privileges, but at the same time enabling them, without molestation, to pursue their own way. I believe young people especially feel put about by the deprivations which they have to suffer in order to save their religious scruples; they are shut off from what their friends and associates enjoy, and they perceive that they are not so well liked as they would be had they less desire to live by conscience and by God's will. They feel ostracized, banished, frowned upon, laid under disabilities; but all this has its compensations: it forms for them a kind of Goshen where they may worship and increase, it runs a fence around them which keeps them apart from much that tempts and from much that enfeebles.

The residence of Israel in Egypt served another important purpose. By contact with the most civilised people of antiquity they emerged from the semi-barbarous condition in which they had previously been living. Going into Egypt mere shepherds, as Jacob somewhat plaintively and deprecatingly says to Pharaoh; not even possessed, so far as we know, of the fundamental arts on which civilisation rests, unable to record in writing the revelations God made, or to read them if recorded; having the most rudimentary ideas of law and justice, and having nothing to keep them together and give them form and strength, save the one idea that God meant to confer on them great distinction; they were transferred into a land where government had been so long established and law had come to be so thoroughly administered that life and property were as safe as among ourselves to-day, where science had made such advances that even the weather-beaten and time-stained relics of it seem to point to regions into which even the bold enterprise of modern investigation has not penetrated, and where all the arts needful for life were in familiar use, and even some practised which modern times have as yet been unable to recover. To no better school could the barbarous sons of Bilhah and Zilpah have been sent; to no more fitting discipline could the lawless spirits of Reuben, Simeon, and Levi have been subjected. In Egypt, where human life was sacred, where truth was worshipped as a deity, and where law was invested with the sanctity which belonged to what was supposed to have descended from heaven, they were brought under influences similar to those which ancient Rome exerted over conquered races.

The unwitting pioneer of this great movement was a man in all respects fitted to initiate it happily. In Joseph we meet a type of character rare in any race, and which, though occasionally reproduced in Jewish history, we should certainly not have expected to meet with at so early a period. For what chiefly strikes one in Joseph is a combination of grace and power, which is commonly looked upon as the peculiar result of civilising influences, knowledge of history, familiarity with foreign races, and hereditary dignity. In David we find a similar flexibility and grace of character, and a similar personal superiority. We find the same bright and humorous disposition helping him to play the man in adverse circumstances; but we miss in David Joseph's self-control and incorruptible purity, as we also miss something of his capacity for difficult affairs of state. In Daniel this latter capacity is abundantly present, and a facility equal to Joseph's in dealing with foreigners, and there is also a certain grace or nobility in the Jewish Vizier; but Joseph had a surplus of power which enabled him to be cheerful and alert in doleful circumstances, which Daniel would certainly have borne manfully, but probably in a sterner and more passive mood. Joseph, indeed, seemed to inherit and happily combine the highest qualities of his ancestors. He had Abraham's dignity and capacity, Isaac's purity and power of self-devotion, Jacob's cleverness and buoyancy and tenacity. From his mother's family he had personal beauty, humour, and management.

A young man of such capabilities could not long remain insensible to his own powers or indifferent to his own destiny. Indeed, the conduct of his father and brothers towards him must have made him self-conscious, even though he had been wholly innocent of introspection. The force of the impression he produced on his family may be measured by the circumstance that the princely dress given him by his father did not excite his brothers' ridicule but their envy and hatred. In this dress there was a manifest suitableness to his person, and this excited them to a keen resentment of the distinction. So too they felt that his dreams were not the mere whimsicalities of a lively fancy, but were possessed of a verisimilitude which gave them importance. In short, the dress and the dreams were insufferably exasperating to the brothers, because they proclaimed and marked in a definite way the feeling of Joseph's superiority which had already been vaguely rankling in their consciousness. And it is creditable to Joseph that this superiority should first have emerged in connection with a point of conduct. It was in moral stature that the sons of Bilhah and Zilpah felt that they were outgrown by the stripling whom they carried with them as their drudge. Neither are we obliged to suppose that Joseph was a gratuitous tale-bearer, or that when he carried their evil report to his father he was actuated by a prudish, censorious, or in any way unworthy spirit. That he very well knew how to hold his tongue no man ever gave more adequate proof; but he that understands that there is a time to keep silence necessarily sees also that there is a time to speak. And no one can tell what torture that pure young soul may have endured in the remote pastures, when left alone to withstand day after day the outrage of these coarse and unscrupulous men. An elder brother, if he will, can more effectually guard the innocence of a younger brother than any other relative can, but he can also inflict a more exquisite torture.

Joseph, then, could not but come to think of his future and of his destiny in this family. That his father should make a pet of him rather than of Benjamin, he would refer to the circumstance that he was the oldest son of the wife of his choice, of her whom first he had loved, and who had no rival while he lived. To so charming a companion as Joseph must always have been, Jacob would naturally impart all the traditions and hopes of the family. In him he found a sympathetic and appreciative listener, who wiled him on to endless narrative, and whose imaginativeness quickened his own hopes and made the future seem grander and the world more wide. And what Jacob had to tell could fall into no kindlier soil than the opening mind of Joseph. No hint was lost, every promise was interpreted by some waiting aspiration. And thus, like every youth of capacity, he came to have his day-dreams. These day-dreams, though derided by those who cannot see the Cæsar in the careless trifler, and though often awkward and even offensive in their expression, are not always the mere discontented cravings of youthful vanity, but are frequently instinctive gropings towards the position which the nature is fitted to fill. "Our wishes," it has been said, "are the forefeeling of our capabilities;" and certainly where there is any special gift or genius in a man, the wish of his youth is predictive of the attainment of manhood. Whims, no doubt, there are, passing phases through which natural growth carries us, flutterings of the needle when too near some powerful influence; yet amidst all variations the true direction will be discernible and ultimately will be dominant. And it is a great art to discover what we are fit for, so that we may settle down to our own work, or patiently wait for our own place, without enviously striving to rob every other man of his crown and so losing our own. It is an art that saves us much fretting and disappointment and waste of time, to understand early in life what it is we can accomplish, and what precisely we mean to be at; "to recognise in our personal gifts or station, in the circumstances and complications of our life, in our relations to others, or to the world—the will of God teaching us what we are, and for what we ought to live." How much of life often is gone before its possessor sees the use he can put it to and ceases to beat the air! How much of life is an ill-considered but passionate striving after what can never be attained, or a vain imitation of persons who have quite different talents and opportunities from ourselves, and who are therefore set to quite another work than ours.

It was because Joseph's dreams embodied his waking ambition that they were of importance. Dreams become significant when they are the concentrated essence of the main stream of the waking thoughts, and picturesquely exhibit the tendency of the character. "In a dream," says Elihu, "in a vision of the night, when deep sleep falleth upon men, in slumberings upon the bed; then He openeth the ears of men, and sealeth their instruction, that He may withdraw man from his purpose." This is precisely the use of dreams; our tendencies, unbridled by reason and fact, run on to results; the purposes which the business and other good influences of the day have kept down act themselves out in our dreams, and we see the character unimpeded by social checks, and as it would be were it unmodified by the restraints and efforts and external considerations of our conscious hours. Our vanity, our pride, our malice, our impurity, our deceit, our every evil passion, has free play, and shows us its finished result, and in so vivid and true though caricatured a form that we are startled and withdrawn from our purpose. The evil thought we have suffered to creep about our heart seems in our dreams to become a deed, and we wake in horror and thank God we can yet refrain. Thus the poor woman, who in utter destitution was beginning to find her child a burden, dreamt she had drowned it, and woke in horror at the fancied sound of the plunge—woke to clasp her little one to her breast with the thrill of a grateful affection that never again gave way. So that while no man is so foolish as to expect instruction from every dream any more than from every thought that visits his waking mind, yet every one who has been accumulating some knowledge of himself is aware that he has drawn a large part of this from his unconscious hours. As the naturalist would know but a small part of the animal kingdom by studying the creatures that show themselves in the daylight, so there are moles and bats of the spirit that exhibit themselves most freely in the darkness; and there are jungles and waste places in the character which, if you look on them only in the sunshine, may seem safe and lovely, but which at night show themselves to be full of all loathsome and savage beasts.

With the simplicity of a guileless mind, and with the natural proneness of members of one family to tell in the morning the dreams they have had, Joseph tells to the rest what seems to himself interesting, if not very suggestive. Possibly he thought very little of his dream till he saw how much importance his brothers attached to it. Possibly there might be discernible in its tone and look some mixture of youthful arrogance. And in his relation of the second dream, there was discernible at least a confidence that it would be realised, which was peculiarly intolerable to his brothers, and to his father seemed a dangerous symptom that called for rebuke. And yet "his father observed the saying;" as a parent has sometimes occasion to check his child, and yet, having done so, feels that that does not end the matter; that his boy and he are in somewhat different spheres, so that while he was certainly justified in punishing such and such a manifestation of his character, there is yet something behind that he does not quite understand, and for which possibly punishment may not be exactly the suitable award.

We fall into Jacob's mistake when we refuse to acknowledge as genuine and God-inspired any religious experience which we ourselves have not passed through, and which appears in a guise that is not only unfamiliar, but that is in some particulars objectionable. Up to the measure of our own religious experience, we recognise as genuine, and sympathise with, the parallel experience of others; but when they rise above us and get beyond us, we begin to speak of them as visionaries, enthusiasts, dreamers. We content ourselves with pointing again and again to the blots in their manner, and refuse to read the future through the ideas they add to our knowledge. But the future necessarily lies, not in the definite and finished attainment, but in the indefinite and hazy and dream-like germs that have yet growth in them. The future is not with Jacob, the rebuker, but with the dreaming, and, possibly, somewhat offensive Joseph. It was certainly a new element Joseph introduced into the experience of God's people. He saw, obscurely indeed, but with sufficient clearness to make him thoughtful, that the man whom God chooses and makes a blessing to others is so far advanced above his fellows that they lean upon him and pay him homage as if he were in the place of God to them. He saw that his higher powers were to be used for his brethren, and that the high destiny he somehow felt to be his was to be won by doing service so essential that his family would bow before him and give themselves into his hand. He saw this, as every man whose love keeps pace with his talent sees it, and he so far anticipated the dignity of Him who, in the deepest self-sacrifice, assumed a position and asserted claims which enraged His brethren and made even His believing mother marvel. Joseph knew that the welfare of his family rested not with the Esau-like good-nature of Reuben, still less with the fanatical ferocity of Simeon and Levi, not with the servile patience of Issachar, nor with the natural force and dignity of Judah, but with some deeper qualities which, if he himself did not yet possess, he at least valued and aspired to.

Whatever Joseph thought of the path by which he was to reach the high dignity which his dreams foreshadowed, he was soon to learn that the path was neither easy nor short. Each man thinks that, for himself at least, an exceptional path will be broken out, and that without difficulties and humiliations he will inherit the kingdom. But it cannot be so. And as the first step a lad takes towards the attainment of his position often involves him in trouble and covers him with confusion, and does so even although he ultimately finds that it was the only path by which he could have reached his goal; so, that which was really the first step towards Joseph's high destiny, no doubt seemed to him most calamitous and fatal. It certainly did so to his brothers, who thought that they were effectually and for ever putting an end to Joseph's pretensions. "Behold, this dreamer cometh; come now therefore, and let us slay him, and we shall see what will become of his dreams." They were, however, so far turned from their purpose by Reuben as to put him in a pit, meaning to leave him to die, and doubtless they thought themselves lenient in doing so. The less violent the death inflicted, the less of murder seems to be in it; so that he who slowly kills the body by only wounding the affections often counts himself no murderer at all, because he strikes no blood-shedding blow, and can deceive himself into the idea that it is the working of his victim's own spirit that is doing the damage.

The tank into which Joseph's brethren cast him was apparently one of those huge reservoirs excavated by shepherds in the East, that they may have a supply of water for their flocks in the end of the dry season, when the running waters fail them. Being so narrow at the mouth that they can be covered by a single stone, they gradually widen and form a large subterranean room; and the facility they thus afford for the confinement of prisoners was from the first too obvious not to be commonly taken advantage of. In such a place was Joseph left to die: under the ground, sinking in mire, his flesh creeping at the touch of unseen slimy creatures, in darkness, alone; that is to say, in a species of confinement which tames the most reckless and maddens the best balanced spirits, which shakes the nerve of the calmest, and has sometimes left the blankness of idiocy in masculine understandings. A few wild cries that ring painfully round his prison show him he need expect no help from without; a few wild and desperate beatings round the shelving walls of rock show him there is no possibility of escape; he covers his face, or casts himself on the floor of his dungeon to escape within himself, but only to find this also in vain, and to rise and renew efforts he knows to be fruitless. Here, then, is what has come of his fine dreams. With shame he now remembers the beaming confidence with which he had related them; with bitterness he thinks of the bright life above him, from which these few feet cut him so absolutely off, and of the quick termination that has been put to all his hopes.

Into such tanks do young persons especially get cast: finding themselves suddenly dropped out of the lively scenery and bright sunshine in which they have been living, down into roomy graves where they seem left to die at leisure. They had conceived a way of being useful in the world; they had found an aim or a hope; they had, like Joseph, discerned their place and were making towards it, when suddenly they seem to be thrown out and are left to learn that the world can do very well without them, that the sun and moon and the eleven stars do not drop from their courses or make wail because of their sad condition. High aims and commendable purposes are not so easily fulfilled as they fancied. The faculty and desire in them to be of service are not recognised. Men do not make room for them, and God seems to disregard the hopes He has excited in them. The little attempt at living they have made seems only to have got themselves and others into trouble. They begin to think it a mistake their being in the world at all; they curse the day of their birth. Others are enjoying this life, and seem to be making something of it, having found work that suits and develops them; but, for their own part, they cannot get fitted into life at any point, and are excluded from the onward movement of the world. They are again and again flung back, until they fear they are not to see the fulfilment of any one bright dream that has ever visited them, and that they are never, never at all, to live out the life it is in them to live, or find light and scope for maturing those germs of the rich human nature that they feel within them.

All this is in the way to attainment. This or that check, this long burial for years, does not come upon you merely because stoppage and hindrance have been useful to others, but because your advancement lies through these experiences. Young persons naturally feel strongly that life is all before them, that this life is, in the first place, their concern, and that God must be proved sufficient for this life, able to bring them to their ideal. And the first lesson they have to learn is, that mere youthful confidence and energy are not the qualities that overcome the world. They have to learn that humility, and the ambition that seeks great things, but not for ourselves, are the qualities really indispensable. But do men become humble by being told to become so, or by knowing they ought to be so? God must make us humble by the actual experience we meet with in our ordinary life. Joseph, no doubt, knew very well, what his aged grandfather must often have told him, that a man must die before he begins to live. But what could an ambitious, happy youth make of this, till he was thrown into the pit and left there? as truly passing through the bitterness of death as Isaac had passed through it, and as keenly feeling the pain of severance from the light of life. Then, no doubt, he thought of Isaac, and of Isaac's God, till between himself and the impenetrable dungeon-walls the everlasting arms seemed to interpose, and through the darkness of his death-like solitude the face of Jacob's God appeared to beam upon him, and he came to feel what we must, by some extremity, all be made to feel, that it was not in this world's life but in God he lived, that nothing could befall him which God did not will, and that what God had for him to do, God would enable him to do.

The heartless barbarity with which the brethren of Joseph sat down to eat and drink the very dainties he had brought them from his father, while they left him, as they thought, to starve, has been regarded by all later generations as the height of hard-hearted indifference. Amos, at a loss to describe the recklessness of his own generation, falls back upon this incident, and cries woe upon those "that drink wine in bowls, and anoint themselves with the chief ointment, but are not grieved for the affliction of Joseph." We reflect, if we do not substantially reproduce, their sin when we are filled with animosity against those who usher in some higher kind of life, effort, or worship, than we ourselves as yet desire or are fit for, and which, therefore, reflects shame on our incapacity; and when we would fain, without using violence, get rid of such persons. There are often schemes set on foot by better men than ourselves, against which somehow our spirit rises, yet which, did we consider, we should at the most say with the cautious Gamaliel, Let us beware of doing anything to hinder this; let us see whether, perchance, it be not of God. Sometimes there are in families individuals who do not get the encouragement in well-doing they might expect in a Christian family, but are rather frowned upon and hindered by the other members of it, because they seem to be inaugurating a higher style of religion than the family is used to, and to be reflecting from their own conduct a condemnation of what has hitherto been current.

This treatment, who among us has not extended to Him who in His whole experience so closely resembles Joseph? So long as Christ is to us merely, as it were, the pet of the family, the innocent, guileless, loving Being on whom we can heap pretty epithets, and in whom we find play for our best affections, to whom it is easier to show ourselves affectionate and well-disposed than to the brothers who mingle with us in all our pursuits; so long as He remains to us as a child whose demands it is a relaxation to fulfil, we fancy that we are giving Him our hearts, and that He, if any, has our love. But when He declares to us His dreams, and claims to be our Lord, to whom with most absolute homage we must bow, who has a right to rule and means to rule over us, who will have His will done by us and not our own, then the love we fancied seems to pass into something like aversion. His purposes we would fain believe to be the idle fancies of a dreamer which He Himself does not expect us to pay much heed to. And if we do not resent the absolute surrender of ourselves to Him which He demands, if the bowing down of our fullest sheaves and brightest glory to Him is too little understood by us to be resented; if we think such dreams are not to come true, and that He does not mean much by demanding our homage, and therefore do not resent the demand; yet possibly we can remember with shame how we have "anointed ourselves with the chief ointment," lain listlesly enjoying some of those luxuries which our Brother has brought us from the Father's house, and yet let Himself and His cause be buried out of sight —enjoyed the good name of Christian, the pleasant social refinements of a Christian land, even the peace of conscience which the knowledge of the Christian's God produces, and yet turned away from the deeper emotions which His personal entreaties stir, and from those self-sacrificing efforts which His cause requires if it is to prosper.

There are, too, unstable Reubens still, whom something always draws aside, and who are ever out of the way when most needed; who, like him, are on the other side of the hill when Christ's cause is being betrayed; who still count their own private business that which must be done, and God's work that which may be done—work for themselves necessary, and God's work only voluntary and in the second place. And there are also those who, though they would be honestly shocked to be charged with murdering Christ's cause, can yet leave it to perish.

CHAPTER XXVI.

JOSEPH IN PRISON.

Genesis xxxix.

"Blessed is the man that endureth temptation: for when he is tried, he shall receive the crown of life."— JAMES i. 12.

DRAMATISTS and novelists, who make it their business to give accurate representations of human life, proceed upon the understanding that there is a plot in it, and that if you take the beginning or middle without the end, you must fail to comprehend these prior parts. And a plot is pronounced good in proportion as, without violating truth to nature, it brings the leading characters into situations of extreme danger or distress, from which there seems no possible exit, and in which the characters themselves may have fullest opportunity to display and ripen their individual excellences. A life is judged poor and without significance, certainly unworthy of any longer record than a monumental epitaph may contain, if there be in it no critical passages, no emergencies when all anticipation of the next step is baffled, or when ruin seems certain. Though it has been brought to a successful issue, yet, to make it worthy of our consideration, it must have been brought to this issue through hazard, through opposition, contrary to many expectations that were plausibly entertained at the several stages of its career. All men, in short, are agreed that the value of a human life consists very much in the hazards and conflicts through which it is carried; and yet we resent God's dealing with us when it comes to be our turn to play the hero, and by patient endurance and righteous endeavour to bring our lives to a successful issue. How flat and tame would this narrative have read had Joseph by easy steps come to the dignity he at last reached through a series of misadventures that called out and ripened all that was manly and strong and tender in his character. And take out of your own life all your difficulties, all that ever pained, agitated, depressed you, all that disappointed or postponed your expectations, all that suddenly called upon you to act in trying situations, all that thoroughly put you to the proof—take all this away, and what do you leave but a blank insipid life that not even yourself can see any interest in?

And when we speak of Joseph's life as typical, we mean that it illustrates on a great scale and in picturesque and memorable situations principles which are obscurely operative in our own experience. It pleases the fancy to trace the incidental analogies between the life of Joseph and that of our Lord. As our Lord, so Joseph was the beloved of his father, sent by him to visit his brethren, and see after their well-being, seized and sold by them to strangers, and thus raised to be their Saviour and the Saviour of the world. Joseph in prison pronouncing the doom of one of his fellow-prisoners and the exaltation of the other, suggests the scene on Calvary where the one fellow-sufferer was taken, the other left. Joseph's contemporaries had of course no idea that his life foreshadowed the life of the Redeemer, yet they must have seen, or ought to have seen, that the deepest humiliation is often the path to the highest exaltation, that the deliverer sent by God to save a people may come in the guise of a slave, and that false accusations, imprisonment, years of suffering, do not make it impossible nor even unlikely that he who endures all these may be God's chosen Son.

In Joseph's being lifted out of the pit only to pass into slavery, many a man of Joseph's years has seen a picture of what has happened to himself. From a position in which they have been as if buried alive, young men not uncommonly emerge into a position preferable certainly to that out of which they have been brought, but in which they are compelled to work beyond their strength, and *that* for some superior in whom they have no special interest. Grinding toil, and often cruel insult, are their portion; and no necklace heavy with tokens of honour that afterwards may be allotted them can ever quite hide the scars made by the iron collar of the slave. One need not pity them over much, for they are young and have a whole life-time of energy and power of resistance in their spirit. And yet they will often call themselves slaves, and complain that all the fruit of their labour passes over to others and away from themselves, and all prospect of the fulfilment of their former dreams is quite cut off. That which haunts their heart by day and by night, that which they seem destined and fit for, they never get time nor liberty to work out and attain. They are never viewed as proprietors of themselves, who may possibly have interests of their own and hopes of their own.

In Joseph's case there were many aggravations of the soreness of such a condition. He had not one friend in the country. He had no knowledge of the language, no knowledge of any trade that could make him valuable in Egypt—nothing, in short, but his own manhood and his faith in God. His introduction to Egypt was of the most dispiriting kind. What could he expect from strangers, if his own brothers had found him so obnoxious? Now when a man is thus galled and stung by injury, and has learned how little he can depend upon finding good faith and common justice in the world, his character will show itself in the attitude he assumes towards men and towards life generally. A weak nature, when it finds itself thus deceived and injured, will sullenly surrender all expectation of good and will vent its spleen on the world by angry denunciations of the heartless and ungrateful ways of men. A proud nature will gather itself up from every blow, and determinedly work its way to an adequate revenge. A mean nature will accept its fate, and while it indulges in cynical and spiteful observations on human life, will greedily accept the paltriest rewards it can secure. But the supreme healthiness of Joseph's nature resists all the infectious influences that emanate from the world around him, and preserves him from every kind of morbid attitude towards the world and life. So easily did he throw off all vain regrets and stifle all vindictive and morbid feelings, so readily did he adjust himself to and so heartily enter into life as it presented itself to him, that he speedily rose to be overseer in the house of Potiphar. His capacity for business, his genial power of devoting himself to other men's interests, his clear integrity, were such, that this officer of Pharaoh's could find no more trustworthy servant in all Egypt—" he left all that he had in Joseph's hand: and he knew not aught he had, save the bread which he did eat."

Thus Joseph passed safely through a critical period of his life—the period during which men assume the attitude towards life and their fellow-men which they commonly retain throughout. Too often we accept the weapons with which the world challenges us, and seek to force our way by means little more commendable than the injustice and coldness we ourselves resent. Joseph gives the first great evidence of moral strength by rising superior to this temptation, to which almost all men in one degree or other succumb. You can hear him saying, deep down in his heart, and almost unconsciously to himself: If the world is full of hatred, there is all the more need that at least one man should forgive and love; if men's hearts are black with selfishness, ambition, and lust, all the more reason for me to be pure and to do my best for all whom my service can reach; if cruelty, lying, and fraud meet me at every step, all the more am I called to conquer these by integrity and guilelessness.

His capacity, then, and power of governing others, were no longer dreams of his own, but qualities with which he was accredited by those who judged dispassionately and from the bare actual results. But this recognition and promotion brought with it serious temptation. So capable a person was he that a year or two had brought him to the highest post he could expect as a slave. His advancement, therefore, only brought his actual attainment into more painful contrast with the attainment of his dreams. As this sense of disappointment becomes more familiar to his heart, and threatens, under the monotonous routine of his household work, to deepen into a habit, there suddenly opens to him a new and unthought-of path to high position. An intrigue with Potiphar's wife might lead to the very advancement he sought. It might lift him out of the condition of a slave. It may have been known to him that other men had not scrupled so to promote their own interests. Besides, Joseph was young, and a nature like his, lively and sympathetic, must have felt deeply that in his position he was not likely to meet such a woman as could command his cordial love. That the temptation was in any degree to the sensual side of his nature there is no evidence whatever. For all that the narrative says, Potiphar's wife may not have been attractive in person. She *may* have been; and as she used persistently, " day by day," every art and wile by which she could lure Joseph to her mind, in some of his moods and under such circumstances as she would study to arrange he may have felt even this element of the temptation. But it is too little observed, and especially by young men who have most need to observe it, that in such temptations it is not only what is sensual that needs to be guarded against, but also two much deeper-lying tendencies—the craving for loving recognition, and the desire to respond to the feminine love for admiration and devotion. The latter tendency may not seem dangerous, but I am sure that if an analysis could be made of the broken hearts and shame-crushed lives around us, it would be found that a large proportion of misery is due to a kind of uncontrolled and mistaken chivalry. Men of masculine make are prone to show their regard for women. This regard, when genuine and manly, will show itself in purity of sympathy and respectful attention. But when this regard is debased by a desire to please and ingratiate one's self, men are precipitated into the unseemly expressions of a spurious manhood. The other craving—the craving for love—acts also in a somewhat latent way. It is this craving which drives men to seek to satisfy themselves with the expressions of love, as if thus they could secure love itself. They do not distinguish between the two; they do not recognise that what they most deeply desire is love, rather than the expression of it; and they awake to find that precisely in so far as they have accepted the expression without the sentiment, in so far have they put love itself beyond their reach.

This temptation was, in Joseph's case, aggravated by his being in a foreign country, unrestrained by the expectations of his own family, or by the eye of those he loved. He had, however, that which restrained him, and made the sin seem to him an impossible wickedness, the thought of which he could not, for a moment, entertain. "Behold, my master wotteth not what is with me in the house, and he hath committed all that he hath to my hand; there is none greater in this house than I; neither hath he kept back anything from me but thee, because thou art his wife: how then can I do this great wickedness, and sin against God?" Gratitude to the man who had pitied him in the slave market, and shown a generous confidence in a comparative stranger, was, with Joseph, a stronger sentiment than any that Potiphar's wife could stir in him. One can well believe it. We know what enthusiastic devotedness a young man of any worth delights to give to his superior who has treated him with justice, generosity, and confidence; who himself occupies a station of importance in public life; and who, by a dignified graciousness of demeanour, can make even the slave feel that he too is a man, and that through his slave's dress his proper manhood and worth are recognised. There are few stronger sentiments than the enthusiasm or quiet fidelity that can thus be kindled, and the influence such a superior wields over the young mind is paramount. To disregard the rights of his master seemed to Joseph a great wickedness and sin against God. The treachery of the sin strikes him; his native discernment of the true rights of every party in the case cannot, for a moment, be hoodwinked. He is not a man who can, even in the excitement of temptation, overlook the consequences his sin may have on others. Not unsteadied by the flattering solicitations of one so much above him in rank, nor sullied by the contagion of her vehement passion; neither afraid to incur the resentment of one who so regarded him, nor kindled to any impure desire by contact with her blazing lust; neither scrupling thoroughly to disappoint her in himself, nor to make her feel her own great guilt, he flung from him the strong inducements that seemed to net him round and entangle him as his garment did, and tore himself, shocked and grieved, from the beseeching hand of his temptress.

The incident is related not because it was the most violent temptation to which Joseph was ever exposed, but because it formed a necessary link in the chain of circumstances that brought him before Pharaoh. And however strong this temptation may have been, more men would be found who could thus have spoken to Potiphar's wife than who could have kept silence when accused by Potiphar. For his purity you will find his equal, one among a thousand; for his mercy scarcely one. For there is nothing more intensely trying than to live under false and painful accusations, which totally misrepresent and damage your character, which effectually bar your advancement, and which yet you have it in your power to disprove. Joseph, feeling his indebtedness to Potiphar, contents himself with the simple averment that he himself is innocent. The word is on his tongue that can put a very different face on the matter, but rather than utter that word, Joseph will suffer the stroke that otherwise must fall on his master's honour; will pass from his high place and office of trust, through the jeering or possibly compassionating slaves, branded as one who has betrayed the frankest confidence, and is fitter for the dungeon than the stewardship of Potiphar. He is content to lie under the cruel suspicion that he had in the foulest way wronged the man whom most he should have regarded, and whom in point of fact he did enthusiastically serve. There was one man in Egypt whose good-will he prized, and this man now scorned and condemned him, and this for the very act by which Joseph had proved most faithful and deserving.

And even after a long imprisonment, when he had now no reputation to maintain, and when such a little bit of court scandal as he could have retailed would have been highly palatable and possibly useful to some of those polished ruffians and adventurers who made their dungeon ring with questionable tales, and with whom the free and levelling intercourse of prison life had put him on the most familiar footing, and when they twitted and taunted him with his supposed crime, and gave him the prison sobriquet that would most pungently embody his villainy and failure, and when it might plausibly have been pleaded by himself that such a woman should be exposed, Joseph uttered no word of recrimination, but quietly endured, knowing that God's providence could allow him to be merciful; protesting, when needful, that he himself was innocent, but seeking to entangle no one else in his misfortune.

It is this that has made the world seem so terrible a place to many—that the innocent must so often suffer for the guilty, and that, without appeal, the pure and loving must lie in chains and bitterness, while the wicked live and see good days. It is this that has made men most despairingly question whether there be indeed a God in heaven Who knows who the real culprit is, and yet suffers a terrible doom slowly to close around the innocent; Who sees where the guilt lies, and yet moves no finger nor speaks the word that would bring justice to light, shaming the secure triumph of the wrongdoer, and saving the bleeding spirit from its agony. It was this that came as the last stroke of the passion of our Lord, that He was numbered among the transgressors; it was this that caused or materially increased the feeling that God had deserted Him; and it was this that wrung from Him the cry which once was wrung from David, and may well have been wrung from Joseph, when, cast into the dungeon as a mean and treacherous villain, whose freedom was the peril of domestic peace and honour, he found himself again helpless and forlorn, regarded now not as a mere worthless lad, but as a criminal of the lowest type. And as there always recur cases in which exculpation is impossible just in proportion as the party accused is possessed of honourable feeling, and where silent acceptance of doom is the result not of convicted guilt, but of the very triumph of self-sacrifice, we must beware of over-suspicion and injustice. There is nothing in which we are more frequently mistaken than in our suspicions and harsh judgments of others.

"But the Lord was with Joseph, and allowed him mercy, and gave him favour in the sight of the keeper of the prison." As in Potiphar's house, so in the king's house of detention, Joseph's fidelity and serviceableness made him seem indispensable, and by sheer force of character he occupied the place rather of governor than of prisoner. The discerning men he had to do with, accustomed to deal with criminals and suspects of all shades, very quickly perceived that in Joseph's case justice was at fault, and that he was a mere scape-goat. Well might Potiphar's wife, like Pilate's, have had warning dreams regarding the innocent person who was being condemned; and probably Potiphar himself had suspicion enough of the true state of matters to prevent him from going to extremities with Joseph, and so to imprison him more out of deference to the opinion of his household, and for the sake of appearances, than because Joseph alone was the object of his anger. At any rate, such was the vitality of Joseph's confidence in God, and such was the light-heartedness that sprang from his integrity of conscience, that he was free from all absorbing anxiety about himself, and had leisure to amuse and help his fellow-prisoners, so that such promotion as a gaol could afford he won, from a dungeon to a chain, from a chain to his word of honour. Thus even in the unlatticed dungeon the sun and moon look in upon him and bow to him; and while his sheaf seems at its poorest, all rust and mildew, the sheaves of his masters do homage.

After the arrival of two such notable criminals as the chief butler and baker of Pharaoh—the chamberlain and steward of the royal household—Joseph, if sometimes pensive, must yet have had sufficient entertainment at times in conversing with men who stood by the king, and were familiar with the statesmen, courtiers, and military men who frequented the house of Potiphar. He had now ample opportunity for acquiring information which afterwards stood him in good stead, for apprehending the character of Pharaoh, and for making himself acquainted with many details of his government, and with the general condition of the people. Officials in disgrace would be found much more accessible and much more communicative of important information than officials in court favour could have been to one in Joseph's position.

It is not surprising that three nights before Pharaoh's birthday these functionaries of the court should have recalled in sleep such scenes as that day was wont to bring round, nor that they should vividly have seen the parts they themselves used to play in the festival. Neither is it surprising that they should have had very anxious thoughts regarding their own fate on a day which was chosen for deciding the fate of political or courtly offenders. But it is remarkable that they having dreamed these dreams Joseph should have been found willing to interpret them. One desires some evidence of Joseph's attitude towards God during this period when God's attitude towards him might seem doubtful, and especially one would like to know what Joseph by this time thought of his juvenile dreams, and whether in the prison his face wore the same beaming confidence in his own future which had smitten the hearts of his brothers with impatient envy of the dreamer. We seek some evidence, and here we find it. Joseph's willingness to interpret the dreams of his fellow-prisoners proves that he still believed in his own, that among his other qualities he had this characteristic also of a steadfast and profound soul, that he " reverenced as a man the dreams of his youth." Had he not done so, and had he not yet hoped that somehow God would bring truth out of them, he would surely have said: Don't you believe in dreams; they will only get you into difficulties. He would have said what some of us could dictate from our own thoughts: I won't meddle with dreams any more; I am not so young as I once was; doctrines and principles that served for fervent romantic youth seem puerile now, when I have learned what human life actually is. I can't ask this man, who knows the world and has held the cup for Pharaoh, and is aware what a practical shape the king's anger takes, to cherish hopes similar to those which often seem so remote and doubtful to myself. My religion has brought me into trouble: it has lost me my situation, it has kept me poor, it has made me despised, it has debarred me from enjoyment. Can I ask this man to trust to inward whisperings which seem to have so misled me? No, no; let every man bear his own burden. If he wishes to become religious, let not me bear the responsibility. If he will dream, let him find some other interpreter.

This casual conversation, then, with his fellow-prisoners was for Joseph one of those perilous moments when a man holds his fate in his hand, and yet does not know that he is specially on trial, but has for his guidance and safe-conduct through the hazard only the ordinary safeguards and lights by the aid of which he is framing his daily life. A man cannot be forewarned of trial, if the trial is to be a fair test of his habitual life. He must not be called to the lists by the herald's trumpet warning him to mind his seat and grasp his weapon; but must be suddenly set upon if his habit of steadiness and balance is to be tested, and the warrior-instinct to which the right weapon is ever at hand. As Joseph, going the round of his morning duty and spreading what might stir the appetite of these dainty courtiers, noted the gloom on their faces, had he not been of a nature to take upon himself the sorrows of others, he might have been glad to escape from their presence, fearful lest he should be infected by their depression, or should become an object on which they might vent their ill-humour. But he was girt with a healthy cheerfulness that could bear more than his own burden; and his pondering of his own experience made him sensitive to all that affected the destinies of other men.

Thus Joseph in becoming the interpreter of the dreams of other men became the fulfiller of his own. Had he made light of the dreams of his fellow-prisoners because he had already made light of his own, he would, for aught we can see, have died in the dungeon. And, indeed, what hope is left for a man, and what deliverance is possible, when he makes light of his own most sacred experience, and doubts whether after all there was any Divine voice in that part of his life which once he felt to be full of significance? Sadness, cynical worldliness, irritability, sour and isolating selfishness, rapid deterioration in every part of the character—these are the results which follow our repudiation of past experience and denial of truth that once animated and purified us; when, at least, this repudiation and denial are not themselves the results of our advance to a higher, more animating, and more purifying truth. We cannot but leave behind us many "childish things," beliefs that we now recognise as mere superstitions, hopes and fears which do not move the maturer mind; we cannot but seek always to be stripping ourselves of modes of thinking which have served their purpose and are out of date, but we do so only for the sake of attaining freer movement in all serviceable and righteous conduct, and more adequate covering for the permanent weaknesses of our own nature —" not for that we would be unclothed, but clothed upon," that truth partial and dawning may be swallowed up in the perfect light of noon. And when a supposed advance in the knowledge of things spiritual robs us of all that sustains true spiritual life in us, and begets an angry contempt of our own past experience and a proud scorning of the dreams that agitate other men; when it ministers not at all to the growth in us of what is tender and pure and loving and progressive, but hardens us to a sullen or coarsely riotous or coldly calculating character, we cannot but question whether it is not a delusion rather than a truth that has taken possession of us.

If it is fanciful, it is yet almost inevitable, to compare Joseph at this stage of his career to the great Interpreter who stands between God and us, and makes all His signs intelligible. Those Egyptians could not forbear honouring Joseph, who was able to solve to them the mysteries on the borders of which the Egyptian mind continually hovered, and which it symbolized by its mysterious sphinxes, its strange chambers of imagery, its unapproachable divinities. And we bow before the Lord Jesus Christ, because He can read our fate and unriddle all our dim anticipations of good and evil, and make intelligible to us the visions of our own hearts. There is that in us, as in these men, from which a skilled eye could already read our destiny. In the eye of One who sees the end from the beginning, and can distinguish between the determining influences of character and the insignificant manifestations of a passing mood, we are already designed to our eternal places. And it is in Christ alone your future is explained. You cannot understand your future without taking Him into your confidence. You go forward blindly to meet you know not what, unless you listen to His interpretation of the vague presentiments that visit you. Without Him what can we make of those suspicions of a future judgment, or of those yearnings after God, that hang about our hearts? Without Him what can we make of the idea and hope of a better life than we are now living, or of the strange persuasion that all will yet be well—a persuasion that seems so groundless, and which yet will not be shaken off, but finds its explanation in Christ? The excess of side light that falls across our path from the present seems only to make the future more obscure and doubtful, and from Him alone do we receive any interpretation of ourselves that even seems to be satisfying. Our fellow-prisoners are often seen to be so absorbed in their own affairs that it is vain to seek light from them; but He, with patient, self-forgetting friendliness, is ever disengaged, and even elicits, by the kindly and interrogating attitude He takes towards us, the utterance of all our woes and perplexities. And it is because He has had dreams Himself that He has become so skilled an interpreter of ours. It is because in His own life He had His mind hard pressed for a solution of those very problems which baffle us, because He had for Himself to adjust God's promise to the ordinary and apparently casual and untoward incidents of a human life, and because He had to wait long before it became quite clear how one Scripture after another was to be fulfilled by a course of simple confiding obedience—it is because of this experience of His own, that He can now enter into and rightly guide to its goal every longing we cherish.

CHAPTER XXVII.

PHARAOH'S DREAMS.

GENESIS xli.

"Thus saith the Lord, that frustrateth the tokens of the liars, and maketh diviners mad; that confirmeth the word of His servant, and performeth the counsel of His messengers; that saith of Cyrus, He is my shepherd, and shall perform all My pleasure."—ISA. xliv. 25, 28.

THE preceding act in this great drama—the act comprising the scenes of Joseph's temptation, unjust imprisonment, and interpretation of his fellow-prisoners' dreams—was written for the sake of explaining how Joseph came to be introduced to Pharaoh. Other friendships may have been formed in the prison, and other threads may have been spun which went to make up the life of Joseph, but this only is pursued. For a time, however, there seemed very little prospect that this would prove to be the thread on which his destiny hung. Joseph made a touching appeal to the Chief Butler: "yet did not the Chief Butler remember Joseph, but forgat him." You can see him in the joy of his release affectionately pressing Joseph's hand as the king's messengers knocked off his fetters. You can see him assuring Joseph, by his farewell look, that he might trust him; mistaking mere elation at his own release for warmth of feeling towards Joseph, though perhaps even already feeling just the slightest touch of awkwardness at being seen on such intimate terms with a Hebrew slave. How could he, when in the palace of Pharaoh and decorated with the insignia of his office and surrounded by courtiers, break through the formal etiquette of the place? What with the pleasant congratulations of old friends, and the accumulation of business since he had been imprisoned, and the excitement of restoration from so low and hopeless to so high and busy a position, the promise to Joseph is obliterated from his mind. If it once or twice recurs to his memory, he persuades himself he is waiting for a good opening to mention Joseph. It would perhaps be unwarrantable to say that he admits the idea that he is in no way indebted to Joseph, since all that Joseph had done was to interpret, but by no means to determine, his fate.

The analogy which we could not help seeing between Joseph's relation to his fellow-prisoners, and our Lord's relation to us, pursues us here. For does not the bond between us and Him seem often very slender, when once we have received from Him the knowledge of the King's goodwill, and find ourselves set in a place of security? Is not Christ with many a mere stepping-stone for their own advancement, and of interest only so long as they are in anxiety about their own fate? Their regard for Him seems abruptly to terminate as soon as they are ushered to freer air. Brought for a while into contact with Him, the very peace and prosperity which that intercourse has introduced them to become opiates to dull their memory and their gratitude. They have received all they at present desire, they have no more dreams, their life has become so plain and simple and glad that they need no interpreter. They seem to regard Him no more than an official is regarded who is set to discharge to all comers some duty for which he is paid; who mingles no love with his work, and from whom they would receive the same benefits whether he had any personal interest in them or no. But there is no Christianity where there is no loving remembrance of Christ. If your contact with Him has not made Him your Friend whom you can by no possibility forget, you have missed the best result of your introduction to Him. It makes one think meanly of the Chief Butler that such a personality as Joseph's had not more deeply impressed him—that everything he heard and saw among the courtiers did not make him say to himself: There is a friend of mine, in prison hard by, that for beauty, wisdom, and vivacity would more than match the finest of you all. And it says very little for us if we can have known anything of Christ without seeing that in Him we have what is nowhere else, and without finding that He has become the necessity of our life to whom we turn at every point.

But, as things turned out, it was perhaps as well for Joseph that his promising friend did forget him. For, supposing the Chief Butler had overcome his natural reluctance to increase his own indebtedness to Pharaoh by interceding for a friend, supposing he had been willing to risk the friendship of the Captain of the Guard by interfering in so delicate a matter, and supposing Pharaoh had been willing to listen to him, what would have been the result? Probably that Joseph would have been sold away to the quarries, for certainly he could not have been restored to Potiphar's house; or, at the most, he might have received his liberty, and a free pass out of Egypt. That is to say, he would have obtained liberty to return to sheep-shearing and cattle-dealing and checkmating his brothers' plots. In any probable case his career would have tended rather towards obscurity than towards the fulfilment of his dreams.

There seems equal reason to congratulate Joseph on his friend's forgetfulness, when we consider its probable effects, not on his career, but on his character. When he was left in prison after so sudden and exciting an incursion of the outer world as the king's messengers would make, his mind must have run chiefly in two lines of thought. Naturally he would feel some envy of the man who was being restored; and when day after day passed and more than the former monotony of prison routine palled on his spirit; when he found how completely he was forgotten, and how friendless and lone a creature he was in that strange land where things had gone so mysteriously against him; when he saw before him no other fate than that which he had seen befall so many a slave thrown into a dungeon at his master's pleasure and never more heard of, he must have been sorely tempted to hate the whole world, and especially those brethren who had been the beginning of all his misfortunes. Had there been any selfishness in solution in Joseph's character, this is the point at which it would have quickly crystallized into permanent forms. For nothing more certainly elicits and confirms selfishness than bad treatment. But from his conduct on his release, we see clearly enough that through all this trying time his heroism was not only that of the strong man who vows that though the whole world is against him the day will come when the world shall have need of him, but of the saint of God in whom suffering and injustice leave no bitterness against his fellows, nor even provoke one slightest morbid utterance.

But another process must have been going on in Joseph's mind at the same time. He must have felt that it was a very serious thing that he had been called upon to do in interpreting God's will to his fellow-prisoners. No doubt he fell into it quite naturally and aptly, because it was liker his proper vocation, and more of his character could come out in it than in anything he had yet done. Still, to be mixed up thus with matters of life and death concerning other people, and to have men of practical ability and experience and high position listening to him as to an oracle, and to find that in very truth a great power was committed to him, was calculated to have *some* considerable result one way or other on Joseph. And these two years of unrelieved and sobering obscurity cannot but be considered most opportune. For one of two things is apt to follow the world's first recognition of a man's gifts. He is either induced to pander to the world's wonder and become artificial and strained in all he does, so losing the spontaneity and naturalness and sincerity which characterise the best work; or he is awed and steadied. And whether the one or the other result follow, will depend very much on the other things that are happening to him. In Joseph's case it was probably well that after having made proof of his powers he was left in such circumstances as would not only give him time for reflection, but also give a humble and believing turn to his reflections. He was not at once exalted to the priestly caste, nor enrolled among the wise men, nor put in any position in which he would have been under constant temptation to display and trifle with his power; and so he was led to the conviction that deeper even than the joy of receiving the recognition and gratitude of men was the abiding satisfaction of having done the thing God had given him to do.

These two years, then, during which Joseph's active mind must necessarily have been forced to provide food for itself, and have been thrown back upon his past experience, seem to have been of eminent service in maturing his character. The self-possessed dignity and ease of command which appear in him from the moment when he is ushered into Pharaoh's presence have their roots in these two years of silence. As the bones of a strong man are slowly, imperceptibly knit, and gradually take the shape and texture they retain throughout; so during these years there was silently and secretly consolidating a character of almost unparalleled calmness and power. One has no words to express how tantalising it must have been to Joseph to see this Egyptian have his dreams so gladly and speedily fulfilled, while he himself, who had so long waited on the true God, was left waiting still, and now so utterly unbefriended that there seemed no possible way of ever again connecting himself with the world outside the prison walls. Being pressed thus for an answer to the question, What does God mean to make of my life? he was brought to see and to hold as the most important truth for him, that the first concern is, that God's purposes be accomplished; the second, that his own dreams be fulfilled. He was enabled, as we shall see in the sequel, to put God truly in the first place, and to see that by forwarding the interests of other men, even though they were but light-minded chief butlers at a foreign court, he might be as serviceably furthering the purposes of God, as if he were forwarding his own interests. He was compelled to seek for some principle that would sustain and guide him in the midst of much disappointment and perplexity, and he found it in the conviction that the essential thing to be accomplished in this world, and to which every man must lay his shoulder, is God's purpose. Let that go on, and all else that should go on will go on. And he further saw that he best fulfils God's purpose who, without anxiety and impatience, does the duty of the day, and gives himself without stint to the "charities that soothe and heal and bless."

His perception of the breadth of God's purpose, and his profound and sympathetic and active submission to it, were qualities too rare not to be called into influential exercise. After two years he is suddenly summoned to become God's interpreter to Pharaoh. The Egyptian king was in the unhappy though not uncommon position of having a revelation from God which he could not read, intimations and presentiments he could not interpret. To one man is given the revelation, to another the interpretation. The official dignity of the king is respected, and to him is given the revelation which concerns the welfare of the whole people. But to read God's meaning in a revelation requires a spiritual intelligence trained to sympathy with His purposes, and such a spirit was found in Joseph alone.

The dreams of Pharaoh were thoroughly Egyptian. The marvel is, that a symbolism so familiar to the Egyptian eye should not have been easily legible to even the most slenderly gifted of Pharaoh's wise men. "In my dream," says the king, "behold, I stood upon the bank of the river: and, behold, there came up out of the river seven kine," and so on. Every land or city is proud of its river, but none has such cause to be so as Egypt of its Nile. The country is accurately as well as poetically called " the gift of Nile." Out of the river do really come good or bad years, fat or lean kine. Wholly dependent on its annual rise and overflow for the irrigating and enriching of the soil, the people worship it and love it, and at the season of its overflow give way to the most rapturous expressions of joy. The cow also was reverenced as the symbol of the earth's productive power. If then, as Joseph avers, God wished to show to Pharaoh that seven years of plenty were approaching, this announcement could hardly have been made plainer in the language of dreams than by showing to Pharaoh seven well-favoured kine coming up out of the bountiful river to feed on the meadow made richly green by its waters. If the king had been sacrificing to the river, such a sight, familiar as it was to the dwellers by the Nile, might well have been accepted by him as a promise of plenty in the land. But what agitated Pharaoh, and gave him the shuddering presentiment of evil which accompanies some dreams, was the sequel. "Behold, seven other kine came up after them, poor and very ill-favoured and lean-fleshed, such as I never saw in all the land of Egypt for badness: and the lean and the ill-favoured kine did eat up the first seven fat kine: and when they had eaten them up it could not be known that they had eaten them; but they were still ill-favoured, as at the beginning,"—a picture which to the inspired dream-reader represented seven years of famine so grievous, that the preceding plenty should be swallowed up and not be known. A similar image occurred to a writer who, in describing a more recent famine in the same land, says: "The year presented itself as a monster whose wrath must annihilate all the resources of life and all the means of subsistence."

It tells in favour of the court magicians and wise men that not one of them offered an interpretation of dreams to which it would certainly not have been difficult to attach some tolerably feasible interpretation. Probably these men were as yet sincere devotees of astrology and occult science, and not the mere jugglers and charlatans their successors seem to have become. When men cannot make out the purpose of God regarding the future of the race, it is not wonderful that they should endeavour to catch the faintest, most broken echo of His voice to the world, wherever they can find it. Now there is a wide region, a borderland between the two worlds of spirit and of matter, in which are found a great many mysterious phenomena which cannot be explained by any known laws of nature, and through which men fancy they get nearer to the spiritual world. There are many singular and startling appearances, coincidences, forebodings, premonitions which men have always been attracted towards, and which they have considered as open ways of communication between God and man. There are dreams, visions, strange apprehensions, freaks of memory, and other mental phenomena, which, when all classed together, assorted, and skilfully applied to the reading of the future, once formed quite a science by itself. When men have no word from God to depend upon, no knowledge at all of where either the race or individuals are going to, they will eagerly grasp at anything that even seems to shed a ray of light on their future. We for the most part make light of that whole category of phenomena, because we have a more sure word of prophecy by which, as with a light in a dark place, we can tell where our next step should be, and what the end shall be. But invariably in heathen countries, where no guiding Spirit of God was believed in, and where the absence of His revealed will left numberless points of duty doubtful and all the future dark, there existed in lieu of this a class of persons who, under one name or other, undertook to satisfy the craving of men to see into the future, to forewarn them of danger, and advise them regarding matters of conduct and affairs of state.

At various points of the history of God's revelation these professors of occult science appear. In each case a profound impression is made by the superior wisdom or power displayed by the "wise men" of God. But in reading the accounts we have of these collisions between the wisdom of God and that of the magicians, a slight feeling of uneasiness sometimes enters the mind. You may feel that these wonders of Joseph, Moses, and Daniel have a romantic air about them, and you feel, perhaps, a slight scruple in granting that God would lend Himself to such displays—displays so completely out of date in our day. But we are to consider not only that there is nothing of the kind more certain than that dreams do sometimes even now impart most significant warning to men; but, also, that the time in which Joseph lived was the childhood of the world, when God had neither spoken much to men, nor could speak much, because as yet they had not learned His language, but were only being slowly taught it by signs suited to their capacity. If these men were to receive any knowledge beyond what their own unaided efforts could attain, they must be taught in a language they understood. They could not be dealt with as if they had already attained a knowledge and a capacity which could only be theirs many centuries after; they must be dealt with by signs and wonders which had perhaps little moral teaching in them, but yet gave evidence of God's nearness and power such as they could and did understand. God thus stretched out His hand to men in the darkness, and let them feel His strength before they could look on His face and understand His nature.

It is the existence at the court of Pharaoh of this highly respected class of dream-interpreters and wise men, which lends significance to the conduct of Joseph when summoned into the royal presence. Such wisdom as he displayed in reading Pharaoh's visions was looked upon as attainable by means within the reach of any man who had sufficient faculty for the science. And the first idea in the minds of the courtiers would probably have been, had Joseph not solemnly protested against it, that he was an adept where they were apprentices and bunglers, and that his success was due purely to professional skill. This was of course perfectly well known to Joseph, who for a number of years had been familiar with the ideas prevalent at the court of Pharaoh; and he might have argued that there could be no great harm in at least effecting his deliverance from an unjust imprisonment by allowing Pharaoh to suppose that it was to him he was indebted for the interpretation of his dreams. But his first word to Pharaoh is a self-renouncing exclamation: "Not in me: *God* shall give Pharaoh an answer of peace." Two years had elapsed since anything had occurred which looked the least like the fulfilment of his own dreams, or gave him any hope of release from prison; and now, when measuring himself with these courtiers and feeling able to take his place with the best of them, getting again a breath of free air and feeling once more the charm of life, and having an opening set before his young ambition, being so suddenly transferred from a place where his very existence seemed to be forgotten to a place where Pharaoh himself and all his court eyed him with the intensest interest and anxiety, it is significant that he should appear regardless of his own fate, but jealously careful of the glory of God. Considering how jealous men commonly are of their own reputation, and how impatiently eager to receive all the credit that is due to them for their own share in any good that is doing, and considering of what essential importance it seemed that Joseph should seize this opportunity of providing for his own safety and advancement, and should use this as the tide in his affairs that led to fortune, his words and bearing before Pharaoh undoubtedly disclose a deeply inwrought fidelity to God, and a magnanimous patience regarding his own personal interests.

For it is extremely unlikely that in proposing to Pharaoh to set a man over this important business of collecting corn to last through the years of famine, it presented itself to Joseph as a conceivable result that he should be the person appointed—he a Hebrew, a slave, a prisoner, cleaned but for the nonce, could not suppose that Pharaoh would pass over all those tried officers and ministers of state around him and fix upon a youth who was wholly untried, and who might, by his different race and religion, prove obnoxious to the people. Joseph may have expected to make interest enough with Pharaoh to secure his freedom, and possibly some subordinate berth where he could hopefully begin the world again; but his only allusion to himself is of a depreciatory kind, while his reference to God is marked with a profound conviction that this is God's doing, and that to Him is due whatever is due. Well may the Hebrew race be proud of those men like Joseph and Daniel, who stood in the presence of foreign monarchs in a spirit of perfect fidelity to God, commanding the respect of all, and clothed with the dignity and simplicity which that fidelity imparted. It matters not to Joseph that there may perhaps be none in that land who can appreciate his fidelity to God or understand his motive. It matters not what he may lose by it, or what he could gain by falling in with the notions of those around him. He himself knows the real state of the case, and will not act untruly to his God, even though for years he seems to have been forgotten by Him. With Daniel he says in spirit, "Let thy gifts be to thyself, and give thy rewards to another. As for me, this secret is not revealed to me for any wisdom that I have more than any living, but that the interpretation may be known to the king, and that thou mayest know the thoughts of thine heart. He that revealeth secrets maketh known to thee what shall come to pass." There is something particularly noble and worthy of admiration in a man thus standing alone and maintaining the fullest allegiance to God, without ostentation and with a quiet dignity and naturalness that show he has a great fund of strength behind.

That we do not misjudge Joseph's character or ascribe to him qualities which were invisible to his contemporaries, is apparent from the circumstance that Pharaoh and his advisers, with little or no hesitation, agreed that to no man could they more safely entrust their country in this emergency. The mere personal charm of Joseph might have won over those experienced advisers of the crown to make compensation for his imprisonment by an unusually handsome reward, but no mere attractiveness of person and manner, nor even the unquestionable guilelessness of his bearing, could have induced them to put such an affair as this into his hands. Plainly they were impressed with Joseph; almost supernaturally impressed, and felt God through him. He stood before them as one mysteriously appearing in their emergency, sent out of unthought-of quarters to warn and save them. Happily there was as yet no jealousy of the God of the Hebrews, nor any exclusiveness on the part of the chosen people: Pharaoh and Joseph alike felt that there was one God over all and through all. And it was Joseph's self-abnegating sympathy with the purposes of this Supreme God that made him a transparent medium, so that in his presence the Egyptians felt themselves in the presence of God. It is so always. Influence in the long run belongs to those who rid their minds of all private aims, and get close to the great centre in which all the race meets and is cared for. Men feel themselves safe with the unselfish, with persons in whom they meet principle, justice, truth, love, God. We are unattractive, useless, uninfluential, just because we are still childishly craving a private and selfish good. We know that a life which does not pour itself freely into the common stream of public good is lost in dry and sterile sands. We know that a life spent upon self is contemptible, barren, empty, yet how slowly do we come to the attitude of Joseph, who watched for the fulfilment of God's purposes, and found his happiness in forwarding what God designed for the people.

CHAPTER XXVIII.

JOSEPH'S ADMINISTRATION.

GENESIS xli. 37-57, and xlvii. 13-26.

"He made him lord of his house, and ruler of all his substance: To bind his princes at his pleasure; and teach his senators wisdom."—PSALM cv. 21, 22.

"MANY a monument consecrated to the memory of some nobleman gone to his long home, who during life had held high rank at the court of Pharaoh, is decorated with the simple but laudatory inscription, ' His ancestors were unknown people' "—so we are told by our most accurate informant regarding Egyptian affairs. Indeed, the tales we read of adventurers in the East, and the histories which recount how some dynasties have been founded, are sufficient evidence that, in other countries besides Egypt, sudden elevation from the lowest to the highest rank is not so unusual as amongst ourselves. Historians have recently made out that in one period of the history of Egypt there are traces of a kind of Semitic mania, a strong leaning towards Syrian and Arabian customs, phrases, and persons. Such manias have occurred in most countries. There was a period in the history of Rome when everything that had a Greek flavour was admired; an Anglomania once affected a portion of the French population, and reciprocally, French manners and ideas have at times found a welcome among ourselves. It is also clear that for a time Lower Egypt was under the dominion of foreign rulers who were in race more nearly allied to Joseph than to the native population. But there is no need that so complicated a question as the exact date of this foreign domination be debated here, for there was that in Joseph's bearing which would have commended him to any sagacious monarch. Not only did the court accept him as a messenger from God, but they could not fail to recognise substantial and serviceable human qualities alongside of what was mysterious in him. The ready apprehension with which he appreciated the magnitude of the danger, the clear-sighted promptitude with which he met it, the resource and quiet capacity with which he handled a matter involving the entire condition of Egypt, showed them that they were in the presence of a true statesman. No doubt the confidence with which he described the best method of dealing with the emergency was the confidence of one who was convinced he was speaking for God. This was the great distinction they perceived between Joseph and ordinary dream-interpreters. It was not guesswork with him. The same distinction is always apparent between revelation and speculation. Revelation speaks with authority; speculation gropes its way, and when wisest is most diffident. At the same time Pharaoh was perfectly right in his inference: "Forasmuch as God hath shewed thee all this, there is none so discreet and wise as thou art." He believed that God had chosen him to deal with this matter because he was wise in heart, and he believed his wisdom would remain because God had chosen him.

At length, then, Joseph saw the fulfilment of his dreams within his reach. The coat of many colours with which his father had paid a tribute to the princely person and ways of the boy, was now replaced by the robe of state and the heavy gold necklace which marked him out as second to Pharaoh. Whatever nerve and self-command and humble dependence on God his varied experience had wrought in him were all needed when Pharaoh took his hand and placed his own ring on it, thus transferring all his authority to him, and when turning from the king he received the acclamations of the court and the people, bowed to by his old masters, and acknowledged the superior of all the dignitaries and potentates of Egypt. Only once besides, so far as the Egyptian inscriptions have yet been deciphered, does it appear that any subject was raised to be Regent or Viceroy with similar powers. Joseph is, as far as possible, naturalised as an Egyptian. He receives a name easier of pronunciation than his own, at least to Egyptian tongues—Zaphnath-Paaneah, which, however, was perhaps only an official title meaning "Governor of the district of the place of life," the name by which one of the Egyptian counties or states was known. The king crowned his liberality and completed the process of naturalisation by providing him with a wife, Asenath, the daughter of Potipherah, priest of On. This city was not far from Avaris or Haouar, where Joseph's Pharaoh, Ra-apepi II., at this time resided. The worship of the sun-god, Ra, had its centre at On (or Heliopolis, as it was called by the Greeks), and the priests of On took precedence of all Egyptian priests. Joseph was thus connected with one of the most influential families in the land, and if he had any scruples about marrying into an idolatrous family, they were too insignificant to influence his conduct, or leave any trace in the narrative.

His attitude towards God and his own family was disclosed in the names which he gave to his children. In giving names which had a meaning at all, and not merely a taking sound, he showed that he understood, as well he might, that every human life has a significance and expresses some principle or fact. And in giving names which recorded his acknowledgment of God's goodness, he showed that prosperity had as little influence as adversity to move him from his allegiance to the God of his fathers. His first son he called Manasseh, *Making to forget*, " for God," said he, " hath made me forget all my toil and all my father's house "—not as if he were now so abundantly satisfied in Egypt that the thought of his father's house was blotted from his mind, but only that in this child the keen longings he had felt for kindred and home were somewhat alleviated. He again found an object for his strong family affection. The void in his heart he had so long felt was filled by the little babe. A new home was begun around him. But this new affection would not weaken, though it would alter the character of, his love for his father and brethren. The birth of this child would really be a new tie to the land from which he had been stolen. For, however ready men are to spend their own life in foreign service, you see them wishing that their children should spend their days among the scenes with which their own childhood was familiar.

In the naming of his second son Ephraim he recognises that God had made him fruitful in the most unlikely way. He does not leave it to us to interpret his life, but records what he himself saw in it. It has been said: "To get at the truth of any history is good; but a man's own history —when he reads that truly, . . . and knows what he is about and has been about, it is a Bible to him." And now that Joseph, from the height he had reached, could look back on the way by which he had been led to it, he cordially approved of all that God had done. There was no resentment, no murmuring. He would often find himself looking back and thinking, Had I found my brothers where I thought they were, had the pit not been on the caravan-road, had the merchants not come up so opportunely, had I not been sold at all or to some other master, had I not been imprisoned, or had I been put in another ward—had any one of the many slender links in the chain of my career been absent, how different might my present state have been. How plainly I now see that all those sad mishaps that crushed my hopes and tortured my spirit were steps in the only conceivable path to my present position.

Many a man has added his signature to this acknowledgment of Joseph's, and confessed a providence guiding his life and working out good for him through injuries and sorrows, as well as through honours, marriages, births. As in the heat of summer it is difficult to recall the sensation of winter's bitter cold, so the fruitless and barren periods of a man's life are sometimes quite obliterated from his memory. God has it in His power to raise a man higher above the level of ordinary happiness than ever he has sunk below it; and as winter and spring-time, when the seed is sown, are stormy and bleak and gusty, so in human life seed-time is not bright as summer nor cheerful as autumn; and yet it is then, when all the earth lies bare and will yield us nothing, that the precious seed is sown: and when we confidently commit our labour or patience of to-day to God, the land of our affliction, now bare and desolate, will certainly wave for us, as it has waved for others, with rich produce whitened to the harvest.

There is no doubt then that Joseph had learned to recognise the providence of God as a most important factor in his life. And the man who does so gains for his character all the strength and resolution that come with a capacity for waiting. He saw, most legibly written on his own life, that God is never in a hurry. And for the resolute adherence to his seven-years' policy such a belief was most necessary. Nothing, indeed, is said of opposition or incredulity on the part of the Egyptians. But was there ever a policy of such magnitude carried out in any country without opposition or without evilly-disposed persons using it as a weapon against its promoter? No doubt during these years he had need of all the personal determination as well as of all the official authority he possessed. And if, on the whole, remarkable success attended his efforts, we must ascribe this partly to the unchallengeable justice of his arrangements, and partly to the impression of commanding genius Joseph seems everywhere to have made. As with his father and brethren he was felt to be superior, as in Potiphar's house he was quickly recognised, as in the prison no prison-garb or slave-brand could disguise him, as in the court his superiority was instinctively felt, so in his administration the people seem to have believed in him.

And if, on the whole and in general, Joseph was reckoned a wise and equitable ruler, and even adored as a kind of saviour of the world, it would be idle in us to canvass the wisdom of his administration. When we have not sufficient historical material to apprehend the full significance of any policy, it is safe to accept the judgment of men who not only knew the facts, but were themselves so deeply involved in them that they would certainly have felt and expressed discontent had there been ground for doing so. The policy of Joseph was simply to economise during the seven years of abundance to such an extent that provision might be made against the seven years of famine. He calculated that one-fifth of the produce of years so extraordinarily plenteous would serve for the seven scarce years. This fifth he seems to have bought in the king's name from the people, buying it, no doubt, at the cheap rates of abundant years. When the years of famine came, the people were referred to Joseph; and, till their money was gone, he sold corn to them, probably not at famine prices. Next he acquired their cattle, and finally, in exchange for food, they yielded to him both their lands and their persons. So that the result of the whole was, that the people who would otherwise have perished were preserved, and in return for this preservation they paid a tax or rent on their farm-lands to the amount of one-fifth of their produce. The people ceased to be proprietors of their own farms, but they were not slaves with no interest in the soil, but tenants sitting at easy rents—a fair enough exchange for being preserved in life. This kind of taxation is eminently fair in principle, securing, as it does, that the wealth of the king and government shall vary with the prosperity of the whole land. The chief difficulty that has always been experienced in working it, has arisen from the necessity of leaving a good deal of discretionary power in the hands of the collectors, who have generally been found not slow to abuse this power.

The only semblance of despotism in Joseph's policy is found in the curious circumstance that he interfered with the people's choice of residence, and shifted them from one end of the land to another. This may have been necessary not only as a kind of seal on the deed by which the lands were conveyed to the king, and as a significant sign to them that they were mere tenants, but also Joseph probably saw that for the interests of the country, if not of agricultural prosperity, this shifting had become necessary for the breaking up of illegal associations, nests of sedition, and sectional prejudices and enmities which were endangering the community.*
Modern experience supplies us with instances in which, by such a policy, a country might be re-

---

* It happened very often that the inhabitants of one district threatened an attack on the occupants of another on account of some dispute about divine or human questions. The hostile feelings of the opponents not unfrequently broke out into a hard struggle, and it required the whole armed power of the king to extinguish at its first outburst the flaming torch of war, kindled by domineering chiefs of nomes or ambitious priests."—Brugsch, *History of Egypt*, i. 16.

generated and a seven years' famine hailed as a blessing if, without famishing the people, it put them unconditionally into the hands of an able, bold, and beneficent ruler. And this was a policy which could be much better devised and executed by a foreigner than by a native.

Egypt's indebtedness to Joseph was, in fact, two-fold. In the first place he succeeded in doing what many strong governments have failed to do: he enabled a large population to survive a long and severe famine. Even with all modern facilities for transport and for making the abundance of remote countries available for times of scarcity, it has not always been found possible to save our own fellow-subjects from starvation. In a prolonged famine which occurred in Egypt during the Middle Ages, the inhabitants, reduced to the unnatural habits which are the most painful feature of such times, not only ate their own dead, but kidnapped the living on the streets of Cairo and consumed them in secret. One of the most touching memorials of the famine with which Joseph had to deal is found in a sepulchral inscription in Arabia. A flood of rain laid bare a tomb in which lay a woman having on her person a profusion of jewels which represented a very large value. At her head stood a coffer filled with treasure, and a tablet with this inscription: " In Thy name, O God, the God of Himyar, I, Tayar, the daughter of Dzu Shefar, sent my steward to Joseph, and he delaying to return to me, I sent my handmaid with a measure of silver to bring me back a measure of flour; and not being able to procure it, I sent her with a measure of gold; and not being able to procure it, I sent her with a measure of pearls; and not being able to procure it, I commanded them to be ground; and finding no profit in them, I am shut up here." If this inscription is genuine—and there seems no reason to call it in question—it shows that there is no exaggeration in the statement of our narrator that the famine was very grievous in other lands as well as in Egypt. And, whether genuine or not, one cannot but admire the grim humour of the starving woman getting herself buried in the jewels which had suddenly dropped to less than the value of a loaf of bread.

But besides being indebted to Joseph for their preservation, the Egyptians owed to him an extension of their influence; for, as all the lands round about became dependent on Egypt for provision, they must have contracted a respect for the Egyptian administration. They must also have added greatly to Egypt's wealth and during those years of constant traffic many commercial connections must have been formed which in future years would be of untold value to Egypt. But above all, the permanent alterations made by Joseph on their tenure of land, and on their places of abode, may have convinced the most sagacious of the Egyptians that it was well for them that their money had failed, and that they had been compelled to yield themselves unconditionally into the hands of this remarkable ruler. It is the mark of a competent statesman that he makes temporary distress the occasion for permanent benefit; and from the confidence Joseph won with the people, there seems every reason to believe that the permanent alterations he introduced were considered as beneficial as certainly they were bold.

And for our own spiritual uses it is this point which seems chiefly important. In Joseph is illustrated the principle that, in order to the attainment of certain blessings, unconditional submission to God's delegate is required. If we miss this, we miss a large part of what his history exhibits, and it becomes a mere pretty story. The prominent idea in his dreams was that he was to be worshipped by his brethren. In his exaltation by Pharaoh, the absolute authority given to him is again conspicuous: " Without thee shall no man lift up hand or foot in all the land of Egypt." And still the same autocracy appears in the fact that not one Egyptian who was helpful to him in this matter is mentioned; and no one has received such exclusive possession of a considerable part of Scripture, so personal and outstanding a place. All this leaves upon the mind the impression that Joseph becomes a benefactor, and in his degree a saviour, to men by becoming their absolute master. When this was hinted in his dreams at first his brothers fiercely resented it. But when they were put to the push by famine, both they and the Egyptians recognised that he was appointed by God to be their saviour, while at the same time they markedly and consciously submitted themselves to him. Men may always be expected to recognise that he who can save them alive in famine has a right to order the bounds of their habitation; and also that in the hands of one who, from disinterested motives, has saved them, they are likely to be quite as safe as in their own. And if we are all quite sure of this, that men of great political sagacity can regulate our affairs with tenfold the judgment and success that we ourselves could achieve, we cannot wonder that in matters still higher, and for which we are notoriously incompetent, there should be One into whose hands it is well to commit ourselves—One whose judgment is not warped by the prejudices which blind all mere natives of this world, but who, separate from sinners yet naturalised among us, can both detect and rectify everything in our condition which is less than perfect. If there are certainly many cases in which explanations are out of the question, and in which the governed, if they are wise, will yield themselves to a trusted authority, and leave it to time and results to justify his measures, any one, I think, who anxiously considers our spiritual condition must see that here too obedience is for us the greater part of wisdom, and that, after all speculation and efforts at sufficing investigation, we can still do no better than yield ourselves absolutely to Jesus Christ. He alone understands our whole position; He alone speaks with the authority that commands confidence, because it is felt to be the authority of the truth. We feel the present pressure of famine; we have discernment enough, some of us, to know we are in danger, but we cannot penetrate deeply either into the cause or the possible consequences of our present state. But Christ—if we may continue the figure—legislates with a breadth of administrative capacity which includes not only our present distress but our future condition, and, with the boldness of one who is master of the whole case, requires that we put ourselves wholly into His hand. He takes the responsibility of all the changes we make in obedience to Him, and proposes so to relieve us that the relief shall be permanent, and that the very emergency which has thrown us upon His help shall be the occasion of our transference not merely out of the present evil, but into the best possible form of human life.

From this chapter, then, in the history of Joseph, we may reasonably take occasion to remind ourselves, first, that in all things pertaining to God unconditional submission to Christ is necessarily required of us. Apart from Christ we cannot tell what are the necessary elements of a permanently happy state; nor, indeed, even whether there is any such state awaiting us. There is a great deal of truth in what is urged by unbelievers to the effect that spiritual matters are in great measure beyond our cognizance, and that many of our religious phrases are but, as it were, thrown out in the direction of a truth but do not perfectly represent it. No doubt we are in a provisional state, in which we are not in direct contact with the absolute truth, nor in a final attitude of mind towards it; and certain representations of things given in the Word of God may seem to us not to cover the whole truth. But this only compels the conclusion that for us Christ is the way, the truth, and the life. To probe existence to the bottom is plainly not in our power. To say precisely what God is, and how we are to carry ourselves towards Him, is possible only to him who has been with God and is God. To submit to the Spirit of Christ, and to live under those influences and views which formed His life, is the only method that promises deliverance from that moral condition which makes spiritual vision impossible.

We may remind ourselves, secondly, that this submission to Christ should be consistently adhered to in connection with those outward occurrences in our life which give us opportunity of enlarging our spiritual capacity. There can be little doubt that there would be presented to Joseph many a plan for the better administration of this whole matter, and many a petition from individuals craving exemption from the seemingly arbitrary and certainly painful and troublesome edict regulating change of residence. Many a man would think himself much wiser than the minister of Pharaoh in whom was the Spirit of God. When we act in a similar manner, and take upon us to specify with precision the changes we should like to see in our condition, and the methods by which these changes might best be accomplished, we commonly manifest our own incompetence. The changes which the strong hand of Providence enforces, the dislocation which our life suffers from some irresistible blow, the necessity laid upon us to begin life again and on apparently disadvantageous terms, are naturally resented; but these things being certainly the result of some unguardedness, improvidence, or weakness in our past state, are necessarily the means most appropriate for disclosing to us these elements of calamity and for securing our permanent welfare. We rebel against such perilous and sweeping revolutions as the basing of our life on a new foundation demands; we would disregard the appointments of Providence if we could; but both our voluntary consent to the authority of Christ and the impossibility of resisting His providential arrangements, prevent us from refusing to fall in with them, however needless and tyrannical they seem, and however little we perceive that they are intended to accomplish our permanent well-being. And it is in after years, when the pain of severance from old friends and habits is healed, and when the discomfort of adapting ourselves to a new kind of life is replaced by peaceful and docile resignation to new conditions, that we reach the clear perception that the changes we resented have in point of fact rendered harmless the seeds of fresh disaster, and rescued us from the results of long bad government. He who has most keenly felt the hardship of being diverted from his original course in life will in after life tell you that had he been allowed to hold his own land, and remain his own master in his old loved abode, he would have lapsed into a condition from which no worthy harvest could be expected. If a man only wishes that his own conceptions of prosperity be realised, then let him keep his land in his own hand and work his material irrespective of God's demands; for certainly, if he yields himself to God, his own ideas of prosperity will not be realised. But if he suspects that God may have a more liberal conception of prosperity and may understand better than he what is eternally beneficial, let him commit himself and all his material of prosperity without doubting into God's hand, and let him greedily obey all God's precepts; for in neglecting one of these, he so far neglects and misses what God would have him enter into.

CHAPTER XXIX.

VISITS OF JOSEPH'S BRETHREN.

GENESIS xlii.-xliv.

"Fear not: for am I in the place of God? But as for you, ye thought evil against me; but God meant it unto good."—GEN. l. 19, 20.

THE purpose of God to bring Israel into Egypt was accomplished by the unconscious agency of Joseph's natural affection for his kindred. Tenderness towards home is usually increased by residence in a foreign land; for absence, like a little death, sheds a halo round those separated from us. But Joseph could not as yet either revisit his old home or invite his father's family into Egypt. Even, indeed, when his brothers first appeared before him, he seems to have had no immediate intention of inviting them as a family to settle in the country of his adoption, or even to visit it. If he had cherished any such purpose or desire he might have sent down wagons at once, as he at last did, to bring his father's household out of Canaan. Why, then, did he proceed so cautiously? Whence this mystery, and disguise, and circuitous compassing of his end? What intervened between the first and last visit of his brethren to make it seem advisable to disclose himself and invite them? Manifestly there had intervened enough to give Joseph insight into the state of mind his brethren were in, enough to satisfy him they were not the men they had been, and that it was safe to ask them and would be pleasant to have them with him in Egypt. Fully alive to the elements of disorder and violence that once existed among them, and having had no opportunity of ascertaining whether they were now altered, there was no course open but that which he adopted of endeavouring in some unobserved way to discover whether twenty years had wrought any change in them.

For effecting this object he fell on the expedient of imprisoning them, on pretence of their being spies. This served the double purpose of detaining them until he should have made up his mind as to the best means of dealing with them, and of securing their retention under his eye until some display of character might sufficiently certify him of their state of mind. Possibly he adopted this expedient also because it was likely deeply to move them, so that they might be expected to exhibit not such superficial feelings as might have been elicited had he set them down to a banquet and entered into conversation with them over their wine, but such as men are surprised to find in themselves, and know nothing of in their lighter hours. Joseph was, of course, well aware that in the analysis of character the most potent elements are only brought into clear view when the test of severe trouble is applied, and when men are thrown out of all conventional modes of thinking and speaking.

The display of character which Joseph awaited he speedily obtained. For so new an experience to these free dwellers in tents as imprisonment under grim Egyptian guards worked wonders in them. Men who have experienced such treatment aver that nothing more effectually tames and breaks the spirit: it is not the being confined for a definite time with the certainty of release in the end, but the being shut up at the caprice of another on a false and absurd accusation; the being cooped up at the will of a stranger in a foreign country, uncertain and hopeless of release. To Joseph's brethren so sudden and great a calamity seemed explicable only on the theory that it was retribution for the great crime of their life. The uneasy feeling which each of them had hidden in his own conscience, and which the lapse of twenty years had not materially alleviated, finds expression: "And they said one to another, We are verily guilty concerning our brother, in that we saw the anguish of his soul, when he besought us, and we would not hear; therefore is this distress come upon us." The similarity of their position to that in which they had placed their brother stimulates and assists their conscience. Joseph, in the anguish of his soul, had protested his innocence, but they had not listened; and now their own protestations are treated as idle wind by this Egyptian. Their own feelings, representing to them what they had caused Joseph to suffer, stir a keener sense of their guilt than they seem ever before to have reached. Under this new light they see their sin more clearly, and are humbled by the distress into which it has brought them.

When Joseph sees this, his heart warms to them. He may not yet be quite sure of them. A prison-repentance is perhaps scarcely to be trusted. He sees they would for the moment deal differently with him had they the opportunity, and would welcome no one more heartily than himself, whose coming among them had once so exasperated them. Himself keen in his affections, he is deeply moved, and his eyes fill with tears as he witnesses their emotion and grief on his account. Fain would he relieve them from their remorse and apprehension—why, then, does he forbear? Why does he not at this juncture disclose himself? It has been satisfactorily proved that his brethren counted their sale of him the great crime of their life. Their imprisonment has elicited evidence that that crime had taken in their conscience the capital place, the place which a man finds some one sin or series of sins will take, to follow him with its appropriate curse, and hang over his future like a cloud—a sin of which he thinks when any strange thing happens to him, and to which he traces all disaster—a sin so iniquitous that it seems capable of producing any results however grievous, and to which he has so given himself that his life seems to be concentrated there, and he cannot but connect with it all the greater ills that happen to him. Was not this, then, security enough that they would never again perpetrate a crime of like atrocity? Every man who has almost at all observed the history of sin in himself, will say that most certainly it was quite insufficient security against their ever again doing the like. Evidence that a man is conscious of his sin, and, while suffering from its consequences, feels deeply its guilt, is not evidence that his character is altered.

And because we believe men so much more readily than God, and think that they do not require, for form's sake, such needless pledges of a changed character as God seems to demand, it is worth observing that Joseph, moved as he was even to tears, felt that common prudence forbade him to commit himself to his brethren without further evidence of their disposition. They had distinctly acknowledged their guilt, and in his hearing had admitted that the great calamity that had befallen them was no more than they deserved; yet Joseph, judging merely as an intelligent man who had worldly interests depending on his judgment, could not discern enough here to justify him in supposing that his brethren were changed men. And it might sometimes serve to expose the insufficiency of our repentance were clear-seeing men the judges of it, and did they express their opinion of its trustworthiness. We may think that God is needlessly exacting when He requires evidence not only of a changed mind about past sin, but also of such a mind being now in us as will preserve us from future sin; but the truth is, that no man whose common worldly interests were at stake would commit himself to us on any less evidence. God, then, meaning to bring the house of Israel into Egypt in order to make progress in the Divine education He was giving to them, could not introduce them into that land in a state of mind which would negative all the discipline they were there to receive.

These men then had to give evidence that they not only saw, and in some sense repented of, their sin, but also that they had got rid of the evil passion which had led to it. This is what God means by repentance. Our sins are in general not so microscopic that it requires very keen spiritual discernment to perceive them. But to be quite aware of our sin, and to acknowledge it, is not to repent of it. Everything falls short of thorough repentance which does not prevent us from committing the sin anew. We do not so much desire to be accurately informed about our past sins, and to get right views of our past selves; we wish to be no longer sinners, we wish to pass through some process by which we may be separated from that in us which has led us into sin. Such a process there is, for these men passed through it.

The test which revealed the thoroughness of his brothers' repentance was unintentionally applied by Joseph. When he hid his cup in Benjamin's sack, all that he intended was to furnish a pretext for detaining Benjamin, and so gratifying his own affection. But, to his astonishment, his trick effected far more than he intended; for the brothers, recognising now their brotherhood, circled round Benjamin, and, to a man, resolved to go back with him to Egypt. We cannot argue from this that Joseph had misapprehended the state of mind in which his brothers were, and in his judgment of them had been either too timorous or too severe; nor need we suppose that he was hampered by his relations to Pharaoh, and therefore unwilling to connect himself too closely with men of whom he might be safer to be rid; because it was this very peril of Benjamin's that matured their brotherly affection. They themselves could not have anticipated that they would make such a sacrifice for Benjamin. But throughout their dealings with this mysterious Egyptian, they felt themselves under a spell, and were being gradually, though perhaps unconsciously, softened, and in order to complete the change passing upon them, they but required some such incident as this of Benjamin's arrest. This incident seemed by some strange fatality to threaten them with a renewed perpetration of the very crime they had committed against Rachel's other son. It threatened to force them to become again the instrument of bereaving their father of his darling child, and bring about that very calamity which they had pledged themselves should never happen. It was an incident, therefore, which, more than any other, was likely to call out their family love.

The scene lives in every one's memory. They were going gladly back to their own country with corn enough for their children, proud of their entertainment by the lord of Egypt; anticipating their father's exultation when he heard how generously they had been treated and when he saw Benjamin safely restored, feeling that in bringing him back they almost compensated for having bereaved him of Joseph. Simeon is revelling in the free air that blew from Canaan and brought with it the scents of his native land, and breaks into the old songs that the strait confinement of his prison had so long silenced—all of them together rejoicing in a scarcely hoped-for success; when suddenly, ere the first elation is spent, they are startled to see the hasty approach of the Egyptian messenger, and to hear the stern summons that brought them to a halt, and boded all ill. The few words of the just Egyptian, and his calm, explicit judgment, "Ye have done evil in so doing," pierce them like a keen blade—that they should be suspected of robbing one who had dealt so generously with them; that all Israel should be put to shame in the sight of the stranger! But they begin to feel relief as one brother after another steps forward with the boldness of innocence; and as sack after sack is emptied, shaken, and flung aside, they already eye the steward with the bright air of triumph; when, as the very last sack is emptied, and as all breathlessly stand round, amid the quick rustle of the corn, the sharp rattle of metal strikes on their ear, and the gleam of silver dazzles their eyes as the cup rolls out in the sunshine. This, then, is the brother of whom their father was so careful that he dared not suffer him out of his sight! This is the precious youth whose life was of more value than the lives of all the brethren, and to keep whom a few months longer in his father's sight Simeon had been left to rot in a dungeon! This is how he repays the anxiety of the family and their love, and this is how he repays the extraordinary favour of Joseph! By one rash childish act had this fondled youth, to all appearance, brought upon the house of Israel irretrievable disgrace, if not complete extinction. Had these men been of their old temper, their knives had very speedily proved that their contempt for the deed was as great as the Egyptian's; by violence towards Benjamin they might have cleared themselves of all suspicion of complicity; or, at the best, they might have considered themselves to be acting in a fair and even lenient manner if they had surrendered the culprit to the steward, and once again carried back to their father a tale of blood. But they were under the spell of their old sin. In all disaster, however innocent they now were, they saw the retribution of their old iniquity; they seem scarcely to consider whether Benjamin was innocent or guilty, but as humbled, God-smitten men, "they rent their clothes, and laded every man his ass, and returned to the city."

Thus Joseph in seeking to gain *one* brother found eleven—for now there could be no doubt that they were very different men from those brethren who had so heartlessly sold into slavery their father's favourite—men now with really brotherly feelings, by penitence and regard for their father so wrought together into one family, that this calamity, intended to fall only on one of their number, did in falling on him fall on them all. So far from wishing now to rid themselves of Rachel's son and their father's favourite, who had been put by their father in so prominent a place in his affection, they will not even give him up to suffer what seemed the just punishment of his theft, do not even reproach him with having brought them all into disgrace and difficulty, but, as humbled men who knew they had greater sins of their own to answer for, went quietly back to Egypt, determined to see their younger brother through his misfortune or to share his bondage with him. Had these men not been thoroughly changed, thoroughly convinced that at all costs upright dealing and brotherly love should continue; had they not possessed that first and last of Christian virtues, love to their brother, then nothing could so certainly have revealed their want of it as this apparent theft of Benjamin's. It seemed in itself a very likely thing that a lad accustomed to plain modes of life, and whose character it was to "ravin as a wolf," should, when suddenly introduced to the gorgeous Egyptian banqueting-house with all its sumptuous furnishings, have coveted some choice specimen of Egyptian art, to carry home to his father as proof that he could not only bring himself back in safety, but scorned to come back from any expedition empty-handed. It was not unlikely either that, with his mother's own superstition, he might have conceived the bold design of robbing this Egyptian, so mysterious and so powerful, according to his brothers' account, and of breaking that spell which he had thrown over them: he may thus have conceived the idea of achieving for himself a reputation in the family, and of once for all redeeming himself from the somewhat undignified, and to one of his spirit somewhat uncongenial, position of the youngest of a family. If, as is possible, he had let any such idea ooze out in talking with his brethren as they went down to Egypt, and only abandoned it on their indignant and urgent remonstrance, then when the cup, Joseph's chief treasure according to his own account, was discovered in Benjamin's sack, the case must have looked sadly against him even in the eyes of his brethren. No protestations of innocence in a particular instance avail much when the character and general habits of the accused point to guilt. It is quite possible, therefore, that the brethren, though willing to believe Benjamin, were yet not so thoroughly convinced of his innocence as they would have desired. The fact that they themselves had found their money returned in their sacks, made for Benjamin; yet in most cases, especially where circumstances corroborate it, an accusation even against the innocent takes immediate hold and cannot be summarily and at once got rid of.

Thus was proof given that the house of Israel was now in truth one family. The men who, on very slight instigation, had without compunction sold Joseph to a life of slavery, cannot now find it in their heart to abandon a brother who, to all appearance, was worthy of no better life than that of a slave, and who had brought them all into disgrace and danger. Judah had no doubt pledged himself to bring the lad back without scathe to his father, but he had done so without contemplating the possibility of Benjamin becoming amenable to Egyptian law. And no one can read the speech of Judah—one of the most pathetic on record—in which he replies to Joseph's judgment that Benjamin alone should remain in Egypt, without perceiving that he speaks not as one who merely seeks to redeem a pledge, but as a good son and a good brother. He speaks, too, as the mouth-piece of the rest, and as he had taken the lead in Joseph's sale, so he does not shrink from standing forward and accepting the heavy responsibility which may now light upon the man who represents these brethren. His former faults are redeemed by the courage, one may say heroism, he now shows. And as he spoke, so the rest felt. They could not bring themselves to inflict a new sorrow on their aged father; neither could they bear to leave their young brother in the hands of strangers. The passions which had alienated them from one another, and had threatened to break up the family, are subdued. There is now discernible a common feeling that binds them together, and a common object for which they willingly sacrifice themselves. They are, therefore, now prepared to pass into that higher school to which God called them in Egypt. It mattered little what strong and equitable laws they found in the land of their adoption, if they had no taste for upright living; it mattered little what thorough national organisation they would be brought into contact with in Egypt, if in point of fact they owned no common brotherhood, and were willing rather to live as units and every man for himself than for any common interest. But now they were prepared, open to teaching, and docile.

To complete our apprehension of the state of mind into which the brethren were brought by Joseph's treatment of them, we must take into account the assurance he gave them, when he made himself known to them, that it was not they but God who had sent him into Egypt, and that God had done this for the purpose of preserving the whole house of Israel. At first sight this might seem to be an injudicious speech, calculated to make the brethren think lightly of their guilt, and to remove the just impressions they now entertained of the unbrotherliness of their conduct to Joseph. And it might have been an injudicious speech to impenitent men; but no further view of sin can lighten its heinousness to a really penitent sinner. Prove to him that his sin has become the means of untold good, and you only humble him the more, and more deeply convince him that while he was recklessly gratifying himself and sacrificing others for his own pleasure, God has been mindful of others, and, pardoning him, has blessed them. God does not need our sins to work out His good intentions, but we give Him little other material; and the discovery that through our evil purposes and injurious deeds God has worked out His beneficent will, is certainly not calculated to make us think more lightly of our sin or more highly of ourselves.

Joseph in thus addressing his brethren did, in fact, but add to their feelings the tenderness that is in all religious conviction, and that springs out of the consciousness that in all our sin there has been with us a holy and loving Father, mindful of His children. This is the final stage of penitence. The knowledge that God has prevented our sin from doing the harm it might have done does relieve the bitterness and despair with which we view our life, but at the same time it strengthens the most effectual bulwark between us and sin—love to a holy, over-ruling God. This, therefore, may always be safely said to penitents: Out of your worst sin God can bring good to yourself or to others, and good of an apparently necessary kind; but good of a permanent kind can result from your sin only when you have truly repented of it, and sincerely wish you had never done it. Once this repentance is really wrought in you, then, though your life can never be the same as it might have been had you not sinned, it may be, in some respects, a more richly developed life, a life fuller of humility and love. You can never have what you sold for your sin; but the poverty your sin has brought may excite within you thoughts and energies more valuable than what you have lost, as these men lost a brother but found a Saviour. The wickedness that has often made you bow your head and mourn in secret, and which is in itself unutterable shame and loss, may, in God's hand, become food against the day of famine. You cannot ever have the enjoyments which are possible only to those whose conscience is laden with no evil remembrances, and whose nature, uncontracted and unwithered by familiarity with sin, can give itself to enjoyment with the abandonment and fearlessness reserved for the innocent. No more at all will you have that fineness of feeling which only ignorance of evil can preserve; no more that high and great conscientiousness which, once broken, is never repaired; no more that respect from other men which for ever and instinctively departs from those who have lost self-respect. But you may have a more intelligent sympathy with other men and a keener pity for them; the experience you have gathered too late to save yourself may put it in your power to be of essential service to others. You cannot win your way back to the happy, useful, evenly-developed life of the comparatively innocent, but the life of the true-hearted penitent is yet open to you. Every beat of your heart now may be as if it throbbed against a poisoned dagger, every duty may shame you, every day bring weariness and new humiliation, but let no pain or discouragement avail to defraud you of the good fruits of true reconciliation to God and submission to His lifelong discipline. See that you lose not both lives, the life of the comparatively innocent and the life of the truly penitent.

CHAPTER XXX.

THE RECONCILIATION.

GENESIS xlv.

"By faith Joseph, when he died, made mention of the departing of the children of Israel; and gave commandment concerning his bones."—HEB. xi. 22.

IT is generally by some circumstance or event which perplexes, troubles, or gladdens us, that new thoughts regarding conduct are presented to us, and new impulses communicated to our life. And the circumstances through which Joseph's brethren passed during the famine not only subdued and softened them to a genuine family feeling, but elicited in Joseph himself a more tender affection for them than he seems at first to have cherished. For the first time since his entrance into Egypt did he feel, when Judah spoke so touchingly and effectively, that the family of Israel was one; and that he himself would be reprehensible did he make further breaches in it by carrying out his intention of detaining Benjamin. Moved by Judah's pathetic appeal, and yielding to the generous impulse of the moment, and being led by a right state of feeling to a right judgment regarding duty, he claimed his brethren as brethren, and proposed that the whole family be brought into Egypt.

The scene in which the sacred writer describes the reconciliation of Joseph and his brothers is one of the most touching on record;—the long estrangement so happily terminated; the caution, the doubts, the hesitation on Joseph's part, swept away at last by the resistless tide of long pent-up emotion; the surprise and perplexity of the brethren as they dared now to lift their eyes and scrutinise the face of the governor, and discerned the lighter complexion of the Hebrew, the features of the family of Jacob, the expression of their own brother; the anxiety with which they wait to know how he means to repay their crime, and the relief with which they hear that he bears them no ill-will—everything, in short, conduces to render this recognition of the brethren interesting and affecting. That Joseph, who had controlled his feeling in many a trying situation, should now have "wept aloud," needs no explanation. Tears always express a mingled feeling; at least the tears of a man do. They may express grief, but it is grief with some remorse in it, or it is grief passing into resignation. They may express joy, but it is joy born of long sorrow, the joy of deliverance, joy that can now afford to let the heart weep out the fears it has been holding down. It is as with a kind of breaking of the heart, and apparent unmanning of the man, that the human soul takes possession of its greatest treasures; unexpected success and unmerited joy humble a man; and as laughter expresses the surprise of the intellect, so tears express the amazement of the soul when it is stormed suddenly by a great joy. Joseph had been hardening himself to lead a solitary life in Egypt, and it is with all this strong self-sufficiency breaking down within him that he eyes his brethren. It is his love for them making its way through all his ability to do without them, and sweeping away as a flood the bulwarks he had built round his heart,—it is this that breaks him down before them, a man conquered by his own love, and unable to control it. It compels him to make himself known, and to possess himself of its objects, those unconscious brethren. It is a signal instance of the law by which love brings all the best and holiest beings into contact with their inferiors, and, in a sense, puts them in their power, and thus eternally provides that the superiority of those that are high in the scale of being shall ever be at the service of those who in themselves are not so richly endowed. The higher any being is, the more love is in him: that is to say, the higher he is, the more surely is he bound to all who are beneath him. If God is highest of all, it is because there is in Him sufficiency for all His creatures, and love to make it universally available.

It is one of our most familiar intellectual pleasures to see in the experience of others, or to read, a lucid and moving account of emotions identical with those which have once been our own. In reading an account of what others have passed through, our pleasure is derived mainly from two sources—either from our being brought, by sympathy with them and in imagination, into circumstances we ourselves have never been placed in, and thus artificially enlarging our sphere of life, and adding to our experience feelings which could not have been derived from anything we ourselves have met with; or, from our living over again, by means of their experience, a part of our life which had great interest and meaning to us. It may be excusable, therefore, if we divert this narrative from its original historical significance, and use it as the mirror in which we may see reflected an important passage or crisis in our own spiritual history. For though some may find in it little that reflects their own experience, others cannot fail to be reminded of feelings with which they were very familiar when first they were introduced to Christ, and acknowledged by Him.

1. The modes in which our Lord makes Himself known to men are various as their lives and characters. But frequently the forerunning choice of a sinner by Christ is discovered in such gradual and ill-understood dealings as Joseph used with those brethren. It is the closing of a net around them. They do not see what is driving them forward, nor whither they are being driven; they are anxious and ill at ease; and not comprehending what ails them, they make only ineffectual efforts for deliverance. There is no recognition of the hand that is guiding all this circuitous and mysterious preparatory work, nor of the eye that affectionately watches their perplexity, nor are they aware of any friendly ear that catches each sigh in which they seem hopelessly to resign themselves to the relentless past from which they cannot escape. They feel that they are left alone to make what they can now of the life they have chosen and made for themselves; that there is floating behind and around them a cloud bearing the very essence exhaled from their past, and ready to burst over them; a phantom that is yet real, and that belongs both to the spiritual and material world, and can follow them in either. They seem to be doomed men—men who are never at all to get disentangled from their old sin.

If any one is in this baffled and heartless condition, fearing even good lest it turn to evil in his hand; afraid to take the money that lies in his sack's mouth, because he feels there is a snare in it; if any one is sensible that life has become unmanageable in his hands, and that he is being drawn on by an unseen power which he does not understand, then let him consider in the scene before us how such a condition ends or may end. It took many months of doubt, and fear, and mystery to bring those brethren to such a state of mind as made it advisable for Joseph to disclose himself, to scatter the mystery, and relieve them of the unaccountable uneasiness that possessed their minds. And your perplexity will not be allowed to last longer than it is needful. But it is often needful that we should first learn that in sinning we have introduced into our life a baffling, perplexing element, have brought our life into connection with inscrutable laws which we cannot control, and which we feel may at any moment destroy us utterly. It is not from carelessness on Christ's part that His people are not always and from the first rejoicing in the assurance and appreciation of His love. It is His carefulness which lays a restraining hand on the ardour of His affection. We see that this burst of tears on Joseph's part was genuine, we have no suspicion that he was feigning an emotion he did not feel; we believe that his affection at last could not be restrained, that he was fairly overcome,—can we not trust Christ for as genuine a love, and believe that His emotion is as deep? We are, in a word, reminded by this scene, that there is always in Christ a greater love seeking the friendship of the sinner than there is in the sinner seeking for Christ. The search of the sinner for Christ is always a dubious, hesitating, uncertain groping; while on Christ's part there is a clear-seeing, affectionate solicitude which lays joyful surprises along the sinner's path, and enjoys by anticipation the gladness and repose which are prepared for him in the final recognition and reconcilement.

2. In finding their brother again, those sons of Jacob found also their own better selves which they had long lost. They had been living in a lie, unable to look the past in the face, and so becoming more and more false. Trying to leave their sin behind them, they always found it rising in the path before them, and again they had to resort to some new mode of laying this uneasy ghost. They turned away from it, busied themselves among other people, refused to think of it, assumed all kinds of disguise, professed to themselves that they had done no great wrong; but nothing gave them deliverance—there was their old sin quietly waiting for them in their tent door when they went home of an evening, laying its hand on their shoulder in the most unlooked-for places, and whispering in their ear at the most unwelcome seasons. A great part of their mental energy had been spent in deleting this mark from their memory, and yet day by day it resumed its supreme place in their life, holding them under arrest as they secretly felt, and keeping them reserved to judgment.

So, too, do many of us live as if yet we had not found the life eternal, the kind of life that we can always go on with—rather as those who are but making the best of a life which can never be very valuable, nor ever perfect. There seem voices calling us back, assuring us we must yet retrace our steps, that there are passages in our past with which we are not done, that there is an inevitable humiliation and penitence awaiting us. It is through that we can alone get back to the good we once saw and hoped for; there were right desires and resolves in us once, views of a well-spent life which have been forgotten and pressed out of remembrance, but all these rise again in the presence of Christ. Reconciled to Him and claimed by Him, all hope is renewed within us. If He makes Himself known to us, if He claims connection with us, have we not here the promise of all good? If He, after careful scrutiny, after full consideration of all the circumstances, bids us claim as our brother Him to whom all power and glory are given, ought not this to quicken within us everything that is hopeful, and ought it not to strengthen us for all frank acknowledgment of the past and true humiliation on account of it?

3. A third suggestion is made by this narrative. Joseph commanded from his presence all who might be merely curious spectators of his burst of feeling, and might, themselves unmoved, criticise this new feature of the governor's character. In all love there is a similar reserve. The true friend of Christ, the man who is profoundly conscious that between himself and Christ there is a bond unique and eternal, longs for a time when he may enjoy greater liberty in uttering what he feels towards his Lord and Redeemer, and when, too, Christ Himself shall by telling and sufficient signs put it for ever beyond doubt that this love is more than responded to. Words sufficiently impassioned have indeed been put into our lips by men of profound spiritual feeling, but the feeling continually weighs upon us that some more palpable mutual recognition is desirable between persons so vitally and peculiarly knit together as Christ and the Christian are. Such recognition, indubitable and reciprocal, must one day take place. And when Christ Himself shall have taken the initiative, and shall have caused us to understand that we are verily the objects of His love, and shall have given such expression to His knowledge of us as we cannot now receive, we on our part shall be able to reciprocate, or at least to accept, this greatest of possessions, the brotherly love of the Son of God. Meanwhile this passage in Joseph's history may remind us that behind all sternness of expression there may pulsate a tenderness that needs thus to disguise itself; and that to those who have not yet recognised Christ, He is better than He seems. Those brethren no doubt wonder now that even twenty years' alienation should have so blinded them. The relaxation of the expression from the sternness of an Egyptian governor to the fondness of family love, the voice heard now in the familiar mother tongue, reveal the brother; and they who have shrunk from Christ as if He were a cold official, and who have never lifted their eyes to scrutinise His face, are reminded that He can so make Himself known to them that not all the wealth of Egypt would purchase from them one of the assurances they have received from Him.

The same warm tide of feeling which carried away all that separated Joseph from his brethren bore him on also to the decision to invite his father's entire household into Egypt. We are reminded that the history of Joseph in Egypt is an episode, and that Jacob is still the head of the house, maintaining its dignity and guiding its movements. The notices we get of him in this latter part of his history are very characteristic. The indomitable toughness of his youth remained with him in his old age. He was one of those old men who maintain their vigour to the end, the energy of whose age seems to shame and overtax the prime of common men; whose minds are still the clearest, their advice the safest, their word waited for, their perception of the actual state of affairs always in advance of their juniors, more modern and fully abreast of the times in their ideas than the latest born of their children. Such an old age we recognise in Jacob's half-scornful chiding of the helplessness of his sons, even after they had heard that there was corn in Egypt. "Why look ye one upon another? Behold! I have heard that there is corn in Egypt; get ye down thither and buy for us from thence." Jacob, the man who had wrestled through life and bent all things to his will, cannot put up with the helpless dejection of this troop of strong men, who have no wit to devise an escape for themselves, and no resolution to enforce upon the others any device that may occur to them. Waiting still like children for some one else to help them, having strength to endure but no strength to undertake the responsibility of advising in an emergency, they are roused by their father, who has been eyeing this condition of theirs with some curiosity and with some contempt, and now breaks in upon it with his " Why look ye one upon another? " It is the old Jacob, full of resources, prompt and imperturbable, equal to every turn of fortune, and never knowing how to yield.

Even more clearly do we see the vigour of Jacob's old age when he comes in contact with Joseph. For many years Joseph had been accustomed to command; he had unusual natural sagacity and a special gift of insight from God, but he seems a child in comparison with Jacob. When he brings his two sons to get their grandfather's blessing, Jacob sees what Joseph has no inkling of, and peremptorily declines to follow the advice of his wise son. With all Joseph's sagacity there were points in which his blind father saw more clearly than he. Joseph, who could teach the Egyptian senators wisdom, standing thus at a loss even to understand his father, and suggesting in his ignorance futile corrections, is a picture of the incapacity of natural affection to rise to the wisdom of God's love, and of the finest natural discernment to anticipate God's purposes or supply the place of a lifelong experience.

Jacob's warm-heartedness has also survived the chills and shocks of a long lifetime. He clings now to Benjamin as once he clung to Joseph. And as he had wrought for Rachel fourteen years, and the love he bare to her made them seem but a few days, so for twenty years now had he remembered Joseph who had inherited this love, and he shows by his frequent reference to him that he was keeping his word and going down to the grave mourning for his son. To such a man it must have been a severe trial indeed to be left alone in his tents, deprived of all his twelve sons; and we hear his old faith in God steadying the voice that yet trembles with emotion as he says, "If I be bereaved of my children, I am bereaved." It was a trial not, indeed, so painful as that of Abraham when he lifted the knife over the life of his only son; but it was so similar to it as inevitably to suggest it to the mind. Jacob also had to yield up all his children, and to feel, as he sat solitary in his tent, how utterly dependent upon God he was for their restoration; that it was not he but God alone who could build the house of Israel.

The anxiety with which he gazed evening after evening towards the setting sun, to descry the returning caravan, was at last relieved. But his joy was not altogether unalloyed. His sons brought with them a summons to shift the patriarchal encampment into Egypt—a summons which evidently nothing would have induced Jacob to respond to had it not come from his long-lost Joseph, and had it not thus received what he felt to be a divine sanction. The extreme reluctance which Jacob showed to the journey, we must be careful to refer to its true source. The Asiatics, and especially shepherd tribes, move easily. One who thoroughly knows the East says: "The Oriental is not afraid to go far, if he has not to cross the sea; for, once uprooted, distance makes little difference to him. He has no furniture to carry, for, except a carpet and a few brass pans, he uses none. He has no trouble about meals, for he is content with parched grain, which his wife can cook anywhere, or dried dates, or dried flesh, or anything obtainable which will keep. He is, on a march, careless where he sleeps, provided his family are around him—in a stable, under a porch, in the open air. He never changes his clothes at night, and he is profoundly indifferent to everything that the Western man understands by 'comfort.'" But there was in Jacob's case a peculiarity. He was called upon to abandon, for an indefinite period, the land which God had given him as the heir of His promise. With very great toil and not a little danger had Jacob won his way back to Canaan from Mesopotamia; on his return he had spent the best years of his life, and now he was resting there in his old age, having seen his children's children, and expecting nothing but a peaceful departure to his fathers. But suddenly the wagons of Pharaoh stand at his tent-door, and while the parched and bare pastures bid him go to the plenty of Egypt, to which the voice of his long-lost son invites him, he hears a summons which, however trying, he cannot disregard.

Such an experience is perpetually reproduced. Many are they who having at length received from God some long-expected good are quickly summoned to relinquish it again. And while the waiting for what seems indispensable to us is trying, it is tenfold more so to have to part with it when at last obtained, and obtained at the cost of much besides. That particular arrangement of our worldly circumstances which we have long sought, we are almost immediately thrown out of. That position in life, or that object of desire, which God Himself seems in many ways to have encouraged us to seek, is taken from us almost as soon as we have tasted its sweetness. The cup is dashed from our lips at the very moment when our thirst was to be fully slaked. In such distressing circumstances we cannot *see* the end God is aiming at; but of this we may be certain, that He does not wantonly annoy, or relish our discomfiture, and that when we are compelled to resign what is partial, it is that we may one day enjoy what is complete, and that if for the present we have to forego much comfort and delight, this is only an absolutely necessary step towards our permanent establishment in all that can bless and prosper us.

It is this state of feeling which explains the words of Jacob when introduced to Pharaoh. A recent writer, who spent some years on the banks of the Nile and on its waters, and who mixed freely with the inhabitants of Egypt, says: "Old Jacob's speech to Pharaoh really made me laugh, because it is so exactly like what a Fellah says to a Pacha, 'Few and evil have the days of the years of my life been,' Jacob being a most prosperous man, but it is manners to say all that." But Eastern manners need scarcely be called in to explain a sentiment which we find repeated by one who is generally esteemed the most self-sufficing of Europeans. "I have ever been esteemed," Goethe says, "one of Fortune's chiefest favourites; nor will I complain or find fault with the course my life has taken. Yet, truly, there has been nothing but toil and care; and I may say that, in all my seventy-five years, I have never had a month of genuine comfort. It has been the perpetual rolling of a stone, which I have always had to raise anew." Jacob's life had been almost ceaseless disquiet and disappointment. A man who had fled his country, who had been cheated into a marriage, who had been compelled by his own relative to live like a slave, who was only by flight able to save himself from a perpetual injustice, whose sons made his life bitter,—one of them by the foulest outrage a father could suffer, two of them by making him, as he himself said, to stink in the nostrils of the inhabitants of the land he was trying to settle in, and all of them by conspiring to deprive him of the child he most dearly loved—a man who at last, when he seemed to have had experience of every form of human calamity, was compelled by famine to relinquish the land for the sake of which he had endured all and spent all, might surely be forgiven a little plaintiveness in looking back upon his past. The wonder is to find Jacob to the end unbroken, dignified, and clear-seeing, capable and commanding, loving and full of faith.

Cordial as the reconciliation between Joseph and his brethren seemed, it was not as thorough as might have been desired. So long, indeed, as Jacob lived, all went well; but "when Joseph's brethren saw that their father was dead, they said, Joseph will peradventure hate us, and will certainly requite us all the evil which we did unto him." No wonder Joseph wept when he received their message. He wept because he saw that he was still misunderstood and distrusted by his brethren; because he felt, too, that had they been more generous men themselves, they would more easily have believed in his forgiveness; and because his pity was stirred for these men, who recognised that they were so completely in the power of their younger brother. Joseph had passed through severe conflicts of feeling about them, had been at great expense both of emotion and of outward good on their account, had risked his position in order to be able to serve them, and here is his reward! They supposed he had been but biding his time; that his apparent forgetfulness of their injury had been the crafty restraint of a deep-seated resentment; or, at best, that he had been unconsciously influenced by regard for his father, and now, when that influence was removed, the helpless condition of his brethren might tempt him to retaliate. This exhibition of a craven and suspicious spirit is unexpected, and must have been profoundly saddening to Joseph. Yet here, as elsewhere, he is magnanimous. Pity for them turns his thoughts from the injustice done to himself. He comforts them, and speaks kindly to them, saying, Fear ye not; I will nourish you and your little ones.

Many painful thoughts must have been suggested to Joseph by this conduct. If, after all he had done for his brethren, they had not yet learned to love him, but met his kindness with suspicion, was it not probable that underneath his apparent popularity with the Egyptians there might lie envy, or the cold acknowledgment that falls far short of love? This sudden disclosure of the real feeling of his brethren towards him must necessarily have made him uneasy about his other friendships. Did every one merely make use of him, and did no one give him pure love for his own sake? The people he had saved from famine, was there one of them that regarded him with anything resembling personal affection? Distrust seemed to pursue Joseph from first to last. First his own family misunderstood and persecuted him. Then his Egyptian master had returned his devoted service with suspicion and imprisonment. And now again, after sufficient time for testing his character might seem to have elapsed, he was still looked upon with distrust by those who of all others had best reason to believe in him. But though Joseph had through all his life been thus conversant with suspicion, cruelty, falsehood, ingratitude, and blindness, though he seemed doomed to be always misread, and to have his best deeds made the ground of accusation against him, he remained not merely unsoured, but equally ready as ever to be of service to all. The finest natures may be disconcerted and deadened by universal distrust; characters not naturally unamiable are sometimes embittered by suspicion; and persons who are in the main high-minded do stoop, when stung by such treatment, to rail at the world, or to question all generous emotion, steadfast friendship, or unimpeachable integrity. In Joseph there is nothing of this. If ever man had a right to complain of being unappreciated, it was he; if ever man was tempted to give up making sacrifices for his relatives, it was he. But through all this he bore himself with manly generosity, with simple and persistent faith, with a dignified respect for himself and for other men. In the ingratitude and injustice he had to endure, he only found opportunity for a deeper unselfishness, a more God-like forbearance. And that such may be the outcome of the sorest parts of human experience we have one day or other need to remember. When our good is evil spoken of, our motives suspected, our most sincere sacrifices scrutinised by an ignorant and malicious spirit, our most substantial and well-judged acts of kindness received with suspicion, and the love that is in them quite rejected, it is then we have opportunity to show that to us belongs the Christian temper that can pardon till seventy times seven, and that can persist in loving where love meets no response, and benefits provoke no gratitude.

How Joseph spent the years which succeeded the famine we have no means of knowing; but the closing act of his life seemed to the narrator so significant as to be worthy of record. "Joseph said unto his brethren, I die: and God will surely visit you, and bring you out of this land unto the land which he sware to Abraham, to Isaac, and to Jacob. And Joseph took an oath of the children of Israel, saying, God will surely visit you, and ye shall carry up my bones from hence." The Egyptians must have chiefly been struck by the simplicity of character which this request betokened. To the great benefactors of our country, the highest award is reserved to be given after death. So long as a man lives, some rude stroke of fortune or some disastrous error of his own may blast his fame; but when his bones are laid with those who have served their country best, a seal is set on his life, and a sentence pronounced which the revision of posterity rarely revokes. Such honours were customary among the Egyptians; it is from their tombs that their history can now be written. And to none were such honours more accessible than to Joseph. But after a life in the service of the state he retains the simplicity of the Hebrew lad. With the magnanimity of a great and pure soul, he passed uncontaminated through the flatteries and temptations of court-life; and, like Moses, "esteemed the reproach of Christ greater riches than the treasures of Egypt." He has not indulged in any affectation of simplicity, nor has he, in the pride that apes humility, declined the ordinary honours due to a man in his position. He wears the badges of office, the robe and the gold necklace, but these things do not reach his spirit. He has lived in a region in which such honours make no deep impression; and in his death he shows where his heart has been. The small voice of God, spoken centuries ago to his forefathers, deafens him to the loud acclaim with which the people do him homage.

By later generations this dying request of Joseph's was looked upon as one of the most remarkable instances of faith. For many years there had been no new revelation. The rising generations, that had seen no man with whom God had spoken, were little interested in the land which was said to be theirs, but which they very well knew was infested by fierce tribes who, on at least one occasion during this period, inflicted disastrous defeat on one of the boldest of their own tribes. They were, besides, extremely attached to the country of their adoption; they luxuriated in its fertile meadows and teeming gardens, which kept them supplied at little cost of labour with delicacies unknown on the hills of Canaan. This oath, therefore, which Joseph made them swear, may have revived the drooping hopes of the small remnant who had any of his own spirit. They saw that he, their most sagacious man, lived and died in full assurance that God would visit His people. And through all the terrible bondage they were destined to suffer, the bones of Joseph, or rather his embalmed body, stood as the most eloquent advocate of God's faithfulness, ceaselessly reminding the despondent generations of the oath which God would yet enable them to fulfil. As often as they felt inclined to give up all hope and the last surviving Israelitish peculiarity, there was the unburied coffin remonstrating; Joseph still, even when dead, refusing to let his dust mingle with Egyptian earth.

And thus, as Joseph had been their pioneer who broke out a way for them into Egypt, so did he continue to hold open the gate and point the way back to Canaan. The brethren had sold him into this foreign land, meaning to bury him for ever; he retaliated by requiring that the tribes should restore him to the land from which he had been expelled. Few men have opportunity of showing so noble a revenge; fewer still, having the opportunity, would so have used it. Jacob had been carried up to Canaan as soon as he was dead: Joseph declines this exceptional treatment, and prefers to share the fortunes of his brethren, and will then only enter on the promised land when all his people can go with him. As in life, so in death, he took a large view of things, and had no feeling that the world ended in him. His career had taught him to consider national interests; and now, on his death-bed, it is from the point of view of his people that he looks at the future.

Several passages in the life of Joseph have shown us that where the Spirit of Christ is present, many parts of the conduct will suggest, if they do not actually resemble, acts in the life of Christ. The attitude towards the future in which Joseph sets his people as he leaves them, can scarcely fail to suggest the attitude which Christians are called to assume. The prospect which the Hebrews had of fulfilling their oath grew increasingly faint, but the difficulties in the way of its performance must only have made them more clearly see that they depended on God for entrance on the promised inheritance. And so may the difficulty of our duties as Christ's followers measure for us the amount of grace God has provided for us. The commands that make you sensible of your weakness, and bring to light more clearly than ever how unfit for good you are, are witnesses to you that God will visit you and enable you to fulfil the oath He has required you to take. The children of Israel could not suppose that a man so wise as Joseph had ended his life with a childish folly, when he made them swear this oath, and could not but renew their hope that the day would come when his wisdom would be justified by their ability to discharge it. Neither ought it to be beyond our belief that, in requiring from us such and such conduct, our Lord has kept in view our actual condition and its possibilities, and that His commands are our best guide towards a state of permanent felicity. He that aims always at the performance of the oath he has taken, will assuredly find that God will not stultify Himself by failing to support him.

CHAPTER XXXI.

THE BLESSINGS OF THE TRIBES.

GENESIS xlviii. and xlix.

JACOB'S blessing of his sons marks the close of the patriarchal dispensation. Henceforth the channel of God's blessing to man does not consist of one person only, but of a people or nation. It is still *one seed*, as Paul reminds us, a unit that God will bless, but this unit is now no longer a single person—as Abraham, Isaac, or Jacob—but one people, composed of several parts, and yet one whole; equally representative of Christ, as the patriarchs were, and of equal effect every way in receiving God's blessing and handing it down until Christ came. The Old Testament Church, quite as truly as the New, formed one whole with Christ. Apart from Him it had no meaning, and would have had no existence. It was the promised seed, always growing more and more to its perfect development in Christ. As the promise was kept to Abraham when Isaac was born, and as Isaac was truly the promised seed—in so far as he was a part of the series that led on to Christ, and was given in fulfilment of the promise that promised Christ to the world—so all through the history of Israel we must bear in mind that in them God is fulfilling this same promise, and that they are the promised seed in so far as they are one with Christ. And this interprets to us all those passages of the prophets regarding which men have disputed whether they are to be applied to Israel or to Christ: passages in which God addresses Israel in such words as, "Behold My servant," "Mine elect," and so forth, and in the interpretation of which it has been thought sufficient proof that they do not apply to Christ, to prove that they do apply to Israel; whereas, on the principle just laid down, it might much more safely be argued that because they apply to Israel, therefore they apply to Christ. And it is at this point—where Israel distributes among his sons the blessing which heretofore had all lodged in himself—that we see the first multiplication of Christ's representatives; the mediation going on no longer through individuals, but through a nation; and where individuals are still chosen by God, as commonly they are, for the conveyance of God's communications to earth, these individuals, whether priests or prophets, are themselves but the official representatives of the nation.

As the patriarchal dispensation ceases, it secures to the tribes all the blessing it has itself contained. Every father desires to leave to his sons whatever he has himself found helpful, but as they gather round his dying bed, or as he sits setting his house in order, and considering what portion is appropriate for each, he recognises that to some of them it is quite useless to bequeath the most valuable parts of his property, while in others he discerns a capacity which promises the improvement of all that is entrusted to it. And from the earliest times the various characters of the tribes were destined to modify the blessing conveyed to them by their father. The blessing of Israel is now distributed, and each receives what each can take; and while in some of the individual tribes there may seem to be very little of blessing at all, yet, taken together, they form a picture of the common outstanding features of human nature, and of that nature as acted upon by God's blessing, and forming together one body or Church. A peculiar interest attaches to the history of some nations, and is not altogether absent from our own, from the precision with which we can trace the character of families, descending often with the same unmistakable lineaments from father to son for many generations.[*] One knows at once to what families to look for restless and turbulent spirits, ready for conspiracy and revolution; and one knows also where to seek steady and faithful loyalty, public-spiritedness, or native ability. And in Israel's national character there was room for the great distinguishing features of the tribes, and to show the richness and variety with which the promise of God could fulfil itself wherever it was received. The distinguishing features which Jacob depicts in the blessings of his sons are necessarily veiled under the poetic figures of prophecy, and spoken of as they would reveal themselves in worldly matters; but these features were found in all the generations of the tribes, and displayed themselves in things spiritual also. For a man has not two characters, but one; and what he is in the world, that he is in his religion. In our own country, it is seen how the forms of worship, and even the doctrines believed, and certainly the modes of religious thought and feeling, depend on the natural character, and the natural character on the local situation of the respective sections of the community. No doubt in a country like ours, where men so constantly migrate from place to place, and where one common literature tends to mould us all to the same way of thinking, you do get men of all kinds in every place; yet even among ourselves the character of a place is generally still visible, and predominates over all that mingles with it. Much more must this character have been retained in a country where each man could trace his ancestry up to the father of the tribe, and cultivated with pride the family characteristics, and had but little intercourse, either literary or personal, with other minds and other manners. As we know by dialect and by the manners of the people when we pass into a new country, so must the Israelite have known by the eye and ear when he had crossed the county frontier, when he was conversing with a Benjamite, and when with a descendant of Judah. We are not therefore to suppose that any of these utterances of Jacob are mere geographical predictions, or that they depict characteristics which might appear in civil life, but not in religion and the Church, or that they would die out with the first generation.

In these blessings, therefore, we have the history of the Church in its most interesting form. In these sons gathered round him, the patriarch sees his own nature reflected piece by piece, and he sees also the general outline of all that must be produced by such natures as these men have. The whole destiny of Israel is here in germ, and the spirit of prophecy in Jacob sees and declares it. It has often been remarked[*] that as a man draws near to death, he seems to see many things in a much clearer light, and especially gets glimpses into the future, which are hidden from others.

"The soul's dark cottage, battered and decayed,
Lets in new light through chinks that time hath made."

Being nearer to eternity, he instinctively measures things by its standard, and thus comes nearer a just valuation of all things before his mind, and can better distinguish reality from appearance. Jacob has studied these sons of his for fifty years, and has had his acute perception of character painfully enough called to exercise itself on them. He has all his life long had a liking for analysing men's inner life, knowing that, when he understands that, he can better use them for his own ends; and these sons of his own have cost him thought over and above that sometimes penetrating interest which a father will take in the growth of a son's character; and now he knows them thoroughly, understands their temptations, their weaknesses, their capabilities, and, as a wise head of a house, can, with delicate and unnoticed skill, balance the one against the other, ward off awkward collisions, and prevent the evil from destroying the good. This knowledge of Jacob prepares

---

[*] Merivale's *Romans under the Empire*, vi. 261.

[*] Plato, *Repub.*, i. 5, etc.

him for being the intelligent agent by whom God predicts in outline the future of His Church.

One cannot but admire, too, the faith which enables Jacob to apportion to his sons the blessings of a land which had not been much of a resting-place to himself, and regarding the occupation of which his sons might have put to him some very difficult questions. And we admire this dignified faith the more on reflecting that it has often been very grievously lacking in our own case—that we have felt almost ashamed of having so little of a present tangible kind to offer, and of being obliged to speak only of invisible and future blessings; to set a spiritual consolation over against a worldly grief; to point a man whose fortunes are ruined to an eternal inheritance; or to speak to one who knows himself quite in the power of sin of a remedy which has often seemed illusory to ourselves. Some of us have got so little comfort or strength from religion ourselves, that we have no heart to offer it to others; and most of us have a feeling that we should seem to trifle were we to offer invisible aid against very visible calamity. At least we feel that we are doing a daring thing in making such an offer, and can scarce get over the desire that we had something to speak of which sight could appreciate, and which did not require the exercise of faith. Again and again the wish rises within us that to the sick man we could bring health as well as the promise of forgiveness, and that to the poor we could grant an earthly, while we make known a heavenly, inheritance. One who has experienced these scruples, and known how hard it is to get rid of them, will know also how to honour the faith of Jacob, by which he assumes the right to bless Pharaoh—though he is himself a mere sojourner by sufferance in Pharaoh's land, and living on his bounty—and by which he gathers his children round him and portions out to them a land which seemed to have been most barren to himself, and which now seemed quite beyond his reach. The enjoyments of it, which he himself had not very deeply tasted, he yet knew were real; and if there were a look of scepticism, or of scorn, on the face of any one of his sons; if the unbelief of any received the prophetic utterances as the ravings of delirium, or the fancies of an imbecile and worn-out mind going back to the scenes of its youth, in Jacob himself there was so simple and unsuspecting a faith in God's promise, that he dealt with the land as if it were the only portion worth bequeathing to his sons, as if every Canaanite were already cast out of it, and as if he knew his sons could never be tempted by the wealth of Egypt to turn with contempt from the land of promise. And if we would attain to this boldness of his, and be able to speak of spiritual and future blessings as very substantial and valuable, we must ourselves learn to make much of God's promise, and leave no taint of unbelief in our reception of it.

And often we are rebuked by finding that when we do offer things spiritual, even those who are wrapped in earthly comforts appreciate and accept the better gifts. So it was in Joseph's case. No doubt the highest posts in Egypt were open to his sons; they might have been naturalised, as he himself had been, and, throwing in their lot with the land of their adoption, might have turned to their advantage the rank their father held, and the reputation he had earned. But Joseph turns from this attractive prospect, brings them to his father, and hands them over to the despised shepherd-life of Israel. One need scarcely point out how great a sacrifice this was on Joseph's part. So universally acknowledged and legitimate a desire is it to pass to one's children the honour achieved by a life of exertion, that states have no higher rewards to confer on their most useful servants than a title which their descendants may wear. But Joseph would not suffer his children to risk the loss of their share in God's peculiar blessing, not for the most promising openings in life, or the highest civil honours. If the thoroughly open identification of them with the shepherds, and their profession of a belief in a distant inheritance, which must have made them appear madmen in the eyes of the Egyptians, if this was to cut them off from worldly advancement, Joseph was not careful of this, for resolved he was that, at any cost, they should be among God's people. And his faith received its reward; the two tribes that sprang from him received about as large a portion of the promised land as fell to the lot of all the other tribes put together.

You will observe that Ephraim and Manasseh were adopted as sons of Jacob. Jacob tells Joseph, "They shall be mine," not my grandsons, but as Reuben and Simeon. No other sons whom Joseph might have were to be received into this honour, but these two were to take their place on a level with their uncle, as heads of tribes, so that Joseph is represented through the whole history by the two populous and powerful tribes of Ephraim and Manasseh. No greater honour could have been put on Joseph, nor any more distinct and lasting recognition made of the indebtedness of his family to him, and of how he had been as a father bringing new life to his brethren, than this, that his sons should be raised to the rank of heads of tribes, on a level with the immediate sons of Jacob. And no higher honour could have been put on the two lads themselves than that they should thus be treated as if they were their father Joseph—as if they had his worth and his rank. He is merged in them, and all that he has earned is, throughout the history, to be found, not in his own name, but in theirs. It all proceeds from him; but his enjoyment is found in their enjoyment, his worth acknowledged in their fruitfulness. Thus did God familiarise the Jewish mind through its whole history with the idea, if they chose to think and have ideas, of adoption, and of an adoption of a peculiar kind, of an adoption where already there was an heir who, by this adoption, has his name and worth merged in the persons now received into his place. Ephraim and Manasseh were not received alongside of Joseph, but each received what Joseph himself might have had, and Joseph's name as a tribe was henceforth only to be found in these two. This idea was fixed in such a way, that for centuries it was steeping into the minds of men, so that they might not be astonished if God should in some other case, say the case of His own Son, adopt men into the rank He held, and let His estimate of the worth of His Son, and the honour He puts upon Him, be seen in the adopted. This being so, we need not be alarmed if men tell us that imputation is a mere legal fiction, or human invention; a legal fiction it may be, but in the case before us it was the never-disputed foundation of very substantial blessings to Ephraim and Manasseh; and we plead for nothing more than that God would act with us as here He did act with these two, that He would make us His direct heirs, make us His own sons, and give us what He who presents us to Him to receive His blessing did earn, and merits at the Father's hand.

We meet with these crossed hands of blessing frequently in Scripture; the younger son blessed above the elder—as was needful, lest grace should become confounded with nature, and the belief gradually grow up in men's minds that natural effects could never be overcome by grace, and that in every respect grace waited upon nature. And these crossed hands we meet still; for how often does God quite reverse *our* order, and bless most that about which we had less concern, and seem to put a slight on that which has engrossed our best affection. It is so, often in precisely the way in which Joseph found it so; the son whose youth is most anxiously cared for, to whom the interests of the younger members of the family are sacrificed, and who is commended to God continually to receive His right-hand blessing, this son seems neither to receive nor to dispense much blessing; but the younger, less thought of, left to work his own way, is favoured by God, and becomes the comfort and support of his parents when the elder has failed of his duty. And in the case of much that we hold dear, the same rule is seen; a pursuit we wish to be successful in we can make little of, and are thrown back from continually, while something else into which we have thrown ourselves almost accidentally prospers in our hand and blesses us. Again and again, for years together, we put forward some cherished desire to God's right hand, and are displeased, like Joseph, that still the hand of greater blessing should pass to some other thing. Does God not know what is oldest with us, what has been longest at our hearts, and is dearest to us? Certainly He does: "I know it, My son, I know it," He answers to all our expostulations. It is not because He does not understand or regard your predilections, your natural and excusable preferences, that He sometimes refuses to gratify your whole desire, and pours upon you blessings of a kind somewhat different from those you most earnestly covet. He will give you the whole that Christ hath merited; but for the application and distribution of that grace and blessing you must be content to trust Him. You may be at a loss to know why He does no more to deliver you from some sin, or why He does not make you more successful in your efforts to aid others, or why, while He so liberally prospers you in one part of your condition, you get so much less in another that is far nearer your heart; but God does what He will with His own, and if you do not find in one point the whole blessing and prosperity you think should flow from such a Mediator as you have, you may only conclude that what is lacking there will elsewhere be found more wisely bestowed. And is it not a perpetual encouragement to us that God does not merely crown what nature has successfully begun, that it is not the likely and the naturally good that are most blessed, but that God hath chosen the foolish things of the world to confound the wise, and the weak things of the world to confound the things that are mighty; and base things of the world and things which are despised hath God chosen, yea, and things which are not, to bring to naught things that are?

In Reuben, the firstborn, conscience must have been sadly at war with hope as he looked at the blind, but expressive, face of his father. He may have hoped that his sin had not been severely thought of by his father, or that the father's pride in his first-born would prompt him to hide, though it could not make him forget it. Probably the gross offence had not been made known to the family. At least, the words " he went up " may be understood as addressed in explanation to the brethren. It may indeed have been that the blind old man, forcibly recalling the long-past transgression, is here uttering a mournful, regretful soliloquy, rather than addressing any one. It may be that these words were uttered to himself as he went back upon the one deed that had disclosed to him his son's real character, and rudely hurled to the ground all the hopes he had built up for his first-born. Yet there is no reason to suppose, on the other hand, that the sin had been previously known or alluded to in the family. Reuben's hasty, passionate nature could not understand that if Jacob had felt that sin of his deeply, he should not have shown his resentment; he had stunned his father with the heavy blow, and because he did not cry out and strike him in return, he thought him little hurt. So do shallow natures tremble for a night after their sin, and when they find that the sun rises and men greet them as cordially as before, and that no hand lays hold on them from the past, they think little more of their sin—do not understand that fatal calm that precedes the storm. Had the memory of Reuben's sin survived in Jacob's mind all the sad events that had since happened, and all the stirring incidents of the emigration and the new life in Egypt? Could his father at the last hour, and after so many thronged years, and before his brethren, recall the old sin? He is relieved and confirmed in his confidence by the first words of Jacob, words ascribing to him his natural position, a certain conspicuous dignity too, and power such as one may often see produced in men by occupying positions of authority, though in their own character there be weakness. But all the excellence that Jacob ascribes to Reuben serves only to embitter the doom pronounced upon him. Men seem often to expect that a future can be *given* to them irrespective of what they themselves are, that a series of blessings and events might be prepared for them, and made over to them; whereas every man's future must be made by himself, and is already in great part formed by the past. It was a vain expectation of Reuben to expect that he, the impetuous, unstable, superficial son, could have the future of a deep, and earnest, and dutiful nature, or that his children should derive no taint from their parent, but be as the children of Joseph. No man's future need be altogether a doom to him, for God may bless to him the evil fruit his life has borne; but certainly no man need look for a future which has no relation to his own character. His future will always be made up of *his* deeds, *his* feelings, and the circumstances which *his* desires have brought him into.

The future of Reuben was of a negative, blank kind—" Thou shalt *not* excel;" his unstable character must empty it of all great success. And to many a heart since have these words struck a chill, for to many they are as a mirror suddenly held up before them. They see themselves when they look on the tossing sea, rising and pointing to the heavens with much noise, but only to sink back again to the same everlasting level. Men of brilliant parts and great capacity are continually seen to be lost to society by instability of purpose. Would they only pursue one direction, and concentrate their energies on one subject, they might become true heirs of promise, blessed and blessing; but they seem to lose relish for every pursuit on the first taste of success—all their energy seems to have boiled over and evaporated in the first glow, and sinks as the water that has just been noisily boiling when the fire is withdrawn from under it. No impression made upon them is permanent: like water, they are plastic, easily impressible, but utterly incapable of retaining an impression; and therefore, like water, they have a downward tendency, or at the best are but retained in their place by pressure from without, and have no eternal power of growth. And the misery of this character is often increased by the *desire* to excel which commonly accompanies instability. It is generally this very desire which prompts a man to hurry from one aim to another, to give up one path to excellence when he sees that other men are making way upon another: having no internal convictions of his own, he is guided mostly by the successes of other men, the most dangerous of all guides. So that such a man has all the bitterness of an eager desire doomed never to be satisfied. Conscious to himself of capacity for something, feeling in him the excellency of power, and having that "excellency of dignity," or graceful and princely refinement, which the knowledge of many things, and intercourse with many kinds of people, have imparted to him, he feels all the more that pervading weakness, that greedy, lustful craving for all kinds of priority, and for enjoying all the various advantages which other men severally enjoy, which will not let him finally choose and adhere to his own line of things, but distracts him by a thousand purposes which ever defeat one another.*

The sin of the next oldest sons was also remembered against them, and remembered apparently for the same reason—because the character was expressed in it. The massacre of the Shechemites was not an accidental outrage that any other of the sons of Jacob might equally have perpetrated, but the most glaring of a number of expressions of a fierce and cruel disposition in these two men. In Jacob's prediction of their future, he seems to shrink with horror from his own progeny—like her who dreamt she would give birth to a firebrand. He sees the possibility of the direst results flowing from such a temper, and, under God, provides against these by scattering the tribes, and thus weakening their power for evil. They had been banded together so as the more easily and securely to accomplish their murderous purposes. "Simeon and Levi are brethren"—showing a close affinity, and seeking one another's society and aid, but it is for bad purposes; and therefore they must be divided in Jacob and scattered in Israel. This was accomplished by the tribe of Levi being distributed over all the other tribes as the ministers

* The subsequent history of the tribe shows that the character of its father was transmitted. "No judge, no prophet, not one of the tribe of Reuben, is mentioned." (*Vide* Smith's Dictionary, *Reuben.*)

of religion. The fiery zeal, the bold independence, and the pride of being a distinct people, which had been displayed in the slaughter of the Shechemites, might be toned down and turned to good account when the sword was taken out of their hand. Qualities such as these, which produce the most disastrous results when fit instruments can be found, and when men of like disposition are suffered to band themselves together, may, when found in the individual and kept in check by circumstances and dissimilar dispositions, be highly beneficial.

In the sin, Levi seems to have been the moving spirit, Simeon the abetting tool, and in the punishment, it is the more dangerous tribe that is scattered, so that the other is left companionless. In the blessings of Moses, the tribe of Simeon is passed over in silence; and that the tribe of Levi should have been so used for God's immediate service stands as evidence that punishments, however severe and desolating, even threatening something bordering on extinction, may yet become blessings to God's people. The sword of murder was displaced in Levi's hand by the knife of sacrifice; their fierce revenge against sinners was converted into hostility against sin; their apparent zeal for the forms of their religion was consecrated to the service of the tabernacle and temple; their fanatical pride, which prompted them to treat all other people as the offscouring of the earth, was informed by a better spirit, and used for the upbuilding and instruction of the people of Israel. In order to understand why this tribe, of all others, should have been chosen for the service of the sanctuary and for the instruction of the people, we must not only recognise how their being scattered in punishment of their sin over all the land fitted them to be the educators of the nation and the representatives of all the tribes, but also we must consider that the sin itself which Levi had committed broke the one command which men had up till this time received from the mouth of God; no law had as yet been published but that which had been given to Noah and his sons regarding bloodshed, and which was given in circumstances so appalling, and with sanctions so emphatic, that it might ever have rung in men's ears, and stayed the hand of the murderer. In saying, "At the hand of every man's brother will I require the life of man," God had shown that human life was to be counted sacred. He Himself had swept the face from the earth, but adding this command immediately after, He showed all the more forcibly that punishment was His own prerogative, and that none but those appointed by Him might shed blood —"Vengeance is Mine, saith the Lord." To take private revenge, as Levi did, was to take the sword out of God's hand, and to say that God was not careful enough of justice, and but a poor guardian of right and wrong in the world; and to destroy human life in the wanton and cruel manner in which Levi had destroyed the Shechemites, and to do it under colour and by the aid of religious zeal, was to God the most hateful of sins. But none can know the hatefulness of a sin so distinctly as he who has fallen into it, and is enduring the punishment of it penitently and graciously, and therefore Levi was of all others the best fitted to be entrusted with those sacrificial symbols which set forth the value of all human life, and especially of the life of God's own Son. Very humbling must it have been for the Levite who remembered the history of his tribe to be used by God as the hand of His justice on the victims that were brought in substitution for that which was so precious in the sight of God.

The blessing of Judah is at once the most important and the most difficult to interpret in the series. There is enough in the history of Judah himself, and there is enough in the subsequent history of the tribe, to justify the ascription to him of all lion-like qualities—a kingly fearlessness, confidence, power, and success; in action a rapidity of movement and might that make him irresistible, and in repose a majestic dignity of bearing. As the serpent is the cognisance of Dan, the wolf of Benjamin, the hind of Naphtali, so is the lion of the tribe of Judah. He scorns to gain his end by a serpentine craft, and is himself easily taken in; he does not ravin like a wolf, merely plundering for the sake of booty, but gives freely and generously, even to the sacrifice of his own person: nor has he the mere graceful and ineffective swiftness of the hind, but the rushing onset of the lion—a character which, more than any other, men reverence and admire—"Judah, *thou* art he whom thy brethren shall praise"—and a character which, more than any other, fits a man to take the lead and rule. If there were to be kings in Israel, there could be little doubt from which tribe they could best be chosen; a wolf of the tribe of Benjamin, like Saul, not only hung on the rear of retreating Philistines and spoiled them, but made a prey of his own people, and it is in David we find the true king, the man who more than any other satisfies men's ideal of the prince to whom they will pay homage;—falling indeed into grievous error and sin, like his forefather, but, like him also, right at heart, so generous and self-sacrificing that men served him with the most devoted loyalty, and were willing rather to dwell in caves with him than in palaces with any other.

The kingly supremacy of Judah was here spoken of in words which have been the subject of as prolonged and violent contention as any others in the Word of God. "The sceptre shall not depart from Judah, nor a lawgiver from between his feet, until Shiloh come." These words are very generally understood to mean that Judah's supremacy would continue until it culminated or flowered into the personal reign of Shiloh; in other words, that Judah's sovereignty was to be perpetuated in the person of Jesus Christ. So that this prediction is but the first whisper of that which was afterwards so distinctly declared, that David's seed should sit on the throne for ever and ever. It was not accomplished in the letter, any more than the promise to David was; the tribe of Judah cannot in any intelligible sense be said to have had rulers of her own up to the coming of Christ, or for some centuries previous to that date. For those who would quickly judge God and His promise by what they could see in their own day, there was enough to provoke them to challenge God for forgetting His promise. But in due time *the* King of men, He to whom all nations have gathered, did spring from this tribe; and need it be said that the very fact of His appearance proved that the supremacy had not departed from Judah? This prediction, then, partook of the character of very many of the Old Testament prophecies; there was sufficient fulfilment in the letter to seal, as it were, the promise, and give men a token that it was being accomplished, and yet so mysterious a falling short, as to cause men to look beyond the literal fulfilment, on which alone their hopes had at first rested, to some far higher and more perfect spiritual fulfilment.

But not only has it been objected that the sceptre departed from Judah long before Christ came, and that therefore the word Shiloh cannot refer to Him, but also it has been truly said that wherever else the word occurs it is the name of a town—that town, viz., where the ark for a long time was stationed, and from which the allotment of territory was made to the various tribes; and the prediction has been supposed to mean that Judah should be the leading tribe till the land was entered. Many objections to this naturally occur, and need not be stated. But it comes to be an inquiry of some interest, How much information regarding a personal Messiah did the brethren receive from this prophecy? A question very difficult indeed to answer. The word Shiloh means "peace-making," and if they understood this as a proper name, they must have thought of a person such as Isaiah designates as the Prince of Peace—a name it was similar to that wherewith David called his son Solomon, in the expectation that the results of his own lifetime of disorder and battle would be reaped by his successor in a peaceful and prosperous reign. It can scarcely be thought likely, indeed, that this single term "Shiloh," which might be applied to many things besides a person, should give to the sons of Jacob any distinct idea of a personal Deliverer; but it might be sufficient to keep before their eyes, and specially before the tribe of Judah, that the aim and consummation of all lawgiving and ruling was peace. And there was certainly contained in this blessing an assurance that the purpose of Judah would not be accomplished, and therefore that the existence of Judah as a tribe would not terminate, until peace had been through its means brought into the world: thus was the assurance given, that the productive power of Judah should not fail until out of that tribe there had sprung that which should give peace.

But to us who have seen the prediction accomplished it plainly enough points to *the* Lion of the tribe of Judah, who in His own person combined all kingly qualities. In Him we are taught by this prediction to discover once more the single Person who stands out on the page of this world's history as satisfying men's ideal of what their King should be, and of how the race should be represented;—the One who without any rival stands in the mind's eye as that for which the best hopes of men were waiting, still feeling that the race could do more than it had done, and never satisfied but in Him.

Zebulun, the sixth and last of Leah's sons, was so called because said Leah, "Now will my husband *dwell with me*" (such being the meaning of the name), "for I have borne him six sons." All that is predicted regarding this tribe is that his *dwelling* should be by the sea, and near the Phœnician city Zidon. This is not to be taken as a strict geographical definition of the tract of country occupied by Zebulun, as we see when we compare it with the lot assigned to it and marked out in the Book of Joshua; but though the border of the tribe did not reach to Zidon, and though it can only have been a mere tongue of land belonging to it that ran down to the Mediterranean shore, yet the situation ascribed to it is true to its character as a tribe that had commercial relations with the Phœnicians, and was of a decidedly mercantile turn. We find this same feature indicated in the blessing of Moses: " Rejoice, Zebulun, in thy *going out*, and Issachar in thy tents "—Zebulun having the enterprise of a seafaring community, and Issachar the quiet bucolic contentment of an agricultural or pastoral population: Zebulun always restlessly eager for emigration or commerce, for *going out* of one kind or other; Issachar satisfied to live and die in his own tents. It is still, therefore, character rather than geographical position that is here spoken of—though it is a trait of character that is peculiarly dependent on geographical position: we, for example, because islanders, having become the maritime power and the merchants of the world; not being shut off from other nations by the encompassing sea, but finding paths by it equally in all directions ready provided for every kind of traffic.

Zebulun, then, was to represent the commerce of Israel, its *outgoing* tendency; was to supply a means of communication and bond of connection with the world outside, so that through it might be conveyed to the nations what was saving in Israel, and that what Israel needed from other lands might also find entrance. In the Church also, this is a needful quality: for our well-being there must ever exist among us those who are not afraid to launch on the wide and pathless sea of opinion, those in whose ears its waves have from their childhood sounded with a fascinating invitation, and who at last, as if possessed by some spirit of unrest, loose from the firm earth, and go in quest of lands not yet discovered, or are impelled to see for themselves what till now they have believed on the testimony of others. It is not for all men to quit the shore, and risk themselves in the miseries and disasters of so comfortless and hazardous a life; but happy the people which possesses, from one generation to another, men who must see with their own eyes, and to whose restless nature the discomforts and dangers of an unsettled life have a charm. It is not the instability of Reuben that we have in these men, but the irrepressible longing of the born seaman, who *must* lift the misty veil of the horizon and penetrate its mystery. And we are not to condemn, even when we know we should not imitate, men who cannot rest satisfied with the ground on which we stand, but venture into regions of speculation, of religious thought which we have never trodden, and may deem hazardous. The nourishment we receive is not all native-grown; there are views of truth which may very profitably be imported from strange and distant lands; and there is no land, no province of thought, from which we may not derive what may advantageously be mixed with our own ideas; no direction in which a speculative mind can go in which it may not find something which may give a fresh zest to what we already use, or be a real addition to our knowledge. No doubt men who refuse to confine themselves to one way of viewing truth—men who venture to go close to persons of very different opinions from their own, who determine for themselves to prove all things, who have no very special love for what they were native to and originally taught, who show rather a taste for strange and new opinions—these persons live a life of great hazard, and in the end are generally, like men who have been much at sea, unsettled; they have not fixed opinions, and are in themselves, as individual men, unsatisfactory and unsatisfied; but still they have done good to the community, by bringing to us ideas and knowledge which otherwise we could not have obtained. Such men God gives us to widen our views; to prevent us from thinking that we have the best of everything; to bring us to acknowledge that others, who perhaps in the main are not so favoured as ourselves, are yet possessed of some things we ourselves would be the better of. And though these men must themselves necessarily hang loosely, scarcely attached very firmly to any part of the Church, like a seafaring population, and often even with a border running very close to heathenism, yet let us own that the Church has need of such—that without them the different sections of the Church would know too little of one another, and too little of the facts of this world's life. And as the seafaring population of a country might be expected to show less interest in the soil of their native land than others, and yet we know that in point of fact we are dependent on no class of our population so much for leal patriotism, and for the defence of our country, so one has observed that the Church also must make similar use of her Zebuluns—of men who, by their very habit of restlessly considering all views of truth which are alien to our own ways of thinking, have become familiar with, and better able to defend us against the error that mingles with these views.

Issachar receives from his father a character which few would be proud of or would envy, but which many are very content to bear. As the strong ass that has its stall and its provender provided can afford to let the free beasts of the forest vaunt their liberty, so there is a very numerous class of men who have no care to assert their dignity as human beings, or to agitate regarding their rights as citizens, so long as their obscurity and servitude provide them with physical comforts, and leave them free of heavy responsibilities. They prefer a life of ease and plenty to a life of hardship and glory. They are not lazy nor idle, but are quite willing to use their strength so long as they are not overdriven out of their sleekness. They have neither ambition nor enterprise, and willingly bow their shoulders to bear, and become the servants of those who will free them from the anxiety of planning and managing, and give them a fair and regular remuneration for their labour. This is not a noble nature, but in a world in which ambition so frequently runs through a thorny and difficult path to a disappointing and shameful end, this disposition has much to say in its own defence. It will often accredit itself with unchallengeable common sense, and will maintain that it alone enjoys life and gets the good of it. They will tell you they are the only true utilitarians, that to be one's own master only brings cares, and that the degradation of servitude is only an idea; that *really* servants are quite as well off as masters. Look at them: the one is as a strong, powerful, well-cared-for animal, his work but a pleasant exercise to him, and when it is over never following him into his rest; he eats the good of the land, and has what all seem to be in vain striving for, rest and contentment: the other, the master, has indeed his position, but that only multiplies his duties; he has wealth, but that proverbially only increases his cares and the mouths that are to consume it; it is *he* who has the air of a bondsman, and never, meet him when you may, seems wholly at ease and free from care.

Yet, after all that can be said in favour of the bargain an Issachar makes, and however he may be satisfied to rest, and in a quiet, peaceful way enjoy life, men feel that at the best there is something despicable about such a character. He gives his labour and is fed, he pays his tribute and is protected; but men feel that they ought to meet the dangers, responsibilities, and difficulties of life in their own persons, and at first hand, and not buy themselves off so from the burden of individual self-control and responsibility. The animal enjoyment of this life and its physical comforts may be a very good ingredient in a national character: it might be well for Israel to have this patient, docile mass of strength in its midst: it may be well for our country that there are among us not only men eager for the highest honours and posts, but a great multitude of men perhaps equally serviceable and capable, but whose desires never rise beyond the ordinary social comforts; the contentedness of such, even though reprehensible, tempers or balances the ambition of the others, and when it comes into personal contact rebukes its feverishness. They, as well as the other parts of society, have amidst their error a truth—the truth that the ideal world in which ambition, and hope, and imagination live is not everything; that the material has also a reality, and that though hope does bless mankind, yet attainment is also something, even though it be a little. Yet this truth is not the whole truth, and is only useful as an ingredient, as a part, not as the whole; and when we fall from any high ideal of human life which we have formed, and begin to find comfort and rest in the mere physical good things of this world, we may well despise ourselves. There is a pleasantness still in the land that appeals to us all; a luxury in observing the risks and struggles of others while ourselves secure and at rest; a desire to make life easy, and to shirk the responsibility and toil that public-spiritedness entails. Yet of what tribe has the Church more cause to complain than of those persons who seem to imagine that they have done enough when they have joined the Church and received their own inheritance to enjoy; who are alive to no emergency, nor awake to the need of others; who have no idea at all of their being a part of the community, for which, as well as for themselves, there are duties to discharge; who couch, like the ass of Issachar, in their comfort without one generous impulse to make common cause against the common evils and foes of the Church, and are unvisited by a single compunction that while they lie there, submitting to whatever fate sends, there are kindred tribes of their own being oppressed and spoiled?

There seems to have been an improvement in this tribe, an infusion of some new life into it. In the time of Deborah, indeed, it is with a note of surprise that, while celebrating the victory of Israel, she names even Issachar as having been roused to action, and as having helped in the common cause—"the princes of Issachar were with Deborah, *even* Issachar;" but we find them again in the days of David wiping out their reproach, and standing by him manfully. And there an apparently new character is given to them—"the children of Issachar, which were men that had understanding of the times, to know what Israel ought to do." This quite accords, however, with the kind of practical philosophy which we have seen to be imbedded in Issachar's character. Men they were not distracted by high thoughts and ambitions, but who judged things according to their substantial value to themselves; and who were, therefore, in a position to give much good advice on practical matters—advice which would always have a tendency to trend too much towards mere utilitarianism and worldliness, and to partake rather of crafty politic diplomacy than of far-seeing statesmanship, yet trustworthy for a certain class of subjects. And here, too, they represent the same class in the Church, already alluded to; for one often finds that men who will not interrupt their own comfort, and who have a kind of stolid indifference as to what comes of the good of the Church, have yet also much shrewd practical wisdom; and were these men, instead of spending their sagacity in cynical denunciation of what the Church does, to throw themselves into the cause of the Church, and heartily advise her what she *ought* to do, and help in the doing of it, their observation of human affairs, and political understanding of the times, would be turned to good account, instead of being a reproach.

Next came the eldest son of Rachel's handmaid, and the eldest son of Leah's handmaid, Dan and Gad. Dan's name, meaning "judge," is the starting point of the prediction—"Dan shall judge his people." This word "judge" we are perhaps somewhat apt to misapprehend; it means rather to defend than to sit in judgment on; it refers to a judgment passed between one's own people and their foes, and an execution of such judgment in the deliverance of the people and the destruction of the foe. We are familiar with this meaning of the word by the constant reference in the Old Testament to God's *judging* His people; this being always a cause of joy as their sure deliverance from their enemies. So also it is used of those men who, when Israel had no king, arose from time to time as the champions of the people, to lead them against the foe, and who are therefore familiarly called "The Judges." From the tribe of Dan the most conspicuous of these arose, Samson, namely, and it is probably mainly with reference to this fact that Jacob so emphatically predicts of *this* tribe, "Dan shall judge his people." And notice the appended clause (as reflecting shame on the sluggish Issachar), "as one of the tribes of Israel," recognising always that his strength was not for himself alone, but for his country; that he was not an isolated people who had to concern himself only with his own affairs, but *one* of the tribes of Israel. The manner, too, in which Dan was to do this was singularly descriptive of the facts subsequently evolved. Dan was a very small and insignificant tribe, whose lot originally lay close to the Philistines on the southern border of the land. It might seem to be no obstacle whatever to the invading Philistines as they passed to the richer portion of Judah, but this little tribe, through Samson, smote these terrors of the Israelites with so sore and alarming a destruction as to cripple them for years and make them harmless. We see, therefore, how aptly Jacob compares them to the venomous snake that lurks in the road and bites the horses' heels: the dust-coloured adder that a man treads on before he is aware, and whose poisonous stroke is more deadly than the foe he is looking for in front. And especially significant did the imagery appear to the Jews, with whom this poisonous adder was indigenous, but to whom the horse was the symbol of foreign armament and invasion. The whole tribe of Dan, too, seems to have partaken of that "grim humour" with which Samson saw his foes walk time after time into the traps he set for them, and give themselves an easy prey to him—a humour which comes out with singular piquancy in the narrative given in the Book of Judges of one of the forays of this tribe, in which they carried off Micah's priest and even his gods.

But why, in the full flow of his eloquent description of the varied virtues of his sons, does the patriarch suddenly check himself, lie back on his pillows, and quietly say, "I have waited for Thy salvation, O God?" Does he feel his strength leave him so that he cannot go on to bless the rest of his sons, and has but time to yield his own spirit to God? Are we here to interpolate one of those scenes we are all fated to witness when some eagerly watched breath seems altogether to fail before the last words have been uttered, when those who have been standing apart, through sorrow and reverence, quickly gather round the bed to catch the last look, and when the dying man again collects himself and finishes his work? Probably Jacob, having, as it were, projected himself forward into those stirring and warlike times he has been speaking of, so realises the danger of his people, and the futility even of such help as Dan's when God does not help, that, as if from the midst of doubtful war, he cries, as with a battle cry, "I have waited for Thy salvation, O God." His longing for victory and blessing to his sons far overshot the deliverance from Philistines accomplished by Samson. That deliverance he thankfully accepts and joyfully predicts, but in the spirit of an Israelite indeed, and a genuine child of the promise, he remains unsatisfied, and sees in all such deliverance only the pledge of God's coming nearer and nearer to His people, bringing with Him *His* eternal salvation. In Dan, therefore, we have not the catholic spirit of Zebulun, nor the practical, though sluggish, temper of Issachar; but we are guided rather to the disposition which ought to be maintained through all Christian life, and which, with special care, needs to be cherished in Church-life—a disposition to accept with gratitude all success and triumph, but still to aim through all at that highest victory which God alone can accomplish for His people.

It is to be the battle-cry with which every Christian and every Church is to preserve itself, not merely against external foes, but against the far more disastrous influence of self-confidence, pride, and glorying in man—"For *Thy* salvation, O God, do we wait."

Gad also is a tribe whose history is to be warlike, his very name signifying a marauding, guerilla troop; and his history was to illustrate the victories which God's people gain by tenacious, watchful, ever-renewed warfare. The Church has often prospered by her Dan-like insignificance; the world not troubling itself to make war upon her. But oftener Gad is a better representative of the mode in which her successes are gained. We find that the men of Gad were among the most valuable of David's warriors, when his necessity evoked all the various skill and energy of Israel. "Of the Gadites," we read, "there separated themselves unto David into the hold of the wilderness men of might, and men of war fit for the battle, that could handle shield and buckler, whose faces were like the faces of lions, and were as swift as the roes upon the mountains: one of the least of them was better than an hundred, and the greatest mightier than a thousand." And there is something particularly inspiriting to the individual Christian in finding this pronounced as part of the blessing of God's people—"a troop shall overcome him, *but he shall* overcome at the last." It is this that enables us to persevere—that we have God's assurance that present discomfiture does not doom us to final defeat. If you be among the children of promise, among those that gather round God to catch His blessing, you shall overcome at the last. You may now feel as if assaulted by treacherous, murderous foes, irregular troops, that betake themselves to every cruel deceit, and are ruthless in spoiling you; you may be assailed by so many and strange temptations that you are bewildered and cannot lift a hand to resist, scarce seeing where your danger comes from; you may be buffeted by messengers of Satan, distracted by a sudden and tumultuous incursion of a crowd of cares so that you are moved away from the old habits of your life amid which you seem to stand safely; your heart may seem to be the rendezvous of all ungodly and wicked thoughts, you may feel trodden under foot and overrun by sin, but, with the blessing of God, you shall overcome at the last. Only cultivate that dogged pertinacity of Gad, which has no thought of ultimate defeat, but rallies cheerfully and resolutely after every discomfiture.

The Book of Exodus
By The Right Reverend G. A. Chadwick, D.D.

DOCTOR CHADWICK was Lord Bishop of Derry and Raphoe, Ireland, from 1896-1915, and previously he was Dean of Armagh Cathedral. He delivered the Donnellan Lectures on "Christ Bearing Witness to Himself," and was the author of several volumes of sermons and the exposition on St. Mark in The Expositor's Bible.

The Book of Exodus deals with a critical period in the history of Israel. It also sets forth principles of permanent significance on questions of leadership and followership. It is specially valuable for its description of the personality and work of Moses. Bishop Chadwick deals with the movement inaugurated by the great lawgiver for emancipation from incredible oppression, with a discerning understanding of its religious and moral bearings for our own day.

PREFACE

MUCH is now denied or doubted, within the Church itself, concerning the Book of Exodus, which was formerly accepted with confidence by all Christians.

But one thing can neither be doubted nor denied. Jesus Christ did certainly treat this book, taking it as He found it, as possessed of spiritual authority, a sacred scripture. He taught His disciples to regard it thus, and they did so.

Therefore, however widely His followers may differ about its date and origin, they must admit the right of a Christian teacher to treat this book, taking it as he finds it, as a sacred scripture and invested with spiritual authority. It is the legitimate subject of exposition in the Church.

Such work this volume strives, however imperfectly, to perform. Its object is to edify in the first place, and also, but in the second place, to inform. Nor has the author consciously shrunk from saying what seemed to him proper to be said because the utterance would be unwelcome, either to the latest critical theory, or to the last sensational gospel of an hour.

But since controversy has not been sought, although exposition has not been suppressed when it carried weapons, by far the greater part of the volume appeals to all who accept their Bible as, in any true sense, a gift from God.

No task is more difficult than to exhibit the Old Testament in the light of the New, discovering the permanent in the evanescent, and the spiritual in the form and type which it inhabited and illuminated. This book is at least the result of a firm belief that such a connection between the two Testaments does exist, and of a patient endeavour to receive the edification offered by each Scripture, rather than to force into it, and then extort from it, what the expositor desires to find. Nor has it been supposed that by allowing the imagination to assume, in sacred things, that rank as a guide which reason holds in all other practical affairs, any honor would be done to Him Who is called the Spirit of knowledge and wisdom, but not of fancy and quaint conceits.

If such an attempt does, in any degree, prove successful and bear fruit, this fact will be of the nature of a scientific demonstration.

If this ancient Book of Exodus yields solid results to a sober devotional exposition in the nineteenth Christian century, if it is not an idle fancy that its teaching harmonises with the principles and theology of the New Testament, and even demands the New Testament as the true commentary upon the Old, what follows? How comes it that the oak is potentially in the acorn, and the living creature in the egg? No germ is a manufactured article: it is a part of the system of the universe.

CONTENTS

CHAPTER I.
	PAGE
The Prologue,	121
God in History,	122
The Oppression,	124

CHAPTER II.
The Rescue of Moses,	127
The Choice of Moses,	129
Moses in Midian,	130

CHAPTER III.
The Burning Bush,	131
A New Name,	134
The Commission,	137

CHAPTER IV.
Moses Hesitates,	138
Moses Obeys,	141

CHAPTER V.
Pharaoh Refuses,	143

CHAPTER VI.
The Encouragement of Moses,	145

CHAPTER VII.
The Hardening of Pharaoh's Heart,	149
The Plagues,	151
The First Plague,	153

CHAPTER VIII.
The Second Plague,	154
The Third Plague,	155
The Fourth Plague,	155

CHAPTER IX.
The Fifth Plague,	156
The Sixth Plague,	157
The Seventh Plague,	157

CHAPTER X.
The Eighth Plague,	159
The Ninth Plague,	161

CHAPTER XI.
The Last Plague Announced,	163

CHAPTER XII.
	PAGE
The Passover,	163
The Tenth Plague,	169
The Exodus,	170

CHAPTER XIII.
The Law of the Firstborn,	171
The Bones of Joseph,	172

CHAPTER XIV.
The Red Sea,	173
On the Shore,	174

CHAPTER XV.
The Song of Moses,	175
Shur,	177

CHAPTER XVI.
Murmuring for Food,	179
Manna,	180
Spiritual Meat,	182

CHAPTER XVII.
Meribah,	183
Amalek,	184

CHAPTER XVIII.
Jethro,	186

THE TYPICAL BEARINGS OF THE HISTORY.

CHAPTER XIX.
At Sinai,	188

CHAPTER XX.
The Law,	191
The Prologue,	192
The First Commandment,	193
The Second Commandment,	194
The Third Commandment,	196
The Fourth Commandment,	197
The Fifth Commandment,	199
The Sixth Commandment,	200
The Seventh Commandment,	201
The Eighth Commandment,	201
The Ninth Commandment,	202
The Tenth Commandment,	203

CONTENTS.

THE LESSER LAW.

	PAGE
I. The Law of Worship,	205

THE LESSER LAW (*Continued*).

CHAPTER XXI.

II. Rights of the Person,	206
III. Rights of Property,	207

THE LESSER LAW (*Continued*).

CHAPTER XXII.

IV. Various Enactments,	208
Sorcery,	208
The Stranger,	209

THE LESSER LAW (*Continued*).

CHAPTER XXIII.

Lesser Law, V. Its Sanctions,	211

CHAPTER XXIV.

The Covenant Ratified. The Vision of God,	213

CHAPTER XXV.

The Shrine and Its Furniture,	215
The Pattern in the Mount,	217

CHAPTER XXVI.

The Tabernacle,	218

CHAPTER XXVII.

	PAGE
The Outer Court,	220

CHAPTER XXVIII.

The Holy Garments,	221
The Priesthood,	222

CHAPTER XXIX.

Consecration Services,	223

CHAPTER XXX.

Incense,	225
A Census,	226
The Laver,	227
Anointing Oil and Incense,	227

CHAPTER XXXI.

Bezaleel and Aholiab,	228

CHAPTER XXXII.

The Golden Calf,	229

CHAPTER XXXIII.

Prevailing Intercession,	229

CHAPTER XXXIV.

The Vision of God,	230

CHAPTERS XXXV.—XL.

Conclusion,	230

THE BOOK OF EXODUS

BY THE VERY REV. G. A. CHADWICK, D. D.

CHAPTER I.

THE PROLOGUE.

EXODUS i. 1-6.

"And these are the names of the children of Israel which came into Egypt."

MANY books of the Old Testament begin with the conjunction And. This fact, it has been often pointed out, is a silent indication of truth, that each author was not recording certain isolated incidents, but parts of one great drama, events which joined hands with the past and future, looking before and after.

Thus the Book of the Kings took up the tale from Samuel, Samuel from Judges, and Judges from Joshua, and all carried the sacred movement forward towards a goal as yet unreached. Indeed, it was impossible, remembering the first promise that the seed of the woman should bruise the head of the serpent, and the later assurance that in the seed of Abraham should be the universal blessing, for a faithful Jew to forget that all the history of his race was the evolution of some grand hope, a pilgrimage towards some goal unseen. Bearing in mind that there is now revealed to us a world-wide tendency toward the supreme consummation, the bringing all things under the headship of Christ, it is not to be denied that this hope of the ancient Jew is given to all mankind. Each new stage in universal history may be said to open with this same conjunction. It links the history of England with that of Julius Cæsar and of the Red Indian; nor is the chain composed of accidents: it is forged by the hand of the God of providence. Thus, in the conjunction which binds these Old Testament narratives together, is found the germ of that instinctive and elevating phrase, the Philosophy of History. But there is nowhere in Scripture the notion which too often degrades and stiffens that Philosophy—the notion that history is urged forward by blind forces, amid which the individual man is too puny to assert himself. Without a Moses the Exodus is inconceivable, and God always achieves His purpose through the providential man.

The Books of the Pentateuch are held together in a yet stronger unity than the rest, being sections of one and the same narrative, and having been accredited with a common authorship from the earliest mention of them. Accordingly, the Book of Exodus not only begins with this conjunction (which assumes the previous narrative), but also rehearses the descent into Egypt. "And these are the names of the sons of Israel which came into Egypt,"—names blotted with many a crime, rarely suggesting any lovable or great association, yet the names of men with a marvellous heritage, as being "the sons of Israel," the Prince who prevailed with God. Moreover they are consecrated: their father's dying words had conveyed to every one of them some expectation, some mysterious import which the future should disclose. In the issue would be revealed the awful influence of the past upon the future, of the fathers upon the children even beyond the third and fourth generation—an influence which is nearer to destiny, in its stern, subtle and far-reaching strength, than any other recognised by religion. Destiny, however, it is not, or how should the name of Dan have faded out from the final list of " every tribe of the children of Israel " in the Apocalypse (Rev. vii. 5-8), where Manasseh is reckoned separately from Joseph to complete the twelve?

We read that with the twelve came their posterity, seventy souls in direct descent from Jacob; but in this number he is himself included, according to that well-known Orientalism which Milton strove to force upon our language in the phrase:

"The fairest of her daughters Eve."

Joseph is also reckoned, although he "was in Egypt already." Now, it must be observed that of these seventy, sixty-eight were males, and therefore the people of the Exodus must not be reckoned to have sprung in the interval from seventy, but (remembering polygamy) from more than twice that number, even if we refuse to make any account of the household which is mentioned as coming with every man. These households were probably smaller in each case than that of Abraham, and the famine in its early stages may have reduced the number of retainers; yet they account for much of what is pronounced incredible in the rapid expansion of the clan into a nation.* But when all allowance has been made, the increase continues to be, such as the narrator clearly regards it, abnormal, well-nigh preternatural, a fitting type of the expansion, amid fiercer persecutions, of the later Church of God, the true circumcision, who also sprang from the spiritual parentage of another Seventy and another Twelve.

"And Joseph died, and all his brethren, and all that generation." Thus the connection with Canaan became a mere tradition, and the powerful courtier who had nursed their interests disappeared. When they remembered him, in the bitter time which lay before them, it was only to reflect that all mortal help must perish. It is thus in the spiritual world also. Paul reminds the Philippians that they can obey in his absence and not in his presence only, working out their own salvation, as no apostle can work it out on their behalf. And the reason is that the one real support is ever present. Work out your own salvation, for it is God (not any teacher) Who worketh in you. The Hebrew race was to learn its need of Him, and in Him to recover its freedom. Moreover, the influences which mould all men's characters, their surroundings and mental atmosphere, were completely changed. These wanderers for pasture were now in the presence of a compact and impressive social system, vast

* Professor Curtiss quotes a volume of family memoirs which shows that 5,564 persons are known to be descended from Lieutenant John Hollister, who emigrated to America in the year 1642 (*Expositor*, Nov., 1887. p. 329). This is probably equal in ratio to the increase of Israel in Egypt.

cities, gorgeous temples, an imposing ritual. They were infected as well as educated there, and we find the men of the Exodus not only murmuring for Egyptian comforts, but demanding visible gods to go before them.

Yet, with all its drawbacks, the change was a necessary part of their development. They should return from Egypt relying upon no courtly patron, no mortal might or wisdom, aware of a name of God more profound than was spoken in the covenant of their fathers, with their narrow family interests and rivalries and their family traditions expanded into national hopes, national aspirations, a national religion.

Perhaps there is another reason why Scripture has reminded us of the vigorous and healthy stock whence came the race that multiplied exceedingly. For no book attaches more weight to the truth, so miserably perverted that it is discredited by multitudes, but amply vindicated by modern science, that good breeding, in the strictest sense of the word, is a powerful factor in the lives of men and nations. To be well born does not of necessity require aristocratic parentage, nor does such parentage involve it: but it implies a virtuous, temperate, and pious stock. In extreme cases the doctrine of race is palpable; for who can doubt that the sins of dissolute parents are visited upon their puny and short-lived children, and that the posterity of the just inherit not only honour and a welcome in the world, "an open door," but also immunity from many a physical blemish and many a perilous craving? If the Hebrew race, after eighteen centuries of calamity, retains an unrivalled vigour and tenacity, be it remembered how its iron sinew has been twisted, from what a sire it sprang, through what ages of more than "natural selection" the dross was thoroughly purged out, and (as Isaiah loves to reiterate) a chosen remnant left. Already, in Egypt, in the vigorous multiplication of the race, was visible the germ of that amazing vitality which makes it, even in its overthrow, so powerful an element in the best modern thought and action.

It is a well-known saying of Goethe that the quality for which God chose Israel was probably toughness. Perhaps the saying would better be inverted: it was among the most remarkable endowments, unto which Israel was called, and called by virtue of qualities in which Goethe himself was remarkably deficient.

Now, this principle is in full operation still, and ought to be solemnly pondered by the young. Self-indulgence, the sowing of wild oats, the seeing of life while one is young, the taking one's fling before one settles down, the having one's day (like "every dog," for it is to be observed that no person says, " every Christian "), these things seem natural enough. And their unsuspected issues in the next generation, dire and subtle and far-reaching, these also are more natural still, being the operation of the laws of God.

On the other hand, there is no youth living in obedience alike to the higher and humbler laws of our complex nature, in purity and gentleness and healthful occupation, who may not contribute to the stock of happiness in other lives beyond his own, to the future well-being of his native land, and to the day when the sadly polluted stream of human existence shall again flow clear and glad, a pure river of water of life.

GOD IN HISTORY.

EXODUS i. 7.

With the seventh verse, the new narrative, the course of events treated in the main body of this book, begins.

And we are at once conscious of this vital difference between Exodus and Genesis,—that we have passed from the story of men and families to the history of a nation. In the first book the Canaanites and Egyptians concern us only as they affect Abraham or Joseph. In the second book, even Moses himself concerns us only for the sake of Israel. He is in some respects a more imposing and august character than any who preceded him; but what we are told is no longer the story of a soul, nor are we pointed so much to the development of his spiritual life as to the work he did, the tyrant overthrown, the nation moulded, the law and the ritual imposed on it.

For Jacob it was a discovery that God was in Bethel as well as in his father's house. But now the Hebrew nation was to learn that He could plague the gods of Egypt in their stronghold, that His way was in the sea, that Horeb in Arabia was the Mount of God, that He could lead them like a horse through the wilderness.

When Jacob in Peniel wrestles with God and prevails, he wins for himself a new name, expressive of the higher moral elevation which he has attained. But when Moses meets God in the bush, it is to receive a commission for the public benefit; and there is no new name for Moses, but a fresh revelation of God for the nation to learn. And in all their later history we feel that the national life which it unfolds was nourished and sustained by these glorious early experiences, the most unique as well as the most inspiring on record.

Here, then, a question of great moment is suggested. Beyond the fact that Abraham was the father of the Jewish race, can we discover any closer connection between the lives of the patriarchs and the history of Israel? Is there a truly spiritual coherence between them, or merely a genealogical sequence? For if the Bible can make good its claim to be vitalised throughout by the eternal Spirit of God, and leading forward steadily to His final revelation in Christ, then its parts will be symmetrical, proportionate, and well designed. If it be a universal book, there must be a better reason for the space devoted to preliminary and half secular stories, which is a greater bulk than the whole of the New Testament, than that these histories chance to belong to the nation whence Christ came. If no such reason can be found, the failure may not perhaps outweigh the great evidences of the faith, but it will score for something on the side of infidelity. But if upon examination it becomes plain that all has its part in one great movement, and that none can be omitted without marring the design, and if moreover this design has become visible only since the fulness of the time is come, the discovery will go far to establish the claim of Scripture to reveal throughout a purpose truly divine, dealing with man for ages, and consummated in the gift of Christ.

Now, it is to St. Paul that we turn for light upon the connection between the Old Testament and the New. And he distinctly lays down two great principles. The first is that the Old Testament is meant to educate men for the New; and especially that the sense of failure, impressed upon men's consciences by the stern demands of the Law, was necessary to make them accept the Gospel.

The law was our schoolmaster to bring us to Christ: it entered that sin might abound. And it is worth notice that this effect was actually wrought, not only upon the gross transgressor by the menace of its broken precepts, but even more perhaps upon the high-minded and pure, by the creation in their breasts of an ideal, inaccessible in its loftiness. He who says, All these things have I kept from my youth up, is the same who feels the torturing misgiving, What good thing must I do to attain life? . . . What lack I yet? He who was blameless as touching the righteousness of the law, feels that such superficial innocence is worthless, that the law is spiritual and he is carnal, sold under sin.

Now, this principle need by no means be restricted to the Mosaic institutions. If this were the object of the law, it would probably explain much more. And when we return to the Old Testament with this clue, we find every condition in life examined, every social and political experiment exhausted, a series of demonstrations made with scientific precision, to refute the arch-heresy which underlies all others—that in favourable circumstances man might save himself, that for the evil of our lives our evil surroundings are more to be blamed than we.

Innocence in prosperous circumstances, unwarped by evil habit, untainted by corruption in the blood, uncompelled by harsh surroundings, simple innocence had its day in Paradise, a brief day with a shameful close. God made man upright, but he sought out many inventions, until the flood swept away the descendants of him who was made after the image of God.

Next we have a chosen family, called out from all the perilous associations of its home beyond the river, to begin a new career in a new land, in special covenant with the Most High, and with every endowment for the present and every hope for the future which could help to retain its loyalty. Yet the third generation reveals the thirst of Esau for his brother's blood, the treachery of Jacob, and the distraction and guilt of his fierce and sensual family. It is when individual and family life have thus proved ineffectual amid the happiest circumstances, that the tribe and the nation essay the task. Led up from the furnace of affliction, hardened and tempered in the stern free life of the desert, impressed by every variety of fortune, by slavery and escape, by the pursuit of an irresistible foe and by a rescue visibly divine, awed finally by the sublime revelations of Sinai, the nation is ready for the covenant (which is also a challenge)—The man that doeth these things shall live by them: if thou diligently hearken unto the voice of the Lord thy God . . . He shall set thee on high above all nations.

Such is the connection between this narrative and what went before. And the continuation of the same experiment, and the same failure, can be traced through all the subsequent history. Whether in so loose an organisation that every man does what is right in his own eyes, or under the sceptre of a hero or a sage,—whether so hard pressed that self-preservation ought to have driven them to their God, or so marvellously delivered that gratitude should have brought them to their knees,—whether engulfed a second time in a more hopeless captivity, or restored and ruled by a hierarchy whose authority is entirely spiritual,—in every variety of circumstances the same melancholy process repeats itself; and lawlessness, luxury, idolatry, and self-righteousness combine to stop every mouth, to make every man guilty before God, to prove that a greater salvation is still needed, and thus to pave the way for the Messiah.

The second great principle of St. Paul is that faith in a divine help, in pardon, blessing, and support, was the true spirit of the Old Testament as well as of the New. The challenge of the law was meant to produce self-despair, only that men might trust in God. Appeal was made especially to the cases of Abraham and David, the founder of the race and of the dynasty, clearly because the justification without works of the patriarch and of the king were precedents to decide the general question (Rom. iv. 1-8). Now, this is pre-eminently the distinction between Jewish history and all others, that in it God is everything and man is nothing. Every sceptical treatment of the story makes Moses to be the deliverer from Egypt, and shows us the Jewish nation gradually finding out God. But the nation itself believed nothing of the kind. It confessed itself to have been from the beginning vagrant and rebellious and unthankful: God had always found out Israel, never Israel God. The history is an expansion of the parable of the good shepherd. And this perfect harmony of a long record with itself and with abstract principles is both instructive and reassuring.

As the history of Israel opens before us, a third principle claims attention—one which the apostle quietly assumes, but which is forced on our consideration by the unhappy state of religious thought in these degenerate days.

"They are not to be heard," says the Seventh Article rightly, "which feign that the old fathers did look only for transitory promises." But certainly they also would be unworthy of a hearing who would feign that the early Scriptures do not give a vast, a preponderating weight, to the concerns of our life on earth. Only very slowly, and as the result of long training, does the future begin to reveal its supremacy over the present. It would startle many a devout reader out of his propriety to discover the small proportion of Old Testament scriptures in which eternity and its prospects are discussed, to reckon the passages, habitually applied to spiritual thraldom and emancipation, which were spoken at first of earthly tyranny and earthly deliverance, and to observe, even in the pious aspirations of the Psalms, how much of the gratitude and joy of the righteous comes from the sense that he is made wiser than the ancient, and need not fear though a host rose up against him, and can break a bow of steel, and has a table prepared for him, and an overflowing cup. Especially is this true of the historical books. God is here seen ruling states, judging in the earth, remembering Israel in bondage, and setting him free, providing supernatural food and water, guiding him by the fiery cloud. There is not a word about regeneration, conversion, hell, or heaven. And yet there is a profound sense of God. He is real, active, the most potent factor in the daily lives of men. Now, this may teach us a lesson, highly important to us all, and especially to those who must teach others. The difference between spirituality and secularity is not the difference between the future life and the present, but between a life that is aware of God and a godless one. Perhaps, when we find our gospel a matter of indifference and weariness to men who are absorbed in the bitter, monotonous, and dreary struggle for existence, we ourselves are most to blame. Perhaps, if Moses had approached the Hebrew drudges as we approach men equally weary and oppressed, they would not have bowed their heads and worshipped. And perhaps we should have better success, if we took care to speak of God in this world, making life a noble struggle, charging with new significance the dull and seemingly degraded lot of all who remember Him, such a God as Jesus revealed when He cleansed the leper, and gave sight to the blind, using one and the same word for the "healing" of diseases and the "saving" of souls, and connecting faith equally with both. Exodus will have little to teach us, unless we believe in that God who knoweth that we have need of food and clothing. And the higher spiritual truths which it expresses will only be found there in dubious and questionable allegory, unless we firmly grasp the great truth, that God is not the Saviour of souls, or of bodies, but of living men in their entirety, and treats their higher and lower wants upon much the same principle, because He is the same God, dealing with the same men, through both.

Moreover, He treats us as the men of other ages. Instead of dealing with Moses upon exceptional and strange lines, He made known His ways unto Moses, His characteristic and habitual ways. And it is on this account that whatsoever things were written aforetime are true admonition for us also, being not violent interruptions but impressive revelations of the steady, silent methods of the judgment and the grace of God.

THE OPPRESSION.

Exodus i. 7-22.

At the beginning of the history of Israel we find a prosperous race. It was indeed their growing importance, and chiefly their vast numerical increase, which excited the jealousy of their rulers, at the very time when a change of dynasty removed the sense of obligation. It is a sound lesson in political as well as personal godliness that prosperity itself is dangerous, and needs special protection from on high.

Is it merely by chance again that we find in this first of histories examples of the folly of relying upon political connections? As the chief butler remembered not Joseph, nor did he succeed in escaping from prison by securing influence at court, so is the influence of Joseph himself now become vain, although he was the father of Pharaoh and lord of all his house. His romantic history, his fidelity in temptation, and the services by which he had at once cemented the royal power and saved the people, could not keep his memory alive. The hollow wraith of dying fame died wholly. There arose a new king over Egypt who knew not Joseph.

Such is the value of the highest and purest earthly fame, and such the gratitude of the world to its benefactors. The nation which Joseph rescued from starvation is passive in Pharaoh's hands, and persecutes Israel at his bidding.

And when the actual deliverer arose, his rank and influence were only entanglements through which he had to break.

Meanwhile, except among a few women, obedient to the woman's heart, we find no trace of independent action, no revolt of conscience against the absolute behest of the sovereign, until selfishness replaces virtue, and despair wrings the cry from his servants, Knowest thou not yet that Egypt is destroyed?

Now, in Genesis we saw the fate of families, blessed in their father Abraham, or cursed for the offence of Ham. For a family is a real entity, and its members, like those of one body, rejoice and suffer together. But the same is true of nations, and here we have reached the national stage in the education of the world. Here is exhibited to us, therefore, a nation suffering with its monarch to the uttermost, until the cry of the maid-servant behind the mill is as wild and bitter as the cry of Pharaoh upon his throne. It is indeed the eternal curse of despotism that unlimited calamity may be drawn down upon millions by the caprice of one most unhappy man, himself blinded and half maddened by adulation, by the absence of restraint, by unlimited sensual indulgence if his tendencies be low and animal, and by the pride of power if he be high-spirited and aspiring.

If we assume, what seems pretty well established, that the Pharaoh from whom Moses fled was Rameses the Great, his spirit was of the nobler kind, and he exhibits a terrible example of the unfitness even of conquering genius for unbridled and irresponsible power. That lesson has had to be repeated, even down to the days of the Great Napoleon.

Now, if the justice of plaguing a nation for the offence of its head be questioned, let us ask first whether the nation accepts his despotism, honours him, and is content to regard him as its chief and captain. According to the principles of the Sermon on the Mount, whoever thinks a tyrant enviable, has already himself tyrannised with him in his heart. Do we ourselves, then, never sympathise with political audacity, bold and unscrupulous "resource," success that is bought at the price of strange compliances, and compromises, and wrongs to other men?

The great national lesson is now to be taught to Israel that the most splendid imperial force will be brought to an account for its treatment of the humblest—that there is a God Who judges in the earth. And they were bidden to apply in their own land this experience of their own, dealing kindly with the stranger in the midst of them, "for thou wast a stranger in the land of Egypt." That lesson we have partly learned, who have broken the chain of our slaves. But how much have we left undone! The subject races were never given into our hands to supplant them, as we have supplanted the Red Indian and the New Zealander, nor to debauch, as men say we are corrupting the African and the Hindoo, but to raise, instruct, and Christianise. And if the subjects of a despotism are accountable for the actions of rulers whom they tolerate, how much more are we? What ought we to infer, from this old-world history, of the profound responsibilities of all free citizens?

We attain a principle which reaches far into the spiritual world, when we reflect that if evil deeds of a ruler can justly draw down vengeance upon his people, the converse also must hold good. Reverse the case before us. Let the kingdom be that of the noblest and purest virtue. Let no subject ever be coerced to enter it, nor to remain one hour longer than while his adoring loyalty consents. And shall not these subjects be the better for the virtues of the Monarch whom they love? Is it mere caprice to say that in choosing such a King they do, in a very real sense, appropriate the goodness they crown? If it be natural that Egypt be scourged for the sins of Pharaoh, is it palpably incredible that Christ is made of God unto His people wisdom and righteousness and sanctification and redemption? The doctrine of imputation can easily be so stated as to become absurd. But the imputation of which St. Paul speaks much can only be denied when we are prepared to assail the principle on which all bodies of men are treated, families and nations as well as the Church of God.

It was the jealous cruelty of Pharaoh which drew down upon his country the very perils he laboured to turn away. There was no ground for his fear of any league with foreigners against him. Prosperous and unambitious, the people would have remained well content beside the flesh-pots of Egypt, for which they sighed even when emancipated from heavy bondage and eating the bread of heaven. Or else, if they had gone forth in peace, from a land whose hospitality had not failed, to their inheritance in Canaan, they would have become an allied nation upon the side where the heaviest blows were afterwards struck by the Asiatic powers. Cruelty and cunning could not retain them, but it could decimate a population and lose an army in the attempt. And this law prevails in the modern world. England paid twenty millions to set her bondmen free. Because America would not follow her example, she ultimately paid the more terrible ransom of civil war. For the same God was in Jamaica and in Florida as in the field of Zoan. Nor was there ever yet a crooked policy which did not recoil either upon its author, or upon his successors when he had passed away. In this case it fulfilled the plans and the prophecies of God, and the wrath of man was made to praise Him.

There is independent reason for believing that at this period one-third at least of the population of Egypt was of alien blood (Brugsch, *History*, ii. 100). A politician might fairly be alarmed, especially if this were the time when the Hittites were threatening the eastern frontier, and had reduced Egypt to stand on the defensive, and erect barrier fortresses. And the circumstances of the country made it very easy to enslave the Hebrews. If any stain of Oriental indifference to the rights of the masses had mingled with the God-given insight of Joseph, when he made his benefactor the owner of all the soil, the Egyptian people were fully avenged upon him now. For this arrangement laid his pastoral race helpless at their oppressor's feet. Forced labour quickly degenerates into slavery, and men who find the story of their misery hard to credit should consider the state of France before the Revolution, and of the Russian serfs before their emancipation. Their wretchedness was probably as bitter as that of the Hebrews at any period but the last climax of their oppression. And they owed it to the same cause—the absolute ownership of the land by others too remote from them to be sympathetic, to take due account of their feelings, to remember that they were their fellow-men. This was enough to slay compassion, even without the aggravation of dealing with an alien and suspected race.

Now, it is instructive to observe these reappearances of wholesale crime. They warn us that the utmost achievements of human wickedness are human still; not wild and grotesque importations by a fiend, originated in the abyss, foreign to the world we live in. Satan finds the material for his master-strokes in the estrangement of class from class, in the drying up of the fountains of reciprocal human feeling, in the failure of real, fresh, natural affection in our bosom for those who differ widely from us in rank or circumstances. All cruelties are possible when a man does not seem to us really a man, nor his woes really woeful. For when the man has sunk into an animal it is only a step to his vivisection.

Nor does anything tend to deepen such perilous estrangement, more than the very education, culture, and refinement, in which men seek a substitute for religion and the sense of brotherhood in Christ. It is quite conceivable that the tyrant who drowned the Hebrew infants was an affectionate father, and pitied his nobles when their children died. But his sympathies could not reach beyond the barriers of a caste. Do *our* sympathies really overleap such barriers? Would God that even His Church believed aright in the reality of a human nature like our own, soiled, sorrowful, shamed, despairing, drugged into that apathetical insensibility which lies even below despair, yet aching still, in ten thousand bosoms, in every great city of Christendom, every day and every night! Would to God that she understood what Jesus meant, when He called one lost creature by the tender name which she had not yet forfeited, saying, "Woman, where are thine accusers?" and when He asked Simon, who scorned such another, "Seest thou this woman!" Would God that when she prays for the Holy Spirit of Jesus she would really seek a mind like His, not only in piety and prayerfulness, but also in tender and heartfelt brotherhood with all, even the vilest of the weary and heavy laden!

Many great works of ancient architecture, the pyramids among the rest, were due to the desire of crushing, by abject toil, the spirit of a subject people. We cannot ascribe to Hebrew labour any of the more splendid piles of Egyptian masonry, but the store cities or arsenals which they built can be identified. They are composed of such crude brick as the narrative describes; and the absence of straw in the later portion of them can still be verified. Rameses was evidently named after their oppressor, and this strengthens the conviction that we are reading of events in the nineteenth dynasty, when the shepherd kings had recently been driven out, leaving the eastern frontier so weak as to demand additional fortresses, and so far depopulated as to give colour to the exaggerated assertion of Pharaoh, "the people are more and mightier than we." It is by such exaggerations and alarms that all the worst crimes of statesmen have been justified to consenting peoples. And we, when we carry what seems to us a rightful object, by inflaming the prejudice and misleading the judgment of other men, are moving on the same treacherous and slippery inclines. Probably no evil is committed without some amount of justification, which the passions exaggerate, while they ignore the prohibitions of the law.

How came it to pass that the fierce Hebrew blood, which was yet to boil in the veins of the Maccabees, and to give battle, not unworthily, to the Roman conquerors of the world, failed to resent the cruelties of Pharaoh?

Partly, of course, because the Jewish people was only now becoming aware of its national existence; but also because it had forsaken God. Its religion, if not supplanted, was at least adulterated by the influence of the mystic pantheism and the stately ritual which surrounded them.

Joshua bade his victorious followers to "put away the gods whom your fathers served beyond the River and in Egypt, and serve ye the Lord" (Josh. xxiv. 14). And in Ezekiel the Lord Himself complains, "They rebelled against Me and would not hearken unto Me: they did not cast away the abominations of their eyes, neither did they forsake the idols of Egypt" (Ezek. xx. 8).

Now, there is nothing which enfeebles the spirit and breaks the courage like religious dependence. A strong priesthood always means a feeble people, most of all when they are of different blood. And Israel was now dependent on Egypt alike for the highest and lowest needs—grass for the cattle and religion for the soul. And when they had sunk so low, it is evident that their emancipation had to be wrought for them entirely without their help. From first to last they were passive, not only for want of spirit to help themselves, but because the glory of any exploit of theirs might have illuminated some false deity whom they adored.

Standing still, they saw the salvation of God, and it was not possible to give His glory to another.

For this cause also, judgment had, first of all, to be wrought upon the gods of Egypt.

In the meantime, without spirit enough to resist, they saw complete destruction drawing nearer to them by successive strides. At first Pharaoh "dealt wisely with them," and they found themselves entrapped into a hard bondage almost unawares. But a strange power upheld them, and the more they were afflicted the more they multiplied and spread abroad. In this they ought to have discerned a divine support, and remembered the promise to Abraham that God would multiply his seed as the stars of heaven. It may have helped them presently to "cry unto the Lord." And the Egyptians were not merely "grieved" because of them: they felt as the Israelites afterwards felt towards that monotonous diet of which they used the same word, and said, "our soul loatheth this light bread." Here it expresses that fierce and contemptuous attitude which the Californian and Australian are now assuming toward the swarms of Chinamen whose labour is so indispensable, yet the infusion of whose blood into the population is so hateful. Then the Egyptians make their service rigorous, and their lives bitter.

And at last that happens which is a part of every downward course: the veil is dropped; what men have done by stealth, and as if they would deceive themselves, they soon do consciously, avowing to their conscience what at first they could not face. Thus Pharaoh began by striving to check a dangerous population; and ended by committing wholesale murder.

Thus men become drunkards through conviviality, thieves through borrowing what they mean to restore, and hypocrites through slightly overstating what they really feel. And, since there are nice gradations in evil, down to the very last, Pharaoh will not yet avow publicly the atrocity which he commands a few humble women to perpetrate; decency is with him, as it is often, the last substitute for a conscience.

Among the agents of God for the shipwreck of all full-grown wrongs, the chief is the revolt of human nature, since, fallen though we know ourselves to be, the image of God is not yet effaced in us. The better instincts of humanity are irrepressible—most so perhaps among the poor. It is by refusing to trust its intuitions that men grow vile; and to the very last that refusal is never absolute, so that no villainy can reckon upon its agents, and its agents cannot always reckon upon themselves. Above all, the heart of every woman is in a plot against the wrong; and as Pharaoh was afterwards defeated by the ingenuity of a mother and the sympathy of his own daughter, so his first scheme was spoiled by the disobedience of the midwives, themselves Hebrews, upon whom he reckoned.

Let us not fear to avow that these women, whom God rewarded, lied to the king when he reproached them, since their answer, even if it were not unfounded, was palpably a misrepresentation of the facts. The reward was not for their falsehood, but for their humanity. They lived when the notion of martyrdom for an avowal so easy to evade was utterly unknown. Abraham lied to Abimelech. Both Samuel and David equivocated with Saul. We have learned better things from the King of truth, Who was born and came into the world to bear witness to the truth. We know that the martyr's bold protest against unrighteousness is the highest vocation of the Church, and is rewarded in the better country. But they knew nothing of this, and their service was acceptable according as they had, not according as they had not. As well might we blame the patriarchs for having been slave-owners, and David for having invoked mischief upon his enemies, as these women for having fallen short of the Christian ideal of veracity. Let us beware lest we come short of it ourselves. And let us remember that the way of the Church through time is the path of the just, beset with mist and vapour at the dawn, but shining more and more unto the perfect day.

In the meantime, God acknowledges, and Holy Scripture celebrates, the service of these obscure and lowly heroines. Nothing done for Him goes unrewarded. To slaves it was written that "From the Lord ye shall receive the reward of the inheritance: ye serve the Lord Christ" (Col. iii. 24). And what these women saved for others was what was recompensed to themselves, domestic happiness, family life and its joys. God made them houses.

The king is now driven to avow himself in a public command to drown all the male infants of the Hebrews; and the people become his accomplices by obeying him. For this they were yet to experience a terrible retribution, when there was not a house in Egypt that had not one dead.

The features of the king to whom these atrocities are pretty certainly brought home are still to be seen in the museum at Boulak. Seti I. is the most beautiful of all the Egyptian monarchs whose faces lie bare to the eyes of modern sight-seers; and his refined features, intelligent, high-bred, and cheerful, resemble wonderfully, yet surpass, those of Rameses II., his successor, from whom Moses fled. This is the builder of the vast and exquisite temple of Amon at Thebes, the grandeur of which is amazing even in its ruins; and his culture and artistic gifts are visible, after all these centuries, upon his face. It is a strange comment upon the modern doctrine that culture is to become a sufficient substitute for religion. And his own record of his exploits is enough to show that the sense of beauty is not that of pity: he is the jackal leaping through the land of his enemies, the grim lion, the powerful bull with sharpened horns, who has annihilated the peoples.

There is no greater mistake than to suppose that artistic refinement can either inspire morality or replace it. Have we quite forgotten Nero, and Lucretia Borgia, and Catherine de Medici?

Many civilisations have thought little of infant life. Ancient Rome would have regarded this atrocity as lightly as modern China, as we may see by the absolute silence of its literature concerning the murder of the innocents—an event strangely parallel with this in its nature and political motives, and in the escape of one mighty Infant.

Is it conceivable that the same indifference should return, if the sanctions of religion lose their power? Every one remembers the callousness of Rousseau. Strange things are being written by pessimistic unbelief about the bringing of more sufferers into the world. And a living writer in France has advocated the legalising of infanticide, and denounced St. Vincent de Paul because, " thanks to his odious precautions, this man deferred for years the death of creatures without intelligence," etc.*

It is to the faith of Jesus, not only revealing by the light of eternity the value of every soul, but also replenishing the fountains of human tenderness that had well-nigh become exhausted, that we owe our modern love of children. In the very helplessness which the ancient masters of the world exposed to destruction without a pang, we see the type of what we must ourselves become, if we would enter heaven. But we cannot afford to forget either the source or the sanctions of the lesson.

CHAPTER II.

THE RESCUE OF MOSES.

EXODUS ii. 1-10.

WE have said that the Old Testament history teems with political wisdom, lessons of permanent instruction for mankind, on the level of this life, yet godly, as all true lessons must be in a world of which Christ is King. These our religion must learn to recognise and proclaim, if it is ever to win the respect of men of affairs, and " leaven the whole lump " of human life with sacred influence.

Such a lesson is the importance of the individual in the history of nations. History, as read in Scripture, is indeed a long relation of

heroic resistance or of base compliance in the presence of influences which are at work to debase modern peoples as well as those of old. The holiness of Samuel, the gallant faith of David, the splendour and wisdom of Solomon, the fervid zeal of Elijah, the self-respecting righteousness of Nehemiah,—ignore these, and the whole course of affairs becomes vague and unintelligible. Most of all this is true of Moses, whose appearance is now related.

In profane history it is the same. Alexander, Mahomet, Luther, William the Silent, Napoleon, —will any one pretend that Europe uninfluenced by these personalities would have become the Europe that we know?

And this truth is not at all a speculative, unpractical theory: it is vital. For now there is a fashion of speaking about the tendency of the age, the time-spirit, as an irresistible force which moulds men like potters' clay, crowning those who discern and help it, but grinding to powder all who resist its course. In reality there are always a hundred time-spirits and tendencies competing for the mastery—some of them violent, selfish, atheistic, or luxurious (as we see with our own eyes to-day)—and the shrewdest judges are continually at fault as to which of them is to be victorious, and recognised hereafter as the spirit of the age.

This modern pretence that men are nothing, and streams of tendency are all, is plainly a gospel of capitulations, of falsehood to one's private convictions, and of servile obedience to the majority and the popular cry. For, if individual men are nothing, what am I? If we are all bubbles floating down a stream, it is folly to strive to breast the current. Much practical baseness and servility is due to this base and servile creed. And the cure for it is belief in another spirit than that of the present age, trust in an inspiring God, who rescued a herd of slaves and their fading convictions from the greatest nation upon earth by matching one man, shrinking and reluctant yet obedient to his mission, against Pharaoh and all the tendencies of the age.

And it is always so. God turns the scale of events by the vast weight of a man, faithful and true, and sufficiently aware of Him to refuse, to universal clamour, the surrender of his liberty or his religion. In small matters, as in great, there is no man, faithful to a lonely duty or conviction, understanding that to have discerned it is a gift and a vocation, but makes the world better and stronger, and works out part of the answer to that great prayer " Thy will be done."

We have seen already that the religion of the Hebrews in Egypt was corrupted and in danger of being lost. To this process, however, there must have been bright exceptions; and the mother of Moses bore witness, by her very name, to her fathers' God. The first syllable of Jochebed is proof that the name of God, which became the keynote of the new revelation, was not entirely new.

As yet the parents of Moses are not named; nor is there any allusion to the close relationship which would have forbidden their union at a later period (chap. vi. 20). And throughout all the story of his youth and early manhood there is no mention whatever of God or of religion. Elsewhere it is not so. The Epistle to the Hebrews declares that through faith the babe was hidden, and through faith the man refused Egyp-

* J. K. Huysmans—quoted in *Nineteenth Century*, May, 1888, p. 673.

tian rank. Stephen tells us that he expected his brethren to know that God by his hand was giving them deliverance. But the narrative in Exodus is wholly untheological. If Moses were the author, we can see why he avoided reflections which directly tended to glorify himself. But if the story were a subsequent invention, why is the tone so cold, the light so colourless?

Now, it is well that we are invited to look at all these things from their human side, observing the play of human affection, innocent subtlety, and pity. God commonly works through the heart and brain which He has given us, and we do not glorify Him at all by ignoring these. If in this case there were visible a desire to suppress the human agents, in favour of the Divine preserver, we might suppose that a different historian would have given a less wonderful account of the plagues, the crossing of the Sea, and the revelation from Sinai. But since full weight is allowed to second causes in the early life of Moses, the story is entitled to the greater credit when it tells of the burning bush and the flaming mountain.

Let us, however, put together the various narratives and their lessons. At the outset we read of a marriage celebrated between kinsfolk, when the storm of persecution was rising. And hence we infer that courage or strong affection made the parents worthy of him through whom God should show mercy unto thousands. The first child was a girl, and therefore safe; but we may suppose, although silence in Scripture proves little, that Aaron, three years before the birth of Moses, had not come into equal peril with him. Moses was therefore born just when the last atrocity was devised, when trouble was at its height.

"At this time Moses was born," said Stephen. Edifying inferences have been drawn from the statement in Exodus that "the woman . . . hid him." Perhaps the stronger man quailed, but the maternal instinct was not at fault, and it was rewarded abundantly. From which we only learn, in reality, not to overstrain the words of Scripture; since the Epistle to the Hebrews distinctly says that he "was hid three months by his parents"—both of them, while naturally the mother is the active agent.

All the accounts agree that he was thus hidden, "because they saw that he was a goodly child" (Heb. xi. 23). It is a pathetic phrase. We see them, before the crisis, vaguely submitting in theory to an unrealised atrocity, ignorant how imperiously their nature would forbid the crime, not planning disobedience in advance, nor led to it by any reasoning process. All is changed when the little one gazes at them with that marvellous appeal in its unconscious eyes, which is known to every parent, and helps him to be a better man. There is a great difference between one's thought about an infant, and one's feeling towards the actual baby. He was their child, their beautiful child; and this it was that turned the scale. For him they would now dare anything, "because they saw he was a goodly child, and they were not afraid of the king's commandment." Now, impulse is often a great power for evil, as when appetite or fear, suddenly taking visible shape, overwhelms the judgment and plunges men into guilt. But good impulses may be the very voice of God, stirring whatever is noble and generous within us. Nor are they accidental: loving and brave emotions belong to warm and courageous hearts; they come of themselves, like song birds, but they come surely where sunshine and still groves invite them, not into clamour and foul air. Thus arose in their bosoms the sublime thought of God as an active power to be reckoned upon. For as certainly as every bad passion that we harbour preaches atheism, so does all goodness tend to sustain itself by the consciousness of a supreme Goodness in reserve. God had sent them their beautiful child, and who was Pharaoh to forbid the gift? And so religion and natural pity joined hands, their supreme convictions and their yearning for their infant. "By faith Moses was hid . . . because they saw he was a goodly child, and they were not afraid of the king's commandment."

Such, if we desire a real and actual salvation, is always the faith which saves. Postpone salvation to an indefinite future; make it no more than the escape from vaguely realised penalties for sins which do not seem very hateful; and you may suppose that faith in theories can obtain this indulgence; an opinion may weigh against a misgiving. But feel that sin is not only likely to entail damnation, but is really and in itself damnable meanwhile, and then there will be no deliverance possible, but from the hand of a divine Friend, strong to sustain and willing to guide the life. We read that Amram lived a hundred and thirty and seven years, and of all that period we only know that he helped to save the deliverer of his race, by practical faith which made him not afraid, and did not paralyse but stimulate his energies.

When the mother could no longer hide the child, she devised the plan which has made her for ever famous. She placed him in a covered ark, or casket,* plaited (after what we know to have been the Egyptian fashion) of the papyrus reed, and rendered watertight with bitumen, and this she laid among the rushes—a lower vegetation, which would not, like the tall papyrus, hide her treasure—in the well-known and secluded place where the daughter of Pharaoh used to bathe. Something in the known character of the princess may have inspired this ingenious device to move her pity; but it is more likely that the woman's heart, in her extremity, prompted a simple appeal to the woman who could help her if she would. For an Egyptian princess was an important personage, with an establishment of her own, and often possessed of much political influence. The most sanguinary agent of a tyrant would be likely to respect the client of such a patron.

The heart of every woman was in a plot against the cruelty of Pharaoh. Once already the midwives had defeated him; and now, when his own daughter † unexpectedly found, in the water at her very feet, a beautiful child sobbing silently (for she knew not what was there until the ark was opened), her indignation is audible enough in the words, "This is one of the Hebrews' children." She means to say, "This is only one specimen of the outrages that are going on."

This was the chance for his sister, who had been set in ambush, not prepared with the exqui-

---

* The same word is used for Noah's ark, but not elsewhere; not, for example, of the ark in the Temple, the name of which occurs elsewhere in Scripture only of the "coffin" of Joseph, and the "chest" for the Temple revenues (Gen. l. 26; 2 Chron. xxiv. 8, 10, 11).

† Or his sister, the daughter of a former Pharaoh.

site device which follows, but simply "to know what would be done to him." Clearly the mother had reckoned upon his being found, and neglected nothing, although unable herself to endure the agony of watching, or less easily hidden in that guarded spot. And her prudence had a rich reward. Hitherto Miriam's duty had been to remain passive—that hard task so often imposed upon the affection, especially of women, by sickbeds, and also in many a more stirring hazard, and many a spiritual crisis, where none can fight his brother's battle. It is a trying time, when love can only hold its breath, and pray. But let not love suppose that to watch is to do nothing. Often there comes a moment when its word, made wise by the teaching of the heart, is the all-important consideration in deciding mighty issues.

This girl sees the princess at once pitiful and embarrassed, for how can she dispose of her strange charge? Let the moment pass, and the movement of her heart subside, and all may be lost; but Miriam is prompt and bold, and asks "Shall I go and call to thee a nurse of the Hebrew women, that she may nurse the child for thee?" It is a daring stroke, for the princess must have understood the position thoroughly, the moment the eager Hebrew girl stepped forward. The disguise was very thin. And at least the heart which pitied the infant must have known the mother when she saw her face, pale with longing. It is therefore only as a form, exacted by circumstances, but well enough though tacitly understood upon both sides, that she bids her nurse the child for her, and promises wages. What reward could equal that of clasping her child to her own agitated bosom in safety, while the destroyers were around?

This incident teaches us that good is never to be despaired of, since this kindly woman grew up in the family of the persecutor.

And the promptitude and success of Miriam suggest a reflection. Men do pity, when it is brought home to them, the privation, suffering, and wrong, which lie around. Magnificent sums are contributed yearly for their relief by the generous instincts of the world. The misfortune is that sentiment is evoked only by visible and pathetic griefs, and that it will not labour as readily as it will subscribe. It is a harder task to investigate, to devise appeals, to invent and work the machinery by which misery may be relieved. Mere compassion will accomplish little, unless painstaking affection supplement it. Who supplies that? Who enables common humanity to relieve itself by simply paying "wages," and confiding the wretched to a painstaking, laborious, loving guardian? The streets would never have known Hospital Saturday, but for Hospital Sunday in the churches. The orphanage is wholly a Christian institution. And so is the lady nurse. The old-fashioned phrase has almost sunk into a party cry, but in a large and noble sense it will continue to be true to nature as long as bereavement, pain, or penitence requires a tender bosom and soothing touch, which speaks of Mother Church.

Thus did God fulfil His mysterious plans. And according to a sad but noble law, which operates widely, what was best in Egypt worked with Him for the punishment of its own evil race. The daughter of Pharaoh adopted the perilous foundling, and educated him in the wisdom of Egypt.

THE CHOICE OF MOSES.

EXODUS ii. 11-15.

God works even His miracles by means. As He fed the multitude with barley-loaves, so He would emancipate Israel by human agency. It was therefore necessary to educate one of the trampled race "in all the learning of Egypt," and Moses was planted in the court of Pharaoh, like the German Arminius in Rome. Wonderful legends may be read in Josephus of his heroism, his wisdom, and his victories; and these have some foundation in reality, for Stephen tells us that he was mighty in his words and works. Might in words need not mean the fluent utterance which he so earnestly disclaimed (iv. 10), even if forty years' disuse of the language were not enough to explain his later diffidence. It may have meant such power of composition as appears in the hymn by the Red Sea, and in the magnificent valediction to his people.

The point is that among a nation originally pastoral, and now sinking fast into the degraded animalism of slaves, which afterwards betrayed itself in their complaining greed, their sighs for the generous Egyptian dietary, and their impure carouse under the mountain, one man should possess the culture and mental grasp needed by a leader and lawgiver. "Could not the grace of God have supplied the place of endowment and attainment?" Yes, truly; and it was quite as likely to do this for one who came down from His immediate presence with his face intolerably bright, as for the last impudent enthusiast who declaims against the need of education in sentences which at least prove that for him the want has by no substitute been completely met. But the grace of God chose to give the qualification, rather than replace it, alike to Moses and St. Paul. Nor is there any conspicuous example among the saints of a man being thrust into a rank for which he was not previously made fit.

The painful contrast between his own refined tastes and habits, and the coarser manners of his nation, was no doubt one difficulty of the choice of Moses, and a lifelong trial to him afterwards. He is an example not only to those whom wealth and power would entangle, but to any who are too fastidious and sensitive for the humble company of the people of God.

While the intellect of Moses was developing, it is plain that his connection with his family was not entirely broken. Such a tie as often binds a foster-child to its nurse may have been permitted to associate him with his real parents. Some means were evidently found to instruct him in the history and messianic hopes of Israel, for he knew that their reproach was that of "the Christ," greater riches than all the treasure of Egypt, and fraught with a reward for which he looked in faith (Heb. xi. 26). But what is meant by naming as part of his burden their "reproach," as distinguished from their sufferings?

We shall understand, if we reflect, that his open rupture with Egypt was unlikely to be the work of a moment. Like all the best workers, he was led forward gradually, at first unconscious of his vocation. Many a protest he must have made against the cruel and unjust policy that steeped the land in innocent blood. Many a jealous councillor must have known how to weaken his dangerous influence by some cautious taunt, some insinuated "reproach" of his own Hebrew origin. The warnings put by Josephus into the lips of the priests in his childhood, were likely enough to have been spoken by some one before he was forty years old. At last, when driven to make his choice, he "refused to be called the son of Pharaoh's daughter," a phrase, especially in its reference to the rejected title as distinguished from "the pleasures of sin," which seems to imply a more formal rupture than Exodus records.

We saw that the piety of his parents was not unhelped by their emotions: they hid him by faith when they saw that he was a goodly child. Such was also the faith by which Moses broke with rank and fortune. He went out unto his brethren, and looked on their burdens, and he saw an Egyptian smiting an Hebrew, one of his brethren. Twice the word of kinship is repeated; and Stephen tells us that Moses himself used it in rebuking the dissensions of his fellow-countrymen. Filled with yearning and pity for his trampled brethren, and with the shame of generous natures who are at ease while others suffer, he saw an Egyptian smiting an Hebrew. With that blended caution and vehemence which belong to his nation still, he looked and saw that there was no man, and slew the Egyptian. Like most acts of passion, this was at once an impulse of the moment, and an outcome of long gathering forces—just as the lightning flash, sudden though it seem, has been prepared by the accumulated electricity of weeks.

And this is the reason why God allows the issues of a lifetime, perhaps of an eternity, to be decided by a sudden word, a hasty blow. Men plead that if time had been given, they would have stifled the impulse which ruined them. But what gave the impulse such violent and dreadful force that it overwhelmed them before they could reflect? The explosion in the coalmine is not caused by the sudden spark, without the accumulation of dangerous gases, and the absence of such wholesome ventilation as would carry them away. It is so in the breast where evil desires or tempers are harboured, unsubdued by grace, until any accident puts them beyond control. Thank God that such sudden movements do not belong to evil only! A high soul is surprised into heroism, as often perhaps as a mean one into theft or falsehood. In the case of Moses there was nothing unworthy, but much that was unwarranted and presumptuous. The decision it involved was on the right side, but the act was self-willed and unwarranted, and it carried heavy penalties. "The trespass originated not in inveterate cruelty," says St. Augustine, "but in a hasty zeal which admitted of correction . . . resentment against injury was accompanied by love for a brother. . . Here was evil to be rooted out, but the heart with such capabilities, like good soil, needed only cultivation to make it fruitful in virtue."

Stephen tells us, what is very natural, that Moses expected the people to accept him as their heaven-born deliverer. From which it appears that he cherished high expectations for himself, from Israel if not from Egypt. When he interfered next day between two Hebrews, his question as given in Exodus is somewhat magisterial: "Wherefore smitest thou thy fellow?" In Stephen's version it dictates less, but it lectures a good deal: "Sirs, ye are brethren, why do ye wrong one to another?" And it was natural enough that they should dispute his pretensions, for God had not yet given him the rank he claimed. He still needed a discipline almost as sharp as that of Joseph, who, by talking too boastfully of his dreams, postponed their fulfilment until he was chastened by slavery and a dungeon. Even Saul of Tarsus, when converted, needed three years of close seclusion for the transformation of his fiery ardour into divine zeal, as iron to be tempered must be chilled as well as heated. The precipitate and violent zeal of Moses entailed upon him forty years of exile.

And yet his was a noble patriotism. There is a false love of country, born of pride, which blinds one to her faults; and there is a loftier passion which will brave estrangement and denunciation to correct them. Such was the patriotism of Moses, and of all whom God has ever truly called to lead their fellows. Nevertheless he had to suffer for his error.

His first act had been a kind of manifesto, a claim to lead, which he supposed that they would have understood; and yet, when he found his deed was known, he feared and fled. His false step told against him. One cannot but infer also that he was conscious of having already forfeited court favour—that he had before this not only made his choice, but announced it, and knew that the blow was ready to fall on him at any provocation. We read that he dwelt in the land of Midian, a name which was applied to various tracts according to the nomadic wanderings of the tribe, but which plainly included, at this time, some part of the peninsula formed by the tongues of the Red Sea. For, as he fed his flocks, he came to the Mount of God.

MOSES IN MIDIAN.

Exodus ii. 16-22.

The interference of Moses on behalf of the daughters of the priest of Midian is a pleasant trait, courteous, and expressive of a refined nature. With this remark, and reflecting that, like many courtesies, it brought its reward, we are often content to pass it by. And yet it deserves a closer examination.

1. For it expresses great energy of character. He might well have been in a state of collapse. He had smitten the Egyptian for Israel's sake: he had appealed to his own people to make common cause, like brethren, against the common foe; and he had offered himself to them as their destined leader in the struggle. But they had refused him the command, and he was rudely awakened to the consciousness that his life was in danger through the garrulous ingratitude of the man he rescued. Now he was a ruined man and an exile, marked for destruction by the greatest of earthly monarchs, with the habits and tastes of a great noble, but homeless among wild races.

It was no common nature which was alert and energetic at such a time. The greatest men have known a period of prostration in calamity: it was enough for honour that they should rally and re-collect their forces. Thinking of Frederick, after Kunersdorf, resigning the command ("I have no resources more, and will not survive the destruction of my country"), and of his subsequent despatch, "I am now recovered from my illness"; and of Napoleon, trembling and weeping on the road to Elba, one turns with fresh admiration to the fallen prince, the baffled liberator, sitting exhausted by the well, but as keen on behalf of liberty as when Pharaoh trampled Israel, though now the oppressors are a group of rude herdsmen, and the oppressed are Midianite women, driven from the troughs which they have toiled to fill. One remembers Another, sitting also exhausted by the well, defying social usage on behalf of a despised woman, and thereby inspired and invigorated as with meat to eat which His followers knew not of.

2. Moreover there is disinterested bravery in the act, since he hazards the opposition of the men of the land, among whom he seeks refuge, on behalf of a group from which he can have expected nothing. And here it is worth while to notice the characteristic variations in three stories which have certain points of contact. The servant of Abraham, servant-like, was well content that Rebekah should draw for all his camels, while he stood still. The prudent Jacob, anxious to introduce himself to his cousin, rolled away the stone and watered her camels. Moses sat by the well, but did not interfere while the troughs were being filled: it was only the overt wrong which kindled him. But as in great things, so it is in small: our actions never stand alone; having once befriended them, he will do it thoroughly, "and moreover he drew water for us, and watered the flock." Such details could hardly have been thought out by a fabricator; a legend would not have allowed Moses to be slower in courtesy than Jacob;* but the story fits the case exactly: his eyes were with his heart, and that was far away, until the injustice of the shepherds roused him.

And why was Moses thus energetic, fearless, and chivalrous? Because he was sustained by the presence of the Unseen: he endured as seeing Him who is invisible: and having, despite of panic, by faith forsaken Egypt, he was free from the absorbing anxieties which prevent men from caring for their fellows, free also from the cynical misgivings which suspect that violence is more than justice, that to be righteous overmuch is to destroy one's self, and that perhaps, after all, one may see a good deal of wrong without being called upon to interfere. It would be a different world to-day, if all who claim to be "the salt of the earth" were as eager to repress injustice in its smaller and meaner forms as to make money or influential friends. If all petty and cowardly oppression were sternly trodden down, we should soon have a state of public opinion in which gross and large tyranny would be almost impossible. And it is very doubtful whether the flagrant wrongs, which must be comparatively rare, cause as much real mental suffering as the frequent small ones. Does mankind suffer more from wild beasts than from insects? But how few that aspire to emancipate oppressed nations would be content, in the hour of their overthrow, to assert the rights of a handful of women against a trifling fraud, to which indeed they were so well accustomed that its omission surprised their father!

Is it only because we are reading a history, and not a biography, that we find no touch of

---

* Nor would it have made the women call their deliverer "an Egyptian," for the Hebrew cast of features is very dissimilar. But Moses wore Egyptian dress, and the Egyptians worked mines in the peninsula, so that he was naturally taken for one of them.

---

tenderness, like the love of Jacob for Rachel, in the domestic relations of Moses?

Joseph also married in a strange land, yet he called the name of his first son Manasseh, because God had made him to forget his sorrows: but Moses remembered his. Neither wife nor child could charm away his home sickness; he called his firstborn Gershom, because he was a sojourner in a strange land. In truth, his whole life seems to have been a lonely one. Miriam is called "the sister of Aaron" even when joining in the song of Moses (xv. 20), and with Aaron she made common cause against their greater brother (Num. xii. 1-2). Zipporah endangered his life rather than obey the covenant of circumcision; she complied at last with a taunt (iv. 24-6), and did not again join him until his victory over Amalek raised his position to the utmost height (xviii. 2).

His children are of no account, and his grandson is the founder of a dangerous and enduring schism (Judges xviii. 30, R. V.).

There is much reason to see here the earliest example of the sad rule that a prophet is not without honour save in his own house; that the law of compensations reaches farther into life than men suppose; and high position and great powers are too often counterbalanced by the isolation of the heart.

CHAPTER III.

THE BURNING BUSH.

EXODUS ii. 23—iii.

"IN process of time the king of Egypt died," probably the great Raamses, no other of whose dynasty had a reign which extended over the indicated period of time. If so, he had while living every reason to expect an immortal fame, as the greatest among Egyptian kings, a hero, a conqueror on three continents, a builder of magnificent works. But he has only won an immortal notoriety. "Every stone in his buildings was cemented in human blood." The cause he persecuted has made deathless the banished refugee, and has gibbeted the great monarch as a tyrant, whose misplanned severities wrought the ruin of his successor and his army. Such are the reversals of popular judgment: and such the vanity of fame. For all the contemporary fame was his.

"The children of Israel sighed by reason of the bondage, and they cried." Another monarch had come at last, a change after sixty-seven years, and yet no change for them! It filled up the measure of their patience, and also of the iniquity of Egypt. We are not told that their cry was addressed to the Lord; what we read is that it reached Him, Who still overhears and pities many a sob, many a lament, which ought to have been addressed to Him, and is not. Indeed, if His compassion were not to reach men until they had remembered and prayed to Him, who among us would ever have learned to pray to Him at all? Moreover He remembered His covenant with their forefathers, for the fulfilment of which the time had now arrived. "And God saw the children of Israel, and God took knowledge of them."

These were not the cries of religious individuals, but of oppressed masses. It is therefore a solemn question to ask How many such appeals ascend from Christian England? Behold, the hire of labourers . . . held back by fraud crieth out. The half-paid slaves of our haste to be rich, and the victims of our drinking institutions, and of hideous vices which entangle and destroy the innocent and unconscious, what cries to heaven are theirs! As surely as those which St. James records, these have entered into the ears of the Lord of Sabaoth. Of these sufferers every one is His own by purchase, most of them by a covenant and sacrament more solemn than bound Him to His ancient Israel. Surely He hears their groaning. And all whose hearts are touched with compassion, yet who hesitate whether to bestir themselves or to remain inert while evil is masterful and cruel, should remember the anger of God when Moses said, "Send, I pray Thee, by whom Thou wilt send." The Lord is not indifferent. Much less than other sufferers should those who know God be terrified by their afflictions. Cyprian encouraged the Church of his time to endure even unto martyrdom, by the words recorded of ancient Israel, that the more they afflicted them, so much the more they became greater and waxed stronger. And he was right. For all these things happened to them for ensamples, and were written for our admonition.

It is further to be observed that the people were quite unconscious, until Moses announced it afterwards, that they were heard by God. Yet their deliverer had now been prepared by a long process for his work. We are not to despair because relief does not immediately appear: though He tarry, we are to wait for Him.

While this anguish was being endured in Egypt, Moses was maturing for his destiny. Self-reliance, pride of place, hot and impulsive aggressiveness, were dying in his bosom. To the education of the courtier and scholar was now added that of the shepherd in the wilds, amid the most solemn and awful scenes of nature, in solitude, humiliation, disappointment, and, as we learn from the Epistle to the Hebrews, in enduring faith. Wordsworth has a remarkable description of the effect of a similar discipline upon the good Lord Clifford. He tells:

"How he, long forced in humble paths to go,
  Was softened into feeling, soothed and tamed.

"Love had he found in huts where poor men lie,
  His daily teachers had been woods and rills,
  The silence that is in the starry sky,
  The sleep that is among the lonely hills.

"In him the savage virtues of the race,
  Revenge, and all ferocious thoughts, were dead;
  Nor did he change, but kept in lofty place
  The wisdom which adversity had bred."

There was also the education of advancing age, which teaches many lessons, and among them two which are essential to leadership,—the folly of a hasty blow, and of impulsive reliance upon the support of mobs. Moses the man-slayer became exceeding meek; and he ceased to rely upon the perception of his people that God by him would deliver them. His distrust, indeed, became as excessive as his temerity had been, but it was an error upon the safer side. "Behold, they will not believe me," he says, "nor hearken unto my voice."

It is an important truth that in very few lives the decisive moment comes just when it is expected. Men allow themselves to be self-indulgent, extravagant, and even wicked, often upon the calculation that their present attitude matters little, and they will do very differently when the crisis arrives, the turning-point in their career to nerve them. And they waken up with a start to find their career already decided, their character moulded. As a snare shall the day of the Lord come upon all flesh; and as a snare come all His great visitations meanwhile. When Herod was drinking among bad companions, admiring a shameless dancer, and boasting loudly of his generosity, he was sobered and saddened to discover that he had laughed away the life of his only honest adviser. Moses, like David, was "following the ewes great with young," when summoned by God to rule His people Israel. Neither did the call arrive when he was plunged in moody reverie and abstraction, sighing over his lost fortunes and his defeated aspirations, rebelling against his lowly duties. The humblest labour is a preparation for the brightest revelations, whereas discontent, however lofty, is a preparation for nothing. Thus, too, the birth of Jesus was first announced to shepherds keeping watch over their flock. Yet hundreds of third-rate young persons in every city in this land to-day neglect their work, and unfit themselves for any insight, or any leadership whatever, by chafing against the obscurity of their vocation.

Who does not perceive that the career of Moses hitherto was divinely directed? The fact that we feel this, although, until now, God has not once been mentioned in his personal story, is surely a fine lesson for those who have only one notion of what edifies—the dragging of the most sacred names and phrases into even the most unsuitable connections. In truth, such a phraseology is much less attractive than a certain tone, a recognition of the unseen, which may at times be more consistent with reverential silence than with obtrusive utterance. It is enough to be ready and fearless when the fitting time comes, which is sure to arrive, for the religious heart as for this narrative—the time for the natural utterance of the great word, God.

We read that the angel of the Lord appeared to him—a remarkable phrase, which was already used in connection with the sacrifice of Isaac (Gen. xxii. 11). How much it implies will better be discussed in the twenty-third chapter, where a fuller statement is made. For the present it is enough to note, that this is one pre-eminent angel, indicated by the definite article; that he is clearly the medium of a true divine appearance, because neither the voice nor form of any lesser being is supposed to be employed, the appearance being that of fire, and the words being said to be the direct utterance of the Lord, not of any one who says, Thus saith the Lord. We shall see hereafter that the story of the Exodus is unique in this respect, that in training a people tainted with Egyptian superstitions, no "similitude" is seen, as when there wrestled a man with Jacob, or when Ezekiel saw a human form upon the sapphire pavement.

Man is the true image of God, and His perfect revelation was in flesh. But now that expression of Himself was perilous, and perhaps unsuitable besides; for He was to be known as the Avenger, and presently as the Giver of Law, with its inflexible conditions and its menaces. Therefore He appeared as fire, which is intense and terrible, even when "the flame of the grace of God does not consume, but illuminates."

There is a notion that religion is languid, repressive, and unmanly. But such is not the scriptural idea. In His presence is the fulness of joy. Christ has come that we might have life, and might have it more abundantly. They who are shut out from His blessedness are said to be asleep and dead. And so Origen quotes this passage among others, with the comment that "As God is a fire, and His angels a flame of fire, and all the saints fervent in spirit, so they who have fallen away from God are said to have cooled, or to have become cold" (*De Princip.*, ii. 8). A revelation by fire involves intensity.

There is indeed another explanation of the burning bush, which makes the flame express only the afflictions that did not consume the people. But this would be a strange adjunct to a divine appearance for their deliverance, speaking rather of the continuance of suffering than of its termination, for which the extinction of such fire would be a more appropriate symbol.

Yet there is an element of truth even in this view, since fire is connected with affliction. In His holiness God is light (with which, in the Hebrew, the very word for holiness seems to be connected); in His judgments He is fire. "The Light of Israel shall be for a fire, and his Holy One for a flame, and it shall burn and devour his thorns and his briers in one day" (Isa. x. 17). But God reveals Himself in this thorn bush as a fire which does not consume; and such a revelation tells at once Who has brought the people into affliction, and also that they are not abandoned to it.

To Moses at first there was visible only an extraordinary phenomenon; He turned to see a great sight. It is therefore out of the question to find here the truth, so easy to discover elsewhere, that God rewards the religious inquirer —that they who seek after Him shall find Him. Rather we learn the folly of deeming that the intellect and its inquiries are at war with religion and its mysteries, that revelation is at strife with mental insight, that he who most stupidly refuses to "see the great sights" of nature is best entitled to interpret the voice of God. When the man of science gives ear to voices not of earth, and the man of God has eyes and interest for the divine wonders which surround us, many a discord will be harmonised. With the revival of classical learning came the Reformation.

But it often happens that the curiosity of the intellect is in danger of becoming irreverent, and obtrusive into mysteries not of the brain, and thus the voice of God must speak in solemn warning: "Moses, Moses, . . . Draw not nigh hither: put off thy shoes from off thy feet, for the place whereon thou standest is holy ground."

After as prolonged a silence as from the time of Malachi to the Baptist, it is God Who reveals Himself once more—not Moses who by searching finds Him out. And this is the established rule. Tidings of the Incarnation came from heaven, or man would not have discovered the Divine Babe. Jesus asked His two first disciples "What seek ye?" and told Simon "Thou shalt be called Cephas," and pronounced the listening Nathaniel "an Israelite indeed," and bade Zaccheus "make haste and come down," in each case before He was addressed by them.

The first words of Jehovah teach something more than ceremonial reverence. If the dust of common earth on the shoe of Moses may not mingle with that sacred soil, how dare we carry into the presence of our God mean passions and selfish cravings? Observe, too, that while Jacob, when he awoke from his vision, said, "How dreadful is this place!" (Gen. xxviii. 17), God Himself taught Moses to think rather of the holiness than the dread of His abode. Nevertheless Moses also was afraid to look upon God, and hid the face which was thereafter to be veiled, for a nobler reason, when it was itself illumined with the divine glory. Humility before God is thus the path to the highest honour, and reverence, to the closest intercourse.

Meantime the Divine Person has announced Himself: "I am the God of thy father" (father is apparently singular with a collective force), "the God of Abraham, the God of Isaac, and the God of Jacob." It is a blessing which every Christian parent should bequeath to his child, to be strengthened and invigorated by thinking of God as his father's God.

It was with this memorable announcement that Jesus refuted the Sadducees and established His doctrine of the resurrection. So, then, the bygone ages are not forgotten: Moses may be sure that a kindly relation exists between God and himself, because the kindly relation still exists in all its vital force which once bound Him to those who long since appeared to die. It was impossible, therefore, our Lord inferred, that they had really died at all. The argument is a forerunner of that by which St. Paul concludes, from the resurrection of Christ, that none who are "in Christ" have perished. Nay, since our Lord was not disputing about immortality only, but the resurrection of the body, His argument implied that a vital relationship with God involved the imperishability of the whole man, since all was His, and in truth the very seal of the covenant was imprinted upon the flesh. How much stronger is the assurance for us, who know that our very bodies are His temple! Now, if any suspicion should arise that the argument, which is really subtle, is over-refined and untrustworthy, let it be observed that no sooner was this announcement made, than God added the proclamation of His own immutability, so that it cannot be said He was, but from age to age His title is I AM. The inference from the divine permanence to the living and permanent vitality of all His relationships is not a verbal quibble, it is drawn from the very central truth of this great scripture.

And now for the first time God calls Israel My people, adopting a phrase already twice employed by earthly rulers (Gen. xxiii. 11, xli. 40), and thus making Himself their king and the champion of their cause. Often afterwards it was used in pathetic appeal:—"Thou hast showed Thy people hard things,"—"Thou sellest Thy people for naught,"—"Behold, look, we beseech Thee; we are all Thy people" (Ps. lx. 3, xliv. 12; Isa. lxiv. 9). And often it expressed the returning favour of their king: "Hear, O My people, and I will speak"; "Comfort ye, comfort ye My people" (Ps. l. 7; Isa. xl. 1).

It is used of the nation at large, all of whom were brought into the covenant, although with many of them God was not well pleased. And since it does not belong only to saints, but speaks of a grace which might be received in vain, it is a strong appeal to all Christian people, all who are within the New Covenant. Them also the Lord claims and pities, and would gladly emancipate: their sorrows also He knows. "I have surely seen the affliction of My people which are in Egypt, and have heard their cry by reason of their taskmasters; for I know their sorrows; and I am come down to deliver them out of the hand of the Egyptians, and to bring them up out of that land unto a good land and a large, unto a land flowing with milk and honey." Thus the ways of God exceed the desires of men. Their subsequent complaints are evidence that Egypt had become their country: gladly would they have shaken off the iron yoke, but a successful rebellion is a revolution, not an Exodus. Their destined home was very different: with the widest variety of climate, scenery, and soil, a land which demanded much more regular husbandry, but rewarded labour with exuberant fertility. Secluded from heathenism by deserts on the south and east, by a sublime range of mountains on the north, and by a sea with few havens on the west, yet planted in the very bosom of all the ancient civilisation which at the last it was to leaven, it was a land where a faithful people could have dwelt alone and not been reckoned among the nations, yet where the scourge for disobedience was never far away.

Next after the promise of this good land, the commission of Moses is announced. He is to act, because God is already active: "*I am come down to deliver them* . . . come now, therefore, and I will send *thee* unto Pharaoh, that thou mayest bring forth My people." And let this truth encourage all who are truly sent of God, to the end of time, that He does not send us to deliver man, until He is Himself prepared to do so; that when our fears ask, like Moses, Who am I, that I should go? He does not answer, Thou art capable, but Certainly I will go with thee. So, wherever the ministry of the word is sent, there is a true purpose of grace. There is also the presence of One who claims the right to bestow upon us the same encouragement which was given to Moses by Jehovah, saying, "Lo, I am with you alway." In so saying, Jesus made Himself equal with God.

And as this ancient revelation of God was to give rest to a weary and heavy-laden people, so Christ bound together the assertion of a more perfect revelation, made in Him, with the promise of a grander emancipation. No man knoweth the Father save by revelation of the Son is the doctrine which introduces the great offer "Come unto Me, all ye that labour and are heavy-laden, and I will give you rest" (Matt. xi. 27, 28). The claims of Christ in the New Testament will never be fully recognised until a careful study is made of His treatment of the functions which in the Old Testament are regarded as Divine. A curious expression follows: "This shall be a token unto thee that I have sent thee: When thou hast brought forth the people out of Egypt, ye shall serve God upon this mountain." It seems but vague encouragement, to offer Moses, hesitating at the moment, a token which could take effect only when his task was wrought. And yet we know how much easier it is to believe what is thrown into distinct shape and particularised. Our trust in good intentions is helped when their expression is detailed and circumstantial, as a candidate for office will reckon all general assurances of support much cheaper than a pledge to canvass certain electors within a certain time. Such is the constitution of human nature; and its Maker has often deigned to sustain its weakness by going thus into particulars. He does the same for us, condescending to embody the most profound of all mysteries in sacramental emblems, clothing his promises of our future blessedness in much detail, and in concrete figures which at least symbolise, if they do not literally describe, the glories of the Jerusalem which is above.

A NEW NAME.

Exodus iii. 14—vi. 2, 3.

"God said unto Moses, I AM THAT I AM: and He said, Thus shalt thou say unto the children of Israel, I AM hath sent me unto you."

We cannot certainly tell why Moses asked for a new name by which to announce to his brethren the appearance of God. He may have felt that the memory of their fathers, and of the dealings of God with them, had faded so far out of mind that merely to indicate their ancestral God would not sufficiently distinguish Him from the idols of Egypt, whose worship had infected them.

If so, he was fully answered by a name which made this God the one reality, in a world where all is a phantasm except what derives stability from Him.

He may have desired to know, for himself, whether there was any truth in the dreamy and fascinating pantheism which inspired so much of the Egyptian superstition.

In that case, the answer met his question by declaring that God existed, not as the sum of things or soul of the universe, but in Himself, the only independent Being.

Or he may simply have desired some name to express more of the mystery of deity, remembering how a change of name had accompanied new discoveries of human character and achievement, as of Abraham and Israel; and expecting a new name likewise when God would make to His people new revelations of Himself.

So natural an expectation was fulfilled not only then, but afterwards. When Moses prayed "Show me, I pray Thee, Thy Glory," the answer was "I will make all My goodness pass before thee, and I will proclaim the name of the Lord." The proclamation was again Jehovah, but not this alone. It was "The Lord, the Lord, a God full of compassion and gracious, slow to anger, and plenteous in mercy and truth" (xxxiii. 18, 19, xxxiv. 6, R. V.). Thus the life of Moses, like the agelong progress of the Church, advanced towards an ever-deepening knowledge that God is not only the Independent but the Good. All sets toward the final knowledge that His highest name is Love.

Meanwhile, in the development of events, the exact period was come for epithets, which were shared with gods many and lords many, to be supplemented by the formal announcement and authoritative adoption of His proper name Jehovah. The infant nation was to learn to think of Him, not only as endowed with attributes of terror and power, by which enemies would be crushed, but as possessing a certain well-defined personality, upon which the trust of man could repose. Soon their experience would enable them to receive the formal announcement that

He was merciful and gracious. But first they were required to trust His promise amid all discouragements; and to this end, stability was the attribute first to be insisted upon.

It is true that the derivation of the word Jehovah is still a problem for critical acumen. It has been sought in more than one language, and various shades of meaning have been assigned to it, some untenable in the abstract, others hardly, or not at all, to be reconciled with the Scriptural narrative.

Nay, the corruption of the very sound is so notorious, that it is only worth mention as illustrating a phase of superstition.

We smile at the Jews, removing the correct vowels lest so holy a word should be irreverently spoken, placing the sanctity in the cadence, hoping that light and flippant allusions may offend God less, so long as they spare at least the vowels of His name, and thus preserve some vestige undesecrated, while profaning at once the conception of His majesty and the consonants of the mystic word.

A more abject superstition could scarcely have made void the spirit, while grovelling before the letter of the commandment.

But this very superstition is alive in other forms to-day. Whenever one recoils from the sin of coarse blasphemy, yet allows himself the enjoyment of a polished literature which profanes holy conceptions,—whenever men feel bound to behave with external propriety in the house of God, yet bring thither wandering thoughts, vile appetites, sensuous imaginations, and all the chamber of imagery which is within the unregenerate heart,—there is the same despicable superstition which strove to escape at least the extreme of blasphemy by prudently veiling the Holy Name before profaning it.

But our present concern is with the practical message conveyed to Israel when Moses declared that Jehovah, I AM, the God of their fathers, had appeared unto him. And if we find in it a message suited for the time, and which is the basis, not the superstructure, both of later messages and also of the national character, then we shall not fail to observe the bearing of such facts upon an urgent controversy of this time.

Some significance must have been in that Name, not too abstract for a servile and degenerate race to apprehend. Nor was it soon to pass away and be replaced; it was His memorial throughout all generations; and therefore it has a message for us to-day, to admonish and humble, to invigorate and uphold.

That God would be the same to them as to their fathers was much. But that it was of the essence of His character to be evermore the same, immutable in heart and mind and reality of being, however their conduct might modify His bearing towards them, this indeed would be a steadying and reclaiming consciousness.

Accordingly Moses receives the answer for himself, " I AM THAT I AM"; and he is bidden to tell his people " I AM hath sent me unto you," and yet again " JEHOVAH the God of your fathers hath sent me unto you." The spirit and tenor of these three names may be said to be virtually comprehended in the first; and they all speak of the essential and self-existent Being, unchanging and unchangeable.

I AM expresses an intense reality of being.

No image in the dark recesses of Egyptian or Syrian temples, grotesque and motionless, can win the adoration of him who has had communion with such a veritable existence, or has heard His authentic message. No dreamful pantheism, on its knees to the beneficent principle expressed in one deity, to the destructive in another, or to the reproductive in a third, but all of them dependent upon nature, as the rainbow upon the cataract which it spans, can ever again satisfy the soul which is athirst for the living God, the Lord, Who is not personified, but is.

This profound sense of a living Person within reach, to be offended, to pardon, and to bless, was the one force which kept the Hebrew nation itself alive, with a vitality unprecedented since the world began. They could crave His pardon, whatever natural retributions they had brought down upon themselves, whatever tendencies of nature they had provoked, because He was not a dead law without ears or a heart, but their merciful and gracious God.

Not the most exquisite subtleties of innuendo and irony could make good for a day the monstrous paradox that the Hebrew religion, the worship of I AM, was really nothing but the adoration of that stream of tendencies which makes for righteousness.

Israel did not challenge Pharaoh through having suddenly discovered that goodness ultimately prevails over evil, nor is it any cold calculation of the sort which ever inspires a nation or a man with heroic fortitude. But they were nerved by the announcement that they had been remembered by a God Who is neither an ideal nor a fancy, but the Reality of realities, beside Whom Pharaoh and his host were but as phantoms.

I AM THAT I AM is the style not only of permanence, but of permanence self-contained, and being a distinctive title, it denies such self-contained permanence to others.

Man is as the past has moulded him, a compound of attainments and failures, discoveries and disillusions, his eyes dim with forgotten tears, his hair gray with surmounted anxieties, his brow furrowed with bygone studies, his conscience troubled with old sin. Modern unbelief is ignobly frank respecting him. He is the sum of his parents and his wet-nurse. He is what he eats. If he drinks beer, he thinks beer. And it is the element of truth in these hideous paradoxes which makes them rankle, like an unkind construction put upon a questionable action. As the foam is what wind and tide have made of it, so are we the product of our circumstances, the resultant of a thousand forces, far indeed from being self-poised or self-contained, too often false to our best self, insomuch that probably no man is actually what in the depth of self-consciousness he feels himself to be, what moreover he should prove to be, if only the leaden weight of constraining circumstance were lifted off the spring which it flattens down to earth. Moses himself was at heart a very different person from the keeper of the sheep of Jethro. Therefore man says, Pity and make allowance for me: this is not my true self, but only what by compression, by starvation and stripes and bribery and error, I have become. Only God says, I AM THAT I AM.

Yet in another sense, and quite as deep a one, man is not the coarse tissue which past circumstances have woven: he is the seed of the future, as truly as the fruit of the past. Strange compound that he is of memory and hope, while half of the present depends on what is over, the other half is projected into the future; and like a bridge, sustained on these two banks, life throws its quivering shadow on each moment that fleets by. It is not attainment, but degradation to live upon the level of one's mere attainment, no longer uplifted by any aspiration, fired by any emulation, goaded by any but carnal fears. If we have been shaped by circumstances, yet we are saved by hope. Do not judge me, we are all entitled to plead, by anything that I am doing or have done: He only can appraise a soul aright Who knows what it yearns to become, what within itself it hates and prays to be delivered from, what is the earnestness of its self-loathing, what the passion of its appeal to heaven. As the bloom of next April is the true comment upon the dry bulb of September, as you do not value the fountain by the pint of water in its basin, but by its inexhaustible capabilities of replenishment, so the present and its joyless facts are not the true man; his possibilities, the fears and hopes that control his destiny and shall unfold it, these are his real self.

I am not merely what I am: I am very truly that which I long to be. And thus, man may plead, I am what I move towards and strive after, my aspiration is myself. But God says, I AM WHAT I AM. The stream hurries forward: the rock abides. And this is the Rock of Ages.

Now, such a conception is at first sight not far removed from that apathetic and impassive kind of deity which the practical atheism of ancient materialists could well afford to grant;—" ever in itself enjoying immortality together with supreme repose, far removed and withdrawn from our concerns, since it, exempt from every pain, exempt from all danger, strong in its own resources and wanting naught from us, is neither gained by favour nor moved by wrath."

Thus Lucretius conceived of the absolute Being as by the necessity of its nature entirely outside our system.

But Moses was taught to trust in Jehovah as intervening, pitying sorrow and wrong, coming down to assist His creatures in distress.

How could this be possible? Clearly the movement towards them must be wholly disinterested, and wholly from within; unbought, since no external influence can modify His condition, no puny sacrifice can propitiate Him Who sitteth upon the circle of the earth and the inhabitants thereof are as grasshoppers: a movement prompted by no irregular emotional impulse, but an abiding law of His nature, incapable of change, the movement of a nature, personal indeed, yet as steady, as surely to be reckoned upon in like circumstances, as the operations of gravitation are.

There is no such motive, working in such magnificent regularity for good, save one. The ultimate doctrine of the New Testament, that God is Love, is already involved in this early assertion, that being wholly independent of us and our concerns, He is yet not indifferent to them, so that Moses could say unto the children of Israel "I AM hath sent me unto you."

It is this unchangeable consistency of Divine action which gives the narrative its intense interest to us. To Moses, and therefore to all who receive any commission from the skies, this title said, Frail creature, sport of circumstances and of tyrants, He who commissions thee sits above the waterfloods, and their rage can as little modify or change His purpose, now committed to thy charge, as the spray can quench the stars. Perplexed creature, whose best self lives only in aspiration and desire, now thou art an instrument in the hand of Him with Whom desire and attainment, will and fruition, are eternally the same. None truly fails in fighting for Jehovah, for who hath resisted His will?

To Israel, and to all the oppressed whose minds are open to receive the tidings and their faith strong to embrace it, He said, Your life is blighted, and your future is in the hand of taskmasters, yet be of good cheer, for now your deliverance is undertaken by Him Whose being and purpose are one, Who *is* in perfection of enjoyment all that He *is* in contemplation and in will. The rescue of Israel by an immutable and perfect God is the earnest of the breaking of every yoke.

And to the proud and godless world which knows Him not, He says, Resistance to My will can only show forth all its power, which is not at the mercy of opinion or interest or change: I sit upon the throne, not only supreme but independent, not only victorious but unassailable; self-contained, self-poised, and self-sufficing, I AM THAT I AM.

Have we now escaped the inert and self-absorbed deity of Lucretius, only to fall into the palsying grasp of the tyrannous deity of Calvin? Does our own human will shrivel up and become powerless under the compulsion of that immutability with which we are strangely brought into contact?

Evidently this is not the teaching of the Book of Exodus. For it is here, in this revelation of the Supreme, that we first hear of a nation as being His: "I have seen the affliction of My people which is in Egypt . . . and I have come down to bring them into a good land." They were all baptised into Moses in the cloud and in the sea. Yet their carcases fell in the wilderness. And these things were written for our learning. The immutability, which suffers no shock when we enter *into* the covenant, remains unshaken also if we depart from the living God. The sun shines alike when we raise the curtain and when we drop it, when our chamber is illumined and when it is dark. The immutability of God is not in His operations, for sometimes He gave His people into the hand of their enemies, and again He turned and helped them. It is in His nature, His mind, in the principles which guide His actions. If He had not chastened David for his sin, then, by acting as before, He would have been other at heart than when He rejected Saul for disobedience and chose the son of Jesse to fulfil all His word. The wind has veered, if it continues to propel the vessel in the same direction, although helm and sails are shifted.

Such is the Pauline doctrine of His immutability. "If we endure we shall also reign with Him: if we shall deny Him, He also will deny us,"—and such is the necessity of His being, for we cannot sway Him with our changes: "if we are faithless, He abideth faithful, for He cannot deny Himself." And therefore it is presently added that "the firm foundation of the Lord standeth sure, having" not only "this seal, that the Lord knoweth those that are His,"—but also this, "Let every one that nameth the name of the Lord depart from unrighteousness" (2 Tim. ii. 12, 13, 19, R. V.).

The Lord knew that Israel was His, yet for their unrighteousness He sware in His wrath that they should not enter into His rest.

It follows from all this that the new name of God was no academic subtlety, no metaphysical refinement of the schools, unfitly revealed to slaves, but a most practical and inspiring truth, a conviction to warm their blood, to rouse their courage, to convert their despair into confidence and their alarms into defiance.

They had the support of a God worthy of trust. And thenceforth every answer in righteousness, every new disclosure of fidelity, tenderness, love, was not an abnormal phenomenon, the uncertain grace of a capricious despot; no, its import was permanent as an observation of the stars by an astronomer, ever more to be remembered in calculating the movements of the universe.

In future troubles they could appeal to Him to awake as in the ancient days, as being He who "cut Rahab and wounded the Dragon." "I am the Lord, I change not, therefore ye sons of Jacob are not consumed."

And as the sublime and beautiful conception of a loving spiritual God was built up slowly, age by age, tier upon tier, this was the foundation which insured the stability of all, until the Head Stone of the Corner gave completeness to the vast design, until men saw and could believe in the very Incarnation of all Love, unshaken amid anguish and distress and seeming failure, immovable, victorious, while they heard from human lips the awful words, "Before Abraham was, I AM." Then they learned to identify all this ancient lesson of trustworthiness with new and more pathetic revelations of affection: and the martyr at the stake grew strong as he remembered that the Man of Sorrows was the same yesterday and to-day and for ever; and the great apostle, prostrate before the glory of his Master, was restored by the touch of a human hand, and by the voice of Him upon Whose bosom he had leaned, saying, Fear not, I am the First and the Last and the Living One.

And if men are once more fain to rend from humanity that great assurance, which for ages, amid all shocks, has made the frail creature of the dust to grow strong and firm and fearless, partaker of the Divine Nature, what will they give us in its stead? Or do they think us too strong of will, too firm of purpose? Looking around us, we see nations heaving with internal agitations, armed to the teeth against each other, and all things like a ship at sea reeling to and fro, and staggering like a drunken man. There is no stability for us in constitutions or old formulæ—none anywhere, if it be not in the soul of man. Well for us, then, that the anchor of the soul is sure and steadfast! well that unnumbered millions take courage from their Saviour's word, that the world's worst anguish is the beginning, not of dissolution, but of the birth-pangs of a new heaven and earth,—that when the clouds are blackest because the light of sun and moon is quenched, then, then we shall behold the Immutable unveiled, the Son of Man, who is brought nigh unto the Ancient of Days, now sitting in the clouds of heaven, and coming in the glory of His Father!

THE COMMISSION.

Exodus iii. 10, 16-22.

We have already learned from the seventh verse that God commissioned Moses, only when He had Himself descended to deliver Israel. He sends none, except with the implied or explicit promise that certainly He will be with them. But the converse is also true. If God sends no man but when He comes Himself, He never comes without demanding the agency of man. The overruled reluctance of Moses, and the inflexible urgency of his commission, may teach us the honour set by God upon humanity. He has knit men together in the mutual dependence of nations and of families, that each may be His minister to all; and in every great crisis of history He has respected His own principle, and has visited the race by means of the providential man. The gospel was not preached by angels. Its first agents found themselves like sheep among wolves: they were an exhibition to the world and to angels and men, yet necessity was laid upon them, and a woe if they preached it not.

All the best gifts of heaven come to us by the agency of inventor and sage, hero and explorer, organiser and philanthropist, patriot, reformer, and saint. And the hope which inspires their grandest effort is never that of selfish gain, nor even of fame, though fame is a keen spur, which perhaps God set before Moses in the noble hope that "thou shalt bring forth the people" (ver. 12). But the truly impelling force is always the great deed itself, the haunting thought, the importunate inspiration, the inward fire; and so God promises Moses neither a sceptre, nor share in the good land: He simply proposes to him the work, the rescue of the people; and Moses, for his part, simply objects that he is unable, not that he is solicitous about his reward. Whatever is done for payment can be valued by its cost: all the priceless services done for us by our greatest were, in very deed, unpriced.

Moses, with the new name of God to reveal, and with the assurance that He is about to rescue Israel, is bidden to go to work advisedly and wisely. He is not to appeal to the mob, nor yet to confront Pharaoh without authority from his people to speak for them, nor is he to make the great demand for emancipation abruptly and at once. The mistake of forty years ago must not be repeated now. He is to appeal to the elders of Israel; and with them, and therefore clearly representing the nation, he is respectfully to crave permission for a three days' journey, to sacrifice to Jehovah in the wilderness. The blustering assurance with which certain fanatics of our own time first assume that they possess a direct commission from the skies, and thereupon that they are freed from all order, from all recognition of any human authority, and then that no considerations of prudence or of decency should restrain the violence and bad taste which they mistake for zeal, is curiously unlike anything in the Old Testament or the New. Was ever a commission more direct than those of Moses and of St. Paul? Yet Moses was to obtain the recognition of the elders of his people; and St. Paul received formal ordination by the explicit command of God (Acts xiii. 3).

Strangely enough, it is often assumed that this

demand for a furlough of three days was insincere. But it would only have been so, if consent were expected, and if the intention were thereupon to abuse the respite and refuse to return. There is not the slightest hint of any duplicity of the kind. The real motives for the demand are very plain. The excursion which they proposed would have taught the people to move and act together, reviving their national spirit, and filling them with a desire for the liberty which they tasted. In the very words which they should speak, "The Lord, the God of the Hebrews, hath met with us," there is a distinct proclamation of nationality, and of its surest and strongest bulwark, a national religion. From such an excursion, therefore, the people would have returned, already well-nigh emancipated, and with recognised leaders. Certainly Pharaoh could not listen to any such proposal, unless he were prepared to reverse the whole policy of his dynasty toward Israel.

But the refusal answered two good ends. In the first place it joined issue on the best conceivable ground, for Israel was exhibited making the least possible demand with the greatest possible courtesy—" Let us go, we pray thee, three days' journey into the wilderness." Not even so much would be granted. The tyrant was palpably in the wrong, and thenceforth it was perfectly reasonable to increase the severity of the terms after each of his defeats, which proceeding in its turn made concession more and more galling to his pride. In the second place, the quarrel was from the first avowedly and undeniably religious: the gods of Egypt were matched against Jehovah; and in the successive plagues which desolated his land Pharaoh gradually learnt Who Jehovah was.

In the message which Moses should convey to the elders there are two significant phrases. He was to announce in the name of God, "I have surely visited you, and seen that which is done unto you in Egypt." The silent observation of God before He interposes is very solemn and instructive. So in the Revelation, He walks among the golden candlesticks, and knows the work, the patience, or the unfaithfulness of each. So He is not far from any one of us. When a heavy blow falls we speak of it as "a visitation of Providence," but in reality the visitation has been long before. Neither Israel nor Egypt was conscious of the solemn presence. Who knows what soul of man, or what nation, is thus visited to-day, for future deliverance or rebuke?

Again it is said, "I will bring you up out of the affliction of Egypt into . . . a land flowing with milk and honey." Their affliction was the divine method of uprooting them. And so is our affliction the method by which our hearts are released from love of earth and life, that in due time He may " surely bring us in " to a better and an enduring country. Now, we wonder that the Israelites clung so fondly to the place of their captivity. But what of our own hearts? Have they a desire to depart? or do they groan in bondage, and yet recoil from their emancipation?

The hesitating nation is not plainly told that their affliction will be intensified and their lives made burdensome with labour. That is perhaps implied in the certainty that Pharaoh "will not let you go, no, not by a mighty hand." But it is with Israel as with us: a general knowledge that in the world we shall have tribulation is enough; the catalogue of our trials is not spread out before us in advance. They were assured for their encouragement that all their long captivity should at last receive its wages, for they should not borrow * but ask of the Egyptians jewels of silver, and gold, and raiment, and they should spoil the Egyptians. So are we taught to have "respect unto the recompense of the reward."

CHAPTER IV.

MOSES HESITATES.

EXODUS iv. 1-17.

HOLY Scripture is impartial, even towards its heroes. The sin of David is recorded, and the failure of Peter. And so is the reluctance of Moses to accept his commission, even after a miracle had been vouchsafed to him for encouragement. The absolute sinlessness of Jesus is the more significant because it is found in the records of a creed which knows of no idealised humanity.

In Josephus, the refusal of Moses is softened down. Even the modest words, "Lord, I am still in doubt how I, a private man and of no abilities, should persuade my countrymen, or Pharaoh," are not spoken after the sign is given. Nor is there any mention of the transfer to Aaron of a part of his commission, nor of their joint offence at Meribah, nor of its penalty, which in Scripture is bewailed so often. And Josephus is equally tender about the misdeeds of the nation. We hear nothing of their murmurs against Moses and Aaron when their burdens are increased, or of their making the golden calf. Whereas it is remarkable and natural that the fear of Moses is less anxious about his reception by the tyrant than bv his own people: "Behold, they will not believe me, nor hearken unto my voice; for they will say, The Lord hath not appeared unto thee." This is very unlike the invention of a later period, glorifying the beginnings of the nation· but it is absolutely true to life. Great men do not fear the wrath of enemies if they can be secured against the indifference and contempt of friends; and Moses in particular was at last persuaded to undertake his mission by the promise of the support of Aaron. His hesitation is therefore the earliest example of what has been so often since observed—the discouragement of heroes, reformers, and messengers from God, less by fear of the attacks of the world than of the contemptuous scepticism of the people of God. We often sigh for the appearing, in our degenerate days, of

"A man with heart, head, hand,
Like some of the simple great ones gone."

Yet who shall say that the want of them is not our own fault? The critical apathy and incredulity, not of the world but of the Church, is what freezes the fountains of Christian daring and the warmth of Christian zeal.

* So much ignorant capital has been made by sceptics out of this unfortunate mistranslation, that it is worth while to inquire whether the word " borrow " would suit the context in other passages. "He *borrowed* water and she gave him milk" (Judges v. 25). "The Lord said unto Solomon, Because thou hast *borrowed* this thing, and hast not *borrowed* long life for thyself, neither hast *borrowed* riches for thyself, nor hast *borrowed* the life of thine enemies" (1 Kings iii. 11). "And Elij ,h said unto Elisha, Thou hast *borrowed* a hard thing" (2 Kings ii. 10). The absurdity of the cavil is self-evident.

For the help of the faith of his people, Moses is commissioned to work two miracles; and he is caused to rehearse them, for his own.

Strange tales were told among the later Jews about his wonder-working rod. It was cut by Adam before leaving Paradise, was brought by Noah into the ark, passed into Egypt with Joseph, and was recovered by Moses while he enjoyed the favour of the court. These legends arose from downright moral inability to receive the true lesson of the incident, which is the confronting of the sceptre of Egypt with the simple staff of the shepherd, the choosing of the weak things of earth to confound the strong, the power of God to work His miracles by the most puny and inadequate means. Anything was more credible than that He who led His people like sheep did indeed guide them with a common shepherd's crook. And yet this was precisely the lesson meant for us to learn—the glorification of poor resources in the grasp of faith.

Both miracles were of a menacing kind. First the rod became a serpent, to declare that at God's bidding enemies would rise up against the oppressor, even where all seemed innocuous, as in truth the waters of the river and the dust of the furnace and the winds of heaven conspired against him. Then, in the grasp of Moses, the serpent from which he fled became a rod again, to intimate that these avenging forces were subject to the servant of Jehovah.

Again, his hand became leprous in his bosom, and was presently restored to health again—a declaration that he carried with him the power of death, in its most dreadful form; and perhaps a still more solemn admonition to those who remember what leprosy betokens, and how every approach of God to man brings first the knowledge of sin, to be followed by the assurance that He has cleansed it.*

If the people would not hearken to the voice of the first sign, they should believe the second; but at the worst, and if they were still unconvinced, they would believe when they saw the water of the Nile, the pride and glory of their oppressors, turned into blood before their eyes. That was an omen which needs no interpretation. What follows is curious. Moses objects that he has not hitherto been eloquent, nor does he experience any improvement "since Thou hast spoken unto Thy servant" (a graphic touch!), and he seems to suppose that the popular choice between liberty and slavery would depend less upon the evidence of a Divine power than upon sleight of tongue, as if he were in modern England.

But let it be observed that the self-consciousness which wears the mask of humility while refusing to submit its judgment to that of God, is a form of selfishness—self-absorption blinding one to other considerations beyond himself—as real, though not as hateful, as greed and avarice and lust.

How can Moses call himself slow of speech

* Tertullian appealed to the second of these miracles to illustrate the possibility of the resurrection. "The hand of Moses is changed and becomes like that of the dead, bloodless, colourless, and stiff with cold. But on the recovery of heat and restoration of its natural colour, it is the same flesh and blood. . . So will changes, conversions and reformation be needed to bring about the resurrection, yet the substance will be preserved safe." (*De Res.*, lv) It is far wiser to be content with the declaration of St. Paul that the identity of the body does not depend on that of its corporeal atoms. "Thou sowest not that body that shall be, but a naked grain. . . . But God giveth . . . to every seed his own body " (1 Cor. xv. 37-8).

and of a slow tongue, when Stephen distinctly declares that he was mighty in word as well as deed? (Acts vii. 22). Perhaps it is enough to answer that many years of solitude in a strange land had robbed him of his fluency. Perhaps Stephen had in mind the words of the Book of Wisdom, that "Wisdom entered into the soul of the servant of the Lord, and withstood dreadful kings in wonders and signs. . . For Wisdom opened the mouth of the dumb, and made the tongues of them that cannot speak eloquent" (Wisdom x. 16, 21).

To his scruple the answer was returned, "Who hath made man's mouth? . . . Have not I the Lord? Now therefore go, and I will be with thy mouth, and teach thee what thou shalt say." The same encouragement belongs to every one who truly executes a mandate from above: "Lo, I am with you alway." For surely this encouragement *is* the same. Surely Jesus did not mean to offer His own presence as a substitute for that of God, but as being in very truth Divine, when He bade His disciples, in reliance upon Him, to go forth and convert the world.

And this is the true test which divides faith from presumption, and unbelief from prudence: do we go because God is with us in Christ, or because we ourselves are strong and wise? Do we hold back because we are not sure of *His* commission, or only because we distrust ourselves? "Humility without faith is too timorous; faith without humility is too hasty." The phrase explains the conduct of Moses both now and forty years before.

Moses, however, still entreats that any one may be chosen rather than himself: "Send, I pray Thee, by the hand of him whom Thou wilt send."

And thereupon the anger of the Lord was kindled against him, although at the moment his only visible punishment was the partial granting of his prayer the association with him in his commission of Aaron, who could speak well, the forfeiting of a certain part of his vocation, and with it of a certain part of its reward. The words, "Is not Aaron thy brother the Levite?" have been used to insinuate that the tribal arrangement was not perfected when they were written, and so to discredit the narrative. But when so interpreted they yield no adequate sense, they do not reinforce the argument; while they are perfectly intelligible as implying that Aaron is already the leader of his tribe, and therefore sure to obtain the hearing of which Moses despaired. But the arrangement involved grave consequences sure to be developed in due time: among others, the reliance of Israel upon a feebler will, which could be forced by their clamour to make them a calf of gold. Moses was yet to learn that lesson which our century knows nothing of,—that a speaker and a leader of nations are not the same. When he cried to Aaron, in the bitterness of his soul, "What did this people to thee, that thou hast brought so great a sin upon them?" did he remember by whose unfaithfulness Aaron had been thrust into the office, the responsibilities of which he had betrayed?

Now, it is the duty of every man, to whom a special vocation presents itself, to set opposite each other two considerations. Dare I undertake this task? is a solemn question, but so is this: Dare I let this task go past me? Am I prepared for the responsibility of allowing it to drift into weaker hands? These are days when the Church of Christ is calling for the help of every one capable of aiding her, and we ought to hear it said more often that one is afraid *not* to teach in Sunday School, and another dares not refuse a proffered district, and a third fears to leave charitable tasks undone. To him that knoweth to do good, and doeth it not, to him it is sin; and we hear too much about the terrible responsibility of working for God, but too little about the still graver responsibility of refusing to work for Him when called.

Moses indeed attained so much that we are scarcely conscious that he might have been greater still. He had once presumed to go unsent, and brought upon himself the exile of half a lifetime. Again he presumed almost to say, I go not, and well-nigh to incur the guilt of Jonah when sent to Nineveh, and in so doing he forfeited the fulness of his vocation. But who reaches the level of his possibilities? Who is not haunted by faces, " each one a murdered self," a nobler self, that might have been, and is now impossible for ever? Only Jesus could say " I have finished the work which Thou gavest Me to do." And it is notable that while Jesus deals, in the parable of the labourers, with the problem of equal faithfulness during longer and shorter periods of employment; and in the parable of the pounds with that of equal endowment variously improved; and yet again, in the parable of the talents, with the problem of various endowments all doubled alike, He always draws a veil over the treatment of five talents which earn but two or three besides.

A more cheerful reflection suggested by this narrative is the strange power of human fellowship. Moses knew and was persuaded that God, Whose presence was even then miraculously apparent in the bush, and Who had invested him with superhuman powers, would go with him. There is no trace of incredulity in his behaviour, but only of failure to rely, to cast his shrinking and reluctant will upon the truth he recognised and the God Whose presence he confessed. He held back, as many a one does, who is honest when he repeats the Creed in church, yet fails to submit his life to the easy yoke of Jesus. Nor is it from physical peril that he recoils: at the bidding of God he has just grasped the serpent from which he fled; and in confronting a tyrant with armies at his back, he could hope for small assistance from his brother. But highly strung spirits, in every great crisis, are aware of vague indefinite apprehensions that are not cowardly but imaginative. Thus Cæsar, when defying the hosts of Pompey, is said to have been disturbed by an apparition. It is vain to put these apprehensions into logical form, and argue them down: the slowness of speech of Moses was surely refuted by the presence of God, Who makes the mouth and inspires the utterance; but such fears lie deeper than the reasons they assign, and when argument fails, will yet stubbornly repeat their cry: " Send, I pray Thee, by the hand of him whom Thou wilt send." Now this shrinking, which is not craven, is dispelled by nothing so effectually as by the touch of a human hand. It is like the voice of a friend to one beset by ghostly terrors: he does not expect his comrade to exorcise a spirit, and yet his apprehensions are dispelled. Thus Moses cannot summon up courage from the protection of God, but when assured of the companionship of his brother he will not only venture to return to Egypt, but will bring with him his wife and children. Thus, also, He Who knew what was in men's hearts sent forth His missionaries, both the Twelve and the Seventy (as we have yet to learn the true economy of sending ours), " by two and two " (Mark vi. 7; Luke x. 1).

This is the principle which underlies the institution of the Church of Christ, and the conception that Christians are brothers, among whom the strong must help the weak. Such help from their fellow-mortals would perhaps decide the choice of many hesitating souls, upon the verge of the divine life, recoiling from its unknown and dread experiences, but longing for a sympathising comrade. Alas for the unkindly and unsympathetic religion of men whose faith has never warmed a human heart, and of congregations in which emotion is a misdemeanour!

There is no stronger force, among all that make for the abuses of priestcraft, than this same yearning for human help becomes when robbed of its proper nourishment, which is the communion of saints and the pastoral care of souls. Has it no further nourishment than these? This instinctive craving for a Brother to help as well as a Father to direct and govern,—this social instinct, which banished the fears of Moses and made him set out for Egypt long before Aaron came in sight, content when assured of Aaron's co-operation,—is there nothing in God Himself to respond to it? He Who is not ashamed to call us brethren has profoundly modified the Church's conception of Jehovah, the Eternal, Absolute, and Unconditioned. It is because He can be touched with the feeling of our infirmities, that we are bidden to draw near with boldness unto the Throne of Grace. There is no heart so lonely that it cannot commune with the lofty and kind humanity of Jesus.

There is a homelier lesson to be learned. Moses was not only solaced by human fellowship, but nerved and animated by the thought of his brother, and the mention of his tribe. " Is not Aaron thy brother the Levite? " They had not met for forty years. Vague rumours of deadly persecution were doubtless all that had reached the fugitive, whose heart had burned, in solitary communion with Nature in her sternest forms, as he brooded over the wrongs of his family, of Aaron, and perhaps of Miriam.

And now his brother lived. The call which Moses would have put from him was for the emancipation of his own flesh and blood, and for their greatness. In that great hour, domestic affection did much to turn the scale wherein the destinies of humanity were trembling. And his was affection well returned. It might easily have been otherwise, for Aaron had seen his younger brother called to a dazzling elevation, living in enviable magnificence, and earning fame by " word and deed "; and then, after a momentary fusion of sympathy and of condition, forty years had poured between them a torrent of cares and joys estranging because unshared. But it was promised that Aaron, when he saw him, should be glad at heart; and the words throw a beam of exquisite light into the depths of the mighty soul which God inspired to emancipate Israel and to found His Church, by thoughts of his brother's joy on meeting him.

Let no man dream of attaining real greatness by stifling his affections. The heart is more important than the intellect; and the brief story of the Exodus has room for the yearning of Jochebed over her infant " when she saw him that he was a goodly child," for the bold inspiration of the young poetess, who " stood afar off to know what should be done to him," and now for the love of Aaron. So the Virgin, in the dread hour of her reproach, went in haste to her cousin Elizabeth. So Andrew " findeth first his own brother Simon." And so the Divine Sufferer, forsaken of God, did not forsake His Mother.

The Bible is full of domestic life. It is the theme of the greater part of Genesis, which makes the family the seed-plot of the Church. It is wisely recognised again at the moment when the larger pulse of the nation begins to beat. For the life-blood in the heart of a nation must be the blood in the hearts of men.

MOSES OBEYS.

Exodus iv. 18-31.

Moses is now commissioned: he is to go to Egypt, and Aaron is coming thence to meet him. Yet he first returns to Midian, to Jethro, who is both his employer and the head of the family, and prays him to sanction his visit to his own people.

There are duties which no family resistance can possibly cancel, and the direct command of God made it plain that this was one of them. But there are two ways of performing even the most imperative obligation, and religious people have done irreparable mischief before now, by rudeness, disregard to natural feeling and the rights of their fellow-men, under the impression that they showed their allegiance to God by outraging other ties. It is a theory for which no sanction can be found either in Holy Scripture or in common sense.

When he asks permission to visit " his brethren " we cannot say whether he ever had brothers besides Aaron, or uses the word in the same larger national sense as when we read that, forty years before, he went out unto his brethren and saw their burdens. What is to be observed is that he is reticent with respect to his vast expectations and designs.

He does not argue that, because a Divine promise must needs be fulfilled, he need not be discreet, wary, and taciturn, any more than St. Paul supposed, because the lives of his shipmates were promised to him, that it mattered nothing whether the sailors remained on board.

The decrees of God have sometimes been used to justify the recklessness of man, but never by His chosen followers. They have worked out their own salvation the more earnestly because God worked in them. And every good cause calls aloud for human energy and wisdom, all the more because its consummation is the will of God, and sooner or later is assured. Moses has unlearned his rashness.

When the Lord said unto Moses in Midian, " Go, return unto Egypt, for all the men are dead which sought thy life," there is an almost verbal resemblance to the words in which the infant Jesus is recalled from exile. We shall have to consider the typical aspect of the whole narrative, when a convenient stage is reached for pausing to survey it in its completeness. But resemblances like this have been treated with so much scorn, they have been so freely perverted into evidence of the mythical nature of the later story, that some passing allusion appears desirable. We must beware equally of both extremes. The Old Testament is tortured, and genuine prophecies are made no better than coincidences, when coincidences are exalted to all the dignity of express predictions. One can scarcely venture to speak of the death of Herod when Jesus was to return from Egypt, as being deliberately typified in the death of those who sought the life of Moses. But it is quite clear that the words in St. Matthew do intentionally point the reader back to this narrative. For, indeed, under both, there are to be recognised the same principles: that God does not thrust His servants into needless or excessive peril; and that when the life of a tyrant has really become not only a trial but a barrier, it will be removed by the King of kings. God is prudent for His heroes.

Moreover, we must recognise the lofty fitness of what is very visible in the Gospels—the coming to a head in Christ of the various experiences of the people of God; and at the recurrence, in His story, of events already known elsewhere, we need not be disquieted, as if the suspicion of a myth were now become difficult to refute; rather should we recognise the fulness of the supreme life, and its points of contact with all lives, which are but portions of its vast completeness. Who does not feel that in the world's greatest events a certain harmony and correspondence are as charming as they are in music? There is a sort of counterpoint in history. And to this answering of deep unto deep, this responsiveness of the story of Jesus to all history, our attention is silently beckoned by St. Matthew, when, without asserting any closer link between the incidents, he borrows this phrase so aptly.

A much deeper meaning underlies the profound expression which God now commands Moses to employ, and although it must await consideration at a future time, the progressive education of Moses himself is meantime to be observed. At first he is taught that the Lord is the God of their fathers, in whose descendants He is therefore interested. Then the present Israel is His people, and valued for its own sake. Now he hears, and is bidden to repeat to Pharaoh, the amazing phrase, " Israel is My son, even My firstborn: let My son go that he may serve Me; and if thou refuse to 'let him go, behold I will slay thy son, even thy firstborn." Thus it is that infant faith is led from height to height. And assuredly there never was an utterance better fitted than this to prepare human minds, in the fulness of time, for a still clearer revelation of the nearness of God to man, and for the possibility of an absolute union between the Creator and His creature.

It was on his way into Egypt, with his wife and children, that a mysterious interposition forced Zipporah reluctantly and tardily to circumcise her son.

The meaning of this strange episode lies perhaps below the surface, but very near it. Danger in some form, probably that of sickness, pressed Moses hard, and he recognised in it the displeasure of his God. The form of the narrative leads us to suppose that he had no previous consciousness of guilt, and had now to infer the nature of his offence without any explicit announcement, just as we infer it from what follows.

If so, he discerned his transgression when trouble awoke his conscience; and so did his wife Zipporah. Yet her resistance to the circumcision of their younger son was so tenacious, with such difficulty was it overcome by her husband's peril or by his command, that her tardy performance of the rite was accompanied by an insulting action and a bitter taunt. As she submitted, the Lord "let him go"; but we may perhaps conclude that the grievance continued to rankle, from the repetition of her gibe, "So she said, A bridegroom of blood art thou because of the circumcision." The words mean, "We are betrothed again in blood," and might of themselves admit a gentler, and even a tender significance; as if, in the sacrifice of a strong prejudice for her husband's sake, she felt a revival of "the kindness of her youth, the love of her espousals." For nothing removes the film from the surface of a true affection, and makes the heart aware how bright it is, so well as a great sacrifice, frankly offered for the sake of love.

But such a rendering is excluded by the action which went with her words, and they must be explained as meaning, This is the kind of husband I have wedded: these are our espousals. With such an utterance she fades almost entirely out of the story: it does not even tell how she drew back to her father; and thenceforth all we know of her is that she rejoined Moses only when the fame of his victory over Amalek had gone abroad.

Their union seems to have been an ill-assorted or at least an unprosperous one. In the tender hour when their firstborn was to be named, the bitter sense of loneliness had continued to be nearer to the heart of Moses than the glad new consciousness of paternity, and he said, "I am a stranger in a strange land." Different indeed had been the experience of Joseph, who called his "firstborn Manasseh, for God, said he, hath made me forget all my toil, and all my father's house" (Gen. xli. 51). The home-life of Moses had not made him forget that he was an exile. Even the removal of imminent death from her husband could not hush these selfish complaints of Zipporah, not because he was a father of blood to her little one, but because he was a bridegroom of blood to her own shrinking sensibilities. It is Miriam the sister, not Zipporah the wife, who gives lyrical and passionate voice to his triumph, and is mourned by the nation when she dies. Both what we read of her and what we do not read goes far to explain the insignificance of their children in history and the more startling fact that the grandson of Moses became the venal instrument of the Danites in their schismatic worship (Judges xviii. 30, R. V.).

Domestic unhappiness is a palliation, but not a justification for an unserviceable life. It is a great advantage to come into action with the dew and freshness of affection upon the soul. Yet it is not once nor twice that men have carried the message of God back from the barren desert and the lonely ways of their unhappiness to the not too happy race of man.

Now, who can fail to discern real history in all this? Is it in such a way that myth or legend would have dealt with the wife of the great deliverer? Still less conceivable is it that these should have treated Moses himself as the narrative hitherto has consistently done. At every step he is made to stumble. His first attempt was homicidal, and brought upon him forty years of exile. When the Divine commission came he drew back wilfully, as he had formerly pressed forward unsent. There is not even any suggestion offered us of Stephen's apology for his violent deed—namely, that he supposed his brethren understood how that God by his hand was giving them deliverance (Acts vii. 25). There is nothing that resembles the eulogium of the Epistle to the Hebrews upon the faith which glorified his precipitancy, like the rainbow in a torrent, because that rash blow committed him to share the affliction of the people of God, and renounced the rank of a grandson of the Pharaoh (Heb. xi. 24-5). All this is very natural, if Moses himself be in any degree responsible for the narrative. It is incredible, if the narrative were put together after the Captivity, to claim the sanction of so great a name for a newly forged hierarchical system. Such a theory could scarcely be refuted more completely, if the narrative before us were invented with the deliberate aim to overthrow it.

But in truth the failures of the good and great are written for our admonition, teaching us how inconsistent are even the best of mortals, and how weak the most resolute. Rather than forfeit his own place among the chosen people, Moses had forsaken a palace and become a proscribed fugitive; yet he had neglected to claim for his child its rightful share in the covenant, its recognition among the sons of Abraham. Perhaps procrastination, perhaps domestic opposition more potent than a king's wrath to shake his purpose, perhaps the insidious notion that one who had sacrificed so much might be at ease about slight negligences,—some such influence had left the commandment unobserved. And now, when the dream of his life was being realised at last, and he found himself the chosen instrument of God for the rebuke of one nation and the making of another, how pardonable it must have seemed to leave an unpleasant small domestic duty over until a more convenient season! How natural it still seems to merge the petty task in the high vocation, to excuse small lapses in pursuit of lofty aims! But this was the very time when God, hitherto forbearing, took him sternly to task for his neglect, because men who are especially honoured should be more obedient and reverential than their fellows. Let young men who dream of a vast career, and meanwhile indulge themselves in small obliquities, let all who cast out demons in the name of Christ, and yet work iniquity, reflect upon this chosen and long-trained, self-sacrificing and ardent servant of the Lord, whom Jehovah seeks to kill because he wilfully disobeys even a purely ceremonial precept.

Moses was not only religious, but "a man of destiny," one upon whom vast interests depended. Now, such men have often reckoned themselves exempt from the ordinary laws of conduct.*

It is not a light thing, therefore, to find God's indignant protest against the faintest shadow of a doctrine so insidious and so deadly, set in the forefront of sacred history, at the very point where national concerns and those of religion begin to touch. If our politics are to be kept pure and clean, we must learn to exact a higher

---

* "I am not an ordinary man," Napoleon used to say, "and the laws of morals and of custom were never made for me."—*Memoirs of Madame de Rémusat*, i. 91.

fidelity, and not a relaxed morality, from those who propose to sway the destinies of nations.

And now the brothers meet, embrace, and exchange confidences. As Andrew, the first disciple who brought another to Jesus, found first his own brother Simon, so was Aaron the earliest convert to the mission of Moses. And that happened which so often puts our faithlessness to shame. It had seemed very hard to break his strange tidings to the people: it was in fact very easy to address one whose love had not grown cold during their severance, who probably retained faith in the Divine purpose for which the beautiful child of the family had been so strangely preserved, and who had passed through trial and discipline unknown to us in the stern intervening years.

And when they told their marvellous story to the elders of the people, and displayed the signs, they believed; and when they heard that God had visited them in their affliction, then they bowed their heads and worshipped.

This was their preparation for the wonders that should follow: it resembled Christ's appeal, "Believest thou that I am able to do this?" or Peter's word to the impotent man, "Look on us."

For the moment the announcement had the desired effect, although too soon the early promise was succeeded by faithlessness and discontent. In this, again, the teaching of the earliest political movement on record is as fresh as if it were a tale of yesterday. The offer of emancipation stirs all hearts: the romance of liberty is beautiful beside the Nile as in the streets of Paris; but the cost has to be gradually learned; the losses displace the gains in the popular attention; the labour, the self-denial, and the self-control grow wearisome, and Israel murmurs for the flesh-pots of Egypt, much as the modern revolution reverts to a despotism. It is one thing to admire abstract freedom, but a very different thing to accept the austere conditions of the life of genuine freemen. And surely the same is true of the soul. The gospel gladdens the young convert: he bows his head and worships; but he little dreams of his long discipline, as in the forty desert years, of the solitary places through which his soul must wander, the drought, the Amalekite, the absent leader, and the temptations of the flesh. In mercy, the long future is concealed; it is enough that, like the apostles, we should consent to follow; gradually we shall obtain the courage to which the task may be revealed.

CHAPTER V.

PHARAOH REFUSES.

EXODUS v. 1-23.

AFTER forty years of obscurity and silence, Moses re-enters the magnificent halls where he had formerly turned his back upon so great a place. The rod of a shepherd is in his hand, and a lowly Hebrew by his side. Men who recognise him shake their heads, and pity or despise the fanatic who had thrown away the most dazzling prospects for a dream. But he has long since made his choice, and whatever misgivings now beset him have regard to his success with Pharaoh or with his brethren, not to the wisdom of his decision.

Nor had he reason to repent of it. The pomp of an obsequious court was a poor thing in the eyes of an ambassador of God, who entered the palace to speak such lofty words as never passed the lips of any son of Pharaoh's daughter. He was presently to become a god unto Pharaoh, with Aaron for his prophet.

In itself, his presence there was formidable. The Hebrews had been feared when he was an infant. Now their cause was espoused by a man of culture, who had allied himself with their natural leaders, and was returned with the deep and steady fire of a zeal which forty years of silence could not quench, to assert the rights of Israel as an independent people.

There is a terrible power in strong convictions, especially when supported by the sanctions of religion. Luther on one side, Loyola on the other, were mightier than kings when armed with this tremendous weapon. Yet there are forces upon which patriotism and fanaticism together break in vain. Tyranny and pride of race have also strong impelling ardours, and carry men far. Pharaoh is in earnest as well as Moses, and can act with perilous energy. And this great narrative begins the story of a nation's emancipation with a human demand, boldly made, but defeated by the pride and vigour of a startled tyrant and the tameness of a downtrodden people. The limitations of human energy are clearly exhibited before the direct interference of God begins. All that a brave man can do, when nerved by lifelong aspiration and by a sudden conviction that the hour of destiny has struck, all therefore upon which rationalism can draw, to explain the uprising of Israel, is exhibited in this preliminary attempt, this first demand of Moses.

Menephtah was no doubt the new Pharaoh whom the brothers accosted so boldly. What we glean of him elsewhere is highly suggestive of some grave event left unrecorded, exhibiting to us a man of uncontrollable temper yet of broken courage, a ruthless, godless, daunted man. There is a legend that he once hurled his spear at the Nile when its floods rose too high, and was punished with ten years of blindness. In the Libyan war, after fixing a time when he should join his vanguard, with the main army, a celestial vision forbade him to keep his word in person, and the victory was gained by his lieutenants. In another war, he boasts of having slaughtered the people and set fire to them, and netted the entire country as men net birds. Forty years then elapse without war and without any great buildings; there are seditions and internal troubles, and the dynasty closes with his son.* All this is exactly what we should expect, if a series of tremendous blows had depopulated a country, abolished an army, and removed two millions of the working classes in one mass.

But it will be understood that this identification, concerning which there is now a very general consent of competent authorities, implies that the Pharaoh was not himself engulfed with his army. Nothing is on the other side except a poetic assertion in Psalm cxxxvi. 15, which is not that God destroyed, but that He "shook off" Pharaoh and his host in the Red Sea, because His mercy endureth for ever.

To this king, then, whose audacious family

* Robinson, "The Pharaohs of the Bondage."

had usurped the symbols of deity for its head-dress, and whose father boasted that in battle "he became like the god Mentu" and "was as Baal," the brothers came as yet without miracle, with no credentials except from slaves, and said, "Thus saith Jehovah, the God of Israel, Let My people go, that they may hold a feast unto Me in the wilderness." The issue was distinctly raised: did Israel belong to Jehovah or to the king? And Pharaoh answered, with equal decision, "Who is Jehovah, that I should hearken unto His voice? I know not Jehovah, and what is more, I will not let Israel go."

Now, the ignorance of the king concerning Jehovah was almost or quite blameless: the fault was in his practical refusal to inquire. Jehovah was no concern of his: without waiting for information, he at once decided that his grasp on his captives should not relax. And his second fault, which led to this, was the same grinding oppression of the helpless which for eighty years already had brought upon his nation the guilt of blood. Crowned and national cupidity, the resolution to wring from their slaves the last effort consistent with existence, such greed as took offence at even the momentary pause of hope while Moses pleaded, because "the people of the land are many, and ye make them rest from their burdens,"—these shut their hearts against reason and religion, and therefore God presently hardened those same hearts against natural misgiving and dread and awe-stricken submission to His judgments.

For it was against religion also that he was unyielding. In his ample Pantheon there was room at least for the possibility of the entrance of the Hebrew God, and in refusing to the subject people, without investigation, leisure for any worship, the king outraged not only humanity, but Heaven.

The brothers proceed to declare that they have themselves met with the deity, and there must have been many in the court who could attest at least the sincerity of Moses; they ask for liberty to spend a day in journeying outward and another in returning, with a day between for their worship, and warn the king of the much greater loss to himself which may be involved in vengeance upon refusal, either by war or pestilence. But the contemptuous answer utterly ignores religion: "Wherefore do ye, Moses and Aaron, loose the people from their work? Get ye unto your burdens."

And his counter-measures are taken without loss of time: "that same day" the order goes out to exact the regular quantity of brick, but supply no straw for binding it together. It is a pitiless mandate, and illustrates the fact, very natural though often forgotten, that men as a rule cannot lose sight of the religious value of their fellow-men, and continue to respect or pity them as before. We do not deny that men who professed religion have perpetrated nameless cruelties, nor that unbelievers have been humane, sometimes with a pathetic energy, a tenacious grasp on the virtue still possible to those who have no Heaven to serve. But it is plain that the average man will despise his brother, and his brother's rights, just in proportion as the Divine sanctions of those rights fade away, and nothing remains to be respected but the culture, power, and affluence which the victim lacks. "I know not Israel's God" is a sure prelude to the refusal to let Israel go, and even to the cruelty which beats the slave who fails to render impossible obedience.

"They be idle, therefore they cry, saying, Let us go and sacrifice to our God." And still there are men who hold the same opinion, that time spent in devotion is wasted, as regards the duties of real life. In truth, religion means freshness, elasticity, and hope: a man will be not slothful in business, but fervent in spirit, if he serves the Lord. But perhaps immortal hope, and the knowledge that there is One Who shall break all prison bars and let the oppressed go free, are not the best narcotics to drug down the soul of a man into the monotonous tameness of a slave.

In the tenth verse we read that the Egyptian taskmasters and the officers combined to urge the people to their aggravated labours. And by the fourteenth verse we find that the latter officials were Hebrew officers whom Pharaoh's taskmasters had set over them.

So that we have here one of the surest and worst effects of slavery—namely, the demoralisation of the oppressed, the readiness of average men, who can obtain for themselves a little relief, to do so at their brethren's cost. These officials were scribes, "writers"; their business was to register the amount of labour due, and actually rendered. These were doubtless the more comfortable class, of whom we read afterwards that they possessed property, for their cattle escaped the murrain and their trees the hail. And they had the means of acquiring quite sufficient skill to justify whatever is recorded of the works done in the construction of the tabernacle. The time is long past when scepticism found support for its incredulity in these details.

One advantage of the last sharp agony of persecution was that it finally detached this official class from the Egyptian interest, and welded Israel into a homogeneous people, with officers already provided. For, when the supply of bricks came short, these officials were beaten, and, as if no cause of the failure were palpable, they were asked, with a malicious chuckle, "Wherefore have ye not fulfilled your task both yesterday and to-day, as heretofore?" And when they explain to Pharaoh, in words already expressive of their alienation, that the fault is with "thine own people," they are repulsed with insult, and made to feel themselves in evil case. For indeed they needed to be chastised for their forgetfulness of God. How soon would their hearts have turned back, how much more bitter yet would have been their complaints in the desert, if it were not for this last experience! But if judgment began with them, what should presently be the fate of their oppressors?

Their broken spirit shows itself by murmuring, not against Pharaoh, but against Moses and Aaron, who at least had striven to help them. Here, as in the whole story, there is not a trace of either the lofty spirit which could have evolved the Mosaic law, or the hero-worship of a later age.

It is written that Moses, hearing their reproaches, "returned unto the Lord," although no visible shrine, no consecrated place of worship, can be thought of.

What is involved is the consecration which the heart bestows upon any place of privacy and prayer, where, in shutting out the world, the soul is aware of the special nearness of its King. In one sense we never leave Him, never return to Him. In another sense, by direct address of the attention and the will, we enter into His presence; we find Him in the midst of us, Who is everywhere. And all ceremonial consecrations do their office by helping us to realise and act upon the presence of Him in Whom, even when He is forgotten, we live and move and have our being. Therefore in the deepest sense each man consecrates or desecrates for himself his own place of prayer. There is a city where the Divine presence saturates every consciousness with rapture. And the seer beheld no temple therein, for the Lord God the Almighty, and the Lamb, are the temple of it.

Startling to our notions of reverence are the words in which Moses addresses God. "Lord, why hast Thou evil entreated this people? Why is it that Thou hast sent me? for since I came to Pharaoh to speak in Thy name, he hath evil entreated this people; neither hast Thou delivered Thy people at all." It is almost as if his faith had utterly given way, like that of the Psalmist when he saw the wicked in great prosperity, while waters of a full cup were wrung out by the people of God (Ps. lxxiii. 3, 10). And there is always a dangerous moment when the first glow of enthusiasm burns down, and we realise how long the process, how bitter the disappointments, by which even a scanty measure of success must be obtained. Yet God had expressly warned Moses that Pharaoh would not release them until Egypt had been smitten with all His plagues. But the warning passed unapprehended, as we let many a truth pass, intellectually accepted it is true, but only as a theorem, a vague and abstract formula. As we know that we must die, that worldly pleasures are brief and unreal, and that sin draws evil in its train, yet wonder when these phrases become solid and practical in our experience, so, in the first flush and wonder of the promised emancipation, Moses had forgotten the predicted interval of trial.

His words would have been profane and irreverent indeed but for one redeeming quality. They were addressed to God Himself. Whenever the people murmured, Moses turned for help to Him Who reckons the most unconventional and daring appeal to Him far better than the most ceremonious phrases in which men cover their unbelief: "Lord, wherefore hast Thou evil entreated this people?" is in reality a much more pious utterance than "I will not ask, neither will I tempt the Lord." Wherefore Moses receives large encouragement, although no formal answer is vouchsafed to his daring question.

Even so, in our dangers, our torturing illnesses, and many a crisis which breaks through all the crust of forms and conventionalities, God may perhaps recognise a true appeal to Him, in words which only scandalise the orthodoxy of the formal and precise. In the bold rejoinder of the Syro-Phœnician woman He recognised great faith. His disciples would simply have sent her away as clamorous.

Moses had again failed, even though Divinely commissioned, in the work of emancipating Israel, and thereupon he had cried to the Lord Himself to undertake the work. This abortive attempt, however, was far from useless: it taught humility and patience to the leader, and it pressed the nation together, as in a vice, by the weight of a common burden, now become intolerable. At the same moment, the iniquity of the tyrant was filled up.

But the Lord did not explain this, in answer to the remonstrance of Moses. Many things happen, for which no distinct verbal explanation is possible, many things of which the deep spiritual fitness cannot be expressed in words. Experience is the true commentator upon Providence, if only because the slow building of character is more to God than either the hasting forward of deliverance or the clearing away of intellectual mists. And it is only as we take His yoke upon us that we truly learn of Him. Yet much is implied, if not spoken out, in the words, "Now (because the time is ripe) shalt thou see what I will do to Pharaoh (I, because others have failed); for by a strong hand shall he let them go, and by a strong hand shall he drive them out of the land." It is under the weight of the "strong hand" of God Himself that the tyrant must either bend or break.

Similar to this is the explanation of many delays in answering our prayer, of the strange raising up of tyrants and demagogues, and of much else that perplexes Christians in history and in their own experience. These events develop human character, for good or evil. And they give scope for the revealing of the fulness of the power which rescues. We have no means of measuring the supernatural force which overcomes but by the amount of the resistance offered. And if all good things came to us easily and at once, we should not become aware of the horrible pit, our rescue from which demands gratitude. The Israelites would not have sung a hymn of such fervent gratitude when the sea was crossed, if they had not known the weight of slavery and the anguish of suspense. And in heaven the redeemed who have come out of great tribulation sing the song of Moses and of the Lamb.

Fresh air, a balmy wind, a bright blue sky—which of us feels a thrill of conscious exultation for these cheap delights? The released prisoner, the restored invalid, feels it:

"The common earth, the air, the skies,
To him are opening paradise."

Even so should Israel be taught to value deliverance. And now the process could begin.

CHAPTER VI.

THE ENCOURAGEMENT OF MOSES.

EXODUS vi. 1-30.

WE have seen that the name Jehovah expresses not a philosophic meditation, but the most bracing and reassuring truth—viz., that an immutable and independent Being sustains His people; and this great title is therefore reaffirmed with emphasis in the hour of mortal discouragement. It is added that their fathers knew God by the name of God Almighty, but by His name Jehovah was He not known, or made known, unto them. Now, it is quite clear that they were not utterly ignorant of this title, for no such theory as that it was hitherto mentioned by anticipation only, can explain the first syllable in the name of the mother of Moses himself, nor the assertion that in the time of Seth men began to call upon the name of Jehovah (Gen. iv. 26), nor the name of the hill of Abraham's sacrifice, Jehovah-jireh (Gen. xxii. 14). Yet the statement cannot be made available for the purpose of any reasonable and moderate scepticism, since the sceptical theory demands a belief in successive redactions of the work in which an error so gross could not have escaped detection.

And the true explanation is that this Name was now, for the first time, to be realised as a sustaining power. The patriarchs had known the name; how its fitness should be realised: God should be known by it. They had drawn support and comfort from that simpler view of the Divine protection which said, "I am the Almighty God: walk before Me and be thou perfect" (Gen. xvii. 1). But thenceforth all the experience of the past was to reinforce the energies of the present, and men were to remember that their promises came from One who cannot change. Others, like Abraham, had been stronger in faith than Moses. But faith is not the same as insight, and Moses was the greatest of the prophets (Deut. xxxiv. 10). To him, therefore, it was given to confirm the courage of his nation by this exalting thought of God. And the Lord proceeds to state what His promises to the patriarchs were, and joins together (as we should do) the assurance of His compassionate heart and of His inviolable pledges: "I have heard the groaning of the children of Israel, ... and I have remembered My covenant."

It has been the same, in turn, with every new revelation of the Divine. The new was implicit in the old, but when enforced, unfolded, re-applied, men found it charged with unsuspected meaning and power, and as full of vitality and development as a handful of dry seeds when thrown into congenial soil. So it was pre-eminently with the doctrine of the Messiah. It will be the same hereafter with the doctrine of the kingdom of peace and the reign of the saints on earth. Some day men will smile at our crude theories and ignorant controversies about the Millennium. We, meantime, possess the saving knowledge of Christ amid many perplexities and obscurities. And so the patriarchs, who knew God Almighty, but not by His name Jehovah, were not lost for want of the knowledge of His name, but saved by faith in Him, in the living Being to Whom all these names belong, and Who shall yet write upon the brows of His people some new name, hitherto undreamed by the ripest of the saints and the purest of the Churches. Meantime, let us learn the lessons of tolerance for other men's ignorance, remembering the ignorance of the father of the faithful, tolerance for difference of views, remembering how the unusual and rare name of God was really the precursor of a brighter revelation, and yet again, when our hearts are faint with longing for new light, and weary to death of the babbling of old words, let us learn a sober and cautious reconsideration, lest perhaps the very truth needed for altered circumstance and changing problem may lie, unheeded and dormant, among the dusty old phrases from which we turn away despairingly. Moreover, since the fathers knew the name Jehovah, yet gained from it no special knowledge of God, such as they had from His Almightiness, we are taught that discernment is often more at fault than revelation. To the quick perception and plastic imagination of the artist, our world reveals what the boor will never see. And the saint finds, in the homely and familiar words of Scripture, revelations for His soul that are unknown to common men. Receptivity is what we need far more than revelation.

Again is Moses bidden to appeal to the faith of his countrymen, by a solemn repetition of the Divine promise. If the tyranny is great, they shall be redeemed with a stretched out arm, that is to say, with a palpable interposition of the power of God, "and with great judgments." It is the first appearance in Scripture of this phrase, afterwards so common. Not mere vengeance upon enemies or vindication of subjects is in question: the thought is that of a deliberate weighing of merits, and rendering out of measured penalties. Now, the Egyptian mythology had a very clear and solemn view of judgment after death. If king and people had grown cruel, it was because they failed to realise remote punishments, and did not believe in present judgments, here, in this life. But there is a God that judgeth in the earth. Not always, for mercy rejoiceth over judgment. We may still pray, "Enter not into judgment with Thy servants, O Lord, for in Thy sight shall no man living be justified." But when men resist warnings, then retribution begins even here. Sometimes it comes in plague and overthrow, sometimes in the worse form of a heart made fat, the decay of sensibilities abused, the dying out of spiritual faculty. Pharaoh was to experience both, the hardening of his heart and the ruin of his fortunes.

It is added, "I will take you to Me for a people, and I will be to you for a God." This is the language, not of a mere purpose, a will that has resolved to vindicate the right, but of affection. God is about to adopt Israel to Himself, and the same favour which belonged to rare individuals in the old time is now offered to a whole nation. Just as the heart of each man is gradually educated, learning first to love a parent and a family, and so led on to national patriotism, and at last to a world-wide philanthropy, so was the religious conscience of mankind awakened to believe that Abraham might be the friend of God, and then that His oath might be confirmed unto the children, and then that He could take Israel to Himself for a people, and at last that God loved the world.

It is not religion to think that God condescends merely to save us. He cares for us. He takes us to Himself. He gives Himself away to us, in return, to be our God.

Such a revelation ought to have been more to Israel than any pledge of certain specified advantages. It was meant to be a silken tie, a golden clasp, to draw together the almighty Heart and the hearts of these downtrodden slaves. Something within Him desires their little human love; they shall be to Him for a people. So He said again, "My son, give Me thine heart." And so, when He carried to the uttermost these unsought, unhoped for, and, alas! unwelcomed overtures of condescension, and came among us, He would have gathered, as a hen gathers her chickens under her wings, those who would not. It is not man who conceives, from definite services received, the wild hope of some spark of real affection in the bosom of the Eternal and Mysterious One. It is not man, amid the lavish joys and splendours of creation, who conceives the notion of a supreme Heart, as the explanation of the universe. It is God Himself Who says, "I will take you to Me for a people, and I will be to you a God."

Nor is it human conversion that begins the process, but a Divine covenant and pledge, by which God would fain convert us to Himself; even as the first disciples did not accost Jesus, but He turned and spoke to them the first question and the first invitation: "What seek ye? . . . Come, and ye shall see."

To-day, the choice of the civilised world has to be made between a mechanical universe and a revealed love, for no third possibility survives.

This promise establishes a relationship, which God never afterwards cancelled. Human unbelief rejected its benefits, and chilled the mutual sympathies which it involved; but the fact always remained, and in their darkest hour they could appeal to God to remember His covenant and the oath which He sware.

And this same assurance belongs to us. We are not to become good, or desirous of goodness, in order that God may requite with affection our virtues or our wistfulness. Rather we are to arise and come to our Father, and to call Him Father, although we are not worthy to be called His sons. We are to remember how Jesus said, "If ye being evil know how to give good gifts unto your children, how much more shall your heavenly Father give His Holy Spirit to them that ask Him!" and to learn that He is the Father of those who are evil, and even of those who are still unpardoned, as He said again, "If ye forgive not . . . neither will your heavenly Father forgive you."

Much controversy about the universal Fatherhood of God would be assuaged if men reflected upon the significant distinction which our Saviour drew between His Fatherhood and our sonship, the one always a reality of the Divine affection, the other only a possibility, for human enjoyment or rejection: "Love your enemies, and pray for them that persecute you, that ye may be sons of your Father Which is in heaven" (Matt. v. 45). There is no encouragement to presumption in the assertion of the Divine Fatherhood upon such terms. For it speaks of a love which is real and deep without being feeble and indiscriminate. It appeals to faith because there is an absolute fact to lean upon, and to energy because privilege is conditional. It reminds us that our relationship is like that of the ancient Israel,—that we are in a covenant, as they were, but that the carcases of many of them fell in the wilderness; although God had taken them for a people, and was to them a God, and said, "Israel is My son, even My firstborn."

It is added that faith shall develop into knowledge. Moses is to assure them now that they "shall know" hereafter that the Lord is Jehovah their God. And this, too, is a universal law, that we shall know if we follow on to know: that the trial of our faith worketh patience, and patience experience, and we have so dim and vague an apprehension of Divine realities, chiefly because we have made but little trial, and have not tasted and seen that the Lord is gracious.

In this respect, as in so many more, religion is analogous with nature. The squalor of the savage could be civilised, and the distorted and absurd conceptions of mediæval science could be corrected, only by experiment, persistently and wisely carried out.

And it is so in religion: its true evidence is unknown to those who never bore its yoke; it is open to just such raillery and rejection as they who will not love can pour upon domestic affection and the sacred ties of family life; but, like these, it vindicates itself, in the rest of their souls, to those who will take the yoke and learn. And its best wisdom is not of the cunning brain but of the open heart, that wisdom from above, which is first pure, then peaceable, gentle, and easy to be entreated.

And thus, while God leads Israel, they shall know that He is Jehovah, and true to His highest revelations of Himself.

All this they heard, and also, to define their hope and brighten it, the promise of Palestine was repeated; but they hearkened not unto Moses for anguish of spirit and for cruel bondage. Thus the body often holds the spirit down, and kindly allowance is made by Him Who knoweth our frame and remembereth that we are dust, and Who, in the hour of His own agony, found the excuse for His unsympathising followers that the spirit was willing although the flesh was weak. So when Elijah made request for himself that he might die, in the utter reaction which followed his triumph on Carmel and his wild race to Jezreel, the good Physician did not dazzle him with new splendours of revelation until after he had slept, and eaten miraculous food, and a second time slept and eaten.

But if the anguish of the body excuses much weakness of the spirit, it follows, on the other hand, that men are responsible to God for that heavy weight which is laid upon the spirit by pampered and luxurious bodies, incapable of self-sacrifice, rebellious against the lightest of His demands. It is suggestive, that Moses, when sent again to Pharaoh, objected, as at first: "Behold, the children of Israel have not hearkened unto me; how then shall Pharaoh hear me, who am of uncircumcised lips?"

Every new hope, every great inspiration which calls the heroes of God to a fresh attack upon the powers of Satan, is checked and hindered more by the coldness of the Church than by the hostility of the world. That hostility is expected, and can be defied. But the infidelity of the faithful is appalling indeed.

We read with wonder the great things which Christ has promised to believing prayer, and, at the same time, although we know painfully that we have never claimed and dare not claim these promises, we wonder equally at the foreboding question, "When the Son of Man cometh, shall He find the faith (faith in its fulness) on the earth?" (Luke xviii. 8). But we ought to remember that our own low standard helps to form the standard of attainment for the Church at large—that when one member suffers, all the members suffer with it—that many a large sacrifice would be readily made for Christ, at this hour, if only ease and pleasure were at stake, which is refused because it is too hard to be called well-meaning enthusiasts by those who ought to glorify God in such attainment, as the first brethren did in the zeal and the gifts of Paul.

The vast mountains raise their heads above mountain ranges which encompass them; and it is not when the level of the whole Church is low, that giants of faith and of attainment may be hoped for. Nay, Christ stipulates for the agreement of two or three, to kindle and make effectual the prayers which shall avail.

For the purification of our cities, for the shaming of our legislation until it fears God as much as a vested interest, for the reunion of those who worship the same Lord, for the conversion of the world, and first of all for the conversion of the Church, heroic forces are demanded. But all the tendency of our half-hearted, abject, semi-Christianity is to repress everything that is unconventional, abnormal, likely to embroil us with our natural enemy, the world; and who can doubt that, when the secrets of all hearts shall be revealed, we shall know of many an aspiring soul, in which the sacred fire had begun to burn, which sank back into lethargy and the commonplace, murmuring in its despair, "Behold, the children of Israel have not hearkened unto me; how then shall Pharaoh hear me?"

It was the last fear which ever shook the great heart of the emancipator Moses.

At the beginning of the grand historical work, of which all this has been the prelude, there is set the pedigree of Moses and Aaron, according to "the heads of their fathers' houses,"—an epithet which indicates a subdivision of the "family," as the family is a subdivision of the tribe. Of the sons of Jacob, Reuben and Simeon are mentioned, to put Levi in his natural third place. And from Levi to Moses only four generations are mentioned, favouring somewhat the briefer scheme of chronology which makes four centuries cover all the time from Abraham, and not the captivity alone. But it is certain that this is a mere recapitulation of the more important links in the genealogy. In Num. xxvi. 58, 59, six generations are reckoned instead of four; in 1 Chron. ii. 3 there are seven generations; and elsewhere in the same book (vi. 22) there are ten. It is well known that similar omissions of obscure or unworthy links occur in St. Matthew's pedigree of our Lord, although some stress is there laid upon the recurrent division into fourteens. And it is absurd to found any argument against the trustworthiness of the narrative upon a phenomenon so frequent, and so sure to be avoided by a forger, or to be corrected by an unscrupulous editor. In point of fact, nothing is less likely to have occurred, if the narrative were a late invention.

Neither, in that case, would the birth of the great emancipator be ascribed to the union of Amram with his father's sister, for such marriages were distinctly forbidden by the law (Lev. xviii. 14).

Nor would the names of the children of the founder of the nation be omitted, while those of Aaron are recorded, unless we were dealing with genuine history, which knows that the sons of Aaron inherited the lawful priesthood, while the descendants of Moses were the jealous founders of a mischievous schism (Judges xviii. 30, R. V.).

Nor again, if this were a religious romance, designed to animate the nation in its later struggles, should we read of the hesitation and the fears of a leader " of uncircumcised lips," instead of the trumpet-like calls to action of a noble champion.

Nor does the broken-spirited meanness of Israel at all resemble the conception, popular in every nation, of a virtuous and heroic antiquity, a golden age. It is indeed impossible to reconcile the motives and the date to which this narrative is ascribed by some, with the plain phenomena, with the narrative itself.

Nor is it easy to understand why the Lord, Who speaks of bringing out " My hosts, My people, the children of Israel " (vii. 4, etc.), should never in the Pentateuch be called the Lord of Hosts, if that title were in common use when it was written; for no epithet would better suit the song of Miriam or the poetry of the Fifth Book.

When Moses complained that he was of uncircumcised lips, the Lord announced that He had already made His servant as a god unto Pharaoh, having armed him, even then, with the terrors which are soon to shake the tyrant's soul.

It is suggestive and natural that his very education in a court should render him fastidious, less willing than a rougher man might have been to appear before the king after forty years of retirement, and feeling almost physically incapable of speaking what he felt so deeply, in words that would satisfy his own judgment. Yet God had endowed him, even then, with a supernatural power far greater than any facility of expression. In his weakness he would thus be made strong; and the less fit he was to assert for himself any ascendency over Pharaoh, the more signal would be the victory of his Lord, when he became " very great in the land of Egypt, in the sight of Pharaoh's servants, and in the sight of the people " (xi. 3).

As a proof of this mastery he was from the first to speak to the haughty king through his brother, as a god through some prophet, being too great to reveal himself directly. It is a memorable phrase; and so lofty an assertion could never, in the myth of a later period, have been ascribed to an origin so lowly as the reluctance of Moses to expose his deficiency in elocution.

Therefore he should henceforth be emboldened by the assurance of qualification bestowed already: not only by the hope of help and achievement yet to come, but by the certainty of present endowment. And so should each of us, in his degree, be bold, who have gifts differing according to the grace given unto us.

It is certain that every living soul has at least one talent, and is bound to improve it. But how many of us remember that this loan implies a commission from God, as real as that of prophet and deliverer, and that nothing but our own default can prevent it from being, at the last, received again with usury?

The same bravery, the same confidence when standing where his Captain has planted him, should inspire the prophet, and him that giveth alms, and him that showeth mercy; for all are members in one body, and therefore animated by one invincible Spirit from above (Rom. xii. 4-9).

The endowment thus given to Moses made him " as a god " to Pharaoh.

We must not take this to mean only that he had a prophet or spokesman, or that he was made formidable, but that the peculiar nature of his prowess would be felt. It was not his own strength. The supernatural would become visible in him. He who boasted " I know not Jehovah " would come to crouch before Him in His agent, and humble himself to the man whom once he contemptuously ordered back to his burdens, with the abject prayer, " Forgive, I pray thee, my sin only this once, and entreat Jehovah your God that He may take away from me this death only."

Now, every consecrated power may bear witness to the Lord: it is possible to do all to the glory of God. Not that every separate action will be ascribed to a preternatural source, but the sum total of the effect produced by a holy life will be sacred. He who said, "I have made thee a god unto Pharaoh," says of all believers, "I in them, and Thou, Father, in Me, that the world may know that Thou hast sent Me."

CHAPTER VII.

THE HARDENING OF PHARAOH'S HEART.

Exodus vii. 3-13.

When Moses received his commission, at the bush, words were spoken which are now repeated with more emphasis, and which have to be considered carefully. For probably no statement of Scripture has excited fiercer criticism, more exultation of enemies and perplexity of friends, than that the Lord said, "I will harden Pharaoh's heart, and he shall not let the people go," and that in consequence of this Divine act Pharaoh sinned and suffered. Just because the words are startling, it is unjust to quote them without careful examination of the context, both in the prediction and the fulfilment. When all is weighed, compared, and harmonised, it will at last be possible to draw a just conclusion. And although it may happen long before then, that the objector will charge us with special pleading, yet he will be the special pleader himself, if he seeks to hurry us, by prejudice or passion, to give a verdict which is based upon less than all the evidence, patiently weighed.

Let us in the first place find out how soon this dreadful process began; when was it that God fulfilled His threat, and hardened, in any sense whatever, the heart of Pharaoh? Did He step in at the beginning, and render the unhappy king incapable of weighing the remonstrances which He then performed the cruel mockery of addressing to him? Were these as insincere and futile as if one bade the avalanche to pause which his own act had started down the icy slopes? Was Pharaoh as little responsible for his pursuit of Israel as his horses were—being, like them, the blind agents of a superior force? We do not find it so. In the fifth chapter, when a demand is made, without any sustaining miracle, simply appealing to the conscience of the ruler, there is no mention of any such process, despite the insults with which Pharaoh then assails both the messengers and Jehovah Himself, Whom he knows not. In the seventh chapter there is clear evidence that the process is yet unaccomplished; for, speaking of an act still future, it declares, "I will harden Pharaoh's heart, and multiply My signs and My wonders in the land of Egypt" (vii. 3). And this terrible act is not connected with the remonstrances and warnings of God, but entirely with the increasing pressure of the miracles.

The exact period is marked when the hand of doom closed upon the tyrant. It is not where the Authorised Version places it. When the magicians imitated the earlier signs of Moses, "his heart was strong," but the original does not bear out the assertion that at this time the Lord made it so by any judicial act of His (vii. 13). That only comes with the sixth plague; and the course of events may be traced, fairly well, by the help of the margin of the Revised Version.

After the plague of blood "Pharaoh's heart was strong" ("hardened"), and this is distinctly ascribed to his own action, because "he set his heart even to this" (vii. 22, 23).

After the second plague, it was still he himself who "made his heart heavy" (viii. 15).

After the third plague the magicians warned him that the very finger of some god was upon him indeed: their rivalry, which hitherto might have been somewhat of a palliation for his obstinacy, was now ended; but yet "his heart was strong" (viii. 19).

Again, after the fourth plague he "made his heart heavy"; and it "was heavy" after the fifth plague (viii. 32, ix. 7).

Only thenceforward comes the judicial infatuation upon him who has resolutely infatuated himself hitherto.

But when five warnings and penalties have spent their force in vain, when personal agony is inflicted in the plague of boils, and the magicians in particular cannot stand before him through their pain, would it have been proof of virtuous contrition if he had yielded then? If he had needed evidence, it was given to him long before. Submission now would have meant prudence, not penitence; and it was against prudence, not penitence, that he was hardened. Because he had resisted evidence, experience, and even the testimony of his own magicians, he was therefore stiffened against the grudging and unworthy concessions which must otherwise have been wrested from him, as a wild beast will turn and fly from fire. He was henceforth himself to become an evidence and a portent; and so "The Lord made strong the heart of Pharaoh, and he hearkened not unto them" (ix. 12). It was an awful doom, but it is not open to the attacks so often made upon it. It only means that for him the last five plagues were not disciplinary, but wholly penal.

Nay, it stops short of asserting even this: they might still have appealed to his reason; they were only not allowed to crush him by the agency of terror. Not once is it asserted that God hardened his heart against any nobler impulse than alarm, and desire to evade danger and death. We see clearly this meaning in the phrase, when it is applied to his army entering the Red Sea: "I will make strong the hearts of the Egyptians, and they shall go in" (xiv. 17). It needed no greater moral turpitude to pursue the Hebrews over the sands than on the shore, but it certainly required more hardihood. But the unpursued departure which the good-will of Egypt refused, their common sense was not allowed to grant. Callousness was followed by infatuation, as even the pagans felt that whom God wills to ruin He first drives mad.

This explanation implies that to harden Pharaoh's heart was to inspire him, not with wickedness, but with nerve.

And as far as the original language helps us at all, it decidedly supports this view. Three different expressions have been unhappily rendered by the same English word, to harden; but they may be discriminated throughout the narrative in Exodus, by the margin of the Revised Version.

One word, which commonly appears without any marginal explanation, is the same which is employed elsewhere about "the cause which is too *hard* for" minor judges (Deut. i. 17, *cf.* xv. 18, etc.). Now, this word is found (vii. 13) in the second threat that "I will harden Pharaoh's heart," and in the account which was to be given to posterity of how "Pharaoh hardened himself to let us go" (xiii. 15). And it is said likewise of Sihon, king of Heshbon, that he "would not let us pass by him, for the Lord thy God hardened his spirit and made his heart strong" (Deut. ii. 30). But since it does not occur anywhere in all the narrative of what God actually did with Pharaoh, it is only just to interpret this phrase in the prediction by what we read elsewhere of the manner of its fulfilment.

The second word is explained in the margin as meaning *to make strong*. Already God had employed it when He said "I will *make strong* his heart" (iv. 21), and this is the term used of the first fulfilment of the menace, after the sixth plague (ix. 12). God is not said to interfere again after the seventh, which had few special terrors for Pharaoh himself; but from henceforth the expression "to make *strong*" alternates with the phrase "to make *heavy*." "Go in unto Pharaoh, for I have made heavy his heart and the heart of his servants, that I might show these My signs in the midst of them" (x. 1).

It may be safely assumed that these two expressions cover between them all that is asserted of the judicial action of God in preventing a recoil of Pharaoh from his calamities. Now, the strengthening of a heart, however punitive and disastrous when a man's will is evil (just as the strengthening of his arm is disastrous then), has in itself no immorality inherent. It is a thing as often good as bad,—as when Israel and Joshua are exhorted to "Be *strong* and of a good courage" (Deut. xxxi. 6, 7, 23), and when the angel laid his hand upon Daniel and said, "Be strong, yea, be strong" (Dan. x. 19). In these passages the phrase is identical with that which describes the process by which Pharaoh was prevented from cowering under the tremendous blows he had provoked.

The other expression is to make heavy or dull. Thus "the eyes of Israel were *heavy* with age" (Gen. xlviii. 10), and as we speak of a *weight* of honour, equally with the heaviness of a dull man, so we are twice commanded, "Make heavy (honour) thy father and thy mother"; and the Lord declares, "I will make Myself heavy (get Me honour) upon Pharaoh" (Deut. v. 16, Exod. xx. 12, xiv. 4, 17, 18). In these latter references it will be observed that the making "strong" the heart of Pharaoh, and the making "Myself heavy" are so connected as almost to show a design of indicating how far is either expression from conveying the notion of immorality, infused into a human heart by God. For one of the two phrases which have been thus interpreted is still applied to Pharaoh; but the other (and the more sinister, as we should think, when thus applied) is appropriated by God to Himself: He makes Himself heavy.

It is also a curious and significant coincidence that the same word was used of the burdens that were made *heavy* when first they claimed their freedom, which is now used of the treatment of the heart of their oppressor (v. 9).

It appears, then, that the Lord is never said to debauch Pharaoh's heart, but only to strengthen it against prudence and to make it dull; that the words used do not express the infusion of evil passion, but the animation of a resolute courage, and the overclouding of a natural discernment; and, above all, that every one of the three words, to make hard, to make strong, and to make heavy, is employed to express Pharaoh's own treatment of himself, before it is applied to any work of God, as actually taking place already.

Nevertheless, there is a solemn warning for all time, in the assertion that what he at first chose, the vengeance of God afterward chose for him. For indeed the same process, working more slowly but on identical lines, is constantly seen in the hardening effect of vicious habit. The gambler did not mean to stake all his fortune upon one chance, when first he timidly laid down a paltry stake; nor has he changed his mind since then as to the imprudence of such a hazard. The drunkard, the murderer himself, is a man who at first did evil as far as he dared, and afterwards dared to do evil which he would once have shuddered at.

Let no man assume that prudence will always save him from ruinous excess, if respect for righteousness cannot withhold him from those first compliances which sap the will, destroy the restraint of self-respect, wear away the horror of great wickedness by familiarity with the same guilt in its lesser phases, and, above all, forfeit the enlightenment and calmness of judgment which come from the Holy Spirit of God, Who is the Spirit of wisdom and of counsel, and makes men to be of quick understanding in the fear of the Lord.

Let no man think that the fear of damnation will bring him to the mercy-seat at last, if the burden and gloom of being "condemned already" cannot now bend his will. "Even as they refused to have God in their knowledge, God gave them up unto a reprobate mind" (Rom. 1. 28). "I gave them My statutes and showed them My judgments, which if a man do, he shall even live in them. . . I gave them statutes that were not good, and judgments wherein they should not live" (Ezek. xx. 11, 25).

This is the inevitable law, the law of a confused and darkened judgment, a heart made heavy and ears shut, a conscience seared, an infatuated will kicking against the pricks, and heaping to itself wrath against the day of wrath. Wilful sin is always a challenge to God, and it is avenged by the obscuring of the lamp of God in the soul. Now, a part of His guiding light is prudence; and it is possible that men who will not be warned by the fear of injury to their conscience, such as they suppose that Pharaoh suffered, may be sobered by the danger of such derangement of their intellectual efficiency as really befel him.

In this sense men are, at last, impelled blindly to their fate (and this is a judicial act of God, although it comes in the course of nature), but first they launch themselves upon the slope which grows steeper at every downward step, until arrest is impossible.

On the other hand, every act of obedience helps to release the will from its entanglement, and to clear the judgment which has grown dull, anointing the eyes with eye-salve that they may see. Not in vain is the assertion of the bondage of the sinner and the glorious liberty of the children of God.

A second time, then, Moses presented himself before Pharaoh with his demands; and, as he had been forewarned, he was now challenged to give a sign in proof of his commission from a god.

And the demand was treated as reasonable; a sign was given, and a menacing one. The peaceable rod of the shepherd, a fit symbol of the meek man who bore it, became a serpent* before the king, as Moses was to become destructive to his realm. But when the wise men of Egypt and the enchanters were called, they did likewise; and although a marvel was added which incontestably declared the superior power of the Deity Whom Aaron represented, yet their rivalry sufficed to make strong the heart of Pharaoh, and he would not let the people go. The issue was now knit: the result would be more signal than if the quarrel were decided at one blow, and upon all the gods of Egypt the Lord would exercise vengeance.

What are we to think of the authentification of a religion by a sign? Beyond doubt, Jesus recognised this aspect of His own miracles, when He said, "If I had not done among them the works that none other man did, they had not had sin" (John xv. 24). And yet there is reason in the objection that no amount of marvel ought to deflect by one hair's breadth our judgment of right and wrong, and the true appeal of a religion must be to our moral sense.

No miracle can prove that immoral teaching is sacred. But it can prove that it is supernatural. And this is precisely what Scripture always proclaims. In the New Testament, we are bidden to take heed, because a day will come when false prophets shall work great signs and wonders, to deceive, if possible, even the elect (Mark xiii. 22). In the Old Testament, a prophet may seduce the people to worship other gods, by giving them a sign or a wonder which shall come to pass, but they must surely stone him: they must believe that his sign is only a temptation: and above whatever power enabled him to work it, they must recognise Jehovah proving them, and know that the supernatural has come to them in judgment, not in revelation (Deut. xiii. 1-5).

Now, this is the true function of the miraculous. At the most, it cannot coerce the conscience, but only challenge it to consider and to judge.

A teacher of the purest morality may be only a human teacher still; nor is the Christian bound to follow into the desert every clamorous innovator, or to seek in the secret chamber every one who whispers a private doctrine to a few. We are entitled to expect that one who is commissioned directly from above will bear special credentials with him; but when these are exhibited, we must still judge whether the document they attest is forged. And this may explain to us why the magicians were allowed for awhile to perplex the judgment of Pharaoh—whether by fraud, as we may well suppose, or by infernal help. It was enough that Moses should set his claims upon a level with those which Pharaoh reverenced: the king was then bound to weigh their relative merits in other and wholly different scales.

* It is true that the word means any large reptile, as when "God created great *whales*"; but doubtless our English version is correct. It was certainly a serpent which he had recently fled from, and then taken by the tail (iv. 4). And unless we suppose the magicians to have wrought a genuine miracle, no other creature can be suggested, equally convenient for their sleight of hand.

THE PLAGUES.

EXODUS vii. 14.

There are many aspects in which the plagues of Egypt may be contemplated.

We may think of them as ranging through all nature, and asserting the mastery of the Lord alike over the river on which depended the prosperity of the realm, over the minute pests which can make life more wretched than larger and more conspicuous ills (the frogs of the water, the reptiles that disgrace humanity, and the insects that infest the air), over the bodies of animals stricken with murrain, and those of man tortured with boils, over hail in the cloud and blight in the crop, over the breeze that bears the locust and the sun that grows dark at noon, and at last over the secret springs of human life itself.

No pantheistic creed (and the Egyptian religion struck its roots deep into pantheistic speculation) could thus completely exalt God above nature, as a superior and controlling Power, not one with the mighty wheels of the universe, of which the height is terrible, but, as Ezekiel saw Him, enthroned above them in the likeness of fire, and yet in the likeness of humanity.

No idolatrous creed, however powerful be its conception of one god of the hills and another of the valleys, could thus represent a single deity as wielding all the arrows of adverse fortune, able to assail us from earth and sky and water, formidable alike in the least things and in the greatest. And presently the demonstration is completed, when at His bidding the tempest heaps up the sea, and at His frown the waters return to their strength again.

And no philosophic theory condescends to bring the Ideal, the Absolute, and the Unconditioned, into such close and intimate connection with the frog-spawn of the ditch and the blain upon the tortured skin.

We may, with ample warrant from Scripture, make the controversial application still more simple and direct, and think of the plagues as wreaking vengeance, for the worship they had usurped and the cruelties they had sanctioned, upon all the gods of Egypt, which are conceived of for the moment as realities, and as humbled, if not in fact, yet in the sympathies of priest and worshipper (xii. 12).

Then we shall see the domain of each impostor invaded, and every vaunted power to inflict evil or to remove it triumphantly wielded by Him Who proves His equal mastery over all, and thus we shall find here the justification of that still bolder personification which says, "Worship Him, all ye gods" (Psalm xcvii. 7).

The Nile had a sacred name, and was adored as "Hapee, or Hapee Mu, the Abyss, or the Abyss of Waters, or the Hidden," and the king was frequently portrayed standing between two images of this god, his throne wreathed with water-lilies. The second plague struck at the goddess HEKT, whose head was that of a frog. The uncleanness of the third plague deranged the whole system of Egyptian worship, with its punctilious and elaborate purifications. In every one there is either a presiding divinity attacked, or a blow dealt upon the priesthood or the sacrifice, or a sphere invaded which some deity should have protected, until the sun himself is darkened, the great god Ra, to whom their sacred city was dedicated, and whose name is incorporated in the title of his earthly representative, the Pharaoh or Ph-ra. Then at last, after all these premonitions, the deadly blow struck home.

Or we may think of the plagues as retributive, and then we shall discover a wonderful suitability in them all. It was a direful omen that the first should afflict the nation through the river, into which, eighty years before, the Hebrew babes had been cast to die, which now rolled bloody, and seemed to disclose its dead. It was fit that the luxurious homes of the oppressors should become squalid as the huts of the slaves they trampled; that their flesh should suffer torture worse than that of the whips they used so unmercifully; that the loss of crops and cattle should bring home to them the hardships of the poor who toiled for their magnificence; that physical darkness should appal them with vague terrors and undefined apprehensions, such as ever haunt the bosom of the oppressed, whose life is the sport of a caprice; and at last that the aged should learn by the deathbed of the prop and pride of their declining feebleness, and the younger feel beside the cradle of the first blossom and fruit of love, all the agony of such bereavement as they had wantonly inflicted on the innocent.

And since the fear of disadvantage in war had prompted the murder of the Hebrew children, it was right that the retributive blow should destroy first their children and then their men of war.

When we come to examine the plagues in detail, we discover that it is no arbitrary fancy which divides them into three triplets, leading up to the appalling tenth. Thus the first, fourth, and seventh, each of which begins a triplet, are introduced by a command to Moses to warn Pharaoh " in the morning " (vii. 15), or " early in the morning " (viii. 20, ix. 13). The third, sixth and ninth, on the contrary, are inflicted without any warning whatever. The story of the third plague closes with the defeat of the magicians, the sixth with their inability to stand before the king, and the ninth with the final rupture, when Moses declares, " Thou shalt see my face no more " (viii. 19, ix. 11, x. 29).

The first three are plagues of loathsomeness—blood-stained waters, frogs, and lice; the next three bring actual pain and loss with them—stinging flies, murrain which afflicts the beasts, and boils upon all the Egyptians; and the third triplet are " nature-plagues "—hail, locusts, and darkness. It is only after the first three plagues that the immunity of Israel is mentioned; and after the next three, when the hail is threatened, instructions are first given by which those Egyptians who fear Jehovah may also obtain protection. Thus, in orderly and solemn procession, marched the avengers of God upon the guilty land.

It has been observed, concerning the miracles of Jesus, that not one of them was creative, and that, whenever it was possible, He wrought by the use of material naturally provided. The waterpots should be filled; the five barley-loaves should be sought out; the nets should be let down for a draught; and the blind man should have his eyes anointed and go wash in the Pool of Siloam.

And it is easily seen that such miracles were a more natural expression of His errand, which was to repair and purify the existing system of things, and to remove our moral disease and death, than any exercise of creative power would have been, however it might have dazzled the spectators.

Now, the same remark applies to the miracles of Moses, to the coming of God in judgment, as to His revelation of Himself in grace; and therefore we need not be surprised to hear that natural phenomena are not unknown which offer a sort of dim hint or foreshadowing of the terrible ten plagues. Either cryptogamic vegetation or the earth borne down from upper Africa is still seen to redden the river, usually dark, but not so as to destroy the fish. Frogs and vermin and stinging insects are the pest of modern travellers. Cattle plagues make ravage there, and hideous diseases of the skin are still as common as when the Lord promised to reward the obedience of Israel to sanitary law by putting upon them none of " the evil diseases of Egypt " which they knew (Deut. vii. 15).* The locust is still dreaded. But some of the other visitations were more direful because not only their intensity but even their existence was almost unprecedented: hail in Egypt was only not quite unknown; and such veiling of the sun as occurs for a few minutes during the storms of sand in the desert ought scarcely to be quoted as even a suggestion of the prolonged horror of the ninth plague.

Now, this accords exactly with the moral effect which was to be produced. The rescued people were not to think of God as one who strikes down into nature from outside, with strange and unwonted powers, superseding utterly its familiar forces. They were to think of Him as the Author of all; and of the common troubles of mortality as being indeed the effects of sin, yet ever controlled and governed by Him, let loose at His will, and capable of mounting to unimagined heights if His restraints be removed from them. By the east wind He brought the locusts, and removed them by the south-west wind. By a storm He divided the sea. The common things of life are in His hands, often for tremendous results. And this is one of the chief lessons of the narrative for us. Let the mind range over the list of the nine which stop short of absolute destruction, and reflect upon the vital importance of immunities for which we are scarcely grateful.

The purity of water is now felt to be among the foremost necessities of life. It is one which asks nothing from us except to refrain from polluting what comes from heaven so limpid. And yet we are half satisfied to go on habitually inflicting on ourselves a plague more foul and noxious than any occasional turning of our rivers into blood. The two plagues which dealt with minute forms of life may well remind us of the vast part which we are now aware that the smallest organisms play in the economy of life, as the agents of the Creator. Who gives thanks aright for the cheap blessing of the unstained light of heaven?

But we are insensible to the every-day teaching of this narrative: we turn our rivers into fluid poison; we spread all around us deleterious influences, which breed by minute forms of para-

---

* To this day, amid squalid surroundings for which nominal Christians are responsible, the immunity of the Jewish race from such suffering is conspicuous, and at least a remarkable coincidence.

sitical life the germs of cruel disease; we load the atmosphere with fumes which slay our cattle with periodical distempers, and are deadlier to vegetation than the hailstorm or the locust; we charge it with carbon so dense that multitudes have forgotten that the sky is blue, and on our Metropolis comes down at frequent intervals the darkness of the ninth plague, and all the time we fail to see that God, Who enacts and enforces every law of nature, does really plague us whenever these outraged laws avenge themselves. The miraculous use of nature in special emergencies is such as to show the Hand which regularly wields its powers.

At the same time there is no more excuse for the rationalism which would reduce the calamities of Egypt to a coincidence, than for explaining away the manna which fed a nation during its wanderings by the drug which is gathered, in scanty morsels, upon the acacia tree. The awful severity of the judgments, the series which they formed, their advent and removal at the menace and the prayer of Moses, are considerations which make such a theory absurd. The older scepticism, which supposed Moses to have taken advantage of some epidemic, to have learned in the wilderness the fords of the Red Sea,[*] to have discovered water, when the caravan was perishing of thirst, by his knowledge of the habits of wild beasts, and finally to have dazzled the nation at Horeb with some kind of fireworks, is itself almost a miracle in its violation of the laws of mind. The concurrence of countless favourable accidents and strange resources of leadership is like the chance arrangement of a printer's type to make a poem.

There is a common notion that the ten plagues followed each other with breathless speed, and were completed within a few weeks. But nothing in the narrative asserts or even hints this, and what we do know is in the opposite direction. The seventh plague was wrought in February, for the barley was in the ear and the flax in blossom (ix. 31); and the feast of passover was kept on the fourteenth day of the month Abib, so that the destruction of the firstborn was in the middle of April, and there was an interval of about two months between the last four plagues. Now, the same interval throughout would bring back the first plague to September or October. But the natural discoloration of the river, mentioned above, is in the middle of the year, when the river begins to rise; and this, it may possibly be inferred, is the natural period at which to fix the first plague. They would then range over a period of about nine months. During the interval between them, the promises and treacheries of the king excited alternate hope and rage in Israel; the scribes of their own race (once the vassals of their tyrants, but already estranged by their own oppression) began to take rank as officers among the Jews, and to exhibit the rudimentary promise of national order and government; and the growing fears of their enemies fostered that triumphant sense of mastery, out of which national hope and pride are born. When the time came for their departure, it was possible to transmit orders throughout all their tribes, and they came out of Egypt by their armies, which would have been utterly im-

[*] But indeed this notion is not yet dead. "A high wind left the shallow sea so low that it became possible to ford it. Moses eagerly accepted the suggestion, and made the venture with success," etc.—*Wellhausen*, "Israel," in *Encyc. Brit.*

possible a few months before. It was with them, as it is with every man that breathes: the delay of God's grace was itself a grace; and the slowly ripening fruit grew mellower than if it had been forced into a speedier maturity.

THE FIRST PLAGUE.

EXODUS vii. 14-25.

It was perhaps when the Nile was rising, and Pharaoh was coming to the bank, in pomp of state, to make official observation of its progress, on which the welfare of the kingdom depended, and to do homage before its divinity, that the messenger of another Deity confronted him, with a formal declaration of war. It was a strange contrast. The wicked was in great prosperity, neither was he plagued like another man. Upon his head, if this were Menephtah, was the golden symbol of his own divinity. Around him was an obsequious court. And yet there was moving in his heart some unconfessed sense of awe, when confronted once more by the aged shepherd and his brother, who had claimed a commission from above, and had certainly met his challenge, and made a short end of the rival snakes of his own seers. Once he had asked "Who is Jehovàh?" and had sent His ambassadors to their tasks again with insult. But now he needs to harden his heart, in order not to yield to their strange and persistent demands. He remembers how they had spoken to him already, "Thus saith the Lord, Israel is My son, My firstborn, and I have said unto thee, Let My son go that he may serve Me; and thou hast refused to let him go: behold, I will slay thy son, thy firstborn" (iv. 22, R. V.). Did this awful warning come back to him, when the worn, solemn, and inflexible face of Moses again met him? Did he divine the connection between this ultimate penalty and what is now announced—the turning of the pride and refreshment of Egypt into blood? Or was it partly because each plague, however dire, seemed to fall short of the tremendous threat, that he hoped to find the power of Moses more limited than his warnings? "Because sentence against an evil work is not executed speedily, therefore the heart of the sons of men is fully set in them to do evil."

And might he, at the last, be hardened to pursue the people because, by their own showing, the keenest arrow in their quiver was now sped? Whatever his feelings were, it is certain that the brothers come and go, and inflict their plagues unrestrained; that no insult or violence is attempted, and we can see the truth of the words "I have made thee as a god unto Pharaoh."

It is in clear allusion to his vaunt, "I know not Jehovah," that Moses and Aaron now repeat the demand for release, and say, "Hitherto thou hast not hearkened: behold, in this thou shalt know that I am Jehovah." What follows, when attentively read, makes it plain that the blow falls upon "the waters that are in the river," and those that have been drawn from it into canals for artificial irrigation, into reservoirs like the lakes Mœris and Mareotis, and even into vessels for immediate use.

But we are expressly told that it was possible to obtain water by digging wells. Therefore there is no point whatever in the cavil that if

Moses turned all the water into blood, none was left for the operations of the magicians. But no comparison whatever existed between their petty performances and the immense and direful work of vengeance which rolled down a putrid mass of corrupt waters through the land, spoiling the great stores of water by which later drought should be relieved, destroying the fish, that important part of the food of the nation, for which Israel afterwards lusted, and sowing the seeds of other plagues, by the pollution of that balmy air in which so many of our own suffering countrymen still find relief, but which was now infected and loathsome. Even Pharaoh must have felt that his gods might do better for him than this, and that it would be much more to the point just then to undo his plague than to increase it—to turn back the blood to water than contribute a few drops more. If this was their best effort, he was already helpless in the hand of his assailant, who, by the uplifting of his rod, and the bold avowal in advance of responsibility for so great a calamity, had formally defied him. But Pharaoh dared not accept the challenge: it was effort enough for him to "set his heart" against surrender to the portent, and he sullenly turned back into the palace from the spot where Moses met him.

Two details remain to be observed. The seven days which were fulfilled do not measure the interval between this plague and the next, but the period of its infliction. And this information is not given us concerning any other, until we come to the three days of darkness.* It is important here, because the natural discoloration lasts for three weeks, and mythical tendencies would rather exaggerate than shorten the term.

Again, it is contended that only with the fourth plague did Israel begin to enjoy exemption, because then only is their immunity recorded.† But it is strange indeed to suppose that they were involved in punishments the design of which was their relief; and in fact their exemption is implied in the statement that the Egyptians (only) had to dig wells. It is to be understood that large stores of water would everywhere be laid up, because the Nile water, however delicious, carries much sediment which must be allowed to settle down. They would not be forced, therefore, to fall back upon the polluted common sources for a supply.

And now let us contrast this miracle with the first of the New Testament. One spoiled the happiness of the guilty; the other rescued the overclouded joy of the friends of Jesus, not turning water into blood but into wine; declaring at one stroke all the difference between the law which worketh wrath, and the gospel of the grace of God. The first was impressive and public, as the revelation upon Sinai; the other appealed far more to the heart than to the imagination, and befitted well the kingdom that was not with observation, the King who grew up like a tender plant, and did not strive nor cry, the redeeming influence which was at first unobtrusive as the least of all seeds, but became a tree, and the shelter of the fowls of heaven.

---

* x. 22. The accurate Kalisch is therefore wrong in speaking of "The duration of the first plague, a statement not made with regard to any of the subsequent inflictions."—Commentary *in loco*.

† *Speaker's Commentary*, i., p. 242; Kalisch on viii. 18; Kiel, i. 484.

CHAPTER VIII.

THE SECOND PLAGUE.

EXODUS viii. 1-15.

ALTHOUGH Pharaoh had warning of the first plague, no appeal was made to him to avert it by submission. But before the plague of frogs he was distinctly commanded, "Let My people go." It is an advancing lesson. He has felt the power of Jehovah: now he is to connect, even more closely, his suffering with his disobedience; and when this is accomplished, the third plague will break upon him unannounced—a loud challenge to his conscience to become itself his judge.

The plague of frogs was far greater than our experience helps us to imagine. At least two cases are on record of a people being driven to abandon their settlements because they had become intolerable; "as even the vessels were full of them, the water infested and the food uneatable, as they could scarcely set their feet on the ground without treading on heaps of them, and as they were vexed by the smell of the great multitude that died, they fled from that region."

The Egyptian species known to science as the Rana Mosaica, and still called by the uncommon epithet here employed, is peculiarly repulsive, and peculiarly noisy too. The superstition which adored a frog as the "Queen of the two Worlds," and placed it upon the sacred lotus-leaf, would make it impossible for an Egyptian to adopt even such forlorn measures of self-defence as might suggest themselves. It was an unclean pest against which he was entirely helpless, and it extended the power of his enemy from the river to the land. The range of the grievance is dwelt upon in the warning: "they shall come up and enter into thine house, and into thy bedchamber, and upon thy bed . . . and into thine ovens, and into thy kneading-troughs" (viii. 3). The most sequestered and the dryest spots alike would swarm with them, thrust forward into the most unsuitable places by the multitude behind.

Thus Pharaoh himself had to share, far more than in the first plague, the misery of his humblest subjects; and, although again his magicians imitated Aaron upon some small prepared plot, and amid circumstances which made it easier to exhibit frogs than to exclude them, yet there was no comfort in such puerile emulation, and they offered no hope of relieving him. From the gods that were only vanities, he turned to Jehovah, and abased himself to ask the intercession of Moses: "Intreat Jehovah that He take away the frogs from me and from my people; and I will let the people go."

The assurance would have been a hopeful one, if only the sense of inconvenience were the same as the sense of sin. But when we wonder at the relapses of men who were penitent upon sick-beds or in adversity, as soon as their trouble is at an end, we are blind to this distinction. Pain is sometimes obviously due to ourselves, and it is natural to blame the conduct which led to it. But if we blame it only for being disastrous, we cannot hope that the fruits of the Spirit will result from a sensation of the flesh. It was so with Pharaoh, as doubtless Moses expected, since God had not yet exhausted His predicted works of retribution. This anticipated fraud is much the simplest explanation of the difficult phrase, "Have thou this glory over me."

It is sometimes explained as an expression of courtesy—"I obey thee as a superior"; which does not occur elsewhere, because it is not Hebrew but Egyptian. But this suavity is quite alien to the spirit of the narrative, in which Moses, however courteous, represents an offended God. It is more natural to take it as an open declaration that he was being imposed upon, yet would grant to the king whatever advantage the fraud implied. And to make the coming relief more clearly the action of the Lord, to shut out every possibility that magician or priest should claim the honour, he bade the king name an hour at which the plague should cease.

If the frogs passed away at once, the relief might chance to be a natural one; and Pharaoh doubtless conceived that elaborate and long protracted intercessions were necessary for his deliverance. Accordingly he fixed a future period, yet as near as he perhaps thought possible; and Moses, without any express authority, promised him that it should be so. Therefore he "cried unto the Lord," and the frogs did not retreat into the river, but suddenly died where they were, and filled the unhappy land with a new horror in their decay.

But "when Pharaoh saw that there was respite, he made his heart heavy and hearkened not unto them." It is a graphic sentence: it implies rather than affirms their indignant remonstrances, and the sullen, dull, spiritless obstinacy with which he held his base and unkingly purpose.

THE THIRD PLAGUE.

Exodus viii. 16-19.

There is no sufficient reason for discarding the ordinary opinion of this plague. Gnats have been suggested (with beetles instead of flies for the fourth, since gnats and flies would scarcely make two several judgments), but these, which spring from marshy ground, would unfitly be connected with the dust whence Aaron was to evoke the pest. Sir Samuel Baker, on the other hand, has said of modern Egypt that "it seemed as if the very dust were turned into lice" (quoted in Speaker's Commentary *in loco*).

Two features in this plague deserve attention. It came without any warning whatever. The faithless king who gave his word and broke it found himself involved in fresh miseries without an opportunity of humbling himself again. He was flung back into deep waters, because he refused to fulfil the terms upon which he had been extricated.

It must be understood that the act of Aaron was a public one, performed in the sight of Pharaoh, and instantly followed by the plague. There was no doubt about the origin of the pest, and the new and alarming prospect was opened up of calamities yet to come, without a chance to avert them by submission.

Again, it will be observed that the magicians are utterly baffled just when there is no warning given, and therefore no opportunity for prearranged sleight of hand. And this surely favours the opinion that they had not hitherto succeeded by supernatural assistance, for there is no such evident reason why infernal aid should cease at this exact point.

It is a mistake to suppose that thereupon they confessed the mission of the brothers. In their agitation they admitted that, on their part at least, no divinity had been at work before. But they rather ascribed what they saw to the action of some vaguely indicated deity, than confessed it to be the work of Jehovah. Again it has to be asked whether this resembles more the vainglorious structure of a myth, or the course of a truthful history.

Nevertheless, their grudging and insufficient avowal was meant to induce a surrender. But "Pharaoh's heart was strong, and he hearkened not unto them." To this statement it is not added, "because the Lord had hardened him," for this had not even yet taken place; but only, "as the Lord had spoken."

THE FOURTH PLAGUE.

Exodus viii. 20-32.

When the third plague had died away, when the sense of reaction and exhaustion had replaced agitation and distress, and when perhaps the fear grew strong that at any moment a new calamity might befal the land as abruptly as the last, God orders a solemn and urgent appeal to be made to the oppressor. And the same occurs three times: after each plague which arrives unexpectedly the next is introduced by a special warning. On each of these occasions, moreover, the appeal is made in the morning, at the hour when reason ought to be clearest and the passions least agitating; and this circumstance is perhaps alluded to in the favourite phrase of Jeremiah when he would speak of condescending earnestness—"I sent my prophets, rising up early and sending them" (Jer. xxv. 4, xxvi. 5, xxix. 19, and many more; cf. also vii. 13, and 2 Chron. xxxvi. 15). So far is the Scripture from regarding Pharaoh as propelled by destiny, as by a machine, down iron grooves to ruin.

We have now come to the group of plagues which inflict actual bodily damage, and not inconvenience and humiliation only: the dogfly (or beetle); the murrain among beasts, which was a precursor of the crowning evil that struck at human life; and the boils. Of the fourth plague the precise nature is uncertain. There is a beetle which gnaws both man and beast, destroys clothes, furniture, and plants, and even now they "are often seen in millions" (Munk, *Palestine*, p. 120). "In a few minutes they filled the whole house. . . Only after the most laborious exertions, and covering the floor of the house with hot coals, they succeeded in mastering them. If they make such attacks during the night, the inmates are compelled to give up the houses, and little children or sick persons, who are unable to rise alone, are then exposed to the greatest danger of life" (Pratte, *Abyssinia*, p. 143, in Kalisch).

Now, this explanation has one advantage over that of dogflies—that special mention is made of their afflicting "the ground whereon they are" (ver. 21), which is less suitable to a plague of flies. But it may be that no one creature is meant. The Hebrew word means "a mixture." Jewish interpreters have gone so far as to make it mean "all kinds of noxious animals and serpents and scorpions mixed together," and although it is palpably absurd to believe that Pharaoh should have survived if these had been upon him and upon his servants, yet the expression "a mixture," following after one kind of vermin had tormented the land, need not be narrowed too exactly. With deliberate particularity the king was warned that they should come "upon thee, and upon thy servants, and upon thy people, and into thine houses, and the houses of the Egyptians shall be full of [them*], and also the ground whereon they are."

It has been supposed, from the special mention of the exemption of the land of Goshen, that this was a new thing. We have seen reason, however, to think otherwise, and the emphatic assertion now made is easy to understand. The plague was especially to be expected in low flat ground: the king may not even have been aware of the previous freedom of Israel; and in any case its importance as an evidence had not been pressed upon him. The spirit of the seventy-eighth Psalm, though not perhaps any one specific phrase, contrasts the earlier as well as the later plagues with the protection of His own people, whom He led like sheep (vers. 42-52).

After the appointed interval (the same which Pharaoh had indicated for the removal of the frogs) the plague came. We are told that the land was corrupted, but it is significant that more stress is laid upon the suffering of Pharaoh and his court in the event than in the menace. It came home to himself more cruelly than any former plague, and he at once attempted to make terms: "Go ye, sacrifice to your God in the land." It is a natural speech, at first not asking to be trusted as before by getting relief before the Hebrews actually enjoy their liberty; and yet conceding as little as possible, and in hot haste to have that little done and the relief obtained. They may even serve their God on the sacred soil, so completely has He already defeated all His rivals. But this was not what was demanded; and Moses repeated the claim of a three days' journey, basing it upon the ground, still more insulting to the national religion, that "We will sacrifice to Jehovah our God the abomination of the Egyptians," that is to say, sacred animals, which it is horror in their eyes to sacrifice. Any faith in his own creed which Pharaoh ever had is surrendered when this argument, instead of making their cause hopeless, forces him to yield—adding, however, like a thoroughly weak man who wishes to refuse but dares not, "only ye shall not go very far away: intreat for me." And again Moses concedes the point, with only the courteous remonstrance, "But let not Pharaoh deal deceitfully any more."

It is necessary to repeat that we have not a shred of evidence that Moses would have violated his compact and failed to return: it would have sufficed as a first step to have asserted the nationality of his people and their right to worship their own God: all the rest would speedily have followed. But the terms which were rejected again and again did not continue for ever to bind the victorious party: the story of their actual departure makes it plain that both sides understood it to be a final exodus; and thence

* The Revised Version has "swarms of flies," which is clearly an attempt to meet the case. But it is worth notice that in the Psalms the expression was twice rendered "divers kinds of flies" (lxviii. c r. 31 A. V.). The word occurs only of this plague.

came the murderous pursuit of Pharaoh (cf. xv. 9), which in itself would have cancelled any compact which had existed until then.

CHAPTER IX.

THE FIFTH PLAGUE.

EXODUS ix. 1-7.

OUR Lord when on earth came not to destroy men's lives. And yet it was necessary, for our highest instruction, that we should not think of Him as revealing a Divinity wholly devoid of sternness. Twice, therefore, a gleam of the fires of justice fell on the eyes which followed Him—through the destruction once of a barren tree, and once of a herd of swine, which property no Jew should have possessed. So now, when half the gloomy round of the plagues was being completed, it was necessary to prove that life itself was staked on this desperate hazard; and this was done first by the very same expedient—the destruction of life which was not human. There is something pathetic, if one thinks of it, in the extent to which domestic animals share our fortunes, and suffer through the brutality or the recklessness of their proprietors. If all men were humane, self-controlled, and (as a natural result) prosperous, what a weight would be uplifted from the lower levels also of created life, all of which groaneth and travaileth in pain together until now! The dumb animal world is partner with humanity, and shares its fate, as each animal is dependent on its individual owner.

We have already seen the whole life of Egypt stricken, but now the lower creatures are to perish, unless Pharaoh will repent. He is once more summoned in the name of "Jehovah, God of the Hebrews," and warned that the hand of Jehovah, even a very grievous murrain (for so the verse appears to say), is "upon thy cattle which is in the field, upon the horses, upon the asses, upon the camels, upon the herds and upon the flocks." Here some particulars need observation. Herds and flocks were everywhere; but horses were a comparatively late introduction into Egypt, where they were as yet chiefly employed for war. Asses, still so familiar to the traveller, were the usual beasts of burden, and were owned in great numbers by the rich, although rash controversialists have pretended that, as being unclean, they were not tolerated in the land.

Camels, it is said, are not to be found on the monuments, but yet they were certainly known and possessed by Egypt, though there were many reasons why they should be held chiefly on the frontiers, and perhaps in connection with the Arabian mines and settlements. Upon all these "in the field" the plague should come.

The murrain still works havoc in the Delta, chiefly at the period, beginning with December, when the floods are down and the cattle are turned out into the pastures, which would this year have been signally unwholesome. It was not, then, the fact of a cattle plague which was miraculous, but its severity, its coming at an appointed time, its assailing beasts of every kind, and its exempting those of Israel. We are told that "all the cattle of Egypt died," and yet that afterwards "the hail . . . smote both man and beast" (ix. 6, 25). It is an inconsistency very serious in the eyes of people who are too stupid or too uncandid to observe that, just before, the mischief was limited to those cattle which were "in the field" (ver. 3). There were great stalls in suitable places, to give them shelter during the inundations; and all that had not yet been driven out to graze are expressly exempted from the plague.

Much of Pharaoh's own property perished, but he was the last man in the country who would feel personal inconvenience by the loss, and therefore nothing was more natural than that his selfish "heart was heavy, and he did not let the people go." Not even such an effort was needed as in the previous plague, when we read that he made his heart heavy, by a deliberate act.

There was nothing to indicate that he had now reached a crisis—that God Himself in His judgment would henceforth make bold and resolute against crushing adversities the heart which had been obdurate against humanity, against evidence, against honour and plighted faith. Nothing is easier than to step over the frontier between great nations. And in the moral world also the Rubicon is passed, the destiny of a soul is fixed, sometimes without a struggle, unawares.

Instead of spiritual conflict, there was intellectual curiosity. "Pharaoh sent, and behold there was not so much as one of the cattle of the Israelites dead. But the heart of Pharaoh was heavy, and he did not let the people go." This inquiry into a phenomenon which was surprising indeed, but yet quite unable to affect his action, recalls the spiritual condition of Herod, who was conscience-stricken when first he heard of Christ, and said, "It is John whom I beheaded" (Mark vi. 16), but afterwards felt merely vulgar curiosity and desire to behold a sign of Him. In the case of Pharaoh it was the next step to judicial infatuation. When Christ confronted Herod, He, Who had explained Himself to Pilate, was absolutely silent. And this warns us not to think that an interest in religious problems is itself of necessity religious. One may understand all mysteries, and yet it may profit him nothing. And many a reprobate soul is controversial, acute, and keenly orthodox.

THE SIXTH PLAGUE.

Exodus ix. 8-12.

At the close of the second triplet, as of the first, stands a plague without a warning, but not without the clearest connection between the blow and Him who deals it.

To the Jews Egypt was a furnace in which they were being consumed—whether literally in human sacrifice, or metaphorically in the hard labour which wasted them (Deut. iv. 20). And now the brothers were commanded to fill both hands with ashes of the furnace and throw them upon the wind,* either to symbolise the suffering which was to be spread wide over the land, or because the ashes of human sacrifices were thus presented to their evil genius, Typhon. If this were its meaning, the irony was keen, when at the same action a feverish inflammation, breaking out in blains, spread over all the nation.

But, apart from any such reference to their cruel idolatry, it was right that they should suffer in the flesh. When the higher nature is dead, there is no appeal so sharp and certain as to the physical sensibility. And moreover, there are other sins which have their root in the flesh besides sloth and bodily indulgence. Wrath and cruelty and pride are strangely stimulated and excited by self-indulgence. Not in vain does St. Paul describe a "mind of the flesh," and reckon among the fruits of the flesh not only uncleanness and drunkenness, but, just as truly, strife, jealousies, wraths, factions, divisions, heresies (Col. ii. 18; Gal. v. 19, 20). From such evil tempers, stimulated by evil appetites, the slaves of Egypt had suffered bitterly; and now the avenging rod fell upon the bodies of their tyrants.

And we may perhaps detect especial suffering, certainly an especial triumph to be commemorated, in the failure of the magicians even to stand before the king. It is implied that they had done so until now, and this confirms the belief that after the third plague they had not acknowledged Jehovah, but merely said in their defeat, "This is the finger of a god." Until now Jannes and Jambres (two, to rival the two brothers) had withstood Moses, but now the contrast between the prophet and his victims writhing in their pain was too sharp for prejudice itself to overlook: their folly was "evident unto all men" (2 Tim. iii. 8, 9). But it was not destined that Pharaoh should yield even to so tremendous a coercion what he refused to moral influences; and as Jesus after His resurrection appeared not unto all the people (hiding this crowning evidence from the eyes which had in vain beheld so much), so "the Lord made strong the heart of Pharaoh, and he hearkened not unto them, as the Lord had spoken unto Moses." In this last expression is the explicit statement that it was now that the prediction attained fulfilment, in the manner which we have discussed already.

But even this strength of heart did not reach the height of attempting any reprisals upon the torturers. The sense of the supernatural was their defence: Moses was as a god unto Pharaoh, and Aaron was his prophet.

In the narrative of this plague there is an expression which deserves attention for another reason. The ashes, it says, "shall become dust." Is there no controversy, turning upon the too rigid and prosaic straining of a New Testament construction, which might be simplified by considering the Hebrew use of language, exemplified in such an assertion as "It shall become dust," and soon after, "It is the Lord's passover"? Do these announce transubstantiations? Did two handfuls of ashes literally become the blains upon the bodies of all the Egyptians?

THE SEVENTH PLAGUE.

Exodus ix. 13-35.

The hardening of Pharaoh's heart, we have argued, was not the debauching of his spirit, but only the strengthening of his will. "Wait on the Lord and *be of good courage*"; "Be strong, O Zerubbabel, saith the Lord; and *be strong*, O

---

* The passage in Deuteronomy had not this event specially in mind, or it would have used the same term for a furnace. The word for ashes implies what can be blown upon the wind.

Joshua, son of Josadak the high priest; and *be strong*, all ye people" (Ps. xxvii. 14; Hag. ii. 4), are clear proofs that what was implied in this word was not wickedness, but only that iron determination which his choice directed in a wicked channel. And therefore it was no mockery, no insincere appeal by one who had provided against the mischance of its succeeding, when God again addressed Himself to the reason, and even to the rational fears of Pharaoh. He had only provided against a terror-stricken submission, as wholly immoral and valueless, as the ceasing to resist of one who has swooned through fright. Now, to give such an one a stimulant and thus to enable him to exercise his volition, would be different from inciting him to rebel.

The seventh plague, then, is ushered in by an expostulation more earnest, resolute, and minatory than attended any of the previous ones. And this is the more necessary because human life is now for the first time at stake. First the king is solemnly reminded that Jehovah, Whom he no longer can refuse to know, is the God of the Hebrews, has a claim upon their services, and demands them. In oppressing the nation, therefore, Pharaoh usurped what belonged to the Lord. Now, this is the eternal charter of the rights of all humanity. Whoever encroaches on the just sphere of the free action of his neighbour deprives him, to exactly the same extent, of the power to glorify God by a free obedience. The heart glorifies God by submission to so hard a lot, but the co-operation of the "whole body and soul and spirit" does not visibly bear testimony to the regulating power of grace. The oppressor may contend (like some slave-owners) that he guides his human property better than it would guide itself. But one assertion he cannot make: namely, that God is receiving the loyal homage of a life spontaneously devoted; that a man and not a machine is glorifying God in this body and spirit which are God's. For the body is but a chattel. This is why the Christian doctrine of the religious equality of all men in Christ carries with it the political assertion of the equal secular rights of the whole human race. I must not transfer to myself the solemn duty of my neighbour to offer up to God the sacrifice not only of his chastened spirit but also of his obedient life.

And these words were also a lifelong admonition to every Israelite. He held his liberties from God. He was not free to be violent and wanton, and to say "I am delivered to commit all these abominations." The dignities of life were bound up with its responsibilities.

Well, it is not otherwise to-day. As truly as Moses, the champions of our British liberties were earnest and God-fearing men. Not for leave to revel, to accumulate enormous fortunes, and to excite by their luxuries the envy and rage of neglected brothers, while possessing more enormous powers to bless them than ever were entrusted to a class,—not for this our heroes bled on the field and on the scaffold. Tyrants rarely deny to rich men leave to be self-indulgent. And self-indulgence rarely nerves men to heroic effort. It is for the freedom of the soul that men dare all things. And liberty is doomed wherever men forget that the true freeman is the servant of Jehovah. On these terms the first demand for a national emancipation was enforced.

And next, Pharaoh is warned that God, who at first threatened to destroy his firstborn, but had hitherto come short of such a deadly stroke, had not, as he might flatter himself, exhausted His power to avenge. Pharaoh should yet experience "*all* My plagues." And there is a dreadful significance in the phrase which threatens to put these plagues, with regard to others, "upon thy servants and upon thy people," but with regard to Pharaoh himself "upon thine heart."

There it was that the true scourge smote. Thence came ruin and defeat. His infatuation was more dreadful than hail in the cloud and locusts on the blast, than the darkness at noon and the midnight wail of a bereaved nation. For his infatuation involved all these.

The next assertion is not what the Authorised Version made it, and what never was fulfilled. It is not, "Now I will stretch out My hand to smite thee and thy people with pestilence, and thou shalt be cut off from the earth." It says, "Now I had done this, as far as any restraint for thy sake is concerned, but in very deed for this cause have I made thee to stand" (unsmitten), "for to show thee My power, and that My name may be declared throughout all the earth" (vers. 15, 16). The course actually taken was more for the glory of God, and a better warning to others, than a sudden stroke, however crushing.

And so we find, many years after all this generation has passed away, that a strangely distorted version of these events is current among the Philistines in Palestine. In the days of Eli, when the ark was brought into the camp, they said, "Woe unto us! who shall deliver us out of the hand of these mighty gods? These are the gods that smote the Egyptians with all manner of plagues in the wilderness" (1 Sam. iv. 8). And this, along with the impression which Rahab declared that the Exodus and what followed it had made, may help us to understand what a mighty influence upon the wars of Palestine the scourging of Egypt had, how terror fell upon all the inhabitants of the land, and they melted away (Josh. ii. 9, 10).

And perhaps it may save us from the unconscious egoism which always deems that I myself shall not be treated quite as severely as I deserve, to mark how the punishment of one affects the interests of all.

Added to all this is a kind of half-ironical clemency, an opportunity of escape if he would humble himself so far as to take warning even to a small extent. The plague was to be of a kind especially rare in Egypt, and of utterly unknown severity—such hail as had not been in Egypt since the day it was founded until now. But he and his people might, if they would, hasten to bring in their cattle and all that they had in the field. Pharaoh, after his sore experience of the threats of Moses, would find it a hard trial in any case, whether to withdraw his property or to brave the stroke. To him it was a kind of challenge. To those of his subjects who had any proper feeling it was a merciful deliverance, and a profoundly skilful education of their faith, which began by an obedience probably hesitating, but had few doubts upon the morrow. We read that he who feared the Lord among the servants of Pharaoh made his servants and his cattle flee into the houses; and this is the first hint that the plagues, viewed as discipline, were not utterly vain. The existence of others who feared Jehovah beside the Jews prepares us for the "mixed multitude" who came up along with them (xii. 38), and whose ill-instructed and probably very selfish adhesion was quite consistent with such sensual discontent as led the whole congregation into sin (Num. xi. 4).

To make the connection between Jehovah and the impending storm more obvious still, Moses stretched his rod toward heaven, and there was hail, and the fire mingled with the hail, such as slew man and beast, and smote the trees, and destroyed all the vegetation which had yet grown up. The heavens, the atmosphere, were now enrolled in the conspiracy against Pharaoh: they too served Jehovah.

In such a storm, the terror was even greater than the peril. When a great writer of our own time called attention to the elaborate machinery by which God in nature impresses man with the sense of a formidable power above, he chose a thunderstorm as the most striking example of his meaning.

"Nothing appears to me more remarkable than the array of scenic magnificence by which the imagination is appalled, in myriads of instances when the actual danger is comparatively small; so that the utmost possible impression of awe shall be produced upon the minds of all, though direct suffering is inflicted upon few. Consider, for instance, the moral effect of a single thunderstorm. Perhaps two or three persons may be struck dead within a space of a hundred square miles; and their death, unaccompanied by the scenery of the storm, would produce little more than a momentary sadness in the busy hearts of living men. But the preparation for the judgment, by all that mighty gathering of the clouds; by the questioning of the forest leaves, in their terrified stillness, which way the winds shall go forth; by the murmuring to each other, deep in the distance, of the destroying angels before they draw their swords of fire; by the march of the funeral darkness in the midst of the noonday, and the rattling of the dome of heaven beneath the chariot wheels of death;—on how many minds do not these produce an impression almost as great as the actual witnessing of the fatal issue! and how strangely are the expressions of the threatening elements fitted to the apprehensions of the human soul! The lurid colour, the long, irregular, convulsive sound, the ghastly shapes of flaming and heaving cloud, are all true and faithful in their appeal to our instinct of danger."—Ruskin, *Stones of Venice*, III. 197-8.

Such a tempest, dreadful anywhere, would be most appalling of all in the serene atmosphere of Egypt, to unaccustomed spectators, and minds troubled by their guilt. Accordingly we find that Pharaoh was less terrified by the absolute mischief done than by the "voices of God," when, unnerved for the moment, he confessed at least that he had sinned "this time" (a singularly weak repentance for his long and daring resistance, even if we explain it, "this time I confess that I have sinned"), and went on in his terror to pour out orthodox phrases and produce confessions with suspicious fluency. The main point was the bargain which he proposed: "Intreat the Lord, for there hath been enough of mighty thunderings and hail: and I will let you go, and ye shall stay no longer."

Looking attentively at all this, we discern in it a sad resemblance to some confessions of these latter days. Men are driven by affliction to acknowledge God: they confess the offence which is palpable, and even add that God is righteous and that they are not. If possible, they shelter themselves from lonely condemnation by general phrases, such as that all are wicked; just as Pharaoh, although he would have scoffed at the notion of any national volition except his own, said, "I and my people are sinners." Above all, they are much more anxious for the removal of the rod than for the cleansing of the guilt; and if this can be accomplished through the mediation of another, they have as little desire as Pharaoh had for any personal approach to God, Whom they fear, and, if possible, repel.

And by these signs, every experienced observer expects that if they are delivered out of trouble they will forget their vows.

Moses was exceedingly meek. And therefore, or else because the message of God implied that other plagues were to succeed this, he consented to intercede, yet adding the simple and dignified protest, "As for thee and thy people, I know that ye will not yet fear Jehovah God." * And so it came to pass. The heart of Pharaoh was made heavy, and he would not let Israel go.

Looking back upon this miracle, we are reminded of the mighty part which atmospheric changes have played in the history of the world. Snowstorms saved Europe from the Turk and from Napoleon: the wind played almost as important a part in our liberation from James, and again in the defeat of the plans of the French Revolution to invade us, as in the destruction of the Armada. And so we read, "Hast thou entered the treasuries of the snow? or hast thou seen the treasuries of the hail, which I have reserved against the time of trouble, against the day of battle and war?" (Job xxxviii. 22-3).

CHAPTER X.

THE EIGHTH PLAGUE.

EXODUS x. 1-20.

THE Lord would not command His servant again to enter the dangerous presence of the sullen prince, without a reason which would sustain his faith: "For I have made heavy his heart." The pronoun is emphatic: it means to say, "His foolhardiness is My doing and cannot go beyond My will: thou art safe." And the same encouragement belongs to all who do the sacred will: not a hair of their head shall truly perish, since life and death are the servants of their God. Thus, in the storm of human passion, as of the winds, He says, "It is I, be not afraid"; making the wrath of man to praise Him, stilling alike the tumult of the waves and the madness of the people.

It is possible that even the merciful mitigations of the last plague were used by infatuated hearts to justify their wilfulness: the most valuable crops of all had escaped; so that these judgments, however dire, were not quite beyond endurance. Just such a course of reasoning deludes all who forget that the goodness of God leadeth to repentance.

Besides the reasons already given for lengthening out the train of judgments, it is added that

---

* Except in one passage (Gen. ii. 4 to iii. 23) these titles of Deity are nowhere else combined in the books of Moses.

Israel should teach the story to posterity, and both fathers and children should "know that I am Jehovah."

Accordingly it became a favourite title—"The Lord which brought thee up out of the land of Egypt." Even the apostates under Sinai would not reject so illustrious a memory: their feast was nominally to Jehovah; and their idol was an image of "the gods which brought thee up out of the land of Egypt" (xxxii. 4, 5).

Has *our* land no deliverances for which to be thankful? Instead of boastful self-assertion, should we not say, "We have heard with our ears, O God, and our fathers have declared unto us, the noble works that Thou didst in their days and in the old time before them"? Have we forgotten that national mercies call aloud for national thanksgiving? And in the family, and in the secret life of each, are there no rescues, no emancipations, no enemies overcome by a hand not our own, which call for reverent acknowledgment? "These things were our examples, and are written for our admonition."

The reproof now spoken to Pharaoh is sterner than any previous one. There is no reasoning in it. The demand is peremptory: "How long wilt thou refuse to humble thyself?" With it is a sharp and short command: "Let My people go, that they may serve Me." And with this is a detailed and tremendous threat. It is strange, in the face of the knowledge accumulated since the objection called for it, to remember that once this narrative was challenged, because locusts, it was said, are unknown in Egypt. They are mentioned in the inscriptions. Great misery was caused by them in 1463, and just three hundred years later Niebuhr was himself at Cairo during a plague of them. Equally arbitrary is the objection that Joel predicted locusts "such as there hath not been ever the like, neither shall be any more after them, even to the years of many generations" (ii. 2), whereas we read of these that "before them there were no such locusts as they, neither after them shall be such" (x. 14). The objection is whimsical in its absurdity, when we remember that Joel spoke distinctly of Zion and the holy mountain (ii. 1), and Exodus of "the borders of Egypt" (x. 14).

But it is true that locusts are comparatively rare in Egypt; so that while the meaning of the threat would be appreciated, familiarity would not have steeled them against it. The ravages of the locust are terrible indeed, and coming just in time to ruin the crops which had escaped the hail, would complete the misery of the land. One speaks of the sudden change of colour by the disappearance of verdure where they alight as being like the rolling up of a carpet; and here we read "they shall cover the eye of the earth," —a phrase peculiar to the Pentateuch (ver. 15; Num. xxii. 5, 11); "and they shall eat the residue of that which has escaped, . . . and they shall fill thy houses, and the . . . houses of all the Egyptians, which neither thy fathers nor thy fathers' fathers have seen."

After uttering the appointed warning, Moses abruptly left, awaiting no negociations, plainly regarding them as vain.

But now, for the first time, the servants of Pharaoh interfered, declared the country to be ruined, and pressed him to surrender. And yet it was now first that we read (ver. 1) that their hearts were hardened as well as his. For that is a hard heart that does not remonstrate against wrong, however plainly God reveals His displeasure, until new troubles are at hand, and which even then has no regard for the wrongs of Israel, but only for the woes of Egypt. It is a hard heart, therefore, which intends to repent upon its deathbed; for its motives are identical with these.

Pharaoh's behaviour is that of a spoiled child, who is indeed the tyrant most familiar to us. He feels that he must yield, or else why should the brothers be recalled? And yet, when it comes to the point, he tries to play the master still, by dictating the terms for his own surrender; and breaks off the negociation rather than do frankly what he must feel that it is necessary to do. Moses laid his finger accurately upon the disease when he reproached him for refusing to humble himself. And if his behaviour seem unnatural, it is worth observation that Napoleon, the greatest modern example of proud, intellectual, godless infatuation, allowed himself to be crushed at Leipsic through just the same reluctance to do thoroughly and without self-deception what he found it necessary to consent to do. "Napoleon," says his apologist, Thiers, "at length determined to retreat—a resolution humbling to his pride. Unfortunately. instead of a retreat frankly admitted . . . he determined on one which from its imposing character should not be a real retreat at all, and should be accomplished in open day." And this perversity, which ruined him, is traced back to "the illusions of pride."

Well, it was quite as hard for the Pharaoh to surrender at discretion, as for the Corsican to stoop to a nocturnal retreat. Accordingly, he asks, "Who are ye that shall go?" and when Moses very explicitly and resolutely declares that they will all go, with all their property, his passion overcomes him, he feels that to consent is to lose them for ever, and he exclaims, "So be Jehovah with you as I will let you go and your little ones: look to it, for evil is before you"— that is to say, Your intentions are bad. "Go ye that are men, and serve the Lord, for that is what ye desire,"—no more than that is implied in your demand, unless it is a mere pretence, under which more lurks than it avows.

But he and they have long been in a state of war: menaces, submissions, and treacheries have followed each other fast, and he has no reason to complain if their demands are raised. Moreover, his own nation celebrated religious festivals in company with their wives and children, so that his rejoinder is an empty outburst of rage. And of a Jewish feast it was said, a little later, "Thou shalt rejoice before the Lord thy God, thou and thy son and thy daughter, and thy manservant and thy maidservant . . . and the stranger, and the fatherless, and the widow" (Deut. xvi. 11). There was no insincerity in the demand; and although the suspicions of the king were naturally excited by the exultant and ever-rising hopes of the Hebrews, and the defiant attitude of Moses, yet even now there is as little reason to suspect bad faith as to suppose that Israel, once released, could ever have resumed the same abject attitude toward Egypt as before. They would have come back victorious, and therefore ready to formulate new demands; already half emancipated, and therefore prepared for the perfecting of the work.

And now, at a second command as explicit as that which bade him utter the warning, Moses, anxiously watched by many, stretched out his hand over the devoted realm. At the gesture, the spectators felt that a fiat had gone forth. But the result was strangely different from that which followed his invocation, both of the previous and the following plague, when we may believe that as he raised his hand, the hail-storm burst in thunder, and the curtain fell upon the sky. Now there only arose a gentle east wind (unlike the "exceeding strong west wind" that followed), but it blew steadily all that day and all the following night. The forebodings of Egypt would understand it well: the prolonged period during which the curse was being steadily wafted toward them was an awful measure of the wide regions over which the power of Jehovah reached; and when it was morning, the east wind brought the locusts, that dreadful curse which Joel has compared to a disciplined and devastating invader, "the army of the Lord," and the first woe that heralds the Day of the Lord in the Apocalypse (Joel ii. 1-11; Rev. ix. 1-11).

The completeness of the ruin brought a swift surrender, but it has been well said that folly is the wisdom which is only wise too late, and, let us add, too fitfully. If Pharaoh had only submitted before the plague instead of after it!* If he had only respected himself enough to be faithful, instead of being too vain really to yield!

It is an interesting coincidence that, since he had this time defied the remonstrances of his advisers, his confession of sin is entirely personal; it is no longer, "I and my people are sinners," but "I have sinned against the Lord your God, and against you." This last clause was bitter to his lips, but the need for their intercession was urgent: life and death were at stake upon the removal of this dense cloud of creatures which penetrated everywhere, leaving everywhere an evil odour, and of which a later sufferer complains, "We could not eat, but we bit a locust; nor open our mouths, but locusts filled them."

Therefore he went on to entreat volubly, "Forgive, I pray thee, my sin only this once, and intreat Jehovah your God that He may take away from me this death only."

And at the prayer of Moses, the Lord caused the breeze to veer and rise into a hurricane: "The Lord turned an exceeding strong west wind." Now, the locust can float very well upon an easy breeze, and so it had been wafted over the Red Sea; but it is at once beaten down by a storm, and when it touches the water it is destroyed. Thus simply was the plague removed.

"But the Lord made strong Pharaoh's heart," and so, his fears being conquered, his own rebellious will went on upon its evil way. He would not let Israel go.

This narrative throws light upon a thousand vows made upon sick beds, but broken when the sufferer recovers; and a thousand prayers for amendment, breathed in all the sincerity of panic, and forgotten with all the levity of security. It shows also, in the hesitating and abortive half-submission of the tyrant, the greater folly of many professing Christians, who will, for Christ's sake, surrender all their sins except one

---

* Oddly enough, the same historian already quoted, relating the story of the same day at Leipsic, says of Napoleon's dialogue with M. de Merfeld, that he "used an expression which, if uttered at the Congress of Prague, would have changed his lot and ours. Unfortunately, it was now too late."

or two, and make any confession except that which really brings low their pride.

Thoroughness, decision, depth, and self-surrender, needed by Pharaoh, are needed by every soul of man.

THE NINTH PLAGUE.

EXODUS x. 21-29.

We have taken it as settled that the Pharaoh of the Exodus was Menephtah, the Beloved of the God Ptah. If so, his devotion to the gods throws a curious light upon his first scorn of Jehovah, and his long-continued resistance; and also upon the threat of vengeance to be executed upon the gods of Egypt, as if they were a resisting power. But there is a special significance in the ninth plague, when we connect it with Menephtah.

In the Tombs of the Kings at Thebes there is to be seen, fresh and lifelike, the admirably sculptured effigy of this king—a weak and cruel face, with the receding forehead of his race, but also their nose like a beak, and their sharp chin. Over his head is the inscription:

"Lord of the Two Lands, Beloved of the God Amen;
Lord of Diadems, Beloved of the God Ptah:
Crowned by Amen with dominion of the world:
Cherished by the Sun in the great abode."

This formidable personage is delineated by the court sculptor with his hand stretched out in worship, and under it is written "He adores the Sun: he worships Hor of the solar horizons."

The worship, thus chosen as the most characteristic of this king, either by himself or by some consummate artist, was to be tested now.

Could the sun help him? or was it, like so many minor forces of earth and air, at the mercy of the God of Israel?

There is a terrible abruptness about the coming of the ninth plague. Like the third and sixth, it is inflicted unannounced; and the parleying, the driving of a bargain and then breaking it, by which the eighth was attended, is quite enough to account for this. Moreover, the experience of every man teaches him that each method has its own impressiveness: the announcement of punishment awes, and a surprise alarms, and when they are alternated, every possible door of access to the conscience is approached. If the heart of Pharaoh was now beyond hope, it does not follow that all his people were equally hardened. What an effect was produced upon those courtiers who so earnestly supported the recent demand of Moses, when this new plague fell upon them unawares!

But not only is there no announcement: the narrative is so concentrated and brief as to give a graphic rendering of the surprise and terror of the time. Not a word is wasted:

"The Lord said unto Moses, Stretch out thine hand toward heaven, that there may be darkness over the land of Egypt, even darkness that may be felt. And Moses stretched forth his hand toward heaven; and there was a thick darkness in all the land of Egypt three days: they saw not one another, neither rose any from his place three days; but all the children of Israel had light in their dwellings" (vers. 21-3). We are not told anything of the emotions of the king, as the prophet strides into his presence, and before the cowering court, silently raises his hand and quenches the day. We may infer his temper, if we please, from the frantic outbreak of menace and rage in which he presently warns the man whose coming is the same thing as calamity to see his face no more. Nothing is said, again, about the evil angels by which, according to later narratives, that long night was haunted.* And after all it is more impressive to think of the blank, utter paralysis of dread in which a nation held its breath, benumbed and motionless, until vitality was almost exhausted, and even Pharaoh chose rather to surrender than to die.

As the people lay cowering in their fear, there was plenty to occupy their minds. They would remember the first dreadful threat, not yet accomplished, to slay their firstborn; and the later assertion that if pestilence had not destroyed them, it was because God would plague them with all His plagues. They would reflect upon all their defeated duties, and how the sun himself was now withdrawn at the waving of the prophet's hand. And then a ghastly foreboding would complete their dread. What was it that darkness typified, in every Oriental nation—nay, in all the world? Death! Job speaks of

> "The land of darkness and of the shadow of death;
> A land of thick darkness, as darkness itself;
> A land of the shadow of death without any order,
> And where the light is as darkness" (x. 21, 22).

With us, a mortal sentence is given in a black cap; in the East, far more expressively, the head of the culprit was covered, and the darkness which thus came upon him expressed his doom. Thus "they covered Haman's face" (Esther vii. 8). Thus to destroy "the face of the covering that is cast over all peoples and the veil that is spread over all nations," is the same thing as to "swallow up death," being the visible destruction of the embodied death-sentence (Isa. xxv. 7, 8). And now this veil was spread over all the radiant land of Egypt. Chill, and hungry, and afraid to move, the worst horror of all that prolonged midnight was the mental agony of dire anticipation.

In other respects there had been far worse calamities, but through its effect upon the imagination this dreadful plague was a fit prelude to the tenth, which it hinted and premonished.

In the Apocryphal Book of Wisdom there is a remarkable study of this plague, regarded as retribution in kind. It avenges the oppression of Israel. "For when unrighteous men thought to oppress the holy nation, they being shut up in their houses, the prisoners of darkness, and fettered with the bonds of a long night, lay exiled from the eternal Providence" (xvii. 2). It expresses in the physical realm their spiritual misery: "For while they supposed to lie hid in their secret sins, they were scattered under a thick veil of forgetfulness" (ver. 3). It retorted on them the illusions of their sorcerers: "as for the illusions of art magick, they were put down. . . . For they, that promised to drive away terrors and troubles from a sick soul, were sick themselves of fear, worthy to be laughed at" (vers. 7, 8). In another place the Egyptians are declared to be worse than the men of Sodom, because they brought into bondage friends and not strangers, and grievously afflicted those whom they had received with feasting; "therefore even with blindness were these stricken, as those were at the doors of the righteous man." (xix. 14-17). And we may well believe that the long night was haunted with special terrors, if we add this wise explanation: "For wickedness, condemned by her own witness, is very timorous, and being pressed by conscience, always forecasteth grievous things. For"—and this is a sentence of transcendent merit—"fear is nothing else than a betrayal of the succours that reason offereth" (xvii. 11, 12). Therefore it is concluded that their own hearts were their worst tormentors, alarmed by whistling winds, or melodious song of birds, or pleasing fall of waters, "for the whole world shined with clear light, and none were hindered in their labour: over them only was spread a heavy night, an image of that darkness which should afterward receive them: yet were they unto themselves more grievous than the darkness" (vers. 20, 21).

Isaiah, too, who is full of allusions to the early history of his people, finds in this plague of darkness an image of all mental distress and spiritual gloom. "We look for light, but behold darkness; for brightness, but we walk in obscurity: we grope for the wall like the blind, yea, we grope as those that have no eyes: we stumble at noonday as in the twilight" (lix. 10). Here the sinful nation is reduced to the misery of Egypt. But if she were obedient she would enjoy all the immunities of her forefathers amid Egyptian gloom: "Then shall thy light rise in darkness and thy obscurity as the noonday" (lviii. 10); "Darkness shall cover the earth, and gross darkness the people, but the Lord shall arise upon thee, and His glory shall be seen upon thee" (lx. 2).

And, indeed, in the spiritual light which is sown for the righteous, and the obscuration of the judgment of the impure, this miracle is ever reproduced.

The history of Menephtah is that of a mean and cowardly prince. Dreams forbade him to share the perils of his army; a prophecy induced him to submit to exile, until his firstborn was of age to recover his dominions for him; and all we know of him is admirably suited to the character represented in this narrative. He will now submit once more, and this time every one shall go; yet he cannot make a frank concession: the flocks and herds (most valuable after the ravages of the murrain and the hail) must remain as a hostage for their return. But Moses is inflexible: not a hoof shall be left behind; and then the frenzy of a baffled autocrat breaks out into wild menaces; "Get thee from me; take heed to thyself; see my face no more; for in the day thou seest my face thou shalt die." The assent of Moses was grim: the rupture was complete. And when they once more met, it was the king that had changed his purpose, and on his face, not that of Moses, was the pallor of impending death.

In the conduct of the prophet, all through these stormy scenes, we see the difference between a meek spirit and a craven one. He was always ready to intercede; he never "reviles the ruler," nor transgresses the limits of courtesy toward his superior in rank; and yet he never falters, nor compromises, nor fails to represent worthily the awful Power he represents.

In the series of sharp contrasts, all the true dignity is with the servant of God, all the meanness and the shame with the proud king, who begins by insulting him, goes on to impose on

---

* Such is probably not the meaning in Ps. lxxviii. 49 (see R. V.), though from it the tradition may have sprung.

him, and ends by the most ignominious of surrenders, crowned with the most abortive of treacheries and the most abject of defeats.

CHAPTER XI.

THE LAST PLAGUE ANNOUNCED.

Exodus xi. 1-10.

The eleventh chapter is, strictly speaking, a supplement to the tenth: the first verses speak, as if in parenthesis, of a revelation made before the ninth plague, but held over to be mentioned in connection with the last, which it now announces; and the conversation with Pharaoh is a continuation of the same in which they mutually resolved to see each other's face no more. To account for the confidence of Moses, we are now told that God had revealed to him the close approach of the final blow, so long foreseen. In spite of seeming delays, the hour of the promise had arrived; in spite of his long reluctance, the king should even thrust them out; and then the order and discipline of their retreat would exhibit the advantages gained by expectation, by promises ofttimes disappointed, but always, like a false alarm which tries the readiness of a garrison, exhibiting the weak points in their organisation, and carrying their preparations farther.

The command given already to the women (iii. 22) is now extended to them all—that they should ask of the terror-stricken people such portable things as, however precious, poorly requited their generations of unpaid and cruel toil. (It has been already shown that the word absurdly rendered "borrow" means to ask; and is the same as when Sisera *asked* water and Jael gave him milk, and when Solomon *asked* wisdom, and did not *ask* long life, neither *asked* riches, neither *asked* the life of his enemies.) They were now to claim such wages as they could carry off, and thus the pride of Egypt was presently dedicated to construct and beautify the tabernacle of Jehovah. We read that the people found favour with the Egyptians, who were doubtless overjoyed to come to any sort of terms with them; "moreover the man Moses was very great in the land of Egypt, in the sight of Pharaoh's servants, and in the sight of the people." This is no unbecoming vaunt: it speaks only of the high place he held, as God's deputy and herald; and this tone of keen appreciation of the rank conceded him, compared with the utter absence of any insistence upon any action of his own, is evidence much rather of the authenticity of the work than the reverse.

By these demands expectation and faith were intensified; while the tidings of such confidence on one side, and such tame submission on the other, goes far to explain the suspicions and the rage of Pharaoh.

With this the narrative is resumed. Moses had said, "Thou shalt see my face no more." Now he adds, "Thus saith Jehovah, About midnight" (but not on that same night, since four days of preparation for the passover were yet to come) "I will go out into the midst of Egypt." This, then, was the meaning of his ready consent to be seen no more: Jehovah Himself, Who had dealt so dreadfully with them through other hands, was now Himself to come. "And all the firstborn of Egypt shall die," from the firstborn and viceroy of the king to the firstborn of the meanest of women, and even of the cattle in their stalls. (It is surely a remarkable coincidence that Menephtah's heroic son did actually sit upon his throne, that inscriptions engraven during his life exhibit his name in the royal cartouche, but that he perished early, and long before his father.) And the wail of demonstrative Oriental agony should be such as never was heard before. But the children of Israel should be distinguished and protected by their God. And all these courtiers should come and bow down before Moses (who even then has the good feeling not to include the king himself in this abasement), and instead of Pharaoh's insulting "Get thee from me—see my face no more," they should pray him saying, "Go hence, thou and thy people that follow thee." And remembering the abject entreaties, the infatuated treacheries, and now this crowning insult, he went out from Pharaoh in hot anger. He was angry and sinned not.

The ninth and tenth verses are a kind of summary: the appeals to Pharaoh are all over, and henceforth we shall find Moses preparing his own followers for their exodus. "And the Lord (had) said unto Moses, Pharaoh will not hearken unto you, that My wonders may be multiplied in the land of Egypt. And Moses and Aaron did all these wonders before Pharaoh; and the Lord made strong Pharaoh's heart, and he did not let the children of Israel go out of his land."

In the Gospel of St. John there comes just such a period. The record of miracle and controversy is at an end, and Jesus withdraws into the bosom of His intimate circle. It is scarcely possible that the evangelist was unconscious of the influence of this passage when he wrote: "But though He had done so many signs before them, yet they believed not on Him, that the word of Isaiah the prophet might be fulfilled which he spoke, Lord, who hath believed our report? . . . For this cause they could not believe, because that Isaiah said again, He hath blinded their eyes and hardened their heart, lest they should see with their eyes and perceive with their heart, and should turn, and I should heal them" (John xii. 37-40).

This is the tragedy of Egypt repeated in Israel; and the fact that the chosen seed is now the reprobate suffices, if any doubt remain, to prove that reprobation itself was not caprice, but retribution.

CHAPTER XII.

THE PASSOVER.

Exodus xii. 1-28.

We have now reached the birthday of the great Hebrew nation, and with it the first national institution, the feast of passover, which is also the first sacrifice of directly Divine institution, the earliest precept of the Hebrew legislation, and the only one given in Egypt.

The Jews had by this time learned to feel that they were a nation, if it were only through the struggle between their champion and the head of the greatest nation in the world. And the first aspect in which the feast of passover presents itself is that of a national commemoration.

This day was to be unto them the beginning of months; and in the change of their calendar to celebrate their emancipation, the device was anticipated by which France endeavoured to glorify the Revolution. All their reckoning was to look back to this signal event. "And this day shall be unto you for a memorial, and ye shall keep it for a feast unto the Lord; throughout your generations ye shall keep it a feast by an ordinance for ever" (xii. 14). "It shall be for a sign unto thee upon thine hand, and for a memorial between thine eyes, that the law of the Lord may be in thy mouth, for with a strong hand hath the Lord brought thee out of Egypt. Thou shalt therefore keep this ordinance in its season from year to year" (xiii. 9, 10).

Now for the first time we read of "the congregation of Israel" (xii. 3, 6), which was an assembly of the people represented by their elders (as may be seen by comparing the third verse with the twenty-first); and thus we discover that the "heads of houses" have been drawn into a larger unity. The clans are knit together into a nation.

Accordingly, the feast might not be celebrated by any solitary man. Companionship was vital to it. At every table one animal, complete and undissevered, should give to the feast a unity of sentiment; and as many should gather around as were likely to leave none of it uneaten. Neither might any of it be reserved to supply a hasty ration amid the confusion of the predicted march. The feast was to be one complete event, whole and perfect as the unity which it expressed. The very notion of a people is that of "community" in responsibilities, joys, and labours; and the solemn law by virtue of which, at this same hour, one blow will fall upon all Egypt, must now be accepted by Israel. Therefore loneliness at the feast of Passover is by the law, as well as in idea, impossible to any Jew. Every one can see the connection between this festival of unity and another, of which it is written, "We, being many, are one body, one loaf, for we are all partakers of that one loaf."

Now, the sentiment of nationality may so assert itself, like all exaggerated sentiments, as to assail others equally precious. In this century we have seen a revival of the Spartan theories which sacrificed the family to the state. Socialism and the *phalanstère* have proposed to do by public organisation, with the force of law, what natural instinct teaches us to leave to domestic influences. It is therefore worthy of notice that, as the chosen nation is carefully traced by revelation back to a holy family, so the national festival did not ignore the family tie, but consecrated it. The feast was to be eaten "according to their fathers' houses"; if a family were too small, it was to the "neighbour next unto his house" that each should turn for co-operation; and the patriotic celebration was to live on from age to age by the instruction which parents should carefully give their children (xii. 3, 26, xiii. 8).

The first ordinance of the Jewish religion was a domestic service. And this arrangement is divinely wise. Never was a nation truly prosperous or permanently strong which did not cherish the sanctities of home. Ancient Rome failed to resist the barbarians, not because her discipline had degenerated, but because evil habits in the home had ruined her population. The same is notoriously true of at least one great nation to-day. History is the sieve of God, in which He continually severs the chaff from the grain of nations, preserving what is temperate and pure and calm, and therefore valorous and wise.

In studying the institution of the Passover, with its profound typical analogies, we must not overlook the simple and obvious fact that God built His nation upon families, and bade their great national institution draw the members of each home together.

The national character of the feast is shown further because no Egyptian family escaped the blow. Opportunities had been given to them to evade some of the previous plagues. When the hail was announced, "he that feared the word of the Lord among the servants of Pharaoh made his servants and his cattle flee into the house"; and this renders the national solidarity, the partnership even of the innocent in the penalties of a people's guilt, the "community" of a nation, more apparent now. There was not a house where there was not one dead. The mixed multitude which came up with Israel came not because they had shared his exemptions, but because they dared not stay. It was an object-lesson given to Israel, which might have warned all his generations.

And if there is hideous vice in our own land to-day, or if the contrasts of poverty and wealth are so extreme that humanity is shocked by so much luxury insulting so much squalor,—if in any respect we feel that our own land, considering its supreme advantages, merits the wrath of God for its unworthiness,—then we have to fear and strive, not through public spirit alone, but as knowing that the chastisement of nations falls upon the corporate whole, upon us and upon our children.

But if the feast of the Passover was a commemoration, it also claims to be a sacrifice, and the first sacrifice which was Divinely founded and directed.

This brings us face to face with the great question, What is the doctrine which lies at the heart of the great institution of sacrifice?

We are not free to confine its meaning altogether to that which was visible at the time. This would contradict the whole doctrine of development, the intention of God that Christianity should blossom from the bud of Judaism, and the explicit assertion that the prophets were made aware that the full meaning and the date of what they uttered was reserved for the instruction of a later period (1 Peter i. 12).

But neither may we overlook the first palpable significance of any institution. Sacrifices never could have been devised to be a blind and empty pantomime to whole generations, for the benefit of their successors. Still less can one who believes in a genuine revelation to Moses suppose that their primary meaning was a false one, given in order that some truth might afterwards develop out of it.

What, then, might a pious and well-instructed Israelite discern beneath the surface of this institution?

To this question there have been many discordant answers, and the variance is by no means confined to unbelieving critics. Thus, a distinguished living expositor says in connection with the Paschal institution, "We speak not of blood as it is commonly understood, but of blood as the life, the love, the heart,—the whole quality of Deity." But it must be answered that Deity is the last suggestion which blood would convey to a Jewish mind: distinctly it is creature-life that it expresses; and the New Testament commentators make it plain that no other notion had even then evolved itself: they think of the offering of the Body of Jesus Christ, not of His Deity.* Neither of this feast, nor of that which the gospel of Jesus has evolved from it, can we find the solution by forgetting that the elements of the problem are, not deity, but a Body and Blood.

But when we approach the theories of rationalistic thinkers, we find a perfect chaos of rival speculations.

We are told that the Hebrew feasts were really agricultural—"Harvest festivals," and that the epithet Passover had its origin in the passage of the sun into Aries. But this great festival had a very secondary and subordinate connection with harvest (only the waving of a sheaf upon the second day) while the older calendar which was displaced to do it honour was truly agricultural, as may still be seen by the phrase, "The feast of ingathering *at the end of the year*, when thou gatherest in thy labours out of the field" (Exod. xxiii. 16).

In dealing with unbelief we must look at things from the unbelieving angle of vision. No sceptical theory has any right to invoke for its help a special and differentiating quality in Hebrew thought. Reject the supernatural, and the Jewish religion is only one among a number of similar creations of the mind of man "moving about in worlds unrecognised." And therefore we must ask, What notions of sacrifice were entertained, all around, when the Hebrew creed was forming itself?

Now, we read that "in the early days ... a sacrifice was a meal. .. Year after year, the return of vintage, corn-harvest, and sheep-shearing brought together the members of the household to eat and drink in the presence of Jehovah. .. When an honoured guest arrives there is slaughtered for him a calf, not without an offering of the blood and fat to the Deity" (Wellhausen, *Israel*, p. 76). Of the sense of sin and propitiation "the ancient sacrifices present few traces. .. An underlying reference of sacrifice to sin, speaking generally, was entirely absent. The ancient sacrifices were wholly of a joyous nature—a merry-making before Jehovah with music" (*ibid.*, p. 81).

We are at once confronted by the question, Where did the Jewish nation come by such a friendly conception of their deity? They had come out of Egypt, where human sacrifices were not rare. They had settled in Palestine, where such idyllic notions must have been as strange as in modern Ashantee. And we are told that human sacrifices (such as that of Isaac and of Jephthah's daughter) belong to this older period (p. 69). Are *they* joyous and festive? are they not an endeavour, by the offering up of something precious, to reconcile a Being Who is estranged? With our knowledge of what existed in Israel in the period confessed to be historical, and of the meaning of sacrifices all around in the period supposed to be mythical, and with the admission that human sacrifices must be taken into account, it is startling to be asked to believe that Hebrew sacrifices, with all their solemn import and all their freight of Christian symbolism, were originally no more than a gift to the Deity of a part of some happy banquet.

It is quite plain that no such theory can be reconciled with the story of the first passover. And accordingly this is declared to be non-historical, and to have originated in the time of the later kings. The offering of the firstborn is only "the expression of thankfulness to the Deity for fruitful flocks and herds. If claim is also laid to the human firstborn, this is merely a later generalisation" (Wellhausen, p. 88).*

But this claim is by no means the only stumbling-block in the way of the theory, serious a stumbling-block though it be. How came the bright festival to be spoiled by bitter herbs and "bread of affliction"? Is it natural that a merry feast should grow more austere as time elapses? Do we not find it hard enough to prevent the most sacred fest vals from reversing the supposed process, and degenerating into revels? And is not this the universal experience, from San Francisco to Bombay? Why was the mandate given to sprinkle the door of every house with blood, if the story originated after the feast had been centralised in Jerusalem, when, in fact, this precept had to be set aside as impracticable, their homes being at a distance? Why, again, were they bidden to slaughter the lamb "between the two evenings" (Exod. xii. 6)—that is to say, between sunset and the fading out of the light— unless the story was written long before such numbers had to be dealt with that the priests began to slaughter early in the afternoon, and continued until night? Why did the narrative set forth that every man might slaughter for his own house (a custom which still existed in the time of Hezekiah, when the Levites only slaughtered "the passovers" for those who were not ceremonially clean, 2 Chron. xxx. 17), if there were no stout and strong historical foundation for the older method?

Stranger still, why was the original command invented, that the lamb should be chosen and separated four days before the feast? There is no trace of any intention that this precept should apply to the first passover alone. It is somewhat unexpected there, interrupting the hurry and movement of the narrative with an interval of quiet expectation, not otherwise hinted at, which we comprehend and value when discovered, rather than anticipate in advance. It is the very last circumstance which the Priestly Code would have invented, when the time which could be conveniently spent upon a pilgrimage was too brief to suffer the custom to be perpetuated. The selection of the lamb upon the tenth day, the slaying of it at home, the striking of the blood upon the door, and the use of hyssop, as in other sacrifices, with which to sprinkle it whether upon door or altar; the eating of the feast standing, with staff in hand and girded loins; the application only to one day of the

---

* Though of course the Person Whose Body was thus offered is Divine (Acts xx. 28), and this gives inestimable value to the offering.

* Here the sceptical theorists are widely divided among themselves. Kuenen has discussed this whole theory, and rejected it as "irreconcilable with what the Old Testament itself asserts in justification of this sacrifice." And he is driven to connect it with the notion of atonement. "Jahveh appears as a severe being who must be propitiated with sacrifices." He has therefore to introduce the notion of human sacrifice, in order to get rid of the connection with the penal death of the Egyptians, and of the miraculous, which this example would establish. (*Religion of Israel*, Eng. Trans., i. 239, 240.)

precept to eat no leavened bread, and the sharing in the feast by all, without regard to ceremonial defilement,—all these are cardinal differences between the first passover and later ones. Can we be blind to their significance? Even a drastic revision of the story, such as some have fancied, would certainly have expunged every divergence upon points so capital as these. Nor could any evidence of the antiquity of the institution be clearer than its existence in a form, the details of which have had to be so boldly modified under the pressure of the exigencies of the later time.

Taking, then, the narrative as it stands, we place ourselves by an effort of the historical imagination among those to whom Moses gave his instructions, and ask what emotions are excited as we listen.

Certainly no light and joyous feeling that we are going to celebrate a feast, and share our good things with our deity. Nay, but an alarmed surprise. Hitherto, among the admonitory and preliminary plagues of Egypt, Israel had enjoyed a painless and unbought exemption. The murrain had not slain their cattle, nor the locusts devoured their land, nor the darkness obscured their dwellings. Such admonitions they needed not. But now the judgment itself is impending, and they learn that they, like the Egyptians whom they have begun to despise, are in danger from the destroying angel. The first paschal feast was eaten by no man with a light heart. Each listened for the rustling of awful wings, and grew cold, as under the eyes of the death which was, even then, scrutinising his lintels and his doorposts.

And this would set him thinking that even a gracious God, Who had "come down" to save him from his tyrants, discerned in him grave reasons for displeasure, since his acceptance, while others died, was not of course. His own conscience would then quickly tell him what some at least of those reasons were.

But he would also learn that the exemption which he did not possess by right (although a son of Abraham) he might obtain through grace. The goodness of God did not pronounce him safe, but it pointed out to him a way of salvation. He would scarcely observe, so entirely was it a matter of course, that this way must be of God's appointment and not of his own invention—that if he devised much more costly, elaborate, and imposing ceremonies to replace those which Moses taught him, he would perish like any Egyptian who devised nothing, but simply cowered under the shadow of the impending doom.

Nor was the salvation without price. It was not a prayer nor a fast which bought it, but a life. The conviction that a redemption was necessary if God should be at once just and a justifier of the ungodly sprang neither from a later hairsplitting logic, nor from a methodising theological science: it really lay upon the very surface of this and every offering for sin, as distinguished from those offerings which expressed the gratitude of the accepted.

We have not far to search for evidence that the lamb was really regarded as a substitute and ransom. The assertion is part and parcel of the narrative itself. For, in commemoration of this deliverance, every firstborn of Israel, whether of man or beast, was set apart unto the Lord. The words are, "Thou shalt cause to PASS OVER unto the Lord all that openeth the womb, and every firstling which thou hast that cometh of a beast; the males shall be the Lord's" (xiii. 12). What, then, should be done with the firstborn of a creature unfit for sacrifice? It should be replaced by a clean offering, and then it was said to be redeemed. Substitution or death was the inexorable rule. "Every firstborn of an ass thou shalt redeem with a lamb, and if thou wilt not redeem it, then thou shalt break its neck." The meaning of this injunction is unmistakable. But it applies also to man: "All my firstborn of man among thy sons thou shalt redeem." And when their sons should ask "What meaneth this?" they were to explain that when Pharaoh hardened himself against letting them go from Egypt, "the Lord slew all the firstborn in the land, . . . therefore I sacrifice to the Lord all that openeth the womb being males; but all the firstborn of my sons I redeem" (xiii. 12-15).

Words could not more plainly assert that the lives of the firstborn of Israel were forfeited, that they were brought back by the substitution of another creature, which died instead, and that the transaction answered to the Passover ("thou shalt cause to pass over unto the Lord"). Presently the tribe of Levi was taken "instead of all the firstborn of the children of Israel." But since there were two hundred and seventy-three of such firstborn children over and above the number of the Levites, it became necessary to "redeem" these; and this was actually done by a cash payment of five shekels apiece. Of this payment the same phrase is used: it is "redemption-money"—the money wherewith the odd number of them is redeemed (Num. iii. 44-51).

The question at present is not whether modern taste approves of all this, or resents it: we are simply inquiring whether an ancient Jew was taught to think of the lamb as offered in his stead.

And now let it be observed that this idea has sunk deep into all the literature of Palestine. The Jews are not so much the beloved of Jehovah as His redeemed—"Thy people whom Thou hast redeemed" (1 Chron. xvii. 21). In fresh troubles the prayer is, "Redeem Israel, O Lord" (Ps. xxv. 22), and the same word is often used where we have ignored the allusion and rendered it "*Deliver* me because of mine enemies . . . *deliver* me from the oppression of men" (Ps. lxix. 18, cxix. 134). And the future troubles are to end in a deliverance of the same kind: "The *ransomed* of the Lord shall return and come with singing unto Zion" (Isa. xxxv. 10, li. 11); and at the last "I will *ransom* them from the power of the grave" (Hos. xiii. 14). In all these places, the word is the same as in this narrative.

It is not too much to say that if modern theology were not affected by this ancient problem, if we regarded the creed of the Hebrews simply as we look at the mythologies of other peoples, there would be no more doubt that the early Jews believed in propitiatory sacrifice than that Phœnicians did. We should simply admire the purity, the absence of cruel and degrading accessories, with which this most perilous and yet humbling and admonitory doctrine was held in Israel.

The Christian applications of this doctrine must be considered along with the whole question of the typical character of the history. But it is not now premature to add, that even in the Old Testament there is abundant evidence that the types were semi-transparent, and behind them something greater was discerned, so that after it was written "Bring no more vain oblations," Isaiah could exclaim, "The Lord hath laid on Him the iniquity of us all. He was led as a lamb to the slaughter. When Thou shalt make His soul a trespass-offering He shall see His seed" (Isa. i. 13, liii. 6, 7, 10). And the full power of this last verse will only be felt when we remember the statement made elsewhere of the principle which underlay the sacrifices: "the life (or soul) of the flesh is in the blood, and I have given it to you upon the altar to make atonement for your souls; for it is the blood that maketh atonement by reason of the life" (or "soul"—Lev. xvii. 11, R. V.). It is even startling to read the two verses together: "Thou shalt make His soul a trespass-offering;" "The blood maketh atonement by reason of the soul . . . the soul of the flesh is in the blood." *

It is still more impressive to remember that a Servant of Jehovah has actually arisen in Whom this doctrine has assumed a form acceptable to the best and holiest intellects and consciences of ages and civilisations widely remote from that in which it was conceived.

Another doctrine preached by the passover to every Jew was that he must be a worker together with God, must himself use what the Lord pointed out, and his own lintels and doorposts must openly exhibit the fact that he laid claim to the benefit of the institution of the Lord Jehovah's passover. With what strange feelings, upon the morrow, did the orphaned people of Egypt discover the stain of blood on the forsaken houses of all their emancipated slaves!

The lamb having been offered up to God, a new stage in the symbolism is entered upon. The body of the sacrifice, as well as the blood, is His: "Ye shall eat it in haste, it is the Lord's passover" (ver. 11). Instead of being a feast of theirs, which they share with Him, it is an offering of which, when the blood has been sprinkled on the doors, He permits His people, now accepted and favoured, to partake. They are His guests; and therefore He prescribes all the manner of their eating, the attitude so expressive of haste, and the unleavened "bread of affliction" and bitter herbs, which told that the object of this feast was not the indulgence of the flesh but the edification of the spirit, "a feast unto the Lord."

And in the strength of this meat they are launched upon their new career, freemen, pilgrims of God, from Egyptian bondage to a Promised Land.

It is now time to examine the chapter in more detail, and gather up such points as the preceding discussion has not reached.

(Ver. 1.) The opening words, "Jehovah spake unto Moses and Aaron in the land of Egypt," have all the appearance of opening a separate document, and suggest, with certain other evidence, the notion of a fragment written very shortly after the event, and afterwards incorporated into the present narrative. And they are, in the same degree, favourable to the authenticity of the book.

---

* The astonishing significance of this declaration would only be deepened if we accepted the theories now so fashionable, and believed that the later passage in Isaiah was the fruit of a period when the full-blown Priestly Code was in process of development out of "the small body of legislation contained in Lev. xvii.–xxvi." What a strange time for such a spiritual application of sacrificial language!

(Ver. 2) The commandment to link their emancipation with a festival, and with the calendar, is the earliest example and the sufficient vindication of sacred festivals, which, even yet, some persons consider to be superstitious and judaical. But it is a strange doctrine that the Passover deserved honour better than Easter does, or that there is anything more servile and unchristian in celebrating the birth of all the hopes of all mankind than in commemorating one's own birth.

(Ver. 5.) The selection of a lamb for a sacrifice so quickly became universal that there is no trace anywhere of the use of a kid in place of it. The alternative is therefore an indication of antiquity, while the qualities required—innocent youth and the absence of blemish—were sure to suggest a typical significance. For, if they were merely to enhance its value, why not choose a costlier animal?

Various meanings have been discovered in the four days during which it was reserved; but perhaps the true object was to give time for deliberation, for the solemnity and import of the institution to fill the minds of the people; time also for preparation, since the night itself was one of extreme haste, and prompt action can only be obtained by leisurely anticipation. We have Scriptural authority for applying it to the Antitype, Who also was foredoomed, "the Lamb slain from the foundation of the world" (Rev. xiii. 8).

But now it has to be observed that throughout the poetic literature the people is taught to think of itself as a flock of sheep. "Thou leddest Thy people like a flock by the hand of Moses and Aaron" (Ps. lxxvii. 20); "We are Thy people and the sheep of Thy pasture" (Ps. lxxix. 13); "All we like sheep have gone astray" (Isa. liii. 6); "Ye, O My sheep, the sheep of My pasture, are men" (Ezek. xxxiv. 31); "The Lord of hosts hath visited His flock" (Zech. x. 3). All such language would make more easy the conception that what replaced the forfeited life was in some sense, figuratively, in the religious idea, a kindred victim. One who offered a lamb as his substitute sang "The Lord is my shepherd." "I have gone astray like a lost sheep" (Ps. xxiii. 1, cxix. 176).

(Ver. 3, 6.) Very instructive it is that this first sacrifice of Judaism could be offered by all the heads of houses. We have seen that the Levites were presently put into the place of the eldest son, but also that this function was exercised down to the time of Hezekiah by all who were ceremonially clean, whereas the opposite holds good, immediately afterwards, in the great passover of Joshua (2 Chron. xxx. 17, xxxv. 11).

It is impossible that this incongruity could be devised, for the sake of plausibility, in a narrative which rested on no solid basis. It goes far to establish what has been so anxiously denied—the reality of the centralised worship in the time of Hezekiah. And it also establishes the great doctrine that priesthood was held not by a superior caste, but on behalf of the whole nation, in whom it was theoretically vested, and for whom the priest acted, so that they were "a nation of priests."

(Ver. 8.) The use of unleavened bread is distinctly said to be in commemoration of their haste—"for thou camest out of Egypt in haste" (Deut. xvi. 3)—but it does not follow that they were forced by haste to eat their bread unleavened at the first. It was quite as easy to prepare leavened bread as to provide the paschal lamb four days previously.

We may therefore seek for some further explanation, and this we find in the same verse in Deuteronomy, in the expression "bread of affliction." They were to receive the meat of passover with a reproachful sense of their unworthiness: humbly, with bread of affliction and with bitter herbs.

Moreover, we learn from St. Paul that unleavened bread represents simplicity and truth; and our Lord spoke of the leaven of the Pharisees and of Herod (Mark viii. 15). And this is not only because leaven was supposed to be of the same nature as corruption. We ourselves always mean something unworthy when we speak of *mixed* motives, possible though it be to act from two motives, both of them high-minded. Now, leaven represents mixture in its most subtle and penetrating form.

The paschal feast did not express any such luxurious and sentimental religionism as finds in the story of the cross an easy joy, or even a delicate and pleasing stimulus for the softer emotions, "a very lovely song of one that hath a pleasant voice, and playeth well on an instrument." No, it has vigour and nourishment for those who truly hunger, but its bread is unfermented, and it must be eaten with bitter herbs.

(Ver. 9.) Many Jewish sacrifices were "sodden," but this had to be roast with fire. It may have been to represent suffering that this was enjoined. But it comes to us along with a command to consume all the flesh, reserving none and rejecting none. Now, though boiling does not mutilate, it dissipates; a certain amount of tissue is lost, more is relaxed, and its cohesion rendered feeble; and so the duty of its complete reception is accentuated by the words "not sodden at all with water." Nor should it be a barbarous feast, such as many idolatries encouraged: true religion civilises; "eat not of it at all raw."

(Ver. 10.) Nor should any of it be left until the morning. At the first celebration, with a hasty exodus impending, this would have involved exposure to profanation. In later times it might have involved superstitious abuses. And therefore the same rule is laid down which the Church of England has carried on for the same reasons into the Communion feast—that all must be consumed. Nor can we fail to see an ideal fitness in the precept. Of the gift of God we may not select what gratifies our taste or commends itself to our desires; all is good; all must be accepted; a partial reception of His grace is no valid reception at all.

(Ver. 12.) In describing the coming wrath, we understand the inclusion equally of innocent and guilty men, because it is thus that all national vengeance operates; and we receive the benefits of corporate life at the cost, often heavy, of its penalties. The animal world also has to suffer with us; the whole creation groaneth together now, and all expects together the benefit of our adoption hereafter. But what were the judgments against the idols of Egypt, which this verse predicts, and another (Num. xxxiii. 4) declares to be accomplished? They doubtless consisted chiefly in the destruction of sacred animals, from the beetle and the frog to the holy ox of Apis—from the cat, the monkey, and the dog, to the lion, the hippopotamus, and the crocodile. In their overthrow a blow was dealt which shook the whole system to its foundation; for how could the same confidence be felt in sacred images when all the sacred beasts had once been slain by a rival invisible Spiritual Being! And more is implied than that they should share the common desolation: the text says plainly, of men and beasts the firstborn must die, but all of these. The difference in the phrase is obvious and indisputable; and in its fulfilment all Egypt saw the act of a hostile and victorious deity.

(Ver. 13.) "And the blood shall be to you for a token upon the houses where ye are." That it was a token to the destroying angel we see plainly; but why *to them?* Is it enough to explain the assertion, with some, as meaning, upon their behalf? Rather let us say that the publicity, the exhibition upon their doorposts of the sacrifice offered within, was not to inform and guide the angel, but to edify the people. They should perform an open act of faith. Their houses should be visibly set apart. "With the mouth confession" (of faith) "is made unto salvation," unto that deliverance from a hundred evasions and equivocations, and as many inward doubts and hesitations, which comes when any decisive act is done, when the die is cast and the Rubicon crossed. A similar effect upon the mind, calming and steadying it, was produced when the Israelite carried out the blood of the lamb, and by sprinkling it upon the door post formally claimed his exemption, and returned with the consciousness that between him and the imminent death a visible barrier interposed itself.

Will any one deny that a similar help is offered to us of the later Church in our many opportunities of avowing a fixed and personal belief? Whoever refuses to comply with an unholy custom because he belongs to Christ, whoever joins heartily in worship at the cost of making himself remarkable, whoever nerves himself to kneel at the Holy Table although he feels himself unworthy, that man has broken through many snares; he has gained assurance that his choice of God is a reality: he has shown his flag; and this public avowal is not only a sign to others, but also a token to himself.

But this is only half the doctrine of this action. What he should thus openly avow was his trust (as we have shown) in atoning blood.

And in the day of our peril what shall be our reliance? That our doors are trodden by orthodox visitants only? that the lintels are clean, and the inhabitants temperate and pure? or that the Blood of Christ has cleansed our conscience?

Therefore (ver. 22) the blood was sprinkled with hyssop, of which the light and elastic sprays were admirably suited for such use, but which was reserved in the Law for those sacrifices which expiated sin (Lev. xiv. 49; Num. xix. 18, 19). And therefore also none should go forth out of his house until the morning, for we are not to content ourselves with having once invoked the shelter of God: we are to abide under its protection while danger lasts.

And (ver. 23) upon the condition of this marking of their doorposts the Lord should *pass over* their houses. The phrase is noteworthy, because it recurs throughout the narrative, being employed nine times in this chapter; and because the same word is found in Isaiah, again in contrast with the ruin of others, and with an interesting and beautiful expansion of the hovering, poised notion which belongs to the word.*

Repeated commandments are given to parents to teach the meaning of this institution to their children, (xii. 26, xiii. 8). And there is something almost cynical in the notion of a later mythologist devising this appeal to a tradition which had no existence at all; enrolling, in support of his new institutions, the testimony (which had never been borne) of fathers who had never taught any story of the kind.

On the other hand, there is something idyllic and beautiful in the minute instruction given to the heads of families to teach their children, and in the simple words put into their mouths, "It is because of that which the Lord did for me when I came forth out of Egypt." It carries us forward to these weary days when children scarcely see the face of one who goes out to labour before they are awake, and returns exhausted when their day is over, and who himself too often needs the most elementary instruction, these heartless days when the teaching of religion devolves, in thousands of families, upon the stranger who instructs, for one hour in the week, a class in Sunday-school. The contrast is not reassuring.

When all these instructions were given to Israel, the people bowed their heads and worshipped. The bones of most of them were doomed to whiten in the wilderness. They perished by serpents and by "the destroyer"; they fell in one day three-and-twenty thousand, because they were discontented and rebellious and unholy. And yet they could adore the gracious Giver of promises and Slayer of foes. They would not obey, but they were quite ready to accept benefits, to experience deliverance, to become the favourites of heaven, to march to Palestine. So are too many fain to be made happy, to find peace, to taste the good word of God and the powers of the age to come, to go to heaven. But they will not take up a cross. They will murmur if the well is bitter, if they have no flesh but only angels' food, if the goodly land is defended by powerful enemies.

On these terms, they cannot be Christ's disciples.

It is apparently the mention of a mixed multitude, who came with Israel out of Egypt, which suggests the insertion, in a separate and dislocated paragraph, of the law of the passover concerning strangers (vers. 38, 43-49).

An alien was not to eat thereof: it belonged especially to the covenant people. But who was a stranger? A slave should be circumcised and eat thereof; for it was one of the benignant provisions of the law that there should not be added, to the many severities of his condition, any religious disabilities. The time would come when all nations should be blessed in the seed of Abraham. In that day the poor would receive a special beatitude; and in the meantime, as the first indication of catholicity beneath the surface of an exclusive ritual, it was announced, foremost among those who should be welcomed within the fold, that a slave should be circumcised and eat the passover.

* So that it is used equally of the slow action of the lame, and of the lingering movements of the false prophets when there was none to answer (2 Sam. iv. 4 ; 1 Kings xviii. 26). "The Lord of Hosts shall come down to fight upon Mount Zion. . . . As birds flying, so will the Lord of Hosts protect Jerusalem; He will PASS OVER and preserve it" (Isa. xxxi. 4, 5).

And if a sojourner desired to eat thereof, he should be mindful of his domestic obligations: all his males should be circumcised along with him, and then his disabilities were at an end. Surely we can see in these provisions the germ of the broader and more generous welcome which Christ offers to the world. Let it be added that this admission of strangers had been already implied at verse 19: while every form of coercion was prohibited by the words "a sojourner and a hired servant shall not eat of it," in verse 45.

THE TENTH PLAGUE.

EXODUS xii. 29-36.

And now the blow fell. Infants grew cold in their mothers' arms; ripe statesmen and crafty priests lost breath as they reposed: the wisest, the strongest, and the most hopeful of the nation were blotted out at once, for the firstborn of a population is its flower.

Pharaoh Menephtah had only reached the throne by the death of two elder brethren, and therefore history confirms the assertion that he "rose up," when the firstborn were dead; but it also justifies the statement that his firstborn died, for the gallant and promising youth who had reconquered for him his lost territories, and who actually shared his rule and "sat upon the throne," Menephtah Seti, is now shown to have died early, and never to have held an independent sceptre.

We can imagine the scene. Suspense and terror must have been wide-spread; for the former plagues had given authority to the more dreadful threat, the fulfilment of which was now to be expected, since all negotiations between Moses and Pharaoh had been formally broken off.

Strange and confident movements and doubtless menacing expressions among the Hebrews would also make this night a fearful one, and there was little rest for "those who feared the Lord among the servants of Pharaoh." These, knowing where the danger lay, would watch their firstborn well, and when the ashy change came suddenly upon a blooming face, and they raised the wild cry of Eastern bereavement, then others awoke to the same misery. From remote villages and lonely hamlets the clamour of great populations was echoed back; and when, under midnight skies in which the strong wind of the morrow was already moaning, the awestruck people rushed into their temples, there the corpses of their animal deities glared at them with glassy eyes.

Thus the cup which they had made their slaves to drink was put in larger measure to their own lips at last, and not infants only were snatched away, but sons around whom years of tenderness had woven stronger ties; and the loss of their bondsmen, from which they feared so much national weakness, had to be endured along with a far deadlier drain of their own life-blood. The universal wail was bitter, and hopeless, and full of terror even more than woe; for they said, "We be all dead men." Without the consolation of ministering by sick beds, or the romance and gallant excitement of war, "there was not a house where there was not one dead," and this is said to give sharpness to the statement that there was a great cry in Egypt.

Then came such a moment as the Hebrew temperament keenly enjoyed, when "the sons of them that oppressed them came bending unto them, and all they that despised them bowed themselves down at the soles of their feet." Pharaoh sent at midnight to surrender everything that could possibly be demanded, and in his abject fear added, "and bless me also"; and the Egyptians were urgent on them to begone, and when they demanded the portable wealth of the land,—a poor ransom from a vanquished enemy, and a still poorer payment for generations of forced labour,—"the Lord gave them favour" (is there not a saturnine irony in the phrase?) "in the sight of the Egyptians, so that they let them have what they asked. And they spoiled the Egyptians."

By this analogy St. Augustine defended the use of heathen learning in defence of Christian truth. Clogged by superstitions, he said, it contained also liberal instruction, and truths even concerning God—"gold and silver which they did not themselves create, but dug out of the mines of God's providence, and misapplied. These we should reclaim, and apply to Christian use" (*De Doct. Chr.*, 60, 61).

And the main lesson of the story lies so plainly upon the surface that one scarcely needs to state it. What God requires *must* ultimately be done; and human resistance, however stubborn and protracted, will only make the result more painful and more signal at the last.

Now, every concern of our obscure daily lives comes under this law as surely as the actions of a Pharaoh.

THE EXODUS.

Exodus xii. 37-42.

The children of Israel journeyed from Rameses to Succoth. Already, at the outset of their journey, controversy has had much to say about their route. Much ingenuity has been expended upon the theory which brought their early journey along the Mediterranean coast, and made the overthrow of the Egyptians take place in "that Serbonian bog where armies whole have sunk." But it may fairly be assumed that this view was refuted even before the recent identification of the sites of Rameses and Pihahiroth rendered it untenable.

How came these trampled slaves, who could not call their lives their own, to possess the cattle which we read of as having escaped the murrain, and the number of which is here said to have been very great?

Just before Moses returned, and when the Pharaoh of the Exodus appears upon the scene, we are told that "their cry came up unto God, . . . and God heard their groaning, and God remembered His covenant . . . and God saw the children of Israel, and God took knowledge of them" (ii. 23).

May not this verse point to something unrecorded, some event before their final deliverance? The conjecture is a happy one that it refers to their share in the revolt of subject races which drove Menephtah for twelve years out of his northern territories. If so, there was time for a considerable return of prosperity; and the retention or forfeiture of their chattels when they were reconquered would depend very greatly upon circumstances unknown to us. At all events, this revolt is evidence, which is amply corroborated by history and the inscriptions, of the existence of just such a discontented and servile element in the population as the "mixed multitude" which came out with them repeatedly proved itself to be.

But here we come upon a problem of another kind. How long was Israel in the house of bondage? Can we rely upon the present Hebrew text, which says that "their sojourning which they sojourned in Egypt, was four hundred and thirty years. And it came to pass at the end of the four hundred and thirty years, even the selfsame day it came to pass, that all the hosts of the Lord came out of the land of Egypt" (xii. 40, 41).

Certain ancient versions have departed from this text. The Septuagint reads, "The sojourning of the children of Israel which they sojourned in Egypt and *in the land of Canaan*, was four hundred and thirty years"; and the Samaritan agrees with this, except that it has "the sojourning of the children of Israel and *of their fathers*." The question is, which reading is correct? Must we date the four hundred and thirty years from Abraham's arrival in Canaan, or from Jacob's descent into Egypt?

For the shorter period there are two strong arguments. The genealogies in the Pentateuch range from four persons to six between Jacob and the Exodus, which number is quite unable to reach over four centuries. And St. Paul says of the covenant with Abraham that "the law which came four hundred and thirty years after" (*i. e.*, after the time of Abraham) "could not disannul it" (Gal. iii. 17).

This reference by St. Paul is not so decisive as it may appear, because he habitually quotes the Septuagint, even where he must have known that it deviates from the Hebrew, provided that the deviation does not compromise the matter in hand. Here, he was in nowise concerned with the chronology, and had no reason to perplex a Gentile church by correcting it. But it was a different matter with St. Stephen, arguing his case before the Hebrew council. And he quotes plainly and confidently the prediction that the seed of Abraham should be four hundred years in bondage, and that one nation should entreat them evil four hundred years (Acts vii. 6). Again, this is the clear intention of the words in Genesis (xv. 13). And as to the genealogies, we know them to have been cut down, so that seven names are omitted from that of Ezra, and three at least from that of our Lord Himself. Certainly when we consider the great population implied in an army of six hundred thousand adult men, we must admit that the longer period is inherently the more probable of the two. But we can only assert with confidence that just when their deliverance was due it was accomplished, and they who had come down a handful, and whom cruel oppression had striven to decimate, came forth, no undisciplined mob, but armies moving in organised and regulated detachments: "the Lord did bring the children of Israel forth by their hosts" (ver. 51). "And the children of Israel went up armed out of the land of Egypt" (xiii. 18).

CHAPTER XIII.

THE LAW OF THE FIRSTBORN.

Exodus xiii. 1.

Much that was said in the twelfth chapter is repeated in the thirteenth. And this repetition is clearly due to a formal rehearsal, made when all "their hosts" had mustered in Succoth after their first march; for Moses says, "Remember this day, in which ye came out" (ver. 3). Already it had been spoken of as a day much to be remembered, and for its perpetuation the ordinance of the Passover had been founded.

But now this charge is given as a fit prologue for the remarkable institution which follows—the consecration to God of all unblemished males who are the firstborn of their mothers—for such is the full statement of what is claimed.

In speaking to Moses the Lord says, "Sanctify unto Me all the firstborn . . . it is Mine." But Moses, addressing the people, advances gradually, and almost diplomatically. First he reminds them of their deliverance, and in so doing he employs a phrase which could only have been used at the exact stage when they were emancipated and yet upon Egyptian soil: "By strength of hand the Lord brought you out *from this place*" (ver. 3). Then he charges them not to forget their rescue, in the dangerous time of their prosperity, when the Lord shall have brought them into the land which He swore to give them; and he repeats the ordinance of unleavened bread. And it is only then that he proceeds to announce the permanent consecration of all their firstborn—the abiding doctrine that these, who naturally represent the nation, are for its unworthiness forfeited, and yet by the grace of God redeemed.

God, Who gave all and pardons all, demands a return, not as a tax which is levied for its own sake, but as a confession of dependence, and like the silk flag presented to the sovereign, on the anniversaries of the two greatest of English victories, by the descendants of the conquerors, who hold their estates upon that tenure. The firstborn, thus dedicated, should have formed a sacred class, a powerful element in Hebrew life enlisted on the side of God.

For these, as we have already seen, the Levites were afterwards substituted (Num. iii. 44), and there is perhaps some allusion to this change in the direction that "all the firstborn of man thou shalt redeem" (ver. 13). But yet the demand is stated too broadly and imperatively to belong to that later modification: it suits exactly the time to which it is attributed, before the tribe of Levi was substituted for the firstborn of all.

"They are Mine," said Jehovah, Who needed not, that night, to remind them what He had wrought the night before. It is for precisely the same reason that St. Paul claims all souls for God: "Ye are not your own, ye are bought with a price; therefore glorify God with your bodies and with your spirits, which are God's."

And besides the general claim upon us all, each of us should feel, like the firstborn, that every special mercy is a call to special gratitude, to more earnest dedication. "I beseech you, by the mercies of God, that ye present your bodies a living sacrifice" (Rom. xii. 1).

There is a tone of exultant confidence in the words of Moses, very interesting and curious. He and his nation are breathing the free air at last. The deliverance that has been given makes all the promise that remains secure. As one who feels his pardon will surely not despair of heaven, so Moses twice over instructs the people what to do when God shall have kept the oath which He swore, and brought them into Canaan, into the land flowing with milk and honey. Then they must observe His passover. Then they must consecrate their firstborn.

And twice over this emancipator and lawgiver, in the first flush of his success, impresses upon them the homely duty of teaching their households what God had done for them (vers. 8, 14; *cf.* xii. 26).

This, accordingly, the Psalmist learned, and in his turn transmitted. He heard with his ears and his fathers told him what God did in their days, in the days of old. And he told the generation to come the praises of Jehovah, and His strength, and His wondrous works (Ps. xliv. 1, lxxviii. 4).

But it is absurd to treat these verses, as Kuenen does, as evidence that the story is mere legend: "transmitted from mouth to mouth, it gradually lost its accuracy and precision, and adopted all sorts of foreign elements." To prove which, we are gravely referred to passages like this. (*Religion of Israel*, i. 22, Eng. Vers.) The duty of oral instruction is still acknowledged, but this does not prove that the narrative is still unwritten.

From the emphatic language in which Moses urged this double duty, too much forgotten still, of remembering and showing forth the goodness of God, sprang the curious custom of the wearing of phylacteries. But the Jews were not bidden to wear signs and frontlets: they were bidden to let hallowed memories be unto them in the place of such charms as they had seen the Egyptians wear, "for a sign unto thee, upon thine hand, and for a frontlet between thine eyes, that the law of the Lord may be in thy mouth" (ver. 9). Such language is frequent in the Old Testament, where mercy and truth should be bound around their necks; their fathers' commandments should be tied around their necks, bound on their fingers, written on their hearts; and Sion should clothe herself with her converts as an ornament, and gird them upon her as a bride doth (Prov. iii. 3, vi. 21, vii. 3; Isa. xlix. 18).

But human nature still finds the letter of many a commandment easier than the spirit, a ceremony than an obedient heart, penance than penitence, ashes on the forehead than a contrite spirit, and a phylactery than the gratitude and acknowledgment which ought to be unto us for a sign on the hand and a frontlet between the eyes.

We have already observed the connection between the thirteenth verse and the events of the previous night. But there is an interesting touch of nature in the words "the firstling of an ass thou shalt redeem with a lamb." It was afterwards rightly perceived that all unclean animals should follow the same rule; but why was only the ass mentioned? Plainly because those humble journeyers had no other beast of burden. Horses pursued them presently, but even the Egyptians of that period used them only in war. The trampled Hebrews would not possess camels. And thus again, in the tenth commandment, when the stateliest of their cattle is specified, no beast of burden is named with it but the ass: "Thou shalt not covet . . . his ox nor his ass." It is an undesigned coincidence of real value; a phrase which would never have been devised by legislators of a later date; a frank and unconscious evidence of the genuineness of the story.

Some time before this, a new and fierce race, whose name declared them to be "emigrants," had thrust itself in among the tribes of Canaan —a race which was long to wage equal war with Israel, and not seldom to see his back turned in battle. They now held all the south of Palestine, from the brook of Egypt to Ekron (Josh. xv. 4, 47). And if Moses in the flush of his success had pushed on by the straight and easy route into the promised land, the first shock of combat with them would have been felt in a few weeks. But "God led them not by the way of the Philistines, though that was near, for God said, Lest peradventure the people repent them when they see war, and they return to Egypt" (ver. 17).

From this we learn two lessons. Why did not He, Who presently made strong the hearts of the Egyptians to plunge into the bed of the sea, make the hearts of His own people strong to defy the Philistines? The answer is a striking and solemn one. Neither God in the Old Testament, nor God manifested in the flesh, is ever recorded to have wrought any miracle of spiritual advancement or overthrow. Thus the Egyptians were but confirmed in their own choice: their decision was carried further. And even Saul of Tarsus was illuminated, not coerced: he might have disobeyed the heavenly vision. He was not an insincere man suddenly coerced into earnestness, nor a coward suddenly made brave. In the moral world, adequate means are always employed for the securing of desired effects. Love, gratitude, the sense of danger and of grace, are the powers which elevate characters. And persons who live in sensuality, fraud, or falsehood, hoping to be saved some day by a sort of miracle of grace, ought to ponder this truth, which may not be the gospel now fashionable, but is unquestionably the statement of a Scriptural fact: *in the moral sphere, God works by means and not by miracle.*

A free life, the desert air, the rejection of the unfit by many visitations, and the growth of a new generation amid thrilling events, in a soul-stirring region, and under the pure influences of the law,—these were necessary before Israel could cross steel with the warlike children of the Philistines; and even then, it was not with them that he should begin.

The other lesson we learn is the tender fidelity of God, Who will not suffer us to be tempted above that we are able to bear. He led them aside into the desert, whither He still in mercy leads very many who think it a heavy judgment to be there.

THE BONES OF JOSEPH.

EXODUS xiii. 19.

It is certain that Moses, in the days of his greatness, must often have mused by the sepulchre of the one Israelite before himself who held high rank in Egypt. The knowledge that Joseph's elevation was providential must have helped him at that time, now many years ago, to think rightly of his own. And now we read that Moses took the bones of Joseph with him. In the Epistle to the Hebrews (xi. 22) it is recorded as the most characteristic example of the faith of the patriarch, that instead of desiring to be carried, like his father, at once to Canaan, he made mention of the departure of the children of Israel, and gave commandment concerning his bones. To him Egypt was no longer an alien land. There only he had known honour without envy, and happiness without betrayal. There his bones could rest in quiet; but not for ever. Personal elevation, which had not rent the cord between him and his unworthy family, could still less sever the bands between him and the sacred race. Let him sleep in Egypt while his grave there was honoured: let the remembrance of him be kept fresh, to protect awhile his kindred; and when the predicted days of evil came, let his ashes share the neglect and dishonour of his people, if only they would remember his remains when the Lord would lead them forth. This confidence in their emancipation was his faith—which meant, here as always, not a clear view of truth, but an assuring grasp of it. He had straitly sworn the children of Israel saying, "God will surely visit you; and ye shall carry up my bones away hence with you."

Many a Christian might well envy a confidence so practical, so thoroughly realised, entering so naturally into the tissue of his thoughts and calculations. And their actual remembrance of him goes to show that the tradition of his faith had never completely died out, but was among the influences which kept alive the nation's hope.

And as the people bore his honoured ashes through the desert, these being dead spoke of bygone times, they linked the present and the past together, they deepened the national consciousness that Israel was a favoured people, called to no common destiny, sustained by no common promises, pressing toward no common goal.

If Israel had been wise, they would have thought of him, the Israelite in heart, though glittering in the splendours of Egypt; and would have considered well that as little as men detected his secret life from his appearance, so little could theirs be judged. To the eye, they were free from the foreign trammels in which he was seemingly entangled, yet many of them in heart turned back to all which strove in vain to bind his affections down. The lesson holds good to-day. Many a modern religionist looks askance at the "worldliness" of high office and rank and state; little dreaming that the "world" he censures is strong in his own ambitious and self-asserting spirit, and is overcome by the gentle and tranquil spirit of hundreds of those whom he condemns.

Bearing this hallowed burden, which might easily have become an object of superstitious regard, the nation moved from Succoth to Etham on the edge of the wilderness. And with them a Presence moved which rebuked all others, however venerable. The Lord went before them. It has already been pointed out that throughout the early history of this nation, just come out of an idolatrous land, and too ready to lapse back into superstition, God never reveals Himself except in fire. To Abraham and to Jacob He appeared in human form, and again to Joshua; but in the interval, never. So now they see Him by day in a pillar of cloud to guide them on the way, and by night in a pillar of fire to give them light. The glory of the nation was that manifested Presence, lacking which, Moses besought Him to carry them up no farther. Nothing in the Exodus is more impressive, and it sank deep into the national heart. Many centuries afterwards, the ideal of a golden age was that the Lord should " create over the whole habitation of Mount Zion, and over her assemblies, a cloud of smoke by day, and the shining of a flaming fire by night " (Isa. iv. 5).

But it has been well observed that, amid the various allusions to it in Hebrew poetry, not one treats it as modern literature has done, with an eye to its marvellous sublimity and picturesque effects:

> "By day, along the astonished lands
> The cloudy pillar glided slow:
> By night, Arabia's crimsoned sands
> Returned the fiery column's glow."

The Hebrew poetry is vivid and passionate, but all its concerns are human or divine—God, and the life of man. It is not artistic, but inspired. "The modern poet is delighting in the scenic effect; the ancient chronicler was wholly occupied with the overshadowing power of God." *

CHAPTER XIV.

THE RED SEA.

EXODUS xiv. 1-31.

It would seem that the Israelites recoiled before a frontier fortress of Egypt at Khetam (Etham). This is probable, whatever theory of the route of the Exodus one may adopt; and it is still open to every reader to adopt almost any theory he pleases, provided that two facts are borne in mind: viz., first, that the narrative certainly means to describe a miraculous interference, not superseding the forces of nature, but wielding them in a fashion impossible to man; and second, that the phrase translated "Red Sea " † (xiii. 18, xv. 4) is the same which is confessed by all persons to have that meaning in chap. xxiii. 31, and in Numbers xxi. 4 and xxxiii. 10.

Checked, without loss or with it, they were bidden to "turn back," and encamp at Pihahiroth, between Migdol and the sea. And since Migdol is simply a watch-tower (there were several in the Holy Land, including that which gave her name to Mary Magdal-ene), we are to infer that from thence their inexplicable movements were signalled back to Pharaoh. It was the natural signal for all the wild passions of a baffled and half-ruined tyrant to leap into flame. We are scarcely able to imagine the mental condition of men who conceived that a God Who had dealt out death and destruction might be far from invincible from another side. But ages after this, a campaign was planned upon the ingenious theory that " Jehovah is a god of the hills but He is not a god of the valleys " (1

---

* Hutton's *Essays*, Vol. ii., *Literary: The Poetry of the Old Test.*
† The Sea of Zuph, or reeds, the word being used of the reeds in which Moses was laid by his mother and found by Pharaoh's daughter (ii. 3, 5), rendered "flags" in the Revised Version.

Kings xx. 28); and plenty of people who would scorn this simple notion are still of opinion that He is a God of eternity and can save them from hell, but a little falsehood and knavery are much better able to save them from want in the meanwhile. Nay, there are many excellent persons who are not at all of opinion that the prince of this world has been dethroned.

Therefore, when his enemies recoiled from his fortresses and wandered away into the wilderness of Egypt, entangling themselves hopelessly between the sea, the mountains, and his own strongholds, it might well appear to Pharaoh that Jehovah was not a warlike deity, that he himself had now found out the weak point of his enemies, and could pursue and overtake and satisfy his lust upon them. There is a significant emphasis in the song of Miriam's triumph— " Jehovah is a man of war." At all events, it was through an imperfect sense of the universal and practical importance of Jehovah as a factor not to be neglected in his calculations, through exactly the same error which misleads every man who postpones religion, or limits the range of its influence in his daily life,—it was thus, and not through any rarer infatuation, that Pharaoh made ready six hundred chosen chariots and all the chariots of Egypt, and captains over all of them. And his court was of the same mind, saying, " What is this that we have done, that we have let Israel go from serving us? "

These words are hard to reconcile with the strange notion that until now a return after three days was expected, despite the torrent of blood which rolled between them, and the demands by which the Israelitish women had spoiled the Egyptians. Upon this theory it is not their own error, but the bad faith of their servants, which they should have cried out against.

At the sight of the army, a panic seized the servile hearts of the fugitives. First they cried out unto the Lord. But how possible it is, without any real faith, to address to Heaven the mere clamours of our alarm, and to mistake natural agitation for earnestness in prayer, we learn by the reproaches with which, after thus crying to the Lord, they assailed His servant. Were there no graves in that land of superb sepulchres— that land, now, of universal mourning? Would God that they had perished with the firstborn! Why had they been treated thus? Had they not urged Moses to let them alone, that they might serve the Egyptians?

And yet these men had lately, for the very promise of so much emancipation as they now enjoyed, bowed their heads in adoring thankfulness. As it was their fear which now took the form of supplication, so then it was their hope which took the form of praise. And we, how shall we know whether that in us which seems to be religious gladness and religious grief, is mere emotion, or is truly sacred? By watching whether worship and love continue, when emotion has spent its force, or has gone round, like the wind, to another quarter.

How did Moses feel when this outcry told him of the unworthiness and cowardice of the nation of his heart? Much as we feel, perhaps, when we see the frailties and failures of converts in the mission-field, and the lapse of the intemperate who have seemed to be reclaimed for ever. We thought that perfection was to be reached at a bound. Now we think that the whole work was unreal. Both extremes are wrong: we have much to learn from the failures of that ancient church, in which was the germ of hero, psalmist, and prophet, which was indeed the church in the wilderness, and whose many relapses were so tenderly borne with by God and His messenger.

The settled faith of Moses, and the assurances which he could give the agitated people,* contrast nobly with their alarm. But his confidence also had its secret springs in prayer, for the Lord said to him, "Wherefore criest thou unto Me? speak unto the children of Israel that they go forward."

The words are remarkable on two accounts. Can prayer ever be out of place? Not if we mean a prayerful dependent mental attitude toward God. But certainly, yes, if God has already revealed that for which we still importune Him, and we are secretly disquieted lest His promise should fail. It is misplaced if our own duty has to be done, and we pass the golden moments in inactivity, however pious. Christ spoke of men who should leave their gift before the altar, unpresented, because of a neglected duty which should be discharged. And perhaps there are men who pray for the conversion of the heathen or of friends at home, to whom God says, Wherefore criest unto Me? because their money and their faithful efforts must be given, as Moses must arouse himself to lead the people forward, and to stretch his wand over the sea.

And again the forces of nature are on the side of God: the strong wind makes the depths of the sea a way for the ransomed to pass over. History has no scene more picturesque than this wild night march, in the roar of tempest, amid the flying foam which "baptised" them unto Moses,† while the glimmering waters stood up like a rampart to protect their flanks; the full moon of passover above them, shown and hidden as the swift clouds raced before the storm, while high and steadfast overhead, unshaken by the fiercest blast, illumined by a mysterious splendour, "stood" the vast cloud which veiled like a curtain their whole host from the pursuer. This it was, and the experience of such protection that the Egyptians, overawed, came not near them, which gave them courage to enter the bed of the sea; and as they trod the strange road they found that not only were the waters driven off the surface, but the sands were left firm to traverse.

But when the blind fury of Pharaoh, "hardened" against everything but the sense that his prey was escaping, sent his army along the same track, and this after long delay, at a crisis when every moment was priceless, then a new element of terrible sublimity was added. Through the pillar of cloud and fire Jehovah looked forth on the Egyptian host, as they pressed on behind, unable to penetrate the supernatural gloom, cold fear creeping into every heart, while the chariot wheels laboured heavily in the wet sand. In that direful vision at last the question was answered, "Who is Jehovah, that I should let His people go?" Now it was the turn of those who said "Israel is entangled in the land, the wilderness hath shut them in," themselves to be taken in a worse net. For at that awful gaze the iron curb of military discipline gave way; their labouring chariots, the pride and defence of the nation, were forsaken; and a wild cry broke out, "Let us fly from the face of Israel, for Jehovah"—He who plagued us—"fighteth for them against the Egyptians." But their humiliation came too late,—for in the morning watch, at a natural time for atmospheric changes, but in obedience to the rod of Moses, the furious wind veered or fell, and the sea returned to its accustomed limits; and first, as the sands beneath became saturated, the chariots were overturned and the mail-clad charioteers went down "like lead," and then the hissing line of foam raced forward and closed around and over the shrieking mob which was the pride and strength of Egypt only an hour before.

But, as the story repeats twice over, with a very natural and glad reiteration, "the children of Israel walked on dry land in the midst of the sea, and the waters were a wall unto them on their right hand, and on their left" (ver. 29, cf. 22).

ON THE SHORE.

EXODUS xiv. 30, 31.

After the haste and agitation of their marvellous deliverance the children of Israel seem to have halted for awhile at the only spot in the neighbourhood where there is water, known as the Ayoun Musa or springs of Moses to this day. There they doubtless brought into some permanent shape their rudimentary organisation. There, too, their impressions were given time to deepen. They "saw the Egyptians dead on the sea-shore," and realised that their oppression was indeed at an end, their chains broken, themselves introduced into a new life,—"baptised unto Moses." They reflected upon the difference between all other deities and the God of their fathers, Who, in that deadly crisis, had looked upon them and their tyrants out of the fiery pillar. "They feared Jehovah, and they believed in Jehovah and in His servant Moses."

"They believed in Jehovah." This expression is noteworthy, because they had all believed in Him already. "By faith 'they' forsook Egypt. By faith 'they' kept the passover and the sprinkling of blood. By faith 'they' passed through the Red Sea." But their former trust was poor and wavering compared with that which filled their bosoms now. So the disciples followed Jesus because they believed on Him; yet when His first miracle manifested forth His glory, "His disciples believed on Him there." And again they said, "By this we believe that Thou camest forth from God." And after the resurrection He said, "Because thou hast seen Me thou hast believed" (John ii. 11, xvi. 30, xx. 29). Faith needs to be edified by successive experiences, as the enthusiasm of a recruit is converted into the disciplined valour of the veteran. From each new crisis of the spiritual life the soul should obtain new powers. And that is a shallow and unstable religion which is content with

---

* But his assurance is, "The Lord shall fight for you, and ye shall hold your peace." When Wellhausen would summarise the work of Moses, he tells us that "he taught them to regard self-assertion against the Egyptians as an article of religion" (*History*, p. 430). It would be impossible, within the compass of so many words, more completely to miss the remarkable characteristic which differentiates this whole narrative from all other revolutionary movements. Expectancy and dependence here take the place of "self-assertion."

† Not the adults only; nor yet by immersion, whether in the rain-cloud or the surf.

the level of its initial act of faith (however genuine and however important), and seeks not to go from strength to strength.

CHAPTER XV.

THE SONG OF MOSES.

Exodus xv. 1-22.

During this halt they prepared that great song of triumph which St. John heard sung by them who had been victorious over the beast, standing by the sea of glass, having the harps of God. For by that calmer sea, triumphant over a deadlier persecution, they still found their adoration and joy expressed in this earliest chant of sacred victory. Because all holy hearts give like thanks to Him Who sitteth upon the throne, therefore " deep answers unto deep," and every great crisis in the history of the Church has legacies for all time and for eternity; and therefore the triumphant song of Moses the servant of God enriches the worship of heaven, as the penitence and hope and joy of David enrich the worship of the Church on earth (Rev. xv. 3).

Like all great poetry, this song is best enjoyed when it is neither commented upon nor paraphrased, but carefully read and warmly felt. There are circumstances and lines of thought which it is desirable to point out, but only as a preparation, not a substitute, for the submission of a docile mind to the influence of the inspired poem itself. It is unquestionably archaic. The parallelism of Hebrew verse is already here, but the structure is more free and unartificial than that of later poetry; and many ancient words, and words of Egyptian derivation, authenticate its origin. So does the description of Miriam, in the fifteenth verse, as "the prophetess, the sister of Aaron." In what later time would she not rather have been called the sister of Moses? But from the lonely youth who found Aaron and Miriam together as often as he stole from the palace to his real home—the lonely man who regained both together when he returned from forty years of exile, and who sometimes found them united in opposition to his authority (Num. xii. 1, 2)—from Moses alone the epithet is entirely natural.

It is also noteworthy that Philistia is mentioned first among the foes who shall be terrified (ver. 14, R. V.), because Moses still expected the invasion to break first on them. But the unbelieving fears of Israel changed the route, so that no later poet would have set them in the forefront of his song. Thus also the terror of the Edomites is anticipated, although in fact they sturdily refused a passage to Israel through their land (Num. xx. 20). All this authenticates the song, which thereupon establishes the miraculous deliverance that inspired it.

The song is divided into two parts. Up to the end of the twelfth verse it is historical: the remainder expresses the high hopes inspired by this great experience. Nothing now seems impossible: the fiercest tribes of Palestine and the desert may be despised, for their own terror will suffice to "melt" them; and Israel may already reckon itself to be guided into the holy habitation (ver. 13).

The former part is again subdivided, by a noble and instinctive art, into two very unequal sections. With amplitude of triumphant adoration, the first ten verses tell the same story which the eleventh and twelfth compress into epigrammatical vigour and terseness. To appreciate the power of the composition, one should read the fourth, fifth, and sixth verses, and turn immediately to the twelfth.

Each of these three divisions closes in praise, and as in the "Israel in Egypt," it was probably at these points that the voices of Miriam and the women broke in, repeating the first verse of the ode as a refrain (vers. 1 and 21). It is the earliest recognition of the place of women in public worship. And it leads us to remark that the whole service was responsive. Moses and the men are answered by Miriam and the women, bearing timbrels in their hands; for although instrumental music had been sorely misused in Egypt, that was no reason why it should be excluded now. Those who condemn the use of instruments in Christian worship virtually contend that Jesus has, in this respect, narrowed the liberty of the Church, and that a potent method of expression, known to man, must not be consecrated to the honour of God. And they make the present time unlike the past, and also unlike what is revealed of the future state.

Moreover there was movement, as in very many ancient religious services, within and without the pale of revelation.* Such dances were generally slow and graceful; yet the motion and the clang of metal, and the vast multitudes congregated, must be taken into account, if we would realise the strange enthusiasm of the emancipated host, looking over the blue sea to Egypt, defeated and twice bereaved, and forward to the desert wilds of freedom.

The poem is steeped in a sense of gratitude. In the great deliverance man has borne no part. It is Jehovah Who has triumphed gloriously and cast the horse and charioteer—there was no "rider"—into the sea. And this is repeated again and again by the women as their response, in the deepening passion of the ode. "With the breath of His nostrils the waters were piled up. . . He blew with His wind and the sea covered them." And such is indeed the only possible explanation of the Exodus, so that whoever rejects the miracle is beset with countless difficulties. One of these is the fact that Moses, their immortal leader, has no martial renown whatever. Hebrew poetry is well able to combine gratitude to God with honour to the men of Zebulun who jeopardised their lives unto the death, to Jael who put her hand to the nail, to Saul and Jonathan who were swifter than eagles and stronger than lions. Joshua and David can win fame without dishonour to God. Why is it that here alone no mention is made of human agency except that, in fact, at the outset of their national existence, they were shown, once for all, the direct interposition of their God?

From gratitude springs trust: the great lesson is learned that man has an interest in the Divine power. "My strength and song is Jah," says the second verse, using that abbreviated form of the covenant name Jehovah, which David also frequently associated with his victories. "And He is become my salvation." It is the same word as when, a little while ago, the trembling

---

* There is no warrant in the use of Scripture for Stanley's assertion that the word translated "dances" should be rendered "guitars." (Smith's *Dict. of Bible*, Article *Miriam*.)

people were bidden to stand still and see the salvation of God. They have seen it now. Now they give the word Salvation for the first time to the Lord as an appellation, and as such it is destined to endure. The Psalmist learns to call Him so, not only when he reproduces this verse word for word (Ps. cxviii. 14), but also when he says, "He only is my rock and my salvation" (lxii. 2), and prays, "Before Ephraim, Benjamin, and Manasseh, come for salvation to us" (lxxx. 2).

And the same title is known also to Isaiah, who says, "Behold God is my salvation," and "Be Thou their arm every morning, our salvation also in the time of trouble" (Isa. xii. 2, xxxiii. 2).

The progress is natural from experience of goodness to appropriation: He has helped me: He gives Himself to me; and from that again to love and trust, for He has always been the same: "my father," not my ancestors in general, but he whom I knew best and remember most tenderly, found Him the same Helper. And then love prompts to some return. My goodness extendeth not to Him, yet my voice can honour Him; I will praise Him, I will exalt His name. Now, this is the very spirit of evangelical obedience, the life-blood of the new dispensation racing in the veins of the old.

Where praise and exaltation are a spontaneous instinct, there is loyal service and every good work, not rendered by a hireling but a child. Had He not said, "Israel is My son"?

From exultant gratitude and trust, what is next to spring? That which is reproachfully called anthropomorphism, something which indeed easily degenerates into unworthy notions of a God limited by such restraints or warped by such passions as our own, yet which is after all a great advance towards true and holy thoughts of Him Who made man after His image and in His likeness.

Human affection cannot go forth to God without believing that like affection meets and responds to it. If He is indeed the best and purest, we must think of Him as sharing all that is best and purest in our souls, all that we owe to His inspiring Spirit.

"So through the thunder comes a human voice,
Saying 'O heart I made, a heart beats here.'"

If ever any religion was sternly jealous of the Divine prerogatives, profoundly conscious of the incommunicable dignity of the Lord our God Who is one Lord, it was the Jewish religion. Yet when Jesus was charged with making Himself God, He could appeal to the doctrine of their own Scripture—that the judges of the people exercised so divine a function, and could claim such divine support, that God Himself spoke through them, and found representatives in them. "Is it not written in your law, I said Ye are gods?" (John x. 34). Not in vain did He appeal to such scriptures—and there are many such—to vindicate His doctrine. For man is never lifted above himself, but God in the same degree stoops towards us, and identifies Himself with us and our concerns. Who then shall limit His condescension? What ground in reason or revelation can be taken up for denying that it may be perfect, that it may develop into a permanent union of God with the creature whom He inspired with His own breath? It is by such steps that the Old Testament prepared Israel for the Incarnation. Since the Incarnation we have actually needed help from the other side, to prevent us from humanising our conceptions overmuch. And this has been provided in the ever-expanding views of His creation given to us by science, which tell us that if He draws nigh to us it is from heights formerly undreamed of. Now, such a step as we have been considering is taken unawares in the bold phrase "Jehovah is a man of war." For in the original, as in the English, this includes the assertion "Jehovah is a man." Of course it is only a bold figure. But such a figure prepares the mind for new light, suggesting more than it logically asserts.

The phrase is more striking when we remember that remarkable peculiarity of the Exodus and its revelations which has been already pointed out. Elsewhere God appears in human likeness. To Abraham it was so, just before, and to Manoah soon afterwards. Ezekiel saw upon the likeness of the throne the likeness of the appearance of a man (Ezek. i. 26). But Israel saw no similitude, only he heard a voice. This was obviously a safeguard against idolatry. And it makes the words more noteworthy, "Jehovah is a man of war," marching with us, our champion, into the battle. And we know Him as our fathers knew Him not,—"Jehovah is His name."

The poem next describes the overthrow of the enemy: the heavy plunge of men in armour into the deeps, the arm of the Lord dashing them in pieces, His "fire" consuming them, while the blast of His nostrils is the storm which "piles up" the waters, solid as a wall of ice, "congealed in the heart of the sea." Then the singers exultantly rehearse the short panting eager phrases, full of greedy expectation, of the enemy breathless in pursuit—a passage well remembered by Deborah, when her triumphant song closed by an insulting repetition of the vain calculations of the mother of Sisera and "her wise ladies."

The eleventh verse is remarkable as being the first announcement of the holiness of God. "Who is like unto Thee, glorious in holiness?" And what does holiness mean? The Hebrew word is apparently suggestive of "brightness," and the two ideas are coupled by Isaiah (x. 17): "The Light of Israel shall be for a fire, and his Holy One for a flame." There is indeed something in the purity of light, in its absolute immunity from stain—no passive cleanness, as of the sand upon the shore, but intense and vital—and in its remoteness from the conditions of common material substances, that well expresses and typifies the lofty and awful quality which separates holiness from mere virtue. "God is called the Holy One because He is altogether pure, the clear and spotless Light; so that in the idea of the holiness of God there are embodied the absolute moral purity and perfection of the Divine nature, and His unclouded glory" (Keil, *Pent.*, ii. 99). In this thought there is already involved separation, a lofty remoteness.

And when holiness is attributed to man, it never means innocence, nor even virtue, merely as such. It is always a derived attribute: it is reflected upon us, like light upon our planet; and like consecration, it speaks not of man in himself, but in his relation to God. It expresses a kind of separation to God, and thus it can reach to lifeless things which bear a true relation to the Divine. The seventh day is thus "hallowed." It is the very name of the "Holy Place," the "Sanctuary." And the ground where Moses was to stand unshod beside the burning bush was pronounced "holy," not by any concession to human weakness, but by the direct teaching of God. Very inseparable from all true holiness is separation from what is common and unclean. Holy men may be involved in the duties of active life; but only on condition that in their bosom shall be some inner shrine, whither the din of worldliness never penetrates, and where the lamp of God does not go out.

It is a solemn truth that a kind of inverted holiness is known to Scripture. Men "sanctify themselves" (it is this very word), "and purify themselves to go into the gardens, . . . eating swine's flesh and the abomination and the mouse" (Isa. lxvi. 17). The same word is also used to declare that the whole fruit of a vineyard sown with two kinds of fruit shall be *forfeited* (Deut. xxii. 9), although the notion there is of something unnatural and therefore interdicted, which notion is carried to the utmost extreme in another derivative from the same root, expressing the most depraved of human beings.

Just so, the Greek word "anathema" means both "consecrated" and "marked out for wrath" (Luke xxi. 5; 1 Cor. xvi. 22: the difference in form is insignificant.) And so again our own tongue calls the saints "devoted," and speaks of the "devoted" head of the doomed sinner, being aware that there is a "separation" in sin as really as in purity. The gods of the heathen, like Jehovah, claimed an appropriate "holiness," sometimes unspeakably degraded. They too were separated, and it was through long lines of sphinxes, and many successive chambers, that the Egyptian worshipper attained the shrine of some contemptible or hateful deity. The religion which does not elevate depresses. But the holiness of Jehovah is noble as that of light, incapable of defilement. "Who among the gods is like Thee . . . glorious in holiness?" And Israel soon learned that the worshipper must become assimilated to his Ideal: "Ye shall be holy men unto Me" (xxii. 31). It is so with us. Jesus is separated from sinners. And we are to go forth unto Him out of the camp, bearing His reproach (Heb. vii. 26, xiii. 13).

The remainder of the song is remarkable chiefly for the confidence with which the future is inferred from the past. And the same argument runs through all Scripture. As Moses sang, "Thou shalt bring them in and plant them in the mountain of Thine inheritance," because "Thou stretchedest out Thy right hand, the earth * swallowed" their enemies, so David was sure that goodness and mercy should follow him all the days of his life, because God was already leading him in green pastures and beside still waters. And so St. Paul, knowing in Whom he had believed, was persuaded that He was able to keep his deposit until that day (2 Tim. i. 12).

So should pardon and Scripture and the means of grace reassure every doubting heart; for "if the Lord were pleased to kill us, He would not have . . . showed us all these things" (Judg. xiii. 23). And in theory, and in good hours, we confess that this is so. But after our song of triumph, if we come upon bitter waters we murmur; and if our bread fail, we expect only to die in the wilderness.

SHUR.

EXODUS xv. 22-7.

From the Red Sea the Israelites marched into the wilderness of Shur—a general name, of Egyptian origin, for the district between Egypt and Palestine, of which Etham, given as their route in Numbers (xxxiii. 8), is a subdivision. The rugged way led over stone and sand, with little vegetation and no water. And the "three days' journey" to Marah, a distance of thirty-three miles, was their first experience of absolute hardship, for not even the curtain of miraculous cloud could prevent them from suffering keenly by heat and thirst.

It was a period of disillusion. Fond dreams of ease and triumphant progress, with every trouble miraculously smoothed away, had naturally been excited by their late adventure. Their song had exulted in the prospect that their enemies should melt away, and be as still as a stone. But their difficulties did not melt away. The road was weary. They found no water. They were still too much impressed by the miracle at the Red Sea, and by the mysterious Presence overhead, for open complaining to be heard along the route; but we may be sure that reaction had set in, and there was many a sinking heart, as the dreary route stretched on and on, and they realised that, however romantic the main plan of their journey, the details might still be prosaic and exacting. They sang praises unto Him. They soon forgat His works. Aching with such disappointments, at last they reached the waters of Marah, and they could not drink, for they were bitter.

And if Marah be indeed Huwara, as seems to be agreed, the waters are still the worst in all the district. It was when the relief, so confidently expected, failed, and the term of their sufferings appeared to be indefinitely prolonged, that their self-control gave way, and they "murmured against Moses, saying, What shall we drink?" And we may be sure that wherever discontent and unbelief are working secret mischief to the soul, some event, some disappointment or temptation, will find the weak point, and the favourable moment of attack, just as the seeds of disease find out the morbid constitution, and assail it.

Now, all this is profoundly instructive, because it is true to the universal facts of human nature. When a man is promoted to unexpected rank, or suddenly becomes rich, or reaches any other unlooked-for elevation, he is apt to forget that life cannot, in any position, be a romance throughout, a long thrill, a whole song at the top note of the voice. Affection itself has a dangerous moment, when two united lives begin to realise that even their union cannot banish aches and anxieties, weariness and business cares. Well for them if they are content with the power of love to sweeten what it cannot remove, as loyal soldiers gladly sacrifice all things for the cause, and as Israel should have been proud to endure forced marches under the cloudy banner of its emancipating God.

---

* This is to be taken literally; it does not mean the waves, but the quicksands in which they "drave heavily," and which, when steeped in the returning waters, engulfed them.

As neither rank nor affection exempts men from the dust and tedium of life, or from its disappointments, so neither does religion. When one is "made happy" he expects life to be only a triumphal procession towards Paradise, and he is startled when "now for a season, if need be, he is in heaviness through manifold temptations." Yet Christ prayed not that we should be taken out of the world. We are bidden to endure hardness as good soldiers, and to run with patience the race which is set before us; and these phrases indicate our need of the very qualities wherein Israel failed. As yet the people murmured not ostensibly against God, but only against Moses. But the estrangement of their hearts is plain, since they made no appeal to God for relief, but assailed His agent and representative. Yet they had not because they asked not, and relief was found when Moses cried unto the Lord. Their leader was "faithful in all his house"; and instead of upbraiding his followers with their ingratitude, or bewailing the hard lot of all leaders of the multitude, whose popularity neither merit nor service can long preserve unclouded, he was content to look for sympathy and help where we too may find it.

We read that the Lord showed him a tree, which when he had cast into the waters, the waters were made sweet. In this we discern the same union of Divine grace with human energy and use of means, as in all medicine, and indeed all uses of the divinely enlightened intellect of man. It would have been easy to argue that the waters could only be healed by miracle, and if God wrought a miracle what need was there of human labour? There was need of obedience, and of the co-operation of the human will with the divine. We shall see, in the case of the artificers of the tabernacle, that God inspires even handicraftsmen as well as theologians—being indeed the universal Light, the Giver of all good, not only of Bibles, but of rain and fruitful seasons. But the artisan must labour, and the farmer improve the soil.

Shall we say with the fathers that the tree cast into the waters represents the cross of Christ? At least it is a type of the sweetening and assuaging influences of religion—a new element, entering life, and as well fitted to combine with it as medicinal bark with water, making all wholesome and refreshing to the disappointed wayfarer, who found it so bitter hitherto.

The Lord was not content with removing the grievance of the hour; He drew closer the bonds between His people and Himself, to guard them against another transgression of the kind: "there He made for them a statute and an ordinance, and there He proved them." It is pure assumption to pretend that this refers to another account of the giving of the Jewish law, inconsistent with that in the twentieth chapter, and placed at Marah instead of Sinai.* It is a transaction which resembles much rather the promises given (and at various times, although confusion and repetition cannot be inferred) to Abraham and Jacob (Gen. xii. 1-3, xv. 1, 18-21, xvii. 1-14, xxii. 15-18, xxviii. 13-15, xxxv. 10-12). He said "If thou wilt diligently hearken to the voice of the Lord thy God, and wilt do that which is right in His eyes, and wilt give ear to His commandments, and wilt keep all His statutes, I will put none of the diseases upon thee which I have put upon the Egyptians, for I am the Lord which healeth thee." It is a compact of obedient trust on one side, and protection on the other. If they felt their own sinfulness, it asserted that He who had just healed the waters could also heal their hearts. From the connection between these is perhaps derived the comparison between human hearts and a fountain of sweet water or bitter (Jas. iii. 11).

But certainly the promised protection takes an unexpected shape. What in their circumstances leads to this specific offer of exemption from certain foul diseases—"the boil of Egypt, and the emerods, and the scurvy, and the itch, whereof thou canst not be healed" (Deut. xxviii. 27)? How does this meet the case? Doubtless by reminding them that there are better exemptions than from hardship, and worse evils than privations. If they do not realise this at the spiritual level, at least they can appreciate the threat that "He will bring upon thee again all the diseases of Egypt which thou wast afraid of" (Deut. xxviii. 60). To be even a luxurious and imperial race, but infected by repulsive and hopeless ailments, is not a desirable alternative. Now, such evils, though certainly not in each individual, yet in a race, are the punishments of non-natural conditions of life, such as make the blood run slowly and unhealthily, and charge it with impure deposits. It was God who put them upon the Egyptians.

If Israel would follow His guidance, and accept a somewhat austere destiny, then the desert air and exercise, and even its privations, would become the efficacious means for their exemption from the scourges of indulgence. A time arrived when they looked back with remorse upon crimes which forfeited their immunity, when the Lord said, "I have sent among you the pestilence after the manner of Egypt; your young men have I slain with the sword" (Amos iv. 10).

But it is a significant fact that at this day, after eighteen hundred years of oppression, hardship, and persecution, of the ghetto and the old-clothes trade, the Hebrew race is proverbially exempt from repulsive and contagious disease. They also "certainly do enjoy immunity from the ravages of cholera, fever, and small-pox in a remarkable degree. Their blood seems to be in a different condition from that of other people. . . . They seem less receptive of disease caused by blood poisoning than others" (*Journal of Victoria Institute*, xxi. 307). Imperfect as was their obedience, this covenant at least has been literally fulfilled to them.

It is by such means that God is wont to reward His children. Most commonly the seal of blessing from the skies is not rich fare, but bread and fish by the lake side with the blessing of Christ upon them; not removal from the desert, but a closer sense of the protection and acceptance of Heaven, the nearness of a loving God, and with this, an elevation and purification of the life, and of the body as well as of the soul. Not in vain has St. Paul written "The Lord for the body." Nor was there ever yet a race of men who accepted the covenant of God, and lived in soberness, temperance, and chastity, without a signal improvement of the national physique, no longer unduly stimulated by passion, jaded by indulgence, or relaxed by the satiety which resembles but is not repose.

From Marah and its agitations there was a journey of but a few hours to Elim, with its

---

* Wellhausen, *Israel*, p. 439.

twelve fountains and seventy palm trees—a fair oasis, by which they encamped and rested, while their flocks spread far and wide over a grassy and luxuriant valley.

The picture is still true to the Christian life, with the Palace Beautiful just beyond the lions, and the Delectable Mountains next after Doubting Castle.

CHAPTER XVI.

MURMURING FOR FOOD.

EXODUS xvi. 1-14.

THE Israelites were now led farther away from all the associations of their accustomed life. From the waters and the palms of Elim they marched deeper into the savage recesses of the desert, haunted by fierce and hostile tribes, such as presently hung upon their rear-guard and cut off their stragglers (Deut. xxv. 18). Nor had they quite emerged from the shadow of their old oppressions, since Egyptian garrisons were scattered, though sparsely, through this district, in which gems and copper were obtained. Here, cut off from all natural modes of sustenance, the hearts of the people failed them. Such is the frequent experience of renewed souls, when privilege and joy are followed by trouble from without or from within, and the peace of God is broken by the strife of tongues, by mental perplexities, by temptations, by physical pain. It is quite as wonderful that paltry disturbances should mar for us the life divine, when once that life has become a realised experience, as that men who moved under the shadow of the marvellous cloud could be agitated by fear for their supplies. And of this our experience, what befel Israel is not a mere type or symbol, it is a case in point, a parallel example. For it also meant the breaking-in of the flesh upon the spirit, the refusal of fallen nature to rise above earthly wants and cravings even in the light of trust and acceptance, the self-assertion of the baser instincts, and the sacrifice to them of the higher life. We recognise the herd of slaves, from whence it must perplex the unbeliever to remember that the seed of immortal heroism and prophetic insight and apostolic service was yet to ripen, in their poor desire, if they must perish, to perish well fed rather than emancipated (ver. 3). Most people, we may fear, would choose to live enslaved rather than to die free men. But there is a special meanness in their regret, since die they must, that they had not died satiated, like the firstborn whom God had slain: "Would that we had died by the hand of Jehovah in the land of Egypt, when we sat by the fleshpots and when we ate bread to the full, for ye have brought us forth into this wilderness to kill this whole assembly with hunger." And to-day, among those who scorn them, how many are far less ambitious of dying holy and pure than rich, famous or powerful, having glutted their vanity if not their appetite. In the sight of angels this is not a much loftier aim; and the apostle reckoned among the works of the flesh, emulation as well as drunkenness (Gal. v. 19-21).

Tertullian draws a striking contrast between Israel, just now baptised into Moses, but caring more for appetite than for God, and Christ, after His baptism, also in the desert, fasting forty days. "The Lord figuratively retorted upon Israel His reproach" (*Baptism*, xx).

We are not to suppose that but for their complaining God would have suffered them to hunger, although Moses declared that the reason why flesh should be given to them in the evening, and in the morning bread to the full, is "for that the Lord heareth your murmurings." But there would have been some difference in the time of the grant, to ripen their faith, some more direct manifestation of His grace, to reward their patience, if unbelief had not precipitated His design. Thus the disciples, when they awakened Jesus in the storm, received the rescue for which they clamoured, but forfeited some higher experience which would have crowned a serener confidence: "Wherefore did ye doubt?" Israel receives what is best in the circumstances, rather than the ideal best, now made unsuitable by their impatience and infidelity. But while the Lord discontinued the test of need and penury, which had proved to be too severe a discipline, He substituted the test of fulness. For we read that the removal of their suspense and anxiety by the gift of manna from heaven was "to prove them whether they will walk in My laws or no" (ver. 4). And in so doing it was seen that worldly and unthankful natures are not to be satisfied; that the disloyal at heart will complain, however favoured. For "the children of Israel wept again and said, Who will give us flesh to eat? We remember the fish which we did eat in Egypt for naught, the cucumbers and the melons and the leeks and the onions and the garlick: but now our soul is dried away; there is nothing at all: we have naught save this manna to look to" (Num. xi. 4-6). Onions and garlick were more satisfactory to gross appetites than angels' food.

At this point we learn that what is called prosperity may indeed be a result of spiritual failure; that God may sometimes abstain from strong measures with a soul because what ought to mould would only crush; and may grant them their hearts' lust, yet send leanness withal into their souls. Perhaps we are allowed to be comfortable because we are unfit to be heroic.

And we also learn, when prosperous, to remember that plenty, equally with want, has its moral aspect. The Lord tries fortunate men whether they will be grateful and obedient, trusting in Him and not in uncertain riches, or whether they will forget Him who has done so great things for them, and so perish in calm weather:

"Like ships that have gone down at sea
 When heaven was all tranquillity."

There is an experiment being tried upon the soul, curious, slow, little-suspected, but incessant, in the giving of daily bread.

In promising relief, God required of them obedience and self-control. They were to respect the Sabbath, and make provision in advance for its requirements. And this direction, given before the Mount of the Lord was reached, has an important bearing upon the question whether the Fourth Commandment was the first institution of a holy day—whether, except as a Church ordinance, the duty of sabbath-keeping has no support beyond the ceremonial law. "For that the Lord hath (already) given you the Sabbath, therefore He giveth you on the sixth day the bread of two days" (ver. 29).

While conveying the promise of relief, Moses

and Aaron rebuked the people, whose murmurs against them were in reality murmurs against God, since they were but His agents, and He had been visibly their Leader. And the same rebuke applies, for exactly the same reason, to many a modern complaint against the weather, against what people call their "luck," against a thousand provoking things in which the only possible provocation must come directly from heaven. It is because our religion is so shallow, and our consciousness of God in His world so dim and rudimentary, that we utter such complaints idly, to relieve our feelings, and hear them spoken without a shock.

Such dulness is not to be removed by sounder views of doctrine, but by a more vivid realisation of God. The Israelites knew by what hand they should have fallen if they had died in Egypt; yet in fact they forgot their true Captain, and upbraided their mortal leaders. So do we confess that afflictions arise not out of the ground, yet lose the impress of divinity upon our daily lives, while we ought, like Moses, to "endure as seeing Him who is invisible."

As our Lord was in the habit of asking for some confession, or demanding some small cooperation from those He was about to bless, so the smoking flax of Hebrew faith is tended: it is a promise, and not the actual relief, which calms them. There is a curious difference in the manner of the communications now made to the people. First of all the two brothers unite their energies to hush their outcries: "At evening ye shall know that Jehovah is your leader from Egypt, and in the morning ye shall behold His glory; and what are we, that ye murmur against us?" Then Moses affirms, with all the energy of his chieftainship, that in the evening they shall eat flesh, and in the morning bread to the full. Again he asks them "What are we?" and more sternly and directly charges them with murmuring against Jehovah. And this is a good example of the true meaning of his "meekness." He is fiery enough, but not for his own greatness; rather because he feels his littleness, and that the offence is entirely against God, does he resent their conduct; absence of self-assertion is his "meekness," and thus we read of it when Miriam and Aaron spake against him, declaring that they were commissioned as well as he (Num. xii. 3). Finally, when order was restored, and some mysterious manifestation was at hand, he resumed the solemn and formal usage of conveying his orders through his brother, and in cold, compact, impressive words, said unto Aaron, "Say unto all the congregation of the children of Israel, Come near before the Lord, for He hath heard your murmurings." All this is very dignified and natural. And so is—what after ages could scarcely have invented—the impressive reticence of what follows. "They looked toward the wilderness, and behold, the glory of the Lord appeared in the cloud."

Were they not then intended to "come near"? and was it as they turned their faces to draw nigh that the Vision revealed itself and stopped them? And what was the untold sight which they beheld? The narrative belongs to a primitive age; it is quite unlike the elaborate symbolisms of Ezekiel and Daniel, or even of Isaiah, but yet this undescribed, mystic, and solitary glory is not less sublime than the train which covered the Temple-floor, while, hovering above it, reverent seraphim veiled their faces and their feet, or the terrible crystal and the wheels of dreadful height, or the throne of flame whence issued a fiery stream, and before which thousands of thousands and myriads of myriads stood (Isa. vi. 2; Ezek. i. 22, 18; Dan. vii. 9, 10). But the point to observe is that it is different, more primitive, an undefined and lonely vision of awe well fitted for the desert wilds and for the gaze of men whose hearts must not be misled by the likeness of anything in heaven or earth; the glory of the Lord appearing in the cloud (most probably, but not of necessity, the cloud which guided them), and in the direction whence they were so fain to turn away.

No later inventor would have known how to say so little, much less to make that little harmonise so exactly with the lessons meant to be suggested by the wild and solemn solitudes into which they were now plunged.

And now the Lord Himself repeats the promise of relief, but first solemnly announces that He is not heedless of their ill-behaviour while He tolerates it. The question is suggested, although not asked, How long will His forbearance last?

Well for them if they learn the lesson, and "know that I am Jehovah your God," mindful of their needs, entitled to their fealty. In the evening, therefore, came a flight of quails; and in the morning they found a small round thing, small as the hoar-frost, upon the ground.

MANNA.

Exodus xvi. 15-36.

The manna which miraculously supplied the wants of Israel was to them an utterly strange food, the use of which they had to learn. Thus it was another means of severing their habitual course of life and association of ideas from their degraded past. And while we may not press too far the assertion that it was the "corn of heaven" and "angels' food" (*i. e.*, "the bread of the mighty"—Psalm lxxviii. 24-5, R. V.), yet the narrative shows, even without help from later scriptures, that it was calculated to sustain their energies and yet to leave their appetites unstimulated and unpampered. For they were now called to purer joys than those of the senses—to liberty, a divine vocation, the presence of God, the revelation of His law, and the unfolding of His purposes. Failing to rise to these heights, they fell far, murmured again, and perished by the destroyer, not merely to avenge the petulance of an hour, but for all that it betrayed, for treason to their vocation and radical inability to even comprehend its meaning. In the language of modern science, it answered to Nature's rejection of the unfit.

Their calling was thus, though under very different forms, that which the apostles found so hard, yet did not quite refuse: it was to mind the things of God and not the things of men.

It is well known that the manna of the Israelites bore some resemblance to a natural product of the wilderness, still exuded by certain plants during the coolness of the night, and formerly more plentiful than now, when all vegetation has been ruthlessly swept away by the Bedouin. But the differences are much greater than the resemblance. The natural product is a drug, and not a food; it is gathered only during some weeks of summer; it is not liable to speedy corruption, nor could there be any reason for preserving a specimen of this common product in the ark; it could not have sufficed, however aided by their herds and flocks, to feed one in a hundred of the Hebrew multitudes, even during the season of its production; nor could it have ceased on the same day when they ate the first ripe corn of Canaan.

And yet the resemblance is suggestive. Unbelievers find, in the links which connect most of our Scripture miracles with nature, in the undefined and gradual transition from one to the other, as from a temperate day to night, an excuse for denying that they are miraculous at all. But the instructed believer finds a confirmation of his faith. He reflects that when Fancy begins to toy with the supernatural, she spurns nature from her: the trammels under which she has long chafed are hateful to her, and she flies from them to the utmost extreme.

It could not be thus with Him by whom the system of the world was framed. He will not wantonly interfere with His own plan. He will regard nature as an elastic band to stretch, rather than as a chain to break. If He will multiply food, in the New Testament, that is no reason why His disciples should fare more delicately than Providence intended for them: they shall still eat barley loaves and fish. And so the winds help to overthrow Pharaoh and to bring the quails; and when a new thing has to be created, it approaches in its general idea to one of the few natural products of that inhospitable region.

Now let it be supposed for a moment that the supply of manna had never ceased, so that until this day men could every morning gather a day's ration off the ground. Such continuance of the provision would not make it any the less a gift; but only a more lavish boon. And yet it would clearly cease to be regarded as miraculous, an exception to the course of nature, miscalled her "laws," since men do strive to subvert the miracle by representing that such manna, however scantily, may still be found. And this may expose the folly of a wish, probably sometimes felt by all men, that some miracle had actually been perpetuated, so that we could strengthen our faith at pleasure by looking upon an exhibition of divine power. In truth, no marvel could excel that which annually multiplies the corn beneath the clod, and by the process of decay in springtime feeds the world in autumn. Only its steady recurrence throws a veil over our eyes; and it is a vain conceit that the same web would not be woven by use between man and the Worker of any other marvel that was perpetuated. Already the earth is full of the goodness of the Lord, for all who have eyes to see.

It is also to be observed that the manna was not given to teach the people sloth. They were obliged to gather it early, before the sun was hot. They had still to endure weary marches, and the care of their flocks and herds.

And, in curious harmony with the manner of all the gifts of nature, the manna sent from heaven had yet to be prepared by man: "bake that which ye will bake, and seethe that which ye will seethe." Thus God, by natural means and by the sweat of our brow, gives us our daily bread; and all knowledge, art, and culture are His gifts, although elaborated by the brain and heart of generations whom He taught.

Moreover, there was a protest against the grasping, unbelieving temper which cannot trust God with to-morrow, but longs to have much goods laid up. That is the temper which forfeits the smile of God, and grinds the faces of the poor, to make an ignoble "provision" for the future. How often, since the time of Moses, has the unblessed accumulation become hateful! How often, since the time of St. James, the rust of such possession has eaten the flesh like fire! Men would be far more generous, the difference between wealth and poverty would be less portentous, and the resources of religion and charity less crippled, if we lived in the spirit of the Lord's prayer, desirous of the advance of the kingdom, but not asking to be given to-morrow's bread until to-morrow. That lesson was taught by the manner of the dispensation of the manna, but the covetousness of Israel would not learn it. The people actually strove to be dishonest in their enjoyment of a miracle. It is no wonder that Moses was wroth with them.

Among the strange properties of their supernatural food not the least curious was this: that when they came to measure what they had collected, and compare it with what Moses had bidden,* the most eager and able-bodied had nothing over, and the feeblest had no lack. Every real worker was supplied, and none was glutted. This result is apparently miraculous. St. Paul's use of it does not, as some have supposed, represent it as a result of Hebrew benevolence, sharing with the weak the more abundant supplies of the strong: the miracle is not cited as an example of charity, but of that practical equality, divinely approved, which Christian charity should reproduce; the Christian Church is bidden to do voluntarily what was done by miracle in the wilderness: "your abundance being a supply at this present time for their want, that their abundance also may become a supply for your want, that there may be equality; as it is written, He that gathered much had nothing over, and he that gathered little had no lack" (2 Cor. viii. 15).

It is quite in vain to appeal to this passage in favour of socialistic theories. In the first place it applies only to the necessities of existence; and even granting that the state should enforce the principle to which it points, the duty would not extend beyound a liberal poor rate. When contributions were afterwards demanded for the sanctuary, there is no trace of a dead level in their resources: the rulers gave the gems and spices and oil, some brought gold, with some were found blue and linen and skins, and others had acacia-wood to offer (xxxv. 22-4).

In the second place, this arrangement was only temporary; and while the soil of Canaan was distinctly claimed for the Lord, the enjoyment of it by individuals was secured, and perpetuated in their families, by stringent legislation. Now, land is the kind of property which socialists most vehemently assail; but persons who appeal to Exodus must submit to the authority of Judges.

Socialism, therefore, and its coercive measures, find no more real sanction here than in the Church of Jerusalem, where the property of Ananias was his own, and the price of it in his own power. But yet it is highly significant that in

* The "omer" of this passage is not mentioned elsewhere in Scripture: it is known to have been the one-hundredth part of the homer with which careless readers sometimes confuse it, and its capacity is variously estimated, from somewhat under half a gallon to somewhat above three-quarters.

both Testaments, as the Church of God starts upon its career, an example should be given of the effacing of inequalities, in the one case by miracle, in the other by such a voluntary movement as best becomes the gospel. Is not such a movement, large and free, the true remedy for our modern social distractions and calamities? Would it not be wise and Christ-like for the rich to give, as St. Paul taught the Corinthians to give, what the law could never wisely exact from them? Would not self-denial, on a scale to imply real sacrifice, and fulfilling in spirit rather than letter the apostle's aspiration for "equality," secure in return the enthusiastic adhesion to the rights of property of all that is best and noblest among the poor?

When will the world, or even the Church, awaken to the great truth that our politics also need to be steeped in Christian feeling—that humanity requires not a revolution but a pentecost —that a millennium cannot be enacted, but will dawn whenever human bosoms are emptied of selfishness and lust, and filled with brotherly kindness and compassion? Such, and no more, was the socialism which St. Paul deduced from the equality in the supply of manna.

SPIRITUAL MEAT.

Exodus xvi. 15-36.

Since the journey of Israel is throughout full of sacred meaning, no one can fail to discern a mystery in the silent ceaseless daily miracle of bread-giving. But we are not left to our conjectures. St. Paul calls manna "spiritual meat," not because it nourished the higher life (for the eaters of it murmured for flesh, and were not estranged from their lust), but because it answered to realities of the spiritual world (1 Cor. x. 3). And Christ Himself said, "It was not Moses that gave you the bread out of heaven, but My Father giveth you the true Bread from heaven," making manna the type of sustenance which the soul needs in the wilderness, and which only God can give (John vi. 32).

We note the time of its bestowal. The soul has come forth out of its bondage. Perhaps it imagines that emancipation is enough: all is won when its chains are broken: there is to be no interval between the Egypt of sin and the Promised Land of milk and honey and repose. Instead of this serene attainment, it finds that the soul requires to be fed, and no food is to be seen, but only a wilderness of scorching heat, dry sand, vacancy, and hunger. Old things have passed away, but it is not yet realised that all things have become new. Religion threatens to become a vast system for the removal of accustomed indulgences and enjoyments, but where is the recompense for all that it forbids? The soul cries out for food: well for it if the cry be not faithless, nor spoken to earthly chiefs alone!

There is a noteworthy distinction between the gift of manna and every other recorded miracle of sustenance. In Eden the fruit of immortality was ripening upon an earthly tree. The widow of Zarephath was fed from her own stores. The ravens bore to Elijah ordinary bread and flesh; and if an angel fed him, it was with a cake baken upon coals. Christ Himself was content to multiply common bread and fish, and even after His resurrection gave His apostles the fare to which they were accustomed. Thus they learned that divine life must be led amid the ordinary conditions of mortality. Even the incarnation of Deity was wrought in the likeness of sinful flesh. But yet the incarnation was the bringing of a new life, a strange and unknown energy, to man.

And here, almost at the beginning of revelation, is typified, not the homely conditions of the inner life, but its unearthly nature and essence. Here is no multiplication of their own stores, no gift, like the quails, of such meat as they were wont to gather. They asked "What is it?" And this teaches the Christian that his sustenance is not of this world. They were fed "with manna which they knew not . . . to make them know that man doth not live by bread only, but by every word that proceedeth out of the mouth of God doth man live" (Deut. viii. 3). The root of worldliness is not in this indulgence or that, in gay clothing or an active career; but in the soul's endeavour to draw its nourishment from things below. And spirituality belongs not to an uncouth vocabulary, nor to the robes of any confraternity, to rigid rules or austere deportment; it is the blessedness of a life nourished upon the bread of heaven, and doomed to starve if that bread be not bestowed. Let not the wealthy find an insuperable bar to spirituality in his condition, nor the poor suppose that indigence cannot have its treasure upon earth; but let each man ask whence come his most real and practical impulses and energies upon life's journey. If these flow from even the purest earthly source—love of wife or child, anything else than communion with the Father of spirits—this is not the bread of life, and can no more nourish a pilgrim towards eternity than the husks which swine eat.

There is no mistaking the doctrine of the New Testament as to what this bread may be. By prayer and faith, by ordinances and sacraments rightly used, the manna may be gathered; but Jesus Himself is the Bread of life, His Flesh is meat indeed and His Blood is drink indeed, and He gives His Flesh for the life of the world. Christ is the Vine, and we are the branches, fruitful only by the sap which flows from Him. As there are diseases which cannot be overcome by powerful drugs, but by a generous and wholesome dietary, so is it with the diseases of the soul—pride, anger, selfishness, falsehood, lust. As the curse of sin is removed by the faith which appropriates pardon, so its power is broken by the steady personal acceptance of Christ; and our Bread and Wine are His new humanity, given to us, until He becomes the second Father of the race, which is begotten again in Him. An easy temper is not Christian meekness; dislike to witness pain is not Christian love. All our goodness must strike root deeper than in the sensibilities, must be nourished by the communication to us of the mind which was in Christ Jesus.

And this food is universally given, and universally suitable. The strong and the weak, the aged chieftain and little children, ate and were nourished. No stern decree excluded any member of the visible Church in the wilderness from sharing the bread from heaven: they did eat the same spiritual meat, provided only that they gathered it. Their part was to be in earnest in accepting, and so is ours; but if we fail, whom shall we blame except ourselves? In the mystery of its origin, in the silent and secret mode of its descent from above, in the constancy of its bestowal, and in its suitability for all the camp, for Moses and the youngest child, the manna prefigured Christ.

Every day a fresh supply had to be laid up, and nothing could be held over from the largest hoard. So it is with us: we must give ourselves to Christ for ever, but we must ask Him daily to give Himself to us. The richest experience, the purest aspiration, the humblest self-abandonment that was ever felt, could not reach forward to supply the morrow. Past graces will become loathsome if used instead of present supplies from heaven. And the secret of many a scandalous fall is that the unhappy soul grew self-confident: unlike St. Paul, he reckoned that he had already attained; and thereupon the graces in which he trusted became corrupt and vile.

The constant supply was not more needful than it was abundant. The manna lay all around the camp: the Bread of Life is He who stands at our door and knocks. Alas for those who murmur for grosser indulgences! Israel demanded and obtained them; but while the flesh was in their nostrils the angel of the Lord went forth and smote them. Is there no plague any longer for the perverse? What are the discords that convulse families, the uncurbed passions to which nothing is sacred, the jaded appetite and weary discontent which hates the world even as it hates itself? what but the judgment of God upon those who despise His provision, and must needs gratify themselves? Be it our happiness, as it is our duty, to trust Him to prepare our table before us, while He leads us to His Holy Land.

The Lord of the Sabbath already taught His people to respect His day. Upon it no manna fell; and we shall hereafter see the bearing of this incident upon the question whether the Sabbath is only an ordinance of Judaism. Meanwhile they who went out to gather had a sharp lesson in the difference between faith, which expects what God has promised, and presumption, which hopes not to lose much by disobeying Him.

Lastly, an omer of manna was to be kept throughout all generations, before the Testimony. Grateful remembrance of past mercies, temporal as well as spiritual, was to connect itself with the deepest and most awful mysteries of religion. So let it be with us. The bitter proverb that eaten bread is soon forgotten must never be true of the Christian. He is to remember all the way that the Lord his God hath led him. He is bidden to "forget not all His benefits, Who forgiveth all thine iniquities, Who healeth all thy diseases . . . Who satisfieth thy mouth with good things." So foolish is the slander that religion is too transcendental for the common life of man.

CHAPTER XVII.

MERIBAH.

Exodus xvii. 1-7.

The people, miraculously fed, are therefore called to exhibit more confidence in God than hitherto, because much is required of him to whom much is given. They have now to plunge deeper into the wilderness; and after two stages which Exodus omits (Num. xxxiii. 12, 13), and just as they approach the mount of God, they find themselves without water. Even the Son of Man Himself was led into the wilderness next after the descent of the Spirit, and the avowal by the voice of God; nor is any true Christian to marvel if his seasons of special privilege are succeeded by special demands upon his firmness.

One finds himself conjecturing, very often, what nobler history, what grander analogies between type and antitype, what more gracious and lavish interpositions might have instructed us, if only the type had been less woefully imperfect—if Israel had been trustful as Moses was, and the crude material had not marred the design.

It would be more practical and edifying to reflect how often we ourselves, like Israel, might have learned and exemplified deep things of the grace of God, when all we really exhibited was the well-worn lesson of human frailty and divine forbearance.

In the story of our Lord, it has been observed that before the Pharisees directly assailed Himself, they found fault with His disciples who fasted not, or accosted them concerning Him Who ate with sinners. And so here the people really tempted God, but openly "strove with Moses," and with Aaron too, for the verb is a plural one: "Give *ye* water" (ver. 2).

But as Aaron is merely an agent and spokesman, the chief value of this tacit allusion to him, besides proving his fidelity, is to refute the notion that he sinks into comparative obscurity only after the sin of the golden calf. Already his position is one to be indicated rather than expressed; and Moses said, "Why do ye quarrel with me? wherefore do ye try the Lord?"

But the frenzy rose higher: it was he, and not a higher One, who had brought them out of Egypt; the upshot of it would only be "to kill us, and our children, and our cattle, with thirst."

Look closely at this expression, and a curious significance discloses itself. Was it mere covetousness, the spirit of the Jew Shylock lamenting in one breath his daughter and his ducats, which introduced the cattle along with the children into this complaint of dying men? Shylock himself, when death actually looked him in the face, readily sacrificed his fortune. Nor is it credible that a large number of people, really believing that a horrible death was imminent, would have spent any complaints upon their property. The language is exactly that of angry exaggeration. They have come through straits quite as desperate, and they know it well. It is not the fear of death, but the painful delay of rescue, the discomfort and misery of their condition in the meanwhile, the contrast between their sufferings and their own conception of the rights of the favourites of heaven, which is audible in this complaint. And thus their "Trial" and "Quarrel" are admirably epitomised in the phrase "Is Jehovah among us or not?" a phrase which has often since been in the heart, if not upon the lips, of men who had supposed the life divine to be one long holiday, the pilgrimage an excursion, when without are fightings and within fears, when they have great sorrow and heaviness in their hearts.

Because God is not a Judge, but a Father, the murmurs of Israel do not prevent Him from showing mercy. Accordingly, when Moses prays, he is bidden to go on before the people, bringing certain of their elders along with him for witnesses of the marvel that was to follow. Such is the Divine method. As soon as unbelief and discontent estranged the Jews of the New Testament from Christ, He would not vulgarise His miracles, nor do many mighty works among the unbelieving. After His resurrection He appeared not unto all the people, but unto witnesses chosen before. And as the Jews were chosen to bear witness to Him among the nations, so were these elders now to bear witness among the Jews, who might without their testimony have fallen into some such rationalising theory as that of Tacitus, who says that Moses discovered a fountain by examining a spot where wild asses lay.

With these witnesses, he is bidden to go to a rock in Horeb (so nearly had these murmurers approached the scene of the most awful of all manifestations of Him whose presence they debated), and there God was to stand before them upon the rock, making His universal presence a localised consciousness in their experience.

A true religion is progressive: every stage of it leans on the past and sustains the future; and so Moses must bring with him " the rod, wherewith thou smotest the river." The dullest can see the fitness of this allusion. Among all the wonders which the shepherd's wand had wrought, the mastery over the Nile, the plague which inflicted an unwonted thirst upon the inhabitants of that well-watered field of Zoan, was most to the purpose now. To kill and to make alive are the functions of the same Being, and He Who spoiled the Egyptian river will now refresh His heritage that is weary. At the touch of the prophetic wand the waters poured forth which thenceforth supplied them through all their desert wanderings.

Reserving the symbolic meaning of this event for a future study, we have to remember meanwhile the warning which the apostle here discovered. All the people drank of the rock, yet with many of them God was not pleased. Privilege is one thing—acceptance is quite another; and it shall be more tolerable at last for Sodom and Gomorrah than for nations, churches, and men, who were content to resemble soil that drinketh in the rain that cometh upon it oft, and yet to remain unfruitful. Already the conduct of Israel was such that the place was named from human worthlessness rather than Divine beneficence. Too often, it is the more conspicuous part of the story of the relations of God and man.

AMALEK.

Exodus xvii. 8-16.

Nothing can be more natural, to those who remember the value of a fountain in the East, than that Amalek should swoop down from his own territories upon Israel, as soon as this abundant river tempted his cupidity. This unprovoked attack of a kindred nation leads to another advance in the education of the people.

They had hitherto been the sheep of God: now they must become His warriors. At the Red Sea it was said to them, " Stand still, and see the salvation of the Lord . . . the Lord shall fight for you, and ye shall hold your peace " (xiv. 13). But it is not so now. Just as the function of every true miracle is to lead to a state of faith in which miracles are not required; just as a mother reaches her hand to a tottering infant, that presently the boy may go alone, so the Lord fought for Israel, that Israel might learn to fight for the Lord. The herd of slaves who came out of Egypt could not be trusted to stand fast in battle; and what a defeat would have done with them we may judge by their outcries at the very sight of Pharaoh. But now they had experience of Divine succor, and had drawn the inspiring breath of freedom. And so it was reasonable to expect that some chosen men of them at least will be able to endure the shock of battle. And if so, it was a matter of the last importance to develop and render conscious the national spirit, a spirit so noble in its unselfish readiness to die, and in its scorn of such material ills as anguish and mutilation compared with baseness and dishonour, that the re-kindling of it in seasons of peril and conflict is more than half a compensation for the horrors of a battle-field.

We do not now inquire what causes avail to justify the infliction and endurance of those horrors. Probably they will vary from age to age; and as the ties grow strong which bind mankind together, the rupture of them will be regarded with an ever-deepening shudder,—just as England to-day would certainly refuse to make war upon our American kinsmen for a provocation which (rightly or wrongly) she would not endure from Russians. But the point to be observed is that war cannot be inherently immoral, since God instructed in war the first nation that He ever trained, not using its experience of His immediate interpositions to supersede all need of human strife, but to make valiant soldiers, and adding some of the most precious lessons of all their later experience on the battle-field and by the sword. Now, it assuredly cannot be shown that anything in itself immoral is fostered and encouraged by the Old Testament. Slavery and divorce, which it was not yet possible to extirpate, were hampered, restricted, and reduced to a minimum, being " suffered " " because of the hardness of ' their ' hearts " (Matt. xix. 8). The wildest assailant of the Pentateuch will scarcely pretend that it fosters and incites either divorce or slavery, as, beyond all question, it encourages the martial ardour of the Jews.

And yet war, though permissible, and in certain circumstances necessary, is only necessary as the lesser of two evils; it is not in itself good. Solomon, not David, could build the temple of the Lord; and Isaiah sharply contrasts the Messiah with even that providentially appointed conqueror, the only pagan who is called by God " My anointed," in that the one comes upon rulers as upon mortar, and as the potter treadeth clay, but the Other breaks not a bruised reed, nor quenches the smoking flax (Isa. xli. 25, xlii. 3, xlv. 1). The ideal of humanity is peace, and also it is happiness, but war may not yet have ceased to be a necessity of life, sometimes as ruinous to evade as any other form of suffering.

Another necessity of national development is the advancement of capable men. The empire of Napoleon would assuredly have withered, if only because its chief was as jealous of commanding genius as he was ready to advance and patronise capacity of the second order. It is a maxim that true greatness finds worthy colleagues and successors, and rejoices in them. And while the guidance of Jehovah is to be assumed throughout, it is significant that the first mention of the splendid commander and godly judge, during all whose days and the days of his contemporaries Israel served Jehovah, comes not in any express revelation or commandment of God; but the narrative relates that Moses said unto Joshua, "Choose out men for us and go out, fight with Amalek: to-morrow I will stand on the top of the hill with the rod of God in my hand." They are the words of one who had noted him already as "a man in whom is the Spirit" (Num. xxvii. 18), of one also who had unlearned, in the experience now of eighty years, the desire of glittering achievement and martial fame, who knew that the deepest fountains of real power are hidden, and was content that another should lead the headlong and victorious charge, if only it were his to hold, upon the top of the hill, the rod of God.

Once it was his own rod: with it the exiled shepherd controlled the sheep of his master; that it should be the medium of the miraculous had appeared to be an additional miracle, but now it was the very rod of God, nor was any cry to heaven more eloquent and better grounded than simply the reaching toward the skies, in long, steady, mute appeal, of that symbol of all His dealings with them—the plaguing of Egypt, the recession of the tide and its wild return, the bringing of water from the rock. Was all to be in vain? Should the wild boar waste the vine just brought out of Egypt before ever it reached the appointed vineyard? And we also should be able to plead with God the noble works that He hath done in our time. For us also there ought to be such experience as worketh hope. As long as the exertion was possible even to the heroic force which age had not abated, Moses thus prayed for his people; for the gesture was a prayer, and a grand one, and must not be criticised otherwise than as the act of a poetic and primitive genius, whose institutions throughout are full of spiritual import. While he did this, Israel prevailed; but the slow progress of the victory reminds us of these dreary centuries during which we are just able to discern some gradual advance of the kingdom of Christ on earth, but no rout, no collapse of evil. And why was this? Because the sustaining and permanent energy was not to flow from the prayers of one, however holy and however eminent; three men were together in the mountain, and the co-operation of them all was demanded; so that only when Aaron and Hur supported the sinking hand of their chief was the decisive victory given.

Now, the lesson from all this does not concern the High-priestly intercession of our Lord, for the office of Moses is consistently distinguished from the priesthood. Nor can the notion be tolerated that if our Lord requires mortal co-operation before asking and being given the heathen for His heritage, which is obviously the case, the reason can be at all expressed by that weakness which needed support.

No, the Lord our Priest is also Himself the dispenser of victory. To Him all power is given on earth, and to Him it is our duty to appeal for the triumph of His own cause. And here and there, doubtless, a Christian heart is fervent and faithful in its intercessions. To these, unknown, unsuspected by the combatants in the heat of battle,—to humble saints, some of them bed-ridden, ignorant, poverty-stricken, despised, holy souls who have no controversial skill, no missionary calling, but who possess the grace habitually to convert their wishes into prayers, —to such, perhaps, it is due that the idols of India and China are now bowing down. And when they cease to be a minority in so doing, when those who now criticise learn to sustain their flagging energies, we shall see a day of the Lord.

Observe, however, that as the active exertion of the host does not displace the silence of intercession, neither is it displaced itself: Joshua really bore his part in the discomfiture of Amalek and his host. And so it is always. The development of human energy to the uttermost is a part of the design of Him Who gave a task even to unfallen man. Let none suppose that to labour is (sufficiently and by itself) to pray; but also let none idly persuade himself that while energies and responsibilities are his, to pray is sufficiently to labour.

Thus it came to pass that Israel won its first victory in battle. Another step was taken toward the fulfilment of the promise to Abraham to make of him a great nation; and also toward the gradual transference of the national faith from a passive reliance in Divine interposition to an abiding confidence in Divine help. Let it be clearly understood that this latter is the nobler and the more mature faith.

With martial ardour, God took care to inculcate the sense of national responsibility, without which warriors become no more than brigands. So it was with Amalek: he had not been attacked or even menaced; he had marched out from his own territories to assail an innocent and kindred race ("then *came* Amalek" ver. 8), and his attack had been cruel and cowardly, he smote the hindmost, all that were feeble and in the rear, when they were faint and weary, and he feared not God (Deut. xxv. 18). Against all such tactics the wrath of God was denounced when, because of them, Amalek was doomed to total extirpation.

Moses now built an altar, to imprint on the mind of the people this new lesson. And he called it, "The Lord is my Banner," a title which called the nation at once to valour and to obedience, which asserted that they were an army, but a consecrated one.

Now let us ask whether this simple story is at all the kind of thing which legend or myth would have created, for the first martial exploit of Israel. The obscure part played by Moses is not what we would expect; nor, even as a mediator, is the position of one whose arms must be held up a very romantic conception. If the object is to inspire the Jews for later struggles with more formidable foes, the story is ill-contrived, for we read of no surprising force of Amalek, and no inspiriting exploit of Joshua. Everything is as prosaic as the real course of events in this poor world is wont to be. And on that account it is all the more useful to us who live prosaic lives, and need the help of God among prosaic circumstances.

CHAPTER XVIII.

JETHRO.

Exodus xviii. 1-27.

The defeat of Amalek is followed by the visit of Jethro; the opposite pole of the relation between Israel and the nations, the coming of the Gentiles to his brightness. And already that is true which repeats itself all through the history of the Church, that much secular wisdom, the art of organisation, the structure and discipline of societies, may be drawn from the experience and wisdom of the world.

Moses was under the special guidance of God, as really as any modern enthusiast can claim to be. When he turned for aid or direction to heaven, he was always answered. And yet he did not think scorn of the counsel of his kinsman. And although eighty years had not dimmed the fire of his eyes, nor wasted his strength, he neglected not the warning which taught him to economise his force; not to waste on every paltry dispute the attention and wisdom which could govern the new-born state.

Jethro is the kinsman, and probably the brother-in-law of Moses; for if he were the father-in-law, and the same as Reuel in the second chapter, why should a new name be introduced without any mark of identification? When he hears of the emancipation of Israel from Egypt, he brings back to Moses his two sons and Zipporah, who had been sent away, after the angry scene at the circumcision of the younger, and before he entered Egypt with his life in his hand. Now he was a great personage, the leader of a new nation, and the conqueror of the proudest monarch in the world. With what feelings would the wife and husband meet? We are told nothing of their interview, nor have we any reason to qualify the unfavourable impression produced by the circumstances of their parting, by the schismatic worship founded by their grandchildren, and by the loneliness implied in the very names of Gershom and Eliezer—" A-stranger-there," and " God-a-Help."

But the relations between Moses and Jethro are charming, whether we look at the obeisance rendered to the official minister of God by him whom God had honoured so specially, by the prosperous man to the friend of his adversity, or at the interest felt by the priest of Midian in all the details of the great deliverance of which he had heard already, or his joy in a Divine manifestation, probably not in all respects according to the prejudices of his race, or his praise of Jehovah as " greater than all gods, yea, in the thing wherein they dealt proudly against them " (ver. 11, R. V.). The meaning of this phrase is either that the gods were plagued in their own domains, or that Jehovah had finally vanquished the Egyptians by the very element in which they were most oppressive, as when Moses himself had been exposed to drown.

There is another expression, in the first verse, which deserves to be remarked. How do the friends of a successful man think of the scenes in which he has borne a memorable part? They chiefly think of them in connection with their own hero. And amid all the story of the Exodus, in which so little honour is given to the human actor, the one trace of personal exultation is where it is most natural and becoming; it is in the heart of his relative: " When Jethro . . . heard of all that the Lord had done *for Moses* and for Israel."

We are told, with marked emphasis, that this Midianite, a priest, and accustomed to act as such with Moses in his family, " took a burnt-offering and sacrifices for God; and Aaron came, and all the elders of Israel, to eat bread with Moses' father-in-law before God." Nor can we doubt that the writer of the Epistle to the Hebrews, who laid such stress upon the subordination of Abraham to Melchizedek, would have discerned in the relative position of Jethro and Aaron another evidence that the ascendency of the Aaronic priesthood was only temporary. We shall hereafter see that priesthood is a function of redeemed humanity, and that all limitations upon it were for a season, and due to human shortcoming. But for this very reason (if there were no other) the chief priest could only be He Who represents and embodies all humanity, in Whom is neither Jew nor Greek, barbarian, Scythian, bond nor free, because He is all and in all.

In the meantime, here is recognised, in the history of Israel, a Gentile priesthood.

And, as at the passover, so now, the sacrifice to God is partaken of by His people, who are conscious of acceptance by Him. Happy was the union of innocent festivity with a sacramental recognition of God. It is the same sentiment which was aimed at by the primitive Christian Church in her feasts of love, genuine meals in the house of God, until licence and appetite spoiled them, and the apostle asked " Have ye not houses to eat and drink in? " (1 Cor. xi. 22). Shall there never come a time when the victorious and pure Church of the latter days shall regain what we have forfeited, when the doctrine of the consecration of what is called " secular life " shall be embodied again in forms like these? It speaks to us meanwhile in a form which is easily ridiculed (as in Lamb's well-known essay), and yet singularly touching and edifying if rightly considered, in the asking for a blessing upon our meals.

On the morrow, Jethro saw Moses, all day long, deciding the small matters and great which needed already to be adjudicated for the nation. He who had striven, without a commission, himself to smite the Egyptian, and lead out Israel, is the same self-reliant, heroic, not too discreet person still.

But the true statesman and administrator is he who employs to the utmost all the capabilities and energies of his subordinates. And Jethro made a deep mark in history when he taught Moses the distinction between the lawgiver and the judge, between him who sought from God and proclaimed to the people the principles of justice and their form, and him who applied the law to each problem as it arose.

" It is supposed, and with probability," writes Kalisch (*in loco*), " that Alfred the Great, who was well versed in the Bible, based his own Saxon constitution of sheriffs in counties, etc., on the example of the Mosaic division (comp. *Bacon on English Government*, i. 70)." And thus it may be that our own nation owes its free institutions almost directly to the generous interest in the well-being of his relative, felt by an Arabian priest, who cherished, amid the growth of idolatries all around him, the primitive belief in God, and who rightly held that the first qualifications of a capable judge were ability, and the fear of God, truthfulness and hatred of unjust gain.

We learn from Deuteronomy (i. 9-15), that Moses allowed the people themselves to elect these officials, who became not only their judges but their captains.

From the whole of this narrative we see clearly that the intervention of God for Israel is no more to be regarded as superseding the exercise of human prudence and common-sense, than as dispensing with valour in the repulse of Amalek, and with patience in journeying through the wilderness.

THE TYPICAL BEARINGS OF THE HISTORY.

We are now about to pass from history to legislation. And this is a convenient stage at which to pause, and ask how it comes to pass that all this narrative is also, in some sense, an allegory. It is a discussion full of pitfalls. Countless volumes of arbitrary and fanciful interpretation have done their worst to discredit every attempt, however cautious and sober, at finding more than the primary signification in any narrative.* And whoever considers the reckless, violent, and inconsistent methods of the mystical commentators may be forgiven if he recoils from occupying the ground which they have wasted, and contents himself with simply drawing the lessons which the story directly suggests.

But the New Testament does not warrant such a surrender. It tells us that leaven answers to malice, and unleavened bread to sincerity; that at the Red Sea the people were baptised; that the tabernacle and the altar, the sacrifice and the priest, the mercy-seat and the manna, were all types and shadows of abiding Christian realities.

It is more surprising to find the return of the infant Jesus connected with the words "When Israel was a child then I loved him, and I called My son out of Egypt,"—for it is impossible to doubt that the prophet was here speaking of the Exodus, and had in mind the phrase "Israel is My son, My first-born: let My son go, that he may serve Me" (Matt. i. 15; Hos. xi. 1; Exod. iv. 22).

How are such passages to be explained? Surely not by finding a superficial resemblance between two things, and thereupon transferring to one of them whatever is true of the other. No thought can attain accuracy except by taking care not to confuse in this way things which superficially resemble each other.

But no thought can be fertilising and suggestive which neglects real and deep resemblances, resemblances of principle as well as incident, resemblances which are due to the mind of God or the character of man.

In the structure and furniture of the tabernacle, and the order of its services, there are analogies deliberately planned, and such as every one would expect, between religious truth shadowed forth in Judaism, and the same truth spoken in these latter days unto us in the Son.

---
* Take as an example the assertion of Bunyan that the sea in the Revelation is a sea of glass, because the laver in the tabernacle was made of the brazen looking-glasses of the women. (*Solomon's Temple*, xxxvi. 1.)

But in the emancipation, the progress, and alas! the sins and chastisements of Israel, there are analogies of another kind, since here it is history which resembles theology, and chiefly secular things which are compared with spiritual. But the analogies are not capricious; they are based upon the obvious fact that the same God Who pitied Israel in bondage sees, with the same tender heart, a worse tyranny. For it is not a figure of speech to say that sin is slavery. Sin does outrage the will, and degrade and spoil the life. The sinner does obey a hard and merciless master. If his true home is in the kingdom of God, he is, like Israel, not only a slave but an exile. Is God the God of the Jew only? for otherwise He must, being immutable, deal with us and our tyrant as He dealt with Israel and Pharaoh. If He did not, by an exertion of omnipotence, transplant them from Egypt to their inheritance at one stroke, but required of them obedience, co-operation, patient discipline, and a gradual advance, why should we expect the whole work and process of grace to be summed up in the one experience which we call conversion? Yet if He did, promptly and completely, break their chains and consummate their emancipation, then the fact that grace is a progressive and gradual experience does not forbid us to reckon ourselves dead unto sin. If the region through which they were led, during their time of discipline, was very unlike the land of milk and honey which awaited the close of their pilgrimage, it is not unlikely that the same God will educate his later Church by the same means, leading us also by a way that we know not, to humble and prove us, that He may do us good at the latter end.

And if He marks, by a solemn institution, the period when we enter into covenant relations with Himself, and renounce the kingdom and tyranny of His foe, is it marvellous that the apostle found an analogy for this in the great event by which God punctuated the emancipation of Israel, leading them out of Egypt through the sea depths and beneath the protecting cloud?

If privilege, and adoption, and the Divine good-will, did not shelter them from the consequences of ingratitude and rebellion, if He spared not the natural branches, we should take heed lest He spare not us.

Such analogies are really arguments, as solid as those of Bishop Butler.

But the same cannot be maintained so easily of some others. When that is quoted of our Lord upon the cross which was written of the paschal lamb, "a bone shall not be broken" (Exod. xii. 46, John xix. 36), we feel that the citation needs to be justified upon different grounds. But such grounds are available. He was the true Lamb of God. For His sake the avenger passes over all His followers. His flesh is meat indeed. And therefore, although no analogy can be absolutely perfect, and the type has nothing to declare that His blood is drink indeed, yet there is an admirable fitness, worthy of inspired record, in the consummating and fulfilment in Him, and in Him alone of three sufferers, of the precept "A bone of Him shall not be broken." It may not be an express prophecy which is brought to pass, but it is a beautiful and appropriate correspondence, wrought out by Providence, not available for the coercion of sceptics, but good for the edifying of believers.

And so it is with the calling of the Son out of Egypt. Unquestionably Hosea spoke of Israel. But unquestionably too the phrase, "My Son, My Firstborn," is a startling one. Here is already a suggestive difference between the monotheism of the Old Testament and the austerer jealous logical orthodoxy of the Koran, which protests "It is not meet for God to have any Son, God forbid" (Sura xix. 36). Jesus argued that such a rigid and lifeless orthodoxy as that of later Judaism ought to have been scandalised, long before it came to consider His claims, by the ancient and recognised inspiration which gave the name of gods to men who sat in judgment as the representatives of Heaven. He claimed the right to carry still further the same principle—namely, that deity is not selfish and incommunicable, but practically gives itself away, in transferring the exercise of its functions. From such condescension everything may be expected, for God does not halt in the middle of a path He has begun to tread.

But if this argument of Jesus were a valid one (and the more it is examined the more profound it will be seen to be), how significant will then appear the term "My Son," as applied to Israel! In condescending so far, God almost pledged Himself to the Incarnation, being no dealer in half measures, nor likely to assume rhetorically a relation to mankind to which in fact He would not stoop.

Every Christian feels, moreover, that it is by virtue of the grand and final condescension that all the preliminary steps are possible. Because Abraham's seed was one, that is Christ, therefore ye (all) if ye are Christ's, are Abraham's seed, heirs according to promise (Gal. iii. 16, 29).

But when this great harmony comes to be devoutly recognised, a hundred minor and incidental points of contact are invested with a sacred interest.

No doctrinal injury would have resulted, if the Child Jesus had never left the Holy Land. No infidel could have served his cause by quoting the words of Hosea. Nor can we now cite them against infidels as a prophecy fulfilled. But when He does return from Egypt our devotions, not our polemics, hail and rejoice in the coincidence. It reminds us, although it does not demonstrate, that He who is thus called out of Egypt is indeed the Son.

The sober historian cannot prove anything, logically and to demonstration, by the reiterated interventions in history of atmospheric phenomena. And yet no devout thinker can fail to recognise that God has reserved the hail against the time of trouble and war.

In short, it is absurd and hopeless to bid us limit our contemplation, in a divine narrative, to what can be demonstrated like the propositions of Euclid. We laugh at the French for trying to make colonies and constitutions according to abstract principles, and proposing, as they once did, to reform Europe "after the Chinese manner." Well, religion also is not a theory: it is the true history of the past of humanity, and it is the formative principle in the history of the present and the future.

And hence it follows that we may dwell with interest and edification upon analogies, as every great thinker confesses the existence of truths, "which never can be proved."

In the meantime it is easy to recognise the much simpler fact, that these things happened unto them by way of example, and they were written for our admonition.

CHAPTER XIX.

AT SINAI.

EXODUS xix. 1-25.

IN the third month from the Exodus, and on the self-same day (which addition fixes the date precisely), the people reached the wilderness of Sinai. This answers fairly to the date of Pentecost, which was afterwards connected by tradition with the giving of the law. And therefore Pentecost was the right time for the gift of the Holy Ghost, bringing with Him the law of the spirit of life in Christ Jesus, and that freedom from servile Jewish obedience which is not attained by violating law, but by being imbued in its spirit, by the love which is the fulfilling of the law.

There is among the solemn solitudes of Sinai a wide amphitheatre, reached by two converging valleys, and confronted by an enormous perpendicular cliff, the Ras Sufsâfeh—a "natural altar," before which the nation had room to congregate, awed by the stern magnificence of the approach, and by the intense loneliness and desolation of the surrounding scene, and thus prepared for the unparalleled revelation which awaited them.

It is the manner of God to speak through nature and the senses to the soul. We cannot imagine the youth of the Baptist spent in Nazareth, nor of Jesus in the desert. Elijah, too, was led into the wilderness to receive the vision of God, and the agony of Jesus was endured at night, and secluded by the olives from the paschal moon. It is by another application of the same principle that the settled Jewish worship was bright with music and splendid with gold and purple; and the notion that the sublime and beautiful in nature and art cannot awaken the feelings to which religion appeals, is as shallow as the notion that when these feelings are awakened all is won.

What happens next is a protest against this latter extreme. Awe is one thing; the submission of the will is another. And therefore Moses was stopped when about to ascend the mountain, there to keep the solemn appointment that was made when God said, "This shall be the token unto thee that I have sent thee: When thou hast brought forth the people out of Egypt, ye shall serve God upon this mountain" (iii. 12). His own sense of the greatness of the crisis perhaps needed to be deepened. Certainly the nation had to be pledged, induced to make a deliberate choice, now first, as often again, under Joshua and Samuel, and when Elijah invoked Jehovah upon Carmel. (Josh. xxiv. 24; 1 Sam. xii. 14; 1 Kings xviii. 21, 39.)

It is easy to speak of pledges and formal declarations lightly, but they have their warrant in many such Scriptural analogies, nor should we easily find a church, careful to deal with souls, which has not employed them in some form, whether after the Anglican and Lutheran fashion, by confirmation, or in the less formal methods of other Protestant communions, or even by delaying baptism itself until it becomes, for the adult in Christian lands, what it is to the convert from false creeds.

Therefore the Lord called to Moses as he climbed the steep, and offered through him a formal covenant to the people.

"Thus shalt thou say to the house of Jacob,[*] and tell the children of Israel: Ye have seen what I did unto the Egyptians, and how I bare you on eagles' wings, and brought you unto Myself."

The appeal is to their personal experience and their gratitude: will this be enough? Will they accept His yoke, as every convert must, not knowing what it may involve, not yet having His demands specified and His commandments before their eyes, content to believe that whatever is required of them will be good, because the requirement is from God? Thus did Abraham, who went forth, not knowing whither, but knowing that he was divinely guided. "Now, therefore, if ye will obey My voice indeed and keep My covenant, then ye shall be a peculiar treasure unto Me from among all peoples; for all the earth is Mine, and ye shall be unto Me a kingdom of priests and a holy nation."

Thus God conveys to them, more explicitly than hitherto, the fact that He is the universal Lord, not ruling one land or nation only, nor, as the Pentateuch is charged with teaching, their tutelary deity among many others. Thus also the seeds are sown in them of a wholesome and rational self-respect, such as the Psalmist felt, who asked "What is man, that Thou art mindful of him?" yet realised that such mindfulness gave to man a real dignity, made him but little lower than the angels, and crowned him with glory and honour.

Abolish religion, and mankind will divide into two classes,—one in which vanity, unchecked by any spiritual superior, will obey no restraints of law, and another of which the conscious pettiness will aspire to no dignity of holiness, and shrink from no dishonour of sin. It is only the presence of a loving God which can unite in us the sense of humility and greatness, as having nothing and yet possessing all things, and valued by God as His "peculiar treasure."[†]

And with a reasonable self-respect should come a noble and yet sober dignity—"Ye shall be a kingdom of priests," a dynasty (for such is the meaning) of persons invested with royal and also with priestly rank. This was spoken just before the law gave the priesthood into the hands of one tribe; and thus we learn that Levi and Aaron were not to supplant the nation, but to represent it.

Now, this double rank is the property of redeemed humanity: we are "a kingdom and priests unto God." Yet the laity of the Corinthian Church were rebuked for a self-asserting and mutinous enjoyment of their rank: "Ye have reigned as kings without us"; and others there were in this Christian dispensation who "perished in the gainsaying of Korah" (1 Cor. iv. 8; Jude 11).

If the words "He hath made us a kingdom and priests" furnish any argument against the existence of an ordained ministry now, then there should have been no Jewish priesthood, for the same words are here. And is it supposed that this assertion only began to be true when the apostles died? Certainly there is a kind of self-assertion in the ministry which they condemn. But if they are opposed to its existence, alas for the Pastoral Epistles! It was because the function belonged to all, that no man might arrogate it who was not commissioned to act on behalf of all.

But while the individual may not assert himself to the unsettling of church order, the privilege is still common property. All believers have boldness to enter into the holiest place of all. All are called upon to rule for God "over a few things," to establish a kingdom of God within, and thus to receive a crown of life, and to sit with Jesus upon His throne. The very honours by which Israel was drawn to God are offered to us all, as it is written, "We are the circumcision," "We are Abraham's seed and heirs according to the promise" (Phil. iii. 3; Gal. iii. 29).

To this appeal the nation responded gladly. They could feel that indeed they had been sustained by God as the eagle bears her young—not grasping them in her claws, like other birds, but as if enthroned between her wings, and sheltered by her body, which interposed between the young and any arrow of the hunter. Thus, say the Rabbinical interpreters, did the pillar of cloud intervene between Israel and the Egyptians. If the image were to be pressed so far, we could now find a much closer analogy for the eagle "preferring itself to be pierced rather than to witness the death of its young" (Kalisch). But far more tender, and very touching in its domestic homeliness, is the metaphor of Him Whose discourses teem with allusions to the Old Testament, yet Who preferred to compare Himself to a hen gathering her chickens under her wing.

With the adhesion of Israel to the covenant, Moses returned to God. And the Lord said, "Lo, I come unto thee in a thick cloud, that the people may hear when I speak with thee, and may also believe thee for ever."

The design was to deepen their reverence for the Lawgiver Whose law they should now receive; to express by lessons, not more dreadful than the plagues of Egypt, but more vivid and sublime, the tremendous grandeur of Him Who was making a covenant with them, Who had borne them on His wings and called them His firstborn Son, Whom therefore they might be tempted to approach with undue familiarity, were it not for the mountain that burned up to heaven, the voice of the trumpet waxing louder and louder, and the Appearance so fearful that Moses said, "I exceedingly fear and quake" ($\tau\grave{o}$ $\phi\alpha\nu\tau\alpha\zeta\acute{o}\mu\epsilon\nu o\nu$—Heb. xii. 21).

When thus the Deity became terrible, the envoy would be honoured also.

But it is important to observe that these terrible manifestations were to cease. Like the impressions produced by sickness, by sudden deaths, by our own imminent danger, the emotion would subside, but the conviction should remain: they should believe Moses for ever. Emotions are like the swellings of the Nile; they subside again; but they ought to leave a fertilising deposit behind.

That the impression might not be altogether

---

[*] This phrase is not found elsewhere in the Pentateuch. Is it fancy which detects in it a desire to remind them of their connection with the least worthy rather than the noblest of the Patriarchs? One would not expect, for instance, to read, Fear not, thou worm Abraham, or even Israel; but the name of Jacob at once calls up humble associations.

[†] This word is the same which occurs in the verse so beautifully but erroneously rendered "They shall be Mine, saith the Lord of hosts, in the day when I make up My Jewels" (Mal. iii. 17, A. V.). "They shall be Mine . . . in the day that I do make, even a peculiar treasure" (R. V.).

passive, and therefore ephemeral, the people were bidden to "sanctify themselves"; all that is common and secular must be suspended for awhile; and it is worth notice that, as when the family of Jacob put away their strange gods, so now the Israelites must wash their clothes (*cf.* Gen. xxxv. 2). For one's vestment is a kind of outer self, and has been with the man in the old occupations from which he desires to purify himself. It was therefore that when Jehu was made king, and when Jesus entered Jerusalem in triumph, men put their garments under their chief to express their own subjection (2 Kings ix. 13; Matt. xxi. 7). Much of the philosophy of Carlyle is latent in these ancient laws and usages.

Moreover, the mountain was to be fenced from the risk of profanation by any sudden impulsive movement of the crowd, and even a beast that touched it should be slain by such weapons as men could hurl without themselves pursuing it. Only when the trumpet blew a long summons might the appointed ones come up to the mount (ver. 13).

On the third day, after a soul-searching interval, there were thunders and lightnings, and a cloud, and the trumpet blast; and while all the people trembled, Moses led them forth to meet with God. Again the narrative reverts to the terrible phenomena—the fire like the smoke of a furnace (called by an Egyptian name which only occurs in the Pentateuch), and the whole mountain quaking. Then, since his commission was now to be established, Moses spake, and the Lord answered him with a voice. And when he again climbed the mountain, it became necessary to send him back with yet another warning, whether his example was in danger of emboldening others to exercise their newly given priesthood, or the very excess of terror exercised its well-known fascinating power, as men in a burning ship have been seen to leap into the flames.

And the priests also, who come near to God, should sanctify themselves. It has been asked who these were, since the Levitical institutions were still non-existent (ver. 22, *cf.* 24). But it is certain that the heads of houses exercised priestly functions; and it is not impossible that the elders of Israel who came to eat before God with Jethro (xviii. 12) had begun to perform religious functions for the people. Is it supposed that the nation had gone without religious services for three months?

It has been remarked by many that the law of Moses appealed for acceptance to popular and even democratic sanctions. The covenant was ratified by a plébiscite. The tremendous evidence was offered equally to all. For, said St. Augustine, "as it was fit that the law which was given, not to one man or a few enlightened people, but to the whole of a populous nation, should be accompanied by awe-inspiring signs, great marvels were wrought . . . before the people" (*De Civ. Dei*, x. 13).

We have also to observe the contrast between the appearance of God on Sinai and His manifestation in Jesus. And this also was strongly wrought out by an ancient father, who represented the Virgin Mary, in the act of giving Jesus into the hands of Simeon, as saying, "The blast of the trumpet does not now terrify those who approach, nor a second time does the mountain, all on fire, cause terror to those who come nigh, nor does the law punish relentlessly those who would boldly touch. What is present here speaks of love to man; what is apparent, of the Divine compassion." (Methodius, *De Sym. et Anna*, vii.)

But we must remember that the Epistle to the Hebrews regards the second manifestation as the more solemn of the two, for this very reason: that we have not come to a burning mountain, or to mortal penalties for carnal irreverence, but to the spiritual mountain Zion, to countless angels, to God the Judge, to the spirits of just men made perfect, and to Jesus Christ. If they escaped not, when they refused Him Who warned on earth, much more we, who turn away from Him Who warneth from heaven (Heb. xii. 18-25).

There is a question, lying far behind all these, which demands attention.

It is said that legends of wonderful appearances of the gods are common to all religions; that there is no reason for giving credit to this one and rejecting all the rest; and, more than this, that God absolutely could not reveal Himself by sensuous appearances, being Himself a Spirit. In what sense and to what extent God can be said to have really revealed Himself, we shall examine hereafter. At present it is enough to ask whether human love and hatred, joy and sorrow, homage and scorn can manifest themselves by looks and tones, by the open palm and the clenched fist, by laughter and tears, by a bent neck and by a curled lip. For if what is most immaterial in our own soul can find sensuous expression, it is somewhat bold to deny that a majesty and power beyond anything human may at least be conceived as finding utterance, through a mountain burning to the summit and reeling to the base, and the blast of a trumpet which the people could not hear and live.

But when it is argued that wondrous theophanies are common to all faiths, two replies present themselves. If all the races of mankind agree in believing that there is a God, and that He manifests Himself wonderfully, does that really prove that there is no God, or even that He never manifested Himself wondrously? We should certainly be derided if we insisted that such a universal belief proved the truth of the story of Mount Sinai, and perhaps we should deserve our fate. But it is more absurd by far to pretend that this instinct, this intuition, this universal expectation that God would some day, somewhere, rend the veil which hides Him, does actually refute the narrative.

We have also to ask for the production of those other narratives, sublime in their conception and in the vast audience which they challenged, sublimely pure alike from taint of idolatrous superstition and of moral evil, profound and far-reaching in their practical effect upon humanity, which deserve to be so closely associated with the giving of the Mosaic law that in their collapse it also must be destroyed, as the fall of one tree sometimes breaks the next. But this narrative stands out so far in the open, and lifts its head so high, that no other even touches a bough of it when overturned.

Is it seriously meant to compare the alleged disappearance of Romulus, or the secret interviews of Numa with his Egeria, to a history like this? Surely one similar story should be produced, before it is asserted that such stories are everywhere.

CHAPTER XX.

THE LAW.

EXODUS xx. 1-17.

We have now reached that great event, one of the most momentous in all history, the giving of the Ten Commandments. And it is necessary to consider what was the meaning of this event, what part were they designed to play in the religious development of mankind.

1. St. Paul tells us plainly what they did *not* effect. By the works of the law could no flesh be justified: to the father of the Hebrew race faith was reckoned instead of righteousness; the first of their royal line coveted the blessedness not of the obedient but of the pardoned; and Habakkuk declared that the just should live by his faith, while the law is not of faith, and offers life only to the man that doeth these things (Rom. iv. 3, 6; Gal. iii. 12). In the doctrinal scheme of St. Paul there was no room for a compromise between salvation by faith and reliance upon our own performance of any works, even those simple and obvious duties which are of world-wide obligation.

2. But he never meant to teach that a Christian is free from the obligation of the moral law. If it is not true that we can keep it and so earn heaven, it is equally false that we may break it without penalty or remorse. What he insisted upon was this: that obligation is one thing, and energy is another; the law is good, but it has not the gift of pardon or of inspiration; by itself it will only reveal the feebleness of him who endeavours to perform it, only force into direst contrast the spiritual beauty of the pure ideal and the wretchedness of the sinner, carnal, sold under sin. In this respect, indeed, the law was its own witness. For if, among all the millions of its children, one had lived by obedience, how could he have shared in its elaborate sacrificial apparatus, in the hallowing of the altar from pollution by the national uncleanness, in the sprinkling of the blood of the offering for sin? Take the case of the highest official. A sinless high priest under the law would have been paralysed by his virtue, for his duty on the greatest day of all the year was to make atonement first for his own sins.

3. The law being an authorised statement of what innocence means, and therefore of the only terms upon which a man might hope to live by works, is an organic whole, and we either keep it as a whole or break it. Such is the meaning of the words, he that offendeth in one point is guilty of all; because He who gave the seventh commandment gave also the sixth—so that if one commit no adultery, yet kill, he has become a transgressor of the law in its integrity (James ii. 11). The challenge of God to human self-righteousness is not one which can be half met. If we have not thoroughly kept it, we have thoroughly failed.

4. But this failure of man does not involve any failure, in the law, to accomplish its intended work. It is, as has been said, a challenge. The sense of our inability to meet it is the best introduction to Him Who came not to call the righteous but sinners to repentance, and thus the law became a tutor to bring men to Christ. It awoke the conscience, brought home the sense of guilt, and entered, that sin might abound in us, whose ignorance had not known sin without it. It was strictly that which Moses most frequently calls it—the Testimony.

5. Finally, however, the teaching of Scripture is not that Christians are condemned to live always in a condition of baffled striving, hopeless longing, conscious transgression of a code which testifies against them. The old and carnal nature gravitates downward, to selfishness and sin, as surely as by a law of the physical universe. But the law of the spirit of life in Christ Jesus emancipates us from that law of sin and death—the higher nature doing, by the very quality of its life, what the lower nature cannot be driven to do, by dread of hell or by desire of heaven. The creature of earth becomes a creature of air, and is at home in a new sphere, poised on its wings upon the breeze. Love is the fulfilling of the law. And the Christian is free from its dictation, as affectionate men are free from any control of the laws which command the maintenance of wife and child, not because they may defy the statutes, but because their volition and the statutes coincide. Liberty is not lawlessness—it is the reciprocal harmony of law and the will.

And thus the grand paradox of Luther is entirely true: "Unless faith be without any, even the smallest works, it does not justify, nay, it is not faith. And yet it is impossible for faith to be without works—earnest, many, and great." We are justified by faith without the works of the law, and yet we do not make void the law by faith—nay, we establish the law.

All this agrees exactly with the contrast, so often urged, between the giving of the Law and the utterance of the Sermon on the Mount. The former echoes across wild heights, and through savage ravines; the latter is heard on the grassy slopes of the hillside which overlooks the smiling Lake of Galilee. The one is spoken in thunder and graven upon stone: the other comes from the lips, into which grace is poured, of Him Who was fairer than the children of men. The former repeats again and again the stern warning, "Thou shalt not!" The latter crowns a sevenfold description of a blessedness, which is deeper than joy, though pensive and even weeping, by adding to these abstract descriptions an eighth, which applies them, and assumes them to be realised in His hearers—"Blessed are *ye*." If so much as a beast touched the mountain it should be stoned. But Simeon took the Divine Infant in his arms.

And this is not because God has become gentler, or man worthier: it is because God the Law-giver upon His throne has come down to be God the Helper. But the beatitudes could never have been spoken, if the law had not been imposed: the blessedness of a hunger and thirst for righteousness was created by the majestic and spiritual beauty of the unattained commandment.

Yes, it had a spiritual beauty. For, however formal, external, and even shallow, the commandments may appear to flippant modern babblers, St. Paul bewailed the contrast between the law, which was spiritual, and his own carnal heart. And he, who had kept all the letter from his youth, was only the more vexed and haunted by the fleeting consciousness of a higher "good thing" unattained. Did not one table say "Thou shalt not covet," and the other promise mercy to thousands of those that love?

This leads us to consider the structure and arrangement of the Decalogue. Scripture itself tells us that there were "ten words" or precepts, written upon both sides of two tables. But various answers have been given at different times, to the question, How shall we divide the ten?

The Jews of a later period made a first commandment of the words, "I am the Lord thy God," which is not a commandment at all. And they restored the proper number, thus exceeded, by uniting in one the prohibition of other gods and of idolatry; although the worship of the golden calf, almost immediately after the law was given, suffices to establish the distinction. For then, as well as under Gideon, Micah, and Jeroboam, the sin of idolatry fell short of apostasy to a wholly different god (Judges viii. 23, 27, xvii. 3, 5; 1 Kings xii. 28). The worship of images dishonours God, even if it be His semblance that they claim. In this arrangement, the tables were allotted five commandments each.

Another curious arrangement was devised, apparently by St. Augustine; and the weight of his authority imposed it upon Western Christianity until the Reformation, and upon the Latin and Lutheran churches unto this day. Like the former, it adds the second commandment to the first, but it divides the tenth. And it gives to the first table three commandments, "since the number of commandments which concern God seem to hint at the Trinity to careful students," while the seven commandments of the second table suggest the Sabbath. Such mystical references are no longer weighty arguments. And the proposed division of the tenth commandment seems quite precluded by the fact that in Exodus we read, "Thou shalt not covet thy neighbour's house nor his wife," while in Deuteronomy the order is reversed; so that its advocates are divided among themselves as to whether the coveting of a house or a wife is to attain the dignity of separate mention.

The ordinary English arrangement assigns to the tables four commandments and six respectively. And the noble catechism of the Church of England appears to sanction this arrangement by including among "my duties to my neighbour" that of loving, honouring, and succouring my father and mother. There are several objections to this arrangement. It is unsymmetrical. There seems to be something more sacred and divine about my relationship with my father and mother than those which connect me with my neighbour. The first table begins with the gravest offence, and steadily declines to the lowest; sin against the unique personality of God being followed by sin against His spirituality of nature, His name, and His holy day. If now the sin against His earthly representative, the very fountain and sanction of all law to childhood, be added to the first table, the same order will pervade those of the second—namely, sin against my neighbour's life, his family, his property, his reputation, and lastly, his interest in my inner self, in the wishes that are unspoken, the thoughts and feelings which

"I wad nae tell to nae man."

We thus obtain both the simplest division and the clearest arrangement. In Romans xiii. 9 the fifth commandment is not enumerated when rehearsing the actions which transgress the second table. In the Hebrew text of Deuteronomy all the later commandments are joined with the sixth by the copulative (represented along with the negative fairly enough in our English by "Neither"), which seems to indicate that these five were united together in the author's mind. But the fifth stands alone, like all those of the first table. Now, it is clear that such an arrangement gives great sanction and weight to the sacred institution of the family.

Finally, the comprehensiveness and spirituality of the law may be observed in this; that the first table forbids sin against God in thought, word, and deed; and the second table forbids sin against man in deed, word, and thought.

THE PROLOGUE.

EXODUS xx. 2.

The Decalogue is introduced by the words "I am the Lord thy God, which brought thee out of the land of Egypt, out of the house of bondage."

Here, and in the previous chapter, is already a great advance upon the time when it was said to them "The God of thy fathers, the God of Abraham, of Isaac, and of Jacob, hath appeared." Now they are expected to remember what He has done for themselves. For, although religion must begin with testimony, it ought always to grow up into an experience. Thus it was that many of the Samaritans believed on Jesus because of the word of the woman; but presently they said, "Now we believe, not because of thy speaking, for we have heard Him ourselves, and know." And thus the disciples who heard John the Baptist speak, and so followed Jesus, having come and seen where He abode, could say, "We have found the Messiah."

This prologue is vitally connected with both tables of the law. In relation to the first, it recognises the instinct of worship in the human heart. In vain shall we say Do not worship idols, until the true object of adoration is supplied, for the heart must and will prostrate itself at some shrine. A leader of modern science confesses "the immovable basis of the religious sentiment in the nature of man," adding that "to yield this sentiment reasonable satisfaction is the problem of problems at the present hour." * It is indeed a problem for the unbelief which, because it professes to be scientific, cannot shut its eyes to the fact that men whose faith in Christ has suffered shipwreck are everywhere seen to be clinging to strange planks—spiritualism, esoteric Buddhism, and other superstitions,— which prove that man must and will reverence something more than streams of tendencies, or beneficial results to the greatest numbers. The Law of Moses abolishes superstition by no mere negation, but by the proclamation of a true God.

Moreover, it declares that this God is knowable, which flatly contradicts the brave assertion of modern agnostics that the notion of a God is not even "thinkable." That assertion is a bald and barren platitude in the only sense in which it is not contrary to the experience of all mankind. As we cannot form a complete and per-

---

* Prof. Tyndall, *Belfast Address*, p. 60. What progress has scientific unbelief made since 1874 in solving this "question of questions for the present hour"? It has perfected the phonograph, but it has not devised a creed.

fect, nor even an adequate notion of God, so no man ever yet conceived a complete and adequate notion of his neighbour, nor indeed of himself. But as we can form a notion of one another, dim and fragmentary indeed, yet more or less accurate and fit to guide our actions, so has every nation and every man formed some notion of deity. Nor could even the agnostic declare that God is unthinkable, unless the word God, of which he makes this assertion, conveyed to him *some* idea, some thought, more or less worthy of the thinking. The ancient Jew never dreamed that he could search out the Almighty to perfection, yet God was known to him by His actions (the only means by which we know our fellow-men); and the combined terror and loving-kindness of these at once warned him against revolt, and appealed to his loyalty for obedience.

In relation to the second table, the prologue was both an argument and an appeal. Why should a man hope to prosper by estranging his best Friend, his Emancipator and Guide? And even if disobedience could obtain some paltry advantage, how base would he be who snatched at it, when forbidden by the God Who broke his chains, and brought him out of the house of bondage—a Benefactor not ungenial and remote, but One Who enters into closest relations with him, calling Himself "Thy God"!

Now, a greater emancipation and a closer personal relationship belong to the Church of Christ. When a Christian hears that God is unthinkable, he ought to be able to answer, "God is my God, and He has brought my soul out of its house of bondage."

Moreover, his emancipation by Christ from many sins and inner slaveries ought to be a fact plain enough to constitute the sorest of problems to the observing world.

It must be observed, besides, that the Law, which was the centre of Judaism, does not appeal chiefly to the meaner side of human nature. Hell is not yet known, for the depths of eternity could not be uncovered before the clouds had rolled away from its heights of love and condescension; or else the sanity and balance of human nature would have been overthrown. But even temporal judgments are not set in the foremost place. As St. Paul, who knew the terrors of the Lord, more commonly and urgently besought men by the mercies of God, so were the ancient Jews, under the burning mountain, reminded rather of what God had bestowed upon them, than of what He might inflict if they provoked Him. And our gratitude, like theirs, should be excited by His temporal as well as His spiritual gifts to us.

THE FIRST COMMANDMENT.

"Thou shalt have none other gods before Me."—xx. 3.

When these words fell upon the ears of Israel, they conveyed, as their primary thought, a prohibition of the formal worship of rival deities, Egyptian or Sidonian gods. Following immediately upon the proclamation of Jehovah, their own God, they declared His intolerance of rivalry, and enjoined a strict and jealous monotheism. For God was a reality. Races who worshipped idealisations or personifications might easily make room for other poetic embodiments of human thought and feeling; but Jehovah would vindicate His rights. He had proved himself very real in Egypt. Other gods would not displace Him: He would observe them: they would be "before Me." * God does not quit the scene when man forgets Him.

Now, it is hard for us to realise the charm which the worship of false gods possessed for ancient Israel. To comprehend it we must reflect upon the universal ignorance which made every phenomenon of nature a portentous manifestation of mysterious and varied power, which they could by no means trace back to a common origin, while the crash and discord of the results appeared to indicate opposing wills behind. We must reflect how closely akin is awe to worship, and how blind and unintelligent was the awe which storm and earthquake and pestilence then excited. We must remember the pressure upon them of surrounding superstitions armed with all the civilisation and art of their world. Above all, we must consider that the gods which seduced them were not of necessity supreme: homage to them was very fairly consistent with a reservation of the highest place for another; so that false worship in its early stages need not have been much more startling than belief in witchcraft, or in the paltry and unimaginative "spirits" which, in our own day, are reputed to play the banjo in a dark room, and to untie knots in a cabinet. Is it for us to deride them?

To oppose all such tendencies, the Lord appealed not to philosophy and sound reason. These are not the parents of monotheism: they are the fruit of it. And so is our modern science. Its fundamental principle is faith in the unity of nature, and in the extent to which the same laws which govern our little world reach through the vast universe. And that faith is directly traceable to the conviction that all the universe is the work of the same Hand.

"One God, one law, one element;"—the preaching of the first was sure to suggest the other two. Nor could any race which believed in a multitude of gods labour earnestly to reduce various phenomena to one cause. Monotheism is therefore the parent of correct thinking, and could not draw its sanctions thence. No: the law appeals to the historical experience of Israel; it is content to stand and fall by that; if they acknowledged the claim of God upon their loyalty, all the rest followed. Their own story made good this claim. And so does the whole story of the Church, and the whole inner life of every man who knows anything of himself, bear witness to the religion of Jesus.

Never let us weary of repeating that while we have ample controversial resource, while no missile can pierce the chain-armour of the Christian evidences connected and interwoven into a great whole, and while the infidelity which is called scientific is really infidel only so far as it begs its case (which is an unscientific thing to do), nevertheless the strength of our position is experimental. If the experience which testifies to Jesus were historical alone, I might refuse to give it credit: if it were only personal, I might ascribe it to enthusiasm. But as long as a great cloud of living witnesses, and all the history of the Church, declare the reality of His salvation, while I myself feel the sufficiency of what He

* "Or *beside me*" (R. V.) The preposition is so vague that either of our English words may suggest quite too definite a meaning as when "before Me" is made to mean "in My angry eyes" or "beside Me" is taken to hint at resentment for intrusion upon the same throne.

offers (or else the bitter need of it), so long the question is not between conflicting theories, but between theories and facts. To have another god is to place him beside One Whom we already have, and Who has wrought for us the great emancipation. It is not an error in theological science: it is ingratitude and treason.

But it very soon became evident that men could apostatise from God otherwise than in formal worship, chant and sacrifice and prostration: "This people honoureth me with their mouths, but their hearts are far from Me." God asks for love and trust, and our litanies should express and cultivate these. Whatever steals away these from the Lord is really His rival, and another god. "What is it to have a God? or what is God?" Luther asks. And he answers, "He is God, and is so called, from Whose goodness and power thou dost confidently promise all good things to thyself, and to Whom thou dost fly from all adverse affairs and pressing perils. So that to have a God is nothing else than to trust Him and believe in Him with all the heart, even as I have often alleged that the reliance of the heart constitutes alike one's God and one's idol. . . In what thing soever thou hast thy mind's reliance and thine heart fixed, that is beyond doubt thy God" (*Larger Catechism*).

And again: "What sort of religion is this, to bow not the knees to riches and honour, but to offer them the noblest part of you, the heart and mind? It is to worship the true God outwardly and in the flesh, but the creature inwardly and in spirit" (*X. Præcepta Witt. Prædicata*).

It was on this ground that he included charms and spells among the sins against this commandment, because, though "they seem foolish rather than wicked, yet do they lead to this too grave result, that men learn to rely upon the creature in trifles, and so fail in great things to rely upon God" (*Ibid.*).

This view of false worship is frequent in Scripture itself. The Chaldeans were idolaters of an elaborate and imposing ritual, but their true deities were not to be found in temples. They adored what they really trusted upon, and that was their military prowess—the god of the modern commander, who said that Providence sided with the big battalions. The Chaldean is " he whose might is his god," whereas the sacred warrior has the Lord for his strength and shield and very present help in battle. Nay, regarding men " as the fishes of the sea," and his own vast armaments as the fisher's apparatus to sweep them away, the Chaldean, it is said, "sacrificeth unto his net, and burneth incense unto his drag; because by them his portion is fat and his meat plenteous" (Hab. i. 11, 14-16). Multitudes of humbler people practise a similar idolatry. They say to God "Give us this day our daily bread"; but they really ascribe their maintenance to their profession or their trade; and so this is the true object of their homage. They, too, burn incense to their drag.

Others had no thought of a higher blessedness than animal enjoyment. Their god was their belly. They set the excitement of wine in the place of the fulness of the Spirit, or preferred some depraved union upon earth to the honour of being one spirit with the Lord (Phil. iii. 19; Eph. v. 18; 1 Cor. vi. 16, 17). And some tried to combine the world and righteousness; not to lose heaven while grasping wealth, and receiving here not only good things, but the only good things they acknowledged—*their* good things (Luke xvi. 25). As the Samaritans feared the Lord and served graven images, so these were fain to serve God and mammon (2 Kings xvii. 41; Matt. vi. 24).

Now, these departures from the true Centre of all love and Source of all light were really a homage to His great rival, "the god of this world." Whenever men seek to obtain any prize by departing from God they do reverence to him who falsely said of all the kingdoms of the earth, and their glory, " These things are delivered unto me, and to whomsoever I will I give them." They deny Him to Whom indeed all power is committed in heaven and earth.

What is the remedy, then, for all such formal or virtual apostasies? It is to "have" the true God—which means, not only to know and confess, but to be in real relationship with Him.

Despite His so-called self-sufficiency, man is not very self-sufficing, after all. The vast endowments of Julius Cæsar did not prevent him from chafing because, at the age when he was still obscure, Alexander had conquered the world. To be Julius Cæsar was not enough for him. Nor is any man able to stand alone. In the Old Testament Joshua said, "If it seem evil unto you to serve the Lord, choose you this day whom ye will serve,"—implying that they must obey some one and will do better to choose a service than to drift into one (Josh. xxiv. 15). And in the New Testament Jesus declared that no man can serve two masters; but added that he would not break with both and go free, he was sure to love and cleave to one of them. Now, he only is proof against apostasy, who has realised the wants of the soul within him, and the powerlessness of all creatures to satisfy or save, and then, turning to the cross of Christ, has found his sufficiency in Him. " Lord, to whom shall we go? Thou hast the words of everlasting life." Marvellous it is to think that underneath the stern words " Thou shalt have none other," lies all the condescension of the privilege " Thou shalt have . . . Me."

THE SECOND COMMANDMENT.

"Thou shalt not make unto thee a graven image, . . . thou shalt not bow down thyself unto them, nor serve them."—xx. 4-6.

How far does the second of these clauses modify the first? Men there are who maintain the severe independence of the former, so that it forbids the presence of any image or likeness in the house of God, even for innocent purposes of adornment. But the Decalogue is not a liturgical directory: what it forbids in church it forbids anywhere; and on this theory the statues in Parliament Square would be idolatrous, as well as those in Westminster Abbey. And such Christians are more Judaical than the Jews, who were taught to place in the very Holy of Holies golden cherubim overshadowing the mercy-seat, and to represent them again upon its curtains.

It is therefore plain that the precept never forbade imagery, but idolatry, which is the making of images to satisfy the craving of men's hearts for a sensuous worship—the making of them " unto thee." The second clause qualifies and elucidates the first. And what the commandment prohibits is any attempt to help our worship by representing the object of adoration to the senses.

The higher and more subtle idolatries do not conceive that wood or gold is actually transformed into their deities; but only that the deities are locally present in the images, which express their attributes—power in a hundred hands, beneficence in a hundred breasts. But in thus expressing, they degrade and cramp the conception.

They may perhaps evade the reproach of Isaiah that they warm themselves with a portion of timber, and roast meat with another portion, and make the remainder a god (Isa. xliv. 15-17), by urging that the timber is not the god, but an abode which he chooses because it expresses his specific qualities. But they cannot evade the reproach of St. Paul, that being ourselves the offspring of God, we ought not to compare Him to the workmanship of our hands, graven with art and man's device (Acts xvii. 29).

A truly spiritual worship is intellectually as well as morally the most elevating exercise of the soul, which it leads onward and upward, making of all that it knows and thinks a vestibule, beyond which lie higher knowledge and deeper feeling as yet unattained.

Why is Gothic architecture better adapted for religious buildings than any Grecian or Oriental style. Because its long aisles, vaulted roofs, and pointed arches, leading the vision up to the unseen, tell of mystery, and draw the mind away beyond the visible and concrete to something greater which it hints; while rounded arches and definite proportions shut in at once the vision and the mind. The difference is the same as between poetry and logic.

And so it is with worship. We fetter and cramp our thoughts of deity when we bind them to even the loftiest conceptions which have ever been shut up in marble or upon canvas. The best image that ever took shape is inferior to the poorest spiritual conception of God, in this respect if in no other—that it has no expansiveness, it cannot grow. And in connecting our prayers with it, we virtually say, "This satisfies my conception of God."

It is not to be condemned merely as inadequate, for so are all our highest thoughts of deity; nor only because average humanity (which is supposed to stand most in need of the help and suggestion of art) will never learn the fine distinctions by which subtle intellects withhold from the image itself the worship which it evokes, and which goes out in its direction. It is still more mischievous because, even for the trained theologian, it is the petrifaction of what is meant to develop and expand, the solidification of the inadequate, the accepting of what is human as our idea of the divine.

Nor will it long continue to be merely inadequate. Experience proves that ideas, like air and water, cannot be confined without stagnating. Idolatries not only fail to develop, they degenerate; and systems, however orthodox they may appear at starting, which connect worship with palpable imagery, are doomed to sink into superstition.

To this precept there is added a startling and painful caution—"For I the Lord thy God am a jealous God." That a man should be jealous is no passport to our friendship: we think of unreasonable estrangements, exaggerated demands, implacable and cruel resentments. It would not enter the average mind to doubt that one is highly praised when another says of him, "I never traced in his words or actions the slightest stain of jealousy." And yet we are to think of God Himself as the jealous God.

Upon reflection, however, we must admit that a man is not condemned as jealous-minded because he is capable of jealousy, but because he has an unjust and unreasonable tendency towards it. It is a narrowing and suspicious quality when it operates without due cause, a vindictive and cruel one when it operates in excessive measure. But what should we think of a parent who felt no jealousy if the heart of his child were stolen from him by intriguing servants or by frivolous comrades? Now, God has called Israel His son, even His firstborn. The truth is that with us jealousy is dangerous and frequently perverted, because we are bad judges of the measure of our own rights, especially when our affections are involved. But some measure of jealousy is the necessary pain of love neglected, love wronged or slighted by those upon whom it has a claim. Jealousy is the shadow thrown where the sunshine of love is intercepted, and it is strong in proportion to the strength of the light. It operates in the heart exactly like the sense of justice in the reason. Justice expects a recompense where it has given service, and jealousy asks for love where it has given affection.

And therefore, when God tells us that He is jealous, He implies that He condescends to love us, to look for a return, to desire more from us than outward service. We cannot be jealous concerning things which are indifferent to us. Even the jealousy of rival competitors for business or for place may be measured by the desire of each for that which the other would engross. The politician is not jealous of the millionaire, nor the capitalist of the prime minister.

Now, if God is jealous when the enemies of our soul would steal away our loyalty, it surely follows that we shall not be left to contend with those enemies alone: He values us; He is upon our side; He will help us to overcome them.

And now we begin to see why this attribute is connected with the second commandment and not the first. The apostate who betakes himself to another god is almost beyond the reach of this tender and intimate emotion: he is still loved, for God loves all men; but yet perhaps the chord is unstrung which trembles responsive to this plaintive note.

When a man who confesses God begins to weary of spiritual intercourse with the Lord of spirits, when he can no longer worship One whose actual presence is realised because His voice is heard within, when the likeness of man or brute, or brightness of morning, or marvel of life or its reproductiveness, contents him as a representation of God the invisible, then his heart is beginning to go after the creature, to content itself with artistic loveliness or majesty, to let go the grasp as upon a living hand, by which alone the soul may be sustained when it stumbles, or guided when it would err.

To those who are within His covenant—to us, therefore, as to His ancient Israel—He says, "I the Lord thy God am a jealous God." Because I am "thy God."

The assertion of a Divine jealousy is but one difficulty of this remarkable verse. The Lord goes on to describe Himself as "visiting the iniquity of the fathers upon the children unto the third and fourth generation of them that hate Me, and showing mercy unto thousands of them that love Me and keep My commandments." And is this reasonable? To punish the child, to be avenged upon the children's children, for sins which are not their own? We know how often the sceptic has made gain out of this representation—which is but his own unauthorised gloss, since in reality God has said nothing about punishing the righteous with the wicked. It is not true that all sad and disastrous consequences are penal; many are disciplinary, and even to the people of God some are surgical, cutting away what would lead to disease and death. Are no evil consequences probable, if men brought up amid scenes dishonouring to God were treated exactly like those who have since childhood felt as it were the hand of a Father upon their head? For themselves it is best and kindest that so deep a loss could come home to their consciousness in pain.

At all events, the assertion so early made in Scripture is confirmed in all the experience of the race. Insanity, idiocy, scrofula, consumption, are too often, though not always, the hereditary results of guilt. Sins of the flesh are visited upon the bodily system. Sins of the temper, such as pride, cynicism, and frivolity, are felt in the mental structure of the race. And the sins which offend directly against God, do they bring no results with them? Ask of the investigators of the new science of heredity and transmitted peculiarities, whether it stops short of the highest and holiest parts of human nature. Or consider the ravages which victory and consequent wealth have made, again and again, in the character of whole nations.

There is no doctrine impugned in Scripture, which men have less prospect of shaking off, even if they close their Bibles for ever, than this. If it were not there, we should be perplexed at a want of conformity between the ways of God in nature and what is asserted of Him in His Book.

But it is either slander or blindness to represent this law, viewed in its entirety, as other than benevolent. The transmission of the result of evil is only a part of the vast law which has bound men together in nations and families, as partners and members with each other. It is clear that distinctive advantages cannot be bestowed upon the children of the good, as such, unless the same advantages be withheld from the evil race beside them. If the prizes of a university are won by knowledge, the result is that ignorance is "visited," in the withholding of them. And if, in the vaster university of life, health, affluence, good repute, and a clear intellect are the transmitted results of virtue, then disease, poverty, neglect, and incompetence become the dire bequest of the unrighteous.

There is no choice, therefore, except either to carry out this law, or else to bid every man in the world begin life, not as "the heir of all the ages," but absolutely destitute of all that has been acquired by his fellow-men.

Sometimes a hint is given us of what this would be. There is brought occasionally into civilised communities, from the depths of forests, a creature without language or decency or intellect, with low forehead and brutal appetites, who in his early childhood had wandered away and been lost,—brought up, men say, by the strange compassion of some lower creature, and now sunken well-nigh to its level. To this degradation we should all come, if it were not for the transmitted inheritance of our fathers. And so vast is the upward force of this grand law, that it is steadily though slowly upheaving the whole mass; and the lowest of to-day, visited for ancestral failings by sinking to the bottom, is higher than if he had been left absolutely alone.

This over-weight of good is clearly seen by comparing the clauses, for the sins of the fathers are visited upon the children to the third and fourth generation, but mercy is shown in them that love God upon a wholly different scale. Even "unto thousands" would enormously counterbalance three generations. But the Revised Version rightly suggests "a thousand generations" in the margin, and supports it by one of its very rare references. It is plainly stated in Deuteronomy vii. 9, that He "keepeth covenant and mercy with them that love Him and keep His commandments unto a thousand generations."

Lastly, it is to be observed that in all this passage the gospel is shining through the law. It is not a question of just dealing, but of emotion. God is not a master exacting taskwork, but a Father, jealous if we refuse our hearts. He visits sin upon the posterity "of them that hate," not only of them that disobey Him. And when our hearts sink, we who are responsible for generations yet to be, as we reflect upon our frailty, our ignorance, and our sins, upon the awful consequences which may result from one heedless act—nay, from a gesture or a look—He reminds us that He does not requite those who serve Him only with a measured wage, but shows "mercy" upon those who love Him unto a thousand generations.

THE THIRD COMMANDMENT.

"Thou shalt not take the name of the Lord thy God in vain."—xx. 7.

What is the precise force of this prohibition? The word used is ambiguous: sometimes it must be rendered as here, as in the verses "*Vain* is the help of man," and "Except the Lord build the house, their labour is but *vain* that build it" (Psalm cviii. 12, cxxvii. 1). But sometimes it clearly means false, as in the texts "Thou shalt not raise a *false* report," and "swearing *falsely* in making a covenant" (Exod. xxiii. 1; Hos. x. 4). Yet again, it hangs midway between the two ideas, as when we read of "*lying* vanities," and again, "trusting in vanity and speaking *lies*" (Psalm xxxi. 6; Isa. lix. 4).

In favour of the rendering "falsely" it is urged that our Lord quotes it as "said to them of old time 'Thou shalt not forswear thyself'" (Matt. v. 33). But it is by no means clear that He quotes this text: the citation is closer to the phraseology of Lev. xix. 12, and it is found in a section of the Sermon which does not confine its citations to the Decalogue (*cf.* ver. 38).

The Authorised rendering seems the more natural when we remember that civic duty had not yet come upon the stage. When we have learned to honour only one God, and not to degrade nor materialise our conception of Him, the next step is to inculcate, not yet veracity toward men when God has been invoked, but reverence, in treating the sacred name.

We have already seen the miserable superstitions by which the Jews endeavoured to satisfy the letter while outraging the spirit of this precept. In modern times some have conceived that all invocation of the Divine Name is unlawful, although St. Paul called God for a witness upon his soul, and the strong angel shall yet swear " by Him Who liveth for ever and ever " (2 Cor. i. 23; Rev. x. 6).

As it is not a temple but a desert which no foot ever treads, so the sacred name is not honoured by being unspoken, but by being spoken aright.

Swearing is indeed forbidden, where it has actually disappeared, namely, in the mutual intercourse of Christian people, whose affirmation should suffice their brethren, while the need of stronger sanctions "cometh of evil," even of the consciousness of a tendency to untruthfulness, which requires the stronger barrier of an oath. But our Lord Himself, when adjured by the living God, responded to the solemn authority of that adjuration, although His death was the result.

The name of God is not taken in vain when men who are conscious of His nearness, and act with habitual reference to His will, mention Him more frequently and familiarly than formalists approve. It is abused when the insincere and hollow professor joins in the most solemn act of worship, honours Him with the lips while the heart is far from Him—nay, when one strives to curb Satan, and reclaim his fellow-sinner, by the use of good and holy phrases, in which his own belief is merely theoretical; and fares like the sons of Sceva, who repeated an orthodox adjuration, but fled away overpowered and wounded. Or if the truth unworthily spoken asserts its inherent power, that will not justify the hollowness of his profession, and in vain will he plead at last, " Lord, Lord, have we not in Thy name cast out devils, and in Thy name done many marvellous acts?"

The only safe rule is to be sure that our conception of God is high and real and intimate; to be habitually humble and trustful in our attitude toward Him; and then to speak sincerely and frankly, as then we shall not fail to do. The words which rise naturally to the lips of men who think thus cannot fail to do Him honour, for out of the fulness of the heart the mouth speaketh.

And the prevalent notion that God should be mentioned seldom and with bated breath is rather an evidence of men's failure habitually to think of Him aright, than of filial and loving reverence. There is a large and powerful school of religion in our own day, whose disciples talk much more of their own emotions and their own souls than St. Paul did, and much less about God and Christ. Some day the proportions will be restored. In the great Church of the future men will not morbidly shrink from confessing their inner life, but neither will it be the centre of their contemplation and their discourse: they will be filled with the fulness of God; out of the abundance of their hearts their mouths will speak; His name shall be continually in their mouth, and yet they shall not take the name of the Lord their God in vain.

THE FOURTH COMMANDMENT.

Exodus xx. 8-11.

It cannot be denied that the commandment to honour the Sabbath day occupies a unique place among the ten. It is, at least apparently, a formal precept embedded in the heart of a moral code, and good men have thought very differently indeed about its obligation upon the Christian Church.

The great Continental reformers, Lutheran and Calvinistic alike, who subscribed the Confession of Augsburg, there affirmed that "Scripture hath abolished the Sabbath by teaching that all Mosaic ceremonies may be omitted since the gospel has been revealed" (II. vii. 28). The Scotch reformers, on the other hand, declared that God "in His Word, by a positive moral and perpetual commandment, binding all men in all ages, hath particularly appointed one day in seven for a Sabbath, to be kept holy unto Him" (*Westminster Confess.*, XXI. vii). They are even so bold as to declare that this day " from the beginning of the world to the resurrection of Christ was the last day of the week, and from the resurrection of Christ was changed into the first day of the week"; but this proposition would be as hard to prove as the contrary assertion, still maintained by some obscure religionists, that the change of day, for however sufficient and sublime a reason, was beyond the capacity of the Church of Christ to enact.

Amid these conflicting opinions the doctrinal formularies of the Church of England are characteristically guarded and prudent; but her worshippers are bidden to seek mercy from the Lord for past violations of this law, and an inclination of heart to keep it in the future; and when the Ten have been recited, they pray that "all these Thy laws" may be written upon their hearts. There is no doubt, therefore, about the opinion of our own Reformers concerning the divine obligation of the commandment.

In examining the problem thus presented to us our chief light must be that of Scripture itself. Is the Sabbath what the Lutheran confession called it, a mere "Mosaic ceremony," or does it rest upon sanctions which began earlier and lasted longer than the precept to abstain from shell-fish, or to sanctify the first-born of cattle? Does its presence in the Decalogue disfigure that great code, as the intrusion of these other precepts would do? When we find a Gentile church reminded that the next precept to this "is the first commandment with promise" (Eph. vi. 2), can we suppose that the tables to which St. Paul appealed, and the promise which he cited at full length, were both cancelled; that in so far as a moral element existed in them, that portion of course survived their repeal, but the code itself was gone? If so, the temporal promise went with it, and its quotation by St. Paul is strange. Strange also, upon this supposition, was the stress which he habitually laid upon the law as a convicting power, and as being only repealed in the letter so far as it was fulfilled by the spontaneous instinct of love which was the fulfilling of the law.

The position of the commandment among a number of moral and universal duties cannot but weigh heavily in its favour. It prompts us to ask whether our duty to God is purely negative, to be fulfilled by a policy of non-intervention, not worshipping idols, nor blaspheming. Something more was already intimated in the promise of mercy to them "that love Me." For love is chiefly the source of active obedience: while fear is satisfied by the absence of provocation, love wants not only to abstain from evil but to do good. And how may it satisfy this instinct when its object is the eternal God, Who, if He were hungry, would not tell us? It finds the necessary outlet in worship, in adoring communion, in the exclusion for awhile of worldly cares, in the devotion of time and thought to Him. Now, the foundation upon which all the institutions of religion may be securely built, is the day of rest. Call it external, formal, unspiritual if you will; say that it is a carnal ordinance, and that he who keeps it in spirit is free from the obligation of the letter. But then, what about the eighth commandment? Are we absolved also from the precept "Thou shalt not steal," because it too is concerned with external actions, because "this . . . thou shalt not steal . . . and if there be any other commandment, it is briefly comprehended in this one saying, Thou shalt love thy neighbour as thyself"? Do we say, the spirit has abolished the letter: love is the rescinding of the law? St. Paul said the very opposite: love is the fulfilling of the law, not its destruction; and thus he re-echoed the words of Jesus, "I am not come to destroy the law, but to fulfil."

All men know that the formal regulations which defend property are relaxed as the ties of love and mutual understanding are made strong; that to enter unannounced is not a trespass, that the same action which will be prosecuted as a theft by a stranger, and resented as a liberty by an acquaintance, is welcomed as a graceful freedom, almost as an endearment, by a friend. And yet the commandment and the rights of property hold good: they are not compromised, but glorified, by being spiritualized. As it is between man and his brother, so should it be between us and our Divine Father. We have learned to know Him very differently from those who shuddered under Sinai: the whole law is not now written upon tables of stone, but upon fleshly tables of the heart. But among the precepts which are thus etherialised and yet established, why should not the fourth commandment retain its place? Why should it be supposed that it must vanish from the Decalogue, unless the gathering of sticks deserves stoning? The institution, and the ceremonial application of it to Jewish life, are entirely different things; just as respect for property is a fixed obligation, while the laws of succession vary.

Bearing this distinction in mind, we come to the question, Was the Sabbath an ordinance born of Mosaism, or not? Grant that the word "Remember," if it stood alone, might conceivably express the emphasis of a new precept, and not the recapitulation of an existing one. Grant also that the mention in Genesis of the Divine rest might be made by anticipation, to be read with an eye to the institution which would be mentioned later. But what is to be made of the fact that on the seventh day manna was withheld from the camp, before they had arrived at Horeb, and therefore before the commandment had been written by the finger of God upon the stone? Was this also done by anticipation? Upon any supposition, it aimed at teaching the nation that the obligation of the day was not based upon the positive precept, but the precept embodied an older and more fundamental obligation.

How is the Sabbath spoken of in those prophecies which set least value upon the merely ceremonial law?

Isaiah speaks of mere ritual as slightly as St. Paul. To fast and afflict one's soul is nothing, if in the day of fasting one smites with the fist and oppresses his labourers. To loose the bonds of wickedness, to free the oppressed, to share one's bread with the hungry, this is the fast which God has chosen, and for him who fasts after this fashion the light shall break forth like sunrise, and his bones shall be strong, and he himself like an unfailing water-spring. Now, it is the same chapter which thus waives aside mere ceremonial in contempt, which lavishes the most ample promises on him who turns away his foot from the Sabbath, and calls the Sabbath a delight, and the holy of the Lord, honourable, and honours it (Isa. lviii. 5-11, 13-14).

There is no such promise in Jeremiah, for the observance of any merely ceremonial law, as that which bids the people to honour the Sabbath day, that there may enter into their gates kings and princes riding in chariots and upon horses, and that the city may remain for ever (Jer. xvii. 24, 25).

And Ezekiel declares that in the day when God made Himself known to His people in the land of Egypt, He gave them statutes and judgments and His sabbaths (Ezek. xx. 11, 12). Now, this phrase is a clear allusion to the word of God in Jeremiah, that "I spake not unto their fathers in the day when I brought them out of Egypt, concerning burnt-offerings or sacrifices, but this thing I commanded them, saying, Hearken unto My voice," etc. (Jer. vii. 23). And it sharply contrasts the sacredness of God's abiding ordinances with the temporary institutions of the sanctuary. But it reckons the Sabbath among the former.

It is objected that our Lord Himself treated the Sabbath lightly, as a worn-out ordinance. But He was "a minister of the circumcision," and always discussed the lawfulness of His Sabbath miracles as a Jew with Jews. Thus He argued that men, admittedly under the law, baked the shewbread, circumcised children, and even rescued cattle from jeopardy upon the seventh day. He appealed to the example of David, who met a sufficiently urgent necessity by eating the consecrated bread, "which was not lawful for him to eat" (Matt. xii. 4).

He did not hint that the law of the Sabbath had disappeared, but insisted that it was meant to serve man and not to oppress him: that "the sabbath was made for man, and not man for the sabbath" (Mark ii. 27).

Now, there is not in the life of Christ an assertion, so broad and strong as that the Sabbath was made for the human race, which can be narrowed down to a discussion of any merely local and temporary institution. He Who stood highest, and saw the widest horizons, declared that the Sabbath was intended for humanity, and not for a section or a sect of it. Not because He was the King of the Jews, but because He was the Son of Man, the ripe fruit and the leader of the world-wide race which it was given to bless, therefore He was also its Lord.

And in Him, so are we. Like all things

present and things to come, it is our help, we are not its slaves.

There is something abject in the notion of a Christian freeman, who has been for a long week imprisoned in some gloomy and ill-ventilated workshop, whose lungs would be purified, and therefore his spirits uplifted, and therefore his reason and his affections invigorated, and therefore his worship rendered more fresh, warm, and reasonable, by the breathing of a purer air, yet whose conception of a day of rest is so slavish that he dares not "rest" from the pollution of an infected atmosphere, and from the closeness of a London court, because he conceives it imperative to "rest" only from that bodily exercise, to enjoy which would be to him the most real and the most delightful repose of all.

But there are other things more abject still; and one of them is the miserable insincerity of the affluent and luxurious, using the exceptional case of him whose week-days are thus oppressed, to excuse their own wanton neglect of religious ordinances, accepting at the hands of Christianity the sacred holiday, but ignoring utterly the fact that the Lord sanctified and hallowed it, that it is to be called the holy of the Lord, and to be honoured, and that we are free from the letter of the precept only in so far as we rise to the spirit of it, in loving and true communion with the Father of spirits.

Another utterance of Jesus throws a strong light upon the nature and the limits of our obligation. "My Father worketh even until now, and I work" (John v. 17) is an appeal to the fact that in the long sabbath of God His world is not deserted; creation may be suspended, but the bounties of Providence go on; and therefore Christ also felt that His day of rest was not one of torpor, that in healing the impotent man upon the Sabbath He was but following the example of Him by whose rest the day was sanctified. All works of beneficent love, all that ministers to human recovery from anguish, and carries out the Divine purposes of grace for body or soul, rescue from danger, healing of disease, reformation of guilt, are sanctioned by this defence of Christ.

They need not plead that the commandment is abrogated, but that Jesus of Nazareth, of the seed of David, found nothing in such liberties inconsistent with the duties of a devout Hebrew.

THE FIFTH COMMANDMENT.

"Honour thy father and thy mother: that thy days may be long upon the land which the Lord thy God giveth thee."—xx. 12.

This commandment forms a kind of bridge between the first table and the second. Obedience to parents is not merely a neighbourly virtue; we do not honour them simply as our fellow-men: they are the vicegerents of God to our childhood; through them He supplies our necessities, defends our feebleness, and pours in light and wisdom upon our ignorance; by them our earliest knowledge of right and wrong is imparted, and upon the sanction of their voice it long depends.

It is clear that parental authority cannot be undermined, nor filial disobedience and irreverence gain ground, without shaking the foundations of our religious life, even more perhaps than of our social conduct.

Accordingly this commandment stands before the sixth, not because murder is a less offence against society, but because it is more emphatically against our neighbour, and less directly against God.

The human infant is dependent and helpless for a longer period, and more utterly, than the young of any other animal. Its growth, which is to reach so much higher, is slower, and it is feebler during the process. And the reason of this is plain to every thoughtful observer. God has willed that the race of man should be bound together in the closest relationships, both spiritual and secular; and family affection prepares the heart for membership alike of the nation and the Church. With this inner circle the wider ones are concentric. The pathetic dependence of the child nourishes equally the strong love which protects and the grateful love which clings. And from our early knowledge of human generosity, human care and goodness, there is born the capacity for belief in the heart of the great Father, from Whom every family in heaven and earth derived its Greek name of Fatherhood (Eph. iii. 15).

Woe to the father whose cruelty, selfishness, or evil passions make it hard for his child to understand the Archetype, because the type is spoiled! or whose tyranny and self-will suggest rather the stern God of reprobation, or of servile, slavish subjection, than the tender Father of freeborn sons, who are no more under tutors and governors, but are called unto freedom.

But how much sorer woe to the son who dishonours his earthly parent, and in so doing slays within himself the very principle of obedience to the Father of spirits!

No earthly tie is perfect, and therefore no earthly obedience can be absolute. Some crisis comes in every life when the most innocent and praiseworthy affection becomes a snare—when the counsel we most relied upon would fain mislead our conscience—when a man, to be Christ's disciple, must "hate father and mother," as Christ Himself heard the temptation of the Evil One speaking through chosen and beloved lips, and said "Get thee behind Me, Satan." Even then we shall respect them, and pray as Christ prayed for His failing apostle, and when the storm has spent itself they shall resume their due place in the loving heart of their Christian offspring.

So Jesus, when Mary would interrupt His teaching, said "Who is My mother?" But imminent death could not prevent Him from pitying her sorrow, and committing her to His beloved disciple as to a son.

From the letter of this commandment streams out a loving influence to sanctify all the rest of our relationships. As the love of God implies that of our brother also, so does the honour of parents involve the recognition of all our domestic ties.

And even unassisted nature will tend to make long the days of the loving and obedient child; for life and health depend far less upon affluence and luxury than upon a well-regulated disposition, a loving heart, a temper which can obey without chafing, and a conscience which respects law. All these are being learned in disciplined and dutiful households, which are therefore the nurseries of happy and righteous children, and so of long-lived families in the next generation also. Exceptions there must be. But the rule is clear, that violent and curbless lives will spend themselves faster than the lives of the gentle, the loving, the law-abiding and the innocent.

THE SIXTH COMMANDMENT.

"Thou shalt do no murder."—xx. 13.

We have now clearly passed to the consideration of man's duty to his fellow-man, as a part of his duty to his Maker. It is no longer as holding a divinely appointed relation to us, but simply as he is a man, that we are bidden to respect his person, his family, his property, and his fair fame.

And the influence of the teaching of our Lord is felt in the very name which we all give to the second table of the law. We call it "our duty to our neighbour." But we do not mean to imply that there lives on the surface of the globe one whom we are free to assault or to pillage. The obligation is universal, and the name we give it echoes the teaching of Him who said that no man can enter the sphere of our possible influence, even as a wounded creature in a swoon whom we may help, but he should thereupon become our neighbour. Or rather, we should become his; for while the question asked of Him was "Who is my neighbour?" (whom should I love?) Jesus reversed the problem when He asked in turn not To whom was the wounded man a neighbour? but Who was a neighbour unto him? (who loved him?)

Social ethics, then, have a religious sanction. It is the constant duty and effort of the Church of God to saturate the whole life of man, all his conduct and his thought, with a sense of sacredness; and as the world is for ever desecrating what is holy, so is religion for ever consecrating what is secular.

In these latter days men have thought it a proof of grace to separate religion from daily life. The Antinomian, who maintains that his orthodox beliefs or feelings absolve him from the obligations of morality, joins hands with the Italian brigand who hopes to be forgiven for cutting throats because he subsidises a priest. The enthusiast who insists that all sins, past and future, were forgiven him when he believed, approaches far nearer than he supposes to the fanatic of another creed, who thinks a formal confession and an external absolution sufficient to wash away sin. All of them hold the grand heresy that one may escape the penalties without being freed from the power of evil; that a life may be saved by grace without being penetrated by religion, and that it is not exactly accurate to say that Jesus saves His people from their sins.

It is scarcely wonderful, when some men thus refuse to morality the sanctions of religion, that others propose to teach morality how she may go without them. In spite of the experience of ages, which proves that human passions are only too ready to defy at once the penalties of both worlds, it is imagined that the microscope and the scalpel may supersede the Gospel as teachers of virtue; that the self-interest of a creature doomed to perish in a few years may prove more effectual to restrain than eternal hopes and fears; and that a scientific prudence may supply the place of holiness. It has never been so in the past. Not only Judea, but Egypt, Greece, and Rome, were strong as long as they were righteous, and righteous as long as their morality was bound up in their religion. When they ceased to worship they ceased to be self-controlled, nor could the most urgent and manifest self-interest, nor all the resources of lofty philosophy, withhold them from the ruin which always accompanies or follows vice.

Is it certain that modern science will fare any better? So far from deepening our respect for human nature and for law, she is discovering vile origins for our most sacred institutions and our deepest instincts, and whispering strange means by which crime may work without detection and vice without penalty. Never was there a time when educated thought was more suggestive of contempt for one's self and for one's fellow-man, and of a prudent, sturdy, remorseless pursuit of self-interest, which may be very far indeed from virtuous. The next generation will eat the fruit of this teaching, as we reap what our fathers sowed. The theorist may be as pure as Epicurus. But the disciples will be as the Epicureans.

Is there anything in the modern conception of a man which bids me spare him, if his existence dooms me to poverty and I can quietly push him over a precipice? It is quite conceivable that I can prove, and very likely indeed that I can persuade myself, that the shortening of the life of one hard and grasping man may brighten the lives of hundreds. And my passions will simply laugh at the attempt to restrain me by arguing that great advantages result from the respect for human life upon the whole. Appetites, greeds, resentments do not regard their objects in this broad and colourless way; they grant the general proposition, but add that every rule has its exceptions. Something more is needed: something which can never be obtained except from a universal law, from the sanctity of all human lives as bearing eternal issues in their bosom, and from the certainty that He who gave the mandate will enforce it.

It is when we see in our fellow-man a divine creature of the Divine, made by God in His own image, marred and defaced by sin, but not beyond recovery, when his actions are regarded as wrought in the sight of a Judge Whose presence supersedes utterly the slightness, heat, and inadequacy of our judgment and our vengeance, when his pure affections tell us of the love of God which passeth knowledge, when his errors affright us as dire and melancholy apostasies from a mighty calling, and when his death is solemn as the unveiling of unknown and unending destinies, then it is that we discern the sacredness of life, and the awful presumption of the deed which quenches it. It is when we realise that he is our brother, holding his place in the universe by the same tenure by which we hold our own, and dear to the same Father, that we understand how stern is the duty of repressing the first resentful movements within our breast which would even wish to crush him, because they are a rebellion against the Divine ordinance and against the Divine benevolence.

Is it asked, how can all this be reconciled with the lawfulness of capital punishment? The death penalty is frequent in the Mosaic code. But Scripture regards the judge as the minister and agent of God. The stern monotheism of the Old Testament "said, Ye are Gods," to those who thus pronounced the behest of Heaven; and private vengeance becomes only more culpable when we reflect upon the high sanction and authority by which alone public justice presumes to act.

Now, all these considerations vanish together, when religion ceases to consecrate morality. The judgment of law differs from my own merely as I like it better, and as I am a party (perhaps unwillingly) to the general consent which creates it; he whom I would assail is doomed in any case to speedy and complete extinction; his longer life is possibly burdensome to himself and to society; and there exists no higher Being to resent my interference, or to measure out the existence which I think too protracted. It is clear that such a view of human life must prove fatal to its sacredness; and that its results would make themselves increasingly felt, as the awe wore away which old associations now inspire.

THE SEVENTH COMMANDMENT.

"Thou shalt not commit adultery."—xx. 14.

This commandment follows very obviously from even the rudest principle of justice to our neighbour. It is among those that St. Paul enumerates as "briefly comprehended in this saying, Thou shalt love thy neighbour as thyself."

And therefore nothing need here be said about the open sin by which one man wrongs another. Wild and evil theories may be abroad, new schemes of social order may be recklessly invented and discussed; yet, when the institution of the permanent family is assailed, every thoughtful man knows full well that all our interests are at stake in its defence, and the nation could no more survive its overthrow than the Church.

But when our Lord declared that to excite desire through the eyes is actually this sin, already ripe, He appealed to some deeper and more spiritual consideration than that of social order. What He pointed to is the sacredness of the human body—so holy a thing that impurity, and even the silent excitement of passion, is a wrong done to our nature, and a dishonour to the temple of the Holy Ghost.

Now, this is a subject upon which it is all the more necessary to write, because it is hard to speak about.

What is the human body, in the view of the Christian? It is the one bond, as far as we know in all the universe, between the material and the spiritual worlds, one of which slopes thence down to inert molecules, and the other upward to the throne of God.

Our brain is the engine-room and laboratory whereby thought, aspiration, worship express themselves and become potent, and even communicate themselves to others.

But it is a solemn truth that the body not only interprets passively but also influences and modifies the higher nature. The mind is helped by proper diet and exercise, and hindered by impure air and by excess or lack of food. The influence of music upon the soul has been observed at least since the time of Saul. And hereafter the Christian body, redeemed from the contagion of the fall, and promoted to a spiritual impressibility and receptiveness which it has never yet known, is meant to share in the heavenly joys of the immortal spirit before God.

This is the meaning of the assertion that it is sown a natural (= *soulish*) body, but shall be raised a spiritual body. In the meantime it must learn its true function. Whatever stimulates and excites the animal at the cost of the immortal within, will in the same degree cloud and obscure the perception that a man's life consisteth not in his pleasures, and will keep up the illusion that the senses are the true ministers of bliss. The soul is attacked through the appetites at a point far short of their physical indulgence. And when lawless wishes are deliberately toyed with, it is clear that lawless acts are not hated, but only avoided through fear of consequences. The reins which govern the life are no longer in the hands of the spirit, nor is it the will which now refuses to sin. How, then, can the soul be alert and pure? It is drugged and stupefied: the offices of religion are a dull form, and its truths are hollow unrealities, assented to but unfelt, because unholy impulses have set on fire the course of nature, in what should have been the temple of the Holy Ghost.

Moreover, the Christian life is not one of mere submission to authority; its true law is that of ceaseless upward aspiration. And since the union of husband and wife is consecrated to be the truest and deepest and most far-reaching of all types of the mystical union between Christ and His Church, it demands an ever closer approach to that perfect ideal of mutual love and service.

And whatever impairs the sacred, mysterious, all-pervading unity of a perfect wedlock is either the greatest of misfortunes or of crimes.

If it be frailty of temper, failure of common sympathies, an irretrievable error recognised too late, it is a calamity which may yet strengthen the character by evoking such pity and helpfulness as Christ the Bridegroom showed for the Church when lost. But if estrangement, even of heart, come through the secret indulgence of lawless reverie and desire, it is treason, and criminal although the traitor has not struck a blow, but only whispered sedition under his breath in a darkened room.

THE EIGHTH COMMANDMENT.

"Thou shalt not steal."—xx. 15.

There is no commandment against which human ingenuity has brought more evasions to bear than this. Property itself is theft, says the communist. "It is no grave sin," says the Roman text-book, "to steal in moderation"; and this is defined to be, "from a pauper less than a franc, from a daily labourer less than two or three, from a person in comfortable circumstances anything under four or five francs, or from a very rich man ten or twelve francs. And a servant whom force or necessity compels to accept an unjust payment, may secretly compensate himself, because the workman is worthy of his hire."[*] A moment's reflection discovers this to be the most naked rationalism, choosing some of the commandments of God for honour, and some for contempt as "not very grave," and wholly ignoring the principle that whoever attacks the code at any one point "is guilty of all," because he has despised it as a code, as an organic system.

[*] Gury, Compend., i., secs. 607, 623.

Nothing is easier than to confuse one's conscience about the ethics of property. For the arrangements of various nations differ: it is a geographical line which defines the right of the elder son against his brothers, of sons against daughters, and of children against a wife; and the demand is still more capricious which the state asserts against them all, under the name of succession duty, and which it makes upon other property in the form of a multitude of imposts and taxes. Can all these different arrangements be alike binding? Add to this variability the immense national revenues, which are apparently so little affected by individual contributions, and it is no wonder if men fail to see that honesty to the public is a duty as immutable and stern as any other duty to their neighbour. Unfortunately the evil spreads. The same considerations which make it seem pardonable to rob the nation apply also to the millionaire; and they tempt many a poor man to ask whether he need respect the wealth of a usurer, or may not adjust the scales of Mine and Thine, which law causes to hang unfairly.

It is forgotten that a nation has at least the same authority as a club to regulate its own affairs, to fix the relative position and the subscription of its members. Common honesty teaches me that I must conform to these rules or leave the club; and this duty is not at all affected by the fact that other associations have different rules. In three such societies God Himself has placed us all—the family, the Church, and the nation; and therefore I am directly responsible to God for due respect to their laws. It is not true that the statute-book is inspired, any more than that the regulations of a household are divinely given. Yet a Divine sanction, such as rests upon the parental rule of fallible human creatures, hallows also national law. I may advocate a change in laws of which I disapprove, but I am bound in the meantime to obey the conditions upon which I receive protection from foreign foes and domestic fraud, and which cannot be subjected to the judgment of every individual, except at the cost of a dissolution of society, and a state of anarchy compared with which the worst of laws would be desirable.

This revolt of the individual is especially tempting when selfishness deems itself wronged, as by the laws of property. And the eighth commandment is necessary to protect society not merely against the violence of the burglar and the craft of the impostor, but also against the deceitfulness of our own hearts, asking What harm is in the evasion of an impost? What right has a successful speculator to his millions? Why should I not do justice to myself when law refuses it?

There is always the simple answer, Who made me a judge in my own case?

But when we regard the matter thus, it becomes clear that honesty is not mere abstinence from pillage. The community has larger claims than this upon us, and is wronged if we fail to discharge them.

The rich man robs the poor if he does not play his part in the great organisation by which he is served so well: every one robs the community who takes its benefits and returns none; and in this sense the bold saying is true, that every man lives by one of two methods—by labour or by theft.

St. Paul does not exhort men to refrain from theft merely in order to be harmless, but to do good. That is the alternative contemplated when he says, "Let the thief steal no more, but rather let him labour, working with his hands the thing that is good, that he may have whereof to give to him that hath need" (Eph. iv. 28).

THE NINTH COMMANDMENT.

"Thou shalt not bear false witness against thy neighbour."—xx. 16.

St. James called the tongue a world of iniquity. And against its lawlessness, which inflames the whole course of nature, each table of the law contains a warning. For it is equally ready to profane the name of God, and to rob our neighbour of his fair fame.

Jesus Christ regarded verbal professions as a very poor thing, and asked, "Why call ye Me Lord, Lord, and do not the things which I command you?" He aimed a parable at the hollowness of merely saying, "I go, sir." But, worthless though such phrases be, the act which substitutes professions for actual service is no trifle; and our Lord felt the importance of words, empty or sincere, so profoundly as to stake upon this one test the eternal destinies of His people: "By thy words thou shalt be justified, and by thy words thou shalt be condemned." Now, the tongue is thus important because it is so prompt and willing a servant of the mind within. We scarcely think of it as a servant at all: our words do not seem to be more than "expressions," manifestations of what is within us.

But a thought, once expressed, is transformed and energetic as a bullet when the charge is fired; it modifies other minds, and the word which we took to be far less potent than a deed becomes the mover of the fateful deeds of many men. And thus, being at once powerful and unsuspected, it is the most treacherous and subtle of all the forces which we wield.

And the ninth commandment does not undertake to bridle it by merely forbidding us in a court of justice to wrong our fellow-man by perjury.

We transgress it whenever we conceive a strong suspicion and repeat it as a thing we know; when we allow the temptation of a biting epigram to betray us into an unkind expression not quite warranted by the facts; when we vindicate ourselves against a charge by throwing blame where it probably but not certainly ought to lie; or when we are not content to vindicate ourselves without bringing a countercharge which it would perplex us to be asked to prove; when we give way to that most shallow and meanest of all attempts at cleverness which claims credit for penetration because it can discover base motives for innocent actions, so that high-mindedness becomes pride, and charity withers up into love of patronising, and forbearance shrivels into lack of spirit. The pattern and ideal of such cleverness is the east wind, which makes all that is fair and sensitive to shut itself up, forbids the bud to expand into a blossom, and puts back the coming of the springtime and of the singing bird.

There are very gifted persons who have never found out that a kindly and winning phrase may have as much literary merit as a stinging one, and it is quite as fine a thing to be like the dew on Hermon as to shoot out arrows, even bitter words.

It is a pity that our harsh judgments always speak more loudly and confidently than our kindly ones, but the reason is plain: angry passion prompts the former, and its voice is loud; while the calm reflection which tones down and sweetens the judgment softens also the expression of it.

It has to be remembered, also, that false witness can reach to nations, organisations, political movements as well as individuals. The habit of putting the worst construction upon the intentions of foreign powers is what feeds the mutual jealousies that ultimately blaze out in war. The habit of thinking of rival politicians as deliberately false and treasonable is what lowers the standard of the noblest of secular pursuits, until each party, not to be undone, protests too much, raises its voice to a falsetto to scream its rival down, and relaxes its standard of righteousness lest it should be outdone by the unscrupulousness of its rival.

And there is yet another neighbour, against whom false witness is wofully rife, both in the Church and in society. That neighbour is mankind at large. There is a prevalent theory of human sinfulness which unconsciously scoffs at the appeals of the gospel, striving indeed to influence me by love, gratitude, admiration for the Perfect One, and desire to be like Him, by the hope of holiness and the shame of vileness, but telling me at the same time that I have no sympathies whatever except with evil. The observation of every day shows that man's nature is corrupt, but it also shows that he is not a fiend—that he has fallen indeed, but remembers yet in what image he was made. But the world cannot upbraid the Church for these exaggerations, since they are but the echo of its own.

> "I do believe,
> Though I have found them not, that there may be
> Words which are things, hopes which will not deceive,
> And virtues which are merciful, nor weave
> Snares for the failing; I would also deem
> O'er others' griefs that some sincerely grieve;
> That two, or one, are almost what they seem,
> That goodness is no name, and happiness no dream."
> *Childe Harold*, III., cxiv.

Cynicism is false witness; and if it does not greatly wrong any one of our fellow-men, it injures both society and the cynic. If he is of a coarse fibre, it excuses him to himself in becoming the hard and unloving creature which he fancies that all men are. If he is too proud or too self-respecting to yield to this temptation, it isolates him, it chills and withers his sympathies for people quite as good as himself, whom he thinks of as the herd.

As for the more flagrant sins, so for this, the remedy is love. Love sympathises, makes allowance for frailty, discovers the germs of good, hopeth all things, taketh not account of evil.

THE TENTH COMMANDMENT.

"Thou shalt not covet . . . anything that is his."—xx. 17.

It will be remembered that the order of the catalogue of objects of desire is different in Exodus and in Deuteronomy. In the latter "thy neighbour's wife" is first, as of supreme importance; and therefore it has been thought possible to convert it into a separate commandment.

But this the order in Exodus forbids, by placing the house first, and then the various living possessions which the householder gathers around him. What is thought of is the gradual process of acquisition, and the right of him who wins first a house, then a wife, servants, and cattle, to be secure in the possession of them all. Now, between foes, we saw that the evil temper is what leads to the evil deed, and the man who nurses hatred is a murderer at heart. Just so the householder is not rendered safe, and certainly not happy in the enjoyment of his rights, by the seventh commandment and the eighth, unless care be taken to prevent the accumulation of those forces which will some day break through them both. To secure cities against explosion, we forbid the storage of gunpowder and dynamite, and not only the firing of magazines.

But the moral law is not given to any man for his neighbour's sake chiefly. It is for me: statutes whereby I myself may live. And as the Psalmist pondered on them, they expanded strangely for his perception. "I have kept Thy testimonies," he says; but presently asks to be quickened,—" So shall I *observe* the testimony of Thy mouth,"—and prays, "Give me understanding, that I may *know* Thy testimonies." And at the last, he confesses that he has "gone astray like a lost sheep" (Ps. cxix. 22, 88, 125, 176). Starting with a literal innocence, he comes to feel a deep inward need, need of vitality to obey, and even of power to understand aright. If the sacrifices of God are a broken spirit, it follows that they are a spirit, and inward loyalty is the necessary condition upon which external obedience can be accepted. The cheers of a traitor, the flattery of one who scorns, the ritual of a hypocrite, these are quite as valuable, as indications of what is within, as a reluctant relinquishment to my neighbour of what is his. I must not covet. Plainly this is the sharpest and most searching precept of all; and accordingly St. Paul asserts that without this he would not have suffered the deep internal discontent, the consciousness of something wrong, which tortured him, even although no mortal could reproach him, even though, touching the righteousness of the law, he was blameless. He had not known coveting except the law had said "Thou shalt not covet."

Here, then, we perceive with the utmost clearness what St. Paul so clearly discerned—the true meaning of the Law, its convicting power, its design to work not righteousness, but self-despair as the prelude of self-surrender. For who can, by resolving, govern his desires? Who can abstain not only from the usurping deed, but from the aggressive emotion? Who will not despair when he learns that God desireth truth in the inward parts? But this despair is the way to that better hope which adds, "In the hidden part Thou shalt make me to know wisdom. Purge me with hyssop, and I shall be clean."

And as a strong interest or affection has power to destroy in the soul many weaker ones, so the love of God and our neighbour is the appointed way to overcome the desire of taking from our neighbour what God has given to him, refusing it to us.

THE LESSER LAW.

Exodus xx. 18—xxiii. 33.

With the close of the Decalogue and its universal obligations, we approach a brief code of laws, purely Hebrew, but of the deepest moral interest, confessed by hostile criticism to bear every mark of a remote antiquity, and distinctly severed from what precedes and follows by a marked difference in the circumstances.

This is evidently the book of the Covenant to which the nation gave its formal assent (xxiv. 7), and is therefore the germ and the centre of the system afterwards so much expanded.

And since the adhesion of the people was required, and the final covenant was ratified as soon as it was given, before any of the more formal details were elaborated, and before the tabernacle and the priesthood were established, it may fairly claim the highest and most unique position among the component parts of the Pentateuch, excepting only the Ten Commandments.

Before examining it in detail, the impressive circumstances of its utterance have to be observed.

It is written that when the law was given, the voice of the trumpet waxed louder and louder still. And as the multitude became aware that in this tempestuous and growing crash there was a living centre, and a voice of intelligible words, their awe became insufferable: and instead of needing the barriers which excluded them from the mountain, they recoiled from their appointed place, trembling and standing afar off. "And they said unto Moses, Speak thou with us and we will hear, but let not God speak with us lest we die." It is the same instinct that we have already so often recognised, the dread of holiness in the hearts of the impure, the sense of unworthiness, which makes a prophet cry, "Woe is me, for I am undone!" and an apostle, "Depart from me, for I am a sinful man."

Now, the New Testament quotes a confession of Moses himself, well-nigh overwhelmed, "I do exceedingly fear and quake" (Heb. xii. 21). And yet we read that he "said unto the people, Fear not, for God is come to prove you, and that His fear may be before your faces, that ye sin not" (xx. 20). Thus we have the double paradox,—that he exceedingly feared, yet bade them fear not, and yet again declared that the very object of God was that they might fear Him.

Like every paradox, which is not a mere contradiction, this is instructive.

There is an abject fear, the dread of cowards and of the guilty, which masters and destroys the will—the fear which shrank away from the mount and cried out to Moses for relief. Such fear has torment, and none ought to admit it who understands that God wishes him well and is merciful.

There is also a natural agitation, at times inevitable though not unconquerable, and often strongest in the highest natures because they are the most finely strung. We are sometimes taught that there is sin in that instinctive recoil from death, and from whatever brings it close, which indeed is implanted by God to prevent foolhardiness, and to preserve the race. Our duty, however, does not require the absence of sensitive nerves, but only their subjugation and control. Marshal Saxe was truly brave when he looked at his own trembling frame, as the cannon opened fire, and said, "Aha! tremblest thou? thou wouldest tremble much more if thou knewest whither I mean to carry thee to-day." Despite his fever-shaken nerves, he was perfectly entitled to say to any waverer, "Fear not."

And so Moses, while he himself quaked, was entitled to encourage his people, because he could encourage them, because he saw and announced the kindly meaning of that tremendous scene, because he dared presently to draw near unto the thick darkness where God was.

And therefore the day would come when, with his noble heart aflame for a yet more splendid vision, he would cry, "O Lord, I beseech Thee show me Thy glory"—some purer and clearer irradiation, which would neither baffle the moral sense, nor conceal itself in cloud.

Meanwhile, there was a fear which should endure, and which God desires: not panic, but awe; not the terror which stood afar off, but the reverence which dares not to transgress. "Fear not, for God is come to prove you" (to see whether the nobler emotion or the baser will survive), "and that His fear may be before your faces" (so as to guide you, instead of pressing upon you to crush), "that ye sin not."

How needful was the lesson may be seen by what followed when they were taken at their word, and the pressure of physical dread was lifted off them. "They soon forgat God their Saviour . . . they made a calf in Horeb, and worshipped the work of their own hands." Perhaps other pressures which we feel and lament to-day, the uncertainties and fears of modern life, are equally required to prevent us from forgetting God.

Of the nobler fear, which is a safeguard of the soul and not a danger, it is a serious question whether enough is alive among us.

Much sensational teaching, many popular books and hymns, suggest rather an irreverent use of the Holy Name, which is profanation, than a filial approach to a Father equally revered and loved. It is true that we are bidden to come with boldness to the throne of Grace. Yet the same Epistle teaches us again that our approach is even more solemn and awful than to the Mount which might be touched, and the profaning of which was death; and it exhorts us to have grace whereby we may offer service well-pleasing to God with reverence and awe, "for our God is a consuming fire" (Heb. iv. 16, xii. 28). That is the very last grace which some Christians ever seem to seek.

When the people recoiled, and Moses, trusting in God, was brave and entered the cloud, they ceased to have direct communion, and he was brought nearer to Jehovah than before.

What is now conveyed to Israel through him is an expansion and application of the Decalogue, and in turn it becomes the nucleus of the developed law. Its great antiquity is admitted by the severest critics; and it is a wonderful example of spirituality and searching depth, and also of such germinal and fruitful principles as cannot rest in themselves, literally applied, but must lead the obedient student on to still better things.

It is not the function of law to inspire men to obey it; this is precisely what the law could not do, being weak through the flesh. But it could arrest the attention and educate the conscience. Simple though it was in the letter, David could meditate upon it day and night. In the New Testament we know of two persons who had scrupulously respected its precepts, but they both, far from being satisfied, were filled with a divine discontent. One had kept all these things from his youth, yet felt the need of doing some good thing, and anxiously demanded what it was that he lacked yet. The other, as touching the righteousness of the law, was blameless, yet when the law entered, sin revived and slew him. For the law was spiritual, and reached beyond itself, while he was carnal, and thwarted by the flesh, sold under sin, even while externally beyond reproach.

This subtle characteristic of all noble law will be very apparent in studying the kernel of the law, the code within the code, which now lies before us.

Men sometimes judge the Hebrew legislation harshly, thinking that they are testing it, as a Divine institution, by the light of this century. They are really doing nothing of the sort. If there are two principles of legislation dearer than all others to modern Englishmen, they are the two which these flippant judgments most ignore, and by which they are most perfectly refuted.

One is that institutions educate communities. It is not too much to say that we have staked the future of our nation, and therefore the hopes of humanity, upon our conviction that men can be elevated by ennobling institutions,—that the franchise, for example, is an education as well as a trust.

The other, which seems to contradict the first, and does actually modify it, is that legislation must not move too far in advance of public opinion. Laws may be highly desirable in the abstract, for which communities are not yet ripe. A constitution like our own would be simply ruinous in Hindostan. Many good friends of temperance are the reluctant opponents of legislation which they desire in theory but which would only be trampled upon in practice, because public opinion would rebel against the law. Legislation is indeed educational, but the danger is that the practical outcome of such legislation would be disobedience and anarchy.

Now, these principles are the ample justification of all that startles us in the Pentateuch.

Slavery and polygamy, for instance, are not abolished. To forbid them utterly would have substituted far worse evils, as the Jews then were. But laws were introduced which vastly ameliorated the condition of the slave, and elevated the status of woman—laws which were far in advance of the best Gentile culture, and which so educated and softened the Jewish character that men soon came to feel the letter of these very laws too harsh.

That is a nobler vindication of the Mosaic legislation than if this century agreed with every letter of it. To be vital and progressive is a better thing than to be correct. The law waged a far more effectual war upon certain evils than by formal prohibition, sound in theory but premature by centuries. Other good things besides liberty are not for the nursery or the school. And "we also, when we were children, were held in bondage" (Gal. iv. 3).

It is pretty well agreed that this code may be divided into five parts. To the end of the twentieth chapter it deals directly with the worship of God. Then follow thirty-two verses treating of the personal rights of man as distinguished from his rights of property. From the thirty-third verse of the twenty-first chapter to the fifteenth verse of the twenty-second, the rights of property are protected. Thence to the nineteenth verse of the twenty-third chapter is a miscellaneous group of laws, chiefly moral, but deeply connected with the civil organisation of the state. And thence to the end of the chapter is an earnest exhortation from God, introduced by a clearer statement than before of the manner in which He means to lead them, even by that mysterious Angel in Whom "is My Name."

PART I.—THE LAW OF WORSHIP.

EXODUS xx. 22-26.

It is no vain repetition that this code begins by reasserting the supremacy of the one God. That principle underlies all the law, and must be carried into every part of it. And it is now enforced by a new sanction,—" Ye yourselves have seen that I have talked with you from heaven: ye shall not make *other* gods with Me; gods of silver or gods of gold ye shall not make unto you" (vers. 22, 23). The costliest material of this low world should be utterly contemned in rivalry with that spiritual Presence revealing Himself out of a wholly different sphere; and in so far as they remembered Him, and the Voice which had thrilled their nature to its core, in so far would they be free from the desire for any carnal and materialised divinity to go before them.

Impressed with such views of God, their service of Him would be moulded accordingly (24, 25). It is true that nothing could be too splendid for His sanctuary, and Bezaleel was presently to be inspired, that the work of the tabernacle might be worthy of its destination. Spirituality is not meanness, nor is art without a consecration of its own. But it must not intrude too closely upon the solemn act wherein the soul seeks the pardon of the Creator. The altar should not be a proud structure, richly sculptured and adorned, and offering in itself, if not an object of adoration, yet a satisfying centre of attention for the worshipper. It should be simply a heap of sods. And if they must needs go further, and erect a more durable pile, it must still be of materials crude, inartistic, such as the earth itself affords, of unhewn stone. A golden casket is fit to convey the freedom of some historic city to a prince, but the noblest offering of man to God is too humble to deserve an ostentatious altar.

"If thou lift up a tool upon it thou hast polluted it:" it has lost its virginal simplicity; it no longer suits a spontaneous offering of the heart, it has become artificial, sophisticated, self-conscious, polluted.

It is vehemently urged that these verses sanction a plurality of altars (so that one might be of earth and another of stone), and recognise the lawfulness of worship in other places than at a central appointed shrine. And it is concluded that early Judaism knew nothing of the exclusive sanctity of the tabernacle and the temple.

This argument forgets the circumstances. The Jews had been led to Horeb, the mount of God. They were soon to wander away thence through the wilderness. Altars had to be set up in many places, and might be of different materials. It was an important announcement that in every place where God would record His name He would come unto them and bless them. But certainly the inference leans rather toward than against the belief that it was for Him to select every place which should be sacred.

The last direction given with regard to worship is a homely one. It commands that the altar must not be approached with steps, lest the clothes of the priest should be disturbed and his limbs uncovered. Already we feel that we have to reckon with the temper as well as the letter of the precept. It is divinely unlike the frantic indecencies of many pagan rituals. It protests against all infractions of propriety, even the slightest, such as even now discredit many a zealous movement, and bear fruit in many a scandal. It rebukes all misdemeanour, all forgetfulness in look and gesture of the Sacred Presence, in every worshipper, at every shrine.

CHAPTER XXI.

THE LESSER LAW (continued).

Part II.—Rights of the Person.

Exodus xxi. 1-32.

The first words of God from Sinai had declared that He was Jehovah Who brought them out of slavery. And in this remarkable code, the first person whose rights are dealt with is the slave. We saw that a denunciation of all slavery would have been premature, and therefore unwise; but assuredly the germs of emancipation were already planted by this giving of the foremost place to the rights of the least of all and the servant of all.

As regards the Hebrew slave, the effect was to reduce his utmost bondage to a comparatively mild apprenticeship. At the worst he should go free in the seventh year; and if the year of jubilee intervened, it brought a still speedier emancipation. If his debt or misconduct had involved a family in his disgrace, they should also share his emancipation, but if while in bondage his master had provided for his marriage with a slave, then his family must await their own appointed period of release. It followed that if he had contracted a degrading alliance with a foreign slave, his freedom would inflict upon him the pang of final severance from his dear ones. He might, indeed, escape this pain, but only by a deliberate and humiliating act, by formally renouncing before the judges his liberty, the birthright of his nation ("they are My servants, whom I brought forth out of Egypt, they shall not be sold as bondservants"—Lev. xxv. 42), and submitting to have his ear pierced, at the doorpost of his master's house, as if, like that, his body were become his master's property. It is uncertain, after this decisive step, whether even the year of jubilee brought him release; and the contrary seems to be implied in his always bearing about in his body an indelible and degrading mark. It will be remembered that St. Paul rejoiced to think that his choice of Christ was practically beyond recall, for the scars on his body marked the tenacity of his decision (Gal. vi. 17). He wrote this to Gentiles, and used the Gentile phrase for the branding of a slave. But beyond question this Hebrew of Hebrews remembered, as he wrote, that one of his race could incur lifelong subjection only by a voluntary wound, endured because he loved his master, such as he had received for love of Jesus.

When the law came to deal with assaults it was impossible to place the slave upon quite the same level as the freeman. But Moses excelled the legislators of Greece and Rome, by making an assault or chastisement which killed him upon the spot as worthy of death as if a freeman had been slain. It was only the victim who lingered that died comparatively unavenged (20, 21). After all, chastisement was a natural right of the master, because he owned him ("he is his money"); and it would be hard to treat an excess of what was permissible, inflicted perhaps under provocation which made some punishment necessary, on the same lines with an assault that was entirely lawless. But there was this grave restraint upon bad temper,—that the loss of any member, and even of the tooth of a slave, involved his instant manumission. And this carried with it the principle of moral responsibility for every hurt (26, 27).

It was not quite plain that these enactments extended to the Gentile slave. But in accordance with the assertion that the whole spirit of the statutes was elevating, the conclusion arrived at by the later authorities was the generous one.

When it is added that man-stealing (upon which all our modern systems of slavery were founded) was a capital offence, without power of commutation for a fine (xxi. 16), it becomes clear that the advocates of slavery appeal to Moses against the outraged conscience of humanity without any shadow of warrant either from the letter or the spirit of the code.

There remains to be considered a remarkable and melancholy sub-section of the law of slavery.

In every age degraded beings have made gain of the attractions of their daughters. With them, the law attempted nothing of moral influence. But it protected their children, and brought pressure to bear upon the tempter, by a series of firm provisions, as bold as the age could bear, and much in advance of the conscience of too many among ourselves to-day.

The seduction of any unbetrothed maiden involved marriage, or the payment of a dowry. And thus one door to evil was firmly closed (xxii. 16).

But when a man purchased a female slave, with the intention of making her an inferior wife, whether for himself or for his son (such only are the purchases here dealt with, and an ordinary female slave was treated upon the same principles as a man), she was far from being the sport of his caprice. If indeed he repented at once, he might send her back, or transfer her to another of her countrymen upon the same terms, but when once they were united she was protected against his fickleness. He might not treat her as a servant or domestic, but must, even if he married another and probably a chief wife, continue to her all the rights and privileges of a wife. Nor was her position a temporary one, to her damage, as that of an ordinary slave was, to his benefit.

And if there was any failure to observe these honourable terms, she could return with unblemished reputation to her father's home, without forfeiture of the money which had been paid for her (xxi. 7-11).

Does any one seriously believe that a system like the African slave trade could have existed in such a humane and genial atmosphere as these enactments breathed? Does any one who knows the plague spot and disgrace of our modern civilisation suppose for a moment that more could have been attempted, in that age, for the great cause of purity? Would to God that the spirit of these enactments were even now respected! They would make of us, as they have made of the Hebrew nation unto this day, models of domestic tenderness, and of the blessings in health and physical vigour which an untainted life bestows upon communities.

By such checks upon the degradation of slavery, the Jew began to learn the great lesson of the sanctity of manhood. The next step was to teach him the value of life, not only in the avenging of murder, but also in the mitigation of such revenge. The blood-feud was too old, too natural a practice to be suppressed at once; but it was so controlled and regulated as to become little more than a part of the machinery of justice.

A premeditated murder was inexpiable, not to be ransomed; the murderer must surely die. Even if he fled to the altar of God, intending to escape thence to a city of refuge when the avenger ceased to watch, he should be torn from that holy place: to shelter him would not be an honour, but a desecration to the shrine (xxi. 12, 14). According to this provision Joab and Adonijah suffered. For the slayer by accident or in hasty quarrel, "a place whither he shall flee" would be provided, and the vague phrase indicates the antiquity of the edict (ver. 13). This arrangement at once respected his life, which did not merit forfeiture, and provided a penalty for his rashness or his passion.

It is because the question in hand is the sanctity of man, that the capital punishment of a son who strikes or curses a parent, the vicegerent of God, and of a kidnapper, is interposed between these provisions and minor offences against the person (15-17).

Of these latter, the first is when lingering illness results from a blow received in a quarrel. This was not a case for the stern rule, eye for eye and tooth for tooth,—for how could that rule be applied to it?—but the violent man should pay for his victim's loss of time, and for medical treatment until he was thoroughly recovered (18, 19).

But what is to be said to the general law of retribution in kind? Our Lord has forbidden a Christian, in his own case, to exact it. But it does not follow that it was unjust, since Christ plainly means to instruct private persons not to exact their rights, whereas the magistrate continues to be "a revenger to execute justice." And, as St. Augustine argued shrewdly, "this command was not given for exciting the fires of hatred, but to restrain them. For who would easily be satisfied with repaying as much injury as he received? Do we not see men slightly hurt athirst for slaughter and blood? . . . Upon this immoderate and unjust vengeance, the law imposed a just limit, not that what was quenched might be kindled, but that what was burning might not spread." (Cont. Faust., xix. 25.)

It is also to be observed that by no other precept were the Jews more clearly led to a morality still higher than it prescribed. Their attention was first drawn to the fact that a compensation in money was nowhere forbidden, as in the case of murder (Num. xxxv. 31). Then they went on to argue that such compensation must have been intended, because its literal observance teemed with difficulties. If an eye were injured but not destroyed, who would undertake to inflict an equivalent hurt? What if a blind man destroyed an eye? Would it be reasonable to quench utterly the sight of a one-eyed man who had only destroyed one-half of the vision of his neighbour? Should the right hand of a painter, by which he maintains his family, be forfeited for that of a singer who lives by his voice? Would not the cold and premeditated operation inflict far greater mental and even physical suffering than a sudden wound received in a moment of excitement? By all these considerations, drawn from the very principle which underlay the precept, they learned to relax its pressure in actual life. The law was already their schoolmaster, to lead them beyond itself (*vide* Kalisch *in loco*).

Lastly, there is the question of injury to the person, wrought by cattle.

It is clearly to deepen the sense of reverence for human life, that not only must the ox which kills a man be slain, but his flesh may not be eaten; thus carrying further the early aphorism "at the hand of every beast will I require . . . your blood" (Gen. ix. 5). This motive, however, does not betray the lawgiver into injustice: "the owner of the ox shall be quit"; the loss of his beast is his sufficient penalty.

But if its evil temper has been previously observed, and he has been warned, then his recklessness amounts to blood-guiltiness, and he must die, or else pay whatever ransom is laid upon him. This last clause recognises the distinction between his guilt and that of a deliberate manslayer, for whose crime the law distinctly prohibited a composition (Num. xxxv. 31).

And it is expressly provided, according to the honourable position of woman in the Hebrew state, that the penalty for a daughter's life shall be the same as for that of a son.

As a slave was exposed to especial risk, and his position was an ignoble one, a fixed composition was appointed, and the amount was memorable. The ransom of a common slave, killed by the horns of the wild oxen, was thirty pieces of silver, the goodly price that Messiah was prized at of them (Zech. xi. 13).

Part III.—Rights of Property.

Exodus xxi. 33—xxii. 15.

The vital and quickening principle in this section is the stress it lays upon man's responsibility for negligence, and the indirect consequences of his deed. All sin is selfish, and all selfishness ignores the right of others. Am I my brother's keeper? Let him guard his own property or pay the forfeit. But this sentiment would quickly prove a disintegrating force in the community, able to overthrow a state. It is the ignoble negative of public spirit, patriotism, all by which nations prosper. And this early legislation is well devised to check it in detail. If an ox fall into a pit or cistern, from which I have removed the cover, I must pay the value of the beast, and take the carcase for what it may be worth. I ought to have considered the public interest (xxi. 33). If I let my cattle stray into my neighbour's field or vineyard, there must be no wrangling about the quality of what he has consumed: I must forfeit an equal quantity of the best of my own field or vineyard (xxii. 5). If a fire of my kindling burn his grain, standing or piled, I must make restitution: I had no right to kindle it where he was brought into hazard (xxii. 6). This is the same principle which had already pronounced it murder to let a vicious ox go loose. And it has to do with graver things than oxen and fires,—with the teachers of principles rightly called incendiary, the ingenious theorists who let loose abstract speculations pernicious when put into practice, the well-behaved questioners of morality, and the law-abiding assailants of the foundations which uphold law.

It is quite in the same spirit that I am accountable for what I borrow or hire, and even for its accidental death (since for the time being it was mine, and so should the loss be); but if I hired the owner with his beast, it clearly continued to be in his charge (14, 15). But again, my responsibility may not be pressed too far. If I have not borrowed property, but consented to keep it for the owner, the risk is fairly his, and if it be stolen, the presumption is not against my integrity, although I may be required to clear myself on oath before the judges (7, 8). But I am accountable in such a case for cattle, because it was certainly understood that I should watch them; and if a wild beast have torn any, I must prove my courage and vigilance by rescuing the carcase and producing it (10-13).

But I must not be plunged into litigation without a compensating hazard on the other side: he whom God shall condemn shall pay double unto his neighbour (9).

It only remains to be observed, with regard to theft, that when cattle were recovered yet alive, the thief restored double, but when his act was consummated by slaughtering what he had taken, then he restored a sheep fourfold, and for an ox five oxen, because his villainy was more high-handed. And we still retain the law which allows the blood of a robber at night to be shed, but forbids it in the day, when help can more easily be had.

All this is reasonable and enlightened law: founded, like all good legislation, upon clear and satisfactory principles, and well calculated to elevate the tone of the public feeling, to be not only so many specific enactments, but also the germinant seeds of good.

CHAPTER XXII.

THE LESSER LAW (continued).

PART IV.

EXODUS xxii. 16—xxiii. 19.

THE Fourth section of this law within the law consists of enactments, curiously disconnected, many of them without a penalty, varying greatly in importance, but all of a moral nature, and connected with the well-being of the state. It is hard to conceive how the systematic revision of which we hear so much could have left them in the condition in which they stand.

It is enacted that a seducer must marry the woman he has betrayed, and if her father refuse to give her to him, then he must pay the same dower as a bridegroom would have done (xxii. 16,17). And presently the sentence of death is launched against a blacker sensual crime (19). But between the two is interposed the celebrated mandate which doomed the sorceress to death, remarkable as the first mention of witchcraft in Scripture, and the only passage in all the Bible where the word is in the feminine form—a witch, or sorceress; remarkable also for a far graver reason, which makes it necessary to linger over the subject at some length.

SORCERY.

"Thou shalt not suffer a sorceress to live."—xxii. 18.

The world knows only too well what sad and shameful inferences have been drawn from these words. Unspeakable terrors, estrangement of natural sympathy, tortures and cruel deaths, have been inflicted on many thousands of the most forlorn creatures upon earth (creatures who were sustained in their sufferings by no high ardour of conviction or fanaticism, not being martyrs but simply victims), because it was held that Moses, in declaring that witches should not live, affirmed the reality of witchcraft. No sooner did the argument cease to be dangerous to old women than it became formidable to religion; for now it was urged that, since Moses was in error about the reality of witchcraft, his legislation could not have been inspired.

What are we to say to this?

In the first place it must be observed that the existence of a sorcerer is one thing, and the reality of his powers is quite another. What was most sad and shameful in the mediæval frenzy was the burning to ashes of multitudes who made no pretensions to traffic with the invisible world, who frequently held fast their innocence while enduring the agonies of torture, who were only aged and ugly and alone. Upon any theory, the prohibition of sorcery by the Pentateuch was no more answerable for these iniquities than its other prohibitions for the lynch law of the backwoods.

On the other hand, there were real professors of the black art: men did pretend to hold intercourse with spirits, and extorted great sums from their dupes in return for bringing them also into communion with superhuman beings. These it is reasonable to call sorcerers, whether we accept their professions or not, just as we speak of thought-readers and of mediums without being understood to commit ourselves to the pretensions of either one or other. In point of fact, the existence, in this nineteenth century after Christ, of sorcerers calling themselves mediums, is much more surprising than the existence of other sorcerers in the time of Moses or of Saul; and it bears startling witness to the depth in human nature of that craving for traffic with invisible powers which the law prohibited so sternly, but the roots of which neither religion nor education nor scepticism has been able wholly to pluck up.

Again, from the point of view which Moses occupied, it is plain that such professors should be punished. They are virtually punished still, whenever they obtain money under pretence of granting interviews with the departed. If we now rely chiefly upon educated public opinion to stamp out such impositions, that is because we have decided that a struggle between truth and falsehood upon equal terms will be advantageous to the former. It is a subdivision of the debate between intolerance and free thought. Our theory works well, but not universally well, even under modern conditions and in Christian lands. And assuredly Moses could not proclaim freedom of opinion, among uneducated slaves, amid the pressure of splendid and of seductive idolatries, and before the Holy Ghost was given. To complain of Moses for proscribing false religions would be to denounce the use of glass for seedlings because the full-grown plant flourishes in the open air.

Now, it would have been preposterous to proscribe false religions and yet to tolerate the sorcerer and the sorceress. For these were the active practitioners of another worship than that of God. They might not profess idolatry; but they offered help and guidance from sources which Jehovah frowned upon, rival sources of defence or knowledge.

The holy people was meant to grow up under the most elevating of all influences, reliance upon a protecting God, Who had bidden His children to subdue the world as well as to replenish it, and of Whom one of their own poets sang that He had put all things under the feet of man. Their true heritage was not bounded by the strip of land which Joshua and his followers slowly conquered; to them belonged all the resources of nature which science, ever since, has wrested from the Philistine hands of barbarism and ignorance. And this nobler conquest depended upon the depth and sincerity of man's feeling that the world is well-ordered and stable and the heritage of man, not a chaos of various and capricious powers, where Pallas inspires Diomed to hunt Venus bleeding off the field, or where the incantations of Canidia may disturb the orderly movements of the skies. Who could hope to discover by inductive science the secrets of such a world as this?

The devices of magic cut the links between cause and effect, between studious labour and the fruits which sorcery bade men to steal rather than to cultivate. What gambling was to commerce, that was witchcraft to philosophy, and the mischief no more depended on the validity of its methods than upon the soundness of the last device for breaking the bank at Monte Carlo.

If one could actually extort their secrets from the dead, or win for luxury and sloth a longer life than is bestowed upon temperance and labour, he would succeed in his revolt against the God of nature. But the revolt was the endeavour; and the sorcerer, however falsely, professed to have succeeded; and preached the same revolt to others. In religion he was therefore an apostate, and in the theocracy a traitor against the King, one whose life was forfeited if it was prudent to exact the penalty.

And when we consider the fascination wielded by such pretensions, even in ages when the stability of nature is an axiom, the dread which false religions all around and their terrible rituals must have inspired, the superstitious tendencies of the people and their readiness to be misled, we shall see ample reasons for treading out the first sparks of so dangerous a fire.

Beyond this it is vain to pretend that the law of Moses goes. It was right in declaring the sorcerer and the sorceress to be real and dangerous phenomena. It never declared their pretensions to be valid though illegitimate. And in one noteworthy passage it proclaims that a real sign or a wonder could only proceed from God, and when it accompanied false teaching was still a sign, though an ominous one, implying that the Lord would prove them (Deut. xiii. 1-3). This does not look very like an admission of the existence of rival powers, inferior though they might be, who could interfere with the order of His world.

Sorcery in all its forms will die when men realise indeed that the world is His, that there is no short or crooked way to the prizes which He offers to wisdom and to labour, that these rewards are infinitely richer and more splendid than the wildest dreams of magic, and that it is literally true that all power, in earth as well as heaven, is committed into the Hands which were pierced for us. In such a conception of the universe, incantations give place to prayers, and prayer does not seek to disturb, but to carry forward and to consummate, the orderly rule of Love.

The denunciation of witchcraft is quite naturally followed, as we now perceive, by the reiteration of the command that no sacrifice may be offered to any god except Jehovah (20). Strange and hateful offerings were an integral part of witchcraft, long before the hags of Macbeth brewed their charm, or the child in Horace famished to yield a spell.

THE STRANGER.

EXODUS xxii. 21, xxiii. 9.

Immediately after this, a ray of sunlight falls upon the sombre page.

We read an exhortation rather than a statute, which is repeated almost literally in the next chapter, and in both is supported by a beautiful and touching reason. "A stranger shalt thou not wrong, neither shall ye oppress him: for ye were strangers in the land of Egypt." "A stranger shall ye not oppress, for ye know the heart of a stranger, seeing ye were strangers in the land of Egypt" (xxii. 21, xxiii. 9).

The "stranger" of these verses is probably the settler among them, as distinguished from the traveller passing through the land. His want of friends and ignorance of their social order would place him at a disadvantage, of which they are forbidden to avail themselves, either by legal process (for the first passage is connected with jurisprudence), or in the affairs of common life. But the spirit of the commandment could not fail to influence their treatment of all foreigners; and simple and commonplace though it appear to us, it would have startled many of the wisest and greatest peoples of antiquity, and would have fallen as strangely upon the ears of the Greeks of Pericles, as of the modern Bedouin, with whom Israel had kinship. A foreigner, as such, was a foe: to wrong him was a paradox, because he had no rights: kinship, or else alliance or treaty was required to entitle the weaker to any better treatment than it suited the stronger to allow.

Yet we find a precept reiterated in this Jewish code which involves, in its inevitable though slow development, the abolition of negro slavery, the respect by powerful and civilised nations of the rights of indigenous tribes, the most boundless advance of philanthropy, through the most generous recognition of the fraternity of man.

However sternly the sword of Joshua might fall, it struck not at the foreigner, as such, but at those tribes, guilty and therefore accursed of God, the cup of whose iniquity was full. And yet there was enough of carnage to prove that so gracious a commandment as this could not have risen spontaneously in the heart of early Judaism. Does it seem to be made more natural, by any proposed shifting of the date?

The reason of the precept is beautifully human. It rests upon no abstract basis of common rights, nor prudential consideration of mutual advantage.

In our time it is sometimes proposed to build all morality upon such foundations; and strange consequences have already been deduced in cases where the proposed sanction has not seemed to apply. But, in fact, no advance in virtue has ever been traced to self-interest, although, after the advance took place, self-interest has always found its account in it. A progressive community is made of good men, and the motive to which Moses appeals is compassion fed by memory: "For ye were strangers in the land of Egypt" (xxii. 21); "For ye know the heart of a stranger, seeing ye were strangers in the land of Egypt" (xxiii. 9).

The point is not that they may again be carried into captivity: it is that they have felt its bitterness, and ought to recoil from inflicting what they writhed under.

Now, this appeal is a master-stroke of wisdom. Much cruelty, and almost all the cruelty of the young, springs from ignorance, and that slowness of the imagination which cannot realise that the pains of others are like our own. Feeling them to be so, the charities of the poor toward one another frequently rise almost to sublimity. And thus, when suffering does not ulcerate the heart and make it savage, it is the most softening of all influences. In one of the most threadbare lines in the classics, the queen of Carthage boasts that

"I, not ignorant of woe,
To pity the distressful know."

And the boldest assertion in Scripture of the natural development of our Saviour's human powers, is that which declares that "In that He Himself hath suffered, being tempted, He is able to succour them that are tempted" (Heb. ii. 18).

To this principle, then, Moses appeals, and by the appeal he educates the heart. He bids the people reflect on their own cruel hardships, on the hateful character of their tyrants, on their own greater hatefulness if they follow the vile example, after such bitter experience of its character. He does not yet rise to the grand level of the New Testament morality, Do all to thy neighbour which it is not servile and dependent to will that he should do for thee. But he attains to the level of that precept of Confucius and Zoroaster which has been so unworthily compared with it: Do not unto thy neighbour what thou wouldest not that he should do to thee—a precept which mere indifference obeys. Nay, he excels it; for the mental and spiritual attitude of one who respects his helpless neighbour because he so much resembles himself, will surely not be content without relieving the griefs that have so closely touched him. Thus again the legislation of Moses looks beyond itself.

Now, if the Jew should be merciful because he had himself known calamity, what implicit confidence may we repose upon the Man of sorrows and acquainted with grief?

In the same spirit they are warned against afflicting the widow or the orphan. And the threat which is added joins hands with the exhortation which preceded. They should not oppress the stranger, because they had been strangers and oppressed. Now the argument advances. The same God Who then heard their cry will hear the cry of the forlorn, and avenge them, according to the judicial fate which He had just announced, in kind, by bringing their own wives to widowhood and their children to orphanage (xxii. 22-4).

To their brethren they should not lend money upon usury; but loans are no more recommended than afterwards by Solomon: the words are "if thou lend" (ver. 25). And if the raiment of the borrower were taken for a pledge, it must be returned for him to use at night, or else God will hear his cry, because, it is added very significantly and briefly, "I am gracious" (ver. 27). It is the most exalting of all motives: Be merciful, for I am merciful: ye shall be the children of your Father.

Again is to be observed the influence reaching beyond the prescription—the motive which cannot be felt without many other and larger consequences than the restoration of pledges at sunset.

How comes this precept to be followed by the words, "Thou shalt not curse God nor blaspheme a ruler" (ver. 28)? and is not this again somewhat strangely followed by the order not to delay to offer the firstfruits of the soil, to consecrate the firstborn son, and to devote the firstborn of cattle at the same age when a son ought to be circumcised? (vers. 29, 30).

If any link can be discovered, it is in the sense of communion with God, suggested by the recent appeal to His character as a motive that should weigh with man. Therefore they must not blaspheme Him, either directly or through His agents, nor tardily yield Him what He claims. Therefore it is added, "Ye shall be holy men unto Me," and from the sense of dignity which religion thus inspires, a homely corollary is deduced—"Ye shall not eat any flesh that is torn of beasts in the field" (ver. 31). The bondmen of Egypt must learn a high-minded self-respect.

CHAPTER XXIII.

THE LESSER LAW (continued).

EXODUS xxiii. 1-19.

THE twenty-third chapter begins with a series of commands bearing upon the course of justice; but among these there is interjected very curiously a command to bring back the stray ox or ass of an enemy, and to help under a burden the over-weighted ass of him that hateth thee, even "if thou wouldest forbear to help him." It is just possible that the lawgiver, urging justice in the bearing of testimony, interrupts himself to speak of a very different manner in which the action may be warped by prejudice, but in which (unlike the other) it is lawful to show not only impartiality but kindness. The help of the cattle of one's enemy shows that in the bearing of testimony we should not merely abstain from downright wrong. And it is a fine example of the spirit of the New Testament, in the Old.

"Thou shalt not take up a false report" (ver. 1) is a precept which reaches far. How many heedless whispers, conjectures lightly spoken because they were amusing, yet influencing the course of lives, and inferences uncharitably drawn, would have been stillborn if this had been remembered!

But when the scandal is already abroad, the temptation to aid its progress is still greater. Therefore it is added, "Put not thine hand with the wicked to be an unrighteous witness." Whatever be the menace or the bribe, however the course of opinion seem to be decided, and the assent of an individual to be harmless because the result is sure, or blameless because the responsibility lies elsewhere, still each man is a unit, not an "item," and must act for himself, as hereafter he must give account. Hence it results inevitably that "Thou shalt not follow a multitude to do evil, neither shalt thou speak in a cause to turn aside after a multitude to wrest judgment" (ver. 2). The blind impulses of a multitude are often as misleading as the solicitations of the bad, and to aspiring temperaments much more seductive. There is indeed a strange magnetism in the voice of the public. Every orator knows that a great assembly acts upon the speaker as really as he acts upon it: its emotions are like a rush of waters to sweep him away, beyond his intentions or his ordinary powers. Yet he is the strongest individual there; no other has at all the same opportunity for self-assertion, and therefore its power over others must be more complete than over him.

This is one reason for the institution of public worship. Men neglect the house of God because they can pray as well at home, and encourage wanton subdivisions of the Church because they think there is no very palpable difference between competing denominations, or even because competition may be as useful in religion as in trade, as if our competition with the world and the devil for souls would not sufficiently animate us, without competing with one another. But in acting thus they weaken the effect for good of one of the mightiest influences which work evil among us, the influence of association. Men are always persuading themselves that they need not be better than their neighbours, nor ashamed of doing what every one does. And yet no voice joins in a cry without deepening it: every one who rushes with a crowd makes its impulse more difficult to stem; his individuality is not lost by its partnership with a thousand more; and he is accountable for what he contributes to the result. He has parted with his self-control, but not with the inner forces which he ought to have controlled.

Against this dangerous influence of the world, Christ has set the contagion of godliness within His Church, and every avoidable subdivision enfeebles this salutary counter-influence.

Moses warns us, therefore, of the danger of being drawn away by a multitude to do evil; but he is thinking especially of the peril of being tempted to "speak" amiss. Who does not know it? From the statesman who outruns his convictions rather than break with his party, and who cannot, amid deafening cheers, any longer hear his conscience speak, down to the humblest who fails to confess Christ before hostile men, and therefore by-and-by denies Him, there is not one whose speech and silence have never been in danger of being set to the sympathies of his own little public like a song to music.

That Moses was really thinking of this tendency to court popularity, is plain from the next clause—"Neither shalt thou favour a poor man in his cause" (ver. 3).

It is an admirable caution. Men there are who would scorn the opposite injustice, and from whom no rich man could buy a wrongful decision with gold or favour, but who are habitually unjust, because they load the other scale. The beam ought to hang straight. When justice is concerned, the poor man's friend is almost as contemptible as his foe, and he has taken a bribe, if not in the mean enjoyment of democratic popularity, yet in his own pride—the fancy that he has done a magnanimous act, the attitude in which he poses.

As in law so in literature. There once was a tendency to describe magnanimous persons of quality, and repulsive clodhoppers and villagers. Times have changed, and now we think it much more ingenious and high-toned to be quite as partial and disingenuous, reversing the cases. Neither is true, and therefore neither is artistic. No class in society is deficient in noble qualities, or in base ones. Nor is the man of letters at all more independent, who flatters the democracy in a democratic age, than he who flattered the aristocracy when they had all the prizes to bestow.

Other precepts forbid bribery, command that the soil shall rest in the seventh year, when its spontaneous produce shall be for the poor, and further recognise and consecrate relaxation, by instituting (or more probably adopting into the code) the three feasts of Passover, Pentecost, and Tabernacles. The section closes with the words "Thou shalt not seethe a kid in his mother's milk" (ver. 19). Upon this clause much ingenuity has been expended. It makes occult reference to some superstitious rite. It is the name for some unduly stimulating compound. But when we remember that, just before, the sabbatical fruit which the poor left ungleaned was expressly reserved for the beasts of the field, that men were bidden to help the overladen ass of their enemies, and that care is taken elsewhere that the ox should not be muzzled when treading out grain, that the birdnester should not take the dam with the young, and that neither cow nor ewe should be slain on the same day with its young (Deut. xxv. 4, xxii. 6; Lev. xxii. 28), the simplest meaning seems also the most probable. Men, who have been taught respect for their fellow-men, are also to learn a fine sensibility even in respect to the inferior animals. Throughout all this code there is an exquisite tendency to form a considerate, humane, delicate and high-minded nation.

It remained, to stamp upon the human conscience a deep sense of responsibility.

Part V.—Its Sanctions.

Exodus xxiii. 20-33.

This summary of Judaism being now complete, the people have to learn what mighty issues are at stake upon their obedience. And the transition is very striking from the simplest duty to the loftiest privilege: "Thou shalt not seethe a kid in his mother's milk. Behold, I send an Angel before thee... Beware of him: for My Name is in him" (19-21).

We have now to ask how much this mysterious phrase involves: who was the Angel of whom it speaks?

The question is not, How much did Israel at that moment comprehend? For we are distinctly told that prophets were conscious of speaking more than they understood, and searched diligently, but in vain, what the spirit that was in them did signify (1 Peter i. 11).

It would, in fact, be absurd to seek the New Testament doctrine of the Logos full-blown in the Pentateuch. But it is mere prejudice, unphilosophical and presumptuous, to shut one's eyes against any evidence which may be forthcoming that the earliest books of Scripture were tending towards the last conclusions of theology; that the slender overture to the Divine oratorio indicates already the same theme which thunders from all the chorus at the close.

It is scarcely necessary to refute the position that a mere "messenger" is intended, because angels have not yet "appeared as personal agents separate from God." Kalisch himself has amply refuted his own theory. For, he says, "we are compelled ... to refer it to Moses and his successor Joshua" (in loco). So then He Who will not forgive their transgressions is he who prayed that if God would not pardon them, his own name might be blotted from the book of life. He, to whom afterwards God said "I will proclaim the name of the Lord before thee" (xxxiii. 19), is the same of Whom God said "My name is in Him." This position needs no examination; but the perplexities of those who reject the deeper interpretation is a strong confirmation of its soundness. We have still to choose between the promise of a created angel, and some manifestation and interposition of God, distinguished from Jehovah and yet one with Him. This latter view is an evident preparation for clearer knowledge yet to come. It is enough to stamp the dispensation which puts it forth as but provisional, and therefore bears witness to that other dispensation which has the key to it. And it is exactly what a Christian would expect to find somewhere in this summary of the law.

What, then, do we read elsewhere about the Angel of Jehovah? What do we find, especially, in these early books?

A difficulty has to be met at the very outset. The issue would be decided offhand, if it could be shown that the Angel of this verse is the same who is offered, as a poor substitute for their Divine protector, in the thirty-third chapter. But no contrast can be clearer than between the encouraging promise before us, and the sharp menace which then plunged Israel into mourning. Here is an Angel who must not be provoked, who will not pardon you, because "My Name is in Him." There is an angel who will be sent because God will not go up, ... lest He consume them (vers. 2, 3). He is not the Angel of God's presence, but of His absence. When the intercession of Moses won from God a reversal of the sentence, He then said "My Presence (My Face) shall go with thee, and I will give thee rest."* but Moses answers, not yet reassured, "If Thy Presence (Thy Face) go not up with us, carry us not up hence. For wherein shall it be known that I have found grace in Thy sight?... Is it not that Thou goest with us? And the Lord said, I will do this thing also that thou hast spoken" (14-17).

Moreover, Isaiah, speaking of this time, says that "In all their affliction He was afflicted, and the Angel of His Presence (His Face) saved them" (Isa. lxiii. 9).

Thus we find that some angel is to be sent because God will not go up: that thereupon the nation mourns, although in this twenty-third chapter they had received as a gladdening promise, the assurance of an Angel escort in Whom is the name of God; that in response to prayer God promises that His Face shall accompany them, so that it may be known that He Himself goes with them; and finally that His Face in Exodus is the Angel of His Face in Isaiah. The prophet at least had no doubt whether the gracious promise in the twenty-third chapter answered, in the thirty-third chapter, to the third verse or the fourteenth—to the menace, or to the restored favour.

This difficulty being now converted into an evidence, we turn back to examine other passages.

When the Angel of the Lord spoke to Hagar, "she called the name of Jehovah that spake unto her El Roi" (Gen. xvi. 11, 13). When God tempted Abraham, "the Angel of Jehovah called unto him out of heaven, and said, ... I know that thou fearest God, seeing thou hast not withheld thy son ... from Me" (Gen. xxii. 11, 12). When a man wrestled with Jacob, he thereupon claimed to have seen God face to face, and called the place Peniel, the Face (Presence) of God (Gen. xxxii. 4, 30). But Hosea tells us that "He had power with God: yea, he had power over the Angel, ... and there He spake with us, even Jehovah, the God of hosts" (Hos. xii. 3, 5). Even earlier, in his exile, the Angel of the Lord had appeared unto him and said, "I am the God of Bethel ... where thou vowedst a vow unto Me." But the vow was distinctly made to God Himself: "I will surely give the tenth to Thee" (xxxi. 11, 13; xxviii. 20, 22). Is it any wonder that when this patriarch blessed Joseph, he said, "The God before whom my fathers Abraham and Isaac did walk, the God which hath fed me all my life long unto this day, the Angel which hath redeemed me from all evil, (may He) bless the lads" (xlviii. 15, 16)?

In Exodus iii. 2 the Angel of the Lord appeared out of the bush. But presently He changes into Jehovah Himself, and announces Himself to be Jehovah the God of their fathers (iii. 2, 4, 15). In Exodus xiii. 21 Jehovah went before Israel, but the next chapter tells how "the Angel of the Lord which went before Israel removed and went behind" (xiv. 19); while Numbers (xx. 16) says expressly that "He sent an Angel and brought us out of Egypt."

By the comparison of these and many later passages (which is nothing but the scientific process of induction, leaning not on the weight of any single verse, but on the drift and tendency of all the phenomena) we learn that God was already revealing Himself through a Medium, a distinct personality whom He could send, yet not so distinct but that His name was in Him,

---

* Even if the rendering were accepted, "Must My Presence (My Face) go with thee?" (Can I not be trusted without a direct Presence?) the argument would not be affected, because Moses presses for the favour and obtains it.

and He Himself was the Author of what He did.

If Israel obeyed Him, He would bring them into the promised land (ver. 23); and if there they continued unseduced by false worships, He would bless their provisions, their bodily frame, their children; He would bring terror and a hornet against their foes; He would clear the land before them as fast as their population could enjoy it; He would extend their boundaries yet farther, from the Red Sea, where Solomon held Ezion Geber (1 Kings ix. 26), to the Mediterranean, and from the desert where they stood to the Euphrates, where Solomon actually possessed Palmyra and Thiphsah (2 Chron. viii. 4; 1 Kings iv. 24).

CHAPTER XXIV.

THE COVENANT RATIFIED. THE VISION OF GOD.

Exodus xxiv.

The opening words of this chapter ("Come up unto the Lord") imply, without explicitly asserting, that Moses was first sent down to convey to Israel the laws which had just been enacted.

This code they unanimously accepted, and he wrote it down. It is a memorable statement, recording the origin of the first portion of Holy Scripture that ever existed as such, whatever earlier writings may now or afterwards have been incorporated in the Pentateuch. He then built an altar for God, and twelve pillars for the tribes, and sacrificed burnt-offerings and peace-offerings unto the Lord. Sin-offerings, it will be observed, were not yet instituted; and neither was the priesthood, so that young men slew the offerings. Half of the blood was poured upon the altar, because God had perfected His share in the covenant. The remainder was not used until the law had been read aloud, and the people had answered with one voice, "All that the Lord hath commanded will we do, and will be obedient." Thereupon they too were sprinkled with the blood, and the solemn words were spoken, "Behold the blood of the covenant which the Lord hath made with you concerning all these words." The people were now finally bound: no later covenant of the same kind will be found in the Old Testament.

And now the principle began to work which was afterwards embodied in the priesthood. That principle, stated broadly, was exclusion from the presence of God, relieved and made hopeful by the admission of representatives. The people were still forbidden to approach, under pain of death. But Moses and Aaron were no longer the only ones to cross the appointed boundaries. With them came the two sons of Aaron, (afterwards, despite their privilege, to meet a dreadful doom,) and also seventy representatives of all the newly covenanted people. Joshua, too, as the servant of Moses, was free to come, although unspecified in the summons (vers. 1, 13).

"They saw the God of Israel," and under His feet the blueness of the sky like intense sapphire. And they were secure: they beheld God, and ate and drank.

But in privilege itself there are degrees: Moses was called up still higher, and left Aaron and Hur to govern the people while he communed with his God. For six days the nation saw the flanks of the mountain swathed in cloud, and its summit crowned with the glory of Jehovah like devouring fire. Then Moses entered the cloud, and during forty days they knew not what had become of him. Was it time lost? Say rather that all time is wasted except what is spent in communion, direct or indirect, with the Eternal.

The narrative is at once simple and sublime. We are sometimes told that other religions besides our own rely for sanction upon their supernatural origin. "Zarathustra, Sâkya-Mooni and Mahomed pass among their followers for envoys of the Godhead; and in the estimation of the Brahmin the Vedas and the laws of Manou are holy, divine books" (Kuenen, *Religion of Israel*, i. 6). This is true. But there is a wide difference between nations which assert that God privately appeared to their teachers, and a nation which asserts that God appeared to the public. It is not upon the word of Moses that Israel is said to have believed; and even those who reject the narrative are not entitled to confound it with narratives utterly dissimilar. There is not to be found anywhere a parallel for this majestic story.

But what are we to think of the assertion that God was seen to stand upon a burning mountain?

He it is Whom no man hath seen or can see, and in His presence the seraphim veil their faces.

It will not suffice to answer that Moses "endured as seeing Him that is invisible" (Heb. xi. 27), for the paraphrase is many centuries later and hostile critics will rule it out of court as an after-thought. At least, however, it proves that the problem was faced long ago, and tells us what solution satisfied the early Church.

With this clue before us, we ask what notion did the narrative really convey to its ancient readers? If our defence is to be thoroughly satisfactory, it must show an escape from heretical and carnal notions of deity, not only for ourselves, but also for careful readers from the very first.

Now it is certain that no such reader could for one moment think of a manifestation thorough, exhaustive, such as the eye receives of colour and of form. Because the effect produced is not satisfaction, but desire. Each new vision deepens the sense of the unseen. Thus we read first that Moses and Aaron, Nadab, and Abihu and the seventy elders, saw God, from which revelation the people felt and knew themselves to be excluded. And yet the multitude also had a vision according to its power to see; and indeed it was more satisfying to them than was the most profound insight enjoyed by Moses. To see God is to sail to the horizon: when you arrive, the horizon is as far in front as ever; but you have gained a new consciousness of infinitude. "The appearance of the glory of the Lord was seen like devouring fire in the eyes of the children of Israel" (ver. 17). But Moses was aware of a glory far greater and more spiritual than any material splendour. When theophanies had done their utmost, his longing was still unslaked, and he cried out, "Show me, I pray Thee, Thy glory" (xxxiii. 18). To his consciousness that glory was still veiled, which the multitude sufficiently beheld in the flaming mountain. And the answer which he received ought to put the question at rest for ever, since, along with the promise "All My goodness shall pass before thee," came the assertion "Thou shalt not see My face, for no man shall see Me and live."

So, then, it is not our modern theology, but this noble book of Exodus itself, which tells us that Moses did not and could not adequately see God, however great and sacred the vision which he beheld. From this book we learn that, side by side with the most intimate communion and the clearest possible unveiling of God, grew up the profound consciousness that only some attributes and not the essence of deity had been displayed.

It is very instructive also to observe the steps by which Moses is led upward. From the burning bush to the fiery cloud, and thence to the blazing mountain, there was an ever-deepening lesson of majesty and awe. But in answer to the prayer that he might really see the very glory of his Lord, his mind is led away upon entirely another pathway: it is "All My goodness" which is now to "pass before" him, and the proclamation is of "a God full of compassion and gracious," yet retaining His moral firmness, so that He "will by no means clear the guilty."

What can cloud and fire avail, toward the manifesting of a God Whose essence is His love? It is from the Old Testament narrative that the New Testament inferred that Moses endured as seeing indeed, yet as seeing Him Who is inevitably and for ever invisible to eyes of flesh: he learned most, not when he beheld some form of awe, standing on a paved work of sapphire stone and as it were the very heaven for clearness, but when hidden in a cleft of the rock and covered by the hand of God while He passed by.

On one hand the people saw the glory of God: on the other hand it was the best lesson taught by a far closer access, still to pray and yearn to see that glory. The seventy beheld the God of Israel: for their leader was reserved the more exalting knowledge, that beyond all vision is the mystic overshadowing of the Divine, and a voice which says "No man shall see Me and live." The difference in heart is well typified in this difference in their conduct, that they saw God and ate and drank, but he, for forty days, ate not. Satisfaction and assurance are a poor ideal compared with rapt aspiration and desire.

Thus we see that no conflict exists between this declaration and our belief in the spirituality of God.

We have still to ask what is the real force of the assertion that God was in some lesser sense seen of Israel, and again, more especially, of its leaders.

What do we mean even by saying that we see each other?—that, observing keenly, we see upon one face cunning, upon another sorrow, upon a third the peace of God? Are not these emotions immaterial and invisible as the essence of God Himself? Nay, so invisible is the reality within each bosom, that some day all that eye hath seen shall fall away from us, and yet the true man shall remain intact.

Man has never seen more than a hint, an outcome, a partial self-revelation or self-betrayal of his fellowman.

"Yes, in the sea of life in-isled,
With echoing straits between us thrown,
Dotting the shoreless watery wild,
We mortal millions live *alone*.
. . . . . .
God bade betwixt 'our' shores to be
The unplumb'd, salt, estranging sea."

And yet, incredible as the paradox would seem, if it were not too common to be strange, the play of muscles and rush of blood, visible through the skin, do reveal the most spiritual and immaterial changes. Even so the heavens declare that very glory of God which baffled the undimmed eyes of Moses. So it was, also, that when rended rocks and burning skies revealed a more imminent action of Him Who moves through all nature always, when convulsions hitherto undreamed of by those dwellers in Egyptian plains overwhelmed them with a new sense of their own smallness and a supreme Presence, God was manifested there.

Not unlike this is the explanation of St. Augustine, "We need not be surprised that God, invisible as He is, appeared visibly to the patriarchs. For, as the sound which communicates the thought conceived in the silence of the mind is not the thought itself, so the form by which God, invisible in His own nature, became visible, was not God Himself. Nevertheless it was He Himself Who was seen under that form, as the thought itself is heard in the sound of the voice; and the patriarchs recognised that, although the bodily form was not God, they saw the invisible God. For, though Moses was conversing with God, yet he said, "If I have found grace in Thy sight, show me Thyself" (*De Civ. Dei*, x. 13). And again: "He knew that he saw corporeally, but he sought the true vision of God spiritually" (*De Trin.*, ii. 27).

It has still to be added that His manifestation is exactly suited to the stage now reached in the education of Israel. Their fathers had already "seen God" in the likeness of man: Abraham had entertained Him; Jacob had wrestled with Him. And so Joshua before Ai, and Manoah by the rock at Zorah, and Ezekiel by the river Chebar, should see the likeness of a man. We who believe the doctrine of a real Incarnation can well perceive that in these passing and mysterious glimpses God was not only revealing Himself in the way which would best prepare humanity for His future coming in actual manhood, but also in the way by which, meanwhile, the truest and deepest light could be thrown upon His nature, a nature which could hereafter perfectly manifest itself in flesh. Why, then, do not the records of the Exodus hint at a human likeness? Why did they "behold no similitude"? Clearly because the masses of Israel were utterly unprepared to receive rightly such a vision. To them the likeness of man would have meant no more than the likeness of a flying eagle or a calf. Idolatry would have followed, but no sense of sympathy, no consciousness of the grandeur and responsibility of being made in the likeness of God. Anthropomorphism is a heresy, although the Incarnation is the crowning doctrine of the faith.

But it is hard to see why the human likeness of God should exist in Genesis and Joshua, but not in the history of the Exodus, if that story be a post-Exilian forgery.

This is not all. The revelations of God in the desert were connected with threats and prohibitions: the law was given by Moses; grace and truth came by Jesus Christ. And with the different tone of the message a different aspect of the speaker was to be expected. From the blazing crags of Sinai, fenced around, the voice of a trumpet waxing louder and louder, said "Thou shalt not!" On the green hill by the Galilean lake Jesus sat down, and His disciples came unto Him, and He opened His mouth and said "Blessed."

Now, the conscience of every sinner knows that the God of the commandments is dreadful. It is of Him, not of hell, that Isaiah said "The sinners in Zion are afraid; trembling hath surprised the godless ones. Who among us shall dwell with the devouring fire? who among us shall dwell with everlasting burnings?" (Isa. xxxiii. 14).

For him who rejects the light yoke of the Lord of Love, the fires of Sinai are still the truest revelation of deity; and we must not deny Sinai because we know Bethlehem. We must choose between the two.

CHAPTER XXV.

THE SHRINE AND ITS FURNITURE.

Exodus xxv. 1-40.

The first direction given to Moses on the mountain is to prepare for the making of a tabernacle wherein God may dwell with man. For this he must invite offerings of various kinds, metals and gems, skins and fabrics, oil and spices; and the humblest man whose heart is willing may contribute toward an abode for Him Whom the heaven of heavens cannot contain.

Strange indeed is the contrast between the mountain burning up to heaven, and the lowly structure of the wood of the desert, which was now to be erected by subscription.

And yet the change marks not a lower conception of deity, but an advance, just as the quiet and serene communion of a saint with God is loftier than the most agitating experience of the convert.

This is the first announcement of a fixed abiding presence of God in the midst of men, and it is therefore the precursor of much. St. John certainly alluded to this earliest dwelling of God on earth when he wrote, "The Word was made flesh, and tabernacled among us" (John i. 14). A little later it was said, "Ye also are builded together for an habitation of God" (Eph. ii. 22); and again the very words used at first of the tabernacle are applied to faithful souls: "We are a temple of the living God, as God said, I will dwell in them and walk in them" (2 Cor. vi. 16; Lev. xxvi. 11). For God dwelt on earth in the Messiah hidden by the veil, that is to say His flesh (Heb. x. 20), and also in the hearts of all the faithful. And a yet fuller communion is to come, of which the tabernacle in the wilderness was a type, even the descent of the Holy City, when the true tabernacle of God shall be with men, and He shall tabernacle with them (Rev. xxi. 3).

It may seem strange that after the commandment "Let them make Me a sanctuary" the whole chapter is devoted to instructions, not for the tabernacle but for its furniture. But indeed the four articles enumerated in this chapter present a wonderfully graphic picture of the nature and terms of the intercourse of God with man. On one side is His revelation of righteousness, but righteousness propitiated and become gracious, and this is symbolised by the ark of the testimony and the mercy-seat. On the other side the consecration both of secular and sacred life is typified by the table with bread and wine, and by the golden candlestick. Except thus, no tabernacle could have been the dwelling of the Lord, nor ever shall be.

And this is the true reason why the altar of incense is not even mentioned until a later chapter (xxx.). We do homage to God because He is present: it is rather the consequence than the condition of His abode with us.

The first step towards the preparation of a shrine for God on earth is the enshrining of His will: Moses should therefore make first of all an ark, wherein to treasure up "the testimony which I shall give thee," the two tables of the law (xxv. 16). In it were also the pot of manna and Aaron's rod which budded (Heb. ix. 4), and beside it was laid the whole book of the law, for a testimony, alas! against them (Deut. xxxi. 26).

Thus the ark was to treasure up the expression of the will of God, and the relics which told by what mercies and deliverances He claimed obedience. It was a precious thing, but not the most precious, as we shall presently learn; and therefore it was not made of pure gold, but overlaid with it. That it might be reverently carried, four rings were cast and fastened to it at the lower corners, and in these four staves, also overlaid with gold, were permanently inserted.

The next article mentioned is the most important of all.

It would be a great mistake to suppose that the mercy-seat was a mere lid, an ordinary portion of the ark itself. It was made of a different and more costly material, of pure gold, with which the ark was only overlaid. There is separate mention that Bezaleel "made the ark, . . . and he made the mercy-seat" (xxxvii. 1, 6), and the special presence of God in the Most Holy Place is connected much more intimately with the mercy-seat than with the remainder of the structure. Thus He promises to "appear in the cloud above the mercy-seat" (Lev. xvi. 2). And when it is written that "Moses heard the voice speaking unto him from above the mercy-seat which is upon the ark of the testimony" (Num. vii. 89), it would have been more natural to say directly "from above the ark" unless some stress were to be laid upon the interposing slab of gold. In reality no distinction could be sharper than between the ark and its cover, from whence to hear the voice of God. And so thoroughly did all the symbolism of the Most Holy Place gather around this supreme object, that in one place it is actually called "the house of the mercy-seat" (1 Chron. xxviii. 11).

Let us, then, put ourselves into the place of an ancient worshipper. Excluded though he is from the Holy Place, and conscious that even the priests are shut out from the inner shrine, yet the high priest who enters is his brother: he goes on his behalf: the barrier is a curtain, not a wall.

But while the Israelite mused upon what was beyond, the ark, as we have seen, suggests the depth of his obligation; for there is the rod of his deliverance and the bread from heaven which fed him; and there also are the commandments which he ought to have kept. And his conscience tells him of ingratitude and a broken covenant; by the law is the knowledge of sin.

It is therefore a sinister and menacing thought that immediately above this ark of the violated covenant burns the visible manifestation of God, his injured Benefactor.

And hence arises the golden value of that which interposes, beneath which the accusing law is buried, by means of which God "hides His face from our sins."

The worshipper knows this cover to be provided by a separate ordinance of God, after the ark and its contents had been arranged for, and finds in it a vivid concrete representation of the idea "Thou hast cast all my sins behind Thy back" (Isa. xxxviii. 17). That this was its true intention becomes more evident when we ascertain exactly the meaning of the term which we have, not too precisely, rendered "mercy-seat."

The word "seat" has no part in the original; and we are not to think of God as reposing on it, but as revealing Himself above. The erroneous notion has probably transferred itself to the type from the heavenly antitype, which is "the throne of grace," but it has no countenance either in the Greek or the Hebrew name of the Mosaic institution. Nor is the notion expressed that of gratuitous and unbought "mercy." When Jehovah showeth mercy unto thousands, the word is different. It is true that the root means "to cover," and is once employed in Scripture in that sense (Gen. vi. 14); but its ethical use is generally connected with sacrifice; and when we read of a "sin-offering for *atonement*," of the half-shekel being an "*atonement*-money," and of "the day of *atonement*," the word is a simple and very similar development from the same root with this which we render *mercy-seat* (Exod. xxx. 10, 16; Lev. xxiii. 27, etc.).

The Greek word is found twice in the New Testament: once when the cherubim of glory overshadow the *mercy-seat*, and again when God hath set forth Christ to be a *propitiation* (Heb. ix. 5; Rom. iii. 25). The mercy-seat is therefore to be thought of in connection with sin, but sin expiated and thus covered and put away.

We know mysteries which the Israelite could not guess of the means by which this was brought to pass. But as he watched the high priest disappearing into that awful solitude, with God, as he listened to the chime of bells, swung by his movements, and announcing that still he lived, two conditions stood out broadly before his mind. One was the bringing in of incense: "Thou shalt bring a censer full of burning coals of fire from before the altar, that the cloud of the incense may cover the mercy-seat" (Lev. xvi. 13). Now, the connection between prayer and incense was quite familiar to the Jew; and he could not but understand that the blessing of atonement was to be sought and won by intense and burning supplication. And the other was that invariable demand, the offering of a victim's blood. All the sacrifices of Judaism culminated in the great act when the high priest, standing in the most holy and the most occult spot in all the world, sprinkled "blood upon the mercy-seat eastwards, and before the mercy-seat sprinkled of the blood with his finger seven times" (Lev. xvi. 14).

Thus the crowning height of the Jewish ritual was attained when the blood of the great national sacrifice was offered not only before God, but, with special reference to the covering up of the broken and accusing law, before the mercy-seat.

No wonder that on either side of it, and moulded of the same mass of metal, were the cherubim in an attitude of adoration, their outspread wings covering it, their faces bent, not only as bowing in reverence before the Divine presence, but, as we expressly read, "toward the mercy-seat shall the faces of the cherubim be." For the meaning of this great symbol was among the things which "the angels desire to look into."

We now understand how much was gained when God said "There will I meet thee, and I will commune with thee from above the mercy-seat" (ver. 22). It was an assurance, not only of the love which desires obedience, but of the mercy which passes over failure.*

Thus far, there has been symbolised the mind of God, His righteousness and His grace.

The next articles have to do with man, his homage to God and his witness for Him.

There is first the table of the shewbread (vers. 23-30), overlaid with pure gold, surrounded, like the ark, with "a crown" or moulding of gold, for ornament and the greater security of the loaves, and strengthened by a border of pure gold carried around the base, which was also ornamented with a crown, or moulding. Close to this border were rings for staves, like those by which the ark was borne. The table was furnished with dishes upon which, every Sabbath day, new shewbread might be conveyed into the tabernacle, and the old might be removed for the priests to eat. There were spoons also, by which to place frankincense upon each pile of bread; and "flagons and bowls to pour out withal." What was thus to be poured we do not read, but there is no doubt that it was wine, second only to bread as a requisite of Jewish life, and forming, like the frankincense, a link between this weekly presentation and the meal-offerings. But all these were subordinate to the twelve loaves, one for each tribe, which were laid in two piles upon the table. It is clear that their presentation was the essence of the rite, and not their consumption by the priests, which was possibly little more than a safeguard against irreverent treatment. For the word shewbread is literally bread of the face or presence, which word is used of the presence of God, in the famous prayer "If Thy presence go not with me, carry us not up hence" (xxxiii. 15). And of whom, other than God, can it here be reasonably understood? Now Jacob, long before, had vowed "Of all that Thou givest me, I will surely give the tenth to Thee" (Gen. xxviii. 22). And it was an edifying ordinance that a regular offering should be made to God of the staple necessaries of existence, as a confession that all came from Him, and an appeal, clearly expressed by covering it with frankincense, which typified prayer (Lev. xxiv. 7) that He would continue to supply their need.

Nor is it overstrained to add, that when this

---

* This investigation offers a fine example of the folly of that kind of interpretation which looks about for some sort of external and arbitrary resemblance, and fastens upon that as the true meaning. Nothing is more common among these expounders than to declare that the wood and gold of the ark are types of the human and Divine natures of our Lord. If either ark or mercy-seat should be compared to Him, it is obviously the latter, which speaks of mercy. But this was of pure gold.

bread was given to their priestly representatives to eat, with all reverence and in a holy place, God responded, and gave back to His people that which represented the necessary maintenance of the tribes. Thus it was, "on the behalf of the children of Israel, an everlasting covenant" (Lev. xxiv. 8).

The form has perished. But as long as we confess in the Lord's Prayer that the wealthiest does not possess one day's bread ungiven—as long, also, as Christian families connect every meal with a due acknowledgment of dependence and of gratitude—so long will the Church of Christ continue to make the same confession and appeal which were offered in the shewbread upon the table.

The next article of furniture was the golden candlestick (vers. 31-40). And this presents the curious phenomenon that it is extremely clear in its typical import, and in its material outline; but the details of the description are most obscure, and impossible to be gathered from the Authorised Version. Strictly speaking, it was not a lamp, but only a gorgeous lampstand, with one perpendicular shaft, and six branches, three springing, one above another, from each side of the shaft, and all curving up to the same height. Upon these were laid the seven lamps, which were altogether separate in their construction (ver. 37). It was of pure gold, the base and the main shaft being of one piece of beaten metal. Each of the six branches was ornamented with three cups, made like almond blossoms; above these a "knop," variously compared by Jewish writers to an apple and a pomegranate, and still higher, a flower or bud. It is believed that there was a fruit and flower above each of the cups, making nine ornaments on each branch. The "candlestick" in ver. 34 can only mean the central shaft, and upon this there were "four cups with their knops and flowers" instead of three. With the lamp were tongs, and snuff-dishes in which to remove the charred wick from the temple.

As we are told that when the Lord called the child Samuel, "the lamp of God was not yet gone out" (1 Sam. iii. 3), it follows that the lights were kept burning only during the night.

We have now to ascertain the spiritual meaning of this stately symbol. There are two other passages in Scripture which take up the figure and carry it forward. In Zechariah (iv. 2-12) we are taught that the separation of the lamps is a mere incident; they are to be conceived of as organically one, and moreover as fed by secret ducts with oil from no limited supply, but from living olive trees, vital, rooted in the system of the universe. Whatever obscurity may veil those "two sons of oil" (and this is not the place to discuss the subject), we are distinctly told that the main lesson is that of lustre derived from supernatural, invisible sources. Zerubbabel is confronted by a great mountain of hindrance, but it shall become a plain before him, because the lesson of the vision of the candlestick is this—"Not by might, nor by power, but by My Spirit, saith the Lord." A lamp gives light not because the gold shines, but because the oil burns; and yet the oil is the one thing which the eye sees not. And so the Church is a witness for her Lord, a light shining in a dark place, not because of its learning or culture, its noble ritual, its stately buildings or its ample revenues. All these things her children, having the power, ought to dedicate. The ancient symbol put art and preciousness in an honourable place, worthily upholding the lamp itself; and in the New Testament the seven lamps of the Apocalypse were still of gold. But the true function of a lamp is to be luminous, and for this the Church depends wholly upon its supply of grace from God the Holy Ghost. It is "not by might, nor by power, but by My Spirit, saith the Lord."

Again, in the Revelation, we find the New Testament Churches described as lamps, among which their Lord habitually walks. And no sooner have the seven churches on earth been warned and cheered, than we are shown before the throne of God seven torches (burning by their own incandescence—*vide* Trench, *N. T. Synonyms*, p. 162), which are the seven spirits of God, answering to His seven light-bearers upon the earth (Rev. iv. 5).

Lastly, the perfect and mystic number, seven, declares that the light of the Church, shining in a dark place, ought to be full and clear, no imperfect presentation of the truth: "they shall light the lamps, to give light over against it."

Because this lamp shines with the light of the Church, exhibiting the graces of her Lord, therefore a special command is addressed to the people, besides the call for contributions to the work in general, that they shall bring pure olive oil, not obtained by heat and pressure, but simply beaten, and therefore of the best quality, to feed its flame.

It is to burn, as the Church ought to shine in all darkness of the conscience or the heart of man, from evening to morning for ever. And the care of the ministers of God is to be the continual tending of this blessed and sacred flame.

THE PATTERN IN THE MOUNT.

Exodus xxv. 9, 40.

Twice over (vers. 9, 40, and *cf.* xxvi. 30, xxvii. 8, etc.) Moses was reminded to be careful to make all things after the pattern shown him in the mount. And these words have sometimes been so strained as to convey the meaning that there really exists in heaven a tabernacle and its furniture, the grand original from which the Mosaic copy was derived.

That is plainly not what the Epistle to the Hebrews understands (Heb. viii. 5). For it urges this admonition as a proof that the old dispensation was a shadow of ours, in which Christ enters into heaven itself, and our consciences are cleansed from dead works to serve the living God. The citation is bound indissolubly with all the demonstration which follows it.

We are not, then, to think of a heavenly tabernacle, exhibited to the material senses of Moses, with which all the details of his own work must be identical.

Rather we are to conceive of an inspiration, an ideal, a vision of spiritual truths, to which all this work in gold and acacia-wood should correspond. It was thus that Socrates told Glaucon, incredulous of his republic, that in heaven there is laid up a pattern, for him that wishes to behold it. Nothing short of this would satisfy the inspired application of the words in the

Epistle to the Hebrews, where the readers, who were Jewish converts, are asked to recognise in this verse evidence that the light of the new dispensation illuminated the institutions of the old.

Without this pervading sentiment, the most elaborate specifications of weight and measurement, of cup and pomegranate and flower, could never have produced the required effect. An ideal there was, a divinely designed suggestiveness, which must be always present to his superintending vigilance, as once it shone upon his soul in sacred vision or trance; a suggestiveness which might possibly be lost amid correct elaborations, like the soul of a poem or a song, evaporating through a rendering which is correct enough, yet in which the spirit, even if that alone, has been forgotten.

It is surely a striking thing to find this need of a pervading sentiment impressed upon the author of the first piece of religious art that ever was recognised by heaven.

For it is the mysterious all-pervading charm of such a dominant sentiment which marks the impassable difference between the lowliest work of art, and the highest piece of art-manufacture which is only a manufactured article.

And assuredly the recognition of this principle among a people whose ancient history shows but little interest in art, calls for some attention from those who regard the tabernacle itself as a fiction, and its details as elaborated in Babylonia, in the priestly interest (Kuenen, *Relig. of Israel*, ii. 148).

The problem of problems for all who deny the divinity of the Old Testament is to explain the curious position which its institutions are consistent in accepting. They rest on the authority of heaven, and yet they are not definitive, but provisional. They are always looking forward to another prophet like their founder, a new covenant better than the present one, a high priest after the order of a Canaanite enthroned at the right hand of Jehovah, a consecration for every pot in the city like that of the vessels in the temple (Deut. xviii. 15; Jer. xxxi. 31; Ps. cx. 1, 4; Zech. xiv. 20). And here, " in the priestly interest," is an avowal that the Divine habitation which they boast of is but the likeness and shadow of some Divine reality concealed. And these strange expectations have proved to be the most fruitful and energetic principles in their religion.

This very presence of the ideal is what will for ever make the highest natures quite certain that the visible universe is no mere resultant of clashing forces without a soul, but the genuine work of a Creator. The universe is charged throughout with the most powerful appeals to all that is artistic and vital within us; so that a cataract is more than water falling noisily, and the silence of midnight more than the absence of disturbance, and a snow mountain more than a storehouse to feed the torrents in summer, being also poems, appeals, revelations, whispers from a spirit, heard in the depth of ours.

Does any one, listening to Beethoven's funeral march, doubt the utterance of a soul, as distinct from clanging metal and vibrating chords? And the world has in it this mysterious witness to something more than heat and cold, moisture and drought: something which makes the difference between a well-filled granary and a field of grain rippling golden in the breeze. This is not a coercive argument for the hostile logic-monger: it is an appeal for the open heart. "He that hath ears to hear, let him hear."

To fill the tabernacle of Moses with spiritual meaning, the ideal tabernacle was revealed to him in the Mount of God.

Let us apply the same principle to human life. There also harmony and unity, a pervading sense of beauty and of soul, are not to be won by mere obedience to a mandate here and a prohibition there. Like Moses, it is not by labour according to specification that we may erect a shrine for deity. Those parables which tell of obedient toil would be sadly defective, therefore, without those which speak of love and joy, a supper, a Shepherd bearing home His sheep, a prodigal whose dull expectation of hired service is changed for investiture with the best robe and the gold ring, and welcome of dance and music.

How shall our lives be made thus harmonious, a spiritual poem and not a task, a chord vibrating under the musician's hand? How shall thought and word, desire and deed, become like the blended voices of river and wind and wood, a witness for the divine? Not by mere elaboration of detail (though correctness is a condition of all true art), but by a vision before us of the divine life, the Ideal, the pattern shown to all, and equally to be imitated (strange though it may seem) by peasant and prince, by woman and sage and child.

CHAPTER XXVI.

THE TABERNACLE.

EXODUS xxvi.

WE now come to examine the structure of the tabernacle for which the most essential furniture has been prepared.

Some confusion of thought exists, even among educated laymen, with regard to the arrangements of the temple; and this has led to similar confusion (to a less extent) concerning the corresponding parts of the tabernacle. "The temple" in which the Child Jesus was found, and into which Peter and John went up to pray, ought not to be confounded with that inner shrine, "the temple," in which it was the lot of the priest Zacharias to burn incense, and into which Judas, forgetful of all its sacredness in his anguish, hurled his money to the priests (Luke ii. 46; Acts iii. 3; Luke i. 9; Matt. xxvii. 5). Now, the former of these corresponded to "the court of the tabernacle," an enclosure open to the skies, and containing two important articles, the altar of burnt sacrifices and the laver. This was accessible to the nation, so that the sinner could lay his hand upon the head of his offering, and the priests could purify themselves before entering their own sacred place, the tabernacle proper, the shrine. But when we come to the structure itself, some attention is still necessary, in order to derive any clear notion from the description; nor can this easily be done by an English reader without substituting the Revised Version for the Authorised. He will then discover that we have a description, first of the " curtains of the tabernacle " (vers. 1-6), and then of other curtains which are not considered to belong to the tabernacle proper, but to "the tent over the tabernacle" (7-13), being no part of the rich ornamental interior, but only a protection spread above it; and over this again were two further screens from the weather (14), and finally, inside all, are "the boards of the tabernacle"—of which boards the two actual apartments were constructed (15-30)—and the veil which divided the Holy from the Most Holy Place (31-3).

"The curtains of the tabernacle" were ten, made of linen, of which every thread consisted of fine strands twisted together, "and blue and purple and scarlet," with cherubim not embroidered but woven into the fabric (1).

These curtains were sewn together, five and five, so as to make two great curtains, each slightly larger than forty-two feet by thirty, being twenty-eight cubits long by five times four cubits broad (2, 3). Finally these two were linked together, each having fifty loops for that purpose at corresponding places at the edge, which loops were bound together by fifty golden clasps (4-6). Thus, when the nation was about to march, they could easily be divided in the middle and then folded in the seams.

This costly fabric was regarded as part of the true tabernacle: why, then, do we find the outer curtains mentioned before the rest of the tabernacle proper is described?

Certainly because these rich curtains lie immediately underneath the coarser ones, and are to be considered along with "the tent" which covered all (7). This consisted of curtains of goats' hair, of the same size, and arranged in all respects like the others, except that their clasps were only bronze, and that the curtains were eleven in number, instead of ten, so that half a curtain was available to hang down over the back, and half was to be doubled back upon itself at the front of "the tabernacle," that is to say, the richer curtains underneath. The object of this is obvious: it was to bring the centre of the goatskin curtains over the edge of the linen ones, as tiles overlap each other, to shut out the rain at the joints. But this implies, what has been said already, that the curtains of the tabernacle should lie close to the curtains of the tent.

Over these again was an outer covering of rams' skins dyed red, and a covering of sealskins above all (14). This last, it is generally agreed, ran only along the top, like a ridge tile, to protect the vulnerable part of the roof. And now it has to be remembered that we are speaking of a real tent with sloping sides, not a flat cover laid upon the flat inner structure of boards, and certain to admit the rain. By calling attention to this fact, Mr. Fergusson succeeded in solving all the problems connected with the measurements of the tabernacle, and bringing order into what was little more than chaos before (*Smith's Bible Dict.*, "Temple").

The inner tabernacle was of acacia wood, which was the only timber of the sanctuary. Each board stood ten cubits high, and was fitted by tenons into two silver sockets, which probably formed a continuous base. Each of these contained a talent of silver, and was therefore more than eighty pounds weight; and they were probably to some extent sunk into the ground for a foundation (xxxviii. 27). There were twenty boards on each side; and as they were a cubit and a half broad, the length of the tabernacle was about forty-five feet (16-18). At the west end there were six boards (22), which, with the breadth of the two posts or boards for the corners (23-4) just gives ten cubits, or fifteen feet, for the width of it. Thus the length of the tabernacle was three times its breadth; and we know that in the Temple (where all the proportions were the same, the figures being doubled throughout) the subdividing veil was so hung as to make the inner shrine a perfect square, leaving the holy place twice as long as it was broad.

The posts were held in their places by wooden bars, which were overlaid with gold (as the boards also were, ver. 29) and fitted into golden rings. Four such bars, or bolts, ran along a portion of each side, and there was a fifth great bar which stretched along the whole forty-five feet from end to end. Thus the edifice was firmly held together; and the wealth of the material makes it likely that they were fixed on the inside, and formed a part of the ornament of the edifice (26-9).

When the two curtains were fastened together with clasps, they gave a length of sixty feet. But we have seen that the length of the boards when jointed together was only forty-five feet. This gives a projection of seven feet and a half (five cubits) for the front and rear of the tent beyond the tabernacle of boards; and when the great curtains were drawn tight, sloping from the ridge-pole fourteen cubits on each side, it has been shown (assuming a right-angle at the top) that they reached within five cubits of the ground, and extended five cubits beyond the sides, the same distance as at the front and rear. The next instructions concern the veil which divided the two chambers of the sanctuary. This was in all respects like "the curtain of the tabernacle," and similarly woven with cherubim. It was hung upon four pillars; and the even number seems to prove that there was no higher one in the centre, reaching to the roof—which seems to imply that there was a triangular opening above the veil, between the Holy and the Most Holy Place (31, 32).

But here a difficult question arises. There is no specific measurement of the point at which this subdividing veil was to stretch across the tent. The analogy of the Temple inclines us to believe that the Most Holy Place was a perfect cube, and the Holy Place twice as long as it was broad and high. There is evident allusion to this final shape of the Most Holy Place in the description of the New Jerusalem, of which the length and breadth and height were equal. And yet there is strong reason to suspect that this arrangement was not the primitive one. For Moses was ordered to stretch the veil underneath the golden clasps which bound together the two great curtains of the tabernacle (ver. 33). But these were certainly in the middle. How, then, could the veil make an unequal division below? Possibly fifteen feet square would have been too mean a space for the dimensions of the Most Holy Place, although the perfect cube became desirable, when the size was doubled.

A screen of the same rich material, but apparently not embroidered with cherubim, was to stretch across the door of the tent; but this was supported on five pillars instead of four, clearly that the central one might support the ridge-bar of the roof. And their sockets were of brass (vers. 36, 37).

The tabernacle, like the Temple, had its entrance on the east (ver. 22); and in the case of the Temple this was the more remarkable, because the city lay at the other side, and the worshippers had to pass round the shrine before they reached the front of it. The object was apparently to catch the warmth of the sun. For a somewhat similar reason, every pagan temple in the ancient world, with a few well-defined exceptions which are easily explained, also faced the east; and the worshippers, with their backs to the dawn, saw the first beams of the sun kindling their idol's face. The orientation of Christian churches is due to the custom which made the neophyte, standing at first in his familiar position westward, renounce the devil and all his works, and then, turning his back upon his idols, recite the creed with his face eastward.

What ideas would be suggested by this edifice to the worshipper will better be examined when we have examined also the external court.

CHAPTER XXVII.

THE OUTER COURT.

Exodus xxvii.

Before describing the tabernacle, its furniture was specified. And so, when giving instructions for the court of the tabernacle the altar has to be described: "Thou shalt make the altar of acacia wood." The definite article either implies that an altar was taken for granted, a thing of course; or else it points back to chap. xx. 24, which said "An altar of earth shalt thou make." Nor is the acacia wood of this altar at all inconsistent with that precept, it being really not an altar but an altar-case, and "hollow" (ver. 8)—an arrangement for holding the earth together, and preventing the feet of the priests from desecrating it. At each corner was a horn, of one piece with the framework, typical of the power which was there invoked, and practically useful, both to bind the sacrifice with cords, and also for the grasp of the fugitive, seeking sanctuary (Ps. cxviii. 27; 1 Kings i. 50). This arrangement is said to have been peculiar to Judaism. And as the altar was outside the tabernacle, and both symbolism and art prescribed simpler materials, it was overlaid with brass (vers. 1, 2). Of the same material were the vessels necessary for the treatment of the fire and blood (ver. 3). A network of brass protected the lower part of the altar; and at half the height a ledge projected, supported by this network, and probably wide enough to allow the priests to stand upon it when they ministered (vers. 4, 5). Hence we read that Aaron "came down from offering" (Lev. ix. 22). Lastly, there was the same arrangement of rings and staves to carry it as for the ark and the table (vers. 6, 7).

It will be noticed that the laver in this court, like the altar of incense within, is reserved for mention in a later chapter (xxx. 18) as being a subordinate feature in the arrangements.

The enclosure was a quadrangle of one hundred cubits by fifty; it was five cubits high, and each cubit may be taken as a foot and a half. The linen which enclosed it was upheld by pillars with sockets of brass; and one of the few additional facts to be gleaned from the detailed statement that all these directions were accurately carried out is that the heads of all the pillars were overlaid with silver (xxxviii. 17). The pillars were connected by rods (fillets) of silver, and a hanging of fine-twined linen was stretched by means of silver hooks (9-13). The entrance was twenty cubits wide, corresponding accurately to the width, not of the tabernacle, but of "the tent" as it has been described (reaching out five cubits farther on each side than the tabernacle), and it was closed by an embroidered curtain (14-17). This fence was drawn firmly into position and held there by brazen tent-pins; and we here incidentally learn that so was the tent itself (19).

[For verses 20, 21, see page 227.]

We are now in a position to ask what sentiment all these arrangements would inspire in the mind of the simple and somewhat superstitious worshippers.

Approaching it from outside, the linen enclosure (being seven feet and a half high) would conceal everything but the great roof of the tent, one uniform red, except for the sealskin covering along the summit. A gloomy and menacing prospect, broken possibly by some gleams, if the curtain of the gable were drawn back, from the gold with which every portion of the shrine within was plated.

So does the world outside look askance upon the Church, discerning a mysterious suggestion everywhere of sternness and awe, yet with flashes of strange splendour and affluence underneath the gloom.

In this place God is known to be: it is a tent, not really "of the congregation," but "of meeting" between Jehovah and His people: "the tent of meeting before the Lord, where I will meet with you, . . . and there I will meet with the children of Israel" (xxix. 42-3). And so the Israelite, though troubled by sin and fear, is attracted to the gate, and enters. Right in front stands the altar: this obtrudes itself before all else upon his attention: he must learn its lesson first of all. Especially will he feel that this is so if a sacrifice is now to be offered, since the official must go farther into the court to wash at the laver, and then return; so that a loss of graduated arrangement has been accepted in order to force the altar to the front. And he will soon learn that not only must every approach to the sacred things within be heralded by sacrifice upon this altar, but the blood of the victim must be carried as a passport into the shrine. Surely he remembers how the blood of the lamb saved his own life when the firstborn of Egypt died: he knows that it is written "The life (or soul) of the flesh is in the blood; and I have given it to you upon the altar to make atonement for your souls (or lives): for it is the blood that maketh atonement by reason of the life (or soul)" (Lev. xvii. 11).

No Hebrew could watch his fellow-sinner lay his hand on a victim's head, and confess his sin before the blow fell on it, without feeling that sin was being, in some mysterious sense, "borne" for him. The intricacies of our modern theology would not disturb him, but this is the sentiment by which the institutions of the tabernacle assuredly ministered comfort and hope to him. Strong would be his hope as he remembered that the service and its solace were not of human devising, that God had "given it to him upon the altar to make atonement for his soul."

Taking courage, therefore, the worshipper dares to lift up his eyes. And beyond the altar he sees a vision of dazzling magnificence. The inner roof, most unlike the sullen red of the exterior, is blazing with various colours, and embroidered with emblems of the mysterious creatures of the sky, winged, yet not utterly afar from human in their suggestiveness. Encompassed and looked down into by these is the tabernacle, all of gold. If the curtain is raised he sees a chamber which tells what the earth should be—a place of consecrated energies and resources, and of sacred illumination, the oil of God burning in the sevenfold vessel of the Church. Is this blessed place for him, and may he enter? Ah, no! and surely his heart would grow heavy with consciousness that reconciliation was not yet made perfect, when he learned that he must never approach the place where God had promised to meet with him.

Much less might he penetrate the awful chamber within, the true home of deity. There, he knows, is the record of the mind of God, the concentrated expression of what is comparatively easy to obey in act, but difficult beyond hope to love, to accept and to be conformed to. That record is therefore at once the revelation of God and the condemnation of His creature. Yet over this, he knows well, there is poised no dead image such as were then adored in Babylonian and Egyptian fanes, but a spiritual Presence, the glory of the invisible God. Nor was He to be thought of as in solitude, loveless, or else needing human love: above Him were the woven seraphim of the curtain, and on either side a seraph of beaten gold—types, it may be, of all the created life which He inhabits, or else pictures of His sinless creatures of the upper world. And yet this pure Being, by Whom the companionship of sinful man is so little needed, is there to meet with man; and is pleased not to look upon His violated law, but to command that a slab, inestimably precious, shall interpose between it and its Avenger. By whom, then, shall this most holy floor be trodden? By the official representative of him who gazes, and longs, and is excluded. He enters not without blood, which he is careful to sprinkle upon all the furniture, but chiefly and seven times upon the mercy-seat.

Thus every worshipper carries away a profound consciousness that he is utterly unworthy, and yet that his unworthiness has been expiated; that he is excluded, and yet that his priest, his representative, has been admitted, and therefore that he may hope. The Holy Ghost did not declare by sign that no way into the Holiest existed, but only that it was not yet made manifest. Not yet.

This leads us to think of the priest.

CHAPTER XXVIII.

"THE HOLY GARMENTS."

Exodus xxviii.

The tabernacle being complete, the priesthood has to be provided for. Its dignity is intimated by the command to Moses to bring his brother Aaron and his sons near to himself (clearly in rank, because the object is defined, "that he may minister unto Me"), and also by the direction to make "holy garments for glory and for beauty." But just as the furniture is treated before the shrine, and again before the court-yard, so the vestments are provided before the priesthood is itself discussed.

The holiness of the raiment implies that separation to office can be expressed by official robes in the Church as well as in the state; and their glory and beauty show that God, Who has clothed His creation with splendour and with loveliness, does not dissever religious feeling from artistic expression.

All that are wise-hearted in such work, being inspired by God as really, though not as profoundly, as if their task were to foretell the advent of Messiah, are to unite their labours upon these garments.

The order in the twenty-eighth chapter is perhaps that of their visible importance. But it will be clearer to describe them in the order in which they were put on.

Next the flesh all the priests were clad from the loins to the thighs in close-fitting linen: the indecency of many pagan rituals must be far from them, and this was a perpetual ordinance, "that they bear not iniquity and die" (xxviii. 42-3).

Over this was a tight-fitting "coat" (a shirt rather) of fine linen, white, but woven in a chequered pattern, without seam, like the robe of Jesus, and bound together with a girdle (39-43).

These garments were common to all the priests; but their "head-tires" differed from the impressive mitre of the high priest. The rest of the vestments in this chapter belong to him alone.

Over the "coat" he wore the flowing "robe of the ephod," all blue, little seen from the waist up, but uncovered thence to the feet, and surrounded at the hem with golden pomegranates, the emblem of fruitfulness, and with bells to enable the worshippers outside to follow the movements of their representative. He should die if this expression of his vicarious function were neglected (31-35).

Above this robe was the ephod itself—a kind of gorgeous jacket, made in two pieces which were joined at the shoulders, and bound together at the waist by a cunningly woven band, which was of the same piece. This ephod, like the curtains of the tabernacle, was of blue and purple and scarlet and fine-twined linen; but added to these were threads of gold, and we read, as if this were a novelty which needed to be explained, that they beat the gold into thin plates and then cut it into threads (xxxix. 3, xxviii. 6-8).

Upon the shoulders were two stones, rightly perhaps called onyx, and set in "ouches"—of filagree work, as the word seems to say. Upon them were engraven the names of the twelve tribes, the burden of whose sins and sorrows he should bear into the presence of his God, "for a memorial" (9-12).

Upon the ephod was the breastplate, fastened to it by rings and chains of twisted gold, made to fold over into a square, a span in measurement, and blazing with twelve gems, upon which were engraved, as upon the onyxes on the shoulders, the names of the twelve tribes. All attempts to derive edification from the nature of these jewels must be governed by the commonplace reflection that we cannot identify them; and many of the present names are incorrect. It is almost certain that neither topaz, sapphire, nor diamond could have been engraved, as these stones were, with the name of one of the twelve tribes (13-30).

"In the breastplate" (that is, evidently, between the folds as it was doubled), were placed those mysterious means of ascertaining the will of God, the Urim and the Thummim, the Lights and the Perfections; but of their nature, or of the manner in which they became significant, nothing can be said that is not pure conjecture (30).

Lastly, there was a mitre of white linen, and upon it was laced with blue cords a gold plate bearing the inscription "HOLY TO JEHOVAH" (36, 37).

No mention is made of shoes or sandals; and both from the commandment to Moses at the burning bush, and from history, it is certain that the priests officiated with their feet bare.

The picture thus completed has the clearest ethical significance. There is modesty, reverence, purity, innocence typified by whiteness, the grandeur of the office of intercession displayed in the rich colours and precious jewels by which that whiteness was relieved, sympathy expressed by the names of the people in the breastplate that heaved with every throb of his heart, responsibility confessed by the same names upon the shoulder, where the government was said to press like a load (Isa. ix. 6); and over all, at once the condition and the explanation of the rest, upon the seat of intelligence itself, the golden inscription on the forehead, "Holy to Jehovah."

Such was the import of the raiment of the high priest: let us see how it agrees with the nature of his office.

THE PRIESTHOOD.

What, then, are the central ideas connected with the institution of a priesthood?

Regarding it in the broadest way, and as a purely human institution, we may trace it back to the eternal conflict in the breast of man between two mighty tendencies—the thirst for God and the dread of Him, a strong instinct of approach and a repelling sense of unworthiness.

In every age and climate, man prays. If any curious inquirer into savage habits can point to the doubtful exception of a tribe seemingly without a ritual, he will not really show that religion is one with superstition; for they who are said to have escaped its grasp are never the most advanced and civilised among their fellows upon that account,—they are the most savage and debased, they are to humanity what the only people which has formally renounced God is fast becoming among the European races.

Certainly history cannot exhibit one community, progressive, energetic, and civilised, which did not feel that more was needful and might be had than its own resources could supply, and stretch aloft to a Supreme Being the hands which were so deft to handle the weapon and the tool. Certainly all experience proves that the foundations of national greatness are laid in national piety, so that the practical result of worship, and of the belief that God responds, has not been to dull the energies of man, but to inspire him with the self-respect befitting a confidant of deity, and to brace him for labours worthy of one who draws, from the sense of Divine favour, the hope of an infinite advance.

And yet, side by side with this spiritual gravitation, there has always been recoil and dread, such as was expressed when Moses hid his face because he was afraid to look upon God.

Now, it is not this apprehension, taken alone, which proves man to be a fallen creature: it is the combination of the dread of God with the desire of Him. Why should we shrink from our supreme Good, except as a sick man turns away from his natural food? He is in an unnatural and morbid state of body, and we of soul.

Thus divided between fear and attraction, man has fallen upon the device of commissioning some one to represent him before God. The priest on earth has come by the same road with so many other mediators—angel and demigod, saint and virgin.

At first it has been the secular chief of the family, tribe, or nation, who has seemed least unworthy to negotiate as well with heaven as with centres of interest upon earth. But by degrees the duty has everywhere been transferred into professional hands, patriarch and king recoiling, feeling the inconsistency of his earthly duties with these sacred ones, finding his hands to be too soiled and his heart too heavily weighted with sin for the tremendous Presence into which the family or the tribe would press him. And yet the union of the two functions might be the ideal; and the sigh of all truly enlightened hearts might be for a priest sitting upon his throne, a priest after the order of Melchizedek. But thus it came to pass that an official, a clique, perhaps a family, was chosen from among men in things pertaining to God, and the institution of the priesthood was perfected.

Now, this is the very process which is recognised in Scripture; for these two conflicting forces were altogether sound and right. Man ought to desire God, for Whom he was created, and Whose voice in the garden was once so welcome: but also he ought to shrink back from Him, afraid now, because he is conscious of his own nakedness, because he has eaten of the forbidden fruit.

Accordingly, as the nation is led out from Egypt, we find that its intercourse with heaven is at once real and indirect. The leader is virtually the priest as well, at whose intercession Amalek is vanquished and the sin of the golden calf is pardoned, who entered the presence of God and received the law upon their behalf, when they feared to hear His voice lest they should die, and by whose hand the blood of the covenant was sprinkled upon the people, when they had sworn to obey all that the Lord had said (xvii. 11, xxxii. 30, xx. 19, xxiv. 8).

Soon, however, the express command of God provided for an orthodox and edifying transfer of the priestly function from Moses to his brother Aaron. Some such division of duties between the secular chief and the religious priest would no doubt have come, in Israel as elsewhere, as soon as Moses disappeared; but it might have come after a very different fashion, associated with heresy and schism. Especially would it have been demanded why the family of Moses, if the chieftainship must pass away from it, could not retain the religious leadership. We know how cogent such a plea would have appeared; for, although the transfer was made publicly and by his own act, yet no sooner did the nation begin to split into tribal subdivisions, amid the confused efforts of each to conquer its own share of the inheritance, than we find the grandson of Moses securely establishing himself and his posterity in the apostate and semi-idolatrous worship of Shechem (Judg. xviii. 30, R. V.).

And why should not this illustrious family have been chosen?

Perhaps because it was so illustrious. A priesthood of that great line might seem to have earned its office, and to claim special access to God, like the heathen priests, by virtue of some special desert. Therefore the honour was transferred to the far less eminent line of Aaron, and that in the very hour when he was lending his help to the first great apostasy, the type of the many idolatries into which Israel was yet to fall. So, too, the whole tribe of Levi was in some sense consecrated, not for its merit, but because, through the sin of its founder, it lacked a place and share among its brethren, being divided in Jacob and scattered in Israel by reason of the massacre of Shechem (Gen. xlix. 7).

Thus the nation, conscious of its failure to enjoy intercourse with heaven, found an authorised expression for its various and conflicting emotions. It was not worthy to commune with God, and yet it could not rest without Him. Therefore a spokesman, a representative, an ambassador, was given to it. But he was chosen after such a fashion as to shut out any suspicion that the merit of Levi had prevailed where that of Israel at large had failed. It was not because Levi executed vengeance on the idolaters that he was chosen, for the choice was already made, and made in the person of Aaron, who was so far from blameless in that offence.

And perhaps this is the distinguishing peculiarity of the Jewish priest among others: that he was chosen from among his brethren, and simply as one of them; so that while his office was a proof of their exclusion, it was also a kind of sacrament of their future admission, because he was their brother and their envoy, and entered not as outshining but as representing them, their forerunner for them entering. The almond rod of Aaron was dry and barren as the rest, until the miraculous power of God invested it with blossoms and fruit.

Throughout the ritual, the utmost care was taken to inculcate this double lesson of the ministry. Into the Holy Place, whence the people were excluded, a whole family could enter. But there was an inner shrine, whither only the high priest might penetrate, thus reducing the family to a level with the nation; " the Holy Ghost this signifying, that the way into the Holy Place hath not yet been made manifest, while as the first tabernacle (the outer shrine—ver. 6) was yet standing" (Heb. ix. 8).

Thus the people felt a deeper awe, a broader separation. And yet, when the sole and only representative who was left to them entered that " shrine, remote, occult, untrod," they saw that the way was not wholly barred against human footsteps: the lesson suggested was far from being that of absolute despair,—it was, as the Epistle to the Hebrews said, " Not yet." The prophet Zechariah foresaw a time when the bells of the horses should bear the same consecrating legend that shone upon the forehead of the priest: HOLY UNTO THE LORD (Zech. xiv. 20).

It is important to observe that the only book of the New Testament in which the priesthood is discussed dwells quite as largely upon the difference as upon the likeness between the Aaronic and the Messianic priest. The latter offered but one Sacrifice for sins, the former offered for himself before doing so for the people (Heb. x. 12). The latter was a royal Priest, and of the order of a Canaanite (Heb. vii. 1-4), thus breaking down all the old system at one long-predicted blow—for if He were on earth He could not so much as be a priest at all (Heb. viii. 4)—and with it all the old racial monopolies, all class distinctions, being Himself of a tribe as to which Moses spake nothing concerning priests (Heb. vii. 14). Every priest standeth, but this priest hath for ever sat down, and even at the right hand of God (Heb. x. 11, 12).

In one sense this priesthood belongs to Christ alone. In another sense it belongs to all who are made one with Him, and therefore a kingly priesthood unto God. But nowhere in the New Testament is the name by which He is designated bestowed upon any earthly minister by virtue of his office. The presbyter is never called *sacerdos*. And perhaps the heaviest blow ever dealt to popular theology was the misapplying of the New Testament epithet (elder, presbyter or priest) to designate the sacerdotal functions of the Old Testament, and those of Christ which they foreshadowed. It is not the word "priest" that is at fault, but some other word for the Old Testament official which is lacking, and cannot now be supplied.

CHAPTER XXIX.

THE CONSECRATION SERVICES.

EXODUS xxix.

THE priest being now selected, and his raiment so provided as that it shall speak of his office and its glory, there remains his consecration.

In our day there is a disposition to make light of the formal setting apart of men and things for sacred uses. If God, we are asked, has called one to special service, is not that enough? What more can earth do to commission the chosen of the sky? But the plain answer which we ought to have the courage to return is that this is not at all enough. For God Himself had already called Paul and Barnabas when He said to such folk as Simeon Niger and Lucius of Cyrene and Manaen, "Separate Me Barnabas and Saul for the work whereunto I have called them" (Acts xiii. 1-4). And these obscure people not only laid their hands upon the great apostle, but actually sent him forth. Now, if he was not exempted from the need of an orderly commission by the marvellous circumstances of his call, by his apostleship not of man, by the explicit announcement that he was a chosen vessel to bear the sacred name before kings and peoples, it is startling to be told of some shallow modern evangelist, who works for no Church and submits to no discipline, that he can dispense with the sanction of human ordination because he is so clearly sent of heaven.

The example of the Old Testament will no doubt be brushed aside as if the religion which Jesus learned and honoured were a mere human superstition. Or else it would be natural to ask, Is it because the offices and functions of Judaism were more formal, more perfunctory than ours, that a greater spiritual grace went with their appointments than with the laying on of hands in the Christian Church, a rite so clearly sanctioned in the New Testament?

It is written of Joshua that Moses was to lay his hands upon him, because already the Spirit was in him; and of Timothy that he had unfeigned faith, and that prophecies went before concerning him (Num. xxvii. 18; 1 Tim. i. 18; 2 Tim. i. 5). But in neither dispensation did special grace fail to accompany the official separation to sacred office: Joshua was full of the Spirit of Wisdom, for Moses had laid his hands upon him; and Timothy was bidden to stir into flame that gift of God which was in him through the laying on of the Apostle's hands (Deut. xxxiv. 9; 2 Tim. i. 6).

Accordingly there is great stress laid upon the orderly institution of the priest. And yet, to make it plain that his authority is only " for his brethren," Moses, the chief of the nation, is to officiate throughout the ceremony of consecration. He it is who shall offer the sacrifices upon the altar, and sprinkle the blood, not upon the first day only, but throughout the ceremonies of the week.

In the first place certain victims must be held in readiness—a bullock and two rams; and with these must be brought in one basket unleavened bread, and unleavened cakes made with oil, and unleavened wafers on which oil is poured. Then, at the door of the tent of the meeting of man with God, a ceremonial washing must follow, in a laver yet to be provided. Here the assertion that purity is needed, and that it is not inherent, is too plain to be dwelt upon.

But such details as the assuming of the existence of a laver, for which no directions have yet been given (and presently also of the anointing oil, the composition of which is still untold), deserve notice. They are much more in the manner of one who is working out a plan, seen already by his mental vision, but of which only the salient and essential parts have been as yet stated, than of any priest of the latter days, who would first have completed his catalogue of the furniture, and only then have described the ceremonies in which he was accustomed to see all this apparatus take its appointed place.

What we actually find is quite natural to a creative imagination, striking out the broad design of the work and its uses first, and then filling in the outlines. It is not natural at a time when freshness and inspiration have departed, and squared timber, as we are told, has taken the place of the living tree.

The priest, when cleansed, was next to be clad in his robes of office, with the mitre on his head, and upon the mitre the golden plate, with its inscription, which is here called, as the culminating object in all his rich array, " the holy crown " (ver. 6).

And then he was to be anointed. Now, the use of oil, in the ceremony of investiture to office, is peculiar to revealed religion. And whether we suppose it to refer to the oil in a lamp, invisible, yet the secret source of all its illuminating power, or to that refreshment and renovated strength bestowed upon a weary traveller when his head is anointed with oil, in either case it expresses the grand doctrine of revealed religion—that no office may be filled in one's own strength, but that the inspiring help of God is offered, as surely as responsibilities are imposed. " The Spirit of the Lord God is upon Me, because He hath anointed Me."

With these three ceremonies—ablution, robing and anointing—the first and most personal section of the ritual ended. And now began a course of sacrifices to God, advancing from the humblest expression of sin, and appeal to heaven to overlook the unworthiness of its servant, to that which best exhibited conscious acceptance, enjoyment of privilege, admission to a feast with God. The bullock was a sin-offering: the word is literally *sin*, and occurs more than once in the double sense: " let him offer for his *sin* which he hath *sinned* a young bullock . . . for a *sin-(offering)* " (Lev. iv. 3, v. 6, etc). And this is the explanation of the verse which has perplexed so many: " He made Him to be sin for us, Who knew no sin " (2 Cor. v. 21). The doctrine that pardon comes not by a cheap and painless overlooking of transgression, as a thing indifferent, but by the transfer of its consequences to a victim divinely chosen, could not easily find clearer expression than in this word. And it was surely a sobering experience, and a wholesome one, when Aaron, in his glorious robes, sparkling with gems, and bearing on his forehead the legend of his holy calling, laid his hand, beside those of his children and successors, upon the doomed creature which was made sin for him. The gesture meant confession, acceptance of the appointed expiation, submission to be freed from guilt by a method so humiliating and admonitory. There was no undue exaltation in the mind of any priest whose heart went with this " remembrance of sins."

The bullock was immediately slain at the door of " the tent of meeting "; and to show that the shedding of his blood was an essential part of the rite, part of it was put with the finger on the horns of the altar, and the remainder was poured out at the base. Only then might the fat and the kidney be burned upon the altar; but it is never said of any sin-offering, as presently of the burnt-offering and the peace-offerings, that it is " a sweet savour before Jehovah " (vers. 18, 25)—a phrase which is only once extended to a trespass-offering for a purely unconscious lapse (Lev. iv. 31). The sin-offering is, at the best, a deplorable necessity. And therefore the notion of a gift, welcome to Jehovah, is carefully shut out: no portion of such an offering may go to maintain the priests: all must be burned " with fire without the camp; it is a sin-offering " (ver. 14). Rightly does the Epistle to the Hebrews emphasise this fact: " The bodies of those beasts whose blood is brought into the Holy Place . . . as an offering for sin " are burned without the camp. The bodies of other sacrifices were not reckoned unfit for food.* And so there is a striking example of humility, as well as an instructive coincidence, in the fact that Jesus suffered without the gate, being the true Sin-offering, " that He might sanctify the people through His own blood " (Heb. xiii. 11, 12).

Thus, by sacrifice for sin, the priest is rendered fit to offer up to God the symbol of a devoted life. Again, therefore, the hands of Aaron and his sons are laid upon the head of the ram, because they come to offer what represents themselves in another sense than that of expiation—a sweet savour now, an offering made by fire unto

---

* Neither, it must be added, were the bodies of certain sin-offerings of the lower grade, and in which the priest was not personally concerned (Lev. x. 17, etc.).

Jehovah (ver. 18). And to show that it is perfectly acceptable to Him, the whole ram shall be burnt upon the altar, and not now without the camp: "it is a burnt-offering unto the Lord." Such is the appointed way of God with man—first expiation, then devotion.

The third animal was a "peace-offering" (ver. 28). This is wrongly explained to mean an offering by which peace is made, for then there could be no meaning in what went before. It is the offering of one who is now in a state of peace with God, and who is therefore himself, in many cases, allowed to partake of what he brings. But on this occasion some quite peculiar ceremonies were introduced, and the ram is called by a strange name—"the ram of consecration." When Aaron and his sons have again declared their connection with the animal by laying their hands upon it, it is slain. And then the blood is applied to the tip of their right ear, the thumb of their right hand, and the great toe of their right foot, that the ear may hearken, and the best energies obey, and their life become as that of the consecrated animal, their bodies being presented, a living sacrifice, holy, acceptable to God. Then the same blood, with the oil which spoke of heavenly anointing, was sprinkled upon them and upon their official robes, and all were hallowed. Then the fattest and richest parts of the animal were taken, with a loaf, a cake, and a wafer from the basket, and placed in the hands of Aaron and his sons. This was their formal investiture with official rights; although not yet performing service, it was as priests that they received these; and their hands, swayed by those of Moses, solemnly waved them before the Lord in formal presentation, after which the pieces were consumed by fire. The breast was likewise waved, and became the perpetual property of Aaron and his sons—although on this occasion it passed from their hands to be the portion of Moses, who officiated. The remainder of the flesh, seethed in a holy place, belonged to Aaron and his sons. No stranger (of another family) might eat it, and what was left until morning should be consumed by fire, that is to say, destroyed in a manner absolutely clean, seeing no corruption.

For seven days this rite of consecration was repeated; and every day the altar also was cleansed, rendering it most holy, so that whatever touched it was holy.

Thus the people saw their representative and chief purified, accepted, and devoted. Thenceforward, when they too brought their offerings, and beheld them presented (in person or through his subordinates) by the high priest with holiness emblazoned upon his brow, they gained hope, and even assurance, since one so consecrated was bidden to present their intercession; and sometimes they saw him pass into secret places of mysterious sanctity, bearing their tribal name on his shoulder and his bosom, while the chime of golden bells announced his movements, ministering there for them.

But the nation as a whole, with which this historical book is chiefly interested, saw in the high priest the means of continually rendering to God the service of its loyalty. Every day began and closed with the burnt-offering of a lamb of the first year, along with a meal-offering of fine flour and oil, and a drink-offering of wine. This would be a sweet savour unto God, not after the carnal fashion in which sceptics have interpreted the words, but in the same sense in which the wicked are a smoke in His nostrils from a continually burning fire.

And where this offering was made, the Omnipresent would meet with them. There He would convey His mind to His priest. There also He would meet with all the people—not occasionally, as amid the more impressive but less tolerable splendours of Sinai, but to dwell among them and be their God. And they should know that all this was true, and also that for this He led them out of Egypt: "I am Jehovah their God."

CHAPTER XXX.

INCENSE.

EXODUS xxx. 1-10.

THE altar of incense was not mentioned when the tent of meeting was being prepared and furnished. But when, in the Divine idea, this is done, when all is ready for the intercourse of God and man, and the priest and the daily victims are provided for, something more than this formal routine of offerings might yet be sought for. This material worship of the senses, this round of splendour and of tragedy, this blaze of gold and gold-encrusted timber, these curtains embroidered in bright colours, and ministers glowing with gems, this blood and fire upon the altar, this worldly sanctuary,—was it all? Or should it not do as nature ever does, which seems to stretch its hands out into the impalpable, and to grow all but spiritual while we gaze; so that the mountain folds itself in vapour, and the ocean in mist and foam, and the rugged stem of the tree is arrayed in fineness of quivering frondage, and it may be of tinted blossom, and around it breathes a subtle fragrance, the most impalpable existence known to sense? Fragrance indeed is matter passing into the immaterial, it is the sigh of the sensuous for the spiritual state of being, it is an aspiration.

And therefore an altar, smaller than that of burnt-offering, but much more precious, being plated all around and on the top with gold (a "golden altar") (xxxix. 38), is now to be prepared, on which incense of sweet spices should be burned whenever a burnt-offering spoke of human devotion, and especially when the daily lamb was offered, every morning and every night.

This altar occupied a significant position. Of necessity it was without the Most Holy Place, or else it would have been practically inaccessible; and yet it was spiritually in the closest connection with the presence of God within. The Epistle to the Hebrews reckons it among the furniture of the inner shrine* (Heb. ix. 4), close to the veil of which it stood, and within which its burning odours made their sweetness palpable. In the temple of Solomon it was "the altar that belonged to the oracle" (1 Kings vi. 22). In Leviticus (xvi. 12) incense was connected especially with that spot in the

---

* For it is incredible that, in a catalogue of furniture which included Aaron's rod and the pot of manna, this altar should be omitted, and "a golden censer," elsewhere unheard of, substituted. The gloss is too evidently an endeavour to get rid of a difficulty But in idea and suggestion this altar belonged to the Most Holy. That shrine "had" it, though it actually stood outside.

Most Holy Place which best expressed the grace that it appealed to, and "the cloud of incense" was to "cover the mercy-seat." Therefore Moses was bidden to put this altar "before the veil that is by the ark of the testimony, before the mercy-seat" (ver. 6).

It can never have been difficult to see the meaning of the rite for which this altar was provided. When Zacharias burned incense the multitude stood without, praying. The incense in the vial of the angel of the Apocalypse was the prayers of the saints (Luke i. 10; Rev. viii. 3). And, long before, when the Psalmist thought of the priest approaching the veil which concealed the Supreme Presence, and there kindling precious spices until their aromatic breath became a silent plea within, it seemed to him that his own heart was even such an altar, whence the perfumed flame of holy longings might be wafted into the presence of his God, and he whispered, "Let my prayer be set forth before Thee as incense" (Ps. cxli. 2).

Such being the import of the type, we need not wonder that it was a perpetual ordinance in their generations, nor yet that no strange perfume might be offered, but only what was prescribed by God. The admixture with prayer of any human, self-asserting, intrusive element, is this unlawful fragrance. It is rhetoric in the leader of extempore prayer; studied inflexions in the conductor of liturgical service; animal excitement, or sentimental pensiveness, or assent which is merely vocal, among the worshippers. It is whatever professes to be prayer, and is not that but a substitute. And formalism is an empty censer.

But, however earnest and pure may seem to be the breathing of the soul to God, something unworthy mingles with what is best in man. The very altar of incense needs to have an atonement made for it once in the year throughout their generations with the blood of the sin-offering of atonement. The prayer of every heart which knows its own secret will be this:

"Forgive what seemed my sin in me,
What seemed my worth since I began;
For merit lives from man to man
And not from man, O Lord, to Thee."

THE CENSUS.

Exodus xxx. 11-16.

Moses by Divine command was soon to number Israel, and thus to lay the foundation for its organisation upon the march. A census was not, therefore, supposed to be presumptuous or sinful in itself; it was the vain-glory of David's census which was culpable.

But the honour of being numbered among the people of God should awaken a sense of unworthiness. Men had reason to fear lest the enrolment of such as they were in the host of God should produce a pestilence to sweep out the unclean from among the righteous. At least they must make some practical admission of their demerit. And therefore every man of twenty years who passed over unto them that were numbered (it is a picturesque glimpse that is here given into the method of enrolment) should offer for his soul a ransom of half a shekel after the shekel of the sanctuary. And because it was a ransom, the tribute was the same for all; the poor might not bring less, nor the rich more. Here was a grand assertion of the equality of all souls in the eyes of God—a seed which long ages might overlook, but which was sure to fructify in its appointed time.

For indeed the madness of modern levelling systems is only their attempt to level down instead of up, their dream that absolute equality can be obtained, or being obtained can be made a blessing, by the envious demolition of all that is lofty, and not by all together claiming the supreme elevation, the measure of the stature of manhood in Jesus Christ.

It is not in any *phalanstère* of Fourier or Harmony Hall of Owen, that mankind will ever learn to break a common bread and drink of a common cup; it is at the table of a common Lord.

And so this first assertion of the equality of man was given to those who all ate the same spiritual meat and drank the same spiritual drink.

This half-shekel gradually became an annual impost, levied for the great expenses of the Temple. Thus Joash made a proclamation throughout Judah and Jerusalem, "to bring in for the Lord the tax that Moses, the servant of God, laid upon Israel in the wilderness" (2 Chron. xxiv. 9).

And it was the claim for this impost, too rashly conceded by Peter with regard to his Master, which led Jesus to distinguish clearly between His own relation to God and that of others, even of the chosen race.

He paid no ransom for His soul. He was a Son, in a sense in which no other, even of the Jews, could claim to be so. Now, the kings of the earth did not levy tribute from their sons; so that, if Christ paid, it was not to fulfil a duty, but to avoid being an offence. And God Himself would provide, directly and miraculously, what He did not demand from Jesus. Therefore it was that, on this one occasion and no other, Christ Who sought figs when hungry, and when athirst asked water at alien hands, met His own personal requirement by a miracle, as if to protest in deed, as in word, against any burden from such an obligation as Peter's rashness had conceded.

And yet, with that marvellous condescension which shone most brightly when He most asserted His prerogative, He admitted Peter also to a share in this miraculous redemption-money, as He admits us all to a share in His glory in the skies. Is it not He only Who can redeem His brother, and give to God a ransom for him?

It is the silver thus levied which was used in the construction of the sanctuary. All the other materials were free-will offerings; but even as the entire tabernacle was based upon the ponderous sockets into which the boards were fitted, made of the silver of this tax, so do all our glad and willing services depend upon this fundamental truth, that we are unworthy even to be reckoned His, that we owe before we can bestow, that we are only allowed to offer any gift because He is so merciful in His demand. Israel gladly brought much more than was needed of all things precious. But first, as an absolutely imperative ransom, God demanded from each soul the half of three shillings and sevenpence.

THE LAVER.

Exodus xxx. 17-21.

For the cleansing of various sacrifices, but especially for the ceremonial washing of the priests, a laver of brass was to be made, and placed upon a separate base, the more easily to be emptied and replenished.

We have seen already that although its actual use preceded that of the altar, yet the other stood in front of it, as if to assert, to the very eyes of all men, that sacrifice precedes purification. But the use of the laver was not by the man as man, but by the priest as mediator. In his office he represented the absolute purity of Christ. And therefore it was a capital offence to enter the tabernacle or to burn a sacrifice without first having washed the hands and feet. At his inauguration, the whole person of the priest was bathed, and thenceforth he needed not save to remove the stains of contact with the world.

When the laver was actually made, an interesting fact was recorded about its materials: "He made the laver of brass, and the base of it of brass, of the mirrors of the serving-women which served at the door of the tent of meeting" (xxxviii. 8). Thus their instruments of personal adornment were applied to further a personal preparation of a more solemn kind, like the ointment with which a penitent woman anointed the feet of Jesus. There is a fitness which ought to be considered in the direction of our gifts; not as a matter of duty, but of good taste and charm. And thus also they continually saw the monument of their self-sacrifice. There is an innocent satisfaction, far indeed from vanity, when one looks at his own work for God.

THE ANOINTING OIL AND THE INCENSE.

Exodus xxx. 22-38.

We have already seen the meaning of the anointing oil and of the incense.

But we have further to remark that their ingredients were accurately prescribed, that they were to be the best and rarest of their kind, and that special skill was demanded in their preparation.

Such was the natural dictate of reverence in preparing the symbols of God's grace to man, and of man's appeal to God.

With the type of grace should be anointed the tent and the ark, and the table of shewbread and the candlestick, with all their implements, and the altar of incense, and the altar of burnt sacrifice and the laver. All the import of every portion of the Temple worship could be realized only by the outpouring of the Spirit of Grace.

It was added that this should be a holy anointing oil, not to be made, much less used, for common purposes, on pain of death. The same was enacted of the incense which should burn before Jehovah: "according to the composition thereof ye shall not make for yourselves; it shall be unto thee holy for the Lord: whosoever shall make like unto that, to smell thereto, he shall be cut off from his people."

And this was meant to teach reverence. One might urge that the spices and frankincense and salt were not in themselves sacred: there was no consecrating efficacy in their combination, no charm or spell in the union of these, more than of any other drugs. Why, then, should they be denied to culture? Why should her resources be thus restricted? Does any one suppose that such arguments belong peculiarly to the New Testament spirit, or that the saints of the older dispensation had any superstitious views about these ingredients? If it was through such notions that they abstained from vulgarising its use, then they were on the way to paganism, through a materialised worship.

But in truth they knew as well as we that gums were only gums, just as they knew that the Most High dwelleth not in temples made with hands. And yet they were bidden to reverence both the shrine and the apparatus of His worship, for their own sakes, for the solemnity and sobriety of their feelings, not because God would be a loser if they did otherwise. And we may well ask ourselves, in these latter days, whether the constant proposal to secularise religious buildings, revenues, endowments, and seasons does really indicate greater religious freedom, or only greater freedom from religious control.

And we may be sure that a light treatment of sacred subjects and sacred words is a very dangerous symptom: it is not the words and subjects alone that are being secularised, but also our own souls.

There is in our time a curious tendency among men of letters to use holy things for a mere perfume, that literature may "smell thereto." A novelist has chosen for the title of a story "Just as I am." An innocent and graceful poet has seen a smile,—

> "'Twas such a smile,
> Aaron's twelve jewels seemed to mix
> With the lamps of the golden candlesticks."

Another is bolder, and sings of the war of love,—

> "In the great battle when the hosts are met
> On Armageddon's plain, with spears beset."

Another thinks of Mazzini as the

> "Dear lord and leader, at whose hand
> The first days and the last days stand."

and again as he who

> "Said, when all Time's sea was foam,
> 'Let there be Rome,' and there was Rome."

And Victor Hugo did not shrink from describing, and that with a strange and scandalous ignorance of the original incidents, the crucifixion by Louis Napoleon of the Christ of nations.

Now, Scripture is literature, besides being a great deal more; and, as such, it is absurd to object to all allusions to it in other literature. Yet the tendency of which these extracts are examples is not merely toward allusion, but desecration of solemn and sacred thoughts: it is the conversion of incense into perfumery.

There is another development of the same tendency, by no means modern, noted by the prophet when he complains that the message of God has become as the "very lovely song of one who hath a pleasant voice and playeth well on an instrument." Wherever divine service is only appreciated in so far as it is "well rendered," as rich music or stately enunciation charms the ear, and the surroundings are æsthetic,—wherever the gospel is heard with enjoyment only of the eloquence or controversial skill of its rendering, wherever religion is reduced by the cultivated to a thrill or to a solace, or by the Salvationist to a riot or a romp, wherever Isaiah and the Psalms are only admired as poetry, and heaven is only thought of as a languid and sentimental solace amid wearying cares,—there again is a making of the sacred balms to smell thereto.

And as often as a minister of God finds in his holy office a mere outlet for his natural gifts of rhetoric or of administration, he also is tempted to commit this crime.

CHAPTER XXXI.

BEZALEEL AND AHOLIAB.

Exodus xxxi. 1-18.

NEXT after this marking off so sharply of the holy from the profane, this consecration of men to special service, this protection of sacred unguents and sacred gums from secular use, we come upon a passage curiously contrasted, yet not really antagonistic to the last, of marvellous practical wisdom, and well calculated to make a nation wise and great.

The Lord announces that He has called by name Bezaleel, the son of Uri, and has filled him with the Spirit of God. To what sacred office, then, is he called? Simply to be a supreme craftsman, the rarest of artisans. This also is a divine gift. "I have filled him with the Spirit of God in wisdom and in understanding and in knowledge and in all manner of workmanship, to devise cunning works, to work in gold and in silver and in brass and in cutting of stones for setting, and in carving of wood, to work in all manner of workmanship,"—that is to say, of manual dexterity. With him God had appointed Aholiab; "and in the hearts of all the wisehearted I have put wisdom." Thus should be fitly made the tabernacle and its furniture, and the finely wrought garments, and the anointing oil and the incense.

So then it appears that the Holy Spirit of God is to be recognised in the work of the carpenter and the jeweller, the apothecary and the tailor. Probably we object to such a statement, so baldly put. But inspiration does not object. Moses told the children of Israel that Jehovah had filled Bezaleel with the Spirit of God, and also Aholiab, for the work "of the engraver . . . and of the embroiderer . . . and of the weaver" (xxxv. 31, 35).

It is quite clear that we must cease to think of the Divine Spirit as inspiring only prayers and hymns and sermons. All that is good and beautiful and wise in human art is the gift of God. We feel that the supreme Artist is audible in the wind among the pines; but is man left to himself when he marshals into more sublime significance the voices of the wind among the organ tubes? At sunrise and sunset we feel that

"On the beautiful mountains the pictures of God are hung;"

but is there no revelation of glory and of freshness in other pictures? Once the assertion that a great masterpiece was "inspired" was a clear recognition of the central fire at which all genius lights its lamp: now, alas! it has become little more than a sceptical assumption that Isaiah and Milton are much upon a level. But the doctrine of this passage is the divinity of all endowment; it is quite another thing to claim Divine authority for a given product sprung from the free human being who is so richly crowned and gifted.

Thus far we have smoothed our way by speaking only of poetry, painting, music—things which really compete with nature in their spiritual suggestiveness. But Moses spoke of the robe-maker, the embroiderer, the weaver, and the perfumer.

Nevertheless, the one is carried with the other. Where shall we draw the line, for example, in architecture or in ironwork? And there is another consideration which must not be overlooked. God is assuredly in the growth of humanity, in the progress of true civilisation—in all, the recognition of which makes history philosophical. It is not only the saints who feel themselves to be the instruments of a Greater than they. Cromwell and Bismarck, Columbus, Raleigh and Drake, William the Silent and William the Third, felt it. Mr. Stanley has told us how the consciousness that he was being used grew up in him, not through fanaticism but by slow experience, groping his way through the gloom of Central Africa.

But none will deny that one of the greatest factors in modern history is its industrial development. Is there, then, no sacredness here?

The doctrine of Scripture is not that man is a tool, but that he is responsible for vast gifts, which come directly from heaven—that every good gift is from above, that it was God Himself Who planted in Paradise the tree of knowledge.

Nor would anything do more to restrain the passions, to calm the impulses, and to elevate the self-respect of modern life, to call back its energies from the base competition for gold, and make our industries what dreamers persuade themselves that the mediæval industries were, than a quick and general perception of what is meant when faculty goes by such names as talent, endowment, gift—of the glory of its use, the tragedy of its defilement. Many persons, indeed, reject this doctrine because they cannot believe that man has power to abase so high a thing so sadly. But what, then, do they think of the human body?

What connection is there between all this and the reiteration of the law of the Sabbath? Not merely that the moral law is now made a civic statute as well, for this had been done already (xxiii. 12). But, as our Lord has taught us that a Jew on the Sabbath was free to perform works of mercy, it might easily be supposed lawful, and even meritorious, to hasten forward the construction of the place where God would meet His people. But He who said "I will have mercy and not sacrifice" said also that to obey was better than sacrifice. Accordingly this caution closes the long story of plans and preparations. And when Moses called the people to the work, his first words were to repeat it (xxxv. 2).

Finally, there was given to Moses the deposit for which so noble a shrine was planned—the two tables of the law, miraculously produced.

If any one, without supposing that they were literally written with a literal finger, conceives that this was the meaning conveyed to a Hebrew by the expression "written with the finger of God," he entirely misses the Hebrew mode of thought, which habitually connects the Lord with an arm, with a chariot, with a bow made naked, with a tent and curtains, without the slightest taint of materialism in its conception. Did not the magicians, failing to imitate the third plague, say " This is the finger of a God " ? Did not Jesus Himself " cast out devils by the finger of God " ? (Ex. viii. 19; Luke xi. 20).

CHAPTER XXXII.

THE GOLDEN CALF.

Exodus xxxii.

While God was thus providing for Israel, what had Israel done with God? They had grown weary of waiting: had despaired of and slighted their heroic leader (" this Moses, the man that brought us up,") had demanded gods, or a god, at the hand of Aaron, and had so far carried him with them or coerced him that he thought it a stroke of policy to save them from breaking the first commandment by joining them in a breach of the second, and by infecting " a feast to Jehovah " with the licentious " play " of paganism. At the beginning, the only fitness attributed to Aaron was that " he can speak well." But the plastic and impressible temperament of a gifted speaker does not favour tenacity of will in danger. Demosthenes and Cicero, and Savonarola, the most eloquent of the reformers, illustrate the tendency of such genius to be daunted by visible perils.

God now rejects them because the covenant is violated. As Jesus spoke no longer of " My Father's house," but " your house, left unto you desolate," so the Lord said to Moses, " thy people which thou broughtest up."

But what are we to think of the proposal to destroy them, and to make of Moses a great nation?

We are to learn from it the solemn reality of intercession, the power of man with God, Who says not that He will destroy them, but that He will destroy them if left alone. Who can tell, at any moment, what calamities the intercession of the Church is averting from the world or from the nation?

The first prayer of Moses is brief and intense; there is passionate appeal, care for the Divine honour, remembrance of the saintly dead for whose sake the living might yet be spared, and absolute forgetfulness of self. Already the family of Aaron had been preferred to his, but the prospect of monopolising the Divine predestination has no charm for this faithful and patriotic heart. No sooner has the immediate destruction been arrested than he hastens to check the apostates, makes them exhibit the madness of their idolatry by drinking the water in which the dust of their pulverised god was strewn; receives the abject apology of Aaron, thoroughly spirit-broken and demoralised; and finding the sons of Levi faithful, sends them to the slaughter of three thousand men. Yet this is he who said " O Lord, why is Thy wrath hot against Thy people?" He himself felt it needful to cut deep, in mercy, and doubtless in wrath as well, for true affection is not limp and nerveless: it is like the ocean in its depth, and also in its tempests. And the stern action of the Levites appeared to him almost an omen; it was their " consecration," the beginning of their priestly service.

Again he returns to intercede; and if his prayer must fail, then his own part in life is over: let him too perish among the rest. For this is evidently what he means and says: he has not quite anticipated the spirit of Christ in Paul willing to be anathema for his brethren (Rom. ix. 3), nor has the idea of a vicarious human sacrifice been suggested to him by the institutions of the sanctuary. Yet how gladly would he have died for his people, who made request that he might die among them!

How nobly he foreshadows, not indeed the Christian doctrine, but the love of Christ Who died for man, Who from the Mount of Transfiguration, as Moses from Sinai, came down (while Peter would have lingered) to bear the sins of His brethren! How superior He is to the Christian hymn which pronounces nothing worth a thought, except how to make my own election sure.

CHAPTER XXXIII.

PREVAILING INTERCESSION.

Exodus xxxiii.

At this stage the first concession is announced. Moses shall lead the people to their rest, and God will send an angel with him.

We have seen that the original promise of a great Angel in whom was the Divine Presence was full of encouragement and privilege (xxiii. 20). No unbiassed reader can suppose that it is the sending of this same Angel of the Presence which now expresses the absence of God, or that He Who then would not pardon their transgression " because My Name is in Him " is now sent because God, if He were in the midst of them for a moment, would consume them. Nor when Moses passionately pleads against this degradation, and is heard in this thing also, can the answer " My Presence shall go with thee " be merely the repetition of those evil tidings. Yet it was the Angel of His Presence Who saved them. All this has been already treated, and what we are now to learn is that the faithful and sublime urgency of Moses did really save Israel from degradation and a lower covenant.

It was during the progress of this mediation that Moses, distracted by a double anxiety—afraid to absent himself from his wayward followers, equally afraid to be so long withdrawn from the presence of God as the descending of Sinai and returning thither would involve—made a noble adventure of faith. Inspired by the conception of the tabernacle, he took a tent, " his tent," and pitched it outside the camp, to express the estrangement of the people, and this he called the Tent of the Meeting (with God), but in the Hebrew it is never called the Tabernacle. And God did condescend to meet him there. The mystic cloud guarded the door against presumptuous intrusion, and all the people, who previously wist not what had become of him, had now to confess the majesty of his communion, and they worshipped every man at his tent door.

It would seem that the anxious vigilance of Moses caused him to pass to and fro between the tent and the camp, " but his minister, Joshua the son of Nun, departed not out of the tent."

The dread crisis in the history of the nation was now almost over. God had said, "My Presence shall go with thee, and I will give thee rest,"—a phrase which the lowly Jesus thought it no presumption to appropriate, saying, "I will give you rest," as He also appropriated the office of the Shepherd, the benevolence of the Physician, the tenderness of the Bridegroom, and the glory of the King and the Judge, all of which belonged to God.

But Moses is not content merely to be secure, for it is natural that he who best loves man should also best love God. Therefore he pleads against the least withdrawal of the Presence: he cannot rest until repeatedly assured that God will indeed go with him; he speaks as if there were no "grace" but that. There are many people now who think it a better proof of being religious to feel either anxious or comforted about their own salvation, their election, and their going to heaven. And these would do wisely to consider how it comes to pass that the Bible first taught men to love and to follow God, and afterwards revealed to them the mysteries of the inner life and of eternity.

CHAPTER XXXIV.

THE VISION OF GOD.

EXODUS xxxiv.

IT was when God had most graciously assured Moses of His affection, that he ventured, in so brief a cry that it is almost a gasp of longing, to ask, "Show me, I pray Thee, Thy glory" (xxxiii. 18).

We have seen how nobly this petition and the answer condemn all anthropomorphic misunderstandings of what had already been revealed; and also how it exemplifies the great law, that they who see most of God know best how much is still unrevealed. The elders saw the God of Israel and did eat and drink: Moses was led from the bush to the flaming top of Sinai, and thence to the tent where the pillar of cloud was as a sentinel; but the secret remained unseen, the longing unsatisfied, and the nearest approach to the Beatific Vision reached by him with whom God spake face to face as with a friend, was to be hidden in a cleft of the rock, to be aware of an awful Shadow, and to hear the Voice of the Unseen.

It was a fit time for the proclamation which was then made. When the people had been righteously punished and yet graciously forgiven, the name of the Self-Existent expanded and grew clearer,—"Jehovah, Jehovah, a God full of compassion and gracious, slow to anger and plenteous in mercy and truth, keeping mercy for thousands, forgiving iniquity and transgression and sin, and that will by no means clear the guilty, visiting the iniquity of the fathers upon the children and upon the children's children, upon the third and upon the fourth generation." And as Moses made haste and bowed himself, it is affecting to hear him again pleading for that beloved Presence which even yet he can scarce believe to be restored, and instead of claiming any separation through his fidelity and his honours, praying "Pardon our iniquity and our sin, and take us for Thine inheritance" (xxxiv. 10).

Thereupon the covenant is given, as if newly, but without requiring its actual re-enactment; and certain of the former precepts are rehearsed, chiefly such as would guard against a relapse into idolatry when they entered the good land where God would bestow on them prosperity and conquest.

As Moses had broken the former tablets, the task was imposed on him of hewing out the slabs on which God renewed His awful sanction of the Decalogue, the fundamental statutes of the nation. And they who had failed to endure his former absence, were required to be patient while he tarried again upon the mountain, forty days and nights.

With his return a strange incident is connected. Unknown by himself, the "skin of his face shone by reason of His speaking with him," and Aaron and the people recoiled until he called to them. And thenceforth he lived a strange and isolated life. At each new interview the glory of his countenance was renewed, and when he conveyed his revelation to the people, they beheld the lofty sanction, the light of God upon his face. Then he veiled his face until next he approached his God, so that none might see what changes came there, and whether—as St. Paul seems to teach us—the lustre gradually waned.

His revelation, the apostle argues, was like this occasional and fading gleam, while the moral glory of the Christian system has no concealments: it uses great frankness; there is nothing withdrawn, no veil upon the face. Nor is it given to one alone to behold as in a mirror the glory of the Lord, and to share its lustre. We all, with face unveiled, share this experience of the deliverer (2 Cor. iii. 12, 18).

But the incident itself is most instructive. Since he had already spent an equal time with God, yet no such results had followed, it seems that we receive what we are adapted to receive, not straitened in Him but in our own capabilities; and as Moses, after his vehemence of intercession, his sublimity of self-negation, and his knowledge of the greater name of God, received new lustre from the unchangeable Fountain of light, so does all true service and earnest aspiration, while it approaches God, elevate and glorify humanity.

We learn also something of the exaltation of which matter is capable. We who have seen coarse bulb and soil and rain transmuted by the sunshine into radiance of bloom and subtlety of perfume, who have seen plain faces illuminated from within until they were almost angelic,—may we not hope for something great and rare for ourselves, and the beloved who are gone, as we muse upon the profound word, "It is raised a spiritual body"?

And again we learn that the best religious attainment is the least self-conscious: Moses wist not that the skin of his face shone.

CHAPTERS XXXV—XL.

THE CONCLUSION.

THE remainder of the narrative sets forth in terms almost identical with the directions already given, the manner in which the Divine injunctions were obeyed. The people, purified in heart by danger, chastisement, and shame, brought much more than was required. A quarter of a million would poorly represent the value of the shrine in which, at the last, Moses and Aaron approached their God, while the cloud covered the tent and the glory filled the tabernacle, and Moses failed to overcome his awe and enter.

Thenceforth the cloud was the guide of their halting and their march. Many a time they grieved their God in the wilderness, yet the cloud was on the tabernacle by day, and there was fire therein by night, throughout all their journeyings.

That cloud is seen no longer; but One has said, " Lo, I am with you all the days." If the presence is less material, it is because we ought to be more spiritual.

Looking back upon the story, we can discern more clearly what was asserted when we began —the forming and training of a nation.

They are called from shameful servitude by the devotion of a patriot and a hero, who has learned in failure and exile the difference between self-confidence and faith. The new name of God, and His remembrance of their fathers, inspire them at the same time with awe and hope and nationality. They see the hollowness of earthly force, and of superstitious worships, in the abasement and ruin of Egypt. They are taught by the Paschal sacrifice to confess that the Divine favour is a gift and not a right, that their lives also are justly forfeited. The overthrow of Pharaoh's army and the passage of the Sea brings them into a new and utterly strange life, in an atmosphere and amid scenes well calculated to expand and deepen their emotions, to develop their sense of freedom and self-respect, and yet to oblige them to depend wholly on their God. Privation at Marah chastens them. The attack of Amalek introduces them to war, and forbids their dependence to sink into abject softness. The awful scene of Horeb burns and brands his littleness into man. The covenant shows them that, however little in themselves, they may enter into communion with the Eternal. It also crushes out what is selfish and individualising, by making them feel the superiority of what they all share over anything that is peculiar to one of them. The Decalogue reveals a holiness at once simple and profound, and forms a type of character such as will make any nation great. The sacrificial system tells them at once of the pardon and the heinousness of sin. Religion is both exalted above the world and infused into it, so that all is consecrated. The priesthood and the shrine tell them of sin and pardon, exclusion and hope; but that hope is a common heritage, which none may appropriate without his brother.

The especial sanctity of a sacred calling is balanced by an immediate assertion of the sacredness of toil, and the Divine Spirit is recognised even in the gift of handicraft.

A tragic and shameful failure teaches them, more painfully than any symbolic system of curtains and secret chambers, how little fitted they are for the immediate intercourse of heaven. And yet the ever-present cloud, and the shrine in the heart of their encampment, assure them that God is with them of a truth.

Could any better system be imagined by which to convert a slavish and superstitious multitude into a nation at once humble and pure and gallant—a nation of brothers and of worshippers, chastened by a genuine sense of ill desert and of responsibility, and yet braced and fired by the conviction of an exalted destiny?

To do this, and also to lead mankind to liberty, to rescue them from sensuous worship, and prepare them for a system yet more spiritual, to teach the human race that life is not repose but warfare, pilgrimage and aspiration, and to sow the seeds of beliefs and expectations which only an atoning Mediator and an Incarnate God could satisfy, this was the meaning of the Exodus.

The Book of Leviticus

By The Reverend S. H. Kellogg, D.D.

DOCTOR KELLOGG was a missionary in India of the American Presbyterian Board, pastor of the Third Presbyterian Church, Pittsburgh, Pennsylvania, and of St. James Square Presbyterian Church, Toronto. He then returned to India to undertake the revision of the Hindi translation of the Old Testament. He wrote "A Grammar of the Hindi Language," "The Light of Asia and the Light of the World," "A Handbook on Comparative Religion," and other works.

The Book of Leviticus exemplifies the origin and growth of Law. What is written about Holiness and Sacrifice, although in a ritualistic setting, is of permanent value. Doctor Kellogg's exposition deals with the elaborate arrangements for Tabernacle worship, in accordance with the method of allegorical interpretation sanctioned by the Epistle to the Hebrews. He brings out some of the essential spiritual truths of Christianity found in germ in this ancient Code.

CONTENTS

PART I.

THE TABERNACLE WORSHIP.
(Lev. i.-x., xvi.)

	PAGE
CHAPTER I. Introductory,	237
CHAPTER II. Sacrifice: The Burnt-Offering,	243
CHAPTER III. The Burnt-Offering (*Concluded*),	248
CHAPTER IV. The Meal-Offering,	252
CHAPTER V. The Peace-Offering,	257
CHAPTER VI. The Sin-Offering,	264
CHAPTER VII. The Ritual of the Sin-Offering,	270
CHAPTER VIII. The Guilt-Offering,	276
CHAPTER IX. The Priests' Portions,	281
CHAPTER X. The Consecration of Aaron and His Sons, and of the Tabernacle,	282
CHAPTER XI. The Inauguration of the Tabernacle Service,	292
CHAPTER XII. Nadab's and Abihu's "Strange Fire,"	296
CHAPTER XIII. The Great Day of Atonement,	301

PART II.

THE LAW OF THE DAILY LIFE.
(Lev. xi.-xv.; xvii.-xxv.)

	PAGE
CHAPTER XIV. Clean and Unclean Animals, and Defilement by Dead Bodies,	306
CHAPTER XV. Of the Uncleanness of Issues,	313
CHAPTER XVI. The Uncleanness of Child-Bearing,	315
CHAPTER XVII. The Uncleanness of Leprosy,	319
CHAPTER XVIII. The Cleansing of the Leper,	323
CHAPTER XIX. Holiness in Eating,	329
CHAPTER XX. The Law of Holiness: Chastity,	332
CHAPTER XXI. The Law of Holiness (*Concluded*),	335
CHAPTER XXII. Penal Sanctions,	342
CHAPTER XXIII. The Law of Priestly Holiness,	345
CHAPTER XXIV. The Set Feasts of the Lord,	349
CHAPTER XXV. The Holy Light and the Shew-Bread: the Blasphemer's End,	356
CHAPTER XXVI. The Sabbatic Year and the Jubilee,	359

PART III.

CONCLUSION AND APPENDIX.
(Lev. xxvi., xxvii.)

CHAPTER XXVII. The Promises and Threats of the Covenant,	367
CHAPTER XXVIII. Concerning Vows,	372

THE BOOK OF LEVITICUS

BY THE REV. S. H. KELLOGG, D. D.

PART I.

THE TABERNACLE WORSHIP.

LEVITICUS i.-x.-xvi.

SECTION 1. The law of the offerings: i.-vi.
SECTION 2. The Institution of the Tabernacle Service: vii.-x.
(1) The Consecration of the Priesthood: vii.
(2) The Induction of the Priesthood: ix., x.
SECTION 3. The day of Atonement: xvi.

CHAPTER I.

INTRODUCTORY.

"And the Lord called unto Moses, and spake unto him out of the tent of meeting."—LEVITICUS i. 1.

PERHAPS no book in the Bible presents to the ordinary reader so many and peculiar difficulties as the book of Leviticus. Even of those who devoutly believe, as they were taught in their childhood, that, like all the other books contained in the Holy Scriptures, it is to be received throughout with unquestioning faith as the very Word of God, a large number will frankly own in a discouraged way that this is with them merely a matter of belief, which their personal experience in reading the book has for the most part failed to sustain; and that for them so to see through symbol and ritual as to get much spiritual profit from such reading has been quite impossible.

A larger class, while by no means denying or doubting the original Divine authority of this book, yet suppose that the elaborate ritual of the Levitical law, with its multiplied, minute prescriptions regarding matters religious and secular, since the Mosaic dispensation has now long passed away, neither has nor can have any living relation to present-day questions of Christian belief and practice; and so, under this impression, they very naturally trouble themselves little with a book which, if they are right, can now only be of special interest to the religious antiquarian.

Others, again, while sharing this feeling, also confess to a great difficulty which they feel in believing that many of the commands of this law can ever have been really given by inspiration from God. The extreme severity of some of the laws, and what seems to them to be the arbitrary and even puerile character of other prescriptions, appear to them to be irreconcilable, in the one case, with the mercy, in the other, with the dignity and majesty, of the Divine Being.

With a smaller, but, it is to be feared, an increasing number, this feeling, either of indifference or of doubt, regarding the book of Leviticus, is further strengthened by their knowledge of the fact that in our day its Mosaic origin and inspired authority are strenuously denied by a large number of eminent scholars, upon grounds which they claim to be strictly scientific. And if such Christians do not know enough to decide for themselves on its merits the question thus raised, they at least know enough to have a very uncomfortable doubt whether an intelligent Christian has any longer a right to regard the book as in any true sense the Word of God; and —what is still more serious—they feel that the question is of such a nature that it is impossible for any one who is not a specialist in Hebrew and the higher criticism to reach any well-grounded and settled conviction, one way or the other, on the subject. Such persons, of course, have little to do with this book. If the Word of God is indeed there, it cannot reach them.

With such mental conditions so widely prevailing, some words regarding the origin, authority, purpose, and use of this book of Leviticus seem to be a necessary preliminary to its profitable exposition.

THE ORIGIN AND AUTHORITY OF LEVITICUS.

As to the origin and authority of this book, the first verse presents a very formal and explicit statement: "The Lord called unto Moses, and spake unto him." These words evidently contain by necessary implication two affirmations: first, that the legislation which immediately follows is of Mosaic origin: "The Lord spake unto *Moses;*" and, secondly, that it was not the product merely of the mind of Moses, but came to him, in the first instance, as a revelation from Jehovah: "*Jehovah* spake unto Moses." And although it is quite true that the words in this first verse strictly refer only to that section of the book which immediately follows, yet, inasmuch as the same or a like formula is used repeatedly before successive sections,—in all, no less than fifty-six times in the twenty-seven chapters,—these words may with perfect fairness be regarded as expressing a claim respecting these two points, which covers the entire book.

We must not, indeed, put more into these words than is truly there. They simply and only declare the Mosaic origin and the inspired authority of the legislation which the book contains. They say nothing as to whether or not Moses wrote every word of this book himself; or whether the Spirit of God directed and inspired other persons, in Moses' time or afterward, to commit this Mosaic law to writing. They give us no hint as to when the various sections which make up the book were combined into their present literary form, whether by Moses himself, as is the traditional view, or by men of God in a later day. As to these and other matters of secondary importance which might be named, the book records no statement. The words used in the text, and similar expressions used elsewhere, simply and only declare the legislation to be of Mosaic origin and of inspired authority. Only, be it observed, so much as this they do affirm in the most direct and uncompromising manner.

It is of great importance to note all this: for in the heat of theological discussion the issue is too often misapprehended on both sides. The real question, and, as every one knows, the burning Biblical question of the day, is precisely this, whether the claim this book contains, thus exactly defined, is true or false.

A certain school of critics, comprising many of the greatest learning, and of undoubted honesty of intention, assures the Church and the world that a strictly scientific criticism compels one to the conclusion that this claim, even as thus sharply limited and defined, is, to use plain words, not true; that an enlightened scholarship must acknowledge that Moses had little or nothing to do with what we find in this book; that, in fact, it did not originate till nearly a thousand years later, when, after the Babylonian captivity, certain Jewish priests, desirous of magnifying their authority with the people, fell on the happy expedient of writing this book of Leviticus, together with certain other parts of the Pentateuch, and then, to give the work a prestige and authority which on its own merits or over their own names it could not have had, delivered it to their countrymen as nearly a thousand years old, the work of their great lawgiver. And, strangest of all, they not only did this, but were so successful in imposing this forgery upon the whole nation that history records not even an expressed suspicion of a single person, until modern times, of its non-Mosaic origin; that is, they succeeded in persuading the whole people of Israel that a law which they had themselves just promulgated had been in existence among them for nearly ten centuries, the very work of Moses, when, in reality, it was quite a new thing.

Astonishing and even incredible as all this may seem to the uninitiated, substantially this theory is held by many of the Biblical scholars of our day as presenting the essential facts of the case; and the discovery of these supposed facts we are called upon to admire as one of the chief literary triumphs of modern critical scholarship!

Now the average Christian, whether minister or layman, though intelligent enough in ordinary matters of human knowledge, or even a well-educated man, is not, and cannot be, a specialist in Hebrew and in the higher criticism. What is he then to do when such a theory is presented to him as endorsed by scholars of the highest ability and the most extensive learning? Must we, then, all learn Hebrew and study this higher criticism before we can be permitted to have any well-justified and decided opinion whether this book, this law of Leviticus, be the Word of God or a forgery? We think not. There are certain considerations, quite level to the understanding of every one; certain facts, which are accepted as such by the most eminent scholars, which ought to be quite sufficient for the maintenance and the abundant confirmation of our faith in this book of Leviticus as the very Word of God to Moses.

In the first place, it is to be observed that if any theory which denies the Mosaic origin and the inspired authority of this book be true, then the fifty-six assertions of such origin and authority which the book contains are unqualifiedly false. Further, however any may seek to disguise the issue with words, if in fact this Levitical ritual and code of laws came into existence only after the Babylonian captivity and in the way suggested, then the book of Leviticus can by no possibility be the Word of God in any sense, but is a forgery and a fraud. Surely this needs no demonstration. "The Lord spake unto Moses," reads, for instance, this first verse; "The Lord did *not* speak these things unto Moses," answer these critics; "they were invented by certain unscrupulous priests centuries afterwards." Such is the unavoidable issue.

Now who shall arbitrate in these matters? who shall settle these questions for the great multitude of believers who know nothing of Hebrew criticism, and who, although they may not well understand much that is in this book, have yet hitherto accepted it with reverent faith as being what it professes to be, the very Word of God through Moses? To whom, indeed, can we refer such a question as this for decision but to Jesus Christ of Nazareth, our Lord and Saviour, confessed of all believers to be in verity the only-begotten Son of God from the bosom of the Father? For He declared that "the Father showed unto Him," the Son, "all things that He Himself did;" He will therefore be sure to know the truth of this matter, sure to know the Word of His Father from the word of man, if He will but speak.

And He has spoken on this matter, He, the Son of God. What was the common belief of the Jews in the time of our Lord as to the Mosaic origin and Divine authority of this book, as of all the Pentateuch, every one knows. Not a living man disputes the statement made by a recent writer on this subject, that "previous to the Christian era, there are no traces of a second opinion" on this question; the book "was universally ascribed to Moses." Now, that Jesus Christ shared and repeatedly endorsed this belief of His contemporaries should be perfectly clear to any ordinary reader of the Gospels.

The facts as to His testimony, in brief, are these. As to the Pentateuch in general, He called it (Luke xxiv. 44) "the law of Moses;" and, as regards its authority, He declared it to be such that "till heaven and earth pass away, one jot or one tittle shall in no wise pass away from the law, till all be fulfilled" (Matt. v. 18). Could this be truly said of this book of Leviticus, which is undoubtedly included in this term, "the law," if it were not the Word of God, but a forgery, so that its fifty-six affirmations of its Mosaic origin and inspired authority were false? Again, Christ declared that Moses in his "writings" wrote of Him,—a statement, which, it should be observed, imputes to Moses foreknowledge, and therefore supernatural inspiration; and further said that faith in Himself was so connected with faith in Moses, that if the Jews had believed Moses, they would have also believed Him (John v. 46, 47). Is it conceivable that Christ should have spoken thus, if the "writings" referred to had been forgeries?

But not only did our Lord thus endorse the Pentateuch in general, but also, on several occasions, the Mosaic origin and inspired authority of Leviticus in particular. Thus, when He healed the lepers (Matt. viii. 4) He sent them to the priests on the ground that Moses had commanded this in such cases. But such a command is found only in this book of Leviticus (xiv. 3-10). Again, in justifying His disciples for plucking the ears of corn on the Sabbath day, He adduces the example of David, who ate the shew-bread when he was an hungered, "which was not lawful for him to eat, but only for the priests" (Matt. xii. 4); thus referring to a law which is only found in Leviticus (xxiv. 9). But the citation was only pertinent on the assumption that He regarded the prohibition of the shew-bread as having the same inspired authority as the obligation of the Sabbath. In John vii. 32, again, He refers to Moses as having renewed the ordinance of circumcision, which at the first had been given to Abraham; and, as usual, assumes the Divine authority of the command as thus given. But this renewal of the ordinance of circumcision is recorded only in Leviticus (xii. 3). Yet once more, rebuking the Pharisees for their ingenious justification of the hard-hearted neglect of parents by undutiful children, He reminds them that Moses had said that he who cursed father or mother should be put to death; a law which is only found in the so-called priest-code, Exod. xxi. 17 and Lev. xx. 9. Further, He is so far from merely assuming the truth of the Jewish opinion for the sake of an argument, that He formally declares this law, equally with the fifth commandment, to be "a commandment of God," which they by their tradition had made void (Matt. xiv. 3-6).

One would suppose that it had been impossible to avoid the inference from all this, that our Lord believed, and intended to be understood as teaching, that the law of Leviticus was, in a true sense, of Mosaic origin, and of inspired, and therefore infallible, authority.

We are in no way concerned, indeed,—nor is it essential to the argument,—to press this testimony of Christ as proving more than the very least which the words fairly imply. For instance, nothing in His words, as we read them, any more than in the language of Leviticus itself, excludes the supposition that in the preparation of the law, Moses, like the Apostle Paul, may have had co-labourers or amanuenses, such as Aaron, Eleazar, Joshua, or others, whose several parts of the work might then have been issued under his endorsement and authority; so that Christ's testimony is in no wise irreconcilable with the fact of differences of style, or with the evidence of different documents, if any think that they discover this, in the book.*

We are willing to go further, and add that in the testimony of our Lord we find nothing which declares against the possibility of one or more redactions or revisions of the laws of Leviticus in post-Mosaic times, by one or more *inspired* men; as, *e. g.*, by Ezra, described (Ezra vii. 6) as "a ready scribe in the law of Moses, which the Lord, the God of Israel, had given;" to whom also ancient Jewish tradition attributes the final settlement of the Old Testament canon down to his time. Hence no words of Christ touch the question as to when the book of Leviticus received its present form, in respect of the order of its chapters, sections, and verses. This is a matter of quite secondary importance, and may be settled any way without prejudice to the Mosaic origin and authority of the laws it contains.

Neither, in the last place, do the words of our Lord, carefully weighed, of necessity exclude even the possibility that such persons, acting under Divine direction and inspiration, may have first reduced some parts of the law given by Moses to writing;* or even, as an extreme supposition, may have entered here and there, under the unerring guidance of the Holy Ghost, prescriptions which, although new as to the letter, were none the less truly Mosaic, in that by necessary implication they were logically involved in the original code.†

We do not indeed here argue either for or against any of these suppositions, which were apart from the scope of the present work. We are only concerned here to remark that Christ has not incontrovertibly settled these questions. These things may be true or not true; the decision of such matters properly belongs to the literary critics. But decide them as one will, it will still remain true that the law is "the law of Moses," given by revelation from God.

So much as this, however, is certain. Whatsoever modifications may conceivably have passed upon the text, all work of this kind was done, as all agree, long before the time of our Lord; and the text to which He refers as of Mosaic origin and of inspired authority, was therefore essentially the text of Leviticus as we have it to-day. We are thus compelled to insist that whatever modifications may have been made in the original Levitical law, they cannot have been, according to the testimony of our Lord, such as in any way conflicted with His affirmation of its Mosaic origin and its inspired authority. They can thus, at the very utmost, only have been, as suggested, in the way of legitimate logical development and application to successive circumstances, of the Levitical law as originally given to Moses; and that, too, under the administration of a priesthood endowed with the possession of the Urim and Thummim, so as to give such official deliverances, whenever required, the sanction of inerrant Divine authority, binding on the conscience as from God. Here, at least, surely, Christ by His testimony has placed an immovable limitation upon the speculations of the critics.

And yet there are those who admit the facts as to Christ's testimony, and nevertheless claim that without any prejudice to the absolute truthfulness of our Lord, we may suppose that in speaking as He did, with regard to the law of Leviticus, He merely conformed to the common usage of the Jews, without intending thereby to endorse their opinion; any more than, when, conforming to the ordinary mode of speech, He spoke of the sun as rising and setting, He meant thereby to be understood as endorsing the common opinion of men of that time that the sun actually passed round the earth every twenty-

---

* "Genesis may be made up of various documents, and yet have been compiled by Moses; and the same thing is possible, even in the later books of the Pentateuch. If these could be successfully partitioned among different writers, on the score of variety in literary execution, why may not these have been engaged jointly with Moses himself in preparing each his appointed portion, and the whole have been finally reduced by Moses to its present form? . . . Why might not these continue their work, and record what occurred after Moses was taken away?"—Professor W. H. Green, *Schaff-Herzog Encyclopædia*; article, "The Pentateuch."

* "If it be proven that a record was committed to writing at a comparatively late date, it does not necessarily follow that the essential part has not been accurately handed down."—Professor Strack, *Ibid*.

† Something like this seems to have been the final position of the late Professor Delitzsch, who said: "We hold firmly that Moses laid the foundation of this codification" (of the "priest-code" of Leviticus, etc.), "but it was continued in the post-Mosaic period within the priesthood, to whom was entrusted the transmission, interpretation, and administration of the law. We admit this willingly; and even the participation of Ezra in this codification in itself furnishes no stumbling block for us. For it is not inconceivable that laws which until then had been handed down orally were fixed by him in writing to secure their judicial authority and execution. The most important thing for us is the historico-traditional character of the Pentateuchal legislation, and especially the occasions for (the laws) and the fundamental arrangements in the history of the times. That which we cannot be persuaded to admit is that the so-called Priestly Code is the work of the free invention of the latest date, which takes on the artificial appearance of ancient history."—*The Presbyterian Review*, July, 1882; article, "Delitzsch on the Origin and Composition of the Pentateuch," p. 578.

four hours. To which it is enough to reply that this illustration, which has so often been used in this argument, is not relevant to the case before us. For not only did our Lord use language which implied the truth of the Jewish belief regarding the origin and authority of the Mosaic law, but He formally teaches it; and—what is of still more moment—He rests the obligation of certain duties upon the fact that this law of Leviticus was a revelation from God to Moses for the children of Israel. But if the supposed facts, upon which He bases His argument in such cases, are, in reality, not facts, then His argument becomes null and void. How, for instance, is it possible to explain away the words in which He appeals to one of the laws of Exodus and Leviticus (Matt. xv. 3-6) as being *not* a Jewish opinion, but, instead, in explicit contrast with the traditions of the Rabbis, "a commandment of God"? Was this expression merely "an accommodation" to the mistaken notions of the Jews? If so, then what becomes of His argument?

Others, again, feeling the force of this, and yet sincerely and earnestly desiring to maintain above possible impeachment the perfect truthfulness of Christ, still assuming that the Jews were mistaken, and admitting that, if so, our Lord must have shared their error, take another line of argument. They remind us of what, however mysterious, cannot be denied, that our Lord, in virtue of His incarnation, came under certain limitations in knowledge; and then urge that without any prejudice to His character we may suppose that, not only with regard to the time of His advent and kingdom (Matt. xxiv. 36), but also with respect to the authorship and the Divine authority of this book of Leviticus, He may have shared in the ignorance and error of His countrymen.

But, surely, the fact of Christ's limitation in knowledge cannot be pressed so far as the argument of such requires, without by logical necessity nullifying Christ's mission and authority as a religious teacher. For it is certain that according to His own word, and the universal belief of Christians, the supreme object of Christ's mission was to reveal unto men through His life and teachings, and especially through His death upon the cross, the Father; and it is certain that He claimed to have, in order to this end, perfect knowledge of the Father. But how could this most essential claim of His be justified, and how could He be competent to give unto men a perfect and inerrant knowledge of the Father, if the ignorance of His humiliation was so great that He was unable to distinguish from His Father's Word a book which, by the hypothesis, was not the Word of the Father, but an ingenious and successful forgery of certain crafty post-exilian priests?

It is thus certain that Jesus must have known whether the Pentateuch, and, in particular, this book of Leviticus, was the Word of God or not; certain also that, if the Word of God, it could not have been a forgery; and equally certain that Jesus could not have intended in what He said on this subject to accommodate His speech to a common error of the people, without thereby endorsing their belief. It thus follows that critics of the radical school referred to are directly at issue with the testimony of Christ regarding this book. It is of immense consequence that Christians should see this issue clearly. While Jesus taught in various ways that Leviticus contains a law given by revelation from God to Moses, these teach that it is a priestly forgery of the days after Ezra. Both cannot be right; and if the latter are in the right, then— we speak with all possible deliberation and reverence—Jesus Christ was mistaken, and was therefore unable even to tell us with inerrant certainty whether this or that is the Word of God or not. But if this is so, then how can we escape the final inference that His claim to have a perfect knowledge of the Father must have been an error; His claim to be the incarnate Son of God, therefore, a false pretension, and Christianity, a delusion, so that mankind has in Him no Saviour?

But against so fatal a conclusion stands the great established fact of the resurrection of Jesus Christ from the dead; whereby He was with power declared to be the Son of God, so that we may know that His word on this, as on all subjects where He has spoken, settles controversy, and is a sufficient ground of faith; while it imposes upon all speculations of men, literary or philosophical, eternal and irremovable limitations.

Let no one think that the case, as regards the issue at stake, has been above stated too strongly. One could not well go beyond the often cited words of Kuenen on this subject: "We must either cast aside as worthless our dearly bought scientific method, or we must for ever cease to acknowledge the authority of the New Testament in the domain of the exegesis of the Old." With good reason does another scholar exclaim at these words, "The Master must not be heard as a witness! We treat our criminals with more respect." So then stands the question this day which this first verse of Leviticus brings before us: In which have we more confidence? in literary critics, like a Kuenen or Wellhausen, or in Jesus Christ? Which is the more likely to know with certainty whether the law of Leviticus is a revelation from God or not?

The devout Christian, who through the grace of the crucified and risen Lord "of whom Moses, in the law, and the prophets did write," and who has "tasted the good word of God," will not long hesitate for an answer. He will not indeed, if wise, timidly or fanatically decry all literary investigation of the Scriptures; but he will insist that the critic shall ever hold his reason in reverent subjection to the Lord Jesus on all points where the Lord has spoken. Such everywhere will heartily endorse and rejoice in those admirable words of the late venerable Professor Delitzsch; words which stand almost as of his last solemn testament:—"The theology of glory, which prides itself upon being its own highest authority, bewitches even those who had seemed proof against its enchantments; and the theology of the Cross, which holds Divine folly to be wiser than men, is regarded as an unscientific lagging behind the steps of progress. . . But the faith which I professed in my first sermons, . . . remains mine to-day, undiminished in strength, and immeasurably higher than all earthly knowledge. Even if in many Biblical questions I have to oppose the traditional opinion, certainly my opposition rests on this side of the gulf, on the side of the theology of the Cross, of grace, of miracles! . . . By this banner let us stand; folding ourselves in it, let us die!"* To

---

* *The Expositor*, January, 1889; article, "The Old Theology and the New," pp. 54, 55.

which truly noble words every true Christian may well say, Amen!

We then stand without fear with Jesus Christ in our view of the origin and authority of the book of Leviticus.

The Occasion and Order of Leviticus.

Before proceeding to the exposition of this book, a few words need to be said regarding its occasion and plan, and its object and present use.

The opening words of the book, "And the Lord said," connect it in the closest manner with the preceding book of Exodus, at the contents of which we have therefore to glance for a moment. The kingdom of God, rejected by corporate humanity in the founding of the Babylonian world-power, but continuing on earth in a few still loyal souls in the line of Abraham and his seed, at last, according to promise, had been formally and visibly re-established on earth at Mount Sinai. The fundamental law of the kingdom, contained in the ten commandments and certain applications of the same, had been delivered in what is called the Book of the Covenant, amid thunders and lightnings, at the holy mount. Israel had solemnly entered into covenant with God on this basis, saying, "All these things will we do and be obedient," and the covenant had been sealed by the solemn sprinkling of blood.

This being done, Jehovah now issued commandment for the building of the tabernacle or "tent of meeting," where He might manifest His glory and from time to time communicate His will to Israel. As mediators between Him and the people, the priesthood was appointed, their vestments and duties prescribed. All this having been done as ordered, the tent of meeting covering the interior tabernacle was set up; the Shekinah cloud covered it, and the glory of Jehovah filled the tabernacle,—the manifested presence of the King of Israel!

Out of the tent of meeting, from this excellent glory, Jehovah now called unto Moses, and delivered the law as we have it in the first seven chapters of the book of Leviticus. To the law of offerings succeeds (viii.-x.) an account of the consecration of Aaron and his sons to the priestly office, and their formal public assumption of their functions, with an account of the very awful sanction which was given to the preceding law, by the death of Nadab and Abihu before the Lord, for offering as He had not commanded them.

The next section of the book contains the law concerning the clean and the unclean, under the several heads of food (xi.), birth-defilement (xii.), leprosy (xiii., xiv.), and unclean issues (xv.); and closes (xvi.) with the ordinance of the great day of atonement, in which the high priest alone, presenting the blood of a sin-offering in the Holy of Holies, was to make atonement once a year for the sins of the whole nation.*

The third section of the book contains the law of holiness,† first, for the people (xvii.-xx.), and then the special laws for the priests (xxi., xxii.). These are followed, first (xxiii.), by the order for the feasts of the Lord, or appointed times of public holy convocation; then (xxiv.), by a historical incident designed to show that the law, as given, must, in several respects noted, be applied in all its strictness no less to the alien than to the native-born Israelite; and finally (xxv.), by the remarkable ordinances concerning the sabbatic year, and the culmination of the sabbatic system of the law in the year of jubilee.

As a conclusion to the whole, the legislation thus given is now sealed (xxvi.) with promises from God of blessing to the nation if they will keep this law, and threats of unsparing vengeance against the people and the land, if they forsake His commandments and break the covenant, though still with a promise of mercy when, having thus transgressed, they shall at any time repent. The book then closes with a supplemental chapter on voluntary vows and dues (xxvii.).

The Purpose of Leviticus.

What now was the purpose of Leviticus? In general, as regards Israel, it was given to direct them how they might live as a holy nation in fellowship with God. The key-note of the book is "Holiness to Jehovah." More particularly, the object of the book was to furnish for the theocracy set up in Israel a code of law which should secure their physical, moral, and spiritual well-being. But the establishment of the theocracy in Israel was itself only a means to an end; namely, to make Israel a blessing to all nations, in mediating to the Gentiles the redemption of God. Hence, the Levitical laws were all intended and adapted to train and prepare the nation for this special historic mission to which God had chosen them.

To this end, it was absolutely necessary, first of all, that Israel should be kept separate from the heathen nations. To effect and maintain this separation, these laws of Leviticus were admirably adapted. They are of such a character that obedience to them, even in a very imperfect way, has made the nation to this day to be, in a manner and degree perfectly unique, isolated and separate from all the peoples in the midst of whom they dwell.

The law of Leviticus was intended to effect this preparation of Israel for its world-mission, not only in an external manner, but also in an internal way; namely, by revealing in and to Israel the real character of God, and in particular His unapproachable holiness. For if Israel is to teach the nations the way of holiness, in which alone they can be blessed, the chosen nation must itself first be taught holiness by the Holy One. A lesson here for every one of us! The revelation of the holiness of God was made, first of all, in the sacrificial system. The great lesson which it must have kept before the most obtuse conscience was this, that "without shedding of blood there is no remission of sin;" that God therefore must be the Most Holy, and sin against Him no trifle. It was made, again, in the precepts of the law. If in some instances these seem to tolerate evils which we should have expected that a holy God would at once have swept away, this is explained by our Lord (Matt. xix. 8) by the fact that some things were of necessity ordained in view of the hardness of men's hearts; while, on the other hand, it is certainly quite plain that the laws of Leviticus constantly held before the Israelite the absolute

---

* From the note in xvi. 1 it would appear that this chapter, so different in subject from the five preceding chapters on "Uncleannesses," originally preceded them, and so followed x., with which it is so closely connected. Its exposition is therefore given immediately after that of x.

† This name is often restricted to xviii.-xx.

holiness of God as the only standard of perfection.

The holiness of God was further revealed by the severity of the penalties which were attached to these Levitical laws. Men often call these harsh, forgetting that we are certain to underestimate the criminality of sin; forgetting that God must, in any case, have rights over human life which no earthly ruler can have. But no one will deny that this very severity of the law was fitted to impress the Israelite, as nothing else could, with God's absolute intolerance of sin and impurity, and make him feel that he could not trifle with God, and hope to sin with impunity.

And yet we must not forget that the law was adapted no less to reveal the other side of the Divine holiness; that "the Lord God is merciful and gracious, and of great kindness." For if the law of Leviticus proclaims that "without shedding of blood there is no remission," with equal clearness it proclaims that with shedding of blood there can be remission of sin to every believing penitent.

And this leads to the observation that this law was further adapted to the training of Israel for its world-mission, in that to every thoughtful man it must have suggested a secret of redeeming mercy yet to be revealed. Every such one must have often said in his heart that it was "not possible that the blood of bulls and of goats should take away sin;" and that as a substitute for human life, when forfeited by sin, more precious blood than this must be required; even though he might not have been able to imagine whence God should provide such a Lamb for an offering. And so it was that the law was fitted, in the highest degree, to prepare Israel for the reception of Him to whom all these sacrifices pointed, the High Priest greater than Aaron, the Lamb of God which should "take away the sins of the world," in whose person and work Israel's mission should at last receive its fullest realisation.

But the law of Leviticus was not only intended to prepare Israel for the Messiah by thus awakening a sense of sin and need, it was so ordered as to be in many ways directly typical and prophetic of Christ and His great redemption, in its future historical development. Modern rationalism, indeed, denies this; but it is none the less a fact. According to the Apostle John (v. 46), our Lord declared that Moses wrote of Him; and, according to Luke (xxiv. 27), when He expounded unto the two walking to Emmaus "the things concerning Himself," He began His exposition with "Moses" and (ver. 44) repeated what He had before His resurrection taught them, that all things "which were written in the law of Moses" concerning Him, must be fulfilled. And in full accord with the teaching of the Master taught also His disciples. The writer of the Epistle to the Hebrews, especially, argues from this postulate throughout, and also explicitly affirms the typical character of the ordinances of this book; declaring, for example, that the Levitical priests in the tabernacle service served "that which is a copy of the heavenly things" (Heb. viii. 5); that the blood with which "the copies of the things in the heavens" were cleansed, prefigured "better sacrifices than these," even the one offering of Him who "put away sin by the sacrifice of Himself" (Heb. ix. 23-6); and that the holy times and sabbatic seasons of the law were "a shadow of the things to come." The fact is familiar, and one need not multiply illustrations. Many, no doubt, in the interpretation of these types, have broken loose from the principles indicated in the New Testament, and given free rein to an unbridled fancy. But this only warns us that we the more carefully take heed to follow the intimations of the New Testament, and beware of mistaking our own imaginings for the teachings of the Holy Ghost. Such interpretations may bring typology into disrepute, but they cannot nullify it as a fact which must be recognised in any attempt to open up the meaning of the book.

Neither is the reality of this typical correspondence between the Levitical ritual and order and New Testament facts set aside, even though it is admitted that we cannot believe that Israel generally could have seen all in it which the New Testament declares to be there. For the very same New Testament which declares the typical correspondence, no less explicitly tells us this very thing: that many things predicted and prefigured in the Old Testament, concerning the sufferings and glory of Christ, were not understood by the very prophets through whom they were anciently made known (1 Peter i. 10-12). We have then carefully to distinguish in our interpretation between the immediate historical intention of the Levitical ordinances, for the people of that time, and their typical intention and meaning; but we are not to imagine with some that to prove the one is to disprove the other.

The Present-day Use of Leviticus.

This very naturally brings us to the answer to the frequent question: Of what use can the book of Leviticus be to believers now? We answer, first, that it is to us, just as much as to ancient Israel, a revelation of the character of God. It is even a clearer revelation of God's character to us than to them; for Christ has come as the Fulfiller, and thus the Interpreter, of the law. And God has not changed. He is still exactly what He was when He called to Moses out of the tent of meeting or spoke to him at Mount Sinai. He is just as holy as then; just as intolerant of sin as then; just as merciful to the penitent sinner who presents in faith the appointed blood of atonement, as He was then.

More particularly, Leviticus is of use to us now, as holding forth, in a singularly vivid manner, the fundamental conditions of true religion. The Levitical priesthood and sacrifices are no more, but the spiritual truth they represented abides and must abide for ever: namely, that there is for sinful man no citizenship in the kingdom of God apart from a High Priest and Mediator with a propitiatory sacrifice for sin. These are days when many, who would yet be called Christians, belittle atonement, and deny the necessity of the shedding of substitutionary blood for our salvation. Such would reduce, if it were possible, the whole sacrificial ritual of Leviticus to a symbolic *self*-offering of the worshipper to God. But against this stands the constant testimony of our Lord and His apostles, that it is only through the shedding of blood *not his own* that man can have remission of sin.

But Leviticus presents not only a ritual, but also a body of civil law for the theocracy. Hence it comes that the book is of use for to-day, as suggesting principles which should guide human legislators who would rule according to the mind of God. Not, indeed, that the laws in their detail should be adopted in our modern states; but it is certain that the principles which underlie those laws are eternal. Social and governmental questions have come to the front in our time as never before. The question of the relation of the civil government to religion, the question of the rights of labour and of capital, of land-holding, that which by a suggestive euphemism we call "the social evil," with its related subjects of marriage and divorce,—all these are claiming attention as never before. There is not one of these questions on which the legislation of Leviticus does not cast a flood of light, into which our modern lawmakers would do well to come and walk.

For nothing can be more certain than this; that if God has indeed once stood to a commonwealth in the relation of King and political Head, we shall be sure to discover in His theocratic law upon what principles infinite righteousness, wisdom, and goodness would deal with these matters. We shall thus find in Leviticus that the law which it contains, from beginning to end, stands in contradiction to that modern democratic secularism, which would exclude religion from government and order all national affairs without reference to the being and government of God; and, by placing the law of sacrifice at the beginning of the book, it suggests distinctly enough that the maintenance of right relation to God is fundamental to good government.

The severity of many of the laws is also instructive in this connection. The trend of public opinion in many communities is against capital punishment, as barbarous and inhuman. We are startled to observe the place which this has in the Levitical law; which exhibits a severity far removed indeed from the unrighteous and undiscriminating severity of the earlier English law, but no less so from the more undiscriminating leniency which has taken its place, especially as regards those crimes in which large numbers of people are inclined to indulge.

No less instructive to modern law-makers and political economists is the bearing of the Levitical legislation on the social question, the relations of rich and poor, of employer and employed. It is a legislation which, with admirable impartiality, keeps the poor man and the rich man equally in view; a body of law which, if strictly carried out, would have made in Israel either a plutocracy or a proletariat alike impossible. All these things will be illustrated in the course of exposition. Enough has been said to show that those among us who are sorely perplexed as to what government should do, at what it should aim in these matters, may gain help by studying the mind of Divine wisdom concerning these questions, as set forth in the theocratic law of Leviticus.

Further, Leviticus is of use to us now as a revelation of Christ. This follows from what has been already said concerning the typical character of the law. The book is thus a treasury of divinely-chosen illustrations as to the way of a sinner's salvation through the priestly work of the Son of God, and as to his present and future position and dignity as a redeemed man.

Finally, and for this same reason, Leviticus is still of use to us as embodying in type and figure prophecies of things yet to come, pertaining to Messiah's kingdom. We must not imagine with some that because many of its types are long ago fulfilled, therefore all have been fulfilled. Many, according to the hints of the New Testament, await their fulfilment in a bright day that is coming. Some, for instance, of the feasts of the Lord have been fulfilled; as passover, and the feast of Pentecost. But how about the day of atonement for the sin of corporate Israel? We have seen the type of the day of atonement fulfilled in the entering into heaven of our great High Priest; but in the type He came out again to bless the people: has that been fulfilled? Has He yet proclaimed absolution of sin to guilty Israel? How, again, about the feast of trumpets, and that of the ingathering at full harvest? How about the Sabbatic year, and that most consummate type of all, the year of jubilee? History records nothing which could be held a fulfilment of any of these; and thus Leviticus bids us look forward to a glorious future yet to come, when the great redemption shall at last be accomplished, and "Holiness to Jehovah" shall, as Zechariah puts it (xiv. 20), be written even "on the bells of the horses."

CHAPTER II.

SACRIFICE: THE BURNT-OFFERING.

LEVITICUS i. 2-4.

THE voice of Jehovah which had spoken not long before from Sinai, now speaks from out "the tent of meeting." There was a reason for the change. For Israel had since then entered into covenant with God; and Moses, as the mediator of the covenant, had sealed it by sprinkling with blood both the Book of the Covenant and the people. And therewith they had professedly taken Jehovah for their God and He had taken Israel for His people. In infinite grace, He had condescended to appoint for Himself a tabernacle or "tent of meeting," where He might, in a special manner, dwell among them, and manifest to them His will. The tabernacle had been made, according to the pattern shown to Moses in the mount; and it had been now set up. And so now, He who had before spoken amid the thunders of flaming, trembling Sinai, speaks from the hushed silence of "the tent of meeting." The first words from Sinai had been the holy law, forbidding sin with threatening of wrath: the first words from the tent of meeting are words of grace, concerning fellowship with the Holy One maintained through sacrifice, and atonement for sin by the shedding of blood. A contrast this which is itself a Gospel!

The offerings of which we read in the next seven chapters are of two kinds, namely, bloody and unbloody offerings. In the former class were included the burnt-offering, the peace-offering, the sin-offering, and the guilt-, or trespass-offering; in the latter, only the meal-offering. The book begins with the law of the burnt-offering.

In any exposition of this law of the offerings, it is imperative that our interpretation shall be determined, not by any fancy of ours as to what the offerings might fitly symbolise, nor yet, on the other hand, be limited by what we may suppose that any Israelite of that day might have thought regarding them; but by the statements concerning them which are contained in the law itself, and in other parts of Holy Scripture, especially in the New Testament.

First of all, we may observe that in the book itself the offerings are described by the remarkable expression, "the bread" or "food of God." Thus, it is commanded (xxi. 6) that the priests should not defile themselves, on this ground: "the offerings of the Lord made by fire, the bread of their God, do they offer." It was an ancient heathen notion that in sacrifice, food was provided for the Deity in order thus to show Him honour. And, doubtless, in Israel, ever prone to idolatry, there were many who rose no higher than this gross conception of the meaning of such words. Thus, in Psalm l. 8-15, God sharply rebukes Israel for so unworthy thoughts of Himself, using language at the same time which teaches the spiritual meaning of the sacrifice, regarded as the "food," or "bread," of God: "I will not reprove thee for thy sacrifices; and thy burnt-offerings are continually before Me. . . . I will take no bullock out of thy house, nor he-goats out of thy stalls. . . . If I were hungry, I would not tell thee; for the world is Mine, and the fulness thereof. Will I eat the flesh of bulls, or drink the blood of goats? Offer unto God the sacrifice of *thanksgiving;* and *pay thy vows* unto the Most High; and call upon Me in the day of trouble: I will deliver thee and thou shalt glorify Me."

Of which language the plain teaching is this: If the sacrifices are called in the law "the bread of God," God asks not this bread from Israel in any material sense, or for any material need. He asks that which the offerings symbolise; thanksgiving, loyal fulfilment of covenant engagements to Him, and that loving trust which will call on Him in the day of trouble. Even so! Gratitude, loyalty, trust! this is the "food of God," this the "bread" which He desires that we should offer, the bread which those Levitical sacrifices symbolised. For even as man, when hungry, craves food, and cannot be satisfied without it, so God, who is Himself Love, desires our love, and delights in seeing its expression in all those offices of self-forgetting and self-sacrificing service in which love manifests itself. This is to God even as is food to us. Love cannot be satisfied except with love returned; and we may say, with deepest humility and reverence, the God of love cannot be satisfied without love returned. Hence it is that the sacrifices, which in various ways symbolise the self-offering of love and the fellowship of love, are called by the Holy Ghost "the food," or "bread of God."

And yet we must, on no account, hasten to the conclusion, as many do, that therefore the Levitical sacrifices were *only* intended to express and symbolise the self-offering of the worshipper, and that this exhausts their significance. On the contrary, the need of infinite Love for this "bread of God" cannot be adequately met and satisfied by the self-offering of any creature, and, least of all, by the self-offering of a sinful creature, whose very sin lies just in this, that he has fallen away from perfect love. The symbolism of the sacrifice as "the food of God," therefore, by this very phrase points toward the self-offering in love of the eternal Son to the Father, and in behalf of sinners, for the Father's sake. It was the sacrifice on Calvary which first became, in innermost reality, that "bread of God," which the ancient sacrifices were only in symbol. It was this, not regarded as satisfying Divine justice (though it did this), but as satisfying the Divine love; because it was the supreme expression of the perfect love of the incarnate Son of God to the Father, in His becoming "obedient unto death, even the death of the cross."

And now, keeping all this in view, we may venture to say even more than at first as to the meaning of this phrase, "the bread of God," applied to these offerings by fire. For just as the free activity of man is only sustained in virtue of and by means of the food which he eats, so also the love of the God of love is only sustained in free activity toward man through the self-offering to the Father of the Son, in that atoning sacrifice which He offered on the cross, and in the ceaseless service of that exalted life which, risen from the dead, Christ now lives unto God for ever. Thus already, this expression, so strange to our ears at first, as descriptive of Jehovah's offerings made by fire, points to the person and work of the adorable Redeemer as its only sufficient explication.

But, again, we find another expression, xvii. 11, which is of no less fundamental consequence for the interpretation of the bloody offerings of Leviticus. In connection with the prohibition of blood for food, and as a reason for that prohibition, it is said: "The life of the flesh is in the blood; and I have given it to you upon the altar to make atonement for your souls; for it is the blood that maketh atonement,"—mark the expression; not, as in the received version, "*for* the soul," which were mere tautology, and gives a sense which the Hebrew cannot have, but, as the Revised Version has it,—"by reason of the life," or "soul" (marg.). Hence, wherever in this law we read of a sprinkling of blood upon the altar, this must be held fast as its meaning, whether it be formally mentioned or not; namely, atonement made for sinful man through the life of an innocent victim poured out in the blood. There may be, and often are, other ideas, as we shall see, connected with the offering, but this is always present. To argue, then, with so many in modern times, that because, not the idea of an atonement, but that of a sacrificial meal given by the worshipper to God, is the dominant conception in the sacrifices of the ancient nations, therefore we cannot admit the idea of atonement and expiation to have been intended in these Levitical sacrifices, is simply to deny, not only the New Testament interpretation of them, but the no less express testimony of the record itself.

But it is, manifestly, in the nature of the case "impossible that the blood of bulls and of goats should take away sins." Hence, we are again, by this phrase also, constrained to look beyond this Levitical shedding of sacrificial blood, for some antitype of which the innocent victims slain at that altar were types; one who, by the shedding of his blood, should do that in reality, which at the door of the tent of meeting was done in symbol and shadow.

What the New Testament teaches on this point is known to every one. Christ Jesus was the Antitype, to whose all-sufficient sacrifice each insufficient sacrifice of every Levitical victim pointed. John the Baptist struck the key-note of all New Testament teaching in this matter, when, beholding Jesus, he cried (John i. 29), "Behold the Lamb of God, which taketh away the sin of the world." Jesus Christ declared **the** same thought again and again, as in His words at the sacramental Supper: "This is My blood of the new covenant, which is shed for many for the remission of sins." Paul expressed the same thought, when he said (Eph. v. 2) that Christ "gave Himself up for us, an offering and a sacrifice to God, for an odour of a sweet smell;" and that "our redemption, the forgiveness of our trespasses," is "through His blood" (Eph. i. 7). And Peter also, speaking in Levitical language, teaches that we "were redeemed . . . with precious blood, as of a lamb without blemish and without spot, even the blood of Christ;" to which he adds the suggestive words, of which this whole Levitical ritual is the most striking illustration, that Christ, although "manifested at the end of the times," "was foreknown" as the Lamb of God "before the foundation of the world" (1 Peter i. 18-20). John, in like manner, speaks in the language of Leviticus concerning Christ, when he declares (1 John i. 7) that "the blood of Jesus . . . cleanseth us from all sin;" and even in the Apocalypse, which is the Gospel of Christ glorified, He is still brought before us as a Lamb that had been slain, and who has thus "purchased with His blood men of every tribe, and tongue, and people, and nation," "to be unto our God a kingdom and priests" (Rev. v. 6, 9, 10).

In this clear light of the New Testament, one can see how meagre also is the view of some who would see in these Levitical sacrifices nothing more than fines assessed upon the guilty, as theocratic penalties. Leviticus itself should have taught such better than that. For, as we have seen, the virtue of the bloody offerings is made to consist in this, that "the life of the flesh is in the blood;" and we are told that "the blood makes atonement for the soul," not in virtue of the monetary value of the victim, in a commercial way, but "by reason of the life" that is in the blood, and is therewith poured out before Jehovah on the altar,—the life of an innocent victim in the stead of the life of the sinful man.

No less inadequate, if we are to let ourselves be guided either by the Levitical or the New Testament teaching, is the view that the offerings only symbolised the self-offering of the worshipper. We do not deny, indeed, that the sacrifice—of the burnt-offering, for example—may have fitly represented, and often really expressed, the self-consecration of the offerer. But, in the light of the New Testament, this can never be held to have been the sole, or even the chief, reason in the mind of God for directing these outpourings of sacrificial blood upon the altar.

We must insist, then, on this, as essential to the right interpretation of this law of the offerings, that every one of these bloody offerings of Leviticus typified, and was intended to typify, our Saviour, Jesus Christ. The burnt-offering represented Christ; the peace-offering, Christ; the sin-offering, Christ; the guilt-. or trespass-offering, Christ. Moreover, since each of these, as intended especially to shadow forth some particular aspect of Christ's work, differed in some respects from all the others, while yet in all alike a victim's blood was shed upon the altar, we are by this reminded that in our Lord's redemptive work the most central and essential thing is this, that, as He Himself said (Matt. xx. 28), He "came to give His life a ransom for many."

Keeping this guiding thought steadily before us, it is now our work to discover, if we may, what special aspect of the one great sacrifice of Christ each of these offerings was intended especially to represent.

Only, by way of caution, it needs to be added that we are not to imagine that every minute circumstance pertaining to each sacrifice, in all its varieties, must have been intended to point to some correspondent feature of Christ's person or work. On the contrary, we shall frequently see reason to believe that the whole purpose of one or another direction of the ritual is to be found in the conditions, circumstances, or immediate intention of the offering. Thus, to illustrate, when a profound interpreter suggests that the reason for the command that the victim should be slain on the north side of the altar, is to be found in the fact that the north, as the side of shadow, signifies the gloom and joylessness of the sacrificial act, we are inclined rather to see sufficient reason for the prescription in the fact that the other three sides were already in a manner occupied: the east, as the place of ashes; the south, as fronting the entrance; and the west, as facing the tent of meeting and the brazen laver.

The Ritual of the Burnt-Offering.

In the law of the offerings, that of the burnt-offering comes first, though in the order of the ritual it was not first, but second, following the sin-offering. In this order of mention we need, however, seek no mystic meaning. The burnt-offering was very naturally mentioned first, as being the most ancient, and also in the most constant and familiar use. We read of burnt-offerings as offered by Noah and Abraham; and of peace-offerings, too, in early times; while the sin-offering and the guilt-offering, in Leviticus treated last, were now ordered for the first time. So also the burnt-offering was still, by Divine ordinance, to be the most common. No day could pass in the tabernacle without the offering of these. Indeed, except on the great day of atonement for the nation, in the ritual for which, the sin-offering was the central act, the burnt-offering was the most important sacrifice on all the great feast-days.

The first law, which applies to bloody offerings in general, was this: that the victim shall be "of the cattle, even of the herd and of the flock" (ver. 2); to which is added, in the latter part of the chapter (ver. 14), the turtledove or young pigeon. The carnivora are all excluded; for these, which live by the death of others, could never typify Him who should come to give life. And among others, only clean beasts could be taken. Israel must not offer as "the food of God" that which they might not eat for their own food; nor could that which was held unclean be taken as a type of the Holy Victim of the future. And, even among clean animals, a further selection is made. Only domestic animals were allowed; not even a clean animal was permitted, if it were taken in hunting. For it was fitting that one should offer to God that which had become endeared to the owner as having cost the most of care and labour in its bringing up. For this, also, we can easily see another reason in the Antitype. Nothing was to mark Him more than this: that He should be subject and obey, and that not of constraint, as the unwilling captive of the chase, but freely and unresistingly.

And now follow the special directions for the burnt-offering. The Hebrew word so rendered means, literally, "that which ascends." It thus precisely describes the burnt-offering in its most distinctive characteristic. Of the other offerings, a part was burned, but a part was eaten; in some instances, even by the offerer himself. But in the burnt-offering all ascends to God in flame and smoke. For the creature is reserved nothing whatever.

The first specification in the law of the burnt-offering is this: "If his oblation be a burnt-offering of the herd, he shall offer it a male without blemish" (ver. 3). It must be a "male," as the stronger, the type of its kind; and "without blemish," that is, ideally perfect.

The reasons for this law are manifest. The Israelite was thereby taught that God claims the best that we have. They needed this lesson, as many among us do still. At a later day, we find God rebuking them by Malachi (i. 6, 13), with indignant severity, for their neglect of this law: "A son honoureth his father: . . . if then I be a Father, where is My honour? . . . Ye have brought that which was taken by violence, and the lame, and the sick; . . . should I accept this of your hand? saith the Lord." And as pointing to our Lord, the command was no less fitting. Thus, as in other sacrifices, it was foreshadowed that the great Burnt-offering of the future would be the one Man without blemish, the absolutely perfect Exemplar of what manhood should be, but is not.

And this brings us now to the ritual of the offering. In the ritual of the various bloody offerings we find six parts. These are: (1) the Presentation; (2) the Laying on of the Hand; (3) the Killing of the Victim; in which three the ritual was the same for all kinds of offerings. The remaining three are: (4) the Sprinkling of Blood; (5) the Burning; (6) the Sacrificial Meal. In these, differences appear in the various sacrifices, which give each its distinctive character; and, in the burnt-offering, the sacrificial meal is omitted,—the whole is burnt upon the altar.

First is given the law concerning

The Presentation of the Victim.

"He shall offer it at the door of the tent of meeting, that he may be accepted before the Lord" (ver. 3).

In this it was ordered, first, that the offerer should bring the victim himself. There were parts of the ceremony in which the priest acted for him; but this he must do for himself. Even so, he who will have the saving benefit of Christ's sacrifice must himself bring this Christ before the Lord. As by so doing, the Israelite signified his acceptance of God's gracious arrangements concerning sacrifice, so do we, bringing Christ in our act of faith before the Lord, express our acceptance of God's arrangement on our behalf; our readiness and sincere desire to make use of Christ, who is appointed for us. And this no man can do for another.

And the offering must be presented for a certain purpose; namely "that he may be accepted before the Lord;"* and that, as the context tells us, not because of a present made to God, but through an atoning sacrifice. And so now it is

* The usage of the common Hebrew phrase so rendered does not warrant the translation in the old version: "of his voluntary will."

not enough that a man make much of Christ, and mention Him in terms of praise before the Lord, as the One whom He would imitate and seek to serve. He must in his act of faith bring this Christ before the Lord, in such wise as to secure thus his personal acceptance through the blood of the Holy Victim.

And, finally, the *place* of presentation is prescribed. It must be "at the door of the tent of meeting." It is easy to see the original reason for this. For, as we learn from other Scriptures, the Israelites were ever prone to idolatry, and that especially at places other than the appointed temple or tent of meeting, in the fields and on high places. Hence the immediate purpose of this order concerning the place, was to separate the worship of God from the worship of false gods. There is now, indeed, no law concerning the place where we may present the great Sacrifice before God. At home, in the closet, in the church, on the street, wherever we will, we may present this Christ in our behalf and stead as a Holy Victim before God. And yet the principle which underlies this ordinance of place is no less applicable in this age than then. For it is a prohibition of all self-will in worship. It was not enough that an Israelite should have the prescribed victim; it is not enough that we present the Christ of God in faith, or what we think to be faith. But we must make no terms or conditions as to the mode or condition of the presentation, other than God appoints. And the command was also a command of publicity. The Israelite was therein commanded to confess publicly, and thus attest, his faith in Jehovah, even as God will now have us all make our confession of Christ a public thing.

The second act of the ceremonial was

The Laying on of the Hand.

It was ordered:

"He shall lay his hand upon the head of the burnt offering; and it shall be accepted for him, to make atonement for him" (ver. 4).

The laying on of the hand was not, as some have maintained, a mere declaration of the offerer's property in that which he offered, as showing his right to give it to God. If this were true, we should find the ceremony also in the bloodless offerings; where the cakes of corn were no less the property of the offerer than the bullock or sheep of the burnt-offering. But the ceremony was confined to these bloody offerings.

It is nearer the truth when others say that this was an act of designation. It is a fact that the ceremony of the laying on of hands in Scripture usage does indicate a designation of a person or thing, as to some office or service. In this book (xxiv. 14), the witnesses are directed to lay their hands upon the blasphemer, thereby appointing him to death. Moses is said to have laid his hands on Joshua, thus designating him in a formal way as his successor; and, in the New Testament, Paul and Barnabas are set apart to the ministry by the laying on of hands. But, in all these cases, the ceremony symbolised more than mere designation; namely, a transfer or communication of something invisible, in connection with this visible act. Thus, in the New Testament the laying on of hands always denotes the communication of the Holy Ghost, either as an enduement for office, or for bodily healing. The laying of the hands of Moses on Joshua, in like manner, signified the transfer to him of the gifts, office, and authority of Moses. Even in the case of the execution of the blaspheming son of Shelomith, the laying on of the hands of the witnesses had the same significance. They thereby designated him to death, no doubt; but therewith thus symbolically transferred to the criminal the responsibility for his own death.

From the analogy of these cases we should expect to find evidence of an ideal transference of somewhat from the offerer to the victim here. And the context does not leave the matter doubtful. It is added (ver. 4), "It shall be accepted for him, to make atonement for him." Hence it appears that while, indeed, the offerer, by this laying on of his hand, did dedicate the victim to death, the act meant more than this. It symbolised a transfer, according to God's merciful provision, of an obligation to suffer for sin, from the offerer to the innocent victim. Henceforth, the victim stood in the offerer's place, and was dealt with accordingly.

This is well illustrated by the account which is given (Numb. viii.) of the formal substitution of the Levites in the place of all the first-born of Israel, for special service unto God. We read that the Levites were presented before the Lord; and that the children of Israel then laid their hands upon the heads of the Levites, who were thus, we are told, "offered as an offering unto the Lord," and were thenceforth regarded and treated as substitutes for the first-born of all Israel. Thus the obligation to certain special service was symbolically transferred, as the context tells us, from the first-born to the Levites; and this transfer of obligation from all the tribes to the single tribe of Levi was visibly represented by the laying on of hands. And just so here: the laying on of the hand designated, certainly, the victim to death; but it did this, in that it was the symbol of a transfer of obligation.

This view of the ceremony is decisively confirmed by the ritual of the great day of atonement. In the sin-offering of that day, in which the conception of expiation by blood received its fullest symbolic expression, it was ordered (xvi. 21) that Aaron should lay his hands on the head of one of the goats of the sin-offering, and "confess over him all the iniquities of the children of Israel." Thereupon the iniquity of the nation was regarded as symbolically transferred from Israel to the goat; for it is added, "and the goat shall bear upon him all their iniquities unto a solitary land." So, while in this ritual for the burnt-offering there is no mention of such confession, we have every reason to believe the uniform Rabbinical tradition, that it was the custom to make also upon the head of the victim for the burnt-offering a solemn confession of sin, for which they give the form to be used.

Such then was the significance of the laying on of hands. But the ceremony meant even more than this. For the Hebrew verb which is always used for this, as the Rabbis point out, does not merely mean to lay the hand upon, but so to lay the hand as to rest or lean heavily upon the victim. This force of the word is well illustrated from a passage where it occurs, in Psalm lxxxviii. 7, "Thy wrath lieth hard upon me." The ceremony, therefore, significantly represented the offerer as resting or relying on the victim to procure that from God for which he presented him, namely, atonement and acceptance.

This part of the ceremonial of this and other sacrifices was thus full of spiritual import and typical meaning. By this laying on of the hand to designate the victim as a sacrifice, the offerer implied, and probably expressed, a confession of personal sin and demerit; as done "before Jehovah," it implied also his acceptance of God's penal judgment against his sin. It implied, moreover, in that the offering was made according to an arrangement ordained by God, that the offerer also thankfully accepted God's merciful provision for atonement, by which the obligation to suffer for sin was transferred from himself, the guilty sinner, to the sacrificial victim. And, finally, in that the offerer was directed so to lay his hand as to rest upon the victim, it was most expressively symbolised that he, the sinful Israelite, rested and depended on this sacrifice as the atonement for his sin, his divinely appointed substitute in penal death.

What could more perfectly set forth the way in which we are for our salvation to make use of the Lamb of God as slain for us? By faith, we lay the hand upon His head. In this, we do frankly and penitently own the sins for which, as the great Burnt-sacrifice, the Christ of God was offered; we also, in humility and self-abasement, thus accept the judgment of God against ourselves, that because of sin we deserve to be cast out from Him eternally; while, at the same time, we most thankfully accept this Christ as "the Lamb of God which taketh away the sins of the world," and therefore our sins also, if we will but thus make use of Him; and so lean and rest with all the burden of our sin on Him.

For the Israelite who should thus lay his hand upon the head of the sacrificial victim a promise follows. "It shall be accepted for him, to make atonement for him."

In this word "atonement" we are introduced to one of the key-words of Leviticus, as indeed of the whole Scripture. The Hebrew radical originally means "to cover," and is used once (Gen. vi. 14) in this purely physical sense. But, commonly, as here, it means "to cover" in a spiritual sense, that is, to cover the sinful person from the sight of the Holy God, who is "of purer eyes than to behold evil." Hence, it is commonly rendered "to atone," or "to make atonement;" also, "to reconcile," or "to make reconciliation." The thought is this: that between the sinner and the Holy One comes now the guiltless victim; so that the eye of God looks not upon the sinner, but on the offered substitute; and in that the blood of the substituted victim is offered before God for the sinner, atonement is made for sin, and the Most Holy One is satisfied.

And when the believing Israelite should lay his hand with confession of sin upon the appointed victim, it was graciously promised: "It shall be accepted for him, to make atonement for him." And just so now, whenever any guilty sinner, fearing the deserved wrath of God because of his sin, especially because of his lack of that full consecration which the burnt-sacrifice set forth, lays his hand in faith upon the great Burnt-offering of Calvary, the blessing is the same. For in the light of the cross, this Old Testament word becomes now a sweet New Testament promise: "When thou shalt rest with the hand of faith upon this Lamb of God, He shall be accepted for thee, to make atonement for thee."

This is most beautifully expressed in an ancient "Order for the Visitation of the Sick," attributed to Anselm of Canterbury, in which it is written:

"The minister shall say to the sick man, Dost thou believe that thou canst not be saved but by the death of Christ? The sick man answereth, Yes. Then let it be said unto him: Go to, then, and whilst thy soul abideth in thee, put all thy confidence in this death alone; place thy trust in no other thing; commit thyself wholly to this death; cover thyself wholly with this alone. . . . And if God would judge thee, say: Lord! I place the death of our Lord Jesus Christ between me and Thy judgment; otherwise I will not contend or enter into judgment with Thee.

"And if He shall say unto thee that thou art a sinner, say: I place the death of our Lord Jesus Christ between me and my sins. If He shall say unto thee, that thou hast deserved damnation, say: Lord! I put the death of our Lord Jesus Christ between Thee and all my sins; and I offer His merits for my own, which I should have, and have not."

And whosoever of us can thus speak, to him the promise speaks from out the shadows of the tent of meeting: "This Christ, the Lamb of God, the true Burnt-offering, shall be accepted for thee, to make atonement for thee!"

CHAPTER III.

THE BURNT-OFFERING (concluded).

LEVITICUS i. 5-17; vi. 8-13.

AFTER the laying on of the hand, the next sacrificial act was—

THE KILLING OF THE VICTIM.

"And he shall kill the bullock before the Lord" (ver. 5).

In the light of what has been already said, the significance of this killing, in a typical way, will be quite clear. For with the first sin, and again and again thereafter, God had denounced death as the penalty of sin. But here is a sinner who, in accord with a Divine command, brings before God a sacrificial victim, on whose head he lays his hand, on which he thus rests as he confesses his sins, and gives over the innocent victim to die instead of himself. Thus each of these sacrificial deaths, whether in the burnt-offering, the peace-offering, or the sin-offering, brings ever before us the death in the sinner's stead of that one Holy Victim who suffered for us, "the just for the unjust," and thus laid down His life, in accord with His own previously declared intention, "as a ransom for many."

In the sacrifices made by and for individuals, the victim was killed, except in the case of the turtle-dove or pigeon, by the offerer himself; but, very naturally, in the case of the national and public offerings, it was killed by the priest. As, in this latter case, it was impossible that all individual Israelites should unite in killing the victim, it is plain that the priest herein acted as the representative of the nation. Hence we may properly say that the fundamental thought of the ritual was this, that the victim should be killed by the offerer himself.

And by this ordinance we may well be reminded, first, how Israel,—for whose sake as a nation the antitypical Sacrifice was offered,—Israel itself became the executioner of the Victim; and, beyond that, how, in a deeper sense, every sinner must regard himself as truly causal of the Saviour's death, in that, as is often truly said, our sins nailed Christ to His cross. But whether such a reference were intended in this law of the offering or not, the great, significant, outstanding fact remains, that as soon as the offerer, by his laying on of the hand, signified the transfer of the personal obligation to die for sin from himself to the sacrificial victim, then came at once upon that victim the penalty denounced against sin.

And the added words, "before the Lord," cast further light upon this, in that they remind us that the killing of the victim had reference to Jehovah, whose holy law the offerer, failing of that perfect consecration which the burnt-offering symbolised, had failed to glorify and honour.

THE SPRINKLING OF BLOOD.

"And Aaron's sons, the priests, shall present the blood, and sprinkle the blood round about upon the altar that is at the door of the tent of meeting" (ver. 5).

And now follows the fourth act in the ceremonial, the Sprinkling of the Blood. The offerer's part is now done, and herewith the work of the priest begins. Even so must we, having laid the hand of faith upon the head of the substituted Lamb of God, now leave it to the heavenly Priest to act in our behalf with God.

The directions to the priest as to the use of the blood vary in the different offerings, according as the design is to give greater or less prominence to the idea of expiation. In the sin-offering this has the foremost place. But in the burnt-offering, as also in the peace-offering, although the conception of atonement by blood was not absent, it was not the dominant conception of the sacrifice. Hence, while the sprinkling of blood by the priest could in no wise be omitted, it took in this case a subordinate place in the ritual. It was to be sprinkled only on the sides of the altar of burnt-offering which stood in the outer court. We read (ver. 5): "Aaron's sons, the priests, shall present the blood, and sprinkle the blood round about upon the altar that is at the door of the tent of meeting."

It was in this sprinkling of the blood that the atoning work was completed. The altar had been appointed as a place of Jehovah's special presence; it had been designated as a place where God would come unto man to bless him. Thus, to present and sprinkle the blood upon the altar was symbolically to present the blood unto God. And the blood represented life,—the life of an innocent victim atoning for the sinner, because rendered up in the stead of his life. And the *priests* were to sprinkle the blood. So, while to bring and present the sacrifice of Christ, to lay the hand of faith upon His head, is our part, with this our duty ends. To sprinkle the blood, to use the blood God-ward for the remission of sin, this is the work alone of our heavenly Priest. We are then to leave that with Him.

Reserving a fuller exposition of the meaning of this sprinkling of blood for the exposition of the sin-offering, in which it was the central act of the ritual, we pass on now to the burning of the sacrifice, which in this offering marked the culmination of its special symbolism.

The Sacrificial Burning.

Leviticus i. 6-9, 12, 13, 17.

"And he shall flay the burnt offering, and cut it into its pieces. And the sons of Aaron the priest shall put fire upon the altar, and lay wood in order upon the fire: and Aaron's sons, the priests, shall lay the pieces, the head, and the fat, in order upon the wood that is on the fire which is upon the altar: but its inwards and its legs shall he wash with water: and the priest shall burn the whole on the altar, for a burnt offering, an offering made by fire, of a sweet savour unto the Lord... And he shall cut it into its pieces, with its head and its fat: and the priest shall lay them in order on the wood that is on the fire which is upon the altar: but the inwards and the legs shall he wash with water: and the priest shall offer the whole, and burn it upon the altar: it is a burnt offering, an offering made by fire, of a sweet savour unto the Lord... And he shall rend it by the wings thereof, but shall not divide it asunder: and the priest shall burn it upon the altar, upon the wood that is upon the fire: it is a burnt offering, an offering made by fire, of a sweet savour unto the Lord."

It was the distinguishing peculiarity of the burnt-offering, from which it takes its name, that in every case the whole of it was burned, and thus ascended heavenward in the fire and smoke of the altar. The place of the burning, in this and other sacrifices, is significant. The flesh of the sin-offering, when not eaten, was to be burned in a clean place without the camp. But it was the law of the burnt-offering that it should be wholly consumed upon the holy altar at the door of the tent of meeting. In the directions for the burning we need seek for no occult meaning; the most of them are evidently intended simply as means to the end; namely, the consumption of the offering with the utmost readiness, ease, and completeness. Hence it must be flayed and cut into its pieces, and carefully arranged upon the wood. The inwards and the legs must be washed with water, that into the offering, as to be offered to the Holy One, might come nothing extraneous, nothing corrupt and unclean.

In vv. 10-13 and 14-17 provision is made for the offering of different victims, of the flock, or of the fowls. The reason for this permitted variation, although not mentioned here, was doubtless the same which is given for a similar permission in chap. v. 7, where it is ordered that if the offerer's means suffice not for a certain offering, he may bring one of less value. Poverty shall be no plea for not bringing a burnt-sacrifice; to the Israelite of that time it thus set forth the truth, that "if there first be a willing heart, it is accepted according to that a man hath, and not according to that he hath not."

The variations in the prescriptions regarding the different victims to be used in the sacrifice are but slight. The bird having been killed by the priest (why this change it is not easy to see), its crop, with its contents of food unassimilated, and therefore not a part of the bird, as also the feathers, was to be cast away. It was not to be divided, like the bullock, and the sheep or goat, simply because, with so small a creature, it was not necessary to the speedy and entire combustion of the offering. In each case alike, the declaration is made that the sacrifice, thus offered and wholly burnt upon the altar, is "an offering made by fire, of a sweet savour unto the Lord."

And now a question comes before us, the answer to which is vital to the right understanding of the burnt-offering, whether in its original or typical import. What was the significance of the burning? It has been very often answered that the consumption of the victim by fire symbolised the consuming wrath of Jehovah, utterly destroying the victim which represented the sinful person of the offerer. And, observing that the burning followed the killing and shedding of blood, some have even gone so far as to say that the burning typified the eternal fire of hell! But when we remember that, without doubt, the sacrificial victim in all the Levitical offerings was a type of our blessed Lord, we may well agree with one who justly calls this interpretation "hideous." And yet many, who have shrunk from this, have yet in so far held to this conception of the symbolic meaning of the burning as to insist that it must at least have typified those fiery sufferings in which our Lord offered up His soul for sin. They remind us how often, in the Scripture, fire stands as the symbol of the consuming wrath of God against sin, and hence argue that this may justly be taken here as the symbolic meaning of the burning of the victim on the altar.

But this interpretation is nevertheless, in every form, to be rejected. As regards the use of fire as a symbol in Holy Scripture, while it is true that it often represents the punitive wrath of God, it is equally certain that it has not always this meaning. Quite as often it is the symbol of God's purifying energy and might. Fire was not the symbol of Jehovah's vengeance in the burning bush. When the Lord is represented as sitting "as a refiner and a purifier of silver," surely the thought is not of vengeance, but of purifying mercy. We should rather say that fire, in Scripture usage, is the symbol of the intense energy of the Divine nature, which continually acts upon every person and on every thing, according to the nature of each person or thing; here conserving, there destroying; now cleansing, now consuming. The same fire which burns the wood, hay, and stubble, purifies the gold and the silver.

Hence, while it is quite true that fire often typifies the wrath of God punishing sin, it is certain that it cannot always symbolise this, not even in the sacrificial ritual. For in the meal-offering of chap. ii. it is impossible that the thought of expiation should enter since no life is offered and no blood is shed; yet this also is presented unto God in fire. The fire then in this case must mean something else than the Divine wrath, and presumably must mean one thing in all the sacrifices. And that not even in the burnt-offering can the burning of the sacrifice symbolise the consuming wrath of God, becomes plain, when we observe that, according to the uniform teaching of the sacrificial ritual, atonement is already fully accomplished, prior to the burning, in the sprinkling of the blood. That the burning, which follows the atonement, should have any reference to Christ's expiatory sufferings, is thus quite impossible.

We must hold, therefore, that the burning can only mean in the burnt-offering that which alone it can signify in the meal-offering; namely, the ascending of the offering in consecration to God, on the one hand; and, on the other, God's gracious acceptance and appropriation of the offering. This was impressively set forth in the case of the burnt-offering presented when the tabernacle service was inaugurated; when, we are told (ix. 24), the fire which consumed it came forth from before Jehovah, lighted by no human hand,

and was thus a visible representation of God accepting and appropriating the offering to Himself.

The symbolism of the burning thus understood, we can now perceive what must have been the special meaning of this sacrifice. As regarded by the believing Israelite of those days, not yet discerning clearly the deeper truth it shadowed forth as to the great Burnt-sacrifice of the future, it must have symbolically taught him that complete consecration unto God is essential to right worship. There were sacrifices having a different special import, in which, while a part was burnt, the offerer might even himself join in eating the remaining part, taking that for. his own use. But, in the burnt-offering, nothing was for himself: all was for God; and in the fire of the altar God took the whole in such a way that the offering for ever passed beyond the offerer's recall. In so far as the offerer entered into this conception, and his inward experience corresponded to this outward rite, it was for him an act of worship.

But to the thoughtful worshipper, one would think, it must sometimes have occurred that, after all, it was not himself or his gift that thus ascended in full consecration to God, but a victim appointed by God to represent him in death on the altar. And thus it was that, whether understood or not, the offering in its very nature pointed to a Victim of the future, in whose person and work, as the One only fully-consecrated Man, the burnt-offering should receive its full explication. And this brings us to the question, What aspect of the person and work of our Lord was herein specially typified? It cannot be the resultant fellowship with God, as in the peace-offering; for the sacrificial feast which set this forth was in this case wanting. Neither can it be expiation for sin; for although this is expressly represented here, yet it is not the chief thing. The principal thing, in the burnt-offering, was the burning, the complete consumption of the victim in the sacrificial fire. Hence what is represented chiefly here, is not so much Christ representing His people in atoning death, as Christ representing His people in perfect consecration and entire self-surrender unto God; in a word, in perfect obedience.

Of these two things, the atoning death and the representative obedience, we think, and with reason, much of the former; but most Christians, though without reason, think less of the latter. And yet how much is made of this aspect of our Lord's work in the Gospels! The first words which we hear from His lips are to this effect, when, at twelve years of age, He asked His mother (Luke ii. 49), "Wist ye not that I must be (lit.) in the things of My Father?" and after His official work began in the first cleansing of the temple, this manifestation of His character was such as to remind His disciples that it was written, "The zeal of Thy house shall eat me up";—phraseology which brings the burnt-offering at once to mind.* And His constant testimony concerning Himself, to which His whole life bare witness, was in such words as these: "I came down from heaven, not to do My own will, but the will of Him that sent Me."

* See Psalm lxix. 9, and compare in the Hebrew such expressions as, "the fire hath consumed the burnt-offering"; and Deut. iv. 24, " thy God is a devouring fire," etc., in all which the verb signifying "to eat" is idiomatically used of fire.

In particular, He especially regarded His atoning work in this aspect. In the parable of the Good Shepherd (John x. 1-18), for example, after telling us that because of His laying down His life for the sheep the Father loved Him, and that to this end He had received from the Father authority to lay down His life for the sheep, He then adds as the reason of this: "This commandment have I received from My Father." And so elsewhere (John xii. 49, 50) He says of all His words, as of all His works: "The Father hath given Me a commandment, what I should say, and what I should speak; . . . the things therefore which I speak, even as the Father hath said unto Me, so I speak." And when at last His earthly work approaches its close, and we see Him in the agony of Gethsemane, there He appears, above all, as the perfectly consecrated One, offering Himself, body, soul, and spirit, as a whole burnt-offering unto God, in those never-to-be-forgotten words (Matt. xxvi. 39), "Father, if it be possible, let this cup pass away from Me; nevertheless, not as I will, but as Thou wilt." And, if any more proof were needed, we have it in that inspired exposition (Heb. x. 5-10) of Psalm xl. 6-8, wherein it is taught that this perfect obedience of Christ, in full consecration, was indeed the very thing which the Holy Ghost foresignified in the whole brunt-offerings of the law: "When He cometh into the world, He saith, Sacrifice and offering Thou wouldest not, but a body didst Thou prepare for Me; in whole burnt-offerings and sacrifices for sin Thou hadst no pleasure: then said I, Lo, I am come (in the roll of the book it is written of Me) to do Thy will, O God."

Thus the burnt-offering brings before us in type, for our faith, Christ as our Saviour in virtue of His being the One wholly surrendered to the will of the Father. Nor does this exclude, but rather defines, the conception of Christ as our substitute and representative. For He said that it was for our sakes that He "sanctified," or "consecrated" Himself (John xvii. 19); and while the New Testament represents Him as saving us by His death as an expiation for sin, it no less explicitly holds Him forth to us as having obeyed in our behalf, declaring (Rom. v. 19) that it is "by the obedience of the One Man" that "many are made righteous." And, elsewhere, the same Apostle represents the incomparable moral value of the atoning death of the cross as consisting precisely in this fact, that it was a supreme act of self-renouncing obedience, as it is written (Phil. ii. 6-9): "Being in the form of God, He yet counted it not a prize to be on an equality with God, but emptied Himself, taking the form of a servant, being made in the likeness of men; . . . becoming obedient even unto death, yea, the death of the cross. Wherefore also God highly exalted Him, and gave unto Him the name which is above every name."

And so the burnt-offering teaches us to remember that Christ has not only died for our sins, but has also consecrated Himself for us to God in full self-surrender in our behalf. We are therefore to plead not only His atoning death, but also the transcendent merit of His life of full consecration to the Father's will. To this, the words, three times repeated concerning the burnt-offering (vv. 9, 13, 17), in this chapter, blessedly apply: it is "an offering made by fire, of a sweet savour," a fragrant odour, "unto the Lord." That is, this full self-surrender of the holy Son of God unto the Father is exceedingly delightful and acceptable unto God. And for this reason it is for us an ever-prevailing argument for our own acceptance, and for the gracious bestowment for Christ's sake of all that there is in Him for us.

Only let us ever remember that we cannot argue, as in the case of the atoning death, that as Christ died that we might not die, so He offered Himself in full consecration unto God, that we might thus be released from this obligation. Here the exact opposite is the truth. For Christ Himself said in His memorable prayer, just before His offering of Himself to death, "For their sakes I sanctify (marg. "consecrate") Myself, *that they also might be sanctified in truth.*" And thus is brought before us the thought, that if the sin-offering emphasised, as we shall see, the substitutionary death of Christ, whereby He became our righteousness, the burnt-offering, as distinctively, brings before us Christ as our sanctification, offering Himself without spot, a whole burnt-offering to God. And as by that one life of sinless obedience to the will of the Father He procured our salvation by His merit, so in this respect He has also become our one perfect Example of what consecration to God really is. A thought this is which, with evident allusion to the burnt-offering, the Apostle Paul brings before us, charging us (Eph. v. 2) that we "walk in love, as Christ also loved us, and gave Himself for us, an offering and a sacrifice to God for an odour of a sweet smell."

And the law further suggests that no extreme of spiritual need can debar any one from availing Himself of our great Burnt-sacrifice. A burnt-offering was to be received even from one who was so poor that he could bring but a turtle-dove or a young pigeon (ver. 14). One might, at first thought, not unnaturally say: Surely there can be nothing in this to point to Christ; for the true Sacrifice is not many, but one and only. And yet the very fact of this difference allowed in the typical victims, when the reason of the allowance is remembered, suggests the most precious truth concerning Christ, that no spiritual poverty of the sinner need exclude him from the full benefit of Christ's saving work. Provision is made in Him for all those who, most truly and with most reason, feel themselves to be poor and in need of all things. Christ, as our sanctification, is for all who will make use of Him; for all who, feeling most deeply and painfully their own failure in full consecration, would take Him, as not only their sin-offering, but also their burnt-offering, both their example and their strength, unto perfect self-surrender unto God. We may well here recall to mind the exhortation of the Apostle to Christian believers, expressed in language which at once reminds us of the burnt-offering (Rom. xii. 1): "I beseech you, brethren, by the mercies of God, to present your bodies a living sacrifice, holy, acceptable to God, which is your reasonable service."

THE CONTINUAL BURNT-OFFERING.

LEVITICUS vi. 8-13.

"And the Lord spake unto Moses, saying, Command Aaron and his sons, saying, This is the law of the burnt offering: the burnt offering shall be on the hearth, upon the altar all night unto the morning; and the fire of the altar shall be kept burning thereon. And the priest shall put on his linen garment, and his linen breeches shall he put upon his flesh; and he shall take up the ashes whereto the fire hath consumed the burnt offering on the altar, and he shall put them beside the altar. And he shall put off his garments, and put on other garments, and carry forth the ashes without the camp unto a clean place. And the fire upon the altar shall be kept burning thereon, it shall not go out; and the priest shall burn wood on it every morning: and he shall lay the burnt offering in order upon it, and shall burn thereon the fat of the peace offerings. Fire shall be kept burning upon the altar continually; it shall not go out."

In chap. vi. 8-13 we have a "law of the burnt-offering" specially addressed to "Aaron and his sons," and designed to secure that the fire of the burnt-offering should be continually ascending unto God. In chap. i. we have the law regarding burnt-offerings brought by the individual Israelite. But besides these it was ordered, Exod. xxix. 38-46, that every morning and evening the priest should offer a lamb as a burnt-offering for the whole people,—an offering which primarily symbolised the constant renewal of Israel's consecration as "a kingdom of priests" unto the Lord. It is to this, the daily burnt-offering, that this supplementary law of chap. vi. refers. All the regulations are intended to provide for the uninterrupted maintenance of this sacrificial fire; first, by the regular removal of the ashes which would else cover and smother the fire; and, secondly, by the supply of fuel. The removal of the ashes from the fire is a priestly function; hence it was ordained that the priest for this service put on his robes of office, "his linen garment and his linen breeches," and then take up the ashes from the altar, and lay them by the side of the altar. But as from time to time it would be necessary to remove them from this place quite without the tent, it was ordered that he should carry them forth "without the camp unto a clean place," that the sanctity of all connected with Jehovah's worship might never be lost sight of; though, as it was forbidden to wear the priestly garments except within the tent of meeting, the priest, when this service was performed, must "put on other garments," his ordinary, unofficial robes. The ashes being thus removed from the altar each morning, then the wood was put on, and the parts of the lamb laid in order upon it to be perfectly consumed. And whenever during the day any one might bring a peace-offering unto the Lord, on this ever-burning fire the priest was to place also the fat, the richest part, of the offering, and with it also the various individual burnt-offerings and meal-offerings of each day. And thus it was arranged by the law that, all day long, and all night long, the smoke of the burnt-offering should be continually ascending unto the Lord.

The significance of this can hardly be missed. By this supplemental law which thus provided for "a continual burnt-offering" to the Lord, it was first of all signified to Israel, and to us, that the consecration which the Lord so desires and requires from His people is not occasional, but continuous. As the priest, representing the nation, morning by morning cleared away the ashes which had else covered the flame and caused it to burn dull, and both morning by morning and evening by evening, laid a new victim on the altar, so will God have us do. Our self-consecration is not to be occasional, but continual and habitual. Each morning we should imitate the priest of old, in putting away all that might dull the flame of our devotion, and, morning by morning, when we arise, and evening by evening, when we retire, by a solemn act of self-consecration give ourselves anew unto the Lord. So shall the word in substance, thrice repeated, be fulfilled in us in its deepest, truest sense: "The fire shall be kept burning on the altar continually: it shall not go out" (vv. 9, 12, 13).

But we must not forget that in this part of the law, as in all else, we are pointed to Christ. This ordinance of the continual burnt-offering reminds us that Christ, as our burnt-offering, *continually* offers Himself to God in self-consecration in our behalf. Very significant it is that the burnt-offering stands in contrast in this respect with the sin-offering. We never read of a continual sin-offering; even the great annual sin-offering of the day of atonement, which, like the daily burnt-offering, had reference to the nation at large, was soon finished, and once for all. And it was so with reason; for in the nature of the case, our Lord's offering of Himself for sin as an expiatory sacrifice was not and could not be a continuous act. But with His presentation of Himself unto God in full consecration of His person as our Burnt-offering, it is different. Throughout the days of His humiliation this self-offering of Himself to God continued; nor, indeed, can we say that it has yet ceased, or ever can cease. For still, as the High Priest of the heavenly sanctuary, He continually offers Himself as our Burnt-offering in constantly renewed and constantly continued devotement of Himself to the Father to do His will.

In this ordinance of the daily burnt-offering, ever ascending in the fire that never went out, the idea of the burnt-sacrifice reaches its fullest expression, the type its most perfect development. And thus the law of the burnt-offering leaves us in the presence of this holy vision: the greater than Aaron, in the heavenly place as our great Representative and Mediator, morning by morning, evening by evening, offering Himself unto the Father in the full self-devotement of His risen life unto God, as our "continual burnt-offering." In this, let us rejoice and be at peace.

CHAPTER IV.

THE MEAL-OFFERING.

Leviticus ii. 1-16; vi. 14-23.

The word which in the original uniformly stands for the English "meal-offering" (A. V. "meat-offering," *i. e.*, "food-offering") primarily means simply "a present," and is often properly so translated in the Old Testament. It is, for example, the word which is used (Gen. xxxii. 13) when we are told how Jacob sent a present to Esau his brother; or, later, of the gift sent by Israel to his son Joseph in Egypt (Gen. xliii. 11); and, again (2 Sam. viii. 2), of the gifts sent by the Moabites to David. Whenever thus used of gifts to men, it will be found that it suggests a recognition of the dignity and authority of the person to whom the present is made, and, in many cases, a desire also to procure thereby his favour.

In the great majority of cases, however, the word is used of offerings to God, and in this use one or both of these ideas can easily be traced. In Gen. iv. 4, 5, in the account of the offerings of Cain and Abel, the word is applied both to the bloody and the unbloody offering; but in the Levitical law, it is only applied to the latter. We thus find the fundamental idea of the meal-offering to be this: it was a gift brought by the worshipper to God, in token of his recognition of His supreme authority, and as an expression of desire for His favour and blessing.

But although the meal-offering, like the burnt-offering, was an offering made to God by fire, the differences between them were many and significant. In the burnt-offering, it was always a life that was given to God; in the meal-offering, it was never a life, but always the products of the soil. In the burnt-offering, again, the offerer always set apart the offering by the laying on of the hand, signifying thus, as we have seen, a transfer of obligation to death for sin; thus connecting with the offering, in addition to the idea of a gift to God, that of expiation for sin, as preliminary to the offering by fire. In the meal-offering, on the other hand, there was no laying on of the hand, as there was no shedding of blood, so that the idea of expiation for sin is in no way symbolised. The conception of a gift to God, which, though dominant in the burnt-offering, is not in that the only thing symbolised, in the meal-offering becomes the *only* thought the offering expresses.

It is further to be noted that not only must the meal-offering consist of the products of the soil, but of such alone as grow, not spontaneously, but by cultivation, and thus represent the result of man's labour. Not only so, but this last thought is the more emphasised, that the grain of the offering was not to be presented to the Lord in its natural condition as harvested, but only when, by grinding, sifting, and often, in addition, by cooking in various ways, it has been more or less fully prepared to become the food of man. In any case, it must, at least, be parched, as in the variety of the offering which is last mentioned in the chapter (vv. 14-16).

With these fundamental facts before us, we can now see what must have been the primary and distinctive significance of the meal-offering, considered as an act of worship. As the burnt-offering represented the consecration of the life, the person, to God, so the meal-offering represented the consecration of the fruit of his labours.

If it be asked, why it was that when man's labours are so manifold, and their results so diverse, the product of the cultivation of the soil should be alone selected for this purpose, for this, several reasons may be given. In the first place, of all the occupations of man, the cultivation of the soil is that of by far the greatest number, and so, in the nature of the case, must continue to be; for the sustenance of man, so far as he is at all above the savage condition, comes, in the last analysis, from the soil. Then, in particular, the Israelites of those days of Moses were about to become an agricultural nation. Most natural and suitable, then, it was that the fruit of the activities of such a people should be symbolised by the product of their fields. And since even those who gained their living in other ways than by the cultivation of the ground, must needs purchase with their earnings grain and oil, the meal-offering would, no less for them than for others, represent the consecration to God of the fruit of their labour.

The meal-offering is no longer an ordinance of worship, but the duty which it signified remains in full obligation still. Not only, in general, are we to surrender our persons without reserve to the Lord, as in the burnt-offering, but unto Him must also be consecrated all our works.

This is true, first of all, regarding our religious service. Each of us is sent into the world to do a certain spiritual work among our fellow-men. This work and all the result of it is to be offered as a holy meal-offering to the Lord. A German writer has beautifully set forth this significance of the meal-offering as regards Israel. "Israel's bodily calling was the cultivation of the ground in the land given him by Jehovah. The fruit of his calling, under the Divine blessing, was corn and wine, his bodily food, which nourished and sustained his bodily life. Israel's spiritual calling was to work in the field of the kingdom of God, in the vineyard of his Lord; this work was Israel's covenant obligation. Of this, the fruit was the spiritual bread, the spiritual nourishment, which should sustain and develop his spiritual life."* And the calling of the spiritual Israel, which is the Church, is still the same, to labour in the field of the kingdom of God, which is the world of men; and the result of this work is still the same, namely, with the Divine blessing, spiritual fruit, sustaining and developing the spiritual life of men. And in the meal-offering we are reminded that the fruit of all our spiritual labours is to be offered to the Lord.

The reminder might seem unneedful, as indeed it ought to be; but it is not. For it is sadly possible to call Christ "Lord," and, labouring in His field, do in His name many wonderful works, yet not really unto Him. A minister of the Word may with steady labour drive the ploughshare of the law, and sow continually the undoubted seed of the Word in the Master's field; and the apparent result of his work may be large, and even real, in the conversion of men to God, and a great increase of Christian zeal and activity. And yet it is quite possible that a man do this, and still do it for himself, and not for the Lord; and when success comes, begin to rejoice in his evident skill as a spiritual husband-man, and in the praise of man which this brings him; and so, while thus rejoicing in the fruit of his labours, neglect to bring of this good corn and wine which he has raised for a daily meal-offering in consecration to the Lord. Most sad is this, and humiliating, and yet sometimes it so comes to pass.

And so, indeed, it may be in every department of religious activity. The present age is without its like in the wonderful variety of its enterprise in matters benevolent and religious. On every side we see an ever-increasing army of labourers driving their various work in the field of the world. City Missions of every variety, Poor Committees with their free lodgings and soup-kitchens, Young Men's Christian Associations, Blue Ribbon Societies, the White Cross Army and the Red Cross Army, Hospital Work, Prison Reform, and so on;—there is no enumerating all the diverse improved methods of spiritual husbandry around us, nor can any one rightly depreciate the intrinsic excellence of all this, or make light of the work or of its good results. But for all this, there are signs that many need to be reminded that all such labour in God's field, however God may graciously make

* Kurtz, "Der Alt-testamentliche Opfercultus," p. 243.

use of it, is not necessarily labour for God; that labour for the good of men is not therefore of necessity labour consecrated to the Lord. For can we believe that from all this the meal-offering is always brought to HIM? The ordinance of this offering needs to be remembered by us all in connection with these things. The fruit of all these our labours must be offered daily in solemn consecration to the Lord.

But the teaching of the meal-offering reaches further than to what we call religious labours. For in that it was appointed that the offering should consist of man's daily food, Israel was reminded that God's claim for full consecration of all our activities covers everything, even to the very food we eat. There are many who consecrate, or think they consecrate, their religious activities; but seem never to have understood that the consecration of the true Israelite must cover the secular life as well,—the labour of the hand in the field, in the shop, the transactions of the office or on 'Change, and all their results, as also the recreations which we are able to command, the very food and drink which we use,—in a word, all the results and products of our labours, even in secular things. And to bring this idea vividly before Israel, it was ordered that the meal-offering should consist of food, as the most common and universal visible expression of the fruit of man's secular activities. The New Testament has the same thought (1 Cor. x. 31): "Whether ye eat or drink, or whatsoever ye do, do all to the glory of God."

And the offering was not to consist of any food which one might choose to bring, but of corn and oil, variously prepared. Not to speak yet of any deeper reason for this selection, there is one which lies quite on the surface. For these were the most common and universal articles of the food of the people. There were articles of food, then as now, which were only to be seen on the tables of the rich; but grain, in some form, was and is a necessity for all. So also the oil, which was that of the olive, was something which in that part of the world, all, the poor no less than the rich, were wont to use continually in the preparation of their food; even as it is used to-day in Syria, Italy, and other countries where the olive grows abundantly. Hence it appears that that was chosen for the offering which all, the richest and the poorest alike, would be sure to have; with the evident intent, that no one might be able to plead poverty as an excuse for bringing no meal-offering to the Lord.

Thus, if this ordinance of the meal-offering taught that God's claim for consecration covers all our activities and all their result, even to the very food that we eat, it teaches also that this claim for consecration covers all persons. From the statesman who administers the affairs of an Empire to the day-labourer in the shop, or mill, or field, all alike are hereby reminded that the Lord requires that the work of every one shall be brought and offered to Him in holy consecration.

And there was a further prescription, although not mentioned here in so many words. In some offerings, barley-meal was ordered, but for this offering the grain presented, whether parched, in the ear, or ground into meal, must be only wheat. The reason for this, and the lesson which it teaches, are plain. For wheat, in Israel, as still in most lands, was the best and most valued of the grains. Israel must not only offer unto God of the fruit of their labour, but the best result of their labours. Not only so, but when the offering was in the form of meal, cooked or uncooked, the best and finest must be presented. That, in other words, must be offered which represented the most of care and labour in its preparation, or the equivalent of this in purchase price. Which emphasises, in a slightly different form, the same lesson as the foregoing. Out of the fruit of our several labours and occupations we are to set apart especially for God, not only that which is best in itself, the finest of the wheat, but that which has cost us the most labour. David finely represented this thought of the meal-offering when he said, concerning the cattle for his burnt-offerings, which Araunah the Jebusite would have him accept without price: " I will not offer unto the Lord my God of that which doth cost me nothing."

But in the meal-offering it was not the whole product of his labour that the Israelite was directed to bring, but only a small part. How could the consecration of this small part represent the consecration of all? The answer to this question is given by the Apostle Paul, who calls attention to the fact that in the Levitical symbolism it was ordained that the consecration of a part should signify the consecration of the whole. For he writes (Rom. xi. 16), " If the first-fruit is holy, then the lump "—the whole from which the first-fruit is taken—" is also holy;" that is, the consecration of a part signifies and symbolically expresses the consecration of the whole from which that part is taken. The idea is well illustrated by a custom in India, according to which, when one visits a man of distinction, he will offer the guest a silver coin; an act of social etiquette which is intended to express the thought that all he has is at the service of the guest, and is therewith offered for his use. And so in the meal-offering. By offering to God, in this formal way, a part of the product of his labour, the Israelite expressed a recognition of His claim upon the whole, and professed a readiness to place, not this part merely, but the whole, at God's service.

But in the selection of the materials, we are pointed toward a deeper symbolism, by the injunction that in certain cases, at least, frankincense should be added to the offering. But this was not of man's food, neither was it, like the meal, and cakes, and oil, a product of man's labour. Its effect, naturally, was to give a grateful perfume to the sacrifice, that it might be, even in a physical sense, " an odour of a sweet smell." The symbolical meaning of incense, in which the frankincense was a chief ingredient, is very clearly intimated in Holy Scripture. It is suggested in David's prayer (Psalm cxli. 2): " Let my prayer be set forth as incense; the lifting up of my hands, like the evening oblation." So, in Luke i. 10, we read of the whole multitude of the people praying without the sanctuary, while the priest Zacharias was offering incense within. And, finally, in the Apocalypse, this is expressly declared to be the symbolical significance of incense; for we read (v. 8), that the four-and-twenty elders " fell down before the Lamb, having . . . golden bowls full of incense, which are the prayers of the saints." So then, without doubt, we must understand it here. In that frankincense was to be added to the meal-offering, it is signified that this offering of the fruit of our labours to the Lord must ever be accompanied by prayer; and, further, that our prayers, thus offered in this daily consecration, are most pleasing to the Lord, even as the fragrance of sweet incense unto man.

But if the frankincense, in itself, had thus a symbolical meaning, it is not unnatural to infer the same also with regard to other elements of the sacrifice. Nor is it, in view of the nature of the symbols, hard to discover what that should be.

For inasmuch as that product of labour is selected for the offering, which is the food by which men live, we are reminded that this is to be the final aspect under which all the fruit of our labours is to be regarded; namely, as furnishing and supplying for the need of the many that which shall be bread to the soul. In the highest sense, indeed, this can only be said of Him who by His work became the Bread of Life for the world, who was at once " the Sower " and " the Corn of Wheat " cast into the ground; and yet, in a lower sense, it is true that the work of feeding the multitudes with the bread of life is the work of us all; and that in all our labours and engagements we are to keep this in mind as our supreme earthly object. Just as the products of human labour are most diverse, and yet all are capable of being exchanged in the market for bread for the hungry, so are we to use all the products of our labour with this end in view, that they may be offered to the Lord as cakes of fine meal for the spiritual sustenance of man.

And the oil, too, which entered into every form of the meal-offering, has in Holy Scripture a constant and invariable symbolical meaning. It is the uniform symbol of the Holy Spirit of God. Isaiah lxi. 1 is decisive on this point, where in prophecy the Messiah speaks thus: " The Spirit of the Lord God is upon me; because the Lord God hath anointed me to preach good tidings." Quite in accord with this, we find that when Jesus reached thirty years of age,—the time for beginning priestly service,—He was set apart for His work, not as the Levitical priests, by anointing with symbolical oil, but by the anointing with the Holy Ghost descending on Him at His baptism. So, also, in the Apocalypse, the Church is symbolised by seven golden candlesticks, or lamp-stands, supplied with oil after the manner of that in the temple, reminding us that as the lamp can give light only as supplied with oil, so, if the Church is to be a light in the world, she must be continually supplied with the Spirit of God. Hence, the injunction that the meal of the offering be kneaded with oil, and that, of whatever form the offering be, oil should be poured upon it, is intended, according to this usage, to teach us, that in all work which shall be offered so as to be acceptable to God, must enter, as an inworking and abiding agent, the life-giving Spirit of God.

It is another direction as to these meal-offerings, as also regarding all offerings made by fire, that into them should never enter leaven (ver. 11). The symbolical significance of this prohibition is familiar to all. For in all leaven is a principle of decay and corruption, which, except its continued operation be arrested betimes in our preparation of leavened food, will soon make that in which it works offensive to the taste. Hence, in Holy Scripture, leaven, without a single exception, is the established symbol of spiritual corruption. It is this, both as considered in itself, and in virtue of its power of self-propagation in the leavened mass. Hence the Apostle Paul, using familiar symbolism, charged the Corinthians (1 Cor. v. 7) that they "purge out from themselves the old leaven; and that they keep festival, not with the leaven of malice and wickedness, but with the unleavened bread of sincerity and truth." Thus, in this prohibition is brought before us the lesson, that we take heed to keep out of those works which we present to God for consumption on His altar the leaven of wickedness in every form. The prohibition, in the same connection, of honey (ver. 11) rests upon the same thought; namely, that honey, like leaven, tends to promote fermentation and decay in that with which it is mixed.

The Revised Version—in this case doubtless to be preferred to the other—brings out a striking qualification of this universal prohibition of leaven or honey, in these words (ver. 12): "As an oblation of first-fruits ye shall offer them unto the Lord; but they shall not come up for a sweet savour on the altar."

Thus, as the prohibition of leaven and honey from the meal-offering burned by fire upon the altar reminds us that the Holy One demands absolute freedom from all that is corrupt in the works of His people; on the other hand, this gracious permission to offer leaven and honey in the first-fruits (which were *not* burned on the altar) seems intended to remind us that, nevertheless, from the Israelite in covenant with God through atoning blood, He is yet graciously pleased to accept even offerings in which sinful imperfection is found, so that only, as in the offering of first-fruits, there be the hearty recognition of His rightful claim, before all others, to the first and best we have.

In ver. 13 we have a last requisition as to the material of the meal-offering: "Every oblation of thy meal-offering shalt thou season with salt." As leaven is a principle of impermanence and decay, so salt, on the contrary, has the power of conservation from corruption. Accordingly, to this day, among the most diverse peoples, salt is the recognised symbol of incorruption and unchanging perpetuity. Among the Arabs of today, for example, when a compact or covenant is made between different parties, it is the custom that each eat of salt, which is passed around on the blade of a sword; by which act they regard themselves as bound to be true, each to the other, even at the peril of life. In like manner, in India and other Eastern countries, the usual word for perfidy and breach of faith is, literally, "unfaithfulness to the salt;" and a man will say, "Can you distrust me? Have I not eaten of your salt?" That the symbol has this recognised meaning in the meal-offering is plain from the words which follow (ver. 13): "Neither shalt thou suffer the salt of the covenant of thy God to be wanting from thy meal-offering." In the meal-offering, as in all offerings made by fire, the thought was this: that Jehovah and the Israelite, as it were, partake of salt together, in token of the eternal permanence of the holy covenant of salvation into which Israel has entered with God.

Herein we are taught, then, that by the consecration of our labours to God we recognise the relation between the believer and his Lord, as not occasional and temporary, but eternal and incorruptible. In all our consecration of our works to God, we are to keep this thought in mind: "I am a man with whom God has entered into an everlasting covenant, 'a covenant of salt.'"

Three varieties of the meal-offering were prescribed: the first (vv. 1-3), of uncooked meal; the second (vv. 4-11), of the same fine meal and oil, variously prepared by cooking; the third (vv. 14-16), of the first and best ears of the new grain, simply parched in the fire. If any special significance is to be recognised in this variety of the offerings, it may possibly be found in this, that one form might be suited better than another to persons of different resources. It has been supposed that the different implements named—the oven, the baking-pan or plate, the frying-pan—represent, respectively, what different classes of the people might be more or less likely to have. This thought more certainly appears in the permission even of parched grain, which then, as still in the East, while used more or less by all, was especially the food of the poorest of the people; such as might even be too poor to own so much as an oven or a baking-pan.

In any case, the variety which was permitted teaches us, that whatever form the product of our labour may take, as determined either by our poverty or our riches, or by whatever reason, God is graciously willing to accept it, so the oil, frankincense, and salt be not wanting. It is our privilege, as it is our duty, to offer of it in consecration to our redeeming Lord, though it be no more than parched corn. The smallness or meanness of what we have to give, need not keep us back from presenting our meal-offering.

If we have rightly understood the significance of this offering, the ritual which is given will now easily yield us its lessons. As in the case of the burnt-offering, the meal-offering also must be brought unto the Lord by the offerer himself. The consecration of our works, like the consecration of our persons, must be our own voluntary act. Yet the offering must be delivered through the mediation of the priest; the offerer must not presume himself to lay it on the altar. Even so still. In this, as in all else, the Heavenly High Priest must act in our behalf with God. We do not, by our consecration of our works, therefore become able to dispense with His offices as Mediator between us and God. This is the thought of many, but it is a great mistake. No offering made to God, except in and through the appointed Priest, can be accepted of Him.

It was next directed that the priest, having received the offering at the hand of the worshipper, should make a twofold use of it. In the burnt-offering the whole was to be burnt; but in the meal-offering only a small part. The priest was to take out of the offering, in each case, "a memorial thereof, and burn it on the altar"; and then it is added (vv. 3-10), "that which is left of the meal offering"—which was always much the larger part—"shall be Aaron's and his sons'." The small part taken out by the priest for the altar was burnt with fire; and its consumption by the fire of the altar, as in the other offerings, symbolised God's gracious acceptance and appropriation of the offering.

But here the question naturally arises, if the total consecration of the worshipper and his full acceptance by God, in the case of the burnt-offering, was signified by the burning of the whole, how is it that, in this case, where also we must think of a consecration of the whole, yet only a small part was offered to God in the fire of the altar? But the difficulty is only in appearance. For, no less than in the burnt-offering, all of the meal-offering is presented to God, and all is no less truly accepted by Him. The difference in the two cases is only in the use to which God puts the offering. A part of the meal-offering is burnt on the altar as "a memorial," to signify that God takes notice of and graciously accepts the consecrated fruit of our labours. It is called "a memorial" in that, so to speak, it reminded the Lord of the service and devotion of His faithful servant. The thought is well illustrated by the words of Nehemiah (v. 19), who said: "Think upon me, O Lord, for good, according to all that I have done for this people;" and by the word of the angel to Cornelius (Acts x. 4): "Thy prayers and thine alms are gone up for a memorial before God;" for a memorial in such wise as to procure to him a gracious visitation.

The remaining and larger portion of the meal-offering was given to the priest, as being the servant of God in the work of His house. To this service he was set apart from secular occupations, that he might give himself wholly to the duties of this office. In this he must needs be supported; and to this end it was ordained by God that a certain part of the various offerings should be given him, as we shall see more fully hereafter.

In striking contrast with this ordinance, which gave the largest part of the meal-offering to the priest, is the law that of the frankincense he must take nothing; "all" must go up to God, with the "memorial," in the fire of the altar (vv. 2, 16). But in consistency with the symbolism it could not be otherwise. For the frankincense was the emblem of prayer, adoration, and praise; of this, then, the priest must take naught for himself. The manifest lesson is one for all who preach the Gospel. Of the incense of praise which may ascend from the hearts of God's people, as they minister the Word, they must take none for themselves. "Not unto us, O Lord, but unto Thy name be the glory."

Such then was the meaning of the meal-offering. It represents the consecration unto God by the grace of the Holy Spirit, with prayer and praise, of all the work of our hands; an offering with salt, but without leaven, in token of our unchanging covenant with a holy God. And God accepts the offerings thus presented by His people, as a savour of a sweet smell, with which He is well pleased. We have called this consecration a duty; is it not rather a most exalted privilege?

Only let us remember, that although our consecrated offerings are accepted, we are not accepted because of the offerings. Most instructive it is to observe that the meal-offerings were not to be offered alone; a bloody sacrifice, a burnt-offering or sin-offering, must always precede. How vividly this brings before us the truth that it is only when first our persons have been cleansed by atoning blood, and thus and therefore consecrated unto God, that the consecration and acceptance of our works is possible. We are not accepted because we consecrate our works, but our consecrated works themselves are accepted because first we have been "accepted in the Beloved" through faith in the blood of the holy Lamb of God.

The Daily Meal-Offering.

Leviticus vi. 14-23.

"And this is the law of the meal-offering: the sons of Aaron shall offer it before the Lord, before the altar. And he shall take up therefrom his handful, of the fine flour of the meal-offering and of the oil thereof, and all the frankincense which is upon the meal-offering, and shall burn it upon the altar for a sweet savour, as the memorial thereof, unto the Lord. And that which is left thereof shall Aaron and his sons eat: it shall be eaten without leaven in a holy place: in the court of the tent of meeting they shall eat it. It shall not be baken with leaven. I have given it as their portion of My offerings made by fire; it is most holy, as the sin-offering, and as the guilt-offering. Every male among the children of Aaron shall eat of it, as a due for ever throughout your generations, from the offerings of the Lord made by fire: whosoever toucheth them shall be holy. And the Lord spake unto Moses, saying, This is the oblation of Aaron and of his sons, which they shall offer unto the Lord in the day when he is anointed; the tenth part of an ephah of fine flour for a meal-offering perpetually, half of it in the morning, and half thereof in the evening. On a baking-pan it shall be made with oil; when it is soaked, thou shalt bring it in: in baken pieces shalt thou offer the meal-offering for a sweet savour unto the Lord. And the anointed priest that shall be in his stead from among his sons shall offer it: by a statute for ever it shall be wholly burnt unto the Lord. And every meal-offering of the priest shall be wholly burnt: it shall not be eaten."

As there were not only the burnt-offerings of the individual Israelite, but also a daily burnt-offering, morning and evening, presented by the priest as the representative of the collective nation, so also with the meal-offering. The law concerning this daily meal-offering is given in chap. vi. 19. The amount in this case was prescribed, being apparently the amount regarded as a day's portion of food—"the tenth part of an ephah of fine flour," half of which was to be offered in the morning and half in the evening, made on a baking pan with oil, "for a sweet savour unto the Lord." Unlike the meal-offering of the individual, it is said, "by a statute for ever, it shall be wholly burnt unto the Lord. . . Every meal-offering of the priest shall be wholly burnt; it shall not be eaten." This single variation from the ordinance of chap. ii. is simply an application of the principle which governs all the sacrifices except the peace-offering, that he who offered any sacrifice could never himself eat of it; and as the priest in this case was the offerer, the symbolism required that he should himself have nothing of the offering, as being wholly given by him to the Lord. And this meal-offering was to be presented, not merely, as some have inferred from ver. 20, on the day of the anointing of the high priest, but, as is expressly said, "perpetually."

The typical meaning of the meal-offering, and, in particular, of this daily meal-offering, which, as we learn from Exod. xxx. 39, 40, was offered with the daily burnt-offering, is very clear. Every meal-offering pointed to Christ in His consecration of all His works to the Father. And as the daily burnt-offering presented by Aaron and his sons typified our heavenly High Priest as offering His person in daily consecration unto God in our behalf, so, in the daily meal-offering, wholly burnt upon the altar, we see Him in like manner offering unto God in perfect consecration, day by day, perpetually, all His works for our acceptance. To the believer, often sorely oppressed with the sense of the imperfection of his own consecration of his daily works, in that because of this the Father is not glorified by him as He should be, how exceedingly comforting this view of Christ! For that which, at the best, we do so imperfectly and interruptedly, He does in our behalf perfectly, and with never-failing constancy; thus at once perfectly glorifying the Father, and also, through the virtue of the boundless merit of this consecration, constantly procuring for us daily grace unto the life eternal.

CHAPTER V.

THE PEACE-OFFERING.

LEVITICUS iii. 1-17; vii. 11-34; xix. 5-8; xxii. 21-25.

IN chap. iii. is given, though not with completeness, the law of the peace-offering. The alternative rendering of this term, "thank-offering" (marg. R. V.), precisely expresses only one variety of the peace-offering; and while it is probably impossible to find any one word that shall express in a satisfactory way the whole conception of this offering, it is not easy to find one better than the familiar term which the Revisers have happily retained. As will be made clear in the sequel, it was the main object of this offering, as consisting of a sacrifice terminating in a festive sacrificial meal, to express the conception of friendship, peace, and fellowship with God as secured by the shedding of atoning blood.

Like the burnt-offering and the meal-offering, the peace-offering had come down from the times before Moses. We read of it, though not explicitly named, in Gen. xxxi. 54, on the occasion of the covenant between Jacob and Laban, wherein they jointly took God as witness of their covenant of friendship; and, again, in Exod. xviii. 12, where "Jethro took a burnt-offering and sacrifices for God; and Aaron came and all the elders of Israel, to eat bread with Moses' father-in-law before God." Nor was this form of sacrifice, any more than the burnt-offering, confined to the line of Abraham's seed. Indeed, scarcely any religious custom has from the most remote antiquity been more universally observed than this of a sacrifice essentially connected with a sacrificial meal. An instance of the heathen form of this sacrifice is even given in the Pentateuch, where we are told (Exod. xxxii. 6) how the people, having made the golden calf, worshipped it with peace-offerings, and "sat down to eat and to drink" at the sacrificial meal which was inseparable from the peace-offering; while in 1 Cor. x. Paul refers to like sacrificial feasts as common among the idolaters of Corinth.

It hardly needs to be again remarked that there is nothing in such facts as these to trouble the faith of the Christian, any more than in the general prevalence of worship and of prayer among heathen nations. Rather, in all these cases alike, are we to see the expression on the part of man of a sense of need and want, especially, in this case, of friendship and fellowship with God; and, seeing that the conception of a sacrifice culminating in a feast was, in truth, most happily adapted to symbolise this idea, surely it were nothing strange that God should base the ordinances of His own worship upon such universal conceptions and customs, correcting in them only, as we shall see, what might directly or indirectly misrepresent truth. Where an alphabet, so to speak, is thus already found existing, whether in letters or in symbols, why should the Lord communicate a new and unfamiliar symbolism, which, because new and unfamiliar, would have been, for that reason, far less likely to be understood?

The plan of chap. iii. is very simple; and there is little in its phraseology requiring explanation. Prescriptions are given for the offering of peace-offerings, first, from the herd (vv. 1-5); then, from the flock, whether of the sheep (vv. 6-11) or of the goats (vv. 12-16). After each of these three sections it is formally declared of each offering that it is "a sweet savour," "an offering made by fire," or "the food of the offering made by fire unto the Lord." The chapter then closes with a prohibition, specially occasioned by the directions for this sacrifice, of all use by Israel of fat or blood as food.

The regulations relating to the selection of the victim for the offering differ from those for the burnt-offering in allowing a greater liberty of choice. A female was permitted, as well as a male; though recorded instances of the observance of the peace-offering indicate that the male was even here preferred when obtainable. The offering of a dove or a pigeon is not, however, mentioned as permissible, as in the case of the burnt-offering. But this is no exception to the rule of greater liberty of choice, since these were excluded by the object of the offering as a sacrificial meal, for which, obviously, a small bird would be insufficient. Ordinarily, the victim must be without blemish; and yet, even in this matter, a larger liberty was allowed (chap. xxii. 23) in the case of those which were termed "free-will offerings," where it was permitted to offer even a bullock or a lamb which might have "some part superfluous or lacking." The latitude of choice thus allowed finds its sufficient explanation in the fact that while the idea of representation and expiation had a place in the peace-offering as in all bloody offerings, yet this was subordinate to the chief intent of the sacrifice, which was to represent the victim as food given by God to Israel in the sacrificial meal. It is to be observed that only such defects are therefore allowed in the victim as could not possibly affect its value as food. And so even already, in these regulations as to the selection of the victim, we have a hint that we have now to do with a type, in which the dominant thought is not so much Christ, the Holy Victim, our representative, as Christ the Lamb of God, the food of the soul, through participation in which we have fellowship with God.

As before remarked, the ritual acts in the bloody sacrifices are, in all, six, each of which, in the peace-offering, has its proper place. Of these, the first four, namely, the presentation, the laying on of the hand, the killing of the victim, and the sprinkling of the blood, are precisely the same as in the burnt-offering, and have the same symbolic and typical significance. In both the burnt-offering and the peace-offering, the innocent victim typified the Lamb of God, presented by the sinner in the act of faith to God as an atonement for sin through substitutionary death; and the sprinkling of the blood upon the altar signifies in this, as in the other, the application of that blood Godward by the Divine Priest acting in our behalf, and thereby procuring for us remission of sin, redemption through the blood of the slain Lamb.

In the other two ceremonies, namely, the burning and the sacrificial meal, the peace-offering stands in strong contrast with the burnt-offering. In the burnt-offering all was burned upon the altar; in the peace-offering all the fat, and that only. The detailed directions which are given in the case of each class of victims are intended simply to direct the selection of those parts of the animal in which the fat is chiefly found. They are precisely the same for each, except in the case of the sheep. With regard to such a victim, the particular is added, according to King James's version, "the whole rump;" but the Revisers have with abundant reason corrected this translation, giving it correctly as "the fat tail entire." The change is an instructive one, as it points to the idea which determined this selection of all the fat for the offering by fire. For the reference is to a special breed of sheep which is still found in Palestine, Arabia, and North Africa. With these, the tail grows to an immense size, sometimes weighing fifteen pounds or more, and consists almost entirely of a rich substance, in character between fat and marrow. By the Orientals in the regions where this variety of sheep is found it is still esteemed as the most valuable part of the animal for food. And thus, just as in the meal-offering the Israelite was required to bring out of all his grain the best, and of his meal the finest, so in the peace-offering he is required to bring the fat, and in the case of the sheep this fat tail, as the best and richest parts, to be burnt upon the altar to Jehovah. And the burning, as in the whole burnt-sacrifice, was, so to speak, the visible Divine appropriation of that which was placed upon the altar, the best of the offering, as appointed to be "the food of God." If the symbolism, at first thought, perplex any, we have but to remember how frequently in Scripture "fat" and "fatness" are used as the symbol of that which is richest and best; as, *e. g.*, where the Psalmist says, "They shall be abundantly satisfied with the fatness of Thy house;" and Isaiah, "Come unto Me, and let your soul delight itself in fatness." Thus when, in the peace-offering, of which the larger part was intended for food, it is ordered that the fat should be given to God in the fire of the altar, the same lesson is taught as in the meal-offering, namely, God is ever to be served first and with the best that we have. "All the fat is the Lord's."

In the burnt-offering, the burning ended the ceremonial: in the nature of the case, since all was to be burnt, the object of the sacrifice was attained when the burning was completed. But in the case of the peace-offering, to the burning of the fat upon the altar now followed the culminating act of the ritual, in the eating of the sacrifice. In this, however, we must distinguish from the eating by the offerer and his household, the eating by the priests; of which only the first-named properly belonged to the ceremonial of the sacrifice. The assignment of certain parts of the sacrifice to be eaten by the priests has the same meaning as in the meal-offering. These portions were regarded in the law as given, not by the offerer, but by God, to His servants the priests; that they might eat them, not as a ceremonial act, but as their appointed sustenance from His table whom they served. To this we shall return in a subsequent chapter, and therefore need not dwell upon it here.

This eating of the sacrifice by the priests has thus not yet taken us beyond the conception of the meal-offering, with a part of which they, in like manner, by God's arrangement, were fed. Quite different, however, is the sacrificial eating by the offerer which follows. He had brought the appointed victim; it had been slain in his behalf; the blood had been sprinkled for atonement on the altar; the fat had been taken off and burned upon the altar; the thigh and breast had been given back by God to the officiating priest; and now, last of all, the offerer himself receives back from God, as it were, the remainder of the flesh of the victim, that he himself might eat it before Jehovah. The chapter before us gives no directions as to this sacrificial eating; these are given in Deut. xii. 6, 7, 17, 18, to which passage, in order to the full understanding of that which is most distinctive in the peace-offering, we must refer. In the two verses last named, we have a regulation which covers, not only the peace-offerings, but with them all other sacrificial eatings, thus: "Thou mayest not eat within thy gates the tithe of thy corn, or of thy wine, or of thy oil, or the firstlings of thy herd or of thy flock, nor any of thy vows which thou vowest, nor thy free-will offerings, nor the heave-offering of thy hand: but thou shalt eat them before the Lord thy God in the place which the Lord thy God shall choose, thou and thy son, and thy daughter, and thy man-servant, and thy maid-servant, and the Levite that is within thy gates; and thou shalt rejoice before the Lord thy God in all that thou puttest thy hand unto."

In these directions are three particulars; the offerings were to be eaten, by the offerer, not at his own home, but before Jehovah at the central sanctuary; he was to include in this sacrificial feast all the members of his family, and any Levite that might be stopping with him; and he was to make the feast an occasion of holy joy before the Lord in the labour of his hands. What was now the special significance of all this? As this was the special characteristic of the peace-offering, the answer to this question will point us to its true significance, both for Israel in the first place, and then for us as well, as a type of Him who was to come.

It is not hard to perceive the significance of a feast as a symbol. It is a natural and suitable expression of friendship and fellowship. He who gives the feast thereby shows to the guests his friendship toward them, in inviting them to partake of the food of his house. And if, in any case, there has been an interruption or breach of friendship, such an invitation to a feast, and association in it of the formerly alienated parties, is a declaration on the part of him who gives the feast, as also of those who accept his invitation, that the breach is healed, and that where there was enmity, is now peace.

So natural is this symbolism that, as above remarked, it has been a custom very widely spread among heathen peoples to observe sacrificial feasts, very like to this peace-offering of the Hebrews, wherein a victim is first offered to some deity, and its flesh then eaten by the offerer and his friends. Of such sacrificial feasts we read in ancient Babylonia and Assyria, in Persia, and, in modern times, among the Arabs, Hindoos, and Chinese, and various native races of the American continent; always having the same symbolic intent and meaning—namely, an expression of desire after friendship and intercommunion with the deity thus worshipped. The existence of this custom in Old Testament days is recognised in Isa. lxv. 11 (R. V.), where God charges the idolatrous Israelites with preparing "a table for the god Fortune," and filling up "mingled wine unto (the goddess) Destiny"—certain Babylonian (?) deities; and in the New Testament, as already remarked, the Apostle Paul refers to the same custom among the idolatrous Greeks of Corinth.

And because this symbolic meaning of a feast is as suitable and natural as it is universal, we find that in the symbolism of Holy Scripture, eating and drinking, and especially the feast, has been appropriated by the Holy Spirit to express precisely the same ideas of reconciliation, friendship, and intercommunion between the giver of the feast and the guest, as in all the great heathen religions. We meet this thought, for instance, in Psalm xxiii. 5: "Thou preparest a table before me in the presence of my enemies;" and in Psalm xxxvi. 8, where it is said of God's people: "They shall be abundantly satisfied with the fatness of Thy house;" and again, in the grand prophecy in Isaiah xxv., of the final redemption of all the long-estranged nations, we read that when God shall destroy in Mount Zion "the veil that is spread over all nations, and swallow up death for ever," then "the Lord of hosts shall make unto all peoples a feast of fat things, a feast of wines on the lees, of fat things full of marrow, of wines on the lees well refined." And in the New Testament, the symbolism is taken up again, and used repeatedly by our Lord, as, for example, in the parables of the Great Supper (Luke xiv. 15-24) and the Prodigal Son (Luke xv. 23), the Marriage of the King's Son (Matt. xxii. 1-14), concerning the blessings of redemption; and also in that ordinance of the Holy Supper, which He has appointed to be a continual reminder of our relation to Himself, and means for the communication of His grace, through our symbolic eating therein of the flesh of the slain Lamb of God.

Thus, nothing in the Levitical symbolism is better certified to us than the meaning of the feast of the peace-offering. Employing a symbol already familiar to the world for centuries, God ordained this eating of the peace-offering in Israel, to be the symbolic expression of peace and fellowship with Himself. In Israel it was to be eaten "before the Lord," and, as well it might be, "with rejoicing."

But, just at this point, the question has been raised: How are we to conceive of the sacrificial feast of the peace-offering? Was it a feast offered and presented by the Israelite to God, or a feast given by God to the Israelite? In other words, in this feast, who was represented as host, and who as guest? Among other nations than the Hebrews, it was the thought in such cases that the feast was given by the worshipper to his god. This is well illustrated by an Assyrian inscription of Esarhaddon, who, in describing his palace at Nineveh, says: "I filled with beauties the great palace of my empire, and I called it 'the Palace which rivals the World.' Ashur, Ishtar of Nineveh, and the gods of Assyria, all of them, I feasted within it. Victims, precious and beautiful, I sacrificed before them, and I caused them to receive my gifts."

But here we come upon one of the most striking and instructive contrasts between the heathen conception of the sacrificial feast and the same symbolism as used in Leviticus and other Scripture. In the heathen sacrificial feasts, it is man who feasts God; in the peace-offering of Leviticus, it is God who feasts man. Some have indeed denied that this is the conception of the peace-offering, but most strangely. It is true that the offerer, in the first instance, had brought the victim; but it seems to be forgotten by such, that prior to the feasting he had already given the victim to God, to be offered in expiation for sin. From that time the victim was no longer, any part of it, his own property, but God's. God having received the offering, now directs what use shall be made of it; a part shall be burned upon the altar; another part He gives to the priests, His servants; with the remaining part He now feasts the worshipper.

And as if to make this clearer yet, while Esarhaddon, for example, gives his feast to the gods, not in their temples, but in his own palace, as himself the host and giver of the feast, the Israelite, on the contrary,—that he might not, like the heathen, complacently imagine himself to be feasting God,—is directed to eat the peace-offering, not at his own house, but at God's house. In this way God was set forth as the host, the One who gave the feast, to whose house the Israelite was invited, at whose table he was to eat.

Profoundly suggestive and instructive is this contrast between the heathen custom in this offering, and the Levitical ordinance. For do we not strike here one of the deepest points of contrast between all of man's religion, and the Gospel of God? Man's idea always is, until taught better by God, "I will be religious and make God my friend, by doing something, giving something for God." God, on the contrary, teaches us in this symbolism, as in all Scripture, the exact reverse; that we become truly religious by taking, first of all, with thankfulness and joy, what He has provided for us. A breach of friendship between man and God is often implied in the heathen rituals, as in the ritual of Leviticus; as also, in both, a desire for its removal, and renewed fellowship with God. But in the former, man ever seeks to attain to this intercommunion of friendship by something that he himself will do for God. He will feast God, and thus God shall be well pleased. But God's way is the opposite! The sacrificial feast at which man shall have fellowship with God is provided not by man for God, but by God for man, and is to be eaten, not in our house, but spiritually partaken in the presence of the invisible God.

We can now perceive the teaching of the peace-offering for Israel. In Israel, as among all the nations, was the inborn craving after fellowship and friendship with God. The ritual of the peace-offering taught him how it was to be obtained, and how communion might be realised. The first thing was for him to bring and present a divinely-appointed victim; and then, the laying of the hand upon his head with confession of sin; then, the slaying of the victim, the sprinkling of its blood, and the offering of its choicest parts to God in the altar fire. Till all this was done, till in symbol expiation had been thus made for the Israelite's sin, there could be no feast which should speak of friendship and fellowship with God. But this being first done, God now, in token of His free forgiveness and restoration to favour, invites the Israelite to a joyful feast in His own house.

What a beautiful symbol! Who can fail to appreciate its meaning when once pointed out? Let us imagine that through some fault of ours a dear friend has become estranged; we used to eat and drink at his house, but there has been none of that now for a long time. We are troubled, and perhaps seek out one who is our friend's friend and also our friend, to whose kindly interest we entrust our case, to reconcile to us the one we have offended. He has gone to mediate; we anxiously await his return; but or ever he has come back again, comes an invitation from him who was estranged, just in the old loving way, asking that we will eat with him at his house. Any one of us would understand this; we should be sure at once that the mediator had healed the breach, that we were forgiven, and were welcome as of old to all that our friend's friendship had to give.

But God is the good Friend whom we have estranged; and the Lord Jesus, His beloved Son, and our own Friend as well, is the Mediator; and He has healed the breach; having made expiation for our sin in offering His own body as a sacrifice, He has ascended into heaven, there to appear in the presence of God for us; He has not yet returned. But meantime the message comes down from Him to all who are hungering after peace with God: "The feast is made; and ye all are invited; come! all things are now ready!" And this is the message of the Gospel. It is the peace-offering translated into words. Can we hesitate to accept the invitation? Or, if we have sent in our acceptance, do we need to be told, as in Deuteronomy, that we are to eat "with rejoicing."

And now we may well observe another circumstance of profound typical significance. When the Israelite came to God's house to eat before Jehovah, he was fed there with the flesh of the slain victim. The flesh of that very victim whose blood had been given for him on the altar, now becomes his food to sustain the life thus redeemed. Whether the Israelite saw into the full meaning of this, we may easily doubt; but it leads us on now to consider, in the clearer light of the New Testament, the deepest significance of the peace-offering and its ritual, as typical of our Lord and our relation to Him.

That the victim of the peace-offering, as of all the bloody offerings, was intended to typify Christ, and that the death of that victim, in the peace-offering, as in all the bloody offerings, foreshadowed the death of Christ for our sins,— this needs no further proof. And so, again, as the burning of the whole burnt-offering represented Christ as accepted for us in virtue of His perfect consecration to the Father, so the peace-offering, in that the fat is burned, represents Christ as accepted for us, in that He gave to God in our behalf the very best He had to offer. For in that incomparable sacrifice we are to think not only of the completeness of Christ's consecration for us, but also of the supreme excellence of that which He offered unto God for us. All that was best in Him, reason, affection, and will, as well as the members of His holy body,—nay, the Godhead as well as the Manhood, in the holy mystery of the Trinity and the Incarnation, He offered for us unto the Father.

This, however, has taken us as yet but little beyond the meaning of the burnt-offering. The closing act of the ritual, the sacrificial eating, however, reaches in its typical significance far beyond this or any of the bloody offerings.

First, in that he who had laid his hand upon the victim, and for whom the blood had been sprinkled, is now invited by God to feast in His house, upon food given by himself, the food of the sacrifice, which is called in the ritual "the bread of God," the eating of the peace-offering symbolically teaches us that if we have indeed presented the Lamb of God as our peace, not only has the Priest sprinkled for us the blood, so that our sin is pardoned, but, in token of friendship now restored, God invites the penitent believer to sit down at His own table,—in a word, to joyful fellowship with Himself! Which means, if our weak faith but take it in, that the Almighty and Most Holy God now invites us to fellowship in all the riches of His Godhead; places all that He has at the service of the believing sinner, redeemed by the blood of the slain Lamb. The prodigal has returned; the Father will now feast him with the best that He has. Fellowship with God through reconciliation by the blood of the slain Lamb,—this then is the first thing shadowed forth in this part of the ritual of the peace-offering. It is a sufficiently wonderful thought, but there is truth yet more wonderful veiled under this symbolism.

For when we ask, what then was the bread or food of God, of which He invited him to partake who brought the peace-offering, and learn that it was the flesh of the slain victim; here we meet a thought which goes far beyond atonement by the shedding of blood. The same victim whose blood was shed and sprinkled in atonement for sin is now given by God to be the redeemed Israelite's food, by which his life shall be sustained! Surely we cannot mistake the meaning of this. For the victim of the altar and the food of the table are one and the same. Even so He who offered Himself for our sins on Calvary, is now given by God to be the food of the believer; who now thus lives by "eating the flesh" of the slain Lamb of God. Does this imagery, at first thought, seem strange and unnatural? So did it also seem strange to the Jews, when in reply to our Lord's teaching they wonderingly asked (John vi. 52), "How can this man give us His flesh to eat?" And yet so Christ spoke; and when He had first declared Himself to the Jews as the Antitype of the manna, the true Bread sent down from heaven, He then went on to say, in words which far transcended the meaning of that type (John vi. 51), "The bread which I will give is My flesh, for the life of the world." How the light begins now to flash back from the Gospel to the Levitical law, and from this, again, back to the Gospel! In the one we read, "Ye shall eat the flesh of your peace-offerings before the Lord with joy;" in the other, the word of the Lord Jesus concerning Himself (John vi. 33, 55, 57): "The bread of God is that which cometh down out of heaven, and giveth life unto the world... My flesh is meat indeed, and My blood is drink indeed... As the living Father sent Me, and I live because of the Father, so he that eateth Me, he also shall live because of Me." And now the Shekinah light of the ancient tent of meeting begins to illumine even the sacramental table, and as we listen to the words of Jesus, "Take, eat! this is My body which was broken for you," we are reminded of the feast of the peace-offerings. The Israel of God is to be fed with the flesh of the sacrificed Lamb which became their peace.

Let us hold fast then to this deepest thought of the peace-offering, a truth too little understood even by many true believers. The very Christ who died for our sins, if we have by faith accepted His atonement and have been for His sake forgiven, is now given us by God for the sustenance of our purchased life. Let us make use of Him, daily feeding upon Him, that so we may live and grow unto the life eternal!

But there is yet one thought more concerning this matter, which the peace-offering, as far as was possible, shadowed forth. Although Christ becomes the bread of God for us only through His offering of Himself first for our sins, as our atonement, yet this is something quite distinct from atonement. Christ became our sacrifice once for all; the atonement is wholly a fact of the past. But Christ is now still, and will ever continue to be unto all His people, the bread or food of God, by eating whom they live. He was the propitiation, as the slain victim; but, in virtue of that, He is now become the flesh of the peace-offering. Hence He must be this, not as dead, but as living, in the present resurrection life of His glorified humanity. Here evidently is a fact which could not be directly symbolised in the peace-offering without a miracle ever repeated. For Israel ate of the victim, not as living, but as dead. It could not be otherwise. And yet there is a regulation of the ritual (chap. vii. 15-18; xix. 6, 7) which suggests this phase of truth as clearly as possible without a miracle. It was ordered that none of the flesh of the peace-offering should be allowed to remain beyond the third day; if any then was left uneaten, it was to be burned with fire. The reason for this lies upon the surface. It was doubtless that there might be no possible beginning of decay; and thus it was secured that the flesh of the victim with which God fed the accepted Israelite should be the flesh of a victim that was not to see corruption. But does not this at once remind us how it was written of the Antitype, "Thou wilt not suffer Thy Holy One to see corruption"? while, moreover, the extreme limit of time allowed further reminds us how it was precisely on the third day that Christ rose from the dead in the incorruptible life of the resurrection, that so He might through all time continue to be the living bread of His people.

And thus this special regulation points us not indistinctly toward the New Testament truth that Christ is now unto us the bread of God, not merely as the One who died, but as the One who, living again, was not allowed to see corruption. For so the Apostle argues (Rom. v. 11), that "being justified by faith," and so having "peace with God through our Lord Jesus Christ," our peace-offering, having been thus "reconciled by His death, we shall now be saved by His life." And thus, as we appropriate Christ crucified as our atonement, so by a like faith we are to appropriate Christ risen as our life, to be for us as the flesh of the peace-offering, our nourishment and strength by which we live.

The Prohibition of Fat and Blood.

Leviticus iii. 16, 17; vii. 22-27; xvii. 10-16.

"And the priest shall burn them upon the altar: it is the food of the offering made by fire, for a sweet savour: all the fat is the Lord's. It shall be a perpetual statute throughout your generations in all your dwellings, that ye shall eat neither fat nor blood. . . . And the Lord spake unto Moses, saying, Speak unto the children of Israel, saying, Ye shall eat no fat, of ox, or sheep, or goat. And the fat of that which dieth of itself, and the fat of that which is torn of beasts, may be used for any other service; but ye shall in no wise eat of it. For whosoever eateth the fat of the beast, of which men offer an offering made by fire unto the Lord, even the soul that eateth it shall be cut off from his people. And ye shall eat no manner of blood, whether it be of fowl or of beast, in any of your dwellings. Whosoever it be that eateth any blood, that soul shall be cut off from his people. . . . And whatsoever man there be of the house of Israel, or of the strangers that sojourn among them, that eateth any manner of blood; I will set My face against that soul that eateth blood, and will cut him off from among his people. For the life of the flesh is in the blood: and I have given it to you upon the altar to make atonement for your souls: for it is the blood that maketh atonement by reason of the life. Therefore I said unto the children of Israel, No soul of you shall eat blood, neither shall any stranger that sojourneth among you eat blood. And whatsoever man there be of the children of Israel, or of the strangers that sojourn among them, which taketh in hunting any beast or fowl that may be eaten; he shall pour out the blood thereof, and cover it with dust. For as to the life of all flesh, the blood thereof is all one with the life thereof: therefore I said unto the children of Israel, Ye shall eat the blood of no manner of flesh: for the life of all flesh is the blood thereof: whosoever eateth it shall be cut off. And every soul that eateth that which dieth of itself, or that which is torn of beasts, whether he be homeborn or a stranger, he shall wash his clothes, and bathe himself in water, and be unclean until the even: then shall he be clean. But if he wash them not, nor bathe his flesh, then he shall bear his iniquity."

The chapter concerning the peace-offering ends (vv. 16, 17) with these words: "All the fat is the Lord's. It shall be a perpetual statute for you throughout your generations, that ye shall eat neither fat nor blood."

To this prohibition so much importance was attached that in the supplemental "law of the peace-offering" (vii. 22-27) it is repeated with added explanation and solemn warning, thus: "And the Lord spake unto Moses, saying, Speak unto the children of Israel, saying, Ye shall eat no manner of fat, of ox, or of sheep, òr of goat. And the fat of the beast that dieth of itself, and the fat of that which is torn with beasts, may be used for any other service: but ye shall in no wise eat of it. For whosoever eateth the fat of the beast, of which men offer an offering made by fire unto the Lord, even the soul that eateth it shall be cut off from his people. And ye shall eat no manner of blood, whether it be of fowl or of beast, in any of your dwellings. Whosoever it be that eateth any blood, that soul shall be cut off from his people."

From which it appears that this prohibition of the eating of fat referred only to the fat of such beasts as were used for sacrifice. With these, however, the law was absolute, whether the animal was presented for sacrifice, or only slain for food. It held good with regard to these animals, even when, because of the manner of their death, they could not be used for sacrifice. In such cases, though the fat might be used for other purposes, still it must not be used for food.

The prohibition of the blood as food appears from xvii. 10 to have been absolutely universal; it is said, "Whatsoever man there be of the house of Israel, or of the strangers that sojourn among them, that eateth any manner of blood, I will set My face against that soul that eateth blood, and will cut him off from among his people."

The reason for the prohibition of the eating of blood, whether in the case of the sacrificial feasts of the peace-offerings or on other occasions, is given (xvii. 11, 12), in these words: "For the life of the flesh is in the blood: and I have given it to you upon the altar to make atonement for your souls: for it is the blood that maketh atonement by reason of the life. Therefore I said unto the children of Israel, No soul of you shall eat blood, neither shall any stranger that sojourneth among you eat blood."

And the prohibition is then extended to include not only the blood of animals which were used upon the altar, but also such as were taken in hunting, thus (ver. 13): "And whatsoever man there be of the children of Israel, or of the strangers that sojourn among them, which taketh in hunting any beast or fowl that may be eaten, he shall pour out the blood thereof, and cover it with dust," as something of peculiar sanctity; and then the reason previously given is repeated with emphasis (ver. 14): "For as to the life of all flesh, the blood thereof is all one with the life thereof: therefore I said unto the children of Israel, Ye shall eat the blood of no manner of flesh: for the life of all flesh is the blood thereof; whosoever eateth it shall be cut off."

And since, when an animal died from natural causes, or through being torn of a beast, the blood would be drawn from the flesh either not at all or but imperfectly, as further guarding against the possibility of eating blood, it is ordered (vv. 15, 16) that he who does this shall be held unclean: "Every soul that eateth that which dieth of itself, or that which is torn of beasts, whether he be home-born or a stranger, he shall wash his clothes, and bathe himself in water, and be unclean until the even. But if he wash them not nor bathe his flesh, then he shall bear his iniquity."

These passages explicitly state the reason for the prohibition by God of the use of blood for food to be the fact that, as the vehicle of the life, it has been appointed by Him as the means of expiation for sin upon the altar. And the reason for the prohibition of the fat is similar; namely, its appropriation for God upon the altar, as in the peace-offerings, the sin-offerings, and the guilt-offerings; "all the fat is the Lord's."

Thus the Israelite, by these two prohibitions, was to be continually reminded, so often as he partook of his daily food, of two things: by the one, of atonement by the blood as the only ground of acceptance; and by the other, of God's claim on the man redeemed by the blood, for the consecration of his best. Not only so, but by the frequent repetition, and still more by the heavy penalty attached to the violation of these laws, he was reminded of the exceeding importance that these two things had in the mind of God. If he eat the blood of any animal claimed by God for the altar, he should be cut off from his people; that is, outlawed, and cut off from all covenant privilege as a citizen of the kingdom of God in Israel. And even though the blood were that of the beast taken in the chase, still ceremonial purification was required as the condition of resuming his covenant position.

Nothing, doubtless, seems to most Christians of our day more remote from practical religion than these regulations touching the fat and the blood which are brought before us with such fulness in the law of the peace-offering and elsewhere. And yet nothing is of more present-day importance in this law than the principles which underlie these regulations. For as with type, so with antitype. No less essential to the admission of the sinful man into that blessed fellowship with a reconciled God, which the peace-offering typified, is the recognition of the supreme sanctity of the precious sacrificial blood of the Lamb of God; no less essential to the life of happy communion with God, is the ready consecration of the best fruit of our life to Him.

Surely, both of these, and especially the first, are truths for our time. For no observing man can fail to recognise the very ominous fact that a constantly increasing number, even of professed preachers of the Gospel, in so many words refuse to recognise the place which propitiatory blood has in the Gospel of Christ, and to admit its pre-eminent sanctity as consisting in this, that it was given on the altar to make atonement for our souls. Nor has the present generation outgrown the need of the other reminder touching the consecration of the best to the Lord. How many there are, comfortable, easy-going Christians, whose principle—if one might speak in the idiom of the Mosaic law—would rather seem to be, ever to give the lean to God, and keep the fat, the best fruit of their life and activity, for themselves! Such need to be most urgently and solemnly reminded that in spirit the warning against the eating of the blood and the fat is in full force. It was written of such as should break this law, "that soul shall be cut off from his people." And so in the Epistle to the Hebrews (x. 26-29) we find one of its most solemn warnings directed to those who "count this blood of the covenant," the blood of Christ, "an unholy (*i. e.*, common) thing;" as exposed by this, their undervaluation of the sanctity of the blood, to a "sorer punishment" than overtook him that "set at naught Moses' law," even the retribution of Him who said, "Vengeance is Mine; I will repay, saith the Lord."

And so in this law of the peace-offerings, which ordains the conditions of the holy feast of fellowship with a reconciled God, we find these two things made fundamental in the symbolism: full recognition of the sanctity of the blood as that which atones for the soul; and the full consecration of the redeemed and pardoned soul to the Lord. So was it in the symbol; and so shall it be when the sacrificial feast shall at last receive its most complete fulfilment in the communion of the redeemed with Christ in glory. There will be no differences of opinion then and there, either as to the transcendent value of that precious blood which made atonement, or as to the full consecration which such a redemption requires from the redeemed.

THANK-OFFERINGS, VOWS, AND FREEWILL OFFERINGS.

LEVITICUS vii. 11-21.

"And this is the law of the sacrifice of peace-offerings which one shall offer unto the Lord. If he offer it for a thanksgiving, then he shall offer with the sacrifice of thanksgiving unleavened cakes mingled with oil, and unleavened wafers anointed with oil, and cakes mingled with oil, of fine flour soaked. With cakes of leavened bread he shall offer his oblation with the sacrifice of his peace-offerings for thanksgiving. And of it he shall offer one out of each oblation for an heave-offering unto the Lord; it shall be the priest's that sprinkleth the blood of the peace-offerings. And the flesh of the sacrifice of his peace-offerings for thanksgiving shall be eaten on the day of his oblation; he shall not leave any of it until the morning. But if the sacrifice of his oblation be a vow, or a freewill offering, it shall be eaten on the day that he offereth his sacrifice: and on the morrow that which remaineth of it shall be eaten: but that which remaineth of the flesh of the sacrifice on the third day shall be burnt with fire. And if any of the flesh of the sacrifice of his peace-offerings be eaten on the third day, it shall not be accepted, neither shall it be imputed unto him that offereth it: it shall be an abomination, and the soul that eateth of it shall bear his iniquity. And the flesh that toucheth any unclean thing shall not be eaten; it shall be burnt with fire. And as for the flesh, everyone that is clean shall eat thereof: but the soul that eateth of the flesh of the sacrifice of peace-offerings, that pertain unto the Lord, having his uncleanness upon him, that soul shall be cut off from his people. And when any one shall touch any unclean thing, the uncleanness of man, or an unclean beast, or any unclean abomination, and eat of the flesh of the sacrifice of peace-offerings, that soul shall be cut off from his people."

According to this supplemental section on the law of the peace-offerings, these were of three kinds; namely, "sacrifices of thanksgiving," "vows," and "freewill-offerings." The first were offered in token of gratitude for mercies received; as in Psalm cxvi. 16, 17, where we read: "Thou hast loosed my bonds; I will offer to Thee the sacrifice of thanksgiving." The second, like these, were offered also in grateful return for prayer answered and mercy received, but with the difference that they were promised before, upon the condition of the prayer for mercy being granted. Lastly, the freewill-offerings were those which had no special occasion, but were merely the spontaneous expression of the love of the offerer to God, and his desire to live in friendship and fellowship with Him. It is apparently these freewill-offerings that we are to recognise in the many instances recorded where the peace-offering was presented in connection with supplication for special help and favour from God; as e. g., when (Judges xx. 26) Israel supplicated mercy from God after their disastrous defeat in the civil war with the tribe of Benjamin; and when David entreated the Lord (2 Sam. xxiv. 25) for the staying of the plague in Israel.

With not only the thank-offering, but all peace-offerings, as is clear from Num. xv. 2-4, a full meal-offering, consisting of three kinds of unleavened cakes, was to be offered, of each of which, one was to be presented as a heave-offering, with the heave-shoulder of the sacrifice, to the Lord (vii. 12). For the sacrificial feast, in which the offerer, his family, and friends were to partake, he was also to bring cakes of leavened bread, which, however, though eaten before God by the offerer, might not be presented unto God for a heave-offering, nor come upon the altar (ver. 13).

From what we have already seen, the spiritual meaning of this will be clear. Thus in symbol the Israelite offered unto God, with his life, the fruit of the labour of his hands, in gratitude to Him, and expressed his happy consciousness of friendship and fellowship with God through atonement, by feasting before Him. The leavened bread is offered simply, as Bähr suggests, as the usual accompaniment to a feast; though regard is still had to the fact, never once forgotten in Holy Scripture, that leaven is nevertheless an element and symbol of corruption; so that however the reconciled Israelite may eat his leavened bread before God, yet it cannot be allowed to come upon the altar of the Most Holy One.

Two slight differences appear in the ritual for the different kinds of peace-offerings. First, in the case of the freewill-offering, a single exception is allowed to the general rule that the victim must be without blemish, in the permission to offer what, otherwise perfect, might have "anything superfluous or lacking" in its parts (xxii. 23); a circumstance which could not affect its fitness as the symbol of spiritual food. For a vow (and, we may infer, for a thank-offering also) such a victim, however, could not be offered; evidently because it would seem peculiarly unsuitable, where the object of the offering was to make in some sense a return for the always perfect and most gracious gifts of God, that anything else than the absolutely perfect should be offered. In the case of the thank-offering, again, an exception is made to the general regulation permitting the eating of the offering on the first and second days, requiring that all be eaten on the day that it is presented, or else be burnt with fire (vii. 15). We need seek for no spiritual meaning in this. A sufficient reason for this special restriction in this case is probably to be found in the consideration that as this was the most common variety of the offering, there was the most danger that the flesh, by some oversight, might be kept too long. The flesh of the victim offered to God, the type of the Victim of Calvary, must on no account be allowed to see corruption; and to this end every needed precaution must be taken, that by no chance it shall remain unconsumed on the third day.

It is easy to connect the special characteristics of these several varieties of the peace-offering with the great Antitype. So may we use Him as our thank-offering; for what more fitting as an expression of gratitude and love to God for mercies received, than renewed and special fellowship with Him through feeding upon Christ as the slain Lamb? So also we may thus use Christ in our vows; as when, supplicating mercy, we promise and engage that if our prayer be heard we will renewedly consecrate our service to the Lord, as in the meal-offering, and anew enter into life-giving fellowship with Him through feeding by faith on the flesh of the Lord. And it is beautifully hinted in the permission of the use of leaven in this feast of the peace-offering, that while the work of the believer, as presented to God in grateful acknowledgment of His mercies, is ever affected with the taint of his native corruption, so that it cannot come upon the altar where satisfaction is made for sin, yet God is graciously pleased, for the sake of the great Sacrifice, to accept such imperfect service offered to Him, and make it in turn a blessing to us, as we offer it in His presence, rejoicing in the work of our hands before Him.

But there was one condition without which the Israelite could not have communion with God in the peace-offering. He must be clean! even as the flesh of the peace-offering must be clean also. There must be in him nothing which should interrupt covenant fellowship with God; as nothing in the type which should make it an unfit symbol of the Antitype. For it was ordered (vii. 19-21), as regards every possible occasion of uncleanness, thus: "The flesh that toucheth any unclean thing shall not be eaten; it shall be burnt with fire. As for the flesh, every one that is clean shall eat thereof; but the soul that eateth of the flesh of the sacrifice of peace-offerings, that pertain unto the Lord, having his uncleanness upon him, that soul shall be cut off from his people. And when any one shall touch any unclean thing, the uncleanness of man, or an unclean beast, or any unclean abomination, and eat of the flesh of the sacrifice of peace-offerings, that soul shall be cut off from his people."

In such cases, he must first go and purify himself, as provided in the law; and then, and then only, presume to come to eat before the Lord. And so Israel was ever impressively reminded that he who would have fellowship with God, and eat in happy fellowship with Him at His table, must keep himself pure. So by the spirit of these commands are we no less warned that we take not encouragement from God's grace, in providing for us the flesh of the Lamb as our food, to be careless in walk and life. If we will use Christ as our peace-offering, we must keep ourselves "unspotted from the world;" must hate "even the garment spotted by the flesh," remembering ever that it is written in the New Testament (1 Peter i. 15, 16), with direct reference to the typical law of Leviticus: "As He which called you is holy, be ye yourselves also holy in all manner of living; because it is written, Ye shall be holy; for I am holy."

CHAPTER VI.

THE SIN-OFFERING.

LEVITICUS iv. 1-35.

BOTH in the burnt-offering and in the peace-offering, Israel was taught, as we are, that all consecration and all fellowship with God must begin with, and ever depends upon, atonement made for sin. But this was not the dominant thought in either of these offerings; neither did the atonement, as made in these, have reference to particular acts of sin. For such, these offerings were never prescribed. They remind us therefore of the necessity of atonement, not so much for what we do or fail to do, as for what we are.

But the sin even of true believers, whether then or now, is more than sin of nature. The true Israelite was liable to be overtaken in some overt act of sin; and for all such cases was ordained, in this section of the law (iv. 1-v. 13), the sin-offering; an offering which should bring out into sole and peculiar prominence the thought revealed in other sacrifices more imperfectly, that in order to pardon of sin, there must be expiation. There was indeed a limitation to the application of this offering; for if a man, in those days, sinned wilfully, presumptuously, stubbornly, or, as the phrase is, "with a high hand," there was no provision made in the law for his restoration to covenant standing. "He that despised Moses' law died without mercy under two or three witnesses;" he was "cut off from his people." But for sins of a lesser grade, such as resulted not from a spirit of wilful rebellion against God, but were mitigated in their guilt by various reasons, especially ignorance, rashness, or inadvertence, God made provision, in a typical way, for their removal by means of the atonement of the sin- and the guilt-offerings. By means of these, accompanied also with full restitution of the wrong done, when such restitution was possible, the guilty one might be restored in those days to his place as an accepted citizen of the kingdom of God.

No part of the Levitical law is more full of deep, heart-searching truth than the law of the sin-offering. First of all, it is of consequence to observe that the sins for which this chief atoning sacrifice was appointed, were, for the most part, sins of ignorance. For so runs the general statement with which this section opens (ver. 2): "If any one shall sin unwittingly, in any of the things which the Lord hath commanded not to be done, and shall do any of them." And to these are afterwards added sins committed through rashness, the result rather of heat and hastiness of spirit than of deliberate purpose of sin; as, for instance, in chap. v. 4: "Whatsoever it be that a man shall utter rashly with an oath, and it be hid from him." Besides these, in the same section (vv. 1-4), as also in all the cases mentioned under the guilt-offering, and the special instance of a wrong done to a slave-girl (xix. 21), a number of additional offences are mentioned which all seem to have their special palliation, not indeed in the ignorance of the sinner, but in the nature of the acts themselves, as admitting of reparation. For all such it was also ordained that the offender should bring a sin- (or a guilt-) offering, and that by this, atonement being made for him, his sin might be forgiven.

All this must have brought before Israel, and is meant to bring before us, the absolute equity of God in dealing with His creatures. We think often of His stern justice in that He so unfailingly takes note of every sin. But here we may learn also to observe His equity in that He notes no less carefully every circumstance that may palliate our sin. We thankfully recognise in these words the spirit of Him of whom it was said (Heb. v. 2, marg.) that in the days of His flesh He could "reasonably bear with the ignorant;" and who said concerning those who know not their Master's will and do it not (Luke xii. 48), that their "stripes" shall be "few;" and who, again, with equal justice and mercy, said of His disciples' fault in Gethsemane (Matt. xxvi. 41), "The spirit indeed is willing, but the flesh is weak." We do well to note this. For in these days we hear it often charged against the holy religion of Christ, that it represents God as essentially and horribly unjust in consigning all unbelievers to one and the same unvarying punishment, the eternal lake of fire; and as thus making no difference between those who have sinned against the utmost light and knowledge, wilfully and inexcusably, and those who may have sinned through ignorance, or weakness of the flesh. To such charges as these we have simply to answer that neither in the Old Testament nor in the New is God so revealed. We may come back to this book of Leviticus, and declare that even in those days when law reigned, and grace and love were less clearly revealed than now, God made a difference, a great difference, between some sins and others; He visited, no doubt, wilful and defiant sin with condign punishment; but, on the other hand, no less justly than mercifully, He considered also every circumstance which could lessen guilt, and ordained a gracious provision for expiation and forgiveness. The God revealed in Leviticus, like the God revealed in the Gospel, the God "with whom we have to do," is then no hard and unreasonable tyrant, but a most just and equitable King. He is no less the Most Just, that He is the Most Holy; but, rather, because He is most holy, is He therefore most just. And because God is such a God, in the New Testament also it is plainly said that ignorance, as it extenuates guilt, shall also ensure mitigation of penalty; and in the Old Testament, that while he who sins presumptuously and with a high hand against

God, shall "die without mercy under two or three witnesses," on the other hand, he who sins unwittingly, or in some sudden rash impulse, doing that of which he afterward truly repents; or who, again, has sinned, if knowingly, still in such a way as admits of some adequate reparation of the wrong,—all these things shall be judged palliation of his guilt; and if he confess his sin, and make all possible reparation for it, then, if he present a sin- or a guilt-offering, atonement may therewith be made, and the sinner be forgiven.

This then is the first thing which the law concerning the sin-offering brings before us: it calls our attention to the fact that the heavenly King and Judge of men is righteous in all His ways, and therefore will ever make all the allowance that strict justice and righteousness demand, for whatever may in any way palliate our guilt.

But none the less for this do we need also to heed another intensely practical truth which the law of the sin-offering brings before us: namely, that while ignorance or other circumstances may palliate guilt, they do not and cannot nullify it. We may have sinned without a suspicion that we were sinning, but here we are taught that there can be no pardon without a sin-offering. We may have sinned through weakness or sudden passion, but still sin is sin, and we must have a sin-offering before we can be forgiven.

We may observe, in passing, the bearing of this teaching of the law on the question so much discussed in our day, as to the responsibility of the heathen for the sins which they commit through ignorance. In so far as their ignorance is not wilful and avoidable, it doubtless greatly diminishes their guilt; and the Lord Himself has said of such that their stripes shall be few. And yet more than this He does not say. Except we are prepared to cast aside the teaching alike of Leviticus and the Gospels, it is certain that their ignorance does not cancel their guilt. That the ignorance of any one concerning moral law can secure his exemption from the obligation to suffer for his sin, is not only against the teaching of all Scripture, but is also contradicted by all that we can see about us of God's government of the world. For when does God ever suspend the operation of physical laws, because the man who violates them does not know that he is breaking them? And so also, will we but open our eyes, we may see that it is with moral law. The heathen, for example, are ignorant of many moral laws; but do they therefore escape the terrible consequences of their law-breaking, even in this present life, where we can see for ourselves how God is dealing with them? And is there any reason to think it will be different in the life hereafter?

Does it seem harsh that men should be punished even for sins of ignorance, and pardon be impossible, even for these, without atonement? It would not seem so, would men but think more deeply. For beyond all question, the ignorance of men as to the fundamental law of God, to love Him with all the heart, and our neighbour as ourselves, which is the sum of all law, has its reason, not in any lack of light, but in the evil heart of man, who everywhere and always, until he is regenerated, loves self more than he loves God. The words of Christ (John iii. 20) apply: "He that doeth evil cometh not to the light;" not even to the light of nature.

And yet, one who should look only at this chapter might rejoin to this, that the Israelite was only obliged to bring a sin-offering, when afterward he came to the knowledge of his sin as sin; but, in case he never came to that knowledge, was not then his sin passed by without an atoning sacrifice? To this question, the ordinance which we find in chapter xvi. is the decisive answer. For therein it was provided that once every year a very solemn sin-offering should be offered by the high priest, for all the multitudinous sins of Israel, which were not atoned for in the special sin-offerings of each day. Hence it is strictly true that no sin in Israel was ever passed over without either penalty or shedding of blood. And so the law keeps it ever before us that our unconsciousness of sinning does not alter the fact of sin, or the fact of guilt, nor remove the obligation to suffer because of sin; and that even the sin of which we are quite ignorant, interrupts man's peace with God and harmony with him. Thus the best of us must take as our own the words of the Apostle Paul (1 Cor. iv. 4, R. V.): " I know nothing against myself; yet am I not hereby justified; He that judgeth me is the Lord."

Nor does the testimony of this law end here. We are by it taught that the guilt of sins unrecognised as sins at the time of their committal, cannot be cancelled merely by penitent confession when they become known. Confession must indeed, be made, according to the law, as one condition of pardon, but, besides this, the guilty man must bring his sin-offering.

What truths can be more momentous and vital than these! Can any one say, in the light of such a revelation, that all in this ancient law of the sin-offering is now obsolete, and of no concern to us? For how many there are who are resting all their hopes for the future on the fact that they have sinned, if at all, then ignorantly; or that they "have meant to do right;" or that they have confessed the sin when it was known, and have been very sorry. And yet, if this law teach anything, it teaches that this is a fatal mistake, and that such hopes rest on a foundation of sand. If we would be forgiven, we must indeed confess our sin and we must repent; but this is not enough. We must have a sin-offering; we must make use of the great Sin-Offering which that of Leviticus typified; we must tell our compassionate High Priest how in ignorance, or in the rashness of some unholy, overmastering impulse, we sinned, and commit our case to Him, that He may apply the precious blood in our behalf with God.

It is a third impressive fact, that after we include all the cases for which the sin-offering was provided, there still remain many sins for the forgiveness of which no provision was made. It was ordered elsewhere, for instance (Numb. xxxv. 31-33) that no satisfaction should be taken for the life of a murderer. He might confess and bewail his sin, and be never so sorry, but there was no help for him; he must die the death. So was it also with blasphemy; so with adultery, and with many other crimes. This exclusion of so many cases from the merciful provision of the typical offering had a meaning. It was intended, not only to emphasise to the conscience the aggravated wickedness of such crimes, but also to develop in Israel the sense of need for a more adequate provision, a better sacrifice than any the Levitical law could offer; blood which should cleanse, not merely in a ceremonial and sacramental way, but really and effectively; and not only from some sins, but from all sins.

The law of the sin-offering is introduced by phraseology different from that which is used in the case of the preceding offerings. In the case of each of these, the language used implies that the Israelites were familiar with the offering before its incorporation into the Levitical sacrificial system. The sin-offering, on the other hand, is introduced as a new thing. And such, indeed, it was. While, as we have seen, each of the offerings before ordered had been known and used, both by the Shemitic and the other nations, since long before the days of Moses, before this time there is no mention anywhere, in Scripture or out of it, of a sacrifice corresponding to the sin- or the guilt-offering. The significance of this fact is apparent so soon as we observe what was the distinctive conception of the sin-offering, as contrasted with the other offerings. Without question, it was the idea of expiation of guilt by the sacrifice of a substituted victim. This idea, as we have seen, was indeed not absent from the other bloody offerings; but in those its place was secondary and subordinate. In the ritual of the sin-offering, on the contrary, this idea was brought out into almost solitary prominence;—sin pardoned on the ground of expiation made through the presentation to God of the blood of an innocent victim.

The introduction of this new sacrifice, then, marked the fact that the spiritual training of man, of Israel in particular, herewith entered on a new stadium; which was to be distinguished by the development, in a degree to that time without a precedent, of the sense of sin and of guilt, and the need therefore of atonement in order to pardon. This need had not indeed been unfelt before; but never in any ritual had it received so full expression. Not only is the idea of expiation by the shedding of blood almost the only thought represented in the ritual of the offering, but in the order afterward prescribed for the different sacrifices, the sin-offering, in all cases where others were offered, must go before them all; before the burnt-offering, the meal-offering, the peace-offering. So again, this new law insists upon expiation even for those sins which have the utmost possible palliation and excuse, in that at the time of their committal the sinner knew them not as sins; and thus teaches that even these so fatally interrupt fellowship with the holy God, that only such expiation can restore the broken harmony. What a revelation was this law, of the way in which God regards sin! and of the extremity, in consequence, of the sinner's need!

Most instructive, too, were the circumstances under which this new offering, with such a special purpose, embodying such a revelation of the extent of human guilt and responsibility, was first ordained. For its appointment followed quickly upon the tremendous revelation of the consuming holiness of God upon Mount Sinai. It was in the light of the holy mount, quaking and flaming with fire, that the eye of Moses was opened to receive from God this revelation of His will, and he was moved by the Holy Ghost to appoint for Israel, in the name of Jehovah, an offering which should differ from all other offerings in this—that it should hold forth to Israel, in solitary and unprecedented prominence, this one thought, that "without shedding of blood there is no remission of sin," not even of sins which are not known as sins at the time of their committal.

Our own generation, and even the Church of to-day, greatly needs to consider the significance of this fact. The spirit of our age is much more inclined to magnify the greatness and majesty of man, than the infinite greatness and holy majesty of God. Hence many talk lightly of atonement, and cannot admit its necessity to the pardon of sin. But can we doubt, with this narrative before us, that if men saw God more clearly as He is, there would be less talk of this kind? When Moses saw God on Mount Sinai, he came down to ordain a sin-offering even for sins of ignorance! And nothing is more certain, as a fact of human experience in all ages, than this, that the more clearly men have perceived the unapproachable holiness and righteousness of God, the more clearly they have seen that expiation of our sins, even of our sins of ignorance, by atoning blood, is the most necessary and fundamental of all conditions, if we will have pardon of sin and peace with a Holy God.

Man is indeed slow to learn this lesson of the sin-offering. It is quite too humbling and abasing to our natural, self-satisfied pride, to be readily received. This is strikingly illustrated by the fact that it is not until late in Israel's history that the sin-offering is mentioned in the sacred record; while even from that first mention till the Exile, it is mentioned only rarely. This fact is indeed often in our day held up as evidence that the sin-offering was not of Mosaic origin, but a priestly invention of much later days. But the fact is quite as well accounted for by the spiritual obtuseness of Israel. The whole narrative shows that they were a people hard of heart and slow to learn the solemn lessons of Sinai; slow to apprehend the holiness of God, and the profound spiritual truth set forth in the institution of the sin-offering. And yet it was not wholly unobserved, nor did every individual fail to learn its lessons. Nowhere in heathen literature do we find such a profound conviction of sin, such a sense of responsibility even for sins of ignorance, as in some of the earliest Psalms, and the earlier prophets. The self-excusing which so often marks the heathen confessions, finds no place in the confessions of those Old Testament believers, brought up under the moral training of that Sinaitic law which had the sin-offering as its supreme expression on this subject. "Search me, O God, and try my heart; and see if there be in me any wicked way" (Psalm cxxxix. 23, 24); "Cleanse Thou me from secret sins." (Psalm xix. 12); "Against Thee only have I sinned, and done this evil in Thy sight" (Psalm li. 4). Such words as these, with many other like prayers and confessions, bear witness to the deepening sense of sin, till at the last the sin-offering teaches, as its own chief lesson, its own inadequacy for the removal of guilt, in those words of the prophetic Psalm (xl. 6), from the man who mourned iniquities more than the hairs of his head: "Sin-offering Thou hast not required."

But, according to the Epistle to the Hebrews, we are to regard David in these words, speaking by the Holy Ghost, as typifying Christ; for we thus read, x. 5-10: "When He cometh into the world He saith, Sacrifice and offering Thou wouldst not, but a body didst Thou prepare for Me; in whole burnt-offerings and sin-offerings Thou hadst no pleasure. Then said I, Lo,

I am come (in the roll of the book it is written of Me) to do Thy will, O God."

Which words are then expounded thus: "Saying above, Sacrifices and offerings, and whole burnt-offerings and sacrifices for sin Thou wouldest not, neither hadst pleasure therein (the which are offered according to the law); then hath He said, Lo, I am come to do Thy will. He taketh away the first that He may establish the second. By which will we have been sanctified through the offering of the body of Jesus Christ once for all."

And so, as the deepest lesson of the sin-offering, we are taught to see in it a type and prophecy of Christ, as the true and one eternally effectual sin-offering for the sins of His people; who, Himself at once High Priest and Victim, offering Himself for us, perfects us for ever, as the old sin-offering could not, giving us therefore "boldness to enter into the holy place by the blood of Jesus." May we all have grace by faith to receive and learn this deepest lesson of this ordinance, and thus in the law of the sin-offering discover Him who in His person and work became the Fulfiller of this law.

Graded Responsibility.

Leviticus iv. 3, 13, 14, 22, 23, 27, 28.

"If the anointed priest shall sin so as to bring guilt on the people; then let him offer for his sin, which he hath sinned, a young bullock without blemish unto the Lord for a sin-offering. . . And if the whole congregation of Israel shall err, and the thing be hid from the eyes of the assembly, and they have done any of the things which the Lord hath commanded not to be done, and are guilty; when the sin wherein they have sinned is known, then the assembly shall offer a young bullock for a sin-offering, and bring it before the tent of meeting. . . When a ruler sinneth, and doeth unwittingly any one of all the things which the Lord his God hath commanded not to be done, and is guilty; if his sin, wherein he hath sinned, be made known to him, he shall bring for his oblation a goat, a male without blemish. . . And if any one of the common people sin unwittingly, in doing any of the things which the Lord hath commanded not to be done, and be guilty; if this sin, which he hath sinned, be made known to him, then he shall bring for his oblation a goat, a female without blemish, for his sin which he hath sinned."

The law concerning the sin-offering is given in four sections, of which the last, again, is divided into two parts, separated by the division of the chapter. These four sections respectively treat of—first, the law of the sin-offering for the "anointed priest" (vv. 3-12); secondly, the law for the offering for the whole congregation (vv. 13-21); thirdly, that for a ruler (vv. 22-26); and lastly, the law for an offering made by a private person, one of "the common people" (iv. 27-v. 16). In this last section we have, first, the general law (iv. 27-35), and then are added (v. 1-16) special prescriptions having reference to various circumstances under which a sin-offering should be offered by one of the people. Under this last head are mentioned first, as requiring a sin-offering, in addition to sins of ignorance or inadvertence, which only were mentioned in the preceding chapter, also sins due to rashness or weakness (vv. 1-4): and then are appointed, in the second place, certain variations in the material of the offering, allowed out of regard to the various ability of different offerers (vv. 5-16).

In the law as given in chap. iv., it is to be observed that the selection of the victim prescribed is determined by the position of the persons who might have occasion to present the offering. For the whole congregation, the victim must be a bullock, the most valuable of all; for the high priest, as the highest religious official of the nation, and appointed also to represent them before God, it must also be a bullock. For the civil ruler, the offering must be a he-goat—an offering of a value less than that of the victim ordered for the high priest, but greater than that of those which were prescribed for the common people. For these, a variety of offerings were appointed, according to their several ability. If possible, it must be a female goat or lamb, or, if the worshipper could not bring that, then two turtle doves, or two young pigeons. If too poor to bring even this small offering, then it was appointed that, as a substitute for the bloody offering, he might bring an offering of fine flour, without oil or frankincense, to be burnt upon the altar.

Evidently, then, the choice of the victim was determined by two considerations: first, the rank of the person who sinned, and, secondly, his ability. As regards the former point, the law as to the victim for the sin-offering was this: the higher the theocratic rank of the sinning person might be, the more costly offering he must bring. No one can well miss of perceiving the meaning of this. The guilt of any sin in God's sight is proportioned to the rank and station of the offender. What truth could be of more practical and personal concern to all than this?

In applying this principle, the law of the sin-offering teaches, first, that the guilt of any sin is the heaviest, when it is committed by one who is placed in a position of religious authority. For this graded law is headed by the case of the sin of the anointed priest, that is, the high priest, the highest functionary in the nation.

We read (ver. 3): "If the anointed priest shall sin so as to bring guilt on the people, then let him offer for his sin which he hath committed, a young bullock without blemish, unto the Lord, for a sin-offering."

That is, the high priest, although a single individual, if he sin, must bring as large and valuable an offering as is required from the whole congregation. For this law there are two evident reasons. The first is found in the fact that in Israel the high priest represented before God the entire nation. When he sinned it was as if the whole nation sinned in him. So it is said that by his sin he "brings guilt on the people"—a very weighty matter. And this suggests a second reason for the costly offering that was required from him. The consequences of the sin of one in such a high position of religious authority must, in the nature of the case, be much more serious and far-reaching than in the case of any other person.

And here we have another lesson as pertinent to our time as to those days. As the high priest, so, in modern time, the bishop, minister, or elder, is ordained as an officer in matters of religion, to act for and with men in the things of God. For the proper administration of this high trust, how indispensable that such a one shall take heed to maintain unbroken fellowship with God! Any shortcoming here is sure to impair by so much the spiritual value of his own ministrations for the people to whom he ministers. And this evil consequence of any unfaithfulness of his is the more certain to follow, because, of all the members of the community, his example has the widest and most effective influence; in whatever that example be bad or defective, it is sure to do mischief in exact proportion to his exalted station. If then such a one sin, the case is very grave, and his guilt proportionately heavy.

This very momentous fact is brought before us in an impressive way in the New Testament, where, in the epistles to the Seven Churches of Asia (Rev. ii., iii.), it is "the angel of the church," the presiding officer of the church in each city, who is held responsible for the spiritual state of those committed to his charge. No wonder that the Apostle James wrote (James iii. 1): "Be not many teachers, my brethren, knowing that we shall receive heavier judgment." Well may every true-hearted minister of Christ's Church tremble, as here in the law of the sin-offering he reads how the sin of the officer of religion may bring guilt, not only on himself, but also "on the whole people"! Well may he cry out with the Apostle Paul (2 Cor. ii. 16): "Who is sufficient for these things?" and, like him, beseech those to whom he ministers, "Brethren, pray for us!"

With the sin of the high priest is ranked that of the congregation, or the collective nation. It is written (vv. 13, 14): "If the whole congregation of Israel shall err, and the thing be hid from the eyes of the assembly, and they have done any one of the things which the Lord hath commanded not to be done, and are guilty, then the assembly shall offer a young bullock for a sin-offering."

Thus Israel was taught by this law, as we are, that responsibility attaches not only to each individual person, but also to associations of individuals in their corporate character, as nations, communities, and—we may add—all Societies and Corporations, whether secular or religious. Let us emphasise it to our own consciences, as another of the fundamental lessons of this law: there is individual sin; there is also such a thing as a sin by "the whole congregation." In other words, God holds nations, communities—in a word, all associations and combinations of men for whatever purpose, no less under obligation in their corporate capacity to keep His law than as individuals, and will count them guilty if they break it, even through ignorance.

Never has a generation needed this reminder more than our own. The political and social principles which, since the French Revolution in the end of the last century, have been, year by year, more and more generally accepted among the nations of Christendom, are everywhere tending to the avowed or practical denial of this most important truth. It is a maxim ever more and more extensively accepted as almost axiomatic in our modern democratic communities, that religion is wholly a concern of the individual; and that a nation or community, as such, should make no distinction between various religions as false or true, but maintain an absolute neutrality, even between Christianity and idolatry, or theism and atheism. It should take little thought to see that this modern maxim stands in direct opposition to the principle assumed in this law of the sin-offering; namely, that a community or nation is as truly and directly responsible to God as the individual in the nation. But this corporate responsibility the spirit of the age squarely denies.

Not that all, indeed, in our modern so-called Christian nations have come to this. But no one will deny that this is the mind of the vanguard of nineteenth century liberalism in religion and politics. Many of our political leaders in all lands make no secret of their views on the subject. A purely secular state is everywhere held up, and that with great plausibility and persuasiveness, as the ideal of political government; the goal to the attainment of which all good citizens should unite their efforts. And, indeed, in some parts of Christendom the complete attainment of this evil ideal seems not far away.

It is not strange, indeed, to see atheists, agnostics, and others who deny the Christian faith, maintaining this position; but when we hear men who call themselves Christians—in many cases, even Christian ministers—advocating, in one form or another, governmental neutrality in religion as the only right basis of government, one may well be amazed. For Christians are supposed to accept the Holy Scriptures as the law of faith and of morals, private and public; and where in all the Scripture will any one find such an attitude of any nation or people mentioned, but to be condemned and threatened with the judgment of God?

Will any one venture to say that this teaching of the law of the sin-offering was only intended, like the offering itself, for the old Hebrews? Is it not rather the constant and most emphatic teaching of the whole Scriptures, that God dealt with all the ancient Gentile nations on the same principle? The history which records the overthrow of those old nations and empires does so, even professedly, for the express purpose of calling the attention of men in all ages to this principle, that God deals with all nations as under obligations to recognise Himself as King of nations, and submit in all things to His authority. So it was in the case of Moab, of Ammon, of Nineveh, and Babylon; in regard to each of which we are told, in so many words, that it was because they refused to recognise this principle of national responsibility to the one true God, which was brought before Israel in this part of the law of the sin-offering, that the Divine judgment came upon them in their utter national overthrow. How awfully plain, again, is the language of the second Psalm on this same subject, where it is precisely this national repudiation of the supreme authority of God and of His Christ, so increasingly common in our day, which is named as the ground of the derisive judgment of God, and is made the occasion of exhorting all nations, not merely to belief in God, but also to the obedient recognition of His only-begotten Son, the Messiah, as the only possible means of escaping the future kindling of His wrath.

No graver sign of our times could perhaps be named than just this universal tendency in Christendom, in one way or another, to repudiate that corporate responsibility to God which is assumed as the basis of this part of the law of the sin-offering. There can be no worse omen for the future of an individual than the denial of his obligations to God and to His Son, our Saviour; and there can be no worse sign for the future of Christendom, or of any nation in Christendom, than the partial or entire denial of national obligation to God and to His Christ. What it shall mean in the end, what is the future toward which these popular modern principles are conducting the nations, is revealed in Scripture with startling clearness, in the warning that the world is yet to see one who shall be in a peculiar and eminent sense "*the* Antichrist" (1 John ii. 18); who shall deny both the Father and Son, and be "the Lawless One," and the "Man of Sin," in that He shall "set Himself forth as God" (2 Thess. ii. 3-8); to whom authority will be given "over every tribe, and people, and tongue, and nation" (Rev. xiii. 7).

The nation, then, as such, is held responsible to God! So stands the law. And, therefore, in Israel, if the nation should sin, it was ordained that they also, like the high priest, should bring a bullock for a sin-offering, the most costly victim that was ever prescribed. This was so ordained, no doubt, in part because of Israel's own priestly station as a "kingdom of priests and a holy nation," exalted to a position of peculiar dignity and privilege before God, that they might mediate the blessings of redemption to all nations. It was because of this fact that, if they sinned, their guilt was peculiarly heavy.

The principle, however, is of present-day application. Privilege is the measure of responsibility, no less now than then, for nations as well as for individuals. Thus national sin, on the part of the British or American nation, or indeed with any of the so-called Christian nations, is certainly judged by God to be a much more evil thing than the same sin if committed, for example, by the Chinese or Turkish nation, who have had no such degree of Gospel light and knowledge.

And the law in this case evidently also implies that sin is aggravated in proportion to its universality. It is bad, for example, if in a community one man commit adultery, forsaking his own wife; but it argues a condition of things far worse when the violation of the marriage relation becomes common; when the question can actually be held open for discussion whether marriage, as a permanent union between one man and one woman, be not "a failure," as debated not long ago in a leading London paper; and when, as in many of the United States of America and other countries of modern Christendom, laws are enacted for the express purpose of legalising the violation of Christ's law of marriage, and thus shielding adulterers and adulteresses from the condign punishment their crime deserves. It is bad, again, when individuals in a State teach doctrines subversive of morality; but it evidently argues a far deeper depravation of morals when a whole community unite in accepting, endowing, and upholding such in their work.

Next in order comes the case of the civil ruler. For him it was ordered: "When a ruler sinneth, and doeth unwittingly any of the things which the Lord his God hath commanded not to be done, and is guilty; if his sin, wherein he hath sinned, be made known to him, he shall bring for his oblation a goat, a male without blemish" (ver. 22). Thus, the ruler was to bring a victim of less value than the high-priest or the collective congregation; but it must still be of more value than that of a private person; for his responsibility, if less than that of the officer of religion, is distinctly greater than that of a man in private life.

And here is a lesson for modern politicians, no less than for rulers of the olden time in Israel. While there are many in our Parliaments and like governing bodies in Christendom who cast their every vote with the fear of God before their eyes, yet, if there be any truth in the general opinion of men upon this subject, there are many in such places who, in their voting, have before their eyes the fear of party more than the fear of God; and who, when a question comes before them, first of all consider, not what would the law of absolute righteousness, the law of God, require, but how will a vote, one way or the other, in this matter, be likely to affect their party? Such certainly need to be emphatically reminded of this part of the law of the sin-offering, which held the civil ruler specially responsible to God for the execution of his trust. For so it is still; God has not abdicated His throne in favour of the people, nor will He waive His crown-rights out of deference to the political necessities of a party.

Nor is it only those who sin in this particular way who need the reminder of their personal responsibility to God. All need it who either are or may be called to places of greater or less governmental responsibility; and it is those who are the most worthy of such trust who will be the first to acknowledge their need of this warning. For in all times those who have been lifted to positions of political power have been under peculiar temptation to forget God, and become reckless of their obligation to Him as His ministers. But under the conditions of modern life, in many countries of Christendom, this is true as perhaps never before. For now it has come to pass that, in most modern communities, those who make and execute laws hold their tenure of office at the pleasure of a motley army of voters, Protestants and Romanists, Jews, atheists, and what not, a large part of whom care not the least for the will of God in civil government, as revealed in Holy Scripture. Under such conditions, the place of the civil ruler becomes one of such special trial and temptation that we do well to remember in our intercessions, with peculiar sympathy, all who in such positions are seeking to serve supremely, not their party, but their God, and so best serve their country. It is no wonder that the temptation too often to many becomes overpowering, to silence conscience with plausible sophistries, and to use their office to carry out in legislation, instead of the will of God, the will of the people, or rather, of that particular party which put them in power.

Yet the great principle affirmed in this law of the sin-offering stands, and will stand for ever, and to it all will do well to take heed; namely, that God will hold the civil ruler responsible, and more heavily responsible than any private person, for any sin he may commit, and especially for any violation of law in any matter committed to his trust. And there is abundant reason for this. For the powers that be are ordained of God, and in His providence are placed in authority; not as the modern notion is, for the purpose of executing the will of their constituents, whatever that will may be, but rather the unchangeable will of the Most Holy God, the Ruler of all nations, so far as revealed, concerning the civil and social relations of men. Nor must it be forgotten that this eminent responsibility attaches to them, not only in their official acts, but in all their acts as individuals. No distinction is made as to the sin for which the ruler must bring his sin-offering, whether public and official, or private and personal. Of whatsoever kind the sin may be, if committed by a ruler, God holds him specially responsible, as being a ruler; and reckons the guilt of that sin, even if a private offence, to be heavier than if it had been committed by one of the common people. And this, for the evident reason that, as in the case of the high priest, his exalted position gives his example double influence and effect. Thus, in all ages and all lands, a corrupt king or nobility have made a corrupt court; and a corrupt court or corrupt legislators are sure to demoralise all the lower ranks of society. But however it may be under the governments of men, under the equitable government of the Most Holy God, high station can give no immunity to sin. And in the day to come, when the Great Assize is set, there will be many who in this world stood high in authority, who will learn, in the tremendous decisions of that day, if not before, that a just God reckoned the guilt of their sins and crimes in exact proportion to their rank and station.

Last of all, in this chapter, comes the law of the sin-offering for one of the common people, of which the first part is given vv. 27-35. The victim which is appointed for those who are best able to give, a female goat, is yet of less value than those ordered in the cases before given; for the responsibility and guilt in the case of such is less. The first prescription for a sin-offering by one of the common people is introduced by these words:—" If any one of the common people sin unwittingly, in doing any of the things which the Lord hath commanded not to be done, and be guilty; if his sin, which he hath sinned, be made known to him, then he shall bring for his oblation a goat, a female without blemish, for his sin which he hath sinned" (vv. 27, 28).

In case of his inability to bring so much as this, offerings of lesser value are authorised in the section following (v. 5-13), to which we shall attend hereafter.

Meanwhile it is suggestive to observe that this part of the law is expanded more fully than any other part of the law of the sin-offering. We are hereby reminded that if none are so high as to be above the reach of the judgment of God, but are held in that proportion strictly responsible for their sin; so, on the other hand, none are of station so low that their sins shall therefore be overlooked. The common people, in all lands, are the great majority of the population; but no one is to imagine that, because he is a single individual, of no importance in a multitude, he shall therefore, if he sin, escape the Divine eye, as it were, in a crowd. Not so. We may be of the very lowest social station; the provision in chapter v. 11 regards the case of such as might be so poor as that they could not even buy two doves. Men may judge the doings of such poor folk of little or no consequence; but not so God. With Him is no respect of persons, either of rich or poor. From all alike, from the anointed high priest, who ministers in the Holy of Holies, down to the common people, and among these, again, from the highest down to the very lowest, poorest, and meanest in rank, is demanded, even for a sin of ignorance, a sin-offering for atonement.

What a solemn lesson we have herein concerning the character of God! His omniscience, which not only notes the sin of those who are in some conspicuous position, but also each individual sin of the lowest of the people! His absolute equity, exactly and accurately grading responsibility for sin committed, in each case, according to the rank and influence of him who commits it! His infinite holiness, which cannot pass by without expiation even the transient act or word of rash hands or lips, not even the sin not known as sin by the sinner; a holiness which, in a word, unchangeably and unalterably requires from every human being, nothing less than absolute moral perfection like His own!

CHAPTER VII.

THE RITUAL OF THE SIN-OFFERING.

LEVITICUS iv. 4-35; v. 1-13; vi. 24-30.

ACCORDING to the Authorised Version (v. 6, 7), it might seem that the section, v. 1-13, referred not to the sin-offering, but to the guilt-offering, like the latter part of the chapter; but, as suggested in the margin of the Revised Version, in these verses we may properly read, instead of " guilt-offering," " for his guilt." That the latter rendering is to be preferred is clear when we observe that in vv. 6, 7, 9 this offering is called a sin-offering; that, everywhere else, the victim for the guilt-offering is a ram; and, finally, that the estimation of a money value for the victim, which is the most characteristic feature of the guilt-offering, is absent from all the offerings described in these verses. We may safely take it therefore as certain that the marginal reading should be adopted in ver. 6, so that it will read, " he shall bring for his guilt unto the Lord;" and understand the section to contain a further development of the law of the sin-offering. In the law of the preceding chapter we have the direction for the sin-offering as graded with reference to the rank and station of the offerer; in this section we have the law for the sin-offering for the common people, as graded with reference to the ability of the offerer.

The specifications (v. 1-5) indicate several cases under which one of the common people was required to bring a sin-offering as the condition of forgiveness. As an exhaustive list would be impossible, those named are taken as illustrations. The instances selected are significant as extending the class of offences for which atonement could be made by a sin-offering, beyond the limits of sins of inadvertence as given in the previous chapter. For however some cases come under this head, we cannot so reckon sins of rashness (ver. 4), and still less, the failure of the witness placed under oath to tell the whole truth as he knows it. And herein it is graciously intimated that it is in the heart of God to multiply His pardons; and, on condition of the presentation of a sin-offering, to forgive also those sins in palliation of which no such excuse as inadvertence or ignorance can be pleaded. It is a faint foreshadowing, in the law concerning the type, of that which should afterward be declared concerning the great Antitype (1 John i. 7), " The blood of Jesus . . . cleanseth from all sin."

When we look now at the various prescriptions regarding the ritual of the offering which are given in this and the foregoing chapter, it is plain that the numerous variations from the ritual of the other sacrifices were intended to withdraw the thought of the sinner from all other aspects in which sacrifice might be regarded, and centre his mind upon the one thought of sacrifice as expiating sin, through the substitution of an innocent life for the guilty. In many particulars, indeed, the ritual agrees with that of the sacrifices before prescribed. The victim must be brought by the guilty person to be offered to God by the priest; he must, as in other cases of bloody offerings, then lay his hand on the head of the victim, and then (a particular not mentioned in the other cases) he must confess the sin which he has committed, and then and thus entrust the victim to the priest, that he may apply its blood for him in atonement before God. The priest then slays the victim, and now comes that part of the ceremonial which by its variations from the law of other offerings is emphasised as the most central and significant in this sacrifice.

The Sprinkling of the Blood.

Leviticus iv. 6, 7, 16-18, 25, 30; v. 9.

"And the priest shall dip his finger in the blood, and sprinkle of the blood seven times before the Lord, before the veil of the sanctuary. And the priest shall put of the blood upon the horns of the altar of sweet incense before the Lord, which is in the tent of meeting; and all the blood of the bullock shall he pour out at the base of the altar of burnt offering, which is at the door of the tent of meeting. . . And the anointed priest shall bring of the blood of the bullock to the tent of meeting, and the priest shall dip his finger in the blood, and sprinkle it seven times before the Lord, before the veil. And he shall put of the blood upon the horns of the altar which is before the Lord, that is in the tent of meeting, and all the blood shall he pour out at the base of the altar of burnt offering, which is at the door of the tent of meeting. . . And the priest shall take of the blood of the sin offering with his finger, and put it upon the horns of the altar of burnt offering, and the blood thereof shall he pour out at the base of the altar of burnt offering. . . And the priest shall take of the blood thereof with his finger, and put it upon the horns of the altar of burnt offering, and all the blood thereof shall he pour out at the base of the altar. . . And he shall sprinkle of the blood of the sin offering upon the side of the altar; and the rest of the blood shall be drained out at the base of the altar; it is a sin offering."

In the case of the burnt-offering and of the peace-offering, in which the idea of expiation, although not absent, yet occupied a secondary place in their ethical intent, it sufficed that the blood of the victim, by whomsoever brought, be applied to the sides of the altar. But in the sin-offering, the blood must not only be sprinkled on the sides of the altar of burnt-offering, but, even in the case of the common people, be applied to the horns of the altar, its most conspicuous and, in a sense, most sacred part. In the case of a sin committed by the whole congregation, even this is not enough; the blood must be brought even into the Holy Place, be applied to the horns of the altar of incense, and be sprinkled seven times before the Lord before the veil which hung immediately before the mercy seat in the Holy of Holies, the place of the Shekinah glory. And in the great sin-offering of the high priest once a year for the sins of all the people, yet more was required. The blood was to be taken even within the veil, and be sprinkled on the mercy seat itself over the tables of the broken law.

These several cases, according to the symbolism of these several parts of the tabernacle, differ in that atoning blood is brought ever more and more nearly into the immediate presence of God. The horns of the altar had a sacredness above the sides; the altar of the Holy Place before the veil, a sanctity beyond that of the altar in the outer court; while the Most Holy Place, where stood the ark, and the mercy-seat, was the very place of the most immediate and visible manifestation of Jehovah, who is often described in Holy Scripture, with reference to the ark, the mercy-seat, and the overhanging cherubim, as the God who "dwelleth between the cherubim."

From this we may easily understand the significance of the different prescriptions as to the blood in the case of different classes. A sin committed by any private individual or by a ruler, was that of one who had access only to the outer court, where stood the altar of burnt-offering; for this reason, it is there that the blood must be exhibited, and that on the most sacred and conspicuous spot in that court, the horns of the altar where God meets with the people. But when it was the anointed priest that had sinned, the case was different. In that he had a peculiar position of nearer access to God than others, as appointed of God to minister before Him in the Holy Place, his sin is regarded as having defiled the Holy Place itself; and in that Holy Place must Jehovah therefore see atoning blood ere the priest's position before God can be re-established.

And the same principle required that also in the Holy Place must the blood be presented for the sin of the whole congregation. For Israel in its corporate unity was "a kingdom of priests," a priestly nation; and the priest in the Holy Place represented the nation in that capacity. Thus because of this priestly office of the nation, their collective sin was regarded as defiling the Holy Place in which, through their representatives, the priests, they ideally ministered. Hence, as the law for the priests, so is the law for the nation. For their corporate sin the blood must be applied, as in the case of the priest who represented them, to the horns of the altar in the Holy Place, whence ascended the smoke of the incense which visibly symbolised accepted priestly intercession, and, more than this, before the veil itself; in other words, as near to the very mercy-seat itself as it was permitted to the priest to go; and it must be sprinkled there, not once, nor twice, but seven times, in token of the re-establishment, through the atoning blood, of God's covenant of mercy, of which, throughout the Scripture, the number seven, the number of sabbatic rest and covenant fellowship with God, is the constant symbol.

And it is not far to seek for the spiritual thought which underlies this part of the ritual. For the tabernacle was represented as the earthly dwelling-place, in a sense, of God; and just as the defiling of the house of my fellow-man may be regarded as an insult to him who dwells in the house, so the sin of the priest and of the priestly people is regarded as, more than that of those outside of this relation, a special affront to the holy majesty of Jehovah, criminal just in proportion as the defilement approaches more nearly the innermost shrine of Jehovah's manifestation.

But though Israel is at present suspended from its priestly position and function among the nations of the earth, the Apostle Peter (1 Peter ii. 5) reminds us that the body of Christian believers now occupies Israel's ancient place, being now on earth the "royal priesthood," the "holy nation." Hence this ritual solemnly reminds us that the sin of a Christian is a far more evil thing than the sin of others; it is as the sin of the priest, and defiles the Holy Place, even though unwittingly committed; and thus, even more imperatively than other sin, demands the exhibition of the atoning blood of the Lamb of God, not now in the Holy Place, but more than that, in the true Holiest of all, where our High Priest is now entered. And thus, in every possible way, with this elaborate ceremonial of sprinkling of blood does the sin-offering emphasise to our own consciences, no less than for ancient Israel, the solemn fact affirmed in the Epistle to the Hebrews (ix. 22), "Without shedding of blood there is no remission of sin."

Because of this, we do well to meditate much and deeply on this symbolism of the sin-offering, which, more than any other in the law, has to do with the propitiation of our Lord for sin. Especially does this use of the blood, in which the significance of the sin-offering reached its supreme expression, claim our most reverent attention. For the thought is inseparable from the ritual, that blood of the slain victim must be presented, not before the priest, or before the offerer, but before Jehovah. Can any one mistake the evident significance of this? Does it not luminously hold forth the thought that atonement by sacrifice has to do, not only with man, but with God?

There is cause enough in our day for insisting on this. Many are teaching that the need for the shedding of blood for the remission of sin, lies only in the nature of man; that, so far as concerns God, sin might as well have been pardoned without it; that it is only because man is so hard and rebellious, so stubbornly distrusts the Divine love, that the death of the Holy Victim of Calvary became a necessity. Nothing less than such a stupendous exhibition of the love of God could suffice to disarm his enmity to God and win him back to loving trust. Hence the need of the atonement. That all this is true, no one will deny; but it is only half the truth, and the less momentous half,—which indeed is hinted in no offering, and in the sin-offering least of all. Such a conception of the matter as completely fails to account for this part of the symbolic ritual of the bloody sacrifices, as it fails to agree with other teachings of the Scriptures. If the only need for atonement in order to pardon is in the nature of the sinner, then why this constant insistence that the blood of the sacrifice should always be solemnly presented, not before the sinner, but before Jehovah? We see in this fact most unmistakably set forth, the very solemn truth that expiation by blood as a condition of forgiveness of sin is necessary, not merely because man is what he is, but most of all because God is what He is. Let us then not forget that the presentation unto God of an expiation for sin, accomplished by the death of an appointed substitutionary victim, was in Israel made an indispensable condition of the pardon of sin. Is this, as many urge, against the love of God? By no means! Least of all will it so appear, when we remember who appointed the great Sacrifice, and, above all, who came to fulfil this type. God does not love us because atonement has been made, but atonement has been made because the Father loved us, and sent His Son to be the propitiation for our sins.

God is none the less just, that He is love; and none the less holy, that He is merciful: and in His nature, as the Most Just and Holy One, lies this necessity of the shedding of blood in order to the forgiveness of sin, which is impressively symbolised in the unvarying ordinance of the Levitical law, that as a condition of the remission of sin, the blood of the sacrifice must be presented, not before the sinner, but before Jehovah. To this generation of ours, with its so exalted notions of the greatness and dignity of man, and its correspondingly low conceptions of the ineffable greatness and majesty of the Most Holy God, this altar truth may be most distasteful, so greatly does it magnify the evil of sin; but just in that degree is it necessary to the humiliation of man's proud self-complacency, that, whether pleasing or not, this truth be faithfully held forth.

Very instructive and helpful to our faith are the allusions to this sprinkling of Blood in the New Testament. Thus, in the Epistle to the Hebrews (xii. 24), believers are reminded that they are come "unto the blood of sprinkling, that speaketh better than that of Abel." The meaning is plain. For we are told (Gen. iv. 10), that the blood of Abel cried out against Cain from the ground; and that its cry for vengeance was prevailing; for God came down, arraigned the murderer, and visited him with instant judgment. But in these words we are told that the sprinkled blood of the holy Victim of Calvary, sprinkled on the heavenly altar, also has a voice, and a voice which "speaketh better than that of Abel;" better, in that it speaks, not for vengeance, but for pardoning mercy; better, in that it procures the remission even of a penitent murderer's guilt; so that, "being now justified through His blood" we may all "be saved from wrath through Him" (Rom. v. 9). And, if we are truly Christ's, it is our blessed comfort to remember also that we are said (1 Peter i. 2) to have been chosen of God unto the sprinkling of this precious blood of Jesus Christ; words which remind us, not only that the blood of a Lamb "without blemish and without spot" has been presented unto God for us, but also that the reason for this distinguishing mercy is found, not in us, but in the free love of God, who chose us in Christ Jesus to this grace.

And as in the burnt-offering, so in the sin-offering, the blood was to be sprinkled by the priest. The teaching is the same in both cases. To present Christ before God, laying the hand of faith upon His head as our sin-offering, this is all we can do or are required to do. With the sprinkling of the blood we have nothing to do. In other words, the effective presentation of the blood before God is not to be secured by some act of our own; it is not something to be procured through some subjective experience, other or in addition to the faith which brings the Victim. As in the type, so in the Antitype, the sprinkling of the atoning blood—that is, its application God-ward as a propitiation—is the work of our heavenly Priest. And our part in regard to it is simply and only this, that we entrust this work to Him. He will not disappoint us; He is appointed of God to this end, and He will see that it is done.

In a sacrifice in which the sprinkling of the blood occupies such a central and essential place in the symbolism, one would anticipate that this ceremony would never be dispensed with. Very strange it thus appears, at first sight, to find that to this law an exception was made. For it was ordained (ver. 11) that a man so poor that "his means suffice not" to bring even two doves or young pigeons, might bring, as a substitute, an offering of fine flour. From this, some have hastened to infer that the shedding of the blood, and therewith the idea of substituted life, was not essential to the idea of reconciliation with God; but with little reason. Most illogical and unreasonable it is to determine a principle, not from the general rule, but from an exception; especially when, as in this case, for the exception a reason can be shown, which is not inconsistent with the rule. For had no such exceptional offering been permitted in the case of the extremely poor man, it would have followed that there would have remained a class of persons in Israel whom God had excluded from the provision of the sin-offering, which He had made the inseparable condition of forgiveness. But two truths were to be set forth in the ritual; the one, atonement by means of a life surrendered in expiation of guilt; the other,—as in a similar way in the burnt-offering,—the sufficiency of God's gracious provision for even the neediest of sinners. Evidently, here was a case in which something must be sacrificed in the symbolism. One of these truths may be perfectly set forth; both cannot be, with equal perfectness; a choice must therefore be made, and is made in this exceptional regulation, so as to hold up clearly, even though at the expense of some distinctness in the other thought of expiation, the unlimited sufficiency of God's provision of forgiving grace.

And yet the prescriptions in this form of the offering were such as to prevent any one from confounding it with the meal-offering, which typified consecrated and accepted service. The oil and the frankincense which belonged to the latter are to be left out (ver. 11); incense, which typifies accepted prayer,—thus reminding us of the unanswered prayer of the Holy Victim when He cried upon the cross, "My God! My God! why hast Thou forsaken Me?" and oil, which typifies the Holy Ghost,—reminding us, again, how from the soul of the Son of God was mysteriously withdrawn in that same hour all the conscious presence and comfort of the Holy Spirit, which withdrawment alone could have wrung from His lips that unanswered prayer. And, again, whereas the meal for the meal-offering had no limit fixed as to quantity, in this case the amount is prescribed—"the tenth part of an ephah" (ver. 11); an amount which, from the story of the manna, appears to have represented the sustenance of one full day. Thus it was ordained that if, in the nature of the case, this sin-offering could not set forth the sacrifice of life by means of the shedding of blood, it should at least point in the same direction, by requiring that, so to speak, the support of life for one day shall be given up, as forfeited by sin.

All the other parts of the ceremonial are in this ordinance made to take a secondary place, or are omitted altogether. Not all of the offering is burnt upon the altar, but only a part; that part, however, the fat, the choicest; for the same reason as in the peace-offering. There is, indeed, a peculiar variation in the case of the offering of the two young pigeons, in that, of the one, the blood only was used in the sacrifice, while the other was wholly burnt like a burnt-offering. But for this variation the reason is evident enough in the nature of the victims. For in the case of a small creature like a bird, the fat would be so insignificant in quantity, and so difficult to separate with thoroughness from the flesh, that the ordinance must needs be varied, and a second bird be taken for the burning, as a substitute for the separated fat of larger animals. The symbolism is not essentially affected by the variation. What the burning of the fat means in other offerings, that also means the burning of the second bird in this case.

The Eating and the Burning of the Sin-Offering without the Camp.

Leviticus iv. 8-12, 19-21, 26, 31; v. 10, 12.

"And all the fat of the bullock of the sin offering he shall take off from it; the fat that covereth the inwards, and all the fat that is upon the inwards, and the two kidneys, and the fat that is upon them, which is by the loins, and the caul upon the liver, with the kidneys, shall he take away, as it is taken off from the ox of the sacrifice of peace offerings: and the priest shall burn them upon the altar of burnt offering. And the skin of the bullock, and all its flesh, with its head, and with its legs, and its inwards, and its dung, even the whole bullock shall he carry forth without the camp unto a clean place, where the ashes are poured out, and burn it on wood with fire: where the ashes are poured out shall it be burnt. . . And all the fat thereof shall he take off from it, and burn it upon the altar. Thus shall he do with the bullock; as he did with the bullock of the sin offering, so shall he do with this: and the priest shall make atonement for them, and they shall be forgiven. And he shall carry forth the bullock without the camp, and burn it as he burned the first bullock: it is the sin offering for the assembly. . . And all the fat thereof shall he burn upon the altar, as the fat of the sacrifice of peace offerings: and the priest shall make atonement for him as concerning his sin, and he shall be forgiven. . . And all the fat thereof shall he take away, as the fat is taken away from off the sacrifice of peace offerings ; and the priest shall burn it upon the altar for a sweet savour unto the Lord ; and the priest shall make atonement for him, and he shall be forgiven. . . And he shall offer the second for a burnt offering, according to the ordinance: and the priest shall make atonement for him as concerning his sin which he hath sinned, and he shall be forgiven. . . And he shall bring it to the priest, and the priest shall take his handful of it as the memorial thereof, and burn it on the altar, upon the offerings of the Lord made by fire: it is a sin offering."

In the ritual of the sin-offering, sacrificial meal, such as that of the peace-offering, wherein the offerer and his house, with the priest and the Levite, partook together of the flesh of the sacrificed victim, there was none. The eating of the flesh of the sin-offerings by the priests, prescribed in chap. vi. 26, had, primarily, a different intention and meaning. As set forth elsewhere (vii. 35), it was "the anointing portion of Aaron and his sons;" an ordinance expounded by the Apostle Paul to this effect, that (1 Cor. ix. 13) they which wait upon the altar should "have their portion with the altar." Yet not of all the sin-offerings might the priest thus partake. For when he was himself the one for whom the offering was made, whether as an individual, or as included in the congregation, then it is plain that he for the time stood in the same position before God as the private individual who had sinned. It was a universal principle of the law that because of the peculiarly near and solemn relation into which the expiatory victim had been brought to God, it was "most holy," and therefore he for whose sin it is offered could not eat of its flesh. Hence the general law is laid down (vi. 30): "No sin offering, whereof any of the blood is brought into the tent of meeting to make atonement in the holy place, shall be eaten; it shall be burnt with fire."

And yet, although, because the priests could not eat of the flesh, it must be burnt, it could not be burnt upon the altar; not, as some have fancied, because it was regarded as unclean, which is directly contradicted by the statement that it is "most holy," but because so to dispose of it would have been to confound the sin-offering with the burnt-offering, which had, as we have seen, a specific symbolic meaning, quite distinct from that of the sin-offering. It must be so disposed of that nothing shall divert the mind of the worshipper from the fact that, not sacrifice as representing full consecration, as in the burnt-offering, but sacrifice as representing expiation, is set forth in this offering. Hence it was ordained that the flesh of these sin-offerings for the anointed priest, or for the congregation, which included him, should be "burnt on wood with fire without the camp" (iv. 11, 12, 21). And the more carefully to guard against the possibility of confounding this burning of the flesh of the sin-offering with the sacrificial burning of the victims on the altar, the Hebrew uses here, and in all places where this burning is referred to, a verb wholly distinct from that which is used of the burnings on the altar, and which, unlike that, is used of any ordinary burning of anything for any purpose.

But this burning of the victim without the camp was not therefore empty of all typical significance. The writer of the Epistle to the Hebrews calls our attention to the fact that in this part of the appointed ritual there was also that which prefigured Christ and the circumstances of His death. For we read (Heb. xiii. 10-12), after an exhortation to Christians to have done with the ritual observances of Judaism regarding meats:—"We," that is, we Christian believers, "have an altar,"—the cross upon which Jesus suffered,—"whereof they have no right to eat which serve the tabernacle;" *i. e.*, they who adhere to the now effete Jewish tabernacle service, the unbelieving Israelites, derive no benefit from this sacrifice of ours. "For the bodies of those beasts whose blood is brought into the Holy Place by the high priest as an offering for sin, are burned without the camp;" the priesthood are debarred from eating them, according to the law we have before us. And then attention is called to the fact that in this respect Jesus fulfilled this part of the type of the sin-offering, thus: "Wherefore Jesus also, that He might sanctify the people with His own blood, suffered without the camp." That is, as Alford interprets (Comm. sub. loc.), in the circumstance that Jesus suffered without the gate, is seen a visible adumbration of the fact that He suffered outside the camp of legal Judaism, and thus, in that He suffered for the sin of the whole congregation of Israel, fulfilled the type of this sin-offering in this particular. Thus a prophecy is discovered here which perhaps we had not else discerned, concerning the manner of the death of the antitypical victim. He should suffer as a victim for the sin of the whole congregation, the priestly people, who should for that reason be debarred, in fulfilment of the type, from that benefit of His death which had else been their privilege. And herein was accomplished to the uttermost that surrender of His whole being to God, in that, in carrying out that full consecration, "He, bearing His cross, went forth," not merely outside the gate of Jerusalem,—in itself a trivial circumstance,—but, as this fitly symbolised, outside the congregation of Israel, to suffer. In other words, His consecration of Himself to God in self-sacrifice found its supreme expression in this, that He voluntarily submitted to be cast out from Israel, despised and rejected of men, even of the Israel of God.

And so this burning of the flesh of the sin-offering of the highest grade in two places, the fat upon the altar, in the court of the congregation, and the rest of the victim outside the camp, set forth prophetically the full self-surrender of the Son to the Father, as the sin-offering, in a double aspect: in the former, emphasising simply, as in the peace-offering, His surrender of all that was highest and best in Him, as Son of God and Son of man, unto the Father as a Sin-offering; in the latter, foreshowing that He should also, in a special manner, be a sacrifice for the sin of the congregation of Israel, and that His consecration should receive its fullest exhibition and most complete expression in that He should die outside the camp of legal Judaism, as an outcast from the congregation of Israel.

Accordingly we find that this part of the type of the sin-offering was formally accomplished when the high priest, upon Christ's confession before the Sanhedrim of His Sonship to God, declared Him to be guilty of blasphemy; an offence for which it had been ordered by the Lord (Lev. xxiv. 14) that the guilty person should be taken "without the camp" to suffer for his sin.

In the light of these marvellous correspondences between the typical sin-offering and the self-offering of the Son of God, what a profound meaning more and more appears in those words of Christ concerning Moses: "He wrote of Me."

The Sanctity of the Sin-Offering.

Leviticus vi. 24-30.

"And the Lord spake unto Moses, saying, Speak unto Aaron and to his sons, saying, This is the law of the sin offering: in the place where the burnt offering is killed shall the sin offering be killed before the Lord: it is most holy. The priest that offereth it for sin shall eat it: in a holy place shall it be eaten, in the court of the tent of meeting. Whatsoever shall touch the flesh thereof shall be holy: and when there is sprinkled of the blood thereof upon any garment, thou shalt wash that whereon it was sprinkled in a holy place. But the earthen vessel wherein it is sodden shall be broken: and if it be sodden in a brasen vessel, it shall be scoured, and rinsed in water. Every male among the priests shall eat thereof: it is most holy. And no sin offering, whereof any of the blood is brought into the tent of meeting to make atonement in the holy place, shall be eaten: it shall be burnt with fire."

In chap. vi. 24-30 we have a section which is supplemental to the law of the sin-offering, in which, with some repetition of the laws previously given, are added certain special regulations, in fuller exposition of the peculiar sanctity attaching to this offering. As in the case of other offerings called "most holy," it is ordered that only the males among the priests shall eat of it; among whom, the officiating priest takes the precedence. Further, it is declared that everything that touches the offering shall be regarded as "holy," that is, as invested with the sanctity attaching to every person or thing specially devoted to the Lord.

Then by way of application of this principle to two of the most common cases in which it could apply, it is ordered, first (ver. 27), with regard to any garment which should be sprinkled with the blood, "thou shalt wash that whereon it was sprinkled in a holy place;" that so by no chance should the least of the blood which had been shed for the remission of sin, come into contact with anything unclean and unholy. And then, again, inasmuch as the flesh which should be eaten by the priest must needs be cooked, and the vessel used by this contact became holy, it is commanded (ver. 28) that, if a brazen vessel, "it shall be scoured" and "then rinsed with water;" that in no case should a vessel in which might remain the least of the sacrificial flesh, be used for any profane purpose, and so the holy flesh be defiled. And because when an (unglazed) earthen vessel was used, even such scouring and rinsing could not so cleanse it, but that something of the juices of the holy flesh should be absorbed into its substance, therefore, in order to preclude the possibility of its ever being used for any common purpose it is directed (ver. 28) that it shall be broken.*

By such regulations as these, it is plain that even in those days of little light the thoughtful Israelite would be impressed with the feeling that in the expiation of sin he came into a peculiarly near and solemn relation to the holiness of God, even though he might not be able to formulate his thought more exactly. In modern times, however, strange to say, these very regulations with regard to the sin-offering, when it has been taken as typical of Christ, have been used as an argument against the New Testament teaching as to the expiatory nature of His death as a true satisfaction to the holy justice of God for the sins of men. For it is argued, that if Christ was really, in a legal sense, regarded as a sinner, because standing in the sinner's place, to receive in His person the wrath of God against the sinner's sin, it could not have been ordered that the blood and the flesh of the typical offering should be thus regarded as of peculiar and pre-eminent holiness. Rather, we are told, should we, for example, have read in the ritual, "No one, and, least of all, the priests, shall eat of it; for it is most unclean." An extraordinary argument and conclusion! For surely it is an utter misapprehension both of the so-called "orthodox" view of the atonement, and of the New Testament teaching on the subject, to represent it as involving the suggestion that Christ, when for us "made sin," and suffering as our substitute, thereby must have been for the time Himself unclean. Surely, according to the constant use of the word, in imputation of sin, of any sin, to any one, there is no conveyance of character; it is only implied that such person is, for whatsoever reason, justly or unjustly, treated as if he were guilty of that sin which is imputed to him. Imputing falsehood to a man who is truth itself, does not make him a liar, though it does involve treating him as if he were. Just so it is in this case.

There is, then, in these regulations which emphasise the peculiar holiness of the sin-offering, nothing which is inconsistent with the strictest juridical view of the great atonement which in type it represented. On the contrary, one can hardly think of anything which should more effectively represent the great truth of the incomparable holiness of the victim of Calvary, than just this strenuous insistence that the blood and the flesh of the typical victim should be treated as of the most peculiar sanctity. If, when we see the victim of the sin-offering slain and its blood presented before God, we behold a vivid representation of Christ, the Lamb of God, "made sin in our behalf;" so when, in these regulations, we see how the flesh and blood of the offered victim is treated as of the most pre-eminent sanctity, we are as impressively reminded how it is written (2 Cor. v. 21) that it was "Him who knew no sin," that God "made to be sin on our behalf." Thus does the type, in order that nothing might be wanting in this law of the offering, insist in every possible way on the holiness of the great Victim who became the Antitype; and most of all in the sin-offering, because in this, where, not consecration of the person or the works, or the impartation and fellowship of the life of Christ, but expiation, was the central idea of the sacrifice, there was a special need for emphasising, in an exceptional way, this thought; that the Victim who bore our sins, although visibly laden with the curse of God, was none the less all the time Himself "most holy;" so that in that unfathomable mystery of Calvary, never was He more truly and really the well-beloved Son of the Father than when He cried out in the extremity of His anguish as "made sin for us," "My God, My God, why hast Thou forsaken Me?"

How wonderfully adapted in all its details was this law of the sin-offering, not only for the education of Israel, but, if we will meditate upon these things, also for our own! How the truths which underlie this law should humble us, even in proportion as they exalt to the uttermost the ineffable majesty of the holiness of God! And, if we will but yield to their teachings, how mightily should they constrain us, in grateful recognition of the love of the Holy One who was "made sin in our behalf," and of the love of the Father who sent Him for this end, to accept Him as our Sin-offering, set forth in the consummation of the ages, "to put away sin by the sacrifice of Himself." No more are offered the sin-offerings of the law of Moses:

> "But Christ, the heavenly Lamb,
> Takes all our sins away;
> A sacrifice of nobler name,
> And richer blood, than they."

If, then, the law of the Levitical sin-offering abides in force no longer, this is not because God has changed, or because the truths which it set forth concerning sin, and expiation, and pardon, are obsolete, but only because the great Sin-offering which the ancient sacrifice typified, has now appeared. God hath "taken away the first, that He may establish the second" (Heb. x. 9). We have thus to do with the same God as the Israelite. Now, as then, He takes account of all our sins, even of sins committed "unwittingly;" He reckons guilt with the same absolute impartiality and justice as then; He pardons sin, as then, only when the sinner who seeks pardon, presents a sin-offering. But He has now Himself provided the Lamb for this offering, and now in infinite love invites us all, without distinction, with whatsoever sins we may be burdened, to make free use of the all-sufficient and most efficient blood of His well-beloved Son. Shall we risk neglecting this Divine provision, and undertake to deal with God by-and-bye, in the great day of judgment, on our own

---

* A striking parallel to this ordinance is found in a caste custom in North India, where the caste Hindoo, as I have often seen, if he give you a drink of water in a vessel, will only use an earthen vessel, which, immediately after you have drunk, he breaks, to preclude the possibility of its accidental use thereafter, by which ceremonial defilement might be contracted. For the Hindoo does not regard it as possible so to cleanse a metallic vessel as to remove the defilement thus caused; and as he could not afford to throw it away, he will give one to drink in the cheap earthen vessel, or else no drink at all.

merits, without a sacrifice for sin? God forbid! Rather let us go on to say in the words of that old hymn:

> "My faith would lay her hand
> On that dear Head of Thine,
> While like a penitent I stand,
> And there confess my sin."

CHAPTER VIII.

THE GUILT-OFFERING.

LEVITICUS v. 14; vi. 7; vii. 1-7.

As in the English version, so also in the Hebrew, the special class of sins for which the guilt-offering * is prescribed, is denoted by a distinct and specific word. That word, like the English "trespass," its equivalent, always has reference to an invasion of the rights of others, especially in respect of property or service. It is used, for instance, of the sin of Achan (Josh. vii. 1), who had appropriated spoil from Jericho, which God had commanded to be set apart for Himself. Thus, also, the neglect of God's service, and especially the worship of idols, is often described by this same word, as in 2 Chron. xxviii. 22, xxix. 6, and many other places. The reason is evident; for idolatry involved a withholding from God of those tithes and other offerings which He claimed from Israel, and thus became, as it were, an invasion of the Divine rights of property. The same word is even applied to the sin of adultery (Numb. v. 12, 27), apparently from the same point of view, inasmuch as the woman is regarded as belonging to her husband, who has therefore in her certain sacred rights, of which adultery is an invasion. Thus, while every " trespass " is a sin, yet every sin is not a " trespass." There are, evidently, many sins of which this is not a characteristic feature. But the sins for which the guilt-offering is prescribed are in every case sins which *may*, at least, be specially regarded under this particular point of view, to wit, as trespasses on the rights of God or man in respect of ownership; and this gives us the fundamental thought which distinguishes the guilt-offering from all others, namely, that for any invasion of the rights of another in regard to property, not only must expiation be made, in that it is a sin, but also satisfaction, and, so far as possible, plenary reparation of the wrong, in that the sin is also trespass.

From this it is evident that, as contrasted with the burnt-offering, which pre-eminently symbolised full consecration of the person, and the peace-offering, which symbolised fellowship with God, as based upon reconciliation by sacrifice, the guilt-offering takes its place, in a general sense, with the sin-offering, as, like that, specially designed to effect the reinstatement of an offender in covenant relation with God. Thus, like the latter, and unlike the former offerings, it was only prescribed with reference to specific instances of failure to fulfil some particular obligation toward God or man. So also, as the express condition of an acceptable offering, the formal confession of such sin was particularly enjoined. And, finally, unlike the burnt-offering, which was wholly consumed upon the altar, or the peace-offering, of the flesh of which, with certain reservations, the worshipper himself partook, in the case of the guilt-offering, as in the sin-offering, the fat parts only were burnt on the altar, and the remainder of the victim fell to the priests, to be eaten by them alone in a holy place, as a thing "most holy." The law is given in the following words (vii. 3-7): "He shall offer of it all the fat thereof; the fat tail, and the fat that covereth the inwards, and the two kidneys, and the fat that is on them, which is by the loins, and the caul upon the liver, with the kidneys, shall he take away: and the priest shall burn them upon the altar for an offering made by fire unto the Lord: it is a guilt-offering. Every male among the priests shall eat thereof: it shall be eaten in a holy place: it is most holy. As is the sin-offering, so is the guilt-offering: there is one law for them: the priest that maketh atonement therewith, he shall have it."

But while, in a general way, the guilt-offering was evidently intended, like the sin-offering, to signify the removal of sin from the conscience through sacrifice, and thus may be regarded as a variety of the sin-offering, yet the ritual presents some striking variations from that of the latter. These are all explicable from this consideration, that whereas the sin-offering represented the idea of atonement by sacrifice, regarded as an *expiation* of guilt, the guilt-offering represented atonement under the aspect of a *satisfaction* and *reparation* for the wrong committed. Hence, because the idea of expiation here fell somewhat into the background, in order to give the greater prominence to that of reparation and satisfaction, the application of the blood is only made, as in the burnt-offering and the peace-offering, by sprinkling "on the altar (of burnt-offering) round about" (vii. 1). Hence, again, we find that the guilt-offering always had reference to the sin of the individual, and never to the congregation; because it was scarcely possible that every individual in the whole congregation should be guilty in such instances as those for which the guilt-offering is prescribed.

Again, we have another contrast in the restriction imposed upon the choice of the victim for the sacrifice. In the sin-offering, as we have seen, it was ordained that the offering should be varied according to the theocratic rank of the offender, to emphasise thereby to the conscience gradations of guilt, as thus determined; also, it was permitted that the offering might be varied in value according to the ability of the offerer, in order that it might thus be signified in symbol that it was the gracious will of God that nothing in the personal condition of the sinner should exclude any one from the merciful provision of the expiatory sacrifice. But it was no less important that another aspect of the matter should be held forth, namely, that God is no respecter of persons; and that, whatever be the condition of the offender, the obligation to plenary satisfaction and reparation for trespass committed, cannot be modified in any way by the circumstances of the offender. The man who, for example, has

---

* It is to be regretted that the Revisers had not allowed in this case the rendering "trespass-offering" to stand, as in the Authorised Version. For, unlike the more generic term "guilt," our word "trespass" very precisely indicates the class of offences for which this particular offering was ordained. It is indeed true that the Hebrew word so rendered is quite distinct from that rendered "trespass;" yet, in this instance, by the attempt to represent this fact in English, more has been lost than gained.

defrauded his neighbour, whether of a small sum or of a large estate, abides his debtor before God, under all conceivable conditions, until restitution is made. The obligation of full payment rests upon every debtor, be he poor or rich, until the last farthing is discharged. Hence, the sacrificial victim of the guilt-offering is the same, whether for the poor man or the rich man, "a ram of the flock."

It was "a ram of the flock," because, as contrasted with the ewe or the lamb, or the dove and the pigeon, it was a valuable offering. And yet it is not a bullock, the most valuable offering known to the law, because that might be hopelessly out of the reach of many a poor man. The idea of value must be represented, and yet not so represented as to exclude a large part of the people from the provisions of the guilt-offering. The ram must be "without blemish," that naught may detract from its value, as a symbol of full satisfaction for the wrong done.

But most distinctive of all the requisitions touching the victim is this, that, unlike all other victims for other offerings, the ram of the guilt-offering must in each case be definitely appraised by the priest. The phrase is (v. 15), that it must be "according to thy estimation in silver by shekels, after the shekel of the sanctuary." This expression evidently requires, first, that the offerer's own estimate of the value of the victim shall not be taken, but that of the priest, as representing God in this transaction; and, secondly, that its value shall in no case fall below a certain standard; for the plural expression, "by shekels," implies that the value of the ram shall not be less than two shekels. And the shekel must be of full weight; the standard of valuation must be God's, and not man's, "the shekel of the sanctuary."

Still more to emphasise the distinctive thought of this sacrifice, that full satisfaction and reparation for all offences is with God the universal and unalterable condition of forgiveness, it was further ordered that in all cases where the trespass was of such a character as made this possible, that which had been unjustly taken or kept back, whether from God or man, should be restored "in full;" and not only this, but inasmuch as by this misappropriation of what was not his own, the offender had for the time deprived another of the use and enjoyment of that which belonged to him, he must add to that of which he had defrauded him "the fifth part more," a double tithe. Thus the guilty person was not allowed to have gained even any temporary advantage from the use for a while of that which he now restored; for "the fifth part more" would presumably quite overbalance all conceivable advantage or enjoyment which he might have had from his fraud. How admirable in all this the exact justice of God! How perfectly adapted was the guilt-offering, in all these particulars, to educate the conscience, and to preclude any possible wrong inferences from the allowance which was made, for other reasons, for the poor man, in the expiatory offerings for sin!

The arrangement of the law of the guilt-offering is very simple. It is divided into two sections, the first of which (v. 14-19) deals with cases of trespass "in the holy things of the Lord," things which, by the law or by an act of consecration, were regarded as belonging in a special sense to Jehovah; the second section, on the other hand (vi. 1-7), deals with cases of trespass on the property rights of man.

The first of these, again, consists of two parts. Verses 14-16 give the law of the guilt-offering as applied to cases in which a man, through inadvertence or unwittingly, trespasses in the holy things of the Lord, but in such manner that the nature and extent of the trespass can afterward be definitely known and valued; verses 17-19 deal with cases where there has been trespass such as to burden the conscience, and yet such as, for whatsoever reason, cannot be precisely measured.

By "the holy things of the Lord" are intended such things as, either by universal ordinance or by voluntary consecration, were regarded as belonging to Jehovah, and in a special sense His property. Thus, under this head would come the case of the man who, for instance, should unwittingly eat the flesh of the firstling of his cattle, or the flesh of the sin-offering, or the shew-bread; or should use his tithe, or any part of it, for himself. Even though he did this unwittingly, yet it none the less disturbed the man's relation to God; and therefore, when known, in order to his reinstatement in fellowship with God, it was necessary that he should make full restitution with a fifth part added, and besides this, sacrifice a ram, duly appraised, as a guilt-offering. In that the sacrifice was prescribed over and above the restitution, the worshipper was reminded that, in view of the infinite majesty and holiness of God, it lies not in the power of any creature to nullify the wrong God-ward, even by fullest restitution. For trespass is not only trespass, but is also sin; an offence not only against the rights of Jehovah as Owner, but also an affront to Him as Supreme King and Lawgiver.

And yet, because the worshipper must not be allowed to lose sight of the fact that sin is of the nature of a debt, a victim was ordered which should especially bring to mind this aspect of the matter. For not only among the Hebrews, but among the Arabs, the Romans and other ancient peoples, sheep, and especially rams, were very commonly used as a medium of payment in case of debt, and especially in paying tribute.

Thus we read (2 Kings iii. 4), that Mesha, king of Moab, rendered unto the king of Israel "an hundred thousand lambs, and an hundred thousand rams, with the wool," in payment of tribute; and, at a later day, Isaiah (xvi. 1, R. V.) delivers to Moab the mandate of Jehovah: "Send ye the lambs for the ruler of the land . . . unto the mount of the daughter of Zion."

And so the ram having been brought and presented by the guilty person, with confession of his fault, it was slain by the priest, like the sin-offering. The blood, however, was not applied to the horns of the altar of burnt-offering, still less brought into the Holy Place, as in the case of the sin-offering; but (vii. 2) was to be sprinkled "upon the altar round about," as in the burnt-offering. The reason of this difference in the application of the blood, as above remarked, lies in this, that, as in the burnt-offering, the idea of sacrifice as symbolising expiation takes a place secondary and subordinate to another thought; in this case, the conception of sacrifice as representing satisfaction for trespass.

The next section (vv. 17-19) does not expressly mention sins of trespass; for which reason some have thought that it was essentially a repetition of the law of the sin-offering. But that it is not to be so regarded is plain from the fact that the victim is still the same as for the guilt-offering, and from the explicit statement (ver. 19) that this "is a guilt-offering." The inference is natural that the prescription still has reference to "trespass in the holy things of the Lord"; and the class of cases intended is probably indicated by the phrase, "though he knew it not." In the former section, the law provided for cases in which though the trespass had been done unwittingly, yet the offender afterward came to know of the trespass in its precise extent, so as to give an exact basis for the restitution ordered in such cases. But it is quite supposable that there might be cases in which, although the offender was aware that there had been a probable trespass, such as to burden his conscience, he yet knew not just how much it was. The ordinance is only in so far modified as such a case would make necessary; where there was no exact knowledge of the amount of trespass, obviously there the law of restitution with the added fifth could not be applied. Yet, none the less, the man is guilty; he "bears his iniquity," that is, he is liable to the penalty of his fault; and in order to the re-establishment of his covenant relation with God, the ram must be offered as a guilt-offering.

It is suggestive to observe the emphasis which is laid upon the necessity of the guilt-offering, even in such cases. Three times, reference is explicitly made to this fact of ignorance, as not affecting the requirement of the guilt-offering: (ver. 17) "Though he knew it not, yet is he guilty, and shall bear his iniquity;" and again (ver. 18), with special explicitness, "The priest shall make atonement for him concerning the thing wherein he erred unwittingly and knew it not;" and yet again (ver. 19), "It is a guilt-offering: he is certainly guilty before the Lord." The repetition is an urgent reminder that in this case, as in all others, we are never to forget that however our ignorance of a trespass at the time, or even lack of definite knowledge regarding its nature and extent, may affect the degree of our guilt, it cannot affect the fact of our guilt, and the consequent necessity for satisfaction in order to acceptance with God.

The second section of the law of the guilt-offering (vi. 1-7) deals with trespasses against man, as also, like trespasses against Jehovah, requiring, in order to forgiveness from God, full restitution with the added fifth, and the offering of the ram as a guilt-offering. Five cases are named (vv. 2, 3), no doubt as being common, typical examples of sins of this character.

The first case is trespass upon a neighbour's rights in "a matter of deposit;" where a man has entrusted something to another to keep, and he has either sold it or unlawfully used it as if it were his own. The second case takes in all fraud in a "bargain," as when, for example, a man sells goods, or a piece of land, representing them to be better than they really are, or asking a price larger than he knows an article to be really worth. The third instance is called "robbery;" by which we are to understand any act or process, even though it should be under colour of legal forms, by means of which a man may manage unjustly to get possession of the property of his neighbour, without giving him due equivalent therefor. The fourth instance is called "oppression" of his neighbour. The English word contains the same image as the Hebrew word, which is used, for instance, of the unnecessary retention of the wages of the *employé* by the employer (xix. 13); it may be applied to all cases in which a man takes advantage of another's circumstances to extort from him any thing or any service to which he has no right, or to force upon him something which it is to the poor man's disadvantage to take. The last example of offences to which the law of the guilt-offering applied, is the case in which a man finds something and then denies it to the rightful owner. The reference to false swearing which follows, as appears from ver. 5, refers not merely to lying and perjury concerning this last-named case, but equally to all cases in which a man may lie or swear falsely to the pecuniary damage of his neighbour. It is mentioned not merely as aggravating such sin, but because in swearing touching any matter, a man appeals to God as witness to the truth of his words; so that by swearing in these cases he represents God as a party to his falsehood and injustice.

In all these cases, the prescription is the same as in analogous offences in the holy things of Jehovah. First of all, the guilty man must confess the wrong which he has done (Numb. v. 7), then restitution must be made of all of which he has defrauded his neighbour, together with one-fifth additional. But while this may set him right with man, it has not yet set him right with God. He must bring his guilt-offering unto Jehovah (vv. 6, 7); "a ram without blemish out of the flock, according to the priest's estimation, for a guilt-offering, unto the priest: and the priest shall make atonement for him before the Lord, and he shall be forgiven; concerning whatsoever he doeth so as to be guilty thereby."

And this completes the law of the guilt-offering. It was thus prescribed for sins which involve a defrauding or injuring of another in respect to material things, whether God or man, whether knowingly or unwittingly. The law was one and unalterable for all; the condition of pardon was plenary restitution for the wrong done, and the offering of a costly sacrifice, appraised as such by the priest, the earthly representative of God, in the shekel of the sanctuary, "a ram without blemish out of the flock."

There are lessons from this ordinance, so plain that, even in the dim light of those ancient days, the Israelite might discern and understand them. And they are lessons which, because man and his ways are the same as then, and God the same as then, are no less pertinent to all of us to-day.

Thus we are taught by this law that God claims from man, and especially from His own people, certain rights of property, of which He will not allow Himself to be defrauded, even through man's forgetfulness or inadvertence. In a later day Israel was sternly reminded of this in the burning words of Jehovah by the prophet Malachi (iii. 8, 9): "Will a man rob God? yet ye rob me. But ye say, Wherein have we robbed thee? In tithes and offerings. Ye are cursed with the curse; for ye rob me, even this whole nation." Nor has God relaxed His claim in the present dispensation. For the Apostle Paul charges the Corinthian Christians (2 Cor. viii. 7), in the name of the Lord, with regard to their gifts, that as they abounded in other graces, so they should "abound in this grace also." And this is the first lesson brought before us in the law of the guilt-offering. God claims His tithe,

His first-fruit, and the fulfilment of all vows. It was a lesson for that time; it is no less a lesson for our time.

And the guilt-offering further reminds us that as God has rights, so man also has rights, and that Jehovah, as the King and Judge of men, will exact the satisfaction of those rights, and will pass over no injury done by man to his neighbour in material things, nor forgive it unto any man, except upon condition of the most ample material restitution to the injured party.

Then, yet again, if the sin-offering called especially for *faith* in an expiatory sacrifice as the condition of the Divine forgiveness, the guilt-offering as specifically called also for *repentance*, as a condition of pardon, no less essential. Its unambiguous message to every Israelite was the same as that of John the Baptist at a later day (Matt. iii. 8, 9): " Bring forth fruit worthy of repentance: and think not to say within yourselves, We have Abraham to our father."

The reminder is as much needed now as in the days of Moses. How specific and practical the selection of the particular instances mentioned as cases for the application of the inexorable law of the guilt-offering! Let us note them again, for they are not cases peculiar to Israel or to the fifteenth century before Christ. "If any one . . . deal falsely with his neighbour in a matter of deposit;" as, *e. g.*, in the case of moneys entrusted to a bank or railway company, or other corporation; for there is no hint that the law did not apply except to individuals, or that a man might be released from these stringent obligations of righteousness whenever in some such evil business he was associated with others; the guilt-offering must be forthcoming, with the amplest restitution, or there is no pardon. Then false dealing in a "bargain" is named, as involving the same requirement; as when a man prides himself on driving "a good bargain," by getting something unfairly for less than its value, taking advantage of his neighbour's straits; or by selling something for more than its value, taking advantage of his neighbour's ignorance, or his necessity. Then is mentioned "robbery;" by which word is covered not merely that which goes by the name in polite circles, but all cases in which a man takes advantage of his neighbour's distress or helplessness, perhaps by means of some technicality of law, to "strip" him, as the Hebrew word is, of his property of any kind. And next is specified the man who may "have oppressed his neighbour," especially a man or woman who serves him, as the usage of the word suggests; grinding thus the face of the poor; paying, for instance, less for labour than the law of righteousness and love demands, because the poor man must have work or starve with his house. What sweeping specifications! And all such in all lands and all ages, are solemnly reminded in the law of the guilt-offering that in these their sharp practices they have to reckon not with man merely, but with God; and that it is utterly vain for a man to hope for the forgiveness of sin from God, offering or no offering, so long as he has in his pocket his neighbour's money. For all such, full restoration with the added fifth, according to the law of the theocratic kingdom, was the unalterable condition of the Divine forgiveness; and we shall find that this law of the theocratic kingdom will also be the law applied in the adjudications of the great white throne.

Furthermore, in that it was particularly enjoined that in the estimation of the value of the guilt-offering, not the shekel of the people, often of light weight, but the full weight "shekel of the sanctuary" was to be held the invariable standard; we, who are so apt to ease things to our consciences by applying to our conduct the principles of judgment current among men, are plainly taught that if we will have our trespasses forgiven, the reparation and restitution which we make must be measured, not by the standard of men, but by that of God, which is absolute righteousness.

Yet again, in that in the case of all such trespasses on the rights of God or man it was ordained that the offering, unlike other sacrifices intended to teach other lessons, should be one and the same, whether the offender were rich or poor; we are taught that the extent of our moral obligations or the conditions of their equitable discharge are not determined by a regard to our present ability to make them good. Debt is debt by whomsoever owed. If a man have appropriated a hundred pounds of another man's money, the moral obligation of that debt cannot be abrogated by a bankrupt law, allowing him to compromise at ten shillings in the pound. The law of man may indeed release him from liability to prosecution, but no law can discharge such a man from the unalterable obligation to pay penny for penny, farthing for farthing. There is no bankrupt law in the kingdom of God. This, too, is evidently a lesson quite as much needed by Gentiles and nominal Christians in the nineteenth century after Christ, as by Hebrews in the fifteenth century before Christ.

But the spiritual teaching of the guilt-offering is not yet exhausted. For, like all the other offerings, it pointed to Christ. He is "the end of the law unto righteousness" (Rom. x. 4), as regards the guilt-offering, as in all else. As the burnt-offering prefigured Christ the heavenly Victim, in one aspect, and the peace-offering, Christ in another aspect, so the guilt-offering presents to our adoring contemplation yet another view of His sacrificial work. While, as our burnt-offering, He became our *righteousness* in full self-consecration; as our peace-offering, our *life;* as our sin-offering, the *expiation* for our sins; so, as our guilt-offering, He made *satisfaction* and plenary reparation in our behalf to the God on whose inalienable rights in us, by our sins we had trespassed without measure.

Nor is this an over-refinement of exposition. For in Isa. liii. 10, where both the Authorised and the Revised Versions read, " shall make his soul *an offering for sin,*" the margin of the latter rightly calls attention to the fact that in the Hebrew the word here used is the very same which through all this Levitical law is rendered " guilt-offering." And so we are expressly told by this evangelic prophet, that the Holy Servant of Jehovah, the suffering Messiah, in this His sacrificial work should make His soul "a guilt-offering." He became Himself the complete and exhaustive realisation of all that in sacrifice which was set forth in the Levitical guilt-offering.

A declaration this is which holds forth both the sin for which Christ atoned, and the Sacrifice itself, in a very distinct and peculiar light. In that Christ's sacrifice was thus a guilt-offering in the sense of the law, we are taught that, in one aspect, our sins are regarded by God, and should therefore be regarded by us, as debts which are due from us to God. This is, indeed, by no means the only aspect in which sin should be regarded; it is, for example, rebellion, high treason, a deadly affront to the Supreme Majesty, which must be expiated with the blood of the sin-offering. But our sins are also of the nature of debts. That is, God has claims on us for service which we have never met; claims for a portion of our substance which we have often withheld, or given grudgingly, trespassing thus in "the holy things of the Lord." Just as the servant who is set to do his master's work, if, instead, he take that time to do his own work, is debtor to the full value of the service of which his master is thus defrauded, so stands the case between the sinner and God. Just as with the agent who fails to make due returns to his principal on the moneys committed to him for investment, using them instead for himself, so stands the case between God and the sinner who has used his talents, not for the Lord, but for himself, or has kept them laid up, unused, in a napkin. Thus, in the New Testament, as the correlate of this representation of Christ as a guilt-offering, we find sin again and again set forth as a debt which is owed from man to God. So, in the Lord's prayer we are taught to pray, "Forgive us our debts;" so, twice the Lord Himself in His parables (Matt. xviii. 23-35; Luke vii. 41, 42) set forth the relation of the sinner to God as that of the debtor to the creditor; and concerning those on whom the tower of Siloam fell, asks (Luke xiii. 4), "Think ye that they were sinners (*Greek* 'debtors,') above all that dwelt in Jerusalem?" Indeed so imbedded is this thought in the conscience of man that it has been crystallised in our word "ought," which is but the old preterite of "owe;" as in Tyndale's New Testament, where we read (Luke vii. 41), "there was a certain lender, which ought him five hundred pence." What a startling conception is this, which forms the background to the great "guilt-offering"! Man a debtor to God! a debtor for service each day due, but no day ever fully and perfectly rendered! in gratitude for gifts, too often quite forgotten, oftener only paid in scanty part! We are often burdened and troubled greatly about our debts to men; shall we not be concerned about the enormous and ever accumulating debt to God! Or is He an easy creditor, who is indifferent whether these debts of ours be met or not? So think multitudes; but this is not the representation of Scripture, either in the Old or the New Testament. For in the law it was required, that if a man, guilty of any of these offences for the forgiveness of which the guilt-offering was prescribed, failed to confess and bring the offering, and make the restitution with the added fifth, as commanded by the law, he should be brought before the judges, and the full penalty of law exacted, on the principle of "an eye for an eye, a tooth for a tooth!" And in the New Testament, one of those solemn parables of the two debtors closes with the awful words concerning one of them who was "delivered to the tormentors," that he should not come out of prison till he had "paid the uttermost farthing." Not a hint is there in Holy Scripture, of forgiveness of our debts to God, except upon the one condition of full restitution made to Him to whom the debt is due, and therewith the sacrificial blood of a guilt-offering. But Christ is our Guilt-Offering. He is our Guilt-Offering, in that He Himself did that, really and fully, with respect to all our debts as sinful men to God, which the guilt-offering of Leviticus symbolised, but accomplished not. His soul He made a guilt-offering for our trespasses! Isaiah's words imply that He should make full restitution for all that of which we, as sinners, defraud God. He did this by that perfect and incomparable service of lowly obedience such as we should render, but have never rendered; in which He has made full satisfaction to God for all our innumerable debts. He has made such satisfaction, not by a convenient legal fiction, or in a rhetorical figure, or as judged by any human standard. Even as the ram of the guilt-offering was appraised according to "the shekel of the sanctuary," so upon our Lord, at the beginning of that life of sacrificial service, was solemnly passed the Divine verdict that with this antitypical Victim of the Guilt-Offering, God Himself was "well pleased" (Matt. iii. 17).

Not only so. For we cannot forget that according to the law, not only the full restitution must be made, but the fifth must be added thereto. So with our Lord. For who will not confess that Christ not only did all that we should have done, but, in the ineffable depth of His self-humiliation and obedience unto death, even the death of the cross, paid therewith the added fifth of the law. Said a Jewish Rabbi to the writer, "I have never been able to finish reading in the Gospel the story of the Jesus of Nazareth; for it too soon brings the tears to my eyes!" So affecting even to Jewish unbelief was this unparalleled spectacle, the adorable Son of God making Himself a guilt-offering, and paying, in the incomparable perfection of His holy obedience, the added fifth in our behalf! Thus has Christ "magnified this law" of the guilt-offering, and "made it honourable," even as He did all law (Isa. xlii. 21).

And, as is intimated, by the formal valuation of the sacrificial ram, in the type, even the death of Christ as the guilt-offering, in one aspect is to be regarded as the consummating act of service in the payment of debts Godward. Just as the sin-offering represented His death in its passive aspect, as meeting the demands of justice against the sinner as a rebel under sentence of death, by dying in his stead, so, on the other hand, the guilt-offering represents that same sacrificial death, rather in another aspect, no less clearly set forth in the New Testament; namely, the supreme act of obedience to the will of God, whereby He discharged "to the uttermost farthing," even with the added fifth of the law, all the transcendent debt of service due from man to God.

This representation of Christ's work has in all ages been an offence, "the offence of the cross." All the more need we to insist upon it, and never to forget, or let others forget, that Christ is expressly declared in the Word of God to have been "a guilt-offering," in the Levitical sense of that term; that, therefore, to speak of His death as effecting our salvation merely through its moral influence, is to contradict and nullify the Word of God. Well may we set this word in Isa. liii. 10, concerning the Servant of Jehovah, against all modern Unitarian theology, and against all Socinianising teaching; all that would maintain any view of Christ's death which excludes or ignores the divinely revealed fact that it was in its essential nature a guilt-offering; and, because a guilt-offering, therefore of the nature of the payment of a debt in behalf of those for whom He suffered.

Most blessed truth this, for all who can receive it! Christ, the Son of God, our Guilt-Offering! Like the poor Israelite, who had defrauded God of that which was His due, so must we do; coming before God, confessing that wherein we have wronged Him, and bringing forth fruit meet for repentance, we must bring and plead Christ in the glory of His person, in all the perfection of His holy obedience, as our Guilt-Offering. And therewith the ancient promise to the penitent Israelite becomes ours (vi. 7), "The priest shall make atonement for him before the Lord, and he shall be forgiven; concerning whatsoever he doeth so as to be guilty thereby."

CHAPTER IX.

THE PRIESTS' PORTIONS.

LEVITICUS vi. 16-18, 26; vii. 6-10, 14, 31-36.

AFTER the law of the guilt-offering follows a section (vi. 8-vii. 38) with regard to the offerings previously treated, but addressed especially to the priests, as the foregoing were specially directed to the people. Much of the contents of this section has already passed before us, in anticipation of its order in the book, as this has seemed necessary in order to a complete exposition of the several offerings. An important part of the section, however, relating to the portion of the offerings which was appointed for the priests, has been passed by until now, and must claim our brief attention.

In the verses indicated above, it is ordered that of the meal-offerings, the sin-offerings, and the guilt-offerings, all that was not burnt, as also the wave-breast and the heave-shoulder of the peace-offerings, should be for Aaron and his sons. In particular, it is directed that the priest's portion of the sin-offering and the guilt-offering shall be eaten by "the priest that maketh atonement therewith" (vii. 7); and that of the meal-offerings prepared in the oven, the frying-pan, or the baking-pan, all that is not burned upon the altar, according to the law of chap. ii., shall be eaten by "the priest that offereth it;" and that of every meal-offering mingled with oil, or dry, the same part "shall all the sons of Aaron have, one as well as another" (vii. 9, 10). Of the burnt-offering, all the flesh being burned, the hide alone fell to the officiating priest as his perquisite (vii. 8).

These regulations are explained in the concluding verses of the section (vii. 35, 36) as follows, "This is the anointing-portion of Aaron, and the anointing-portion of his sons, out of the offerings of the Lord made by fire, in the day when he presented them to minister unto the Lord in the priest's office; which the Lord commanded to be given them of the children of Israel, in the day that he anointed them. It is a due for ever throughout their generations."

Hence, it is plain that this use which was to be made of certain parts of certain offerings does not touch the question of the consecration of the whole to God. The whole of each offering is none the less wholly accepted and appropriated by God, that He designates a part of it to the maintenance of the priesthood. That even as thus used by the priest it is used by him as something belonging to God, is indicated by the phrase used, "it is most holy" (vi. 17); expressive words, which in the law of the offerings always have a technical use, as denoting those things of which only the sons of Aaron might partake, and that only in the holy place. In the case of the meal-offering, its peculiarly sacred character as belonging, the whole of it, exclusively to God, is further marked by the additional injunctions that it should be "eaten *without leaven* in a holy place" (vi. 16); and that whosoever touched these offerings should be holy (vi. 18); that is, he should be as a man separated to God, under all the restrictions (doubtless, without the privileges), which belonged to the priesthood, as men set apart for God's service. In the eating of their portion of the various offerings by the priests, we are to recognise no official act: we simply see the servants of God supported by the bread of His table.

This last thought, which is absent in the case of no one of the offerings,* is brought out with special clearness and fulness in the ceremonial connected with the peace-offerings (vii. 28-34). In this case, certain parts, the right thigh (or shoulder?) and the breast, are set apart as the due of the priest. The selection of these is determined by the principle which marks all the Levitical legislation: God and those who represent Him are to be honoured by the consecration of the best of everything. In the animals used upon the altar, these were regarded as the choice parts, and are indeed referred to as such in other Scriptures. But, in order that neither the priest nor the people may imagine that the priest receives these as a man from his fellowmen, but may understand that they are given to God, and that it is from God that the priest now receives them, as His servant, fed from His table; to this end, certain ceremonies were ordained to be used with these parts; the breast was to be "heaved," the thigh was to be "waved," before the Lord. What was the meaning of these actions?

The breast was to be "heaved;" that is, elevated heavenward. The symbolic meaning of this act can scarcely be missed. By it, the priest acknowledged his dependence upon God for the supply of this sacrificial food, and, again, by this act consecrated it anew to Him as the One that sitteth in the heavens.

But God is not only the One that "sitteth in the heavens;" He is the God who has condescended also to dwell among men, and especially in the tent of meeting in the midst of Israel. And thus, as by the elevation of the breast heavenward, God, the Giver, was recognised as the One enthroned in heaven, so by the "waving" of the thigh, which, as the rabbis tell us, was a movement backward and forward, to and from the altar, He was recognised also as Jehovah, who had condescended from heaven to dwell in the midst of His people. Like the "heaving," so the "waving," then, was an act of acknowledgment and consecration to God; the former, to God, as in heaven, the God of creation; the other, to God, as the God of the altar, the God of redemption. And that this is

* Even in the burnt-offering, the hide of the victim was assigned to the priest (vii. 8).

the true significance of these acts is illustrated by the fact that in the Pentateuch, in the account of the gold and silver brought by the people for the preparation of the tabernacle (Exod. xxxv. 22), the same word is used to describe the presentation of these offerings which is here used of the wave-offering.

And so in the peace-offering the principle is amply illustrated upon which the priests received their dues. The worshippers bring their offerings, and present them, not to the priest, but through him to God; who, then, having used such parts as He will in the service of the sanctuary, gives again such parts of them as He pleases to the priests.

The lesson of these arrangements lies immediately before us. They were intended to teach Israel, and, according to the New Testament, are also designed to teach us, that it is the will of God that those who give up secular occupations to devote themselves to the ministry of His house should be supported by the freewill offerings of God's people. Very strange indeed it is to hear a few small sects in our day denying this. For the Apostle Paul argues at length to this effect, and calls the attention of the Corinthians (1 Cor. ix. 13, 14) to the fact that the principle expressed in this ordinance of the law of Moses has not been set aside, but holds good in this dispensation. "Know ye not that they which . . . wait upon the altar have their portion with the altar? Even so did the Lord ordain that they which proclaim the Gospel should live of the Gospel." The principle plainly covers the case of all such as give up secular callings to devote themselves to the ministry of the Word, whether to proclaim the Gospel in any of the great mission fields, or to exercise the pastorate of the local church. Such are ever to be supported out of the consecrated offerings of God's people.

To point in disparagement of modern "hireling" ministers and missionaries, as some have done, to the case of Paul, who laboured with his own hands, that he might not be chargeable to those to whom he ministered, is singularly inapt, seeing that in the chapter above referred to he expressly vindicates his right to receive of the Corinthians his support, and in this Second Epistle to them even seems to express a doubt (2 Cor. xii. 13) whether in refusing, as he did, to receive support from them, he had not done them a "wrong," making them thus "inferior to the rest of the churches," from whom, in fact, he did receive such material aid (Phil. iv. 10, 16).

And if ever claims of this kind upon our benevolence and liberality seem to be heavy, and if to nature the burden is sometimes irksome, we shall do well to remember that the requirement is not of man, and not of the Church, but of God. It comes to us with the double authority of the Old and New Testament, of the Law and the Gospel. And it will certainly help us all to give to these ends the more gladly, if we keep that in mind which the Levitical law so carefully kept before Israel, that the giving was to be regarded by them as not to the priesthood, but to the Lord, and that in our giving outwardly to support the ministry of God's Word, we give, really, to the Lord Himself. And it stands written (Matt. x. 42): "Whosoever shall give to drink unto one of these little ones a cup of cold water only, . . . he shall in no wise lose his reward."

CHAPTER X.

THE CONSECRATION OF AARON AND HIS SONS, AND OF THE TABERNACLE.

LEVITICUS viii. 1-36.

THE second section of the book of Leviticus (viii. 1-x. 20) is historical, and describes (viii.) the consecration of the tabernacle and of Aaron and his sons, (ix.) their induction into the duties of their office, and, finally (x.), the terrible judgment by which the high sanctity of the priestly office and of the tabernacle service was very solemnly impressed upon them and all the people.

First in order (chap. viii.) is described the ceremonial of consecration. We read (vv. 1-4): "And the Lord spake unto Moses, saying, Take Aaron and his sons with him, and the garments, and the anointing oil, and the bullock of the sin offering, and the two rams, and the basket of unleavened bread; and assemble thou all the congregation at the door of the tent of meeting. And Moses did as the Lord commanded him; and the congregation was assembled at the door of the tent of meeting."

These words refer us back to Exod. xxviii., xxix., in which are recorded the full directions previously given for the making of the garments and the oil of anointing, and for the ceremonial of the consecration of the priests. The law of offerings having been delivered, Moses now proceeds to consecrate Aaron and his sons to the priestly office, according to the commandment given; and to this end, by Divine direction, he orders "all the congregation" to be assembled "at the door of the tent of meeting." In this last statement some have seen a sufficient reason for rejecting the whole account as fabulous, insisting that it is palpably absurd to suppose that a congregation numbering some millions could be assembled at the door of a single tent! But, surely, if the words are to be taken in the ultra-literal sense required in order to make out this difficulty, the impossibility must have been equally evident to the supposed fabricator of the fiction; and it is yet more absurd to suppose that he should ever have intended his words to be pressed to such a rigid literality. Two explanations lie before us, either of which meets the supposed difficulty; the one, that endorsed by Dillmann,[*] that the congregation was gathered in their appointed representatives; the other, that which refuses to see in the words a statement that every individual in the nation was literally "at the door," and further reminds us that, inasmuch as the ceremonies of the consecration are said to have continued seven days, we are not, by the terms of the narrative, required to believe that all, in any sense, were present, either at the very beginning or at any one time during that week. It is not too much to say that by a captious criticism of this kind, any narrative, however sober, might be shown to be absurd.

The consecration ceremonial was introduced by a solemn declaration made by Moses to assembled Israel, that the impressive rites which they were now about to witness, were of Divine appointment. We read (ver. 5), "Moses said

[*] See "Die Bücher Exodus und Leviticus," 2 Aufl., p. 462.

unto the congregation, This is the thing which the Lord hath commanded to be done."

Just here we may pause to note the great emphasis which the narrative lays upon this fact of the Divine appointment of all pertaining to these consecration rites. Not only is this Divine ordination of all thus declared at the beginning, but in connection with each of the chief parts of the ceremonial the formula is repeated, "as the Lord commanded Moses." Also, at the close of the first day's rites, Moses twice reminds Aaron and his sons that this whole ritual, in all its parts, is for them an ordinance of God, and is to be regarded accordingly, upon pain of death (vv. 34, 35). And the narrative of the chapter closes (ver. 36) with the words, "Aaron and his sons did all the things which the Lord commanded by the hand of Moses." Twelve times in this one chapter is reference thus made to the Divine appointment of these consecration rites.

This is full of significance and instruction. It is of the highest importance in an apologetic way. For it is self-evident that this twelvefold affirmation, twelve times directly contradicts the modern theory of the late origin and human invention of the Levitical priesthood. There is no evading of the issue which is thus placed squarely before us. To talk of the inspiration from God, in any sense possible to that word, of a writing containing such affirmations, so numerous, formal, and emphatic, if the critics referred to are right, and these affirmations are all false, is absurd. There is no such thing as inspired falsehood.

Again, a great spiritual truth is herein brought before us, which concerns believers in all ages. It is set forth in so many words in Heb. v. 4, where the writer, laying down the essential conditions of priesthood, specially mentions Divine appointment as one of these; which he affirms as satisfied in the high-priesthood of Christ: "No man taketh the honour unto himself, but when he is called of God, even as was Aaron. So Christ also glorified not Himself to be made a high priest." Fundamental to Christian faith and life is this thought: priesthood is not of man, but of God. In particular, in all that Christ has done and is still doing as the High Priest, in the true holiest, He is acting under Divine appointment.

And we are hereby pointed to the truth of which some may need to be reminded, that the work of our Lord in our behalf, and that of the whole universe into which sin has entered, has its cause and origin in the mind and gracious will of the Father. It was in His incomprehensible love, who appointed the priestly office, that the whole work of atonement, and therewith purification and full redemption, had its mysterious origin. The thoughtful reader of the Gospels will hardly need to be reminded how constantly our blessed Lord, in the days of His high-priestly service upon earth, acted in all that He did under the consciousness, often expressed, of His appointment by the Father to this work. Thus, Aaron in the solemn ceremonial of those days of consecration, as ever afterward, doing "all the things which the Lord commanded by the hand of Moses," in so doing fitly represented Him who should come afterward, who said of Himself (John vi. 38), "I came down from heaven, not to do Mine own will, but the will of Him that sent Me."

The Levitical Priesthood and Tabernacle as Types.

In order to any profitable study of the following ceremonial, it is indispensable to have distinctly before us the New Testament teaching as to the typical significance of the priesthood and the tabernacle. A few words on this subject, therefore, seem to be needful as preliminary to more detailed exposition. As to the typical character of Aaron, as high priest, the New Testament leaves us no room for doubt. Throughout the Epistle to the Hebrews, Christ is held forth as the true and heavenly High Priest, of whom Aaron, with his successors, was an eminent type.

As regards the other priests, while it is true that, considered in themselves, and without reference to the high priest, each of them also, in the performance of his daily functions in the tabernacle, was a lesser type of Christ, as is intimated in Heb. x. 11, yet, as contrasted with the high priest, who was ever one, while they were many, it is plain that another typical reference must be sought for the ordinary priesthood. What that may be is suggested to us in several New Testament passages; as, especially, in Rev. v. 10, where the whole body of believers, bought by the blood of the slain Lamb, is said to have been made "unto our God a kingdom and priests;" with which may be compared Heb. xiii. 10, where it is said, "We have an altar, whereof they have no right to eat which serve the tabernacle"; words which plainly assume the priesthood of all believers in Christ, as the antitype of the priesthood of the Levitical tabernacle.*

As to the typical meaning of the tabernacle, which also is anointed in the consecration ceremonial, there has been much difference of opinion. That it was typical is declared, in so many words, in the Epistle to the Hebrews (viii. 5), where the Levitical priests are said to have served "that which is a copy and shadow of the heavenly things;" as also ix. 24, where we read, "Christ entered not into a holy place made with hands, like in pattern to the true; but into heaven itself, now to appear before the face of God for us." But when we ask what then were "the heavenly things" of which the tabernacle was "the copy and shadow," we have different answers.

Many have replied that the antitype of the tabernacle, as of the temple, was the Church of believers; and, at first thought, with some apparent Scriptural reason. For it is certain that Christians are declared (1 Cor. iii. 16) to be the temple of the living God; where, however, it is to be noted that the original word denotes, not the temple or tabernacle in general, but the "sanctuary" or inner shrine—the "holy of holies." More to the point is 1 Peter ii. 5, where it is said to Christians, "Ye also, as living stones, are built up a spiritual house." Such passages as these do certainly warrant us in saying that the tabernacle, and especially the inner sanctuary, as the special place of the Divine habitation and manifestation, did in so far typify the Church.

But when we consider the tabernacle, not in

---

* Especially striking in this connection is the expression used by the Apostle Paul (Rom. xv. 16), where he speaks of himself as "a minister of Christ Jesus unto the Gentiles, ministering the Gospel of God;" in which last phrase, the Greek word denotes "ministration as a priest." See R. V., margin.

itself, but in relation to its priesthood and ministry, the explanation fails, and we fall into confusion. As when the priests are considered, not in themselves, but in their relation to the high priest, we are compelled to seek an antitype different from the Antitype of the high priest, so in this case. To identify the typical meaning of the tabernacle, considered as a part of a whole system and order, with that of the priesthood who serve in it, is to throw that whole typical system into confusion. Furthermore, this cannot be harmonised with a number of New Testament expressions with regard to the tabernacle and temple, as related to the high priesthood of our Lord. It is hard to see, for example, how the Church of believers could be properly described as "things in the heavens." Moreover, we are expressly taught (Heb. ix. 24), that the Antitype of the Holy Place into which the high priest entered every year, with blood, was "heaven itself," "the presence of God;" and again, His ascension to the right hand of God is described (Heb. iv. 14, R. V.), with evident allusion to the passing of the high priest through the Holy Place into the Holiest, as a passing "*through* the heavens;" and also (Heb. ix. 11). as an entering into the Holy Place, "through the greater and more perfect tabernacle." These expressions exclude reference to the Church of Christ as the antitype of the earthly tabernacle.

Others, again, have regarded the tabernacle as a type of the human nature of Christ, referring in proof to John ii. 19-21, where our Lord speaks of "the temple of His body;" and also to Heb. x. 19, 20, where it is said that believers have access to the Holiest "by a new and living way, which He dedicated for us through the veil, that is to say, His flesh."

As regards the first of these passages, we should note that the original word is, again, not the word for the temple in general, but that which is invariably used to denote the inner sanctuary, as the special shrine of Jehovah's presence: so that it really gives us no warrant for affirming that the tabernacle, *as a whole*, was a type of our Lord's humanity; nor, on that supposition, does it seem possible to explain the meaning of the three parts into which the tabernacle was divided. And the second passage referred to is no more to the point. For the writer had only a little before described the tabernacle as a "pattern of things in the heavens;" words which, surely, could not be applied to the humanity in which our Lord appeared in His incarnation and humiliation,—a humanity which was not a thing "of the heavens," but of the earth. The reference to the "flesh" of Christ, as being the veil through which He passed into the Holiest (Heb. x. 19, 20) is merely by way of illustration, and not of typical interpretation. The thought of the inspired writer appears to be this. Just as, in the Levitical tabernacle, the veil must be parted before the high priest could go into the Holiest Place, even so was it necessary that the flesh of our Lord should be rent in order that thus, through death, it might be possible for Him to enter into the true holiest. The thought has been happily expressed by Delitzsch, thus: "While He was with us here below, the weak, limit-bound, and mortal flesh which He had assumed for our sakes hung like a curtain between Him and the Divine sanctuary into which He would enter; and in order to such entrance, this curtain had to be withdrawn by death, even as the high priest had to draw aside the temple veil in order to make his entry to the Holy of Holies." *

Not to review other opinions on this matter, the various expressions used constrain us to regard the tabernacle as typifying the universe itself, measured and appointed in all its parts by infinite wisdom, as the abode of Him who "filleth immensity with His presence," the place of the Divine manifestation, and the abode of His holiness. In the outer court, where the victims were offered, we have this world of sense in which we live, in which our Lord was offered in the sight of all; in the Holy Place, and the Holy of Holies, the unseen and heavenly worlds, through the former of which our Lord is represented as having passed (Heb. iv. 14, ix. 11) that He might appear with His blood in the true Holiest, where God in the innermost shrine of His glory "covereth Himself with light as with a garment." For this cosmical dwelling-place of the Most High God has been defiled by sin, which, as it were, has profaned the whole sanctuary; for we read (Col. i. 20), that not only "things upon the earth," but also "things in the heavens," are to be "reconciled" through Christ, even "through the blood of His cross;" and, still more explicitly, to the same effect (Heb. ix. 23), that as the typical "copies of the things in the heavens" needed to be cleansed with the blood of bullocks and of goats, so "it was necessary that . . . the heavenly things themselves should be cleansed with better sacrifices than these." And so, at this present time, Christ, as the High Priest of this cosmical tabernacle, "not made with hands," having offered His great sacrifice for sins for ever, is now engaged in carrying out His work of cleansing the people of God, and the earthly and the heavenly sanctuary, to the uttermost completion.

With these preliminary words, which have seemed essential to the exposition of these chapters, we are now prepared to consider the ceremonial of the consecration of the priesthood and tabernacle, and the spiritual meaning which it was intended to convey.

The Washing with Water.

Leviticus viii. 6.

"And Moses brought Aaron and his sons, and washed them with water."

The consecration ceremonies consisted of four parts, namely, the Washing, the Investiture, the Anointing, and the Sacrifices. Of these, first in order was the *Washing*. We read that "Moses" —acting throughout, we must remember, as Mediator, representing God—"brought Aaron and his sons, and washed them with water." The meaning of this act is so evident as not to have been called in question. Washing ever signifies cleansing; the ceremonial cleansing of the body, therefore, in symbol ever represents the inward purification of the spirit.

Of this usage the Biblical illustrations are very numerous. Thus, the spiritual purification of Israel in the latter day is described (Isa. iv. 4) by the same word as is used here, as a washing away

* "Commentary on the Epistle to the Hebrews," vol. ii., p. 172.

of "the filth of the daughters of Zion" by the Lord. So, again, in the New Testament, we read that Christ declared unto Nicodemus that in order to see the kingdom of God a man must be born again, "of water and the Spirit," and in the Epistle to Titus (iii. 5) we read of a cleansing of the Church "with the washing (*marg.*, laver) of water, by the Word," even the "washing of regeneration." The symbolism in this case, therefore, points to cleansing from the defilement of sin as a fundamental condition of priesthood. As regards our Lord indeed, such cleansing was no more needed for His high priesthood than was the sin-offering for Himself; for in His holy incarnation, though He took our nature indeed with all the consequences and infirmities consequent on sin, He was yet "without sin." But all the more it was necessary in the symbolism that if Aaron was to typify the sinless Christ of God he must be cleansed with water, in type of the cleansing of human nature, without which no man can approach to God. And in that not only Aaron, but also his sons, the ordinary priests, were thus cleansed, we are in the ordinance significantly pointed to the deep spiritual truth that they who are called to be priests to God must be qualified for this office, first of all, by the cleansing of their human nature through the washing of regeneration, by the power of the Holy Ghost.

The Investiture.

Leviticus viii. 7-9.

"And he put upon him the coat, and girded him with the girdle, and clothed him with the robe, and put the ephod upon him, and he girded him with the cunningly woven band of the ephod, and bound it unto him therewith. And he placed the breastplate upon him: and in the breastplate he put the Urim and the Thummim. And he set the mitre upon his head: and upon the mitre, in front, did he set the golden plate, the holy crown; as the Lord commanded Moses."

The next ceremony of the consecration was the Investiture of Aaron with his official high-priestly robes, as they had been appointed of God to be made (Exod. xxviii.). The investiture of the sons of Aaron significantly takes place only after the anointing of the tabernacle, and of Aaron as high priest. Of the investiture of Aaron we read in vv. 7-9, above.

As these garments were official, we must needs regard them as symbolical; a thought which is the more emphasised by the very minute and special directions given by the Lord for making them. Nothing was left to the fancy of man; all was prescribed by the Lord. The official robes of the high priest consisted of eight pieces, four of which, the coat, the girdle, the turban (or "mitre"), and the breeches, were, with the exception of the turban, of white linen, and identical in every respect with the official dress of the ordinary priests.

Four pieces more were peculiar to himself, the special insignia of his office, and unlike the dress of the ordinary priest, were richly made in gold and various colours, "garments for glory and for beauty." These were: the robe of the ephod, made all of blue, with a border of pendant pomegranates and golden bells in alternation; the ephod itself consisting of two pieces, broidered in gold and blue, purple, scarlet, and fine white linen, the one hanging in front, the other behind, over the robe of the ephod, and joined on the shoulders with two onyx stones, on which were graven the names of the twelve tribes, six on the one shoulder and six on the other; it was girt about him with a girdle of the same material and colours. The third was the breastplate, which was a double square of the same material and colours as the ephod, within the fold of which, as it hung from his shoulders by golden chains, was placed the Urim and the Thummim, whatever these may have been, and upon the front of which were set twelve precious stones, on which, severally, were engraved the names of the twelve tribes of the children of Israel. And the fourth and last article of his attire was "the golden plate, the holy crown;" a band of gold bound about his forehead over the turban, with blue lace, on which were engraven the words, "Holiness to Jehovah."

This dress of the high priest represented him, in the first place, as the appointed minister of the *tabernacle*. The number of pieces, twice four, like the four of the common priests' attire, answered to the four which was represented in the ground plan of the tabernacle, quadrangular both in its form as a whole and in its several parts, the Holy of Holies being a perfect cube; four being in Scripture constantly the number which symbolises the universe, as created by God and bearing witness to Him. So also the garments of the high priest marked him as the minister of the tabernacle by their colours, also four in number, and the same as those of the latter, namely, blue, purple, scarlet, and white.

But the official robes of the high priest marked him, in the second place, as the servant of *the God of the tabernacle*, whose livery he wore. For these colours, various modifications of light, all thus had a symbolic reference to the God of light, who made the universe of which the Mosaic tabernacle was a type. Of these, the blue, the colour of the overarching heaven, has been in many lands and religions naturally regarded as the colour symbolising God, as the God of the heaven, bowing to the earth in condescending love and self-revelation. In like manner, we find it repeatedly recurring in the symbolic manifestations of Jehovah in the Holy Scriptures, where it always brings God before us with special reference to His condescending love as entering into covenant with man, and revealing for their good His holy law.* The purple, as will occur to every one, is everywhere recognised as the colour of royalty, and therefore symbolised the kingly exaltation and majesty of God, as the Ruler of heaven and earth. The scarlet reminds us at once of the colour of blood, which stands in the very foreground of the Mosaic symbolism as the symbol of life, and thus points us to the conception of God, as the essentially Living One, who is Himself the sole primal source of all life, whether physical or spiritual, in the creature. No one can mistake, again, the symbolic meaning of the white, which, not only in the Scripture, but among all nations, has ever been the symbol of purity and holiness, and thus represented the high priest as the minister of God, as the Most Holy One. By this investiture, therefore, Aaron was symbolically constituted the minister of the tabernacle, on the one hand, and of God, on the other; and, in particular, of God as the God of revelation, in covenant with Israel; of God as the Most High, the King of Israel; of God as

* See, *e. g.*, Exod. xxiv. 10; Ezek. i. 26.

the God of life, the Giver of life in the redemption of Israel; and, finally, of God as the Most Holy, the God "who is light," and "with whom is no darkness at all."

The "robe of the ephod" was woven in one piece, and all of blue. In that it was thus without seam, was symbolised the wholeness and absolute integrity necessary to him who should bear the high-priestly office. In that it was made all of blue, the colour which symbolised the God of heaven as manifesting Himself to Israel in condescending love, in the holy law and covenant, this robe of the ephod specially marked the high priest as the minister of Jehovah and of His revealed law.

The ephod, which depended from the shoulders before and behind, according to the usage of Scripture, was the garment specially significant of rule and authority; a thought which reached full expression in the breastplate which was fastened to it, which contained the Urim and Thummim, by which God's will was made known to Israel in times of perplexity, and was called "the breast-plate of judgment."

The ornamentation of these garments had also a symbolic meaning, though it may not be in each instance equally clear. In that the high priest, as thus robed, bore upon the ephod and the breast-plate of judgment, graven on precious stones, the names of the twelve tribes of Israel, he was marked as one who in all his high-priestly work before and with God, presented and represented Israel. In that the names were engraven upon precious stones was signified the exceeding preciousness of Israel in God's sight, as His "peculiar treasure." In that, again, they were worn upon his shoulders, Aaron was represented to Israel as upholding and bearing them before God in the strength of his office; in that he wore their names upon his breast, he was represented as also bearing them upon his heart in love and affection.

The symbolic meaning of the pomegranates and golden bells, which formed the border of the robe of the ephod, is not quite so clear. But we may probably find a hint as to their significance in the Divine direction as to the border of blue which every Israelite was to wear upon the bottom of his garment (Numb. xv. 39). The purpose of this is said to be that it might be for a continual reminder of the law: "It shall be unto you for a fringe, that ye may look upon it, and remember all the commandments of the Lord, and do them." If then this border in the garment of each individual member of the priestly nation was designed symbolically to mark them as the keepers of the law of the God of heaven, we may safely infer an analogous meaning in the similar border to the official garment of the high priest. And if so, then we shall perhaps not be far out of the way if in this case we follow Jewish tradition in regarding the pomegranate, a fruit distinguished by being filled to the full with seeds, as the symbol, *par excellence*, of the law of commandments, the words of the living God, as "incorruptible seed," endowed by Him with vital energy and power.*

As for the bells, we naturally think at once of the common use of the bell to give a signal, and announce what one may be concerned to know.

So we read of these golden bells (Exod. xxviii. 35), "the sound thereof shall be heard when he goeth in unto the holy place before the Lord . . . that he die not."

These golden bells in the border of his garment, between each pair of pomegranates, thus announced him as officially appearing before God as the fulfiller of the law of commandments, and as, for this reason, acceptable to God in the execution of his high-priestly functions.

As to the Urim and Thummim, "Light and Perfection," which were apparently placed within the fold of the breast-plate of judgment, as the tables of the law within the ark of the covenant, there has been in all ages much debate; but what they were cannot be said to have been certainly determined. Most probable appears the opinion that they were two sacred lots which on solemn occasions were used by the high priest for determining the will of God. So much, in any case, is clear from the Scripture, that in some way through them the will of God as the King of Israel was made known to the high priest, for the direction of the nation in doubtful matters. Most fitly, therefore, they were placed within the breast-plate of judgment, which, indeed, may have received this name from this circumstance. The high priest, therefore, as the bearer of the Urim and Thummim, was set forth, in accordance with the meaning of these words, as one who in virtue of his office received perfect enlightenment from God as to His will, in all that concerned Israel's action.

The plate of graven gold, called the "holy crown" was bound by Moses with a lace of blue upon the mitre of Aaron in front. The precious metal here, as elsewhere in the official garments of the high priest, and in the tabernacle, was symbolic of the boundless riches of the glory of the God of Israel, whose minister the high priest was. The special significance, however, of this holy crown, is found in the words which appeared upon it, "Holiness to Jehovah." This was a continual visible mark and reminder of the fact that the high priest, in all that he was, and in all that he did, was a person in the highest possible sense consecrated to Jehovah, the heavenly King of Israel, whose livery he wore. And in that this golden plate with this inscription is called his "crown," it is further suggested that in this last-named fact is found the crowning glory and dignity of the high priest's office. He is the minister of the God of Israel, Jehovah, whose own supreme glory is just this, that He is holy. In the directions given for this crown in Exod. xxviii. 36-38 it is said that in virtue of his wearing this, or, rather in virtue of the fact thus set forth, "Aaron shall bear the iniquity of the holy things which the children of Israel shall hallow in all their holy gifts; and it shall always be upon his forehead, that they may be accepted before the Lord." That is, even Israel's consecrated things, their holiest gifts, are yet defiled by the ever abiding sinfulness of those who offer them; but they are nevertheless graciously accepted, as being offered by Aaron, himself "holy to the Lord."

Such then appears to have been the symbolic meaning of these "garments for glory and for beauty," with which Moses now robed Aaron, in token of his investiture with the manifold dignities of the exalted office to which God had called him. But we must not forget that we are not, in all this, dealing merely with matters of anti-

---

* Thus, *e. g.*, in Cant. iv. 13, where the Revised Version reads, "Thy shoots are an orchard of pomegranates," the Jewish paraphrast in the Chaldee Targum renders, "Thy young men are filled with the commandments (of God) like unto pomegranates (*sc.* with their seeds)."

quarian or archæological interest. Nothing is plainer than the teaching of the New Testament, that Aaron, as the high priest, not by accident, but by Divine intention, prefigured Christ. In all the directions given concerning his investiture with his office, and the work which, as high priest, he had to do, the Holy Ghost intended to prefigure, directly or indirectly, something concerning the person, office, and work of Jesus Christ, as our heavenly High Priest, the Fulfiller of all these types. As Aaron appears in his fourfold high-priestly garments of four colours, which represented him as the minister, on the one hand, of the tabernacle, and, on the other, of the God of Israel, the Inhabitant of the tabernacle, so are we reminded how Christ is appointed as the "Minister of the greater and more perfect tabernacle, not made with hands" (Heb. ix. 11), the earth, the heaven, and the heaven of heavens, to reconcile, by the offering of His blood, "both the things which are on earth and those which are in the heavens" (Col. i. 20). We look upon the blue robe of the ephod, and remember how Christ is made a minister of "a better covenant, enacted upon better promises" (Heb. viii. 6), representing, as that old covenant did not, the fulness of the revelation of God's condescending love and saving mercy. So also the inwoven scarlet reminds us how Christ, again, as the great High Priest, is the minister of the God of life, and is also Himself life and the Giver of life to all His people. We look upon the high priest's purple and gold, and are reminded again that Christ, the High Priest, is also invested with regal power and dominion, all authority being given unto Him in heaven and on earth (Matt. xxviii. 18).

Again, we look on the ephod of fine linen, inwoven with blue, and scarlet, and purple, and gold, with its girdle, symbolising service, and its pendant breast-plate of judgment, and are reminded how Christ in all the relations thus pertaining to Him as High Priest, is the Ruler and the Judge of His people, who, as the bearer of the true Urim and Thummim, is not only Priest, and King, and Judge, but also, and in order to the salvation of His people, their Prophet, continually revealing unto those who seek Him, the will of God for their direction and guidance in every emergency of life. The girdle, the symbol of service, brings to mind, again, how in all this He is the Servant of the Lord, serving the Father in saving us.

The symbolism of the pomegranates and the golden bells reminds us, for the strengthening of our faith, how our exalted High Priest, who appears before God in our behalf in the Holiest, appears there as the great Preserver and Fulfiller of the Divine law, supremely qualified, no less by His supreme merit than by Divine appointment, to urge our needs with prevalence before God, His very presence in the heavenly sanctuary vocal with sweet music. Did Aaron bear the names of the twelve tribes of Israel on his shoulders and on his breast before God continually? Even so does his great Antitype bear continually all His people before God, as He executes His high-priestly office; and this, too, not merely in a vague and general way, but tribe by tribe, community by community, each with its peculiar case and special need; nay, we may say even more;. each individual, as such, is thus borne continually on the shoulders and the breast of the heavenly Priest; on His shoulders He bears them, to support them by His power; on His heart, in tenderest love and sympathy. And so often as we are distressed and discouraged by the consciousness of defilement still pertaining even to the holiest of our holy things, consecration ever imperfect at the best, we may bethink ourselves of the golden crown which Aaron wore, and its inscription, and remember how the Lord Jesus is in fullest reality "holy to the Lord;" so that we may take heart of grace as, with full reason and right, we apply to Him what is said of this crown of holiness on Aaron's brow: "The crown of holiness is ever on His forehead, and He shall bear the iniquity of the holy things which we shall hallow in all our holy gifts; it is always on His forehead, that our works may be accepted before the Lord." And so we are taught by this symbolism ever to look away from all conscious defilement and sin to the infinite holiness of the person of the Lord Jesus, as He continually appears before God as High Priest in our behalf, the all-sufficient Surety for the acceptance of our persons and of our imperfect works, for His own sake.

The investiture, as also the anointing, of the sons of Aaron, followed the robing and anointing of Aaron. We read (ver. 13): "Moses brought Aaron's sons, and clothed them with coats, and girded them with girdles, and bound head-tires upon them; as the Lord commanded Moses."

To the three articles of their attire here mentioned, must be added the "linen breeches" (Exod. xxviii. 42, 43); so that they also, in the several parts of their official vestments, bore the number four, the signature of the creaturely, as represented in the tabernacle. All was of pure white linen, signifying the holiness and righteousness of those who should act as priests before God. So once and again in the Apocalypse, the same symbol is used to denote the spotless holiness and righteousness of the blood-bought saints, who are made "a kingdom and priests" unto God: as, for instance, it is said of that same holy body, symbolised as the bride of the Lamb, that "it was given unto her that she should array herself in fine linen, bright and pure: for the fine linen is the righteous acts of the saints" (Rev. xix. 8).

The Anointing.

Leviticus viii. 10-12.

"And Moses took the anointing oil, and anointed the tabernacle and all that was therein, and sanctified them. And he sprinkled thereof upon the altar seven times, and anointed the altar and all its vessels, and the laver and its base, to sanctify them. And he poured of the anointed oil upon Aaron's head, and anointed him, to sanctify him."

Next in order came the anointing, first of the tabernacle and all that pertained to its service, and then the anointing of Aaron.

The anointing oil was made (Exod. xxx. 22-23) with a perfume of choice spices, their number, four, the sacred number so constantly recurring in the tabernacle. To make or use this oil, except for the sacred purposes of the sanctuary, was forbidden under penalty of being cut off from the holy people. The purpose of the anointing of the tabernacle and all within it, is declared to be its consecration thereby to the service of Jehovah. The altar, as a place of special sanctity, the place where God had covenanted to meet with Israel, was anointed seven times. For the number seven, compounded of three, the signet number of the Godhead, and four, the constant symbol of the creaturely, is thus by eminence the sacred number, the number, in particular, which is the sign and reminder of the covenant of redemption; and so here it is with special meaning that the altar, as being the place where God had specially covenanted to meet with Israel as reconciled through the blood of atonement, should receive a sevenfold anointing.

After this, the anointing oil was poured on the head of Aaron, to sanctify him.

As to the meaning of this part of the symbolic service, there is little room for doubt. The "anointing" is said to have been "to sanctify" or set apart to the service of Jehovah him that was anointed. And, inasmuch as oil, in the Holy Scriptures, is the constant symbol of the Holy Spirit, it is taught hereby that consecration is secured only through the anointing with the Holy Ghost.

The direct typical reference of this part of the ceremonial to Christ, will not be denied by any one for whom the Scripture any longer has authority. For Christ Himself quoted the words we find in Isa. lxi. 1, as fulfilled in Himself: "The Spirit of the Lord God is upon Me, because the Lord God hath anointed Me." And the Apostle Peter afterward taught (Acts x. 38) that God had "anointed Jesus with the Holy Ghost and with power;" while the most common title of our Lord, as "the Messiah" or "Christ," as we all know, though often forgetful of its meaning, simply means "the Anointed One." So every time we use the word, we unconsciously testify to the fulfilment of this type of the anointing of Aaron as priest, as, afterward, of the anointing of David as king, in Him. And as the anointing of Aaron took place in the sight of all Israel, assembled at the door of the tent of meeting, so in the fulness of time was Jesus, in the sight of all the multitude that waited on the baptism of John, after having been washed with water, "to fulfil all righteousness," anointed from heaven, as "the Holy Ghost descended in bodily form, as a dove," and abode upon him (Luke iii. 22). And while, according to Jewish tradition, the anointing oil was applied to the ordinary priests only in small quantity and by the finger, on the head of Aaron it was "poured;" in which word, as suggested in Psalm cxxxiii. 2, we are to understand a reference to the great copiousness with which it was used. In which, again, the type exactly corresponds to the Antitype. For while it is true of all believers that they "have an anointing from the Holy One" (1 John ii. 20), even as their Lord, yet of Him alone is it true that unto Him the Spirit "was not given by measure" (John iii. 34). And by this Divine anointing with the Holy Spirit without limit, was Jesus sanctified and qualified for the office of High Priest for all His people.

The anointing of the tabernacle with the same holy oil was according to a custom long before prevalent, and however it may seem strange to any of us now, will not have seemed strange to Israel. We read, for instance (Gen. xxviii. 18), of the anointing of the stone at Bethel by Jacob, by which he thus consecrated it to be a stone of remembrance of the revelation of God to him in that place. So, by this anointing, the tabernacle, with all that it contained, was "sanctified;" that is, consecrated that so the use of these might be made, through the power of the Holy Ghost, a means of grace and blessing to Israel. And it was thus anointed, and for this purpose, as being a "copy and pattern of the heavenly things." By the ceremony is signified to us, that by the power of the Holy Ghost, through the high-priesthood of our Lord, the whole universe and all that is in it has been consecrated and endowed by God with virtue, to become a means of grace and blessing to all believers, by His grace and might who works "in all things and through all things" to this end.

THE CONSECRATION SACRIFICES.

LEVITICUS viii. 14-32.

"And he brought the bullock of the sin offering: and Aaron and his sons laid their hands upon the head of the bullock of the sin offering. And he slew it; and Moses took the blood, and put it upon the horns of the altar round about with his finger, and purified the altar, and poured out the blood at the base of the altar, and sanctified it, to make atonement for it. And he took all the fat that was upon the inwards, and the caul of the liver, and the two kidneys, and their fat, and Moses burnt it upon the altar. But the bullock, and its skin, and its flesh, and its dung, he burnt with fire without the camp; as the Lord commanded Moses. And he presented the ram of the burnt offering; and Aaron and his sons laid their hands upon the head of the ram. And he killed it; and Moses sprinkled the blood upon the altar round about. And he cut the ram into its pieces; and Moses burnt the head, and the pieces, and the fat. And he washed the inwards and the legs with water; and Moses burnt the whole ram upon the altar; it was a burnt offering for a sweet savour: it was an offering made by fire unto the Lord; as the Lord commanded Moses. And he presented the other ram, the ram of consecration; and Aaron and his sons laid their hands upon the head of the ram. And he slew it, and Moses took of the blood thereof, and put it upon the tip of Aaron's right ear, and upon the thumb of his right hand, and upon the great toe of his right foot. And he brought Aaron's sons, and Moses put of the blood upon the tip of their right ear, and upon the thumb of their right hand, and upon the great toe of their right foot: and Moses sprinkled the blood upon the altar round about. And he took the fat, and the fat tail, and all the fat that was upon the inwards, and the caul of the liver, and the two kidneys and their fat, and the right thigh; and out of the basket of unleavened bread, that was before the Lord, he took one unleavened cake, and one cake of oiled bread, and one wafer, and placed them on the fat, and upon the right thigh; and he put the whole upon the hands of Aaron, and upon the hands of his sons, and waved them for a wave offering before the Lord. And Moses took them from off their hands, and burnt them on the altar upon the burnt offering: they were a consecration for a sweet savour: it was an offering made by fire unto the Lord. And Moses took the breast, and waved it for a wave offering before the Lord: it was Moses' portion of the ram of consecration; as the Lord commanded Moses. And Moses took of the anointing oil, and of the blood which was upon the altar, and sprinkled it upon Aaron, upon his garments, and upon his sons, and upon his sons' garments with him; and sanctified Aaron, his garments, and his sons, and his sons' garments with him. And Moses said unto Aaron and to his sons, Boil the flesh at the door of the tent of meeting; and there eat it and the bread that is in the basket of consecration, as I commanded, saying, Aaron and his sons shall eat it. And that which remaineth of the flesh and of the bread shall ye burn with fire."

The last part of the consecration ceremonial was the sacrifices. Each of the chief sacrifices of the law were offered in order; first, a sin-offering; then, a burnt-offering; then, a peace-offering, with some significant variations from the ordinary ritual, adapting it to this occasion; with which was conjoined, after the usual manner, a meal-offering. A sin-offering was offered, first of all; there had been a symbolical cleansing with water, but still a sin-offering is required.

It signified, what so many in these days seem to forget, that in order to our acceptableness before God, not only is needed a cleansing of the defilement of nature by the regeneration of the Holy Ghost, but also expiation for the guilt of our sins. The sin-offering was first, for the guilt of Aaron and his sons must be thus typically removed, before their burnt-offerings and their meal- and peace-offerings can be accepted.

The peculiarities of the offerings as rendered on this occasion are easily explained from the circumstances of their presentation. Moses officiates, for this time only, as specially delegated for this occasion, inasmuch as Aaron and his sons are not yet fully inducted into their office. The victim for the sin-offering is the costliest ever employed: a bullock, as ordered for the sin of the anointed priest. But the blood is not brought into the Holy Place, as in the ritual for the offering for the high priest, because Aaron is not yet fully inducted into his office. Nor do Aaron and his sons eat of the flesh of the sin-offering, as ordered in the case of other sin-offerings whose blood is not brought within the Holy Place; obviously, because of the principle which rules throughout the law, that he for whose sin the sin-offering is offered, must not himself eat of the flesh; it is therefore burnt with fire, without the camp, that it may not see corruption.

By this sin-offering, not only Aaron and his son were cleansed, but we read that hereby atonement was also made " for the altar;" a mysterious type, reminding us that, in some way which we cannot as yet fully understand, sin has affected the whole universe: in such a sense, that not only for man himself who has sinned, is propitiation required, but, in some sense, even for the earth itself, with the heavens. That in expounding the meaning of this part of the ritual we do not go beyond the Scripture is plain from such passages as Heb. ix. 23, where it is expressly said that even as the tabernacle and the things in it were cleansed with the blood of the bullock, so was necessary that, not merely man, but " the heavenly things themselves," of which the tabernacle and its belongings were the " copies," should be cleansed with better sacrifices than these," even the offering of Christ's own blood. So also we read in Col. i. 20, before cited, that through Christ, even through the blood of His cross, not merely persons, " but all *things*, whether things on the earth, or things in the heavens," should be reconciled unto God. Mysterious words these, no doubt; but words which teach us at least so much as this, how profound and far-reaching is the mischief which sin has wrought, even our sin. Not merely the sinning man must be cleansed with blood before he can be made a priest unto God, but even nature, " made subject to vanity " (Rom. viii. 20), for man's sin, needs the reconciling blood before redeemed man can exercise his priesthood unto God in the heavenly places. Evidently we have here an estimate of the evil of sin which is incomparably higher than that which is commonly current among men; and we shall do well to conform our estimate to that of God, who required atonement to be made even for the earthen altar, to sanctify it.

Reconciliation being made by the sin-offering, next in order came the burnt-offering, symbolic, as we have seen, of the full consecration of the person of the offerer to God; in this case of the full consecration of Aaron and his sons to the service of God in the priesthood. The ritual was according to the usual law, and requires no further exposition.

The ceremonial culminated and was completed in the offering of " the ram of consecration." The expression is, literally, " the ram of fillings;" in which phrase there is a reference to the peculiar ceremony described in vv. 27, 28, in which certain portions of the victim and of the meal-offering were placed by Moses on the hands of Aaron and his sons, and waved by them for a wave-offering; and afterwards burnt wholly on the altar upon the burnt-offering, in token of their full devotement to the Lord. Of these it is then added, " they were a consecration " (*lit.* " fillings," *sc.* of hands, " were these "). The meaning of the phrase and the action it denoted is determined by its use in 1 Chron. xxix. 5 and 2 Chron. xxix. 31, where it is used of the bringing of the freewill-offerings by the people for Jehovah. The ceremonial in this case therefore signified the formal making over of the sacrifices into the charge of Aaron and his sons, which henceforth they were to offer; that they received them to offer them to and for Jehovah, was symbolised by their presentation to be waved before Jehovah, and further by their being burnt upon the altar, as a sacrifice of sweet savour.

Another thing peculiar to this special consecration sacrifice, was the use which was made of the blood, which (ver. 23) was put upon the tip of Aaron's right ear, upon the thumb of his right hand, and upon the great toe of his right foot. Although the solution is not without difficulty, we shall probably not err in regarding this as distinctively an act of consecration, signifying that in virtue of the sacrificial blood, Aaron and his sons were set apart to sacrificial service. It is applied to the ear, to the hand, and the foot, and to the most representative member in each case, to signify the consecration of the whole body to the Lord's service in the tabernacle; the ear is consecrated by the blood to be ever attentive to the word of Jehovah, to receive the intimations of His will; the hand, to be ever ready to do the Lord's work; and the foot, to run on His service.

Another peculiarity of this offering was in the wave-offering of Aaron and his sons. Not the breast, but the thigh, and that together with the fat (ver. 27) was waved before the Lord; and, afterward, not only the fat was burnt upon the altar, according to the law, but also the thigh, which in other cases was the portion of the priest, was burnt with the fat and the memorial of the meal-offering. The breast was afterward waved, as the law commanded in the case of the peace-offerings, but was given to Moses as his portion. The last particular is easy to understand; Moses in this ceremonial stands in the place of the officiating priest, and it is natural that he should thus receive from the Lord his reward for his service. As for the thigh, which, when the peace-offering was offered by one of the people, was presented to the Lord, and then given to the officiating priest to be eaten, obviously the law could not be applied here, as the priests themselves were the bringers of the offering; hence the only alternative was, as in the case of sin-offerings of the holy place, to burn the flesh with fire upon the altar. as " the food of Jehovah." The remainder of the flesh was to be eaten by the priests alone as the offerers, under the regulation for the thank-offering, except that whatever remained until the next day was to be burnt; a direction which is explained by the fact that the sacrifice was to be repeated for seven days, so that there could be no reason for keeping the flesh until the third day. Last of all, it is to be noted that whereas in the thank-offerings of the people, the offerer was allowed to bring leavened bread for the sacrificial feast, in the feast of the consecration of priests this was not permitted; no doubt to emphasise the peculiar sanctity of the office to which they were inducted.

With these modifications, it is plain that the sacrifice of consecration was essentially, not a guilt-offering, as some have supposed, but a peace-offering. It is true that a ram was enjoined as the victim instead of a lamb, but the correspondence here with the law of the guilt-offering is of no significance when we observe that rams were also enjoined or used for peace-offerings on other occasions of exceptional dignity and sanctity, as in the peace-offerings for the nation, mentioned in the following chapter, and the peace-offerings for the princes of the tribes (Numb. vii.). Unlike the guilt-offering, but after the manner of the other, the sacrifice was followed by a sacrificial feast. That participation in this was restricted to the priests is sufficiently explained by the special relation of this sacrifice to their own consecration.

Before the sacrificial feast, however, one peculiar ceremony still remained. We read (ver. 30): "Moses took of the anointing oil, and of the blood (of the peace-offering) which was upon the altar, and sprinkled it upon Aaron, upon his garments, and upon his sons, and upon his sons' garments with him; and sanctified Aaron, his garments, and his sons, and his sons' garments with him."

This sprinkling signified that now, through the atoning blood which had been accepted before God upon the altar, and through the sanctifying Spirit of grace, which was symbolised by the anointing, thus inseparably associated each with the other, they had been brought into covenant relation with God regarding the office of the priesthood. That this their covenant relation to God concerned them, not merely as private persons, but in their official character, was intimated by the sprinkling, not only of their persons, but of the garments which were the insignia of their priestly office.

All this completed, now followed the sacrificial feast. We read that Moses now ordered Aaron and his sons (ver. 31): "Boil the flesh at the door of the tent of meeting: and there eat it and the bread that is in the basket of consecration, as I commanded, saying, Aaron and his sons shall eat it. And that which remaineth of the flesh and of the bread shall ye burn with fire."

This sacrificial feast most fitly marked the conclusion of the rites of consecration. Hereby it was signified, first, that by this solemn service they were now brought into a relation of peculiarly intimate fellowship with Jehovah, as the ministers of His house, to offer His offerings, and to be fed at His table. It was further signified, that strength for the duties of this office should be supplied to them by Him whom they were to serve, in that they were to be fed of His altar. And, finally, in that the ritual took the specific form of a thank-offering, was thereby expressed, as was fitting, their gratitude to God for the grace which had chosen them and set them apart to so holy and exalted service.

These consecration services were to be repeated for seven consecutive days, during which time they were not to leave the tent of meeting,—obviously, that by no chance they might contract any ceremonial defilement; so jealously must the sanctity of everything pertaining to the service be guarded.

The commandment was (vv. 33-35): "Ye shall not go out from the door of the tent of meeting seven days, until the days of your consecration be fulfilled: for he shall consecrate you seven days. As hath been done this day, so the Lord hath commanded to do, to make atonement for you. And at the door of the tent of meeting shall ye abide day and night seven days, and keep the charge of the Lord, that ye die not: for so I am commanded."

By the sevenfold repetition of the consecration ceremonies was expressed, in the most emphatic manner known to the Mosaic symbolism, the completeness of the consecration and qualification of Aaron and his sons for their office, and the fact also that, in virtue of this consecration, they had come into a special covenant relation with Jehovah concerning the priestly office.

That these consecration sacrifices by which Aaron and his sons were set apart to the priesthood, no less than the preceding part of the ceremonial, pointed forward to Christ and His priestly people as the Antitype, it will be easy to see. As regards our Lord, in Heb. vii. 28, the sacred writer applies to the consecration of our Lord as high priest the very term which the Seventy had used long before in this chapter of Leviticus to denote this formal consecration, and represents the consecration of the Son as the antitype of the consecration of Aaron by the law: " the law appointeth men high priests, having infirmity; but the word of the oath, which was after the law, appointeth a Son, perfected for evermore."

An exception, indeed, must be made, as regards our Lord, in the case of the sin-offering; of whom it is said (Heb. vii. 27), that He "needeth not . . . like those high priests, to offer up sacrifices, first for His own sins." But as regards the other two sacrifices, we can see that in their distinctive symbolical import they each bring before us essential elements in the consecration of our Lord Jesus Christ as High Priest. In the burnt-offering, we see Him consecrating Himself by the complete self-surrender of Himself to the Father. In the offering of consecrations, we see Him in the meal-offering of unleavened bread, offering in like manner His most holy works unto the Father; and in the sacrifice of the peace-offering, wherein Aaron ate of the food of God's house in His presence, we see Jesus in like manner as qualified for His high-priestly work by His admission into terms of the most intimate fellowship with the Father, and sustained for His work by the strength given from Him, according to His own word, "The living Father hath sent Me, and I live because of the Father." In the formal "filling of the hands" of Aaron with the sacrificial material, in token of his endowment with the right to offer sacrifices for sin for the sake of sinful men, we are reminded how our Lord refers to the fact that He had received in like manner authority from the Father to lay down His life for His sheep, emphatically adding the words (John x. 18), "This commandment have I received of My Father."

So also was the meaning of the collateral ceremonies fully realised in Him. If Aaron was anointed with the blood on ear, hand, and foot, by way of signifying that the members of his body should be wholly devoted unto God in priestly service, even so we are reminded (Heb. x. 5, 7), that "when He cometh into the world He saith, ... Sacrifice and offering thou wouldest not, but a body didst thou prepare for Me; ... Lo, I am come to do Thy will, O God."

And so, as Aaron was at the end of the sacrifice sprinkled with blood and oil, in token that God had now, through the blood and the oil, entered into a covenant of priesthood with him, so we find repeated reference to the fact of such a solemn covenant and compact between God and the High Priest of our profession summed up in the words of prophecy, "The Lord hath sworn, and will not repent, Thou art a priest for ever after the order of Melchizedek."

So did this whole consecration ceremony, with the exception only of such parts of it as had reference to the sin of Aaron, point forward to the future investiture of the Son of God with the high-priestly office, by God the Father, that He might act therein for our salvation in all matters between us and God. How can any who have eyes to see all this, as opened out for us in the New Testament, fail with fullest joy and thankfulness to accept Christ, the Son of God, now passed into the Holiest, as the High Priest of our profession? How naturally to all such come the words of exhortation with which is concluded the great argument upon Christ's high-priesthood in the Epistle to the Hebrews (x. 19-23): "Having therefore, brethren, boldness to enter into the holy place by the blood of Jesus; ... and having a great priest over the house of God; let us draw near with a true heart, in fulness of faith, having our hearts sprinkled from an evil conscience, and our body washed with pure water: let us hold fast the confession of our hope that it waver not; for He is faithful that promised."

But not only was Aaron thus consecrated to be high priest of the tabernacle, but his sons also, to be priests under him in the same service. In this also the type holds good. For when in Heb. ii. Christ is brought before us as "the High Priest of our confession," He is represented as saying (ver. 13), "Behold, I and the children which God hath given me!" As Aaron had his sons appointed to perform priestly functions under him in the earthly tabernacle, so also his great Antitype has "sons," called to priestly office under Him in the heavenly tabernacle. Accordingly, we find that in the New Testament, not any caste or class in the Christian Church, but all believers, are represented as "a holy priesthood, to offer up spiritual sacrifices, acceptable to God through Jesus Christ" (1 Peter ii. 5). To the testimony of Peter corresponds that of John in the Apocalypse, where in like manner believers are declared to be priests unto God, and represented as also acting as priests of God and of Christ in the age which is to come after "the first resurrection"* (Rev. xx. 6). Hence it is plain that according to the New Testament we shall rightly regard the consecration of the sons of Aaron as no less typical than that of Aaron himself. It is typical of the consecration of all believers to priesthood under Christ. It thus sets forth in symbol the fact and the manner of our own consecration to ministrations between lost men and God, in the age which now is and that which is to come, in things pertaining to sin and salvation, according to the measure to each one of the gift of Christ.

As the consecration of Aaron's sons began with the washing with pure water, so ours with "the washing of regeneration and the renewing of the Holy Ghost" (Titus iii. 5). As Aaron's sons, thus washed, were then invested in white linen, clean and pure, so for the believer must the word be fulfilled (Isa. lxi. 10): "He hath covered me with the robe of righteousness, as a bridegroom decketh himself" (marg. "decketh as a priest"). That is, the reality of our appointment of God unto this high dignity must be visibly attested unto men by the righteousness of our lives. But whereas the sons of Aaron were not clothed until first Aaron himself had been clothed and anointed, it is signified that the robing and anointing of Christ's people follows and depends upon the previous robing and anointing of their Head. Again, as Aaron's sons were also anointed with the same holy oil as was Aaron, only in lesser measure, so are believers consecrated to the priestly office, like their Lord, by the anointing with the Holy Ghost. The anointing of Pentecost follows and corresponds to the anointing of the High Priest at the Jordan with one and the same Spirit. This is another necessary consecration mark, on which the New Testament Scriptures constantly insist. As Jesus was "anointed with the Holy Ghost and (thereby) with power," so He Himself said to His disciples (Acts i. 8), "Ye shall receive power, when the Holy Ghost is come upon you;" which promise being fulfilled, Paul could say (2 Cor. i. 21), "He that ... anointed us is God;" and John (1 John ii. 20), to all believers, "Ye have an anointing from the Holy One." And the sacrificial symbols are also all fulfilled in the case of the Lord's priestly people. For them, no less essential to their consecration than the washing of the Holy Ghost, is the removal of guilt by the great Sin-offering of Calvary; which same offering, and true Lamb of God, has also become their burnt-offering, their meal-offering, and their sacrifice of consecrations, as it is written (Heb. x. 10), that, by the will of God, "we have been sanctified through the offering of the body of Jesus Christ once for all;" and that He also is become "our peace," in that He has expiated our sins, and also given Himself to us as our spiritual food; that so we may derive daily strength for the daily service in the priest's office, by feeding on the Lamb of God, the true food of the altar, given by God for our support. Also, as the sons of Aaron, like Aaron himself, were anointed with the blood of the peace-offering of consecration, on the ear, the hand, and the foot, so has the blood of the Lamb, in that it has brought us into peace with God, set apart every true believer unto full surrender of all the members of his body unto Him; ears, that they may be quick to hear God's word; hands, that they may be quick to do it; feet, that they may only run in the way of His command-

---

* Not, however, as many imagine, in behalf of those who have in this age died in sin, but in ministrations to the living nations in the flesh, in the age to come. We find no ground of hope, in Holy Scripture, for the impenitent dead.

ments. And finally, whereas the solemn covenant of priesthood into which Aaron and his sons had entered with God, was sealed and ratified by the sprinkling with the oil and the blood, so by the unction of the Holy Spirit given to believers, and the cleansing of the conscience by the blood, is it witnessed and certified that they are a people called out to enter into covenant of priestly service with the God of all the earth and the heavens.

What searching questions as to personal experience all this raises! What solemn thoughts throng into the mind of every thoughtful reader! All this essential, if we are to be indeed members of that royal priesthood, who shall reign as priests of God and of Christ? Have we then the marks, all of them? Let us not shrink from the questions, but probe with them the innermost depths of our hearts. Have we had the washing of regeneration? If we think that we have had this, then let us also remember that after the washing came the investiture in white linen. Let us ask, Have we then put on these white garments of righteousness? All that were washed, were also clad in white; these were their official robes, without which they could not act as priests unto God. And there was also an anointing. Have we, in like manner, received the anointing with the Holy Ghost, endowing us with power and wisdom for service? Then, the sin-offering, the burnt-offering, the peace-offering of consecration,—has the Lamb of God been used by us in all these various ways, as our expiation, our consecration, our peace, and our life? And has the blood which consecrates also been applied to ear, hand, and foot? Are we consecrated in all the members of our bodies?

What questions these are! Truly, it is no light thing to be a Christian; to be called and consecrated to be, with and under the great High Priest, Jesus Christ, a "priest unto God" in this life and in that of "the first resurrection;" to deal between God and men in matters of salvation. Have we well understood what is our "high calling," and what the conditions on which alone we may exercise our ministry? To this may God give us grace, for Jesus' sake. Amen.

CHAPTER XI.

THE INAUGURATION OF THE TABERNACLE SERVICE.

LEVITICUS ix. 1-24.

AARON and his sons having now been solemnly consecrated to the priestly office by the ceremonies of seven days, their formal assumption of their daily duties in the tabernacle was marked by a special service suited to the august occasion, signalised at its close by the appearance of the glory of Jehovah to assembled Israel, in token of His sanction and approval of all that had been done. It would appear that the daily burnt-offering and meal-offering had been indeed offered before this, from the time that the tabernacle had been set up; in which service, however, Moses had thus far officiated. But now that Aaron and his sons were consecrated, it was most fitting that a service should thus be ordered which should be a complete exhibition of the order of sacrifice as it had now been given by the Lord, and serve, for Aaron and his sons in all after time, as a practical model of the manner in which the divinely-given law of sacrifice should be carried out.

The order of the day began with a very impressive lesson of the inadequacy of the blood of beasts to take away sin. For seven consecutive days a bullock had been offered for Aaron and his sons, and so far as served the typical purpose, their consecration was complete. But still Aaron and his sons needed expiating blood; for before they could offer the sacrifices of the day for the people, they are ordered yet again first of all to offer a sin-offering for themselves. We read (vv. 1, 2): "And it came to pass on the eighth day, that Moses called Aaron and his sons, and the elders of Israel; and he said unto Aaron, Take thee a bull calf for a sin-offering, and a ram for a burnt-offering, without blemish, and offer them before the Lord."

And then Aaron was commanded (vv. 3-5): "Unto the children of Israel thou shalt speak, saying, Take ye a he-goat for a sin-offering; and a calf and a lamb, both of the first year, without blemish, for a burnt-offering; and an ox and a ram for peace-offerings, to sacrifice before the Lord; and a meal-offering mingled with oil: for to-day the Lord appeareth unto you. And they brought that which Moses commanded before the tent of meeting: and all the congregation drew near and stood before the Lord."

There is little in these directions requiring explanation. Because of the exceptional importance of the occasion, therefore, as in the feasts of the Lord, a special sin-offering was ordered, and a burnt-offering, besides the regular daily burnt-offering, meal-offering, and drink-offering; and, in addition, peculiar to this occasion, a peace-offering for the nation; which last was evidently intended to signify that now on the basis of the sacrificial worship and the mediation of a consecrated priesthood, Israel was privileged to enter into fellowship with Jehovah, the Lord of the tabernacle. No peace-offering was ordered for Aaron and his sons, as, according to the law of the peace-offering, they would themselves take part in that of the people. The sin-offering prescribed for the people was, not a kid, as in King James's version, but a he-goat, which, with the exception of the case of a sin of commission as described in chap. iv. 13, 14, appears to have been the usual victim. For the selection of such a victim, no reason appears more probable than that assigned by rabbinical tradition, namely, that it was intended to counteract the tendency of the people to the worship of shaggy he-goats, referred to in chap. xvii. 7, "They shall no more sacrifice their sacrifices unto the he-goats (R. V.), after whom they go a whoring."

THE ORDER OF THE OFFERINGS.

LEVITICUS ix. 7-21.

"And Moses said unto Aaron, Draw near unto the altar, and offer thy sin offering, and thy burnt offering, and make atonement for thyself, and for the people: and offer the oblation of the people, and make atonement for them; as the Lord commanded. So Aaron drew near unto the altar, and slew the calf of the sin offering, which was for himself. And the sons of Aaron presented the blood unto him: and he dipped his finger in the blood, and put it upon the horns of the altar, and poured out the blood at the base of the altar: but the fat, and the kidneys, and the caul from the liver of the sin offering, he burnt upon the altar; as the Lord commanded Moses. And the flesh and the skin he burnt with fire without the camp. And he slew the burnt offering; and Aaron's sons delivered unto him the blood, and he sprinkled it upon the altar round about. And they delivered the burnt offering unto him, piece by piece, and the head; and he burnt them upon the altar. And he washed the inwards and the legs, and burnt them upon the burnt offering on the altar. And he presented the people's oblation, and took the goat of the sin offering which was for the people, and slew it, and offered it for sin, as the first. And he presented the burnt offering, and offered it according to the ordinance. And he presented the meal offering, and filled his hand therefrom, and burnt it upon the altar, besides the burnt offering of the morning. He slew also the ox and the ram, the sacrifice of peace offerings, which was for the people: and Aaron's sons delivered unto him the blood, and he sprinkled it upon the altar round about, and the fat of the ox; and of the ram, the fat tail and that which covered the inwards, and the kidneys, and the caul of the liver: and they put the fat upon the breasts and he burnt the fat upon the altar; and the breast and the right thigh Aaron waved for a wave offering before the Lord; as Moses commanded."

Verses 7-21 detail the way in which this commandment of Moses was carried out in the offerings, first, for Aaron and his sons, and then for all the people; but, as the peculiarities of these several offerings have been already explained, they need not here detain us. That which is new, and of profound spiritual and typical meaning, is the *order* of the sacrifices as here enjoined; an order which, as we learn from many Scriptures, represented what was intended to be the permanent and invariable law. The appointed order of the offerings was as follows: first, whenever presented, came the sin-offering, as here; then, the burnt-offering, with its meal-offering; and last, always, the peace-offering, with its characteristic sacrificial feast.

The significance of this order will readily appear if we consider the distinctive meaning of each of these offerings. The sin-offering had for its central thought, expiation of sin by the shedding of blood; the burnt-offering, the full surrender of the person symbolised by the victim, to God; the meal-offering, in like manner, the consecration of the fruit of his labours; the peace-offering, sustenance of life from God's table, and fellowship in peace and joy with God and with one another. And the great lesson for us now from this model tabernacle service is this: that this order is determined by a law of the spiritual life.

So much as this, even without clear prevision of the Antitype of all these sacrifices, the thoughtful Israelite might have discerned; and even though the truth thus symbolised is placed before us no more in rite and symbol, yet it abides, and ever will abide, a truth. Man everywhere needs fellowship with God, and cannot rest without it; to attain such fellowship is the object of all religions which recognise the being of a God at all. Even among the heathen, we are truly told, there are many who are feeling after God " if haply they may find Him;" and, among ourselves in Christian lands, and even in the external fellowship of Christian churches, there are many who with aching hearts are seeking after an unrealised experience of peace and fellowship with God. And yet God is " not far from any one of us;" and the whole Scripture represent Him as longing on His part with an incomprehensible condescension and love after fellowship with us, desiring to communicate to us His fulness; and still so many seek and find not!

We need not go further than this order of the offerings, and the spiritual truth it signifies regarding the order of grace, to discover the secret of these spiritual failures.

The peace-offering, the sacrificial feast of fellowship with God, the joyful banqueting on the food of His table, was always, as on this day, in order. Before this must ever come the burnt-offering. The ritual prescribed that the peace-offering should be burnt " upon the burnt-offering;" the presence of the burnt-offering is thus presupposed in every acceptable peace-offering. But what if one had ventured to ignore this divinely-appointed order, and had offered his peace-offering to be burnt alone; can we imagine that it would have been accepted?

These things are a parable, and not a hard one. For the burnt-offering with its meal-offering symbolised full consecration of the person and the works to the Lord. Remembering this, we see that the order is not arbitrary. For, in the nature of the case, full consecration to God must precede fellowship with God; he who would know what it is to have God give Himself to him, must first be ready to give himself to God. And that God should enter into loving fellowship with any one who is holding back from loving self-surrender is not to be expected. This is not merely an Old Testament law, still less merely a fanciful deduction from the Mosaic symbolism; everywhere in the New Testament is the thought pressed upon us, no longer indeed in symbol, but in plainest language. It is taught by precept in some of the most familiar words of the great Teacher. There is promise, for example, of constant supply of sufficient food and raiment, fellowship with God in temporal things; but only on condition that " we seek first the kingdom of God, and His righteousness," shall " all these things be added unto us " (Matt. vi. 33). There is a promise of " a hundred-fold in this life, and in the world to come, eternal life;" but it is prefaced by the condition of surrender of father, mother, brethren, sisters, of houses and lands, for the Lord's sake (Matt. xix. 29). Not, indeed, that the actual parting with these is enjoined in every case; but, certainly, it is intended that we shall hold all at the Lord's disposal, possessing, but " as though we possessed not;"—this is the least that we can take out of these words.

Full consecration of the person and the works, this then is the condition of fellowship with God; and if so many lament the lack of the latter, it is no doubt because of the lack of the former. We often act strangely in this matter; half unconsciously, searching, perhaps, every corner of our life but the right one, from looking into which by the clear light of God's Word we instinctively shrink, conscience softly whispering that just there is something about which we have a lurking doubt, and which therefore, if we will be fully consecrated, we must at once give up, till we are sure that it is right, and right for us; and for that self-denial, that renunciation unto God, we are not ready. Is it a wonder that, if such be our experience, we lack that blessed, joyful fellowship with the Lord, of which some tell us? Is it not rather the chief wonder that we should wonder at the lack, when yet we are not ready to consecrate all, body, soul, and spirit, with all our works, unto the Lord? Let us then remember the law of the offerings upon this point. No Israelite could have the blessed feast of the peace-offering, except, first the burnt-offering and the meal-offering, symbolising full consecration, were smoking on the altar.

But this full consecration seems to many so exceeding hard,—nay, we may say more, to many it is utterly impossible. A consecration of some things, especially those for which they care little, this they can hear of; but a consecration of *all*, that the whole may be consumed upon the altar before and unto God, this they cannot think of. Which means—can we escape the conclusion?—that the love of God does not yet rule supreme. How sad! and how strange! But the law of the offerings will again declare the secret of the strange holding back from full consecration. For it was ordained, that wherever there was sin in the offerer, unconfessed and unforgiven, before even the burnt-offering must go the sin-offering, expiating sin by blood presented on the altar before God. And here we come upon another law of the spiritual life in all ages. If fellowship with God in peace and joy is conditioned by the full consecration of person and service to Him, this consecration, even as a possibility for us, is in turn conditioned by the expiation of sin through the great Sin-offering. So long as conscience is not satisfied that the question of sin has been settled in grace and righteousness with God, so long it is a spiritual impossibility that the soul should come into that experience of the love of God, manifested through atonement, which alone can lead to full consecration.

This truth is always of vital importance; but it is, if possible, more important than ever to insist upon it in our day, when, more and more, the doctrine of the expiation of sin through the blood of the Lamb of God is denied, and that, forsooth, under the claim of superior enlightenment. Men are well pleased to hear of a burnt-offering, so long especially as it is made to signify no more than the self-devotement of the offerer; but for a sin-offering, much modern theology has no place. So soon as we begin to speak of the sacrifice of our Lord for sin in the dialect of the ancient altar—which, it must never be forgotten, is that of Christ and His apostles—we are told that "it would be better for the world if the Christian doctrine of sacrifice could be presented to men apart from the old Jewish ideas and terms, which only serve to obscure the simplicity that is in Christ(!)" And so men, under the pretext of magnifying the love of God, and laying a truer basis for spiritual life, in effect deny the supreme and incomparable manifestation of that love, that God made "Him who knew no sin to be sin on our behalf" (2 Cor. v. 21).

Very different is the teaching, not merely of the law of Moses, but of the whole New Testament; which, in all it has to say of the Christian life as proceeding from full self-surrender, ever represents this full consecration as inspired by the believing recognition and penitent acceptance of Christ, not merely as the great Example of perfect consecration, but as a sin-offering, reconciling us first of all by His death, before He saves us by His life (Rom. v. 10). The expiation of sin by the sin-offering, before the consecration which burnt-offering and meal-offering typify, this is the invariable order in both Testaments. The Apostle Paul, in his account of his own full consecration, is in full accord with the spiritual teaching of the Mosaic ritual when he gives this as the order. He describes himself, and that in terms of no undue exaggeration, as so under the constraint of the love of Christ as to seem to some beside himself; and then he goes on to explain the secret of this consecration, in which he had placed himself and all he had upon God's altar, as a whole burnt-sacrifice, as consisting just in this, that he had first apprehended the mystery of Christ's death, as a substitution so true and real of the sinless Victim in the place of sinful men, that it might be said that "one died for all, therefore all died;" whence he thus judged, "that they which live should no longer live unto themselves, but unto Him who for their sakes died and rose again" (2 Cor. v. 13-15). To the same effect is the teaching of the Apostle John. For all true consecration springs from the thankful recognition of the love of God; and, according to this Apostle also, the Divine love which inspires the consecration is manifest in this, that "He sent His Son to be the propitiation for our sins" (1 John iv. 10). The apprehension, then, of the reality of the expiation made by the great Sin-offering, and the believing appropriation of its virtue to the cancelling of our guilt, this is the inseparable previous condition of full consecration of person and work unto the Lord. It is so, because only the apprehension of the need of expiation by the blood of the Son of God, as the necessary condition of forgiveness, can give us any adequate measure of the depth of our guilt and ruin, as God sees it; and, on the other hand, only when we remember that God spared not His only-begotten Son, but sent Him to become, through death upon the cross, a propitiation for our sins, can we begin to have such an estimate of the love of God and of Christ His Son as shall make full consecration easy, or even possible.

Let us then, on no account, miss this lesson from the order of this ritual; before the peace-offering, the burnt-offering; before the burnt-offering, the sin-offering. Or, translating the symbolism, perfect fellowship with God in peace and joy and life, only after consecration; and the consecration only possible in fulness, and only accepted of God, in any case, when the great Sin-offering has been first believingly appropriated, according to God's ordination, as the propitiation for our sins, for the cancelling of our guilt.

But there is yet more in this order of the offerings. For, as the New Testament in every way teaches us, the Antitype of every offering was Christ. As we have already seen, in the Sin-offering we have the type of Christ as our propitiation, or expiation; in the burnt-offering, of Christ as consecrating Himself unto God in our behalf; in the meal-offering, as, in like manner, consecrating all His works in our behalf; in the peace-offering, as imparting Himself to us as our life, and thus bringing us into fellowship of peace and love and joy with the Father.

Now this last is, in fact, the ultimate aim of salvation; rather, indeed, we may say, it is salvation. For life in its fulness means the cancelling of death; death spiritual, and bodily death also, in resurrection from the dead; it means also perfect fellowship with the living God, and this, attained, is heaven. Hence it must needs be that the peace-offering which represents Christ as giving Himself to us as our life, and introducing us into this blessed state, comes last.

But before this, in order, not of time, but of grace, as also of logic, must be Christ as Sin-offering, and Christ as Burnt-offering. And, first of all, Christ as Sin-offering. For God's way of peace puts the cancelling of guilt, the satisfaction of His holy law and justice, and therewith the restoration of our right relation to Him, first, and in order to a holy life and fellowship; while man will ever put these last, and regard the latter as the means to obtaining a right standing with God. Hence, inasmuch as Christ, coming to save us, finds us under a curse, the first thing in order is, and must be, the removal of that curse of the holy wrath of God, against every one that " continueth not in all things that are written in the book of the law, to do them." And so, first in order in the typical ritual is the sin-offering which represents Christ as made " a curse for us," that He might thus redeem us from the curse of the law (Gal. iii. 13).

But this is not a complete account of the work of our Lord for us in the days of His flesh. His work indeed was one, but the Scriptures set it forth in a twofold aspect. On the one hand, He is the Sinless One, bearing the curse for us; but also, in all His suffering for our sins, He is also manifested as the Righteous One, making many righteous by His obedience, even an obedience unto the death of the cross (Rom. v. 19; Phil. ii. 8). And if we ask what was the essence of this obedience of our Lord for us, what was it, indeed, but that which is the essence of all obedience to God, namely, full, unreserved, uninterrupted consecration and self-surrender to the will of the Father? And as, by His suffering, Christ endured the curse for us, so by all His obedience and suffering in full submission to the will of God, He became also " the Lord our righteousness." And this, as repeatedly remarked, is the central thought of the burnt-offering and the meal-offering,—full consecration of the person and the work to God.

In the sin-offering, then, we see Christ as our propitiation; in the burnt-offering, we see Him rather as our righteousness; but the former is presupposed in the latter; and apart from this, that in His death He became the expiation of our sins, His obedience could have availed us nothing. But given now Christ as our propitiation and also our righteousness, the whole question of the relation of Christ's people to God in law and righteousness is settled, and the way is now clear for the communication of life which the peace-offering symbolised. Thus, as by faith in Christ as the Sin-offering, our propitiation and righteousness, we are " justified freely by grace," " apart from the works of the law," so now the way is open, by the appropriation of Christ as our life in the peace-offering, for our sanctification and complete redemption. In a word, the law of the order of the offerings teaches, symbolically and typically, exactly what, in Rom. vi. and vii., the Apostle Paul teaches dogmatically, namely, that the order of grace is first justification, then sanctification; but both by the same crucified Christ, our propitiation, our righteousness, and our life: in whom we come to have fellowship in all good and blessing with the Father.

It is interesting to observe that after the analogy of this order of the offerings, is the most usual order of the development of Christian experience. For the awakened soul is usually first of all concerned about the question of forgiveness of sin and acceptance; and hence, most commonly, faith first apprehends Christ in this aspect, as the One who " bare our sins in His Body," by whose stripes we are healed; and then, at a later period of experience, as the One who also, in lowly consecration to the Father's will, obeyed for us, that we might be made righteous through His obedience. But no one who is truly justified by faith in Christ as our propitiation and righteousness, can long rest with this. He very quickly finds what he had little thought of before, that the evil nature abides even in the justified and accepted believer; nay, more, that it has still a terrible strength to overcome him and lead him into sin, even often when he would not. And this prepares the believer, still in accord with the law of the order of grace here set forth, to lay hold also on Christ by faith as His Peace-offering, by feeding on whom we receive spiritual strength, so that He thus, in a word, becomes our sanctification and, at last, full redemption.

The Double Benediction.

Leviticus ix. 22-24.

" And Aaron lifted up his hands toward the people, and blessed them ; and he came down from offering the sin offering, and the burnt offering, and the peace offerings. And Moses and Aaron went into the tent of meeting, and came out and blessed the people ; and the glory of the Lord appeared unto all the people. And there came forth fire from before the Lord, and consumed upon the altar the burnt offering and the fat; and when all the people saw it, they shouted, and fell on their faces."

The sacrifices having now been made, and the offerings presented in this divinely-appointed order, by the ordained and consecrated priesthood, two things followed: a double benediction was pronounced upon the people, and Jehovah manifested to them His glory. We read (ver. 22), " And Aaron lifted up his hands toward the people, and blessed them; and he came down from offering the sin-offering, and the burnt-offering, and the peace-offerings."

Presumably, the form of benediction which Aaron used was that which, according to Numb. vi. 24-27, the priests were commanded by the Lord to use: " The Lord bless thee, and keep thee: the Lord make His face to shine upon thee, and be gracious unto thee: the Lord lift up His countenance upon thee, and give thee peace." It was not an empty form; for the Lord at that time also promised Himself to make this blessing efficient, saying thereafter, " So shall they put My Name "—Jehovah, the name of God in covenant,—" upon the children of Israel; and I will bless them."

So also the Lord Jesus, just before withdrawing from the bodily sight of His disciples after the completion of His great sacrifice, " lifted up His hands, and blessed them;" and thereupon disappeared from their sight, ascending into heaven. Even so was it in the typical service of this day; for when Aaron had thus lifted up his hands and blessed the people (ver. 23), " Moses and Aaron went into the tent of meeting."

The work of Aaron in the outer court had been finished, and now he disappears from Israel's sight; for he must, in like manner, be inducted into the priestly work within the Holy Place. He must there be shown all those things to which, in his priestly ministrations, the blood must be applied; and, especially, must also offer the sweet incense at the golden altar which was before the veil which enshrined the immediate presence of Jehovah. But this offering of incense, as all have agreed, typifies the precious and most effective intercession of the great Antitype; so that thus it was shown in a figure, how the Christ of God, having finished His sacrificial work in the sight of men, and having ascended into heaven, should there for a season abide, hidden from human sight, making intercession for His waiting people.

After an interval—we are not told how long—Moses and Aaron again (vv. 23, 24), "came out, and blessed the people: and the glory of the Lord appeared unto all the people. And there came forth fire from before the Lord, and consumed upon the altar the burnt-offering and the fat: and when all the people saw it, they shouted, and fell on their faces."

This second blessing, by Moses and Aaron conjointly, followed Aaron's reappearance to Israel, and marked the completion of these inauguration services, the intercession within the veil, as well as the sacrifices. And the revelation in a visible way of the glory of the Lord added what now was alone required, the manifest attestation by the Lord of the tabernacle of His approval of all that had been done in these memorable eight days. This appearance of the Shekinah glory was followed by a flash of fire which, in token of the Divine appropriation of the sacrifices, consumed in an instant the burnt-offering on the altar with the fat of the sin-offering and the peace-offering, which had been laid upon it. We cannot follow here the Jewish tradition, which has it that with this act the sacrificial fire which was never to go out upon the altar, was originated. On the contrary, as we have seen, the offerings had before this been made by Moses, and even on this day the fire had been kindled before (ver. 10, *et seq.*). Nor is there any necessary inconsistency here; for we have but to suppose that the burning of the sacrifices which had been kindled by Aaron was not yet complete, when the flash from the cloud of glory in an instant consummated the burning, teaching in a most august and impressive manner the symbolic meaning of the burning of the sacrifices on the altar, as signifying the acceptance and appropriation of that which was offered, by the Lord who had commanded all, and thereby endorsing all that had been done, as according to His mind and will.

And even so, according to the sure Word of prophecy, our heavenly High Priest has yet in reserve for His people a second benediction. His first blessing upon leaving the world was followed by Pentecost; the second, on His reappearing, shall bring in resurrection and full salvation. And in that day, when He "shall appear a second time, apart from sin, to them that wait for Him unto salvation" (Heb. ix. 28), therewith shall appear the glory which on that day, long ago, appeared to Israel; for He "shall come in the glory of His Father," and thus shall God, the Most High and the Most Holy, testify before the universe His gracious acceptance of the service of the true Aaron and His "many sons," the priestly people of God, through all the Christian ages. Thus, the services and events of that day of induction, in their order from beginning to end, were not only a parable of the order of grace, but also, as it were, a typical epitome of the whole work of redemption. They are thus a prophecy that the work which began when Christ made His soul an offering for sin, and to perfect which He is now withdrawn from our sight for a season, shall be consummated at last by His reappearing in glory for the final blessing of His waiting people.

And if we look at other and subordinate aspects of this inauguration service, we shall still find this sequel of all, no less richly suggestive. Expiation, righteousness, fellowship in peace with God, shall bring with it the blessing of the Lord, and finally issue in the revelation of His glory in the sight of all who accept this great redemption through sacrifice. And so also in the personal life. As the trustful acceptance and use of the appointed Sin-offering leads to the consecration of the person and the life, and as by this consecration we come into conscious fellowship with God in joy and peace, as we feed on the flesh of the slain Lamb, so, as the blessed result, unto every true believer, according to the measure of his faith, this is followed by the double benediction of the Lord; one for this life, and a larger, for the life which is to come. The Lord blesses him, and keeps him: the Lord makes His face to shine upon him, and is gracious unto him: the Lord lifts up His countenance upon him, and gives him peace, according to that word of the great High Priest: "Peace I leave with you; My peace I give unto you" (John xiv. 27). And then, after the present peace, is yet to follow, as the final issue of the expiated sin, and the consecrated life, and fellowship in peace with the God of life and love, the beholding of the glory of the Lord; according to that highpriestly prayer of our Redeemer, "That which Thou hast given Me, I will that, where I am, they also may be with Me: that they may behold My glory" (John xvii. 24). Even here some know a little of this, and find that expiated sin and full consecration are followed here and now by bright glimpses of the Glory of the Lord. But what is now seen thus in part shall then be seen fully and face to face. Who would not make sure of that beatific vision of the glory of the Lord?

CHAPTER XII.

NADAB'S AND ABIHU'S "STRANGE FIRE."

Leviticus x. 1-20.

The solemn and august ceremonies of the consecration of the priests, and the tabernacle, and the inauguration of the tabernacle service, had a sad and terrible termination. The sacrifices of the inauguration day had been completed, the congregation had received the priestly benediction, the glory of Jehovah had appeared unto the people, and, in token of His acceptance of all that had been done, consumed the victims on the altar. This manifestation of the glory of the Lord so affected the people—as well it might—that when they saw it, "they shouted, and fell on their faces." It was, probably, under the influence of the excitement of this occasion that (vv. 1, 2), "Nadab and Abihu, the sons of Aaron, took each of them his censer, and put fire therein, and laid incense thereon, and offered strange fire before the Lord, which He had not commanded them. And there came forth fire from before the Lord, and devoured them, and they died before the Lord."

There has been no little speculation as to what it was, precisely, which they did. Some will have it, that they lighted their incense, not from the altar fire, but elsewhere. As to this, while it is not easy to prove that to light the incense at the altar fire was an invariable requirement, yet it is certain that this was commanded for the great day of atonement (xvi. 12); and also, that when Aaron offered incense in connection with the plague which broke out upon the rebellion of Korah, Dathan, and Abiram, Moses commanded him to take the fire for the censer from off the altar (Numb. xvi. 46); so that, perhaps this is not unlikely to have been one element, at least, in their offence. Others, again, have thought that their sin lay in this, that they offered their incense at a time not commanded in the order of worship which God had just prescribed; and this, too, may very probably have been another element in their sin, for it is certain that the divinely-appointed order of worship for the day had been already completed. Yet again, others have supposed that they rashly and without Divine warrant pressed within the veil, into the immediate presence of the Shekinah glory of God, to offer their incense there. For this, too, there is evidence, in the fact that the institution of the great annual day of atonement, and the prohibition of entrance within the veil at any other time, even to the high priest himself, is said to have followed "after the death of the two sons of Aaron, when they drew near before the Lord, and died" (xvi. 1, 2).

It is perfectly possible, and even likely, that all these elements were combined in their offence. In any case, the gravamen of their sin is expressed in these words; they offered "fire which the Lord had not commanded them:" offered it, either in a way not commanded, or at a time not commanded, or in a place not commanded; or, perhaps, in each and all of these ways, offered "fire which the Lord had not commanded." This was their sin, and one which brought instant and terrible judgment.

It is easy enough to believe that yet they meant well in what they did. It probably seemed to them the right thing to do. After such a stupendous display as they had just witnessed, of the flaming glory of Jehovah, why should they not, in token of reverence and adoration, offer incense, even in the most immediate presence of Jehovah? And why should such minor variations from the appointed law, as to manner, or time, or place, matter very much, so the motive was worship? So may they probably have reasoned, if indeed they thought at all. But, nevertheless, this made no difference; all the same, "fire came forth from Jehovah, and devoured them." They had been but so lately consecrated! and—as we learn from ver. 5—their priestly robes were on them at the time, in token of their peculiar privilege of special nearness to God! But this, too, made no difference; "there came forth fire from before the Lord and devoured them."

Their sin, in the form in which it was committed, can never be repeated; but as regards its inner nature and essence, no sin has been in all ages more common. For the essence of their sin was this, that it was will-worship; worship in which they consulted not the revealed will of God regarding the way in which He would be served, but their own fancies and inclinations. The directions for worship had been, as we have seen, exceedingly full and explicit; but they apparently imagined that the fragrance of their incense, and its intrinsic suitableness as a symbol of adoration and prayer, was sufficient to excuse neglect of strict obedience to the revealed will of God touching His own worship. Their sin was not unlike that of Saul in a later day, who thought to excuse disobedience by the offering of enormous sacrifices. But he was sharply reminded that "to obey is better than sacrifice" (1 Sam. xv. 22); and the priesthood were in like manner on this occasion very terribly taught that obedience is also better than incense, even the incense of the sanctuary.

In all ages, men have been prone to commit this sin, and in ours as much as any. It is true that in the present dispensation the Lord has left more in His worship than in earlier days to the sanctified judgment of His people, and has not minutely prescribed details for our direction. It is true, again, that there is, and always will be, room for some difference of judgment among good and loyal servants of the Lord, as to how far the liberty left us extends. But we are certainly all taught as much as this, that wherever we are not clear that we have a Divine warrant for what we do in the worship of God, we need to be exceeding careful, and to act with holy fear, lest possibly, like Nadab and Abihu, we be chargeable with offering "strange fire," which the Lord has not commanded. And when one goes into many a church and chapel, and sees the multitude of remarkable devices by which, as is imagined, the worship and adoration of God is furthered, it must be confessed that it certainly seems as if the generation of Nadab and Abihu was not yet extinct; even although a patient God, in the mystery of His long-suffering, flashes not instantly forth His vengeance.

This then is the first lesson of this tragic occurrence. We have to do with a God who is very jealous; who will be worshipped as He wills, or not at all. Nor can we complain. If God be such a Being as we are taught in the Holy Scripture, it must be His inalienable right to determine and prescribe how He will be served.

And it is a second lesson, scarcely less evident, that with God, intention of good, though it palliate, cannot excuse disobedience where He has once made known His will. No one can imagine that Nadab and Abihu meant wrong; but for all that, for their sin they died.

Again, we are herein impressively taught that, with God, high position confers no immunity when a man sins; least of all, high position in the Church. On the contrary, the greater the exaltation in spiritual honour and privilege, the more strictly will a man be held to account for every failure to honour Him who exalted him. We have seen this illustrated already by the law of the sin-offering; and this tragic story illustrates the same truth again.

But the question naturally arises, How could these men, who had been so exalted in privilege, who had even beheld the glory of the God of Israel in the holy mount (Exod. xxiv. 1, 9, 10), have ventured upon such a perilous experiment? The answer is probably suggested by the warning which immediately followed their death (vv. 8, 9): "The Lord spake unto Aaron, saying, Drink no wine nor strong drink, . . . when ye go into the tent of the meeting, that ye die not." It is certainly distinctly hinted by these words, that it was under the excitement of strong drink that these men so fatally sinned.

If so, then, although their sin may not be repeated in its exact form among us, yet the fact points a very solemn warning, not only regarding the careless use of strong drink, but, more than that, against all religious worship and activity which is inspired by other stimulus than by the Holy Spirit of God. Of this every age of the Church's history has furnished sad examples. Sometimes we see it illustrated in "revivals," even in such as may be marked by some evidence of the presence of the Spirit of God; when injudicious speakers seek by various methods to work up what is, after all, merely a physical excitement of a strange, infectious kind, though too often mistaken for the work of the Holy Spirit of God. More subtle and yet more common is the sin of such as in preaching the Word find their chief stimulation in the excitement of a crowded house, or the visible signs of approbation on the part of the hearers; and perhaps sometimes mistake the natural effect of this influence for the quickening power of the Holy Ghost, and go on to offer before the Lord the incense of their religious service and worship, but with "strange fire." Of this all need to beware; and most of all, ministers of the Word.

The penalty of sin is often long delayed, but it did not lag in this case. The strange fire in the hands of Nadab and Abihu was met by a flash of flame that instantly withered their life; and, just as they were, their priestly robes upon them unconsumed, their censers in their hands, they dropped dead before the fatal bolt.

In reading this account and other similar narratives in Holy Scripture, of the deadly outbreak of God's wrath, many have felt not a little disquieted in mind because of the terrific severity of the judgment, which to them seems so out of all proportion to the guilt of the offender. And so, in many hearts, and even to many lips, the question has perforce arisen: Is it possible to believe that in this passage, for instance, we have a true representation of the character of God? In answering such a question we ought always to remember, first of all, that, apart from our imperfect knowledge, just because we all are sinners, we are, by that fact, all more or less disqualified and incapacitated for forming a correct and unbiassed judgment regarding the demerit of sin. It is quite certain that every sinful man is naturally inclined to take a lenient view of the guilt of sin, and, by necessary consequence, of its desert in respect of punishment. In approaching this question, here and elsewhere in God's Word, it is imperative that we keep this fact in mind.

Again, it is not unnecessary to remark, that we must be careful and not read into this narrative what, in fact, is not here. For it is often assumed without evidence, that when we read in the Bible of men being suddenly cut off by death for some special sin, we are therefore required to believe that the temporal judgment of physical death must have been followed, in each instance, by the judgment of the eternal fire. But always to infer this in such cases, when, as here, nothing of the kind is hinted in the text, is a great mistake, and introduces a difficulty which is wholly of our own making. That sometimes, at least, the facts are quite the opposite, is expressly certified to us in 1 Cor. xi. 30-32, where we are told that among the Christians of Corinth, many, because of their irreverent approach to the Holy Supper of the Lord, slept the sleep of death; but that these judgments from the Lord, of bodily death, instead of being necessarily intended for their eternal destruction, were sent that they might not finally perish. For the Apostle's words are most explicit; for it is with reference to these cases of sickness and death of which he had spoken, that he adds (ver. 32): "But when we are (thus) judged, we are chastened of the Lord, that we may not be condemned with the world."

What we have here before us, then, is not the question of the eternal condemnation of Nadab and Abihu for their thoughtless, though perhaps not so intended, profanation of God's worship, —a point on which the narrative gives us no information,—but, simply and only, the inflicting on them, for this sin, of the judgment of temporal death. And if this yet seem to some undue severity, as no doubt it will, there remain other considerations which deserve to have great weight here. In the first place, if this reveal God as terribly severe in His judgment, even upon what, compared with other crimes, may seem a small sin, we have to remember that, after all, this God of the Bible, this Jehovah of the Old Testament, is only herein revealed as in this respect like the God whose working we see in nature and in history. Was the God of Nadab and Abihu a severe God? Is not the God of nature a terribly severe God? Who then is it that has so appointed the economy of nature that even for one thoughtless indulgence by a young man, he shall be racked with pain all his life thereafter? It is a law of nature, one says. But what is a law of nature but the ordinary operation of the Divine Being who made nature? So let us not forget that the reasoning which, because of the confessed severity of this judgment on the sons of Aaron, argues God out of the tenth of Leviticus, and refuses to believe that this can be a revelation of His mind and character, by parity of reasoning must go on to argue God out of nature and out of history. But if one be not yet ready for the latter, let him take heed how he too hastily decide on this ground against the verity of the history and the truth of the revelation in the case before us.

Then, again, we need to be careful that we pass not judgment before considering all that was involved in this act of sin. We cannot look upon the case as if the act of Nadab and Abihu had been merely a private matter, personal to themselves alone. This it was not, and could not be. They did what they did in their official robes; moreover, it was a peculiarly public act: it took place before the sanctuary, where all the people were assembled. What was the influence of this their act, if it passed unrebuked and unpunished, likely to be? History shows that nothing was more inbred in the nature of the people than just this tendency to will-worship. For centuries after this, notwithstanding many like terrible judgments, it mightily prevailed, taking the form of numberless attempted improvements on the arrangements of worship appointed by God, and introducing, under such pretexts of expediency, often the grossest idolatry. And although the Babylonian judgment made an end of the idolatrous form of will-worship, the old tendency persisted, and worked on under a new form till, as we learn from our Lord's words in the Gospel, the people were in His day utterly overwhelmed with "heavy burdens and grievous to be borne," rabbinical additions to the law, attempted improvements on Moses, under pretext of honouring Moses, all begotten of this same inveterate spirit of will-worship. Nor are such things of little consequence, as some seem to imagine, whether we find them among Jews or in Christian communions. On the contrary, all will-worship, in all its endless variety of forms, tends to confuse conscience, by confounding with the commandments of God the practices and traditions of men; and all history, no less of the Church than of Israel, shows that the tendency of all such will-worship is to the subversion alike of morality and religion, occasioning, too often, total misapprehension as to what indeed is the essence of religion well pleasing to God.

Was the sin of the priests, Nadab and Abihu, then, committed in such a public manner, such a trifling matter after all? And when we further remember the peculiar circumstances of the occasion,—that the whole ceremonial of the day was designed in a special manner to instruct the people as to the manner in which Jehovah, their King and their God, would be worshipped,—it certainly is not so hard, after all, to see how it was almost imperative that in the very beginning of Israel's national history, God should give them a lesson on the sanctity of His ordinances and His hatred of will-worship, which should be remembered to all time.

The solemn lesson of the terrible judgment, Moses, as Prophet and Interpreter of God's will to the people, declares in these words (ver. 3): "This is it that the Lord spake, saying, I will be sanctified in them that come nigh Me, and before all the people I will be glorified."

If God separate a people to be specially near unto Him, it is that, admitted to such special nearness to Himself, they shall ever reverently recognise His transcendent exaltation in holiness, and take care that He be ever glorified in them before all men. But if any be careless of this, God will nevertheless not be defrauded. If they will recognise His august holiness, in the reverence of loyal service, well; God shall thus glorify Himself in them before all. But if otherwise, still God will be glorified in them before all people, though now in their chastisement and in retribution. The principle is that which is announced by Amos (iii. 2): "You only have I known of all the families of the earth; *therefore* I will visit upon you all your iniquities." And when we remember that the sons of Aaron typically represent the whole body of believers in Christ, as a priestly people, it is plain that the warning of this judgment comes directly home to us all. If, as Christians, we have been brought into a relation of special nearness and privilege with God, we have to remember that the place of privilege is, in this case, a place of peculiar danger. If we forget the reverence and honour due to His name, and insist on will-worship of any kind, we shall in some way suffer for it. God may wink at the sins of others, but not at ours. He is a God of love, and desires not our death, but that He may be glorified in our life; but if any will not have it so, He will not be robbed of his glory. Hence the warning of the Apostle Peter, who was so filled with these Old Testament conceptions of God and His worship: "It is written, Ye shall be holy, for I am holy. And if ye call on Him as Father, who without respect of persons judgeth according to each man's work, pass the time of your sojourning in fear" (1 Peter i. 17).

Ver. 3: "And Aaron held his peace."

For rebellion were useless; nay, it had been madness. Even the tenderest natural affection must be silent when God smites for sin; and in this case the sin was so manifest, and the connection therewith of the judgment so evident, that Aaron could say nothing, though his heart must have been breaking.

MOURNING IN SILENCE.
LEVITICUS x. 4-7.

"And Moses called Mishael and Elzaphan, the sons of Uzziel the uncle of Aaron, and said unto them, Draw near, carry your brethren from before the sanctuary out of the camp. So they drew near, and carried them in their coats out of the camp; as Moses had said. And Moses said unto Aaron, and unto Eleazar and unto Ithamar, his sons, Let not the hair of your heads go loose, neither rend your clothes; that ye die not, and that He be not wroth with all the congregation: but let your brethren, the whole house of Israel, bewail the burning which the Lord hath kindled. And ye shall not go out from the door of the tent of meeting, lest ye die: for the anointing oil of the Lord is upon you. And they did according to the word of Moses."

Even in ordinary cases, restrictions were placed upon Aaron and his sons as regards the outward signs of mourning; but exceptions were made in the case of the nearest relations, and, in particular, of the death of a son, or a brother (chap. xxi. 2). In this case, however, this permission could not be given; and they are warned that by public expressions of grief they would not only bring death from the Lord upon themselves, but also bring His wrath upon the whole congregation which they represented before God. They are not indeed forbidden to mourn in their hearts, but from all the outward and customary signs of mourning they must abstain. And the reason for this is given; "The anointing oil of the Lord is upon you." That is, by the anointing they had been set apart to represent God before Israel. Hence, when God had thus manifested His holy wrath against sin, for them to have exhibited the public signs of mourning for this, even though the stroke of wrath had fallen into their own family, would have been a visible contradiction between their actions and their priestly position. To others, indeed, these outward tokens of mourning are expressly permitted, for they stood in no such special relation to God; their brethren, "the whole house of Israel," might bewail the burning which the Lord had kindled, but they, although nearest of kin to the dead, are not permitted even to follow the slain of the Lord to the grave, and (vv. 4, 5) the sad duty is assigned to their cousins, who bear the dead, in their white priestly robes, just as they had fallen, out of the camp to burial, while Aaron and his sons mourn silently within the tent of meeting.

This has seemed hard to many, and has furnished some another illustration of the hardness and severity of the character of God as held up in the Pentateuch. But we shall do well to remember that in all this we have nothing which in any respect goes beyond the very solemn words of the tender-hearted and most compassionate Saviour, who said, for example, "If any man cometh unto Me, and hateth not his own father, and mother, and wife, and children, and brethren, and sisters, . . . he cannot be My disciple" (Luke xiv. 26). In language such as this, we cannot but recognise the same character as in this command unto Aaron and his sons; and if such "hard sayings" are to be held reason for rejecting the revelation of the character of God as given in the Old Testament, the same logic, in the presence of similar words, will require us also to reject the revelation of God's character as given by Christ in the New Testament.

The teaching of both Testaments on this matter is plain. Natural affection is right; it is indeed implanted in our hearts by the God who made us in all our human relations. But none the less, whenever the feelings which belong even to the nearest and tenderest earthly relations come into conflict with absolute fealty and submission to the will of God, and unswerving loyalty to the will of Christ, then, hard though indeed it may be, natural affection must give way, and mourn within the tent in the silence of a holy submission to the Lord.

CAREFULNESS AFTER JUDGMENT.
LEVITICUS x. 8-20.

"And the Lord spake unto Aaron, saying, Drink no wine nor strong drink, thou, nor thy sons with thee, when ye go into the tent of meeting, that ye die not: it shall be a statute for ever throughout your generations: and that ye may put difference between the holy and the common, and between the unclean and the clean; and that ye may teach the children of Israel all the statutes which the Lord hath spoken unto them by the hand of Moses. And Moses spake unto Aaron, and unto Eleazar and unto Ithamar, his sons that were left, Take the meal offering that remaineth of the offerings of the Lord made by fire, and eat it without leaven beside the altar: for it is most holy: and ye shall eat it in a holy place, because it is thy due, and thy sons' due, of the offerings of the Lord made by fire: for so I am commanded. And the wave breast and the heave thigh shall ye eat in a clean place; thou, and thy sons, and thy daughters with thee: for they are given as thy due, and thy sons' due, out of the sacrifices of the peace offerings of the children of Israel. The heave thigh and the wave breast shall they bring with the offerings made by fire of the fat, to wave it for a wave offering before the Lord: and it shall be thine, and thy sons' with thee, as a due for ever; as the Lord hath commanded. And Moses diligently sought the goat of the sin offering, and, behold it was burnt: and he was angry with Eleazar and with Ithamar, the sons of Aaron that were left, saying, Wherefore have ye not eaten the sin offering in the place of the sanctuary, seeing it is most holy, and He hath given it you to bear the iniquity of the congregation, to make atonement for them before the Lord? Behold, the blood of it was not brought into the sanctuary within: ye should certainly have eaten it in the sanctuary, as I commanded. And Aaron spake unto Moses, Behold, this day have they offered their sin offering and their burnt offering before the Lord; and there have befallen me such things as these: and if I had eaten the sin offering to-day, would it have been well-pleasing in the sight of the Lord? And when Moses heard that, it was well-pleasing in his sight."

Such a judgment as the foregoing ought to have had a good effect, and it did. This appeared in renewed carefulness to secure the most exact obedience hereafter in all their official duties. To this end, the Lord Himself now laid down a law evidently designed to preclude, as far as possible, every risk of any such fault in the priestly service as might again bring down judgment. It is not only holiness, but considerate and anxious love, which speaks in the next words, addressed to Aaron (vv. 8, 9): "Drink no wine nor strong drink, thou, nor thy sons with thee, when ye go into the tent of meeting, that ye die not: it shall be a statute for ever throughout your generations."

And for this prohibition the reason is given (vv. 10, 11): "That ye may put difference between the holy and the common, and between the unclean and the clean; and that ye may teach the children of Israel all the statutes which the Lord hath spoken unto them by the hand of Moses."

It was not then that the use of wine was in itself sinful; for this is taught nowhere in the Old or New Testament, and as a doctrine of religion is characteristic, not of Judaism or Christianity, but only of Mohammedanism, of Buddhism and other heathen religions. The ground of this command of abstinence, as of the New Testament counsel (Rom. xiv. 20, 21), is that of expediency. Because, in the use of wine or strong drink, there was involved a certain risk, that by undue indulgence, the judgment might be confused or the memory weakened, so that something might be done amiss; therefore the priests, who were specially commissioned to teach the statutes of the Lord to Israel, and this most of all, by their own carefulness to obey all the least of His commandments, are here warned to abstain whenever about engaging in their official duties. As suggested above, it is at least very natural to infer, from the historical setting of this prohibition, that the fatal offence of Nadab and Abihu was occasioned by such an indulgence in wine or strong drink as made it possible for impulse to get the better of knowledge and judgment.

But, however this may be, the lesson for us abides the same; a lesson which each one according to his circumstances must faithfully apply to his own case. For the Christian it is not enough that he shall abstain from what is in its own nature always sinful; it must be the law of our life that we abstain also from whatever may needlessly become occasion of sin. In this we cannot, indeed, lay down a universal code of law. Heathen reformers have done this, and their imitators in the Church, but never Christ or His Apostles. And this with reason. For that which for one carries with it inevitable risk of sin, is not always fraught with the same danger to another person with a different temperament, or even to the same person under different circumstances. In each instance we must judge for ourselves, taking heed not to abuse our liberty to another's harm; and also, on the other hand, being careful how we judge others in regard to things which in their essential nature are neither right nor wrong. But we shall be wise to recognise the fact that it is just in such things that many Christians do most harm, both to their own souls and to those of others. And in regard to the drinking of wine in particular, one must be blind indeed not to perceive it to be the fact that, whatever the reason may be, the English-speaking peoples seem to be peculiarly susceptible to the danger of undue indulgence in wine and strong drink. On both sides of the Atlantic, drunkenness must be set down as one of the most prevalent national sins.

In deciding the question of personal duty in this and like cases, all believers are bound, as the Lord's priestly people, to remember that He has appointed them that they should walk before Him as a separated people, who, by their daily walk, above all, are to teach others to "put a difference between holy and common, and unclean and clean, and to observe all the statutes which the Lord hath spoken."

In vv. 12-15 we have a repetition of the commandments previously given, concerning the use to be made of the meal-offering and the peace-offering. From this it apears that Moses himself, in view of the tragic occurrence of the day, was stirred up to charge Aaron and his sons anew on matters on which he had already commanded them. And with this intensified care on his part is evidently connected the incident recorded in the verses which follow, where we read that, having repeated the directions as to the meal-offering and the peace-offering (vv. 16, 17), "Moses diligently sought the goat of the sin offering, and, behold, it was burnt; and he was angry with Eleazar and with Ithamar, the sons of Aaron that were left, saying, Wherefore have ye not eaten the sin offering in the place of the sanctuary, seeing it is most holy, and He hath given it you to bear the iniquity of the congregation, to make atonement for them before the Lord?"

It had indeed been commanded, in the case of those sin-offerings of which the blood was brought into the holy place, that their flesh should not be eaten; but that the flesh of all others should be eaten, as belonging to the class of things "most holy," by the priests alone within the Holy Place. Hence Moses continued (ver. 18): "Behold, the blood of it was not brought into the sanctuary within: ye should certainly have eaten it in the sanctuary, as I commanded."

What had been done, as it appears, had been done with Aaron's knowledge and sanction; for Aaron then answered in behalf of his sons (ver. 19): "Behold, this day have they offered their sin offering and their burnt offering before the Lord; and there have befallen me such things as these: and if I had eaten the sin offering to-day, would it have been well-pleasing in the sight of the Lord?"

Of which answer, the intention seems to have been this. In this day of special exaltation and privilege, when for the first time they had performed their solemn priestly duties, when most of all there should have been the utmost care to please the Lord in the very smallest things, His holy Name had been profaned by the will-worship of his sons, and the wrath of God had broken out against them, and, in them, against their father's house. Could it be the will of God that a house in which was found the guilt of such a sin, should yet partake of the most holy things of God in the sanctuary?

From this it appears that the judgment sent into the house of Aaron had had a most wholesome spiritual effect. They had received such an impression of their own profound sinfulness as they had never had before. And it is very instructive to observe that they assume to themselves a part in the sinfulness which had been shown in the sin of Nadab and Abihu. It did not occur to Aaron or his remaining sons to say, in the spirit of Israel in the day of our Lord, "If we had been in their place, we would not have done so." Rather their consciences had been so awakened to the holiness of God and their own inborn evil, that they coupled themselves with the others as under the displeasure of God. Was it possible, even though they personally had not sinned, that such as they should eat that which was most holy unto God? They had thus in the letter disobeyed the law; but because their offence was begotten of a misapprehension, and only showed how deeply and thoroughly they had taken to heart the lesson of the sore judgment, we read that "when Moses heard" their explanation, "it was well pleasing in his sight."

All this which followed the sin of Nadab and Abihu, and the judgment which fell on them, and thus upon the whole house of Aaron, is a most instructive illustration of the working of the chastising judgments of the Lord, when rightly received. Its effect was to awaken the utmost solicitude that nothing else might be found about the tabernacle service, even through oversight, which was not according to the mind of God; and, in those immediately stricken, to produce a very profound sense of personal sinfulness and unworthiness before God. The New Testament gives us a graphic description of this effect of the chastisement of God on the believer, in the account which we have of the result of the discipline which the Apostle Paul inflicted on the sinning member of the Church of Corinth; concerning which he afterward wrote to them (2 Cor. vii. 11) "Behold, this selfsame thing, that ye were made sorry after a godly sort, what earnest care it wrought in you, yea, what clearing of yourselves, yea, what indignation, yea, what fear, yea, what longing, yea, what zeal, yea, what avenging!"

A good test is this, which, when we have passed under the chastising hand of God, we may well apply to ourselves: this "earnest care," this "clearing of ourselves," this holy fear of a humbled heart,—have we known what it means? If so, though we sorrow, we may yet rejoice that by grace we are enabled to sorrow "after a godly sort," with "a repentance which bringeth no regret."

CHAPTER XIII.

THE GREAT DAY OF ATONEMENT.

LEVITICUS xvi. 1-34.

IN the first verse of chapter xvi., which ordains the ceremonial for the great annual day of atonement, we are told that this ordinance was delivered by the Lord to Moses "after the death of the two sons of Aaron, when they drew near before the Lord, and died."* Because of the close historical connection thus declared between this chapter and chapter x., and also because in this ordinance the Mosaic sacrificial worship, which has been the subject of the book thus far, finds its culmination, it seems most satisfactory to anticipate the order of the book by taking up at this point the exposition of this chapter, before proceeding in chapter xi. to a wholly different subject.

This ordinance of the day of atonement was perhaps the most important and characteristic in the whole Mosaic legislation. In the law of the offerings, the most distinctive part was the law of the sin-offering; and it was on the great annual day of atonement that the conceptions embodied in the sin-offering obtained their most complete development. The central place which this day occupied in the whole system of sacred times is well illustrated in that it is often spoken of by the rabbis, without any more precise designation, as simply "*Yomā.*" "The Day." It was "*the* day" because, on this day, the idea of sacrificial expiation and the consequent removal of all sin, essential to the life of peace and fellowship

---

* The interposition of chapters xi.-xv. on ceremonial uncleanness, between chapters x. and xvi., which are so closely connected by this historical note in xvi. 1, certainly suggests an editorial redaction—as the phrase is—in which the latter chapter, for whatsoever reason, has been removed from its original context. But that such a redaction, of which we have in the book other traces, does not of necessity affect in the slightest degree the question of its inspiration and Divine authority, should be self-evident.

with God, which was set forth imperfectly, as regards individuals and the nation, by the daily sin-offerings, received the highest possible symbolical expression. It is plain that countless sins and transgressions and various defilements must yet have escaped unrecognised as such, even by the most careful and conscientious Israelite; and that, for this reason, they could not have been covered by any of the daily offerings for sin. Hence, apart from this full, solemn, typical purgation and cleansing of the priesthood and the congregation, and the holy sanctuary, from the uncleannesses and transgressions of the children of Israel, "even all their sins" (ver. 16), the sacrificial system had yet fallen short of expressing in adequate symbolism the ideal of the complete removal of all sin. With abundant reason then do the rabbis regard it as the day of days in the sacred year.

It is insisted by the radical criticism of our day that the general sense of sin and need of expiation which this ordinance expresses could not have existed in the days of Moses; and that since, moreover, the later historical books of the Old Testament contain no reference to the observance of the day, therefore its origin must be attributed to the days of the restoration from Babylon, when, as such critics suppose, the deeper sense of sin, developed by the great judgment of the Babylonian captivity and exile, occasioned the elaboration of this ritual.

To this one might reply that the objection rests upon an assumption which the Christian believer cannot admit, that the ordinance was merely a product of the human mind. But if, as our Lord constantly taught, and as the chapter explicitly affirms, the ordinance was a matter of Divine, supernatural revelation, then naturally we shall expect to find in it, not man's estimate of the guilt of sin, but God's, which in all ages is the same.

But, meeting such objectors on their own ground, we need not go into the matter further than to refer to the high authority of Dillmann, who declares this theory of the post-exilian origin of this institution to be "absolutely incredible;" and in reply to the objection that the day is not alluded to in the whole Old Testament history, justly adds that this argument from silence would equally forbid us to assign the origin of the ordinance to the days of the return from Babylon, or any of the pre-Christian centuries! for "one would then have to maintain that the festival first arose in the first Christian century; since only out of that age do we first have any explicit testimonies concerning it."*

Again, the first verse of the chapter gives as the occasion of the promulgation of this law, "the death of the two sons of Aaron," Nadab and Abihu, "when they drew near before the Lord and died;" a historical note which is perfectly natural if we have here a narrative dating from Mosaic days, but which seems most objectless and unlikely to have been entered, if the law were a late invention of rabbinical forgers. On that occasion it was, as we read (v. 2), that "the Lord said unto Moses, Speak unto Aaron thy brother, that he come not at all times into the holy place within the veil, before the mercy-seat which is upon the ark; that he die not: for I will appear in the cloud upon the mercy-seat."

Into this place of Jehovah's most immediate earthly manifestation, even Aaron is to come

* "Die Bücher Exodus und Leviticus," 2 Aufl., p. 525.

only once a year, and then only with atoning blood, as hereinafter prescribed.

The object of the whole service of this day is represented as atonement; expiation of sin, in the highest and fullest sense then possible. It is said to be appointed to make atonement for Aaron and for his house (ver. 6), for the holy place, and for the tent of meeting (vv. 15-17); for the altar of burnt-offering in the outer court (vv. 18, 19); and for all the congregation of Israel (vv. 20-22, 33); and this, not merely for such sins of ignorance as had been afterward recognised and acknowledged in the ordinary sin-offerings of each day, but for "*all* the iniquities of the children of Israel, and *all* their transgressions, even all their sins:" even such as were still unknown to all but God (ver. 21). The fact of such an ordinance for such a purpose taught a most impressive lesson of the holiness of God and the sinfulness of man, on the one hand, and, on the other, the utter insufficiency of the daily offerings to cleanse from all sin. Day by day these had been offered in each year; and yet, as we read (Heb. ix. 8, 9), the Holy Ghost this signified by this ordinance, "that the way into the holy place hath not yet been made manifest;" it was "a parable for the time now present;" teaching that the temple sacrifices of Judaism could not "as touching the conscience, make the worshipper perfect" (Heb. ix. 9). We may well reverse the judgment of the critics, and say—not that the deepened sense of sin in Israel was the cause of the day of atonement; but rather, that the solemn observances of this day, under God, were made for many in Israel a most effective means to deepen the conviction of sin.

The time which was ordained for this annual observance is significant—the tenth day of the seventh month. It was appointed for the seventh month, as the sabbatic month, in which all the related ideas of rest in God and with God, in the enjoyment of the blessings of a now complete redemption, received in the great feast of tabernacles their fullest expression. It was therefore appointed for that month, and for a day which shortly preceded this greatest of the annual feasts, to signify in type the profound and most vital truth, that the full joy of the sabbatic rest of man with God, and the ingathering of the fruits of complete redemption, is only possible upon condition of repentance and the fullest possible expiation for sin. It was appointed for the tenth day of this month, no doubt, because in the Scripture symbolism the number ten is the symbol of completeness; and was fitly thus connected with a service which signified expiation completed for the sins of the year.

The observances appointed for the day had regard, first, to the people, and, secondly, to the tabernacle service. As for the former, it was commanded (ver. 29) that they should "do no manner of work," observing the day as a *Sabbath Sabbathon*, "a high Sabbath," or "Sabbath of solemn rest," (ver. 31); and, secondly, that they should "afflict their souls" (ver. 31), namely, by solemn fasting, in visible sign of sorrow and humiliation for sin. By which it was most distinctly taught, that howsoever complete atonement may be, and howsoever, in making that atonement through a sacrificial victim, the sinner himself have no part, yet apart from his personal repentance for his sins, that atonement shall profit him nothing; nay, it was declared (xxiii. 29), that if any man should fail on this point, God would cut him off from his people. The law abides as regards the greater sacrifice of Christ; except we repent, we shall, even because of that sacrifice, only the more terribly perish; because not even this supreme exhibition of the holy love and justice of God has moved us to renounce sin.

As regards the tabernacle service for the day, the order was as follows. First, as most distinctive of the ritual of the day, only the high-priest could officiate. The other priests, who, on other occasions, served continually in the holy place, must on this day, during these ceremonies, leave it to him alone; taking their place, themselves as sinners for whom also atonement was to be made, with the sinful congregation of their brethren. For it was ordered (ver. 17): "There shall be no man in the tent of meeting when the high priest goeth in to make atonement in the holy place, until he come out," and the work of atonement be completed.

And the high priest could himself officiate only after certain significant preparations. First (ver. 4), he must "bathe in water" his whole person. The word used in the original is different from that which is used of the partial washings in connection with the daily ceremonial cleansings; and, most suggestively, the same complete washing is required as that which was ordered in the law for the consecration of the priesthood, and for cleansing from leprosy and other specific defilements. Thus was expressed, in the clearest manner possible, the thought, that the high priest, who shall be permitted to draw near to God in the holiest place, and there prevail with Him, must himself be wholly pure and clean.

Then, having bathed, he must robe himself in a special manner for the service of this day. He must lay aside the bright-coloured "garments for glory and beauty" which he wore on all other occasions, and put on, instead, a vesture of pure, unadorned white, like that of the ordinary priest; excepting only that for him, on this day, unlike them, the girdle also must be white. By this substitution of these garments for his ordinary brilliant robes was signified, not merely the absolute purity which the white linen symbolised, but especially also, by the absence of adornment, humiliation for sin. On this day he was thus made in outward appearance essentially like unto the other members of his house, for whose sin, together with his own, he was to make atonement.

Thus washed and robed, wearing on his white turban the golden crown inscribed "Holiness to Jehovah" (Exod. xxviii. 38), he now took (vv. 3, 5-7), as a sin-offering for himself and for his house, a bullock; and for the congregation, "two he-goats for a sin offering;" with a ram for himself, and one for them, for a burnt-offering. The two goats were set "before the Lord at the door of the tent of meeting." The bullock was the offering before prescribed for the sin-offering for the high priest (iv. 3), as being the most valuable of all sacrificial victims. For the choice of the goats many reasons have been given, none of which seem wholly satisfactory. Both of the goats are equally declared (ver. 5) to be "for a sin offering;" yet only one was to be slain.

The ceremonial which followed is unique; it is without its like either in Mosaism or in heathenism. It was ordered (ver. 8): "Aaron shall cast lots upon the two goats; one lot for the Lord, and the other lot for Azazel;" an expression to which we shall shortly return. Only the goat on whom the lot fell for the Lord was to be slain.

The two goats remain standing before the Lord; while now Aaron kills the sin-offering for himself and for his house (ver. 11); then enters, first, the Holy of Holies within the veil, having taken (ver. 12) a censer "full of coals of fire from off the altar before the Lord," with his hands full of incense (ver. 13), "that the cloud of the incense may cover the mercy-seat that is upon the testimony (*i. e.*, the two tables of the law within the ark), that he die not." Then (ver. 13) he sprinkles the blood "upon the mercy-seat on the east"—by which was signified the application of the blood God-ward, accompanied with the fragrance of intercession, for the expiation of his own sins and those of his house; and then "seven times, before the mercy-seat,"—evidently, on the floor of the sanctuary, for the symbolic cleansing of the holiest place, defiled by all the uncleannesses of the children of Israel, in the midst of whom it stood. Then, returning, he kills the goat of the sin-offering "for Jehovah," and repeats the same ceremony, now in behalf of the whole congregation, sprinkling, as before, the mercy-seat, and, seven times, the Holy of Holies, thus making atonement for it, "because of the uncleannesses of the children of Israel, and because of their transgressions, even all their sins" (ver. 16). In like manner, he was then to cleanse, by a seven-fold sprinkling, the Holy place; and then again going into the outer court, also the altar of burnt-offering; this last, doubtless, as in other cases, by applying the blood to the horns of the altar.

In all this it will be observed that the difference from the ordinary sin-offerings and the wider reach of its symbolical virtue is found, not in that the offering is different from or larger than others, but in that, symbolically speaking, the blood is brought, as in no other offering, into the most immediate presence of God; even into the secret darkness of the Holy of Holies, where no child of Israel might tread. For this reason did this sin-offering become, above all others, the most perfect type of the one offering of Him, the God-Man, who reconciled us to God by doing that in reality which was here done in symbol, even entering with atoning blood into the very presence of God, there to appear in our behalf.

AZAZEL.

LEVITICUS xvi. 20-28.

"And when he hath made an end of atoning for the holy place, and the tent of meeting, and the altar, he shall present the live goat: and Aaron shall lay both his hands upon the head of the live goat, and confess over him all the iniquities of the children of Israel and all their transgressions, even all their sins; and he shall put them upon the head of the goat, and shall send him away by the hand of a man that is in readiness into the wilderness: and the goat shall bear upon him all their iniquities unto a solitary land: and he shall let go the goat in the wilderness. And Aaron shall come into the tent of meeting, and shall put off the linen garments, which he put on when he went into the holy place, and shall leave them there: and he shall bathe his flesh in water in a holy place, and put on his garments, and come forth, and offer his burnt offering and the burnt offering of the people, and make atonement for himself and for the people And the fat of the sin offering shall he burn upon the altar. And he that letteth go the goat for Azazel shall wash his clothes, and bathe his flesh in water, and afterward he shall come into the camp. And the bullock of the sin offering, and the goat of the sin offering, whose blood was brought in to make atonement in the holy place, shall be carried forth without the camp; and they shall burn in the fire their skins, and their flesh, and their dung. And he that burneth them shall wash his clothes, and bathe his flesh in water, and afterward he shall come into the camp."

And now followed the second stage of the ceremonial, a rite of the most singular and impressive character. The live goat, during the former part of the ceremony, had been left standing before Jehovah, where he had been placed after the casting of the lot (ver. 10.) The rendering of King James' version, that the goat was so placed, "to make an atonement *with* him," assumes a meaning to the Hebrew preposition here which it never has. Usage demands either that which is given in the text or the margin of the Revised Version, to make atonement "*for* him" or "*over* him." But to the former the objection seems insuperable that there is nothing in the whole rite suggesting an atonement as made for this living goat; while, on the other hand, if the rendering "over" be adopted from the margin, it may not unnaturally be understood of the performance *over* this goat of that part of the atonement ceremonial described as follows:—

Vv. 20-22: "When he hath made an end of atoning for the holy place, and the tent of meeting, and the altar, he shall present the live goat . . . and confess over him all the iniquities of the children of Israel, and all their transgressions, even all their sins; and he shall put them upon the head of the goat, and shall send him away by the hand of a man that is in readiness into the wilderness: and the goat shall bear upon him all their iniquities unto a solitary land: and he shall let go the goat in the wilderness." And with this ceremony the atonement was completed. Aaron now laid aside the robes which he had put on for this service, bathed again, and put on again his richly coloured garments of office, came forth and offered the burnt-offering for himself and for the people, and burnt the fat of the sin-offering as usual on the altar (vv. 23-25), while its flesh was burned, according to the law for such sacrifices, without the camp (ver. 27).

What was the precise significance of this part of the service, is one of the most difficult questions which arises in the exposition of this book; the answer to which chiefly turns upon the meaning which is attached to the expression, "for Azazel" (O.V., "for a scapegoat"). What is the meaning of "Azazel"?

There are three fundamental facts which stand before us in this chapter, which must find their place in any explanation which may be adopted. 1. Both of the goats are declared to be "a sin-offering;" the live goat, no less than the other. 2. In consistency with this, the live goat, no less than the other, was consecrated to Jehovah, in that he was "set alive before the Lord." 3. The function expressly ascribed to him in the law is the complete removal of the transgressions of Israel, symbolically transferred to him as a burden, by the laying on of hands with confession of sin. Passing by, then, several interpretations, which seem intrinsically irreconcilable with one or other of these facts, or are, for other reasons, to be rejected, the case seems to be practically narrowed down to this alternative. Either Azazel is to be regarded as the name of an evil spirit, conceived of as dwelling in the wilderness, or else it is to be taken as an abstract noun, as in the margin (R.V.), signifying "removal," "dismissal." That the word may have this meaning is very commonly admitted even by those who deny that meaning here; and if, with Bähr* and others, we adopt it in this passage, all that follows is quite clear. The goat "for removal" bears away all the iniquities of Israel, which are symbolically laid upon him, into a solitary land; that is, they are taken wholly away from the presence of God and from the camp of His people. Thus, as the killing and sprinkling of the blood of the first goat visibly set forth the *means* of reconciliation with God, through the substituted offering of an innocent victim, so the sending away of the second goat, laden with those sins, the expiation of which had been signified by the sacrifice of the first, no less vividly set forth the *effect* of that sacrifice, in the complete removal of those expiated sins from the holy presence of Jehovah. That this effect of atonement should have been adequately represented by the first slain victim was impossible; hence the necessity for the second goat, ideally identified with the other, as jointly constituting with it one sin-offering, whose special use it should be to represent the blessed effect of atonement. The truth symbolised, as the goat thus bore away the sins of Israel, is expressed in those glad words (Psalm ciii. 12), "As far as the east is from the west, so far hath He removed our transgressions from us;" or, under another image, by Micah (vii. 19), "Thou wilt cast all their sins into the depth of the sea."

So far all seems quite clear, and this explanation, no doubt, will always be accepted by many.

And yet there remains one serious objection to this interpretation; namely, that the meaning we thus give this word "Azazel" is not what we would expect from the phrase which is used regarding the casting of the lots (ver. 8): "One lot for the Lord, and the other lot for Azazel." These words do most naturally suggest that Azazel is the name of a person, who is here contrasted with Jehovah; and hence it is believed by a large number of the best expositors that the term must be taken here as the name of an evil spirit, represented as dwelling in the wilderness, to whom this goat, thus laden with Israel's sins, is sent. In addition to this phraseology, it is urged, in support of this interpretation, that even the Scripture lends apparent sanction to the Jewish belief that demons are, in some special sense, the inhabitants of waste and desolate places; and, in particular, that Jewish demonology does in fact recognise a demon named Azazel, also called Sammael. It is admitted, indeed, that the name Azazel does not occur in the Scripture as the name of Satan or of any evil spirit; and, moreover, that there is no evidence that the Jewish belief concerning the existence of a demon called Azazel dates nearly so far back as Mosaic days; and, again, that even the rabbis themselves are not agreed on this interpretation here, many of them rejecting it, even on traditional grounds. Still the interpretation has secured the support of the majority of the best modern expositors, and must claim respectful consideration.

But if Azazel indeed denotes an evil spirit to whom the second goat of the sin-offering is thus sent, laden with the iniquities of Israel, the ques-

* "Symbolik des Mosäischen Cultus," 2 Band., p. 668.

tion then arises: How then, on this supposition, is the ceremony to be interpreted?

The notion of some, that we have in this rite a relic of the ancient demon-worship, is utterly inadmissible. For this goat is expressly said (ver. 5) to have been, equally with the goat that was slain, "a sin-offering," and (vv. 10, 20) it is placed "before the Lord," as an offering to Him; nor is there a hint, here or elsewhere, that this goat was sacrificed in the wilderness to this Azazel; while, moreover, in this very priest-code (xvii. 7-9, R.V.) this special form of idolatry is forbidden, under the heaviest penalty.

That the goat sent to Azazel personified, by way of warning and in a typical manner, Israel, as rejecting the great Sin-offering, and thus laden with iniquity, and therefore delivered over to Satan, is an idea equally untenable. For the goat, as we have seen, is regarded as ideally one with the goat which is slain; they jointly constitute one sin-offering. If, therefore, the slain goat represented in type Christ as the Lamb of God, our Sin-offering, so also must this goat represent Him as our Sin-offering. Further, the ceremonial which is performed over him is explicitly termed an "atonement;" that is, it was an essential part of a ritual designed to symbolise, not the condemnation of Israel for sin, but their complete deliverance from the guilt of their sins.

Not to speak of other explanations, more or less untenable, which have each found their advocates, the only one which, upon this understanding of the meaning of Azazel, the context and the analogy of the Scripture will both admit, appears to be the following. Holy Scripture teaches that Satan has power over man, only because of man's sin. Because of his sin, man is judicially left by God in Satan's power (1 John v. 19, R.V.). When as "the prince of this world" he came to the sinless Man, Jesus Christ, he had nothing in Him, because He was the Holy One of God; while, on the other hand, he is represented (Heb. ii. 14) as having over men under sin "the authority of death." In full accord with this conception, he is represented, both in the Old and the New Testament, as the accuser of God's people. He is said to have accused Job before God (Job i. 9-11; ii. 4, 5). When Zechariah (iii. 1) saw Joshua the high-priest standing before the angel of Jehovah, he saw Satan also standing at his right hand to be his "adversary." So, again, in the Apocalypse (xii. 10) he is called " the Accuser of our brethren, which accuseth them before our God day and night," and who is only overcome by means of "the blood of the Lamb."

To this Evil One, then, the Accuser and Adversary of God's people in all ages—if we assume the interpretation before us—the live goat was symbolically sent, bearing on him the sins of Israel. But does he bear their sins as forgiven, or as unforgiven? Surely, as forgiven; for the sins which he symbolically carries are those very sins of the bygone year for which expiating blood had just been offered and accepted in the Holy of Holies. Moreover, he is sent as being ideally one with the goat that was slain. As sent to Azazel, he therefore symbolically announces to the Evil One that with the expiation of sin by sacrificial blood the foundation of his power over forgiven Israel is gone. His accusations are now no longer in place; for the whole question of Israel's sin has been met and settled in the atoning blood. Thus, as the acceptance of the blood of the one goat offered in the Holiest symbolised the complete propitiation of the offended holiness of God and His pardon of Israel's sin, so the sending of the goat to Azazel symbolised the *effect* of this expiation, in the complete removal of all the penal effects of sin, through deliverance by atonement from the power of the Adversary as the executioner of God's wrath.

Which of these two interpretations shall be accepted must be left to the reader: that neither is without difficulty, those who have most studied this very obscure question will most readily admit; that either is at least consistent with the context and with other teachings of Scripture, should be sufficiently evident. In either case, the symbolic intention of the first part of the ritual, with the first goat, was to symbolise the *means* of reconciliation with God; namely, through the offering unto God of the life of an innocent victim, substituted in the sinner's place: in either case alike, the purpose of the second part of the ceremonial, with the second goat, was to symbolise the blessed *effect* of this expiation; either, if the reading of the margin be taken, in the complete removal of the expiated sin from the presence of the Holy God, or, if Azazel be taken as a proper name, in the complete deliverance of the sinner, through expiatory blood presented in the Holiest, from the power of Satan. If in the former case, we think of the words already cited, " As far as the east is from the west, so far hath He removed our transgressions from us;" in the latter the words from the Apocalypse (xii. 10, 11) come to mind, " The Accuser of our brethren is cast down, which accuseth them before our God day and night. And they overcame him because of the blood of the Lamb."

On other particulars in the ceremonial of the day we need not dwell, as they have received their exposition in earlier chapters of the law of the offerings. Of the burnt-offerings, indeed, which followed the dismissal of the living goat of the sin-offering, little is said; it is, emphatically, the sin-offering, upon which, above all else, it was designed to centre the attention of Israel on this occasion.

And so, with an injunction to the perpetual observance of this day, this remarkable chapter closes. In it the sacrificial law of Moses attains its supreme expression; the holiness and the grace alike of Israel's God, their fullest revelation. For the like of the great day of atonement, we look in vain in any other people. If every sacrifice pointed to Christ, this most luminously of all. What the fifty-third of Isaiah is to his Messianic prophecies, that, we may truly say, is the sixteenth of Leviticus to the whole system of Mosaic types,—the most consummate flower of the Messianic symbolism. All the sin-offerings pointed to Christ, the great High Priest and Victim of the future; but this, as we shall now see, with a distinctness found in no other.

As the unique sin-offering of this day could only be offered by the one high-priest, so was it intimated that the High Priest of the future, who should indeed make an end of sin, should be one and only. As once only in the whole year, a complete cycle of time, this great atonement was offered, so did it point toward a sacrifice which should indeed be "once for all" (Heb. ix. 26; x. 10); not only for the lesser æon of the year, but for the æon of æons which is the lifetime of humanity. In that the high-priest, who was on all other occasions conspicuous among his sons by his bright garments made for glory and for beauty, on this occasion laid them aside, and assumed the same garb as his sons for whom he was to make atonement; herein was shadowed forth the truth that it behoved the great High Priest of the future to be "in all things made like unto His brethren" (Heb. ii. 17). When, having offered the sin-offering, Aaron disappeared from the sight of Israel within the veil, where in the presence of the unseen glory he offered the incense and sprinkled the blood, it was presignified how "Christ having come a High Priest of the good things to come, through the greater and more perfect tabernacle, not made with hands, . . . nor yet through the blood of goats and calves, but through His own blood, entered in once for all into the holy place," even "into heaven itself, now to appear before the face of God for us" (Heb. ix. 11, 12, 24). And, in like manner in that when the sin-offering had been offered, the blood sprinkled, and his work within the veil was ended, arrayed again in his glorious garments, he reappeared to bless the waiting congregation; it was again foreshown how yet that must be fulfilled which is written, that this same Christ, "having been once offered to bear the sins of many, shall appear a second time, apart from sin, to them that wait for Him, unto salvation" (Heb. ix. 28).

To all this yet more might be added of dispensational truth typified by the ceremonial of this day, which we defer to the exposition of chap. xxv., where its consideration more properly belongs. But even were this all, what a marvellous revelation here of the Lord Jesus Christ! The fact of these correspondences between the Levitical ritual and the New Testament facts, let it be observed, is wholly independent of the questions as to the date and origin of this law; and every theory on this subject must find a place for these correspondences and account for them. But how can any one believe that all these are merely accidental coincidences of a post-exilian forgery with the facts of the incarnation, and the high-priestly work of Christ in death and resurrection as set forth in the Gospels? How can they all be adequately accounted for except by assuming that to be true which is expressly taught in the New Testament concerning this very ritual: that in it the Holy Ghost presignified things that were to come; that, therefore, the ordinance must have been, not of man, but of God; not a mere product of the human mind, acting under the laws of a religious evolution, but a revelation from Him unto whom "known are all His works from the foundation of the world"?

Nor must we fail to take in the blessed truth so vividly symbolised in the second part of the ceremonial. When the blood of the sin-offering had been sprinkled in the Holiest, the sins of Israel were then, by the other goat of the sin-offering, borne far away. Israel stood there still a sinful people; but their sin, now expiated by the blood, was before God as if it were not. So does the Holy Victim in the Antitype, who first by His death expiated sin, then as the Living One bear away all the believer's sins from the presence of the Holy One into a land of forgetfulness. And so it is that, as regards acceptance with God, the believing sinner, though still a sinner, stands as if he were sinless; all through the great Sin-offering. To see this, to believe in it, and rest in it, is life eternal; it is joy, and peace, and rest! IT IS THE GOSPEL!

PART II.

THE LAW OF THE DAILY LIFE.

LEVITICUS xi.-xv., xvii.-xxv.

SECTION 1. The Law Concerning the Clean and the Unclean: xi.-xv.
SECTION 2. The Law of Holiness: xvii-xxii.
SECTION 3. The Law Concerning Sacred Times (with Episode, xxiv.): xxiii.-xxv.

CHAPTER XIV.

CLEAN AND UNCLEAN ANIMALS, AND DEFILEMENT BY DEAD BODIES.

LEVITICUS xi. 1-47.

WITH chap. xi. begins a new section of this book, extending to the end of chap. xv., of which the subject is the law concerning various bodily defilements, and the rites appointed for their removal.

The law is given under four heads, as follows:
I. Clean and Unclean Animals, and Defilement by Dead Bodies: chap. xi.
II. The Uncleanness of Child-birth: chap. xii.
III. The Uncleanness of Leprosy: chaps. xiii., xiv.
IV. The Uncleanness of Issues: chap. xv.

From the modern point of view this whole subject appears to many, with no little reason, to be encompassed with peculiar difficulties. We have become accustomed to think of religion as a thing so exclusively of the spirit, and so completely independent of bodily conditions, provided that these be not in their essential nature sinful, that it is a great stumbling-block to many that God should be represented as having given to Israel an elaborate code of laws concerning such subjects as are treated in these five chapters of Leviticus: a legislation which, to not a few, seems puerile and unspiritual, if not worse. And yet, for the reverent believer in Christ, who remembers that our blessed Lord did repeatedly refer to this book of Leviticus as, without any exception or qualification, the Word of His Father, it should not be hard, in view of this fact, to infer that the difficulties which most of us have felt are presumably due to our very imperfect knowledge of the subject. Remembering this, we shall be able to approach this part of the law of Moses, and, in particular, this chapter, with the spirit, not of critics, but of learners, who know as yet but little of the mysteries of God's dealings with Israel or with the human race.

Chap. xi. may be divided into two sections, together with a concluding appeal and summary (vv. 41-47). The first section treats of the law of the clean and the unclean in relation to eating (vv. 1-23). Under this head, the animals which are permitted or forbidden are classified, after a fashion not scientific, but purely empirical and practical, into (1) the beasts which are upon the earth (vv. 2-8); (2) things that are in the waters

(vv. 9-12); (3) flying things,—comprising, first, birds and flying animals like the bat (vv. 13-19); and, secondly, insects, "winged creeping things that go upon all four" (vv. 20-23).

The second section treats of defilement by contact with the dead bodies of these, whether unclean (vv. 24-38), or clean (vv. 39, 40).

Of the living things among the beasts that are upon the earth (vv. 2-8), those are permitted for food which both chew the cud and divide the hoof; every animal in which either of these marks is wanting is forbidden. Of the things which live in the waters, those only are allowed for food which have both fins and scales; those which lack either of these marks, such as, for example, eels, oysters, and all the mollusca and crustacea, are forbidden (vv. 9-12). Of flying things (vv. 13-19) which may be eaten, no special mark is given; though it is to be noted that nearly all of those which are by name forbidden are birds of prey, or birds reputed to be unclean in their habits. All insects, "winged creeping things that go upon all four" (ver. 20), or "whatsoever hath many feet," or "goeth upon the belly," as worms, snakes, etc., are prohibited (ver. 42). Of insects, a single class, described as those "which have legs above their feet, to leap withal upon the earth," is excepted (vv. 21, 22): these are known to us as the order *Saltatoria*, including, as typical examples, the cricket, the grasshopper, and the migratory locust; all of which, it may be noted, are clean feeders, living upon vegetable products only. It is worthy of notice that the law of the clean and the unclean in food is not extended, as it was in Egypt, to the vegetable kingdom.

The second section of the chapter (vv. 24-40) comprises a number of laws relating chiefly to defilement by contact with the dead bodies of animals. In these regulations, it is to be observed that the dead body, even of a clean animal, except when killed in accordance with the law, so that its blood is all drained out (xvii. 10-16), is regarded as defiling him who touches it; while, on the other hand, even an unclean animal is not held capable of imparting defilement by mere contact, so long as it is living. Very minute charges are given (vv. 29-38) concerning eight species of unclean animals, of which six (vv. 29, 30, R. V.) appear to be different varieties of the lizard family. Regarding these, it is ordered that not only shall the person be held unclean who touches the dead body of one of them (ver. 31), but also anything becomes unclean on which such a dead body may fall, whether household utensil, or food, or drink (vv. 32-35). The exception only is made (vv. 36-38), that fountains, or wells of water, or dry seed for sowing, shall not be held to be by such defiled.

That which has been made unclean must be put into water, and be unclean until the even (ver. 32); with the exception that nothing which is made of earthenware, whether a vessel, or an oven, or a range, could be thus cleansed; for the obvious reason that the water could not adequately reach the interior of its porous material. It must therefore be broken in pieces (vv. 33, 34). If a person be defiled by any of these, he remained unclean until the even (ver. 31). No washing is prescribed, but, from analogy, is probably to be taken for granted.

Such is a brief summary of the law of the clean and the unclean as contained in this chapter. To preclude adding needless difficulty to a difficult subject, the remark made above should be specially noted,—that so far as general marks are given by which the clean is to be distinguished from the unclean, these marks are evidently selected simply from a practical point of view, as of easy recognition by the common people, for whom a more exact and scientific mode of distinction would have been useless. We are not therefore for a moment to think of cleanness or uncleanness as causally determined, for instance, by the presence or absence of fins or scales, or by the habit of chewing the cud, and the dividing of the hoof, or the absence of these marks, as if they were themselves the ground of the cleanness or uncleanness, in any instance. For such a fancy as this, which has diverted some interpreters from the right line of investigation of the subject, there is no warrant whatever in the words of the law, either here or elsewhere.

Than this law concerning things clean and unclean nothing will seem to many, at first, more alien to modern thought, or more inconsistent with any intelligent view of the world and of man's relation to the things by which he is surrounded. And, especially, that the strict observance of this law should be connected with religion, and that, upon what professes to be the authority of God, it should be urged on Israel on the ground of their call to be a holy people to a holy God,—this, to the great majority of Bible readers, certainly appears, to say the least, most extraordinary and unaccountable. And yet the law is here, and its observance is enforced by this very consideration; for we read (vv. 43, 44): "Ye shall not make yourselves abominable with any creeping thing that creepeth, neither shall ye make yourselves unclean with them, that ye should be defiled thereby. For I am the Lord your God: sanctify yourselves therefore, and be ye holy; for I am holy." And, in any case, explain the matter as we may, many will ask, How, since the New Testament formally declares this law concerning clean and unclean beasts to be no longer binding (Col. ii. 16, 20-23), is it possible to imagine that there should now remain anything in this most perplexing law which should be of spiritual profit still to a New Testament believer? To the consideration of these questions, which so naturally arise, we now address ourselves.

First of all, in approaching this subject it is well to recall to mind the undeniable fact, that a distinction in foods as clean and unclean, that is, fit and unfit for man's use, has a very deep and apparently irremovable foundation in man's nature. Even we ourselves, who stumble at this law, recognise a distinction of this kind, and regulate our diet accordingly; and also, in like manner, feel, more or less, an instinctive repugnance to dead bodies. As regards diet, it is true that when the secondary question arises as to what particular animals shall be reckoned clean or unclean, fit or unfit for food, nations and tribes differ among themselves, as also from the law of Moses, in a greater or less degree; nevertheless, this does not alter the fact that such a distinction is recognised among all nations of culture; and that, on the other hand, in those who recognise it not, and who eat, as some do, without discrimination, whatever chances to come to hand,—insects, reptiles, carrion, and so on,—this revolting indifference in the matter of food is always associated with gross intellectual and moral degradation. Certainly these indisputable facts should suffice to dispose of the charge of puerility, as sometimes made against the laws of this chapter.

And not only this, but more is true. For while even among nations of the highest culture and Christian enlightenment many animals are eaten, as, *e. g.*, the oyster, the turtle, the flesh of the horse and the hog, which the law of Moses prohibits; on the other hand, it remains true that, with the sole exception of creatures of the locust tribe, the animals which are allowed for food by the Mosaic code are reckoned suitable for food by almost the entire human family. A notable exception to the fact is indeed furnished in the case of the Hindoos, and also the Buddhists (who follow an Indian religion), who, as a rule, reject all animal food, and especially, in the case of the former, the flesh of the cow, as not to be eaten. But this exception is quite explicable by considerations into which we cannot here enter at length, but which do not affect the significance of the general fact.

And, again, on the other hand, it may also be said that, as a general rule, the appetite of the great majority of enlightened and cultivated nations revolts against using as food the greater part of the animals which this code prohibits. Birds of prey, for instance, and the carnivora generally, animals having paws, and reptiles, for the most part, by a kind of universal instinct among cultivated peoples, are judged unfit for human food.

The bearing of these facts upon our exposition is plain. They certainly suggest, at least, that this law of Lev. xi. may, after all, very possibly have a deep foundation both in the nature of man and that of the things permitted or forbidden; and they also raise the question as to how far exceptions and divergencies from this law, among peoples of culture, may possibly be due to a diversity in external physical and climatic conditions, because of which that which may be wholesome and suitable food in one place—the wilderness of Sinai, or Palestine, for instance—may not be wholesome and suitable in other lands, under different physical conditions. We do not yet enter into this question, but barely call attention to it, as adapted to check the hasty judgment of many, that such a law as this is necessarily puerile and unworthy of God.

But while it is of no small consequence to note this agreement in the fundamental ideas of this law with widely extended instincts and habits of mankind, on the other hand, it is also of importance to emphasise the contrast which it exhibits with similar codes of law among other peoples. For while, as has just been remarked, there are many most suggestive points of agreement between the Mosaic distinctions of clean and unclean and those of other nations, on the other hand, remarkable contrasts appear, even in the case of those people with whom, like the Egyptians, the Hebrews had been most intimately associated. In the Egyptian system of dietary law, for instance, the distinction of clean and unclean in food was made to apply, not only in the animal, but also in the vegetable world; and, again, while all fishes having fins and scales are permitted as food in the Mosaic law, no fishes whatever are permitted by the Egyptian code. But more significant than such difference in details is the difference in the religious conception upon which such distinctions are based. In Egypt, for example, animals were reckoned clean or unclean according as they were supposed to have more predominant the character of the good Osiris or of the evil Typhon. Among the ancient Persians, those were reckoned clean which were supposed to be the creation of Ormazd, the good Spirit, and those unclean whose origin was attributed to Ahriman, the evil Spirit. In India, the prohibition of flesh as food rests on pantheistic assumptions. Not to multiply examples, it is easy to see that, without anticipating anything here with regard to the principle which determined the Hebrew distinctions, it is certain that of such dualistic or pantheistic principles as are manifested in these and other instances which might be named, there is not a trace in the Mosaic law. How significant and profoundly instructive is the contrast here, will only fully appear when we see what in fact appears to have been the determining principle in the Mosaic legislation.

But when we now seek to ascertain upon what principle certain animals were permitted and others forbidden as food, it must be confessed that we have before us a very difficult question, and one to which, accordingly, very diverse answers have been given. In general, indeed, we are expressly told that the object of this legislation, as of all else in this book of laws, was moral and spiritual. Thus, we are told in so many words (vv. 43-45) that Israel was to abstain from eating or touching the unclean, on the ground that they were to be holy, because the Lord their God was holy. But to most this only increases the difficulty. What possible connection could there be between eating, or abstinence from eating, animals which do not chew the cud, or fishes which have not scales, and holiness of life?

In answer to this question, some have supposed a mystical connection between the soul and the body, such that the former is defiled by the food which is received and assimilated by the latter. In support of this theory, appeal has been made to ver. 44 of this chapter, which, in the Septuagint translation, is rendered literally: "Ye shall not defile your souls." But, as often in Hebrew, the original expression here is simply equivalent to our compound pronoun "yourselves," and is therefore so translated both in the Authorised and the Revised Versions. As for any other proof of such a mystical evil influence of the various kinds of food prohibited in this chapter, there is simply none at all.

Others, again, have sought the explication of these facts in the undoubted Divine purpose of keeping Israel separate from other nations; to secure which separation this special dietetic code, with other laws regarding the clean and the unclean, was given them. That these laws have practically helped to keep the children of Israel separate from other nations, will not be denied; and we may therefore readily admit, that inasmuch as the food of the Hebrews has differed from that of the nations among whom they have dwelt, this separation of the nation may therefore have been included in the purpose of God in these regulations. However, it is to be observed that in the law itself the separation of Israel from other nations is represented, not as the end to be attained by the observance of these food laws, but instead, as a fact already existing, which is given as a reason why they should keep these laws (xx. 24, 25). Moreover, it will be found impossible, by reference to this principle alone, to account for the details of the laws before us. For the question is not merely why there should have been food laws, but also why these laws should have been such as they are? The latter question is not adequately explained by reference to God's purpose of keeping Israel separate from the nations.

Some, again, have held that the explanation of these laws was to be found simply in the design of God, by these restrictions, to give Israel a profitable moral discipline in self-restraint and control of the bodily appetites; or to impose, in this way, certain conditions and limitations upon their approach to Him, which should have the effect of deepening in them the sense of awe and reverence for the Divine majesty of God, as their King. Of this theory it may be said, as of the last-named, that there can be no doubt that in fact these laws did tend to secure these ends; but that yet, on the other hand, the explanation is still inadequate, inasmuch as it only would show why restrictions of some kind should have been ordered, and not, in the least, why the restrictions should have been such, in detail, as we have here.

Quite different from any of these attempted explanations is that of many who have sought to explain the law allegorically. We are told by such that Israel was forbidden the flesh of certain animals, because they were regarded as typifying by their character certain sins and vices, as, on the other hand, those which were permitted as food were regarded as typifying certain moral virtues. Hence, it is supposed by such that the law tended to the holiness of Israel, in that it was, so to speak, a continual object-lesson, a perpetually acted allegory, which should continually remind them of the duty of abstaining from the typified sins and of practising the typified virtues. But, assuredly, this theory cannot be carried out. Animals are in this law prohibited as food whose symbolic meaning elsewhere in Scripture is not always bad, but sometimes good. The lion, for example, as having paws, is prohibited as food; and yet it is the symbol of our blessed Lord, "the Lion of the tribe of Judah." Nor is there the slightest evidence that the Hebrews ever attached any such allegorical significance to the various prescriptions of this chapter as the theory would require. Other expositors allegorise in a different but no more satisfactory manner. Thus a popular, and, it must be added, most spiritual and devout expositor, sets forth the spiritual meaning of the required conjunction of the two marks in clean animals of the chewing of the cud and the dividing of the hoof in this wise: "The two things were inseparable in the case of every clean animal. And as to the spiritual application, it is of the very last importance in a practical point of view... A man may profess to love and feed upon, to study and ruminate over, the Word of God—the pasture of the soul; but if his footprints along the pathway of life are not such as the Word requires, he is not clean."

But it should be evident that such allegorising interpretation as this can carry with it no authority, and sets the door wide open to the most extravagant fancy in the exposition of Scripture.

Others, again, find the only principle which has determined the laws concerning defilement by the dead, and the clean and unclean meats, to be the presence in that which was reckoned unclean, of something which is naturally repulsive to men; whether in odour, or in the food of a creature, or its other habits of life. But while it is true that such marks distinguish many of the creatures reckoned unclean, they are wanting in others, and are also found in a few animals which are nevertheless permitted. If this had been the determining principle, surely, for example, the law which permitted for food the he-goat and forbade the horse, would have been exactly the opposite; while, as regards fishes and insects permitted and forbidden, it is hard to see any evidence whatever of the influence of this principle.

Much more plausible, at first sight, and indeed much more nearly approaching the truth, than any of the theories above criticised, is one which has been elaborated with no little learning and ingenuity by Sommer,* according to which the laws concerning the clean and the unclean, whether in regard to food or anything else, are all grounded in the antithesis of death and life. Death, everywhere in Holy Scripture, is set in the closest ethical and symbolical connection with sin. Bodily death is the wages of sin; and inasmuch as it is the outward physical expression and result of the inner fact that sin, in its very nature, is spiritual death, therefore the dead is always held to be unclean; and the various laws enforcing this thought are all intended to keep before the mind the fact that death is the visible representation and evidence of the presence of sin, and the consequent curse of God. Hence, also, it will follow that the selection of foods must be governed by a reference to this principle. The carnivora, on this principle, must be forbidden,—as they are,—because they live by taking the life of other animals; hence, also, is explained the exclusion of the multitudinous varieties of the insect world, as feeding on that which is dead and corrupt. On the other hand, the animals which chew the cud and divide the hoof are counted clean; inasmuch as the sheep and the cattle, the chief representatives of this class, were by every one recognised as at the furthest possible remove from any such connection with death and corruption in their mode of life; and hence the familiar marks which distinguish them, as a matter merely of practical convenience, were taken as those which must distinguish every animal lawful for food.

But while this view has been elaborated with great ability and skill, it yet fails to account for all the facts. It is quite overlooked that if the reason of the prohibition of carnivorous birds and quadrupeds is to be found in the fact that they live by the destruction of life, the same reason should have led to the prohibition of all fishes without exception, as in Egypt; inasmuch as those which have fins and scales, no less than others, live by preying on other living creatures. On the other hand, by the same principle, all insects which derive their sustenance from the vegetable world should have been permitted as food, instead of one order only of these.

Where so much learning and profound thought has been expended in vain, one might well hesitate to venture anything in exposition of so difficult a subject, and rest content, as some have, with declaring that the whole subject is utterly inexplicable. And yet the world advances in knowledge, and we are therefore able to approach the subject with some advantage in this respect over earlier generations. And in the

* "Biblische Abhandlungen," pp. 239-270.

light of the most recent investigations, we believe it highly probable that the chief principle determining the laws of this chapter will be found in the region of hygiene and sanitation, as relating, in this instance, to diet, and to the treatment of that which is dead. And this in view of the following considerations.

It is of much significance to note, in the first place, that a large part of the animals which are forbidden as food are unclean feeders. It is a well-ascertained fact that even the cleanest animal, if its food be unclean, becomes dangerous to health if its flesh be eaten. The flesh of a cow which has drunk water contaminated with typhoid germs, if eaten, especially if insufficiently cooked, may communicate typhoid fever to him who eats it. It is true, indeed, that not all animals that are prohibited are unclean in their food; but the fact remains that, on the other hand, among those which are allowed is to be found no animal whose ordinary habits of life, especially in respect of food, are unclean.

But, in the second place, an animal which is not unclean in its habits may yet be dangerous for food, if it be, for any reason, specially liable to disease. One of the greatest discoveries of modern science is the fact that a large number of diseases to which animals are liable are due to the presence of low forms of parasitic life. To such diseases those which are unclean in their feeding will be especially exposed, while none will perhaps be found wholly exempt.

Another discovery of recent times which has a no less important bearing on the question raised by this chapter is the now ascertained fact that many of these parasitic diseases are common to both animals and men, and may be communicated from the former to the latter. All are familiar with the fact that the small-pox, in a modified and mild form, is a disease of cattle as well as of men, and we avail ourselves of this fact in the practice of vaccination. Scarcely less familiar is the communication of the parasitic trichinæ, which often infest the flesh of swine, to those who eat such meat. And research is constantly extending the number of such diseases. Turkeys, we are now told, have the diphtheria, and may communicate it to men; men also sometimes take from horses the loathsome disease known as the glanders. Now in the light of such facts as these, it is plain that an ideal dietary law would, as far as possible, exclude from human food all animals which, under given conditions, might be especially liable to these parasitic diseases, and which, if their flesh should be eaten, might thus become a frequent medium of communicating them to men.

Now it is a most remarkable and significant fact that the tendency of the most recent investigations of this subject has been to show that the prohibitions and permissions of the Mosaic law concerning food, as we have them in this chapter, become apparently explicable in view of the above facts. Not to refer to other authorities, among the latest competent testimonies on this subject is that of Dr. Noel Gueneau de Mussy, in a paper presented to the Paris Academy of Medicine in 1885, in which he is quoted as saying: "There is so close a connection between the thinking being and the living organism in man, so intimate a solidarity between moral and material interests, and the useful is so constantly and so necessarily in harmony with the good, that these two elements cannot be separated in hygiene... It is this combination which has exercised so great an influence on the preservation of the Israelites, despite the very unfavourable external circumstances in which they have been placed... The idea of parasitic and infectious maladies, which has conquered so great a position in modern pathology, appears to have greatly occupied the mind of Moses, and to have dominated all his hygienic rules. He excludes from Hebrew dietary *animals particulary liable to parasites;* and as it is in the blood that the germs or spores of infectious disease circulate, he orders that they must be drained of their blood before serving for food."

If this professional testimony, which is accepted and endorsed by Dr. Behrends, of London, in his remarkable paper on "Diseases caught from Butcher's Meat,"* be admitted, it is evident that we need look no further for the explanation of the minute prescriptions of these dietary laws which we find here and elsewhere in the Pentateuch.

And, it may be added, that upon this principle we may also easily explain, in a rational way, the very minute prescriptions of the law with regard to defilement by dead bodies. For immediately upon death begins a process of corruption which produces compounds not only obnoxious to the senses, but actively poisonous in character; and what is of still more consequence to observe, in the case of all parasitic and infectious diseases, the energy of the infection is specially intensified when the infected person or animal dies. Hence the careful regulations as to cleansing of those persons or things which had been thus defiled by the dead; either by water, where practicable; or where the thing could not be thus thoroughly cleansed, then by burning the article with fire, the most certain of all disinfectants.

But if this be indeed the principle which underlies this law of the clean and the unclean as here given, it will then be urged that since the Hebrews have observed this law with strictness for centuries, they ought to show the evidence of this in a marked immunity from sickness, as compared with other nations, and especially from diseases of an infectious character; and a consequent longevity superior to that of the Gentiles who pay no attention to these laws. Now it is the fact, and one which evidently furnishes another powerful argument for this interpretation of these laws, that this is exactly what we see. In this matter we are not left to guessing; the facts are before the world, and are undisputed. Even so long ago as the days when the plague was desolating Europe, the Jews so universally escaped infection that, by this their exemption, the popular suspicion was excited into fury, and they were accused of causing the fearful mortality among their Gentile neighbours by poisoning the wells and springs. In our own day, in the recent cholera epidemic in Italy, a correspondent of the *Jewish Chronicle* testifies that the Jews enjoyed almost absolute immunity, at least from fatal attack.

Professor Hosmer says: "Throughout the entire history of Israel, the wisdom of the ancient lawgivers in these respects has been remarkably shown. In times of pestilence the Jews have suffered far less than others; as regards longevity and general health, they have in every age been noteworthy, and, at the present day, in the life-insurance offices, the life of a Jew is said

* In *The Nineteenth Century*, September, 1889.

to be worth much more than that of men of other stock."

Of the facts in the modern world which sustain these statements, Dr. Behrends gives abundant illustration in the article referred to, such as the following: "In Prussia, the mean duration of Jewish life averages five years more than that of the general population. In Furth, the average duration of Jewish life is 37, and of Christians 26 years. In Hungary, an exhaustive study of the facts shows that the average duration of life with the Croats is 20.2, of the Germans 26.7, but of the Jews 46.5 years, and that although the latter generally are poor, and live under much more unfavourable sanitary conditions than their Gentile neighbours."

In the light of such well-certified facts, the conclusion seems certainly to be warranted, that at least one chief consideration which, in the Divine wisdom, determined the allowance or prohibition, as the food of Israel, of the animals named in this chapter, has been their fitness or unfitness as diet from a hygienic point of view, especially regarding their greater or less liability to have, and to communicate to man, infectious, parasitic diseases.

From this position, if it be justified, we can now perceive a secondary reference in these laws to the deeper ethical truth which, with much reason, Sommer has so emphasised; namely, the moral significance of the great antithesis of death to life; the former being ever contrasted in Holy Scripture with the latter, as the visible manifestation of the presence of sin in the world, and of the consequent curse of God. For whatever tends to weakness or disease, by that fact tends to death,—to that death which, according to the Scriptures, is, for man, the penal consequence of sin. But Israel was called to be a people redeemed from the power of death to life, a life of full consecration to God. Hence, because redeemed from death, it was evidently fitting that the Israelite should, so far as possible in the flesh, keep apart from death, and all that in its nature tended, or might specially tend, to disease and death.

It is very strange that it should have been objected to this view, that since the law declares the reason for these regulations to have been religious, therefore any supposed reference herein to the principles of hygiene is by that fact excluded. For surely the obligation so to live as to conserve and promote the highest bodily health must be regarded, both from a natural, and a Biblical and Christian point of view, as being no less really a religious obligation than truthfulness or honesty. If there appear sufficient reason for believing that the details of these laws are to be explained by reference to hygienic considerations, surely this, so far from contradicting the reason which is given for their observance, helps us rather the more clearly to see how, just because Israel was called to be the holy people of a holy God, they must needs keep this law. For the central idea of the Levitical holiness was consecration unto God, as the Creator and Redeemer of Israel,—consecration in the most unreserved, fullest possible sense, for the most perfect possible service. But the obligation to such a consecration, as the essence of a holy character, surely carried with it by necessary consequence, then, as now, the obligation to maintain all the powers of mind and body also in the highest possible perfection.

That, as regards the body, and, in no small degree, the mind as well, this involves the duty of the preservation of health so far as in our power; and that this, again, is conditioned by the use of a proper diet, as one factor of prime importance, will be denied by no one. If, then, sufficient reason can be shown for recognising the determining influence of hygienic considerations in the laws of this chapter concerning the clean and the unclean, this fact will only be in the fullest harmony with all that is said in this connection, and elsewhere in the law, as to the relation of their observance to Israel's holiness as a consecrated nation.

It may very possibly be asked, by way of further objection to this interpretation of these laws: Upon this understanding of the immediate purpose of these laws, how can we account for the selection of such test marks of the clean and the unclean as the chewing of the cud, and the dividing of the hoof, or having scales and fins? What can the presence or absence of these peculiarities have to do with the greater or less freedom from parasitic disease of the animals included or excluded in the several classes? To which question the answer may fairly be given, that the object of the law was not to give accurately distributed categories of animals, scientifically arranged, according to hygienic principles, but was purely practical; namely, to secure, so far as possible, the observance by the whole people of such a dietary as in the land of Palestine would, on the whole, best tend to secure perfect bodily health. It is not affirmed that every individual animal which by these tests may be excluded from permitted food is therefore to be held specially liable to disease; but only that the limitation of the diet by these test marks, as a practical measure, would, *on the whole*, secure the greatest degree of immunity from disease to those who kept the law.

It may be objected, again, by some who have looked into this question, that, according to recent researches, it appears that cattle, which occupy the foremost place in the permitted diet of the Hebrews, are found to be especially liable to tubercular disease, and capable, apparently, under certain conditions, of communicating it to those who feed upon their flesh. And it has been even urged that to this source is due a large part of the consumption which is responsible for so large part of our mortality. To which objection two answers may be given. First, and most important, is the observation that we have as yet no statistics as to the prevalence of disease of this kind among cattle in Palestine and that, presumably, if we may argue from the climatic conditions of its prevalence among men, it would be found far less frequently there among cattle than in Europe and America. Further, it must be remembered that, in the case even of clean cattle, the law very strictly provides elsewhere that the clean animal which is slain for food shall be absolutely free from disease; so that still we see here, no less than elsewhere, the hygienic principles ruling the dietary law.

It will be perhaps objected, again, that if all this be true, then, since abstinence from unwholesome food is a moral duty, the law concerning clean and unclean meats should be of universal and perpetual obligation; whereas, in fact, it is explicitly abrogated in the New Testament, and is not held to be now binding on any one. But the abrogation of the law of Moses touching clean and unclean food can be easily explained, in perfect accord with all that has been said as to its nature and intent. In the first place, it is to be remembered that it is a fundamental characteristic of the New Testament law as contrasted with that of the Old, that on all points it leaves much more to the liberty of the individual, allowing him to act according to the exercise of an enlightened judgment, under the law of supreme love to the Lord, in many matters which, in the Old Testament day, were made a subject of specific regulation. This is true, for instance, regarding all that relates to the public worship of God, and also many things in the government and administration of the Church, not to speak of other examples. This does not indeed mean that it is of no consequence what a man or a Church may do in matters of this kind; but it is intended thus to give the individual and the whole Church a discipline of a higher order than is possible under a system which prescribes a large part of the details of human action. Subjection to these "rudiments" of the law, according to the Apostle, belongs to a condition of religious minority (Gal. iv. 1-3), and passes away when the individual, or the Church, so to speak, attains majority. Precisely so it is in the case of these dietary and other laws, which, indeed, are selected by the Apostle Paul (Col. ii. 20-22) in illustration of this characteristic of the new dispensation. That such matters of detail should no longer be made matter of specific command is only what we should expect according to the analogy of the whole system of Christian law. This is not, indeed, saying that it is of no consequence in a religious point of view what a man eats; whether, for instance, he eat carrion or not, though this, which was forbidden in the Old Testament, is nowhere expressly prohibited in the New. But still, as supplying a training of higher order, the New Testament uniformly refrains from giving detailed commandments in matters of this kind.

But, aside from considerations of this kind, there is a specific reason why these laws of Moses concerning diet and defilement by dead bodies, if hygienic in character, should not have been made, in the New Testament, of universal obligation, however excellent they might be. For it is to be remembered that these laws were delivered for a people few in number, living in a small country, under certain definite climatic conditions. But it is well known that what is unwholesome for food in one part of the world may be, and often is, necessary to the maintenance of health elsewhere. A class of animals which under the climatic conditions of Palestine may be specially liable to certain forms of parasitic disease, under different climatic conditions may be comparatively free from them. Abstinence from fat is commanded in the law of Moses (iii. 17), and great moderation in this matter is necessary to health in hot climates; but, on the contrary, to eat fat largely is necessary to life in the polar regions. From such facts as these it would follow, of necessity, that when the Church of God, as under the new dispensation, was now to become a worldwide organisation, still to have insisted on a dietetic law perfectly adapted only to Palestine would have been to defeat the physical object, and by consequence the moral end for which that law was given. Under these conditions, except a special law were to be given for each land and climate, there was and could be, if we have before us the true conception of the ground of these regulations, no alternative but to abrogate the law.

This exposition has been much prolonged; but not until we have before us a definite conception as to the principle underlying these regulations, and the relation of their observance to the holiness of Israel, are we in a position to see and appreciate the moral and spiritual lessons which they may still have for us. As it is, if the conclusions to which our exposition has conducted be accepted, such lessons lie clearly before us. While we have here a law which, as to the letter, is confessedly abrogated, and which is supposed by the most to be utterly removed from any present-day use for practical instruction, it is now evident that, annulled as to the letter, it is yet, as to the spirit and intention of it, in full force and vital consequence to holiness of life in all ages.

In the first place, this exposition being granted, it follows, as a present-day lesson of great moment, that the holiness which God requires has to do with the body as well as the soul, even with such commonplace matters as our eating and drinking. This is so, because the body is the instrument and organ of the soul, with which it must do all its work on earth for God, and because, as such, the body, no less than the soul, has been redeemed unto God by the blood of His Son. There is, therefore, no religion in neglecting the body, and ignoring the requirements for its health, as ascetics have in all ages imagined. Neither is there religion in pampering, and thus abusing, the body, after the manner of the sensual in all ages. The principle which inspires this chapter is that which is expressed in the New Testament by the words: "Whether therefore ye eat, or drink, or whatsoever ye do, do all to the glory of God" (1 Cor. x. 31). If, therefore, a man needlessly eats such things, or in such a manner, as may be injurious to health, he sins, and has come short of the law of perfect holiness. It is therefore not merely a matter of earthly prudence to observe the laws of health in food and drink and recreation, in a word, in all that has to do with the appetite and desires of the body, but it is essential to holiness. We are in all these things to seek to glorify God, not only in our souls, but also in our bodies.

The momentous importance of this thought will the more clearly appear when we recall to mind that, according to the law of Moses (v. 2), if a man was defiled by any unclean thing, and neglected the cleansing ordered by this law, even though it were through ignorance or forgetfulness, he was held to have incurred guilt before God. For it was therein declared that when a man defiled by contact with the dead, or any unclean thing, should for any reason have omitted the cleansing ordered, his covenant relation with God could only be re-established on his presentation of a sin-offering. By parity of reasoning it follows that the case is the same now; and that God will hold no man guiltless who violates any of those laws which He has established in nature as the conditions of bodily health. He who does this is guilty of a sin which requires the application of the great atonement.

How needful it is even in our day to remind men of all this, could not be better illustrated than by the already mentioned argument of many expositors, that hygienic principles cannot have dominated and determined the details of these laws, because the law declares that they are grounded, not in hygiene, but in religion, and have to do with holiness. As if these two were exclusive, one of the other, and as if it made no difference in respect to holiness of character whether a man took care to have a sound body or not!

No less needful is the lesson of this law to many who are at the opposite extreme. For as there are those who are so taken up with the soul and its health, that they ignore its relation to the body, and the bearing of bodily conditions upon character; so there are others who are so preoccupied with questions of bodily health, sanitation, and hygiene, regarded merely as prudential measures, from an earthly point of view, that they forget that man has a soul as well as a body, and that such questions of sanitation and hygiene only find their proper place when it is recognised that health and perfection of the body are not to be sought merely that man may become a more perfect animal, but in order that thus, with a sound mind in a sound body, he may the more perfectly serve the Lord in the life of holiness to which we are called. Thus it appears that this forgotten law of the clean and the unclean in food, so far from being, at the best, puerile, and for us now certainly quite useless, still teaches us the very important lesson that a due regard to wholeness and health of body is essential to the right and symmetrical development of holiness of character. In every dispensation, the law of God combines the bodily and the spiritual in a sacred synthesis. If in the New Testament we are directed to glorify God in our spirits, we are no less explicitly commanded to glorify God in our bodies (1 Cor. vi. 20). And thus is given to the laws of health the high sanction of the Divine obligation of the moral law, as summed up in the closing words of this chapter: "Be ye holy; for I am holy."

This law concerning things unclean, and clean and unclean animals, as thus expounded, is also an apologetic of no small value. It has a direct and evident bearing on the question of the Divine origin and authority of this part of the law. For the question will at once come up in every reflecting mind: Whence came this law? Could it have been merely an invention of crafty Jewish priests? Or is it possible to account for it as the product merely of the mind of Moses? It appears to have been ordered with respect to certain facts, especially regarding various invisible forms of noxious parasitic life, in their bearing on the causation and propagation of disease,—facts which, even now, are but just appearing within the horizon of modern science. Is it probable that Moses knew about these things three thousand years ago? Certainly, the more we study the matter, the more we must feel that this is not to be supposed.

It is common, indeed, to explain much that seems very wise in the law of Moses by referring to the fact that he was a highly educated man, "instructed in all the wisdom of the Egyptians." But it is just this fact of his Egyptian education that makes it in the last degree improbable that he should have derived the ideas of this law from Egypt. Could he have taken his ideas with regard, for instance, to defilement by the dead, from a system of education which taught the contrary, and which, so far from regarding those who had to do with the dead as unclean, held them especially sacred? And so with regard to the dietetic laws: these are not the laws of Egypt; nor have we any evidence that those were determined, like these Hebrew laws, by such scientific facts as those to which we have referred.* In this day, when, at last, men of all schools, and those with most scientific knowledge, most of all, are joining to extol the exact wisdom of this ancient law, a wisdom which has no parallel in like laws among other nations, is it not in place to press this question? Whence had this man this unique wisdom, three thousand years in advance of his times? There are many who will feel compelled to answer, even as Holy Scripture answers; even as Moses, according to the record, answers. The secret of this wisdom will be found, not in the court of Pharaoh, but in the holy tent of meeting; it is all explained if we but assume that what is written in the first verse of this chapter is true: "The Lord spake unto Moses and unto Aaron."

CHAPTER XV.

OF THE UNCLEANNESS OF ISSUES.

LEVITICUS xv. 1-33.

INASMUCH as the law concerning defilement from issues is presupposed and referred to in that concerning the defilement of child-bearing, in chap. xii., it will be well to consider this before the latter. For this order there is the more reason, because, as will appear, although the two sections are separated, in the present arrangement of the book, by the law concerning defilement by leprosy (xiii., xiv.), they both refer to the same general topic, and are based upon the same moral conceptions.

The arrangement of the law in chap. xv. is very simple. Verses 2-18 deal with the cases of ceremonial defilement by issues in men; vv. 19-30, with analogous cases in women. The principle in both classes is one and the same; the issue, whether normal or abnormal, rendered the person affected unclean; only, when abnormal, the defilement was regarded as more serious than in other cases, not only in a physical, but also in a ceremonial and legal aspect. In all such cases, in addition to the washing with water which was always required, it was commanded that on the eighth day from the time of the cessation of the issue, the person who had been so affected should come before the priest and present for his cleansing a sin-offering and a burnt-offering.

What now is the principle which underlies these regulations?

In seeking the answer to this question, we at once note the suggestive fact that this law concerning issues takes cognisance only of such as are connected with the sexual organisation. All others, however, in themselves, from a merely physical point of view, equally unwholesome or loathsome, are outside the purview of the Mosaic code. They do not render the person affected, according to the law, ceremonially unclean. It is therefore evident that the lawgiver must have had before him something other than merely the physical peculiarities of these defilements, and that, for the true meaning of this part of the law, we must look deeper than the surface. It

* See above, p. 310.

should also be observed here that this characteristic of the law just mentioned, places the law of issues under the same general category with the law (chap. xii.) concerning the uncleanness of child-bearing, as indeed the latter itself intimates (xii. 2). The question thus arises: Why are these particular cases, and such as these only, regarded as ceremonially defiling?

To see the reason of this, we must recur to facts which have already come before us. When our first parents sinned, death was denounced against them as the penalty of their sin. Such had been the threat: " In the day that thou eatest thereof, thou shalt die." The death denounced indeed affected the whole being, the spiritual as well as the physical nature of man; but it comprehended the death of the body, which thus became, what it still is, the most impressive manifestation of the presence of sin in every person who dies. Hence, as we have seen, the law kept this connection between sin and death steadily before the mind, in that it constantly applied the principle that the dead defiles. Not only so, but, for this reason, such things as tended to bring death were also reckoned unclean; and thus the regulations of the law concerning clean and unclean meats, while strictly hygienic in character, were yet grounded in this profound ethical fact of the connection between sin and death; had man not sinned, nothing in the world had been able to bring in death, and all things had been clean. For the same reason, again, leprosy, as exemplifying in a vivid and terrible way disease as a progressive death, a living manifestation of the presence of the curse of God, and therefore of the presence of sin, a type of all disease, was regarded as involving ceremonial defilement and therefore as requiring sacrificial cleansing.

But in the curse denounced upon our first parents was yet more. It was specially taught that the curse should affect the generative power of the race. For we read (Gen. iii. 16): " Unto the woman He said, I will greatly multiply thy sorrow and thy conception; in sorrow thou shalt bring forth children." Whatever these words may precisely mean, it is plain that they are intended to teach that, because of sin, the curse of God fell in some mysterious way upon the sexual organisation. And although the woman only is specifically mentioned, as being " first in the transgression," that the curse fell also upon the same part of man's nature is plain from the words in Gen. v. 3, where the long mortuary record of the antediluvians is introduced by the profoundly significant statement that Adam began the long line, with its inheritance of death, by begetting a son " in his own likeness, after his image." Fallen himself under the curse of death, physical and spiritual, he therewith lost the capacity to beget a creature like himself in his original state, in the image of God, and could only be the means of bringing into the world a creature who was an inheritor of physical weakness and spiritual and bodily death.

In the light of this ancient record, which must have been before the mind of the Hebrew lawgiver, we can now see why the law concerning unclean issues should have had special relation to that part of man's physical organisation which has to do with the propagation of the race. Just as death defiled, because it was a visible representation of the presence of the curse of God, and thus of sin, as the ground of the curse, even so was it with all the issues specified in this law. They were regarded as making a man unclean, because they were manifestations of the curse in a part of man's nature which, according to the Word of God, sin has specially affected. For this reason they fell under the same law as death. They separated the person thus affected from the congregation, and excluded him from the public worship of a holy God, as making him " unclean."

It is impossible now to miss the spiritual meaning of these laws concerning issues of this class. In that these alone, out of many others, which from a merely physical point of view are equally offensive, were taken under the cognisance of this law, the fact was thereby symbolically emphasised that the fountain of life in man is defiled. To be a sinner were bad enough, if it only involved the voluntary and habitual practice of sin. But this law of issues testifies to us, even now, that, as God sees man's case, it is far worse than this. The evil of sin is so deeply seated that it could lie no deeper. The curse has in such manner fallen on our being, as that in man and woman the powers and faculties which concern the propagation of their kind have fallen under the blight. All that any son of Adam can now do is to beget a son in his own physical and moral image, an heir of death, and by nature unclean and unholy. Sufficiently distasteful this truth is in all ages; but in none perhaps ever more so than our own, in which it has become a fundamental postulate of much popular theology, and of popular politics as well, that man is naturally not bad, but good, and, on the whole, is doing as well as under the law of evolution, and considering his environment, can reasonably be expected. The spiritual principle which underlies the law concerning defilement by issues, as also that concerning the uncleanness of child-bearing, assumes the exact opposite.

It is indeed true that similar causes of ceremonial uncleanness have been recognised in ancient and in modern times among many other peoples. But this is no objection to the truth of the interpretation of the Mosaic law here given. For in so far as there is genuine agreement, the fact may rather confirm than weaken the argument for this view of the case, as showing that there is an ineradicable instinct in the heart of man which connects all that directly or indirectly has to do with the continuance of our race, in a peculiar degree, with the ideas of uncleanness and shame. And, on the other hand, the differences in such cases from the Mosaic law show us just what we should expect,—a degree of moral confusion and a deadening of the moral sense among the heathen nations, which is most significant. As has been justly remarked, the Hindoo has one law on this subject for the Brahman, another for others; the outcast for some deadly sin, often of a purely frivolous nature, and a new-born child, are reckoned equally unclean. Or,—to take the case of a people contemporary with the Hebrews,—among the ancient Chaldeans, while these same issues were accounted ceremonially defiling, as in the law of Moses, with these were also reckoned in the same category, as unclean, whatsoever was separated from the body, even to the cuttings of the hair and the parings of the nails. Evidently, we thus have here, not likeness, but a profound and most suggestive moral contrast between the Chaldean and the Hebrew law. Of the profound ethical truth which vitalises and gives deep significance to the law of Moses, we find no trace in the other system. And it is no wonder if, indeed, the one law is, as declared, a revelation from the holy God, and the other the work of sinful and sin-blinded man.

It is another moral lesson which is brought before us in these laws that, as God looks at the matter, sin pertains not only to action, but also to being. Not only actions, from which we can abstain, but operations of nature which we cannot help, alike defile; defile in such a manner and degree as to require, even as voluntary acts of sin, the cleansing of water, and the expiatory blood of a sin-offering. One could not avoid many of the defilements mentioned in this chapter, but that made no difference; he was unclean. For the lesser grades of uncleanness it sufficed that one be purified by washing with water; and a sin-offering was only required when this purification had been neglected; but in all cases where the defilement assumed its extreme form, the sin-offering and the burnt-offering must be brought, and be offered for the unclean person by the priest. So is it, we are taught, with that sin of nature which these cases symbolised; we cannot help it, and yet the washing of regeneration and the cleansing of the blood of Christ is required for its removal. Very impressive in its teaching now becomes the miracle in which our Lord healed the poor woman afflicted with the issue of blood (Mark v. 25-34), for which she had vainly sought cure. It was a case like that covered by the law in chap. xv. 25-27; and he who will read and consider the provisions of that law will understand, as otherwise he could not, how great her trial and how heavy her burden must have been. He will wonder also, as never before, at the boldness of her faith, who, although, according to the law, her touch should defile the Lord, yet ventured to believe that not only should this not be so, but that the healing power which went forth from Him should neutralise the defilement, and carry healing virtue to the very centre of her life. Thus, if other miracles represent our Lord as meeting the evil of sin in its various manifestations in action, this miracle represents His healing power as reaching to the very source and fountain of life, where it is needed no less.

The law concerning the removal of these defilements, after all that has preceded, will admit only of one interpretation. The washing of water is the uniform symbol of the cleansing of the soul from pollution by the power of the Holy Ghost; the sacrifices point to the sacrifice of Christ, in its twofold aspect as burnt-offering and sin-offering, as required by and availing for the removal of the sinful defilement which, in the mind of God, attaches even to that in human nature which is not under the control of the will. At the same time, whereas in all these cases the sin-offering prescribed is the smallest known to the law, it is symbolised, in full accord with the teaching of conscience, that the gravity of the defilement, where there has not been the active concurrence of the will, is less than where the will has seconded nature. In all cases of prolonged defilement from these sources, it was required that the affected person should still be regarded as unclean for seven days after the cessation of the infirmity, and on the eighth day came the sacrificial cleansing. The significance of the seven as the covenant number, the number also wherein was completed the old creation, has been already before us: that of "the eighth" will best be considered in connection with the provisions of chap. xii., to which we next turn our attention.

The law of this chapter has a formal closing, in which are used these words (ver. 31): "Thus shall ye separate the children of Israel from their uncleanness; that they die not in their uncleanness, when they defile My tabernacle that is in the midst of them."

Of which the natural meaning is this, that the defilements mentioned, as conspicuous signs of man's fallen condition, were so offensive before a holy God, as apart from these purifications to have called down the judgment of death on those in whom they were found. In these words lies also the deeper spiritual thought—if we have rightly apprehended the symbolic import of these regulations—that not only, as in former cases mentioned under the law of offerings, do voluntary acts of sin separate from God and if unatoned for call down His judgment, but that even our infirmities and the involuntary motions of sin in our nature have the same effect, and, apart from the cleansing of the Holy Spirit and the blood of the Lord Jesus Christ, ensure the final judgment of death.

CHAPTER XVI.

THE UNCLEANNESS OF CHILD-BEARING.

LEVITICUS xii. 1-8.

THE reference in xii. 2 to the regulations given in xv. 19, as remarked in the preceding chapter, shows us that the author of these laws regarded the circumstances attending child-birth as falling under the same general category, in a ceremonial and symbolic aspect, as the law of issues. As a special case, however, the law concerning child-birth presents some very distinctive and instructive features.

The period during which the mother was regarded as unclean, in the full comprehension of that term, was seven days, as in the analogous case mentioned in xv. 19, with the remarkable exception, that when she had borne a daughter this period was doubled. At the expiration of this period of seven days, her ceremonial uncleanness was regarded as in so far lessened that the restrictions affecting the ordinary relations of life, as ordered, xv. 19-23, were removed. She was not, however, yet allowed to touch any hallowed thing or to come into the sanctuary, until she had fulfilled, from the time of the birth of the child, if a son, forty days; if a daughter, twice forty, or eighty days. At the expiration of the longer period, she was to bring, as in the law concerning the prolonged issue of blood (xv. 25-30), a burnt-offering and a sin-offering unto the door of the tent of meeting, wherewith the priest was to make an atonement for her; when first she should be accounted clean, and restored to full covenant privileges. The only difference from the similar law in chap. xv. is in regard to the burnt-offering commanded, which was larger and more costly,—a lamb, instead of a turtle dove, or a young pigeon. Still, in the same spirit of gracious accommodation to the poor which was illustrated in the general law of the sin-offering, it was ordered (ver. 8.): "If her means suffice not for a lamb, then she shall take two turtledoves, or two young pigeons; the one for a burnt-offering, and the other for a sin-offering." The law then applied, according to xv. 29, 30. A gracious provision this was, as all will remember, of which the mother of our Lord availed herself (Luke ii. 22-24), as being one of those who were too poor to bring a lamb for a burnt-offering.

To the meaning of these regulations, the key is found in the same conceptions which we have seen to underlie the law concerning issues. In the birth of a child, the special original curse against the woman is regarded by the law as reaching its fullest, most consummate and significant expression. For the extreme evil of the state of sin into which the first woman, by that first sin, brought all womanhood, is seen most of all in this, that now woman, by means of those powers given her for good and blessing, can bring into the world only a child of sin. And it is, apparently, because we here see the operation of this curse in its most conspicuous form, that the time of her enforced separation from the tabernacle worship is prolonged to a period either of forty or eighty days.

It has been usual to speak of the time of the mother's uncleanness, and subsequent continued exclusion from the tabernacle worship, as being doubled in the case of the birth of a daughter; but it were, perhaps, more accurate to regard the normal length of these periods as being respectively fourteen and eighty days, of which the former is double of that required in xv. 28. This normal period would then be more properly regarded as shortened by one half in the case of a male child, in virtue of his circumcision on the eighth day.

The Ordinance of Circumcision.

Leviticus xii. 3.

"And in the eighth day the flesh of his foreskin shall be circumcised."

Although the rite of circumcision here receives a new and special sanction, it had been appointed long before by God as the sign of His covenant with Abraham (Gen. xvii. 10-14). Nor was circumcision, probably, even then a new thing. That the ancient Egyptians practised it is well known; so also did the Arabs and Phœnicians; in fact, the custom has been very extensively observed, not only by nations with whom the Israelites came in contact, but by others who have not had, in historic times, connection with any civilised peoples; as, for example, the Congo negroes, and certain Indian tribes in South America.

The fundamental idea connected with circumcision, by most of the peoples who have practised it, appears to have been physical purification; indeed, the Arabs call it by the name *tatur*, which has this precise meaning. And it deserves to be noticed that for this idea regarding circumcision there is so much reason in fact, that high medical authorities have attributed to it a real hygienic value, especially in warm climates.

No one need feel any difficulty in supposing that this common conception attached to the rite also in the minds of the Hebrews. Rather all the more fitting it was, if there was a basis in fact for this familiar opinion, that God should thus have taken a ceremony already known to the surrounding peoples, and in itself of a wholesome physical effect, and constituted it for Abraham and his seed a symbol of an analogous spiritual fact; namely, the purification of sin at its fountain-head, the cleansing of the evil nature with which we all are born. It should be plain enough that it makes nothing against this as the true interpretation of the rite, even if that be granted which some have claimed, that it has had, in some instances, a connection with the phallic worship so common in the East, or that it has been regarded by some as a sacrificial ceremony. Only the more noteworthy would it thus appear that the Hebrews should have held strictly to that view of its significance which had a solid basis in physical fact,—a fact, moreover, which made it a peculiarly fitting symbol of the spiritual grace which the Biblical writers connect with it. For that it was so regarded by them will not be disputed. In this very book (xxvi. 41) we read of an "uncircumcised heart;" as also in Deuteronomy, the prophecies of Jeremiah and Ezekiel, and other books of Scripture.

All this, as intimating the signification of circumcision as here enjoined, is further established by the New Testament references. Of these the most formal is perhaps that in Col. ii. 10, 11, where we read that believers in Christ, in virtue of their union with Him in whom the unclean nature has been made clean, are said to be "circumcised with a circumcision not made with hands, in the putting off of the body of the flesh, in the circumcision of Christ;" so that Paul elsewhere writes to the Philippians (iii. 3): "We are the circumcision, who worship by the Spirit of God, and glory in Christ Jesus, and have no confidence in the flesh."

And that God, in selecting this ancient rite to be the sign of His covenant in the flesh of Abraham and his seed (Gen. xvii. 13), had regard to the deep spiritual meaning which it could so naturally carry is explicitly declared by the Apostle Paul (Rom. iv. 11), who tells us that this sign of circumcision was "a seal of the righteousness of faith," even the righteousness and the faith concerning which, in the previous context, he was arguing; and which are still, for all men, the one, the ground, and the other, the condition, of salvation. It is truly strange that, in the presence of these plain words of the Apostle, any should still cling to the idea that circumcision had reference only to the covenant with Israel as a nation, and not, above all, to this profound spiritual truth which is basal to salvation, whether for the Jew or for the Gentile.

And so, when the Hebrew infant was circumcised, it signified for him and for his parents these spiritual realities. It was an outward sign and seal of the covenant of God with Abraham and with his seed, to be a God to him and to his seed after him; and it signified further that this covenant of God was to be carried out and made effectual only through the putting away of the flesh, the corrupt nature with which we are born, and of all that belongs to it, in order that, thus circumcised with the circumcision of the heart, every child of Abraham might indeed be an Israelite in whom there should be no guile.

And the law commands, in accord with the original command to Abraham, that the circumcision should take place on the eighth day. This is the more noticeable, that among other nations which practised, or still practise, the rite, the time is different. The Egyptians, for example, circumcised their sons between the sixth and tenth years, and the modern Mohammedans between the twelfth and fourteenth year. What is the significance of this eighth day?

In the first place, it is easy to see that we have in this direction a provision of God's mercy; for if delayed beyond infancy or early childhood, as among many other peoples, the operation is much more serious, and may even involve some danger; while in so early infancy it is comparatively trifling, and attended with no risk.

Further, by the administration of circumcision at the very opening of life, it is suggested that in the Divine ideal the grace which was signified thereby, of the cleansing of nature, was to be bestowed upon the child, not first at a late period of life, but from its very beginning, thus anticipating the earliest awakening of the principle of inborn sin. It was thus signified that before ever the child knew, or could know, the grace that was seeking to save him, he was to be taken into covenant relation with God. So even under the strange form of this ordinance we discover the same mind that was in Him who said concerning infant children (Luke xviii. 16): "Suffer the little children to come unto Me, and forbid them not: for of such is the kingdom of God." Thus we may well recollect, in passing, that, although the law has passed away in the Levitical form, the mind of the Lawgiver concerning the little children of His people is still the same.

But the question still remains, Why was the eighth day selected, and not rather, for instance, the sixth or the seventh, which would have no less perfectly represented these ideas? The answer is to be found in the symbolic significance of the eighth day. As the old creation was completed in six days, with a following Sabbath of rest, so that six is ever the number of the old creation, as under imperfection and sin; the eighth day, which is the first day of a new week, everywhere in Scripture appears as the number symbolic of the new creation, in which all things shall be restored in the great redemption through the Second Adam. The thought finds its fullest expression in the resurrection of Christ, as the First-born from the dead, the Beginning and the Lord of the new creation, who in His resurrection-body manifested the first-fruits in physical life of the new creation, rising from the dead on the first, or, in other words, the day after the seventh, the eighth day. This gives the key to the use of the number eight in the Mosaic symbolism. Thus in the law of the cleansing of the man or the woman that had an issue, the sacrifices which effectuated their formal deliverance from the curse under which, through the weakness of their old nature, they had suffered, were to be offered on the eighth day (xv. 14, 29); the priestly cleansing of the leper from the taint of his living death was also effected on the eighth day (xiv. 10); so also the cleansing of the Nazarite who had been defiled by the dead (Numb. vi. 10). So also the holy convocation which closed the feast of tabernacles or ingathering—the feast which, as we shall see, typically prefigured the great harvest of which Christ was the First-fruits—was ordained, in like manner, for the eighth day (xxiii. 36). With good reason, then, was circumcision ordered for the eighth day, seeing that what it symbolically signified was precisely this: the putting off of the flesh with which we are born through the circum-cision of Christ, and therewith the first beginning of a new and purified nature—a change so profound and radical, and in which the Divine efficiency is so immediately concerned, that Paul said of it that if any man was in Christ, in whose circumcision we are circumcised (Col. ii. 11), "there is a new creation" (2 Cor. v. 17, margin, R. V.).

Purification after Child-birth.

Leviticus xii. 4-8.

"And she shall continue in the blood of her purifying three and thirty days; she shall touch no hallowed thing, nor come into the sanctuary, until the days of her purifying be fulfilled. But if she bear a maid child, then she shall be unclean two weeks, as in her impurity: and she shall continue in the blood of her purifying threescore and six days. And when the days of her purifying are fulfilled, for a son, or for a daughter, she shall bring a lamb of the first year for a burnt offering, and a young pigeon, or a turtledove, for a sin offering, unto the door of the tent of meeting, unto the priest: and he shall offer it before the Lord, and make atonement for her; and she shall be cleansed from the fountain of her blood. This is the law for her that beareth, whether a male or a female. And if her means suffice not for a lamb, then she shall take two turtledoves, or two young pigeons; the one for a burnt offering, and the other for a sin offering: and the priest shall make atonement for her, and she shall be clean."

Until the circumcision of the new-born child, on the eighth day, he was regarded by the law as ceremonially still in a state of nature, and therefore as symbolically unclean. For this reason, again, the mother who had brought him into the world, and whose life was so intimately connected with his life, was regarded as unclean also. Unclean, under analogous circumstances, according to the law of xv. 19, she was reckoned doubly unclean in this case,—unclean because of her issue, and unclean because of her connection with this child, uncircumcised and unclean. But when the symbolic cleansing of the child took place by the ordinance of circumcision, then her uncleanness, so far as occasioned by her immediate relation to him, came to an end. She was not indeed completely restored; for, according to the law, in her still continuing condition, it was impossible that she should be allowed to come into the tabernacle of the Lord, or touch any hallowed thing; but the ordinance which admitted her child, admitted her also again to the fellowship of the covenant people.

The longer period of forty—or, in the case of the birth of a female child, of twice forty—days must also be explained upon symbolical grounds. Some have indeed attempted to account for these periods, as also for the difference in their length in the two cases, by a reference to beliefs of the ancients with regard to the physical condition of the mother during these periods; but such notions of the ancients are not justified by facts; nor, especially, would they by any means account for the greatly prolonged period of eighty days in the case of the female child. It is possible that in the forty, and twice forty, we may have a reference to the forty weeks during which the life of the unborn child had been identified with that of the mother,—a child which, it must be remembered, according to the uniform Biblical view, was not innocent, but conceived in sin; for each week of which connection of life, the mother suffered a judicial exclusion of one, or, in the case of the birth of a daughter, of two days; the time being doubled in the latter case with allusion to the double curse which, according to Genesis, rested upon the woman, as "first in the transgression." But, apart from this, however difficult it may be to give a satisfactory explanation of the fact, it is certain that throughout Scripture the number forty appears to have a symbolic meaning; and one can usually trace in its application a reference, more or less distinct, to the conception of trial or testing. Thus for forty days was Moses in the mount,—a time of testing for Israel, as for him: forty days, the spies explored the promised land; forty years, Israel was tried in the wilderness; forty days, abode Elijah in the wilderness; forty days, also, was our Lord fasting in the wilderness; and forty days, again, He abode in resurrection life upon the earth.

The forty (or eighty) days ended, the mother was now formally reinstated in the fulness of her privileges as a daughter of Israel. The ceremonial, as in the law of issues, consisted in the presentation of a burnt-offering and a sin-offering, with the only variation that, wherever possible, the burnt-offering must be a young lamb, instead of a dove or pigeon; the reason for which variation is to be found either in the fact that the burnt-offering was to represent not herself alone, but also her child, or, possibly, as some have suggested, it was because she had been so much longer excluded from the tabernacle service than in the other case.*

The teaching of this law, then, is twofold: it concerns, first, the woman; and, secondly, the child which she bears. As regards the woman, it emphasises the fact that, because "first in the transgression," she is under special pains and penalties in virtue of her sex. The capacity of motherhood, which is her crown and her glory, though still a precious privilege, has yet been made, because of sin, an inevitable instrument of pain, and that because of her relation to the first sin. We are thus reminded that the specific curse denounced against the woman, as recorded in the book of Genesis, is no dead letter, but a fact. No doubt, the conception is one which raises difficulties which in themselves are great, and to modern thought are greater than ever. Nevertheless, the fact abides unaltered, that even to this day woman is under special pains and disabilities, inseparably connected with her power of motherhood. Modern theorists, men and women with nineteenth-century notions concerning politics and education, may persist in ignoring this; but the fact abides, and cannot be got rid of by passing resolutions in a mass-meeting, or even by Act of Parliament or Congress.

And so, as it is useless to object to facts, it is only left to object to the Mosaic view of the facts, which connects them with sin, and, in particular, with the first sin. Why should all the daughters of Eve suffer because of her sin? Where is the justice in such an ordinance? A question this is to which we cannot yet give any satisfactory answer. But it does not follow that because in any proposition there are difficulties which at present we are unable to solve, therefore the proposition is false. And, further, it is important to observe that this law, under which womanhood abides, is after all only a special case under that law of the Divine government which is announced in the second commandment, by which the iniquities of the fathers are visited upon the children. It is most certainly a law which, to our apprehension, suggests great moral difficulties, even to the most reverent spirits; but it is no less certainly a law which represents a conspicuous and tremendous fact, which is illustrated, for instance, in the family of every drunkard in the world. And it is well worth observing, that while the ceremonial law, which was specially intended to keep this fact before the mind and the conscience, is abrogated, the fact that woman is still under certain Divinely imposed disabilities because of that first sin, is reaffirmed in the New Testament, and is by apostolic authority applied in the administration of Church government. For Paul wrote to Timothy (1 Tim. ii. 12, 13): "I permit not a woman to teach, nor to have dominion over a man. . . For Adam was not beguiled, but the woman being beguiled hath fallen into transgression." Modern theorists, and so-called "reformers" in Church, State, and society, busy with their social, governmental, and ecclesiastical novelties, would do well to heed this apostolic reminder.

All the more beautiful, as against this dark background of mystery, is the word of the Apostle which follows, wherein he reminds us that, through the grace of God, even by means of those very powers of motherhood on which the curse has so heavily fallen, has come the redemption of the woman; so that "she shall be saved through the childbearing, if they continue in faith and love and sanctification with sobriety" (1 Tim. ii. 15, R. V.); seeing that "in Christ Jesus," in respect of the completeness and freeness of salvation, "there can be no male and female" (Gal. iii. 28, R. V.).

But, in the second place, we may also derive abiding instruction from this law, concerning the child which is of man begotten and of woman born. It teaches us that not only has the curse thus fallen on the woman, but that, because she is herself a sinful creature, she can only bring forth another sinful creature like herself; and if a daughter, then a daughter inheriting all her own peculiar infirmities and disabilities. The law, as regards both mother and child, expresses in the language of symbolism those words of David in his penitential confession (Psalm li. 5): "Behold, I was shapen in iniquity; and in sin did my mother conceive me." Men may contemptuously call this "theology," or even rail at it as "Calvinism;" but it is more than theology, more than Calvinism; it is a *fact*, to which until this present time history has seen but one exception, even that mysterious Son of the Virgin, who claimed, however, to be no mere man, but the Christ, the Son of the Blessed!

And yet many, who surely can think but superficially upon the solemn facts of life, still object to this most strenuously, that even the new-born child should be regarded as in nature sinful and unclean. Difficulty here we must all admit,—difficulty so great that it is hard to overstate it—regarding the bearing of this fact on the character of the holy and merciful God, who in the beginning made man. And yet surely, deeper thought must confess that herein the Mosaic view of infant nature—a view which is assumed and taught throughout Holy Scripture—however humbling to our natural pride, is only in strictest accord with what the admitted principles of the most exact science compel us to admit. For

---

* This latter reason, however, would rather appear to have demanded, as in the case of the leper, a guilt-offering.

whenever, in any case, we find all creatures of the same class doing, under all circumstances, any one thing, we conclude that the reason for this can only lie in the nature of such creatures, antecedent to any influence of a tendency to imitation. If, for instance, the ox everywhere and always eats the green thing of the earth, and not flesh, the reason, we say, is found simply in the nature of the ox as he comes into being. So when we see all men, everywhere, under all circumstances, as soon as ever they come to the time of free moral choice, always choosing and committing sin, what can we conclude—regarding this, not as a theological, but merely as a scientific question—but that man, as he comes into the world, must have a sinful nature? And this being so, then why must not the law of heredity apply, according to which, by a law which knows of no exceptions, like ever produces its like?

Least of all, then, should those object to the view of child-nature which is represented in this law of Leviticus, who accept these commonplaces of modern science as representing facts. Wiser it were to turn attention to the other teaching of the law, that, notwithstanding these sad and humiliating facts, there is provision made by God, through the cleansing by grace of the very nature in which we are born, and atonement for the sin which without our fault we inherit, for a complete redemption from all the inherited corruption and guilt.

And, last of all, especially should Christian parents with joy and thankfulness receive the manifest teaching of this law,—teaching reaffirmed by our blessed Lord in the New Testament,—that God our Father offers to parental faith Himself to take in hand our children, even from the earliest beginning of their infant days, and, purifying the fountain of their life through "a circumcision made without hands," receive the little ones into covenant relation with Himself, to their eternal salvation. And thus is the word of the Apostle fulfilled. "Where sin abounded, grace did abound more exceedingly: that, as sin reigned in death, even so might grace reign through righteousness unto eternal life through Jesus Christ our Lord."

CHAPTER XVII.

THE UNCLEANNESS OF LEPROSY.

LEVITICUS xiii. 1-46.

THE interpretation of this chapter presents no little difficulty. The description of the diseases with which the law here deals is not given in a scientific form; the point of view, as the purpose of all, is strictly practical. As for the Hebrew word rendered "leprosy," it does not itself give any light as to the nature of the disease thus designated. The word simply means "a stroke," as also does the generic term used in ver. 2 and elsewhere, and translated "plague." Inasmuch as the Septuagint translators rendered the former term by the Greek word "*lepra*" (whence our word "leprosy"), and as, it is said, the old Greek physicians comprehended under that term only such scaly cutaneous eruptions as are now known as *psoriasis* (*vulg.*, "salt-rheum"), and for what is now known as leprosy reserved the term "elephantiasis,"* it has been therefore urged by high authority that in these chapters is no reference to the leprosy of modern speech, but only to some disease or diseases much less serious, either *psoriasis* or some other, consisting, like that, of a scaly eruption on the skin.† To the above argument it is also added that the signs which are given for the recognition of the disease intended, are not such as we should expect if it were the modern leprosy; as, for example, there is no mention of the insensibility of the skin, which is so characteristic a feature of the disease, at least, in a very common variety; moreover, we find in this chapter no allusion to the hideous mutilation which so commonly results from leprosy.

When the use of the Hebrew term rendered "leprosy" is examined, in this law and elsewhere, it certainly seems to be used with great definiteness to describe a disease which had as a very characteristic feature a whitening of the skin throughout, together with other marks common to the early stages of leprosy as given in this chapter. Only in ver. 12 does the Hebrew word appear to be applied to a disease of a different character, though also marked by the whitening of the skin. As for the symptoms indicated, the undoubted absence of many conspicuous marks of leprosy may be accounted for by the following considerations. In the first place, with a single exception (vv. 9-11), the earliest stages of the disease are described; and, secondly, it may reasonably be assumed that, through the desire to ensure the earliest possible separation of a leprous man from the congregation, signs were to be noted and acted upon, which might also be found in other forms of skin disease. The aim of the law is that, if possible, the man shall be removed from the camp before the disease has assumed its most unambiguous and revolting form. As for the omission to mention the insensibility of the skin of the leper, this seems to be sufficiently explained when we remember that this symptom is characteristic of only one, and that not the most fatal, variety of the disease.

But, it has also been urged, that elsewhere in the Scripture the so-called lepers appear as mingling with other people—as, for example, in the case of Naaman and Gehazi—in a way which shows that the disease was not regarded as contagious; whence it is inferred, again, that the leprosy of which we read in the Bible cannot be the same with the disease which is so called in our time. But, in reply to this objection, it may be answered that even modern medical opinion has been by no means as confident of the contagiousness of the disease—at least, until quite recently—as were people in the middle ages; nor, moreover, can we assume that the prevention of contagion must have been the chief reason for the segregation of the leper, according to the Levitical law, seeing that a like separation was enjoined in many other cases of ceremonial uncleanness where any thought of contagion or infection was quite impossible.

In further support of the more common opinion, which identifies the disease chiefly re-

---

* This word, it should be noted, is now popularly used to denote a disease quite distinct from leprosy, known also as "Barbadoes leg," which consists essentially of an elephantine enlargement of the lower extremities.

† This opinion has been ably argued by Sir Risdon Bennett, M.D., LL. D., F. R. S., in "By-paths of Bible Knowledge," vol. ix., "The Diseases of the Bible."

ferred to in this chapter with the leprosy of modern times, the following considerations appear to be of no little weight. In the first place, the words themselves which are applied to the disease in these chapters and elsewhere,—*tsara'ath* and *nega'*, both meaning, etymologically, "a stroke," *i. e.*, a stroke in some eminent sense,*—while peculiarly fitting if the disease be that which we now know as leprosy, seem very strangely chosen if, as Sir Risdon Bennett thinks, they only designate varieties of a disease of so little seriousness as *psoriasis*. Then, again, the words used by Aaron to Moses (Numb. xii. 12), referring to the leprosy of Miriam, deserve great weight here: "Let her not, I pray, be as one dead, of whom the flesh is half consumed." These words sufficiently answer the allegation that there is no certain reference in Scripture to the mutilation which is so characteristic of the later stages of the disease. It would not be easy to describe in more accurate language the condition of the leper as the plague advances; while, on the other hand, if the leprosy of the Bible be only such a light affection as "salt-rheum," these words and the evident horror which they express, are so exaggerated as to be quite unaccountable.

Then, again, we cannot lose sight of the place which the disease known in Scripture language as leprosy holds in the sight of the law. As a matter of fact, it is singled out from a multitude of diseases as the object of the most stringent and severe regulations, and the most elaborate ceremonial, known to the law. Now, if the disease intended be indeed the awful *elephantiasis Græcorum* of modern medical science, popularly known as leprosy, this is most natural and reasonable; but if, on the other hand, only some such non-malignant disease as *psoriasis* be intended, this fact is inexplicable. Further, the tenour of all references to the disease in the Scripture implies that it was deemed so incurable that its removal in any case was regarded as a special sign of the exercise of Divine power. The reference of the Hebrew maid of Naaman to the prophet of God (2 Kings v. 3), as one who could cure him, instead of proving that it was thought curable—as has been strangely urged—by ordinary means, surely proves the exact opposite. Naaman, no doubt, had exhausted medical resources; and the hope of the maid for him is not based on the medical skill of Elisha, but on the fact that he was a prophet of God, and therefore able to draw on Divine power. To the same effect is the word of the King of Israel, when he received the letter of Naaman (2 Kings v. 7): "Am I God, to kill and to make alive, that this man doth send unto me to recover a man of his leprosy?" In full accord with this is the appeal of our Lord (Matt. xi. 5) to His cleansing of the lepers, as a sign of His Messiahship which He ranks for convincing power along with the raising of the dead.

Nor is it a fatal objection to the usual understanding of this matter, that because the Levitical law prescribes a ritual for the ceremonial cleansing of the leper in case of his cure, therefore the disease so called could not be one of the gravity and supposed incurability of the true leprosy. For it is to be noted, in the first place, that there is no intimation that recovery from the leprosy was a common occurrence, or even that it was to be expected at all, apart from the direct

* Compare our frequent use of the word to denote paralysis.

power of God; and, in the second place, that the Scriptural narrative represents God as now and then—though very rarely—interposing for the cure of the leper. And it may perhaps be added, that while a recent authority writes, and with truth, that "medical skill appears to have been more completely foiled by this than by any other malady," it is yet remarked that, when of the anæsthetic variety, "some spontaneous cures are recorded."

The chapter before us calls for little detailed exposition. The diagnosis of the disease by the priest is treated under four different heads: (1) the case of a leprosy rising spontaneously (vv. 1-17, 38, 39); (2) leprosy rising out of a boil (vv. 18-24); (3) rising out of a burn (vv. 24-28); (4) leprosy on the head or beard (vv. 29-37, 40-44). The indications which are to be noted are described (vv. 2, 3, 24-27, etc.) as a rising of the surface, a scab (or scale), or a bright spot (very characteristic), the presence in the spot of hair turned white, the disease apparently deeper than the outer or scarf skin, a reddish-white colour of the surface, and a tendency to spread. The presence of "raw flesh" is mentioned (ver. 10) as an indication of a leprosy already somewhat advanced, "an old leprosy." In cases of doubt, the suspected case is to be isolated for a period of seven or, if need be, fourteen days, at the expiration of which the priest's verdict is to be given, as the symptoms may then indicate.

Two cases are mentioned which the priest is not to regard as leprosy. The first (vv. 12, 13) is that in which the plague "covers all the skin of him that hath the plagues from his head even to his feet, as far as appeareth to the priest," so that he "is all turned white." At first thought, this seems quite unaccountable, seeing that leprosy finally affects the whole body. But the solution of the difficulty is not far to seek. For the next verse provides that, in such a case, if "raw flesh" appear, he shall be held to be unclean. The explanation of this provision of ver. 12 is therefore apparently this: that if an eruption had so spread as to cover the whole body, turning it white, and yet no raw flesh had appeared in any place, the disease could not be true leprosy as, if it were, then, by the time that it had so extended, "raw flesh" would certainly have appeared somewhere. The disease indicated by this exception was indeed well known to the ancients, as it is also to the moderns as the "dry tetter;" which, although an affection often of long duration, frequently disappears spontaneously, and is never malignant.

The second case which is specified as not to be mistaken for leprosy is mentioned in vv. 38, 39, where it is described as marked by bright spots of a dull whiteness, but without the white hair, and other characteristic signs of leprosy. The Hebrew word by which it is designated is rendered in the Revised Version "tetter;" and the disease, a non-malignant tetter or *eczema*, is still known in the East under the same name (*bohak*) which is here used.

Verses 45, 46, give the law for him who has been by the priest adjudged to be a leper. He must go with clothes rent, with his hair neglected, his lip covered, crying, "Unclean! unclean!" without the camp, and there abide alone for so long as he continues to be afflicted with the disease. In other words, he is to assume all the ordinary signs of mourning for the dead; he is to regard himself, and all others are to regard him, as a dead man. As it were, he is a continual mourner at his own funeral.

Wherein lay the reason for this law? One might answer, in general, that the extreme loathsomeness of the disease, which made the presence of those who had it to be abhorrent even to their nearest friends, would of itself make it only fitting, however distressing might be the necessity, that such persons should be excluded from every possibility of appearing, in their revolting corruption, in the sacred and pure precincts of the tabernacle of the holy God, as also from mingling with His people. Many, however, have seen in the regulation only a wise law of public hygiene. That a sanitary intent may very probably have been included in the purpose of this law, we are by no means inclined to deny. In earlier times, and all through the middle ages, the disease was regarded as contagious; and lepers were accordingly segregated, as far as practicable, from the people. In modern times, the weight of opinion until recent years has been against this older view; but the tendency of medical authority now appears to be to reaffirm the older belief. The alarming increase of this horrible disease in all parts of the world, of late, following upon a general relaxation of those precautions against contagion which were formerly thought necessary, certainly supports this judgment; and it may thus be easily believed that there was just sanitary ground for the rigid regulations of the Mosaic code. And just here it may be remarked, that if indeed there be any degree of contagiousness, however small, in this plague, no one who has ever seen the disease, or understands anything of its incomparable horror and loathsomeness, will feel that there is any force in the objections which have been taken to this part of the Mosaic law as of inhuman harshness toward the sufferers. Even were the risk of contagion but small, as it probably is, still, so terrible is the disease that one would more justly say that the only inhumanity were to allow those afflicted with it unrestricted intercourse with their fellow-men. The truth is, that the Mosaic law concerning the treatment of the leper, when compared with regulations touching lepers which have prevailed among other nations, stands contrasted with them by its comparative leniency. The Hindoo law, as is well known, even insists that the leper ought to put himself out of existence, requiring that he shall be buried alive.

But if there be included in these regulations a sanitary intent, this certainly does not exhaust their significance. Rather, if this be admitted, it only furnishes the basis, as in the case of the laws concerning clean and unclean meats, for still more profound spiritual teaching. For, as remarked before, it is one of the fundamental thoughts of the Mosaic law, that death, as being the extreme visible manifestation of the presence of sin in the race, and a sign of the consequent holy wrath of God against sinful man, is inseparably connected with legal uncleanness. But all disease is a forerunner of death, an incipient dying; and is thus, no less really than actual death, a visible manifestation of the presence and power of sin working in the body through death. And yet it is easy to see that it would have been quite impracticable to carry out a law that therefore all disease should render the sick person ceremonially unclean; while, on the other hand, it was of consequence that Israel, and we as well, should be kept in remembrance of this connection between sin and disease, as death beginning. What could have been more fitting, then, than this, that the one disease which, without exaggeration, is of all diseases the most loathsome, which is most manifestly a visible representation of that which is in a measure true of all disease, that it is death working in life, that disease which is, not in a merely rhetorical sense, but in fact, a living image of death,—should be selected from all others for the illustration of this principle: to be to Israel and to us, a visible, perpetual, and very awful parable of the nature and the working of sin?

And this is precisely what has been done. This explains, as sanitary considerations alone do not, not merely the separation of the leper from the holy people, but also the solemn symbolism which required him to assume the appearance of one mourning for the dead; as also the symbolism of his cleansing, which, in like manner, corresponded very closely with that of the ritual of cleansing from defilement by the dead. Hence, while all sickness, in a general way, is regarded in the Holy Scriptures as a fitting symbol of sin, it has always been recognised that, among all diseases, leprosy is this in an exceptional and pre-eminent sense. This thought seems to have been in the mind of David, when, after his murder of Uriah and adultery with Bathsheba, bewailing his iniquity (Psalm li. 7), he prayed, "Purge me with hyssop, and I shall be clean." For the only use of the hyssop in the law, which could be alluded to in these words is that which is enjoined (xiv. 4-7) in the law for the cleansing of the leper, by the sprinkling of the man to be cleansed with blood and water with a hyssop branch.

And thus we find that, again, this elaborate ceremonial contains, not merely an instructive lesson in public sanitation, and practical suggestions in hygiene for our modern times; but also lessons, far more profound and momentous, concerning that spiritual malady with which the whole human race is burdened,—lessons therefore of the gravest personal consequence for every one of us.

From among all diseases, leprosy has been selected by the Holy Ghost to stand in the law as the supreme type of sin, as seen by God! This is the very solemn fact which is brought before us in this chapter. Let us well consider it and see that we receive the lesson, however humiliating and painful, in the spirit of meekness and penitence. Let us so study it that we shall with great earnestness and true faith resort to the true and heavenly High Priest, who alone can cleanse us of this sore malady. And in order to this, we must carefully consider what is involved in this type.

In the first place, leprosy is undoubtedly selected to be a special type of sin, on account of its extreme *loathsomeness*. Beginning, indeed, as an insignificant spot, "a bright place," a mere scale on the skin, it goes on spreading, progressing ever from worse to worse, till at last limb drops from limb, and only the hideous mutilated remnant of what was once a man is left. A vivid picture of the horrible reality has been given by that veteran missionary and very accurate observer, the Rev. William Thomson, D. D., who writes thus: "As I was approaching Jerusalem, I was startled by the sudden apparition of a crowd of beggars, sans eyes, sans nose, sans hair, sans everything... They held up their handless arms, unearthly sounds gurgled through throats without palates,—in a word, I was horrified."* Too horrible is this to be repeated or thought of? Yes! But then all the more solemnly instructive is it that the Holy Spirit should have chosen this disease, the most loathsome of all, as the most fatal of all, to symbolise to us the true nature of that spiritual malady which affects us all, as it is seen by the omniscient and most holy God.

But it will very naturally be rejoined by some: Surely it were gross exaggeration to apply this horrible symbolism to the case of many who, although indeed sinners, unbelievers also in Christ, yet certainly exhibit truly lovely and attractive characters. That this is true regarding many who, according to the Scriptures, are yet unsaved, cannot be denied. We read of one such in the Gospel,—a young man, unsaved, who yet was such that "Jesus looking upon him loved him" (Mark x. 21). But this fact only makes the leprosy the more fitting symbol of sin. For another characteristic of the disease is its *insignificant and often even imperceptible beginning*. We are told that in the case of those who inherit the taint, it frequently remains quite dormant in early life, only gradually appearing in later years. How perfectly the type, in this respect, then, symbolises sin! And surely any thoughtful man will confess that this fact makes the presence of the infection not less alarming, but more so. No comfort then can be rightly had from any complacent comparison of our own characters with those of many, perhaps professing more, who are much worse than we, as the manner of some is. No one who knew that from his parents he had inherited the leprous taint, or in whom the leprosy as yet appeared as only an insignificant bright spot, would comfort himself greatly by the observation that other lepers were much worse; and that he was, as yet, fair and goodly to look upon. Though the leprosy were in him but just begun, that would be enough to fill him with dismay and consternation. So should it be with regard to sin.

And it would so affect such a man the more surely, when he knew that the disease, however slight in its beginnings, was certainly *progressive*. This is one of the unfailing marks of the disease. It may progress slowly, but it progresses surely. To quote again the vivid and truthful description of the above-named writer, "It comes on by degrees in different parts of the body: the hair falls from the head and eyebrows; the nails loosen, decay, and drop off; joint after joint of the fingers and toes shrinks up and slowly falls away; the gums are absorbed, and the teeth disappear; the nose, the eyes, the tongue, and the palate are slowly consumed; and, finally, the wretched victim sinks into the earth and disappears."

In this respect again the fitness of the disease to stand as an eminent type of sin is undeniable. No man can morally stand still. No one has ever retained the innocence of childhood. Except as counteracted by the efficient grace of the Holy Spirit in the heart, the Word (2 Tim. iii. 13) is ever visibly fulfilled, "evil men wax worse and worse." Sin may not develop in all with equal rapidity, but it does progress in every natural man, outwardly or inwardly, with equal certainty.

It is another mark of leprosy that sooner or later it *affects the whole man;* and in this, again, appears the sad fitness of the disease to stand as a symbol of sin. For sin is not a partial disorder, affecting only one class of faculties, or one part of our nature. It disorders the judgment; it obscures our moral perceptions; it either perverts the affections, or unduly stimulates them in one direction, while it deadens them in another; it hardens and quickens the will for evil, while it paralyses its power for the volition of that which is holy. And not only the Holy Scripture, but observation itself, teaches us that sin, in many cases, also affects the body of man, weakening its powers, and bringing in, by an inexorable law, pain, disease, and death. Sooner or later, then, sin affects the whole man. And for that reason, again, is leprosy set forth as its pre-eminent symbol.

It is another remarkable feature of the disease that, as it progresses from bad to worse, the victim becomes more and more *insensible*. This numbness or insensibility of the spots affected— in one most common variety at least—is a constant feature. In some cases it becomes so extreme that a knife may be thrust into the affected limb, or the diseased flesh may be burnt with fire, and yet the leper feels no pain. Nor is the insensibility confined to the body, but, as the leprosy extends, the mind is affected in an analogous manner. A recent writer says: "Though a mass of bodily corruption, at last unable to leave his bed, the leper seems happy and contented with his sad condition." Is anything more characteristic than this of the malady of sin? The sin which, when first committed, costs a keen pang, afterward, when frequently repeated, hurts not the conscience at all. Judgments and mercies, which in earlier life affected one with profound emotion, in later life leave the impenitent sinner as unmoved as they found him. Hence we all recognise the fitness of the common expression, "a seared conscience," as also of the Apostle's description of advanced sinners as men who are "past feeling" (Eph. iv. 19). Of this moral insensibility which sin produces, then, we are impressively reminded when the Holy Spirit in the Word holds before us leprosy as a type of sin.

Another element of the solemn fitness of the type is found in the persistently *hereditary* nature of leprosy. It may indeed sometimes arise of itself, even as did sin in the case of certain of the holy angels, and with our first parents; but when once it is introduced, in the case of any person, the terrible infection descends with unfailing certainty to all his descendants; and while, by suitable hygiene, it is possible to alleviate its violence, and retard its development, it is not possible to escape the terrible inheritance. Is anything more uniformly characteristic of sin? We may raise no end of metaphysical difficulties about the matter, and put unanswerable questions about freedom and responsibility; but there is no denying the hard fact that since sin first entered the race, in our first parents, not a child of man, of human father begotten, has escaped the taint. If various external influences, as in the case of leprosy, may, in some instances, modify its manifestations, yet no individual, in any class or condition of mankind, escapes the taint. The most cultivated and the most barbarous alike, come into the world so constituted that, quite antecedent to any act of free choice on their part, we know that it is not more certain that they will

* "The Land and the Book," vol. i., pp. 530, 531.

eat than that, when they begin to exercise freedom, they will, each and every one, use their moral freedom wrongly,—in a word, will sin. No doubt, then, when such prominence is given to leprosy among diseases, in the Mosaic symbolism and elsewhere, it is with intent, among other truths, to keep before the mind this very solemn and awful fact with regard to the sin which it so fitly symbolises.

And, again, we find yet another analogy in the fact that, among the ancient Hebrews, the disease was regarded as *incurable* by human means; and, notwithstanding occasional announcements in our day that a remedy has been discovered for the plague, this seems to be the verdict of the best authorities in medical science still. That in this respect leprosy perfectly represents the sorer malady of the soul, every one is witness. No possible effort of will or fixedness of determination has ever availed to free a man from sin. Even the saintliest Christian has often to confess with the Apostle Paul (Rom. vii. 19), "The evil which I would not, that I practise." Neither is culture, whether intellectual or religious, of any more avail. To this all human history testifies. In our day, despite the sad lessons of long experience, many are hoping for much from improved government, education, and such like means; but vainly, and in the face of the most patent facts. Legislation may indeed impose restrictions on the more flagrant forms of sin, even as it may be of service in restricting the devastations of leprosy, and ameliorating the condition of lepers. But to do away with sin, and abolish crime by any conceivable legislation, is a dream as vain as were the hope of curing leprosy by a good law or an imperial proclamation. Even the perfect law of God has proved inadequate for this end; the Apostle (Rom. viii. 3) reminds us that in this it has failed, and could not but fail, "in that it was weak through the flesh." Nothing can well be of more importance than that we should be keenly alive to this fact; that so we may not, through our present apparently tolerable condition, or by temporary alleviations of the trouble, be thrown off our guard, and hope for ourselves or for the world, upon grounds which afford no just reason for hope.

Last of all, the law of leprosy, as given in this chapter, teaches the supreme lesson, that as with the symbolic disease of the body, so with that of the soul, sin *shuts out from God and from the fellowship of the holy.* As the leper was excluded from the camp of Israel and from the tabernacle of Jehovah, so must the sinner, except cleansed, be shut out of the Holy City, and from the glory of the heavenly temple. What a solemnly significant parable is this exclusion of the leper from the camp! He is thrust forth from the congregation of Israel, wearing the insignia of mourning for the dead! Within the camp, the multitude of them that go to the sanctuary of God, and that joyfully keep holy day; without, the leper dwelling alone, in his incurable corruption and never-ending mourning! And so, while we do not indeed deny a sanitary intention in these regulations of the law, but are rather inclined to affirm it; yet of far more consequence is it that we heed the spiritual truth which this solemn symbolism teaches. It is that which is written in the Apocalypse (xxi. 27; xxii. 15) concerning the New Jerusalem: "There shall in no wise enter into it anything unclean... Without are the dogs, and the sorcerers, and the fornicators, and the murderers, and the idolaters, and every one that loveth and maketh a lie."

In view of all these correspondences, one need not wonder that in the symbolism of the law leprosy holds the place which it does. For what other disease can be named which combines in itself, as a physical malady, so many of the most characteristic marks of the malady of the soul? In its intrinsic loathsomeness, its insignificant beginnings, its slow but inevitable progress, in the extent of its effects, in the insensibility which accompanies it, in its hereditary character, in its incurability, and, finally, in the fact that according to the law it involved the banishment of the leper from the camp of Israel,—in all these respects, it stands alone as a perfect type of sin; it is sin, as it were, made visible in the flesh.

This is indeed a dark picture of man's natural state, and very many are exceedingly loth to believe that sin can be such a very serious matter. Indeed, the fundamental postulate of much of our nineteenth-century thought, in matters both of politics and religion, denies the truth of this representation, and insists, on the contrary, that man is naturally not bad, but good; and that, on the whole, as the ages go by, he is gradually becoming better and better. But it is imperative that our views of sin and of humanity shall agree with the representations held before us in the Word of God. When that Word, not only in type, as in this chapter, but in plain language (Jer. xvii. 9, R. V.), declares that "the heart is deceitful above all things, and it is *desperately sick,*" it must be a very perilous thing to deny this.

It is a profoundly instructive circumstance that, according to this typical law, the case of the supposed leper was to be judged by the priest (vv. 2, 3, *et passim*). All turned for him upon the priest's verdict. If he declared him clean, it was well; but if he pronounced him unclean, it made no difference that the man did not believe it, or that his friends did not believe it; or that he or they thought better in any respect of his case than the priest,—out of the camp he must go. He might plead that he was certainly not nearly in so bad a case as some of the poor, mutilated, dying creatures outside the camp; but that would have no weight, however true. For still he, no less really than they, was a leper; and, until made whole, into the fellowship of lepers he must go and abide. Even so for us all; everything turns, not on our own opinion of ourselves, or on what other men may think of us; but solely on the verdict of the heavenly Priest.

The picture thus set before us in the symbolism of this chapter is sad enough; but it would be far more sad did the law not now carry forward the symbolism into the region of redemption, in making provision for the cleansing of the leper, and his re-admission into the fellowship of the holy people. To this our attention is called in the next chapter.

CHAPTER XVIII.

THE CLEANSING OF THE LEPER.

Leviticus xiv. 1-32.

The ceremonies for the restoration of the leper, when healed of his disease, to full covenant privileges, were comprehended in two distinct series. The first part of the ceremonial took place without the camp, and sufficed only to terminate his condition as one ceremonially dead, and allow of his return into the camp, and his association, though still under restriction, with his fellow-Israelites. The second part of the ceremonial took up his case on the eighth day thereafter, where the former ceremonial had left him, as a member, indeed, of the holy people, but a member still under defilement such as debarred him from approach to the presence of Jehovah; and, by a fourfold offering and an anointing, restored him to the full enjoyment of all his covenant privileges before God.

This law for the cleansing of the leper certainly implies that the disease, although incurable by human skill, yet, whether by the direct power of God, as in several instances in Holy Scripture, or for some cause unknown, might occasionally cease its ravages. In this case, although the visible effects of the disease might still remain, in mutilations and scars, yet he would be none the less a healed man. That occasionally instances have occurred of such arrest of the disease, is attested by competent observers, and the law before us thus provides for the restoration of the leper in such cases to the position from which his leprosy had excluded him.

The first part of the ceremonial (vv. 3-9) took place without the camp; for until legally cleansed the man was in the sight of the law still a leper, and therefore under sentence of banishment from the congregation of Israel. Thus, as the outcast could not go to the priest, the priest, on receiving word of his desire, went to him. For the ceremony which was to be performed, he provided himself with two living, clean birds, and with cedar-wood, and scarlet, and hyssop; also he took with him an earthen vessel filled with living water,—*i. e.*, with water from some spring or flowing stream, and therefore presumably pure and clean. One of the birds was then killed in such a manner that its blood was received into the vessel of water; then the living bird and the hyssop—bound, as we are told, with the scarlet band to the cedar-wood—were dipped into the mingled blood and water, and by them the leper was sprinkled therewith seven times by the priest, and was then pronounced clean; when the living bird, stained with the blood of the bird that was killed, was allowed to fly away. Thereupon, the leper washed his clothes, shaved off all his hair, bathed in water, and entered the camp. This completed the first stadium of his restoration.

Certain things about this symbolism seem very clear. First of all, whereas the leper, afflicted, as it were, with a living death, had become, as regards Israel, a man legally dead, the sprinkling with blood, in virtue of which he was allowed to take his place again in the camp as a living Israelite, symbolised the impartation of life; and, again, inasmuch as death is defiling, the blood was mingled with water, the uniform symbol of cleansing. The remaining symbols emphasise thoughts closely related to these. The cedar-wood (or juniper), which is almost incorruptible, signified that with this new life was imparted also freedom from corruption. Scarlet, as a colour, is the constant symbol, again, like the blood, of life and health. What the hyssop was is still in debate; but we can at least safely say that it was a plant supposed to have healing and purifying virtues.

So far all is clear. But what is the meaning of the slaying of the one bird, and the loosing afterward of the other, moistened with the blood of its fellow? Some have said that both of the birds symbolised the leper: the one which was slain, the leper as he was,—namely, as one dead, or under sentence of death by his plague; the other, naturally, then, the leper as healed, who, even as the living bird is let fly whither it will, is now set at liberty to go where he pleases. But when we consider that it is by means of being sprinkled with the blood of the slain bird that the leper is cleansed, it seems quite impossible that this slain bird should typify the leper in his state of defilement. Indeed, if this bird symbolised him as under his disease, this supposition seems even absurd; for the blood which cleansed must then have represented his own blood, and his blood as diseased and unclean!

Neither is it possible that the other bird, which was set at liberty, should represent the leper as healed, and its release, his liberation; however plausible, at first thought, this explanation may seem. For the very same ceremony as this with the two birds was also to be used in the cleansing of a leprous house (vv. 50-53), where it is evident that the loosing of the living bird could not have any such significance; since the notion of a liberty given would be wholly inapplicable in the case of a house. But whatever the true meaning of the symbolism may be, it is clear that it must be one which will apply equally well in each of the two cases, the cleansing of the leprous house, no less than that of the leprous person.

We are therefore compelled to regard the slaying of the one bird as a true sacrifice. No doubt there are difficulties in the way, but they do not seem insuperable, and are, in any case, less than those which beset other suppositions. It is true that the birds are not presented before Jehovah in the tabernacle; but as the ceremony took place outside the camp, and therefore at a distance from the tabernacle, this may be explained as merely because of the necessity of the case. It is true, again, that the choice of the bird was not limited, as in the tabernacle sacrifices, to the turtle-dove or pigeon; but it might easily be that when, as in this case, the sacrifice was elsewhere than at the tabernacle, the rules for service there did not necessarily apply. Finally and decisively, when we turn to the law for the cleansing of the leprous house, we find that atoning virtue is explicitly ascribed to this rite with the birds (ver. 53): "He shall make atonement for the house."

But sacrifice is here presented in a different aspect from elsewhere in the law. In this ceremonial the central thought is not consecration through sacrifice, as in the burnt-offering; nor expiation of guilt through sacrifice, as in the sin-offering; nor yet satisfaction for trespass committed, as in the guilt-offering. It is sacrifice as procuring for the man for whom it is offered purity and life, which is the main thought.

But, according to vv. 52, 53, the atonement is made with both the dead and the living bird. The special thought which is emphasised by the use of the latter, seems to be merely the full completeness of the work of cleansing which has been accomplished through the death of the other bird. For the living bird was represented as ideally identified with the bird which was slain, by being dipped in its blood; and in that it was now loosed from its captivity, this was in token of the fact that the bird, having now given its life to impart cleansing and life to the leper, has fully accomplished that end.

Obviously, this explanation is one that will apply no less readily to the cleansing of the leprous house than of the leprous person. For the leprosy in the house signifies the working of corruption and of decay and death in the wall of the house, in a way adapted to its nature, as really as in the case of the person; and the ceremonial with the birds and other material prescribed means the same with it as with the other,—namely, the removal of the principle of corruption and disease, and impartation of purity and wholesomeness. In both cases the sevenfold sprinkling, as in analogous cases elsewhere in the law, signified the completeness of the cleansing, to which nothing was lacking, and also certified to the leper that by this impartation of new life, and by his cleansing, he was again brought into covenant relations with Jehovah.

With these ceremonies, the leper's cleansing was now in so far effected that he could enter the camp; only he must first cleanse himself and his clothes with water and shave his hair,—ceremonies which, in their primary meaning, are most naturally explained by the importance of an actual physical cleansing in such a case. Every possible precaution must be taken that by no chance he bring the contagion of his late disease into the camp. Of what special importance in this connection, besides the washing, is the shaving of the hair, will be apparent to all who know how peculiarly retentive is the hair of odours and infections of every kind.

The cleansed man might now come into the camp; he is restored to his place as a living Israelite. And yet he may not come to the tabernacle. For even an Israelite might not come, if defiled for the dead; and this is precisely the leper's status at this point. Though delivered from the power of death, there is yet persisting such a connection of his new self with his old leprous self as precludes him from yet entering the more immediate presence of God. The reality of this analogy will appear to any one who compares the rites which now follow (vv. 10-20) with those appointed for the Nazarite, when defiled by the dead (Numb. vi. 9-12).

Seven days, then, as in that case, he remains away from the tabernacle. On the seventh day, he again shaves himself even to the eyebrows, thus ensuring the most absolute cleanness, and washes himself and his clothes in water. The final restoration ceremonial took place on the eighth day,—the day symbolic of the new creation,—when he appeared before Jehovah at the tent of meeting with a he-lamb for a guilt-offering, and another for a sin-offering, and a ewe-lamb for a burnt-offering; also a meal-offering of three tenth-deals, one tenth for each sacrifice, mingled with oil, and a log (3.32 qts.) of oil. The oil was then waved for a wave-offering before the Lord, as also the whole lamb of the guilt-offering (an unusual thing), and then the lamb was slain and offered after the manner of the guilt-offering.

And now followed the most distinctive part of the ceremonial. As in the case of the consecration of the priests was done with the blood of the peace-offering and with the holy oil, so was it done here with the blood of the guilt-offering and with the common oil—now by its waving consecrated to Jehovah—which the cleansed leper had brought. The priest anoints the man's right ear, the thumb of his right hand, and the great toe of his right foot, first with the blood of the guilt-offering, and then with the oil, having previously sprinkled of the oil seven times with his finger before the Lord. The remnant of the oil in the hand of the priest he then pours upon the cleansed leper's head; then offers for him the sin-offering, the burnt-offering, and the meal-offering; and therewith, at last, the atonement is complete, and the man is restored to his full rights and privileges as a living member of the people of the living God.

The chief significance of this ceremonial lies in the prominence given to the guilt-offering. This is evidenced, not only by the special and peculiar use which is made of its blood, in applying it to the leper, but also in the fact that in the case of the poor man, while the other offerings are diminished, there is no diminution allowed as regards the lamb of the guilt-offering, and the log of oil. Why should the guilt-offering have received on this occasion such a place of special prominence? The answer has been rightly given by those who point to the significance of the guilt-offering as representing reparation and satisfaction for loss of service due. By the fact of the man's leprosy, and consequent exclusion from the camp of Israel, God had been, for the whole period of his excision, defrauded, so to speak, of His proper dues from him in respect of service and offerings; and the guilt-offering precisely symbolised satisfaction made for this default in service which he had otherwise been able to render.

Nor is it a fatal objection to this understanding of the matter that, on this principle, he also that for a long time had had an issue should have been required, for his prolonged default of service, to bring a guilt-offering in order to his restoration; whereas from him no such demand was made. For the need, before the law, for the guilt-offering lay, not in the duration of the leprosy, as such apprehend it, but in the nature of the leprosy, as being, unlike any other visitation, in a peculiar sense, a death in life. Even when the man with an issue was debarred from the sanctuary, he was not, like the leper, regarded by the law as a dead man; but was still counted among them that were living in Israel. And if precluded for an indefinite time from the service and worship of God at the tabernacle, he yet, by his public submission to the demands of the law, in the presence of all, rendered still to God the honour due from a member of the living Israel. But in that the leper, unlike any other defiled person, was reckoned ceremonially dead, obviously consistency in the symbolism made it impossible to regard him as having in any sense rendered honour or service to God so long as he continued a leper, any more than if he had been dead and buried. Therefore he must bring a guilt-offering, as one who had, however unavoidably, committed "a trespass in the holy things of the Lord." And so this guilt-offering, in the case of the leper, as in all others, represented the satisfaction of debt; and as the reality or the amount of a debt cannot be affected by the poverty of the debtor, the offering which symbolised satisfaction for the debt must be the same for the poor leper as for the rich leper.

And the application of the blood to ear, hand, and foot meant the same as in the case of the consecration of the priests. Inducted, as one now risen from the dead, into the number of the priestly people, he receives the priestly consecration, devoting ear, hand, and foot to the service of the Lord. And as it was fitting that the priests, because brought into a relation of special nearness to God, in order to be ministers of reconciliation to Israel, should therefore be consecrated with the blood of the peace-offering, which specially emphasised the realisation of reconciliation,—so the cleansed leper, who was re-established as a living member of the priestly nation, more especially by the blood of the guilt-offering, was therefore fittingly represented as consecrated in virtue, and by means of that fact.

So, like the priests, he also was anointed by the priest with oil; not indeed with the holy oil, for he was not admitted to the priestly order; yet with common oil, sanctified by its waving before God, in token of his consecration as a member of the priestly people. Especially suitable in his case was this anointing, that the oil constantly stands as a symbol of healing virtue, which in his experience he had so wondrously received.

Remembering in all this how the leprosy stands as a pre-eminent type of sin, in its aspect as involving death and corruption, the application of these ceremonies to the antitypical cleansing, at least in its chief aspects, is almost self-evident. As in all the Levitical types, so in this case, at the very entrance on the redeemed life stands the sacrifice of a life, and the service of a priest as mediator between God and man. Blood must be shed if the leper is to be admitted again into covenant standing with God; and the blood of the sacrifice in the law ever points to the sacrifice of Christ. But that great Sacrifice may be regarded in various aspects. Sin is a many-sided evil, and on every side it must be met. As often repeated, because sin as guilt requires expiation, hence the type of the sin-offering; in that it is a defrauding of God of His just rights from us, satisfaction is required, hence the type of the guilt-offering; as it is absence of consecration, life for self instead of life for God, hence the type of the burnt-offering. And yet the manifold aspects of sin are not all enumerated. For sin, again, is spiritual death; and, as death, it involves corruption and defilement. It is with special reference to this fact that the work of Christ is brought before us here. In the clean bird, slain that its blood may be applied to the leper for cleansing, we see typified Christ, as giving Himself, that His very life may be imparted to us for our life. In that the blood of the bird is mingled with water, the symbol of the Word of God, is symbolised the truth, that with the atoning blood is ever inseparably united the purifying energy of the Holy Ghost through the Word. Not the water without the blood, nor the blood without the water, saves, but the blood with the water, and the water with the blood. So it is said of Him to whom the ceremony pointed (1 John v. 6): "This is He that came by water and blood, even Jesus Christ; not with the water only, but with the water and with the blood."

But the type yet lacks something for completeness; and for this reason we have the second bird, who, when by his means the blood has been sprinkled on the leper, and the man is now pronounced clean, is released and flies away heavenward. What a beautiful symbol of that other truth, without which even the atonement of the Lord were naught, that He who died, having by that death for us procured our life, was then released from the bonds of death, rising from the dead on the third day, and ascending to heaven, like the freed bird, in token that His life-giving, cleansing work was done. Thus the message which, as the liberated bird flies carolling away, sweet as a heavenly song, seems to fall upon the ear, is this, " Delivered up for our trespasses, and raised for our justification " (Rom. iv. 25; see *Gr.*).

But although thus and then restored to his standing as a member of the living people of God, not yet was the cleansed leper allowed to appear in the presence of God at the tent of meeting. There was a delay of a week, and only then, on the eighth day, the day typical of resurrection and new creation, does He appear before God. Is there typical meaning in this delay? We would not be too confident. It is quite possible that this delay of a week, before the cleansed man was allowed to present himself for the completion of the ceremonial which reinstated him in the plenary enjoyment of all the rights and privileges of a child of Israel, may have been intended merely as a precautionary rule, of which the purpose was to guard against the possibility of infection, and the defilement of the sanctuary by his presence, through renewed activity of the disease; while, at the same time, it would serve as a spiritual discipline to remind the man, now cleansed, of the extreme care and holy fear with which, after his defilement, he should venture into the presence of the Holy One of Israel; and thus, by analogy, it becomes a like lesson to the spiritually cleansed in all ages.

But perhaps we may see a deeper significance in this week of delay, and his appointed appearance before the Lord on the eighth day. If the whole course of the leper, from the time of his infection till his final reappearing in the presence of Jehovah at the tent of meeting, be intended to typify the history and experience of a sinner as saved from sin; and if the cleansing of the leper without the camp, and his reinstatement thereupon as a member of God's Israel, represents in type the judicial reinstatement of the cleansed sinner, through the application of the blood and Spirit of Christ, in the number of God's people; one can then hardly fail to recognise in the week's delay appointed to him, before he could come into the immediate presence of God, an adumbration of the fact that between the sinner's acceptance and the appointed time of his appearing, finally and fully cleansed, before the Lord, on the resurrection morning, there intervenes a period of delay, even the whole lifetime of the believer here in the flesh and in the disembodied state. For only thereafter does he at last, wholly perfected, appear before God in the heavenly Zion. But before thus appearing, the accepted man once and again had to cleanse his garments and his person, that so he might remove everything in which by any chance uncleanness might still lurk. Which, translated into New Testament language, gives us the charge of the Apostle Paul (2 Cor. vii. 1) addressed to those who had indeed received the new life, but were still in the flesh: " Let us cleanse ourselves from all defilement of flesh and spirit, perfecting holiness in the fear of God."

But, at last, the week of delay is ended. After its seventh day follows an eighth, the first-day morning of a new week, the morning typical of resurrection and therewith completed redemption, and the leper now, completely restored, appears before God in the holy tabernacle. Even so shall an eighth-day morning dawn for all who by the cleansing blood have been received into the number of God's people. And when that day comes, then, even as when the cleansed man appeared at the tent of meeting, he presented guilt-offering, sin-offering, and burnt-offering, as the warrant for his presence there, and the ground of his acceptance, so shall it be in that day of resurrection, when every one of God's once leprous but now washed and accepted children shall appear in Zion before Him. They will all appear there as pleading the blood, the precious blood of Christ; Christ, at last apprehended and received by them in all His fulness, as expiation, satisfaction, and righteousness. For so John represents it in the apocalyptic vision of the blood-washed multitude in the heavenly glory (Rev. vii. 14, 15): "These are they which come out of the great tribulation, and they washed their robes, and made them white in the blood of the Lamb. *Therefore* are they before the throne of God; and they serve Him day and night in His temple."

And as it is written (Rom. viii. 11) that the final quickening of our mortal bodies shall be accomplished by the Spirit of God, so the leper, now in God's presence, receives a special anointing; a type of the unction of the Holy Ghost in resurrection power, consecrating the once leprous ear, hand, and foot, and therewith the whole body, now cleansed from all defilement, to the glad service of Jehovah our God and our Redeemer.

Such, in outline at least, appears to be the typical significance of this ceremonial of the cleansing of the leper. Some details are indeed still left unexplained, but, probably, the whole reason for some of the regulations is to be found in the immediate practical necessities of the leper's condition.

Of Leprosy in a Garment or House.

Leviticus xiii. 47-59; xiv. 33-53.

"The garment also that the plague of leprosy is in, whether it be a woollen garment, or a linen garment; whether it be in warp, or woof; of linen, or of woollen; whether in a skin, or in any thing made of skin; if the plague be greenish or reddish in the garment, or in the skin, or in the warp, or in the woof, or in any thing of skin; it is the plague of leprosy, and shall be shewed unto the priest: and the priest shall look upon the plague, and shut up that which hath the plague seven days: and he shall look on the plague on the seventh day: if the plague be spread in the garment, either in the warp, or in the woof, or in the skin, whatever service skin is used for; the plague is a fretting leprosy; it is unclean. And he shall burn the garment, whether the warp or the woof, in woollen or in linen, or any thing of skin, wherein the plague is: for it is a fretting leprosy; it shall be burnt in the fire. And if the priest shall look, and, behold, the plague be not spread in the garment, either in the warp, or in the woof, or in any thing of skin; then the priest shall command that they wash the thing wherein the plague is, and he shall shut it up seven days more: and the priest shall look, after that the plague is washed: and, behold, if the plague have not changed its colour, and the plague be not spread, it is unclean; thou shalt burn it in the fire: it is a fret, whether the bareness be within or without. And if the priest look, and, behold, the plague be dim after the washing thereof, then he shall rend it out of the garment, or out of the skin, or out of the warp, or out of the woof: and if it appear still in the garment, either in the warp, or in the woof, or in any thing of skin, it is breaking out: thou shalt burn that wherein the plague is with fire. And the garment, either the warp, or the woof, or whatsoever thing of skin it be, which thou shalt wash, if the plague be departed from them, then it shall be washed the second time, and shall be clean. This is the law of the plague of leprosy in a garment of woollen or linen, either in the warp, or the woof, or any thing of skin, to pronounce it clean, or to pronounce it unclean. . . . And the Lord spake unto Moses and unto Aaron, saying, When ye be come into the land of Canaan, which I give to you for a possession, and I put the plague of leprosy in a house of the land of your possession; then he that owneth the house shall come and tell the priest, saying, There seemeth to me to be as it were a plague in the house: and the priest shall command that they empty the house, before the priest go in to see the plague, that all that is in the house be not made unclean: and afterward the priest shall go in to see the house: and he shall look on the plague, and, behold, if the plague be in the walls of the house with hollow strakes, greenish or reddish, and the appearance thereof be lower than the wall; then the priest shall go out of the house to the door of the house, and shut up the house seven days: and the priest shall come again the seventh day, and shall look: and, behold, if the plague be spread in the walls of the house; then the priest shall command that they take out the stones in which the plague is, and cast them into an unclean place without the city: and he shall cause the house to be scraped within round about, and they shall pour out the mortar that they scrape off without the city into an unclean place: and they shall take other stones, and put them in the place of those stones; and he shall take other mortar and shall plaister the house. And if the plague come again, and break out in the house, after that he hath taken out the stones, and after he hath scraped the house, and after it is plaistered; then the priest shall come in and look, and, behold, if the plague be spread in the house, it is a fretting leprosy in the house: it is unclean. And he shall break down the house, the stones of it, and the timber thereof, and all the mortar of the house; and he shall carry them forth out of the city into an unclean place. Moreover he that goeth into the house all the while that it is shut up shall be unclean until the even. And he that lieth in the house shall wash his clothes; and he that eateth in the house shall wash his clothes. And if the priest shall come in, and look, and, behold, the plague hath not spread in the house, after the house was plaistered; then the priest shall pronounce the house clean, because the plague is healed. And he shall take to cleanse the house two birds, and cedar wood, and scarlet, and hyssop: and he shall kill one of the birds in an earthen vessel over running water: and he shall take the cedar wood, and the hyssop, and the scarlet, and the living bird, and dip them in the blood of the slain bird, and in the running water, and sprinkle the house seven times: and he shall cleanse the house with the blood of the bird, and with the running water, and with the living bird, and with the cedar wood, and with the hyssop, and with the scarlet: but he shall let go the living bird out of the city into the open field: so shall he make atonement for the house: and it shall be clean."

There has been much debate as to what we are to understand by the leprosy in the garment or in a house. Was it an affection identical in nature with the leprosy of the body? or was it merely so called from a certain external similarity to that plague?

However extraordinary the former supposition might once have seemed, in the present state of medical science we are at least able to say that there is nothing inconceivable in it. We have abundant experimental evidence that a large number of diseases, and, not improbably, leprosy among them, are caused by minute parasitic forms of vegetable life; and, also, that in many cases these forms of life may, and do, exist and multiply in various other suitable media besides the fluids and tissues of the human body. If, as is quite likely, leprosy be caused by some such parasitic life in the human body, it is then evidently possible that such parasites, under favourable conditions of heat, moisture, etc., should exist and propagate themselves, as in other analogous cases, outside the body; as, for instance, in cloth, or leather, or in the plaster of a house; in which case it is plain that such garments or household implements, or such dwellings, as might be thus infected, would be certainly unwholesome, and presumably capable of communicating the leprosy to the human subject. But we have not yet sufficient scientific observation to settle the question whether this is really so; we can, however, safely say that, in any case, the description which is here given indicates a growth in the affected garment or house of some kind of mould or mildew; which, as we know, is a form of life produced under conditions which always imply an unwholesome state of the article or house in which it appears. We also know that if such growths be allowed to go on unchecked, they involve more or less rapid processes of decomposition in that which is affected. Thus, even from a merely natural point of view, one can see the high wisdom of the Divine King of Israel in ordering that, in all such cases, the man whose garment or house was thus affected should at once notify the priest, who was to come and decide whether the appearance was of a noxious and unclean kind or not, and then take action accordingly.

Whether the suspicious spot were in a house or in some article it contained, the article or house (the latter having been previously emptied) was first shut up for seven days (xiii. 50; xiv. 38). If in the garment or other article affected it was found then to have spread, it was without any further ceremony to be burnt (xiii. 51, 52). If it had not spread, it was to be washed and shut up seven days more, at the end of which time, even though it had not spread, if the greenish or reddish colour remained unchanged, it was still to be adjudged unclean, and to be burned (xiii. 55). If, on the other hand, the colour had somewhat "dimmed," the part affected was to be cut out; when, if it spread no further, it was to be washed a second time and be pronounced clean (xiii. 58). If, however, after the excision of the affected part, the spot appeared again, the article, without further delay, was to be burned (xiii. 57).

The law, in the case of the appearing of a leprosy in a house (xiv. 33-53), was much more elaborate. As in the former case, when the occupant of the house suspects, "as it were a plague in the house," he is to go and tell the priest; who is, first of all, to order the emptying of the house before he goes in, lest that which is in the house, should it prove to be the plague, be made unclean (ver. 36). The diagnosis reminds us of that of the leprosy in the body; greenish or reddish streaks, in appearance "lower than the wall," i. e., deep-seated (ver. 37). Where this is observed, the empty house is to be shut up for seven days (ver. 38); and at the end of that time, if the spot has spread, "the stones in which the plague is" are to be taken out, the plaster scraped off the walls of the house, and all carried out into an unclean place outside of the city, and new stones and new plaster put in the place of the old (vv. 40-42). If, after this, the plague yet reappear, the house is to be adjudged unclean, and is to be wholly torn down, and all the material carried into an unclean place without the city (vv. 44, 45). If, on the other hand, after this renewal of the interior of the house, the spots do not reappear, the priest "shall pronounce the house clean, because the plague is healed" (ver. 48). But, unlike the case of the leprous garment, this does not end the ceremonial. It is ordered that the priest shall take to cleanse (lit. "to purge the house from sin") (ver. 49) two birds, scarlet, cedar, and hyssop, which are then used precisely as in the case of the purgation of the leprous man; and at the end, "he shall let go the living bird out of the city into the open field: so shall he make atonement for the house: and it shall be clean" (vv. 50-53).

For the time then present, one can hardly fail to see in this ceremonial, first, a merciful sanitary intent. By the observance of these regulations not only was Israel to be saved from many sicknesses and various evils, but was to be constantly reminded that Israel's God, like a wise and kind Father, had a care for everything that pertained to their welfare; not only for their persons, but also for their dwellings, and even all the various articles of daily use. The lesson is always in force, for God has not changed. He is not a God who cares for the souls of men only, but for their bodies also, and everything around them. His servants do well to remember this, and in this imitate Him, as happily many are doing more and more. Bibles and tracts are good, and religious exhortation; but we have here left us a Divine warrant not to content ourselves with these things alone, but to have a care for the clothing and the homes of those we would reach with the Gospel. In all the large cities of Christendom it must be confessed that the principle which underlies these laws concerning houses and garments, is often terribly neglected. Whether the veritable plague of leprosy be in the walls of many of our tenement houses or not, there can be no doubt that it could not be much worse if it were; and Christian philanthropy and legislation could scarcely do better in many cases than vigorously to enforce the Levitical law, tear down, re-plaster, or, in many cases, destroy from the foundation, tenement houses which could, with little exaggeration, be justly described as leprous throughout.

But all which is in this law cannot be thus explained. Even the Israelite must have looked beyond this for the meaning of the ordinance of the two birds, the cedar, scarlet, and hyssop, and the "atonement" for the house. He would have easily perceived that not only leprosy in the body, but this leprosy in the garment and the house, was a sign that both the man himself, and his whole environment as well, was subject to death and decay; that, as already he would have learned from the Book of Genesis, even nature was under a curse because of man's sin; and that, as in the Divine plan, sacrificial cleansing was required for the deliverance of man, so also it was somehow mysteriously required for the cleansing of his earthly abode and surroundings, in default of which purgation they must be destroyed.

And from this to the antitypical truth prefigured by these laws it is but a step; and a step which we take with full New Testament light to guide us. For if the leprosy in the body visibly typified the working of sin and death in the soul of man, then, as clearly, the leprosy in the house must in this law be intended to symbolise the working of sin in the material earthly creation, which is man's abode. The type thus brings before us the truth which is set forth by the Apostle Paul in Rom. viii. 20-22, where we are taught in express words that, not man alone, but the whole creation also, because of sin, has come under a "bondage of corruption." "The creation was subjected to vanity, not of its own will, but by reason of him who subjected it. . . For we know that the whole creation groaneth and travaileth in pain together until now." This is one truth which is shadowed forth in this type.

But the type also shows us how, as Scripture elsewhere clearly teaches, if after such partial purgation as was effected by means of the deluge the bondage of corruption still persist, then the abode of man must itself be destroyed; "the earth and the works that are therein shall be burned up" (2 Peter iii. 10). Nothing less than fire will suffice to put an end to the working in material nature of this mysterious curse. And yet beyond the fire is redemption. For the atonement shall avail not only for the leprous man, but for the purifying of the leprous abode. The sprinkling of sacrificial blood and water by means of the cedar, and hyssop, and scarlet, and the living bird, which effected the deliverance of the leper, are used also in the same way and for the same end, for the leprous house. And so "according to his promise, we look for new heavens and a new earth, wherein dwelleth righteousness" (2 Peter iii. 13); and it shall be brought in through the virtue of atonement made by a Saviour slain, and applied by a Saviour alive from the dead; so that, as the free bird flies away in token of the full completion of deliverance from the curse, so "the creation itself also shall be delivered from the bondage of corruption into the liberty of the glory of the children of God" (Rom. viii. 21).

But there was also a leprosy of the garment. If the leprosy in the body typified the effect of sin in the soul, and the leprosy in the house, the effect of sin in the earthly creation, which is man's home; the leprosy of the garment can scarcely typify anything else than the presence and effects of sin in those various relations in life which constitute our present environment. Whenever, in any of these, we suspect the working of sin, first of all we are to lay the case before the heavenly Priest. And then, if He with the "eyes like a flame of fire" (Rev. i. 14, ii. 18) declare anything unclean, then that in which the stain is found must be without hesitation cut out and thrown away. And if still, after this, we find the evil reappearing, then the whole garment must go, fair and good though the most of it may still appear. In other words, those relations and engagements in which, despite all possible care and precaution, we find manifest sin persistently reappearing, as if there were in them, however inexplicably, an ineradicable tendency to evil,—these we must resolutely put away, "hating even the garment spotted by the flesh."

The leprous garment must be burnt. For its restoration or purification the law made no provision. For here, in the antitype, we are dealing with earthly relationships, which have only to do with the present life and order. "The fashion of this world passeth away" (1 Cor. vii. 31). There shall be "new heavens and a new earth," but in that new creation the old environment shall be found no longer. The old garments, even such as were best, shall be no longer used. The redeemed shall walk with the King and Redeemer, clothed in the white robes which He shall give. No more leprosy then in person, house, or garment! For we shall be set before the presence of the Father's glory, without blemish, in exceeding joy, "not having spot, or wrinkle, or any such thing." Wherefore "to the only God our Saviour, through Jesus Christ our Lord, be glory, majesty, dominion, and power, before all time, and now, and for evermore. Amen."

CHAPTER XIX.

HOLINESS IN EATING.

LEVITICUS xvii. 1-16.

WITH this chapter begins another subdivision of the law. Hitherto we have had before us only sacrificial worship and matters of merely ceremonial law. The law of holy living contained in the following chapters (xvii.-xx.), on the other hand, has to do for the most part with matters rather ethical than ceremonial, and consists chiefly of precepts designed to regulate morally the ordinary engagements and relationships of every-day life. The fundamental thought of the four chapters is that which is expressed, e. g., in xviii. 3: Israel, redeemed by Jehovah, is called to be a holy people; and this holiness is to be manifested in a total separation from the ways of the heathen. This principle is enforced by various specific commands and prohibitions, which naturally have particular regard to the special conditions under which Israel was placed, as a holy nation consecrated to Jehovah, the one, true God, but living in the midst of nations of idolaters.

The whole of chapter xvii., with the exception of vv. 8, 9, has to do with the application of this law of holy living to the use even of lawful food. At first thought, the injunctions of the chapter might seem to belong rather to ceremonial than to moral law; but closer observation will show that all the injunctions here given have direct reference to the avoidance of idolatry, especially as connected with the preparation and use of food.

It was not enough that the true Israelite should abstain from food prohibited by God, as in chap. xii.; he must also use that which was permitted in a way well-pleasing to God, carefully shunning even the appearance of any complicity with surrounding idolatry, or fellowship with the heathen in their unholy fashions and customs. Even so for the Christian: it is not enough that he abstain from what is expressly forbidden; even in his use of lawful food, he must so use it that it shall be to him a means of grace, in helping him to maintain an uninterrupted walk with God.

In vv. 1-7 is given the law to regulate the use of such clean animals for food as could be offered to God in sacrifice; in vv. 10-16, of such as, although permitted for food, were not allowed for sacrifice.

The directions regarding the first class may be summed up in this: all such animals were to be treated as peace-offerings. No private person in Israel was to slaughter any such animal anywhere in the camp or out of it, except at the door of the tent of meeting. Thither they were to be brought "unto the priest," and offered for peace-offerings (ver. 5); the blood must be sprinkled on the altar of burnt-offering; the fat parts burnt "for a sweet savour unto the Lord" (ver. 6); and then only, the priest having first taken his appointed portions, the remainder might now be eaten by the Israelite, as given back to him by God, in peaceful fellowship with Him.

The law could not have been burdensome, as some might hastily imagine. Even when obtainable, meat was probably not used as food by them so freely as with us; and in the wilderness the lack of flesh, it will be remembered, was so great as to have occasioned at one time a rebellion among the people, who fretfully complained (Numb. xi. 4): "Who shall give us flesh to eat?"

Even the uncritical reader must be able to see how manifest is the Mosaic date of this part of Leviticus. The terms of this law suppose a camp-life; indeed, the camp is explicitly named (ver. 3). That which was enjoined was quite practicable under the conditions of life in the wilderness, when, at the best, flesh was scarce, and the people dwelt compactly together; but would have been utterly inapplicable and impracticable at a later date, after they were settled throughout the land of Canaan, when to have slaughtered all beasts used for food at the central sanctuary would have been impossible. Hence we find that, as we should expect, the modified law of Deuteronomy (xii. 15, 16, 20-24), assuming the previous existence of this earlier law, explicitly repeals it. To suppose that forgers of a later day, as, for instance, of the time of Josiah, or after the Babylonian exile, should have needlessly invented a law of this kind, is an hypothesis which is rightly characterised by Dillmann as "simply absurd." *

This regulation for the wilderness days is said (vv. 5, 7) to have been made " to the end that the children of Israel may bring their sacrifices, which they sacrifice in the open field . . . unto the Lord, . . . and sacrifice them for sacrifices of peace offerings unto the Lord. . . . And they shall no more sacrifice their sacrifices unto the he-goats, after whom they go a whoring."

There can be no doubt that in the last sentence, "he-goats," as in the Revised Version, instead of "devils," as in the Authorised, is the right rendering. The worship referred to was still in existence in the days of the monarchy; for it is included in the charges against "Jeroboam, the son of Nebat, who made Israel to sin" (2 Chron. xi. 15), that "he appointed him priests, . . . for the he-goats, and for the calves which he had made." Nor can here we agree with Dillmann † that in this worship of he-goats here referred to, there is "no occasion to think of the goat-worship of Egypt." For inasmuch as we know that the worship of the sacred bull and that of the he-goat prevailed in Egypt in those days, and inasmuch as in Ezekiel xx. 6, 7, 15-18, repeated reference is made to Israel's having worshipped "the idols of Egypt," one can hardly avoid combining these two facts, and thus connecting the goat-worship to which allusion is here made, with that which prevailed at Mendes, in Lower Egypt. This cult at that place was accompanied with nameless revolting rites, such as give special significance to the description of this worship (ver. 7) as "a whoring" after the goats; and abundantly explain and justify the severity of the penalty attached to the violation of this law (ver. 4) in cutting off the offender from this people; all the more when we observe the fearful persistency of this horrible goat-worship in Israel, breaking out anew, as just remarked, some five hundred years later, in the reign of Jeroboam.

The words imply that the ordinary slaughter of animals for food was often connected with some idolatrous ceremony related to this goat-worship. What precisely it may have been, we know not; but of such customs, connecting the preparation of the daily food with idolatry, we have abundant illustration in the usages of the ancient Persians, the Hindoos, and the heathen Arabs of the days before Mohammed. The law was thus intended to cut out this every-day idolatry by the root. With these "field-devils," as Luther renders the word, the holy people of the Lord were to have nothing to do.

Very naturally, the requirement to present all slaughtered animals as peace-offerings to Jehovah gives occasion to turn aside for a little from the matter of food, which is the chief subject of the chapter, in order to extend this principle beyond animals slaughtered for food, and insist particularly that all burnt-offerings and sacrifices of every kind should be sacrificed at the door of the tent of meeting, and nowhere else. This law, we are told (ver. 8), was to be applied, not only to the Israelites themselves, but also to "strangers" among them; such as, *e. g.*, were the Gibeonites. No idolatry, nor anything likely to be associated with it, was to be tolerated from any one in the holy camp.

The principle which underlies this stringent law, as also the reason which is given for it, is of constant application in modern life. There was nothing wrong in itself in slaying an animal in one place more than another. It was abstractly possible—as, likely enough, many an Israelite may have said to himself—that a man could just as really "eat unto the Lord" if he slaughtered and ate his animal in the field, as anywhere else. Nevertheless this was forbidden under the heaviest penalties. It teaches us that he who will be holy must not only abstain from that which is in itself always wrong, but must carefully keep himself from doing even lawful or necessary things in such a way, or under such associations and circumstances, as may outwardly compromise his Christian standing, or which may be proved by experience to have an almost unavoidable tendency toward sin. The laxity in such matters which prevails in the so-called "Christian world" argues little for the tone of spiritual life in our day in those who indulge in it, or allow it, or apologise for it. It may be true enough, in a sense, that as many say, there is no harm in this or that. Perhaps not; but what if experience have shown that, though in itself not sinful, a certain association or amusement almost always tends to worldliness, which is a form of idolatry? Or—to use the apostle's illustration—what if one be seen, though with no intention of wrong, "sitting at meat in an idol's temple," and he whose conscience is weak be thereby emboldened to do what to him is sin? There is only one safe principle, now as in the days of Moses: everything must be brought "before the Lord;" used as from Him and for Him, and therefore used under such limitations and restrictions as His wise and holy law imposes. Only so shall we be safe; only so abide in living fellowship with God.

Very beautiful and instructive, again, was the direction that the Israelite, in the cases specified, should make his daily food a peace-offering. This involved a dedication of the daily food to the Lord; and in his receiving it back again then from the hand of God, the truth was visibly represented that our daily food is from God; while also, in the sacrificial acts which preceded the eating, the Israelite was continually reminded

---

* "Die Bücher Exodus und Leviticus," 2 Aufl., p. 535.
† *Ibid.*, p. 537.

that it was upon the ground of an accepted atonement that even these every-day mercies were received. Such also should be, in spirit, the often neglected prayer before each of our daily meals. It should be ever offered with the remembrance of the precious blood which has purchased for us even the most common mercies; and should thus sincerely recognise what, in the confusing complexity of the second causes through which we receive our daily food, we so easily forget: that the Lord's prayer is not a mere form of words when we say, "Give us this day our daily bread;" but that working behind, and in, and with, all these second causes, is the kindly Providence of God, who, opening His hand, supplies the want of every living thing. And so, eating in grateful, loving fellowship with our Heavenly Father that which His bounty gives us, to His glory, every meal shall become, as it were, a sacramental remembrance of the Lord. We may have wondered at what we have read of the world-wide custom of the Mohammedan, who, whenever the knife of slaughter is lifted against a beast for food, utters his "*Bism allah*," "In the name of the most merciful God;" and not otherwise will regard his food as being made *halal*, or "lawful;" and, no doubt, in all this, as in many a Christian's prayer, there may often be little heart. But the thought in this ceremony is even this of Leviticus, and we do well to make it our own, eating even our daily food "in the name of the most merciful God," and with uplifting of the heart in thankful worship toward Him.

But there were many beasts which, although they might not be offered to the Lord in sacrifice, were yet "clean," and permitted to the Israelites as food. Such, in particular, were clean animals that are taken in the hunt or chase. In vv. 10-16 the law is given for the use of these. It is prefaced by a very full and explicit prohibition of the eating of blood;* for while, as regards the animals to be offered to the Lord, provision was made with respect to the blood, that it was to be sprinkled around the altar, there was the danger that in other cases, where this was not permissible, the blood might be used for food. Hence the prohibition against eating "any manner of blood," on a twofold ground: first (vv. 11, 14), that the life of the flesh is the blood; and second (ver. 11), that, for this reason, God had chosen the blood to be the symbol of life substituted for the life of the guilty in atoning sacrifice: "I have given it to you upon the altar to make atonement for your souls." Hence, in order that this relation of the blood to the forgiveness of sins might be constantly kept before the mind, it was ordained that never should the Israelite eat of flesh except the blood should first have been carefully drained out. And it was to be treated with reverence, as having thus a certain sanctity; when the beast was taken in hunting, the Israelite must (ver. 13) "pour out the blood thereof, and cover it with dust;"—an act by which the blood, the life, was symbolically returned to Him who in the beginning said (Gen. i. 24), "Let the earth bring forth the living creature after its kind." And because, in the case of "that which dieth of itself," or is "torn of beasts," the blood would not be thus carefully drained off, all such animals (ver. 15) are prohibited as food.

It is profoundly instructive to observe that here, again, we come upon declarations and a command, the deep truth and fitness of which is only becoming clear now after three thousand years. For, as the result of our modern discoveries with regard to the constitution of the blood, and the exact nature of its functions, we in this day are able to say that it is not far from a scientific statement of the facts, when we read (ver. 14), "As to the life of all flesh, the blood thereof is all one with the life thereof." For it is in just this respect that the blood is most distinct from all other parts of the body; that, whereas it conveys and mediates nourishment to all, it is itself nourished by none; but by its myriad cells brought immediately in contact with the digested food, directly and immediately assimilates it to itself. We are compelled to say that as regards the physical life of man—which alone is signified by the original term here—it is certainly true of the blood, as of no other part of the organism, that "the life of all flesh is the blood thereof."

And while it is true that, according to the text, a spiritual and moral reason is given for the prohibition of the use of blood as food, yet it is well worth noting that, as has been already remarked in another connection, the prohibition, as we are now beginning to see, had also a hygienic reason. For Dr. de Mussy, in his paper before the French Academy of Medicine already referred to,* calls attention to the fact that, not only did the Mosaic laws exclude from the Hebrew dietary animals "particularly liable to parasites;" but also that "it is in the blood," so rigidly prohibited by Moses as food, "that the germs or spores of infectious disease circulate." Surely no one need fear, with some expositors, lest this recognition of a sanitary intent in these laws shall hinder the recognition of their moral and spiritual purport, which in this chapter is so expressly taught. Rather should this cause us the more to wonder and admire the unity which thus appears between the demands and necessities of the physical and the moral and spiritual life; and, in the discovery of the marvellous adaptation of these ancient laws to the needs of both, to find a new confirmation of our faith in God and in His revealed Word. For thus do they appear to be laws so far beyond the wisdom of that time, and so surely beneficent in their working, that in view of this it should be easy to believe that it must indeed have been the Lord God, the Maker and Preserver of all flesh, who spake all these laws unto His servant Moses.

The moral and spiritual purpose of this law concerning the use of blood was apparently twofold. In the first place, it was intended to educate the people to a reverence for life, and purify them from that tendency to bloodthirstiness which has so often distinguished heathen nations, and especially those with whom Israel was to be brought in closest contact. But secondly, and chiefly, it was intended, as in the former part of the chapter, everywhere and always to keep before the mind the sacredness of the blood as being the appointed means for the expiation of sin; given by God upon the altar to make atonement for the soul of the sinner, "by reason of the life" or soul with which it stood in such immediate relation. Not only were they

---

* These verses have been partially expounded, indeed, before, in so far as was necessary to a complete exposition of the sin-offering; but in this context the subject is brought forward in another relation, which renders necessary this additional exposition.

* See p. 310.

therefore to abstain from the blood of such animals as could be offered on the altar, but even from that of those which could not be offered. Thus the blood was to remind them, every time that they ate flesh, of the very solemn truth that without shedding of blood there was no remission of sin. The Israelite must never forget this; even in the heat and excitement of the chase, he must pause and carefully drain the blood from the creature he had slain, and reverently cover it with dust;—a symbolic act which should ever put him in mind of the Divine ordinance that the blood, the life, of a guiltless victim must be given, in order to the forgiveness of sin.

A lesson lies here for us regarding the sacredness of all that is associated with sacred things. All that is connected with God, and with His worship, especially all that is connected with His revelation of Himself for our salvation, is to be treated with the most profound reverence. Even though the blood of the deer killed in the chase could not be used in sacrifice, yet, because it was blood, was in its essential nature like unto that which was so used, therefore it must be treated with a certain respect, and be always covered with earth. It is the fashion of our age —and one which is increasing in an alarming degree—to speak lightly of things which are closely connected with the revelation and worship of the holy God. Against everything of this kind the spirit of this law warns us. Nothing which is associated in any way with what is sacred is to be spoken of or treated irreverently, lest we thus come to think lightly of the sacred things themselves. This irreverent treatment of holy things is a crying evil in many parts of the English-speaking world, as also in continental Christendom. We need to beware of it. After irreverence, too often, by no obscure law, comes open denial of the Holy One and of His Holy Son, our Lord and Saviour. The blood of Christ, which represented that holy life which was given on the cross for our sins, is holy—an infinitely holy thing! And what is God's estimate of its sanctity we may perhaps learn—looking through the symbol to that which was symbolised—from this law; which required that all blood, because outwardly resembling the holy blood of sacrifice, and, like it, the seat and vehicle of life, should be treated with most careful reverence. And it is safe to say that just those most need the lesson taught by this command who find it the hardest to appreciate it, and to whom its injunctions still seem regulations puerile and unworthy, according to their fancy, of the dignity and majesty of God.

CHAPTER XX.

THE LAW OF HOLINESS: CHASTITY.

Leviticus xviii. 1-30.

Chapters xviii., xix., and xx., by a formal introduction (xviii. 1-5) and a formal closing (xx. 22-26), are indicated as a distinct section, very commonly known by the name, "the Law of Holiness." As this phrase indicates, these chapters—unlike chap. xvii., which as to its contents has a character intermediate between the ceremonial and moral law—consist substantially of moral prohibitions and commandments throughout. Of the three, the first two contain the prohibitions and precepts of the law; the third (xx.), the penal sanctions by which many of these were to be enforced.

The section opens (vv. 1, 2) with Jehovah's assertion of His absolute supremacy, and a reminder to Israel of the fact that He had entered into covenant relations with them: " I am the Lord your God." With solemn emphasis the words are again repeated, ver. 4; and yet again in ver. 5: " I am the Lord."* They would naturally call to mind the scene at Sinai, with its august and appalling grandeur, attesting amid earthquake and fire and tempest at once the being, power, and unapproachable holiness of Him who then and there, with those stupendous solemnities, in inexplicable condescension, took Israel into covenant with Himself, to be to Himself " a kingdom of priests and a holy nation." There could be no question as to the right of the God thus revealed to impose law; no question as to the peculiar obligation upon Israel to keep His law; no question as to His intolerance of sin, and full power and determination, as the Holy One, to enforce whatever He commanded. All these thoughts—thoughts of eternal moment—would be called up in the mind of every devout Israelite, as he heard or read this preface to the law of holiness.

The prohibitions which we find in chap. xviii. are not given as an exhaustive code of laws upon the subjects traversed, but rather deal with certain gross offences against the law of chastity, which, as we know from other sources, were horribly common at that time among the surrounding nations. To indulgence in these crimes, Israel, as the later history sadly shows, would be especially liable; so contagious are evil example and corrupt associations! Hence the general scope of the chapter is announced in this form (ver. 3): " After the doings of the land of Egypt, wherein ye dwelt, shall ye not do: and after the doings of the land of Canaan, whither I bring you, shall ye not do: neither shall ye walk in their statutes."

Instead of this, they were (ver. 4) to do God's judgments, and keep His statutes, to walk in them, bearing in mind whose they were. And as a further motive it is added (ver. 5): " which if a man do, he shall live in them;" that is, as the Chaldee paraphrast, Onkelos, rightly interprets in the Targum, " with the life of eternity." Which far-reaching promise is sealed by the repetition, for the third time, of the words, " I am the Lord." That is enough; for what Jehovah promises, that shall certainly be!

The law begins (ver. 6) with a general statement of the principle which underlies all particular prohibitions of incest: " None of you shall approach to any that is near of kin to him, to uncover their nakedness;" and then, for the fourth time, are iterated the words, " I am the Lord." The prohibitions which follow require little special explanation. As just remarked, they are directed in particular to those breaches of the law of chastity which were most common with the Egyptians, from the midst of whom Israel had come; and with the Canaanites, to whose land they were going. This explains, for

---

* It deserves to be noticed that in this phrase, which recurs with such frequency in this "Law of Holiness," the original, with evident allusion to Exod. iii. 15 ; vi. 2-4, always has the covenant name of God, commonly anglicised "Jehovah." The retention of the term "Lord" here, as in many other places, is much to be regretted, as seriously weakening and obscuring the sense to the ordinary reader.

instance, the fulness of detail in the prohibition of incestuous union with a sister or half-sister (vv. 9, 11),—an iniquity very common in Egypt, having the sanction of royal custom from the days of the Pharaohs down to the time of the Ptolemies. The unnatural alliance of a man with his mother prohibited in ver. 8, of which Paul declared (1 Cor. v. 1) that in his day it did not exist among the Gentiles, was yet the distinguishing infamy of the Medes and Persians for many centuries. Union with an aunt, by blood or by marriage, prohibited in vv. 12-14,—a connection less gross, and less severely to be punished than the preceding,—seems to have been permitted even among the Israelites themselves while in Egypt, as is plain from the case of Amram and Jochebed (Exod. vi. 20). To the law forbidding connection with a brother's wife (ver. 16), the later Deuteronomic law (Deut. xxv. 5-10), made an exception, permitting that a man might marry the widow of his deceased brother, when the latter had died without children, and "raise up seed unto his brother." In this, however, the law but sanctioned a custom which—as we learn from the case of Onan (Gen. xxxviii.)—had been observed long before the days of Moses, both by the Hebrews and other ancient nations, and, indeed, even limited and restricted its application; with good reason providing for exemption of the surviving brother from this duty, in cases where for any reason it might be repugnant or impracticable.

The case of a connection with both a woman and her daughter or granddaughter is next mentioned (ver. 17); and, with special emphasis, is declared to be "wickedness," or "enormity."

The prohibition (ver. 18) of marriage with a sister-in-law, as is well known, has been, and still is, the occasion of much controversy, into which it is not necessary here to enter at length. But, whatever may be thought for other reasons as to the lawfulness of such a union, it truly seems quite singular that this verse should ever have been cited as prohibiting such an alliance. No words could well be more explicit than those which we have here, in limiting the application of the prohibition to the life-time of the wife: "Thou shalt not take a woman to her sister, *to be a rival to her*, to uncover her nakedness, beside the other *in her life time*" (R.V.). The law therefore does not touch the question for which it is so often cited, but was evidently only intended as a restriction on prevalent polygamy. Polygamy is ever likely to produce jealousies and heart-burnings; but it is plain that this phase of the evil would reach its most extreme and odious expression when the new and rival wife was a sister to the one already married; when it would practically annul sisterly love, and give rise to such painful and peculiarly humiliating dissensions as we read of between the sisters Leah and Rachel. The sense of the passage is so plain, that we are told that this interpretation "stood its ground unchallenged from the third century B. C. to the middle of the sixteenth century A. D." Whatever opinion any may hold therefore as to the expediency, upon other grounds, of this much debated alliance, this passage, certainly, cannot be fairly cited as forbidding it; but is far more naturally understood as by natural implication permitting the union, after the decease of the first wife. The laws concerning incest therefore terminate with ver. 17; and ver. 18, according to this interpretation, must be regarded as a restriction upon polygamous connections, as ver. 19 is upon the rights of marriage.

It seems somewhat surprising that the question should have been raised, even theoretically, whether the Mosaic law, as regards the degrees of affinity prohibited in marriage, is of permanent authority. The reasons for these prohibitions, wherever given, are as valid now as then; for the simple reason that they are grounded fundamentally in a matter of fact,—namely, the nature of the relation between husband and wife, whereby they become "one flesh," implied in such phraseology as we find in ver. 16; and also the relation of blood between members of the same family, as in vv. 10, etc. Happily, however, whatever theory any may have held, the Church in all ages has practically recognised every one of these prohibitions, as binding on all persons; and has rather been inclined to err, if at all, by extending, through inference and analogy, the prohibited degrees even beyond the Mosaic code. So much, however, by way of guarding against excess in such inferential extensions of the law, we must certainly say: according to the law itself, as further applied in chap. xxi. 1-4, and limited in Deut. xxv. 5-10, relationship by marriage is not to be regarded as precisely equivalent in degree of affinity to relationship by blood. We cannot, for instance, conceive that, under any circumstances, the prohibition of the marriage of brothers and sisters should have had any exception; and yet, as we have seen, the marriage between brother and sister-in-law is explicitly authorised, in the case of the levirate marriage, and by implication allowed in other cases, by the language of ver. 18 of this chapter.

But in these days, when there is such a manifest inclination in Christendom, as especially in the United States and in France, to ignore the law of God in regard to marriage and divorce, and regulate these instead by a majority vote, it assuredly becomes peculiarly imperative that, as Christians, we exercise a holy jealousy for the honour of God and the sanctity of the family, and ever refuse to allow a majority vote any authority in these matters, where it contravenes the law of God. While we must observe caution that in these things we lay no burden on the conscience of any, which God has not first placed there, we must insist—all the more strenuously because of the universal tendency to license—upon the strict observance of all that is either explicitly taught or by necessary implication involved in the teachings of God's Word upon this question. Nothing more fundamentally concerns the well-being of society than the relation of the man and the woman in the constitution of the family; and while, unfortunately, in our modern democratic communities, the Church may not be able always to control and determine the civil law in these matters, she can at least utterly refuse any compromise where the civil law ignores what God has spoken; and with unwavering firmness deny her sanction, in any way, to any connection between a man and a woman which is not according to the revealed will of God, as set before us in this most holy, good, and beneficent law.

The chapter before us casts a light upon the moral condition of the most cultivated heathen peoples in those days, among whom many of the grossest of these incestuous connections, as already remarked, were quite common, even among those of the highest station. There are many in our day more, or less affected with the present fashion of admiration for the ancient (and modern) heathenisms, who would do well to heed this light, that their blind enthusiasm might thereby be somewhat tempered.

On the other hand, these laws show us, in a very striking contrast, the estimate which God puts upon the maintenance of holiness, purity, and chastity between man and woman; and His very jealous regard for the sanctity of the family in all its various relations. Even in the Old Testament we have hints of a reason for this, deeper than mere expediency,—hints which receive a definite form in the clearer teaching of the New Testament, which tells us that in the Divine plan it is ordained that in these earthly relations man shall be the shadow and image of God. If, as the Apostle tells us (Eph. iii. 15, R.V.), " every family in heaven and on earth " is named from the Father; and if, as he again teaches (Eph. v. 29-32), the relation of husband and wife is intended to be an earthly type and symbol of the relation between the Lord Jesus Christ and His Church, which is His Bride,—then we cannot wonder at the exceedingly strong emphasis which marks these prohibitions. Everything must be excluded which would be incompatible with this holy ideal of God for man; that not only in the constitution of his person, but in these sacred relations which belong to his very nature, as created male and female, he should be the image of the invisible God.

Thus, he who is a father is ever to bear in mind that in his fatherhood he is appointed to shadow forth the ineffable mystery of the eternal relation of the only-begotten and most holy Son to this everlasting Father. As husband, the man is to remember that since he who is joined to his wife becomes with her " one flesh," therefore this union becomes, in the Divine ordination, a type and pattern of the yet more mysterious union of life between the Son of God and the Church, which is His Bride. As brothers and sisters, again, the children of God are to remember that brotherly love, in its purity and unselfish devotion, is intended of God to be a living illustration of the love of Him who has been made of God to be " the firstborn among many brethren " (Rom. viii. 29). And thus, with the family life pervaded through and through by these ideas, will license and impurity be made impossible, and, as happily now in many a Christian home, it will appear that the family, no less truly than the Church, is appointed of God to be a sanctuary of purity in a world impure and corrupt by wicked works, and, no less really than the Church, to be an effective means of Divine grace, and of preparation for the eternal life of the heavenly kingdom, when all of God's " many sons " shall have been brought to glory, the " many brethren " of the First-Begotten, to abide with Him in the Father's house for ever and ever.

After the prohibition of adultery in ver. 20, we have what at first seems like a very abrupt introduction of a totally different subject; for ver. 21 refers, not to the seventh, but to the second, and, therewith also, to the sixth commandment. It reads: " Thou shalt not give any of thy seed to make them pass through the fire to Molech, neither shalt thou profane the name of thy God."

But the connection of thought is found in the historical relation of the licentious practices prohibited in the preceding verses to idolatry, of which this Molech-worship is named as one of the most hideous manifestations. Some, indeed, have supposed that this frequently recurring phrase does not designate an actual sacrifice of the children, but only their consecration to Molech by some kind of fire-baptism. But certainly such passages as 2 Kings xvii. 31, Jer. vii. 31, xix. 5, distinctly require us to understand an actual offering of the children as " burnt-offerings." They were not indeed burnt alive, as a late and untrustworthy tradition has it, but were first slain, as in the case of all burnt-sacrifices, and then burnt. The unnatural cruelty of the sacrifice, even as thus made, was such, that both here and in xx. 3 it is described as in a special sense a " profaning " of God's holy name,—a profanation, in that it represented Him, the Lord of love and fatherly mercy, as requiring such a cruel and unnatural sacrifice of parental love, in the immolation of innocent children.

The inconceivably unnatural crimes prohibited in vv. 22, 23 were in like manner essentially connected with idolatrous worship: the former with the worship of Astarte or Ashtoreth; the latter with the worship of the he-goat at Mendes in Egypt, as the symbol of the generative power in nature. What a hideous perversion of the moral sense was involved in these crimes, as thus connected with idolatrous worship, is illustrated strikingly by the fact that men and women, thus prostituted to the service of false gods, were designated by the terms qâdesh and qâdeshâh, " sacred," " holy " !* No wonder that the sacred writer brands these horrible crimes as, in a peculiar and almost solitary sense, " abomination," " confusion."

In these days of ours, when it has become the fashion among a certain class of cultured writers —who would still, in many instances, apparently desire to be called Christian—to act as the apologist of idolatrous, and, according to Holy Scripture, false religions, the mention of these crimes in this connection may well remind the reader of what such seem to forget, as they certainly ignore; namely, that in all ages, in the modern heathenism no less than in the ancient, idolatry and gross licentiousness ever go hand in hand. Still, to-day, even in Her Majesty's Indian Empire, is the most horrible licentiousness practised as an office of religious worship. Nor are such revolting perversions of the moral sense confined to the " Maharájás " of the temples in Western India, who figured in certain trials in Bombay a few years ago; for even the modern " reformed " Hindooism, from which some hope so much, has not always been able to shake itself free from the pollution of these things, as witness the argument conducted in recent numbers of the *Árya Patriká* of Lahore, to justify the infamous custom known as *Niyoga*, practised to this day in India, *e. g.*, by the Panday Brahmans of Allahabad;—a practice which is sufficiently described as being adultery arranged for, under certain conditions, by a wife or husband, the one for the other. One would fain charitably hope, if possible, that our modern apologists for Oriental idolatries are unaccountably ignorant of what all history should have taught them as to the inseparable connection between idolatry and licentiousness. Both Egypt and Canaan, in the olden time,—as this chap-

---

* See, for example, in the Hebrew text, 1 Kings xiv. 24; Gen. xxxviii. 21 ; Hosea iv. 14, *et passim*.

ter with all contemporaneous history teaches,—and also India in modern times, read us a very awful lesson on this subject. Not only have these idolatries led too often to gross licentiousness of life, but in their full development they have, again and again, in audacious and blasphemous profanation of the most holy God, and defiance even of the natural conscience, given to the most horrible excesses of unbridled lust the supreme sanction of declaring them to be religious obligations. Assuredly, in God's sight, it cannot be a trifling thing for any man, even through ignorance, to extol, or even apologise for, religions with which such enormities are both logically and historically connected. And so, in these stern prohibitions, and their heavy penal sanctions, we may find a profitable lesson for even the cultivated intellect of the nineteenth century!

The chapter closes with reiterated charges against indulgence in any of these abominations. Israel is told (vv. 25, 28) that it was because the Canaanites practised these enormities that God was about to scourge them out of their land;—a judicial reason which, one would think, should have some weight with those whose sympathies are so drawn out with commiseration for the Canaanites, that they find it impossible to believe that it can be true, as we are told in the Pentateuch, that God ordered their extermination. Rather, in the light of the facts, would we raise the opposite question: whether, if God indeed be a holy and righteous Governor among the nations, He could do anything else either in justice toward the Canaanites, or in mercy toward those whom their horrible example would certainly in like manner corrupt, than, in one way or another, effect the extermination of such a people?

Israel is then solemnly warned (ver. 28) that if they, notwithstanding, shall practise these crimes, God will not spare them any more than He spared the Canaanites. No covenant of His with them shall hinder the land from spueing them out in like manner. And though the nation, as a whole, give not itself to these things, each individual is warned (ver. 29), "Whosoever shall commit any of these abominations, even the souls that do them shall be cut off from among their people;" that is, shall be outlawed and shut out from all participation in covenant mercies. And therewith this part of the law of holiness closes, with those pregnant words, repeated now in this chapter for the fifth time: "I am the Lord (Heb. Jehovah) your God!"

CHAPTER XXI.

THE LAW OF HOLINESS (CONCLUDED).

Leviticus xix. 1-37.

WE have in this chapter a series of precepts and prohibitions which from internal evidence appear to have been selected by an inspired redactor of the canon from various original documents, with the purpose, not of presenting a complete enumeration of all moral and ceremonial duties, but of illustrating the application in the everyday life of the Israelite of the injunction which stands at the beginning of the chapter (ver. 2): "Ye shall be holy: for I the Lord your God am holy."

Truly strange it is, in the full light of Hebrew history, to find any one, like Kalisch, representing this conception of holiness, so fundamental to this law, as the "ripest fruit of Hebrew culture"! For it is insisted by such competent critics, as Dillmann, that we have not in this chapter a late development of Hebrew thought, but "ancient," "the most ancient" material;*—we shall venture to say, dating even from the days of Moses, as is declared in ver. 1. And we may say more. For if such be the antiquity of this law, it should be easy even for the most superficial reader of the history to see how immeasurably far was that horde of almost wholly uncultured fugitives from Egyptian bondage from having attained through any culture this Mosaic conception of holiness. For "Hebrew culture," even in its latest maturity, has, at the best, only tended to develop more and more the idea, not of holiness, but of legality—a very different thing! The ideal expressed in this command, "Ye shall be holy," must have come, not from Israel, not even from Moses, as if originated by him, but from the Holy God Himself, even as the chapter in its first verse testifies.

The position of this command at the head of the long list of precepts which follows, is most significant and instructive. It sets before us the object of the whole ceremonial and moral law, and, we may add, the supreme object of the Gospel also, namely, to produce a certain type of moral and spiritual character, a HOLY manhood; it, moreover, precisely interprets this term, so universally misunderstood and misapplied among all nations, as essentially consisting in a spiritual likeness to God: "Ye shall be holy: for I the Lord your God am holy." These words evidently at once define holiness and declare the supreme motive to the attainment and maintenance of a holy character. This then is brought before us as the central thought in which all the diverse precepts and prohibitions which follow find their unity; and, accordingly, we find this keynote of the whole law echoing, as it were, all through this chapter, in the constant refrain, repeated herein no less than fourteen—twice seven—times: "I am the Lord (Heb. Jehovah)!" "I am the Lord your God!"

The first division of the law of holiness which follows (vv. 3-8) deals with two duties of fundamental importance in the social and the religious life: the one, honour to parents; the other, reverence to God.

If we are surprised, at first, to see this place of honour in the law of holiness given to the fifth commandment (ver. 3), our surprise will lessen when we remember how, taking the individual in the development of his personal life, he learns to fear God, first of all, through fearing and honouring his parents. In the earliest beginnings of life, the parent—to speak with reverence—stands to his child, in a very peculiar sense, for and in the place of God. We gain the conception of the Father in heaven first from our experience of fatherhood on earth; and so it may be said of this commandment, in a sense in which it cannot be said of any other, that it is the foundation of all religion. Alas for the child who contemns the instruction of his father and the command of his mother! for by so doing he puts himself out of the possibility of coming into the knowledge and experience of the Fatherhood of God.

The principle of reverence toward God is inculcated, not here by direct precept, but by three

* "Die Bücher Exodus und Leviticus," 2 Aufl., p. 550.

injunctions, obedience to which presupposes the fear of God in the heart. These are, first (ver. 3), the keeping of the sabbaths; the possessive, "My sabbaths," reminding us tersely of God's claim upon the seventh part of all our time as His time. Then is commanded the avoidance of idolatry (ver. 4); and, lastly (vv. 5-8), a charge as to the observance of the law of the peace-offering.

One reason seems to have determined the selection of each of these three injunctions, namely, that Israel would be more liable to fail in obedience to these than perhaps any other duties of the law. As for the sabbath, this, like the law of the peace-offering, was a positive, not a moral law; that is, it depended for its authority primarily on the explicit ordinance of God, instead of the intuition of the natural conscience. Hence it was certain that it would only be kept in so far as man retained a vivid consciousness of the Divine personality and moral authority. Moreover, as all history has shown, the law of the sabbath rest from labour constantly comes into conflict with man's love of gain and eager haste to make money. It is a life-picture, true for men of every generation, when Amos (viii. 5) brings before us the Israelites of his day as saying, in their insatiate worldly greed, "When will the sabbath be gone, that we may set forth wheat?" As regards the selection of the second commandment, one can easily see that Israel's loyalty, surrounded as they were on every side with idolaters, was to be tested with peculiar severity on this point, whether they would indeed worship the living God alone and without the intervention of idols.

The circumstances, as regards the peace-offering, were different; but the same principle of choice can be discovered in this also. For among all the various ordinances of sacrificial worship there was none in which the requisitions of the law were more likely to be neglected; partly because these were the most frequent of all offerings, and also because the Israelite would often be tempted, through a short-sighted economy and worldly thriftiness, to use the meat of the peace-offering for food, if any remained until the third day, instead of burning it, in such case, as the Lord commanded. Hence the reminder of the law on this subject, teaching that he who will be holy must not seek to save at the expense of obedience to the holy God.

The second section of this chapter (vv. 9-18) consists of five groups, each of five precepts, all relating to duties which the law of holiness requires from man to man, and each of them closing with the characteristic and impressive refrain, "I am the Lord."

The first of these pentads (vv. 9, 10) requires habitual care for the poor: we read, "Thou shalt not wholly reap the corners of thy field, neither shalt thou gather the gleaning of thy harvest. And thou shalt not glean thy vineyard, neither shalt thou gather the fallen fruit of thy vineyard; thou shalt leave them for the poor and for the stranger."

The law covers the three chief products of their agriculture: the grain, the product of the vine, and the fruit of the trees,—largely olive-trees, which were often planted in the vineyard. So often as God blessed them with the harvest, they were to remember the poor, and also "the stranger," who according to the law could have a legal claim to no land in Israel. Apart from the benefit to the poor, one can readily see what an admirable discipline against man's natural selfishness, and in loyalty to God, this regulation, faithfully observed, must have been. Behind these commands lies the principle, elsewhere explicitly expressed (xxv. 23), that the land which the Israelite tilled was not his own, but the Lord's; and it is as the Owner of the land that He thus charges them that as His tenants they shall not regard themselves as entitled to everything that the land produces, but bear in mind that He intends a portion of every acre of each Israelite to be reserved for the poor. And so the labourer in the harvest-field was continually reminded that in his husbandry he was merely God's steward, bound to apply the product of the land, the use of which was given him, in such a way as should please the Lord.

If the law is not in force as to the letter, let us not forget that it is of full validity as to its spirit. God is still the God of the poor and needy; and we are still every one, as truly as the Hebrew in those days, the stewards of God. And the poor we have with us always; perhaps never more than in these days, in which so great masses of helpless humanity are crowded together in our immense cities, did the cry of the poor and needy so ascend to heaven. And that the Apostles, acting under Divine direction, and abolishing the letter of the theocratic law, yet steadily maintained the spirit and intention of that law in care for the poor, is testified with abundant fulness in the New Testament. One of the firstfruits of Pentecost in the lives of believers was just this, that "all that believed . . . had all things common" (Acts ii. 44, 45), so that, going even beyond the letter of the old law, "they sold their possessions and goods, and parted them to all, according as any man had need." And the one only charge which the Apostles at Jerusalem gave unto Paul is reported by him in these words (Gal. ii. 10): "Only they would that we should remember the poor; which very thing I was also zealous to do." Let the believer then remember this who has plenty: the corners of his fields are to be kept for the poor, and the gleanings of his vineyards; and let the believer also take the peculiar comfort from this law, if he is poor, that God, his heavenly Father, has a kindly care, not merely for his spiritual wants, but also for his temporal necessities.

The second pentad (vv. 11, 12) in the letter refers to three of the ten commandments, but is really concerned, primarily, with stealing and defrauding; for the lying and false swearing is here regarded only as commonly connected with theft and fraud, because often necessary to secure the result of a man's plunder. The pentad is in this form: "Ye shall not steal; neither shall ye deal falsely, nor lie one to another. And ye shall not swear by My name falsely, so that thou profane the name of thy God: I am the Lord!"

Close upon stinginess and the careless greed which neglects the poor, with eager grasping after the last grape on the vine, follows the active effort to get, not only the uttermost that might by any stretch of charity be regarded as our own, but also to get something more that belongs to our neighbour. There is thus a very close connection in thought, as well as in position, in these two groups of precepts. And the sequence of thought in this group suggests what is, indeed, markedly true of stealing, but also of other sins. Sin rarely goes alone; one sin, by almost a necessity, leads straight on to another sin. He who steals, or deals falsely in regard to anything committed to his trust, will most naturally be led on at once to lie about it; and when his lie is challenged, as it is likely to be, he is impelled by a fatal pressure to go yet further, and fortify his lie, and consummate his sin, by appealing by an oath to the Holy God, as witness to the truth of his lie. Thus, the sin which in the beginning is directed only toward a fellow-man, too often causes one to sin immediately against God, in profanation of the name of the God of truth, by calling on Him as witness to a lie! Of this tendency of sin, stealing is a single illustration; but let us ever remember that it is a law of all sin that sin ever begets more sin.

This second group has dealt with injury to the neighbour in the way of guile and fraud; the third pentad (vv. 13, 14), progressing further, speaks of wrong committed in ways of oppression and violence. "Thou shalt not oppress thy neighbour, nor rob him: the wages of a hired servant shall not abide with thee all night until the morning. Thou shalt not curse the deaf, nor put a stumbling-block before the blind, but thou shalt fear thy God: I am the Lord!" In these commands, again it is still the helpless and defenceless in whose behalf the Lord is speaking. The words regard a man as having it in his power to press hard upon his neighbour; as when an employer, seeing that a man must needs have work at any price, takes advantage of his need to employ him at less than fair wages; or as when he who holds a mortgage against his neighbour, seeing an opportunity to possess himself of a field or an estate for a trifle, by pressing his technical legal rights, strips his poor debtor needlessly. No end of illustrations, evidently, could be given out of our modern life. Man's nature is the same now as in the days of Moses. But all dealings of this kind, whether then or now, the law of holiness sternly prohibits.

So also with the injunction concerning the retention of wages after it is due. I have not fulfilled the law of love toward the man or woman whom I employ merely by paying fair wages; I must also pay promptly. The Deuteronomic law repeats the command, and, with a peculiar touch of sympathetic tenderness, adds the reason (xxiv. 15): "for he is poor, and setteth his heart upon it." I must therefore give the labourer his wages "in his day." A sin this is, of the rich especially, and, most of all, of rich corporations, with which the sense of personal responsibility to God is too often reduced to a minimum. Yet it is often, no doubt, committed through sheer thoughtlessness. Men who are themselves blessed with such abundance that they are not seriously incommoded by a delay in receiving some small sum, too often forget how a great part of the poor live, as the saying is, "from hand to mouth," so that the failure to get what is due to them at the exact time appointed is frequently a sore trial; and, moreover, by forcing them to buy on credit instead of for cash, of necessity increases the expense of their living, and so really robs them of that which is their own.

The thought is still of care for the helpless, in the words concerning the deaf and the blind, which, of course, are of perpetual force, and, in the principle involved, reach indefinitely beyond these single illustrations. We are not to take advantage of any man's helplessness, and, especially, of such disabilities as he cannot help, to wrong him. Even the common conscience of men recognises this as both wicked and mean; and this verdict of conscience is here emphasised by the reminder "I am the Lord,"—suggesting that the labourer who reaps the fields, yea, the blind also and the deaf, are His creatures; and that He, the merciful and just One, will not disown the relation, but will plead their cause.

Each of these groups of precepts has kept the poor and the needy in a special way, though not exclusively, before the conscience. And yet no man is to imagine that therefore God will be partial toward the poor, and that hence, although one may not wrong the poor, one may wrong the rich with impunity. Many of our modern social reformers, in their zeal for the betterment of the poor, seem to imagine that because a poor man has rights which are too frequently ignored by the rich, and thus often suffers grievous wrongs, therefore a rich man has no rights which the poor man is bound to respect. The next pentad of precepts therefore guards against any such false inference from God's special concern for the poor, and reminds us that the absolute righteousness of the Holy One requires that the rights of the rich be observed no less than the rights of the poor, those of the employer no less than those of the employed. It deals especially with this matter as it comes up in questions requiring legal adjudication. We read (vv. 15, 16), "Ye shall do no unrighteousness in judgment: thou shalt not respect the person of the poor, nor honour the person of the mighty: but in righteousness shalt thou judge thy neighbour. Thou shalt not go up and down as a talebearer among thy people: neither shalt thou stand against the blood of thy neighbour: I am the Lord!"

A plain warning lies here for an increasing class of reformers in our day, who loudly express their special concern for the poor, but who in their zeal for social reform and the diminishing of poverty are forgetful of righteousness and equity. It applies, for instance, to all who would affirm and teach with Marx that "capital is robbery;" or who, not yet quite ready for so plain and candid words, yet would, in any way, in order to right the wrongs of the poor, advocate legislation involving practical confiscation of the estates of the rich.

In close connection with the foregoing, the next precept forbids, not precisely "tale-bearing," but "slander," as the word is elsewhere rendered, even in the Revised Version. In the court of judgment, slander is not to be uttered nor listened to. The clause which follows is obscure; but means either, "Thou shalt not, by such slanderous testimony, seek in the court of judgment thy neighbour's life," which best suits the parallelism; or, perhaps, as the Talmud and most modern Jewish versions interpret, "Thou shalt not stand silent by, when thy neighbour's life is in danger in the court of judgment, and thy testimony might save him." And then again comes in the customary refrain, reminding the Israelite that in every court, noting every act of judgment, and listening to every witness, is a judge unseen, omniscient, absolutely righteous, under whose final review, for confirmation or reversal, shall come all earthly decisions: "I," who thus speak, "am the Lord!"

The fifth and last pentad (vv. 17, 18) fitly

closes the series, by its five precepts, of which, three, reaching behind all such outward acts as are required or forbidden in the foregoing, deal with the state of the heart toward our neighbour which the law of holiness requires, as the soul and the root of all righteousness. It closes with the familiar words, so simple that all can understand them, so comprehensive that in obedience to them is comprehended all morality and righteousness toward man: "Thou shalt love thy neighbour as thyself." The verses read, "Thou shalt not hate thy brother in thine heart: thou shalt surely rebuke thy neighbour, and not bear sin because of him. Thou shalt not take vengeance, nor bear any grudge against the children of thy people, but thou shalt love thy neighbour as thyself: I am the Lord!"

Most instructive it is to find it suggested by this order, as the best evidence of the absence of hate, and the truest expression of love to our neighbour, that when we see him doing wrong we shall rebuke him. The Apostle Paul has enjoined upon Christians the same duty, indicating also the spirit in which it is to be performed (Gal. vi. 1): "Brethren, even if a man be overtaken in any trespass, ye which are spiritual, restore such a one in a spirit of meekness; looking to thyself, lest thou also be tempted." Thus, if we will be holy, it is not to be a matter of no concern to us that our neighbour does wrong, even though that wrong do not directly affect our personal well-being. Instead of this, we are to remember that if we rebuke him not, we ourselves "bear sin, because of him;" that is, we ourselves, in a degree, become guilty with him, because of that wrong-doing of his which we sought not in any way to hinder. But although, on the one hand, I am to rebuke the wrong-doer, even when his wrong does not touch me personally, yet, the law adds, I am not to take into my own hands the avenging of wrongs, even when myself injured; neither am I to be envious and grudge any neighbour the good he may have; no, not though he be an ill-doer and deserve it not; but be he friend or foe, well-doer or ill-doer, I must love him as myself.

What an admirable epitome of the whole law of righteousness! a Mosaic anticipation of the very spirit of the Sermon on the Mount. Evidently, the same mind speaks in both alike; the law the same, the object and aim of the law the same, both in Leviticus and in the Gospel. In this law we hear: "Ye shall be holy: for I the Lord your God am holy;" in the Sermon on the Mount: "Ye shall be perfect, as your heavenly Father is perfect."

The third division of this chapter (vv. 19-32) opens with a general charge to obedience: "Ye shall keep My statutes;" very possibly, because several of the commands which immediately follow might seem in themselves of little consequence, and so be lightly disobeyed. The law of ver. 19 prohibits raising hybrid animals, as, for example, mules; the next command apparently refers to the chance, through sowing a field with mingled seed, of giving rise to hybrid forms in the vegetable kingdom. The last command in this verse is obscure both in meaning and intention. It reads (R.V.), "Neither shall there come upon thee a garment of two kinds of stuff mingled together." Most probably the reference is to different materials, interwoven in the yarn of which the dress was made; but a difficulty still remains in the fact that such admixture was ordered in the garments of the priests. Perhaps the best explanation is that of Josephus, that the law here was only intended for the laity; which, as no question of intrinsic morality was involved, might easily have been. But when we inquire as to the reason of these prohibitions, and especially of this last one, it must be confessed that it is hard for us now to speak with confidence. Most probable it appears that they were intended for an educational purpose, to cultivate in the mind of the people the sentiment of reverence for the order established in nature by God. For what the world calls the order of nature is really an order appointed by God, as the infinitely wise and perfect One; hence, as nature is thus a manifestation of God, the Hebrew was forbidden to seek to bring about that which is not according to nature, unnatural commixtures; and from this point of view, the last of the three precepts appears to be a symbolic reminder of the same duty, namely, reverence for the order of nature, as being an order determined by God.

The law which is laid down in vv. 20-22, regarding the sin of connection with a bond-woman betrothed to a husband, apparently refers to such a case as is mentioned in Exod. xxi. 7, 8, where the bond-maid is betrothed to her master, while yet, because of her condition of bondage, the marriage has not been consummated. For the same sin in the case of a free woman, where both were proved guilty, for each of them the punishment was death (Deut. xxii. 23, 24). In this case, because the woman's position, inasmuch as she was not free, was rather that of a concubine than of a full wife, the lighter penalty of scourging is ordered for both of the guilty persons. Also, since this was a case of trespass as well, in which the rights of the master to whom she was espoused were involved, a guilt-offering was in addition required, as the condition of pardon.

It will be said, and truly, that by this law slavery and concubinage are to a certain extent recognised by the law; and upon this fact has been raised an objection bearing on the holiness of the law-giver, and, by consequence, on the Divine origin and inspiration of the law. Is it conceivable that the holy God should have given a law for the regulation of two so evil institutions? The answer has been furnished us, in principle, by our Lord (Matt. xix. 8), in that which He said concerning the analogous case of the law of Moses touching divorce; which law, He tells us, although not according to the perfect ideal of right, was yet given "because of the hardness of men's hearts." That is, although it was not the best law ideally, it was the best practically, in view of the low moral tone of the people to whom it was given. Precisely so it was in this case. Abstractly, one might say that the case was in nothing different from the case of a free woman, mentioned Deut. xxii. 23, 24, for which death was the appointed punishment; but practically, in a community where slavery and concubinage were long-settled institutions, and the moral standard was still low, the cases were not parallel. A law which would carry with it the moral support of the people in the one case, and which it would thus be possible to carry into effect, would not be in like manner supported and carried into effect in the other; so that the result of greater strictness in theory would, in actual practice, be the removal thereby of all restriction on license. On the other hand, by thus appointing herein a penalty for both the guilty parties such as the public conscience would approve, God taught the Hebrews the fundamental lesson that a slave-girl is not regarded by God as a mere chattel; and that if, because of the hardness of their hearts, concubinage was tolerated for a time, still the slave-girl must not be treated as a thing, but as a person, and indiscriminate license could not be permitted. And thus, it is of greatest moment to observe, a principle was introduced into the legislation, which in its ultimate logical application would require and effect—as in due time it has—the total abolition of the institution of slavery wherever the authority of the living God is truly recognised.

The principle of the Divine government which is here illustrated is one of exceeding practical importance as a model for us. We live in an age when, everywhere in Christendom, the cry is "Reform;" and there are many who think that if once it be proved that a thing is wrong, it follows by necessary consequence that the immediate and unqualified legal prohibition of that wrong, under such penalty as the wrong may deserve, is the only thing that any Christian man has a right to think of. And yet, according to the principle illustrated in this legislation, this conclusion in such cases can by no means be taken for granted. That is not always the best law practically which is the best law abstractly. That law is the best which shall be most effective in diminishing a given evil, under the existing moral condition of the community; and it is often a matter of such exceeding difficulty to determine what legislation against admitted sins and evils may be the most productive of good in a community whose moral sense is dull concerning them, that it is not strange that the best of men are often found to differ. Remembering this, we may well commend the duty of a more charitable judgment, in such cases, than one often hears from such radical reformers, who seem to imagine that in order to remove an evil all that is necessary is to pass a law at once and for ever prohibiting it; and who therefore hold up to obloquy all who doubt as to the wisdom and duty of so doing, as the enemies of truth and of righteousness. Moses, acting under direct instruction from the God of supreme wisdom and of perfect holiness, was far wiser than such well-meaning but sadly mistaken social reformers, who would fain be wiser than God.

Next follows a law (vv. 23-25) directing that when any fruit tree is planted, the Israelite shall not eat of its fruit for the first three years; that the fruit of the fourth year shall be wholly consecrated to the Lord, "for giving praise unto Jehovah;" and that only after that, in the fifth year of its bearing, shall the husbandman himself first eat of its fruit.

The explanation of this peculiar regulation is to be found in a special application of the principle which rules throughout the law; that the first-fruit, whether the first-born of man or beast, or the first-fruits of the field, shall always be consecrated unto God. But in this case the application of the principle is modified by the familiar fact that the fruit of a young tree, for the first few years of its bearing, is apt to be imperfect; it is not yet sufficiently grown to yield its best possible product. Because of this, in those years it could not be given to the Lord, for He must never be served with any but the best of everything; and thus until the fruit should reach its best, so as to be worthy of presentation to the Lord, the Israelite was meanwhile debarred from using it. During these three years the trees are said to be "as uncircumcised;" *i. e.*, they were to be regarded as in a condition analogous to that of the child who has not yet been consecrated, by the act of circumcision, to the Lord. In the fourth year, however, the trees were regarded as having now so grown as to yield fruit in perfection; hence, the principle of the consecration of the first-fruit now applies, and all the fourth year's product is given to the Lord, as an offering of thankful praise to Him whose power in nature is the secret of all growth, fruitfulness, and increase. The last words of this law, "that it may yield unto you its increase," evidently refer to all that precedes. Israel is to obey this law, using nothing till first consecrated to the Lord, in order to a blessing in these very gifts of God.

The moral teaching of this law, when it is thus read in the light of the general principle of the consecration of the first-fruits, is very plain. It teaches, as in all analogous cases, that God is always to be served before ourselves; and that not grudgingly, as if an irksome tax were to be paid to the Majesty of heaven, but in the spirit of thanksgiving and praise to Him, as the Giver of "every good and perfect gift." It further instructs us in this particular instance, that the people of God are to recognise this as being true even of all those good things which come to us under the forms of products of nature.

The lesson is not an easy one for faith; for the constant tendency, never stronger than in our own time, is to substitute "Nature" for the God of nature, as if nature were a power in itself and apart from God, immanent in all nature, the present and efficient energy in all her manifold operations. Very fittingly, thus, do we find here again (ver. 25) the sanction affixed to this law, "I am the Lord your God!" Jehovah, your God who redeemed you, who therefore am worthy of all thanksgiving and praise! Jehovah, your God in covenant, who gives the fruitful seasons! filling your hearts with joy and gladness! Jehovah, your God, who as the Lord of Nature, and the Power in nature, am abundantly able to fulfil the promise affixed to this command!

The next six commands are evidently grouped together as referring to various distinctively heathenish customs, from which Israel, as a people holy to the Lord, was to abstain. The prohibition of blood (ver. 26) is repeated again, not, as has been said, in a stronger form than before, but, probably, because the eating of blood was connected with certain heathenish ceremonies, both among the Shemitic tribes and others. The next two precepts (ver. 26) prohibit every kind of divination and augury; practices notoriously common with the heathen everywhere, in ancient and modern times. The two precepts which follow, forbidding certain fashions of trimming the hair and beard, may appear trivial to many, but they will not seem so to any one who will remember how common among heathen peoples has been the custom, as in those days among the Arabs, and in our time among the Hindoos, to trim the hair or beard in a particular way, in order thus visibly to mark a person as of a certain religion, or as a worshipper of a certain god. The command means that the Israelite was not only to worship God alone, but he was not to adopt a fashion in dress which, because commonly associated with idolatry, might thus misrepresent his real position as a worshipper of the only living and true God.

"Cutting the flesh for the dead" (ver. 28) has been very widely practised by heathen peoples in all ages. Such immoderate and unseemly expressions of grief were prohibited to the Israelite, as unworthy of a people who were in a blessed covenant relation with the God of life and of death. Rather, recognising that death is of God's ordination, he was to accept in patience and humility the stroke of God's hand; not, indeed, without sorrow, but yet in meekness and quietness of spirit, trusting in the God of life. The thought is only a less clear expression of the New Testament word (1 Thess. iv. 13) that the believer "sorrow not, even as the rest, which have no hope." Also, probably, in this prohibition, as certainly in the next (ver. 28), it is suggested that as the Israelite was to be distinguished from the heathen by full consecration, not only of the soul, but also of the body, to the Lord, he was by that fact inhibited from marring or defacing in any way the integrity of his body.

In general, we may say, then, that the central thought which binds this group of precepts together, is the obligation, not merely to abstain from everything directly idolatrous, but also from all such customs as are, in fact, rooted in or closely associated with idolatry. On the same principle, the Christian is to beware of all fashions and practices, even though they may be in themselves indifferent, which yet, as a matter of fact, are specially characteristic of the worldly and ungodly element in society. The principle assumed in these prohibitions thus imposes upon all who would be holy to the Lord, in all ages, a firm restriction. The thoughtless desire of many, at any risk, to be "in the fashion," must be unwaveringly denied. The reason which is so often given by professing Christians for indulgence in such cases, that "all the world does so," may often be the strongest possible reason for declining to follow the fashion. No servant of God should ever be seen in any part of the livery of Satan's servants. That God does not think these "little things" always of trifling consequence, we are reminded by the repetition here, for the tenth time in this chapter, of the words, "I am the Lord!"

Next (ver. 29) follows the prohibition of the horrible custom, still practised among heathen peoples, of the prostitution of a daughter by a parent. It is here enforced by the consideration of the public weal: "lest the land fall to whoredom, and the land become full of wickedness." Assuredly, that a land in which such harlotry as this, in which all the most sacred relations of life are trampled in the mire, would be nothing less than a land full of wickedness, is so evident as to require no comment.

Herewith now begins the fourth and last division of this chapter (vv. 30-37), with a repetition of the injunction to keep the Sabbaths of the Lord, and reverence His sanctuary. The emphasis on this command, shown by its repetition in this chapter, and the very prominent place which it occupies both in the law and the prophets, certainly suggest that in the mind of God, reverence for the Sabbath and for the place where God is worshipped, has much to do with the promotion of holiness of life, and the maintenance of a high degree of domestic and social morality. Nor is it difficult to see why this should be so. For however the day of holy rest may be kept, and the place of Divine worship be regarded with only an outward reverence by many, yet the fact cannot be disputed, that the observance of a weekly sabbatic rest from ordinary secular occupations, and the maintenance of a spirit of reverence for sacred places or for sacred times, has, and must have, a certain and most happy tendency to keep the God of the Sabbath and the God of the sanctuary before the mind of men, and thus imposes an effective check upon unrestrained godlessness and reckless excesses of iniquity. The diverse condition of things in various parts of modern Christendom, as related to the more or less careful observance of the weekly religious rest, is full of both instruction and warning to any candid mind upon this subject. There is no restraint on immorality like the frequent remembrance of God and the spirit of reverence for Him.

Verse 31 prohibits all inquiring of them that "have familiar spirits," and of "wizards," who pretend to make revelations through the help of supernatural powers. According to 1 Sam. xxviii. 7-11, and Isa. viii. 19, the "familiar spirit" is a supposed spirit of a dead man, from whom one professes to be able to give communications to the living. This pretended commerce with the spirits of the dead has been common enough in heathenism always, and it is not strange to find it mentioned here, when Israel was to be in so intimate relations with heathen peoples. But it is truly most extraordinary that in Christian lands, as especially in the United States of America, and that in the full light, religious and intellectual, of the last half of the nineteenth century, such a prohibition should be fully as pertinent as in Israel! For no words could more precisely describe the pretensions of the so-called modern spiritualism, which within the last half century has led away hundreds of thousands of deluded souls, and those, in many cases, not from the ignorant and degraded, but from circles which boast of more than average culture and intellectual enlightenment. And inasmuch as experience sadly shows that even those who profess to be disciples of Christ are in danger of being led away by our modern wizards and traffickers with familiar spirits, it is by no means unnecessary to observe that there is not the slightest reason to believe that this which was rigidly forbidden by God in the fifteenth century B. C., can now be well-pleasing to Him in the nineteenth century A. D. And those who have most carefully watched the moral developments of this latter-day delusion, will most appreciate the added phrase which speaks of this as "defiling" a man.

Verse 32 enjoins reverence for the aged, and closely connects it with the fear of God. "Thou shalt rise up before the hoary head, and honour the face of the old man, and thou shalt fear thy God: I am the Lord."

A virtue this is which—it must be with shame confessed—although often displayed in an illustrious manner among the heathen, in many parts of Christendom has sadly decayed. In many lands one only needs to travel in any crowded conveyance to observe how far it is from the thoughts of many of the young "to rise up before the hoary head, and honour the face of the old man." So manifest are the facts that one hears from competent and thoughtful observers of the tendencies of our times no lamentation more frequently than just this, for the concurrent decay of reverence for the aged and reverence for God. No more beautiful remarks on these words have we found than the words quoted by Dr. H. Bonar, commenting on this verse: "Lo! the shadow of eternity! for one cometh who is almost in eternity already. His head and his beard, white as snow, indicate his speedy appearance before the Ancient of Days, the hair of whose head is as pure wool."

In this last command is also, no doubt, contained the thought of the comparative weakness and physical infirmity of the aged, which is thus commended in a special way to our tender regard. And thus this sentiment of kindly sympathy for all who are subject to any kind of disability naturally prepares the way for the injunction (vv. 33, 34) to regard "the stranger" in the midst of Israel, who was debarred from holding land, and from many privileges, with special feelings of good-will. "If a stranger sojourn with thee in your land, ye shall not do him wrong. The stranger that sojourneth with you shall be unto you as the homeborn among you, and thou shalt love him as thyself; for ye were strangers in the land of Egypt: I am the Lord your God."

The Israelite was not to misinterpret, then, the restrictions which the theocratic law imposed upon such. These might be no doubt necessary for a moral reason; but, nevertheless, no man was to argue that the law justified him in dealing hardly with aliens. So far from this, the Israelite was to regard the stranger with the same kindly feelings as if he were one of his own people. And it is most instructive to observe that this particular case is made the occasion of repeating that most perfect and comprehensive law of universal love, "Thou shalt love thy neighbour as thyself;" and this the more they were to do that they too had been "strangers in the land of Egypt."

Last of all the injunctions in this chapter (vv. 35, 36) comes the command to absolute righteousness in the administration of justice, and in all matters of buying and selling; followed (ver. 37) by a concluding charge to obedience, thus: "Ye shall do no unrighteousness in judgment, in meteyard, in weight, or in measure. Just balances, just weights, a just ephah, and a just hin, shall ye have: I am the Lord your God, which brought you out of the land of Egypt. And ye shall observe all My statutes, and all My judgments, and do them: I am the Lord."

The ephah is named here, of course, as a standard of dry measure, and the hin as a standard of liquid measure. These commandments are illustrated in a graphic way by the parallel passage in Deut. xxv. 13, 14, which reads: "Thou shalt not have in thy bag divers weights, a great and a small. Thou shalt not have in thine house divers measures, a great and a small;" *i. e.*, one set for use in buying, and another set for use in selling. This charge is there enforced by the same promise to honesty in trade which is annexed to the fifth commandment, namely, length of days; and, furthermore, by the declaration that all who thus cheat in trade "are an abomination unto the Lord."

How much Israel needed this law all their history has shown. In the days of Amos it was a part of his charge against the ten tribes (viii. 5), for which the Lord declares that He will "make the land to tremble, and every one in it to mourn," that they "make the ephah small, and the shekel great," and "deal falsely with balances of deceit." So also Micah, a little later, represents the Lord as calling Judah to account for supposing that God, the Holy One, can be satisfied with burnt-offerings and guilt-offerings; indignantly asking (vi. 10, 11), "Are there yet the treasures of wickedness in the house of the wicked, and the scant measure that is abominable?"

But it is not Israel alone which has needed, and still needs, to hear iterated this command, for the sin is found in every people, even in every city, one might say in every town, in Christendom; and—we have to say it—often with men who make a certain profession of regard for religion. All such, however religious in certain ways, have special need to remember that "without holiness no man shall see the Lord;" and that holiness is now exactly what it was when the Levitical law was given out. As, on the one side, it is inspired by reverence and fear toward God, so, on the other hand, it requires love to the neighbour as to one's self, and such conduct as that will secure. It is of no account, therefore, to keep the Sabbath—in a way—and reverence—outwardly—the sanctuary, and then on the week-day water milk, adulterate medicines, sugars, and other foods, slip the yard-stick in measuring, tip the balance in weighing, and buy with one weight or measure and sell with another, "water" stocks and gamble in "margins," as the manner of many is. God hates, and even honest atheists despise, religion of this kind. Strange notions, truly, of religion have men who have not yet discovered that it has to do with just such commonplace, every-day matters as these, and have never yet understood how certain it is that a religion which is only used on Sundays has no holiness in it; and therefore, when the day comes, as it is coming, that shall try every man's work as by fire, it will, in the fierce heat of Jehovah's judgment, be shrivelled into ashes as a spider's web in a flame, and the man and his work shall perish together.

And herewith this chapter closes. Such is the law of holiness! Obligatory, let us not forget, in the spirit of all its requirements, to-day, unchanged and unchangeable, because the Holy God, whose law it is, is Himself unchangeable. Man may be sinful, and because of sin be weak; but there is not a hint of compromise with sin, on this account, by any abatement of its claims. At every step of life this law confronts us. Whether we be in the House of God, in acts of worship, it challenges us there; or in the field, at our work, it commands us there; in social intercourse with our fellow-men, in our business in bank or shop, with our friends or with strangers and aliens, at home or abroad, we are never out of the reach of its requirements. We can no more escape from under its authority than from under the overarching heaven! What sobering thoughts are these for sinners! What self-humiliation should this law cause us, when we think what we are! what intensity of aspiration, when we think of what the Holy One would have us be, holy like Himself!

The closing words above given (ver. 37) assert the authority of the Law-giver, and, by their reminder of the great deliverance from Egypt, appeal, as a motive to faithful and holy obedience, to the purest sentiment of grateful love for undeserved and distinguishing mercy. And this is only the Old Testament form of a New Testament argument. For we read, concerning our deliverance from a worse than Egyptian bondage (1 Peter i. 15-19): "Like as He which called you is holy, be ye yourselves also holy in all manner of living; because it is written, Ye shall be holy; for I am holy. And if ye call on Him as Father, who without respect of persons judgeth according to each man's work, pass the time of your sojourning in fear: knowing that ye were redeemed, not with corruptible things, as silver or gold, . . . but with precious blood, as of a lamb without blemish and without spot, even the blood of Christ."

CHAPTER XXII.

PENAL SANCTIONS.

LEVITICUS xx. 1-27.

IN no age or community has it been found sufficient, to secure obedience, that one should appeal to the conscience of men, or depend, as a sufficient motive, upon the natural painful consequences of violated law. Wherever there is civil and criminal law, there, in all cases, human government, whether in its lowest or in its most highly developed forms, has found it necessary to declare penalties for various crimes. It is the peculiar interest of this chapter that it gives us certain important sections of the penal code of a people whose government was theocratic, whose only King was the Most Holy and Righteous God. In view of the manifold difficulties which are inseparable from the enactment and enforcement of a just and equitable penal code, it must be to every man who believes that Israel, in that period of its history, was, in the most literal sense, a theocracy, a matter of the highest civil and governmental interest to observe what penalties for crime were ordained by infinite wisdom, goodness, and righteousness as the law of that nation.

This penal code (vv. 1-21) is given in two sections. Of these, the first (vv. 1-6) relates to those who give of their seed to Molech, or who are accessory to such crime by their concealment of the fact; and also to those who consult wizards or familiar spirits. Under this last head also comes ver. 27, which appears to have become misplaced, as it follows the formal conclusion of the chapter, and by its subject—the penalty for the wizard, or him who claims to have a familiar spirit—evidently belongs immediately after ver. 6.

The second section (vv. 9-21) enumerates, first (vv. 9-16), other cases for which capital punishment was ordered: and then (vv. 17-21) certain offences for which a lesser penalty is prescribed. These two sections are separated (vv. 7, 8) by a command, in view of these penalties, to sanctification of life, and obedience to the Lord, as the God who has redeemed and consecrated Israel to be a nation to Himself.

These penal sections are followed (vv. 22-26) by a general conclusion to the whole law of holiness, as contained in these three chapters, as also to the law concerning clean and unclean meats (xi.); which would thus appear to have been originally connected more closely than now with these chapters. This closing part of the section consists of an exhortation and argument against disobedience, in walking after the wicked customs of the Canaanitish nations; enforced by the declaration that their impending expulsion was brought about by God in punishment for their practice of these crimes; and, also, by the reminder that God in His special grace had separated them to be a holy nation to Himself, and that He was about to give them the good land of Canaan as their possession.

It is perhaps hardly necessary to observe that the law of this chapter does not profess to give the penal code of Israel with completeness. Murder, for example, is not mentioned here, though death is expressly denounced against it elsewhere (Numb. xxxv. 31). So, again, in the Book of Exodus (xxi. 15) death is declared as the penalty for smiting father or mother. Indeed, the chapter itself contains evidence that it is essentially a selection of certain parts of a more extended code, which has been nowhere preserved in its entirety.

In this chapter death is ordained as the penalty for the following crimes: viz., giving of one's seed to Molech (vv. 2-5); professing to be a wizard, or to have dealings with the spirits of the dead (ver. 27); adultery, incest with a mother or step-mother, a daughter-in-law or mother-in-law (vv. 10-12, 14); and sodomy and bestiality (ver. 13). In a single case—that of incest with a wife's mother—it is added (ver. 14) that both the guilty parties shall be burnt with fire; i. e., after the usual infliction of death by stoning. Of him who becomes accessory by concealment to the crime of sacrifice to Molech, it is said (ver. 5) that God Himself will set His face against that man, and will cut off both the man himself and his family. The same phraseology is used (ver. 6) of those who consult familiar spirits: and the cutting off is also threatened, ver. 18. The law concerning incest with a full- or half-sister requires (ver. 17) that this excision shall be "in the sight of the children of their people;" i. e., that the sentence shall be executed in the most public way, thus to affix the more certainly to the crime the stigma of an indelible ignominy and disgrace. A lesser grade of penalty is attached to an alliance with the wife of an uncle or of a brother; in the latter case (ver. 21) that they shall be childless, in the former (ver. 20), that they shall die childless; that is, though they have children, they shall all be prematurely cut off; none shall outlive their parents. To incest with an aunt by blood no specific penalty is affixed; it is only said that "they shall bear their iniquity," i. e., God will hold them guilty.

The chapter, directly or indirectly, casts no little light on some most fundamental and practical questions regarding the administration of justice in dealing with criminals.

We may learn here what, in the mind of the King of kings, is the primary object of the punishment of criminals against society. Certainly there is no hint in this code of law that these penalties were specially intended for the reformation of the offender. Were this so, we should not find the death-penalty applied with such unsparing severity. This does not indeed mean that the reformation of the criminal was a matter of no concern to the Lord; we know to the contrary. But one cannot resist the conviction in reading this chapter, as also other similar portions of the law, that in a governmental point of view this was not the chief object of punishment. Even where the penalty was not death, the reformation of the guilty persons is in no way brought before us as an object of the penal sentence. In the governmental aspect of the case, this is, at least, so far in the background that it does not once come into view.

In our day, however, an increasing number maintain that the death-penalty ought never to be inflicted, because, in the nature of the case, it precludes the possibility of the criminal being reclaimed and made a useful member of society; and so, out of regard to this and other like humanitarian considerations, in not a few instances, the death penalty, even for wilful murder, has been abrogated. It is thus, to a Christian citizen, of very practical concern to observe that in this theocratic penal code there is not so much as an allusion to the reformation of the criminal, as one object which by means of punishment it was intended to secure. Penalty was to be inflicted, according to this code, without any apparent reference to its bearing on this matter. The wisdom of the Omniscient King of Israel, therefore, must certainly have contemplated in the punishment of crime some object or objects of more weighty moment than this.

What those objects were, it does not seem hard to discern. First and supreme in the intention of this law is the satisfaction of outraged justice and of the regal majesty of the supreme and holy God, defiled; the vindication of the holiness of the Most High against that wickedness of men which would set at nought the Holy One and overturn that moral order which He has established. Again and again the crime itself is given as the reason for the penalty, inasmuch as by such iniquity in the midst of Israel the holy sanctuary of God among them was profaned. We read, for example, "I will cut him off . . . because he hath defiled My sanctuary, and hath profaned My holy name;" "they have wrought confusion," i. e., in the moral and physical order of the family; "their blood shall be upon them;" "they have committed abomination; they shall surely be put to death;" "it is a shameful thing; they shall be cut off." Such are the expressions which again and again ring through this chapter; and they teach with unmistakable clearness that the prime object of the Divine King of Israel in the punishment was, not the reformation of the individual sinner, but the satisfaction of justice and the vindication of the majesty of broken law. And if we have no more explicit statement of the matter here, we yet have it elsewhere; as in Numb. xxxv. 33, where we are expressly told that the death-penalty to be visited with unrelenting severity on the murderer is of the nature of an expiation. Very clear and solemn are the words, "Blood, it polluteth the land: and no expiation can be made for the land for the blood that is shed therein, but by the blood of him that shed it."

But if this is set forth as the fundamental reason for the infliction of the punishment, it is not represented as the only object. If, as regards the criminal himself, the punishment is a satisfaction and expiation to justice for his crime, on the other hand, as regards the people, the punishment is intended for their moral good and purification. This is expressly stated, as in ver. 14: "They shall be burnt with fire, that there be no wickedness among you." Both of these principles are of such a nature that they must be of perpetual validity. The government or legislative power that loses sight of either of them is certain to go wrong, and the people will be sure, sooner or later, to suffer in morals by the error.

In the light we have now, it is easy to see what are the principles according to which, in various cases, the punishments were measured out. Evidently, in the first place, the penalty was determined, even as equity demands, by the intrinsic heinousness of the crime. With the possible exception of a single case, it is easy to see this. No one will question the horrible iniquity of the sacrifice of innocent children to Molech; or of incest with a mother, or of sodomy, or bestiality. A second consideration which evidently had place, was the danger involved in each crime to the moral and spiritual well-being of the community; and, we may add, in the third place, also the degree to which the people were likely to be exposed to the contagion of certain crimes prevalent in the nations immediately about them.

But although these principles are manifestly so equitable and benevolent as to be valid for all ages, Christendom seems to be forgetting the fact. The modern penal codes vary as widely from the Mosaic in respect of their great leniency, as those of a few centuries ago in respect of their undiscriminating severity. In particular, the past few generations have seen a great change with regard to the infliction of capital punishment. Formerly, in England, for example, death was inflicted, with intolerable injustice, for a large number of comparatively trivial offences; the death-penalty is now restricted to high treason and killing with malice aforethought; while in some parts of Christendom it is already wholly abolished. In the Mosaic law, according to this chapter and other parts of the law, it was much more extensively inflicted, though, it may be noted in passing, always without torture. In this chapter it is made the penalty for actual or constructive idolatry, for sorcery, etc., for cursing father or mother, for adultery, for the grosser degrees of incest, and for sodomy and bestiality. To this list of capital offences the law elsewhere adds, not only murder, but blasphemy, sabbath-breaking, unchastity in a betrothed woman when discovered after marriage, rape, rebellion against a priest or judge, and man-stealing.

As regards the crimes specified in this particular chapter, the criminal law of modern Christendom does not inflict the penalty of death in a single possible case here mentioned; and, to the mind of many, the contrasted severity of the Mosaic code presents a grave difficulty. And yet, if one believes, on the authority of the teaching of Christ, that the theocratic government of Israel is not a fable, but a historic fact, although he may still have much difficulty in recognising the righteousness of this code, he will be slow on this account either to renounce his faith in the Divine authority of this chapter, or to impugn the justice of the holy King of Israel in charging Him with undue severity; and will rather patiently await some other solution of the problem, than the denial of the essential equity of these laws. But there are several considerations which, for many, will greatly lessen, if they do not wholly remove, the difficulty which the case presents.

In the first place, as regards the punishment of idolatry with death, we have to remember that, from a theocratic point of view, idolatry was essentially high treason, the most formal repudiation possible of the supreme authority of Israel's King. If even in our modern states, the gravity of the issues involved in high treason has led men to believe that death is not too severe a penalty for an offence aimed directly at the subversion of governmental order, how much more must this be admitted when the government is not of fallible man, but of the most holy and infallible God? And when, besides this, we recall the atrocious cruelties and revolting impurities which were inseparably associated with that idolatry, we shall have still less difficulty in seeing that it was just that the worshipper of Molech should die. And as decreeing the penalty of death for sorcery and similar practices, it is probable that the reason for this is to be found in the close connection of these with the prevailing idolatry.

But it is in regard to crimes against the integrity and purity of the family that we find the most impressive contrast between this penal code and those of modern times. Although, unhappily, adultery and, less commonly, incest, and even, rarely, the unnatural crimes mentioned in this chapter, are not unknown in modern Christendom, yet, while the law of Moses punished all these with death, modern law treats them with comparative leniency, or even refuses to regard some forms of these offences as crimes. What then? Shall we hasten to the conclusion that we have advanced on Moses? that this law was certainly unjust in its severity? or is it possible that modern law is at fault, in that it has fallen below those standards of righteousness which rule in the kingdom of God?

One would think that by any man who believes in the Divine origin of the theocracy only one answer could be given. Assuredly, one cannot suppose that God judged of a crime with undue severity; and if not, is not then Christendom, as it were, summoned by this penal code of the theocracy—after making all due allowance for different conditions of society—to revise its estimate of the moral gravity of these and other offences? In these days of continually progressive relaxation of the laws regulating the relations of the sexes, this seems indeed to be one of the chief lessons from this chapter of Leviticus; namely, that in God's sight sins against the seventh commandment are not the comparative trifles which much over-charitable and easy-going morality imagines, but crimes of the first order of heinousness. We do well to heed this fact, that not merely unnatural crimes, such as sodomy, bestiality, and the grosser forms of incest, but adultery, is by God ranked in the same category as murder. Is it strange? For what are crimes of this kind but assaults on the very being of the family? Where there is incest or adultery, we may truly say the family is murdered; what murder is to the individual, that, precisely, are crimes of this class to the family. In the theocratic code these were, therefore, made punishable with death; and, we venture to believe, with abundant reason. Is it likely that God was too severe? or must we not rather fear that man, ever lenient to prevailing sins, in our day has become falsely and unmercifully merciful, kind with a most perilous and unholy kindness?

Still harder will it be for most of us to understand why the death-penalty should have been also affixed to cursing or smiting a father or a mother, an extreme form of rebellion against parental authority. We must, no doubt, bear in mind, as in all these cases, that a rough people like those just emancipated slaves, required a severity of dealing which with finer natures would not be needed; and, also, that the fact of Israel's call to be a priestly nation bearing salvation to mankind, made every disobedience among them the graver crime, as tending to so disastrous issues, not for Israel alone, but for the whole race of man which Israel was appointed to bless. On an analogous principle we justify military authority in shooting the sentry found asleep at his post. Still, while allowing for all this, one can hardly escape the inference that, in the sight of God, rebellion against parents must be a more serious offence than many in our time have been wont to imagine. And the more that we consider how truly basal to the order of government and of society is both sexual purity and the maintenance of a spirit of reverence and subordination to parents, the easier we shall find it to recognise the fact that if in this penal code there is doubtless great severity, it is yet the severity of governmental wisdom and true paternal kindness on the part of the high King of Israel: who governed that nation with intent, above all, that they might become in the highest sense "a holy nation" in the midst of an ungodly world, and so become the vehicle of blessing to others. And God thus judged that it was better that sinning individuals should die without mercy, than that family government and family purity should perish, and Israel, instead of being a blessing to the nations, should sink with them into the mire of universal moral corruption.

And it is well to observe that this law, if severe, was most equitable and impartial in its application. We have here, in no instance, torture; the scourging which in one case is enjoined, is limited elsewhere to the forty stripes save one. Neither have we discrimination against any class, or either sex; nothing like that detestable injustice of modern society which turns the fallen woman into the street with pious scorn, while it often receives the betrayer and even the adulterer—in most cases the more guilty of the two—into "the best society." Nothing have we here, again, which could justify by example the insistence of many, through a perverted humanity, when a murderess is sentenced for her crime to the scaffold, her sex should purchase a partial immunity from the penalty of crime. The Levitical law is as impartial as its Author; even if death be the penalty, the guilty one must die, whether man or woman.

Quite apart, then, from any question of detail, as to how far this penal code ought to be applied under the different conditions of modern society, this chapter of Leviticus assuredly stands as a most impressive testimony from God against the humanitarianism of our age. It is more and more the fashion, in some parts of Christendom, to pet criminals; to lionize murderers and adulterers, especially if in high social station. We have even heard of bouquets and such-like sentimental attentions bestowed by ladies on blood-red criminals in their cells awaiting the halter; and a maudlin pity quite too often usurps among us the place of moral horror at crime and intense sympathy with the holy justice and righteousness of God. But this Divine government of old did not deal in flowers and perfumes; it never indulged criminals, but punished them with an inexorable righteousness. And yet this was not because Israel's King was hard and cruel. For it was this same law which with equal kindness and equity kept a constant eye of fatherly care upon the poor and the stranger, and commanded the Israelite that he love even the stranger as himself. But, none the less, the Lord God who declared Himself as merciful and gracious and of great kindness, also herein revealed Himself, according to his word, as one who would "by no means clear the guilty." This fact is luminously witnessed by this penal code; and, let us note, it is witnessed by that penal law of God which is revealed in nature also. For this too punishes without mercy the drunkard, for example, or the licentious man, and never diminishes one stroke because by the full execution of penalty the sinner must suffer often so terribly. Which is just what we should expect to find, if indeed the God of nature is the One who spake in Leviticus.

Finally, as already suggested, this chapter gives a most weighty testimony against the modern tendency to a relaxation of the laws which regulate the relations of the sexes. That such a tendency is a fact is admitted by all; by some with gratulation, by others with regret and grave concern. French law, for instance, has explicitly legalized various alliances which in this law God explicitly forbids, under heavy penal sanctions, as incestuous; German legislation has moved about as far in the same direction; and the same tendency is to be observed, more or less, in all the English-speaking world. In some of the United States, especially, the utmost laxity has been reached, in laws which, under the name of divorce, legalise gross adultery,—laws which had been a disgrace to pagan Rome. So it goes. Where God denounced the death-penalty, man first apologises for the crime, then lightens the penalty, then abolishes it, and at last formally legalises the crime. This modern drift bodes no good; in the end it can only bring disaster alike to the well-being of the family and of the State. The maintenance of the family in its integrity and purity is nothing less than essential to the conservation of society and the stability of good government.

To meet this growing evil, the Church needs to come back to the full recognition of the principles which underlie this Levitical code; especially of the fact that marriage and the family are not merely civil arrangements, but Divine institutions; so that God has not left it to the caprice of a majority to settle what shall be lawful in these matters. Where God has declared certain alliances and connections to be criminal, we shall permit or condone them at our peril. God rules, whether modern majorities will it or not; and we must adopt the moral standards of the kingdom of God in our legislation, or we shall suffer. God has declared that not merely the material well-being of man, but *holiness*, is the moral end of government and of life; and He will find ways to enforce His will in this respect. "The nation that will not serve Him shall perish." All this is not theology, merely, or ethics, but history. All history witnesses that moral corruption and relaxed legislation, especially in matters affecting the relations of the sexes, bring in their train sure retribution, not in Hades, but here on earth. Let us not miss of taking the lesson by imagining that this law was for Israel, but not for other peoples. The contrary is affirmed in this very chapter (vv. 23, 24), where we are reminded that God visited His heavy judgments upon the Canaanitish nations precisely for this very thing, their doing of these things which are in this law of holiness forbidden. Hence "the land spued them out." Our modern democracies, English, American, French, German, or whatever they be, would do well to pause in their progressive repudiation of the law of God in many social questions, and heed this solemn warning. For, despite the unbelief of multitudes, the Holy One still governs the world, and it is certain that He will never abdicate his throne of righteousness to submit any of his laws to the sanction of a popular vote.

CHAPTER XXIII.

THE LAW OF PRIESTLY HOLINESS.

LEVITICUS xxi. 1-xxii. 33.

THE conception of Israel as a kingdom of priests, a holy nation, was concretely represented in a threefold division of the people,—the congregation, the priesthood, and the high priest. This corresponded to the threefold division of the tabernacle into the outer court, the holy place, and the holy of holies, each in succession more sacred than the place preceding. So while all Israel was called to be a priestly nation, holy to Jehovah in life and service, this sanctity was to be represented in degrees successively higher in each of these three divisions of the people, culminating in the person of the high priest, who, in token of this fact, wore upon his forehead the inscription, "HOLINESS TO JEHOVAH."

Up to this point the law of holiness has dealt only with such obligations as bore upon all the priestly nation alike; in these two chapters we now have the special requirements of this law in its yet higher demands upon, first, the priests, and, secondly, the high priest.

Abolished as to the letter, this part of the law still holds good as to the principle which it expresses, namely that special spiritual privilege and honour places him to whom it is given under special obligations to holiness of life. As contrasted with the world without, it is not then enough that Christians should be equally correct and moral in life with the best men of the world; though too many seem to be living under that impression. They must be more than this; they must be holy: God will wink at things in others which He will not deal lightly with in them. And, so, again, within the Church, those who occupy various positions of dignity as teachers and rulers of God's flock are just in that degree laid under the more stringent obligation to holiness of life and walk. This most momentous lesson confronts us at the very opening of this new section of the law, addressed specifically to "the priests, the sons of Aaron." How much it is needed is sufficiently and most sadly evident from the condition of baptized Christendom to-day. Who is there that will heed it?

Priestly holiness was to be manifested, first (vv. 1-15), in regard to earthly relations of kindred and friendship. This is illustrated under three particulars, namely, in mourning for the dead (vv. 1-6), in marriage (vv. 7, 8), and (ver. 9) in the maintenance of purity in the priest's family. With regard to the first point, it is ordered that there shall be no defilement for the dead, except in the case of the priest's own family,—father, mother, brother, unmarried sister, son, or daughter.* That is, with the exception of these cases, the priest, though he may mourn in his heart, is to take no part in any of those last offices which others render to the dead. This were "to profane himself." And while the above exceptions are allowed in the case of members of his immediate household, even in these cases he is specially charged (ver. 5) to remember, what was indeed elsewhere forbidden to every Israelite, that such excessive demonstrations of grief as shaving the head, cutting the flesh, etc., were most unseemly in a priest. These restrictions are expressly based upon the fact that he is "a chief man among his people," that he is holy unto God, appointed to offer "the bread of God, the offerings made by fire." And inasmuch as the high priest, in the highest degree of all, represents the priestly idea, and is thus admitted into a peculiar and exclusive intimacy of relation with God, having on him "the crown of the anointing oil of his God," and having been consecrated to put on the "garments for glory and for beauty," worn by none other in Israel, with him the prohibition of all public acts of mourning is made absolute (vv. 10-12). He may not defile himself, for instance, by even entering the house where lies the dead body of a father or a mother!

These regulations, at first thought, to many will seem hard and unnatural. Yet this law of holiness elsewhere magnifies and guards with most jealous care the family relation, and commands that even the neighbour we shall love as ourselves. Hence it is certain that these regulations cannot have been intended to condemn the natural feelings of grief at the loss of friends, but only to place them under certain restrictions. They were given, not to depreciate the earthly relationships of friendship and kindred, but only to magnify the more the dignity and significance of the priestly relation to God, as far transcending even the most sacred relations of earth. As priest, the son of Aaron was the servant of the Eternal God, of God the Holy and the Living One, appointed to mediate from Him the grace of pardon and life to those condemned to die. Hence he must never forget this himself, nor allow others to forget it. Hence he must maintain a special, visible separation from death, as everywhere the sign of the presence and operation of sin and unholiness; and while he is not forbidden to mourn, he must mourn with a visible moderation; the more so that if his priesthood had any significance, it meant that death for the believing and obedient Israelite was death in hope. And then, besides all this, God had declared that He Himself would be the portion and inheritance of the priests. For the priest therefore to mourn, as if in losing even those nearest and dearest on earth he had lost all, were in outward appearance to fail in witness to the faithfulness of God to His promises, and His all-sufficiency as his portion.

Standing here, will we but listen, we can now hear the echo of this same law of priestly holiness from the New Testament, in such words as these, addressed to the whole priesthood of believers: "He that loveth father or mother more than Me is not worthy of Me;" "Let those that have wives be as though they had none, and those that weep as though they wept not;" "Concerning them that fall asleep . . . sorrow not, even as the rest, which have no hope." As Christians we are not forbidden to mourn; but because a royal priesthood to the God of life, who raised up the Lord Jesus, and ourselves looking also for the resurrection, ever with moderation and self-restraint. Extravagant demonstrations of sorrow, whether in dress or in prolonged separation from the sanctuary and active service of God, as the manner of many is, are all as contrary to the New Testament law of holiness as to that of the Old. When bereaved, we are to call to mind the blessed fact of our priestly relation to God, and in this we shall find a restraint and a remedy for excessive and despairing grief. We are to remember that the law for the High Priest is the law for all His priestly house; like Him, they must all be perfected for the priesthood by sufferings; so that, in that they themselves suffer, being tried, they may be able the better to succour others that are tried in like manner (2 Cor. i. 4; Heb. ii. 18). We are also to remember that as priests to God, this God of eternal life and love is Himself our satisfying portion, and with holy care take heed that by no immoderate display of grief we even seem before men to traduce His faithfulness and belie to unbelievers His glorious all-sufficiency.

The holiness of the priesthood was also to be represented visibly in the marriage relation. A priest must marry no woman to whose fair fame attaches the slightest possibility of suspicion,—no harlot, or fallen woman,* or a woman divorced (ver. 7); such an alliance were manifestly most unseemly in one "holy to his God." As in the former instance, the high priest is still further restricted; he may not marry a widow, but only "a virgin of his own people" (ver. 14); for virginity is always in Holy Scripture the peculiar type of holiness. As a reason it is added that this were to "profane his seed among his people;" that is, it would be inevitable that by neglect of this care the people would come to regard his seed with a diminished reverence as the separated priests of the holy God. From observing the practice of many who profess to be Christians, one would naturally infer that they can never have suspected that there was anything in this part of the law which concerns the New Testament priesthood of believers. How often we see a young man or a young woman professing to be a disciple of Christ, a member of Christ's royal priesthood, entering into marriage alliance with a confessed unbeliever in Him! And yet the law is laid down as explicitly in the New Testament as in the Old (1 Cor. vii. 39), that marriage shall be only "in the Lord;" so that one principle rules in both dispensations. The priestly line must, as far as possible, be kept pure; the holy man must have a holy wife. Many, indeed, feel this deeply and marry accordingly; but the apparent thoughtlessness on the matter of many more is truly astonishing, and almost incomprehensible.

And the household of the priest were to remember the holy standing of their father. The sin of the child of a priest was to be punished more severely than that of the children of others; a single illustration is given (ver. 9): "The daughter of any priest, if she profane herself by

---

* The wife is not mentioned, but that she would also be included in the exception, in view of her being always regarded in the law as yet nearer to her husband than father or mother, may be safely taken for granted.

* See margin (R. V.).

playing the harlot, ... shall be burnt with fire."* And the severity of the penalty is justified by this, that by her sin "she profaneth her father." From which it appears that, as a principle of the Divine judgment, if the children of believers sin, their guilt will be judged more heavy than that of others; and that justly, because to their sin this is added, over like sin of others, that they thereby cast dishonour on their believing parents, and in them soil and defame the honour of God. How little is this remembered by many in these days of increasing insubordination even in Christian families!

The priestly holiness was to be manifested, in the second place, in physical, bodily perfection. It is written (ver. 17): "Speak unto Aaron, saying, Whosoever he be of thy seed throughout their generations that hath a blemish, let him not approach to offer the bread of his God."

And then follows (vv. 18-20) a list of various cases in illustration of this law, with the proviso (vv. 21-23) that while such a person might not perform any priestly function, he should not be debarred from the use of the priestly portion, whether of things "holy" or "most holy," as his daily food. The material and bodily is ever the type and symbol of the spiritual; hence, in this case, the spiritual purity and perfection required of him who would draw near to God in the priests' office must be visibly signified by his physical perfection; else the sanctity of the tabernacle were profaned. Moreover, the reverence due from the people toward Jehovah's sanctuary could not well be maintained where a dwarf, for instance, or a humpback, were ministering at the altar. And yet the Lord has for such a heart of kindness; in kindly compassion He will not exclude them from His table. Like Mephibosheth at the table of David, the deformed priest may still eat at the table of God.

There is a thought here which bears on the administration of the affairs of God's house even now. We are reminded that there are those who, while undoubtedly members of the universal Christian priesthood, and thus lawfully entitled to come to the table of the Lord, may yet be properly regarded as disabled and debarred by various circumstances, for which, in many cases, they may not be responsible, from any eminent position in the Church.

In the almost unrestrained insistence of many in this day for "equality," there are indications not a few of a contempt for the holy offices ordained by Christ for His Church, which would admit an equal right on the part of almost any who may desire it, to be allowed to minister in the Church in holy things. But as there were dwarfed and blinded sons of Aaron, so are there not a few Christians who—evidently, at least to all but themselves—are spiritually dwarfs or deformed; subject to ineradicable and obtrusive constitutional infirmities, such as utterly disqualify, and should preclude, them from holding any office in the holy Church of Christ. The presence of such in her ministry can only now, as of old, profane the sanctuaries of the Lord.

The next section of the law of holiness for the priests (xxii. 1-16) requires that the priests, as holy unto Jehovah, treat with most careful reverence all those holy things which are their lawful portion. If, in any way, any priest have incurred ceremonial defilement,—as, for instance, by an issue, or by the dead,—he is not to eat

* That is, not burnt alive, but after execution.

until he is clean (vv. 2-7). On no account must he defile himself by eating of that which is unclean, such as that which has died of itself, or has been torn by beasts (ver. 8), which indeed was forbidden even to the ordinary Israelite. Furthermore, the priests are charged that they preserve the sanctity of God's house by carefully excluding all from participation in the priests' portion who are not of the priestly order. The stranger or sojourner in the priest's house, or a hired servant, must not be fed from this "bread of God;" not even a daughter, when, having married, she has left the father's home to form a family of her own, can be allowed to partake of it (ver. 12). If, however (ver. 13), she be parted from her husband by death or divorce, and have no child, and return to her father's house, she then becomes again a member of the priestly family, and resumes the privileges of her virginity.

All this may seem, at first, remote from any present use; and yet it takes little thought to see that, in principle, the New Testament law of holiness requires, under a changed form, even the same reverent use of God's gifts, and especially of the holy Supper of the Lord, from every member of the Christian priesthood. It is true that in some parts of the Church a superstitious dread is felt with regard to approach to the Lord's Table, as if only the conscious attainment of a very high degree of holiness could warrant one in coming. But, however such a feeling is to be deprecated, it is certain that it is a less serious wrong, and argues not so ill as to the spiritual condition of a man as the easy carelessness with which multitudes partake of the Lord's Supper, nothing disturbed, apparently, by the recollection that they are living in the habitual practice of known sin, unconfessed, unforsaken, and therefore unforgiven. As it was forbidden to the priest to eat of those holy things which were his rightful portion, with his defilement or uncleanness on him, till he should first be cleansed, no less is it now a violation of the law of holiness for the Christian to come to the Holy Supper having on his conscience unconfessed and unforgiven sin. No less truly than the violation of this ancient law is this a profanation, and who so desecrates the holy food must bear his sin.

And as the sons of Aaron were charged by this law of holiness that they guard the holy things from the participation of any who were not of the priestly house, so also is the obligation on every member of the New Testament Church, and especially on those who are in official charge of her holy sacraments, that they be careful to debar from such participation the unholy and profane. It is true that it is possible to go to an extreme in this matter which is unwarranted by the Word of God. Although participation in the Holy Supper is of right only for the regenerate, it does not follow, as in some sections of the Church has been imagined, that the Church is therefore required to satisfy herself as to the undoubted regeneration of those who may apply for membership and fellowship in this privilege. So to read the heart as to be able to decide authoritatively on the regeneration of every applicant for Church membership is beyond the power of any but the Omniscient Lord, and is not required in the Word. The Apostles received and baptised men upon their credible profession of faith and repentance, and entered into no inquisitorial cross-examination as to the details of the religious experience of the candidate. None the less, however, the law of holiness requires that the Church, under this limitation, shall to the uttermost of her power be careful that no one unconverted and profane shall sit at the Holy Table of the Lord. She may admit upon profession of faith and repentance, but she certainly is bound to see to it that such profession shall be credible; that is, such as may be reasonably believed to be sincere and genuine. She is bound, therefore, to satisfy herself in such cases, so far as possible to man, that the life of the applicant, at least externally, witnesses to the genuineness of the profession. If we are to beware of imposing false tests of Christian character, as some have done, for instance, in the use or disuse of things indifferent, we are, on the other hand, to see to it that we do apply such tests as the Word warrants, and firmly exclude all such as insist upon practices which are demonstrably, in themselves always wrong, according to the law of God.

No man who has any just apprehension of Scriptural truth can well doubt that we have here a lesson which is of the highest present-day importance. When one goes out into the world and observes the practices in which many whom we meet at the Lord's Table habitually indulge, whether in business or in society,—the crookedness in commercial dealings and sharp dealing in trade, the utter dissipation in amusement, of many Church members,—a spiritual man cannot but ask, Where is the discipline of the Lord's house? Surely, this law of holiness applies to a multitude of such cases; and it must be said that when such eat of the holy things, they "profane them;" and those who, in responsible charge of the Lord's Table, are careless in this matter, "cause them to bear the iniquity that bringeth guilt, when they eat their holy things" (ver. 16). That word of the Lord Jesus certainly applies in this case (Matt. xviii. 7): "It must needs be that occasions of stumbling come; but woe to that man through whom the occasion cometh!"

The last section of the law concerning priestly holiness (xxii. 17-33) requires the maintenance of jealous care in the enforcement of the law of offerings. Inasmuch as, in the nature of the case, while it rested with the sons of Aaron to enforce this law, the obligation concerned every offerer, this section (vv. 17-25) is addressed also (ver. 18) "unto all the children of Israel." The first requirement concerned the perfection of the offering; it must be (vv. 19, 20) "without blemish." Only one qualification is allowed to this law, namely, in the case of the free-will offering (ver. 23), in which a victim was allowed which, otherwise perfect, had something "superfluous or lacking in his parts." Even this relaxation of the law was not allowed in the case of an offering brought in payment of a vow; hence Malachi (i. 14), in allusion to this law, sharply denounces the man who "voweth, and sacrificeth unto the Lord a blemished thing." Verse 25 provides that this law shall be enforced in the case of the foreigner, who may wish to present an offering to Jehovah, no less than with the Israelite.

A third requirement (ver. 27) sets a minimum limit to the age of a sacrificial victim; it must not be less than eight days old. The reason of this law, apart from any mystic or symbolic meaning, is probably grounded in considerations of humanity, requiring the avoidance of giving unnecessary suffering to the dam. A similar intention is probably to be recognised in the additional law (ver. 28) that the cow, or ewe, and its young should not both be killed in one day; though it must be confessed that the matter is somewhat obscure. Finally, the law closes (vv. 29, 30) with the repetition of the command (vii. 15) requiring that the flesh of the sacrifice of thanksgiving be eaten on the same day in which it is offered. The slightest possibility of beginning corruption is to be precluded in such cases with peculiar strictness.

This closing section of the law of holiness, which so insists that the regulations of God's law in regard to sacrifice shall be scrupulously observed, in its inner principle forbids all departures in matter of worship from any express Divine appointment or command. We fully recognise the fact that, as compared with the old dispensation, the New Testament allows in the conduct and order of worship a far larger liberty than then. But, in our age, the tendency, alike in politics and in religion, is to the confounding of liberty and license. Yet they are not the same, but are most sharply contrasted. Liberty is freedom of action within the bounds of Divine law; license recognises no limitation to human action, apart from enforced necessity, —no law save man's own will and pleasure. It is therefore essential lawlessness,[*] and therefore is sin in its most perfect and consummate expression. But there is law in the New Testament as well as in the Old. Because the New Testament lays down but few laws concerning the order of Divine worship, it does not follow that these few are of no consequence, and that men may worship in all respects just as they choose, and equally please God.

To illustrate this matter. It does not follow, because the New Testament allows large liberty as regards the details of worship, that therefore we may look upon the use of images or pictures in connection with worship as a matter of indifference. If told that these are merely used as an aid to devotion,—the very argument which in all ages has been used by all idolaters,—we reply that, be that as it may, it is an aid which is expressly prohibited under the heaviest penal sanctions in both Testaments. We may take another present-day illustration, which, especially in the American Church, is of special pertinence. One would say that it should be self-evident that no ordinance of the Church should be more jealously guarded from human alteration or modification than the most sacred institution of the sacramental Supper. Surely it should be allowed that the Lord alone should have the right to designate the symbols of His own death in this most holy ordinance. That He chose and appointed for this purpose bread and wine, even the fermented juice of the grape, has been affirmed by the practically unanimous consensus of Christendom for almost nineteen hundred years; and it is not too much to say that this understanding of the Scripture record is sustained by the no less unanimous judgment of truly authoritative scholarship even to-day. Neither can it be denied that Christ ordained this use of wine in the Holy Supper with the most perfect knowledge of the terrible evils connected with its abuse in all ages. All this being

[*] See 1 John iii. 4 and 2 Thess. ii. 3, 4, 7, 8,—passages which, in view of this most manifest and characteristic tendency of our times, are pregnant with very solemn warning.

so, how can it but contravene this principle of the law of holiness, which insists upon the exact observance of the appointments which the Lord has made for His own worship, when men, in the imagined interest of " moral reform," presume to attempt improvements in this holy ordinance of the Lord, and substitute for the wine which He chose to make the symbol of His precious blood, something else, of different properties, for the use of which the whole New Testament affords no warrant? We speak with full knowledge of the various plausible arguments which are pressed as reasons why the Church should authorise this nineteenth-century innovation. No doubt, in many cases, the change is urged through a misapprehension as to the historical facts, which, however astonishing to scholars, is at least real and sincere. But whenever any, admitting the facts as to the original appointment, yet seriously propose, as so often of late years, to improve on the Lord's arrangements for His own Table, we are bold to insist that the principle which underlies this part of the priestly law of holiness applies in full force in this case, and cannot therefore be rightly set aside. Strange, indeed, it is that men should unthinkingly hope to advance morality by ignoring the primal principle of all holiness, that Christ, the Son of God, is absolute and supreme Lord over all His people, and especially in all that pertains to the ordering of His own house!

We have in these days great need to beseech the Lord that He may deliver us, in all things, from that malign epidemic of religious lawlessness which is one of the plagues of our age; and raise up a generation who shall so understand their priestly calling as Christians, that, no less in all that pertains to the offices of public worship, than in their lives as individuals they shall take heed, above all things, to walk according to the principles of this law of priestly holiness. For, repealed although it be as to the outward form of the letter, yet in the nature of the case, as to its spirit and intention, it abides, and must abide, in force unto the end. And the great argument also, with which, after the constant manner of this law, this section closes, is also, as to its spirit, valid still, and even of greater force in its New Testament form than of old. For we may now justly read it in this wise: " Ye shall not profane My holy name, but I will be hallowed among My people: I am the Lord that hallow you, *that have redeemed you by the cross*, to be your God."

CHAPTER XXIV.

THE SET FEASTS OF THE LORD.

LEVITICUS xxiii. 1-44.

IT is ever an instinct of natural religion to observe certain set times for special public and united worship. As we should therefore anticipate, such observances are in this chapter enjoined as a part of the requirement of the law of holiness for Israel.

It is of consequence to observe that the Revisers have corrected the error of the Authorised Version, which renders two perfectly distinct words alike as " feasts;" and have distinguished the one by the translation, " set feasts," the other by the one word, " feasts." The precise sense of the former word is given in the margin " appointed seasons," and it is naturally applied to all the set times of special religious solemnity which are ordained in this chapter. But the other word translated " feast,"—derived from a root meaning " to dance," whence " feast " or " festival,"—is applied to only three of the former six " appointed seasons," namely, the feasts of Unleavened Bread, of Pentecost, and of Tabernacles; as intended to be, in a special degree, seasons of gladness and festivity.

The indication of this distinction is of importance, as completely meeting the allegation that there is in this chapter evidence of a later development than in the account of the feasts given in Exod. xxxiv., where the number of the " feasts," besides the weekly Sabbath, is given as three, while here, as it is asserted, their number has been increased to six. In reality, however, there is nothing here which suggests a later period. For the object of the former law in Exodus was only to name the "feasts " (*haggim*); while that of the chapter before us is to indicate not only these,—which here, as there, are three, —but, in addition to these, all " appointed seasons " for " holy convocations," which, although all *mo'adim*, were not all *haggim*.

The observance of public religious festivals has been common to all the chief religions of the world, both ancient and modern. Very often, though not in all cases, these have been determined by the phases of the moon; or by the apparent motion of the sun in the heavens, as in many instances of religious celebrations connected with the period of the spring and autumnal equinoxes; and thus, very naturally, also with the times of harvest and ingathering. It is at once evident that of these appointed seasons of holy convocation, the three feasts (*haggim*) of the Hebrews also fell at certain points in the harvest season; and with each of these, ceremonies were observed connected with harvest and ingathering; while two, the feast of weeks and that of tabernacles, take alternate names, directly referring to this their connection with the harvest; namely, the feast of firstfruits and that of ingathering. Thus we have, first, the feast of unleavened bread, following passover, which was distinguished by the presentation of a sheaf of the firstfruits of the barley harvest, in the latter part of March, or early in April; then, the feast of weeks, or firstfruits, seven weeks later, marking the completion of the grain harvest with the ingathering of the wheat; and, finally, the feast of tabernacles or ingathering, in the seventh month, marking the harvesting of the fruits, especially the oil and the wine, and therewith the completed ingathering of the whole product of the year.

From these facts it is argued that in these Hebrew feasts we have simply a natural development, with modifications, of the ancient and widespread system of harvest feasts among the heathen; to which the historical element which appears in some of them was only added as an afterthought, in a later period of history. From this point of view, the idea that these feasts were a matter of supernatural revelation disappears; what religious character they have belongs originally to the universal religion of nature.

But it is to be remarked, first, that even if we admit that in their original character these were simply and only harvest feasts, it would not follow that therefore their observance, with certain prescribed ceremonies, could not have been matter of Divine revelation. There is a religion of nature; God has not left Himself without a witness, in that He has given men "rains and fruitful seasons," filling their hearts with food and gladness. And, as already remarked in regard to sacrifice, it is no part of the method of God in revelation to ignore or reject what in this religion of nature may be true and right; but rather to use it, and build on this foundation.

But, again, the mere fact that the feast of unleavened bread fell at the beginning of barley harvest, and that one—though only one—ceremony appointed for that festive week had explicit reference to the then beginning harvest, is not sufficient to disprove the uniform declaration of Scripture that, as observed in Israel, its original ground was not natural, but historical; namely, in the circumstances attending the birth of the nation in their exodus from Egypt.

But we may say more than this. If the contrary were true, and the introduction of the historical element was an afterthought, as insisted by some, then we should expect to find that in accounts belonging to successive periods, the reference to the harvest would certainly be more prominent in the earlier, and the reference of the feast to a historical origin more prominent in the later, accounts of the feasts. Most singular it is then, upon this hypothesis, to find that even accepting the analysis, *e. g.*, of Wellhausen, the facts are the exact reverse. For the only brief reference to the harvest in connection with this feast of unleavened bread is found in this chap. xxiii. of Leviticus, composed, it is alleged, about the time of Ezekiel; while, on the other hand, the narrative in Exod. xii., regarded by all the critics of this school as the earliest account of the origin of the feast of unleavened bread, refers only to the historical event of the exodus, as the occasion of its institution. If we grant the asserted difference in age of these two parts of the Pentateuch, one would thus more naturally conclude that the historical events were the original occasion of the institution of the festival, and that the reference to the harvest, in the presentation of the sheaf of firstfruits, was the later introduction into the ceremonies of the week.

But the truth is that this naturalistic identification of these Hebrew feasts with the harvest feasts of other nations is a mistake. In order to make it out, it is necessary to ignore or pervert most patent facts. These so-called harvest feasts in fact form part of an elaborate system of sacred times,—a system which is based upon the Sabbath, and into which the sacred number seven, the number of the covenant, enters throughout as a formative element. The weekly Sabbath, first of all, was the seventh day; the length of the great festivals of unleavened bread and of tabernacles was also, in each case, seven days. Not only so, but the entire series of sacred times mentioned in this chapter and in chap. xxv. constitutes an ascending series of sacred septenaries, in which the ruling thought is this: that the seventh is holy unto the Lord, as the number symbolic of rest and redemption; and that the eighth, as the first of a new week, is symbolic of the new creation. Thus we have the seventh day, the weekly Sabbath, constantly recurring, the type of each of the series; then, counting from the feast of unleavened bread,—the first of the sacred year,—the fiftieth day, at the end of the seventh week, is signalised as sacred by the feast of firstfruits or of "weeks;" the seventh month, again, is the sabbatic month, of special sanctity, containing as it does three of the annual seasons of holy convocation,—the feast of trumpets on its first day, the great day of atonement on the tenth, and the last of the three great annual feasts, that of tabernacles or ingathering, for seven days from the fifteenth day of the month. Beyond this series of sacred festivals recurring annually, in chap. xxv., the seventh year is appointed to be a sabbatic year of rest to the land, and the series at last culminates at the expiration of seven sevens of years, in the fiftieth year,—the eighth following the seventh seven,—the great year of jubilee, the supreme year of rest, restoration, and release. All these sacred times, differing in the details of their observance, are alike distinguished by their connection with the sacred number seven, by the informing presence of the idea of the Sabbath, and therewith always a new and fuller revelation of God as in covenant with Israel for their redemption.

Now, like to this series of sacred times, in heathenism there is absolutely nothing. It evidently belongs to another realm of thought, ethics, and religion. And so, while it is quite true that in the three great feasts there was a reference to the harvest, and so to fruitful nature, yet the fundamental, unifying idea of the system of sacred times was not the recognition of the fruitful life of nature, as in the heathen festivals, but of Jehovah, as the Author and Sustainer of the life of His covenant people Israel, as also of every individual in the nation. This, we repeat, is the one central thought in all these sacred seasons; not the life of nature, but the life of the holy nation, as created and sustained by a covenant God. The annual processes of nature have indeed a place and a necessary recognition in the system, simply because the personal God is active in all nature; but the place of these is not primary, but secondary and subordinate. They have a recognition because, in the first place, it is through the bounty of God in nature that the life of man is sustained; and, secondly, also because nature in her order is a type and shadow of things spiritual. For in the spiritual world, whether we think of it as made up of nations or individuals, even as in the natural, there is a seedtime and a harvest, a time of firstfruits and a time of the joy and rest of the full ingathering of fruit, and oil, and wine. Hence it was most fitting that this inspired rubric, as primarily intended for the celebration of spiritual things, should be so arranged and timed, in all its parts, as that in each returning sacred season, visible nature should present itself to Israel as a manifest parable and eloquent suggestion of those spiritual verities; the more so that thus the Israelite would be reminded that the God of the Exodus and the God of Sinai was also the supreme Lord of nature, the God of the seed-time and harvest, the Creator and Sustainer of the heavens and the earth, and of all that in them is.

THE WEEKLY SABBATH.

LEVITICUS xxiii. 1-3.

"And the Lord spake unto Moses, saying, Speak unto the children of Israel, and say unto them, The set feasts of the Lord, which ye shall proclaim to be holy convocations, even these are My set feasts. Six days shall work be done: but on the seventh day is a sabbath of solemn rest, an holy convocation; ye shall do no manner of work: it is a sabbath unto the Lord in all your dwellings."

The first verse of this chapter announces the purpose of the section as not to give a complete calendar of sacred times or of seasons of worship,—for the new moons and the sabbatic year and the jubilee are not mentioned,—but to enumerate such sacred times as are to be kept as "holy convocations." The reference in this phrase cannot be to an assembling of the people at the central sanctuary which is elsewhere ordered (Exod. xxxiv. 23) only for the three feasts of passover, weeks, and atonement; but rather, doubtless, to local gatherings for purposes of worship, such as, at a later day, took form in the institution of the synagogues.

The enumeration of these "set times" begins with the Sabbath (ver. 3), as was natural; for, as we have seen, the whole series of sacred times was sabbatic in character. The sanctity of the day is emphasised in the strongest terms, as a *shabbath shabbathon*, a "sabbath of sabbatism,"— a "sabbath of solemn rest," as it is rendered by the Revisers. While on some other sacred seasons the usual occupations of the household were permitted, on the Sabbath "no manner of work" was to be done; not even was it lawful to gather wood or to light a fire.

For this sanctity of the Sabbath two reasons are elsewhere given. The first of these, which is assigned in the fourth commandment, makes it a memorial of the rest of God, when having created man in Eden, He saw His work which He had finished, that it was very good, and rested from all His work. As created, man was participant in this rest of God. He was indeed to work in tilling the garden in which he had been placed; but from such labour as involves unremunerative toil and exhaustion he was exempt. But this sabbatic rest of the creation was interrupted by sin; God's work, which He had declared "good," was marred; man fell into a condition of wearying toil and unrest of body and soul, and with him the whole creation also was "subjected to vanity" (Gen. iii. 17, 18; Rom. viii. 20). But in this state of things the God of love could not rest; it thus involved for Him a work of new creation, which should have for its object the complete restoration, both as regards man and nature, of that sabbatic state of things on earth which had been broken up by sin. And thus it came to pass that the weekly Sabbath looked not only backward, but forward; and spoke not only of the rest that was, but of the great sabbatism of the future, to be brought in through a promised redemption. Hence, as a second reason for the observance of the Sabbath, it is said (Exod. xxxi. 13) to be a sign between God and Israel through all their generations, that they might know that He was Jehovah which sanctified them, *i. e.*, who had set them apart for deliverance from the curse, that through them the world might be saved.

These are thus the two sabbatic ideas; rest and redemption. They everywhere appear, in one form or another, in all this sabbatic series of sacred times. Some of them emphasise one phase of the rest and redemption, and some another; the weekly Sabbath, as the unit of the series, presents both. For in Deuteronomy (v. 15) Israel was commanded to keep the Sabbath in commemoration of the exodus, as the time when God undertook to bring them into His rest; a rest of which the beginning and the pledge was their deliverance from Egyptian bondage; a rest brought in through a redemption.*

* See the inspired comment in Heb. iv.

THE FEAST OF PASSOVER AND UNLEAVENED BREAD.

LEVITICUS xxiii. 4-14.

"These are the set feasts of the Lord, even holy convocations, which ye shall proclaim in their appointed season. In the first month, on the fourteenth day of the month at even, is the Lord's passover. And on the fifteenth day of the same month is the feast of unleavened bread unto the Lord: seven days ye shall eat unleavened bread. In the first day ye shall have an holy convocation: ye shall do no servile work. But ye shall offer an offering made by fire unto the Lord seven days: in the seventh day is an holy convocation; ye shall do no servile work. And the Lord spake unto Moses, saying, Speak unto the children of Israel, and say unto them, When ye be come into the land which I give unto you, and shall reap the harvest thereof, then ye shall bring the sheaf of the firstfruits of your harvest unto the priest: and he shall wave the sheaf before the Lord, to be accepted for you: on the morrow after the sabbath the priest shall wave it. And in the day when ye wave the sheaf, ye shall offer a he-lamb without blemish of the first year for a burnt offering unto the Lord. And the meal offering thereof shall be two tenth parts of an ephah of fine flour mingled with oil, an offering made by fire unto the Lord for a sweet savour: and the drink offering thereof shall be of wine, the fourth part of an hin. And ye shall eat neither bread, nor parched corn, nor fresh ears, until this selfsame day, until ye have brought the oblation of your God: it is a statute for ever throughout your generations in all your dwellings."

Verses 5-8 give the law for the first of the annual feasts, the passover and unleavened bread. The passover lamb was to be slain and eaten on the evening of the fourteenth day; and thereafter, for seven days, they were all to eat unleavened bread. The first and seventh days of unleavened bread were to be kept as an "holy convocation;" in both of which "servile work," *i. e.*, the usual occupations in the field or in one's handicraft, were forbidden. Further than this the restriction did not extend.

The utter impossibility of making this feast of passover also to have been at first merely a harvest festival is best shown by the signal failure of the many attempts to explain on this theory the name "passover" as applied to the sacrificial victim, and the exclusion of leaven for the whole period. Admit the statements of the Pentateuch on this subject, and all is simple. The feast was a most suitable commemoration by Israel of the solemn circumstances under which they began their national life; their exemption from the plague of the death of the first-born, through the blood of a slain victim; and their exodus thereafter in such haste that they stopped not to leaven their bread.

And there was a deeper spiritual meaning than this. Whereas, secured by the sprinkling of blood, they then fed in safety on the flesh of the victim, by which they received strength for their flight from Egypt, the same two thoughts were thereby naturally suggested which we have seen represented in the peace-offering; namely, friendship and fellowship with God secured through sacrifice, and life sustained by His bounty. And the unleavened bread, also, had more than a historic reference; else it had sufficed to eat it only on the anniversary night, and it had not been commanded also to put away the leaven from their houses. For leaven is the established symbol of moral corruption; and in that, the passover lamb having been slain, Israel must abstain for a full septenary period of a week from every use of leaven, it was signified in symbol that the redeemed nation must not live by means of what is evil, but be a holy people, according to their calling. And the inseparable connection of this with full consecration of person and service, and with the expiation of sin, was daily symbolised (ver. 8) by the "offerings made by fire," burnt-offerings, meal-offerings, and sin-offerings, "offerings made by fire unto the Lord."

On "the morrow after the Sabbath" (ver. 15) of this sacred week, it was ordered (ver. 10) that "the sheaf of the firstfruits of the (barley) harvest" should be brought "unto the priest;" and (ver. 11) that he should consecrate it unto the Lord, by the ceremony of waving it before Him. This wave-offering of the sheaf of firstfruits was to be accompanied (vv. 12, 13) by a burnt-offering, a meal-offering, and a drink-offering of wine. Until all this was done (ver. 14) they were to "eat neither bread, nor parched corn, nor fresh ears" of the new harvest. By the consecration of the firstfruits is ever signified the consecration of the whole, of which it is the first part, unto the Lord. By this act, Israel, at the very beginning of their harvest, solemnly consecrated the whole harvest to the Lord; and are only permitted to use it, when they receive it thus as a gift from Him. This ethical reference to the harvest is here expressly taught; but still more was thereby taught in symbol.

For Israel was declared (Exod. iv. 22) to be God's first-born; that is, in the great redemptive plan of God, which looks forward to the final salvation of all nations, Israel ever comes historically first. "The Jew first, and also the Greek," is the New Testament formula of this fundamental dispensational truth. The offering unto God, therefore, of the sheaf of firstfruits, at the very beginning of the harvest,—in fullest harmony with the historic reference of this feast, which commemorated Israel's deliverance from bondage and separation from the nations, as a firstfruits of redemption,—symbolically signified the consecration of Israel unto God as the firstborn unto Him from the nations, the beginning of the world's great harvest.

But this is not all. For in these various ceremonies of this first of the feasts, all who acknowledge the authority of the New Testament will recognise a yet more profound, and prophetic, spiritual meaning. Passover and unleavened bread not only looked backward, but forward. For the Apostle Paul writes, addressing all believers (1 Cor. 7, 8): "Purge out the old leaven, that ye may be a new lump, even as ye are unleavened. For our passover also hath been sacrificed, even Christ: wherefore let us keep the feast, not with old leaven, neither with the leaven of malice and wickedness, but with the unleavened bread of sincerity and truth;"—an exposition so plain that comment is scarcely needed. And as following upon the passover, on the morrow after the Sabbath, the first day of the week, the sheaf of firstfruits was presented before Jehovah, so in type is brought before us that of which the same Apostle tells us (1 Cor. xv. 20), that Christ, in that He rose from the dead on the first day after the Sabbath, became "the firstfruits of them that are asleep;" thus, for the first time, finally and exhaustively fulfilling this type, in full accord also with His own representation of Himself (John xii. 24) as "a grain of wheat," which should "fall into the earth and die," and then, living again, "bear much fruit."

The Feast of Pentecost.

Leviticus xxiii. 15-21.

"And ye shall count unto you from the morrow after the sabbath, from the day that ye brought the sheaf of the wave offering; seven sabbaths shall there be complete: even unto the morrow after the seventh sabbath shall ye number fifty days; and ye shall offer a new meal offering unto the Lord. Ye shall bring out of your habitations two wave loaves of two tenth parts of an ephah : they shall be of fine flour, they shall be baken with leaven, for firstfruits unto the Lord. And ye shall present with the bread seven lambs without blemish of the first year, and one young bullock, and two rams : they shall be a burnt offering unto the Lord, with their meal offering, and their drink offerings, even an offering made by fire, of a sweet savour unto the Lord. And ye shall offer one he-goat for a sin offering, and two he-lambs of the first year for a sacrifice of peace offerings. And the priest shall wave them with the bread of the firstfruits for a wave offering before the Lord, with the two lambs : they shall be holy to the Lord for the priest. And ye shall make proclamation on the selfsame day ; there shall be an holy convocation unto you : ye shall do no servile work : it is a statute for ever in all your dwellings throughout your generations."

Next in order came the feast of firstfruits, or the feast of weeks, which, because celebrated on the fiftieth day after the presentation of the wave-sheaf in passover week, has come to be known as Pentecost, from the Greek numeral signifying fifty. It was ordered that the fiftieth day after this presentation of the first sheaf of the harvest should be kept as a day of "holy convocation," with abstinence from all "servile work." The former festival had marked the absolute beginning of the harvest with the first sheaf of barley; this marked the completion of the grain harvest with the reaping of the wheat. In the former, the sheaf was presented as it came from the field; in this case, the offering was of the grain as prepared for food. It was ordered (ver. 16) that on this day "a new meal offering" should be offered. It should be brought out of their habitations and be baken with leaven. In both particulars, it was unlike the ordinary meal-offerings, because the offering was to represent the ordinary food of the people. Accompanied with a sevenfold burnt-offering, and a sin-offering, and two lambs of peace-offerings, these were to be waved before the Lord for their acceptance, after the manner of the wave-sheaf (vv. 18-20). On the altar they could not come, because they were baken with leaven.

This festival, as one of the sabbatic series, celebrated the rest after the labours of the grain harvest, a symbol of the great sabbatism to follow that harvest which is "the end of the age" (Matt. xiii. 39). As a consecration, it dedicated unto God the daily food of the nation for the coming year. As passover reminded them that God was the Creator of Israel, so herein, receiving their daily bread from Him, they were reminded that He was also the Sustainer of Israel; while the full accompaniment of burnt-offerings and peace-offerings expressed their full consecration and happy state of friendship with Jehovah, secured through the expiation of the sin-offering.

Was this feast also, like passover, prophetic? The New Testament is scarcely less clear than in the former case. For after that Christ, first having been slain as "our Passover," had then risen from the dead as the "Firstfruits," fulfilling the type of the wave-sheaf on the morning of the Sabbath, fifty days passed; "and when the day of Pentecost was fully come," came that great outpouring of the Holy Ghost, the conversion of three thousand out of many lands (Acts ii.), and therewith the formation of that Church of the New Testament whose members the Apostle James declares (i. 18) to be "a kind of firstfruits of God's creatures." Thus, as the sheaf had typified Christ as "the First-born from the dead," the presentation on the day of Pentecost of the two wave loaves, the product of the sheaf of grain, no less evidently typified the presentation unto God of the Church of the first-born, the firstfruits of Christ's death and resurrection, as constituted on that sacred day. This then was the complete fulfilment of the feast of weeks regarded as a redemptive type, showing how, not only rest, but also redemption was comprehended in the significance of the sabbatic idea. And yet, that complete redemption was not therewith attained by that Church of the firstborn on Pentecost was presignified in that the two wave-loaves were to be baken with leaven. The feast of unleavened bread had exhibited the ideal of the Christian life; that of firstfruits, the imperfection of the earthly attainment. On earth the leaven of sin still abides.

The Feast of Trumpets.
Leviticus xxiii. 23-25.

"And the Lord spake unto Moses, saying, Speak unto the children of Israel, saying, In the seventh month, in the first day of the month, shall be a solemn rest unto you, a memorial of blowing of trumpets, an holy convocation. Ye shall do no servile work : and ye shall offer an offering made by fire unto the Lord."

By a very natural association of thought, in ver. 22 the direction to leave the gleaning of the harvest for the poor and the stranger is repeated verbally from chap. xix. 9, 10. Thereupon we pass from the feast of the seventh week to the solemnities of the seventh month, in which the series of annual sabbatic seasons ended. It was thus, by eminence, the sabbatic season of the year. Of the "set times" of this chapter, three fell in this month, and of these, two—the day of atonement and tabernacles—were of supreme significance: the former being distinguished by the most august religious solemnity of the year, the entrance of the high priest into the Holy of Holies to make atonement for the sins of the nation; the latter marking the completion of the ingathering of the products of the year, with the fruit, the oil, and the wine. Of this sabbatic month, it is directed (vv. 23-25) that the first day be kept as a *shabbathon*, "a solemn rest," marked by abstinence from all the ordinary business of life, and a holy convocation. The special ceremony of the day, which gave it its name, is described as a "memorial of blowing of trumpets." This "blowing of trumpets" was a reminder, not from Israel to God, as some have fancied, but from God to Israel. It was an announcement from the King of Israel to His people that the glad sabbatic month had begun, and that the great day of atonement, and the supreme festivity of the feast of tabernacles, was now at hand.

That the first day of this sabbatic month should be thus sanctified was but according to the Mosaic principle that the consecration of anything signifies the consecration unto God of the whole. "If the firstfruit is holy, so also the lump;" in like manner, if the first day, so is the month. Trumpets—though not the same probably as used on this occasion—were also blown on other occasions, and, in particular, at the time of each new moon; but, according to tradition, these only by the priests and at the central sanctuary; while in this feast of trumpets every one blew who would, and throughout the whole land.

The Day of Atonement.
Leviticus xxiii. 26-32.

"And the Lord spake unto Moses, saying, Howbeit on the tenth day of this seventh month is the day of atonement : it shall be an holy convocation unto you, and ye shall afflict your souls; and ye shall offer an offering made by fire unto the Lord. And ye shall do no manner of work in that same day : for it is a day of atonement, to make atonement for you before the Lord your God. For whatsoever soul it be that shall not be afflicted in that same day, he shall be cut off from his people. And whatsoever soul it be that doeth any manner of work in that same day, that soul will I destroy from among his people. Ye shall do no manner of work : it is a statute for ever throughout your generations in all your dwellings. It shall be unto you a sabbath of solemn rest, and ye shall afflict your souls : in the ninth day of the month at even, from even unto even, shall ye keep your sabbath."

After this festival of annunciation, followed, on the tenth day of the month, the great annual day of atonement. This has already come before us (chap. xiii.) in its relation to the sacrificial system, of which the sin-offering of this day was the culmination. But this chapter brings it before us in another aspect, namely, in its relation to the annual septenary series of sacred seasons, the final festival of which it preceded and introduced.

Its significance, as thus coming in this final seventh and sabbatic month of the ecclesiastical year, lay not merely in the strictness of the rest which was commanded (vv. 28-30) from every manner of work, but, still more, in that it expressed in a far higher degree than any other festival the other sabbatic idea of complete restoration brought in through expiation for sin. This was indeed the central thought of the whole ceremonial of the day,—the complete removal of all those sins of the nation which stood between them and God, and hindered complete restoration to God's favour. And while this restoration was symbolised by the sacrifice of the sin-offering, and its presentation and acceptance before Jehovah in the Holy of Holies; yet, that none might hence argue from the fact of atonement to license to sin, it was ordained (ver. 27) that the people should "afflict their souls," namely, by fasting,* in token of their penitence for the sins for which atonement was made; and the absolute necessity of this condition of repentance in order to any benefit from the high-priestly sacrifice and intercession was further emphasised by the solemn threat (ver. 29): "Whatsoever soul it be that shall not be afflicted in that same day, he shall be cut off from his people."

These then were the lessons—lessons of transcendent moment for all people and all ages—which were set forth in the great atonement of the sabbatic month,—the complete removal of sin by an expiatory offering, conditioned on the part of the worshipper by the obedience of faith and sincere repentance for the sin, and issuing in rest and full establishment in God's loving favour.

* Compare Isa. lviii. 3-7. Zech. vii. 5, where the necessity of the inward sorrow for sin and turning unto God, in connection with this fast of the seventh month, is solemnly urged upon Israel.

The Feast of Tabernacles.

Leviticus xxiii. 33-43.

"And the Lord spake unto Moses, saying, Speak unto the children of Israel, saying, On the fifteenth day of this seventh month is the feast of tabernacles for seven days unto the Lord. On the first day shall be an holy convocation: ye shall do no servile work. Seven days ye shall offer an offering made by fire unto the Lord: on the eighth day shall be an holy convocation unto you; and ye shall offer an offering made by fire unto the Lord: it is a solemn assembly; ye shall do no servile work. These are the set feasts of the Lord, which ye shall proclaim to be holy convocations, to offer an offering made by fire unto the Lord, a burnt offering, and a meal offering, a sacrifice, and drink offerings, each on its own day: beside the sabbaths of the Lord, and beside your gifts, and beside all your vows, and beside all your freewill offerings, which ye give unto the Lord. Howbeit on the fifteenth day of the seventh month, when ye have gathered in the fruits of the land, ye shall keep the feast of the Lord seven days: on the first day shall be a solemn rest, and on the eighth day shall be a solemn rest. And ye shall take you on the first day the fruit of goodly trees, branches of palm trees, and boughs of thick trees, and willows of the brook; and ye shall rejoice before the Lord your God seven days. And ye shall keep it a feast unto the Lord seven days in the year: it is a statute for ever in your generations: ye shall keep it in the seventh month. Ye shall dwell in booths seven days; all that are homeborn in Israel shall dwell in booths: that your generations may know that I made the children of Israel to dwell in booths, when I brought them out of the land of Egypt: I am the Lord your God."

The sin of Israel having been thus removed, the last and the greatest of all the feasts followed—the feast of tabernacles or ingathering. It occupied a full week (ver. 34), from the fifteenth to the twenty-second of the month, the first day being signalised by a holy convocation and abstinence from all servile work (ver. 35). Two reasons are indicated, here and elsewhere, for the observance: the one, natural (ver. 39), the completed ingathering of the products of the year; the other, historical (vv. 42, 43),—it was to be a memorial of the days when Israel dwelt in booths in the wilderness. Both ideas were represented in the direction (ver. 40) that they should take on the first day "the fruit of goodly trees, branches of palm trees, and boughs of thick trees, and willows of the brook," fitly symbolising the product of the vine and the fruit-trees which were harvested in this month; and, making booths of these, all were to dwell in these tabernacles, and "rejoice before the Lord their God seven days." And to this the historical reason is added, "that your generations may know that I made the children of Israel to dwell in booths, when I brought them out of the land of Egypt."

No one need feel any difficulty in seeing in this a connection with similar harvest and vintage customs among other peoples of that time. That other nations had festivities of this kind at that time, was surely no reason why God should not order these to be taken up into the Mosaic law, elevated in their significance, and sanctified to higher ends. Nothing could be more fitting than that the completion of the ingathering of the products of the year should be celebrated as a time of rejoicing and a thanksgiving day before Jehovah. Indeed, so natural is such a festivity to religious minds, that—as is well known—in the first instance, New England, and then, afterward, the whole United States, and also the Dominion of Canada, have established the observance of an annual "Thanksgiving Day" in the latter part of the autumn, which is observed by public religious services, by suspension of public business, and as a glad day of reunion of kindred and friends. It is interesting to observe how this last feature of the day is also mentioned in the case of this Hebrew feast, in the later form of the law (Deut. xvi. 13-15): "After that thou hast gathered in from thy threshing-floor and from thy winepress . . . thou shalt rejoice in thy feast, thou, and thy son, and thy daughter, and thy manservant, and thy maidservant, and the Levite, and the stranger, and the fatherless, and the widow, that are within thy gates, . . . and thou shalt be altogether joyful."

The chief sentiment of the feast was thus joy and thanksgiving to God as the Giver of all good. Yet the joy was not to be merely natural and earthly, but spiritual; they were to rejoice (ver. 40) "before the Lord." And the thanksgiving was not to be expressed merely in words, but in deeds. The week, we are elsewhere told, was signalised by the largest burnt-offerings of any of the feasts, consisting of a total of seventy bullocks, beginning with thirteen on the first day, and diminishing by one each day; while these again were accompanied daily by burnt-offerings of fourteen lambs and two rams, the double of what was enjoined even for the week of unleavened bread, with meal-offerings and drink-offerings in proportion. Nor was this outward ritual expression of thanksgiving enough; for their gratitude was to be further attested by taking into their glad festivities the Levite who had no portion, the fatherless and the widow, and even the stranger.

It is not hard to see the connection of all this with the historical reference to the days of their wilderness journeyings. Lest they might forget God in nature, they were to recall to mind, by their dwelling in booths, the days when they had no houses, and no fields nor crops, when, notwithstanding, none the less easily the Almighty God of Israel fed them with manna which they knew not, that He might make them to "know that man doth not live by bread only, but by every thing that proceedeth out of the mouth of the Lord" (Deut. viii. 3). There is, indeed, no better illustration of the intention of this part of the feast than those words with their context as they occur in Deuteronomy.

The ceremonies of the feast of tabernacles having been completed with the appointed seven days, there followed an eighth day,—an holy convocation, a festival of solemn rest (vv. 36, 39). This last day of holy solemnity and joy, to which a special name is given, is properly to be regarded, not as a part of the feast of tabernacles merely, but as celebrating the termination of the whole series of sabbatic times from the first to the seventh month. No ceremonial is here enjoined except the holy convocation, and the offering of "an offering made by fire unto the Lord," with abstinence from all servile work.

Typical Meaning of the Feasts of the Seventh Month.

We have already seen that the earlier feasts of the year were also prophetic; that Passover and Unleavened Bread pointed forward to Christ, our Passover, slain for us; Pentecost, to the spiritual ingathering of the firstfruits of the world's harvest, fifty days after the presentation of our Lord in resurrection, as the wave-sheaf of the firstfruits. We may therefore safely infer that these remaining feasts of the seventh month must be typical also. But, if so, typical of what? Two things may be safely said in this matter. The significance of the three festivals of this seventh month must be interpreted in harmony with what has already passed into fulfilment; and, in the second place, inasmuch as the feast of trumpets, the day of atonement, and the feast of tabernacles all belong to the seventh and last month of the ecclesiastical year, they must find their fulfilment in connection with what Scripture calls "the last times."

Keeping the first point in view, we may then safely say that if Pentecost typified the first-fruits of the world's harvest in the ingathering of an election from all nations, the feast of tabernacles must then typify the completion of that harvest in a spiritual ingathering, final and universal. Not only so, but, inasmuch as in the antitypical fulfilment of the wave-sheaf in the resurrection of our Lord, we were reminded that the consummation of the new creation is in resurrection from the dead, and that in regeneration is therefore involved resurrection, hence the feast of tabernacles, as celebrating the absolute completion of the year's harvest, must typify also the resurrection season, when all that are Christ's shall rise from the dead at His coming. And, finally, whereas this means for the now burdened earth permanent deliverance from the curse, and the beginning of a new age thus signalised by glorious life in resurrection, in which are enjoyed the blessed fruits of life's labours and pains for Christ, this was shadowed forth by the ordinance that immediately upon the seven days of tabernacles should follow a feast of the eighth day, the first day of a new week, in celebration of the beginning season of rest from all the labours of the field.

Most beautifully, thus regarded, does all else connected with the feast of tabernacles correspond, as type to antitype, to the revelation of the last things, and therein reveal its truest and deepest spiritual significance: the joy, the reunion, the rejoicing with son and with daughter, the fulness of gladness also for the widow and the fatherless; and this, not only for those in Israel, but also for the stranger, not of Israel, —for Gentile as well as Israelite was' to have part in the festivity of that day; and, again, the full attainment of the most complete consecration, signified in the tenfold burnt-offering—all finds its place here. And so now we can see why it was that our Saviour declared (Matt. xiii. 39) that the end of this present age should be the time of harvest; and how Paul, looking at the future spiritual ingathering, places the ingathering of the Gentiles (Rom. xi. 25) as one of the last things. In full accord with this interpretation of the typical significance of this feast it is that in Zech. xiv. we find it written that in the predicted day of the Lord, when (ver. 5) the Lord "shall come, and all the holy ones" with Him, and (ver. 9) "the Lord shall be King over all the earth; . . . the Lord . . . one, and His name one," then (ver. 16) "every one that is left of all the nations . . . shall go up from year to year to worship the King, the Lord of hosts, and to keep the feast of tabernacles;" and, moreover, that so completely shall consecration be realised in that day that (ver. 20) even upon the bells of the horses shall the words be inscribed, "HOLY UNTO THE LORD!"

But before the joyful feast of tabernacles could be celebrated, the great, sorrowful day of atonement must be kept,—a season marked, on the one hand, by affliction of soul throughout all Israel; on the other, by the complete putting away of the sin of the nation for the whole year, through the presentation of the blood of the sin-offering by the high priest, within the veil before the mercy-seat. Now, if the feast of tabernacles has been correctly interpreted, as presignifying in symbol the completion of the great world harvest in the end of the age, does the prophetic word reveal anything in connection with the last things as preceding that great harvest, and, in some sense, preparing for and ushering in that day, which should be the antitype of the great day of atonement?

One can hardly miss of the answer. For precisely that which the prophets and apostles both represent as the event which shall usher in that great day of final ingathering and of blessed resurrection rest and joy in consummated redemption, is the national repentance of Israel, and the final cleansing of their age-long sin. In the type, two things are conspicuous: the great sorrowing of the nation and the great atonement putting away all Israel's sin. And two things, in like manner, are conspicuous in the prophetic pictures of the antitype, namely, Israel's heart-broken repentance, and the removal thereupon of Israel's sin; their cleansing in the "fountain opened for sin and for uncleanness." As Zechariah puts it (xii. 10, xiii. 1), "I will pour upon the house of David, and upon the inhabitants of Jerusalem, the spirit of grace and of supplication; and they shall look unto me whom they have pierced: and they shall mourn for him, as one mourneth for his only son;" and "in that day there shall be a fountain opened to the house of David and to the inhabitants of Jerusalem for sin and for uncleanness." And the relation of this cleansing of Israel to the days of blessing which follow is most explicitly set forth by the Apostle Paul, in these words concerning Israel (Rom. xi. 12, 15), "If their fall is the riches of the world, and their loss the riches of the Gentiles; how much more their fulness? If the casting away of them is the reconciling of the world, what shall the receiving of them be, but life from the dead?"

So far, then, all seems clear. But the feast of trumpets yet remains to be explained. Has Holy Scripture predicted anything falling in the period between Pentecost and the repentance of Israel, but specially belonging to the last things, which might with reason be regarded as the antitype of this joyful feast of trumpets? Here, again, it is not easy to go far astray. For the essential idea of the trumpet call is announcement, proclamation. From time to time all through the year the trumpet-call was heard in Israel; but on this occasion it became the feature of the day, and was universal throughout their land. And as we have seen, its special significance for that time was to announce that the day of atonement and the feast of ingathering, which typified the full consummation of the kingdom of God, were now at hand. One can thus hardly fail to think at once of that other event which, according to our Lord's express word (Matt. xxiv. 14), is immediately to precede "the end," namely, the universal proclamation of the Gospel: "This gospel of the kingdom shall be preached in the whole world for a testimony unto all the nations; and then shall the end come." As throughout the year, from time to time, the trumpet call was heard in Israel, but only in connection with the central sanctuary; but now in all the land, as the chief thing in the celebration of the day which ushered in the final sabbatic month, precisely so in the antitype. All through the ages has the Gospel been sounded forth, but in a partial and limited way; but at "the time of the end" the proclamation shall become universal. And thus and then shall the feast of trumpets also, like Passover and Pentecost, pass into complete fulfilment, and be swiftly followed by Israel's repentance and restoration, and the consequent reappearing, as Peter predicts (Acts iii. 19-21 R. V.), of Israel's High Priest from within the veil, and thereupon the harvest of the world, the resurrection of the just, and the consummation upon earth of the glorified kingdom of God.

Of many thoughts of a practical kind which this chapter suggests, we may perhaps well dwell especially on one. The ideal of religious life, which these set times of the Lord kept before Israel, was a religion of joy. Again and again is this spoken of in the accounts of these feasts. This is true even of Passover, with which we oftener, though mistakenly, connect thoughts of sadness and gloom. Yet Passover was a feast of joy; it celebrated the birthday of the nation, and a deliverance unparalleled in history. The only exception to this joyful character in all these sacred times is found in the day of atonement; but it is itself instructive on the same point, teaching most clearly that in the Divine order, as in the necessity of the case, the joy in the Lord, of which the feast of ingathering was the supreme expression, must be preceded by and grounded in an accepted expiation and true penitence for sin.

So it is still with the religion of the Bible: it is a religion of joy. God does not wish us to be gloomy and sad. He desires that we should ever be joyful before Him, and thus find by blessed experience that "the joy of the Lord is our strength." Also, in particular, we do well to observe further that, inasmuch as all these set times were sabbatic seasons, joyfulness is inseparably connected with the Biblical conception of the Sabbath. This has been too often forgotten; and the weekly day of sabbatic rest has sometimes been made a day of stern repression and forbidding gloom. How utterly astray are such conceptions from the Divine ideal, we shall perhaps the more clearly see when we call to mind the thought which appears more or less distinctly in all these sabbatic seasons, that every Sabbath points forward to the eternal joy of the consummated kingdom, the sabbath rest which remaineth for the people of God (Heb. iv. 9).

CHAPTER XXV.

THE HOLY LIGHT AND THE SHEWBREAD: THE BLASPHEMER'S END.

LEVITICUS xxiv. 1-23.

It is not easy to determine with confidence the association of thought which occasioned the interposition of this chapter, with its somewhat disconnected contents, between chap. xxiii., on the set times of holy convocation, and chap. xxv., on the sabbatic and jubilee years, which latter would seem most naturally to have followed the former immediately, as relating to the same subject of sacred times. Perhaps the best explanation of the connection with the previous chapter is that which finds it in the reference to the olive oil for the lamps and the meal for the shewbread. The feast of tabernacles, directions for which had just been given, celebrated the completed ingathering of the harvest of the year, both of grain and of fruit; and here Israel is told what is to be done with a certain portion of each.

THE ORDERING OF THE LIGHT IN THE HOLY PLACE.

LEVITICUS xxiv. 1-4.

"And the Lord spake unto Moses, saying, Command the children of Israel, that they bring unto thee pure olive oil beaten for the light, to cause a lamp to burn continually. Without the veil of the testimony, in the tent of meeting, shall Aaron order it from evening to morning before the Lord continually: it shall be a statute for ever throughout your generations. He shall order the lamps upon the pure candlestick before the Lord continually."

First (vv. 1-4) is given the direction for the ordering of the daily light, which was to burn from evening until morning in the holy place continually. The people themselves are to furnish the oil for the seven-branched candlestick out of the product of their olive yards. The oil is to be "pure," carefully cleansed from leaves and all impurities; and "beaten," that is, not extracted by heat and pressure, as are inferior grades, but simply by beating and macerating the olives with water,—a process which gives the very best. The point in these specifications is evidently this, that for this, as always, they are to give to God's service the very best,—an eternal principle which rules in all acceptable service to God. The oil is to come from the people in general, so that the illuminating of the Holy Place, although specially tended by the high priest, is yet constituted a service in which all the children of Israel have some part. The oil was to be used to supply the seven lamps upon the golden candlestick which was placed on the south side of the Holy Place, without the veil of the testimony, in the tent of meeting. This Aaron was to "order from evening to morning before the Lord continually." According to Exod. xxv. 31-40, this candlestick—or, more properly, lampstand—was made of a single shaft, with three branches on either side, each with a cup at the end like an almond blossom; so that, with that on the top of the central shaft, it was a stand of seven lamps, in a conventional imitation of an almond tree.

The significance of the symbol is brought clearly before us in Zech. iv. 1-14, where the seven-branched candlestick symbolises Israel as the congregation of God, the giver of the light of life to the world. And yet a lamp can burn only as it is supplied with oil and trimmed and cared for. And so in the symbol of Zechariah the prophet sees the golden candlestick supplied with oil conveyed through two golden pipes into which flowed the golden oil, mysteriously self-distilled from two olive trees on either side the candlestick. And the explanation given is this: "Not by might, nor by power, but by My Spirit," saith the Lord. Thus we learn that the golden seven-branched lampstand denotes Israel, more precious than gold in God's sight, appointed of Him to be the giver of light to the world. And yet by this requisition of oil for the golden candlestick the nation was reminded that their power to give light was dependent upon the supply of the heavenly grace of God's Spirit, and the continual ministrations of the priest in the Holy Place. And how this ordering of the light might be a symbolic act of worship, we can at once see, when we recall the word of Jesus (Matt. v. 14, 16): "Ye are the light of the world. . . . Let your light shine before men, that they may see your good works, and glorify your Father which is in heaven."

How pertinent for instruction still in all its deepest teaching is this ordinance of the lamp continually burning in the presence of the Lord, is vividly brought before us in the Apocalypse (i. 12, 13), where we read that seven candlesticks appeared in vision to the Apostle John; and Christ, in His glory, robed in high-priestly vesture, was seen walking up and down, after the manner of Aaron, in the midst of the seven candlesticks, in care and watch of the manner of their burning. And as to the significance of this vision, the Apostle was expressly told (ver. 20) that the seven candlesticks were the seven Churches of Asia,—types of the collective Church in all the centuries. Thus, as in the language of this Levitical symbol, we are taught that in the highest sense it is the office of the Church to give light in darkness; but that she can only do this as the heavenly oil is supplied, and each lamp is cared for, by the high-priestly ministrations of her risen Lord.

The "Bread of the Presence."

Leviticus xxiv. 5-9.

"And thou shalt take fine flour, and bake twelve cakes thereof: two tenth parts of an ephah shall be in one cake. And thou shalt set them in two rows, six on a row, upon the pure table before the Lord. And thou shalt put pure frankincense upon each row, that it may be to the bread for a memorial, even an offering made by fire unto the Lord. Every sabbath day he shall set it in order before the Lord continually; it is on the behalf of the children of Israel, an everlasting covenant. And it shall be for Aaron and his sons; and they shall eat it in a holy place: for it is most holy unto him of the offerings of the Lord made by fire by a perpetual statute."

Next follows the ordinance for the preparation and presentation of the "shew-bread," lit., "bread of the Face," or "Presence," sc. of God. This was to consist of twelve cakes, each to be made of two tenth parts of an ephah of fine flour, which were to be placed in two rows or piles, "upon the pure table" of gold that stood before the Lord, in the Holy Place, opposite to the golden candlestick. On each pile was to be placed (ver. 7) "pure frankincense,"—doubtless, as tradition says, placed in the golden spoons, or little cups (Exod. xxxvii. 16). Every sabbath (vv. 8, 9) fresh bread was to be so placed, when the old became the food of Aaron and his sons only, as belonging to the order of things "most holy;" the frankincense which had been its "memorial" having been first burned, "an offering made by fire unto the Lord" (ver. 7). Tradition adds that the bread was always unleavened; a few have called this in question, but this has been only on theoretic grounds, and without evidence; and when we remember how stringent was the prohibition of leaven even in any offerings made by fire upon the altar of the outer court, much less is it likely that it could have been tolerated here in the Holy Place immediately before the veil.

This bread of the Presence must be regarded as in its essential nature a perpetual meal-offering,—the meal-offering of the Holy Place, as the others were of the outer court.* The material was the same, cakes of fine flour; to this frankincense must be added as a "memorial," as in the meal-offerings of the outer court. Such part of the offering as was not burned, as in the case of the others, was to be eaten by the priests only, as a thing "most holy." It differed from those in that there were always the twelve cakes, one for each tribe; and in that while they were repeatedly offered, this lay before the Lord continually. The altar of burnt-offering might sometimes be empty of the meal-offering, but the table of shew-bread, "the table of the Presence," never.

In general, therefore, the meaning of the offering of the shew-bread must be the same as that of the meal-offerings; like them it symbolised the consecration unto the Lord of the product of the labour of the hands, and especially of the daily food as prepared for use. But in this, by the twelve cakes for the twelve tribes it was emphasised that God requires, not only such consecration of service and acknowledgment of Him from individuals, as in the law of chap. ii., but from the nation in its collective and organised capacity; and that not merely on such occasions as pious impulse might direct, but continuously.

In these days, when the tendency among us is to an extreme individualism, and therewith to an ignoring or denial of any claim of God upon nations and communities as such, it is of great need to insist upon this thought thus symbolised. It was not enough in God's sight that individual Israelites should now and then offer their meal-offerings; the Lord required a meal-offering "on behalf of the children of Israel" *as a whole*, and of each particular tribe of the twelve, each in its corporate capacity. There is no reason to think that in the Divine government the principle which took this symbolic expression is obsolete. It is not enough that individuals among us consecrate the fruit of their labours to the Lord. The Lord requires such consecration of every nation collectively; and of each of the subdivisions in that nation, such as cities, towns, states, provinces, and so on. Yet where in the wide world can we see one such consecrated nation? Can we find one such consecrated province or state, or even such a city or town? Where then, from this biblical and spiritual point of view, is the ground for the religious boasting of the Christian progress of our day which one sometimes hears? Must we not say, "It is excluded"?

Typically, the shew-bread, like the other meal-offerings with their frankincense, must foreshadow the work of the Messiah in holy consecration; and, in particular, as the One in whom the ideal of Israel was perfectly realised, and who thus represented in His person the whole Israel of God. But the bread of the Presence represents His holy obedience in self-consecration, not merely, as in the other meal-offerings, presented in the outer court, in the sight of men, as in His earthly life; but here, rather, as con-

---

* See Kurtz, "Der Alttestamentliche Opfercultus," p. 271.

tinually presented before the "Face of God," in the Holy Place, where Christ appears in the presence of God for us. And in this symbolism, which has been already justified, we may recognise the element of truth that there is in the view held by Bähr,* apparently, as by others, that the shew-bread typified Christ Himself regarded as the bread of life to His people. Not indeed, precisely, that Christ Himself is brought before us here, but rather His holy obedience, continually offered unto God in the heavenly places, in behalf of the true Israel, and as sealing and confirming the everlasting covenant;—this is what this symbol brings before us. And it is as we by faith appropriate Him, as thus ever presenting His holy life to God for us, that He becomes for us the Bread of Life.

THE PENALTY OF BLASPHEMY.

LEVITICUS xxiv. 10-23.

"And the son of an Israelitish woman, whose father was an Egyptian, went out among the children of Israel: and the son of the Israelitish woman and a man of Israel strove together in the camp; and the son of the Israelitish woman blasphemed the Name, and cursed: and they brought him unto Moses. And his mother's name was Shelomith, the daughter of Dibri, of the tribe of Dan. And they put him in ward, that it might be declared unto them at the mouth of the Lord. And the Lord spake unto Moses, saying, Bring forth him that hath cursed without the camp; and let all that heard him lay their hands upon his head, and let all the congregation stone him. And thou shalt speak unto the children of Israel, saying, Whosoever curseth his God shall bear his sin. And he that blasphemeth the name of the Lord, he shall surely be put to death; all the congregation shall certainly stone him: as well the stranger, as the homeborn, when he blasphemeth the name of the Lord, shall be put to death. And he that smiteth any man mortally shall surely be put to death; and he that smiteth a beast mortally shall make it good: life for life. And if a man cause a blemish in his neighbour; as he hath done, so shall it be done to him; breach for breach, eye for eye, tooth for tooth: as he hath caused a blemish in a man, so shall it be rendered unto him. And he that killeth a beast shall make it good: and he that killeth a man shall be put to death. Ye shall have one manner of law, as well for the stranger, as for the homeborn: for I am the Lord your God. And Moses spake to the children of Israel, and they brought forth him that had cursed out of the camp, and stoned him with stones. And the children of Israel did as the Lord commanded Moses."

The connection of this section with the preceding context is now impossible to determine. Very possibly its insertion here may be due to the occurrence here described having taken place at the time of the delivery of the preceding laws concerning the oil for the golden lampstand and the shew-bread. However, the purport and intention of the narrative is very plain, namely, to record the law delivered by the Lord for the punishment of blasphemy; and therewith also His command that the penalty of broken law, both in this case and in others specified, should be exacted both from native Israelites and from foreigners alike.

The incident which was the occasion of the promulgation of these laws was as follows. The son of an Israelitish woman by an Egyptian husband fell into a quarrel in the camp. As often happens in such cases, the one sin led on to another and yet graver sin; the half-caste man "blasphemed the Name, and cursed;" whereupon he was arrested and put into confinement until the will of the Lord might be ascertained in his case. "The Name" is of course the name of God; the meaning is that he used the holy

* "Symbolik des Mosäischen Cultus," erster Band, pp. 428-432.

name profanely in cursing. The passage, together with ver. 16, is of special and curious interest, as upon these two the Jews have based their well-known belief that it is unlawful to utter the Name which we commonly vocalise as Jehovah; whence it has followed that wherever in the Hebrew text the Name occurs it is written with the vowels of *Adonây* "Lord," to indicate to the reader that this word was to be substituted for the proper name,—a usage which is represented in the Septuagint by the appearance of the Greek word *Kurios*, "Lord," in all places where the Hebrew has Jehovah (or Yâhveh); and which, in both the authorised and revised versions, is still maintained in the retention of "Lord" in all such cases,—a relic of Jewish superstition which one could greatly wish that the Revisers had banished from the English version, especially as in many passages it totally obscures to the English reader the exact sense of the text, wherever it turns upon the choice of this name. It is indeed true that the word rendered "blaspheme" has the meaning "to pronounce," as the Targumists and other Hebrew writers render it; but that it also means simply to "revile," and in many places cannot possibly be rendered "to pronounce," is perforce admitted even by Jewish scholars.* To give it the other meaning here were so plainly foreign to the spirit of the Old Testament, debasing reverence to superstition, that no argument against it will be required with any but a Jew.

And this young man, in the heat of his passion, "reviled the Name." The words "of the Lord" are not in the Hebrew; the name "Jehovah" is thus brought before us expressively as THE NAME, *par excellence*, of God, as revealing Himself in covenant for man's redemption.† Horrified at the man's wickedness, "they brought him unto Moses;" and "they put him in ward" (ver. 12), "that it might be declared unto them at the mouth of the Lord" what should be done unto him. This was necessary because the case involved two points upon which no revelation had been made: first, as to what should be the punishment of blasphemy; and secondly, whether the law in such cases applied to a foreigner as well as to the native Israelite. The answer of God decided these points. As to the first (ver. 15), "Whosoever curseth his God shall bear his sin," *i. e.*, he shall be held subject to punishment; and (ver. 16), "He that blasphemeth the name of the Lord, he shall surely be put to death; all the congregation shall certainly stone him." And as to the second point, it is added, "as well the stranger, as the homeborn, when he blasphemeth the Name, shall be put to death."

Then follows (vv. 17-21) a declaration of penalties for murder, for killing a neighbour's beast, and for inflicting a bodily injury on one's neighbour. These were to be settled on the principle of the *lex talionis*, life for life, "breach for breach, eye for eye, tooth for tooth;" in the case of the beast killed, its value was to be made good to the owner. All these laws had been previously given (Exod. xxi. 12, 23-36); but are repeated here plainly for the purpose of expressly ordering that these laws, like that now declared

* See, *e.g.*, Rabbi Dr. J. Levy, "Chaldäisches Wörterbuch," zweiter Band, pp. 301, 302; and compare Numb. xxiii. 8, Prov. xi. 26, xxiv. 24, where the same Hebrew word is used.
† *Cf.* the expression used with reference to Jesus Christ, Phil. ii. 9 (R.V.), "the name which is above every name."

for blasphemy, were to be applied alike to the home-born and the stranger (ver. 22).

Much cavil have these laws occasioned, the more so that Christ Himself is cited as having condemned them in the Sermon on the Mount (Matt. v. 38-42). But how little difficulty really exists here will appear from the following considerations. The Jews from of old have maintained that the law of "an eye for eye," as here given, was not intended to authorise private and irresponsible retaliation in kind, but only after due trial and by legal process. Moreover, even in such cases, they have justly remarked that the law here given was not meant to be applied always with the most exact literality; but that it was evidently intended to permit the commutation of the penalty by such a fine as the judges might determine. They justly argue from the explicit prohibition of the acceptance of any such satisfaction in commutation in the case of a murderer (Numb. xxxv. 31, 32) that this implies the permission of it in the instances here mentioned;—a conclusion the more necessary when it is observed that the literal application of the law in all cases would often result in defeating the very ends of exact justice which it was evidently intended to secure. For instance, the loss by a one-eyed man of his only eye, under such an interpretation, would be much more than an equivalent for the loss of an eye which he had inflicted upon a neighbour who had both eyes. Hence, Jewish history contains no record of the literal application of the law in such cases; the principle is applied as often among ourselves, in the exaction from an offender of a pecuniary satisfaction proportioned to the degree of the disability he has inflicted upon his neighbour. Finally, as regards the words of our Saviour, that He did not intend His words to be taken in their utmost stretch of literality in all cases, is plain from His own conduct when smitten by the order of the high priest (John xviii. 23), and from the statement that the magistrate is endowed with the sword, as a servant of God, to be a terror to evil-doers (Rom. xiii. 4); from which it is plain that Christ did not mean to prohibit the resort to judicial process under all circumstances, but rather the spirit of retaliation and litigation which sought to justify itself by a perverse appeal to this law of "an eye for eye;" —a law which, in point of fact, was given, as Augustine has truly observed, not "as an incitement to, but for the mitigation of wrath."

The narrative then ends with the statement (ver. 23) that Moses delivered this law to the children of Israel, who then, according to the commandment of the Lord, took the blasphemer out of the camp, when all that heard him blaspheme laid their hands upon his head, in token that they thus devolved on him the responsibility for his own death; and then the congregation stoned the criminal with stones that he died (ver. 23).

The chief lesson to be learned from this incident and from the law here given is very plain. It is the high criminality in God's sight of all irreverent use of His holy name. To a great extent in earlier days this was recognised by Christian governments; and in the Middle Ages the penalty of blasphemy in many states of Christendom, as in the Mosaic code and in many others, although not death, was yet exceedingly severe. The present century, however, has seen a great relaxation of law, and still more of public sentiment, in regard to this crime,—a change which, from a Christian point of view, is a matter for anything but gratulation. Reverence for God lies at the very foundation of even common morality. Our modern atheism and agnosticism may indeed deny this, and yet, from the days of the French Revolution to the present, modern history has been presenting, in one land and another, illustrations of the fact which are pregnant with most solemn warning. And while no one could wish that the crime of blasphemy should be punished with torture and cruelty, as in some instances in the Middle Ages, yet the more deeply one thinks on this subject in the light of the Scripture and of history, the more, if we mistake not, will it appear that it might be far better for us, and might argue a far more hopeful and wholesome condition of the public sentiment than that which now exists, if still, as in Mosaic days and sometimes in the Middle Ages, death were made the punishment for this crime;—a crime which not only argues the extreme of depravity in the criminal, but which, if overlooked by the State, or expiated with any light penalty, cannot but operate most fatally by breaking down in the public conscience that profound reverence toward God which is the most essential condition of the maintenance of all private and public morality.

In this point of view, not to speak of other considerations, it is not surprising that the theocratic law here provides that blasphemy shall be punished with death in the case of the foreigner as well as the native Israelite. This sin, like those of murder and violence with which it is here conjoined, is of such a kind that to every conscience which is not hopelessly hardened, its wickedness must be manifest even from the very light of nature. Nature itself is sufficient to teach any one that abuse and calumny of the Supreme God, the Maker and Ruler of the world,— a Being who, if He exist at all, must be infinitely good,—must be a sin involving quite peculiar and exceptional guilt. Hence, absolute equity, no less than governmental wisdom, demanded that the law regarding blasphemy, as that with respect to the other crimes here mentioned, should be impartially enforced upon both the native Israelite and the foreigner.

CHAPTER XXVI.

THE SABBATIC YEAR AND THE JUBILEE.

Leviticus xxv. 1-55.

The system of annually recurring sabbatic times, as given in chap. xxiii., culminated in the sabbatic seventh month. But this remarkable system of sabbatisms extended still further, and besides the sacred seventh day, the seventh week, and seventh month, included also a sabbatic seventh year; and beyond that, as the ultimate expression of the sabbatic idea, following the seventh seven of years, came the hallowed fiftieth year, known as the jubilee. And the law concerning these two last-named periods is recorded in this twenty-fifth chapter of Leviticus.

First (vv. 1-5), is given the ordinance of the sabbatic seventh year, in the following words: "When ye come into the land which I give you, then shall the land keep a sabbath unto the

Lord. Six years thou shalt sow thy field, and six years thou shalt prune thy vineyard, and gather in the fruits thereof; but in the seventh year shall be a sabbath of solemn rest for the land, a sabbath unto the Lord: thou shalt neither sow thy field, nor prune thy vineyard. That which groweth of itself of thy harvest thou shalt not reap, and the grapes of thy undressed vine thou shalt not gather: it shall be a year of solemn rest for the land."

This sacred year is thus here described as a sabbath for the land unto the Lord,—a *shabbath shabbathon;* that is, a sabbath in a special and eminent sense. No public religious gatherings were ordered, however, neither was labour of every kind prohibited. It was strictly a year of rest for the land, and for the people in so far as this was involved in that fact. There was to be no sowing or reaping, even of what might grow of itself; no pruning of vineyard or fruit trees, nor gathering of their fruit. These regulations thus involved the total suspension of agricultural labour for this entire period.

It was further ordered (vv. 6, 7) that during this year the spontaneous produce of the land should be equally free to all, both man and beast: "The sabbath of the land shall be for food for you; for thee, and for thy servant and for thy maid, and for thy hired servant and for thy stranger that sojourn with thee; and for thy cattle, and for the beasts that are in thy land, shall all the increase thereof be for food."

That this cannot be regarded as merely a regulation of a communistic character, designed simply to affirm the absolute equality of all men in right to the product of the soil, is evident from the fact that the beasts also are included in the terms of the law. The object was quite different, as we shall shortly see.

That it should be regarded as possible for a whole people thus to live off the spontaneous produce of self-sowed grain may seem incredible to us who dwell in less propitious lands; and yet travellers tell us that in the Palestine of to-day, with its rich soil and kindly climate, the various food grains continuously propagate themselves without cultivation; and that in Albania, also, two and three successive harvests are sometimes reaped as the result of one sowing. So, even apart from the special blessing from the Lord promised to them if they would obey this command, the supply of at least the necessities of life was possible from the spontaneous product of the sabbath of the land. Though less than usual, it might easily be sufficient. In Deut. xv. 1-11 it is ordered also that the seventh year should be "a year of release" to the debtor; not indeed as regards all debts, but loans only; nor, apparently, that even these should be released absolutely, but that throughout the seventh year the claim of the creditor was to be in abeyance. The regulation may naturally be regarded as consequent upon this fundamental law regarding the sabbath of the land. The income of the year being much less than usual, the debtor, presumably, might often find it difficult to pay; whence this restriction on collection of debt during this period.

The central thought of this ordinance then is this, that man's right in the soil and its product, originally granted from God, during this sabbatic year reverted to the Giver; who, again, by ordering that all exclusive rights of individuals in the produce of their estates should be suspended for this year, placed, for so long, the rich and the poor on an absolute equality as regards means of sustenance.

THE JUBILEE.

LEVITICUS xxv. 8-12.

"And thou shalt number seven sabbaths of years unto thee, seven times seven years; and there shall be unto thee the days of seven sabbaths of years, even forty and nine years. Then shalt thou send abroad the loud trumpet on the tenth day of the seventh month ; in the day of atonement shall ye send abroad the trumpet throughout all your land. And ye shall hallow the fiftieth year, and proclaim liberty throughout the land unto all the inhabitants thereof : it shall be a jubilee unto you ; and ye shall return every man unto his possession, and ye shall return every man unto his family. A jubilee shall that fiftieth year be unto you : ye shall not sow, neither reap that which groweth of itself in it, nor gather the grapes in it of the undressed vines. For it is a jubilee ; it shall be holy unto you : ye shall eat the increase thereof out of the field."

The remainder of this chapter, vv. 8-55, is occupied with this ordinance of the jubilee year; an observance absolutely without a parallel in any nation, and which has to do with the solution of some of the most difficult social problems, not only of that time, but also of our own. Seven weeks of years, each terminating with the sabbatic year of solemn rest for the land, were to be numbered, *i. e.*, forty-nine full years, of which the last was a sabbatic year, beginning, as always, with the feast of atonement in the tenth day of the seventh month. And then when, at its expiration, the day of atonement came round again, at the beginning of the fiftieth year of this reckoning, at the close, as would appear, of the solemn expiatory ritual of the day, throughout all the land of Israel the loud trumpet was to be sounded, proclaiming "liberty throughout the land unto all the inhabitants thereof." The ordinance is given in vv. 8-12 above.

It appears that the liberty thus proclaimed was threefold: (1) liberty to the man who, through the reverses of life, had become dispossessed from his family inheritance in the land, to return to it again; (2) liberty to every Hebrew slave, so that in the jubilee he became a free man again; (3) the liberty of release from toil in the cultivation of the land,—a feature, in this case, even more remarkable than in the sabbatic year, because already one such sabbatic year had but just closed when the jubilee year immediately succeeded.

Why this year should be called a jubilee (Heb. *yobel*) is a vexed question, on which scholars are far from unanimous; but as it is of no practical importance, there is no need to enter on the discussion here. To suppose that these enactments should have originated, as the radical critics claim, in post-exilian days, when, under the existing social and political conditions, their observance was impossible, is utterly absurd.* Not only so, but in view of the admitted neglect even of the sabbatic year,—an ordinance certainly less difficult to carry out in practice,—during four

---

* Thus Dillmann writes: "That the law (of the jubilee) in its principal features was already issued by Moses does not admit of demonstration to him who wills not to believe it ; but that it cannot have been in the first instance the invention of a post-exilian scribe is certain. Only in the simpler communal relations of the more ancient time could a law of such an ideal character have seemed practicable; after the exile, all the presuppositions involved in its promulgation are wanting" ("Die Bücher Exodus und Leviticus," 2 Aufl., p. 608).

hundred and ninety years of Israel's history, the supposition that the law of the jubilee should have been first promulgated at any earlier post-Mosaic period is scarcely less incredible.

The Jubilee and the Land.

Leviticus xxv. 13-28.

"In this year of jubilee ye shall return every man unto his possession. And if thou sell aught unto thy neighbour, or buy of thy neighbour's hand, ye shall not wrong one another: according to the number of years after the jubilee thou shalt buy of thy neighbour, and according unto the number of years of the crops he shall sell unto thee. According to the multitude of the years thou shalt increase the price thereof, and according to the fewness of the years thou shalt diminish the price of it; for the number of the crops doth he sell unto thee. And ye shall not wrong one another; but thou shalt fear thy God: for I am the Lord your God. Wherefore ye shall do My statutes, and keep My judgments and do them; and ye shall dwell in the land in safety. And the land shall yield her fruit, and ye shall eat your fill, and dwell therein in safety. And if ye shall say, What shall we eat the seventh year? behold, we shall not sow, nor gather in our increase: then I will command My blessing upon you in the sixth year, and it shall bring forth fruit for the three years. And ye shall sow the eighth year, and eat of the fruits, the old store; until the ninth year, until her fruits come in, ye shall eat the old store. And the land shall not be sold in perpetuity; for the land is Mine: for ye are strangers and sojourners with Me. And in all the land of your possession ye shall grant a redemption for the land. If thy brother be waxen poor, and sell some of his possession, then shall his kinsman that is next unto him come, and shall redeem that which his brother hath sold. And if a man have no one to redeem it, and he be waxen rich and find sufficient to redeem it; then let him count the years of the sale thereof, and restore the overplus unto the man to whom he sold it; and he shall return unto his possession. But if he be not able to get it back for himself, then that which he hath sold shall remain in the hand of him that hath bought it until the year of jubilee: and in the jubilee it shall go out, and he shall return unto his possession."

The remainder of the chapter (vv. 13-55) deals with the practical application of this law of the jubilee to various cases. In vv. 13-28 we have the application of the law to the case of property in *land;* in vv. 29-34, to sales of *dwelling houses;* and the remaining verses (35-55) deal with the application of this law to the institution of *slavery.*

As regards the first matter, the transfers of right in land, these in all cases were to be governed by the fundamental principle enounced in ver. 23: "The land shall not be sold in perpetuity; for the land is Mine: for ye are strangers and sojourners with Me."

Thus in the theocracy there was no such thing as either private or communal ownership in land. Just as in some lands to-day the only owner of the land is the king, so it was in Israel; but in this case the King was Jehovah. From this it follows evidently, that properly speaking, according to this law, there could be no such thing in Israel as a sale or purchase of land. All that any man could buy or sell was the right to its products, and that, again, only for a limited time; for every fiftieth year the land was to revert to the family to whom its use had been originally assigned. Hence the regulations (vv. 14-19) regarding such transfers of the right to the use of the land. They are all governed by the simple and equitable principle that the price paid for the usufruct of the land was to be exactly proportioned to the number of years which were to elapse between the date of the sale and the reversion of the land, which would take place in the jubilee. Thus, the price for such transfer of right in the first year of the jubilee period would be at its maximum, because the sale covered the right to the produce of the land for forty-nine years; while, on the other hand, in the case of a transfer made in the forty-eighth year, the price would have fallen to a very small amount, as only the product of one year's cultivation remained to be sold, and after the ensuing sabbatic year the land would revert in the jubilee to the original holder. The command to keep in mind this principle, and not wrong one another, is enforced (vv. 17-19) by the injunction to do this because of the fear of God; and by the promise that if Israel will obey this law, they shall dwell in safety, and have abundance.

In vv. 24-28, after the declaration of the fundamental law that the land belongs only to the Lord, and that they are to regard themselves as simply His tenants, "sojourners with Him," a second application of the law is made. First, it is ordered that in every case, and without reference to the year of jubilee, every landholder who through stress of poverty may be obliged to sell the usufruct of his land shall retain the right to redeem it. Three cases are assumed. First (ver. 25), it is ordered that if the poor man have lost his land, and have a kinsman who is able to redeem it, he shall do so. Secondly (ver. 26), if he have no such kinsman, but himself become able to redeem it, it shall be his privilege to do so. In both cases alike, "the overplus," *i. e.*, the value of the land for the years still remaining till the jubilee, for which the purchaser had paid, is to be restored to him, and then the land reverts at once, without waiting for the jubilee, to the original proprietor. The third case (ver. 28) is that of the poor man who has no kinsman to buy back his landholding, and never becomes able to do so himself. In such a case, the purchaser was to hold it until the jubilee year, when the land reverted without compensation to the family of the poor man who had transferred it. That this was strictly equitable is self-evident, when we remember that, according to the law previously laid down, the purchaser had only paid for the value of the product of the land until the jubilee year; and when he had received its produce for that time, naturally and in strict equity his right in the land terminated.

The Jubilee and Dwelling Houses.

Leviticus xxv. 29-34.

"And if a man sell a dwelling house in a walled city, then he may redeem it within a whole year after it is sold; for a full year shall he have the right of redemption. And if it be not redeemed within the space of a full year, then the house that is in the walled city shall be made sure in perpetuity to him that bought it, throughout his generations: it shall not go out in the jubilee. But the houses of the villages which have no wall round about them shall be reckoned with the fields of the country: they may be redeemed, and they shall go out in the jubilee. Nevertheless the cities of the Levites, the houses of the cities of their possession, may the Levites redeem at any time. And if one of the Levites redeem [not], then the house that was sold, and the city of his possession, shall go out in the jubilee: for the houses of the cities of the Levites are their possession among the children of Israel. But the field of the suburbs of their cities may not be sold; for it is their perpetual possession."

In vv. 29-34 is considered the application of the jubilee ordinance to the sale of dwelling houses: first (vv. 29-31), to such sale in case of the people generally; secondly (vv. 32-34), to sales of houses by the Levites. Under the former head we have first the law as regards sales of dwelling houses in "walled cities;" to which it is ordered that the law of reversion in the jubilee shall not apply, and for which the right of redemption was only to hold valid for one year. The obvious reason for exempting houses in cities from the law of reversion is that the law has to do only with land such as may be used in a pastoral or agricultural way for man's support. And this explains why, on the other hand, it is next ordered (ver. 31) that in the case of houses in unwalled villages the law of redemption and reversion in the jubilee shall apply as well as to the land. For the inhabitants of the villages were the herdsmen and cultivators of the soil; and the house was regarded rightly as a necessary attachment to the land, without which its use would not be possible. But inasmuch as God had assigned no landholding to the Levites in the original distribution of the land,—and apart from their houses they had no possession (ver. 33),—in order to secure them in the privilege of a permanent holding, such as others enjoyed in their lands, it was ordered that in their case their houses, as being their only possession in real estate, should be treated as were the landholdings of members of the other tribes.*

The relation of the jubilee law to personal rights in the land having been thus determined and expounded, in the next place (vv. 35-55) is considered the application of the law to slavery. Quite naturally, this section begins (vv. 35-37) with a general injunction to assist and deal mercifully with any brother who has become poor. "If thy brother be waxen poor, and his hand fail with thee; then thou shalt uphold him: as a stranger and a sojourner shall he live with thee. Take thou no usury of him or increase; but fear thy God: that thy brother may live with thee. Thou shalt not give him thy money upon usury, nor give him thy victuals for increase."

The evident object of this law is to prevent, as far as possible, that extreme of poverty which might compel a man to sell himself in order to live. Debt is a burden in any case, to a poor man especially; but debt is the heavier burden when to the original debt is added the constant payment of interest. Hence, not merely "usury" in the modern sense of *excessive* interest, but it is forbidden to claim or take any interest whatever from any Hebrew debtor. On the same principle, it is forbidden to take increase for food which may be lent to a poor brother; as when one lets a man have twenty bushels of wheat on condition that in due time he shall return for it twenty-two. This command is enforced (ver. 38) by reminding them from whom they have received what they have, and on what easy terms, as a gift; from their covenant God, who is Himself their security that by so doing they shall not lose: "I am the Lord your God, which brought you forth out of the land of Egypt, to give you the land of Canaan, to be your God." They need not therefore have recourse to the exaction of interest and increase from their poor brethren in order to make a living, but are to be merciful, even as Jehovah their God is merciful.

The Jubilee and Slavery.

Leviticus xxv. 39-55.

"And if thy brother be waxen poor with thee, and sell himself unto thee ; thou shalt not make him to serve as a bondservant : as an hired servant, and as a sojourner, he shall be with thee ; he shall serve with thee unto the year of jubilee : then shall he go out from thee, and he and his children with him, and shall return unto his own family, and unto the possession of his fathers shall he return. For they are My servants, which I brought forth out of the land of Egypt: they shall not be sold as bondmen. Thou shalt not rule over him with rigour ; but shalt fear thy God. And as for thy bondmen, and thy bondmaids, which thou shalt have ; of the nations that are round about you, of them shall ye buy bondmen and bondmaids. Moreover of the children of the strangers that do sojourn among you, of them shall ye buy, and of their families that are with you, which they have begotten in your land : and they shall be your possession. And ye shall make them an inheritance for your children after you, to hold for a possession ; of them shall ye take your bondmen for ever : but over your brethren the children of Israel ye shall not rule, one over another, with rigour. And if a stranger or sojourner with thee be waxen rich, and thy brother be waxen poor beside him, and sell himself unto the stranger or sojourner with thee, or to the stock of the stranger's family : after that he is sold he may be redeemed ; one of his brethren may redeem him : or his uncle, or his uncle's son, may redeem him, or any that is nigh of kin unto him of his family may redeem him ; or if he be waxen rich, he may redeem himself. And he shall reckon with him that bought him from the year that he sold himself to him unto the year of jubilee : and the price of his sale shall be according unto the number of years ; according to the time of an hired servant shall he be with him. If there be yet many years, according unto them he shall give back the price of his redemption out of the money that he was bought for. And if there remain but few years unto the year of jubilee, then he shall reckon with him ; according unto his years shall he give back the price of his redemption. As a servant hired year by year shall he be with him : he shall not rule with rigour over him in thy sight. And if he be not redeemed by these means, then he shall go out in the year of jubilee, he, and his children with him. For unto Me the children of Israel are servants ; they are My servants whom I brought forth out of the land of Egypt : I am the Lord your God."

Even with the burdensomeness of debt lightened as above, it was yet possible that a man might be reduced to poverty so extreme that he should feel compelled to sell himself as a slave. Hence arises the question of slavery, and its relation to the law of the jubilee. Under this head two cases were possible: the first, where a man had sold himself to a fellow-Hebrew (vv. 39-46); the second, where a man had sold himself to a foreigner resident in the land (vv. 47-55).

With the Hebrews and all the neighbouring peoples, slavery was, and had been from of old, a settled institution. Regarded simply as an abstract question of morals, it might seem as if the Lord might once for all have abolished it by an absolute prohibition; after the manner in which many modern reformers would deal with such evils as the liquor traffic, etc. But the Lord was wiser than many such. As has been remarked already, in connection with the question of concubinage, that law is not in every case the best which may be the best intrinsically and ideally. That law is the best which can be best enforced in the actual moral status of the people, and consequent condition of public opinion. So the Lord did not at once prohibit slavery; but He ordained laws which would restrict it, and modify and ameliorate the condition of the slave wherever slavery was permitted to exist; laws, moreover, which have had such an educational

---

* The interpretation of ver. 33 presents a difficulty which, if the rendering retained in the text by the Revisers be accepted, is hard to resolve. But if we assume that a negative has fallen out of the first clause in the received text, and read with the Vulgate, as given in the margin of the Revised Version, "if one of the Levites redeem *not*," all becomes clear. In the exposition we have ventured to assume in this instance the correctness of the Vulgate.

power as to have banished slavery from the Hebrew people.

In the first place, slavery, in the unqualified sense of the word, is allowed only in the case of non-Israelites. That it was permitted to hold these as bondmen is explicitly declared (vv. 44-46). It is, however, important, in order to form a correct idea of Hebrew slavery, to observe that, according to Exod. xxi. 16, man-stealing was made a capital offence; and the law also carefully guarded from violence and tyranny on the part of the master the non-Israelite slave lawfully gotten, even decreeing his emancipation from his master in extreme cases of this kind (Exod xxi. 20, 21, 26, 27).

With regard to the Hebrew bondman, the law recognises no property of the master in his person; that a servant of Jehovah should be a slave of another servant of Jehovah is denied; because they are His servants, no other can own them (vv. 42, 55). Thus, while the case is supposed (ver. 39) that a man through stress of poverty may sell himself to a fellow-Hebrew as a bondservant, the sale is held as affecting only the master's right to his service, but not to his person. "Thou shalt not make him to serve as a bondservant: as an hired servant, and as a sojourner, he shall be with thee."

Further, it is elsewhere provided (Exod. xxi. 2) that in no case shall such sale hold valid for a longer time than six years; in the seventh year the man was to have the privilege of going out free for nothing. And in this chapter is added a further alleviation of the bondage (vv. 40, 41): "He shall serve with thee unto the year of jubilee: then shall he go out from thee, he and his children with him, and shall return unto his own family, and unto the possession of his fathers shall he return. For they are My servants, which I brought forth out of the land of Egypt: they shall not be sold as bondmen."

That is, if it so happened that before the six years of his prescribed service had been completed the jubilee year came in, he was to be exempted from the obligation to service for the remainder of that period.

The remaining verses of this part of the law (vv. 44-46) provide that the Israelite may take to himself bondmen of "the children of the strangers" that sojourn among them; and that to such the law of the periodic release shall not be held to apply. Such are "bondmen for ever." "Ye shall make them an inheritance for your children after you, to hold for a possession; of them shall ye take your bondmen for ever."

It is to be borne in mind that even in such cases the law which commanded the kind treatment of all the strangers in the land (xix. 33, 34) would apply; so that even where permanent slavery was allowed it was placed under humanising restriction.

In vv. 47-55 is taken up, finally, the case where a poor Israelite should have sold himself as a slave to a foreigner resident in the land. In all such cases it is ordered that the owner of the man must recognise the right of redemption. That is, it was the privilege of the man himself, or of any of his near kindred, to buy him out of bondage. Compensation to the owner is, however, enjoined in such cases according to the number of the years remaining to the next jubilee, at which time he would be obliged to release him (ver. 54), whether redeemed or not. Thus we read (vv. 50-52): "He shall reckon with him that bought him from the year that he sold himself to him unto the year of jubilee: and the price of his sale shall be according unto the number of years; according to the time of an hired servant shall he be with him. If there be yet many years, according unto them he shall give back the price of his redemption out of the money that he was bought for. And if there remain but few years unto the year of jubilee, then he shall reckon with him; according unto his years shall he give back the price of his redemption. As a servant hired year by year shall he be with him."

Furthermore, it is commanded (ver. 53) that the owner of the Israelite, for so long time as he may remain in bondage, shall "not rule over him with rigour;" and by the addition of the words "in thy sight" it is intimated that God would hold the collective nation responsible for seeing that no oppression was exercised by any alien over any of their enslaved brethren. To which it should also be added, finally, that the regulations for the release of the slave carefully provided for the maintenance of the family relation. Families were not to be parted in the emancipation of the jubilee: the man who went out free was to take his children with him (vv. 41, 54). In the case, however, where the wife had been given him by his master, she and her children remained in bondage after his emancipation in the seventh year; but of course only until she had reached her seventh year of service. But if the slave already had his wife when he became a slave, then she and their children went out with him in the seventh year (Exod. xxi. 3, 4). The contrast in the spirit of these laws with that of the institution of slavery as it formerly existed in the Southern States of America, and elsewhere in Christendom, is obvious.

These, then, were the regulations connected with the application of the ordinance of the jubilee year to rights of property, whether in real estate or in slaves. In respect to the cessation from the cultivation of the soil which was enjoined for the year, the law was essentially the same as that for the sabbatic year, except that, apparently, the right of property in the spontaneous produce of the land, which was in abeyance in the former case, was in so far recognised in the latter that each man was allowed to "eat the increase of the jubilee year out of the field" (ver. 12).

Practical Objects of the Sabbatic Year and Jubilee Law.

Such was this extraordinary legislation, the like of which will be sought in vain in any other people. It is indeed true that, in some instances, ancient lawgivers decreed that land should not be permanently alienated, or that individuals should not hold more than a certain amount of land. Thus, for example, the Lacedemonians were forbidden to sell their lands, and the Dalmatians were wont to redistribute their lands every eight years. But laws such as these only present accidental coincidences with single features of the jubilee year; an agreement to be accounted for by the fact that the aim of such lawgivers was, in so far, the same as that of the Hebrew code, that they sought thus to guard against excessive accumulations of property in the hands of individuals, and those consequent great inequalities in the distribution of wealth which, in all lands and ages, and never more clearly than in our own, have been seen to be fraught with the gravest dangers to the highest interests of society. Beyond this single point we shall search in vain the history of any other people for an analogy to these laws concerning the sabbatic and the jubilee year.

What was the immediate object of this remarkable legislation? It is not irrelevant to observe that in so far as regards the prescription of a periodic rest to the land, agricultural science recognises that this is an advantage, especially in places where it may be difficult to obtain fertilisers for the soil in adequate amount. But it cannot be supposed that this was the chief object of these ordinances, not even in so far as they had respect to the land. We shall not err in regarding them as intended, like all in the Levitical system, to make Israel to be in reality, what they were called to be, a people holy, *i. e.*, fully consecrated to the Lord. The bearing of these laws on this end is not hard to perceive.

In the first place, the law of the sabbatic year and the jubilee was a most impressive lesson as to the relation of God to what men call their property; and, in particular, as to His relation to man's property in land. By these ordinances every Israelite was to be reminded in a most impressive way that the land which he tilled, or on which he fed his flocks and herds, belonged, not to himself, but to God. Just as God taught him that his time belonged to Him, by putting in a claim for the absolute consecration to Himself of every seventh day, so here He reminded Israel that the land belonged to Him, by asserting a similar claim on the land every seventh year, and twice in a century for two years in succession.

No one will pretend that the law of the sabbatic year or the jubilee is binding on communities now. But it is a question for our times as to whether the basal principle regarding the relation of God to land, and by necessary consequence the right of man regarding land, which is fundamental to these laws, is not in its very nature of perpetual force. Surely, there is nothing in Scripture to suggest that God's ownership of the land was limited to the land of Palestine, or to that land only during Israel's occupancy of it. Instead of this, Jehovah everywhere represents Himself as having given the land to Israel, and therefore by necessary implication as having a like right over it while as yet the Canaanites were dwelling in it. Again, the purpose of God's dealing with Egypt is said to be that Pharaoh might know this same truth: that the earth (or land) was the Lord's (Exod. ix. 29); and in Psalm xxiv. 1 it is stated, as a broad truth, without qualification or restriction, that the earth is the Lord's, as well as that which fills it. It is true that there is no suggestion in any of these passages that the relation of God to the earth or to the land is different from His relation to other property; but it is intended to emphasise the fact that in the use of land, as of all else, we are to regard ourselves as God's stewards, and hold and use it as in trust from Him.

The vital relation of this great truth to the burning questions of our day regarding the rights of men in land is self-evident. It does not indeed determine how the land question should be dealt with in any particular country, but it does settle it that if in these matters we will act in the fear of God, we must keep this principle steadily before us, that, primarily, the land belongs to the Lord, and is to be used accordingly. How, as a matter of fact, God did order that the land should be used, in the only instance when He has condescended Himself to order the political government of a nation, we have already seen, and shall presently consider more fully.

It is obvious that the natural and therefore intended effect of these regulations, if obeyed, would have been to impose a constant and powerful check upon man's natural covetousness and greed of gain. Every seventh year the Hebrew was to pause in his toil for wealth, and for one whole year he was to waive even his ordinary right to the spontaneous produce of his fields; which year of abstinence from sowing and reaping once in fifty years was doubled. Add to this the strict prohibition of lending money upon interest to a fellow-Israelite, and we can see how far-reaching and effective, if obeyed, were such regulations likely to be in restraining that insatiate greed for riches which ever grows the more by that which feeds it.

Yet again; the law of the sabbatic year and the jubilee was adapted to serve also as a singularly powerful discipline in that faith toward God which is the soul of all true religion. In this practical way every Hebrew was to be taught that "man doth not live by bread alone, but by every word that proceedeth out of the mouth of God." The lesson is ever hard to learn, though none the less necessary. This thought is alluded to in ver. 20, where it is supposed that a man might raise the very natural objection to these laws, "What shall we eat the seventh year?" To which the answer is given, with reference even to the extreme case of the jubilee year: "I will command My blessing upon you in the sixth year, and it shall bring forth fruit for the three years; until the ninth year . . . ye shall eat the old store."

But probably the most prominent and important object of the regulations in this chapter was to secure, as far as possible, the equal distribution of wealth, by preventing excessive accumulations either of land or of capital in the hands of a few, while the mass should be sunk in poverty. It is certain that these laws, if carried out, would have had a marvellous effect in this respect. As for capital, we all know what an important factor in the production of wealth is accumulation by interest on loans, especially when the interest is constantly compounded. There can be no doubt of its immense power as an instrument for at once enriching the lender and in proportion impoverishing the borrower. But among the Israelites, to receive interest or its equivalent was prohibited. One other chief cause of the excessive wealth of individuals among us, as in all ages, is the acquirement in perpetuity by individuals of a disproportionate amount of the public land. The condition of things in the United Kingdom is familiar to all, with its inevitable effect on the condition of large masses of people; and in parts of the United States there are indications of a like tendency working toward the similar disadvantage of many small landholders and cultivators. But in Israel, if these laws should be carried into effect, such a state of things, so often witnessed among other nations, was made for ever impossible. Individual ownership in the land itself was forbidden; no man was allowed more than a leasehold right; nor could he, even by adding largely to his leaseholds, increase his wealth indefinitely, so as to transmit a fortune to his children, to be still further augmented by a similar process in the next and succeeding generations; for every fifty years the jubilee came around, and whatever leaseholds he might have acquired from less fortunate brethren, reverted unconditionally to the original owner or his legal heirs.

However impracticable such arrangements may seem to us under the conditions of modern life, yet it must be confessed that in the case of a nation just starting on its career in a new country, as was Israel at that time, nothing could well be thought of more likely to be effective toward securing, along with careful regard to the rights of property, an equal distribution of wealth among the people, than the legislation which is placed before us in this chapter.

It deserves to be specially noticed by how exact equity the laws are distinguished. While, on the one hand, excessive accumulations, either of capital or of land, were thus made impossible, there is here nothing of the destructive communism advocated by many in our day. These laws put no premium on laziness; for if a man, through indolence or vice, was compelled to sell out his right in his land, he had no security of obtaining it again until the jubilee; that is to say, upon an average, during his working lifetime. On the other hand, encouragement was given to industry, as a man who was thrifty might, by purchase of leaseholds, materially increase his wealth and comfort in life. And the effect on inheritance is evident. There could, on the one hand, be no inheritance of such colossal and overgrown fortunes as are possible in our modern states,—no blessing, certainly, in many cases, to the heirs; and neither, on the other hand, could there be any inheritance of hopeless and degrading poverty. A man might have had an indolent or a vicious father, who had thus forfeited his landholding; but while the father would doubtless suffer deserved poverty during his active life, the young man, when the jubilee returned, and the lost paternal inheritance reverted to him, would have the opportunity to see whether he might not, with his father's experience before him as a warning, do better, and retrieve the fortunes of the family. In any case, he would not start upon the work of life weighted, as are multitudes among us, with a crushing and almost irremovable burden of poverty.

It is certain, no doubt, that these laws are not morally binding now; and no less certain, probably, that failing, as they did, to secure observance in Israel, such laws, even if enacted, could not in our day be practically carried out any more than then. Nevertheless, so much we may safely say, that the intention and aim of these laws as regards the equal distribution of wealth in the community ought to be the aim of all wise legislation now. It is certain that all good government ought to seek in all righteous and equitable ways to prevent the formation in the community of classes, either of the excessively rich or of the excessively poor. Absolute equality in this respect is doubtless unattainable, and in a world intended for purposes of moral training and discipline were even undesirable; but extreme wealth or extreme poverty are certainly evils to the prevention of which our legislators may well give their minds. Only it needs also to be kept in mind that these Hebrew laws no less distinctly teach us that this end is to be sought only in such a way as shall neither, on the one hand, put a premium on laziness and vice, nor, on the other, deny to the virtuous and industrious the advantage which industry and virtue deserve, of additional wealth, comfort, and exemption from toilsome drudgery.

In close connection with all this it will be observed that all this legislation, while guarding the rights of the rich, is evidently inspired by that same merciful regard for the poor which marks the Levitical law throughout. For in all these regulations it is assumed that there would still be poor in the land; but the law secured to the poor great mitigations of poverty. Every seventh year the produce of the land was to be free alike to all; if one were poor his brother was to uphold him; when lending him, he was not to add to the debt the burden of interest or increase. And then there was to the poor man the ever-present assurance, which alone would take off half the bitterness of poverty, that through the coming of the jubilee the children at least would have a new chance, and start life on an equality, in respect of inheritance in land, with the sons of the richest. And when we remember the close connection between extreme poverty and every variety of crime, it is plain that the whole legislation is as admirably adapted to the prevention of crime as of abject and hopeless poverty. Well might Asaph use the words which he employs, with evident allusion to the trumpet sound which ushered in the jubilee: "Happy the people that know the joyful sound!" *i. e.*, that have the blessed experience of the jubilee, that supreme earthly sabbatism of the people of God.*

Most significant and full of instruction, no less to us than to Israel, was the ordinance that both the sabbatic and the jubilee years should date from the day of Atonement. It was when, having completed the solemn ritual of that day, the high priest put on again his beautiful garments and came forth, having made atonement for all the transgressions of Israel, that the trumpet of the jubilee was to be sounded. Thus was Israel reminded in the most impressive manner possible that all these social, civil, and communal blessings were possible only on condition of reconciliation with God through atoning blood; atonement in the highest and fullest sense, which should reach even to the Holy of Holies, and place the blood on the very mercy-seat of Jehovah. This is true still, though the nations have yet to learn it. The salvation of nations, no less than that of individuals, is conditioned by national fellowship with God, secured through the great Atonement of the Lord. Not until the nations learn this lesson may we expect to see the crying evils of the earth removed, or the questions of property, of land-holding, of capital and labour, justly and happily solved.

Typical Significance of the Sabbatic and Jubilee Years.

But we must not forget that the sabbatic year and the year of jubilee, following the seventh seven of years, are the two last members of a

---
* See Psalm lxxxix. 15.

sabbatic system of septenary periods, namely, the sabbath of the seventh day, the feast of Pentecost, following the expiry of the seventh week from Passover, and then the still more sacred seventh month, with its two great feasts, and the day of atonement intervening. But, as we have seen, we have good scriptural authority for regarding all these as typical. Each in succession brings out another stage or aspect of the great Messianic redemption, in a progressive revelation historically unfolding. In all of these alike we have been able to trace thoughts connected with the sabbatic idea, as pointing forward to the final rest, redemption, and consummated restoration, the sabbatism that remaineth to the people of God. To these preceding sabbatic periods these last two are closely related. Both alike began on the great day of atonement, in which all Israel was to afflict their souls in penitence for sin; and on that day they both began when the high priest came out from within the veil, where, from the time of his offering the sin-offering, he had been hidden from the sight of Israel for a season; and both alike were ushered in with a trumpet blast.

We shall hardly go amiss if we see in both of these—first in the sabbatic year, and still more clearly in the year of jubilee—a prophetic foreshadowing in type of that final repentance of the children of Israel in the latter days, and their consequent re-establishment in their land, which the prophets so fully and explicitly predict. In that day they are to return, as the prophets bear witness, every man to the land which the Lord gave for an inheritance to their fathers. Indeed, one might say with truth that even the lesser restoration from Babylon was prefigured in this ordinance; but, without doubt, its chief and supreme reference must be to that greater restoration still in the future, of which we read, for example, in Isa. xi. 11, when "the Lord shall set His hand again the *second* time to recover the remnant of His people, which shall remain, from Assyria, and from Egypt, . . . and from the islands of the sea."

But the typical reference of these sacred years of sabbatism reaches yet beyond what pertains to Israel alone. For not only, according to the prophets and apostles, is there to be a restoration of Israel, but also, as the Apostle Peter declared to the Jews (Acts iii. 19-21), closely connected with and consequent on this, a "restoration of all things." And it is in this great, final, and exceedingly glorious restoration of the time of the end that we recognise the ultimate antitype of these sabbatic seasons. When read in the light of later predictions they appear to point forward with singular distinctness to what, according to the Holy Word, shall be when Jesus Christ, the heavenly High Priest, shall come forth from within the veil; when the last trumpet shall sound, and He who was "once offered to bear the sins of many" shall appear a second time, apart from sin, to them that wait for Him, unto salvation (Heb. ix. 28).

Even in the beginning of the Pentateuch (Gen. iii. 17-19) it is explicitly taught that because of Adam's sin, the curse of God, in some mysterious way, fell even upon the material earthly creation. We read that the Lord said unto Adam: "Cursed is the ground for thy sake; in toil shalt thou eat of it all the days of thy life; thorns also and thistles shall it bring forth to thee; and thou shalt eat the herb of the field; in the sweat of thy face shalt thou eat bread, till thou return unto the ground." It is because of sin, then, that man is doomed to labour, toilsome and imperfectly requited by an unwilling soil. It lies immediately before us that both the sabbatic year and the year of jubilee, by the ordinance regarding the rest for the land, and the special promise of sufficiency without exhausting labour, involved for Israel a temporary suspension of the full operation of this curse. The ordinance therefore points unmistakably in a prophetic way to what the New Testament explicitly predicts—the coming of a day when, with man redeemed, material nature also shall share the great deliverance. In a word, in the sabbatic year, and in a yet higher form in the year of jubilee, we have in symbol the wonderful truth which in the most didactic language is formally declared by the Apostle Paul in these words (Rom. viii. 19-22): "The earnest expectation of the creation waiteth for the revealing of the sons of God. For the creation was subjected to vanity, not of its own will, but by reason of him who subjected it, in hope that the creation itself also shall be delivered from the bondage of corruption into the liberty of the glory of the children of God. For we know that the whole creation groaneth and travaileth in pain together until now."

The jubilee year contained in type all this, and more. Where the sabbatic year had typically pointed only to a coming rest of the earth from the primeval curse, the jubilee, falling, not on a seventh, but on an eighth year, following immediately on the sabbatic seventh, pointed also to the permanence of this blessed condition. It is the festival, by eminence, of the new creation, of paradise completely and for ever restored.

Moreover, as falling in the fiftieth year, and therefore on an eighth year of the sabbatic calendar, the jubilee was to the week of years as the Lord's day to the week of days. Like that, it is the festival of resurrection. This is as clearly foreshadowed in the type as the other. For in the year of jubilee not only was the land to rest, but every bond-slave was to be released, and to return to his inheritance and to his family. In the light of what has preceded, and of other revelations of Scripture, we can hardly miss of perceiving the typical meaning of this. For what is the great event which the Apostle Paul, in the passage just cited, associates in time with the deliverance of the earthly creation, but "the redemption of the body," as the final issue of the atoning work of Christ? For as yet even believers are in bondage to death and the grave; but the day which is coming, the day of earth's redemption, shall bring to all that are Christ's, all that are Israelites indeed, deliverance "from the bondage of corruption into the liberty of the glory of the children of God."

And as the slave who was freed in the year of jubilee therewith also returned to his forfeited inheritance, so also shall it be in that day. For precisely this is given us by the Holy Spirit in the New Testament (1 Peter i. 4, 5), as another aspect of the day when the heavenly Aaron shall come forth from the Holiest. For we are begotten *unto an inheritance*, reserved in heaven for us, "who by the power of God are guarded through faith unto a salvation ready to be revealed in the last time." Cast out through death from the inheritance of the earth, which in the beginning was given by God to our first father, and to his seed in him, but which was lost to him and to his children through his sin, the great jubilee of the future shall bring us again, every man who is in Christ by faith, into the lost inheritance, redeemed and glorified citizens of a redeemed and glorified earth. Hence it is that in Rev. xxii. we are shown in vision, first, the new earth, delivered from the curse, and then the New Jerusalem, the Church of the risen and glorified saints of God, descending from God out of heaven, to assume possession of the purchased inheritance.

And the law adds also: "Ye shall return every man unto his family;" which gives the last feature here prefigured of that supreme sabbatism which remaineth for the people of God (Heb. iv. 9). It shall bring the reunion of those who had been parted and scattered. The day of resurrection is accordingly spoken of (2 Thess. ii. 1) as a day of "gathering together" of all who, though one in Christ, have been rudely parted by death. And yet more, it will be "the day of our gathering together unto Him," even the blessed Lord Jesus Christ, the "*Goel*," the Kinsman-Redeemer of the ruined bondsmen and their lost inheritance: "Whom not having seen, we love," but then expect to see even as He is, and beholding Him, be like Him, and be with Him for ever and for ever. Who should not long for the day?—the day when for the first time, this last type of Leviticus shall pass into complete fulfilment in the antitype: the day of "the restoration of all things;" the day of the deliverance of the material creation from her present bondage to corruption; the day also of the release of every true Israelite from the bondage of death, and the eternal establishment of all such with the Elder Brother, the First-begotten, in the enjoyment of the inheritance of the saints in light.

> "Love, rest, and home!
> Sweet hope!
> Lord! tarry not, but COME!"

PART III.

CONCLUSION AND APPENDIX.

LEVITICUS xxvi., xxvii.

1. CONCLUSION: Promises and Threatenings: xxvi.
2. APPENDIX: Concerning Vows: xxvii.

CHAPTER XXVII.

THE PROMISES AND THREATS OF THE COVENANT.

LEVITICUS xxvi. 1-46.

ONE would have expected that this chapter would have been the last in the book of Leviticus, for it forms a natural and fitting close to the whole law as hitherto recorded. But whatever may have been the reason of its present literary form, the fact remains that while this chapter is, in outward form, the conclusion of the Levitical law, another chapter follows it in the manner of an appendix.

Chapter xxvi. opens with these words (vv. 1, 2): "Ye shall make you no idols, neither shall ye rear you up a graven image, or a pillar, neither shall ye place any figured stone in your land, to bow down unto it: for I am the Lord your God. Ye shall keep My sabbaths, and reverence My sanctuary: I am the Lord."

These verses, as they stand in the English versions as a preface to this chapter, at first sight seem but distantly related to what follows; and the Chaldee paraphrast and others have therefore appended them to the preceding chapter. But with that they have even less evident connection. The thought of the editor of this part of the canon, however, seems to have been that the three commands which are here repeated might be regarded as presenting a compendious summary, in its fundamental principles, of the whole law, the promises and threatenings attached to which immediately follow. And the more we think upon these commands and what they involve, the more evident will appear the fitness of their selection from the whole law to introduce this chapter.

The commands which are here repeated are three: namely, (1) a detailed prohibition of idolatry in the forms then chiefly prevalent; (2) an injunction to observe God's sabbaths; and (3) to reverence His sanctuary. Inasmuch as the various forms of idol-worship, which are here forbidden, all involved the recognition of gods other than Jehovah, it is plain that ver. 1 is in effect inclusive of the first and second commandments of the decalogue. The injunction to keep God's sabbaths, although in principle including all the sabbatic times previously appointed, evidently refers especially to the weekly sabbath of the fourth commandment; while the command to reverence the sanctuary of Jehovah covers in principle the ground of the third. And thus, in fact, these three injunctions essentially include the four commands of the decalogue which have to do with man's duty to God, and are thus fundamental to all other duties, both to God and man. Very appropriately, then, are these verses given here as a brief summary of the law to which the following promises and threatenings are annexed. And their suitableness to that which follows is the more clear when we remember that the weekly sabbath, in particular, is elsewhere (Exod. xxxi. 12-17) declared to be a sign of God's covenant with Israel, to which these promises and threats belong; and that the presence of Jehovah's sanctuary also, which they are here charged to reverence, was a continual visible witness among them of the special presence of God in Israel in pursuance of that covenant.

After this pertinent summation of the most fundamental commands of the law, the remainder of the chapter contains, first (vv. 3-13), promises of blessing from God, in case they shall obey this law; secondly (vv. 14-39), threats of chastising judgment, in case they disobey: and, thirdly (vv. 40-45), a prediction of their final repentance, and promise of their gracious restoration thereupon to the favour of God, and the everlasting endurance of God's covenant to preserve them in existence as a nation. The chapter then closes (ver. 46) with the declaration: "These are the statutes and judgments and laws, which the Lord made between Him and the children of Israel in mount Sinai by the hand of Moses."

THE PROMISES OF THE COVENANT.

LEVITICUS xxvi. 3-13.

"If ye walk in My statutes, and keep My commandments, and do them; then I will give your rains in their season, and the land shall yield her increase, and the trees of the field shall yield their fruit. And your threshing shall reach unto the vintage, and the vintage shall reach unto the sowing time: and ye shall eat your bread to the full, and dwell in your land safely. And I will give peace in the land, and ye shall lie down, and none shall make you afraid: and I will cause evil beasts to cease out of the land, neither shall the sword go through your land. And ye shall chase your enemies, and they shall fall before you by the sword. And five of you shall chase an hundred, and an hundred of you shall chase ten thousand: and your enemies shall fall before you by the sword. And I will have respect unto you, and make you fruitful, and multiply you; and I will establish My covenant with you. And ye shall eat old store long kept, and ye shall bring forth the old because of the new. And I will set My tabernacle among you: and My soul shall not abhor you. And I will walk among you, and will be your God, and ye shall be My people. I am the Lord your God, which brought you forth out of the land of Egypt, that ye should not be their bondmen; and I have broken the bars of your yoke, and made you go upright."

The promises of the covenant are thus to the effect that if Israel shall keep the law, God will give them rain and fruitful seasons, harvests so abundant that the "threshing shall reach unto the vintage, and the vintage shall reach unto the sowing time;" internal security; deliverance from the wild beasts, which are still such a scourge in many parts of the East; and such power and spirit, that no enemy shall be able to stand before them, but five of them shall chase an hundred, and an hundred chase ten thousand. Then (ver. 9) is renewed the promise, given long before to Abraham, of a great increase in their numbers; and thereupon, very naturally, is repeated the promise of abundant harvests, so that notwithstanding they shall be so multiplied, one year's harvest should not be consumed before it would have to be removed from the granaries to make room for the new (ver. 10). And then this section ends with the assurance which secures all other blessings, temporal and spiritual, that God will abide among them in His tabernacle, and will be their God, and they shall be His people. And the fulfilment of all this is guaranteed by the person, the purpose, and the past dealing of the Promiser; Himself, Jehovah; His purpose, to deliver them from bondage; and His past mercy, in breaking the bands of their yoke.

"The Vengeance of the Covenant."

Leviticus xxvi. 14-46.

"But if ye will not hearken unto Me, and will not do all these commandments; and if ye shall reject My statutes, and if your soul abhor My judgments, so that ye will not do all My commandments, but break My covenant; I also will do this unto you; I will appoint terror over you, even consumption and fever, that shall consume the eyes, and make the soul to pine away: and ye shall sow your seed in vain, for your enemies shall eat it. And I will set My face against you, and ye shall be smitten before your enemies: they that hate you shall rule over you; and ye shall flee when none pursueth you. And if ye will not yet for these things hearken unto me, then I will chastise you seven times more for your sins. And I will break the pride of your power; and I will make your heaven as iron, and your earth as brass: and your strength shall be spent in vain: for your land shall not yield her increase, neither shall the trees of the land yield their fruit. And if ye walk contrary unto Me, and will not hearken unto Me; I will bring seven times more plagues upon you according to your sins. And I will send the beast of the field among you, which shall rob you of your children, and destroy your cattle, and make you few in number; and your ways shall become desolate. And if by these things ye will not be reformed unto Me, but will walk contrary unto Me; then will I also walk contrary unto you; and I will smite you, even I, seven times for your sins. And I will bring a sword upon you, that shall execute the vengeance of the covenant; and ye shall be gathered together within your cities: and I will send the pestilence among you; and ye shall be delivered into the hand of the enemy. When I break your staff of bread, ten women shall bake your bread in one oven, and they shall deliver your bread again by weight: and ye shall eat, and not be satisfied. And if ye will not for all this hearken unto Me, but walk contrary unto Me; then I will walk contrary unto you in fury; and I also will chastise you seven times for your sins. And ye shall eat the flesh of your sons, and the flesh of your daughters shall ye eat. And I will destroy your high places, and cut down your sun-images, and cast your carcases upon the carcases of your idols; and My soul shall abhor you. And I will make your cities a waste, and will bring your sanctuaries unto desolation, and I will not smell the savour of your sweet odours. And I will bring the land into desolation: and your enemies which dwell therein shall be astonished at it. And you will I scatter among the nations, and I will draw out the sword after you: and your land shall be a desolation, and your cities shall be a waste. Then shall the land enjoy her sabbaths, as long as it lieth desolate, and ye be in your enemies' land; even then shall the land rest, and enjoy her sabbaths. As long as it lieth desolate it shall have rest; even the rest which it had not in your sabbaths, when ye dwelt upon it. And as for them that are left of you I will send a faintness into their heart in the lands of their enemies: and the sound of a driven leaf shall chase them; and they shall flee, as one fleeth from the sword; and they shall fall when none pursueth. And they shall stumble one upon another, as it were before the sword, when none pursueth: and ye shall have no power to stand before your enemies. And ye shall perish among the nations, and the land of your enemies shall eat you up. And they that are left of you shall pine away in their iniquity in your enemies' lands; and also in the iniquities of their fathers shall they pine away with them. And they shall confess their iniquity, and the iniquity of their fathers, in their trespass which they trespassed against Me, and also that because they have walked contrary unto Me, I also walked contrary unto them, and brought them into the land of their enemies: if then their uncircumcised heart be humbled, and they then accept of the punishment of their iniquity; then will I remember My covenant with Jacob; and also My covenant with Isaac, and also My covenant with Abraham will I remember; and I will remember the land. The land also shall be left of them, and shall enjoy her sabbaths, while she lieth desolate without them; and they shall accept of the punishment of their iniquity: because, even because they rejected My judgments, and their soul abhorred My statutes. And yet for all that, when they be in the land of their enemies, I will not reject them, neither will I abhor them, to destroy them utterly, and to break My covenant with them: for I am the Lord their God: but I will for their sakes remember the covenant of their ancestors, whom I brought forth out of the land of Egypt in the sight of the nations, that I might be their God: I am the Lord. These are the statutes and judgments and laws, which the Lord made between Him and the children of Israel in mount Sinai by the hand of Moses."

So, if Israel should not obey the commandments of the Lord, but break that covenant which they had made with Him, when they had said unto the Lord (Exod. xxiv. 7): "All that the Lord hath spoken will we do, and will be obedient;" then they are threatened, first in a general way (vv. 14-17) with terrible judgments, which shall reverse, and more than reverse, all the blessings. God will appoint over them "terror;" disease shall ravage them, consumption and fever; their enemies shall lay waste the land, defeat them in battle, and rule over them; and instead of five of them chasing an hundred, they should flee when none was pursuing (vv. 17, 18). Then follow four series of threats, each conditioned by the supposition that through what they should have already experienced of Jehovah's judgment they should not repent; each also introduced by the formula, "I will chastise (or "smite") you seven times for your sins." In these four times repeated series of denunciations, thus introduced, we are not to insist that numerical precision was intended; neither can we, with some, give to the "seven times" a numerical or temporal reference. The thought which runs through all these denunciations, and determines the form which they take, is this: that the judgments threatened as to follow each new display of hardness and impenitence on the part of Israel shall be marked by continually increasing severity;

and the phrase "seven times," by the reference to the sacred number "seven," intimates that the vengeance should be "the vengeance of the covenant" (ver. 25), and also the awful thoroughness and completeness with which the threatened judgments, in case of their continued obduracy, would be inflicted.

This interpretation is sustained by the details of each section. The first series (vv. 18-20), in which the threatenings of vv. 14-17 are developed, adds to what had been previously threatened, the withholding of harvest for lack of rain. He who had promised to send the rains "in their season," if they were obedient, now declares that if they will not hearken unto Him for the other chastisements before denounced, He will "make their heaven as iron, and their earth as brass." The second series threatens in addition their devastation by wild beasts, which shall rob them of their children and their cattle; and also, in consequence of these great judgments, with a great diminution of their numbers. The third series (vv. 23-26) repeats under forms still more intense, the threats of sword, pestilence, and famine. The staff of bread shall be broken, and when, stricken with pestilence, they are gathered together in their cities, one oven shall suffice ten women for their baking, and bread shall be distributed by rations and in insufficient quantity (vv. 25, 26).

It is intimated that with these extraordinary judgments it shall become increasingly evident that it is Jehovah who is thus dealing with them for the breach of His covenant. This is suggested (ver. 24) by the emphatic use of the personal pronoun in the Hebrew, only to be rendered in English by a stress of voice; and by the declaration (ver. 25) that the sword which should be brought upon them should "execute the vengeance of the covenant."

The same remark applies with still more emphasis to the next and last of these sub-sections (vv. 27-39), the terrific denunciations of which are introduced by these words, which almost seem to flash with the fire of God's avenging wrath: "If . . . ye will walk contrary unto Me; then I will walk contrary unto you in fury (*lit.*, "I will walk with you in fury of opposition"); and I also will chastise you seven times for your sins." All that has been threatened before is here repeated with every circumstance which could add terror to the picture. Was famine threatened? it shall be so awful in its severity that they shall eat the flesh of their own sons and daughters. The high places which had been the scenes of their licentious worship should be destroyed, and the "sun-images" which they had worshipped, going after Baal, should be cut down; and, in visible sign of the Divine wrath and of God's holy contempt for the impotent idols for which they had forsaken the Lord, upon the fallen idols should lie the dead corpses of their worshippers. The sanctuaries (with special,—though, perhaps, not exclusive,—reference, as the following words show, to the holy places of Jehovah's tabernacle or temple) should become a desolation; the sweet savour of their sacrifices should be rejected. The holy people should be scattered into other lands; the land should become so desolate that those of their enemies who should dwell in it should themselves be astonished at its transformation. And so, while they should be scattered in their enemies' land, the land would "enjoy her sabbaths;"* *i. e.*, it should thus, untilled and desolate, enjoy the rest which Jehovah had commanded them to give the land each seventh year, which they had not observed. Meanwhile, the condition of the banished nation in the lands of their captivity should be most pitiful: minished in number, those that were left alive should pine away in their iniquities, and in the iniquity of their fathers; timid and broken-spirited, they should flee before the sound of a broken leaf, and the land of their enemies should "eat them up."

And herewith ends the second section of this remarkable prophecy. Promising Israel the highest prosperity in the land of Canaan, if they will keep the words of this covenant, it threatens them with successive judgments of sword, famine, and pestilence, of continually increasing severity, to culminate, if they yet persist in disobedience, in their expulsion from the land for a prolonged period; and predicts their continued existence, despite the most distressing conditions, in the lands of their enemies, while their own land meanwhile lies desolate and untilled without them.

The fundamental importance and instructiveness of this prophecy is evident from the fact that all later predictions concerning the fortunes of Israel are but its more detailed exposition and application to successive historical conditions. Still more evident is its profound significance when we recall to mind the fact, disputed by none, that not only is it an epitome of all later prophecy of Holy Scripture concerning Israel, but, no less truly, an epitome of Israel's history. So strictly true is this that we may accurately describe the history of that nation, from the days of Moses until now, as but the translation of this chapter from the language of prediction into that of history.

The facts which illustrate this statement are so familiar that one scarcely needs to refer to them. The numerous visitations in the days of the Judges, when again and again the people were given into the hands of their enemies for their sins, and so often as then they repented, were again and again delivered; the heavier judgments of later days, first in the days of the earlier kings, and afterwards culminating in the captivity of the ten tribes, following the siege and capture of Samaria, 721 B. C., and, still later, the terrible siege and capture of Jerusalem by Nebuchadnezzar, 586 B. C., to the horrors of which the Lamentations of Jeremiah bear most sorrowful witness;—what were all these events, with others of lesser importance, but an historical unfolding of this twenty-sixth chapter of Leviticus?

And how, since Old Testament days, this prophecy has been continually illustrated in Israel's history, is, or should be, familiar to all. As apostasy has succeeded to apostasy, judgment has followed upon judgment. To a Nebu-

---

* Much has been made of this reference to the neglect of the sabbatic years as evidence of the late composition of the chapter; but surely in this argument there is little force. For, even apart from any question of inspiration, the ordinance of the sabbatic year was of such an extraordinary character, so opposed alike to human selfishness and eagerness for gain, and calling for such faith in God, that it would require no great knowledge of human nature to anticipate its probable neglect, even on natural grounds. But, even were this not so, still an argument of this kind against the Mosaic origin of this minatory section of the covenant can have decisive force for those only who, for whatsoever reason, have come to disbelieve that God can tell beforehand what free agents will do, or that, if He know, He can impart that knowledge to His servants.

chadnezzar succeeded an Antiochus Epiphanes; and, after the Greco-Syrian judgment, then, following the supreme national crime of the rejection and crucifixion of their promised Messiah, came the Roman captivity, the most terrible of all; a judgment continued even until now in the eighteen hundred years of Israel's exile from the land of the covenant, and their scattering among the nations,—eighteen hundred years of tragic suffering, such as no other nation has ever known, or, knowing, has yet survived; sufferings which are still exhibited before the eyes of all the world to-day in the bitter experiences of the four millions of Jews in the Empire of the Czar, and the persecutions of Anti-Shemitism in other lands.

Existing, rather than living, under such conditions for centuries, as a natural result, the Jewish people became few in number, as here predicted; having been reduced from not less than seven or eight millions in the days of the kingdom, to a minimum, about two hundred years ago, of not more than three millions.* And, strangest of all, throughout this time the once fertile land has lain desolate, for the Gentiles have never settled in it in any great number; and in place of a population of five hundred to the square mile in the days of Solomon, we find now only a few hundred thousand miserable people, and the most of the land, for lack of cultivation, in such a condition that nothing can easily exceed its desolation. And when we have said all this, and much more that might be said without exaggeration, we have but simply testified that vv. 31-34 of this chapter have in the fullest possible sense become historical fact. For it was written (vv. 32-34): "I will bring the land into desolation: and your enemies which dwell therein shall be astonished at it. And you will I scatter among the nations, and I will draw out the sword after you: and your land shall be a desolation, and your cities shall be a waste. Then shall the land enjoy her sabbaths, as long as it lieth desolate, and ye be in your enemies' land; even then shall the land rest, and enjoy her sabbaths."

These facts make this chapter to be an apologetic of prime importance. It is this, because we have here evidence of foreknowledge, and therefore of the supernatural inspiration of the Holy Spirit of God in the prophecy here recorded. The facts cannot be adequately explained, either on the supposition of fortunate guessing or of accidental coincidence. It was not indeed impossible to forecast on natural grounds that Israel would become corrupt, or that, if so, they should experience disaster in consequence of their moral depravation. For God has not one law for Israel and another for other nations. Nor does the argument rest on the details of these threatened judgments, as consisting in the sword, famine, and pestilence; for other nations have experienced these calamities, though, indeed, few in equal measure with Israel; and of these one has a natural dependence on another.

But setting aside these elements of the prophecy, as of less apologetic significance, two particulars yet remain in which this predicted experience has been unique, and antecedently to the event in so high degree improbable, that we can reasonably think here neither of shrewd human forecast nor of chance agreement of prediction and fulfilment. The one is the predicted survival of exiled Israel as a nation in the land of their enemies, their indestructibility throughout centuries of unequalled suffering; the other, the extraordinary fact that their land, so rich and fertile, which was at that time and for centuries afterwards one of the principal highways of the world's commerce and travel, the coveted possession of many nations from a remote antiquity, should during the whole period of Israel's banishment remain comparatively unoccupied and untilled.

As regards the former particular, we may search history in vain for a similar phenomenon. Here is a people who, at their best, as compared with many other nations, such as the Egyptians, Babylonians, and Romans, were few in number and in material resources; who now have been scattered from their land for centuries, crushed and oppressed always, in a degree and for a length of time never experienced by any other people; yet never merging in the nations with whom they were mingled, or losing in the least their peculiar racial characteristics and distinct national identity. This, although now for a long time matter of history, was yet, *à priori*, so improbable that all history records no other instance of the kind; and yet all this had to be if those words of ver. 44 were to prove true: "When they be in the land of their enemies, I will not reject them, neither will I abhor them, to destroy them utterly." With abundant reason has Professor Christlieb referred to this fact as an unanswerable apologetic, thus: "We point to the people of Israel as a perennial historical miracle. The continued existence of this nation up to the present day, the preservation of its national peculiarities throughout thousands of years, in spite of all dispersion and oppression, remains so unparalleled a phenomenon, that without the special providential preparation of God, and His constant interference and protection, it would be impossible for us to explain it. For where else is there a people over which such judgments have passed, and yet not ended in destruction?"*

No less remarkable and significant is the long-continued depopulation of the land of Israel. For it was and is by nature a richly fertile land; and at the time of this prediction—whether it be assigned to an earlier or later period—it was upon one of the chief commercial and military routes of the world, and its possession has thus been an object of ambition to all the dominant nations of history. Surely, one would have expected that if Israel should be cast out of such a land, it would at once and always be occupied by others who should cultivate its proverbially productive soil. But it was not to be so, for it had been otherwise written. And yet it seems as if it had scarcely been possible that through all these later centuries of the history of Christendom, the land could have thus lain desolate, except for the so momentous discovery in 1497 of the Cape route to India, by which event—which no one could in so remote days have well anticipated—the tide of commerce with the East was turned away from Egypt, Syria, and Palestine, to the Atlantic and the Indian Oceans; so that the land of Israel was left, like a city made to

---

* So Basnage ("History of the Jews," London, 1700, chap. xxviii., sec. 15) estimated it in his day. Since then, however, their number has materially increased, and is still increasing; a fact the significance of which has been pointed out by the present writer in "The Jews; or, Prediction and Fulfilment" (New York, 1883, pp. 178-83).

* "Modern Doubt and Christian Belief," p. 333.

stand solitary in a desert by the shifting of the channel of a river; and its predicted desolation thus went on to receive its most complete, consummate, and now long-realised fulfilment.

So, then, stands the case. It is truly difficult to understand how one can fairly escape the inference from these facts, namely, that they imply in this chapter such a prescience of the future as is not possible to man, and therefore demonstrate that the Spirit of God must, in the deepest and truest sense, have been the author of these predictions of the future of the chosen people and their land.

And it is of the very first importance, with reference to the controversies of our day regarding this question, that we note the fact that the argument is of such a nature that it is not in the least dependent upon the date that any may have assigned to the origin of this chapter. Even though we should, with Graf and Wellhausen, attribute its composition to exilian or post-exilian times, it would still remain true that the chapter contained unmistakable predictions regarding the nation and the land; predictions which, if fulfilled, no doubt, in a degree, in the days of the Babylonian exile and the return, were yet to receive a fulfilment far more minute, exhaustive, and impressive, in centuries which then were still in a far distant future. But if this be granted, it is plain that these facts impose a limitation upon the conclusions of criticism. That only is true science which takes into view *all* the facts with respect to any phenomenon for which one seeks to account; and in this case the facts which are to be explained by any theory, are not merely peculiarities of style and vocabulary, etc., but also this phenomenon of a demonstrably predictive element in the chapter; a phenomenon which requires for its explanation the assumption of a supernatural inspiration as one of the factors in its authorship. But if this is so, how can we reconcile with such a Divine inspiration any theory which makes the last statement of the chapter, that " these are the statutes which the Lord made . . . in mount Sinai by the hand of Moses," to be untrue, and the preceding " laws " to be thus, in plain language, a forgery of exilian or post-exilian times?

The Promised Restoration.

Leviticus xxvi. 40-45.

"And they shall confess their iniquity, and the iniquity of their fathers, in their trespass which they trespassed against Me, and also that because they have walked contrary unto Me, I also walked contrary unto them, and brought them into the land of their enemies: if then their uncircumcised heart be humbled, and they then accept of the punishment of their iniquity; then will I remember My covenant with Jacob; and also My covenant with Isaac, and also My covenant with Abraham will I remember; and I will remember the land. The land also shall be left of them, and shall enjoy her sabbaths, while she lieth desolate without them; and they shall accept of the punishment of their iniquity: because, even because they rejected My judgments, and their soul abhorred My statutes. And yet for all that, when they be in the land of their enemies, I will not reject them, neither will I abhor them, to destroy them utterly, and to break My covenant with them: for I am the Lord their God: but I will for their sakes remember the covenant of their ancestors, whom I brought forth out of the land of Egypt in the sight of the nations, that I might be their God: I am the Lord."

This closing section of this extraordinary chapter yet remains to be considered. It is the most remarkable of all, whether from a historical or a religious point of view. It declares that even under so extreme visitations of Divine wrath, and howsoever long Israel's stubborn rebellion and impenitence should continue, yet the nation should never become extinct and pass away. Very impressive are the words (vv. 43-45) which emphasise this prediction: " The land also shall be left of them, and shall enjoy her sabbaths, while she lieth desolate without them; and they shall accept* of the punishment of their iniquity: because, even because they rejected My judgments, and their soul abhorred My statutes. And yet for all that, when they be in the land of their enemies, I will not reject them, neither will I abhor them, to destroy them utterly, and to break My covenant with them: for I am the Lord their God: but I will for their sakes remember the covenant of their ancestors, whom I brought forth out of the land of Egypt in the sight of the nations, that I might be their God: I am the Lord."

As to what is included in this promise of everlasting covenant mercy, we are told explicitly (ver. 40)† that as the final result of these repeated and long-continued judgments, the children of Israel " shall confess their iniquity, and the iniquity of their fathers, in their trespass which they trespassed " against the Lord. Also they will acknowledge (ver. 41) that all these calamities have been sent upon them by the Lord; that it is because they have walked contrary unto Him that He has also walked contrary unto them, and brought them into the land of their enemies. And then follows the great promise (vv. 41, 42): " If then their uncircumcised heart be humbled, and they then accept of the punishment of their iniquity; then will I remember My covenant with Jacob; and also My covenant with Isaac, and also My covenant with Abraham will I remember; and I will remember the land."

These words are very full and explicit. That they have had already a partial and inadequate fulfilment in the restoration from Babylon, and the spiritual quickening by which it was accompanied, is not to be denied. But one only needs to refer to the covenants to which reference is made, and especially the covenant with Abraham, as recorded in the book of Genesis,‡ to see that by no possibility can that Babylonian restoration be said to have exhausted this prophecy. Since those earlier days Israel has again forsaken the Lord, and committed the greatest of all their national sins in the rejection and crucifixion of the promised Messiah; and therefore, again, according to the threat of the earlier part of this chapter, they have been cast out of their land and scattered among the nations, and the land, again, for centuries has been left a desolation. But for all this, God's covenant with Israel has not lapsed, nor, as we are here formally assured, can it ever lapse. To imagine, with some, that because of the new dispensation of grace to the Gentiles which has come in, therefore the promises of this covenant have become

---

* It is the same Hebrew word which is rendered "enjoy" when applied to the land and "accept" when applied to Israel: it might thus be rendered "enjoy" in the latter case—"they shall enjoy the punishment of their iniquity," when the words would express a severe irony, a figure of which we have examples elsewhere in the Scriptures.

† The "if" which introduces ver. 40 in the Authorised version has no equivalent in the Hebrew, and should therefore be omitted, as in the revision.

‡ See Gen. xii. 1-3; xiii. 14-17; xv. 5-21; xvii. 2-11; xxii. 15-18.

void, is a mistake which is fatal to all right understanding of the prophetic word. As for the spiritual blessing of true repentance and a national turning unto God, Zechariah, after the Babylonian captivity, represents the prediction as yet to have a larger and far more blessed fulfilment, in a day which, beyond all controversy, has never yet risen on the world. For it is written (Zech. xii. 8-14; xiii. 1): "In that day . . . I will pour upon the house of David, and upon the inhabitants of Jerusalem, the spirit of grace and of supplication; and they shall look unto Me whom they have pierced: and they shall mourn for Him, as one mourneth for his only son, and shall be in bitterness for Him, as one that is in bitterness for his firstborn; . . . all the families that remain, every family apart, and their wives apart. In that day there shall be a fountain opened to the house of David and to the inhabitants of Jerusalem, for sin and for uncleanness." And that this great promise, which implies by its very terms the previous "piercing" of the Messiah, is still valid for the nation in the new dispensation, is expressly testified by the Apostle Paul, who formally teaches, with regard to Israel, that "God did not cast off His people which He foreknew;" that "the gifts and calling of God are without repentance;" and that therefore the days are surely coming when "all Israel shall be saved" (Rom. xi. 2, 29, 26).

And while nothing is said in this chapter of Leviticus as to the relation of this future repentance of Israel to the establishment of the kingdom of God, we only speak according to the express teaching both of the later prophets and of the apostles, when we add that we are not to think of this covenant of God concerning Israel as of little consequence to our faith and hope as Christians. For we are plainly taught, with regard to the present exclusion and impenitence of Israel (Rom. xi. 15), that "the receiving of them" again shall be as "life from the dead;" which, again, is only what long before had been declared in the Old Testament (Psalm cii. 13-16); that when God shall arise and have mercy upon Zion, and the set time to have pity upon her shall come, the nations shall fear the name of the Lord, and all the kings of the earth His glory.

And while we may grant that the matter is in itself of less moment, it is yet of importance to observe that the very covenant which promises spiritual mercy to the people, as explicitly assures us (ver. 42) that, when Israel confesses its sin, God "will remember the land" as well as the people. All that has been said for the present and unchangeable validity of the former part of this promise, is of necessity true for this latter part also. To affirm the former, and on that ground maintain the faith and expectation of the future repentance of Israel, and yet deny the latter part of this promise, which is no less verbally explicit, regarding the land of Israel, is an inconsistency of interpretation which is as astonishing as it is common. For the restoration of the scattered nation to their land is repeatedly promised, as here, in connection with, and yet in clear distinction from, their conversion, by both the pre- and post-exilian prophets. And if, for reasons not hard to discover, the promise concerning the land is not in so many words repeated in the New Testament, its future fulfilment is yet, to say the least, distinctly assumed in the prediction of Christ (Luke xxi. 24), that Israel, because of their rejection of Him, should be "led captive into all the nations, and Jerusalem be trodden down of the Gentiles,"—not for ever, but only—"until the times of the Gentiles be fulfilled." Surely these words of our Lord imply that, whenever these "times of the Gentiles" shall have run their course, their present domination over the Holy City and the Holy Land shall end.

Nor is such a restoration of Israel to their land, with all that it implies, inconsistent, as some have urged, with the spirit and principles of the Gospel. Many a Gentile nation is greatly favoured of the Lord, and, as one mark of that favour, is permitted to abide in peace and prosperity in their own land. Why should it be any more alien to the spirit of the Gospel that penitent Israel should be blessed in like manner, and, upon their turning unto the Lord, also, like many other nations, be permitted to dwell in peace and safety in that land which lies almost empty and desolate for them until this day? And if it be urged that, admitting this interpretation, we shall also be obliged to admit that Israel is in the future to be exalted to a position of preeminence among the nations, which, again, is inconsistent, it is said, with the principles of the Gospel dispensation, we must again deny this last assertion, and for a similar reason. If not inconsistent with the Gospel that the British nation, for example, should to-day hold a position of exceptional eminence and world-wide influence among the nations, how can it be inconsistent with the Gospel that Israel, when repentant before God, should be in like manner exalted of Him to national eminence and glory?

While in itself this question may be of little consequence, yet in another aspect it is of no small moment that we steadfastly affirm the permanent validity of this part of the promise of the covenant with Israel as given in this chapter. For it is not too much to say that the logic and the exegesis which make the promise to have become void with regard to Israel's land, if accepted, would equally justify one in affirming the abrogation of the promise of Israel's final repentance, if the exigencies of any eschatological theory should seem to require it. Either both parts of this promise in ver. 42 are still valid, or neither is now valid; and if either is still in force, the other is in force also. These two, the promise concerning the people, and the promise concerning the land, stand or fall together.

CHAPTER XXVIII.

CONCERNING VOWS.

LEVITICUS xxvii. 1-34.

As already remarked, the book of Leviticus certainly seems, at first sight, to be properly completed with the previous chapter; and hence it has been not unnaturally suggested that this chapter has by some editor been transferred, either of intention or accident, from an earlier part of the book—as, *e. g.*, after chapter xxv. The question is one of no importance; but it is not hard to perceive a good reason for the position of this chapter after not only the rest of the law, but also after the words of promise and threatening which conclude and seal its prescriptions. For what has preceded has concerned duties of religion which were obligatory upon all Israelites; the regulations of this chapter, on the contrary, have to do with special vows, which were obligatory on no one, and concerning which it is expressly said (Deut. xxiii. 22): "If thou shalt forbear to vow, it shall be no sin in thee." To these, therefore, the promises and threats of the covenant could not directly apply, and therefore the law which regulates the making and keeping of vows is not unfitly made to follow, as an appendix, the other legislation of the book.

Howsoever the making of vows be not obligatory as a necessary part of the religious life, yet, in all ages and in all religions, a certain instinct of the heart has often led persons, either in order to procure something from God, or as a thank-offering for some special favour received, or else as a spontaneous expression of love to God, to "make a special vow." But just in proportion to the sincerity and depth of the devout feeling which suggests such special acts of worship and devotion, will be the desire to act in the vow, as in all else, according to the will of God, so that the vow may be accepted of Him. What then may one properly dedicate to God in a vow? And, again, if by any stress of circumstances a man feels compelled to seek release from a vow, is he at liberty to recall it? and if so, then under what conditions? Such are the questions which in this chapter were answered for Israel.

As for the matter of a vow, it is ruled that an Israelite might thus consecrate unto the Lord either persons, or of the beasts of his possession, or his dwelling, or the right in any part of his land. On the other hand, "the firstling among beasts" (vv. 26, 27), any "devoted thing" (vv. 28, 29), and the tithe (vv. 30-33) might not be made the object of a special vow, for the simple reason that on various grounds each of these belonged unto the Lord as His due already. Under each of these special heads is given a schedule of valuation, according to which, if a man should wish for any reason to redeem again for his own use that which, either by prior Divine claim or by special vow, had been dedicated to the Lord, he might be permitted to do so.

Of the Vowing of Persons.

Leviticus xxvii. 1-8.

"And the Lord spake unto Moses, saying, Speak unto the children of Israel, and say unto them, When a man shall accomplish a vow, the persons shall be for the Lord by thy estimation. And thy estimation shall be of the male from twenty years old even unto sixty years old, even thy estimation shall be fifty shekels of silver, after the shekel of the sanctuary. And if it be a female, then thy estimation shall be thirty shekels. And if it be from five years old even unto twenty years old, then thy estimation shall be of the male twenty shekels, and for the female ten shekels. And if it be from a month old even unto five years old, then thy estimation shall be of the male five shekels of silver, and for the female thy estimation shall be three shekels of silver. And if it be from sixty years old and upward; if it be a male, then thy estimation shall be fifteen shekels, and for the female ten shekels. But if he be poorer than thy estimation, then he shall be set before the priest, and the priest shall value him; according to the ability of him that vowed shall the priest value him."

First, we have the law (vv. 2-8) concerning the vowing of persons. In this case it does not appear that it was intended that the personal vow should be fulfilled by the actual devotement of the service of the person to the sanctuary. For such service abundant provision was made by the separation of the Levites, and it can hardly be imagined that under ordinary conditions it would be possible to find special occupation about the sanctuary for all who might be prompted thus to dedicate themselves by a vow to the Lord. Moreover, apart from this, we read here of the vowing to the Lord of young children, from five years of age down to one month, from whom tabernacle service is not to be thought of.

The vow which dedicated the person to the Lord was therefore usually discharged by the simple expedient of a commutation price to be paid into the treasury of the sanctuary, as the symbolic equivalent of the value of his self-dedication. The persons thus consecrated are said to be "for the Lord," and this fact was to be recognised and their special dedication to Him discharged by the payment of a certain sum of money. The amount to be paid in each instance is fixed by the law before us, with an evident reference to the labour value of the person thus given to the Lord in the vow, as determined by two factors—the sex and the age. Inasmuch as the woman is inferior in strength to the man, she is rated lower than he is. As affected by age, persons vowed are distributed into four classes: the lowest, from one month up to five years; the second, from five years to twenty; the third, from twenty to sixty; the fourth, from sixty years of age and upwards.

The law takes first (vv. 3, 4) the case of persons in the prime of their working powers, from twenty to sixty years old, for whom the highest commutation rate is fixed; namely, fifty shekels for the male and thirty for a female, "after the shekel of the sanctuary," *i. e.*, of full standard weight. If younger than this, obviously the labour value of the person's service would be less; it is therefore fixed (ver. 5) at twenty shekels for the male and ten for the female, if the age be from five to twenty; and if the person be over sixty, then (ver. 7), as the feebleness of age is coming on, the rate is fifteen shekels for the male and ten for the female.* In the case of a child from one month to five years old, the rate is fixed (ver. 6) at five, or, in a female, then at three shekels. In this last case it will be observed that the rate for the male is the same as that appointed (Numb. xviii. 15, 16) for the redemption of the firstborn, "from a month old," in all cases. As in that ordinance, so here, the payment was merely a symbolic recognition of the special claim of God on the person, without any reference to a labour value.

But although the sum was so small that even at the most it could not nearly represent the actual value of the labour of such as were able to labour, yet one can see that cases might occur when a man might be moved to make such a vow of dedication of himself or of a child to the Lord, while he was yet too poor to pay even such a small amount. Hence the kindly provision (ver. 8) that if any person be poorer than this estimation, he shall not therefore be excluded from the privilege of self-dedication to the Lord, but "he

---

* These commutation rates are so low that it is plain that they could not have represented the actual value of the individual's labour. The highest sum which is named—fifty shekels—as the rate for a man from twenty to sixty years of age, taking the shekel as 2s. 3.37d., or $0.5474, would only amount to £5 14s. 0¾d., or $27.375. Even from this alone it is clear that, as stated above, the chief reference in these figures must have been symbolic of a claim of God upon the person, graded according to his capacity for service.

Of the Vowing of Domestic Animals.

Leviticus xxvii. 9-13.

"And if it be a beast, whereof men offer an oblation unto the Lord, all that any man giveth of such unto the Lord shall be holy. He shall not alter it, nor change it, a good for a bad, or a bad for a good: and if he shall at all change beast for beast, then both it and that for which it is changed shall be holy. And if it be any unclean beast, of which they do not offer an oblation unto the Lord, then he shall set the beast before the priest: and the priest shall value it, whether it be good or bad: as thou the priest valuest it, so shall it be. But if he will indeed redeem it, then he shall add the fifth part thereof unto thy estimation."

This next section concerns the vowing to the Lord of domestic animals (vv. 9-13). If the animal thus dedicated to the Lord were such as could be used in sacrifice, then the animal itself was taken for the sanctuary service, and the vow was unalterable and irrevocable. If, however, the animal vowed was "any unclean beast," then the priest (ver. 12) was to set a price upon it, according to its value; for which, we may infer, it was to be sold and the proceeds devoted to the sanctuary.

In this case, the person who had vowed the animal was allowed to redeem it to himself again (ver. 13) by payment of this estimated price and one-fifth additional, a provision which was evidently intended to be of the nature of a fine, and to be a check upon the making of rash vows.

Of the Vowing of Houses and Fields.

Leviticus xxvii. 14-25.

"And when a man shall sanctify his house to be holy unto the Lord, then the priest shall estimate it, whether it be good or bad: as the priest shall estimate it, so shall it stand. And if he that sanctified it will redeem his house, then he shall add the fifth part of the money of thy estimation unto it, and it shall be his. And if a man shall sanctify unto the Lord part of the field of his possession, then thy estimation shall be according to the sowing thereof: the sowing of a homer of barley shall be valued at fifty shekels of silver. If he sanctify his field from the year of jubilee, according to thy estimation it shall stand. But if he sanctify his field after the jubilee, then the priest shall reckon unto him the money according to the years that remain unto the year of jubilee, and an abatement shall be made from thy estimation. And if he that sanctified the field will indeed redeem it, then he shall add the fifth part of the money of thy estimation unto it, and it shall be assured to him. And if he will not redeem the field, or if he have sold the field to another man, it shall not be redeemed any more: but the field, when it goeth out in the jubilee, shall be holy unto the Lord, as a field devoted; the possession thereof shall be the priest's. And if he sanctify unto the Lord a field which he hath bought, which is not of the field of his possession; then the priest shall reckon unto him the worth of thy estimation unto the year of jubilee: and he shall give thine estimation in that day, as a holy thing unto the Lord. In the year of jubilee the field shall return unto him of whom it was bought, even to him to whom the possession of the land belongeth. And all thy estimations shall be according to the shekel of the sanctuary: twenty gerahs shall be the shekel."

The law regarding the consecration of a man's house unto the Lord by a vow (vv. 14, 15) is very simple. The priest is to estimate its value, without right of appeal. Apparently, the man might still live in it, if he desired, but only as one living in a house belonging to another; presumably, a rental was to be paid, on the basis of the priest's estimation of value, into the sanctuary treasury. If the man wished again to redeem it, then, as in the case of the beast that was vowed, he must pay into the treasury the estimated value of the house, with the addition of one-fifth.

In the case of the "sanctifying" or dedication of a field by a special vow two cases might arise, which are dealt with in succession. The first case (vv. 16-21) was the dedication to the Lord of a field which belonged to the Israelite by inheritance; the second (vv. 22-24), that of one which had come to him by purchase. In the former case, the priest was to fix a price upon the field on the basis of fifty shekels for so much land as would be sown with a *homer*—about eight bushels—of barley. In case the dedication took effect from the year of jubilee, this full price was to be paid into the Lord's treasury for the field; but if from a later year in the cycle, then the rate was to be diminished in proportion to the number of years of the jubilee period which might have already passed at the date of the vow. Inasmuch as in the case of a field which had been purchased, it was ordered that the price of the estimation should be paid down to the priest " in that day " (ver. 23) in which the appraisal was made, it would appear as if, in the present case, the man was allowed to pay it annually, a shekel for each year of the jubilee period, or by instalments otherwise, as he might choose, as a periodic recognition of the special claim of the Lord upon that field, in consequence of his vow. Redemption of the field from the obligation of the vow was permitted under the condition of the fifth added to the priest's estimation, *e. g.*, on the payment of sixty instead of fifty shekels (ver. 19).

If, however, without having thus redeemed the field, the man who vowed should sell it to another man, it is ordered that the field, which otherwise would revert to him again in full right of usufruct when the jubilee year came round, should be forfeited; so that when the jubilee came the exclusive right of the field would henceforth belong to the priest, as in the case of a field devoted by the ban. The intention of this regulation is evidently penal; for the field, during the time covered by the vow, was in a special sense the Lord's; and the man had the use of it for himself only upon condition of a certain annual payment; to sell it, therefore, during that time, was, in fact, from the legal point of view, to sell property, absolute right in which he had by his vow renounced in favour of the Lord.

The case of the dedication in a vow of a field belonging to a man, not as a paternal inheritance, but by purchase (vv. 22-24), only differed from the former in that, as already remarked, immediate payment in full of the sum at which it was estimated was made obligatory; when the jubilee year came, the field reverted to the original owner, according to the law (xxv. 28). The reason for thus insisting on full immediate payment, in the case of the dedication of a field acquired by purchase, is plain, when we refer to the law (xxv. 25), according to which the original owner had the right of redemption guaranteed to him at any time before the jubilee. If, in the case of such a dedicated field, any part of the amount due to the sanctuary were still unpaid, obviously this, as a lien upon the land, would stand in the way of such redemption. The regulation of immediate payment is therefore intended to protect the original owner's right to redeem the field.

Ver. 25 lays down the general principle that in all these estimations and commutations the shekel must be "the shekel of the sanctuary," twenty gerahs to the shekel;—words which are not to be understood as pointing to the existence of two distinct shekels as current, but simply as meaning that the shekel must be of full weight, such as only could pass current in transactions with the sanctuary.

The "Vow" in New Testament Ethics.

Not without importance is the question whether the vow, as brought before us here, in the sense of a voluntary promise to God of something not due to Him by the law, has, of right, a place in New Testament ethics and practical life. It is to be observed in approaching this question, that the Mosaic law here simply deals with a religious custom which it found prevailing, and while it gives it a certain tacit sanction, yet neither here or elsewhere ever recommends the practice; nor does the whole Old Testament represent God as influenced by such a voluntary promise, to do something which otherwise He would not have done. At the same time, inasmuch as the religious impulse which prompts to the vow, howsoever liable to lead to an abuse of the practice, may be in itself right, Moses takes the matter in hand, as in this chapter and elsewhere, and deals with it simply in an educational way. If a man will vow, while it is not forbidden, he is elsewhere (Deut. xxiii. 22) reminded that there is no special merit in it; if he forbear, he is no worse a man.

Further, the evident purpose of these regulations is to teach that, whereas it must in the nature of the case be a very serious thing to enter into a voluntary engagement of anything to the holy God, it is not to be done hastily and rashly; hence a check is put upon such inconsiderate promising, by the refusal of the law to release from the voluntary obligation, in some cases, upon any terms; and by its refusal, in any case, to release except under the condition of a very material fine for breach of promise. It was thus taught clearly that if men made promises to God, they must keep them. The spirit of these regulations has been precisely expressed by the Preacher (Eccl. v. 5, 6): "Better is it that thou shouldst not vow, than thou shouldst vow and not pay. Suffer not thy mouth to cause thy flesh to sin; neither say thou before the messenger [of God],* that it was an error: wherefore should God be angry at thy voice, and destroy the work of thine hands?" Finally, in the careful guarding of the practice by the penalty attached also to change or substitution in a thing vowed, or to selling that which had been vowed to God, as if it were one's own; and, last of all, by insisting that the full-weight shekel of the sanctuary should be made the standard in all the appraisals involved in the vow,—the law kept steadily and uncompromisingly before the conscience the absolute necessity of being strictly honest with God.

But in all this there is nothing which necessarily passes over to the new dispensation, except the moral principles which are assumed in these regulations. A hasty promise to God, in an inconsiderate spirit, even of that which ought to be freely promised Him, is sin, as much now as then; and, still more, the breaking of any promise to Him when once made. So we may take hence to ourselves the lesson of absolute honesty in all our dealing with God,—a lesson not less needed now than then.

Yet this does not touch the central question: Has the vow, in the sense above defined— namely, the promise to God of something not due to Him in the law—a place in New Testament ethics? It is true that it is nowhere forbidden; but as little is it approved. The reference of our Lord (Matt. xv. 5, 6) to the abuse of the vow by the Pharisees to justify neglect of parental claims does not imply the propriety of vows at present; for the old dispensation was then still in force. The vows of Paul (Acts xviii. 18; xxi. 24-26) apparently refer to the vow of a Nazarite, and in no case present a binding example for us, inasmuch as they are but illustrations of his frequent conformity to Jewish usages in things involving no sin, in which he became a Jew that he might gain the Jews. On the other hand, the New Testament conception of Christian life and duty seems clearly to leave no room for a voluntary promise to God of what is not due, seeing that, through the transcendent obligation of grateful love to the Lord for His redeeming love, there is no possible degree of devotement of self or of one's substance which could be regarded as not already God's due. "He died for all, that they which live should no longer live unto themselves, but unto Him who for their sakes died and rose again." The vow, in the sense brought before us in this chapter, is essentially correlated to a legal system such as the Mosaic, in which dues to God are prescribed by rule. In New Testament ethics, as distinguished from those of the Old, we must therefore conclude that for the vow there is no logical place.

The question is not merely speculative and unpractical. In fact, we here come upon one of the fundamental points of difference between Romish and Protestant ethics. For it is the Romish doctrine that, besides such works as are essential to a state of salvation, which are by God made obligatory upon all, there are other works which, as Rome regards the matter, are not commanded, but are only made matters of Divine counsel, in order to the attainment, by means of their observance, of a higher type of Christian life. Such works as these, unlike the former class, because not of universal obligation, may properly be made the subject of a vow. These are, especially, the voluntary renunciation of all property, abstinence from marriage, and the monastic life. But this distinction of precepts and counsels, and the theory of vows, and of works of supererogation, which Rome has based upon it, all Protestants have with one consent rejected, and that with abundant reason. For not only do we fail to find any justification for these views in the New Testament, but the history of the Church has shown, with what should be convincing clearness, that, howsoever we may gladly recognise in the monastic communities of Rome, in all ages, men and women living under special vows of poverty, obedience, and chastity, whose purity of life and motive, and sincere devotion to the Lord, cannot be justly called in question, it is none the less clear that, on the whole, the tendency of the system has been toward either

---

* So certainly should we render instead of "angel," in accordance with the suggestion of the margin (R.V.). The reference is to the priest, as Mal. ii. 7 makes very clear: "He [the priest] is the messenger of the Lord."

legalism on the one hand, or a sad licentiousness of life on the other. In this matter of vows, as in so many things, it has been the fatal error of the Roman Church that, under the cover of a supposed Old Testament warrant, she has returned to "the weak and beggarly elements" which, according to the New Testament, have only a temporary use in the earliest childhood of religious life.

Exclusions from the Vow.

Leviticus xxvii. 26-33.

"Only the firstling among beasts, which is made a firstling to the Lord, no man shall sanctify it ; whether it be ox or sheep, it is the Lord's. And if it be of an unclean beast, then he shall ransom it according to thine estimation, and shall add unto it the fifth part thereof : or if it be not redeemed, then it shall be sold according to thy estimation. Notwithstanding, no devoted thing, that a man shall devote unto the Lord of all that he hath, whether of man or beast, or of the field of his possession, shall be sold or redeemed : every devoted thing is most holy unto the Lord. None devoted, which shall be devoted of men, shall be ransomed ; he shall surely be put to death. And all the tithe of the land, whether of the seed of the land, or of the fruit of the tree, is the Lord's : it is holy unto the Lord. And if a man will redeem aught of his tithe, he shall add unto it the fifth part thereof. And all the tithe of the herd or the flock, whatsoever passeth under the rod, the tenth shall be holy unto the Lord. He shall not search whether it be good or bad, neither shall he change it : and if he change it at all, then both it and that for which it is changed shall be holy ; it shall not be redeemed."

The remaining verses of this chapter specify three classes of property which could not be dedicated by a special vow, namely, "the firstling among beasts" (ver. 26); any "devoted thing" (vv. 28, 29), *i. e.*, anything which had been devoted to the Lord by the ban—as, *e. g.*, all the persons and property in the city of Jericho by Joshua (vii. 17); and, lastly, "the tithe of the land" (ver. 30). The reason for prohibiting the vowing of any of these is in every case one and the same; either by the law or by a previous personal act they already belonged to the Lord. To devote them in a vow would therefore be to vow to the Lord that over which one had no right. As for the firstborn, the Lord had declared His everlasting claim on these at the time of the Exodus (Exod. xiii. 12-15); to vow to give the Lord His own, had been absurd. To the law previously given, however, concerning the firstling of unclean beasts (Exod. xiii. 13), it is here added that, if a man wish to redeem such a firstling, the same law shall apply as in the redemption of what has been vowed; namely, the priest was to appraise it, and then the man whose it had been might redeem it by the payment of the amount thus fixed, increased by one-fifth.

The Law of the Ban.

Leviticus xxvii. 28, 29.

"Notwithstanding, no devoted thing, that a man shall devote unto the Lord of all that he hath, whether of man or beast, or of the field of his possession, shall be sold or redeemed : every devoted thing is most holy unto the Lord. None devoted, which shall be devoted of men, shall be ransomed ; he shall surely be put to death."

Neither could any "devoted thing" be given to the Lord by a vow, and for the same reason—that it belonged to Him already. But it is added that, unlike that which has been vowed, the Lord's firstlings and the tithes, that which has been devoted may neither be sold nor redeemed. If it be a person which is thus "devoted," "he shall surely be put to death" (ver. 29). The reason of this law is found in the nature of the *herem* or ban. It devoted to the Lord only such persons and things as were in a condition of irreformable hostility and irreconcilable antagonism to the kingdom of God. By the ban such were turned over to God, in order to the total nullification of their power for evil; by destroying whatever was capable of destruction, as the persons and all living things that belonged to them; and by devoting to the Lord's service in the sanctuary and priesthood such of their property as, like silver, gold, and land, was in its nature incapable of destruction. In such devoted persons or things no man therefore was allowed to assert any personal claim or interest, such as the right of sale or of redemption would imply. Elsewhere the Israelite is forbidden even to desire the silver or gold that was on the idols in devoted cities (Deut. vii. 25), or to bring it into his house or tent, on penalty of being himself banned or devoted like them; a threat which was carried out in the case of Achan (Josh. vii.), who, for appropriating a wedge of gold and a garment which had been devoted, according to the law here and elsewhere declared, was summarily put to death.

This is not the place to enter fully into a discussion of the very grave questions which arise in connection with this law of the ban, in which it is ordered that "none devoted," "whether of man or beast," "shall be ransomed," but "shall be surely put to death." The most familiar instance of its application is furnished by the case of the Canaanitish cities, which Joshua, in accordance with this law of Lev. xxvii. 28, 29, utterly destroyed, with their inhabitants and every living thing that was in them. There are many sincere believers in Christ who find it almost impossible to believe that it can be true that God commanded such a slaughter as this; and the difficulty well deserves a brief consideration. It may not indeed be possible wholly to remove it from every mind; but one may well call attention, in connection with these verses, to certain considerations which should at least suffice very greatly to relieve its stress.

In the first place, it is imperative to remember that, if we accept the teaching of Scripture, we have before us in this history, not the government of man, but the government of God, a true theocracy. Now it is obvious that if even fallible men may be rightly granted power to condemn men to death, for the sake of the public good, much more must this right be conceded, and that without any limitation, to the infinitely righteous and infallible King of kings, if, in accord with the Scripture declarations, He was, literally and really, the political Head (if we may be allowed the expression) of the Israelitish nation. Further, if this absolute right of God in matters of life and death be admitted, as it must be, it is plain that He may rightly delegate the execution of His decrees to human agents. If this right is granted to one of our fellow-men, as to a king or a magistrate, much more to God.

Granting that the theocratic government of Israel was a historical fact, the only question then remaining as to the right of the ban, concerns the justice of its application in particular cases. With regard to this, we may concede that it was quite possible that men might sometimes apply this law without Divine authority; but we are not required to defend such cases, if any be shown, any more than to excuse the infliction of capital punishment in America sometimes by lynch law. These cases furnish no argument against its infliction after due legal process, and by legitimate governmental authority. As to the terrible execution of this law of the ban, in the destruction of the inhabitants of the Canaanitish cities, if the fact of the theocratic authority be granted, it is not so difficult to justify this as some have imagined. Nor, conversely, when the actual facts are thoroughly known, can the truth of the statement of the Scripture that God commanded this terrible destruction, be regarded as irreconcilable with those moral perfections which Scripture and reason alike attribute to the Supreme Being.

The researches and discoveries of recent years have let in a flood of light upon the state of society prevailing among those Canaanitish tribes at the date of their destruction; and they warrant us in saying that in the whole history of our race it would be hard to point to any civilised community which has sunken to such a depth of wickedness and moral pollution. As we have already seen, the book of Leviticus gives many dark hints of unnamable horrors among the Canaanitish races: the fearful cruelties of the worship of Molech, and the unmentionable impurities of the cult of Ashtoreth; the prohibition among some of these of female chastity, requiring that all be morally sacrificed*—one cannot go into these things. And when now we read in Holy Scripture that the infinitely pure, holy and righteous God commanded that these utterly depraved and abandoned communities should be extirpated from the face of the earth, is it, after all, so hard to believe that this should be true? Nay, may we not rather with abundant reason say that it would have been far more difficult to reconcile with the character of God if He had suffered them any longer to exist?

Nor have we yet fully stated the case. For we must, in addition, recall the fact that these corrupt communities, which by this law of the ban were devoted to utter destruction, were in no out-of-the-way corner of the world, but on one of its chief highways. The Phœnicians, for instance, more than any people of that time, were the navigators and travellers of the age; so that from Canaan as a center this horrible moral pestilence was inevitably carried by them hither and thither, a worse than the "black death," to the very extremities of the known world. Have we then so certainly good reason to call in question the righteousness of the law which here ordains that no person thus devoted should be ransomed, but be surely put to death? Rather are we inclined to see in this law of the theocratic kingdom, and its execution in Canaan—so often held up as an illustration of the awful cruelty of the old theocratic *regime*—not only a conspicuous vindication of the righteousness and justice of God, but a no less illustrious manifestation of His mercy;—of His mercy, not merely to Israel, but to the whole human race of that age, who because of this deadly infection of moral evil had otherwise again everywhere sunk to such unimaginable depths of depravity as to have required a second flood for the cleansing of the world. This certainly was the way in which the Psalmist regarded it, when (Psalm cxxxvi. 17-22) he praised Jehovah as One who "smote

* On this subject, among other authorities, see Ebrard, "Apologetik," 2 Theil, pp. 167-90, especially p. 173.

great kings, and slew famous kings, and gave their land for an heritage, even an heritage unto Israel His servant: for HIS MERCY endureth for ever;" a thought which is again more formally expressed (Psalm lxii. 12) in the words: "Unto Thee, O Lord, belongeth mercy: for Thou renderest to every man according to his work."

Nor can we leave this law of the ban without noting the very solemn suggestion which it contains that there may be in the universe persons who, despite the great redemption, are morally irredeemable, hopelessly obdurate; for whom, under the government of a God infinitely righteous and merciful, nothing remains but the execution of the ban—the "eternal fire which is prepared for the devil and his angels" (Matt. xxv. 41); "a fierceness of fire which shall devour the adversaries" (Heb. x. 27). And this, not merely although, but BECAUSE God's "mercy endureth for ever."

THE LAW OF THE TITHE.

LEVITICUS xxvi. 30-33.

"And all the tithe of the land, whether of the seed of the land, or of the fruit of the tree, is the Lord's: it is holy unto the Lord. And if a man will redeem aught of his tithe, he shall add unto it the fifth part thereof. And all the tithe of the herd or the flock, whatsoever passeth under the rod, the tenth shall be holy unto the Lord. He shall not search whether it be good or bad, neither shall he change it: and if he change it at all, then both it and that for which it is changed shall be holy; it shall not be redeemed."

Last of all these exclusions from the vow is mentioned the tithe. "Whether of the seed of the land, or of the herd, or of the flock," it is declared to be "holy unto the Lord;" "it is the Lord's." That because of this it cannot be given to the Lord by a special vow, although not formally stated, is self-evident. No man can give away what belongs to another, or give God what He has already. In Numb. xviii. 21 it is said that this tenth should be given "unto the children of Levi . . . for the service of the tent of meeting."

Most extraordinary is the contention of Wellhausen and others, that since in Deuteronomy no tithe is mentioned other than of the product of the land, therefore, because of the mention here also of a tithe of the herd and the flock, we must infer that we have here a late interpolation into the "priest-code," marking a time when now the exactions of the priestly caste had been extended to the utmost limit. This is not the place to go into the question of the relation of the law of Deuteronomy to that which we have here; but we should rather, with Dillmann,* from the same premisses argue the exact opposite, namely, that we have here the very earliest form of the tithe law. For that an ordinance so extending the rights of the priestly class should have been "smuggled" into the Sinaitic laws after the days of Nehemiah, as Wellhausen, Reuss, and Kuenen suppose, is simply "unthinkable;"† while, on the other hand, when we find already in Gen. xxviii. 22 Jacob promising unto the Lord the tenth of all that He should give him, at a time when he was living the life of a nomad herdsman, it is inconceivable that he should have meant "all, *excepting* the increase of the flocks and herds," which were his chief possession.

* See "Die Bücher Exodus und Leviticus," pp. 635-638.
† See "Undenkbar:" so Dillmann, *op. cit.*, p. 638.

The truth is that the dedication of a tithe, in various forms, as an acknowledgment of dependence upon and reverence to God, is one of the most widely-spread and best-attested practices of the most remote antiquity. We read of it among the Romans, the Greeks, the ancient Pelasgians, the Carthaginians, and the Phœnicians; and in the Pentateuch, in full accord with all this, we find not only Jacob, as in the passage cited, but, at a yet earlier time, Abraham, more than four hundred years before Moses, giving tithes to Melchizedek. The law, in the exact form in which we have it here, is therefore in perfect harmony with all that we know of the customs both of the Hebrews and surrounding peoples, from a time even much earlier than that of the Exodus.

Very naturally the reference to the tithe, as thus from of old belonging to the Lord, and therefore incapable of being vowed, gives occasion to other regulations respecting it. Like unclean animals, houses, and lands which had been vowed, so also the tithe, or any part of it, might be redeemed by the individual for his own use, upon payment of the usual mulct of one-fifth additional to its assessed value. So also it is further ordered, with special regard to the tithe of the herd and the flock, "that whatsoever passeth under the rod," *i. e.*, whatever is counted, as the manner was, by being made to pass into or out of the fold under the herdsman's staff, "the tenth"—that is, every tenth animal as in its turn it comes—"shall be holy to the Lord." The owner was not to search whether the animal thus selected was good or bad, nor change it, so as to give the Lord a poorer animal, and keep a better one for himself; and if he broke this law, then, as in the case of the unclean beast vowed, as the penalty he was to forfeit to the sanctuary both the original and its attempted substitute, and also lose the right of redemption.

A very practical question emerges just here, as to the continued obligation of this law of the tithe. Although we hear nothing of the tithe in the first Christian centuries, it began to be advocated in the fourth century by Jerome, Augustine, and others, and, as is well known, the system of ecclesiastical tithing soon became established as the law of the Church. Although the system by no means disappeared with the Reformation, but passed from the Roman into the Reformed Churches, yet the modern spirit has become more and more adverse to the mediæval system, till, with the progressive hostility in society to all connection of the Church and the State, and in the Church the development of a sometimes exaggerated voluntaryism, tithing as a system seems likely to disappear altogether, as it has already from the most of Christendom.

But in consequence of this, and the total severance of the Church from the State, in the United States and the Dominion of Canada, the necessity of securing adequate provision for the maintenance and extension of the Church, is more and more directing the attention of those concerned in the practical economics of the Church, to this venerable institution of the tithe as the solution of many difficulties. Among such there are many who, while quite opposed to any enforcement of a law of tithing for the benefit of the Church by the civil power, nevertheless earnestly maintain that the law of the tithe, as we have it here, is of permanent obligation and binding on the conscience of every Christian. What is the truth in the matter? In particular, what is the teaching of the New Testament?

In attempting to settle for ourselves this question, it is to be observed, in order to clear thinking on this subject, that in the law of the tithe as here declared there are two elements—the one moral, the other legal,—which should be carefully distinguished. First and fundamental is the principle that it is our duty to set apart to God a certain fixed proportion of our income. The other and—technically speaking—*positive* element in the law is that which declares that the proportion to be given to the Lord is precisely one-tenth. Now, of these two, the first principle is distinctly recognised and reaffirmed in the New Testament as of continued validity in this dispensation; while, on the other hand, as to the precise proportion of our income to be thus set apart for the Lord, the New Testament writers are everywhere silent.

As regards the first principle, the Apostle Paul, writing to the Corinthians, orders that "on the first day of the week"—the day of the primitive Christian worship—"every one" shall "lay by him in store, as God hath prospered him." He adds that he had given the same command also to the Churches of Galatia (1 Cor. xvi. 1, 2). This most clearly gives apostolic sanction to the fundamental principle of the tithe, namely, that a definite portion of our income should be set apart for God. While, on the other hand, neither in this connection, where a mention of the law of the tithe might naturally have been expected, if it had been still binding as to the letter, nor in any other place does either the Apostle Paul or any other New Testament writer intimate that the Levitical law, requiring the precise proportion of a tenth, was still in force;—a fact which is the more noteworthy that so much is said of the duty of Christian benevolence.

To this general statement with regard to the testimony of the New Testament on this subject, the words of our Lord to the Pharisees (Matt. xxiii. 23), regarding their tithing of "mint and anise and cummin"—"these ye ought to have done"—cannot be taken as an exception, or as proving that the law is binding for this dispensation; for the simple reason that the present dispensation had not at that time yet begun, and those to whom He spoke were still under the Levitical law, the authority of which He there reaffirms. From these facts we conclude that the law of these verses, in so far as it requires the setting apart to God of a certain definite proportion of our income, is doubtless of continued and lasting obligation; but that, in so far as it requires from all alike the exact proportion of one-tenth, it is binding on the conscience no longer.

Nor is it difficult to see why the New Testament should not lay down this or any other precise proportion of giving to income, as a universal law. It is only according to the characteristic usage of the New Testament law to leave to the individual conscience very much regarding the details of worship and conduct, which under the Levitical law was regulated by specific rules; which the Apostle Paul explains (Gal. iv. 1-5) by reference to the fact that the earlier method was intended for and adapted to a lower and more immature stage of religious development; even as a child, during his minority, is kept under guardians and stewards, from whose authority, when he comes of age, he is free.

But, still further, it seems to be often forgotten by those who argue for the present and permanent obligation of this law, that it was here for the first time formally appointed by God as a binding law, in connection with a certain divinely instituted system of theocratic government, which, if carried out, would, as we have seen, effectively prevent excessive accumulations of wealth in the hands of individuals, and thus secure for the Israelites, in a degree the world has never seen, an equal distribution of property. In such a system it is evident that it would be possible to exact a certain fixed and definite proportion of income for sacred purposes, with the certainty that the requirement would work with perfect justice and fairness to all. But with us, social and economic conditions are so very different, wealth is so very unequally distributed, that no such law as that of the tithe could be made to work otherwise than unequally and unfairly. To the very poor it must often be a heavy burden; to the very rich, a proportion so small as to be a practical exemption. While, for the former, the law, if insisted on, would sometimes require a poor man to take bread out of the mouth of wife and children, it would still leave the millionaire with thousands to spend on needless luxuries. The latter might often more easily give nine-tenths of his income than the former could give one-twentieth.

It is thus no surprising thing that the inspired men who laid the foundations of the New Testament Church did not reaffirm the law of the tithe as to the letter. And yet, on the other hand, let us not forget that the law of the tithe, as regards the moral element of the law, is still in force. It forbids the Christian to leave, as so often, the amount he will give for the Lord's work, to impulse and caprice. Statedly and conscientiously he is to "lay by him in store as the Lord hath prospered him." If any ask how much should the proportion be, one might say that by fair inference the tenth might safely be taken as an *average minimum* of giving, counting rich and poor together. But the New Testament (2 Cor. viii. 7, 9) answers after a different and most characteristic manner: "See that ye abound in this grace. . . . For ye know the grace of our Lord Jesus Christ, that, though He was rich, yet for your sakes He became poor, that ye through His poverty might become rich." Let there be but regular and systematic giving to the Lord's work, under the law of a fixed proportion of gifts to income, and under the holy inspiration of this sacred remembrance of the grace of our Lord, and then the Lord's treasury will never be empty, nor the Lord be robbed of His tithe.

And so hereupon the book of Leviticus closes with the formal declaration—referring, no doubt, strictly speaking, to the regulations of this last chapter—that "these are the commandments, which the Lord commanded Moses for the children of Israel in mount Sinai." The words as explicitly assert Mosaic origin and authority for these last laws of the book, as the opening words asserted the same for the law of the offerings with which it begins. The significance of these repeated declarations respecting the origin and authority of the laws contained in this book has been repeatedly pointed out, and nothing further need be added here.

To sum up all:—what the Lord, in this book of Leviticus, has said, was not for Israel alone. The supreme lesson of this law is for men now, for the Church of the New Testament as well. For the individual and for the nation, HOLINESS, consisting in full consecration of body and soul to the Lord, and separation from all that defileth, is the Divine ideal, to the attainment of which Jew and Gentile alike are called. And the only *way* of its attainment is through the atoning Sacrifice, and the mediation of the High Priest appointed of God; and the only *evidence* of its attainment is a joyful obedience, hearty and unreserved, to all the commandments of God. For us all it stands written: "YE SHALL BE HOLY; FOR I, JEHOVAH, YOUR GOD, AM HOLY."

The Book of Numbers
By The Reverend Robert A. Watson, M.A., D.D.

DOCTOR WATSON was pastor of the Free Church, Dundee, Scotland. He was the author of "Gospels of Yesterday," "In the Apostolic Age," the volumes in THE EXPOSITOR'S BIBLE on Judges and Ruth and Job. He also collaborated with his wife, who was well known to readers of *The British Weekly* under the pen name of Deas Cromarty.

The Book of Numbers is concerned largely with the sojourn of the Israelites in the wilderness, and with their experiences of divine discipline and of human progress, while in a state of warfare with alien tribes. The lessons from this transition time are forcibly expounded by Doctor Watson, who combines the gifts of spiritual insight and of fine literary expression.

CONTENTS

CHAPTER I.	PAGE
Introductory, ...	385
CHAPTER II.	
The Census and the Camp, . . .	389
CHAPTER III.	
Priests and Levites, ...	392
CHAPTER IV.	
Defilement and Purgation, . . .	396
CHAPTER V.	
Nazaritism : The Blessing of Aaron, .	399
CHAPTER VI.	
Sanctuary and Passover, ...	403
CHAPTER VII.	
The Cloud and the March, . . .	407
CHAPTER VIII.	
Hobab the Kenite, ...	411
CHAPTER IX.	
The Strain of the Desert Journey, . .	414
CHAPTER X.	
The Jealousy of Miriam and Aaron, . .	418
CHAPTER XI.	
The Spies and Their Report, . . .	422
CHAPTER XII.	
The Doom of the Unbelieving, . .	426
CHAPTER XIII.	
Offerings : Sabbath-Keeping : Dress, .	429

CHAPTER XIV.	PAGE
Korah, Dathan, and Abiram, . . .	433
CHAPTER XV.	
Tithes and Cleansings, ...	437
CHAPTER XVI.	
Sorrow and Failure at Kadesh, . .	440
CHAPTER XVII.	
The Last March and the First Campaign,	445
CHAPTER XVIII.	
Balaam Invoked, ...	449
CHAPTER XIX.	
Balaam on the Way, ...	453
CHAPTER XX.	
Balaam's Parables, ...	457
CHAPTER XXI.	
The Matter of Baal-Peor, . . .	461
CHAPTER XXII.	
A New Generation, ...	465
CHAPTER XXIII.	
Offerings and Vows, ...	470
CHAPTER XXIV.	
War and Settlement, ...	475
CHAPTER XXV.	
The Way and the Lot, ...	480
CHAPTER XXVI.	
The Cities of Refuge, ...	483

THE BOOK OF NUMBERS

BY THE REV. ROBERT A. WATSON, M. A., D. D.

CHAPTER I.

INTRODUCTORY.

To summon from the past and reproduce with any detail the story of Israel's life in the desert is now impossible. The outlines alone remain, severe, careless of almost everything that does not bear on religion. Neither from Exodus nor from Numbers can we gather those touches that would enable us to reconstruct the incidents of a single day as it passed in the camp or on the march. The tribes move from one "wilderness" to another. The hardship of the time of wandering appears unrelieved, for throughout the history the doings of God, not the achievements or sufferings of the people, are the great theme. The patriotism of the Book of Numbers is of a kind that reminds us continually of the prophecies. Resentment against the distrustful and rebellious, like that which Amos, Hosea, and Jeremiah express, is felt in almost every portion of the narrative. At the same time the difference between Numbers and the books of the prophets is wide and striking. Here the style is simple, often stern, with little emotion, scarcely any rhetoric. The legislative purpose reacts on the historical, and makes the spirit of the book severe. Seldom does the writer allow himself respite from the grave task of presenting Israel's duties and delinquencies, and exalting the majesty of God. We are made continually to feel the burden with which the affairs of the people are charged; and yet the book is no poem: to excite sympathy or lead up to a great climax does not come within the design.

Nevertheless, so far as a book of incident and statute can resemble poetry, there is a parallel between Numbers and a form of literature produced under other skies, other conditions—the Greek drama. The same is true of Exodus and Deuteronomy; but Numbers will be found especially to bear out the comparison. The likeness may be traced in the presentation of a main idea, the relation of various groups of persons carrying out or opposing that main idea, and the Puritanism of form and situation. The Book of Numbers may be called eternal literature more fitly than the *Iliad* and *Æneid* have been called eternal poems; and the keen ethical strain and high religious thought make the movement tragical throughout. Moses the leader is seen with his helpers and opponents, Aaron and Miriam, Joshua and Hobab, Korah, Dathan, and Abiram, Balak and Balaam. He is brought into extremity; he despairs and appeals passionately to Heaven; in an hour of pride he falls into sin which brings doom upon him. The people, murmuring, craving, suffering, are always a vague multitude. The tent, the cloud, the incense, the wars, the strain of the wilderness journey, the hope of the land beyond—all have a dim solemnity. The occupying thought is of Jehovah's purpose and the revelation of His character. Moses is the prophet of this Divine mystery, stands for it almost alone, urges it upon Israel, is the means of impressing it by judgments and victories, by priestly law and ceremony, by the very example of his own failure in sudden trial. With a graver and bolder purpose than any embodied in the dramatic masterpieces of Greece, the story of Numbers finds its place not in literature only, but in the development of universal religion, and breathes that Divine inspiration which belongs to the Hebrew and to him alone among those who speak of God and man.

The Divine discipline of human life is an element of the theme, but in contrast to the Greek dramas the books of the exodus are not individualistic. Moses is great, but he is so as the teacher of religion, the servant of Jehovah, the lawgiver of Israel. Jehovah, His religion, His law, are above Moses. The personality of the leader stands clear; yet he is not the hero of the Book of Numbers. The purpose of the history leaves him, when he has done his work, to die on Mount Abarim, and presses on, that Jehovah may be seen as a man of war, that Israel may be brought to its inheritance and begin its new career. The voice of men in the Greek tragedy is, as Mr. Ruskin says, "We trusted in the gods; we thought that wisdom and courage would save us. Our wisdom and courage deceive us to our death." When Moses despairs, that is not his cry. There is no Fate stronger than God; and He looks far into the future in the discipline He appoints to men, to His people Israel. The remote, the unfulfilled, gleams along the desert. There is a light from the pillar of fire even when the pestilence is abroad, and the graves of the lustful are dug, and the camp is dissolved in tears because Aaron is dead, because Moses has climbed the last mountain and shall never again be seen.

In respect of content, one point shows likeness between the Greek drama and our book—the vague conception of death. It is not an extinction of life, but the human being goes on into an existence of which there is no definite idea. What remains has no reckoning, no object. The recoil of the Hebrew is not indeed piteous, and fraught with horror, like that of the Greek, although death is the last punishment of men who transgress. For Aaron and Moses, and all who have served their generation, it is a high and venerated Power that claims them when the hour of departure comes. The God they have obeyed in life calls them, and they are gathered to their people. No note of despair is heard like that in the *Iphigenia in Aulis*,—

> "He raves who prays
> To die. 'Tis better to live on in woe
> Than to die nobly."

Dying as well as living men are with God; and this God is the Lord of all. Immense is the difference between the Greek who trusts or dreads many powers above, beneath, and the Hebrew realising himself, however dimly, as the servant of Jehovah the holy, the eternal. This great idea, seized by Moses, introduced by him into the faith of his people, remained it may be indefinite, yet always present to the thought of Israel with many implications till the time of full revelation came with Christ, and He said: "Now that the dead are raised, even Moses showed, in the bush, when he called the Lord the God of Abraham, and the God of Isaac, and the God of Jacob. For He is not the God of the dead, but of the living." The wide interval between a people whose religion contained this thought, in whose history it is interwoven, and a people whose religion was polytheistic and natural is seen in the whole strain of their literature and life. Even Plato the luminous finds it impossible to overpass the shadows of pagan interpretations. "In regard to the facts of a future life, a man," said Phædo, "must either learn or find out their nature; or, if he cannot do this, take at any rate the best and least assailable of human words, and, borne on this as on a raft, perform in peril the voyage of life, unless he should be able to accomplish the journey with less risk and danger on a surer vessel—some word Divine." Now Israel had a Divine word; and life was not perilous.

The problem which appears again and again in Moses' relation with the people is that of the theocratic idea as against the grasping at immediate success. At various points, from the start in Egypt onwards, the opportunity of assuming a regal position comes to Moses. He is virtually dictator, and he might be king. But a rare singleness of mind keeps him true to Jehovah's lordship, which he endeavours to stamp on the conscience of the people and the course of their development. He has often to do so at the greatest risk to himself. He holds back the people in what seems the hour of advance, and it is the will of Jehovah by which they are detained. The Unseen King is their Helper and equally their Rhadamanthine Judge; and on Moses falls the burden of forcing that fact upon their minds.

Israel could never, according to Moses' idea, become a great people in the sense in which the nations of the world were great. Amongst them greatness was sought in despite of morality, in defiance of all that Jehovah commanded. Israel might never be great in wealth, territory, influence, but she was to be true. She existed for Jehovah, while the gods of other nations existed for them, had no part to play without them. Jehovah was not to be overborne either by the will or the needs of His people. He was the self-existent Lord. The Name did not represent a supernatural assistance which could be secured on terms, or by any authorised person. Moses himself, though he entreated Jehovah, did not change Him. His own desire was sometimes thwarted; and he had often to give the oracle with sorrow and disappointment.

Moses is not the priest of the people: the priesthood comes in as a ministering body, necessary for religious ends and ideas, but never governing, never even interpreting. It is singular from this point of view that the so-called Priests' Code should be attributed confidently to a caste ambitious of ruling or practically enthroned. Wellhausen ridicules the "fine" distinction between hierocracy and theocracy. He affirms that government of God is the same thing as rule of priest; and he may affirm this because he thinks so. The Book of Numbers, as it stands, might have been written to prove that they are not equivalent; and Wellhausen himself shows that they are not by more than one of his conclusions. The theocracy, he says, is in its nature intimately allied to the Roman Catholic Church, which is, in fact, its child; and on the whole he prefers to speak of the Jewish Church rather than the theocracy. But if any modern religious body is to be named as a child of the Hebrew *theocracy*, it must not be one in which the priest intervenes continually between faith and God. Wellhausen says again that "the sacred constitution of Judaism was an artificial product" as contrasted with the broadly human indigenous element, the real idea of man's relation to God; and when a priesthood, as in later Judaism, becomes the governing body, God is, so far, dethroned. Now Moses did not give to Aaron greater power than he himself possessed, and his own power is constantly represented, as exercised in submission to Jehovah. A theocracy might be established without a priesthood; in fact, the mediation of the prophet approaches the ideal far more than that of the priest. But in the beginnings of Israel the priesthood was required, received a subordinate place of its own, to which it was throughout rigidly confined. As for priestly government, that, we may say, has no support anywhere in the Pentateuch.

The Book of Numbers, called also "In the wilderness," opens with the second month of the second year after the exodus, and goes on to the arrival of the tribes in the plains of Moab by the Jordan. As a whole it may be said to carry out the historical and religious ideas of Exodus and Leviticus: and both the history and the legislation flow into three main channels. They go to establish the separateness of Israel as a people, the separateness of the tribe of Levi and the priesthood, and the separateness and authority of Jehovah. The first of these objects is served by the accounts of the census, of the redemption of the first-born, the laws of national atonement and distinctive dress, and generally the Divine discipline of Israel recorded in the course of the book. The second line of purpose may be traced in the careful enumeration of the Levites; the minute allocation of duties connected with the tabernacle to the Gershonites, the Kohathites, and the Merarites; the special consecration of the Aaronic priesthood; the elaboration of ceremonials requiring priestly service; and various striking incidents, such as the judgment of Korah and his company, and the budding of Aaron's almond twig. Lastly, the institution of some cleansing rites, the sin offering of chap. xix. for example, the details of punishment that fell upon offenders against the law, the precautions enjoined with regard to the ark and the sanctuary, together with the multiplication of sacrifices, went to emphasise the sanctity of worship and the holiness of the unseen King. The book is sacerdotal; it is marked even more by a physical and moral Puritanism, exceedingly stringent at many points.

The whole system of religious observance and priestly ministration set forth in the Mosaic books may seem difficult to account for, not indeed as a national development, but as a moral and religious gain. We are ready to ask how God could in any sense have been the author of a code of laws imposing so many intricate ceremonies, which required a whole tribe of Levites and priests to perform them. Where was the spiritual use that justified the system, as necessary, as wise, as Divine? Inquiries like these will arise in the minds of believing men, and sufficient answer must be sought for.

In the following way the religious worth and therefore the inspiration of the ceremonial law may be found. The primitive notion that Jehovah was the exclusive property of Israel, the pledged patron of the nation, tended to impair the sense of His moral purity. An ignorant people inclined to many forms of immorality could not have a right conception of the Divine holiness; and the more it was accepted as a commonplace of faith that Jehovah knew them alone of all the families of the earth, the more was right belief towards Him imperilled. A psalmist who in the name of God reproves " the wicked" indicates the danger: "Thou thoughtest that I was altogether such an one as thyself." Now the priesthood, the sacrifices, all provisions for maintaining the sanctity of the ark and the altar, and all rules of ceremonial cleansing, were means of preventing that fatal error. The Israelites began without the solemn temples and impressive mysteries that made the religion of Egypt venerable. In the desert and in Canaan, till the time of Solomon, the rude arrangements of semi-civilised life kept religion at an everyday level. The domestic makeshifts and confusion of the early period, the frequent alarms and changes which for centuries the nation had to endure, must have made culture of any kind, even religious culture, almost impossible to the mass of the people. The law in its very complexity and stringency provided a needful safeguard and means of education. Moses had been acquainted with a great sacerdotal system. Not only would it appear to him natural to originate something of a like kind, but he would see no other means of creating in rude times the idea of the Divine holiness. For himself he found inspiration and prophetic power in laying the foundation of the system; and once initiated, its development necessarily followed. With the progress of civilisation the law had to keep pace, meeting the new circumstances and needs of each succeeding period. Certainly the genius of the Pentateuch, and in particular of the Book of Numbers, is not liberating. The tone is that of theocratic rigour. But the reason is quite clear; the development of the law was determined by the necessities and dangers of Israel in the exodus, in the wilderness, and in idolatrous, seductive Canaan.

Opening with an account of the census, the Book of Numbers evidently stood, from the first, quite distinct from the previous books as a composition or compilation. The mustering of the tribes gave an opportunity of passing from one group of documents to another, from one stage of the history to another. But the memoranda brought together in Numbers are of various character. Administrative, legislative, and historical sources are laid under contribution. The records have been arranged as far as possible in chronological order; and there are traces, as for instance in the second account of the striking of the rock by Moses, of a careful gathering up of materials not previously used, at least in the precise form they now have. The compilers collected and transcribed with the most reverent care, and did not venture in any case to reject. The historical notices are for some reason anything but consecutive, and the greater part of the time covered by the book is virtually passed over. On the other hand some passages repeat details in a way that has no parallel in the rest of the Mosaic books. The effect generally is that of a compilation made under difficulties by a scribe or scribes who were scrupulous to preserve everything relating to the great lawgiver and the dealings of God with Israel.

Recent criticism is positive in its assertion that the book contains several strata of narrative; and there are certain passages, the accounts of Korah's revolt and of Dathan and Abiram, for instance, where without such a clew the history must seem not a little confused. In a sense this is disconcerting. The ordinary reader finds it difficult to understand why an inspired book should appear at any point incomplete or incoherent. The hostile critic again is ready to deny the credibility of the whole. But the honesty of the writing is proved by the very characteristics that make some statements hard to interpret and some of the records difficult to receive. The theory that a journal of the wanderings was kept by Moses or under his direction is quite untenable. Dismissing that, we fall back on the belief that contemporary records of some incidents, and traditions early committed to writing, formed the basis of the book. The documents were undoubtedly ancient at the time of their final recension, whensoever and by whomsoever it was made.

By far the greater part of Numbers refers to the second year after the exodus from Egypt, and to what took place in the fortieth year, after the departure from Kadesh. Regarding the intermediate time we are told little but that the camp was shifted from one place to another in the wilderness. Why the missing details have not survived in any form cannot now be made out. It is no sufficient explanation to say that those events alone are preserved which struck the popular imagination. On the other hand, to ascribe what we have to unscrupulous or pious fabrication is at once unpardonable and absurd. Some may be inclined to think that the book consists entirely of accidental scraps of tradition, and that inspiration would have come better to its end if the religious feelings of the people had received more attention, and we had been shown the gradual rise of Israel out of ignorance and semi-barbarism. Yet even for the modern historical sense the book has its own claim, by no means slight, to high estimation and close study. These are venerable records, reaching back to the time they profess to describe, and presenting, though with some traditional haze, the important incidents of the desert journey.

Turning from the history to the legislation, we have to inquire whether the laws regarding priests and Levites, sacrifices and cleansings, bear uniformly the colour of the wilderness. The origins are certainly of the Mosaic time, and some of the statutes elaborated here must be founded on customs and beliefs older even than the exodus. Yet in form many enactments are apparently later than the time of Moses; and it does not seem well to maintain that laws requiring what was next to impossible in the wilderness were, during the journey, given and enforced as they now stand by a wise legislator. Did Moses require, for instance, that five shekels, " of the shekel of the sanctuary," should be paid for the ransom of the first-born son of a household, at a time when many families must have had no silver and no means of obtaining it? Does not this statute, like another which is spoken of as deferred till the settlement in Canaan, imply a fixed order and medium of exchange? For the sake of a theory which is intended to honour Moses as the only legislator of Israel, is it well to maintain that he imposed conditions which could not be carried out, and that he actually prepared the way for neglect of his own code?

It is beyond our range to discuss the date of the compilation of Numbers as compared with the other Pentateuchal books, or the age of the "Jehovistic" documents as compared with the "Priests' Code." This, however, is of less moment, since it is now becoming clear that attempts to settle these dates can only darken the main question—the antiquity of the original records and enactments. The assertion that Exodus, Leviticus, and Numbers belong to an age later than Ezekiel is of course meant to apply to the present form of the books. But even in this sense it is misleading. Those who make it themselves assume that many things in the law and in the history are of far older date, based indeed on what at the time of Ezekiel must have been immemorial usage. The main legislation of the Pentateuch must have existed in the time of Josiah, and even then possessed the authority of ancient observance. The priesthood, the ark, sacrifice and feast, the shewbread, the ephod, can be traced back beyond the time of David to that of Samuel and Eli, quite apart from the testimony of the Books of Moses. Moreover, it is impossible to believe that the formula "The Lord said unto Moses" was invented at a late date as the authority for statutes. It was the invariable accompaniment of the ancient rule, the mark of an origin already recognised. The various legislative provisions we shall have to consider had their sanction under the great ordinance of the law and the inspired prophetism which directed its use and maintained its adaptation to the circumstances of the people. The religious and moral code as a whole, designed to secure profound reverence towards God and the purity of national faith, continued the legislation of Moses, and at every point was the task of men who guarded as sacred the ideas of the founder and were themselves taught of God. The entire law was acknowledged by Christ in this sense as possessing the authority of the great lawgiver's own commission.

It has been said that "the inspired condition would seem to be one which produces a generous indifference to pedantic accuracy in matters of fact, and a supreme absorbing concern about the moral and religious significance of facts." If the former part of this statement were true, the historical books of the Bible, and, we may say, in particular the Book of Numbers, would deserve no attention as history. But nothing is more striking in a survey of our book than the clear unhesitating way in which incidents are set forth, even where moral and religious ends could not be much served by the detail that is freely used. The account of the muster-roll is a case in point. There we find what may be called "pedantic accuracy." The enumeration of each tribe is given separately, and the formula is repeated, "by their families, by their fathers' houses, according to the number of the names from twenty years old and upward, all that were able to go forth to war." Again, the whole of the seventh chapter, the longest in the book, is taken up with an account of the offerings of the tribes, made at the dedication of the altar. These oblations are presented day after day by the heads of the twelve tribes in order, and each tribe brings precisely the same gifts—"one silver charger, the weight thereof was an hundred and thirty shekels, one silver bowl of seventy shekels after the shekel of the sanctuary, both of them full of fine flour mingled with oil for a meal offering; one golden spoon of ten shekels full of incense; one young bullock, one ram, one he-lamb of the first year for a burnt offering; one male of the goats for a sin offering; and for the sacrifice of peace offerings, two oxen, five rams, five he-goats, five he-lambs of the first year." Now the difficulty at once occurs that in the wilderness, according to Exod. xvi., there was no bread, no flour, that manna was the food of the people. In Numb. xi. 6 the complaint of the children of Israel is recorded: "Now our soul is dried away; there is nothing at all: we have nought save this manna to look to." In Josh. v. 10 ff. it is stated that, after the passage of the Jordan, "they kept the passover on the fourteenth day of the month at even in the plains of Jericho. And they did eat of the old corn of the land on the morrow after the passover, unleavened cakes and parched corn in the self-same day. And the manna ceased on the morrow after they had eaten of the old corn of the land." To the compilers of the Book of Numbers the statement that tribe after tribe brought offerings of fine flour mingled with oil, which could only have been obtained from Egypt or from some Arabian valley at a distance, must have been as hard to receive as it is to us. Nevertheless, the assertion is repeated no less than twelve times. What then? Do we impugn the sincerity of the historians? Are we to suppose them careless of the fact? Do we not rather perceive that in the face of what seemed insuperable difficulties they held to what they had before them as authentic records? No writer could be inspired and at the same time indifferent to accuracy. If there is one thing more than another on which we may rely, it is that the authors of these books of Scripture have done their very utmost by careful inquiry and recension to make their account of what took place in the wilderness full and precise. Absolute sincerity and scrupulous carefulness are essential conditions for dealing successfully with moral and religious themes; and we have all evidence that the compilers had these qualities. But in order to reach historical fact they had to use the same kind of means as we employ; and this qualifying statement, with all that it involves, applies to the whole contents of the book we are to consider. Our dependence with regard to the events recorded is on the truthfulness but not the omniscience of the men, whoever they were, who from traditions, records, scrolls of law, and venerable memoranda compiled this Scripture as we have it. They wrought under the sense of sacred duty, and found through that the inspiration which gives perennial value to their work. With this in view we shall take up the various matters of history and legislation.

Recurring now, for a little, to the spirit of the Book of Numbers, we find in the ethical passages its highest note and power as an inspired writing. The standard of judgment is not by any means that of Christianity. It belongs to an age when moral ideas had often to be enforced with indifference to human life; when, conversely, the plagues and disasters that befell men were always connected with moral offences. It belongs to an age when the malediction of one who claimed supernatural insight was generally believed to carry power with it, and the blessing of God meant earthly prosperity. And the notable fact is that, side by side with these beliefs, righteousness of an exalted kind is strenuously taught. For example, the reverence for Moses and Aaron, usually so characteristic of the Book of Numbers, is seen falling into the background when the Divine judgment of their fault is recorded; and the earnestness shown is nothing less than sublime. In the course of the legislation Aaron is invested with extraordinary official dignity; and Moses appears at his best in the matter of Eldad and Medad when he says, "Enviest thou for my sake? Would God that all the Lord's people were prophets, and that the Lord would put His Spirit upon them." Yet Numbers records the sentence pronounced upon the brothers: "Because ye believe Me not, to sanctify Me in the eyes of the children of Israel, therefore ye shall not bring this congregation into the land which I have given them." And more severe is the form of the condemnation recorded in chap. xxvii. 14: "Because ye rebelled against My word in the wilderness of Zin, in the strife of the congregation, to sanctify Me at the waters before their eyes." The moral strain of the book is keen in the punishment inflicted on a Sabbath-breaker, in the destination to death of the whole congregation for murmuring against God—a judgment which, at the entreaty of Moses, was not revoked, but only deferred—and again in the condemnation to death of every soul that sins presumptuously. On the other hand, the provision of refuge cities for the unwitting man-slayer shows the Divine righteousness at one with mercy.

It must be confessed the book has another note. In order that Israel might reach and conquer Canaan there had to be war; and the warlike spirit is frankly breathed. There is no thought of converting enemies like the Midianites into friends; every man of them must be put to the sword. The census enumerates the men fit for war. The primitive militarism is consecrated by Israel's necessity and destiny. When the desert march is over, Reuben, Gad, and the half-tribe of Manasseh must not turn peacefully to their sheep and cattle on the east side of Jordan; they must send their men of war across the river to maintain the unity of the nation by running the hazard of battle with the rest. Experience of this inevitable discipline brought moral gain. Religion could use even war to lift the people into the possibility of higher life.

CHAPTER II.

THE CENSUS AND THE CAMP.

1. THE MUSTERING.

NUMBERS i. 1-46.

FROM the place of high spiritual knowledge, where through the revelation of God in covenant and law Israel has been constituted His nation and His Church, the tribes must now march with due order and dignity. The sense of a Divine calling and of responsibility to the Highest will react on the whole arrangements made for the ordinary tasks and activities of men. Social aims may unite those who have them in common, and the emergencies of a nation will lay constraint on patriotic souls. But nothing so binds men together as a common vocation to do God's will and maintain His faith. These ideas are to be traced in the whole account of the mustering of the warriors and the organisation of the camp. We review it feeling that the dominating thought of a Divine call to spiritual duty and progress is far from having control of modern Christendom. Under the New Covenant there is a distribution of grace to every one, an endowment of each according to his faith with priestly and even kingly powers. No chief men swear fealty to Christ on behalf of the tribes that gather to His standard; but each believer devotes himself to the service and receives his own commission. Yet, while the first thought is that of personal honour and liberty, there should follow at once the desire, the determination, to find one's fit place in the camp, in the march, in the war. The unity is imperative, for there is one body and one spirit, even as we are called in one hope of our calling. The commission each receives is not to be a free-lance in the Divine warfare, but to take his right place in the ranks; and that place he must find.

The enumeration, as recorded in chap. i., was not to be of all Israelites, but of men from twenty years old and upward, all that were able to go forth to war. From Sinai to Canaan was no long journey, and fighting might soon be required. The muster was by way of preparation for conflicts in the wilderness and for the final struggle. It is significant that Aaron is shown associated with Moses in gathering the results. We see not only a preparation for war, but also for the poll tax or tithe to be levied in support of the priests and Levites. A sequel to the enumeration is to be found in chap. xviii. 21: "And unto the children of Levi, behold, I have given all the tithe in Israel for an inheritance, in return for their service which they serve, even the service of the tent of meeting." The Levites again were to give, out of what they received, a tenth part for the maintenance of the priests. The enactment when carried into effect would make the support of those who ministered in holy things a term of the national constitution.

Now taking the census as intended to impress the personal duties of service in war and contribution for religious ends, we find in it a valuable lesson for all who acknowledge the Divine authority. Not remotely may the command be interpreted thus. Take the sum of them, that they may realise that God takes the sum of them and expects of every man service commensurate with his powers. The claim of Jehovah went side by side with the claim on behalf of the nation, for He was Head of the nation. But God is equally the Head of all who have their life from Him; and this numbering of the Hebrews points to a census which is accurately registered and never falls short of the sum of a people by a single unit. Whoever can fight the battle of righteousness, serve the truth by witness-bearing, aid in relieving the weak, or help religion by personal example and willing gift—every possible servant of God, who is also by the very possession of life and privilege a debtor of God, is numbered in the daily census of His providence. The measure of the ability of each is known. "To whomsoever much is given, of him shall much be required." The Divine regard of our lives and estimate of our powers, and the accompanying claim made upon us, are indeed far from being understood; even members of the Church are strangely ignorant of their duty. But is it thought that because no Sinai shrouded in awful smoke towers above us, and now we are encamped at the foot of Calvary, where one great offering was made for our redemption, therefore we are free in any sense from the service Israel was expected to render? Do any hold themselves relieved from the tithe because they are Christ's freemen, and shirk the warfare because they already enjoy the privileges of the victors? These are the ignorant, whose complacent excuses show that they do not understand the law of Divine religion.

True, the position of the Church among us is not of the kind which the Mosaic law gave to the priesthood in Israel. Tithes are gathered, not from those only who are numbered within the Church and acknowledge obligations, but also from those outside, and always by another authority than that of Divine commandment. In this way the whole matter of the support of religion is confused in these lands both for members of the national Churches and for those beyond their borders. Successfully as the old Hebrew scheme may once have wrought, it is now hopelessly out of line with the development of society. The census does not in any way determine what a national Church can claim. Aaron does not stand beside Moses to watch the enrollment of the tribes, families, and households as they come to be numbered. Yet, by the highest law of all, which neither Church nor State can alter, the demand for service is enforced. There is a warlike duty from which none are exempt, from which there is no discharge. Although the ideal of an organised humanity appears as yet far off in our schemes of government and social melioration, providentially it is being carried into effect. Laws are at work that need no human administration. By the Divine ordinance generous effort for the common good and the ends of religion is made imperative. Obedience brings its reward: "The liberal deviseth liberal things, and by liberal things shall he stand." Neglect is also punished: the sure result of selfishness is an impoverished life.

The census is described as having been thoroughly organised. Keil and Delitzsch think that the registering may have taken place "according to the classification adopted at Jethro's suggestion for the administration of justice—viz., in thousands, hundreds, fifties, and tens." They also defend the total of six hundred and three thousand five hundred and fifty, which is precisely the same as that reached apparently nine months before. It is an obvious explanation of what appears a perplexing agreement, that the enumeration may have occupied nine months. But the number is certainly large, much larger than the muster-rolls of the Book of Judges would lead us to expect, if we reckon back from them. Nor can any explanation be given that is satisfactory in all respects. We may shrink from interfering with these numerical statements carefully set down thousands of years ago. Yet we feel that the haze of remoteness hangs over this roll of the tribes and all after-reckonings based upon it.

Of the twelve princes named in chap. i. 5-15, as overseers of the census, Nahshon, son of Amminadab, of the tribe of Judah, has peculiar distinction. His name is found in the genealogy of David given in the Book of Ruth (chap. iv. 20). It also appears in the "book of the generation of Jesus Christ" (Matt. i.) and the roll of Joseph's ancestry recorded by St. Luke. One after another in that honourable line which gave the Hebrews their Psalmist and the world its Saviour is but a name to us. Yet the life represented by the name Nahshon, spent mainly in the wilderness, had its part in far-off results; and so had many a life, not even named—the hard lives of brave fathers and burdened mothers in Israel, who, on the weary march through the desert, had their sorrow and pain, their scanty joy and hope. Far away is the endurance of those Hebrew men and women, yet it is related to our own religion, our salvation. The discipline of the wilderness made men of courage, women great in faith. Beneath their feet the Arabian sand burned, above them the sun flamed; they heard alarms of war, and followed the pillar of smoke for their appointed time, looking, even when they knew they looked in vain, for the land beyond of which Jehovah had spoken. Unaware of their nation's destiny, they toiled and suffered to serve a great Divine plan which in the course of the ages came to ripeness. And the thought brings help to ourselves. We too have our desert journey, our duty and hardship, with an outlook not merely personal. It is our privilege, if we will take it so, to aid the Divine plan for the humanity that is to be, the great brotherhood in which Christ shall see of the travail of His soul and be satisfied. Like a prince of Judah, or a humble nameless mother in Israel, each may find abiding dignity of life in doing well some allotted part in the great enterprise.

The age of service fixed for the men of the tribes may yield suggestions for our time. It is not of warlike service we have to think, but of that which depends on spiritual influence and intellectual power. And we may ask whether the limits on one side and the other have any parallel for us. Young men and women, having reached the age of bodily and mental vigour, are to hold themselves enrolled in the ranks of the army of God. There is a time of learning and preparation, when knowledge is to be acquired, when the principles of life are to be grasped, and the soul is to find its inspiration through personal faith. Then there should come that self-consecration by which response is made to the claim of God. Neither should that be premature, nor should it be deferred. When an aimless, irresolute adolescence is followed by years of drifting and experimenting without clear religious purpose, the best opportunity of life is thrown away. And this far too frequently occurs among those on whom parental influence and the finest Christian teaching have been expended. The time arrives when such young men and women should begin to serve the Church and the world; but they are still unprepared because they have not considered the great questions of duty, and seen that they have a part to play on the field of endeavour. It is true, no time can be fixed. The public service of Christ has been begun by some in very early youth; and the results have justified their adventure. From the humble tasks they first undertook they have gone on steadily to places of high responsibility, never once looking back, learning while they taught, gaining faith while they imparted it to others. Each for himself or herself, in this matter of supreme importance, must seek the guidance and realise the vocation of God. But delay is often indulged, and the twentieth, even the thirtieth year, passes without a single effort in the holy service. One could wish for a Divine conscription, a command laid on every one in youth to be ready at a certain day and hour to take the sword of the Spirit.

On the other side also many need to reconsider. No time was fixed for the end of the service to which the Israelites were summoned. As long as a man could carry arms he was to hold himself ready for the field. Not the increasing cares of his family, not the disinclination which comes with years, was to weigh against the ordinance of Jehovah. But service now, however cheerfully it may be rendered in early manhood and womanhood, is often renounced altogether when knowledge and power are coming to ripeness with the experience of life. Doubtless there are many excuses to be made for heads of households who are leaving their young folk to represent them in religion, and pretty much in everything outside the mere maintaining of existence or the enjoyment of it. The demands of public service all round are sometimes quite out of proportion to the available time and strength. Yet the Christian duty never lapses; and it is a great evil when the balance is wanting between old and young, tried and untried.

2. The Tribe of Levi.

Numbers i. 47-54.

The tribe of Levi is not numbered with the rest. No warlike service, no half-shekel for the sanctuary, is to be exacted from the Levite. His contribution to the general good is to be of another kind. Pitching their tents about the tabernacle, the men of this tribe are to guard the sanctuary from careless or rude intrusion, and minister unto it, taking charge of its parts and furniture, dismantling it when it is to be removed, setting it up again when another stage of the march is over.

In this order it is implied that, although according to the ideal of the Mosaic law Israel was to be a holy nation, yet the reality fell very far short of it. "The Lord spake unto Moses, saying, Speak unto all the congregation of the children of Israel, and say unto them, Ye shall be holy: for I the LORD your God am holy" (Lev. xix. 1, 2). Again and again this command of consecration is given. But neither in the wilderness, nor throughout the pre-exilic history, nor after the Babylonian affliction had purged the nation of idolatry, was Israel so holy that access to the sanctuary could be allowed to the men of the tribes. Rather, as time went by, did the need for special consecration of those about the temple become more evident. Although by statute the tribe of Levi was well provided for, it cannot be said that the life of the Levite was at any time enviable from a worldly point of view; at the best it was a kind of honourable poverty. Something else than mere priest-craft upheld the system which separated the whole tribe; something else made the Levites content with their position. There was a real and imperative sense of need to guard the sanctities of religion, a jealousy for the honour of God, which, originating with Moses and the priesthood, was felt throughout the whole nation.

As we have seen, the scheme of Israel's religion required this array of servants of the sanctuary. Under Christianity the ideal of the life of faith and the manner of worship are entirely different. A way into the holy place of the Divine presence is now open to every believer, and each may have boldness to enter it. But even under Christianity there is a general failure from holiness, from the spiritual worship of God. And as among the Hebrews, so among Christians, the need for a body of guardians of sacred truth and pure religion has been widely acknowledged. Throughout the Church generally down to the Reformation, and still in countries like Russia and Spain, we may even say in England, the condition of things is like that in Israel. A people conscious of ignorance and secularity, feeling nevertheless the need of religion, willingly supports the "priests," sometimes a great army, who conduct the worship of God. There is nothing to wonder at here, in a sense; much, indeed, for which to be thankful. Yet the system is not the New Testament one; and those who endeavour to realise the ideal are not to be branded and scorned as schismatics. They should be honoured for their noble effort to reach and use the holy consecration of the Christian.

3. The Camp.

Numbers ii.

The second chapter is devoted to the arrangement of the camp and the position of the various tribes on the march. The front is eastward, and Judah has the post of honour in the van; at its head Nahshon son of Amminadab. Issachar and Zebulun, closely associated with Judah in the genealogy as descended from Leah, are the others in front of the tabernacle. The right wing, to the south of the tabernacle, is composed of Reuben, Simeon, and Gad, again connected by the hereditary tie, Gad by descent from the "handmaid of Leah." The seniority of Reuben is apparently acknowledged by the position of the tribe at the head of the right wing, which would sustain the first attack of the desert clans; for dignity and onerous duty go together. The rear is formed by Ephraim, Manasseh, and Benjamin, connected with one another by descent from Rachel. Northward, on the left of the advance, Dan, Asher, and Naphtali have their position. Standards of divisions and ensigns of families are not forgotten in the description of the camp; and Jewish tradition has ventured to state what some of these were. Judah is said to have been a lion (compare "the lion that is of the tribe of Judah," Rev. v. 5); Reuben, the image of a human head; Ephraim, an ox; and Dan an eagle. If this tradition is accepted, it will connect the four main ensigns of Israel with the vision of Ezekiel in which the same four figures were united in each of the four living creatures that issued from the fiery cloud.

The picture of the great organised camp and orderly march of Israel is interesting; but it presents a contrast to the disorganised, disorderly condition of human society in every land and every age. While it may be said that there are nations leagued in creed, allied by descent, which form the van; that others, similarly connected more or less, constitute the right and left wings of the advancing host; and the rest, straggling far behind, bring up the rear—this is but a very imaginative representation of the fact. No people advances as with one mind and one heart; no group of nations can be said to have a single standard. Time and destiny urge on the host, and all is to be won by steady resolute endeavour. Yet some are encamped, while others are moving about restlessly or engaged in petty conflicts that have nothing to do with moral gain. There should be unity; but one division is embroiled with another, tribe crosses swords with tribe. The truth is that as Israel came far short of real spiritual organisation and due disposition of its forces to serve a common end, so it is still with the human race. Nor do the schemes that are occasionally tried to some extent promise a remedy for our disorder. For the symbol of our most holy faith is not set in the midst by most of those who aim at social organisation, nor do they dream of seeking a better country, that is, a heavenly. The description of the camp of Israel has something to teach us still. Without the Divine law there is no progress, without a Divine rallying-point there is no unity. Faith must control, the standard of Christianity must show the way; otherwise the nations will only wander aimlessly, and fight and die in the desert.

CHAPTER III.

PRIESTS AND LEVITES.

1. THE PRIESTHOOD.

NUMBERS iii. 1-10.

IN the opening verse of this chapter, which relates to the designation of the priesthood, Moses is named, for once, after his brother. According to the genealogy of Exod. vi., Aaron was the elder; and this may have led to the selection of his as the priestly house—which again would give him priority in a passage relating to the hierarchy. If Moses had chosen, his undoubted claims would have secured the priestly office for his family. But he did not desire this; and indeed the duties of administrative head of the people were sufficiently heavy. Aaron was apparently fitted for the sacerdotal office, and without peculiar qualifications for any other. He seems to have had no originating power, but to have been ready to fall in with and direct the routine of ceremonial worship. And we may assume that Moses knew the surviving sons of Aaron to be of the stamp of their father, likely to inaugurate a race of steady, devoted servants of the altar.

Yet all Aaron's sons had not been of this quiet disposition. Nadab and Abihu, the two eldest, had sinned presumptuously, and brought on themselves the doom of death. No fewer than five times is their fall referred to in the books of Leviticus and Numbers. Whatever that strange fire was which they put in their censers and used before the Lord, the judgment that befell them was signal and impressive. And here reference is made to the fact that they died without issue, as if to mark the barrenness of the sacrilegious. Did it not appear that inherent disqualification for the priesthood, the moral blindness or self-will which was shown in their presumptuous act, had been foreseen by God, who wrote them childless in His book? This race must not be continued. Israel must not begin with priests who desecrate the altar.

Whether the death of those two sons of Aaron came by an unexpected stroke, or was a doom inflicted after judgment in which their father had to acquiesce, the terrible event left a most effectual warning. The order appointed for the incense offering, and all other sacred duties, would thenceforth be rigidly observed. And the incident—revived continually for the priests when they studied the Law—must have had especial significance through their knowledge of the use and meaning of fire in idolatrous worship. The temptation was often felt, against which the fate of Nadab and Abihu set every priest on his guard, to mingle the supposed virtue of other religious symbols with the sanctities of Jehovah. Who can doubt that priests of Israel, secretly tempted by the rites of sun-worship, might have gone the length of carrying the fire of Baal into Jehovah's temple, if the memory of this doom had not held back the hand? Here also the degradation of the burnt offering by taking flame from a common fire was by implication forbidden. The source of that which is the symbol of Divine purity must be sacredly pure.

Those who minister in holy things have still a corresponding danger, and may find here a needed warning. The fervour shown in sacred worship and work must have an origin that is purely religious. He who pleads earnestly with God on behalf of men, or rises to impassioned appeal in beseeching men to repent, appearing as an ambassador of Christ urged by the love of souls, has to do not with symbols, but with truths, ideas, Divine mysteries infinitely more sacred than the incense and fire of Old Testament worship. For the Hebrew priest outward and formal consecration sufficed. For the minister of the New Testament, the purity must be of the heart and soul. Yet it is possible for the heat of alien zeal, of mere self-love or official ambition, to be carried into duties the most solemn that fall to the lot of man; and if it is not in the Spirit of God a preacher speaks or offers the sacrifice of thanksgiving, if some other inspiration makes him eloquent and gives his voice its tremulous notes, sin like that of Nadab and Abihu is committed, or rather a sin greater than theirs. With profound sorrow it must be confessed that the "strange fire" from idolatrous altars too often desecrates the service of God. Excitement is sought by those who minister in order that the temperament may be raised to the degree necessary for free and ardent speech; and it is not always of a purely religious kind. Those who hear may for a time be deceived by the pretence of unction, by dramatic tones, by alien fire. But the difference is felt when it cannot be defined; and on the spiritual life of the ministrant the effect is simply fatal.

The surviving sons of Aaron, Eleazar and Ithamar, were anointed and "consecrated to minister in the priest's office." The form of designation is indicated by the expression, "whose hand he filled to exercise priesthood." This has been explained as referring to a portion of the ceremony described in Lev. viii. 26 f. "And out of the basket of unleavened bread, that was before the Lord, he took one unleavened cake, and one cake of oiled bread, and one wafer, and placed them on the fat, and upon the right thigh: and he put the whole upon the hands of

Aaron, and upon the hands of his sons, and waved them for a wave offering before the Lord." The explanation is scarcely satisfactory. In the long ceremony of consecration this incident was not the only one to which the expression "filling the hand" was applied; and something simpler must be found as the source of an idiomatic phrase. To fill the hand would naturally mean to pay or hire, and we seem to be pointed to the time when for the patriarchal priesthood there was substituted one that was official, supported by the community. In Exod. xxviii. 41 and in Lev. viii. 33, the expression in question is used in a general sense incompatible with its reference to any particular portion of the ceremony of consecration. It is also used in Judges xvii., where to all appearance the consecration of Micah's Levite implied little else than the first payment on account of a stipulated hire. The phrase, then, appears to be a mark of history, and carries the mind back to the simple origin of the priestly office.

Eleazar and Ithamar "ministered in the priest's office in the presence of Aaron their father." So far as the narrative of the Pentateuch gives information, there were originally, and during the whole of the wilderness journey, no other priests than Aaron and his sons. Nadab and Abihu having died, there remained but the two besides their father. Phinehas the son of Eleazar appears in the history, but is not called a priest, nor has he any priestly functions. What he does is indeed quite apart from the holy office. And this early restriction of the number is not only in favour of the Pentateuchal history, but partly explains the fact that in Deuteronomy the priests and Levites are apparently identified. Taking at their very heaviest the duties specially laid on the priests, much must have fallen to the share of their assistants, who had their own consecration as ministers of the sanctuary. It is certain that members of the Levitical families were in course of time admitted to the full status of priests.

The direction is given in ver. 10, "Thou shalt appoint Aaron and his sons, and they shall keep their priesthood; and the stranger that cometh nigh shall be put to death." This is rigorously exclusive, and seems to contrast with the statements of Deuteronomy, "At that time the Lord separated the tribe of Levi to bear the ark of the covenant of the Lord, to stand before the Lord to minister unto Him and to *bless in His name* unto this day" (x. 8); and again, "The priests the Levites, even all the tribe of Levi, shall have no portion nor inheritance with Israel; they shall eat the offerings of the Lord made by fire, and His inheritance" (xviii. 1); and once more, "Moses wrote the law and delivered it unto the priests, the sons of Levi, which bore the ark of the covenant of the Lord, and unto all the elders of Israel" (xxxi. 9). Throughout Deuteronomy the priests are never called sons of Aaron, nor is Aaron called a priest. Whether the cause of this apparent discrepancy is that Deuteronomy regarded the arrangements for the priestly service in a different light, or that the distinction of priests from Levites fell into abeyance and was afterwards revived, the variation cannot be ignored. In the book of Joshua "the children of Aaron the priest" appear on a few occasions, and certain of the duties of high priest are ascribed to Eleazar. Yet even in Joshua the importance attached to the Aaronic house is far less than in Exodus, Leviticus, and Numbers; and the expression "the priests the Levites" occurs twice. If we regard the origin of the Aaronic priesthood as belonging to the Mosaic period, then the wars and disturbances of the settlement in Canaan must have entirely disorganized the system originally instituted. In the days of the judges there seems to have been no orderly observance of those laws which gave the priesthood importance. Scattered Levites had to do as they best could what was possible in the way of sacrifice and purification. And this confusion may have begun in the plain of Moab. The death of Aaron, the personal insignificance of his sons, and still more the death of Moses himself, would place the administration of religious as well as secular affairs on an entirely different footing. Memoranda preserved in Leviticus and Numbers may therefore be more ancient than those of Deuteronomy; and Deuteronomy, describing the state of things before the passage of Jordan, may in regard to the priesthood reflect the conditions of new development, the course of which did not blend with the original design till after the captivity.

The tribe of Levi is, according to ver. 6 ff., appointed to minister to Aaron, and to keep his charge and that of the congregation before the "tent of meeting," to do the service of the tabernacle. For all the necessary work connected with the sanctuary the Levites are "wholly given unto Aaron on behalf of the children of Israel." It was of course in accordance with the patriarchal idea that each clan should have a hereditary chief. Here, however, an arbitrary rule breaks in. For Aaron was not by primogeniture head of the tribe of Levi. He belonged to a younger family of the tribe. The arrangements made by Moses as the representative of God superseded the succession by birthright. And this is by no means the only case in which a law usually adhered to was broken through. According to the history the high-priesthood did not invariably follow the line of Eleazar. At a certain point a descendant of Ithamar was for some reason raised to the dignity. Samuel, too, became virtually a priest, and rose higher than any high-priest before the captivity, although he was not even of the tribe of Levi. The law of spiritual endowment in his case set the other aside. And is it not often so? The **course** of providence brings forward the man who can guide affairs. While his work lasts he is practically supreme. It is useless to question or rebel. Neither in religion nor in government can the appeal to Divine right or to constitutional order alter the fact. Korah need not revolt against Moses; nor may Aaron imagine that he can push himself into the front. And Aaron, as head of the tribe of Levi, and of the religious administration, is safe in his own position so long only as his office is well served. It is to responsibility he is called, rather than to honour. Let him do his duty, otherwise he will surely become merely a name or a figure.

2. THE FIRST-BORN.

NUMBERS iii. 11-13, 40-51.

These two passages supplement each other and may be taken together. Jehovah claims the first-born in Israel. He hallowed them unto Himself on the day when He smote all the first-born in the land of Egypt. They are now numbered from a month old and upward. But instead of their being appointed personally to holy service, the Levites are substituted for them. The whole account supplies a scheme of the origin of the sacerdotal tribe.

It has been questioned whether the number of the first-born, which is 22,273, can in any way be made to agree with the total number of the male Israelites, previously stated at 603,550. Wellhausen is specially contemptuous of a tradition or calculation which, he says, would give an average of forty children to each woman. But the difficulty partly yields if it is kept in view that the Levites were separated for the service of the sanctuary. Naturally it would be the heir-apparent alone of each family group whose liability to this kind of duty fell to be considered. The head of a household was, according to the ancient reckoning, its priest. In Abraham's family no one counted as a first-born but Isaac. Now that a generation of Israelites is growing up sanctified by the covenant, it appears fit that the presumptive priest should either be devoted to sacerdotal duty, or relieved of it by a Levite as his substitute. Suppose each family had five tents, and suppose further that the children born before the exodus are not reckoned, the number will not be found at all disproportionate. The absolute number remains a difficulty.

Dr. Robertson Smith argues from his own premises about the sanctity of the first-born. He repudiates the notion that at one time the Hebrews actually sacrificed all their first-born sons; yet he affirms that "there must have been some point of attachment in ancient custom for the belief that the Deity asked for such a sacrifice."* "I apprehend," he proceeds, "that all the prerogatives of the first-born among Semitic peoples are originally prerogatives of sanctity; the sacred blood of the kin flows purest and strongest in him (Gen. xlix. 3). Neither in the case of children nor in that of cattle did the congenital holiness of the first-born originally imply that they must be sacrificed or given to the Deity on the altar, but only that if sacrifice was to be made, they were the best and fittest because the holiest victims." The passage in Numbers may be confidently declared to be far from any such conception. The special fitness for sacrifice of the first-born of an animal is assumed: the fitness of the heir of a family, again, is plainly not to *become* a sacrifice, but to offer sacrifice. The first-born of the Egyptians died. But it is the life, the holy activity of His own people, not their death, God desires. And this holy activity, rising to its highest function in the first-born, is according to our passage laid on the Levites to a certain extent. Not entirely indeed. The whole congregation is still consecrated and must be holy. All are bound by the covenant. The head of each family group will still have to officiate as a priest in celebrating the passover. Certain duties, however, are transferred for the better protection of the sanctities of worship.

The first-born are found to exceed the number of the Levites by two hundred and seventy-three; and for their redemption Moses takes "five shekels apiece by the poll; after the shekel of the sanctuary." The money thus collected is given unto Aaron and his sons.

The method of redemption here presented, purely arbitrary in respect of the sum appointed for the ransom of each life, is fitly contrasted by

* "Religion of the Semites," p. 445.

the Apostle Peter with that of the Christian dispensation. He adopts the word *redeem*, taking it over from the old economy, but says, "Ye were redeemed not with corruptible things, with silver or gold, from your vain manner of life handed down from your fathers." And the difference is not only that the Christian is redeemed with the precious blood of Christ, but this also, that, while the first-born Israelite was relieved of certain parts of the holy service which might have been claimed of him by Jehovah, it is for sacred service, "to be a holy priesthood to offer up spiritual sacrifices," Christians are redeemed. In the one case exemption, in the other case consecration is the end. The difference is indeed great, and shows how much the two covenants are in contrast with each other. It is not to enable us to escape any of the duties or obligations of life Christ has given Himself for us. It is to make us fit for those duties, to bring us fully under those obligations, to purify us that we may serve God with our bodies and spirits which are His.

A passage in Exodus (xiii. 11 f.) must not be overlooked in connection with that presently under consideration. The enactment there is to the effect that when Israel is brought into the land of the Canaanites every first-born of beasts shall be set apart unto the Lord, the firstling of an ass shall be redeemed with a lamb or killed, and all first-born children shall be redeemed. Here the singular point is that the law is deferred, and does not come into operation till the settlement in Canaan. Either this was set aside for the provisions made in Numbers, or these are to be interpreted by it. The difficulties of the former view are greatly increased by the mention of the "shekel of the sanctuary," which seems to imply a settled medium of exchange, hardly possible in the wilderness.

In Numb. viii. 18, 19, the subject of redemption is again touched, and the additions are significant. Now the service of the Levites "in the tent of meeting" is by way of atonement for the children of Israel, "that there be no plague among the children of Israel when the children of Israel come nigh unto the sanctuary." Atonement is not with blood in this case, but by the service of the living substitute. While the general scope of the Mosaic law requires the shedding of blood in order that the claim of God may be met, this exception must not be forgotten. And in a sense it is the chief instance of atonement, far transcending in expressiveness those in which animals were slaughtered for propitiation. The whole congregation, threatened with plagues and disasters in approaching God, has protection through the holy service of the Levitical tribe. Here is substitution of a kind which makes a striking point in the symbolism of the Old Testament in its relation to the New. The principle may be seen in patriarchal history. The ten in Sodom, if ten righteous men could have been found, would have saved it, would have been its atonement in a sense, not by their death on its behalf but by their life. And Moses himself, standing alone between God and Israel, prevails by his pleading and saves the nation from its doom. So our Lord says of His disciples, "Ye are the salt of the earth." Their holy devotion preserves the mass from moral corruption and spiritual death. Again, "for the elect's sake," the days of tribulation shall be shortened (Matt. xxiv. 22).

The ceremonies appointed for the cleansing and consecration of the Levites, described in viii. 5-26, may be noticed here. They differ considerably from those enjoined for the consecration of priests. Neither were the Levites anointed with sacred oil, for instance, nor were they sprinkled with the blood of sacrifices; nor, again, do they seem to have worn any special dress, even in the tabernacle court. There was, however, an impressive ritual which would produce in their minds a consciousness of separation and devotion to God. The water of expiation, literally of *sin*, was first to be sprinkled upon them, a baptism not signifying anything like regeneration, but having reference to possible defilements of the flesh. A razor was then to be made to pass over the whole body, and the clothes were to be washed, also to remove actual as well as legal impurity. This cleansing completed, the sacrifices followed. One bullock for a burnt offering, with its accompanying meal offering, and one for a sin offering were provided. The people being assembled towards the door of the tent of meeting, the Levites were placed in front of them to be presented to Jehovah. The princes probably laid their hands on the Levites, so declaring them the representatives of all for their special office. Then Aaron had to offer the sacrifices for the Levites, and the Levites themselves as living sacrifices to Jehovah. The Levites laid their hands on the bullocks, making them their substitutes for the symbolic purpose. Aaron and his sons slew the animals and offered them in the appointed way, burning the one bullock upon the altar, around which its blood had been sprinkled, of the other burning only certain portions called the fat. Then the ceremony of waving was performed, or what was possible in the circumstances, each Levite being passed through the hands of Aaron or one of his sons. So set apart, they were, according to viii. 24, required to wait upon the work of the tent of meeting, each from his twenty-fifth to his fiftieth year. The service had been previously ordered to begin at the thirtieth year (iv. 3). Afterwards the time of ministry was still further extended (1 Chron. xxiii. 24-27).

Such is the account of the symbolic cleansing and the representative ministry of the Levites; and we see both a parallel and a contrast to what is demanded now for the Christian life of obedience and devotion to God. Purification there must be from all defilement of flesh and spirit. With the change which takes place when by repentance and faith in Christ we enter into the free service of God there must be a definite and earnest purging of the whole nature. "As ye presented your members as servants to uncleanness and to iniquity unto iniquity, even so now present your members as servants to righteousness unto sanctification" (Rom. vi. 19). "Mortify therefore your members which are upon the earth; fornication, uncleanness, passion, evil desire, and covetousness, the which is idolatry, . . . put ye also away all these: anger, wrath, malice, railing, shameful speaking out of your mouth: lie not one to another; seeing that ye have put off the old man with his doings, and have put on the new man" (Col. iii. 5, 8, 9). Thus the purity of heart and soul so imperfectly represented by the cleansings of the Levites is set forth as the indispensable preparation of the Christian. And the contrast lies in this, that the purification required by the New Testament law is for all, and is the same for each. Whether one is to serve in the ministry of the Gospel or sweep a room as for God's cause, the same profound purity is needful. All in the Kingdom of God are to be holy, for He is holy.

3. LEVITICAL SERVICE.

NUMBERS iii. 14-39; iv.

The sacred service of the Levites is described in detail. There are three divisions, the Gershonites, the Kohathites, the Merarites. The Gershonites, from a month old and upward, numbered 7,500; the Kohathites, 8,600; the Merarites, 6,200. Eleazar, son of Aaron, is prince of the princes of the Levites.

The office of the Kohathites is of peculiar sanctity, next to that of Aaron and his sons. They are not "cut off" or specially separated from among the Levites (iv. 18); but they have duties that require great care, and they must not venture to approach the most holy things till preparation has been made by the priests. The manner of that preparation is fully described. When order has been given for the setting forward of the camp, Aaron and his sons cover the ark of the covenant first with the veil of the screen, then with a covering of sealskin, and lastly with a cloth of blue; they also insert in the rings the long staves with which the ark is to be carried. Next the table of shewbread is covered with a blue cloth; the dishes, spoons, bowls, and cups are placed on the top, over them a scarlet cloth, and above that a sealskin covering; the staves of the table are also placed in readiness. The candlestick and its lamps and other appurtenances are wrapped up in like manner and put on a frame. Then the golden altar by itself, and the vessels used in the service of the sanctuary by themselves are covered with blue cloth and sealskin and made ready for carriage. Finally, the great altar is cleansed of ashes, covered up with purple cloth and sealskin, and its staves set in their rings. When all this is done the sons of Kohath may advance to bear the holy things, never touching them lest they die.

The question arises, why so great care is considered necessary that none but the priests should handle the furniture of the sanctuary. We have learned to think that a real religion should avoid secrecy, that everything connected with it should be done in the open light of day. Why, then, is the shrine of Jehovah guarded with such elaborate precaution? And the answer is that the idea of mystery appears here as absolutely needful, in order to maintain the solemn feelings of the people and their sense of the holiness of God. Not only because the Israelites were rude and earthly, but also because the whole system was symbolic, the holy things were kept from common sight. In this respect the worship described in these books of Moses resembled that of other nations of antiquity. The Egyptian temple had its innermost shrine where the arks of the gods were placed; and into that most holy place with its silver soil the priests alone went. But even Egyptian worship, with all its mystery, did not always conceal the arks and statues of the gods. When those gods were believed to be favourable, the arks were carried in procession, the images so far unveiled that they could be seen by the people. It was entirely different in the case of the sacred symbols and instruments of Hebrew worship, according to the ideal of the law. And the elaborate precautions are to be regarded as indicating the highest tidemark of symbolised sanctity. Jehovah was not like Egyptian or Assyrian or Phœnician gods. These might be represented by statues which the people could see. But everything used in His worship must be kept apart. The worship must be of faith; and the ark which was the great symbol must remain always invisible. The effect of this on the popular mind was complex, varying with the changing circumstances of the nation; and to trace it would be an interesting piece of study. It may be remembered that in the time of most ardent Judaism the want of the ark made no difference to the veneration in which the temple was held and the intense devotion of the people to their religion. The ark was used as a talisman in Eli's time; in the temple erected after the captivity there was no ark; its place in the holy of holies was occupied by a stone.

The Gershonites had as their charge the screens and curtains of the tabernacle, or most holy place, and the tent of meeting or holy place, also the curtains of the court of the tabernacle. The boards, bars, pillars, and sockets of the tabernacle and of the court were to be entrusted to the Merarites.

In the whole careful ordering of the duties to be discharged by these Levites we see a figure of the service to be rendered to God and men in one aspect of it. Organisation, attention to details, and subordination of those who carry out schemes to the appointed officials, and of all, both inferior and superior, to law—these ideas are here fully represented. Assuming the incapacity of many for spontaneous effort, the principle that God is not a God of confusion but of order in the churches of the saints may be held to point to subordination of a similar kind even under Christianity. But the idea carried to its full limit, implies an inequality between men which the free spirit of Christianity will not admit. It is an honour for men to be connected with any spiritual enterprise, even as bearers of burdens. Those who take such a place may be spiritual men, thoughtful men, as intelligent and earnest as their official superiors. But the Levites, according to the law, were to be bearers of burdens, menials of the sanctuary from generation to generation. Here the parallel absolutely fails. No Christian, however cordially he may fill such a place for a time, is bound to it in perpetuity. His way is open to the highest duties and honours of a redeemed son of God. In a sense Judaism even did not prevent the spiritual advancement of any Levite, or any man. The priesthood was practically closed, but the office of the prophet, really higher than that of the priest, was not. From the routine work of the priesthood men like Jeremiah and Ezekiel were called by the Spirit of God to speak in the name of the Highest. The word of the Lord was put into their mouths. Elijah, who was apparently of the tribe of Manasseh, Amos and Daniel, who belonged to Judah, became prophets. The open door for the men of the tribes was into this calling. Neither in Israel nor in Christendom is priesthood the highest religious function. The great servants of God might well refuse it or throw aside its shackles.

CHAPTER IV.

DEFILEMENT AND PURGATION.

NUMBERS V.

THE separation of Israel as a people belonging to Jehovah proceeded on ideas of holiness which excluded from privilege many of the Hebrews themselves. The law did not ordain that in cases of defilement there might be immediate purification by washing or sacrifice. So far as ceremonial uncleanness was concerned, we may think this might have been provided for, and moral offences alone might have involved the offender in continued defilement. But just as idolatry, blasphemy, and murder caused pollution which could not be removed by sacrifice, but only by the capital punishment of the guilty, so certain bodily conditions and defects, and certain diseases, chiefly leprosy and those akin to it, were held to cause a defilement which could not be purged by any ceremony. A high standard of bodily health and purity was required for the priesthood; a lower standard was to be applied to the people. And the system declaring the uncleanness of many animals, and of the person under various conditions, touched at countless points the life of society. An Israelite who was unclean for one or other of a hundred reasons could not approach the sanctuary. He had his portion in God after a sense; yet for a time, it might be for life, the peculiar blessings of holy fellowship were denied him. He could celebrate no feast. He had no share in the great atonement. The precautions and terms to be observed were of such a nature that if the law had been at any time stringently enforced a very large percentage of the people would have been denied access to the altar.

It may appear a strange thing that the precept, "Ye shall be holy; for I am holy," was affixed not only to moral duties but with almost the same force to ceremonial duties. We can understand this, however, when we trace the result of the priestly ordinances. They created religious care and feeling; and the end was gained not so much by directing attention, as we now do, to faults of conduct, defects of will, sins of injustice, impurity, intemperance, and the like, but by keeping up a scrupulous attention to matters not, properly speaking, either moral or immoral, not ethical as we say, which were yet declared to be of moment in religion. The moral law did its part. But to make the enforcement of moral statutes, many of which bore on desire and will, the only means of urging the fear of God, would have resulted practically in a very bare and desultory cultus. Among a comparatively rude people like the Israelites it would have been absurd to institute a religion consisting of "morality touched by emotion." For the mass of people still it is equally hopeless. There must be ordinances of prayer, praise, sacrament, and the duties which reach Godward through the Church. The value of the whole ceremonial system of the Mosaic law is clear from this point of view; and we need not wonder in the least at the nature of many provisions which, without grasp of the principle, we might reckon irksome and useless. The origin of some of the statutes is apparently hygienic; others again reach back to customs and beliefs of a very primitive world.

But they are made part of the sacred law in order to enforce the conviction that the judgment of God enters into the whole of life, follows men wherever they go, decides as to their state with relation to Him hour by hour, almost moment by moment. The ceremonial law was a constant and strenuous lesson in regard to the omnipresence of God, and the oversight of human affairs by Him. It created a conscience of God's existence, His control, His superintendence of each life. And for a certain stage of the education of Israel this could be achieved in no other way. The moral and spiritual progress of a people, depending on the recognition of the authority of One who is of purer eyes than to behold iniquity, depends also, of necessity, on the sense of His oversight of human life at every point.

1. Exclusion from the Camp.

Numbers v. 1-4.

The rigidness of the law which excluded lepers from the camp and afterwards from the cities had its necessity in the presumed nature of their disease. Leprosy was regarded as contagious, and practically incurable by any medical appliances, requiring to be kept in check by strenuous measures. Care for the general health meant hardship to the lepers; but this could not be avoided. From friends and home they were sent forth to live together as best they might, and spend what remained of life in almost hopeless separation. The authority of Moses is attached to the statute of exclusion, and there can be no doubt of its great antiquity. In Leviticus there are detailed enactments regarding the disease, some of which contemplate its decay and provide for the restoration to privilege of those who had been cured. The ceremonies were complicated, and among them were sacrifices to be offered by way of "atonement." The leper was alienated from God, severed from the congregation as one guilty in the eye of the law (Lev. xiv. 12); and there can be no wonder that with this among other facts before him the writer of the Epistle to the Hebrews speaks of the law as having a mere "shadow of the good things to come."

And yet, in view of the malignant nature of the disease and the peril it caused to the general health, we must admit the wisdom of segregating those afflicted with leprosy. That Israel might be a robust people capable of its destiny, a rule like this was needful. It anticipated our modern laws made in harmony with advanced medical science, which require segregation or isolation in cases of virulent disease.

It has been affirmed that leprosy was from the first regarded as symbolic of moral disease, and that the legislation was from this point of view. There is, however, no evidence to support the theory. Indeed the conception of moral evil would have been confused rather than helped by any such idea. For although evil habits taint the mind and vice ruins it as leprosy taints and destroys the body; although the infectious nature of sin is fitly indicated by the insidious spread of this disease—one point in which there is no resemblance would make the symbol dangerously misleading. A few here and there were attacked by leprosy, and these with their blotched disfigured bodies were easily distinguished from the healthy. But this was in contrast with the secret moral malady by which all were tainted. The teaching that leprosy is a type of sin would make, not for morality, but for hypocrisy. The symptoms of a bad nature, like the signs of leprosy, would be looked for and found by every man in his neighbour, not in his own heart. The hypocrite would be encouraged in his self-satisfaction because he escaped the judgment of his fellow men. But the disease of sin is endemic, universal. The whole congregation was by reason of that excluded from the sanctuary of God.

According to the idea which underlies the priest law, leprosy did not typify sin; it meant sin. In no single place, indeed, is this directly affirmed. Yet the belief connecting bodily afflictions and calamities with transgressions implied it, and the fact that guilt-offerings had to be made for the leper when he was cleansed. Again, in the cases of Miriam, of Gehazi, and of Uzziah, the punishment of sin was leprosy. Under the conditions of climate which often prevailed, the germs of this disease might rapidly be developed by excitement, especially by the excitement of immoral rashness. Here we may find the connection which the law assumes between leprosy and guilt, and the origin of the statute which made the intervention of the priests necessary. In their poor dwellings beyond camp and city wall the lepers lay under a double reproach. They were not only tainted in body but appeared as sinners above others, men on whom some divine judgment had fallen, as the very name of their disease implied. And not till One came who did not fear to lay His hand on the leprous flesh, whose touch brought healing and life, was the pressure of the moral condemnation taken away. Of many cases of leprosy He would have said, as of the blindness He cured: "Neither did this man sin, nor his parents."

Now is the law to be charged with creating a class of social pariahs? Is there any reason for saying that in some way the legislation should have expressed pity rather than the rigour which appears in the passage before us and other enactments regarding leprosy? It would be easy to bring arguments which would seem to prove the law defective here. But in matters of this kind civilisation and Christian culture could not be forestalled. What was possible, what in the conditions that existed could be carried into effect, this only was commanded. These old enactments sprang out of the best wisdom and religion of the age. But they do not represent the whole of the Divine will, the Divine mercy, even as they were contemporaneously revealed. Add to the statutes regarding leprosy the other, "Thou shalt love thy neighbour as thyself," and those that enjoined kindness to the poor and provision for their needs, and the true tenor of the legislation will be understood. According to these laws there were to be no pariahs in Israel. It was a sad necessity if any were excluded from the congregation of God's people. The laws of brotherhood would insure for the wretched colony outside the camp every possible consideration. Denied access to God in festival and sacrifice, the lepers appealed to the humane feelings of the people. With their pathetic cry, "Unclean, unclean!" their loose hair and rent clothes, they confessed a miserable state that touched every heart. As time went on, the law of segregation was interpreted liberally. Even in the synagogues a place was set apart for the lepers. The kindly disposition promoted by the Mosaic institutions was shown thus, and in many other ways.

The lepers banished outside the camp remind us of those who have for no wrong-doing of their own to endure social reproach. Were sometimes good men and women among the Hebrews, men with kind hearts, good mothers and daughters, attacked by this disease and compelled to betake themselves to the squalid tents of the lepers? That decree of rigorous precaution is outdone by the strange fact that under the providence of God, in His world, the best have often had to undergo opprobrium and cruelty; that Jesus Himself was crucified as a malefactor, bore the curse of him that "hangeth upon a tree." We see great suffering which is not due to moral delinquency; and we see the sting of it taken quite away. The stern ordinances of nature have light thrown upon them from a higher world. "Himself took our infirmities and bare our sicknesses." For our sakes He was the object of brutal mockery, the sufferer, the sacrifice.

Besides the lepers and those who had an issue, every one who was unclean by reason of touching a dead body was to be excluded from the camp. This provision appears to rest on the idea that death was no "debt of nature," but unnatural, the result of the curse of God. Associated, however, in the statute before us with leprosy, defilement from the dead may have been decreed to prevent the spread of disease. Many maladies too well known to us have an infectious character; and those who were present at a death would be most exposed to their influence. Pathological explanations do not by any means account for all the kinds and causes of defilement; but exclusion from the camp is the special point here; and the cases may be classed together as having a common origin. The notion that some demon or fallen spirit was at work both in producing leprosy and in causing death, was involved in the customs of some barbarous tribes and entered into the beliefs of the Egyptians and Assyrians. This explanation, however, is too remote and alien from Judaism to be applied to these statutes regarding uncleanness, at least in the form they have in the Mosaic books. The few hints surviving in them, as where a bird was to be allowed to fly away when the leper was pronounced clean, cannot be permitted to fix a charge of superstition on the whole code.

A singular point in the statute regarding uncleanness "by the dead" is that the word נֶפֶשׁ (*nephesh*) stands apparently for the dead body. Of this some other explanation is needed than the free transference of meanings in Hebrew. Here and elsewhere in the Book of Numbers (vi. 11; ix. 6, 7, 10; xix. 13), as well as in various passages in Leviticus, defilement is attributed to the *nephesh*. Commonly the word means *soul* or animal life-principle. When connected with death it corresponds to our word "ghost," as in Job xi. 20; Jer. xv. 9. Now the law was that not only those who touched a dead body, but all present in a house when death took place in it, were unclean. The question occurs whether the *nephesh*, or soul escaping at death, was believed to defile. As if in doubt here a rabbi said, "The body and the soul may plead successfully not guilty by charging their sinful life each upon the other. The body may say: 'Since that guilty soul parted with me, I have been lying in the grave as harmless as a stone.' The soul may plead: 'Since that depraved body separated from me, I flutter about in the air like an innocent bird.'" Is it not possible that the *nephesh* meant the effluvium of the dead body, the active element which, springing from corruption, diffused uncleanness through the whole house of death? It seems quite in harmony with other uses of the word, and with the idea of defilement, to interpret "was unclean by the *nephesh*," "sinned by the *nephesh*," as technical expressions carrying this meaning. The passage Numb. xix. 13 is peculiarly instructive—בְּמֵת בְּנֶפֶשׁ הָאָדָם אֲשֶׁר־יָמוּת בְּכָל־הַנֹּגֵעַ —"Every one coming in contact with the dead, with the *nephesh* of a man who has died." To translate, "with the corpse of a man who has died," would fix on the language the fault of tautology. In Psalm xvii. 9 *nephesh* has the meaning of *deadly*, that is to say *breathing death*; and the idea here points to the meaning suggested.

The reason given for the banishment of the unclean is the presence of God in the congregation—"That they defile not their camp, in the midst whereof I dwell." All that are unhealthy, and those who have been in contact with death, which is the result of irremediable disease or accident, must be withdrawn from the precincts that belong to the Holy God. Human maladies are in contrast with the Divine health, death is in contrast to the Divine life. Here the whole scope of the legislation regarding defilement has its highest range of suggestion. It was a part of moral education to realise that God was separate from all distortion, wasting, and decay. In glad and deathless power He reigned in the midst of Israel. From the living God man received life which had to be kept pure and disciplined. Among the Egyptians it was held to be sacrilege when the operator, in the process preparatory to embalming, opened a human body. He who made the incision was driven out of the room by his assistants with abuse and violence. Quite different is the idea of the Mosaic law which makes the holiness belong entirely to God, and requires of men the preservation of the clean life He has given. Every statute suggests that there is a tendency in the creature to fall away from purity and become unfit for fellowship with the Most Holy.

2. ATONEMENT FOR TRESPASS.

NUMBERS v. 5-10.

The enactment of this passage refers to the sin of theft or any other breach of the eighth commandment which involved trespass not only against man, but also against God—"When a man or woman shall commit any sin that men commit to do a trespass against the Lord, and that soul be guilty; then shall they confess their sin which they have done." The statute supplements one given in Lev. vi. 1-4, omitting some details, but adding the provision that if the person defrauded has died, restitution shall be made to the *goël*, and if there is no surviving relation, to the priest. The cases specified in Leviticus are those of false dealing in regard to a deposit or a bargain, robbery, oppression,—probably in the way of withholding hire from a labourer,—finding what was lost and denying it; but in each instance false swearing is added to the offence and constitutes it a trespass against the Lord. Restitution to man must be made by returning the amount and one-fifth in addition; to God by bringing a ram without blemish, with which the priest makes atonement.

In this statute the punishment does not seem severe. But the penalty is imposed after confession when the offence has been for some time undetected. The ordinary law required for the theft of an ox, if the animal had not been slaughtered, double restitution; and if it had been slaughtered or sold, fivefold restitution. In the case of a sheep slaughtered or sold the restitution was to be fourfold. Confession of the theft, according to the present statute, diminishes the penalty.

Noticeable particularly is the provision for atonement, which is nowhere else admitted in connection with a serious breach of the moral law. Any offence against the first four commandments was to be punished with death; so also were murder, adultery, and certain other crimes. It might have been expected that false swearing by any one in regard to theft or valuables intrusted to him would add to his guilt. Here, however, by means of the ram of atonement even that offence is apparently expiated. Possibly the confession is held to mitigate the crime. Still the nature of the statute is surprising and exceptional.

3. The Water of Jealousy.

Numbers v. 11-31.

The long and remarkable statute regarding the water of jealousy seems to have been interposed to prevent, by means of an ordeal, that cruel practice of peremptory divorce which had been in vogue at some period among the Hebrews. The position given to woman by the old customs must have been exceedingly low. Under polygamy a wife was in constant danger of suspicions and accusations and had no means of removing. The whole scope of this enactment and the means used for deciding between the husband and a suspected wife point to the frequency and general groundlessness of charges made by men in the "hardness of their hearts," or by other women in the hardness of theirs.

The ordeal to which the wife was to be subjected was twofold. One point was the imprecation of the Divine curse upon herself if she had been guilty. This oath was administered in terms and with ceremonies fitted to produce the most profound impression. She is set "before the Lord"—probably in the court of the sanctuary. Her hair is loose. She has the offering of jealousy in her hand—the tenth part of an ephah of barley-meal. The priest holds a basin of the "water of jealousy." The terms of the curse with its frightful consequences are not only repeated in her hearing, but written on a scroll which is dropped into the water. The second thing is her drinking of the "water of jealousy," "holy water" mingled with dust from the floor of the sanctuary, and with the terms of the curse. The nature of the ordeal was such that few guilty persons would have braved it. The only thing which appears wanting is a provision for the punishment of the man whose wife had passed the terrible test. Since the punishment of this crime was death, and he made the accusation without cause, his own judgment should have followed. Here, however, deference had to be paid to the notions of the time, as our Lord clearly indicates. The absolute right, the just equality between husband and wife, could not be established. Nor indeed, with all our progress, is it yet secured.

The ordeal of the water of jealousy must have saved many an innocent life from wreck. In one sense it was part of a system designed to maintain a high standard of morality, and in that system it had a place which at the time could not be filled in any other way. The main stress lies on the oath of purgation; and to the present day in certain ecclesiastical courts this is in use for the purpose of bringing to an end processes not otherwise capable of solution. It must be noted that our marriage laws, lax as they are thought to be, do not give to a husband anything like the power or allow divorce with anything like the facility admitted by the Mosaic law as some of the Rabbis interpreted it. And this ordeal was of such a nature that if those in use throughout Europe only a century ago or thereby, in the trial of witches for instance, be compared with it, we can at once see its superiority. Those barbarous tests, not used by the vulgar alone, but by religious men and Church authorities, made escape from false accusation next to impossible. Here there is absolutely nothing required which could in any sense injure or imperil an innocent woman. She might take her oath, see it written, and drink the water without the least fear or hesitation. The beneficence of the law is strongly marked along with its wisdom. It was a wonderful provision for the time.

CHAPTER V.

NAZARITISM: THE BLESSING OF AARON.

Numbers vi.

1. The custom of Nazaritism, which tended to form a semi-religious caste, is obscure in its origin. The cases of Samson and Samuel imply that before birth some were bound in terms of this vow by their parents. In the passage before us nothing whatever is said as to the reasons which the law recognised for the practice of Nazaritism. We may believe, however, that it was from the first, like many votive customs, distinctly religious. One who had been delivered from some danger or restored to health might adopt this method of showing his thankfulness to God. It is impossible to connect Nazaritism with any sacerdotal duty. A man under the vow had no function, no privilege, that in the least approached that of the priest. Nor can we trace any parallel between the Nazarite rule and that of the fakirs of India or the dervishes of Egypt and Arabia, whose poverty is their mark of consecration. There is, however, some resemblance to the vow of the Arab pilgrim, who, on his way to the holy place, must not cut or dress his hair, and must abstain from bloodshed. The prophet Amos (ii. 11) claims that God had raised up young men to be Nazarites, and he places their influence almost on a

level with that of the prophets as a means of blessing to the people. We may believe, therefore, that they helped both morality and religion; and the conditions of their vow seem to have given them fine bodily health and personal appearance.

When the Nazarite vow was undertaken for a term, say thirty, sixty, or a hundred days, the law assumed its religious character, prescribed the conditions to be observed, the means of removing accidental defilement, and the ceremonies to be performed when the period of separation closed. Any man might devote himself without appealing to the priest or going through any religious rite; and in general his own conscience was depended on to make him rigidly attentive to his vow. There was to be no monastic association of Nazarites, no formal watch kept over their conduct. They mingled with others in ordinary life, and went about their business as at other times. But the unshorn hair distinguished them; they felt that the eye of God as well as the eyes of men were upon them, and walked warily under the sense of their pledge. The discharge which had to be given by the priest was a further check; it would have been withheld if any charge of laxity had been made against the Nazarite. The ceremonies of release were of a kind fitted to attract general attention.

The modern pledge of abstinence bears in various points resemblance to the Nazarite vow. We can easily believe that indulgence in strong drink was one of the principal sins against which Nazaritism testified. And as in ancient Israel that body of abstainers from the fruit of the vine, honourably known as a caste, acknowledged by the Divine law, formed a constant check on intemperance, so the existence of a large class among ourselves, bound to abstinence, aids most effectually in restraining the drinking customs of the present age. When we add to the approval of Nazaritism which is before us here the fact that priests in the discharge of their ministry were required to forego the use of wine, the sanction of Hebrew legislation on its moral side may certainly be claimed for the total abstinence pledge. No doubt the circumstances differ greatly. Wine was the common beverage in Palestine. It was in general so slightly intoxicating that the use of it brought little temptation. But our distilled liquors and fermented drinks are so strongly alcoholic, so dangerous to health and morals, that the argument for abstinence is now immensely greater than it was among the Hebrews. Not only as an example of self-restraint, but as a safeguard against constant peril, the pledge of abstinence deservedly enjoys the sanction of the Churches of Christ.

On the other hand, the pledge of the total abstainer, like the vow of the Nazarite, carries with it a certain moral danger. One who, having come voluntarily under such a pledge, allows himself to break it, suffers a serious loss of spiritual power. The abstainer, like the Nazarite, is his own witness, his own judge. But if his pledge has been sacredly undertaken, solemnly made, any breach of it is an offence to conscience, a denial of obligation to God which must react on the will and life. It was not by using strong drink that Samson broke his vow of Nazaritism, but in a far less serious manner— by allowing his hair to be cut off. Still his case is an instructive parable. The Spirit of the Lord passed from him; he became weak as other men, the prey of his enemies. The man who has come under the bond of total abstinence, especially in a religious way, and breaks it, becomes weaker than others. To confess his fault and resume his resolution may not lift him up again. The will is less capable, the sense of sacredness less imperative and potent.

It is hard to say why the peculiar defilement caused by touching a dead body or being present at a death is that alone on which special attention is fixed in the Nazarite law (vi. 9 ff.). One would have expected the other offence of using wine to be dealt with rather than mere accidents, so to speak. We can see that the law as it stands is one of many that must have preceded the prophetic period. If Amos, for example, had influenced the nature of the legislation regarding Nazaritism, it would have been in the direction of making drunkenness rather than ceremonial uncleanness a special point in the statutes. From beginning to end of his prophecy he makes no distinct reference to ceremonial defilement. But injustice, intemperance, disaffection to Jehovah, are constantly and vehemently denounced. Hosea, again, does refer to unclean food, the necessity of eating which would be part of Israel's punishment in exile. But he too, unless in this casual reference, is a moralist—cares nothing, so far as his language goes, for the contact with dead bodies or any other ceremonial defilement. Judging a Nazarite, he would certainly have regarded sobriety and purity of life as the tests of consecration—drunkenness and neglect of God as the sins that deserved punishment. Hosea's condemnation of Israel is: " They have left off to take heed to Jehovah. Whoredom and wine and new wine take away the understanding." In Ezekiel, whose schemes of worship and of priestly work are declared to have been the origin of the Priests' Code, the same tendency is to be found. He has a passage regarding unclean foods, which assumes the existence of statutes on the subject. But as a legislator he is not concerned with ceremonial transgressions, the defilement caused by dead bodies, and the like. Take into account the whole of his prophecy, and it will be seen that the new heart and the right spirit are for Ezekiel the main things, and the worship of the temple he describes is to be that of a people not ceremonially consecrated, but spiritually pure, and so in moral unity with God. He adopts the old forms of worship along with the priesthood, but his desire is to give the ritual an ethical basis and aim.

The statute which applies to the discharge of the Nazarite from his rule (vi. 13-21) is exceedingly detailed, and contains provisions which on the whole seem fitted to deter rather than encourage the vow. The Nazarite could not escape from obligation as he had entered upon it, without priestly intervention and mediation. He had to offer an oblation,—one he-lamb of the first year for a burnt offering; one ewe-lamb of the first year for a sin offering; and for peace offerings a ram, with a basket of unleavened bread, cakes of fine flour mingled with oil, unleavened wafers anointed with oil; and meal offerings and drink offerings. These had to be presented by the priest in the prescribed manner. In addition to the possible cost of repeated cleansings which might be needful during the period of separation, the expense of those offerings must have been to many in a humble station almost prohibitory. We cannot help concluding that under this law, at whatever time it prevailed, Nazaritism became the privilege of the more wealthy. Those who took the vow under the appointed conditions must have formed a kind of puritan aristocracy.

The final ceremonies included burning of the hair, which was carefully removed at the door of the tent of meeting. It was to be consumed in the fire under the peace offering, the idea being that the obligation of the vow and perhaps its sanctity had been identified with the flowing locks. The last rite of all was similar to that used in the consecration of priests. The sodden shoulder of the ram, an unleavened cake, and an unleavened wafer were to be placed on the hands of the Nazarite, and waved for a wave offering before the Lord—thereafter, with other parts of the sacrifice, falling to the priest. After that the man might drink wine, perhaps in a formal way at the close of the ceremonies.

To explain this elaborate ritual of discharge it has been affirmed that the idea of the vow "culminated in the sacrificial festival which terminated the consecration, and in this attained to its fullest manifestation." If this were so, ritualism was indeed predominant. To make such the underlying thought is to declare that the abstinence of the Nazarite from strong drink and dainties, to which a moralist would attach most importance, was in the eye of the law nothing compared to the symbolic feasting with God and the sacerdotal functions of the final ceremony. Far more readily would we assume that the ritual of the discharge was superfluously added to the ancient law at a time when the hierarchy was in the zenith of its power. But, as we have already seen, the final rites were of a kind fitted to direct public attention to the vow, and may have had their use chiefly in preventing any careless profession of Nazaritism, tending to bring it into contempt.

One other question still demands consideration: What was meant by the "sin offering" which had to be presented by the Nazarite when he had unintentionally incurred uncleanness, and the sin offering which had to be offered at the time of his discharge—what, in short, was the idea of sin to which this oblation corresponded? The case of the Nazarite is peculiarly instructive, for the point to be considered is seen here entirely free from complications. The Nazarite does not undertake the obligation of his vow as an acknowledgment of wrong he has done, nor does he place himself under any moral disadvantage by assuming it. There is no reason why in becoming a Nazarite or ceasing to be a Nazarite he should appear as a transgressor; rather is he honouring God by what he does. Suppose he has been present at a death which has unexpectedly taken place—that involves no moral fault by which a man's conscience should be burdened. Deliberately to touch a dead body might, under the law, have brought the sense of wrongdoing; but to be casually in a defiled house could not. Yet an atonement was necessary (vi. 11). It is expressly said that a sin offering and a burnt offering must be presented to "make atonement for him, for that he sinned by reason of the dead." And again, when he has kept the terms of his vow to the last, honouring Jehovah by his devotion, commending morality by his abstinence, maintaining more rigidly than other Israelites the idea of consecration to Jehovah, he cannot be released from his obligation till a sin offering is made for him. There is no moral offence to be expiated. Rather, to judge in an ordinary human way, he has carried obedience farther than his fellow-Israelites.

The whole circumstances show that the sin-offering has no reference to moral pollution. The idea is not that of removing a shadow from the conscience, but taking away a taint of the flesh, or, in certain cases, of the mind which has become aware of some occult injury. A clear division was made between the moral and the immoral; and it was assumed that all Israelites were keeping the moral commandments of the law. Then moral persons were divided into those who were clean and those who were unclean; and the ceremonial law alone determined the conditions of undefiled and acceptable life. If the law declared that a sin offering was necessary, it meant not that there had been immorality, but that some specified or unspecified taint lay upon a man. No doubt there were principles according to which the law was framed. But they might not be apparent; and no man could claim to have them explained. Now with regard to Nazaritism, the idea was that of a vivid and pure form of life to which a man might attain if he would discipline himself. And it seems to have been understood that in returning from this to the common life of the race an apology, so to speak, had to be made to Jehovah and to religion. The higher range of life during the term of separation was peculiarly sensitive to invasions of earthly circumstance, and especially of the defilement caused by death; and for anything of this sort there was needed more than apology, more than trespass offering. The Nazarite going back to ordinary life was regarded in more senses than one as a sinner. The conditions of his vow had been difficult to keep, and, presumably, had been broken. He was all the more under the suspicion of defilement that he had undertaken special obligations of purity. A peculiar form of mysticism is involved here, an effort of humanity to reach transcendental holiness. And the law seemed to give up each experiment with a sigh. In the story of Samson we have only the popular pictorial elements of Nazaritism. The statutes convey hints of deeper thought and feeling.

Generally speaking the whole system of purification enjoined by the ceremonial law, the constant succession of cleansings and sacrifices, must have appeared to be arbitrary. But it would be a mistake to suppose that there was no esoteric meaning, no purpose beyond that of keeping up the sense of religious duty and the need of mediation. Some intangible defilement seems to have been associated with everything mundane, everything human. The aim was to represent sanctity of a transcendent kind, the nature of which no words could express, for which the shedding of blood alone supplied a sufficiently impressive symbol.

2. The blessing which the priests were commissioned to pronounce on the people (vi. 24-26) was in the following terms:

"Jehovah bless thee, and keep thee:
Jehovah make His face to shine upon thee, and be gracious unto thee:
Jehovah lift up His countenance upon thee, and give thee peace."

By means of this threefold benediction the name of Jehovah was to be put upon the children of

Israel—that is to say, their consecration to Him as His accepted flock and their enjoyment of His covenant grace were to be signified. In a sense the invocation of this blessing was the highest function of the priest: he became the channel of spiritual endowment in which the whole nation shared.

It is a striking fact that the distinctive ideas conveyed in the three portions of the blessing—Preservation, Enlightenment, Peace—bear a relation, by no means fanciful, to the work of the Father, the Son, and the Holy Spirit. First are invoked the providential care and favour of God, as Ruler of the universe, Arbiter among the nations, Source of creaturely life, Upholder of human existence. Israel as a whole, and each individual Israelite as a member of the sacred community, should in terms of the covenant enjoy the guardianship of the Almighty. The idea is expanded in Psalm cxxi.:

"Jehovah is thy keeper:
Jehovah is thy shade upon thy right hand.
The sun shall not smite thee by day,
Nor the moon by night.
Jehovah shall keep thee from all evil;
He shall keep thy soul.
Jehovah shall keep thy going out and thy coming in,
From this time forth and for evermore."

And in almost every Psalm the theme of Divine preservation is touched on either in thanksgiving, prayer, or exultant hope.

"For God will save Zion, and build the cities of Judah;
And they shall abide there, and have it in possession.
The seed also of His servants shall inherit it;
And they that love His name shall dwell therein."

Often sorely pressed by the nations around, their land made the battle-field of empires, the Hebrews could comfort themselves with the assurance that Jehovah of Hosts was with them, that the God of Jacob was their refuge. And each son of Abraham had his own portion in the blessing.

"I will say of Jehovah, He is my refuge and my fortress,
My God in whom I trust."

The keynote of joyful confidence in the unseen King was struck in the benediction which, pronounced by Aaron and by the high-priests after him, associated Israel's safety with obedience to all the laws and forms of religion.

The second member of the blessing indicates under the figure of the shining of Jehovah's face the revelation of enlightening truth. Here are implied the unfolding of God's character, the kindly disclosure of His will in promise and prophecy, the opening to the minds of men of those high and abiding laws that govern their destiny. There is a forth-shining of the Divine countenance which troubles and dismays the human heart: "The face of the Lord is against them that do evil." But here is denoted that gracious radiance which came to its fulness in Christ. And of this Divine shining Jacob Boehme writes: "As the sun in the visible world ruleth over evil and good, and with its light and power and all whatsoever itself is, is present everywhere, and penetrates every being, and yet in its image-like [symbolic] form doth not withdraw again to itself with its efflux, but wholly giveth itself into every being, and yet ever remaineth whole, and nothing of its being goeth away therewith: thus also it is to be understood concerning Christ's power and office which ruleth in the inward spiritual world visibly, and in the outward world invisibly, and thoroughly penetrateth the faithful man's soul, spirit, and heart. . . And as the sun worketh through and through an herb so that the herb becometh solar (or filled with the virtue of the sun, and as it were so converted by the sun that it becometh wholly of the nature of the sun): so Christ ruleth in the resigned will in soul and body over all evil inclinations, over Satan's introduced lust, and generateth the man to be a new heavenly creature and wholly floweth into him." *

For the Hebrew people that shining of the face of God became spiritual and potent for salvation less through the law, the priesthood, and the ritual, than through psalm and prophecy. Of the revelation of the law Paul says, "The ministration of death written and engraven on stones came with glory, so that the children of Israel could not look steadfastly upon the face of Moses, for the glory of his face." With such holy and awful brightness did God appear in the law, that Moses had to cover his face from which the splendour was reflected. But the psalmist, pressing towards the light with fine spiritual boldness and humility, could say, "When Thou saidst, Seek ye My face; my heart said unto Thee, Thy face, Lord, will I seek" (Psalm xxvii. 8); and again, "Turn us again, O God of hosts, and cause Thy face to shine; and we shall be saved" (Psalm lxxx. 7). And in an oracle of Isaiah (liv. 8), Jehovah says, "In overflowing wrath I hid My face from thee for a moment; but with everlasting kindness shall I have mercy on thee."

In the third clause of the benediction the peace of God, that calm of mind, conscience, and life which accompanies salvation, is invoked. From the trouble and sorrow and tumult of existence, from the fear of hostile power, from evil influences seen and unseen, the Divine hand will give salvation. It seems indeed to be the meaning that the gracious regard of God is enough. Are His people in affliction and anxiety? Jehovah's look will deliver them. They will feel calmly safe as if a shield were interposed between them and the keen arrows of jealousy and hatred. "In covert of Thy presence shalt Thou hide them from the plottings of man: Thou shalt keep them secretly in a pavilion from the strife of tongues." Their tranquillity is described by Isaiah: "In righteousness shalt thou be established: thou shalt be far from oppression, for thou shalt not fear; and from terror, for it shall not come near thee . . . no weapon that is formed against thee shall prosper; and every tongue that shall rise against thee in judgment thou shalt condemn. This is the heritage of the servants of the Lord, and their righteousness which is of Me, saith the Lord."

The peace of the human soul is not, however, entirely provided for by the assurance of Divine protection from hostile force. A man is not in perfect tranquillity because he belongs to a nation or a church defended by omnipotence. His own troubles and fears are the main causes of unrest. And the Spirit of God, who cleanses and renews the soul, is the true Peace-giver. "To win true peace a man needs to feel himself directed, pardoned, and sustained by a supreme power, to feel himself in the right road, at the point where God would have him to be—in order with God and the universe." In his heart the note of harmony must be struck deep and true, in profound

* "Concerning the Holy Baptism," chap. i.

reconciliation and unity with God. With this in view the oracles of Ezekiel connect renewal and peace. "I will put My Spirit in you, and ye shall live . . . I will make a covenant of peace with them; it shall be an everlasting covenant with them . . . and I will set My sanctuary in the midst of them for evermore."

The protection of God the Father, the grace and truth of the Son, the comfort and peace of the Spirit—were these, then, implied in Israel's religion and included in this blessing of Aaron? Germinally, at least, they were. The strain of unity running through the Old and New Testaments is heard here and in the innumerable passages that may be grouped along with the threefold benediction. The work of Christ, as Revealer and Saviour, did not begin when He appeared in the flesh. As the Divine Word He spoke by every prophet and through the priest to the silent congregations age after age. Nor did the dispensation of the Spirit arise on the world like a new light on that day of Pentecost when the disciples of Christ were gathered in their upper chamber and the tongues of fire were seen. There were those even in the old Hebrew days on whom the Spirit was poured from on high, with whom "judgment dwelt in the wilderness, and righteousness in the fruitful field: and the work of righteousness was peace, and the effect of righteousness quietness and assurance for ever." He who is our peace came in the appointed time to fill with eternal meaning the old benedictions, and set our assurance on the immovable rock of His own sacrifice and power.

CHAPTER VI.

SANCTUARY AND PASSOVER.

I. THE OFFERINGS OF THE PRINCES.

NUMBERS vii.

THE opening verses of the chapter seem to imply that immediately after the erection of the tabernacle the gifts of the princes were brought by way of thank offering. The note of time, "on the day that Moses had made an end of setting up the tabernacle," appears very precise. It has been made a difficulty that, according to the narrative of Exodus, a considerable time had elapsed since the work was finished. But this account of the oblations of the princes, like a good many other ancient records incorporated in the present book, has a place given it from the desire to include everything that seemed to belong to the time of the wilderness. All incidents could not be arranged in consecutive order, because, let us suppose, the Book of Exodus to which this and others properly belonged was already complete. Numbers is the more fragmentary book. The expression, "on the day," must apparently be taken in a general sense as in Gen. ii. 4: "These are the generations of the heavens and of the earth in the day that the Lord God made earth and heaven." In Numb. ix. 15 the same note of time, "on the day that the tabernacle was reared up," marks the beginning of another reminiscence or tradition. The setting up of the tabernacle and consecration of the altar gave occasion presumably for this manifestation of generosity. But the offerings described could not be provided immediately; they must have taken time to prepare. Golden spoons of ten shekels' weight were not to be found ready-made in the camp; nor were the oil and fine flour to be had at a day's notice. Of course the gifts might have been prepared in anticipation.

The account of the bringing of the offerings by the princes on twelve successive days, one Sabbath at least included, gives the impression of a festival display. The narrator dwells with some pride on the exhibition of religious zeal and liberality, a fine example set to the people by men in high position. The gifts had not been asked by Moses; they were purely voluntary. Considering the value of precious metals at the time, and the poverty of the Israelites, they were handsome, though not extravagant. It is estimated that the gold and silver of each prince would equal in value about seven hundred and thirty of our shillings, and so the whole amount contributed, without regarding the changed value of the metals, would be equivalent to some four hundred and thirty-eight pounds sterling. In addition there were the fine flour and oil, and the bullocks, rams, lambs, and kids for sacrifice.

It is an obvious remark here that spontaneous liberality has in the very form of the narrative the very highest commendation. Nothing could be more fitted to create in the minds of the people respect for the sanctuary and the worship associated with it than this hearty dedication of their wealth by the heads of the tribes. As the people saw the slow processions moving day by day from the different parts of the camp, and joined in raising their hallelujahs of joy and praise, a spirit of generous devotion would be kindled in many hearts. It appears a singular agreement that each prince of a tribe gave precisely the same as his neighbour. But by this arrangement one was not put to shame by the greater liberality of another. Often, as we know, there is in giving, quite as much of human rivalry as of holy generosity. One must not be outdone by his neighbour, would rather surpass his neighbour. Here all appears to be done in the brotherly spirit.

Does the author of Numbers present an ideal for us to keep in view in our dedication of riches to the service of the Gospel? It was in full accord with the symbolic nature of Hebrew religion that believers should enrich the tabernacle and give its services an air of splendour. Almost the only way for the Israelites to honour God in harmony with their separation from others as His people, was that of making glorious the house in which He set His name, the whole arrangements for sacrifice and festival and priestly ministration. In the temple of Solomon that idea culminated which on this occasion fixed the value and use of the princes' gifts. But under Christianity the service of God is the service of mankind. When the thought and labour of the disciples of Christ are devoted to the needs of men there is a tribute to the glory of God. "It has been said—it is true—that a better and more honourable offering is made to our Master in ministry to the poor, in extending the knowledge of His name, in the practice of the virtues by which that name is hallowed, than in material gifts to His temple. Assuredly it is so: woe to all who think that any other kind or manner of offering may in any way take the place of these."* The decoration of the

* Ruskin, "Seven Lamps of Architecture."

house used for worship, its stateliness and charm, are secondary to the upbuilding of that temple of which believing men and women are the eternal stones, for basement, pillar, and wall. In the development of Judaism the temple with its costly sacrifices and ministries swallowed up the means and enthusiasm of the people. Israel recognised no duty to the outside world. Even its prophets, because they were not identified with the temple worship, were in the main neglected and left to penury. It is a mistaken use of the teaching of the Old Testament to take across its love of splendour in sanctuary and worship, while the spread of Christian truth abroad and among the poor is scantily provided for.

But the liberality of the leaders of the tribes, and of all who in the times of the old covenant gave freely to the support of religion, stands before us to-day as a noble example. In greater gratitude for a purer faith, a larger hope, we should be more generous. Devoting ourselves first as living sacrifices, holy and acceptable to God, we should count it an honour to give in proportion to our ability. One after another, every prince, every father of a family, every servant of the Lord, to the poorest widow, should bring a becoming gift.

The chapter closes with a verse apparently quite detached from the narrative as well as from what follows, which, however, has a singular importance as embodying the law of the oracle. "And when Moses went into the tent of meeting to speak with Him, then he heard the Voice speaking unto him from above the mercy-seat that was upon the ark of the testimony, from between the two cherubim: and he spake unto Him." At first this may seem exceedingly anthropomorphic. It is a human voice that is heard by Moses speaking in response to his inquiries. One is there, in the darkness behind the veil, who converses with the prophet as friend communicates with friend. Yet, on reflection, it will be felt that the statement is marked by a grave idealism and has an air of mystery befitting the circumstances. There is no form or visible manifestation, no angel or being in human likeness, representing God. It is only a Voice that is heard. And that Voice, as proceeding from above the mercy-seat which covered the law, is a revelation of what is in harmony with the righteousness and truth, as well as the compassion, of the Unseen God. The separateness of Jehovah is very strikingly suggested. Here only, in this tent of meeting, apart from the common life of humanity, can the one prophet-mediator receive the sacred oracles. And the veil still separates even Moses from the mystic Voice. Yet God is so akin to men that He can use their words, make His message intelligible through Moses to those who are not holy enough to hear for themselves, but are capable of responding in obedient faith.

Whatever is elsewhere said in regard to the Divine communications that were given through Moses must be interpreted by this general statement. The revelations to Israel came in the silence and mystery of this place of audience, when the leader of the people had withdrawn from the bustle and strain of his common tasks. He must be in the exalted mood this highest of all offices requires. With patient, earnest soul he must wait for the Word of God. There is nothing sudden, no violent flash of light on the ecstatic mind. All is calm and grave.

2. The Candelabrum.

Numbers viii. 1-4.

The seven-branched candlestick with its lamps stood in the outer chamber of the tabernacle into which the priests had frequently to go. When the curtain at the entrance of the tent was drawn aside during the day there was abundance of light in the Holy Place, and then the lamps were not required. It may indeed appear from Exod. xxvii. 20, that one lamp of the seven fixed on the candelabrum was to be kept burning by day as well as by night. Doubt, however, is thrown on this by the command, repeated in Lev. xxiv. 1-4, that Aaron shall order it "from evening to morning;" and Rabbi Kimchi's statement that the "western lamp" was always found burning cannot be accepted as conclusive. In the wilderness, at all events, no lamp could be kept always alight; and from 1 Sam. iii. 3 we learn that the Divine voice was heard by the child-prophet when Eli was laid down in his place, "and the lamp of God was not yet gone out" in the temple where the ark of God was. The candelabrum therefore seems to have been designed not specially as a symbol, but for use. And here direction is given, "When thou lightest the lamps, the seven lamps shall give light in front of the candlestick." All were to be so placed upon the supports that they might shine across the Holy Place, and illuminate the altar of incense and the table of shewbread.

The text goes on to state that the candlestick was all of beaten work of gold; "unto the base thereof and unto the flowers thereof, it was beaten work," and the pattern was that which Jehovah had showed Moses. The material, the workmanship, and the form, not particularly important in themselves, are anew referred to because of the special sacredness belonging to all the furniture of the tabernacle.

The attempt to fasten typical meanings to the seven lights of the candelabrum, to the ornaments and position, and especially to project those meanings into the Christian Church, has little warrant even from the Book of Revelation, where Christ speaks as "He that walketh in the midst of the seven golden candlesticks." There can be no doubt, however, that symbolic references may be found, illustrating in various ways the subjects of revelation and the Christian life.

The "tent of meeting" may represent to us that chamber or temple of reverent inquiry where the voice of the Eternal is heard, and His glory and holiness are realised by the seeker after God. It is a chamber silent, solemn, and dark, curtained in such gloom, indeed, that some have maintained there is no revelation to be had, no glimpse of Divine life or love. But as the morning sunshine flowed into the Holy Place when the hangings were drawn aside, so from the natural world light may enter the chamber in which fellowship with God is sought. "The invisible things of Him since the creation of the world are clearly seen, being perceived through the things that are made, even His everlasting power and divinity." The world is not God, its forces are not in the true sense elemental—do not belong to the being of the Supreme. But it bears witness to the infinite mind, the omnipotent will it cannot fitly represent. In the silence of the tent of meeting, when the light of nature shines through the door that opens to the sunrise, we realise that the inner mystery must be in profound accord with the outer revelation—that He who makes the light of the natural world must be in Himself the light of the spiritual world; that He who maintains order in the great movements and cycles of the material universe, maintains a like order in the changes and evolutions of the immaterial creation.

Yet the light of the natural world shining thus into the sacred chamber, while it aids the seeker after God in no small degree, fails at a certain point. It is too hard and glaring for the hour of most intimate communion. By night, as it were, when the world is veiled and silent, when the soul is shut alone in earnest desire and thought, then it is that the highest possibilities of intercourse with the unseen life are realised. And then, as the seven-branched candlestick with its lamps illuminated the Holy Place, a radiance which belongs to the sanctuary of life must supply the soul's need. On the curtained walls, on the altar, on the veil whose heavy folds guard the most holy mysteries, this light must shine. Nature does not reveal the life of the Ever-Living, the love of the All-Loving, the will of the All-Holy. In the conscious life and love of the soul, created anew after the plan and likeness of God in Christ,—here is the light. The unseen God is the Father of our spirits. The lamps of purified reason, Christ-born faith and love, holy aspiration, are those which dispel the darkness on our side the veil. The Word and the Spirit give the oil by which those lamps are fed.

Must we say that with the Father, Christ also, who once lived on earth, is in the inner chamber which our gaze cannot penetrate? Even so. A thick curtain is interposed between the earthly and the heavenly. Yet while by the light which shines in his own soul the seeker after God regards the outer chamber—its altar, its shewbread, its walls, and canopy—his thought passes beyond the veil. The altar is fashioned according to a pattern and used according to a law which God has given. It points to prayer, thanksgiving, devotion, that have their place in human life because facts exist out of which they arise—the beneficence, the care, the claims of God. The table of shewbread represents the spiritual provision made for the soul which cannot live but by every word that cometh out of the mouth of God. The continuity of the outer chamber with the inner suggests the close union there is between the living soul and the living God—and the veil itself, though it separates, is no jealous and impenetrable wall of division. Every sound on this side can be heard within; and the Voice from the mercy seat, declaring the will of the Father through the enthroned Word, easily reaches the waiting worshipper to guide, comfort, and instruct. By the light of the lamps kindled in our spiritual nature the things of God are seen; and the lamps themselves are witnesses to God. They burn and shine by laws He has ordained, in virtue of powers that are not fortuitous nor of the earth. The illumination they give on this side the veil proves clearly that within it the Parent Light, glorious, never-fading, shines—transcendent reason, pure and almighty will, unchanging love—the life which animates the universe.

Again, the symbolism of the candlestick has an application suggested by Rev. i. 20. Now, the outer chamber of the tabernacle in which the lamps shine represents the whole world of human life. The temple is vast; it is the temple of the universe. Still the veil exists; it separates the life of men on earth from the life in heaven, with God. Isaiah in his oracles of redemption spoke of a coming revolution which should open the world to Divine light. " He will destroy in this mountain the face of the covering that is cast over all people, and the veil that is spread over all nations." And the light itself, still as proceeding from a Hebrew centre, is described in the second book of the Isaian prophecies: " For Zion's sake will I not hold my peace, and for Jerusalem's sake I will not rest, until her righteousness go forth as brightness and her salvation as a lamp that burneth. And the nations shall see thy righteousness and all kings thy glory." But the prediction was not fulfilled until the Hebrew merged in the human and He came who, as the Son of Man, is the true light which lighteth every man coming into the world.

Dark was the outer chamber of the great temple when the Light of life first shone, and the darkness comprehended it not. When the Church was organised, and the apostles of our Lord, bearing the gospel of Divine grace, went through the lands, they addressed a world still under the veil of which Isaiah spoke. But the spiritual enlightenment of mankind proceeded; the lamps of the candlestick, set in their places, showed the new altar, the new table of heavenly bread, a feast spread for all nations, and made the ignorant and earthly aware that they stood within a temple consecrated by the offering of Christ. St. John saw in Asia, amid the gross darkness of its seven great cities, seven lamp-stands with their lights, some increasing, some waning in brightness. The sacred flame was carried from country to country, and in every centre of population a lamp was kindled. There was no seven-branched candelabrum merely, but one of a hundred, of a thousand arms. And all drew their oil from the one sacred source, cast more or less bravely the same Divine illumination on the dark eye of earth.

True, the world had its philosophy and poetry, using, often with no little power, the themes of natural religion. In the outer chamber of the temple the light of nature gleamed on the altar, on the shewbread, on the veil. But interpretation failed, faith in the unseen was mixed with dreams, no real knowledge was gained of what the folds of the curtain hid—the mercy-seat, the holy law that called for pure worship and love of one Living and True God. And then the darkness that fell when the Saviour hung on the cross, the darkness of universal sin and condemnation, was made so deeply felt that in the shadow of it the true light might be seen, and the lamp of every church might glow, a beacon of Divine mercy shining across the troubled life of man. And the world has responded, will respond, with greater comprehension and joy, as the Gospel is proclaimed with finer spirit, embodied with greater zeal in lives of faith and love. Christ in the truth, Christ in the sacraments, Christ in the words and deeds of those who compose His Church—this is the light. The candlestick of every life, of every body of believers, should be as of beaten gold, no base metal mixed with that which is precious. He who fashions his character as a Christian is to have the Divine idea before him and re-think it; those who build the Church are to seek its purity, strength, and grace. But still the light must come from God, not from man, the light that burned on the altar of the Divine sacrifice and shines from the glorious personality of the risen Lord.

3. THE PASSOVER.

NUMBERS ix. 1-14.*

The day fixed by statute for the feast which commemorated the deliverance from Egypt was the fourteenth of the first month—the year beginning with the month of the exodus. Chap. ix. opens by reiterating this statute, already recorded in Exod. xii. and Lev. xxiii., and proceeds to narrate the observance of the Passover in the second year. A supplementary provision follows which met the case of those excluded from the feast through ceremonial uncleanness. In one passage it is assumed that the statutes and ordinances of the celebration are already known. The feast proper, ordered to be kept between the two evenings of the fourteenth day, is, however, alone spoken of; there is no mention of the week of unleavened bread (Exod. xii. 15; Lev. xxiii. 6), nor of the holy convocations with which that week was to open and close. It is almost impossible to avoid the conclusion that the Passover in the wilderness was a simple family festival at which every head of a household officiated in a priestly capacity. The supplementary Passover of this chapter was, according to the rabbis, distinguished from the great feast by the rites lasting only one day instead of seven, and by other variations. There is, however, no trace of such a difference between the one observance and the other. What was done by the congregation on the fourteenth of Abib was apparently to be done at the "Little Passover" of the following month.

On every male Israelite old enough to understand the meaning of the Passover, the observance of it was imperative. Lest the supplementary feast should be made an excuse for failure to keep the fourteenth day of the first month, it is enacted (ix. 13) that he who wilfully neglects shall be "cut off from his people." For strangers who sojourn among the Israelites provision is made that if they wish to keep the feast they may do so under the regulations applied to the Hebrews; these, of course, including the indispensable rite of circumcision, which had to precede any observance of a feast in honour of God. Noticeable are the terms with which this statute concludes: "Ye shall have one statute, both for the stranger and for him that is born in the land." The settlement in Canaan is assumed.

Regarding the Passover in the wilderness, difficulties have been raised on the ground that a sufficient number of lambs, males of the first year, could scarcely have been provided, and that the sacrificing of the lambs by Aaron and his two sons within the prescribed time would have been impossible. The second point of difficulty disappears if this Passover was, as we have seen reason to believe, a family festival like that observed on the occasion of the exodus. Again, the number of yearling male lambs required would depend on the number who partook of the feast. Calculations made on the basis that one lamb sufficed for about fifteen, and that men alone ate the Passover, leave the matter in apparent doubt. Some fifty thousand lambs would still be needed. Keeping by the enumeration of the Israelites given in the muster-roll of Numbers, some writers explain that the desert tribes might supply large numbers of lambs, and that kids also were available. The difficulty, however, remains, and it is one of those which point to the conclusion that the numbers given have somehow been increased in the transcription of the ancient records century after century.

The case of certain men who could not partake of the Passover in the first month, because they were unclean through the dead, was brought before Moses and Aaron. The men felt it to be a great loss of privilege, especially as the march was about to begin, and they might not have another opportunity of observing the feast. Who indeed could tell whether in the first conflict it might not be his lot to fall by the sword? "We are unclean by the *nephesh* of a man," they said: "wherefore are we kept back, that we may not offer the oblation of the Lord in its appointed season among the children of Israel?" The result of the appeal was the new law providing that two disabilities, and two only, should be acknowledged. The supplementary Passover of the second month was appointed for those unclean by the dead, and those on a journey who found themselves too far off to reach in time the precincts of the sanctuary. Those unclean would be in a month presumably free from defilement; those on a journey would probably have returned. The concession is a note of the gracious reasonableness that in many ways distinguished the Hebrew religion; and the Passover observances of Jews at the present day are based on the conviction that what is practicable is accepted by God, though statute and form cannot be kept.

The question presents itself, why keeping of the Passover should be necessary to covenant union with Jehovah. And the reply bears on Christian duty with regard to the analogous sacrament of the Lord's Supper, for it rests on the historical sanction and continuity of faith. If God was to be trusted as a Saviour by the Hebrew, certain facts in the nation's history had to be known, believed, and kept in clear remembrance; otherwise no reality could be found in the covenant. And under the new covenant the same holds good. The historical fact of Christ's crucifixion must be kept in view, and constantly revived by the Lord's Supper. In either case redemption is the main idea presented by the commemorative ordinance. The Hebrew festival is not to be held on the anniversary of the giving of the law; it recalls the great deliverance connected with the death of the first-born in Egypt. So the Christian festival points to the deliverance of humanity through the death of Christ.

Remarkable is the congruity between the view of the law presented by Paul and the fact that the great commemorative feast of Hebraism is attached, not to the legislation of Sinai, but to the rescue from Egyptian bondage. The law kept the Hebrew nation in ward (Gal. iii. 23); "it was added because of transgressions, till the seed should come to whom the promise had been made" (Gal. iii. 19); it "came in beside, that the trespass might abound" (Rom. v. 20). The He-

---

* For chap. viii. 5-26 see p. 392.

brews were not required to commemorate that ordinance which laid on them a heavy burden and was found, as time went on, to be "unto death" (Rom. vii. 10). And, in like manner, the feast of Christianity does not recall the nativity of our Lord, nor that agony in the garden which showed Him in the depths of human sorrow, but that triumphant act of His soul which carried Him, and humanity with Him, through the shadow of death into the free life of spiritual energy and peace. The Sacrament of the Lord's Supper is the commemoration of a victory by which we are enfranchised. Partaking of it in faith, we realise our rescue from the Egypt of slavery and fear, our unity with Christ and with one another as "an elect race, a royal priesthood, a holy nation, a people for God's own possession." The wilderness journey lies before us still; but in liberty we press on as the ransomed of the Lord.

Mr. Morley has said, not without reason, that "the modern argument in favour of the supernatural origin of the Christian religion, drawn from its suitableness to our needs and its Divine response to our aspirations," is insufficient to prove it the absolute religion. "The argument," he says, "can never carry us beyond the relativity of religious truth."* Christians may not assume that "their aspirations are the absolute measure of those of humanity in every stage." To dispense with faith in the historical facts of the life of Christ, His claims, and the significance of His cross, to leave these in the haze of the past as doubtful, incapable of satisfactory proof, and to rest all on the subjective experience which any one may reckon sufficient, is to obliterate the covenant and destroy the unity of the Church. Hence, as the Hebrews had their Passover, and the observance of it gave them coherence as a people and as a religious body, so we have the Supper. No local centre, indeed, is appointed at which alone our symbolic feast can be observed. Wherever a few renew their covenant with God in proclaiming the Lord's death till He come, there the souls of the faithful are nourished and inspired through fellowship with Him who brought spiritual life and liberty to our world.

CHAPTER VII.

THE CLOUD AND THE MARCH.

1. THE GUIDING CLOUD.

NUMBERS ix. 15-23.

THE pillar of cloud, the ensign of Jehovah's royalty among the Hebrews, and for us one of the most ancient symbols of His grace, is first mentioned in the account of the departure from Egypt. "Jehovah went before them by day in a pillar of cloud, to lead them the way; and by night in a pillar of fire, to give them light." At the passage of the Red Sea this murky cloud removed and came between the host of Israel and their pursuers. In the morning watch "Jehovah looked unto the host of the Egyptians through the pillar of fire and of the cloud, and troubled the host of the Egyptians." On that occasion it followed or represented "the angel of God." There is nowhere any attempt to give a complete account of the symbol. We read of its

* "Voltaire," by John Morley, ed. 1891, pp. 254, 255.

glory filling the inner shrine and even the holy place. At other times it only hovers above the western end of the tabernacle, marking the situation of the ark. Now and again it moves from that position, and covers the door of the tent of meeting into which Moses has entered. The targums use the term *Shechinah* to indicate what it was conceived to be—a luminous cloud, the visible manifestation of the Divine presence; and Philo speaks of the fiery appearance of the Deity shining forth from a cloud. But these are glosses on the original descriptions and cannot be altogether harmonised. In one passage only (Isa. iv. 5) do we find a reference which appears to throw any light on the real nature of the symbol. Evidently recalling it, the prophet says, "Jehovah will create over the whole habitation of Mount Zion, and over her assemblies, a cloud and smoke by day, and the shining of a flaming fire by night." To him the cloud is one of smoke rising from a fire which at night sends up tongues of flame; and the reflection of the bright fire on the overhanging cloud resembles a canopy of glory.

Ewald's view is that the smoke of the altar which went up in a thick column, visible at a great distance by day, ruddy with flame by night, was the origin of the conception. There are various objections to this theory, which the author of it himself finds difficult to reconcile with many of the statements. At the same time the pillar of cloud does not need to be thought of as in any respect a more Divine symbol than others which were associated with the tabernacle. Certainly the ark of the covenant which Bezaleel made according to the instructions of Moses was, far beyond anything else, the sacred centre around which the whole of the worship gathered, the mysterious emblem of Jehovah's character, the guarantee of His presence with Israel. It was from the space above the mercy-seat, as we have seen, that the Voice proceeded, not from the pillar of cloud. The sanctity of the ark was so great that it was never exposed to the view of the people, nor even of the Levites who were set apart to carry it. The cloud, on the other hand, was seen by all, and had its principal function in showing where the ark was in the camp or on the march.

Now assuming, in harmony with the reference in Isaiah, that the cloud was one of smoke, some may be disposed to think that, like the ark of the covenant, the holiest symbol of all, this was produced by human intervention, yet in a way not incompatible with its sacredness, its mystery, and value as a sign of Jehovah's presence. Where Moses was as leader, law-giver, prophet, mediator, there God was for this people: what Moses did in the spirit of Divine zeal and wisdom was done for Israel by God. Through his inspiration the ritual and its elaborate symbolism had their origin. And is it not possible that after the manner of the emblem of Jehovah which appeared in the desert of Horeb the fire and cloud were now realised? While some may adopt this explanation, others again will steadily believe that the appearance and movements of the cloud were quite apart from human device or agency.

Scarcely any difficulty greater than that connected with the pillar of cloud presents itself to thoughtful modern readers of the Pentateuch. The traditional view, apparently involved in the narrative, is that in this cloud and in this alone Jehovah revealed Himself in the interval between His appearance to Jacob and, long afterwards, to Joshua in angelic form. Many will maintain that unless the cloud was of supernatural origin the whole relation of the Israelites to their Divine King must fall into shadow. Was not this one of the miracles which made Hebrew history different in kind from that of every other nation? Is it not one of the revelations of the Unseen God on which we must build if we are to have sure faith in the Old Testament economy, and indeed in Christianity itself, as of superhuman revelation? If we are not to interpret literally what is said in Exodus—"The Lord went before them by day in a pillar of cloud, to lead them the way; and by night in a pillar of fire, to give them light"—shall we not practically abandon the whole Divine element in the history of Israel's deliverance and education? Thus the difficulty stands.

Yet, it may be argued, since we have now the revelation of God in the human life of Christ and the gospel of salvation through the ministry of men, what need is there to doubt that, for the guidance of a people from place to place in the wilderness, the wisdom, foresight, and faithfulness of an inspired man were the appointed means? It is admitted that in many things Moses acted for Jehovah, that his mind received in idea, and his intellectual skill expressed in verbal form, the laws and statutes which were to maintain Israel's relation to God as a covenant people. We follow our Lord Himself in saying that Moses gave Israel the law. But the legislation of the Decalogue was far more of the nature of a disclosure of God, and had far higher aims and issues than could be involved in the guidance through the desert. The law was for the spiritual nature of the Hebrews. It brought them into relation with God as just, pure, true, the sole source of moral life and progress. As the nucleus of the covenant it was symbolic in a sense that fire could never be. It may be asked, then, What need is there to doubt that Moses had his part in this symbol which has so long appeared, more than the other, important as a nexus between heaven and earth? To interpret the words "whenever the cloud was taken up from over the tent," as meaning that it was self-moved, would imply that Moses, though he is called the leader, did not lead but was led like the rest. And this would reduce his office to a point to which no prophet's work is reduced throughout the entire Old Testament. Was he unable to direct the march from Moseroth to Bene-jaakan? An inspired man, on whom, according to the will of God, lay the whole responsibility for Israel's national development, was he unable to determine when the pastures in one region were exhausted and others had to be sought? Then indeed the mediation of his genius would be so minimised that our whole idea of him must be changed. Especially would we have to set aside that prediction applied to Christ: "A prophet shall the Lord raise up unto you, from your brethren, like unto me."

And further, it may be said, the pillar of cloud and fire retains the whole of its value as a symbol when the intervention of Moses is admitted; and this may be proved by the analogy of other emblems. Almost parallel to the cloud, for instance, is the serpent of brass, which became a sign of Jehovah's healing power, and conveyed new life to those who looked towards it in faith. The fact that this rude image of a serpent was made by human hands did not in the least impair its value as an instrument of deliverance, and the efficacy of that particular symbol was selected by Christ as an illustration of His own redeeming energy which was to be gained through the cross: "As Moses lifted up the serpent in the wilderness, even so must the Son of man be lifted up." For certain occasions and needs of a people one symbol avails; in other circumstances there must be other signs. The smoke-cloud was not enough when the serpents terrified the host. Elijah in this same desert saw a flashing fire; but Jehovah was not in the fire. Natural symbols, however impressive, do not avail by themselves; and when God by His prophet says, "This cloud, this fire, symbolise My presence," and the people believe, is it not sufficient? The Divine Friend is assuredly there. The symbol is not God; it represents a fact, impresses a fact which altogether apart from the symbol would still hold good.

In the course of the passage (ix. 17-23) the manner of the guidance given by means of the cloud is carefully detailed. Sometimes the tribes remained encamped for many days, sometimes only from evening to morning. "Whether it were two days, or a month, or a year, that the cloud tarried on the tabernacle, abiding thereon, the children of Israel remained encamped, and journeyed not: but when it was taken up, they journeyed." Here is emphasised the authority which lay in "the commandment of the Lord *by the hand of Moses*" (ver. 23). For Israel, as for every nation that is not lost in the desert of the centuries, and every society that is not on the way to confusion, there must be wise guidance and cordial submission thereto. We are not, however, saved now, as the Israelites were, by a great movement of society, or even of the Church. Individually we must see the signal of the Divine will, and march where it points the way. And in a sense there are no rests of many days. Each morning the cloud moves forward; each morning we must strike our tents. Our march is in the way of thought, of moral and spiritual progress; and if we live in any real sense, we shall press on along that way. The indication of duty, the guidance in thought which we are to follow, impose a Divine obligation none the less that they are communicated through the instrumentality of men. For every group of travellers, associated in worship, duty, and aim, there is some spiritual authority pointing the direction to be followed. As individuals we have our separate calling, our responsibility to Christ, with which nothing is to interfere. But the unity of Christians in the faith and work of the kingdom of God must be kept; and for this one like Moses is needed, or at least a consensus of judgment, a clear expression of the corporate wisdom. The standard must be carried forward, and where it moves on to quiet pasturage or grim conflict the faithful are to advance.

> "Ye armies of the living God,
>   His sacramental host,
> Where hallowed footsteps never trod
>   Take your appointed post.
>
> "Follow the cross; the ark of peace
>   Accompany your path."

Thus, we may say, the general direction runs; and in the changing circumstances of the Church submission is given by its members to those who hold command at once from the Lord Himself and from His people. But in the details of duty each must follow the guidance of a cloud that marks his own path to his own eye.

2. The Silver Trumpets.

Numbers x. 1-10.

An air of antique simplicity is felt in the legislation regarding the two trumpets of silver, yet we are not in any way hindered from connecting the statute with the idea of claiming human art for Divine service. Instrumental music was of course rudimentary in the wilderness; but, such as it was, Jehovah was to control the use of it through the priests; and the developed idea is found in the account of the dedication of the temple of Solomon, as recorded in 2 Chron. v., where we are told that besides the Levites, who had cymbals, psalteries, and harps, a hundred and twenty priests sounding with trumpets took part in the music.

There is no need to question the early use of these instruments; nevertheless, the legislation in our passage assumes the settlement in Canaan, and times when defensive war became necessary and the observance of the sacred feasts fell into a fixed order. The statute is instructive as to the meaning of the formula "The Lord spake unto Moses," and not less as to the gradual accretion of particulars around an ancient nucleus. We cannot set aside the sincere record, though it may seem to make Jehovah speak on matters of small importance. But interpretation must spring from a right understanding of the purpose suggested to the mind of Moses. Uses found for the trumpets in the course of years are simply extensions of the germinal idea of reserving for sacred use those instruments and the art they represented. It was well that whatever fear or exhilaration the sounding of them caused should be controlled by those who were responsible to God for the moral inspiration of the people.

According to the statute, the two trumpets, which were of very simple make, and capable of only a few notes, had their use first in calling assemblies. A long peal blown on one trumpet summoned the princes who were the heads of the thousands of Israel: a long peal on both trumpets called the whole congregation to the "tent of meeting." There were occasions when these assemblies were required not for deliberation, but to hear in detail the instructions and orders of the leader. At other times the convocations were for prayer or thanksgiving; or, again, the people had to hear solemn reproofs and sentences of punishment. We may imagine that with varying sound, joyful or mournful, the trumpets were made to convey some indication of the purpose for which the assembly was called.

A sacred obligation lay on the Israelites to obey the summons, whether for joy or sorrow. They heard in the trumpet-blast the very voice of God. And upon us, bound to His service by a more solemn and gracious covenant, rests an obligation even more commanding. The unity of the tribes of Israel, and their fellowship in the obedience and worship of Jehovah, could never be of half so much importance as the unity of Christians in declaring their faith and fulfilling their vocation. To come together at the call of recurring opportunity, that we may confess Christ and hear His word anew, is essential to our spiritual life. Those who hear the call should know its urgency and promptly respond, lest in the midst of the holiest light there come to be a shadow of deep darkness, the midnight gloom of paganism and death.

Again, in the wilderness, the trumpets gave the signal for striking the camp and setting out on a new stage of the journey. Blown sharply by way of alarm, the peals conveyed now to one, now to another part of the host the order to advance. The movement of the pillar of cloud, we may assume, could not be seen everywhere, and this was another means of direction, not only of a general kind, but with some detail.

Taking vv. 5, 6, along with the passage beginning at ver. 14, we have an ideal picture of the order of movement. One peal, sharply rung out from the trumpets, would signify that the eastern camp, embracing the tribes of Judah, Issachar, and Zebulun, should advance. Then the tabernacle was to be taken down, and the Levites of the families of Gershon and Merari were to set forward with the various parts of the tent and its enclosure. Next two alarms gave the signal to the southern camp, that of Reuben, Simeon, and Gad. The Levites of the family of Kohath followed, bearing the ark, the altar of incense, the great altar, the table of shewbread, and other furniture of the sanctuary. The third and fourth camps, of which Ephraim and Benjamin were the heads, brought up the rear. In these movements the trumpets would be of much use. But it is quite clear that the real difficulty was not to set the divisions in motion each at a fit time. The camps were not composed only of men under military discipline. The women and children, the old and feeble, had to be cared for. The flocks and herds also had to be kept in hand. We cannot suppose that there was any orderly procession; rather was each camp a straggling multitude, with its own delays and interruptions.

And so it is in the case of every social and religious movement. Clear enough may be the command to advance, the trumpet of Providence, the clarion of the Gospel. But men and women are undisciplined in obedience and faith. They have many burdens of a personal kind to bear, many private differences and quarrels. How very seldom can the great Leader find prompt response to His will, though the terms of it are distinctly conveyed and the demand is urgent! God makes a plan for us, opens our way, shows us our need, proclaims the fit hours; but our unbelief and fear and incapacity impede the march. Nevertheless, through the grace of His providence, as Israel slowly made its way across the desert and reached Canaan at last, the Church moves, and will continue to move, towards the holy future, the millennial age.

Turning now to the uses of the silver trumpets after the settlement in Canaan, there is first that connected with war. The people are presumed to be living peaceably in their country; but some neighbouring power has attacked them. The sounding of the trumpets then is to be of the nature of a prayer to the Divine Protector of the nation. The cry of the dependent tribes will be gathered up, as it were, into the shrill blast which carries the alarm to the throne of the Lord of Hosts. To the army and to the nation assurance is given that the old promise of Jehovah's favour remains in force, and that the promise, claimed by the priests according to the covenant, will be fulfilled. And this will make the trumpet-blast exhilarating, a presage of victory. The claim and hope of the nation rise heavenward. The men of war stand together in faith, and put to flight the armies of the aliens.

For the battles we have to fight, the conflicts of faith with unbelief, and righteousness with aggressive iniquity, an inspiration is needed like that conveyed to Israel in the peal of the silver trumpets. Have we any means of assurance resembling that which was to animate the Hebrews when the enemy came upon them? Even the need is often unrecognised. Many take for granted that religion is safe, that the truth requires no valour of theirs in maintaining it, and the Gospel of Christ no spirited defence. The trumpet is not heard because the duty to which all Christians are called as helpers of the Gospel is never considered. Messages are accepted as oracles of God only when they tell the trustful of safety and confirm them in easy enjoyment of spiritual privilege and hope. One kind of trumpet peal alone is liked—that which sounds an alarm to the unconverted, and bids them prepare for the coming of the Judge.

But there are for all Christians frequent calls to a service in which they need the courage of faith and every hope the covenant can give. At the present time no greater mistake is possible than to sit in comfort under the shadow of ancient forms and creeds. We cannot realise the value of the promise given to genuine faith unless we abandon the crumbling walls and meet our assailants in the open ground, where we can see them face to face, and know the spirit with which they fight, the ensigns of their war. There is no brave thinking now in those old shelters, no room to use the armour of light. Christianity is one of the free forces of human life. Its true inspiration is found only when those who stand by it are bent on securing and extending the liberties of men. The trumpets that lift to heaven the prayers of the faithful and fill the soldiers of the Cross with the hope of victory can never be in the hands of those who claim exclusive spiritual authority, nor will they ever again sound the old Hebrew note. They inspire those who are generous, who feel that the more they give the more they are blessed, who would impart to others their own life that God's love to the world may be known. They call us not to defend our own privileges, but to keep the way of salvation open to all, to prevent the Pharisee and the unbeliever from closing against men the door of heavenly grace.

Once more; in the days of gladness and solemn feasting the trumpets were to be blown over the burnt offerings and peace offerings. The joy of the Passover, the hope of the new-moon festival, especially in the beginning of the seventh month, were to be sent up to heaven with the sound of these instruments, not as if Jehovah had forgotten His people and His covenant, but for the assurance and comfort of the worshippers. He was a Friend before whom they could rejoice, a King whose forgiveness was abundant, who showed mercy unto the thousands who loved Him and kept His commandments. The music, loud, and clear, and bold, was to carry to all who heard it the conviction that God had been sought in the way of His holy law, and would cause blessing to descend upon Israel.

We claim with gentler sounds, those of lowly prayer and pleading, the help of the Most High. Even in the secret chamber when the door is shut we can address our Father, knowing that our claim will be answered for the sake of Christ. Yet there are times when the loud and clear hallelujahs, borne heavenward by human voices and pealing organ, seem alone to express our exultation. Then the instruments and methods of modern art may be said to bind the old Hebrew times, the ancient faith of the wilderness and of Zion, to our own. We carry out ideas that lie at the heart of the race; we realise that human skill, human discovery, find their highest use and delight when they make beautiful and inspiring the service of God.

3. The Order of March.

Numbers x. 11-28.

The difficulties connected with the order of march prescribed in this passage have been often and fully rehearsed. According to the enumeration given in chap. ii., the van of the host formed by the division of Judah, men, women, and children, must have reached some six hundred thousand at least. The second division, headed by Reuben, would number five hundred thousand. The Levites, with their wives and children, according to the same computation would be altogether about seventy thousand. Then came the two remaining camps, about nine hundred thousand souls. At the first signal six hundred thousand would have to get into marching order and move off across the desert. There could be no absolute separation of the fighting men from their families and flocks, and even if there were no narrow passes to confine the vast multitude, it would occupy miles of road. We must not put a day's journey at more than ten miles. The foremost groups would therefore have reached the camping ground, let us say, when the last ranks of the second division were only beginning to move; and the rear would still be on its way when night had long fallen upon the desert. Whatever obstacles were removed for the Israelites, the actual distance to be traversed could not be made less; and the journey is always represented as a stern and serious discipline. When we take into account the innumerable hindrances which so vast a company would certainly have to contend with, it seems impossible that the order of march as detailed in this passage could have been followed for two days together.

Suppose we receive the explanation that the numbers have been accidentally increased in the transcription of records. This would relieve the narrative, not only here but at many points, of a burden it can hardly carry. And we remember that according to the Book of Nehemiah less than fifty thousand Jews, returning from Babylon at the close of the captivity, reconstructed the nation, so that it soon showed considerable spirit and energy. If the numbers as they stand in the Pentateuch were reduced, divided by ten, as some propose, the desert journey would appear less of a mere marvel. It would remain one of the most striking and important migrations known to history; it would lose none of its religious significance. No religious idea is affected by the numbers who receive it; nor do the great purposes of God depend on multitudes for their fulfilment. We can view with composure the criticism which touches the record on its numerical side, because we know the prophetic work of Moses and the providential education of Israel to be incontrovertible facts.

It has been suggested that the order of march as described did not continue to be kept throughout the whole of the wilderness journey; that in point of fact it may have been followed only so far as Kadesh. Whether this was so or not it must be taken into account that for the greater part of the forty years there was absolutely no travelling: the tribes were settled in the wilderness of Paran. The proofs are incidental but conclusive. From a central point, where the cloud rested (Numb. x. 12), the people spread themselves, we may suppose, in various directions, seeking grass for their cattle, and living for the most part like the other inhabitants of the district. Even if there were but three years of travelling in all, before and after the sojourn in the neighbourhood of Kadesh, there would be ample time for the movement from one place to another mentioned in the records.

CHAPTER VIII.

HOBAB THE KENITE.

Numbers x. 29-36.

The Kenites, an Arab tribe belonging to the region of Midian, and sometimes called Midianites, sometimes Amalekites, were already in close and friendly relation with Israel. Moses, when he went first to Midian, had married a daughter of their chief Jethro, and, as we learn from Exod. xviii., this patriarch, with his daughter Zipporah and the two sons she had borne to Moses, came to the camp of Israel at the mount of God. The meeting was an occasion of great rejoicing; and Jethro, as priest of his tribe, having congratulated the Hebrews on the deliverance Jehovah had wrought for them, "took a burnt offering and sacrifices for God," and was joined by Moses, Aaron, and all the elders of Israel in the sacrificial feast. A union was thus established between Kenites and Israelites of the most solemn and binding kind. The peoples were sworn to continual friendship.

While Jethro remained in the camp his counsel was given in regard to the manner of administering justice. In accordance with it rulers of thousands, hundreds, fifties, and tens were chosen, "able men, such as feared God, men of truth, hating covetousness"; and to them matters of minor importance were referred for judgment, the hard causes only being brought before Moses. The sagacity of one long experienced in the details of government came in to supplement the intellectual power and the inspiration of the Hebrew leader.

It does not appear that any attempt was made to attach Jethro and the whole of his tribe to the fortunes of Israel. The small company of the Kenites could travel far more swiftly than a great host, and, if they desired, could easily overtake the march. Moses, we are told, let his father-in-law depart, and he went to his own place. But now that the long stay of the Israelites at Sinai is over and they are about to advance to Canaan, the visit of a portion of the Kenite tribe is made the occasion of an appeal to their leader to cast in his lot with the people of God. There is some confusion in regard to the relationship of Hobab with Jethro or Raguel. Whether Hobab was a son or grandson of the chief cannot be made out. The word translated father-in-law (Numb. x. 29), means a relation by marriage. Whatever was the tie between Hobab and Moses, it was at all events so close, and the Kenite had so much sympathy with Israel, that it was natural to make the appeal to him: "Come thou with us, and we will do thee good." Himself assured of the result of the enterprise, anticipating with enthusiasm the high destiny of the tribes of Israel, Moses endeavours to persuade these children of the desert to take the way to Canaan.

There was a fascination in the movement of that people who, rescued from bondage by their Heavenly Friend, were on their journey to the land of His promise. This fascination Hobab and his followers appear to have felt; and Moses counted upon it. The Kenites, used to the wandering life, accustomed to strike their tents any day as occasion required, no doubt recoiled from the thought of settling even in a fertile country, still more from dwelling in any walled town. But the south of Canaan was practically a wilderness, and there, keeping to a great extent their ancestral habits, they might have had the liberty they loved, yet kept in touch with their friends of Israel. Some aversion from the Hebrews, who still bore certain marks of slavery, would have to be overcome. Yet, with the bond already established, there needed only some understanding of the law of Jehovah, and some hope in His promise to bring the company of Hobab to decision.

And Moses had right in saying, "Come with us, and we will do thee good; for Jehovah hath spoken good concerning Israel." The outlook to a future was something which the Kenites as a people had not, never could have in their desultory life. Unprogressive, out of the way of the great movements of humanity, gaining nothing as generations went by, but simply reproducing the habits and treasuring the beliefs of their fathers, the Arab tribe might maintain itself, might occasionally strike for righteousness in some conflict, but otherwise had no prospect, could have no enthusiasm. They would live their hard life, they would enjoy freedom, they would die—such would be their history. Compared with that poor outlook, how good it would be to share the noble task of establishing on the soil of Canaan a nation devoted to truth and righteousness, in league with the living God, destined to extend His kingdom and make His faith the means of blessing to all. It was the great opportunity of these nomads. As yet, indeed, there was no courage of religion, no brightness of enthusiasm among the Israelites. But there was the ark of the covenant, there were the sacrifices, the law; and Jehovah Himself, always present with His people, was revealing His will and His glory by oracle, by discipline and deliverance.

Now these Kenites may be taken as representing a class, in the present day to a certain extent attracted, even fascinated, by the Church, who standing irresolute are appealed to in terms like those addressed by Moses to Hobab. They feel a certain charm, for in the wide organisation and vast activity of the Christian Church, quite apart from the creed on which it is based, there are signs of vigour and purpose which contrast favourably with endeavours directed to mere material gain. In idea and in much of its effort the Church is splendidly humane, and it provides interests, enjoyments, both of an intellectual and artistic kind, in which all can share. Not so much its universality nor its mission of converting the world, nor its spiritual worship, but rather the social advantages and the culture it offers draw towards it those minds and lives. And to them it extends, too often without avail, the invitation to join its march.

Is it asked why many, partly fascinated, remain proof against its appeals? why an increasing number prefer, like Hobab, the liberty of the desert, their own unattached, desultory, hopeless way of life? The answer must partly be that, as it is, the Church does not fully commend itself by its temper, its enthusiasm, its sincerity and Christianity. It attracts but is unable to command, because with all its culture of art it does not appear beautiful, with all its claims of spirituality it is not unworldly; because, professing to exist for the redemption of society, its methods and standards are too often human rather than Divine. It is not that the outsider shrinks from the religiousness of the Church as overdone; rather does he detect a lack of that very quality. He could believe in the Divine calling and join the enterprise of the Church if he saw it journeying steadily towards a better country, that is a heavenly. Its earnestness would then command him; faith would compel faith. But social status and temporal aims are not subordinated by the members of the Church, nor even by its leaders. And whatever is done in the way of providing attractions for the pleasure-loving, and schemes of a social kind, these, so far from gaining the undecided, rather make them less disposed to believe. More exciting enjoyments can be found elsewhere. The Church offering pleasures and social reconstruction is attempting to catch those outside by what, from their point of view, must appear to be chaff.

It is a question which every body of Christians has need to ask itself—Can we honestly say to those without, Come with us, and we will do you good? In order that there may be certainty on this point, should not every member of the Church be able to testify that the faith he has gives joy and peace, that his fellowship with God is making life pure and strong and free? Should there not be a clear movement of the whole body, year by year, towards finer spirituality, broader and more generous love? The gates of membership are in some cases opened to such only as make very clear and ample profession. It does not, however, appear that those already within have always the Christian spirit corresponding to that high profession. And yet as Moses could invite Hobab and his company without misgiving because Jehovah was the Friend and Guide of Israel and had spoken good concerning her, so because Christ is the Head of the Church, and Captain of her salvation, those outside may well be urged to join her fellowship. If all depended on the earnestness of our faith and the steadfastness of our virtue we should not dare to invite others to join the march. But it is with Christ we ask them to unite. Imperfect in many ways, the Church is His, exists to show His death, to proclaim His Gospel and extend His power. In the whole range of human knowledge and experience there is but one life that is free, pure, hopeful, energetic in every noble sense, and at the same time calm. In the whole range of human existence there is but one region in which the mind and the soul find satisfaction and enlargement, in which men of all sorts and conditions find true harmony. That life and that region of existence are revealed by Christ; into them He only is the Way. The Church, maintaining this, demonstrating this, is to invite all who stand aloof. They who join Christ and follow Him will come to a good land, a heavenly heritage.

The first invitation given to Hobab was set aside. "Nay," he said, "I will not go; but I will depart to my own land and to my kindred." The old ties of country and people were strong for him. The true Arab loves his country passionately. The desert is his home, the mountains are his friends. His hard life is a life of liberty. He is strongly attached to his tribe, which has its own traditions, its own glories. There have been feuds, the memory of which must be cherished. There are heirlooms that give dignity to those who possess them. The people of the clan are brothers and sisters. Very little of the commercial mingles with the life of the desert; so perhaps family feeling has the more power. These influences Hobab felt, and this besides deterred him, that if he joined the Israelites he would be under the command of Moses. Hobab was prospective head of his tribe, already in partial authority at least. To obey the word of command instead of giving it was a thing he could not brook. No doubt the leader of Israel had proved himself brave, resolute, wise. He was a man of ardent soul and fitted for royal power. But Hobab preferred the chieftainship of his own small clan to service under Moses; and, brought to the point of deciding, he would not agree.

Freedom, habit, the hopes that have become part of life—these in like manner interpose between many and a call which is known to be from God. There is restraint within the circle of faith; old ideas, traditional conceptions of life, and many personal ambitions have to be relinquished by those who enter it. Accustomed to that Midian where every man does according to the bent of his own will, where life is hard but uncontrolled, where all they have learned to care for and desire may be found, many are unwilling to choose the way of religion, subjection to the law of Christ, the life of spiritual conflict and trial, however much may be gained at once and in the eternal future. Yet the liberty of their Midian is illusory. It is simply freedom to spend strength in vain, to roam from place to place where all alike are barren, to climb mountains lightning-riven, swept by interminable storms. And the true liberty is with Christ, who opens the prospect of the soul, and redeems the life from evil, vanity, and fear. The heavenward march appears to involve privation and conflict, which men do not care to face. But is the worldly life free from enemies, hardships, disappointments? The choice is, for many, between a bare life over which death triumphs, and a life moving on over obstacles, through tribulations, to victory and glory. The attractions of land and people, set against those of Christian hope, have no claim. "Every one," says the Lord, "that hath left houses, or brethren, or sisters, or father, or mother, or children, or lands, for My sake, shall receive a hundredfold, and shall inherit eternal life."

Passing on, the narrative informs us that

Moses used another plea: "Leave us not, I pray thee; forasmuch as thou knowest how we are to encamp in the wilderness, and thou shalt be to us instead of eyes." Hobab did not respond to the promise of advantage to himself; he might be moved by the hope of being useful. Knowing that he had to deal with a man who was proud, and in his way magnanimous, Moses wisely used this appeal. And he used it frankly, without pretence. Hobab might do real and valuable service to the tribes on their march to Canaan. Accustomed to the desert, over which he had often travelled, acquainted with the best methods of disposing a camp in any given position, with the quick eye and habit of observation which the Arab life gives, Hobab would be the very adjutant to whom Moses might commit many details. If he joins the tribes on this footing it will be without pretence. He professes no greater faith either in Israel's destiny or in Jehovah's sole Godhead than he really feels. Wishing Israel well, interested in the great experiment, yet not bound up in it, he may give his counsel and service heartily so far as they avail.

We are here introduced to another phase of the relation between the Church and those who do not altogether accept its creed, or acknowledge its mission to be supernatural, Divine. Confessing unwillingness to receive the Christian system as a whole, perhaps openly expressing doubts of the miraculous, for example, many in our day have still so much sympathy with the ethics and culture of Christianity that they would willingly associate themselves with the Church, and render it all the service in their power. Their tastes have led them to subjects of study and modes of self-development not in the proper sense religious. Some are scientific, some have literary talent, some artistic, some financial. The question may be, whether the Church should invite these to join her ranks in any capacity, whether room may be made for them, tasks assigned to them. On the one hand, would it be dangerous to Christian faith? on the other hand, would it involve them in self-deception? Let it be assumed that they are men of honour and integrity, men who aim at a high moral standard and have some belief in the spiritual dignity man may attain. On this footing may their help be sought and cordially accepted by the Church?

We cannot say that the example of Moses should be taken as a rule for Christians. It was one thing to invite the co-operation with Israel for a certain specified purpose of an Arab chief who differed somewhat in respect of faith; it would be quite another thing to invite one whose faith, if he has any, is only a vague theism, to give his support to Christianity. Yet the cases are so far parallel that the one illustrates the other. And one point appears to be this, that the Church may show itself at least as sympathetic as Israel. Is there but a single note of unison between a soul and Christianity? Let that be recognised, struck again and again till it is clearly heard. Our Lord rewarded the faith of a Syrophœnician woman, of a Roman centurion. His religion cannot be injured by generosity. Attachment to Himself personally, disposition to hear His words and accept His morality, should be hailed as the possible dawn of faith, not frowned upon as a splendid sin. Every one who helps sound knowledge helps the Church. The enthusiast for true liberty has a point of contact with Him whose truth gives freedom. The Church is a spiritual city with gates that stand wide open day and night towards every region and condition of human life, towards the north and south, the east and west. If the wealthy are disposed to help, let them bring their treasures; if the learned devote themselves reverently and patiently to her literature, let their toil be acknowledged. Science has a tribute that should be highly valued, for it is gathered from the works of God; and art of every kind—of the poet, the musician, the sculptor, the painter—may assist the cause of Divine religion. The powers men have are given by Him who claims all as His own. The vision of Isaiah in which he saw Tarshish and the isles, Sheba and Seba offering gifts to the temple of God, did not assume that the tribute was in all cases that of covenant love. And the Church of Christ has broader human sympathy and better right to the service of the world than Isaiah knew. For the Church's good, and for the good of those who may be willing in any way to aid her work and development, all gifts should be gladly received, and those who stand hesitating should be invited to serve.

But the analogy of the invitation to Hobab involves another point which must always be kept in view. It is this, that the Church is not to slacken her march, not divert her march in any degree because men not fully in sympathy with her join the company and contribute their service. The Kenite may cast in his lot with the Israelites and aid them with his experience. But Moses will not cease to lead the tribes towards Canaan, will not delay their progress a single day for Hobab's sake. Nor will he less earnestly claim sole Godhead for Jehovah, and insist that every sacrifice shall be made to Him and every life kept holy in His way, for His service. Perhaps the Kenite faith differed little in its elements from that which the Israelites inherited. It may have been monotheistic; and we know that part of the worship was by way of sacrifice not unlike that appointed by the Mosaic law. But it had neither the wide ethical basis nor the spiritual aim and intensity which Moses had been the means of imparting to Israel's religion. And from the ideas revealed to him and embodied in the moral and ceremonial law he could not for the sake of Hobab resile in the least. There should be no adjustment of creed or ritual to meet the views of the new ally. Onward to Canaan, onward also along the lines of religious duty and development, the tribes would hold their way as before.

In modern alliances with the Church a danger is involved, sufficiently apparent to all who regard the state of religion. History is full of instances in which, to one company of helpers and another, too much has been conceded; and the march of spiritual Christianity is still greatly impeded by the same thing. Money contributed, by whomsoever, is held to give the donors a right to take their place in councils of the Church, or at least to sway decision now in one direction, now in another. Prestige is offered with the tacit understanding that it shall be repaid with deference. The artist uses his skill, but not in subordination to the ideas of spiritual religion. He assumes the right to give them his own colour, and may even, while professing to serve Christianity, sensualise its teaching. Scholarship offers help, but is not content to submit to Christ. Having been allowed to join itself with the Church, it proceeds, not infrequently, to play the traitor's part, assailing the faith it was invoked to serve. Those who care more for pleasure than for religion may within a certain range find gratification in Christian worship; they are apt to claim more and still more of the element that meets their taste. And those who are bent on social reconstruction would often, without any thought of doing wrong, divert the Church entirely from its spiritual mission. When all these influences are taken into account, it will be seen that Christianity has to go its way amid perils. It must not be unsympathetic. But those to whom its camp is opened, instead of helping the advance, may neutralise the whole enterprise.

Every Church has great need at present to consider whether that clear spiritual aim which ought to be the constant guide is not forgotten, at least occasionally, for the sake of this or that alliance supposed to be advantageous. It is difficult to find the mean, difficult to say who serve the Church, who hinder its success. More difficult still is it to distinguish those who are heartily with Christianity from those who are only so in appearance, having some nostrum of their own to promote. Hobab may decide to go with Israel; but the invitation he accepts, perhaps with an air of superiority, of one conferring a favour, is really extended to him for his good, for the saving of his life. Let there be no blowing of the silver trumpets to announce that a prince of the Kenites henceforth journeys with Israel; they were not made for that! Let there be no flaunting of a gay ensign over his tent. We shall find that a day comes when the men who stand by true religion have—perhaps through Kenite influence—the whole congregation to face. So it is in Churches. On the other hand, Pharisaism is a great danger, equally tending to destroy the value of religion; and Providence ever mingles the elements that enter into the counsels of Christianity, challenging the highest wisdom, courage, and charity of the faithful.

The closing verses of chap. x. (33-6), belonging, like the passage just considered, to the prophetic narrative, affirm that the ark was borne from Sinai three days' journey before the host to find a halting-place. The reconciliation between this statement and the order which places the ark in the centre of the march, may be that the ideal plan was at the outset not observed, for some sufficient reason. The absolute sincerity of the compilers of the Book of Numbers is shown in their placing almost side by side the two statements without any attempt to harmonise. Both were found in the ancient documents, and both were set down in good faith. The scribes into whose hands the old records came did not assume the *rôle* of critics.

At the beginning of every march Moses is reported to have used the chant: "Rise up, O Jehovah, and let Thine enemies be scattered; and let them that hate Thee flee before Thee." When the ark rested he said: "Return, O Jehovah, unto the ten thousands of the thousands of Israel." The former is the opening strain of Psalm lxviii., and its magnificent strophes move towards the idea of that rest which Israel finds in the protection of her God. Part of the ode returns upon the desert journey, adding some features and incidents, omitted in the narrations of the Pentateuch—such as the plentiful rain which refreshed the weary tribes, the publishing by women of some Divine oracle. But on the whole the psalm agrees with the history, making Sinai the scene of the great revelation of God, and indicating the guidance He gave through the wilderness by means of the cloudy pillar. The chants of Moses would be echoed by the people, and would help to maintain the sense of constant relation between the tribes and their unseen Defender.

Through the wilderness Israel went, not knowing from what quarter the sudden raid of a desert people might be made. Swiftly, silently, as if springing out of the very sand, the Arab raiders might bear down upon the travellers. They were assured of the guardianship of Him whose eye never slumbered, when they kept His way and held themselves at His command. Here the resemblance to our case in the journey of life is clear; and we are reminded of our need of defence and the only terms on which we may expect it. We may look for protection against those who are the enemies of God. But we have no warrant for assuming that on whatever errand we are bound we have but to invoke the Divine arm in order to be secure. The dreams of those who think their personal claim on God may always be urged have no countenance in the prayer, "Rise up, O Jehovah, and let Thine enemies be scattered." And as Israel settling to rest after some weary march could enjoy the sense of Jehovah's presence only if the duties of the day had been patiently done, and the thought of God's will had made peace in every tribe, and His promise had given courage and hope—so for us, each day will close with the Divine benediction when we have "fought a good fight and kept the faith." Fidelity there must be; or, if it has failed, the deep repentance that subdues wandering desire and rebellious will, bringing the whole of life anew into the way of lowly service.

CHAPTER IX.

THE STRAIN OF THE DESERT JOURNEY.

NUMBERS xi.

THE narrative has accompanied the march of Israel but a short way from the mount of God to some spot marked for an encampment by the ark of the covenant, and already complaining has to be told of, and the swift judgment of those who complained. The Israelites have made a reservation in their covenant with God, that though obedience and trust are solemnly promised, yet leave shall be taken to murmur against His providence. They will have God for their Protector, they will worship Him; but let Him make their life smooth. Much has had to be borne which they did not anticipate; and they grumble and speak evil.

Generally men do not realise that their murmuring is against God. They have no intention to accuse His providence. It is of other men they complain, who come in their way; of accidents, so called, for which no one seems to be responsible; of regulations, well enough meant, which at some point prove vexatious; the obtuseness and carelessness of those who undertake but do not perform. And there does seem to be a great difference between displeasure with human agents whose follies and failures provoke us, and discontent with our own lot and its trials. At the same time, this has to be kept in view, that while we carefully refrain from criticising Providence, there may be, underlying our complaints, a tacit opinion that the world is not well made nor well ordered. To a certain extent the persons who irritate us are responsible for their mistakes; but just among those who are prone to err our discipline has been appointed. To gird at them is as much a revolt against the Creator as to complain of the heat of summer or the winter cold. With our knowledge of what the world is, of what our fellow-creatures are, should go the perception that God rules everywhere and stands against us when we resent what, in His world, we have to do or to suffer. He is against those who fail in duty also. Yet it is not for us to be angry. Our due will not be withheld. Even when we suffer most it is still offered, still given. While we endeavour to remedy the evils we feel, it must be without a thought that the order appointed by the Great King fails us at any point.

The punishment of those who complained is spoken of as swift and terrible. "The fire of the Lord burnt among them, and devoured in the uttermost part of the camp." This judgment falls under a principle assumed throughout the whole book, that disaster must overtake transgressors, and conversely that death by pestilence, earthquake, or lightning is invariably a result of sin. For the Israelites this was one of the convictions that maintained a sense of moral duty and of the danger of offending God. Again and again in the wilderness, where thunderstorms were common and plagues spread rapidly, the impression was strongly confirmed that the Most High observed everything that was done against His will. The journey to Canaan brought in this way a new experience of God to those who had been accustomed to the equable conditions of climate and the comparative health enjoyed in Egypt. The moral education of the people advanced by the quickening of conscience in regard to all that befell Israel.

From the disaster at Taberah the narrative passes to another phase of complaint in which the whole camp was involved. The dissatisfaction began amongst the "mixed multitude"—that somewhat lawless crowd of low-caste Egyptians and people of the Delta and the wilderness who attached themselves to the host. Among them first, because they had absolutely no interest in Israel's hope, a disposition to quarrel with their circumstances would naturally arise. But the spirit of dissatisfaction grew apace, and the burden of the new complaint was: "We have nought but this manna to look to." The part of the desert into which the travellers had now penetrated was even more sterile than Midian. Hitherto the food had been varied somewhat by occasional fruits and the abundant milk of kine and goats. But pasturage for the cattle was scanty in the wilderness of Paran, and there were no trees of any kind. Appetite found nothing that was refreshing. Their soul was dried away.

It was a common belief in our Lord's time that the manna, falling from heaven, very food of the angels, had been so satisfying, so delicious, that no people could have been more favoured than those who ate of it. When Christ spoke of the meat which endureth unto eternal life, the thought of His hearers immediately turned to the manna as the special gift of God to their fathers, and they conceived an expectation that Jesus would give them that bread of heaven, and so prove Himself worthy of their faith. But He replied, "Moses gave you not that bread out of heaven, but My Father giveth you the true bread out of heaven. I am the Bread of Life."

In the course of time the manna had been, so to speak, glorified. It appeared to the later generations one of the most wonderful and impressive things recorded in the whole history of their nation, this provision made for the wandering host. There was the water from the rock, and there was the manna. What a benignant Providence had watched over the tribes! How bountiful God had been to the people in the old days! They longed for a sign of the same kind. To enjoy it would restore their faith and put them again in the high position which had been denied for ages.

But these notions are not borne out by the history as we have it in the passage under notice. Nothing is said about angels' food—that is a poetical expression which a psalmist used in his fervour. Here we read, as to the coming of the manna, that when the dew fell upon the camp at night the manna fell upon it, or with it. And so far from the people being satisfied, they complained that instead of the fish and onions, cucumbers and melons of Egypt, they had nothing but manna to eat. The taste of it is described as like that of fresh oil. In Exodus it is said to have resembled wafers mixed with honey. It was not the privilege of the Israelites in the wilderness but their necessity to live on this somewhat cloying food. In no sense can it be called ideal. Nevertheless, complaining about it, they were in serious fault, betraying the foolish expectation that on the way to liberty they should have no privations. And their discontent with the manna soon became alarming to Moses. A sort of hysteria spread through the camp. Not the women only, but the men at the doors of their tents bewailed their hard lot. There was a tempest of tears and cries.

God, through His providence, determining for men, carrying out His own designs for their good, does not allow them to keep in the region of the usual and of mere comfort. Something is brought into their life which stirs the soul. In new hope they begin an enterprise the course and end of which they cannot foresee. The conventional, the pleasant, the peace and abundance of Egypt, can be no longer enjoyed if the soul is to have its own. By Moses Jehovah summoned the Israelites from the land of plenty to fulfil a high mission and when they responded, it was so far a proof that there was in them spirit enough for an uncommon destiny. But for the accomplishment of it they had to be nerved and braced by trial. Their ordeal was that mortifying of the flesh and of sensuous desire which must be undergone if the hopes through which the mind becomes conscious of the will of God are to be fulfilled.

In our personal history God, reaching us by His word, enlightening us with regard to the true ends of our being, calls us to begin a journey which has no earthly terminus and promises no earthly reward. We may be quite sure that we have not yet responded to His call if there is nothing of the wilderness in our life, no hardship, no adventure, no giving up of what is good in a temporal sense for what is good in a spiritual sense. The very essence of the design of God concerning a man is that he leave the lower and seek the higher, that he deny himself that which according to the popular view is his life, in order to seek a remote and lofty goal. There will be duty that calls for faith, that needs hope and courage. In doing it he will have recurring trials of his spirit, necessities of self-discipline, stern difficulties of choice and action. Every one of these he must face.

What is wrong with many lives is that they have no strain in them as of a desert journey towards a heavenly Canaan, the realisation of spiritual life. Adventure, when it is undertaken, is often for the sake of getting fish and melons and cucumbers by-and-by in greater abundance and of better kinds. Many live hardly just now, not because they are on the way to spiritual freedom and the high destiny of life in God, but because they believe themselves to be on the way to better social position, to wealth or honour. But take the life that has begun its high enterprise at the urgency of a Divine vocation, and that life will find hardness, deprivations, perils, of its own. It is not given to us to be absolutely certain in decision and endeavour. Out in the wilderness, even when manna is provided, and the pillar of cloud seems to show the way, the people of God are in danger of doubting whether they have done wisely, whether they have not taken too much upon themselves or laid too much upon the Lord. The Israelites might have said, We have obeyed God: why, then, should the sun smite us with burning heat, and the dust-storms sweep down upon our march, and the night fall with so bitter a chill? Interminable toil, in travelling, in attending to cattle and domestic duties, in pitching tents and striking them, gathering fuel, searching far and wide through the camp for food, helping the children, carrying the sick and aged, toil that did not cease till far into the night and had to be resumed with early morning—such, no doubt, were the things that made life in the wilderness irksome. And although many now have a lighter burden, yet our social life, adding new difficulties with every improvement, our domestic affairs, the continual struggle necessary in labour and business, furnish not a few causes of irritation and of bitterness. God does not remove annoyances out of the way even of His devoted servants. We remember how Paul was vexed and burdened while carrying the world's thought on into a new day. We remember what a weight the infirmities and treacheries of men laid upon the heart of Christ.

Let us thank God if we feel sometimes across the wilderness a breeze from the hills of the heavenly Canaan, and now and then catch glimpses of them far away. But the manna may seem flat and tasteless, nevertheless; the road may seem long; the sun may scorch. Tempted to despond, we need afresh to assure ourselves that God is faithful who has given us His promise. And although we seem to be led not towards the heavenly frontier, but often aside through close defiles into some region more barren and dismal than we have yet crossed, doubt is not for us. He knoweth the way that we take; when He has tried us, we shall come forth where He appoints.

From the people we turn to Moses and the strain he had to bear as leader. Partly it was due to his sense of the wrath of God against Israel. To a certain extent he was responsible for those he led, for nothing he had done was apart from his own will. The enterprise was laid on him as a duty certainly; yet he undertook it freely. Such as the Israelites were, with that mixed multitude among them, a dangerous element enough, Moses had personally accepted the leadership of them. And now the murmuring, the lusting, the childish weeping, fall upon him. He feels that he must stand between the people and Jehovah. The behaviour of the multitude vexes him to the soul; yet he must take their part, and avert, if possible, their condemnation.

The position is one in which a leader of men often finds himself. Things are done which affront him personally, yet he cannot turn against the wayward and unbelieving, for, if he did, the cause would be lost. The Divine judgment of the transgressors falls on him all the more because they themselves are unaware of it. The burden such an one has to sustain points directly to the sin-bearing of Christ. Wounded to the soul by the wrong-doing of men, He had to interpose between them and the stroke of the law, the judgment of God. And may not Moses be said to be a type of Christ? The parallel may well be drawn; yet the imperfect mediation of Moses fell far short of the perfect mediation of our Lord. The narrative here reflects that partial knowledge of the Divine character which made the mediation of Moses human and erring for all its greatness.

For one thing Moses exaggerated his own responsibility. He asked of God: "Why hast Thou evil entreated Thy servant? Why dost Thou lay the burden of all this people upon me? Am I their father? Am I to carry the whole multitude as a father carries his young child in his bosom?" These are ignorant words, foolish words. Moses is responsible, but not to that extent. It is fit that he should be grieved when the Israelites do wrong, but not proper that he should charge God with laying on him the duty of keeping and carrying them like children. He speaks unadvisedly with his lips.

Responsibility of those who endeavour to lead others has its limits; and the range of duty is bounded in two ways—on the one hand by the responsibility of men for themselves, on the other hand by God's responsibility for them, God's care of them. Moses should see that no law or ordinance makes him chargeable with the childish lamentations of those who know they should not complain, who ought to be manly and endure with stout hearts. If persons who can go on their own feet want to be carried, no one is responsible for carrying them. It is their own fault when they are left behind. If those who can think and discover duty for themselves, desire constantly to have it pointed out to them, crave daily encouragement in doing their duty, and complain because they are not sufficiently considered, the leader, like Moses, is not responsible. Every man must bear his own burden— that is, must bear the burden of duty, of thought, of effort, so far as his ability goes.

Then, on the other side, the power of God is beneath all, His care extends over all. Moses ought not for a moment to doubt Jehovah's mindfulness of His people. Men who hold office in society or the Church are never to think that their effort is commensurate with God's. Proud indeed he would be who said: "The care of all these souls lies on me: if they are to be saved,

I must save them; if they perish, I shall be chargeable with their blood." Speaking ignorantly and in haste, Moses went almost that length; but his error is not to be repeated. The charge of the Church and of the world is God's; and He never fails to do for all and for each what is right. The teacher of men, the leader of affairs, with full sympathy and indefatigable love, is to do all he can, yet never trench on the responsibility of men for their own life, or assume to himself the part of Providence.

Moses made one mistake and went on to another. He was on the whole a man of rare patience and meekness; yet on this occasion he spoke to Jehovah in terms of daring resentment. His cry was to get rid of the whole enterprise: "If Thou deal thus with me, kill me, I pray Thee, out of hand, and let me not see my wretchedness." He seemed to himself to have this work to do and no other, apparently imagining that if he was not competent for this, he could be of no use in the world. But even if he had failed as a leader, highest in office, he might have been fit enough for a secondary place, under Joshua or some other whom God might inspire: this he failed to see. And although he was bound up in Israel's well-being, so that if the expedition did not prosper he had no wish to live, and was so far sincerely patriotic, yet what good end could his death serve? The desire to die shows wounded pride. Better live on and turn shepherd again. No man is to despise his life, whatever it is, however it may seem to come short of the high ambition he has cherished as a servant of God and men. Discovering that in one line of endeavour he cannot do all he would, let him make trial of others, not pray for death.

The narrative represents God as dealing graciously with his erring servant. Help was provided for him by the appointment of seventy elders, who were to share the task of guiding and controlling the tribes. These seventy were to have a portion of the leader's spirit—zeal and enthusiasm like his own. Their influence in the camp would prevent the faithlessness and dejection which threatened to wreck the Hebrew enterprise. Further, the murmuring of the people was to be effectually silenced. Flesh was to be given them till they loathed it. They should learn that the satisfaction of ignorant desire meant punishment rather than pleasure.

The promise of flesh was speedily fulfilled by an extraordinary flight of quails, brought up, according to the seventy-eighth Psalm, by a wind which blew from the south and east—that is, from the Elanitic Gulf. These quails cannot sustain themselves long on the wing, and after crossing the desert some thirty or forty miles they would scarcely be able to fly. The enormous numbers of them which fluttered around the camp are not beyond ordinary possibility. Fowls of this kind migrate at certain seasons in such enormous multitudes that in the small island of Capri, near Naples, one hundred and sixty thousand have been netted in one season. When exhausted, they would easily be taken as they flew at a height of about two cubits above the ground. The whole camp was engaged in capturing quails from one morning to the evening of the following day; and the quantity was so great that he who gathered least had ten homers, probably a heap estimated to be of that measure. To keep them for further use the birds were prepared and spread on the ground to dry in the sun.

When the epidemic of weeping broke out through the camp, the doubt occurred to Moses whether there was any spiritual quality in the people, any fitness for duty or destiny of a religious kind. They seemed to be all unbelievers on whom the goodness of God and the sacred instruction had been wasted. They were earthly and sensual. How could they ever trust God enough to reach Canaan?—or if they reached it, how would their occupation of it be justified? They would but form another heathen nation, all the worse that they had once known the true God and had abandoned Him. But a different view of things was presented to Moses when the chosen elders, men of worth, were gathered at the tent of meeting, and on a sudden impulse of the Spirit began to prophesy. As these men in loud and ecstatic language proclaimed their faith, Moses found his confidence in Jehovah's power and in the destiny of Israel re-established. His mind was relieved at once of the burden of responsibility and the dread of an extinction of the heavenly light he had been the means of kindling among the tribes. If there were seventy men capable of receiving the Spirit of God, there might be hundreds, even thousands. A spring of new enthusiasm is opened, and Israel's future is again possible.

Now there were two men, Edad and Medad, who were of the seventy, but had not come to the tent of meeting, where the prophetic spirit fell upon the rest. They had not heard the summons, we may suppose. Unaware of what was taking place at the tabernacle, yet realising the honour conferred upon them, they were perhaps engaged in ordinary duties, or, having found some need for their interference, they may have been rebuking murmurers and endeavouring to restore order among the unruly. And suddenly they also, under the same influence as the other sixty-eight, began to prophesy. The spirit of earnestness caught them. With the same ecstasy they declared their faith and praised the God of Israel.

There was in one sense a limitation of the spirit of prophecy, whatever it was. Of all the host only the seventy received it. Other good men and true in Israel that day might have seemed as capable of the heavenly endowment as those who prophesied. It was, however, in harmony with a known principle that the men designated to special office alone received the gift. The sense of a choice felt to be that of God does unquestionably exalt the mind and spirit of those chosen. They realise that they stand higher and must do more for God and men than others, that they are inspired to say what otherwise they could not dare to say. The limitation of the Spirit in this sense is not invariable, is not strict. At no time in the world's history has the call to office been indispensable to prophetic fervour and courage. Yet the sequence is sufficiently common to be called a law.

But while in a sense there is restriction of the spiritual influence, in another sense there is no restraint. The Divine afflatus is not confined to those who have gathered at the tabernacle. It is not place or occasion that makes the prophets; it is the Spirit, the power from on high entering into life; and out in the camp the two have their portion of the new energy and zeal. Spiritual influence, then, is not confined to any particular place. Neither was the neighbourhood of the tabernacle so holy that there alone the elders could receive their gift; nor is any place of meeting, any church, capable of such consecration and singular identification with the service of God that there alone the power of the Divine Spirit can be manifested or received. Let there be a man chosen of God, ready for the duties of a holy calling, and on that man the Spirit will come, wherever he is, in whatever he is engaged. He may be employed in common work, but in doing it he will be moved to earnest service and testimony. He may be labouring, under great difficulties, to restore the justice that has been impaired by social errors and political chicanery—and his words will be prophetic; he will be a witness for God to those who are without faith, without holy fear.

While Eldad and Medad prophesied in the camp, a young man who heard them ran officiously to inform Moses. To this young man as to others—for no doubt there were many who loved and revered the Usual—the two elders were presumptuous fools. The camp was, as we say, secular: was it not? People in the camp looked after ordinary affairs, tended their cattle, chaffered and bargained, quarrelled about trifles, murmured against Moses and against God. Was it right to prophesy there, carrying religious words and ideas into the midst of common life? If Eldad and Medad could prophesy, let them go to the tabernacle. And besides, what right had they to speak for Jehovah, in Jehovah's name? Was not Moses the prophet, the only prophet? Israel was accustomed to think him so, would keep to that opinion. It would be confusing if at any one's tent door a prophet might begin to speak without warning. So the young man thought it his duty to run and tell Moses what was taking place. And Joshua, when he heard, was alarmed, and desired Moses to put an end to the irregular ministry. "My lord Moses, forbid them," he said. He was jealous not for himself and the other elders, but for Moses' sake. So far the leader alone held communication with Jehovah and spoke in His name; and there was perhaps some reason for the alarm of Joshua, more than was apparent at the time. To have one central authority was better and safer than to have many persons using the right to speak in any sense for God. Who could be sure that these new voices would agree with Moses in every respect? Even if they did, might there not be divisions in the camp, new priesthoods as well as new oracles? Prophets might not be always wise, always truly inspired. And there might be false prophets by-and-by, even if Eldad and Medad were not false.

In like manner it might be argued now that there is danger when one here and another there assume authority as revealers of the truth of things. Some, full of their own wisdom, take high ground as critics and teachers of religion. Others imagine that with the right to wear a certain dress there has come to them the full equipment of the prophet. And others still, remembering how Elijah and John the Baptist arrayed themselves in coarse cloth and leathern girdle, assume that garb, or what corresponds to it, and claim to have the prophetic gift because they express the voice of the people. So in our days there is a question whether Eldad or Medad, prophesying in the camp, ought to be trusted or even allowed to speak. But who is to decide? Who is to take upon him to silence the voices? The old way was rough and ready. All who were in office in a certain Church were commissioned to interpret Divine mysteries; the rest were ordered to be silent on pain of imprisonment. Those who did not teach as the Church taught, under her direction, were made offenders against the public well-being. That way, however, has been found wanting, and "liberty of prophesying" is fully allowed. With the freedom there have come difficulties and dangers enough. Yet to "try the spirits whether they are of God" is our discipline on the way to life.

The reply of Moses to Joshua's request anticipates, in no small degree, the doctrine of liberty. "Art thou jealous for my sake? Would God that all the Lord's people were prophets, and that the Lord would put His Spirit upon them." His answer is that of a broad and magnanimous toleration. Moses cannot indeed have believed that great religious truths were in the reach of every man, and that any earnest soul might receive and communicate those truths. But his conception of a people of God is like that in the prophecy of Joel, where he speaks of all flesh being endued with the Spirit, the old men and young men, the sons and daughters, alike made able to testify of what they have seen and heard. The truly great man entertains no jealousy of others. He delights to see in other eyes the flash of heavenly intelligence, to find other souls made channels of Divine revelation. He would have no monopoly in knowledge and sacred prophecy. Moses had instituted an exclusive priesthood; but here he sets the gate of the prophetical office wide open. All whom God endows are declared free in Israel to use that office.

We can only wonder that still any order of men should try in the name of the Church to shut the mouths of those who approve themselves reverent students of the Divine Word. At the same time let it not be forgotten that the power of prophesying is no chance gift, no easy faculty. He who is to speak on God's behalf must indeed know the mind of God. How can one claim the right to instruct others who has never opened his mind to the Divine voice, who has not reverently compared Scripture with Providence and all the phases of revelation that are unfolded in conscience and human life? Men who draw a narrow circle and keep their thoughts within it can never become prophets.

The closing verses of the chapter tell of the plague that fell on the lustful, and the burial of those who died of it, in a place thence called Kibroth-hattaavah. The people had their desire, and it brought judgment upon them. Here in Israel's history a needful warning is written; but how many read without understanding! And so, every day the same plague is claiming its victims, and "graves of lust" are dug. The preacher still finds in this portion of Scripture a subject that never ceases to claim treatment, let social conditions be what they may.

CHAPTER X.

THE JEALOUSY OF MIRIAM AND AARON.

NUMBERS xii.

It may be confidently said that no representative writer of the post-exilic age would have invented or even cared to revive the episode of this chapter. From the point of view of Ezra and his fellow-reformers, it would certainly appear a blot on the character of Moses that he passed by the women of his own people and took a Cushite or Ethiopian wife. The idea of the "holy seed," on which the zealous leaders of new Judaism insisted after the return from Babylon, was exclusive. It appeared an abomination for Israelites to intermarry either with the original inhabitants of Canaan, or even with Moabites, Ammonites, and Egyptians. At an earlier date any disposition to seek alliance with Egypt or hold intercourse with it was denounced as profane. Isaiah and Jeremiah alike declare that Israel, whom Jehovah led forth from Egypt, should never think of returning to drink of its waters or trust in its shadow. As the necessity of separateness from other peoples became strongly felt, revulsion from Ethiopia would be greater than from Egypt itself. Jeremiah's inquiry, "Can the Ethiopian change his skin?" made the dark colour of that race a symbol of moral taint.

To be sure, the prophets did not all adopt this view. Amos, especially, in one of his striking passages, claims for the Ethiopians the same relation to God as Israel had: "Are ye not as the children of the Ethiopians unto Me, O children of Israel, saith the Lord?" No reproach to the Israelites is intended; they are only reminded that all nations have the same origin and are under the same Divine providence. And the Psalms in their evangelical anticipations look once and again to that dark land in the remote south: "Princes shall come out of Egypt; Ethiopia shall soon stretch out her hands unto God"; "I will make mention of Rahab and Babylon to them that know Me: behold Philistia, and Tyre, with Ethiopia; this man was born there." The zeal of the period immediately after the captivity carried separateness far beyond that of any earlier time, surpassing the letter of the statute in Exod. xxxiv. 11 and Deut. vii. 2. And we may safely assert that if the Pentateuch did not come into existence till after the new ideas of exclusion were established, and if it was written then for the purpose of exalting Moses and his law, the reference to his Cushite wife would certainly have been suppressed.

All the more may this be maintained when we take into account the likelihood that it was not entirely without reason Aaron and Miriam felt some jealousy of the woman. The story is usually taken to mean that there was no cause whatever for the feeling entertained; and if Miram alone had been involved, we might have regarded the matter as without significance. But Aaron had hitherto acted cordially with the brother to whom he owed his high position. Not a single disloyal word or deed had as yet separated him in the least, personally, from Moses. They wrought together in the promulgation of law, they were together in transgression and judgment. Aaron had every reason for remaining faithful; and if he was now moved to a feeling that the character and reputation of the lawgiver were imperilled, it must have been because he saw reason. He could approach Moses quietly on this subject without any thought of challenging his authority as leader. We see that while he accompanied Miriam he kept in the background, unwilling, himself, to appear as an accuser, though persuaded that the unpleasant duty must be done.

So far as Moses is concerned these thoughts, which naturally arise, go to support the genuineness of the history. And in like manner the condemnation of Aaron bears out the view that the episode is not of legendary growth. If priestly influence had determined to any extent the form of the narrative, the fault of Aaron would have been suppressed. He agrees with Miriam in making a claim the rejection of which involves him and the priesthood in shame. And yet, again, the theory that here we have prophetic narrative, critical of the priesthood, will not stand; for Miriam is a prophetess, and language is used which seems to deny to all but Moses a clear and intimate knowledge of the Divine will.

Miriam was the spokeswoman. She it was, as the Hebrew implies, who "spake against Moses because of the Cushite woman whom he had married." It would seem that hitherto in right of her prophetical gift she was to some extent an adviser of her brother, or had otherwise a measure of influence. It appeared to her not only a bad thing for Moses himself but absolutely wrong that a woman of alien race, who probably came out of Egypt with the tribes, one among the mixed multitude, should have anything to say to him in private, or should be in his confidence. Miriam maintained, apparently, that her brother had committed a serious mistake in marrying this wife, and still more in denying to Aaron and to herself that right of advising which they had hitherto used. Was not Moses forgetting that Miriam had her share in the zeal and inspiration which had made the guidance of the tribes so far successful? If Moses stands aloof, consults only with his alien wife, will he not forfeit position and authority and be deprived of help with which he has no right to dispense?

Miriam's is an instance, the first instance we may say, of the woman's claim to take her place side by side with the man in the direction of affairs. It would be absurd to say that the modern desire has its origin in a spirit of jealousy like that which Miriam showed; yet, parallel to her demand, "Hath the Lord indeed spoken only by Moses? Hath he not also spoken by us?" is the recent cry, "Has man a monopoly either of wisdom or of the moral qualities? Are not women at least equally endowed with ethical insight and sagacity in counsel?" Long excluded from affairs by custom and law, women have become weary of using their influence in an unrecognised, indirect way, and many would now claim an absolute parity with men, convinced that if in any respect they are weak as yet they will soon become capable. The claim is to a certain extent based on the Christian doctrine of equality between male and female, but also on the acknowledged success of women who, engaging in public duties side by side with men, have proved their aptitude and won high distinction.

At the same time, those who have had experience of the world and the many phases of human life must always have a position which the inexperienced may not claim; and women, as compared with men, must continue to be at a certain disadvantage for this reason. It may be supposed that intuition can be placed against experience, that the woman's quick insight may serve her better than the man's slowly acquired knowledge. And most will allow this, but only to a certain point. The woman's intuition is a fact of her nature—to be trusted often and along many ways. It is, indeed, her experience, gained half unconsciously. But the modern claim is assuming far more than this. We are told that the moral sense of the race comes down through women. They conserve the moral sense. This is no Christian claim, or Christian only in outdoing Romanism and setting Mary far above her Son. Seriously put forward by women, this will throw back their whole claim into the middle ages again. That a finer moral sense often forms part of their intuition is admitted: that as a sex they lead the race must be proved where, as yet, they do not prove it. Nevertheless, the world is advancing by the advance of women. There is no need any longer for that jealous intriguing which has often wrecked governments and homes. Christianity, ruling the questions of sex, means a very stable form of society, a continuous and calm development, the principle of charity and mutual service.

Miriam claimed the position of a prophet or *nabi* for herself, and endeavoured to make her gift and Aaron's as revealers of truth appear equal to that of Moses. At the Red Sea she led the chorus "Sing ye to the Lord, for He hath triumphed gloriously. The horse and his rider hath He thrown into the sea." That, so far as we know, was her title to count herself a prophetess. As for Aaron, we often find his name associated with his brother's in the formula, "The Lord spake unto Moses and Aaron." He had also been the *nabi* of Moses when the two went to Pharaoh with their demand on behalf of Israel. But the claim of equality with Moses was vain. Poor Miriam had her one flash of high enthusiasm, and may have now and again risen to some courage and zeal in professing her faith. But she does not seem to have had the ability to distinguish between her fitful glimpses of truth and Moses' Divine intelligence. Aaron, again, must have been half ashamed when he was placed beside his brother. He had no genius, none of the elevation of soul that betokens an inspired man. He obeyed well, served the sanctuary well; he was a good priest, but no prophet.

The little knowledge, the small gifts, appear great to those who have them, so great as often to eclipse those of nobler men. We magnify what we have,—our power of vision, though we cannot see far; our spiritual intelligence, though we have learned the first principles only of Divine faith. In the religious controversies of to-day, as in those of the past, men whose claims are of the slightest have pushed to the front with the demand, Hath not the Lord spoken by us? But there is no Moses to be challenged. The age of the revealers is gone. He who seems to be a great prophet may be taken for one because he stands on the past and invokes voluminous authority for all he says and does. In truth, our disputations are between the modern Eliphaz, Bildad, and Job—all of them to-day men of limited view and meagre inspiration, who repeat old hearsays with wearisome pertinacity, or inveigh against the old interpretations with infinite assurance. Jehovah speaks from the storm; but there is no heed paid to His voice. By some the Word is declared unintelligible; others deny it to be His.

While Moses kept silence, ruling his spirit in the meekness of a man of God, suddenly the command was given, "Come out, ye three, unto the tent of meeting." Possibly the interview had been at Moses' own tent in the near portion of the camp. Now judgment was to be solemnly given; and the circumstances were made the more impressive by the removal of the cloud-pillar from above the tabernacle to the door of the tent, where it seems to have intervened between Moses on the one side and Miriam and Aaron on the other; then the Voice spoke, requiring these two to approach, and the oracle was heard. The subject of it was the position of Moses as the interpreter of Jehovah's will. He was distinguished from any other prophet of the time.

We are here at a point where more knowledge is needful to a full understanding of the revelation: we can only conjecture. Not long is it since the seventy elders belonging to different tribes were endowed with the spirit of prophecy. Already there may have been some abuse of their new power; for though God bestows His gifts on men, they have practical liberty, and may not always be wise or humble in exercising the gifts. So the need of a distinction between Moses and the others would be clear. As to Miriam and Aaron, their jealousy may have been not only of Moses, but also of the seventy. Miriam and Aaron were prophets of older standing, and would be disposed to claim that the Lord spoke by them rather in the way He spoke by Moses than after the manner of His communications through the seventy. Were members of the sacred family to be on a level henceforth with any persons who spoke ecstatically in praise of Jehovah? Thus claim asserted itself over claim. The seventy had to be informed as to the limits of their office, prevented from taking a place higher than they had been assigned: Miriam and Aaron also had to be instructed that their position differed entirely from their brother's, that they must be content so far as prophecy was concerned to stand with the rest whose inspiration they may have despised. With this view the general terms of the deliverance appear to correspond.

The Voice from the tent of meeting was heard through the cloud; and on the one hand the function of the prophet or *nabi* was defined, on the other the high honour and prerogative of Moses were announced. The prophet, said the Voice, shall have Jehovah made known to him "in vision, or in dream,"—in his waking hours, when the mind is on the alert, receiving impressions from nature and the events of life; when memory is occupied with the past and hope with the future, the vision shall be given. Or again, in sleep, when the mind is withdrawn from external objects and appears entirely passive, a dream shall open glimpses of the great work of Providence, the purposes of judgment or of grace. In these ways the prophet shall receive his knowledge; and of necessity the revelation will be to some extent shadowed, difficult to interpret. Now the name prophet, *nabi*, is continually applied throughout the Old Testament, not only to the seventy and others who like them spoke in ecstatic language, and those who afterwards used musical instruments to help the rapture with which the Divine utterance came, but also to men like Amos and Isaiah. And it has been made a question whether the inspiration of these prophets is to come under the general law of the oracle we are considering. The answer in one sense is clear. So far as the word *nabi* designates all, they are all of one order. But it is equally certain, as Kuenen has pointed out, that the later prophets were not always in a state of ecstasy when they gave their oracles, nor simply reproducing thoughts of which they first became conscious in that state. They had an exalting consciousness of the presence and enlightening Spirit of Jehovah bestowed on them, or the burden of Jehovah laid on them. The visions were often flashes of thought; at other times the prophet seemed to look on a new earth and heaven filled with moving symbols and powers. But the whole development of national faith and knowledge affected their flashes of thought and visions, lifting prophetic energy into a higher range.

Now, returning to the oracle, we find that Moses is not a prophet or *nabi* in this sense. The words that relate to him carefully distinguish between his illumination and that of the *nabi*. "My servant Moses is not so; he is faithful in all Mine house: with him will I speak mouth to mouth, even manifestly, and not in dark speeches; and the form of Jehovah shall he behold." Every word here is chosen to exclude the idea of ecstasy, the idea of vision or dream, which leaves some shadow of uncertainty upon the mind, and the idea of any intermediate influence between the human intelligence and the disclosure of God's will. And when we try to interpret this in terms of our own mental operations, and our consciousness of the way in which truth reaches our minds, we recognise for one thing an impression made distinctly word by word of the message to be conveyed. There is given to Moses not only a general idea of the truth or principle to be embodied in his words, but he receives the very terms. They come to him in concrete form. He has but to repeat or write what Jehovah communicates. Along with this there is given to Moses a power of apprehending the form or similitude of God. His mind is made capable of singular precision in receiving and transmitting the oracle or statute. There is complete calmness and what we may call self-possession when he is in the tent of meeting face to face with the Eternal. And yet he has this spiritual, transcendent symbol of the Divine Majesty before him. He is no poet, but he enjoys some revelation higher and more exalting to mind and soul than poet ever had.

The paradox is not inconceivable. There is a way to this converse with God "mouth to mouth" along which the patient, earnest soul can partly travel. Without rhapsody, with full effort of the mind that has gathered from every source and is ready for the Divine synthesis of ideas, the Divine illumination, the Divine dictation, if we may so speak, the humble intelligence may arrive where, for the guidance of the personal life at least, the very words of God are to be heard. Beyond, along the same way, lies the chamber of audience which Moses knew. We think it an amazing thing to be sure of God and of His will to the very words. Our state is so often that of doubt, or of self-absorption, or of entanglement with the affairs of others, that we are generally incapable of receiving the direct message. Yet of whom should we be sure if not of God? Of what words should we be more certain than those pure, clear words that come from His mouth? Moses heard on great themes, national and moral—he heard for the ages, for the world: there lay his unique dignity. We may hear only for our own guidance in the next duty that is to be done. But the Spirit of God directs those who trust Him. It is ours to seek and to receive the very truth.

With regard to the *similitude* of Jehovah which Moses saw, we notice that there is no suggestion of human form; rather would this seem to be carefully avoided. The statement does not take us back to the appearance of the angel Jehovah to Abraham, nor does it point to any manifestation like that of which we read in the history of Joshua or of Gideon. Nothing is here said of an angel. We are led to think of an exaltation of the spiritual perception of Moses, so that he knew the reality of the Divine life, and was made sure of an originative wisdom, a transcendent source of ideas and moral energy. He with whom Moses holds communion is One whose might and holiness and glory are seen with the spiritual eye, whose will is made known by a voice entering into the soul. And the distinction intended between Moses and all other prophets corresponds to a fact which the history of Israel's religion brings to light. The account of the way in which Jehovah communicated with Moses remains subject to the condition that the expressions used, such as "mouth to mouth," are still only symbols of the truth. They mean that in the very highest sense possible to man Moses entered into the purposes of God regarding His people. Now Isaiah certainly approached this intimate knowledge of the Divine counsel when long afterwards he said in Jehovah's name: "Behold My Servant, whom I uphold; Mine Elect, in whom My soul delighteth; I have put My Spirit upon Him: He shall bring forth judgment unto the Gentiles. He shall not cry, nor lift up, nor cause His voice to be heard in the street." Yet between Moses and Isaiah there is a difference. For Moses is the means of giving to Israel pure morality and true religion. By the inspiration of God he brings into existence that which is not. Isaiah foresees; Moses, in a sense, creates. And the one parallel with Moses, according to Scripture, is to be found in Christ, who is the creator of the new humanity.

When the oracle had spoken, there was a movement of the cloud from the door of the tent of meeting, and apparently from the tabernacle—a sign of the displeasure of God. Following the idea that the cloud was connected with the altar, this withdrawal has been interpreted by Lange as a rebuke to Aaron. "He was inwardly crushed; the fire on his altar went out; the pillar of smoke no longer mounted up as a token of grace; the cultus was for a moment at a standstill, and it was as if an interdict of Jehovah lay on the cultus of the sanctuary." But the cloud-pillar is not, as this interpretation would imply, associated with Aaron personally; it is always the symbol of the Divine will "by the hand of Moses." We must suppose therefore that the movement of the cloud conveyed in some new and unexpected way a sense of the Divine support which Moses enjoyed. He was justified in all he had done: condemnation was brought home to his accusers.

And Miriam, who had offended most, was punished with more than a rebuke. Suddenly she was found to be covered with leprosy. Aaron, looking upon her, saw that morbid pallor which was regarded as the invariable sign of the disease. It was seen as a proof of her sin and of the anger of Jehovah. Himself trembling as one who had barely escaped, Aaron could not but confess his share in the transgression. Addressing Moses with the deepest reverence, he said, "Oh my lord, lay not, I pray thee, sin upon us, for that we have done foolishly, and for that we have sinned." The leprosy is the mark of sin. Let it not be stamped on her indelibly, nor on me. Let not the disease run its course to the horrible end. With no small presumption the two had ventured to challenge their brother's conduct and position. They knew indeed, yet from their intimacy with him did not rightly apprehend, the "divinity that hedged" him. Now for the first time its terror is disclosed to themselves; and they shrink before the man of God, pleading with him as if he were omnipotent.

Moses needs no second appeal to his compassion. He is a truly inspired man, and can forgive. He has seen the great God merciful and gracious, longsuffering, slow to anger, and he has caught something of the Divine magnanimity. This temper was not always shown throughout Israel's history by those who had the position of prophets. And we find that men who claim to be religious, even to be interpreters of the Divine will, are not invariably above retaliation. They are seen to hate those who criticise them, who throw doubt upon their arguments. A man's claim to fellowship with God, his professed knowledge of the Divine truth and religion, may be tested by his conduct when he is under challenge. If he cannot plead with God on behalf of those who have assailed him, he has not the Spirit; he is as "sounding brass, or a clanging cymbal."

Even in response to the prayer of Moses, Miriam could not be cured at once. She must go aside bearing her reproach. Shame for her offence, apart from the taint of leprosy, would make it fitting that she should withdraw seven days from camp and sanctuary. A personal indignity, not affecting her character in the least, would have been felt to that extent. Her transgression is to be realised and brooded over for her spiritual good. The law is one that needs to be kept in mind. To escape detection and leave adverse judgment behind is all that some offenders against moral law seem to desire. They dread the shame and nothing besides. Let that be avoided, or, after continuing for a time, let the sense of it pass, and they feel themselves free. But true shame is towards God; and from the mind sincerely penitent that does not quickly pass away. Those only who are ignorant of the nature of sin can soon overcome the consciousness of God's displeasure. As for men, no doubt they should forgive; but their forgiveness is often too lightly granted, too complacently assumed, and we see the easy self-recovery of one who should be sitting in sackcloth and ashes. God forgives with infinite depth of tenderness and grace of pardon. But His very generosity will affect the truly contrite with poignant sorrow when His name has by their act been brought into dishonour.

The offence of Miriam was only jealousy and presumption. She may scarcely seem so great a sinner that an attack of leprosy should have been her punishment, though it lasted for no more than seven days. We make so much of bodily maladies, so little of diseases of the soul, that we would think it strange if any one for his pride should be struck with paralysis, or for envy should be laid down with fever. Yet beside the spiritual disorder that of the body is of small moment. Why do we think so little of the moral taint, the falsehood, malice, impurity, and so much of the ills our flesh is heir to? The bad heart is the great disease.

Miriam's exclusion from the camp becomes a lesson to all the people. They do not journey while she is separated as unclean. There may have been other lepers in the outlying tents; but her sin has been of such a kind that the public conscience is especially directed to it. And the lesson had particular point with reference to those who had the prophetic gift.

Modern society, making much of sanitation and all kinds of improvements and precautions intended to prevent the spread of epidemics and mitigate their effects, has also some thought of moral disease. Persons guilty of certain crimes are confined in prisons or "cut off from the people." But of the greater number of moral maladies no account is taken. And there is no widespread gloom over the nation, no arrest of affairs, when some hideous case of social immorality or business depravity has come to light. It is but a few who pray for those who have the evil heart, and wait sympathetically for their cleansing. Ought not the reorganisation of society to be on a moral rather than an economic basis? We should be nearer the general well-being if it were reckoned a disaster when any employer oppressed those under him, or workmen were found indifferent to their brothers, or a grave crime disclosed a low state of morality in some class or circle. It is the defeat of armies and navies, the overthrow of measures and governments, that occupy our attention as a people, and seem often to obscure every moral and religious thought. Or if injustice is the topic, we find the point of it in this: that one class is rich while another is poor; that money, not character, is lost in shameful contention.

CHAPTER XI.

THE SPIES AND THEIR REPORT.

NUMBERS xiii.; xiv. 1-10.

Two narratives at least appear to be united in the thirteenth and fourteenth chapters. From xiii. 17, 22, 23, we learn that the spies were despatched by way of the south, and that they went to Hebron and a little beyond, as far as the valley of Eshcol. But ver. 21 states that they spied out the land from the wilderness of Zin, south of the Dead Sea, to the entering in of Hamath. The latter statement implies that they traversed what were afterwards called Judæa, Samaria, and Galilee, and penetrated as far as the valley of the Leontes, between the southern ranges of Libanus and Antilibanus. The one account taken by itself would make the journey of the spies northward about a hundred miles; the other, three times as long.

A further difference is this: According to one of the narratives Caleb alone encourages the people (xiii. 30; xiv. 24). But according to the other (xiii. 8, 16; xiv. 6, 7), Joshua, as well as Caleb, is among the twelve, and reports favourably as to the possibility of conquering and possessing Canaan.

Without deciding on the critical points involved, we may find a way of harmonising the apparent differences. It is quite possible, for instance, that while some of the twelve were instructed to keep in the south of Canaan, others were sent to the middle district and a third company to the north. Caleb might be among those who explored the south; while Joshua, having gone to the far north, might return somewhat later and join his testimony to that which Caleb had given. There is no inconsistency between the portions ascribed to the one narrative and those referred to the other; and the account, as we have it, may give what was the gist of several co-ordinate documents. As to any variance in the reports of the spies, we can easily understand how those who looked for smiling valleys and fruitful fields would find them, while others saw only the difficulties and dangers that would have to be faced.

The questions occur, why and at whose instance the survey was undertaken. From Deuteronomy we learn that a demand for it arose among the people. Moses says (i. 22): "Ye came near unto me every one of you, and said, Let us send men before us, that they may search the land for us, and bring us word again of the way by which we must go up, and the cities unto which we shall come." In Numbers the expedition is undertaken at the order of Jehovah conveyed through Moses. The opposition here is only on the surface. The people might desire, but decision did not lie with them. It was quite natural when the tribes had at length approached the frontier of Canaan that they should seek information as to the state of the country. And the wish was one which could be sanctioned, which had even been anticipated. The land of Canaan was already known to the children of Abraham, Isaac, and Jacob, and the praise of it as a land flowing with milk and honey mingled with their traditions. In one sense there was no need to send spies, either to report on the fertility of the land or on the peoples dwelling in it. Yet Divine Providence, on which men are to rely, does not supersede their prudence and the duty that rests with them of considering the way they go. The destiny of life or of a nation is to be wrought out in faith; still we are to use all available means in order to ensure success. So personality grows through providence, and God raises men for Himself.

To the band of pioneers each tribe contributes a man, and all the twelve are headmen, whose intelligence and good faith may presumably be trusted. They know the strength of Israel; they should also be able to count upon the great source of courage and power—the unseen Friend of the nation. Remembering what Egypt is, they know also the ways of the desert; and they have seen war. If they possess enthusiasm and hope, they will not be dismayed by the sight of a few walled towns or even of some Anakim. They will say, "The Lord of hosts is with us, the God of Jacob is our refuge." Yet there is danger that old doubts and new fears may colour their report. God appoints men to duty; but their personal character and tendencies remain. And the very best men Israel can choose for a task like this will need all their faithfulness and more than all their faith to do it well.

The spies were to climb the heights visible in the north, and look forth towards the Great Sea and away to Moriah and Carmel. They were also to make their way cautiously into the land itself and examine it. Moses anticipates that all he has said in praise of Canaan will be made good by the report, and the people will be encouraged to enter at once on the final struggle. When the desert was around them, unfruitful, seemingly interminable, the Israelites might have been disposed to fear that journeying from Egypt they were leaving the fertility of the world farther and farther behind. Some may have thought that the Divine promise had misled and deceived them, and that Canaan was a dream. Even although they had now overpassed that dreary region covered with coarse gravel, black flints, and drifting sand, "the great and terrible wilderness," what hope was there that northward they should reach a land of olives, vineyards, and flowing streams? The report of the spies would answer this question.

Now in like manner the future state of existence may seem dim and unreal, scarcely credible, to many. Our life is like a series of marches hither and thither through the desert. Neither as individuals nor as communities do we seem to approach any state of blessedness and rest. Rather, as years go by, does the region become more inhospitable. Hopes once cherished are one after another disappointed. The stern mountains that overhung the track by which our forefathers went still frown upon us. It seems impossible to get beyond their shadow. And in a kind of despair some may be ready to say: There is no promised land. This waste, with its sere grass, its burning sand, its rugged hills, makes the whole of life. We shall die here in the wilderness like those who have been before us; and when our graves are dug and our bodies laid in them, our existence will have an end. But it is a thoughtless habit to doubt that of which we have no full experience. Here we have but begun to learn the possibilities of life and find a clew to its Divine mysteries. And even as to the Israelites in the wilderness there were not wanting signs that pointed to the fruitful and pleasant country beyond, so for us, even now, there are previsions of the higher world. Some shrubs and straggling vines grew in sheltered hollows among the hills. Here and there a scanty crop of maize was reared, and in the rainy season streams flowed down the wastes. From what was known the Israelites might reason hopefully to that which as yet was beyond their sight. And are there not fore-signs for the soul, springs opened to the seekers after God in the desert, some verdure of righteousness, some strength and peace in believing?

Science and business and the cares of life absorb many and bewilder them. Immersed in the work of their world, men are apt to forget that deeper draughts of life may be drunk than they obtain in the laboratory or the counting-house. But he who knows what love and worship are, who finds in all things the food of religious thought and devotion, makes no such mistake. To him a future in the spiritual world is far more within the range of hopeful anticipation than Canaan was to one who remembered Egypt and had bathed in the waters of the Nile. Is the heavenly future real? It is: as thought and faith and love are real, as the fellowship of souls and the joy of communion with God are realities. Those who are in doubt as to immortality may find the cause of that doubt in their own earthliness. Let them be less occupied with the material, care more for the spiritual possessions, truth, righteousness, religion, and they will begin to feel an end of doubt. Heaven is no fable. Even now we have our foretaste of its refreshing waters and the fruits that are for the healing of the nations.

The spies were to climb the hills which commanded a view of the promised land. And there are heights which must be scaled if we are to have previsions of the heavenly life. Men undertake to forecast the future of the human race who have never sought those heights. They may have gone out from camp a few miles or even some days' journey, but they have kept in the plain. One is devoted to science, and he sees as the land of promise a region in which science shall achieve triumphs hitherto only dreamt of, when the ultimate atoms shall disclose their secrets and the subtle principle of life shall be no longer a mystery. The social reformer sees his own schemes in operation, some new adjustment of human relations, some new economy or system of government, the establishment of an order that shall make the affairs of the world run smoothly, and banish want and care and possibly disease from the earth. But these and similar previsions are not from the heights. We have to climb quite above the earthly and temporal, above economics and scientific theories. Where the way of faith rises, where the love of men becomes perfect in the love of God, not in theory but in the practical endeavour of earnest life, there we ascend, we advance. We shall see the coming kingdom of God only if we are heartily with God in the ardour of the redeemed soul, if we follow in the footsteps of Christ to the summits of Sacrifice.

The spies went forth from among tribes which had so far made a good journey under the Divine guidance. So well had the expedition sped that a few days' march would have brought the travellers into Canaan. But Israel was not a hopeful people nor a united people. The thoughts of many turned back; all were not faithful to God nor loyal to Moses. And as the people were, so were the spies. Some may have professed to be enthusiastic who had their doubts regarding Canaan and the possibility of conquering it. Others may have even wished to find difficulties that would furnish an excuse for returning even to Egypt. Most were ready to be disenchanted at least and to find cause for alarm. In the south of Canaan a pastoral district, rocky and uninviting towards the shore of the Dead Sea, was found to be sparsely occupied by wandering companies of Amalekites, Bedawin of the time, probably with a look of poverty and hardship that gave little promise for any who should attempt to settle where they roamed. Towards Hebron the aspect of the country improved; but the ancient city, or at all events its stronghold, was in the hands of a class of bandits whose names inspired terror throughout the district—Ahiman, Sheshai, and Talmai, sons of Anak. The great stature of these men, exaggerated by common report, together with stories of their ferocity, seem to have impressed the timid Hebrews beyond measure. And round Hebron the Amorites, a hardy highland race, were found in occupation. The report agreed on was that the people were men of great stature; that the land was one which ate up its inhabitants—that is to say, yielded but a precarious existence. Just beyond Hebron vineyards and olive-groves were found; and from the valley of Eschol one fine cluster of grapes was brought, hung upon a rod to preserve the fruit from injury, an evidence of capabilities that might be developed. Still the report was an evil one on the whole.

Those who went farther north had to tell of strong peoples—the Jebusites and Amorites of the central region, the Hittites of the north, the Canaanites of the seaboard, where afterwards Sisera had his headquarters. The cities, too, were great and walled. These spies had nothing to say of the fruitful plains of Esdraelon and Jezreel, nothing to tell of the flowery meadows, the "murmuring of innumerable bees," the terraced vineyards, the herds of cattle and flocks of sheep and goats. They had seen the strong, resolute holders of the soil, the fortresses, the difficulties; and of these they brought back an account which caused abundant alarm. Joshua and Caleb alone had the confidence of faith, and were assured that Jehovah, if He delighted in His people, would give them Canaan as an inheritance.

The report of the majority of the spies was one of exaggeration and a certain untruthfulness. They must have spoken altogether without knowledge, or else allowed themselves to magnify what they saw, when they said of the children of Anak, "We were in our own sight as grasshoppers, and so we were in their sight." Possibly the Hebrews were at this time somewhat ill-developed as a race, bearing the mark of their slavery. But we can hardly suppose that the Amorites, much less the Hittites, were of overpassing stature. Nor could many cities have been so large and strongly fortified as was represented, though Lachish, Hebron, Shalim, and a few others were formidable. On the other hand, the picture had none of the attractiveness it should have borne. These exaggerations and defects, however, are the common faults of misbelieving and therefore ignorant representation. Are any disposed to leave the wilderness of the world and possess the better country? A hundred voices of the baser kind will be heard giving warning and presage. Nothing is said about its spiritual fruit, its joy, hope, and peace. But its hardships are detailed, the renunciations, the obligations, the conflicts necessary before it can be possessed. Who would enter on the hopeless task of trying to cast out the strong man armed, who sits entrenched—of holding at bay the thousand forces that oppose the Christian life? Each position must be taken after a sore struggle and kept by constant watchfulness. Little know they who think of becoming religious how hard it is to be Christians. It is a life of gloom, of constant penitence for failures that cannot be helped, a life of continual trembling and terror. So the reports go that profess to be those of experience and knowledge of men and women who understand life.

Observe also that the account given by those who reconnoitred the land of promise sprang from an error which has its parallel now. The spies went supposing that the Israelites were to conquer Canaan and dwell there purely for their own sake, for their own happiness and comfort. Had not the wilderness journey been undertaken for that end? It did not enter into the consideration either of the people as a whole or of their representatives that they were bound for Canaan in order to fulfil the Divine purpose of making Israel a means of blessing to the world. Here, indeed, a spirituality of view was needful which the spies could not be expected to have. Breadth of foresight, too, would have been required which in the circumstances scarcely lay within human power. If any of them had taken account of Israel's spiritual destiny as a witness for Jehovah in the midst of the heathen, could they have told whether this land of Syria or some other would be a fit theatre for the fulfilment of that high destiny?

And in ignorance like theirs lies the source of mistakes often made in judging the circumstances of life, in deciding what will be wisest and best to undertake. We, too, look at things from the point of view of our own happiness and comfort, and, in a higher range, of our religious enjoyment. If we see that these are to be had in a certain sphere, by a certain movement or change, we decide on that change, we choose that sphere. But if neither temporal well-being nor enjoyment of religious privilege appears to be certain, our common practice is to turn in another direction. Yet the truth is that we are not here, and we shall never be anywhere, either in this world or another, simply to enjoy, to have the milk and honey of a smiling land, to fulfil our own desires and live to ourselves. The question regarding the fit place or state for us depends for its answer on what God means to do through us for our fellow-men, for the truth, for His kingdom and glory. The future which we with greater or less success attempt to conquer and secure will, as the Divine hand leads us on, prove different from our dream in proportion as our lives are capable of high endeavour and spiritual service. We shall have our hope, but not as we painted it.

Who are the Calebs and Joshuas of our time? Not those who, forecasting the movements of society, see what they think shall be for their people a region of comfort and earthly prosperity, to be maintained by shutting out as far as possible the agitation of other lands; but those who realise that a nation, especially a Christian nation, has a duty under God to the whole human race. Those are our true guides and come with inspiration who bid us not be afraid in undertaking the world-wide task of commending truth, establishing righteousness, seeking the enfranchisement and Christianisation of all lands.

Notwithstanding the efforts of Caleb and afterwards of Joshua to controvert the disheartening reports spread by their companions, the people were filled with dismay; and night fell upon a weeping camp. The pictures of those Anakim and of the tall Amorites, rendered more terrible by imagination, appear to have had most to do with the panic. But it was the general impression also that Canaan offered no attractions as a home. There was murmuring against Moses and Aaron. Disaffection spread rapidly, and issued in the proposal to take another leader and return to Egypt. Why had Jehovah brought them across the desert to put them under the sword at last? The tumult increased, and the danger of a revolt became so great that Moses and Aaron fell on their faces before the assembly.

Always and everywhere *faithless* means foolish, *faithless* means cowardly. By this is explained the dejection and panic into which the Israelites fell, into which men often fall. Our life and history are not confided to the Divine care; our hope is not in God. Nothing can save a man or a nation from vacillation, despondency, and defeat but the conviction that Providence opens the way and never fails those who press on. No doubt there are considerations which might have made Israel doubtful whether the conquest of Canaan lay in the way of duty. Some modern moralists would call it a great crime—would say that the tribes could look for no success in endeavouring to dispossess the inhabitants of Canaan, or even to find a place among them. But this thought did not enter into the question. Panic fell on the host, because doubt of Jehovah and His purpose overcame the partial faith which had as yet been maintained with no small difficulty.

Now it was by the mouth of Moses Israel had been assured of the promise of God. Broadly speaking, faith in Jehovah was faith in Moses, who was their moralist, their prophet, their guide. Men here and there, the seventy who prophesied for instance, had their personal consciousness of the Divine power; but the great mass of the people had the covenant, and trusted it through the mediation of Moses. Had Moses then, as the Israelites could judge, a right to command unquestionable authority as a revealer of the will of the unseen God? Take away from the history every incident, every feature, that may appear doubtful, and there remains a personality, a man of distinguished unselfishness, of admirable patience, of great sagacity, who certainly was a patriot, and as certainly had greater conceptions, higher enthusiasms, than any other man of Israel. It was perhaps difficult for those who were gross in nature and very ignorant to realise that Moses was indeed in communication with an unseen, omnipotent Friend of the people. Some might even have been disposed to say: What if he is? What can God do for us? If we are to get anything, we must seek and obtain it for ourselves. Yet the Israelites as a whole held the almost universal belief of those times, the conviction that a Power above the visible world does rule the affairs of earth. And there was evidence enough that Moses was guided and sustained by the Divine hand. The sagacious mind, the brave, noble personality of Moses, made for Israel, at least for every one in Israel capable of appreciating character and wisdom, a bridge between the seen and the unseen, between man and God.

We must not indeed deny that this conviction was liable to challenge and revision. It must always be so when a man speaks for God, represents God. Doubt of the wisdom of any command meant doubt whether God had really given it by Moses. And when it seemed that the tribes had been unwisely brought to Canaan, the reflection might be that Moses had failed as an interpreter. Yet this was not the common conclusion. Rather, from all we learn, was it the conclusion that Jehovah Himself had failed the people or deceived them. And there lay the error of unbelief which is constantly being committed still.

For us, whatever may be said as to the composition of the Bible, it is supremely, and as no other sacred book can be, the Word of God. As Moses was the one man in Israel who had a right to speak in Jehovah's name, so the Bible is the one book which can claim to instruct us in faith, duty, and hope. Speaking to us in human language, it may of course be challenged. At one point and another, some even of those who believe in Divine communication to men may question whether the Bible writers have always caught aright the sound of the heavenly

Word. And some go so far as to say: There is no Divine Voice; men have given as the Word of God, in good faith, what arose in their own mind, their own exalted imagination. Nevertheless, our faith, if faith we are to have at all, must rest on this Book. We cannot get away from human words. We must rely on spoken or written language if we are to know anything higher than our own thought. And what is written in the Bible has the highest marks of inspiration—wisdom, purity, truth, power to convince and convert and to build up a life in holiness and in hope.

It remains true accordingly that doubt of the Bible means for us, must mean, not simply doubt of the men who have been instrumental in giving us the Book, but doubt of God Himself. If the Bible did not speak in harmony with nature and reason and the widest human experience when it lays down moral law, prescribes the true rules and unfolds the great principles of life, the affirmation just made would be absurd. But it is a book of breadth, full of wisdom which every age is verifying. It stands an absolute, the manifest embodiment of knowledge drawn from the highest sources available to men—from sources not earthly nor temporary, but sublime and eternal. Faith, therefore, must have its foundation on the teaching of this Book as to " what man is to believe concerning God and what duty God requires of man." And on the other hand infidelity is and must be the result of rejecting the revelation of the Bible, denying that here God speaks with supreme wisdom and authority to our souls.

The Israelites doubting Jehovah who had spoken through Moses, that is to say, doubting the highest, most inspiring word it was possible for them to hear, turning away from the Divine reason that spoke, the heavenly purpose revealed to them, had nothing to rely upon. Confused inadequate counsels, chaotic fears, waited immediately upon their revolt. They sank at once to despondency and the most fatuous and impossible projects. The men who stood against their despair were made offenders, almost sacrificed to their fear. Joshua and Caleb, facing the tumult, called for confidence. " Fear not ye the people of the land," they said, " for they are bread for us: their defence is removed from over them, and Jehovah is with us: fear them not." But all the congregation bade stone them with stones; and it was only the bright glow of the pillar of fire shining out at the moment that prevented a dreadful catastrophe.

So the faithless generations fell back still into panic, fatuity, and crime. Trusting in their resources, men say, " No change need trouble us; we have courage, wisdom, power, sufficient for our needs." But have they unity, have they any scheme of life for which it is worth while to be courageous? The hope of bare continuance, of ignoble safety and comfort will not animate, will not inspire. Only some great vision of Duty seen along the track of the eternally right will kindle the heart of a people; the faith that goes with that vision will alone sustain courage. Without it, armies and battle-ships are but a temporary and flimsy defence, the pretext of a self-confidence, while the heart is clouded with despair. Whether men say, We will return to Egypt, refusing the call of Providence which bids us fulfil a high destiny, or, still refusing to fulfil it, We will maintain ourselves in the wilderness—they have in secret the conviction that they are failures, that their national organisation is a hollow pretence. And the end, though it may linger for a time, will be dismemberment and disaster.

Modern nations, nominally Christian, are finding it difficult to suppress disorder, and occasionally we are almost thrown into a state of panic by the activity of revolutionists. Does the cause not lie in this, that the *en avant* of Providence and Christianity is not obeyed either in the politics or social economy of the people? Like Israel, a nation has been led so far through the wilderness, but advance can only be into a new order which faith perceives, to which the voice of God calls. If it is becoming a general conclusion that there is no such country, or that the conquest of it is impossible, if many are saying, Let us settle in the wilderness, and others, Let us return to Egypt, what can the issue be but confusion? This is to encourage the anarchist, the dynamiter. The enterprise of humanity, according to such counsels, is so far a failure, and for the future there is no inspiring hope. And to make economic self-seeking the governing idea of a nation's movement is simply to abandon the true leader and to choose another of some ignominious order. Would it have been possible to persuade Moses to hold the command of the tribes, and yet remain in the desert or return to Egypt? Neither is it possible to retain Christ as our captain and also to make this world our home, or return to a practical heathenism, relieved by abundance of food, the Hellenic worship of beauty, the organisation of pleasure. For the great enterprise of spiritual redemption alone will Christ be our leader. We lose Him if we turn to the hopes of this world and cease to press the journey towards the city of God.

CHAPTER XII.

THE DOOM OF THE UNBELIEVING.

NUMBERS xiv.

THE spirit of revolt which came to a head in the proposal to put Joshua and Caleb to death was quelled by the fiery splendour that flashed out at the tent of meeting; but disaffection continued, and Moses realised with horror that immediate destruction threatened the tribes. Jehovah would smite them with pestilence, disinherit them, and raise up a new nation greater and mightier than they. Moses himself should be the father of the destined race.

The thought was one at which an ambitious man would have grasped; and to entertain it might well seem a good man's duty. In what better way could one of earnest and courageous spirit serve the world and the Divine purpose of grace? Moses stood as a representative of Abraham, to whom the promise had been first given, and of Jacob, to whom it had been renewed. If the will of Heaven was that a fresh beginning in the old succession should be made, the honour was not lightly to be put aside. Moses now saw, as Abraham saw, a great possibility. The Divine purpose did not fail, though Israel proved unfit to serve it; in the field of a more instructed age that magnificent hope which made Abraham great would blossom more generously and yield its fruit of blessing. With the sense of this possible honour to himself, there came, however, to Moses other and arresting thoughts. For Abraham had become great by sacrifice, and only one spiritually greater even than he could found a worthier race. Did Moses not think of that scene on Moriah, when the son of the promise lay stretched on the altar, and feel himself inspired for a sacrifice of his own? Yet what could it be? Nothing but the silent inward refusal of that great honour which was being put in his power, the honour of becoming even higher than Abraham in the line of originators. True, it seemed that necessity was laid on him. Yet might not Jehovah intervene on Israel's behalf as once before on Isaac's when the moment of his death had almost come? Not to sacrifice Israel was the call Moses heard when he listened in the silence, but to sacrifice his own hope, though it seemed to be pressed on him by Providence. And this began to prove itself the necessity. On the one hand he could not hide the fear that even if the Israelites were settled in Canaan a long period of education would be required to fit them for national life and power; after many generations they would be still incapable of any high spiritual task. But if Israel perished, what would happen? The faith of Jehovah, already established as an influence in the world, would fall into abeyance. When doom fell on Israel, the Egyptians would hear of it, Canaan would hear of it. The desert, the valley of the Nile, the hills of the Promised Land, would ring with the exultant cry that Jehovah had failed. And then—how long would the world have to wait till this seeming defeat could be retrieved? Century after century had passed since Abraham left his own land to fulfil the vocation of God. Century after century would have to pass before the sons of Moses could attain to any greatness, any power to move the world. The instrument Jehovah had meanwhile to use was imperfect; the tribes were not like a strong two-edged sword in the hand of the King. Yet they existed; they could be used, and Divine might, Divine grace, could overcome their imperfection. Ere the world grew older in ignorance and idolatry, Moses would have the heavenly purpose wrought. For this he will renounce, for this he must renounce, the honour possible to himself. Let Jehovah do all.

His choice made, Moses intercedes with God. The prayer has an air of simple anthropomorphism. He appears to plead that Jehovah should not imperil His own fame. The underlying thought is partly concealed by the form of expression; but the meaning is clear. It is the dawning power of the religion of God for which Moses is concerned. He would not have that lost to men which by the events of the exodus and the wilderness journey has been so far secured. Egypt is half persuaded; Canaan is beginning to see that Jehovah is greater than Anubis and Thoth, than Moloch and Baal. Was that impression to fade and to be succeeded by doubt, possibly contempt of Jehovah as Israel's God? He had brought His people into the wilderness, but He could not establish them in Canaan; therefore He slew them: if that were said, would not the loss to mankind be incalculable? "Thou, Jehovah, art seen face to face, and Thy cloud standeth over them, and Thou goest before them in a pillar of cloud by day, and in a pillar of fire by night." The astonished lands have seen this; let them not return with greater trust than ever to their own poor idols.

In the report of Moses' intercession words are quoted which were part of the revelation of the Divine character at Sinai: "Jehovah slow to anger, and plenteous in mercy, forgiving iniquity and transgression, and that will by no means clear the guilty; visiting the iniquity of the fathers upon the children, upon the third and fourth generation." The prayer quoting these latter clauses is abundantly sincere; and it proceeds on the belief that mercy rather than judgment is the delight of God. The greatness of the Divine compassion, already shown time after time since the people left Egypt, is still relied upon. And the desire of Moses is granted so far as it is in harmony with the character and purpose of God. "Thou wast a God that forgavest them, though Thou tookest vengeance of their doings" (Psalm xcix. 8).

Jehovah says, "I have pardoned according to My word." The national sin is not to be visited with destruction of the nation. No pestilence shall exterminate the murmurers, nor shall they be left without the guidance of Moses and of the cloud to melt away in the plagues of the wilderness. But yet the power of Jehovah shall be shown in their punishment; the manner of it shall be such that the earth shall be filled with the glory of the Lord. The men who came out of Egypt and have tempted Jehovah ten times shall never see Canaan. Their carcases shall fall in the desert. For forty years shall the Israelites wander as shepherds till the evil generation shall have disappeared.

Divine Providence judges the pusillanimity of men. Their fear deprives them of that which is offered and actually put within their grasp. They prove themselves incapable when the time of decisive endeavour comes, and a new generation must arise before the ripeness of circumstance again opens the way. The case of the Israelites shows that rebuke and disappointment are necessary in the Divine discipline of human life. Defects of character, of faith, are not overborne by a *tour de force* in order that the development of a heavenly purpose may be hastened. It would indeed cease to be a heavenly purpose, if with easy forgiveness God gave miraculous success. The result would be no gain in the long-run to any good cause. If men fail, God can wait for others who shall not fail. We are apt to forget this; we think that we show proper trust in the fulness of Divine pardon when we insist that men who have erred and been forgiven, who have faithlessly missed their opportunity and passed through penitence into new zeal, shall be hurried on to the duties they refused to face. But now, as in the times of Israel, the law of adequate discipline forbids, the law of punishment forbids. Humanity is not to be cheated of its Divine instruction, nor shall any pretext of generosity or necessity be urged in order that certain men may enter a Canaan they once refused to possess. We see a term set to a probation.

Does it appear an inordinate punishment, this denial of Canaan to the unbelieving? There is no need to think so. For the men and women who held back in doubt of God, the wilderness, quite as well as Canaan, would serve the main end, to teach them trust. Life went on still under the protection of the Almighty. The desert was His, as well as the land flowing with milk and honey. Yea, in the desert they had, being such as they were, fewer temptations to question the power of God and their own need of Him than they would have found in the land of promise. May we not say that men who had been so ready to receive an evil report of the land would have been confirmed in their doubt of Jehovah if they had been allowed to cross the frontier? Better for them to remain in the desert that made no pretence to be anything else, than to enter Canaan and find excuses for calling it a desert. No individual was prevented from learning to know God and trust Him; of that we may be sure. The way of instruction was that of penitence and sorrow and continued hardships. But there would have been no other way for those unbelievers even if they had entered on the promised inheritance. In Canaan, as well as in the desert, they would have had to learn contrition, to advance in moral life by means of temporal hardships and defeat.

And there was a limitation of the judgment. Only those from twenty years old and upward were included. The young men and young women, presumably because they had not bewailed their lot and cried against Moses and God, having too much of the hopeful spirit of youth, were not condemned to die in the wilderness. A difference was there, and by the terms of the deliverance was made clear, which often comes to light in human history. The old, who should know most of the goodness of God and His unfailing power, draw back; the young and inexperienced are ready to advance. Men who are occupied with affairs tend to think that their wise management brings success, and they place Divine Providence secondary to their own wisdom. Shall we be able for this? they ask. Does this approve itself to us as men of the world, responsible men? If not, they think it would be folly to go forward even at the call of God. But the young are not so wise in their own experience; they are in the mood to dare: the young and the trustful—men like Joshua and Caleb, who have learned that power and success are of God, and that His way is always safe. To calculate and act on the basis of expediency is not the failing of the young. Let us pray for men who have faith in the future of humanity and of the Church to stand forth and rally about them the youths, not spoiled by over-wise theories of life, who have still in their souls the heavenly instinct of hope.

Caleb has here and elsewhere in the history peculiar honour, all the more remarkable that he was, properly speaking, no Israelite. The narrative at this point associates his family with the tribe of Judah. But Caleb was a Kenizzite (Numb. xxxii. 12); and Kenaz appears in Gen. xxxvi. 11, 15, as an Edomite or descendant of Esau. At what time this particular Kenizzite family joined the expedition of Israel we have no hint. As yet, however, there was no intermarriage; and it should be noticed that the district which in consideration of his fidelity Caleb has for his inheritance in Canaan is the same as was occupied by Kenizzites before the conquest. There is, of course, no improbability in this; it may rather appear to give proof of the genuineness of the narrative. Caleb joins the Israelites, attaches himself to Judah in the camp and on the march, proves himself a faithful servant of God and of the host, and has the promise of his forefathers' inheritance when the distribution of Canaan shall be made. He reported favourably of the region about Hebron; and Hebron became his city, as we learn from Josh. xiv.

In contrast to the special promise made to Joshua and Caleb is the fate of the other ten whose report brought "a slander upon the land." These "died by the plague before Jehovah." It would seem that before Moses appealed to God on behalf of the people, the pestilence was spreading which might have swept the Israelites down like Sennacherib's army in after-times. And the ten false spies had been among the first to die. Little indeed know men how soon providence will convict them of their faithlessness and rebellion. Let us save our lives, they say, by holding back from duties that involve difficulty and danger. Why advance where we are sure to fall by the sword? But the sword finds them nevertheless, or the plague lays hold of them; and where then is the life they were so careful to preserve? The men of Israel who said, "Let us not go to Canaan, but return to Egypt," neither see Canaan nor Egypt. They gain nothing they desire; they lose all they were so careful to keep.

Suddenly at ver. 40 we are brought to a new development. The people no sooner hear their doom than they resolve to take the future into their own hands. They acknowledge that they have sinned, meaning, however, only that they have fallen into a mistake the consequences of which they had not foreseen; and with this inadequate confession of fault they decide to make the advance into Canaan forthwith. They do not see that instead of recovering their hope in God by any such attempt they will really deepen the alienation between themselves and Him. Submission is indeed hard, but it is their one grace, their one duty. If they press on into Canaan, they must go without the Lord, as Moses warns them, and they shall not prosper.

It is not enough when men have discovered an evil heart of unbelief, and turned again in repentance, that they take up the thread of life which has become ravelled. Perverse faithlessness cannot be cured by a sudden decision to resume the duty which was abandoned in fear. The refusal was no superficial thing, but had its source in the springs of will, the character and habits of life. We are apt to judge otherwise, and to suppose that we can alter the whole current of our nature by a single act of choice. To-day the trend is strongly in one direction, along a channel which has been forming for many years; to-morrow we think it possible to become other men, strong where we were weak, determined upon that which we abhorred. But something must intervene; some change must take place deeper than our impulse. We must have the new heart and the right spirit; and in proportion to the gravity of the situation and the importance of the duty to be done must the time of discipline be long. The wilderness wandering had to be for many years because the temper of a whole people was to be altered. For a single person a far shorter ordeal may suffice. He may pass through the stages of conviction, repentance, and new creation in a few weeks or even days. Nay, sometimes the regenerating Spirit brings about the change apparently in a moment. Yet the rule is that stability in faith must come slowly, that the way of trial cannot be hastened. A great task, therefore, the right doing of which is necessary to the open vindication of religion, may not be gone about in a sudden change of mind. We are not to take lightly, into untried hands, the massive plough of the kingdom of God.

In Canaan, the Amalekites and Canaanites, Moses said, would dispute the advance of Israel, —Amalekites skilled in desultory war, Canaanites long trained in military art. These would fight without any sense of the support of the true God. But how would the Hebrews speed, meeting them on the same footing? The contest would be then between human skill and daring on either side; and there could be no doubt as to the issue. Bands of men acquainted with the country, disciplined in war as the tribes of Israel were not, fighting for their fields and homes with a defence of walled cities to fall back upon, would certainly win. If the Hebrews went up, it would be without the sign of Jehovah's presence; the ark of the covenant could not be borne with the army on such an expedition. Their attempt, being presumptuous, must end in disaster.

Too often the conflicts in which the Church is involved are of this very kind. There is profession of high moral design and Christian principle. Ostensibly it is for the sake of true religion that something is undertaken. But in reality the affair is not one that belongs to the essence of faith. It is perhaps a question of prestige, of exclusive claim to certain rights or moneys, the very last thing a Christian church should insist upon. Then the contest is between human diplomacy and resolution, whether on the one side or the other. It is idle to call a campaign like this a holy war. The ark of the covenant does not accompany the army that calls itself Jehovah's. As Israel found that even Amalekites and Canaanites were too strong for her, so has the Church often found that men whom she termed unbelievers were superior to her in the arms she chose to use. Again and again have her forces had to retire smitten even unto Hormah. For those who are called unbelievers and atheists have their rights; and they will always be able to maintain their rights against a presumptuous church which " goes up into the mountain " without the sanction of its living Head.

It was no general advance of the tribes that on this occasion ended in defeat. The solid, resolute march of the whole people was a very different thing from the half-hearted sally of some hundreds of fighting men. When the host of the Israelites, men, women, and children, moved together, the men of war had support in the sympathy of those they defended, in the prayers of the priest and of the people. They were nerved to play the part of heroes by the thought that all depended upon them, that if they failed their wives and children would be put to the sword. And again there is a parallel in the advance of the Church against her adversaries. If the officials only go out to fight, if it is their affair, their expedition, if there is no strong onward movement of the whole host, what is there to give support to the enterprise? The fighting men may seem to have heart enough for their battle; but the underlying feeling that they are not engaged in the defence of the Gospel itself, or in guarding any position on which the power and success of the Gospel depend, must always, and properly, weaken their arms. There is all the difference in the world between an ecclesiastical battle and the contest for vital faith. And it is a matter of regret that so much of the strength and ardour of good men should be wasted in downright earthly fighting, when the feeling of the Church as a whole is not with those who claim to be her army. Let all the tribes, that is to say all the churches of Christ that are of one mind as to vital truth, advance together, without jealousy, without mutual contempt, and the opposition to Christianity will practically melt away.

From the twenty-first chapter, which appears to open with a reminiscence of the first attack on Canaan, we gather that one of those who opposed the expedition was the Canaanite King of Arad. The advance appears therefore to have been made by way of Hezron and Beersheba. The mountains visible from the camp were likely the chalk hills beyond the " Ascent of Akrabbim." These passed, probably near Hezron, a valley opened, stretching away towards Hebron. The Amalekites gathering from every wady, and the Canaanites from the ridge to the right, where Arad lay, seem to have fallen upon the Hebrews with a sudden onset. While many escaped others were slain or taken captive. A keen memory of the defeat survived; but it was not till long afterwards, in the days of the judges, that the strongholds of the region were reduced.

CHAPTER XIII.

OFFERINGS: SABBATH-KEEPING: DRESS.

NUMBERS XV.

THE enactments of this chapter regarding meal offerings and drink offerings, the heave offerings of the first dough, and the atonement for unwitting errors belong to the cultus of Canaan. Nothing generic distinguishes the first and third of these statutes from some that were presumably to be observed in the desert; but the note is explicit, " When ye be come into the land of your habitations which I give unto you," " When ye be come into the land whither I bring you." The whole chapter, with its instance of presumptuous sin introduced by the clause, " And while the children of Israel were in the wilderness," marking a return to that time, and its commandment regarding the fringes or tassels of blue to be attached to the dress as remembrances of obligations, may appear at first sight without any reference either to what has preceded or what follows. The compilers, however, have a definite purpose in view. The presumption of Korah and his company, and of Dathan and Abiram, is in contrast to the unwitting faults for which atonement is provided, and it comes under the category of what is " done with a high hand "—a form of blasphemy which is to be punished with death. The case of the Sabbath-breaker is an instance of this unpardonable sin, and sends its light on to the incidents that follow. Even the memorial fringes or tassels, and the prophetic sentences that accompany the command to wear them, seem to be forewarnings of the doom of sacrilegious men.

1. MEAL AND DRINK OFFERINGS.—The statute regarding offerings " to make a sweet savour unto Jehovah " is specially occupied with prescribing the proportion of flour and oil and wine to be presented along with the animal brought for a burnt offering or sacrifice. Any

one separating himself in terms of a vow, or desiring to express gratitude for some Divine favour, or again on the occasion of a sacred festival when he had special cause of rejoicing before God, might bring a lamb, a ram, or an ox as his oblation; and the meal and drink offerings were to vary with the value of the animal brought for sacrifice. The law does not demand the same offering of every person under similar circumstances. According to his means or his gratitude he may give. But deciding first as to his burnt or slain offering, he must add to it, for a lamb, the tenth of an ephah of fine flour mixed with a quarter of a hin of oil, and also a quarter of a hin of wine. For a bullock, the quantities were to be three-tenths of an ephah of fine flour, with half a hin of oil, and, as a drink offering, half a hin of wine.

The provision is a singular one, based on some sense of what was becoming which we cannot pretend to revive. But it points to a rule which the Apostle Paul may have recognised in this and other Jewish statutes as belonging to universal morality: "Take thought for things honourable in the sight of all men." To make a show of generosity by giving a bullock, while the flour and oil and wine were withheld, was not seemly. Neither is it seemly for a Christian to be lavish in his gifts to the Church, but withhold the meal offering and drink offering he owes to the poor. Throughout the whole range of use and expenditure, personal and of the family, a proportion is to be found which it is one of the Christian arts to determine, one of the Christian duties to observe. And nothing is right unless all is right. The penny saved here takes away the sweet savour of the pound given there. No man is in this to be a law to himself. Public justice and Divine are to be satisfied.

The presence or absence of oil in an oblation marked its character. The sin offering and the jealousy offering were without oil. The "oil of joy" (Isa. lxi. 3) accompanied festal and peace offerings. All ordinances prescribing the oblation of wine and oil necessarily belonged to the cultus of Canaan, for in the wilderness neither of these elements of the sacrifice could be always had. The idea underlying the peace offerings, with their accompanying meal and drink offerings, was unquestionably that of feasting with Jehovah, enjoying His bounty at His table. Acknowledgment was made that the cattle on the hills were His, that it was He who gave the harvest, the vintage, and the fruit of the olive-grove. Confession of man's indebtedness to Jehovah as Lord of nature was interwoven with the whole sacrificial system.

In connection with this ordinance of meal and drink offerings, and that of atonement for unintentional failures in duty (ver. 22 ff.), it is very carefully enacted that the law shall be the same for the "homeborn" and the "stranger." "For the assembly there shall be one statute for you and for the stranger that sojourneth with you, a statute for ever throughout your generations: as ye are, so shall the stranger be before the Lord." The design is to secure religious unity, and by means of it gradually to incorporate with Israel all dwellers in the land. While certain ordinances were intended to make Israel a holy nation separated and consecrated to Jehovah, this admission of strangers to the privileges of the covenant has another design. In the Book of Deuteronomy (vii. 2) a statute occurs that entirely excludes from citizenship and incorporation all Canaanites, Hittites, Jebusites, Amorites, Hivites, Girgashites, and Perizzites. There was to be no intermarriage with them, no toleration of them, lest they led Israel away into idolatry. The statute is enforced by the words, "For thou art an holy people unto the Lord thy God: the Lord thy God hath chosen thee to be a peculiar people unto Himself, above all peoples that are upon the face of the earth." With this emphatic assertion of the severance of the Hebrews from other races the strain of Numbers, as well as Exodus and Leviticus, generally agrees. When we endeavour to harmonise with it the admission of strangers to the right and joy of sacrificial festivals, we at once meet the difficulty that no other races were fitter to be received into religious confraternity than those of Canaan. Neither Babylonians, Syrians, Phœnicians, nor Philistines were free from the taint of idolatry; and however degrading the rites of the Canaanites were, some of the other nations followed practices quite as revolting.

We know that for a long period of Israel's history strangers were, according to the statute presently under consideration, admitted to the fellowship of religion, as well as to high office in the state. "We have only to study the Book of Joshua to discover that the Israelites, like the Saxons in Britain, destroyed the cities and not the population of the country, and that the number of cities actually overthrown was not very large. We have only to turn to the list of the 'mighty men' of David to learn how many of them were foreigners, Hittites, Ammonites, Zobahites, and even Philistines of Gath (2 Sam. xv. 18, 19; vi. 10). Nor must it be forgotten that David himself was partly a Moabite by descent."[*] In accordance with this large tolerance we might be disposed to include among the "strangers" admitted to privilege men belonging to races that inhabited Canaan before the conquest. Even Deuteronomy seems in one passage to exclude none but Ammonites and Moabites; and the covenant law of Exod. xxiii. commands generous treatment of the stranger. In contrast to the "homeborn," strangers may appear to mean those only who had come from other countries and chosen to identify themselves with the faith and fortunes of Israel; still this passage attempts no such definition, and on the whole we must allow that the Mosaic law in regulating the political and social position of resident non-Israelites showed "a spirit of great liberality." They had, of course, to conform to many laws—those, for instance, of marriage, and those which forbade the eating of blood and the flesh of animals not properly slaughtered. If uncircumcised, they could not keep the Passover; but being circumcised, they had equal rights with the Hebrews. The purpose evidently was to make an open way to the benefits of Israel's government and religion.

The heave offering of the first dough is placed (ver. 20) side by side with the heave offering of the threshing-floor of the first sheaves. In Leviticus (xxiii. 17) a harvest oblation is ordered—two wave-loaves of fine flour baken with leaven. Here the heave offering of a cake made from the first dough is not accompanied with sacrifices of animals, but is of a simple kind, mainly a tribute to

[*] Sayce, "The Higher Criticism and the Verdict of the Monuments," p. 359.

the priests. The Deuteronomic statute regarding firstfruits, which were to be put in a basket and set down before the altar, prescribed a formula of dedication beginning, "An Aramean ready to perish was my father, and he went down into Egypt": and the offering of these firstfruits was to be an occasion of joy—"Thou shalt rejoice in all the good which the Lord thy God hath given unto thee and unto thine house, thou and the Levite, and the stranger that is in the midst of thee." There can be no question that the most developed statute regarding these harvest offerings is that given in Leviticus, where the exact time for the presentation of the loaves is fixed, the fiftieth day after the Sabbath, from the day when the sheaf was brought. The feast accompanying the offering of the loaves came to be known as that of Pentecost.

Passing now to the law of atonement for unintentional omissions of duty, we notice that the introductory sentences (vv. 22, 23) have a peculiar retrospective cast. They seem to point back to the time when the Lord gave commandment by the hand of Moses. It would appear that in course of years discovery was made that portions of the law were neglected, and the provisions of this statute were to relieve the nation and individuals of accumulating defilement. "When ye shall err, and not observe all these commandments which the Lord hath spoken unto Moses, even all that the Lord hath commanded you by the hand of Moses, from the day that the Lord gave commandment, and onward throughout your generations; then it shall be, if it be done unwittingly, without the knowledge of the congregation"—so runs the preamble. A series of statutes in Lev. iv. contemplates offences of a like kind, when something has been done which the Lord commanded not to be done. The enactment of Numbers appears to point to a "complete falling away of the congregation from the whole of the law," an unconscious apostasy. Maimonides understands the provision as relating to guilt incurred by the people in adopting customs and usages of the heathen that seemed to be reconcilable with the law of Jehovah, though they really led to contempt and neglect of His commandments.*

For the nation as a whole, under these circumstances, atonement was to be made by the burnt offering of a young bullock with its meal offering and drink offering, and the sin offering of a he-goat. In this purgation all strangers resident with Israel are specially included. When any person discovered that he had neglected a precept, he was to offer a she-goat of the first year for a sin offering. The Israelite and the stranger alike had in this way access to the sanctuary. But in contrast to unintentional omission of duty was set deliberate neglect of it. For this there was no atonement. Whether the highhanded transgressor was homeborn or a stranger, he was to be utterly cut off as a blasphemer; his iniquity rested upon him. The distinction is morally sound; and the punishment of the rebel against authority—apparently nothing less than death, or perhaps, if he has fled the land, outlawry—is such as the theocratic idea obviously required. It was Jehovah Himself who was defied. A man who, as it were, shook his fist in rebellion against God had no right to live in His world, under the protection of His beneficent laws.

* See Keil and Delitzsch *in loco*.

The distinction between unwitting neglect and open rejection runs through the whole range of duty, natural, Hebrew, Christian. What a man knows to be right he has before him as a Divine law of moral conduct. By the highest obligations, under which he lies to the Lord of conscience, to his fellow-men, and to himself, he is bound to obey. Judaism added the authority of revelation—the Mosaic law, the prophetic word. Christianity still further adds the authority of the word spoken by the Son of God, and the obligation imposed by His death as the manifestation of eternal love. In proportion as the Divine will is made clear, and the law enforced by revelation and grace, the sin of rejection becomes greater and more blasphemous. But, on the other hand, the unwitting transgressor, be he heathen or imperfectly instructed Christian, has under the new covenant, in which mercy and justice go hand in hand, no less consideration than the Hebrew who unintentionally erred. There is no law that cuts him off from his people. Wide as this principle may reach, it must be that according to which men are judged. Many, knowing the invisible things of God "through the things that are made," are without excuse. They "hold down the truth in unrighteousness"; they are high-handed transgressors. But others who have no knowledge of the Divine law, and break it unwittingly, have their atonement: God provides it. Nor are we to impeach Divine Providence by judging before the time.

It may be asked, Why, since defiant rejection of Christian law is more blasphemous than highhanded breach of the old Hebrew law, the providence of God does not punish it? If any one with Christ and His cross in view is guilty of injustice, or of hatred which is murder, does he not prove himself unworthy to live in God's world? And why, then, does he not suffer at once the doom of his rebellion? The theory of some stern moralists has been that human government should administer the justice of Heaven and cut off the unbeliever. In many a notable case this has been done, and has caused a righteous horror which continues to be felt. But although men cannot safely undertake the punishment of such offenders, why does not God? Christ boldly stated that here and now this is not the method of the Divine government, but that men enjoy the Father's mercy even when they are unjust, unthankful, and evil. Yet He spoke of judgment universal—judgment and retribution that shall not miss a single sinner, a single secret sin. And His view of the theocracy clearly is that meanwhile God by mercy to the defiant desires to train men in mercy, by forbearance towards the unthankful and evil commends to us like patience and endurance. Transgressors are to have their full opportunity of repentance, to which the very goodness of God calls them. But justice which delays is not unobservant. Though He who reigns moves slowly to His end, He will not fail to reach it. "He hath appointed a day in the which He will judge the world in righteousness." As for human law, its sphere is fixed. Society must protect itself against crime, and is to do so in the name of God, in conformity with the eternal principles of righteousness. The Hebrew temper may seem to have carried this principle into a range that was perilous to enter, as in the instance immediately to be considered; yet the protection of society was even then the immediate motive, not vain jealousy for the honour of God. For ourselves, we have a duty which must be done without assumption or hypocrisy.

The various subjects of thought suggested here should be followed out. For us, they are complicated on the social as well as the religious side by certain theories that are in vogue. The duty of civil government, for example, is on one side extended beyond its proper range by the attempt to give it authority in the domain of religious truth; on the other hand it is unduly restricted by toleration of what is against the well-being of society. The Christian moralist has much to ponder in relation to popular opinions and the trend of modern legislation.

2. THE SABBATH-BREAKER.—If the actual sequence of events is followed in the narrative of Numbers, it must have been after the condemnation of the adult Israelites that judgment of the man who was found infringing the Sabbath law had to be executed; and some who were themselves under reprobation took part in convicting and punishing this offender. There is a difficulty here which on high moral grounds it is impossible to explain away. Disaffection and revolt had brought on the mass of the people the sentence of destruction; and this had only been exchanged on Moses' intercession for the forty years of wandering. Should not sins that were visited with this penalty have excluded all who were guilty of them from any judicial act? But the same objection would, if admitted, prevent all of us from taking part in the execution of law. Neither the judge nor the jury, neither those who legislate nor those who administer law, are free from moral fault. The whole system dealing with crime has this defect; and Israel in the wilderness was as much entitled as modern society to take in hand the correction of offenders, the maintenance of public well-being.

The law which had been broken was one specially connected with duty to God. Sabbath-keeping might indeed seem to belong to worship rather than to social morality. The seventh day was the Sabbath of Jehovah. It was to be kept holy to Him, made a delight for His sake. The statute regarding it belonged to the first table of the Decalogue. Still, the commandment had a social as well as a religious side. In good will to men Jehovah required the day to be kept holy to Him. Had one and another like this offender been allowed to set aside the fourth commandment, the interests of the whole congregation would soon have suffered. It was for the good of the race, physically as well as intellectually and spiritually, the Sabbath was to be kept. Those who guarded the sanctity of the Sabbath were guarding not the honour of God alone, though they may have thought that the chief merit of their watchfulness, but the interests of the people, a precious heritage of the nation.

It is not necessary to maintain that judgment was given by Moses solely on the ground that the man who gathered sticks on the Sabbath was an offender against the public well-being. The thought of Jehovah's "jealousy" was constantly kept before the mind of Israel, for by that idea, better than any other, beneficent legislation was supported in a rude age; and judgment no doubt rested mainly on this. Yet the interference of the people and their share in the execution of punishment are to be justified by the undoubted fact that Israel could not afford to let the Sabbath be lost. Even those who were to a great extent earthly could perceive this. And if the punishment seems disproportionate, we must remember that it was the presumptuous temper of the man rather than his actual fault that was judged criminal. St. James said, no doubt from this point of view, "Whosoever shall keep the whole law, and yet offend in one point, he is become guilty of all." The criminal act was that of breaking down, with daring hand, the safeguard of social and religious prosperity.

And there is a sense in which without Phariseeism those who are concerned for the public well-being may still insist on the strict enforcement of the laws that guard the day of rest. Though all days are alike sacred to spiritually minded persons, yet bodily health and mental soundness are bound up more than men in general know with the Sabbatic interval between labour and labour. The Puritanism often scoffed at is far more philanthropic than the humanitarianism, so-called, which derides it. And when any one enforces the duty of Sabbath-keeping by insisting on God's claim to the seventh day, his belief is no superstition. Convict him first of advocating what is against the good of men, irrational, absurd, before venturing to call him superstitious. If what is advanced as a claim of God can be proved to be really for the good of men, it is a virtue to insist that for God's sake as well as the sake of men it should be rendered. There were persons in our Lord's time who made Sabbath-keeping a superstition. Against them He testifieth. But it is in His name who was the great Friend of men the Sabbath law is now insisted on; and the day of rest has all the higher sanction that it commemorates His resurrection from the dead, His promise of that new life which relief from labour enables us to pursue.

The institution of the Sabbath and the scrupulous observance of it were, for Israel, and are still for all believers in Divine religion, most important means of maintaining unity in the faith. Now that many causes interfere with the simultaneous exhibition of regard for other symbols of Christian belief, the day of rest and worship gives a universal opportunity which it would be fatal to neglect. It has the advantage of beginning to claim men on the ground where religion first appeals to them, that of God's care for their temporal well-being. Those with whom religious feeling is quite elementary must see that a boon of incalculable value is offered in this recurring refreshment to the wearied body and strained mind. And with progress in religious culture the benefit of the day of rest is found to advance. The opportunities of worship, of religious meditation and service, which it brings, will be esteemed as the value of Christian fellowship, the importance of Christian knowledge, and the duty of Christian endeavour are successively understood. On all these grounds the Sabbath, or Lord's Day, is for modern religion, as for that of the old covenant, a great declaration, a means of unity and development which the spiritual will earnestly uphold. Let it fail, and distinction between religious and non-religious will be without a sign. No doubt the reality is more by far than the symbol. Yet fellowship, for which in many cases the Sabbath alone gives opportunity, is far more than a symbol: and unity requires an outward manifestation. Nothing could be more perilous to the religious life of our people than the tendency, shown by many who profess Christianity and sanctioned by some of its teachers, to make the Sabbath a day of self-pleasing, of mere individualism, and incoherent secularity.

3. THE MEMORIAL TASSELS.—The unique sumptuary law with which the chapter closes may be regarded as a sequence of the Sabbath-breaker's conviction. That Israelites might never be without a reminder of their duty, and of the Divine laws they were scrupulously to observe, these tassels with a band of blue were to be constantly worn. It appears to us singular that men should be expected to pay heed to such mementoes as these. We are apt to say, If the laws of God were not in their hearts, the *zizith* would scarcely make them more attentive; and if they had the laws in their hearts, they would need no memorials of obligation. But the ornament was something more than a reminder of duty. It was a badge of honour, and became more so as the Israelites understood their high position among the peoples. The *zizith* would be like an order, a mark of rank; or like the uniform of his regiment, which to the good soldier recalls its history. The Hebrew would have to live up to his duty as signified by these attachments of his dress.

And Israelites were to be distinguished by the *zizith* from those who were of other races, not under law to Jehovah. Every man who wore this badge would be able to count on the sympathy of every other Israelite. The symbol became a means of rousing the *esprit* of the nation, and binding it together in a zealous fraternity. The nature of the badge appears to us peculiar; but the value of it cannot be denied. The modern peoples, far as they have travelled from the old ways of the Hebrews, retain the use of symbolic dress, the liking for ornaments, by which a man's life may be known.

The name *zizith* is derived from a word meaning blossom. The tassel was formed of twisted threads bound by a cord or ribbon of blue to the garment. It was the blossom of the robe, so to speak, hanging by a blue stem. The ornament is again mentioned in Deut. xxii. 12, where it has another name, *gedilim*, enlargements. With extraordinary pride the Jews of our own time still wear the *talith*, which is a fantastical development of the *zizith* of Numbers. "The rabbins observe that each string consisted of eight threads, which, with the number of knots and the numerical value of the letters in the word, make 613, which, according to them, is the exact number of the precepts in the law." The Pharisees in Christ's time enlarged their phylacteries, displaying superfluously the proofs of their Hebrew orthodoxy and zeal. It is the danger of all symbols. In the youth of a people they have meaning; they express fact, they give honour. The Israelite, wearing his, felt himself reminded, put on his honour, not to go about "according to his own heart and his own eyes by which he used to go a-whoring." But afterwards the zeal became that of pride, the symbol a mere amulet or a token of self-sufficiency. The Jew of to-day is partly kept separate by his talith, and because he wears it, feels himself in touch with the fathers and heroes and prophets of his people. But he also feels, what is not always good, his remoteness from heathen and Christian "dogs."

And Christian symbols, the few sanctioned by Scripture, the others that have crept into use in the course of history, bring with their use a similar danger. In many cases they are signs of privilege rather than memorials of duty. They minister to pride, rather than stimulate zeal in the service of God and men. The crucifix itself, with consummate superstition, is worn and kissed as a talisman.

CHAPTER XIV.

KORAH, DATHAN, AND ABIRAM.

NUMBERS xvi., xvii.

BEHIND what appears in the history, there must have been many movements of thought and causes of discontent which gradually led to the events we now consider. Of the revolts against Moses which occurred in the wilderness, this was the most widely organised and involved the most serious danger. But we can only conjecture in what way it arose, how it was related to previous incidents and tendencies of popular feeling. It is difficult to understand the report, in which Korah appears at one time closely associated with Dathan and Abiram, at other times quite apart from them as a leader of disaffection. According to Wellhausen and others, three narratives are combined in the text. But without going so far in the way of analysis we clearly trace two lines of revolt: one against Moses as leader; the other against the Aaronic priesthood. The two risings may have been distinct; we shall however deal with them as simultaneous and more or less combined. A great deal is left unexplained, and we must be guided by the belief that the narrative of the whole book has a certain coherency, and that facts previously recorded must have had their bearing on those now to be examined.

The principal leader of revolt was Korah, son of Izhar, a Levite of the family of Kohath; and with him were associated two hundred and fifty "princes of the congregation, called to the assembly, men of renown," some of them presumably belonging to each of the tribes as is shown incidentally in xxvii. 3. The complaint of this company—evidently representing an opinion widely held—was that Moses and Aaron took too much upon them in reserving to themselves the whole arrangement and control of the ritual. The two hundred and fifty, who according to the law had no right to use censers, were so far in opposition to the Aaronic priesthood that they were provided with the means of offering incense. They claimed for themselves on behalf of the whole congregation, whom they declared to be holy, the highest function of priests. With Korah were specially identified a number of Levites who, not content with being separated to do the service of the tabernacle, demanded the higher sacerdotal office. It might seem from vv. 10, 11, that all the two hundred and fifty were Levites; but this is precluded by the earlier statement that they were princes of the congregation, called to the assembly. So far as we can gather, the tribe of Levi did not supply princes, "men of renown," in this sense. While Moses deals with Korah and his company, Dathan, Abiram, and On, who belong to the tribe of Reuben, stand in the background with their grievance. Invited to state it, they complain that Moses has not only brought the congregation out of a land "flowing with milk and honey," to kill them in the wilderness, failing to give them the inheritance he promised; but he has made himself a prince over the host, determining everything without consulting the heads of the tribes. They ask if he means " to put out the eyes of these men,"—that is, to blind them to the real purpose he has in view, whatever it is, or to make them his slaves after the Babylonian fashion, by actually boring out the eyes of each tenth man, perhaps. The two hundred and fifty are called by Moses to bring their censers and the incense and fire they have been using, that Jehovah may signify whether He chooses to be served by them as priests, or by Aaron. The offering of incense over, the decree against the whole host as concerned in this revolt is made known, and Moses intercedes for the people. Then the Voice commands that all the people shall separate themselves from the "tabernacle" of Korah, Dathan, and Abiram, apparently as if some tent of worship had been erected in rivalry of the true tabernacle. Dathan and Abiram are not at the "tabernacle," but at some little distance, in tents of their own. The people remove from the "tabernacle of Korah, Dathan, and Abiram," and on the terrible invocation of judgment pronounced by Moses, the ground cleaves asunder and all the men that appertain unto Korah go down alive into the pit. Afterwards, it is said, "fire came forth from the Lord and devoured the two hundred and fifty men that offered the incense." "The men that appertained unto Korah" may be the presumptuous Levites, most closely identified with his revolt. But the two hundred and fifty consumed by the fire are not said to have been swallowed by the cleaving earth; their censers are taken up "out of the burning," as devoted or sacred, and beaten into plates for a covering of the altar.

On the morrow the whole congregation, even more disaffected than before, is in a state of tumult. The cry is raised that Moses and Aaron "have killed the people of Jehovah." Forthwith a plague, the sign of Divine anger, breaks out. Atonement is made by Aaron, who runs quickly with his burning censer "into the midst of the assembly," and "stands between the dead and the living." But fourteen thousand seven hundred die before the plague is stayed. And the position of Aaron as the acknowledged priest of Jehovah is still further confirmed. Rods or twigs are taken, one for each tribe, all the tribes having been implicated in the revolt; and these rods are laid up in the tent of meeting. When a day has passed, the rod of Aaron for the tribe of Levi is found to have put forth buds and borne almonds. The close of the whole series of events is an exclamation of amazed anxiety by all the people: "Behold, we perish, we are undone, we are all undone. Every one that cometh near unto the tabernacle of Jehovah dieth: shall we perish all of us?"

Now throughout the narrative, although other issues are involved, there can be no question that the main design is the confirmation of the Aaronic priesthood. What happened conveyed a warning of most extraordinary severity against any attempt to interfere with the sacerdotal order as established. And this we can understand. But it becomes a question why a revolt of Reubenites against Moses was connected with that of Korah against the sole priesthood of the Aaronic house. We have also to consider how it came about that princes out of all the tribes were to be found provided with censers, which they were apparently in the habit of using to burn incense to Jehovah. There is a Levitical revolt; there is an assumption by men in each tribe of priestly dignity; and there is a protest by men representing the tribe of Reuben against the dictatorship of Moses. In what way might these different movements arise and combine in a crisis that almost wrecked the fortunes of Israel?

The explanation supplied by Wellhausen on the basis of his main theory is exceedingly laboured, at some points improbable, at others defective. According to the Jehovistic tradition, he says,[*] the rebellion proceeds from the Reubenites, and is directed against Moses as leader and judge of the people. The historical basis of this is dimly discerned to be the fall of Reuben from its old place at the head of the brother tribes. Out of this story, says Wellhausen, at some time or other not specified, "when the people of the congregation, *i. e.*, of the Church, have once come on the scene," there arises a second version. The author of the agitation is now Korah, a prince of the tribe of Judah, and he rebels not only against Moses but against Moses and Aaron as representing the priesthood. "The jealousy of the secular grandees is now directed against the class of hereditary priests instead of against the extraordinary influence on the community of a heaven-sent hero." Then there is a third addition which "belongs likewise to the Priestly Code, but not to its original contents." In this, Korah the prince of the tribe of Judah is replaced by another Korah, head of a "post-exilic Levitical family"; and "the contest between clergy and aristocracy is transformed into a domestic strife between the higher and inferior clergy which was no doubt raging in the time of the narrator." All this is supposed to be a natural and easy explanation of what would otherwise be an "insoluble enigma." We ask, however, at what period any family of Judah would be likely to claim the priesthood, and at what post-exilic period there was "no doubt" a strife between the higher and inferior clergy. Nor is there any account here of the two hundred and fifty princes of the congregation, with their partially developed ritual antagonistic to that of the tabernacle.

We have seen that according to the narrative of Numbers seventy elders of the tribes were appointed to aid Moses in bearing the heavy burden of administration, and were endowed with the gift of prophecy that they might the more impressively wield authority in the host. In the first instance, these men might be zealous helpers of Moses, but they proved, like the rest, angry critics of his leadership when the spies returned with their evil report. They were included with the other men of the tribes in the doom of the forty years' wandering, and might easily become movers of sedition. When the ark was stationed permanently at Kadesh, and the tribes spread themselves after the manner of shepherds over a wide range of the surrounding district, we can easily see that the authority of the seventy would increase in proportion to the need for direction felt in the different groups to which they belonged. Many of the scattered

[*] Prolegomena to the "History of Israel," p. 354.

companies too were so far from the tabernacle that they might desire a worship of their own, and the original priestly function of the heads of tribes, if it had lapsed, might in this way be revived. Although there were no altars, yet with censers and incense one of the highest rites of worship might be observed.

Again, the period of inaction must have been galling to many who conceived themselves quite capable of making a successful assault on the inhabitants of Canaan, or otherwise securing a settled place of abode for Israel. And the tribe of Reuben, first by birthright, and apparently one of the strongest, would take the lead in a movement to set aside the authority of Moses. We have also to keep in mind that though Moses had pressed the Kenizzites to join the march and relied on their fidelity, the presence in the camp of one like Hobab, who was an equal not a vassal of Moses, must have been a continual incentive to disaffection. He and his troops had their own notions, we may believe, as to the delay of forty years, and would very likely deny its necessity. They would also have their own cultus, and religiously, as well as in other ways, show an independence which encouraged revolt.

Once more, as to the Levites, it might seem unfair to them that Aaron and his two sons should have a position so much higher than theirs. They had to do many offices in connection with sacrifice, and other parts of the holy service. On them, indeed, fell the burden of the duties, and the ambitious might expect to force their way into the higher office of the priesthood, at a time when rebellion against authority was coming to a head. We may suppose that Korah and his company of Levites, acting partly for themselves, partly in concert with the two hundred and fifty who had already assumed the right to burn incense, agreed to make their demand in the first instance, that as Levites they should be admitted priests. This would prepare the way for the princes of the tribes to claim sacerdotal rights according to the old clan idea. And at the same time, the priority of Reuben would be another point, insistence upon which would strike at the power of Moses. If the princes of Reuben had gone so far as to erect a "tabernacle" or *mishcan* for their worship, that may have been, for the occasion, made the headquarters of revolt, perhaps because Reuben happened at the time to be nearest the encampment of the Levites.

A widespread rebellion, an organised rebellion, not homogeneous, but with many elements in it tending to utter confusion, is what we see. Suppose it to have succeeded, the unity of worship would have been destroyed completely. Each tribe with its own cultus would have gone its own way so far as religion was concerned. In a very short time there would have been as many debased cults as there were wandering companies. Then the claim of autonomy, if not of right to lead the tribes, made on behalf of Reuben, involved a further danger. Moses had not only the sagacity but the inspiration which ought to have commanded obedience. The princes of Reuben had neither. Whether all under the lead of Reuben or each tribe led by its own princes, the Israelites would have travelled to disaster. Futile attempts at conquest, strife or alliance with neighbouring peoples, internal dissension, would have worn the tribes piecemeal away. The dictatorship of Moses, the Aaronic priesthood, and the unity of worship stood or fell together. One of the three removed, the others would have given way. But the revolutionary spirit, springing out of ambition and a disaffection for which there was no excuse, was blind to consequences. And the stern suppression of this revolt, at whatever cost, was absolutely needful if there was to be any future for Israel.

It has been supposed that we have in this rebellion of Korah the first example of ecclesiastical dissension, and that the punishment is a warning to all who presumptuously intrude into the priestly office. Laymen take the censer; and the fire of the Lord burns them up. So, let not laymen, at any time in the Church's history, venture to touch the sacred mysteries. If ritual and sacramentarian miracle were the heart of religion; if there could be no worship of God and no salvation for men now unless through a consecrated priesthood, this might be said. But the old covenant, with its symbols and shadows, has been superseded. We have another censer now, another tabernacle, another way which has been consecrated for ever by the sacrifice of Christ, a way into the holiest of all open to every believer. Our unity does not depend on the priesthood of men, but on the universal and eternal priesthood of Christ. The co-operation of Aaron as priest was needful to Moses, not that his power might be maintained for his own sake, but that he might have authority over the host for Israel's sake. It was not the dignity of an order or of a man that was at stake, but the very existence of religion and of the nation. This bond snapped at any point, the tribes would have been scattered and lost.

A leader of men, standing above them for their temporal interests, can rarely take upon him to be the instrument of administering the penalty of their sins. What king, for instance, ever invoked an interdict on his own people, or in his own right of judging for God condemned them to pay a tax to the Church, because they had done what was morally wrong? Rulers generally have regarded disobedience to themselves as the only crime it was worth their while to punish. When Moses stood against the faithless spirit of the Israelites and issued orders by way of punishing that bad spirit, he certainly put his authority to a tremendous test. Without a sure ground of confidence in Divine support, he would have been foolhardy in the extreme. And we are not surprised that the coalition against him represented many causes of discontent. Under his administration the long sojourn in the desert had been decreed, and a whole generation deprived of what they held their right—a settlement in Canaan. He appeared to be tyrannising over the tribes; and proud Reubenites sought to put an end to his rule. The priesthood was his creation, and seemed to be made exclusive simply that through Aaron he might have a firmer hold of the people's liberties. Why was the old prerogative of the headmen in religious matters taken from them? They would reclaim their rights. Neither Levi nor Reuben should be denied its priestly autonomy any longer. In the whole rebellion there was one spirit, but there were also divided counsels; and Moses showed his wisdom by taking the revolt not as a single movement, but part by part.

First he met the Levites, with Korah at their head, professing great zeal for the principle that all the congregation were holy, every one of them. A claim made on that ground could not be disproved by argument, perhaps, although the holiness of the congregation was evidently an ideal, not a fact. Jehovah Himself would have to decide. Yet Moses remonstrated in a way that was fitted to move the Levites, and perhaps did touch some of them. They had been honoured by God in having a certain holy office assigned to them. Were they to renounce it in joining a revolt which would make the very priesthood they desired common to all the tribes? From Jehovah Himself the Levites had their commission. It was against Jehovah they were fighting; and how could they speed? They spoke of Aaron and his dignity. But what was Aaron? Only a servant of God and of the people, a man who personally assumed no great airs. By this appeal some would seem to have been detached from the rebellion, for in xxvi. 9-11, when the judgment of Korah and his company is referred to, it is added, "Notwithstanding the children of Korah died not." From 1 Chron. vi. we learn that in the line of Korah's descendants appeared certain makers and leaders of sacred song, Heman among them, one of David's singers, to whom Psalm lxxxviii. is ascribed.

With the Reubenites Moses deals in the next place, taking their cause of discontent by itself. Already one of the three Reubenite chiefs had withdrawn, and Dathan and Abiram stood by themselves. Refusing to obey the call of Moses to a conference, they stated their grievance roughly by the mouth of a messenger; and Moses could only with indignation express before God his blamelessness in regard to them: "I have not taken one ass from them, neither have I hurt one of them." Neither for his own enrichment, nor in personal ambition had he acted. Could they maintain, did the people think, that the present revolt was equally disinterested? Under cover of opposition to tyranny, are they not desiring to play the part of tyrants and aggrandise themselves at the expense of the people?

It is singular that not a word is said in special condemnation of the two hundred and fifty because they were in possession of censers and incense. May it be the case that the complete reservation of the high-priestly duties to the house of Aaron had not as yet taken effect, that it was a purpose rather than a fact? May it not further be the case that the rebellion partly took form and ripened because an order had been given withdrawing the use of censers from the headmen of the tribes? If there had as yet been a certain temporary allowance of the tribal priesthood and ritual, we should not have to ask how incense and censers were in the hands of the two hundred and fifty, and why the brass of their vessels was held to be sacred and put to holy use.

The prayer of Moses in which he interceded for the people, ver. 22, is marked by an expression of singular breadth, "O God, the God of the spirits of all flesh." The men, misled on the fleshly side by appetite (ver. 13), and shrinking from pain, were against God. But their spirits were in His hand. Would He not move their spirits, redeem and save them? Would He not look on the hearts of all and distinguish the guilty from the innocent, the more rebellious from the less? One man had sinned, but would God burst out on the whole congregation? The form of the intercession is abrupt, crude. Even Moses with all his justice and all his pity could not be more just, more compassionate, than Jehovah. The purpose of destruction was not as the leader thought it to be.

Regarding the judgments, that of the earthquake and that of the fire, we are too remote in time to form any proper conception of what they were, how they were inflicted. "Moses," says Lange, "appears as a man whose wonderful presentiment becomes a miraculous prophecy by the Spirit of revelation." But this is not sufficient. There was more than a presentiment. Moses knew what was coming, knew that where the rebels stood the earth would open, the consuming fire burn. The plague, on the other hand, which next day spread rapidly among the excited people and threatened to destroy them, was not foreseen. It came as if straight from the hand of Divine wrath. But it afforded an opportunity for Aaron to prove his power with God and his courage. Carrying the sacred fire into the midst of the infected people he became the means of their deliverance. As he waved his censer, and its fumes went up to heaven, faith in Jehovah and in Aaron as the true priest of Jehovah was revived in the hearts of men. Their spirits came again under the healing power of that symbolism which had lost its virtue in common use, and was now associated in a grave crisis with an appeal to Him who smites and heals, who kills and makes alive.

It has been maintained by some that the closing sentences of chap. xvii. should follow chap. xvi. with which they appear to be closely connected, the incident of the budding of Aaron's rod seeming to call rather for a festal celebration than a lament. The theory of the Book of Numbers we have seen reason to adopt would account for the introduction of the fresh episode, simply because it relates to the priesthood and tends to confirm the Aaronites in exclusive dignity. The symbolic test of the claim raised by the tribes corresponds closely to the signs that were used by some of the prophets, such as the girdle laid up by the river Euphrates, and the basket of summer fruits. The rod on which Aaron's name was written was of almond, a tree for which Syria was famous. Like the sloe it sends forth blossoms before the leaves; and the unique way in which this twig showed its living vigour as compared with the others was a token of the choice of Levi to serve and Aaron to minister in the holiest office before Jehovah.

The whole circumstances, and the closing cry of the people, leave the impression of a grave difficulty found in establishing the hierarchy and centralising the worship. It was a necessity—shall we call it a sad necessity?—that the men of the tribes should be deprived of direct access to the sanctuary and the oracle. Earthly, disobedient, and far from trustful in God, they could not be allowed, even the hereditary chiefs among them, to offer sacrifices. The ideas of the Divine holiness embodied in the Mosaic law were so far in advance of the common thought of Israel, that the old order had to be superseded by one fitted to promote the spiritual education of the people, and prepare them for a time when there shall be "on the bells of the horses, HOLY UNTO THE LORD; and every pot in Judah shall be holy unto the Lord of hosts, and all they that sacrifice shall come and take of them and seethe therein." The institution of the Aaronic priesthood was a step of progress indispensable to the security of religion and the brotherhood of the tribes in that high sense for which they were made a nation. But it was at the same time a confession that Israel was not spiritual, was not the holy congregation Korah declared it to be. The greater was the pity that afterwards in the day of Israel's opportunity, when Christ came to lead the whole people into the spiritual liberty and grace for which prophets had longed, the priestly system was held tenaciously as the pride of the nation. When the law of ritual and sacrifice and priestly mediation should have been left behind as no longer necessary because the Messiah had come, the way of higher life was opened in vain. Sacerdotalism held its place with full consent of those who guided affairs. Israel as a nation was blinded, and its day shone in vain.

Of all priesthoods as corporate bodies, however estimable, zealous, and spiritually-minded individual members of them may be, must it not be said that their existence is a sad necessity? They may be educative. A sacerdotal system now may, like that of the Mosaic law, be a tutor to bring men to Christ. Realising that, those who hold office under it may bring help to men not yet fit for liberty. But priestly dominance is no perpetual rule in any church, certainly not in the Kingdom of God. The freedom with which Christ makes men free is the goal. The highest duty a priest can fulfil is to prepare men for that liberty; and as soon as he can he should discharge them for the enjoyment of it. To find in episodes like those of Korah's revolt and its suppression a rule applicable to modern religious affairs is too great an anachronism. For whatever right sacerdotalism now has is purely of the Church's tolerance, in the measure not of Divine right, but of the need of uninstructed men. To the spiritual, to those who know, the priestly system with its symbols and authoritative claim is but an interference with privilege and duty.

Can any Aaron now make an atonement for a mass of people, or even in virtue of his office apply to them the atonement made by Christ? How does his absolution help a soul that knows Christ the Redeemer as every Christian soul ought to know Him? The great fault of priesthoods always is, that having once gained power, they endeavour to retain it and extend it, making greater claims the longer they exist. Affirming that they speak for the Church, they endeavour to control the voice of the Church. Affirming that they speak for Christ, they deny or minimise His great gift of liberty. Freedom of thought and reason was to Cardinal Newman, for example, the cause of all deplorable heresies and infidelities, of a divided Church and a ruined world. The candid priest of our day is found making his claim as largely as ever, and then virtually explaining it away. Should not the vain attempt to hold by Judaic institutions cease? And although the Church of Christ early made the mistake of harking back to Mosaism, should not confession now be made that priesthood of the exclusive kind is out of date, that every believer may perform the highest functions of the consecrated life?

The Divine choice of Aaron, his confirmation in high religious office by the budding of the almond twig as well as by the acceptance of his intercession, have their parallels now. The realities of one age become symbols for another. Like the whole ritual of Israel, these particular incidents may be turned to Christian use by way of illustration. But not with regard to the prerogative of any arch-hierarch. The availing intercession is that of Christ, the sole headship over the tribes of men is that which He has gained by Divine courage, love, and sacrifice. Among those who believe there is equal dependence on the work of Christ. When we come to intercession which they make for each other, it is of value in consideration not of office but of faith. "The effectual fervent prayer of a righteous man availeth much." It is as "righteous" men, humble men, not as priests they prevail. The sacraments are efficacious, "not from any virtue in them or in him that administers them," but through faith, by the energy of the omnipresent Spirit.

Yet there are men chosen to special duty, whose almond twigs bud and blossom and become their sceptres. Appointment and ordination are our expedients; grace is given by God in a higher line of calling and endowment. While there are blessings pronounced that fall upon the ear or gratify the sensibility, theirs reach the soul. For them the world has need to thank God. They keep religion alive, and make it bourgeon and yield the new fruits for which the generations hunger. They are new branches of the Living Vine. Of them it has often to be said, as of the Lord Himself, "The stone which the builders rejected the same has become head of the corner; this is the Lord's doing, and it is marvellous in our eyes."

CHAPTER XV.

TITHES AND CLEANSINGS.

NUMBERS xviii., xix.

1. DUTIES AND SUPPORT OF THE MINISTRY.—The statutes of chap. xviii. are related to the rebellion of Korah by a clause in ver. 9, "Ye shall keep the charge of the sanctuary and the charge of the altar: that there be wrath no more upon the children of Israel." The enactments are directed anew against any intrusion into the sacred service by those who are not Levites, and into the priesthood by those who are not Aaronites. It is clearly implied that the ministry of the tabernacle is held under a grave responsibility. The "iniquity of the sanctuary" and the "iniquity of the priesthood" have to be borne; and the Aaronites alone are commissioned to bear that iniquity. The Levites, though they serve, are not to touch the holy vessels lest they die. The priesthood, "for everything of the altar, and for that within the veil," is given to the Aaronites as a service of gift.

A certain "iniquity," corresponding to the holiness of the tabernacle and its vessels, attends the service which is to be done by the priests. Their entrance into the sacred tent is an approach to Jehovah, and from His purity there is thrown a defilement on human life. The idea thus represented is capable of fine spiritual realisation. With this embodied in the law and worship, there is no need to look in any other direction for that evangelical poverty of spirit which the better Israelites of an after time knew. Here prophecy found in the law a germ of deep religious feeling which, rising above tabernacle and altar, became the holy fear of Him who inhabits eternity. The creation throughout its whole range, in the very act of receiving existence, comes into contrast with the creative Will and is on a lower moral plane, to which the Divine purity does not accompany it. The seraphim of Isaiah's vision feel this severance to a certain extent. They are so far apart from God that His holiness is not enjoyed unconsciously, as the element of life. It shines above them and determines their attitude and the terms of their praise. With their wings they cover their faces, and they cry to each other, "Holy, holy, holy is Jehovah of hosts: the whole earth is full of His glory." Even they "bear the iniquity" of the great temple of the world in which they minister. On fallen man that iniquity lies with almost crushing weight. "Woe is me!" says the prophet, "for I am undone; because I am a man of unclean lips, and I dwell in the midst of a people of unclean lips: for mine eyes have seen the King, Jehovah of hosts." Thus the soul is brought into that profound consciousness of defect and pollution which is the preparation for reverent service of the Highest. The attribute of holiness remains with God always, and His mercy in forgiving sin in no way detracts from it. The eternity of God sets Him so far above transitory men that He can extend compassion to them. "Art Thou not from everlasting, O Jehovah my God, mine Holy One? We shall not die." But His touch is, to the sinful earth, almost destruction. When the Lord the God of hosts toucheth the land it melteth, and all that dwell therein mourn (Amos ix. 12). When a people falls from righteousness the Divine holiness burns against it like a consuming fire. "We are all become as one that is unclean, and all our righteousnesses are as a polluted garment: and we all do fade as a leaf, and our iniquities like the wind take us away.... Thou hast hid Thy face from us, and hast consumed us by means of our iniquities" (Isa. lxiv. 6, 7).

The idea of the identification with the Holy God of the sanctuary dedicated to Him, so that from the porch of it falls the shadow of iniquity, is still further carried out in Numb. xviii. 1, where it is declared that Aaron and his sons shall "bear the iniquity" of their priesthood. The meaning is that the priesthood as an abstract thing, an office held from Jehovah and for Him, has a holiness like the sanctuary, and that the entrance into it of a man like Aaron brings to light his human imperfection and taint. And this corresponds to a consciousness which every one who deals with sacred truth and undertakes the conduct of Divine worship in the right spirit is bound to have. Entering on those exalted duties he "bears his iniquity." The sense of daring intrusion may almost keep back a man who knows that he has received a Divine call. To the heavenly muse the poet can but reply:—

> "I am not worthy even to speak
> Of Thy prevailing mysteries;
> For I am but an earthly muse . . .
> And darken sanctities with song."

With regard to the Levites whom Aaron is to bring near "that they may be joined unto him," it is singular that their duties and the restrictions put on them are detailed here as if now for the first time this branch of the sacred ministry was being organised. In the actual development of things this may be true. Difficulties had to be overcome, the nature of the statutes and ordinances had to be explained. Now the time of practical initiation may have arrived. On the other hand, the attempt of Korah to press into the priesthood may have made necessary a recapitulation of the law of Levitical service.

For the support of the Aaronites the heave offerings, "even all the hallowed things of the children of Israel" were to be given "by reason of the anointing." The meal offerings, sin offerings, and guilt offerings, as most holy, were to be for the male Aaronites alone: heave offerings of sacrifice, again, "all the wave offerings," were to be used by the Aaronites and their families, the reservation being made that only those without ceremonial defilement should eat of them. The first-fruits of the oil and vintage and the first ripe of all fruits in the land were other perquisites. Further, the first-born of man and of beast were to be nominally devoted; but first-born children were to be redeemed for five shekels, and the firstlings of unclean beasts were also to be redeemed. The children of Aaron were to have no inheritance in the land. In these ways however, and by the payment to the priests of the tenth part of the tithes collected by the Levites, ample provision was made for them.

For the Levites, nine-tenths of all tithes of produce would appear to have been not only sufficient, but far more than their proportion. According to the numbers reported in this book, twenty-two thousand Levites—about twelve thousand of them adult men—were to receive tithes from six hundred thousand. This would make the provision for the Levite as much as for any five men of the tribes. An explanation is suggested that the regular payment of tithes could not be reckoned upon. There would always be Israelites who resented an obligation like this; and as the duty of paying tithes, though enjoined in the law, was a moral one, not enforced by penalty, the Levites were really in many periods of the history of Israel in a state of poverty. It was a complaint of Malachi even after the captivity, when the law was in force, that the tithes were not brought to the temple storehouses. The Deuteronomic laws of tithing, moreover, are different from those given in Numbers. While here we read of a single tithe which is to be for the Levites, which, if paid, would be more than sufficient for them, Deuteronomy speaks of an annual tithe of produce to be eaten by the people at the central sanctuary by way of a festival, to which children, servants, and Levites were to be invited. Each third year a special tithe was to be used in feasting, not necessarily at the sanctuary, and again the Levites were to have their share. It is supposed by some that there were two annual tithings and in the third year three tithings of the produce of the land. But this seems far more than even a specially fertile country could bear. There was no rent to be paid, of course; and if the tithes were used in a festival no great difficulty might be found. But it is clear at all events that more dependence was placed on the free will of the people than on the law; and the Levites and priests must have suffered when religion fell into neglect. Israel was not ideally generous.

2. WATER OF PURIFICATION.—The statute of xix. 1-22 is peculiar, and the rites it enjoins are full of symbolism. It is implied that water alone was unable to remove the defilement caused by

touching a dead body; but at the same time the taint was so common and might be incurred so far from the sanctuary that sacrifice could not always be exacted. In order to meet the case an animal was to be offered, and the residue of its burning was to be kept for use whenever the defilement of death had to be taken away.

A red heifer was to be chosen, the colour of the animal pointing to the hue of blood. The heifer was to be free from blemish, a type of vigorous and prolific life. The charge of the sacrifice was to be given to Eleazer the priest, for the high-priest himself might not undertake a duty the performance of which caused uncleanness. The ceremonies must take place not only outside the tabernacle court, but outside the camp, that the intensity of the uncleanness to be transferred to the animal and purged by the sacrifice may be clearly understood. The heifer being slain, the priest takes of its blood and sprinkles it towards the tent of meeting seven times, in lieu of the ordinary sprinkling on the altar. The whole animal is then burnt, and while the flame ascends the virtue of the residuent ashes is symbolically increased by certain other elements. These are cedar wood, which was believed to have special medicinal qualities, and also may have been chosen on account of the long life of the tree; some threads of scarlet wool which would represent the arterial blood, instinct with vital power; and hyssop which was employed in purification.

The priest, having presided at the sacrifice, was to wash his clothes in water and bathe his flesh and hold himself unclean till the even. The assistant who fed the fire was in like manner unclean. These were both to withdraw; and one who was clean was to gather the ashes of the burning and, having provided some clean vessel within the camp, he was to store up the purifying ashes for future use by the people. Finally, the person who did this last duty, having become tainted like the others, was to wash his clothes and be unclean for the day. The ashes were to be used by mixing them with water to make "water for pollution"; that is, water to take away pollution. Special care was to be exercised that only living water, or water from a flowing stream, should be used for this purpose. It was to be applied to the defiled person, vessel, or tent, by means of hyssop. But, again, the man who used the water of purification in this way was to wash his clothes and be unclean until even.

Here we have an extra-sacerdotal rite, not of worship—for as ordinarily used there was no prayer to God, nor perhaps even the thought of appeal to God. It was religious, for the sense of defilement belonged to religion; but when under the necessity of the occasion any one applied the water of purification, his sense of acting the priestly part was reduced to the lowest point. The efficacy came through the action of the accredited priest when the heifer was sacrificed, it might be a year previously. So, although provision was made for needs occurring far from the sanctuary, no opening was left for any one to claim the power belonging to the sacerdotal office. And in order to make this still more sure it was enacted (ver. 21), that though the sprinkled water of purification cleansed the unclean, any one who touched it being himself clean should *de facto* be defiled. The water was declared so sacred that unless in cases where it was really required no one would be disposed to meddle with it. The sanctity of the tabernacle and the priesthood was symbolically carried forth to the most distant parts of the land. All were to be on their guard lest they should incur the judgment of God by abusing that which had ceremonial holiness and power.

The idea here is in a sense directly opposite to that which we associate with the sacred word, by which Divine will is communicated and souls are begotten anew. To use that word, to make it known abroad is the duty of every one who has heard and believed. He diffuses blessing and is himself blessed. There is no strict law hedging about with precautions the happy privilege of conveying to the sin-defiled the message of forgiveness and life. And yet may we not call to recollection here the words of Paul, "I buffet my body, and bring it into bondage; lest by any means, after that I have preached to others, I myself should be rejected." In a spiritual sense they should be clean who bear the vessels of the Lord; and every deed done, every word spoken in the sacred Name, if not with purity of purpose and singleness of heart, involves in guilt him who acts and speaks. The privilege has its accompanying danger; and the more widely it is used in the thousand organisations within and without the Church, the more carefully do all who use it need to guard the sanctity of the message and the Name. "In a great house there are not only vessels of gold and silver, but also of wood and of earth; and some unto honour, and some unto dishonour. If a man therefore purge himself from these"—the profane babblings of those who do not handle the word of God aright—"he shall be a vessel unto honour, sanctified, meet for the Master's use, prepared unto every good work."

3. DEFILEMENT BY THE DEAD.—The statute of the water of purification stands closely related to one form of uncleanness, that occasioned by death. When death took place in a tent, every one who came into the tent and every one who was in the tent, every open vessel that had no covering bound upon it, and the tent itself (ver. 18) were defiled; and the taint could not be removed in less than seven days. Whoever in the open field touched one who had been slain with a sword, or had otherwise died, or touched the bone of a man, or a grave—contracted like defilement. For purification the sacred water had to be sprinkled on the defiled person, on the third day and again on the seventh day. Not only the aspersion with sacred water, but, in addition, cleansing of clothes and of the body was necessary, in order to complete the removal of the taint. And further, while any one was unclean from this cause, if he touched another, his touch carried defilement that continued to the close of the day. To neglect the statute of purification was to defile the tabernacle of Jehovah: he who did so was to be cut off from his people.

The law was made stringent, as we have already seen, partly no doubt for the purpose of preventing the spread of disease. And to that extent the preservation of health was presented as a religious duty; for only in that sense can we understand the statement that he who did not purify himself defiled the tabernacle of Jehovah. Yet the stringency cannot be altogether due to this, for a bone or a grave would not often communicate infection. The general principle must be received by way of explanation, that death is peculiarly repugnant to the life of God, and therefore contact with it, in any form, takes away the right of approach to the sanctuary. That this idea goes back to the fall and the death penalty then pronounced might seem a reasonable conclusion. But the same thought does not apply to the defilement connected with birth. If the statute regarding uncleanness by death rested on the connection of death with sin, making "death and mortal corruption an embodiment of sin," the thought was obscured by many other laws regarding uncleanness. The aim we must believe was to make the theocratic oversight of the people penetrate as many as possible of the incidents and contingencies of their existence.

CHAPTER XVI.

SORROW AND FAILURE AT KADESH.

NUMBERS XX.

THERE is a mustering at Kadesh of the scattered tribes, for now the end of the period of wandering approaches, and the generation that has been disciplined in the wilderness must prepare for a new advance. The spies who searched Canaan were sent from Kadesh (xiii. 26), to which, in the second year from the exodus, the tribes had penetrated. Now, in the first month of the fortieth year it would seem, Kadesh is again the headquarters. The adjacent district is called the desert of Zin. Eastward, across the great plain of the Arabah, reaching from the Dead Sea to the Elanitic Gulf, are the mountains of Seir, the natural rampart of Edom. To the head of the Gulf at Elath the distance is some eighty miles in a straight line southward; to the southern end of the Dead Sea it is about fifty miles. Kadesh is almost upon the southern border of Canaan; but the way of the Negeb is barred by defeat, and Israel must enter the Promised Land by another route. In preparation for the advance the tribes gather from the wadies and plateaus in which they have been wandering, and at Kadesh or near it the earlier incidents of this chapter occur.

First among them is the death of Miriam. She has survived the hardships of the desert and reached a very great age. Her time of influence and vigour past, all the joys of life now in the dim memories of a century, she is glad, no doubt, when the call comes. It was her happiness once to share the enthusiasm of Moses and to sustain the faith of the people in their leader and in God. But any service of this kind she could render has been left behind. For some time she has been able only now and then with feeble steps to move to the tent of meeting that she might assure herself of the welfare of Moses. The tribes will press on to Canaan, but she shall never see it.

How is a life like this of Miriam's to be reckoned? Take into account her faith and her faithfulness; but remember that both were maintained with some intermixture of poor egotism; that while she helped Moses she also claimed to rival and rebuke him; that while she served Jehovah it was with some of the pride of a prophetess. Her devotion, her endurance, the long interest in her brother's work, which indeed led to the great error of her life—these were her virtues, the old great virtues of a woman. So far as opportunity went she doubtless did her utmost, with some independence of thought and decision of character. Even though she gave way to jealousy and passed beyond her right, we must believe that, on the whole, she served her generation in loyalty to the best she knew, and in the fear of the Most High. But into what a strange disturbed current of life was her effort thrown! Downcast, sorely burdened women, counting for very little when they were cheerful or when they complained, heard Miriam's words and took them into their narrow thoughts, to resent her enthusiasm, perhaps, when she was enthusiastic, to grudge her the power she enjoyed, which to herself seemed so slight. In the camp generally she had respect, and perhaps, once and again, she was able to reconcile to Moses and to one another those whose quarrels threatened the common peace. When she was put forth from the camp in the shame of her leprosy, all were affected, and the march was stayed till her time of separation was over. Was she one of those women whose lot it is to serve others all their lives and to have little for their service? Still, like many another, she helped to make Israel. Of good and evil, of Divine elements and some that are anything but Divine, lives are made up. And although we cannot gather the results of any one and tell its worth, the stream of being retains and the unerring judgment of God accepts whatever is sincere and good. Miriam from first to last fills but a few lines of sacred history; yet of her life, as of others, more has to be told; the end did not come when she died at Kadesh and was buried outside Canaan.

Spread through a diversified and not altogether barren region, over many square miles, the tribes have been able during the thirty-seven years to provide themselves with water. Gathered more closely now, when the dry season begins they are in want. And at once complaints are renewed. Nor can we wonder much. In flaming sunshine, in the parched air of the heights and the stifling heat of the narrow valleys, the cattle gasping and many of them dying, the children crying in vain for water, the little that is to be had, hot and almost putrid, carefully divided, yet insufficient to give each family a little,—the people might well lament their apparently inevitable fate. It may be said, "They should have confided in God." But while that might apply in ordinary circumstances, would not be out of place if the whole history were ideal, the reality, once understood, forbids so easy a condemnation of unbelief. Nothing is more terrible to endure, nothing more fitted to make strong men weep or turn them into savage critics of a leader and of Providence, than to see their children in the extremity of want which they cannot relieve. And a leader like Moses, patient as he may have been of other complaints, should have been most patient of this. When the people chode with him and said, "Would God that we had died when our brethren died before the Lord! And why have ye brought the assembly of the Lord into this wilderness, that we should die, we and our cattle?" they ought surely to have been met with pity and soothing words.

It is indeed a tragedy we are to witness when we come to the rock; and one element of it is the old age and the weary spirit of the leader.

Who can tell what vexed his soul that day? how many cares and anxieties burdened the mind that was clear yet, but not so tolerant, perhaps, as once it had been? The years of Moses, his long and arduous service of the people, are not remembered as they ought to be. Even in their extremity the men of the tribes ought to have appealed to their great chief with all respect, instead of breaking in upon him with reproaches. Was no experience sufficient for these people? After the discipline of the wilderness, was the new generation, like that which had died, still a mere horde, ungrateful, rebellious? From the leader's point of view this thought could not fail to arise, and the old magnanimity did not drive it away.

Another point is the forbearance of Jehovah, who has no anger with the people. The Divine Voice commands Moses to take his rod and go forth to the rock and speak to it before the assembly. This does not fall in with Moses' mood. Why is God not indignant with the men of this new generation who seize the first opportunity to begin their murmuring? Relapsing from his high inspiration to a poor human level, Moses begins to think that Jehovah, whose forgiveness he has often implored on Israel's behalf, is too ready now to forgive. It is a failing of the best men thus to stand for the prerogative of God more than God Himself; that is, to mistake the real point of the circumstances they judge and the Divine will they should interpret. The story of Jonah shows the prophet anxious that Nineveh, the inveterate foe of Israel, the centre of proud, God-defying idolatry, should be destroyed. Does God wish it to be spared, to repent and obtain forgiveness? So does not Jonah. His creed is one of doom for wickedness. He resents the Divine mercy and, in effect, exalts himself above the Most High. In like temper is Moses when he goes out followed by the crowd. There is the rock from which water shall be made to flow. But with the thought in his mind that the people do not deserve God's help, Moses takes the affair upon himself. The tragedy is fulfilled when his own feelings guide him more than the Divine patience, his own displeasure more than the Divine compassion; and with the words on his lips, "Hear now, ye rebels: shall we bring you forth water out of this rock?" he smites it twice with his rod.

For the moment, forgetting Jehovah the merciful, Moses will himself act God; and he misrepresents God, dishonours God, as every one who forgets Him is sure to do. Is he confident in the power of his wonder-working rod? Does he wish to show that its old virtue remains? He will use it as if he were smiting the people as well as the rock. Is he willing that this thirsting multitude should drink? Yet he is determined to make them feel that they offend by the urgency with which they press upon him for help. There have been crises in the lives of leaders of men when, with all the teaching of the past to inspire them, they should have risen to a faith in God far greater than they ever exercised before; and more or less they have failed. This is not the will of Providence, they have thought, though they should have known that it was. They have said, "Advance: but God goes not with you," when they should have seen the heavenly light moving on. So Moses failed. He touched his limit; and it was far short of that breadth of compassion which belongs to the Most Merciful. He stood as God, with the rod in his hand to give the water, but with the condemnation upon his lips which Jehovah did not speak.

In this mood of assumed majesty, of moral indignation which has a personal source, with an air of superiority not the simplicity of inspiration, a man may do what he will for ever regret, may betray a habit of self-esteem which has been growing upon him and will be his ruin if it is not checked. In the strong mind of Moses there had lain the germs of hauteur. The early upbringing in an Egyptian court could not fail to leave its mark, and the dignity of a dictator could not be sustained, after the anxieties of the first two years in the desert, without some slight growth of a tendency or disposition to look down on people so spiritless, and play among them the part of Providence, the decrees of which Moses had so often interpreted. But pride, even beginning to show itself towards men, is an aping of God. Unconsciously the mind that looks down on the crowd falls into the trick of a superhuman claim. Moses, great as he is, without personal ambition, the friend of every Israelite, reaches unaware the hour when a habit long suppressed lifts itself into power. He feels himself the guardian of justice, a critic not only of the lives of men but of the attitude of Jehovah towards them. It is but for an hour; yet the evil is done. What appears to the uplifted mind justice, is arrogance. What is meant for a defence of Jehovah's right, is desecration of the highest office a man can hold under the Supreme. The words are spoken, the rock is struck in pride; and Moses has fallen.

Think of the realisation of this which comes when the flush of hasty resentment dies, and the true self which had been suppressed revives in humble thought. "What have I done?" is the reflection—"What have I said? My rod, my hand, my will, what are they? My indignation! Who gave me the right to be indignant? A king against whom they have revolted! A guardian of the Divine honour! Alas! I have denied Jehovah. I, who stood for Him in my pride, have defamed Him in my vanity. The people who murmured, whom I rebuked, have sinned less than I. They distrusted God, I have declared Him unmerciful, and thereby sown the seeds of distrust. Now I, too, am barred from Israel's inheritance. Unworthy of the promise, I shall never cross the border of God's land. Aaron my brother, we are the transgressors. Because we have not honoured God to sanctify Him in the eyes of the children of Israel, therefore we shall not bring this assembly unto the land He gives them." By the lips of Moses himself the oracle was given. It was tragical indeed.

But how could the brothers who had yielded to this dictatorial hierarchical temper be men of God again, fit for another stroke of work for Him, unless, coming forth into action, their pride had disclosed itself, and with whatever bad result shown its real nature? We deplore the pride; we almost weep to see its manifestation; we hear with sorrow the judgment of Moses and Aaron. But well is it that the worst should come to light, that the evil thing should be seen, God-dishonouring, sacrilegious; should be judged, repented of, punished. Moses must "feel himself and find the blessedness of being little." "By that sin fell the angels," that sin unconfessed.

Here in open sight of all, in hearing of all, Moses lays down the godhead he had assumed, acknowledges unworthiness, takes his place humbly among those who shall not inherit the promise. The worst of all happens to a man when his pride remains unrevealed, uncondemned; grows to more and more, and he never discovers that he is attempting to carry himself with the air of Providence, of Divinity.

The error of Moses was great, yet only showed him to be a man of like passions with ourselves. Who can realise the mercy and lovingkindness that are in the heart of God, the danger of limiting the Holy One of Israel? The murmuring of the Israelites against Jehovah had often been rebuked, had often brought them into condemnation. Moses had once and again intervened as their mediator and saved them from death. Remembering the times when he had to speak of Jehovah's anger, he feels himself justified in his own resentment. He thought the murmuring was over; it is resumed unexpectedly, the same old complaints are made and he is carried away by what appears zeal for Jehovah. Yet there is in him even, the man, much more in God, a better than the seeming best. Pathetic indeed is it to find Moses judged as one who has failed from the high place he could have reached by a final effort of self-mastery, one more generous thought. And we see him fail at a point where we often fail. Sternly to judge our own right of condemning before we speak sternly in the name of God; neither to do nor say anything which implies the assumption of knowledge, justice, charity we do not possess—how few of us are in these respects blameless for a day! Far back in sacred history this high duty is presented so as to evoke the best endeavour of the Christian soul and warn it from the place of failure.

There is preserved in the Book of Exodus (xxxvi.) a list of the Kings of Edom reaching down apparently to about the establishment of the monarchy of Israel. Recent archæology sees no reason to question the genuineness of this historical notice or the names of the Dukes of Edom given in the same passage. With varying boundaries the region over which they ruled extended southward from Moab and the Dead Sea as far as the Elanitic Gulf. Kadesh, considerably west of the Arabah, is described as being on its uttermost border. But the district inhabited by the Edomites proper was a narrow strip of rugged country eastward of the range of Mount Seir. One pass giving entrance to the heart of Edom led by the base of Mount Hor towards Selah, afterwards called Petra, which occupied a fine but narrow valley in the heart of broken mountains. To reach the south of Moab the Israelites desired probably to take a road a good deal farther north. But this would have led them by Bozrah the capital, and the king who reigned at the time refused them the route. The message sent him in Moses' name was friendly, even appealing. The brotherhood of Edom and Israel was claimed; the sore travail of the tribes in Egypt and the deliverance wrought by Jehovah were given as reasons; promise was made that no harm should be done to field or vineyard: Israel would journey by the king's way, turning neither to the right nor the left. When the first request was refused Moses added that if his people drank of the water while passing through Edom they would pay for it. The appeal, however, was made in vain. An attempt to advance without permission was repelled. An armed force barred the way, and most reluctantly the desert road was again taken.

We can easily understand the objection of the King of Edom. Many of the defiles through which the main road wound were not adapted for the march of a great multitude. The Israelites could scarcely have gone through Edom without injuring the fields and vineyards; and though the undertaking was given in good faith by Moses, how could he answer for the whole of that undisciplined host he was leading towards Canaan? The safety of Edom lay in denying to other peoples access to its strongholds. The difficulty of approaching them was their main security. Israel might go quietly through the land now; but its armies might soon return with hostile intent. Water, too, was very precious in some parts of Edom. Enough was stored in the rainy season to supply the wants of the inhabitants; beyond that there was none to spare, and for this necessary of life money was no equivalent. A multitude travelling with cattle would have made scarcity, or famine,—might have left the region almost desolate. With the information they had, Moses and Joshua may have believed that there were no insuperable difficulties. Yet the best generalship might have been unequal to the task of controlling Israel in the passes and among the cultivated fields of that singular country.

There is no need to go back on the history of Jacob and Esau in order to account for the apparent incivility of the King of Edom to the Israelites and Moses. That quarrel had surely been long forgotten! But we need not wonder if the kinship of the two peoples was no availing argument in the case. Those were not times when covenants like that proposed could be easily trusted, nor was Israel on an expedition the nature of which could reassure the Idumæans. And we have parallels enough in modern life to show that from the only point of view the king could take he was amply justified. There are demands men make on others without perceiving how difficult it will be to grant them, demands on time, on means, on good-will, demands that would involve moral as well as material sacrifice. The foolish intrusions of well-meaning people may be borne for a time, but there is a limit beyond which they cannot be suffered. Our whole life cannot be exposed to the derangements of every scheme-maker, every claimant. If we are to do our own work well, it is absolutely necessary that a certain space shall be jealously guarded, where the gains of thought may be kept safely and the ideas revealed to us may be developed. That any one's life should be open so that travellers, even with some right of close fraternity, may pass through the midst of it, drink of the wells, and trample down the fields of growing purpose or ripening thought, this is not required. Good-will makes an open gate; Christian feeling makes one still wider and bids many welcome. But he who would keep his heart in fruitfulness must be careful to whom he grants admission. There is beginning to be a sort of jealousy of any one's right to his own reserve. It is not a single Israel approaching from the West, but a score, with their different schemes, who come from every side demanding right of way and even of abode. Each presses a Christian claim on whatever is wanted of our hospitality. But if all had what they desire there would be no personal life left.

On the other hand, some whose highways are broad, whose wells and streams are overflowing, whose lives are not fully engaged, show themselves exclusive and inhospitable—like those proprietors of vast moors who refuse a path to the waterfall or the mountain-top. Without Edom's excuse, some modern Idumæans warn every enterprise off their bounds. Neither brotherhood nor any other claim is acknowledged. They would find advantage, not injury, in the visit of those who bring new enthusiasms and ideas to bear on existence. They would learn of other aims than occupy them, a better hope than they possess. Their sympathy would be enlisted in heavenly or humane endeavours, and new alliances would quicken as well as broaden their life. But they will not listen; they continue selfish to the end. Against all such Christianity has to urge the law of brotherhood and of sacrifice.

We have assumed that Kadesh was on the western side of the Arabah, and it is necessary to take ver. 20 as referring to an incident that occurred after the Israelites had crossed the valley. Not otherwise can we explain how they came to encamp among the mountains on the eastern side. The repulse must have been sustained by the tribes after they had left Kadesh and penetrated some distance into the northern defiles of Idumæa. Bozrah, the capital, appears to have been situated about half way between Petra and the southern extremity of the Dead Sea, and a force issuing from that stronghold would divert the march southward so that the Israelites could safely encamp only when they reached the open plain near Mount Hor. Hither therefore they retreated: and here it was that Moses and Aaron were parted. The time had come for the high priest to be gathered to his people.

Scarcely any locality in the whole track of the wandering is better identified than this. From the plain of the Arabah the mountains rise in a range parallel to the valley, in ridges of sandstone, limestone, and chalk, with cliffs and peaks of granite. The defile that leads by Mount Hor to Petra is peculiarly grand, for here the range attains its greatest height. "Through a narrow ravine," says one traveller, "we ascended a steep mountain side, amid a splendour of colour from bare rock or clothing verdure, and a solemnity of light on the broad summits, of shade in the profound depths—a memory for ever. . . . It was the same narrow path through which in old times had passed other trains of camels laden with the merchandise of India, Arabia, and Egypt. And thus having ascended, we had next a long descent to the foot of Mount Hor, which stands isolated." The mountain rises about four thousand feet above the Arabah and has a peculiar double crest. On its green pastures there graze flocks of sheep and goats; and inhabited caves—used perhaps since the days of the old Horites—are to be seen here and there. The ascent of the mountain is aided by steps cut in the rock, "indeed a tolerably complete winding staircase," for the chapel or mosque on the summit, said to cover the grave of Aaron, is a notable Arab sanctuary, resorted to by many pilgrims. "From the roof of the tomb—now only an ordinary square building with a dome—northward and southward, a hilly desert; eastward, the mountains of Edom, within which Petra lies hid; westward, the desert of the Arabah, or wilderness of Zin; beyond that, the desert of Et-Tih; beyond that again, in the far horizon, the blue-tinted hills of the Land of Promise."

Such is the mountain at the foot of which Israel lay encamped when the Lord said unto Moses, " Take Aaron and Eleazar his son, and bring them up unto Mount Hor; and strip Aaron of his garments, and put them upon Eleazar his son: and Aaron shall be gathered unto his people and shall die there." We imagine the sorrowful gaze of the multitude following the three climbers, the aged brothers who had borne so long the burden and heat of the day, and Eleazar, already well advanced in life, who was to be invested with his father's office. Coming soon after the death of Miriam, this departure of Aaron broke sharply one other link that still bound Israel with its past. The old times were receding, the new had not yet come into sight.

The life of a good man may close mournfully. While some in leaving the world cross cheerfully the river beyond which the smiling fields of the heavenly land are full in view, others there are who, even with the faith of the Conqueror of death to sustain them, have no gladdening prospect at the last. Only from a distance Aaron saw the Land of Promise; from so great a distance that its beauty and fruitfulness could not be realised. The sullen gleam of the Lake of Sodom, lying in its grim hollow, was visible away to the north. Besides that the dim eyes could make out little. But Edom lay below; and the tribes would have a great circuit round that inhospitable land, would have to traverse another desert beyond the horizon to the east, ere they could reach Moab and draw near to Canaan. A true patriot, Aaron would think more of the people than of himself. And the confidence he had in the friendliness of God and the wisdom of his brother would scarcely dispel the shadow that settled on him as he forecast the journey of the tribes and saw the difficulties they were yet to meet. So not a few are called away from the world when the great ends for which they have toiled are still remote. The cause of liberty or of reformation with which life has been identified may even appear farther from success than years before. Or again, the close of life may be darkened by family troubles more pressing than any that were experienced earlier. A man may be heavily burdened without distrusting God on his own account, or doubting that in the long run all shall be well. He may be troubled because the immediate prospect shows no escape from painful endurance for those he loves. He does not sorrow perhaps that he has found the promises of life to be illusory; but he is grieved for dear friends who must yet make that discovery, who shall travel many a league and never win the battle or pass beyond the wilderness.

The mind of Aaron as he went to his death was darkened by the consciousness of a great failure. Kadesh lay westward across the valley, and the thought of what took place there was with the brothers as they climbed Mount Hor and stood upon its summit. They had repented, but they had not yet forgiven themselves. How could they, when they saw in the temper of the people too plain proofs that their lese-majesty had borne evil fruit? It needs much faith to be sure that God will remedy the evil we have done; and so long as the means cannot be seen, the shadow of self-reproach must remain. Many a good man, climbing the last slope, feels the burden of transgressions committed long before. He has done his utmost to restore the defences of truth and rebuild the altars of witness which in thoughtless youth or proud manhood he cast down. But circumstances have hindered the work of reparation; and many who saw his sin have passed far beyond the reach of his repentance. The thought of past faults may sadly obscure the close of a Christian life. The end would indeed be hopeless often were it not for trust in the omnipotent grace which brings again that which was driven away and binds up that which was broken. Yet since the very work of God and the victory of Christ are made more difficult by things a believer has done, is it possible that he should always have happy recollections of the past as life draws near its end?

It was no doubt honourable to Aaron that his death was appointed to be on that mountain in Seir. Old as he was, he would never think of complaining that he was ordained to climb it. Yet to the tired limbs it was a steep, difficult path, a way of sorrow. Here, also, we find resemblance to the close of many a worthy life. High office in the Church has been well served, overflowing wealth has been used in beneficence; but at the last reverses have come. The man who was always prosperous is now stripped of his possessions. Darkened in mind by successive losses, bereaved of friends and of power, he has to climb a dreary mountain-path to the sharp end. It may be really honourable to such a man th t God has thus appointed his death to be not in the midst of luxury, but on the rugged peak of loss. Understanding things aright, he should say: "The Lord gave, and the Lord hath taken away; blessed be the name of the Lord." But if dependence is felt as shame, if he who gave freely to others feels it a sore thing to receive from others, who can have the heart to blame the good man because he does not triumph here? And if he has to climb alone, no Eleazar with him, scarcely one human aid, what shall we say? Now life must gird itself and go whither it would not. Sad is the journey, but not into night. The Christian does not impeach Divine providence nor grieve that earthly good is finally taken away. Though his life has been in his generosity, not in his possessions, yet he will confess that the last bitter trial is needful to the perfecting of faith.

Should the believer triumph over death through Christ? It is his privilege; but some display unwarranted complacency. They have confidence in the work of Christ; they boast that they rest everything on Him. But is it well with them if they have no sorrow because of days and years that ran to waste? Is it well with them if they deplore no failure in Christian effort when the reason is that they never gave heart and strength to any difficult task? Who can be satisfied with the apparent victory of faith at the last of one who never had high hopes for himself and others, and therefore was never disappointed? Better the sorrowful ending to a life that has dared great things and been defeated, that has cherished a pure ideal and come painfully short of it, than the exultation of those who even as Christians have lived to themselves.

Perhaps the circumstances that attended the death of Aaron were to him the finest discipline of life. Climbing the steep slope at the command of God, would he not feel himself brought into a closer relation with the Eternal Will? Would he not feel himself separated from the world and gathered up into the quiet massiveness of life with Him who is from everlasting to everlasting? The years of a high priest, dealing constantly with sacred things and symbols, might easily fall into a routine not more helpful to generous thought and spiritual exaltation than the habits of secular life. One might exist among sacrifices and purifications till the mind became aware of nothing beyond ritual and its orderly performance. True, this had not been the case with Aaron during a considerable portion of the time since he began his duties. There had been many events by means of which Jehovah broke in upon the priests with His great demands. But thirty-seven years had been comparatively uneventful. And now the little world of camp and tabernacle court, the sacred shrine with its ark, the symbolic dwelling-place of God, must have their contrast in the broad spaces filled with gleaming light, the blue vault, the widespread hills and valleys, the heavens which are Jehovah's throne, the earth which is His footstool. The bustle of Israel's little life is left behind for the calm of the mountain land. The high priest finds another vestibule of the dwelling of Jehovah than that which he has been accustomed to enter with sprinkled blood and the pungent fumes of the incense.

Is it not good thus to be called away from the business of the world, immersed in which every day men have lost the due proportions of things, both of what is earthly and what is spiritual? They have to leave the computations recorded in their books, and what bulks largely in the gossip of the way and the news of the town; they are to climb where greater spaces can be seen, and human life, both as brief and as immortal, shall be understood in its relations to God. Often those who have this call addressed to them are most unwilling to obey. It is painful to lose the old standards of proportion, to hear no longer the familiar noise of wheels, to see no machinery, no desks, no ledgers, to read no newspapers, to have the quiet, the slow-moving days, the moonless or moonlit nights. But if reflection follows, as it should, and brings wisdom, the change has saved a man who was near to being lost. The things he toiled for once, as well as the things he dreaded,—that success, this breath of adverse opinion,—seem little in the new light, scarcely disturb the new atmosphere. One thus called apart with God, learning what are the real elements of life, may look with pity on his former self, yet gather out of the experience that had small value, for the most part, here and there a jewel of price. And the wise, becoming wiser, will feel preparation made for the greater existence that lies beyond.

Moses accompanied his brother to the mountain top. By his hands, with all considerateness, the priestly robes were taken from Aaron's shoulders and put on Eleazar. The true friend he had all along relied upon was with the dying man at the last, and closed his eyes. In this there was a palliation of the decree under which it would have been terrible to suffer alone; yet in the end the loneliness of death had to be felt. We know a Friend who passed through death for us, and made a way into the higher life, but still we have our dread of the solitude. How much heavier must it have weighed when no clear hope of immortality shone upon the hill. The vastness of nature was around the dying priest of Israel, his face was turned to the skies. But the thrill of Divine love we find in the touch of Christ did not reassure him. "These all . . . received not the promise, God having provided some better thing concerning us, that apart from us they should not be made perfect."

Eleazar followed Aaron and took up the work of the priesthood, not less ably, let us believe, yet not precisely with the same spirit, the same endowments. And indeed to have one in all respects like Aaron would not have served. The new generation, in new circumstances, needs a new minister. Office remains; but, as history moves on, it means always something different. When the hour comes that requires a clear step to be taken away from old notions and traditions of duty, neither he who holds the office nor those to whom he has ministered should complain or doubt. It is not good that one should cling to work merely because he has served well and may still seem able to serve; often it is the case that before death commands a change the time for one has come. Even the men who are most useful to the world, Paul, Apollos, Luther, do not die too soon. It may appear to us that a man who has done noble work has no successor. When, for instance, England loses its Dr. Arnold, Stanley, Lightfoot, and we look in vain for one to whom the robes are becoming, we have to trust that by some education they did not foresee the Church has to be perfected. The same theory, nominally, is not the same when others undertake to apply it. The same ceremonies have another meaning when performed by other hands. There are ways to the full fruition of Christ's government which go as far about as Israel's to Canaan round the land of Moab, for a time as truly retrogressive. But the great Leader, the one High Priest of the new covenant, never fails His Church or His world, and the way that does not hasten, as well as that which makes straight for the goal, is within His purpose, leads to the fulfilment among men of His mediatorial design.

CHAPTER XVII.

THE LAST MARCH AND THE FIRST CAMPAIGN.

NUMBERS xxi.

IT has been suggested in a previous chapter that the repulse of the Israelites by the King of Arad took place on the occasion when, after the return of the spies, a portion of the army endeavoured to force its way into Canaan. If that explanation of the passage with which chap. xxi. opens cannot be accepted, then the movements of the tribes after they were driven back from Edom must have been singularly vacillating. Instead of turning southward along the Arabah they appear to have moved northward from Mount Hor and made an attempt to enter Canaan at the southern end of the Dead Sea. Arad was in the Negeb or South Country, and the Canaanites there, keeping guard, must have descended from the hills and inflicted a defeat which finally closed that way.

From the time of the departure from Kadesh onward no mention is made of the pillar of cloud. It may have still moved as the standard of the host; yet the unsuccessful attempt to pass through Edom, followed possibly by a northward march, and then by a southward journey to the Elanitic Gulf when they "compassed Mount Seir many days" (Deut. ii. 1), would appear to prove that the authoritative guidance had in some way failed. It is a suggestion, which, however, can only be advanced with diffidence, that after the day at Kadesh when the words fell from Moses' lips, "Hear now, ye rebels," his power as a leader declined, and that the guidance of the march fell mainly into the hands of Joshua,—a brave soldier indeed, but no acknowledged representative of Jehovah. It is at all events clear that attempts had now to be made in one direction and another to find a feasible route. Moses may have retired from the command, partly on account of age, but even more because he felt that he had in part lost his authority. Israel, moreover, had to become a military nation: and Moses, though nominally the head of the tribes, had to stand aside to a great extent that the new development might proceed. In a short time Joshua would be sole leader; already he appears to hold the military command.

The journey from Mount Hor to the borders of Moab by way of the Red Sea, or Yâm-Suph, is very briefly noticed in the narrative. Oboth, Iye-abarim, Zared, are the only three names mentioned in chap. xxi. before the border of Moab is reached. Chap. xxxiii. gives Zalmonah, Punon, Oboth, and lastly Iye-abarim, which is said to be in the border of Moab. The mention of these names suggests nothing as to the extremely trying nature of the journey; that is only indicated by the statement, "the soul of the people was much discouraged because of the way." The truth is, that of all the stages of the wandering, these along the Arabah, and from the Elanitic Gulf eastward and northward to the valley of Zared, were perhaps the most difficult and perilous. The Wady Arabah is "an expanse of shifting sands, broken by innumerable undulations, and countersected by a hundred watercourses." Along this plain the route lay for fifty miles, in the track of the furious sirocco and amidst terrible desolation. Turning eastward from the palm-groves of Elath and the beautiful shores of the Gulf, the way next entered a tract of the Arabian wilderness outside the border of Edom. Oboth lay, perhaps, east from Maan, still an inhabited city, and the point of departure for one who journeys from Palestine into central Arabia. Out from Maan this desert lies, and is thus described:—"Before and around us extended a wide and level plain, blackened over with countless pebbles of basalt and flint, except when the moonbeams gleamed white on little intervening patches of clear sand, or on yellowish streaks of withered grass, the scanty produce of the winter rains, and now dried into hay. Over all a deep silence which even our Arab companions seemed fearful of breaking; when they spoke it was in a half whisper and in few words, while the noiseless tread of our camels sped stealthily but rapidly through the gloom without disturbing its stillness." * For one hundred miles the route for Israel lay through this wilderness: and it is hardly possible to escape the conviction that although little is said of the ex-

* Palgrave, "Central and Eastern Arabia," p. 2.

periences of the way the tribes must have suffered enormously and been greatly reduced in number. As for cattle, we must conclude that hardly any survived. Where camels sustain themselves with the greatest difficulty, oxen and sheep would certainly perish. There had come the necessity for a rapid advance, to be made at whatever hazard. All that would retard the progress of the people had to be sacrificed. There is indeed some ground for the supposition that part of the tribes remained near Kadesh while the main body made the long and perilous detour. The army entering Canaan by way of Jericho would as soon as possible open communication with those who had been left behind.

The only recorded episode belonging to the period of this march is that of the fiery serpents. In the Arabah and the whole North Arabian region the cobra, or *naja haie*, is common, and is superstitiously dreaded. Other serpents are so innocuous by comparison that this chiefly receives the attention of travellers. One incident is recorded thus by Mr. Stuart-Glennie:—" Two cobras have been caught, and one, which has been dexterously pinned by the neck in the slit end of a stick, its captor comes up triumphantly to exhibit. . . After a time the fellow let it go, refusing to kill it, and permitting it to glide away unharmed. This I understood to be from fear—fear of the vengeance after death of what, in life, had been incapable of defending itself. At Petra . . . the snakes which Hamilton, a fearless hunter of them, killed, the Arabs would not allow to lie within the encampment, asserting that we should thus bring the whole snake-tribe to which the individual belonged to avenge the death of their kinsman." Whether all the serpents that attacked the Israelites were cobras is doubtful; but the description " fiery " seems to point to the effects of the cobra-poison, which produces an intense burning sensation in the whole body. Another explanation of the adjective is found in the metallic sparkle of the reptiles.

" Much people of Israel died " of the bites of these serpents, which, disturbed by the travellers as they went sullenly and carelessly along, issued from crevices of the ground and from the low shrubs in which they lurked, and at once fastened on feet and hands. The peculiar character of the new enemy caused universal alarm. As one and another fell writhing to the ground, and after a few convulsive movements died in agony, a feeling of terrified revulsion spread through the ranks. Pestilence was natural, familiar, as compared with this new punishment which their murmuring about the light food and the thirst of the desert had brought on them. The serpent, lithe and subtle, scarcely seen in the twilight, creeping into the tents at night, quick at any moment, without provocation, to use its poisoned fangs, has appeared the hereditary enemy of man. As the instrument of the Tempter it was connected with the origin of human misery; it appeared the embodied evil which from the very dust sprang forth to seek the evil-doer. Many ways had Jehovah of reaching men who showed distrust and resented His will. This was in a sense the most dreadful.

The serpents that lurked in the Israelites' way and darted suddenly upon them are always felt to be analogues of the subtle sins that spring on man and poison his life. What traveller knows the moment when he may feel in his soul the sharp sting of evil desire that will burn in him to a deadly fever? Men who have been wounded can, for a time, hide from fellow-travellers their mortal hurt. They keep on the march and make shift to look like others. Then the madness reveals itself. Words are spoken, deeds are done, that show the vile inoculation taking effect. By-and-by there is another moral death. Humanity may well fear the power of evil thoughts, of lusts, of envious feelings, that serpent-like attack and madden the soul; may well look up and cry aloud to God for a sufficient remedy. No herb nor balm to be found in the gardens or fields of earth is an antidote to this poison; nor can the surgeon excise the tainted flesh, or destroy the virus by any brand of penance.

Resuming his generous part as intercessor for the people, Moses sought and found the means to help them. He was to make a serpent of brass, an image of the foe, and erect it on a standard full in sight of the camp, and to it the eyes of the stricken people were to be turned. If they realised the Divine purpose of grace and trusted Jehovah while they looked, the power of the poison would be destroyed. The serpent of brass was nothing in itself, was, as long afterwards Hezekiah declared it to be, *nehushtan*; but as a symbol of the help and salvation of God it served the end. The stricken revived: the camp, almost in a panic through superstitious fear, was calmed. Once more it was known that He who smote the sinful, in wrath remembered mercy. It must be assumed that there was repentance and faith on the part of those who looked. The serpents appear as the means of punishment, and the poison loses its effect with the growth of the new spirit of submission. It has rightly been pointed out that the heathen view of the serpent as a healing power has no countenance here. That singular belief must have had its origin in the worship of the serpent which arose from dread of it as an embodiment of demoniacal energy. Our passage treats it as a creature of God, ready, like the lightning and the pestilence, or like the frogs and insects of the Egyptian plagues, to be used as an instrument in bringing home to men their sins.

And when our Lord recalled the episode of the healing of Israel by means of the brazen serpent, He certainly did not mean that the image in itself was in any sense a type or even symbol of Him. It was lifted up; He was to be lifted up: it was to be looked upon with the gaze of repentance and faith; He is to be regarded, as He hangs on the cross, with the contrite, believing look: it signified the gracious interposition of God, who was Himself the True Healer; Christ is lifted up and gives Himself on the cross in accordance with the Father's will, to reveal and convey His love—these are the points of similarity. " As Moses lifted up the serpent in the wilderness, even so must the Son of Man be lifted up." The uplifting, the healing, are symbolic. The serpent-image fades out of sight. Christ is seen giving Himself in generous love, showing us the way of life when He dies, the just for the unjust. He is the power of God unto salvation. With Him we die that He may live in us. He judges us, condemns us as sinners, and at the same time turns our judgment into acquittal, our condemnation into liberty. Israel's past and the grace of Jehovah to the stricken tribes are connected by our Lord's words with the redemption provided through His own sacrifice. The Divine Healer of humanity is there and here; but here in spiritual life, in quickening grace, not in an empirical symbol. Christ on the cross is no mere sign of a higher energy; the very energy is with Him, most potent when He dies.

Like the serpent poison, that of sin creates a burning fever, a mortal disease. But into all the springs and channels of infected life the renovating grace of God enters through the long deep look of faith. We see the Man, our brother full of sympathy, the Son of God our sin-bearer. The pity is profound as our need; the strong spiritual might, sin-conquering, life-giving, is enough for each, more than sufficient for all. We look—to wonder, to hope, to trust, to love, to rejoice with joy unspeakable and full of glory. We see our condemnation, the handwriting of ordinances that is against us—and we see it cancelled through the sacrifice of our Divine Redeemer. Is it the death that moves us first? Then we perceive love stronger than death, love that can never die. Our souls go forth to find that love, they are bound by it for ever to the Infinite Truth, the Eternal Purity, the Immortal Life. We find ourselves at length whole and strong, fit for the enterprises of God. The trumpet call is heard; we respond with joy. We will fight the good fight of faith, suffering and achieving all through Christ.

At Iye-abarim, the Heaps of the Outlands, "which is toward the sunrising," the worst of the desert march was over. That the long and dreary wilderness did not swallow up the host is, humanly speaking, matter of astonishment. Yet singular light is thrown on the journey by an incident recorded by Mr. Palmer. In the midst of the broken country extending from the neighbourhood of the ancient Kadesh to the Arabah, he and his companions encamped at the head of the Wady Abu Taraimeh, which slopes to the south-east. Here in the midst of the desolate mountains a quite young girl, small, solitary traveller, was found. She was on her way to Abdeh, some twenty miles behind, and had come from a place called Hesmeh, six days' journey beyond Akabah, a distance of some hundred and fifty miles. "She had been without bread or water, and had only eaten a few herbs to support herself by the way." The simple trust of the child could achieve what strong men might have pronounced impossible. And the Israelites, knowing little of the road, trusted and hoped and pressed on till the green hills of Moab were at last in sight. The march was eastward of the present highway, which keeps within the border of Edom and passes through El Buseireh, the ancient Bozrah. We may suppose that the Israelites followed a track afterwards chosen for a Roman road and still traceable. The valley of Zared, perhaps the modern Feranjy, would be reached about fifteen miles east from the southern gulf of the Dead Sea. Thence, striking on a watercourse and keeping to the desert side of Ar, the modern Rabba, the Hebrews would have a march of about twenty miles to the Arnon, which at that time formed the boundary between Moab and the Amorites.

At this point the history incorporates, why we cannot tell, part of an old song from the "Book of the Wars of Jehovah."

> "Vaheb in Suphah,
> And the valleys of Arnon,
> And the slope of the valleys
> That inclineth toward the dwelling of Ar,
> And leaneth upon the border of Moab."

The picturesque topography of this chant, the meaning of which as a whole is obscured for us by the first line, may be the sole reason of its quotation. If we read "Vaheb in storm" we have a word-picture of the scene under impressive conditions; and if the storm is that of war the relique may belong to the time of the contest described in ver. 26 when the Amorite chief, crossing Jordan, gained the northern heights and drove the Moabites in confusion across the Arnon toward the stronghold of Ar, some twelve or fifteen miles to the south. Yet another ancient song is connected with a station called Beer, or the Well, some spot in the wilderness north of the Arnon valley. Moses points out the place where water may be found, and as the digging goes on the chant is heard:

> "Spring up, O well; sing ye unto it:
> The well which the princes digged,
> Which the nobles of the people delved,
> With the sceptre, and with their staves."

The seeking of the precious water by rude art in a thirsty valley kindles the mind of some poet of the people. And his song is spirited, with ample recognition of the zeal of the princes who themselves take part in the labour. While they dig he chants, and the people join in the song till the words are fixed in their memory, so as to become part of the traditions of Israel.

The finding of a spring, the discovery that by their own effort they can reach the living water laid up for them beneath the sand, is an event to the Israelites, worth preserving in a national ballad. What does this imply? That the resources of nature and the means of unlocking them were still only beginning to be understood? We are almost compelled to think so, whatever conclusions this may involve. And Israel, slowly finding out the Divine provision lying beneath the surface of things, is a type of those who very gradually discover the possibilities that are concealed beneath the seemingly ordinary and unpromising. By the beaten tracks of life, in its arid valleys, there are, for those who dig, wells of comfort, springs of truth and salvation. Men are athirst for inspiration, for power. They think of these as endowments for which they must wait. In point of fact they have but to open the fountains of conscience and of generous feeling in order to find what they desire. Multitudes faint by the way because they will not seek for themselves the water of Divine truth that would reinvigorate their being. When we trust to wells opened by others we cannot obtain the supply suited to our special need. Each for himself must discover Divine providence, duty, conviction, the springs of repentance and of love. The many wait, and never get beyond spiritual dependence. The few, some with sceptre, some with staff, dig for themselves and for the rest wells of new ardour and sustaining thought. The whole of human life, we may say, has beneath its surface veins and rills of heavenly water. In heart and conscience we can find the will of our Maker, the springs of His promises, revelations of His power and love. More than we know of the living water that flows through the world of humanity like a river has its source in springs that have been dug in waste places by those who reflected, who saw in man's world and man's soul the work of the "faithful Creator."

From Beer in the wilderness the march skirted the green fields and valleys of the country once held by the Moabites, now under Sihon the Amorite. When they had gone but a few stages along this route the leaders of the host found it necessary to enter into negotiations. They were now some twenty miles only by road from the fords of Jordan, but Heshbon, a strong fortress, confronted them. The Amorites must be either conciliated or attacked. This time there was no circuitous way that could be taken; a critical hour had come.

The presence of the Amorites on the eastern side of Jordan is accounted for in a passage extending from vv. 26-30. Moab had apparently, as at a later time referred to by one of the prophets, been at ease, resting securely behind her mountain rampart. Suddenly the Amorite warriors, crossing the ford of Jordan and pressing up the defile, had attacked and taken Heshbon; and with the loss of that fortress Moab was practically defenceless. Field by field the old inhabitants had been driven back, out into the desert, southward beyond the Arnon. Even as far as Ar itself the victors had carried fire and sword. Retiring, they left all south of the Arnon to the Moabites, and themselves occupied the country from Arnon to Jabbok, a stretch of sixty miles. The song of vv. 27-30 commemorates this ancient war:

> "Come ye to Heshbon,
> Let the city of Sihon be built and established;
> For a fire is gone out of Heshbon,
> A flame from the city of Sihon:
> It hath devoured Ar of Moab,
> The Lords of the High Places of Arnon.
> Woe to thee, Moab!
> Thou art undone, O people of Chemosh."

The chant rejoicing over the defeated goes on to tell how the sons of Moab fled, and her daughters were taken captive; how the arms of the Amorite were victorious from Heshbon to Dibon, over Nophah and Medeba. The Israelites arriving soon after this sanguinary conflict, found the conquered region immediately beyond the Arnon open to their advance. The Amorites had not yet occupied the whole of the land; their power was concentrated about Heshbon, which according to the song had been rebuilt.

The request made of Sihon to allow the passage of a people on its way to Jordan and the country beyond came possibly at a time when the Amorites were scarcely prepared for resistance. They had been successful, but their forces were insufficient for the large district they had taken, larger considerably than that on the other side of Jordan from which they had migrated. In the circumstances Sihon would not grant the request. These Israelites were bent on establishing themselves as rivals: the answer accordingly was a refusal, and war began. Refreshed by the spoil of the fields of Arnon, and now almost within sight of Canaan, the Hebrew fighting men were full of ardour. The conflict was sharp and decisive. Apparently in a single battle the power of Sihon was broken. Leaving his fortress the Amorite chief had gone out against Israel "into the wilderness"; and at Jahaz the fight went against him. From Arnon to Jabbok his land lay open to the conquerors.

And having once tasted success the warriors of Israel did not sheathe their swords. The fortress of Amman guarded the land of the Ammonites so strongly that it seemed for the time perilous to strike in that direction. Crossing the valley of the Jabbok, however, and leaving the fierce Ammonites unattacked, the Israelites had Bashan before them; a fertile region of innumerable streams, populous, and with many strongholds and cities. There was hesitation for a time, but the oracle of Jehovah reassured the army. Og the king of Bashan waited the attack at Edrei in the north of his kingdom, about forty miles east from the Sea of Galilee. Israel was again victorious. The king of Bashan, his sons, and his army were cut to pieces.

Such was the rapid success the Israelites had in their first campaign, amazing enough, though partly explained by the strifes and wars which had reduced the strength of the peoples they attacked. We must not suppose, however, that though the Amorites and the people of Bashan were defeated, their lands were occupied or could be occupied at once. What had been done was rather in the way of defending the passage of the Jordan than providing a settlement for any of the tribes. When the Reubenites, Gadites, and Manassites came to dwell in those districts east of the Jordan, they had to make good their ground against the old inhabitants who remained.

The army had passed into the north, but the main body of the people descended from the neighbourhood of Heshbon by a pass leading to the Jordan Valley. The return of the victorious troops after a few months gave them the assurance that at last they could safely prepare for the long expected entrance into the Land of Promise.

Suffering and the discipline of the wilderness had educated the Israelites for the day of action. By what a long and tedious journey they reached their success! Behind them, yet with them still, was Sinai, whose lightnings and awful voices made them aware of the power of Jehovah into covenant with whom they entered, whose law they received. As a people bound solemnly to the unseen Almighty God they left that mountain and journeyed towards Kadesh. But the covenant had neither been thoroughly accepted nor thoroughly understood. They began their march from the mountain of the Lord as the people of Jehovah, yet expecting that He was to do all for them, require little at their hands. The other side of privilege, the duty they owed to God, had to be impressed by many a painful chastisement, by the sorrows and disasters of the way. Wonderfully, all things considered, had they sped, though their murmurings were the sign of an ignorant rebellious temper which was incompatible with any moral progress. By the long delay in the wilderness of Kadesh that disposition had to be cured. In a region not fertile like Canaan itself, yet capable of supporting the tribes, they had to forget Egypt, realise that forward not backward was their only way, that while desert after desert intervened now between them and Goshen, they were within a day's march of the Promised Land. But even this was not enough. Perhaps they might have crept gradually northward; shifting their headquarters a few miles at a time till they had taken possession of the Negeb and made a settlement of some kind in Canaan. But if they had done so, as a nation of shepherds, advancing timorously, not boldly, they would have had no strength at the opening of their career. And it was decreed that by another door, in another spirit, they should enter. Edom refused them access to the east country. They had again to gird up their loins for a long journey. And that last terrible march was the discipline they required. Resolutely kept to it by their leader, on through the Arabah, across the desert, to the "Heaps of the Outlands towards the sunrising" they went, with new need for courage, a new call to endure hardness every day. Did they faint once, and turn murmurers again? The serpents stung them in judgment, and the cure was provided in grace. They learned once more that it was One they could not elude with whom they had to do, One who could be severe and also kind, who could strike and also save. Decimated, but knit together, as they had never been, the tribes reached the Arnon. And then, the first trial of their arms made, they knew themselves a conquering people, a people with power, a people with a destiny.

It is so in the making of manhood, in the discipline of the soul. Sinai, and the awful declarations of duty and of the Divine claim there, must enter into our life; it would be light, frivolous, and incapable otherwise. But the revelation of power and righteousness does not insure our submission to the power, our conformity to the righteousness. Divine words have to be followed by Divine deeds; we have to learn that in God's kingdom there is to be no murmuring, no shrinking even from death, no turning back. It is a lesson that tries the generations. How many will not learn it! In society, in the Church, the rebellious spirit is shown and has to be corrected. At the "Graves of Lust," at the "Place of Burning," murmurers are judged, those who refuse God's way fall and are left behind. And when the Land of Promise is in sight possession of it shall not be easily obtained by those who are still half-wedded to the old life, distrustful of the righteousness of God and His demand on the whole love and service of the soul. There is indeed no heaven for those who look back, who even if angels were to hurry them onward would still lament the losses of this life as irremediable. There must be the courage of the daring soul that adventures all on faith, on the Divine promise, on the eternity of the spiritual.

Wherefore, that the earthly temper may be taken out of us, we have to cross desert after desert, to make long circuits through the hot and thirsty wilderness even when we think our faith complete and our hope nigh its fulfilment. It is as those who overcome we are to enter the kingdom. Not as "the world's poor routed leavings," not obtaining permission from Edomites or Amorites to slip ingloriously through their land, but as those who with the sword of the Spirit can hew our own way through falsehoods and bring down the lusts of the flesh and of the mind, as warriors of God we are to reach and cross the border. How many survive, having gone through discipline like this? How many overcome and have the right to pass through the gate into the city?

CHAPTER XVIII.

BALAAM INVOKED.

NUMBERS xxii. 1-19.

WHILE a part of the army of Israel was engaged in the campaign against Bashan, the tribes remained "in the plains of Moab beyond the Jordan at Jericho." The topography is given here, as elsewhere, from the point of view of one dwelling in Canaan; and the locality indicated is a level stretch of land, some five or six miles broad, between the river and the hills. In this plain there was ample room for the encampment, while along the Jordan and on the slopes to the east all the produce of field and garden, the spoil of conquest, was at the disposal of the Israelites. They rested therefore, after their long journey, in sight of Canaan, waiting first for the return of the troops, then for the command to advance; and the delay may very likely have extended to several months.

Now the march of Israel had kept to the desert side of Moab, so that the king and people of that land had no reason to complain. But the campaign against the Amorites, ending so quickly and decisively for the invaders, showed what might have taken place if they had attacked Moab, what might yet come to pass if they turned southward instead of crossing the Jordan. And there was great dismay. "Moab was sore afraid of the people, because they were many; and Moab was distressed because of the children of Israel." Manifestly it would have been unwise for Balak the king of the Moabites to attack Israel single-handed. But others might be enlisted against this new and vigorous enemy, among them the Midianites. And to these Balak turned to consult in the emergency.

By the "Midianites" we must understand the Bedawin of the time, the desert tribes which possibly had their origin in Midian, east of the Elanitic Gulf, but were now spread far and wide. On the borders of Moab a large and important clan of this people fed their flocks; and to their elders Balak appealed. "Now," he said, "shall this multitude lick up all that is round about us, as the ox licketh up the grass of the field." The result of the consultation was not an expedition of war but one of a quite different kind. Even the wild Bedawin had been dismayed by the firm resolute tread of the Israelites, a people marching on, as no people had ever been seen to march, from far-away Egypt to find a new home. The elders of Moab and of Midian cannot decide on war; but superstition points to another means of attack. May they not obtain a curse against Israel, under the influence of which its strength shall decay? Is there not in Pethor one who knows the God of this people and has the power of dreadful malediction? They will send for him; Balaam shall invoke disaster on the invaders, then peradventure Balak will prevail, and smite them, and drive them out of the land.

There can be no doubt in what direction we are to look for Pethor, the dwelling-place of the great diviner. It is "by the River," that is to say, by the River Euphrates. It is in Aram, for thence Balaam says Balak has brought him. It is in "the land of the children of Ammo" (xxii. 5), for such is the preferable translation of the words rendered "children of his people." The situation of Pethor has been made out. "At an early period in Assyrian research," says Mr. A. H. Sayce,[*] "Pethor was identified by Dr. Hincks with the Pitru of the cuneiform inscriptions. Pitru stood on the western bank of the Euphrates, close to its junction with the Sajur, and a little to the north of the latter. It was consequently only a few miles to the south of the Hittite capital Carchemish. Indeed, Shalman-

[*] "The Higher Criticism and the Monuments," p. 274.

eser II. tells us explicitly that the city was called Pethor by 'the Hittites.' It lay on the main road from east to west, and so occupied a position of military and commercial importance." Originally an Aramæan town, Pethor had received, on its conquest by the Hittites, a new element of population from that race, and the two peoples lived in it side by side. The Aramæans of Pethor called themselves "the sons of (the god) Ammo"; and, according to Mr. Sayce, Dr. Neubauer is right in explaining the name of Balaam as a compound of Baal with Ammi, which occurs as a prefix in the Hebrew names Ammiel, Amminadab, and others. It is also worthy of mention that the name of Balak's father—Zippor, or "Bird"—occurs in the notice, still extant, of a despatch sent by the Egyptian government to Palestine in the third year of Menephtah II.

It may be further said with regard to Mr. Sayce's valuable work, that he does not attempt to deal particularly with the prophecies of Balaam. "They must," he says, "be explained by Hebrew philology before the records of the monuments can be called upon to illustrate them. It may be that the text is corrupt; it may be that passages have been added at various times to the original prophecy of the Aramæan seer; these are questions which must be settled before the Assyriologist can determine when it was that the Kenite was carried away captive, or when Asshur himself was 'afflicted.'"

The divination of which so great things were expected by Balak is amply illustrated in the Babylonian remains. Among the Chaldeans the art of divination rested "on the old belief in every object of inanimate nature being possessed or inhabited by a spirit, and the later belief in a higher power, ruling the world and human affairs to the smallest detail, and constantly manifesting itself through all things in nature as through secondary agents, so that nothing whatever could occur without some deeper significance which might be discovered and expounded by specially trained and favoured individuals." The Chaldeo-Babylonians "not only carefully noted and explained dreams, drew lots in doubtful cases by means of inscribed arrows, interpreted the rustle of trees, the plashing of fountains and murmur of streams, the direction and form of lightnings, not only fancied that they could see things in bowls of water, and in the shifting forms assumed by the flame which consumed sacrifices and the smoke which rose therefrom, and that they could raise and question the spirits of the dead, but drew presages and omens, for good or evil, from the flight of birds, the appearance of the liver, lungs, heart, and bowels of the animals offered in sacrifice and opened for inspection, from the natural defects or monstrosities of babies or the young of animals—in short, from any and everything that they could possibly subject to observation." There were three classes of wise men, astrologers, sorcerers, and soothsayers; all were in constant demand, and all used rules and principles settled for them by the so-called science which was their study.

We cannot of course affirm that Balaam was one of these Chaldeans, or that his art was precisely of the kind described. He is declared by the narrative to have received communications from God. There can, however, be no doubt that his wide reputation rested on the mystical rites by which he sought his oracles, for these, and not his natural sagacity, would impress the common mind. When the elders of Moab and Midian went to seek him they carried the "rewards of divination" in their hands. It was believed that he might obtain from Jehovah the God of the Israelites some knowledge concerning them on which a powerful curse might be based. If then, in right of his office, he pronounced the malediction, the power of Israel would be taken away. The journey to Pethor was by the oasis of Tadmor and the fords at Carchemish. A considerable time, perhaps a month, would be occupied in going and returning. But there was no other man on whose insight and power dependence could be placed. Those who carried the message were men of rank, who might have gone as ambassadors to a king. It was confidently expected that the soothsayer would at once undertake the important commission.

Arriving at Pethor they find Balaam and convey the message, which ends with the flattering words, "I know that he whom thou blessest is blessed, and he whom thou cursest is cursed." But they have to treat with no vulgar thaumaturgist, no mere weaver of spells and incantations. This is a man of intellectual power, a diplomatist, whose words and proceedings have a tone of high purpose and authority. He hears attentively, but gives no immediate answer. From the first he takes a position fitted to make the ambassadors feel that if he intervenes it will be from higher motives than desire to earn the rewards with which they presume to tempt him. He is indeed a prince of his tribe, and will be moved by nothing less than the oracle of that unseen Being whom the chiefs of Moab and Midian cannot approach. Let the messengers wait, that in the shadow and silence of night Balaam may inquire of Jehovah. His answer shall be in accordance with the solemn, secret word that comes to him from above.

Three of the New Testament writers, the Apostles Peter, John, and Jude, refer to Balaam in terms of reprobation. He is "Balaam the son of Beor who loved the hire of wrongdoing"; he "taught Balak to cast a stumbling-block before the children of Israel, to eat things sacrificed to idols, and to commit fornication"; he is the type of those who run riotously in the way of error for hire. Gathering up the impressions of his whole life, these passages declare him avaricious and cunningly malignant, a prophet who, perverting his gifts, brought on himself a special judgment. At the outset, however, Balaam does not appear in this light. The pictorial narrative shows a man of imposing personality, who claims the "vision and the faculty Divine." He seems resolute to keep by the truth rather than gratify any dreams of ambition or win great pecuniary rewards. It is worth while to study a character so mingled, in circumstances that may be called typical of the old world.

Did Balaam enjoy communications with God? Had he real prophetic insight? Or must we hold with some that he only professed to consult Jehovah, and found the answer to his inquiries in the conclusions of his own mind?

It would appear at first sight that Balaam, as a heathen, was separated by a great gulf from the Hebrews. But at the time to which the narrative of Numbers refers, if not at the period of its composition, the boundary line implied by the word "gentile" did not exist. Moses had clearly taught to the Hebrews ethical and religious truths which neighbouring nations saw very indistinctly; and the Israelites were beginning to know themselves a chosen race. Yet Abraham was their father, and other peoples could claim descent from him. Edom, for example, is in Numbers xx. acknowledged as Israel's brother.

At the stage of history, then, to which our passage belongs, the strongly marked differences between nation and nation afterwards insisted upon were not realised. And this is so far true in respect of religion, that though the Kenites, a Midianite tribe, did not follow the way of Jehovah, Moses, as we have seen, had no difficulty in joining with them in a sacrificial feast in honour of the Lord of Heaven. If beyond the circle of the tribes any one, impressed by their history, attributing their rescue from Egypt and their successful march towards Canaan to Jehovah, acknowledged His greatness and began to approach Him with sacred rites, no doubt would have existed among the Hebrews generally that by such a man their God could be found and His favour won. The narrative before us, stating that Jehovah called Balaam and communicated with him, simply declares what the more patriotic and religious Israelites would have had no difficulty whatever in receiving. This diviner of Pethor had heard of Israel's deliverance at the Red Sea, had followed with keen interest the progress of the tribes, had made himself acquainted with the law of Jehovah given at Sinai. Why, then, should he not worship Jehovah? And why should not Jehovah speak to him, make revelations to him of things still in the future?

So far, however, we touch only the beliefs, or possible beliefs, of the Israelites. The facts may be quite different. We are in the way of considering revelations of the Divine will to have been so uncommon and sacred that a man of very high character alone could have enjoyed them. If indeed God spoke to Balaam, it must have been in another way than to Abraham, Moses, Elijah. Especially since his history shows him to have been a man bad at heart, we are inclined to pronounce his consultation of God mere pretence; and as for his prophecies, did he not simply hear of Israel's greatness and forecast the future with the prescience of a clear calculator, who used his eyes and reason to good purpose? But with this the gist of the Bible narrative cannot be said to agree. It seems to be certainly implied that God did speak to Balaam, open his eyes, unfold to him things far off in the future. Although many cases might be adduced which go to prove that an acute man of the world, weighing causes and tracing the drift of things, may show wonderful foresight, yet the language here used points to more than that. It seems to mean that Divine illumination was given to one beyond the circle of the chosen people, to one who from the first was no friend of God and at the last showed himself a malicious enemy of Israel. And the doctrine must be that any one who, looking beneath the surface of things, studying the character of men and peoples, connects the past and the present and anticipates events which are still far off, has his illumination from God. Further it is taught that in a real sense the man who has some conception of Providence, though he is false at heart, may yet, in the sincerity of an hour, in the serious thought roused at some crisis, have a word of counsel, a clear indication of duty, a revelation of things to come which others do not receive. Still we must interpret the words, "God said to Balaam," in a way which will not lift him into the ranks of the heaven-directed who are in any sense mediators, prophets of the age and the world. This man has his knowledge so far from above, has his insight as a true gift, receives the word of prohibition, of warning, veritably from a Divine source. Yet he does not stand in a high position, lifted above other men. The whole history is of value for our instruction, because as surely as Balaam received directions from God, we also receive them through conscience; because as he opposed God so we also may oppose Him in self-will or the evil mind. When we are urged to do what is right the urgency is Divine, as certainly as if a voice from heaven fell on our ears. Only when we realise this do we feel aright the solemnity of obligation. If we fail to ascribe our knowledge and our sense of duty to God, it will seem a light thing to neglect the eternal laws by which we should be ruled.

Reaching Pethor the messengers of Balak state their request. Instead of going with them at once, as a false man might be expected to do, Balaam declares that he must consult Jehovah; and the result of his consultation is that he declines. In the morning he says to the princes of Moab, "Get you into your land, for Jehovah refuseth to give me leave to go with you." The question whether Israel was a fit subject for blessing or for cursing has been practically settled in his mind. When he lays the matter before Jehovah, as he knows Him through His law and the history of Israel, it is made unmistakable that no malediction is to be pronounced. But what, then, was the secret of Balaam's delay, of his consultation of the oracle? If it had been an absolute determination to serve the interests of righteousness, he could now frame his reply to the princes in such a way that they would understand it to be final. He would not say demurely, "Jehovah refuseth to give me leave," for these words allow the belief that somehow the power to curse may yet be obtained. Balaam permits himself to hope that he will find some flaw in Israel's relation to Jehovah which will leave room for a malediction. He delays, and professes to consult God, diplomatically, that even by the refusal his fame as a diviner acquainted with the Unseen Power may be established. And the answer he returns means that his own reputation is not to be hazarded by any divination which Jehovah will discredit.

Had not the future proceedings of Balaam cast their shadow back on his career and words, he might have been pronounced at the outset a man of integrity. The rewards offered him were probably large. We may believe that whatever reputation Balaam had previously enjoyed this embassy was the most important ever sent to him, the greatest tribute to his fame. And we would have been inclined to say, Here is an example of conscientiousness. Balaam might go with the princes at least, though he can pronounce no curse on Israel; but he does not; he is too honourable even to profess the desire to gratify his patrons. This favourable judgment, however, is forbidden. It was of himself, of his fame and position, he was thinking. He would not have gone in any case unless it had precisely suited his purpose. Understanding that Israel is not to be cursed, he manages so that his refusal shall enhance his own reputation.

Still, the small amount of sincerity there is in Balaam, superimposed on his self-love and diplomacy, is in contrast to the utter want of it which men often show. They are of a party, and at the first call they will make shift to denounce whatever their leaders bid them denounce. There is no pretence even of waiting for a night to have time for quiet reflection; much less any anxious thought regarding Divine providence, righteousness, mercy, by means of which duty may be discovered. It is possible for men to appear earnest defenders of religion who never go even as far as Balaam went in seeking the guidance of truth and principle. They pass judgments with a haste that shows the shallow heart. Tempted by some envious Balak within, even when no appeal is made, they set up as soothsayers and take on them to prophesy evil.

The messengers of Balak returned with the report of their disappointment; but what they had to say caused, as Balaam no doubt intended, greater anxiety than ever to secure his services. One who was so lofty, and at the same time so much in the secrets of the God Israel worshipped, was indeed a most valuable ally, and his help must be obtained at any price. Did he say that Jehovah refused to give him leave? Balak will assure him of rewards which no God of Israel can give, very great recompense, tangible, immediate. Other messengers are sent, more, and more honourable than the former, and they carry very flattering offers. If he will curse Israel, Balak the son of Zippor will do for him whatever he desires. Nothing is to hinder him from coming; neither the prohibition of Jehovah nor anything else.

The conduct of Balaam when he is appealed to the second time confirms the judgment it has been found necessary to pronounce on his character. He behaves like a man who has been expecting, and yet, with what conscience he has, dreading, the renewed invitation. He appears indeed to be emphatic in declaring his superiority to the offer of reward: "If Balak would give me his house full of silver and gold, I cannot go beyond the word of the Lord my God, to do less or more." The air of incorruptible virtue is kept. The Moabites and Midianites are to understand that they have to do with a man whose whole soul is set on truth. And the protestation would deceive us—only Balaam does not dismiss the men. Giving him all credit for an intention still to keep right with the Almighty, or, shall we say? allowing that he was too clever a man to imperil his reputation by intending a curse which would not be followed by any ill effects, we find immediately that he is unwilling to let the opportunity pass. He asks the messengers to tarry for the night, that he may again consult Jehovah in the matter. He has already seen the truth as to Israel, the promise of its splendid career. Yet he will repeat the inquiry, ask once more regarding the prospect he has distinctly seen. It is ambition that moves him, and perhaps, along with that, avarice. May he not be able to say something that will sound like a curse, something on which Balak shall fasten in the belief that it gives him power against Israel? It would, at all events, be a gratification to travel in state across the desert, to appear amongst the princes of Midian and Moab as the man after whom kings had to run. And there was the possibility that without absolutely forfeiting his reputation as a seer of things to come he might obtain at least a portion of the reward. He will at all events do the messengers the honour of seeking another oracle for their sakes, though he dishonours the name of God from whom he seeks it.

It was possible for Balaam during the interval of the two embassies to recover himself. He was one who could understand integrity, who knew enough of the conditions of success to see that absolute consistency is the only strength. There was a straight way which he might have followed. But temptation pressed on him. Tired of the narrow field within which he had as yet exercised his powers, he saw one wider and more splendid open to him. The wealth was no small inducement. He was in the way of divining for reward; this was the greatest ever in his reach. And Balaam, knowing well how base and vain his pretext was, resigned his integrity, even the pretence of it, when he bade the messengers wait.

Yet was his fault a singular one? We cannot say that he showed extraordinary covetousness in desiring Balak's silver and gold. For the time, in the circumstances, scarcely anything else could be expected of a man like him. To judge Balaam by modern Christian rules is an anachronism. The remarkable thing is to find one of his class at all scrupulous about the means he employs to promote himself. We say that he was guilty of perverting conscience; and so he was. But his conscience did not see or speak so clearly as ours. And are not Christian men liable to have their heads turned by the countenance of those in a higher rank than their own, and to succumb to the enticement of great wealth? When they are asked to reconsider a decision they know to be right, do they never tamper with conscience? It is one of the commonest things to find persons nominally religious indulging in the same desires and acting in the same way as Balaam. But the earthly craving that makes any one go back to God a second time about a matter which ought to have been settled once for all, involves the greatest moral hazard. No human being, in any situation, has spiritual strength to spare. There is a point where he who hesitates casts the whole of his life into the balance. For young persons, especially, a great warning, often needed, lies here.

The fault of Balaam, a fault of which he could not fail to be conscious, was that of tampering with his inspiration. The insight he possessed— and which he valued—had come through his sincere estimate of things and men apart from any pressure brought to bear on him to take a side either for money or for fame. His mind using perfect freedom, travelling in a way of sincere judgment, had reached a height from which he enjoyed wide prospects. As a man and a prophet he had his standing through this superiority to the motives that swayed vulgar minds. The admission of sordid influences, whether it began with the visit of Balak's messengers or had been previously allowed, was perhaps the first great error of his life. And it is so in the case of every man who has found the strength of integrity and reached the vision of the true. The Christian who has held himself free from the entanglements of the world, refusing to touch its questionable rewards, or to be influenced by its jealousy and envy, has what may be called his inspiration, though it lifts him to no prophetic height. He has a clear mind, a clear eye. His own way is plain, and he can also see the crookedness of paths which others follow and reckon straight enough. He can go with a firm step and say fearlessly, "Be ye followers of me." But if the base considerations of gain and loss, of ease or discomfort, of the applause or enmity of other men, intrude, if even in a small way he becomes a man of the world, at once there is declension. He may not be ambitious nor covetous. Yet the withdrawal of his mind from its sole allegiance to God and the righteousness of God tells at once on his moral vision. It is clouded. The oracle becomes ambiguous. He hears two voices, many voices; and the counsels of his mind are confused. Like others, he now takes a crooked course, he feels that he has lost the old firmness of speech and action.

It is a sad thing when one who has felt himself "born to the good, to the perfect," who has gained the power that comes through reverence, and sees greater power before him, yields to that which is not venerable, not pure. The beginnings of the fatal surrender may be small. Only a throb of self-consciousness and satisfaction when some one speaks a word of flattery or with show of much deference prefers an astute request. Only a disposition to listen when in seeming friendship counsel of a plausible kind is offered, and milder ways of judging are recommended to lessen friction and put an end to discord. Even the strong are so weak, and those who see are so easily blinded, that no one can count himself safe. And indeed it is not the great temptations, like that which came to Balaam, we have chiefly to dread. The very greatness of a bribe and magnificence of an opportunity put conscience on its guard. Peril comes rather when the appeal for charity, or the casuistry of protesting virtue, sends one to reconsider judgment that has been solemnly pronounced by a voice we cannot mistake; when we forget that the matter is only rightly determined for men when it is clearly and irrevocably decided by the law of God, whatever men may think, however they may deplore or rebel.

> "Thou and God exist—
> So think!—for certain; think the mass—mankind—
> Disparts, disperses, leaves thyself alone!
> Ask thy lone soul what laws are plain to thee—
> Thee and no other,—stand or fall by them!
> That is the part for thee: regard all else
> For what it may be—Time's illusion."

Men in their need, in their sorrow, their self-esteem, would have the true man revoke his judgment, yield a point at least to their entreaties. He will do them kindness, he will show himself human, reasonable, judicious. But on the other side are those to whom, in showing this consideration, he will be unjust, declaring their honour worthless, their sore struggle a useless waste of strength; and he himself stands before the Judge. The one sure way is that which keeps the life in the line of the statutes of God, and every judgment in full accord with His righteousness.

CHAPTER XIX.
BALAAM ON THE WAY.
NUMBERS xxii. 20-38.

THE history is moving towards a great vindication of Israel and prediction of its coming power, all the more impressive that they are to be wrung from an unwilling witness, a man who would pronounce a curse rather than a blessing; all the more impressive, too, because the enemies of Israel will themselves arrange on a mountain pinnacle the scene of the revelation, with smoking altars and princely spectators. The great Actor in the drama is unseen; but His voice is heard. However tractable the omens may have been under other circumstances in the hands of the soothsayer, he now finds a Master. As the story unfolds, Balaam is seen attempting the impossible, endeavouring to force the hands of Providence, held as in a chain at every stage. There is a Power that treats him as if he were a child. Finally, with most unwilling eloquence, he is compelled to fling far and wide a challenge to Israel's enemies, the praises of her rising star.

In harmony with this general movement is the result of Balaam's second appeal for permission to take the journey to Moab. He receives it, but with a reservation. Fear of the great God whom he invokes holds him to the conviction that whatever he may do no word must pass his lips other than Jehovah gives him to speak. In repeating his inquiry he has assumed that the God of Israel is amenable to human urgency; and as he will have Jehovah to be, so within limits he seems to find Him. Yet there is more to reckon with than a dubious oracle, discovered through signs and portents of the sky or whisperings of the breeze at night. Jehovah has brought His people from Egypt, fed them in the desert, given them victory. Balaam finds that this God can send angels upon His errands, that there is no escape from His presence nor evasion of His will.

It was in a kind of madness the diviner set out from Pethor by the way of the Euphrates' ford. Excited by the hope of gaining the rewards and enjoying the fame awaiting him in Moab, he was at the same time conscious of being in opposition to the God of Israel, and committed to an adventure that might end disastrously. He went in a mood of wilfulness, hoping and yet half doubting that his way would become clear, irritable therefore, ready to resent every hindrance. A diviner of repute, credited with powers of blessing and cursing, he perhaps felt himself safe on ordinary occasions, especially among his own people, even when he went against those who consulted him. But could he count on the forbearance of the king of Moab into whose country he was venturing? Jehovah might be opening his way only to destruction. Such fears could hardly be avoided.

And men who have gone back to conscience endeavouring to extort from it a sanction or permission previously denied, who, with some half assurance that the way is open, set out on a desired course, are practically in the same mad mood, have equal reason to dread the issue. Is this understood? It may be safely asserted that half the wrong things men do—taking an average of human action, half at least—are done not in despite of conscience, but with its dubious consent, when the first clear decision has been set aside. No doubt the urgency is often very great, as it was in Balaam's case, and frequently of a less questionable kind. Not the desire of envious persons to have others cursed or evil intreated, but possibly the desire of some to have the shadow of adverse judgment taken away, may be the plea, and be supported by the promise of large reward. The first word of conscience is distinct—Have nothing whatever to do with the matter: the shadow has fallen on the wrongdoer; he has not repented; let him suffer still. But his agents come with gold and silver, with plausible words, with seeming Christian arguments. Then the appeal to conscience is renewed, and he who should be firm in judgment finds a false permission. Or the case may be of one in business, tempted to some practice, common enough, but dishonest, vile. His first feeling has been that of disgust. He could not for a moment contemplate a thing so base. But under the pressure of what appears to be necessity, plausible arguments and pretexts gain ground. The fact that reputable men find no difficulty about the matter, the notion that a custom is excusable because it is followed by most if not by all, along with other considerations of a personal kind, are allowed to have some weight, and then to overbalance the sense of duty. And the result is that the moral atmosphere is confused. The man sets out on a way which appears to be opened for him; but he goes under the shadow of a haunting fear.

Like Balaam, one who thus extorts from conscience, that is from God, permission to go where he himself desires, knowing it to be a wrong way, is quite aware, may indeed be eager to acknowledge to himself, that he is still held by a Divine command extending over a part of his conduct. He will not speak a word that shall be against truth. He will resume friendship with the rich transgressor; but he will not in words excuse or palliate his crime. He will adulterate certain commodities in which he deals, but he will never assert that they are genuine. This is the tribute to religion and to conscience that sustains decaying self-respect. By this the man who passes for a Christian endeavours to keep himself separate from those who have no conscience. The most is made of the difference. As compared with those who unblushingly defend the wrong, this man may think himself a saint. He would on no account speak a falsehood. Does he not fear God? Is he a dog that he should do this thing? Nevertheless, the way leads into a bottomless quagmire. For a time the waning light of religion may shine. It may even burst before it dies into a bright flame of indignation against sin—the crimes others commit—or of loud protestation against what are called false charges. But the man dies a Balaam, with a perverted conscience, and must face the dreadful result.

Well has it been said that no virtue is safe without enthusiasm. A man cannot be true to the highest law unless he has the motive within him of pure devotion to God as his personal Redeemer, unless he recognises that his joy in God and his salvation are bound up with fidelity to the moral ideal which is presented to him. Faith, hope, love must inspire and keep the soul in fervour of desire to reach the heights to which it is called by the Divine voice. But the most of men come far short of this enthusiasm. It is rather with reluctance, after a kind of struggle with themselves, that they look duty in the face. And even when they do they find no pleasure in resolving to press on where the absolutely right is seen. Their pleasure lies in doing less than that. They seek accordingly some way of observing the letter of duty while they avoid its spirit. But the sense of having come short in a matter that involves their highest wellbeing, their standing before God, their very right to hope and to live, remains with them. Marriage, for example, is often entered upon after a struggle with conscience in which a clear mandate has been set aside. The desire to please self is allowed to overcome the conviction that the new bond will keep life on the low worldly ground, or drag it back from spirituality. The merely expedient is chosen rather than the ideal of moral independence and power. And of this come fretfulness, dissatisfaction with self, with others, with Providence. All the sophistries that can be used fail to set the mind at rest. Events continually occur which throw flashes of light on the past and reveal the lost hope, the forfeited vision.

God does not make the wrong way smooth for one who has extorted permission to follow it. A man desiring to enter on a course which he sees to be dishonourable or at least dubious may be absolutely prevented at first. His appeal is to Providence. If circumstances allowed his plan he would reckon the Divine will favourable to it. But they do not. Every door he tries in the direction he wishes to take is barred against him. Afterwards one yields to pressure, or is thrown wide because he knocks at it persistently. Then he advances, taking for granted that he has obtained permission from God. But he does not go far till he is undeceived. So, Balaam sets out on his adventure, riding on his ass and attended by his two servants. Yet he does not get clear of the vineyards of Pethor without hindrance. Obstacles to his journey which do not appear in the narrative may have at first stood in his way, certain political complications, we may suppose. Now they are removed. But he is met by others. The angel of the Lord opposes him, one who stands with a drawn sword in hand in a hollow way between the vineyards, a path closely fenced on the one side and the other. Balaam fails to see the adversary; he is absorbed in his own thoughts. But the ass sees, and will not go forward, and as Balaam becomes aware of resistance his anger is kindled.

The narrative here is confessedly difficult. One of the most reverent commentators on the passage declares that he feels too deeply the essential veracity of the story to be troubled with minute questions about its details. "I would not," he says, "force them upon any one's belief merely by uttering the coarse sentence, that they are in the Bible and therefore must be received. One is afraid of leading people to fancy that they do believe what they do not believe, and so of propagating hypocrisy under the name of faith." To some the narrative may present no serious difficulty. They accept it literally at every point. Others again are not so easily satisfied that the occasion called for miracles like those which appear on the face of the history. It seems to them of no great moment whether Balaam went or did not go to Moab, whether he cursed Israel or blessed it. Neither the curse nor the blessing of a man of Balaam's sort could make the least difference to Israel. These readers accordingly would find a parabolical or pictorial explanation of the incidents. Literal belief, in any case, need not be made a test of reverence; the spirit is surely more than the letter. The point of greatest importance is to believe that God dealt with this man, opposed his perverse will by gracious influences and unexpected protests. To Balaam, no doubt, the angel's appearance and the ass's rebuke were real, as real and impressive as any experiences he ever had. He was humbled; he acknowledged his sin and offered to return. When he reached the land of Moab, the recollection of what befell him by the way had a salutary influence on all he said and did.

In many unforeseen, singular, and often homely ways, men are checked in the endeavour to carry out the schemes which ambition and avarice prompt. The angel of the Lord who opposes one bent on a bad enterprise often appears in familiar guise. To some men their wives stand in the way, some are challenged by their children. What in voluntary blindness they have declined to see—the madness of the wrong course, the intrinsic baseness of the thing undertaken—those who look with pure eyes perceive clearly and are brave enough to condemn. At other times obstacles are placed in the way by the simple ordinary duties which claim attention, occupy thought and time, and tend to bring back the mind to humility and saneness. Yet covetousness can make men very blind. Under the influence of it they suppose themselves to be acting cleverly, while all the time those whom they think they are outwitting see them posting on the way to bankruptcy and shame.

Even a good man may lose his spiritual discrimination occasionally when he fancies himself called to curse not Israel but Moab, and sets out in heat upon the errand. He fails to see that the case of Balaam is so far parallel to his own that he ought to expect an angel to oppose him. The critical Balaam who feels it his high duty to pronounce maledictions on some theological opponent, not for silver and gold, but for the cause of God, is resisted by many an angel bearing the sharp sword of the Word, set to declare the great tolerance of Christ, and to vindicate the liberty that is in Him. That men fail to see these angels, or else ride past them, is abundantly evident, for the altars smoke on many a height, and scrolls of futile condemnation are flung upon the breeze.

Balaam smites the ass even when she falls down under him in her abject terror. He endeavours to force her on till at last he is put to shame by her rebuke. We are pointed to the irrational way in which those act whose moral judgment is blinded. Their course being wrong, they do not turn against themselves, but rise in passion against every person or thing that hinders. The husband who is resolved to take a wrong path thrusts away his faithful wife; the son bent on what will be his ruin pushes off his weeping mother when she pleads before him. Often an apparently inexplicable fit of temper in public or in private means that a man is in the wrong and is aware of a mistake, from the consequences of which he would fain escape. One's heart bleeds for none more than for those victims of selfish anger who suffer under the abuse of the Balaams of society. They have seen the angel in the way. They have sought by a gesture or a warning word to arrest the friend who would go on to evil. Then the cruel strokes fall on them, curses, foul abuse, taunts often directed against their religion. They are charged with setting themselves up as holier and better than other people. They are denounced as meddlers and fools. They protest without effect often, and suffer apparently to no purpose. Yet shall we suppose their endeavours altogether lost? Good is surely stronger than evil. Every right act and word is germinal. After long years it bears fruit.

In Balaam's case there was a happier issue than is often seen. The protest against his cruelty opened his eyes to the truth that a messenger of God stood in his way. The rebuke came home to him. So might a hard, self-willed man who rode rough-shod over the feelings and rights of others be brought suddenly to a sense of his cruelty by the look on the face of a dog. Bad as men and women may be, violent and abusive as they may become in times of anger and impatience, there are ways of softening their hearts. They go on for years attempting to justify themselves in a rough and selfish course. But who shall say that even the seeming worst are beyond recovery? When there appears to be no redeeming feature left in the character, the crisis may be at hand, the transgressor may be so taught by the piteous look of a dumb animal that his infatuation will come to an end. Recoiling from himself he will acknowledge his perversity and turn to better thoughts.

How far did Balaam's repentance go? There can be little doubt the motive of it was the sudden discovery that the God of Israel was mightier and more observant than he had imagined; in short, that Jehovah was his master. Balaam yields, changes his mind, not because he is in the least degree more disposed to do what is right, but because he finds the antagonism of God falling suddenly upon his life. To the angel he says: "I have sinned: for I knew not that thou stoodest in the way against me: now therefore, if it displease thee, I will get me back again." This is an acknowledgment of authority, but not of an obligation into which any sense of God's goodness enters. It is the sullen acquiescence of a foiled adventurer, who at the very outset is made to understand the terms and narrow limits of his power. He has his knowledge, his vision. When he set out he intended to use them, if possible, under such conditions as would secure his own liberty. He is now made to understand that he is not free. The angel with the drawn sword will be in Moab before him, ready to cut him down if he should do or say anything opposed to the mind of the God of Israel. He is cowed, not converted.

And so it often is with men who find their schemes counteracted, and are made to feel their weakness in presence of the forces of human government, or of the natural world. Their confession of sin is really a sullen acknowledgment of impotence. Sift their feelings and you discover no sense of guilt. They miscalculated, and they regret having done so, because it is to their shame. They will go back to make other plans, to lay the foundations deeper with greater subtlety, and by-and-by, if they can, to carry out their ideas and gratify their covetousness and ambition in other ways. Sometimes indeed it may become clear to a man that his efforts to advance himself, such as he is, cannot prosper because Omnipotence is against him. Then acknowledgment of defeat is confession of despair. Of this we see an example in the first Napoleon after his final capture when he was on the voyage to St. Helena. He had forced his way over obstacles enough, leaving blood and ruin behind him. But at length the stronger power came down to meet him, and he knew that the game was lost. Beneath the seeming acquiescence there lurked rebellion. He often spoke as a believer in God; but the God he knew was one he could have wished to foil. In the island to which he was confined he schemed desperately to regain his freedom that he might renew the vain conflict with Providence for his own glory and the glory of France. "I have sinned: I will get me back again." Yes. But will it be to lay other and more cunning plots for self-aggrandisement, and recover the lost ground by some daring stroke? Then it will be also to meet other angels, and at the last the minister who bears the sword of doom.

Balaam will return, confessing himself defeated for the time. But he learns that he may not. He has come so far with designs of his own; he must now go on to Moab to serve the purposes of God. The permission he wrested, so to speak, from Providence, was not wrested after all. There are deeper schemes than Balaam can form, the great far-reaching plans of the God of Israel, and by these, however unwillingly, the soothsayer of Pethor is now bound. This journey has been of his own perverse choosing; now he must finish it, feeling himself at every point a servant, an instrument; and if danger and even death await him, still he must proceed. Easy it is to begin in the craftiness of human purpose and the foolishness of earthly hope; but the end is not under the control of him who begins. There is One who orders all things so that the gifts of men and their perversity and their wrath shall all praise Him, shall all be woven into the web of His evolving purpose, universal, holy, sure.

It is a startling thought that in a sense whatever we begin in pride or self-will, playing, as it were, the first act of the drama on some stage we ourselves select, the movement cannot be arrested when we choose. In one way or another, act after act must proceed to the very end which God foreordains. Many human purposes appear to be sharply and completely broken off. In the midst of his days man hears the call he cannot disobey. His tools, his hopes, his declared intentions must be laid aside. But the end is not yet. The curtain has fallen here. It will be raised again. And in many unfoldings of Divine purpose we witness scene after scene, in scene after scene have to play our part. One who has begun ill may sincerely repent, and then the development takes a direction which will be to the glory of Divine grace. That act of repentance over, another comes, in which the humble thought of the penitent reveals itself. He is seen a new man, timorous where he was bold, bold where he was timorous. Beyond there are other scenes, in which he shall be found endeavouring to repair the evil he has done, to gather the poisoned arrows he has strewed about the world. And the consummation shall be reached when the task at which he has vainly laboured is completed for him by Christ, and his recovery and the restitution he toiled for shall be complete.

But if there is no penitence, still the drama must go on to its finish. The man resenting, yet unable to resist, shall do what God requires, what God permits. He shall attempt to curse, yet be constrained to bless. He shall in bitterness of anger frame new devices and carry them out. Then, when the cup of his iniquity is full, and all is done Providence allows, retribution shall overtake him. In the thick of battle the sword of the angel shall smite him to the ground. For each man, under God's rule, in the midst of the forces He upholds, there is a destiny, some stages of which we can trace. Entering on life we of necessity become subject to great laws which our revolt cannot in the least affect. And these are moral laws. The seeming success of the immoral who are intellectually or brutally strong is within the narrow limits of time and space. In the breadths of eternity and infinity there is no strength for any but the good.

There is a purpose of God which Balaam is unwilling to subserve; and of that the man becomes gradually aware. When he is met by Balak and his train and upbraided with his reluctance to come where honours and rewards are to be had, the soothsayer realises his peril and begins at once to prepare the Moabite king for disappointment. "Lo, I am come unto thee," he says: "have I now any power at all to speak anything? The word that God putteth in my mouth, that shall I speak." What we see now is a contest between the influence of Balak, with his power to reward and also to punish, and the consciousness of a constraint which had entered deeply into Balaam's mind. The sense of Jehovah's authority over him on this occasion was indeed supported by another strong motive which the diviner never allowed to fall into the background. He had his reputation to maintain. At whatever hazard, he must show himself to Moabites, Midianites, Aramæans, a man who knew the knowledge of the Most High. The ignorance of Balak is seen in his absurd hope that for the sake of some bribe of his the prophet of Pethor will be induced to fling away his fame.

There are things which even money cannot buy. There is a limit beyond which even a false and avaricious man cannot venture for the sake of honours and rewards. It is a vulgar judgment that every man has his price. One who is not particularly conscientious on most occasions will sometimes touch the bounds of concession and take his stand for what is left, all the self he has in any true sense. Neither will money buy nor threats compel his further acquiescence in what he deems wrong. Again, as in Balaam's case, the limit of the power of gold or of threats may be fixed by pride. There are gifts, qualities, distinctions possessed by some, in virtue of which they seem to themselves to occupy a place which all might covet. The veteran has his decoration, once attached to his uniform by some honoured commander under whom he served. No money could buy that. He would die rather than part with it. Another is proud of his name. To dishonour that would be treachery to his ancestors. Balaam has his unique power of vision, and for a while at least he preserves it. A man like Balak, measuring others by himself, regards a diviner as one of a lower order who may be moved by menaces and promises. He finds that Balaam has pride enough to lift him above them. Thus vanity counteracts vanity; the comparatively base keeps the base in check.

CHAPTER XX.

BALAAM'S PARABLES.

NUMBERS xxii. 39-xxiv. 9.

THE scene is now on some mountain of Moab from which the encampment of the Hebrew tribes in the plain of the Jordan is fully visible. At Kiriath-huzoth, possibly the modern Shihan, about ten miles east of the Dead Sea, and to the south of the Arnon valley, preparation for the attempt against Israel's destiny has been made by a great sacrifice of oxen and sheep intended to secure the good-will of Chemosh, the Baal or Lord of Moab. On the range overhanging the Dead Sea, somewhat to the north of the Arnon, perhaps, are the Bamoth-Baal, or high places of Baal, and the "bare height" where Balaam is to seek his auguries and will be met by God.

The evening of Balaam's arrival has been spent in the sacrificial festival, and in the morning Balak and his princes escort the diviner to the Bamoth-Baal that he may begin his experiment. After his usual manner, Balaam pompously requires that great arrangements be made for the trial of auguries by means of which his oracle is to be found. Balak has offered sacrifices to Chemosh; now Jehovah must be propitiated, and seven altars have to be built, and on each of them a bullock and a ram offered by fire. The altars erected, the carcases of the animals prepared, Balaam does not remain beside them to take actual part in the sacrifice. It is, in fact, to be Balak's, not his; and if the God of Israel should refuse His sanction to the curse, that will be because the offering of the king of Moab has not secured His favour. Accordingly, while the seven wreaths of smoke ascend from the altars, and the invocations of the Divine power which usually accompany sacrifice are chanted by the king and his princes, the soothsayer withdraws to a peak at some distance that he may read the omens. "Peradventure," he says, "Jehovah will come to meet me."

It was now a critical hour for the ambitious prophet. He had indeed already found distinction, for who in Moab or Midian could have commanded with so royal an air and received attention so obsequious? But the reward remained to be won. Yet may we not assume that when Balaam reached Moab and saw the pitiable state of what had been once a strong kingdom, the cities half ruined, filled with poor and dejected inhabitants, he conceived a kind of contempt for Balak and perceived that his offers must be set aside as worthless? God met Balaam, we are told. And this may have been the sense in which God met him and put a word into his mouth. What was Moab compared with Israel? A glance at Kiriath-huzoth, a little experience of Balak's empty boastfulness and the entreaties and anxiety which betrayed his weakness, would show Balaam the vanity of proposing to reinvigorate Moab at the expense of Israel. His way led clearly enough where the finger of the God of Israel pointed, and his mind almost anticipated what the Voice he heard as Jehovah's declared. He saw the smoke streaming south-eastward, and casting a black shadow between him and Moab; but the sun shone on the tents of Israel, right away to the utmost part of the camp (xxii. 41). The mind of Balaam was made up. It would be better for him in a worldly sense to win some credit with Israel than to have the greatest honour Moab could offer. Chemosh was in decline, Jehovah in the ascendant. Perhaps the Hebrews might need a diviner when their great Moses was dead, and he, Balaam, might succeed to that exalted office. We never can tell what dreams will enter the mind of the ambitious man, or rather, we do not know on what slender foundations he builds the most extravagant hopes. There was nothing more unlikely, the thing indeed was absolutely impossible, yet Balaam may have imagined that his oracle would come to the ears of the Israelites, and that they would send for him to give favourable auguries before they crossed the Jordan.

Rapidly the diviner had to form his decision. That done, the words of the oracle could be trusted to the inspiration of the moment, inspiration from Jehovah, whose superiority to all the gods of Syria Balaam now heartily acknowledged. He accordingly left his place of vision and returned to the Bamoth where the altars still smoked. Then he took up his parable and spoke.

"From Aram Balak brought me,
Moab's king from the mountains of the east;
'Come, curse for me Jacob,
And come, menace Israel.'
How can I curse whom God hath not cursed?
And how can I menace whom God hath not menaced?
For from the head of the rocks I see him,
And from the hills I behold him.

Lo, a people apart he dwells,
And among the nations he is not counted.
Who can reckon the dust of Jacob,
And in number the fourth of Israel?
Let my soul die the death of the righteous;
And be my last end like his!"

In this parable, or *mashal*, along with some elements of egotism and self-defence, there are others that have the ring of inspiration. The opening is a vaunt, and the expression, "How can I curse whom God hath not cursed?" is a form of self-vindication which savours of vanity. We see more of the cowed and half-resentful man than of the prophet. Yet the vision of a people dwelling apart, not to be reckoned among the others, is a real revelation, boldly flung out. Something of the difference already established between Israel and the *goim*, or peoples of the Syrian district, had been caught by the seer in his survey of past events, and now came to clear expression. For a moment, at least, his soul rose almost into spiritual desire in the cry that his last end should be of the kind an Israelite might have; one who with calm confidence laid himself down in the arms of the great God, the Lord of providence, of death as well as life.

A man has learned one lesson of great value for the conduct of life when he sees that he cannot curse whom God has not cursed, that he would be foolish to menace whom God has not menaced. Reaching this point of sight, Balaam stands superior for the time to the vulgar ideas of men like the king of Moab, who have no conception of a strong and dominant will to which human desires are all subjected. However reluctantly this confession is made, it prevents many futile endeavours and much empty vapouring. There are some indeed whose belief that fate must be on their side is simply immovable. Those whom they choose to reckon enemies are established in the protection of heaven; but they think it possible to wrest their revenge even from the Divine hand. Not till the blow they strike recoils with crushing force on themselves do they know the fatuity of their hope. In his "Instans Tyrannus" Mr. Browning pictures one whose persecution of an obscure foe ends in defeat.

> "I soberly laid my last plan
> To extinguish the man.
> Round his creep-hole, with never a break,
> Ran my fires for his sake;
> Overhead, did my thunder combine
> With my underground mine:
> Till I looked from my labour, content
> To enjoy the event.
> When sudden . . . how think ye, the end?
> Did I say, 'Without friend'?
> Say rather from marge to blue marge
> The whole sky grew his targe,
> With the sun's self for visible boss,
> While an Arm ran across,
> Which the earth heaved beneath, like a breast
> Where the wretch was safe prest!
> Do you see? Just my vengeance complete,
> The man sprang to his feet,
> Stood erect, caught at God's skirts and prayed!
> —So, I was afraid!"

In smaller matters, the attempts at impudent detraction which are common, when the base, girding at the good, think it possible to bring them to contempt, or at least stir them to unseemly anger, or prick them to humiliating self-defence, the law is often well enough understood, yet neither the assailants nor those attacked may be wise enough to recognise it. A man who stands upon his faithfulness to God does not need to be vexed by the menaces of the base; he should despise them. Yet he often allows himself to be harassed, and so yields all the victory hoped for by his detractor. Calm indifference, if one has a right to use it, is the true shield against the arrows of envy and malice.

Balaam's vision of Israel as a separated people, a people dwelling alone, had singular penetration. The others he knew—Amorites, Moabites, Ammonites, Midianites, Hittites, Aramæans—went together, scarcely distinguishable in many respects, with their national Baals all of the same kind. Was Ammon or Chemosh, Melcarth or Sutekh, the name of the Baal? The rites might differ somewhat, there might be more or less ferocity ascribed to the deities; but on the whole their likeness was too close for any real distinction. And the peoples, differing in race, in habit, no doubt, were yet alike in this, that their morality and their mental outlook passed no boundary, were for the most part of the beaten, crooked road. Strifes and petty ambitions here and there, temporary combinations for ignoble ends, the rise of one above another for a time under some chief who held his ground by force of arms, then fell and disappeared—such were the common events of their histories. But Israel came into Balaam's sight as a people of an entirely different kind, generically distinct. Their God was no Baal ferocious by report, really impotent, a mere reflection of human passion and lust. Jehovah's law was a creation, like nothing in human history ascribed to a God. His worship meant solemn obligation, imposed, acknowledged, not simply to honour Him, but to be pure and true and honest in honouring Him. Israel had no part in the orgies that were held in professed worship of the Baals, really to the disgrace of their devotees. The lines of the national development had been laid down, and Balaam saw to some extent how widely they diverged from those along which other peoples sought power and glory. Amorites and Hittites and Canaanites might keep their place, but Israel had the secret of a progress of which they never dreamed. Wherever the tribes settled, when they advanced to fulfil their destiny, they would prove a new force in the world.

For the time Israel might be called the one spiritual people. It was this Balaam partly saw, and made the basis of his striking predictions. The modern nations are not to be distinguished by the same testing idea. The thoughts and hopes of Christianity have entered more or less into all that are civilised, and have touched others that can scarcely be called so. Yet if there is any oracle for the peoples of our century it is one that turns on the very point which Balaam seems to have had in view. But it is, that not one of them, as a nation, is distinctly moved and separated from others by spirituality of aim. Of not one can it be said that it is confessedly, eagerly, on the way to a Canaan where the Living and True God shall be worshipped, that its popular movements, its legislation, its main endeavours look to such a heavenly result. If we saw a people dwelling apart, with a high spiritual aim, resolutely excluding those ideas of materialism which dominate the rest, of them it would not be presumptuous to prophesy in the high terms to which the oracles of Balaam gradually rose.

Regarding the wish with which the diviner closed his first *mashal*, hard things have been said, as for example, that "even in his sublimest visions his egotism breaks out; in the sight of God's Israel he cries, 'Let me die the death of the righteous.'" Here, however, there may be personal sorrow and regret, a pathetic confession of human fear by one who has been brought to serious thought, rather than any mere egoistic craving. Why should he speak of death? That is not the theme of the egotist. We hear a sudden ejaculation that seems to open a glimpse of his heart. For this man, like every son of Adam, has his burden, his secret trouble, from which all the hopes and plans of his ambition cannot relieve his mind. Now for the first time he speaks in a genuinely religious strain. "There are the righteous whom the Great Jehovah regards with favour, and gathers to Himself. When their end comes they rest. Alas! I, Balaam, am not one of them; and the shadows of my end are not far away! Would that by some mighty effort I could throw aside my life as it has been and is, revoke my destiny, and enter the ranks of Jehovah's people—were it only to die among them."

Wistfully, men whose life has been on the low ground of mere earthly toil and pleasure may, in like manner, when the end draws near, envy the confidence and hope of the good. For the old age of the sensualist, and even of the successful man of the world, is under a dull wintry sky, with no prospect of another morning, or even of a quiet night of dreamless sleep.

> "The weariest and most loathed worldly life,
> That age, ache, penury, and imprisonment
> Can lay on nature, is a paradise
> To what we fear of death."

Courage and peace at the last belong to those alone who have kept in the way of righteousness. To them and no others light shall arise in the darkness. The faithfulness of God is their refuge even when the last shadows fall. He whom they trust goes before them in the pillar of fire when night is on the world, as well as in the pillar of cloud by day. To the man of this earth even the falling asleep of the good is enviable, though they may not anticipate a blessed immortality. Their very grave is a bed of peaceful rest, for living or dying they belong to the great God.

It was with growing dissatisfaction, rising to anxiety, Balak heard the first oracle that fell from the diviner's lips. Despite the warning he had received that only the words which Jehovah gave should be spoken, he hoped for some kind of a curse. His altars had been built, his oxen and rams sacrificed, and surely, he thought, all would not be in vain! Balaam had not travelled from Pethor to mock him. But the prophecy carried not a single word of heartening to the enemies of Israel. The camp lay in the full sunshine of fortune, unobscured by the least cloud. It was the first blow to Balak's malignant jealousy, and might well have put him to confusion. But men of his sort are rich in conjectures and expedients. He had set his mind on this as the means of finding advantage in a struggle that was sure to come; and he clung to his hope. Although the curse would not light on the whole camp of Israel, yet it might fall on a part, the remote outlying portion of the tribes. In superstition men are for ever catching at straws. If the anger of some heavenly power, what power mattered little to Balak, could be once enlisted against the tribes, even partially, the influence of it might spread. And it would at least be something if pestilence or lightning smote the utmost part of that threatening encampment.

One must be sorry for men whose impotent anger has to fall on expedients so miserably inadequate. Moab defeated by the Amorites sees them in turn vanquished and scattered by this host which has suddenly appeared, and to all ordinary reckoning has no place nor right in the region. Sad as was the defeat which deprived Balak of half his land and left his people in poverty, this incursion and its success foreboded greater trouble. The king was bound to do something, and, feeling himself unable to fight, this was his scheme. The utter uselessness of it from every point of view gives the story a singular pathos. But the world under Divine providence cannot be left in a region where superstition reigns and progress is impossible—simply that a people like the Moabites may settle again on their lees, and that others may continue to enjoy what seem to them to be their rights. There must be a stirring of human existence, a new force and new ideas introduced among the peoples, even at the expense of war and bloodshed. And our sympathy with Balak fails when we recollect that Israel had refrained from attacking Moab in its day of weakness, had even refrained from asking leave to pass through its impoverished territory. The feelings of the vanquished had been respected. Perhaps Balak, with the perversity of a weak man and an incompetent prince, resented this as much as anything.

Balaam was now brought into the field of Zophim, or the Watchers, to the "top of Pisgah," whence he could see only a part of the camp of Israel. The Hebrew here as well as in xxii. 41 is ambiguous. It has even been interpreted as meaning that on the first occasion part of the encampment only was in view, and on the second occasion the whole of it (so Keil *in loco*). But the tenor of the narrative corresponds better with the translation given in the English Version. The precise spot here called the top of Pisgah has not been identified. In the opinion of some the name Pisgah survives in the modern Siaghah; but even if it does we are not helped in the least. Others take Pisgah as meaning simply "hill," and read "the field of Zophim on the top of the hill." The latter translation would obviate the difficulty that in Deut. xxxiv. 1 it is said that Moses, when the time of his death approached, "went up from the plains of Moab unto Mount Nebo, to the top of Pisgah that is over against Jericho." Pisgah may have been the name of the range; yet again in Numb. xxvii. 12, and Deut. xxxii. 49, Abarim is given as the name of the range of which Nebo is a peak. We are led to the conclusion that Pisgah was the name in general use for a hill-top of some peculiar form. The root meaning of the word is difficult to make out. It may at all events be taken as certain that this top of Pisgah is not the same as that to which Moses ascended to die. Balak and his princes had not as yet ventured so far beyond the Arnon.

At Balaam's request the same arrangements were made as at Bamoth-Baal. Seven altars were built, and seven bullocks and seven rams were offered; and again the diviner withdrew to some distance to seek omens. This time his meeting with Jehovah gave him a more emphatic message. It would seem that with the passing of the day's incidents the vatic fire in his mind burned more brightly. Instead of endeavouring to conciliate Balak he appears to take delight in the oracle that dashes the hopes of Moab to the ground. He has looked from the new point of vision and seen the great future that awaits Israel. It is vain to expect that the decree of the Almighty One can be revoked. Balak must hear all that the spirit of Elohim has given to the seer.

"Up, Balak, and hear;
Hearken to me, son of Zippor:
No man is God, that He should lie;
And no son of man, that He should repent.
Hath He said, and shall He not do it?
And spoken, and shall He not make good?
Behold to bless I have received;
And He hath blessed and I cannot undo.
He hath not beheld iniquity in Jacob,
Nor seen perverseness in Israel.
Jehovah his God is with him;
And the shout of a King is with him.
God brings them forth from Egypt:
Like the horns of the wild ox are his.
Surely no snake-craft is in Jacob,
And no enchantment with Israel.
At the time it shall be said of Jacob and Israel,
What hath God wrought?
Behold the people as a lioness arises,
And as a lion lifts himself up;
He shall not lie down till he eat the prey,
And drink the blood of the slain."

The confirmation of the first oracle by what Balaam has realised on his second approach to Jehovah compels the question which rebukes the king's vain desire. "Hath He said, and shall He not do it?" Balak did not know Jehovah as Balaam knew Him. This God never went back from His decision, nor recalled His promises. And He is able to do whatever He wills. Not only does He refuse to curse Israel, but He has given a blessing which Balaam even, powerful as he is, cannot possibly hinder. It has become manifest that the judgment of God on His people's conduct is in no respect adverse. Reviewing their past, the diviner may have found such failure from the covenant as would give cause for a decision against them, partial at least, if not general. But there is no excuse for supposing that Jehovah has turned against the tribes. Their recent successes and present position are proofs of His favour unrevoked, and, it would seem, irrevocable. There is a King with this people, and when they advance it is with a shout in His honour. The King is Jehovah their God; mightier far than Balak or any ruler of the nations. When the loud Hallelujah rose from the multitude at some sacred feast, it was indeed the shout of a monarch.

Singular is it to find a diviner like Balaam noting as one of the great distinctions of Israel that the nation used neither augury nor divination. The hollowness of his own arts in presence of the God of Israel who could not be moved by them, who gave His people hope without them, would seem to have impressed Balaam profoundly. He speaks almost as if in contempt of the devices he himself employs. Indeed, he sees that his art is not art at all, as regards Israel. The Hebrews trust no omens; and either for or against them omens give no sign. It was another mark of the separateness of Israel. Jehovah had fenced His people from the spells of the magician. True to Him, they could defy all the sorcery of the East. And when the time for further endeavour came, the nations around should have to hear of the God who had brought the Hebrew tribes out of Egypt. With a lion-like vigour they would rise from their lair by the Jordan. The Canaanites and Amorites beyond should be their prey. Already perhaps tidings had come of the defeat of Bashan: the cities on the other side of Jordan should fall in their turn.

As yet there is nothing in the predictions of Balaam that can be said to point distinctly to any future event in Israel's history. The oracles are of that general kind which might be expected from a man of the world who has given attention to the signs of the times and perceived the value to a people of strong and original faith. But taking them in this sense they may well rebuke that modern disbelief which denies the inspiring power of religion and the striking facts which come to light not only in the history of nations like Israel but in the lives of men whose vigour springs from religious zeal. Balaam saw what any whose eyes are open will also see, that when the shout of the Heavenly King is among a people, when they serve a Divine Master, holy, just, and true, they have a standing ground and an outlook not otherwise to be reached. The critics of religion who take it to be a mere heat of the blood, a transient emotion, forget that the grasp of great and generous principles, and the thought of an Eternal Will to be served, give a sense of right and freedom which expediency and self-pleasing cannot supply. However man comes to be what he is, this is certain, that for him strength depends not so much on bodily physique as on the soul, and for the soul on religious inspiration. The enthusiasm of pleasure-seeking has never yet made a band of men indomitable, nor need it be expected to give greatness; we cannot persuade ourselves that apart from God our blessedness is a matter of surpassing importance. We are a multitude whose individual lives are very small, very short, very insignificant, unless they are known to serve some Divine end.

It has been seen by one philosopher that if the religious sanction be taken away from morality some other must be provided to fill up the vacuum. Further, it may be said that if the religious support and stimulus of human energy be withdrawn there will be a greater vacuum more difficult to fill. The would-be benefactors of our race, who think that the superstition of a personal God is effete and should be swept away as soon as possible, so that man may return to nature, might do well to return to Balaam. He had a penetration which they do not possess. And singularly, the very apostle of that impersonal "stream of tendency making for righteousness," which was once to be put in the place of God, did on one occasion unwittingly remind us of this prophet. Mr. Matthew Arnold had a difficult thing to do when he tried to encourage a toiling population to go on toiling without hope, to plod on in the underground while a select few above enjoyed the sunlight. The part was that of a diviner finding auguries for the inevitable. But he spoke as one who had to pity a poor blind Israel, no longer inspired by the shout of a king or the hope of a promised land, an Israel that had lost its faith and its way and seemed about to perish in the desert. Well did he know how difficult it is for men under this dread to endure patiently when those above have abolished God and the future life; men, who are disposed to say, yet must be told that they say vainly, "If there is nothing but this life, we must have it. Let us help ourselves, whenever we can, to all we desire." Was that Israel to be blessed or cursed? There was no oracle. Yet the cultured Balak, hoping for a spell at least against the revolutionaries, had a rebuke. The prophet did not curse; he had no power to bless. But Moab was shown to be in peril, was warned to be generous.

Balaams enough there are, after a sort, with more or less penetration and sincerity. But what the peoples need is a Moses to revive their faith. The hollow maledictions and blessings that are now launched incessantly from valley to hill, from hill to valley, would be silenced if we found the leader who can re-awaken faith. It would be superfluous, then, for the race in its fresh hope to bless itself, and vain for the pessimists to curse it. With the ensign of Divine love leading the way, and the new heavens and earth in view, all men would be assured and hopeful, patient in suffering, fearless in death.

The second oracle produced in the mind of Balak an effect of bewilderment, not of complete discomfiture. He appears to be caught so far in the afflatus that he must hear all the prophet has to tell. He desires Balaam neither to curse nor bless; neutrality would be something. Yet, with all he has already heard giving clear indication what more is to be expected, he proposes another place, another trial of the auguries. This time the whole of Israel shall again be seen. The top of Peor that looketh down upon Jeshimon, or the desert, is chosen. On this occasion when the altars and sacrifices are prepared the order is not the same as before. The diviner does not retire to a distance to seek for omens. He makes no profession of mystery now. The temperature of thought and feeling is high, for the spot on which the company gathers is almost within range of the sentinels of Israel. The adventure is surely one of the strangest which the East ever witnessed. In the dramatic

The third prophetic chant repeats several of the expressions contained in the second, and adds little; but it is more poetical in form. The prophet standing on the height saw "immediately below him the vast encampment of Israel amongst the acacia groves of Abel Shittim—like the water-courses of the mountains, like the hanging gardens beside his own river Euphrates, with their aromatic shrubs and their wide-spreading cedars. Beyond them on the western side of Jordan rose the hills of Palestine, with glimpses through their valleys of ancient cities towering on their crested heights. And beyond all, though he could not see it with his bodily vision, he knew well that there rolled the deep waters of the great sea, with the Isles of Greece, the Isle of Chittim—a world of which the first beginnings of life were just stirring, of which the very name here first breaks upon our ears." From the deep meditation which passed into a trance the diviner awoke to gaze for a little upon that scene, to look fixedly once more on the camp of the Hebrew tribes, and then he began:

> "Balaam the son of Beor saith,
> And the man whose eye was closed saith :
> He saith who heareth the words of El,
> Who seeth the vision of Shaddai,
> Falling down and having his eyes opened."

Thus in the consciousness of an exalted state of mind which has come with unusual symptoms, the ecstasy that overpowers and brings visions before the inward eye, he vaunts his inspiration. There is no small resemblance to the manner in which the afflatus came to seers of Israel in aftertimes; yet the description points more distinctly to the rapture of one like King Saul, who has been swept by some temporary enthusiasm into a strain of thought, an emotional atmosphere, beyond ordinary experience. The far-reaching encampment is first poetically described, with images that point to perennial vitality and strength. Then as a settled nation Israel is described, irrigating broad fields and sowing them to reap an abundant harvest. Why comparison is made between the power of Israel and Agag one can only guess. Perhaps the reigning chief of the Amalekites was at this time distinguished by the splendour of his court, so that his name was a type of regal magnificence. The images of the wild ox and the lion are repeated with additional emphasis; and the strain rises to its climax in the closing apostrophe:

> "Blessed be every one that blesseth thee
> And cursed be every one that curseth thee."

So strongly is Israel established in the favour of Shaddai, the Almighty One, that attempts to injure her will surely recoil on the head of the aggressor. And on the other hand, to help Israel, to bid her God-speed, will be a way to blessedness. Jehovah will make the overflowing of His grace descend like rain on those who take Israel's part and cheer her on her way.

In the light of what afterwards took place, it is clear that Balaam was in this last ejaculation carried far beyond himself. He may have seen for a moment, in the flash of a heavenly light, the high distinction to which Israel was advancing. He certainly felt that to curse her would be perilous, to bless her meritorious. But the thought, like others of a more spiritual nature, did not enter deeply into his mind. Balaam could utter it with a kind of strenuous cordiality, and then do his utmost to falsify his own prediction. What matter fine emotions and noble protestations if they are only momentary and superficial? Balak's open jealousy and hatred of Israel were, after all, more complimentary to her than the high-sounding praises of Balaam, who spoke as enjoying the elation of the prophet, not as delighting in the tenor of his message. Israel was nothing to him. Soon the prosperity to which she was destined became like gall and wormwood to his soul. The encampment roused his admiration at the time, but afterwards, when it became clear that the Israelites would have none of him, his mood changed towards them. Ambition ruled him to the end; and if the Hebrews did not offer in any way to minister to it, a man like Balaam would by-and-by set himself to bring down their pride. Weak humanity gives many examples of this. The man who has been an expectant flatterer of one greater than himself, but is denied the notice and honour he looks for, becomes, when his hopes have finally to be renounced, the most savage assailant, the most bitter detractor of his former hero. And so strong often are the minds which fall in this manner, that we look sometimes with anxiety even to the highest.

CHAPTER XXI.

THE MATTER OF BAAL-PEOR.

Numbers xxiv. 10-xxv. 18.

The last oracle of Balaam, as we have it, ventures into far more explicit predictions than the others, and passes beyond the range of Hebrew history. Its chief value for the Israelites lay in what was taken to be a Messianic prophecy contained in it, and various bold denunciations of their enemies. Whether the language can bear the important meanings thus found in it is a matter of considerable doubt. On the whole, it appears best not to make over-much of the prescience of this *mashal*, especially as we cannot be sure that we have it in the original form. One fact may be given to prove this. In Jeremiah xlviii. 45, an oracle regarding Moab embodies various fragments of the Book of Numbers, and one clause seems to be a quotation from chap. xxiv. 17. In Numbers the reading is, "and break down [וְקַרְקַר], all the sons of tumult [שֵׁת] ;" in Jeremiah it is, "and the crown of the head [וְקָדְקֹד] of the sons of tumult [שָׁאוֹן]." The resemblance leaves little doubt of the derivation of the one expression from the other, and at the same time shows diversity in the text.

The earlier deliverances of Balaam had disappointed the king of Moab; the third kindled his anger. It was intolerable that one called to curse his enemies should bless them again and again. Balaam would do well to get him back to his own place. That Jehovah of whom he spake had kept him from honour. If he delayed he might find himself in peril. But the diviner did not retire. The word that had come to him should be spoken. He reminded Balak of the terms on which he had begun his auguries, and, perhaps to embitter Moab against Israel, persisted in advertising Balak "what this people should do to his people in the latter days."

The opening was again a vaunt of his high authority as a seer, one who knew the knowledge of Shaddai. Then, with ambiguous forms of speech covering the indistinctness of his outlook, he spoke of one whom he saw far away, in imagination, not reality, a personage bright and powerful, who should rise star-like out of Jacob, bearing the sceptre of Israel, who should smite through the corners of Moab and break down the sons of tumult. Over Edom and Seir he should triumph, and his dominion should extend to the city which had become the last refuge of a hostile people. Of spiritual power and right there is not a trace in this prediction. It is unquestionably the military vigour of Israel gathered up into the headship of some powerful king Balaam sees on the horizon of his field of view. But he anticipates with no uncertainty that Moab shall be attacked and broken, and that the victorious leader shall even penetrate to the fastnesses of Edom and reduce them. A people like Israel, with so great vitality, would not be content to have jealous enemies upon its very borders, and Balak is urged to regard them with more hatred and fear than he has yet shown.

The view that this prophecy "finds its preliminary fulfilment in David, in whom the kingdom was established, and by whose victories the power of Moab and Edom was broken, but its final and complete fulfilment only in Christ," is supported by the unanimous belief of the Jews, and has been adopted by the Christian Church. Yet it must be allowed that the victories of David did not break the power of Moab and Edom, for these peoples are found again and again, after his time, in hostile attitude to Israel. And it is not to the purpose to say that in Christ the kingdom reaches perfection, that He destroys the enemies of Israel. Nor is there an argument for the Messianic reference worth considering in the fact that the pseudo-Messiah in the reign of Hadrian styled himself Barcochba, son of the star. A pretender to Messiahship might snatch at any title likely to secure for him popular support; his choice of a name proves only the common belief of the Jews, and that was very ignorant, very far from spiritual. There is indeed more force in the notion that the star by which the wise men of the East were guided to Bethlehem is somehow related to this prophecy. Yet that also is too imaginative. The oracle of Balaam refers to the virility and prospective dominance of Israel, as a nation favoured by the Almighty and destined to be strong in battle. The range of the prediction is not nearly wide enough for any true anticipation of a Messiah gaining universal sway by virtue of redeeming love. It is becoming more and more necessary to set aside those interpretations which identify the Saviour of the world with one who smites and breaks down and destroys, who wields a sceptre after the manner of Oriental despots.

In Balaam's vision small nations with which he happens to be acquainted bulk largely—the Kenites, Amalek, Moab, and Edom. To him the Amalekites appear as having once been "the first of the nations." We may explain, as before, that he had been impressed on some occasion by what he had seen of their force and the royal state of their king. The Kenites, dwelling either among the cliffs of Engedi or the mountains of Galilee, were a very small tribe; and the Amalekites, as well as the people of Moab and Edom, were of little account in the development of human history. At the same time the prophecy looks in one direction to a power destined to become very great, when it speaks of the ships of Chittim. The course of empire is seen to be westward. Asshur, or Assyria, and Eber—the whole Abrahamic race, perhaps, including Israel—are threatened by this rising power, the nearest point of which is Cyprus in the Great Sea. Balaam is, we may say, a political prophet: to class him among those who testified of Christ is to exalt far too much his inspiration and read more into his oracles than they naturally contain. There is no deep problem in the narrative regarding him—as, for instance, how a man false at heart could in any sense enter into those gracious purposes of God for the human race which were fulfilled by Christ.

Balaam, we are told, "rose up and returned to his own place"; and from this it would seem that with bitterness in his heart he betook himself to Pethor. If he did so, vainly hoping still that Israel would appeal to him, he soon returned to give Balak and the Midianites advice of the most nefarious kind. We learn from xxxi. 16, that through his counsel the Midianite women caused the children of Israel to commit trespass against Jehovah in the matter of Peor. The statement is a link between chaps. xxiv. and xxv. Vainly had Balaam as a diviner matched himself against the God of Israel. Resenting his defeat, he sought and found another way which the customs of his own people in their obscure idolatrous rites too readily suggested. The moral law of Jehovah and the comparative purity of the Israelites as His people kept them separate from the other nations, gave them dignity and vigour. To break down this defence would make them like the rest, would withdraw them from the favour of their God and even defeat His purposes. The scheme was one which only the vilest craft could have conceived; and it shows us too plainly the real character of Balaam. He must have known the power of the allurements which he now advised as the means of attack on those he could not touch with his maledictions nor gain by his soothsaying. In the shadow of this scheme of his we see the diviner and all his tribe, and indeed the whole morality of the region, at their very worst.

The tribes were still in the plain of Jordan; and we may suppose that the victorious troops had returned from the campaign against Bashan, when a band of Midianites, professing the utmost friendliness, gradually introduced themselves into the camp. Then began the temptation to which the Midianitish women, some of them of high rank, willingly devoted themselves. It was to impurity and idolatry, to degradation of manhood in body and soul, to abjuration at once of faith and of all that makes individual and social life. The orgies with which the Midianites were familiar belonged to the dark side of a nature-cultus which carried the distinction between male and female into religious symbolism, and made abject prostration of life before the Divinity a crowning act of worship. Surviving still, the same practices are in India and elsewhere the most dreadful and inveterate barriers which the Gospel and Christian civilisation encounter. The Israelites were assailed unexpectedly, it would appear, and in a time of comparative inaction. Possibly, also, the camp was composed to some extent of men whose families were still in Kadesh waiting the conquest of the land of Canaan to cross the border. But the fact need not be concealed that the polygamy which prevailed among the Hebrews was an element in their danger. That had not been forbidden by the law; it was even countenanced by the example of Moses. The custom, indeed, was one which at the stage of development Israel had reached implied some progress; for there are conditions even worse than polygamy against which it was a protest and safeguard. But like every other custom falling short of the ideal of the family, it was one of great peril; and now disaster came. The Midianites brought their sacrifices and slew them; the festival of Baal-peor was proclaimed. "The people did eat and bowed down to their gods." It was a transgression which demanded swift and terrible judgment. The chief men of the tribes who had joined in the abominable rites were taken and "hanged up before the Lord against the sun"; the "judges of Israel" were commanded to slay "every one his men that were joined unto Baal-peor."

The narrative of the "Priests' Code," beginning at ver. 6, and going on to the close of the chapter, adds details of the sin and its punishment. Assuming that the row of stakes with their ghastly burden is in full view, and the dead bodies of those slain by the executioners are lying about the camp, this narrative shows the people gathered at the tent of meeting, many of them in tears. There is a plague, too, which is rapidly spreading and carrying off the transgressors. In the midst of the sorrow and wailing, when the chief men should have been bowed down in repentance, one of the princes of Simeon is seen leading by the hand his Midianitish paramour, herself a chief's daughter. In the very sight of Moses and the people the guilty persons enter a tent. Then Phinehas, son of Eleazar the priest, following them, inflicts with a javelin the punishment of death. It is a daring but a true deed; and for it Phinehas and his seed after him are promised the "covenant of peace," even the "covenant of an everlasting priesthood." His swift stroke has vindicated the honour of God, and "made an atonement for the children of Israel." An act like this, when the elemental laws of morality are imperilled and a whole people needs a swift and impressive lesson, is a tribute to God which He will reward and remember. True, one of the priestly house should keep aloof from death. But the emergency demands immediate action, and he who is bold enough to strike at once is the true friend of men and of God.

The question may be put, whether this is not justice of too rude and ready a kind to be praised in the name of religion. To some it may seem that the honour of God could not be served by the deed attributed to Phinehas; that he acted in passion rather than in the calm deliberation without which justice cannot be dealt out by man to man. Would not this excuse the passionate action of a crowd, impatient of the forms of law, that hurries an offender to the nearest tree or lamp-post? And the answer cannot be that Israel was so peculiarly under covenant to God that its necessity would exonerate a deed otherwise illegal. We must face the whole problem alike of personal and of united action for the vindication of righteousness in times of widespread license.

It is not necessary now to slay an offender in order clearly and emphatically to condemn his crime. In that respect modern circumstances differ from those we are discussing. Upon Israel, as it was at the time of this tragedy, no impression could have been made deep and swift enough for the occasion otherwise than by the act of Phinehas. But for an offender of the same rank now, there is a punishment as stern as death, and on the popular mind it produces a far greater effect—publicity, and the reprobation of all who love their fellowmen and God. The act of Phinehas was not assassination; a similar act now would be, and it would have to be dealt with as a crime. The stroke now is inflicted by public accusation, which results in public trial and public condemnation. From the time to which the narrative refers, on to our own day, social conditions have been passing through many phases. Occasionally there have been circumstances in which the swift judgment of righteous indignation was justifiable, though it did seem like assassination. And in no case has such action been more excusable than when the purity of family life has been invaded, while the law of the land would not interfere. We do not greatly wonder that in France the avenging of infidelity is condoned when the sufferer snatches a justice otherwise unattainable. That is not indeed to be praised, but the imperfection of law is a partial apology. The higher the standard of public morality the less needful is this venture on the Divine right to kill. And certainly it is not private revenge that is ever to be sought, but the vindication of the elemental righteousness on which the well-being of humanity depends. Phinehas had no private revenge to seek. It was the public good.

It is confidently affirmed by Wellhausen that the "Priestly Code" makes the cultus the principal thing, and this, he says, implies retrogression from the earlier idea. The passage we are considering, like many others ascribed to the "Priests' Code," makes something else than the cultus the principal thing. We are told that in the teaching of this code "the bond between cultus and sensuality is severed; no danger can arise of an admixture of impure, immoral elements, a danger which was always present in Hebrew antiquity." But here the danger is admitted, the cultus is entirely out of sight, and the sin of sensuality is conspicuous. When Phinehas intervenes, moreover, it is not in harmony with any statute or principle laid down in the "Priests' Code"—rather, indeed, against its general spirit, which would prohibit an Aaronite from a deed of blood. According to the whole tenor of the law the priesthood had its duties, carefully prescribed, by doing which faithfulness was to be shown. Here an act of spontaneous zeal, done not "on the positive command of a will outside," but on the impulse arising out of a fresh occasion,* receives the approval of Jehovah, and the "covenant of an everlasting priesthood" is confirmed for the sake of it. Was Phinehas in any sense carrying out statutory instructions for atonement on behalf of Israel when he inflicted the punishment of death on Zimri and his paramour? To identify the

* Wellhausen, "Prolegomena," p. 424.

"Priestly Code" with "cultus legislation," and that with theocracy, and then declare the cultus to have become a "pedagogic instrument of discipline," "estranged from the heart," is to make large demands on our inattention.

In the closing verses of the chapter another question of a moral nature is involved. It is recorded that after the events we have considered Jehovah spake unto Moses, saying, "Vex the Midianites, and smite them; for they vex you with their wiles, wherewith they have beguiled you in the matter of Peor, and in the matter of Cozbi, the daughter of the prince of Midian, their sister, which was slain on the day of the plague in the matter of Peor." Now is it for the sake of themselves and their own safety the Israelites are to smite Midian? Is retaliation commanded? Does God set enmity between the one people and the other, and so doing make confession that Israel has no duty of forgiveness, no mission to convert and save?

There is difficulty in pronouncing judgment as to the point of view taken by the narrator. Some will maintain that the historian here, whoever he was, had no higher conception of the command than that it was one which sanctioned revenge. And there is nothing on the face of the narrative which can be brought forward to disprove the charge. Yet it must be remembered that the history proceeds on the theocratic conception of Israel's place and destiny. To the writer Israel is of less account in itself than as a people rescued from Egypt and called to nationality in order to serve Jehovah. The whole tenor of the "Priests' Code" narrative, as well as of the other, bears this out. There is no patriotic zeal in the narrow sense,—" My country right or wrong." Scarcely a passage can be pointed to implying such a sentiment, such a drift of thought. The underlying idea in the whole story is the sacredness of morality, not of Israel; and the suppression or extinction of this tribe of Midianites with their obscene idolatry is God's will, not Israel's. Too plain, indeed, is it that the Israelites would have preferred to leave Midian and other tribes of the same low moral cast unmolested, free to pursue their own ends.

And Jehovah is not revengeful, but just. The vindication of morality at the time the Book of Numbers deals with, and long afterwards, could only be through the suppression of those who were identified with dangerous forms of vice. The forces at command in Israel were not equal to the task of converting; and what could be achieved was commanded—opposition, enmity; if need were, exterminating war. The better people has a certain spiritual capacity, but not enough to make it fit for what may be called moral missionary work. It would suffer more than it would gain if it entered on any kind of intercourse with Midian with the view of raising the standard of thought and life. All that can be expected meanwhile is that the Israelites shall be at issue with a people so degraded; they are to be against the Midianites, keep them from power in the world, subject them by the sword.

Our judgment, then, is that the narrative sustains a true theocracy in this sense, exhibits Israel as a unique phenomenon in human history, not impossible,—there lies the clear veracity of the Bible accounts,—but playing a part such as the times allowed, such as the world required. From a passage like that now before us, and the sequel, the war with Midian, which some have regarded as a blot on the pages of Scripture, an argument for its inspiration may be drawn. We find here no ethical anachronisms, no impracticable ideas of charity and pardon. There is a sane and strenuous moral aim, not out of keeping with the state of things in the world of that time, yet showing the rule and presenting the will of a God who makes Israel a protesting people. The Hebrews are men, not angels; men of the old world, not Christians—true! Who could have received this history if it had represented them as Christians, and shown us God giving them commands fit for the Church of to-day? They are called to a higher morality than that of Egypt, for theirs is to be spiritual; higher than that of Chaldea or of Canaan, for Chaldea is shrouded in superstition, Canaan in obscene idolatry. They can do something; and what they can do Jehovah commands them to do. And He is not an imperfect God because His prophet does not give from the first a perfect Christian law, a redeeming gospel. He is the "I Am." Let the whole course of Old Testament development be traced, and the sanity and coherency of the theocratic idea as it is presented in law and prophecy, psalm and parable, cannot fail to convince any just and frank inquirer.

The end of Balaam's life may be glanced at before the pages close that refer to his career. In xxxi. 8, it is stated that in the battle which went against the Midianites Balaam was slain. We do not know whether he was so maddened by his disappointment as to take the sword against Jehovah and Israel, or whether he only joined the army of Midian in his capacity of augur. F. W. Robertson imagines "the insane frenzy with which he would rush into the field, and finding all go against him, and that lost for which he had bartered heaven, after having died a thousand worse than deaths, find death at last upon the spears of the Israelites". It is of course possible to imagine that he became the victim of his own insane passion. But Balaam never had a profound nature, was never more than within sight of the spiritual world. He appears as the calculating, ambitious man, who would reckon his chances to the last, and with coolness, and what he believed to be sagacity, decide on the next thing to attempt. But his penetration failed him, as at a certain point it fails all men of his kind. He ventured too far, and could not draw back to safety.

The death he died was almost too honourable for this false prophet, unless, indeed, he fell fleeing like a coward from the battle. One who had recognised the power of a higher faith than his country professed, and saw a nation on the way to the vigour that faith inspired, who in personal spleen and envy set in operation a scheme of the very worst sort to ruin Israel, was not an enemy worth the edge of the sword. Let us suppose that a Hebrew soldier found him in flight, and with a passing stroke brought him to the ground. There is no tragedy in such a death; it is too ignominious. Whatever Balaam was in his boyhood, whatever he might have been when the cry escaped him, "Let me die the death of the righteous," selfish craft had brought him below the level of the manhood of the time. Balak with his pathetic faith in cursing and incantation now seems a prince beside the augur. For Balaam, though he knew Jehovah after a manner, had no religion, had only the envy of the religion of others. He came on the stage with an air that almost deceived Balak and has deceived many. He leaves it without one to lament him. Or shall we rather suppose that even for him, in Pethor beyond the Euphrates, a wife or child waited and prayed to Sutekh and, when the tidings of his death were brought, fell into inconsolable weeping? Over the worst they think and do men draw the veil to hide it from some eyes. And Balaam, a poor, mean tool of the basest cravings, may have had one to believe in him, one to love him. He reminds us of Absalom in his character and actions—Absalom, a man void of religion and morals; and for him the father he had dethroned and dishonoured wept bitterly in the chamber over the gate of Mahanaim, "My son Absalom! would God I had died for thee, O Absalom, my son, my son!" So may some woman in Pethor have wailed for Balaam fallen under the spear of a Hebrew warrior.

CHAPTER XXII.

A NEW GENERATION.

NUMBERS xxvi., xxvii.

THE numbering at Sinai before the sojourn in the Desert of Paran has its counterpart in the numbering now recorded. In either case those reckoned are the men able to go forth to war, from twenty years old and upward. Once, an easy entrance into the land of promise may have been expected; but that dream has long passed away. Now the Israelites are made clearly to understand that the last effort will require the whole warlike energy they can summon, the best courage of every one who can handle sword or spear. There has been hitherto comparatively little fighting. The Amalekites at an early stage, afterwards the Amorites and the Bashanites, have had to be attacked. Now, however, the serious strife is to begin. Peoples long established in Canaan have to be assailed and dispossessed. Let the number of capable men be reckoned that there may be confidence for the advance.

Nothing is to be won without energy, courage, unity, wise preparation and adjustment of means to ends. True, the battle is the Lord's and He can give victory to the few over the many, to the feeble over the strong. But not even in the case of Israel are the ordinary laws suspended. This people has an advantage in its faith. That is enough to support the army in the coming struggle; and the Israelites must make Canaan theirs by force of arms. For, surely, in a sense, there is right on the other side, the right of prior possession at least. The Canaanites, Hittites, Jebusites, Hivites have tilled the land, planted vineyards, built cities, and fulfilled, so far, their mission in the world. They, indeed, never feel themselves secure. Often one tribe falls on the territory of another, and takes possession. The right to the soil has to be continually guarded by military power and courage. It is not wonderful to Amorites that another race should attempt the conquest of their land. But it would be strange, humanly speaking impossible, that a weaker, less capable people should master those who are presently in occupation. By the great laws that govern human development, the dominant laws of God we may call them, this could not be. Israel must show itself powerful, must prove the right of might, otherwise it shall not even yet obtain the inheritance it has long been desiring. The might of some nations is purely that of animal physique and dogged determination. Others rise higher in virtue of their intellectual vigour, splendid discipline, and ingenious appliances. Man for man, Israelites should be a match for any people, because there is trust in Jehovah, and hope in His promise. Now the trial of battle is to be made; the Hebrews are to realise that they will need all their strength.

Do we ever imagine that the law of endeavour shall be relaxed for us, either in the physical or in the spiritual region? Is it supposed that at some point, when after struggling through the wilderness we have but a narrow stream between us and the coveted inheritance, the object of our desire shall be bestowed in harmony with some other law, having been procured by other efforts than our own? Thinking so, we only dream. What we gain by our endeavour—physical, intellectual, spiritual—can alone become a real possession. The future discipline of humanity is misunderstood, the forecast is altogether wrong, when this is not comprehended. In this world we have that for which we labour; nothing more. So-called properties and domains do not belong to their nominal owners, who have merely "inherited." The literature of a country does not belong to those who possess books in which it is contained; it is the domain of men and women who have toiled for every ell and inch of ground. And spiritually, while all is the gift of God, all has to be won by efforts of the soul. Before humanity lies a Canaan, a Paradise. But no easy way of acquisition shall ever be found, no other way indeed than has all along been followed. The men of God able to go forth to war need to be numbered and brought under discipline for the conquests that remain. And what is yet to be won by moral courage and devotion to the highest shall have to be kept in like manner.

The second numbering of the people showed that a new generation filled the ranks. Plagues that swept away thousands, or the slow, sure election of death, had taken all who left Egypt excepting a few. It was the same Israel, yet another. Is, then, the nation of account, and not the individuals who compose it? Perhaps the two numberings may be intended to guard us against this error; at all events, we may take them so. Man by man, the host was reckoned at Sinai; man by man it is reckoned again in the plains of Moab. There were six hundred and three thousand five hundred and fifty: there are six hundred and one thousand seven hundred and thirty. The numberings by the command of Jehovah could not but mean that His eye was upon each. And when the new race looked back along the wilderness way, each group remembering its own graves over which the sand of the desert was blown, there might at least be the thought that God also remembered, and that the mouldering dust of those who, despite their transgression, had been brave and loving and honest, was in His keeping. Israel was experiencing a singular break in its history. It would begin its new career in Canaan without memorials, except that cave at Machpelah where, centuries before, Abraham and Sarah, Isaac and Jacob, had been buried, and the field at Shechem where the body of Joseph was laid. No graves but these would be the monuments of Israel. In Jehovah, the Ancient of Days, lay the history, with Him the career of the tribes.

The past receding, the future advancing, and God the sole abiding link between them. For us, as for Israel, notwithstanding all our care of the monuments and gains of the past, that is the one sustaining faith; and it is adequate, inspiring. The swift decay of life, the constant flux of humanity, would be our despair if we had not God.

"Thou carriest them away as with a flood; they are as a sleep:
In the morning they are like grass which groweth up,
In the morning it flourisheth and groweth up;
In the evening it is cut down and withereth."

So the "Prayer of Moses the man of God," under the saddening thought of mortality. But God is "from everlasting to everlasting," "the dwelling place of His people in all generations." The life that begins in the Divine will, and enjoys its day under the Divine care, blends with the current, yet is not absorbed. A generation or a people lives only as the men and women that compose it live. Such is the final judgment, Christ's judgment, by which all providence is to be interpreted. An Israelite might enter much into the national hope, and to some extent forget himself for the sake of it. But his proper life was never in that forgetfulness: it was always in personal energy of will and soul that contributed to the nation's strength and progress. The tribes, Reuben, Simeon, Judah, and the rest, are mustered. But the men make the tribes, give them quality, value; or rather, of the men, those who are brave, faithful, and true.

That each life is a fact in the Eternal overflowing Life, conscious of all—in this there is comfort for us who are numbered among the millions, with no particular claim to reminiscence, and aware, at any rate, that when a few years pass the world will forget us. In vain the most of us seek a niche in the Valhalla of the race, or the record of a single line in the history of our time. Whatever our suffering or achieving, are we not doomed to oblivion? The grave-yard will keep our dust, the memorial stone will preserve our names—but for how long? Until in the evolutions that are to come the ploughshare of a covetous age tears up the soil we imagine to be consecrated for ever. But there is a memory that does not grow old, in which for good or evil we are enshrined. "We all live unto God." The Divine consciousness of us is our strength and hope. It alone keeps the soul from despair —or, if the life has not been in faith, stings with a desperate reassurance. Does God remember us with the love He beareth to His own? In any case each human life is held in an abiding consciousness, a purpose which is eternal.

The page of Israel's history we are reading preserves many names. It is in outline a genealogy of the tribes. Reuben's sons are Hanoch, Pallu, Hezron, Carmi. The son of Pallu is Eliab. The sons of Eliab are Nemuel, Dathan, and Abiram. And of Dathan and Abiram we are reminded that they strove against Moses and Aaron in the company of Korah; and the earth opened her mouth and swallowed them up. The judgment of evildoers is commemorated. The rest have their praise in this alone, that they held aloof from the sin. Turn to other tribes, Zebulun, Asher, Naphtali, for instance, and in the case of each the names of those who were heads of families are given. In the First Book of Chronicles the genealogy is extended, with various details of settlement and history. In what are we to find the explanation of this attempt to preserve the lineage of families, and the ancestral names? If the progenitors were great men distinguished by heroism, or by faith, the pride of the descendants might have a show of reason. Or again, if the families had kept the pure Hebrew descent we should be able to understand. But no greatness is assigned to the heads of families, not a single mark of achievement or distinction. And the Israelites did not preserve their purity of race. In Canaan, as we learn from the Book of Judges, they "dwelt among the Canaanites, the Hittite, and the Amorite, and the Perizzite, and the Hivite, and the Jebusite: and they took their daughters to be their wives, and gave their own daughters to their sons, and served their gods" (iii. 5, 6).

The sole reason we can find for these records is the consciousness of a duty which the Israelites felt, but did not always perform—to keep themselves separate as Jehovah's people. In the more energetic minds, through all national defection and error, that consciousness survived. And it served its end. The Bene-Israel, tracing their descent through the heads of families and tribes to Jacob, Isaac, Abraham, realised their distinctness from other races and entered upon a unique destiny which is not yet fulfilled. It is a singular testimony to what on the human side appears as an idea, a sentiment; to what on the Divine side is a purpose running through the ages. Because of this human sentiment and this Divine purpose, the former maintained apparently by the pride of race, by genealogies, by traditions often singularly unspiritual, but really by the over-ruling providence of God, Israel became unique, and filled an extraordinary place among the nations. Many things co-operated to make her a people regarding whom it could be said: "Israel never stood quietly by to see the world badly governed, under the authority of a God reputed to be just. Her sages burned with anger over the abuses of the world. A bad man, dying old, rich, and at ease, kindled their fury; and the prophets in the ninth century B. C. elevated this idea to the height of a dogma... The childhood of the elect is full of signs and prognostics, which are only recognised afterwards." A race may treasure its ancient records and venerated names to little purpose, may preserve them with no other result than to mark its own degeneracy and failure. Israel did not. The Unseen King of this people so ordered their history that greater and still greater names were added to the rolls of their leaders, heroes, and prophets, until the Shiloh came.

By the computations that survive, a diminished yet not greatly diminished number of fighting men was reckoned in the plains of Moab. Some tribes had fallen away considerably, others had increased; Simeon notably among the former, Judah and Manasseh among the latter. The causes of diminution and increase alike are purely conjectural. Simeon may have been involved in the sin of Baal-peor more than the others and suffered proportionately. Yet we cannot suppose that, on the whole, character had much to do with numerical strength. Assuming the transgressions of which the history informs us and the punishments that followed them, we must believe that the tribes were on much the same moral plane. In the natural course of things there would have been a considerable increase in the numbers of men. The hardships and judgments of the desert and the defection of some by the way are general causes of diminution. We have also seen reason to believe that a proportion, not perhaps very great, remained at Kadesh, and did not take the journey round Edom. It is certainly worthy of notice with regard to Simeon that the final allocation of territory gave to this tribe the district in which Kadesh was situated. The small increase of the tribe of Levi is another fact shown by the second census; and we remember that Simeon and Levi were brethren (Gen. xlix. 5).

The numbering in the plains of Moab is connected in vv. 52-6 with the division of the land among the tribes. "To the more thou shalt give the more inheritance, and to the fewer thou shalt give the less inheritance: to every one according to those that were numbered of him shall his inheritance be given." The principle of allocation is obvious and just. No doubt the comparative value of different parts of Canaan was to be taken into account. There were fertile plains on the one hand, barren highlands on the other. These reckoned for, the greater the tribe the larger was to be the district assigned to it. An elementary rule; but how has it been set aside! Vast districts of Great Britain are almost without inhabitants; others are overcrowded. An even distribution of people over the land capable of tillage is necessary to the national health. In no sense can it be maintained that good comes of concentrating population in immense cities. But the policy of proprietors is not more at fault than the ignorant rush of those who desire the comforts and opportunities of town life.

The twenty-seventh chapter is partly occupied with the details of a case which raised a question of inheritance. Five daughters of one Zelophehad of the tribe of Manasseh appealed to Moses on the ground that they were the representatives of the household, having no brother. Were they to have no possession because they were women? Was the name of their father to be taken away because he had no son? It was not to be supposed that the want of male descendants had been a judgment on their father. He had died in the wilderness, but not as a rebel against Jehovah, like those who were in the company of Korah. He had "died in his own sins." They petitioned for an inheritance among the brethren of their father.

The claim of these women appears natural if the right of heirship is acknowledged in any sense, with this reservation, however, that women might not be able properly to cultivate the land, and could not do much in the way of defending it. And these, for the time, were considerations of no small account. The five sisters may of course have been ready to undertake all that was necessary as occupiers of a farm, and no doubt they reckoned on marriage. But the original qualification that justified heirship of land was ability to use the resources of the inheritance and take part in all national duties. The decision in this case marks the beginning of another conception—that of the personal development of women. The claim of the daughters of Zelophehad was allowed, with the result that they found themselves called to the cultivation of mind and life in a manner which would not otherwise have been open to them. They received by the judgment here recorded a new position of responsibility as well as privilege. The law founded on their case must have helped to make the women of Israel intellectually and morally vigorous.

The rules of inheritance among an agricultural people, exposed to hostile incursions, must, like that of ver. 8, assume the right of sons in preference to daughters; but under modern social conditions there are no reasons for any such preference, except indeed the sentiment of family, and the maintenance of titles of rank. But the truth is that inheritance, so-called, is every year becoming of less moral account as compared with the acquisitions that are made by personal industry and endeavour. Property is only of value as it is a means to the enlargement and fortifying of the individual life. The decision on behalf of the daughters of Zelophehad was of importance for what it implied rather than for what it actually gave. It made possible that dignity and power which we see illustrated in the career of Deborah, whose position as a "mother in Israel" does not seem to have depended much, if at all, on any accident of inheritance; it was reached by the strength of her character and the ardour of her faith.

The generation that came from Egypt has passed away, and now (xxvii. 12) Moses himself receives his call. He is to ascend the mountain of Abarim and look forth over the land Israel is to inhabit; then he is to be gathered to his people. He is reminded of the sin by which Aaron and he dishonoured God when they failed to sanctify Him at the waters of Meribah. The burden of the Book of Numbers is revealed. The brooding sadness which lies on the whole narrative is not cast by human mortality but by moral transgression and defect. There is judgment for revolt, as of those who followed Korah. There are men who like Zelophehad die "in their own sins," filling up the time allowed to imperfect obedience and faith, the limit of existence that falls short of the glory of God. And Moses, whose life is lengthened that his honourable task may be fully done, must all the more conspicuously pay the penalty of his high misdemeanour. With the goal of Israel's great destiny in view the narrative moves from shadow to shadow. Here and throughout, this is a characteristic of Old Testament history. And the shadows deepen as they rest on lives more capable of noble service, more guilty in their disbelief and defiance of Jehovah.

The rebuke which darkens over Moses at the close and lies on his grave does not obscure the greatness of the man; nor have all the criticisms of the history in which he plays so great a part overclouded his personality. The opening of Israel's career may not now seem so marvellous in a sense as once it seemed, nor so remote from the ordinary course of Providence. Development is found where previously the complete law, institution, or system appeared to burst at once into maturity. But the features of a man look clearly forth on us from the Pentateuchal narrative; and the story of the life is so coherent as to compel a belief in its veracity, which at the same time is demanded by the circumstances of Israel. A beginning there must have been, in the line which the earliest prophets continued, and that beginning in a single mind, a single will. The Moses of these books of the exodus is one who could have unfolded the ideas from which the nationality of Israel sprang: a man of smaller mind would have made a people of more ordinary frame. Institutions that grow in the course of centuries may reflect their perfected form on the story of their origin; it is, however, certain this cannot be true of a faith. That does not develop. What it is at its birth it continues to be; or, if a change takes place, it will be to the loss of definiteness and power. Kuenen himself makes the three universal religions to be Judaism, Mohammedanism, and Christianity. The analogy of the two latter is conclusive with regard to the first—that Moses was the author of Israel's faith in Jehovah.

And this involves much, both with regard to the human characteristics and the Divine inspiration of the founder, much that an after-age would have been utterly incapable of imagining. When we find a life depicted in these Pentateuchal narratives, corresponding in all its features with the place that has to be filled, revealing one who, under the conditions of Israel's nativity, might have made a way for it into sustaining faith, it is not difficult to accept the details in their substance. The records are certainly not Moses' own. They are exoteric, now from the people's point of view, now from that of the priests. But they present with wonderful fidelity and power what in the life of the founder went to stamp his faith on the national mind. And the marvellous thing is that the shadows as well as the lights in the biography serve this great end. The gloom that falls at Meribah and rests on Nebo tells of the character of Jehovah, bears witness to the Supreme Royalty which Moses lived and laboured to exalt. A living God, righteous and faithful, gracious to them that trusted and served Him, who also visited iniquity—such was the Jehovah between whom and Israel Moses stood as mediator, such the Jehovah by whose command he was to ascend the height of Abarim to die.

To die, to be gathered to his people—and what then? It is at death we reckon up the account and estimate the value and power of faith. Has it made a man ready for his change, ripened his character, established his work on a foundation as of rock? The command which at Horeb Moses received long ago, and the revelation of God he there enjoyed, have had their opportunity; to what have they come?

The supreme human desire is to know the nature, to understand the distinctive glory of the Most High. At the bush Moses had been made aware of the presence with him of the God of his fathers, the Fear of Abraham, Isaac, and Jacob. His duty also had been made clear. But the mystery of being was still unsolved. With sublime daring, therefore, he pursued the inquiry: "Behold when I come unto the children of Israel, and shall say unto them, The God of your fathers hath sent me unto you; and they shall say to me, What is His name? what shall I say unto them?" The answer came in apocalypse, in a form of simple words:—"I AM THAT I AM." The solemn Name expressed an intensity of life, a depth and power of personal being, far transcending that of which man is conscious. It belongs to One who has no beginning, whose life is apart from time, above the forces of nature, independent of them. Jehovah says, "I am not what you see, not what nature is, standing forth into the range of your sight; I Am in eternal separation, self-existent, with underived fulness of power and life." The remoteness and incomprehensibility of God remain, although much is revealed. Whatever experience of life each man sums up for himself in saying "I am," aids him in realising the life of God. Have we aspired? have we loved? have we undertaken and accomplished? have we thought deeply? Does any one in saying "I am" include the consciousness of long and varied life?—the "I AM" of God comprehends all that. And yet He changes not. Beneath our experience of life which changes there is this great Living Essence. "I AM THAT I AM," profoundly, eternally true, self-consistent, with whom is no beginning of experience or purpose, yet controlling, harmonising, yea, originating all in the unfathomable depths of an eternal Will.

Ideas like these, we must believe, shaped themselves, if not clearly, at least in dim outline before the mind of Moses, and made the faith by which he lived. And how had it proved itself as the stay of endeavour, the support of a soul under heavy burdens of duty, trial, and sorrowful consciousness? The reliance it gave had never failed. In Egypt, before Pharaoh, Moses had been sustained by it as one who had a sanction for his demands and actions which no king or priest could claim. At Sinai it had given spiritual strength and definite authority to the law. It was the spirit of every oracle, the underlying force in every judgment. Faith in Jehovah, more than natural endowments, made Moses great. His moral vision was wide and clear because of it, his power among the people as a prophet and leader rested upon it. And the fruit of it, which began to be seen when Israel learned to trust Jehovah as the one living God and girt itself for His service, has not even yet been all gathered in. We pass by the theories of philosophy regarding the unseen to rest in the revelation of God which embodies Moses' faith. His inspiration, once for all, carried the world beyond polytheism to monotheism, unchallengeably true, inspiring, sublime.

There can be no doubt that death tested the faith of Moses as a personal reliance on the Almighty. How he found sufficient help in the thought of Jehovah when Aaron died, and when his own call came, we can only surmise. For him it was a familiar certainty that the Judge of all the earth did right. His own decision went with that of Jehovah in every great moral question; and even when death was involved, however great a punishment it appeared, however sad a necessity, he must have said, Good is the will of the Lord. But there was more than acquiescence. One who had lived so long with God, finding all the springs and aims of life in Him, must have known that irresistible power would carry on what had been begun, would complete to its highest tower that building of which the foundation had been laid. Moses had wrought not for self but for God; he could leave his work in the Divine hand with absolute assurance that it would be perfected. And as for his own destiny, his personal life, what shall we say? Moses had been what he was through the grace of Him whose name is "I AM THAT I AM." He could at least look into the dim region beyond and say, "It is God's will that I pass through the gate. I am spiritually His, and am strong in mind for His service. I have been what He has willed, excepting in my transgression. I shall be what He wills; and that cannot be ill for me; that will be best for me." God was gracious and forgave sin, though He could not suffer it to pass unjudged. Even in appointing death the Merciful One could not fail to be merciful to His servant. The thought of Moses might not carry him into the future of his own existence, into what should be after he had breathed his last. But God was His; and he was God's.

So the personal drama of many acts and scenes draws to a close with forebodings of the end, and yet a little respite ere the curtain falls. The music is solemn as befits the night-fall, yet has a ring of strong purpose and inexhaustible sufficiency. It is not the "still sad music of humanity" we hear with the words, "Get thee up into this mountain of Abarim, and behold the land which I have given unto the children of Israel. And when thou hast seen it, thou also shalt be gathered unto thy people, as Aaron thy brother was gathered." It is the music of the Voice that awakens life, commands and inspires it, cheers the strong in endeavour and soothes the tired to rest. He who speaks is not weary of Moses, nor does He mean Moses to be weary of his task. But this change lies in the way of God's strong purpose, and it is assumed that Moses will neither rebel nor repine. Far away, in an evolution unforeseen by man, will come the glorification of One who is the Life indeed; and in His revelation as the Son of the Eternal Father Moses will share. With Christ he will speak of the change of death and that faith which overcomes all change.

The designation of Joshua, who had long been the minister of Moses, and perhaps for some time administrator of affairs, is recorded in the close of the chapter. The prayer of Moses assumes that by direct commission the fitness of Joshua must be signified to the people. It might be Jehovah's will that, even yet, another should take the headship of the tribes. Moses spake unto the Lord, saying, "Let Jehovah, the God of the spirits of all flesh, appoint a man over the congregation which may go out before them, and which may come in before them, and which may lead them out and which may bring them in; that the congregation of Jehovah be not as sheep which have no shepherd." One who has so long endeavoured to lead, and found it so difficult, whose heart and soul and strength have been devoted to make Israel Jehovah's people, can relax his hold of things without dismay only if he is sure that God will Himself choose and endow the successor. What aimless wandering there would be if the new leader proved incompetent, wanting wisdom or grace! How far about might Israel's way yet be, in another sense than the compassing of Edom! Before the Friend of Israel Moses pours out his prayer for a shepherd fit to lead the flock.

And the oracle confirms the choice to which Providence has already pointed. Joshua the son of Nun, "a man in whom is the spirit," is to have the call and receive the charge. His investiture with official right and dignity is to be in the sight of Eleazar the priest and all the congregation. Moses shall put of his own honour upon Joshua and declare his commission. Joshua shall not have the whole burden of decision resting upon him, for Jehovah will guide him. Yet he shall not have direct access to God in the tent of meeting as Moses had. In the time of special need Eleazar "shall inquire for him by the judgment of the Urim before Jehovah." Thus instructed, he shall exercise high authority.

"A man in whom is the spirit"—such is the one outstanding personal qualification. "The God of the spirits of all flesh" finds in Joshua the sincere will, the faithful heart. The work that is to be done is not of a spiritual kind, but grim fighting, control of an army and of a people not yet amenable to law, under circumstances that will try a leader's firmness, sagacity, and courage. Yet, even for such a task, allegiance to Jehovah and His purpose regarding Israel, the enthusiasm of faith, high spirit, not experience—these are the commendations of the chief. Qualified thus, Joshua may occasionally make mistakes. His calculations may not always be perfect, nor the means he employs exactly fitted to the end. But his faith will enable him to recover what is momentarily lost; his courage will not fail. Above all, he will be no opportunist guided by the turn of events, yielding to pressure or what may appear necessity. The one principle of faithfulness to Jehovah will keep him and Israel in a path which must be followed, even if success in a worldly sense be not immediately found.

The priest who inquires of the Lord by Urim has a higher place under Joshua's administration than under that of Moses. The theocracy will henceforth have a twofold manifestation, less of unity than before. And here the change is of a kind which may involve the gravest consequences. The simple statement of ver. 21 denotes a very great limitation of Joshua's authority as leader. It means that though on many occasions he can both originate and execute, all matters of moment shall have to be referred to the oracle. There will be a possibility of conflict between him and the priest with regard to the occasions that require such a reference to Jehovah. In addition there may be the uncertainty of responses through the Urim, as interpreted by the priest. It is easy also to see that by this method of appealing to Jehovah the door was opened to abuses which, if not in Joshua's time, certainly in the time of the judges, began to arise.

It may appear to some absolutely necessary to refer the Urim to a far later date. The explanation given by Ewald, that the inquiry was always by some definite question, and that the answer was found by means of the lot, obviates this difficulty.* The Urim and Thummim, which mean "clearness and correctness," or as in our passage the Urim alone, may have been pebbles of different colours, the one representing an affirmative, the other a negative reply. But inquiry appears to have been made by these means after certain rites, and with forms which the priest alone could use. It is evident that absolute sincerity on his part, and unswerving loyalty to Jehovah, were an important element in the whole administration of affairs. A priest who became dissatisfied with the leader might easily

* "Antiquities of Israel": "The Priesthood."

frustrate his plans. On the other hand, a leader dissatisfied with the responses would be tempted to suspect and perhaps set aside the priest. There can be no doubt that here a serious possibility of divided counsels entered into the history of Israel, and we are reminded of many after events. Yet the circumstances were such that the whole power could not be committed to one man. With whatever element of danger, the new order had to begin.

Moses laid his hands on Joshua and gave him his charge. As one who knew his own infirmities, he could warn the new chief of the temptations he would have to resist, the patience he would have to exercise. It was not necessary to inform Joshua of the duties of his office. With these he had become familiar. But the need for calm and sober judgment required to be impressed upon him. It was here he was defective, and here that his "honour" and the maintenance of his authority would have to be secured. Deuteronomy mentions only the exhortation Moses gave to be strong and of a good courage, and the assurance that Jehovah would go before Joshua, would neither fail him nor forsake him. But though much is recorded, much also remains untold. An education of forty years had prepared Joshua for the hour of his investiture. Yet the words of the chief he was so soon to lose must have had no small part in preparing him for the burden and duty which he was now called by Jehovah to sustain as leader of Israel.

CHAPTER XXIII.

OFFERINGS AND VOWS.

NUMBERS xxviii.-xxx.

THE legislation of chapters xxviii.-xxx. appears to belong to a time of developed ritual and organised society. Parallel passages in Exodus and Leviticus treating of the feasts and offerings are by no means so full in their details, nor do they even mention some of the sacrifices here made statutory. The observances of New Moon are enjoined in the Book of Numbers alone. In chapter xv. they are simply noticed; here the order is fixed. The purpose of chapters xxviii., xxix. is especially to prescribe the number of animals that are to be offered throughout the year at a central altar, and the quantities of other oblations which are to accompany them. But the rotation of feasts is also given in a more connected way than elsewhere; we have, in fact, a legislative description of Israel's Sacred Year. Daily, weekly, monthly, and at the two great festal seasons, Jehovah is to be acknowledged by the people as the Redeemer of life, the Giver of wealth and blessedness. Of their cattle and sheep, and the produce of the land, they are to bring continual oblations, which are to be their memorial before Him. By their homage and by their gladness, by afflicting themselves and by praising God, they shall realise their calling as His people.

The section regarding vows (ch. xxx.) completes the legislation on that subject supplementing Lev. xxvii. and Numb. vi. It is especially interesting for the light it throws on the nature of family life, the position of women and the limitations of their freedom. The link between the law of offerings and the law of vows is hard to find; but we can easily understand the need for rules concerning women's vows. The peace of families might often be disturbed by lavish promises which a husband or a father might find it impossible or inconvenient to fulfil.

1. THE SACRED YEAR.

NUMBERS xxviii.-xxix.

Throughout the year, each day, each sabbath, and each month is to be consecrated by oblations of varying value, forming a routine of sacrifice. First the Day, bringing duty and privilege, is to have its morning burnt offering of a yearling lamb, by which the Divine blessing is invoked on the labour and life of the whole people. A meal offering of flour and oil and a drink offering of "strong drink"—that is, not of water or milk, but wine—are to accompany the sacrifice. Again in the evening, as a token of gratitude for the mercies of the day, similar oblations are to be presented. Of this offering the note is made: "it is a continual burnt offering, which was ordained in Sinai for a sweet savour, a sacrifice made by fire unto the Lord."

In these sacrifices the whole of time, measured out by the alternation of light and darkness, was acknowledged to be God's; through the priesthood the nation declared His right to each day, confessed obligation to Him for the gift of it. The burnt offering implied complete renunciation of what was represented. No part of the animal was kept for use, either by the worshipper or the priest. The smoke ascending to heaven dissipated the entire substance of the oblation, signifying that the whole use or enjoyment of it was consecrated to God. In the way of impressing the idea of obligation to Jehovah for the gifts of time and life the daily sacrifices were valuable; yet they were suggestive rather than sufficient. The Israelites throughout the land knew that these oblations were made at the altar, and those who were pious might at the times appointed offer each his own thanksgivings to God. But the individual expression of gratitude was left to the religious sense, and that must often have failed. At a distance from the sanctuary, where the ascending smoke could not be seen, men might forget; or again, knowing that the priests would not forget, they might imagine their own part to be done when offering was made for the whole people. The duty was, however, represented and kept before the minds of all.

In the Psalms and elsewhere we find traces of a worship which had its source in the daily sacrifice. The author of Psalm cxli., for example, addresses Jehovah:

"Give ear unto my voice when I cry unto Thee.
Let my prayer be set forth as incense before Thee;
The lifting up of my hands as the evening sacrifice."

Less clearly in the fifth, the fifty-ninth, and the eighty-eighth psalms, the morning prayer appears to be connected with the morning sacrifice:

"O Lord, in the morning shalt Thou hear my voice;
In the morning will I order my prayer unto Thee,
and will keep watch" (Psalm v. 3).

The pious Hebrew might naturally choose the morning and the evening as his times of special approach to the throne of Divine grace, as every believer still feels it his duty and privilege to begin and close the day with prayer. The appropriateness of dawn and sunset might determine both the hour of sacrifice and the hour of private worship. Yet the ordinance of the daily oblations set an example to those who would otherwise have been careless in expressing gratitude. And earnestly religious persons learned to find more frequent opportunities. Daniel in Babylon is seen at the window open towards Jerusalem, kneeling upon his knees three times a day, praying and giving thanks to God. The author of Psalm cxix. says:

> "Seven times a day do I praise Thee,
> Because of Thy righteous judgments."

The grateful remembrance of God and confession of His right to the whole of life were thus made a rule with which no other engagements were allowed to interfere. It is by facts like these the power of religion over the Hebrews in their best time is explained.

We pass now to the Sabbath and the sacrifices by which it was distinguished. Here the number seven which recurs so frequently in the statutes of the sacred year appears for the first time. Connection has been found between the ordinances of Israel and of Chaldea in the observance of the seventh day as well as at many other points. According to Mr. Sayce, the origin of the Sabbath went back to pre-Semitic days, and the very name was of Babylonian origin. "In the cuneiform tablets the *sabbatu* is described as a 'day of rest for the soul.' . . . The Sabbath was also known, at all events in Accadian times, as a *dies nefastus*, a day on which certain work was forbidden to be done; and an old list of Babylonian festivals and fast-days tells us that on the seventh, fourteenth, nineteenth, twenty-first, and twenty-eighth days of each month the Sabbath rest had to be observed. The king himself, it is stated, 'must not eat flesh that has been cooked over the coals or in the smoke, he must not change the garments of his body, white robes he must not wear, sacrifices he may not offer, in a chariot he must not ride.'" The soothsayer was forbidden on that day "to mutter in a secret place." In this observance of a seventh day of rest, specially sacred, for the good of the soul, ancient Accadians and Babylonians prepared the way for the Sabbath of the Mosaic law.

But while the days of the Chaldean week were devoted each to a separate divinity, and the seventh day had its meaning in relation to polytheism, the whole of time, every day alike, and the Sabbaths with greater strictness than the others, were, in Israel's law, consecrated to Jehovah. This difference also deserves to be noticed, that, while the Chaldean seventh days were counted from each new moon, in the Hebrew year there was no such astronomical date for reckoning them. Throughout the year, as with us, each seventh day was a day of rest. While we find traces of old religious custom and observance that mingled with those of Judaism and cannot but recognise the highly humane, almost spiritual character those old institutions often had, the superiority of the religion of the One Living and True God clearly proves itself to us. Moses, and those who followed him, felt no need of rejecting an idea they met with in the ancient beliefs of Chaldea, for they had the Divine light and wisdom by which the earthly and evil could be separated from the kernel of good. And may we not say that it was well to maintain the continuity of observance so far as thoughts and customs of the far past could be woven into the worship of Jehovah's flock? Neither was Israel nor is any people to pretend to entire separation from the past. No act of choice or process of development can effect it. Nor would the severance, if it were made, be for the good of men. Beyond the errors and absurdities of human belief, beyond the perversions of truth due to sin, there lie historical and constitutional origins. The Sabbaths, the sacrifices, and the prayers of ancient Chaldea had their source in demands of God and needs of the human soul, which not only entered into Judaism, but survive still, proving themselves inseparable from our thought and life.

The special oblations to be presented on the Sabbath were added to those of the other days of the week. Two lambs of the first year in the morning and two in the evening were to be offered with their appropriate meal and drink offerings. It may be noted that in Ezekiel where the Sabbath ordinances are detailed the sacrifices are more numerous. After declaring that the eastern gate of the inner court of the temple, which is to be shut on the six working days, shall be opened on the Sabbath and in the day of the new moon, the prophet goes on to say that the prince, as representing the people, shall offer unto the Lord in the Sabbath day six lambs without blemish and a ram without blemish. In the legislation of Numbers, however, the higher consecration of the Sabbath as compared with the other days of the week did not require so great a difference as Ezekiel saw it needful to make. And, indeed, the law of Sabbath observance assumes in Ezekiel an importance on various grounds which passes beyond the high distinction given it in the Pentateuch. Again and again in chapter xx. the prophet declares that one of the great sins of which the Israelites were guilty in the wilderness was that of polluting the Sabbath which God had given to be a sign between Himself and them. The keeping holy of the seventh day had become one of the chief safeguards of religion, and for this reason Ezekiel was moved to prescribe additional sacrifices for that day.

We find as we go on that the week of seven days, ended by the recurring day of rest, is an element in the regulations for all the great feasts. Unleavened bread was to be eaten for seven days. Seven weeks were then to be counted to the day of the firstfruits and the feast of weeks. The feast of tabernacles, again, ran for seven days and ended on the eighth with a solemn assembly. The whole ritual was in this way made to emphasise the division of time based on the fourth commandment.

The New Moon ritual consecrating the months was more elaborate. On the day when the new moon was first seen, or should by computation be seen, besides the continual burnt offering two young bullocks, one ram, and seven lambs of the first year, with meal and drink offerings, were to be presented. These animals were to be wholly offered by fire. In addition, a sin offering was to be made, a kid of the goats. Why this guilt sacrifice was introduced at the new moon service is not clear. Keil explains that "in consideration of the sins which had been committed in the course of the past month, and had remained without expiation," the sin offering was needed. But this might be said of the week in its degree, as well as of the month. It is certain that the opening of each month was kept in other ways than the legislation of the Pentateuch seems to require. In Numbers it is prescribed that the silver trumpets shall be blown over the new moon sacrifices for a memorial before God, and this must have given the observances a festival air. Then we learn from 1 Sam. xx. that when Saul was king a family feast was observed in his house on the first day of the month, and that this day also, in some particular month, was generally chosen by a family for the yearly sacrifice to which all were expected to gather (1 Sam. xx. 5, 6). These facts and the festal opening of Psalm lxxxi., in which the timbrel, harp, and psaltery, and joyful singing in praise of God, are associated with the new moon trumpet, imply that for some reason the occasion was held to be important. Amos (viii. 5) implies further that on the day of new moon trade was suspended; and in the time of Elisha it seems to have been common for those who wished to consult a prophet to choose either the Sabbath or the day of new moon for enquiring of him (2 Kings iv. 23). There can be little doubt that the day was one of religious activity and joy, and possibly the offering of the kid for expiation was intended to counteract the freedom the more thoughtless might permit themselves.

There are good reasons for believing that in pre-Mosaic times the day of new moon was celebrated by the Israelites and all kindred peoples, as it is still among certain heathen races. Originally a nature festival, it was consecrated to Jehovah by the legislation before us, and gradually became of account as the occasion of domestic gatherings and rejoicings. But its religious significance lay chiefly in the dedication to God of the month that had begun and expiation of guilt contracted during that which had closed.

We come now to the great annual festivals. These were arranged in two groups, which may be classed as vernal and autumnal, the one group belonging to the first and third months, the other to the seventh. They divided the year into two portions, the intervals between them being the time of great heat and the time of rain and storm. The month Abib, with which the year began, corresponded generally to our April; but its opening, depending on the new moon, might be earlier or later. One of the ceremonies of the festival season of this month was the presentation, on the sixteenth day, of the first sheaf of harvest; and seven weeks afterwards, at Pentecost, cakes made from the first dough were offered. The explanation of what may appear to be autumnal offerings in spring is to be found in the early ripening of corn throughout Palestine. The cereals were all reaped during the interval between Passover and Pentecost. The autumnal festival celebrated the gathering in of the vintage and fruits.

The Passover, the first great feast, a sacrament rather, is merely mentioned in this portion of Numbers. It was chiefly a domestic celebration —not priestly—and had a most impressive significance, of which the eating of the lamb with bitter herbs was the symbol. The day after it, the "feast of unleavened bread" began. For a whole week leaven was to be abjured. On the first day of the feast there was to be a holy convocation, and no servile work was to be done. The closing day likewise was to be one of holy convocation. On each of the seven days the offerings were to be two young bullocks, one ram, and seven yearling he-lambs, with their meal and drink offerings, and for sin one he-goat to make atonement.

The week of this festival, commencing with the paschal sacrament, was made to bear peculiarly on the national life, first by the command that all leaven should be rigidly kept out of the houses. As the ceremonial law assumed more importance with the growth of Pharisaism, this cleansing was sought quite fanatically. Any crumb of common bread was reckoned an accursed thing which might deprive the observance of the feast of its good effect. But even in the time of less scrupulous legalism the effort to extirpate leaven from the houses had its singular effect on the people. It was one of the many causes which made Jewish religion intense. Then the daily sacrificial routine, and especially the holy convocations of the first and seventh days, were profoundly solemnising. We may picture thus the ceremonies and worship of these great days of the feast. The people, gathered from all parts of the land, crowded the outer court of the sanctuary. The priests and Levites stood ready around the altar. With solemn chanting the animals were brought from some place behind the temple where they had been carefully examined so that no blemish might impair the sacrifice. Then they were slain one by one, and prepared, the fire on the great altar blazing more and more brightly in readiness for the holocaust, while the blood flowed away in a red stream, staining the hands and garments of those who officiated. First the two bullocks, then the ram, then the lambs were one after another placed on the flames, each with incense and part of the meal offering. The sin offering followed. Some of the blood of the he-goat was taken by the priest and sprinkled on the inner altar, on the veil of the Holy of Holies, and on the horns of the great altar, around which the rest was poured. The fat of the animal, including certain of the internal parts, was thrown on the fire; and this portion of the observances ended with the pouring out of the last drink offering before the Lord. Then a chorus of praise was lifted up, the people throwing themselves on the ground and praying in a low, earnest monotone.

To this followed in the later times singing of chants and psalms, led by the chorus of Levites, addresses to the people, and shorter or longer prayers to which the worshippers responded. The officiating priest, standing beside the great altar in view of all, now pronounced the appointed blessing on the people. But his task was still not complete. He went into the sanctuary, and, having by his entrance and safe return from the holy place shown that the sacrifice had been accepted, he spoke to the assembly a few words of simple and sublime import. Finally, with repeated blessing, he gave the dismissal. On one or both of these occasions the form of benediction used was that which we have found preserved in the sixth chapter of this book.*

It is evident that celebrations like these, into which, as time went on, the mass of worshippers entered with increased fervour, gave the feast of unleavened bread an extraordinary importance

* See Ewald's "Antiquities," p. 131, Solly's translation.

in the national life. The young Hebrew looked forward to it with the keenest expectancy, and was not disappointed. So long as faith remained, and especially in crises of the history of Israel, the earnestness that was developed carried every soul along. And now that the Israelites bewail the loss of temple and country, reckoning themselves a martyred people, this feast and the more solemn day of atonement nerve them to endurance and reassure them of their hope. They are separate still. They are Jehovah's people still. The covenant remains. The Messiah will come and bring them new life and power. So they vehemently cling to the past and dream of a future that shall never be.

"The day of the firstfruits" was, according to Lev. xxiii. 15, the fiftieth day from the morrow after the passover sabbath. The special harvest offering of this "feast of weeks" is thus enjoined: "Ye shall bring out of your habitations two wave loaves of two tenth parts of an ephah; they shall be of fine flour, they shall be baken with leaven, for firstfruits unto the Lord" (Lev. xxiii. 17). According to Leviticus one bullock, two rams, and seven lambs; according to Numbers two bullocks, one ram, and seven lambs, were to be sacrificed as whole offerings; the difference being apparently that of varying usage at an earlier and later time. The sin offering of the he-goat followed the burnt offerings. The day of the feast was one of holy convocation; and it has peculiar interest for us as the day on which the pentecostal effusion of the Spirit came on the gathering of Christians in the upper room at Jerusalem. The joyous character of this festival was signified by the use of leaven in the cakes or loaves that were presented as firstfruits. The people rejoiced in the blessing of another harvest, the fulfilment once more by Jehovah of His promise to supply the needs of His flock. It will be seen that in every case the sin offering prescribed is a single he-goat. This particular sacrifice was distinguished from the whole offerings, the thank offerings, and the peace offerings, which were not limited in number. "It must stand," says Ewald, "in perfect isolation, as though in the midst of sad solitude and desolation, with nothing similar or comparable by its side." Why a he-goat was invariably ordered for this expiatory sacrifice it is difficult to say. And the question is not made easy by the peculiar rite of the great day of atonement, when besides the goat of the sin offering for Jehovah another was devoted to "Azazel." Perhaps the choice of this animal implied its fitness in some way to represent transgression, wilfulness, and rebellion. The he-goat, more wild and rough than any other of the flock, seemed to belong to the desert and to the spirit of evil.

From the festivals of spring we now pass to those of autumn, the first of which coincided with the New Moon of the seventh month. This was to be a day of holy convocation, on which no servile work should be done, and it was marked by a special blowing of trumpets over the sacrifices. From other passages it would appear that the trumpets were used on the occasion of every new moon; and there must have been a longer and more elaborate service of festival music to distinguish the seventh. The offerings prescribed for it were numerous. Those enjoined for the opening of the other months were two bullocks, one ram, seven he-lambs, and the he-goat of the sin offering. To these were now added one bullock, one ram, and seven he-lambs. Altogether, including the daily sacrifices which were never omitted, twenty-two animals were offered; and with each sacrifice, except the he-goat, fine flour mingled with oil and a drink offering of wine had to be presented.

There seems no reason to doubt that the seventh month was opened in this impressive way because of the great festivals ordained to be held in the course of it. The labour of the year was practically over, and more than any other the month was given up to festivity associated with religion. It was the seventh or sabbath month, forming the "exalted summit of the year, for which all preceding festivals prepared the way, and after which everything quietly came down to the ordinary course of life." The trumpets blown in joyful peals over the sacrifices, the offering of which must have gone on for many hours, inspired the assembly with gladness, and signified the gratitude and hope of the nation.

But the joy of the seventh month thus begun did not go on without interruption. The tenth day was one of special solemnity and serious thought. It was the great day of confession, for on it, in the holy convocation, the people were to "afflict their souls." The transgressions and failures of the year were to be acknowledged with sorrow. From the evening of the ninth day to the evening of the tenth there was to be a rigid fast—the one fast which the law ordained. Before the full gladness of Jehovah's favour can be realised by Israel all those sins of neglect and forgetfulness which have been accumulating for twelve months must be confessed, bewailed, and taken away. There are those who have become unclean without being aware of their defilement; those who have unwittingly broken the Sabbath law; those who have for some reason been unable to keep the passover, or who have kept it imperfectly; others again have failed to render tithes of all the produce of their land according to the law; and priests and Levites called to a high consecration have come short of their duty. With such defects and sins of error the nation is to charge itself, each individual acknowledging his own faults. Unless this is done a shadow must lie on the life of the people; they cannot enjoy the light of the countenance of God.

For this day the whole offerings are, one young bullock, one ram, seven he-lambs; and there is this peculiarity, that, besides a he-goat for a sin offering, there is to be provided another he-goat, "for atonement." Maimonides says that the second he-goat is not that "for Azazel," but the fellow of it, the one on which the lot had fallen "for Jehovah." Leviticus again informs us that Aaron was to sacrifice a bullock as a sin offering for himself and his house. And it was the blood of this bullock and of the second he-goat he was to take and sprinkle on the ark and before the mercy-seat. Further, it is prescribed that the bodies of these animals are to be carried forth without the camp and wholly burned—as if the sin clinging to them had made them unfit for use in any way.

The great atonement thus made, the reaction of joy set in. Nothing in Jewish worship exceeded the solemnity of the fast, and in contrast with that the gladness of the forgiven multitude. Another crisis was past, another year of Jehovah's favour had begun. Those who had been prostrate in sorrow and fear rose up to sing their hallelujahs. "The deep seriousness of the Day of Atonement," says Delitzsch, "was transformed on the evening of the same day into lighthearted merriment. The observance in the temple was accomplished in a significant drama which was fascinating from beginning to end. When the high priest came forth from the Most Holy Place, after the performance of his functions there, this was for the people a consolatory, gladsome sight, for which poetry can find no adequate words: 'Like the peace-proclaiming arch in painted clouds; like the morning star, when he arises from the eastern twilight; like the sun, when opening his bud, he unfolds in roseate hue.' When the solemnity was over, the high priest was escorted with a guard of honour to his dwelling in the city, where a banquet awaited his more immediate friends." The young people repaired to the vineyards, the maidens arrayed in simple white, and the day was closed with song and dancing.*

This description reminds us of the mingling of elements in the old Scottish fast-days, closing as they did with a simple entertainment in the manse.

The feast of tabernacles continued the gladness of the ransomed people. It began on the fifteenth day of the seventh month, with a holy convocation and a holocaust of no fewer than twenty-nine animals, in addition to the daily sacrifice, and a he-goat for a sin offering. The number of bullocks, which was thirteen on this opening day of the feast, was reduced by one each day till on the seventh day seven bullocks were sacrificed. But two rams and fourteen he-lambs were offered each day of the feast, and the he-goat for expiation, besides the continual burnt offering. The celebration ended, so far as sacrifices were concerned, on the eighth day with a special burnt offering of one bullock, one ram, and seven he-lambs, returning thus to the number appointed for New Moon.

It will be noticed that on the closing day there was to be a "solemn assembly." It was "the great day of the feast" (John vii. 37). The people who during the week had lived in the booths or arbours which they had made, now dismantled them and went on pilgrimage to the sanctuary. The opening of the festival came to be of a striking kind. "One could see," says Professor Franz Delitzsch, "even before the dawn of the first day of the feast, if this was not a Sabbath, a joyous throng pouring forth from the Jaffa Gate at Jerusalem. The verdure of the orchards, refreshed with the first showers of the early rain, is hailed by the people with shouts of joy as they scatter on either side of the bridge which crosses the brook fringed with tall poplar-osiers, some in order with their own hands to pluck branches for the festal display, others to look at the men who have been honoured with the commission to fetch from Kolonia the festal leafy adornment of the altar. They seek out right long and goodly branches of these poplar-osiers, and cut them off, and then the reunited host returns in procession, with exultant shouts and singing and jesting, to Jerusalem, as far as the Temple hill, where the great branches of poplar-osier are received by the priests and set upright around the sides of the altar, so that they bend over it with their tips. Priestly trumpet-clang resounded during this decoration of the altar with foliage, and they went on that feast day once, on the seventh day seven times, around the altar with willow branches, or the festive posy entwined of a palm branch and branches of myrtles and willows, amidst the usual festive shouts of Hosanna; exclaiming after the completed encircling, 'Beauty becomes thee, O Altar! Beauty becomes thee, O Altar!'" So, in later times, the festival began and was sustained, each worshipper carrying boughs and fruit of the citron and other trees. But the eighth day brought all this to a close. The huts were taken down, the worshippers sought the house of God for prayer and thanksgiving. The reading of the Law which had been going on day by day concluded; and the sin offering fitly ended the season of joy with expiation of the guilt of the people in their holy things.

The series of sacrifices appointed for days and weeks and months and years required a large number of animals and no small liberality. They did not, however, represent more than a small proportion of the offerings which were brought to the central sanctuary. Besides, there were those connected with vows, the free-will offerings, meal offerings, drink offerings, and peace offerings (xxix. 39). And taking all together it will be seen that the pastoral wealth of the people was largely claimed. The explanation lies partly in this, that among the Israelites, as among all races, "the things sacrificed were of the same kind as those the worshippers desired to obtain from God." The sin offering, however, had quite a different significance. In this the sprinkling of the warm blood, representing the life blood of the worshipper, carried thought into a range of sacred mystery in which the awful claim of God on men was darkly realised. Here sacrifice became a sacrament binding the worshippers by the most solemn symbol imaginable—a vital symbol—to fidelity in the service of Jehovah. Their faith and devotion expressed in the sacrifice secured for them the Divine grace on which their well-being depended, the blood-bought pardon that redeemed the soul. Among the Israelites alone was expiation by blood made fully significant as the center of the whole system of worship.*

2. THE LAW OF VOWS.

NUMBERS xxx.

The general command regarding vows is that whosoever binds himself by one, or takes an oath in regard to any promise, must at all hazards keep his word. A man is allowed to judge for himself in vowing and undertaking by oath, but he is to have the consequences in view, and especially keep in mind that God is his witness. The matter scarcely admitted of any other legislation, and neither here nor elsewhere is any attempt made to lay penalties on those who broke their vows. To use the Divine Name in an oath which was afterwards falsified brought a man under the condemnation of the third commandment, a spiritual doom. But the authorities could not give it effect. The transgressor was left to the judgment of God.

With regard to vows and oaths the sophistry

---

* *Expositor*, 3d Series, vol. iv., p. 88.   * Ewald's "Antiquities," p. 40.

of the Jews and their rabbis led them so far astray that our Lord had to lay down new rules for the guidance of His followers. No doubt cases arose in which it was exceedingly difficult to decide. One might vow with good intention and find himself utterly unable to keep his promise, or might find that to keep it would involve unforeseen injury to others. But apart from circumstances of this sort there came to be such a net-work of half-legalised evasions, and so many unseemly discussions, that the purpose of the law was destroyed. Absolution from vows was claimed as a prerogative by some rabbis; against this, others protested. One would say that if a man vowed by Jerusalem or by the Law he had said nothing; but if he vowed by what is written in the Law, his words stood. The " wise men " declared four kinds of vows not binding—incentive vows, as when a buyer vows that he will not give more than a certain price in order to induce the seller to take less; meaningless vows; thoughtless and compulsory vows. In such ways the practice was reduced to ignominy. It even came to this, that if a man wished to neutralise all the vows he might make in the course of a year he had only to say at the beginning of it, on the eve of the Day of Atonement, " Let every vow which I shall make be of none effect," and he would be absolved. This immoral tangle was cut through by the clear judgment of Christ: " Ye have heard that it was said to them of old time, Thou shalt not forswear thyself, but shalt perform unto the Lord thine oaths: but I say unto you, Swear not at all; neither by the heaven, for it is the throne of God; nor by the earth, for it is the footstool of His feet; nor by Jerusalem, for it is the city of the great King. Neither shalt thou swear by thy head, for thou canst not make one hair white or black. But let your speech be, Yea, yea; Nay, nay: and whatsoever is more than these is of the evil one." In ordinary conversation and dealings Christ will have no vows and oaths. Let men promise and perform, declare and stand to their word. He lifts even ordinary life to a higher plane.

With regard to women's vows, four cases are made the subject of enactment. First, there is the case of a young woman living in her father's house, under his authority. If she vow unto the Lord, and bind herself by a bond in the hearing of her father and he do not forbid, her vow shall stand. It may involve expense to the father, or put him and the family to inconvenience, but by silence he has allowed himself to be bound. On the other hand, if he interpose and forbid the vow, the daughter is released. The second case is that of a woman who at the time of marriage is under a vow; and this is decided in the same way. Her betrothed husband's silence, if he hears the promise, sanctions it; his refusal to allow it gives discharge. The third instance is that of a widow or a divorced woman, who must perform all she has solemnly engaged to do. The last case is that of the married woman in her husband's house, concerning whom it is decreed: " Every vow and every binding oath to afflict the soul, her husband may establish it, or her husband may make it void. . . . If he shall make them null and void after he hath heard them, then he shall bear her iniquity."

These regulations establish the headship of the father and the husband in regard to matters which belong to religion. And the significance of them lies in this, that no intrusion of the priest is permitted. If the " Priests' Code " had been intended to set up a hierocracy, these vows would have given the opportunity of introducing priestly influence into family life. The provisions appear to be designed for the very purpose of disallowing this. It was seen that in the ardour of religious zeal women were disposed to make large promises, dedicating their means, their children, or perhaps their own lives to special service in connection with the sanctuary. But the father or husband was the family head and the judge. No countenance whatever is given to any official interference.

It would have been well if the wisdom of this law had ruled the Church, preventing ecclesiastical dominance in family affairs. The promises, the threats of a domineering Church have in many cases introduced discord between daughters and parents, wives and husbands. The amenability of women to religious motives has been taken advantage of, always indeed with a plausible reason,—the desire to save them from the world, —but far too often, really, for political-ecclesiastical ends, or even from the base motive of revenge. Ecclesiastics have found the opportunity of enriching the Church or themselves, or under cover of confession have become aware of secrets that placed families at their mercy. No practice followed under the shield of religion and in its name deserves stronger reprobation. The Church should, by every means in its power, purify and uphold family life. To undermine the unity of families by laying obligations on women, or obtaining promises apart from the knowledge of those to whom they are bound in the closest relationship, is an abuse of privilege. And the whole custom of auricular confession comes under the charge. It may occasionally or frequently be used with good intention, and lonely women without trusted advisers among their kindred may see no other resource in times of peculiar difficulty and trial. But the submission that forms part of it is debasing, and the secrecy gives priesthood a power that should belong to no body of men in dealing with the souls of their fellow-creatures, and fellow-sinners. At the very best, confession to a priest is a weak expedient.

CHAPTER XXIV.

WAR AND SETTLEMENT.

1. THE WAR WITH MIDIAN.

NUMBERS xxxi.

THE command to vex and smite the Midianites (xxv. 16) has already been considered. Israel had not the spiritual power which would have justified any attempt to convert that people. Degrading idolatry was to be held in abhorrence, and those who clung to it suppressed. Now the time comes for an exterminating war. While hordes of Bedawin occupy the hills and the neighbouring desert, there can be no security either for morals, property, or life. Balaam is among them plotting against Israel; and his restless energy, we may suppose, precipitates the conflict. Moses conveys the command of God that the attack on Midian shall be immediately made, and himself directs the campaign.

The details of the enterprise are given somewhat fully. A thousand fighting men are called from each tribe. The religious purpose of the war is signified by the presence in the host of Phinehas, whose zeal has given him a name among the warriors. He is allowed to carry with him the "vessels of the sanctuary"; and the silver trumpets are to be sounded on the march and in the attack. The Midianitish clan apparently gives way at once before the Hebrews, and either makes no stand or is totally defeated in a single battle. All the men are put to the sword, including Balaam and five chiefs, whose names are preserved. The women and children are taken; the whole of the cattle and goods becomes the prey of the victors; the cities and encampments are burned with fire. On the return of the army with the large band of captives, Moses is greatly displeased. He demands of the officers why the women have been spared,—the very women who caused the children of Israel to trespass against the Lord. Then he orders all above a certain age, and the male children, to be put to death. The young girls alone are to be kept alive.

The purification of those who have been engaged in the war is next commanded. For seven days the army must remain outside the camp. Those who have touched any dead body and all the captives are to be ceremonially cleansed on the third and seventh days. Every article of raiment, everything made of skins and goats' hair, and all woollen articles, are to be purified by means of the water of expiation. Whatever is made of metal is to be passed through the fire.

Details of the quantity and division of the prey, and the voluntary oblations made as an "atonement for their souls" by the officers and soldiers out of their booty, occupy the rest of the chapter. The numbers of oxen, sheep, and asses are great —six hundred and seventy-five thousand sheep, seventy-two thousand beeves, sixty-one thousand asses. No mention is made of horses or camels. The girls saved alive are thirty-two thousand. The army takes one half, and those who remained in the camp receive the other. But of the soldiers' portion, one in five hundred both of the persons and of the animals is given to the priests, and of the people's portion one in fifty to the Levites. The jewels of gold, ankle-chains, bracelets, signet-rings, earrings and armlets offered by the men of war as their "atonement," not one of them having fallen in the battle, amount in weight to sixteen thousand seven hundred and fifty shekels, the value of which may be estimated at some thirty thousand of our pounds. The gold is brought into the tent of meeting for a memorial before the Lord.

Now here we have to deal with an accumulation of statements, every one of which raises some question or other. The war of national and moral antipathy is itself easily understood. But the slaughter of so many in battle and so many others in cold blood, the statement that not a single Israelite fell, the number and kinds of the animals captured, the order given by Moses to put all the women to death, the quantity of gold taken, of which the offering appears only to have been a part—all of these points have been criticised in a more or less incredulous spirit. In apology it has been said, with regard to the slaughter of the women, that when brought as captives by the soldiers they could not be received into the camp, and there was only this way of dealing with them, unless indeed they had been sent back to their ruined encampments, where they would have slowly died. Again, it has been explained that the Midianites were so debased and enfeebled as to have no power to withstand the onset of the Hebrews. The droves of oxen, sheep, and asses are held to be not greater than a wealthy nomadic clan, numbering perhaps two hundred thousand, would be likely to own; and the quantity of gold is likewise accounted for by the well-known fact that among Orientals the wealth represented by precious metals is fashioned into ornaments for the women.

In detail the difficulties may thus be partly overcome; yet the whole account remains so singular, both in its spirit and incidents, that Wellhausen has roundly declared it to be fictitious, and others have had no resource but to fall back, even for the slaughter of the women, on the Divine command. It is true there were other peoples, the Moabites, for instance, as idolatrous, and almost as degraded. But a terror of Jehovah's name had to be created for the moral good of the whole region, and the Midianites, it is said, who had so grossly assailed the purity of Israel, were fitly selected for Divine chastisement. The opinion that the whole account is an invention of the "Priests' Code" may be at once dismissed. The ideas of national purity that prevailed after the exile and are insisted upon in the books of Ezra and Nehemiah would not have countenanced the dedication of any spared from the slaughter, even young girls, as a tribute to Jehovah. The attack and the issue of it were, no doubt, recorded in the ancient documents of which the compilers of the Book of Numbers made use. And the fact must be held to stand, that there was a grim slaughter relentlessly carried out at the command of Moses in accordance with the moral and theocratic ideas that ruled his mind.

But it remains doubtful whether the numbers can be trusted, even although they appear to be in the substance of the narrative. The disproportion is enormous between the twelve thousand Israelites sent against Midian and the number of men who, if we accept the figures given, must have fallen without striking one effective blow for their lives. Of these there would have been some forty thousand at least. Assuming that somehow the numbers are exaggerated, we find the story a good deal cleared. It was entirely in harmony with the spirit of the age that a war à outrance should have been commanded in the circumstances. If, then, an adequate force of Hebrews marched against the Midianites and took them at unawares, perhaps by night, or when they were engaged in some idolatrous orgy, their defeat and slaughter would be comparatively easy. The Hebrews with Phinehas among them were, we may believe, filled with patriotic and religious ardour, assured that they were commissioned to execute Divine justice and must not shrink from any work that lay in their way, however dreadful. Does the thing they did still seem incredible? Perhaps the recollection of what took place after the Indian Mutiny, when Great Britain was in the same temper, may throw light upon the question. The soldiers then, bent on punishing the cruelty and lust of the rebels, partly in patriotism, partly in revenge, set mercy altogether aside. If we had the whole history of the war with Midian, instead of the mere outlines preserved in Numbers, we might find that, apart from figures, the statements are by no means over-coloured. Moses had the entire responsibility of ordering the women to be put to death. When he saw the train of female captives, some of them possibly using their arts of blandishment not without success, he might well be afraid that the very end for which the war had been undertaken was to be frustrated. He was a man who did not scruple to shed blood when the law of God and the purity of morals and religion seemed to be endangered. He knew Jehovah to be gracious—gracious to those who loved Him and kept His commandments. But was He not also a jealous God, visiting the iniquity of the fathers upon the children unto the third and fourth generations of them that hated Him? It was this God Moses sought to serve when in the heat of his indignation, and not without reason, he gave the terrible order.

The appropriation of some of the captive girls to the priests and Levites as "Jehovah's tribute," the offering by the soldiers of part of their booty as an "atonement" for their souls, the presence of Phinehas with the "vessels of the sanctuary," and the sacred trumpets in the ranks—these manifestly belong to the time to which the history refers. And it may be said in closing that circumstances might be well known to Moses on account of which the attack had to be made promptly and the dispersion of the Midianites had to be complete. We cannot tell what Balaam may have been plotting; but we may be pretty sure there was nothing too base for him to scheme and the Midianites to carry into effect. They knew themselves to be under suspicion, perhaps in danger. With what craft and vehemence the Bedawin can act we are well aware. Life even yet is of no account among them. Another day, perhaps, and the ark might have been carried off or Moses put to death in his tent. But the nature of the wrong done to Israel is a sufficient explanation of the war. And we can also see that the Hebrews themselves had a lesson in moral severity when their soldiers went forth to the massacre and returned red with blood. They learned that the sin of Midian was abominable in the sight of God and should be abominable in theirs. They were taught, whether they received the teaching or not, that they were to be enemies for ever of those who practised idolatry so vile. A deep gulf was made between them and all who sympathised with the worship and customs of the tribe they destroyed.

And the whole circumstances, remote as they are from our own time, may bring home even to Christians the duty of moral decision and relentless war against the vices and lusts with which too many are inclined to make terms. We wrestle not against flesh and blood, but against the "wiles of error," the "lusts of deceit," against "fornication, uncleanness, lasciviousness, enmities, strife, jealousies, wraths, factions, divisions, heresies, envyings, drunkenness, revellings and such like,"—the works of the flesh. These Midianites are with us, would draw our hearts away from religion and destroy our souls. Not only are we to assail the grosser forms of sin and exterminate them, but we are with equal severity to strike down the fair-seeming vices that come with blandishment and insidious appeal. This is our holy war. The old form of it required the suppression or extermination of those identified with vice, men and women, all in whom the impurity was rooted. Young girls alone could be spared, whose character might still be shaped by a higher morality. Even yet, to a certain extent, that way of dealing with evil has to be followed. We imprison felons and put murderers to death; but the new power that has come with Christianity enables us to deal with many transgressors as capable of reformation and a new life. And this power is far as yet from being fully developed.

It is the fault of our age to be on one side too lenient, on another wanting in patience, charity, and hope. Excuses are found for sin on the ground that it is useless to fight against nature, that we must not be hypocritical nor puritanical. Temptations that come with mincing gait, cajolery, and smiles, are allowed to disport themselves untouched. Why, it is asked, should life be made sombre? A stern religion that would banish gaiety is declared to be no friend of the race. Under cover of art—pictorial, dramatic, literary—the customs of Midian are not only admitted but allowed to have authority. And religion even is invoked. Are not all things pure to the pure? Should not life be as free and joyous as the Maker clearly intends in giving us the capacity for those gratifications to which art of every kind ministers? Is not full freedom indispensable to the highest religion? Ought not genius, in every department, to have complete liberty in guiding and developing the race?

Without hypocrisy, without banishing the sunshine of life or denying the freedom which is necessary to progress and vigour, we are to be jealous for morality, severe against all that threatens it. And here our age is impatient of direction. The tendency is to a civilisation without morality, that is, a new barbarism. The strenuous mind of the old theocratic leaders is required anew, with a difference. Life and thought have so far advanced under Christianity that liberty is good in things which once had to be sternly reprobated; but only the same guidance will carry us higher. To those who lead in arts and literature the appeal has to be made in the name of God and men to regard the fitness of things The old ideas of Puritanism are not to be the standard? True. Neither are the tastes of Greece nor the manners of Pompeii. Every artist must, it appears, be his own censor. Let each, then, use his right under a sense of responsibility to the God who would have all to be pure and free. There are pictures exhibited, and poems sent out from the press, and novels published, which, for all the skill and charm that are in them, ought to have been cast into the fire. In private life, too, the Midianitish talk, the jest, the anecdote, the innuendo, all but indecent, the hint, the laugh that breaks down the barriers of integrity and sobriety, show the license of a barbarism which is bent on conquest. Every Christian is called to wage against these immoralities an exterminating war.

On the other hand, charity and patience are needed. It is difficult to forbear with those who seem to find their pleasure in what is evil, more difficult to continue the efforts necessary to win them to religion, purity, and honour. We feel it a hard task to track our own unholy desires to their retreats and slay them there. Proteus-like they elude us; when we think they have been destroyed, a passing word or thought revives them. And if in the task of our own purification we need long patience, it is not wonderful that even more should be required in the attempt to set others free from their besetting sins. Much of our philanthropy, again, is useless because we try to cover too large a field. Few are engaged in comparison with the enormous region over which effort has to extend, and we treat the hurt slightly, with too much haste. Then we grow despondent. Impatience, hopelessness, should never be known among those who undertake the Divine work of saving men and women from their sins. But to cure this, new ideas on the whole subject of Christian endeavour and new methods of work are required. The evil forces, a host arrayed against true life, must be followed into the desert places where they lurk, and there, with the sword of the Spirit, which is the bright strong word of God, attacked and slain. When Christians are brave and loving enough, when they have patience enough, the gospel of purity will begin to have its power.

2. Settlement.

Numbers xxxii.

The request of the men of Reuben and Gad that they should be allowed to settle on the eastern side of Jordan in the land of Jazer and the land of Gilead was at first refused by Moses with warm displeasure. They appeared to wish exemption from further military duty, if indeed they had not almost formed the intention of parting altogether with the rest of the tribes. Moses asked of them, "Shall your brethren go to the war and shall ye sit here? And wherefore discourage ye the heart of the children of Israel from going over into the land which the Lord hath given them?" He recalled the spies and the evil report they brought, by which a former generation had been disheartened and made to murmur against the Lord. The forty years of wandering had intervened since that error—a long period of suffering and punishment. And now with this request the men of Reuben and Gad were playing the same dangerous part. "Behold, ye are risen up in your fathers' stead, an increase of sinful men, to augment yet the fierce anger of the Lord toward Israel."

It is somewhat surprising to find the proposal met in this way. But Moses had doubtless good cause for his condemnation of the two tribes. For some time, we can believe, the notion had been entertained, and already the cattle were driven northwards and scattered over the pastures of Gilead. The people felt that the confraternity which had survived the test of the wilderness journey was now about to break up. And as the two clans that proposed to settle in Eastern Palestine were strong and could send a large number of warriors into the field, there was reason to fear that the want of them would make the conquest of the great tribes beyond Jordan too heavy a task.

The circumstances were of a kind resembling those of a Church when the enjoyment of privilege and of the gains of the past is chosen by many of its members, and the rest, discouraged by this moral unbrotherliness, have to maintain the aggressive work which ought to be shared by all. The force of unity lost, the Christian energy of large numbers lying unemployed, the rest overburdened, Churches often come far short of the success they might attain. When Reubenites and Gadites devote themselves to building houses, cultivating fields, and rearing cattle, neglecting altogether the command of God to conquer the territory still in the hands of His enemies, the spirit of religion cannot but decay. The selfishness of worldly Christians reacts on those who are not worldly, so that they feel its subtle influence, even although they scorn to yield. And when there is some great task to be done which requires the personal service and contributions of all, withdrawal of the less zealous may in this way make victory impossible. True, we have on the other side the case of Gideon and his rejection of the great bulk of his army, that he might take the field with a few who were brave and ready. Numbers of half-hearted people do not help an enterprise. Still, the duties of the Church of Christ are so great that all are required for them. It is no apology to say that men are apathetic, and therefore useless. They ought to be eager for the Divine war.

It was not at all wonderful that the men of Reuben and Gad proposed to settle on the east of Jordan. The soil of that region, extending from the Jabbok Valley northwards, and including the whole district watered by the Yarmuk and its tributaries, was exceedingly fertile, with fine forests of oak, and stretches of meadow and arable land. What could be seen of Judæa from the heights of Moab appeared poor and barren in comparison with that green and fertile country. There was abundance of room there, not only for the two tribes, but for more; and besides the half of Manasseh which finally joined Reuben and Gad, other clans may have begun to think that they might rest content without venturing across Jordan. But Moses had good reasons for resisting as far as possible this desire. There was no natural boundary on the east of Gilead and Bashan. Moab, in a similar situation, was exposed to the attacks and perhaps corrupted by the influence of the Midianites. If Israel had taken up its abode in this region which joined on to the desert, it too would have become half a desert people. The Jordan came, as no doubt Moses foresaw, to be the real boundary of the nation which maintained the faith of Jehovah and carried on His purposes.

In danger of losing all because they had been too selfish, the men of Reuben and Gad made a new proposal. They would go with the rest to the conquest of Canaan; yea, they would form the van of the army. If Moses would only allow them to provide sheep-folds for their flocks and cities for their families, they would take the field and never think of returning till the other tribes had all found settlement. The offer was one which Moses saw fit to accept; but with a caution to the Reubenites. If they fulfilled the promise, he said, they should be guiltless before the Lord; but if they did not, their sin would be written against them. Foreseeing the result of a division between the east and west which any such faithless conduct would certainly cause, he added the warning, "Be sure your sin will find you out." The time would come when, if they refused to do their part in helping the rest, they should find themselves, in some day of extreme peril, without the sympathy of their brethren, the prey of enemies who came from the east and north.

Earthly comfort and the means of material prosperity can never be enjoyed without spiritual disadvantage, or at least the risk of spiritual loss. The whole region of ease and wealth lies towards the desert in which the adversaries of the soul have their lurking-places, from which they come stealthily or even boldly in open day to make their assaults. A man who has large means is exposed to the envy of others; his life may be embittered by their designs upon him; his nature may be seriously injured by the flattery of those who have no power but only the base cunning to which narrow self-love may descend. These, however, are not the assailants that are most to be dreaded. Rather should the man who is rich fear the danger to his religion and his soul which draws near in other ways. The wealthy who have no religion court his friendship and propose to him schemes for increasing his wealth. Alliances are urged upon him which stir and partly gratify his ambition. He is pointed to honours that can only be had through abandoning the great ideas of life by which he should be ruled. He is served obsequiously, and is tempted to think that the world goes very well because he enjoys all he desires, or is in the way to obtain the fulfilment of his highest earthly hopes. The curse of egotism hangs over him, and to escape it he needs a double portion of the spirit of humility. Yet how is that to come to him?

It is well for a man when, before enjoying the good things of this life in abundance, he has taken the field with those who have to fight a hard battle, and has done his share of common work. But even that is not enough to guard him against pride and self-sufficiency for the whole term of his existence. Better is it when by his own choice the hardness is retained in his experience, when he never discharges himself from the duty of fighting side by side with others, that he may help them to their inheritance. That and that alone will save his life. He is called as a soldier of God to maintain the holy war for human rights, for the social well-being and spiritual good of mankind. Every rich man should be a friend of the people, a reformer, taking the part of the multitude against his own tendency and the tendency of his class to exclusiveness and self-indulgence. The warning given by Moses to Reuben and Gad in accepting their proposals should linger with those who are rich and in high station. If they fail to do their duty to the general mass of their fellow-men, if they leave the rest to fight, at disadvantage, for their human inheritance, they sin against God's law, which calls for brotherhood, and that sin will surely find them out. In the end no sin is more sure to come home in judgment. And it is not by some miserable gifts to religious objects or some patronage of philanthropic schemes the prosperous can discharge the great debt laid upon them. In whatever way the inequalities of life, the disabilities of privilege and wealth, hinder the realisation of brotherhood, there lie opportunity and need for men's personal effort. Would this imply sacrifice of what are called rights, of perhaps no small amount of substance? That is precisely the saving of a rich man's life. To that Christ pointed the rich young ruler who came to Him seeking salvation—from that the inquirer turned away.

And how does the sin of those who neglect such high duties find them out? Perhaps in the loss of the possessions they have selfishly guarded, and their reduction to the level of those whom they kept at arm's-length and treated as inferiors or as enemies. Perhaps in the harshness of temper and bitterness of spirit the proud, friendless rich man may find growing upon him in old age, the horrible feeling that he has not one brother where he should have had thousands, no one to care—except selfishly—whether he lives or dies. To come to that, so far as a man is concerned with his fellow-men, is to be indeed lost. But these retributions may be artfully escaped. What then? Is not One to be reckoned with who is the Guardian of the human family and gives men power and wealth only as His stewards, to be used in His service? The future life does not obliterate society, but it destroys the class separations, the factitious distinctions, that exist now. It brings a man face to face with the fact that he is but a man, like others, responsible to God. Is not the result indicated by our Lord when He says to exclusive Pharisaical men, "They shall come from the east and west, and from the north and south, and shall sit down in the kingdom—ye yourselves cast forth without"? Brotherhood here, not in name, but in deed and truth, means brotherhood above. Denial of it here means unfitness for the society of heaven.

We learn from ver. 19 that the Reubenites and Gadites confidently affirmed, even when they made their request to Moses, that their inheritance had fallen to them on the east side of Jordan. It may be asked how they knew, since the division was not yet made. And the answer appears to be that they had made up their minds on the subject. Without waiting for the lot, they seem to have said, This is nobody's land now that the Amorites and Midianites are dispossessed. We will have it. And there was no sufficient reason for refusing them their choice when they accepted the conditions. At the same time, these tribes did not act fairly and honourably. And the result was that, although they gained the fat land and the good pastures, they lost the close fellowship with the other tribes which was of greater value. Reuben, the premier tribe, could no longer keep its position. It was by-and-by succeeded by Judah. Neither Reuben nor Gad made any great figure in the subsequent history. The half-tribe of Manasseh, which was settled, not on its own request, but by authority, in the northern part of Gilead towards the Argob, had greater distinction. Gad has some notice. We read of eleven valiant men of this tribe who swam the Jordan at its highest to join David in his trouble. "But no person, no incident is recorded to place Reuben before us in any distincter form than as a member of the community (if community it can be called) of the Reubenites, the Gadites, and the half-tribe of Manasseh. The very towns of his inheritance—Heshbon, Aroer, Kiriathaim, Dibon, Baalmeon, Sibmah, Jazer—are familiar to us as Moabite, not as Israelite, towns." The Reubenites, in fact, under the influence of their wild neighbours, gradually lost touch with their brethren and fell away from the religion of Jehovah.

It is a parable of the degeneration of life.—Earthly choice rules and heavenly faith is hazarded for the sake of a temporal advantage. Men have their will because they insist upon it. They do not consult the prophet, but make terms with him, that they may gain their end. But as they place themselves, so they have to live, not on the soil of the promised land, no integral part of Israel.

CHAPTER XXV.

THE WAY AND THE LOT.

NUMBERS xxxiii., xxxiv.

1. THE itinerary of xxxiii. 1-49 is one of the passages definitely ascribed to Moses. It opens with the departure from Rameses in Egypt on the morrow after the passover, when the children of Israel "went out with an high hand in the sight of all the Egyptians." The exodus is made singularly impressive in this narrative by the addition that it took place "while the Egyptians were burying all their firstborn, which the Lord had smitten among them." The Divine salvation of Israel begins when the dark shadow of loss and judgment rests on their oppressors. The gods of Egypt are discredited by the triumph of Jehovah's people. They can neither save their own worshippers nor prevent the servants of another from obtaining liberty.

From Rameses, the place of departure, to Abel-shittim, in the plains of Moab, forty-two stations in all are given at which the Israelites pitched. Of these about twenty-four are named either in Exodus, in other parts of the Book of Numbers, or in Deuteronomy. Some eighteen, therefore, are mentioned in this passage and nowhere else. Of the whole number, comparatively few have as yet been identified. The Egyptian localities, at least Rameses and Succoth, are known. With the exit from Egypt, at the crossing of the Red Sea difficulty begins. Our passage says that the Israelites went three days' journey into the wilderness of Etham; Exodus calls it the wilderness of Shur. Then Marah and Elim bring the travellers, according to chap. xxxiii., to the Red Sea, the *Yâm Suph*. Ordinarily, this is supposed to be the Gulf of Suez, alongside which the route would have lain from the day it was crossed. There are, however, the best reasons for believing that this "Red Sea" is the eastern gulf, the Elanitic, as it must be in xiv. 25, where, after the evil report of the spies, the Divine command is given: "To-morrow turn ye, and get you into the wilderness by the way to the Red Sea." From this identification of the *Yâm Suph* many things follow. And one is the rejection of the ordinary opinion regarding the position of Sinai. The mountain of the law-giving is always described as situated in Midian. Now, Midian is beyond Elath, on the eastern side of the Yâm Suph, not in the peninsula between the Gulfs of Suez and Akabah. Elim and Elath, or Eloth, appear to be names for the same place, at the head of the Gulf of Akabah. We have therefore to look for Sinai either among the southern hills of Seir or those lying more southward still, towards the desert. In Deborah's song (Judg. v. 4, 5) occur the following verses:

"Lord, when Thou wentest out of Seir,
  When Thou marchedst out of the field of Edom,
  The earth trembled, the heavens also dropped,
  Yea, the clouds dropped water;
  The mountains flowed down at the presence of the Lord,
  Even yon Sinai at the presence of the Lord, the God of Israel."

In the same direction the "Prayer of Habbakkuk" points (iii. 3, 7):

"God came from Teman,
  And the Holy One from Mount Paran.
  His glory covered the heavens,
  And the earth was full of His light...
  I saw the tents of Cushan in affliction,
  The curtains of the land of Midian did tremble."

The tradition which places Sinai in the south of the peninsula between the two gulfs "is of later origin than the lifetime of St. Paul, and can claim no higher authority than the interested fancies of ignorant cœnobites. It throws into confusion both the geography and the history of the Pentateuch, and contradicts the definite statements of the Old Testament." So the most recent inquiry.

If Mount Sinai was somewhere to the south of Edom, the journey thence to Kadesh by way of Kibroth-hattaavah and Hazeroth, localities mentioned both in Num. xi. and xxxiii., may have had other stations; and these may be named in ver. 19 of our passage and onward. But identification of the places is exceedingly doubtful till we come to Ezion-geber, in the Arabah, and Mount Hor. Deut. x. places the scene of Aaron's death at Mosera, which seems to be the same as Moseroth, and is there given along with other stations named in the itinerary—Bene-jaakan, Gudgodah (= Hor-haggidgad), Jotbathah. And this seems to prove that these localities were in or near the Arabah, Moseroth being in the region of Mount Hor. But where Kadesh is to be found between Rithmah and Moseroth, and under what name, it is impossible to say. Keil argues for Rithmah itself. Palmer reckons twenty stations to the first arrival at Kadesh. His map, however, shows a Mount Sheraif, which may be the same as Shepher, not far from Gadis, which he identifies with Kadesh. For the rest we are left in great ignorance, relieved only by this, that at the most there are but eighteen stations given, more probably thirteen, for the whole thirty-seven years between the first arrival at Kadesh and the death of Aaron at Mount Hor; and five or six of these were on the Arabah. During the whole of that long period there were only a few removals of the tabernacle, and those apparently within a limited area near Kadesh.

A list of names with only three historical notes appears a singular memorial of the forty years. Time was, no doubt, when the places named were all well known, and any Israelite desiring to satisfy himself as to the route by which his forefathers went could make it out by help of this passage. To us the interest of the subject is partly the same as that which might have been found by a Hebrew, say, of the time of Hezekiah, for whom the verification of the wilderness journey might be a help to faith. But the impossibility of identifying the localities shows that there are matters in the history of Israel which are of no particular importance now. There is more danger in seeking to gratify mere curiosity, than profit in any possible discoveries. Why should not the mountain of the law-giving be hid in the shadows as well as the grave in which Moses was laid? Why should not the places at which Israel encamped be to us mere names, since, if we could identify them, it might only be to add fresh difficulties instead of clearing away those that exist? The Israelites who entered Canaan had not seen all the way by which Jehovah led His people. When they crossed the Jordan, present duty was to engage them, not the mere names that belonged to the past. They were to forget the things behind, and stretch forward to the things which were before. And duty is the same still. Our backward glance, especially on the actual path from one spot of earth to another by which men have gone in trial and anticipation, must not hinder the efforts called for by the circumstances of our own time. The way of the desert, especially, may well lie half obliterated in the distance, since we know the spiritual fruit of the dealings of God with Israel, and can bear it with us as we follow our own road.

The ideas of change and urgency are in our passage. The wilderness journey was taken by a people on whom Divine influences had laid hold, who of themselves would have remained content in Egypt, but were not suffered, because God had some greater thing in store for them. The urgency throughout was His. And so is that which we ourselves feel hurrying us from change to change, from place to place. We may not be in the wilderness, but in a spot of shelter and comfort; and it may be no house of bondage, but a vantage-ground for generous effort. Even when we are thus happily settled, as we imagine, the call comes, and we must strike our tents. At other times our own anxiety anticipates the command. But we know that always, whether we pass into sterner conditions of life or escape to more pleasant circumstances, the times and changes that happen to us are of God's appointing, that His providence urges us toward a goal. And this means that our reaching the goal must be by His way, although properly we endeavour to find it for ourselves.

The number of the stations at which Israel encamped in the course of forty years can scarcely be taken as representing the number of changes from dwelling to dwelling any pilgrim through this world shall have to make. But if we think of halting-places and movements of thought, we shall have a fruitful parallel. From the twentieth to the sixtieth year—may we not say?—is the time of journeying that takes the mind from its first freedom to comparative rest. Not far on the Divine law-giving impresses itself on the conscience; and hence a direct road may appear to lead into the peace of obedience. But the stations successively reached, Kibroth-hattaavah, Hazeroth, Rithmah, and the rest, represent each a peculiar difficulty encountered, a barrier to our steady progress towards the settled mind. St. Paul indicates one he found when he says: "I had not known coveting, except the law had said, Thou shalt not covet." Another halt is imposed when it is found that the law appears to forbid what is according to nature; still another when obedience requires separation from those who have been valued friends and pleasant companions. These hindrances left behind as the soul, still confiding and hopeful, is urged on towards the goal, a great trial like that of Kadesh follows. We are not far from the frontier of promise; and anticipations are formed of many delights for heart and life. Is not obedience to bring felicity, an easy salvation from doubt and fear? But it becomes plain that there are enemies to faith and peace beyond the border as well as in the region already crossed. Complete conformity to the Divine will has not been achieved. Will it ever be achieved? We begin to doubt the result of law-keeping. There is perhaps a backward look to Sinai, implying a question whether God spoke there, or beyond Sinai, to the old traditional way of life. And so another term of difficult inquiry begins.

In this way many find themselves held for a long period of middle life. Their minds move from one point to another without seeming to make any progress. But neither does rest come. It is seen that partial obedience, a measure of nearness to the perfection once dreamed of, will not suffice. Then arises the question whether obedience can ever save. There is return almost to Sinai itself, at least to a place from which its peak is seen and the mind is confirmed as to the inexorability of law. So the urgency of the Divine will is felt, and the way is fixed. If the soul would make its own way into peace, it is driven back. For, perhaps, it would have the difficulty solved by taking the way of a Church, accepting a creed—as Israel would have passed through the territory of Edom. This also is forbidden. Trusted helpers fall by the way, as Aaron died at Hor, and there is sorrowful delay. But movement is enforced; and, finally, it is by a road that reveals Sinai and the law in quite another aspect, showing vital faith, not mere obedience, to be the means of salvation, our progress is made. Round the borders of Edom, not by trust in creed or Church, but by confidence in God Himself, the soul must advance. Then strength comes. Point after point is reached and passed. Self-righteousness, pride, and Pharisaism—Amorites of the mountain land —are overcome. At length through the faith of Christ peace is found, the peace that is possible on this side of the river.

It is our high privilege to be urged and led on thus by Him who knows the way we should take, who tries us that we may come forth purified as gold. Without Divine pressure we should content ourselves in the desert and never see the real good of life. So many lose themselves because they will not admit that to be of the truth is necessary to salvation. There is a way of thinking, or rather refusing to think, of spiritual verities which keeps the soul unaware of the purpose God would carry into effect, or indifferent to it. The mind refuses its duty; and in the midway of life the spiritual goal fades from view. To guard against this taking place in the case of any one is the office of the Gospel ministry. If evangelical preaching does not keep thought awake and attentive to Divine inspirations, if it does not speak to those who are in every stage of perplexity, at every possible camping-ground, it fails of its high purpose.

2. Commandment is given that when the Israelites pass over Jordan they shall use effectual means for establishing themselves as the people of Jehovah in Canaan. They are, for one thing, to drive out before them all the inhabitants of the land. Nothing is here said of putting them all to the sword; only they are not to be left even in partial occupation. The plan of Israel's settlement in its new territory requires that it shall be subject to no alien influence, and shall have the field entirely to itself for the development of customs, civilisation, and religion. And in this there is nothing either impossible or, as the ideas of the time went, strange and cruel. We do not need to take refuge in the command of God and defend it by saying that He had absolute right over the lives of the Canaanites. The tides of

war and population were continually flowing and receding. When the Israelites reached Canaan, they had the same right as others to occupy it, provided they could make their right good at the point of the sword. Yet for their own special consciousness the command given by Moses in Jehovah's name was most important. It was only as His people they were to advance, and as His people they were to dwell separate in Canaan.

To drive out all the inhabitants of the land was, however, a difficult task; and even Moses might not intend the order to be literally obeyed. We have seen that he did not require the destruction of the Midianites to be absolute. In the wars of conquest in Canaan cases of a similar kind would necessarily arise. When a tribe was driven out of its cities many would be left behind, some of whom would conceal themselves and gradually venture from their hiding-places. The command was general, and could scarcely be supposed to require the putting to death of all children. And again, as we know, there were fortresses which for a long time defied attempts to reduce them. The Israelites were not so faithful to God that Moses could expect their success to be insured by supernatural aid. It is the constant purpose they are to have in view, to sweep the land clear of those presently in occupation. As they establish themselves, this will be carried out; and if they fail, allowing any of the tribes to remain, these will be as pricks in their eyes and as thorns in their sides.

The will of God that Israel, called to special duty in the world, was to keep itself separate, is here strongly emphasised. It was the only way by which faith could be preserved and made fruitful. For the Canaanites, already civilised and in many of the arts superior to the Hebrews, had gross polytheistic beliefs imbedded in their customs, and a somewhat elaborate cultus which was observed throughout the whole land. "Figured stones," which by their shape or incised emblems conveyed religious ideas; molten images, probably of bronze, like those found at Tel el Hesy, which were for household use, or of a larger size for tribal adoration; "high places" crowned by altars and sacrificial stones, were especially to be destroyed. The tendency to polytheism required to be carefully guarded against, for the gods of Canaan represented the powers of nature, and their rites celebrated the fruitfulness of earth under the lordship of Baal or Bel, and the mysterious processes of life associated with the influence of Astarte, the moon. The divinities of Egypt also appear to have had their worshippers; and, indeed, the mixed population of the land had drawn from every neighbouring region symbols, rites, and practices supposed to propitiate the unseen powers on whose favour human life must depend. Israel could prosper only by rejecting and extirpating this idolatry. Allowed to survive in any degree, it would be the cause of physical suffering and spiritual decay.

The command thus ascribed to Moses was again one which he must have known the Israelites would find difficult to carry out, even if they were cordially disposed to obey it. The sacred places of a country like Canaan tend to retain their reputation even when the rites fall into disuse; and however expeditiously the work of sweeping away the original inhabitants might be done, there was no small danger that knowledge of the cult as well as veneration for the high places would be learned by the Hebrews. The command was made clear and uncompromising so that every Israelite might know his duty; but the difficulty and the peril remained. And as we know from the Book of Judges and subsequent history, the law, especially in regard to the demolition of high places, became practically a dead letter. Jehovah was worshipped at the ancient places of sacrifice; and so far were even pious Israelites of the next few centuries from thinking they did wrong in using those old altars, that Samuel fell in with the custom. It was true in regard to this commandment as it is with regard to many others,—the high mark of duty is presented, but few aim at it. Expediency rules, the possible is made to suffice instead of the ideal. There is reason to believe, not only that the images and stone symbols of Canaan were venerated, but that Jehovah Himself was worshipped by many of the Hebrews under the form of some animal. And the Canaanites became to those who fraternised with them as pricks in their eyes. Spiritual vision failed; faith fell back on the coarse emblems used by the old inhabitants of the land. Then the vigour of the tribes decayed and they were judged and punished.

3. The boundaries of the land in which the Israelites were to dwell are laid down in ch. xxxiv.; but, as elsewhere, there is difficulty in following the geography and identifying the old names. The south quarter is to be "from the wilderness of Zin along by the side of Edom" —that is to say, it is to include the region of Zin near Kadesh and extend to the mountains of Seir. The "ascent of Akrabbim" is apparently the Ghor rising southwards from the Dead Sea. The line then runs along the Arabah for some distance, say fifty miles, across by the south of the Azazimeh hills and of Kadesh Barnea towards the stream called the river or brook of Egypt, which it followed to its debouchment in the Mediterranean. The western boundary was the Mediterranean or Great Sea for a distance of perhaps one hundred and sixty miles. The northern boundary is exceedingly obscure. They were to keep in view a "mount Hor" as a landmark; but no two geographers can be said to agree where it was. The "entering in of Hamath" is also a locality greatly disputed. Most likely it was some well-known part of the road leading along the Leontes valley to that of the Orontes. If we take the mount Hor here indicated to be Hermon, a line running west and striking the Mediterranean somewhere north of Tyre would be a natural boundary, and would correspond fairly with the actual partition and occupation of the country. It is certain, however, that both the Philistines and Phœnicians, especially the latter, were so strongly established in the southern and northern parts of the seaboard that any attempt to dispossess them was soon discovered to be futile. And even in the limited central range from Kedesh Naphtali to Beersheba the settlement was only effected gradually.

The Canaan of the Divine promise marked out, yet never fully possessed, is a symbol of the region of this life which those who believe in God have assigned to them, but never entirely enjoy. There are boundaries within which there is abundant room for the development of the life of faith. It is not, as the world reckons, a district of great resources. As Canaan had neither gold nor silver, neither coal nor iron mines, as its seaboard was not well supplied with harbours, nor its rivers and lakes of great use for inland navigation, so we may say the life open to the Christian has its limitations and disabilities. It does not invite those who seek pleasure, wealth, or dazzling exploits. Within it, discipline is to be found rather than enjoyment of earthly good. The "milk and honey" of this land are spiritual symbols, Divine sacraments. There is room for the development of life in every branch of study and culture, but in subordination to the glory of God, and for the testimony that should be borne to His majesty and truth.

Many of us affect to despise so narrow a range of thought and endeavour, and persist in believing that something more than discipline may be looked for in this world. Is there not a proper kingdom of humanity better than any kingdom of God? May not the race of men, apart from any service paid to an Unseen God, attain dignity of its own, power, gladness, magnificence? It is supposed that by rejecting all the limitations of religion and refusing the outlook to another life the united labour of men will make this life free and this earth a paradise. But it remains true that men must limit their hopes with regard to their own future here as individuals and the future of the race. We must accept the boundaries God has fixed, on one side the swift Jordan, on the other the Great Sea. There are seemingly rich fields beyond, wide regions that invite the tastes and senses, but these are no part of the soul's inheritance; to explore and reduce them would bring no real gain.

The range that lies open to us as servants of God, and affords ample space for the discipline of life, is often not used and therefore not enjoyed. When people will not accept the inevitable fixed limits within which their time and vigour can be occupied to the best advantage, when they look covetously to districts of experience not meant for them, as Israel did at certain periods of her history, their life is spoiled. Discontent begins, envy follows. Where in seeking and reaching moral gains, purity, courage, love, there would have been a continual sense of adequate result and encouraging prospect, there is now no gain, no pleasure. The appointed lot is despised, and all it can yield held in contempt. How many there are who, with a full river of Divine bounty on one side their life, and the great ocean of the Divine faithfulness ebbing and flowing on the other, with the pastures and olive-groves of the Word of God to nourish their soul, with access to His city and sanctuary, and an outlook from summits like Tabor and Hermon to a transfigured life in the new heavens and earth, speak nevertheless with scorn and bitterness of their heritage! They might be reaching "the measure of the stature of the fulness of Christ," but they remain graceless and discontented to the end. Israel, understanding its destiny and using its opportunities aright, might well say—and so may every one who knows the truth as it is in Jesus Christ—"the lines are fallen unto me in pleasant places; yea, I have a goodly heritage." But this gladness of heart has its root in believing content. The restricted land is full of God's promise: "Thou maintainest my lot." The security of Jehovah's word encompasses the man of faith.

CHAPTER XXVI.

THE CITIES OF REFUGE.

NUMBERS xxxv., xxxvi.

1. THE INHERITANCE OF THE LEVITES. The order relating to the Levitical cities may be said to describe an ideal settlement. We have, at all events, no evidence that the command was ever fully carried out. It was to the effect that in forty-eight cities, scattered throughout the whole of the tribes in proportion to their population, dwellings were to be allotted to the Levites, who were also to have the suburbs of those cities; that is to say, the fields lying immediately about them, "for their cattle, and for their substance, and for all their beasts." It is assumed that closely surrounding each of the cities there shall be pasturage, and that a regular or fairly regular boundary can be made at the distance of one thousand cubits from the city. Singularly, nothing whatever is said as to the duties of the Levites thus distributed throughout the land on both sides Jordan, from Kedesh Naphtali in the north, to Debir in the south, according to Josh. xxi. It is not said that they were to perform any ecclesiastical functions or instruct the people in the Divine Law. Yet something of the kind must have been intended, since many of them were at a great and inconvenient distance from Shiloh and other places at which the ark was stationed.

According to this statute, there is, for one thing, to be no seclusion of the Levites from the rest of the people. If clergy and laity, as we say, are distinguished, the distinction is made as small as possible. From the terms of the present order (xxxv. 2, ff.) it might appear that the towns given to the Levites were to be occupied by them exclusively. In parallel passages, however, it is clear that the Levites dwelt along with others in the cities; and in this way, as well as by engaging in pastoral work, they were kept closely in touch with the men of the tribes. The land allotted to them was not sufficient for farms; but the tithes and offerings were to a large extent for their support. And the arrangement thus sketched is held with some reason to be an ideal for every order of men called to similar duty. The Levites, indeed, were not at first spiritual. Neither the nature of their work at the sanctuary, nor the conditions of their life, implied any special consecration of heart. But the general tone of a religious ministry advances; and even in David's time there were Levites who served God in no mere routine, but with earnest mind, with a measure of inspiration. The ordinance here is in behalf of a consecrated order devoted to the service of God.

The suburbs, or pasture lands about the cities, are measured a thousand cubits broad, and are to be two thousand cubits along each of the four boundaries. If the figures given are correct it would seem that, although the wall of the city is spoken of, the measurement must really have begun in the centre of the city; otherwise there could never have been a square of land, cities not taking that form; nor could a boundary of two thousand cubits on each aspect, north, south, east, and west, be made out. The cities must often have been small, a cluster of poor huts built of clay or rude brick, with a wall of similar material. We need imagine no stately dwellings or fine pleasure grounds when we read here of the provision for the Levites. Within the wall they had their bare, mean cottages; outside, there might be a breadth of perhaps four hundred yards of poor enough ground which they could claim. But as the tithes were not always paid, so the dwellings and the pasturage may not always have been allotted. There is not much reason to wonder that in a short time after the settlement in Canaan the Levites, finding no special work at the sanctuary, and obtaining little support from the offerings, gradually became part of the tribes in which they happened to have their abode. Hence we read in Judges (xvii. 7) of "a young man out of Bethlehem-judah, of the family of Judah, who was a Levite."

The main purpose of the present statute, so far as it refers to the dwellings of the Levites, would appear to have been economic, not religious. It was that all the tribes might have their share of maintaining the servants of the sanctuary. But it seems likely that a class half priestly would, in lack of other duty, attach itself to the high places, and set up a worship not contemplated by the law. And if this is to be regarded as a misfortune, the choice of the Levitical cities is in some cases difficult to account for. Kedesh in Naphtali had been a famous holy place of the Canaanites; so probably were others, as Gibeon, Shechem, Gath-rimmon. The special symbol of Jehovah was the ark; and where the ark was the principal national rites were always performed. But in a time of pioneer work and constant alarms the central sanctuary could not always be visited, and the Levites appear to have lent themselves to worship of a local kind.

An ecclesiastical order needs great faithfulness if it is not to become irreligious through poverty, or proud and domineering through assumption of power with God. To live poorly as those Levites were expected to live, without the opportunity of earthly gain, while often the share of national support which was due fell to a very low and wholly inadequate amount, would try the fidelity of the best of them. No large claim need be made in behalf of men specially engaged in the work of the Christian Church; and great wealth seems inappropriate to those who represent Christ. But what is their due should at least be paid cheerfully, and the more so if they give earnest minds to the service of God and man. With all faults that have at various periods of the Church's history stained the character of the clergy, they have maintained a testimony on behalf of the higher life, and the sacredness of duty to God. A materialistic age will make light of that service, and point to ecclesiastical pride and covetousness as more than counterbalancing any good that is done. But a broad and fair survey of the course of events will show that the witness-bearing of a special class to religious ideas has kept alive that reverence on which morality depends. True, the ideal of a theocracy would dispense with an order set apart to teach the law of God and to enforce His claims on men. But for the times that now are, even in the most Christian country, the witness-bearing of a gospel ministry is absolutely needful. And we may take the statute before us as anticipating a general necessity, that necessity which the apostles of our Lord met when they ordained presbyters in every Church, and gave them commission to feed the flock of God.

2. THE CITIES OF REFUGE. Among the forty-eight cities that provide dwellings for the Levites, six are to be cities of refuge, "that the man-slayer which killeth any person unwittingly may flee thither." Three of these cities are to be on the east and three on the west side of Jordan. According to other enactments they are to be distributed so as to be reached quite easily from all parts of the country. They were sanctuaries for any one fleeing from the "avenger of blood"; but the protection found in them was not by any means absolute. Only if there appeared to be good cause for admitting a fugitive was he afforded refuge even for a time, and his trial followed as soon as possible. The laws of protection and judgment are here laid down not fully, though with some detail.

We notice first that the statutes regarding the manslayer are frankly based on the primitive practice of blood revenge. It was the duty of the nearest male relation of one who had been slain to seek the blood of the man who slew him. The duty was held to be one which he owed to his brother, to the community, and to God; and the principle of retribution in such cases was embodied in the saying, "Whoso sheddeth man's blood, by man shall his blood be shed." The goël, or redeemer, whose part it was to recover for a family land that had been alienated, or a member of the family who had fallen into slavery, had it also laid on him to seek justice on behalf of the family when one belonging to it had been killed. The evils of this method of punishing crime are very evident. All the heat of personal affection for the man put to death, the keen desire to maintain the honour of family or clan, and the bitter hatred of the tribe to which the homicide belonged, made the pursuit of the criminal swift and the stroke fierce and unrelenting. A goël put on a false track might easily strike to the ground an innocent person; and he would feel himself bound to incur all risks in avenging his kinsman. Often whole tribes of Arabs are involved in the blood feud beginning in a single stroke, and wherever the custom prevails there is the gravest danger of wide and sanguinary strife. The enactments of our passage are intended to counteract in part these abuses and dangers.

We may wonder that the Hebrew law, enlightened on many points, did not wholly abolish the practice of blood revenge. Justice is not the private affair of any man, even the nearest kinsman of one who has been injured. We have learned that the administration of law, especially in cases of murder or supposed murder, is best taken out of the hands of a private avenger, whose aim is to strike as soon and as effectually as possible. It remains of course for those whose friend has died by violence to institute inquiries and do their utmost to bring the criminal to justice. But even when a man's guilt seems clear his trial is before an impartial judge by whom all relevant facts are elicited. In Hebrew law there was no complete provision for such an administration of justice. The ancient custom could not be easily set aside, for one thing; the passionate Oriental nature would cling to it. And for another, there was no organisation for repressing disorder and dealing with crime. A certain risk had to be run, in order that the sanctity of human life might be clearly kept before a people too ready to strike as well as to curse. But if the man-slayer was able to reach a city of refuge he had his trial. The old custom was checked by the right of the fugitive to claim sanctuary and to have his case investigated.

As for the sanctuary cities, there may also have been some imperfect custom which anticipated them. In Egypt there certainly was; and the Canaanites, who had learned not a little from Egypt, may have had sacred places that afforded protection to the fugitive. But the Mosaic law prevented abuse of the means of evading justice. He who had killed another was a criminal before God. The blood of the brother he had slain defiled the land and cried to Heaven. No sanctuary must protect a man who had with homicidal purpose struck another. There was to be neither priestly protection, nor sanctuary, nor ransom for him. The Divine principle of justice took up the cause.

In vv. 16 ff. there are examples of cases which are adjudged to be murder. To smite one with an instrument of iron, or with a stone grasped in the hand presumably large enough to kill, or with a weapon of wood, a heavy club or bar, is adjudged to be deliberate homicide. Then if hatred can be proved, and one known to have cherished enmity towards another is shown to have thrust him down, or hurled at him, lying in wait, or to have smitten him with the hand, such a one is to be allowed no sanctuary. On the other hand, the cases of inadvertent homicide are defined: "if he thrust him suddenly without enmity, or hurled upon him anything without lying in wait, or with any stone, whereby a man may die, seeing him not." These, of course, are simply instances, not exhaustive categories.

It is not here stated, but in Josh. xx. 4 the statute runs that the man-slayer who fled to a sanctuary city was to state his cause before the elders, no doubt at the gate. Their preliminary decision had to be given in his favour before he could be admitted. But the real trial was by the "congregation," Numb. xxxv. 24, some assembly representing the tribe within whose territory the crime has been committed, or more likely a gathering of headmen of the whole nation. Further, at ver. 30 it is enacted that the charge of the avenger of blood against any one must be substantiated by two witnesses at least. These provisions form the basis of a sound judicial method. The rights of refuge and of revenge stand opposed to each other, and between the two a large and authoritative court gives judgment. It will be observed, moreover, that the judiciary was not ecclesiastical. Where power was to be exercised in the name of God, the priests were not to wield it, but the people. The form of government is far nearer a democracy than a hierocracy.

A singular point in the law is the term during which the unwitting man-slayer who had been acquitted by the court of justice must remain in sanctuary. He is in danger of being put to death by the avenger of blood until the acting high priest dies. Till that event he must keep within the border of his city of refuge. And here the idea seems to be that the official memory of the crime which had ceremonially defiled the land rested with the high priest. He was supposed to keep in mind, on God's behalf, the bloodshed which even though unintentional was still polluting. His death accordingly obliterated the recollection that kept the man-slayer under peril of the goël's revenge. The high priest had no power to acquit or condemn a criminal, nor to enforce against him the punishment of his fault. But he was the guardian of the sacredness of the land in the midst of which Jehovah dwelt.

With regard to the symbolical meaning of the cities of refuge, it is needful to exercise great care at every point. The man-slayer, for instance, fleeing from the avenger of blood, is not a type of the sinner fleeing for his life from the justice of God. If guilty of murder, a man could find no safety even in the city of refuge. It was only if he was not guilty of premeditated crime that he found sanctuary. The refuge cities, however, represented Divine justice as in contrast to the justice or rather the vengeance of man—that Divine justice which Christ came to reveal, giving Himself for us upon the cross. Human righteousness errs sometimes by excess, sometimes by defect. Certain offences it would never condemn, others it would passionately and remorselessly punish. The sanctuary cities show a higher idea of justice. But all men are guilty before God. And there is mercy with Him not only for the unwitting transgressor, but for the man who has to confess deliberate sin, the forfeiture of his life to Divine law.

The singular opinion has been expressed that the death of the high priest was expiatory. This is said to be "unmistakably evident" from the addition of the clause, "who has been anointed with the holy oil" (ver. 25). The argument is that as the high priest's life and work "acquired a representative signification through this anointing with the Holy Ghost, his death might also be regarded as a death for the sins of the people by virtue of the Holy Ghost imparted to him, through which the unintentional man-slayer received the benefits of the propitiation for his sins before God, so that he could return cleansed to his native town without further exposure to the vengeance of the avenger of blood." And thus, it is said, "The death of the earthly high priest became a type of that of the Heavenly One, who through the eternal Spirit offered Himself without spot to God, that we might be redeemed from our transgressions." But although many of the Rabbins and fathers held this view as to the expiatory nature of the high priest's death, there is absolutely nothing in Scripture or reason to support it. All the expiation, moreover, which the Mosaic law provided for was ceremonial. If the death of the high priest was efficacious only so far as his functions were, then there could be no atonement or appearance of atonement for moral guilt, even that of culpable homicide for instance. The death of the high priest was therefore in no sense a type of the death of Christ, the whole meaning of which lies in relation to moral, not ceremonial, offences.

While it cannot be said that "light is thrown by the provisions regarding cities of refuge on the atonement of Christ"—for that would be the morning star shedding light on the sun—still there are some points of illustration; and one of these may be noted. As the protection of the sanctuary city extended only to the boundaries or precincts belonging to it, so the defence the sinner has in Christ can be enjoyed only so far as life is brought within the range of the influence and commands of Christ. He who would be safe must be a Christian. It is not mere profession of faith—" Lord, Lord, have we not prophesied in Thy name?"—but hearty obedience to the laws of duty coming from Christ that gives safety. "Who shall lay any thing to the charge of God's elect?"—and the elect are those who yield the fruit of the Spirit, who are lovers of God and their fellow-men, who show their faith by their works. It is a misrepresentation of the whole teaching of Scripture to declare that salvation can be had, apart from life and practice, in some mystical relation with Christ which is hardly even to be stated in words.

3. TRIBAL INHERITANCE. Already we have heard the appeal of the daughters of Zelophehad to be allowed an inheritance as representing their father. Now a question which has arisen regarding them must be solved. The five women have not cared to undertake the work of the upland farm allotted to them, somewhere about the head waters of the Yarmuk. They have, in fact, as heiresses been somewhat in request among the young men of different tribes; and they are almost on the point of giving their hands to husbands of their choice. But the chiefs of the family of Manasseh to which they belong find a danger here. The young women may perhaps choose men of Gad, or men of Judah. Then their land, which is part of the land of Manasseh, will go over to the tribes of the husbands. There will be a few acres of Judah or of Gad in the north of Manasseh's land. And if other young women throughout the tribes, who happen to be heiresses, marry according to their own liking, by-and-by the tribe territories will be all confused. Is this to be allowed? If not, how is the evil to be prevented?

The national centre and general unity of Israel could not in the early period be expected to suffice. Without tribal coherence and a sense of corporate life in each family the Israelites would be lost among the people of the land. Especially would this tend to take place on the eastern side of Jordan and in the far north. Now the clan unity went with the land. It was as those dwelling in a certain district the descendants of one progenitor realised their brotherhood. Hence there was good reason for the appeal of the Manassites and the legislation that followed. Women who succeeded to land were to marry within the families of their fathers. Men were apparently not forbidden to marry women of another tribe if they were not heiresses. But the possession of land by women carried with it a responsibility and deprived them of a certain part of freedom. Every daughter who had an inheritance was to be wife to one of her near kin; so should no inheritance remove from one family to another; the tribes should cleave every one to his own inheritance.

The exigencies of the early settlement appear to have required this law; and it was maintained as far as possible, so that he who lived in a certain region might know himself not only a Reubenite or a Benjamin as the case might be, but a son of Hanoch of the Reubenites, or a son of Ard among the Benjamites. But we may doubt whether the unity of the nation was not delayed by the means used to keep the land for each tribe and each tribe on its own land. The arrangement was perhaps inevitable; yet it certainly belonged to a primitive social order. The homogeneity of the people would have been helped and the tribes held more closely together by interchange of land. In every law made at an early stage of a people's development there is involved something unsuitable to after periods. And perhaps one error made by the Israelites was to cling too long and too closely to tribal descent and make too much of genealogy. The enactment regarding the marriage of heiresses within their own families was an old one, bearing the authority of Moses. There came a time when it should have been revoked and everything done that was possible to weld the tribes together. But the old customs held; and what was the result? The tribes east of Jordan, as well as Dan and Asher, were well-nigh lost to the Confederacy at an early date. Subsequently a division began between the northern and southern peoples. We cannot doubt that partly for want of family alliances between Judah and Ephraim, and subordination of tribal to national sentiment, there came the separation into two kingdoms.

For the tribe idea and the other of making inheritance of land a governing matter, the Israelites would seem to have paid dearly. And there is danger still in the attempt to make a nation cohere on any mere territorial basis. It is the spirit, the fidelity to a common purpose, and the pervasive enthusiasm that give real unity. If these are wanting, or if the general aim is low and material, the security of families in the soil may be exceedingly mischievous. At the same time the old feeling is proved to have a deep root in fact. Territorial solidarity is indispensable to a nation; and the exclusion of a people from large portions of its land is an evil intolerable. Christianity has not done its work where the Church, the teacher of righteousness, is unconcerned for this great matter. How can religion flourish where brotherhood fails? And how can brotherhood survive in a nation when the right of occupying the soil is practically denied? First among the economic questions which claim Christian settlement is that of land tenure, land right. Christianity carries forward the principles of the Mosaic law into higher ranges, where justice is not less, but more—where brotherhood has a nobler purpose, a finer motive.

The Book of Deuteronomy
By Principal Andrew Harper, M.A., D.D.

DOCTOR HARPER was Professor of Hebrew and Old Testament Exegesis, Ormond College, University of Melbourne, Professor of Hebrew, and later, Principal of St. Andrew's College, University of Sydney. He was one of the brilliant students of Professor A. B. Davidson of New College, to whom he dedicated his exposition on Deuteronomy.

This fifth book of the Bible has been well called "that glorious sermon on the love of God." Doctor Harper deals thoroughly with the many issues relating to faith and loyalty, as dramatically set forth in this comprehensive summary of the Mosaic Law. His historical survey of the origin and development of this Law is the basis for a lucid exposition of Deuteronomy. It offers needed counsel to counteract the dangers, to emphasize the duties, and to multiply the privileges of our own age.

PREFACE

An adequate exposition of Deuteronomy requires the discussion of many topics. The author has endeavoured to keep these various claims in view: at the same time the limits of the volume have dictated selection and compression. In particular, a chapter on miracle in the Old Testament has been wholly omitted. That topic cannot be said to have a peculiar or exclusive relation to Deuteronomy. Yet the writer would have wished to include in the volume a reasoned statement of the grounds on which he owns and asserts the supernatural in Old Testament history; all the more because he admits critical views which have sometimes been associated, and still oftener supposed to be associated, with rationalistic views generally. For the present this discussion is postponed. In some instances, also, the writer has been obliged to content himself with statements on critical questions more brief than he could have desired; but it is hoped that enough has been said to explain the position assumed, and to make clear the main lines of argument.

The task of adjusting the matter to the space would have been easier if it had seemed legitimate to omit the critical and archæological questions on the one hand, or, on the other, to leave untouched the bearing of the thoughts and Laws of Deuteronomy on the religious history of the race, and on the dangers and duties of our own age. But an exposition of Deuteronomy must endeavour to open the appropriate outlooks in all these directions.

CONTENTS

	PAGE
CHAPTER I.	
The Authorship and Age of Deuteronomy,	493
CHAPTER II.	
The Historic Setting of Deuteronomy,	503
CHAPTER III.	
The Divine Government,	505
CHAPTER IV.	
The Decalogue—Its Form,	509
CHAPTER V.	
The Decalogue—Its Substance,	512
CHAPTER VI.	
The Mediatorship of Moses,	521
CHAPTER VII.	
Love to God the Law of Life,	524
CHAPTER VIII.	
Education—Mosaic View,	532
CHAPTER IX.	
The Ban,	538
CHAPTER X.	
The Ban in Modern Life,	542
CHAPTER XI.	
The Bread of the Soul,	547
CHAPTER XII.	
Israel's Election, and Motives for Faithfulness,	551
CHAPTER XIII.	
Law and Religion,	557

	PAGE
CHAPTER XIV.	
Laws of Sacrifice,	561
CHAPTER XV.	
The Relation of Old Testament Sacrifice to Christianity,	565
CHAPTER XVI.	
Laws Against Idolatrous Acts and Customs,	568
CHAPTER XVII.	
The Speakers for God—I. The King,	573
CHAPTER XVIII.	
Speakers for God—II. The Priest,	576
CHAPTER XIX.	
Speakers for God—III. The Prophet,	583
CHAPTER XX.	
The Economic Aspects of Israelite Life,	589
CHAPTER XXI.	
Justice in Israel,	595
CHAPTER XXII.	
Laws of Purity (Chastity and Marriage),	601
CHAPTER XXIII.	
Laws of Kindness,	605
CHAPTER XXIV.	
Moses' Farewell Speeches,	611
CHAPTER XXV.	
The Song and Blessing of Moses,	616
CHAPTER XXVI.	
Moses' Character and Death,	621

THE BOOK OF DEUTERONOMY

BY ANDREW HARPER, B. D.

CHAPTER I.

THE AUTHORSHIP AND AGE OF DEUTERONOMY.

In approaching a book so spiritually great as Deuteronomy, it might seem superfluous to allude to the critical questions which have been raised concerning it. On any supposition as to origin and authorship, its spiritual elevation and the moral impulse it gives are always there; and it might consequently seem sufficient to expound and illustrate the text as we have it. Minute and vexatious inquiry into details, such as any adequate treatment of the critical question demands, tends to draw away the mind in a disastrous way, from the spiritual and moral purpose of the book. That, however, is precisely what the expositor has to elucidate and apply; and so it might seem to be an error in method to enter upon extraneous matters such as those with which criticism has mainly to do.

On the other hand, this has to be taken into account. The truth about the composition of a book, about the authorities it is founded on, about the times in which and the circumstances under which it was composed, if it be attainable, often throws a very welcome light upon the meaning. It clears up obscurities, removes chances of error, and often, when two or three possible paths have opened before us, it shuts us up to the right one. But if that is the case when no special conflict of opinion has arisen, it is much more so when a revolution of opinion concerning the whole religious life of a nation has been caused by the critical view of a book adopted by able men. Now that is plainly the case here. Deuteronomy has been the key of the position, the centre of the conflict, in the battle which has been waged so hotly as to the growth of religion in Israel. The attack upon the views hitherto generally held within the Church in regard to that matter has rested more upon the character and date of Deuteronomy than upon anything else. Consequently every part of the book has been the object of intense and microscopic scrutiny, and there is scarcely a cardinal point in it which must not be regarded differently, according as we accept or reject the strictly Mosaic origin of the book as a whole, or even of the legal portions. The difference is probably never absolutely fundamental. On either supposition, as we have said, the spiritual and moral teaching remains the same; but the mind is apt to be clouded with harassing doubt as to many important points, until clear views on the critical question have been attained. This is felt more or less acutely by all readers of the Old Testament who are touched by recent debates, and they expect that any new exposition shall help them to a clearer view. Many will even demand that some effort in that direction should be made; and, as we think, they rightly demand it.

But there is still another reason for dealing with the questions gathering round the authorship and age of our book, and it is decisive.

The debate concerning the critical views of the Old Testament has reached a stage at which it is no longer confined to the professed teachers and students of the Old Testament. It has filtered down, through magazines first, and then through newspapers, into the public mind, and opinions are becoming current concerning the results of criticism which are so partial and ill-informed that they cannot but produce evil results of a formidable kind in the near future. By those who are sceptically inclined, as well as by those who cling most closely to the teaching of the Churches, it is loudly proclaimed that the acceptance of the critical view—viz. that the Levitical law, as a written code, came into existence after the Exile, and that Deuteronomy, written in the royal period of Israelite history, occupies a middle position between the first legislation (Exod. xx.-xxiii.) and this latest—destroys the character of the Old Testament as a record of Revelation, and undermines Christianity itself. The former class rejoice that this should be so, and think their scepticism is thereby justified. The latter, on the contrary, reject the critical conclusions with vehemence. They have found God through the Scripture, and, resting upon this experience, they turn away from theories which they believe to be in direct conflict with it. To write an exposition of Deuteronomy therefore, without correcting the false impression that the critical view as to its age, etc., is incompatible with faith in a Divine revelation, would be to miss one of the great opportunities which fall to writers on the Old Testament in our day. Questions regarding the age, authorship, and literary form of the books of Scripture cannot ultimately be so decided as to nullify the testimony borne to them by the experience of so many generations of Christian men and women. Whatever makes itself ultimately credible to the human mind in regard to such matters, will always be capable of being held along with a belief in the manifestation of Himself which God has given in the history and literature of Israel. But nothing will make that fact so readily apprehensible, nothing will make it stand out so clearly, as an exposition of a book like Deuteronomy, which takes account of all that seems established in the critical view. Even the most extreme critical positions, when separated from the totally irrelevant assumption (which too often accompanies them) that miracle is unhistorical, are compatible with a real faith in Revelation and Inspiration. It is not the fact of Revelation, but the common conception of its method, which is challenged by the critical theories. We shall therefore only try to meet a clamant need of our time, if we take with us into the explanation of the Deuteronomic teaching a definite conclusion as to the authorship, age, and literary character of the book.

As regards authorship, the ordinary opinion still is that Deuteronomy was written by Moses. This was the view handed over to Christianity in pre-critical ages by the Jews, and accepted as the natural one. But if the Mosaic authorship of the whole contents of the other books of the Pentateuch is now given up, much more should it be given up in the case of Deuteronomy. For Deuteronomy does not even claim to be written by Moses. It is not merely that in it Moses is often spoken of in the third person; that, if it were carried out consistently, as it is, for instance, in Cæsar's Commentaries, would be compatible with Mosaic authorship. But what we find is that the author, "whenever he speaks himself, purports to give a description in the third person of what Moses did or said," * while Moses, when he speaks, always uses the first person. The book, consequently, falls naturally into two portions: the subsidiary, introductory framework of statement, in which Moses is always spoken of in the third person, together with the historical portions and the utterances of Moses himself, which these introduce and hold together, and in which Moses always uses the first person.† Again, wherever the expression "beyond Jordan" is used in the portions where the author speaks for himself, it signifies the land of Moab.‡ Wherever, on the contrary, Moses is introduced speaking in the first person, "beyond Jordan" denotes the land of Israel.§ The only exception is iii. 8, where at the beginning of a long archæological note, which cannot have originally formed part of the speech of Moses, and consequently must be a comment of the writer, or of a later editor of Deuteronomy, "beyond Jordan" signifies the land of Moab. If, consequently, the book be taken at its word, there can be no doubt that it professes to be an account of what Moses did and said on a certain day in the land of Moab, before his death, written by another person, who lived to the west of the Jordan. The author must consequently have lived after Moses' day; and he has taken pains by his use of language to distinguish himself from Moses in a most unmistakable way. It is no doubt possible, though not probable, that Moses might have written of himself in the third person in the connecting passages, and in the first person in the remainder of his book: but that he should have made the anxious distinction we have seen as to the phrase "beyond Jordan" does not seem possible.

But if our book, as we have it, is not by Moses, but is an account by another person of what Moses did and said on a certain occasion, that fact has a very important bearing upon the speeches reported as Mosaic. For the style of the whole book up to the end of the twenty-eighth chapter is, for all practical purposes, one. The parts where the author speaks, and the parts where Moses speaks, are all alike in style, and that style is in all respects different from the style of the speeches attributed to Moses in other parts of the Pentateuch. Consequently we cannot accept the speeches and laws as being in the very words of Moses. They may contain the exact ideas of Moses, but these have manifestly passed through the mind and clothed themselves in the vocabulary of the author of Deuteronomy. Even Delitzsch is quite decisive on this point.‖ In the tenth of his "Pentateuch Kritische Studien" after distinguishing the Deuteronomist from Moses, he continues thus: "The addresses are freely reproduced, and he who reproduces them is the same who also contributed the historical framework and the historical details between the addresses. The same colouring, though in a less degree, may also be remarked in the repetition of the law in chapters xii.-xxvi. to which the book owes its name. All the component parts of Deuteronomy, not excepting the legal prescriptions, are woven through and through with the favourite phrases of the Deuteronomist."

Under these circumstances, the question immediately suggests itself to what degree this representation of Moses' legislation can be regarded as purely and unmixedly Mosaic. Was this legislation given in the main or entirely by Moses, and, if it was so given, may there not be mingled with what he gave inferences drawn by the author in whose style the book is written, and adaptations demanded by the exigencies of his later times? A full discussion of this point would, of course, be out of the question here, and it would, moreover, be superfluous. In Dr. Driver's article on "Deuteronomy" in Smith's "Dictionary of the Bible," and in his "Introduction to Hebrew Literature," detailed discussions will be found. All that is necessary here is that one or two large and salient aspects of the question should be looked at.

In the first place, it is important to know whether the author of Deuteronomy can have been a contemporary of Moses, or a younger contemporary of his contemporaries. If he were, the relation between the speeches and legislation in his book and that which Moses actually uttered would be similar to that between the speeches of Christ reported by St. John in his Gospel and the actual words of our Lord. They might, in fact, be taken to be in all respects a reliable, though not a verbal, representation of what Moses actually said or commanded. If, on the contrary, it should be proved, either from the character of the legislation itself, or from the evidence we have as to the date of the authorities whom the Deuteronomist quotes, and upon whom he relies, that he must have lived centuries later, then any such confidence would be materially weakened. Now there can be no doubt, to take the last point first, that Deuteronomy, taken as a legal code, though not wanting in laws which have been first formulated by its author, is mainly intended to be a repetition and a reinforcement of what we find in the book of the Covenant (Exod. xx.-xxiii.). The result of Driver's careful tabulation of the subjects dealt with in the two codes is "that the laws in JE,* viz. Exod. xx.-xxiii. (repeated partially in xxxiv. 10-26) and the kindred section xiii. 3-16, *form the foundations of the Deuteronomic legislation.* This is evident as well from the numerous verbal coincidences as from the fact that nearly the whole ground covered by Exod.

---

* Driver, "Introduction," 5th Ed., p. 84.
† Cf. Deut. i. 1-5, iv. 41-43, iv. 44, v. 1, xxvii. 1, 9-11, xxix. 1, xxxi. 1-30.
‡ Cf. Deut. i. 1, 5, iv. 41, 46, 47, 49.
§ iii. 20, 25, and xi. 30.
‖ Cf. "Pentateuch Kritische Studien," in Luthardt's *Zeitschrift,* 1880.

* It is scarcely necessary to remind readers that, from the point of view of the critics, J signifies one of the constituent documents of the Pentateuch which uses the name Yahweh for God. Its date is about 850 B.C. E is that document which uses the name Elohim, and may be dated about the same period as J. D is the author of Deuteronomy, who wrote, it is supposed, in the reign of Manasseh, perhaps about 670 B.C. P is the Priestly document, which Dillmann dates before Deuteronomy, but which most critics think was brought substantially into its present shape by Ezra. The portions of the Pentateuch assigned to these various documents will be found in Driver's "Introduction."

xx.-xxiii. is included in it; almost the only exception being the special compensations to be paid for various injuries (Exod. xxi. 18, xxii. 15), which would be less necessary in a manual intended for the people." This is also the conclusion of other scholars, and indeed is plainly demanded by the facts. It is, moreover, what may be called the Biblical hypothesis, for Moses is supposed to have been renewing the covenant made at Horeb, and repeating its conditions.

But in the present condition of our knowledge, the fact of Deuteronomy's dependence upon the Book of the Covenant brings into view unexpected consequences. It is true, certainly, that the laws of the latter code existed before they were incorporated in the text where we now find them. Consequently no verbal coincidences would give us the assurance that the Deuteronomist had before him the actual book in which these laws have come down to us. But a conclusion may be reached in another way. A comparison of the historical portions of Deuteronomy with the corresponding narrative in the previous four books of our Bible shows that for his history also the author of Deuteronomy relies upon these earlier narratives, and that he must have had portions at least of them before him in the same text as we have now. The verbal coincidences tabulated in Driver, pp. 75 f., as well as the general and exact agreement in the events recorded in Deuteronomy with those recorded in the earlier books, show that the author has not only drawn his information from the same sources as those of the earlier books, but that he must have had before him at least that section which contains the laws.

Now, as it happens, in the course of the analysis of the Pentateuch it has come to be all but universally acknowledged that Exod. xx.-xxiii. form part of a document which can be traced, dovetailed into others, from Genesis to Joshua, and perhaps beyond it. This document has been called by Wellhausen the Jehovist document, and in all critical books it is referred to as JE, as being made up of two sections, one of which uses Yahweh for the Divine name, and the other Elohim. The only generally known scholar who denies the existence of JE is Professor Green, of Princeton in America, who, rightly enough, sees that the Mosaic authorship of the Pentateuch cannot be held, if these separate component documents are acknowledged. But the separate existence and character of JE may be regarded as demonstrated, and also that it has been interwoven with another narrative, largely parallel, but which deals of preference with priestly matters, and has consequently been called the Priest codex, or P. Together these make up the first four books of the Pentateuch; and the remarkable thing is that, both as regards law and history, Deuteronomy is dependent upon JE. "Throughout the parallels just tabulated," says Driver,* "(as well as in the others occurring in the book), not the allusions only, but the words cited, will be found, all but uniformly, to be in JE, not in P. An important conclusion follows from this fact. Inasmuch as, in our existing Pentateuch, JE and P repeatedly cross one another, the constant absence of any reference to P can only be reasonably explained by one supposition, viz. that when Deuteronomy was composed JE and P were not yet united into a single work, and JE alone formed the basis of Deuteronomy." And this is not Driver's conclusion only. Dillmann, who argues with splendid ability against Wellhausen for the dating of P in the ninth century B. C. instead of after the Exile, and consequently considers that it was in existence before Deuteronomy, still holds that in general JE is the Deuteronomist's authority both for law and history, contenting himself with affirming that D shows undoubted acquaintance with laws, etc., known *to us* only in P. Clearly, therefore, Deuteronomy must have been written after JE had been made public, or at least after J and E had been written.

The question therefore arises, what is their date? An answer can be gradually approached in this way. As JE reappear as an element in the Book of Joshua,* and contribute to it an account of Joshua's death and burial, they cannot have been written by him, nor before his death. That is the first fixed point. Then we may proceed a step further. In various parts of JE there occur phrases which cannot all be later glosses, and which imply that the land, when the writer lived, had long ceased to be in possession of the Canaanites, if some of them do not even presuppose a time when the original inhabitants had been absorbed into Israel, as Solomon attempted to absorb them by making them slaves of the State. Such passages are Gen. xii. 6. "And the Canaanite was then in the land"; Gen. xiii. 7, "Moreover the Canaanites and the Perizzites dwelled then in the land"; Gen. xl. 15, in which Joseph says of himself, "I was stolen away out of the land of the Hebrews," a name which the country could not have acquired till some little time at least after the conquest. Further, in Numbers xxxii. 41, which belongs to J or E, probably the latter, we have an account of the rise of the name Hawwoth Jair. Now in Judges x. 3-5 we are informed that the Jair from whom the Hawwoth Jair had their name was a judge in Israel after the time of Abimelech, who made new conquests for his tribe east of the Jordan. Unless, therefore, the unlikely hypothesis be accepted that both the district bearing this name in Judges and its conqueror are other than those mentioned in Numbers, the verse brings down JE at least to the period of Abimelech, which Kautzsch in his "View of the History of the Israelites," appended to his translation of the Old Testament, states as about 1120 B. C., *i. e.*, two hundred years after the Exodus.

The next step is suggested by Gen. xxxvi. 31-39, a passage from JE in which a list of Edomite kings is given with this heading: "These are the kings that reigned in the land of Edom before there reigned any king over the children of Israel." That sentence clearly cannot have been written before kings arose in Israel; consequently JE must be later than the days of Saul, and probably than David, since the Israelite kingship appears to the author's mind here as a firmly established institution. The author of Deuteronomy must have lived and written at a still later date, and we are thus gradually brought down to the time of Solomon, or perhaps even later.

And the literary indications of date confirm this conclusion. For instance, two books are quoted occasionally in JE as authorities, which must consequently have existed before that work

---

* Driver, "Introduction," p. 76.

* Josh. xxiv. 30.

—the Book of the Wars of Yahweh (Numb. xxi. 14, 15), and the Book of Yashar (Josh. x. 12 f.). The former has indeed been declared by Geiger to be the product of false punctuation; but soberer critics have accepted it and date it in Solomon's day. However that may be, there can be no doubt that the latter actually existed, and was probably a collection of songs, since from it the verses describing the standing still of the sun and moon are quoted. But we learn from 2 Sam. i. 18 that David's beautiful lament for Saul and Jonathan was contained in this book, and was quoted from it by the sacred historian. The book must therefore have been compiled, or at least completed, after David's lament. As it was manifestly a compilation, and the poems it contained may have been of very various ages, much stress in our search for dates cannot be laid upon it. It is still of some weight, however, that this post-Davidic book is quoted by JE; so far as it goes, that fact confirms the conclusion arrived at from other indications.

In the same way, the linguistic indications, though not of themselves conclusive, point towards the same period. It is, of course, true that we are as yet far from having a general agreement as to the history of the Hebrew language. That can only be established along with the history of the Hebrew literature and the Hebrew people; and perhaps we never shall be able to fix any definite stages in the growth and decay of the language. Nevertheless no careful reader of JE will deny what Professor Driver says regarding them: "Both belong to the golden period of Hebrew literature. They resemble the best parts of Judges and Samuel (much of which cannot be greatly later than David's own time); but whether they are actually earlier or later than these, the language and style do not enable us to say. There is at least no *archaic* flavour perceptible in the style of JE."* That is an admirably balanced judgment, and we may rely upon the indication it gives as an additional confirmation of what we have already seen to be probable.

It is impossible that these various lines of inquiry should converge, as they have done, towards the early centuries of the kingship as the date of JE, if Moses had written Deuteronomy, in which JE is drawn upon at every moment. We may consequently dismiss that view finally, and admit that the author of Deuteronomy cannot well have written before the middle of the kingly period. But we have still to inquire what the character of the Mosaic speeches and the Mosaic writings given in Deuteronomy is in that case. Had the author lived and written near the time of Moses, we might, as has been said, have accepted them as the Church generally accepts the Johannine speeches of Christ. But if the Deuteronomist wrote four, or five, or six centuries after Moses, what are we to say? In one view it must be granted that his account may be as accurate as if it had been written within fifty years of Moses' death. For an author of our own day, by keeping close to original written authorities, and strenuously endeavouring to keep out of his mind any information he may have as to later times, may reproduce with marvellous correctness the actual state of things, as regards law and other departments of public life, which existed in England, say, five hundred years ago. Similarly the author of Deuteronomy *may* have handed on to us, without flaw or defect, the information as to Moses' sayings and doings in the plains of Moab which he had received from the written accounts of Moses' contemporaries. He may have done so; but when we consider that his authorities may have been in part not much earlier than his own time, that the critical sifting of history was then unknown, and finally and most important of all, that the Deuteronomist has hortatory much more than purely historical aims, we cannot evade the question whether a good deal that is here set down to Moses may not turn out to be additions to and deductions from the original Mosaic germs of law, made by inspired lawgivers and prophets who took up and carried on Moses' work. Many assert that this is so, and we must face and try to settle the question they raise.

The theory held by those who most strenuously deny this assertion is that all the laws in the Pentateuch are Mosaic in the strict sense, that the codes were given by Moses in the order in which they now stand in the Pentateuch, and that they were enacted with all their modifications in a period of not more than forty years, all of which was spent in the desert. In order to ascertain whether this view is tenable, we shall take one or two of the more important matters, such as the place of worship, the agents of worship, and the support of the cultus; and we shall compare the provisions of the various codes in order to see whether they can be supposed to belong to so short a period, or to have been all enacted by one man.

Let us take first the place of worship. The three codes—that called the Book of the Covenant (Exod. xx.-xxiii.), that contained in Leviticus and Numbers and called the Levitical code, and that in Deuteronomy—all contain directions about this. In the first the prescriptions are (Exod. xx. 24): "An altar of earth shalt thou make to Me, and thou shalt sacrifice upon it thy burnt offerings and thy peace offerings, thy sheep and thy oxen. In every place where I cause My name to be remembered I will come unto and bless thee." In the Levitical law "the altar" is to be of Shittim or acacia wood overlaid with copper, and the place for it is to be in the court of the Tabernacle. There all sacrifices are to be offered, and thither every slaughtered animal is to be brought (Lev. xvii. 1 ff.), and this is to be a statute for ever unto them throughout their generations. In Deuteronomy again (chap. xii.) it is enacted that all sacrifices are to be brought "unto the place which Yahweh your God shall choose out of all your tribes to put His name there," and ver. 21, "If the place which Yahweh thy God hath chosen to put His name there be too far from thee, then thou shalt kill of thy herd and of thy flock" and eat them as game was eaten without bringing it to the Sanctuary. But Moses is not represented as ordering this law to be introduced immediately. It is only when they go over Jordan and dwell in the land which Yahweh their God giveth them, and when He giveth them rest from all their enemies round about so that they dwell in safety, that they are to do this. Nay, according to ver. 20 the new order is to be fully introduced only when Yahweh their God shall enlarge their border as He had promised, *i. e.*, when their boundaries should

* "Introduction," p. 117.

be (xi. 24) the wilderness on the south and Lebanon on the north, the Euphrates on the east and the Mediterranean on the west. Now these boundaries were attained only in David's day, and the rest from all their enemies round about was, as Dillmann says, given as a matter of fact only in the times of David and Solomon (*cf.* 2 Sam. vii. 11 and 1 Kings v. 18), notwithstanding Josh xxi. 42. Consequently the Temple at Jerusalem must have been the place referred to. This is distinctly the view of 1 Kings iii. 3 and viii. 16. The latter passage is peculiarly emphatic. Solomon says, at the dedication of the Temple, "Since the day that I brought forth My people Israel out of Egypt, I chose no city out of all the tribes of Israel to build an house that My name might be therein." The Deuteronomic view consequently is that the law requiring sacrifice at *one* sole altar was intended by Moses to be enforced only after the Temple at Jerusalem had been built.

These are the provisions of the three codes. Can they have been the successive ordinances of a man legislating under the influence of Divine inspiration within a period of less than forty years? Let us see. The first legislation was given at Sinai, in the third month after the Exodus: the Levitical legislation on the matter was given about nine months later when the Tabernacle was finished, and during that time they had not removed from Sinai: thirty-eight years afterward the Deuteronomic code was given in the plains of Moab. Let us look at the character of the legislation given first of all at Sinai. The meaning of the decisive phrase, "In every place where I cause My name to be remembered I will come unto thee and bless thee," has been much discussed; yet taken as it stands, without reference to laws which on any supposition are later, it cannot mean that sacrifices were to be offered only at one central shrine. It specially provides for sacrifices being offered at different places, but restricts them to places which Yahweh Himself has chosen. At every such place He promises to come to them and bless them. So much, men of all schools admit; difference of opinion arises only as to whether these places are meant to be successive, or whether they may be simultaneous. The view of those who accept all the legislation of the Pentateuch as Mosaic in the strict sense is that the places could only be successive, since otherwise the words would imply that originally worship at one altar was not prescribed. Delitzsch, for example, maintains that these words imply necessarily only this, that the place of sacrifice would, in the course of time, be altered by Divine appointment, and he declares that to be their meaning. Others, again, suppose that the command was meant only to justify worship at the various places where the Tabernacle was called to halt on the people's journeyings, whether in the wilderness or in Palestine. Now it cannot be denied that only on some such interpretation can Exodus be brought into harmony with Leviticus, and that undoubtedly has influenced, and rightly so, the scholars who take this view. If it were tenable it would be by far the most satisfactory interpretation. But it can hardly be considered tenable if we look at the time at which this law was given. There was as yet no other law, and this was given as soon as the people came to Mount Sinai. The law in Leviticus was not on any supposition given till nine months later. Now, if Exod. xx. 24 was meant for immediate use only, and was superseded by the Levitical law after so short a time, it is difficult to understand why it was given, and still more difficult to conceive why it was preserved. In any case it cannot have been understood to command worship at only one place. It could have no other sense than that the people, so long as they were at Sinai, were to sacrifice only at Sinai where Yahweh had revealed Himself, or at other places in the neighbourhood which He should sanctify, or had sanctified, by revealing His presence at them. At any such place, if there He had once revealed Himself, He would continue to meet them. Without the colour thrown upon them by succeeding laws, that is surely the only meaning that *could* be put upon the words, and so understood they undoubtedly authorise sacrifice at two or more places simultaneously. If, on the other hand, this law was meant more for the future than the present, as some of the laws in the Book of the Covenant undoubtedly were, it must have been intended to be in force concurrently with Lev. i. f. But if so, the " places " it refers to cannot be the mere halting-places on the wilderness journey. No doubt these were determined by Yahweh, and the tabernacle was set up at places He may be said to have chosen, but the places themselves were of no consequence at all. The Divine presence is declared to be always in the Tabernacle. That was certainly a place where Yahweh caused His name to be remembered, and without further inquiry about place, the men of Israel knew that He would always meet them and bless them in sacrifice there. The different character of the altar in the Book of the Covenant too, a mere heap of earth or unhewn stone, and that in the Tabernacle, made of acacia wood overlaid with copper, corroborates the view that the altar aimed at in Exod. xxiv. is not the Tabernacle altar. The only coherent view, on the supposition of the concurrence of the two laws, is therefore that while, as a rule, sacrifice was to be offered at the Tabernacle, yet if the people came to any place where Yahweh had caused His name to be remembered, sacrifice might be offered there on an altar of earth or unhewn stone, as well as at the Tabernacle. Either way therefore there is permission to worship at more than one place. But then the difficulty is that Leviticus appears to denounce upon pain of being " cut off from the people " absolutely every sacrifice not offered at the Tabernacle.

Now if so far matters have been far from clear on the traditional supposition of the date and order of these codes, a glance at Deuteronomy will produce absolute confusion in every mind. As we have seen, Deuteronomy represents Moses as restricting sacrifice most rigorously to one altar after the building of the Temple at Jerusalem, but virtually declaring that worship at various shrines was to be blameless until that time. We have also seen that that is the view taken by the author of the Book of Kings. Now this might be regarded as a temporary relaxation of the law, intended to meet the difficult circumstances of a period of war and conquest, were it not for one thing. That is, that Moses in Deut. xii. 8, after prescribing worship at one altar, adds, " Ye shall not do after all that *we* do here this day, every man whatsoever is right in his own eyes," and as if to render mistake as to the meaning impossible, in ver. 13 he explains ver. 8 thus: "Take heed to thyself that thou offer not thy burnt offerings in every place that thou seest." Notwithstanding the efforts of conservative scholars like Keil and Bredenkamp to explain ver. 8 as a reference to the intermissions in, *e. g.*, the daily sacrifice, brought about by the desert wanderings, or to the arbitrariness and illegality of the generation which had brought judgment upon themselves by refusal to obey Yahweh in attacking Canaan, it still seems impossible to accept that view. Of course if we knew that Moses was the giver of all these laws, these words would have to be explained away in some such fashion. But if they are approached by an inquirer seeking to discover whether they all are Mosaic, sound exegesis demands that they should be taken as Dillmann and others take them. In the plain sense of words Moses here admits that, up till the time at which he is speaking, sacrifices were offered wherever men chose, and that he had participated in the practice. And observe, he does not refer to the Levitical law. He does not say this conduct of ours is a sin which we must repent of and turn from at once. He calmly permits this state of things to continue after Israel is in Canaan, and looks forward with equanimity to its continuance till the Temple shall be erected in Jerusalem. With this passage before us we ask, Can this be the same inspired legislator who thirty-eight years before compelled sacrifice at one central altar on pain of death?

The traditional hypothesis being thus encompassed with difficulties, students of the Old Testament have sought another which would correspond better with all the data. Relying upon the fact that the author of Deuteronomy founds his book almost entirely on JE, and that if he knows some of the laws and some of the facts mentioned in P only, there are no proofs that he knew that book as we have it, they put it aside in this matter also. Immediately, when that is done, light breaks in upon our problem. If we take Exod. xxiv. 20 in the natural sense given to it above, sacrifice at various altars was permitted from Sinai onwards, the only limitation being that there should have been, at the place chosen, authentic proof of a theophany or some other manifestation of the Divine presence. That is the state of things out of which Moses speaks in Deuteronomy. It will be noticed, however, that there is a slight contradiction of Exod. xx. 24. The Moses of Deuteronomy speaks as if every man's arbitrary choice had been his only guide. Probably, however, with his mind full of the stringent unity he desires to see, he speaks hyperbolically of the looseness of the former law, and means nothing else than the practice prescribed by it. In all ways this view is supported by the history. From the patriarchs till the time of Samuel, the practice was to sacrifice at various altars.* Consequently, according to both the Book of the Covenant and Deuteronomy, and according to the history, the worship of Yahweh at sacred places throughout the land was legal, until the Temple was erected at Jerusalem. The centralisation of worship was, consequently, a new thing when the division of the kingdoms took place, and was not an express law till Deuteronomy. If that book was not written till perhaps Hezekiah's day, the fact will account as nothing else will do for Elijah's words (1 Kings xix. 10), "The children of Israel have forsaken Thy covenant, thrown down Thine altars, and slain Thy prophets with the sword." Even in the presence of Yahweh he, without rebuke, calls the altars in the Northern Kingdom His.

The first attempt we know of to centralise worship was made by Hezekiah; a second and more strenuous attempt was made under Josiah, but the work was not actually accomplished till after the Return from the Captivity. All the facts taken together suggest that the movement towards centralisation was an age-long development. At first all holy places might be sacrificed at, though a certain primacy belonged to a central sanctuary, and this may have been stamped by Moses with approval. When the Solomonic Temple was built the primacy began to take the form of a claim for exclusive validity. The experiences in both kingdoms strengthened that claim, by showing that if Yahwism was to be kept pure the worship at the High Places must be abolished. The inspired writer of Deuteronomy then completed Moses' work by embodying that which had been always a tendency of the Mosaic system, and had now become a necessity, in his revisal of the Mosaic legislation. This was adopted by the nation under Josiah, and the Priest Codex must in that case represent a later stage of the development, when the centralisation was neither a tendency nor a demand, but a realised fact. Such a process accounts much better for the facts than the traditional belief; and though it is not free from difficulties it at least releases us from the confusion of mind which the ordinary supposition forces upon us.

The inquiry as to the agents of the cultus need not detain us so long. In the Book of the Covenant no priests are mentioned at all. The person addressed, the "thou" of these chapters, which is either the individual Israelite or the whole community, has been held by some to indicate that the individual offerer was the only agent in sacrifice. But that is to press the word too far. Even in Leviticus, while the whole people are addressed, the actions enjoined or prohibited are such as are done by "any man of them," and in Deut. xii. 13 we have precisely the same expression, "Take heed to thyself that thou offer not thy burnt offerings in every place that thou seest," used at a time when there was undeniably a priestly tribe and even the High Places had a regular priesthood. But while in Exod. xx.-xxiii. there is no evidence to show whether a priesthood existed, in the previous chapter (xix. 22, 24) priests who "come near to Yahweh" are twice mentioned. This would be a fact of the first importance were it not that the words occur in a passage which is admitted to be in its present shape the work of the later editor. Dillmann maintains, and with good reason, that he has inserted and adapted here a fragment of J. If so, then J may have held the view that there were priests before Sinai was reached, but under the circumstances we cannot be certain that the mention of them may not be an anachronism introduced by the later hand. In favour of the view that it is so is the fact that in the account given by JE of the ratification of the Covenant between Yahweh and the people (Exod. xxiv. 1 ff.), Moses erected an altar and then "sent the young men of the children of Israel which offered burnt offerings and sacri-

---

* *Cf.* for the passages on which this statement is founded Driver's "Introduction," p. 80, and note in small print.

ficed peace-offerings of oxen unto Yahweh." He himself however performed the specially priestly act of sprinkling the blood upon the altar. Had there been priests or Levites accustomed to perform priestly functions, we should have expected them to act, instead of "the young men of the children of Israel." But, on the other hand, we must not omit to notice that the Levites occupy in all these transactions, as narrated by JE, a very prominent position. Dillmann,* as we have seen, separating J and E, considers that the passages in which priests before the Sinaitic legislation are spoken of belong to J, and adds: "Indeed, it appears from Exod. iv. 14, 'Is not Aaron the Levite thy brother?' and xxiv. 1, 9, that for him even then the Levites were the priestly persons." To these passages Driver adds Exod. xviii. 12: "And Jethro, Moses' father-in-law, took a burnt offering and sacrifices for God; and Aaron came, and all the elders of Israel, to eat bread with Moses' father-in-law before God." Further, Nadab and Abihu are Levites, nay, sons of Aaron, and in Exod. xxiv. 1 and 9 they go with Moses, Aaron, and the seventy elders as the complete representation of the people, and Moses, himself a Levite, performs all the greater priestly acts.† Moreover JE knows of the ark, and speaks frequently of the "tent of meeting" (Exod. xxxiii. 7 ff.; Numb. xi. 24 f., xii. 4 ff. and Deut. xxxi. 14 ff.). But a very notable thing in connection with the inquiry as to the performers of priestly duties appears in Exod. xxxiii. 7 ff., where E's account of the "tent of meeting" is given. When Moses turned again into the camp "his minister (*mesharetho*) Joshua, the son of Nun, a young man, departed not out of the tent," yet Joshua was an Ephraimite (1 Chron. vii. 22-27). In Exod. xxxii. 29, however, the same authority describes the consecration of the Levites to the priesthood, after the apostasy of the golden calf.

In Deuteronomy, on the contrary, the priests are very prominent; they are called, however, the Levitical priests, or priests simply, but never sons of Aaron. The whole tribe of Levi is regarded as priestly in some sense. They constitute, in fact, a clerical order, though there are clear indications of ranks, of men being assigned to special duties. Curiously enough, the tribe thus highly honoured is spoken of as being notoriously and all but universally poor. No sacrifice can legitimately be offered without them; and, though the question of the place of sacrifice has not yet been finally settled, the position of the Levitical priests as sacrificers is so entirely established that it is regarded as needing neither assertion nor justification. Nay, in one passage, Deut. x. 6—which there is no valid reason, except the wish to get rid of its contents, for supposing to belong to another authority than D ‡—the hereditary succession to the chief place among the priesthood is assigned to the family of Aaron. In xviii. 5 also the hereditary character of the priesthood is asserted in the words, "For Yahweh thy God hath chosen him—*i. e.*, the priest—out of all thy tribes, to stand to minister in the name of Yahweh, *him and his sons for ever.*" As for the body of the Levites, their position is somewhat ill-defined. On the authority of xviii. 6 ff. many claim that at the date of Deuteronomy every Levite was, at least potentially, a priest, that in fact Levite and priest were synonymous. But, as will appear in the exposition of the verses referred to, that is a very questionable proposition. Nevertheless it cannot be denied that in Deuteronomy the line between priests and Levites is a very indistinct one; there is *prima facie* reason to believe that it could be passed, and the gap between the two is certainly not nearly so wide as it appears to be in the undeniably post-exilic literature.

In the Priest Codex again, the priesthood is confined exclusively to the house of Aaron, with the high priest at their head. The Levites have no possible way of entrance into the priesthood. They are Yahweh's gift to the priests, and are confined most strictly to the duty of waiting upon these in the ministration of the Sanctuary. They have none but the most subordinate share in the sacrifices; they are shut out from the holy places of the Tabernacle; and they have assigned to them cities in which they may dwell together when they are not on duty at the Sanctuary. There is no word there of Levites being poor, and altogether the position of the tribe is, through the priests, much more dignified and prosperous in a worldly sense than we found it to be in Deuteronomy.

Now, taking all these data together, we find here, just as we did in the previous section, that the Levitical law is a disturbing element between Exodus and Deuteronomy. If we take it out of the way, J, E, and D harmonise well enough. The main difference is that the latter shows the same fundamental conditions as we find in the former, only consolidated and developed by time, but by a longer time than forty years. In fact D makes explicit that importance of the Levites which is only hinted at and foreshadowed in JE. They have come to be the only authorised agents of sacrifice; they have a hereditary headship in the house of Aaron; various orders and degrees must be held to exist (*cf.* Deut. xviii. 1 ff.). Compared with this state of things, the Levitical arrangements of P, supposed to have been given thirty-eight years before, are very different. In every respect they are more definite, more detailed, and show a much more differentiated organisation than those sketched in Deuteronomy. These latter indicate a state of matters which would suit admirably as an embryonic stage of the full-grown Levitical system, and which can hardly be fitted into their place otherwise.

It is suggested, in reply, that allusions in Deuteronomy *imply* the existence of a system of a much more elaborate kind than any that we could construct from the explicit statements of the book, and that is certainly true. But no reasonable interpretation of these allusions can lead us to a system identical with that in P. Nor can Deuteronomy's use of the name Levites (though undoubtedly it has been pressed by some too far) be held to be consistent with the public recognition of the "great gulf fixed" in P between the Aaronic priests and the Levites as a body. Nor will the fact that Deuteronomy is the people's book, and is consequently not called upon to go into technical details, cover the difference. Indeed nothing will, short of recognising the fact that, as publicly acknowledged organisations, the tribe of Levi in P and the tribe

---
* Dillmann, "Exodus and Leviticus," p. 199.
† Josh. iii. 14-17 and *passim*.
‡ Driver, "Introduction," p. 145; Oettli, "Deuteronomy," p. 7; Kuenen, "H.K.O.," p. 113.

of Levi in D are different, and that the state of things in D's day is earlier than that in P. If this is not so, then the Levitical legislation, conceived as given by Moses, must be held to have proved impracticable, and Deuteronomy must then be regarded as an abrogation of it for the time.

And the same conclusions suggest themselves if we look more closely into the curious fact that Deuteronomy always speaks of the Levites as poor. Some have supposed that this poverty is the result of the centralisation of the cultus which the author demands, and that the constant insistence that the Levite shall be invited to all sacrificial feasts, along with the widow and the orphan, and other helpless classes, is a provision against the poverty to be brought upon them by the abolition of the High Places. But that is not so. We know the manner of the Deuteronomist when he is providing for contingencies arising from the new state of things he wishes to bring about, and it is quite different from his manner here. Clearly, the Levites were poor before the suppression of the High Places, and were so, as Deuteronomy tells us, from the fact that they had no inheritance in the land. But that poverty is not consistent with their whole position as sketched in the Levitical legislation. There we have the Levites launched as a regularly organised priestly corporation, endowed with ample revenues, and ruled and represented by a high priest of the family of Aaron, clothed with powers almost royal, surrounded by a priestly nobility of his own family and by a bodyguard of tribesmen entirely at his disposal. Such a body never has remained chronically and notoriously poor. In the wilderness they would not be so in contrast with others, for all were poor, and there was nothing to hinder the Levites having cattle as the other tribes had, and being on the same level as they. In the promised land, instead of becoming poor, they would at once enter upon the enjoyment of their various tithes and dues, and would moreover have such a share in the booty of Canaan as would more than make up at first for their want of a heritage. The priests were to receive one five-hundredth part of the army's half, and the Levites the fiftieth share of the people's half (Numb. xxxi. 28 ff.). Gradually, too, they would be put in possession of the priestly cities. Evidently, therefore, if the Levites were ever poor, it cannot have been till some time after Israel had been settled in the land, and then only if P's laws and organisations of the tribe were not enforced.

Deuteronomy supports the same argument. Since want of a heritage was the cause of the Levites' poverty, they cannot have been *exceptionally* poor in the wilderness. Nor can they have been poor during the time of the conquest; for even if the Levitical law was in force and the tribe was then wholly organised for the priesthood, they must have shared in the fighting and the spoil. But if the order of legislation, as we maintain, was (1) Exodus xx.-xxiii., (2) Deuteronomy, (3) the Priest Codex, then as the booty from war ceased to be a source of income, the Levites as a body remaining nomads, while the other tribes became agricultural, would necessarily become poor in comparison with their fellow-countrymen. It is out of that state of things the Deuteronomist speaks.*

* See further in exposition of chapter xvii.; xviii.

The same conclusions follow when the regulations are examined which bear upon the support of the priestly tribe. The outstanding matters in this department are tithes and firstlings. Space will not admit of a full discussion of these topics, but if the reader will compare, in regard to tithes, Numb. xviii. 21-24 and Lev. xxvii. 30, 32, with Deut. xii. 17, and in regard to firstlings Numb. xviii. 18 with Deut. xii. 6, 17 f., and xv. 19 f., he will see that the application of tithes and of firstlings according to Deuteronomy is quite different from that in the Levitical legislation. The difference is such as will not comport with the hypothesis of a single legislator and a consistent legislation. Expedients with a view to solve the difficulty have been suggested by Keil and others; but each of those expedients is burdened with specific difficulties of its own.

The inevitable conclusion from all this would seem to be that in the Deuteronomic as in the Levitical laws we have not the legislation of Moses or of his age alone. The roots of all the legislative codes are Mosaic, but in all save perhaps the Book of the Covenant the trunk and branches are of much later growth. The authors of them are not careful to distinguish what came from Moses himself from that which had been developed out of it under the influence of the same inspiration. In both D and P there were Mosaic elements, and in both there are laws not given by him. To disentangle these completely now is impossible, and it is probably best for expository purposes to take the codes as giving what the Mosaic legislation had become at the time of the writer. What we have in Deuteronomy therefore cannot be better described than in Driver's words ("Introduction," p. 85), as "the prophetic re-formulation and adaptation to new needs of an older legislation." Its relations to the other codes are as the same critic states (p. 71): "It is an *expansion* of that in JE (Exod. xx.-xxiii.); it is, in several features, *parallel* to that in Lev. xvii.-xxvi.; it contains *allusions* to laws such as those codified in some parts of P, while from those contained in other parts of P it differs widely." And the state of things in which these various codes originated is more and more coming to be conceived in the manner stated by Dr. A. B. Davidson.* "It is evident," he says, "that two streams of thought, both issuing from a fountain as high up as the very origin of the nation, ran side by side down the whole history of the people, the prophetic and the priestly. In the one Jehovah is a moral ruler, a righteous king and judge, who punishes iniquity judicially or forgives sins freely of His mercy. In the other He is a Person dwelling among His people in a house, a Holy Being or Nature, sensitive to every uncleanness in all that is near Him, and requiring its removal by lustrations and atonement. Those cherishing the latter circle of conceptions might be as zealous for the Lord of Hosts as the prophets. And the developments of the national history would extend their conceptions and lead to the amplification of practices embodying them, just as they extended the conceptions of the prophets. A growth of priestly ideas is quite as probable as a growth of prophetic ideas. That the streams ran apart is no evidence that they were not equally ancient and always contemporaneous, for we see Jeremiah and Ezekiel both flourishing in one age. At one point in the history the

* "Ezekiel," Introduction, p. liv. f.

prophetic stream was swelled by an inflow from the priestly, as is seen in Deuteronomy, and from the Restoration downwards both streams appear to coalesce."

The actual date of Deuteronomy still remains to be settled. Already it has been brought down to post-Solomonic days. How much later must it probably be put? The book must have been written before the eighteenth year of Josiah, 621 B. C., for the Book of the Law which was then found in the Temple was undoubtedly not the whole Pentateuch, but approximately Deut. i.-xxvi. But it can hardly have been produced in Josiah's reign, because it would never have been permitted to drop out of sight had it been known to that pious king and the reforming high priest Hilkiah. On the other hand, it can hardly have been written or known before Hezekiah's reforms, for otherwise it would have been made the basis of them, as it was made the basis of Josiah's. Probably, therefore, we may date it between Hezekiah and Josiah. Indeed we may with great likelihood affirm, as Robertson Smith suggests, that it was the need of guidance caused by Hezekiah's reforms which suggested and called out this book.*

But, say some, if the body of the book is not Mosaic, then this is nothing else but forgery, and no forged or even pseudonymous book can be inspired! Others again, most gratuitously, suppose that Hilkiah found the book only because he had forged it and put it where it was found. But there is neither need nor room for such suppositions; and our effort must be to conceive to ourselves the means by which such a book could come into existence, and be found as it was, without fraud on the part of any one.

To modern, and especially Western notions, it seems difficult to conceive any legitimate process by which a book of comparatively modern date could be attributed, so far as its main part is concerned, to Moses, and published as Mosaic. But if we take into account the character of Deuteronomy as only an extension and adaptation of the Book of the Covenant set in a framework of affectionate exhortation, and that all men then believed that the Book of the Covenant was Mosaic, we can see better how such action might be considered legitimate. Even on modern and Western principles we can see that; but at that early time and in the East, literary methods and literary ideas were so different from ours that there may have been customs which made the publication of a book in this way not only natural but right. An example from modern India will make this clear. Among the sacred books of the Hindus one of the most famous is the "Laws of Manu." This is a collection of religious, moral, and ceremonial laws much like the Book of Leviticus. It is generally admitted that it was not the work of any one man, but of a school of-legal writers and law-givers who lived at very various times, each of whom, with a clear conscience and as a matter of course, adapted the works of his predecessors to the need of his own day. And this practice, together with the belief in its legitimacy, survives to this day. In his "Early Law and Custom" (p. 161) Sir Henry Maine tells us that " A gentleman in a high official position in India has a native friend who has devoted his life to preparing a new Book of Manu. He does not,

* "Additional Answer to the Libel," p. 80.

however, expect or care that it should be put in force by any agency so ignoble as a British-Indian Legislature, deriving its powers from an Act of Parliament not a century old. He waits till there arises a king in India who will serve God and take the law from the new 'Manu' when he sits in his Court of Justice." There is here no question of fraud. This Indian gentleman considers that his book *is* the Book of Manu, and would be amazed if any one should question its identity because he had edited it; and he supposes that the king he looks for, if he should come in his day, would accept and act upon it as a Divine authority. So strangely different are Eastern notions from those of the West. It is legitimate to suppose that *this* Eastern book originated in something of the same fashion. In the evil days of persecution, when all the prophetic spokesmen were cut off, and when the priests were occupying the chief position among the supporters of pure religion, some pious man, inspired, but not with the prophetic inspiration, set himself, like this modern Hindu, to re-write and adapt the legislation which he believed to be Mosaic to the needs of his own day. Altering the fundamental points as little as might be, he developed it to meet the evils which were threatening the Mosaic religion; and he inspired it with the passion for righteousness and the love of God which had already thrilled the hearts of faithful men in Israel through the ministry of the great prophets. Hoping for the coming of a king who should serve God and judge Israel out of this new Book of Moses, but while the darkness still clouded the future, he died, committing his book to some temple chamber where he might hope that it would be discovered when God's set time should come. In such a supposition there is perhaps something to shock the conventional theories of our time. But, so far as can be seen, there is nothing to shock any open-minded man who knows how widely ancient and Eastern thought differs from modern and Western thought. It is certain that at this day Eastern men of the highest character and of the most burning zeal for religion would act in this manner without a qualm of conscience. We may well believe, therefore, that in ancient days it was the same. If so, this was a literary method which inspiration might well use; and the supposition that Deuteronomy was so produced is certainly more consistent with its history and character than any other. It explains how it so exactly met the needs of the time and summed up all its aspirations; and it gives to its claim of inspiration a new support by laying bare the circumstances of its birth and its psychological pre-suppositions.

But it may still be asked, what are we to think of the Mosaic speeches, which, as has been seen, contain, to say the least, much non-Mosaic matter? The answer probably is that in these, as in the laws, the author relies upon earlier documents. From the appearance in the codes of laws which would have little or no meaning if originated in the time of the Deuteronomist, it has rightly been concluded that there are very ancient and Mosaic elements in them. So, in the speeches there are references and allusions that suggest an ancient tradition of a final address of Moses, and perhaps a written account of its general purport, in which even a hope that the worship might be centralised may have been contained.* This the author has adapted to his purpose of inciting his contemporaries to be faithful to the Mosaic teaching, and has woven into it all that later experience could suggest as effective ground of exhortation. So much as that all ancient historians would have done, and some moderns would do, without the faintest intention to deceive, or any feeling of guilt; and so much may probably have been done here. Delitzsch,† Robertson Smith,‡ and Driver § are all at one as to this, and in the proofs they produce of the necessity of accepting this view. In the words of Driver, "It is the uniform practice of the Biblical historians in both the Old and New Testaments to represent their characters as speaking in words and phrases which cannot have been those actually used, but which they themselves select and frame for them." The speeches of David in Samuel and Chronicles serve for examples. In Samuel he speaks in the language of Samuel, in Chronicles in the language of Chronicles. "In some of these cases," Driver continues, "the authors no doubt had information as to what was actually said on the occasions in question, which they recast in their own words, only preserving, perhaps, a few characteristic expressions; in other cases, they merely gave articulate expression to the thoughts and feelings which it was presumed that the persons in question would have entertained. In the Deuteronomic speeches both these characteristic methods have probably been employed, and we must just accept the inspired record for what it reveals itself to be, setting aside, with the inevitable sighs, our own *à priori* assumptions of what it ought to be."

These then are the conclusions regarding Deuteronomy on which the exposition offered here will rest. They have been reached after a careful consideration of the evidence on both sides, and are stated here not altogether without regret. For, as Robertson Smith has well said,|| "to the ordinary believer the Bible is precious as the practical rule of faith and life in which God still speaks directly to his heart. No criticism can be otherwise than hurtful to faith if it shakes the confidence with which the simple Christian turns to his Bible, assured that he can receive every message which it brings to his soul as a message from God Himself." Now, though it can be demonstrated that the view of Scripture which permits of such conclusions as those stated above is quite compatible with this believing confidence, there can be little doubt that Christian people will for a time find great difficulty in accepting this assurance. The transition from the old view of inspiration, so complete, comprehensible, and effective as it is, to the newer and less definite doctrine, cannot fail to be trying, and the introduction of it here cannot but be a disturbing influence which it would have been greatly preferable to avoid.

It is not to be wondered at, therefore, that to the minds of the working ministry and of their earnest fellow-labourers, who come into constant contact with the actual needs of men, the change should be unwelcome. But it cannot now, in my judgment, be avoided. Even the best and most scholarly work of those who still hold the traditional view does not convince. Rather it is their writings, more even than those on the modern side, which make it clear that the traditional view can no longer be held. These writers admit the facts upon which their opponents' case rests, and then explain them all away, harmonising everything by a crowd of hypotheses, often scholarly, generally acute, but almost always such as can be accepted only if we know beforehand that the view they support is true. But far too many hypotheses are needed. Each case has to be set right by a special effort of the imagination; while the new view has this great advantage, that it makes room for all the facts, by a hypothesis, suggested not by one difficulty, but by almost all the discrepancies and difficulties which are encountered. And, after all, this view does not move men away from the central truth of inspiration, even as it was conceived by the last generation. Apart from any care for averting errors in detail which can be ascribed to Divine wisdom according to the old view or the new, the central thing in both surely is the revelation of God Himself. It was always God that was held to be revealed, and this the advocates of the newer view insist upon most strenuously. They hold that chosen men, the wisest, best, most truthful of their respective generations, those who travailed most in thought, received exceptional impressions of the Divine nature. They saw God, and their whole being bore the impress henceforth of this illumination. In every word and act the light they had received found expression for itself. They did not receive this revelation in mere propositions about God, which had to be carefully repeated with minute verbal accuracy. They saw, and their natures were in their degree uplifted, changed, and harmonised with the Divine. They could no more be false in speaking of what they had thus experienced, than a sincere and tender nature can be false in speech or thought about death, when it once has found its love frustrated and overborne by that dread messenger of God. The impression in both cases is true as it is final, and it will triumphantly convey itself to others with substantial and effective truth, whatever the man's knowledge or ignorance otherwise may be. When a man has received an impression, or a sight of God which has shaken his very soul, will it be lost in its essential parts because in the speech in which he utters it he shows ignorance of science, or accepts as simply true the historic knowledge of his day? The thing is impossible. The light that is within him must shine out, even though the medium through which it shines be here and there blackened by imperfection. In the fundamental point, therefore, the old school of critics and the new are entirely at one. On the basis of this essential harmony it should be possible for each to speak to the other for edification. This is what has been attempted here; and if those who hold by the Mosaic authorship of Deuteronomy will tolerate the opposite view, they will find that in dealing with the Scriptures as a revelation of God, and as an infallible guide in all that concerns religious and moral truth, there is no difference. To make the sacred word living and powerful as an instrument of spiritual regeneration is our common effort; and our common hope must be that, if in anything we have been led into error, the mistake may be discovered

---

* *Cf.* Driver, art. "Deuteronomy," Smith's "Dictionary," p. 770.
† "Pentateuch Kritische Studien," X.
‡ "Answer to the Form of Libel," p. 34. Note: where Arnold and Masson's "Life of Milton," are referred to.
§ Art. "Deuteronomy," Smith's "Bible Dict.," pp. 769 ff.
|| "Answer," pp. 41 f.

CHAPTER II.

THE HISTORIC SETTING OF DEUTERONOMY.

WHATEVER may be the date of the first publication of Deuteronomy, there can be no doubt that it was accepted by Josiah and the people of his time with an energy and thoroughness of which we find no previous example. Its main lessons were learnt and put into practice by them, and from that period the religious conceptions of Deuteronomy dominated and formed the Hebrew mind in a manner of which we have no earlier trace. For practical purposes, therefore, we may say that this was the Deuteronomic period. The book gathered up and embodied the higher strivings of that time; and to understand it thoroughly we need to know the history of which it was, in part at least, the outcome. Indeed, on any supposition as to age and authorship, a study of the history of Judah from the end of the eighth century B. C. to the end of the seventh is indispensable if we would adequately understand our book, for that was the time when the book is seen entering as a living force into the history of Israel.

Unfortunately, however, there are few periods of Israelite history as to which we have less of reliable information. During much of the period the main currents of the national life ran contrary to all better influences, and in such epochs the compilers of the Book of Kings took no interest. For the most part they were content to "look and pass," gathering up the results of such times of declension in a few condemnatory words. It is only when the nation is on the upward slope that they enter into details. They wrote at a time when the purpose of God in their national life was becoming clear, and the splendour of it possessed them so that nothing else but the increase of this purpose seemed worthy of any intenser contemplation. Victories and defeats, successes and failures, and last of all the tremendous catastrophe of the Exile, had taught them this discernment; and they pressed forward so eagerly to record the deeds and thoughts of those who had learned the secret of Yahweh that they had eyes for nothing else. Consequently the eighty years after the fall of Samaria, which for our purpose would be so extremely instructive, are passed over in all our sources, almost without mention. But there are some facts and events of which we can be entirely sure; and from these it is possible to conceive in outline the way in which things must have shaped themselves in these eventful years.

Brought about as it had been by the appeal of Ahaz to the king of Assyria for help against the continual aggressions of Syria and Israel, the fall of Samaria must have come to the king and people of Judah as a relief. Their enemy had fallen, and they would henceforth be free from the anxiety and harassment which Israel's enmity had caused. But those must have been blind indeed with whom this feeling was permanent. Very soon it must have become apparent to all thoughtful men in Judah that, if they had been freed from the worrying and exasperating enmity of their kindred, their very success had brought them into the presence of a much more serious foe. With Assyria on their immediate frontier, settled in the lands both of Damascus and Samaria, they must have felt themselves exposed to chances and dangers they had never hitherto had to face. Under the old conditions, except during comparatively short periods when there was actual war between the two kingdoms, Israel had stood between Judah and any danger from the North. But now the people of the Southern Kingdom were summoned from "the safe glad rear to the dreadful van." Henceforth no patriot could fail to be haunted by fear of that ambitious and conquering Assyrian nation. The whole of Hezekiah's reign was filled with more or less convulsive efforts to maintain the independence of Judah. These were giving but faint promise of success, when the great deliverance of Jerusalem foretold by Isaiah gave the king a breathing space, and raised the highest hopes in the minds of his people. It seemed for a little quite possible that the ancient independence of Israel might be restored. To many it seemed that the Messianic times were at hand; faith in Yahweh carried all before it. But Hezekiah died not long after; and in the succeeding reigns of Manasseh and Amon the whole temper and policy of Israel underwent a most serious and reactionary change.

The causes of this are not far to seek. During the greater part of Hezekiah's reign Isaiah had received only moderate support. According to his own vision of his future work, he was to preach without success; he was to say, "Hear ye indeed, but understand not; and see ye, but perceive not"; and, so far as the mass of the people were concerned, that prevision was justified. Only the astounding success with which his opposition to the Assyrians had been crowned had turned the tide of popular opinion in his favour. It was probably, therefore, only then that Hezekiah's reforms were instituted. They had been too short a time in force at his death to have sent out their roots into the national life. But that was not all. One of the most characteristic points in all prophecy was that the *time* when the full Messianic Kingdom should appear was never clearly defined. Neither the Prophet nor his hearers knew when it would be. It loomed always as a bright but vague background to the deliverance which lay immediately before them; and in almost every case neither speaker nor hearers had any conception of the long and weary way which divided those sunlit mountain peaks from the dark and threatening pass which they were approaching. Now the literal interpretation of Isaiah's prophecies with regard to the deliverance from Assyria had inevitably led the mass of the people to believe that the raising of the siege of Jerusalem would mean the immediate destruction of Assyria, and the advent of the Messianic day of peace and glory for Israel. But the facts completely falsified that expectation. Instead of being destroyed Assyria only grew more powerful, and instead of the Messianic time there was only the old position of vassalage to Assyria. So men grew weary, and said then as they have said so often since, "All things are as they have been from the beginning, and where is the promise of His coming?" The true-hearted said it with sadness; and the false-hearted, saying it in mockery and unbelief, fell back upon the old heathenish test, and said, "The gods of Assyria are stronger than Yahweh, and we must give them a place in our adoration." With the bulk of the people this required no really great change in their point of view. They had believed in Yahweh and agreed to purify His worship, because He had proved Himself stronger than Sennacherib and his gods; and now when, in the long run, Assyria was triumphing, they must have seemed to themselves only to be following the teachings of experience in giving the host of heaven equal honour with their own ancestral God. The reaction, therefore, was more in the outward expression than in principle, and we can easily understand how it was so swift and so universal. Manasseh, Hezekiah's son, had probably opposed his father's policy, as the heir-apparent has so often opposed the policy of the reigning monarch; and if, as many suppose, Hezekiah lived for sixteen years after the destruction of Sennacherib's host, Manasseh came to the throne just when men's minds were most weary with hope deferred, and when the Assyrian success was about to reach its highest point before its final fall.

Accordingly Manasseh would seem to have undone at once all that his father and Isaiah had accomplished. Nay, he went further in the introduction of idolatry than any even of the idolatrous kings who had preceded him. In the Book of Kings the charges made against him are three:—1st, that he introduced the worship of the host of heaven according to the Assyrian ritual; 2d, that he took part in the Moloch-worship; and 3d, that he restored the old semi-Canaanite worship which it had been Isaiah's most strenuous effort to root out. And this policy, evil as it was in the eyes of all who cared for the higher destinies of Israel, had at once great and striking external success. For it meant complete submission to Assyria, a willing vassalage from which even the wish for independence had disappeared. The heart of the old Israelite independence had been faith in Yahweh and confidence in Israel's calling as His people. Even so late as Isaiah's day it had been faith in Yahweh which had kept Hezekiah steady in his opposition to apparently overwhelming force. But now Manasseh and the people who supported him exalted the gods of Assyria as an even surer refuge than Yahweh had been. Having made that admission, there was nothing left for them but to humble themselves under the mighty hand of the great king and his great gods. And this Israel under Manasseh did most thoroughly. As Stade has strikingly said, "The Temple of the one God of Israel became a Pantheon." The feeble attempts which Ahaz had made in the same direction were utterly swept out of men's memory by the completeness of Manasseh's apostasy. With this degradation of the religious faith there also came, naturally, an intellectual degradation. Superstition, baser even than idolatry, seized upon the minds of men, and illegitimate efforts to pry into the future or to influence the destinies of men by magic and incantations became part of the popular fashion of the day. The old religion of Israel had sternly set itself against all such debasing practices. Alone amid the religions of the ancient world, it had relentlessly refused the help of necromancy and magic generally. But the barrier the religion of Yahweh had erected fell at once when its purity and uniqueness had been sacrificed, and Manasseh gave himself up to "practise augury and to use enchantments, and to deal with them that had familiar spirits and with wizards." And to superstition he also added cruelty. Not content with his signal victory over all the best impulses of the past, not content with the applause of the multitude who gladly followed him to do evil, he endeavoured to force those whose work he had destroyed to bow before the gods they both hated and despised. We know too little of the circumstances of the time to be sure of his motives, but his action may have been founded upon a craven fear that if he did not suppress the voices of those who spoke for freedom, he might be visited with the anger of the Assyrian king. Or it may have been that feeling, so powerfully expressed in Browning's poem "Instans Tyrannus," which makes a tyrant feel that all his life is made bitter to him if there remain within his power one free man whom he cannot bend to his will. In any case it is certain that he attacked the prophetic party with sanguinary fury. Though he had the gods of the great battalions on his side, he was dimly afraid of the power of ideas; and, so far as faithful men were concerned, he instituted a "reign of terror." According to the graphic statement of the historian, "he filled Jerusalem with innocent blood from lip to lip," and for the time at least was able to silence righteousness so far as public utterance was concerned. There is a tradition that even Isaiah fell a victim to his fury, being sawn asunder between two planks at his command. It is perhaps not likely that Isaiah had survived so long. But, beyond all doubt, many suffered for their faithfulness to God; and it seems probable that the wonderful picture of the Suffering Servant in the Deutero-Isaiah owes much of its colour to the pathetic and painful memories of this evil time.

All this apostasy brought with it worldly success. Manasseh reigned long, and under him the land had peace. Assyria *could* have no quarrel with a people and a king who anticipated its very desire by eager submission. Peace brought material prosperity. The land was so naturally fertile that it always grew rich when war was kept from its borders. We may surmise, too, that a kind of bastard culture became popular when the Jewish mind had opened to it, for good and evil, a world of myth and song and legend which, if known before, had until now been barred from complete and triumphant entrance by faith in a living God. Once only would Manasseh appear to have asserted himself, and, according to the Book of Chronicles, he was taken prisoner in Jerusalem by the master he had served so well, and learned to know in the bitterness of a Babylonian prison that sycophancy does not always lead to safety. And the wisdom he learned went further even than that. At the end of his life he appears to have wished to undo, at least in some measure, the evil he had laboured throughout his reign to establish and make strong. But he found that to be impossible; and if his repentance was deep and sincere he must have learned how severely the heavenly powers can punish, by opening a man's eyes to the evil he has done when it cannot be undone. Nor did his late repentance affect his son, for under Amon all things continued in their previous evil course. Indeed the prevailing idolatry had rooted itself so firmly that even in the early years of Josiah, when the prophetic influence was beginning to reappear, it still retained its hold with unshaken power.

But what of the prophetic party during those evil days? Precipitated from power in an instant at Hezekiah's death, it had at once become feeble and obscure. Its leading supporters, we may well believe, had to seek safety in hiding or in flight; and after some of its chief speakers had been cut off, the once dominant party had to take the position of persecuted remnants for whom all public work was impossible. Under such circumstances what could these faithful men do? They could only wait and pray, and prepare for that better day of whose return their faith in Yahweh would not suffer them to despair.

From the position afterwards taken up by the high priest, it would seem probable that the Temple clergy were in full sympathy with the prophetic movement. We need not suppose that that sympathy arose wholly from the tendency of prophetic thought and effort towards the suppression of the High Places. We should probably do the better spirits among the priesthood grievous wrong if we thought that their personal interest was their main motive in supporting even that reform. Notwithstanding the earlier prophets' denunciation of the priests as a class, there can be little doubt that they had advanced, with the better classes of their nation generally, in their appreciation of spiritual religion. And we may well believe that the sight of the havoc which the now degraded worship at the High Places was working in the popular mind made them earnest in their endeavours to restore the true faith. Privileged as they were, they would naturally be sheltered from the full fury of the persecution. Consequently, when the time came for the supporters of true religion to take their place in public life again, it was natural and inevitable that the priests should be at their head. The fact, too, that Josiah at his accession was a child, for whose guardian no fitter person could be found than the chief priest, gave the future into their hands. But they did not move prematurely. So long as Josiah was a minor they contented themselves with instilling their principles into the mind of the king. In outward political life, so far as we can ascertain, they did not interfere at all, and the ground was moved away from beneath the feet of the idolatrous party, while they thought themselves firmly established. In Josiah's eighteenth year the results of this quiet preparation appeared. In that year Hilkiah, the high priest, told Shaphan the scribe that he had found "the Book of the Law" in the Temple. That this was Deuteronomy, if not altogether, yet practically, as we have it now, there can be but little doubt; and it immediately became the text-book of religion for all that remained of Israel.

Now it is obvious that the whole hopes of the religious party would naturally be fixed upon it. They would turn to it as eagerly as the Reformers turned to the Bible, after it had been rediscovered by Luther at Erfurt. For obviously, if the people could be got to acknowledge the law, the axe would be laid at the root of every evil which they deplored. The High Places would be destroyed; the primacy of the Temple at Jerusalem would be secured; and the prophetic teaching, with its insistence upon judgment and the love of God as the essentials of true worship, would, for the first time, become the dominant influence in civil and religious life. Never since Israel was a nation had the condition of the people called so loudly for the enforcement of such a law, and now for the first time was there hope that it might be actually enforced. The character of the evils that afflicted the nation, the history of the last half-century, and the teachings of the great canonical prophets had all converged, as it were, to this one point, and we can understand how all who strove for the higher life of Israel would strive that Deuteronomy, whether ancient or modern, should be neglected no longer. The result was that the whole power of the State was thrown into the struggle against idolatry and the half-heathen Bamoth-worship. The prophets and the priests joined hands to spread the principles of the true religion, as voiced by Deuteronomy. Professor Cheyne, in his "Jeremiah," conjectures, with considerable likelihood, that the break in that prophet's activity which occurred at this time is to be accounted for by the zeal with which he devoted himself to Deuteronomic propaganda throughout the land. In any case, for the moment the purer worship obtained a completer victory than ever before. Unfortunately it came too late and proved too evanescent. But in the inward sphere, the Deuteronomic view of religion as having its centre in love to God, the tender, thoughtful evangelical spirit which distinguishes the whole outlook of its author, laid hold upon all the higher minds that came after it. To Jeremiah and to St. Paul alike, it, *par excellence*, represented the law of God. Produced, or at any rate first prized, at a time when Israel had fallen very low, when evil was triumphant and good persecuted, it recommended and exemplified a cheerful courage, born of faith in the high destiny of Israel and the truth of God. That, more than anything else, helped to bear the ark of the Church over the tumultuous centuries which separated those two great servants of God, and when Christ appeared it was seen that this book, more than any in the Old Testament save perhaps the Psalms, had anticipated His cardinal teachings regarding the attitude of man to God and of man to man. The conflicts and needs of the seventh century B. C., which are so clearly reflected in it, gave inspiration the opportunity it needed to reveal that inner secret of God's Kingdom. Out of defeat and disaster this revelation came, and through times of defeat and backsliding it proved its Divine origin by keeping steadfast and calm those who specially waited for the coming of the Messiah.

CHAPTER III.

THE DIVINE GOVERNMENT.

DEUTERONOMY i.-iii.

AFTER these preliminary discussions we now enter upon the exposition. With the exception of the first two verses of chapter i., concerning which there is a doubt whether they do not belong to Numbers, these three chapters stand out as the first section of our book. Examination shows that they form a separate and distinct whole, not continued in chapter iv.; but there has been a great diversity of opinion as to their authorship and the intention with which they have been placed here. The vocabulary and the style so resemble those of the main parts of the book that they cannot be entirely separated from them; yet, at the same time, it seems unlikely that the original author of the main trunk of Deuteronomy can have begun his book with this introductory speech from Moses, followed it up with another Mosaic speech, still introductory, in chapter iv., and in chapter v. begun yet another introductory speech running through seven chapters, before he comes to the statutes and judgments which are announced at the very beginning. The current supposition about these chapters, therefore, is that they are the work of a Deuteronomist, a man formed under the influence of Deuteronomy and filled with its spirit, but not the author of the book. This seems to account for the resemblances, and would also explain to some extent the existence of such a superfluous prologue. But the hypothesis is, nevertheless, not entirely satisfactory. The resemblances are closer than we should expect in the work of different authors; and one feels that the supposed Deuteronomist must have been less sensitive in a literary sense than we have any right to suppose him if he did not feel the incongruity of such a speech in this place. Professor Dillmann has made a very acute suggestion, which meets the whole difficulty in a more natural way. Feeling that the style and language were in all essentials one with those of the central Deuteronomy, he seeks for some explanation which would permit him to assign this section to the author of the book himself. He suggests that as originally written this was a historical introduction leading up to the central code of laws; a historical preface, in fact, which the author of Deuteronomy naturally prefixed to his book. *Ex hypothesi* he had not the previous books, Exodus, Leviticus, and Numbers, before him as we have them. These now form a historical introduction to Deuteronomy of a very minute and elaborate kind; but he had to embody in his own book all of the past history of his people that he wished to emphasise. But when the editor who arranged the Pentateuch as we now have it inserted Deuteronomy in its present place, he found that he had a double historical preface, that in the previous books and this in Deuteronomy itself. As reverence forbade the rejection of these chapters, he took refuge in the expedient of turning the originally impersonal narrative into a speech of Moses; which he could all the more blamelessly do as the probability is that the whole book was regarded in his time as the work of Moses. This hypothesis, if it can be accepted, certainly accounts for all the phenomena presented by these chapters—the similarity of language, the archæological notes in the speech, and the historic colour in the statements regarding Edom, for example, which corresponds to early feeling, not to post-exilic thought at all. It has besides the merit of reducing the number of anonymous writers to be taken account of in the Pentateuch, a most desirable thing in itself. Lastly, it gives us in Deuteronomy a compact whole more complete in all its parts than almost any other portion of the Old Testament, certainly more so than any of the books containing legislation.

Moreover, that the Deuteronomic reinforcement and expansion of the Mosaic legislation, as contained in the Book of the Covenant, should begin with such a history of Yahweh's dealings with His people, is entirely characteristic of Old Testament Revelation. In the main and primarily, what the Old Testament writers give us is a history of how God wrought, how He dealt with the people He had chosen. In the view of the Hebrew writers, God's first and main revelation of Himself is always in conduct. He showed Himself good and merciful and gentle to His people, and then, having so shown Himself, He has an acknowledged right to claim their obedience. As St. Paul has so powerfully pointed out, the law was secondary, not primary. Grace, the free love and choice of God, was always the beginning of true relations with Him, and only after that had been known and accepted does He look for the true life which His law is to regulate. Naturally, therefore, when the author of Deuteronomy is about to press upon Israel the law in its expanded form, to call them back from many aberrations, to summon them to a reformation and new establishment of the whole framework of their lives, he turns back to remind them of what their past had been. Law, therefore, is only a secondary deposit of Revelation. If we are true to the Biblical point of view we shall not look for the Divine voice only, or even chiefly, in the legal portions of the Scripture. God's full revelation of Himself will be seen in the process and the completion of that age-long movement, which was begun when Israel first became a nation by receiving Yahweh as their God, and which ended with the life and death of Him who summed up in Himself all that Israel was called, but failed, to be.

That is the ruling thought in Scripture about Revelation. God reveals Himself in history; and by the persistent thoroughness with which the Scriptural writers grasp this thought, the unique and effective character of the Biblical Revelation is largely accounted for. Other nations, no doubt, looked back at times upon what their gods had done for them, and those who spoke for these gods may often have claimed obedience and service from their people on the ground of past favour and under threats of its withdrawal. But earlier than any other people which has affected the higher races of mankind, Israel conceived of God as a moral power with a will and purpose which embraced mankind. Further, in the belief which appears in their earliest records, that through them the nations were to be blessed, and that in the future One was coming who would in Himself bring about the realisation of Israel's destiny, they were provided with a philosophy of history, with a conception which was fitted to draw into organic connection with itself all the various fortunes of Israel and of the nations.

Of course, at first much that was involved in their view was not present to any mind. It was the very merit of the germinal revelation made through Moses that it had in it powers of growth and expansion. In no other way could it be a true revelation of God, a revelation which should have in it the fulness, the flexibility, the aloofness from mere local and temporary peculiarities, which would secure its fitness for universal mankind. Any revelation that consists only of words, of ideas even, must, to be received, have some kind of relation to the minds that are to receive it. If the words and ideas are revealed, as they must be, at a given place and a given time, they must be in such a relation to that place and time that at some period of the world's history they will be found inadequate, needing expansion, which does not come naturally, and then they have to be laid aside as insufficient. But a revelation which consists in acts, which reveals God in intimate, age-long, constant dealings with mankind, is so many-sided, so varied, so closely moulded to the actual and universal needs of man, that it embraces all the fundamental exigencies of human life, and must always continue to cover human experience. From it men may draw off systems of doctrines, which may concentrate the revelation for a particular generation, or for a series of generations, and make it more potently active in these circumstances. But unless the system be kept constantly in touch with the revelation as given in the history, it must become inadequate, false in part, and must one day vanish away.

The revelation then in life is the only possible form for a real revelation of God; and that the writers of the Old Testament in their circumstances and in their time felt and asserted this, is in itself so very great a merit that it is almost of itself sufficient to justify any claims they may make to special inspiration. The greatest of them saw God at work in the world, and had experience of His influence in themselves, so that they had their eyes opened to His actions as other men had not. The least of them, again, had been placed at the true point of view for estimating aright the significance of the ordinary action of the Divine Providence, and for tracing the lines of Divine action where they were to other men invisible, or at least obscure. And in the records they have left us they have been entirely true to that supremely important point of view. All they deal with in the history is the moral and spiritual effects of God's dealing; and the great interests, as the world reckons them, of war and conquest, of commerce and art, are referred to only briefly and often only in the way of allusion. To many moderns this is an offence, which they avenge by speaking contemptuously of the mental endowment of the Biblical writers as historians. On the contrary, that these should have kept their eyes fixed only upon that which concerned the religious life of their people, that they should have kept firm hold of the truth that it was there the central importance of the people lay, and that they have given us the material for the formation of that great conception of supernatural revelation by history in which God Himself moves as a factor, is a merit so great that even if it were only a brilliant fancy they might surely be pardoned for ignoring other things. But if, as is the truth, they were tracing the central stream of God's redemptive action in the world, were laying open to our view the steps by which the unapproachably lofty conception of God was built up, which their nation alone has won for the human race, then it can hardly seem a fault that nothing else appealed to them. They have given God to those who were blindly groping for Him, and they have established the standard by which all historic estimates of even modern life are ultimately to be measured.

For though there were in the history of that particular nation, and in the line of preparation for Christ, special miraculous manifestations of God's power and love, which do not now occur, yet no judgment of the course of history is worth anything, even to-day, which does not occupy essentially the Biblical position. Ultimately the thing to be considered is, what hath God wrought? If that be ignored, then the stable and instructive element in history has been kept out of sight, and the mind loses itself hopelessly amid the weltering chaos of second causes. Froude, in his "History of England," has noted this, and declares that in the period he deals with it was the religious men who alone had any true insight into the tendency of things. They measured all things, almost too crudely, by the Biblical standard; but so essentially true and fundamental does that show itself to be, that their judgment so formed has proved to be the only sound one. This is what we should expect if God's power and righteousness are the great factors in the drama which the history of man and of the world unfolds to us. That being so, the suicidal folly of the policy of any Church or party which shuts the Bible away from popular use is manifest. It is nothing short of a blinding of the people's eyes, and a shutting of their ears to warning voices which the providential government of the world, when viewed on a large scale, never fails to utter. It renders sound political judgment the prerogative only of the few, and sets them among a people who will turn to any charlatans rather than believe their voice.

It was natural and it was inevitable, therefore, that the author of Deuteronomy, standing, as he did, on the threshold of a great crisis in the history of Israel, should turn the thoughts of his people back to the history of the past. To him the great figure in the history of Israel in those trying and eventful years during which they wandered between Horeb, Kadesh-Barnea, and the country of the Arnon, is Yahweh their God. He is behind all their movements, impelling and inciting them to go on and enjoy the good land He had promised to their fathers. He went before them and fought for them. He bare them in the wilderness, as a man doth bear his son. He watched over them and guided their footsteps in cloud and fire by day and night. Moreover all the nations by whom they passed had been led by Him and assigned their places, and only those nations whom Yahweh chose had been given into Israel's hand. In the internal affairs of the community, too, He had asserted Himself. They were Yahweh's people, and all their national action was to be according to His righteous character. Especially was the administration of justice to be pure and impartial, yielding to neither fear nor favour because the "judgment is God's." And how had they responded to all this loving favour on the part of God? At the first hint of serious conflict they shrank back in fear. Notwithstanding that the land which God had given them was a good and fruitful country, and notwithstanding the promises of Divine help, they refused to incur the necessary toils and risks of the conquest. Every difficulty they might encounter was exaggerated by them; their very deliverance from Egypt, which they had been wont to consider "their crowning mercy," became to their faithless cowardice an evidence of hatred for them on the part of God.

To men in such a state of mind conquest was impossible; and though, in a spasmodic revulsion from their abject cowardice, they made an attack upon the people they were to dispossess, it ended, as it could not but end, in their defeat and rout. They were condemned to forty years of wandering, and it was only after all that generation was dead that Israel was again permitted to approach the land of promise. But Yahweh had been faithful to them, and when the time was come He opened the way for their advance and gave them the victory and the land. For His love was patient, and always made a way to bless them, even through their sins.

That was the picture the Deuteronomist spread out before the eyes of his countrymen, to the intent that they might know the love of God, and might see that safety lay for them in a willing yielding of themselves to that love. The disastrous results of their wayward and faint-hearted shrinking from this Divine calling is the only direct threat he uses, but in the passage there is another warning, all the more impressive that it is vague and shadowy. God is to the Deuteronomist the universal ruler of the world. The nations are raised up and cast down according to His will, and until He wills it they cannot be dispossessed. But He had willed that fate for many, and at every step of Israel's progress they come upon traces of vanished peoples whom for their sins He had suffered others to destroy. The Emim in Moab, the Zamzummim in Ammon, the Horites in Seir, and the Avvims in Philistia, had all been destroyed before the people who now occupied these lands, and the whole background of the narrative is one of judgment, where mercy had been of no avail. The sword of the Lord is dimly seen in the archæological notes which are so frequent in this section of our book and thus the final touch is given to the picture of the past which is here drawn to be an impulse for the future. While all the foreground represents only God's love and patience overcoming man's rebellion, the background is, like the path of the great pilgrim caravans which year by year make their slow and toilsome way to Mohammedan holy places, strewn with the remains of predecessors in the same path. With stern, menacing finger this great teacher of Israel points to these evidences that the Divine love and patience may be, and have been, outworn, and seems to re-echo in an even more impressive way the language of Isaiah: "The anger of Yahweh was kindled (against these peoples), and He stretched forth His hand (against them) and smote (them); and the hills did tremble, and (their) carcases were as refuse in the midst of the streets. For all this His anger is not turned away, but His hand is stretched out still." Without a word of direct rebuke he opens his people's eyes to see that shadowy outstretched hand. Behind all the turmoil of the world there is a presence and a power which supports all who seek good, but which is sternly set against all evil, ready, when the moment comes, "to strike once and strike no more."

Yet another glimpse is given us in these chapters of God's manner of dealing with men. We have seen how He guides and rules His chosen ones. We have seen how He punishes those who have set themselves against the Divine law. And in chapter ii. 30 we are told how men become hardened in their sin, so as to render destruction inevitable. Of Sihon, king of Heshbon, who would not let the Israelites pass by him, the writer says: "Yahweh thy God hardened his spirit, and made his heart obstinate, that He might deliver him into thy hand, as appeareth this day." But he does not mean by these expressions to lay upon God the causation of Sihon's obstinacy, so as to make the man a mere helpless victim. His thought rather is, that as God rules all, so to Him must be ultimately traced all that happens in the world. In some sense all acts, whether good or bad, all agencies, whether beneficent or destructive, have their source in and their power from Him. But nevertheless men have moral responsibility for their acts, and are fully and justly conscious of ill desert. Consequently that hardening of spirit or of heart, which at one moment may be attributed solely to God, may at another be ascribed solely to the evil determination of man. The most instructive instance of this is to be found in the history of Pharaoh, when he was commanded to let Israel go. In that narrative, from Exodus iv. to xi., there is repeated interchange of expression. Now it is Yahweh hardened Pharaoh's heart; now, as in viii. 15 and 32, Pharaoh hardened his own heart; and, again, Pharaoh's heart was hardened. In each case the same thing is meant, and the varying expressions correspond only to a difference of standpoint. When Yahweh foretells that the signs He authorises Moses to show will fail of their effect, it is always "Yahweh will harden Pharaoh's heart," since the main point in contemplation is His government of the world. If, on the other hand, it is the sinful obstinacy of Pharaoh which is prominent in the passage, we have the self-determination of Pharaoh alone set before us. But it is to be noted, and this is indeed the cardinal fact, that Yahweh never is said to harden the heart of a good man, or a man set mainly upon righteousness. It is always those who are guilty of palpable wrongs and acts of evil-doing upon whom God thus works.

Now we know that the author of Deuteronomy had two at least of the ancient historical narratives before him which are combined in Exod. iv.-xi., and he takes up their thinking. Expressed in modern language, the thought is this. When men are found following their own will in defiance of all law and all the restraints of righteousness, that is manifestly not the first stage in their moral declension. This obstinacy in evil is the result and the wages of former evil deeds, beginning perhaps only with careless laxity, but gathering strength and virulence with every wilful sin. Until near the end of a completed growth in wickedness no man deliberately says, " Evil, be thou my good." Nevertheless each act of sin involves a step towards that, and the sinner in this manner hardens himself against all warning. Like the sins which work this obduracy, this hardening is the sinner's own act. The ruin which falls upon his moral nature is his own work. That is the inexorable result of the moral order of the universe, and from it no exception is possible. But if so, God too has been active in all such catastrophes. He has so framed and ordered the world that indulgence in evil must harden in evil. This it was which the Israelite religious mind saw and dwelt upon, as well as upon man's share in the dread process of moral decay. We also do well to take heed to this aspect of the truth. When we do, we have solved the Scriptural difficulty regarding the Divine hardening of man's heart. It is simply the ancient formula for what every mind that is ethically trained recognises in the world to-day. Those who recognise themselves as children of God, and acknowledge the obligations of His law, are dealt with in the way of discipline with infinite love and patience. Those who definitely set themselves against the moral order of the world which God has established are broken in pieces and destroyed. Between these two classes there are the morally undetermined, who ultimately turn either to the right hand or to the left. The process by which these pass on to be numbered among the rebellious is pictured in Scripture with extraordinary moral insight. The only difference from a present-day description of it is, that here God is kept constantly present to the mind as the chief factor in the development of the soul. To-day, even those who believe in God are apt to forget Him in tracing His laws of action. But that is an error of the first magnitude. It darkens the hope of man; for without a sure promise of Divine help there is no certainty of moral victory either for the race or the individual. It narrows our view of the awful sweep of sin; for unless we see that sin affects even the Ruler of the universe, and defies His unchanging law, its results are limited to the evil that we do our fellow-men, which, as we see it, is of little importance. Further, it degrades moral law to a mere arbitrary dictum of power, or to an opinion founded upon man's purblind experience. The acknowledgment of God, on the contrary, makes morality the very essence of the Divine nature, and the unchangeable rule for the life of man.

CHAPTER IV.

THE DECALOGUE—ITS FORM.

DEUTERONOMY v. 1-21.

As the fourth chapter belongs to the speech which concludes the legislative portion of Deuteronomy both in contents and language (see chapter xxiii.), we shall pass on now to the fifth chapter, which begins with a recital of the Decalogue. As has already been pointed out, the main trunk of the Book of Deuteronomy is a repetition and expansion of the Law of the Covenant contained in Exod. xx.-xxiii.* Now, both in Exodus and Deuteronomy, before the more general and detailed legislation, we have the Decalogue, or the Ten Words, as it is called, substantially the same form; and the question immediately arises as to the age at which this beautifully systematised and organised code of fundamental laws came into existence. Whatever its origin, it is an exceedingly remarkable document. It touches the fundamental principles of religious and moral life with so sure a hand that at this hour, for even the most civilised nations, it sums up the moral code, and that so effectively that no change or extension of it has ever been proposed. That being its character, it becomes a question of exceeding interest to decide whether it can justly be referred to so early a time as the days of Moses. In both the passages where it occurs it is represented as having been given to the people at Horeb by Yahweh Himself, and it is made the earliest and most fundamental part of the covenant between Him and Israel. It would accordingly seem as if a claim were made for it as a specially early and specially sacred law. Now, much as critics have denied, there have been found very few who deny that in the main some such law as this must have been given to Israel in Moses' day. Even Kuenen admits as much as that in his "History of the Religion of Israel." The only commandment of the ten he has difficulty in accepting is the second, which forbids the making of any graven image for worship. That, he thinks, cannot have been in the original Decalogue, not because of any peculiarity of language, or because of any incoherency in composition, but simply because he cannot believe that at that early day the religion of Yahweh could have been so spiritual as to demand the prohibition of images. But his reasons are extremely inadequate; more especially as he admits that the Ark was the Mosaic Sanctuary, and that in it there was no image, as there was none in the Temple at Jerusalem. That Yahweh was worshipped under the form of a calf at Horeb, and afterwards in Northern Israel at Bethel and elsewhere, proves nothing. A law does not forthwith extinguish that against which it is directed, for idolatry continued even after Deuteronomy was accepted as the law. Moreover, if, as Kuenen thinks, calf-worship had existed in Israel before Moses, it was not unnatural that it took centuries before the higher view superseded the lower. Even by Christianity the ancient superstitions and religious practices of heathenism were not thoroughly overcome for centuries. Indeed in many places they have not yet been entirely suppressed. Nor does Wellhausen* make a better case for a late Decalogue. His hesitation about it is most remarkable, and the reasons he gives for tending to think it may be late are singularly unsatisfactory. His first reason is that "according to Exodus xxxiv. the commandments which stood upon the two tables were quite different." He relies on the words in ver. 28 of that chapter—"And he (Moses) was there with the Lord forty days and forty nights; he did neither eat bread nor drink water. And he wrote upon the tables the words of the covenant, the ten words"—taking them to imply that the immediately preceding commandments, which are of the same ritual character with those which follow the Decalogue in Exodus xx., are here called the ten words. But it is not necessary to take the passage so. According to ver. 1 it was Yahweh who was to write the words on the tables, and we cannot suppose that so flagrant a contradiction should occur in a single chapter as that here it should be said that Moses wrote the tables. Yahweh, who is mentioned in the previous verse, must therefore be the subject of *wayyikhtobh* (ver. 28), and the ten words consequently are different from the words (up to ver. 27) which Yahweh commanded Moses to write, somewhere, but not on the tables. Besides, every one who attempts to make ten words of the commands before ver. 27 brings out a different result, and that of itself, as Dillmann says, is sufficient to show that the second Decalogue in chapter xxxiv. is entirely fanciful. Wellhausen's second reason is this: "The prohibition of images was quite unknown during the other period: Moses himself is said to have made a brazen serpent, which down to Hezekiah's time continued to be worshipped as an image of Jehovah." But the Decalogue does not prohibit the making of every image; it pro-

---

* See this brought out in detail in Robertson Smith, "Old Testament in Jewish Church," p. 431.

* Wellhausen, "Prolegomena," p. 439.

hibits the making of images for worship. Therefore Moses might quite well have made a figure of a serpent, even though he wrote the Decalogue, if it was not meant for worship. But there is nothing said to lead us to believe that the serpent was regarded as an image of Yahweh. Indeed the very contrary is asserted; and if Israel in later times made a bad use of this ancient relic of a great deliverance, Moses can hardly be held responsible for that. In the third place, Wellhausen says: "The essentially and necessarily national character of the older phases of the religion of Yahweh completely disappears in the quite universal code of morals which is given in the Decalogue as the fundamental law of Israel; but the entire series of religious personalities throughout the period of the Judges and Kings—from Deborah, who praised Jael's treacherous act of murder, to David, who treated his prisoners of war with the utmost cruelty—make it very difficult to believe that the religion of Israel was from the outset one of a specifically moral character." Surely this is very feeble criticism. On the same grounds we might declare, because of the Massacre of St. Bartholomew, or on account of Napoleon's reported poisoning of his own wounded at Acre, that Christianity was not a religion of a "specifically moral character" at this present moment. Surely the facts that people never live at the level of their ideals, and that the lifting of a nation's life is a process which is as slow as the raising of the level of the delta of the Nile, should be too familiar to permit any one to be misled by difficulties of this kind. Nor is his last ground in any degree more convincing. "It is extremely doubtful," he says, "whether the actual monotheism which is undoubtedly presupposed in the universal moral precepts of the Decalogue could have formed the foundation of a national religion. It was first developed out of the national religion at the downfall of the nation." The obvious reply is that this is a *petitio principii*. The whole debate in regard to this question is whether Moses was a monotheist, or at least the founder of a religion which was implicitly monotheistic from the beginning; and the date of the Decalogue is interesting mainly because of the light it would throw upon that question. To decide this date therefore by the assertion that, being monotheistic, the Decalogue cannot be Mosaic, is to assume the very thing in dispute. Wellhausen himself, elsewhere (p. 434), seems to favour the opposite view. In speaking of what Moses did for Israel he says that through "the Torah," in the sense of decisions given by lot from the Ark, "he gave a definite positive expression to their sense of nationality and their idea of God. Yahweh was not merely the God of Israel; as such He was the God at once of Law and of Justice, the basis, the informing principle, and the implied postulate of their national consciousness"; and again (p. 438), "As God of the nation Yahweh became the God of Justice and of Right; as God of Justice and Right, He came to be thought of as the highest, and at last as the only power in heaven and earth." In the Mosaic conception of God, therefore, Wellhausen himself being witness, there lay implicitly, perhaps even explicitly, the conception of Yahweh as "the only power in heaven and earth." In that case, is it reasonable to put the Decalogue late, because being moral it is universal, and so implies monotheism?

But there is still other, and perhaps stronger evidence, that the universality of the Decalogue is no indication of a late date. On the contrary it would seem, from Professor Muirhead's account of the Roman *fas*, that universality in legal precept may be a mark of very primitive laws. Speaking of Rome in its earliest stages of growth, when the circumstances of the people in very many respects resembled those of the Hebrews in Mosaic times,* he says: "We look in vain for, and it would be absurd to expect, any definite system of law in those early times. What passed for it was a composite of *fas*, *jus*, and *boni mores*, whose several limits and characteristics it is extremely difficult to define." He then proceeds to describe *fas*: "By *fas* was understood the will of the gods, the laws given by Heaven for men on earth, much of it regulative of ceremonial, but a by no means insignificant part embodying rules of conduct. It appears to have had a wider range than *jus*. There were few of its commands, prohibitions, or precepts that were addressed to men as citizens of any particular state; *all mankind came within its scope*. It forbade that a war should be undertaken without the prescribed fetial ceremonial, and required that faith should be kept with even an enemy—when a promise had been made to him under sanction of an oath. It enjoined hospitality to foreigners, because the stranger guest was presumed, equally with his entertainer, to be an object of solicitude to a higher power. It punished murder, for it was the taking of a God-given life; the sale of a wife by her husband, for she had become his partner in all things human and Divine; the lifting of a hand against a parent, for it was subversive of the first bond of society and religion, the reverence due by a child to those to whom he owed his existence; incestuous connections, for they defiled the altar; the false oath, and the broken vow, for they were an insult to the divinities invoked," etc. In fact, the Roman *fas* had much the same character as the Decalogue and the legislation of the first code (Exod. xx.-xxiii.). Consequently those who have thought that all early legislation must be concrete, narrow, particularistic, bounded at widest by the direct needs of the men making up the clan, tribe, or petty nationality, are wrong. The early history of law shows that, along with that, there is also a demand for some expression of the laws of life seen from the point of view of man's relation to God. That fact greatly strengthens the case for the early date of the Decalogue. For practically it is the Hebrew *fas*. If it has a higher tone and a wider sweep if it provides a framework into which human duty can, even now, without undue stretching of it, be securely fitted, that is only what we should expect, if God was working in the history and development of this nation as nowhere else in the world. In short, the history of primitive Roman law shows that, without inspiration, a feeble wavering step would have been taken to the development of a code of moral duty, within the scope of which all mankind should come. With inspiration, surely this effort would also be made, and made with a success not elsewhere attained.

In none of the reasons which have been advanced, therefore, is there anything to set against the Biblical statement that the ten words were older and more sacred than any other por-

* "Ency. Brit.," vol. xx., p. 670.

tion of the Israelite legislation, and that they were Mosaic in origin. The universal hesitation shown by the greater among the most advanced critics in definitely removing the Decalogue from the foundations of Israel's history, although its presence there is so great an embarrassment to them, lets us see how strong the case for the Mosaic origin is, and assures us that the evidence is all in favour of this view.

But if it be Mosaic, at first sight the conclusion would seem to be that the form of the Decalogue given in Exodus is the more ancient, and that the text in Deuteronomy is a later and somewhat extended version of that. Closer examination, however, tends to suggest that the original ten words, in their Mosaic form, differed from any of the texts we have, and that of these the Exodus text in its present form is later than that in Deuteronomy. The great difference in length between the two halves of the Decalogue suggests the probability that originally all the commandments were short, and much the same in style and character as the last half, "Thou shalt not steal," and so on. Further, when the reasons and inducements given for the observance of the longer commands are set aside, just such short commands are left to us as we find in the second table. Lastly, differences between the versions in Exodus and Deuteronomy occur in almost every case in those parts of the text which may be regarded as appendices. In fact there are only two variations in the proper text of the commands. In the fourth, we have in Exodus "Remember the Sabbath day," while in Deuteronomy we have "Observe the Sabbath day"; but the meaning is the same in both cases. In the tenth, in Exodus the command is "Thou shalt not covet thy neighbour's house"; and the "house" is explained by the succeeding clause, "Thou shalt not covet thy neighbour's wife, nor his manservant," etc., to mean "household" in its widest sense. In Deuteronomy the old meaning of "house" as household and goods has fallen out of use, and the component parts of the neighbour's household possessions are named, beginning with his wife. Then follows the "house" in its narrow meaning, as the mere dwelling, grouped along with the slaves and cattle, and with *tithawweh* substituted in Hebrew for *tachmodh*. Fundamentally therefore the two recensions are the same. Even in the reasons and explanations there is only one really important variation. In Exod. xx. 11 the reason for the observance of the fourth commandment is stated thus: "For in six days Yahweh made heaven and earth, the sea and all that in them is, and rested the seventh day; therefore Yahweh blessed the Sabbath day, and hallowed it." In Deuteronomy, on the other hand, that reason is omitted, and in its place we find this: "And thou shalt remember that thou wast a servant in the land of Egypt, and Yahweh thy God brought thee out thence by a mighty hand, and by a stretched out arm; therefore Yahweh thy God commanded thee to keep the Sabbath." Now if the reference to the creation had formed part of the original text of the Decalogue in the days of the author of Deuteronomy, if he had that before him as actually spoken by Yahweh, it is difficult to believe that he would have left it out and substituted another reason in its stead. He would have no object in doing so, for he could have added his own reason after that given in Exodus, had he so desired. It is likely, therefore, that in the original text no reason appeared; that Deuteronomy first added a reason; while ver. 11 in Exod. xx. was probably inserted there from a combination of Exod. xxxi. 17*b* and Gen. ii. 2*b*,—"For in six days Yahweh made heaven and earth, and on the seventh day He rested and was refreshed"; "and He rested on the seventh day from all His work which He had made." Both these texts belong to P and differ in style altogether from JE, with whose language all the rest of the setting of the Decalogue corresponds. On these suppositions Exod. xx. 11 would necessarily be the latest part of the two texts. Originally, therefore, the Mosaic commands probably ran thus:

"I am Yahweh thy God, which brought thee out of the land of Egypt, out of the house of bondage.

"I. Thou shalt not have any other gods before Me.

"II. Thou shalt not make unto thee any graven image.

"III. Thou shalt not take the name of Yahweh thy God in vain.

"IV. Remember (*or* Keep) the day of rest to sanctify it.

"V. Honour thy father and thy mother.

"VI. Thou shalt not kill.

"VII. Thou shalt not commit adultery.

"VIII. Thou shalt not steal.

"IX. Thou shalt not bear false witness against thy neighbour.

"X. Thou shalt not covet thy neighbour's house."

In that shape they contain everything that is fundamentally important, and exhibit the foundations of the Mosaic religion and polity in an entirely satisfactory and credible form.

But, before passing on to consider the substance of the Decalogue, it will be worth our while to consider what the full significance of these differing recensions of the Decalogue is. In both places the words are quoted directly as having been spoken by Yahweh to the people, and they are introduced by the quoting word "saying." Now if we do not wish to square what we read with any theory, the slight divergences between the two recensions need not trouble us, for we have the substance of what was said, and in the main the very words, and that is really all we need to be assured of. But if, on the contrary, we are going to insist that, this being part of an inspired book, every word must be pressed with the accuracy of a masoretic scribe, then we are brought into inextricable difficulties. It cannot be true that at Horeb Yahweh said two different things on this special occasion. One or both of these accounts must be inaccurate, in the pedantic sense of accuracy, and yet both have the same claim to be inspired. In fact both *are* inspired; it is the theory of inspiration which demands for revelation this kind of accuracy that must go to the wall.

It will be seen that this instance is very instructive as to the method of the ancient Hebrews in dealing with legislation which was firmly held to be Mosaic, or even directly Divine. If we are right in holding that originally the ten words were, as we have supposed, limited to definite short commands, this example teaches us that where there could be no question of deceit, or even an object for deceiving, additions calculated to meet the needs and defects of the particular period at which the laws are written down, are inserted without any hint that they did not form part of the original document. If this has been done, even to the extent we have seen reason to infer, in a small, carefully ordered, and specially ancient and sacred code, how much more freely may we expect the same thing to have been done in the looser and more fluid regulations of the large political and ceremonial codes, which on any supposition were posterior, and much less fundamental and sacred. That there is for *us* something disappointing, and even slightly questionable, in such action is really nothing to the purpose. We have to learn from the actual facts of revelation how revelation may be, or perhaps even must be, conveyed; and we cannot too soon learn the lesson that to a singular degree, and in many other directions than their notions of accuracy, the ancient mind differs from the modern mind, and that at any period there is a great gulf to be crossed before a Western mind can get into any intimate and sure *rapport* with an Eastern mind.

One other thing is noteworthy. Wellhausen has already been quoted as to the quite universal and moral character of the Decalogue; and his view, that a code so free from merely local and ceremonial provisions can hardly be Mosaic, has been discussed. But, while rejecting his conclusion, we must adhere to his premisses. By emphasising the universal nature of the ten commandments, and by showing that they preceded the ceremonial law by many centuries, the critical school have cut away the ground from under the semi-antinomian views once so prevalent, and always so popular, with those who call themselves advanced thinkers. It is now no longer possible to maintain that the Decalogue was part of a purely Jewish law, binding only upon Jews and passing away at the advent of Christianity as the ceremonial law did. Of course this view was never really taken seriously in reference to murder or theft; but it has always been a strong point with those who have wished to secularise the Sunday. Now if the advanced critical position be in any degree true, then the ten commandments stand quite separate from the ceremonial law, have nothing in common with it, and are handed down to us in a document written before the conception even of a binding ceremonial law had dawned upon the mind of any man in Israel. Nor is there anything ceremonial or Jewish in the command, Remember *or* Observe the rest-day to keep it holy. In the reasons given in Exodus and Deuteronomy we have the two principles which make this a moral and universal command—the necessity for rest, and the necessity of an opportunity to cultivate the spiritual nature. Nothing indeed is said about worship; but it lies in the nature of the case that if secular work was rigorously forbidden, mere slothful abstinence from activity cannot have been all that was meant. Worship, and instruction in the things of the higher life, must certainly have been practised in such a nation as Israel on such a day; and we may therefore say that they were intended by this commandment. Understood in that way, the fourth commandment shows a delicate perception of the conditions of the higher life which surpasses even the prohibition of covetousness in the tenth. In the words of a working man who was advocating its observance, " It gives God a chance "; that is, it gives man the leisure to attend to God. But the moral point of view which it implies is so high, and so difficult of attainment, that it is only now that the nations of Europe are awaking to the inestimable moral benefits of the Sabbath they have despised. Because of this difficulty too, many who think themselves to be leaders in the path of improvement, and are esteemed by others to be so, are never weary of trying to weaken the moral consciousness of the people, until they can steal this benefit away, on the ground that Sabbath-keeping is a mere ceremonial observance. So far from being that, it is a moral duty of the highest type; and the danger in which it seems at times to stand is due mainly to the fact that to appreciate it needs a far more trained and sincere conscience than most of us can bring to the consideration of it.

CHAPTER V.

THE DECALOGUE—ITS SUBSTANCE.

THAT the Decalogue in any of its forms must have been the work of one mind, and that a very great and powerful mind, will be evident on the most cursory inspection. We have not here, as we have in other parts of Scripture, fragments of legislation supplementary to a large body of customary law, fragments which, because of their intrinsic importance or the necessities of a particular time, have been written down. We have here an extraordinarily successful attempt to bring within a definite small compass the fundamental laws of social and individual life. The wonder of it does not lie in the individual precepts. All of them, or almost all of them, can be paralleled in the legislation of other peoples, as indeed could not fail to be the case if the *fundamental* laws of society and of individual conduct were aimed at. These must be obeyed, more or less, in every society that survives. It is the wisdom with which the selection has been made; it is the sureness of hand which has picked out just those things which were central, and has laid aside as irrelevant everything local, temporary, and purely ceremonial; it is the relation in which the whole is placed to God,—these give this small code its distinction. In these respects it is like the Lord's Prayer. It is vain for men to point out this petition of that unique prayer as occurring here, that other as occurring there, and a third as found in yet another place. Even if every single petition contained in it could be unearthed somewhere, it would still remain as unique as ever; for where can you find a prayer which, like it, groups the fundamental cries of humanity to God in such short space and with so sure a touch, and brings them all into such deep connection with the Fatherhood of God? In both cases, in the prayer and in the Decalogue alike, we must recognise that the grouping is the work of one mind; and in both we must recognise also that, whatever were the natural and human powers of the mind that wrought the code and prayer respectively, the main element in the success that has attended their work is the extraordinary degree in which they were illumined by the Divine Spirit. But where, between the time of Moses and the time when Deuteronomy first laid hold upon the life of the nation, are we to look for a legislator of this pre-eminence? So far as we know the history, there is no name that would occur to us. So far as can be seen, Moses alone has been marked out for us in the history of his people as equal to, and likely to undertake, such a task. Everything, therefore, concurs to the conclusion that in the Decalogue we have the first, the most sacred, and the fundamental law in Israel. Here Moses spoke for God; and whatever additions to his original ten words later times may have made, they have not obscured or overlaid what must be ascribed to him. He may not have been the author of much that bears his name, for unquestionably there were developments later than his time which were called Mosaic because they were a continuation and adaptation of his work; but we are justified in believing that here we have the first law he gave to Israel; and in it we should be able to see the really germinal principles of the religion he taught.

Now, manifestly, a religion which spoke its first word in the ten commandments, even in their simplest form, must have been in its very heart and core moral. It must always have been a heresy therefore, a denial of the fundamental Mosaic conception, to place ritual observance *per se* above moral and religious conduct, as a means of approach to Yahweh. On any reading of the commandments only the third and fourth (two out of ten) refer to matters of mere worship; and even these may more correctly be taken to refer primarily to the moral aspects of the cultus. All the rest deal with fundamental relations to God and man. Consequently the prophets who, after the manner of Amos and Hosea, denounce the prevailing belief that Yahweh's help could be secured for Israel, whatever its moral state, by offerings and sacrifices, were not teaching a new doctrine, first discovered by themselves. They were simply reasserting the fundamental principles of the Mosaic religion. Reverence and righteousness—these from the first were the twin pillars upon which it rested. Before ever the ceremonial law, even in its most rudimentary form, had been given, these were emphasised in the strongest way as the requirements of Yahweh; and the people whom the prophets reproved, instead of being the representatives of the ancient Yahwistic faith, had rejected it. Whether the popular view was a falling away from a truer view which had once been popular, or whether it represented a heathen tendency which remained in Israel from pre-Mosaic times and had not even in the days of Amos been overcome, it seems undeniable that it was entirely contrary to the fundamental principles of Yahwism as given by Moses. Even by the latest narrators, those who brought our Pentateuch into its present shape, and who were, it is supposed, completely under the influence of ceremonial Judaism, the primarily moral character of Yahweh's religion was acknowledged by the place they gave to the ten commandments. They alone are handed down as spoken by Yahweh Himself, and as having preceded all other commands; and the terrors of Sinai, the thunder and the earthquake, are made more intimately the accompaniments of this law than of any other. Unquestionably the mind of Israel always was, that here, and not in the ceremonial law, was the centre of gravity of Yahwism. In the view of that fact it is somewhat hard to understand how so many writers of our times, who admit the Decalogue to have been Mosaic, or at any rate pre-prophetic, yet deny the prevailingly moral character of the early religion of Israel. When this law was once promulgated, the old naturalism in which Israel, like other ancient races, had been entangled was repudiated, and the relation between Yahweh and His people was declared to be one which rested upon moral conduct in the widest sense of that term. And the ground of this fact is plainly declared here to be the character of Yahweh: "I am the Lord thy God, that brought thee out of the land of Egypt, out of the house of bondage." He was their deliverer, He had a right to command them, and His commands revealed His nature to His people.

The first four commandments show that Yahweh was already conceived as a spiritual being, removed by a whole heaven from the gods of the Canaanite nations by whom Israel was surrounded. These were mere representatives of the powers of nature. As such they were regarded as existing in pairs, each god having his female counterpart; and their acts had all the indifference to moral considerations which nature in its processes shows. They dwelt in mountain tops, in trees, in rude stones, or in obelisks, and they were worshipped by rites so sanguinary and licentious that Canaanite worship bore everywhere a darker stain than even nature-worship elsewhere had disclosed. In contrast to all this the Yahweh of the Decalogue is "alone," in solitary and unapproachable separation. Amid all the unbridled speculation that has been let loose on this subject, no one, I think, has ever ventured to join with Him any name of a goddess, and He sternly repudiates the worship of any other god besides Him. Now, though there is nothing said of monotheism here, *i. e.*, of the doctrine that no god but one exists, yet, in contrast to the hospitality which distinguished and distinguishes nature-worship in all its forms, Yahweh here claims from His people worship of the most exclusive kind. Besides Him they were to have no object of worship. He, in His unapproachable separateness, had alone a claim upon their reverence. Further, in contrast to the gods who dwelt in trees and stones and pillars, and who could be represented by symbols of that kind, Yahweh sternly forbade the making of any image to represent Him. Thereby He declared Himself spiritual, in so far as He claimed that no visible thing could adequately represent Him. In contrast to the ethnic religions in general, even that of Zarathushtra, the noblest of all, where only the natural element of fire was taken to be the god or his symbol, this fundamental command asserts the supersensuous nature of the Deity, thereby rising at one step clear above all naturalism.

So great is the step indeed, that Kuenen and others, who cannot escape the evidence for the antiquity of the other commandments, insist that this at least cannot be pre-prophetic, since we have such numerous proofs of the worship of Yahweh by images, down at least to the time of Josiah's reform. But, by all but Stade, it is admitted that there was at Shiloh under Eli, and at Jerusalem under David and Solomon, no visible representation of Deity. Now the same writers who tell us this everywhere represent the worship of Yahweh by images as existing among the people. According to their view, the nation had a continual and hereditary tendency to slip into image-worship, or to maintain it as pre-Mosaic custom. And it is quite certain that up even to the Captivity, and after, when, according to even the very boldest negative view, this command had been long known, image-worship, not only of Yahweh, but also of false gods and of the host of heaven, was largely prevalent. Only the Captivity, with its hardships and trials, brought Israel to see that image-worship was incompatible with any true belief in Yahweh. Undeniably, therefore, the existence of an authoritative prohibition does not necessarily produce obedience; and the Biblical view that the Decalogue is Israel's earliest law proves to be the more reasonable, as well as the better authenticated of the two. If, after the command beyond all doubt existed in Israel, it needed the calamities of Israel's last days, and the hardships and griefs of the Exile, to get it completely observed, and if in Jerusalem and at Shiloh in the pre-prophetic time Yahweh was worshipped without images, there can hardly be a doubt that this command must have existed in the earliest period. For no religion is to be judged by the actual practice of the multitude. The true criterion is its highest point; and the imageless worship of Jerusalem is much more difficult to understand if the second commandment was not acknowledged previously in Israel, than it would be if the Decalogue, essentially as we now have it, was acknowledged in the days before the kingship at least.*

The arguments advanced by Kuenen and Wellhausen for a contrary view, beyond those we have just been considering, rest on an undue extension of the prohibition to make any likeness of anything. They adduce the brazen serpent of Moses, and the Cherubim, and the brazen bulls that bore the brazen laver in the court of the Temple at Jerusalem, and the ornaments of that building, as a proof that even in Jerusalem this commandment cannot have been known. But, as we have seen, the original command prohibited only the making of a *pesel*, *i. e.*, of an image for worship. The making of likenesses of men and animals for mere purposes of art and adornment was never included; and the whole objection falls to the ground unless it be asserted that the bulls under the basin were actually worshipped by those who came into the Temple!

The supersensuous nature of Yahweh must, therefore, be taken to be a fundamental part of the Mosaic religion. But besides being solitary and supersensuous, Yahweh was declared by Moses, perhaps by His very name, to be not only mighty, but helpful. The preface to the whole series of commandments is, "I am Yahweh thy God, who brought thee forth out of the land of Egypt." Now of all the derivations of Yahweh, that which most nearly commands universal acceptance is its derivation from *hayah*, to be. And the probabilities are all in favour of the view that it does not imply mere timeless existence, as the translation of the explanation in Exodus† has led many to believe. That is a purely philosophical idea entirely outside of morality, and it can hardly be that the introduction to this moral code, which announces the author of it, should contain no moral reference. If the name be from Qal, and be connected with *ehyeh*, then it means, as Dillmann says ("Exodus and Leviticus," p. 35), that He will be what He has been, and the name involves a reference to all that the God of Israel has been in the past. Such He will be in the future, for He is what He is, without variableness or shadow of turning. If, on the other hand, it be from Hiphil, it will mean "He who causes to be," the creator. In either case there is a clear rise above the ordinary Semitic names for God, Baal, Molech, Milkom, which all express mere lordship. No doubt Yahweh was also called Baal, or Lord, just as we find Him in the Psalms addressed as "my King and my God"; but the specially Mosaic name, the personal name of the God of Israel, does undoubtedly imply quite another quality in God. It is the Helper who has revealed Himself to Israel who here speaks. Hence the addition, "who brought thee out of the land of Egypt." It is as a Saviour that Yahweh addresses His people. By His very name He lifts all the commands He gives out of the region of mere might, or the still lower region of gratification at offerings and precious things bestowed, into the region of gratitude and love.

Further, by issuing this code under the name of Yahweh Moses claimed for Him a moral character. Whether the Hebrew word for holy, *qādhōsh*, implied more in those days than mere separateness, may be doubted; but it is impossible that the idea which we now connect with the word "holy" should not have been held to be congruous to, and expressive of, the nature of Yahweh. Here morality in its initial and fundamental stages is set forth as an expression of His will. And similarly, righteousness must also be an attribute of His, for justice between man and man is made to be His demand upon men. He Himself, therefore, must be faithful as well as holy, and His emancipation from the clinging chain of mere naturalism was thereby completed. The Yahweh of the Decalogue is therefore absolutely alone. He is supersensuous. He is the Helper and Saviour, and He is holy and true. These are His fundamental qualities. Such qualities may be supposed to be present only in their elements, even to the mind of Moses himself: yet the fundamental germinal point was there: and all that has grown out of it may be justly put to the credit of this first revelation.

A moment's thought will show how the teaching that Yahweh alone was to be worshipped broke away from the main stream of Semitic belief, and prepared the way for the ultimate prevalence of the belief that God was one. That He was supersensuous, so that He could not rightly or adequately be represented by any likeness of anything in heaven or earth or sea, left no possible outlet for thought about Him, save in the direction that He was a Spirit. In essence consequently the spirituality of God was thereby secured. Still more important perhaps was the conception of Yahweh as the Helper and Deliverer, the Saviour of His people; for this at once suggested the thought that the true bond between God and man was not mere necessity, nor mere dependence upon resistless power, but love—love to a Divine Helper who revealed Himself in gracious acts and providences, and who longed after and cared for His people with a perfectly undeserved affection. Lastly, His holiness and faithfulness, His righteousness in fact, held implicit in it His supremacy and uni-

---

* Granting that the commandment did not exist, one asks, *What* was it in Yahwism which determined the Jerusalem Sanctuary to be imageless?
† iii. 14.

versality. As Wellhausen has said, "As God of justice and right, Yahweh came to be thought of as the highest, and at last as the only power in heaven and earth." Whether that last stage was present to the mind of Moses, or of any who received the commandments in the first place, is of merely secondary importance. At the very least, the way which must necessarily lead to that stage was opened here, and the mind of man entered upon the path to a pure monotheism, a monotheism which separated God from the world, and referred to His will all that happened in the world of created things. God is One, God is a Spirit, God is Love, and God rules over all—these are the attributes of Yahweh as the Decalogue sets them forth; and in principle the whole higher life of humanity was secured by the great synthesis.

Like all beginnings, this was an achievement of the highest kind. Nowhere but in the soul of one Divinely enlightened man could such a revelation have made itself known; and the solitude of a lonely shepherd's life, following upon the stir and training of a high place in the cultured society of Egypt, gave precisely the kind of environment which would prepare the soul to hear the voice by which God spoke. For we are not to suppose that this revelation came to Moses without any effort or preparation on his part. God does not reveal His highest to the slothful or the debased. Even when He speaks from Sinai in thunder and in flame, it is only the man who has been exercising himself in these great matters who can understand and remember. All the people had been terrified by the Divine Presence, but they forgot the law immediately and fell back into idolatry. It was Moses who retained it and brought it back to them again. His personality was the organ of the Divine will; and in this law which he promulgated Moses laid the foundation of all that now forms the most cherished heritage of men. The central thing in religion is the character of God. Contrary to the prevailing feeling, which makes many say that they know nothing of God, but are sure of their duty to man, history teaches that, in the end, man's thought of God is the decisive thing. Everything else shapes itself according to that; and by taking the first great steps, which broke through the limits of mere naturalism, Moses laid the foundation of all that was to come. There was here the promise and the potency of all higher life: love and holiness had their way prepared, so that they should one day become supreme in man's conception of the highest life: the confused halting between the material and the spiritual, which can be traced in the very highest conceptions of merely natural religions, was in principle done away. And what was here gained was never lost again. Even though the multitude never really grasped all that Moses had proclaimed Yahweh to be; and though it should be proved, which is as yet by no means the case, that even David thought of Him as limited in power and claims by the extent of the land which Israel inhabited; and though, as a matter of fact, the full-orbed universality which the ten commandments implicitly held in them was not attained under the old covenant at all; yet these ten words remained always an incitement to higher thoughts. No advance made in religion or morals by the chosen people ever superseded them. Even when Christ came, He came not to destroy but to fulfil. The highest reach of even his thoughts as regards God could be brought easily and naturally under the terms of this fundamental revelation to Israel.

The remaining commands, those which deal with the relations of men to each other, are naturally introduced by the fifth commandment, which, while it deals with human relations, deals with those which most nearly resemble the relations between God and man. Reverence for God, the deliverer and forgiver of men, is the sum of the commandments which precede; and here we have inculcated reverence for those who are, under God, the source of life, upon whose love and care all, at their entrance into life, are so absolutely dependent. Love is not commanded; because in such relations it is natural, and moreover it cannot be produced at will. But reverence is; and from the place of the command, manifestly what is required is something of that same awful respect which is due to Yahweh Himself. The power which parents had over their children in Israel was extensive, though much less so than that possessed, for example, by Roman parents. A father could sell his daughters to be espoused as subordinate wives;* he could disallow any vows a daughter might wish to take upon her;† and both parents could bring an incorrigible rebellious son to the elders of the city‡ and have him stoned publicly to death. But, according to Moses, the main restraining forces in the home should be love and reverence, guarded only by the solemn sanction of death to the openly irreverent, just as reverence for Yahweh was guarded.

There was here nothing of the sordid view, repudiated so energetically by Jewish scholars like Kalisch,§ that we ought "to weigh and measure filial affection after the degree of enjoyed benefits." No; to this law "the relation between parents and children is holy, religious, godly, not of a purely human character"; and it is a mere profanation to regard it as we in modern times too often do. In our mad pursuit after complete individual liberty we have fallen back into a moral region which it was the almost universal merit of the ancient civilisations to have left behind them. It is true, certainly, that there were reasons for this advance then which we could not now recognise without falling back from our own attainments in other directions; but it was the saving salt of the ancient civilisations that the parents in a household were surrounded with an atmosphere of reverence, which made transgressions against them as rare as they were considered horrible. The modern freedom may in favourable circumstances produce more intimate and sympathetic intercourse between parents and children; but in the average household it has lowered the whole tone of family life; and it threatens sooner or later, if the ancient feeling cannot be restored, to destroy the family, the very keystone of our religion and civilisation. This commandment is not conditioned on the question whether parents have been more or less successful in giving their children what they desire, or whether they have been wise and unselfish in their dealing with their children. As parents they have a claim upon their respect,

* Exod. xxi. 7.
† Numb. xxx. 6.
‡ Deut. xxi. 8.
§ Kalisch, "Exodus," p. 364:—yet taught in all Victorian State schools under the vicious system at present admitted.

their tenderness, their observance, which can be neglected only at the children's peril. Even the average parent gives quite endless thought and care to his children, and almost unconsciously falls into the habit of living for them. That brings with it for the children an indelible obligation; and along with the new and wiser freedom which is permitted in the modern home, this reverence should grow, just as the love and reverence for God on the part of those who have been made the free children of God through Christ ought far to exceed that to which the best of the Old Testament saints could attain.

Want of reverence for parents is, in the Decalogue, made almost one with want of reverence toward God, and, in the case of this human duty alone, there is a promise annexed to its observance. The duty runs so deep into the very core of human life, that its fulfilment brings wholesomeness to the moral nature; this health spreads into the merely physical constitution, and long life becomes the reward. But apart from the quietude of heart and the power of self-restraint which so great a duty rightly fulfilled brings with it, we must also suppose that in a special manner the blessing of God does rest upon dutiful children. Even in the modern world, amid all its complexity, and though in numberless instances it may seem to have been falsified, this promise verifies itself on the large scale. In the less complex life of early Israel we may well believe that its verification was even more strikingly seen. In both ancient and modern times, moreover, the human conscience has leaped up to justify the belief that of all the sins committed without the body this is the most heinous, and that there does rest upon it in a peculiar manner the wrath of Almighty God. It is a blasphemy against love in its earliest manifestations to the soul, and only by answering love with love and reverence can there be any fulfilling of the law.

After the fifth, the commandments deal with the purely human relations; but in coming down from the duties which men owe to God, this law escapes the sordidness which seems to creep over the laws of other nations, when they have to deal with the rights and duties of men. The human rights are taken up rather into their relation to God, and cease to be mere matters of bargain and arrangement. They are viewed entirely from the religious and moral standpoint. For example, the destruction of human life, which in most cases was in ancient times dealt with by private law, and was punished by fines or money payments, is here regarded solely as a sin, an act forbidden by God. The will of a holy God is the source of these prohibitions, however much the idea of property may extend in them beyond the limits which to us now seem fitting. They begin with the protection of a man's life, the highest of his possessions. Next, they prohibit any injury to him through his wife, who next to his life is most dear to him. Then property in our modern sense is protected; and lastly, rising out of the merely physical region, the ninth commandment prohibits any attack upon a man's civil standing or honour by false witness concerning him in the courts of justice. To that crime Easterns are prone to a degree which Westerns, whom Rome has trained to reverence for law, can hardly realise. In India, at this hour, false witnesses can be purchased in the open market at a trifling price; and under native government the whole forces of civil justice become instruments of the most remediless and exasperating tyranny. So long as the law has not spoken its last word *against* the innocent, there is hope of remedy; justice may at last assert itself. But when, either by corrupt witnesses or by a corrupt judge, the law itself inflicts the wrong, then redress is impossible, and we have the oppression which drives a wise man mad. Both murder and robbery, moreover, may be perpetrated by false swearing; and the trust, the confidence that social life demands, is utterly destroyed by it.

But it is in the tenth commandment especially that this code soars most completely away beyond others. In four short words the whole region of neighbourly duty, so far as acts are concerned, has been covered, and with that other codes have been content. But the laws of Yahweh must cover more than that. Out of the heart proceed all these acts which have been forbidden, and Yahweh takes knowledge of its thoughts and intents. The covetous desire, the grasping after that which we cannot lawfully have, that, too, is absolutely forbidden. It has been pointed out that the first commandment also deals with the thoughts. "Thou shalt have no other gods before Me," separated from the prohibition of idol-worship, can refer only to the inward adoration or submission of the heart. And in this last commandment also it is the evil desire, the lust which "bringeth forth sin," which is condemned. In its beginning and ending, therefore, this code transcends the limits ordinarily fixed for law; it leads the mind to a view of the depth and breadth of the evil that has to be coped with, which the other precepts, taken by themselves and understood in their merely literal sense, would scarcely suggest.

This fact should guard us against the common fallacy that Moses and the people of his day could not have understood these commandments in any sense except the barely literal one. In the first and tenth commandments there is involved the whole teaching of our Lord that he that hateth his brother is a murderer. The evil thought that first stirs the evil desire is here placed on the same interdicted level as the evil deed; and though until our Lord had spoken none had seen all that was implied, yet here too He was only fulfilling, bringing to perfection, that which the law as given by Moses had first outlined. With this in view, it seems difficult to justify that interpretation of the commandments which refuses all depth of meaning to them. The initial and final references to the inner thoughts of men, the delicate moral perception which puts so unerring a finger on the sources of sin, show that such literalism is out of place. No interpretation can do this law justice which treats it superficially; and instead of feeling safest when we find least in these commandments, we should welcome from them all the correction and reproof which a reasonable exegesis will sustain.

Some of those who adopt the other view do so in the interests of the authenticity of the commandments. They say, We must be careful not to put into them any idea which transcends what was possible in the days of Moses; otherwise we must agree with those who bring down the date of these marvellous ten words to the middle of the seventh century B. C. But there is much ground for distrusting modern judgments as to what men can have thought and felt in earlier and ruder stages of society. So long as the *naïve* interpretation of the state of man before the fall prevailed, which Milton has made so widely popular, the tendency was to exaggerate the early man's moral and spiritual attainments. Now, when the most degraded savages are taken as the truest representatives of primitive man, the temptation is to minimise both unduly. How often have we been told, for example, that the Australian is the lowest of mankind, and that he has no other idea of a spiritual world than that when he dies he will "jump up" a white man! Yet Mr. A. W. Howitt,* an unexceptionable authority, as having himself been "initiated" among the Australian blacks, tells us that they give religious and moral instruction to their boys when they receive the privileges of manhood. His words are: "The teachings of the initiation are in a series of 'moral lessons,' pantomimically displayed in a manner intended to be so impressive as to be indelible. There is clearly a belief in a Great Spirit, or rather an anthropomorphic Supernatural Being, the 'Master of all,' whose abode is above the sky, and to whom are attributed powers of omnipotence and omnipresence, or, at any rate, the power 'to do anything and to go anywhere.' The exhibition of his image to the novices, and the magic dances round it, approach very near to idol-worship. The wizards who profess to communicate with him, and to be the mediums of communication between him and his tribe, are not far removed from an organised priesthood. To his direct ordinance are attributed the spiritual and moral laws of the community. Although there is no worship of Daramülun, as, for instance, by prayer, yet there is clearly an invocation of him by name, and a belief that certain acts please while others displease him." To most it would have seemed absurd to attribute religious ideas of such a kind to a people in the social and moral condition of the Australian aborigines. Yet here we have the testimony of a perfectly competent and reliable witness, who, moreover, has no personal bias in favour of theologic notions, to prove that even in their present state their theology is of this comparatively advanced kind.

Many critics like Stade, and even Kuenen, would deny to Israel in the days of Moses any conception of Yahweh which would equal the Australian conception of Daramülun! Not to speak of the "regrettable vivacities" of Renan in regard to Yahweh, Kuenen would deny to the Mosaic Yahweh the title of Lord of all; he would deny to Him the power "to go anywhere and to do anything," binding Him strictly to His tribe and His land; he would make His priests little more than the Australian wizards; and purely moral laws like the Decalogue Wellhausen would remove to a late date mainly because such laws transcend the limits of the thought and knowledge of the Mosaic time. But can any one believe that Israel in the Mosaic time had lower beliefs than those of the Australian aborigines? In every other respect they had left far behind them the social state and the merely embryonic culture of the Australian tribes. Moses himself is an irrefragable proof of that. No such man as he could have arisen among a people in the state of the Australians. Even the fact that the Hebrews had lived in Egypt, and had been compelled to do forced labour for a long series of years, would of itself have raised them to a higher stage of culture. Moreover they built houses, and owned sheep and cattle, and must have known at least the rudiments of agriculture. Indeed Deut. xi. 10 asserts this, and the testimony of travellers as to the habits of the tribes in the wilderness of the wanderings now confirms it. Further, they had been in contact with Egyptian religion, and they had been surrounded by cults having more or less relation to the ancient civilisations of Mesopotamia. Under such circumstances, even apart from all revelation, it could not be assumed that their religious ideas must needs correspond to modern notions of the low type of primitive religions. On the contrary, nothing but the clearest proof that their religious conceptions were so surprisingly low should induce us to believe it. On any supposition, they had in the Mosaic time the first germs of what is now universally admitted to be the highest form of religion. Can we believe that only 1300 years B. C., in the full light of history, coming out of a land where the religion of the people had been systematised and elaborated, not for centuries, but for millenniums, and only 600 years before the monotheistic prophets, a people at such a stage of civilisation as the Hebrews can have had cruder notions of Deity than the Wiraijuri and Wolgal tribes of New South Wales!* It may have been so; but before we take it to have been so, we have a right to demand evidence of a stringent kind, evidence which leaves us no way of escape from a conclusion so improbable.

Moreover the acceptance of the view now opposed does not get rid of the necessity for supernatural enlightenment in Israel. It only transfers it from an earlier to a later time. For if the knowledge of Israel in Moses' day was below the Wolgal standard, then it would seem inexplicable that the ethical monotheism of the prophets should have grown out of it by any merely natural process. If there were no inspiration before the prophets, though they believed and asserted there was, then their own inspiration only becomes the more marvellous. It is not needful to deny that the Hebrew tribes may at some time have passed through the low stage of religious belief of which these writers speak. But they err conspicuously in regarding every trace of animistic and fetichistic worship which can be unearthed in the language, the ceremonies, and the habits of the Hebrews at the Exodus, as evidence of the highest beliefs of the people at that time. As a matter of fact, these were probably mere survivals of a state of thought and feeling then either superseded or in the process of being so. Besides, the mass of any people always lag far behind the thoughts and aspirations of the highest thinkers of their nation; and if we admit inspiration at all as a factor in the religious development of Israel, the distance between what Moses taught and believed himself, and what he could get the mass of the people to believe and practise, must have been still greater. If he gave the people the ten commandments, he must have been far above them, and dogmatic assertions as to what he can have thought and believed ought to be abandoned.

Granting, however, that all we have found in the Decalogue's conception of Yahweh was

* *Journal Anthropological Institute*, May, 1884, p. 28.

* See Page Renouf, "Hibbert Lectures."

present to the mind of Moses, and granting that the commands which deal with the relations of men to each other are not mere isolated prohibitions, but are founded upon moral principles which were understood even then to have much wider implications, there still remains a gap between the widest meaning that early time could put into them, and that which Luther's Catechism, or the Catechism of the Westminster Divines, for example, asserts. The question therefore arises whether these wider and more detailed explanations, which make the Decalogue cover the whole field of the moral and religious life, are legitimate, and if so, on what principle can they be justified? The reply would seem to be that they are legitimate, and that the ten words did contain much more than Moses or any of his nation for many centuries after him understood. For any fruitful thought, any thought which really penetrates the heart of things, must have in it wider implications than the first thinker of it can have conceived. If by any means a man has had insight to see the central fact of any domain of thought and life, its applications will not be limited to the comparatively few cases to which he may apply it. He will generally be content to deduce from his discovery just those conclusions which in his circumstances and in his day are practically useful and are most clamorously demanded. But those who come after, pressed by new needs, challenged by new experiences, and enlightened by new thoughts in related regions, will assuredly find that more was involved in that first step than any one had seen. The scope of the fruitful principle will thus inevitably widen with the course of things, and inferences undreamed of by those who first enunciated the principle will be securely drawn from it by later generations. Now if that be true in regard to truths discovered by the unassisted intellect of man, how much more true will it be of thoughts which have first been revealed to man under the influence of inspiration? Behind the human mind which received them and applied them to the circumstances which then had to be dealt with, there is always the infinite mind which sees that

"Far-off Divine event
To which the whole creation moves."

The Divine purpose of the revelation must be the true measure of the thoughts revealed, and the Divine purpose can best be learned by studying the results as they have actually evolved themselves in the course of ages. Consequently, while the fundamental point in sound interpretation of a book such as the Bible is to ascertain *first* what the statements made therein signified to those who heard them first, the second point is not to shut the mind to the wider and more extensive applications of them which the thought and experience of men, taught by the course of history, have been induced, or even compelled, to make. Both the narrower and the wider meanings are there, and were meant to be found there. No exposition which ignores either can be adequate.

That all works of God are to be dealt with in this way is beautifully demonstrated by Ruskin (*Fors Clavigera*, Vol. I., Letter V.). In criticising the statement of a botanist that "there is no such thing as a flower," after admitting that in a certain sense the lecturer was right, he goes on to say: "But in the deepest sense of all, he was to the extremity of wrongness wrong; for leaf and root and fruit exist, all of them, only—that there may be flowers. He disregarded the life and passion of the creature, which were its essence. Had he looked for these, he would have recognised that in the thought of nature herself, there is, in a plant, nothing else but flowers." That means, of course, that the final perfection of a development is the real and final meaning of it all. Now any thought given by God in this special manner which we call "inspiration" has in it a manifold and varied life, and an end in view, which God alone foresees. It works like leaven, it grows like a seed. It is supremely living and powerful; and though it may have begun its life, like the mustard seed, in a small and lowly sphere, it casts out branches on all sides till its entire allotted space is filled. So in the Decalogue; the central chord in all the matters dealt with has been touched with Divine skill, and all that has further to be revealed or learned on that matter must lie in the line of the first announcement.

It is not, therefore, an illegitimate extension of the meaning of the first commandment to say that it teaches monotheism, nor of the second that it teaches the spirituality of God, nor of the seventh that it forbids all sensuality in thought or word or deed. It is true that probably only the separateness of God was originally seen to be asserted in the first, and the words may possibly have been understood to mean that the "other gods" referred to had some kind of actual life. The second, too, may have seemed to be fulfilled when no earthly thing that was made by man was taken to represent Yahweh. Lastly, those who say that nothing is forbidden in the seventh commandment but literal adultery have much to say for themselves. In a polygamous society concubinage always exists. The absence of the more flagrant of what in monogamous societies are called social evils does not in the least imply the superior morality, such as many who wish to disparage our Christian civilisation have ascribed, for instance, to Mohammedans. The degraded class of women who are the reproach and the despair of our large towns are not so frequent in those societies, because all women are degraded to nearer their level than in monogamous lands. Both lust and vice are more prevalent: and they are so because the whole level of thought and feeling in regard to such matters is much lower than with us.

Now, undoubtedly, ancient Israel was no exception to this rule. In it, as a polygamous nation, there was a license in regard to sexual relations with women who were neither married nor betrothed which would be impossible now in any Christian community. It may be, therefore, that only the married woman was specially protected by this law. But in none of these cases did the more rudimentary conception of the scope of the commandments last. By imperceptible steps the sweep of them widened, until finally the last consequences were deduced from them, and they were seen to cover the whole sphere of human duty. It may have been a long step from the prohibition to put other gods along with Yahweh to St. Paul's decisive word "An idol is nothing in the world," but the one was from the first involved in the other. Between "Thou shalt not make unto thee a graven image" and our Lord's declaration "God is a Spirit, and must be worshipped in spirit and in truth," there lies a long and toilsome upward movement; but the first was the gate into the path which must end in the second. Similarly, the commandment which affirmed so strongly the sacredness of the family, by hedging round the housemother with this special defence held implicit in it all that rare and lovely purity which the best type of Christian women exhibits. The principles upon which the initial prohibitions were founded were true to fact and to the nature both of God and man. They were, therefore, never found at fault in the advancing stages of human experience; and the meaning which a modern congregation of Christians finds in these solemn "words," when they are read before them, is as truly and justly their meaning as the more meagre interpretation which alone ancient Israel could put upon them.

How gradually, and how naturally, the advancing thoughts and changed circumstances of Israel affected the Decalogue may be seen most clearly in the differences between its form as originally given, and as it is set forth in Exodus and in Deuteronomy. If the original form of these commandments was what we have indicated (p. 511), they corresponded entirely to the circumstances of the wilderness. There is no reference in them which presupposes any other social background than that of a people dwelling together according to families, possessing property, and worshipping Yahweh. None of the commandments involves a social state different from that. But when Israel had entered upon its heritage, and had become possessed of the oxen and asses which were needed in agricultural labour and in settled life, this stage of their progress was reflected in the reasons and inducements which were added to the original commands. In the fourth and tenth commandments of Exodus we have consequently the essential commandments of the earlier day adapted to a new state of things, *i. e.*, to a settled agricultural life. Then, even as between the Exodus and Deuteronomic texts, a progress is perceptible. The reasons for keeping the Sabbath which these two recensions give are different, as we have seen, and it is probable that the reason given in Deuteronomy was first. To the people in the wilderness came the bare Divine command that this one day was to be sacred to Yahweh. In both Exodus and Deuteronomy we have additions, going into details which show that when these versions were prepared Israel had ceased to be nomadic and had become agricultural. In Deuteronomy we find that the importance and usefulness of this command from a humane point of view had been recognised, and one at least of the grounds upon which it should be held a point of morality to keep it is set forth in the words "that thy manservant and thy maidservant may rest as well as thou." Finally, if the critical views be correct, in Exodus we have the motive for the observance of the Sabbath raised to the universal and eternal, by being brought into connection with the creative activity of God.

If the progression now traced out be real, then we have in it a classical instance of the manner in which Divine commands were given and dealt with in Israel. Given in the most general form at first, they inevitably open the way for progress, and as thought and experience grow in volume and rise in quality, so does the understanding of the law as given expand. Under the influence of this expansion addition after addition is made, till the final form is reached; and the whole is then set forth as having been spoken by Yahweh and given by Moses when the command was first promulgated. In such cases literary proprietorship was never in question. Each addition was sanctioned by revelation, and those by whom it came were never thought of. It would seem, indeed, that nothing but modern sceptical views as to the reality of revelation, the feeling that all this movement to a higher faith was merely natural, and that the hand of God was not in it, could have suggested to the ancient Hebrew writers the wish to hand on the names of those by whom such changes were made. Yahweh spoke at the beginning, Moses mediated between the people and Yahweh, and the law thus mediated was in all forms equally Mosaic, and in all forms equally Divine.

One other thing remains to be noticed, and that is the prevailing negative form of the commandments. Of the ten only the fourth and fifth are in the affirmative. All the others are prohibitions, and we who have been taught by Christianity to put emphasis upon the positive aspects of duty as the really important aspects of it, may not improbably feel chilled and repelled by a moral code which so definitely and prevailingly forbids. But the cause of this is plain. A code like that of the Twelve Tables published in early Rome is only occasionally negative, because it rises to no great height in its demands, and is intent only upon ordering the life of the citizens in their outward conduct. But this code, which seeks to raise the whole of life into the sacredness of a continual service of God and man, must forbid, because the first condition of such a life is the renunciation and the restriction of self. Benevolent dreamers and theorists of all ages, and men of the world whose moral standard is merely the attainment of the average man, have denied the evil tendency in man's nature. They have asserted that man is born good; but the facts of experience are entirely against them. Whenever a serious effort has been made to raise man to any conspicuous height of moral goodness, it has been found necessary to forbid him to follow the bent of his nature. "Thou shalt not" has been the prevailing formula; and in this sense original sin has always been witnessed to in the world. Hence the Old Testament, in which the most strenuous conflict for goodness which the world in those ages knew was being carried on, could not fail, in every part of it, to proclaim that man is not born good. However late we may be compelled to put the writing of the story of the fall as it stands in Genesis, there can be no question that it represents the view of the Old Testament at all times. Man is fallen; he is not what he ought to be, and the evil taint is handed on from one generation to another. Every generation, therefore, is called, by prophet and priest and lawgiver alike, to the conflict against the natural man.

The truth is that all along the leaders of Israel had a quite overawing sense of the moral greatness of Yahweh and of the stringency of His demands upon them. "Be ye holy, for I am holy," was His demand; and so among this people, as among no other, the sense of sin was heightened, till it embittered life to all who seriously took to heart the religion they professed. This feeling sought relief in expiatory sacrifices, like the sin offering and the guilt offering; but in vain. It then led to Pharisaic hedging of the law, to seeking a positive precept for every moment of time, to binding upon men's consciences the most minute and burdensome prescriptions, as a means of making them what they must be if they were to meet the Divine requirements. But that too failed. It became a slavery so intolerable that, when St. Paul received the power of a new life, his predominant feeling was that for the first time he knew what liberty meant. He was set free from both the bondage of sin and the bondage of ritual.

To the religious man of the Old Testament life was a conflict against evil tendencies, a conflict in which defeat was only too frequent, but from which there was no discharge. It was fitting, therefore, that at the very beginning of Israel's history, as the people of God, this stern prohibition of the rougher manifestations of the natural man should stand.

But it is characteristic of the Old Testament that it states the fundamental fact, without any of the over-refinements and exaggerations by which later doctrinal developments have discredited it. There is no appearance here, or anywhere in the Old Testament, of the Lutheran exaggeration that man is by nature impotent to all good, as a stock or a stone is. Keeping close to the testimony of the universal conscience, the Decalogue, and the Old Testament generally, speaks to men as those who can be otherwise if they will. There is, further, a robust assertion of righteous intention and righteous act on the part of those whose minds are set to be faithful to God. This may have been partly due to a blunter feeling in regard to sin, and a less highly developed conscience, but it was mainly a healthy assertion of facts which ought not to be ignored. Yet, with all that, original sin was too plain a fact ever to be denied by the healthy-minded saints of the Old Testament. Fundamentally, they held that human nature needed to be restrained, its innate lawlessness needed to be curbed, before it could be made acceptable to God.

Among the heathen nations that was not so. Take the Greeks, for instance, as the highest among them. Their watchword in morals was not repression, but harmonious development. Every impulse of human nature was right, and had the protection of a deity peculiarly its own. Restraint, such as the Israelite felt to be his first need, would have been regarded as mutilation by the Greek, for he was dominated by no higher ideal than that of a fully developed man. There was no vision of unattainable holiness hovering always before his mind, as there was before the mind of the Israelite. God had not revealed Himself to him in power and unalloyed purity, with a background of infinite wisdom and omnipotence, so that unearthly love and goodness were seen to be guiding and ruling the world. As a consequence, the calling and destiny of man were conceived by the Greeks in a far less soaring fashion than by Israel. To put the difference in a few words, man, harmoniously developed in all his powers and passions and faculties, with nothing excessive about him, was made God by the Greeks; whereas in Israel God was brought down into human life to bear man's burden and to supply the strength needed that man might become like God in truth and mercy and purity. It is of course true that both conceived of God under human categories. They could not conceive God save by attributing to Him that which they looked upon as highest in man. It is also true that the higher natures in both nations, starting thus differently, did in much approach each other. Still, the immense difference remains, that the impulse in the one case was given from the earth by dreams of human perfection, in the other it came from above through men who had seen God. The Greeks had seen only the glory of man; Israel had seen the glory of God.

The result was that human nature as it is seemed to the one much more worthy of respect and much less seriously compromised than it did to the other. Comparing man as he is, only with man as he easily might be, the Greeks took a much less serious view of his state than the Hebrews, who compared him with God as He had revealed Himself. The former never attained any clear conception of sin, and regarded it as a passing weakness which could without much trouble be overcome. The latter saw that it was a radical and now innate want of harmony with God, which could only be cured by a new life being breathed into man from above. And when Europe became Christian, this difference made itself felt in very widespread religious and theological divergences. In the South and among the Latin races the less strenuous view of human disabilities—the view which naturally grew out of the heathen conception of man as, on the whole, born good, with no very arduous moral heights to scale—has prevailed, and in those regions the Pelagian form of doctrine has mastered the Christian Church. But the Teutonic races have, in this matter, shown a remarkable affinity with the Hebrew mind and teaching. The deeper and more tragic view of the state of man has commended itself to the Teutonic mind, and the depth of the moral taint in the natural man has been estimated according to the Biblical standard. It is not only theologians among the Northern races who have been thus affected. The higher imaginative literature of England gives the same impression; and in our own day Browning, our greatest poet, has emphasised his acceptance of the Augustinian view of human nature by making its teaching as to original sin a proof of the truth of Christianity.* At the end of his poem "Gold Hair: a Story of Pornic," in which he tells how a girl of angelic beauty, and of angelic purity of nature as was supposed, is found after her death to have sold her soul to the most gruesome avarice, he says:

"The candid incline to surmise of late
That the Christian faith may be false, I find;
For our Essays and Reviews' debate
Begins to tell on the public mind,
And Colenso's words have weight:

I still, to suppose it true, for my part,
See reasons and reasons; this, to begin:
'Tis the faith that launched point-blank her dart
At the head of a lie—taught original sin,
The corruption of man's heart."

But the Pagan view always reasserts itself; and modern Hellenists especially, in their admiration of the grace which does undoubtedly go with such conceptions of goodness as the Greeks could attain, are apt to look askance at the harshness and strenuousness which they find in the

* Browning's "Poetical Works," vol. vi., p. 69.

Old Testament. For the most pathetic and pure of the Greek conceptions of the gods are those which, like Demeter, embody mother's love or some other natural glory of humanity. Being thus natural, they are set before us by the Greek imagination with an unconstrained and graceful beauty which makes goodness appeal to the æsthetic sense. To do this seems to many the supreme achievement. Without this they hold that Christianity would fail to meet the requirements of the modern heart and mind, for to interest "taste" on the side of goodness is, apparently, better than to let men feel the compulsion of duty. Reasoning on such premisses, they claim that Greek religion gave to Christianity its completion and its crown. This is the claim advanced by Dyer in his "Gods of Greece" (p. 19). "The Greek poets and philosophers," he says, "are among our intellectual progenitors, and therefore the religion of to-day has requirements which include all that the noblest Greeks could dream of, requirements which the aspirations of Israel alone could not satisfy. Our complex life had need, not only of a supreme God of power, universal and irresistible, of a jealous God beside whom there was no other God, but also of a God of love and grace and purity. To these ideal qualities, present in the Diviner godhead of the Gospels, the evolution of Greek mythology brought much that satisfies our hearts." The best answer to that is to read Deuteronomy. The Hebrews had no need to borrow "a God of love and grace and purity" from Greek mythology. Centuries before they came in contact with Greeks, their inspired men had painted the love and grace and purity of God in the most attractive colours. Nor did they ever need to unlearn the belief that Yahweh was merely a supreme God of power. In the course of our exposition we shall have occasion to see that the worship of mere power was superseded by the religion of Yahweh from the first, and that the author of Deuteronomy gives his whole strength to demonstrate that the God of Israel is a "God of love and grace and purity." But perhaps "grace" means to Mr. Dyer "gracefulness." In that case we would deny that "the Diviner godhead of the Gospels," as revealed in Jesus Christ, had that æsthetic quality either. There is no word of an appeal to the sense of the artistically beautiful in anything recorded of Him; but neither in the Old Testament nor the New is there any want of moral beauty in the representation given of God. Moral beauty alone has a central place in religion; and when beauty that appeals to the senses intrudes into religion, it becomes a source of weakness rather than of strength. There may be a few people who can trust to their taste to keep them firm in the pursuit of goodness, but the bulk of men have always needed, and will always need, the severer compulsion of duty. They need an objective standard; they need a God, the embodiment and enforcer of all that duty demands of them; and when they bend themselves to the yoke of obligation thus imposed, they enter into a world of heavenly beauty which seizes and enraptures the soul. The mere æsthetic beauty of Greek mythology pales, for the more earnest races of mankind at least, before this Diviner loveliness, and it is the special gift of the Hebrew as well as of the Teutonic races to be sensitive to it, just as they fall behind others in æsthetic sensitiveness. Wordsworth felt this, and has expressed it inimitably in his "Ode to Duty"—

"Stern Lawgiver! yet Thou dost wear
The Godhead's most benignant grace,
Nor know we anything so fair
As is the smile upon Thy face."

That expresses the Hebrew feeling also. Drawn upwards by the infinite and unchangeable love and goodness of Yahweh, the Hebrews felt the clog of their innate sinfulness as no other race has done. The stern "thou shalt nots" of the Decalogue consequently found an echo in their hearts. Won by the beauty of holiness, they gladly welcomed the discipline of the Divine law, and by doing so they established human goodness on a foundation immeasurably more stable than any the gracefulness of Greek imaginations could hope to lay.

CHAPTER VI.

THE MEDIATORSHIP OF MOSES.

DEUTERONOMY v. 22-23.

AFTER the ten commandments, Deuteronomy, like Exodus, next indicates that for all of legislation, exhortation, and advice that follows, Moses was to be the mediator between God and the people. He is represented as Yahweh's prophet or speaker in all that succeeds; the Decalogue alone is set forth as the direct Divine command. Evidently a great distinction is here notified, and what it exactly was may be best explained by reference to the history of Roman law. In the earliest times that consisted of *Fas*, *Jus*, and *Jus moribus constitutum*. In chapter iv. Professor Muirhead's description of *fas* has been given at length, so that we need not repeat it here. The point to remember is that it consisted of universal precepts such as the Decalogue contains, given direct by God. *Jus* again was, according to Breal, the Divine will declared by human agency, and it occupied much the position which law does in civilised states now. Finally, *jus moribus constitutum*, or *boni mores*, was customary law, which had a twofold function. "It was (1) a restraint upon the law, condemning, though it could not prevent, the ruthless and unnecessary exercise of legal right. (2) It was a supplement to law (*jus*), requiring things law did not, *e. g.*, dutiful service, respect and obedience, chastity, fidelity to engagements, etc." Now it is a striking fact that, though there can be no question of imitation here, the legislation of Deuteronomy falls naturally into these very divisions; and that fact of itself gives strong support to the belief that here in Israel, as there in Rome, we have the recorded facts of the earliest efforts at the regulation of national life. The *fas*, then, corresponds to the Decalogue. The *jus* runs exactly parallel with the laws in the strict sense of the term, those which Moses received from Yahweh and afterwards promulgated. Lastly, the *boni mores* are represented in Deuteronomy by those beautiful precepts which limited the exercise of legal right, and, going far beyond law, demanded of Israel that they should make good their claim to be Yahweh's people by justice, charity, and purity.

To some it may seem that we do no service to Scripture by insisting upon such a parallel. They will feel as if thereby the unique character of the religion of Israel as a revealed religion were obscured, if not obliterated. But nothing can be imagined which could confirm us in belief of the substantial accuracy of what we find narrated of early times in Scripture, more than the discovery that, without any possibility of collusion, the earliest records of civilisation elsewhere give us precisely the same account of the forms in which law first makes its appearance. Surely we ought now to have learned this lesson at least, that it is no disparagement to a Divinely given system of law and religion, that its growth and development run in the same channels as the growth and development of similar systems which have none of the marks of a Divine origin. Revelation always seizes upon mind as it is, and makes that a sufficient and effective channel for itself. However it is to be explained, it is true that Divine action generally seeks to hide itself in the ordinary course of human things as quickly as possible. It is only at the moment of contact, or at the moment when it has burst forth in some flower of more than earthly grace and loveliness, or when it has overturned and overturned until that state of things which has a right to endure has been attained, that the Divine force reveals itself. For the most part it sinks into the general sum of forces that are making for the progress of humanity, and clothes itself gladly in the uniform of other beneficent but natural influences. Consequently it ought to be a welcome fact that so close a parallel exists between the origins of Roman law and the origins of Hebrew law. The one great gain already mentioned, that it explains the early appearance of the Decalogue, and shows that some such laws would naturally be among the primary laws of Israel, would be sufficient to justify that view; while in addition the distinctions from the early laws of Rome help us to classify in clear broad masses the somewhat disordered series of Deuteronomic laws.

On one point only does the parallel seem questionable. If we followed it alone as our guide, we should have to set down the mediatorship of Moses, as a mere part of the method, as belonging to the formal side only of the great revelation. In other words, we should have to ask whether the statement we have in Deut. v. 22-30 is only an emotional and pictorial way of setting forth the fact that, following and supplementing the elementary and Divinely given Hebrew *fas*, there was also a Divinely given but humanly mediated *jus*. But clearly it means much more than that. By the earlier prophets, and generally in all earlier delineations of him, Moses is regarded as a prophet who had more direct and continuous access to the Divine presence than any other prophet of Israel. Moreover he had always been represented from the earliest times as standing between Yahweh and His people, holding on to the one and refusing to let the other go. In the great scene, taken from the earliest constituents of the Pentateuch and narrated in Exod. xxxii., we see him anticipating by centuries the wonderful picture of the Servant of God in Isa. liii., and by a still more amazing stretch of time, that Divinest wish of St. Paul, that he himself might be accursed even from Christ for his brethren's sake. He thus stood between Yahweh and His people both as the organ of Revelation and as the self-forgetting intercessor, who suffered for sins not his own, as well as for sins which his connection with his nation had brought upon him; who, instead of repining, was willing to be blotted out of God's book if that could benefit his people.

This representation of Moses is not accidental. It is in complete accord with a characteristic of Israelite literature from beginning to end. In the earliest historical records we find that the chief heroes of the nation are mediators, standing for God in the face of evil men, and pleading with God for men when they are broken and penitent, or even when they are only terrified and restrained by the terror of the Lord. At the beginning of the national history we see the noble figure of Abraham in an agony of supplication and entreaty before God on behalf of the cities of the plain. At the end of it, we see the Christ, the supreme "mediator between God and man," pouring out His soul unto death for men "while they were yet sinners," dying, the just for the unjust, taking upon Himself the responsibility for the sin of man, and refusing to let him wander away into permanent separation from God. And all between is in accord with this. For it is not Moses only who is regarded as having a mediatorial office. The very people itself is set, by the promise given to Abraham, in the same position. As early at least as the eighth century it was put before Israel, that their calling was not for their own sakes only, but that in them all nations of the earth might be blessed. And at their highest moments the prophets and teachers of Israel always recognise this as their nation's part. Even when they were being scattered among the heathen, it was that they might be the means of bringing the knowledge of Yahweh to the nations. From end to end of Scripture, therefore, this conception is wrought into the very fibre of its utterances. It is of the essence of the Biblical conception of God that He should work among men by mediators. In no other way could the primary Divine message be set forth than by the prophetic voice; in no other way than by the intercession and the suffering of those most in harmony with the Divine will could any effective hold upon God be given to His people. Only by those who thus proved that they had seen Yahweh could His character be expressed. Further, it was in this way that Moses and the prophets, the rulers and the saints of Israel, were types of Christ. They were not mere puppets set forth in certain crises of Israel's history to go through a certain career, live a certain life, and pass into and out of a number of scenes, in order that they might afford us, upon whom the end of the world has come, pictorial proofs that all things in this history were pressing towards and converging upon Christ. That would be a very artificial way of conceiving the matter. No, each of these types was a real man, with real tasks of his own to accomplish in the world. Not only were they all real men, they were the leading men of their various times. They bore the burden of their day more than others; they were the special organs of Divine power and grace; and their lives were spent in giving impulse and direction to the movements of their people's life towards the strange, unlooked-for consummation appointed for it. They were types of Christ, they gave promise of Him, not because of mere arbitrary appointment or selection, but because they did in their day, in a lower degree and at an earlier stage, the very same work that He did. Further, the whole nation was a type of Christ in so far as it was true to its calling at all. It was the prophet and the priest among nations. It spread abroad the knowledge of Him, and it died at last as a nation that life might be given to the world. Both Israel and all the men who truly represented it were partakers in the labours and in the sufferings of Christ beforehand, just as Christians are said to fill up the measure of His sufferings now. The mediatorial character of Moses, therefore, was essential. It is no merely formal thing, nor an afterthought. He would have been no fit founder of the mediatorial nation had he not been a mediator himself, for not otherwise could he have helped to realise the Abrahamic promise.

But there is another subsidiary reason why a mediator was necessary to Israel at this stage. Behind all that Moses taught his people lay necessarily the ancient popular religion of the Hebrews. Now, except in so far as it may have been changed in Egypt, that was in its main features the same as the religion of the other nomadic tribes of Semitic stock, for the Abrahamic faith was, clearly, known but to few. But the names given to their deities by these people —such as Baal, Adhonai, Milcom, etc.—" all expressed submission to the irresistible power revealing itself in nature," just as " Islam," which means " submission," indicates that Mohammedanism is a mere perpetuation of this view.* Consequently the Israelite people were unable to conceive God save as a devouring presence, before which no man could live. The Mosaic view was, in itself, immeasurably higher, and, besides that, it opened up the path to attainments then inconceivable. Moses therefore had to stand alone in his new relation to God, while the people cowered away in terror, dominated entirely by the lower conception. They could not stand where he stood. They were unable to believe that power was not Yahweh's only attribute; while Moses had had revealed to him, in germ at least, that God was " merciful and gracious, long-suffering and slow to anger," and that a life passed in His presence was the ideal life for man. Both the Yahwistic narrative in Exodus and the repetition of it in Deuteronomy give the same representation of the events at Sinai, and indicate quite clearly that, while the old relation to God was in itself good so far, it was to be superseded by that higher relation in which Moses stood. That is the meaning of the words in Deut. v. 28, 29: " And Yahweh said unto me, I have heard the voice of the words of this people which they have spoken unto thee; they have well said all that they have spoken. Oh that there were such a heart in them, that they would fear Me and keep all My commandments, always, that it might be well with them and with their children for ever!" The parallel passage in Exodus is xx. 20: " And Moses said unto the people, Fear not: for God is come to prove you, and that His fear may be before you, that ye sin not." In both, the standpoint of fear is approved as relatively good and wholesome. It was well that the people should have this awestruck fear of the Divine, for it would act as a deterrent from sin. But it was not sufficient. It was only the starting-point for the attainments which Yahweh by Moses, and in Moses, was about to call and incite them to. Moses therefore had to stand between Israel and Yahweh in this too,

* *Cf*. Schultz, " Alttestamentliche Theologie," p. 92.

that he had entered into and lived in relations with his God which they were as yet unable either to conceive or to endure.

It is well to add, also, that in giving approval of this kind to fear as a religious motive these early teachers were entirely in accord with the final development of Israelite religion in the New Testament. The modern view that any appeal to fear in religion or morality is degrading would have been simply unintelligible to the Biblical writers. Even now, the whole fabric of society, the state with its officials and the law with its penalties, are a continual protest against it in the realm of practical morality. In truth the conflict raised about this matter in modern times is simply a conflict between superfine theories and facts. Now the Old Testament is throughout supremely true to the facts of human nature and human experience. It is practically a transcript of them as seen in the light of revelation. In a time, therefore, when in morals and religion physical fact is being allowed to override or pervert psychical fact, the Old Testament view is peculiarly wholesome. It helps to restore the balance and to keep man's thoughts sane.

Another point on which this narrative of Deuteronomy corrects and restores that which the tendency of modern thought has perverted is an even more important one. We have seen that the Old Testament view, as stated here, and as it is interwoven with the central fibres of the Old Testament conception, is that all men who are called to the task of permanently raising the level of human life and thought must give not only their light to, but their life for, those whom they seek to win for God. They must ask nothing from mankind but ever widening opportunities for service and self-sacrifice. But in our modern day this has been precisely reversed, and men like Goethe and Schopenhauer, and even Carlyle, have demanded that mankind should yield service to them, and then, by the furtherance and development they thereby attain, they promise to work out the deliverance of men from superstition and unreality and the bondage of ignorance. Goethe in this matter is typical. He preached and practised in the most uncompromising manner the doctrine of self-development. He thought that he could serve humanity in no way so well as by making every one he met, and all the experiences he encountered, minister to his own intellectual growth. Instead of saying with Moses, " Blot me out of Thy book," but spare these dim idolatrous masses, he would have said, " Let them all perish, and let me become the origin of a wiser, more intellectual, more self-restrained race than they." He consequently pursued his own ends relentlessly from his early years, and attained results so immense that almost every domain of thought, speculation, and science is now under some debt to him. But for all purposes of inspiring moral and spiritual enthusiasm he is practically useless. His selfishness, however high its kind, accomplished its work and left him cold, unapproachable, isolated. This want of love for men made him the accurate critic of human nature, but left him blind in great degree and hopeless altogether in regard to those possibilities of better things which are never wholly wanting to it. The result is that, notwithstanding his heroic powers, his influence is to-day rather a minus quantity in the spiritual and moral life. No one who has not warmth from other sources pouring in upon him can have much communion with Goethe without losing vitality, and in his presence the Divine passion of self-sacrificing love looks out of place, or even slightly absurd. His power is fascinating, but it freezes all the sources of the nobler spiritual emotions, and ultimately must tend to the impoverishing of human nature and the lowering of the level of human life. No; men are not to be reached so if it is wished to raise them to their highest powers, and all experience proves that the New Testament was right in summing up the teaching of the Old by the words, " He that saveth his life shall lose it, and he that loseth his life for My sake shall find it."

> "That is the doctrine, simple, ancient, true;
> Such is life's trial, as old earth smiles and knows.
> If you loved only what were worth your love,
> Love were clear gain, and wholly well for you;
> Make the low nature better by your throes!
> Give earth yourself, go up for gain above!"*

CHAPTER VII.

LOVE TO GOD THE LAW OF LIFE.

DEUTERONOMY vi. 4, 5.

IN these verses we approach " the commandments, the statutes, and the judgments " which it was to be Moses' duty to communicate to the people, *i. e.*, the second great division of the teaching and guidance received at Sinai. But though we approach them we do not come to them for a number of chapters yet. We reach them only in chapter xii., which begins with almost the same words as chapter vi. What lies between is a new exhortation, very similar in tone and subject to that into which chapters i.-iii. have been transformed.

To some readers in our day this repetition, and the renewed postponement of the main subject of the book, have seemed to justify the introduction of a new author here. They are scornfully impatient of the repetition and delay, especially those of them who have themselves a rapid, dashing style; and they declare that the writer of the laws, etc., from chapter xii. onwards cannot have been the writer of these long double introductions. *They* would not have written so; consequently no one else, however different his circumstances, his objects, and his style may be, can have written so. It is true, they admit, that the style, the grammar, the vocabulary are all exactly those of the purely legal chapters, but that matters not. Their irritation with this delay is decisive; and so they introduce us, entirely on the strength of it, to another Deuteronomist, second or third or fourth—who knows? But all this is too purely subjective to meet with general acceptance, and we may without difficulty decide that the linguistic unity of the book, when chapters vi. to xii. are compared with what we find after xii., is sufficient to settle the question of authorship.

But we have now to consider the possible reasons for this second long introduction. The first introduction has been satisfactorily explained in a former chapter; this second one can, I think, quite as easily be accounted for. The object of the book is in itself a sufficient explanation. To modern critical students of the Old Testament the laws are the main interest of Deuteronomy. They are the material they need for their reconstruction of the history of Israel, and they feel as if all besides, though it may contain beautiful thoughts, were irrelevant. But that was not the writer's point of view at all. For him it was not the main thing to introduce new laws. He was conscious rather of a desire to bring old laws, well known to his fellow-countrymen, but neglected by them, into force again. Anything new in his version of them was consequently only such an adaptation of them to the new circumstances of his time as would tend to secure their observance. Even if Moses were the author of the book this would be true; but if a prophetic man in Manasseh's day was the author, we can see how naturally and exclusively that view would fill his mind. He had fallen upon evil times. The best that had been attained in regard to spiritual religion had been deliberately abandoned and trodden under foot. Those who sympathise with pure religion could only hope that a time would come when Hezekiah's work would be taken up again. If Deuteronomy was written in preparation for that time, the legal additions necessary to ward off the evils which had been so nearly fatal to Yahwism would seem to the author much less important than they appear to us to be. His object was to retrieve what had been lost, to rouse the dead minds of his countrymen, to illustrate that on which the higher life of the nation depended, and to throw light upon it from all the sources of what then was modern thought. His mind was full of the high teaching of the prophets. He was steeped in the history of his people, which was then receiving, or was soon to receive, its all but final touches. He was intensely anxious that in the later time for which he was writing all men should see how Providence had spoken for the Mosaic law and religion, and what the great principles were which had always underlain it, and which had now at last been made entirely explicit.

Under these circumstances, it was not merely natural that the author of Deuteronomy should dwell with insistence upon the hortatory part of his book; it was necessary. He could not feel Wellhausen's haste to approach his restatement of the law. To him the exhortation was, in fact, the important thing. Every day he lived he must have seen that it was not want of knowledge that misled his contemporaries. He must have groaned too often under the weight of the indifference even of the well disposed not to be aware that that was the great hindrance to the restoration of the better thoughts and ways of Hezekiah's day.

He had learned by bitter experience, what every man who is in earnest about inducing masses of men to take a step backward or forward to a higher life always learns, that nothing can be accomplished till a fire has been kindled in the hearts of men which will not let them rest. To this task the author of Deuteronomy devotes himself. And whatever impatient theorists of to-day may say, he succeeds amazingly. His exhortation touches men from one end of the world to the other, even to this day, by its affectionate impressiveness. This exhibition of the principles underlying the law is so true that, when our Lord was asked, " Which is the first commandment of all? " He answered from this chapter of

---

* Browning, " James Lee's Wife," VII.

Deuteronomy: "The first of all the commandments is this, The Lord our God is one Lord: and thou shalt love the Lord thy God with all thy heart, and with all thy soul, and with all thy strength. The second is this, Thou shalt love thy neighbour as thyself. There is none other commandment greater than these." Now these are precisely the truths Deuteronomy exhibits in these prefatory chapters, and it is by them that the after-treatment of the law is permeated. The author of Deuteronomy by announcing these truths brought the Old Testament faith as near to the level of the New Testament faith as was possible; and we may well believe that he saw his work in its true relative proportions. The hortatory chapters are really the most original part of the book, and exhibit what was permanent in it. The mere fact that the author lingers over it, therefore, is entirely inadequate to justify us in admitting a later hand. Indeed, if criticism is to retain the respect of reasonable men, it will have to be more sparing than it has hitherto been with the "later hand"; to introduce it here under the circumstances is nothing short of a blunder.

In our verses, therefore, we have to deal with the main point of our book. Coming immediately after the Decalogue, these words render explicit the principle of the first table of that law. In them our author is making it clear that all he has to say of worship, and of the relation of Israel to Yahweh, is merely an application of this principle, or a statement of means by which a life at the level of love to God may be made possible or secured. This section, therefore, forms the bridge which connects the Decalogue with the legal enactments which follow; and it is on all accounts worthy of very special attention. Our Lord's quotation of it as the supreme statement of the Divine law, in its Godward aspect, would in itself be an overwhelmingly special reason for thorough study of it, and would justify us in expecting to find it one of the deepest things in Scripture.

The translation of the first clause presents difficulties. The Authorised Version gives us, "Hear, O Israel: The Lord our God is one Lord," but that can no longer be accepted, since it rests upon the Jewish substitution of Adhonai for Yahweh. Taking this view of the construction, it should be rendered, "Hear, O Israel: Yahweh our God is one Yahweh"; and this is the meaning which most recent authorities—*e. g.*, Knobel, Keil, and Dillmann—put upon it. But equally good authorities—such as Ewald and Oehler—render, "Yahweh our God—Yahweh is one." This is unobjectionable grammatically. Still another translation, "Hear, O Israel: Yahweh is our God, Yahweh alone," has been received by the most recent and most scholarly German translation of the Scripture, that edited by Kautzsch. But the objection that in that case *l' bhaddo*, not *'echādh*, should have been used, seems conclusive against it. The two others come very much to the same thing in the end, and were it not for the time at which Deuteronomy was written, Ewald's translations would be the simpler and more acceptable. But the first—"Yahweh our God is one Yahweh"—exactly meets the circumstances of that time, and moreover emphasises that in Israel's God which the writer of Deuteronomy was most anxious to establish. As against the prevailing tendency of the time, he not only denies polytheism, or, as Dillmann puts it, asserts the concrete fact that the true God cannot be resolved in the polytheistic manner into various kinds and shades of deity, like the Baalim, but he also prohibits the amalgamation or partial identification of Him with other gods. Though very little is told us concerning Manasseh's idolatry, we know enough to feel assured that it was in this fashion he justified his introduction of Assyrian deities into the Temple worship. Moloch, for example, must in some way have been identified with Yahweh, since the sacrifices of children in Tophet are declared by Jeremiah to have been to Yahweh. Further, the worship at the High Places had led, doubtless, to belief in a multitude of local Yahwehs, who in some obscure way were yet regarded as one, just as the multitudinous shrines of the Virgin in Romanist lands lead to the adoration of our Lady of Lourdes, our Lady of Étaples, and so on, though the Church knows only one Virgin Mother. This incipient and unconscious polytheism it was our author's purpose to root out by his law of one altar; and it seems congruous, therefore, that he should sum up the first table of the Decalogue in such a way as to bring out its opposition to this great evil. Of course the oneness of deity as such is involved in what he says; but the aspect of this truth which is specially put forward here is that Yahweh, being God, is one Yahweh, with no partners, nor even with variations that practically destroy unity. No proposition could have been framed more precisely and exactly to contradict the general opinion of Manasseh and his followers regarding religion; and in it the watchword of monotheism was spoken. Since it was uttered, this has been the rallying point of monotheistic religion, both among Jews and Mohammedans. For "there is no God but God" is precisely the counterpart of "Yahweh is one Yahweh"; and from one end of the civilised world to the other this strenuous confession of faith has been heard, both as the tumultuous battleshout of victorious armies, and as the stubborn and immovable assertion of the despised, and scattered, and persecuted people to whom it was first revealed. Even to-day, though in the hands of both Jews and Mohammedans it has been hardened into a dogma which has stripped the Mosaic conception of Yahweh of those elements which gave it possibilities of tenderness and expansion, it still has power over the minds of men. Even in such hands, it incites missionary effort, and it appeals to the heart at some stages of civilisation as no other creed does. It makes men, nay, even civilised men, of the wild fetich-worshipping African; but for want of what follows in our context it leaves them stranded—at a higher level, it is true, but stranded nevertheless—without possibilities of advance, and exposed to that terrible decay in their moral and spiritual conceptions which sooner or later asserts itself in every Mohammedan community.

Israel was saved from the same spiritual disease by the great words which succeed the assertion of Yahweh's oneness. The writer of Deuteronomy did not desire to set forth this declaration as an abstract statement of ultimate truth about God. He makes it the basis of a quite new, a quite original demand upon his countrymen. Because Yahweh thy God is one Yahweh, "thou shalt love Yahweh thy God with all thine heart, and with all thy soul, and with all thy might." To us, who have inherited all that was attained by Israel in their long and eventful history as a nation, and especially in its disastrous close, it may have become a commonplace that God demands the love of His people. But if so, we must make an effort to shake off the dull yoke of custom and familiarity. If we do, we shall see that it was an extraordinarily original thing which the Deuteronomist here declares. In the whole of the Old Testament there are, outside of Deuteronomy, thirteen passages in which the *love* of men to Yahweh is spoken of. They are Exod. xx. 6; Josh. xxii. 5, xxiii. 11; Judges v. 31; 1 Kings iii. 3; Neh. i. 5; Psalms xviii. 2, xxxi. 24, xci. 14, xcvii. 10, cxvi. 1, cxlv. 20; and Dan. ix. 4. Now of these the verses from Nehemiah and Daniel are manifestly later than Deuteronomy, and of the Psalms only the eighteenth can with any confidence be assigned to a time earlier than the seventh century B. C. All the others may with great probability be assigned at earliest to the times of Jeremiah and the post-exilic period. Three of the passages from the historic books again—Josh. xxii. 5, xxiii. 11; 1 Kings iii. 3—are attributed, on grounds largely apart from the use of this expression, to the Deuteronomic editor, *i. e.*, the writer who went over the historical books about 600 B. C., and made slight additions here and there, easily recognisable by their differing in tone and feeling from the surrounding context. Indeed Josh. xxii. 5 is a palpable quotation from Deuteronomy itself.

Of the thirteen passages, therefore, only three —Exod. xx. 6, Judges v. 31, and Psalm xviii. 2—belong to the time previous to Deuteronomy, and in all three the mention of love to God is only allusive, and, as it were, by the way. Before Deuteronomy, consequently, there is little more than the mere occurrence of the word. There is nothing of the bold and decisive demand for love to the one God as the root and ground of all true relations with Him which Deuteronomy makes. At most, there is the hint of a possibility which might be realised in the future; of love to God as the permanent element in the life of man there is no indication; and it is this which the author of Deuteronomy means, and nothing less than this. He makes this demand for love the main element of his teaching. He returns to it again and again, so that there are almost as many passages bearing on this in Deuteronomy as in the whole Old Testament besides; and the particularity and emphasis with which he dwells upon it are immeasurably greater. Only in the New Testament do we find anything quite parallel to what he gives us; and there we find his view taken up and expanded, till love to God flashes upon us from almost every page as the test of all sincerity and the guarantee of all success in the Christian life.

To proclaim this truth was indeed a great achievement; and when we remember the abject fear with which Israel had originally regarded Yahweh, it will appear still more remarkable that the book embodying this should have been adopted by the whole people with enthusiasm, and that with it should begin the Canon of Holy Scripture; for Deuteronomy, as all now recognise, was the first book which became canonical. And I have said that the conception was an extraordinarily original one, and have pointed out that it had not been traceable to any extent previously in Israel's religious books or its religious men. It will appear still more original, I think, if we consider what a growth in moral and spiritual stature separates the Israel of Moses' day and that of Josiah's; what the attitude of other nations to their gods was in contrast to this; and, lastly, what it involves and implies, as regards the nature of both God and man.

As we have already seen, the earlier narratives represent the men to whom Moses spoke as acknowledging that they could not, as yet at any rate, bear to remain in the presence of Yahweh. Between their God and them, therefore, there could be no relation of love properly so called. There was reverence, awe, and chiefly fear, tempered by the belief that Yahweh as their God was on their side. He had proved it by delivering them from the oppressions of Egypt, and they acknowledged Him and were jealous for His honour and submissive to His commands. So far as the record goes, that would seem to have been their religious state. Progress from that state of mind to a higher, to a demand for direct personal relations between each individual Israelite and Yahweh, was not easy. It was hindered by the fact that Israel as a whole, and not the individual, was for a long time regarded as the subject of religion. That, of course, was no hindrance to the development of the thought that Yahweh loved Israel; but so long as that conception dominated religious thought in Israel, so long was it impossible to think of individual love and trust as the element in which each faithful man should live.

But the love of Yahweh was declared, century after century, by prophet and priest and psalmist, to be set upon His people, and so the way for this demand for love on man's part was opened. Man's relations with God began to grow more intimate. The distance lessened, as the use of the words "them that love Me" in the song of Deborah and the Davidic word in Psalm xviii., "I love thee, Yahweh my rock," clearly show. Hosea next took up the strain, and intensified and heightened it in a wonderful manner, but the nation failed to respond adequately. In the later prophets the love and grace and long-suffering of Yahweh and His ceaseless efforts on behalf of Israel are continually made the ground of exhortations, entreaties, and reproaches; but, as a whole, the people still did not respond. We may be sure, however, that an ever increasing minority were affected by the clearness and intensity of the prophetic testimony. To this minority, the Israel within Israel, the remnant that was to return from exile and become the seed of a people that should be all righteous, the love of Yahweh tended to become His main characteristic. That love sustained their hopes; and though the awe and reverence which were due to His holiness, and the fear called forth by His power, still predominated, there grew up in their hearts a multitude of thoughts and expectations tending more and more to the love of God.

As yet it was only a timid reaching out towards Him, a hope and longing which could hardly justify itself. Yet it was robust enough not to be killed by disappointment, by hope deferred, or even by crushing misfortune; and in the furnace of affliction it became stronger and more pure. And in the heart of the author of Deuteronomy it grew certain of itself, and soared up with an eagerness that would not be denied. Then, as always where God is the object of it, love that dares was justified; and out of its restless and timid longings it came to the "place of rest imperturbable, where love is not forsaken if itself forsaketh not."* From knowledge, confirmed by the answering love and inspiration of God, and impelled consciously by Him, he then in this book made and reiterated his great demand. All spiritual men found in it the word they had needed. They responded to it eagerly when the book was published; and their enthusiasm carried even the torpid and careless masses with them for a time. The nation, with the king at their head, accepted the legislation of which this love to God was the underlying principle, and so far as public and corporate action can go, Israel adopted the deepest principle of spiritual life as their own.

Of course with the mass this assent had little depth; but in the hearts of the true men in Israel the joy and assurance of their great discovery, that Yahweh their God was open to, nay, desired and commanded, their most fervent affection, soon produced its fruit. From the fragments of the earliest legislation which have come down to us, it is obvious that the Mosaic principles had led to a most unwonted consideration for the poor. In later days, though the ingrained tendency to oppression, which those who have power in the East seem quite unable to resist, did its evil work in both Israel and Judah, there were never wanting prophetic voices to denounce such villainy in the spirit of these laws. The public conscience was thereby kept alive, and the ideal of justice and mercy, especially to the helpless, became a distinguishing mark of Israelite religion. But it was in the minds of those who had learned the Deuteronomist's great lesson, and had taken example by him, that the love which came from God, and had just been answered back by man, overflowed in a stream of blessing to man's "neighbours." Deuteronomy had uttered the first and great commandment! but it is in the Law of Holiness, that complex of ancient laws brought together by the author of P, and found now mainly in Lev. xvii.-xxvi., that we find the second word, "Thou shalt love thy neighbour as thyself."† If we ask, Who is my neighbour? we find that not even those beyond Israel are excluded, for in Lev. xix. 34 we read, "The stranger that sojourneth with you shall be unto you as the homeborn among you, and thou shalt love him as thyself." The idea still needed the expansion which it received from our Lord Himself in the parable of the Good Samaritan; but it is only one step from these passages to the New Testament.

From the standpoint of mere fear, then, to the standpoint of love which casteth out fear, even the masses of Israel were lifted, in thought at least, by the love and teaching of God. And the process by which Israel was led to this height has proved ever since to be the only possible way to such an attainment. It began in the free favour of God, it was continued by the answer of love on the part of man, and these antecedents had as their consequence the proclamation of that law of liberty—for self-renouncing love is liberty—"Thou shalt love thy neighbour as thyself." Without the first, the second was impossible; and the last without the other two would have been only a satire upon the incurable selfishness of man. It is worthy of remark, at least, that only on the critical theory of the Old Testament is each of these steps in the moral and religious education of Israel found in its right place, with its right antecedents; only when taken so do the teachers who were inspired to make each of these attainments find circumstances suited to their message, and a soil in which the germs they were commissioned to plant could live.

But great as is the contrast between the Israel of Moses' day and that of Josiah's, it is not so great as the contrast between the religion of Israel in the Deuteronomic period and the religion of the neighbouring nations. Among them, at our date 650 B. C., there was, so far as we know them, no suggestion of personal love to God as an effective part of religion. In the chapters on the Decalogue the main ideas of the Canaanites in regard to religion have been described, so that they need not be repeated here. I shall add only what E. Meyer says of their gods: "With advancing culture the cultus loses its old simplicity and homeliness. A fixed ritual was developed—founded upon old hereditary tradition. And here the gloomier conception became the ruling one, and its consequences were inexorably deduced. The great gods, even the protecting gods of the tribe or the town, are capricious and in general hostile to man—possibly to some degree because of the mythological conception of Baal as sun-god—and they demand sacrifices of blood that they may be appeased. In order that evil may be warded off from those with whom they are angry, another human being must be offered to them as a substitute in propitiatory sacrifice—nay, they demand the sacrifice of the firstborn, the best-loved son. If the community be threatened with the wrath of the deity, then the prince or the nobility as a whole must offer up their children on its behalf."* This also is the view of Robertson Smith,† who considers that while in their origin the Semitic religions involved kindly relations and continual intercourse between the gods and their worshippers, these gradually disappeared as political misfortune began to fall upon the smaller Semitic peoples. Their gods were angry and in the vain hope of appeasing them men had recourse to the direst sacrifices. Hints concerning these had survived from times of savagery; and to the diseased minds of these terror-stricken peoples the more ancient and more horrible a sacrifice was the more powerful did it seem. At this time, therefore, the course of the Canaanite religions was away from love to their gods. The decay of nationality brought despair, and the frantic efforts of despair, into the religion of the Canaanite peoples; but to Israel it brought this higher demand for more intimate union with their God. Whatever elements tending towards love the Canaanite religions originally may have had, they had either been mingled with the corrupting sensuality which seems inseparable from the worship of female deities, or had been limited to the mere superficial good understanding which their participation in the same common life established between the people and their gods. Their union was largely independent of moral considerations on either side. But in Israel there had grown up quite a different state of things. The union between Yahweh and His people had from the days of the Decalogue taken a moral turn; and gradually it had become clear that to

---

* Augustine's "Confessions," p. 64.
† Lev. xix. 18, 34.

* "Geschichte des Alterthums," p. 249.
† "Religion of the Semites," p. 330.

have Abraham for their father and Yahweh for their God would profit them little, if they did not stand in right moral relations and in moral sympathy with Him. Now, in Deuteronomy, that fundamentally right conception of the relation between God and man received its crown in Yahweh's claim to the love of His people. No contrast could be greater than that which common misfortune and a common national ruin produced between the surrounding Semitic peoples and Israel.

But besides the small kingdoms which immediately surrounded Palestine, Israel had for neighbours the two great empires of Egypt and Assyria. She was exposed therefore to influence from them in even a greater degree. Long before the Exodus, the land which Israel came afterwards to occupy had been the meeting-place of Babylonian and Egyptian power and culture. In the fifteenth century B. C. it was under the suzerainty if not the direct sovereignty of Egypt; but its whole culture and literature, for it must have had books, as the name Kirjath-Sepher (Book-town) shows, was Babylonian. Throughout Israel's history, moreover, Assyrian and Egyptian manners and ways of thought were pressed upon the people; and we cannot doubt that in regard to religion also their influence was felt. But at this period, as in the Canaanite religions, so also in those of Assyria and Egypt, the tendency was altogether different from what Deuteronomy shows it to have been in Israel.

In regard to Egypt this is somewhat difficult to prove, for the Egyptian religion is so complicated, so varied, and so ancient, that men who have studied it despair of tracing any progress in it. A kind of monotheism, polytheism, fetichism, animism, and nature-worship such as we find in the Vedas, have in turn been regarded as its primitive state; but as a matter of fact all these systems of religious thought and feeling are represented in the earliest records, and they remained constant elements of it till the end.* Whatever had once formed part of it, Egyptian religion clung to with extraordinary tenacity. As time went on, however, the accent was shifted from one element to the other, and after the times of the XIXth dynasty, *i. e.*, after the time of the Exodus, it began to decay. A systematised pantheism, of which sun-worship was the central element, was elaborated by the priests; the moral element, which had been prominent in the days when the picture of the judgment of the soul after death was so popular in Thebes, retired more into the background, and the purely magical element became the principal one. Instead of moral goodness and the fulfilment of duty being the main support of the soul in its dread and lonely journeys in the "world of the Western sky," knowledge of the proper formulas became the chief hope, and the machinations of evil demons the main danger. In the royal tombs at Thebes the walls of the long galleries are covered with representations of these demons, and the accompanying writing gives directions as to the proper formulas by knowledge of which deliverance can be secured. This, of course, confined the benefits of religion, so far as they related to the life to come, to the educated, and the wealthy. For these secret spells were hard to obtain, and had to be purchased at a high price. As Wiedemann says, "Still more important than in this world was the knowledge of the correct magical words and formulas in the other world. No door opened here if its name was not known, no dæmon let the dead pass in if he did not address him in the proper fashion, no god came to his help so long as his proper title was not given him, no food could be procured so long as the exactly prescribed words were not uttered."* The people were therefore thrown back upon the ancient popular faith, which needed gods only for practical life, and honoured them only because they were mighty.† Some of them were believed to be friendly; but others were malevolent deities who would destroy mankind if they did not mollify them by magic, or render them harmless by the greater power of the good gods. Consequently Set, the unconquerable evil demon, was worshipped with zeal in many places. With him there were numerous demons, "the enemies," "the evil ones," which lie in wait for individuals, and threaten their life and weal. The main thing, therefore, was to bring the correct sacrifices, to use such formulas and perform such acts as would render the gods gracious and turn away evil. Moreover the whole of nature was full of spirits, as it is to the African of to-day, and in the mystic texts of the Book of the Dead, there is constant mention made of the "mysterious beings whose names, whose ceremonials are not known," which thirst for blood, which bring death, which go about as devouring flame, as well as of others which do good. At all times this element existed in Egypt; but precisely at this time, in the reign of Psamtik, Brugsch‡ declares that new force was given to it, and on the monuments there appear, along with the "great gods," monstrous forms of demons and genii. In fact the higher religion had become pantheistic, and consequently less rigidly moral. Magic had been taken up into it for the life beyond the grave, and became the only resource of the people in this life. Fear, therefore, necessarily became the ruling religious motive, and instead of growing toward love of God, men in Egypt at this time were turning more decisively than ever away from it.

Of the Assyrian religion and its influence it is also difficult to speak in this connection, for notwithstanding the amount of translation that has been done, not much has come to light in regard to the personal religion of the Assyrians. On the whole it seems to be established that in its main features the religion of both Babylon and Assyria remained what the non-Semitic inhabitants of Akkad had made it. Originally it had consisted entirely of a spirit and demon worship not one whit more advanced than the religion of the South Sea islanders to-day. As such it was in the main a religion of fear. Though some spirits were good, the bulk were evil, and all were capricious. Men were consequently all their lifetime subject to bondage, and love as a religious emotion was impossible. When the Semites came at a later time into the country their star-worship was amalgamated with this mere Shamanism of the Akkadians. In the new faith thus evolved the great gods of the Semites were arranged in a hierarchy, and the spirits, both good and evil, were subordinated to them. But even the great gods remain within the sphere of nature, and have in full measure the defects and

---

* *Cf.* Wiedemann, *Religion der alten Aegypter*, p. 3.

* Wiedemann, p. 1, 35.
† *Cf.* Meyer, p. 71.
‡ "Egypt under the Pharaohs," Brodick's edition, p. 423.

limitations of nature-gods everywhere.* They are not entirely beneficent powers, nor are they even moral beings. Some have special delight in blood and destruction, while the cruel Semitic child-sacrifice was practised in honour of others. Again, their displeasure has no necessary or even general connection with sin. Their wrath is generally the outcome of mere arbitrary whim. Indeed it may be doubted whether the conception of sin or of moral guilt ever had a secure footing in this religion. It certainly had none in the terror-struck hymn to the seven evil spirits who are described thus:—

"Seven (are) they, seven (are) they.
Male they (are) not, female they (are) not;
Moreover the deep is their pathway.
Wife they have not, child is not born to them.
Law (and) order they know not,
Prayer and supplication hear they not.
Wicked (are) they, wicked (are) they." †

There is here an accent of genuine terror, which involved not love, but hatred. Even in what Sayce calls a "Penitential Psalm," and which he compares to the Biblical Psalms, there is nothing of the gratitude to God as a deliverer from sin which in Israel was the chief factor in producing the response to Yahweh's demand for the love of man. Morally, it contains nothing higher than is contained in the hymn of the spirits. The transgressions which are so pathetically lamented, and from the punishment of which deliverance is so earnestly sought, are purely ceremonial and involuntary. The author of the prayer conceives that he has to do with a god whose wrath is a capricious thing, coming upon men they know not why. So conceived God cannot be loved. It is entirely in accord with this that in the great flood epic no reason is given for the destruction of mankind save the caprice of Bel.‡ The few expressions quoted by Sayce from a hymn to the sun-god—such as this, "Merciful God, that liftest up the fallen, that supportest the weak. . . . Like a wife, thou submittest thyself, cheerful and kindly. . . . Men far and wide bow before thee and rejoice"—cannot avail to subvert a conclusion so firmly fixed. These are simply the ordinary expressions which the mere physical pleasure of the sunlight brings to the lips of sun-worshippers of all ages and of all climes. At best they could only be taken as germs out of which a loving relation between God and man might have been developed. But though they were ancient they never were developed. At the end as at the beginning the Assyrio-Babylonian religion moves on so low a level, even in its more innocent aspects, that a development like that in Deuteronomy is absolutely impossible. In its worse aspects Assyrian religion was unspeakable. The worship of Ishtar at Nineveh outdid everything known in the ancient world for lust and cruelty.

On this side too, therefore, we find no parallel to Israel's new outgrowth of higher religion. Comparison only makes it stand out more boldly in its splendid originality; and we are left with the fruitful question, "What was the root of the astonishing difference between Yahweh and every other god whom Israel had heard of?" Precisely at this time and under the same circumstances, the ethnic religions around Israel were developing away from any higher elements they had contained, and were thereby, as we know now, hastening to extinction. Under the inspired prophetic influence, Israel's religion turned the loss of the nation into gain; it rose by the darkness of national misfortune into a nobler phase than any it had previously known.

But perhaps the crowning merit of this demand for love of God is the emphasis it lays upon personality in both God and man, and the high level at which it conceives their mutual relations. From the first, of course, the personal element was always very strongly present in the Israelite conception of God. Indeed personality was the dominating idea among all the smaller nations which surrounded Israel. The national god was conceived of mainly as a greater and more powerful man, full of the energetic self-assertion without which it would be impossible for any man to reign over an Eastern community. The Moabite stone shows this, for in it Chemosh is as sharply defined a person as Mesha himself. The Canaanite gods, therefore, might be wanting in moral character; their existence was doubtless thought of in a limited and wholly carnal manner; but there never was, apparently, the least tendency to obscure the sharp lines of their individuality. In Israel, *a fortiori*, such a tendency did not exist; and that a writer of Matthew Arnold's ability should have persuaded himself, and tried to persuade others, that under the name of Yahweh Israel understood anything so vague as his "stream of tendency which makes for righteousness," is only another instance of the extraordinarily blinding effects of a preconceived idea. So far from Yahweh being conceived in that manner, it would be much easier to prove that, whatever aberrations in the direction of making God merely "a non-natural man" may be charged upon Christianity, they have been founded almost exclusively upon Old Testament examples and Old Testament texts. If there was defect in the Old Testament conception of God, it was, and could not but be, in the direction of drawing Him down too much into the limits of human personality.

But though the gods were always thought of by the Canaanites as personal, their character was not conceived as morally high. Moral character in Chemosh, Moloch, or Baal was not of much importance, and their relations with their peoples were never conditioned by moral conduct. How deeply ingrained this view was in Palestine is seen in the persistency with which even Yahweh's relation to His people was viewed in this light. Only the continual outcry of the prophets against it prevented this idea becoming permanently dominant even in Israel. Nay, it often deceived would-be prophets. Clinging to the idea of the national God, and forgetting altogether the ethical character of Yahweh, without, perhaps, conscious insincerity, they prophesied peace to the wicked, and so came to swell the ranks of the false prophets. But from very early times another thought was cherished by Israel's representative men in regard to their relations with God. Yahweh was righteous, and demanded righteousness in His people. Obla-

---

* Meyer, p. 117.
† Sayce, "Babylonian Literature," p. 36. Both poems here referred to are pre-Assyrian, being found as translations in the library of Assurbanipal. But Assyrian religion made no progress; it seems to have remained always dependent on Babylonian, even in details.
‡ Meyer, p. 178. *Cf.* however Sayce, "The Higher Criticism and the Monuments," p. 114. Sayce maintains that the Assyrian epic attributes the flood to the moral guilt of men. But that is by no means proved, for it is more than doubtful whether sin to the Assyrian was not always mainly a ceremonial matter.

tions were vain if offered as a substitute for this. All the prophets reach their greatest heights of sublimity in preaching this ethically noble doctrine; and the love to God which Deuteronomy demands is to be exhibited in reverent obedience to moral law.

Moreover, that God should seek or even need the love of man threw other light on the Old Testament religion. If, without revelation, Israel had widened its mental horizon so as to conceive Yahweh as Lord of the world, it may be questioned whether it could have kept clear of the gulf of pantheism. But by the manifestation of God in their special history, the Israelites had been taught to rise step by step to the higher levels, without losing their conception of Yahweh as the living, personal, active friend of their people. Moreover they had been early taught, as we have seen, that the deep design of all that was wrought for them was the good of all men. The love of God was seen pressing forward to its glorious and beneficent ends; and both by ascribing such far-reaching plans to Yahweh, and by affirming His interest in the fate of men, Israel's conception of the Divine personality was raised alike in significance and power; for anything more personal than love planning and working towards the happiness of its objects cannot be conceived. But the crown was set upon the Divine personality by the claim to the love of man. This signified that to the Divine mind the individual man was not hid from God by his nation, that he was not for Him a mere specimen of a genus. Rather each man has to God a special worth, a special character, which, impelled by His free personal love, He seeks to draw to Himself. At every step each man has near him "the great Companion," who desires to give Himself to him. Nay, more, it implies that God seeks and needs an answering love; so that Browning's daring declaration, put into the mouth of God when the song of the boy Theocrite is no more heard, "I miss My little human praise," is simple truth.*

But if the demand illustrates and illuminates the personality of God, it throws out in a still more decisive manner the personality of man. In a rough sense, of course, there never could have been any doubt of that. But children have to grow into full self-determining personality, and savages never attain it. Both are at the mercy of caprice, or of the needs of the moment, to which they answer so helplessly that in general no consistent course of conduct can be expected of them. That can be secured only by rigorous self-determination. But the power of self-determination does not come at once, nor is acquired without strenuous and continued effort; it is, in fact, a power which in any full measure is possessed only by the civilised man. Now the Israelites were not highly civilised when they left Egypt. They were still at the stage when the tribe overshadowed and absorbed the individual, as it does to-day among the South Sea islanders. The progress of the prophetic thought towards the demand for personal love has already been traced. Here we must trace the steps by which the personal element in each individual was strengthened in Israel, till it was fit to respond to the Divine demand.

The high calling of the people reacted on the individual Israelites. They saw that in many respects the nations around them were inferior to them. Much that was tolerated or even respected among them was an abomination to Israel; and every Israelite felt that the honour of his people must not be dragged in the dust by him, as it would be if he permitted himself to sink to the heathen level. Further, the laws regarding even ceremonial holiness which in germ certainly, and probably in considerable extension also, existed from the earliest time, made him feel that the sanctity of the nation depended upon the care and scrupulosity of the individual. And then there were the individual spiritual needs, which could not be suppressed and would not be denied. Though one sees so little explicit provision for restoration of individual character in early Yahwism, yet in the course of time—who can doubt it?—the personal religious needs of so many individual men would necessarily frame for themselves some outlet. Building upon the analogy of the relation established between Yahweh and Israel, they would hope for the satisfaction of their individual needs through the infinite mercy of God. The Psalms, such of them as can fairly be placed in the pre-Deuteronomic time, bear witness to this; and those written after that time show a hopefulness, and a faith in the reality of individual communion with God which show that such communion was not then a new discovery.

In all these ways the religious life of the individual was being cultivated and strengthened; but this demand made in Deuteronomy lifts that indirect refreshment of soul, for which the cultus and the covenants made no special provision, into a recognised position, nay, into the central position in Israelite religion. The word, "Thou shalt love Yahweh thy God," confirmed and justified all these persistent efforts after individual life in God, and brought them out into the large place which belongs to aspirations that have at last been authorised. By a touch, the inspired writer transformed the pious hopes of those who had been the chosen among the chosen people into certainties. Each man was henceforth to have his own direct relation to God as well as the nation; and the national hope, which had hitherto been first, was now to depend for its realisation upon the fulfilment of the special and private hope. Thus the old relation was entirely reversed by Deuteronomy. Instead of the individual holding "definite place in regard to Yahweh only through his citizenship," now the nation has its place and its future secured only by the personal love of each citizen to God. For that is obviously what the demand here made really means. Again and again the inspired writer returns to it; and his persistent endeavour is to connect all else that his book contains—warning, exhortation, legislation—with this as the foundation and starting-point. Here, as elsewhere, we can trace the roots of the new covenant which Jeremiah and Ezekiel saw afar off and rejoiced at, and which our blessed Lord has realised for us. The individual religious life is for the first time fully recognised for what ever since it has been seen to be, the first condition of any attempt to realise the kingdom of God in the life of a nation.

And not only thus does our text emphasise individuality. Love with all the heart, and all the mind, and all the soul is possible only to a fully developed personality; for, as Roth says, "We love only in the measure in which personality is developed in us. Even God can love only in so

---

* Browning's Poems, "The Boy and the Angel."

far as He is personal."* Or, as Julius Muller says in his "Doctrine of Sin," "The association of personal beings in love, while it involves the most perfect distinction of the I and Thou, proves itself to be the highest form of unity."† Unless other counteracting circumstances come in, therefore, the more highly developed individuality is, the more entirely human beings are determined from within, the more entirely will union among men depend upon free and deliberate choice, and the more perfect will it be. In being called to love God men are dealt with as those who have attained to complete self-determination, who have come to completed manhood in the moral life. For all that could mix love with alloy, mere sensuous sympathy, and the insistent appeal of that which is materially present, are wanting here. Here nothing is involved but the free outgoing of the heart to that which is best and highest; nothing but loyalty to that vision of Good which, amid all the ruin sin has wrought in human nature, dominates us so that " we needs must love the highest when we see it." The very demand is a promise and a prophecy of completed moral and religious liberty to the individual soul. It rests upon the assurance that men have at last been trained to walk alone, that the support of social life and external ordinances has become less necessary than it was, and that one day a new and living way of access to the Father will bring every soul into daily intercourse with the source of all spiritual life.

But this demand, in affirming personality of so high a kind, also re-created duty. Under the national dispensation the individual man was a *servant*. To a large extent he knew not what his Lord did, and he ruled his life by the commands he received without understanding, or perhaps caring to understand, their ultimate ground and aim. Much too of what he thus laid upon himself was mere ancient custom, which had been a protection to national and moral life in early days, but which had survived, or was on the point of surviving, its usefulness. Now, however, that man was called upon to love God with all his heart and mind and soul, the step was taken which was to end in his becoming the consciously free *son* of God. For to love in this fashion means, on the one hand, a willingness to enter into communion with God and to seek that communion; and on the other it implies a throwing open of the soul to receive the love which God so persistently has pressed upon men. In such a relation slavery, blind or constrained obedience, disappears, and the motives of right action become the purest and most powerful that man can know.

In the first place, selfishness dies out. Those to whom God has given Himself have no more to seek. They have reached the dwelling "of peace imperturbable," and know that they are secure. Nothing that they do can win more for them; and they do those things that please God with the free, uncalculating, ungrudging forgetfulness of self, which distinguishes those fortunate children who have grown up into a perfect filial love. Of course it was only the elect in Israel who in any great degree realised this ideal. But even those who neglected it had for a moment been illuminated by it; and the record of it remained to kindle the nobler hearts of every generation. Even the legalism of later days could not obscure it. In the case of many it bore up and transfigured the dry details of Judaism, so that even amid such surroundings the souls of men were kept alive. The later Psalms prove this beyond dispute, and the advanced view which brings the bulk of the Psalter down to the post-exilic period only emphasises the more this aspect of pre-Christian Judaism. In Christianity of course the ideal was made infinitely more accessible: and it received in the Pauline doctrine, the Evangelical doctrine, of Justification by Faith, a form which more than any other human teaching has made unselfish devotion to God a common aim. It would hardly be too much to say that those philosophical and religious systems which have preached the unworthiness of looking for a reward of well-doing, which have striven to set up the doing of good for its own sake as the only morality worthy of the name, have failed, just because they would not begin with the love of God. To Christianity, especially to Evangelical Christianity, they have assumed to speak from above downwards; but it alone has the secret they strove in vain to learn. Men justified by faith have peace with God, and do good with passionate fervour without hope or possibility of further reward, just because of their love and gratitude to God, who is the source of all good. This plan has succeeded, and no other has; for to teach men on any other terms to disregard reward is simply to ask them to breathe in a vacuum.

In the second place, those who rose to the height of this calling had duty not only deepened but extended. It was natural that they should not seek to throw off the obligations of worship and morality as they had been handed down by their ancestors. Only an authoritative voice which they were separated from by centuries could say, "It hath been said by them of old time, . . . but *I* say unto you"; and men would be disposed rather to fulfil old obligations with new zeal, while they added to them the new duties which their widened horizon had brought into view. It is true that in course of time the Pharisaic spirit laid hold of the Jews, and that by it they were led back into a slavery which quite surpassed the half-conscious bondage of their earlier time. It is one of the mysteries of human nature that it is only the few who can live for any time at a high level, and hold the balance between extremes. The many cannot choose but follow those few; and the dumb, half-reluctant, half-fascinated way in which they are drawn after them is a most pathetic thing to see. But too often they avenge themselves for the pressure put upon them, by taking up the teaching they receive in a perverted or mutilated form, dropping unawares the very soul of it, and suiting it to the average man. When that is done the bread from heaven becomes a stone; the message of liberty is turned into a summons to the prison house; and the darkness becomes of that opaque sort which is found only where the light within men is darkness. That tragedy was enacted in Judaism as rarely elsewhere. The free service of sons was exchanged for the timorous, anxious scrupulosity of the formalist. How could men love a God whom they pictured as inexorable in claiming the mint and cummin of ceremonial worship, and as making life a burden for all who had a conscience? They could not, and they did not. Most substituted a merely formal compli-

* "Theol., Ethik," i., p. 515.
† "Doctrine of Sin," vol. i., p. 114.

ance with the externalities of worship for the love to God and man which was the presupposition of the true Israelite's life, and the mass of the nation fell away from true faith. Strangely enough, therefore, the strength of men's love for God, and of their belief in His love, gave an impulse to the legalistic Pharisaism which our Lord denounced as the acme of loveless irreligion.

But it was not so perverted in all. There always was an Israel within Israel that refused to let go the truths they had learned, and kept up the succession of men inspired by the free spirit of God. Even among the Pharisees there were such—witness St. Paul—men who, though they were entangled in the formalism of their time, found it at last a pedagogue to bring them unto Christ. We must believe therefore that at the beginning the attainment marked by the demands of Deuteronomy and the Law of Holiness existed and was carried over into the daily life. As the national limits of religion were broken down, the word "neighbour" received an ever wider definition in Israel. At first only a man's fellow-tribesman or fellow-countryman was included; then the stranger; later, as in Jonah's picture of the conduct of the sailors, it was hinted that even among the heathen brethren might be found. Finally, in our Lord's parable of the Good Samaritan the last barrier was broken down. But it needed all St. Paul's lifework, and the first and most desperate inner conflict Christianity had to live through, to initiate men into anything like the full meaning of what Christ had taught. Then it was seen that as there was but one Father in heaven, so there was but one family on earth. Then too, though the merely ceremonial duties by which the Jew had been bound ceased to be binding on Christians, the sphere for the practice of moral duty was immensely widened. Indeed, had it not been for the free, joyous spirit with which they were inspired by Christ, they must have shrunk from the immensity of their obligation. For not only were men's neighbours infinitely more numerous now, but their relations with them became vastly more complicated. To meet all possible cases that might arise in the great and elaborate civilisations Christianity had to face and save, our Lord deepened the meaning of the commandments; and so far from Christians being free from the obligation to law, immeasurably more was demanded of them. To them first was the full sweep of moral obligation revealed, for they first had reached the full moral stature of men in Jesus Christ.

CHAPTER VIII.

EDUCATION—MOSAIC VIEW.

Deuteronomy vi. 6-25.

Those great verses, Deut. vi. 4, 5, form the central truth of the book. Everything else in it proceeds from and is informed by them, and they are dwelt upon and enforced with a clear perception of their radical importance. There is something of the joy of discovery in the way in which the unity of Yahweh and exclusive love to Him are insisted upon, not only in verses 6-25 of this chapter, but in xi. 13-20. The same strongly worded demand to lay to heart Yahweh's command to love Him and Him only, and to teach it strenuously to their children—to make it "a sign upon their hand," and "as a frontlet between their eyes"—is found in both passages. It is worthy of remark also that nearly the same words are found in Exod. xiii. 9, 16. Presumably on account of this, some have ascribed that section of Exodus to the author of Deuteronomy. But both Dillmann and Driver ascribe these passages to J and E, and with good reason. Indeed, apart from the purely literary grounds for thinking that these formulas were first used by the earlier writers and were copied by the author of Deuteronomy, another line of argument points in the same direction. In Exodus the thing to be remembered and taught to the children was the meaning and origin of the Passover and the consecration of the firstborn, i. e., the meaning and origin of some of their ritual institutions. Here in Deuteronomy, on the contrary, that which is to be written on the heart and taught to the children is moral and spiritual truth about God, and love to God. Now the probable explanation of this likeness and difference is, not that the author of Deuteronomy, after using this insistive phrase only of high spiritual truths in his own book, inserted it in Exodus with regard to mere institutions of the cultus; rather, the writers of Exodus had used it of that which was important in their day, and the Deuteronomist borrowed it from them to emphasise his own most cherished revelation. In the earlier stages of a religious movement, the establishment of institutions which shall embody and perpetuate religious truth, is one of the first necessities. It has become a commonplace of Christian defence, for example, that Baptism and the Lord's Supper were made the most successful vehicles for conveying fundamental Christian truth, and that the celebration of these two rites from the first days even until now is one of the most convincing proofs of the continuity of Christianity. Naturally, therefore, the establishment of the Passover was specially marked out as the *palladium* of Israelite religion in the earlier days. But in the time after Isaiah, when Deuteronomy was written, the institutions needed no longer such insistence. They had indeed become so important to the people that the mere observance of them threatened to become a substitute for religious and even moral feeling. The Deuteronomist's great message was, consequently, a reiteration of the prophetic truths as to the supremacy of the spiritual; and for the object of the warm exhortation of the earlier writings he substituted the proclamation of Yahweh's oneness, and of His demand for His people's love. This seems a reasonable and probable explanation of the facts as we find them. If true, it is a proof that the need of ritual institutions, and the danger of unduly exalting them, was not peculiar to post-exilic times. In principle the temptation was always present; and as living faith rose and fell it came into operation, or was held in abeyance, throughout the whole of Israel's history. Hence the mention of this kind of formalism or the denunciation of it must be very cautiously used as a criterion by which to date any Scriptural writings.

It is therefore with a full consciousness of its fundamental importance that the author of Deuteronomy follows the great passage chapter vi. 4, 5, with this solemn and inspiring exhortation. It is from no mere itch for religious improvement of the occasion that he presses home his message thus. Nor is it love for the mere repetition of an ancient formula of exhortation that dictates its use. He knew and understood the work of Moses, and felt that the moulding power in Israel's life as a nation, the unifying element in it, had been the religion of Yahweh. Whatever else may have been called in question, it has never been doubted that the salt which kept the political and social life of the people from rotting through many centuries was the always advancing knowledge of God. At each great crisis of Israel's history the religion of Yahweh had met the demands for direction, for inspiration, for uplifting which were made upon it. With Protean versatility it had adapted itself to every new condition. In all circumstances it had provided a lamp for the feet and a light for the path of the faithful; and in meeting the needs of generation after generation it had revealed elements of strength and consolation which, without the commentary of experience, could never have been brought out. Now the author of Deuteronomy felt that in these short sentences the high-water mark of Israelite religion so far had been reached, and that in renewing the work of Moses, and adapting it to his own time, the principles here enunciated must be the main burden of his message. Further progress depended, he obviously felt, upon the absorption and assimilation of these truths by his people, and he felt he must provide for the perpetuation of them in that better time he was preparing for. This he did by providing for the religious education of the young. Whatever else Israel had gained it had been careful to hand on from generation to generation. The land flowing with milk and honey was still in the possession of the descendants of the first conquerors. The literature, the science, the wisdom that the fathers had gathered, had been carefully passed down to the children; and a precious deposit of enriching experience in the form of history had reached to the elect even among the common people, as the example of Amos shows. But the most valuable heritage of Israel was that continually growing deposit of religious truth which had been the life-blood of its master-spirits. From generation to generation the noblest men in the nation, those most sensitive to the touch of the Divine, had been casting soundings into the great deep of the hidden purposes of God. With sore travail of both mind and spirit, they had found solutions of the great problems which no living soul can escape. These were no doubt more or less partial, but they were sufficient for their day, and were always in the line of the final answer. As the sum of experience widened, the scope of the solutions widened also, and in the course of Providence these issued in a conception of God which elsewhere was never approached. This of all national treasures was the most priceless, and to preserve and hand on this was simply to keep the national soul alive. Compared with this, every other heritage from the past was as nothing; and so, with a simple directness which must amaze the legislators of modern states, the inspired lawgiver arranged for a religious education.

To him, as to all ancient lawgivers, a commonwealth without religion was simply inconceivable, and the hampering, confusing, and confused difficulties of to-day lay far beyond his horizon. Parents must take over this great heritage and lay it deeply to heart. They must then make it the subject of their common talk. They must write the profound words which summed it up upon the doorposts of their houses. They must let it fill their minds at their down-sitting and their uprising, and while they walked by the way. Further, as the crown of their work, they were to teach it diligently to their children, already accustomed by their parents' continual interest to regard this as the worthiest object of human thought. But though the parents were to be the chief instructors of children in religion, the State or the community was also to do its part. As the private citizen was to write, " Hear, O Israel: Yahweh our God is one Yahweh; and thou shalt love Yahweh thy God with all thine heart, and with all thy soul, and with all thy might," on the posts of his door, so the representatives of the community were to write them upon the town or village gates. In those early days schools were unknown, as State-regulated schools are still unknown in all purely Eastern countries. Consequently there was no sphere for the State in the direct religious teaching of the young. But so far as it could act, the State was to act. It was to commit itself to the religious principles that underlay the life of the people, and to proclaim them with the utmost publicity. It was to secure that none should be ignorant of them, so far as proclamation by writing in the most public place could secure knowledge, for on this the very existence of the State depended.

But the religious instruction was not to be limited to the reiteration of these great sentences; in that case they would have become a mere form of words. In the last verses of the chapter, vv. 20-25, we find a model of the kind of explanatory comment which was to be given in addition: " When thy son asketh thee in time to come, saying, What mean the testimonies, and the statutes, and the judgments, which Yahweh our God hath commanded you? then thou shalt say unto thy son, We were Pharaoh's bondmen in the land of Egypt; and Yahweh brought us out of Egypt with a mighty hand," and so on. That means that the *history* of Yahweh's dealings with His people was to be taught, to show the reasonableness of the Divine commands, to exhibit the love-compelling character of God. And this was entirely in accord with the Biblical conception of God. Neither here nor elsewhere in the Old Testament are there any abstract definitions of His character, His spirituality, His omnipresence, or His omnipotence. Nor is there anywhere any argument to prove His existence. All that is postulated, presupposed, as that which all men believe, except those who have wilfully perverted themselves. But the existence of God with all these great and necessary attributes is undoubtedly implied in what is narrated of Yahweh's dealings with His people. As we have seen, too, the very name of Yahweh implies that His nature should not be limited by any definition. He was what He would prove Himself to be, and throughout the Old Testament the *gesta Dei* through and for the Israelites, and the prophetic promises made in Yahweh's name, represented all that was known of God. This gave a peculiarly healthy and robust tone to Old Testament piety. The subjective, introspective element which in modern times is so apt to take the upper hand, was kept in due subordination by making history the main nourishment of religious thought. In constant contact with external fact, Israelite piety was simple, sincere, and practical; and men's thoughts being turned away from themselves to the Divine action in the world, they were less touched by the disease of self-consciousness than modern believers in God. In every sphere of human life, too, they looked for God, and traced the working of His hand. The later distinction between the sacred and secular parts of life, which has been often pushed to disastrous extremes, was to them unknown. For these among many other reasons, the Old Testament must always remain of vital importance to the Church of God. It can fall into neglect only when the religious life is becoming unhealthy and one-sided.

Further, its qualities especially fit it for use in the education of children. In many respects a child's mind resembles the mind of a primitive people. It has the same love of concrete examples, the same incapacity to appreciate abstract ideas, and it has the same susceptibility to such reasoning as this: God has been very loving and gracious to men, especially to our forefathers, and we are therefore bound to love Him and to obey Him with reverence and fear. To the children of a primitive people such teaching would therefore be doubly suitable; but the Deuteronomist's anxiety in regard to it has been justified by its results in times no longer primitive. Through ages of persecution and oppression, often amid a social environment of the worst sort, there has been little or no wavering in the fundamental points of Jewish faith. Scattered and peeled, slaughtered and decimated, as they have been through blood-stained centuries, this nation have held fast to their religion. Not even the fact that, through their refusal to accept their Messiah when He came, the most tender, the most expansive, the most highly spiritual elements of the Old Testament religion have escaped them, has been able to neutralise the benefit of the truth they have so tenaciously held. Of non-Christian nations they stand by far the highest; and among the orthodox Jews who still keep firm to the national traditions, and teach the ancient Scriptures diligently to their children, there is often seen a piety and a confidence in God, a submission and a hopefulness which put to shame many who profess to have hope in Christ. Even in our day, when agnosticism and denial of the supernatural is eating into Judaism more than into almost any other creed,[*] a book like Friedländer's "The Jewish Religion" gives us a very favourable idea of the spirit and teachings of orthodox Judaism. And its main stay is, and always has been, the religious training of the young. "In obedience to the precept 'Thou shalt speak of them,' *i. e.*, of 'the words which I command thee this day,'" says Friedländer, "'when thou liest down and when thou risest up,' three sections of the law are read daily, in the morning and in the evening, viz. (1) Deut. vi. 4-9, beginning 'Hear'; (2) Deut. xi. 13-21, beginning 'And it shall be if ye diligently hearken'; (3) Numb. xv. 37-41, beginning 'And the Lord said.' The first section teaches the unity of God, and our duty to love this one God with all our heart, to make His word the subject of our constant meditation and to instil it into the heart of the young. The second section contains the lesson of reward and punishment, that our success depends on our obedience to the will of God. This important truth must constantly be kept before our eyes, and before the eyes of our children. The third section contains the commandments of Tsitsith, the object of which is to remind us of God's precepts." To-day, therefore, as so many centuries ago, these great words are uttered daily in the ears of all pious Jews, and they are as potent to keep them steady to their faith now as they were then. For in most cases where a drift towards the fashionable agnosticism of the day or to atheistic materialism is observable among Jews, it will be found to have been preceded either by neglect or formalism in regard to this fundamental matter. Briefly, without this teaching they cease to be Jews; with it they remain steadfast as a rock. Uprooted as they are from their country, their national coherence endures and seems likely to endure till their set time has come. So triumphantly has the enforcement of religious education vindicated itself in the case of God's ancient people.

In the remaining verses of the chapter, vv. 10-19, we have a warning against neglect and forgetfulness of their God, and an indication of the circumstances under which it would be most difficult to remain true to Him. These are uttered entirely from the Mosaic standpoint, and are among the passages which it is most difficult to reconcile with the later authorship; for there would appear to be no motive for the later writer to go back upon the exceptional circumstances of the early days in Canaan. His object must have been to warn and guide and instruct the people of *his* time in the face of their difficulties and temptations, to adapt Mosaic legislation and Mosaic teaching to the needs of his own day. Now on any supposition he must have written when all conquest on Israel's part had long ceased. It is most probable too that in his day the prosperity of his people was on the wane. They were not looking forward to a time of special temptation from riches; rather they were dreading expatriation and decay. Consequently this reference to the ease with which they became rich by occupying the cities and villages and farms of those they had conquered is quite out of place, unless we are to regard the author as a skilled and artistic writer who deliberately set himself to reproduce in all respects the mind and thoughts of a man of an earlier day, as Thackeray, for instance, does in his "Henry Esmond." But that is not credible; and the explanation is that given in chapter i., that the addresses here attributed to Moses are free reproductions of earlier traditions or narratives concerning what Moses actually said. If we know anything about Moses at all, it is in the highest degree probable that he left his people some parting charge. He longed to pass the Jordan with them. He could not fail to see that an immense revolution in their habits and manner of life was certain to occur when they entered the promised land. That must have appeared to him fraught with varied dangers, and words of warning and instructions would rush even unbidden to his lips.

There can be no doubt, at any rate, that this passage is true to human nature in regarding the sudden acquirement of great and goodly cities which they did not build, and houses full of good things which they filled not, and cisterns hewn out which they did not hew, vineyards and olive trees

---

[*] *Jewish Quarterly Review*, October, 1888, p. 55, where Professor Schechter finds himself compelled to discuss the question whether a man may be a good Jew and yet deny the existence of God.

which they did not plant, as a great temptation to forgetfulness of God. At all times prosperity, especially if it come suddenly, and without being won by previous toil and self-denial, has tended to deteriorate character. When men have no changes or vicissitudes, then they fear not God. It is for help in trouble when the help of man is vain, or for a deliverance in danger, that average men most readily turn to God. But when they feel fairly safe, when they have raised themselves, as they think, "beyond all storms of chance," when they have built up between themselves and poverty or failure a wall of wealth and power, then the impulse that drives them upward ceases to act. It becomes strangely pleasant, and it seems safe, to get rid of the strain of living at the highest attainable level, and with a sigh of relief men stretch themselves out to rest and to enjoy. These are the average men; but there are some in every age, the elect, who have had the love of God shed abroad in their hearts, who have had such real and intimate communion with God that separation from Him would turn all other joys into mockery. They cannot yield to this temptation as most do, and in the midst of wealth and comfort keep alive their aspirations. In Israel these two classes existed; and to the former, *i. e.*, to the great bulk of both rulers and people, the stimulus administered by the conquest to the material side of their nature must have been potent indeed.

It is here implied that the Israelite people when they entered Canaan had some moral education to lose. Whether that could be so is the question asked by many critics, and their answer is an emphatic No. They were, say they, a rude, desert people, without settled habits of life, without knowledge of agriculture, and possessed of a religion which in all outward respects was scarcely, if at all, higher than that of the surrounding nations. What happened to them in Canaan, therefore, was not a lapse, but a rise. They advanced from being a wandering pastoral people to become settled agriculturists. They gained knowledge of the arts of life by their contact with the Canaanites, and they lost little or nothing in religion; for they were themselves only image-worshippers and looked upon Yahweh as on a level with the Canaanite Baals. But if the Decalogue belongs, in any form, to that early time, and if the character of Moses be in any degree historical, then, of course, this mode of view is false. Then Israel worshipped a spiritual God, who was the guardian of morals; and there was in the mind of their leader and legislator a light which illuminated every sphere of life, both private and national. Consequently there could be a falling away from a higher level of religious life, as the Scriptures consistently say there was. Without perhaps having understood and made their own the fundamental truths of Yahwism, the people had had their whole social and political life remodelled in accordance with its principles. They had, moreover, had time to learn something of its inner meaning, and in forty years we may well believe that the more spiritually minded among them had become imbued with the higher religious spirit. Add to that the union, the movement, the excitement of a successful advance, crowned by conquest, and we have all the elements of a revived religious and national life among Eastern people.

Similar causes have produced precisely similar effects since. In important respects the origin of Mohammedanism repeats the same story. A semi-nomadic people, divided into clans and tribes, related by blood but never united, were unified by a great religious idea vastly in advance of any they had hitherto known. The religious reformer who proclaimed this truth, and those who belonged to the inner circle of his friends and counsellors, were turned from many evils, and exhibited a moral force and enthusiasm corresponding, in some degree at least, to the sublimity of the religious doctrine they had embraced. The masses, on their part, received and submitted to a revised and improved scheme of social life. Then they moved forward to conquest, and in their first days not only trampled down opposition, but deserved to do so, for in most respects they were superior to the ignorant and degraded Christians they overthrew. They came out of the desert, and were at first soldiers only. But in a generation or two they largely settled to purely agricultural life, as landowners for whom the native population laboured; and they gained in knowledge of the arts of life from the more civilised peoples they conquered. But in religious and moral character imitations of the conquered peoples involved, for the conquerors, a loss. And soon they did lose. The violence accompanying successful war produced arrogance and injustice; the immense wealth thrown into their hands so suddenly gave rise to luxury and greed. Within twenty-five years from the flight of Mohammed from Mecca, relaxation of manners manifested itself. Sensuality and drunkenness were rife; with Ali's death the Caliphate passed into the hands of Muawia, the leader of the still half-heathen part of the Koreish; and the secular, indifferent portion of Mohammed's followers ruled in Islam.*

Allowing all that can be allowed for exceptional influences in Israel, we may well believe that the circumstances of the first invaders were such as would strain the influence of the higher religion upon the nation. And after the conquest and settlement the strain would necessarily be greater still. Whatever drawbacks warfare may have, it at least keeps men active and hardy, but the rest of a conqueror after warfare is a temptation to luxury and corruption which has been very rarely resisted. Even to-day, when men enter upon new and vacant lands, and that without war and under Christian influences, the plenty which the first immigrants soon gather about them proves adverse to higher thought. In America in its earlier days, and in new American territories and Australia now, our civilisation at that stage always takes a materialistic turn. Every man may hope to become rich, the resources of the country are so great and those who are to share them are so few. In order to develop them, all concerned must give their time and thoughts to the work, and must become absorbed in it. The result is that, though the religious instinct asserts itself in sufficient strength to lead to the building of churches and schools, and men are too busy to be much influenced by theoretical unbelief, yet the pulse of religion beats feebly and low. The feeling spreads, under many disguises it is true, but still it spreads, that a man's life does "con-

---

* For an illustration of the way in which land-hunger and the rush to satisfy it operate on men, see the account of "The Invasion of Oklahoma" (a territory lately thrown open to occupation in the United States), *Spectator*, April 27th, 1889.

sist in the abundance of the things which he possesseth"; and the heroic element of Christianity, the impulse to self-sacrifice, falls into the background. The result is a social life respectable enough, save that the social blots due to self-indulgence are a good deal more conspicuous than they should be; a very high average of general comfort, with its necessary drawback of a self-satisfied and somewhat ignoble contentment; and a religious life that prides itself mainly in avoiding the falsehood of extremes. In such an atmosphere true and living religion has great difficulty in asserting itself. Each individual is drawn away from the region of higher thought more powerfully than in the older lands where ambitions are for most men less plausible; and so the struggle to keep the soul sensitive to spiritual influences is more hard. As for the national life, public affairs in those circumstances tend to be ruled simply by the standard of immediate expediency, and strenuousness of principle or practice tends to be regarded as an impossible ideal.

To all this Israel was exposed, and to more. There are doubts as to the extent of their conquests when they settled down; but there are none that when they did so they still had heathen Canaanites among them. Throughout almost the whole country the population was mixed and constant intercourse with the conquered peoples was unavoidable. At first these were either Israel's teachers in many of the arts of settled life, or they must have carried on the work of agriculture for their Israelite lords. Moreover many of the sacred places of the land, the sanctuaries which from time immemorial had been resorted to for worship, were either taken over by the Israelites or were left in Canaanite hands. In either case they opened a way for malign influences upon the purer faith. Gradually, too, the tribal feeling asserted itself. The tribal heads regained the position they had held before the domination of Moses and his successor, just as the tribal heads of the Arabs asserted themselves after the death of Mohammed and his immediate successors, and plunged into fratricidal war with the companions of their prophet. The only difference was that, while the circumstances of the Arabs compelled them to retain a supreme head, the circumstances of the Israelites permitted them to fall back into the tribal isolation from which they had emerged. The national life was broken up, the religious life followed in the same path, until, as the Book of Judges graphically says in narrating how Micah set up an Ephod and Teraphim for himself and made his son a priest, "every man did that which was right in his own eyes." With a people so recently won for a higher faith, there could not but follow a recrudescence of heathen or semi-heathen beliefs and practices.

To sum up, given a great truth revealed to one man, which, though accepted by a nation, is only half understood by the bulk of them, and given also a great national deliverance and expansion brought about by the same leader, you have there the elements of a great enthusiasm with the seeds of its own decay within it. Such a nation, especially if plied with external temptation, will fall back, not into its first state certainly, but into a condition much below its highest level, so soon as the leader and those who had really comprehended the new truth are removed to a distance or are dead.

In the case of Mohammedanism this was instinctively felt. We find the Governor of Bassorah writing thus to Omar, the third Khalif: "Thou must strengthen my hands with a company of the Companions of the Prophet, for verily they are as salt in the midst of the people."* The same thing is expressly asserted of Israel also by the later editor in Josh. xxiv. 31: "And Israel served the Lord all the days of Joshua, and all the days of the elders that outlived Joshua, and had known all the work of the Lord, that He had wrought for Israel." It would almost seem as if Semitic peoples were specially liable to such oscillations, if Palgrave's account of the people of Nejed before the rise of the Wahabbis in the middle of last century can be trusted. "Almost every trace of Islam," he says,† "had long since vanished from Nejed, where the worship of the Djann, under the spreading foliage of large trees, or in the cavernous recesses of Djebel Toweyk, along with the invocation of the dead and sacrifices at their tombs, was blended with remnants of old Sabæan superstition. The Coran was unread, the five daily prayers forgotten, and no one cared where Mecca lay, east or west, north or south; tithes, ablutions, and pilgrimages were things unheard of."‡ If that was the state of things in a country exposed to no extraneous influences after a thousand years of Islam, we may well believe that the state of Israel in the time of the Judges was a fall from a better state religiously as well as politically. Looking to the future, Moses might well foresee the danger; and looking back the author of Deuteronomy would have reasons, many of them now unknown, for knowing that what was feared had occurred.

It is striking to see that both know but one security against such lapses in the life of a nation, and that is education. Nowadays we are inclined to ask if this was not a delusion on their part. The boundless faith in education as a moral, religious, and national restorative which filled men's minds in the early part of this century, has given place to disquieting questions as to whether it can do anything so high. Many begin to doubt whether it does more than restrain men from the worst crimes, by pointing out their consequences. And in the case of ordinary secular education that doubt is only too well founded. But it was not mere secular education the Old Testament relied on. Reading, writing, and arithmetic, valuable as these are as gateways to knowledge, were not in its view at all. What it was felt necessary to do was to keep alive an ideal view of life; and that was done by pouring into the young the history of their people, with the best that their highest minds had learned and thought of God. The demand is that parents shall first of all give themselves up to the love of God, without any reserve, and then that they shall teach this diligently to their children as the substance of the Divine demand upon *them*. Evidently by the words, "Thou shalt talk of them

---

* "The Caliphate," by Sir William Muir, p. 185.
† "Central and Eastern Arabia," vol. i., p. 373.
‡ This shows how precarious the fundamental principle of much new criticism is. The non-observance of rites laid down as Divine commands, and the appearance of ancient superstitions such as the worship of the dead at any period, are held sufficient in the history of Israel to prove that monotheism did not then exist, and that ancestor-worship was then the prevailing cult. If applied to Islam that principle would lead to utterly false conclusions. Is there any reason for thinking that it may not give similar results when applied to the history of Israel?

when thou sittest in thine house, and when thou walkest by the way, and when thou liest down and when thou risest up," it is meant that the truth about God and the thought of God should be a subject on which conversation naturally turned, and to which it gladly returned continually. Words about these things were to flow from a genuine delighted interest in them, which made speech a necessity and a joy. Further, parents were to meet the *naïve* and questioning curiosity of their children as to the meaning of religious and moral ordinances of their people, with grave and extended teaching as to the work of God among them in the past. They were to point out, vv. 21-25, all the grace of God, and to show them that the statutes, which to young and undisciplined minds might seem a heavy burden, were really God's crowning mercy: they marked out the lines upon which alone good could come to man: they were the directions of a loving guide anxious to keep their feet from paths of destruction, "for their good always." Such education as this might prove adequate to overcome even stronger temptations than those to which Israel was exposed. For see what it means. It means that all the garnered religious thought and emotion of past generations, which the experiences of life and the felt presence of God in them had borne in upon the deepest minds of Israel, was to be made the bounding horizon for the opening mind of every Israelite child. When the child looked beyond the desires of its physical nature, it was to see this great sight, this panorama of the grace of Yahweh. To compensate for the restrictions which the Decalogue puts upon the natural impulses, Yahweh was to be held up to every child as an object of love, no desire after which could be excessive. Love to Yahweh, drawn out by what He had shown Himself to be, was to turn the energies of the young soul outward, away from self, and direct them to God, who works and is the sum of all good. Obviously those upon whom such education had its perfect work would never be fettered by the material aspects of things. Their horizon could never be so darkened that the twilight gods worshipped by the Canaanites should seem to them more than dim and vanishing shadows. Every evil, incident to their circumstances as conquerors, would fall innocuous at their feet.

The instrument put into the hands of Israel was, viewed ideally, quite adequate for the work it had to do. But the history of Israel shows that the effort to keep Yahweh continually present to the mind of the people failed; and the question arises, why did it fail? If, as we have every reason to believe, the main tendencies of human nature then were what they are now, the first cause of failure would be with the parents. Many, probably the most of them, would observe to do all that Moses commanded, but they would do it without themselves keeping alive their spiritual life. Wherever that was the case, though the prayers should be scrupulously rehearsed, though the religious talk should be increasing, though the instruction about the past should be exact and regular, the highest results of it all would cease to appear. The best that would be done would be to keep alive knowledge of what the fathers had told them. The worst would be to render the child's mind so familiar with all aspects of the truth, and with all the phases of religious emotion, that throughout life this would always seem a region already explored, and in which no water for the thirsty soul had been found.

But in the children, too, there would be fatal hindrances. One would almost expect, *a priori*, that when one generation had won in trial and hardship and conquest a fund of moral and spiritual wisdom, their children would be able to take it to themselves, and would start from the point their fathers had attained. But in experience that is not found to be so. The fathers may have gained a sane and strong manhood through the training and teaching of Divine Providence, but their children do not start from the level their fathers have gained. They begin with the same passions, and evil tendencies, and illusions, as their fathers began with, and against these they have to wage continual war. Above all, each soul for itself must take the great step by which it turns from evil to good. No rise in the general level of life will ever enable men to dispense with that. The will must determine itself morally by a free choice, and the Divine grace must play its part, before that union with God which is the heart of all religion can be brought about. No mechanical keeping up of good habits or fairer forms of social life can do much at this crucial point; and so each generation finds that there is no discharge in the war to which it is committed. As in all wars, many fall; sometimes the battle goes sorely against the kingdom of God, and the majority fall. The strength and beauty of a whole generation turns to the world and away from God, and the labours and prayers of faithful men and women who have taught them seem to be in vain.

The method of warding off evil by even high religious education is consequently very imperfect and uncertain in its action. Nevertheless this relative uncertainty is bound up with the very nature of moral influence and moral agency. Professor Huxley, in a famous passage of one of his addresses, says that if any being would offer to wind him up like a clock, so that he should always do what is right, and think what is true, he would close with the offer, and make no mourning about his moral freedom. Probably this was only a vehement way of expressing a desire for righteousness in deed, and truth in thought, somewhat pathetic in such a man. But if we are to take it literally, it is a singularly unwise declaration. The longing which gives pathos to the professor's words would on his hypothesis be a lunacy: for in the realm of morals mechanical compulsion has no meaning. Even God must give room to His creature, that he may exercise the spiritual freedom with which he is endowed. Even God, we may say without irreverence, must sometimes fail in that which He seeks to accomplish, in the field of moral life. Philosophically speaking, perhaps, this statement cannot be defended. But it is not the Absolute of Philosophy which can touch the hearts and draw the love of men. It is the living, personal God, of whom we gain our best working conception by boldly transferring to Him the highest categories predicable of our humanity. He is, doubtless, much more than we; but we can only ascribe to Him our own best and highest. When we have done that we have approached Him as near as we can ever do. The Scriptural writers, therefore, have no pedantic scruples in their speech about God. They constantly represent Him as pleading with men, desiring to influence them, and yet sometimes as being driven back defeated by the obstinate sin of man. The Bible is full of the failures of God in this sense; and God's greatest failure, that which forms the burden and inspires the pathos of the bulk of the Old Testament, is His failure with His chosen people. They *would* not be saved, they *would* not be faithful; and God had to accomplish His work of planting the true and spiritual religion in the world by means of a mere remnant of faithful men chosen from a faithless multitude.

But though this plan failed miserably in one way, in the way of gaining the bulk of the people, it succeeded in another. As has just been said, *the* purpose of God was in any case accomplished. But even apart from that, the religious education that was given was of immense importance. It raised the level of life for all; like the Nile mud in the inundation, it fertilised the whole field of this people's life. It kept an ideal, too, before men, without which they would have fallen even lower than they did. And it lay in the minds of even the worst, ready to be changed into something higher; for without previous intellectual acquaintance with the facts, the deeper knowledge was impossible. Moreover the ordinary civil morality of the people rested upon it. Without their religion and the facts on which it was based, the moral code had no hold upon them, and could have none. That had grown up in one complex tangle with religion; it had received its highest inspiration from the conception of God handed down from the fathers; and apart from that it would have fallen into an incoherent mass of customs unable to justify or account for their existence. In every community the same principle holds. Hence whatever the theory of the relation of the State to religion which may prevail, no State can, without much harm, ignore the religion of the people. It may sometimes even be wise and right for a government to introduce or to encourage a higher religion at the expense of a lower. But it can never be either wise or right to be inadvertent of religion altogether. In accordance with this precept, the rulers of Israel never were so. They not only encouraged parents to be strenuous, as this passage demands of them, but on more than one occasion they made definite provision for the religious instruction of the people. In a formal sense that grew into a habit which even yet has not lost its hold; and hence, as we have seen, the Jews have been kept true in an unexampled manner to their racial and religious characteristics.

CHAPTER IX.

THE BAN.

Deuteronomy vii.

As in the previous chapter we have had the Mosaic and Deuteronomic statement of the internal and spiritual means of defending the Israelite character and faith from the temptations which the conquest in Canaan would bring with it, in this we have strenuous provision made against the same evil by external means. The mind first was to be fortified against the temptation to fall away: then the external pressure from the example of the peoples they were to conquer was to be minimised by the practice of the ban. The first five verses, and the last two deal emphatically with that, as also does ver. 16, and what lies between is a statement of the grounds upon which a strict execution of this dreadful measure was demanded. These, as is usual in Deuteronomy, are dealt with somewhat discursively; but the command as to the ban, coming as it does at the beginning, middle, and end, gives this chapter unity, and suggests that it should be treated under this head as a whole. There are besides other passages which can most conveniently be discussed in connection with chapter vii. These are the historic statements as to the ban having been laid upon the cities of Sihon (Deut. ii. 34) and Og (Deut. iii. 6); the provision for the extirpation of idolatrous persons and communities (Deut. xiii. 15); and lastly, that portion of the law of war which treats of the variations in the execution of the ban which circumstances might demand (Deut. xx. 13-18). These passages, taken together, give an almost exhaustive statement in regard to the nature and limitations of the Cherem, or ban, in ancient Israel, a statement much more complete than is elsewhere to be found; and they consequently suggest, if they do not demand, a complete investigation of the whole matter.

It is quite clear that the Cherem, or ban, by which a person or thing, or even a whole people and their property, were devoted to a god, was not a specially Mosaic ordinance, for it is a custom known to many half-civilised and some highly civilised nations. In Livy's account of early Rome we read that Tarquinius, after defeating the Sabines, burned the spoils of the enemy in a huge heap, in accordance with a vow to Vulcan, made before advancing into the Sabine country. The same custom is alluded to in Vergil, *Æn.* viii. 562, and Cæsar, *B. G.* vi. 17, tells us a similar thing of the Gauls. The Mexican custom of sacrificing all prisoners of war to the god of war was of the same kind. But the most complete example of the ban in the Hebrew sense, occurring among a foreign people, is to be found in the Moabite stone which Mesha, king of Moab, erected in the ninth century B. C., *i. e.*, in the days of Ahab. Of course Moab and Israel were related peoples, and it might in itself be possible that Moab during its subjection to Israel had adopted the ban from Israel. But that is highly improbable, considering how widespread this custom is, and how deeply its roots are fixed in human nature. Rather we should take the Moabite ban as an example of its usual form among the Semitic peoples. "And Chemosh said to me, Go, take Nebo against Israel. And I went by night and fought against it from the break of morn until noon, and took it and killed them all, seven thousand men and boys, and women and girls and maid-servants, for I had devoted it to 'Ashtor-Chemosh'; and I took thence the vessels" (so Renan) "of Yahweh, and I dragged them before Chemosh."* The ordinary Semitic word for the ban is *Cherem*. It denotes a thing separated from or prohibited to common use, and no doubt it indicated originally merely that which was given over to the gods, separated for their exclusive use for ever. In this way it was distinguished from that which was "sanctified" to Yahweh, for that could be redeemed; devoted things could not.

* Driver, "Notes on Hebrew Text of the Books of Samuel," p. 101, note.

In the ancient laws repeated in Lev. xxvii. 28, 29, two classes of devoted things seem to be referred to. First of all, we have the things which an individual may devote to God, "whether of man or beast, or of the field of his possession." The provision made in regard to them is that they shall not be sold or redeemed, but shall become in the highest degree sacred to Yahweh. Men so devoted, therefore, became perpetual slaves at the holy places, and other kinds of property fell to the priests. In the next verse, 29, we read, "None devoted which shall be devoted of" (*i. e.*, from among) "men shall be ransomed; he shall surely be put to death," but that must refer to some other class of men devoted to Yahweh. It is inconceivable that in Israel individuals could at their own will devote slaves or children to death. Moreover, if every man devoted must be killed, the provision of Numb. xviii. 14, according to which everything devoted in Israel is to be Aaron's, could not be carried out. Further, there is a difference in expression in the two verses: in 28 we have things "devoted to Yahweh," in 29 we have simply men "devoted."* There can be little doubt, therefore, that we have in ver. 29 the case of men condemned for some act for which the punishment prescribed by the law was the ban (as in Exod. xxii. 19, "He that sacrificeth unto any god save unto Yahweh only shall be put to the ban"), or which some legal tribunal considered worthy of that punishment. In such cases, the object of the ban being something offensive, something which called out the Divine wrath and abhorrence, this "devotion" to God meant utter destruction. Just as *anathēma*, a thing set up in a temple as a votive offering, became *anathēma*, an accursed thing, and as *sacer*, originally meaning sacred, came to mean devoted to destruction, so *Cherem*, among the Semites, came to have the meaning of a thing devoted to destruction by the wrath of the national gods. From ancient days it had been in use, and in Israel it continued to be practised, but with a new moral and religious purpose which antiquity could know nothing of. No more conspicuous instance of that transformation of ancient customs of a doubtful or even evil kind by the spirit of the religion of Yahweh, which is one of the most remarkable characteristics of the history of Israel, can be conceived than this use of the ban for higher ends.

As the fundamental idea of the *Cherem* was the devoting of objects to a god, it is manifest that the whole inner significance of the institution would vary with the conception of the Deity. Among the worshippers of cruel and sanguinary gods, such as the gods of the heathen Semites were, the ends which this practice was used to promote would naturally be cruel and sanguinary. Moreover, where it was thought that the gods could be bought over by acceptable sacrifices, where they were conceived of as non-moral beings, whose reasons for favour or anger were equally capricious and unfathomable, it was inevitable that the *Cherem* should be mainly used to bribe these gods to favour and help their peoples. Where victory seemed easy and within the power of the nation, the spoil and the inhabitants of a conquered city or country would be taken by the conquerors for their own use. Where, on the other hand, victory was difficult and doubtful, an effort would be made to win the favour of the

Cf. Dillmann, "Exodus and Leviticus," p. 634.

god, and wring success from him by promising him all the spoil. The slaughter of the captives would be considered the highest gratification such sanguinary gods could receive, while their pride would be held to be gratified by the utter destruction of the seat of the worship of other gods. Obviously it was in this way that the Gauls and Germans worked this institution; and the probability is that the heathen Semites would view the whole matter from an even lower standpoint. But to true worshippers of Yahweh such thoughts must have grown abhorrent. From the moment when their God became the centre and the norm of moral life to Israel, acts which had no scope but the gratification of a thirst for blood, or of a petty jealous pride, could not be thought acceptable to Him. Every institution and custom, therefore, which had no moral element in it, had either to be swept away, or moralised in the spirit of the purer faith. Now the ban was not abolished in Israel; but it was moralised, and turned into a potent and terrible weapon for the preservation and advancement of true religion.

By the Divine appointment the national life of Israel was bound up with the foundation and progress of true religion. It was in this people that the seeds of the highest religion were to be planted, and it was by means of it that all the nations of the earth were to be blessed. But as the chief means to this end was to be the higher ethical and religious character of the nation as such, the preservation of that from depravation and decay became the main anxiety of the prophets and priests and lawgivers of Israel. Just as in modern days the preservation and defence of the State is reckoned in every country the supreme law which overrides every other consideration, so in Israel the preservation of the higher life was regarded. Rude and half-civilised as Israel was at the beginning of its career, the Divinely revealed religion had made men conscious of that which gave this people its unique value both to God and men. They recognised that its glory and strength lay in its thought of God, and in the character which this impressed upon the corporate life, as well as on the life of each individual. As we have seen, this bred in them a consciousness of a higher calling, of a higher obligation resting on them than upon others. They consequently felt the necessity of guarding their special character, and used the ban as their great weapon to ward off the contagion of evil, and to give this character room to develop itself. Its tremendous, even cruel, power was directed in Israel to this end; it was from this point of view alone that it had value in the eyes of the fully enlightened man of Israel. Stade in his history (vol. i., p. 490) holds that this distinction did not exist, that the Israelite view differed in little, if anything, from that of their heathen kinsmen, and that the ban resulted from a vow intended to gratify Yahweh and win His favour by giving Him the booty. But it is undeniable that in the earliest statement in regard to it (Exod. xx.) there is a distinct legislative provision that the ban should be proclaimed and executed irrespective of any vow; and in the later, but still early, notices of it in Joshua, Judges, and 1 Samuel the command to execute it comes in every case from Yahweh. In Deuteronomy, again, the ethical purpose of the ban is always insisted upon, most emphatically perhaps in chap. xx. 17 ff., where the *Cherem* is laid down as a regular practice in war against the heathen inhabitants of Canaan: "But thou shalt utterly destroy them, . . . that they teach you not to do after all their abominations, which they have done unto their gods; so should ye sin against Yahweh your God." Whatever hints or appearances there may be in the Scripture narratives that the lower view still clung to some minds are not to be taken as indicating the normal and recognised view. They were, like much else of a similar kind, mere survivals, becoming more and more shadowy as the history advances, and at last entirely vanishing away. The new and higher thought which Moses planted was the rising and prevailing element in the Israelite consciousness. The lower thought was a decaying reminiscence of the state of things which the Mosaic revelation had wounded to the death, but which was slow in dying.

In Israel, therefore, the ban was, on the principles of the higher religion, legitimate only where the object was to preserve that religion when gravely endangered. If any object could justify a measure so cruel and sweeping as the ban, this could, and this is the only ground upon which the Scriptures defend it. That the danger was grave and imminent, when Israel entered Canaan, cannot be doubted. As we have seen, the Israelite tribes were far from being of one blood or of one faith. There was a huge mixed multitude along with them; and even among those who had unquestioned title to be reckoned among Israelites, many were gross, carnal, and slavish in their conceptions of things. They had not learned thoroughly nor assimilated the lessons they had been taught. Only the elect among them had done that; and the danger from contact with races, superior in culture, and religiously not so far below the position occupied by the multitude of Israel, was extreme. The nation was born in a day, but it had been educated only for a generation; it was raw and ignorant in all that concerned the Yahwistic faith. In fact it was precisely in the condition in which spiritual disease could be most easily contracted and would be most deadly. The new religion had not been securely organised; the customs and habits of the people still needed to be moulded by it, and could not, consequently, act as the stay and support of religion as they did at later times. Further, the people were at the critical moment when they were passing from one stage of social life to another. At such moments there is immense danger to the health and character of a nation, for there is no unity of ideal present to every mind. That which they are moving away from has not ceased to exert its influence, and that *to* which they are moving has not asserted itself with all its power. At such crises in the career of peoples emerging from barbarism, even physical disease is apt to be deadlier and more prevalent than it is among either civilised or entirely savage men. The old Semitic heathenism had not been entirely overcome, and the new and higher religion had not succeeded in establishing full dominion. Contact with the Canaanites in almost any shape would under such circumstances be like the introduction of a contagious disease, and at almost any price it had to be avoided. The customs of the world at that time, and of the Semitic nations in particular, offered this terribly effective weapon of the "ban," and for this higher purpose it was accepted; and it was enforced with a stringency which nothing would justify short of the fact that life or death to the great hope of mankind was involved in it.

But it may be and should be asked, Would any circumstances justify Christian men, or a Christian nation, in entering upon a war of extermination now? and if not, how can a war of extermination against the Canaanites have been sanctioned by God? In answer to the first question, it must be said that, while circumstances can be conceived under which the extermination of a race would certainly be carried out by nations called Christian, it is hardly possible to imagine Christian men taking part in such a massacre. Even the supposed command of God could not induce them to do so.* It would be so contrary to all that they have learned of God's will, both as regards themselves and others, that they would hesitate. Almost certainly they would decide that they were bound to be faithful to what God had revealed of Himself; they would feel that He could not wish to blunt their moral sense and undo what He had done for them, and they would put aside the command as a temptation. But the case with the Israelites was altogether different. The question is not, how could God destroy a whole people? Were it only that, there would be little difficulty. Everywhere in His action through nature God is ruthless enough against sin. Vice and sin are every day bringing men and women and innocent children to death, and to suffering worse than death. For that every believer in God holds the Divine law responsible. And when the Divine command was laid upon the Israelites to do, more speedily, and in a more awe-inspiring way, what Canaanite vices were already doing, there can be no difficulty except in so far as the effect upon the Israelites is concerned. It is by death, inflicted as the punishment of vice, and sparing neither woman nor child, that nations have, as a rule, been blotted out; and, except to the confused thinker, so far as the Divine action is concerned there is no difference between such cases and this of the Canaanites. The real question is, Can a living, personal God deliberately set to men a task which can only lower them in the scale of humanity—brutalise them, in fact? No, is of course the only possible answer; therefore a supposed Divine command coming to us to do such things would rightly be suspected. We could not, we feel sure, be called upon by God to slay the innocent with the guilty, to overwhelm in one common punishment individual beings who have each of them an inalienable claim to justice at our hands. But the Israelites had not and could not have the feeling we have on the subject. The feeling for the individual did not exist in early times. The clan, the tribe, the nation was everything, and the individual nothing. Consequently there was not existent in the world that keen feeling in regard to individual rights, which dominates us so completely that we can with difficulty conceive any other view. In this world the early Israelite scarcely perceived the individual man, and beyond this world he knew of no certain career for him. He consequently dealt with him only as part of his clan or tribe. His tribe suffered for him and he for his tribe, and in early penal law the two could hardly be separated. Indeed it may almost be said that, when the individual suffered for his own sin, the satisfaction felt by the

* Mozley's "Lectures on the Old Testament," p. 102.

wronged was rather due to the tribe having suffered so much loss in the individual's death than to the retribution which fell upon him. Moreover war was the constant employment of all, and death by violence the most common of all forms of death. Manners and feelings were both rude, and the pains as well as the pleasures of civilised and Christian men lay largely beyond their horizon. There was consequently no danger of doing violence to nobler feelings or of leaving a sting in the conscience by calling such men to such work. The stage of moral development they had reached did not forbid it, and the work therefore might be given them of God.

But the grounds for the action were immeasurably raised. Instead of being left on the heathen level, "the usage was utilised so as to harmonise with the principles of their religion, and to satisfy its needs. It became a mode of secluding and rendering harmless anything which peculiarly imperilled the religious life of either an individual or the community, such objects being withdrawn from society at large, and presented to the sanctuary, which had power, if needful, to authorise their destruction."* The Deuteronomic command is not given shamefacedly. The interests at stake are too great for that. Israel is utterly to smite the Canaanite nations, to put them to the ban, to make no covenant with them nor to intermarry with them. "Thus shall ye deal with them: ye shall break down their altars, and dash in pieces their obelisks, and hew down their Asherim, and burn their graven images with fire." There is a fierce, curt energy about the words which impresses the reader with the vigour needed to defend the true religion. The danger was seen to be great, and this tremendous weapon of the ban was to be wielded with unsparing rigour, if Israel was to be true to its highest call. "For," ver. 6 goes on to say, "thou art a holy people unto Yahweh thy God; Yahweh thy God hath chosen thee to be a peculiar people unto Himself, out of all peoples that are upon the face of the earth." They were the elect of God; they were a holy people, a people separated unto their God, and the Divine blessing was to come upon all nations through them if they remained true. Their separateness must therefore be maintained. As a people marked out by the love of God, they could not share in the common life of the world as it then was. They could not lift the Canaanites to their level by mingling with them. So they would only obscure, nay, in so far as this rigorous command was not carried out, they did all but fatally obscure, the higher elements of national and personal life which they had received. They were too recently converted to be the people of Yahweh, too weak in their own faith, to be able to do anything but stand in this austere and repellent attitude towards the world. Centuries passed before they could relax without danger. It may even be said that until the coming of our Lord they dared not take up any other than this separatist position, though as the ages passed and the prophetic influence grew, the yearning after a gathering in of the Gentiles, and the promise of it in the Messianic day, became more markedly prominent. Only when men could look forward to being made perfect in Jesus Christ did they receive the command to go unreservedly out into the world, for only then had they an anchor which no storm in the world could drag.

But we must be careful not to exaggerate the separation called for here. It does not authorise anything like the fierce, intolerant thirst for conquest and domination which was the very keynote of Islam.* In Deut. ii. 5, 6, 19, the lands of Edom, Moab, and Ammon are said to be Yahweh's gift to these peoples in the same way as Canaan was to Israel. Nor did the law ever authorise the bitter and contemptuous feeling with which Pharisaic Israelites often regarded all men beyond the pale of Judaism. There was no general prohibition against friendly intercourse with other peoples. It was against those only, whose presence in Canaan would have frustrated the establishment of the theocracy, and whose influence would have been destructive of it when established, that the "ban" was decreed. When war arose between Israel and cities farther off than those of Canaan, they were not to be put to the "ban." Though they were to be hardly treated according to our ideas, they were to suffer only the fate of cities stormed in those days, for the danger of corruption was proportionately diminished (Deut. xx. 17) by their distance. The right of other peoples to their lands was to be respected, and friendly intercourse might be entered on with them. But the right of Israel to the free and unhindered development to which it had been called by Yahweh was the supreme law. The suspicion of danger to that was to make things otherwise harmless, or even useful, to be abhorred. If men are to live nearer to God than others, they must sacrifice much to the higher call.

To press home this, to induce Israel to respond to this demand, to convince them anew of their obligation to go any length to keep their position as a people holy to Yahweh, our chapter urges a variety of reasons. The first (vv. 7-11) is that the history and grounds of their election exhibit the character of Yahweh in such a way as to heighten their sense of their privileges and the danger of losing them. He had chosen them, only because of His own love to them; and having chosen them and sworn to their fathers, He is true to His covenant. He brought them out of the house of bondage, and has led them until now. In Yahweh they had a spiritual ideal, whose characteristics were love and faithfulness. But though He loves He can be wrathful, and though He has made a covenant with Israel, it must be fulfilled in accordance with righteousness. In dealing with such a God they must beware of thinking that their election is irrespective of moral conditions, or that His love is mere good nature. He can and does smite the enemies of good, for anger is always possible where love is. It is only with good nature that anger is not compatible, just as warm and self-sacrificing affection also is. Those who turn away from Him, therefore, He requites immediately to their face, as surely as "He keepeth covenant and mercy with them that love Him and keep His commandments." All the blessed and intimate relations which He has opened up with them, and in which their safety and their glory lie, can be dissolved by sin. They are, therefore, to strike fiercely at temptation, to regard neither their own lives nor the lives of others when that has to be put out of the way, to smite and spare not, for the very love of God.

---

* Driver, "Notes on the Hebrew Text of the Books of Samuel," p. 101.

* Riehm, "Old Testament Theology," p. 98.

A second reason why they should obey the Divine commands, as in other matters, so in this terrible thing, is this. If they be willing and obedient, then God will bless them in temporal ways as well as with spiritual blessings. Even for their earthly prosperity a loyal attitude to Yahweh would prove decisive. "Thou shalt be blessed above all peoples; there shall not be a male or female barren among you, or among your cattle. And Yahweh will take away from thee all sickness, and He will put none of the evil diseases of Egypt which thou knowest upon thee; but will lay them upon all them that hate thee." The same promises are renewed in more detail and with greater emphasis in the speech contained in chapters xxviii. and xxix. There the significance of such a view, and the difficulties involved in it for us, will be fully discussed. Here it will be sufficient to note that the profit of obedience is brought in to induce Israel to enforce the "ban" most rigorously.

The last verses of our chapter, vv. 17-26, set before Israel a third incitement and encouragement. Yahweh, who had proved His might and His favour for them by His mighty deeds in Egypt, would be among them, to make them stronger than their mightiest foes (ver. 21): "Thou shalt not be affrighted at them, for Yahweh thy God is in the midst of thee, a great God and a terrible." The previous inducements to obey Yahweh their God and be true to Him were founded on His character and on His acts. He was merciful; but He could be terrible, and He would reward the faithful with prosperity. Now His people are encouraged to go forward because His presence will go with them. In the conflicts which obedience to Him would provoke, He would be with them to sustain them, whatever stress might come upon them. Step by step they would drive out those very peoples whom they had dreaded so when the spies brought back their report of the land. The terror of their God would fall upon all these nations. A great God and a terrible He would prove Himself to be, and with Him in their midst they might go forth boldly to execute the ban upon the Canaanites. The sins and vices of these peoples had brought this upon them; their horrible worship left an indelible stain wherever its shadow fell. Israel, led and directed by Yahweh Himself, was to fall upon them as the scourge of God.

Notwithstanding the Divine urgency, the command to destroy the Canaanites and their idols was not carried out. After a victory or two the enemy began to submit. Glad to be rid of the toils of war, Israel settled down among the people of the land. All central control would seem to have disappeared. The Canaanite worship and the Canaanite customs attracted and fascinated the people, and enemy after enemy broke in upon them and triumphed over them. The half-idolatrous masses were led away into depraved forms of worship, and for a time it looked as if the work of Moses would be utterly undone. Had the purer faith he taught them not been revived, Israel would probably not have survived the period of the Judges. As it was they just survived; but by their lapse the leavening of the whole of the nation with the pure principles of Yahweh-worship had been stopped. Instead of being cured, the idolatrous inclinations they had brought with them from the pre-Mosaic time had been revived and strengthened. Multitudes, while calling Yahweh their God, had sunk almost to the Canaanite level in their worship, and during the whole period of their existence as a nation Israel as a whole never again rose clear of half-heathen conceptions of their God. The prophets taught and threatened them in vain, until at last ruin fell upon them and the Divine threats of punishment were fulfilled.

CHAPTER X.

THE BAN IN MODERN LIFE.

IN our modern time this practice of the ban has, of course, become antiquated and impossible. The *Cherem*, or ban, of the modern synagogue is a different thing, based upon different motives, and is directed to the same ends as Christian excommunication. But though the thing has ceased, the principles underlying it, and the view of life which it implies, are of perpetual validity. These belong to the essential truths of religion, and especially need to be recalled in a time like ours, when men tend everywhere to a feeble, lax, and cosmopolitan view of Christianity. As we have seen, the fundamental principle of the *Cherem* was that, however precious, however sacred, however useful and helpful in ordinary circumstances a thing might be, whenever it became dangerous to the higher life it should at once be given up to Yahweh. The lives of human beings, even though they were men's dearest and nearest, should be sacrificed; the richest works of art, the weapons of war, and the wealth which would have adorned life and made it easy, were equally to be given up to Him, that He might seclude them and render them harmless to men's highest interests. Neighbourliness to the Canaanites was absolutely forbidden, and the Church of the Old Testament was commanded to take up a position of hostility, or at best of armed neutrality, to all the pleasures, interests, and concerns of the peoples who surrounded them. Now the prevailing modern view is that not only the ban itself, but these principles have become obsolete. Notwithstanding that the Church of the New Testament is the bearer of the higher interests of humanity, we are taught that when it is least definite in its direction as to conduct, when it is most tolerant of the practices of the world, then it is most true to its original conception. We are told that an indulgent Church is what is wanted; rigour and religion are now supposed to be finally divorced in all enlightened minds. This view is not often categorically expressed, but it underlies all fashionable religion, and has its apostles in the golden youth who forward enlightenment by playing tennis on Sundays. Because of it too, Puritan has become a name of scorn, and careless self-gratification a mark of cultured Christianity. Not only asceticism, but ἄσκησις has been discredited, and the moral tone of society has perceptibly fallen in consequence. In wide circles both within and without the Church it seems to be held that pain is the only intolerable evil, and in legislation as well as in literature that idea has been registering itself.

For much of this progress, as some call it, no reasoned justification has been attempted, but it has been defended in part by the allegation that the circumstances which make the "ban" necessary to the very life of the ancient people of God have passed away, now that social and political life has been Christianised. Even those who are outside the Church in Christian lands are no longer living at a moral and spiritual level so much below that of the Church. They are not heathen idolaters, whose moral and religious ideas are contagiously corrupting, and nothing but Pharisaism of the worst type, it is said, can justify the Church in taking up a position to society in any degree like that which was imposed upon ancient Israel. Now it cannot be denied that there is truth here, and in so far as the Christian Church or individual Christians have taken up precisely the same position to those without as is implied in the Old Testament ban, they are not to be defended. Modern society, as at present constituted, is not corrupting like that of Canaan. No one in a modern Christian state has been brought up in an atmosphere of heathenism, and what an incredible difference that involves only those who know heathenism well can appreciate. If spiritual life is neither understood nor believed in by all, yet the rules of morals are the same in every mind, and these rules are the product of Christianity. As a consequence, the Church is not endangered in the same way and to the same degree by contact with the world as in the ancient days. Indeed to the Israelite of the post-Mosaic time our "world," which some sects at least would absolutely ignore and shut out, would seem a very definite and legitimate part of the church. The Jewish Church was certainly to a very large extent made up of precisely such elements, while those who were to be put to the ban were far more remote than any citizens of a modern state, except a portion of the criminal class. Further, those not actively Christian are, on account of this community of moral sentiments, open to appeal from the Church as the heathen Canaanites were not. In English-speaking lands, while there are multitudes indifferent to Christianity, most acknowledge the obligation of the Christian motives. In nations at least nominally Christian, therefore, both because the danger of corruption is greatly less, and because the world is more accessible to the leaven of Christian life, no Church can, or dare, without incurring terrible loss and responsibility, withdraw from or show a merely hostile front to the world. The sects which do so live an invalid life. Their virtues take on the sickly look of all "fugitive and cloistered virtue." Their doctrines become full of the "idols of the cave," and they cease to have any perception of the real needs of men.

Nevertheless the austere spirit inculcated in this chapter must be kept alive, if the Church is to be the spiritual leader of humanity, for strenuousness is the great want of modern life. Dr. Pearson, whose book on "National Life and Character" has lately expounded the theory that the Church, "being too inexorable in its ideal to admit of compromises with human frailty, is precisely on this account unfitted for governing fallible men and women," *i. e.*, governing them in the political sense, has elsewhere stated his view of the remedy for one of the great evils of modern life.* "The disproportionate growth of the distributing classes, as compared with the producing, is due, I believe, to two moral causes—the love of amusement and the passion for speculation. Men flock out of healthy country lives in farms or mines into our great cities, because they like to be near the theatre and the racecourse, or because they hope to grow rich suddenly by some form of gambling. The cure for a taint of this kind is not economical but religious, and can only be found, I am convinced, in a return to the masculine asceticism that has distinguished the best days of history, Puritan or Republican." This is emphatically true of Australia, where and of which the words were first spoken; and masculine asceticism of the Puritan type would cure many another evil there besides these. But the same thing is true everywhere; and if religion is to cure slackness in social or political life, how much more must it cultivate this austere spirit for itself! The function of the Church is not to govern the world; it seeks rather to inspire the world. It should lead the advance to a higher, more ennobling life, and should exhibit that in its own collective action and in the kind of character it produces. Its greatest gift to the world should be itself, and it is useful only when it is true to its own *ethos* and spirit. To keep that unimpaired must therefore be its first duty, and to fulfil that duty it must keep rigorously back from everything which, in relation to its own existing state, would be likely to lower the power of its peculiar life. The State must often compromise with human frailty. Often there will be before the legislator and the statesman only a choice between two evils, or at least two undesirable courses, unless a worse thing is to be tolerated. The Church, on the other hand, should keep close to the ideal as it sees it. Its reason for existence is that it may hold up the ideal to men, and exhibit it as far as that may be. Compromise in regard to that is impossible for the Church, for that would be nothing else than disloyalty to its own essential principle. The spirit, therefore, that inspired the "ban" must always be living and powerful in the Church. Whatever is dangerous to the special Christian life must cease to exist for Christians. It should be laid at the feet of their Divine Head, that He may seclude it from His people and render it innocuous. Many things that are harmless or even useful at a lower level of life must be refused a place by the Christian. Gratifications that cannot but seem good to others must be refused by him; for he seeks to be in the forefront of the battle against evil, to be the pioneer to a more whole-hearted spiritual life.

But that does not imply that we should seek to renew the various imperfect and external devices by which past times sought to attain this exceedingly desirable end. Experience has taught the folly and futility of sumptuary laws, for example. Their only effect was to do violence to the inwardness which belongs of necessity to spiritual life. They externalised and depraved morality, and finally defeated themselves. Nor would the later Puritanism, with its rigidity as regards dress and deportment, and its narrow and limited view of life, help us much more. It began doubtless with the right principle; but it sought to bind all to its observances, whether they cared for the spirit of them or not; and it showed a measureless intemperance in regard to the things which it declared hostile to the life of faith. In that form it has been charged with "isolation from human history, human enjoyment, and all the manifold play and variety of

---

* "The Social Movements of the Age," by Professor Pearson, Melbourne Church Congress, 1882.

human character." For a short time, however, Puritanism did strike the golden mean in this matter, and probably we could not in this present connection find a better example for modern days than in the Puritanism of Spenser, of Colonel Hutchinson (one of the regicides so called), and of Milton. Their united lives covered the heroic period of Puritanism, and taken in their order they represent very fairly its rise, its best estate, and its tendencies towards harsh extremes, when as yet it was but a tendency.

Spenser, born in the "spacious times of great Elizabeth," was politically and nationally a Puritan, and in aim and ideal, at least, was so in his stern view of life and religion.* His attachment to Lord Grey of Wilton, that personally kind yet absolutely ruthless executor of the English "ban" against the untamable Irish, and his defence of his policy, show the one; while his "Fairy Queen," with its representation of religion as "the foundation of all nobleness in man" and its dwelling upon man's victory over himself, reveals the other. But he had in him also elements belonging to that strangely mingled world in which he lived, and which came from an entirely different source. He had the Elizabethan enthusiasm for beauty, the large delight in life as such even where its moral quality was questionable, and the artist's sensitiveness and adaptability in a very high degree. These diverse elements were never fully interfused in him. Amid all the gracious beauty of his work, there is the trace of discord and the mark of conflict; and at times perhaps his life fell into courses which spoke little of self-control. But his face was always in the main turned upwards. In the main, too, his life corresponded with his aspirations. He combined his poetic gift, his love of men and human life, with a faithfulness to his ideal of conduct which, if not always perfect, was sincere, and was, too, as we may hope, ultimately victorious. The Puritan in him had not entire victory over the worldling, but it had the mastery; and the very imperfection of the victory kept the character in sympathy with the whole of life.

In Colonel Hutchinson,† as depicted in that stately and tender panegyric which speaks to us across more than two centuries so pathetically of his wife's almost adoring love, we see the Puritan character in its fullest and most balanced form. We do not, of course, mean that his mind had the imaginative power of Spenser's, or his character the force of Milton's; but partly from circumstances, partly by singular grace of nature, his character possessed a stability and an equilibrium which had not come when Spenser lived, and which was beginning to go in the evil days upon which Milton fell. At the root of all his virtues his wife sets "that which was the head and spring of them all, his Christianity." "By Christianity," she says, "I intend that universal habit of grace which is wrought in a soul by the regenerating Spirit of God, whereby the whole creature is resigned up into the Divine will and love, and all its actions designed to the obedience and glory of its Maker." He had been trained in a Puritan home, and though when he went out into the world he had to face quite the average temptations of a rich and well-born youth, he fled all youthful lusts. But he did not retire from the world. "He could dance admirably well, but neither in youth nor riper years made any practice of it; he had skill in fencing such as became a gentleman; he had a great love to music, and often diverted himself with a viol, on which he played masterly; he had an exact ear, and judgment in other music; he shot excellently in bows and guns, and much used them for his exercise; he had great judgment in painting, graving, sculpture, and all liberal arts, and had many curiosities of value in all kinds. He took much pleasure in improvement of grounds, in planting groves and walks and fruit-trees, in opening springs and making fishponds. Of country recreations he loved none but hawking, and in that was very eager, and much delighted for the time he used it." Hutchinson was no ascetic, therefore, in the wrong sense, but lived in and enjoyed the world as a man should. But perhaps his greatest divergence from the lower Puritanism lay in this, that "everything that it was necessary for him to do he did with delight, free and unconstrained." Moreover, though he adopted strong Puritan opinions in theology, "he hated persecution for religion, and was always a champion for all religious people against all their great oppressors. Nevertheless self-restraint was the law of his life, and he many times forbore things lawful and delightful to him, rather than he would give any one occasion of scandal." In public affairs he took the courageous part of a man who sought nothing for himself, and was moved only by his hatred of wrong to leave the prosperity and peace of his home life. He became a member of the Court which tried the King against his will, but signed the warrant for his death, simply because he conceived it to be his duty. When the Restoration came and he was challenged for his conduct, scorning the subterfuges of some who declared they signed under compulsion, he quietly accepted the responsibility for his acts. This led to his death in the flower of his age, through imprisonment in the Tower; but he never flinched, "having made up his accounts with life and death, and fixed his purpose to entertain both honourably." From the beginning of his life to the end there was a consistent sanity, which is rare at any time, and was especially rare in those days. His loyalty to God kept him austerely aloof from unworthiness, while it seemed to add zest to the sinless joys which came in his way. Above all, it never suffered him to forget that the true Christian temper and character was the pearl of price which all else he had might lawfully be sacrificed to purchase.

In the character of Milton we find the same essential elements, the same purity in youth, which, with his beauty, won for him the name of the Lady of his College; the same courage and public spirit in manhood; the same love of music and of culture. After his University career he retired to his father's house, and read all Greek and Latin literature, as well as Italian, and studied Hebrew and some other Oriental languages. All the culture of his time, therefore, was absorbed by him, and his mind and speech were shot through and through with the brilliant colours of the history and romance of many climes. Almost no kind of beauty failed to appeal to him, but the austerity of his views of life kept him from being enslaved by it. In his earlier works even, he caught in a surprising way all the glow, and splendour, and poetic fervour of the English Renaissance; but he

---

* *Vide* Church's "Spenser," p. 16.
† "Memoirs of Colonel Hutchinson," by his wife.

joined with it the sternest and most uncompromising Puritan morality, not only in theory and desire like Spenser, but in the hard practice of actual life. When the idea of duty comes to dominate a man, the grace and impetuosity of youth, the overmastering love of beauty, and the appreciation of the mere joy of living are apt to die away, and the poetic fire burns low. But it was not so with Milton. To the end of his life he remained a true Elizabethan, but an Elizabethan who had always kept himself free from the chains of sensual vice, and had never stained his purity of soul. That fact makes him unique almost in English history, and has everywhere added a touch of the sublime to all that his works have of beauty. " His soul was like a star, and dwelt apart: " and we may entirely believe what he tells us of himself when he returned from his European travels: " In all the places in which vice meets with so little discouragement, and is protected with so little shame, I never once turned from the path of integrity and virtue, and perpetually reflected that, though my conduct might escape the notice of men, it could not elude the inspection of God." Like the true Puritan he was, Milton not only overcame evil in himself, but he thought his own life and health a cheap price to pay for the overthrow of evil wherever he saw it. When the civil war broke out, he returned at once from his travels, to help to right the wrongs of his country. In the service of the Government he sacrificed his poetic gift, his leisure for twenty years, and finally his sight, to the task of defending England from her enemies. But he did not stop there. His severity became excessive, at times almost vindictive. When he wrote prose he scarcely ever wrote without having an enemy to crush, and much that he uttered in this vein cannot possibly be approved. His pamphlets are unfair to a degree which shows that his mind had lost balance in the turmoil of the great struggle, so that he approached at moments the narrower Puritanism. But he still proved himself too great for that, and emerged anew as a great and lofty spirit, held down very little by earthly bonds, and strenuously set against evil as a true servant of God.

Now the temper of Puritanism such as this of these old English worthies is precisely what Christians need most to cultivate in these days. They must be animated by the spirit which refuses to touch, and refers to God, whatever proves hostile to life in God; but they must also combine with this aloofness a sympathetic hold on ordinary life. It is easy on the one hand to solve all problems by cutting oneself off from any relation with the world, lest the inner life should suffer. It is also easy to let the inner life take care of itself, and to float blithely on with all the currents of life which are not deadly sins. But it is not easy to keep the mind and life open to all the great life-streams which tend to deepen and enrich human nature, and yet to stand firm in self-control, determined that nothing which drags down the soul shall be permitted to fascinate or overpower. To this task Christian men and the Christian Church seem at present to be specially called. It is admitted on all hands that the ordinary Puritanism became too intolerant of all except spiritual interests; so that it could not, without infinite loss, have been accepted as the guide for all life. But hence what was good in it has been rejected along with the bad; and it needs to be restored, if a weak, self-indulgent temper, which resents hardship or even discipline, is not to gain the upper hand. In social life especially this is needful, otherwise so much debate would never have been expended on the question of amusements. On the face of it, a Christianity which can go with the world in all those of its amusements which are not actually forbidden by the moral law must be a low type of Christianity. It can be conscious of no special character which it has to preserve, of no special voice which it has to utter in the antiphony of created things. Whatever others allow themselves, therefore, the vigilant Christian must see to it that he does nothing which will destroy his special contribution to the world he lives in. It is precisely by that that he is the salt of the earth; and if the salt have lost its savour wherewith will you season it? No price is too great for the preservation of this savour, and in reference to the care of it each man must ultimately be a law unto himself. No one else can really tell where his weakness lies. No one else can know what the effect of this or that recreation upon that weakness is.

When men lose spiritual touch with their own character they are apt to throw themselves back for guidance in such matters upon the general opinion of the Christian community, or the tradition of the elders. In doing so they are in danger of losing sincerity in a mass of formalism. But if a vivid apprehension of the need of individuality in the regulation of life is maintained, the formulated Christian objection to certain customs or certain amusements may be a most useful substitute for painful experience of our own. Some such amusements may have been banned in the past without sufficient reason; or they may have been excluded only because of the special openness to temptation of a certain community; or they may have so changed their character that they do not now deserve the ban which was laid upon them once justly enough. Any plea, therefore, for the revisal or abolition of standing conventions on such grounds must be listened to and judged, But, on the whole, these standing prohibitions of the Church represent accumulated experience, and all young people especially will do wisely not to break away from them. What the mass of Christians in the past have found hurtful to the Christian character will in most cases be hurtful still. For if it can be said of the secular world in all matters of experience that " this wise world is mainly right," it may surely be said also of the Christian community. In our time there is a quite justifiable distrust of conventionality in morals and in religion; but it should not be forgotten that conventions are not open to the same objection. They represent, on the whole, merely the registered results of actual experience, and they may be estimated and followed in an entirely free spirit. It is not wise, therefore, to revolt against them indiscriminately, merely because they may be used cruelly against others, or may be taken as a substitute for a moral nature by oneself. Thackeray in his constant railing at the judgment of the world seems to make this mistake. He is never weary in pointing out how unjust the broad general judgments of the world are to specially selected individuals. Harry Warrington in " The Virginians," for instance, though innocent, lives in a manner and with associates which the world has generally found to indicate intolerable moral laxity; and because the world was wrong in thinking that to be true in his case which would have been true in ninety-five out of a hundred similar cases, the moralist rails at the evil-hearted judgments of the world. But "this wise world is mainly right," and its rough and indiscriminating judgments fit the average case. They are part of the great sanitary provision which society makes for its own preservation. And the case is precisely similar with the conventions of the religious life. They too are in the main sanitary precautions which a conscience thoroughly alive and a strong intelligence may make superfluous, but for which for the unformed, the half-ignorant, the less original natures, in a word, for average men and women, are absolutely necessary. Spontaneity and freedom are admirable qualities in morals and religion. They are even the conditions of the highest kinds of moral and religious life, and the necessary presuppositions of health and progress. But something is due to stability as well; and a world of original and spontaneous moralists, trusting only to their own "genial sense" of truth, would be a maddening chaos. In other words, conventions if used unconventionally, if not exalted into absolute moral laws disobedience to which excludes from reputable society, if taken simply as indications of the paths in which least danger to the higher life has been found to lie, are guides for which men may well be thankful.

In the world of thought too, as well as in the world of action, a wise austerity of self-control is absolutely necessary. The prevailing theory is that every one, young men more especially, should read on all sides on all questions, and that they should know and sympathise with all modes of thought. This is advocated in the supposed interests of freedom from external domination and from internal prejudice. But in a great number of cases the result does not follow. Such catholicity of taste does produce a curious *dilettante* interest in lines of thought, but as a rule it weakens interest in truth as such. It delivers from the domination of a Church or other historic authority; but only, in most cases, to hand over the supposed freeman to the narrower domination of the thinker or school by which he happens to be most impressed. For it is vain and impotent to suppose that in regard to morals and religion every mind is able to find its way by free thought, when in regard to bodily health, or even in questions of finance, the free thought of the amateur is acknowledged to end usually in confusion. Those only can usefully expose their minds to all the various currents of modern thought who have a clear footing of their own. Whatever that may be, it gives them a point on which to stand, and a vantage-ground from which they can gather up what widens or corrects their view. But to leave the land altogether, and commit oneself to the currents, is to render any after-landing all but impossible. With regard to the books read, the lines of thought followed, and the associations formed, the Christian must exercise self-denial and self-examination. Whatever is manifestly detrimental to his best life, whatever he feels to be likely to taint the purity of his mind or lower his spiritual vitality, should be put under the "ban," should be resolutely avoided in all ordinary cases. Of course modes of thought that deserve to be weighed may be found mingled with such elements; also views of life which have a truth and importance of their own, though their setting is corrupt. But it is not every one's business to extricate and discuss these. Those who are called to it will have to do it; and in doing it as a duty they may expect to be kept from the lurking contagion. Every one else who investigates them runs a risk which he was not called upon to run. The average Christian should, therefore, note all that tends to stunt or deprave him spiritually, and should avoid it. It is not manliness but folly which makes men read filthy literature because of its style, or sceptical literature because of its ability, when they are not called upon to do so, and when they have not fortified themselves by the purity of the Scriptures and the power of prayer. To make such literature or such modes of thought our staple mental food, or to make the writers or admirers of such books our intimate friends, is to sap our own best convictions and to disregard our high calling.

Lastly, however common it may be for men to sit down in selfish isolation and devote themselves to their own interests, even though these be spiritual, in the face of remediable evils, that is not the Christian manner of acting. Of the great Puritans we mentioned, Spenser endured hardness in that terrible Irish war which the men of Elizabeth's day regarded as the war of good against evil; Hutchinson fought for and died in the cause of political and religious freedom; and Milton devoted his life and health to the same cause. All of them, the two latter especially, might have kept out of it all, in the peace and comfort of private life; but they judged that the destruction of evil was their first duty. At the trumpet call they willingly took their side, and prepared to give their lives, if necessary, for the righteous cause. Now it is not enough for us to avoid evil any more than it was for them. Though personal influence and example are undoubtedly among the most potent weapons in the warfare for the Kingdom of God, there must be, besides these, the power and the will to put public evils under the ban. Whatever institution or custom or law is ungodly, whatever in our social life is manifestly unjust, should stir the Christian Church to revolt against it, and should fill the heart of the individual Christian with an undying energy of hatred. It is not meant that the Christian Churches as such should transform themselves into political societies or social clubs. To do that would simply be to abdicate their only real functions. But they should be the sources of such teaching as will turn men's thoughts towards social justice and political righteousness, and should prepare them for the sacrifice which any great improvement in the social state must demand of some. Further, every individual Christian should feel that his responsibility for the condition of his brethren, those of his own nation, is very great and direct; that to discharge municipal and political duty with conscientious care is a primary obligation. Only so can the power be gained to "ban" the bad laws, the unjust practices, the evil social customs, which disfigure our civilisation, which degrade and defraud the poor.

A militant Puritanism here is not only a necessity for further social progress, but it is also a necessity for the full exhibition of the power and the essential sympathies of Christianity.

For want of it the working classes in their movement upward have not only been alienated from the Churches, but they have learned to demand of their leaders that they shall "countenance the poor man in his cause." They are tempted to require their leaders to share not only their common principles, but their prejudices; and they often look with suspicion upon those who insist upon applying the plumb-line of justice to the demands of the poor as well as to the claims of the rich. The whole popular movement suffers, for it is degraded from its true position. From being a demand for justice, it becomes a scramble for power—power too which, when gained, is sometimes used as selfishly and tyrannically by its new possessors as it sometimes was by those who previously exercised it. Into all branches of public life there is needed an infusion of a new and higher spirit. We want men who hate evil and will destroy it where they can, who seek nothing for themselves, who feel strongly that the kind of life the poor in civilised countries live is intolerably hard, and are prepared to suffer, if by any means they may improve it. But we want at the same time a type of reformer who, by his hold upon a power lying beyond this world, is kept steady to justice even where the poor are concerned, who, though he passionately longs for a better life for them, does not make more food, more leisure, more amusement, his highest aim. Men are needed who think more nobly of their brethren than that: men, on the one hand, who know that the Christian character and the Christian virtues may exist under the hardest conditions, and that the Christian Church exists mainly to brighten and rob of its degradation the otherwise cheerless life of the multitude; but, on the other, who recognise that our present social state is fatal in many ways to moral and spiritual progress for the mass of men, and must be in some way recast.

All this means the entrance into public life of Christian men of the highest type. Such men the Christian community must supply to the State in great numbers, if the higher characteristics of our people are not to be lost. Through a long and eventful history, by the manifold training afforded by religion and experience, the English nation has become strong, patient, hopeful, and self-reliant, with an instinct for justice and a hatred of violence which cannot easily be paralleled. It has, too, retained a faith in and respect for religion which many other nations seem to have lost. That character is its highest achievement, and its decay would be deplorable. Christianity is specially called to help to preserve it, by bringing to its aid the power of its own special character, with its great spiritual resources. The sources of its life are hid, and must be kept pure; the power of its life must be made manifest in actual union with the higher elements in the national character for mutual defence. Above all, Christianity must not, timidly or sluggishly, draw upon itself the curse of Meroz by not coming to the help of the Lord against the mighty. Nor can it permit the immediate interests of the respectable to blind or hold it back. That which is best in its own nature demands all this; and in seeking to answer that demand the Churches will attain to a quite new life and power. The Lord their God will be in the midst of them, and they will feel it; for they will then have made themselves channels for the Divine purity and power.

CHAPTER XI.

THE BREAD OF THE SOUL.

DEUTERONOMY viii.

In the chapters which follow, viz. viii., ix., and x. 1-11, we have an appeal to history as a motive for fulfilling the fundamental duty of loving God and keeping His commandments. In its main points it is substantially the same appeal which is made in chapters i.-iii., is, in fact, a continuation of it. Its main characteristics, therefore, have already been dealt with; but there are details here which deserve more minute study. Coming after Yahweh's great demand for the love of His people, the references to the Divine action in the past assume a deeper and more affectionate character than when they were mere general exhortations to obedience and submission. They become inducements to the highest efforts of love; and the first appeal is naturally made to the gracious and fatherly dealing of Yahweh with His people in their journey through the wilderness. Of all the traditions or reminiscences of Israel, this of the wilderness was the most constantly present to the popular mind, and it is always referred to as the most certain, the most impressive, and the most touching of all Israel's historic experiences. Yet Stade and others push the whole episode aside, saying, if any Israelites came out of Egypt, we do not know who they were. Such a mode of dealing with clear, coherent, and in themselves not improbable historical memories, is too arbitrary to have much effect, and the wilderness journey remains, and is likely to remain, one of the indubitable facts which modern critical research has established rather than shaken.

To this, then, our author turns, and he deals with it in a somewhat unusual way. As we have seen, the prevalent notion that piety and righteousness are rewarded with material prosperity is firmly rooted in his mind. But he did not feel himself limited to that as the solitary right way of regarding the providence of God. Men's minds are never quite so simple and direct in their action as many students and critics are tempted to suppose. Every great conception which holds the minds of men produces its effects, even from the first moment it is grasped, by *all* that is in it. Implications and developments which are made explicit, or are called out into visibility, only by the friction of new environments, have been there from the beginning; and minds have been secretly moulded by them though they were not conscious of them. Hard and fast lines, then, are not to be drawn between the stages of a great development, so that one should say that before such and such a moment, when a new aspect of the old truth has emerged into consciousness, that aspect was not effective in any wise. The outburst of waters from a reservoir is indubitable evidence of steady, persistent pressure from within in that direction before the overflow. Similarly, in the region of thought and feeling the emergence of a new aspect of truth is of itself a proof that the holders of the root conception were already swayed in that direction.

The history of Christianity affords proof of this. It is a commonplace to-day that the world is only beginning to do justice to some aspects of the teaching of our Lord. But the teaching, always present, always exerted its influence, and was felt before it could be explained. In the Old Testament development the same thing was most emphatically true. Individual responsibility to God was not, so far as we can now see, distinctly present in Israelite religious thought till the time of Jeremiah, but it would be absurd to say that any mind that accepted the religion of Yahweh had ever been without that feeling. So with the doctrine of God's providence over men: we are not to say that before the Book of Job the explanation of suffering as testing discipline had been entirely hid from Israel, by the view that material prosperity and adversity were regulated in the main according to moral and religious life. Consequently, notwithstanding previous strong assertions of the latter view which we find in Deuteronomy, we need not be in the least surprised to find that here the hardships of the wilderness journey are regarded, not as a punishment for Israel's sins, but simply as a trial or test to see what their heart was towards Him. This is essentially the point of view of the Book of Job, the only difference being that here it is applied to the nation, there to the individual. But our chapter rises even above that, for the first verses of it plainly teach that the experiences of the wilderness were made to be what they were, in order that the people might learn to know the spiritual forces of the world to be the essential forces, and that they might be induced to throw themselves back upon them as that which is alone enduring. In the words of ver. 3, they were taught by this training that man does not live by bread alone, but by everything that proceeds from the mouth of God.

These two then, that hardship was testing discipline for Israel, and that it was also intended to be the means of revealing spirit as the supreme force even in the material world, are the main lessons of the eighth chapter. Of these the last is by far the most important. Casting back his eye upon the past, the author of Deuteronomy teaches that the trials and the victories, the wonders and the terrors of their wilderness time were meant to humble them, to empty them of their own conceits, and to make them know beyond all doubting that God alone was their portion, and that apart from Him they had no certainty of continuance in the future and no sustainment in the present. "All the commandment which I command thee this day shall ye observe to do, *that ye may live,*" is the fundamental note, and the physical needs and trials of the time are cited as an object-lesson to that effect. "He humbled thee, and suffered thee to hunger, and fed thee with manna which thou knewest not; that He might make thee to know that man doth not live by bread alone, but by everything that proceedeth out of the mouth of Yahweh doth man live." Of course the first reference of the "everything that proceedeth" is to the creative word of Yahweh. The meaning is that the sending of the manna was proof that the ordinary means of living, *i. e.,* bread, could be dispensed with when Yahweh chose to make use of His creative power. Many commentators think that this exhausts the meaning of the passage, and they regard our Lord's use of these words in the Temptation as limited in the same fashion. But both here and in the New Testament more must be intended. Here we have the statement in the first verse that Israel is to keep the commandments, which certainly are a part of "all that proceeds" from the mouth of God, that they may *live*. This implies that the mere possession of material sustenance is not enough for even earthly life. Impalpable spiritual elements must be mingled with "bread" if life is not to decay. This, our chapter goes on to say, would be plain to them if they would carefully consider God's dealing with them in the wilderness, for the sending of the manna was meant to emphasise and bring home to them that very truth. It was meant, in short, to convey a double lesson—the direct one above referred to, and the more remote but deeper one which had been asserted in the first verse.

In the Temptation narrative the same deeper meaning is surely implied. The temptation suggested to Jesus was that He should use the miraculous powers given to Him for special purposes to make stones into bread for Himself. Now that would have been precisely an instance of the literal primary meaning of our passage; it would have been a case of supplying the absence of bread by the use of the creative word of God. To meet that temptation and to put it aside our Lord uses these words: "It is written, Man shall not live by bread alone, but by every word that proceedeth out of the mouth of God." Thereupon He was no more importuned to supply the place of bread by a creative word. The implication is that the life of the Son of God found sustenance in spiritual strength derived from His Father. In other words, the passage is really parallel to John iv. 31 ff: "In the mean while the disciples prayed Him, saying, Rabbi, eat. But He said unto them, I have meat to eat that ye know not. The disciples therefore said one to another, Hath any man brought Him to eat? Jesus saith unto them, My meat is to do the will of Him that sent Me, and to accomplish His work." Understanding it thus, the Temptation passage is entirely in accord with that from which it is quoted, if the first and third verses be taken together. Both teach that abundance of material resources, all that visibly sustains the material life, is not sufficient for the life of such a creature as man. Not only his inner life, but his outer life, is dependent for its permanence upon the inflow of spiritual sustenance from the spiritual God. For animals, bread might be enough; but man holds of both the spiritual and the material as animals do not. It is not mere mythical dreaming when man is said to be made in the image of God; it expresses the essential fact of his being. Consequently, without inbreathings from the spiritual, even his physical life pines and dies. But how wonderful is this insight in a writer so ancient, belonging to so obscure a people as the Jews! How can we account for it? There was nothing in their character or destiny as a people to explain it, apart from the supernatural link that binds them and their thoughts at all times to the coming Christ, and draws them, notwithstanding all aberrations, even when they know it not, towards Him.

How great an attainment it is we may see, if we reflect for a moment upon the state of Christian Europe at the present day. Nowhere among the masses of the most cultured nations is this deeply simple truth accepted by the vast majority of men. Nowhere do we find that history has succeeded in bringing it home to the conscience as a commonplace. The rich or well-to-do cling to riches, the means of material enjoyment, as if their life did consist in the abundance of things they possess. They strive and struggle for them with an industry, a forethought, a perseverance, which would be justified only if man could live by bread alone. That is largely the condition of those who have bread in abundance or hope to gain it abundantly. With those who do not have it the case is perhaps even worse. Worn and fretted by the hopeless struggle against poverty, driven wild by the exigencies of a daily life so near starvation point that a strike, a fall in prices, a month's sickness, bring them face to face with misery, the toiling masses in Europe have turned with a kind of wolfish impatience upon those who talk of God to them, and demand "bread." As a German Socialist mother said publicly some years ago, "He has never given me a mouthful of bread, or means to gain it: what have I to do with your God?" Their only hope for the future is that they may eat and be full; and of this they have made a political and religious ideal which is attracting the European working classes with most portentous power.

In all countries men are passionately asserting that man *can* live by bread alone, and that he will. For this dreadful creed increasing numbers are prepared to sacrifice all that humanity thought it had gained, and shut their ears to any who warn them that, if they had all they seek, earth might be still more of a Pandemonium than they think it at present. But they have much excuse. They have never had wealth so as to know how very little it can do for the deepest needs of men; and their faith in it, their belief that if they were assured of a comfortable maintenance all would be right with the world, is pathetic in its simplicity. Yet the secret that is hid to-day from the mass of men was known among the small Israelite people two thousand five hundred years ago. Since then it has formed the very keynote of the teaching of our Lord; but save by the generations of Christians who have found in it the key to much of the riddle of the world it has been learned by nobody.

Yet history has never wearied in proclaiming the same truth. Israel, as we have seen, had verified it in the history of the pre-Canaanite races whose disappearance is recorded in the first section of our book, and in the doom which was impending over the Canaanites. But to our wider experience, enriched by the changes of more than two thousand years, and by the still more striking vicissitudes of ancient days revealed by archæology, the fact that intelligence of the highest kind, practical skill, and the courage of conquerors cannot secure "life," is only more impressively brought home. If we go back to the pre-Semitic empire of Mesopotamia, to what is called the Akkadian time, we find that, before the days of Abraham, a great civilisation had arisen, flourished for more than one thousand years, and then decayed so utterly that the very language in which its records were written had to be dealt with by the Semites, who inherited the former culture, as we deal with Latin. Yet these early people had made a most astonishing advance into the ocean of unknown truth. They had invented writing; they had elaborate systems of law and social life; they had in other directions made remarkable discoveries in science, especially in mathematical and astronomical science, and had built great cities in which the refinement and art of modern times was in many directions anticipated. In all ways they stood far higher above neighbouring peoples than any civilised nation of Europe stands now in comparison with its neighbours. But if they were at all inclined to put their trust in the immortality of science, if they ever valued themselves, as we do, on the strength of the advances they had made, time has had them in derision. Very much of what they knew had to be rediscovered painfully in later times. Their very name perished out of the earth; and it has been discovered now to make them an object of abiding interest only to the few who make ethnology their study. Neither material wealth and comfort nor assiduous culture of the mind could save them. For their religion and morals were, amid all this material success, of the lowest type. They heard little of what issues from the mouth of God in the specially Divine sphere of morality, and did not give heed to that little, and they perished. For man does not live by bread alone, but by that also, and neglect of it is fatal.

It may be said that they flourished for more than a thousand years, and neglect of the Divine word, if it be a poison, must (as Fénelon said of coffee) be a very slow one, so far as nations are concerned. But it has always been a snare to men to mistake the Divine patience for Divine indifference and inaction. The movement, though to us creatures of a day it seems slow, is as continuous, as crushing, and as relentless as the movement of a glacier. "The mills of God grind slowly, but they grind exceeding small," and all along the ages they have thrown out the crushed and scattered fragments of the powers that were deaf to the Divine voice. So persistently has this appeared that it would by this time have passed beyond the region of faith into that of sight, were it not always possible to ignore the moral cause and substitute for it something mechanical and secondary. The great world-empires of Egypt and Assyria passed away, primarily owing to neglect of the higher life. Secondarily, no doubt, the ebbs and flows of their power, and their final extinction, were influenced by the course of the Indian trade; and many wise men think they do well to stop there. But in truth we do not solve the difficulty by resting in this secondary cause; we only shift it a step backwards. For the question immediately arises, Why did the trade change its course from Assyria to Egypt, and back again from Egypt to Assyria? Why did a rivulet of it flow through the land of Israel in Solomon's day and afterwards cease? The answer must be that it was when the character of these various nations rose in vigour by foresight and moral self-restraint that they drew to themselves this source of power. They "lived," in fact, by giving heed to some word of God. Nor does the history of Greek supremacy in Europe and Asia, or the rise and fall of the Roman Empire, contradict that view. The modern historian, whatever his faith or unfaith may be, is driven to find the motive power which wrought in these stupendous movements in the moral and spiritual sphere. This transforms history from being merely secular into a Bible, as Mommsen finely says,* "And if she cannot any more than the Bible hinder the fool from misunderstanding and the devil from quoting her, she too will be able to bear with and to

* "History of Rome," vol. iv., Part II., p. 467.

requite them both." She utters her voice in the streets, and in the end makes her meaning clear. For she gives us ever new examples.

Probably her grandest object-lesson at present is the wasting and paralysis that is slowly withering up all Mohammedan states. Where they have been left to themselves, as in Morocco and Persia, depopulation and the break-up of society has come upon them, and where Muslim populations are really prospering it is under the influence of Christian Powers. And the reason is plain. Islam is a revolt from, and a rejection of, the higher principles of life contained in Christianity, and a return to Judaism. But the Judaism to which it returned had already lost its finest bloom. All that was left to it of tenderness or power of expansion Islam rejected, and of the driest husks of Old Testament religion it made its sole food. Naturally and necessarily, therefore, it has been found inadequate. It cannot permanently live under present conditions, and it is capable of no renewal. Here and there, especially in India, attempts to break out of the prison house which this system builds around its votaries are being made, but in the opinion of experts like Mr. Sell* they cannot succeed. "Such a movement," he tells us, "may elevate individuals and purify the family life of many, but it will, like all reform movements of the past, have very little real effect on Islam as a polity and as a religion." If he be right, we learn from a Mohammedan whom he quotes, the Naual Mulisin-ul-Mulk, what alone can be looked for. "To me it seems," he says, "that as a nation and a religion we are dying out; our day is past, and we have little hope of the future." More conspicuously and deliberately perhaps than any one did Mohammed choose to go back from the best light that shone in the world of his day. Some at least of his contemporaries knew what a spiritual religion meant. He was guilty, therefore, of the "great refusal"; and his work, great as it was, seems to some even of his own disciples to be hastening to its end. Material success, bread in all senses, the kingdoms founded by him and his successors had in abundance, and still might have. But man cannot live by that alone, and the absence of the higher element has taken even that away.

In Christendom, too, the same lesson is being taught. Of all European countries France perhaps is that where the corroding power of materialistic thought has been most severely felt. Yet few countries are so rich in material wealth, and if bread was all that "life" demanded, no country should be so full of it. But it is in no sense so. Even its intellectual life is drooping, and its population, if not decreasing, is standing still. This, all serious writers deplore; and the dawn of what may perhaps be a new era is seen in the earnestness with which the sources of this evil are sought out and discussed. Men like the Vicomte de Vogüé† depict the new generation as weary of negations, sick of the material positivism of their immediate predecessors, disgusted with "realism," which, as another recent writer defines it, "in thought is mere provincialism, in affection absolute egoism, in politics the deification of brute force; in the higher grades of society tyranny; in the lower, unbridled license." And the only cure is faith and moral idealism.

* *Contemporary Review*, August, 1893, p. 293.
† "Heures d'Histoire."

"Society can apply to itself to-day," says De Vogüé, "the beautiful image of Plotinus; it resembles those travellers lost in the night, seated in silence on the shore of the sea, waiting for the sun to rise above the billows." In Germany similar conditions have produced similar though much mitigated results. Yet even there, Lange, the historian of materialism, tells us that there runs through all our modern culture a tendency to materialism, which carries away every one who has not found somewhere a sure anchor. "The ideal has no currency; all that cannot prove its claim on the basis of natural science and history is condemned to destruction, though a thousand joys and refreshments of the masses depend upon it." He concludes by saying that "ideas and sacrifices may still save our civilisation, and change the path of destructive revolution into a path of beneficent reforms." Through all history, then, and loudest in our own day, the cry of our passage goes up; and where the path marked out by the faith of Israel, and carried to its goal by Jesus Christ, has been forsaken, the peoples are resting in hungry expectation. Words from the mouth of God can alone save them; and if the Churches cannot make them hear, and no new voice brings it home to them, there would seem to be nothing before them but a slower or quicker descent into death.

But it may be that the nations are deaf to the Churches' voice because these have not learned thoroughly that life for them too is conditioned in the same fashion. They can live truly, fully, triumphantly only when they take up and absorb "everything that issues from the mouth of God." All Christians must admit this; but most proceed at once to annul what they have stated by the limitations of meaning they impose upon it. An older generation vehemently affirmed this faith, meaning by it every word and letter which Scripture contained. We do not find fault with what they assert, for the first necessity of spiritual life is the study and love of the Holy Scriptures. No one who knows what the higher life in Christ is, needs to be told that the very bread of life is in the Bible. Neglect it, or, what is perhaps worse, study it only from the scientific and intellectual point of view, and life will slowly ebb away from you, and your religion will bring you none of the joy of living. Bring your thoughts, your hopes, your fears, and your aspirations into daily contact with it, and you will feel a vigour in your spiritual nature which will make you "lords over circumstance." Every part of it contributes to this effect when it is properly understood, for experience proves the vanity of the attempt to distinguish between the Bible and the word of God. As it stands, wrought into one whole by labours the strenuousness, the multiplicity, the skill, and the religious spirit of which we are only now coming to understand, it is the word of God; it has issued from His mouth, and from it, searched out and understood, the most satisfying "bread" of the soul must come. Only by use of it can the Christian soul live. But though the Bible is the word of God *par excellence*, it is not the only word that issues from the mouth of God to man. Because the Church has often too much refused to listen to any other word of God, those who are without are "sitting looking out over the sea towards the west for the rising of the sun which is behind them." For if it is death to the spirit to turn away from Scripture, it means sickness and disease to refuse to learn the other lessons which are set for us by the God of truth. All true science must contain a revelation of Him, for it is an exposition of the manner of His working. History too is a Bible, which has been confirming with trumpet tongue the truths of Scripture as we have seen. Nay, it is a commentary upon the special revelation given to us through Israel, set for our study by the Author of that revelation. Further, we may say that the progress of our Christian centuries has shown us heights and depths of wisdom in the revelation mankind has received in Christ which, without its light, we should not have known.

The spirit of Christ in regard to slavery, for instance, was made manifest fully only in our day. The true relations of men to each other, as conceived by our blessed Lord, are evidently about to be forced home upon the world by the turmoils, the strikes, and the outrages, by the wild demands, and the wilder hopes which are the characteristic of our epoch. In the future, too, there must lie experiences which will make manifest to men the brand which the spirit of Christ puts upon war, with its savagery and its folly. These are only noteworthy instances of the explanation of revelation by the developments of the Divine purpose in the world. But in countless ways the same process is going on, and the Church which refuses to regard it is preparing a decay of its own life. For man lives by *every* word that proceedeth out of the mouth of God, and every such word missed means a loss of vitality. The Christian Church, therefore, if it is to be true to its calling, should be seriously watchful lest any Divinely sent experience should be lost to it. It cannot be indifferent, much less hostile, to discoveries in physical science; it cannot ignore any fact or lesson which history reveals; it cannot sit apart from social experiments, as if holding no form of creed in such things, without seriously impairing its chances of life. For all these things are pregnant with most precious indications of the mind of God, and to turn from them is to sit in darkness and the shadow of death. In the most subtle and multifarious way, the inner spiritual life of man is being modified by the discoveries of scientists, historians, philologists, archæologists, and critics, and by the new attention which is being given to the foundations of society and social life. All the truth that is in these discoveries issues from the mouth of God. They too are a Bible, as Mommsen says, and if the Christian Church cannot "hinder the fool from misunderstanding and the devil from quoting them," it can itself listen with open ear to these teachings, and work them into coherent unity with the great spiritual Revelation. This is the perennial task which awaits the Church at every stage of its career, for on no other terms can it live a healthy life.

Here we find the answer to timid Christians who address petulant complaints to those who are called to attempt this work. If, say they, these new thoughts are not essential to faith, if in the forms to which we have been accustomed the essence of true religion has been preserved, why do you disturb the minds of believers by outside questions? The reply is that we dare not refuse the teaching which God is sending us in these ways. To refuse light is to blaspheme light. Though we might save our generation some trouble by turning our back upon this light, though we might even save some from manifest shipwreck of faith, we should pay for that by sacrificing all the future, and by rendering faith impossible perhaps for greater multitudes of our successors.

Yet this does not imply that the Church is to be driven about by every wind of doctrine. Some men of science demand, apparently, that every new discovery, in its first crude form, should be at once adopted by the Church, and that all the inferences unfavorable to received views of religion, which occur to men accustomed to think only truths that can be demonstrated by experiment, should be registered in its teachings. But such a demand is mere folly. The Church has in its possession a body of truth which, if not verifiable by experiment, has been verified by experience as no other body of truth has been. Even its enemies being judges, no other system of a moral or spiritual kind has risen above the horizon which can for a moment be compared with Christianity as the guide of men for life and death.* Through all changes of secular thought, and amid all the lessons which the world has taught the Church, the fundamental doctrines have remained in essence the same, and by them the whole life of man, social, political, and scientific, has ultimately been guided. Immense practical interests have therefore been committed to the Church's keeping, the interests primarily of the poor and the obscure. She ought never to be tempted, consequently, to think that she is moving and acting in a vacuum, or manage her affairs after the manner of a debating society. It is no doubt a fault to move too slowly; but in circumstances like that of the Church, it can never be so destructive to the best interests of mankind as to move with wanton instability. Her true attitude must be to prohibit no lines of inquiry, to open her mind seriously to all the demonstrated truths of science with gladness, to be tolerant of all loyal effort to reform Christian thought in accordance with the new light, when that has become at all possible. For her true food is everything that issues from the mouth of God; and only when she receives with gratitude her daily bread in this way also, can her life be as vigorous and as elevated as it ought to be.

CHAPTER XII.

ISRAEL'S ELECTION, AND MOTIVES FOR FAITHFULNESS.

DEUTERONOMY ix.-xi.

THE remaining chapters of this special introduction to the statement of the actual laws beginning with chapter xii., contain also an earnest insistence upon other motives why Israel should remain true to the covenant of Yahweh. They are urged to this, not only because life both spiritual and physical depended upon it, as was shown in the trials of the wilderness, but they are also to lay it to heart that in the conquests which assuredly await them, it will be Yahweh alone to whom they will owe them. The spies had declared, and the people had accepted their report, that these peoples were far mightier than they, and that no one could stand before the children of Anak. But the victory over them

*Cf. Lange, "Geschichte des Materialismus," vol. ii., pp. 510, 528.

would show that Yahweh had been among them like a consuming fire, before which the Canaanite power would wither as brushwood in the flame.

Under these circumstances the thought would obviously lie near that, as they had been defeated and driven back in their first attempt upon Canaan because of their unrighteousness and unbelief, so they would conquer now because of their righteousness and obedience. But this thought is sternly repressed. The fundamental doctrine which is here insisted on is that Israel's consciousness of being the people of God must at the same time be a consciousness of complete dependence upon Him. If His gifts were ultimately to be the reward of human righteousness, then obviously that feeling of complete dependence could not be established. They are to move so completely in the shadow of God that they are to see in their successes only the carrying out of the Divine purposes. Instead of feeling fiercely contemptuous of the Canaanites they destroy, because they stand on a moral and spiritual height which gives them a right to triumph, the Israelites are to feel that, while it is for wickedness that the Canaanite people are to be punished, they themselves had not been free from wickedness of an aggravated kind. Their different treatment, therefore, rests upon the fact that they are to be Yahweh's chosen instruments. In the patriarchs he chose them to become the means, the vehicle, by which salvation and blessing were to be brought to all nations. While, therefore, the evil that comes upon the peoples they are to conquer is deserved, the good they themselves are to receive is equally undeserved. That which alone accounts for the difference is the faithfulness of God to the promises He made for the sake of His purposes. He needs an instrument through which to bless mankind. He has chosen Israel for this purpose, partly doubtless because of some qualities, not necessarily spiritual or moral, which they have come to have, and partly because of their historical position in the world. These taken together make them at this precise moment in the history of the world's development the fittest instruments to carry out the Divine purpose of love to mankind. And they are elected, made to enter into more constant and intimate communion with God than other nations, on that account. In the words of Rothe, " God chooses or elects at each historical moment from the totality of the sinful race of mankind that nation by whose enrolment among the positive forces which are to develop the kingdom of God the greatest possible advance towards the complete realisation of it may be attained, under the historical circumstances of that moment." Whether that completely covers the individual election of St. Paul, as Rothe thinks, or not, it certainly precisely expresses the national election of the Old Testament, and exhausts the meaning of our passage. Israelite particularism had universality of the highest kind as its background, and here the latter comes most insistently to its rights.

It was not only the election of Israel to be a peculiar people which depended upon the wise and loving purpose of God; the providences which befell them also had that as their source. To fit them for their mission, and to give them a place wherein they could develop the germs of higher faith and nobler morality which they had received, Yahweh gave them victory over those greater nations, and planted them in their place. This, and this only, was the reason of their success; and with scathing irony the author of Deuteronomy stamps under his feet (ix. 7 ff.) any claim to superior righteousness on their part. He points back to their continuous rebellions during the forty years in the wilderness. From the beginning to the end of their journey towards the promised land, they are told, they have been rebellious and stiff-necked and unprofitable. They have broken their covenant with their God. They have caused Moses to break the tables of stone containing the fundamental conditions of the covenant, because their conduct had made it plain that they had not seriously bound themselves to it. But the mercy of God had been with them. Notwithstanding their sin, Yahweh had been turned to mercy by the prayer of Moses (vv. 25 ff.), and had repented of His design to destroy them. A new covenant was entered into with them (chap. x.) by means of the second tables, which contained the same commands as were engraven on the first. The renewal, moreover, was ratified by the separation of the tribe of Levi (x. 8 ff.) to be the specially priestly tribe, " to bear the Ark of the Covenant of the Lord, to stand before the Lord to minister unto Him and to bless in His name." From beginning to end it was always Yahweh, and again Yahweh, who had chosen and loved and cared for them. It was He who had forgiven and strengthened them; but always for reasons which reached far beyond, or even excluded, any merit on their part.

The grounds of Moses' successful intercession for them (ix. 25 ff.) are notable in this connection. They have no reference at all to the needs, or hopes, or expectations of the people. These are all brushed aside, as being of no moment after such unfaithfulness as theirs had been. The great object before his mind is represented to be Yahweh's glory. If this stiff-necked people perish, then the greatness of God will be obscured and His purposes will be misunderstood. Men will certainly think, either that Yahweh, Israel's God, attempted to do what He was not able to do, or that He was wroth with His people, and drew them out into the wilderness to slay them there. It is God's purpose with them, God's purpose for the world through them, which alone gives them importance. Were it not for that, they would be as little worth saving as they have deserved to be saved. For his people, and, we may be sure, for himself, Moses recognises no true worth save in so far as he or they were useful in carrying out Divine purposes of good to the world. Nor is the absence of any plea on Israel's behalf, that it is miserable or unhappy, due merely to a desire to keep the rebellious people in the background for the moment, and to appeal only to the Divine self-love for a pardon which would, on the merits of the case, be refused. It is the God of the whole earth, before whom " the inhabitants of the earth are as grasshoppers," who is appealed to; a God removed far above the petty motives of self-interested men, and set upon the one great purpose of establishing a kingdom of God upon the earth into which all nations might come. If His glory is appealed to, that is only because it is the glory of the highest good both for the individual and for the world. If fear lest doubt should be cast upon His power is put forward as a reason for His having mercy, that is because to doubt His power is to doubt the supremacy of goodness. If the Divine promise to the patriarchs is set forth here, it is because that promise was the assurance of the Divine interest in and Divine love of the world.

Under such circumstances it would need a very narrow-hearted literalism, such as only very "liberal" theologians and critics could favour, to reduce this appeal to a mere attempt to flatter Yahweh into good-humour. It really embodies all that can be said in justification of our looking for answers to prayer at all; and rightly understood it limits the field of the answer as strictly as the expressed or implied limitations of the New Testament, viz. that effectual prayer can only be for things according to the will of God. Moreover it expresses an entirely natural attitude towards God. Before Him, the sum of all perfections, the loving and omniscient and omnipresent God, what is man that he should assert himself in any wise? When the height and the depth, the sublimity and the comprehensiveness of the Divine purpose is considered, how can a man do aught save fall upon his face in utter self-forgetfulness, immeasurably better even than self-contempt? The best and holiest of mankind have always felt this most; and the habit of measuring their attainments by the faithfulness and knowledge, the virtue and power which is in God, has impressed some of the greatest minds and purest souls with such humility, that to men without insight it has seemed mere affectation. But the pity, the condescension, the love of Christ has so brought God down into our human life, that we are apt at times to lose our awe of God as seen in Him. Were we children of the spirit we should not fall into that sin. We cannot, consequently, be too frequently or too sharply recalled to the more austere and remote standpoint of the Old Testament. For many even of the most pious it would be well if they could receive and keep a more just impression of their own worthlessness and nullity before God.

In the section from the twelfth verse of chapter x. to the end of chapter xi. the hortatory introduction is summed up in a final review of all the motives to and the results of obedience and love to God. The fundamental exhortation as to love to God is once more repeated; only here fear is joined with love and precedes it; but the necessity of love to God is expanded and dwelt upon, as at the beginning, with a zeal that never wearies. The Deuteronomist illustrates and enforces it with old reasons and new, always speaking with the same pleading and heartfelt earnestness. He does not fear the tedium of repetition, nor the accusation of moving in a narrow round of ideas. Evidently in the evil time when he wrote this love towards God had come to be his own support and his consolation; and it had been revealed to him as the source of a power, a sweetness, and a righteousness which could alone bring the nation into communion with God. In affecting words resembling very closely the noble exhortation in Micah vi., "He hath showed thee, O man, what is good; and what doth Yahweh require of thee, but to do justly, and to love mercy, and to walk humbly with thy God?" he teaches much the same doctrine as his contemporary: "And now, Israel, what doth Yahweh thy God require of thee, but to fear Yahweh thy God, to walk in all His ways, and to love Him, and to serve Yahweh thy God with all thy heart and with all thy soul, to keep the commandments of Yahweh and His statutes which I command thee this day for thy good?" *

In spirit these passages seem identical; but it is held by many writers on the Old Testament that they are not so, that they represent, in fact, opposite poles of the faith and life of Israel. Micah is supposed by Duhm, for instance, to mean by his threefold demand that justice between man and man, love and kindliness and mercy towards others, and humble intercourse with God are, in *distinction from sacrifice*, true religion and undefiled. Robertson Smith also considers that these verses in Micah contain a repudiation of sacrifice. In Deuteronomy, on the contrary, fear and love of God and walking in His ways are placed first, but they are joined with a demand for the heartfelt service of God and the keeping of His statutes as about to be set forth. Now these certainly include ritual and sacrifice. The one passage, written by a prophet, excludes sacrifice as binding and acceptable service of God; the other, written perhaps by a priest, certainly by a man upon whom no prophetic lessons of the past had been lost, includes it. To use the words of Robertson Smith in discussing the requisites of forgiveness in the Old Testament, "According to the prophets Yahweh asks only a penitent heart and desires no sacrifice; according to the ritual law, He desires a penitent heart approaching Him in certain sacrificial sacraments." † The author of Deuteronomy teaches the second view; the author of Micah, chap. vi., who is probably his contemporary, teaches the former. How is such divergence accounted for? The answer generally made is that Deuteronomy was the product of a close alliance between priests and prophets. A common hatred of Manasseh's idolatry and a common oppression had brought them together as never perhaps before. With one heart and mind they wrought in secret for the better day which they saw approaching, and Deuteronomy was a reissue of the ancient Mosaic law adapted to the prophetic teaching. It represented a compromise between, or an amalgamation of, two entirely distinct positions.

But even on this view it would follow that from the time of Josiah, when Deuteronomy was accepted as the completest expression of the will of God, the doctrine that ritual and sacrifice as well as penitence were essential things in true religion was known, and not only known but accepted as the orthodox opinion. Putting aside, then, the question whether sacrifice was acknowledged by the prophets before this or not, they must have accepted it from this point onward, unless they denied to Deuteronomy the authority which it claimed and which the nation conceded to it. Jeremiah clearly must have assented to it, for his style and his thought have been so closely moulded on this book that some have thought he may have been its author. In any case he did not repudiate its authority; and all the prophets who followed him must have known of this view, and also that it had been sanctioned by that book which was made the first Jewish Bible.

We have here, at all events, the keynote of the supremacy of moral duty over Divine commands concerning ritual which distinguishes the prophetic teaching in Micah and elsewhere,

* Chap. x. 12.
† "Old Testament in Jewish Church," 2d edition, p. 308.

joined with the enforcement of ritual observances. But there are few purely prophetic passages which raise the higher demand so high as it is raised here.

To love and fear God are anew declared to be man's supreme duties, and the author presses these home by arguments of various kinds. Again he returns to the election of Israel by Yahweh, without merit of theirs; and to bring home to them how much this means, the Deuteronomist exhibits the greatness of their God, His might, His justice, and His mercy, which, great as it is to His chosen people, is not confined to them, but extends to the stranger also. This most gracious One they are to serve by deeds, to Him they are to cleave, and they are to swear by Him only, that is, they are solemnly to acknowledge Him to be their God in return for His undeserved favour. For their very existence as a nation is a wonder of His power, since they were only a handful when they went down to Egypt, and now were "as the stars of heaven for multitude."

Then once more, in chapter xi., he repeats his one haunting thought that love is to be the source of all worthy fulfilment of the law; and he endeavours to shed abroad this love to God in their hearts by reminding them once more of all the marvels of their deliverance from Egypt, and of their wilderness journey. Their God had delivered them first, then chastised them for their sins, and had trained them for the new life that awaited them in the land promised to their fathers.

Even in the security of the land they were to find themselves not less dependent upon God than before. Rather their dependence would be more striking and more impressive than in Egypt. As we have seen repeatedly, this inspired writer belonged in many respects to the childhood of the world, and the people he addressed were primitive in their ideas. Yet his thoughts of God in their highest flight were so essentially true and deep, that even to-day we can go back upon them for edification and inspiration. But here we have an appeal based upon a distinction which to-day should have almost entirely lost its meaning. The Deuteronomist yields quite simply and unreservedly to the feeling that the regular, unvarying processes of nature are less Divine, or at least are less immediately significant of the Divine presence, than those which cannot be foreseen, which vary, and which defy human analysis. For he here contrasts Egypt and Canaan, in both of which he represents Israel as having been engaged in agricultural pursuits, and speaks as if in the former all depended upon human industry and ingenuity, and might be counted upon irrespective of moral conduct, while in the latter all would depend upon Divine favour and a right attitude towards God. It is quite true that in preceding chapters he has been teaching that, even for worldly material success, the higher life is necessary, that man nowhere lives by bread alone; and that we may assuredly assume is his deepest, his ultimate thought. But he has a practical end in view at this moment. He wishes to persuade his people, and he appeals to what both he and they felt, though in the last resort it might hardly perhaps be justified. In Egypt, he says, your agricultural success was certain if only you were industrious. The great river, of which the land itself is the gift, came down in flood year after year, and you had only to store and to guide its waters to ensure you a certain return for your labour. You had not to look to uncertain rains, but could by diligence always secure a sufficiency of the life-giving element. In Canaan it will not be so. It "drinketh water only of the rain of heaven." God's eye has to be upon it continually to keep it fertile, and the sense of dependence upon Him will force itself upon you more constantly and powerfully in consequence. They could hope to prosper only if they never forgot, never put away His exhortations out of their sight. Otherwise, he says, the life-giving showers will not fall in their due season. Your land will not yield its fruits, and "ye shall perish quickly off the good land which Yahweh giveth you."

Now what are we to say of this appeal? There can be no doubt that the Divine omnipotence was really, in the Deuteronomist's view as well as in ours, as irresistible in Egypt as in Canaan. Fundamentally, no doubt, life or death, prosperity or adversity, were as much in the hand of God in the one case as in the other; and the Deuteronomist, at least, had no doubt that rebellion against God could and would destroy Egypt's prosperity as much as Canaan's. But he felt that somehow there was a tenderer and more intimate communion of love between Yahweh and His people under the one set of circumstances than under the other. We are not entitled to impute to him a questionable distinction which modern minds are apt to make, viz. that where long experience has taught men to regard the course of providence as fixed, there the sphere of prayer for material benefit ends, and that only in the region where the Divine action in nature seems to us more spontaneous, and less capable of being foreseen, can prayer be heartily, because hopefully, made. But the feeling that suggests that was certainly in his mind. He felt the difference between the fixed conditions of life in Egypt and the more variable conditions in Canaan, to be much the same as the difference between the circumstances of a son receiving a fixed yearly allowance from his father, in an independent and perhaps distant home, and those of a son in his father's house, who receives his portion day by day as the result and evidence of an ever-present affection. Both are equally dependent upon the father's love, and both should theoretically be equally filled with loving gratitude. But as a fact, the latter would be more likely to be so, and would be held more guilty if he were not so. Upon that actual fact the Deuteronomist takes his stand. As they were now to enter into Yahweh's land, His chosen dwelling-place, he sees in the different material conditions of the new country that which should make the union between Yahweh and His people more intimate and more secure, and He presses home upon them the greater shame of ingratitude, if under such circumstances they should forget God and His laws.

Finally (xi. 22-25) he promises them the victorious extension of their dominion if they will love Yahweh and keep His laws. From Lebanon to the southern wilderness, from the Euphrates to the western sea, they should rule, if they would cleave unto their God. At no time was this promise fulfilled save in the days of David and Solomon. For only then had Lebanon and the wilderness, the Euphrates and the sea, been the boundaries of Israel. This must, then, be regarded as the time of Israel's greatest faithfulness. But it is striking that it is in Josiah's day, after the adoption of Deuteronomy as the national law, that we meet with a conscious effort to realise this condition of things once more. There would seem to be little doubt that the good king took an equally literal view of what the book commanded and of what it promised. He inaugurated a period of complete external compliance with the law, and like the young and inexperienced man he was, he regarded that as the fulfilment of its requirements, and looked for a similar instantaneous fulfilment of the promises. Bit by bit he had absorbed the ancient territory of the Northern Kingdom; and in the decay of the Assyrian power he saw the opportunity for the enlargement of his dominion to the limit here defined. He consequently went out against Pharaoh Necho in the full confidence that he would be victorious. But if the Divine promise and its conditions were taken up too superficially by him, Divine providence soon and terribly corrected the error. The defeat and death of Josiah revealed that the reformation had not been real and deep enough, and that the nation was not faithful enough to make such triumph possible. Indeed, so far as we can see, the time for any true fulfilment of Israel's calling in that fashion had then passed by. The harvest was past, and Israel was not saved, and could not now be saved, for it was in its deepest heart unfaithful.

It may be questioned by some, of course, whether an Israel faithful even in the highest degree could at any time have kept possession of so wide a dominion in the face of the great empires of Assyria and Egypt. These were rich, and had a far larger command both of territory and men: how then could the Israelites ever have maintained themselves in face of them? But the question is how to measure the power of the higher ideas they held. It is not force but truth that rules the world; and absolutely no limit can be set to the possibilities which open out to a free, morally robust, and faithful people, who have become possessed of higher spiritual ideas than the peoples that surround them. Even in this sceptical modern day the transformation as regards physical strength which takes place when certain classes of Hindus become either Mohammedans or Christians is so startling and so rapid that it appears almost a miracle. As regards courage, too, it is even more rapid and equally remarkable. The great majority of the struggles of nations are fought out on the level of mere physical force and for material ends, and the strongest and richest wins: but whenever a people possessed of higher ideas and absolutely faithful to them does appear, the opposing power, however great it may be in wealth and numbers, is whirled away in fragments as by a tornado, or it dissolves like ice before the sun. What Israel might have been, therefore, had it been penetrated by the principles of the higher religion, and been passionately true to it, can in no way be judged by that which it actually was. Among the untried possibilities which it was too unfaithful to realise, the possession of such an empire as Deuteronomy promises would seem to be one of the least.

Our chapter sums up what precedes with the declaration on the part of Yahweh, "See, I am setting before you this day a blessing and a curse," according as they might obey or disobey the Divine command. It is stated, in short, that the whole future of the people is to be determined by their attitude to Yahweh and the commands He has given them. In these two words "blessing" and "curse," as Dillmann observes, He sets before them the greatness of the decision they are called upon to make. Just as at the end of chapter iii. the vision of Yahweh's stretched-out hand, which has strewn the world with the wrecks and fragments of destroyed nations, is relied on to prepare the people for contemplating their own calling, so here the gain or loss which would follow their decision is solemnly set before them. By Dillmann and others it is supposed that vv. 29 and 31, which instruct the people to "lay the blessing upon Mount Gerizim and the curse upon Mount Ebal," have been transferred by the later editor from chapter xxvii., where they would come in very fittingly after ver. 3. But whether that be so or not, they are evidently so far in place here that they add to the solemnity with which the fate of the nation in the future is insisted upon. Their "choice is brief and yet endless"; it can be made in a moment, but in its consequence it will endure.

But here a difficulty arises. Dr. Driver in his "Introduction" says of this hortatory section of our book that its teaching is that "duties are not to be performed from secondary motives, such as fear or dread of consequences; they are to be the spontaneous outcome of a heart from which every taint of worldliness has been removed, and which is penetrated by an all-absorbing sense of personal devotion to God." Yet in these later chapters we have had little else but appeals to the gratitude and hopes and fears of Israel. Chapters viii. to xi. are wholly taken up with incitements to love and obey God, because He has been immeasurably good to them, never letting their ingratitude overcome His lovingkindness; because they are wholly dependent upon Him for prosperity and the fertility of their land; and because evil will come upon them if they do not. That would seem to be the opposite of what Driver has declared to be the informing spirit and the fundamental teaching of Deuteronomy.

Yet his view is the true one. Even if the Deuteronomist had added these lower motives to attract and gain over those who were not so open to the higher, that would not deprive him of the glory of having set forth disinterested love as the really impelling power in true religion. We are not required to lower our esteem of that achievement, even if, like the reasonable and wise teacher he is, he boldly uses every motive that actually influences men, whether it should do so or not, to win them to the higher life. But it is not necessary to suppose that he does so. His demand is that men shall love Yahweh their God with all their heart and strength, and to win them to that he sets forth what their God has revealed Himself to be. Men cannot love one whom they do not know; they cannot love one who has not proved himself lovable to them. As his whole effort is to get men to love God, and show their love by obedience to His expressed will, the Deuteronomist brings to mind all His loving thoughts and acts towards them, and so continually keeps his appeal at the highest level. He does not ask men to serve God because it will be profitable to them, but because they love God; and he endeavours to make them love God by reciting all His love and friendliness and patience to His people, and by pointing out the evil which His love is seeking to ward off. The plea is not the ignoble one that they must serve Yahweh for what they can gain by it, but that they should love Yahweh for His love and graciousness, and that out of this love continual obedience should flow as a necessary result. That is his central position; and if he points out the necessary results of a refusal to turn to God in this way, he does not thereby set forth slavish fear or calculating prudence as in themselves religious motives. They are only natural and reasonable means of turning men to view the other side. He uses them to bring the people to a pause, during which he may win them by the love of God. That is always the true appeal; and Christianity when it is at its finest can do nothing but follow in this path. Having before his mind the results of evil conduct, he does urge men to escape from the wrath that may rest upon them. But the only means so to escape is to yield to the love of God. No self-restraint dictated by fear of consequences, no turning from evil because of the lions that are seen in the path, satisfies the demand of either Old Testament or New Testament religion. Both raise the truly religious life above that into the region of self-devoting love; and they both deny spiritual validity to all acts, however good they may be in themselves, which do not follow love as its free and uncalculating expression. Yet they both deal with men as rational beings who can estimate the results of their acts, and warn them of the death which must be the end of every other way of supposed salvation. In this manner they keep the path between extremes, ignoring neither the inner heart of religion nor winding themselves too high for sinful men.

How hard it is to keep to this reasonable but spiritual view is seen by popular aberrations both within and without the Church. At times in the history of the Church Christian teachers have allowed their minds to be so dominated by the terror of judgment that judgment has seemed to the world to be the sole burden of their message. As a reaction from that again, other teachers have arisen who put forward the love of God in such a one-sided way as to empty it of all its severe but glorious sublimity; as if, like Mohammed, they believed God was minded mainly "to make religion easy" unto men. Outside the Church the same discord prevails. Some secular writers praise those religions which declare that a man's fate is decided at the judgment by the balance of merit over demerit in his acts; while others mock at any judgment, and commit themselves with a light heart to the half-amused tolerance of the Divine good nature. But the teaching which combines both elements can alone sustain and bear up a worthy spiritual life. To rely upon terror only, is to ignore the very essence of true religion and the better elements in the nature of man; for that *will* not be dominated by fear alone. To think of the Divine love as a lazy, self-indulgent laxity, is to degrade the Divine nature, and to forget that the possibility of wrath is bound up in all love that is worthy of the name.

One other point is worthy of remark. In these chapters, which deal with the history of God's chosen people in their relations with Him, there come out the very elements which distinguish the personal religion of St. Paul. The beginning and end of it all is the free grace of God. God elected His people that they might be His instrument for blessing the world, not because of any goodness in them, for they were perverse and rebellious, but because He had so determined and had promised to the fathers. He had delivered them from the bondage of Egypt by His mighty power, and dwelt among them thenceforth as among no other people. He gave them a land to dwell in, and there as in His own house He watched and tended them, and strove to lead them upwards to the height of their calling as the people of God by demanding of them faith and love. It is a very enlightening remark of Robertson Smith's that the deliverance out of Egypt was to Israel in the Old Testament what conversion is to the individual Christian according to the New Testament. Taking that as our starting-point, we see that the thought of Deuteronomy is precisely the thought of Romans. It is said, and truly enough, that the Pauline theology was a direct transcript of Paul's own experience; but we see from this that he did not need to form the moulds for his own fundamental thoughts. Long before him the author of Deuteronomy had formed these, and they must have been familiar to every instructed Jew. But the recognition of this is not a loss but a gain. If St. Paul had founded a theory of the universal action of God upon the soul only on the grounds of his own very peculiar experience, it might be argued that the basis of his teaching had been too personal to permit us to feel sure that his view was really as exhaustive as he thought. We see, however, that what he experienced the Deuteronomist had long before traced in the history of his people; and most probably he would not have traced it with so firm a hand had he not himself had experience of a similar kind in his personal relations with God. This method of conceiving the relation of God to the higher life of man, therefore, is stated by the Scriptures as normal. The free grace of God is the source and the sustainer of all spiritual life, whether in individuals or communities. Ultimately, behind all the successful or unsuccessful efforts of the human heart and will, we are taught to see the great Giver, waiting to be gracious, willing that all men should be saved, but acting with the strangest reserves and limitations, choosing Israel among the nations, and even within Israel choosing *the* Israel in whom alone the promises can be realised. Made to serve by human sin, He waits upon the caprices of the wills He has created. He does not force them; but with compassionate patience He builds up His Holy Temple of such living stones as offer themselves, and "without haste as without rest" prepares for the consummation of His work in the redemption of a people that shall be all prophets, a kingdom of priests, a holy nation unto whom all nations shall join themselves when they see that God is in them of a truth. That is the Old Testament conception of the source, and guarantee, and goal of all spiritual life in the world, and St. Paul's view is merely a more mature and definite form of the same thing. And wherever spiritual life has manifested itself with unusual power, the same consciousness of utter unworthiness on the part of man, and entire dependence upon the grace and favour of God, has also manifested itself. The intellectual difficulties connected with this view, great as they are, have never suppressed it; the pride of man and his faith in himself have not been able permanently to obscure it. The greater men are, the more entirely do they dread any approach to that self-exaltation which puts away as unnecessary the Divine hand stretched out to them. As Dean Church points out,* "not Hebrew prophets only, but the heathen poets of Greece looked with peculiar and profound alarm upon the haughty self-sufficiency of men." Nothing can, they think, ward off evil from the man who makes the mistake of supposing, even when carrying out the Divine will, that he needs only his own strength of brain and will and arm to succeed, that he is accountable to no one for the character which he permits success to build up within him.

Even the agnostic of to-day, as represented by Professor Huxley, cannot do without some modicum of "grace" in his conception of man's relation to the powers of nature, though to admit this is to run a rift of inconsistency through his whole system of thought. "Suppose," he says in his "Lay Sermons," "it were perfectly certain that the life and future of every one of us would, one day or other, depend on his winning or losing a game at chess. . . The chessboard is the world, the pieces are the phenomena of the universe, the rules of the game are what we call the laws of nature. The player on the other side is hidden from us. We know that his play is always fair, just, patient. But we know to our cost that he never overlooks a mistake, or makes the smallest allowance for ignorance. To the man who plays well the highest stakes are paid with that overflowing generosity with which the strong shows delight in strength, and one who plays ill is checkmated without haste, but without remorse. My metaphor will remind you of the famous picture in which the Evil One is depicted playing a game of chess with man for his soul. Substitute for the mocking fiend in that picture a calm, strong angel, playing, as we say, for love, and who would rather lose than win, and I should accept it as the image of human life." Even in a world without God, therefore, the facts of life suggest "justice," "patience," "generosity," and a pity which "would rather lose than win." With all the inexorable rigour and hardness of man's lot there is mingled something that suggests "grace" in the power that rules the world; and from the Deuteronomist to St. Paul, from Augustine to Calvin and Professor Huxley, the resolutely thorough thinkers have found, in the last analysis, these two elements, the rigour of law and the election of grace, working together in the moulding of mankind.

The statement of these facts in Deuteronomy is as thorough as any that succeeded it. The rigour of law could not be more precisely and pathetically declared than in this insistence on the blessing or the curse which must inevitably follow right choice or wrong. But the tenderness of grace could not be more attractively displayed than in this picture of Yahweh's dealings with Israel. Love never faileth here, no more than elsewhere. It persists, notwithstanding stiff-necked rebellion, and in spite of coarse materialism of nature. Even a childish fickleness, more utterly trying than any other weakness or defect, cannot wear it out. But inexorable blessing or curse is blended with it, and helps

* "Cathedral Sermons," p. 26.

to work out the final result for Israel and mankind. That is the manner of the government of God, according to the Scriptures. History in its long course as known to us now confirms the view; and the author of Deuteronomy, in thus blending love and law together in the end of this great exhortation, has rested the obligation to obedience on a foundation which cannot be moved.

CHAPTER XIII.

LAW AND RELIGION.

DEUTERONOMY xii.-xxvi.

WITH this section (chapters xii.-xxvi.) we have at length reached the legislation to which all that has gone before is, in form at least, a prelude. But in its general outline this code, if it can be so called, has a very unexpected character. When we speak of a code of laws in modern days, what we mean is a series of statutes, carefully arranged under suitable heads, dealing with the rights and duties of the people, and providing remedies for all possible wrongs. Then behind these laws there is the executive power of the Government, pledged to enforce them, and ready to punish any breaches of them which may be committed. In most cases, too, definite penalties are appointed for any disregard or transgression of them. Each word has been carefully selected, and it is understood that the very letter of the laws is to be binding. Every one tried by them knows that the exact terms of the laws are to be pressed against him, and that the thing aimed at is a rigorous, literal enforcement of every detail. Tried by such a conception, this Deuteronomic legislation looks very extraordinary and unintelligible.

In the first place, there is very little of orderly sequence in it. Some large sections of it have a consecutive character; but there is no perceptible order in the succession of these sections, and there has been very little attempt to group the individual precepts under related heads. Moreover in many sections there is no mention of a penalty for disobedience, nor is there any machinery for enforcing the prescriptions of the code. There is, too, much in it that seems rather to be good advice, or direction for leading a righteous life, a life becoming an Israelite and a servant of Yahweh, than law. For instance, such a prescription as this, "If there be with thee a poor man, one of thy brethren, within any of thy gates, in thy land which Yahweh thy God giveth thee, thou shalt not harden thine heart nor shut thine hand from thy poor brother," can in no sense be treated as a law, in the hard technical sense of that word. It stands exactly on a level with the exhortations of the New Testament, e. g., "Be not wise in your own conceits," "Render to no man evil for evil," and rather sets up an ideal of conduct which is to be striven after than establishes a law which must be complied with. There is no punishment prescribed for disobedience. All that follows if a man do harden his heart against his poor brother is the sting of conscience, which brings home to him that he is not living according to the will of God. In almost every respect, therefore, this Deuteronomic code differs from a modern code, and in dealing with it we must largely dismiss the ideas which naturally occur to us when we speak of a code of laws. Our conception of that is, clearly, not valid for these ancient codes; and we need not be surprised if we find that they will not bear being pressed home in all their details, as modern codes must be, and are meant to be. Great practical difficulties have arisen in India, Sir Henry Maine assures us, from applying the ideas of Western lawyers to the ancient and sacred codes of the East. He says that the effect of a procedure under which all the disputes of a community must be referred to regular law-courts is to stereotype ascertained usages, and to treat the oracular precepts of a sacred book as texts and precedents that must be enforced. The consequence is that vague and elastic social ordinances, which have hitherto varied according to the needs of the people, become fixed and immutable, and an Asiatic society finds itself arrested and, so to speak, imprisoned unexpectedly within its own formulas. Inconsistencies and contradictions, which were never perceived when these laws were worked by Easterns, who had a kind of instinctive perception of their true nature, became glaring and troublesome under Western rule, and much unintentional wrong has resulted. May it not be that the same thing has happened in the domain of literature in connection with these ancient Hebrew laws? Discrepancies, small and great, have been the commonplace of Pentateuch criticism for many years past, and on them very far-reaching theories have been built. It may easily be that some of these are the result rather of our failure to take into account the elastic nature of Asiatic law, and that a less strained application of modern notions would have led to a more reasonable interpretation.

But granting that ordinary ancient law is not to be taken in our rigorous modern sense, yet the fact that what we are dealing with here is Divine law may seem to some to imply that in all its details it was meant to be fulfilled to the letter. If not, then in what sense is it inspired, and how can we be justified in regarding it as Divinely given? The reply to that is, of course, simply this, that inspiration makes free use of all forms of expression which are common and permissible at the time and place at which it utters itself. From all we know of the Divine methods of acting in the world, we have no right to suppose that in giving inspired laws God would create entirely new and different forms for Himself. On the contrary, legislation in ancient Israel, though Divine in its source, would naturally take the ordinary forms of ancient law. Moreover in this case it could hardly have been otherwise. As has already been pointed out, a large part of the Mosaic legislation must have been adopted from the customs of the various tribes who were welded into one by Moses. It cannot be conceived that the laws against stealing, for example, the penalties for murder, or the prescriptions for sacrifice, can have been first introduced by the great Lawgiver. He made much ancient customary law to be part and parcel of the Yahwistic legislation by simply taking it over. If so, then all that he added would naturally, as to form, be moulded on what he found pre-existing. Consequently we may apply to this law, whether Divinely revealed or adopted, the same tests and methods of interpretation as we should apply to any other body of ancient Eastern law.

Now of ancient Eastern codes the laws of Manu are the nearest approach to the Mosaic codes, and their character is thus stated by themselves (chap. i., ver. 107): "In this work the sacred law has been fully stated, as well as the good and bad qualities of human actions and the immemorial rule of conduct to be followed by all." That means that in the code are to be found ritual laws, general moral precepts, and a large infusion of immemorial customs. And its history, as elicited by criticism, has very interesting hints to give us as to the probable course of legal development in primitive nations. It is sometimes said that the results of the criticism of the Old Testament, if true, present us with a literature which has gone through vicissitudes and editorial processes for which literary history elsewhere affords absolutely no parallel. However that may be as regards the historical and prophetical books, it is not true with regard to the legal portions of the Pentateuch. The very same processes are followed in Professor Buhler's Introduction to his translation of the "Laws of Manu," forming Vol. XXV. of "The Sacred Books of the East," as are followed in the critical commentaries on the Old Testament law codes. Pages lxvii. *seq.* of Buhler's Introduction read exactly like an extract from Kuenen or Dillmann; and the analysis of the text, with its resultant list of interpolations, runs as much into detail as any similar analysis in the Old Testament can do. Moreover the conjectures as to the growth of Manu's code are, in many places, parallel to the critical theories of the growth of the Mosaic codes. The foundation of Manu is, in the last resort, threefold—the teaching of the Vedas, the decisions of those acquainted with the law, and the customs of virtuous Aryas. At a later time the teachers of the Vedic schools gathered up the more important of these precepts, decisions, and customs into manuals for the use of their pupils, written at first in aphoristic prose, and later in verse. These, however, were not systematic codes at all. As the name given them implies, they were strings of maxims or aphorisms. Later, these were set forth as binding upon all, and were revised into the form of which the "Laws of Manu" is the finest specimen.

In Israel the process would appear to have been similar, though much simpler. It was similar; for though there are radical differences between the Aryan and the Semitic mind which must not be overlooked, the former being more systematic and fond of logical arrangement than the latter, a great many of the things which are common to Moses and Manu are quite independent of race, and are due to the fact that both legislations were to regulate the lives of men at the same stage of social advancement. But Manu was much later than Moses. Indeed, as we now have them, the laws of Manu are as late as the post-Ezraite Judaic code, and in temper and tone these two codes very nearly resemble each other. Consequently the earlier codes of the Pentateuch are simpler than Manu. When Israel left Egypt, custom must have been almost alone the guide of life. Moses' task was to promulgate and force home his fundamental truths; in this view he must adopt and remodel the customary law so as to make it innocuous to the higher principles he introduced, or even to make it a vehicle for the popularising of them. So far as he made codes, he would make them with that end. Consequently he would take up mainly such prominent points as were most capable of being, or which most urgently needed to be, moralised, leaving all the rest to custom where it was harmless. This is the reason, too, most probably, why the earlier codes are so short and so unsystematic. They are selections which needed special attention, not complete codes covering the whole of life. In fact the form and contents of all the Old Testament codes can be accounted for only on this supposition. As the codes lengthen, they do so simply by taking up, in a modified or unmodified form, so much more of the custom; and under the pressure of Yahwistic ideas these selected codes became more and more weighted with spiritual significance and power.

That would seem to have been the process by which the inspired legislators of Israel did their work; and if it be so, some of the variations which are now taken to be certain indications of different ages and circumstances may simply represent local varieties of the same custom. Custom tends always to vary with the locality within certain narrow limits. It would be quite in accord with the general character of ancient customary law to believe that, provided the law was on the whole observed, there would be no inclination to insist upon excluding small local variations; and equally so that in a collection like the Pentateuch the custom of one locality should appear in one place, that of another in another. In that case, to insist that a certain sacrifice, for example, shall always consist of the same number of animals, and that any variation means a new and later legislation on the subject, is only to make a mistake. The discrepancy is made important only by applying modern English views of law to ancient law. Professor A. B. Davidson has shown in the Introduction to his "Ezekiel" (p. liii.) that this latter was probably Ezekiel's view. "On any hypothesis of priority," he says, "the differences in details between him (*i. e.*, Ezekiel) and the law (*i. e.*, P) may be easiest explained by supposing that, while the sacrifices in general and the ideas which they expressed were fixed and current, the particulars, such as the kind of victims and the number of them, the precise quantity of meal, oil, and the like, were held non-essential and alterable when a change would better express the idea." The same principle would apply to the differences between Ezekiel and Deuteronomy, *e. g.*, the omission of the feast of weeks and of the law of the offering of the firstlings of the flock. If so, then obviously Ezekiel must have thought that the previous ritual law was not meant to be as binding as we make it.

But, as has already been remarked, this law was elastic in more important matters; often, even when it seems to legislate, it is only setting up ideals of conduct. Before we leave this subject an example should be given, and the law of war may serve, especially if we compare it with the corresponding section of Manu. The provisions in Deuteronomy, chap. xx., according to which on the eve of a battle the officers should proclaim to the army that any man who had built a new house and had not dedicated it, or who had planted a vineyard and had not yet used the fruit of it, or who had betrothed a wife and not yet taken her, or who was afraid, should retire from the danger, as also the provisions that forbid the destruction of fruit-trees belonging to a besieged city, cannot have been meant as absolute laws. Yet that is no ground for supposing that they could have been introduced only after Israel, having ceased to be a sovereign state, waged no war, and that consequently they are interpolations in the original Deuteronomy. For the similar provisions of the laws of Manu were given while kings reigned, and were addressed to men constantly engaged in war. Yet this is what we find: "When he (the king) fights with his foes in battle, let him not strike him with weapons concealed (in wood), nor with (such as are) barbed, poisoned, or the points of which are blowing with fire. Let him not strike one who (in flight) has climbed on an eminence, nor a eunuch, nor one who joins the palms of his hands (in supplication), nor one (who flees) with flying hair, nor one who sits down, nor one who says 'I am thine,' nor one who sleeps, nor one who has lost his coat of mail, nor one who is naked, nor one who is disarmed, nor one who looks on without taking part in the fight, nor one who is fighting with another foe, nor one whose weapons are broken, nor one afflicted (with sorrow), nor one who has been grievously wounded, nor one who is in fear, nor one who has turned to flight; but in all these cases let him remember the duty (of honourable warriors)." With an exact and unremitting obligation to observe these precepts war would be impossible, and we may be sure that in neither case were they meant in that sense. They simply set forth the conduct which a chivalrous soldier would desire to follow, and would on fitting occasions actually follow; but by no means what he must do, or else break with his religion. Only by hypotheses like these can the form and the character of such laws be properly explained, and if we keep them constantly in mind, some at least of the difficulties which result from a comparison of the law and the histories may be mitigated.

Such being the character of the Deuteronomic code, the question has been raised whether its introduction and acceptance by Josiah was not a falling away from the spirituality of ancient religion. Many modern writers, supported by St. Paul's *dicta* concerning the law, say that it was. Indeed the very mention of law seems to depress writers on religion in these days, and Deuteronomy appears to be to them a name of fear. But whatever tendencies of modern thinking may have brought this about, it is nevertheless true that experience embodied in custom and law is the kindly nurse, not the deadly enemy, of moral and spiritual life. Without law a nation would be absolutely helpless; and it is inconceivable that at any stage of Israel's history they were without this guide and support. As we have seen, they never were. First they had customary law; then along with that short special codes, *e. g.*, the Book of the Covenant and the Deuteronomic code; and even when the whole Pentateuchal law as we have it had been elaborated, a good deal must still have been left to custom. Consequently there was nothing so startling and revolutionary in the introduction of Deuteronomy as many have combined to represent. Indeed it is difficult to see how it altered anything in this respect. Of all forms of law, customary law is perhaps that which demands and receives most unswerving obedience. Under it, therefore, the pressure of law was heavier than it could be in any other form. It does not appear how the fact that those observing it did not think of that which they obeyed as law, but simply custom, altered the essential nature of their relation to it. They were guided by ordinances which did not express their own inward conviction, and were not a product of their own thought. They obeyed ordinances from without, and these ought therefore to have had the same effect upon the moral and spiritual life as written laws. For they cannot be said to have regulated only civil life. Religious life (even if the Book of the Covenant be Mosaic or sub-Mosaic, as I believe; much more if it be post-Davidic, as many say) must have been largely regulated by the customs of Israel. If law then be in its own nature, as the antinomians tell us, destructive of spontaneity and progress, if it necessarily externalises religion, then there would have been as little room for the religion of the prophets before Deuteronomy as after it.

But, as a matter of fact, no falling off in spirituality took place after Deuteronomy. Wellhausen says that with law freedom came to an end, and this was the death of prophecy. But he can support his thesis only by denying the name of prophet to all the prophets after Jeremiah. It is difficult to see the basis of such a distinction. It is judged by this, if by nothing else—that it compels Wellhausen to deny that the author of Second Isaiah is a prophet. That he wrote anonymously is held to prove that he felt this himself. Now a view so extraordinarily superficial has no root, and every reader of that most touching and sublime of all the Old Testament books will simply stand amazed at the depth of the critical prejudice which could dictate such a judgment. If the post-Deuteronomic prophets are not prophets, then there are no prophets at all, and the whole discussion becomes a useless logomachy. But even if Ezekiel and Second Isaiah and the rest are not prophets, they are at least full of spiritual life and power, so that the decay of spiritual religion which the adoption of Deuteronomy is supposed to have brought about must be considered purely imaginary on that ground also. And this contention is strengthened by the theories of the critical school themselves. If the bulk of the Psalms, as all critics incline to believe, or all of them, as some say, are post-exilic, then the first centuries of the post-exilic period must have been the most spiritually minded epoch in Israelite history. The depth of religious feeling exhibited in the Psalms, and the comprehension of the inwardness of man's true relation to God by which they are penetrated, are the exact contrary of the externality and superficiality which the introduction of written law is said to have produced. So long as the Psalms were being written religious life must have been vigorous and healthy, and to date the beginnings of Pharisaic externalism from Josiah's day must consequently be an error.

After what has been said it is scarcely necessary to discuss Duhm's views of the opposition between prophecy and Deuteronomy. It will be sufficient to ask how the latter can have turned against prophecy, when it is in its essence an embodiment of prophetic principles in law, and was introduced and supported by prophets. But, it may be said, after all prophecy did decay, and ultimately die, and that too during the period after Deuteronomy. Is there not in that admitted fact a presumption that this law did work against prophecy? If so, then it is more than met by the fact that the decay of spiritual religion became noticeable only some centuries after this, and that the immediate effect of Deuteronomy was rather to deepen and intensify religion, and to keep it alive amid all the vicissitudes of the Captivity and Return. Moreover the break-up of the national life was sufficient to account for the slow decay and final cessation of prophecy. From the first, prophecy had been concerned with the building up of a nation which should be faithful to Yahweh. Its main function had been to interpret and to foretell the great movements and crises of national life—to read God's purpose in the great world-movements and to proclaim it. With Israel's death as a nation the field of prophecy became gradually circumscribed, and ultimately its voice ceased. Consequently, though in the main the final cessation of prophecy was connected with the rise of externalism in religion and with the great decay of spiritual life in the two or three centuries before Christ, the destruction of the nation would account for the feebleness of prophecy during a period when the inner spiritual life was flourishing as it flourished after Deuteronomy. Moreover, as religion became more inward and personal, prophecy, in the Old Testament sense, had less place. Though in New Testament times spiritual life and spiritual originality and power were more present than at any time in the world's history, prophecy did not revive. In the whole New Testament there is not one purely prophetic book save the Revelation, and that is apocalyptic more than simply prophetic; and though there was an order of prophets in the early Church, if they had any special function other than that of preachers their office soon died out. If then the denationalising of religion and its growth in individualism and inwardness in New Testament times prevented the revival of prophecy, we may surely gather that the same things, and not the introduction of written law, brought it to an end in the Old Testament.

Nor does St. Paul's judgment as to the meaning and use of law, in Galatians, when rightly understood, contradict this. No doubt he seems to say that the Mosaic law by its very nature as law is incompatible with grace, that it necessarily stands out of relation to faith, and that its principle is a purely external one, so much wages for so much work. Further, he clearly regards it as having been interpolated into the history of Israel between the promises given to Abraham and the fulfilment of them in the redemption by Christ, and as having served only to increase sin and to drive men thus to Christ. But when he says this he is replying mainly to the Pharisaic view of the law which was represented by the Judaizers, and finds himself all the more at home in refuting it that it was his own view before he became a Christian. According to that view, the whole law, both the moral and ceremonial provisions of it, was necessary to obtain moral righteousness, and the mere doing of the legally prescribed things gave a claim to the promised reward. So interpreted, law had all the evil qualities he states, and stood in absolute hostility to grace and faith, the great Christian principles. The only difficulty is that St. Paul does not say, as we should expect him to do, that originally the law was not meant to be so regarded. He seems to admit by his silence that the Pharisaic view of the law was the right one. But if he does, he cannot have meant to include Deuteronomy. For there law is made to have its root and ground in grace. It is given to Israel as a token of the free love of God, and it is a law of life which, if kept, would make them a peculiar people unto God. Further, love to God is to be the motive from which all obedience springs, so that this law is bound up with both grace and faith. But the probability is that St. Paul admits the Pharisaic view only because it is that view with which alone he has to contend in the case in hand. For in Romans vii. he gives us quite another conception of the Mosaic law.* There he is thinking of it mainly from an ethical point of view, and he regards it as full of the Spirit of God, as a norm of moral life which not only continues to be valid in Christianity, but which finds in the Christian life the very fulfilment which it was intended to have. It presses home too the moral ideal upon the man with extraordinary power, and marks and emphasises the terrible divergence between his aspirations and his actual performance. This is a much higher office than that which he assigns to law in Galatians; and hence one gathers that he is not speaking in Galatians exhaustively and conclusively, but is condemning rather a way of regarding the Mosaic law with which he had once sympathised than that law in its own essential character. In its moral aspects, as represented by the Decalogue, the law is of eternal obligation. From it comes the light which brings to the Christian that moral unrest and dissatisfaction which is one of God's Divinest gifts to His people. In this aspect, the law is holy and just and good: instead of favouring the critical view St. Paul leaves it without any fragment of real support.

Our conclusion is, therefore, that the antinomianism, which makes the acknowledgment of Deuteronomy by Josiah and his people the turning-point for the worse in the religious history of Israel, is unfounded. The nation had always been under law, and previous to Deuteronomy under even written law. This code was not in any previously unheard-of way made the law of the kingdom. Its very contents are conclusive against that view, for it contains much that could not be enforced by the State. Instead of trying to do by external means that which the persuasions of the prophets had failed to do, Josiah and his people did just what they would have had to do, when they became convinced that the prophetic principles ought to be carried out. They made an agreement to follow these Divine commands, these God-given principles, in actual life. But there is no hint that they regarded Deuteronomy as the sum of the Divine ordinances for the life of men. Indeed there are many references to other Divine laws; and the priestly oracle remained, after Deuteronomy as before it, a source of Divine guidance. Deuteronomy therefore did not destroy prophecy; the post-exilic Psalms are proof that it did not destroy spiritual life: and the Pauline view of the law, in at least one series of passages, coincides entirely with the view that law stated as it is stated in Deuteronomy may be one of the mightiest influences to mould, and enrich, and deepen, moral and spiritual life.

* Ritschl's "Rechtfertigung und Versöhnung," vol. ii., pp. 311ff.

CHAPTER XIV.

LAWS OF SACRIFICE.

DEUTERONOMY xii.

It is a characteristic of all the earlier codes of law—the Book of the Covenant, the Deuteronomic Code, and the Law of Holiness—that at the head of the series of laws which they contain there should be a law of sacrifice. Probably, too, each of the three had, as first section of all, the Decalogue. The Book of the Covenant and Deuteronomy undeniably have it so, and the earlier element which forms the basis of Lev. xvii.-xxvi. not improbably had originally the same form. If so, we may assume that the order of the precepts has in a measure been determined by the order of the commandments. On this account the laws for the cultus would naturally come first. For just as the first commandment is, "Thou shalt have no other god before Me," and the second forbids all idolatrous images, so the laws begin with provisions meant in the main to ward off idolatry. Israel's great calling was to receive and to spread the truth concerning God. That was the centre of the sacred deposit of Divine and revealed truth committed to that nation; and it is most instructive to see how, not only in historical statements, but even in the form in which early Israelite legislation is handed down to us, the Decalogue dominates all the details of it. It formulated in as concrete a shape as was possible the Divine demand that Israelites should love God and their neighbour, and *therefore* the legislative provisions and statutes begin with ordinances dealing with sacrifice.

To us in modern times it may seem almost bathos to connect such an antecedent with such a consequent; but it seems so, only because we have difficulty in apprehending the meaning and importance of sacrifice in primitive religion. For sacrifice had in Israel a meaning and importance of its own, and a present value at every period, which in no way depended upon its typical or prophetic value as pointing forward to the sacrifice of Christ. It supplied the religious needs of men even apart from the clearness of their knowledge about its ultimate purpose. Sacrifice, especially in its simplest meaning, was in heathenism absolutely essential as a means of approach to God. To come before a great *man* without a gift was in ancient days an outrage. It was therefore inevitable that men should approach their gods in the same manner. Sacrificial gifts expressed the dependent's joy in a gracious lord, and also the homage and reverence due from a subject to a king. Further, as all good things were regarded as the gifts of the gods to their worshippers, the sacrifices conveyed thanks for good gifts received, and joined the gods and their worshippers by a common participation in the Divine gift which connected them as eaters at the same table. But sacrifices had a higher reach of expression even than that. As they were brought to the gods they were the symbols of the self-devotion of the offerer to the service of his god; and where there was need of propitiation because of offence consciously given, or offence felt by the deity for unknown reasons, these gifts took on in some measure a reconciling or propitiatory quality.

Now the Old Testament sacrifices had in them, unquestionably, all these elements: but as Yahweh was high above all heathen deities in moral character, they also took on a depth and intensity of meaning which they could never have on the soil of heathen religious conceptions. Along this line of sacrificial ritual, therefore, all the spiritual emotions of Israel flowed; and to hold that sacrifice had no real place in the religion of Yahweh would be almost equivalent to saying that neither love, nor penitence, nor prayer, had any real place in it either. All these found utterance in sacrifice and along with it; and it has yet to be shown that they had any regular and acceptable utterance otherwise. To regulate sacrifice and keep it pure must, therefore, have been one chief means of guarding against the degradation of Yahweh to the level of the gods of the heathen.

But there is another and very important reason for it. Both in the days when Moses parted from his people, and also in the time of Manasseh, the people stood confronted by very special danger just at this point.

At the earlier period they were about to enter upon intimate contact with the Canaanites, their superiors in culture and in all the arts of civilised life, but corrupted to the core. Further, the Canaanite corruption was focussed in their religious rites and worship, and evil could not fail to follow if the people suffered themselves to be drawn into any participation in it. For if Professor Robertson Smith be right, the central point of ancient sacrifice was the communion between the god and his worshippers in the sacrificial feast. They became of one kin with each other and with the god, and this close relationship made the communication of spiritual and moral infection almost a certainty.

In Manasseh's day again it was natural that legislation on the same subject, and warnings of even a more solemn kind, should be repeated. A prophetic lawgiver writing at that date had before him, not only the possibility of evil, but actual experience of it. The laws and warnings of the earlier code had been defied and neglected. The faith of the chosen people had been miserably perverted by contact with the Canaanites; the whole history of prophecy had been a struggle against corrupt and insincere worship; and now the monstrous sacrifices to Moloch and the invasion of Assyrian idolatry had degraded Yahweh and destroyed His people, so that scarce any hope of recovery remained. In bracing himself for one more struggle with this desperate corruption, the Deuteronomist naturally repeated in deeper tones the Mosaic warnings. The command utterly to uproot and trample under foot the symbols and instruments of Canaanite worship, he brings, from the less prominent place it occupies in the Book of the Covenant, to the first place in his own code. To break with that and all other forms of idolatry, utterly and decisively, had come to be the first condition of any upward movement. The degrading and defiling bondage to idolatry into which his people had fallen must end. With trumpet tongue he calls upon them to break down the Canaanite altars, dash in pieces their obelisks, and burn their Asherim with fire.

To some moderns it may seem that such excessive energy might, with better effect, have been expended upon the denunciation of moral evils, such as cruelty and lust and oppression, rather than of idolatry. We have grown so accustomed to the distinctions drawn by the Church of Rome, and in later times by the neo-classicists, between worshipping God through an image or a picture, or in any natural object or natural force, and the actual worship of the image or picture or natural object itself, that we have sophisticated our minds. But the author of Deuteronomy knew by bitter experience that such subtle, and, in great part, sophistical distinctions had no application to his people and his time. Their worst immoralities were, he knew well, rooted in their idol-worship. For idolatry in any form binds all that is highest in man to the sphere of nature, *i. e.*, of moral indifference. Just as a conception of God which rigorously separated Him from nature, which made His will the supreme impelling force in the world, and which conceived His essential attributes to be entirely ethical, was the fountain of the higher life in Israel, so a lapse into idolatry of any kind was the negation of it all. No doubt some moral life would have remained in Israel, even if the lapse had become universal. But, even at its best, this natural morality of self-preservation has no future and no goal. It does not lead the van of human progress; it merely comes after, to ratify the results of it. Only when social morality is taken up into a wider sphere than its own,—only when it is conceived as the path by which man can co-operate with a sublime purpose lying beyond himself,—can it maintain itself as the inspiration of human life, impelling to progress and guiding it.* Now, so far as history teaches, this energy of moral life has been attained only where the conception of God which makes moral perfection to be His essential nature has been accepted and cherished. But no natural religion can rise to that; hence idolatry must always be destructive of ethical religion. It must destroy faith in the moral character of God.

Further, it must destroy the moral character of man. In the last resort all idolaters are equally acceptable to their god, if only they bring the prescribed gifts and accurately perform the prescribed ceremonies. The lewd and the chaste, the cruel and the merciful, the revengeful and the forgiving, are all equally accepted when they sacrifice. Non-moral or positively immoral gods can care nothing about such differences. Of this fact and its results no man acquainted with the history of Israel could doubt. The main zeal of the prophets was at all times directed against those who were steeped in moral evil, but were zealous in all that concerned sacrifice, and against the amazing folly of a people who thought to bind the living God to their cause and their interests by mere bribes, in the shape of thousands of bullocks and ten thousand rivers of oil. This conception was bound up essentially with idolatry. But the evil of it was intensified in the Semitic idolatries with which Israel specially defiled itself. Their cruelty and obscenity were unspeakable. Now by Israel's idolatry Yahweh was made to appear tolerant of Moloch and Baal, as if they were equals. Every quality which the Mosaic revelation had set forth as essential to the character of Yahweh—His purity, His mercy, His truth—was outraged by the society which His worshippers in Manasseh's days had thrust upon Him. No reform, then, had the least chance of stability

* *Cf.* Riehm, "Old Testament Theology," p. 25.

till the axe was laid at the root of this wide-spreading upas tree.

Deuteronomy, therefore, grapples first and grapples thoroughly with the evil, and strikes it a blow from which it was never to recover. The inspired writer repeats with new energy the old decrees of utter destruction against the Canaanite sanctuaries; for though these were for the most part no longer in Canaanite hands, the High Places still existed; and the principle of that old prohibition was more clamant for recognition and realisation than it had ever been in the history of Israel before.

Then he goes on to proclaim the new law, that no sacrifice should any longer be offered save at the one central sanctuary chosen by Yahweh. There is no such provision in the Book of the Covenant, and there is no hint in the legislation of Deuteronomy that its author knew of the Tabernacle and its sole right as a place of sacrifice. From beginning to end of the code he never mentions the Tabernacle nor the sacrifices there; and in the very terms in which he permits the slaughter of animals for food in vv. 15, 16, and 20-25, though he obviously repeals a custom which has been embodied in the Priestly Code as a law (Lev. xvii. 3 ff.), he makes no reference to that passage. Consequently this at least may be said, that he may quite conceivably have been ignorant of Lev. xvii. 3 ff. In ignorance of it, he might write as he has done; and if not ignorant, it would be much more natural to refer to it. When we add to this negative testimony the positive testimony of verses 8 and 13, which we have already discussed in Chapter I., there would seem to be little room for doubt that the priestly law on this subject was not before the writer of Deuteronomy. Consequently we are justified in regarding this as the first written law actually promulgated on this subject. Hezekiah had attempted the same reform; but he had, so far as we know, neither published nor referred to any law commanding it, and his work was entirely undone. The Deuteronomist, more convinced than he that this step was absolutely necessary to complete the Mosaic legislation on idolatry, and filled with the same inspiration of the Almighty, completed it; and though a reaction followed Josiah's enforcement of this law also, its existence saved the life of the nation. Its principles kept the nation holy, *i. e.*, separate to their God, during the Exile, and at the return they were dominant in the formation of the "congregation."

Certainly there is no lack of earnestness in the way in which these principles are urged. With that love of repetition which is a distinguishing mark of this writer, he expresses the commandment first positively, then negatively. Then he brings in the consequential alteration in the law regarding the slaughtering of animals for food. Again he returns to the command, explaining, enlarging, insisting, and concludes with a reiteration of the permission to slaughter. Efforts, of course, have been made to show that this repetition is due to the amalgamation here of no fewer than seven separate documents! But little heed need be given to such fantastic attempts. It is, once for all, a habit of this writer's mind to shrink from no monotony of this kind. There is not one important idea in his book which he does not repeat again and again; and where repetition is so constant a feature, and where the language and thought is so consistent as it is here, it is worse than useless to assert separate documents. The writer's earnestness is sufficient explanation. He saw plainly that, so long as the provincial High Places existed and were popular, it would be impossible to secure purity of worship. The heathen conceptions of the Canaanites clung about their ancient sanctuaries, and, like the mists from a fever swamp, infected everything that came near. Inspection sufficiently minute and constant to be of use was impracticable; there remained nothing but to decree their abandonment. When the whole worship of the people was centred at Jerusalem, corruption of the idolatrous kind would, it was hoped, be impossible. There, a pious king could watch over it; there, the Temple priesthood had attained to worthier ideas in regard to sacrifice and the fulfilment of the law than the priests elsewhere. Josiah accordingly rigorously enforced this new law.

Such a change, aimed solely at religious ends, did not stop there. In many ways it affected the social life of the people; in vv. 15, 16, and 20, 24, the author meets one hardship connected with the new law, by allowing men to slay for food at a distance from the altar. According to ancient custom, no flesh could be eaten by any Israelite, save when the fat and the blood had been presented at the altar. During the wilderness journey there would be little difficulty regarding this. In the desert very little meat is eaten; and so long as life was nomadic there would be no hardship in demanding that those who wished to make sacrificial feasts should wander towards the central place of worship rather than from it. It has been disputed whether there was in those days a tabernacle such as the Priestly Code describes; but there certainly was, according to the earliest documents, a tent in which Yahweh revealed Himself and gave responses. As we have seen, there must have been sacrifice in connection with it; and though worship at other places where Yahweh had made His name to be remembered was permitted, this sanctuary in the camp must have had a certain pre-eminence. A tendency, but according to the words of Deuteronomy nothing stronger than a tendency, must have shown itself to make this the main place of worship.

When the people crossed the Jordan into the land promised to the fathers, and had abandoned the nomadic life, great difficulty must have arisen. For those at a distance from the place where the Tabernacle was set up, the eating of meat and the enjoyment of sacrificial feasts would, by this ancient customary law, have been rendered impossible, if the attendance at one sanctuary had been obligatory. Only if men could come to local sanctuaries, each in his own neighbourhood, could the religious character of the festivals at which meat was eaten be preserved. The nature of men's occupations, now that they had become settled agriculturists, and the dangers from the Canaanites so long as they were not entirely subdued and absorbed, alike forbade such long and frequent journeys to a central sanctuary. The conquest must consequently at once have checked any tendency to centralisation that may have existed; and there is reason to believe that the acceptance of the Canaanite High Places as sanctuaries of Yahweh was in great part caused by the demands of this ancient law concerning the "zebhach." In any case it must have helped to overcome any scruples that may have existed. But when the Tabernacle and Ark were brought to Zion, and still more when the Temple was built, the centripetal tendency, never altogether dead, must have revived. For there was peace throughout the land and beyond it. No danger from the Canaanites existed; and the political centralisation which Solomon aimed at, and actually carried out, as well as the superior magnificence of the Solomonic Temple and its priests, must have attracted to Jerusalem the thoughts and the reverence of the whole people. What Deuteronomy now makes law may have then first arisen as a demand of the Jerusalem priests. At all events, the very existence of the Temple must have been a menace to the High Places; and we may be sure that among the motives which led the ten tribes to reject the Davidic house, jealousy for the local sanctuaries must have been prominent.

But the separation of the ten tribes would only strengthen the claim of the Temple on Zion to be for Judah the one true place of worship. The territory ruled from Jerusalem was now so small that resort to the central sanctuary was comparatively easy. The glorious memories of the Davidic and Solomonic time would centre round Jerusalem. Any local sanctuaries would be entirely dwarfed and overshadowed by the splendour and the, at least comparative, purity of the worship there. Priests of local altars too must inevitably have sunk in the popular estimation, and even in their own, to a secondary and subordinate position, as compared with the carefully organised and strictly graded Jerusalem priests. Even without a positive command, therefore, the people of Judah must have been gradually growing into the habit of seeking Yahweh at Jerusalem on all more solemn religious occasions; and though the High Places might exist, their repute in the Southern Kingdom must have been decreasing. Of course if a command was given in the Mosaic time which had been neglected, the tendencies here traced must have been stronger and more definite than we have depicted them. When the prophetic teachings of Isaiah which proclaimed Jerusalem to be "Ariel," the "sacrificial hearth," or "the hearth of God," were so wondrously confirmed by the destruction of Sennacherib's host before the city, the unique position of Zion must have been secured; and after that only those who were set upon idolatry can have had much interest in the High Places. Hezekiah's effort to abolish these latter is quite intelligible in these circumstances; and we may feel assured that, as Wellhausen says,* "The Jewish royal temple had early overshadowed the other sanctuaries, and in the course of the seventh century they were extinct or verging on extinction."

Along with this there must have grown up a measure of laxity in regard to the provision that all slaughtering for food should take place at the sanctuary. Many would doubtless go to Zion, many would continue to resort to the High Places, and a number, from a mere halting between two opinions, would probably take their "zebhachim" to neither. Consequently the law before us would by no means be so revolutionary as Duhm, for instance, pictures it. He says: "I do not know if in the whole history of the world a law can be pointed to which was so fitted to change a whole people in its innermost nature and in its outward appearance, at one stroke, as

* Wellhausen, "History," p. 420.

this was. The Catholic Church even has never by all her laws succeeded in anything in the least like it." But we have seen evidence of a very strong and continuous pressure to this point, at least in Judah. History during centuries had justified and intensified it; so that in all probability the true worshippers of Yahweh found in the new law not so much a revolution as a ratification of their already ancient practice. To idolaters, of course, its adoption must have meant a cessation of their idolatry; but the change in the people and in their life would, though extensive, be only such as any ordinary reform would produce. Duhm overlooks altogether the very small territory which the law affected. A long day's walk would bring men from Jericho, from Hebron, from the borders of the Philistine country, and from Shechem and Samaria to Jerusalem. If Deuteronomy made a revolution, it must have been confined within the modest limits of substituting a whole for a half-day's journey to the Sanctuary.

Moreover it is a mistake to say that sacrifice at one central sanctuary "took religion away from the people," as Duhm says. If spiritual religion be meant, it ultimately brought religion more vitally home to them. For when the priestly system was fully carried out, the demands of household religion were met, as the post-exilic Psalms show, by the adoption of the practice of household prayer without reference to sacrifice, and finally by the institution of the synagogue. A more spiritual method of approach to God was substituted for a less spiritual in the remote places and in the homes of the people. And the public worship even gained. It became deeper, and more penetrated with a sense of the necessity of deliverance from sin. It is true, of course, that in the end Pharisaic legalism perverted the new forms of worship, as heathen externalism had perverted the old. But in neither case was the perversion a necessity. In both it was simply a manifestation of the materialistic tendency which dogs the footsteps of even the most spiritual religion, when it has to realise itself in the life of man. It is enough for the justification of the whole movement led by Josiah to say that it held the Judæan exiles together; that it kept alive in their hearts, as nothing else did, their faith in God and in their future; and that on their return it gave them the form which their institutions could most profitably take. Further, under the forms of religious and social life which this movement generated, the true, heartfelt piety which the prophets so mourned the want of became more common than ever it had been before.

The establishment of the central altar as the only one was the main object of this law; but there is much to be learned from the very terms in which this is expressed. They breathe the same love for man and sympathy with the poor which forms one of the most attractive characteristics of our book. The gracious bonds of family affection, the kindly feeling that should unite masters and servants, the helpfulness which ought to distinguish the conduct of the rich to the poor, and above all the cheerful enjoyment of the results of honest labour, are to be preserved and sanctified even in the ritual of sacrifice. "Thou shalt rejoice before Yahweh in all that thou puttest thine hand unto," is here the motto, if we may so speak, of religious service. That, indeed, is to be made the opportunity for the discharge of all humane and brotherly duties; and the religious life is at its highest when the worshipper rejoices himself, and shares and sheds abroad his joy upon others. The love of God is here most intimately blended with love of the brethren. Masters and servants, slaves and free, the high and the low, are to be reminded of their equal standing in the sight of God, by their common participation in the sacrificial meals; and the poorest are to be permitted an equal enjoyment of the luxuries of the rich in these solemn approaches to Yahweh. The Deuteronomist here reaches the highest stage of religious life, in that he shows himself in nowise afraid of human joy. As we have seen, he knows the value of austerity in religion. He is well enough aware that war against evil is not made with rose-water. But then he is equally far from the extreme of suspecting all affection not directly turned to God, of regarding natural gladness as a ruinous snare to the soul. This finely balanced, this just attitude to all aspects of life, is a most notable thing at this epoch in the history of the world, and considering the circumstances of the time it is little short of a marvel. It is true, of course, that the religion of Israel was always finely human. It could run into excesses, and was marked by many imperfections; but asceticism, the doctrine which holds pain and self-denial to be in themselves good, when it did intrude into Israel, always came from without. Nevertheless the heartiness and thoroughness with which all gracious human feelings and all kindly human relations are here taken up into religion is remarkable, even in the Old Testament. More, perhaps, than anything else in this book, it shows the sweetening and wholesome effect of demanding supreme love to God as man's first duty. "If any man come to Me and hate not his father and mother," says Christ, "he cannot be My disciple,"* and many purblind critics have found this to be a hard saying. But all who know men know, that when God in Christ is made so much the supreme object of love that even the most sacred human obligations seem to be disregarded in comparison, the human affection so thrust into the background is only made richer far than it otherwise could be.

CHAPTER XV.

THE RELATION OF OLD TESTAMENT SACRIFICE TO CHRISTIANITY.

But it may be asked, What is the relation of this Divinely sanctioned ritual law of sacrifice to our religion in its present phase? To that question various answers are being returned, and indeed it may be said that on this point almost all the main differences of Christians turn. The Church of Rome maintains in essence the sacerdotal view of the later Old Testament times, though in a spiritualised Christian shape, and to this the High Anglican view is a more or less pronounced return. The Protestant Churches, on the other hand, regard priests and sacrifices as anachronisms since the death of Christ. In that, for the most part, they regard the significance of sacrifice as being summed up and completed; and the present dispensation is for them the realisation in embryo of that which Old Testament

* Luke xiv. 26.

saints looked forward to—a people of God, every true member of which is both priest and prophet, *i. e.*, has free and unrestricted access to God, and is authorised and required to speak in His name. The interest of Protestant Christians, therefore, in priesthood and sacrifice in the Old Testament sense, though very great and enduring, has no connection with the continuation of sacrifice. They look upon the Old Testament ritual as wholly obsolete now. It was simply a stage in the religious development of the chosen people, and as such it has no claim to be continued among Christians.

By a curious allegorical process, however, some devout Protestants keep alive their interest in Old Testament ritual by finding in it an elaborate symbolism covering the whole field of evangelical theology. But this revivification of the old law is too arbitrary and subjective, as well as too improbable, to have an abiding place in Christianity. It is, moreover, useless for the guidance of life; for all that is thus ingeniously put into the Levitical ordinances is found more clearly and directly expressed elsewhere. The amount of religious symbolism in the earlier stages of Israelite religion is small, and very simple and direct. Even in the most elaborate parts of the Levitical legislation, *e. g.*, in the directions regarding the Tabernacle, the purposely allegorical element is kept within comparatively narrow limits; and we may boldly say that the mind which delights in finding spiritual mysteries in every detail of the sacrificial ritual is Rabbinical rather than Christian. On the other hand we need not enter upon a discussion of the view held by "Modern" or Broad Church theologians and by Unitarians, that sacrifice was merely a heathen form taken over into Mosaism, that it had no special significance there, and that the ideas connected with it have absolutely no place in enlightened Christian theology. The Christianity which attaches no sacrificial signification to the death of Christ has, so far as I know, never shown itself to be a type of religion able to create a future, and it is only with types of Christianity that do and can live we have to do. Our question here therefore is limited to this, Which of the two types of view, the Roman Catholic or the Protestant, is truest to the Old Testament teaching?

Externally, perhaps, the evidence seems to favour the Roman Catholic position; for the prophets either directly say, or imply, that sacrifice shall be restored with new purity and power in the Messianic time. This is so patent a fact that it led Edward Irving to say that it was the Old Testament economy that should abide, and that of the New Testament which should pass away. But the inner progress and development of Old Testament religion is quite as decisively on the other side. As we have seen, Old Testament piety had at the beginning almost no recognised expression save in connection with sacrifice, and the Exile first trained the people to faithfulness to God without it, sowing the seed of a religious life largely separate from the sacrificial ritual. Then the ordinance demanding sacrifice at one central altar, which, though introduced by Deuteronomy, was made the exclusive law only by the post-exilic community, furthered the growth of these germs, so that they produced the synagogue system. This completed the severance of the ordinary daily religion of the bulk of the people from sacrificial ritual, so far as that was attained within the limits of Judaism, and prepared the way for Pauline Christianity, in which all allegiance to ritual Judaism is cast off. Now, as between the external and internal evidence, there can be little doubt that the latter has by far the greater weight, especially as the external evidence can, perfectly well, be read in a different sense. The Old Testament promises that sacrifice should be restored may be held to have been fulfilled by the sacrificial death of Christ, which completed and filled up all that had gone before. In that case the evidence that sacrifice and ritual are now obsolete for Christians is left standing alone, and the Protestant view is justified.

And the case for this view is strengthened immeasurably by observing that the modern sacerdotalism has taken up as essential what was the main vice of sacrificial worship in the old economy. That was, as we have seen, the tendency to rest on the mere performance of the external rite, without reference to the disposition of the heart or even to conduct. Rivers of oil and hecatombs of victims were thought sufficient to meet all possible demands on God's part, and against this the polemic of the prophets is unceasing. Now in almost all modern sacerdotalism the doctrine of the efficacy of sacraments duly administered, apart from right dispositions in either him who administers them or in him who receives them, has been affirmed. It is not now, as it was in the "old time," an evil tendency which had to be assiduously fought against, but which could not be overcome. It is openly incorporated in the orthodox teaching and is distinctly provided for in the ideal of Christian worship. That marks a considerable falling away from the prophetic ideal: it can hardly be regarded as the appointed end of that great religious movement which the prophets dominated and directed for so long. The teaching of Deuteronomy certainly is, that wherever mere external acts are supposed to have power to secure entrance into the spiritual world of life and peace, there the character of God is misconceived and religion degraded. What it demands is the inward and spiritual allegiance of faithful men to God. What it depicts as the essence of religious life is a set of the whole nature Godward, as deep and irresistible as the set of the tides—

> "Such a tide as moving seems asleep,
> Too full for sound and foam."

Under no sacerdotal system can that view be unreservedly accepted, and therein lies the condemnation of every such system. So far as it is allowed to prevail, the force of the prophetic polemic has to be ignored or evaded, and in greater or less degree the same spiritual decay which the prophets mourned over in Israel must appear.

But it is not only where trust in the mere *opus operatum* is theoretically justified that it makes its baleful presence felt. It may surreptitiously creep in where the door is theoretically shut against it. The tendency is very deepseated in human nature; and many evangelical preachers, who repudiate all sacramentarianism, and throw the full emphasis of Christian religious life upon grace and faith, yet bring back again in subtler shape that very thing which they have rejected. For example, instead of the reception of the sacrament at the hands of ordained ministers, a man's acceptance with God is sometimes made to depend upon a declaration of belief that Christ has died for him, or that he has been redeemed and saved by Christ. Wherever such statements are forced upon men, there is a tendency to assume that a decisive step in the spiritual life is taken by the mere utterance of them. The motives which actuate the utterer are taken for granted; the existence of such a set of the spiritual nature to God as Deuteronomy demands is supposed to be proved by the mere spoken words; and men who cannot or will not say such things glibly are unchurched without mercy. What is that but the *opus operatum* in its most offensive shape? But in whatever shape it appears, the Deuteronomic demand for love to God, with the heart and soul and strength, as essential to all true spiritual service and sacrifice, condemns it. Love to God and love to men are the main things in true religion. All else is subordinate and secondary. Sacrifice and ritual without these are dead forms. That is the Deuteronomic teaching, and by it, once for all, the true relation of the cultus to the life is fixed.

Nevertheless the priestly and sacrificial system of the Old Testament has even for Christians a present importance, for it is an adumbration of that which was to be done in the death of Christ. It has an unspeakable value, when rightly used, as an object-lesson in the elements which are essential to a right approach to a Holy God on the part of sinful men. Even in heathenism there were such foreshadowings; and nothing is more fitted to exalt our views of the Divine wisdom than to trace, as we can now do, the ways in which man's seekings after God, even beyond the bounds of the chosen people, took forms that were afterwards absorbed and justified in the redeeming work of our Blessed Lord. For example, Professor Robertson Smith says of certain ancient heathen piacular sacrifices, "The dreadful sacrifice is performed, not with savage joy, but with awful sorrow, and in the mystic sacrifices the deity himself suffers with and for the sins of his people and lives again in their new life." Now if we admit that he is not unduly importing into these sacrifices ideas which are really foreign to them, surely awe is the only adequate emotion wherewith a believer in Christ can meet such a strange prophecy, in the lowest religion, of that which is deepest in the highest.*

The sacrificial system in general was founded, in part at least, on belief in the possibility and desirability of communion with God. In the sacrificial feasts this was supposed to be attained, and the essential religious needs of mankind found expression in much of the ritual. If the death of the god, and his returning to life again in his people found a prominent place in piacular sacrifices in various lands, that suggests that in some dim way even heathen men had learned that sin cannot be removed and forgiven without cost to God as well as to man, and that communion in suffering as well as in joy is a necessary element of life with God. The human heart, Divinely biassed, asserted itself in effort after such association with Deity, and in the feeling that sin was that element in life which it would make the highest demand upon the Divine love to set effectively aside.

But if such preparation for the fulness of the time was going on in heathenism, if the mind and heart of man, driven forward by Divinely

* "Ency. Brit.," vol. xxi., p. 138.

ordered experience and its own needs, could produce such forecasts in the ritual of heathen religion, we surely must admit that the religious ritual in Israel had an even more intimate connection with that which was to come. For we claim that in guiding the destinies of Israel God was, in an exceptional manner, revealing Himself, that among them He established the true religion, unfolded it in their history, and prepared as nowhere else for the advent of Him who should make real and objective the union of God and man. Here consequently, if anywhere, we should expect to find the permanent factors in religion recognised even in the forms of worship, and the less permanent allowed to fall away. We should also expect the ritual of the cultus to grow in depth of meaning with time, and that it would more and more recognise the moral and spiritual elements in life. Finally, we should expect that it would be the parent of conceptions rising above and beyond itself, and more fully consonant with the revelation given by Christ than anything in heathenism.

Now all these expectations would seem to have been fulfilled; and it is reasonable to assume that those sacrificial ideas which corresponded to the deepened consciousness of sin, and synchronised apparently with the decay of Israel's political independence, are rightly applied to the elucidation of the meaning of Christ's death. Of course mistakes may be and have been made in the application of this principle; the most common being that of forcing every detail of the imperfect and temporary provision into the interpretation of the perfect and eternal. Sometimes, too, the significance of the life and coming of Christ are obscured by a too exclusive attention to His sacrificial death. But the principle in itself must be sound, if Christianity is in any sense to be regarded as the completion and full development of the Old Testament religion. Besides the immediate significance of sacrifice which the worshippers perceived and by which they were edified, there was another significance which belonged to it as a step in the long progress which had been marked out for this people in the Divine purpose. Regarded from that standpoint, the sacrifices, and the ritual connected with them, had a meaning for the future also, were in fact typical of the final sacrifice which would need to be offered only once for all. How much of this was understood by the men of ancient Israel we have no means of knowing. Some, doubtless, had a faint perception of it; but at its clearest it was probably more a dissatisfaction with what they had, leading them to look for some better sacrifice, than any more definite understanding. But what they only dimly guessed was, as we can now see, the inner meaning of all; and it is perfectly legitimate to use both the provisional and the perfected revelations to explain each other. On these grounds the New Testament freely makes use of the ancient ritual to bring out the full significance of the sacrifice of Christ.

No doubt a different view has to be reckoned with. Many say that the whole of this typical reference is a begging of the question. In the infancy of mankind sacrifice was a natural way of expressing adoration and of seeking the favour of the gods. In the heathen world it reached its highest manifestation in those piacular sacrifices of which Robertson Smith speaks, but which nevertheless were merely an outgrowth of Totemism. In Israel sacrifice was taken up by the religion of Yahweh and embodied in it. The spiritual forces which were at work in that nation used it as a means whereby to express themselves; and when Christ came to complete the revelation, His purely ethical and spiritual work was unavoidably expressed in sacrificial terms. But that is no guarantee that the essential thing in the work of Christ was sacrifice. On the contrary, the sacrificial language used about it is of no real importance. It is simply the natural and unavoidable form of expression, in that place and at that time, for any spiritual deliverance. In short, had there been really nothing sacrificial in the death of Christ, the religious meaning and significance of it would have been expressed in sacrificial language, for no other was available. Consequently the presence of such language in the New Testament does not prove that the sacrificial meaning belongs to its main and permanent significance. The sacrificial idea, on this view of things, belongs, both in Israel and in heathenism, to the elements which Christianity superseded and did away with; and it is consequently an anachronism to bring it in to explain and elucidate anything done or taught under this new dispensation.

But such a view is singularly narrow, and unjust to the past. It surely is more honouring to both God and man to suppose that the capital religious ideas of the race, those ideas which have been everywhere present and have been seen to deepen and refine with every advance man has made, have permanent value. Moreover, on any view, it is probable that in them the essential religious needs of human nature have found expression. If so, we should expect that they would in the end be met, and that the perfect religion, when it did come, would not ignore but satisfy the demand which the nature of man and the providence of God had originated and combined to strengthen. Further, it is the very essence of the Scriptural view of Christ that He perfected and carried to their highest power all the essential features in the religious constitution of Israel. He *was* indeed the true Israel, and all Israel's tasks fell to Him. As Prophet, Priest, and Messianic King alike, He excelled all His predecessors, who were what they were only because they had, in their degree, done part of the work which He was to come to finish. Apart from the religion of the Old Testament, therefore, Christ is unintelligible, and that, in turn, without Him, has neither a progress nor a goal. Belief in a Divine direction of the world would in itself be sufficient to forbid the separation of one from the other. If so, it will follow that the sacrificial idea is essential to the interpretation of our Lord's work. That idea grew in complexity with the growth of the higher religion. It was at its deepest when religious thought and feeling had done its most perfect work; and on every principle of evolution we should expect that, instead of disappearing at the next stage, it would, though transformed, be more influential than ever. It is so if Christ's death is regarded from the point of view of sacrifice; whereas, if that is laid aside like a worn-out garment, it can never have been anything anywhere but an excrescence and a superstition. That has not been so; the essential ideas connected with sacrifice, and forgiveness by means of it, were lessons Divinely taught in the childhood of the world, to prepare men to understand the Divinest mystery of history when it should be manifested to the world.

CHAPTER XVI.

LAWS AGAINST IDOLATROUS ACTS AND CUSTOMS.

Deuteronomy xiii., xiv.

Having thus set forth the law which was to crown and complete the long resistance of faithful Israel to idolatry, our author goes on to prohibit and to decree punishment for any action likely to lead to the worship of false gods. He absolutely forbids any inquiry into the religions of the Canaanites. "Take heed to thyself that thou inquire not after their gods, saying, How do these nations serve their gods? even so will I do likewise." All that was acceptable to Yahweh was included in the law of Israel, and beyond that they were on no account to go in their worship. "What thing soever I command you, that shall ye observe to do: thou shalt not add thereto nor diminish from it." But it should be observed that the inquiry here forbidden has nothing in common with the scientific inquiries of Comparative Religion in our time. Curiosity of that kind, supported by the motive of discovering how religion had grown, was unknown at that early age of the world, probably everywhere, certainly in Israel. The only curiosity powerful enough to result in action then was that which tried to learn how the ritual might be made more potent in its influence over Yahweh by gathering attractive features from every known religion. That was one of the distinguishing characteristics of Manasseh's reign. The Canaanite religions, the religions of Egypt and Assyria, were all laid under contribution; and wherever there was a feature which promised additional power with God or the gods, that was eagerly adopted. Israel had lost faith in Yahweh, owing to the successes of Assyria. In unbelieving terror men were wildly grasping at any means of safety. They worshipped Yahweh, lest He should do them harm, but they joined with Him the gods of their foes, to secure if possible their favour also. Inquiry into other religions, with the intent of adopting something from them which would make either Yahweh or the strange gods, or both, propitious to them, was rife. Like the heathen population who had been transported by Assyria into the territory of the ten tribes, men "feared Yahweh, and served their graven images." All that is here sternly condemned, and Judah is taught to look only to the Divine commands for effective means of approach to their God. The prohibition, therefore, does not import mere fanatical opposition to knowledge. It is a necessary practical measure of defence against idolatry; and only those who can disapprove of it who are incapable of estimating the value which the true religion in its Old Testament shape had and has for the world. To preserve that was the high and unique calling of Israel. Any narrowness, real or supposed, which this great task imposed upon that people, is amply compensated for by their guardianship of the spiritual life of mankind.

But if inquiry into lower religions was forbidden, there could be nothing but the sternest condemnation for those who had inquired, and then endeavoured to seduce the chosen people. Deuteronomy, therefore, takes three typical cases—first, seduction by one who was respected because of high religious office, then seduction by one who had influence because of close bonds of natural affection, and lastly that of a community which would be likely to have influence by force of numbers—and gives inexorably stern directions how such evil is to be met. There can be little doubt that the cases are not imaginary. In the evil days which the Deuteronomist had fallen upon they were probably of frequent occurrence, and they are, consequently, provided against as real and present evils. Naturally the writer takes the most difficult case first. If an Israelite prophet, with all his religious prestige as a confidant of Yahweh, and still more with the prestige of successful prediction in his favour, shall attempt to lead men to join other gods to Yahweh in their worship—for that and not rejection of Yahweh for the exclusive service of strange gods is almost certainly meant—then they were not to listen to him. They were to fall back upon the original principle of the Mosaic teaching as it was restated in Deuteronomy, that Yahweh alone was to be their God. Some lynx-eyed critics have discovered here the cloven hoof of legalism. They think they see here the free spirit of prophecy, to which untrammelled initiative was the very breath of life, subjected to the bondage of written law, and so doomed to death. But probably such a mood is unnecessarily elegiac. It is not to written law that prophecy is subjected here. It is the actual life-principle of Yahwism in its simplest form which prophecy is required to respect; that is, ultimately, it is called upon simply to respect itself. Its own existence depended upon faithfulness to Yahweh. If it had a mission at all, it was to proclaim Him and to declare His character. If it had a distinction which severed it from mere heathen soothsaying, it was that it had been raised by the inspiration of Yahweh into the region of "the true, the good, the eternal," and its whole power lay in its keeping open the communication with that region. It is therefore only the law of its own inner being to which prophecy is here bound; and the people are instructed that, whatever reputation or even supernatural power it might have attained to, it was to be obeyed only when true to itself and to the faith. Nothing was to make men stagger from that foundation. Not even the working of miracles was to mislead the people, for only on the plane of Yahweh's revelation had even miracle any worth. This is the sound and wholesome doctrine of true prophecy, and other utterances on the subject in our book must be taken in conjunction with it. Religious faithfulness, not foretelling, is the essence of it, and by that the prophet is to be inexorably judged. If any prophet, therefore, leads men to strange gods, his character and his powers only make him more dangerous and his punishment more inexorable. "That prophet, or that dreamer of dreams, shall be put to death." He comes under the ban. "So shalt thou put away the evil from the midst of thee."

Similarly, when family ties and family affection are perverted to be instruments of seduction, they are to be disregarded, just as religious reputation and miraculous power were to be set aside. If a brother, or a son, or a daughter, or a wife, or a friend, shall secretly entice a man to "serve other gods," then he shall not only not yield, but he must slay the tempter. It is characteristic of the Deuteronomist that, by the qualifications of the various relationships he mentions, he should show his sympathy and his insight into the depths of both family affection and friendship. "Thy brother, the son of thy mother," "the wife of thy bosom," "the friend which is as thine own soul," even these, near as they are to thee, must be sacrificed if they are false to Israel and to Israel's God. Nay more, "Thou shalt surely kill him; thine hand shall be upon him to put him to death, and afterwards the hand of all the people, and thou shalt stone him with stones that he die." Upon him, too, the ban shall be laid.

Nor, finally, shall their multitude shield those who suffered themselves to be perverted. If a city should have been led away by sons of Belial, *i. e.*, by worthless men, to worship strange gods, then the whole city was to be put to the ban. It was to be immediately stormed, every living creature put to death, and all the spoil of it burnt "unto Yahweh their God."; and the ruins were to be a "mound for ever"—that is, a place accursed. Only on these terms could Yahweh be turned away from the fierceness of His anger at such treason and unfaithfulness among His people. The Canaanites had been condemned to death that their idolatries and vices might not corrupt the spiritual faith of Israel. There was no other way, if the treasure which had been committed to this nation was to be preserved. As Robertson Smith has said, "Experience shows that primitive religious beliefs are practically indestructible except by the destruction of the race in which they are engrained." But if so, it was perhaps even more necessary that idolaters within Israel should be also extirpated. We may think the punishment harsh; and our modern doctrines concerning toleration can by no ingenuity be brought into harmony with it. But the times were fierce, and men were not easily restrained. In more civilised communities excessive severity in punishment defeats itself, for it enlists sympathy on the side of the criminal. But among a people like the Hebrews, probably severity succeeded where mercy would have been flouted. In India our administrators have had to confess that the horrible recklessness and severity of punishment in the Mahratta states of the old type suppressed crime as the infinitely more just and better organised but milder British police organisations could not then do. "Probably the success of barbarous methods of repressing crime is best explained by their origin in and close connection with a primitive state of society. Because punishments were inhuman, they struck terror where no other motive would deter from crime."[*] In other and Scriptural words, the hardness of men's hearts made such harshness unavoidable.

Taking the whole of this thirteenth chapter into consideration, therefore, we see how high and severe were the demands which Old Testament religion, as taught in Deuteronomy, made upon its votaries. It presupposes on the part of the people an insight into the fundamentally spiritual nature of their faith entirely unobscured by ritual and sacrifice. They were expected to pass beyond the teachings of accredited spiritual guides, beyond even the evidence of supernatural power, and to test all by the moral and spiritual truth, once delivered to them by prophet and by miracle, and now a secure possession. Spiritual truth received and lived by is thus set above everything else as the test and the judge of all. Other things were merely ladders by which men had been brought to the truth in religion. Once there, nothing should move them; and any further guidance which purported to come from even the heavenly places was to be tried and accepted, only if it corroborated the fundamental truths already received and attested by experience in actual life. Loyalty to ascertained truth, that is, is greater than loyalty to teachers, or to that which seems to be supernatural; and the chief power for which a prophet is to be reverenced is not that by which he gives a true forecast of the future, but that which impels him to speak the truth about God.

Even at this day, and for believers in Christ, after all the teaching and experience of eighteen Christian centuries, this is a high, almost an unattainable, standard to set up. Even to-day it is thought an advanced position that miracles as a security for truth are subordinate and inferior to the light of the truth itself as exhibited in the lives of faithful men. Yet that is precisely what the Deuteronomist teaches. He has no doubt about miracles. He regards them as being Divinely sent, even when they might be made use of to mislead; but he calls upon his people to disregard them if they seem to point towards unfaithfulness to God. Their supreme trust is to be that Yahweh cannot deny Himself. If he seem to do so by giving the sanction of miracle to teaching which denies Him, that is only to prove men, to know whether they love Yahweh their God with all their heart and with all their soul. The inner certainty of those who have had communion with Yahweh is to override everything else. "Whosoever loves God with a pure heart," says Calvin, "is armed with the invincible power of the Divine Spirit, that he should not be ensnared by falsehoods."[*] This has always been the confidence of religious reformers who have had real power. Luther, for example, took his stand upon the New Testament and his own personal experience; and by what he *knew* of God he judged all that the most venerable tradition, and the authority of the Church, and the examples of saintly men claimed to set forth as binding upon him. "Here stand I: I can do no other: God help me." He felt that he had hold of the heart of the revelation of God as it was made in Christ, and he rejected, without scruple, whatever in itself or in its results contradicted or obscured that. Inspired and upheld by this consciousness, he faced a hostile world and a raging Church with equanimity. It is always so that abuses have been removed and innovations that are hurtful warded off in the Church of God.

But there is a difficulty here. As against the historical examples which show how much good may be wrought by this unshaken mind when accompanied by adequate insight, many, perhaps even more, instances can be adduced where unbending assertion of individual conviction has led to fanaticism and irreligion; or, as has even more frequently been the case, has blinded men's eyes, and made them resist with immovable obstinacy teachings on which the future of religion

---

[*] Tupper, "Our Indian Protectorate," p. 248.

[*] "Commentary on Pentateuch," vol. i., p. 448.

depended. On the altar of uncompromising fidelity to the letter of the faith delivered to them, men in all ages have offered up love and gentleness and fairness, and that open mind to which alone God can speak. How then can they be sure, when they disregard their teachers and defy even signs from heaven, that they are really only holding up the banner of faith in an evil day, and are not hardening themselves against God? The answer is that, since the matter concerns the spiritual life, there are no clear, mechanical dividing lines which can be pointed out and respected. Nothing but spiritual insight can teach a man what the absolutely essential and the less essential elements of religion are. Nothing else can give him that power of distinguishing great things from small which here is of such cardinal importance. Probably the nearest approach to effective guidance may be found in this principle, that when all points in a man's faith are to him equally important, when he frets as much in regard to divergence from his own religious practices as in regard to denial of the faith altogether, he must certainly be wrong. Such a temper must necessarily resist all change; and since progress is as much a law in the religious life as in any other, it must be found at times fighting against God. Otherwise, stagnation would be the test of truth, and the principles of the Christian faith would be branded as so shallow and so easily exhausted, that their whole significance could be seized and set forth at once by the generation which heard the apostles. That was far from being the case. The post-apostolic Church, for instance, did not understand St. Paul. It turned rather to the simpler ideas of the mass of Christians, and elaborated its doctrines almost entirely on that basis. During the centuries since then many lessons of unspeakable value have been learned by the Christian world. The Church has been enriched by the thoughts and teachings of multitudes of men of genius. The providential chances and changes of all these centuries have immensely widened and deepened Christian experience. Stagnation consequently cannot be made the test of Christian truth. We must be open to new light on the meaning of Divine revelation, or we fail altogether, as the Israelites would have done had they refused to accept the teaching of any prophet after the first. This much may, however, be said on the affirmative side, that when a man has thoughtfully and prayerfully decided that the central element of his faith is attacked, he cannot but resist, and if he is faithful he will resist in the spirit of the passage we are discussing. His assertion of his individual conviction, even if it be mistaken, will do little harm. Time will be in favour of the truth. But mistake will be rare, indeed, when men are taught to assert in this manner only the things by which the soul lives, when only the actual channels of communion with God are thus defended to the uttermost. These any thoughtful, patient man who looks for and yields to the guidance of the Holy Spirit of Christ will almost infallibly recognise, and by these he will take his stand, for he can do no other.

But precautions against idolatry are not exhausted by the war declared upon men who might attempt to lead the Israelite into evil. Besides insidious human enemies, there were also insidious customs originating in heathenism, and still redolent of idolatry even when they were severed from any overt connection with it. Ancient rituals, ancient superstitions, hateful remnants of bloodthirsty pagan rites, were being revived in the Deuteronomist's day on every hand, because faith in the higher religion that had superseded them had been shaken. Like streams from hidden reservoirs suddenly reopened, idolatrous and magical practices were overflowing the land, and were finding in popular customs, harmless in better days, channels for their return into the life of those who had formerly risen above them.

Some of these were more hurtful than others, and two are singled out at the beginning of chapter xiv. as those which a people holy unto Yahweh must specially avoid: "Ye shall not cut yourselves, nor make any baldness between your eyes for the dead." The grounds for avoiding these practices are first given, and we may probably assume that they are the grounds also for the other enactments which follow. They are these: "Ye are the children of Yahweh your God," and "Thou art a holy people unto Yahweh thy God, and Yahweh hath chosen thee to be a peculiar people unto Himself, out of all peoples that are upon the face of the earth." The last of these reasons is common to the Exodus code with Deuteronomy, and comes even more prominently into view in the Levitical law. Just as Yahweh alone was to be their God, they alone were to be Yahweh's people, and they were to be holy to Him, *i. e.*, were to separate themselves to Him; for in its earliest meaning to be holy is simply to be separate to Yahweh. This whole dispensation of law, that is, was meant to separate the people of Israel from the idolatrous world, and in this separation we have the key to much that would otherwise be hard to comprehend. Looked at from the point of view of revelation, petty details about tonsure, about clean and unclean animals, and so on, seem incredibly unworthy; and many have said to themselves, How can the God of the whole earth have really been the author of laws dealing with such trivialities? But when we regard these as provisions intended to secure the separation of the chosen people, they assume quite another aspect. Then we see that they had to be framed in contrast to the idolatries of the surrounding nations, and are not meant to have further spiritual or moral significance.

But the first reason given is a higher and more important one, which occurs here for the first time in Deuteronomy: "Ye are the children of Yahweh your God." In heathen lands such a title of honour was common, because physically most worshippers of false gods were regarded as their children. But in Israel, where such physical sonship would have been rejected with horror as impairing the Divine holiness, the spiritual sonship was asserted of the individual much more slowly. In Yahweh's command to Moses to threaten Pharaoh with the death of his firstborn son, and in Hosea xi. 1, Israel collectively is called Yahweh's firstborn and His son. In Hosea i. 10 it is prophesied that in the Messianic time, "in the place where it was said unto them, Ye are not My people, it shall be said unto them, Ye are the sons of the living God." But here for the first time this high title is bestowed upon the actual individual Israelites. It was perhaps implied in the Deuteronomist's view of God's fatherly treatment of the nation in the desert, and still more in his demand for the love of the individual heart. Yet only here is it brought plainly forth as a ground for the regulation of life according to Yahweh's commands. Each son of Israel is also a son of God; and by none of his acts or habits should he bring disgrace upon his spiritual Father. Likeness to God is expected and demanded of him. It is his function in the world to represent Him, to give expression to the Divine character in all his ways. This is the Israelite's high calling, and the religious application of *noblesse oblige* to such matters as follow, gives a dignity and importance to all of them such as in their own nature they could hardly claim.

"Ye shall not cut yourselves, nor make any baldness between your eyes for the dead." Israel was not to express grief for the dead in these ways, first because that was the custom of other nations, and secondly still more because the origin and meaning of such rites was idolatrous, and as such altogether unworthy of Yahweh's sons. "Both," says Robertson Smith, "occur not only in mourning, but in the worship of the gods, and belong to the sphere of heathen superstition."* Elsewhere he explains the cutting of themselves to be the making of a blood covenant with the dead, just as the priests of Baal in their worship tried to get their god to come to their help by making a covenant of blood with him at his altar.† This naturally tended to bring in the superstitions of necromancy, and opened the way also for the worship of the dead. Many traces of its previous existence among the Israelite tribes are to be found in the Scriptures; and the probability is that as ancestor-worship ruled the life and shaped the thoughts of Greeks and Romans till Christianity appeared, so Yahwism alone had broken its power over Israel. But such superstitions die hard, and in the general recrudescence of almost forgotten forms of heathenism at this time, this cult may very well have been reasserting itself. As for the shaving of the front part of the head, that had a precisely similar import. "It had exactly the same sense as the offering of the mourner's blood."‡ "When the hair of the living is deposited with the dead, and the hair of the dead remains with the living, a permanent bond of connection unites the two."

The prohibition as food of the animals and birds called "unclean" was another measure obviously of the same nature as the prohibition of heathen mourning practices; but in its details it is more difficult to explain. Probably, however, it was a more potent instrument of separation than any other. In India to-day the gulf between the flesh-eater and the orthodox vegetarian Hindu is utterly impassable; and in the east of Europe and in Palestine, where the Jewish restrictions as to food are still regarded, the orthodox Jew is separated from all Gentiles as by a wall. In travelling he never appears at meals with his fellow-travellers. All the food he requires he carries with him in a basket; and at every place where he stops it is the duty of the Jewish community to supply him with proper food, that he may not be tempted to defile himself with anything unclean. But it is very difficult for us now to bring the individual prohibitions under one head, and it seems impossible to explain them from any one point of view.

* "The Old Testament in the Jewish Church," p. 366.
† "Religion of the Semites," p. 304.
‡ *Ibid.*, p. 306.

Some of the animals and birds prohibited were probably, then, animals eaten in connection with idolatrous feasts by the neighbouring heathen. Isa. lxv. 4 shows that swine's flesh was eaten at sacrificial meals by idolaters, and from the expression "broth of abominable things is in their vessels" it is clear that the flesh of other animals was so used. All these would necessarily be prohibited to Israel; but beyond a few, such as the swine, which was sacrificed to Tammuz or Adonis, and the mouse and the wild ass, we have no means of knowing what they were. That this is a *vera causa* of such prohibitions is shown by the facts mentioned by Professor Robertson Smith, that "Simeon Stylites forbade his Saracen converts to eat the flesh of the camel, which was the chief element in the sacrificial meals of the Arabs, and our own prejudice against the use of horse-flesh is a relic of an old ecclesiastical prohibition framed at the time when the eating of such food was an act of worship to Odin." The very ancient and stringent prohibition of blood as an article of diet is probably to be accounted for in this way also. Blood was eaten at heathen sacrificial feasts; without other reason that would be sufficient. These are the general lines which must have determined the list of clean animals in the view of the lawgiver, since he brings them in under the head of idolatry and under the two general grounds we have discussed.

Jewish writers, however, especially since Maimonides, have regarded these prohibitions as aiming primarily at sanitary ends, and as a proof of their efficacy have adduced the unusually high average health of the Jews, and their almost complete exemption from certain classes of disease. No such point of view is suggested in the Scriptures themselves, for it would surely be rather far-fetched to class possible disease as an infringement of the holiness demanded of Israel, or as a thing unworthy of Yahweh's sons. Nevertheless a general view of the list of clean animals here given would support the idea that sanitary considerations also had *something* to do with the classification. The practical effect of the rule laid down is to exclude all the *carnivora* among quadrupeds, and so far as we can interpret the nomenclature, the *raptores* among birds.* "Amongst fish, those which were allowed contain unquestionably the most wholesome varieties." Further, the nations of antiquity which developed such categories of clean and unclean animals seem in the main to have taken the same line. The ground of this probably is the natural disgust with which unclean feeders are always regarded. Animals and birds especially which feed, or may be supposed to feed, on carrion, are everywhere disliked, and as a rule they are unsuitable for food. Grass-eating animals, on the other hand, are always regarded as clean. Scaleless fish, too, are generally more or less slimy to the touch, and with them reptiles are altogether forbidden. All this seems to show that a natural sentiment of disgust, for whatever reason felt, was active in the selection of the animals marked unclean by men of every race. The pre-Mosaic customary law on this subject would, of course, have this characteristic in common with similar laws of primitive nations. When the worship of Yahweh was introduced, most of this would be taken over, only such modifications being introduced as the

* Smith's "Dictionary of the Bible," vol. iii. p. 1589.

higher religion demanded. In some main elements, therefore, the Mosaic law on this subject would be a repetition of what is to be found elsewhere. Hence a general tendency to health may be expected; for besides the guidance which healthy disgust would give, a long experience must also have been registered in such laws. The influence of them in promoting health has recently been acknowledged by the *Lancet;* and though that reason for observing them is not mentioned in Scripture, we may view it as a proof that the Jewish legislators were under an influence which brought them, perhaps even when they knew it not, into relation with what was wholesome in the practices and customs of their place and time.

Beyond these three reasons for the laws regarding food, all is the wildest speculation. If other reasons underlie these laws, we cannot now ascertain what they were. For a time it was the custom to ascribe the Jewish laws to Persian influence, though from the nature of the case such laws must have been part of the heritage of Israel from pre-Mosaic time. Even to-day Jewish writers ascribe them to the evil effect which bad food has upon the soul, either by infecting it with the characteristics of the unclean beasts, or by rendering it impenetrable to good influences.* But, as usual, it is the allegorical interpreters who carry off the palm. Animals that chew the cud were to be eaten, because they symbolised those who "read, mark, learn, and inwardly digest" the Divine law: those which divide the hoof are examples of those who distinguish between good and bad actions; and in the ostrich one interpreter finds an analogue to the bad commentators who pervert the words of Holy Scripture.

Hitherto in chapter xiv. we have been dealing with material to which a parallel can be found only in the small code of laws contained in Lev. xvii.-xxvi., commonly called the Law of Holiness, and in the Priestly Code.† But the two remaining directions regarding food, which are contained in the twenty-first verse, are parallel to prohibitions in the Law of the Covenant. The first, "Ye shall not eat of anything that dieth of itself . . . for thou art an holy people unto Yahweh thy God," is parallel to Exod. xxii. 31. "And ye shall be holy men unto Me: therefore ye shall not eat any flesh that is torn of beasts in the field," and to Lev. xvii. 15, "Every soul that eateth that which dieth of itself, or that which is torn of beasts, whether he be homeborn or a stranger, he shall wash his clothes, and bathe himself in water, and be unclean until the evening." The ground for prohibiting such food, was, of course, that the blood was in it. But there is a divergence between the parallel laws, which is seen clearly when we take into account the destination of the flesh of the animal so dying. In Exodus it is said, "To the dogs shall ye cast it." In Deuteronomy the command is, "To the stranger within thy gates ye shall give it, and he shall eat of it, or ye may sell it unto a foreigner." In Leviticus it is taken for granted that an Israelite and also a stranger may eat either of the *nebhelah,* that which dieth of itself, or the *terephah,* that which is torn; and if either do so it is prescribed only that he should wash, and should be unclean until the evening.

Here, therefore, we have one of the cases in which the traditional hypothesis—that the Law of the Covenant was given at Sinai when Israel arrived there, the laws of the Priestly Code probably not many weeks after, and the code of Deuteronomy only thirty-eight or thirty-nine years later, but before the laws had come fully into effect by the occupation of Canaan—raises a difficulty. Why should the Sinaitic law say that *terephah* is not to be eaten by any one, but cast to the dogs, and the Levitical law in so short a time after make the eating of that and *nebhelah* mere cause of subordinate uncleanness to both Israelite and stranger, while Deuteronomy permits the Israelite either to give the *nebhelah* to the stranger that he may eat it, or to make it an article of traffic with the foreigner? Keil's explanation is certainly feasible, that in Exodus we have the law, in Leviticus the provision for accidental, or perhaps wilful, disobedience of it under the pressure of hunger, while in Deuteronomy we have a permission to sell, lest on the plea of waste the law might be ignored. But the position of the "$g\bar{e}r$," or stranger, is not accounted for. In Leviticus he is bound to the worship of Yahweh, and can no more eat *nebhelah* or *terephah* than the native Israelite can, while in Deuteronomy he is on a lower stage than the Israelite as regards ceremonial cleanness, and much on the same level as the *nokhri,* the foreigner, who in Deuteronomy is dealt with as an inferior, not bound to the same scrupulosity as the Israelite (Deut. xv. 3, 23, 29). There does not appear to be any explanation of such a change in less than forty years; more especially as the moment at which the change would on that hypothesis be made was precisely the moment when the stranger was about for the first time to become an important element in Israelite life. If, on the other hand, the order of the codes be Exodus, Deuteronomy, Leviticus, then the Exodus law, which does not consider the stranger, would suit the earliest stage of Israel's history, when the stranger would generally be a spy. Later, he crept into Israelite life, and gradually received more and more consideration; especially in the days of Solomon, when the Chronicler estimates the number of the strangers at over a hundred and fifty thousand. But he was not recognised at that stage as fully bound to all an Israelite's duties, or as possessed of all an Israelite's privileges, and that is precisely the position he occupies in Deuteronomy. In the Priestly Code, however, at a time when the stranger had practically become a proselyte, the ideal Kingdom of God includes the "stranger," and gives him a position which differs little from that of the homeborn. That would make these different laws answer to different periods of Israel's history, and would coincide with what has been otherwise found to be the order of Israel's legal development.

The second prohibition, which runs parallel to what we find in Exodus, is the somewhat enigmatical one that a kid should not be sodden in its mother's milk. What it was in this act which made it seem necessary to issue such a command cannot now be ascertained with any certainty. Most probably it was connected in some way with heathen ceremonies, perhaps at a har-

---

* Dillmann, "Deuteronomy," p. 483.
† This, of course, does not show that P must have been known to D, but it proves that as regards material P and D have drawn from the same source, and that older documents, or customs at least, underlie both.

vest feast; for, as we have seen, it is a ruling motive throughout all this section that the Israelites should reject everything which among their neighbours was connected with idolatry.

CHAPTER XVII.

THE SPEAKERS FOR GOD—I. THE KING.

DEUTERONOMY xvii. 14-20.

IN approaching the main section of the legislation it will be necessary, in accordance with the expository character of the series to which this volume belongs, to abandon the consecutive character of the comment. It would lead us too far into archæology to discuss the meaning and origin of all the legal provisions which follow. Moreover nothing short of an extensive commentary would do them justice, and for our purpose we must endeavour to group the prescriptions of the code, and discuss them so. As it stands there is no arrangement traceable. So utterly without order is it, that it can hardly be thought that it is in the exact shape in which it left its author's hands. Transpositions and misplacements must, one thinks, have taken place to some extent. We are thus left free to make our own arrangements, and it would appear most fitting to discuss the code under the five heads of National Life, Economic Life, and three fundamental qualities of a healthy national life—Purity, Justice, and the Treatment of the Poor. Every phase of the laws which remain for discussion can easily be brought under these heads, and this chapter will discuss the first of them, the organisation of the national life.

It is a striking instance of the accuracy of the national memory that there is a clear and conscious testimony to the fact that for long there was no king in Israel. Had the later historians been at the mercy of a tradition so deeply influenced by later times as it pleases some critics to suppose, it would seem inexplicable that Moses should not have been represented as a king, and especially that the conquest should not have been represented as a king's work. Evidently there was a perfectly clear national consciousness of the earlier circumstances of the nation, and it presents us with an outline of the original constitution which is very simple and credible. According to this the tribes whom Moses led were ruled in the main by their own sheikhs or elders. Under these again were the clans or fathers' houses similarly governed; and lastly, there were the families in the wider sense, made up of the individual households and governed by their heads. So far as can be gathered, Moses did not interfere with this fundamental organisation at all. He added to it only his own supremacy, as the mediator and means of communication between Yahweh and His people. As such, his decision was final in all matters too difficult for the sheikhs and judges. But the fundamental point never lost sight of was that Yahweh alone was their ruler, their legislator, their leader in war, and the doer of justice among His people. From the very first moment of Israel's national existence therefore, from the moment that it passed the Red Sea, Yahweh was acknowledged as King, and Moses was simply His representative. That is the cardinal fact in this nation's life, and amid all the difficulties and changes of its later history that was always held to. Even when kings were appointed, they were regarded only as the viceroys of Yahweh. In this way the whole of the national affairs received a religious colour; and those who look at them from a religious standpoint have a justification which would have been less manifest under other circumstances.

It is, therefore, no delusion of later times which finds in Israelite institutions a deep religious meaning. Nor is the persistence with which the Scriptural historians regard only the religious aspects of national life to be laid as a fault to their charge. It is nothing to the purpose to say that the bulk of the people had no thoughts of that kind, that the whole fabric of the national institutions appeared to them in a different light. We have no right to lower the meaning of things to the gross materialism of the populace. One would almost think, to hear some Old Testament critics speak, that in this most ideal realm of religion we can be safe from illusion only when ideal points of view are abandoned, that only in the commonest light of common day have we any security that we are not deceiving ourselves. But most of these same men would resent it bitterly if that standard were applied to the history of the lands they themselves love. What Englishman would think that Great Britain's career and destiny were rightly estimated if imperial sentiment and humanitarian aims were thrust aside in favour of purely material considerations? Why then should it be supposed that the views and opinions of the multitude are the only safe criterion to be applied to the institutions of God's ancient people?

In truth, there is no reason why we should think so. The Divine kingship made it impossible that the higher minds should be content with the low aims of the opportunists of their day, whether these were of the multitude or not. Even the entrance into Canaan, which to the mass of the people was, in the first place, a mere acquisition of territory and wealth, was idealised for the leaders of the people by the thought that it was the land promised by Yahweh to their fathers, the land in which they should live in communion with Him. Generally, it may be said that the desire for communion with God was the impelling and formative power in Israel. The thoughts of even the dullest and most earthly were touched by that ideal at times; and no leader, whether royal, or priestly, or prophetic, ever really succeeded among this people who did not keep that persistently in view as the true goal of his efforts. Moreover this gave its depth of meaning to the whole movement of history in Israel. Every triumph and defeat, every lapse and every reform had, owing to this direction of the people's efforts, a significance far beyond itself. These were not merely incidents in the history of an obscure people; they were the pulsations and movements of the world's advance to the full revelation of God. All that would have been wholly national or tribal in the institutions and arrangements of an ordinary people was in Israel lifted up into the religious sphere; and the orders of men who spoke for the invisible King—the earthly king, the priest, and the prophet—became naturally the organs of the national life.

The king's position was entirely dependent upon Yahweh. He was to be chosen by Yahweh, he was to act for Yahweh, and no king could rightly fill his place in Israel who was not loyal to that conception. It is in this sense that David was the man after God's own heart. He, in contrast to Saul and to many of the later kings, accepted with entire loyalty, notwithstanding his great natural powers, the position of viceroy for Yahweh. It is, therefore, an essential truth which underlies the Scriptural judgment that the kings who made themselves, or attempted to make themselves, independent of Yahweh, were false to Israel and to their true calling. And this is why Samuel, when the people demanded a king, regarded the movement with stern disapproval, and why he received an oracle denouncing the movement as a falling away from Yahweh. For, in the first place, the motive for the people's request, their desire to be like other nations, was in itself a rejection of their God. It repudiated, in part at least, the position of Israel as His peculiar people, and implied that an earthly king would do more for them than Yahweh had done; whereas if they had been faithful and united enough in spirit they would have found victory easy. In the second, the request in itself was a confession of unfitness for their high national calling; it was a confession of failure under the conditions which had been Divinely appointed for them. Not only in the eyes of the Biblical historian therefore, but as a plain matter of fact, the demand was an expression of dissatisfaction on the people's part with their invisible King. They needed something less spiritual than Yahweh's invisible presence and the prophetic word to guide them. But since they had declared themselves thus unfaithful, Yahweh had to deal with them at that level, and granted their request as a concession to their unbelief and hardness of heart.

That is the representation of the Books of Samuel; and the absence of any similar law from the codes before Deuteronomy confirms the view that the earthly kingship was not an essential part of the polity of Israel, but a mere episode. Nowhere in legislation save here in Deuteronomy is the king ever mentioned, and nowhere, not even here, is any provision made for his maintenance. No civil taxes are appointed by any law, while the most ample provision is made for the presentation direct to Yahweh, as Lord paramount, of tithes and firstfruits.

The history and the law alike agree therefore in regarding the kingship as somewhat of an excrescence upon the national polity; and this law, where alone the king's existence is recognised, confines itself strictly to securing the theocratic character of the constitution. He must be chosen by Yahweh; he must be a born worshipper of Yahweh, not a foreigner; and he must rule in accordance with the law given by Yahweh. Further, the ideal Israelite king must be on his guard against the grossly voluptuous luxury which Oriental sovereigns have never been able to resist, either in ancient or modern times; and also against the lust for war and conquest which was the ruling passion of Assyrian and Egyptian kings. Evidently too the ideal king of Israel was, like Bedouin sheikhs now, expected to be rich, able to maintain his state out of his own revenues. The tribute paid by subject peoples, together with the booty taken in war and the profits of trade, were his only legitimate sources of income beyond his own wealth. Every other exaction was more or less of an oppression. He had no right to make any claims upon the land, for that was held direct of Yahweh. Nor were there any regular taxes, so far as the Old Testament informs us. The only approach to that would appear to be that the presents with which his subjects voluntarily approached the king were sometimes and by some rulers made permanent demands; at least that would seem to be the meaning of the somewhat obscure statement in 1 Sam. xvii. 25 that King Saul would reward the slayer of Goliath by making "his father's house free in Israel." Some kind of regular exaction from which the victorious champion's family should be free must here be referred to; but it would not be safe, in the absence of all other evidence, to suppose that regular taxes in the modern sense are referred to. More probably something of the nature of the "benevolences" which Edward IV. introduced into England as a source of revenue is meant. If a popular and powerful king of Israel was in want of money, he could always secure it by ordering those able to afford handsome presents to appear yearly before him with such gifts as a loyal subject should offer. For the convenience of all parties an indication of how much would be expected might be made, and then he would have what to all intents and purposes would be a tax. Along with this he might also enforce the *corvée;* but such things were always regarded as excesses of despotic power. That Samuel in his *mishpat hammelekh* (1 Sam. viii. 15) warns the people that the king would demand of them a tithe of their cereal crops and of the fruit of their vineyards and of their sheep, does not contradict this reading of the passage in 1 Sam. xvii. For though chapter viii. belongs to the later portion of 1 Samuel and may therefore represent what the kings had actually claimed, yet it in no way endorses such demands. On the contrary, it indicates that such exactions would bring the people into slavery to the king by the phrase "And ye shall be to him for slaves." All that is mentioned there, consequently, is part of the evil the kingship would bring with it, and cannot in any way be regarded as a legal provision for the maintenance of royalty.

It is not probable, therefore, that in these prescriptions the author of Deuteronomy is repeating a more ancient law. No such law has come down to us. Dillmann supposes the provision that the king should always be an Israelite to be ancient; and indeed at first sight it is difficult to see why such a provision should be introduced for the first time in the last days of the Southern Kingdom, where the kingship had so long been confined, not only to Israelites, but to the Davidic line. But Jer. xxxii. 21—"Their potentate shall be of themselves, and their governor shall proceed from the midst of them"—shows that, whatever the cause might be, there was in the first years of the sixth century a longing for a native king similar to that here expressed. In any case, as the obvious intention here is to make entire submission to Yahweh the condition of any legitimate kingship, it was only consistent to require expressly that the king should be one of Yahweh's people. That motive would be quite sufficient to account for raising what had been the invariable practice into a formulated law; and no other of the prescriptions need have been ancient. On the other hand, the curious phrase "Only he shall not multiply horses to himself, nor cause the people to return to Egypt to the end that he should multiply horses; forasmuch as Yahweh hath said unto you, Ye shall henceforth return no more that way," can hardly belong to the Mosaic time. There was no doubt then much danger that the people should wish to return to Egypt; but that a king should cause them to return for horses, is too much of a subordinate detail to have been portion of a Mosaic prophecy. If, as is most probable, the phrase condemns the sending of Israelites into Egypt to buy horses and chariots, it can have been written only after Solomon's days. Before that time Israel, as an almost exclusively mountain people, regarded horses and chariots with dislike, and usually destroyed them when they fell into their hands. With the extension of their power over the plains and the growth of a lust for conquest, they sought after chariots eagerly. To procure them they entered into alliances with Egypt which the prophets denounced, and which brought to the nation nothing but evil. It was natural, therefore, that the Deuteronomist should specially mention this detail, and should support it by reference to a Divine promise, which does not appear in our Bible, but which probably was found in either the Yahwistic or the Elohistic narrative.

But whether the whole is Deuteronomic or not, there can be no question that the command that the king shall have "a copy of this law" prepared for him and shall read constantly therein is so; and perhaps of all the prescriptions this is the most important. In purely Eastern states there is no legislature at all, and the greater part of the criminal jurisdiction especially is carried on without any reference to fixed law save in cases affecting religion. This was the case in the Mahratta states in India so long as they were independent. The ruler and the officers he appointed administered justice, solely according to custom and their own notions of rectitude, "without advertence to any law except the popular notions of customary law."* Now in Israel the state of things was entirely similar, save in so far as the fundamental principles of Yahwistic religion had been formulated. In all other respects customary law ruled everything. But it was the religious influence that gave its highest and best developments to the life of Israel. It was this, too, which brought to such early maturity in Israel the principles of justice, mercy, and freedom. Elsewhere these were of exceedingly slow growth. In Israel, the influence of the lofty religious ideas implanted in the nation by Moses did for them what the influence of the higher political and social ideas of the governing Englishmen are said to do, under favourable circumstances, for the Indian peoples. Without disturbing the general harmony which must subsist between all parts of the organism of the State if the nation's life is to be healthy, and without putting it out of relation with its surroundings, that influence has been, and is still, moving the more backward Indian societies along the natural paths of human progress at a greatly accelerated speed.† In a similar way the Israelite people was moved by the Mosaic influence, in its aspirations at least, with an elsewhere unexampled speed and certainty, towards an ideal of national life which no nation since has even endeavoured to realise. But whenever the kings threw off the yoke of Yahweh and plunged into idolatry, then the evils of despotic Oriental rule made their appearance unchecked. These evils have been enumerated in the following words by one well acquainted with Oriental states: "Cruelty, superstition, callous indifference to the security of the weaker and poorer classes, avarice, corruption, disorder in all public affairs, and open brigandage." With the exception perhaps of the last, these are precisely the sins which the prophets are continually denouncing. Long before Hezekiah they were rampant, especially in the Northern Kingdom, and in the evil days between Hezekiah and Josiah, when we suppose Deuteronomy to have been written, they were indulged in without shame or compunction.

The result was that an inarticulate cry, like that we hear to-day from Persia in the articulate form of newspaper articles, must have filled the hearts of all righteous men and the multitude of the oppressed. What it would be we may learn from the following extract from a letter written from Persia to the *Kamin*, *i. e.*, "Law," a Persian newspaper published in London, and translated by Arminius Vambéry in the *Deutsche Rundschau* for October, 1893: "Oh, brothers, behold how deeply we have sunk into the sea of ignominy and shame. Tyranny, famine, disease, poverty, calamity, decay of character, and all the misery in the world has overflowed our country. The cause of all this misfortune lies in this, that we have no laws; only in this, that our conscienceless and foolish great ones have wilfully and purposely rejected, trodden under foot, and destroyed the laws of the sacred code, . . . We are men, and would have laws! It is not new laws we ask for, but we desire that our secular and spiritual heads should assemble and press for the enforcement of the holy laws of the sacred code. Therefore we ask of you this one thing, that you should proclaim: 'We are men, and would have laws.'" The East is so perennially the same, that the two thousand five hundred years which separate that pathetic cry from the prayers of the true Israel in Manasseh's and Amon's days make no radical difference. The situation was the same, and the need was the same. Hence came this prophetic and priestly redaction of the Law of the Covenant. "They were men, and would have laws." They sought to be freed from the greed, the cruelty, and the lawlessness of their rulers; and having produced their revised code, they wished to secure that it should not disappear from memory, as the more ancient law had been suffered to do. It must be kept continually before the king's mind. "It shall be with him, and he shall read therein all the days of his life; that he may learn to fear Yahweh his God, to keep all the words of this law and these statutes to do them." In this way it was thought that future "great ones" would be prevented from "rejecting, treading under foot, and destroying the laws of the sacred code."

But the king of Israel was not only to be a law-abiding and a law-enforcing king. He was to learn from this new law even a deeper lesson. He was to read daily in the law, "that his heart might not be lifted up above his brethren." Oriental despots either openly claim that they are of higher and purer blood than their subjects, or they deal with these latter as if they had

* Tupper, "Our Indian Protectorate," pp. 248, 249.
† *Ibid.*, p. 321.

nothing in common with them. In the laws of Manu it is said, "Even an infant king must not be despised (from an idea) that he is a (mere) mortal; for he is a great deity in human form." It was not to be so in Israel. His subjects were the Israelite king's "brethren." They all stood in the same relation to their God. All equally had shared Yahweh's favour in being delivered from the bondage of Egypt. Each had the same rights, the same privileges, the same claims to justice and consideration as the king himself had. That, this law was to teach the king; and when he had learned the lesson, it is taken for granted that the root from which the other evils spring would be destroyed.

Such, then, the ruler of Israel was to be. He was to feel, first of all his responsibility to God. Then he was to deny himself to the lust of conquest, to the voluptuous pleasures of the flesh, to the most devouring lust of all, the love of money. Last of all, and above all, he was to acknowledge his equality with the poorest of the people in the sight of God. Could there be even yet a nobler ideal set before the kings of the world than this? The reign of only one king of Israel, Josiah, promised its realisation. That seemed, indeed, to be "the fair beginning of a time." But it was not so; it proved to be only an afterglow, a mere prelude to the night. None of his successors made even an attempt to imitate him, and the destruction of the Jewish State put an end to all hope of the appearance of the Yahwistic king in Israel. Elsewhere, before the coming of Christ, he did not appear. Since Christ's coming, here and there, at rare intervals, such rulers have been found. But in the East perhaps the only rulers who can be said to have made any attempt in this direction are the best of the great uncrowned kings of India, the British viceroys.

Such, for example, was Lord Lawrence's aim, and his reward. From the beginning to the end of his Indian career he lived a pure and simple life, laboured with untiring energy for the good of the people, and kept in his mind, as his aspirations for his Punjaub peasantry show, the Old Testament ideal of both ruler and ruled. He was, too, entirely free from the lust of conquest, as some Indian viceroys have not perhaps been; and he did all his work under a solemn sense of responsibility to God. To a large extent, the Biblical ideal made him what he was as a ruler, and the life and power of that ideal now, in such men, sufficiently show the truth of the prophetic and priestly insight which is embodied here. Many who have disregarded these rules have done great things for the world; but we are only the more sure, after two thousand five hundred years, that on these lines alone can the ruler attain his highest and purest eminence. All the aspirations of men to-day are towards a state of things in which rulers, whether they be any longer kings or no, shall stand on a level of brotherhood with their subjects, and shall set the good of the ruled before them as their sole aim. All men are dreaming now of a future in which personal ambition shall have little scope, in which none will be for himself or for a party, but "all will be for the State." If ever that good dream be realised, rulers of the Deuteronomic type will be universal; and the depth of wisdom embodied in the laws of this small and obscure Oriental people, so many ages ago, will be manifested in a general political and social happiness such as has never yet been seen, on any large scale at least, in the history of men.

CHAPTER XVIII.

SPEAKERS FOR GOD.—II. THE PRIEST.

DEUTERONOMY xviii. 1-8.

THE priesthood naturally follows the kingship in the regulations regarding the position of the governing classes. But it was an older and much more radical constituent in the polity of Israel than we have seen the kingship to be. Originally, the priests were the normal and regular exponents of Yahweh's will. They received and gave forth to the people oracles from Him, and they were the fountain of moral and spiritual guidance. The Torah of the priests, which on the older view was the Pentateuch as we have it, or its substance at least, which Moses had put into their hands, is much more probably now regarded as the guidance given by means of the sacred lot and the Urim and Thummim. Because of their special nearness to and intimacy with God, the priests were in contact with the Divine will and could receive special Divine guidance; and in days when the voice of prophecy was dumb, or in matters which it left untouched, the priestly Torah, or direction, was the one authorised Divine voice. But this was not the only function of the priests. Sacrificial worship was a more fundamental function. Wellhausen and his school indeed seem inclined to deny that as priests of Yahweh they had any Divinely ordered connection with sacrifice. But the truer view is that their power to give Torah to Israel depended entirely upon their being the custodians of the places where Yahweh had caused His name to be remembered. The theory was that, as they approached Him with sacrifices in His sanctuaries, they consequently could speak for Him; so that the guarding of His shrines, and the offering of the people's sacrifices there were their first duties. In fact they were the mediators between Yahweh and Israel. Yahweh was King, but He was invisible, and the priests were His visible earthly representatives. The dues, which in a merely secular state would have gone to the king, as rent for the lands held of him, were employed for their appointed uses by the priests, as the servants and representatives of the heavenly King who had bestowed the land upon Israel and allotted to each family its portion. Occupying a middle position, then, between the two parties to the Covenant by which Israel had become Yahweh's chosen people, they spoke for the people when they appeared before Yahweh, and for Him when they came forth to the people. They were, as we have said, the oldest and most important of the ruling classes, and must have been from early times a special order set apart for the service of Israel's God.

The main passages in Deuteronomy which bear upon the position and character of the priesthood and of the tribe of Levi are the following. In chaps. xviii. 1-8, x. 6-9, and xxvii. 9-14 the strictly priestly functions of the tribe of Levi are dealt with; in xvii. 9 ff., xix. 17, the judicial functions; in xxi. 1-5 their function in connection with sanitary matters is referred to. Besides these there are the various injunctions to invite the Levites to the sacrificial feasts, because they have no inheritance, and a number of references to the priesthood as a well-known body, the constitution and duties of which did not need special treatment. These last are of themselves sufficient to prove beyond question that in dealing with the priests and Levites the author of this book writes from out of the midst of a long established system. He does not legislate for the introduction of priests, neither does he refer to a priestly system recently elaborated by himself, and only now coming into operation. He does not tell us how priests are to be appointed, nor from whom, nor with what ceremonies of consecration they are to be inducted into their office. In fact the writer speaks of what concerns the priests and Levites in a manner which makes it certain that in his day there were, and had long been, Levites who were priests, and Levites of whom it may at least be said that they were probably nothing more than subordinates in regard to religious duty. In a word, while presupposing an established system of priestly and Levitical service, he nowhere attempts to give any clear or complete view of that system. His whole mind is turned towards the people. It is about their duties and their rights he is anxious, about their duties perhaps more than their rights; and he touches upon matters connected with others than the people only in a cursory way. In this matter, especially, he clearly needs to be supplemented by information drawn from other sources, and his every word about it shows that he is not introducing or referring to anything new. Any modifications he makes are plainly stated and are limited to a few special points.

The chief passage for our purpose is, however, xviii. 1-8, where we have the agents of the cultus defined, and directions for the dues to be given them. In ver. 1 these agents are clearly said to be the whole tribe of Levi; for the phrase "The priests, the Levites, the whole tribe of Levi," cannot mean the priests and the Levites who together make up the whole tribe of Levi. Notwithstanding the arguments of Keil and Curtiss and other ingenious scholars, the unprejudiced mind must, I think, accept Dillmann's rendering, "The Levitical priests, the whole tribe of Levi," the latter clause standing in apposition to the former. In that case Deuteronomy must be held to regard every Levite as in some sense priestly. This view is confirmed by x. 8 f., where distinctly priestly duties are assigned to the "tribe of Levi." Some indeed assert that this verse was written by a later editor, but valid reasons for the assertion are somewhat difficult to find.* Neither Kuenen nor Oettli nor Dillmann find any. We may, then, accept it as Deuteronomic since critics of such various leanings do so. To quote Dillmann, " Beyond question, therefore, the tribe as a whole appears here as called to sacred, especially priestly service; only it does not follow from that that every individual member of the tribe could exercise these functions at his pleasure, without there being any organisation and gradation among these servants of God." No, that does not follow; and this very passage (Deut. xviii. 1-8) shows that it does not, for it makes a very clear distinction. In vv. 3 ff. the dues of the priest are dealt with, while in vv. 6 ff. those of the Levite in one special case are provided for. As if to emphasise the distinction between them, the priest in

* Kuenen, "H. K. O.," Eerste Deel, p. 113.

ver. 3 is not called " Levitical," as he is in other passages.

Further, the verses concerning the Levite also emphasise the distinction; for few will be able to adopt the view that here in vv. 6 ff. every Levite who chooses is authorised to become a priest, by the mere process of presenting himself at the central sanctuary. The author of Deuteronomy must have known, better probably than any one now considering this matter, that the priests in the central sanctuary would never consent to divide their privileges and their income with every member of their tribe who might choose to come up to Jerusalem. Indeed, if they had received each and every one, the crowd would have been an embarrassment instead of a help. As a matter of fact, when the Deuteronomic reform came to be put in practice, this free admission of every Levite to the service of the Jerusalem Temple was not adopted, and it is *prima facie* improbable that the author of it can have meant his provision in that sense. The meaning seems to be that, as only those Levites who were employed in the central sanctuary could be *de facto* priests, those living in the country were not priests in the same sense; and the regulation made is that if any Levite came up to Jerusalem and was received into the ranks of the Temple Levites, i. e., the sacrificial priests, he should receive the same dues as the others performing the same work did. But though no conditions of admission to the Temple service are mentioned, obviously there must have been some conditions, some division of labour, some organisation involving gradations in rank, and perhaps also some limitation as to time in the case of such voluntary service as is here dealt with. For, as Dillmann points out, it is not said that the service of every Temple Levite is the same; numbers of them may have had no higher work than the Levites under the laws of the Priest Codex.

Moreover the other functions assigned to the priests confirm the argument, and prove that in the time of Deuteronomy distinctions of rank among the Levites must have been firmly established. They had a place in the public justiciary, even in the supreme court, " in the place which Yahweh their God" had chosen (Deut. xvii. 9, xix. 17). Not only so, the law concerning a man found slain in chap. xxi., vv. 1-5, implies that there were in the cities throughout the land priests, the sons of Levi, whom " Yahweh thy God hath chosen to minister unto Him and to bless in the name of Yahweh, and according to their word shall every controversy and every stroke be." Now it cannot possibly have been the intention of the author of Deuteronomy that every member of the tribe of Levi should have equal power to decide such matters. If in his view every Levite was a priest, then we should have this impossible state of affairs, that the highest courts for judicial process should be in the hands of a class which was more largely indebted to the generosity of the rich for its maintenance than any other in the country. It seems plain therefore that every Levite could not exercise *full* priestly functions because of his birth. Clearly, if any Levite might become a priest it was only in the same sense in which every Napoleonic soldier was said to carry a marshal's baton in his knapsack.*

* The same conclusion must be come to in connection with the sanitary duties of the priesthood as laid down, or

Finally, in this passage (ver. 5), by the words "him and his sons for ever," which refer back to "the priest," a hereditary character of the priesthood is asserted. This phrase is remarkably parallel to that so frequently used by P, "Aaron and his sons"; and though we are not told in what family or families the priesthood was hereditary, it must have been so in some. But in x. 6, 7, the family of Aaron is mentioned by the Deuteronomist as having hereditary right to the priesthood at the central shrine. There can therefore be no doubt that in the time of the author of Deuteronomy priesthood was hereditary, perhaps in several families, but certainly in the family of Aaron.

The remaining point in these verses of chap. xviii. is the dues. As the whole tribe had no land, so the whole tribe had a share in the dues paid by the people to their Divine King. In vv. 3 ff. we have a statement of what these were. The whole tribe of Levi are to eat "the offerings of Yahweh made by fire, and His inheritance. And they shall have no inheritance among their brethren: Yahweh is their inheritance, as He hath spoken unto them." The only place in Scripture in which such a promise is given is Numb. xviii. 20, 24, so that these passages, if not referred to by the author of Deuteronomy, must be founded upon a tradition already old in his time. As the servants of Yahweh, the Levites were to be wholly Yahweh's care; as His representatives, they were to use for the supply of their needs all such portions of the offerings made to Him by fire as were not to be consumed on the altar. Their remaining provision was to be "His," *i. e.*, Yahweh's "inheritance," or rather "portion," or that which belongs to Him. Now Yahweh's "portion" consisted of all the other sacred dues (besides the sacrifices) which should be paid to Yahweh, such as the tithes, the firstlings, and the firstfruits. On these the whole tribe of Levi was to live, and so be free to give their time to the special business of the sanctuary, and to related duties, in so far as they were called upon.

But there were to be distinctions. In vv. 3-5 we have a special statement of what was to be paid by the people to the priests, *i. e.*, the sacrificing priests. Of every animal offered in sacrifice, except those offered as whole burnt-offerings, they were to receive "the shoulder, the two cheeks, and the maw," all choice pieces. Further, they were to receive the "firstfruits of corn, wine, oil, and the first of the fleece of the sheep." For the priests of one sanctuary these would be quite provision enough, though the word translated "firstfruits," *rēshith*, is very indefinite, and probably meant much or little, according as the donor was liberal or churlish. But how does this agree with that which is bestowed upon the priests according to the Priest Codex? In the passage corresponding to this (Lev. vii. 31-34) the wave breast and the heave thigh are the portions which are to be bestowed upon "Aaron the priest and his sons, as a due

for ever from the children of Israel"; and where the firstfruits are dealt with (Numb. xviii. 12 ff.) "the first of the fleece of the sheep" is not mentioned. That is an addition made by the author of Deuteronomy; but what of "the shoulder, the two cheeks, and the maw"? Are they a substitute for the "wave breast and the heave thigh," or are they an addition? If we hold that the laws in the Pentateuch were all given by Moses in the wilderness, and in the order in which they stand, it will be most natural to think that what we have here is meant to be an addition to what Numbers prescribes. But if it is established that Deuteronomy is a distinct work, written at a different period from the other books of the Pentateuch, then, though there is not sufficient evidence to justify a dogmatic decision on either side, the weight of probability is in favour of the supposition that the Deuteronomic provision is a substitute, or at least an alternative, for what we have in Numbers. The fact that the prescription in Numbers is not repeated makes for that view, as well as the fact that Deuteronomy does not as a rule tend to increase the burdens on the people. Keil's view, that Deuteronomy and Numbers are dealing with quite different sacrifices, will hardly stand examination. He thinks that the feasts at which the firstlings, turned into money, and the third-year tithes were eaten, are referred to here, while in Numbers it is the ordinary peace-offerings which are dealt with. But the postponed firstlings were eaten at the sanctuary, and would consequently come under the head of ordinary sacrifices; and the third-year tithes were eaten in the local centres, so that the bringing of the priestly portions would be as difficult in this case as in the case of the slaughterings for ordinary meals, which Keil, partly for that reason, thinks cannot be referred to here. On the whole, the best opinion seems to be that Deuteronomy has here different prescriptions from those in Numbers, and that probably there is a considerable interval of time between the two.

In vv. 6-8 the Levite as distinguished from the priest is dealt with, though by no means fully. Only in one respect are special regulations given. When such an one came to do duty at the central sanctuary, he was to receive his share of the sacrifices with the rest.

In Chapter I. the main outlines of the Deuteronomic system of priestly arrangements have been placed alongside those of the Book of the Covenant and JE, and those of P, with a view to decide whether they could all have been the work of one lawgiver's life. Here they must be compared in order that we may ascertain whether a view of the development of the priestly tribe which will do justice to these various documents and their provisions can be suggested.

Some schools of critics offer the hypothesis that there was no special priesthood till late in the time of the kings. From the beginning, they say, the head of each household was the family priest, and secular men, such as the kings, and men of other tribes than the Levites, could be and were priests, and offered sacrifice even at Jerusalem. With Deuteronomy the tribe of Levi was established as the priestly tribe, and only after the Exile was priesthood restricted to the sons of Aaron. But this scheme does justice to one set of passages only at the expense of another. It accounts for all that is anoma-

rather as alluded to, in Deut. xxiv. 8, 9. This implies that the Levitical priests had special duties in connection with such matters, duties which, if not precisely the same as those laid down in the Law of Leprosy (Lev. xiii., xiv.), must have nearly resembled them. Semi-medical skill must have been necessary for the satisfactory discharge of these duties, and we must suppose that the priests who discharged them were selected from the tribe of Levi on some principle either of special proved knowledge and fitness, or on the ground of hereditary devotion to such work.

lous in the history, and pushes aside the main and consistent affirmation of all our authorities, that from the earliest days the tribe of Levi had a special connection with sacred things and a special position in Israel. To what straits its advocates are reduced may be seen in the fact that Wellhausen has to declare that there were two tribes of Levi, one purely secular that was all but destroyed in an attack upon Shechem, and which afterwards disappeared, and a later ecclesiastical and somewhat factitious tribe, or caste, which "towards the end of the monarchy arose out of the separate priestly families of Judah."* A more improbable suggestion than that can hardly be conceived.

But historical analogy, the favourite weapon of these very critics, also condemns it. Let us look at the growth of the priesthood in other ancient nations. In small and isolated communities the head of the household was generally the family priest, and in all probability this was the case in the various separate tribes of which Israel was composed; at least it was so in the households of the patriarchs. But, in communities formed by amalgamation of different tribes—and according to modern ideas Israel was so formed—there was almost always superinduced upon that more primitive state of things another and different arrangement. In antiquity no bond could hold together tribes or families conscious of different descent, save the bond of religion. Consequently, whenever such an amalgamation took place, the very first thing which had to be done was to establish religious rites common to the whole new community, which of course were not the care of the heads of households as such. Each separate section of the composite body kept up, no doubt, the family rites; but there had to be a common worship, and of course a special priesthood, for the new community. This is sufficiently attested for the Greeks and Romans by De Coulanges, who in his "La Cité Antique" gathers together such a mass of authorities in regard to this matter that few will be inclined to dispute his conclusion. On page 146 he says: "Several tribes might unite, on condition that the worship of each was respected. When such an alliance was entered into, the city or state came into existence. It is of little importance to inquire into the causes which induced several tribes to unite; what is certain is that the bond of the new association was again a religion. The tribes which grouped themselves to form a state never failed to light a sacred fire, and to set up a common religion." But the family and tribal rites continued to exist as *sacra privata*, just as the central government dominated but did not destroy the family and tribal governments.†

It may be objected that these customs are proved only for the Aryan races, and that, though proved for them, they form no valid analogy for Semitic peoples. But besides the fact that part of the statements we have quoted are obviously true of Israel, we have a guarantee that the principle enunciated is also valid for it. The whole process traced in the religious progress of the Aryan nations is based upon the worship of ancestors. Now one of the critical discoveries is that ancestor-worship was a part of the religion of the tribes which afterwards united to form the Israelite nation. Some, like Stade, tell us that that was the early religion of Israel itself. In that form the theory is, I think, to be rejected; but there would seem to be little doubt that, before the birth of the nation, ancestor-worship was much practised by the Hebrew tribes. If so, we may quite safely take over the analogy we have established, and believe that when Moses united the tribes into a nation, the religion of Yahweh was the absolutely necessary connecting link which bound them together. For though the tribes were related, and are represented as the descendants of Abraham, they must have varied considerably from each other in religious beliefs and usages. By Moses these variations were extinguished, as far as that was possible, by the establishment of an exclusive Yahweh-worship as the national cult; and to carry on this, not the heads of households, but a priesthood that represented the nation, must have been selected. But if so, who would most naturally be selected for this duty? A sentence from De Coulanges will show that in this case the tribe of Levi would almost necessarily be chosen. Speaking of cases in which a composite state relieved itself of the trouble of inventing a new worship by adopting the special god of one of the component tribes, he says: "But when a family consented to share its god in this fashion it reserved for itself at least the priesthood." Now if that was the case in Israel, the priesthood of the tribe of Levi would at once become a necessity. Whether Yahweh had been ever known to the other tribes or not, there can be little doubt that the knowledge of Him which made them a nation and started them on their unique career of spiritual discovery came from the Mosaic tribe and family.

The God whom the family worshipped became the God of the confederacy, and they would be the natural guardians of His sanctuary. This would not in the least involve special sanctity and meekness on the part of the tribe, as some insist. They would remain a tribe like the others; but their leading men would discharge the functions of priests for the confederated nation. It is difficult, indeed, to see why any one else should have been thought of: most likely the arrangement was made as a thing of course.

But if there was such a common worship, there must have been a sanctuary for it, and at it the Levitic priests must have discharged their functions. Now though the Tabernacle, as P knows it, is not spoken of either in JE or in Deuteronomy, a "tent of meeting" at which Jehovah revealed Himself to Moses and to which the people went to seek Yahweh (Exod. xxxiii. 7 ff.) is known to all our authorities. Further, Wellhausen himself says, "If Moses did anything at all he certainly founded the sanctuary at Qadesh and the Torah there, which the priests of the ark carried on after him," so that even he recognises the necessity we have pointed out. From the days of Moses onwards, therefore, there must have been special priests of Yahweh, a special Yahwistic sanctuary, ritual with a special sacrifice presented to Yahweh, and lastly a central oracle, which is precisely what the passages explained away by Wellhausen assert. But of course at that early time, even if the ultimate purpose was to have an exclusively Levitical priesthood, concessions to the old state of

---

* "History of Israel," p. 145.
† *Cf.* also Muirhead, article "Roman Law," in "Ency. Brit.," vol. xx. p. 669, 2d col., and Ramsay, "Church in Roman Empire," p. 190.

things would have to be made. The Passover was left in the hands of the household priest, and in other ways probably he would be considered. The old order would insist on surviving, and the rigour of the later arrangements cannot then have been attained. In other respects we know that it was so; and we may well believe that the priesthood of the individual householder and of the rulers was tolerated, and as far as possible regulated, so as to offer no public scandal to the religion of Yahweh. So, among the Homeric Greeks special hereditary priesthoods coexisted with a political priesthood of the head of the State, and with the household priesthood.*

The laxity on these points ascribed to Moses is, however, less than has been supposed. At Mount Sinai he certainly did appoint the "young men of the children of Israel" † to slaughter the beasts for sacrifice; but he reserved for himself, a Levite, the sprinkling of the blood on the altar.‡ He also made Joshua his servant, an Ephraimite, the keeper of the sanctuary; but even under the Levitical law, a priest's slave was reckoned to be of his household and could eat of the holy things. These were not very great laxities, and there is nothing in them to make us suppose that a regular priesthood did not exist from Sinai. Moreover, that a special place should be assigned to Aaron and his sons was natural. He was the brother of Moses, and would be the natural representative of the tribe, since Moses was removed from it as being leader of all. Everything therefore concurs to confirm the Biblical view that the Levitic priesthood had its origin at Sinai, and that at the chief sanctuary and oracle the chief place in the priesthood fell to Aaron and his sons. Worship at other sanctuaries was permitted, and there the heads of households may have performed priestly functions, or in later times in Canaan some other Levitic families; but that there was a central sanctuary in the hands of Levitic priests, among whom the family of Aaron had a chief place, is what the circumstances, the historical data we have, and all historical analogy alike demand.

For the discharge of their sacred functions certain dues were doubtless assigned to the priests, and the Levites sharing in the subordinate duties of the sanctuary would share also in the emoluments. In other respects Levi in the wilderness would differ in nothing from other tribes. But in preparation for the arrival in Canaan, it was decreed that Levi should "have no part or inheritance in Israel." Yahweh was to be their inheritance.

The point to notice here is that this tribe was to retain the nomadic life when the other tribes became agricultural. The reason for it is plain. That ancient manner of life was looked upon as superior in a religious aspect to the agricultural life. In the first place, the ancestral life of Israel had been of that kind. Abraham, Isaac, and Jacob had been heads of nomadic families or tribes; and the pure and peaceful religious life, the intimate communion with God which they enjoyed, always dominated the imagination of the pious Israelite. Moreover the fundamental revelation had come to Moses when he was a shepherd in the waste. Further, the life of the shepherd is necessarily less continuously busy than that of the agriculturist; it has, therefore, more scope in it for contemplation; and in many countries and at various times shepherds have been a specially thoughtful, as well as a specially pious class. But, perhaps the chief reason was that the shepherd life was not only simple and frugal in itself, but it was also by its very conditions free from some of the greatest dangers to which the religious life of the Israelite in Canaan was exposed. When the bulk of the people adopted the settled life, they were not only thrown among the Canaanites, but they went to school to them in all that concerned elaborate agriculture. This necessarily made the intercourse and connection between the two peoples extremely intimate, and was fruitful in evil results. From this the semi-nomadic portions of the people were to a great extent free, and they would seem to have been regarded as the guardians of a higher life and a purer tradition than others. They represented to the popular mind the Israel of ancient days, which had known nothing of the vices of cities, and in which the pure, uncorrupted religion of Yahweh had held exclusive sway.

A remarkable narrative of the Old Testament establishes this. When Jehu was engaged in his sanguinary suppression of the house of Ahab, and the Baal-worship which they had introduced, we read in 2 Kings x. 15 ff. that he lighted on Jonadab the son of Rechab coming to meet him. This Jonadab was the chief of the Rechabites, a nomadic clan, who were bound by oath to drink no wine, nor to build houses, nor sow seed, nor plant vineyards, and to dwell in tents all their days (Jer. xxxv. 6, 7). This was clearly intended as a protest against the prevailing corruption of manners, and was founded on a special zeal for the uncorrupted religion of Yahweh. Recognising Jonadab's position as a champion of true religion, Jehu anxiously seeks his approval and co-operation. He says, "Is thine heart right, as my heart is with thy heart?" And Jonadab answered, "It is." "If it be," said Jehu, "give me thine hand." And he gave him his hand, and he took him up to him into the chariot. And he said, "Come with me, and see my zeal for Yahweh." At a much later time, Jeremiah, at the Divine command, used the faithfulness of these nomads to the ordinances of their chiefs to put to shame the unfaithfulness of Israel to Yahweh's ordinances; and promises (Jer. xxxv. 19) that because of it "Jonadab the son of Rechab shall never want a man to stand before Yahweh," *i. e.*, as His servant. The Nazarites, again, were in some measure an indication of the same thing. Their rigorous abstinence from the fruit of the vine (the special sign and gift of a settled life in a country like Palestine) was their great distinguishing mark, as persons peculiarly set apart to the service of God. Something analogous is seen in that other desert faith, Mohammedanism. When the great reformer, Abd-el-Wahab, attempted to bring back Islam to its primitive power, he fell back largely upon the simplicity of the desert life, though he did not insist upon the abandonment of agriculture and fixed habitations.

It is, therefore, not surprising that the priestly tribe was kept to the nomadic life by the ordinance that they should not have a portion in the distribution of the Canaanite territory. But according to the narrative of the attack upon Shechem by Levi and Simeon, and the verses

---

* Rägelsbach, "Homerische Theologie," p. 198.
† Exod. xxiv. 5.
‡ Exod. xxxiii. 11.

in the blessing of Jacob (Gen. xlix.) dealing with these tribes, the course of history reinforced this command. Whether the treachery at Shechem occurred, as the Genesis narrative places it, before the Exodus, when Israel was only a family, or was an incident in the history of the two tribes after Canaan had been invaded, as many critics think,[*] the significance of it is that because of an historical exhibition of fierce and intolerant zeal on the part of Levi and Simeon, which the other tribes would not defend, their settlement in that part of the land was rendered difficult, if not impossible. Hence Simeon had to seek other settlements, while Levi fell back to the position assigned to it by its priestly character. It is not a valid exception to this view—which reconciles the two statements that Levi had no inheritance with the other tribes because of its specially near relation to Yahweh, and also because of its cruel treachery at Shechem—that a priestly tribe is likely to have been not more, but rather less, fierce than the others. That would entirely depend upon the cause or occasion which called out the fierceness. In all that concerned religion Levi would naturally be more inclined to extreme measures than the other tribes, and in this case the higher morality, secured by the separateness of Israel, might easily appear to be at stake.[†] It is, therefore, quite credible that the excessive vengeance taken should have been planned mainly by Levi, and that the resulting hatred should have broken up Simeon, and driven back Levi with emphasis to its higher call.

In any case there never was again any doubt that the Levites were to be excluded from the number of land-owning tribes. Even in the legislation regarding the forty-eight priestly cities this principle asserts itself. The keeping of sheep and cattle on the pastures, which were the only lands attached to these cities, was to be the Levites' only secular occupation, and they were neither to own nor work agricultural land. But to compensate for any hardship this arrangement might bring with it, the Levites, as the special servants of Yahweh, were to have Him for their inheritance, *i. e.*, as we have seen, the dues coming to Yahweh were to become the property of the Levites in great part. I say in great part, because the gift to the Levites exclusively of a tithe of the income of the people is thought by many to be only a late provision.

After Canaan had been conquered, the state of things in connection with the priesthood would be something like this. The tent with the ark would be the principal sanctuary, served by a hereditary Levitic priesthood, at the head of which would be a descendant of Aaron. The tribe of Levi, being nomadic, would probably encamp in the neighbourhood of the central sanctuary in part, and recruits for the priestly work would be taken occasionally from them, while other sections would gravitate to the neighbourhood of other sanctuaries. As we see from the story of Micah in Judges, it was considered desirable to have a Levite for priest everywhere, and consequently there would arise at all the High Places Levitic priesthoods, most probably in part hereditary. But notwithstanding their dues, the bulk of the tribe, being nomads, would be looked upon by the agricultural population as poor, just as the Bedouin, in Palestine now are, comparatively speaking, very poor. This state of things would correspond entirely with what Deuteronomy tells us; and after that legislation the position of the Levites as a priestly body would be more assured than ever. In the post-exilic period all that had been regulated by practice in earlier days found written expression. Differentiation of function was minutely carried out. The priesthood was confined rigorously to the Aaronic house, and the other Levites were given to them as attendants. In this way the whole Levitic system was introduced, and with the exclusive altar came the exclusive priesthood. So far as I can see, it is only by some such hypothesis that justice can be done to *all* the statements of Scripture; and considering the elastic nature of Old Testament law, there is nothing improbable in it. In any case there is an amount of evidence of various kinds for the Mosaic origin of the Levitic, and even the Aaronic priesthood, which no proof of irregularities can overturn.

In the Divinely sanctioned arrangements of the Old Testament Church, therefore, the existence of a body of ecclesiastical persons, having little share in the ordinary pursuits of their neighbours, and dependent upon their clerical duties for a large part of their maintenance, was deemed necessary to secure the continuity of worship and religious belief. As has been already pointed out, the priesthood was necessarily more conservative than progressive. As an institution, it was suited rather to gather up and perpetuate the results of religious movements otherwise originated, than to originate them itself. But in that sphere it was an absolutely necessary element in the life of Israel. Difficult as it was to permeate the people with the truths of revealed religion, it would have been impossible without the services of the priestly tribe. Wherever they went they were a visible embodiment of the demand for faithfulness to Yahweh, and, with all their aberrations, they probably lived at a higher spiritual level than the average layman. As has been well said, though Malachi had much reason to complain of the priests in his own day, his estimate of what Levi had been in the past is no exaggeration (ii. 6): "The law of truth was in his mouth, and unrighteousness was not found in his lips: he walked with Me in peace and uprightness, and did turn many away from iniquity." But such a body as the Levites could not have been kept thus spiritually alive, unless the members of it had lived somewhat aloof from the strifes and envies of the market-place, and this they could not have done had they not lived by their sacred function. The prophets, under the power and impulse of new truth adapted to their own time, did not need this protection; consequently some of them were called from ordinary secular work—from the plough, like Elisha, or from the midst of the rich and high-born inhabitants of Jerusalem, like Isaiah. If one may so say, they were men of religious genius; while the bulk of the priests and Levites must always have been commonplace men in comparison. Yet even of the prophets a number were trained in the nomadic life; others were priests who were shut off also from agriculture. Clearly, therefore, some measure of separation from the full pulsing life of the world was, even in the most favourable circumstances, helpful in developing religious character. For the ordinary average ecclesiastic it was indispensable;

---

[*] *Cf.* Kittel's "Geschichte der Hebräer," II., p. 63.
[†] *Cf.* Exod. xxxii. 15-20.

and that he should exist, and should live at as high a level as possible, was as much a condition of Israel's discharge of her great mission, as that the voice of the prophet should be heard at all the great turning-points of her career.

The modern tendency in Old Testament study is to depreciate the priest and to exalt the prophet, just as in ecclesiastical life we tend to make much of those who are or give themselves out to be religious reformers and thinkers, and to make little of the ordinary parish or congregational ministry. But the good done by the latter is, and must be, for each individual generation more than that done by the former. No one can estimate too highly the conserving and elevating effect of a faithful high-minded spiritual minister. Often without genius either intellectual or religious, without much speculative power, with so firm a hold of the old truth, which has been their own guiding star, that they cannot readily see the good in anything new, such men, when faithful to the light they have, are the stable, restful, immediately effective element in all Church life. And such a body can be best spiritualised by being separated somewhat from the stress and strain of competition in the race of life. Being what they are, the necessity of taking their full part in the business of the world would inevitably secularise them, to the great and lasting damage of all spiritual interests. For though to modern students of Old Testament religion, who are interested most in its growth and progress towards its consummation in Christianity, the prophet is by far the most interesting figure, to the ancient people itself it must have seemed that the priests and Levites, if they in any degree deserved Malachi's eulogy, were the entirely indispensable element in their religious life. They gave the daily bread of religion to the people. They embodied the principles which came to them from prophetic inspiration in ceremonies and institutions; they treasured up whatever had been gained, and kept the people nurtured in it and admonished by it. In short, they prepared the soil and cultivated the roots from which alone the consummate flower of prophecy could spring; and when the voice of prophecy was dying away they brought the piety of the average Israelite to the highest point it ever reached.

In modern times the necessity for such a body of special churchmen is challenged from two opposite sides. There is, on the one hand, the body of over-spiritualised believers who abhor organisation, and the machinery of organisation, as if it were an intolerable evil. Conscious very often of quick spiritual impulse and vivid life in themselves, they fret against the slow movements of large bodies of men; they separate themselves from all the organised Churches and reject a regular ministry. All the Lord's people are now under the Christian dispensation, priests and prophets, they say, and a separate paid ministry in sacred things they refuse to hear of. For spiritual nourishment they rely solely upon the prophetic gifts of their members, and are satisfied that thus they are preparing the way for the universal prevalence of a higher form of Church life. But, so far as can be judged, their experiment has not prospered, nor is it likely to do so. For these separatist Christians have found that spiritual life, like other kinds of life, cannot express itself without an organism. That implies organisation; and though they do with less of it than other Christians, still they are often driven into arrangements which really bring back the regular ministry with its separate position; and in other respects they are saved from the inconveniences they have fled from, only by their want of success. If their system ever became general, it would necessarily drift into organisation, for only at that price can any coherent, continuous, and lasting effect be produced. Unfettered by the dull, the critical, and the judicious, the impulsive and enthusiastic would always be outrunning the possibilities of the present time. In the interests of the best, they would be continually ignoring or destroying the good. To prevent that, a special body of religious men set apart for sacred services, and freed from the rough struggle for existence so far as a maintenance from funds devoted to religious purposes can free them, is one of the best provisions known. Where in the mass they are really religious men, they secure that the pressure upward, which the Church exerts upon the lives of its own members and upon the community in general, shall be effective to the highest degree then possible, and shall be exerted in the directions in which such pressure will most fully answer to the needs and aspirations of the time. Where, on the contrary, the mass of them are secularised, they no doubt are a power for evil; but the contrast between their profession and their practice in that case is so shocking, that unless they be supported by the " dead hand " of endowments with no living spiritual demand behind them, they soon sink by their own weight, to give place to a better type. And even when they are thus supported, though unfaithful, their calling in name at least remains spiritual, and sooner than the other elements in the nation they are apt to be stirred by breathings of a new life.

The other objectors to the regular ministry are those, in the press and elsewhere, who demand of all ministers that they should be prophets, or inspired religious geniuses, and, because they are not, deny their right to exist. According to this view every sermon that is not a new revelation is a failure, every minister of the sanctuary who is not a discoverer in religion is a pretender, every one who only exemplifies and lives by the power of the Gospel, as it was last formulated so as to lay hold upon the popular mind, is an obscurantist. But no reasonable man really believes this. Such reproaches are merely the penalty which must be paid for claiming so high a calling as that of an ambassador for Christ. No man can quite adequately fill such a position; and the bulk of ministers of Christ know better than others how much below their ideal their real service is. But this also is true, that, take them all in all, no class of men are doing anything like so much as Christian ministers throughout the world are doing to keep up the standard of morals and to keep alive faith in that which is spiritual. We have no right to complain that in their sphere they are conservative of that which has been handed on to them. They have tried and proved that teaching; they know that wherever it secures a foothold it lifts men up to God, and they are naturally doubtful whether new and untried teaching will do as much. They have pressing upon them, too, as others have not, the interest of individual men and women whom they see and know, men and women who for the most part, and so far as they can see, are accessible to spiritual impulse only on lines with which they are familiar; and they dread the diversion of their thoughts from their real spiritual interests, to matters which, for them at least, must remain largely intellectual and speculative. No doubt it would be well if all pastors could, as the most highly endowed do, look beyond that narrower field; could take account of the movements which are drifting men into new positions, from which the old landmarks cannot be seen and consequently exert no influence; and could endeavour to rethink their Christianity from new points of view, which may be about to become the orthodoxy of the next generation. But no ministry will ever be a ministry of prophets. It may even be doubted whether such a ministry could be borne if it ever should arise. Under it one might fear that spiritual repose and spiritual growth would alike be impossible for the average man, in his breathless race after teachers each of whom was always catching sight of new lights. The mass of men need, first of all, teachers who have firmly seized the common truth by which the Church of their day lives, who live conspicuously nearer the Christian ideal, as generally conceived, than others do, who devote themselves in sincerity and self-sacrifice to the work of making the things that are most surely believed among Christians a common and abiding possession. Such men need never be ashamed of themselves or of their calling. Theirs is the foundation work, so far as any attempt to realise the Kingdom of God on earth is concerned; for without the general acceptance of the truth attained which they bring about, no further attainment would be possible. The very environment out of which alone the prophet could be developed would be wanting, and stagnation and death would certainly and necessarily follow.

One other thing remains to be said. Though we have taken these significant words of ver. 2—" And they shall have no inheritance among their brethren: Yahweh is their inheritance, as He hath spoken unto them "—in their first and most obvious reference, it is not to be supposed that that meaning has exhausted all that the words conveyed to ancient Israel. The perpetuation of the nomadic form of life among the Levites, and the bestowal of tithes and sacrificial meats upon them, was undoubtedly the first purpose of this command. But it had, even for ancient Israel, a more spiritual meaning. Just as in the promise of Canaan as a dwelling-place the spiritual Israelite never regarded *merely* the gift of wealth and the prospect of comfort,—Canaan was always for them Yahweh's land, the land where they would specially live near Him and find the joy of His presence,—so in this case the spiritual gift, of which the material was only an expression, is the main thing. To have Yahweh for their heritage can never have meant *only* so much money and provisions, so much leisure and opportunity for contemplation, to any true son of Levi. Otherwise it is inexplicable how the words used to indicate this very earthly thing should have become so acceptable a formula for the deepest spiritual experience of Christian men. It meant also a spiritual bond between Yahweh and His servants—a special nearness on their part, and a special condescension on His. To the other tribes Yahweh had given His land, to them He had given Himself as a heritage; and though doubtless any unspiritual son of Levi must have thought the tangible advantages of a fertile farm more attractive than visionary nearness to God, the spiritual among the Levites must have felt that they had received the really good part, which no hostile invasion, no oppression of the rich, could ever take away. Their ordinary life-work brought them more into contact with sacred things than others. The goodness, the mercy, the love of God were, or at least ought to have been, clearer to them than to their brethren; and the joy of doing good to men for God's sake, the rapture of contemplation which possessed them when they were privileged to see the face of God, must have made all the coarser benefits of the earthly heritage seem worse than nothing, and vanity. Of course there was the danger that familiarity with religious things should dull instead of quickening the insight; and many passages in the Old Testament show that this danger was not always escaped. But often, and for long periods, it must have been warded off; and then the superiority of God's gift of Himself must have been manifest, not only to the chosen tribe, but to all Israel. For the nature of man is too intrinsically noble ever to be quite satisfied with the world, and the riches and comforts of the world, for its inheritance. At no time has man ever failed to do homage to spiritual gifts. Even to-day, in spheres outside of religion, there are multitudes of men and women who would put aside without a sigh any wealth the world could give, if it were offered as a substitute for their delight in poetry, or for their power to rethink and re-enjoy the ideas of those whose "thoughts have wandered through eternity." And the power to follow and to yield oneself up to the thoughts of the Eternal God Himself is a reward far above these. To the faithful servant of God at all times and in all lands that joy has been open, for God Himself has been their heritage; and though in ancient Israel the beauty of "Yahweh their God" was not quite unveiled, yet we know from the Psalms that many penetrated even then to the inner glory where God meets His chosen, and there, though having nothing, yet found that in Him they had all.

CHAPTER XIX.

SPEAKERS FOR GOD—III. THE PROPHET.

DEUTERONOMY xviii. 9-22.

THE third of the Divine voices to this nation was the prophet. Just as in the other Semitic nations round about Israel there were kings and priests and soothsayers, there were to be in Israel kings and priests and prophets; and the first two orders having been discussed, there remains for consideration the prophet, in so far at least as he was to be the substitute for the soothsayer. That this parallel was in the mind of the writer, and that he probably intended only to deal with certain aspects of the prophetic office, is witnessed by the fact that he introduces what he has to say regarding the prophet by a stern and detailed denunciation of any dealings with soothsayers and wizards. In the earlier codes the same denunciation is found, but the catalogue of names for those who practised such arts is nowhere so extensive as it is here. In the Book of the Covenant the *mekhashsheph*, or magician, alone is mentioned (Exod. xxii. 17); while the peculiar code which is contained in the last chapters of Leviticus,* mentions only five varieties of sorcerers. The Deuteronomic list of eight is thus the most complete; and Dillmann may be right in regarding it as also the latest. But the special indignation of the writer of Deuteronomy against these forms of superstition would be quite sufficient to account for his elaborate detail. If he lived in the days of Manasseh, he would have before his eyes the passing of children through the fire to Moloch. That was connected with soothsaying and was the crowning horror of Israel's idolatry. The author of Deuteronomy might, therefore, well be more passionate and detailed in his denunciations than others, whether earlier or later.

Nor let any one imagine that in this he was wrong and unenlightened. Whether we believe in the occasional appearance of abnormal powers of the soothsaying kind or not, it is evident that in every nation's life there has been a time in which faith in the existence of such powers was universal, and in which the moral and spiritual life of men has been threatened in the gravest way by the proceedings of those who claimed to possess them. At this hour the witch-doctor, with his cruelties and frauds, is the incubus that rests upon all the semi-civilised or wholly uncivilised peoples of Africa. Even British justice has to lay hands upon him in New Guinea, as the following extract from a Melbourne newspaper will show: "Divination by means of evil spirits is practised to such an extent and with such evil effects by the natives of New Guinea that the Native Regulation Board of British New Guinea has found it necessary to make an ordinance forbidding it. The regulation opens with the statement, 'White men know that sorcery is only deceit, but the lies of the sorcerer frighten many people; the deceit of the sorcerer should be stopped.' It then proceeds to point out that it is forbidden for any person to practise or to pretend to practise sorcery, or for any person to threaten any other person with sorcery, whether practised by himself or any one else. Any one found guilty of sorcery may be sentenced by a European magistrate to three months' imprisonment, or by a native magistrate to three days' imprisonment, and he will be compelled to work in prison without payment." Through the sorcerer attempts at advance to a higher life are in our own day being rendered futile; at his instigation the darkest crimes are committed; and because of him and the beliefs he inculcates men are kept all their lives subject to bondage. So also of old. The ancient soothsayer might be an impostor in everything, but he was none the less dangerous for that. To what depths of wickedness his practices can bring men is seen in the horrors of the secret cult of the negroes of Hayti. Even when soothsaying and magic were connected with higher religions than the fetichism of the Haytian negro, they were still detrimental in no ordinary degree. No worthy conception of God could grow up where these were dominant, and toleration of them was utterly impossible for the religion of Yahweh.

The justice of the punishment of death decreed against wizards and witches in Scripture was, therefore, quite independent of the reality of

* Only two in any one law; Lev. xviii. 21, xix. 26, 31, xx. 6, 27.

the powers such persons claimed. They professed and were believed to have them, and thus they acquired an influence which was fatal to any real belief in a moral and spiritual government of the world. They must therefore be an "abomination" to Yahweh; and as, in any case, by the very fact that they were soothsayers and diviners they practised low forms of idolatry, those who sought them must share the condemnation of the idolater in Israel. In the earlier days of the sacred history there was no enemy so subtle, so insidious, so difficult to meet as magic and soothsaying. Only by actual prohibition, on pain of death, could the case be adequately met; and under these circumstances there is no need for us to apologise for the Old Testament law, "Thou shalt not suffer a witch to live" (Exod. xxii. 17). What is aimed at here is the profession on the part of any woman that she had and used these supernatural powers. This was a crime against Israel's higher life. The punishment of it had no resemblance to the judicial cruelties perpetrated in comparatively modern times, when the charge of being a witch became a weapon against people, who for the most part were guilty only of being helpless and lonely.

But it is characteristic of the large outlook of Deuteronomy that not only is the evil protested against; the universal human need which underlay it is acknowledged and supplied. Behind all the terrible aberrations of heathen soothsaying and divination the author saw hunger for a revelation of the will and purpose of God. That was worthy of sympathy, however inadequate and evil the substitutes elaborated for the really Divine means of enlightenment were. So he promises that the real need will be supplied by God's holy prophets. Nothing that savoured of ignorance or misapprehension of God's spirituality, or of unfaithfulness to Yahweh, could be tolerated; for Israel's God would supply all their need by a prophet from the midst of them, of their brethren, like unto Moses, in whose mouth Yahweh would put His words, and who should speak unto them all that He should command him. This is the broadest and most general legitimation of the prophet, as a special organ of revelation in Israel, that the Scripture contains. By it he is made one of the regularly constituted channels of Divine influence for his people. For it is evidently not one single individual, such as the Messiah, who is here foretold. That has been the interpretation received from the earlier Jews, and cherished in the Church up till quite modern times. But as Keil rightly says, the fact that this promise is set against any supposed need to have recourse to diviners and wizards, is in itself sufficient proof that the prophetic order is meant. It was not only in the far-off Messianic time that Israel was to find in this Divinely sent prophet that knowledge of God's will and purposes which it needed. Israel of all times, tempted by the customs of its heathen neighbours to go to the diviners, was to have in Yahweh's prophet a continual deliverance from the temptation. That implies that this *Nabhi*, or prophet like unto Moses, was to be continually recurring, at every turn and crisis of this nation's career.

Further, the direction in the end of the passage for testing the prophets, whether they were really sent of God or not, confirms this view. It would be singularly out of place in a promise which referred to the Messiah in an exclusive and primary fashion. He would never need testing of this sort, for He was to be the realisation and embodiment of Israel's highest aspirations. But if the passage means to give the prophets a place among the national organs of intercourse with Yahweh alongside of the priests, the necessity of distinguishing these true and Divinely given prophets from pretenders was urgent. The context, both before and after the promise, seems, therefore, to be decisively in favour of the general reference; and the phrases "like unto me," "like unto thee," *i. e.*, Moses, when carefully examined, instead of weakening that inference, strengthen it. They are not used here as the similar phrase is used in Deut. xxxiv. 10: "And there hath not arisen a prophet since in Israel like unto Moses, whom Yahweh knew face to face." There the closeness of Moses' approach to Yahweh is the point in hand, and it is clearly stated that in that regard Moses was more favoured than any who had succeeded him. But here the comparison is between Moses and the prophets, in so far as mediation between Yahweh and His people was concerned. At Israel's own wish Moses had been appointed to hear the Divine voice. Israel had said "Let me not hear again the voice of Yahweh my God, neither let me see this great fire any more, that I die not." The prophet here promised was to be like Moses in that respect, but there is nothing to assert that he would be equal to Moses in power and dignity. On all grounds, therefore, the reference to the line of prophets is to be maintained.

Still, the interpretation thus reached does not exclude—it distinctly includes—the Messianic reference. If the passage promises that at all moments of difficulty and crisis in Israel's history, the will of God would be made known by a Divinely sent prophet, that would be specially true of the last and greatest crisis, the birth of the new time which the Messiah was to inaugurate. Whatever fulfilment the promise might receive previously to that, it could not be perfectly fulfilled without the advent of Him whose office it was to close up the history of the present world, and bring all things by a safe transition into the new Messianic world. That was the greatest crisis; and necessarily the prophet who spoke for Yahweh in it must be the crown of the long line of prophets. There is still a higher sense in which this promise has reference to the Messiah. He was to sum up and realise in Himself all the possibilities of Israel. Now they were the prophetic nation, the people who were to reveal God to mankind; and when they proved prevailingly false to their higher calling, the hopes of all who remained faithful turned to that "true" Israel which alone would inherit the promises. At one period, just before and in the Exile, the prophetic order would appear to have been looked upon as the Israel within Israel, to whom it would fall to accomplish the great things to which the seed of Abraham had been called. But the author of Second Isaiah, despairing even of them, saw that the destiny of Israel would be accomplished by one great Servant of Yahweh, who should outshine all other prophets, as He would surpass all other Israelite priests and Davidic kings. As the crown and embodiment of all that the prophets had aspired to be, the Messiah alone completely fulfilled this promise, and consequently the Messianic reference is organically one with the primary reference. They are so intimately interwoven that nothing but violence can separate them; and thus we gain a deeper insight into the wide reach of the Divine purposes, and the organic unity of the Divine action in the world. These form a far better guarantee for the recognition of Messianic prophecy here than the supposed direct and exclusive reference did. By not grasping too desperately at the view which more strikingly involves the supernatural, we have received back with "full measure pressed down and running over" the assurance that God was really speaking here, and that this, like all the promises of the Old Testament when rightly understood, is yea and amen in Christ.

But for our present purpose the primary reference of this passage to the prophetic line is even more important than the secondary but most vital reference to the Messiah. For it sets forth prophecy as the most potent instrument for the growth and furtherance of the religion of Israel. The prophet is here declared to be the successor of Moses, to be the inspired declarer of the Divine will to His people in cases which did not come within the sphere or the competency of the priest. The latter was, as we have seen, bound to work within the limits and on the basis of the revelation given by Moses. He was to carry out into execution what had been commanded, to keep alive in the hearts of the people the knowledge of their God as Moses had given it, to give "Torah" from the sanctuary in accordance with its principles. But here a nobler office is assigned to the prophet. He is to enlarge and develop the work of Moses. The Mosaic revelation is here viewed as fundamental and normative, but, in contrast to the views of later Judaism, as by no means complete. For the completion of it the prophet is here declared to be the Divinely chosen instrument, and he is consequently assigned a higher position in the purpose of God than either king or priest. He is raised far above the diviners by having his calling lifted into the moral sphere; and he excels both the other organs of national life in that, while they are largely bound by the past, he is called of God to initiate new and higher stages in the life of the chosen people. The ascending steps of the revelation begun by Moses were to be in his hands, and through him God was to reveal Himself in ever fuller measure.

Viewed thus, the prophetic order in Israel has a quite unique character. It is a provision for religious progress such as had no parallel elsewhere in the world; and this public acknowledgment of its Divine right is almost more remarkable. Wherever elsewhere in the world religion has been supposed to be Divinely given through one man, though modifications have indeed been made in later times, yet they have never been anticipated and provided for beforehand. Save in the case of Mohammedanism, which borrowed its idea of the office of the prophet from Judaism, there has never been a deliberate admission that God had yet higher things to reveal concerning Himself, still less has provision been made for the coming of that which was new to fulfil the old. And in modern times the revealer of new aspects of truth finds nowhere a welcome. Instead of being received as a messenger of God, even in the Christian Church he has always to face neglect, often persecution, and only if he be unusually fortunate does he live to see his message received. But in Israel, even in such ancient days as those we are dealing with, the progressive nature of God's Revelation of Himself was acknowledged, the reception of new truth was legitimised and looked for, and the highest place in the earthly kingdom of God was reserved for those whom God had enlightened by it. It is true of course that the nation as a whole never acted in accordance with this teaching. They did not obey the command given here, "Unto him shall ye hearken," and reiterated still more solemnly in the words, "And it shall come to pass, that whosoever will not hearken unto My words, which he shall speak in My name, I will require of him." The prophets for the most part spoke to their contemporaries in vain. Where they were not neglected they were persecuted, and many sealed their testimony with their blood. But the thought that Yahweh was educating His people step by step, and that at all times in their history He would have further revelations of Himself to make, is familiar to this writer. Therefore he welcomes the thought of advance in this region of things, and here solemnly enrols those who are to be the instruments of it among the ruling powers of the nation.

Now in religious thought this is quite unparalleled. Tenacious conservatism, based on the conviction that full truth has already been attained, has always been the mark of religious thinking. That a religious teacher should be able to see that the light of revelation, like the natural light, must come gradually, broadening by degrees into perfect day, and that he himself was standing only in the morning twilight, is a thing so remarkable that one is at a loss to account for it, save on the ground of the special nature of prophetic enlightenment. It was part of the office of the prophets to foresee and foretell the future. Smend is certainly in the right, as against those who have been teaching that the prophet was merely a preacher of genius, when he says that "in Amos and his successors prophecy is the starting-point of their whole discourse and action," and that "all new knowledge which they preach comes to them from the action of Yahweh which they foretell. . . Consequently the greatness of a prophet is to be gathered from the measure in which he foresees the future."* This statement gives us the truth that lies between the two other extremes; for according to it the prophet proclaims and preaches religious truth, but he does so on the basis of what he perceives that God is about to do in the future. In other words, he proclaims new truth on the ground of the revelation God is about to make of Himself, which he is inspired to foresee and to interpret. His business is neither all foreseeing nor all teaching; it is teaching grounded upon foresight. Consequently it was impossible for the prophet to believe that change in religion was in itself evil. He *knew* to the contrary. Only change which should remove men from the Divinely given basis of the faith was evil; and such change, whatever credentials might accompany it, even though they might be miraculous, every faithful Israelite had been already warned most sternly to reject (Deut. xiii. 5). But when the impulse to advance came from Yahweh's manifestation of Himself, change was not only good, it was the indispensable test of faithfulness. They were not the true followers of Isaiah who, on the ground of his prophecy that Zion, as Yahweh's dwelling-place, should be delivered from destruction, rejected the prophecy of Jeremiah that Zion would fall before the Chaldeans. The really faithful men were those who had taken to heart the lessons Yahweh had set for His people in the century that lay between these two prophets; who saw that the time when the deliverance of Zion was necessary to the safety of the true religion was past, and that now the capture of Zion was necessary to its true development. And that is not a solitary case; it is an example of what was normal in the religious history of this people.

This did not escape the quick eye of John Stuart Mill. He says the religion of Israel "gave existence to an inestimably precious unorganised institution—the order (if it may be so termed) of prophets. . . Religion, consequently, was not there, what it has been in so many other places, a consecration of all that was once established, and a barrier against further improvement." There always was the movement of pulsing life within it, and under the Divine guidance that movement was always upward. At some times it was comparatively shallow and slow, at others it was a deep and rushing tide. But it was always moving in directions which led straight to the great consummation of itself in the coming of Christ, who gathered up into His own life all the varied streams of revelation, and crowned and fulfilled them all. At no point in the progress from Moses to the Messiah do we touch rounded and completed truth; nor, according to the teaching of Scripture in this passage, were we meant to do so. The faithful among Israel had as their watchword the *disio* and *pace* of Dante. They saw before them a world of Divine "peace," which they knew lay still in the future, and the "desire" and yearning of their souls were always directed towards it. With inextinguishable hope they marched onward with uplifted faces, to which light reflected from that future gave at times a radiant gladness; and always they kept an open ear for those who saw what God was about to do at each turning of the way.

But granting that religion was thus progressive before men were spoken unto "by the Son," can we say or believe that, now that He has spoken, progress in this way is still possible? At first sight it would seem necessary to answer that question in the negative. The progressive revelation of God has come to its perfection in Jesus Christ: what then remains to us but to cling to that? Are we not bound to make resistance to progress, to any new view in religion, our first duty? Many act and speak as if that were the only possible course consistent with faithfulness. But we must distinguish. The revelation of God has, according to our Christian faith, reached not only its highest actual point, but also its highest possible point in Christ. God can do nothing more for His vineyard than He has done. As a manifestation of God, revelation is completed and closed in Christ. For it is impossible to manifest God to men more fully than in a man who reveals God in every thought and word and act.

But it is quite otherwise with the interpretation of the manifestation. In the earlier days this was provided for by a special inspiration of God, which made the holy men of old infallible in their interpretation of the revelation received

---

*"Lehrbuch der Alt-Testamentlichen Religion's Geschichte," pp. 169 ff.

up to their day, and that continued till the establishment of the Church. Since then the Holy Spirit is to be the guide of faithful men into all truth. Now in the way of interpreting Christ and His message progress is as much open to us as it was to Israel. A complete revelation of God must necessarily, at any given time up till the consummation of all things, contain in it a residuum of significance which, at that point of their experience, mankind has not felt the need of, nor has had the capacity to understand. As the world grows older, however, new outlooks, new environments, new circumstances continually appear, and they all insist upon being dealt with by the Church. In order to deal with them adequately and worthily, a faithful Church must turn to Christ to see what God would have it do; and if Christ be what we take Him to be, there will issue from Him a light, unseen or unnoticed before, to meet the hitherto unfelt need. Moreover, while our Lord Jesus Christ reveals God completely as the God of Redemption, and throws light upon all God's relations to man, a light which needs and admits of no supplementary addition, there are other aspects of the Divine character which He does not so entirely reveal. For example, God's relations to the world of nature, which are now being unveiled in a most striking manner, are dealt with comparatively rarely in the Gospels. Are we to shut our eyes to these as of no importance, and to allow them no influence upon our thoughts? Surely that cannot be demanded of us; for, to speak plainly, it is impossible. No one can remain unmoved when God and man are revealing themselves in the wondrous panorama of the world's life.

Even those who most profess to do so in no case take their stand simply and solely upon the truths believed and held by the first Christians. All of them have adopted later developments as part of their indefeasible treasure. Some go back to the theology of the great Evangelical Revival only; some to the Reformation; some to the pre-Reformation Scholastics; others to the first five centuries. But whatever the point may be at which they take up Christian theology, they take up, along with the original creed of the first believers, some truths or doctrines which emerged and were accepted at a later date. Themselves being judges, therefore, additions to the primitive deposit of faith have to be admitted; and it is a purely arbitrary proceeding on their part to say that now we have attained to all truth, and stolid conservatism is henceforth the only faithful attitude. No, we have still a living God and a living Church, and a multifarious and wonderful world to deal with. Interaction of these cannot be avoided, nor can it occur without new truth being evolved. To have ears and not to hear, to have eyes and not to see, must be as offensive to God now as it was in Old Testament times. Though we have now no inspired prophets to foresee and interpret, we have in all our Churches men whose ears are better attuned to the celestial harmony than others, whose eyes have a keener and surer insight into what God the Lord would speak; and we ought to hear them, to see at least whether they can make their position good. To reject their teaching, only because some element or aspect of it is new, is to deny the guiding providence of God, to turn our back upon the rich stores of instruction which the facts of history, both secular and religious, are fitted to impart. That can never be a Christian duty. Even if it were possible it would be futile. The light will be received by the younger, the fresher and less stereotyped natures in all the Churches; and those who refuse it, in holding obstinately and with exclusive devotion to what they have, will find it shrink and shrivel in their hand. Only in the rush and conflict, only amid the impulses and the powers which are moving in the world, can a healthy religion breathe. Doubtless new teaching will come to *us* in ways congruous to the completed Revelation of our Redeeming God; but it will come; and it should be welcomed as gladly as the teaching of the prophets was welcomed by faithful men in Israel. If it be not, then the Divine threat will apply in this case as fully as in the other: "Whosoever will not hearken unto My words which he shall speak in My name, I will require it of him."

Many say now, and at all times many have said, to those who had caught glimpses of some new lesson God was desiring to teach: "You admit that souls have been renewed and character built up and spiritual life preserved without this new teaching. Why then can you not let us alone? In your pursuit of the best you may destroy the good; and no harm can happen if you keep the improved faith to yourself." But they have forgotten Yahweh's solemn "whosoever will not hearken, I will require it of him." If we refuse to hear when the Lord hath spoken, evil must come of it. Indeed, though the evils of heresy may be more dramatically and strikingly manifest, those of stagnation and a refusal to learn may be much more destructive of the common faith. For refusal to acknowledge truth has far wider issues than the loss of any particular truth. It indicates and reinforces an attitude of soul which, if persisted in, will allow the Church that adopts it to drift slowly away from living contact with the minds of men. So drifting, it shrinks into a *coterie*, and its every activity becomes infected with the curse of futility.

On both sides, therefore, there is danger for us, as there was for the Old Testament Church; and we turn with quickened interest to the test, the criterion, by which Deuteronomy would have the prophets tried. It puts the very question which the line of thought we have been pursuing could not fail to suggest: "How shall we know the word which Yahweh hath not spoken?" If a prophet spoke in the name of other gods he was to die; that had already been determined in the thirteenth chapter, and it is repeated here. But the prophet who should speak a word presumptuously in the name of Yahweh, which He had not commanded, was to be in the same condemnation. It was, therefore, of the last importance that there should be means of detecting when this last evil occurred. The test is this: "When a prophet speaketh in the name of Yahweh, if the thing follow not, nor come to pass, that is the thing which Yahweh hath not spoken." The strange notions of Duhm and others in regard to this have been already dealt with (*vide* pp. 560 f.). There, too, it has been shown that the prophecy here spoken of must have been prophecy in its narrower sense, prophecy dealing with promises of *immediate* judgment and deliverance. Furthermore, this is set forth here as a test applicable to prophets in all ages of the history of Israel. It lies, too, in the nature of the case that it must always have been the popular test. The announcement of things to come before they came was made, at least partially, with the view of impressing the populace, and of gaining their confidence and attention. They must consequently have been continually on the alert to apply this test, and all that is here done is to acknowledge it in the fullest manner as a right and Divinely approved criterion.

But the way in which it ought to be applied is best exemplified by Jeremiah's own method of applying it, which, as Dr. Edersheim* has pointed out, is to be found in the twenty-eighth chapter of that prophet's book. There we read of Jeremiah's conflict with "Hananiah the son of Azzur the prophet," in the beginning of the reign of Zedekiah. Just previously Nebuchadnezzar had carried away Jeconiah the king of Judah, with all the treasures of the house of Yahweh and the strength of the people. Jeremiah had prophesied that they would not return; nay, he had foretold a further calamity, viz. that Nebuchadnezzar would come again and would take away the people and the vessels of the house which still remained. In opposition to that, Hananiah declared, as a word of Yahweh, "Within two full years will I bring again into this place all the vessels of Yahweh's house that Nebuchadnezzar king of Babylon took away from this place, and carried them to Babylon; and I will bring again to this place Jeconiah the son of Jehoiakim king of Judah, with all the captives of Judah that went to Babylon, saith Yahweh." Jeremiah's conduct under these circumstances is noteworthy. He did not immediately denounce his rival as prophesying falsely. He seems to have thought that possibly he might have a true word from Yahweh, since, as we see in the Book of Jonah, the most positive prophecies were conditional, and Jeremiah would seem to have thought it possible that personal repentance was about to bring upon the captive king and people a blessing, instead of the evil he had foreseen. He consequently expressed a fervent wish that Hananiah's prophecy might come true, but reminded his rival that the causes of the evil prophecies of himself and previous prophets were far wider than the ground which the personal repentance of the captives could cover. Because of that he evidently felt the gravest doubt about Hananiah; but he disposes of the matter by saying, "The prophet which prophesieth of peace, when the word of the prophet shall come to pass, then shall the prophet be known, that Yahweh hath truly sent him." Only afterwards, when he had himself received a special revelation concerning Hananiah, did he denounce him as an impostor and a false prophet.

The whole narrative is of extreme importance, for it shows us how the prophets themselves regarded their own supernatural powers, and how they used the tests supplied in Deuteronomy. In the first place, they asked how the new word of Yahweh stood in regard to the older words which He had certainly spoken. If there was any possible way in which the new and the old could be reconciled, they gave the new the benefit of the doubt, and left the decision to the event. Obviously had there been no way of reconciling Hananiah's prophecy with the mass of contrary prophecy which had gone before, Jeremiah would have denounced him under the law of Deut. xiii. 5 as leading away from Yahweh. As it was, he fell back upon the test in this twenty-eighth chapter, and would have maintained an attitude of watchful neutrality until the event had justified or condemned his rival, had not Yahweh Himself settled the question.

For our own day and in our different circumstances the tests are radically the same, though, as prophecy is extinct in the Church, they must to some extent act differently. The New Testament parallel to the criterion in Deut. xiii. 5 is to be found in 1 John iv. 1, 2, and 3: "Prove the spirits, whether they are of God: because many false prophets are gone out into the world. Hereby know ye the Spirit of God: every spirit which confesseth that Jesus Christ is come in the flesh is of God: and every spirit which confesseth not Jesus is not of God: and this is the spirit of the antichrist, whereof ye have heard that it cometh." Under the Christian dispensation to deny "that Jesus Christ is come in the flesh" is the same as it was to say under the earlier dispensation "Let us go after other gods," so completely do God and Christ coincide in our most holy faith. In each case the ultimate test of prophecy is to be the fundamental principle of the faith. Whatever credentials teachers who deny that may bring, they are to be unhesitatingly rejected. They belong to the world, that scheme and fabric of things which rejects allegiance to the Spirit of God. Least of all is popularity with the world as distinguished from the Church, or with the worldly portion of the Church, to stand in the way of its rejection. That is only the natural consequence of its being "of the world." Within the Church no quarter is to be shown to such teaching, for it really carries with it the absolute negation of the faith.

But what of erroneous teaching which acknowledges that "Jesus Christ is come in the flesh"? To it the Old Testament parallel is the utterance of the prophet who "speaketh in the name of Yahweh, and the thing followeth not nor comes to pass." According to Old Testament precept and example, that was to be left to the judgment of time. In our day a corresponding course must be found. The case supposed is that of teaching believed to be erroneous, but neither fundamentally subversive of Christianity nor destructive of the special principles of a Church. If so, earnest opposition by those who hold the opposite view, and adequate discussion, are the true way of meeting the case. For the rest, the final decision should be left to experience. In time, even subsidiary error of this kind, if important, will manifest itself by weakening spiritual life in those who hold it; they will gradually dwindle in numbers and their influence in the Church will die away. They begin by promising renewed strength and insight in spiritual things, renewed energy in the spiritual life. If that "follow not nor come to pass," when due time has been given for any such development, then that is the thing which the Lord hath not spoken, and it should be dealt with as the fundamental heresy is to be dealt with. But probably by that time it will have judged itself, and will need no judgment of men at all.

These then were the connecting links between Yahweh and His people, and the organs by which the life of the Israelite nation was guided: the Kingship, the Priesthood, and the Prophetic Order. The first gave visibility to the Divine

---

* "Prophecy and History in Relation to the Messiah," p. 150.

rule, and stability to national and social life; the second secured the stability of religion, and built up the moral life of the nation on the basis of Mosaic law; the third secured progress and averted stagnation, both in religion and in social and individual morals. In fact, order and progress, the two things Positivist thinkers have set forth as those which can alone secure health to a community, are provided for here with a directness and success which it would be difficult to parallel elsewhere. When we remember how small, how obscure, and how uncivilised the people was to whom this scheme of things was given, and how little their surroundings or circumstances were calculated to suggest such far-reaching provisions, we see that the source of it all was the Revelation of the Divine character given by Moses. Yahweh as revealed through him did not permit His worshippers to believe that they could, at one moment, receive all that was to be known about Him. They were taught to found their conduct and their polity upon what they did know, and to be eagerly on the watch for that which might be revealed at new crises of their history. Now that teaching finds its most complete expression in the laws concerning the three institutions we have been reviewing. Behind all healthy national life and all stable institutions there was, so had this people learned, the power and the righteousness of Almighty God. In His eagerness to draw near to men, He had changed the priest, the king, the prophet from being, as they were among the heathen, merely political and religious officials appointed for purely earthly ends, into channels of communication with Him. Through them there were poured into the life of this nation wholesome and varied streams of Divine grace and enlightenment, and a just balance between conservatism and reform in religion was admirably secured. Consequently, amid all drawbacks, the Israelites became an instrument of the finest power for good in the hands of their Almighty King; and even when their outward glory faded, they were inwardly renewed and pressed onward age after age. "Without hasting and without resting," the purpose of God was realised in their history, guided by these three organs of their national life. Each contributed its share in preparing for the fulness of the time when He came who was the Salvation of God, and each supplied elements of the most essential kind to the mingled expectation which was so marvellously satisfied by the life and work of Christ. They wrought together in the fullest harmony, moreover, though they were not always conscious of doing so. For they all moved at the bidding of the still small voice wherewith God speaks most effectively to the souls of men. Because of this their purposes took a wider sweep than they knew, their hopes received wings which carried them far away beyond the horizon of Old Testament time; and, starting from the remotest points, all the streams of the national life converged, till, at the close of the Old Testament time, they were running in such directions that they could not fail in little space to meet. It was therefore no surprise to the faithful in Israel when, at the beginning of the New Testament, they were found to have met in Jesus the Christ. Once that point was reached, the whole former history, which was now lying completed before the eyes of all, could be fully appreciated. Everything in the past seemed to speak of Him. If, in that first burst of joyous surprise, Messianic references of the most definite kind were found where we now can see only faint hints and adumbrations, we need not wonder. So much more had been spoken of Him than they had thought, it would have been strange had they not swung a little to the opposite extreme. But that need not hinder us from acknowledging that the history of Israel, viewed from their standpoint, was and is the most conspicuous, the most convincing, the most inspiring proof of the Divine action in the world. The finger of God was so manifestly *here*, harmonising, directing, impelling, that the evidence for Divine guidance in much more obscure regions becomes irresistible. With this history before us we can believe that it was not only in those far-off days, and in that little corner of Asia that God was active for the production of good. Now and here, as well as then and there, there are Divine and guiding forces at work in the world; and the only safe politics, the only truly prosperous peoples, are those in which rulers and priests and prophets are secured, to whom the secret of God is open.

CHAPTER XX.

THE ECONOMIC ASPECTS OF ISRAELITE LIFE.

It has often and justly been said that the life of Israel is so entirely founded on the grace and favour of God that no distinction is made between the secular and the religious laws. Whatever their origin may have been, whether they had been part of the tribal constitution before Moses' day or not, they were all regarded as Divinely given. They had been accepted as fit building stones for the great edifice of that national life in which God was to reveal Himself to all mankind, and behind them all was the same Divine authority. That being so, it is not wonderful, in times like these, when the air is full of plans and theories for the reconstruction of society in the interest of the toiling masses of men, that believers in the Scriptures should turn with hope to the legislation of the Old Testament. In the present state of things the material conditions of life are far more deadening and demoralising for the multitude in civilised countries than they are in many uncivilised lands. That this should be so is intolerable to all who think and feel; and men turn with hope to a scene where God is teaching and training men, not merely in regard to their individual life, as in the New Testament, but also in regard to national life. It is seen, too, that the tone and feeling of these laws are sympathetic for the poor as no other code has ever been; and many maintain that, if we would only return to the provisions of these laws, the social crisis which is as yet only in its beginning, and which threatens to darken and overshadow all lands, would be at once and wholly averted. Men consequently are diligently inquiring what the land tenure of ancient Israel was, what its trade laws were, how the poor were dealt with, and how and to what extent pauperism was averted or provided for. Many say, If God has spoken in and by this people, so that their first steps in religion and morals have been the starting-point for the highest life of humanity, may we not expect that their first steps in political and social life will have the same abiding value, if rightly understood? Now the main thing in regard to which the economical arrangements of a nation are important is land. In modern times there may be some exceptionally situated communities, such as the British people, among whom commerce and manufactures are more important than agriculture; but in ancient times no such case could arise. In every community the land and the land tenure were the fundamentally important things.

Now the fundamental thing concerning it was that Yahweh, being the King of Israel, who had formed and was guiding this people as His instrument for saving the world, and who had bestowed their country upon them, was regarded as the sole owner of the soil. It is not necessary to quote texts to prove this, since it is the fundamental assumption throughout the Old Testament Scriptures that the Israelite title to their land was the gift of Yahweh. He had promised it to the fathers. He had driven out the Canaanite nations before Israel. He had by His mighty hand and His stretched-out arm established His chosen people in the place which He had chosen, and He had granted them the use and enjoyment of it so long as they proved faithful to Him. Consequently, in a quite real and palpable sense, there was no owner of land in Israel save Yahweh. And this thought was not without practical consequences of great moment. It was not a mere religious sentiment, it was a hard and palpable fact, that Yahweh ruled. Absolute proprietorship could never be built up on that basis, and never, as a matter of fact, was acknowledged in Israel. All were tenants, who held their places only so long as they obeyed the statutes of Yahweh. The sale in perpetuity of that which had been portioned out to tribes and families was consequently entirely prohibited. As against other nations, indeed, Israel was to possess this land, so that no heathen could be permitted to buy and possess even a scrap of it; but as against Yahweh and the purposes for which He had chosen Israel, all were equally strangers and sojourners, practically tenants at will, who could neither give nor take their holdings as if they were absolutely theirs. Yet, relatively, the land was given to the community as a whole, and according to Joshua xiii. 7 sqq. (a passage generally assigned to the Deuteronomic editor) it was parcelled out by lot to the various tribes just before Joshua's death, according to their respective numbers.* Then within the tribal domain the families in the wider sense had their portion, and within these family domains again the individual households. In this way the Israelite tenure of land occupies a middle point between the theories of Socialism and the high doctrine of private property in land which declares that the individual owner can do what he will with his own. The nation as a whole claimed rights over all the land, but it did not attempt to manage the public estate for the common good. It delegated its powers to the tribes. But not even they undertook the burdens of proprietorship. Under them the families undertook a general superintendence; but the true proprietary rights, the cultivation of the soil, and the drawing of profit from it, subject only to deductions made by the larger bodies, the families, the tribes, and the nation, were exercised only by individuals. The nation took care that none of its territory should be sold to foreigners, lest the national inheritance should be diminished, and the tribes did the same for the tribal heritage, as we see from the narrative concerning the daughters of Zelophehad. It was only within limits, therefore, and the individual proprietor was free; and though the rights of property were respected, the corresponding duties of property were set forth with irresistible clearness. The community, in fact, never abandoned its claims upon the common heritage, any more than Israel's Divine King did, and consequently the field within which proprietary rights were exercised was more restricted here than in any modern state.

Further, besides the prohibition of absolute sale which flowed from the recognition of Yahweh's ownership, and the limitations which tribal and family claims involved, there were distinct provisions in which the national ownership under Yahweh was plainly asserted. For example, it is enacted in Deut. xxiii. 24—" When thou comest into thy neighbour's vineyard, then thou mayest eat grapes thy fill at thine own pleasure; but thou shalt not put any in thy vessel. When thou comest into thy neighbour's standing corn, then thou mayest pluck the ears with thine hand; but thou shalt not move a sickle unto thy neighbour's standing corn." Allied to these were the provisions (Lev. xix. 9 ff., xxiii. 10) concerning gleaning, and not reaping the corners of the field. It will be observed that, though these latter may be discounted as intended for the relief of the poor alone, the former provision was for all, and that consequently it may be regarded as an undoubted assertion of the common ownership, or common *usufruct*, which, though latent, was always held to be a fact. In other ways also the same hint is given. The provisions for letting the land lie fallow in the seventh year and in the jubilee year, and for securing the use of what grew in the field for all who chose to take it, were interferences with the free-will of the individual owners or occupiers, which find their justification only in the fact that the general ownership was never suffered entirely to fall into the background.

To sum up then: this system aimed at securing the advantages both of the socialist view and of the individualistic view while avoiding the evils of both. Private enterprise was encouraged, by the individual being guaranteed possession of his land against any other individual; while public spirit and a regard for general interests were promoted by the restrictions which limited the private ownership. Further, and more important still, the whole relation of the nation and of the individual to the land was raised out of the merely sordid region of material gain into the spiritual and moral region, by the principle that Yahweh their God alone had full proprietary rights over the soil. All were "sojourners" with Him. He had promised this land to their fathers as the place wherein He should specially reveal Himself to them. Here, communion with Him was to be established, and to each household there had been assigned by Yahweh a special portion of it, which it would be equally a sin and an unspeakable loss to part with. Compulsion alone could justify such a surrender; and the completed legislation, whatever its date, and even if it remained always an unrealised ideal,

---

* *Cf.* Numb. xxvi. 53-55 from P and Josh. xvii. 14 ff. from JE.

shows how determined the effort was to secure the perpetuity of the tenure in the original hands. The ideal of Israelite life was consequently that the land should remain in the hands of the hereditary owners, and that the main support of all the people should be agricultural labour.*

The hypothesis that this was the case is strengthened to a certainty by the manner in which commerce, one of the other main sources of wealth, is dealt with in the Israelite law. There is but little sympathy expressed with it, and some of the regulations issued are such as to render trade on any very large scale within Palestine itself impossible. From the use of the word "Canaanite" in the Old Testament (*cf.* Job xli. 6; Prov. xxxi. 24; Zeph. i. 11; Ezek. xvii. 4, and Isa. xxiii. 8) it is clear that, even in the later periods of Israelite history, the merchants were so prevailingly Canaanites that the two words are synonymous. Nay, more; there can be no doubt that the commercial career was looked down upon. Even as early as the prophet Hosea the Canaanite name is connected with false weights and vulgar commercial cheating (Hos. xii. 7), and it is looked upon as a last degradation that Ephraim should take delight in similar pursuits. In all that we read of merchants in the Old Testament we seem to hear the expression of a feeling that commerce, with its necessary wanderings, its temptations to dishonesty, its constant contact with heathen peoples, was an occupation that was unworthy of a son of Israel. Even Solomon's success as a royal merchant would not seem to have overcome this feeling, nor did the later commercial successes of kings like Jehoshaphat. In fact the ordinary Israelite had the home-staying farmer's contempt and suspicion of these far-wandering commercial people, so much more nimble-witted than himself, who were therefore to be regarded with half-admiring wariness.

But the very sinews of extensive commerce were cut by the law against the taking of interest from a brother Israelite.† Without credit, or the lending of money, or what is called sleeping partnership (and all these are bound up with receiving interest), it is impossible to have extensive trade. Without them every merchant would have to limit his operations to cash transactions and to his own immediate capital, and the great combinations which especially bring wealth would be impossible. Now we do not need at present to discuss the wisdom of prohibiting the taking of interest, nor the still more debated question whether that ancient prohibition would be wise or advantageous now. It is enough for our purpose that usury in its literal sense was actually forbidden among Israelites, and that they were thus shut out from the developed commercial life of the surrounding nations. As a result trade remained in a merely embryonic condition.

But in still other ways the Sinaitic legislation interfered with its development. The inculcation of ceremonial purity, especially in food, and the effort to make Israel a peculiar people unto Yahweh, which distinguishes even the earlier forms of the law, made intercourse with foreigners and living abroad always difficult and under some circumstances impossible. Consequently all the legislation that can possibly be considered commercial was of a very rudimentary character. From every point of view it is clear that ancient Israel was not a commercial people, and that the Divine law was intended to restrain them from commercial pursuits. They could not have been the holy and peculiar people they were meant to be, had they become a nation of traffickers.

With regard to manufacturing industries the case was not essentially different. Such pursuits were, it is true, more honoured than commerce was, for skill in all arts, whether agricultural or industrial, was regarded as a special gift of the Almighty. But so far as the records go, there is no evidence that a manufacturing industry existed, beyond what the very limited needs of the nation itself demanded. From the fact that, according to Prov. xxxi. 24, which was probably written late in the history of Israel, the manufacturing of linen garments for sale and of girdles for the Canaanites was the business of the thrifty and virtuous housewife, we may gather that systematic wholesale manufacture of such things was unknown. Probably the case was not otherwise in regard to all branches of industry. There are no traces of trade castes, nor of manufacturing towns; so that the manufacturing industries, so far as they existed, had no other place than that of handmaids to agriculture, by which the nation really lived.

According to the Old Testament, then, the ideal state of things for a people like Israel was that every household should be settled upon the land, that permanent eviction from or even alienation of the holdings should be impossible, and that the whole population should have a common interest in agriculture, that most honourable and fundamental of all human pursuits. There were, of course, some men in Israel more prominent than others, and some richer, but there was to be no impassable barrier between classes such as we find in Eastern countries where caste prevails, or in Western countries where the aristocratic principle has drawn a deep dividing line between those of "good" blood and all others. So far as is known, there were no class barriers to intermarriage. From the highest to the lowest, all were servants of Yahweh, and were consequently equal. The conditions of the land tenure were such that it was impossible, if they were respected, that large estates should accumulate in the hands of individuals, and a landless proletariate could not arise. The very rich and the very poor were alike legislated out of existence,

---

* The questions connected with the jubilee year are numerous and intricate, and it may be for ever impossible, from lack of data, to decide at what period in Israelite history it originated, or whether it was ever actually observed; but it undoubtedly expressed the spirit of the Israelite legislation and customary law at all times. It is the natural culmination of tendencies and ideas which were always present. That it is not mentioned in Deuteronomy at all is surprising, if it had been previously to Manasseh's day embodied either in custom or in law; yet, on the other hand, there are references in Ezekiel and other exilic books which are almost unintelligible except on the supposition that the jubilee year was a perfectly well-known institution (*cf.* Jer. xxxiv. 8 ff.; Ezek. vii. 12 f.; Ezek. xlvi. 16 ff.; Isa. lxi. 1 ff.). It is referred to in a merely allusive way, which implies that every hearer or reader of the prophetic warnings would know at once the full scope and meaning of the reference. Now, had the jubilee year been unknown before the exile, had it been introduced by the author of Lev. xxv. just before Ezekiel, no such assumption could have been made. It would, therefore, seem necessary to suppose that the ordinance for a jubilee year must have existed in pre-exilic time; for, strange as Deuteronomy's silence in regard to it is, the *argumentum e silentio* cannot weigh against indications of a positive kind, were they even fainter than those we have in regard to this matter.

† *Cf.* Kübel, "Die sociale und wirthschaftliche Gesetzgebung des Alten Testaments," p. 47.

and a sufficient provision for all was that which was aimed at. By the cycle of Sabbatic periods (the weekly Sabbath, the Sabbatic year, and the year of jubilee) ample rest for the land and its inhabitants was secured; and in the limits set upon the period for which a Hebrew slave might be retained, in the release, whatever that was, which the seventh year brought to the debtor, and in the restoration of land to the impoverished owner in the year of jubilee, such a series of breakwaters were erected against the inrushing flood of pauperism, that, had they been maintained, the world would have seen for the first time a fairly civilised community in which even moderate ill-desert in a man could not bring irretrievable ruin upon his posterity. The prodigal was hindered from selling his heritage; he could only sell the use of it for a number of years. He could not ruin himself by borrowing at extravagant rates of interest, for no one was tempted to lend him, and usury was forbidden. He might indeed run into debt and be sold into slavery along with his family, but that could only be for a few years, and then they all resumed their former position. In this very land where the fact, Divinely impressed upon human life, that the sins of the fathers were visited on the children was most unflinchingly taught, the most elaborate precautions were taken to mitigate the severity of this necessary law. From the first the ideal was that there should be no son or daughter of Israel oppressed or impoverished permanently; and whatever the stages of advance in Israelite law may have been, and whatever the date of particular ordinances may be, there is an admirable consistency of aim throughout. Even should it be proved that the Sabbatic ordinances remained mere generous aspirations, which never entered into the practical life of the people at all, that fact would only emphasise the earnestness and persistency with which the inspired legislators pursued their generous aim. No change in circumstances turned them aside. The glitter of the wealth acquired by Solomon and other kings by commerce never seduced them. No ideal but that early one of every man sitting under his own vine and his own fig-tree, with none to make him afraid, which is witnessed to before the Exile (Micah iv. 4), in the Exile (1 Kings iv. 25), and after the Exile (Zech. iii. 10), was ever cherished by them; and the whole economic legislation is entirely consistent with what we know of the earliest time. And the deepest roots of it all were religious. The Biblical writers have no doubt at all that the ideal economic state can be reached only by a people attuned by religion to self-sacrifice, to pity, and to justice. In this they differ radically from the socialists or semi-socialists of to-day. These imagine that man needs only a favourable environment to become good; whereas the Scriptural writers know that to use well the best environment is a task which, more than anything, puts strain upon the moral and spiritual nature. For to deal in a supremely wise fashion with great opportunities is the part only of a nature perfectly moralised. Consequently all the social laws of Israel are made to have their root in the relation of the people to their God.

There was only one power that could secure that this admirable machinery would move, and keep it moving. That was the love and fear of God. The conduct prescribed was the conduct befitting the *true* Israelite, the man who was faithful in all his ways. The laws marked out the paths wherein he should walk if he willed to do God's will. They were, therefore, ideal in all their highest prescriptions, and could never become real except where the true religion had had its perfect work. In that respect the Sermon on the Mount resembles the Israelite law. It presupposes a completely Christian society, just as the old law presupposes a completely Yahwistic society, *i. e.*, a society made up of men who made devotion to their God the chief motive of their lives. In such a community there would have been no difficulty in entirely realising the state of things aimed at here, just as in a community penetrated by the love of Christ the Sermon on the Mount would be not only practicable but natural. But without that supreme motive much that the enactments of both the Old Testament and the New demand must remain mere aspiration. Just in proportion as Israel was true to Yahweh was the law realised, and the demands of the law always acted as a spur to the better part of the people to enter into fuller sympathy and communion with Him in order that they might respond to them. The law and the religion of the people acted and reacted upon one another, but the greater of these two elements was religion.

It was not wonderful, therefore, that to a large extent this legislation failed, as men measure failure. The religious state of the nation never was what it should have been; and the law, though it was held to be Divine, was never wholly observed. In the Northern Kingdom, by the time of the Syrian wars, the old constitution of Israel had broken up. The hardy yeomanry had been ruined and dispersed. Their lands had been seized or bought by the rich, and every law that had been made to ensure restoration was habitually disregarded. As Robertson Smith states it [*] : "The unhappy Syrian wars sapped the strength of the country, and gradually destroyed the old peasant proprietors who were the best hope of the nation. The gap between the many poor and the few rich became wider and wider. The landless classes were ground down by usury and oppression, for in that state of society the landless man had no career in trade, and was at the mercy of the land-holding capitalist." And in Judah the state of things, though not so bad, was similar. In the days of Zedekiah we know that Hebrew slaves were held for life, instead of being released in the seventh year.[†] The properties of those compelled to sell were never returned to the owners, and all the laws that were meant to secure the welfare and prosperity of the masses of Israel were contemptuously disregarded. In short, the worst features of a purely competitive civilisation, with materialism eating into its soul, became glaringly manifest. All the canonical prophets without exception denounce the vices and tyrannies of the rich.[‡] As far as can be learned, moreover, the year of release and the Sabbatic year were not regularly or generally observed, while the jubilee year would seem never to have been kept after the Exile. The laws regarding taking interest were also evaded.[§]

Nevertheless it would be a great error to suppose that these Divinely given social laws should be branded as a failure. They were not lived up to, and it is not improbable that the corruption

---

[*] "Prophets of Israel," p. 88.   [‡] *Cf.* Amos ii. 6 ff.
[†] *Cf.* Jer. xxxiv. 8 ff.   [§] Neh. v. 1 seq.

of the people's life was in a degree intensified by the reaction from so high an ideal. But the axiom which is current now in all the newspapers, that laws too far above the general level of the national conscience cannot be enforced, and becoming a dead letter tend to produce lawlessness, does not apply to such codes as those of Israel. These, as has more than once been pointed out, were not of the same character as our legal codes are. Among us, laws are meant to be observed with minute and careful diligence, and any breach of them is punished by the courts, which, on the whole, can be easily set in motion. Ancient religious codes are never of that kind. They do contain laws of that character, but the bulk of the provisions are not laws which the executive is to enforce, but ideals of conduct which the true worshipper of God ought to strive to attain to. It is, therefore, of their very essence that they should be far above the average national conscience. Nations whose ideals soar no higher than the possible attainment of the average man as he is, have virtually no ideals at all, and are cut off from all enduring upward impulses. Those, on the contrary, who have a vision of the perfect life, are certain to be both humbler, and at the same time more sure to persist in the painful path of moral discipline. As "a man's reach should exceed his grasp," so also should a nation's; and though it is almost always forgotten, it is precisely Israel's glory that she set up for herself and exhibited to the world an ideal of brotherhood, of love to God and man, to which she could not attain. Great as the practical failure in Israel was, therefore, no fault can be found in the legislation. It moulded the characters of men who were sensitive to the influences coming from God, so that they became fit instruments of inspiration; and it made their lives examples of the highest virtue that the ancient world knew. Further, it gave shape to the hopes and aspirations of the people, especially where it was not realised. The year of jubilee, for example, is the groundwork of that great and affecting promise contained in Isa. lxi.: "The Spirit of the Lord Yahweh is upon me, because Yahweh hath anointed me to preach good tidings unto the meek; He hath sent me to bind up the broken-hearted, to proclaim liberty (*deror*) to the captives, and the opening of the prison to them that are bound; to proclaim the acceptable year of Yahweh and the day of vengeance of our God; to comfort all that mourn." That which was unattainable here, amid the greeds and lusts of an unspiritual generation, gave colour to the Messianic future; and men were taught to look and wait for a kingdom of God in which a peace and truth that could not as yet be reached would be the certain possession of all.

When we turn to modern times and modern circumstances, it is not easy to see how this ancient law can be applicable to them. In the first place, much of it was made binding upon Israel only because of its peculiar character as the people to whom the true religion was revealed. As custodians of that, they were justified in keeping up walls of partition between themselves and the world, which if universally accepted would only be hurtful to the highest interests of mankind. On the contrary, the development of the true religion having been completed by the coming of Christ, it is the duty of those nations which enjoy the light to spread abroad the "good news" of God which they have received, and to exhibit its power among all the nations of the earth. The highest and most Divine call which can now come to any people must, therefore, be radically different in some chief aspects from that of Israel. In the second place, the civilisation and culture of the great nations of to-day are far more complicated than any ancient civilisation ever was, and the general level is fixed by an action and reaction extending over the whole civilised world. No successes can be achieved, no blunders can be committed, in any part of the world which do not affect almost immediately the farthest ends of the earth. Moreover the intimate and universal correlation of interest makes interference with any part of the complicated whole an exceedingly perilous matter. Any proposal that this law, as being Divinely given, ought in its economic aspect to be made universally binding, should therefore be met by a demand for a careful inquiry into possible differences between ancient life and modern, which might make guidance Divinely given to the one inapplicable to the other. It is not necessarily true that because Israel by Divine command established every household upon the soil, forbade interest, and did nothing to encourage trade and manufactures, we should do these things. Take, for instance, the case of interest. In our day, and in civilisations of a high type, lending money to a person not in distress at all, but who sees an opportunity of making enough by the use of borrowed money to pay the interest and make a profit, is often a most praiseworthy and charitable act.

But if the Israelite legislation in regard to interest cannot justly be taken as a law for all time, still less can any great modern state neglect or discourage commerce and manufactures. The merely embryonic character of commercial legislation, and the contempt for the merchant which did in ancient days exist, would be exceedingly out of place now. There is no career more honourable than that of the merchant of our day when he carries on his business in a high-minded fashion, nor is there any member of the community whose calling is more beneficent than his. So long as he looks for gain to himself in ways which, taken on the great scale, bring benefit both to producer and consumer, his activity is purely beneficial. There is absolutely no reason why commercial life should not be as honest, as sound, as much in accord with the mind of God, in itself, as any other manner of life. For in many ways it has been a civilising agent of the highest power. Of course, if the charges brought against merchants by Ruskin, for example, who seizes upon and believes every story which involves charges of fraud against modern commerce, were true; if it were impossible, as he says it is, for an honest man to prosper in trade, then we might have some ground for condemning this branch of human activity. But happily only a confirmed and incorrigible pessimist can believe that. In our time some of the noblest men of whom we have any knowledge have been merchants, and among no class has so much princely generosity been exhibited. If mercantile help had been withdrawn from the poor, if the time, the money, the organising skill which merchants have freely expended upon charities were suddenly to fail them, the case against our modern civilisation would be indefinitely stronger than it is. Moreover the immense expansion of credit which is at once the glory and the danger of modern commerce, is itself a proof that such wholesale condemnation as we have spoken of is unwarrantable. The bulk of commerce must, after all, be fairly sound, otherwise it could not continue and spread as it does. And, as against the evils which affect it in common with all human activities, we must put the fact that it brings the produce of all lands to the door even of the poor, and by the constant contact between nations which it causes it is influencing the thought as well as the lives of men. Human brotherhood is being furthered by it, slowly, it is true, but surely, and the barriers which separate the nations are being sapped by its influence. These are indispensable services for the future progress of mankind, and make commerce now as much the necessary handmaid of the highest life as it would have been a hindrance to it in the case of the chosen people, before they had assimilated the truths of which they were to be the bearers to the world. That commerce, and trade in general, need to be purified goes without saying. That it may, of late years, have deteriorated, as the general decay of faith and the pursuit of luxury have weakened the sanctions of morality, is not improbable. But in itself it is not only a legitimate human activity; it is also an admirable instrument for bringing home to the consciences of men the truth that they are all their brothers' keepers. It presses home as nothing else could do the great truth proclaimed by St. Paul in regard to the Church, as true also of the world, that if one member suffers all the body suffers with it. Every day through this channel men are receiving lessons, which they cannot choose but hear, to the effect that no permanent benefit can come from the loss and suffering of men in any part of the world; that peace and righteousness and good faith are things which have supreme value even in the mercantile sense; and that, conversely, the merchant's pursuit of wealth, if carried on in accord with the fundamental truths of morality, inevitably becomes a potent factor in that advance to a world-wide knowledge of the Lord, which gleamed before the eyes of prophets and seers as the

"Far-off Divine event,
To which the whole creation moves."

But if we cannot make the Old Testament our law in regard to commerce, we must ask whether the legislation in regard to land has for us any binding force? Viewing it with this question in our minds, I think we must be struck by one fact, this namely, that the universal possession of land which was provided for in Israel and so anxiously maintained is the only provision known against the growth of a wage-earning class largely, if not entirely, at the mercy of the employer. In Greece and Rome the population at first were all settled on their own lands, and it was only when by money-lending the small properties were bought up and turned into huge farms, worked by farm-bailiffs and slaves, that misery began to invade all parts of the social fabric. In mediæval and feudal England, on the other hand, and indeed wherever the feudal system existed, the cultivators, even when they were serfs, had an inalienable right to the land. They could not be evicted if they rendered certain not very burdensome services to the lord. "As long as these dues were satisfied, it is plain the tenant was secure from dispossession," says Professor Thorold Rogers ("Six Centuries," etc., p. 44). But in time that system was broken down; and ever since, until within the last half-century, the course of things with the labouring classes in England has been one long descent. So long as the people were attached to the soil, and so long as all alike practised agriculture, as in Palestine under the Mosaic law, Englishmen lived in rough plenty, and were for the most part content. The fifteenth century was the golden age of mediæval agriculture; but a change for the worse came in with the seventeenth, and it continued.*

Two measures—the introduction of competitive rents with its corollary, eviction, and the enclosure of the common lands—worked gradually on until they have entirely divorced the workman from the soil, and Professor Cairnes [†] has told us clearly what that means. "In a contest between vast bodies of people so circumstanced and the owners of the soil the negotiation could have but one issue, that of transferring to the owners of the soil the whole produce, *minus* what was sufficient to maintain in the lowest state of existence the race of cultivators. This is what has happened wherever the owners of the soil, discarding all considerations but those dictated by self-interest, have really availed themselves of the full strength of their position. It is what has happened under rapacious governments in Asia; it is what has happened under rapacious landlords in Ireland; it is what now happens under the bourgeois proprietors of Flanders; it is, in short, the inevitable result which cannot but happen in the great majority of all societies now existing on earth where land is given up to be dealt with on commercial principles unqualified by public opinion, custom, or law." The result is that the labourers have only their daily wages to depend upon. "They have no means of productive home industry; they have not even a home from which they cannot be ejected at any moment on failure to pay the weekly rent; they have no land, garden, or domestic animals, the produce of which might support them till fresh work could be obtained." [‡] We need not wonder that this question of the occupancy of land as the only visible remedy for the hideous social state of the most highly civilised nations of the world is gradually becoming *the* question of our time. A great reaction against the purely commercial theory of land tenure has taken place. The land legislation in Ireland has been based on the doctrines that the nation cannot permit absolute property in land, and that there is no hope for any permanent improvement in the condition of the poor until labourers have land of their own. Now these are precisely the principles of the Scriptural land legislation. Under it landlords with absolute rights over land were impossible, and the rise of a proletariate at the mercy of the capitalist was also impossible. It is not so strange, therefore, as it might at first sight appear, that the demands of advanced land reformers, as they are voiced in Mr. Wallace's book (p. 192) are *mutatis mutandis*, identical with the provisions of the Israelite law. He demands (1) that landlordism

---

* *Contemp. Rev.*, 1880, April, p. 681.
† "Essays on Political Economy," p. 201.
‡ Wallace, "Land Nationalisation," p. 16.

shall be superseded by occupying ownership; (2) that the tenure of the holders of land must be made secure and permanent; (3) that arrangements must be made by which every British subject may secure a portion of land for personal occupation at its fair agricultural value; and (4) that in order that these conditions be rendered permanent sub-letting must be absolutely prohibited, and mortgages strictly limited. This essential oneness of view in the modern land reformer and in the ancient law is all the more remarkable that, so far as can be gathered from his book, Mr. Wallace has never regarded the Old Testament from this point of view. He never quotes it, and is apparently quite unconscious that the plan which experience of present evils, and acute and disinterested reflection on them, has suggested to him, was set forth thousands of years ago as the only righteous one.

But this is not by any means the end of the matter. Even if the social reformers of our day could restore society to the conditions set forth so emphatically and so long ago in Israel, history proves that nothing more than a temporary improvement might be accomplished. In Israel, as we have seen, with the decay of religion came the decay of this righteous social state. Human selfishness then shook off the curb of religion, and gave itself without restraint to the oppression of the poor. Have we any reason to believe that now human selfishness would do less? There appears little ground to think so; and though we may believe that without the acceptance of Deuteronomic principles in modern life we cannot restrain the growth of poverty, even with Deuteronomic principles embodied in our laws nothing will be done if the people turn their backs upon religion, make selfish enjoyment their highest good, and the comforts and pleasures of a merely material life their only heart-warming aspiration. In that fact we have an indication of the true functions of the Church and of religious teachers in the social and political life of our time and of times to come. As individuals, religious men should certainly be found always among the advocates of all laws and plans which tend to justice and mercy, and to the raising of the toilers everywhere to a higher standard of living. Further, at no time should the Church be found committed to a purely conservative policy, of retaining things as they are. The undeniable facts as to the condition of the poor are so utterly unjustifiable, that to leave things as they are is to fall into the treason of despair in regard to the future of our race, and into scarcely veiled disbelief of the essential truth of Christianity. No Church whose heart has not been corrupted by worldliness can think for a moment that the present state of things in all highly civilised communities is even tolerable. It cannot last, and it ought not to last; the Church that timidly supports it, lest worst things should come, is named and known thereby for recreant to Christ and to the highest hopes of His Gospel. But, on the other hand, it is only in very exceptional circumstances, and for short intervals, that the Churches and their ministers can ever be called upon to make the external, material condition of the people their first and chief care. They have a place of their own to fill, a function of their own to discharge; and upon their efficiency and diligence in these the stability and permanence of all that politicians and publicists can accomplish ultimately depends. They must keep alive and nourish the religious life, as that life has been shaped and constituted by our Lord Jesus Christ. Their province is to witness, in season and out of season, for a life of purity and love, for the Divine and ideal sides of things, for the necessity, for man's highest well-being, of a life hid with Christ in God. If they do not keep up this testimony, no others will; and if it be dropped out of sight, then the social agony and struggle, the patriotic and humanitarian strivings of all the reformers, will lack their final sanction. Men will inevitably come to think that man's life does consist in the abundance of the things that he possesses, the leisure, the amusement, the culture which by combining material resources he may attain to. But it is to deny and denounce that view that the Church exists in the world. It was to lift men out of it, to set them above it for ever, that Christ died. It is finally only by abandoning it that the highest social condition can be reached and made permanent for the multitudes of men. In no way therefore can the Church so dangerously betray the cause of the poor and the oppressed as by plunging into the heat of the social and political struggle. She has to witness to higher things than that involves, and her silence in the ideal region which would certainly follow her devotion to material interests, however unselfish, would be but ill compensated for by any imaginable success she might attain.

CHAPTER XXI.

JUSTICE IN ISRAEL.

AMONG the nations of the modern world one of the most vital distinctions is the degree in which just judgment is estimated and provided for. Indeed, according to modern ideas, life is tolerable only where all men are equal before the law; where all are judged by statutes which are known, or at least may be known, by all; where corruption or animus in a judge is as rare as it is held to be dishonourable. But we cannot forget that in the majority of even the more advanced countries of the world these three conditions are not yet found, and that where they do exist they are only recent acquirements. In the latest born, and in many respects the most advanced of the great commonwealths, in the United States of America, the corruption of a number of the inferior courts is undeniable, and is tolerated with a most disappointing patience by the people. In England Judge Jeffries is no very remote memory, and Lord Bacon's acceptance of presents from litigants in his court has only been made more certain by recent investigations. An absolutely honest intention to give even-handed justice to all is, therefore, even in England, only a recent attainment, and in no country is the honest intention always successful in realising itself. But if this be so among the civilised nations of the West, we may say that in Oriental countries there has been little of systematic and continuous effort to give even-handed justice at all. Yet nowhere has the sinfulness and the destructiveness of corruption in judgment been more impassionedly and more frequently set forth by the highest authorities in religion and morals, than in the East. Tupper, our most recent authority, in writing of "Our Indian Protectorate,"

p. 289, describes the Indian attitude to law thus: "There was not that reverence for law which in Europe is in all probability very largely due to the influence of the Roman law, and to the teaching of the Roman Catholic and other Christian Churches. So far as there was a germ out of which the respect for law ought to have grown, it was to be found in dislike to actions plainly opposed to custom and tradition. There was a deeply rooted and widespread conviction that there could be no rule to which exceptions could not be made, if agreeable to the discretion of the chief or any of his delegates. The chief was set above the law; it did not limit his authority by any constitution. There was no legislation for the improvement of law. The administration of justice was extremely imperfect." The same writer describes the result of such a state of mind in his picture of Mahratta rule (p. 247). "There was," he says, "no prescribed form of trial. Men were seized on slight suspicions. Presumptions of guilt were freely made. Torture was employed to compel confession. Prisoners for theft were often whipped at intervals to make them discover where the stolen property was hidden. *Ordinarily no law was referred to except in cases affecting religion.*" That there were both Hindu codes and Mohammedan codes in existence which claimed and were believed to have Divine authority made no difference in India. Nor does it make any in Persia to-day.*

Now, in coming to the consideration of the views of justice embodied in Old Testament law, and the quality of the judiciary in ancient Israel, we must take not Western but Eastern ideas as our standard. Judging from that point of view, it should create no prejudice in our minds if we find on the first glance that all men were not equal before the ancient law of Israel; that for a considerable period, if not during the whole political existence of Israel, there was no very extensive written law; and that arbitrary and corrupt judgment was only too common at all times. For none of these defects would indicate in ancient Israel the same evils as similar defects in nations of our time would indicate. They are rather defects in the process of being overcome, than defects arising from feeble or vitiated life. If there was a constant movement towards the highest state of things, that is all we can demand or expect to find.

Now there does seem to have been that. As has been well pointed out by Dr. Oort,† in the tribes which became Israel justice must have been administered by the heads of the various bodies which went to make these up. The household was ruled even in matters of life and death solely by the father; the family, in the wider sense, was judged by its own heads; the tribes by the elders of the tribes, and there probably was no appeal from one tribunal to another. Each tribunal was final in its own domain. It may be, also, that the judicial function was in all these bodies exercised in the lax and timid fashion common among Bedouin tribes to-day.‡ In all cases, too, it is probable that in the pre-Mosaic time the standard of judgment was customary law. Only with this very great modification can Oort's epigrammatic description of the situation—"There was no law, but there were givers of legal decisions"—be accepted. So far as can be ascertained, the customs according to which men were expected to live were perfectly well known, and within certain narrow limits of variation were extraordinarily stable. How stable customary law may be made, even in the midst of a society governed in the main according to written law in its strictest sense, may be seen in the execration which any breach of the Ulster custom of tenant right met with, before that custom was embodied in any statutes. And in antiquity the stringency of custom can hardly be exaggerated. Under it, when thoroughly established, there was, in all the cases covered by it, only this one way of acting for all, both men and women, who were fit for society at all. Any alternative course was probably inconceivable in the tribal stage of the Israelites' existence.

But a change would doubtless be wrought whenever the appointment of a king took place. Then national law would appear, in embryo at least; and at first, until custom had grown up in this region also, it would largely be an expression of the will of the king, and of the royal officers instructed and trained by the king. But it would have free and unchallenged course only when it claimed authority in matters lying outside of the family and tribal jurisdictions. Wherever it attempted to interfere with tribal or family rights, danger to the kingship of the most acute kind would be sure to arise. In all probability, it was disregard of this axiomatic truth which made Solomon's reign so burdensome to the people and tore the kingdom asunder under Rehoboam. Ahab too fell a victim to his disregard of it. Lastly, the introduction of elaborate written codes of law would, if it came as the crown of such a development, depose custom from its supremacy, though it would not abolish it; and would substitute for it as the main element in all judicial matters the written prescription, which is the necessary presupposition of a fully organised judiciary of the modern type, with a regulated and definite power of appeal.

But in the case of ancient Israel there is a distinguishing element which has to be fitted into this ordinary scheme of progression, and that is the Divine revelation to Moses. Taken up at the tribal stage by the Mosaic revelation, the Israelite tribes were touched and welded into coherence, if not quite as a nation, at least as the people of Yahweh, so that during all the distracting days of the Judges they kept up in essentials their social and religious unity.* And with the religious union there must have come administrative uniformity to some considerable extent. The jurisdiction of the heads of households, of heads of families, and of the tribal elders would be as little interfered with as possible; but, as we have seen, all customs and rights had to be reviewed from the point of view of the new religion, and appeal to Moses as the prophet of it must have often been unavoidable. Just as his first followers were continually coming to Mohammed, to ask whether this or that ancient custom could be followed by professors of Islam, so there must have been constant appeals to Moses. So long as he lived, therefore, he, and after him Joshua and Moses' fellow-tribesmen the sons of Levi, as being specially zealous for the religion of Yahweh, must have been constantly called in to assist the customary judges; and so the habit of appeal must have

---

* See *ante*, p. 575.
† *Cf.* "Oud-Israël Rechtswezen," pp. 10 ff.
‡ *Cf.* Doughty, "Arabia Deserta," vol. i., p. 249.

* *Cf.* Nowack, "Die sozialen Probleme in Israel," p. 5.

grown in Israel long before there was any king. Thus also a common standard of judgment would be established. That standard must necessarily have been the law of Yahweh, *i. e.*, the new Yahwistic principles and all that might *prima facie* be deduced from them, together with so much of custom and tradition as had been accepted as compatible with these principles. We have stated the reasons for holding that the Decalogue was Mosaic, and the Book of the Covenant may be taken also to represent what the current law in Mosaic or sub-Mosaic time was held to be. As Oort well says (*loc. cit.*), when we know that the Hittites about the middle of the fourteenth century B. C. concluded a treaty with Rameses II. of Egypt the terms of which were written upon a silver plate, "why may there not also have been written statements regarding the mutual rights and duties of the people of a town, engraved upon stone or metal, and set forth openly for inspection?" What he confines to mere town business and refers to the time of the Judges, we may without risk extend to a general fundamental law like the Decalogue, or even to the Book of the Covenant, and date it in the time of Moses. Writing was so common an accomplishment in Canaan before the Exodus, that such a supposition is not in the least improbable. These written laws formed the crown of the law of Yahweh, and by them all the rest was raised to a higher level and transformed.

As new men, new times, and new difficulties arose, the priest became the special organ of Divine direction. It may be that the priestly Torah was largely the result of the sacred lot; but the questions that were put, and the manner in which they were put, would be decided ultimately by the conception the priest had of the truth about God. The teaching of the Decalogue would therefore be the dominant and formative power in all that was spoken by the priest and for Yahweh. In the disorganised state into which Israel fell during the time of the Judges, when, as Deuteronomy takes for granted, and as 1 Kings iii. 2 and 3 asserts, the legitimate worship of Yahweh was carried on at many centres, the substantial sameness of the tradition as to the history of Israel, in all the varied forms in which we encounter it, is proof sufficient that at each of the great sanctuaries (which were certainly in the hands of Levitical priests) the treasure of ancient knowledge, both in law and history, was carefully and accurately preserved.* New decisions would be given, but they came through men penetrated with the high thoughts of God, and of His people's destiny, which Moses had so fruitfully set forth. This was the element in the life of the people which all the higher minds strove to perpetuate, and, being spiritual, it spiritualised and raised all accessory things. Consequently there was, long before the kingship, what was equivalent to a national feeling of the highest kind, and the conception of justice and its administration corresponded to that.

In the Book of the Covenant, which in this matter represents so early a period that there is no mention of "judges," only of Pelilim,† *i. e.*, arbitrators (Exod. xxi. 22), so that the tribal and family heads can alone have exercised judicial functions, we find the most solemn warnings against any legal perversion of right to gain popularity, against yielding to the vulgar temptation to oppress the poor, or to the subtler and, for generous minds, more insidious temptation, to give an unjust judgment out of pity for the poor. Israel was, moreover, to keep far from bribery, "which blindeth them that have sight, and perverteth righteous causes." In no way was the law to be used for criminal or oppressive purposes. From the very first, therefore, in Israel the higher principles of faith and life set themselves to combat *à outrance* the tendency to unjust judgment, which seems now, at least, quite ineradicable in the East, save among the Bedouin.*

A still higher note is struck in the repetition of the law in the Book of Deuteronomy. In chap. i., originally part of a historic introduction to the book proper, we read: "Hear the causes between your brethren, and judge righteously between a man and his brother, and the stranger that is with him. Ye shall not respect persons in judgment; ye shall hear the small and the great alike; ye shall not be afraid of the face of man; for the judgment (*i. e.*, the whole judicial process and function) is God's; and the cause that is too hard for you ye shall bring unto me (Moses), and I will hear it." Yes, the judgment is God's. Just as the whole of moral duty towards man was raised by the Decalogue to a new and more intimate relation with God, so here justice, the fundamental necessity of a sound and stable political state, is lifted out of the conflict of mean and selfish motives, in which it must eventually go down, and is set on high as a matter in which the righteous God is supremely concerned. In this, as in all things, Israel was called to a lonely eminence of ideal perfection by the character of the God whom they were bound to serve. Therefore it strikes us with no surprise that justice is insisted upon almost with passion in Deut. xvii. 20: "Justice, justice shalt thou pursue after, that thou mayest live and possess the land which Yahweh thy God giveth thee"; or that it is made one of the conditions of Israel's permanence as a nation. In chap. xxiv. 17 we read, "Thou shalt not wrest the judgment of the stranger, nor of the fatherless; nor take the widow's raiment to pledge"; in xxv. 1 and 2, "If there be a plea between men, . . . then they (*i. e.*, the judges) shall justify the righteous and condemn the wicked." For any other course of conduct would bring guilt upon the nation in the sight of Yahweh; and how jealously that was guarded against is seen in the sacrifice and ritual imposed for the purification of the people from the guilt of a murder the perpetrator of which was unknown (Deut. xxi. 1-9). Unatoned for and disregarded, such a crime brought disturbance into those relations between Israel and their God upon which their very existence as a nation depended; and the disregard of justice, where wrongs were committed by known persons and were left unpunished, was of course more deadly. So the author of Deuteronomy looked upon it; and the prophets, from the first of them to the last, brand unjust judgment, the perverting the course of legal justice, as the most alarming sign of national decay. The righteous God, with whom there was no respect of persons, could not permanently

---

* Oort, "Oud-Israël Rechtswezen," p. 14.
† A probable parallel to these may be found in the non-official arbiters mentioned by Doughty. "Arabia Deserta," vol. i., pp. 145 and 502-3.

* Doughty, vol. i., p. 249.

favour a people whose judges and rulers disregarded righteousness; and when destruction actually came upon this people, it was proclaimed to be God's doing, "because there was no truth nor justice nor knowledge of God in the land."

Nowhere in the world, therefore, has the demand for justice been made more central than here, and nowhere has injustice been more passionately fought against. Nor have the sanctions binding to a pursuit of justice been at any period more nobly or more vividly conceived. In this main point, therefore, Israel's law stands irreproachable—marvellously so, considering its great antiquity. But we have still to inquire whether any really adequate provision was made for the general and inexpensive administration of justice. To take the latter first, law was in old Israel probably *as cheap* as it would be in the primitive East to-day, if bribery were to be stopped. To advise as to the sacred law, to plead for justice according to it, did not then, and does not now in similar circumstances, belong to any special professional class who live by it. The priest could be appealed to freely by all; and the heads of fathers' houses, as well as the tribal heads, were, by the very fact that they were such, bound to give judgment among their people, and to appear for and take responsibility for them when they had a cause with persons beyond the limits of the particular families and tribes. Justice, consequently, was in ordinary circumstances perfectly free to all.

And from a very early time earnest efforts were made to make it equally *accessible*. At first, when the people were in one army or train, before they came to Sinai, an overwhelming burden was laid upon Moses. As the prophet of the new dispensation all difficulties were brought to him. But at Jethro's suggestion, as JE tells us in Exod. xviii. 13 ff., and as Deuteronomy repeats in chap. i. 16, he chose men of each tribe, or took the heads of each tribe, and set them as captains of thousands and hundreds and fifties and tens. Not improbably this was primarily a military organisation, but to these captains was committed also jurisdiction over those under them. In all ordinary cases they judged them and their families in the spirit of Yahwism, as well as commanded them; and in this way, as has already been pointed out, the customary law was revised in accordance with Yahwistic principles. Justice too was brought to every man's door. The only question that suggests itself is whether these captain-judges were the ordinary family and tribal heads, organised for this purpose by Moses. On the whole this would seem to have been so, and it may well be that Jethro's suggestion had in view the danger of ignoring them, as well as the burden which Moses' sole judgeship laid upon him. But with the advance to the conquest of Canaan a new situation emerged, and the probability is that more and more, as the tribes fell into entire or semi-isolation, the tribal organisation in its natural shape would come to the front again. Deuteronomy, however, tells us little if anything of this. In the main passage regarding this matter (xvii. 8-13), where provision is made for an appeal to a central court, the legislation is entirely for a period much later than Moses. Like the law regarding sacrifice at one altar, the judicial provisions of Deuteronomy seem all to be bound up with the place which Yahweh shall choose, viz. the Solomonic Temple in Jerusalem.

We may consequently conclude that the judicial arrangements to which Deuteronomy alludes existed only after the Israelite kingship had been for some time established at Jerusalem. We have no distinct evidence for the existence of a central high court in David's days; and from the story of Absalom's rebellion we should gather that the old, simple Oriental method still prevailed, according to which the king, like the heads of tribes, families, etc., judged every one who came to him, personally, at the gate of the royal city. But Samuel is said in 1 Sam. vii. 16 to have annually gone on circuit to Bethel, Gilgal, and Mizpah. According to the school of Wellhausen, nearly the whole of this chapter is the work of a Deuteronomic writer about the year 600. In that case, of course, it would be difficult to prove that the arrangement attributed to Samuel was not a mere echo of what was done in Josiah's day; though, if the Deuteronomic prescriptions were carried out then, there would be no need for such a system. On the other hand, if Budde and Cornill be right in tracing the chapter back to JE, this habit of going on circuit must have been an ancient one, possibly dating from Samuel's time. That this latter view is the correct one is in a degree confirmed by the statement in viii. 2 that Samuel's sons were installed by him as judges in Israel, at Beersheba. This belongs to E, and it would seem to indicate the beginnings of such a system as Deuteronomy presupposes.

But it is only in the days of Jehoshaphat (873-849 B.C.) that an arrangement like that in Deuteronomy is mentioned. From 2 Chron. xix. 5 ff. we learn that "he set judges in the land throughout all the fenced cities of Judah, city by city. Moreover in Jerusalem did Jehoshaphat set of the Levites and of the priests, and of the heads of the fathers' houses, for the judgment of Yahweh and for controversies." Further, it is stated that Amariah the chief priest was set over the judges in Jerusalem in all Yahweh's matters, *i.e.*, in all religious questions, and Zebadiah the son of Ishmael the prince of the house of Judah in all the king's matters, *i.e.*, in all secular affairs. Of course few advanced critics will admit that the Books of Chronicles are reliable in such matters. But that judgment is altogether too sweeping, and here we would seem to have a well-authenticated record of what Jehoshaphat actually did.

For it will be observed, that when we take up the various notices in regard to the administration of justice, we have a well-defined progress from Moses to Jehoshaphat. Moses was chief judge and committed ordinary cases to the tribal and family heads who were chosen as military leaders, each judging his own detachment. After passing the Jordan, the whole matter would seem to have fallen back into the hands of the tribal heads, with the occasional help of the heroes who delivered and judged Israel. At the end of this period Samuel, as head of the State, went on circuit, and appointed his sons judges in Beersheba, thus initiating a new system, which, had it been successful, might have superseded the tribal and family heads altogether. But it was a failure, and was not repeated. With the rise of the kingship the courts received further organisation. If the Chronicler can be trusted, Levites to the number of six thousand were appointed to be judges and Shoterim. The number seems excessive; but the appointment of Levites to act as assessors with the tribal and other heads would be a natural expedient for a king like David to have recourse to, if he desired to secure uniformity of judgment, and to bring the courts under his personal influence. The next step would naturally be that which is attributed to Jehoshaphat, and it is precisely that which Deuteronomy points to as being already at work in his time. We have, consequently, more than the late authority of the Chronicler for Jehoshaphat's high court. The probabilities of the case point so strongly to the rise of some such judicial system about that period, that it would require some positive proof, not mere negative suspicion, to lead us to reject the narrative. In any case this must have been the system in Josiah's day, and afterwards. For when Jeremiah was arraigned for prophesying destruction to the Temple and to Jerusalem, the process against him was conducted on similar lines to those laid down in Deuteronomy. The princes judged, the priests (curiously enough along with the false prophets) made the charge, *i. e.*, stated that the prophet's conduct was worthy of death, and the princes acquitted. During the Exile it is probable that the "elders" of the people were permitted to judge them in all ordinary cases, but we have no certain proof that this was so. After the return from Babylon, however, the local courts were re-established, probably in the very form in which they appear in the New Testament (Matt. v. 22, x. 17; Mark xiii. 9; Luke xii. 14-58).

Throughout the whole history of Israel, therefore, courts of justice were easily accessible to every man, whether he were rich or poor. No doubt the free, open-air, Eastern manner of administering justice was favourable to that; but from the days of Moses onward we have fairly conclusive proof that the leaders of the people made it their continual care that wherever a wrong was suffered there should be some court to which an appeal for redress could be made.

The justice aimed at in Israel was, therefore, *impartial* and *accessible*. We have still to inquire whether it was *merciful* or cruel in its infliction of punishment. Dr. Oort says it was a hard law in this respect, but one is at a loss to see how that view can be sustained. There is no mention of torture in connection with legal proceedings, either in the history or in the legislation. Nor is there any instance mentioned in which an accused person was imprisoned until he confessed. Indeed imprisonment would not appear to have been a legal punishment in Israel, nor in any antique state. The idea of providing maintenance for those who had offended against the law was one which could never have occurred to any one in antiquity. Prisons are, of course, frequently mentioned in Scripture; but they were used, up to the time of Ezra, only for the safekeeping of persons charged with crime till they could be brought before the judges. Sometimes, as in the case of the prophets, men were imprisoned to prevent them from stirring up the people; but this procedure was nowhere sanctioned by law. Further, the crimes for which the punishment prescribed in the ancient law was death were few. Idolatry, adultery, unnatural lust, sorcery, and murder or manslaughter, together with striking or cursing parents and kidnapping—these were all. Considering that idolatry and sorcery were high treason in its worst form, so far as this people was concerned, and that impurity threatened the family in a much more direct and immediate fashion then than it does now, while the people were naturally inclined to it, one must wonder that the list of capital crimes is so short. Contrast this with Blackstone's statement in regard to England (quoted "Ency. Brit.," iv., p. 589): "Among the variety of actions which men are daily liable to commit, no less than one hundred and sixty have been declared by Act of Parliament to be felonies without benefit of clergy, or, in other words, to be worthy of instant death." It is only in comparatively recent years that the punishment of death has been practically restricted to murder in England. Yet that is almost the case in the ancient Jewish law; for the exceptions are such as would reappear in England if it were more sparsely populated and manners were rougher. In Australia, for example, highway robbery under arms and violence to women are capital crimes, just because the country is sparsely inhabited and the households unprotected. Nor were the modes of death inflicted cruel. Only three—viz. impalement, and burning, and stoning—appear to be so. But it may be believed that in the cases contemplated by the law death in some less painful manner had preceded the two former, as is certainly the case in Josh. vii. 15 and 25, and in Deut. xxi. 22. As for the latter, it must have been horrible to look upon, but in all probability the criminal's agony was rarely a prolonged one. The other method of execution, by the sword namely, was humane enough. Dr. Oort tells us that mutilations were common; but his proof is only this, that in the treaty between the Hittite king and Rameses II. we read, concerning inhabitants of Egypt who have fled to the land of the Hittites and have been returned, "His mother shall not be put to death; he shall not be punished in his eyes, nor on his mouth, nor on the soles of his feet." The same provision is made for Hittite fugitives. From this evidence of the custom of surrounding peoples, and from the fact that the *jus talionis* is announced in the Scriptures by the familiar formula, "Eye for eye, tooth for tooth, hand for hand, foot for foot," Dr. Oort draws this conclusion. But he appears to forget that the *jus talionis* was common to almost all the peoples of the ancient world, and is referred to in the Pentateuch, not as a new principle, but as a custom coming down from immemorial time. Consequently, though there must once have been a time in which it was carried out in its literal form, that time probably was past when the laws referring to it were written. In Rome, and probably in other lands where this custom existed, it early gave place to the custom of giving and receiving money payments. Most probably this was the case in Israel, at least from the time of the Exodus. For the new religion introduced by Moses was merciful. But these references to the principle of retaliation tell us nothing as to the frequency or otherwise of mutilation as a punishment. No instance of mutilation being inflicted either as a retaliation or as a punishment occurs in the Old Testament, and the probability is that cases were never numerous. Apart from retaliation they are never mentioned; and we may, I think, set it down as one of the distinctive merits of the Israelite law that it never was betrayed into sanctioning the cutting off of hands or feet or ears or noses as general punishment for crime. But so far as the principle of the *lex talionis* was retained, its effect was wholesome. It was a continual reminder that all free Israelites were equals in the sight of Yahweh. And not only so, it enforced as well as asserted equality. Any poor man mutilated by a rich man could demand the infliction of the same wound upon his oppressor. He could reject his excuses, and refuse his money, and bring home to him the truth that they had equal rights and duties.

In this way this seemingly harsh law helped to lay the foundation for our modern conception of humanity, which regards all men as brethren. For the teaching of our Lord, which fulfilled all that the polity and religion of ancient Israel had foreshadowed of good, broke down the walls of partition between Jew and Gentile, and made all men brethren by revealing to them a common Father. It surely is strange and sad that those who specially make liberty, equality, and fraternity their watchwords, have received so false an impression of the religion of both the Old and New Testaments, that they pride themselves on rejecting both. When all is said, the levelling of barriers which the crushing weight of Roman power brought about, and the common methods and elements of thought which the Greek conquest had spread all over the civilised world, would never have made the brotherhood of man the universally accepted doctrine it is. The truths which made it credible came from the revelation given by God to His chosen people, and its final and conclusive impulse was given to it by the lips of Christ.

In face of that cardinal fact it is vain to point out as one of the defects of this law that all men were not equal before it. Women were not equal with men, nor were foreigners nor slaves equal with freeborn Israelites; but the seed of all that later times were to bring was already there. The principles which at the long end of the day have abolished slavery, raised women to the equal position they now occupy, and made peace with foreigners increasingly the desire of all nations, had their first hold upon men given them here. In all these directions the Mosaic law was epoch-making. In the fifth commandment, as well as in the legislation regarding the punishment of a rebellious son, the mother is put upon the same level as the father. However subordinate woman's position in the larger public life might be, within the home she was to be respected. There, in her true domain, she was man's equal, and was acknowledged to have an equal claim to reverence from her children.

In precisely the same way the "stranger" was freed from disability and protected. In the earliest days, when the Israelite community was still being formed, whole groups of strangers were received into it and obtained full rights, as for example the Kenites and Kenizzites. But though this was a promise of what Israel was ultimately to be to the world, the necessities of the situation, the need to keep intact the treasure of higher religion which was committed to this people, compelled the adoption of a more separatist policy. Yet "in no other nation of antiquity were strangers received and treated with such liberality and humanity as in Israel." They were freely afforded the protection of the law; they were, in short, received as "a kind of half-citizens, with definite rights and duties."*

* Riehm, "Handwörterbuch," Baethgen, vol. i., p. 463.

Further, though the *ger* was not bound to all the religious practices and rites of the Israelite, yet he was permitted, and in some cases commanded, to take part in their religious worship. If he consented to circumcise all his house he might even share in the Passover feast. All oppression of such an one was also rigorously forbidden, and to a large extent the stranger shared in the benefits conferred by the provision for the poor of the land which the law made compulsory.

Nor was the case otherwise with slaves. Equality there was not, and could not be; but in the provisions for the emancipation of the Israelite slave and the introduction of penalties for undue harshness, it began to be recognised that the slave stood, in some degree at least, on the same level as his master—he too was a man.

Taking it as a whole, therefore, the ancient world will be searched in vain for any legislation equal to this in the "promise and the potency" of its fundamental ideas as to justice. Here, as nowhere else, we can see the radical principles which should dominate in the administration of justice laying hold upon mankind, and that there was a living will and power behind these principles is shown in the steady movement toward something higher which characterised Israelite law. In the pursuit of impartiality, accessibility, and humanity, the teachers of Israel were untiring, and the sanctions by which they surrounded and guarded all that tended to make the administration of justice effective in the high sense were unusually solemn and powerful. The result has been most remarkable. All the ages of civilised men since have been the heirs of Israel in this matter. Roman influence and the influence of the Christian Church have no doubt been powerful, and the manifold exigencies of life have drawn out and made explicit much which was only implicit in the ancient days. But the higher qualities of our modern administration of justice can be traced back step by step to Biblical principles, and the course of development laid bare. When that is done, it is seen that the almost ideal purity and impartiality of the best modern tribunals is the completion of what the Israelite law and methods began. In this one instance at least the great Mosaic principles have come to fruition; and from the security and peace, the contentment and the confidence, with which impartial justice has filled the minds of men, we can estimate how potent to cure the ills of our social and moral state the realisation of the other great Mosaic ideals would be. It should be a source of encouragement to all who look for a time when "the kingdoms of this world shall become the kingdoms of our Lord and of His Christ," that something like the ideal of justice has so far been realised. It has no doubt been a weary time in coming, and it has as yet but a narrow and perhaps precarious footing in the world. But it is here, with its healing and beneficent activity; and in that fact we may well see a pledge that all the rest of the Divinely given ideals for the Kingdom of God will one day be realised also. Such a consummation, however remote it may seem to our human impatience, however devious and winding the paths by which alone it can draw near, will come most surely, and in our approach to the ideal in our judicial system we may well see the firstfruits of a richer and more plentiful harvest.

CHAPTER XXII.

LAWS OF PURITY (CHASTITY AND MARRIAGE).

In dealing with the ten commandments it has been already shown that, though these great statements of religious and moral truth were to some extent inadequate as expressions of the highest life, they yet contained the living germs of all that has followed. But we cannot suppose that the reality of Israelite life from the first corresponded with them. They contained much that only the experience and teaching of ages could fully bring to light; therefore we cannot expect that the actual laws in regard to the relations of the sexes and the virtue of chastity should stand upon the same high level as the Decalogue. The former represent the reality, this the ultimate ideal of Israelite law on these subjects. But neither is unimportant in forming an estimate of the value of the revelation given to Israel, and of the moral condition of early Israel itself, nor can either be justly viewed altogether alone. The actual law at any moment in the history of Israel must be regarded as inspired and upborne by the ideal set forth in the ten commandments. But it must, at the same time, be a very incomplete realisation of these, and its various stages will be best regarded as instalments of advance towards that comparative perfection.

In regard to the relations of the sexes and the virtue of purity this must be peculiarly the case. For though chastity has been safeguarded by almost all nations up to a certain low point, it has never been really cherished by any naturalistic system. Nor has it ever been favoured by mere humanism.* Consequently there is no point of morals in regard to which man has more conspicuously failed to work out the merely animal impulse from his nature than in this. And yet, for all the higher ends of life, as well as for the prosperity and vigour of mankind, purity in the sexual relations is entirely vital. One great cause of the decay of nations, nay, even of civilisations, has been the abandonment of this virtue. This was the main cause of the destruction of the Canaanites. It may even be said to have been the cause of the wreck of the whole ancient world. We should consequently measure what the Mosaic influence did for purity of life, not by comparing early Israelite laws with what has been accomplished by Christianity, but with the condition of the Semitic peoples surrounding Israel, in and after the Mosaic times.

What that was we know. Their religions, far from discouraging sexual immorality, made it a part of their holiest rites. Both men and women gave themselves up to natural and unnatural lusts, in honour of their gods. To the north, and south, and east, and west of Israel these practices prevailed, and as a natural result the moral fabric of these nations' life fell into utter ruin. In private life adultery, and the still more degrading sin of Sodom were common. The man had a right to indiscriminate divorce and remarriage, and marriage connections now reckoned incestuous, such as those between brother and sister, were entirely approved. In all these points Israel as a nation was without reproach. The higher teaching this people had received in respect to the character of God, and it may be some reminiscence of Egyptian custom, which was in some respects purer than that of the Semitic peoples, raised them to a higher level. Yet in the main the early Israelite view of women was fundamentally the uncivilised one.

But at all periods of Israelite history, even the earliest, women had asserted their personality. In the eye of the law they might be the chattels of their male relatives, but as a fact they were dealt with as persons, with many personal rights. They had no independent position in the community, it is true. They could take no part in a festival so important as the Passover, nor were they free to make vows without the consent of their husbands. In other ways also social restraints were laid upon them. Nevertheless their position in early Israel was much higher than it is in the East to-day, and their liberty was in no wise unreasonably abridged. In David's day women could appear in public to converse with men without scandal.* They also took part in religious festivals and processions, giving life to them by beating their timbrels, by singing, and by dancing.† They could be present also at all ordinary sacrifices and at sacrificial feasts; and, as we see in the case of Deborah and others, they could occupy a high, almost a supreme, position as prophetesses. In the main, too, the relations between husband and wife were loving and respectful, and in Israel's best days, when the people still remained landed yeomanry, the wife, by her industry within the house, supplemented and completed her husband's labour in the fields. The Israelite woman was consequently a very important person in the community, whatever her status in law might be; and if she had not the full rights which are now granted to her sex in Western and Christian lands, her position was for the times a noble and independent one. That all this was so was largely due to the improvements which Mosaism wrought on the basis of that ancient Semitic custom which we sketched at the beginning of this chapter, and with which it seems natural to suppose the Israelite tribes had also begun.

Bearing these preliminary considerations in mind, we now go on to consider the actual legislation in regard to the relations of the sexes. But here we must once more recall the fact that, in regard to all matters vitally affecting the community, there had always been a custom, and even before written law appears that custom had been adopted and modified in Yahwism by Moses himself. That this was actually the case here is rendered highly probable by the history of legislation in this matter. In the Book of the Covenant there is no mention of sexual sin, save in one passage (Exod. xxii. 16), where the penalty for seduction of a virgin who is not betrothed is that the seducer shall offer a "*mohar*" for her, and marry her without possibility of divorce, if her father consent. If he will not, then the "*mohar*" is forfeited to the father nevertheless, as compensation for the degradation of his daughter. But it is obvious that there must have been laws or customs regulating marriage other than this, for without them there could have been no such

---

* Cf. Renan, *Philosophic Dialogues*, iii. p. 26: "La nature a intérêt à ce que la femme soit chaste et à ce que l'homme ne le soit pas trop. De là un ensemble d'opinions qui couvre d'infamie la femme non chaste, et frappe presque de ridicule l'homme chaste. Et l'opinion quand elle est profonde, obstinée, c'est la nature même."

* Cf. 1 Sam. xxv. 18 ff.; 2 Sam. xiv. 1 ff.
† Cf. Exod. xv. and 1 Sam. xviii. 6 f.

crime as is here punished. Obviously, also, there must have been laws or customs of divorce. But of what these laws of marriage and divorce were Exodus gives us no hint. Deuteronomy, the next code, which on the critical hypothesis arose at a much later time as a revision of the Book of the Covenant, contains much more, *i. e.*, it draws out of the obscurity of unwritten custom a more extensive series of provisions in regard to purity. The Law of Holiness then adds largely to Deuteronomy, and with it the main points of the law of purity have attained to written expression. But the influence of the higher standard set in the Decalogue also makes itself felt,—not in the law so much as in the historic books and the prophets—and our task now is to trace out first the legal development, then the prophetical, and to show how the whole movement culminated and was crowned in the teaching of Christ.

Beginning then with Deuteronomy, we find that the chastity of women was surrounded by ample safeguards. Religious prostitution was absolutely prohibited (Deut. xxiii. 18). Further, if any violence was done to a woman who had been betrothed, the punishment of the wrong was death; if done to a woman who was not betrothed, the wrong was atoned for by payment of fifty shekels of silver to her father, and by offering marriage without possibility of divorce. If marriage was refused, then the fifty shekels was retained by the father in consideration of the wrong done him. When the woman was a sharer in the guilt the punishment in all cases was death; while pre-nuptial unchastity, when discovered after marriage, was punished, as adultery also was, with the same severity.* In women who were free, therefore, purity was demanded in Israel as strenuously as it ever has been anywhere, though in man the only limit to sexual indulgence was the demand, that in seeking it he should not infringe upon the father's property in his daughter, or the husband's in his wife or his betrothed bride.

Admittedly the original underlying motive for this moral severity was a low one, the mere proprietary rights of the father or husband. But it would be a mistake to suppose that purely ethical and religious motives had no place in establishing the customs or enactments which we find in Deuteronomy. With the lapse of time higher motives entwined themselves with the coarse strand of personal proprietary interest, which had originally, though perhaps never alone, been the line of limitation. Gradually there grew up a standard of higher purity; and when Deuteronomy was written, though the original line was still clearly visible, it was justified by appeals to a moral sense which reached far beyond the original motives of the customary law. The continually recurring burden of Deuteronomy in dealing with these matters is that to work "folly in Israel" is a crime for which only the severest punishment can atone. To "extinguish the evil from Israel," and to put away such things as were "abominations to Yahweh their God," are the great reasons on which the writer of Deuteronomy founds the claim for obedience in these cases. Obviously, therefore, by his time, under the teaching of the religion of Yahweh, Israel had risen to a moral height which took account of graver interests than the rights of property

* Chap. xxii. 13-18.

in legislating for female purity. The cases included in the law had been determined by considerations of that kind; but the sanctions by which the commands were buttressed had entirely changed their character. The holiness of God and the dignity of man, the consideration of what alone was worthy of a "son of Israel," have taken the place of the coarser sanctions. In this way a possibility of unlimited moral progress was secured, since the cause of purity was indissolubly bound to the general and irresistible advance of religious and moral enlightenment in the chosen people.

Moreover the personality of the woman was acknowledged in the entire acquittal of the betrothed woman who had been exposed to outrage in the country, where her cries could bring no help. In the earliest times most probably the punishment of death would have been inflicted equally in that case, since the husband's property had been deteriorated to such a degree as to make it unworthy of him. But in the Deuteronomic provision quite other things are drawn into the estimate. The moral guilt of the person concerned is now the decisive consideration. The woman has ceased to be a mere chattel, and the full claims of her personality are in the way to be recognised. These were great advances, and for these it is vain to seek for other causes than the persistent upward pressure of the Mosaic religion. The moral superiority of Israel at the time of the conquest over the much more cultured Canaanites, as also over the nomadic tribes to which they were more nearly related, is due, as Stade says, ultimately to their religion; and no reader of the Old Testament, in our time at least, can fail to see that their moral progress in the land they conquered depended entirely upon the same cause. At the Deuteronomic epoch purity had already been placed upon a worthy basis, as a moral achievement of the first importance, and impurity had taken its proper place as a degrading sin. But much still remained to be done before these principles could be extended into all domains of life equally.

How far they had penetrated in early times may perhaps best be seen in the Deuteronomic references to divorce. Before Deuteronomy there is no law of divorce, nor indeed is there any after it. We may perhaps even say that there is in it not so much the statement of a law of divorce, as a reference to custom which the writer wishes to correct or reinforce in one particular respect only. Notwithstanding the Jewish view, therefore, which finds in Deut. xxiv. 1-4 a divorce law, we must adduce the passage as a new and striking proof of what we have all along asserted, that neither Deuteronomy nor any other of the legal codes can be taken as complete statements of what was legally permitted or forbidden in Israel. Behind all of them there is a vast mass of unwritten customary law, and divorce was doubtless always determined by it. That this was the case will be seen at once if the passage we are now concerned with be rightly translated. It runs thus: " When a man taketh a wife and marrieth her, and it shall be (if she find no favour in his eyes, because he hath found in her some unseemly thing) that he writeth her a bill of divorcement, and giveth it into her hand, and sendeth her out of his house, and she go forth out of his house and goeth and becometh the wife of another man, and if the latter husband also hate her, and write her a bill of divorcement, and give it in her hand and send her out of his house, or if the latter husband die who took her to him to wife, then her former husband who sent her away may not take her again to be his wife after that she has permitted herself to be defiled." All the passage provides for, therefore, is that a divorced woman shall not be remarried to the divorcing man after she has been married again, even though she be separated from her second husband by divorce or death. There is consequently no law of divorce here stated. There is merely a reference to a general law or custom by which divorce was permitted for "any unseemly thing," and according to which a chief wife at any rate could be divorced only by a "bill of divorcement," and not by mere word of mouth, as is common in many Eastern lands to-day. Mosaic influence may have procured this last slight increase in rigour, and Deuteronomy certainly adds three other restrictions, viz. that after remarriage a woman cannot be again married to her first husband, and that pre-nuptial wrong done to a woman by her husband, or a false accusation by him after marriage, takes away his right of divorce altogether. But the woman has no right of divorce at all, so firmly fixed throughout all Old Testament time was the belief in the inferiority of women. On the whole, therefore, divorce in Israel remained, after the law had dealt with it, much on the level to which the tribal customs had brought it. So far as the legislation dealt with it, it tended to restriction; but when all is said it remains true that the Israelite *law* of divorce was in the main much what it would have been had there been no revelation. But the *spirit* of the religion of Yahweh was against laxity in this matter, and this more rigorous feeling finds expression in the evident distaste for the remarriage of a divorced woman which is expressed in Deut. xxiv. 4. Remarriage is not forbidden; but the woman who remarries is spoken of as one who has "let herself be defiled." No such expression could have been used, had not remarriage after divorce been looked upon as something which detracted from perfect feminine purity. The legislator evidently regarded it as the higher way for a divorced woman to remain unmarried so long at least as the divorcing husband lived. If she remained so, the possibility of reunion was always kept open, and the law evidently looked upon the ultimate annulment of the divorce as the course which was most consonant with the ideal of marriage.

It is thus clearly seen how our Lord's statement (Matt. xix. 8)—"Moses because of the hardness of your hearts suffered you to put away your wives, but from the beginning it hath not been so"—is true.

And when we leave the law and come to history and prophecy, we find this view to have been a prevalent one from early times. In one of the earliest connected historical narratives, that of J (Gen. ii. 24), the union of husband and wife is said to be so peculiarly intimate that it makes them one body, so that separation is equivalent to mutilation. And the prophets remain true to this conception of marriage, as the one which fitted best into their deeper and loftier views of morality. From Hosea onwards* they represent the indissoluble bond between Yahweh and His people as a marriage relation, founded on free choice and unchangeable love. The possibility of divorce is no doubt often admitted, and the conduct of Israel is represented as justifying that course. But the prophetic message always is that the love of God will never permit Him to put away His people; and the people are often addressed as faithless and faint-hearted, because they yield to the temptation of believing that He has cast them off (Isa. l. 1). Evidently, therefore, the prophetic ideal of marriage was that it should be indissoluble, that it should be founded upon free mutual love, and that such a love should make it impossible for either husband or wife to give the other up, however desperate the errors of the guilty one might have been.

Perhaps the finest expression of this view occurs in Isa. liv., in the exhortation addressed to exiled Israel and beginning, "Sing, O barren, thou that didst not bear." There the ideal Israel is urged to lay aside all her fears with this assurance: "For thy Maker is thine husband; Yahweh of Hosts is His name: and thy Redeemer, the Holy One of Israel, the God of the whole earth shall He be called. For Yahweh hath called thee as a woman forsaken and grieved in spirit; how can a wife of youth be rejected? saith thy God." The full meaning of this last touching question has been well brought out by Prof. Cheyne (*Isaiah*, ii., p. 55): "Even many an earthly husband (how much more then Yahweh!) cannot bear to see the misery of his divorced wife, and therefore at length recalls her; and when his wife is one who has been wooed and won in youth, how impossible is it for her to be absolutely dismissed." The rising tide of prophetic feeling on this subject culminates in the pathetic scene depicted by Malachi, who in chap. ii. 12 ff. reproves his people for their cruel and frivolous use of divorce. Drawn away by love of idolatrous women, they had divorced their Hebrew wives; and these in their misery crowded the Temple, covering the altar of Yahweh with "tears and weeping and sobbing," till He could endure it no more. He had been witness of the covenant made between each of these men and the wife of his youth; yet they had broken this Divinely sanctioned bond. He therefore warns them to take heed, "for Yahweh the God of Israel saith, I hate putting away, and him who covers his garment with violence." The Rabbinic interpreters, not being minded to give up the privilege of divorce, have wrested these words into "for Yahweh the God of Israel saith, If he hate her put her away." But, so wrested, the words bring down the whole context in one ruin. They are intelligible only if they denounce divorce, and in this sense they must undoubtedly be taken.

There remains for consideration, however, a marriage which the Deuteronomist permits, which seems to run counter to all the finer feelings and instincts of his later time. It is dealt with in chap. xxv. 5-10, and is notable because it is a clear breach of the definite rule that a man should not marry his deceased brother's wife. But it will be obvious at once that the permission of this marriage stands upon quite a different footing from the prohibition. It is permitted only in a special case for definite ends; and while the sanction of the prohibition is the infliction of childlessness (Lev. xx. 21), the man who refuses to enter upon marriage with his de-

* Hosea ii. 19.

ceased brother's wife is punished only by being put to shame by her before the elders of his city. We have not here, therefore, a law in the strict sense. It is only a recognition of a very ancient custom which is not yet abolished, though evidently public feeling was beginning to make light of the obligation. Its place in the twenty-fifth chapter, away from the marriage laws (which are given in xxi. 10 ff., xxii. 13 ff., and xxiv. 1-4), and among duties of kindness, seems to hint this, and we may consequently take the law as a concession. That the custom was ancient in the time of Deuteronomy may be gathered from the fact that in Hebrew there is a special technical term, *yibbēm*, for entering on such a marriage. The probability is, indeed, that levirate marriage was a pre-Mosaic custom connected with ancestor-worship. It certainly is practised by many other races, *e. g.*, the Hindus and Persians, whose religions can be traced to that source. Under that system, it was necessary that the male line of descent should be kept up in order that the ancestral sacrifices might be continued, and to bear the expense of this the property of the brother dying childless was jealously preserved. In India, at present, both purposes are served by adoption, either by the childless man or by the widow. In earlier times, when fatherhood was to a large extent a merely juridical relationship,* when, that is to say, it was a common thing for a man to accept as his son any child born of women under his control, whether he were the father or not, the same end was also attained by this marriage.† Originating in this way, the practice was carried over into the Israelite social life when it changed its form, and the motives for it were then brought into line with the new and higher religion. The motive of keeping alive the name and memory of the childless man was substituted for that of securing the continuance of his worship; and the purpose of securing the permanence of property, landed property especially, in each household, was substituted for that of supplying means for the sacrifice. Later, the motive connected with the transmission of property possibly became the main one. For, since the levirate marriage came in, according to the strict wording of our passage, whenever a man died without a son, whether he had daughters or not, this marriage would seem to have been an alternative means of keeping the property in the family to that of letting the daughters inherit.‡ But the spirit of the higher religion, as well as a more advanced civilisation, was unfavourable to it. The custom evidently was withering when Deuteronomy was written, though in Judaism it was not disallowed till post-Talmudic times.

The impression, therefore, which the laws and customs regulating the relations of men and women in Israel give to the candid student must be pronounced to be a strangely mixed one. It would probably not be too much to say that it is at first a deeply disappointing one. We have been accustomed to fill all the Old Testament utterances on this subject with the suffused light of Gospel precept and example, till we have lost sight of the lower elements undeniably present in the Old Testament laws and ideas concerning purity. But that is no longer possible. Whether of enmity or of zeal for the truth, these less worthy elements have been dragged forth into the broad light of day, and in that light we are called upon to readjust our thoughts so as to accept and account for them. Evidently at the beginning the Israelite tribes accepted the uncivilised idea of woman. On that as a basis, however, customs and laws regarding chastity, marriage, and divorce were adopted, which transcended and passed beyond that fundamental idea. The moral complicity of woman, or her innocence, in cases where her chastity had been attacked, came to be taken into account. Polygamy, though never forbidden, received grievous wounds from prophets and others of the sacred writers; and as marriage with one became more and more the ideal, the higher teachers of the people kept the indissolubleness of marriage before the public mind, till Malachi denounced divorce in Yahweh's name. In regard to the bars to marriage there was little change, probably, from the days of Moses; but the old family rules were reinforced by a deep and delicate regard for even the less palpable affections and relations which grew up in the home.

The final attainment, therefore, was great and worthy enough; but the cruder and less refined ideas, which had been inherited from pre-Mosaic custom, always make themselves felt, and have even dominated some of the laws. They dominated, even more, the practice of the people and the theory of the scribes; so that on the very eve of His coming who was to proclaim decisively the indissolubility of marriage, the great Jewish schools were wrangling whether mere caprice, or some immodesty only could justify divorce. Nevertheless the Decalogue, with its deep and broad command, culminating in prohibition even of inward evil desire, had always had its own influence. The teachings of the prophets, which breathe passionate hatred of impurity, had taught all men of good-will in Israel that the wrath of God surely burned against it. But the stamp of imperfection was upon Old Testament teaching here as elsewhere. Like the Messianic hope, like the future of Israel, like all Israel's greatest destinies, the promise of a higher life in this respect was darkened by the inconsistencies of general practice; and uncertainty prevailed as to the direction in which men were to look for the harmonious development of the higher potencies which were making their presence felt. It was in them rather than in the law, in the ideals rather than in the practice of the people, that the hidden power was silently doing its regenerating work. The religion of Yahweh in its central content surrounded all laws and institutions with an atmosphere which challenged and furthered growth of every wholesome kind. The axe and hammer of the legislative builder was rarely heard at work; but in the silence which seems to some so barren, there slowly grew a fabric of moral and spiritual ideas and aspirations, which needed only the coming of Christ to make it the permanent home of all morally earnest souls.

---

* "The Primitive Family," Starcke, p. 141.
† Indeed in India it was not only the widow of the childless man who might bear him a son whose real father was a near relation, but his childless wife also.—Maine, "Early Law," p. 102.
‡ That the latter course may in some cases have been unpopular with the sonless man's nearest kin is clear, since under it the inheritance must be divided, and it might pass to remoter connections, though not beyond the tribe. The nearer relations would, therefore, probably prefer that their brother's property should be kept intact and be transmitted with his name, and this ancient custom, sanctioned and modified by Mosaism, would give them that choice.

With Him all that the past generations "had willed, or hoped, or dreamed of good" came actually to exist. He made what had been aspiration only the basis of an actual Kingdom of God. As one of its primary moral foundations He laid down the radical indissolubility of marriage, and made visible to all men the breadth of the law given in the Decalogue by forbidding even wandering desires. In doing this He completely surpassed all Old Testament teaching, and set up a standard which Christian communities as such have held to hitherto, but which from lack of elevation and earnestness they seem inclined in these days to let slip. That such a standard was ever set up was the work of a Divine revelation of a perfectly unique kind, working through long ages of upward movement. Humanity has been dragged upwards to it most unwillingly. Men have found difficulty in living at that height, and nothing is easier than to throw away all the gain of these many centuries. All that is needed is a plunge or two downwards. But if ever these plunges are taken, the long, slow effort upwards will only have to be begun again, if family life is to be firmly established, and purity is to become a permanent possession of men.

CHAPTER XXIII.

LAWS OF KINDNESS.

With the commands we now have to consider, we leave altogether the region of strict law, and enter entirely upon that of aspiration and of feeling. Kindness, by its very nature, eludes the rude compulsion of law, properly so called. It ceases to be kindness when it loses spontaneity and freedom. Precept, therefore, not law, is the utmost that any lawgiver can give in respect to it; and this is precisely what we have in Deuteronomy, so far as it endeavours to incite men to gentleness, goodness, and courtesy to one another. The author gives his people an ideal of what they ought to be in these respects, and presses it home upon them with the heartfelt earnestness which distinguishes him. That is all; but yet, if we are to do justice to him as a lawgiver, we must consider and estimate the moral value of these precepts; for, properly speaking, they are the flower of his legal principles, and they reveal in detail, and therefore, for the average man, most impressively, the spirit in which his whole legislation was conceived. In the abstract no doubt he had told us that love —love to Yahweh—was to be the fundamental thing, and we have seen how deep and wide-reaching that announcement was. But a review of the precepts which indicate how he conceived that love to God should affect men's relations with men, will give that general principle a definiteness and a concreteness more impressive than a thousand homilies. For the conception that a relation of love is the only fit relation between man and God, could not, if it were sincerely taken up, fail to throw light upon men's true relations to each other. Consequently the great declaration of the sixth chapter was bound to re-echo in the precepts to guide conduct, giving new sanctity and breadth to all man's duty to his fellows.

Of course the risk of great failure was nigh at hand: for men may be intellectually convinced that love is the element in which life ought to be lived, and may proclaim it, who are far from being actually penetrated and filled with love, tested and increased by communion with God. As a result, much talk about love and kindly human duty has fallen with but little impulsive power upon the hearts of men. When, however, it is felt to be the expression of a present experience, such exhortation has power to move men as no other words can do. And the author of Deuteronomy was one of those who had this divinely given secret. In all parts of his book you find his words becoming winged with power, wherever love to God and man is even remotely touched upon. If our hypothesis as to the age in which he lived and wrote be correct, his must have been one of those high and rare natures which are not embittered by persecution or contemptuous neglect. Long before our Lord had spoken His decisive words on our duty to our neighbour, or St. Paul had written his great hymn to love, this man of God had been chosen to feel the truth, and had suffused his book with it, so that the only principle which can be recognised as binding together all his precepts is the central principle of the New Testament. Of course that made his ideal too high for present realisation; but he gained more than he lost; for, from Jeremiah and Josiah downwards through the years, all the noblest of his people responded to him. The splendour of his thought cast reflections upon their minds, and these glowed and shone amid the meaner lights which Pharisaism kindled and cherished, till He came whose right it was to reign. Then Deuteronomy's true rank was seen; for from it Christ took the answers by which He repelled Satan in the temptation, and from it, too, He took that commandment which He called the first and greatest. Of course the humanity of the book had not, in expression at least, the imperial sweep of Christian brotherhood which makes all men equal, so that for it there is neither Jew nor Gentile, neither wise nor unwise, neither male nor female, neither bond nor free. But *all* the chosen people are included in its sympathy; and in this field, without undue interference with private life, the author sets forth by specimen cases how the fraternal feeling should manifest itself in loving, neighbourly kindness.

As these laws or precepts of kindness are not systematically arranged, it will be necessary to group them, and we shall take first those in which it is prescribed that injury to others should be avoided. Of course criminal wrongs are not dealt with here. They have already been forbidden in the strictly legal portions of the book, and penalties have been attached to them. But in the region beyond law, there are many acts in which the difference between a good, and kindly, and sympathetic man, and a morose, and sullen, and unkindly one, can be even more clearly seen. In that region Deuteronomy is unmistakably on the side of sympathy. The poor, the slave, the helpless should, it teaches, be objects of special care to the true son of Israel. They should be treated, it shows, with a generous perception of the peculiar difficulties of their lot; and pressure upon them at these special points where their lot is hard should be abhorrent to every Israelite.

The first in order of the precepts which we are considering (chap. xxii. 8)—"When thou buildest a new house, then thou shalt make a railing for thy roof, that thou bring not blood upon thine house, if any man fall from thence"

—reveals the fatherly and loving temper which it is the author's delight to attribute to Yahweh. As earthly parents guard their children from accidents and dangers, so Yahweh thinks of possible danger to the lives of His people, and calls for even minute precautions. The habit of sitting and sleeping upon the flat roofs of the houses has always been, and is now, prevalent in the East. Many accidents take place through this habit. In recent years Emin Pasha, who ruled so long at Wadelai, nearly lost his life by one; and here the house-owner is required in Yahweh's name to minimise that danger, "that he bring not blood upon his house." The life of each one of Yahweh's people is precious to Him; therefore it is that He will have them to guard one another. This is the principle which runs through all these precepts. In the sphere of ritual and religion the Deuteronomist does not transcend Old Testament conditions. For him as for others it is the nation which is the unit. But in the region now before us he virtually goes beyond that limitation, and emphasises the care of Yahweh for the individual, just as in the demand for love to God he had already made Israel's relation to their God depend upon each man's personal attitude. The thought that the Divine care was exerted over even " such a set of paltry ill-given animalcules as himself and his nation were," according to Carlyle's phrase, does not stagger him as it staggered Frederick the Great.

In matters like these, the unsophisticated religion of the Old Testament is most helpful to us to-day. We have analysed, and refined, and dimmed all things into abstractions, God and man among the rest. The fearless simplicity of the Old Testament restores us to ourselves, and pours fresh blood into the veins of our religion. No faith in God as the living orderer of all the circumstances of our lives can be too strong or too detailed. The stronger and more definite it becomes, the nearer will it approach the truth. Only one danger can threaten us on that line, the danger of taking all our own plans and desires for the Divinely appointed path for us. But most men will by natural humility be saved from that presumption; and the glad assurance that they are wrapped about with the love of God is perhaps the greatest need of God's people in their many sceptical and unspiritual hours.

We cannot, therefore, be surprised that, in connection with debts and pledges for payment, the same kindness in the Divine commands should be observable. As usury was forbidden in Israel, and precautions against excessive indebtedness were exceedingly elaborate, the possibilities of oppression in connection with debt in Israel were much more limited than in most ancient communities. Nevertheless there was here a region of life in which great wrongs could still be done by a harsh and unscrupulous creditor. In order that the creditor might have some security for what he had lent, it was permitted to receive and give pledges. The precepts regarding these are contained in chap. xxiv., vv. 6, 10 ff. and 17, and express a considerate brotherly spirit, for which it would be hard to find a parallel either in ancient or modern times. The creditor who has taken a poor man's upper garment as a pledge is commanded, both in the Book of the Covenant and in Deuteronomy, to restore the garment to its owner in the evening, that he may sleep in it. In Palestine for much of the year the nights are cold enough, and the poor man has no covering save his ordinary clothes. To deprive him of these, therefore, is to inflict punishment upon him, whereas all that should be aimed at is the creditor's security. This was peculiarly offensive to Israelite feeling, as we see from the mention in Amos ii. 8 of the breach of this prescription as one of the sins for which Yahweh would not turn away Israel's punishment. Further, in no case was a widow's garment to be taken in pledge, nor the handmill used for preparing the daily flour, for that is taking " life " in pledge, as the Deuteronomist says with the feeling for the conditions of the poor man's life which he always shows.

But the crown of all this kindness is found in the beautiful tenth verse: " When thou dost lend thy neighbour any manner of loan, thou shalt not go into his house to fetch his pledge; thou shalt stand without, and the man to whom thou dost lend shall bring forth the pledge without unto thee." Not only does Yahweh care for external and physical pain, He sympathises with those deeper wrongs and pains which may hurt a man's feelings. If a pledge to satisfy the lender had to be given, scruples of delicacy on the part of the borrower would appear to the " practical " man, as he would call himself, contemptibly misplaced. If the man's feelings were so very superfine, why did he borrow? But the author of Deuteronomy knew the heart of God better. With the fine tact of a man of God, he knew how even the well-meaning rich man's amused contempt for the poor man's few household treasures would cut like a whip, and he knew that Yahweh, who was " very pitiful and of tender mercy," would desire no son of Israel to be exposed to it. He knew, too, how human greed might dispose the lender to seize upon the thing of greatest value in the poor house, whether its price was in excess of the loan or not. Finally, he knew how it deteriorates the poor to be dealt with in an unceremonious, tactless way even by the benevolent. And in the name and with the authority of God he forbids it. The poor man's home, the home of the man whom we desire to help especially, is to be sacred. In our dealing with him of all men the finest courtesy is to be brought into play. Just because he needs our help, we are to stand on points of ceremony with him, which we might dispense with in dealing with friends and equals. " Thou shalt stand without," unless he asks thee to enter; and thou shalt show thereby, in a deeper way than any gifts or loans can show, that the fraternal tie is acknowledged and reverenced.

In two other precepts the same delicate regard for the finer feelings finds expression. In the fifth verse it is commanded that " When a man taketh a new wife, he shall not go out in the host, neither shall he be charged with any business: he shall be free at home one year, and shall cheer his wife that he hath taken." The strangeness and loneliness which everywhere make themselves felt as a formidable drawback to a young wife's joy, and which in a polygamous family, where jealousies are bitter, must often have reached the point of being intolerable, are provided for. In chap. xxv. 1-3 again, which deals with the punishment of criminals by beating, it is provided that in no case shall the number of blows exceed forty, and that they shall be given in the presence of the judge. This in itself was a measure of humanity, but the reason given for the direction is greatly more humane. "Forty stripes he may give him," says ver. 3; "he shall not exceed; lest, if he should exceed, and beat him above these with many stripes, then thy brother should seem vile unto thee." Even in the case of the criminal care is to be taken that he be not made an object of contempt. Punishment has gone beyond its true aim when it makes a man seem vile unto his neighbours by attacking his dignity as a man; for that should be inalienable even in a criminal. A man may have all his material wants satisfied, and yet be sorely vexed and injured. God sympathises with these hurts of the soul, and defends His people against them.

After the lovingkindness of these commands, it seems almost needless to say that the smaller social wrongs which men may inflict upon each other are sternly forbidden. Often, the rich from want of thought about the life of the poor carelessly do them wrong. Such a case is that dealt with in chap. xxiv. 14 f.: "Thou shalt not oppress an hired servant that is poor and needy, whether he be of thy brethren, or of thy strangers (*gerim*) that are in thy land within thy gates: in his day thou shalt give him his hire, neither shall the sun go down upon it; for he is poor, and setteth his heart upon it: lest he cry against thee unto Yahweh, and it be sin unto thee." The same command is given in Lev. xix. 13, and Dillmann is probably right in regarding this as a Deuteronomic repetition of that, since there the precept forms part of a pentad of commands dealing with similar things, while here it stands alone. From early times, therefore, Yahweh had revealed Himself as considering the poor and the necessities of their position. Further, the poor man or the wayfarer was permitted to satisfy his hunger by taking fruit or grain in his hands as he passed through the fields. No one was to die of starvation if the fields were "yielding meat." Last of all, estrangement between brethren, *i. e.*, all Israelites, was not to free them from duties of neighbourly love. If a man find a stray ox or sheep or ass, or a garment or any other lost thing, he is not to leave it where he finds it. He is to restore it to the owner; and if the owner is unknown or too far off, the finder is to keep that which he has found till it is inquired after. Then if he see his brother's, *i. e.*, his neighbour's, ass or ox fallen by the way, he must not pass by, but must help the owner to set it on its feet again. That an estranged "brother" was especially in view is shown by the fact that in the parallel passage (Exod. xxiii. 4) "thine enemy's ox" and "the ass of him that hateth thee" are mentioned.

Now, we have called these precepts and provisions the flower and blossom of the Deuteronomic legislation, because they reveal in their greatest perfection that sympathy with the commonest and the innermost cares of men which is the moving impulse of it all. But they reveal more than that. They show that already in those far-off days the secret of God's love to man had been made known. Its universality so far as Israel was concerned, its penetrative sympathy, its quality of regarding no human interest as outside its scope, its superhuman impartiality —all are here. They are not of course present in their full sweep and power, as Christ made them known. Outside of Israel there were the Gentiles, who had a share only in the "uncovenanted mercies" of God; and even among the chosen people there were the slaves and the strangers, who had a comparatively insecure relation to Him. Further, the thought of the self-sacrifice of God, though soon to have its dawning in the later chapters of Isaiah, was not as yet an appreciable element in the Israelite theology. Nevertheless the passages we have been considering throw a light upon social duty, as seen by this inspired servant of God, which puts to shame the state of the Christian mind on these subjects even now.

The great principles underlying right relations between men of different social status are, according to these precepts, courtesy and consideration. Now it is precisely the want of these which lies at the root of the bitterness which is so alarming a symptom of our social state at present. There is not, we are willing to believe, much of intentional, deliberate oppression exercised by the strong upon the weak. The injustice that is done is probably inherent in the present social system, for the character of which no one living is responsible. But one reason why reform comes so slowly, and why patience till it can come dies out among the masses of men, is that the employing classes, and those who have inherited privileges, often convey to those they employ the impression that they are beyond the pale of the courtesies which are recognised as binding between men of the same class. Often without intending it, their manner when they are approached by those they employ, their short and half-aggrieved replies, reveal to the latter that they are regarded much more as parts of the machinery, than as men who might naturally be expected to claim, and who have a right to, the recognition of their rights as men.

Of course there are excuses. There is the long tradition of subordination to arbitrary power, from which none in earlier ages of the world have been free. There is the impatience with which a governing and organising mind listens to grievances which it sees either to be inevitable under the circumstances, or to be compensated by some corresponding privilege, which stands or falls with the thing complained of. And then there is the absence of outlook, which is the foible of the directing mind. It is set to rule and make successful a large and intricate business under given circumstances. The more effective such a mind is for practical purposes, the more thoroughly will it limit itself to working out the problem committed to it. When grievances have to be dealt with which have their root in the present circumstances, and which imply changes more or less radical in his fixed point if they are to be redressed, it is hard for the employer to persuade himself that his employees are not merely crying for the moon. If he think so, he will probably say so; and working men go away from such interviews with the feeling that it is vain to expect from employers any sympathy for their aspirations towards a better social state, which yet they cannot give up without a slur upon their manhood.

But though these are excuses for the attitude we have been describing, there can be no question that the fine and delicate courtesy which Deuteronomy prescribes is indispensable in order to avert class hostility. Courtesy cannot, of course, change our social state, and where it works badly evils that produce friction will remain. But the first condition of a successful solution of our difficulties is, that evil tempers should as far as possible be banished, and for that purpose courtesy even under provocation is the one sovereign remedy. For it means that you convey to your neighbour that you consider him in all essentials your equal. It means, too, that you are willing to recognise his rights and to respect them. Though power may be on your side, and weakness on his, that will only make it more incumbent upon you to show that mere external circumstances cannot impair your reverence for him as man. If that be sincerely felt, it opens a way, otherwise absolutely closed, to mutual confidence and mutual understanding. These once established, light on all parts of the social problem (which, be it remembered, employers and employed must solve together if it is to be solved at all) will break in upon the minds of both classes. In spite of the diversity of their immediate interests, the ultimate interest of all is the same. If contempt and suspicion were excluded, eyes which are now holden would be opened, and a common effort to reach a social state in which all men shall have the opportunity of living lives worthy of men would become possible. If all would learn to treat those of other classes with the courtesy which they constantly show to those of their own, a great step in the right direction would be taken. Men overlook much and forgive much to their fellows when these recognise their equality, and show that they attach importance to having good relations with them.

But much more is to be aimed at than that. The esteem for man as man has great conquests yet to make before even the Deuteronomic courtesy becomes common. But if these nobler manners are to come in, then the motives suggested by Deuteronomy will have to be made effective for our day. What these were it is not difficult to see. They all had their source in the author's own relations and the relations of his people to God. Each of his brethren of the chosen people was a friend of Yahweh. There was no difference between Israelite men before Him. He had brought them all, the poor and the weak, as well as the rich and the strong, out of the house of bondage; He had guided them all through the wilderness, and had appointed each household a place in His land where full communion with Him was to be had. He had thought many thoughts about them, had given them laws and statutes dictated by loving insight, so as to fill their life with the consciousness that Yahweh loved them, condescended to them, and even allowed Himself to be made to serve by their sins. Whatever else they might be, they were friends of God, and had a right to respect on that ground. And for us who are Christians all these motives have been intensified and raised to a higher power. It is not lawful for us to call any man common or unclean. It is not lawful to overwhelm and bear down the minds of others by sheer energy and power. Those "for whom Christ died" are not to be dealt with save on the worthy plane of moral and spiritual conviction. That is the law of Christ; and so long as it is broken in our labour troubles by contemptuous refusal of conference when it can be granted without compromising principle, or by slighting references to labour leaders and a refusal to meet them, when leaders of another class would be courteously met, so long will the bitterness which inevitably springs up trouble us.

It is not, however, to be supposed that only the rich can sin in this respect. The labour organisations are becoming in many places, the stronger,* and so far they have learned the law of courtesy no better than their opponents. Opprobrious epithets and injurious suspicions and accusations are the stock-in-trade of some who lead the labour cause. That is as unworthy in them as it would be in others; it is not only a crime, but a blunder.

But the practice of courtesy does not end with itself. It opens the way for that consideration of the circumstances of the poor which we have found so conspicuous in Deuteronomy. As we have seen, Yahweh's precepts contemplate with the nicest care the unavoidable necessities of the poor man's life. So He stirs us to endeavour to realise the conditions of our poorer brethren, and by doing so to avoid the blunders which well-meaning people make by assuming that the conditions of their own life are the norm. There are vast varieties of circumstance in the world; and from lack of consideration those more favourably situated excite envies and hatreds the bitterness of which they cannot conceive, by simply taking it for granted that every one has the same opportunities for recreation, the same possibilities of rest. To realise clearly what life and death mean to the toiling millions of men; to see that matters which are small to those who live the materially larger and freer life of the class above them are of vital moment to the poor; to consider and allow for all such things in their dealings with them,—this is the teaching of Deuteronomy. Hence the command to pay the labourer his wages in the same day. The heart of man responds when this note is struck. In nothing is the story of Gautama the Buddha more true to the best instincts of humanity than in this, that it represents him as making his great renunciation through coming into intimate contact with the pain and misery of ordinary life.† That gave him insight, and insight wrought sympathy, and sympathy transformed him from being a petty prince of Northern India into the consoler and helper of millions in all Eastern lands. Even hopeless pessimism, when born of sympathy, has an immense consoling power. Much more should the inextinguishable hope given by Christ, combined as it is with the same sympathetic insight, console men and uplift them.

But the sixteenth verse of chap. xxiii. reminds us that in that ancient Deuteronomic world there were sad limitations to these lofty sympathies and hopes. If intensively Deuteronomy almost reaches the Gospel, extensively it shows the whole difference between Judaism at its best and Christianity. Below the world of free-born members of the Israelite community, to whom the precepts we have hitherto been considering alone apply, there was the class of slaves, who in many respects lay beyond the region of the finer charities. The origin of slavery we need not discuss. It was a quite universal feature in all ancient communities, and was doubtless a step upwards from the custom of destroying all prisoners taken in war. Among the Hebrews it had always been customary; but in historic times it was not among them the all-important matter it was in Greek and Roman polity. Had it been

---

* Especially in some of the Southern Colonies, in one of which this exposition is written.
† "Buddhism," by T. W. Rhys Davids, p. 29.

so, it would have been impossible to discuss the economic ideals of Israel without taking this social feature into consideration first. But slaves were comparatively few in Israel, and the slave trade can never have been extensive, since no slave markets are mentioned in the Old Testament. Moreover the social state of the country made owners of slaves share in the slaves' work, and that of itself prevented the growth of the worst abuses. But the most powerful element in making the lot of the slave tolerable was undoubtedly the just and pitiful character of the Israelite religion.

The fundamental position with regard to him was, however, the common one: he was the property of his master. He could be sold, pledged, given away as a present, and inherited, and could even be sold to foreigners. But a female slave, if taken as a subordinate wife, could not be sold, but only freed if she ceased to occupy that position. Exclusive of the Canaanites, subject to forced labour, and the Nethinim, the servants of the Sanctuary, who occupied much the same place as the *servi publici* in Rome, there were two classes of slaves, non-Israelites and Israelites. The ways in which a non-Israelite slave could come into Israelite hands were just what they were elsewhere. They might be prisoners of war, they might be purchased from travelling merchants, they might voluntarily have sold themselves from poverty in a strange land, or might have been sold for debt, and finally they might be children born of slaves. Their lot was of course the hardest. Yet even they were not so entirely unprotected by the law as slaves were among Greeks and Romans. They were recognised as men, having certain general human rights. The master had no right to kill; and if he maimed his slave he had to give him his freedom, according to the oldest law (Exod. xvi. 20 f.). The law regarding the killing of a slave has often been quoted as singularly harsh, especially that clause which says that if a slave when fatally smitten lives for some days after the blow, his death shall not be avenged, " for he is his (the master's) money." But it ought, notwithstanding the harshness of the expression, to be judged quite otherwise. The fact that death was not immediate was taken to indicate that death was not intended, and consequently the loss of the slave was thought a sufficient punishment. But the prohibition of the deliberate murder of a slave was a humane provision which could not be paralleled in the Græco-Roman world. Moreover these laws would not seem to have been widely called into action. The humane spirit became so general in Israel that slaves were generally well treated. In Prov. xxix. 21 overindulgence to a slave is deprecated, as if it were a common error; and during the whole history there is no mention of evils resulting from cruel treatment of slaves, much less any record of servile insurrection. Nor is there very frequent mention even of runaway slaves. On the other hand, we read of slaves who were stewards of their masters' houses; others probably were entrusted with the charge of the education of children.

In Deuteronomy we find, as we should expect, that the movement towards humanity in dealing with slaves is greatly furthered. In chap. xxi. 10 ff. the hardship of a woman's lot when she was taken captive in war is mitigated with sympathetic insight. To modern women of the Western world the lot of such an one seems so dreadful that no mitigation of it can make any difference. The current teaching among even religious men is that rather than submit to it a woman is justified in suicide. But in antiquity the personality of woman was undeveloped, the chances of life constantly passed her from one master to another, and things intolerable now were tolerable then. Making even these allowances, however, if we look at the law of the Old Testament as being in all its provisions and *ab initio* Divine, it seems impossible to praise it. A law which graciously permitted a captive woman to mourn for her people for a month, and only then allowed her captor to marry her, but if he wished afterwards to get rid of her provided that he should not sell her, but should let he go whither she would, cannot be said to be in itself compassionate. But, if the customary law of the Israelite tribes, restrained and purified by the higher spirit, be regarded as the basis of Old Testament legislation, then the leaven of religion and humanity can be seen working nobly, and in a manner worthy of revelation, even in such cases as these. Long after the Christian era we see what the ordinary fate of a captive woman was, in the conduct of Khalid the " sword of the Lord," one of the first great Mohammedan soldiers. When he had captured Malik ibn Noweira, who had resisted Islam, along with his wife, he gave orders which led to Malik's death, and the same night he married his widow.* Shortly afterwards, at the battle of Yemama, he demanded the daughter of his captive Mojda, and married her, as the Caliph wrote in reproof, " whilst the ground beneath the nuptial couch was yet moistened with the blood of twelve hundred." Horrors like these Deuteronomy forbids. The frenzied moments of a captive's first grief are respected, and some tenderness is shown to woman in a world where her lot at its best had always in it possibilities which cannot now be even thought of with equanimity. The same steady pressure to a nobler form of life is likewise seen in the Deuteronomic law dealing with the case of a foreign slave who had taken refuge in Israel (Deut. xxiii. 15 f.). In the words, " Thou shalt not deliver unto his master the slave which is escaped from his master unto thee; he shall dwell with thee, in the midst of thee, in the place which he shall choose within one of thy gates, where it liketh him best; thou shalt not oppress him," we have, thus early, the same legislation which it is the peculiar boast of England to have introduced into the modern world. " Slaves cannot breathe in England," and the moment they touch British soil in any part of the world they are free. This was the case with the land of Israel according to the Deuteronomic conception of what it ought to be.

But the highest points of privilege come to the non-Israelite slave in a way which disturbs the modern conscience, for they came by means of compulsion in religion. In contrast to the day labourer and the " Toshab " or sojourner, the slave *must* be of his master's religion. For a heathen, however, that was not a difficulty. His gods were gods of his land; and when he left his land and was carried into a foreign country, he had no scruple about worshipping the god of the new land. A typical case of this is found in the narrative 2 Kings xvii., where the im-

* Sir W. Muir, " Caliphate," pp. 26 and 33.

migrants whom the king of Assyria had settled in Samaria after Israel had been carried captive besought him to send some one to teach them how to worship Yahweh. This adoption of the master's religion secured equality of slave and free to a degree which could not otherwise have been attained, and brought the slaves fully within the humanity of the Hebrew law. It gave them the Sabbath (chap. v. 14). It gave a full share in all the religious festivals and a part in the sacrificial feasts (Deut. xii. 12 and xvi. 11, 14). Such slaves were, in fact, fully adopted into the family of God, and became brethren, poorer and more unfortunate, but still brethren, of their masters. They had indeed no claim to freedom, as Israelite slaves had; they were slaves in perpetuity. But their slavery was of a kind that did not degrade them beneath the condition of man.

With regard to Israelite slaves the beneficence of the law was naturally still greater. The fullest statement in regard to them is found, not in Deuteronomy, but in Lev. xxv. 39-46; but in the main we may suppose that in its larger outlines the distinction between Israelite and non-Israelite slaves there insisted on was always acknowledged. They were not to be thrust down into the lowest depth of slavery, and they were not to be set to the lowest kinds of labour, rather to that which hired labourers were wont to do, because they were of the children of Israel, of the nation whom Yahweh had brought out of the house of bondage. Further, they had a right to emancipation every seventh year, that is to say, whenever they had served six full years they could claim freedom in the seventh. Their original property was meant to be restored to them in the Sabbatic year, and so their degradation could last only for a very limited time. In Exod. xxi. 2 ff. we find the original provisions concerning the Israelite slave. Deuteronomy simply took these up, and modified them in certain respects. It extends all that Exodus says of the slave to the female slave also, and, in its care for and understanding of the difficulties of the poor, enacts that a slave when set free shall receive a fresh start in life from the cattle, the barn, and the winepress of the former owner. But this anticipation of discharged prisoners' aid societies was too high a demand upon a faithless generation. Even Jeremiah could not get it carried out; and the probability is that none but the most spiritually minded of the Jews ever regarded it as binding law.

The love which love of Yahweh inspired spread still more widely. It took in not only the poor and the slave, but it took account also of the lower animals. It has been often made a reproach to Christianity that it makes no such appeal on behalf of the lower creation as Buddhism does. But that reproach (like the kindred one brought by J. S. Mill, that in comparison with the Qur'an the New Testament is defective in not pressing civil duty) is tenable only if the New Testament be absolutely severed from the Old. Taken as the completion of the moral and religious development begun in Israel, Christianity takes up into itself all the experience, and all the teaching by example, which the Old Testament contains. It does not repeat it, because to the first Christians the Old Testament was the Divinely inspired guide. It was at first their whole Bible, and to take the New Testament by itself as an independent product is to mutilate both the Old and the New. When the Old Testament, therefore, enjoins kindness to animals we may set down all that it prescribes to the credit of Christianity. So much, at least, the latter must be held to teach; and if we consider the spirit as well as the letter of this law, there is no exaggeration in saying that it covers all the ground. Here, as in the case of slaves and the poor, the fundamental reason for kindness is relation to God. In the Yahwist's narrative in Gen. ii. all creatures are formed by God, and God Himself shows kindness to them. Indeed in passages like Psalm xxxvi. 7, as Cheyne well remarks, there is an implication "that morally speaking there is no complete break of continuity in the scale of sentient life," and that, as is seen by passages like Jer. xxi. 6, and Isa. iv. 11, the mild domesticated animals "are in fact regarded as a part of the human community." In the Decalogue the animals that labour with and for man have their share in the Sabbath rest, and the produce of the fields during the Sabbatic year (Exod. xxiii. 11; Lev. xxv. 7) is to be for them as well as for the poor. That they were mere machines of flesh and blood, to be driven till they were worn out, and were then to be cast aside, seems never to have occurred to the Israelite mind. These helpful creatures had made a covenant with man, and had a share in the consideration which the sons of Israel were taught to have for one another. In reaching that attainment Israel had reached the only effective ground for dealing with animals, as Cheyne says, "without inhumanity and without sentimentalism." The individual prescriptions of Deuteronomy emphasise and bring down these principles into the practical life. It is probable that the precept not to seethe a kid in its mother's milk (Deut. xiv. 21) was, in part at least, a law of kindness, founded upon a reverential feeling for the parental relationship even in this lower sphere. The command in Deut. xxii. 6 is certainly so. We read there: "If a bird's nest chance to be before thee in the way, in any tree or on the ground, with young ones or eggs, and the dam sitting upon the young, or upon the eggs, thou shalt not take the dam with the young; thou shalt in any wise let the dam go, but the young thou mayest take unto thyself; that it may be well with thee, and that thou mayest prolong thy days." Evidently the ground of sympathy here is the existence and the sacredness of the parental relationship. The mother bird is sacred as a mother; and length of days is promised to those who regard the sanctity of motherhood in this sphere, as it is promised to those who observe the fifth commandment of the Decalogue. Thus intimately the lower creation is drawn into the human sphere.

The only other precepts under this head are that a fallen animal is always to be lifted (Deut. xxii. 4), and the ox is not to be muzzled when it is treading out the corn (Deut. xxv. 4). These were ordinary prescriptions of humanity, but they too rest upon the sympathetic identification of the sufferings and wants of all sentient beings with those of mankind. It may be objected, however, that St. Paul denies that the last precept really was due to pity for the oxen. In 1 Cor. ix. 9, referring to it, he says, "Is it for the oxen that God careth, or saith He it altogether for our sake? Yea, for our sake it was written." But there is no real contradiction here. It is quite impossible that a devout Jew like St. Paul did not believe that God's "tender mercies are over all His works" (Psalm cxlv. 9). He would have been false to all his training had he not accepted that as a fundamental axiom. His apparent denial does not refer at all to the historic fact that the precept *was* given because of God's care for oxen. It only signifies that, when taken in its highest sense, it was meant to form character in *men*. St. Paul argues, as Alford says, "that not the oxen, but those for whom the law was given, were its objects. Every duty of *humanity* has for its ultimate ground, not the mere welfare of the animal concerned, but its welfare in that system of which man is the head, and therefore man's welfare." In fact St. Paul understood the Old Testament as we have seen it demands to be understood, and places the duty of kindness to animals in its right relation to man.

In all relations, therefore, Deuteronomy insists that life's main principle shall be love illumined by sympathy. Beginning with God and giving man's unquiet heart a firm anchorage there, it commands that all creatures about us shall be embraced in the same sympathising tenderness. It forbids us to look upon any of them as mere instruments for our use, for all of them have ends of their own in the loving thought of God. God is for it the great unifying, harmonising power in the world, and from a right conception of Him all right living flows. If the New Testament asks with wonder how a man who loves not his brother whom he hath seen can love God whom he hath not seen, the Old Testament teaches with equal emphasis the complementary truth that he who loves not God whom he hath not seen will never love as he ought his brother whom he hath seen. For to it Yahweh is the first and last word; and all the growth in kindness, gentleness, consideration, and goodness which can be traced in the revelation given to Israel, has its source in a conception of the Divine character which from the first was spiritual, and was moreover unique in the world.

CHAPTER XXIV.

MOSES' FAREWELL SPEECHES.

DEUTERONOMY iv. 1-40, xxvii.-xxx.

WITH the twenty-sixth chapter the entirely homogeneous central portion of the Book of Deuteronomy ends, and it concludes it most worthily. It prescribes two ceremonies which are meant to give solemn expression to the feeling of thankfulness which the love of God, manifested in so many laws and precepts, covering the commonest details of life, should have made the predominant feeling. The first is the utterance of what we have called the "liturgy of gratitude" at the time of the feast of firstfruits; and the second is the solemn dedication of the third year's tithe to the poor and the fatherless, and the disclaimer of any misuse of it. Further notice of either after what has already been said in reference to them would be superfluous. The closing verses (16-19) of the chapter are a solemn reminder that all these transactions with God had bound the people to Yahweh in a covenant. "Thou hast avouched Yahweh this day to be thy God" and, "Yahweh hath avouched thee this day to be a peculiar people ('*am segullāh*) unto Himself." By this they were bound to keep Yahweh's statutes and judgments, and do them with all their heart and with all their soul, while He, on His part, undertakes on these terms to set them "high above all nations which He hath made in praise, and in name, and in honour," and to make them a holy people unto Himself.

But the original Deuteronomy as read to King Josiah cannot have ended with chapter xxvi., for the thing that awed him most was the threat of evil and desolation which were to follow the non-observance of this covenant. Now though there are indications of such dangers in the first twenty-six chapters of Deuteronomy, yet threats are not, so far, a prominent part of this book. The book as read must consequently have contained some additional chapters, which, in part at least, must have contained threats. Now this is what we have in our Biblical Deuteronomy. But in chapters xxvii. and xxviii. there are reduplications which can hardly have formed part of the original author's work. An examination of these has led every one who admits composite authorship in the Pentateuch to see that from chapter xxvii. onwards the original work has been broken up and dovetailed again with the works of JE and P; so that component parts of the first four books of the Hexateuch appear along with elements which the author of Deuteronomy has supplied. We have, in fact, before us, from this point, the work of the editor who fitted Deuteronomy into the framework of the Pentateuch; and it is of importance, from an expository point of view even, to endeavour to restore Deuteronomy to its original form, and to follow out the traces of it that are left.

As we have said, we must look for the threats and promises which undoubtedly formed part of it. These are contained in chapters xxvii. and xxviii. But a careful reader will feel at once that chapter xxvii. disturbs the connection, and that xxviii. should follow xxvi. In chapter xxvii., vv. 9 and 10 alone seem necessary to give a transition to chapter xxviii.; and if all the rest were omitted we should have exactly what the narrative in Kings would lead us to expect, a coherent, natural sequence of blessings and curses, which should follow faithfulness to the covenant, or unfaithfulness. The rest of chapter xxvii. is not consistent either with itself or with Josh. viii. 30, where the accomplishment of that which is commanded here is recorded. In vv. 1-3 Moses and the elders command the people to set up great stones and plaister them with plaister and write upon them all the words of this law, on the day when they shall pass over Jordan, that they may go in unto the land. In ver. 4 it is said that these stones are to be set up in Mount Ebal, and there an altar of unhewn stones is to be built, and sacrifices offered, "and thou shalt write upon the stones very plainly." From the position of this last clause and the mention of Mount Ebal, the course of events would be quite different from that which vv. 1-3 suggest. The stones were, according to the verses 4 ff., to be set up in Mount Ebal; out of these an altar of unhewn stones was to be built; and on them the law was to be inscribed, and this is what Joshua says was done. But if we take all the verses, 1-8, together, we can reconcile them only by the hypothesis that the stones were set up as soon as Jordan was crossed, plaistered, and inscribed with the law; that afterwards they were removed to Mount Ebal and built into an altar "of unhewn stone," upon which sacrifices were offered. But that surely is in the highest degree improbable; and since we know that in other cases two narratives have been combined in the sacred text, that would seem the most probable solution here. Verses 4-8 will in that case be a later insertion, probably from J. In the same connection vv. 15-26 contain a list of crimes which are visited with a curse and no blessings; this cannot be the proclamation of blessing and cursing which is here required. Further, this list must be by a different author, for it affixes curses to some crimes which are not mentioned in Deuteronomy, and omits such sins as idolatry, which are continually mentioned there. This section must consequently have been inserted here by some later hand. It must probably have been later even than the time of the writer of Josh. viii. 33 ff., since the arrangement as reported there differs from what is prescribed here. Moreover, as there is nothing new in these sections, and all they say is repeated substantially in chapter xxviii., we may give our attention wholly to chapter xxviii. 1-68, as being the original proclamation of blessing and curse.

But other entanglements follow. Chapters xxix. and xxx. manifestly contained an adieu on the part of Moses, who turns finally to the people with an affecting and solemn speech of farewell. That appears in chapters xxix. and xxx. But for many reasons it is impossible to believe that these chapters as they stand are the original speech of Deuteronomy.* The language is in large part different, and there are references to the Book of the Law as being already written out (chap. xxix. 19 f. 26, and chap. xxx. 10). It is probably therefore an editor's rewriting of the original speech, and from the fact that "it contains many points of contact with Jeremiah in thoughts and words," it is probably to be dated in the Exile. But there is another noticeable thing in connection with it. It has a remarkable resemblance in these and other respects to chapter iv. 1-40. That passage can hardly have originally followed chapters i.-iii., if as is most probable these were at first an historic introduction to Deuteronomy. The hortative character of iv. 1-40 shows that it must have been placed where it is by a reviser. But the language, though not altogether that of Deuteronomy, is like it, and the thought is also Deuteronomic. Probably the passage must have been transferred from some other part of Deuteronomy and adapted by the editor. A clue to its true place may perhaps be found in ver. 8, where "all this law" is spoken of as if it were already given, and in ver. 5, where we read, "Behold, I have taught you statutes and judgments." These passages imply that the law of Deuteronomy had been given, and in that case chapter iv. must belong to a closing speech. We probably shall not be in error, therefore, in thinking that chapters iv. 1-40 and xxix. and xxx. are all founded on an original farewell speech which stood in Deuteronomy after the blessing and the curse.

But it may be asked, if that be so, why did an editor make these changes? The answer is to be found in two passages in chapters xxxi. and xxxii. which cannot be harmonised as they stand. In xxxi. 19 we are told that Yahweh commanded Moses to write "this song" and teach it to the children of Israel, "that this song may be a witness for Me against the children of Israel," and ver. 22, "So Moses wrote this song." But in vv. 28 f. we read that "Moses said, Assemble unto me all the elders of the tribes and your officers, that I may speak these words in their ears, and call heaven and earth to witness against them." Obviously "these words" are different from "this song," and are meant for a different purpose. The same ambiguity occurs at the end of the song in vv. 44 ff., where we first read of Moses ending "this song," and in the next verse we read, "And Moses made an end of speaking all these words to all Israel." Now what has become of "*these words*"? In all probability they were the substance of chapters iv. and xxix. and xxx., and were separated and amplified, because the editor who fitted Deuteronomy into the Pentateuch took over the song in chapter xxxii., as well as those passages of xxxi. and xxxii. that speak of this song, from JE. He accepted them as a fitting conclusion for the career of Moses, and transferred the original speech, which we suppose to have been the last great utterance of the original Deuteronomy, putting the main part of it immediately before the song, but taking parts out of it to form a hortatory ending (such as the other Moses' speeches have) to that first one which he had formed out of the historic introduction. This may seem a very complicated process and an unlikely one; but after the foundation had been built by Dillmann, Westphal has elaborated the whole matter with such luminous force that it seems hardly possible to doubt that the facts can be accounted for only in this way. By piecing together iv., xxx., and xxxi. he produces a speech so thoroughly coherent and consistent that the mere reading of it becomes the most cogent proof of the substantial truth of his argument.*

An analysis of it will show this. (1) There is the introduction; up till now the people have understood neither the commands nor the love of Yahweh (xxix. 1-9). (2) There is the explanation of the Covenant (xxix. 10-15); (3) A command to observe the Covenant (iv. 1, 2); (4) Warning against individual transgression, which will be punished by the destruction of the rebel (xxix. 16-21, iv. 3, 4); (5) Warning against collective transgression, which will be punished by the ruin of the people (iv. 5-26). The author, from this point regarding the transgression as an accomplished fact, announces: (6) The dispersion and exile of the people (iv. 27, 28); (7) The impression produced on future generations by the horror of this dispersion (xxix. 22-28); (8) The conversion of the exiles to God (iv. 30, 31); (9) Their return to the land of their fathers (xxx. 1-10). (10) In conclusion, it is stated that the power of Yahweh to sustain the faith of His people and to save them is guaranteed by the past (iv. 32-40); and there is no reason therefore that the people should shrink from obeying the commandment prescribed to them. It is a matter of will. Life and death are before them; let them choose (xxx. 11-20).

The analysis of the remaining chapters is not difficult. Chapter xxxi., vv. 14-23 and 30, form the introduction to the song, chapter xxxii., vv. 1-43, just as ver. 44 is the conclusion of it. Both introduction and song are extracted prob-

---

* *Cf.* Dillmann, "Deuteronomy," pp. 178 ff.

* *Le Deuteronome* (Toulouse, 1891), pp. 62-75. The order in which he disposes of the verses is as follows: Deut. xxxi. 24-29, xxix. 1-15, iv. 1, 2, xxix. 16-21, iv. 3-30, xxix. 22-28, iv. 30, 31, xxx. 1-10, iv. 32-40, xxx. 11-20, xxxii. 45-47. If before this we place xxxi. 1-13, we shall probably have the original sequence fully restored.

ably from J and E. Verses 48-52 are after P. Then follows the blessing of Moses, chapter xxxiii. Finally, chapter xxxiv. contains an account of Moses' death and a final eulogy of him, in which all the sources JE, P, and D have been called into requisition. The threefold cord which runs through the other books of the Pentateuch was untwisted to receive Deuteronomy, and has been retwisted so as to bind the Pentateuch into one coherent whole. That is the result of the microscopic examination which the text as it stands has undergone, and we may pretty certainly accept it as correct. But we should not lose sight of the fact that, as the book is now arranged, it has a notable coherence of its own, and the impression of unity which it conveys is in itself a result of great literary skill. Not only has the editor combined Deuteronomy into the other narratives most successfully, but he has done so not only without falsifying, but so as to confirm and enhance the impression which the original book was meant to convey.

We turn now to the substance of the two speeches—the proclamation of the blessing and the curse, and the great farewell address. As we have seen, the first is contained in chapter xxviii. If any evidence were now needed that this chapter was written later than the Mosaic time, it might be found in the space given to the curses, and the much heavier emphasis laid upon them than upon the blessings. Not that Moses might not have prophetically foretold Israel's disregard of warnings. But if the heights to which Israel was actually to rise had been before the author's mind as still future, instead of being wrapped in the mists of the past, he could not but have dwelt more equally upon both sides of the picture. Whatever supernatural gifts a prophet might have, he was still and in all things a man. He was subject to moods like others, and the determination of these depended upon his surroundings. He was not kept by the power of God beyond the shadows which the clouds in his sky might cast; and we may safely say that if the curses which are to follow disobedience are elaborated and dwelt upon much more than the blessings which are to reward obedience, it is because the author lived at a time of unfaithfulness and revolt. Obviously his contemporaries were going far in the evil way, and he warns them with intense and eager earnestness against the dangers they are so recklessly incurring.

But after all we have seen of the spirituality of the Deuteronomic teaching, and its insistence upon love as the true bond between men and God and the true motive to all right action, it is perhaps disappointing to some to find how entirely these promises and threats have their centre in the material world. Probably nowhere else will the truth of Bacon's famous saying that "Prosperity is the blessing of the Old Testament" be more conspicuously seen than here. If Israel be faithful she is promised productivity, riches, success in war. Even when it is promised that she shall be established by Yahweh as a holy people unto Himself, the meaning seems to be that the people shall be separated from others by these earthly favours, rather than that they shall have the moral and spiritual qualities which the word "holy" now connotes. Other nations shall fear Israel because of the Divine favour. Israel shall be raised above them all. If it become unfaithful, on the other hand, it is to be visited with pestilence, consumption, fever, inflammation, sword, blasting, mildew. The earth is to be iron beneath them, and the heaven above them brass. Instead of rain they are to have dust; they are to be visited with more than Egyptian plagues. Their minds are to refuse to serve them; they are to be defeated in war; their country is to be overrun by marauders; their wives and children, their cattle and their crops, are to fall into the enemy's hands. Locusts and all known pests are to fall upon their fields; and they themselves are to be carried away captive, after having endured the worst horrors of siege, and been compelled by hunger to devour their own children. And in exile they shall be an astonishment, a proverb, and a by-word, and shall be ruled by oppressive aliens. Worst of all, they shall there lose hope in God and "shall serve other gods, even wood and stone." Their lives shall hang in doubt before them. In the morning they shall say, "Would God it were evening," and at even they shall say, "Would God it were morning." All the deliverance Yahweh had wrought for them by bringing them out of Egypt would be undone, and once more they should go back into Egyptian bondage.

All that is materialistic enough; but there is no need to make apology for Deuteronomy, nevertheless. The prophet has taught the higher law; he has rooted all human duty, both to God and man, in love to God, and now he tries to enlist man's natural fear and hope as allies of his highest principle. How justifiable that is we have already seen in chapter xii., pp. 551 ff.

But a more serious question is raised when it is asked, does Nature, in definite sober truth, lend itself, in the manner implied throughout this chapter, to the support of religious and moral fidelity? At a time when imaginative literature is largely devoting itself to an angry or querulous denial of any righteous force working for the unfortunate and the faithful,* there can be no question what the popular answer to such a question would be. But from the ranks of literature itself we may summon testimony on the other side. Mr. Hall Caine, in his address at the Edinburgh Philosophical Institution, maintains in a wider and more general way the essence of the Deuteronomic thesis when he says, "I count him the greatest genius who touches the magnetic and Divine chord in humanity which is always waiting to vibrate to the sublime hope of recompense; I count him the greatest man who teaches men that the world is ruled in righteousness." And his justification of that position is too admirable not to be quoted: "Life is made up of a multitude of fragments, a sea of many currents, often coming into collision and throwing up breakers. We look around and see wrong-doing victorious, and right-doing in the dust; the evil man growing rich and dying in his bed, the good man becoming poor and dying in the street; and our hearts sink and we say, What is God doing after all in this world of His children? But our days are few, our view is limited, we cannot watch the event long enough to see the end which Providence sees." "It is the very province of imaginative genius," he goes on to say, "to see that which the common mind cannot see, to offer to it at least suggestions of how these triumphs of unrighteousness may be accounted for in accordance with the law that righteousness rules

* Cf. recent fiction, e. g., "The African Farm," "Tess of the D'Urbevilles," "The Heavenly Twins."

in the world." We would go further. It is one of the main purposes of inspiration to go beyond even imaginative genius, to point out in history not only how right may perhaps ultimately triumph, but how it has been in reality and must be victorious. For it will not do to shut off the world of material things from the working of this great and universal law. Owing to the narrow fanaticism of science, modern men have become sceptical, not only of miracle, but even of the fundamental truth that righteousness is profitable for the life that now is, that in following righteousness men are co-operating with the deepest law of the universe. But it remains a truth for all that. It is written deep in the heart of man; and in more wavering lines perhaps, but still most legibly, it is written on the face of things. With the limitations of his time and place, this is what the Deuteronomist preaches. Doubtless he has not faced, as Job does, the whole of the problem; still less has he attained to the final insight exhibited in the New Testament, that temporal gifts may be curses in disguise, that the highest region of recompense is in the eternal life, in the domain of things which are invisible but eternal. He does not yet *know*, though he has perhaps a presentiment of it, that being completely stripped of all earthly good may be the path to the highest victory—the victory which makes men more than conquerors through Christ. Nevertheless he is, making these allowances, right, and the moderns are wrong. In many ways obedience to spiritual inspirations does bring worldly prosperity. The absence of moral and spiritual faithfulness does affect even the fruitfulness of the soil, the fecundity of animals, the prevalence of disease, the stability of ordered life, and success in war. This was visible to the ancient world generally in a dim way; but by the inspired men of the Old Covenant it was clearly seen, for they were enlightened for the very purpose of seeing the hand of God where others saw it not. But they never thought of tracing out the chain of intermediate causes by which such results were connected with men's spiritual state. They saw the facts, they recognised the truth, and they threw themselves back at once upon the will of God as the sufficient explanation.

We, on the other hand, have been so diligent in tracing out the immediately preceding links of natural causation that, for the most part, we have been fatigued before we reached God. We consequently have lost view of Him; and it is wholesome for us to be brought sharply into contact with the ancient Oriental mind as we are here, in order that we may be forced to go the whole way back to Him. For the fact is that much of that very process of decay and destruction from moral causes is going on before us in countries like Turkey and Morocco, where social righteousness is all but unknown, and private morality is low. A truly modern mind scorns the idea that the fertility of the soil can be affected by immorality. Yet there is the whole of Mesopotamia to show that misgovernment can make a garden into a desert. Where teeming populations once covered the country with fruitful gardens and luxurious cities, there are now in the lands of the Tigris and Euphrates a few handfuls of people, and all the fertility of the country has disappeared. Irrigation channels which made all things live have been choked up and have been gradually filled with drifting sand, and one of the most populous and fertile countries of the world has become a desert. In Palestine the same thing may be seen. Under Turkish domination the character of the soil has been entirely changed. In many places where in ancient days the hills were terraced to the top the sweeping rains have had their way, and the very soil has been carried off, leaving only rocks to blister in the pitiless sun. Even in the less likely sphere of animal fecundity modern science shows that peace and good government and righteous order are causes of extraordinary power. And the movements which are going on around us at this day in the elevation and depression of nations and races have a visible connection with fidelity or lack of fidelity to known principles of order and justice. This can be said without concealing how scanty and partial in most cases such attainments are. Prevailing principles can be discerned in the providence which rules the world. And these are of such a kind that the connection which obedience to the highest known rules of life has with fertility, success, and prosperity, is constant and intimate. It is, too, far wider reaching than at first sight would seem possible. To this extent, even modern knowledge justifies these blessings and curses of Deuteronomy.

But it may be asked, Is this all the Old Testament means by such threats and promises? Does it recognise any even self-imposed limitations to the direct action of Divine power? Most probably it does not. Though always keeping clear of Pantheism, the Old Testament is so filled and possessed by the Divine Presence that all second causes are ignored, and the action of God upon nature was conceived, as it could not fail to be, on the analogy of a workman using tools. Now that the methods of Divine action in nature have been studied in the light of science, they have been found to be more fixed and regular than was supposed. The extent of their operation, too, has been found to be immeasurably wider, and the purposes which have to be cared for at every moment are now seen to be infinitely various. As a result, human thought has fallen back discouraged, and takes refuge more and more in a conception of nature which practically deifies it, or at least entirely separates it from any intimate relation to the will of God. It is even denied that there is any purpose in the world at all, or any goal, and to chance or fate all the vicissitudes of life and the mechanical changes of nature are attributed. But though we must recognise, as the Old Testament does not, that ordinary Divine action flows out in perfectly well-defined channels, and is so stable in its movement that results in the sphere of physical nature may be predicted with certainty; and though we see, as was not seen in ancient days, that even God does not always approach His ends by direct and short-cut paths,—these considerations only make the Old Testament view more inspiring and more healthful for us. We may gather from it the inference that if the fertility of a land, the frequency of disease, and success in war are so powerfully affected by the moral and spiritual quality of a people, it is very likely that in subtler and less palpable ways the same influences produce similar effects, even in regions where they cannot be traced. If so, whatever allowance may be required for the inevitable simplicity of Old Testament conceptions on this subject, however much we miss the limitations we have learned to regard as necessary, the Deuteronomic view as to the effects of moral and spiritual declension upon the material fortunes of a people is much nearer the truth than our timorous and hesitating half-belief. To find these effects emphasised and affirmed as they are here, therefore, acts as a much needed tonic in our spiritual life. Coming too from a man who possessed, if ever man did, Divinely inspired insight into the process of the world and the ideal of human life, these promises and warnings bring God near. They dissipate the mists which obscure the workings of God's Providence, and keep before us aspects of truth which it is the present tendency of thought to ignore too much. They declare in accents which carry conviction that, even in material things, the Lord reigneth; and for that the world has reason to be supremely glad.

Certainly Christians now know that prosperity in material things is by no means God's best gift. That great principle must be held to firmly, as well as the legitimacy of the vivid hopes and fears of Old Testament times regarding the material rewards of right-doing. In many ways the new principle must overrule and modify for us those hopes and fears. But with this limitation we are justified in occupying the Deuteronomic standpoint and in repeating the Deuteronomic warnings. For to its very core the world is God's; and those who find His working everywhere are those whose eyes have been opened to the inmost truth of things.

With regard to the farewell speech contained in chapters xxix. and xxx. and the related parts of chapter iv. and chapter xxxi. there is not much to be said. Taken as a whole, it develops the promises and threats of the previous chapters, and repeats again with affectionate hortatory purpose much of the history. But there is not a great deal that is new; most of the underlying principles of the address have been already dealt with. Taken according to the reconstruction of the speech and its reinsertion in its original framework, the course of things would seem to have been this. After the threats and promises had been concluded, Moses, carrying on the injunction of iii. 28, addressed (chapter xxxii. 8) all the people and appointed Joshua to be his successor; then he wrote out "this law," and produced it before the priests and elders of the people, with the instruction that at the end of every seven years, at the feast of release, in the feast of tabernacles, it should be read before all Israel, men, women, and children (chapter xxxi., vv. 9-13). Then he gave the book to the Levites, that they might "lay it up" by the side of the Ark of the Covenant of Yahweh their God, that it might be there for a witness against them when they became unfaithful, as he foresaw they would. He next summons all Israel to him, and delivers the farewell address contained in chapters iv., xxix., and xxx., an outline of which has already been given (p. 612), according to Westphal's recombination. This would seem to indicate that Moses himself inaugurated the custom of reading the law and giving instruction to all the people, which he prescribed for the feast of tabernacles in the year of release. After the law had been given he addressed the whole people in this farewell speech.

But though on the whole there is no need for detailed exposition here, there are one or two things which ought to be noticed, things which express the spirit of Deuteronomy so directly and so sincerely that they can be identified as forming part of the original Deuteronomic speech. One of these is unquestionably xxx. 11-20. At the end of the farewell address a return is made to the core of the whole Deuteronomic teaching: "Thou shalt love Yahweh thy God with all thy heart, and with all thy soul, and with all thy might." This was announced with unique emphasis at the beginning; it has lain behind all the special commands which have been insisted upon since; and now it emerges again into view as the conclusion of the whole matter. For beyond doubt this, and not the whole series of legal precepts, is what is meant by "this commandment" in verse 11. Both before it, in the sixth and tenth verses, and after it, in the sixteenth and twentieth verses, this precept is repeated and insisted on as the Divine command. Had the individual commands or the whole mass of them together been meant, the phrase used would have been different. It would have been that in ver. 10, where they are called "His commandments and His statutes which are written in this book of the law," or something analogous. No, it is the central command of love to God, without which all external obedience is vain, which is the theme of this last great paragraph; and a clear perception of this will carry us through both the obscurities of it, and the difficulties of St. Paul's application of it in the Romans.

Of this then the author of Deuteronomy says: "It is not too hard for thee, neither is it far off. It is not in heaven, that thou shouldest say, Who shall go up for us to heaven, and bring it unto us, and make us to hear it, that we may do it? Neither is it beyond the sea, that thou shouldest say, Who shall go over the sea for us, and bring it unto us, and make us to hear it, that we may do it? But the word is very nigh unto thee, in thy mouth, and in thy heart, that thou mayest do it." That is to say, there is no mystery or difficulty about this commandment of love. Neither have you to go to the uttermost parts of the sea to hear it, nor need you search into the mysteries of heaven. It has been brought near to you by all the mercy and forgiveness and kindness of Yahweh; it has been made known to you now by my mouth, even in its pettiest applications. But that is not all; it is graven on your own heart, which leaps up in glad response to this demand, and in answer to the manifestation of God's love for you. It is really the fundamental principle of your own nature that is appealed to. You should clearly feel that life in the love of God and man is the only fit life for you who are made in the image of God. If you do, then the fulfilment of all the Divine precepts will be easy, and your lives will lighten more and more unto the perfect day.

Now, for an Oriental of the pre-Christian era such teaching is most marvellous. How marvellous it is Christians perhaps find it difficult to see. In point of fact, many have denied that Old Testament teaching ever had this character. Misled by the doctrines of Islam, the great Semitic religion of to-day, many assert that the religion of ancient Israel called upon men to submit to mere power in submitting to God. But the appeal of our text to the heart of man shows that this is an error. No such appeal has ever been made to Mohammedans. Their state of mind in regard to God is represented by the remark of a recent traveller in Persia. Speaking of the Persian Babis, who may be described roughly as an heretical sect whose minds have been formed by Mohammedanism, he says: "They seemed to have no conception of absolute good, or absolute truth; to them good was merely what God chose to ordain, and truth what He chose to reveal, so that they could not understand how any one could attempt to test the truth of a religion by an ethical and moral standard."[*] Now that is precisely the opposite of the Deuteronomic attitude. Israel is encouraged and incited to right action by having it pointed out that not only experience, not only Divinely given statutes and judgments, but the very nature of man itself guarantees the truth of this supreme law of love. The law laid upon men is nothing strange to, or incongruous with, their own better selves. It is the very thing which their hearts have cried out for; when it is proclaimed the higher nature in man recognises it and bows before it. It is not received because of fear, nor is it bowed before because it is backed by power which can smite men to the dust. No; even in its ruins human nature is nobler than that; and Deuteronomy everywhere teaches with burning conviction that God is too ethical and spiritual in nature to accept the submission of a slave.

This reading of our passage is plainly that which St. Paul takes in Rom. x. 5 and 6. He perceives, what so many fail to do, that the spirit and scope of the Deuteronomic teaching is different from that of the purely legal sections of the Pentateuch. Paul therefore quotes the Pentateuch as having already made the distinction between works and faith which he wishes to emphasise, and as having distinctly given preference to the latter. Leviticus keeps men at the level of the worker for wages, while Deuteronomy in this passage, by making love to God the essence of all true observance of the law, raises them almost to the level of sons. And just as in those ancient days the highest manifestations of God had not to be laboured for and sought by impotent strivings, but had plainly been made known to them and had found an echo in their hearts, so now the highest revelation had been brought near to men in Christ, and had found a similar response. They did not need to seek it in heaven, for it had been brought to earth in the Incarnation. They did not need to descend into the abyss, for all that was needed had been brought thence by Christ at His resurrection. And in the New Testament as in the Old, the simplicity of the entrance into true relations with God is emphasised. Love and faith are the fundamental conditions. From them obedience will naturally issue, since "to faith all things are possible, and to love all things are easy."

CHAPTER XXV.

THE SONG AND BLESSING OF MOSES.

(A) THE SONG OF MOSES.

DEUTERONOMY xxxii.

CRITICS have debated the date, authorship, and history of this song. For the present pur-

[*] "A Year Among the Persians," E. G. Browne, p. 406.

pose it is sufficient, perhaps, to refer to the statement on these points in the note below.[*]

But in discussing the meaning and contents of the song the differences referred to cause no difficulties. On any supposition the time and circumstances, whether assumed as present, or actually and really present to the prophet's mind, can clearly be identified as not earlier than those of the Syrian wars. Accepted as dealing with that time, this poem takes its place among the Psalms of that period. Its subject is a very common one in Scripture: the goodness of Yahweh to his people, and their unfaithfulness to Him; His grief at their rebellion; His punishment of them by heathen oppressors; and His turning in love to them, along with His destruction of the nations who had prematurely

[*] The song is described, in the narrative framework, as delivered through Moses to the children of Israel. On the other hand, internal evidence points to a date after the establishment of the monarchy—when the days of Moses and the events of the wilderness were old, when the fruits of the land were gifts of God in present use, and when ingratitude and rebellion had become conspicuous, so that judgment was impending. Either, then, Moses took his stand, in the spirit, at a point of time long subsequent to his own death, adapted the song to its circumstances, and spoke not to his own generation but to one much later; or a later prophet must be the writer. The objection to the former view is supported by arguments drawn from various features in the language and the allusions of the song, which are asserted to be indicative of the later origin. On the detail of these we cannot dwell. But the most interesting part of the argument is the position that the transference of the prophetic consciousness to a remote future period, in order to give hope and guidance to a generation not the prophet's own, is too improbable to be admitted.

Such a process is now generally regarded as not impossible indeed, but unheard of in the history of prophecy. The examination of the prophets of the Old Testament has convinced students that the prophet's vision starts from his own time, and is primarily for the comfort and warning of his contemporaries. His words may have a more remote reference, but must have the nearer one. Hence Isa. xl.–lxvi. is now ascribed to a prophet or prophets of the Exile. The principle is really the same as that which determines the authorship of Deut. xxxiv. 5-12. No one now holds the view of some Jews, that Moses by the spirit of prophecy wrote this himself. Yet if Moses could in a poem address his people as sinning and suffering through rebellions induced by their prosperity in Canaan, which they had not entered when he died, one might as well believe him to describe his own decease. In both cases we have to suppose the mind of Moses transported to a period when he had been removed by death, that he might look back upon and speak of events which when he wrote were still future. Now in both cases a reason is lacking. Every one accepts the view that since Joshua or Eleazar was there to write the account of Moses' death, it is unlikely the lawgiver should have been inspired to write it himself. Just so, since Yahweh inspired new prophets at every crisis of His people's history, it seems unlikely that the spirit of Moses should be transferred to, and made at home in, the circumstances of a distant generation, in order to deliver to it a message which could have been made known by a prophet to whom the time was present. Neither Kamphausen nor Oettli nor Dillmann nor the English expositors who accept the non-Mosaic authorship of the song have any doubt as to the supernatural character of prophecy. They found upon observations as to the manner of Old Testament prophecy, which ought to regulate interpretation.

According to critical views the ascription to Moses of the reception and delivery of this song was taken by the Deuteronomist from JE. Kautzsch supposes that an editor to whom the song was known as passing under the name of Moses may have inserted it. Dillmann suggests grounds for believing that several prayers and poems ascribed to Moses (including Psalm xc.) were in circulation in prophetic circles in the Northern Kingdom, and that this one of them was inserted here as its appropriate place. The case would be parallel to the ascription of various later Psalms to David. Compare also the discussions as to the song of Hannah, 1 Sam. ii.

The view that a mistake as to the Mosaic authorship, for which the writers of JE were not responsible, was handed on in perfect good faith, is compatible with the doctrine of inspiration as held by representatives of the orthodox Evangelical school in Germany, and by the newer Evangelicals in England. Cf. Oettli, "Deuteronomy," p. 22, and Sanday's "Bampton Lecture."

triumphed over the people of God. Practically this is the burden of all the prophecies, as indeed it may be said to be the burden of the whole Book of Deuteronomy itself. Here it is stated and elaborated with great poetic skill; but in the main, the essential thought, there is little that has not already been elucidated.

As regards form the poem is among the finest specimens of Hebrew literary art which the Old Testament contains. Every verse contains at least two parallel clauses of three words or word-complexes each, and the parallelism in the great majority of instances is of the "Synonymous" kind; that is to say, "the second line enforces the thought of the first by repeating, and as it were *echoing* it in a varied form." * But into this as a foundation there is wrought a great deal of pleasing variation. The two-clause verses are varied by single instances or couplets or triplets of four-clause verses; while in two cases, at the emphatic end of sections, in vv. 14 and 39, the rare five-clause verse is found. Further, the synonymous parallelism is relieved by occasional appearances of the "synthetic" parallelism, in which "the second line contains neither a repetition nor a contrast to the thought of the first, but in different ways supplements and completes it," † *e. g.*, vv. 8, 19, and 27.

The contents of the song are in every way worthy of the origin assigned to it, and higher praise than that it is impossible to conceive. Beginning with a fine exordium calling upon heaven and earth to give ear, the inspired poet expresses the hope that his teaching may fall with refreshing and fertilising power upon the hearts of men, for he is about to proclaim the name of Yahweh, to whom all greatness is to be ascribed. In vv. 4 ff. the character and dealings of Yahweh are set over against those of the people:—

"The Rock! His deeds are perfect,
For all His ways are judgment;
A God of faithfulness and without falsity,
Just and upright is He."

They, on the contrary, were perverse and crooked; and, acting corruptly, they requited all Yahweh's benefits with rebellion. To win them from that perverseness, he calls upon his people to look back upon the whole course of God's dealings with them. Even before Israel had appeared among the nations, Yahweh had taken thought for His people. When He assigned their lands to the various nations of the world He had always before Him the provision that must be made for the children of Israel, and had left a space for them from which none but Yahweh could ever drive them out. For He had the same need of and delight in His people as the nations had in the lands assigned to them, the lot of their inheritance. And not only had He thus prepared a place for Israel from the beginning, but He had led him through the wilderness, through "the waste, the howling desert."

"He compassed him about, He cared for him,
He kept him as the apple of His eye."

To depict the Divine care worthily, he ventures upon a simile of a specially tender kind, rare in the Old Testament, but to which our Lord's comparison of His own brooding affection for Jerusalem to that of a "hen gathering her chickens under her wing" is parallel.

"As an eagle stirs up her nest,
Flutters above her young;
He, Yahweh, spread abroad His wings, He took him,
He bore him upon His pinions."

All the hardship and the toil were of God's appointment to drive His beloved people upwards and onwards. Whatever they might think or believe now, it was Yahweh alone, without companion or ally, who had done this for them, borne them up through it, and had bestowed upon them all the luxury of the goodly land once promised to their fathers. Even from the rocks He had given them honey, and the rocky soil had produced the olive tree. They had, too, all the luxuries of a pastoral people in abundance, and the wheat and foaming wine which were the finest products of agriculture.

In every way their God had blessed them. They had all the prosperity which a complete fulfilment of the will of God could have brought, but the result of it all was unfaithfulness and rejection of Him. Jeshurun, the upright people, as the sacred singer in bitter irony calls Israel, waxed fat and wanton. Instead of being drawn to God by His benefits, they had been puffed up with conceit concerning their own power and discernment. Full of these, they had mingled idolatrous rites with their worship of Yahweh. He had suffered them to read the results of their own unfaithfulness in defeat at the hands of their foes.

Instead of seeking the cause of their ill-success in themselves, they had found it in the weakness of their God. All the victories Yahweh had given them over foes whose strength they had feared were forgotten, and they "despised the Rock of their salvation." They had adopted new and upstart deities whom their fathers had never heard of, who as they had come up in a day might disappear in a day, and neglected the Rock who begat them.

Yahweh on His part saw all this, and scorned His people and their doings. In a vivid imaginative picture the poet represents Him as resolving to hide His face from them, to see what their end would be. Without the shining of God's countenance there could be but one issue for a people who were so faithless and perverse. He will recompense them for their doings.

"They made Me jealous with a no-God,
They vexed Me with their vain idols,
And I will make them jealous with a no-people,
With a foolish nation will I vex them."

For the fire of Divine wrath is kindled against them. It burns in Yahweh with an all-consuming power, and fills the universe even to the lowest depths of Sheol. Upon this sinful people it is about to burst forth; Yahweh will exhaust all His arrows upon them. By famine and drought; by disease and the rage of wild beasts, and of "the crawlers of the dust"; by giving them up to their enemies, and by overwhelming them with terror. He will destroy this people, "the young man and the virgin, the suckling and the man of grey hairs" alike. Nothing could save them, save Yahweh's respect for His own name.

"I had said, I shall blow them away,
I shall make their memory to cease from among men:
Were it not that I feared vexation from the enemy,
Lest their adversaries should misdeem,

---

* *Cf.* Driver's "Introduction," 5th edition, p. 340.
† *Cf.* Driver, *cit. loc.*

> Lest they should say, *Our* hand is exalted,
> And Yahweh hath not done all this."

Nothing but that stood between them and utter destruction, for as a nation they had no capacity for receiving and profiting by instruction. If they had been wise they would have known that there was but a step between them and death; they would have seen that their deeds had separated them from Yahweh, and could have but one issue. Their frequent and shameful defeats should have taught them that, for

> "How could one chase a thousand,
> And two put to flight ten thousand,
> Were it not that their Rock had sold them,
> And that Yahweh had delivered them up?"

There was no possible explanation of Israel's defeats but this; for neither in the gods of the heathen nor in the heathen nations themselves was there anything to account for them. Their gods were not comparable to the Rock of Israel; even Israel's enemies knew as much as that. Israel might forget and doubt Yahweh's power, but those who had been smitten before Him in Israel's happier days knew that He was above all their gods. Nor was the explanation to be sought in the heathen nations themselves. For they were not vines of Yahweh's planting, but shoots from the vine of Sodom, tainted by the soil of Gomorrah. They were, perhaps, in race, of the old Canaanite stock; in any case they were morally and spiritually related to them, and their acts were such as brought death and destruction with them. In themselves, consequently, they could not have been strong enough to discomfit the people of God as they were doing, nor could they have been helped to that by any favour of His. Only the determination of Yahweh to chastise His people could explain Israel's unhappy fate in war.

But Yahweh's purpose was only to chastise. He was in no way finally forgetful of His chosen, nor of the ineradicable evil of their enemies' nature. The inner character of men and things is always present to Him, and their deeds are laid up with Him as that which must be dealt with, for it is one of the glories of Deity to sweep evil away and to restore anything that has good at its heart. Recompense is God's great function in the world, and evil, however strong it may be, and however long it may triumph, must one day be dealt with by Him. It is laid up and sealed

> "Against the day of vengeance and of recompense,
> Against the time when their foot shall slip;
> For the day of their calamity is at hand,
> And hastening are the things prepared for them."

Without that, justice could never be done to the people of God; and justice should be done to them when they had been brought to the verge of extinction, when, according to the antique Hebrew phrase, there "was none fettered or set free," none left under or over age. Then when all but the worst had come, Yahweh would demand, "Where are their gods, with whom they took refuge, and who have eaten the fat of their sacrifices, and drunk the wine of their drink offerings?" He will challenge them to arise and help in this last disastrous state of their votaries.

But there will be no response, and it will be made clear beyond all doubting that Yahweh alone is God. He will declare Himself, saying:—

> "See now that I, I, am He,
> And there is no god with Me:
> *I* kill, and *I* make alive;
> I wound, and I heal:
> And there is none that delivereth out of My hand."

In that great day of Yahweh's manifested glory He will stand forth in the fulness of avenging power. Before the universe He will pledge Himself by the most solemn oath to bring down the pride of His enemies. In a death-dealing judgment, such as is seen only when the evil elements in the world have brought about a mere carnival of wickedness, and only universal death can cleanse, He will recompense upon evil-doers the evil they have wrought, and to a renovated world bring peace. There are few finer or more impressive imaginative passages in Scripture than this:—

> "For I lift up My hand to heaven,
> And say, (As) I live for ever,
> If I whet My gleaming sword,
> And My hand take hold on judgment,
> I will take vengeance upon Mine enemies,
> And I will recompense them that hate Me.
> I will make Mine arrows drunk with blood,
> And My sword shall devour flesh,
> With the blood of the slain and the captives,
> From the chief of the leaders of the enemy."

With this great vision of judgment the poet leaves his people. For them the first necessity evidently was that they should be assured that Yahweh reigned, that evil could not ultimately prosper. With their whole horizon dominated and illumined by this tremendous figure of the ever living and avenging God, their faith in the moral government of the world and in the ultimate deliverance of their nation would be restored.

The poem closes with a stanza in which the seer and singer calls upon the nations to rejoice because of Yahweh's people. The deliverance worked for them will be so great and so memorable that even the heathen who see it must rejoice. They will see His justice and His faithfulness, and will gain new confidence in the stability and the moral character of the forces which rule the world.

(B) The Blessing of Moses.

Deuteronomy xxxiii.

Besides the farewell speeches and the farewell song, we have in this chapter yet another closing utterance attributed to Moses. Here, as in the case of the song, we relegate critical matters to the note below.*

---

* The blessing of Moses was certainly not written by the author of Deuteronomy: the vocabulary and the style are different from his. Nor probably was the poem inserted here by him, but rather by the final editor of the Pentateuch who is believed to have brought these closing chapters into their present shape (*cf.* chap. xxiv.). The authority on which he relied may have been E.

As to the authorship of the blessing, Volck and Keil ascribe it to Moses. The great majority of recent students regard it, at all events in its present form, as post-Mosaic, on grounds drawn from features in the poem, and from the principles of prophetic exegesis referred to in the note (p. 616). Opinions differ much as to the date to be assigned, varying from the time of David to that of Jeroboam II. The general assumption is that the blessing is the work of a Northern Israelite; and the feeling for the tribes of Levi and Judah which it embodies is the chief indication on which a conjecture can be hazarded. That would agree with a date later than Solomon and not later than Jehoshaphat—a period when many in the Northern Kingdom still looked with reverence to the sanctuary at Jerusalem, and when the Northern Levites still resented the intrusion by Jeroboam of a mixed multitude into the priesthood.

As to form, and partly as to contents, the blessing of

We must notice in the first place the remarkable difference in tone and outlook between the blessing and the song of Moses. In the latter evil-doing and approaching judgment are the burden; here the outward and inward condition of Israel leaves little to be desired. Satisfaction is breathed in every line, for both temporally and spiritually the state of the people is almost ideally happy. Nowhere is there a shadow; even on the horizon there is scarcely a cloud. Now even an optimist would need a background of actual prosperity to draw such a picture of idyllic happiness for any nation, and we may therefore conclude that the poem has in view one of the few halcyon periods of Israel, before social wrongs had ruined the yeomen farmers, or war and conquest had corrupted the powerful. The nation is as yet faithful to Yahweh, and possesses in peace the land which He had given them to inherit.

The central part of the poem is of course the ten blessings promised to the various tribes, but these are preceded by an introduction (vv. 2-5), in which the formation of the people is traced to Yahweh's revelation of Himself and His coming forth as their King. They are followed also by a concluding section (vv. 26-29), in which the God of Jeshurun is declared to be incomparable, and His people are depicted as supremely happy under His protecting care. The language is in parts obscure, and though the general scope is always plain, yet there are verses the meaning of which can only be conjectured. This is especially the case in the introduction. Of the five lines of ver. 2, the fourth and fifth as they stand are hardly intelligible; the fifth indeed is not intelligible at all. In ver. 3 again, while the first and second clauses are fairly clear, the third and fourth are as they stand untranslatable. But the general signification of the introductory verses (2-5) is that the Divine revelation of Himself which Yahweh bestowed upon His people as He came with them from Sinai, Paran, and Seir through the wilderness, and the establishment of the covenant which made Yahweh Israel's King, together with the bestowal of an inheritance upon them, is the foundation and beginning of that happiness which is to be described. It is all traced back to the "dawning" of God upon them, His "shining out" upon them from Sinai, and Seir, and Paran. These are named simply as the most prominent points in that region whence the people came out into Canaan, and where the great revelation had been bestowed. God had risen like the sun and had shed forth light upon them there, so that they walked no more in darkness. The sight of God was, on this view, the great and fundamental fact in the history of the chosen people. They, like all who have seen that great sight, were henceforth separate from others, with different duties and obligations, with hopes and desires and joys unknown to all beside. And the ground of this condescension on the part of God was His love for His people. He loved them, and the saints among them were upheld by Him. By Moses He gave them a law, which was to hold from generation to generation; and He had crowned His gifts to them by becoming their King when the heads of the people entered into covenant with Him.

Then follow the blessings, beginning with good wishes for Reuben as the firstborn. But the tribe is not highly favoured. It is however less severely dealt with than in Jacob's blessing. There instability and obscurity are foretold of it. Here it would seem as if the fortunes of the tribe were at the lowest ebb, and a wish is expressed that it may not be suffered to die out. From the earliest times the tribe of Reuben seems to have been tending to decay. At the first census taken under Moses the number of Reubenites capable of bearing arms was 46,500 men (Numb. i. 21), at the second 43,730 (Numb. xxvi. 7). Both passages are from P, and consequently this decadence of the tribe must have been present to that author's mind. In David's day they had still possession of part of their heritage, but even then their best estate was past. They had allowed many Moabites to remain in the territory they conquered. These most certainly caused trouble and gained the upper hand in places, until before the days of Mesa, king of Moab, as we learn from his inscription,* a great part of the cities formerly Reubenite were in Moabite or Gadite hands. In Isaiah xv. and xvi. again, Heshbon and Elealeh, cities still Reubenite in Mesa's day, appear as Moabite, so that the bulk of the territory assigned to the tribe must have been lost.† This record confirms the view that the blessing was written between Rehoboam and Jehoshaphat, and throws light upon our verse:—

"May Reuben live, and not die,
So that his men be few."

The blessing of Judah follows, but in contrast with the great destiny foretold for this tribe in Jacob's blessing what is here said is strangely short and unenthusiastic:—

"Hear, O Yahweh, Judah's voice,
And bring him to his people;
With his hands has he striven for it (his people);
And a help against his enemies be thou."

Some whose opinions we are bound to respect, as Oettli, think this refers merely to Judah's being appointed to lead the van of the invasion, as in Judges i. 1 and xx. 8. In that case we should have to conceive that on some occasion Judah was absent leading the conquest, and got into dangerous circumstances, which are here referred to. But it would seem that any such temporary danger could hardly have a place here. In all the other blessings permanent conditions only are regarded; and the sole historical fact we really know that would explain this reference is the division of the kingdom. But, it may be said, all critics agree that the author of the blessing is a Northern Israelite: now we cannot suppose a Northern man to speak in this way of Judah, for it was the ten tribes that revolted from the house of David, not Judah from them. We must remember, however, that though that is how Scripture, which in this matter represents the Southern view, regards the matter, the Northern Israelites could look at the separation from another standpoint. To those even who

---

Moses is modelled on the blessing of Jacob (Gen. xlix). One conspicuous difference is the introduction into that before us of a prose heading before most of the sections, analogous to the headings which appear in Arabic poetry (as the "Hamasa") before each quatrain or longer poem. There is no ground for treating these as later insertions, nor for separating other portions, as some have proposed, as later than the main composition.

* Dillmann, "Deuteronomy," p. 420.
† Baethgen's Riehm, "Handwörterbuch," p. 1321.

were favourable to the Davidic house, and regretted the folly of Rehoboam, it might seem that Judah had first broken away from the kingdom as united under Saul; and the revolt under Jeroboam would appear to be only a resumption of the older state of things, from which Judah had again separated itself. What circumstance can be referred to in the request to hear Judah's voice cannot now be ascertained; but it is not at all unlikely that some indication of a wish for reunion, perhaps expressed in some public prayer, may have been given in the first period of the separation. The rest of the verse would fit this hypothesis as well as it fits the other, and I think with the light we at present have we must hold the reference to be as suggested.

With the eighth verse the blessing of Levi (one of the two most heartfelt and sympathetic) begins. In it Yahweh is addressed thus:—

"Thy Urim and thy Thummim be to the men (*i.e.*, tribe) of
thy devoted one (*i.e.*, Moses or Aaron),
Whom thou didst prove at Massah,
With whom thou didst strive at the waters of Meribah."

In the last lines the relative pronoun is ambiguous, as it may refer either to "men," for which in Hebrew we have the collective singular *'ish*, or to "thy devoted one." The last is the more probable; but in either case there is a superficial discrepancy here between the historical books and this statement. In Exod. xvii. 1-7, as well as in Deuteronomy itself, it is the people who strove with Moses and proved or tempted Yahweh. On this account some would have us believe that a different account of the events at Massah and Meribah was in this writer's mind. But that is the result of a mere itch for discovering discrepancies. It lies in the very nature of the case that there should be another side to it. The beginning was with the people; but just as the wandering in the wilderness is said to have been meant by God to prove Israel, so this insubordination of the people was meant to prove Moses or Aaron, and their failure to stand the proof made Yahweh strive with them. The verse, then, founds Levi's claim to possess the chief oracle and to instruct Israel first of all upon their connection with Moses or Aaron, or both, since they had been exceptionally tried and had proved their devotion. The next verse, then, goes on to found it also on the faithfulness of the Levites, when they were called upon by Moses (Exod. xxxii. 26-29) to punish the people for their worship of the golden calf. In vv. 27 and 29 of that chapter we find the same phrases,

9 "Who (*i.e.*, the tribe) said unto his father and to his
mother,
I have not seen him;
Who recognised not his brother, and would know
nought of his son?
For they kept Thy commandment,
And kept guard over Thy covenant."

Being such—

10 "Let them teach Jacob Thy judgments,
And Israel Thy Torah;
Let them put incense in Thy nostrils,
And whole burnt-offerings upon Thine altars."

Here we have the whole priestly duties assigned to the Levites. They are to perform judicial functions; to give Torah, or instruction, by means of the Urim and Thummim and otherwise; to offer incense in the Holy Place, and sacrifices in the court of the Temple. As early as this, therefore (on any supposition we need regard, long before Deuteronomy), we find the Levites fully established as the priestly tribe. Before the earliest writing prophets this was so— a fact of the greatest importance for the history of Israelite religion. The remaining verse beseeches Yahweh to accept the work of Levi's hands, and to smite down his enemies. Evidently when this was written special enmity was being shown to this tribe; and, as has been said already, the religious proceedings of Jeroboam I. would be sufficient to call forth such a cry to Yahweh.

In ver. 12 the tribe of Benjamin is dealt with, and it is depicted as specially blessed by the Divine favour and the Divine presence. Yahweh covers him all the day long, and dwells between his shoulders. There can hardly be a doubt that the reference is to the situation of the Temple at Jerusalem, on the hill of Zion, towards the loftier boundary of Benjamin's territory.

Verses 13-17 contain the blessing of Joseph, *i. e.*, of the two tribes Ephraim and Manasseh.

13 "Blessed of Yahweh be his land
By the precious things of heaven from above,
By the deep which crouches beneath;

14 "By the precious things of the sun,
And the precious things of the moons;

15 "And by the (precious things of the) tops of the ancient
mountains
And by the precious things of the everlasting hills;

16 "And by the precious things of the earth and its fulness.
And may the good-will of Him that dwelt in the bush
Come upon Joseph's head,
And upon the top of the head of the crowned among
his brethren.

17 "May the firstborn of his ox be glorious;
And the horns thereof like the horns of the wild-ox;
With them may he gore the peoples, even all the
earth's ends together.
These (*i. e.*, thus blessed) are the myriads of Ephraim,
And these the thousands of Manasseh."

Supreme fertility is to be his, and the favour of Yahweh is to rest upon him as the kingly tribe in Israel. The curious phrase at the beginning of the seventeenth verse has been supposed to be a reference to some individual, Joshua, Jeroboam II., or to the Ephraimite kings as a whole. But the subject of the blessing is the Josephite tribes, and there seems to be no good reason why the reference should be changed here. It cannot, therefore, refer to less than a whole tribe, and as according to Gen. xlviii. 14 Ephraim received the blessing of the firstborn, it must be Ephraim which is Joseph's firstborn ox. This view is confirmed by the last clause of the verse, in which the myriads of Ephraim are spoken of, and only the thousands of Manasseh. Obviously this must refer to times like those of Omri, when the Israelite kingship was in its first youthful energy, and was extending conquest on every hand.

The benedictions which remain are addressed to Zebulun, Issachar, Gad, Dan, Naphtali, and Asher. They need little comment beyond close translation.

18 "And of Zebulun he said,
Rejoice, Zebulun, in thy going out;
And, Issachar, in thy tents.

19 "They shall call the peoples unto the mountain;
They shall offer sacrifices of righteousness:
For they shall suck the abundance of the seas,
And the hidden treasures of the sand."

The territory of Zebulun stretched from the Sea of Galilee to the Mediterranean, probably quite down to the sea near Akko, in any case near enough to give it an active share in the sea traffic. Issachar, whose tribal land was the plain of Esdraelon, also shares in it; but the contrast between "thy going out" and "thy tents" implies that Zebulun took the more active part in the traffic. The reference in verse 19, clauses *a* and *b*, is obscure. As the Septuagint reads "they shall destroy" instead of "unto the mountain," the text may be corrupt. It may perhaps be an allusion to the sacrificial feasts at inaugurated fairs to which surrounding peoples were called, as Stade suggests.

20 "And of Gad he said,
   Blessed be the enlarger of Gad :
   He dwelleth as a lioness,
   And teareth the arm, yea, the crown of the head.

21 "And he looked out the first part for himself,
   Because there a (tribal) ruler's portion lay ready ;
   And he came with the heads of the people,
   He executed the justice of Yahweh,
   And His judgments in company with Israel."

At this time Gad was in possession of a wide territory, and was famed for courage and success in war. His foresight in choosing the first of the conquered land as a worthy tribal portion is praised, and his faithfulness in carrying out his bargain to accompany the nation in its attack on the west Jordan land.

22 "And of Dan he said,
   Dan is a lion's whelp,
   Leaping forth from Bashan."

This does not mean that Dan's territory was Bashan, but only that his attack was as fierce and unexpected as that of a lion leaping forth from the crevices and caves of the rocks in Bashan.

23 "And of Naphtali he said,
   O Naphtali, sated with favour,
   And full of the blessing of Yahweh :
   Possess thou the sea and the south."

The soil in the territory of Naphtali was specially fruitful, in the region of Huleh and on the shore of the Sea of Gennesaret. These are the sea and the hot south part which the tribe is called upon to take as a possession, and because of which the favour of Yahweh and His blessing specially rested upon it.

24 "And of Asher he said,
   Blessed above children be Asher ;
   May he be the favoured of his brethren,
   And dip his feet in oil.

25 "Iron and brass (be) thy bars ;
   And as thy days (so may) thy strength (be)."

The last line is extremely doubtful. The word translated "thy strength" is really not known, and that meaning probably implies another reading; "thy bars" in the previous line is also doubtful. The reference to oil probably implies that the olive tree was specially fruitful, in the country inhabited by Asher, but why he should be specially favoured of his brethren can now hardly be conjectured.

In the concluding verses we have an exaltation of Israel's God and of His people. Speaking out of the time when Israel had driven out its enemies and was in full and undisturbed possession of its heritage (ver. 28), the poet declares to Jeshurun how incomparable God is. He rides upon the heaven to bring help to them, and He comes in the clouds with majesty. The God of old time is Israel's refuge or dwelling, covering him from above, and beneath, *i. e.*, on the earth. His everlasting arms bear His people up in their weariness, and shelter them there against all foes. He has proved this by thrusting out before them, and by commanding them to destroy, their enemies.

28 "And so Israel came to dwell in safety,
   The fountain of Jacob alone,
   In a land of corn and wine ;
   Yea, His heavens drop down dew.

29 "Happy art thou, O Israel :
   Who is like unto thee ?
   A people saved by Yahweh,
   The shield of thy help
   And the sword of thy majesty !
   Thine enemies shall feign friendship to thee ;
   And thou shalt tread upon their high places."

CHAPTER XXVI.

MOSES' CHARACTER AND DEATH.

IT has been often said, and it has even become a principle of the critical school, that the historical notices in the earlier documents of the Old Testament represent nothing but the ideas current at the time when they were written. Whether they depict an Abraham, a Jacob, or a Moses, all they really tell us is the kind of character which at such times was held to be heroic. In this way the value of the historic parts of Deuteronomy has been called in question, and we have been told that all we can gather from them about Moses is the kind of character which the pious, in the age of Manasseh, would feel justified in attributing to their great religious hero. But it is manifestly unfair to estimate the statements of men who write in good faith, as if they were only projecting their own desires and prejudices upon a past which is absolutely dark. It may be true that such writers might be unwilling to narrate stories concerning the great men of the past which were inconsistent with the esteem in which they were held; but it is much more certain that their narratives will represent the tradition and the current knowledge of their time regarding the heroes of their race. Unless this be true, no reliance could be placed upon anything but absolutely contemporary documents; even these would be open to suspicion, if the human mind were so lawless as to have no scruple in filling up all gaps in its knowledge by imaginations. We must protest, therefore, against the notion that what J and E and D tell us concerning the life and character of Moses must be discounted in any effort we make to represent to ourselves the life and thought of that great leader of Israel. They tell us much more than what was thought fitting for a leader of the people in the ninth and eighth and seventh centuries B. C. They tell us what was *believed* in those times about Moses; and much of what was believed about him must have rested upon good authority, upon entirely reliable tradition, or upon previous written narratives concerning him.

Up till recently it was held, by men as eminent even as Reuss, that writing was unknown in the days of Moses, and that for long afterwards oral tradition alone could be a source of knowledge of the past. But recent discoveries have shown that this is an entire mistake. Long before

Moses writing was a common accomplishment in Canaan; and it seems almost ridiculous to suppose that the man who left his mark so indelibly upon this nation should have been ignorant of an art with which every master of a village or two was thoroughly conversant. Moreover the fact that the same root (k-t-b) occurs in every Semitic tongue with the meaning "to write," would seem to indicate that before their separation from one another the art of writing was known to all the Semitic tribes. The new facts enormously strengthen that probability, and make the arguments advanced by those who hold the opposite view look even absurd. But if writing were known and practised in Moses' day in Canaan, it would be marvellous if many of the great events of the early days had not been recorded. It would be still more marvellous if the comparatively late writings, which alone we have at our disposal, had not embodied and absorbed much older documents.

But for still another reason the critical dictum must be held to be false. Applied in other fields and in regard to other times, this same principle would deprive us of almost every character which has been considered the glory of humanity. Zarathustra and Buddha have alike been sacrificed to this prejudice, and there are men living who say that we know so little about our Lord Jesus Christ that it is doubtful whether He ever existed. A method which produces such results *must* be false. The great source of progress and reform has always been some man possessed by an idea or a principle. Even in our own days, when the press and the facilities for communication have given general tendencies a power to realise themselves which they never had in the world's history before, great men are the moving factors in all great changes. In earlier ages this was still more the case. It is an utterly unjustifiable scepticism which makes men contradict the grateful recollection of mankind, in regard to those who have raised and comforted humanity. Through all obscurities and confusions we can reach that Indian Prince for whom the sight of human misery embittered his own brilliant and enjoyable life. We refuse to give up Zarathustra, though his story is more obscure and entangled than that of almost any other great leader of mankind. Especially in a history like that of Israel, which purports to have been guided in a special manner by revelations of the will of God, the individual man filled with God's spirit is quite indispensable. Even if mythical elements in the story could be proved, that would not shake our faith in the existence of Moses; for as Steinthal, who holds the very "advanced" opinion that solar myths have strayed into the history of Moses, wisely says, it is quite as possible to distinguish between the mythical and the historical Moses as it is to distinguish between the historical Charlemagne and the mythical. Because of the general reliability of tradition regarding great men therefore, and because also of the proofs we have that writing was common before Moses' day, we need not burden ourselves with the assumption or the fear that the Deuteronomic character of Moses may be unreliable.

But in endeavouring to set forth this conception of the character of Moses, we cannot confine ourselves to what appears in this book. It is generally acknowledged that the author had at least the Yahwist and the Elohist documents in their entirety before him, and regarded them with respect, not to say reverence. Consequently we must believe that he accepted what they said of Moses as true. The only document in the Pentateuch that he may not have known in any shape was the Priest Codex, but that makes no attempt to depict the inner or outer life of Moses. All the personal life and colour in the Biblical narrative belongs to the other sources. For a personal estimate, therefore, we lose little by excluding P. Only one other cause of suspicion in regard to the historical parts of Deuteronomy *could* arise. If it, comparatively modern as it is, contained much that was new, if it revealed aspects of character for which no authority was quoted, and of which there was no trace in the earlier narratives, there might be reasonable doubt whether these new details were the product of imagination, But there is very little more in Deuteronomy than there is in the historical parts of the other books, though the older narratives are repeated with a vivid and insistive pathos which almost seems to make them new.

Combining then what the Deuteronomist himself says with what the Yahwist and Elohist documents contain, we find that the claim usually made for Moses, that he was the founder of an entirely new religion, is not sustained. Again and again it is asserted that Yahweh had been the God of their fathers, of Abraham, Isaac, and Jacob—so that Moses was simply the renewer of a higher faith which for a time had been corrupted. Some have even asserted that there had been all down the ages to Moses the memory of a primeval revelation. But if there ever was such a thing, we learn from Josh. xxiv. 2, a verse acknowledged to be from the Elohist, that that "fair beginning of a time" had been entirely eclipsed, for Terah, the father of Abraham, had served other gods beyond the flood. Abraham, therefore, rather than Moses, is regarded as the founder of the religion of Yahweh. Whether the word Yahweh (Exod. vi. 3) was known or not makes little difference, for all our four authorities teach that Moses' work was the revival of faith in that which Abraham, Isaac, and Jacob had believed. But the bulk of the people would appear to have been ignorant regarding the God of their fathers; and probably the conception which Deuteronomy shares with J and E is that in Moses' day Yahweh was the special God of a small circle, perhaps of the tribe of Levi, among whom a more spiritual conception of God than was common among their countrymen had either been retained, or had arisen anew. Probably then we ought to conceive the circumstances of Moses' early life somewhat in this way. A number of Semitic tribes, more or less nearly related to each other and to Edom and Moab, had settled in Egypt as semi-agricultural nomads. At first they were tolerated; but they were now being worn down and oppressed by forced labour of the most brutal sort. Either a tribe or a clan among them had the germs of a purer conception of God, and in this tribe or clan Moses, the deliverer of his people, was born. Providentially he escaped the death which awaited all Israelite boys in those days, and grew up in the camp of the enemies of his people. By this means he received all the culture that the best of the oppressors had, while the tie to Israel was neither obscured nor weakened in his mind. At the court of Pharaoh he could not fail to acquire some notions of statecraft, and he must have seen that the first step towards anything great for his people must be their union and consolidation. But his earliest effort on their behalf showed that he had not really considered and weighed the magnitude of his task. Killing an Egyptian oppressor might conceivably have served as a signal for revolt. But in point of fact it frustrated any plans Moses might have had for the good of his people, and drove him into the wilderness. Here the germs of various thoughts which education and experience of life had deposited in his mind had time to develop and grow. According to the narrative, it was only at the end of his long sojourn in Midian that he had direct revelation from God. But amid the wide and awful solitudes of that wilderness land, as General Gordon said of himself in the kindred solitudes of the Soudan, he learned himself and God. Whatever deposits of higher faith he had received from his family, no doubt the long, silent broodings inseparable from a shepherd's life had increased and vivified it. Every possible aspect of it must have been reckoned with, all its consequences explored; and his great and solitary soul, we may be sure, had many a time let down soundings into the deeps which were, as yet, dark to him. And then—for it is to souls that have yearned after Him in the travail of intellectual and spiritual longing that God gives His great and splendid revelations—Yahweh revealed Himself in the flame of the bush, and gave him the final assurance and the first impulse for his life's work. It is a touch of reality in the narrative which can hardly be mistaken, that it represents Moses as shrinking from the responsibility which his call must lay upon him. Behind the few and simple objections in the narrative, we must picture to ourselves a whole world of thoughts and feelings into which the call of God had brought tumult and confusion. One would need to be a dry-as-dust pedant not to see here, as in the case of Isaiah's call, the triumphant issue of a long conflict and the decisive moment of a victory over self, which had had already many stages of defeat and only partial success. It is perennially true to human nature and to the Divine dealings with human nature, that help from on high comes to establish and touch to finer issues that which the true man has striven for with all his powers.

Enlightened and assured by this great revelation of God, Moses left the quiet of the desert to undertake an extraordinarily difficult task. He had to weld jealous tribes into a nation; he had to rouse men whose courage had been broken by slavery and cruelty to undertake a dangerous revolt; and he had to prepare for the march of a whole population, burdened with invalids and infants, the feeble and the old, through a country which even to-day tries all but the strongest. These things had to be done; and the mere fact that they were accomplished would be inexplicable, without the domination of a great personality inspired by great ideas of a religious kind. For, in antiquity, the only bond able to hold incongruous elements together in one nationality was religion. With the people whom Moses had to lead the necessity would be the same, or even greater. But the political work which must have preceded any common action likewise demanded a great personality. Though no doubt a common misery might silence jealousies and make men eager to listen to any promises of deliverance, yet many troublesome negotiations must have been carried through successfully before these sentences could have been written with truth: "And Moses and Aaron went and gathered together all the elders of the children of Israel, and the people believed, and bowed their heads and worshipped."

Many conjectures have been hazarded as to what the centre of Moses' message at this time really was. Some, like Stade, bring it down to this, that Yahweh was the God of Israel. Others add to this somewhat meagre statement another equally meagre, that Israel was the people of Yahweh. But unless the character of Yahweh had been previously expounded to the people, there seems little in these two declarations to excite any enthusiasm or to kindle faith. The mere fact of inducing the tribes to put all other gods aside is insufficient to account for any of the results that followed, if to Moses Yahweh had remained simply a tribal God, of the same type as the gods of the Canaanites. On the other hand, if he had risen to the conception of God as a spirit, of Yahweh as the only living God, as the inspirer and defender of moral life, or even if he had made any large approach to these conceptions, it is easy to understand how the hearts of the mass of the people were stirred and filled, even though things so high were not, by the generality, thoroughly understood or long retained. But the hearts of all the chosen, the spiritually elect, would be moved by them as the leaves are moved by the wind. These, with Moses at their head, formed a nucleus which bore the people on through all their trials and dangers, and gradually leavened the mass to some extent with the same spirit.

Even after this had been accomplished, the main work remained to be done. We cannot agree indeed with many writers who seem to think that the whole life of the Israelite people was started anew by Moses. That would involve that every regulation for the most trivial detail of ordinary life was directly revealed, and that *Moses* made a *tabula rasa* of their minds, rubbing out all previous laws and customs, and writing a God-given constitution in their place. Obviously, that could hardly be; but still a task very different, yet almost as difficult, remained for Moses after his first success. His final aim was to make a virtually new nation out of the Hebrew tribes; and their whole constitution and habits had, consequently, to be revised from the new religious standpoint. He and the nation alike had inherited a past, and it was no part of his mission to delete that. Reforms, to be stable, must have a root in the habits and thoughts of the people whom they concern. Moses would, consequently, uproot nothing that could be spared; he would plant nothing anew which was already flourishing, and was compatible with the new and dominant ideas he had introduced. A great mass of the laws and customs of the Hebrews must have been good, and suitable to the stage of moral advancement they had reached before Moses came to them. Any measure of civilised life involves so much as that. Another great mass, while lying outside of the religious sphere, must have been at least compatible with Yahwism. All laws and customs coming under these two categories, Moses would naturally adopt as part of the legislation of the new nation, and would stamp them with his approval as being in accord with the religion of Yahweh. They would thus acquire the same authority as if they were entirely new, given for the first time by the Divinely inspired lawgiver.

But besides these two classes of laws and customs there must have been a number which were so bound up with the lower religion that they could not be adopted. They would either be obstructive of the new ideas, or they would be positively hostile to them; for on any supposition heathenism of various sorts was largely mingled with the religion of the Israelite people before their deliverance and even after it. To sift these out, and to replace them by others more in accord with the will of Yahweh as now revealed, must have been the chief work of the lawgiver. In that more or less protracted period before Israel came to Sinai, during which Moses burdened himself with judging the people personally, he must have been doing this work. His reflections in the wilderness had doubtless prepared him for it. In a mind like his, the fruitful principles received by the inspiration of the Almighty could not be merely passively held. Like St. Paul in his Arabian sojourn, we must believe that Moses in Midian would work out the results of these principles in many directions; and when he led Israel forth, he must have been clearly conscious of changes that were indispensable. But it needed close every-day contact with the life of the people to bring out all the incompatibilities which he would have to remove. Every day unexpected complications would arise; and the people at any rate, if Moses himself be supposed to be raised by his inspiration above the needs of experience, would be able to receive the instruction they needed only in concrete examples, here a little and there a little. When they came to "seek Yahweh" in any matter which perplexed them, Moses gave them Yahweh's mind on the subject; and each decision tended to purify and render innocuous to their higher life some department of public or private affairs. Every day at that early time must have been a day of instruction how to apply the principles of the higher faith just revived. The better minds among the chiefs were thereby trained to an appreciation of the new point of view; and when Jethro suggested that the burden of this work should be divided, quite a sufficient number were found prepared to carry it on. After this it must have gone on with tenfold speed, and we may believe that when Sinai was reached the preliminaries on the human side to the great revelation had been thoroughly elaborated. The Divine presence had been with Moses day by day, judging, deciding, inspiring in all their individual concerns as well as in their common affairs. But that would only bring out more clearly the extent of the reformation that remained to be wrought; doubtless too it had revealed the dulness of heart in regard to the Divine which has always characterised the mass of men. The need for a more complete revelation, a more extended and detailed legislation on the new basis, must have been greatly felt. In the great scene at Sinai, a scene so strange and awe-inspiring that to the latest days of Israel the memory of it thrilled every Israelite heart and exalted every Israelite imagination, this need was adequately met.

In connection with it Moses rose to new heights of intimacy with the Divine. What he had already done was ratified, and in the Decalogue the great lines of moral and social life were marked out for the people. But the most remarkable thing to us, in the narrative of the circle of events which made the mountain of the law for ever memorable, is the sublimity attributed to the character of Moses. From the day when he smote the Egyptian, at every glimpse we have of him we find him always advancing in power of character. The shepherd of Midian is nobler, less self-assertive, more overawed by communion with God, than the son of Pharaoh's daughter, noble as he was. Again, the religious reformer, the popular leader, who needs the very insistence of God to make him lead, who speaks for God with such courageous majesty, who teaches, inspires, and manages a turbulent nation with such conspicuous patience, self-repression, and success, is greatly more impressive than the Moses of Midianite days. But it is here, at Sinai, that his rank among the leaders of men is fixed for ever. To the people of that time God was above all things terrible; and when they came to the mount and found that "there were thunders and lightnings and a thick cloud upon the mount, and the voice of the trumpet exceeding loud," they could only tremble. Their very fear made it impossible for them to understand what God desired to reveal concerning Himself. But in Moses love had cast out fear. Even to him, doubtless, the darkness was terrible, because it expressed only too well the mystery which enwrapped the end of the Divine purposes of which he alone had seen the beginnings; even his mind must have been clouded thick with doubts as to whither Yahweh was leading him and his people; yet he went boldly forth to seek God, venturing all upon that errand.

In previous perplexities the narrative represents Moses as calling instantly upon Yahweh; but now, when experience had taught him the formidable nature of his task, when difficulties had increased upon him, when his perplexities of all kinds must have been simply overwhelming, he heard the voice of Yahweh calling him to Himself. Straightway he went into solitary communion with Him; and when he passed with satisfied heart from that communion, he brought with him those immortal words of the Decalogue which, amid all changes since, have been acknowledged to be the true foundation for moral and spiritual life. He brought too a commission authorising him to give laws and judgments to his people in accord with what he had heard and seen on the mount. However we are to understand the details of the narrative therefore, its meaning is that at this time, and under these circumstances, Moses attained his maximum of inspiration as a seer or prophet, and from that time onward stood in a more intimate relation to God than any of the prophets and saints of Israel who came after him. He had found God; and from where he stood with God he saw the paths of religious and political progress plainly marked out.

Henceforth he was competent to guide the nation he had made as he had not yet been, and with his power to help them his eagerness to do so grew. Twice during this great crisis of his life the people broke away into evil, and national death was threatened. But with passionate supplications for their pardon he threw himself down between God and them. At precisely the moment when his communion with God was most complete, he rose to the loving recklessness of desiring that if they were to be destroyed he might perish with them. Strangely enough, though the author of Deuteronomy had this before him, he does not mention it. It cannot have struck even him as the crowning point of Moses' career, as it does us. Even in his day the fitness, nay, the necessity, of this self-sacrificing spirit as the fruit of deeper knowledge of God, was not yet felt; much less could it have been felt in the days of the earlier historians. There must, therefore, be reliable information here as to what Moses actually did. Such love as this was not part of the Israelite ideal at the time of our narrative, and from nothing but knowledge of the fact could it have been attributed to Moses. We may rank this enthusiasm of love, therefore, as a reliable trait in his character. But if it be so, how far must he in his highest moments have transcended his contemporaries, and even the best of his successors, in knowledge of the inmost nature of God! His thought was so far above them that it remained fruitless for many centuries. Jeremiah's life and death first prepared the way for its appreciation, but only in the character of the Servant of Yahweh in Second Isaiah is it surpassed. Now if in this deepest part of true religion Moses possessed such exceptional spiritual insight, it is vain to attempt to show that his conception of God was so low, and his aim for man so limited, as modern theorists suppose. The truth must lie rather with those who, like Dr. A. B. Davidson,* see in him "a profoundly reverential ancient mind with thoughts of God so broad that mankind has added little to them. Nothing in the way of sublimity of view would be incongruous with such a character, while nothing could be more grotesque than to shut it up within the limits of the gross conceptions of the mass of the people. He was their guiding star, not their fellow, in all that concerned God, and his religious conceptions were by a whole heaven removed from theirs. The entire tragedy of his life just consisted in this, that he had to strive with a turbulent and gainsaying people, had to bear with them and train them, had to be content with scarcely perceptible advances, where his strenuous guidance and his patient love should have kindled them to *run* in the way of God's commandments. But though their progress was lamentably slow, he gave them an impulse they were never to lose. Under the inspiration of the Almighty he so fixed their fundamental ideas about God that they never henceforth could get free of his spiritual company. In all their progress afterwards they felt the impress of his mind, moulding and shaping them even when they knew it not, and through them he started in the world that redemptive work of God which manifested its highest power in Jesus Christ."

From this point onward the idea of Moses that Deuteronomy gives us is that of a great popular leader, meeting with extraordinary calmness all the crises of government, and guiding his people with unwavering steadfastness. Without power, except that which his relation to God and the choice of the people gave him, without any official title, he simply dominated the Israelites as long as he lived. And the secret of his success is plainly told us in the narrative. He would not move a single step without Divine guidance (Exod. xxxiii. 12): "And Moses said unto the Lord, See, Thou sayest unto me, Bring up this people: but Thou hast not let me know whom Thou wilt send with me." (Ver. 14) "And He said, Must I go in person with thee and bring thee to thy place of rest? And Moses said, If Thou dost not go with us in person, then rather lead us not away hence." That can only mean that he laid aside self-will, that he put away personal sensitiveness, that he had learned to feel himself unsafe when vanity or self-regard asserted themselves in his decisions, that he sought continually that detachment of view which absolute devotion to the Highest always gives. It means also that he knew how dark and dull his own vision was, that clouds and darkness would always be about him, and that it would be impossible for him to choose his path, unless he knew what the Divine plan for his people was. And all that is narrated of him afterward shows that his prayer was granted. His patience under trial has been handed down to us as a marvel. Though his brother and sister rebelled against him, he won them again entirely to himself. Though a faction among the people rose against his authority under Dathan and Abiram, his power was not even shaken. Amid all the perversity and childish fickleness of Israel he kept them true to their choice of the desert, "that great and terrible wilderness," as against Egypt with the flesh-pots. He kept alive their faith in the promise of Yahweh to give them a land flowing with milk and honey, and what was more and greater than that, their faith in Him as their Redeemer. By his intercourse with Yahweh he was upheld from falling away from his own ideals, as so many leaders of nations have done, or from despairing of them.

The complaints and perversities of the people did however force him into sin; and perhaps we may take it that the outbreak of petulance when he smote the rock was only one instance of some general decay of character on that side, or perhaps one should rather say, of some general falling away from the self-restraint which had distinguished him. It seems strange that this one failure should have been punished in him, by exclusion from the land he had so steadfastly believed in, the land which most of those who actually entered it would never have seen but for him. And it is pathetic to find him among that great company of martyrs for the public good, those who in order to serve their people have neglected their own characters. Under the stress of public work and the pressure of the stupidity and greed of those whom they have sought to guide, many leaders of men have been tempted, and have yielded to the temptation, to forget the demands of their better nature. But whatever their services to the world, such unfaithfulness does not pass unpunished. They have to bear the penalty, whosoever they be; and Moses was no more an exception than Cromwell or Savonarola was, to mention only some of the nobler examples. He had been courageous when others had faltered. He had been pre-eminently just; for in founding the judicial system of Israel he had guarded alike against the tyranny of the great and against unjust favour to the small. He had laid a firm hand upon the education of youth, determined that the best inheritance of their people, the knowledge of the laws of Yahweh and of His providences, should not be lost to them. He had cleared their religion in principle of all that

* "Moses' God," *British Weekly*, February 2, 1893.

was unworthy of Yahweh, and he had by resolute valour, and by uncompromising sternness to enemies, brought his great task to a successful issue. But the reward of it all, the entrance into the land he had virtually won for his people, was denied to him. It is one of the laws of the Divine government of the world, that with those to whom God specially draws near He is more rigorous than with others. Amos clearly saw and proclaimed this principle (Amos iii. 2). "Hear this word that Yahweh hath spoken against you, children of Israel," he says; "You only have I known of all the families of the earth: *therefore* I will visit upon you all your iniquities." The pathetic picture of the aged lawgiver, judge, and prophet, beseeching God in vain that he might share in the joy which was freely bestowed upon so many less known and less worthy than he, pushes home that strenuous teaching. For his sin he died with his last earnest wish unfulfilled, and it was sadly longing eyes that death's finger touched. We remember also that, so far as we can judge, he had no certain hope of a future life other than the shadowy existence of Hades. "Though he slay me yet will I trust him" had a much more tragic meaning for Old Testament saints than it can ever have for us, for whom Christ has brought life and immortality to light. Yet, with a so much heavier burden, and with so much less of gracious support, they played their high part. That solitary figure on the mountain-top, about to die with the fulfilment of his passionate last wish denied him by his God, must shame us into silence when we fret because our hopes have perished. All those nations which have had that figure on their horizon have been permanently enriched in nature by it. In a thousand ways it has shot forth instructions; but, above all, it has made men worthy in their own eyes; for it has been a continuous reminder that God can and ought to be served unfalteringly, even when the reward we wish is denied us, and when every other consolation is dim.

But the question may now arise, Is not this character of Moses which the author of Deuteronomy partly had before him and partly helped to elaborate, too exalted to be reliable? Can we suppose that a man in Moses' day and circumstances could actually have entertained such thoughts, and have possessed such a character as we have been depicting? In essentials it would appear to be quite possible. Putting aside all distracting questions about details, and remembering that it is a mere superstition to suppose that the wants and appliances of civilisation are necessary to loftiness of character and depth of thought, where is there anything in the situation of Moses which should make this view of him incredible? No doubt there was a rudeness in his surroundings which must necessarily have affected his nature; and the forms of his thinking in that early, though by no means primitive, time must have differed greatly from ours. Moreover, as an instrument for scientific inquiry and for the verification of facts, the human mind must have been greatly less effective then than it is to-day. But none of these things have much influence upon a man's capacity to receive a new and inspiring revelation as to God. Otherwise no child could be a Christian. As regards the rudeness of his surroundings, we must not consciously or unconsciously degrade him to the level of a modern Bedouin. Among the host he led, some doubtless were at that level; but the bulk of Israel must have been above it; and Moses himself, from his circumstances and his natural endowment, must have stood side by side with the most cultured men of his time. Whatever ignorance or error in science he may have been capable of, and however rude, according to our ideas, his manner of life, there was nothing in these to shut him out from spiritual truth. That which Prof. Henry Morley has finely said of Dante[*] must have been true, *mutatis mutandis*, of a man like Moses. "Dante's knowledge is the knowledge of his time," but "if spiritual truth only came from right and perfect knowledge, this would have been a world of dead souls from the first to now, for future centuries in looking back at us will wonder at the little faulty knowledge that we think so much. But let the *known* be what it may, the true soul rises from it to a sense of the Divine mysteries of wisdom and love. Dante's knowledge may be full of ignorance, and so is ours. But he fills it as he can with the spirit of God." In the East this is even more conspicuously true, even to this day. What an Israelite under similar conditions might be is seen in the prophet Amos. His external condition was of the poorest—a gatherer of sycamore fruit must have been poor even for the East— yet he knew accurately the history, not only of his own people, but of the surrounding nations, and brooded on the purpose of God in regard to his own people and the world, till he became a fit recipient of prophetic inspirations. But indeed the whole history of Christianity is a demonstration of this truth. From the first days, when "not many mighty, not many noble were being called," when it was specially the message to listening slaves, the religion of Christ has had its greatest triumphs among the "poor of the world, rich in faith," but in nothing else. These have not only believed it, but they have lived it, and amid the meanest and rudest surroundings, with the most limited outlook, have built up characters often of even resplendent virtue. Whatever primitiveness we may fairly ascribe, therefore, to the life and surroundings of Moses, that is no reason why we should think it incredible that he had received lofty spiritual truth from God. If he did such things for Israel as we have seen, if, as almost all admit, he actually made a nation, and planted the seeds of a religion of which Christianity is the natural complement and crown, then the 'view that he had a greatly higher idea of God than those about him is not only credible but necessary. If his teaching concerning Yahweh had amounted only to this, that He was the only God Israel was to worship, and that they were to be solely His people, then on such a basis nothing more than the ordinary heathen civilisations of the Semitic people could have been built. But if he had the thought of God which is embodied in the Decalogue, that could bring with it everything in the character of Moses that seems too high for those early days. The knowledge of God as a spiritual and moral being could not fail to moralise and spiritualise the man. The lofty conception of human duty, the submission to the will of God, the passionate love for his nation which made personal loss nothing to Moses, may well have been evoked by the great truth which formed his prophetic revelation.

[*] "Convito of Dante," Morley's "Universal Library," Introduction, pp. 6 ff.

But the narrative itself, considered merely as a history, is of such a nature as to give confidence that it rests upon some record of an actual life. Ideal sketches of great men (setting aside the products of modern fictive art) are much more uniform and superficially coherent than this character of Moses. The purpose of the writer either to exalt or to decry carries all before it, and we get from such a source pictures of character so consistent that they cannot possibly be true. Here, however, we have nothing of that kind. Rashnesses and weaknesses are narrated, and even Moses' good qualities are manifested in unexpected ways in response to unexpected evils in the people. The mere fact, also, that his grave was unknown is indicative of truth. Though it would be absurd to say that wherever we have the graves of great men pointed out, there we have a mythical story, it is nevertheless true that in the case of every name or character which has come largely under the influence of the myth-making spirit, the grave has been made much of. The Arabian imagination here seems to be typical of the Semitic imagination; and in all Moslem lands the graves of the prophets and saints of the Old Testament are pointed out with great reverence, even, or perhaps we should say especially, if they be eighty feet long. Though a well-authenticated tomb of Moses, therefore, would have been a proof of his real existence and life among men, the absence of any is a stronger proof of the sobriety and truth of the narrative. That with the goal in sight, and with his great work about to come to fruition, he should have turned away into the solitude of the mountains to die, is so very unlikely to occur to the mind of the writer of an ideal life of an ideal leader, that only some tradition of this as a fact can account for it. The unexpectedness of such an end to a hero's career is the strongest evidence of its truth.

The result of all the indications is that the story of Moses, as the author of Deuteronomy knew it, rests upon authentic information handed down somehow, probably in written documents, from the earliest time. Apart from the question of inspiration, therefore, we may rest upon it as reliable in all essentials. Only in him, and the revelation he received, have we an adequate cause for the great upheaval of religious feeling which shaped and characterised all the after-history of Israel.

The Book of Joshua

By Professor William Garden Blaikie, D.D., LL.D.

DOCTOR BLAIKIE was Professor of Theology, New College, Edinburgh, from 1868 to 1897. In addition to the work of his chair, and of frequent preaching, he wrote "For the Work of the Ministry," "The Personal Life of David Livingstone," "Heroes of Israel," "The Life of Chalmers," the volumes on Samuel in The Expositor's Bible, and many other books.

The Book of Joshua is a history of the period of colonization in Canaan under the leadership of the man whose name it bears. The religious and economic problems incident to such a time, and the crusades against infidelity and immorality due to contacts with foreign peoples, presented a truly complicated situation. Doctor Blaikie expounds its significance with a wealth of historical and biographical illustration, and throws light on the solution of our own difficulties in this day of conflict and confusion.

CONTENTS

	PAGE
CHAPTER I.	
Introductory :—The Book of Joshua,	633
CHAPTER II.	
Joshua's Antecedents,	638
CHAPTER III.	
A Successor to Moses,	642
CHAPTER IV.	
Joshua's Call,	644
CHAPTER V.	
Joshua's Encouragement,	647
CHAPTER VI.	
Joshua's Charge to the People,	650
CHAPTER VII.	
The Spies in Jericho,	653
CHAPTER VIII.	
Jordan Reached,	656
CHAPTER IX.	
Jordan Divided,	659
CHAPTER X.	
Circumcision and Passover—Manna and Corn,	662
CHAPTER XI.	
The Captain of the Lord's Host,	664
CHAPTER XII.	
The Fate of Jericho,	668
CHAPTER XIII.	
Rahab Saved,	671
CHAPTER XIV.	
Achan's Trespass,	674
CHAPTER XV.	
Achan's Punishment,	677
CHAPTER XVI.	
The Capture of Ai,	680
CHAPTER XVII.	
Ebal and Gerizim,	683

	PAGE
CHAPTER XVIII.	
The Stratagem of the Gibeonites,	685
CHAPTER XIX.	
The Battle of Bethhoron,	688
CHAPTER XX.	
The Battle of Merom,	692
CHAPTER XXI.	
Joshua's Old Age—Division for the Eastern Tribes,	695
CHAPTER XXII.	
The Inheritance of Caleb,	698
CHAPTER XXIII.	
The Distribution of the Land,	701
CHAPTER XXIV.	
The Inheritance of Judah,	704
CHAPTER XXV.	
The Inheritance of Joseph,	708
CHAPTER XXVI.	
The Distribution Completed,	711
CHAPTER XXVII.	
The Cities of Refuge,	714
CHAPTER XXVIII.	
The Inheritance of the Levites,	718
CHAPTER XXIX.	
No Failure of God's Promise,	721
CHAPTER XXX.	
The Altar Ed,	724
CHAPTER XXXI.	
Jehovah the Champion of Israel,	727
CHAPTER XXXII.	
Joshua's Last Appeal,	730
CHAPTER XXXIII.	
Joshua's Work for Israel,	733

THE BOOK OF JOSHUA.

BY WILLIAM GARDEN BLAIKIE, D. D., LL. D.

CHAPTER I.

INTRODUCTORY: THE BOOK OF JOSHUA.

WITH a purely historical book like Joshua before us, it is of importance to keep in view two ways of regarding Old Testament history, in accordance with one or other of which any exposition of such a book must be framed.

According to one of these views, the historical books of Scripture, being given by inspiration of God, have for their *main* object not to tell the story or dwell on the fortunes of the Hebrew nation, but to unfold God's progressive revelation of Himself made to the seed of Abraham, and to record the way in which that revelation was received, and the effects which it produced. The story of the Hebrew nation is but the frame in which this Divine revelation is set. It was God's pleasure to reveal Himself not through a formal treatise, but in connection with the history of a nation, through announcements and institutions and practical dealings bearing in the first instance on them. The historical books of the Hebrews therefore, while they give us an excellent view of the progress of the nation, must be studied in connection with God's main purpose, and the supernatural interpositions by which from time to time it was carried out.

The other view regards the historical books of the Hebrews in much the same light as we look on those of other nations. Whatever may have been their origin, they are, as we find them, like other books, and our purpose in dealing with them should be the same as in dealing with books of similar contents. We are to deal with them, in the first instance at least, from a natural point of view. We are to regard them as recording the history and development of an ancient nation—a very remarkable nation, no doubt, but a nation whose progress may be referred to ascertainable causes. If we find natural causes sufficient to account for that progress, we are not to call in supernatural. It is an acknowledged law, at least as old as Lord Bacon, that no more causes are to be assigned for phenomena than are true and sufficient to account for them. This law, and the investigations which have taken place under it, have expunged much that used to be regarded as supernatural from the history of other nations; and it will only be according to analogy if the same result is reached in connection with the history of Israel.

In this spirit we have recently had several treatises dealing with that history from a purely natural standpoint. Very earnest endeavours have been made to clear the atmosphere, to expiscate facts, to apply the laws of history, to weigh statements in the balances of probability, to reduce the Hebrew history to the principles of science. The general effect of this method has been to bring out results very different from those previously accepted. In particular, there has been a thorough elimination of the supernatural from Hebrew history. Natural causes have been judged sufficient to explain all that occurred. The introduction of the supernatural in the narrative was due to those obvious causes that have operated in the case of other nations and other religions:—love of the mythical, a patriotic desire to glorify the nation, the exaggerating tendency of tradition, and readiness to translate symbolical pictures into statements of literal occurrences. Hebrew historians were not exempted from the tendencies and weaknesses of other historians, and were ready enough to colour and apply their narratives according to their own views. It is when we subject the Hebrew books to such principles as these (such writers tell us) that we get at the real history of the nation, deprived no doubt of much of the glory with which it has usually been invested, but now for the first time reliable history, on which the most scientific may depend. And as to its moral purpose, it is just the moral purpose that runs through the scheme of the world, to show that, amid much conflict and confusion, the true, the good, the just, and the merciful become victorious in the end over the false and the evil.

The difference between the two methods, as an able writer remarks, is substantially this, that "the one regards the Hebrew books as an unfolding of God's nature, and the other as an unfolding of the nature of man."

The naturalistic method claims emphatically to be scientific. It reduces all events to historical law, and finds for them a natural explanation. But what if the natural explanation is no explanation? What becomes of the claim to be scientific if the causes assigned are not sufficient to account for the phenomena? If science will not tolerate unnatural causes, no more should it tolerate unnatural effects. A truly scientific method must show a fit proportion between cause and effect. Our contention is that, in this respect, the naturalistic method is a failure. In many instances its causes are wholly inadequate to the effects. We are compelled to fall back on the supernatural, otherwise we are confronted with a long series of occurrences for which no reasonable explanation can be found.

We are reminded of an incident which a popular writer, under the *nom de plume* of Edna Lyall, has introduced in a novel, bearing the title "We Two." Erica, the daughter of an atheist, assists her father in conducting a journal. She gets from him for review a Life of David Livingstone, with instructions to leave his religion entirely out. As she proceeds with the work, she becomes convinced that the condition is impossible. To describe Livingstone without his religion would be like playing "Hamlet" without the part of Hamlet. Not only does she find her task impossible, but when she comes to an incident where Livingstone, in most imminent danger of his life, gets entire composure of mind from an act of devotion, she becomes convinced that this could not have happened had there not been an objective reality corresponding to his belief; and she is an atheist no more. Erica now believes in God. *Se non e vero e ben trovato.*

In like manner, we believe that to delineate

Old Testament history without reference to the supernatural is as impossible as to describe Livingstone apart from his religion. You are baffled in trying to explain actual events. Long ago, Edward Gibbon tried to account for the rapid progress and brilliant success of Christianity in the early centuries by what he called secondary causes. It was really an attempt to eliminate the supernatural from early Christian history. But the five causes which he specified were really not causes, but effects,—effects of that supernatural action which had its source in the supernatural person of Jesus Christ. These "secondary causes" never could have existed had not Jesus Christ already commended Himself to all sorts of men as a Divine Saviour, sent by God to bless the world. In like manner we maintain that behind the causes by which our naturalistic historians attempt to explain the remarkable history of the Jewish people, there lay a supernatural force, but for which the Hebrews would not have been essentially different from the Edomites, the Ammonites, the Moabites, or any other Semitic tribe in their neighbourhood. It was the supernatural element underlying Hebrew history that made it the marvellous development it was; and that element began at the beginning and continued more or less actively till Jesus Christ came in the flesh.

Let us try to make good this position. Let us select a few of the more remarkable occurrences of early Hebrew history, and, in the language of Gibbon, make "a candid and reasonable inquiry" whether or not they can be accounted for, on the ordinary principles of human nature, without a supernatural cause.

1. It is certain that from the earliest times, and during at least the first four centuries of their history, the Hebrew people had an immovable conviction that the land of Canaan was divinely destined to be theirs. Of the singular hold which this conviction took of the minds of the patriarchs, we have innumerable proofs. Abraham leaves the rich plains of Chaldæa to dwell in Canaan, and spends a hundred years in it, a stranger and a pilgrim, without having a single acre of his own. When he sends to Padan Aram for a wife to Isaac he conjures his servant on no account to listen to any proposal that Isaac should settle there; the damsel must at all hazards come to Canaan. When Jacob determines to part from Laban, he sets his face resolutely towards his native land across the Jordan, although his injured brother is there, thirsting as he knows for his blood. When Joseph sends for his father to go down to Egypt, Jacob must get Divine permission at Beersheba before he can comfortably go. Joseph, for his services to Egypt, might reasonably have looked for a magnificent tomb in that country to cover his remains and perpetuate his memory; but, strange to say, he prefers to remain unburied for an indefinite time, and leaves a solemn charge to his people to bury him in Canaan, carrying his bones with them when they leave Egypt. In the bitterness of their oppression by Pharaoh it would have been much more feasible for their champions, Moses and Aaron, to try to obtain a relaxation of their burdens; but their demand was a singular one—liberty to go into the wilderness, with the hardly concealed purpose of escaping to the land of their affections. Goshen was a goodly land, but Canaan had a dearer name— it was the land of their fathers, and of their brightest hopes. The uniform tradition was, that the God whom Abraham worshipped had promised to give the land to his posterity, and along with the land other blessings of mysterious but glorious import. With this promise was connected that Messianic hope which like a golden thread ran through all Hebrew history and literature, brightening it more and more as the ages advanced.

It is vain to account for this extraordinary faith in the land as theirs, and this remarkable assurance that it would be the scene of unwonted blessing, apart from a supernatural communication from God. To suppose that it originated in some whim or fancy of Abraham's or in the saga of some old bard like Thomas the Rhymer, and continued unimpaired century after century, is to suppose what was never realised in the history of any people. In vain do we look among natural causes for any that could have so impressed itself on a whole nation, and swayed their whole being for successive ages with irresistible force. That "God spake to Abraham to give him the land" was the indefeasible conviction of his descendants; nor could any consideration less powerful have sustained their hopes, or nerved them to the efforts and perils needful to realize it.

2. No more can the leaving of Egypt, with all that followed, be accounted for without supernatural agency. It is the contention of the naturalistic historian that the Israelites were very much fewer in number than the Scripture narrative alleges. But if so, how could an empire, with such immense resources as the monuments show Egypt to have had, have been unable to retain them? Wellhausen affirms that at the time Egypt was weakened by a pestilence. We know not his authority for the statement; but if the Egyptians were weakened, the Israelites (unless supernaturally protected) must have been weakened too. Make what we may of the contest between Moses and Pharaoh, it is beyond dispute that Pharaoh's pride was thoroughly roused, and that his firm determination was not to let the children of Israel go. And if we grant that his six hundred chariots were lost by some mishap in the Red Sea, what were these to the immense forces at his disposal, and what was there to hinder him from mustering a new force, and attacking the fugitives in the wilderness of Sinai? Pharaoh himself does not seem to have entered the sea with his soldiers, and was therefore free to take other steps. How, then, are we to account for the sudden abandonment of the campaign?

3. And as to the residence in the wilderness, even if we suppose that the Israelites were much fewer in number than is stated, they were far too great a multitude to be supported from the scanty resources of the desert. The wilderness already had its inhabitants, as Moses knew right well from his experience as a shepherd; it had its Midianites and Amalekites and other pastoral tribes, by whom the best of its pastures were eagerly appropriated for the maintenance of their flocks. How, in addition to these, were the hosts of Israel to obtain support?

4. And how are we to explain the extraordinary route which they took? Why did they not advance towards Canaan by the ordinary way—the wilderness of Shur, Beersheba, and Hebron? Why cross the Red Sea at all, or have anything to do with Mount Sinai and its awful cliffs, which

INTRODUCTORY: THE BOOK OF JOSHUA.

a glance at the map will show was entirely out of their way? And when they did take that route, what would have been easier than for Pharaoh, if he had chosen to follow them with a new force, to hem them in among these tremendous mountains, and massacre or starve them at his pleasure? If the Israelites had no supernatural power to fall back on, their whole course was simply madness. We may talk of good fortune extricating men from difficulties, but what fortune that can be conceived could have availed a people, professing to be bound for the land of Canaan, that, without food or drink or stores of any kind, had wandered into the heart of a vast labyrinth, for no reasonable purpose under the sun?

5. Nor can the career of Moses be made intelligible without a supernatural backing. The contention is, that the desire of the people in Egypt for deliverance having become very strong, especially in the tribe of Levi, they sent Aaron to find Moses, remembering his former attempt on their behalf; and that, under the able leadership of Moses, their deliverance was secured by natural means. But does this explain the actual campaign in Sinai? Who ever heard of a leader that, after he had roused the enthusiasm of his people by a brilliant deliverance, arrested their further progress in order to preach to them for a twelvemonth, and give them a system of law? Did Moses not possess that instinct of a general that must have urged him to push on the moment the Egyptians were drowned, and amid the enthusiasm of his own troops and the consternation of the Canaanites, fling his army upon the seven nations, and seize their land by a *coup de main?* Abraham before him and Joshua after him found the value of such prompt, sudden movements. Never had a leader a more splendid opportunity. What could have induced Moses to throw away his chance, bury his people among the mountains, and remain inactive for months upon months? Is there any conceivable explanation but that he acted by supernatural direction? The Divine plan was entirely different from any that human wisdom would have contrived. It is as clear as day that, had there been no Divine power controlling the movement, the course taken by Moses would have been simply insane.

6. Nor could the law of Moses, first given in such circumstances, have acquired the glory which surrounded it ever after, had there been no manifestation of the Divine presence at Sinai. The people were greatly dissatisfied, especially at their delays. The only course that would have quieted them was to push on towards Canaan, so that their minds might be animated by the enthusiasm of hope. Under their detentions they greedily seized every occasion that presented itself for growling against Moses. How little they were in sympathy with his ideas of religion and worship was apparent from the affair of the golden calf. The history of the time is an almost unbroken record of murmuring, complaining, and rebellion. Yet the law which originated with Moses in these circumstances became the very idol of the people, and, according to the naturalistic historians, was the means of creating the nation, and welding the tribes into a living unity! We can quite easily understand how, in spite of all their growlings, the law as given at Sinai should have taken the firmest hold of their imagination and kindled their utmost enthusiasm in the end, if it was accompanied by those tokens of the Divine presence which the whole literature of the Hebrews assumes. And if Moses was closely identified with the Divine Being, the surpassing glory of the occasion must have been reflected on him. But to suppose that a discontented people should have had their enthusiasm roused for the law simply because this Moses commanded them to observe it, and that they should ever after have counted it the holiest, the most Divine law that men had ever known, is again to postulate an effect without a cause, and to suppose a whole people acting in disregard of the strongest propensities of human nature.

7. Then, as to the generalship of Moses. How are we to explain the further detention of the people in the wilderness for nearly forty years? If this was not the result of a supernatural Divine decree, it must have proceeded from the inability of Moses to lead the people to victory. No people who had struggled out of bondage in order to enter a land flowing with milk and honey, would of their own accord have spent forty years in the wilderness. At Hormah, they were willing to fight, but Moses would not lead them, and they were beaten. Either the wandering of the forty years was a Divine punishment, or the generalship of Moses was at fault. He abandoned himself to inaction for an unprecedented period. There was no shadow of benefit to be gained by this delay; nothing could come of it (apart from the Divine purpose) but wearing out the patience of the people, and killing them with the sickness of hope deferred. And if it should be said that the forty years' wandering was a myth, and that probably the wilderness sojourn did not exceed a year or two at most, is it conceivable that any people in its senses would invent such a legend?—a legend that covered them with shame, and that was felt to be so disgraceful that the whole region was shunned by them; insomuch that with the exception of Elijah, we do not read of any member of the nation ever making a pilgrimage to the spot which otherwise must have had overwhelming attractions.

8. At last Moses suddenly awakes to activity and courage. And the next difficulty is to account for his success at the eleventh hour of his life, if he had no supernatural help. No phrase occurs more frequently in naturalistic explanations than " it is likely." Likelihood is the touchstone to which all extraordinary statements are brought, although, as Lord Beaconsfield used to tell us, " it is the unexpected that happens." Borrowing the touchstone for the nonce, we may ask, Is it likely that, after a sleep of eight-and-thirty years, Moses of his own accord, without any apparent change of circumstances, sprang suddenly to his feet, and urged the people to attempt the invasion of the land? Is it likely that all the inertia and fears of the people vanished in a moment, as if at the touch of a magician's wand? And when it came to actual fighting, is it likely that these shepherds of the desert were able of themselves not only to stand before a trained and successful warrior like Sihon King of the Amorites, who had so lately overrun the country, but to defeat him utterly and take possession of his whole territory? Is it likely that Sihon's neighbour, Og King of Bashan, though warned by the fate of Sihon, and therefore sure to make a more careful defence, shared the fate

of the other king? Or if Og was a mere myth, as Wellhausen strangely maintains, is it likely that the Israelites got possession of the powerful cities and well-defended kingdom of Bashan without striking a blow? Is it likely that, after this brilliant victory, Moses, who was still in full vigour, detained them again for weeks to preach old sermons, and sing them songs, and make pathetic speeches, instead of dashing at once at the petrified people on the other side, and acquiring the great prize—Western Palestine? Strange mortal this Moses must have been!—wise enough to give the people an unexampled constitution and system of laws, and yet blind to the most obvious laws of military science, and the most elementary perceptions of common sense.

And now we come to Joshua, and to the book that records his achievements.

Joshua was no prophet; he made no claim to the prophetic character; he succeeded Moses only as military leader. Consequently the Book of Joshua contains little matter that would fall under the term "revelation." But both the work of Joshua and the book of Joshua served an important purpose in the plan of Divine manifestation, inasmuch as they showed God fulfilling His old promises, vindicating His faithfulness, and laying anew a foundation for the trust of His people. In this point of view, both the work and the book have an importance that cannot be exaggerated. The naturalistic historian regards the book as merely setting forth, with sundry traditional embellishments, the manner in which one people ousted another from their country, much as those who were then evicted had dispossessed the previous inhabitants. But whoever believes that, centuries before, God made a solemn promise to Abraham to give that land to his seed, must see in the story of the settlement the unfolding of a Divine purpose, and a solemn pledge of blessings to come. "The Ancient of days," who "declares the end from the beginning," is seen to be faithful to His promises; and if He has been thus faithful in the past, he may surely be trusted to be faithful in the future.

If, then, Joshua's work was a continuation of the work of Moses, and his book of the books of Moses, both must be regarded from the same point of view. You cannot explain either of them reasonably in a merely rationalistic sense. Joshua could no more have settled the people in Canaan by merely natural means than Moses could have delivered them from Pharaoh and maintained them for years in the wilderness. In the history of both you see a Divine arm, and in the books of both you find a chapter of Divine revelation. It is this that gives full credibility to the miracles which they record. What happened under Joshua formed a most important chapter of the process of revelation by which God made Himself known to Israel. In such circumstances, miracles were not out of place. But if the Book of Joshua is nothing more than the record of a raid by one nation on another, miracles were uncalled for, and must be given up.

Rationalists may count us wrong in believing that the Hebrew historical books are more than Hebrew annals—are the records of a Divine manifestation. But they cannot hold us unreasonable or inconsistent if, believing this, we believe in the miracles which the books record. Miracles assume a very different character when they are connected into a sublime purpose in the economy of God; when they signalize a great epoch in the history of revelation—the completion of a great era of promise, the fulfilment of hopes delayed for centuries. The Book of Joshua has thus a far more dignified place in the history of revelation than a superficial observer would suppose. And those historians who bring it down to the level of a mere record of an invasion, and who leave out of account its bearing on Divine transactions so far back as the days of Abraham, spoil it of its chief glory and value for the Church in every age. There is nothing of more importance, whether for the individual believer or for the Church collectively, than a firm conviction, such as the Book of Joshua emphatically supplies, that long delays on God's part involve no forgetfulness of His promises, but that whenever the destined moment comes "no good thing will fail of all that He hath spoken."

The Book of Joshua consists mainly of two parts; one historical, the other geographical. It was the old belief that it was the work of a single writer, with such slight revision at an after time as a writing might receive without essential interference with its substance. The author was sometimes supposed to be Joshua himself, but more commonly one of the priests or elders who outlived Joshua, and who might therefore fitly record his death. It has been remarked that there are several traces in the book of contemporary origin, like the remark on Rahab—"She dwelleth in Israel even unto this day" (vi. 25). It must be allowed, we think, that there is not much in this book to suggest to the ordinary reader either the idea of a late origin or of the use of late materials.

But recent critics have taken a different view. Ewald maintained that, besides the Jehovist and Elohist writers of whose separate contributions in Genesis the evidence seems incontrovertible, there were three other authors of Joshua, with one or more redactors or revisers. The view of Kuenen and Wellhausen is similar, but with this difference, that the Book of Joshua shows so much affinity, both in object and style, to the preceding five books, that it must be classed with them, as setting forth the origin of the Jewish nation, which would not have been complete without a narrative of their settlement in their land. The composition of Joshua is therefore to be brought down to a late date; we owe it to the documents, writers, and editors concerned in the composition of the Pentateuch; and instead of following the Jews in classing the first five books by themselves, we ought to include Joshua along with them, and in place of the Pentateuch speak of the Hexateuch. Canon Driver substantially accepts this view; in his judgment, the first part of the book rests mainly on the JE (Jehovist-Elohist) document, with slight additions from P (the priestly code) and D² (the second Deuteronomist). The second half of the book is derived mainly from the priestly code. But Canon Driver has the candour to say that it is much more difficult to distinguish the writers in Joshua than in the earlier books; and so little is he sure of his ground that even such important documents as J and E have to be designated by new letters, a and b. But, all the same, he goes right on with his scheme, furnishing us with tables all through, in which he shows that the Book of Joshua consists of ninety different pieces, no two consecutive pieces being by the same author. Most of it he refers to three earlier writings, but some of these were composite, and it is hard to say how many hands were engaged in putting together this simple story.

One is tempted to say of this complicated but confidently maintained scheme, that it is just too complete, too wonderfully finished, too clever by half. Allowing most cordially the remarkable ability and ingenuity of its authors, we can hardly be expected to concede to them the power of taking to pieces a book of such vast antiquity, putting it in a modern mincing machine, dividing it among so many supposed writers, and settling the exact parts of it written by each! Is there any ancient writing that might not yield a similar result if the same ingenuity were exercised upon it?

To judge of the source of writings by apparent varieties of style, and call in a different writer for every such variety, is to commit oneself to a very precarious rule. There are doubtless cases where the diversity of style is so marked that the inference is justified, but in these the evidence is unmistakably clear. Often the evidence against identity of authorship *appears* very clear, while it is absolutely worthless. Suppose that three thousand years hence an English book should be found, consisting, first, of an eloquent exposition of a parliamentary budget; secondly, a scheme for Home Rule in Ireland; thirdly, a dissertation on Homer; and fourthly, essays on the "Impregnable Rock of Holy Scripture"—how convincingly might the critics of the day demonstrate, beyond possibility of contradiction, that the book could not be the work of the single man who bore the name of William E. Gladstone! In like manner, it might be made very plain that Milton could never have written both "L'Allegro" and "Il Penseroso," or "Paradise Lost" and the "Defence of the English People." Cowper could not have written "John Gilpin" and "God moves in a mysterious way." Samuel Rutherford could not have written his "Letters" and his "Divine Right of Church Government." Moreover, in the course of years a writer may change his style, even when his subject is the same. The earlier essays of Mr. Carlyle show no traces of that most quaint, terse, graphic style which became one of his outstanding characteristics in later years. Perhaps the most remarkable instance of change of style in a great writer is that of Jeremy Bentham. In Sir James Mackintosh's Dissertation prefixed to the "Encyclopædia Britannica" (eighth edition) he says: "The style of Mr. Bentham underwent a more remarkable revolution than perhaps befell that of any other celebrated writer. In his early works, it was clear, free, spirited, often and seasonably eloquent. . . . He gradually ceased to use words for conveying his thoughts to others, but merely employed them as a short-hand to preserve his meaning for his own purpose. It is no wonder that his language thus became obscure and repulsive. Though many of his technical terms are in themselves exact and pithy, yet the overflow of his vast nomenclature was enough to darken his whole diction."

If we compare the criticism of the Book of Joshua with that (let us say) of Genesis, the difference in the clearness of the conclusions is very great. By far the most striking basis of the criticism of Genesis is the feature that was noticed first—the occurrence of different Divine names, Elohim and Jehovah, in different portions of the book. Now, although it is held that the *combined* JE document was used in compiling Joshua, there is no trace of this distinction of names in that book. Nor is there much trace of other distinctions found in Genesis. So that it is no great wonder that Canon Driver is uncertain whether, after all, that was the document that was used in compiling Joshua. Then, as to the grounds on which the Deuteronomist is supposed to have had a share in the book. Wherever anything is said indicating that under Joshua the Divine purposes and ordinances enjoined by God on Moses were fulfilled, that is referred to the Deuteronomist writer, as if it would have been unnatural for an ordinary historian to call attention to such a circumstance. For instance, the remark of Rahab that as soon as the Canaanites heard what God had done to Egypt, and to the two kings of the Amorites on the other side of Jordan, their hearts fainted, is referred to the Deuteronomist, as if it had rather been an idea of his than a statement of Rahab's. It is strange that Canon Driver should not have seen that this is the very hinge of Rahab's speech, because it gives us the explanation of the remarkable faith that had taken possession of her polluted heart. The truth is, we can hardly conceive that any part of the book should have been written by one who did not connect Joshua with Moses, and both of them with the patriarchs, and who was not impressed by the vital connection of the earlier with the later transactions, and likewise by the single Divine purpose running through the whole history.

But we are far from thinking that there is no foundation for any of the conclusions of the critics regarding the Book of Joshua. What seems their great weakness is the confidence with which they assign this part to one writer and that part to another, and bring down the composition of the book to a late period of the history. That various earlier documents were made use of by the author of the book seems very plain. For instance, in the account of the crossing of the Jordan, use seems to have been made of two documents, not always agreeing in minute details, and pieced together in a primitive fashion characteristic of a very early period of literary composition. The record of the delimitation of the possessions of the several tribes must have been taken from the report of the men that were sent to survey the country, but it is not a complete record. There are other traces of different documents in other parts of the book, but any diversities between them are quite insignificant, and in no degree impair its historical trustworthiness.

As to the hand of a reviser or revisers in the book, we see no difficulty in allowing for such. We can conceive an authorised reviser expanding speeches, but thoroughly in the line of the speakers, or inserting explanatory remarks as to places, or as to practices that had prevailed "unto this day." But it is atrocious to be told of revisers colouring statements and modifying facts in the interests of religious parties, or even in the interest of truth itself. Any alterations in the way of revision seem to have been very limited, otherwise we should not find in the existing text those awkward joinings of different documents which are not in perfect accord. Whoever the revisers were, they seem to have judged it best to leave these things as they found them, rather than incur the responsibility of altering what had already been written.

It has generally been assumed by spiritual expositors that there must be something profoundly symbolical in a book that narrates the work of Joshua, or Jesus, the first, so far as we know, to bear the name that is "above every name." The subject is considered with some fulness in Pearson's "Exposition of the Creed," and various points of resemblance, not all equally valid,* are noted between Joshua and Jesus.

The one point of resemblance on which we seem to be warranted to lay much stress is, that Joshua gave the people REST. Again and again we read—"The land rested from war" (xi. 23), "The land had rest from war" (xiv. 15), "The Lord gave them rest round about" (xxi. 44), "The Lord your God hath given rest unto your brethren" (xxii. 4), "The Lord had given rest unto Israel from all their enemies round about" (xxiii. 1). That was Joshua's great achievement, as the instrument of God's purpose. Yet in Hebrews we read that this was not the real rest—it was only a symbol of it: "If Joshua had given them rest, then would God not afterward have spoken of another day." The real rest was the rest arising from faith in Jesus Christ. Many persons look on Joshua as a somewhat dry book, full of geographical names, as unsuggestive as they are hard and unfamiliar. Yet on every one of the places so named faith may see inscribed, as in letters from heaven, the sweet word REST. Each of these places became a home for men who had been wandering for some forty years in a waste howling wilderness. At last they reached a spot where they did not fear the long familiar summons to "arise and depart." The sickly mother, the consumptive maiden, the paralysed old man might rest in peace, no longer terrified at the prospect of journeys which only increased their ailments and aggravated their sufferings.

The spiritual lesson of this book then is, that in Jesus Christ there is rest for the pilgrim. It is no slight or unevangelical lesson. It is the echo of His own glorious words, "Come unto Me, all ye that labour and are heavy laden, and I will give you rest." Whosoever is weary—whether under the burden of care, or the sense of guilt, of the bitterness of disappointment, or the anguish of a broken heart, or the conviction that all is vanity—the message of this book to him is,—"There remaineth a rest to the people of God." Even now, the rest of faith; and hereafter, that rest of which the voice from heaven proclaimed—"Blessed are the dead which die in the Lord from henceforth: yea, saith the Spirit, that they may rest from their labours; and their works do follow them."

CHAPTER II.

JOSHUA'S ANTECEDENTS.

FOUR hundred years is a long way to go back in tracing a pedigree. Joshua's might have been traced much farther back than that—back to Noah, or for that matter to Adam; but Israelites usually counted it enough to begin with that son of Jacob who was the head of their tribe. It could be no small gratification to Joshua that he had Joseph for his ancestor, and that of the two sons of Joseph he was sprung from the one whom the dying Jacob so expressly placed before the other as the heir of the richer blessing (1 Chron. vii. 20-27). It is remarkable that the descendants of Joseph attached no consequence to the fact that on the side of Joseph's wife they were sprung from one of the highest functionaries of Egypt (Gen. xli. 45), any more than the children of Mered, of the tribe of Judah, whose wife, Bithiah, was a daughter of Pharaoh (1 Chron. iv. 18), gained rank in Israel from the royal blood of their mother. The glory of high connections with the heathen counted for nothing; it was entirely eclipsed by the glory of the chosen seed. To be of the household of God was higher than to be born of kings.

Joshua appears to have come of the principal family of the tribe, for his grandfather, Elishama (1 Chron. vii. 26), was captain and head of his tribe (Num. i. 10, ii. 18), and in the order of march through the wilderness marched at the head of the forty thousand five hundred men that constituted the great tribe of Ephraim; while his son, Nun, and his grandson, Joshua, would of course march beside him. Not only was Elishama at the head of the tribe, but apparently also of the whole "camp of Ephraim," which, besides his own tribe, embraced Manasseh and Benjamin, being the whole descendants of Rachel (Num. ii. 24). Under their charge in all likelihood was a remarkable relic that had been brought very carefully from Egypt—the bones of Joseph (Exod. xiii. 19). Great must have been the respect paid to the coffin which contained the embalmed body of the Governor of Egypt, and which was never lost sight of during all the period of the wanderings, till at length it was solemnly deposited in its resting-place at Shechem (Josh. xxiv. 32). Young Joshua, grandson of the prince of the tribe, must have known it well. For Joshua was himself cast in the mould of Joseph, an ardent, courageous, God-fearing, patriotic youth. Very interesting to him it must have been to recall the romance of Joseph's life, his grievous wrongs and trials, his gentle spirit under them all, his patient and invincible faith, his lofty purity and self-control, his intense devotion to duty, and finally his marvellous exaltation and blessed experience as the saviour of his brethren! And that coffin must have seemed to Joshua ever to preach this sermon,—"God will surely visit you." With Joseph, young Joshua believed profoundly in his nation, because he believed profoundly in his nation's God; he felt that no other people in the world could have such a destiny, or could be so worthy of the service of his life.

This sense of Israel's relation to God raised in him an enthusiastic patriotism, and soon brought

---

* "The hand of Moses and Aaron brought the people out of Egypt, but left them in the wilderness, and could not seat them in Canaan. . . . Joshua, the successor, only could effect that in which Moses failed. . . . The death of Moses and the succession of Joshua pre-signified the continuance of the law till Jesus came. . . . Moses must die that Joshua might succeed. . . . If we look on Joshua as the judge and ruler of Israel, there is scarce an action which is not predictive of our Saviour. He begins his office at the banks of the Jordan where Christ is baptised, and enters upon the public exercise of his prophetical office. He chooseth there twelve men out of the people to carry twelve stones over with them; as our Jesus thence began to choose His twelve apostles. . . . It hath been observed that the saving Rahab the harlot alive foretold what Jesus once should speak to the Jews—'Verily I say unto you, that the publicans and the harlots go into the kingdom of God before you.' . . ."

him under the notice of Moses, who quickly discerned in the grandson a spirit more congenial to his own than that of either the father or the grandfather. Not even Moses himself had a warmer love than Joshua for Israel, or a more ardent desire to serve the people that had such a blessed destiny. In all likelihood the first impression Joshua made on Moses might have been described in the words—"It came to pass that the soul of Moses was knit with the soul of Joshua, and Moses loved him as his own soul."

In no other way can we account for the extraordinary mark of confidence with which Joshua was honoured when he was selected in the early days of the wilderness sojourn, not only to repel the attack which the Amalekites had made upon Israel, but to choose the men by whom this was to be done. Why pass over father and grandfather, if this youth, Joshua, had not already displayed qualities that fitted him for this difficult task better than either of them? We cannot but note, in passing, the proof we have of the contemporaneousness of the history, that no mention is made of the reasons why Joshua of all men was appointed to this command. If the history was written near the time, with Joshua's splendid career fresh in the minds of the people, the reasons would be notorious and did not need to be given; if it was written long afterwards, what more natural than that something should be said to explain the remarkable choice?

On whatever grounds Joshua was appointed, the result amply vindicated the selection. On Joshua's part there is none of that hesitation in accepting his work which was shown even by Moses himself when he got his commission at the burning bush. He seems to have accepted the appointment with humble faith and spirited enthusiasm, and prepared at once for the perilous enterprise.

And he had little enough time to prepare, for a new attack of the Amalekites was to be made next day. We may conceive him, after prayer to his Lord, setting out with a few chosen comrades to invite volunteers to join his corps, rousing their enthusiasm by picturing the dastardly attack that the Amalekites had made on the sick and infirm (Deut. xxv. 17, 18), and scattering their fears by recalling the promise to Abraham, "I will bless them that bless thee, and curse him that curseth thee." That Moses knew him to be a man of faith whose trust was in the living God was shown by his promise to stand next morning on the hill top with the rod of God in his hand. Yes, the rod of God! Had not Joshua seen it stretched out over the Red Sea, first to make a passage for Israel, and thereafter to bring back the waters on Pharaoh's host? Was he not just the man to value aright that symbol of Divine power? The troop selected by Joshua may have been small as the band of Gideon, but if it was as full of faith and courage it was abundantly able for its work!

The Amalekites are sometimes supposed to have been descendants of an Amalek who was the grandson of Esau (Gen. xxxvi. 12), but the name is much older (Gen. xiv. 7), and was applied at an early period to the inhabitants of the tract of country stretching southwards from the Dead Sea to the peninsula of Sinai. Whatever may have been their origin, they were old inhabitants of the wilderness, well acquainted probably with every mountain and valley, and well skilled in that Bedouin style of warfare which even practised troops are little able to meet. They were therefore very formidable opponents to the raw levy of Israelites, who could be but little acquainted with weapons of war, and were wholly unaccustomed to battle.

The Amalekites could not have been ignorant of the advantage of a good position, and they probably occupied a post not easy to attack and carry. Evidently the battle was a serious one. The practised and skilful tactics of the Amalekites were more than a match for the youthful valour of Joshua and his comrades; but as often as the uplifted rod of Moses was seen on the top of the neighbouring hill, new life and courage rushed into the souls of the Israelites, and for the time the Amalekites retreated before them. Hour after hour the battle raged, till the arm of Moses became too weary to hold up the rod. A stone had to be found for him to sit on, and his comrades, Aaron and Hur, had to hold up his hands. But even then, though the advantage was on the side of Joshua, it was sunset before Amalek was thoroughly defeated. The issue of the battle was no longer doubtful—"Joshua discomfited Amalek and his people with the edge of the sword" (Exod. xvii. 13).

It was a memorable victory, due in effect to the hand of God as really as the destruction of the Egyptians had been, but due instrumentally to the faith and fortitude of Joshua and his troop, whose ardour could not be quenched by the ever-resumed onslaughts of Amalek. And when the fight was over, Joshua could not but be the hero of the camp and the nation, as really as David after the combat with Goliath. Congratulations must have poured on him from every quarter, and not only on him, but on his father and grandfather as well. To Joshua these would come with mingled feelings; gratification at having been able to do such a service for his people, and gratitude for the presence of Him by whom alone he had prevailed. "Not unto us, Lord, not unto us, but to Thy name be the glory." It was a splendid beginning for Israel's wilderness history, if only it had been followed up by the people in a kindred spirit. But there were not many Joshuas in the camp, and the spirit did not spread.

It is remarkable what a hold that incident at Rephidim has taken on the Christian imagination. Age after age, for more than three thousand years, its influence has been felt. Nor can it ever cease to impress believing men that, so long as Moses holds out his rod, so long as active trust is placed in the power and presence of the Most High in the great battle with sin and evil, Israel must prevail; but if this trust should fail, if Moses should let down his rod, Amalek will conquer. It was well that Moses was instructed to write the transaction in a book and rehearse it before Joshua. Well also that it should be commemorated by another memorial, an altar to the Lord with the name of "Jehovah-nissi," the Lord my banner. How often has faith looked out towards that unknown mountain where Aaron and Hur held up the weary arms of Moses, and what a new thrill of courage and hope has the spectacle sent through hearts often "faint yet pursuing"! Happily on Joshua the effect was wholesome; a less spiritual man would have been puffed up by his remarkable victory; but in him its only effect, as was shown by the whole tenor of his future life, was a firmer trust in God, and a deeper determination to wait only on Him.

It was no wonder that after this Joshua was selected by Moses to be his personal comrade and attendant in connection with that most solemn of all his duties—the receiving of the law on the top of the mount. Here again was a most distinguished honour for so young a man. Aaron, and Nadab, and Abihu, with seventy of the elders, were summoned to ascend to a certain height and worship afar off; while Moses, accompanied by Joshua, went up into the mount of God (Exod. xxiv. 13). What became of Joshua while Moses was in immediate fellowship with God is not very apparent. The first impression we derive from the narrative is that he was with Moses all the time, for when Moses begins his descent Joshua is at his side (Exod. xxxii. 17). Yet we cannot suppose that in that most solemn transaction of Moses with Jehovah when the law was given any third party was present. On a careful study of the narrative throughout it will probably be seen that when, after going up a certain distance in company with Aaron and his sons and the seventy elders, Moses was called to a higher part of the mount, Joshua accompanied Moses (Exod. xxiv. 13), and that he was with Moses during the six days when the glory of God abode on Mount Sinai and a cloud covered the mount (ver. 15); but that when God again, after these six days, called to Moses to ascend still higher, and Moses "went into the midst of the cloud, and gat him up to the mount" (ver. 18), Joshua remained behind. His place of rest would thus be half-way between the spot where the elders saw God's glory and the summit where God talked with Moses. But the remarkable thing is, that from that place Joshua would seem never to have moved all the forty days and forty nights when Moses was with God. We can hardly conceive a case of more remarkable obedience, a more striking instance of the quiet waiting of faith. To a youth of his spirit and habits the restraint must have been somewhat trying. We know that Aaron did not remain long on the hill, for he was at hand when the people cried for "gods to go before them" (Exod. xxxii. 1). Impatience of God's slow methods had been a snare to the fathers—to Abraham and Sarah in the matter of Hagar; to Rachel when she raised the petulant cry, "Give me children, or else I die"; to Jacob when the promises seemed broken to atoms, and "all things" seemed "against him." Joseph alone had stood the trial of patience, and now Joshua showed himself of the like spirit. The word of Moses to him was like an anchor holding the ship firmly against the force of wind and tide. What a solemn time it must have been, and what a precious lesson it must have taught him for the whole future of his life!

More than three thousand years have sped away, but have the servants of God on an average reached the measure of Joshua's patience? Prayers unanswered, promises unfulfilled, sickness protracted during weary years of pain, disappointments and trials coming in troops as if all God's waves and billows were passing over them, active persecution bringing all the devices of torture to bear upon them,—how have such things tried the patience, the waiting power of the servants of God! But let them remember that if the trial be severe the recompense is great, and that in the end nothing will grieve them more than to have distrusted their Master and thought it possible that His promises would fail. "God is not unrighteous to forget." Richard Cecil tells that once, when walking with his little son, he bade him wait for him at a certain gate till he should return. He thought he would be back in a few minutes, but meanwhile an unexpected occurrence constrained him to go into the city, where, under an engrossing piece of business, he remained all day utterly forgetful of his charge to the boy. On his return at night to his suburban home, the boy was nowhere to be found. In a moment the order to remain at the gate flashed on his father's memory. Was it possible he should still be there? He hurried back and found him—he had been told to wait till his father returned, and he had done as he had been told. The boy that could act thus must have been made of no common stuff. So are they who can say, "I waited patiently for the Lord, and He inclined unto me, and heard my cry."

At last Joshua rejoins his master, and they proceed towards the foot of the mount. As they approach the camp, a noise is heard from afar. His military instinct finds an explanation,— "There is a noise of war in the camp." No, says the more experienced Moses; it is neither the shout of victors nor of vanquished, it is the noise of singing I hear; and so it was. For when they reached the camp, the people were at the very height of the idolatrous revelling that followed the construction and worship of the golden calf, and the sounds that fell on the ears of Moses and Joshua were the bacchanalian shouts of unholy and shameful riot. What a contrast to the solemn and holy scene on the top! What a gulf lies between the holy will of God and the polluted passions of men!

During the painful scenes that ensued, Joshua continued in faithful attendance on Moses; and when Moses removed the tabernacle (the temporary structure hitherto used for sacred services) and placed it outside the camp, Joshua was with him, and departed not out of the tabernacle (Exod. xxxiii. 11). We are not told whether he ascended the mount the second time with Moses, but it is likely that he did. At all events he was much with Moses at this early and susceptible period of his life. The young man did not recoil from the company of the old, nor did he who had been commander in the battle of Rephidim shrink from the duty of a servant. Deeper and deeper, as he kept company with Moses, must have been his impression of his wisdom, his faith, his loyalty to God, and his entire devotion to the welfare of his people; and stronger and stronger must have waxed his own desire that if ever he should be called to a similar service he might show the same spirit and fulfil the same high end!

The next time that Joshua comes into notice is not so flattering to himself. It is on that occasion when the Spirit descended on the seventy elders that had been appointed to assist Moses, and they prophesied round about the tabernacle. Two of the seventy were not with the rest, but nevertheless they got the spirit and were prophesying in the camp. The military instinct of Joshua was hurt at the irregularity, and his concern for the honour of Moses was roused by their apparent indifference to the presence of their head. He hurried to inform Moses, not doubting but he would interfere to correct the irregularity. But the narrow spirit of youth met with a memorable rebuke from the larger and more noble spirit of the leader,—" Enviest thou for my sake? Would God that all the Lord's people were prophets, and that the Lord would put His Spirit upon them!"

Not long after this Joshua was appointed to another memorable service. After the law-giving had been brought to an end, and the host of Israel had removed from the mountain to the borders of the promised land, he was appointed one of the twelve spies that were sent forward to explore the country. Formerly his name had been Oshea; it was now changed to Jehoshua or Joshua. The changing of the name was in itself significant, and still more the character of the change, by which a syllable of the Divine name was inserted in it. For, by the practice of the nation, the changing of a name denoted a man's entrance on a new chapter of his history, or his coming out before the world in a new character. So it was when Abram's name was changed to Abraham, Sarai's to Sarah, and Jacob's to Israel; so also when Simon became Cephas, and Saul Paul. But the new name given to Joshua was in itself more remarkable—Joshua, that is, Jehovah saves: in the New Testament, Jesus. No doubt it looked back on the victory of Rephidim when the Lord wrought such a deliverance in Israel through Joshua. But it indicated that the feature that had appeared at Rephidim would continue to characterise him during his life. It was a testimony from Moses, and from Him who inspired Moses, to the character of Joshua, as it had come out during all the close intercourse of Moses with him. And it invested Joshua with a dignity that ought to have raised him very highly in the eyes of the other spies, and of all the congregation of Israel. Who could be more worthy of their respect than the young man who had shown himself so faithful in all his previous history, and who had now received a name that indicated that it would be the distinction of his life, like Him whom he prefigured, to lead his people to the enjoyment of God's salvation?

The forty days spent by the twelve men in exploring the land were a great contrast to the forty days spent by Joshua on the mount. All was inactivity and patient waiting in the one case; all was activity and bustle in the other. For there is a time to work and a time to rest. If at the one period Joshua had to put a restraint on his natural activity, at the other he could give it full swing.

Apart from its more immediate object, this early tour through Palestine must have been one of surpassing interest. To witness each spot that had been made memorable and classical by the lives of his forefathers; to sit by the well of Beersheba, and recall all that had happened there; to repose under Abraham's oak at Mamre; to bow at the cave of Machpelah; to recall the visits of angels at Bethel, and the ladder which had been seen going up to heaven,—was not only most thrilling, but to a man of Joshua's faith most inspiring; because every spot that had such associations was a witness that God had given them the land, and a proof that even though the sons of Anak were there, and their cities were walled up to heaven, the God of Abraham and Isaac and Jacob would be faithful to His promise, and, if the people would only trust Him, would right speedily place them in full possession.

Caleb and Joshua were the only two men whose faith stood the test of this survey; the rest were thoroughly cowed by the greatness of the difficulties. And Caleb seems to have been the foremost of the two, for in some places he is named as if he stood alone. Probably he was the one who came forward and spoke; but even if Joshua's faith was not so strong at first, it was no dishonour to be indebted to the greater courage and confidence of his brother.

We can hardly doubt that in their long marches and quiet encampments the twelve men had many a discussion as to what they would advise, and that the ten felt themselves beaten both in argument and in faith by the two. Long before they returned to the camp of Israel they had taken their sides, and by the sides they had taken they were determined to abide.

When they come back, the ten open the business and give their decided judgment against any attempt to take possession of the land. Impatient of their misrepresentations, Caleb perhaps strikes in, repudiates the notion that the people are not able to take possession, and urges them in God's name to go up at once. But it is easier far to stir up discontent and fear than to stimulate faith. The cry of the congregation, "Up, make us a captain, and let us return to Egypt," shows how strongly the tide of unbelief is flowing. Moses and Aaron are overwhelmed. The two leaders fall on their faces before the congregation. But neither the cry of the congregation nor the attitude of Moses and Aaron daunts the two faithful spies. With clothes rent they rush in, renewing their commendations of the land, laying hold of the Almighty Protector, and scorning the opposition of the inhabitants, whose hearts were cowed with terror and whose defence was departed from them. It was a fine spectacle,—the two against the million—the little remnant "faithful found among the faithless." But it was all in vain. " All the congregation bade stone them with stones." And in their impulsive and excitable temper the horrible cry would have been obeyed had not the glory of the Lord shone out and arrested the infatuated people (Num. xiv. 10).

For this shameless sin the penalty was very heavy. The congregation were to wander in the wilderness for forty years till all that generation should die off; the ten unfaithful spies were to die at once of a plague before the Lord; and not one of the generation that left Egypt was to enter the promised land. How easily can God defeat the purposes of man! Where is now the proposal to make a captain and return to Egypt? " How art thou fallen from heaven, O Lucifer, son of the morning!"

Joshua and Caleb are doubly honoured; their lives are preserved when the other ten die of the plague; and they alone, of all the grown men of that generation, are to be allowed to enter and obtain homes in the land of promise.

For eight-and-thirty years we hear nothing more of Joshua. Like Moses, he has an interesting youth, then a long burial in the wilderness, and then he emerges from his obscurity and does a great work, second only to that of Moses himself. The first mention of him after his long eclipse is immediately before the death of Moses. God virtually appoints him to be his successor, and directs both of them to present themselves in the tabernacle of the congregation (Deut. xxxi. 14). And Moses calls him to his office, gives him a charge and says, "Be strong and of a good courage: for thou shalt bring the children of Israel into the land which I sware unto them: and I will be with thee" (Deut. xxxi. 23).

We might earnestly desire, in entering on the study of Joshua's life, to draw aside the veil that covers the eight-and-thirty years, and see how he was further prepared for his great work. We might like to look into his heart, and see after what fashion this man was made to whom the destruction of the Canaanites was entrusted. A religious warrior is a peculiar character; a Gustavus Adolphus, an Oliver Cromwell, a Henry Havelock, a General Gordon; Joshua was of the same mould, and we should have liked to know him more intimately; but this is denied to us. He stands out to us simply as one of the military heroes of the faith. In depth, in steadiness, in endurance, his faith was not excelled by that of Abraham or of Moses himself. The one conviction that dominated all in him was, that he was called by God to his work. If that work was often repulsive, let us not on that account withhold our admiration from the man who never conferred with flesh and blood, and who was never appalled either by danger or difficulty, for he "saw Him who is invisible."

CHAPTER III.

A SUCCESSOR TO MOSES.

JOSHUA i. 2.

THERE are some men to whom it is almost impossible to find successors. Men of imperial mould; Nature's primates, head and shoulders above other men, born to take the lead. Not only possessed of great gifts originally, but placed by Providence in situations that have wonderfully expanded their capacity and made their five talents ten. Called to be leaders of great movements, champions of commanding interests, often gifted with an imposing presence, and with a magnetic power that subdues opposition and kindles enthusiasm as if by magic. What a bereavement when such men are suddenly removed! How poor in comparison those who come next them, and from among whom successors have to be chosen! When the Hebrews mourned the death of Samson, the difference in physical strength between him and his brethren could not have appeared greater than the intellectual and moral gulf appears between a great king of men, suddenly removed, and the bereaved children that bend helpless over his grave.

A feeling of this sort must have spread itself through the host of Israel when it was known that Moses was dead. Speculation as to his successor there could be none, for not only had God designated Joshua, but before he died Moses had laid his hands upon him, and the people had acknowledged him as their coming leader. And Joshua had already achieved a record of no common order, and had been favoured with high tokens of the Divine approval. Yet what a descent it must have seemed from Moses to Joshua! From the man who had so often been face to face with God, who had commanded the sea to make a way for the redeemed of the Lord to pass over, who had been their legislator and their judge ever since they were children, to whom they had gone in every difficulty, and who for wisdom and disinterestedness had gained the profound confidence of every one of them;—what a descent, we say, to this son of Nun, known hitherto as but the servant of Moses—an intrepid soldier, no doubt, and a man of unfaltering faith, but whose name seemed as if it could not couple with that of their imperial leader!

Well though Joshua did his work in after life, and bright though the lustre of his name ultimately became, he never attained to the rank of Moses. While the name of Moses is constantly reappearing in the prophets, in the Psalms, in the Gospels, in the Epistles, and in the Apocalypse, that of Joshua is not found out of the historical books except in the speech of Stephen and that well-known passage in the Hebrews (iv. 8), where the received version perplexes us by translating it Jesus. But it was no disparagement of him that he was so far surpassed by the man to whom, under God, the very existence of the nation was due. And in some respects, Joshua is a more useful example to us than Moses. Moses seems to stand half-way in heaven, almost beyond reach of imitation. Joshua is more on our own level. If not a man of surpassing genius, he commends himself as having made the best possible use of his talents, and done his part carefully and well.

The remark has been made that eras of great creative vigour are often succeeded by periods dull and commonplace. The history of letters and of the fine arts shows that bursts of artistic splendour like the Renaissance, or of literary originality like the Augustan age in Roman or the Elizabethan in English literature, are not followed by periods of equal lustre. And the same phenomenon has often been found in the Christian Church. In more senses than one the Apostles had no successors. Who in all the sub-apostolic age was worthy even to untie the latchet of Peter, or John, or Paul? The inferiority is so manifest that had there been nothing else to guide the Church in framing the canon of the New Testament, the difference between the writings of the Apostles and their companions on the one hand, and of men like Barnabas, Clement of Rome, Polycarp, Ignatius, and Hermes on the other, would have sufficed to settle the question. So also at the era of the Reformation. Hardly a country but had its star or its galaxy of the first magnitude. Luther and Melancthon, Calvin and Coligny, Farel and Viret, John à-Lasco and John Knox, Latimer and Cranmer,—what incomparable men they were! But in the age that followed what names can we find to couple with theirs?

Of other sections of the Church the same remark has been made, and sometimes it has been turned to an unfair use. If in the second generation, after a great outburst of power and grace, there are few or no men of equal calibre, it does not follow that the glory has departed, and that the Church is to droop her head, and wonder to what unworthy course on her part the degeneracy is to be ascribed. We are not to expect in such a case that the laws of nature will be set aside to gratify our pride. We are to recognise a state of things which God has ordained for wise purposes, although it may not be flattering to us. We are to place ourselves in the attitude in which Joshua was called to place himself when the curt announcement of the text as to Moses was followed by an equally curt order to him—"Moses My servant is dead; now therefore arise."

The question for Joshua is not whether he is a fit person to succeed Moses. His mental exercise is not to compare himself with Moses, and note the innumerable points of inferiority on every side. His attitude is not to bow down his head like a bulrush, mourning over the departed glory of Israel, grieving for the mighty dead, on whose like neither he nor his people will ever look again. If there ever was a time when it might seem excusable for a bereaved nation and a bereaved servant to abandon themselves to a sense of helplessness, it was on the death of Moses. But even at that supreme moment the command to Joshua is, "Now therefore arise." Gird yourself for the new duties and responsibilities that have come upon you. Do not worry yourself with asking whether you are capable of doing these duties, or with vainly looking within yourself for the gifts and qualities which marked your predecessor. It is enough for you that God in His providence calls you to take the place of the departed. If He has called you, He will equip you. It is not His way to send men a warfare on their own charges. The work to which He calls you is not yours but His. Remember He is far more interested in its success than you can be. Think not of yourself, but of Him, and go forth under the motto, "We will rejoice in Thy salvation, and in the name of our God we will set up our banners."

In many different situations of life we may hear the same exhortation that was now addressed to Joshua. A wise, considerate, and honoured father is removed, and the eldest son, a mere stripling, is called to take his place, perhaps in the mercantile office or place of business, certainly in the domestic circle. He is called to be the comforter and adviser of his widowed mother, and the example and helper of his brothers and sisters. Well for him when he hears a voice from heaven, "Your father is dead; now therefore arise!" Rouse yourself for the duties that now devolve upon you; onerous they may be and beyond your strength, but not on that account to be evaded or repudiated; rather to be looked on as spurs provided and designed by God, that you may apply yourself with heart and soul to your duties, in the belief that faithful and patient application shall not be without its reward!

Or it may be that the summons comes to some young minister as successor to a father in Israel, whose ripe gifts and fragrant character have won the confidence and the admiration of all. Or to some teacher in a Sunday-school, where the man of weight, of wise counsel, and holy influence has been suddenly snatched away. But be the occasion what it may, the removal of any man of ripe character and gifts always comes to the survivor with the Divine summons, "Now therefore arise!" That is the one way in which you must try to improve this dispensation; the world is poorer for the loss of his gifts—learn you to make the most of yours!

It was no mean impression of Moses that God meant to convey by the designation, "Moses My servant." It was not a high-sounding title, certainly. A great contrast to the long list of honourable titles sometimes engraved on men's coffins or on their tombs, or proclaimed by royal herald or king-at-arms over departed kings or nobles. One of the greatest of men has no handle to his name—he is simply Moses. He has no titles of rank or office—he is simply "My servant." But true greatness is "when unadorned adorned the most." Moses is a real man, a man of real greatness; there is no occasion therefore to deck him out in tinsel and gilt; he is gold to the core.

But think what is really implied in this designation, "My servant." Even if Moses had not been God's servant in a sense and in a degree in which few other men ever were, it would have been a glorious thing to obtain that simple appellation. True indeed, the term "servant of God" is such a hackneyed one, and often so little represents what it really means, that we need to pause and think of its full import. There may be much honour in being a servant. Even in our families and factories a model servant is a rare and precious treasure. For a real servant is one that has the interest of his master as thoroughly at heart as his own, and never scruples, at any sacrifice of personal interest or feeling, to do all that he can for his master's welfare. A true servant is one of whom his master may say, "There is absolutely no need for me to remind him what my interest requires; he is always thinking of my interest, always on the alert to attend to it, and there is not a single thing I possess that is not safe in his hands."

Does God possess many such servants? Who among us can suppose God saying this of him? Yet this was the character of Moses, and in God's eyes it invested him with singular honour. It was his distinction that he was "faithful in all his house." His own will was thoroughly subdued to the will of God. The people of whom God gave him charge were dear to him as a right hand or a right eye. All personal interests and ambitions were put far from him. To aggrandise himself or to aggrandise his house never entered into his thoughts. Never was self more thoroughly crucified in any man's breast. Beautiful and delightful in God's eyes must have seemed this quality in Moses,—his absolute disinterestedness, his sensibility to every hint of his Master's will, his consecration of all he was and had to God, and to his people for God's sake!

It was thus no unsuggestive word that God used of Moses, when he told Joshua that "His servant" was dead. It was a significant indication of what God had valued in Moses and now expected of Joshua. The one thing for Joshua to remember about Moses is, that he was the servant of God. Let him take pains to be the same; let him have his ear as open as that of Moses to every intimation of God's will, his will as prompt to respond, and his hand as quick to obey.

Was not this view of the glory of Moses as God's servant a foreshadow of what was afterwards taught more fully and on a wider scale by our Lord? "The Son of man came not to be ministered unto, but to minister, and to give His life a ransom for many." Jesus sought to reverse the natural notions of men as to what constitutes greatness, when He taught that, instead of being measured by the number of servants who wait on us, it is measured rather by the number of persons to whom we become servants. And if it was a mark of Christ's own humiliation that "He took on Him the form of a servant," did not this redound to His highest glory? Was it not for this that God highly exalted Him and gave Him a name that is above every name? Happy they who are content to be God's SERVANTS in whatsoever sphere of life He may place them; seeking not their own, but always intent upon their Master's business!

And now Joshua must succeed Moses and be God's servant as he was. He must aim at this as the one distinction of his life; he must seek in every action to know what God would have him to do. Happy man if he can carry out this ideal of life! No conflicting interests or passions will distract his soul. His eye being single, his whole body will be full of light. The power that nerves his arm will not be more remarkable than the peace that dwells in his soul. He will show to all future generations the power of a "lost will,"—not the suppression of all desire, according to the Buddhist's idea of bliss, but all lawful natural desires in happy and harmonious action, because subject to the wise, holy, and loving guidance of the will of God.

Thus we see among the other paradoxes of His government, how God uses death to promote life. The death of the eminent, the aged, the men of brilliant gifts makes way for others, and stimulates their activity and growth. When the champion of the forest falls the younger trees around it are brought more into contact with the sunshine and fresh air, and push up into taller and more fully developed forms. If none of the younger growth attains the size of the champion, a great many may be advanced to a higher average of size and beauty. If in the second generation of any great religious movement few or none can match the "mighties" of the previous age, there may be a general elevation, a rise of level, an increase of efficiency among the rank and file.

In many ways death enters into God's plans. Not only does it make way for the younger men,* but it has a solemnizing and quickening effect on all who are not hardened and dulled by the wear and tear of life.

What a memorable event in the spiritual history of families is the first sudden affliction, the first breach in the circle of loving hearts! First, the new experience of intense tender longing, baffled by the inexorable conditions of death; then the vivid vision of eternity, the reality of the unseen flashing on them with living and awful power, and giving an immeasurable importance to the question of salvation; then the drawing closer to one another, the forswearing of all animosities and jealousies, the cordial desire for unbroken peace and constant co-operation; and if it be the father or the mother that has been taken, the ambition to be useful,—to be a help not a burden to the surviving parent, and to do what little they can of what used to be their father's or their mother's work. Death becomes actually a quickener of the vital energies; instead of a withering influence, it drops like the gentle dew, and becomes the minister of life.

And death is not alone among the destructive agencies that are so often directed to life-giving ends. What a remarkable place is that which is occupied by Pain among God's instruments of good! How many are there who, looking back on their lives, have to confess, with a mixture of sadness and of joy, that it is their times of greatest suffering that have been the most decisive in their lives,—marked by their best resolutions,—followed by their greatest advance! And it sometimes would seem as if the acuter the suffering the greater the blessing. How near God seems at times to come to the height of cruelty when really He is overflowing with love! He seems to select the very tenderest spots on which to inflict His blows, the very tenderest and purest affections of the heart. It is a wonderful triumph of faith and submission when the sufferer stands firm and tranquil amidst it all. And still more when he can find consolation in the analogy which was supplied by God's own act,—"He that spared not His own Son, but delivered Him up for us all, how shall He not with Him also freely give us all things?"

And this brings us to our last application. Our Lord Himself, by a beautiful analogy in nature, showed the connection, in the very highest sense, between death and life—" Except a grain of wheat fall into the earth and die, it abideth alone; but if it die it beareth much fruit." " Without shedding of blood there is no remission of sin." When Jesus died at Calvary, the headquarters of death became the nursery of life. The place of a skull, like the prophet's valley of dry bones, gave birth to an exceeding great army of living men. Among the wonders that will bring glory to God in the highest throughout eternity, the greatest will be this evolution of good from evil, of happiness from pain, of life from death. And even when the end comes, and death is swallowed up of victory, and death and hell are cast into the lake of fire, there will abide with the glorified a lively sense of the infinite blessing that came to them from God through the repulsive channel of death, finding its highest expression in that anthem of the redeemed—" THOU WAST SLAIN, AND HAST REDEEMED US TO GOD BY THY BLOOD."

CHAPTER IV.

JOSHUA'S CALL.

JOSHUA i. 2-5.

JOSHUA has heard the Divine voice summoning him to the attitude of activity—" Arise!" Directions follow immediately as to the course which his activity is to take. His first step is to be a very pronounced one—" Go over this Jordan ": enter the land, not by yourself, or with a handful of comrades, as you did forty years ago, but " thou and all this people." Take the bold step, cross the river; and when you are across the river, take possession of the country which I now give to your people. The time has come for decided action; it is for you to show the way, and summon your people to follow.

It was a very solemn and striking moment,

---

* " Can death itself when seen in the light of this truth [the adjustment of every being in animated nature to every other] be denied to be an evidence of benevolence? I think not. The law of animal generation makes necessary the law of animal death, if the largest amount of animal happiness is to be secured. If there had been less death there must also have been less life, and what life there was must have been poorer and meaner. Death is a condition of the prolificness of nature, the multiplicity of species, the succession of generations, the co-existence of the young and the old; and these things, it cannot reasonably be doubted, add immensely to the sum of animal happiness."—Flint's " Theism," p. 251.

second only in interest to that when, forty years before, their fathers had stood at the edge of the sea, with the host of Pharaoh hurrying on behind. At length the hour has come to take possession of the inheritance! At length the promise made so many hundred years ago to Abraham, Isaac, and Jacob is ripe for fulfilment! You, children of Israel, have seen that God is in no haste to fulfil His promises, and your hearts may have known much of the sickness of hope deferred. But now you are to see that after all God is faithful. He never forgets. He makes no mistakes. His delays are all designed for good, either to chasten or to try, and thus confirm and bless His people. He will now bring forth your righteousness as the light and your judgment as the noon-day.

There were two things that might make Joshua and the people hesitate to cross the Jordan. In the first place, the river was in flood; it was the time when the Jordan overflowed its banks (Josh. iii. 15), and, being a rapid river, crossing it in such circumstances might well seem out of the question. But in the second place, to cross the Jordan was to throw down the gauntlet to the enemy. It was a declaration of war, and a challenge to them to do their worst. It was a signal for them to assemble, fight for their hearths and homes, and strain every nerve to annihilate this invader who made such a bold claim to their possessions. All the children of Anak whom Joshua had seen on his former visit would now range themselves against Israel; all the seven nations would muster their bravest forces, and the contest would not be like Joshua's battle with Amalek, finished in a single day, but a long succession of battles, in which all the resources of power and skill, of craft and cunning would be brought to bear against Israel. According to appearances, nothing short of this would be the result of compliance with the command, "Go over this Jordan."

On the one hand, therefore, compliance was physically impossible, and on the other, even if possible, it would have been fearfully perilous. But it is never God's method to give impossible commands. The very fact of His commanding anything is a proof of His readiness to make it possible, nay, to make it easy and simple to those who have faith to attempt it. "Stretch out thy hand," said Christ to the man with the withered hand. "Stretch out my hand?" the man might have said in astonishment,—"why, it is the very thing I am unable to do." "Rise up and walk," said Peter to the lame man at the Beautiful gate. "How can I do that?" he might have replied; "don't you see that I have no use of my limbs?" But in these cases the helpless men had faith in those who bade them exert themselves; they believed that if they tried they would be helped, and helped accordingly they were. So too in the present case. Joshua knew that he and the host could not have crossed the Jordan as it then was by any contrivance in his power; but he knew that it was God's command, and he was sure that He would provide the means. He felt as if God and the people were in partnership, each equally interested in the result, and equally desirous to bring it about. Whatever it was necessary for God to do he was assured would be done, provided he and the people entered into the Divine plan, and threw all their energies into the work. Not a word of remonstrance did Joshua offer, not a word of explanation of the Divine plan did he ask; he acted as a servant should;

"His not to make reply,
His not to reason why;"

his only to trust and obey.

This faith in Divine power qualifying feeble mortals for the hardest tasks has originated some of the noblest enterprises in the history of the world. It was a Divine voice Columbus seemed to hear bidding him cross the wild Atlantic, for he desired to bring the natives of the distant shores beyond it into the pale of the Church; and it was his faith that sustained him when his crew became mutinous and his life was not safe for an hour. It was a Divine voice Livingstone seemed to hear bidding him cross Africa, strike up into the heart of the continent, examine its structure, and throw it open from shore to shore; and never was there a faith stronger or steadier than that which bore him on through fever and famine, through pain and sickness, through disappointment and anguish, and, even when the cold hand of death was on him, would not let him rest until his work was done.

Often in the spiritual warfare it is useful to apply this principle. Are we called to believe? Are we called to make ourselves a new heart and a new spirit? Are we summoned to fight, to wrestle, to overcome? Certainly we are. But is not this to tantalize us by ordering us to do what we cannot do? Is not this like telling a sick man to get well, or a decrepit old creature to skip and frisk like a child? It would be so if the principle of partnership between God and us did not come into play. Faith says, God is my partner in this matter. Partners even in an ordinary business put their resources together, each doing what his special abilities fit him for. In the partnership which faith establishes between God and you, the resources of the infinite Partner become available for the needs of the finite. It is God's part to give orders, it is your part to execute them, and it is God's part to strengthen you so to do. It is this that makes the command reasonable, "Work out your salvation with fear and trembling; for it is God that worketh in you both to will and to do of His good pleasure." Faith rejoices in the partnership, and goes forward in the confidence that the strength of the Almighty will help its weakness, not by one sudden leap, but by that steady growth in grace that makes the path of the just like the shining light, that shineth more and more unto the perfect day.

It was a great thing for God to announce that He was now in the act of turning His old, old promise into reality,—that the land pledged to Abraham centuries ago was now at length to become the possession of his descendants. But the gift could be of no avail unless it was actually appropriated. God gave the people the right to the land; but their own energy, made effectual through His grace, could alone secure the possession. In a remarkable way they were made to feel that, while the land was God's gift, the appropriation and enjoyment of the gift must come through their own exertions. Just as in a higher sphere we know that our salvation is wholly the gift of God; and yet the getting hold of this gift, the getting linked to Christ, the entrance as it were into the marriage covenant with Him involves the active exertion of our own will and energy, and the gift never can be ours if we fail thus to appropriate it.

As soon as God mentions the land, He expatiates on its amplitude and its boundaries. It was designed to be both a comfortable and an ample possession. In point of extent it was a spacious region,—" from the wilderness and this Lebanon, even unto the great river, the river Euphrates, all the land of the Hittites, and unto the great sea, towards the going down of the sun." And it was not merely bits or corners of this land that were to be theirs, they were not designed to share it with other occupants, but "every place that the sole of your foot shall tread upon, to you have I given it, as I spake unto Moses." It was in no meagre or stingy spirit that God was now to fulfil His ancient promise, but in a way corresponding to the essential bountifulness of His nature. For it is a delightful truth that God's heart is large and liberal, and that He delights in large and bountiful gifts. Has He not made this plain to all in the arrangements of nature? What more lavish than the gift of light, ever streaming from the sun in silver showers? What more abundant than the fresh air that, like an inexhaustible ocean, encompasses our globe, or the rivers that carry their fresh and fertilizing treasures unweariedly through every meadow? What more productive than the vegetable soil that under favourable conditions teems with fruits and flowers and the elements of food for the use and enjoyment of man?

And when we turn to God's provision in grace we find glorious proofs of the same abundance and generosity. We see this symbolized by the activity and generosity of our Lord, as He went about "preaching the gospel of the kingdom, and healing all manner of sickness and all manner of disease among the people." We understand the spiritual reality of which this was the symbol, when we call to mind the Divine generosity that receives the vilest sinners; the efficacy of the blood that cleanses from all sin; the power of the Spirit that sanctifies soul, body, and spirit; the wisdom of the providence that makes all things work together for good; the glory of the love that makes us now "sons of God, and it doth not yet appear what we shall be; but we know that when He shall appear we shall be like Him, for we shall see Him as He is." And once more it appears in the glory and amplitude of the inheritance, of which the land of Canaan was but the type, prepared of God's infinite bounty for all who are His children by faith. Our Father's house is both large and well furnished; it is a house of many mansions; and the inheritance which He has promised is incorruptible and undefiled and fadeth not away.

It is a grand truth, of which we never can make too much, this bountifulness of God, and the delight which He has in being bountiful. It is emphatically a truth for faith to apprehend and enjoy, because appearances are so often against it. Appearances were fearfully against it while the Israelites were groaning in their Egyptian bondage, and hardly less so, despite the manna and the water from the rock, during the forty years' wandering in the desert. But that was a period of correction and of training, and in such circumstances lavish bounty was out of the question.

The most bountiful man on earth could not pour out all the liberality of his heart on the inmates of a hospital for the sick; he may give all that sick men need, but he must wait till they are well before he can give full scope to his generosity. While we are in the body we are like patients in a hospital, and the kindest feelings from God toward us must often take the form of bitter medicines, painful operations, close restraint, stinted diet, and it may be silence and darkness. But wait till we are well, and then we shall see what God hath prepared for him that waiteth for Him! Wait till we go over Jordan and take possession of the land! Two things will be seen in the clearest light—the supreme bountifulness of God, and the sinfulness of that impatient and suspicious spirit to which we are so prone. What a humiliation, if humiliation be possible in heaven, to discover that all the time when we were fretting and grumbling, God was working out His plans of supreme beneficence and love, waiting only till we should come of age to make us heirs of the universe!

It is natural to ask why, if the boundaries of the promised land were so extensive, if they reached so far on the north-east as the Euphrates, and if they extended from Lebanon on the north to the confines of Egypt on the south, there should have been any difficulty about the two and a half tribes occupying the land east of the Jordan, where only by a special permission they obtained their settlement. For it is plain from the narrative that it was contrary to God's first intention, so to speak, that they should settle there, and that the land west of the Jordan was that to which the promise was held specially to apply. It will hardly do to say, as some have said, that the extension of the land to the Euphrates was a figure of speech, a poetical fringe or ornament as it were, intended to show that places adjacent to the land of Israel would share in some degree the radiance of its light and the influence of the Divine presence among its people. For the promise of God was really of the nature of a charter, and figures of poetry are not suitable in charters. It is rather to be understood that, in the *final* purpose of God, the possession included the whole of the ample domain contained within the specified boundaries, but that at first it would be confined within a narrower space. If the people should prove faithful to the covenant, the wider dominion would one day be conferred on them; but they were to start and get consolidated in a narrower territory. And the narrower space was that which had already been consecrated by the residence of the fathers Abraham, Isaac, and Jacob. The country west of Jordan was the land of *their* pilgrimage; and even when Lot and Abraham had to separate, it was not proposed that either should cross the river. The little strip lying between the Jordan and the sea was judged most suitable for the preparatory stage of Israel's history; but had the nation served God with fidelity, their country would have been extended—as in the days of David and Solomon it really was—to the dimensions of an empire. The rule afterwards announced was to be virtually brought into operation—"To him that hath shall be given." Hence the view taken of the settlement of the two and a half tribes east of the Jordan. It was not illegitimate; it was not inconsistent with the covenant made with the fathers; but it was for the time inexpedient, seeing that it exposed them to risks, both material and spiritual, which it would have been better for them to avoid.

One geographical expression, in the delimitation of the country, demands a brief explanation. While the country is defined as embracing the whole territory from Lebanon to the Euphrates, it is also defined as consisting in that direction of "all the land of the Hittites." But were not the Hittites one of the seven nations whose land was promised to Abraham and the fathers, and not even the first in the enumeration of these? Why should this great north-eastern section of the promised domain be designated "the land of the Hittites"?

The time was when it was a charge against the accuracy of the Scripture record that it ascribed to the Hittites this extensive dominion. That time has passed away, inasmuch as, within quite recent years, the discovery has been made that in those distant times a great Hittite empire did exist in the very region specified, between Lebanon and the Euphrates. The discovery is based on twofold data: references in the Egyptian and other monuments to a powerful people, called the Khita (Hittites), with whom even the great kings of Egypt had long and bloody wars; and inscriptions in the Hittite language found in Hamah, Aleppo, and other places in Syria. There is still much obscurity resting on the history of this people. That the Hittites proper prevailed so extensively has been doubted by some; a Hittite confederacy has been supposed, and sometimes a Hittite aristocracy exercising control over a great empire. The only point which it is necessary to dwell on here is, that in representing the tract between Lebanon and Euphrates as equivalent to "all the land of the Hittites," the author of the Book of Joshua made a statement which has been abundantly verified by recent research.*

To encourage and animate Joshua to undertake the work and position of Moses it is very graciously promised—"There shall not any man be able to stand before thee all the days of thy life: as I was with Moses, so will I be with thee: I will not fail thee, nor forsake thee." The invariable success promised was a greater boon than the greatest conquerors had been able to secure. Uniform success is a thing hardly known to captains of great expeditions, even though in the end they may prevail. But the promise to Joshua is, that all his enemies shall flee before him. None of his battles shall be even neutral, his opponents must always give way.† No son of Anak shall be able to oppose his onward march; no giant, like Og King of Bashan, shall terrify either him or his troops. He will "onward still to victory go,"—the Lord of hosts ever with him, the God of Jacob ever his defence.

And this was no vague, indefinite assurance. It was sharply defined by a well-known example in the immediate past—"As I was with Moses, so I will be with thee." In what a remarkable variety of dangers and trials God was with Moses! Now he had to confront the grandest monarch on earth, supported by the strongest armies, and upheld by what claimed to be the mightest gods. Again he had to deal with an apostate people, mad upon idols, and afterwards with an excited mob, ready to stone him. Anon he had to overcome the forces of nature and bend them to his purposes; to call water

* See "The Empire of the Hittites." By William Wright, D. D., F. R. G. S. London, 1885.
† The promise is not inconsistent with the fact that Joshua's troops were defeated by the men of Ai. In such promises there is an implied condition of steadfast regard to God's will on the part of those who receive them, and this condition was violated at Ai, not by Joshua, indeed, but by one of his people.

from the rock, to sweeten the bitter fountain, to heal the fiery bite, to cure his sister's leprous body, to bring down bread from heaven, and people the air with flocks of birds. Moreover, he had to be the messenger of the covenant between God and Israel, to unfold God's law in its length and breadth and in all its variety of application, and to obtain from the people a hearty compliance—"All that the Lord hath said unto us, that will we do." What a marvellous work Moses did! What a testimony his life presented to the reality of the Divine presence and guidance, and what a solid and indefeasible ground of trust God gave to Joshua when He said, "As I was with Moses, so will I be with thee."

And this is crowned with the further assurance, "I will not fail thee, nor forsake thee,"—an assurance which is extended in the Epistle to the Hebrews to all who believe. We are so apt to view these promises as just beautiful expressions that we need to pause and think what they really mean. A promise of Divine presence, Divine protection and guidance and blessing all the days of our life, is surely a treasure of inexpressible value. It is no slight matter to realise that this is in God's heart—that He has a constant, unvarying feeling of love toward us, and readiness to help; but we must believe this in order to get the benefit of it; and, moreover, He must be left to determine the time, the manner, and the form in which His help is to come. Alas for the unbelief, the suspicion, the fear that is so prone to eat out the spirit of trust, and in our trials and difficulties make us tremble as if we were alone! What a profound peace, what calm enjoyment and blessed hope fall to the lot of those who can believe in a God ever near, and in His unfailing faithfulness and love! Was it not the secret alike of David's calmness, of our Lord's serenity, and of the cheerful composure of many a martyr and many a common man and woman who have gone through life undisturbed and happy, that they could say—"I have set the Lord always before me; because He is at my right hand, I shall not be moved"? God grant us all that, like Abraham, we may "stagger not at the promise of God through unbelief, but that being strong in faith we may give glory to God, and believe that what He hath promised He is able also to perform."

CHAPTER V.

JOSHUA'S ENCOURAGEMENT.

JOSHUA i. 6-9.

GOD has promised to be with Joshua, but Joshua must strive to act like one in partnership with God. And that He may do so, God has just two things to press on him: in the first place, to be strong and of a good courage; and in the second place, to make the book of the law his continual study and guide. In this way he shall be able to achieve the specific purpose to which he is called, to divide the land for an inheritance to the people, as God hath sworn to their fathers; and likewise, more generally, to fulfil the conditions of a successful life—" then shalt thou make thy way prosperous, and then thou shalt have good success."

First, Joshua must be strong and very courageous. But are strength and courage really within our own power? Is strength not absolutely a Divine gift, and as dependent on God in its ordinary degrees as it was in the case of Samson in its highest degree? No doubt in a sense it is so; and yet the amount even of our bodily strength is not wholly beyond our own control. As bodily strength is undoubtedly weakened by careless living, by excess of eating and drinking, by all irregular habits, by the breathing of foul air, by indolence and self-indulgence of every kind, so undoubtedly it is increased and promoted by attention to the simple laws of health, by activity and exercise, by sleep and sabbatic rest, by the moderate use of wholesome food, as well as by abstinence from hurtful drinks and drugs. And surely the duty of being strong, in so far as such things can give strength, is of far more importance than many think; for if we can thus maintain and increase our strength we shall be able to serve both God and man much better and longer than we could otherwise have done. On the other hand, the feebleness and fitfulness and querulousness often due to preventable illness must increase the trouble which we give to others, and lessen the beneficent activity and the brightening influence of our own lives.

But in Joshua's case it was no doubt strength and courage of soul that was mainly meant. Even that is not wholly independent of the ordinary conditions of the body. On the other hand, there are no doubt memorable cases where the elasticity and power of the spirit have been in the very inverse ratio to the strength of the body. By cheerful views of life and duty, natural depression has been counteracted, and the soul filled with hope and joy. "The joy of the Lord," said Nehemiah, "is the strength of His people." Fellowship with God, as our reconciled God and Father in Christ, is a source of perpetual strength. Who does not know the strengthening and animating influence of the presence even of a friend, when we find his fresh and joyous temperament playing on us in some season of depression? The radiance of his face, the cheeriness of his voice, the elasticity of his movements seem to infuse new hope and courage into the jaded soul. When he is gone, we try to shake off the despondent feeling that has seized us, and gird ourselves anew for the battle of life. And if such an effect can be produced by fellowship with a fellow-creature, how much more by fellowship with the infinite God!—especially when it is His work we are trying to do, and when we have all His promises of help to rest on. "God is near thee, therefore cheer thee" is a perpetual solace and stimulus to the Christian soul.

But even men who are full of Christian courage need props and bulwarks in the hour of trial. Ezra and Nehemiah were bold, but they had ways of stimulating their courage, which they sometimes needed to fall back on, and they could find allies in unlikely quarters. Ezra could draw courage even from his shame, and Nehemiah from his very pride. "I was ashamed," said Ezra, "to require of the king a band of soldiers and horsemen to help us against the enemy in the way;" therefore he determined to face the danger with no help but the unseen help of God. And when Nehemiah's life was in danger from the cunning devices of the enemy, and his friends advised him to hide himself, he repelled the advice with high-minded scorn—"Should such a man as I flee?"

But there is no source of courage like that which flows from the consciousness of serving God, and the consequent assurance that He will sustain and help His servants. Brief ejaculatory prayers, constantly dropping from their lips, often bring the courage which is needed. "Now, therefore, O God, strengthen my hands," was Nehemiah's habitual exclamation when faintness of heart came over him. No doubt it was Joshua's too, as it has always been of the best of God's servants. Again and again, amid the murderous threats of cannibals in the New Hebrides, the missionary Paton must have sunk into despair but for his firm belief in the protection of God.

The other counsel to Joshua was to follow in all things the instructions of Moses, and for this end, not to let "the book of the law depart out of his mouth, but to meditate on it day and night, that he might observe to do all that was written therein."

For Joshua was called to be the executor of Moses, as it were, not to start on an independent career of his own; and that particular call he most humbly and cheerfully accepted. Instead of breaking with the past, he was delighted to build on it as his foundation, and carry it out to its predestined issues. It was no part of his work to improve on what Moses had done; he was simply to accept it and carry it out. He had his brief, he had his instructions, and these it was his one business to fulfil. No puritan ever accepted God's revelation with more profound and unquestioning reverence than Joshua accepted the law of Moses. No Oliver Cromwell or General Gordon ever recognised more absolutely his duty to carry out the plan of another, and, undisturbed himself, leave the issue in His hands. He was to be a very incarnation of Moses, and was so to meditate on his law day and night that his mind should be saturated with its contents.

This, indeed, was a necessity for Joshua, because he required to have a clear perception of the great purpose of God regarding Israel. Why had God taken the unusual course of entering into covenant with a single family out of the mass of mankind? A purpose deliberately formed and clung to for more than four hundred years must be a grand object in the Divine mind. It was Joshua's part to keep the people in mind of the solemnity and grandeur of their mission and to call them to a corresponding mode of life. What can more effectually give dignity and self-respect to men than to find that they have a part in the grand purposes of God? To find that God is not asleep; that He has neither given up the world to chance nor bound it with a chain of irreversible law, but that He calls us to be fellow-workers with Him in a great plan which shall in the end tend gloriously to advance the highest welfare of man?

This habit of meditation on the law which Joshua was instructed to practise was of great value to one who was to lead a busy life. No mere cursory perusal of a book of law can secure the ends for which it is given. The memory is treacherous, the heart is careless, and the power of worldly objects to withdraw attention is proverbial. We must be continually in contact with the Book of God. The practice enjoined on Joshua has kept its ground among a limited class during all the intervening generations. In every age of the Church it has been impressed on all devout and earnest hearts that there can be no spiritual prosperity and progress without daily meditation on the Word of God. It would be hard to believe in the genuine Christianity of any one who did not make a practice morning and evening of bringing his soul into contact with some portion of that Word. And wherever an eminent degree of piety has been reached, we shall find that an eminently close study of the Word has been practised. Where the habit is perfunctory, the tendency is to omit the meditation and to be content with the reading. Even in pious families there is a risk that the reading of the Scriptures morning and evening may push the duty of meditation aside, though even then we are not to despise the benefit that arises from the familiarity gained with their contents.

But, on the other hand, the instances are numberless of men attaining to great intimacy with the Divine will and to a large conformity to it, through meditation on the Scriptures. To many the daily portion comes fresh as the manna gathered each morning at the door of Israel's camp. Think of men like George Müller of Bristol reading the Bible from beginning to end as many as a hundred times, and finding it more fresh and interesting at each successive perusal. Think of Livingstone reading it right on four times when detained at Manyuema, and Stanley three times during his Emin expedition. What resources must be in it, what hidden freshness, what power to feed and revive the soul! The sad thing is that the practice is so rare. Listen to the prophet-like rebuke of Edward Irving to the generation of his time: "Who feels the sublime dignity there is in a fresh saying descended from the porch of heaven? Who feels the awful weight there is in the least iota that hath dropped from the lips of God? Who feels the thrilling fear or trembling hope there is in words whereon the eternal destinies of himself do hang? Who feels the swelling tide of gratitude within his breast for redemption and salvation, instead of flat despair and everlasting retribution? . . . This book, the offspring of the Divine mind and the perfection of heavenly wisdom, is permitted to lie from day to day, perhaps from week to week, unheeded and unperused; never welcome to our happy, healthy, and energetic moods; admitted, if admitted at all, in seasons of weakness, feeble-mindedness, and disabling sorrow. . . . Oh, if books had but tongues to speak their wrongs, then might this book exclaim, Hear, O heavens, and give ear, O earth! I came from the love and embrace of God, and mute nature, to whom I brought no boon, did me rightful homage. . . . I set open to you the gates of salvation and the way of eternal life, heretofore unknown. . . . But ye requited me with no welcome, ye held no festivity on my arrival; ye sequester me from happiness and heroism, closeting me with sickness and infirmity; ye make not of me, nor use me as your guide to wisdom and prudence, but press me into your list of duties, and withdraw me to a mere corner of your time, and most of you set me at nought and utterly disregard me. . . . If you had entertained me, I should have possessed you of the peace which I had with God when I was with Him and was daily His delight rejoicing always before Him. . . . Because I have called and ye refused . . . I also will laugh at your calamity and mock when your fear cometh." *

It is no excuse for neglecting this habitual reading of the Book of God that He places us now more under the action of principles than the discipline of details. For the glory of principles is that they have a bearing on every detail of our life. "Whatsoever ye do in word or in deed, do all in the name of the Lord Jesus, giving thanks unto God and the Father by Him." What could be more comprehensive than this principle of action—a principle that extends to "whatsoever we do"? There is not a moment of our waking life, not an action great or small we ever perform where the influence of this wide precept ought not to be felt. And how can it become thus pervasive unless we make it a subject of continual meditation?

In the case of Joshua, all the strenuous exhortations to him to be strong and of a good courage, and to meditate on the Divine law as given by Moses by day and by night, were designed to qualify him for his great work—"to divide the land for an inheritance to the people as God had sworn to their fathers." First of all, the land had to be conquered; and there is no difficulty in seeing how necessary it was for one who had this task on hand to be strong and of a good courage, and to meditate on God's law. Then the land had to be divided, and the people settled in their new life, and Joshua had to initiate them, as it were, in that life; he had to bind on their consciences the conditions on which the land was to be enjoyed, and start them in the performance of the duties, moral, social, and religious, which the Divine constitution required. Here lay the most difficult part of his task. To conquer the country required but the talent of a military commander; to divide the country was pretty much an affair of trigonometry; but to settle them in a higher sense, to create a moral affinity between them and their God, to turn their hearts to the covenant of their fathers, to wean them from their old idolatries and establish them in such habits of obedience and trust that the doing of God's will would become to them a second nature,—here was the difficulty for Joshua. They had not only to be planted physically in groups over the country, but they had to be married to it morally, otherwise they had no security of tenure, but were liable to summary eviction. It was no land of rest for idolaters; all depended on the character they attained; loyalty to God was the one condition of a happy settlement; let them begin to trifle with the claims of Jehovah, punishment and suffering, to be followed finally by dispersion and captivity, was the inevitable result.

It was thus that Joshua had to justify his name,—to show that he was worthy to be called by the name of Jesus. The work of Jesus may be said to have been symbolised both by that of Moses and that of Joshua. Moses symbolised the Redeemer in rescuing the people from Egypt and their miserable bondage there; as "Christ hath redeemed us from the curse of the law." Joshua symbolised Him as He renews our hearts and makes us "meet to be partakers of the inheritance of the saints in light." For there are conditions moral and spiritual essential to our dwelling in the heavenly Canaan. "Lord, who shall abide in Thy tabernacle? and who shall dwell in Thy holy hill? He that hath clean

* "For the Oracles of God: four Orations." Pp. 3-6.

hands, and a pure heart; who hath not lifted up his soul to vanity, nor sworn deceitfully." The atmosphere of heaven is too pure to be breathed by the unregenerate and unsanctified. There must be an adaptation between the character of the inhabitant and the place of his habitation. "Verily, verily, I say unto you, Except a man be born of water and of the Spirit, he cannot see the kingdom of God."

Thus we see the connection between Joshua's devotion to the book of the law, and success in the great work of his life—" then thou shalt make thy way prosperous, and then thou shalt have good success." No doubt he would have the appearance of success if he simply cleared out the inhabitants who were so degraded by sin that God was compelled to sweep them off, and settled His people in their room. But that, after all, was but a small matter unless accompanied by something more. It would not secure the people from at last sharing the fate of the old inhabitants; so far at least that though they should not be exterminated, yet they would be scattered over the face of the globe. How could Joshua get rid of these ominous words in the song of Moses to which they had so lately listened?—"They provoked Him to jealousy with strange gods, with abominations provoked they Him to anger. They sacrificed to devils, not to God; to gods whom they knew not, to new gods that came newly up, whom your fathers feared not. . . . And He said, I will hide My face from them, I will see what their end shall be; for they are a very froward generation, children in whom is no faith." But even if in the end of the day it should come to this, nevertheless Joshua might so move and impress the people for the time being, that in the immediate future all would be well, and the dreaded consummation would be put off to a distant day.

And so at all times, in dealing with human beings, we can obtain no adequate and satisfying success unless their hearts are turned to God. Your children may be great scholars, or successful merchants, or distinguished authors, or brilliant artists, or even statesmen; what does it come to if they are dead to God, and have no living fellowship with Jesus Christ? Your congregation may be large and influential, and wealthy, and liberal; what if they are worldly, proud, and contentious? We must aim at far deeper effects, effects not to be found without the Spirit of God. The more we labour in this spirit, the more shall our way be made prosperous, the better shall be our success. "For them that honour Me I will honour; but they that despise Me shall be lightly esteemed."

CHAPTER VI.

JOSHUA'S CHARGE TO THE PEOPLE.

JOSHUA i. 10-18.

GOD has spoken to Joshua; it is now Joshua's part to speak to the people. The crossing of the Jordan must be set about at once, and in earnest, and all the risks and responsibilities involved in that step firmly and fearlessly encountered.

And in the steps taken by Joshua for this purpose we see, what we so often see, how the natural must be exhausted before the supernatural is brought in. Thus, in communicating with the people through the *shoterim*, or officers, the first order which he gives is to "command the people to prepare them victuals." "Victuals" denotes the natural products of the country, and is evidently used in opposition to "manna." In another passage we read that "the manna ceased on the very morning after they had eaten of the old corn of the land" (chap. v. 12). This may have been a considerable time before, for the conquest of Sihon and Og would give the people possession of ample stores of food out of the old corn of the land. The manna was a provision for the desert only, where few or no natural supplies of food could be found. But the very day when natural stores become available, the manna is discontinued. One cannot but contrast the carefully limited use of the supernatural in Scripture with its arbitrary and unstinted employment in mythical or fictional writings. Often in such cases it is brought in with a wanton profusion, simply to excite wonder, sometimes to gratify the love of the grotesque, not because natural means could not have accomplished what was sought, but through sheer love of revelling in the supernatural. In Scripture the natural is never superseded when it is capable of either helping or accomplishing the end. The east wind helps to dry the Red Sea, although the rod of Moses has to be stretched out for the completion of the work. The angel of God knocks Peter's chains from his limbs and opens the prison gates for him, but leaves him to find his way thereafter as best he can. So now. It is now in the power of the people to prepare them victuals, and though God might easily feed them as He has fed them miraculously for forty years, He leaves them to find food for themselves. In all cases the co-operation of the Divine and the human is carried out with an instructive combination of generosity and economy; man is never to be idle; alike in the affairs of the temporal and the spiritual life, the Divine energy always stimulates to activity, never lulls to sleep.

A little explanation is needed respecting the time when Joshua said the Jordan must be crossed—" within three days." If the narrative of the first two chapters be taken in chronological order, more than three days must have elapsed between the issuing of this order and the crossing of the river, because it is expressly stated that the two spies who were sent to examine Jericho hid themselves for three days in the mountains, and thereafter recrossed the Jordan and returned to Joshua (ii. 22). But it is quite in accordance with the practice of Scripture narrative to introduce an episode out of its chronological place so that it may not break up the main record. It is now generally held that the spies were sent off before Joshua issued this order to the people, because it is not likely that he would have committed himself to a particular day before he got the information which he expected the spies to bring. In any case, it is plain that no needless delay was allowed. Half a week more and Jordan would be crossed, although the means of crossing it had not yet been made apparent; and then the people would be actually in their own inheritance, within the very country which in the dim ages of the past had been promised to their fathers.

Yes, the people generally; but already an arrangement had been made for the Reubenites, the Gadites, and the half-tribe of Manasseh on the east side of the river. How, then, were they to act in the present crisis? That had been determined between them and Moses when they got leave to occupy the lands of Sihon and Og, on account of their suitableness for their abundant flocks and herds. It had been arranged then that, leaving their cattle and their children, a portion of the men likewise, the rest would cross the river with their brethren and take their share of the toils and risks of the conquest of Western Canaan. All that Joshua needs to do now is to remind them of this arrangement. Happily there was no reluctance on their part to fulfil it. There was no going back from their word, even though they might have found a loophole of escape. They might have said that as the conquest of Sihon and Og had been accomplished so easily, so the conquest of the western tribes would be equally simple. Or they might have said that the nine tribes and a half could furnish quite a large enough army to dispossess the Canaanites. Or they might have discovered that their wives and children were exposed to dangers they had not apprehended, and that it would be necessary for the entire body of the men to remain and protect them. But they fell back on no such after thought. They kept their word at no small cost of toil and danger, and furnished thereby a perpetual lesson for those who, having made a promise under pressure, are tempted to resile from it when the pressure is removed. Fidelity to engagements is a noble quality, just as laxity in regard to them is a miserable sin. Even Pagan Rome could boast of a Regulus who kept his oath by returning to Carthage, though it was to encounter a miserable death. In the fifteenth psalm it is a feature in the portrait of the man who is to abide in God's tabernacle and dwell in His holy hill, that he "sweareth to his own hurt, and changeth not."

One arrangement was made by these transjordanic tribes that was perfectly reasonable—a portion of the men remained to guard their families and their property. The number that passed over was forty thousand (Josh. iv. 13), whereas the entire number of men capable of bearing arms (dividing Manasseh into two) was a hundred and ten thousand (Num. xxvi. 7, 18, and 34). But the contingent actually sent was amply sufficient to redeem the promise, and, consisting probably of picked men, was no doubt a very efficient portion of the force. The actual fighting force of the other tribes would probably be in the same proportion to the whole; and there, too, a section would have to be left to guard the women, children, and flocks, so that in point of fact the labours and dangers of the conquest were about equally divided between all the tribes.

Here, then, was an edifying spectacle: those who had been first provided for did not forget those who had not yet obtained any settlement; but held themselves bound to assist their brethren until they should be as comfortably settled as themselves.

It was a grand testimony against selfishness, a grand assertion of brotherhood, a beautiful manifestation of loyalty and public spirit; and, we may add, an instructive exhibition of the working of the method by which God's providence seeks to provide for the dissemination of many blessings among the children of men. It was an act of socialism, without the drawbacks which most forms of socialism involve.

God has allowed many differences in the lots of mankind, bestowing on some ample means, for which they toiled not neither did they spin; bestowing, often on the same individuals, a higher position in life, with corresponding social influence; setting some nations in the van of the world's march, bestowing on some churches very special advantages and means of influence; and it is a great question that arises—what obligations rest on these favoured individuals and communities? Does God lay any duty on them toward the rest of mankind?

The inquiry in its full scope is too wide for our limits; let us restrict ourselves to the element in respect of which the transjordanic tribes had the advantage of the others—the element of time. What do those who have received their benefits early owe to those who are behind them in time?

The question leads us first to the family constitution, but there is really no question here. The obligations of parents to their children are the obligations of those who have already got their settlement to those who have not; of those who have already got means, and strength, and experience, and wisdom to those who have not yet had time to acquire them. It is only the vilest of our race that refuse to own their obligations here, and this only after their nature has been perverted and demonised by vice. To all others it is an obligation which amply repays itself. The affection between parent and child in every well-ordered house sweetens the toil that often falls so heavily on the elders; while the pleasure of seeing their children filling stations of respectability and usefulness, and the enjoyment of their affection, even after they have gone out into the world, amply repay their past labours, and greatly enrich the joys of life.

We advance to the relation of the rich to the poor, especially of those who are born to riches to those who are born to obscurity and toil. Had the providence of God no purpose in this arrangement? You who come into the world amid luxury and splendour, who have never required to work for a single comfort, who have the means of gratifying expensive tastes, and who grudge no expenditure on the objects of your fancy:—was it meant that you were to sustain no relation of help and sympathy to the poor, especially your neighbours, your tenants, or your workpeople? Do you fulfil the obligations of life when, pouring into your coffers the fruits of other men's toil, you hurry off to the resorts of wealth and fashion, intent only on your own enjoyment, and without a thought of the toiling multitude you leave at home? Is it right of you to leave deserving people to fall peradventure into starvation and despair, without so much as turning a finger to prevent it? What are you doing for the widows and orphans? Selfish and sinful beings! let these old Hebrews read you a lesson of condemnation! They could not selfishly enjoy their comfortable homes till they had done their part on behalf of their brethren, for wherever there is a brotherly heart a poor brother's welfare is as dear as one's own.

Then there is the case of nations, and pre-eminently of our own. Some races attain to civilisation, and order, and good government sooner than others. They have all the benefit of settled institutions and enlightened opinion, of discoveries in the arts and sciences, and of the manifold comforts and blessings with which life is thus enriched, while other nations are sunk in barbarism and convulsed by disorder. But how much more prone are such nations to claim the rights of superiority than to play the part of the elder brother! We are thankful for the great good that has been done in India, and in other countries controlled by the older nations. But even in the case of India, how many have gone there not to benefit the natives, but with the hope of enriching themselves. How ready have many been to indulge their own vices at the cost of the natives, and how little has it pained them to see them becoming the slaves of new vices that have sunk them lower than before. Our Indian opium traffic, and our drink traffic generally among native races—what is their testimony to our brotherly feeling? What are we to think of the white traders among the South Sea islands, stealing and robbing and murdering their feebler fellow-creatures? What are we to think of the traffic in slaves, and the inconceivable brutalities with which it is carried on? Or what are we to think of our traders at home, sending out in almost uncountable profusion the rum, and the gin, and the other drinks by which the poor weak natives are at once enticed, enslaved, and destroyed? Is there any development in selfishness that has ever been heard of more heartless and horrible? Why can't they let them alone, if they will not try to benefit them? What can come to any man in the end but the well-merited punishment of those who out of sheer greed have made miserable savages tenfold more the children of hell than before?

We pass over the case of the early settlers in colonies, because there is hardly any obligation more generally recognised than that of such settlers to lend a helping hand to new arrivals. We go on to the case of Churches. The light of saving truth has come to some lands before others. We in this country have had our Christianity for centuries, and in these recent years have had so lively a dispensation of the gospel of Christ that many have felt more than ever His power to forgive, to comfort, to lift us up and bless us. Have we no duty to those parts of the earth which are still in the shadow of death? If we are not actually settled in the Promised Land, we are as good as settled, because we have the Divine promise, and we believe in that promise. But what of those who are yet " without Christ, alienated from the commonwealth of Israel, and strangers to the covenants of promise, having no hope, and without God in the world "? Have we no responsibility for them? Have we no interest in that Divine plan which seeks to use those who first received the light as instruments of imparting it to the rest? Infidels object that Christianity cannot be of God, because if Christianity furnishes the only Divine remedy for sin it would have been diffused as widely as the evil for which it is the cure. Our reply is, that God's plan is to give the light first to some, and to charge them to give it freely and cordially to others. We say, moreover, that this plan is a wholesome one for those who are called to work it, because it draws out and strengthens what is best and noblest in them, and because it tends to form very loving bonds between those who give and those who get the benefit. But what if the first recipients of the light fold their hands, content to have got the blessing themselves, and decline to do their part in sending it to the rest? Surely there is here no ordinary combination of sins! Indolence and selfishness at the root, and, with these, a want of all public spirit and beneficent activity; and, moreover, not mere neglect but contempt of the Divine plan by which God has sought the universal diffusion of the blessing. Again we say, look to these men of Reuben, Gad, and Manasseh. They were not the *élite* of the race of Israel. Their fathers, at least in the case of Reuben and Dan, were not among the more honoured of the sons of Jacob. And yet they had the grace to think of their brethren, when so many among us are utterly careless of ours. And not only to think of them, but to go over the Jordan and fight for them, possibly die for them; nor would they think of returning to the comfort of their homes till they had seen their brethren in the west settled in theirs.

And this readiness of Reuben, Gad, and the half-tribe of Manasseh to fulfil the engagement under which they had come to Moses, was not the only gratifying occurrence which Joshua met with on announcing the impending crossing of the Jordan. For the whole people declared very cordially their acceptance of Joshua as their leader, vowed to him the most explicit fidelity, declared their purpose to pay him the same honour as they had paid to Moses, and denounced a sentence of death against any one that would not hearken to his words in all that he commanded them.

Joshua, in fact, obtained from them a promise of loyalty beyond what they had ever given to Moses till close on his death. It was the great trial of Moses that the people so habitually complained of him and worried him, embittering his life by ascribing to him even the natural hardships of the wilderness, as well as the troubles that sprang directly from their sins. It is the unwillingness of his people to trust him, after all he has sacrificed for them, that gives such a pathetic interest to the life of Moses, and makes him, more than perhaps any other Old Testament prophet, so striking an example of unrequited affection. After crossing the Red Sea, all the marvels of that deliverance from Pharaoh of which he had been the instrument are swallowed up and forgotten by the little inconveniences of the journey. And afterwards, when they are doomed to the forty years' wandering, they are ready enough to blame him for it, forgetting how he fell down before God and pled for them when God threatened to destroy them. Moreover, his enactments against the idolatry they loved so well made him anything but popular, to say nothing of the burdensome ceremonial which he enjoined them to observe. The time of real loyalty to Moses was just the little period before his death, when he led them against Sihon and Og, and a great stretch of fertile and beautiful land fell into their hands. Moses had just gained the greatest victory of his life, he had just become master of the hearts of his people, when he was called away. For Moses at last did gain the people's hearts, and those to whom Joshua appealed could say without irony or sarcasm, " According as we hearkened unto Moses in all things, so will we hearken unto thee."

In point of fact a great change had been effected on the people at last. Moses had laboured, and Joshua now entered into his labours. The same thing has often occurred in history, and notably in our own. In civil life how much do we owe to the noble champions of freedom of other days, through whose patriotism, courage, and self-denial the hard fight was fought and the victory won that enables us to sit under our vine and under our fig tree. In ecclesiastical life is it not the blood of the martyrs and the struggles of those of whom the world was not worthy, who wandered in deserts and in mountains and in dens and caves of the earth, that won for us the freedom and the peace in which we now rejoice? What blessings we owe to those that have gone before us! And how can we better discharge our obligations to them than by hastening to the aid of those who have but emerged from the period of struggle and suffering, like the Christians of Madagascar or of Uganda, whose fearful sufferings and awful deaths under the merciless rule of heathen kings made Christendom stand aghast, and drew a wail of anguish from her bosom?

The unanimity of the people in their loyalty to Joshua is a touching sight. So far as appears there was not one discordant note in that harmonious burst of loyalty. No Korah, Dathan, or Abiram rose up to decline his rule and embarrass him in his new position. It is a beautiful sight, the united loyalty of a great nation. Nothing more beautiful has ever been known in the long reign of Queen Victoria than the crowding of her people in hundreds of thousands to witness her procession to St. Paul's on that morning when she went to return thanks for the rescue of her eldest son from the very jaws of death. Not one discordant note was uttered, not one disloyal feeling was known; the vast multitude were animated by the spirit of sympathy and affection for one who had tried to do her duty as a queen and as a mother. It was a sight not unlike to this that was seen in the streets of New York at the centennial celebration of the inauguration of George Washington as first President of the United States. One was thrilled by the thought that not only the multitude that thronged the streets, but the representatives of the whole nation, gathered in their churches throughout the land, were animated by a common sentiment of gratitude to the man whose wisdom and courage had laid the foundation of all the prosperity and blessing of the last hundred years. Are not such scenes the pattern of that spirit of loyalty which the entire race of man owes to Him who by His blood redeemed the world, and whose rule and influence, if the world would but accept of it, are so beneficent and so blessed? Yet how far are we from such a state! How few are the hearts that throb with true loyalty to the Saviour, and whose most fervent aspiration for the world is, that it would only throw down its weapons of rebellion, and give to him its hearty allegiance! Strange that the Old Testament Joshua should have got at once what eighteen hundred years have failed to bring to the New Testament Jesus! God hasten the day of universal light and universal love, when He shall reign from sea to sea, and from the river to the ends of the earth!

"One song employs all nations, and all cry
  'Worthy the Lamb, for He was slain for us!'
The dwellers in the vales and on the rocks
Shout to each other, and the mountain tops
From distant mountains catch the flying joy,
Till nation after nation taught the strain
Earth rolls the rapturous Hosanna round."

CHAPTER VII.

THE SPIES IN JERICHO.

JOSHUA ii.

IT was not long ere Joshua found an occasion not only for the exercise of that courage to which he had been so emphatically called both by God and the people, but for calling on others to practise the same manly virtue. For the duty which he laid on the two spies—detectives we should now call them—to enter Jericho and bring a report of its condition, was perhaps the most perilous to which it was possible for men to be called. It was like sending them into a den of lions, and expecting them to return safe and sound. Evidently he was happy in finding two men ready for the duty and the risk. Young men they are called further on (vi. 23), and it is quite likely that they were leading men in their tribes. No doubt they might disguise themselves, they might divest themselves of anything in dress that was characteristically Hebrew, they might put on the clothes of neighbouring peasants, and carry a basket of produce for sale in the city; and as for language, they might be able to use the Canaanite dialect and imitate the Canaanite accent. But if they did try any such disguise, they must have known that it would be of doubtful efficacy; the officials of Jericho could not fail to be keenly on the watch, and no disguise could hide the Hebrew features, or divest them wholly of the air of foreigners. Nevertheless the two men had courage for the risky enterprise. Doubtless it was the courage that sprang from faith! it was in God's service they went, and God's protection would not fail them. To be able to find agents so willing and so suitable was a proof to Joshua that God had already begun to fulfil His promises.

Joshua had been a spy himself, and it was natural enough that he should think of the same mode of reconnoitring the country, now that they were again on the eve of making the entrance into it which they should have made nearly forty years before. There is no reason to think that in taking this step Joshua acted presumptuously, proceeding on his own counsel when he should have sought counsel of God. For Joshua might rightly infer that he ought to take this course inasmuch as it had been followed before with God's approval in the case of the twelve. Its purpose was twofold—to obtain information and confirmation. Information as to the actual condition and spirit of the Canaanites, as to the view they took of the approaching invasion of the Israelites, and the impression that had been made on them by all the remarkable things that had happened in the desert; and confirmation,—new proof for his own people that God was with them, fresh encouragement to go up bravely to the attack, and fresh assurance that not one word would ever fail them of all the things which the Lord had promised.

We follow the two men as they leave Shittim, so named from the masses of bright acacia which shed their glory over the plain; then cross the river at "the fords," which flooded though they were, were still practicable for swimmers; enter the gates of Jericho, and move along the streets. In such a city as Jericho, and among such an immoral people as the Canaanites, it was not strange that they should fall in with a woman of Rahab's occupation, and should receive an invitation to her house. Some commentators have tried to make out that she was not so bad as she is represented, but only an innkeeper; but the meaning of the word both here and as translated in Heb. xi. and James ii. is beyond contradiction. Others have supposed that she was one of the harlot-priestesses of Ashtoreth, but in that case she would have had her dwelling in the precincts of a temple, not in an out-of-the-way place on the walls of the city. We are to remember that in the degraded condition of public opinion in Canaan, as indeed much later in the case of the Hetairai of Athens, her occupation was not regarded as disgraceful, neither did it banish her from her family, nor break up the bonds of interest and affection between them, as it must do in every moral community.* It was not accompanied with that self-contempt and self-loathing which in other circumstances are its fruits. We may quite easily understand how the spies might enter her house simply for the purpose of getting the information they desired, as modern detectives when tracking out crime so often find it necessary to win the confidence and worm out the secrets of members of the same wretched class. But the emissaries of Joshua were in too serious peril, in too devout a mood, and in too high-strung a state of nerve to be at the mercy of any Delilah that might wish to lure them to careless pleasure. Their faith, their honour, their patriotism, and their regard to their leader Joshua, all demanded the extremest circumspection and self-control; they were, like Peter, walking on the sea; unless they kept their eye on their Divine protector, their courage and presence of mind would fail them, they would be at the mercy of their foes.

Whether disguised or not, the two men had evidently been noticed and suspected when they entered the city, which they seem to have done in the dusk of evening. But, happily for them, the streets of Jericho were not patrolled by policemen ready to pounce on suspicious persons, and run them in for judicial examination. The king or burgomaster of the place seems to have been the only person with whom it lay to deal with them. Whoever had detected them, after following them to Rahab's house, had then to resort to the king's residence and give their information to him. Rahab had an inkling of what was likely to follow, and being determined to save the men, she hid them on the roof of the house, and covered them with stalks of flax, stored there for domestic use. When, after some interval, the king's messengers came, commanding her to bring them forth since they were Israelites come to search the city, she was ready with her plausible tale. Two men had indeed come to her, but she could not tell who they were,—it was no business of hers to be inquisitive about them; the men had left just before the gates were shut, and doubtless, if they were alert and pursued after them, they would overtake them, for they could not be far off. The king's messengers had not half the wit of the woman; they took her at her word, made no search of her house, but set out on the wild-goose chase on which she had sent them. Sense and spirit failed them alike.

We are not prepared for the remarkable development of her faith that followed. This first Canaanite across the Jordan with whom the Israelites met was no ordinary person. Rays of Divine light had entered that unhallowed soul, not to be driven back, not to be hidden under a bushel, but to be welcomed, and ultimately improved and followed. Our minds are carried forward to what was so impressive in the days of our Lord, when the publicans and the harlots entered into the kingdom before the scribes and the pharisees. We are called to admire the riches of the grace of God, who does not scorn the moral leper, but many a time lays His hand upon him, and says "I will, be thou clean." "They shall come from the east, and from the west, and from the north, and from the south, and shall enter into the kingdom of heaven; but the children of the kingdom shall be cast into outer darkness; there shall be weeping and gnashing of teeth."

In the first place, Rahab made a most explicit confession of her faith, not only in Jehovah as the God of the Hebrews, but in Him as the one only God of heaven and earth. It would have been nothing had she been willing to give to the Hebrew God a place, a high place, or even the highest place among the gods. Her faith went much further. "The Lord your God, He is God in heaven above and in earth beneath." This is an exclusive faith—Baal and Ashtoreth are nowhere. What a remarkable conviction to take hold of such a mind! All the traditions of her youth, all the opinions of her neighbours, all the terrors of her priests set at nought, swept clean off the board, in face of the overwhelming evidence of the sole Godhead of Jehovah!

Again, she explained the reason for this faith. "We have heard how the Lord dried up the water of the Red Sea for you, when ye came out of Egypt; and what ye did unto the two kings of the Amorites, that were on the other side Jordan, Sihon and Og, whom ye utterly destroyed." The woman has had an eye to see and an ear to hear. She has not gazed in stupid amazement on the marvellous tokens of Divine power displayed before the world, nor accepted the sophistry of sceptics referring all these marvels to accidental thunderstorms and earthquakes and high winds. She knew better than to suppose that a nation of slaves by their own resources could have eluded all the might of Pharaoh, subsisted for forty years in the wilderness, and annihilated the forces of such renowned potentates as Sihon and Og. She was no philosopher, and could not have reasoned on the doctrine of causation, but her common sense taught her that you cannot have extraordinary effects without corresponding causes. It is one of the great weaknesses of modern unbelief that with all its pretensions to philosophy, it is constantly accepting effects without an adequate cause. Jesus Christ, though He revolutionised the world, though He founded an empire to which that of the Cæsars is not

---

* It is somewhat remarkable that the present village of Riha, at or near the site of the ancient Jericho, is noted for its licentiousness. The men, it is said, wink at the infidelity of the women, a trait of character singularly at variance with the customs of the Bedouin. "At our encampment over 'Ain Terâbeh (says Robinson) the night before we reached this place, we overheard our Arabs asking the Khatib for a paper or written charm to protect them from the women of Jericho; and from their conversation it seemed that illicit intercourse between the latter and strangers that come here is regarded as a matter of course. Strange that the inhabitants of the valley should have retained this character from the earliest ages; and that the sins of Sodom and Gomorrah should still flourish upon the same accursed soil."—"Researches in Palestine," i. 553.

for a moment to be compared, though all that were about Him admitted His supernatural power and person, after all, was nothing but a man. The gospel that has brought peace and joy to so many weary hearts, that has transformed the slaves of sin into children of heaven, that has turned cannibals into saints, and fashioned so many an angelic character out of the rude blocks of humanity, is but a cunningly devised fable. What contempt for such sophistries, such vain explanations of facts patent to all would this poor woman have shown! How does she rebuke the many that keep pottering in poor natural explanations of plain supernatural facts, instead of manfully admitting that it is the Arm of God that has been revealed, and the Voice of God that has spoken!

Further, Rahab informed the spies that when they heard these things the inhabitants of the land had become faint, their hearts melted, and there remained no more courage in them because of the Israelites. For they felt that the tremendous Power that had desolated Egypt and dried up the sea, that had crushed Sihon King of the Amorites and Og King of Bashan like nuts under the feet of a giant, was now close upon themselves. What could they do to arrest the march of such a power, and avert the ruin which it was sure to inflict? They had neither resource nor refuge—their hearts melted in them. It is when Divine Power draws near to men, or when men draw near to Divine Power that they get the right measure of its dimensions and the right sense of their own impotence. Caligua could scoff at the gods at a distance, but in any calamity no man was more prostrate with terror. It is easy for the atheist or the agnostic to assume a bold front when God is far off, but woe betide him when He draws near in war, in pestilence, or in death!

If we ask, How could Rahab have such a faith and yet be a harlot? or how could she have such faith in God and yet utter that tissue of falsehoods about the spies with which she deluded the messengers of the king? we answer that light comes but gradually and slowly to persons like Rahab. The conscience is but gradually enlightened. How many men have been slaveholders after they were Christians! Worse than that, did not the godly John Newton, one of the two authors of the Olney hymns, continue for some time in the slave trade, conveying cargoes of his fellow-creatures stolen from their homes, before he awoke to a sense of its infamy? Are there no persons among us calling themselves Christians engaged in traffic that brings awful destruction to the bodies and souls of their fellow-men? That Rahab should have continued as she was after she threw in her lot with God's people is inconceivable; but there can be no doubt how she was living when she first comes into Bible history. And as to her falsehoods, though some have excused lying when practised in order to save life, we do not vindicate her on that ground. All falsehood, especially what is spoken to those who have a right to trust us, must be offensive to the God of truth, and the nearer men get to the Divine image, through the growing closeness of their Divine fellowship, the more do they recoil from it. Rahab was yet in the outermost circle of the Church, just touching the boundary; the nearer she got to the centre the more would she recoil alike from the foulness and the falseness of her early years.

We have to notice further in Rahab a determination to throw in her lot with the people of God. In spirit she had ceased to be a Canaanite and become an Israelite. She showed this by taking the side of the spies against the king, and exposing herself to certain and awful punishment if it had been found out that they were in her house. And her confidential conversation with them before she sent them away, her cordial recognition of their God, her expression of assurance that the land would be theirs, and her request for the protection of herself and her relations when the Israelites should become masters of Jericho, all indicated one who desired to renounce the fellowship of her own people and cast in her lot with the children of God. That she was wholly blameless in the way in which she went about this, in favouring the spies against her own nation in this underhand way, we will not affirm; but one cannot look for a high sense of honour in such a woman. Still, whatever may be said against her, the fact of her remarkable faith remains conspicuous and beyond dispute, all the more striking, too, that she is the last person in whom we should have expected to find anything of the kind. That faith beyond doubt was destined to expand and fructify in her heart, giving birth to virtues and graces that made her after life a great contrast to what it had been. No doubt the words of the Apostle might afterwards have been applied to her—"Such were some of you: but ye are washed, but ye are sanctified, but ye are justified in the name of the Lord Jesus, and by the Spirit of the Lord."

And yet, though her faith may at this time have been but as a grain of mustard seed, we see two effects of it that are not to be despised. One was her protection of the Lord's people, as represented by the spies; the other was her concern for her own relations. Father, mother, brothers, and sisters and all that they had, were dear to her, and she took measures for their safety when the destruction of Jericho should come. She exacted an oath of the two spies, and asked a pledge of them, that they would all be spared when the crisis of the city arrived. And the men passed their oath and arranged for the protection of the family. No doubt it may be said that it was only their temporal welfare about which she expressed concern, and for which she made provision. But what more could she have been expected to do at that moment? What more could the two spies have engaged to secure? It was plain enough that if they were ever to obtain further benefit from fellowship with God's people, their lives must be preserved in the first instance from the universal destruction which was impending. Her anxiety for her family, like her anxiety for herself, may even then have begun to extend beyond things seen and temporal, and a fair vision of peace and joy may have begun to flit across her fancy at the thought of the vile and degrading idolatry of the Canaanites being displaced in them by the service of a God of holiness and of love. But neither was she far enough advanced to be able as yet to give expression to this hope, nor were the spies the persons to whom it would naturally have been communicated. The usual order in the Christian life is, that as anxiety about ourselves begins in a sense of personal danger and a desire for deliverance therefrom, so spiritual anxiety about the objects of our affection has usually the same beginning. But as it would be a miserable thing for the new life to stand still as soon as our personal safety was secured, so it would be a wretched affection that sought nothing more on behalf of our dearest friends. When, by accepting Christ, we get the blessing of personal safety, we only reach a height from which we see how many other things we need. We become ashamed of our unholy passions, our selfish hearts, our godless ways, and we aspire, with an ardour which the world cannot understand, to purity and unselfishness and consecration to God. For our friends we desire the same; we feel for them as for ourselves, that the bondage and pollution of sin are degrading, and that there can be neither peace, nor happiness, nor real dignity for the soul until it is created anew after the image of God.

Some commentators have laid considerable stress on the line of scarlet thread that was to be displayed in the window by which the spies had been let down, as a token and remembrance that that house was to be spared when the victorious army should enter Jericho. In that scarlet thread they have seen an emblem of atonement, an emblem of the blood of Christ by which sinners are redeemed. To us it seems more likely that, in fixing on this as the pledge of safety, the spies had in view the blood sprinkled on the lintels and door posts of the Hebrew houses in Egypt by which the destroying angel was guided to pass them by. The scarlet rope had some resemblance to blood, and for this reason its special purpose might be more readily apprehended. Obviously the spies had no time to go into elaborate explanations at the moment. It is to be observed that, as the window looked to the outside of the city, the cord would be observed by the Israelites and the house recognised as they marched round and round, according to the instructions of Joshua. Not a man of all the host but would see it again and again, as they performed their singular march, and would mark the position of the house so carefully that its inmates, gathered together like the family of Noah in the ark, would be preserved in perfect safety.

The stratagem of Rahab, and the mode of flight which she recommended to the spies, fruits of woman's ready wit and intuitive judgment, were both successful. She reminds us of the self-possession of Jael, or of Abigail, the wife of Nabal. In the dark, the spies escaped to the mountain,—the rugged rampart which bounded the valley of the Jordan on the west. Hiding in its sequestered crevices for three days, till the pursuit of the Jerichonians was over, they stole out under cover of darkness, recrossed the Jordan, told Joshua of their stirring and strange adventure, and wound up with the remark that the hearts of the people of the country were melting because of them. How often is this true, though unbelief cannot see it! When Jesus told His disciples that He beheld Satan fall as lightning from heaven, He taught us that those who set themselves against Him and His cause are fallen powers, no longer flushed with victory and hope, but defeated and dejected, and consciously unable to overcome the heaven-aided forces that are against them. Well for all Christian philanthropists and missionaries of the Cross, and brave assailants of lust and greed and vice and error, to bear this in mind! The cause of darkness never can triumph in the end, it has no power to rally and rush against the truth; if only the servants of Christ would be strong and of a good courage, they too would find that the boldest champions of the world do faint because of them.

When the spies return to Joshua and tell him all that has befallen them, he accepts their adventure as a token for good. They have not given him any hint how Jericho is to be taken; but, what is better, they have shown him that the outstretched arm of God has been seen by the heathen, and that the inhabitants of the country are paralysed on account of it. The two spies were a great contrast to the ten that accompanied Joshua and Caleb so long before: the ten declared the land unassailable; the two looked on it as already conquered—"The Lord hath delivered into our hands all the land." Children of Israel, you must not be outdone in faith by a harlot; believe that God is with you, go up, and possess the land!

CHAPTER VIII.

JORDAN REACHED.

JOSHUA iii. 1-7.

THE host of Israel had been encamped for some time at Shittim on the east side of the river Jordan. It is well to understand the geographical position. The Jordan has its rise beyond the northern boundary of Palestine in three sources, the most interesting and beautiful of the three being one in the neighbourhood of Cæsarea Philippi. The three streamlets unite in the little lake now called Huleh, but Merom in Bible times. Issuing from Merom in a single stream the Jordan flows on to the lake of Galilee or Gennesareth, and from thence, in a singularly winding course to the Dead Sea. Its course between the lake of Galilee and the Dead Sea is through a kind of ravine within a ravine; the outer ravine is the valley or plain of Jordan, now called by the Arabs El Ghor, which is about six miles in width at its northern part, and considerably more at its southern, where the Israelites now were. Within this "El Ghor" is a narrower ravine about three-quarters of a mile in width, in the inner part of which flows the river, its breadth varying from twenty to sixty yards. Some travellers say that the Jordan does not now rise so high as formerly, but others tell us they have seen it overflowing its banks at the corresponding season. But "the plain" is not fertilised by the rising waters: hence the reason why the banks of the river are not studded with towns as in Egypt. It is quite possible, however, that in the days of Abraham and Lot artificial irrigation was made use of: hence the description given of it then that it was "like the land of Egypt" (Gen. xiii. 10). If it be remarked as strange that Jordan should have overflowed his banks "in time of harvest" (Josh. iii. 15) when usually rain does not fall in Palestine, it is to be remembered that all the sources of the Jordan are fountains, and that fountains do not usually feel the effects of the rain until some time after it has fallen. The harvest referred to is the barley harvest, and near Jericho that harvest must have occurred earlier than throughout the country on account of the greater heat.

The host of Israel lay encamped at Shittim, or

Abel Shittim, "the shadow or moist place of the acacias," somewhere in the Arboth-Moab or fields of Moab. The exact spot is unknown, but it was near the foot of the Moabite mountains, where the streams, coming down from the heights on their way to the Jordan, caused a luxuriant growth of acacias, such as are still found in some of the adjacent parts. Sunk as this part of the plain is far below the level of the Mediterranean, and enclosed by the mountains behind it as by the walls of a furnace, it possesses an almost tropical climate which, though agreeable enough in winter and early spring, would have been unbearable to the Israelites in the height of summer. It was while Israel "abode in Shittim," during the lifetime of Moses, that they were seduced by the Moabites to join in the idolatrous revels of Baal-peor and punished with the plague. The acacia groves gave facilities for the unhallowed revelling. That chastisement had brought them into a better spirit, and now they were prepared for better things.

The Jordan was not crossed then by bridges nor by ferry boats; the only way of crossing was by fords. The ford nearest to Jericho, now called El Mashra'a, is well known; it was the ford the Israelites would have used had the river been fordable; and perhaps the tradition is correct that there the crossing actually took place. When the spies crossed and recrossed the river it must have been by swimming, as it was too deep for wading at the time; but though this mode of crossing was possible for individuals, it was manifestly out of the question for a host. That the Israelites could by no possibility cross at that season must have been the forlorn hope of the people of Jericho; possibly they smiled at the folly of Joshua in choosing such a time of the year, and asked in derision, How is he ever to get over?

The appointed day for leaving Shittim has come, and Joshua, determined to lose no time, rises "early in the morning." Nor is it without a purpose that so often in the Old Testament narrative, when men of might commence some great undertaking, we are told that it was early in the morning. In all hot climates work in the open air, if done at all, must be done early in the morning or in the evening. But, besides this, morning is the appropriate time for men of great energy and decision to be astir; and it readily connects itself with the New Testament text—"Not slothful in business, fervent in spirit, serving the Lord." The benefits of an early start for all kinds of successful work are in the proverbs of all nations; and we may add that few have reached a high position in the Christian life who could not say, in the spirit of the hymn, "early in the morning my song shall rise to Thee." Nor can it easily be understood how under other conditions the precept could be fulfilled—"Whatsoever thy hand findeth to do, do it with thy might."

From Shittim to the banks of the Jordan is an easy journey of a few miles, the road being all over level ground, so that the march was probably finished before the sun had risen high. However strong their faith, it could not be without a certain tremor of heart that the people would behold the swollen river, and mark the walls and towers of Jericho a few miles beyond. Three days are to be allowed, if not for physical, certainly for moral and spiritual preparation for the crossing of the river. The three days are probably the same as those adverted to before (chap. i. 3), just as the order to select twelve men to set up twelve stones (chap. iii. 12) is probably the same as that more fully detailed in chap. iv. 2. The host is assembled in orderly array on the east bank of the Jordan, when the officers pass through to give instructions as to their further procedure. Three such instructions are given.

First, they are to follow the ark. Whenever they see the priests that bear it in motion, they are to move from their places and follow it. There was no longer the pillar of fire to guide them—that was a wilderness-symbol of God's presence, now superseded by a more permanent symbol—the ark. Both symbols represented the same great truth—the gracious presence and guidance of God, and both called the people to the same duty and privilege, and to the same assurance of absolute safety so long as they followed the Lord. Familiar sights are apt to lose their significance, and the people must have become so familiar with the wilderness-pillar that they would hardly think what it meant. Now a different symbol is brought forward. The ark carried in solemn procession by the priests is now the appointed token of God's guidance, and therefore the object to be unhesitatingly followed. A blessed truth for all time was clearly shadowed forth. Follow God implicitly and unhesitatingly in every time of danger, and you are safe. Set aside the counsels of casuistry, of fear, and of worldly wisdom; find out God's will and follow it through good report and through evil report, and you will be right. It was thus that Joshua and Caleb did, and counselled the people to do, when they came back from exploring the land; and now these two were reaping the benefit; while the generation, that would have been comfortably settled in the land if they had done the same, had perished in the wilderness on account of their unbelief.

Secondly, a span of two thousand cubits was to be left between the people and the ark. Some have thought that this was designed as a token of reverence; but this is not the reason assigned. Had it been designed as a token of reverence, it would have been prescribed long before, as soon as the ark was constructed, and began to be carried with the host through the wilderness. The intention was, "that ye may know the way by which you must go" (ver. 4). If this arrangement had not been made, the course of the ark through the flat plains of the Jordan would not have been visible to the mass of the host, but only to those in the immediate neighbourhood, and the people would have been liable to straggle and fall into confusion, if not to diverge altogether. In all cases, when we are looking out for Divine guidance, it is of supreme importance that there be nothing in the way to obscure the object or to distort our vision. Alas, how often is this direction disregarded! How often do we allow our prejudices, or our wishes, or our worldly interests to come between us and the Divine direction we profess to desire! At some turn of our life we feel that we ought not to take a decisive step without asking guidance from above. But our own wishes bear strongly in a particular direction, and we are only too prone to conclude that God is in favour of our plan. We do not act honestly; we lay stress on all that is in favour of what we like; we think little of considerations of the opposite kind. And when we announce our decision, if the matter concern others, we are at pains to tell them that we have made it matter of prayer. But why make it matter of prayer if we do so with prejudiced minds? It is only when our eye is single that the whole body is full of light. This clear space of two thousand cubits between the people and the ark deserves to be remembered. Let us have a like clear space morally between us and God when we go to ask His counsel, lest peradventure we not only mistake His directions, but bring disaster on ourselves and dishonour on His name.

Thirdly, the people were instructed,—"Sanctify yourselves, for to-morrow the Lord will do wonders among you." It is an instinct of our nature that when we are to meet with some one of superior worldly rank preparation must be made for the meeting. When Joseph was summoned into the presence of Pharaoh, and they brought him hastily out of the dungeon, "he shaved himself, and changed his raiment, and came in unto Pharaoh." The poorest subject of the realm would try to wear his best and to look his best in the presence of his sovereign. But while "man looketh on the outward appearance the Lord looketh on the heart." And our very instincts teach us, that the heart needs to be prepared when God is drawing near. It is not in our ordinary careless mood that we ought to stand before Him who "sets our iniquities before Him, our secret sins in the light of His countenance." Grant that we can neither atone for our sin, nor cleanse our hearts without His grace; nevertheless, in God's presence everything that is possible ought to be done to remove the abominable thing which He hates, so that He may not be affronted and offended by its presence. Most appropriate, therefore, was Joshua's counsel,—" Sanctify yourselves, for to-morrow the Lord will do wonders among you." He will surpass all that your eyes have seen since that night, much to be remembered, when He divided the sea. He will give you a token of His love and care that will amaze you, much though you have seen of it in the wilderness, and in the country of Sihon and Og. Expect great things, prepare for great things; and let the chief of your preparations be to sanctify yourselves, for "the foolish shall not stand in His sight, and He hateth all workers of iniquity."

Next day (compare ver. 5, "to-morrow," and ver. 7, "this day") Joshua turns to the priests and bids them "take up the ark of the covenant." The priests obey; "they take up the ark, and go before the people."

Shall we take notice of the assertion of some that all those parts of the narrative which refer to priests and religious service were introduced by a writer bent on glorifying the priesthood? Or must we repel the insinuation that the introduction of the ark, and the miraculous effects ascribed to its presence, are mere myths? If they are mere myths, they are certainly myths of a very peculiar kind. Twice only in this book is the ark associated with miraculous events—at the crossing of the Jordan and at the taking of Jericho. If these were myths, why was the myth confined to these two occasions? When mythical writers find a remarkable talisman they introduce it at all sorts of times. Why was the ark not brought to the siege of Ai? Why was it absent from the battles of Bethhoron and Merom? Why was its presence restricted to the Jordan and Jericho, unless it was God's purpose to inspire confidence at first through the visible symbol of His presence, but leave the people afterwards to infer His presence by faith?

The taking up of the ark by the priests was a decisive step. There could be no resiling now from the course entered on. The priests with the ark must advance, and it will be seen whether Joshua has been uttering words without foundation, or whether he has been speaking in the name of God. Shall mere natural forces be brought into play, or shall the supernatural might of heaven come to the conflict, and show that God is faithful to His promise?

Let us put ourselves in Joshua's position. We do not know in what manner the communications were carried on between him and Jehovah of which we have the record under the words "the Lord spake unto Joshua." Was it by an audible voice? Or was it by impressions on Joshua's mind of a kind that could not have originated with himself, but that were plainly the result of Divine influence? In any case, they were such as to convey to Joshua a very clear knowledge of the Divine will. Yet even in the best of men nature is not so thoroughly subdued in such circumstances but that the shadow of anxiety and fear is liable to flit across them. They crave something like a personal pledge that all will go well. Hence the seasonableness of the assurance now given to Joshua—" This day will I begin to magnify thee in the sight of all Israel, that they may know that, as I was with Moses, so I will be with thee." How full and manifold the assurance! First, I will magnify thee. I will endue thee with supernatural might, and that will give you authority and weight, corresponding to the position in which you stand. Further, this shall be but the beginning of a process which will be renewed as often as there is occasion for it. "This day I will *begin*." You are not to go a warfare on your own charges, but "as your days, so shall your strength be." Moreover, this exaltation of your person and office will take place "in the sight of all Israel," so that no man of them shall ever be justified in refusing you allegiance and obedience. And to sum up—you shall be just as Moses was; the resources of My might will be as available for you as they were for him. After this, what misgivings could Joshua have? Could he doubt the generosity, the kindness, the considerateness of his Master? Here was a promise for life; and no doubt the more he put it to the test in after years the more trustworthy did he find it, and the more convincing was the proof it supplied of the mindfulness of God.

It is an experience which has been often repeated in the case of those who have had to undertake difficult work for their Master. Of all our misapprehensions, the most baseless and the most pernicious is, that God does not care much about us, and that we have not much to look for from Him. It is a misapprehension which dishonours God greatly, and which He is ever showing Himself most desirous to remove. It stands fearfully in the way of that spirit of trust by which God is so much honoured, and which He is ever desirous that we should show. And those who have trusted God, and have gone forward to their work in His strength, have always found delightful evidence that their trust has not been in vain. What is the testimony of our great Christian philanthropists, our most successful missionaries, and other devoted Christian workers? Led to undertake enterprises far beyond their strength, and undergo responsibilities far beyond their means, we know not a single case in which they have not had ample proof of the mindfulness of their Master, and found occasion to wonder at the considerateness and the bountifulness which He has brought to bear upon their position. And is it not strange that we should be so slow to learn how infinite God is in goodness? That we should have no difficulty in believing in the goodness of a parent or of some kind friend who has always been ready to help us in our times of need, but so slow to realise this in regard to God, though we are constantly acknowledging in words that He is the best as well as the greatest of beings? It is a happy era in one's spiritual history when one escapes from one's contracted views of the love and liberality of God, and begins to realise that "as far as heaven is above the earth, so far are His ways above our ways, and His thoughts above our thoughts"; and when one comes to find that in one's times of need, whether arising from one's personal condition or from the requirements of public service, one may go to God for encouragement and help with more certainty of being well received than one may go to the best and kindest of friends.

It is sometimes said that the Old Testament presents us with a somewhat limited view of God's love. Certainly it is in the New Testament that we see it placed in the brightest of all lights—the Cross, and that we find the argument in its most irresistible form—" He that spared not His own Son, but delivered Him up for us all, how shall He not, with Him also, freely give us all things?" But one must have read the Old Testament in a very careless spirit if one has not been struck with its frequent and most impressive revelations of God's goodness. What scenes of gracious intercourse with His servants does it not present from first to last, what outpourings of affection, what yearnings of a father's heart! If there were many in Old Testament times whom these revelations left as heedless as they found them, there were certainly some whom they filled with wonder and roused to words of glowing gratitude. The Bible is not wont to repeat the same thought in the same words. But there is one truth and one only which we find repeated again and again in the Old Testament, in the same words, as if the writers were never weary of them—" For His mercy endureth for ever." Not only is it the refrain of a whole psalm (cxxxvi.), but we find it at the beginning of three other psalms (cvi., cvii., cxviii.), we find it in David's song of dedication when the ark was brought up to Jerusalem (1 Chron. xvi. 34), and we find also that on the same occasion a body of men, Heman and Jeduthun and others, were told off expressly " to give thanks to the Lord, because His mercy endureth for ever " (1 Chron. xvi. 41). This, indeed, is the great truth which gives the Old Testament its highest interest and beauty. In the New Testament, in its evangelical setting, it shines with incomparable brightness. Vividly realised, it makes the Christian's cup to flow over; as it fills him likewise with the hope of a joy to come—" a joy unspeakable and full of glory."

CHAPTER IX.

JORDAN DIVIDED.

JOSHUA iii.

AT Joshua's command, the priests carrying the ark are again in motion. Bearing the sacred vessel on their shoulders, they make straight for the bank of the river. " The exact spot is unknown; it certainly cannot be that which the Greek tradition has fixed, where the eastern banks are sheer precipices of ten or fifteen feet high. Probably it was either immediately above or below, where the cliffs break away; above at the fords, or below where the river assumes a tamer character on its way to the Dead Sea." * Following the priests, at the interval of a full half-mile, was the host of Israel. " *There* was the mailed warrior with sword and shield, and the aged patriarch, trembling on his staff. Anxious mothers and timid maidens were there, and helpless infants of a day old; and there, too, were flocks and herds and all the possessions of a great nation migrating westward in search of a home. Before them lay their promised inheritance,

'While Jordan rolled between,'

full to the brim, and overflowing all its banks. Nevertheless, through it lies their road, and God commands the march. The priests take up the sacred ark and bear it boldly down to the brink; when lo! 'the waters which came down from above stood and rose up upon a heap very far from the city Adam, that is before Zaretan: and those that came down toward the sea of the plain, even the Salt Sea, failed, and were cut off: and the people passed over right against Jericho.' And thus, too, has all-conquering faith carried the thousand times ten thousand of God's people in triumph through the Jordan of death to the Canaan of eternal rest." †

The description of the parting of the waters is clear enough in the main, though somewhat obscure in detail. The obscurity arises from the meaningless expression in the Authorized Version, " very far from the city Adam, which is beside Zaretan." The Revised rendering gives a much more natural meaning—" rose up in one heap, very far off, at Adam, the city that is beside Zarethan." The names Adam and Zaretan occur nowhere else in Scripture, nor are they mentioned by Josephus; some think we have a relic of Adam in the first part of ed-Damieh, the name of a ford, and others, following the rendering of the Septuagint, which has ἕως μέρους Καριαθιαρίμ, consider the final " arim " to be equivalent to " adim " or " adam," the Hebrew letter " r " being almost the same as " d." What we are taught is, that the waters were cut off from the descending river a long way up, while down below the whole channel was laid bare as far as the Dead Sea. The miracle involved an accumulation of water in the upper reaches of the river, and as it was obviously undesirable that this should continue for a long time, enough of the channel was laid bare to enable the great host to cross rapidly in a broad belt, and without excitement or confusion. The sceptical objection is completely obviated that it

---

* Stanley's " Sinai and Palestine," p. 303.
† " Land and Book," vol. ii., pp. 460-61.

was physically impossible for so vast a host to make the passage in a short time.

As soon as the waters began to retreat, after the feet of the priests were planted in them, the priests passed on to the middle of the channel, and stood there "firm, on dry ground," until all the people were passed clean over. The vast host crossed at once, and drew up on the opposite bank. That no attempt was made by the men of Jericho, which was only about five miles off, to attack them and stop their passage, can be explained only on the supposition that they were stricken with panic. One inhabitant undoubtedly heard of the passage without surprise. Rahab could feel no astonishment that the arm of God should thus be made bare before the people whom He was pledged to protect and guide. As little could she wonder at the paralysis which had petrified her own people.

The priests passed on before the people, and stood firm in the midst of the river until the whole host had passed. It was both a becoming thing that they should go before, and that they should stand so firm. It is not always that either priests or Christian ministers have set the example of going before in any hazardous undertaking. They have not always moved so steadily in the van of great movements, nor stood so firmly in the midst of the river. What shall we say of those whose idea, whether of Hebrew priesthood or of Christian ministry, has been that of a mere office, that of men ordained to perform certain mechanical functions, in whom personal character and personal example signified little or nothing? Is it not infinitely nearer to the Bible view that the ministers of religion are the leaders of the people, and that they ought as such to be ever foremost in zeal, in holiness, in self-denial, in victory over the world, the flesh, and the devil? And of all men ought they not to stand firm? Where are Mr. Byends, and Mr. Facing-Both-Ways, and Mr. Worldly-Wiseman more out of place than in the ministry? Where does even the world look more for consistency and devotion and fearless regard to the will of God? What should we think of an army where the officers counted it enough to see to the drill and discipline of the men, and in the hour of battle confined themselves to mere mechanical duties, and were outstripped in self-denial, in courage, in dash and daring by the commonest of their soldiers? Happy the Church where the officers are officers indeed! Feeling ever that their place is in the front rank of the battle and in the vanguard of every perilous enterprise, and that it is their part to set the men an example of unwavering firmness even when the missiles of death are whistling or bursting on every side!

Who shall try to picture the feelings of the people during that memorable crossing? The outstretched arm of God was even more visibly shown than in the crossing of the Red Sea, for in that case a natural cause, the strong east wind, contributed something to the effect, while in this case no secondary cause was employed, the drying up of the channel being due solely to miracle. Who among all that host could fail to feel that God was with them? And how solemn yet cheering must the thought have been alike to the men of war looking forward to scenes of danger and death, and to the women and children, and the aged and infirm, dreading otherwise lest they should be trampled down amid the tumult! But of all whose hearts were moved by the marvellous transaction, Joshua must have been pre-eminent. "As I was with Moses, so I will be with thee." At the dividing of the sea the leadership of Moses began, and they were all baptised unto him in the cloud and in the sea. And now, in like manner, the leadership of Joshua begins at the dividing of the river, and baptism unto Joshua takes the place of baptism unto Moses. A new chapter of an illustrious history begins as its predecessor had begun, but not to be marred and rendered abortive by unbelief and disobedience like the last. How true God has been to his word! What wonders He has done among the people! What honour He has put upon Joshua! How worthy He is to be praised! Will disloyalty to Him ever occur again, will this marvellous deed be forgotten, and the miserable gods of the heathen be preferred to Jehovah? Will any future prophet have cause to say, "O Ephraim, what shall I do unto thee? O Judah, what shall I do unto thee? For your goodness is as a morning cloud, and as the early dew, it goeth away"?

It is to be especially remarked that God took into His own hands the prescription of the method by which this great event was to be commemorated. It seems as if He could not trust the people to do it in a way that would be free from objection and from evil tendency. It was assumed that the event was worthy of special commemoration. True, indeed, there had been no special commemoration of the passage of the sea, but then the Passover was instituted so near to that event that it might serve as a memorial of it as well as of the protection of the Israelites when the firstborn of the Egyptians was slain. And generally the people had been taught, what their own hearts in some degree recognised, that great mercies should be specially commemorated. The Divine method of commemorating the drying up of the Jordan was a very simple one. In the first place, twelve men were selected, one from every tribe, to do the prescribed work. The democratic constitution of the nation was recognised —each tribe was to take part in it; and as it was a matter in which all were concerned, each person was to take part in the election of the representative of his tribe. Then each of these twelve representatives was to take from the bed of the river, from the place where the priests had stood with the ark, a stone, probably as large as he could carry. The twelve stones were to be carried to the place where the host lodged that night, and to be erected as a standing memorial of the miracle. It was a very simple memorial, but it was all that was needed. It was not like the proud temples or glorious pyramids of Egypt, reared as these were to give glory to man more than to God. It was like Jacob's pillar before, or Samuel's Ebenezer afterwards; void of every ornament or marking that could magnify man, and designed for one single purpose—to recall the goodness of God.

It would appear, from chap. iv. 9, that two sets of stones were set up; Joshua, following the spirit of the Divine direction, having caused a second set to be erected in the middle of the river on the spot where the priests had stood. Some have supposed that that verse is an interpolation of later date; but, as it occurs in all the manuscripts, and as it is expressly stated in the Septuagint and Vulgate versions that this was a different transaction from the other, we must accept it as such. The one memorial stood on the spot where the ark had indicated the presence of God, the other where the first encampment of the host had shown God's faithfulness to His word. Both seemed to proclaim the great truth afterwards brought out in the exquisite words of the psalm—"God is our refuge and strength; a very present help in time of trouble." They might not be needed so much for the generation that experienced the deliverance; but in future generations they would excite the curiosity of the children, and thus afford an opportunity to the parents to rehearse the transactions of that day, and thrill their hearts with the sense of God's mercy.

Among devout Israelites, that day was never forgotten. The crossing of the Jordan was coupled with the crossing of the sea, as the two crowning tokens of God's mercy in the history of Israel, and the most remarkable exhibitions of that Divine power which had been so often shown among them. In that wailing song, the seventy-fourth psalm, where God's wonderful works of old are contrasted in a very sad spirit with the unmitigated desolations that met the writer's eye, almost in the same breath in which he extols the miracle of the sea, "Thou didst divide the sea by Thy strength," he gives thanks for the miracle of the river, "Thou didst cleave the fountain and the flood: Thou driedst up mighty rivers." And in a song, not of wailing, but of triumph, the hundred and fourteenth psalm, we have the same combination:—

"When Israel went forth out of Egypt,
The house of Jacob from a people of strange language;
Judah became His sanctuary,
Israel His dominion.
The sea saw it, and fled;
Jordan was driven back.
The mountains skipped like rams,
The little hills like lambs.
What aileth thee, O thou sea, that thou fleest?
Thou Jordan, that thou turnest back?
Ye mountains, that ye skip like rams;
Ye little hills like lambs?
Tremble, thou earth, at the presence of the Lord,
At the presence of the God of Jacob;
Which turned the rock into a pool of water,
The flint into a fountain of waters."

The point of this psalm lies in the first verse—in the reference to the time "when Israel came out of Egypt, the house of Jacob from a people of strange language." Israel on that occasion gave a signal proof of his trust in God. At God's bidding, and with none but God to trust in, he turned his back on Egypt, and made for the wilderness. It was a delight to God to receive this mark of trust and obedience, and in recognition of it the mightiest masses and forces of nature were moved or arrested. The mountains and hills skipped like living creatures, and the sea saw it and fled. It seemed as if God could not do too much for His people. It was the same spirit that was shown when they followed Joshua to the river. They showed that they trusted God. They renounced the visible and the tangible for the invisible and the spiritual. They rose up at Joshua's command, or rather at the command of God by Joshua; and, pleased with this mark of trust, God caused the waters of the Jordan to part asunder. Surely there is something pathetic in this; the Almighty is so pleased when His children trust Him, that to serve them the strongest forces are moved about as if they were but feathers.

In many ways the truth has been exemplified in later times. When a young convert, at home or abroad, takes up decided ground for Christ, coming out from the world and becoming separate, very blessed tokens of God's nearness and of God's interest are usually given him. And Churches that at the call of Christ surrender their worldly advantages, receive tokens of spiritual blessing that infinitely outweigh in sweetness and in spiritual value all that they lose. "Them that honour Me, I will honour."

Occurrences of more recent times show clearly that God did well in taking into His own hands the prescription of the way in which the crossing of the Jordan was to be commemorated. Tradition has it that it was at the same place where Joshua crossed that Jesus was baptised by John. That may well be doubted, for the Bethabara where John was baptising was probably at a higher point of the river. But it is quite possible that it was at this spot that Elijah's mantle smote the river, and he and his servant passed over on dry ground. Holding that all these events occurred at the same place, tradition has called in the aid of superstition, and given a sacred character to the waters of the river at this spot. Many have seen, and every one has read of the pilgrimage to the Jordan, performed every spring, from which many hope to reap such advantage. "In the mosaics of the earliest churches at Rome and Ravenna," says Dean Stanley, "before Christian and pagan art were yet divided, the Jordan appears as a river god pouring his streams out of his urn. The first Christian emperor had always hoped to receive his long-deferred baptism in the Jordan, up to the moment when the hand of death struck him at Nicomedia. . . . Protestants, as well as Greeks and Latins, have delighted to carry off its waters for the same sacred purpose to the remotest regions of the West."

No doubt the expectation of spiritual benefit from the waters of the Jordan is one cause of the annual pilgrimage thither, and of the strange scene that presents itself when the pilgrims are bathing. It seems impossible for man, except under the influence of the strongest spiritual views, to avoid the belief that somehow mechanical means may give rise to spiritual results. There is nothing from which he is naturally more averse than spiritual activity. Any amount of mechanical service he will often render to save him from spiritual exercise. Symbols without number he will willingly provide, if he thereby escape the necessity of going into the immediate presence of God, and worshipping Him who is a spirit in spirit and in truth. But can mechanical service or material symbols be anything but an evil, if the would-be worshipper is thereby prevented from recognising the necessity of a heart-to-heart fellowship with the living God? Must we not be in living touch with God if the stream of Divine influence is to reach our hearts, and we are to be changed into His image? In the Psalms, which express the very essence of Hebrew devotion, spiritual contact with God is the only source of blessing. "O God, Thou art my God; early will I seek Thee: my soul thirsteth for Thee, my flesh longeth for Thee in a dry and thirsty land, where there is no water. To see Thy power and Thy glory, so as I have seen Thee in the sanctuary."

Thus it was that by God's prescription the twelve plain stones taken out of the Jordan were the only memorial of the great deliverance. There was no likeness on them of the Divine Being by whom the miracle had been performed. There was nothing to encourage acts of reverence or worship directed toward the memorial. Twelve rough stones, with no sculptured figures or symbols, not even dressed by hammer and chisel, but simply as they were taken out of the river, were the memorial. They were adapted for one purpose, and for one only: "When your children shall ask their fathers in time to come, saying, What mean these stones? then ye shall let your children know, saying, Israel came over this Jordan on dry land. For the Lord your God dried up the waters of the Jordan from before you, until ye were passed over, as the Lord your God did to the Red Sea, which He dried up from before us, until we were gone over: that all the people of the earth might know the hand of the Lord, that it is mighty: that ye might fear the Lord your God for ever."

CHAPTER X.

CIRCUMCISION AND PASSOVER—MANNA AND CORN.

Joshua v. 1-12.

The first two facts recorded in this chapter seem to be closely connected with each other. One is, that when all the Amorite and Canaanite kings on the west side of the Jordan heard of the miraculous drying up of the waters and the passage of the Israelites, "their heart melted, neither was there spirit in them any more." The other is, that the opportunity was taken then and there to circumcise the whole of the generation that had been born after leaving Egypt. But for the fact recorded in the first verse, it would have been the most unsuitable time that could be conceived for administering circumcision. The whole male population would have been rendered helpless for the time, and an invitation would have been given to the men of Jericho to commit such a massacre as in the like circumstances the sons of Jacob inflicted on the men of Shechem (Gen. xxxiv. 25). Why was not this business of circumcising performed while the host were lying inactive on the other side, and while the Jordan ran between Israel and his foes? It was because the kings of the Canaanites were petrified. It is true they plucked up courage by-and-by, and many of the kings entered into a league against Joshua. But this was after the affair of Ai, after the defeat of the Israelites before that city had showed that, as in the case of Achilles, there was a vulnerable spot somewhere, notwithstanding the protection of their God. Meanwhile the people of Jericho were paralysed, for though the whole male population of Israel under forty lay helpless in their tents, not a finger was raised by the enemy against them.

It is with no little surprise that we read that circumcision had been suspended during the long period of the wilderness sojourn. Why was this? Some have said that, owing to the circumstances in which the people were, it would not have been convenient, perhaps hardly possible, to administer the rite on the eighth day. Moving as they were from place to place, the administration of circumcision would often have caused so much pain and peril to the child, that it is no wonder it was delayed. And once delayed, it was delayed indefinitely. But this explanation is not sufficient. There were long, very long periods of rest, during which there could have been no difficulty. A better explanation, brought forward by Calvin, leads us to connect the suspension of circumcision with the punishment of the Israelites, and with the sentence that doomed them to wander forty years in the wilderness. When the worship of the golden calf took place, the nation was rejected, and the breaking by Moses of the two tables of stone seemed an appropriate sequel to the rupture of the covenant which their idolatry had caused. And though they were soon restored, they were not restored without certain drawbacks,—tokens of the Divine displeasure. Afterwards, at the great outburst of unbelief in connection with the report of the spies, the adult generation that had come out of Egypt were doomed to perish in the wilderness, and, with the exception of Joshua and Caleb, not one of them was permitted to enter the land of promise. Now, though it is not expressly stated, it seems probable that the suspension of circumcision was included in the punishment of their sins. They were not to be allowed to place on their children the sign and seal of a covenant which in spirit and in reality they had broken.

But it was not an abolition, but only a suspension of the sacrament for a time that took place. The time might come when it would be restored. The natural time for this would be the end of the forty years of chastisement. These forty years had now come to an end. Doubtless it would have been a great joy to Moses if it had been given him to see the restoration of circumcision, but that was not to take place until the people had set foot on Abraham's land. Now they have crossed the river. They have entered on the very land which God sware to Abraham and Isaac and Jacob to give it them. And the very first thing that is done after this is to give back to them the holy sign of the covenant, which was now administered to every man in the congregation who had not previously received it. We may well think of it as an occasion of great rejoicing. The visible token of his being one of God's children was now borne by every man and boy in the camp. In a sense they now served themselves heirs to the covenant made with their fathers, and might thus rest with firmer trust on the promise—"I will bless them that bless thee, and curse him that curseth thee."

Two other points in connection with this transaction demand a word of explanation. The first is the statement that "all the people that were born in the wilderness by the way as they came forth out of Egypt, them they had not circumcised" (ver. 5). If the view be correct that the suspension of circumcision was part of the punishment for their sins, the prohibition would not come into operation for some months, at all events, after the exodus from Egypt. We think, with Calvin, that for the sake of brevity the sacred historian makes a general statement without waiting to explain the exceptions to which it was subject. The other point needing explanation is the Lord's statement after the circumcision—"This day have I rolled the reproach of Egypt from off you. Wherefore the name of the place is called Gilgal (*i. e.*, Rolling) unto this day." How could the suspension of circumcision be called the reproach of Egypt? The words imply that, owing to the want of this sacrament, they had lain exposed to a reproach from the Egyptians, which was now rolled away. The brevity of the statement, and our ignorance of what the Egyptians were saying of the Israelites at the time, make the words difficult to understand. What seems most likely is, that when the Egyptians heard how God had all but repudiated them in the wilderness, and had withdrawn from them the sign of His covenant, they malignantly crowed over them, and denounced them as a worthless race, who had first rejected their lawful rulers in Egypt under pretext of religion, and, having shown their hypocrisy, were now scorned and cast off by the very God whom they had professed themselves so eager to serve. We may be sure that the Egyptians would not be slow to seize any pretext for denouncing the Israelites, and would be sure to make their jibes as sharp and as bitter as they could. But now the tables are turned on the Egyptians. The restoration of circumcision stamps this people once more as the people of God. The stupendous miracle just wrought in the dividing of the Jordan indicates the kind of protection which their God and King is sure to extend to them. The name of Gilgal will be a perpetual testimony that the reproach of Egypt is rolled away.

Circumcision being now duly performed, the way was prepared for another holy rite for which the appointed season had arrived—the Passover. Some have supposed that the Passover as well as circumcision was suspended after the sentence of the forty years' wandering, the more especially that it was expressly enacted that no uncircumcised person was to eat the Passover. We know (Num. ix. 5) that the Passover was kept the second year after they left Egypt, but no other reference to it occurs in the history. On this, as on many other points connected with the wilderness history, we must be content to remain in ignorance. We are not even very sure how far the ordinary sacrifices were offered during that period. It is quite possible that the considerations that suspended the rite of circumcision applied to other ordinances. But whether or not the Passover was observed in the wilderness, we may easily understand that after being circumcised the people would observe it with a much happier and more satisfied feeling. There were many things to make this Passover memorable. The crossing of the Jordan was so like the crossing of the Red Sea that the celebration in Egypt could not fail to come back vividly to all the older people,—those that were under twenty at the exodus, to whom the sentence of exclusion from Canaan did not apply (Num. xiv. 29). Many of these must have looked on while their fathers sprinkled the lintels and door posts with the blood of the lamb, and must have listened to the awful death-cry of the firstborn of the Egyptians. They must have remembered well that memorable midnight when all were in such excitement marching away from Egypt; and not less vividly must they have remembered the terror that seized them when the Egyptian host was seen in pursuit; and then again the thrill of triumph with which they passed between the crystal walls, under the glow of the fiery pillar; and once more the triumphant notes of Miriam's timbrel and the voices of the women, "Sing unto the Lord, for He hath triumphed gloriously; the horse and his rider He hath cast into the sea." And now these days of glory were coming back! As surely as the passage of the sea had been followed by the destruction of the Egyptians, so surely would the passage of the Jordan be followed by the destruction of the Canaanites. Glorious things were spoken of the city of their God. The benediction of Moses was about to receive a new fulfilment—"Happy art thou, O Israel: who is like unto thee, O people saved by the Lord, the shield of thy help, and who is the sword of thy excellency! and thine enemies shall be found liars unto thee; and thou shalt tread upon their high places."

The remembrance of the past is often an excellent preparation for the trials of the future, and as often it proves a remarkable support under them. It was the very nature of the Passover to look back to the past, and to recall God's first great interposition on behalf of His people. It was a precious encouragement both to faith and hope. So also is our Christian Passover. It is a connecting link between the first and second comings of our Lord. The first coming lends support to faith, the second to hope. No exercise of soul can be more profitable than to go back to that memorable day when Christ our Passover was sacrificed for us. For then the price of redemption was paid in full, and the door of salvation flung wide open. Then the Son sealed His love by giving Himself to the cross for us. What blessing, whether for this life or the life to come, was not purchased by that transaction? Life may be dark and stormy, but hope foresees a bright tomorrow. "When Christ, who is our life, shall appear, then shall ye also appear with Him in glory."

Yet another incident is connected with this transition period of the history. "They did eat of the old corn of the land on the morrow after the passover, unleavened cakes, and parched corn in the selfsame day. And the manna ceased on the morrow after they had eaten of the old corn of the land; neither had the children of Israel manna any more; but they did eat of the fruit of the land of Canaan that year." It is not necessary to suppose that they did not partake at all of the fruits of the land till the morning after that Passover. The conquest of Sihon and Og must have put a large share of produce in their hands, and we can hardly suppose that they did not make some use of it. The narrative is so brief that it does not undertake to state every modification that may be applicable to its general statements. The main thing to be noticed is, that while the manna continued to descend, it was the staple article of food; but when the manna was withdrawn, the old corn and other fruits of the country took its place. In other words, the miracle was not continued when it ceased to be necessary. The manna had been a provision for the wilderness, where ordinary food in sufficient quantity could not be obtained; but now that they were in a land of fields and orchards and vineyards the manna was withdrawn.

We have already adverted to the Bible law of the supernatural. No sanction is given to the idea of a lavish and needless expenditure of supernatural power. A law of economy, we might almost say parsimony, prevails, side by side with the exercise of unbounded liberality. Jesus multiplies the loaves and fishes to feed the multitude, but He will not let one fragment be lost that remains after the feast. A similar law guides the economy of prayer. We have no right to ask that mercies may come to us through extraordinary channels, when it is in our power to get them by ordinary means. If it is in our power to procure bread by our labour, we dare not ask it to be sent direct. We are only too prone to make prayer at the eleventh hour an excuse for want of diligence or want of courage in what bears on the prosperity of the spiritual life. It may be that of His great generosity God sometimes blesses us, even though we have made a very inadequate use of the ordinary means. But on that we have no right to presume. We are fond of short and easy methods where the natural method would be long and laborious. But here certainly we find the working of natural law in the spiritual world. We cannot look for God's blessing without diligent use of God's appointed means.

More generally, this occurrence in the history of Israel, the cessation of one provision when another comes into operation, exemplifies a great law in providence by which the loss of one kind of advantage is compensated by the advent of another. In childhood and early youth we depend for our growth in knowledge on the instructions of our teachers. What puzzles us we refer to them, and they guide us through the difficulty. If they are wise teachers they will not tell us everything, but they will put us on the right method to find out. Still they are there as a court of appeal, so to speak, and we have always the satisfaction of a last resort. But the time comes when we bid farewell to teachers. Happily it is the time when the judgment becomes self-reliant, independent, penetrating. We are thrown mainly upon our own resources. And the very fact of our having to depend on our own judgment fosters and promotes independence, and fits us better for the responsibilities of life. When we become men we put away childish things. A habit of leaning on others keeps us children; but grappling with difficulties as we find them, and trying to make our way through them and over them, promotes manliness. The manna ceases, and we eat the fruit of the land.

So in family life. The affection that binds parents and children, brothers and sisters to one another in the family is both beautiful and delightful; and it were no wonder if, on the part of some, there were the desire that their intercourse should suffer no rude break, but go on unchanged for an indefinite time. But it is seldom God's will that family life shall remain unbroken. Often the interruption comes in the rudest and most terrible form—by the death of the head of the house. And the circumstances of the family may require that all who are capable of earning anything shall turn out to increase the family store. It is often a painful and distressing change. But at least it wakens up all who can do anything, it rescues them from the temptation of a slumbering, aimless life, and often draws out useful gifts that turn their lives into a real blessing. And there are other compensations. When Sarah died, Isaac was left with an empty heart; but when Rebecca came to him, he was comforted. The precise blank that death leaves may never be wholly filled, but the heart expands in other directions, and with new objects of affection the gnawing void ceases to be acutely felt. As old attachments are snapped, new are gradually formed. And even in old age a law of compensation often comes in; children and children's children bring new interests and pleasures, and the green hues of youth modify the grey of age.

Then there is the happy experience by which the advent of spiritual blessings compensates the loss of temporal. Nothing at first appears more desolate than loss of fortune, loss of health, or loss of some principal bodily sense—like sight or hearing. But in a Milton intellectual vigour, patriotic ardour, and poetic sensibility attain their noblest elevation, though

"Cloud and ever-during dark
Surrounds me, from the cheerful ways of men
Cut off, and, for the book of knowledge fair,
Presented with a universal blank
Of nature's works, to me expunged and rased,
And wisdom at one entrance quite shut out."

It is the total loss of hearing, the result of a sudden accident, that turns the slater, John Kitto, into a most instructive and interesting Oriental scholar and writer. How often temporal loss has proved in a higher sense spiritual gain, all Christian biography testifies. Such instances are not uncommon as that which the Rev. Charles Simeon gives, in speaking of some blind men from Edinburgh whom nearly a century ago he found at work in a country house in Scotland: "One of the blind men, on being interrogated with respect to his knowledge of spiritual things, answered, 'I never saw till I was blind; nor did I ever know contentment while I had my eyesight, as I do now that I have lost it; I can truly affirm, though few know how to credit me, that I would on no account change my present situation and circumstances with any that I ever enjoyed before I was blind.' He had enjoyed eyesight till twenty-five, and had been blind now about three years."*

Lastly, of all exchanges in room of old provisions the most striking is that which our Lord thus set forth: "It is expedient for you that I go away: for if I go not away, the Comforter will not come unto you; but if I depart, I will send Him to you." If we should think of life, even the Christian life, as a mere time of enjoyment, albeit spiritual enjoyment, no statement could be more paradoxical or unpalatable. It is because life is a training school, and because what we most need in that school is the immediate action of the Divine Spirit on our spirits, purifying, elevating, strengthening, guiding all that is deepest in our nature, that our Lord's words are true. Very precious had been the manna that ceased when Jesus left. But more nourishing is the new corn with which the Spirit feeds us. Let us prize it greatly so long as we are in the flesh. We shall know the good of it when we enter on the next stage of our being. Then, in the fullest sense, the manna will cease, and we shall eat the corn of the land.

CHAPTER XI.

THE CAPTAIN OF THE LORD'S HOST.

JOSHUA v. 13-15, vi. 1.

THE process of circumcision is over, and the men are well; the feast of unleavened bread has come to an end; all honour has been paid to

* "Life of Rev. Charles Simeon," p. 125.

these sacred ordinances according to the appointment of God; the manna has ceased, and the people are now depending on the corn of the land, of which, in all probability, they have but a limited supply. Everything points to the necessity of further action, but it is hard to say what the next step is to be. Naturally it would be the capture of Jericho. But this appears a Quixotic enterprise. The city is surrounded by a wall, and its gates are " straitly shut up," barred, and closely guarded to prevent the entrance of a single Israelite. Joshua himself is at a loss. No Divine communication has yet come to him, like that which came as to the crossing of the Jordan. See him walking all alone " by Jericho," as near the city as it is safe for him to go. With mind absorbed in thought and eyes fixed on the ground, he is pondering the situation, but unable to get light upon it, when something comes athwart his sphere of vision. He lifts his eyes, and right against him perceives a soldier, brandishing his sword.

A less courageous man would have been startled, perhaps frightened. His first thought is, that it is an enemy. None of his own soldiers would have ventured there without his orders, or would have dared to take up such an attitude towards his commander-in-chief. With a soldier's presence of mind, instead of moving off, he assumes an aggressive attitude, challenges this warrior, and demands whether he is friend or foe. If friend, he must explain his presence; if foe, prepare for battle. Joshua is himself a thorough soldier, and will allow no one to occupy an ambiguous position. "And Joshua went unto him, and said unto him, Art thou for us, or for our adversaries?"

If the appearance of the soldier was a surprise, his answer to the question must have been a greater. "Nay; but as Captain of the host of the Lord am I now come." The "nay" deprecates his being either friend or foe in the common sense, but especially his being foe. His position and his office are far more exalted. As Captain of the host of the Lord, he is at the head, not of human armies, but of all the principalities and powers of heavenly places,

"The mighty regencies
Of seraphim, and potentates and thrones."

And now the real situation flashes on Joshua. This soldier is no other than the Angel of the Covenant, the same who came to Abraham under the oak at Mamre, and that wrestled with Jacob on the banks of this very Jordan at Peniel. Joshua could not but remember, when God threatened to withdraw from Israel after the sin of the golden calf, and send some created angel to guide them through the wilderness, how earnestly Moses remonstrated, and how his whole soul was thrown into the pleading—"If Thy presence go not with us, carry me not up hence." He could not but remember the intense joy of Moses when this pleading proved successful— "My presence shall go with thee, and I will give thee rest." There could be little doubt in his mind who this "Captain of the host of Jehovah" was, and no hesitation on his part in yielding to Him the Divine honour due to the Most High. And then he must have felt warmly how very kind and seasonable this appearance was, just at the very moment when he was in so great perplexity, and when his path was utterly dark. It was a new proof that man's extremity is God's opportunity. It was just like what used to happen afterwards, when "the Word became flesh and dwelt among us," and was so promptly at hand for His disciples in all times of their tribulation. It was an anticipation of the scene when the ship was tossed so violently on the waves, and Jesus appeared with His "Peace, be still." Or, on that dreary morning, soon after the crucifixion, after they had spent the whole night on the lake and caught nothing, when Jesus came and brought the miraculous draught of fishes to their nets. It is the truth with which all His suffering and stricken children have been made so familiar in all ages of the Church's history:—that, however He may seem to hide Himself and stand afar off in times of trouble, He is in reality ever near, and can never forget that last assurance to His faithful people—"Lo, I am with you alway, even to the end of the world."

It is not likely that Joshua found any cause to discuss the question that modern criticism has so earnestly handled, whether this being that now appeared in human form really was Jehovah. And as little does it seem necessary for us to discuss it. There seems no good reason to reject the view that these theophanies, though not incarnations, were yet foreshadows of the incarnation,—hints of the mystery afterwards to be realised when Jesus was born of Mary. If these appearances looked like incarnations, it was incarnation after the pagan, not the Christian type; momentary alliances of the Divine being with the human form or appearance, assumed merely for the occasion, and capable of being thrown aside as rapidly as they were assumed. This might do very well to foreshadow the incarnation, but it fell a long way short of the incarnation itself. The Christian incarnation was after a type never dreamt of by the pagan mind. That the Son of God should be born of a woman, His body formed in the womb by the slow but wonderful process which "fashioned all His members in continuance, when as yet there was none of them" (Psalm cxxxix. 16), and that He should thus stand in relations to His fellow-men that could not be obliterated, was very wonderful; but most wonderful of all that the manhood once assumed could never be thrown off, but that the Son of God must continue to be the Son of man, in two distinct natures and one person for ever. The fact that all this has taken place is well fitted to give us unshaken confidence in the love and sympathy of our Elder Brother. For He is as really our Brother as He ever was in the days of His flesh, and as full of the care and thoughtful interest that the kindest of elder brothers takes in the sorrows and struggles of his younger brethren.

It has often been remarked as an instructive circumstance, that now, as on other occasions, the Angel of the Lord appeared in the character most adapted to the circumstances of His people. He appeared as a soldier with a drawn sword in His hand. A long course of fighting lay before the Israelites ere they could get possession of their land, and the sword in the hand of the Angel was an assurance that He would fight with them and for them. It was also a clear intimation that in the judgment of God, it was necessary to use the sword. But it was not the sword of the ambitious warrior who falls upon men simply because they are in his way, or because he covets their territories for his country. It was the judicial sword, demanding the death of men who had been tried for their sins, long warned, and at last judicially condemned. The iniquity of the Amorites was now full. We know what kind the people were who dwelt near Jericho four or five hundred years before, while the cities of Sodom and Gomorrah stood in the plain, cities that even then were reeking with the foulest corruption. It is true the judgment of God came down on these cities, but bare judgments have never reformed the world. The destruction of Sodom and Gomorrah removed the foulest stain-spot for the time, but it did not change the hearts nor the habits of the nations. It has seemed good to the Spirit of God to give us one glimpse of the foulness that had been reached at that early period, but not to multiply the filthy details at a future time,—after the long interval between Abraham and Joshua. But we know that if Sodom was bad, Jericho was no better. The country as a whole, which had now filled up its cup of iniquity, was no better. No wonder that the Angel bore a drawn sword in His hand. The long-suffering of the righteous God was exhausted, and Joshua and his people were the instruments by whom the judicial punishment was to be inflicted. The Captain of the Lord's host had drawn His sword from its scabbard to show that the judgment of that wicked people was to slumber no more.

It was not in this spirit nor in this attitude that the Angel of the Covenant had met with Jacob, centuries before, a little higher up the river, at the confluence of the Jabbok. Yet there was not a little that was similar in the two meetings. Like Joshua now, Jacob was then about to enter the land of promise. Like him, he was confronted by an enemy in possession, who, in Jacob's case, was bent on avenging the wrong of his youth. How that enemy was to be overcome Jacob knew not, just as Joshua knew not how Jericho was to be taken. But there was this difference between the two, that in Jacob's case the Angel dealt with him as an opponent; in Joshua's He avowed Himself a friend. The difference was no doubt due to the different dispositions of the two men. Jacob does not seem to have felt that it was only in God's name, and in God's strength, and under God's protection that he could enter Canaan; he appears to have been trusting too much to his own devices,—especially to the munificent present which he had forwarded to his brother. He must be taught the lesson "Not by might, nor by power, but by My Spirit, saith the Lord." At first Jacob dealt with his opponent simply as an obstructionist; then he discovered His Divine rank, and immediately he became the aggressor, and, spite of his dislocated thigh, held on to his opponent, declaring that he would not let Him go except He blessed him. It is otherwise with Joshua. He has no personal matter to settle with God before he is ready to advance into the land. He is in perplexity, and the Angel comes to relieve him. It is neither for reproof nor correction but simply for blessing that He is there.

The appearance of the Angel denoted a special method of communication with Joshua. We have already remarked that we do not know in what manner God's communications to His servant were made before. This incident shows that the ordinary method was not that of personal intercourse,—probably it was that of impressions made supernaturally on Joshua's mind. Why, then, is the method changed now? Why does this Warrior-angel present Himself in person? Probably because the way in which Jericho was to be taken was so extraordinary that, to encourage the faith of Joshua and the people, a special mode of announcement had to be used. One might have thought this unnecessary after the display of Divine power at the crossing of the Jordan. But steadiness of faith was no characteristic of the Israelites, and such as it was it was as liable to fail after crossing the Jordan as it had been after crossing the sea. Special means were taken to invigorate it and fit it for the coming strain. It was one of those rare occasions when a personal visit from the Angel of the Covenant was desirable. Something visible and tangible was needed, something which might be spoken of and readily understood by the people, and which could not possibly be gainsaid.

The moment that Joshua understood with whom he was conversing, he fell on his face, and offered to his visitor not only obeisance but worship, which the visitor did not decline. And then came a question indicating profound regard for his Lord's will, and readiness to do whatsoever he might be told—"What saith my Lord unto His servant?" It cannot but remind us of the question put by Saul to the Lord while yet lying on the ground on the way to Damascus —"Lord, what wilt Thou have me to do?" Joshua compares favourably with Moses at the burning bush, not only now, but throughout the whole interview. No word of remonstrance does he utter, no token of unwillingness or unbelief does he show. And it cannot be said that the instructions which the Angel gave him respecting the taking of Jericho were of a kind to be easily accepted. The course to be followed seemed to human wisdom the very essence of silliness. To all appearance there was not a vestige of adaptation of means to the end. Yet so admirable is the temper of Joshua, that he receives all with absolute and perfect submission. The question "What saith my Lord unto His servant?" is very far from mere matter of courtesy. It is a first principle with Joshua that when the mind of God is once indicated there is nothing for him but to obey. What is he that he should dare to criticise the plans of omnipotence? that he should propose to correct and improve the methods of Divine wisdom? Anything of the kind was alike preposterous and irreverent. "Let all the earth fear the Lord; let all the inhabitants of the world stand in awe of Him. For He spake, and it was done; He commanded, and it stood fast." "Thus saith the high and lofty One that inhabiteth eternity, and whose name is Holy: I dwell in the high and holy place, and with him also who is of a humble and contrite spirit, and who trembleth at My word."

The first answer to the question "What saith my Lord unto His servant?" is somewhat remarkable. "Put off thy shoes from off thy feet, for the place whereon thou standest is holy." Rationalists have explained this as meaning that this was an ancient shrine of the Canaanites, and therefore a place holy in the eyes of Israel; but such an idea needs no refutation. Others conceive it to mean that Joshua, having crossed the Jordan, had now set foot on the land promised to the fathers, and that the soil for that reason was called holy. But if that was the reason for his putting off his shoes, it is difficult to see how he could ever have been justified in again putting them on. And when God called to Moses out of the bush and bade him do the very same thing, it surely was not because the peninsula of Sinai was holy; it was because Moses stood in the immediate presence of the holy God. And it is simply to remind Joshua of the Divine presence that this command is given; and being given it is no sooner uttered than obeyed.

And then follow God's instructions for the taking of Jericho. Never was such a method propounded to reasonable man, or one more open to the objections and exceptions of worldly wisdom. No arrangement of his forces could have been more open to objection than that which God required of him. He was to march round Jericho once a day for six successive days, and seven times on the seventh day, the priests carrying the ark and blowing with trumpets, the men of war going before, and others following the ark, making a long narrow line round the place. We know that the city was provided with gates, like other fortified cities. What was there to prevent the men of Jericho from sallying out at each of the gates, breaking up the line of Israel into sections, separating them from each other, and inflicting dreadful slaughter on each? Such a march round the city seems to be the very way to invite a murderous attack. But it is the Divine command. And this process of surrounding the city is to be carried on in absolute silence on the part of the people, with no noise save the sounding of trumpets until a signal is given; then a great shout is to be raised, and the walls of Jericho are to fall down flat on the ground. Who would have thought it strange if Joshua had been somewhat staggered by so singular directions, and if, like Moses at the bush, he had suggested all manner of objections, and shown the greatest unwillingness to undertake the operation? The noble quality of his faith is shown in his raising no objection at all. After God has thus answered his question, "What saith my Lord unto His servant?" he is just as docile and submissive as he was before. True faith is blind to everything except the Divine command. When God has given him his orders, he simply communicates them to the priests and to the people. He leaves the further development of the plan in God's hands, assured that He will not leave His purpose unfulfilled.

Nor do the priests or the people appear to have made any objection on their part. The plan no doubt exposed them to two things which men do not like, ridicule and danger. Possibly the ridicule was as hard to bear as the danger. God would protect them from the danger, but who would shield them from the ridicule? Even if at the end of the seven days, the promised result should take place, would it not be hard to make themselves for a whole week the sport of the men of Jericho, who would ask all that time whether they had lost their senses, whether they imagined that they would terrify them into surrender by the sound of their rams' horns? How often, especially in the case of young persons, do we find this dread of ridicule the greatest obstacle to Christian loyalty? And even where they have the strongest conviction that ere long the laugh, if laughter may be spoken of in the case, will be turned against their tormentors, and that it will be clearly seen who the men are whom the King delighteth to honour, what misery is caused for the time by ridicule, and how often do the young prove traitors to Christ rather than endure it? All the more remarkable is the steadiness of the priests and people on this occasion. We cannot think that this was due simply and solely to their loyalty to the leader to whom they had recently sworn allegiance. We cannot but believe that personal faith animated many of them, the same faith as that of Joshua himself. Their wilderness training and trials had not been in vain; the manifest interposition of God in the defeat of Sihon and Og had sunk into their hearts; the miraculous passage of the river had brought God very near to them; and it was doubtless in a large measure their conviction that He who had begun the work of conquest for them would carry it on to the end, that procured for Joshua's announcement the unanimous acquiescence and hearty support alike of priests and people.

And hence, too, the reason why, in the eleventh chapter of Hebrews, the falling down of the walls of Jericho is specially accounted for as the result of faith: "By faith the walls of Jericho fell down, after they were compassed about seven days" (ver. 30). The act of faith lay in the conviction that God, who had prescribed the method of attack, foolish though it seemed, would infallibly bring it to a successful issue. It was not merely Joshua's faith, but the priests' faith, and the people's faith, that shone in the transaction. Faith repelled the idea that the enemy would sally forth and break their ranks; it triumphed over the scorn and ridicule which would certainly be poured on them; it knew that God had given the directions, and it was convinced that He would bring all to a triumphant issue. Never had the spiritual thermometer risen so high in Israel, and seldom did it rise so high at any future period of their history. That singular week, spent in marching round Jericho again and again and again, was one of the most remarkable ever known; the people were near heaven, and the grace and peace of heaven seem to have rested on their hearts.

We sometimes speak of "ages of faith." There have been times when the disposition to believe in the unseen, in the presence and power of God, and in the certain success at last of all that is done in obedience to His will, has dominated whole communities, and led to a wonderful measure of holy obedience. Such a period was this age of Joshua. We cannot say, thinking of ourselves, that the present is an age of faith. Rather, on the part of the masses, it is an age when the secular, the visible, the present lords it over men's minds. Yet we are not left without splendid examples of faith. The missionary enterprise that contemplates the conquest of the whole world for Christ, because God has given to His Messiah the heathen for His inheritance and the uttermost part of the earth for His possession, and that looks forward to the day when this promise shall be fulfilled to the letter, is a fruit of faith. And the ready surrender of so many young lives for the world's evangelisation, as missionaries, and teachers, and medical men and women, is a crowning proof that faith is not dead among us. Would only it were a faith that pervaded the whole community,—princes, priests, and people alike; and that there were a harmony among us in the attack on the strongholds of sin and Satan as great as there was in the host of Israel when the people, one in heart and one in hope, marched out, day after day, round the walls of Jericho!

CHAPTER XII.

THE FATE OF JERICHO.

JOSHUA vi. 8-27.

THE instructions of Joshua to the priests and the people are promptly obeyed. In the bright rays of the morning sun, on the day when Jericho is to be surrounded, the plain between the Jordan and Jericho, a space of some five miles, may be seen dotted over with the tents of Israel, arranged in that orderly manner which had been prescribed by Moses in the wilderness. The whole encampment is astir in the prospect of great events. The erect carriage, the flashing eye, the compressed lip of the soldiers show that something great and unusual is expected. By-and-by, there is a stir near the spot where the ark rests, and, borne on the shoulders of the priests, the sacred vessel is seen in motion in the direction of Jericho. Right in front of it are seven priests carrying trumpets of rams' horns, or, as some render it, jubilee horns. The procession of the ark halts a little, till a body of armed men advance and form in front of it. Others of the people take up their places in the rear. The seven priests sound their trumpets, and the procession moves on. Their course is round the walls of Jericho, far enough removed to be beyond the reach of the arrows of its defenders. Not a shout is raised. Not a sound is heard, save that of the trumpets of the seven priests. At last the procession returns to the camp, leaving Jericho just as it found it. Next day the same process is repeated; and the next, and the next, on to the sixth. On the seventh day, the march begins early and is continued late. The spirits of the people are sustained during their weary, monotonous tramp by the expectation of a crisis. At length, when the seventh circuit has been made, the signal is given by Joshua. The air is rent with the shouts of the people and the noise of the trumpets, and immediately, all round, the wall falls flat to the ground, and the people march straight into the city. Paralysed with astonishment and terror, the inhabitants are unable to resist, and lie, men, women and children, at the mercy of their assailants. And the instructions to the Israelites are to destroy everything that is in the city, both man and woman, young and old, ox and sheep and ass, with the edge of the sword. As for the more solid part of the spoil, the silver and the gold and the vessels of brass and iron, they are "devoted" to the service of God (the Authorised translation unhappily uses the word "accursed"). No one is to appropriate a single article to his own use. An exception to the universal massacre was to take place only in the case of the harlot Rahab, who was to be saved, with all her relations, in accordance with the solemn promise of the spies.

There is no difficulty in perceiving the great lesson for all time to be derived from this extraordinary transaction, or the great law of the kingdom of God that was made so conspicuous by it. When we have clear indications of the Divine mind as to any course of action, we are to advance to it promptly and without fear, even though the means at our disposal appear utterly inadequate to the object sought to be gained. No man goeth a warfare at his own charges in the service of God. The resources of infinite power avail for that service, and they are sure to be brought into play if it be undertaken for God's glory, and in accordance with His will. Who could have supposed that the fishermen of Galilee would in the end triumph over all the might of kings and rulers; over all the influence of priesthoods and systems of worship enshrined in the traditions of centuries; over all the learning and intellect of the philosopher, and over all the prejudices and passions of the multitude? The secret lay manifestly in the promise of Jesus —" Lo, I am with you alway, even to the end of the world." Who could have thought that the efforts of a poor German student in Berlin, on behalf of some neglected children, would expand into the widespread and well-rooted "Inner Mission" of Wichern? Or that the concern of a prison chaplain for the welfare of some of the prisoners after their release would develop into the worldwide work of Fliedner? Or that the distress of a kind-hearted medical student in London for a batch of poor boys who "didn't live nowhere," and whose pale faces, as they lay on a cold night on the roof of a shed, stirred in him an irrepressible compassion, would give birth to one of the marvels of London philanthropy,—Dr. Barnardo's twenty institutions, caring for three to four thousand children, in connection with which the announcement could be made that no really destitute child was ever turned from its doors? When Carey on his shoemaker's stool contemplated the evangelisation of India, there was as great a gulf between the end and the apparent means, as when the priests blew with their rams' horns round the walls of Jericho. But Carey felt it to be a Divine command, and Joshua-like set himself to obey it, leaving to God from whom it came to furnish the power by which the work was to be done. And wherever there have been found men and women of strong faith in God, who have looked on His will as recorded in the Scriptures with as much reverence as if it had been announced personally to themselves, and who have set themselves to obey that will with a sense of its reality, and a faith in God's promised help, like that of Joshua as the priests marched round Jericho, the same result has been realised; before Zerubbabel the great mountain has become a plain, and success has been achieved worthy of the acknowledgment—"The Lord hath done great things for us, whereof we are glad."

Far more effectual has this brave and thorough method of doing the Divine will proved than all the contrivances of compromise and worldly wisdom. The attempt to serve two masters has never proved either dignified or permanently successful. "If the Lord be God, follow Him; but if Baal, then follow him;" but do not attempt to combine in one what will please God and Baal too. It is the single eye that is full of light, and full of blessing. If God really is our Master, all the resources of heaven and earth are at our back. If we are able to go forward in sole and simple reliance on His might, as David did in the conflict with Goliath, all will go well. If we waver in our trust in Him, if we fly to the resources of human policy, if we seek deliverance from present evil at whatever cost, we arrest, as it were, the electric current flowing from Heaven, and become weak as other men. Still more if we are guilty of deceit and cunning. How different was David confronting Goliath, and David feigning madness before King Achish! In the one case a noble hero, in the other a timid, faltering child. It is a dear price we pay for present safety or convenience when we forfeit the approval of our conscience and the favour of God. It is a sublime attitude that faith takes up even in the face of overwhelming danger—"Lord, it is nothing with Thee to help, whether with many, or with them that have no power: help us, O Lord our God; for we rest on Thee, and in Thy name we go against this multitude. O Lord, Thou art our God; let not man prevail AGAINST THEE" (2 Chron. xiv. 11).

This, however, is but one half of the lesson of the siege of Jericho. The other and not less valuable lesson is, that in many good enterprises, all that is done may appear for a long time to be labour lost, and not to advance us by one step nearer to the object in view. For six days the priests carried the ark round Jericho, but not one stone was loosened from the walls, not by one iota did the defences seem to yield. Six times on the seventh day there was an equally complete want of result. Nay, the seventh perambulation on the seventh day appeared to be equally unsuccessful, until the very last moment; but when that moment came, the whole defences of the city came tumbling to the ground. It is often God's method to do a great deal of work unseen, and then on a sudden effect the consummation. And whenever we are working in accordance with God's will, it is our encouragement to believe that though our visible success is hardly appreciable, yet good and real work is done. For one day is with the Lord as a thousand years, and a thousand years as one day. Sometimes in a thousand years God does not seem to accomplish a good day's work, but at other times in a single day He does the work of a thousand years. The reformation of the Church in the Middle Ages,—how little progress it seemed to make during weary centuries; and even when victory seemed to be drawing nigh, how thoroughly was it arrested by the martyrdom of Huss and Jerome in Bohemia, the extinction of the light of Wicliffe in England, and the suppression of the Lollards in Scotland! And when in Providence some causes began to operate that seemed to have a bearing on the desired consummation, such as the invention of printing, the revival of learning, and the love of freedom, how feebly they seemed to operate in opposition to that overwhelming force which the Papacy had been accumulating for centuries, and which nothing seemed able to touch! But when Luther appeared, nailed his theses to the door of the church at Wittenberg, and took up the bold attitude of an out-and-out opponent to Rome, in one hour the Church was struck as with an earthquake; it reeled to its foundations, and half of the proud structure fell. The conflict with American slavery, how slowly it advanced for many a year, nay, at times it seemed to be even losing ground; till in the midst of the great Civil War the President signed a certain proclamation, and in one moment American slavery received its death blow. An eminent historian of England has a striking picture of the slow, steady, awful triumph of iniquity in the career of Cardinal Wolsey, and the sudden collapse of the structure built up so carefully by that wicked man. Speaking of the final retribution, he says: "The time of reckoning at length was arrived. Slowly had the hand crawled along the dial plate, slowly as if the event would never come, and wrong was heaped on wrong, and oppression cried, and it seemed as if no ear had heard its voice, till the measure of the wickedness was at length fulfilled; the finger touched the hour, and as the strokes of the great hammer rang out above the nation, in an instant the mighty fabric of iniquity was shivered to ruins."

It is the prerogative of faith to believe that the same law of Providence is ever in operation, and that the rapidity with which some great drama is to be wound up may be as striking as the slowness of its movement was trying in its earlier stages. May we not be living in an age destined to furnish another great example of this law? The years as they pass seem laden with great events, and we seem to hear the angel that hath power over fire calling to the angel with the sharp sickle,—"Thrust in thy sharp sickle, and gather the clusters of the vine of the earth, for the grapes thereof are fully ripe." We cannot tell but before a year ends some grand purpose of Providence shall be accomplished, the death blow given to some system of force or of fraud that has scourged the earth for centuries, or some great prophetic cycle completed for which Simeons and Annas have been watching more than they that watch for the morning. God hasten the day when on every side truth shall finally triumph over error, good over evil, peace over strife, love over selfishness, and order over confusion; and when from every section of God's great but scattered family the shout of triumph shall go up, "Alleluia: for the Lord God omnipotent reigneth."

But let us return to the narrative of the fall of Jericho, and advert to two of the difficulties that have occurred to many minds in connection with it; one of comparatively little moment, but another of far more serious import.

The lesser difficulty is connected with the order to march round Jericho for seven successive days. Was it not contrary to the spirit of the law to make no difference on the Sabbath? As the narrative reads we are led to think that the Sabbath was the last of the seven days, in which case, instead of a cessation of labour, there was an increase of it sevenfold. Possibly this may be a mistake; but at the least it seems as if, all days being treated alike, there was a neglect of the precept, "In it thou shalt not do any work."

To this it has usually been replied that the law of the Sabbath being only a matter of arrangement, and not founded on any unchangeable obligation, it was quite competent for God to suspend it or for a time repeal it, if occasion required. The present instance has been viewed as one of those exceptional occasions when the obligation to do no work was suspended for a time. But this is hardly a satisfactory explanation. Was it likely that immediately after God had so solemnly charged Joshua respecting the book of the law, that it was "not to depart out of his mouth, but he was to meditate therein day and night, to observe to do according to all that was written therein," that almost on the first occurrence of a public national interest He would direct him to disregard the law of the Sabbath? Or was it likely that now that the people were about to get possession of the land, under the most sacred obligation to frame both their national and their personal life by the Divine law, one of the most outstanding requirements of that law should be even temporarily superseded? We cannot help thinking that it is in another direction that we must look for the solution of this difficulty.

And what seems the just explanation is, that this solemn procession of the ark was really an act of worship, a very public and solemn act of worship, and that therefore the labour which it involved was altogether justifiable, just as the Sabbath labour involved in the offering of the daily sacrifices could not be objected to. It was a very solemn and open demonstration of honour to that great Being in whom Israel trusted—of obedience to His word, and unfaltering confidence that He would show Himself the God of His chosen people. At every step of their march they might well have sung—"I will lift up mine eyes unto the hills, from whence cometh my help." The absurdity of their proceeding to the eye of flesh invested with a high sanctity, because it testified to a conviction that the presence of that God who dwelt symbolically in the ark would more than compensate for all the feebleness and even apparent silliness of the plan. It was indeed an exception to the usual way of keeping the Sabbath, but an exception that maintained and exalted the honour of God. And, in a sense, it might be called resting, inasmuch as no aggressive operations of any kind were carried on; it was simply a waiting on God, waiting till He should arise out of His place, and cause it to be seen that "Israel got not the land in possession by their own sword, neither did their own arm save them: but Thy right hand, and Thine arm, and the light of Thy countenance, because Thou hadst a favour unto them" (Psalm xliv. 3).

A more serious objection in the eyes of many is that which is founded on the promiscuous massacre of the people of Jericho, which, according to the narrative, the Israelites were ordered to make. And it is not wonderful that, with the remarkable sense of the sanctity of human life attained in our country and in our age, and the intense horror which we have at scenes of blood and death, the idea of this slaughter should excite a strong feeling of repugnance. For in truth human life has never been held so sacred among men as it is in these our days and in this our island, where by the mercy of God war and bloodshed have been unknown for nearly a century and a half. We must remember that three thousand years ago, and in the tumultuous regions of the East, such a sentiment was unknown. The massacre of one tribe by another was an event of frequent occurrence, and so little thought of that a year or two after its occurrence the survivors of the massacre might be found on perfectly good terms with those who had committed it. This of course does not affect the righteousness of the sentence executed on the men of Jericho, but it shows that as executioners of that sentence the Israelites were not exposed either to the harrowing or the hardening influence which would now be inseparable from such a work.

We reserve the general question for consideration further on.* We confine ourselves for the present to the inquiry, Why was Jericho singled out for treatment so specially severe? Not only were all its inhabitants put to the sword, as indeed the inhabitants of other cities were too, but the city was burnt with fire, and a special curse was pronounced upon any one that should set up its gates and its walls. Of only two other cities do we read that they were destroyed in this way —Ai and Hazor (viii. 28, xi. 13). And in regard to all the three we may see special considerations dictating Joshua's course. Jericho and Ai were the first two cities taken by him, and it may have been useful to set an example of severity in their case. Hazor was the centre of a conspiracy, and being situated in the extreme north, its fate might read a lesson to those who were too far from Jericho and Ai to see what had happened there. But in the case of Jericho there was another consideration. Gilgal, which Joshua had made his headquarters, was but three or four miles distant. At that place there were no doubt gathered a great part of the flocks and herds of the Israelites, with the women and children, as well as the ark and the sacred tabernacle. It was necessary to prevent the possibility of a fortress being again erected at Jericho. For if it should fall into the enemy's hands, it would endanger the very existence of Gilgal. We shall see in the after part of the narrative that the policy of sparing the towns even when the inhabitants were destroyed proved a mistake, and was very disastrous to the Israelites. We shall find that in very many cases, while Joshua was occupied elsewhere, the towns were taken possession of anew by the Canaanites, and new troubles befell the Israelites. For Joshua's conquest was not a complete subjugation, and much remained to be done by each tribe in its settlement in order to get quit of the old inhabitants. It was the failure of most of the tribes to do their part in this process that led to most of the troubles in the future history of Israel, both in the way of temptation to idolatry and in the form of actual war.

The only things saved from utter destruction at Jericho were the gold and the silver and other metallic substances, which were put into the treasury of the house of the Lord. The fact that the "house of the Lord," situated at this time at Gilgal, was an establishment of such size as to be able to employ all these things in its service refutes the assertion of those critics who would make out that at the settlement in Canaan there was no place that might be called emphatically "*the* house of the Lord." It indicates that the arrangements for worship were on a large scale, —a fact which is confirmed afterwards by the circumstance that the Gibeonites were assigned by Joshua to be "hewers of wood and drawers of water *for the house of my God*." If little is said about the arrangements for worship in the Book of Joshua, it is because the one object of the book is to record the settlement of the nation in the country. If it were true that the book was overhauled by some priestly writer who took every opportunity of magnifying his office, he must have done his work in a strange manner. We find in it such hints as we have noticed showing that the service of the sanctuary was not neglected, but we have none of those full or formal details that would have been given if a

* See chapter xxxi., "Jehovah the Champion of Israel."

writer with such a purpose had worked over the book.

We hear of Jericho from time to time as a place of abode both in the Old Testament and in the New; but when Hiel the Bethelite rebuilt it with walls and gates, "he laid the foundation thereof in Abiram his firstborn, and set up the gates thereof in his youngest son Segub, according to the word of the Lord, which He spake by Joshua the son of Nun" (1 Kings xvi. 34). It was ordained that that first fortress which had withstood the people of God on the west of Jordan should remain a perpetual desolation. As the stones set up in the channel and on the banks of the river witnessed to future generations of God's care for His own people, so the stones of Jericho cast down and lying in ruined heaps were designed to testify to the dread retribution that overtook the guilty. The two great lessons of Providence from Jericho are, the certainty of the reward of faith and obedience on the one hand, and of the punishment of wickedness on the other. The words which Balaam had proclaimed from the top of the mountain on the other side now received their first fulfilment:

"How goodly are thy tents, O Jacob,
Thy tabernacles, O Israel! . . . .
God bringeth him forth out of Egypt;
He hath, as it were, the strength of the wild ox;
He shall eat up the nations his adversaries,
And shall break their bones in pieces,
And smite them through with His arrows."

CHAPTER XIII.

RAHAB SAVED.

Joshua vi. 17, 22-25.

It has not been the lot of Rahab to share the devout interest which has been lavished on Mary Magdalene. Our Correggios, Titians, and Carlo Dolcis have not attempted to represent the spirit of contrition and devotion transfiguring the face of the Canaanite girl. And this is not surprising. Rahab had never seen the human face of Jesus, nor heard the words that dropped like honey from His lips. She had never come under that inexpressible charm which lay in the bearing of the living Jesus, the charm that made so remarkable a change not only on the "woman that was a sinner," but on Zaccheus, on Peter in the high priest's hall, on the penitent thief, and on Saul of Tarsus on the way to Damascus. For there was a wonderful power in the very looks and tones of Jesus to touch the heart, and thereby to throw a new light on all one's past life, making sin look black and odious, and inspiring an intense desire for resemblance to Him who was so much fairer than all the children of men. Rahab had never seen the Divine image in any purer form than it appeared in Joshua and men and women like-minded with him.

But though she was not one of those whose contrite and holy love painters delight to represent, she belonged to the same order, and in some respects is more remarkable than any of the New Testament penitents. For her light was much dimmer than theirs who lived in the days of the Son of man. She was utterly without support or sympathy from those among whom she lived, for with the exception of her own relations, who seem to have been influenced by herself, not a creature in Jericho shared her faith, or showed the slightest regard for the God of Israel.

But the time has now come for her to reap the reward of her faith and its works. In her case there was but a short interval between the sowing and the reaping. And God showed Himself able to do in her exceeding abundantly above what she could ask or think. For she was not only protected when Jericho and all its people were destroyed, but incorporated with the children of Israel. She became an heir of Abraham's blessing; she came among those "to whom pertained the adoption, and the glory, and the covenants, and the giving of the law, and the service of God, and the promises." An old tradition made her the wife of Joshua, but, according to the genealogies she married Salmon (Matt. i. 5), prince of the imperial tribe of Judah, great-grandfather of David, and ancestor of the Messiah. In the golden roll of the eleventh chapter of Hebrews, she is the only woman who shares with Sarah, the great mother of the nation, the honour of a place among the heroes of the faith. Such honours could not have been attained by her had she not been a changed character,—one of those who erewhile "had lain among the pots, but who became like the wings of a dove covered with silver and her feathers with yellow gold."

Very special mention is made of her in the narrative of the destruction of Jericho. In the first place, before the overthrow of the city, Joshua gives particular instructions regarding her, accepting very readily the promise that had been made to her by the two spies. If Joshua had been a man of unreasonable temper, he might have refused to ratify their action in her case. He might have said that God had doomed the whole inhabitants of the city to destruction, and as no instructions had been given by Him to spare Rahab, she must share the doom of the rest. But Joshua at once recognised the propriety of an exception in favour of one who had shown such faith, and who had rendered such service to the spies and to the nation; and, moreover, he looked on the promise made by the spies as reasonable, for it would have been gross tyranny to send them on such an errand without power to make fair compensation for any assistance they might receive. Yet how often have promises made in danger been broken when the danger was past! Rahab must have known that had it been some Canaanite chief and not Joshua that had to decide her fate, he would have scorned the promise of the spies, and consigned her to the general doom. She must have been impressed with the honourable conduct of Joshua in so cordially endorsing the promise of the spies, and thought well of his religion on that account. Honour and religion go well together; meanness and religion breed contempt. We see meanness with a religious profession culminating in the treachery of Judas. We see honour in alliance with religion culminating in the Garden of Gethsemane, when the bleeding Sufferer rallied His fainting courage and stood firm to His undertaking—"The cup which My Father hath given Me, shall I not drink it?"

No doubt the scarlet cord was hung from her window, as had been arranged with the spies, and the Israelites, when they saw it, would be reminded of the blood of the lamb sprinkled on their door posts and lintels when the destroying angel passed through Egypt. It was the two men who had acted as spies that Joshua instructed to enter her house, and bring out the woman and all that she had. And a happy woman she no doubt was when she saw the faces of her old guests, and under their protection was brought out with all her kindred and all that she had and led to a place of safety. It is a blessed time, after you have stood fast to duty while many have failed, when the hour comes that brings you peace and blessing, while it carries confusion and misery to the faithless. How thankful one is at such a moment for the grace that enabled one to choose the right! With what awe one looks into the gulf on whose edge one stood, and thanks God for the grace that brought the victory! And how often is the welfare of a lifetime secured in some crisis by the firm attitude of an hour. What do we not gain by patience when we do the right and wait for the reward? One of the pictures in the Interpreter's House is that of "a little room where sat two little children, each in his chair. The name of the eldest was Passion, and of the other Patience. Passion seemed much discontent, but Patience was very quiet. Then asked Christian, What is the reason of the discontent of Passion? The Interpreter answered, The Governor of them would have them stay for his best things till the beginning of the next year; but he will have them all now; but Patience is willing to wait." How invaluable is the spirit that can wait till the beginning of the next year! And especially with reference to the awards of eternity. The rush for good things now, the desire at all hazards to gratify inclination as it rises, the impatience that will not wait till next year—how many lives they wreck, what misery they gender for eternity! But when you do choose that good part that shall not be taken away, and count all things but loss for the excellency of the knowledge of Christ Jesus, what ecstatic bliss you make sure of in that solemn hour when the dead, small and great, shall stand before God; and, amid weeping and wailing inexpressible on the left hand, the Judge shall pronounce the words, "Come, ye blessed of My Father, inherit the kingdom prepared for you from the foundation of the world."

The case of Rahab was one of those where whole families were saved on account of the faith of one member. Such was the case of Noah, whose faith secured the exemption of himself and all his family from the flood. Such, hypothetically, was the case of Lot, whose whole family would have been preserved from the fire and brimstone, if only they had received his warning and left Sodom with him. On the other hand, there were cases, like that of Korah in the wilderness, and of Achan, near this very place, Jericho, where the sin of the father involved the death of the whole family. In the case of Rahab, we find a family saved, not through the faith of the head of the house, but of a member of it, and that member a woman. The head of a Hebrew house was eminently a representative man, and by a well-understood and recognised law his family were implicated in his acts, whether for good or for evil. But in this case the protector of the family, the member of it that determines the fate of the whole, is not the one whom the law recognises, but his child, his daughter. A woman occupies here a higher and more influential place, in relation to the rest of the family, than she has ever held at any previous time. The incident comes in as a kind of foreshadow of what was to be abundantly verified in after times. For it is in Christian times that woman has most conspicuously attained that position of high influence on the welfare of the family, and especially its eternal welfare, which Rahab showed in delivering her house from the destruction of Jericho.

At a very early period in the history of the Christian Church, the great influence of godly women on the welfare of their male relations began to be seen. About the fourth century we can hardly peruse the biography of any eminent Christian father, without being struck with the share which the prayers and efforts of some pious female relative had in his conversion. Monica, the mother of Augustine, is held in reverence all over Christendom for her tears and wrestling prayers on behalf of her son; and the name of Anthusa, the mother of Chrysostom, is hardly less venerable. Nonna, the mother of Gregory Nazianzen; Macrina and Emmelia, the mother and the grandmother of Basil the Great and Gregory of Nyssa, as well as their sister, also called Macrina; Theosebia too, the wife of Gregory, and Marallina, the sister of Ambrose, all share a similar renown. And in more recent times, how many are the cases where sisters and daughters have exercised a blessed influence on brothers and fathers! Every right-hearted sister has a peculiarly warm and tender interest in the welfare of her brothers. It is a feeling not to be neglected, but carefully nursed and deepened. This narrative shows it to be in the line of God's providence that sisters and daughters shall prove instruments of deliverance to their relations. It is blessed when they are so even in earthly things, but far more glorious when, through faith and prayer and unwearied interest, they are enabled to win them to Christ, and turn them into living epistles for Him.

It can hardly be necessary to dwell at length on the commentary which we find in the Epistle of James on the faith of Rahab. For it is not so much anything personal to her that he handles, but an important quality of all true faith, and of her faith as being true. "Was not Rahab the harlot justified by works when she had received the messengers, and had sent them out another way?" No intelligent person needs to be told that the view of justification here given is in no wise at variance with that of St. Paul. Paul's doctrine was propounded in the early years of the Church, when, in opposition to the notion prevalent among the Gentiles, it was necessary to show clearly that there was no justifying merit in works. The doctrine of James was propounded at a later period, when men, presuming on free grace, were beginning to get lax in their practice, and it was necessary to insist that faith could not be true faith if it was not accompanied by corresponding works. The case of Rahab is employed by St. James to illustrate this latter position. If Rahab had merely professed belief in the God of Israel as the only true God, and in the certainty that Israel would possess the land, according to God's promise, her faith would have been a barren or dead faith; in other words, it would have been no true faith at all. It was her taking up the cause of the spies, protecting them, endangering her life for them, and then devising and executing a scheme for their safety, that showed her faith to be living, and therefore real. Let it be true that faith is only the instrument of justification, that it possesses no merit, and that its value lies solely in its uniting us to Christ, so that we get justification and all other blessings from Him; still that which really unites us to Christ must be living. Dr. Chalmers used to sum up the whole doctrine in the formula, "We are justified by faith alone, but not by a faith which is alone."

But let us now advert to the reception of Rahab into the nation and church of the Israelites. "They brought out all her kindred, and left them without the camp of Israel... And Joshua saved Rahab the harlot alive, and her father's household, and all that she had; and she dwelleth in Israel even unto this day; because she hid the messengers which Joshua sent to spy out Jericho." First, they left them without the camp. At first they could be treated only as unclean until the rites of purification should be performed. In the case of Rahab this was doubly necessary—owing to her race, and owing to her life. Thereafter they were admitted to the commonwealth of Israel, and had an interest in the covenants of promise. The ceremonial purification and the formal admission signified little, except in so far as they represented the washing of regeneration and the renewal of the Holy Ghost. Whether this vital change took place we are not told, but we seem justified in inferring it both from what we read in Hebrews and from the fact that Rahab was one of the ancestors of our Lord. It is interesting and instructive to think of her as exemplifying that law of grace by which the door of heaven is flung open even to the vilest sinner. "Where sin abounded grace did much more abound." When the enemy ensnares a woman, wiles her into the filthiest chambers of sin, and so enchains her there that she cannot escape, but must sink deeper and deeper in the mire, the case is truly hopeless. More rapidly and more thoroughly than in the case of a man, the leprosy spreads till every virtuous principle is rooted out, and every womanly feeling is displaced by the passions of a sensual reprobate. "Son of man, can these bones live?" Is there any art to breathe the breath of purity and pure love into that defiled soul? Can such a woman ever find her home on the mountains of spices, and hear a loving bridegroom say, "My love, my undefiled is but one"? It is just here that the religion of the Bible achieves its highest triumphs. We say the religion of the Bible, but we should rather say, that gracious Being whose grace the Bible unfolds. "The things that are impossible with men are possible with God." Jesus Christ is the prince of life. Experience of His saving grace, living fellowship with Him, can so change "fornicators and idolaters, and adulterers and effeminate and abusers of themselves with mankind, and thieves and covetous and drunkards and revilers and extortioners," that it may be said of them, "But ye are washed, but ye are sanctified, but ye are justified in the name of the Lord Jesus, and by the Spirit of our God." Living faith in a living and loving Saviour can do all things.

Ten thousand times has this truth been illustrated in evangelistic addresses, in sermons, and in tracts innumerable from the case of the prodigal son. And what imagination can estimate the good which that parable has done? In this point of view it is strange that little use has been made of an Old Testament passage, in which the same truth is unfolded with touching beauty from the case of a faithless woman. We refer to the second chapter of Hosea. It is the case of a guilty and apparently shameless wife. Impelled by greed, meanest of all motives, she has gone after this lover and that, because they seemed able to gratify her love of finery and luxury, and all the vain show of the world. But the time comes when her eyes are opened, her lovers are brought to desolation, she sees that they have all been a lie and a deception, and that no real good has ever come to her save from the husband whom she has forsaken and insulted. And now when she turns to him she is simply overwhelmed by his graciousness and generosity. He does all that can be done to make her forget her past miseries, all her past life, and he succeeds. The valley of Achor becomes a door of hope; she is so transformed inwardly, and her outward surroundings are so changed, that "she sings as in the days of her youth." The happy feelings of her unpolluted childhood return to her, as if she had drunk the waters of Lethe, and she sings like a light-hearted girl once more. The allegory is hardly an allegory,—it is Divine love that has effected the change; that love that many waters cannot quench and floods cannot drown.

We wonder whether Rahab obtained much help in her new life from the fellowship of those among whom she came when she joined the Church. If the Church then was what the Church ever ought to be, if its outstanding members were like the three fair damsels, Prudence, Piety, and Charity, in the Palace Beautiful, no doubt she would be helped greatly. But it is not very often that that emblem is realised. And strange to say, among the members of our Churches now, we usually find a very imperfect sense of the duty which they owe to those who come among them from without, and especially out of great wickedness. It is quite possible that Rahab was chilled by the coldness of some of her Hebrew sisters, looking on her as an intruder, looking on her as a reprobate, and grieved because their select society was broken in upon by this outlandish woman. And it is quite possible that she was disappointed to find that, though they were nominally the people of God, there was very little of what was divine or heavenly about them. So it often happens that what ought to be the greatest attraction in a Church, the character of its members, is the greatest repellent. If all sin-worn and world-worn souls, weary of the world's ways, and longing for a society more loving, more generous, more pure, more noble, could find in the Christian Church their ideal fulfilled, could find in the fellowship of Christians the reality of their dreams, how blessed would be the result! Alas, in too many cases they find the world's bitterness and meanness and selfishness reproduced under the flag of Christ! If all so-called Christians, it has been said, should live for but one year in accordance with the thirteenth chapter of 1st Corinthians, unbelief would vanish. Will the day ever be when every one that names the name of Christ shall be a living epistle, known and read of all men?

But, however she may have been affected by the spirit of those among whom she came, Rahab undoubtedly attained to a good degree before God, and a place of high honour in the Hebrew community. It was well for her that what at first arrested and impressed her was not anything in the people of Israel; it was the glorious attributes of their God. For this would preserve her substantially from disappointment. Men might change, or they might pass away, but God remained the same yesterday and to-day and for ever. If she kept looking to Him, admiring His grace and power, and drawing from His inexhaustible fulness, she would be able to verify one at least of the prophet's pictures: " Cursed be the man that trusteth in man, and maketh flesh his arm, and whose heart departeth from the Lord: for he shall be like the heath in the desert, and shall not see when good cometh; but shall inhabit the parched places in the wilderness, in a salt land and not inhabited. Blessed is the man that trusteth in the Lord, and whose hope the Lord is: for he shall be as a tree planted by the waters, and that spreadeth out her roots by the river, and shall not see when heat cometh, but her leaf shall be green; and shall not be careful in the year of drought, neither shall cease from yielding fruit."

CHAPTER XIV.

ACHAN'S TRESPASS.

JOSHUA vii.

A VESSEL in full sail scuds merrily over the waves. Everything betokens a successful and delightful voyage. The log has just been taken, marking an extraordinary run. The passengers are in the highest spirits, anticipating an early close of the voyage. Suddenly a shock is felt, and terror is seen on every face. The ship has struck on a rock. Not only is progress arrested, but it will be a mercy for crew and passengers if they can escape with their lives.

Not often so violently, but often as really, progress is arrested in many a good enterprise that seemed to be prospering to a wish. There may be no shock, but there is a stoppage of movement. The vital force that seemed to be carrying it on towards the desired consummation declines, and the work hangs fire. A mission, that in its first stages was working out a beautiful transformation, becomes languid and advances no further. A Church, eminent for its zeal and spirituality, comes down to the ordinary level, and seems to lose its power. A family that promised well in infancy and childhood fails of its promise, its sons and daughters waver and fall. A similar result is often found in the undertakings of common life. Something mysterious arrests progress in business or causes a decline. In " enterprises of great pith and moment," " the currents turn awry, and lose the name of action."

In all such cases we naturally wonder what can be the cause. And very often our explanation is wide of the mark. In religious enterprises, we are apt to fall back on the sovereignty and inscrutability of God. " He moves in a mysterious way, His wonders to perform." It seems good to Him, for unknown purposes of His own, to subject us to disappointment and trial. We do not impugn either His wisdom or His goodness; all is for the best. But, for the most part, we fail to detect the real reason. That the fault should lie with ourselves is the last thing we think of. We search for it in every direction rather than at home. We are ingenious in devising far-off theories and explanations, while the real offender is close at hand— "*Israel hath sinned.*"

It was an unexpected obstacle of this kind that Joshua now encountered in his next step towards possessing the land. Let us endeavour to understand his position and his plan. Jericho lay in the valley of the Jordan, and its destruction secured nothing for Joshua save the possession of that low-lying valley. From the west side of the valley rose a high mountain wall, which had to be ascended in order to reach the plateau of Western Palestine. Various ravines or passes ran down from the plateau into the valley; at the top of one of these, a little to the north of Jericho, was Bethel, and farther down the pass, nearer the plain, the town or village of Ai. No remains of Ai are now visible, nor is there any tradition of the name, so that its exact position cannot be ascertained. It was an insignificant place, but necessary to be taken, in order to give Joshua command of the pass, and enable him to reach the plateau above. The plan of Joshua seems to have been to gain command of the plateau about this point, and thereby, as it were, cut the country in two, so that he might be able to deal in succession with its southern and its northern sections. If once he could establish himself in the very centre of the country, keeping his communications open with the Jordan valley, he would be able to deal with his opponents in detail, and thus prevent those in the one section from coming to the assistance of the other. Neither Ai nor Bethel seemed likely to give him trouble; they were but insignificant places, and a very small force would be sufficient to deal with them.

Hitherto Joshua had been eminently successful, and his people too. Not a hitch had occurred in all the arrangements. The capture of Jericho had been an unqualified triumph. It seemed as if the people of Ai could hardly fail to be paralysed by its fate. After reconnoitring Ai, Joshua saw that there was no need for mustering the whole host against so poor a place—a detachment of two or three thousand would be enough. The three thousand went up against it as confidently as if success were already in their hands. It was probably a surprise to find its people making any attempt to drive them off. The men of Israel were not prepared for a vigorous onslaught, and when it came thus unexpectedly they were taken aback and fled in confusion. As the men of Ai pursued them down the pass, they had no power to rally or retrieve the battle; the rout was complete, some of the men were killed, while consternation was carried into the host, and their whole enterprise seemed doomed to failure.

And now for the first time Joshua appears in a somewhat humiliating light. He is not one of the men that never make a blunder. He rends his clothes, falls on his face with the elders before the ark of the Lord till even, and puts dust upon his head. There is something too abject in this prostration. And when he speaks to God, it is in the tone of complaint and in the language of unbelief. " Alas, O Lord God, wherefore hast Thou at all brought this people over Jordan, to deliver us into the hand of the Amorites, to destroy us? would to God we had been content, and dwelt on the other side Jordan!

O Lord, what shall I say, when Israel turneth their backs before their enemies! For the Canaanites and all the inhabitants of the land shall hear of it, and shall environ us round, and cut off our name from the earth: and what wilt Thou do unto Thy great name?" Thus Joshua almost throws the blame on God. He seems to have no idea that it may lie in quite another quarter. And very strangely, he adopts the very tone and almost the language of the ten spies, against which he had protested so vehemently at the time: "Would God that we had died in the land of Egypt, or would God we had died in this wilderness! And wherefore hath the Lord brought us unto this land, to fall by the sword, that our wives and our children should be a prey?" What has become of all your courage, Joshua, on that memorable day? Is this the man to whom God said so lately, "Be strong, and of good courage; as I was with Moses, so I will be with thee. I will not fail thee nor forsake thee"? Like Peter on the waters, and like so many of ourselves, he begins to sink when the wind is contrary, and his cry is the querulous wail of a frightened child! After all he is but flesh and blood.

Now it is God's turn to speak. "Get thee up; wherefore liest thou thus upon thy face?" Why do you turn on Me as if I had suddenly changed, and become forgetful of My promise? Alas, my friends, how often is God slandered by our complaints! How often do we feel and even speak as if He had broken His word and forgotten His promise, as if He had induced us to trust in Him, and accept His service, only to humiliate us before the world, and forsake us in some great crisis! No wonder if God speak sharply to Joshua, and to us if we go in Joshua's steps. No wonder if He refuse to be pleased with our prostration, our wringing of our hands and sobbing, and calls us to change our attitude. "Get thee up; wherefore liest thou thus upon thy face?"

Then comes the true explanation—"Israel hath sinned." Might you not have divined that this was the real cause of your trouble? Is not sin directly or indirectly the cause of all trouble? What was it that broke up the joy and peace of Paradise? Sin. What brought the flood of waters over the face of the earth to destroy it? Sin. What caused the confusion of Babel and scattered the inhabitants over the earth in hostile races? Sin. What brought desolation on that very plain of Jordan, and buried its cities and its people under an avalanche of fire and brimstone? Sin. What caused the defeat of Israel at Hormah forty years ago, and doomed all the generation to perish in the wilderness? Sin. What threw down the walls of Jericho only a few days ago, gave its people to the sword of Israel, and reduced its homes and its bulwarks to the mass of ruins you see *there?* Again, sin. Can you not read the plainest lesson? Can you not divine that this trouble which has come on you is due to the same cause with all the rest? And if it be a first principle of Providence that all trouble is due to sin, would it not be more suitable that you and your elders should now be making diligent search for it, and trying to get it removed, than that you should be lying on your faces and howling to me, as if some sudden caprice or unworthy humour of mine had brought this distress upon you?

"Behold, the Lord's ear is not heavy that it cannot hear, nor His arm shortened that it cannot save. But your iniquities have separated between you and your God." What a curse that sin is, in ways and forms, too, which we do not suspect! And yet we are usually so very careless about it. How little pains we take to ascertain its presence, or to drive it away from among us! How little tenderness of conscience we show, how little burning desire to be kept from the accursed thing! And when we turn to our opponents and see sin in them, instead of being grieved, we fall on them savagely to upbraid them, and we hold them up to open scorn. How little we think if they are guilty, that their sin has intercepted the favour of God, and involved not them only, but probably the whole community in trouble! How unsatisfactory to God must seem the bearing even of the best of us in reference to sin! Do we really think of it as the object of God's abhorrence? As that which destroyed Paradise, as that which has covered the earth with lamentation and mourning and woe, kindled the flames of hell, and brought the Son of God to suffer on the cross? If only we had some adequate sense of sin should we not be constantly making it our prayer—" Search me, O God, and know my heart; try me, and know my thoughts; and see if there be any wicked way in me, and lead me in the way everlasting"?

The peculiar covenant relation in which Israel stood to God caused a method to be fallen on for detecting their sin that is not available for us. The whole people were to be assembled next morning, and inquiry was to be made for the delinquent in God's way, and when the individual was found condign punishment was to be inflicted. First the tribe was to be ascertained, then the family, then the man. For this is God's way of tracking sin. It might be more pleasant to us that He should deal with it more generally, and having ascertained, for example, that the wrong had been done by a particular tribe or community, inflict a fine or other penalty on that tribe in which we should willingly bear our share. For it does not grieve us very much to sin when every one sins along with us. Nay, we can even make merry over the fact that we are all sinners together, all in the same condemnation, in the same disgrace. But it is a different thing when we are dealt with one by one. The tribe is taken, the family is taken, but that is not all; the household that God shall take shall come MAN BY MAN! It is that individualising of us that we dread; it is when it comes to that, that "conscience makes cowards of us all." When a sinner is dying, he becomes aware that this individualising process is about to take place, and hence the fear which he often feels. He is no longer among the multitude, death is putting him by himself, and God is coming to deal with him by himself. If he could only be hid in the crowd it would not matter, but that searching eye of God—who can stand before it? What will all the excuses or disguises or glosses he can devise avail before Him who "sets our iniquities before Him, our secret sins in the light of His countenance"? "Neither is there any creature that is not manifest in His sight; for all things are naked, and opened unto the eyes of Him with whom we have to do." Happy, in that hour, they who have found the Divine covering for sin: " Blessed is he whose transgression is forgiven, whose sin is covered. Blessed is the man to whom the Lord imputeth not iniquity, and in whose spirit there is no guile."

But before passing on to the result of the scrutiny, we find ourselves face to face with a difficult question. If, as is here intimated, it was one man that sinned, why should the whole nation have been dealt with as guilty? Why should the historian, in the very first verse of this chapter, summarise the transaction by saying: " But the *children of Israel* committed a trespass in the devoted thing: for *Achan*, the son of Carmi, the son of Zabdi, the son of Zerah, of the tribe of Judah, took of the devoted thing; and the anger of the Lord was kindled against the children of Israel"? Why visit the offence of Achan on the whole congregation, causing a peculiarly humiliating defeat to take place before an insignificant enemy, demoralising the whole host, driving Joshua to distraction, and causing the death of six-and-thirty men?

In dealing with a question of this sort, it is indispensable that we station ourselves at that period of the world's history; we must place before our minds some of the ideas that were prevalent at the time, and abstain from judging of what was done then by a standard which is applicable only to our own day.

And certain it is that, what we now call the *solidarity* of mankind, the tendency to look on men rather as the members of a community than as independent individuals, each with an inalienable standing of his own, had a hold of men's minds then such as it has not to-day, certainly among Western nations. To a certain extent, this principle of solidarity is inwoven in the very nature of things, and cannot be eliminated, however we may try. Absolute independence and isolation of individuals are impossible. In families, we suffer for one another's faults, even when we hold them in abhorrence. We benefit by one another's virtues, though we may have done our utmost to discourage and destroy them. In the Divine procedure toward us, the principle of our being a corporate body is often acted upon. The covenant of Adam was founded on it, and the fall of our first parents involved the fall of all their descendants. In the earlier stages of the Hebrew economy, wide scope was given to the principle. It operated in two forms: sometimes the individual suffered for the community, and sometimes the community for the individual. And the operation of the principle was not confined to the Hebrew or to other Oriental communities. Even among the Romans it had a great influence. Admirable though Roman law was in its regulation of property, it was very defective in its dealings with persons. " Its great blot was the domestic code. The son was the property of the father, without rights, without substantial being, in the eye of Roman law. . . The wife again was the property of her husband, an ownership of which the moral result was most disastrous."*

We are to remember that practically the principle of solidarity was fully admitted in Joshua's time among his people. The sense of injustice and hardship to which it might give rise among us did not exist. Men recognised it as a law of wide influence in human affairs, to which they were bound to defer. Hence it was that when it became known that one man's offence lay at the foundation of the defeat before Ai, and of the displeasure of God toward the people at large,

* See Mozley's "Ruling Ideas in the Early Ages," p. 40.

there was no outcry, no remonstrance, no complaint of injustice. This could hardly take place if the same thing were to happen now. It is hard to reconcile the transaction with our sense of justice. And no doubt, if we view the matter apart and by itself, there may be some ground for this feeling. But the transaction will assume another aspect if we view it as but a part of a great whole, of a great scheme of instruction and discipline which God was developing in connection with Israel. In this light, instead of a hardship it will appear that in the end a very great benefit was conferred on the people.

Let us think of Achan's temptation. A large amount of valuable property fell into the hands of the Israelites at Jericho. By a rigorous law, all was devoted to the service of God. Now a covetous man like Achan might find many plausible reasons for evading this law. "What I take to myself (he might say) will never be missed. There are hundreds of Babylonish garments, there are many wedges of gold, and silver shekels without number, amply sufficient for the purpose for which they are devoted. If I were to deprive another man of his rightful share, I should be acting very wickedly; but I am really doing nothing of the kind. I am only diminishing imperceptibly what is to be used for a public purpose. Nobody will suffer a whit by what I do,—it cannot be very wrong."

Now the great lesson taught very solemnly and impressively to the whole nation was, that this was just awfully wrong. The moral benefit which the nation ultimately got from the transaction was, that this kind of sophistry, this flattering unction which leads so many persons ultimately to destruction, was exploded and blown to shivers. A most false mode of measuring the criminality of sin was stamped with deserved reprobation. Every man and woman in the nation got a solemn warning against a common but ruinous temptation. In so far as they laid to heart this warning during the rest of the campaign, they were saved from disastrous evil, and thus, in the long run, they profited by the case of Achan.

That sin is to be held sinful only when it hurts your fellow-creatures, and especially the poor among your fellow-creatures, is a very common impression, but surely it is a delusion of the devil. That it has such effects may be a gross aggravation of the wickedness, but it is not the heart and core of it. And how can you know that it will not hurt others? Not hurt your fellow-countrymen, Achan? Why, that secret sin of yours has caused the death of thirty-six men, and a humiliating defeat of the troops before Ai. More than that, it has separated between the nation and God. Many say, when they tell a lie, it was not a malignant lie, it was a lie told to screen some one, not to expose him, therefore it was harmless. But you cannot trace the consequences of that lie, any more than Achan could trace the consequences of his theft, otherwise you would not dare to make that excuse. Many that would not steal from a poor man, or waste a poor man's substance, have little scruple in wasting a rich man's substance, or in peculating from Government property. Who can measure the evil that flows from such ways of trifling with the inexorable law of right, the damage done to conscience, and the guilt contracted before God? Is there safety for man or woman except in the most rigid regard to right and truth, even in the smallest portions of them with which they have to do? Is there not something utterly fearful in the propagating power of sin, and in its way of involving others, who are perfectly innocent, in its awful doom? Happy they who from their earliest years have had a salutary dread of it, and of its infinite ramifications of misery and woe!

How well fitted for us, especially when we are exposed to temptation, is that prayer of the psalmist: "Who can understand his errors? cleanse Thou me from secret faults. Keep back Thy servant also from presumptuous sins; let them not have dominion over me: then shall I be perfect, and I shall be clear of great transgression."

CHAPTER XV.
ACHAN'S PUNISHMENT.
JOSHUA vii.

"BE sure your sin will find you out." It has an awful way of leaving its traces behind it, and confronting the sinner with his crime. "Though he hide himself in the top of Carmel, I will search and take him out thence; and though he be hid from My sight in the bottom of the sea, thence will I command the serpent, and he shall bite him" (Amos ix. 3). "For God shall bring every work into judgment, with every secret thing, whether it be good, or whether it be evil" (Eccles. xii. 14).

When Achan heard of the muster that was to take place next morning, in order to detect the offender, he must have spent a miserable night. Between the consciousness of guilt, the sense of the mischief he had done, the dread of detection, and the foreboding of retribution, his nerves were too much shaken to admit the possibility of sleep. Weariedly and anxiously he must have tossed about as the hours slowly revolved, unable to get rid of his miserable thoughts, which would ever keep swimming about him like the changing forms of a kaleidoscope, but with the same dark vision of coming doom.

At length the day dawns, the tribes muster, the inquiry begins. It is by the sure, solemn, simple, process of the lot that the case is to be decided. First the lot is cast for the tribes, and the tribe of Judah is taken. That must have given the first pang to Achan. Then the tribe is divided into its families, and the family of the Zarhites is taken; then the Zarhite family is brought out man by man, and Zabdi, the father of Achan, is taken. May we not conceive the heart of Achan giving a fresh beat as each time the casting of the lot brought the charge nearer and nearer to himself? The coils are coming closer and closer about him; and now his father's family is brought out, man by man, and Achan is taken. He is quite a young man, for his father could only have been a lad when he left Egypt. Look at him, pale, trembling, stricken with shame and horror, unable to hide himself, feeling it would be such a relief if the earth would open its jaws and swallow him up, as it swallowed Korah. Look at his poor wife; look at his father; look at his children. What a load of misery he has brought on himself and on them! Yes, the way of transgressors *is* hard.

Joshua's heart is overcome, and he deals gently with the young man. "My son, give, I pray thee, glory to the Lord God of Israel, and make confession unto Him; and tell me now what thou hast done; hide it not from me." There was infinite kindness in that word "my son." It reminds us of that other Joshua, the Jesus of the New Testament, so tender to sinners, so full of love even for those who had been steeped in guilt. It brings before us the Great High Priest, who is touched with the feeling of our infirmities, seeing He was in all things tempted like as we are, yet without sin. A harsh word from Joshua might have set Achan in a defiant attitude, and drawn from him a denial that he had done anything amiss. How often do we see this! A child or a servant has done wrong; you are angry, you speak harshly, you get a flat denial. Or if the thing cannot be denied, you get only a sullen acknowledgment, which takes away all possibility of good arising out of the occurrence, and embitters the relation of the parties to each other.

But not only did Joshua speak kindly to Achan, he confronted him with God, and called on him to think how He was concerned in this matter. "Give glory to the Lord God of Israel." Vindicate Him from the charge which I and others have virtually been bringing against Him, of proving forgetful of His covenant. Clear Him of all blame, declare His Glory, declare that He is unsullied in His perfections, and show that He has had good cause to leave us to the mercy of our enemies. No man as yet knew what Achan had done. He might have been guilty of some act of idolatry, or of some unhallowed sensuality like that which had lately taken place at Baal-peor; in order that the transaction might carry its lesson, it was necessary that the precise offence should be known. Joshua's kindly address and his solemn appeal to Achan to clear the character of God had the desired effect. "Achan answered Joshua, and said, Indeed I have sinned against the Lord God of Israel, and thus and thus have I done: when I saw among the spoils a goodly Babylonish garment, and two hundred shekels of silver, and a wedge of gold of fifty shekels weight, then I coveted them, and took them; and, behold, they are hid in the earth in the midst of my tent, and the silver under it."

The confession certainly was frank and full; but whether it was made in the spirit of true contrition, or whether it was uttered in the hope that it would mitigate the sentence to be inflicted, we cannot tell. It would be a comfort to us to think that Achan was sincerely penitent, and that the miserable doom which befell him and his family ended their troubles, and formed the dark introduction to a better life. Where there is even a possibility that such a view is correct we naturally draw to it, for it is more than our hearts can well bear to think of so awful a death being followed by eternal misery.

Certain it is that Joshua earnestly desired to lead Achan to deal with God in the matter. "Make confession," he said, "unto Him." He knew the virtue of confession to God. For "he that covereth his sins shall not prosper; but whoso confesseth and forsaketh them shall have mercy" (Prov. xxviii. 13). "When I kept silence, my bones waxed old through my roaring all the day... I acknowledged my sin unto Thee, and mine iniquity have I not hid. I said, I will confess my transgressions unto the Lord;

and Thou forgavest the iniquity of my sin" (Psalm xxxii. 3, 5). It is a hopeful circumstance in Achan's case that it was after this solemn call to deal with God in the matter that he made his confession. One hopes that the sudden appearance on the scene of the God whom he had so sadly forgotten, led him to see his sin in its true light, and drew out the acknowledgment,— "Against Thee, Thee only, have I sinned." For no moral effect can be greater than that arising from the difference between sin covered and sin confessed to God. Sin covered is the fruitful parent of excuses, and sophistries, and of all manner of attempts to disguise the harsh features of transgression, and to show that, after all, there was not much wrong in it. Sin confessed to God shows a fitting sense of the evil, of the shame which it brings, and of the punishment which it deserves, and an earnest longing for that forgiveness and renewal which, the gospel now shows us so clearly, come from Jesus Christ. For nothing becomes a sinner before God so well as when he breaks down. It is the moment of a new birth when he sees what miserable abortions all the refuges of lies are, and, utterly despairing of being able to hide himself from God in his filthy rags, unbosoms everything to Him with whom "there is mercy and plenteous redemption, and who will redeem Israel from all his transgressions."

It is a further presumption that Achan was a true penitent, that he told so frankly where the various articles that he had appropriated were to be found. "Behold, they are hid in the midst of my tent." They were scalding his conscience so fearfully that he could not rest till they were taken away from the abode which they polluted and cursed. They seemed to be crying out against him and his with a voice which could not be silenced. To bring them away and expose them to public view might bring no relaxation of the doom which he expected, but it would be a relief to his feelings if they were dragged from the hiding hole to which he had so wickedly consigned them. For the articles were now as hateful to him as formerly they had been splendid and delightful. The curse of God was on them now, and on him too on their account. Is there anything darker or deadlier than the curse of God?

And now the consummation arrives. Messengers are sent to his tent, they find the stolen goods, they bring them to Joshua, and to all the children of Israel, and they lay them out before the Lord. We are not told how the judicial sentence was arrived at. But there seems to have been no hesitation or delay about it. "Joshua and all the children of Israel took Achan the son of Zerah, and the silver, and the garment, and the wedge of gold, and his sons, and his daughters, and his oxen, and his asses, and his sheep, and his tent, and all that he had: and they brought them unto the valley of Achor. And Joshua said, Why hast thou troubled us? the Lord shall trouble thee this day. And all Israel stoned him with stones, and they burned him with fire, after they had stoned them with stones. And they raised over him a great heap of stones unto this day. So the Lord turned from the fierceness of His anger. Therefore the name of that place was called, The valley of Achor, unto this day."

It seems a terrible punishment, but Achan had already brought defeat and disgrace on his countrymen, he had robbed God, and brought the whole community to the brink of ruin. It must have been a strong lust that led him to play with such consequences. What sin is there to which covetousness has not impelled men? And, strange to say, it is a sin which has received but little check from all the sad experience of the past. Is it not as daring as ever to-day? Is it not the parent of that gambling habit which is the terror of all good men, sapping our morality and our industry, and disposing tens of thousands to trust to the bare chance of an unlikely contingency, rather than to God's blessing on honest industry? Is it not sheer covetousness that turns the confidential clerk into a robber of his employer, who uses all the devices of cunning to discover how long he can carry on his infamous plot, till the inevitable day of detection arrive and he must fly, a fugitive and a vagabond, to a foreign land? Is it not covetousness that induces the blithe young maiden to ally herself to one whom she knows to be a moral leper, but who is high in rank and full of wealth? Is it not the same lust that induces the trader to send his noxious wares to savage countries and drive the miserable inhabitants to a deeper misery and degradation than ever? Catastrophes are always happening: the ruined gambler blows out his brains; the dishonest clerk becomes a convict, the unhappy young wife gets into the divorce court, the scandalous trader sinks into bankruptcy and misery. But there is no abatement of the lust which makes such havoc. If the old ways of indulging it are abandoned, new outlets are always being found. Education does not cripple it; civilisation does not uproot it; even Christianity does not always overcome it. It goeth about, if not like a roaring lion, at least like a cunning serpent intent upon its prey. Within the Church, where the minister reads out "Thou shalt not covet," and where men say with apparent devoutness, "Lord, have mercy upon us, and incline our hearts to keep this law" —as soon as their backs are turned, they are scheming to break it. Still, as of old, "love of money is the root of all evil, which while some coveted after they erred from the faith, and pierced themselves through with many sorrows."

Achan's sin has found him out, and he suffers its bitter doom. All his visions of comfort and enjoyment to be derived from his unlawful gain are rudely shattered. The pictures he has been drawing of what he will do with the silver and the gold and the garment are for ever dispersed. He has brought disaster on the nation, and shame and ruin on himself and his house. In all coming time, he must stand in the pillory of history as the man who stole the forbidden spoil of Jericho. That disgraceful deed is the only thing that will ever be known of him. Further, he has sacrificed his life. Young though he is, his life will be cut short, and all that he has hoped for of enjoyment and honour will be exchanged for a horrible death and an execrable memory. O sin, thou art a hard master! Thou draggest thy slaves, often through a short and rapid career, to misery and to infamy!

Nevertheless, the hand of God is seen here. The punishment of sin is one of the inexorable conditions of His government. It may look dark and ugly to us, but it is there. It may create a very different feeling from the contemplation of His love and goodness, but in our present condition that feeling is wholesome and necessary. As we follow unpardoned sinners into the future world, it may be awful, it may be dismal to think of a state from which punishment will never be absent; but the awfulness and the dismalness will not change the fact. It is the mystery of God's character that He is at once infinite love and infinite righteousness. And if it be unlawful for us to exclude His love and dwell only on His justice, it is equally unlawful to exclude His justice and dwell only on His love. Now, as of old, His memorial is, "The Lord, the Lord God merciful and gracious, longsuffering and abundant in mercy and truth, forgiving iniquity and transgression and sin, and that will by no means clear the guilty."

But if it be awful to contemplate the death, and the mode of death of Achan, how much more when we think that his wife and his sons and his daughters were stoned to death along with him! Would that not have been a barbarous deed in any case, and was it not much more so if they were wholly innocent of his offence? To mitigate the harshness of this deed, some have supposed that they were privy to his sin, if not instigators of it. But of this we have not a tittle of evidence, and the whole drift of the narrative seems to show that the household suffered in the same manner and on the same ground as that of Korah (Num. xvi. 31-33). As regards the mode of death, it was significant of a harsh and hard-tempered age. Neither death nor the sufferings of the dying made much impression on the spectators. This callousness is almost beyond our comprehension, the tone of feeling is so different now. But we must accept the fact as it was. And as to the punishment of the wife and children, we must fall back on that custom of the time which not only gave to the husband and father the sole power and responsibility of the household, but involved the wife and children in his doom if at any time he should expose himself to punishment. As has already been said, neither the wife nor the children had any rights as against the husband and father; as his will was the sole law, so his retribution was the common inheritance of all. With him they were held to sin, and with him they suffered. They were considered to belong to him just as his hands and his feet belonged to him. It may seem to us very hard, and when it enters, even in a modified form, into the Divine economy we may cry out against it. Many do still, and ever will cry out against original sin, and against all that has come upon our race in consequence of the sin of Adam.

But it is in vain to fight against so apparent a fact. Much wiser surely it is to take the view of the Apostle Paul, and rejoice that, under the economy of the gospel, the principle of imputation becomes the source of blessing infinitely greater than the evil which it brought at the fall. It is one of the greatest triumphs of the Apostle's mode of reasoning that, instead of shutting his eyes to the law of imputation, he scans it carefully, and compels it to yield a glorious tribute to the goodness of God. When his theme was the riches of the grace of God, one might have thought that he would desire to give a wide berth to that dark fact in the Divine economy—the imputation of Adam's sin. But instead of desiring to conceal it, he brings it forward in all its terribleness and universality of application; but with the skill of a great orator, he turns it round to his side by showing that the imputation of Christ's righteousness has secured results that outdo all the evil flowing from the imputation of Adam's sin. "Therefore as by the offence of one judgment came upon all men to condemnation; even so by the righteousness of one the free gift came upon all men unto justification of life. For as through the one man's disobedience the many were made sinners, even so through the obedience of the one shall the many be made righteous. Moreover the law entered that the offence might abound; but where sin abounded, grace did much more abound: that, as sin reigned in death, even so might grace reign through righteousness unto eternal life, through Jesus Christ our Lord" (Rom. v. 18-21).

Very special mention is made of the place where the execution of Achan and his family took place. "They brought them unto the valley of Achor, . . . and they raised over him a great heap of stones, . . . wherefore the name of that place is called, The valley of Achor, unto this day." Achor, which means *trouble*, seems to have been a small ravine near the lower part of the valley in which Ai was situated, and therefore near the scene of the disaster that befell the Israelites. It was not an old name, but a name given at the time, derived from the occurrence of which it had just been the scene. It seemed appropriate that poor Achan should suffer at the very place where others had suffered on his account. It is subsequently referred to three times in Scripture. Later in this book it is given as part of the northern boundary of the tribe of Judah (chap. xv. 7); in Isaiah (lxv. 10) it is referred to on account of its fertility; and in Hosea (ii. 15) it is introduced in the beautiful allegory of the restored wife, who has been brought into the wilderness, and made to feel her poverty and misery, but of whom God says, "I will give her vineyards from thence, and the valley of Achor for a door of hope." The reference seems to be to the evil repute into which that valley fell by the sin of Achan, when it became the valley of trouble. For, by Achan's sin, what had appeared likely to prove the door of access for Israel into the land was shut; a double trouble came on the people—partly because of their defeat, and partly because their entrance into the land appeared to be blocked. In Hosea's picture of Israel penitent and restored, the valley is again turned to its natural use, and instead of a scene of trouble it again becomes a door of hope, a door by which they may hope to enter their inheritance. It is a door of hope for the penitent wife, a door by which she may return to her lost happiness. The underlying truth is, that when we get into a right relation to God, what were formerly evils become blessings, hindrances are turned into helps. Sin deranges everything, and brings trouble everywhere. The ground was cursed on account of Adam: not literally, but indirectly, inasmuch as it needed hard and exhausting toil, it needed the sweat of his face to make it yield him a maintenance. "We know," says the Apostle, "that the whole creation groaneth and travaileth in pain together until now." "For the creation was subjected to vanity, not of its own will, but by reason of Him who subjected it, in hope that the creation itself also shall be delivered out of the bondage of corruption into the glorious liberty of the children of God."

No man can tell all the "trouble" that has come into the world by reason of sin. As little can we know the full extent of that deliverance that shall take place when sin comes to an end. If we would know anything of this we must go to those passages which picture to us the new heavens and the new earth: " in the midst of the street of it, and on either side of the river, was there the tree of life, which bare twelve manner of fruits, and yielded her fruit every month: and the leaves of the tree were for the healing of the nations. And there shall be no more curse: but the throne of God and of the Lamb shall be in it; and His servants shall serve Him: and they shall see His face; and His name shall be in their foreheads. And there shall be no night there; and they need no candle, neither light of the sun; for the Lord God giveth them light: and they shall reign for ever and ever."

CHAPTER XVI.

THE CAPTURE OF AI.

JOSHUA viii. 1-29.

Joshua, having dealt faithfully with the case of Achan, whose sin had intercepted the favour of God, is again encouraged, and directed to renew, but more carefully, his attack on Ai. That word is addressed to him which has always such significance when coming from the Divine lips— " Fear not." How much of our misery arises from fear! How many a beating heart, how many a shaking nerve, how many a sleepless night have come, not from evil experienced, but from evil apprehended! To save one from the apprehension of evil is sometimes more important, as it is usually far more difficult, than to save one from evil itself. An affectionate father finds that one of his most needed services to his children is to allay their fears. Never is he doing them a greater kindness than when he uses his larger experience of life to assure them, in some anxiety, that there is no cause for fear. Our heavenly Father finds much occasion for a similar course. He has indeed got a very timid family. It is most interesting to mark how the Bible is studded with " fear nots," from Genesis to Revelation; from that early word to Abraham —" Fear not, I am thy shield, and thy exceeding great reward "—to that most comforting assurance to the beloved disciple, " Fear not; I am the first and the last: I am He that liveth, and was dead; and, behold, I am alive for evermore, Amen; and have the keys of hades and of death." If only God's children could hear Him uttering that one word, from how much anxiety and misery would it set them free!

Virtually the command to Joshua is to " try again." Success, though denied to the first effort, often comes to the next, or at least to a subsequent one. Even apart from spiritual considerations, it is those who try oftenest who succeed best. There is little good in a man who abandons an undertaking simply because he has tried once and failed. Who does not recall in this connection the story of Alfred the Great? Or of Robert the Bruce watching the spider in the barn that at last reached the roof after sixteen failures? Or, looking to what has a more immediate bearing on the kingdom of God, who has not admired the perseverance of Livingstone, undaunted by fever and famine, and the ferocity of savage chiefs; unmoved by his longings for home and dreams of plenty and comfort that mocked him when he awoke to physical wretchedness and want? Such perseverance gives a man the stamp of true nobility; we are almost tempted to fall down and worship. If failure be humiliating, it is redeemed by the very act and attitude of perseverance, and the self-denial and scorn of ease which it involves. In the Christian warfare no man is promised victory at the first. " Let us not be weary in well-doing, for in due season we shall reap if we faint not."

To Christian men especially, failure brings very valuable lessons. There is always something to be learned from it. In our first attempt we were too self-confident. We went too carelessly about the matter, and did not sufficiently realise the need of Divine support. Never was there a servant of God who learned more from his failures than St. Peter. Nothing could have been more humiliating than his thrice-repeated denial of his Lord. But when Peter came to himself, he saw on what a bruised reed he had been leaning when he said, " Though I should die with Thee yet will I not deny Thee." How miserably misplaced that self-confidence had been! But it had the effect of startling him, of showing him his danger, and of leading him to lift up his eyes to the hills from whence came his help. It might have seemed a risky, nay reckless thing for our Lord to commit the task of steering His infant Church over the stormy seas of her first voyage to a man who, six weeks before, had proved so weak and treacherous. But Peter was a genuine man, and it was that first failure that afterwards made him so strong. It is no longer Peter, but Christ in Peter that directs the movement. And thus it came to pass that, during the critical period of the Church's birth, no carnal drawback diminished his strength or diluted his faith; all his natural rapidity of movement, all his natural outspokenness, boldness, and directness were brought to bear without abatement on the advancement of the young cause. He conducted himself during this most delicate and vital period with a nobility beyond all praise. He took the ship out into the open sea amid raging storms without touching a single rock. And it was all owing to the fact that by God's grace he profited by his failure!

In the case of Joshua and his people, one of the chief lessons derived from their failure before Ai was the evil of covering sin. Alas, this policy is the cause of failures innumerable in the spiritual life! In numberless ways it interrupts Divine fellowship, withdraws the Divine blessing, and grieves the Holy Spirit. We have not courage to cut off a right hand and pluck out a right eye. We leave besetting sins in a corner of our hearts, instead of trying to exterminate them, and determining not to allow them a foothold there. The acknowledgment of sin, the giving up of all leniency towards it, the determination, by God's grace, to be done with it, always go before true revivals, before a true return of God to us in all His graciousness and power. Rather, we should say, they are the beginning of revival. In Israel of old the land had to be purged of every vestige of idolatry under Hezekiah and other godly kings, before the light of God's countenance was again lifted upon it. " To this man will I look, even to him that is poor and of a contrite spirit, and that trembleth at My word."

Joshua is instructed to go up again against Ai,

but in order to interest and encourage the people, he resorts to a new plan of attack. A stratagem is to be put in operation. An ambuscade is to be stationed on the west side of the city, while the main body of the assaulting force is to approach it, as formerly, from the east. There is some obscurity and apparent confusion in the narrative, confined, however, to one point, the number composing the ambuscade and the main body respectively. Some error in the text appears to have crept in. From the statement in ver. 3 we might suppose that the men who were to lie in ambush amounted to thirty thousand; but in ver. 12 it is expressly stated that only five thousand were employed in this way. There can be little doubt (though it is not according to the letter of the narrative) that the whole force employed amounted to thirty thousand, and that, of these, five thousand formed the ambush. Indeed, in such a valley, it would not have been possible for thirty thousand men to conceal themselves so as to be invisible from the city. It would appear (ver. 17) that the people of Bethel had left their own village and gone into Ai. Bethel, as we have said, was situated higher up; in fact, it was on the very ridge of the plateau of Western Palestine. It must have been but a little place, and its people seem to have deemed it better to join those of Ai, knowing that if the Israelites were repulsed from the lower city, the upper was safe.

The *ruse* was that the ambush should be concealed behind the city; that Ai, as before, should be attacked from the east by the main body of troops; that on receiving the onslaught from the city they should seem to be defeated as before; that Joshua, probably standing on some commanding height, should give a signal to the men in ambush by raising his spear; whereupon these men should rush down on the now deserted place and set it on fire. On seeing the flames, the pursuers would naturally turn and rush back to extinguish them; then the main body of Israel would turn likewise, and thus the enemy would be caught as in a trap from which there was no escape, and fall a victim to the two sections of Israel.

To plots of this kind, the main objection in a strategical sense lies in the risk of detection. For the five thousand who went to station themselves in the west it was a somewhat perilous thing to separate themselves from the host, and place themselves in the heart of enemies both in front and in rear. It needed strong faith to expose themselves in such a situation. Suppose they had been detected as they went stealing along past Ai in the darkness of the night; suppose they had come on some house or hamlet, and wakened the people, so that the alarm should have been carried to Ai, what would have been the result? It was well for Israel that no such mishap occurred, and that they were able in silence to reach a place where they might lie concealed. The ground is so broken by rocks and ravines that this would not have been very difficult; the people of Ai suspected nothing; probably the force on the east were at pains, by camp-fires and otherwise, to engage their attention, and whenever that force began to move, as if for the attack, every eye in the city would be fixed intently upon it.

The plot was entirely successful; everything fell out precisely as Joshua had desired. A terrible slaughter of the men of Ai took place, caught as they were on the east of the city between the two sections of Joshua's troops, for the Israelites gave no quarter either to age or sex. The whole number of the slain amounted to twelve thousand, and that probably included the people of Bethel too. We see from this what an insignificant place Ai must have been, and how very humiliating was the defeat it inflicted at first. With reference to the spoil of the city, the rigid law prescribed at Jericho was not repeated; the people got it for themselves. Jericho was an exceptional case; it was the firstfruits of the conquest, therefore holy to the Lord. If Achan had but waited a little, he would have had his share of the spoil of Ai or some other place. He would have got legitimately what he purloined unlawfully. In the slaughter, the king, or chief of the place, suffered a more ignominious doom than his soldiers; instead of being slain with the sword, he was hanged, and his body was exposed on a tree till sunset. Joshua did not want some drops of Oriental blood; he had the stern pleasure of the Eastern warrior in humbling those who were highest in honour. What remained of the city was burned; it continued thereafter a heap of ruins, with a great cairn of stones at its gate, erected over the dead body of the king.

We see that already light begins to be thrown on what at the time must have seemed the very severe and rigid order about the spoil of Jericho. Although Achan was the only offender, he was probably far from being the only complainer on that occasion. Many another Israelite with a covetous heart must have felt bitterly that it was very hard to be prevented from taking even an atom to oneself. " Were not our fathers allowed to spoil the Egyptians—why, then, should we be absolutely prevented from having a share of the spoil of Jericho?" It might have been enough to answer that God claimed the firstfruits of the land for Himself. Or to say that God designed at the very entrance of His people into Canaan to show that they were not a tumultuous rabble, rushing greedily on all they could lay their hands on, but a well-trained, well-mannered family, in whom self-restraint was one of the noblest virtues. But to all this it might have been added, that the people's day was not far off. It is not God's method to muzzle the ox that treadeth out the corn. And so to all who rush tumultuously upon the good things of this life, He says, " Seek first the kingdom of heaven and His righteousness, and all these things shall be added unto you." Let God arrange the order in which His gifts are distributed. Never hurry Providence, as Sarah did when she gave Hagar to Abraham. Sarah had good cause to repent of her impetuosity; it brought her many a bitter hour. Whereas God was really kinder to her than she had thought, and in due time He gave her Isaac, not the son of the bondwoman, but her own.

A question has been raised respecting the legitimacy of the stratagem employed by Joshua in order to capture Ai. Was it right to deceive the people; to pretend to be defeated while in reality he was only executing a *ruse*, and thus draw on the poor men of Ai to a terrible death? Calvin and other commentators make short work of this objection. If war is lawful, stratagem is lawful. Stratagem indeed, as war used to be conducted, was a principal part of it; and even now the term " strategic," derived from it, is often used to denote operations designed for a different purpose from that which at first appears. It is needless to discuss here the lawfulness of war, for the Israelites were waging war at the express command of the Almighty. And if it be said that when once you allow the principle that it is lawful in war to mislead the enemy, you virtually allow perfidy, inasmuch as it would be lawful for you, after pledging your word under a flag of truce, to disregard your promise, the answer to that is, that to mislead in such circumstances would be infamous. A distinction is to be drawn between acts where the enemy has no right to expect that you will make known your intention, and acts where they have such a right. In the ordinary run of strategic movements, you are under no obligation to tell the foe what you are about. It is part of their business to watch you, to scrutinise your every movement, and in spite of appearances to divine your real purpose. If they are too careless to watch, or too stupid to discern between a professed and a real plan, they must bear the consequences. But when a flag of truce is displayed, when a meeting takes place under its protection, and when conditions are agreed to on both sides, the case is very different. The enemy is entitled now to expect that you will not mislead them. Your word of honour has been passed to that effect. And to disregard that pledge, and deem it smart to mislead thereby, is a proceeding worthy only of the most barbarous, the most perfidious, the most shameless of men.

Thus far we may defend the usages of war; but at best it is a barbarous mode of operation. Very memorable was the observation of the Duke of Wellington, that next to the calamity of suffering a defeat was that of gaining a victory. To look over a great battlefield, fresh from the clash of arms; to survey the trampled crops, the ruined houses, the universal desolation; to gaze on all the manly forms lying cold in death, and the many besides wounded, bleeding, groaning, perhaps dying; to think of the illimitable treasure that has been lavished on this work of destruction and the comforts of which it has robbed the countries engaged; to remember in what a multitude of cases, death must carry desolation and anguish to the poor widow, and turn the remainder of life into a lonely pilgrimage, is enough surely to rob war of the glory associated with it, and to make good the position that on the part of civilised and Christian men it should only be the last desperate resort, after every other means of effecting its object has failed. We are not forgetful of the manly self-sacrifice of those who expose themselves so readily to the risk of mutilation and death, wherever the rulers of their country require it, for it is the redeeming feature of war that it brings out so much of this high patriotic devotion; but surely they are right who deem arbitration the better method of settling national differences; who call for a great disarmament of the European nations, and would put a stop to the attitude of every great country shaking its fist in the face of its neighbours. What has become of the prophecy "They shall beat their swords into ploughshares and their spears into pruning hooks"? Or the beautiful vision of Milton on the birth of the Saviour?—

"No war, or battle's sound,
    Was heard the world around;
The idle spear and shield were high uphung;
    The hookèd chariot stood
    Unstained with hostile blood,
The trumpet spake not to the armèd throng;
And kings sat still with awful eye
As if they surely knew their sovran Lord was by."

One lesson comes to us with pre-eminent force from the operations of war. The activity displayed by every good commander is a splendid example for all of us in spiritual warfare. "Joshua arose"; "Joshua lodged that night among the people"; "Joshua rose up early in the morning"; "Joshua went that night into the middle of the valley"; "Joshua drew not his hand back wherewith he stretched out the spear, until he had utterly destroyed all the inhabitants of Ai." Such expressions show how intensely in earnest he was, how unsparing of himself, how vigilant and indefatigable in all that bore upon his enterprise. And generally we still see that, wherever military expeditions are undertaken, they are pushed forward with untiring energy, and the sinews of war are supplied in unstinted abundance, whatever grumbling there may be afterwards when the bill comes to be paid. Has the Christian Church ever girded herself for the great enterprise of conquering the world for Christ with the same zeal and determination? What are all the sums of money contributed for Christian missions, compared to those spent annually on military and naval forces, and multiplied indefinitely when active war goes on! Alas, this question brings out but one result of a painful comparison—the contrast between the ardour with which secular results are pursued by secular men, and spiritual results by spiritual men. Let the rumour spread that gold or diamonds have been found at some remote region of the globe, what multitudes flock to them in the hope of possessing themselves of a share of the spoil! Not even the prospect of spending many days and nights in barbarism, amid the misery of dirt and heat and insects, and with company so rude and rough and reckless that they have hardly the appearance of humanity, can overcome the impetuous desire to possess themselves of the precious material, and come home rich. What crowds rush in when the prospectus of a profitable brewery promises an abundant dividend, earned too often by the manufacture of drunkards! What eager eyes scan the advertisements that tell you that if persons bearing a certain name, or related to one of that name, would apply at a certain address, they would hear of something to their advantage. Once we knew of a young man who had not even seen such an advertisement, but had been told that it had appeared. There was a vague tradition in his family that in certain circumstances a property would fall to them. The mere rumour that an advertisement had appeared in which he was interested set him to institute a search for it. He procured a file of the *Times* newspaper, reaching over a series of years, and eagerly scanned its advertisements. Failing to find there what he was in search of, he procured sets of other daily newspapers and subjected them to the same process. And thus he went on and on in his unwearied search, till first he lost his situation, then he lost his reason, and then he lost his life. What will men not do to obtain a corruptible crown? Could it be supposed from *our* attitude and ardour that we are striving for the incorruptible? Could it be thought that the riches which we are striving to accumulate are not those which moth and rust do corrupt, but the treasures that endure for evermore? Surely "it is high time for us to awake out of sleep." Surely we ought to lay to heart that "the things which are seen are temporal, but the things which are not seen are eternal." Memorable are the poet's words respecting the great objects of human desire:

> "The cloud-capt towers, the gorgeous palaces,
> The solemn temples, the great globe itself,
> Yea, all which it inherit, shall dissolve:
> And like this unsubstantial pageant faded,
> Leave not a rack behind."

CHAPTER XVII.

EBAL AND GERIZIM.

Joshua viii. 30-35.

Commentators on Joshua have been greatly perplexed by the place which this narrative has in our Bibles. No one can study the map, and take into account the circumstances of Joshua and the people, without sharing in this perplexity. It will be observed from the map that Ebal and Gerizim, rising from the plain of Shechem, are a long way distant from Ai and Bethel. If we suppose Joshua and not his army only, but the whole of his people (ver. 33), to have gone straight from Gilgal to Mount Ebal after the capture of Ai, the journey must have occupied several days each way, besides the time needed for the ceremony that took place there. It certainly would have needed an overwhelming reason to induce him at such a time, first to march a host like this all the way to Mount Ebal, and then to march them back to their encampment at Gilgal. Hence many have come to believe that, in some way which we cannot explain, this passage has been inserted out of its proper place. The most natural place for it would be at the end of chap. xi. or chap. xii., after the conquest of the whole country, and before its division among the tribes. Nearly all the manuscripts of the Septuagint insert it between vv. 2 and 3 of the ninth chapter, but this does not go far to remove the difficulty. It has been thought by some that Joshua left the original Gilgal in the plain of Jordan, and fixed his camp at another Gilgal, transferring the name of his first encampment to the second. Mention is certainly made in Scripture of another Gilgal in the neighbourhood of Bethel (2 Kings ii. 2), but nothing is said to lead us to suppose that Joshua had removed his encampment thither.

Some have thought that no record has been preserved of one of Joshua's great campaigns, the campaign in which he subdued the central part of the country. A good deal may be said for this supposition. In the list of the thirty-one kings whom he subdued over the country (chap. xii.) we find several whose dominions were in this region. For instance, we know that Aphek, Taanach, and Megiddo were all situated in the central part of the country, and probably other cities too. Yet, while the fact is recorded that they were defeated, no mention is made of any expedition against them. They belonged neither to the confederacy of Adonizedec in the south nor to that of Jabin in the north, and they must have been subdued on some separate occasion. It is just possible that Joshua defeated them before encountering the confederacy of Adonizedec at Gibeon and Bethhoron. But it is far more likely that it was after that victory that he advanced to the central part of the country.

On the whole, while admitting the perplexity of the question, we incline to the belief that the passage has been transferred from its original place. This in no way invalidates the authority of the book, or of the passage, for in the most undoubtedly authentic books of Scripture we have instances beyond question—very notably in Jeremiah—of passages inserted out of their natural order.

It has been said that the passage in Deuteronomy (xxvii. 4-19) could not have been written by Moses, because he had never set foot in Canaan, and therefore could not have been acquainted with the names or the locality of Ebal and Gerizim. On the contrary, we believe that he had very good reason to be acquainted with both. For at the foot of Ebal lay the portion of ground which Jacob gave to his son Joseph, and where both Jacob's well and Joseph's tomb are pointed out at the present day. That piece of ground must have been familiar to Jacob, and carefully described to Joseph by its great natural features when he made it over to him. And as Joseph regarded it as his destined burial-place, the tradition of its situation must have been carefully transmitted to those that came after him, when he gave commandment concerning his bones. Joseph was not the oldest son of Jacob, any more than Rachel was his oldest wife, and for these reasons neither of them was buried in the cave of Machpelah. Moses therefore had good reasons for being acquainted with the locality. Probably it was at the time of the ceremony at Ebal that the bones of Joseph were buried, although the fact is not recorded till the very end of the book (Josh. xxiv. 32). But that passage, too, is evidently not in its natural place.

It was a most fitting thing that when he had completed the conquest of the country, Joshua should set about performing that great national ceremony, designed to rivet on the people's hearts the claims of God's law and covenant, which had been enjoined by Moses to be performed in the valley of Shechem. For though Joshua was neither priest nor prophet, yet as a warm believer and earnest servant of God, he felt it his duty on all suitable occasions to urge upon the people that there was no prosperity for them save on condition of loyalty to Him. He sought to mingle the thought of God and of God's claims with the very life of the nation; to make it run, as it were, in their very blood; to get them to think of the Divine covenant as their palladium, the very pledge of all their blessings, their one only guarantee of prosperity and peace.

When therefore Joshua conducted his people to the Mounts Ebal and Gerizim, in order that they might have the obligations of the law set before them in a form as impressive as it was picturesque, he was not merely fulfilling mechanically an injunction of Moses, but performing a transaction into which he himself entered heart and soul. And when the writer of the book records the transaction, it is not merely for the purpose of showing us how certain acts prescribed in a previous book were actually performed, but for the purpose of perpetuating an occurrence which in the whole future history of the nation would prove either a continual inspiration for good, or a testimony against them, so that out of their own life they should be condemned. Knowing Joshua as we do, we can easily believe that all along it was one of his most cherished projects to implement the legacy of Moses, and superintend this memorable covenanting act. It must have been a great relief from the bloody scenes and awful experiences of war to assemble his people among the mountains and engage them in a service which was so much more in harmony with the beauty and sublimity of nature. No critic or writer who has any sense of the fitness of things can coolly remove this transaction from the sphere of history into that of fancy, or deprive Joshua of his share in a transaction into which his heart was doubtless thrown as enthusiastically as that of David in after times when the ark was placed upon Mount Zion.

It could not be without thrilling hearts that Joshua and all of his people who were likeminded entered the beautiful valley of Shechem, which had been the first resting-place in Canaan of their father Abraham, the first place where God appeared to him, and the first place where "he builded an altar unto the Lord" (Gen. xii. 6, 7). By general consent the valley of Shechem holds the distinction of being one of the most beautiful in the country. "Its western side," says Stanley, "is bounded by the abutments of two mountain ranges, running from west to east. These ranges are Gerizim and Ebal; and up the opening between them, not seen from the plain, lies the modern town of Nablous [Neapolis = Shechem]. . . . A valley green with grass, grey with olives, gardens sloping down on each side, fresh springs running down in all directions; at the end a white town embosomed in all this verdure, lodged between the two high mountains which extend on each side of the valley—that on the south Gerizim, that on the north Ebal;—this is the aspect of Nablous, the most beautiful, perhaps it might be said the only very beautiful spot in Central Palestine."

If the host of Israel approached Ebal and Gerizim from the south, they would pass along the central ridge or plateau of the country till they reached the vale of Shechem, where the mountain range would appear as if it had been cleft from top to bottom by some great convulsion of nature. Then, as now, the country was studded thickly with villages, the plains clothed with grass and grain, and the rounded hills with orchards of fig, olive, pomegranate, and other trees. On either side of the fissure rose a hill of about eight hundred feet, about the height of Arthur's Seat at Edinburgh, Ebal on the north and Gerizim on the south. It was not like the scene at Sinai, where the bare and desolate mountains towered up to heaven, their summits lost among the clouds. This was a more homely landscape, amid the fields and dwellings where the people were to spend their daily life. If the proclamation of the law from Sinai had something of an abstract and distant character, Ebal and Gerizim brought it home to the business and bosoms of men. It was now to be the rule for every day, and for every transaction of every day; the bride was now to be settled in her home, and if she was to enjoy the countenance and the company of her heavenly Bridegroom, the law of His house must be fully implemented, and its every requirement riveted on her heart.

The ceremony here under Joshua was twofold: first, the rearing of an altar; and second, the proclamation of the law.

1. The altar, as enjoined in Exod. xx. 24, was of whole, undressed stones. In its simple structure it was designed to show that the Most High dwelleth not in temples made with hands. In its open position it demonstrated that the most fitting place for His worship was not the secret recesses of the woods, but the open air and full light of heaven, seeing that He is light, and in Him is no darkness at all. On this altar were offered burnt offerings and peace offerings to the Lord. The sacrificial system had been little attended to amid the movements of the wilderness, and the warlike operations in which the people had been more or less engaged ever since their entrance on the land; but now was the beginning of a more regular worship. The first transaction here performed was the sacrificial. Here sin was called to mind, and the need of propitiation. Here it was commemorated that God Himself had appointed a method of propitiation; that He had thereby signified His gracious desire to be at peace with His people; that He had not left them to sigh out, "Oh that we knew where we might find Him, that we might come even to His seat!"—but had opened to His people the gates of righteousness, that they might go in and praise the Lord.

Moreover, we read in Joshua, that "he wrote there upon the stones a copy of the law of Moses, which he wrote in the presence of the children of Israel." There is sufficient difference between the passages in Deuteronomy and Joshua to show that the one was not copied from the other. From Joshua we might suppose that it was on the stones of the altar that Joshua wrote, and there is no reference to the command given in Deuteronomy to plaister the stones with plaister. But from Deuteronomy it is plain that it was not the stones of the altar that were plaistered over, but memorial stones set up for the purpose. There has been no little controversy as to the manner in which this injunction was carried out. According to Dr. Thomson, in the "Land and the Book," the matter is very simple. The difficulty in the eyes of commentators has arisen from the idea that plaister is altogether too soft a substance to retain the impression of what is written on it. This Dr. Thomson wholly disputes: "A careful examination of Deut. xxvii. 4, 8 and Josh. viii. 30-32 will lead to the opinion that the law was written upon and in the plaister with which these pillars were coated. This could easily be done; and such writing was common in ancient times. I have seen numerous specimens of it certainly more than two thousand years old, and still as distinct as when they were first inscribed upon the plaister. . . In this hot climate, where there is no frost to dissolve the cement, it will continue hard and unbroken for thousands of years,—which is certainly long enough. The cement on Solomon's pools remains in admirable preservation, though exposed to all the vicissitudes of the climate and with no protection. . . What Joshua did, therefore, when he erected those great stones on Mount Ebal, was merely to write *in* the still soft cement with a style, or more likely *on* the polished surface when dry, with red paint, as in ancient tombs. If properly sheltered, and not broken by violence, they would have remained to this day."

Joshua could not have written the whole of the law on his pillars; it was probably only the ten commandments. As we shall see, another arrangement was made for the rehearsal of the whole law; it was solemnly read out afterwards. But now the entire nation, with all the strangers and followers, took up their position in the valley between the two mountains. Half of the tribes separated from the rest to the slopes of Gerizim, and the other half to those of Ebal. From Deuteronomy we gather that those who were grouped on Gerizim were far the more important and numerous tribes. They embraced Simeon, Levi, Judah, Issachar, Joseph, and Benjamin. On Mount Ebal were stationed Reuben, Gad and Asher, Zebulun, Dan, and Naphtali. The priests stood between, and read out blessings and curses. When blessings were read out the tribes on Gerizim shouted Amen. When curses were read out those on Ebal did the same. Let us imagine the scene. A mountain side covered with people is always a picturesque sight, and the effect is greatly heightened when the clothing of the multitude is of light, bright colours, as probably it was on this occasion. "It was," says Dr. Thomson, "beyond question or comparison the most august assembly the sun has ever shone upon; and I never stand in the narrow plain, with Ebal and Gerizim rising on either hand to the sky, without involuntarily recalling and reproducing the scene. I have shouted to hear the echo, and then fancied how it must have been when the loud-voiced Levites proclaimed from the naked cliffs of Ebal, 'Cursed is the man that maketh any graven image, an abomination to Jehovah.' And then the tremendous AMEN! tenfold louder from the united congregation, rising and swelling and re-echoing from Ebal to Gerizim, and from Gerizim to Ebal. AMEN! Even so, let him be accursed. No, there never was an assembly to compare with this."

Very explicit mention is made of the fact that "there was not a word of all that Moses commanded which Joshua read not before all the congregation of the children of Israel, with the women and the little ones and the strangers that were conversant among them." This obviously implies that the law of Moses was in definite form, and that the reading of it took up a considerable portion of time.

The order of events had been very significant. First, a great work of destruction—the dispossession of the Canaanites. Next, the erection of an altar, and the offering up of sacrifices. And, lastly, the inscribing and proclamation of the law. "The surgeon has done his duty, and now nature will proceed to heal and comfort and bless. The enemy has been driven off the field. Now the altar is put up and the law is promulgated. Society without law is chaos. An altar without righteousness is evaporative sentiment. Prayer without duty may be a detachment of the wings from the bird they were designed to assist. . . . Having done the destructive work, do not imagine that the whole programme is complete; now begins the construction of the altar. And having made a place for prayer, do not imagine that the whole duty of man has been perfected; next put up the law; battle, prayer, law; law, prayer, battle." *

If the conjecture that this passage originally occupied a later place in the book be correct, the army was now about to be disbanded, and the people were about to be settled in homes of their own. It was a momentous crisis. They were

* "The People's Bible," by Joseph Parker, D. D.

about to lose, in a great degree, the influence of union, and the presence of men like Joshua and the godly elders, whose noble example and stirring words had ever been a power for what was good and true. Scattered over the land, they would now be more at the control of their own hearts, and often of what in them was least noble and least godly. On the part of Joshua everything had been done, by this solemn gathering, to secure that they should separate with the remembrance of God's mighty works on their behalf filling their hearts, and the words of God's law ringing in their ears.

CHAPTER XVIII.

THE STRATAGEM OF THE GIBEONITES.

JOSHUA ix.

WE now resume the thread of the story interrupted by the narrative of the transaction at Ebal and Gerizim. We learn from the testimony of Rahab of Jericho, as uttered to the spies (chap. ii. 9), that the terror of Israel had caused the hearts of the inhabitants of the country to faint, and that the fame of all that had been done for them by Jehovah had quite paralysed them. But when the host of Israel actually entered Western Palestine, and began their conquest by the destruction of Jericho and Ai, the inhabitants seem to have plucked up courage, and begun to consider what could be done in self-defence. It is very probable that they found considerable encouragement from what happened at Ai. There it had been seen that Israel was not invincible. Insignificant though Ai was, its people had been able to repel with great success the first attack of the Israelites. And though they had been destroyed in the second, this was achieved only by the combined influence of stratagem and an overwhelming force. The supernatural power under which Jericho had fallen had not been shown at Ai, and might not come into play in the future. There was therefore yet a chance for the Canaanites, if they should combine and act in concert. Steps were therefore taken for such a union. The kings or chiefs who occupied the hills, or central plateau of the country; those of the valleys, interspersed between the mountains; and those occupying the Shephelah, or maritime plains of Philistia, Sharon, and Phœnicia;—all the nations comprised under the well-known names Hittites, Amorites, Canaanites, Perizzites, Hivites, and Jebusites, entered into a league of defence, and prepared to confront Joshua and the Israelites with a determined resistance. The news of the confederacy would bring a tremor over some timid hearts in the camp of Israel, but would cause no serious anxiety to Joshua and all the men of faith, who, like him, felt assured that the Lord was with them.

There was one native community, however, that determined to follow another course. The Gibeonites were a branch of the Hivite race, inhabiting the town of Gibeon, and some other prominent towns in the great central plateau of the country. Gibeon is undoubtedly represented now by the village of El Jib, situated about halfway between Jerusalem and Bethel, four or five miles distant from each. Dr. Robertson describes El Jib as situated in a beautiful plain of considerable extent, on an oblong hill or ridge, composed of layers of limestone, rising as if by regular steps out of the plain. In the days of Joshua, it was a place of great importance, a royal city, and it had under its jurisdiction the towns of Beeroth, Chephirah, and Kirjath-jearim. Its inhabitants were in no humour to fight with Joshua. They had faith enough to understand what would be the inevitable result of that, and therein they were right, and the confederate kings were wrong. On the other hand, they were not prepared to make an honest and unconditional surrender. They probably knew that the orders under which Joshua was acting called on him to destroy all the people of the land, and they had no assurance that, being of the doomed nations, open submission would secure their lives. They resolved therefore to proceed by stratagem. A detachment was appointed to wait on Joshua at his camp at Gilgal, as if they were ambassadors from a distant country, and represent to him in pious tone that they had come from afar, "because of the name of the Lord his God, having heard the fame of Him, and all that He did in Egypt, and all that He did to the two kings of the Amorites that were beyond Jordan, to Sihon King of Heshbon, and to Og King of Bashan." They came with the desire to show respect to the people whose God was so powerful, and to be allowed, though far off, to live at peace with them. Then they presented their credentials, as it were; showing the old sacks, the shrivelled bottles, the musty bread they had brought with them, and the clouts upon their feet and ragged garments which attested the great length of their journey. "Those old Gibeonites," says the "Land and the Book," "did indeed 'work wilily' with Joshua. Nothing could be better calculated to deceive than their devices. I have often thought that their ambassadors, as described in the narrative, furnish one of the finest groups imaginable for a painter; with their old sacks on their poor asses; their wine bottles of goat skin, patched and shrivelled up in the sun, old, rent, and bound up; old shoes and clouted upon their feet; old garments, ragged and bedraggled, with bread dry and mouldy,—the very picture of an over-travelled and wearied caravan from a great distance. It is impossible to transfer to paper the ludicrous appearance of such a company. No wonder that, having tasted their mouldy victuals, and looked upon their soiled and travel-worn costume, Joshua and the elders were deceived, especially as they did not wait to ask counsel at the mouth of the Lord."

It was just the completeness of the disguise that threw Joshua and the men of Israel off their guard. For at first the idea did occur to them that the strangers might be neighbours, and therefore of the nations that they were called on to destroy. On closer inspection, however, that seemed out of the question; indeed, the supposition was so utterly preposterous that it was deemed hardly fitting to bring the matter before the Lord. It is as plain as day, Joshua and the elders would reason; the evidence of what they say is beyond question; theirs is no case of perplexity requiring us to go to God; we may surely exercise our common sense and make a league with these far-travelled men. In a short time they will be back in their own country, far beyond our boundaries, and the only effect of their visit and of our league will be a fresh tribute to the name and power of Jehovah, a fresh testimony to His presence with us, and a fresh pledge that He will bear us to success in the enterprise in which we are engaged. And when the confederate kings that are now leaguing against us hear that this distant people have come to us to propitiate our favour, they will be struck by a new terror and will be the more easily subdued.

We see in all this the simple, unsuspecting spirit of men who have spent their lives in the wilderness. As for the Gibeonites, there was a combination of good and bad in their spirit. They remind us in a measure of the woman with the issue of blood. In her there was certainly faith; but along with the faith, extraordinary superstition. In the Gibeonites there was faith —a belief that Israel was under the protection of a remarkable Divine power, under a Divine promise the truth of which even Balaam had very recently acknowledged—" I will bless them that bless thee, and curse him that curseth thee." Undoubtedly a religious feeling lay at the bottom of the proceeding. A great divine Being was seen to be involved, who was on Israel's side and against his enemies, and it would not do to trifle with Him. But in their way of securing exemption from the effects of His displeasure, the grossest superstition appeared. They were to gain their object by deceit. They were to get Him to favour them above their neighbours through an elaborate system of fraud, through a tissue of lies, through unmitigated falsehood. What a strange conception of God! What blindness to His highest attributes, —His holiness and His truth! What amazing infatuation to suppose that they could secure His blessing through acts fitted to provoke His utmost displeasure! What a miserable God men fashion to themselves when they simply invest Him with almighty power, or perhaps suppose Him to be moved by whims and prejudices and favouritisms like frail man, but omit to clothe Him with His highest glory—forget that "justice and judgment are the habitation of His throne, mercy and truth go before His face."

The conduct of the men was the more strange that it was impossible that they should not be speedily found out. And it was quite possible that, when found out, they would be dealt with more severely than ever. True, indeed, Joshua, when he did detect their plot, did not so act; he acted on a high, perhaps a mistaken sense of honour; but they had no right to count on that. Timidity is a poor adviser. All it can do is to turn the next corner. True faith, resting on eternal truth, acts for eternity. True faith is often blind, but in the deepest darkness it knows that it is on the right track, and under the guidance of the eternal light. Blind faith is very different from blind fear. Faith holds on in full expectation of deliverance; fear trembles and stumbles, in perpetual dread of exposure and humiliation.

"A lying tongue is but for a moment;" and the Gibeonite fraud lived just three days. Then it was discovered by Joshua that the Gibeonites lived in the immediate neighbourhood. But before that, he had made peace with them, and entered into a league to let them live, and the princes of the congregation had confirmed it by an oath. Nothing could have been more provoking than to discover that they had been duped and swindled. It is always a very bitter experience to find that our confidence has been misplaced. Men whom we thought trustworthy, and whom we commended to others as trustworthy, have turned out knaves. It is hard to bear, for we have committed ourselves to our friends in the matter. What would Joshua and his people think now of the supposed tribute to the God of Israel, and the impression expected to be made on the confederate kings? Before all the inhabitants of Canaan he and his people were befooled, humiliated. Not a man in all the country but would be making merry at their expense. Yet even that was not the worst of it. They had been guilty of over-confidence, and of neglect of means that were in their hands; they had neglected to get counsel of their God. They had trusted in their own hearts when they ought to have sought guidance from above. The trouble was their own creation; they were alone to blame.

We cannot but respect the way in which Joshua and the princes acted when they discovered the fraud. It might have been competent to repudiate the league on the ground that it was agreed to by them under false pretences. It was made on the representation that the Gibeonites had come from a far country, and when that was seen to be utterly untrue there would have been an honourable ground for repudiating the transaction. But Joshua did not avail himself of this loophole. He and the princes had such respect for the sanctity of an oath that, even when they discovered that they had been grossly deceived, they would not resile from it. It seems to have been the princes that took up this ground, and they did so in opposition to the congregation (ver. 18). The fact that the name of the Lord God of Israel had been invoked in the oath sworn to the Gibeonites constrained them to abide by the transaction. It is a good sign of their spirit that they were so jealous of the honour of their God, and of the sanctity of their oath. They came out of the transaction with more honour than we should have expected. Personal interests were subordinated to higher considerations. They carried out that great canon of true religion—first and foremost giving "glory to God in the highest."

But though the lives of the Gibeonites were spared, that was all. They were to be reduced to a kind of slavery—to be "hewers of wood and drawers of water for the congregation and the altar of God." The expression has become a household word to denote a life of drudgery, but perhaps we fail to recognise the full significance of the terms. "I was forcibly reminded of this," says the author of "The Land and the Book," "by long files of women and children (near El Jib) carrying on their heads heavy bundles of wood. . . It is the severest kind of drudgery, and my compassion has often been enlisted in behalf of the poor women and children, who daily bring loads of wood to Jerusalem from these very mountains of the Gibeonites. To carry water, also, is very laborious and fatiguing. The fountains are far off, in deep wadies with steep banks, and a thousand times have I seen the feeble and the young staggering up long and weary ways with large jars of water on their heads. It is the work of slaves, and of the very poor, whose condition is still worse. Among the pathetic lamentations of Jeremiah there is nothing more affecting than this: 'They took the young men to grind, and the children fell under the wood' (i. 16). Grinding at the hand-mill is a low, menial work, assigned to female slaves, and therefore utterly humiliating to the young men of Israel. And the delicate children of Zion falling under the loads of hard, rough wood, along the mountain paths! Alas! 'for these things I weep; mine eye, mine eye runneth down with water, because the comforter that should relieve my soul is far from me: my children are desolate, because the enemy prevailed.'"

Respecting the after history of Gibeon and the Gibeonites we find some notices in the Old Testament, but none in the New. At one time there was a sanctuary at Gibeon, even after the ark had been removed to Mount Zion; for it was at Gibeon that Solomon offered his great sacrifice of a thousand burnt offerings, and had that remarkable dream in which, in reply to the Divine offer of a choice of gifts, he chose wisdom in preference to any other (1 Kings iii. 4 sq.). But the most remarkable reappearance of the Gibeonites in history is in the reigns of Saul and David. For some unknown reason, and probably quite unjustly, Saul had put some of them to death. And in the reign of David, probably the early part of it, when a succession of famines desolated the land, and inquiry was made as to the cause, the reply of the oracle was: "It is for Saul and his bloody house, because he slew the Gibeonites." And it was to avenge this unjust slaughter that seven descendants of Saul were put to death, on that occasion when Rizpah, the mother of two of them, showed such remarkable affection by guarding their dead bodies from the beasts and birds of prey. It is possible that even after the Babylonian captivity some Gibeonites survived under their old name, because it is said in Nehemiah that among the others who repaired the wall of Jerusalem were "Melatiah the Gibeonite, and Jadon the Meronothite, the men of Gibeon, and of Mizpah" (iii. 7). Only it is uncertain whether Melatiah was of the old Gibeonite stock, or an Israelite who had Gibeon for his city. While the old Gibeonites did survive they seem to have had a miserable lot, and the question might have been often asked by them—Did our fraud bring us any real good? Is life worth living?

Does anything resembling this fraud of the Gibeonites ever take place among ourselves? In answer, let us ask first of all, what is the meaning of pious frauds? Are they not transactions where fraud is resorted to in order to accomplish what are supposed to be religious ends? Granting that the fraud of the Gibeonites was not for a religious but for a secular object—their deliverance from the sword of Joshua—still they professed, in practising it, to be doing honour to God. It is the part of superstition at once to lower the intellectual and the moral attributes of God. It often represents that the most frivolous acts, the uttering of mysterious words, or the performance of senseless acts have such a power over God as to bring about certain desired results. More frequently it holds that cruelty, falsehood, injustice, and other crimes, if brought to bear on religious or ecclesiastical ends, are pleasing in God's sight. Is there anything more truly odious than this severance of religion from morality and humanity,—this representation that fraud and other immoral acts have value before God? How can anything be a real religious gain to a man, how can it be otherwise than disastrous in the last degree, if it develops a fraudulent spirit, if it perverts his moral nature, if it deepens and intensifies the moral disorder of his heart? If men saw "the beauty of holiness," "the beauty of the Lord," they could never bring their minds to such miserable distortions. It is pure blasphemy to suppose that God could thus demean Himself. It is self-degradation to imagine that anything that can be gained by oneself through such means, could make up for what is lost, or for the guilt incurred by such wickedness.

And this suggests a wider thought—the fearful miscalculation men make whensoever they resort to fraud in the hope of reaping benefit by means of it. Yet what practice is more common? The question is, Does it really pay? Does it pay, for instance, to cheat at cards? Have we not seen recently what swift and terrible retribution that may bring, making us feel for the culprit as we might have felt for Cain. Does it pay the merchant to cheat as to the quality of his goods? Does it not leak out that he is not to be trusted, and does not that suspicion lose more to him in the long run than it gains? Does it pay the preacher to preach another man's sermon as his own? Or, to vary the illustration. When one has entrapped a maiden under false promises, and then forsakes her; or when he conceals the fact that he is already married to another; or when he controls himself for a time, to conceal from her his ill temper, or his profligate habits, or his thirst for strong drink, does it pay in the end? The question is not, Does he succeed in his immediate object? but, How does the matter end? Is it a comfortable thought to any man that he has broken a trustful heart, that he has brought misery to a happy home, that he has filled some one's life with lamentation and mourning and woe? We are not thinking only of the future life, when so many wrongs will be brought to light, and so many men and women will have to curse the infatuation that made fraud their friend and evil their good. We think of the present happiness of those who live in an atmosphere of fraud, and worship daily at its shrine. Can such disordered souls know aught of real peace and solid joy? In the case of some of them, are there not occasional moments of sober feeling, when they think what their life was given them for, and contrast their selfish and heartless devices with the career of those who deal truly and live to do good? Bitter, very bitter is the feeling which the contrast raises. It is bitter to think how unfit one is for the society of honest men; how the master one is serving is the father of lies; and how, even when the master does grant one a momentary success, it is at the sacrifice of all self-respect and conscious purity, and with a dark foreboding of wrath in the life to come.

All Eastern nations get the character of being deceitful; but indeed the weed may be said to flourish in every soil where it has not been rooted out by living Christianity. But if it be peculiarly characteristic of Eastern nations, is it not remarkable how constantly it is rebuked in the Bible, even though that book sprang from an Eastern soil? No doubt the record of the Bible abounds with *instances* of deceit, but its voice is always against them. And its instances are always instructive. Satan gained nothing by deceiving our first parents. Jacob was well punished for deceiving Isaac. David's misleading of the high priest when he fled from Saul involved ultimately the slaughter of the whole priestly household. Ananias and Sapphira had an awful experience when they lied unto the Holy Ghost. All through the Bible it is seen that lying lips are an abomination to the Lord, but they that deal truly are His delight. And when our blessed Lord comes to show us the perfect life, how free He is from the slightest taint or vestige of deceit! How beautifully transparent is His whole life and character! No little child with his honest smile and open face was ever more guileless. In the light of that perfect example, who among us does not blush for our errors—for our many endeavours to conceal what we have done, to appear better than we were, to seem to be pleasing God when we were pleasing ourselves, or to be aiming at God's glory when we were really consulting for our own interests? Is it possible for us ever to be worthy of such a Lord? First, surely, we must go to His cross, and, bewailing all our unworthiness, seek acceptance through His finished work. And then draw from His fulness, even grace for grace; obtain through the indwelling of His Spirit that elixir of life which will send a purer life-blood through our souls, and assimilate us to Him of whom His faithful apostle wrote: "He did not sin, *neither was guile found in His mouth.*"

CHAPTER XIX.

THE BATTLE OF BETHHORON.

JOSHUA x.

OUT of the larger confederacy of the whole Canaanite chiefs against Joshua and his people recorded in the beginning of chap. ix., a smaller number, headed by Adonizedec, undertook the special task of chastising the Gibeonites, who had not only refused to join the confederacy, but, as it was thought, basely and treacherously surrendered to Joshua. It is interesting to find the King of Jerusalem, Adonizedec, bearing a name so similar to that of Melchizedek, King of Salem, in the days of Abraham. No doubt, since the days of Jerome, there have been some who have denied that the Salem of Melchizedek was Jerusalem. But the great mass of opinion is in favour of the identity of the two places. Melchizedek means King of Righteousness; Adonizedec, Lord of Righteousness; in substance the same. It was a striking name for a ruler, and it was remarkable that it should have been kept up so long, although in the time of Adonizedec its significance had probably been forgotten. Jerusalem was but five miles south of Gibeon; the other four capitals, whose chiefs joined in the expedition, were farther off. Hebron, eighteen miles south of Jerusalem, was memorable in patriarchal history as the dwelling-place of Abraham and the burial-place of his family; Jarmuth, hardly mentioned in the subsequent history, is now represented by Yarmuk, six miles from Jerusalem; Lachish, of which we have frequent mention in Scripture, is probably represented by Um Lakis, about fifteen miles south-west of Jerusalem; and Eglon by Ajlan, a little farther west. The five little kingdoms embraced most of the territory afterwards known as the tribe of Judah, and they must have been far more than a match for Gibeon. Their chiefs are called "the five Amorite kings," but this does not imply that they were exclusively of the

Amorite race, for "Amorite," like "Canaanite," is often used generically to denote the whole inhabitants (as in Gen. xv. 16). The five chiefs were so near Gibeon that it was quite natural for them to undertake this expedition. No doubt they reckoned that, by making a treaty with Joshua, the Gibeonites had strengthened his hands and weakened those of his opponents; they had made resistance to Joshua more difficult for the confederacy, and therefore they deserved to be chastised. To turn their arms against Gibeon, when they had Joshua to deal with, was probably an unwise proceeding; but to their resources it would seem a very easy task. Gibeon enjoyed nothing of that aid from a great unseen Power that made Joshua so formidable; little could they have dreamt that Joshua would come to the assistance of his new allies, and with God's help inflict on them a crushing defeat. "The Lord bringeth the counsel of the heathen to naught, He maketh the devices of the people of none effect. The counsel of the Lord standeth for ever, the thoughts of His heart to all generations."

The case was very serious for the Gibeonites. As Gibeon lay so near Jerusalem and the cities of the other confederates, it is likely that the appearance of the enemy before its walls was the first, or nearly the first, intimation of the coming attack. In their extremity they sent to Joshua imploring help, and the terms in which they besought him not to lose a moment, but come to them at his utmost speed, show the urgency of their danger. To appeal to Joshua at all after their shameful fraud was a piece of presumption, unless—and this is very unlikely—the treaty between them had promised protection from enemies. Had Joshua been of a mean nature he would have chuckled over their distress, and congratulated himself that now he would get rid of these Gibeonites without trouble on his part. But the same generosity that had refused to take advantage of their fraud when it was detected showed itself in this their time of need. Joshua was encamped at Gilgal on the banks of the Jordan; for the arguments that suppose him to have been at another Gilgal are not consistent with the terms used in the narrative (e. g., ver. 9, "went up from Gilgal all night"). From Gilgal to Gibeon the distance is upwards of twenty miles, and a great part of the way is steep and difficult.

Encouraged by the assurance of Divine protection and favoured by the moonlight, Joshua, by a marvellous act of pluck and energy, went up by night, reached Gibeon in the morning, fell upon the army of the assembled kings, possibly while it was yet dark, and utterly discomfited them. It would have been natural for the routed armies to make for Jerusalem, only five miles off, by the south road, but either Joshua had occupied that road, or it was too difficult for a retreat. The way by which they did retreat, running west from Gibeon, is carefully described. First they took the way " that goeth up to Bethhoron." As soon as they had traversed the plain of Gibeon, they ascended a gentle slope leading towards Bethhoron the upper, then fled down the well-known pass, through the two Bethhorons, upper and nether, making for Jarmuth, Lachish, and other towns at the bottom of the hills. In the course of their descent a hailstorm overtook them, one of those terrific storms which seem hardly credible to us, but are abundantly authenticated both in ancient and modern times, and " they which died with hailstones were more than they whom the children of Israel slew with the sword." The Israelites, exhausted, no doubt, with their night march and morning exertions, seem to have been outstripped by the flying army, and in this way to have escaped the shower of hail. By the time the five kings, who had had to fly on foot, reached Makkedah at the foot of the mountains, they were unable to go farther and hid themselves in a cave. As Joshua passed he was informed of this, but, unwilling to stop the pursuit of the fugitives, he ordered large stones to be rolled to the door of the cave, locking the kings up as it were in a prison, and no doubt leaving a guard in charge. Then, when the pursuit had been carried to the very gates of the walled cities, he returned to the cave. The five kings were brought out, and the chiefs of the Israelite army put their feet upon their necks. The kings were slain, and their bodies hanged on trees till the evening.

Thereafter Joshua attacked the chief cities of the confederates, and took in succession Makkedah, Libnah, Lachish, Eglon, Hebron, and Debir. Nothing is said of his taking Jerusalem; indeed it appears from the after history that the stronghold of Jerusalem on Mount Zion remained in Jebusite hands up to the time of David. Many of the inhabitants were able to escape destruction, but substantially Joshua was now in possession of the whole southern division of the land, from the Jordan on the east to the borders of the Philistines on the west, and from Gibeon on the north to the wilderness on the south. It does not appear, however, that he retained full possession; while he was occupied in other parts of the country the people returned and occupied their cities. The clemency of Joshua in not destroying the inhabitants proved the source of much future trouble.

In all the subsequent history of the country, the victory of Gibeon was looked back on, and justly, as one of the most memorable that had ever been known. For promptitude, dash, and daring it was never eclipsed by any event of the kind; while the strength of the confederate army, the completeness of its defeat, and the picturesqueness of the whole situation constantly supplied materials for wonder and delight. Moreover, the hand of God had been conspicuously shown in more ways than one. The hailstorm that wrought such havoc was ascribed to His friendly hand, but a far more memorable token of His interest and support lay in the miracle that arrested the movements of the sun and the moon, in order that victorious Israel might have time to finish his work. And after the victory the capture of the fortified towns became comparatively easy. The remnant that had escaped could have no heart to defend them. Joshua must have smiled at the fate of the " cities walled up to heaven" that had so greatly distressed his brother spies when they came up to examine the land. And as he found them one by one yield to his army, as though their defence had really departed from them, he must have felt with fresh gratitude the faithfulness and lovingkindness of the Lord, and earnestly breathed the prayer that neither his faith nor that of his people might ever fail until the whole campaign was brought to an end.

In some respects this victory had a special significance. In the first place, it had a most important bearing on the success of the whole enterprise; its suddenness, its completeness, its manifold grandeur being admirably fitted to paralyse the enemy in other parts of the country, and open the whole region to Joshua. By some it has been compared to the battle of Marathon, not only on account of the suddenness with which the decisive blow was struck, but also on account of the importance of the interests involved. It was a battle for freedom, for purity, for true religion, in opposition to tyranny, idolatry, and abominable sensuality; for all that is wholesome in human life, in opposition to all that is corrupt; for all that makes for peaceful progress, in opposition to all that entails degradation and misery. The prospects of the whole world were brighter after that victory of Bethhoron. The relation of heaven to earth was more auspicious, and more full of promise for the days to come. Had any hitch occurred in the arrangements; had Israel halted half-way up the eastern slopes, and the troops of Adonizedec driven them back; had the tug of war in the plain of Gibeon proved too much for them after their toilsome night march; had no hailstorm broken out on the retreating enemy; had he been able to form again at the western foot of the hills and arrest the progress of Joshua in pursuit, the whole enterprise would have had a different complexion. No doubt the Divine arm might have been stretched out for Israel in some other way; but the remarkable thing was, that no such supplementary mode of achieving the desired result was required. At every point the success of Israel was complete, and every obstacle opposed to him by the enemy was swept away for the time being as smoke before the wind.

In the next place, the tokens of Divine aid were very impressive. After the experience which Joshua had had of the consequences of failing to ask God for direction when first the Gibeonites came to him, we may be very sure that on the present occasion he would be peculiarly careful to seek Divine counsel. And he was well rewarded. For "the sun stood still, and the moon stayed, until the people had avenged themselves upon their enemies." It does not need to be said that this miraculous incident has from first to last given birth to an immensity of perplexity and discussion. It will be observed that the record of it does not come in as part of the narrative, but as a quotation from a pre-existing book. Concerning that book we know very little. From its name, Jashar, "The upright," we may believe it to have been a record of memorable deeds of righteous men. In form it was poetical, the extract in the present case being of that rhythmical structure which was the mark of Hebrew poetry. The only other occasion on which it is mentioned is in connection with the song composed by David, after the death of Saul and Jonathan (2 Sam. i. 18). "David" (as the Revised Version puts it) "bade them teach the children of Israel the song of the bow; behold, it is written in the book of Jashar." As to the origin and nature of this book we can only conjecture. It may have been a public record, contributed to from time to time by various writers, under conditions and arrangements which at this distance of time, and under the obscurity of the whole subject, we cannot ascertain.

Then as to the miracle of the sun and the moon standing still. It is well known that this was one of the passages brought forward by the Church of Rome to condemn Galileo, when he affirmed that the earth and the moon revolved round the sun, and that it was not the motion of the sun round the earth, but the rotation of the earth on her own axis that produced the change of day and night. No one would dream now of making use of this passage for any such purpose. Whatever theory of inspiration men may hold, it is admitted universally that the inspired writers used the popular language of the day in matters of science, and did not anticipate discoveries which were not made till many centuries later. That expressions occur in Scripture which are not in accord with the best established conclusions of modern science would never be regarded by any intelligent person as an argument against the Scriptures as the inspired records of God's will, designed especially to reveal to us the way of life and salvation through Jesus Christ, and to be an infallible guide to us on all that "man is to believe concerning God, and the duty that God requires of man."

A far more serious question has been raised as to whether this miracle ever occurred, or could have occurred. To those who believe in the possibility of miracles, it can be no conclusive argument that it could not have occurred without producing injurious consequences the end of which can hardly be conceived. For if the rotation of the earth on its axis was suddenly arrested, all human beings on its surface, and all loose objects whatever must have been flung forward with prodigious violence; just as, on a small scale, on the sudden stoppage of a carriage, we find ourselves thrown forward, the motion of the carriage having been communicated to our bodies. But really this is a paltry objection; for surely the Divine power that can control the rotation of the earth is abundantly able to obviate such effects as these. We can understand the objection that God, having adjusted all the forces of nature, leaves them to operate by themselves in a uniform way without disturbance or interference; but we can hardly comprehend the reasonableness of the position that if it is His pleasure miraculously to modify one arrangement, he is unable to adjust all relative arrangements, and make all conspire harmoniously to the end desired.

But was it a miracle? The narrative, as we have it, implies not only that it was, but that there was something in it stupendous and unprecedented. It comes in as a part of that supernatural process in which God had been engaged ever since the deliverance of His people from Egypt, and which was to go on till they should be finally settled in the land. It naturally joins on to the miraculous division of the Jordan, and the miraculous fall of the walls of Jericho. We must remember that the work in which God was now engaged was one of peculiar spiritual importance and significance. He was not merely finding a home for His covenant people; He was making arrangements for advancing the highest interests of humanity; He was guarding against the extinction on earth of the Divine light which alone could guide man in safety through the life that now is, and in preparation for that which is to come. He was taking steps to prevent a final and fatal severance of the relation between God and man, and He was even preparing the way for a far more complete and glorious development of that relation

—to be seen in the person of His Incarnate Son, the spiritual Joshua, and made possible for men through that great work of propitiation which He was to accomplish on the cross. Who will take upon him to say that at an important crisis in the progress of the events which were to prepare the way for this grand consummation, it was not fitting for the Almighty to suspend for a time even the ordinances of heaven, in order that a day's work, carrying such vast consequences, might not be interrupted before its triumphant close?

There are commentators worthy of high respect who have thought that the fact of this incident being noticed in the form of a quotation from the Book of Jashar somewhat diminishes the credit due to it. It looks as if it had not formed part of the original narrative, but had been inserted by a subsequent editor from a book of poetry, expressed with poetic license, and perhaps of later date. They are disposed to regard the words of Joshua, "Sun, stand thou still upon Gibeon; and thou, Moon, in the valley of Ajalon," as a mere expression of his desire that the light would last long enough to allow the decisive work of the day to be brought to a thorough conclusion. They look on it as akin to the prayer of Agamemnon ("Iliad," ii. 412 *sq.*) that the sun might not go down till he had sacked Troy; and the form of words they consider to be suited to poetical composition, like some of the expressions in the eighteenth psalm —" There went up a smoke out of His nostrils, and fire out of His mouth devoured: coals were kindled by it. He bowed the heavens also, and did come down: He rode upon a cherub, and did fly."

But whatever allowance we may make for poetical license of speech, it is hardly possible not to perceive that the words as they stand imply a miracle of extraordinary sublimity; nor do we see any sufficient ground for resisting the common belief that in whatsoever way it was effected, there was a supernatural extension of the period of light, to allow Joshua to finish his work.*

One other notable feature in the transaction of this day was the completeness of the defeat inflicted by Joshua on the enemy. This defeat went on in successive stages from early morning till late at night. First, there was the slaughter in the plain of Gibeon. Then the havoc produced by the hail and by Joshua on the retreating army. Then the destruction caused as Joshua followed the enemy to their cities. And the work of the day was wound up by the execution of the five kings. Moreover, there followed a succession of similar scenes at the taking and sacking of their cities. When we try to realise all this in detail, we are confronted with a terrible scene of blood and death, and possibly we may find ourselves asking, Was there a particle of humanity in Joshua, that he was capable of such a series of transactions? Certainly Joshua was a great soldier, and a great religious soldier, but he was in many ways like his time. He had many of the qualities of Oriental commanders, and one of these qualities has ever been to carry slaughter to the utmost limit that the occasion allows. His treatment of the conquered kings, too, was marked by characteristic Oriental barbarity, for he caused his captains to put their feet upon their necks, needlessly embittering their dying moments, and he exposed their dead bodies to the needless humiliation of being hanged on a tree. But it must be said, and said firmly for Joshua, that there is no evidence of his acting on this or on other such occasions in order to gratify personal feelings; it was not done either to gratify a thirst for blood, or to gratify the pride of a conqueror. Joshua all through gives us the impression of a man carrying out the will of another; inflicting a judicial sentence, and inflicting it thoroughly at the first so that there might be no need for a constant series of petty executions afterwards. This certainly was his aim; but the enemy showed themselves more vital than he had supposed.

And when we turn to ourselves and think what we may learn from this transaction, we see a valuable application of his method to the spiritual warfare. God has enemies still, within and without, with whom we are called to contend. "For we wrestle not against flesh and blood, but against principalities and powers, against the rulers of the darkness of this world, against spiritual wickedness in high places." When we are fighting with the enemy within our own hearts leniency is our great temptation, but at the same time our greatest snare. What we need here is, courage to slay. We content ourselves with confessions and regrets, but the enemy lives, returns to the attack, and keeps us in perpetual discomfort. Oh, that in this battle we resembled Joshua, aiming at killing the enemy outright, and leaving nothing belonging to him that breathes!

And in reference to the outside world, want of thoroughness in warfare is still our besetting sin. We play at missions; we trifle with the awful drunkenness and sensuality around us; we look on, and we see rural districts gradually depopulated; and we wring our hands at the mass of poverty, vice, and misery in our great crowded cities. How rare is it for any one to arise among us like General Booth, to face prevailing evils in all their magnitude, and even attempt to do battle with them along the whole line! Why should not such a spirit be universal in the Christian Church? Who can tell the evil done by want of faith, by languor, by unwillingness to be disturbed in our quiet, self-indulged life, by our fear of rousing against us the scorn and rage of the world? If only the Church had more faith, and, as the fruit of faith, more courage and more enterprise, what help from heaven might not come to her! True, she would not see the enemy crushed by hailstones, nor the sun standing in Gibeon, nor the moon in the valley of Ajalon; but she would see grander sights; she would see men of spiritual might raised up in her ranks; she would see tides of strong spiritual influence overwhelming her enemies. Jerichos dismantled, Ais captured, and the champions of evil falling like Lucifer from heaven to make way for the King of kings and Lord of lords.

Let us go to the cross of Jesus to revive our faith and recruit our energies. The Captain of our salvation has not only achieved salvation for

---

* It seems hardly necessary to notice an explanation of the phenomenon that has been made lately—to the effect that it was in the morning, not the evening of the day, that Joshua expressed his wish. It was to prevent the allied kings about Gibeon knowing of his approach that he desired the sun to delay his rising in the east, a desire which was virtually fulfilled by that dark, cloudy condition of the sky which precedes a thunderstorm. The natural sense of the narrative admits neither of this explanation of the time nor of the miracle itself.

us, but He has set us a blessed example of the spirit and life of true Christian warriors.

> "At the Name of Jesus
>   Satan's legions flee;
> On then, Christian soldiers,
>   On to victory.
> Hell's foundations quiver
>   At the shout of praise;
> Brothers, lift your voices,
>   Loud your anthems raise!"

CHAPTER XX.

THE BATTLE OF MEROM.

JOSHUA xi., xii.

THERE is some appearance of confusion in the terms in which the great confederacy of native princes against Israel is brought in. In the beginning of the ninth chapter, a combination that embraced the whole country, north and south, east and west, is described as gathered together to fight with Joshua and with Israel. Nothing more is said till after the treaty with the Gibeonites, when five of these confederate kings residing in the south not far from Gibeon muster their forces to besiege that city. Of the utter rout and ruin of these five kings and of some of their neighbours we have just been reading. And now we read that, after these things, Jabin, King of Hazor, sent to his neighbours, and to all the princes in the northern part of the country, and organised a combined movement against Israel, for which the appointed rendezvous was at the waters of Merom, in the extreme north of the country. The statement at the beginning of the ninth chapter that the confederates "gathered themselves together," seems to be made proleptically; the actual gathering together not having taken place till the occasions specified in the tenth and eleventh chapters respectively. The plan of the confederacy was no doubt formed soon after the fall of Jericho and Ai, and the arrangements for a vast united movement began to be made then. But it would necessarily consume a considerable time to bring so vast a host together. Meanwhile, another event had taken place. The Gibeonites had refused to join the confederacy and had made peace with Joshua. Their neighbours were intensely provoked, especially Adonizedec of Jerusalem, and without waiting for the general movement proceeded at once to chastise their treachery. As we have said already, they doubtless thought it would be an easy task. To the surprise of them all, Joshua, with an activity which they could not have looked for, hastened to the relief of Gibeon, and inflicted a defeat on the confederates which amounted to absolute ruin.

It has not been generally noticed how remarkably the Gibeonite fraud, and the honourable action of Joshua in connection with it, tended in the end to the good of Israel. Had Joshua, after the discovery of the fraud, repudiated his treaty and attacked and exterminated the Gibeonites, or had he disregarded their appeal to him for help and suffered them to be crushed by Adonizedec, there would have been nothing to hinder the southern kings from uniting with the northern, and thus presenting to Joshua the most formidable opposition that was ever mustered in defence of a country. The magnificent exploit of Joshua in the plain of Gibeon, down the pass of Bethhoron, and in the valley of Ajalon entirely frustrated any such arrangement. The armies of the southern kings were destroyed or demoralised. And though the united forces in the north, with their vast resources of war, still formed a most formidable opponent, the case would have been very different if the two had combined, or if one of them had hung on Joshua's rear while he was engaged in front with the other. Nothing could have fallen out more for the advantage of Israel than the procedure of the Gibeonites, which drew off so large and powerful a section of the confederates, and exposed them thus separate to the sword of Joshua.

Joshua was not allowed a long rest at Gilgal after his dealings with Adonizedec and his brethren. No doubt the news of that tremendous disaster would quicken the energies of the northern kings. The head of the new conspiracy was Jabin, King of Hazor. Jabin was evidently an official name borne by the chief ruler of Hazor, like Pharaoh in Egypt, for when, at a subsequent period, the place has recovered somewhat of its importance, and comes again into view as a Canaanite capital, Jabin is again the name of its chief ruler (Judg. iv. 2).

The situation of Hazor has been disputed by geographers, and Robinson, who is usually so accurate, differs from other authorities. He assigns it to a ruinous city on a hill called Tell Khuraibeh, overhanging the Lake Merom, for little other reason than that it seems to answer the conditions of the various narratives where Hazor is introduced. On the other hand, the author of "The Land and the Book," assigns it to a place still called Hazere, a little west of Merom, the remains of which lie in a large natural basin, and spread far up the hill, toward the south. "Heaps of hewn stone, old and rotten; open pits, deep wells, and vast cisterns cut in the solid rock—these are the unequivocal indications of an important city. . . I inquired of an old sheikh what saint was honoured there. In a voice loud and bold, as if to make a doubtful point certain, he replied, Neby Hazûr, who fought with Yeshua Ibn Nun." The matter is of no great moment; all that it is important to know is that Hazor was situated near Lake Merom, and was the capital of a powerful kingdom.

The cities of some of the other confederates are named, but it is not easy to identify them all. The sites of Madon, Shimron, and Achshaph, are unknown, but they were apparently not far from Hazor. "The Arabah south of Chinneroth" (ver. 2, R. V.) denotes the plain of Jordan south of the lake of Galilee; the valley, or "lowland" (R. V.), denotes the maritime plain from the Philistines northward; "the heights of Dor on the west" (R. V.), or Highlands of Dor ("Speaker's Commentary"), the hills about a city on the sea coast, near the foot of Carmel, prominent in after history, but now reduced to a village with a few poor houses. The sacred historian, however, does not attempt to enumerate all the places from which the confederacy was drawn, and falls back on the old comprehensive formula—"Canaanites on the east and on the west, Amorites, Hittites, the Jebusites in the hill country, and the Hivite under Hermon in the land of Mizpeh." "The Canaanites on the west" embraced the people of Zidon, for Joshua is expressly stated to have followed a band of the fugitives to that city (ver. 8). The muster must have been an extraordinary one, as numerous "as the sand that is upon the sea shore in multitude." Josephus gives the numbers as 300,000 footmen, 10,000 horsemen, and 20,000 chariots; but we can hardly attach much value to his figures. "Horses and chariots" was an arm unknown to the Israelites, with which hitherto they had never contended. This vast host came together and pitched at the waters of Merom. Merom, now called Huleh, is the little lake where, as already stated, the three streamlets that form the Jordan unite. It varies in size in summer and winter. To the north, a large plain spreads itself out, sufficient for the encampment of a great army. It was at or near this plain that Abraham overtook the five kings of Mesopotamia and defeated them, rescuing Lot, and all that had been taken from Sodom (Gen. xiv. 14, 15). Now again it is crowded with a mighty host: far as the eye can reach, the plain is darkened by the countless squadrons of the enemy. Probably, after mustering here, their intention was to bear down the Jordan valley, till they came on Joshua at Gilgal, or such other place as he might choose to meet them. But if this was their intention they were outwitted by the activity and intrepidity of Joshua, who resolved, in spite of their overwhelming numbers, to take the aggressive; and, marching, as before, with extraordinary rapidity, to fall on them by surprise and throw them at once into confusion so that they should be unable to bring their chariots and horses into the action.

It was a very serious undertaking for Joshua, and before attempting it he stood much in need of the encouragement of Jehovah—"Be not afraid because of them: for to-morrow about this time will I deliver them up all slain before Israel: thou shalt hough their horses, and burn all their chariots with fire." Not on the number nor on the bravery of his own people, though they had stood by him most nobly, was he to place his reliance, but on the power of God. "Rule thou in the midst of thine enemies" was his *mot d'ordre*, as it was afterwards of that other Joshua, whose battles were not with confused noise nor with garments rolled in blood, but were triumphs of truth and love. Where else should the true warrior be found but in the midst of his enemies? Joshua knew it, and with the promised help of God, did not flinch from the position, though his opponents were like the sand of the seaside, with a corresponding multitude of chariots and horses. Jesus, too, knew it, and resting on the same promise did not shrink from the conflict in His own person; nor did He hesitate to send His apostles into all the world to preach the gospel to every creature, and look forward to a victory not less complete than that of Joshua, when the hordes of the Canaanites were scattered before him.

"To-morrow about this time will I deliver them up all slain before Israel." When he got that assurance, Joshua must already have left Gilgal some days before, and was now within a moderate distance of Merom. There was to be no delay in the completing of the enterprise. "To-morrow about this time." Though, as a rule, the mills of God grind slowly, there are times when their velocity is wonderfully accelerated. He has sometimes wonderful to-morrows. When Hezekiah was gazing appalled on the hosts of Sennacherib as they lay coiled round Jerusalem, God had a "to-morrow about this time" when the terror would be exchanged for a glorious relief. When the apostles met in the upper chamber, and were wondering how they were ever to conquer the world for their Master, there was a "to-morrow" at hand, when the Spirit was to "come down like rain on the mown grass, and like showers that water the earth." When, at the end of the world, iniquity abounds and faith is low, and scoffers are asking, "Where is the promise of His coming?" there will come a "to-morrow about this time" when the heavens will pass away with a great noise, and the elements shall melt with fervent heat, the earth also and all that is therein shall be destroyed. Hold on, brave Joshua, for a little longer; hold on too, ye soldiers of the Lord Jesus, though all the powers of darkness are leagued against you; hold on, ye suffering saints, whose days of pain and nights of waking are such a weariness to your flesh; the glorious "to-morrow" may be at hand which is to end your troubles and bring you the victory!

"We expect a bright to-morrow,
All will be well."

And all was well with Joshua. Arriving suddenly at the waters of Merom, he fell on the mighty host of the enemy, who, taken by surprise, seem not to have struck one blow, but to have been seized at once with that panic which so thoroughly demoralises Eastern hordes, and to have fled in consternation. In three great streams the fugitives sought their homes. One portion made for Misrephothmaim in the southwest, now, it is thought, represented by Musheirifeh on the north border of the plain of Acre; another struck in a northeasterly direction through the valley of the upper Jordan, or east of Hermon to the valley of Mizpeh; a third, passing through the gorge of the Litany, made for great Zidon, in the distant north. Joshua himself would seem to have pursued this column of fugitives, and, passing over a rough path of more than forty miles, not to have abandoned them till they took refuge within the walls of Zidon. If he had attacked and destroyed that stronghold, it might have changed for the better much of the future history of his country; for the Jezebels and Athaliahs of after days were among the worst enemies of Israel. But he did not deem himself called to that duty. It seemed more urgent that he should demolish Hazor, the capital of the confederacy that he had just scattered. So "he turned back and took Hazor, and smote the king thereof with the sword; for Hazor beforetime was the head of all those kingdoms." For this reason Hazor was treated like Jericho, utterly destroyed, as were also the other cities of the confederate kings. One class of cities was spared, called in our version "the cities that stood still in their strength," but better in the Revised—"the cities that stood on their mounds." The custom referred to is that of building cities on mounds or hills for the sake of protection. With the exception of Hazor, none of these were destroyed. The reason probably was, that it would have cost too much time. But it was in such places that the old inhabitants rallied and entrenched themselves, and from them they were able in after years to inflict much loss and give great trouble to Israel. Joshua, however, had not received instructions to destroy them; they were left to serve a purpose in God's plan of discipline (Judg. ii. 3), and while

Israel was often humbled under them their attacks proved occasions of rallying, bringing them back to God, whose worship they were so ready to neglect.

The conquest of Western Palestine was thus virtually completed. First, by taking Jericho, Joshua had possessed himself of the Jordan valley, and established a clear communication with Bashan and Gilead, which the two and a half tribes had received for their inheritance. By the conquest of Ai and Bethel, he had made a way to the great plateau of Western Palestine, and by his treaty with the Gibeonites he had extended his hold a considerable way farther to the south and the west. Then, by the great victory of Bethhoron, he had crushed the southern chiefs and possessed himself, for the time at least, of all that quarter. As to the inhabitants of the central part, we know not (as we have already said) how they were dealt with, but most probably they were too frightened to resist him. (See p. 683.)

The northern section had been subdued at Merom, and much crippled through the pursuit of Joshua after the battle there. The only important parts of the country of which he did not gain possession were the land of the Philistines, the strip of sea coast held by Tyre and Zidon, and some small kingdoms on the northeast. It would seem that in the instructions received by him from Moses, these were not included, for it is expressly said of him that "he left nothing undone of all that the Lord commanded Moses." Emphasis is laid on the fact that his conquests were not confined to one section or denomination of territory, but embraced the whole. "Joshua took all that land, the hill country, and all the South, and all the land of Goshen, and the lowland, and the Arabah, and the hill country of Israel, and the lowland of the same; from Mount Halak (or, the bare mountain) [on the south], that goeth up to Seir [the land of Edom], even unto Baalgad in the valley of Lebanon under Mount Hermon [in the north]: and all their kings he took, and smote them, and put them to death" (R. V.). The "Goshen" here spoken of cannot, of course, be the Egyptian Goshen, for this city was in the neighbourhood of Gibeon (chap. x. 41); but its site has not been identified.

We are told that the wars of Joshua occupied a long time. Probably from five to seven years were consumed by them, for though the pitched battles of Bethhoron and Merom virtually decided the mastership of the country, there must have been a large amount of guerilla warfare, and the sieges of the various cities may have required much time. The list of kings subdued, as given in chap. xii., is a remarkable document. Granting that though called kings they were mostly but little chieftains, still they were formidable enough to a pastoral people unused to the pursuits of war; and it was very striking that not one of them by himself, nor all of them combined, were equal to Joshua. If Joshua was not divinely aided, the conquest of all these chieftains and the capture of their cities is the most inexplicable event in history.

Two additional statements are made towards the close of the eleventh chapter. One is, that with the single exception of Gibeon, no attempt was made by any of the chiefs or cities to make peace with Joshua. "For it was of the Lord to harden their hearts that they should come against Israel in battle, that he might destroy them utterly, and that they might have no favour, but that he might destroy them, as the Lord commanded Moses." It would have been very embarrassing to Joshua if they had submitted spontaneously, and cast themselves on his generosity, for his orders were to destroy them. But this difficulty did not arise. None of the cities seem to have shared the conviction of the Gibeonites that opposition was needless, that Israel was sure to prevail, and get possession of the country. When men's backs are up, to use a common phrase, they will do wonders in the way of facing danger and enduring suffering. Even the resistance of the martyrs cannot be wholly ascribed to holy faith and loyalty to God; in many cases, no doubt, something was due to that dogged spirit that won't submit, that won't be beat, that will endure incredible privation rather than give in. The effect of this resistance by the Canaanites was, that while Joshua's task was increased in one way, it was simplified in another. Ages before, God had given the country to the fathers of the Hebrew nation. That people now came and demanded in God's name possession of the land which He had given them. Had the nations submitted voluntarily they must have left the country to seek new settlements elsewhere. By resisting, they compelled Joshua to meet them with the sword; and having resisted Israel with all their might, nothing remained but that they should encounter the doom which they had so fiercely provoked.

That some of the Canaanites did leave the country seems very probable, although little importance is to be attached to the statement of Procopius that after trying Egypt they settled in Libya, and overspread Africa as far as the Pillars of Hercules. At a fortress in Numidia called Tigisis or Tingis he says that so late as the sixth century after Christ there were discovered near a great wall two pillars of white stone bearing, in Phœnician, the inscription, "We are those who fled before the robber Jeshus, son of Nane." Ewald and others by whom this tradition is noticed are not disposed, owing to its late date, to attach to it any weight.

The other statement relates to the Anakim. Sometime, not precisely defined, while engaged in his conflicts Joshua "cut off the Anakims from the mountains, from Hebron, from Debir, from Anab, and from all the mountains of Judah, and from all the mountains of Israel," leaving none of them except in Gaza, in Gath, and in Ashdod (xi. 21). Afterwards it is said (xv. 14) that it was Caleb that drove from Hebron the three sons of Anak, Sheshai, Ahiman, and Talmai; but this cannot be counted a contradiction inasmuch as "Joshua," being the leader of the army, must be held to represent and include all who fought in connection with his enterprise. These Anakim were the men that had so terrified the ten spies. "And there we saw the giants, the sons of Anak, which come of the giants: and we were in our own sight as grasshoppers, and so we were in their sight" (Num. xiii. 33). To men of little faith, giants, whether physical or moral, are always formidable. Kings, with the resources of an empire at their back; generals, at the head of mighty battalions; intellectual chiefs, with all their talent and brilliancy, their wit, their irony, their power to make the worse appear the better reason, are more than a match for the obscure handfuls to whom the battles of the faith are often left. But if the obscure handfuls are allied with the Lord of hosts, their victory is sure; the triumphant experience of the forty-sixth psalm awaits them: "God is in the midst of her, she shall not be moved; God shall help her, and that right early."

We are weary of the din of arms, and come at last to the refreshing statement: "And the land rested from war." The annals of peace are always more brief than the records of war; and when we reach this short but welcome clause we might wish that it were so expanded as to fill our eyes and our hearts with the blessings which peace scatters with her kindly hand. For that impression we need only to turn to another page of our Bible, and read of the campaigns of another Joshua. "And Jesus went about all Galilee, teaching in their synagogues, and preaching the gospel of the kingdom, and healing all manner of sickness, and all manner of disease among the people." The contrast is very glorious. In His Galilee journeys, Jesus traversed the very region where Joshua had drawn his sword against the confederate kings. Joshua had pursued them as far as Zidon, leaving marks of bloodshed along the whole way; Jesus, when "He departed to the coasts of Tyre and Sidon," went to reward faith, to dispossess devils, and to kindle in a desolate heart thanksgiving and joy. Everywhere, throughout all Galilee and the regions beyond, His advent was accompanied with benedictions, and blessings were scattered by Him in His path.

But let us not indulge in too complete a contrast between the two conquerors. Joshua's rough ploughshare prepared the way for Jesus' words of mercy and deeds of love. God's message to man is not all in honeyed words. Even Jesus, as He went through Galilee, proclaimed, "Repent, for the kingdom of heaven is at hand." And it was those only who gave heed to the call to repent that became possessors of the kingdom.

CHAPTER XXI.

JOSHUA'S OLD AGE—DIVISION FOR THE EASTERN TRIBES.

Joshua xiii., xiv. 1-5.

"The Lord said unto Joshua, Thou art old and stricken in years." To many men and women this would not be a welcome announcement. They do not like to think that they are old. They do not like to think that the bright, joyous, playful part of life is over, and that they are arrived at the sombre years when they must say, "There is no pleasure in them." Then, again, there are some who really find it hard to believe that they are old. Life has flown past so swiftly that before they thought it was well begun it has gone. It seems so short a time since they were in the full play of their youthful energies, that it is hardly credible that they are now in the sere and yellow leaf. Perhaps, too, they have been able to keep their hearts young all the time, and still retain that buoyant sensation which seems to indicate the presence of youth. And are there not some who have verified the psalm—"They that are planted in the house of the Lord shall flourish in the courts of our God. They shall still bring forth fruit in old age, they shall be fat and flourishing"?

But however much men may like to be young, and however much some may retain in old age of the feeling of youth, it is certain that the period of strength has its limit, and the period of life also. To the halest and heartiest, if he be not cut off prematurely, the time must come when God will say to him, "Thou art old." It is a solemn word to hear from the lips of God. God tells me my life is past; what use have I made of it? And what does God think of the use I have made of it? And what account of it shall I be able to give when I stand at His bar?

Let the young think well of this, before it is too late to learn how to live.

To Joshua the announcement that he was old and stricken in years does not appear to have brought any painful or regretful feeling. Perhaps he had aged somewhat suddenly; his energies may have failed consciously and rapidly, after his long course of active and anxious military service. He may have been glad to hear God utter the word; he may have been feeling it himself, and wondering how he should be able to go through the campaigns yet necessary to put the children of Israel in full possession of the land. That word may have fallen on his ear with the happy feeling—how considerate God is! He will not burden my old age with a load not suited for it. Though *His* years have no end, and He knows nothing of failing strength, "He knoweth *our* frame, He remembereth that we are dust." He will not "cast me off in the time of old age, nor forsake me when my strength faileth." Happy confidence, especially for the aged poor! It is the want of trust in the heavenly Father that makes so many miserable in old age. When you will not believe that He is considerate and kind, you are left to your own resources, and often to destitution and misery. But when between Him and you there is the happy relation of father and child; when through Jesus Christ you realise His fatherly love and pity, and in real trust cast yourselves on Him who clothes the lilies and feeds the ravens, your trust is sure to be rewarded, for your heavenly Father knoweth what things you have need of before you ask them.

So Joshua finds that he is now to be relieved by his considerate Master of laborious and anxious service. Not of all service, but of exhausting service, unsuited to his advancing years. Joshua had been a right faithful servant; few men have ever done their work so well. From that day when he stood against Amalek from morning to night, while the rod of Moses was stretched out over him on the hill; thereafter, during all his companionship with Moses on the mount; next in that search-expedition when Caleb and he stood so firm, and did not flinch in the face of the congregation, though every one was for stoning them; and now, from the siege of Jericho to the victory of Merom, and all through the trying and perilous sieges of city after city, year after year, Joshua has proved himself the faithful servant of God and the devoted friend of Israel. During these last years he has enjoyed supreme power, apparently without a rival and without a foe; yet, strange to say, there is no sign of his having been corrupted by power, or made giddy by elevation. He has led a most useful and loyal life, which there is some satisfaction in looking back on. No doubt he is well aware of unnumbered failings: "Who can understand his errors?" But he has the rare satisfaction—oh! who would not wish to share it?—of looking back on a well-spent life, habitually and earnestly regulated amid many infirmities by regard to the will of God. Neither he, nor St. Paul after him, had any trust in their own good works, as a basis of salvation; yet Paul could say, and Joshua might have said it in spirit: "I have fought the good fight, I have finished my course, I have kept the faith: henceforth there is laid up for me a crown of righteousness."

Yet Joshua was not to complete that work to which he had contributed so much: "there remaineth yet very much land to be possessed." At one time, no doubt, he thought otherwise, and he desired otherwise. When the tide of victory was setting in for him so steadily, and region after region of the land was falling into his hands, it was natural to expect that before he ended he would sweep all the enemies of Israel before him, and open every door for them throughout the land, even to its utmost borders. Why not make hay when the sun shone? When God had found so apt an instrument for His great design, why did He not employ him to the end? If the natural term of Joshua's strength had come, why did not that God who had supernaturally lengthened out the day for completing the victory of Bethhoron, lengthen out Joshua's day that the whole land of Canaan might be secured?

Here comes in a great mystery of Providence. Instead of lengthening out the period of Joshua's strength, God seems to have cut it short. We can easily understand the lesson for Joshua himself. It is the lesson which so many of God's servants have had to learn. They start with the idea they are to do everything; they are to reform every abuse, overthrow every stronghold of evil, reduce chaos to order and beauty; as if each were

"the only man on earth
Responsible for all the thistles blown
And tigers couchant, struggling in amaze
Against disease and winter, snarling on
For ever, that the world's not paradise."

Sooner or later they find that they must be satisfied with a much humbler *rôle*. They must learn to

"be content in work,
To do the thing we can, and not presume
To fret because it's little. 'Twill employ
Seven men, they say, to make a perfect pin, . . .
Seven men to a pin, and not a man too much!
Seven generations, haply to this world,
To right it visibly a finger's breadth,
And mend its rents a little."

Joshua must be made to feel—perhaps he needs this—that this enterprise is not his, but God's. And God is not limited to one instrument, or to one age, or to one plan. Never does Providence appear to us so strange, as when a noble worker is cut down in the very midst of his work. A young missionary has just shown his splendid capacity for service, when fever strikes him low, and in a few days all that remains of him is rotting in the ground. What can God mean? we sometimes ask impatiently. Does He not know the rare value and the extreme scarcity of such men, that He sets them up apparently just to throw them down? But "God reigneth, let the people tremble." All that bears on the Christian good of the world is in God's plan, and it is very dear to God, and "precious in the sight of the Lord is the death of His saints." But He is not limited to single agents. When Stephen died, He raised up Saul. For Wicliffe He gave Luther. When George Wishart was burnt He raised up John Knox. Kings, it is said, die, but the king never. The herald that announces "The king is dead," proclaims in the same breath, "God save the king!" God's workers die, but His work goes on. Joshua is superannuated, so far as the work of conquest is concerned, and that work for a time is suspended. But the reason is that, at the present moment, God desires to develop the courage and energy of each particular tribe. And when the time comes to extend still farther the dominion of Israel, an agent will be found well equipped for the service. From the hills of Bethlehem, a godly youth of dauntless bearing will one day emerge, under whom every foe to Israel shall be brought low, and from the river of Egypt to the great river, the river Euphrates, the entire Promised Land shall come under Israel's dominion. And the conquests of David will shine with a brighter lustre than Joshua's, and will be set, as it were, to music of a higher strain. Associated with David's holy songs and holy experience, and with his early life of sadness and humiliation, crowned at last with glory and honour, they will more fitly symbolise the work of the great Joshua, and there will then be diffused over the world a more holy aroma than that of Joshua's conquests,—a fragrance sweet and refreshing to souls innumerable, and fostering the hope of glory,—the rest that remaineth for the people of God, the inheritance incorruptible, and undefiled, and that fadeth not away.

So Joshua must be content to have done his part, and done it well, although he did not conquer all the land, and there yet remained much to be possessed. Without entering in detail into all the geographical notices of this chapter, it will be well to note briefly what parts of the country were still unsubdued.

First, there were all the borders of the Philistines, and all Geshuri; the five lords of the Philistines, dwelling in Gaza, Ashdod, Ascalon, Gath, and Ekron; and also the Avites. This well defined country consisted mainly of a plain "remarkable in all ages for the extreme riches of its soil; its fields of standing corn, its vineyards and oliveyards, are incidentally mentioned in Scripture (Judg. xv. 5); and in the time of famine the land of the Philistines was the hope of Palestine (2 Kings viii. 2). . . . It was also adapted to the growth of military power; for while the plain itself permitted the use of war chariots, which were the chief arm of offence, the occasional elevations which rise out of it offered secure sites for towns and strongholds. It was, moreover, a commercial country; the great thoroughfare between Phœnicia and Syria on the north and Egypt and Arabia on the south. Ashdod and Gaza were the keys of Egypt, and commanded the transit trade, and the stores of frankincense and myrrh which Alexander captured in the latter place prove it to have been a depôt of Arabian produce." *

Geshuri lay between Philistia and the desert, and the Avites were probably some remainder of the Avims, from whom the Philistines conquered the land (Deut. ii. 23).

In many respects it would have been a great boon for the Israelites if Joshua had conquered a people that were so troublesome to them as the Philistines were for many a day. What

* Smith's "Bible Dictionary."

Joshua left undone, Saul began, but failed to achieve, and at last David accomplished. The Geshurites were subdued with the Amalekites while he was dwelling at Ziklag as an ally of the Philistines (1 Sam. xxvii. 8), and the Philistines themselves were brought into subjection, and had to yield to Israel many of their cities (1 Sam. vii. 14; 2 Sam. viii. 1, 12).

Another important section of the country unsubdued was the Phœnician territory—the land of the Sidonians (vv. 4, 6). Also the hilly country across Lebanon, embracing the valley of Cœle-Syria, and apparently the region of Mount Carmel ("from Lebanon unto Misrephothmaim," ver. 6, and comp. chap. xi. 8). No doubt much of this district was recovered in the time of the Judges, and still more in the time of David; but David made peace with the King of Tyre, who still retained the rocky strip of territory that was so useful to a commercial nation, but would have been almost useless to an agricultural people like the Israelites.

Joshua was not called on to conquer these territories in the sense of driving out all the old inhabitants; but he was instructed to divide the whole land among his people—a task involving, no doubt, its own difficulties, but not the physical labour which war entailed. And in this division he was called first to recognise what had already been done by Moses with the part of the country east of the Jordan. That part had been allotted to Reuben, Gad, and half the tribe of Manasseh; and the allotment was still to hold good.

It is remarkable with what fulness the places are described. First, we have the boundaries of that part of the country generally (vv. 9-12); then of the allotments of each of the two and a half tribes (vv. 15-31). With regard to the district as a whole, the conquest under Moses was manifestly complete, from the river Arnon on the south, to the borders of the Geshurites and Maachathites on the north. The only part not subdued were the territories of these Geshurites and Maachathites. The Geshurites here are not to be confounded with the people of the same name mentioned in ver. 2, who were at the opposite extreme—the southwest instead of, as here, the northeast of the land. But no doubt the Syrian Geshurites and Maachathites were brought into subjection by David, with all the other tribes in that region, in his great Syrian war, "when he went to recover his border at the river Euphrates" (2 Sam. viii. 3). But instead of expelling or exterminating them, David seems to have allowed them to remain in a tributary condition, for Geshur had its king in the days of Absalom (2 Sam. xiii. 37), to whom that prince fled after the murder of Amnon. With the Maachathites also David had a family connection (2 Sam. iii. 3).

But though the subjugation and occupation of the eastern part of the land was thus tolerably complete (with the exceptions just mentioned), it remained in the undisturbed possession of Israel for the shortest time of any. From Moabites and Ammonites on the south, Canaanites and Syrians on the north and the east, as well as the Midianites, Amalekites, and other tribes of the desert, it was subject to continual invasions. In fact, it was the least settled and least comfortable part of all the country; and doubtless it became soon apparent that though the two tribes and a half had seemed to be very fortunate in having their wish granted to settle in this rich and beautiful region, yet on the whole they had been penny-wise and pound-foolish. Not only were they incessantly assailed and worried by their neighbours, but they were the first to be carried into captivity, when the King of Assyria directed his eyes to Palestine. They had shown somewhat of the spirit of Lot, and they suffered somewhat of his punishment. It is worthy of remark that even at this day this eastern province is the most disturbed part of Palestine. The Bedouins are ever liable to make their attacks wherever there are crops or cattle to tempt their avarice. People will not sow where they have no chance of reaping; and thus it is that much of that productive region lies waste. The moral is not far to seek: in securing wealth, look not merely at the apparent productiveness of the investment, but give heed to its security, its stability. It is not all gold that glitters either on the stock-exchange or anywhere else. And even that which is real gold partakes of the current instability. We must come back to our Saviour's advice to investors, if we would really be safe: "Lay not up for yourselves treasures on earth, where moth and rust do corrupt, and where thieves break through and steal. But lay up for yourselves treasures in heaven, where moth and rust do not corrupt, and where thieves do not break through nor steal."

The specification of the allotments need not detain us long. Reuben's was the farthest south. His southern and eastern flanks were covered by the Moabites, who greatly annoyed him. "Unstable as water, he did not excel." Gad settled north of Reuben. In his lot was the southern part of Gilead; Mahanaim, and Peniel, celebrated in the history of Jacob, and Ramothgilead, conspicuous in after times. East of Gad were the Ammonites, who proved as troublesome to that tribe as Moab did to Reuben. To the half-tribe of Manasseh the kingdom of Og fell, and the northern half of Gilead. Jabesh-gilead, where Saul routed the Ammonites, was in this tribe (1 Sam. xi.). Here also were some of the places on the lake of Galilee mentioned in the gospel history; here the "desert place" across the sea to which our Lord used to retire for rest; here He fed the multitude; here He cured the demoniac; and here were some of the mountains where He would spend the night in prayer.

In our Lord's time this portion of Palestine was called Perea. Under the dominion of the Romans, it was comparatively tranquil, and our Lord would sometimes select it, on account of its quiet, as his route to Jerusalem. And many of His gifts of love and mercy were doubtless scattered over its surface.

Two statements are introduced parenthetically in this chapter which hardly belong to the substance of it. One of these, occurring twice, respects the inheritance of the Levites (vv. 14, 33). No territorial possessions were allotted to them corresponding to those of the other tribes. In the one place it is said that "the sacrifices of the Lord God of Israel made by fire were their inheritance"; in the other, that "the Lord God of Israel was their inheritance." We shall afterwards find the arrangements for the Levites more fully detailed (chaps. xx., xxi.). This early allusion to the subject, even before the allotments in Western Palestine begin to be described, shows that their case had been carefully considered, and that it was not by oversight but deliberately that the country was divided without any section being reserved for them.

The other parenthetical statement respects the death of Balaam. " Balaam also, the soothsayer, did the children of Israel slay with the sword among them that were slain by them " (ver. 22). It appears from Numb. xxxi. 8 that the slaughter of Balaam took place in the days of Moses, by the hands of the expedition sent by him to chastise the Midianites for drawing the Israelites into idolatry. That the fact should be again noticed here is probably due to the circumstance that the death of Balaam occurred at the place which had just been noted—the boundary line between Reuben and Gad. It was a fact well worthy of being again noted. It was a fact never to be forgotten that the man who had been sent for to curse was constrained to bless. As far as Balaam's public conduct was concerned, he behaved well to Israel. He emphasised their Divine election and their glorious privileges. He laid especial stress upon the fact that they were not a Bedouin horde, rushing about in search of plunder, but a sacramental host, executing the judgments of a righteous God—" The Lord his God is with him, and the shout of a king is among them." This was a valuable testimony, for which Israel might well be grateful. It was when Balaam took part in that disgraceful plot to entice Israel into sensuality and idolatry that he came out in his real colours. It seemed to him very clever, no doubt, to obey the Divine command in the letter by absolutely refusing to curse Israel, while at the same time he accomplished the object he was sent for by seducing them into sins which brought down on them the judgments of God. Nevertheless, he reckoned without his host. Possibly he gained his reward, but he did not live to enjoy it; and " what shall a man be profited if he gain the whole world and forfeit his own life?" (Matt. xvi. 26, R. V.).

The two and a half tribes were well taught by the fate of Balaam that, in the end, however cunningly a man may act, his sin will find him out. They were emphatically reminded that the sins of sensuality and idolatry are exceedingly hateful in the sight of God, and certain to be punished. They were assured by the testimony of Balaam, that Israel, if only faithful, would never cease to enjoy the Divine protection and blessing. But they were reminded that God is not mocked: that whatsoever a man soweth, that shall he also reap. Balaam had sown to the flesh; of the flesh it behoved him to reap corruption. And so must it ever be; however ingeniously you may disguise sin, however you may conceal it from yourself, and persuade yourself to believe that you are not doing wrong, sin must show itself ultimately in its true colours, and your ingenious disguises will not shield it from its doom:—" The wages of sin is DEATH."

CHAPTER XXII.

THE INHERITANCE OF CALEB.*

JOSHUA xiv. 6-15.

CALEB is one of those men whom we meet with seldom in Bible history, but whenever we do meet them we are the better for the meeting.

* There is some difficulty in adjusting the three passages in which the settlement of Caleb is referred to. From this

Bright and brave, strong, modest and cheerful, there is honesty in his face, courage and decision in the very pose of his body, and the calm confidence of faith in his very look and attitude. It is singular that there should be cause to doubt whether his family were *originally* of the promised seed. When introduced to us in the present passage he is emphatically called " Caleb, the son of Jephunneh the Kenezite" (R. V., Kenizzite, rightly, same as Kenizzite in Gen. xv. 19), as if he had been a descendant of Kenaz, a son of Esau (Gen. xxxvi. 11 and 15), and a member of the Kenizzite tribe. It was not customary to distinguish Israelites in this way, but only those who had come among them from other tribes, like " Heber the Kenite," " Jael, the wife of Heber the Kenite" (Judg. iv. 11, 17), Uriah the Hittite, Hushai the Archite, etc. Moreover, Othniel, Caleb's younger brother, is called the son of Kenaz (Josh. xv. 17); and further, when it is recorded in the fourteenth verse of this chapter that Hebron became the possession of Caleb, the reason assigned is that he " wholly followed the Lord God *of Israel.*" On the other hand, in the genealogical list of 1 Chron. iv. 13, 15, Othniel and Caleb occur as if they were regular members of the tribe; but that list shows obvious signs of imperfection. On the whole, the preponderance of evidence is in favour of the opinion that Caleb's family were originally outside the covenant, but had become proselytes, like Hobab, Rahab, Ruth, and Heber. Their faith was preeminently the fruit of conviction, and not the accident of heredity. It had a firmer basis than that of most Israelites. It was woven more closely into the texture of their being, and swayed their lives more powerfully. It is pleasing to think that there may have been many such proselytes; that the promise to Abraham may have attracted souls from the east, and the west, and the north, and the south; that even beyond the limits of the twelve tribes many hearts may have been cheered, and many lives elevated and purified by the promise to him, " In thee and in thy seed shall all the families of the earth be blessed."

Caleb and Joshua had believed and acted alike, in opposition to the other ten spies; but Caleb occupies the more prominent place in the story of their heroism and faith. It was he that " stilled the people before Moses, and said, Let us go up at once, and possess it; for we are well able to overcome it" (Numb. xiii. 30); and at first his name occurs alone, as exempted from the sentence of exclusion against the rest of his generation: " But my servant Caleb, because he had another spirit with him, and hath followed Me fully, him will I bring into the land whereinto he went: and his seed shall possess it" (Numb. xiv. 24). As we have said before, it is

first passage of the three, we are led to think that it was before the tribe of Judah obtained its portion. Again, from chap. xv. 13 we might suppose that it was simultaneously with the rest of the tribe. From Judg. i. 10, again, it might be thought that the subduing of the natives in Hebron was effected, not by Caleb alone, but by the tribe of Judah, and that it took place "after the death of Joshua" (Judg. i. 1). Putting all these together, it would appear that Hebron was assigned to Caleb before the tribe of Judah was settled ; that this allocation was ratified at the general settlement ; that as Caleb was a member of the tribe, his services against the Canaanites, and especially the Anakim, were ascribed to his tribe ; and that the process of dispossessing the Canaanites went on for some time after the death of Joshua. The repetitions in the narrative concerning Caleb form one of the considerations that favour the idea of more sources than one having been made use of in the composition of this book.

probable that Caleb was the readier speaker, and it is possible that he was the firmer man. Joshua seems to have wanted that power of initiation which Caleb had. It was because he had always been a good follower that Joshua in his old age was fitted to be a leader. Because he had been a good servant he became a good master. As long as Moses lived, Joshua was his servant. After Moses died, Joshua set himself simply to carry out his instructions. It was a happy thing for him on the return of the ten spies that Caleb was one of them, otherwise he might have found himself in a condition of embarrassment. Caleb was evidently the man who led the opposition to the ten, not only asserting the course of duty, but manifesting the spirit of contempt and defiance toward the faithless cowards that forgot that God was with them. In his inmost heart Joshua was quite of his mind, but probably he wanted the energetic manner, the ringing voice, the fearless attitude of his more demonstrative companion. Certain it is that Caleb reaped the chief honour of that day.*

It is beautiful to see that there was no rivalry between them. Not only did Caleb interpose no remonstrance when Joshua was called to succeed Moses, but he seems all through the wars to have yielded to him the most loyal and hearty submission. God had set His seal on Joshua, and the people had ratified the appointment, and Caleb was too magnanimous to allow any poor ambition of his, if he had any, to come in the way of the Divine will and the public good. His affectionate and cordial bearing on the present occasion seems to show that not even in the corner of his heart did there linger a trace of jealousy toward the old friend and companion whom on that occasion he had surpassed, but who had been set so much higher than himself. He came to him as the recognised leader of the people—as the man whose voice was to decide the question he now submitted, as the judge and arbiter in a matter which very closely concerned him and his house.

And yet there are indications of tact on the part of Caleb, of a thorough understanding of the character of Joshua, and of the sort of considerations by which he might be expected to be swayed. There were two grounds on which he might reasonably look for the conceding of his request—his personal services, and the promise of Moses. Caleb knows well that the promise of Moses will influence Joshua much more than any other consideration; therefore he puts it in the foreground. "Thou knowest the thing that the Lord said unto Moses, the man of God, concerning me and thee in Kadesh-barnea." "Moses, the man of God." Why does Caleb select that remarkable epithet? Why add anything to the usual name, Moses? The use of the epithet was honouring to all the three. That which constituted the highest glory of Moses was that he was so much at one with God. God's will was ever his law, and he was in such close sympathy with God that whatever instructions he gave on any subject might be assumed to be in accordance with God's will. Moreover, in calling him "the man of God" when addressing Joshua, Caleb assumed that Joshua would be impressed by this consideration, and would be disposed to agree to a request which was not only sanctioned by the will of Moses, but by that higher will which Moses constantly recognised. In short, when Joshua considered that the particular wish of Moses which Caleb now recalled was only the expression of the Divine will, Caleb felt assured that he could not withhold his consent. The three men were indeed a noble trio, worthy descendants of their father Abraham, even if one of the three was no son of Jacob. Long before our Lord taught the petition "Thy will be done on earth as it is in heaven," it had become habitual to them all. Moses was indeed "the man of God,"—pre-eminently in fellowship with Him; in a lower sphere both Caleb and Joshua were of the same order, men who tried to live their lives, and every part of them, only in God.

Having fortified his plea with this strong reference at once to Moses and to God, Caleb proceeds to rehearse the service which had led to the promise of Moses. The facts could not but be well known to Joshua. "Forty years old was I when Moses, the servant of the Lord, sent me from Kadesh-barnea to spy out the land, and I brought him word again as it was in my heart. Nevertheless, my brethren that went up with me made the heart of the people melt; but I wholly followed the Lord my God." Why does Caleb put the matter in this way? Why does he not couple Joshua with himself as having been faithful on that never-to-be-forgotten occasion? The only explanation that seems feasible is, that from the pre-eminent position of Joshua this was unnecessary, perhaps it might have appeared even unbecoming. A soldier making a request of the Duke of Wellington, and recalling some service he had done at the battle of Waterloo, would hardly think it necessary, or even becoming, to say how the Duke, too, had been there, and what surpassing service he had rendered on that day. A soldier like the Duke, occupying a position of unrivalled pre-eminence on account of long and brilliant service, does not need to be told what he has done. Joshua was now the leader of Israel, and the last few years had crowned him with such manifold glory that his whole life was transfigured, and individual acts of service did not need to be spoken of. Caleb was comparatively an obscure individual, whose fame rested on a single service now nearly half a century old, which could not, indeed, be quite forgotten, but amid the brilliant events of later times might easily pass out of sight and out of mind. There was no disparagement of Joshua, therefore, in his not being mentioned by Caleb, but, on the contrary, a silent tribute to his exalted office as chief ruler of Israel, and to his all but unparalleled services, especially during these later years.

"I brought him word again, *as it was in my heart.*" The statement is made in no boasting spirit, and yet what a rare virtue it denotes! Caleb, as we now say, had the courage of his convictions. He had both an honest heart and an honest tongue. We can have but little idea what temptations he lay under *not* to speak what was in his heart. For six weeks these ten men had been his close companions. They had eaten together, slept under the same canvas, walked by the same paths, beguiled the long way by story and anecdote, and no doubt by joke and play of humour, and done kind offices to each other as circumstances required. To break away from

---

* Some readers may no doubt prefer the explanation that when Caleb is mentioned alone one document was followed, and when Caleb and Joshua are coupled, another.

your own set, from the comrades of your campaign, to upset their plans, and counsel those in power to a course diametrically opposed to theirs, is one of the most difficult of social duties. And in these days of ours there is no duty more commonly set aside. Moral cowardice has been well said to be one of the most common vices of our age.

What more common in Parliament, for example, than for men to differ strongly from some of the measures of their party, and yet, because it is their party, support them by their votes? And in the ranks of the Church and of its various sections the same tendency prevails, though it may be in a less degree. Of the many able and seemingly honest prelates of the Roman Church who dissented, often with vehemence, from the Vatican decree of the pope's infallibility, what became finally of their opposition? Were there more than one or two who did not surrender in the end, and agree to profess what they did not believe? And to come to more ordinary matters, when our opinions on religious subjects are at a discount, when they are met with ridicule, how often do we conceal them, or trim and modify them in order that we may not share in the current condemnation? The men that have the courage of their convictions are often social martyrs, shut out from the fellowship of their brethren, shut out from every berth of honour or emolument, and yet, for their courage and honesty, worthy of infinitely higher regard than whole hundreds of the time-servers that "get on" in the world by humouring its errors and its follies.

Nevertheless, though most of us show ourselves miserably weak by *not* speaking out all that is "in our hearts," especially when the honour of our Lord and Master is concerned, we are able to appreciate and cannot fail to admire the noble exhibitions of courage that we sometimes meet with. That beautiful creation of Milton's, the Seraph Abdiel, "faithful found among the faithless, faithful only he," is the type and ideal of the class. Shadrach, Meshach, and Abednego resisting the enthusiasm of myriads and calmly defying the fiery furnace; the Apostle Paul clinging to his views of the law and the gospel when even his brother Peter had begun to waver; Martin Luther, with his foot on the Bible, confronting the whole world; John Knox defying sovereign and nobles and priests alike, determined that the gospel should be freely preached; Carey going out as a missionary to India amid the derision of the world, because he could not get the words out of his head, "Go ye into all the world, and preach the gospel unto every creature,"—have all exemplified the Caleb spirit that must utter what is in the heart; nor has any new idea commonly laid hold of mankind till the struggles of some great hero or the ashes of some noble martyr have gone to sanctify the cause.

"He that believeth shall not make haste." Caleb believed, and therefore he was patient. Five-and-forty long years had elapsed since Moses, the man of God, speaking in the Spirit of God, had promised him a particular inheritance in the land. It was a long time for faith to live on a promise, but, like a tree in the face of a cliff that seems to grow out of the solid rock, it derived nourishment from unseen sources. It was a long time to be looking forward; but Caleb, though he did not receive the promise during all that time, was persuaded of it and embraced it, and believed that at last it would come true. He did not anticipate the proper time, though he might have had as plausible reasons for doing so as the two tribes and a half had for asking leave to settle on the east side of the river. He bore his share of warlike work, bore the burden and heat of the day, waited till the proper time for dividing the land. Nor did he rush forward selfishly by himself, disregarding the interests of the rest of his tribe; for the children of Judah, recognising his claim, draw near to Joshua along with him. Nor was it a portion of the land which any tribe might be eager to enter upon that he asked; for it was still so harassed by the Anakim, that there would be no peace till that formidable body of giants were driven out.

It seems that when acting as one of the twelve spies, Caleb had in some emphatic way taken his stand on Hebron. "The land *on which thy foot hath trodden* will be an inheritance to thee." Perhaps the spies were too terrified to approach Hebron, for the sons of the Anakim were there, and, in the confidence of faith, Caleb, or Caleb and Joshua, had gone into it alone. Moses had promised him Hebron, and now he came to claim it. But he came to claim it under circumstances that would have induced most men to let it alone. The driving out of the Anakim was a formidable duty, and the task might have seemed more suitable for one who had the strength and enthusiasm of youth on his side. But Caleb, though eighty-five, was yet young. Age is not best measured by years. He was a remarkable instance of prolonged vigour and youthful energy. "As yet I am as strong this day as I was in the day that Moses sent me; as my strength was then, even so is my strength now, for war, and to go out and to come in." Faith, and temperance, and cheerfulness are wonderful aids to longevity. As one reads these words of Caleb, one recalls the saying of a well-known physician, Dr. Richardson, that the human frame might last for a hundred years if it were only treated aright.

There is something singularly touching in Caleb's asking as a favour what was really a most hazardous but important service to the nation. Rough though these Hebrew soldiers were, they were capable of the most gentlemanly and chivalrous acts. There can be no higher act of courtesy than to treat as a favour to yourself what is really a great service to another. Well done, Caleb! You do not ask for a berth which there will be no trouble in taking or in keeping. You are not like Issachar, the strong ass couching between the sheepfolds: "and he saw a resting-place that it was good, and the land that it was pleasant; and he bowed his shoulder to bear, and became a servant under task-work." The dew of youth is yet upon you, the stirring of lofty purpose and noble endeavour; you are like the warhorse of Job—" he paweth in the valley and rejoiceth in his strength; he mocketh at fear, and is not dismayed; he smelleth the battle afar off, the thunder of the captains and the shouting."

There is nothing we admire more in military annals than a soldier volunteering for the most hazardous and difficult of posts,—showing

"That stern joy which warriors feel
In foemen worthy of their steel."

In the spiritual warfare, too, we do not want instances of the same spirit. We recall Captain Allan Gardiner choosing Tierra del Fuego as his mission sphere just because the people were so ferocious, the climate so repulsive, and the work so difficult that no one else was likely to take it up. We think of the second band who went out after Gardiner and his companions had been starved to death; and still more after these were massacred by the natives, of the third detachment who were moved simply by the consideration that the case was seemingly so desperate. Or we think of Livingstone begging the directors of the London Missionary Society, wherever they sent him, to be sure that it was "Forward"; turning aside from all previous mission stations, and the comparative ease they afforded, to grapple with the barbarian where he had never begun to be tamed; his eyes thirsting for unknown scenes and untried dangers, because he scorned to build on the foundation of others, and thirsted for "fresh woods and pastures new." We think of him persevering in his task from year to year in the same lofty spirit; disregarding the misery of protracted pain, the intense longings of his weary heart for home, the repulsive society of savages and cannibals, the vexations, disappointments, and obstacles that seemed to multiply every day, the treachery of so-called friends whom he had helped to raise, the indifference of a careless world, and of a languid Church; but ever girding himself with fresh energy for the task which he had undertaken, and of which the difficulties and trials had never been absent from his thoughts. We think of many a young missionary turning away from the comfortable life which he might lead at home and which many of his companions will lead, that he may go where the need is greatest and the fight is hottest, and so render to his Master the greatest possible service. A crowd of noble names comes to our recollection—Williams, and Judson, and Morrison, and Burns, and Patteson, and Keith-Falconer, and Hannington, and Mackay—men for whom even the Anakim had no terrors, but rather an attraction; but who, serving under another Joshua, differed from Caleb in this, that what they desired was not to destroy these ferocious Anakim, but to conquer them by love, and to demonstrate the power of the gospel of Jesus Christ to change the vilest reprobates into sons of God.

And even now there are other Anakim among us for whom the fate of the Canaanite giants ought to be reserved. Anakim within us—greed, selfishness, love of ease, lust, passion, cruelty—all, if we are faithful, to be put to the edge of the sword. And there are Anakim, tremendous Anakim, around us—drunkenness, and all that fosters it, despite the paltry excuses we so often hear; sensuality, that vile murderer of soul and body together; avarice, so cruelly unjust, and content to gather its hoard from the thews and sinews of men and women to whom life has become worse than slavery; luxurious living, that mocks the struggles of thousands to whom one crumb from the table or one rag from the wardrobe would bring such a blessed relief. With giants like these we need to wage incessant war, and for the necessary spirit we need constant supplies of the faith and courage that were so remarkable in Caleb. He followed the Lord *fully;* believing that if the Lord deserved to be followed at all, He deserved to be followed in full. What was there to gain by following Him one half, and surrendering the other half to the world? Could he count on God helping him if he went with but half his heart into His service, and, like Lot's wife, looked back even when flying from Sodom? "Thou shalt love the Lord thy God with all thy heart, and with all thy soul, and with all thy strength, and with all thy might."

The tendency to compromise is one of the besetting sins of the day. In the army or the navy, if one is to serve God at all, one must serve Him wholly. Decision is eminently requisite there, and Christians there are commonly more whole-hearted and consistent than in many circles nominally Christian. Decision is manly, is noble; it brings rest within, and in the end it conciliates the respect of the bitterest foes. Courage is the ornament of Christianity, and the crown of the Christian youth. "FEAR NOT" is one of the brightest gems of the Bible.

CHAPTER XXIII.

THE DISTRIBUTION OF THE LAND.

JOSHUA xv.-xix.

WE come now in earnest to the distribution of the land. The two and a half tribes have already got their settlements on the other side of Jordan; but the other side of Jordan, though included in the land of promise, was outside the part specially consecrated as the theatre of Divine manifestation and dealing. From Dan to Beersheba and from Jordan to the sea was *par excellence* the land of Israel; it was here the patriarchs had dwelt; it was here that most of the promises had been given; it was here that Abraham, Isaac, and Jacob had been buried; and here also, though in another tomb, that the bones of Joseph had been laid. This portion was the kernel of the inheritance, surrounded by a wide penumbra of more feeble light and fewer privileges. In due time there arose a holy of holies within this consecrated region, when Jerusalem became the capital, the focus of blessing and holy influence.

Now that the distribution of this part of the country begins, we must give special attention to the operation. The narrative looks very bare, but important principles and lessons underlie it. These lists of unfamiliar names look like the *débris* of a quarry—hard, meaningless, and to us useless. But nothing is inserted in the Bible without a purpose,—a purpose that in some sense bears on the edification of the successive generations and the various races of men. We are not to pass the distribution over because it looks unpromising, but rather to inquire with all the greater care what the bearing of it is on ourselves.

1. Now, in the first place, there is something to be learned from the maintenance of the distinction of the twelve tribes, and the distribution of the country into portions corresponding to each. In some degree this was in accordance with Oriental usage; for the country had already been occupied by various races, dwelling in a kind of unity—the Canaanites, Amorites, Hittites, Hivites, Jebusites, Perizzites, and Girgashites. What was peculiar to Israel was, that each of the tribes was descended from one of Jacob's sons,

and that their relation to each other was conspicuously maintained, though their dwelling-places were apart. It was an arrangement capable of becoming a great benefit under a right spirit, or a great evil under the opposite. As in the case of the separate States of North America, or the separate cantons of Switzerland, it provided for variety in unity; it gave a measure of local freedom and independence, while it maintained united action; it contributed to the life and vigour of the commonwealth, without destroying its oneness of character, or impairing its common purpose and aim. It promoted that picturesque variety often found in little countries, where each district has a dialect, or a pronunciation, or traditions, or a character of its own; as Yorkshire differs from Devon, or Lancashire from Cornwall; Aberdeenshire from Berwick, or Fife from Ayr. As in a garden, variety of species enlivens and enriches the effect, so in a community, variety of type enriches and enlivens the common life. A regiment of soldiers clothed in the same uniform, measuring the same stature, marching to the same step, may look very well as a contrast to the promiscuous crowd; but when a painter would paint a striking picture it is from the promiscuous crowd in all their variety of costume and stature and attitude that his figures are drawn. In the case of the Hebrew commonwealth, the distinction of tribes became smaller as time went on, and in New Testament times the three great districts Judæa, Samaria, and Galilee showed only the survival of the fittest. A larger individuality and a wider variety would undoubtedly have prevailed if a good spirit had continued to exist among the tribes, and if all of them had shown the energy and the enterprise of some.

But the wrong spirit came in, and came in with a witness, and mischief ensued. For distinctions in race and family are apt to breed rivalry and enmity, and not only to destroy all the good which may come of variety, but to introduce interminable mischief. For many a long day the Scottish clans were like Ishmael, their hand against every man, and every man's hand against them; or at least one clan was at interminable feud with another, and the country was wretched and desolate. Among the twelve tribes of Israel the spirit of rivalry soon showed itself, leading to disastrous consequences. In the time of the judges, the men of Ephraim exhibited their temper by envying Gideon when he subdued the Midianites, and Jephthah when he subdued the Ammonites; and under Jephthah a prodigious slaughter of Ephraimites resulted from their unreasonable spirit. In the time of the kings, a permanent schism was caused by the revolt of the ten tribes from the house of David. Thus it is that the sin of man often perverts arrangements designed for good, and so perverts them that they become sources of grievous evil. The family order is a thing of heaven; but let a bad spirit creep into a family, the result is fearful. Let husband and wife become alienated; let father and son begin to quarrel; let brother set himself against brother, and let them begin to scheme not for mutual benefit but for mutual injury, no limits can be set to the resulting mischief and misery.

Many arrangements of our modern civilisation that conduce to our comfort when in good order, become sources of unexampled evil when they go wrong. The drainage of houses conduces much to comfort while it works smoothly; but let the drains become choked, and send back into our houses the poisonous gases bred of decomposition, the consequences are appalling. The sanitary inspector must be on the alert to detect mischief in its very beginnings, and apply the remedy before we have well become conscious of the evil. And so a vigilant eye needs ever to be kept on those arrangements of providence that are so beneficial when duly carried out, and so pernicious when thoughtlessly perverted. What a wonderful thing is a little forbearance at the beginning of a threatened strife! What a priceless blessing is the soft answer that turneth away wrath! There is a pithy tract bearing the title "The Oiled Feather." The oiled feather has a remarkable power of smoothing surfaces that would otherwise grate and grind upon each other, and so of averting evil. Among Christians it should be always at hand; for surely, if the forbearance and love that avert quarrels ought to be found anywhere, it is among those who have received the fulness of Divine love and grace in Jesus Christ. Surely among them there should be no perversion of Divine arrangements; in their homes no quarrels, and in their hearts no rivalry. They ought, instead, to be the peacemakers of the world, not only because they have received the peace that passeth understanding, but because their Master has said, "Blessed are the peacemakers, for they shall be called the children of God."

2. Again, in the allocation of the tribes in their various territories we have an instance of a great natural law, the law of distribution, a law that, on the whole, operates very beneficially throughout the world. In society there is both a centripetal and a centrifugal force; the centripetal chiefly human, the centrifugal chiefly Divine. Men are prone to cluster together; God promotes dispersion. Through the Divine law of marriage, a man leaves his father's house and cleaves to his wife; a new home is established, a new centre of activity, a new source of population. In the early ages they clustered about the plain of Shinar; the confusion of tongues scattered them abroad. And generally, in any fertile and desirable spot, men have been prone to multiply till food has failed them, and either starvation at home or emigration abroad becomes inevitable. And so it is that, in spite of their cohesive tendency, men are now pretty well scattered over the globe. And when once they are settled in new homes, they acquire adaptation to their locality, and begin to love it. The Esquimaux is not only adapted to his icy home, but is fond of it. The naked negro has no quarrel with the burning sun, but enjoys his sunny life. We of the temperate zone can hardly endure the heat of the tropics, and we shiver at the very thought of Lapland. It is a proof of Divine wisdom that a world that presents such a variety of climates and conditions has, in all parts of it, inhabitants that enjoy their life.

The same law operates in the vegetable world. Everywhere plants seem to discover the localities where they thrive best. Even in the same country you have one flora for the valley and another for the mountain. The lichen spreads itself along the surface of rocks, or the hard bark of ancient trees; the fungus tarries in damp, unventilated corners; the primrose settles on open banks; the fern in shady groves. There is always a place for the plant, and a plant for the place. And it is so with animals too. The elephant in the spreading forest, the rabbit in the sandy down, the beaver beside the stream, the caterpillar in the leafy garden. If we could explore the ocean we should find the law of distribution in full activity there. There is one great order of fishes for fresh water, another for salt; one great class of insects in hot climates, another in temperate; birds of the air, from the eagle to the humming-bird, from the ostrich to the bat, in localities adapted to their habits. We ask not whether this result was due to creation or to evolution. There it is, and its effect is to cover the earth. All its localities, desirable and undesirable, are more or less occupied with inhabitants. Some of the great deserts that our imagination used to create in Africa or elsewhere do not exist. Barren spots there are, and "miry places and marshes given to salt," but they are not many. The earth has been replenished, and the purpose of God so far fulfilled.

And then there is a distribution of talents. We are not all created alike, with equal dividends of the gifts and faculties that minister in some way to the purposes of our life. We depend more or less on one another; women on men, and men on women; the young on the old, and sometimes the old on the young; persons of one talent on those of another talent, those with strong sinews on those with clear heads, and those with clear heads on those with strong sinews; in short, society is so constituted that what each has he has for all, and what all have they have for each. The principle of the division of labour is brought in; and in a well-ordered community the general wealth and well-being of the whole are better promoted by the interchange of offices, than if each person within himself had a little stock of all that he required.

The same law of distribution prevails in the Church of Christ. It was exemplified in an interesting way in the case of our Lord's apostles. No one of these was a duplicate of another. Four of them, taking in Paul, were types of varieties which have been found in all ages of the Church. In a remarkable paper in the *Contemporary Review*, Professor Godet of Neuchâtel, after delineating the characteristics of Peter, James, John, and Paul, remarked what an interesting thing it was, that four men of such various temperaments should all have found supreme satisfaction in Jesus of Nazareth, and should have yielded up to Him the homage and service of their lives. And throughout the history of the Church, the distribution of gifts has been equally marked. Chrysostom and Augustine, Jerome and Ambrose, Bernard and Anselm, were all of the same stock, but not of the same type. At the Reformation men of marked individuality were provided for every country. Germany had Luther and Melancthon; France, Calvin and Coligny; Switzerland, Zwingle and Farel, Viret and Œcolampadius; Poland, A-Lasco; Scotland, Knox; England, Cranmer, Latimer, and Hooper. The missionary field has in like manner been provided for. India has had her Schwartz, her Carey, her Duff, and a host of others; China her Morrison, Burmah her Judson, Polynesia her Williams, Africa her Livingstone. The most unattractive and inhospitable spots have been supplied. Greenland was not too cold for the Moravians, nor the leper-stricken communities of India or Africa too repulsive. And never were Christian men more disposed than to-day to honour that great Christian law of distribution—"Go ye into all the world, and preach the gospel to every creature."

It was a great providential law, therefore, that was recognised in the partition of the land of Canaan among the tribes. Provision was thus made for so scattering the people that they should occupy the whole country, and become adapted to the places where they settled, and to the pursuits proper to them. Even where there seems to us to have been a mere random distribution of places, there may have been underlying adaptations for them, or possibilities of adaptation known only to God; at all events the law of adaptation would take effect, by which a man becomes adapted and attached to the place that not only gives him a home but the means of living, and by which, too, he becomes a greater adept in the methods of work which ensure success.

3. Still further, in the allocation of the tribes in their various territories we have an instance of the way in which God designed the earth to minister most effectually to the wants of man. We do not say that the method now adopted in Canaan was the only plan of distributing land that God ever sanctioned; very probably it was the same method as had prevailed among the Canaanites; but it is beyond doubt that, such as it was, it was sanctioned by God for His chosen people.

It was a system of peasant proprietorship. The whole landed property of the country was divided among the citizens. Each freeborn Israelite was a landowner, possessing his estate by a tenure, which, so long as the constitution was observed, rendered its permanent alienation from his family impossible. At the fiftieth year, the year of jubilee, every inheritance returned, free of all encumbrance, to the representatives of the original proprietor. The arrangement was equally opposed to the accumulation of overgrown properties in the hands of the few, and to the loss of all property on the part of the many. The extremes of wealth and poverty were alike checked and discouraged, and the lot eulogised by Agur—a moderate competency, neither poverty nor riches, became the general condition of the citizens.

It is difficult to tell what extent of land fell to each family. The portion of the land divided by Joshua has been computed at twenty-five million acres.* Dividing this by 600,000, the probable number of *families* at the time of the settlement, we get forty-two acres as the average size of each property. For a Roman citizen, seven acres was counted enough to yield a moderate maintenance, so that even in a country of ordinary productiveness the extent of the Hebrew farms would, before further subdivision became necessary, have been ample. When the population increased the inheritance would of course have to be subdivided. But for several generations this, so far from an inconvenience, would be a positive benefit. It would bring about a more complete development of the resources of the soil. The great rule of the Divine economy was thus honoured—nothing was lost.

There is no reason to suppose that the peasant proprietorship of the Israelites induced a stationary and stagnant condition of society, or reduced it to one uniform level—a mere con-

* See Wines on the "Laws of the Ancient Hebrews," p. 388.

glomeration of men of uniform wealth, resources, and influence. Though the land was divided equally at first, it could not remain so divided long. In the course of providence, when the direct heirs failed, or when a man married a female proprietor, two or more properties would belong to a single family. Increased capital, skill, and industry, or unusual success in driving out the remaining Canaanites, would tend further to the enlargement of properties. Accordingly we meet with "men of great possessions," like Jair the Gileadite, Boaz of Bethlehem, Nabal of Carmel, or Barzillai the Gileadite, even in the earlier periods of Jewish history.* There was a sufficient number of men of wealth to give a pleasing variety and healthful impulse to society, without producing the evils of enormous accumulation on the one hand, or frightful indigence on the other.†

We in this country, after reaching the extreme on the opposite side, are now trying to get back in the direction of this ancient system. All parties seem now agreed that something of the nature of peasant proprietorship is necessary to solve the agrarian problem in Ireland and in Great Britain too. It is only the fact that in Britain commercial enterprise and emigration afford so many outlets for the energies of our landless countrymen that has tolerated the abuses of property so long among us,—the laws of entail and primogeniture, the accumulation of property far beyond the power of the proprietor to oversee or to manage, the employment of land agents acting solely for the proprietor, and without that sense of responsibility or that interest in the welfare of the people which is natural to the proprietor himself. It is little wonder that theories of land-possession have risen up which are as impracticable in fact as they are wild and lawless in principle. Such desperate imaginations are the fruit of despair—absolute hopelessness of getting back in any other way to a true land law,—to a state of things in which the land would yield the greatest benefit to the whole nation. Not only ought it to supply food and promote health, but also a familiarity with nature, and a sense of freedom, and thus produce contentment and happiness, and a more kindly feeling among all classes. It seems to us one of the most interesting features of the land law recently brought in for Ireland that it tends towards an arrangement of the land in the direction of God's early designs regarding it. If it be feasible for Ireland, why not have it for England and Scotland? Some may scout such matters as purely secular, and not only unworthy of the interference of religious men, but when advocated by them as fitted to prejudice spiritual religion. It is a narrow view. All that is right is religious; all that is according to the will of God is spiritual. Whatever tends to realise the prayer of Agur is good for rich and poor alike: "Give me neither poverty nor riches; feed me with food convenient for me."

4. Lastly, in the arrangements for the distribution of the land among the twelve tribes we may note a proof of God's interest in the temporal comfort and prosperity of men. It is not God that has created the antithesis of secular and spiritual, as if the two interests were like a see-saw, so that whenever the one went up the other must go down. Things in this world are made to be enjoyed, and the enjoyment of them is agreeable to the will of God, provided we use them as not abusing them. If Scripture condemns indulgence in the pleasures of life, it is when these pleasures are preferred to the higher joys of the Spirit, or when they are allowed to stand in the way of a nobler life and a higher reward. In ordinary circumstances God intends men to be fairly comfortable; He does not desire life to be a perpetual struggle, or a dismal march to the grave. The very words in which Christ counsels us to consider the lilies and the ravens, instead of worrying ourselves about food and clothing, show this; for, under the Divine plan, the ravens are comfortably fed, and the lilies are handsomely clothed.

This is the Divine plan; and if those who enjoy a large share of the comforts of life are often selfish and worldly, it is only another proof how much a wrong spirit may pervert the gifts of God and turn them to evil. The characteristic of a good man, when he enjoys a share of worldly prosperity, is, that he does not let the world become his idol,—it is his servant, it is under his feet; he jealously guards against its becoming his master. His effort is to make a friend of the mammon of unrighteousness, and to turn every portion of it with which he may be entrusted to such a use for the good of others, that when at last he gives in his account, as steward to his Divine Master, he may do so with joy, and not with grief.

CHAPTER XXIV.

THE INHERITANCE OF JUDAH.*

JOSHUA xv.

JUDAH was the imperial tribe, and it was fitting that he should be planted in a conspicuous territory. Even if the republic had not been destined to give place to the monarchy, some pre-eminence was due to the tribe which had inherited the patriarchal blessing, and from which He was to come in whom all the families of the earth were to be blessed. Judah and the sons of Joseph seem to have obtained their settlements not only before the other tribes, but in a different manner. They did not obtain them by lot, but apparently by their own choice and by early possession. Judah was not planted in the heart of the country. That position was gained

---

* Judg. x. 4; Ruth ii. 1; 1 Sam. xxv. 2; 2 Sam. xvii. 27.
† See the author's essay "An Old Key to our Social Problems" in "Counsel and Cheer for the Battle of Life."

* We do not encumber our exposition with a discussion of the extraordinary theory of Wellhausen, to the effect that Judah and Simeon, with Levi, were the first to cross the Jordan and attack the Canaanites; that Simeon and Levi were all but annihilated; that Joshua, who belonged to the tribe of Ephraim, did little more than settle that tribe; and that there was hardly such a thing as united action by the tribes, most of them having acted and fought at their own hand. This theory rests professedly on the ground that Judges i. is a more true and trustworthy account of the settlement than the narrative of Joshua. It is a strange proof of the greater truthfulness of Judges that, according to this theory, its very first statement should be a lie—"It came to pass *after the death of Joshua!*" The narrative of Judges naturally follows that of Joshua because it is plain that while Joshua secured for his people standing ground in the country, he did not secure undisturbed possession. Joshua set them an example of faith and courage which, if followed up by them, would have secured undisturbed possession; but with few exceptions they preferred to tolerate the Canaanites at their side, instead of making a vigorous effort to dispossess them wholly.

by Ephraim and Manasseh, the children of Joseph, while Judah obtained the southern section. In this position his influence was not so commanding at first as it would have been had he occupied the centre. The portion taken possession of by Judah had belonged to the first batch of kings that Joshua subdued,—the kings that came up to take vengeance on the Gibeonites. What was first assigned to Judah was too large, and the tribe of Simeon got accommodation within his lot (chap. xix. 9). Dan also obtained several cities that had first been given to Judah (comp. chaps. xv. 21-62 and xix. 40-46). In point of fact, Judah ere long swallowed up a great part of Simeon and Dan, and Benjamin was so hemmed in between him and Ephraim that, while Jerusalem was situated within the limits of Benjamin, it was, for all practical purposes, a city of Judah.

The territory of Judah was not pre-eminently fruitful; it was not equal in this respect to that of Ephraim and Manasseh. It had some fertile tracts, but a considerable part of it was mountainous and barren. It was of four descriptions —the hill country, the valley or low country, the south, and the wilderness. "The hill country," says Dean Stanley, "is the part of Palestine which best exemplifies its characteristic scenery; the rounded hills, the broad valleys, the scanty vegetation, the villages and fortresses sometimes standing, more frequently in ruins, on the hill tops; the wells in every valley, the vestiges of terraces whether for corn or wine." Here the lion of the tribe of Judah entrenched himself, to guard the southern frontier of the Chosen Land, with Simeon, Dan, and Benjamin nestled around him. Well might he be so named in this wild country, more than half a wilderness, the lair of savage beasts, of which the traces gradually disappear as we advance into the interior. Fixed there, and never dislodged, except by the ruin of the whole nation, " he lay down, he couched as a lion, and as an old lion; who shall rouse him up?"

Many parts of Judah were adapted for the growth of corn; witness Bethlehem, "the house of bread." But the cultivation of the vine was pre-eminently the feature of the tribe. "Here more than elsewhere in Palestine are to be seen on the sides of the hills the vineyards, marked by their watch-towers and walls, seated on their ancient terraces, the earliest and latest symbol of Judah. The elevation of the hills and tablelands of Judah is the true climate of the vine. He 'bound his foal unto the vine, and his ass's colt unto the choice vine; he washed his garments in wine, and his clothes in the blood of grapes.' It was from the Judæan valley of Eshcol, 'the torrent of the cluster,' that the spies cut down the gigantic cluster of grapes. 'A vineyard on a "hill of olives"' with the 'fence,' and 'the stones gathered out,' and the tower in 'the midst of it,' is the natural figure which both in the prophetical and evangelical records represents the kingdom of Judah. The 'vine' was the emblem of the nation on the coins of the Maccabees, and in the colossal cluster of golden grapes which overhung the porch of the second Temple; and the grapes of Judah still mark the tombstones of the Hebrew race in the oldest of their European cemeteries at Prague."*

The chapter now before us has a particularly barren look; but if we examine it with care

* Stanley's "Sinai and Palestine."

we shall find it not deficient in elements of interest.

1. First, we have an elaborate delineation of the boundaries of the territory allotted to Judah. It is not difficult to follow the boundary line in the main, though some of the names cannot be identified now. The southern border began at the wilderness of Zin, where the host had been encamped more than forty years before, when the twelve spies returned with their report of the land. The line moved in a southwesterly course till it reached "the river of Egypt" and the sea shore. What this "river of Egypt" was is far from clear. Naturally one thinks of the Nile, the only stream that seems to be entitled to such an appellation. On the other hand, the term translated "river" is commonly though not always, applied to brooks or shallow torrents, and hence it has been thought to denote a brook, now called El Arish, about midway in the desert between Gaza and the Pelusiac mouth of the Nile. While we incline to the former view, we own that practically the question is of little consequence; the only difference being that if the boundary reached to the Nile, it included a larger share of the desert than if it had a more northerly limit. The Dead Sea was the chief part of the eastern frontier. The northern boundary began near Gilgal, and stretched westwards to the Mediterranean by a line that passed just south of Jerusalem.

The position of Judah was peculiar, in respect of the enemies by whom he was surrounded. On his eastern frontier, close to the Dead Sea, he was in contact with Moab, and on the south with Edom, the descendants of Esau. On the southwest were the Amalekites of the desert; and on the west the Philistines, and pre-eminent among them, until Caleb subdued them, the sons of Anak, the giants. On his extreme north, but within the tribe of Benjamin, was the great fortress of the Jebusites. It was no bed of roses that was thus prepared for the lion of the tribe of Judah. If he should rule at all, he must rule in the midst of his enemies. Hemmed in by fierce foes on every side, he needed to show his prowess if he was to prevail against them. It was the necessity of contending with these and other enemies that developed the military genius of David (1 Sam. xvii. 50, xviii. 5, 17, 27, xxvii. 8), and made him the fitting type of the heavenly warrior who goes forth "conquering and to conquer." The vigilance that was needed to keep these enemies at bay was one means of preserving the vigour and independence of the tribe. Living thus in the very heart of foes, Judah was the better fitted to symbolise the Church of Christ, as she is usually found when faithful to her high calling. "Behold, I send you forth as sheep in the midst of wolves." "We wrestle not against flesh and blood, but against principalities and powers, against the rulers of the darkness of this world, against spiritual wickedness in high places." As long as the Church is militant, it cannot be otherwise; and it little becomes her either to complain on the one hand, or be despondent on the other, however strong and bitter the opposition or even the persecution of her foes.

2. Next, a little episode comes into our narrative (vv. 13-19), in connection with a special allocation of territory within the tribe. The incident of Caleb is rehearsed, as an introduction to the narrative that follows. Caleb, on the strength

of his promise to drive out the Anakim, had got Hebron for his inheritance, and a portion of the country around. Near to Hebron, but on a site now unknown, stood Debir, or Kirjath-sepher, apparently a stronghold of the Anakim. We do not know the circumstances that induced Caleb to put this place up, as it were, to public competition. Whoever should capture it was promised his daughter Achsah in marriage. Othniel, who is called his younger brother, which may perhaps mean his brother's son, took the place, and, according to the bargain, got Achsah for his wife. The capture of Debir is recorded twice, here and in Judges i. 14, 15, and in the latter case with the addition of an incident that followed the marriage, as if in both cases it had been copied from an older record. Achsah was evidently a woman who could look well after her interests. She was not satisfied with the portion of land that fell to Othniel. There was a certain field besides, on which she had set her affection, and which she induced her husband to ask of Caleb. This he appears to have obtained. Then she herself turned supplicant, and having gone to Caleb and lighted down from off her ass,* and Caleb having said to her, "What wouldest thou?" she said unto her father, "Give me a blessing; for thou hast given me a south land; give me also springs of water." ["And she said, Give me a blessing (*margin*, present); for thou hast set me in the land of the south; give me also springs of water," R. V.] Her request was granted:—" he gave her the upper springs and the nether springs."

The incident, though picturesque, is somewhat strange, and we naturally ask, why should it have a place in the dry narrative of the settlement? Possibly for the very reason that what concerns the settlement was very dry, and that an incident like this gave it something of living interest. Those who lived at the time must have had a special interest in the matter, for in Judges i. 14 it is said that Achsah moved Othniel to ask of her father "*the* field" (Heb.), implying that it was a particular field, well known to the public. The moral interest of the narrative is the light it throws on the generosity of Caleb. His son-in-law asked of him a field, a field apparently of special value; he got it: his daughter asked springs of water, and she too gained her request. We contrast Caleb with Saul, as we afterwards read of him. In no such fashion was David treated by his father-in-law, after his brilliant victories over the Philistines. So far was he from acquiring field or fountain, that he did not even acquire his wife:—" It came to pass at the time when Merab, Saul's daughter, should have been given to David, that she was given unto Adriel the Meholathite to wife" (1 Sam. xviii. 19). Caleb had another spirit with him. He had the heart of a father, he had a genuine interest in his daughter and son-in-law, and desired to see them comfortable and happy. Kindly and large-hearted, he at once transferred to them valuable possessions that a greedier man would have kept for himself. Evidently he was one of those godlike men that enjoy giving, that have more pleasure in making others happy than in multiplying their own store. "The liberal man deviseth liberal things, and by liberal things shall he stand." "There is that scattereth, and yet increaseth; and there is that withholdeth more than is meet, and it tendeth to poverty."

It is no great wonder that an incident which reveals the flowing generosity of a godlike heart should sometimes be turned to account as a symbol of the liberality of God. All human generosity is but a drop from the ocean of the Divine bounty, a faint shadow of the inexhaustible substance. "If ye that are evil know how to give good gifts to your children, how much more shall your Father in heaven give good things to them that ask Him?" If in the earthly father's bosom there be that interest in the welfare of his children which is eager to help them where help is needed and it is in his power to give it, how much more in the bosom of the Father in heaven? Why should any be backward to apply to Him—to say to Him, like Achsah, " Give me a blessing"? It pleases Him to see His children reposing trust in Him, believing in His infinite love. All that He asks of us is to come to Him through Jesus Christ, acknowledging our unworthiness, and pleading the merit of His sacrifice and intercession, as our only ground of acceptance in His sight. After His revelation of His grace in Christ our requests cannot be restricted to mere temporal things; when we ask a blessing it must be one of higher scope and quality. Yet such is His bounty that nothing can be withheld that is really for our good. "No good thing will the Lord withhold from them that walk uprightly." "Prove me now herewith, saith the Lord; if I will not open to you the windows of heaven, and pour you out a blessing that there shall not be room enough to receive it."

3. We leave this picturesque incident to re-enter the wilderness of unfamiliar names. We find a list of no fewer than a hundred and fifteen cities which lay within the confines of the tribe of Judah (vv. 21-32). They fall into four divisions. First, twenty-nine cities belonged to "the south"—the "Negeb" of the Hebrews, the part of the country which bordered on the desert, and to some degree partook of its character. Cities they are called, but few of them were more than villages, and hardly any were important enough to leave their mark on the history. There are two, however, having memorable associations with men of mark, the one carrying us back to a glorious past, the other forward to a disgraceful future. Strange association—Abraham and Judas Iscariot! With Beersheba the name of Abraham is imperishably associated, as well as the name of Isaac. And to this day the very name Beersheba seems to emit a holy fragrance. With Kerioth (ver. 25) we connect the traitor Judas—the Is-cariot of the New Testament being equivalent to Ish-Kerioth, a man of Kerioth, of the Old. Our heart fills with a sense of nausea as we recall the association. The traitor was doubly connected with the tribe of Judah,—by his name and by his birthplace. What mockery of a noble name! "Judah, thou art he whom thy brethren shall praise." What contrast could be greater than that between the Judah who surrendered himself to slavery to set his brother free, and the Judah who sold his Lord for thirty pieces of silver! What extremes

---

* Founding on the expression, "having lighted off her ass," some have thought that she feigned to fall off, and that her father coming to help her in the compassionate spirit one shows in a case of accident, she took the opportunity to ask and obtain this gift. The explanation is far-fetched if not foolish. Her dismounting is explained by the universal custom when one met a person of superior rank. Comp. Gen. xxiv. 64. See Kitto's "Pictorial Commentary."

of character may we find under the same name, and often in the same family! Strange that so few are drawn by the example of the noble, and so many follow the course of the vile!

The next division, "the valley," the lowland, or Shephelah, embraced three subdivisions—the northeastern Shephelah with her fourteen towns (vv. 33-36), the middle, with sixteen (vv. 37-41), and the southern, with nine (vv. 42-44); to which are added three of the cities of the Philistines, —Ekron, Ashdod, and Gaza (vv. 45-47). Many of the places in this list became famous in the history. Eshtaol and Zorah were of note in the history of Samson, but in his time they were Danite settlements. Jarmuth, Lachish, Eglon, and Makkedah had been conspicuous in Joshua's great battle of Bethhoron. Adullam and Keilah figured afterwards in David's outlaw history, and Ashdod and Ekron were two of the Philistine cities to which the ark was taken after the battle of Ebenezer and Aphek (1 Sam. iv. 1, v. 1, 10). In later years Lachish and Libnah were among the places attacked by Sennacherib, King of Assyria, in his great raid upon the country (Isa. xxxvii. 8).

The third great group of cities were those of "the mountain," or highlands. These were mostly in the central part of the territory, on the plateau or ridge that runs along it, rising up from the valley of the Dead Sea on the east, and the Shephelah, or "valley," on the west. Here there were four groups of cities: eleven on the southwest (vv. 48-51), nine farther north (vv. 52-54), ten to the east (vv. 55-57), and six to the north (vv. 58, 59), along with Kirjath-baal and Rabbah in the same neighbourhood. This group included Hebron, of which we hear so much; also Carmel, Maon, and Ziph, conspicuous in the outlaw life of David. It is remarkable that there is no mention of Bethlehem, which lay in "the mountain"; it probably had not yet attained to the rank of a town. But its very omission may be regarded as a proof of the contemporaneous date of the book; for soon after Bethlehem was a well-known place (Ruth i.-iv.), and if the Book of Joshua had been written at the late date sometimes assigned to it, that city could not have failed to have a place in the enumeration.

A fourth group of cities were in "the wilderness" or Migdar. This was a wild rocky region extending between the Dead Sea and the mountains of Hebron. "It is a plateau of white chalk, terminated on the east by cliffs which rise vertically from the Dead Sea shore to a height of about two thousand feet. The scenery is barren and wild beyond all description. The chalky ridges are scored by innumerable torrents, and their narrow crests are separated by broad, flat valleys. Peaks and knolls of fantastic forms rise suddenly from the swelling downs, and magnificent precipices of rugged limestone stand up like fortress walls above the sea. Not a tree nor a spring is visible in the waste; and only the desert partridge and the ibex are found ranging the solitude." * This district was in large measure the scene of David's wanderings, and well might he call it "a dry and thirsty land where there is no water" (Psalm lxiii. 1). It was also the scene of the preaching of John the Baptist, at least at the beginning (Matt. iii. 1); for when the administration of baptism became common, it was necessary for him to remove to a better-watered region (John iii. 23). There is some reason to believe that it was also the scene of our Lord's temptation (Matt. iv. 1), the more especially because one of the Evangelists has said that "He was there with the wild beasts" (Mark i. 12).

Only six cities are enumerated as "in the wilderness" (vv. 61, 62), so that its population must have been very small. And of those mentioned some are wholly unknown. The most interesting of the six is Engedi, which derived its name from a celebrated fountain, meaning "fountain of the kid." It is noted as one of the hiding-places of David; Saul pursued him to it, and it was there that David spared his life when he found him in a cave (1 Sam. xxiv.). Solomon extols its vineyards and its camphire (Song of Solomon i. 14) [henna-flowers, R. V.], Josephus its balsam (Ant., ix. 1, § 2), and Pliny its palms (v. 17). In ancient times it was the site of a town, and in the fourth century, in Jerome's time, there was still a considerable village; now, however, there is no trace of anything of the kind. Sir Walter Scott, in the "Talisman," makes it the abode of a Christian hermit—Theodoric of Engaddi. It is situated near the middle of the western shore of the Dead Sea. A rich plain, half a mile square, slopes gently from the base of the mountains to the sea; and about a mile up the western acclivity, four hundred feet above the plain, is the fountain of Ain Jiddy, from which the place gets its name.

Such, then, was the distribution of the cities of Judah over the four sections of the territory, the south, the Shephelah, the highlands, and the wilderness. It was an ample and varied domain, and after Caleb expelled the Anakim, there seems to have been little or no opposition to the occupation of the whole by the tribe. But "the crook in the lot" was not wanting. The great Jebusite fortress, Jerusalem, was on the very edge of the northern boundary of Judah. Nominally, as we have said, Jerusalem was in the territory of Benjamin, but really it was a city of Judah. For it is said (ver. 63), "As for the Jebusites, the children of Judah could not drive them out; but the Jebusites dwell with the children of Judah at Jerusalem unto this day." * For some reason Joshua had omitted to take possession of this stronghold after the battle of Bethhoron. The stream of pursuit had gone westward, and the opportunity of taking Jerusalem when the king had been slain and his army cut to pieces, was lost. And just as in modern history, when the opportunity of taking Sebastopol was lost after the battle of the Alma, and a long, harassing, and most disastrous siege had to be resorted to, so it was with Jerusalem; the Jebusites, recovering their spirits after the defeat, were able to hold it, and to defy the tribe of Judah, and all the tribes, for many a long year. While the fortress was held by the Jebusites, Jew and Jebusite dwelt together in the city, leading no doubt a comfortless life, neither the one nor the other feeling truly at home.

The moral is not far to seek. There is a crisis in some men's lives, when they come under the power of religion, and feel the obligation to live to God. If they had decision and courage enough at this crisis to break off all sinful habits and connections, to renounce all unchristian ways of life, to declare with Joshua, "As for me

---

* Conder's "Handbook to the Bible," pp. 213, 214.

* A proof that Joshua was written before the time of David.

and my house, we will serve the Lord,"—they would no doubt experience a sharp opposition, but it would pass over, and peace would come. But often they hesitate, and shrink, and cower; they cannot endure opposition and ridicule; they retain religion enough to appease their consciences, but not to give them satisfaction and joy. It is another case of the men of Judah dwelling with the Jebusites, and with the same result; they are not happy, they are not at rest; they bring little or no honour to their Master, and they have little influence on the world for good.

CHAPTER XXV.

THE INHERITANCE OF JOSEPH.

JOSHUA xvi., xvii.

NEXT to Judah, the most important tribe was Joseph; that is, the double tribe to which his two sons gave names, Ephraim and Manasseh. In perpetual acknowledgment of the service rendered by Joseph to the family, by keeping them alive in the famine, it was ordained by Jacob that his two sons should rank with their uncles as founders of tribes (Gen. xlviii. 5). It was also prophetically ordained by Jacob that Ephraim, the younger son, should take rank before Manasseh (Gen. xlviii. 19). The privilege of the double portion, however, remained to Manasseh as the elder son. Hence, in addition to his lot in Gilead and Bashan, he had also a portion in Western Palestine. But Ephraim was otherwise the more important tribe; and when the separation of the two kingdoms took place, Ephraim often gave his name to the larger division. And in the beautiful prophetic vision of Ezekiel, when the coming re-union of the nation is symbolised, it is on this wise: "Son of man, take thou one stick and write upon it, For Judah, and for the children of Israel his companions; then take another stick and write upon it, For Joseph, the stick of Ephraim, and for all the house of Israel his companions, and join them for thee one to another into one stick, that they may become one in thine hand" (xxxvii. 16, 17). The superiority allotted to Ephraim was not followed by very happy results; it raised an arrogant spirit in that tribe, of which we find some indications in the present chapter, but more pronounced and mischievous manifestations further on.

The delimitation of the tribes of Ephraim and Manasseh is not easy to follow, particularly in the Authorised Version, which not only does not translate very accurately, but uses some English expressions of uncertain meaning. The Revised Version is much more helpful, correcting both classes of defects in its predecessor. Yet even the Revised Version sometimes leaves us at a loss. It has been supposed, indeed, that some words have dropped out of the text. Moreover, it has not been found possible to ascertain the position of all the places mentioned. Uncertainty as to the precise boundaries cannot but prevail, and differences of opinion among commentators. But the uncertainty applies only to the minuter features of the description, it bears chiefly on the points at which one tribe adjoined another. The portion of the land occupied by Ephraim and Manasseh is, on the whole, very clearly known, just as their influence on the history of the country is very distinctly marked.

In point of fact, the lot of Joseph in Western Palestine was, in many respects, the most desirable of any. It was a fertile and beautiful district. It embraced the valley of Shechem, the first place of Abraham's sojourn, and reckoned by travellers to be one of the most beautiful spots, some say the most beautiful spot, in Palestine. Samaria, at the head of another valley celebrated for its "glorious beauty," and for its "fatness" or fertility (Isa. xxviii. 1), was at no great distance. Tizrah, a symbol of beauty, in the Song of Solomon (vi. 4) was another of its cities, as was also Jezreel, "a lovely position for a capital city" (*Tristram*). On the other hand, this portion of the country laboured under the disadvantage of not having been well cleared of its original inhabitants. The men of Ephraim did not exert themselves as much as the men of Judah. This is apparent from what is said in chap. xvi. 10, "They drove not out the Canaanites that dwelt in Gezer"; and also from Joshua's answer to the request of Ephraim for more land (xvii. 15-18).

As we have said already, we have no information regarding Joshua's conquest of this part of the country. It seems to have been run over more superficially than the north and the south. Consequently the ancient inhabitants were still very numerous, and they were formidable likewise, because they had chariots of iron.

In the definition of boundaries we have first a notice applicable to Joseph as a whole, then specifications applicable to Ephraim and Manasseh respectively. The southern border is delineated twice with considerable minuteness, and its general course, extending from near the Jordan at Jericho, past Bethel and Luz, and down the pass of Bethhoron to the Mediterranean, is clear enough. The border between Ephraim and Manasseh is not so clear, nor the northern border of Manasseh. It is further to be remarked that, while we have an elaborate statement of boundaries, we have no list of towns in Ephraim and Manasseh such as we have for the tribe of Judah. This gives countenance to the supposition that part of the ancient record has somehow dropped out. We find, however, another statement about towns which is of no small significance. At chap. xvi. 9 we find that several cities were appropriated to Ephraim that were situated in the territory of Manasseh. And in like manner several cities were given to Manasseh which were situated in the tribes of Issachar and Asher. Of these last the names are given. They were Bethshean, Ibleam, Dor, Endor, Taanach, and Megiddo. Some of them were famous in after history. Bethshean was the city to whose wall the bodies of Saul and his sons were fixed after the fatal battle of Gilboa; Ibleam was in the neighbourhood of Naboth's vineyard (2 Kings ix. 25, 27); Endor was the place of abode of the woman with a familiar spirit whom Saul went to consult; Taanach was the battle-field of the kings of Canaan whom Barak defeated, and of whom Deborah sung:

"The kings came and fought;
Then fought the kings of Canaan,
In Taanach by the waters of Megiddo:
They took no gain of money" (Judg. v. 19).

As for Megiddo, many a battle was fought in its plain. So early as the days of Thotmes III. of

Egypt (about 1600 B. C.) it was famous in battle, for in an inscription on the temple of Karnak, containing a record of his conquests in Syria, Megiddo flourishes as the scene of a great conflict. The saddest and most notable of its battles was that between King Josiah and the Egyptians, in which that good young king was killed. In fact, Megiddo obtained such notoriety as a battle-field that in the Apocalypse (xvi. 16) Ar-Mageddon (Har-magedon, R. V.) is the symbol of another kind of battle-ground—the meeting-place for "the war of the great day of God the Almighty."

We can only conjecture why these cities, most of which were in Issachar, were given to Manasseh. They were strongholds in the great plain of Esdraelon, where most of the great battles of Canaan were fought. For the defence of the plain it seemed important that these places should be held by a stronger tribe than Issachar. Hence they appear to have been given to Manasseh. But, like Ephraim, Manasseh was not able to hold them at first. "The children of Manasseh could not drive out the inhabitants of those cities; but the Canaanites would dwell in that land. And it came to pass, when the children of Israel were waxen strong that they put the Canaanites to task-work, and did not utterly drive them out" (R. V.). This last verse appears to have been inserted at a later date, and it agrees with 1 Chron. vii. 29, where several of the same towns are enumerated, and it is added, "In these dwelt the children of Joseph, the son of Israel."

Undoubtedly these sons of Joseph occupied a position which gave them unrivalled opportunities of benefiting their country. But with the exception of the splendid exploit of Gideon, a man of Manasseh, and his little band, we hear of little in the history that redounded to the credit of Joseph's descendants. Nobility of character is not hereditary. Sometimes nature appears to spend all her intellectual and moral wealth on the father, and almost to impoverish the sons. And sometimes the sons live on the virtues of their fathers, and cannot be roused to the exertion or the sacrifice needed to continue their work and maintain their reputation. A humorous saying is recorded of an eminent pastor of the Waldensian Church who found his people much disposed to live on the reputation of their fathers, and tried in vain to get them to do as their fathers did; he said that they were like the potato—the best part of them was under the ground. If you say, "We have Abraham for our father," take care that you say it in the proper sense. Be sure that you are following hard in his footsteps, and using his example as a spur to move your languid energies, and not as a screen to conceal your miserable defects. If you think of Abraham or of any forefather or body of forefathers as a cover for your nakedness, or a compensation for your defects, you are resorting to a device which has never proved successful in past ages, and is not likely to change its character with you.

After the division, the vain, self-important spirit of Ephraim broke out in a characteristic way. "Why," said he to Joshua, "hast thou given me but one lot and one part for an inheritance, seeing I am a great people, forasmuch as hitherto the Lord hath blessed me?" A grumbling reference seems to be made here to his brother Manasseh, who had received two lots, one on each side of the Jordan. At first it appears that there was some reason in the complaint of Ephraim. The *free* part of his lot seems to have been small, that is, the part not occupied by Canaanites. But we cannot think that the whole inheritance of Ephraim was so small as we find represented in the map of Major Conder, of the Palestine Exploration Fund, in his "Handbook to the Bible," because it is said, both in the Authorised and in the Revised Version, that his western boundary extended to the sea, while Major Conder makes it cease much sooner. But, looking at the whole circumstances, it is probable that Ephraim's complaint was dictated by jealousy of Manasseh, who certainly had received the double inheritance.

Alas, how apt is the spirit of discontent still to crop up when we compare our lot with that of others! Were we quite alone, or were there no case for comparison, we might be content enough; it is when we think how much more our brother has than we, that we are most liable to murmur. And, bad though murmuring and grieving at the good of our brother may be, it is by no means certain that the evil spirit will stop there. At the very dawn of history we find Cain the murderer of his brother because the one had the favour of God and not the other. What an evil feeling it is that grudges to our brother a larger share of God's blessing; if at the beginning it be not kept under it may carry us on to deeds that may well make us shudder.

Joshua dealt very wisely and fearlessly with the complaint of Ephraim, though it was his own tribe. You say you are a great people—be it so; but if you are a great people, you must be capable of great deeds. Two great undertakings are before you now. There are great woodlands in your lot that have not been cleared—direct your energies to them, and they will afford you more room for settlements. Moreover, the Canaanites are still in possession of a large portion of your lot; up and attack them and drive them out, and you will be furnished with another area for possession. Joshua accepted their estimate of their importance, but gave it a very different practical turn. What they had wished him to do was to take away a portion from some other tribe and give it as an extra allotment to them, so that it would be theirs without labour or trouble. What Joshua did was to spur them to courageous and self-denying exertion, in order that their object might be gained through the instrumentality of their own labour. For the sickly sentiment that desires a mine of gold to start into being and scatter its untold treasure at our feet, he substituted the manly sentiment of the proverb, "No gains without pains." "The soul of the sluggard desireth and hath nothing; but the hand of the diligent maketh rich." If they wished more land they must work for it; they must not take idleness for their patron-saint.

We have all heard of the dying father who informed his sons that there was a valuable treasure in a certain field, and counselled them to set to work to find it. With great care they turned up every morsel of the soil; but no treasure appeared, till, observing in autumn what a rich crop covered the field, they came to understand that the fruit of persevering labour was the treasure which their father meant. We have heard, too, of a physician who was consulted by a rich man suffering cruelly from gout, and asked if he had any cure for it. "Yes," said the doctor, "live on sixpence a day, and work for it." The same principle underlay the counsel of Joshua. Of course it gratifies a certain part of our nature to get a mass of wealth without working for it. But this is not the best part of our nature. Probably in no class has the great object of life been so much lost, and the habit of indolence and self-indulgence become so predominant as in that of young men born to the possession of a great fortune, and never requiring to turn a hand for anything they desired. After all, the necessity of work is a great blessing. We speak of the curse of toil, but except when the labour is excessive, or unhealthy in its conditions, or when it has to be prosecuted in sickness or failing strength, it is not a curse but a blessing. Instead of being ashamed of labour, we have cause rather to be proud of it. It guards from numberless temptations; it promotes a healthy body and a healthy mind; it increases the zest of life; it promotes cheerfulness and flowing spirits; it makes rest and healthy recreation far sweeter when they come, and it gives us affinity to the great Heavenly Worker, by whom, and through whom, and for whom are all things.

This great principle of ordinary life has its place too in the spiritual economy. The age is now past that had for its favourite notion, that seclusion from the world and exemption from all secular employment was the most desirable condition for a servant of God. The experiment of the hermits was tried, but it was a failure. Seclusion from the world and the consecration of the whole being to private acts of devotion and piety were no success. He who moves about among his fellows, and day by day knows the strain of labour, is more likely to prosper spiritually than he who shuts himself up in a cell, and looks on all secular work as pollution. It is not the spiritual invalid who is for ever feeling his pulse and whom every whiff of wind throws into a fever of alarm, that grows up to the full stature of the Christian; but the man who, like Paul, has his hands and his heart for ever full, and whose every spiritual fibre gains strength and vitality from his desires and labours for the good of others. And it is with churches as with individuals. An idle church is a stagnant church, prone to strife, and to all morbid experiences. A church that throws itself into the work of faith and labour of love is far more in the way to be spiritually healthy and strong. It was not for the good of the world merely, but of the church herself likewise, that our Lord gave out that magnificent *mot d'ordre*,—" Go ye into all the world, and preach the gospel to every creature."

Before we pass from the inheritance of the sons of Joseph, it is proper that we should direct attention to an incident which may seem trifling to us, but which was evidently regarded as of no little moment at the time. What we refer to is the petition presented by the five daughters of Zelophehad, a member of the tribe of Manasseh, for an inheritance in their tribe. Their father had no son, so that the family was represented wholly by daughters. No fewer than four times the incident is referred to, and the names of the five girls given in full (Numb. xxvi. 33, xxvii. 1-11, xxxvi. 11; Josh. xvii. 3). We know not if there be another case in Scripture of such prominence given to names for no moral or spiritual quality, but simply in connection with a law of property.

The question decided by their case was the right of females to inherit property in land when there were no heirs male in the family. We find that the young women themselves had to be champions of their own cause. Evidently possessed of more than ordinary spirit, they had already presented themselves before Moses, Eleazar the priest, and the princes of the congregation, at the door of the tabernacle, and formally made a claim to the inheritance that would have fallen to their father had he been alive. The case was deemed of sufficient importance to be laid before the Lord, because the decision on it would settle similar cases for the whole nation and for all time. The decision was, that in such cases the women should inherit, but under the condition that they should not marry out of their own tribe, so that the property should not be transferred to another tribe. In point of fact, the five sisters married their cousins and thus kept the property in the tribe of Manasseh.

The incident is interesting, because it shows a larger regard to the rights of women than was usually conceded at the time. Some have, indeed, found fault with the decision as not going far enough. Why, they have asked, was the right of women to inherit land limited to cases in which there were no men in the family? The decision implied that if there had been one brother, he would have got all the land; the sisters would have been entitled to nothing. The answer to this objection is, that had the rights of women been recognised to this extent, it would have been too great an advance on the public opinion of the time. It was not God's method to enjoin laws absolutely perfect, but to enjoin what the conscience and public opinion of the time might be fairly expected to recognise and support. It may be that under a perfect system women ought to inherit property on equal terms with men. But the Jewish nation was not sufficiently advanced for such a law. The benefit of the enactment was that, when propounded, it met with general approval.

Certainly it was a considerable advance on the ordinary practice of the nations. It established the principle that woman was not a mere chattel, an inferior creature, subject to the control of the man, with no rights of her own. But it was far from being the first time when this principle obtained recognition. The wives of the patriarchs —Sarah, Rebekah, Rachel—were neither chattels, nor drudges, nor concubines. They were ladies, exerting the influence and enjoying the respect due to cultivated, companionable women. And though the law of succession did not give the females of the family equal rights with the males, it recognised them in another way. While the eldest son succeeded to the family home and a double portion of the land, he was expected to make some provision for his widowed mother and unmarried sisters. In most cases the sisters came to be provided for by marriage. It is the circumstance that among us so many women remain unmarried that has drawn so keen attention to their rights, and already caused so much to be done, as no doubt more will be done speedily, for enlarging their sphere and protecting their interests.

No doubt these spirited daughters of Zelophehad conferred a great benefit on their sex in Israel. Their names are entitled to grateful remembrance, as the names of all are who bring about beneficial arrangements that operate in many directions and to all time. Yet one would be sorry to think that this was the only service which they rendered in their day. One would like to think of them as shedding over their households and friends the lustre of those gentle, womanly qualities which are the glory of the sex. Advocacy of public rights may be a high duty, for the faithful discharge of which the highest praise is due; but such a career emits little of the fragrance which radiates from a female life of faithful love, domestic activity, and sacred devotion. What blessed ideals of life Christianity furnishes for women even of middling talent and ordinary education! It is beautiful to see distinguished talents, high gifts, and persuasive elements directed to the advocacy of neglected claims. "And yet I show unto you a more excellent way."

CHAPTER XXVI.

THE DISTRIBUTION COMPLETED.

JOSHUA xviii., xix.

AN event of great importance now occurs; the civil arrangements of the country are in a measure provided for, and it is time to set in order the ecclesiastical establishment. First, a place has to be found as the centre of the religious life; next, the tabernacle has to be erected at that place—and this is to be done in the presence of all the congregation. It is well that a godly man like Joshua is at the head of the nation; a less earnest servant of God might have left this great work unheeded. How often, in the emigrations of men, drawn far from their native land in search of a new home, have arrangements for Divine service been forgotten! In such cases the degeneracy into rough manners, uncouth ways of life, perhaps into profanity, debauchery, and lawlessness, has usually been awfully rapid. On the other hand, when the rule of the old puritan has been followed, "Wherever I have a house, there God shall have an altar"; when the modest spire of the wooden church in the prairie indicates that regard has been had to the gospel precept—" Seek ye first the kingdom of God and His righteousness, and all these things shall be added unto you,"—a touch of heaven is imparted to the rude and primitive settlement; we may believe that the spirit of Christ is not unknown; the angels of virtue and piety are surely hovering around it.

The narrative is very brief, and no reason is given why Shiloh was selected as the religious centre of the nation. We should have thought that the preference would be given to Shechem, a few miles north, in the neighbourhood of Ebal and Gerizim, which had already been consecrated in a sense to God. That Shiloh was chosen by Divine direction we can hardly doubt, although there may have been reasons of various kinds that commended it to Joshua. Josephus says it was selected for the beauty of the situation; but if the present Seilûn denotes its position, as is generally believed, there is not much to corroborate the assertion of Josephus. Its locality is carefully defined in the book of Judges (xxi. 19),—" on the north side of Bethel, on the east side of the highway that goeth up from Bethel to Shechem, and on the south of Lebonah." As for its appearance, Dean Stanley says, "Shiloh is so utterly featureless that had it not been for the preservation of its name, Seilûn, and for the extreme precision with which its situation is described in the Book of Judges, the spot could never have been identified; and, indeed, from the time of Jerome till the year 1838 [when Robinson identified it], its real site was completely forgotten." Robinson does not think so poorly of it as Stanley, describing it as "surrounded by hills, and looking out into a beautiful oval basin" ("Biblical Researches," ii. 268).

From the days of Joshua, all through the period of the Judges, and on to the last days of Eli the high priest, Shiloh continued to be the abode of the tabernacle, and the great national sanctuary of Israel. Situated about half-way between Bethel and Shechem, in the tribe of Ephraim, it was close to the centre of the country, and, moreover, not difficult of access for the eastern tribes. Here for many generations the annual assemblies of the nation took place. Here came Hannah from her home in Mount Ephraim to pray for a son; and here little Samuel, "lent to the Lord," spent his beautiful childhood. Through that opening in the mountains, old Eli saw the ark carried by the rash hands of his sons into the battle with the Philistines, and there he sat on his stool watching for the messenger that was to bring tidings of the battle. After the ark was taken by the Philistines, the city that had grown up around the tabernacle appears to have been taken and sacked and the inhabitants massacred (Psalm lxxviii. 60-64). We hear of it in later history as the abode of Ahijah the prophet (1 Kings xi. 29); afterwards it sinks into obscurity. It is to be noted that its name occurs nowhere among the towns of the Canaanites; it is likely that it was a new place, founded by Joshua, and that it derived its name, Shiloh, "rest," from the sacred purpose to which it was now devoted.

Here, then, assembled the whole congregation of the children of Israel, to set up the tabernacle, probably with some such rites as David performed when it was transferred from the house of Obed-Edom to Mount Zion. Hitherto it had remained at Gilgal, the headquarters and depôt of the nation. The "whole congregation" that now assembled does not necessarily mean the whole community, but only selected representatives, not only of the part that had been engaged in warfare, but also of the rest of the nation.

If we try to form a picture of the state of Israel while Joshua was carrying on his warlike campaigns, it will appear that his army being but a part of the whole, the rest of the people were occupied in a somewhat random manner, here and there, in providing food for the community, in sowing and reaping the fields, pasturing their flocks, and gathering in the fruits. And from the tone of Joshua it would appear that many of them were content to lead this somewhat irregular life. In a somewhat sharp and reproachful tone he says to them, " How long are ye slack to go to possess the land which the Lord God of your fathers has given you?" One of Joshua's great difficulties was to organise the vast mass of people over whom he presided, to prevent them from falling into careless, slatternly ways, and to keep them up to the mark of absolute regularity and order. Many of them would have been content to jog on carelessly as they had been doing in the desert, in a sort of confused jumble, and to forage about, here and there, as the case might be, in pursuit of the necessaries of life. Their listlessness was provoking. They knew that the Divine plan was quite different, that each tribe was to have a territory of its own, and that measures ought to be taken at once to settle the boundaries of each tribe. But they were taking no steps for this purpose; they were content with social hugger-mugger.

Joshua is old, but his impatience with laziness and irregularity still gives sharpness to his remonstrance, "How long are ye slack to possess the land?" The ring of authority is still in his voice; it still commands obedience. More than that, the organising faculty is still active—the faculty that decides how a thing is to be done. "Give out from among you three men for each tribe; and I will send them, and they shall rise and go through the land and describe it according to the inheritance of them."

The men are chosen, three from each of the seven tribes that are not yet settled; and they go through and make a survey of the land. Judah and Joseph are not to be disturbed in the settlements that have already been given to them; but the men are to divide the rest of the country into seven parts, and thereafter it is to be determined by lot to which tribe each part shall belong. It would appear that special note was to be taken of the cities, for when the surveyors returned and gave in their report they "described the land by cities into seven parts in a book." Each city had a certain portion of land connected with it, and the land always went with the city. The art of writing was sufficiently practised to enable them to compose what has been called the "Domesday Book" of Canaan, and the record being in writing was a great safeguard against the disputes that might have arisen had so large a report consisted of mere oral statement. When the seven portions had been balloted for, there was no excuse for any of the tribes clinging any longer to that nomad life, for which, while in the wilderness, they seem to have acquired a real love.

And now we come to the actual division. The most interesting of the tribes yet unsupplied was Benjamin, and the region that fell to him was interesting too. It may be remarked as an unusual arrangement, that when portions were allotted to Judah and to Ephraim, a space was allowed to remain between them, so that the northern border of Judah was at some distance from the southern border of Ephraim. As Judah and Ephraim were the two leading tribes, and in some respects rivals, the benefit of this intervening space between them is apparent. But for this, whenever their relations became strained, hostilities might have taken place.

Now it was this intervening space that constituted the inheritance of the tribe of Benjamin. For the most part it consisted of deep ravines running from west to east, from the central tableland down to the valley of the Jordan, with mountains between. Many of its cities were perched high in the mountains, as is shown by the commonness of the names Gibeon, Gibeah, Geba, or Gaba, all of which signify "hill"; while Ramah is a "high place," and Mizpeh a "tower." In the wilderness, Benjamin had marched along with Ephraim and Manasseh, all the descendants of Joseph forming a united company; and after the settlement Benjamin naturally inclined towards fellowship with these tribes. But, as events went on, he came more into fellowship with the tribe of Judah, and though Saul, Shimei, and Sheba, the bitterest enemies of the house of David, were all Benjamites, yet, when the separation of the two kingdoms took place under Rehoboam, Benjamin took the side of Judah (1 Kings xii. 21). On the return from the captivity it was the tribes of Judah and Benjamin that took the lead (Ezra i. 5), and throughout the Book of Ezra the returned patriots are usually spoken of as "the men of Judah and Benjamin."

The cities of Benjamin included several of the most famous. Among them was Jericho, the rebuilding of which as a fortified place had been forbidden, but which was still in some degree inhabited; Bethel, which was already very famous in the history, but which, after the separation of the kingdoms, was taken possession of by Jeroboam, and made the shrine of his calves; Gibeon, the capital of the Gibeonites, and afterwards a shrine frequented by Solomon (1 Kings iii. 5); Ramah, afterwards the dwelling-place of Samuel (1 Sam. vii. 17); Mizpeh, one of the three places where he judged Israel (1 Sam. vii. 16); Gibeath, or Gibeah, where Saul had his palace (1 Sam. x. 26); and last, not least, Jerusalem. As to Jerusalem, some have thought that it lay partly in the territory of Judah, and partly in that of Benjamin. When certain terms in the description of the boundaries are studied there are difficulties that might suggest this solution. But we have seen that in practice there was a considerable amount of giving and taking among the tribes with reference to particular cities, and that sometimes a city, locally within one tribe, belonged to the people of another. So it was with Jerusalem; locally within the inheritance of Benjamin, it was practically occupied by the men of Judah (see chap. xv. 63).

Benjamin was counted the least of the tribes (1 Sam. ix. 31), and when, with other tribes, it was represented by its chief magistrate, it was rather disparagingly distinguished as "little Benjamin with their ruler" (Psalm lxviii. 27). Yet it was strong enough, on one occasion, to set at defiance for a time the combined forces of the other tribes (Judg. xx. 12, etc.). It was distinguished for the singular skill of its slingers; seven hundred, who were left-handed, "could every one sling stones at an hair-breadth and not miss" (Judg. xx. 16). The character of its territory, abounding in rocky mountains, and probably in game, for the capture of which the sling was adapted, might, in some degree, account for this peculiarity.

Many famous battles were fought on the soil of Benjamin. The battle of Ai; that of Gibeon, followed by the pursuit through Bethhoron, both under Joshua; Jonathan's battle with the Philistines at Michmash (1 Sam. xiv.); and the duel at Gibeon between twelve men of Saul and twelve of David (2 Sam. ii. 15, 16); were all fought within the territory of Benjamin. And when Sennacherib approached Jerusalem from the north, the places which were thrown into panic as he came near were in this tribe. "He is come to Aiath, he is passed through Migron; at Michmash he layeth up his baggage: they are gone over the pass; they have taken up their lodging at Geba: Ramah trembleth; Gibeah of Saul is fled. Cry aloud with thy voice, O daughter of

Gallim! hearken, O Laishah! O thou poor Anathoth! Madmenah is a fugitive; the inhabitants of Gebim gather themselves to flee. This very day shall he halt at Nob: he shaketh his hand at the mount of the daughter of Zion, the hill of Jerusalem" (Isa. x. 28-32, R. V.). In later times Judas Maccabeus gained a victory over the Syrian forces at Bethhoron; and, again, Cestius and his Roman troops were defeated by the Jews; and, once more, centuries later, Richard Cœur de Lion and the flower of English chivalry, when they pushed up through Bethhoron in the hope of reaching Jerusalem, were compelled to retire.

Even down to New Testament times, as Dean Stanley remarks, the influence of Benjamin remained, for the name of Saul, the king whom Benjamin gave to the nation, was preserved in Hebrew families; and when a far greater of that name appeals to his descent, or to the past history of his nation, a glow of satisfaction is visible in the marked emphasis with which he alludes to "the stock of Israel, the tribe of Benjamin" (Phil. iii. 5), and to God's gift of "Saul the son of Kish, a man of the tribe of Benjamin" (Acts xiii. 21).

There is little to be said of Simeon, the second of the seven that drew his lot. It is admitted that his portion was taken out of the first allotment to Judah (ver. 9), which was found to be larger than that tribe required, and many of his cities are contained in Judah's list. One act of valour is recorded of Simeon in the first chapter of Judges; after the first settlement, he responded to the appeal of Judah and accompanied him against the Canaanites. But the history of this tribe as a whole might be written in the words of Jacob's prophecy—" I will divide them in Jacob, and scatter them in Israel." There is no historical reason for the supposition of Wellhausen that Simeon and Levi were all but annihilated on occasion of their attack on the Canaanites. If Simeon had been virtually extinguished, it would not have had a territory assigned to it in the ideal division of the country by Ezekiel (xlviii. 24), nor would it have afforded the twelve thousand of the "sealed" in the symbolical vision of St. John (Rev. vii. 7). While the tribe was scattered, the name of its founder survived, and both as Simeon and Simon it was crowned with honour. It was the name of one of the family of Maccabean patriots; it was borne by the just and devout man that waited in the temple for the consolation of Israel; and it was the Hebrew name of the great Apostle whose honour it was to lay the foundation of the Christian Church.

Next came the tribe of Zebulun, the boundaries of which are given with much precision; but as most of the names are now unknown, and there are also appearances of imperfection in the text, the delineation cannot be followed. "The brook that is before Jokneam" is supposed to be the Kishon, and Chisloth-Tabor, or the flanks of Tabor, points to the mountain which is the traditional, though probably not the real scene of our Lord's transfiguration. Gittah-hepher, or Gath-hepher, was the birthplace of the prophet Jonah. Bethlehem, now Beit-Lahm, is a miserable village, not to be confounded with the Bethlehem of Judah. As no mention is made either of the sea or the lake of Galilee as a boundary, it is probable that Zebulun was wholly an inland tribe. Strange to say, there is no mention, either here or in any part of the Old Testament, of by far the most famous place in the tribe,—Nazareth, the early residence of our Lord. Yet its situation would indicate that it must have been a very ancient place. Nor is it likely to have escaped the notice of the surveyors when they went through the land. The omission of this name has given rise to the opinion that the list is incomplete.

Issachar occupied an interesting and important site. Jezreel, the first name in the definition of its boundaries, is also the most famous. Jezreel, now represented by Zerin, was situated on a lofty height, and gave name to the whole valley around. Here Ahab had his palace in the days of Elijah. By its association with the worship of Baal, Jezreel got a bad reputation, and in the prophet Hosea degenerate Israel is called Jezreel, a name somewhat similar, but with very different associations (chap. i. 4). Shunem was the place of encampment of the Philistine army before the battle of Gilboa, and also the residence of the woman whose son Elisha restored to life. Bethshemesh must not be confounded with the town of the same name in Judah, nor with that in the tribe of Naphtali. Signifying "house of the sun," it was a very common name among the Canaanites, as being noted for the worship of the heavenly bodies. As we have already remarked in connection with Megiddo which belonged to Manasseh, the valley of Jezreel, now usually called the plain of Esdraelon, was noted as the great battlefield of Palestine.

Asher also had an interesting territory. Theoretically it extended from Carmel to Sidon, embracing the whole of the Phœnician strip; but practically it did not reach so far. Naphtali was adjacent to Asher, and had the Jordan and the lakes of Merom and Galilee for its eastern boundary. It is in the New Testament that Naphtali enjoys its greatest distinction, the lake of Galilee and the towns on its banks, so conspicuous in the gospel history, having been situated there.

These northern tribes, as is well known, constituted the district of Galilee. The contrast between its early insignificance and its later glory is well brought out in the Revised Version of Isa. ix. 1, 2: " But there shall be no gloom to her that was in anguish. In the former time He brought into contempt the land of Zebulun and the land of Naphtali, but in the latter time hath He made it glorious, by the way of the sea, beyond Jordan, Galilee of the nations. The people that walked in darkness have seen a great light: they that dwelt in the land of the shadow of death, upon them hath the light shined."

Dan was the last tribe whose lot was drawn. And it really seemed as if the least desirable of all the portions fell to him. He was hemmed in between Judah on the one hand and the Philistines on the other, and the Philistines were anything but comfortable neighbours. The best part of the level land was no doubt in their hands, and Dan was limited to what lay at the base of the mountains (see Judg. i. 34, 35). Very early, therefore, in the history, a colony of Dan went out in search of further possessions, and, having dispossessed some Sidonians at Laish in the extreme north, gave their name to that city, which proverbially denoted the most northerly city in the country, as Beersheba, in like manner, denoted the most southerly.

The division of the country was now completed, save that one individual was still unprovided for. And that was Joshua himself. As in a shipwreck, the captain is the last to leave the doomed vessel, so here the leader of the nation was the last to receive a portion. With rare self-denial he waited till every one else was provided for. Here we have a glimpse of his noble spirit. That there would be much grumbling over the division of the country, he no doubt counted inevitable, and that the people would be disposed to come with their complaints to him followed as matter of course. See how he circumvents them! Whoever might be disposed to go to him complaining of his lot, knew the ready answer he would get—you are not worse off than I am, for as yet I have got none! Joshua was content to see the fairest inheritances disposed of to others, while as yet none had been allotted to him. When, last of all, his turn did come, his request was a modest one—"They gave him the city that he asked, even Timnath-serah in the hill country of Ephraim." He might have asked for an inheritance in the fertile and beautiful vale of Shechem, consecrated by one of the earliest promises to Abraham, near to Jacob's well and his ancestor Joseph's tomb, or under shadow of the two mountains, Ebal and Gerizim, where so solemn a transaction had taken place after his people entered the land. He asks for nothing of the kind, but for a spot on one of the highland hills of Ephraim, a place so obscure that no trace of it remains. It is described in Judg. ii. 9 as "Timnath-heres, in the hill country of Ephraim, on the north of the mountain of Gaash." The north side of the mountain does not indicate a spot remarkable either for amenity or fertility. In the days of Jerome, his friend Paula is said to have expressed surprise that the distributer of the whole country reserved so wild and mountainous a district for himself.

Could it have been that it was a farm rejected by every one else? that the head of the nation was content with what no one else would have? If it was so, how must this have exalted Joshua in the eyes of his countrymen, and how well fitted it is to exalt him in ours! Whether it was a portion that every one else had despised or not, it undoubtedly was comparatively a poor and far-off inheritance. His choice of it was a splendid rebuke to the grumbling of his tribe, to the pride and selfishness of the "great people" who would not be content with a single lot, and wished an additional one to be assigned to them. "Up with you to the mountain" was Joshua's spirited reply; "cut down the wood, and drive out the Canaanites!"

And Joshua was not the man to give a prescription to others that he was not prepared to take himself. Up to the mountain he certainly did go; and as he was now too old to fight, he quite probably spent his last years in clearing his lot, cutting down timber, and laboriously preparing the soil for crops. In any case, he set a splendid example of disinterested humility. He showed himself the worthy successor of Moses, who had never hinted at any distinction for his family or any possession in the country beyond what might be given to an ordinary Levite. How nobly both contrasted with men like Napoleon, who used his influence so greedily for the enrichment and aggrandisement of every member of his family! Joshua came very near to the spirit of our blessed Lord, who "though He was in the form of God, and thought it no robbery to be equal with God, made Himself of no reputation, and took on Him the form of a servant, and was made in the likeness of man." As we see the Old Testament Jesus retiring in His old age, not to a paradise in some fertile and flowery vale, but to a bleak and rocky farm on the north side of the mountain of Gaash, or to a shaggy forest, still held by the wolf and the bear, we are reminded of the Joshua of the New Testament: "Foxes have holes, and the birds of the air have nests; but the Son of man hath not where to lay his head."

CHAPTER XXVII.

THE CITIES OF REFUGE.

JOSHUA xx.

CITIES of refuge had a very prominent place assigned to them in the records of the Mosaic legislation. First, in that which all allow to be the earliest legislation (Exod. xx.-xxiii.) intimation is given of God's intention to institute such cities (Exod. xxi. 13): then in Numbers (xxxv. 9-34) the plan of these places is given in full, and all the regulations applicable to them; again in Deuteronomy (xix. 1-13) the law on the subject is rehearsed; and finally, in this chapter, we read how the cities were actually instituted, three on either side of Jordan. This frequent introduction of the subject shows that it was regarded as one of great importance, and leads us to expect that we shall find principles underlying it of great value in their bearing even on modern life.*

Little needs to be said on the particular cities selected, except that they were conveniently dispersed over the country. Kedesh in Galilee in the northern part, Shechem in the central, and Hebron in the south, were all accessible to the people in these regions respectively; as were also on the other side the river, Bezer in the tribes of Reuben, Ramoth in Gilead, and Golan in Bashan. Those who are fond of detecting the types of spiritual things in material, and who take a hint from Heb. vi. 18, connecting these cities with the sinner's refuge in Christ, naturally think in this connection of the nearness of the Saviour to all who seek Him, and the certainty of protection and deliverance when they put their trust in Him.

1. The first thought that naturally occurs to us when we read of these cities concerns the sanctity of human life; or, if we take the material symbol, the preciousness of human blood. God wished to impress on His people that to put an end to a man's life under any circumstances, was a serious thing. Man was something higher than the beasts that perish. To end a human career,

---

* These frequent references do not prevent modern critics from affirming that the cities of refuge were no part of the Mosaic legislation. They found this view upon the absence throughout the history of all reference to them as being in actual use. They were not instituted, it is said, till after the Exile. But the very test that rejects them from the early legislation fails here. There is no reference to them as actually occupied in the post-exilian books, amounting, as these are said to do, to half the Old Testament. Their occupation, it is said, with the other Levitical cities, was postponed to the time of Messiah. The shifts to which the critics are put in connection with this institution do not merely indicate a weak point in their theory; they show also how precarious is the position that when you do not *hear* of an institution as in actual operation you may conclude that it was of later date.

to efface by one dread act all the joys of a man's life, all his dreams and hopes of coming good; to snap all the threads that bound him to his fellows, perhaps to bring want into the homes and desolation into the hearts of all who loved him or leant on him—this, even if done unintentionally, was a very serious thing. To mark this in a very emphatic way was the purpose of these cities of refuge. Though in certain respects (as we shall see) the practice of avenging blood by the next-of-kin indicated a relic of barbarism, yet, as a testimony to the sacredness of human life, it was characteristic of civilisation. It is natural for us to have a feeling, when through carelessness but quite unintentionally one has killed another; when a young man, for example, believing a gun to be unloaded, has discharged its contents into the heart of his sister or his mother, and when the author of this deed gets off scot-free,—we may have a feeling that something is wanting to vindicate the sanctity of human life, and bear witness to the terribleness of the act that extinguished it. And yet it cannot be denied that in our day life is invested with pre-eminent sanctity. Never, probably, was its value higher, or the act of destroying it wilfully, or even carelessly, treated as more serious. Perhaps, too, as things are with us, it is better in cases of unintentional killing to leave the unhappy perpetrator to the punishment of his own feelings, rather than subject him to any legal process, which, while ending with a declaration of his innocence, might needlessly aggravate a most excruciating pain.

It is not a very pleasing feature of the Hebrew economy that this regard to the sanctity of human life was limited to members of the Hebrew nation. All outside the Hebrew circle were treated as little better than the beasts that perish. For Canaanites there was nothing but indiscriminate slaughter. Even in the times of King David we find a barbarity in the treatment of enemies that seems to shut out all sense of brotherhood, and to smother all claim to compassion. We have here a point in which even the Hebrew race were still far behind. They had not come under the influence of that blessed Teacher who taught us to love our enemies. They had no sense of the obligation arising from the great truth that "God hath made of one blood all the nations of men for to dwell on all the face of the earth." This is one of the points at which we are enabled to see the vast change that was effected by the spirit of Jesus Christ. The very psalms in some places reflect the old spirit, for the writers had not learned to pray as He did— "Father, forgive them; for they know not what they do."

2. Even as apportioned to the Hebrew people, there was still an uncivilised element in the arrangements connected with these cities of refuge. This lay in the practice of making the go-el, or nearest of kin, the avenger of blood. The moment a man's blood was shed, the nearest relative became responsible for avenging it. He felt himself possessed by a spirit of retribution, which demanded, with irrepressible urgency, the blood of the man who had killed his relation. It was an unreasoning, restless spirit, making no allowance for the circumstances in which the blood was shed, seeing nothing and knowing nothing save that his relative had been slain, and that it was his duty, at the earliest possible moment, to have blood for blood. Had the law been perfect, it would have simply handed over the killer to the magistrate, whose duty would have been calmly to investigate the case, and either punish or acquit, according as he should find that the man had committed a crime or had caused a misfortune. But, as we have seen, it was characteristic of the Hebrew legislation that it adapted itself to the condition of things which it found, and not to an ideal perfection which the people were not capable of at once realising. In the office of the go-el there was much that was of wholesome tendency. The feeling was deeply rooted in the Hebrew mind that the nearest of kin was the guardian of his brother's life, and for this reason he was bound to avenge his death; and instead of crossing this feeling, or seeking wholly to uproot it, the object of Moses was to place it under salutary checks, which should prevent it from inflicting gross injustice where no crime had really been committed. There was something both sacred and salutary in the relation of the go-el to his nearest of kin. When poverty obliged a man to dispose of his property, it was the go-el that was bound to intervene and "redeem" the property. The law served as a check to the cold spirit that is so ready to ask, in reference to one broken down, "Am I my brother's keeper?" It maintained a friendly relation between members of families that might otherwise have been entirely severed from each other. The avenging of blood was regarded as one of the duties resulting from this relation, and had this part of the duty been rudely or summarily superseded, the whole relationship, with all the friendly offices which it involved, might have suffered shipwreck.

3. The course to be followed by the involuntary manslayer was very minutely prescribed. He was to hurry with all speed to the nearest city of refuge, and stand at the entering of the gate till the elders assembled, and then to declare his cause in their ears. If he failed to establish his innocence, he got no protection; but if he made out his case he was free from the avenger of blood, so long as he remained within the city or its precincts. If, however, he wandered out, he was at the mercy of the avenger. Further, he was to remain in the city till the death of the high priest. Some have sought a mystical meaning in this last regulation, as if the high priest figured the Redeemer, and the death of the high priest the completion of redemption by the death of Christ. But this is too far-fetched to be of weight. The death of the high priest was probably fixed on as a convenient time for releasing the manslayer, it being probable that by that time all keen feeling in reference to his deed would have subsided, and no one would then think that justice had been defrauded when a man with blood on his hands was allowed to go at large.

4. As it was, the involuntary manslayer had thus to undergo a considerable penalty. Having to reside in the city of refuge, he could no longer cultivate his farm or follow his ordinary avocations; he must have found the means of living in some new employment as best he could. His friendships, his whole associations in life, were changed; perhaps he was even separated from his family. To us all this appears a harder line than justice would have prescribed. But, on the one hand, it was a necessary testimony to the strong, though somewhat unreasonable, feeling respecting the awfulness, through whatever cause,

of shedding innocent blood. A man had to accept of this quietly, just as many a man has to accept the consequences—the social outlawry, it may be, and other penalties—of having had a father of bad character, or of having been present in the company of wicked men when some evil deed was done by them. Then, on the other hand, the fact that the involuntary destruction of life was sure, even at the best, to be followed by such consequences, was fitted to make men very careful. They would naturally endeavour to the utmost to guard against an act that might land them in such a situation; and thus the ordinary operations of daily life would be rendered more secure. And perhaps it was in this way that the whole appointment secured its end. Some laws are never broken. And here may be the explanation of the fact that the cities of refuge were not much used. In all Bible history we do not meet with a single instance; but this might indicate, not the non-existence of the institution, but the indirect success of the provision, which, though framed to cure, operated by preventing. It made men careful, and thus in silence checked the evil more effectually than if it had often been put in execution.

The desire for vengeance is a very strong feeling of human nature. Nor is it a feeling that soon dies out; it has been known to live, and to live keenly and earnestly, even for centuries. We talk of ancient barbarism; but even in comparatively modern times the story of its deeds is appalling. Witness its operation in the island of Corsica. The historian Filippini says that in thirty years of his own time 28,000 Corsicans had been murdered out of revenge. Another historian calculates that the number of the victims of the Vendetta from 1359 to 1729 was 330,000.* If an equal number be allowed for the wounded, we have 660,000 Corsicans victims of revenge. And Corsica was but one part of Italy where the same passion raged. In former ages Florence, Bologna, Verona, Padua, and Milan were conspicuous for the same wild spirit. And, however raised, even by trifling causes, the spirit of vengeance is uncontrollable. The causes, indeed, are often in ludicrous disproportion to the effects. "In Ireland, for instance, it is not so long since one of these blood-feuds in the county of Tipperary had acquired such formidable proportions that the authorities of the Roman Catholic Church there were compelled to resort to a mission in order to put an end to it. A man had been killed nearly a century before in an affray which commenced about the age of a colt. His relatives felt bound to avenge the murder, and their vengeance was again deemed to require fresh vengeance, until faction fights between the 'Three Year Olds' and the 'Four Year Olds' had grown almost into petty wars." † When we find the spirit of revenge so blindly fierce even in comparatively modern times, we can the better appreciate the necessity of such a check on its exercise as the cities of refuge supplied. The mere fact that blood had been shed was enough to rouse the legal avenger to the pitch of frenzy; in his blind passion he could think of nothing but blood for blood; and if, in the first excitement of the news, the involuntary manslayer had crossed his path, nothing could have restrained him from falling on him and crimsoning the ground with his blood.

* Gregorovius, "Wanderings in Corsica."
† "Pulpit Comment.," *in loco*.

In New Testament times the practice that committed the avenging of blood to the nearest of kin seems to have fallen into abeyance. No such keen desire for revenge was prevalent then. Such cases as those now provided for were doubtless dealt with by the ordinary magistrate. And thus our Lord could grapple directly with the spirit of revenge and retaliation in all its manifestations. "Ye have heard that it was said of old time, An eye for an eye, and a tooth for a tooth; but I say unto you, Resist not him that is evil; but whosoever smiteth thee on thy right cheek, turn to him the other also" (R. V.). The old practice was hurtful, because, even in cases where punishment was deserved, it made vengeance or retribution so much a matter of personal feeling. It stimulated to the utmost pitch what was fiercest in human temper. It is a far better system that commits the dealing with crime to the hands of magistrates, who ought to be, and who are presumed to be, exempt from all personal feeling in the matter. And now, for those whose personal feelings are roused, whether in a case of premeditated or of unintended manslaughter, or of any lesser injury done to themselves, the Christian rule is that those personal feelings are to be overcome; the law of love is to be called into exercise, and retribution is to be left in the hands of the great Judge:—"Vengeance is Mine; I will recompense, saith the Lord."

The attempt to find in the cities of refuge a typical representation of the great salvation fails at every point but one. The safety that was found in the refuge corresponds to the safety that is found in Christ. But even in this point of view the city of refuge rather affords an illustration that constitutes a type. The benefit of the refuge was only for unintentional offences; the salvation of Christ is for all. What Christ saves from is not our misfortune but our guilt. The protection of the city was needed only till the death of the high priest; the protection of Christ is needed till the great public acquittal. All that the manslayer received in the city was safety; but from Christ there is a constant flow of higher and holier blessings. His name is called Jesus because He saves His people from their sins. Not merely from the penalty, but from the sins themselves. It is His high office not only to atone for sin, but to destroy it. "If the Son makes you free, ye shall be free indeed." The virtue that goes out of Him comes into contact with the lust itself and transforms it. The final benefit of Christ is the blessing of transformation. It is the acquisition of the Christlike spirit. "Moreover whom He did foreknow, them He also did predestinate to be conformed to the image of His Son, that He might be the firstborn of many brethren."

In turning an incident like this to account, as bearing on our modern life, we are led to think how much harm we are liable to do to others without intending harm, and how deeply we ought to be affected by this consideration, when we discover what we have really done. We may be helped here by thinking of the case of St. Paul. What harm he did in the unconverted period of his life, without intending to do harm, cannot be calculated. But when he came to the light, nothing could have exceeded the depth of his contrition, and, to his last hour, he could not think of the past without horror. It was his great joy to know that his Lord had pardoned him, and that he had been able to find one good use of the very enormity of his conduct—to show the exceeding riches of His pardoning love. But, all his life long, the Apostle was animated by an overwhelming desire to neutralise, as far as he could, the mischief of his early life, and very much of the self-denial and contempt of ease that continued to characterise him was due to this vehement feeling. For though Paul felt that he had done harm in ignorance, and for this cause had obtained mercy, he did not consider that his ignorance excused him altogether. It was an ignorance that proceeded from culpable causes, and that involved effects from which a rightly ordered heart could not but recoil.

In the case of His own murderers our blessed Lord, in His beautiful prayer, recognised a double condition,—they were ignorant, yet they were guilty, "Father, forgive them; for they know not what they do." They were ignorant of what they were doing, and yet they were doing what needed forgiveness, because it involved guilt. And what we admire in Paul is, that he did not make his ignorance a self-justifying plea, but in the deepest humility owned the inexcusableness of his conduct. To have done harm to our fellow-creatures under any circumstances is a distressing thing, even when we meant the best; but to have done harm to their moral life owing to something wrong in our own, is not only distressing, but humiliating. It is something which we dare not lightly dismiss from our minds, under the plea that we meant the best, but unfortunately we were mistaken. Had we been more careful, had our eye been more single, we should have been full of light, and we should have known that we were not taking the right way to do the best. Errors in moral life always resolve themselves into disorder of our moral nature, and, if traced to their source, will bring to light some fault of indolence, or selfishness, or pride, or carelessness, which was the real cause of our mistaken act.

And where is the man—parent, teacher, pastor, or friend—that does not become conscious, at some time or other, of having influenced for harm those committed to his care? We taught them, perhaps, to despise some good man whose true worth we have afterwards been led to see. We repressed their zeal when we thought it misdirected, with a force which chilled their enthusiasm and carnalised their hearts. We failed to stimulate them to decision for Christ, and allowed the golden opportunity to pass which might have settled their relation to God all the rest of their life. The great realities of the spiritual life were not brought home to them with the earnestness, the fidelity, the affection that was fitting. "Who can understand his errors?" Who among us but, as he turns some new corner in the path of life, as he reaches some new viewpoint, as he sees a new flash from heaven reflected on the past,—who among us but feels profoundly that all his life has been marred by unsuspected flaws, and almost wishes that he had never been born? Is there no city of refuge for us to fly to, and to escape the condemnation of our hearts?

It is here that the blessed Lord presents Himself to us in a most blessed light. "Come unto Me, all ye that labour and are heavy laden, and I will give you rest." Do we not labour indeed, are we not in truth very heavy laden, when we feel the burden of unintentional evil, when we feel that unconsciously we have been doing hurt to others, and incurring the curse of him who causeth the blind to stumble? Are we not heavy laden indeed when we cannot be sure that even yet we are thoroughly on the right track —when we feel that peradventure we are still unconsciously continuing the mischief in some other form? Yet is not the promise true?—"I will give you rest." I will give you pardon for the past, and guidance for the future. I will deliver you from the feeling that you have been all your life sowing seeds of mischief, sure to spring up and pervert those whom you love most dearly. I will give you comfort in the thought that as I have guided you, I will guide them, and you shall have a vision of the future, that may no doubt include some of the terrible features of the shipwreck of St. Paul, but of which the end will be the same—" and so it came to pass that they escaped all safe to land."

And let us learn a lesson of charity. Let us learn to be very considerate of mischief done by others either unintentionally or in ignorance. What more inexcusable than the excitement of parents over their children or of masters over their servants, when, most undesignedly and not through sheer carelessness, an article of some value is broken or damaged? Have you never done such a thing yourself? And if a like torrent fell on you then from *your* parent or master, did you not feel bitterly that it was unjust? And do you not even now have the same feeling when your temper cools? How bitter the thought of having done injustice to those dependent on you, and of having created in their bosoms a sullen sense of wrong! Let them have their city of refuge for undesigned offences, and never again pursue them or fall on them in the excited spirit of the avenger of blood!

So also with regard to opinions. Many who differ from us in religious opinion differ through ignorance. They have inherited their opinions from their parents or their other ancestors. Their views are shared by nearly all whom they love and with whom they associate; they are contained in their familiar books; they are woven into the web of their daily life. If they were better instructed, if their minds were more free from prejudice, they might agree with us more. Let us make for them the allowance of ignorance, and let us make it not bitterly but respectfully. They are doing much mischief, it may be. They are retarding the progress of beneficent truth, they are thwarting your endeavours to spread Divine light. But they are doing it ignorantly. If you are not called to provide for them a city of refuge, cover them at least with the mantle of charity. Believe that their intentions are better than their acts. Live in the hope of a day "When perfect light shall pour its rays," when all the mists of prejudice shall be scattered, and you shall perhaps find that in all that is vital in Christian truth and for the Christian life, you and your brethren were not so far separate after all.

CHAPTER XXVIII.

THE INHERITANCE OF THE LEVITES.

JOSHUA xxi. 1-42.

ONCE and again we have found reference made to the fact that Levites received no territorial inheritance among their brethren (xiii. 14, 33, xiv. 3, 4). They had a higher privilege: the Lord was their inheritance. In the present chapter we have an elaborate account of the arrangements for their settlement; it will therefore be suitable here to rehearse their history, and ascertain the relation they now stood in to the rest of the tribes.

In the days of the patriarchs and during the sojourn in Egypt there were no official priests. Each head of a house discharged the duties of the priesthood in patriarchal times, and a similar arrangement prevailed during the residence in Egypt. The whole nation was holy; in this sense it was a nation of priests; all were set apart for the service of God. By-and-by it pleased God to select a portion of the nation specially for His service, to establish, as it were, a holy of holies within the consecrated nation. The first intimation of this was given on that awful occasion when the firstborn of the Egyptians was slain. In token of His mercy in sparing Israel on that night, all the firstborn of Israel, both of man and beast, were specially consecrated to the Lord. The animals were to be offered in sacrifice, except in the case of some, such as the ass, not suited for sacrifice; these were to be redeemed by the sacrifice of another animal. Afterwards a similar arrangement was made with reference to the firstborn of men, the tribe of Levi being substituted for them (see Numb. iii. 12). But this arrangement was not made till after the tribe of Levi had shown, by a special act of service, that they were fitted for this honor.

Certainly we should not have thought beforehand that the descendants of Levi would be the specially sacred tribe. Levi himself comes before us in the patriarchal history in no attractive light. He and Simeon were associated together in that massacre of the Shechemites, which we can never read of without horror (Gen. xxxiv. 25). Levi was likewise an accomplice with his brethren in the lamentable tragedy of Joseph. And as nothing better is recorded of him, we are apt to think of him as through life the same. But this were hardly fair. Why should not Levi have shared in that softening influence which undoubtedly came on the other brethren? Why may he not have become a true man of God, and transmitted to his tribe the memory and the example of a holy character? Certain it is that we find among his descendants in Egypt some very noble specimens of godliness. The mother of Moses, a daughter of the house of Levi, is a woman of incomparable faith. Moses, her son, is emphatically "the man of God." Aaron, his brother, moved by a Divine influence, goes to the wilderness to find him when the very crisis of oppression seems to indicate that God's time for the deliverance of Israel is drawing nigh. Miriam, his sister, though far from faultless, piously watched his bulrush-cradle, and afterwards led the choir whose praises rose to God in a great volume of thanksgiving after crossing the sea.

The first honour conferred on Levi in connection with religious service was the appointment of Aaron and his sons to the special service of the priesthood (Exod. xxviii.; Numb. xviii. 1). This did not necessarily involve any spiritual distinction for the whole tribe of which Aaron was a member, nor was that distinction conferred at that time. It was after the affair of the golden calf that the tribe of Levi received this honour. For when Moses, in his holy zeal against that scandal, called upon all who were on the Lord's side to come to him, "all the sons of Levi gathered themselves unto him" (Exod. xxxii. 26). This seems to imply that that tribe alone held itself aloof from the atrocious idolatry into which even Aaron had been drawn. And apparently it was in connection with this high act of service that Levi was selected as the sacred tribe, and in due time formally substituted for the firstborn in every family (Numb. iii. 12, *sqq*., viii. 6 *sqq*., xviii. 2 *sqq*.). From this time the tribe of Levi stood to God in a relation of peculiar honour and sacredness, and had duties assigned to them in harmony with this eminent position.

The tribe of Levi consisted of three main branches, corresponding to Levi's three sons—Kohath, Gershon, and Merari. The Kohathites, though apparently not the oldest (see Numb. iii. 17) were the most distinguished, Moses and Aaron being of that branch. As Levites, the Kohathites had charge of the ark and its sacred furniture, guarding it at all times, and carrying it from place to place during the journeys of the wilderness. The Gershonites had charge of the tabernacle, with its cords, curtains, and coverings. The sons of Merari had charge of the more solid parts of the tabernacle, "its boards and bars, its pillars and its pins, and all the vessels thereof." Korah, the leader of the rebellion against Moses and Aaron, was, like them, of the family of Kohath, and the object of his rebellion was to punish what he considered the presumption of the two brothers in giving to Aaron the special honours of a priesthood which, in former days, had belonged alike to all the congregation (Numb. xvi. 3). We are accustomed to think that the supernatural proofs of the Divine commission to Moses were so overwhelming that it would have been out of the question for any man to challenge them. But many things show that, though we might have thought opposition to Moses impossible, it prevailed to a great extent. The making of the golden calf, the report of the spies and the commotion that followed, the rebellion of Korah, and many other things, prove that the prevalent spirit was usually that of unbelief and rebellion, and that it was only after many signal miracles and signal judgments that Moses was enabled at last to exercise an unchallenged authority. The rationalist idea, that it was enthusiasm for Moses that led the people to follow him out of Egypt, and endure all the hardships of the wilderness, and that there is nothing more in the Exodus than the story of an Eastern nation leaving one country under a trusted leader to settle in another, is one to which the whole tenor of the history offers unqualified contradiction. And not the least valid ground of opposition is the bitter, deadly spirit in which attempts to frustrate Moses were so often made.

Many of the duties of the Levites as detailed in the Pentateuch were duties for the wilderness. After the settlement in Canaan, and the establishment of the tabernacle at Shiloh, these duties would undergo a change. The Levites were not all needed to be about the tabernacle. The Gibeonites indeed had been retained as "hewers of wood and drawers of water for the congregation and for the altar of the Lord," so that the more laborious part of the work at Shiloh would be done by them. If the Levites had clustered like a swarm of bees around the sacred establishment, loss would have been sustained alike by themselves and by the people. It was desirable, in accordance with the great law of distribution already referred to, that they should be dispersed over the whole country. The men that stood nearest to God, and who were a standing testimony to the superiority of the spiritual over the secular, who were Divine witnesses, indeed, to the higher part of man's nature, as well as to God's pre-eminent claims, must have failed egregiously of their mission had they been confined to a single city or to the territory of a single tribe. Jacob had foretold both of Simeon and Levi that they would be "divided in Jacob and scattered in Israel." In the case of Levi, the scattering was overruled for good. Designed to point God-wards and heavenwards, the mission of Levi was to remind the people over the whole country that they were not mere earth-worms, created to grub and burrow in the ground, but beings with a nobler destiny, whose highest honour it was to be in communion with God.

The functions of the Levites throughout the country seem to have differed somewhat in successive periods of their history. Here, as in other matters, there was doubtless some development, according as new wants appeared in the spiritual condition of the people, and consequently new obligations for the Levites to fulfil. When the people fell under special temptations to idolatry, it would naturally fall to the Levites, in connection with the priesthood, to warn them against these temptations, and strive to keep them faithful to their God. But it does not appear that even the Levites could be trusted to continue faithful. It is a sad and singular fact that a grandson of Moses was one of the first to go astray. The Authorized Version, indeed, says that the young man who became a priest to the Danites when they set up a graven image in the city of Dan, was Jonathan, the son of Gershom, the son of Manasseh (Judg. xviii. 30). But the Revised Version, not without authority, calls him Jonathan, the son of Gershom, the son of Moses. Here we have a glimpse of two remarkable facts: in the first place, that a grandson of Moses, a Levite, was located in so confined a place that he had to leave it in search of another, "to sojourn where he could find a place"—so entirely had Moses abstained from steps to secure superior provision for his own family; and, in the second place, that even with his remarkable advantages and relations, this Jonathan, in defiance of the law, was tempted to assume an office of priesthood, and to discharge that office at the shrine of a graven image. We are far indeed from the truth when we suppose that the whole nation of Israel submitted to the law of Moses from the beginning with absolute loyalty, or when we accept the prevalent practice among them at any one period as undoubted evidence of what was then the law.

But let us now turn our attention to the distribution of the Levites as it was planned. We say deliberately "as it was planned," because there is every reason to believe that the plan was not effectually carried out. In no case does there seem to have been such a failure of official arrangements as in the case of Levi. And the reason is not difficult to find. Few of the cities allotted to them were free of Canaanites at the time. To get actual possession of the cities they must have dispossessed the remaining Canaanites. But, scattered as they were, this was peculiarly difficult. And the other tribes seem to have been in no humour to help them. Hence it is that in the early period of the Judges we find Levites wandering here and there seeking for a settlement, and glad of any occupation they could find (Judg. xviii. 7, xix. 1).

The provision made by Joshua for the Levites was that out of all the other tribes, forty-eight cities with their suburbs, including the six cities of refuge, were allotted to them. It is necessary for us here to call to mind how much Canaan, like other Eastern countries and some countries not Eastern, was a land of towns and villages. Cottages and country-houses standing by themselves were hardly known. A house in its own grounds—"a lodge in a garden of cucumbers"—might shelter a man for a time, but could not be his permanent home. The country was too liable to hostile raids for its inhabitants to dwell thus unprotected. Most of the people had their homes in the towns and villages with which their fields were connected. In consequence of this each town had a circuit of land around it, which always fell to the conquerors when the town was taken. And it is this fact that sometimes makes the boundaries of the tribes so difficult to follow, because these boundaries had to embrace all the lands connected with the cities which they embraced. If it be asked, Did the Levites receive as part of their inheritance all the lands adjacent to their cities, the answer is, No. For in that case the only difference between them and the other tribes would have been that the Levites had forty-eight little territories instead of one large possession, and there would have been no ground for the distinction so emphatically made that "the Lord was their inheritance," or "the sacrifices of the Lord made by fire."

The cities given to the Levites, even when cleared of Canaanites, were not possessed by Levites alone. We may gather the normal state of affairs from what is said regarding Hebron and Caleb. Hebron was a Levitical city, a city of the priests, a city of refuge; they gave to the Kohathites the city, with the suburbs thereof roundabout; "but the fields of the city, and the villages thereof, gave they to Caleb the son of Jephunneh for his possession" (vv. 11, 12). What are called "suburbs," or, as some prefer to render, "cattle-drives," extended for two thousand cubits round about the city on every side (Numb. xxxv. 5), and were used only for pasture. It behoved the Levites to have cattle of some kind to supply them with their food, the main part of which, besides fruit, was milk and its produce. But, beyond this, the Levites were not entangled with the business of husbandry. They were left free for more spiritual service. It was their part to raise the souls of the people above the level of earth, and, like the angel in the "Pilgrim's Progress," call on those who might otherwise have worshipped the mud-rake to lift up their eyes to the crown of glory, and accept the heavenly gift.

In fact, the whole function of the Levites, ideally at least, was as Moses sung:—

"And of Levi he said,
Let thy Urim and thy Thummim be with thy godly one,
Whom thou didst prove at Massah,
With whom thou didst strive at the waters of Meribah;
Who said of his father, and of his mother, I have not seen him;
Neither did he acknowledge his brethren,
Nor knew his own children:
For they have observed Thy word,
And kept Thy covenant.
*They shall teach Jacob Thy judgments,
And Israel Thy law:*
They shall put incense before Thee,
And whole burnt offering upon Thine altar.
Bless, Lord, his substance,
And accept the work of his hands:
Smite through the loins of them that rise up against him,
And of them that hate him, that they rise not again."
Deut. xxxiii. 8-11 (R.V.).

But to come now to the division itself. The Kohathites, or leading family, had no fewer than thirteen cities in the tribes of Judah, Benjamin, and Simeon, and ten more in Ephraim, Dan, and Manasseh. The thirteen in Judah, Benjamin, and Simeon were for the priests; the other ten were for the other branches of the Kohathites. At first the priests, strictly so called, could not occupy them all. But, as the history advances, the priests become more and more prominent, while the Levites as such seem to hold a less and less conspicuous place. In the Psalms, for example, we sometimes find the house of Levi left out when all classes of worshippers are called on to praise the Lord. In the 135th Psalm all are included:—

"O house of Israel, bless ye the Lord:
O house of Aaron, bless ye the Lord:
O house of Levi, bless ye the Lord:
Ye that fear the Lord, bless ye the Lord."

But in the 115th the Levites are left out:—

"O Israel, trust thou in the Lord:
He is their help and their shield.
O house of Aaron, trust ye in the Lord:
He is their help and their shield.
Ye that fear the Lord, trust in the Lord:
He is their help and their shield."

And in the 118th:—

"Let Israel now say
That His mercy endureth for ever.
Let the house of Aaron now say
That His mercy endureth for ever.
Let them now that fear the Lord say
That His mercy endureth for ever."

There is this to be said for the region where the priests, the house of Aaron, had their cities, viz., the tribe of Judah, that it maintained its integrity longest of any; nor did it thoroughly succumb to idolatry till the dark days of Manasseh, one of its later kings. But, on the other hand, in New Testament times, Judæa was the most bigoted part of the country, and the most bitterly opposed to our Lord. And the explanation is, that the true spirit of Divine service had utterly evaporated from among the priesthood, and the miserable spirit of formalism had come in. The living sap of the institution had been turned into stone, and the plant of renown of early days had become a stony fossil. So true is it that the best institutions, when perverted from their true end, become the sources of greatest evil, and the highest gifts of heaven, when seized by the devil and turned to his purposes, become the most efficient instruments of hell.

The other portions of the family of Kohath were distributed in ten cities over the central part of Western Palestine. Some of them were important centers of influence, such as Bethhoron, Shechem, and Taanach. But the influence of the Levites for good seems to have been feeble in this region, for it was here that Jeroboam reigned, and here that Ahab and Jezebel all but obliterated the worship of Jehovah. It is commonly believed that Samuel was a member of the tribe of Levi, although there is some confusion in the genealogy as given in 1 Chron. vi. 28, 34; yet Ramathaim Zophim, his father's place of abode, was not one of the Levitical cities. And Samuel's influence was exerted more on the southern than the central district; for, after the destruction of Shiloh, Mizpeh appears to have been his ordinary residence (1 Sam. vii. 6), and afterwards Ramah* (vii. 17). It would indeed be a pleasant thought that the inefficiency of the Kohathites as a whole was in some measure redeemed by the incomparable service of Samuel. If Samuel was a Levite, he was a noble instance of what may be done by one zealous and consecrated man, amid the all but universal defection of his official brethren.

The Gershonites were placed in cities in eastern Manasseh, Issachar, Asher, and Naphtali; while the Merarites were in Zebulun, and in the transjordanic tribes of Gad and Reuben. They thus garrisoned the northern and eastern districts. Those placed in the north ought to have been barriers against the gross idolatry of Tyre and Sidon, and those in the east, besides resisting the idolatry of the desert tribes, should have held back that of Damascus and Syria. But there is very little to show that the Levites as a whole rose to the dignity of their mission in these regions, or that they formed a very efficient barrier against the idolatry and corruption which they were designed to meet. No doubt they did much to train the people to the outward observance of the law. They would call them to the celebration of the great annual festivals, and of the new moons and other observances that had to be locally celebrated. They would look after cases of ceremonial defilement, and no doubt they would be careful to enjoin payment of the tithes to which they had a claim. They would do their best to maintain the external distinctions in religion, by which the nation was separated from its neighbours. But, except in rare cases, they do not appear to have been spiritually earnest, nor to have done much of that service which Samuel did in the southern part of the country. Externalism and formalism seem to have been their most frequent characteristics; and externalism and formalism are poor weapons when the enemy cometh in like a flood.

And, whatever may have been the usual life and work of the Levites over the country, they never seem to have realised the glory of the distinction divinely accorded to them—" The Lord is their inheritance." Few, indeed, in any age or country have come to know what is meant by having God for their portion. Unbelief can never grasp that there is a life in God—a real life, so full of enjoyment that all other happiness may be dispensed with; a real property, so rich in every blessing, that the goods and chattels of this world

* Ramathaim and Ramah are used interchangeably (1 Sam. i. 1 and 19, ii. 11).

are mere shadows in comparison. Yet that there have been men profoundly impressed by these convictions, in all ages and in many lands, amid prevailing ungodliness, cannot be denied. How otherwise is such a life as that of St. Bernard or that of St. Francis to be accounted for? Or that of St. Columba and the missionaries of Iona? Or, to go farther back, that of St. Paul? There is a magic virtue, or rather a Divine power, in real consecration. "Them that honour Me, I will honour." It is the want of such men that makes our churches feeble. It is our mixing up our own interests with the interests of God's kingdom and refusing to leave self out of view while we profess to give ourselves wholly to God, that explains the slowness of our progress. If the Levites had all been consecrated men, idolatry and its great brood of corruptions would never have spread over the land of Israel. If all Christian ministers were like their Master, Christianity would spread like wildfire, and in a very little time the light of salvation would brighten the globe.

NOTE.—In this chapter we have accepted the statements of the Pentateuch regarding the Levites as they stand. We readily own that there are difficulties not a few connected with the received view. The modern critical theory that maintains that the Levitical order was a much later institution would no doubt remove many of these difficulties, but only by creating other difficulties far more serious. Besides, the hypothesis of Wellhausen that the tribe of Levi was destroyed with Simeon at the invasion of Canaan—having no foundation to rest on, except the assumption that the prophecy ascribed to Jacob was written at a later date—is ludicrously inadequate to sustain the structure made to rest on it. Nor is it conceivable that, after the captivity, the priests should have been able to make the people believe a totally different account of the history of one of the tribes from that which had previously been received. It is likewise incredible that the Levites should have been "annihilated" or "extinguished" in the days of Joshua, without a single allusion in the history to so terrible a fact. How inconsistent with the concern expressed when the tribe of Benjamin was in danger of extinction (Judg. xxi. 17). The loss of a tribe was like the loss of a limb; it would have marred essentially the symmetry of the nation.

CHAPTER XXIX.

NO FAILURE OF GOD'S PROMISE.

Joshua xxi. 43-45.

THE historian has reached a point where he may stand still and look back. One look is comparatively limited; another reaches very far. The immediate survey extends only over the last few years; the remote embraces centuries, and goes back to the time of Abraham.

The historian sees the venerable patriarch of the nation among his flocks and herds in Ur of the Chaldees; receiving there a Divine summons to remove to an unknown land; obeying the call, tarrying at Haran, then traversing the desert, and crossing the Jordan. At Shechem, at Bethel, at Mamre, and at Beersheba, he perceives him listening to the Divine voice that promises that, stranger and pilgrim though he was, the Lord would give his posterity all that land; that he would bless those that blessed him, and curse those that cursed him; and that in him and in his seed all the nations of the earth should be blessed.

For one hundred long years Abraham had wandered over the country without so much as a house or homestead in it. Isaac had come after him, living the same pilgrim life. Jacob, with a much more stirring and troubled life, had in his old age gone down to Joseph in Egypt, leaving but one field in the country which he could call his own.

Then came the long centuries of Egyptian bondage. At last the Divine call is heard to leave Egypt, but after this, forty long years have still to be spent in the wilderness. Then Moses, the great leader of the people, dies—dies at the very time when he is apparently most needed, just at the very crisis of Israel's history.

But Joshua comes in Moses' room, and the Lord is with Joshua; He rewards his faith and gives him victory over all his enemies. And now at last comes the fulfilment of the promises to the fathers, hoary with age, and seemingly long forgotten. The bill has at last matured and fallen due. After so many generations, it might be thought that it would have been enough to discharge the main substance of the obligation or that some compromise might have been proposed reducing the claim. After having lain long out of their money, creditors are usually ready to accept a composition. But this was not God's method of settlement. During the whole period of Joshua's leadership, God had been doing nothing but discharging old obligations. Not one word of the original bill had been obliterated; not one item had been allowed to lapse through time. East and west and north and south He had been giving what He had promised to give. And now, as the transaction comes to an end, it is seen that nothing has been omitted or forgotten. "There failed not ought of any good thing which the Lord had spoken concerning Israel; all came to pass." He proved Himself, as Moses had said, "the faithful God, which keepeth covenant and mercy with them that love Him, and keep His commandments to a thousand generations."

Three gifts are specified which God bestowed on Israel: possessions, rest, and victory. First, He gave them the land which He had sworn to give unto their fathers, and they possessed it; next, He gave them rest round about, according to all that He had sworn to their fathers; and, lastly, He gave them victory over all their enemies. "He satisfied the longing soul, and filled the hungry soul with goodness." He brought His bride to her home, and surrounded her with comforts. And had the bride only been as faithful to her obligations as the Divine bridegroom, it might have been said that

"Time had run back, and fetched the age of gold."

But, it may perhaps be said,—this is only the historian's view of the matter, and it is hardly in accordance with facts. Are we not told that, at an early period, a colony of the tribe of Dan had to go elsewhere in search of land, because they were too hampered in the allotment they had received? And, in the beginning of Judges, are we not told that after the death of Joshua, Judah and Simeon had a desperate tussle with Canaanites and Perizzites who were still in their territories, and that in Bezek alone there were slain of them ten thousand men? And is not the whole of the first chapter of Judges a record of the relations of Israel in various places to the original inhabitants, from which it appears that very many of the Canaanites continued to dwell in the land? Surely this was not what God's promise to the fathers was fitted to convey. Had not God promised that He would "drive out" the seven nations, and give the seed of Abraham possession of the whole? How then could His word be said to be implemented when so many of the original inhabitants remained? And, in particular, how could the historian of Joshua say so explicitly that "there failed not ought of any good thing which the Lord had spoken unto the house of Israel."

In answer to this objection it is to be remarked that God had never promised to give the people full possession of the land *save through their own exertions made in dependence on Him.* Their possessions were not to fall into their hands as the manna fell in the wilderness or as the water gushed from the rock. The seven nations were not to rush from before them the moment they crossed the Jordan. God always meant that they were to be His instruments for clearing the country. Now, that clearance was evidently designed to be effected in two ways. First, under Joshua, a general encounter with the former possessors was to take place, their confederacies were to be shattered, their spirit was to be broken, and to a certain extent their lands were to be set free. But beyond this, there was to be a further process of clearing out. When each tribe was settled in its lot, it was to address itself, in detail, to the task of dispossessing such Canaanites as yet lingered there. It might not be expedient that all should be engaged in this task together, for this would necessarily interfere with the ordinary operations of agriculture. It was judged better that it should be done piecemeal, and therefore God was asked to say which of the tribes ought to begin it. Judah was named, and Judah aided by Simeon did his work well, and set a good example to the rest. But the other tribes did not act with Judah's spirit, and therefore they did not enjoy his reward. The testimony of the historian is, that nothing failed of any good thing which *the Lord had spoken* unto the house of Israel. The Lord faithfully performed every part of His obligation. He did not add Israel's obligations to His own, and discharge them too, when they were remiss concerning them. The ultimate result of the whole business was, that trouble befell Israel, inasmuch as he neglected his obligations, while the Lord faithfully performed every one of His. Time therefore did not run back and fetch the age of gold. Israel did not enjoy all the possessions that had been allotted to him. Canaanites remained in the country to torment him like thorns in his sides. But this was Israel's fault, not God's. Though you were to give a lazy farmer the finest farm in the country, you could not make him prosperous if he neglected his fields and idled away the time that should be spent in continuous labour. You cannot keep a man in health if he breathes unwholesome air or drinks water poisoned with putrid matter. No more could Israel be wholly prosperous if he allowed Canaanites to settle quietly at his side. If he had roused himself, and attacked them with courage and in faith, God would have made him to prevail. But, since he preferred ease and quiet to the painfulness of duty, God left him to reap as he had sowed, and suffer the consequences of his neglect. He had seldom long periods of prosperity, and often he had very bitter experiences of calamity and distress.

Certainly God had furnished His people with the materials for a happy and prosperous life, if only they had used them aright. There was first the element of possessions. They had comfortable homes and all the requisites of a comfortable life. It is most true that "a man's life consisteth not in the abundance of the things which he possesseth." But moderate possessions are one element, though not the chief or most essential of human prosperity. Possessions, however rich or manifold, in connection with a discontented temper, an ungodly spirit, or a selfish nature, can bring no genuine pleasure. In addition to possessions, the Lord had given Israel rest. Their enemies were not disposed to attack them even when dwelling by their side. True it is that the rest into which Joshua brought them was not the true, the ultimate rest. If Joshua had given them that rest, the Holy Spirit would not have spoken of a rest that was still to come (Heb. iv. 8). But external rest, like external possessions, though not all, was one contribution towards prosperity. Moreover, none of their enemies had been able to stand before them; in every encounter that had yet taken place the Lord had delivered them into their hand.

This was a blessed presage for the future. Whatever encounters might yet remain, they might count on the same result, if they lifted up their eyes to God. Their life in the future would not be without toil, without anxiety, without danger. But if they looked to Him and made the requisite efforts, God was ready to bless their toil, He was able to overcome their anxieties, He was sure as in the past to subdue their enemies. The gifts that God had conferred on them, and the materials of enjoyment with which He had surrounded them, were not designed to make them independent, as if they could now do everything for themselves. God's purpose was the very reverse. He wished to keep up the sense of dependence on Him, and to encourage at every turn the habit that seeks unto God, and goes to Him for help.

For this, after all, is the great lesson for all human beings. The great thing for us all is to keep up a living connection with God, so that our whole nature shall be replenished out of His fulness, and purified and elevated by His Divine influence. Whatever draws us to God draws us to the fountain of all that is best and purest and noblest. God would have conferred but a poor blessing on Israel if He had just settled them in the land, and then left them to themselves, without any occasion or inducement to fellowship with Him. The inducements to resort to Him which they were to be continually under were by far the most valuable part of what God now conferred upon them. The certainty that all would go wrong, that their possessions would be invaded and their rest disturbed, and that their enemies would prove victorious unless they sought continually to their God, fostered the most precious of all habits—that drawing near to God which brings with it all spiritual blessing.

> "Nearer, my God, to Thee,
> Nearer to Thee!
> E'en though it be a cross
> That raiseth me,
> Still all my song would be
> Nearer, my God, to Thee,
> Nearer to Thee!"

There is no small amount of instruction to be drawn by all of us from this record of Israel's experience.

First, it is of supreme importance for us all to

have our hearts firmly established in the conviction of the faithfulness of God. It should be our habit to regard this as an attribute on which we not only may, but must rely. To ascribe to God any laxity as to His word or promises were to cast a fearful imputation on His holy nature. "Heaven and earth shall pass away, but My word shall not pass away." "He is not a man that he should lie, or the son of man that he should repent." Nothing can be conceived that could make it better to God to break His word than to keep it. This is the root of all religion; it is the basis of faith, the true ground of trust. To train our minds to habitual reliance on all that God has said, is one of the most vital and blessed exercises of spiritual religion. It is alike honouring to God and beneficial to ourselves. To search out from the body of Scripture the promises of God; to fasten our attention on them one by one; and to exercise our minds on the thought that in Christ Jesus they are yea, and in Him Amen, is a most blessed help to spiritual stability and spiritual growth. And in our prayers there is nothing more fitted to give us confidence than to plead in this spirit the promises that God has made. No plea is more powerful than the Psalmist's—"Remember Thy word unto Thy servant, upon which Thou hast caused me to hope." How many sadly perplexed men have found rest from the words: "Commit thy way unto the Lord; trust also in Him, and He shall bring it to pass." "Faithful is He that calleth you, who also will do it."

But secondly, we may learn from this passage that, wherever the promises of God *seem* to fail, the fault is not His, but ours. On the one hand, we are taught clearly that delay is not failure, and on the other that where there does seem to be failure there is none really on the part of God. At least five-and-twenty long years elapsed between God's first promise to Abraham and the birth of Isaac. Four hundred years were to be spent by the chosen seed in bondage in Egypt. And even after the deliverance from Egypt there came the sojourn in the wilderness of other forty years. Yet God was faithful all the time. How often we need to recall the text, that one day is with the Lord as a thousand years, and a thousand years as one day! "Though the vision tarry," do not give it up in despair, but "wait for it" (Hab. ii. 3).

Perhaps it is in the matter of answers to prayer that we are most liable to the temptation that God forgets His promises. Have we not the most explicit and abundant promises that prayer will be answered? Yet how many have prayed, and seemingly prayed in vain! Nay, does not the very opposite of what we pray for often come? We entreat God to spare a beloved life; that life is taken away. We pray for victory over temptation; the temptation seems to acquire a redoubled force. We pray for success in business; the clouds seem to thicken the more. We ask, "Has God forgotten to be gracious? Is His mercy clean gone for ever? Does His promise fail for evermore?" Nay, let us rally our faith. "Then I said, This is my infirmity: but I will remember the years of the right hand of the Most High" (Psalm lxxvii. 10). If my prayer was not answered, it was not God's fault. It may be that, like Israel, I failed in my part. I may have been laying the whole burden on God, and omitting something that it fell to me to do. I may have been asking for something that would not have been for my good or for God's glory. I may have failed in that spirit of affectionate trust which is a requisite of acceptable prayer. Let us remember that God knows what things we have need of before we ask Him. And God is infinitely kind and willing to bless us. What He longs for on our part is the spirit of filial trust. What He values prayer for is that it is the channel of this spirit. We can never say that God disregards prayer unless we can say that we approached Him, and spoke to Him like confiding children dealing with a loving father, and He cast us off. But how often do we go to the footstool half hoping, half doubting, instead of going in the full conviction,—"Our gracious Father is sure to hear us; and if He do not give us the precise thing we ask, He is sure to give us something better." Let prayer ever be the outcome of a profound belief in the infinite love of God, and His constant readiness to bless us in Christ; let it be the communing of a child with his father; and let it never be darkened by a shade of suspicion that the Hearer of prayer will not be faithful to His word.

It is the happy experience both of individuals and the Church to have occasional periods of fulfilment—it may be after long periods of expectation and trial. The patriarch Job had a terrible time of trial, when God seemed so untrue to His promises that he was sometimes on the very edge of blaspheming His name. But a time of fulfilment came at last, and through all the mystery of the past Job at length saw "the end of the Lord, that the Lord is very pitiful and of tender mercy" (James v. 11). The aged Simeon and the aged Anna in the temple had waited long, but the hour came at last when all that they had been looking for was accomplished, and with a feeling of perfect satisfaction they could sing their "Nunc dimittis." The souls under the altar of them that were slain for the word of God and for the testimony which they held, when they groaned out their sad "How long?" had still to wait a little season; but the time came when, clothed in white robes and with palms in their hands, they attained complete satisfaction, crying with a loud voice, "Salvation to our God that sitteth on the throne, and to the Lamb" (Rev. vi. 10, vii. 10). And in more recent times there have been eras of fulfilment and corresponding rejoicing. When St. Augustine, after year upon year of restless tossing, at length found pardon and peace in Christ; when Columbus, after perils and privations innumerable, at length saw the dim coast which he had often prayed to behold; when Wilberforce heard the slave trade declared an illegal traffic, and Fowell Buxton saw the last fetter struck from the slave in the dominions of Great Britain; when Lord Shaftesbury found the ten hours factory bill turned into law; or when the friends of the slaves learned that the President of the United States had signed the proclamation which set four millions at liberty—the old experience of Joshua's days seemed to be repeated, and gratitude to Him who had failed in no good thing was the one feeling that filled the heart. Sometimes the death-bed affords a retrospect that kindles the same emotion. The dying man looks along the way by which he has been led, and, with the walls of the New Jerusalem gleaming before him, he owns that he has been conducted by the right way to the city of habitation. The objects of earth and heaven are seen by him in a truer light. Valuations are made more accurately on the margin of eternity. The things that have been shaken and that have perished —of how little value are they seen to be, compared to the things that cannot be shaken! The loving purpose of Divine providence in shattering so many hopes, in defeating so many projects, in inflicting so much pain, is clearly apprehended. The heart is grieved that it was so near charging God foolishly when His purpose was really so merciful and so kind. The bright era of fulfilment is at hand; and even already, while the day is only dawning, the soul can give forth its testimony that "no good thing has failed of all that the Lord hath spoken."

And then at last will come the end of the mystery. The Lord shall send His angels with a great sound of a trumpet, and they shall gather together his elect from the four winds, from the one end of heaven to the other. On the sea of glass mingled with fire they take their stand, having the harps of God, and sing the song of Moses, the servant of God, and the song of the Lamb; "Great and marvellous are Thy works, Lord God Almighty; just and true are Thy ways, Thou King of saints." What a scene and what a sensation! What joy in entering on possession of the Promised Land, in experiencing the rest of the redeemed, and in the consciousness that not a single enemy survives to annoy! What delight in the harmonious working of the new nature, in the free and happy play of all its faculties and feelings, and in the conscious presence of a God and Saviour to whose image you have been thoroughly conformed! The last shadow that dimmed your vision on earth shall have fled away; the last vestige of complaint of your earthly lot shall have vanished. Whatever you may have thought once, no other feeling will now occupy your heart but gratitude to Him who has not only not failed to fulfil all His promises, but has done in you exceeding abundantly above all that ye could ask or think!

CHAPTER XXX.

THE ALTAR ED.

JOSHUA xxii.

THE two tribes and a half had behaved well. They had kept their word, remained with their brethren during all Joshua's campaign, and taken their part in all the perils and struggles through which the host had passed. And now they receive the merited reward of honourable conduct. They are complimented by their general; their services are rehearsed with approval; their threefold fidelity, to God, to Moses, and to Joshua, is commended; they are dismissed with honour, and they receive as their reward a substantial share of the spoil which had been taken from the enemy. "Return," said Joshua, "with much riches unto your tents, and with very much cattle, with silver and with gold, and with brass, and with iron, and with very much raiment; divide the spoil of your enemies with your brethren." It thus appeared that honour, like honesty, is the best policy. Had these two tribes and a half chosen the alternative of selfishness, refused to cross the Jordan to help their brethren, and devoted their whole energies at once to their fields and flocks, they would have fared worse in the end. No doubt as they recrossed the Jordan, bearing with them the treasure which had been acquired on the western side, their hearts would be full of that happy feeling which results from duty faithfully performed, and honourable conduct amply rewarded. They brought back "peace with honour," and prosperity into the bargain. After all, it is high principle that pays. It demands a time of patient working and of patient waiting, but its bills are fully implemented in the end.

In sending away the two tribes and a half Joshua pressed two counsels on them. One was that they were to divide the spoil with those of their brethren that had remained at home. Here, again, selfishness might possibly have found a footing. Why should the men that had incurred none of the labour and the peril enjoy any of the spoil? Would it not have been fair that those who had borne the burden and heat of the day should alone enjoy its rewards? But, in point of fact, there had been good reason why a portion should remain at home. To leave the women and children wholly undefended would have been recklessness itself. Some arrangement, too, had to be made for looking after the flocks and herds. And as the supply of manna had ceased, the production of food had to be provided for. The men at home had been doing the duty assigned to them as well as the men abroad. If they could not establish a claim in justice to a share of the spoil, the spirit of brotherhood and generosity pleaded on their behalf. The soldier-section of the two and a half tribes had done their part honourably and generously to the nine and a half; let them act in the same spirit to their own brethren. Let them share in the good things which they had brought home, so that a spirit of joy and satisfaction might be diffused throughout the community, and the welcome given to those who had been absent might be cordial and complete, without one trace of discontent or envy.

Occasions may occur still on which this counsel of Joshua may come in very suitably. It does not always happen that brothers or near relatives who have prospered abroad are very mindful of those whom they have left at home. They like to enjoy their abundance, and if the case of their poor relations comes across their minds, they dismiss it with the thought that men's lots must differ, and that they are not going to lose all the benefit of their success by supporting other families besides their own. Yet, how much good might accrue from a little generosity, though it were but an occasional gift, towards those who are straitened? And how much better it would be to kindle by this means a thankful and kindly feeling, than to have envy and jealousy rankling in their hearts!

The other counsel of Joshua bore upon that which was ever uppermost in his heart—loyalty to God. "Take diligent heed to do the commandment and the law, which Moses the servant of the Lord charged you, to love the Lord your God, and to walk in all His ways, and to keep all His commandments, and to cleave unto Him, and to serve Him with all your heart and with all your soul." It is evident that Joshua poured his whole heart into this counsel. He was evidently anxious as to the effect which their separation from their brethren would have on their religious condition. It was west of the Jordan that the sanctuary had been placed, and that the great central influence in support of the national worship would mainly operate. Would not these eastern tribes be in great danger of drifting away from the recognised worship of God, and becoming idolaters? Joshua knew well that as yet the nation was far from being weaned from idolatry (see xxiv. 14). He knew that among many there were strong propensities towards it. He had something of the feeling that an earnest Christian parent would have in sending off a son, not very decided in religion, to some colony where the public sentiment was loose, and where the temptations to worldliness and religious indifference were strong. He was therefore all the more earnest in his exhortations to them, for he felt that all their prosperity, all their happiness, their very life itself, depended on their being faithful to their God.

We cannot tell how long time had elapsed when word was brought to the western side that the two and a half tribes had built a great altar on the edge of Jordan, apparently as a rival to the ecclesiastical establishment at Shiloh. That this was their intention seems to have been taken for granted, for we find the congregation or general assembly of Israel assembled at Shiloh to prepare for war with the schismatical tribes. War had evidently become a familiar idea with them, and at first no other course suggested itself for arresting the proposal. It was one of the many occasions of unreasoning impetuosity which the history of Israel presents.

No mention is made of Joshua in the narrative of this transaction; he had retired from active life, and perhaps what is here recorded did not take place for a considerable time after the return of the two and a half tribes. It may be that we have here an instance of the method so often pursued in Hebrew annals, of recording together certain incidents pertaining to the same transaction, or to the same people, though these incidents were separated from each other by a considerable interval of time.

It was well that the congregation assembled at Shiloh. They would be reminded by the very place that great national movements were not to be undertaken rashly, since God was the supreme ruler of the nation. We are not told whether the usual method of asking counsel of God was resorted to, but certainly the course followed was more reasonable than rushing into war. It was resolved to begin by remonstrating with the two and a half tribes. The idea that their proposal was schismatical, nay, even idolatrous, was not given up, but it was thought that if a solemn remonstrance and warning were addressed to them, they might be induced to abandon their project.

A deputation was sent over, consisting of Phinehas, the son of Eleazar the priest, as representing the religious interest, and ten princes, representing the ten tribes, to have an interview with the heads of the two and a half tribes. When they met, the deputation opened very fiercely on their brethren. They charged them with unheard-of wickedness. What they had done was a daring act of rebellion. It was worthy to be classed with the iniquity of Peor —one of the vilest deeds that ever disgraced the nation. It was fitted to bring down God's judgments on the whole nation, and would certainly do so. If the secret act of Achan involved the congregation in wrath, what calamity to the whole people would not result from this daring and open deed of rebellion? They were not safe for a single day. The vials of the Divine wrath could not but be ready, and in twenty-four hours the whole congregation of Israel might be overwhelmed by the tokens of His displeasure.

One should have said that if anything was fitted to have a bad effect on the two and a half tribes, it was this mode of dealing. It is not wise to assume that your brother is a villain. And scolding, as has been well said, does not make men sorry for their sins. But one thing was said by the deputation that was fitted to have a different effect. "Notwithstanding, if the land of your possession be unclean, then pass ye over unto the land of the possession of the Lord, wherein the Lord's tabernacle dwelleth, and take possession among us: but rebel not against the Lord, nor rebel against us, in building you an altar beside the altar of the Lord our God."

Here was a generous, a self-denying proposal; the ten tribes were some of them in straits themselves, finding the room available for them far too narrow; nevertheless they were prepared to divide what they had with their brethren, if their real feeling was that the east side of the Jordan was outside the hallowed and hallowing influence of the presence of the Lord.

Instead, therefore, of firing up at the fierce reproof of their brethren, the two and a half tribes were softened by this really kind proposal and returned a reassuring answer. They solemnly repudiated all idea of a rival establishment. They knew that there was but one place where the tabernacle and the ark of the covenant could be, and they had not the remotest intention of interfering with the spot that had been chosen for that purpose. They had never entertained the thought of offering burnt offerings, or meat offerings, or peace offerings on their altar. They solemnly abjured all intention to show disrespect to the Lord, or to His law. The altar which they had built had a very different purpose. It was occasioned by the physical structure of the country, and the effect which that might have on their children in years to come. "In time to come your children might speak unto our children, saying, What have ye to do with the Lord God of Israel? For the Lord hath made Jordan a border between us and you, ye children of Reuben and children of Gad; ye have no part in the Lord: so shall your children make our children cease from fearing the Lord. Therefore we said, Let us now prepare to build us an altar, not for burnt offering, nor for sacrifice; but that it may be a witness between us, and you, and our generations after us." It was not a rival, but a witness, a pattern; a reminder to the two and a half tribes that the true altar, the Divine sanctuary, hallowed by the token of God's presence, was elsewhere, and that there, and only there, were the public sacrifices to be offered.

The acquaintance with the physical structure of Palestine which we have obtained in recent years enables us to appreciate the feeling of the two and a half tribes better than could have been done before. The mere fact that a river separated the east from the west of Palestine would not have been enough to account for the sense of isolation and the fear thence arising which had taken hold of the heads of the two and a half tribes. It is the peculiar structure of the valley in which the river runs that explains the story. The Jordan valley, as has already been mentioned, is depressed below the level of the Mediterranean Sea, the depression increasing gradually as the river flows towards the Dead Sea, where it amounts to 1300 feet. In addition to this, the mountainous plateau on each side of the Jordan valley rises to the height of 2000 or 2500 feet above the sea, so that the entire depression, counting from the top of the plateau to the edge of the river, is between three and four thousand feet. On each side the approach to the Jordan is difficult, while, during the warm season, the great heat increases the fatigue of travelling and discourages the attempt. All these things make the separation between the two parts of the country caused by the river and its valley much more complete than in ordinary cases of river boundaries. There can be no doubt now that the heads of the two and a half tribes had considerable ground for their apprehensions. There was some risk that they should cease to be regarded as part of the nation; and their explanation of the altar seems to have been an honest one. It was designed simply as a memorial, not for sacrifices. We see what a happy thing it was for the whole nation that the deputation was sent across before resorting to arms. A new light was thrown on what had seemed a daring sin; it was but an innocent arrangement; and the terrible forebodings which it awakened are at once scattered to the winds.

But who can estimate all the misery that has come in almost every age, in circles both public and private, from hasty suspicions of evil, which a little patience, a little inquiry, a little opportunity of explanation, might have at once averted? History, tradition, fiction, alike furnish us with instances. We recall the story of Llewellyn and his dog Gelert, stabbed by his master, who thought the stains upon his mouth were the blood of his beloved child; while, on raising the cradle which had been turned over, he found his child asleep and well, and a huge wolf dead, from whose fangs the dog had delivered him. We remembered the tragedy of Othello and Desdemona; we see how the fondest love may be poisoned by hasty suspicion, and the dearest of wives murdered, when a little patience would have shown her innocent—shown her all too pure to come in contact with even a vestige of the evil thing. We think of the many stories of crusaders and others leaving their homes with their love pledged to another, detained in distant lands without means of communication, hearing a rumour that their beloved one had turned false, and doing some rash and irrevocable deed, while a little further waiting would have realised all their hopes. But perhaps it is in less tragic circumstances that the spirit of suspicion and unjust accusation is most commonly manifested. A rumour unfavorable to your character gets into circulation; you suspect some one of being the author, and deal fiercely with him accordingly; it turns out that he is wholly innocent. A friend has apparently written a letter against you which has made you furious; you pour a torrent of reproaches upon him; it turns out that the letter was written by some one else with a similar name. But indeed there is no end to the mischief that is bred by impatience, and by want of inquiry, or of waiting for explanations that would put a quite different complexion on our matters of complaint. True charity "thinketh no evil," for it "rejoiceth not in iniquity, but rejoiceth in truth. It beareth all things, believeth all things, hopeth all things, endureth all things." If its gentle voice were more regarded, what a multitude of offences would vanish, and how much wider would be the reign of peace!

The explanation that had been offered by Reuben, Gad, and Manasseh proved satisfactory to Phinehas and the princes of the congregation, and likewise to the people of the west generally, when the deputation reported their proceedings. The remark of Phinehas before he left his eastern brethren was a striking one: "This day do we perceive that the Lord is among us, because ye have not committed this trespass against the Lord; now ye have delivered the children of Israel out of the hand of the Lord." There was a great difference between the Lord being among them, and their being in the hand of the Lord. If the Lord were among them they were under all manner of gracious influence; if they were in the hand of the Lord they were exposed to the utmost visitations of His wrath. It was the joy of Phinehas to find not only that no provocation had been given to God's righteous jealousy, but that proof had been afforded that He was graciously blessing them. If God often departs from us without our suspecting it, He is sometimes graciously present with us when we have been fearing that He was gone. So it was now. Phinehas in imagination had seen the gathering of a terrible storm, as if the very enemy of man had been stirring up his countrymen to rebellion and contempt of God; but in place of that, he sees that they have been consulting for God's honour, for the permanence of His institutions, and for the preservation of unity between the two sections of the nation; and in this he finds a proof that God has been graciously working among them. For God is the God of peace, not of strife, and the Spirit is the spirit of order, and not of confusion. And when two sections of a community are led to desire the advancement of His service and the honour of His name, even by methods which are not in all respects alike, it is a proof that he is among them, drawing their hearts to Himself and to one another.

Perhaps the common adage might have been applied to the case—that there were faults on both sides. If the ten tribes were too hasty in preparing for war, the two and a half tribes had been too hasty in deciding on the erection of their altar, without communication with the priests and the civil heads of the nation. In a matter so sacred, no such step should have been taken without full consultation and a clear view of duty. The goodness of their motive did not excuse them for not taking all available methods to carry out their plan in a way wholly unexceptional. As it was, they ran a great risk of kindling a fire which might have at once destroyed themselves and weakened the rest of the nation through all time. In their effort to promote unity, they had almost occasioned a fatal schism. Thus both sections of the nation had been on the edge of a fearful catastrophe.

But now it appeared that the section that had seemed to be so highly offending were animated by a quite loyal sentiment. Phinehas gladly seized on the fact as a proof that God was among them. A less godly man would not have thought of this as of much importance. He would hardly have believed in it as anything that could exist except in a fanatical imagination. But the more one knows of God the more real does the privilege seem, and the more blessed.

Nay, it comes to be felt as that which makes the greatest conceivable difference between one individual or one community and another. The great curse of sin is that it has severed us from God. The glory of the grace of God in Christ is that we are brought together. Man without God is like the earth without the sun, or the body without the soul. Man in fellowship with God is man replenished with all Divine blessings and holy influences. A church in which God does not dwell is a hold of unclean spirits and a cage of every unclean and hateful bird. A church inhabited by God, like the bride in the Song of Solomon, "looketh forth as the morning, fair as the moon, clear as the sun, and terrible as an army with banners."

CHAPTER XXXI.

JEHOVAH THE CHAMPION OF ISRAEL.

Joshua xxiii.

The last two chapters of Joshua are very like each other. Each professes to be a report of the aged leader's farewell meeting with the heads of the people. No place of meeting is specified in the one; Shechem is the place named in the other. The address reported in the twenty-third chapter is in somewhat general terms; in the twenty-fourth, we have more of detail. The question arises, Were there two meetings, or have we in these chapters different reports of the same? The question is of no great importance in itself; but it bears on the structure of the book. In our judgment, both reports bear on the same occasion; and if so, all that needs to be said as to their origin is, that the author of the book, having obtained two reports from trustworthy sources, did not adopt the plan of weaving them into one, but gave them separately, just as he had received them. The circumstance is a proof of the trustworthiness of the narrative; had the writer put on record merely what Joshua might be *supposed* to have said, he would not have adopted this twofold form of narrative.

Joshua had been a close follower of Moses in many things, and now he follows him by calling the people together to hear his closing words. On the edge of the future life, on the eve of giving in his own account, in the crisis when men are most disposed to utter the truth, the whole truth, and nothing but the truth, he calls his children around him to hear his parting words. He knows, as Moses also knew, the impulsive, fitful temper of the people. All the more did he regard it as desirable not to omit such an opportunity of impression. "All pathetic occasions," it has been well said, "should be treasured in the memory; the last interview, the last sermon, the last prayer, the last fond, lingering look; all these things may be frivolously treated as sentimental; but he who treats them so is a fool in his heart. Whatever can subdue the spirit, chasten the character, and enlarge the charity of the soul, should be encouraged as a ministry from God."*

What was the burden of Joshua's address? What was alike the keynote, and the central note, and the closing note—the beginning, and the middle, and the end? You have it in the words

* "The People's Bible," by Joseph Parker.

—"The Lord your God is He that fighteth for you"; therefore "cleave unto the Lord your God." You owe everything to the Lord; therefore render to Him all His due. Let Him receive from you in the proportion in which He has given to you; let Him be honoured by you in the ratio in which you have been blessed by Him; and see that none of you ever, to the last day of your lives, give the faintest countenance to the idolatry of your neighbours, or consent to any entangling connection that would furnish a temptation to join in their wickedness.

This starting-point of Joshua's address—"The Lord your God is He that fighteth for you"—is a serious one, and demands careful investigation. God is expressly set forth as the champion of Israel, fighting for him against the Canaanites, and driving them out. He is here the God of battles; and the terrible desolation that followed the track of Israel is here ascribed to the championship of the Most High.

There are some expositors who explain these sayings in a general sense. There are great laws of conquest, they say, roughly sanctioned by Providence, whereby one race advances upon another. Nations enervated through luxury and idleness are usually supplanted by more vigorous races. The Goths and Vandals overcame the Romans; the Anglo-Saxons subdued the Britons, to be in time conquered by the Normans; Dutch rule has prevailed over the negro, English over the Hindu, American over the native Indian. In the treatment of the conquered races by the conquerors, there has often been much that is gross and objectionable. Even when a civilised and cultured race has had to deal with a barbarous one, instead of the sweetness and light of culture you have often had the devices of injustice and oppression. We cannot vindicate all the rule of the British in India; greed, insolence, and lust have left behind them many a stain. Still, the result on the whole has been for good. The English have a higher conception of human life than the Hindus. They have a higher sense of order, of justice, of family life, of national well-being. There is a vigour about them that will not tolerate the policy of drifting; that cannot stand still or lie still and see everything going wrong; that strives to remedy injustice, to reform abuse, to correct what is vicious and disorderly, and foster organisation and progress. In these respects British rule has been a benefit to India. There may have been deeds of oppression and wrong that curdle the blood, or habits of self-indulgence may have been practised at the expense of the natives that shock our sense of humanity, as if the inferior race could have no rights against the superior; but these are but the eddies or by-play of a great beneficent current, and in the summing up of the long account they hold but an insignificant place. In themselves, they are to be detested and denounced; but when you are estimating great national forces, when you are trying the question whether on the whole these forces have been beneficent or evil, whether they have been of heaven or of the devil, these episodes of wrong are not to be allowed to determine the whole question. You are constrained to take a wider view. And when you survey the grand result; when you see a great continent like India peaceable and orderly that used to be distracted on every side by domestic warfare; when you see justice carefully administered, life and property protected, education and civilisation advanced, to say nothing of the spirit of Christianity introduced, you are unable to resist the conclusion that the influence of its new masters has been a gain to India, and therefore that the British rule has had the sanction of heaven.

We say there are some expositors who hold that it is only in a way parallel to this that the conquest of Canaan by the Israelites enjoyed the sanction of God. Without making a great deal of the wickedness of the Canaanite tribes, they dwell on their weakness, their poor ideas of life, their feeble aims, their want of developing power, their inability to rise. Into the heart of these tribes there comes a race that somehow possesses extraordinary capabilities and force. History has shown it to be one of the great dominant races of the world. The new people apply themselves with extraordinary energy to acquire the country of the other. Dispossession of one race by another was the common practice of the times, and in a moral point of view was little thought of. The times were rude and wild, property had not become sacred, human life was cheap, pain and suffering got small consideration. Having spent some centuries in Egypt, the new race brought with it a share of Egyptian culture and accomplishment; but its great strength lay in its religious ardour, and in the habits of order and self-control which its religion fostered. The memory of their ancestors, who had dwelt as pilgrims in that country, but under the strongest promises on the part of God that He would give it as an inheritance to their descendants, increased the ardour of the invasion and the confidence of the invaders. With all the enthusiasm of a heaven-guided race, they dashed against the old inhabitants, who staggered under the blow. To a large extent the former occupants fell under the usual violence of invaders—the sword of battle and the massacre after victory. The process was accompanied by many wild deeds, which in these days of ours would excite horror. Had it been completely successful it would have utterly annihilated the native races; but the courage and perseverance of the invaders were not equal to this result; many of the original inhabitants remained, and were finally amalgamated with their conquerors.

Now, in this case, as in the conquest of India by Britain, a process went on which was a great benefit on a large scale. It was not designed to be of benefit to the original inhabitants, as was the British occupation of India, for they were a doomed race, as we shall immediately see. But the settlement of the people of Israel in Canaan was designed and was fitted to be a great benefit to the world. Explain it as we may, Israel had higher ideas of life than the other nations, richer gifts of head and heart, more capacity of governing, and a far purer religious sentiment. Wherever Israel might be planted, if he remained in purity, mankind must be benefited. A people so gifted, with such intellectual capacity, with such moral and spiritual power, with such high ideals, and producing from time to time men of such remarkable character and influence, could not but help to elevate other races. That such a people should prevail over tribes emasculated by vice, degraded by idolatrous superstition, and enfeebled and stunted through mutual strife, was only in accordance with the nature of things. On the principle that a race like this must necessarily prevail over such tribes as had occupied Palestine before, the conquest of Joshua might well be said to have Divine approval. God might truly be said to go forth with the armies of Israel, and to scatter their enemies as smoke is scattered by the wind.

But this was not all. There was already a judicial sentence against the seven nations of which Israel was appointed to be the executioner. Even in Abraham's time we have abundant proof that they were far gone in corruption, and the destruction of Sodom and Gomorrah was but an early stroke of that holy sword which was to come down over a far wider area when the iniquity of the Amorites should become full. We have no elaborate account of the moral and religious condition of the people in Joshua's time, but we have certain glimpses which tell much. In the story of Baal-peor we have an awful picture of the idolatrous debauchery of the Moabites; and the Moabites were not so sunk in vice as the Canaanites. The first Canaanite house that any of the Israelites entered was that of an immoral woman, who, however, was saved by her faith, as any and every Canaanite would have been had he believed. The most revolting picture we have of Canaanite vice is connected with the burning of children alive in sacrifice to the gods. What a hideous practice it was! Who can estimate its effect on the blithe nature of children, or tell how the very thought of it and the possibility of suffering from it must have weighed like a nightmare on many a child, converting the season of merry childhood into a time of dreadful foreboding, if not for themselves, at least for some of their companions. Loathsome vice, consecrated by the seal of religion; unnatural lust, turning human beings into worse than beasts; natural affection, converted into an instrument of the most horrid cruelty—could any practices show more powerfully the hopeless degradation of these nations in a moral and religious sense, or their ripeness for judgment? Israel was the appointed executioner of God's justice against them, and in order that Israel might fulfil that function, God went before him in his battles and delivered his enemies into his hands. And what Israel did in this way was done under a solemn sense that he was inflicting Divine retribution. That the process was carried out with something of the solemnity of an execution appears, as we have already seen, from the injunction at Jericho, which forbade all on pain of death to touch an atom of the spoil. And this lesson was burnt into their inmost souls by the terrible fate of Achan. Afterwards, it is true, they were allowed to appropriate the spoil, but not till after they had been taught most impressively at Jericho that the spoil was God's, so that, even when it became theirs, it was as if they had received it from His hand.

We cannot suppose that the people uniformly acted with the moderation and self-restraint becoming God's executioners. No doubt there were many instances of unwarrantable and inhuman violence. Such excesses are unavoidable when human beings are employed as the executioners of God. To charge these on God is not fair. They were the spots and stains that ever indicate the hand of man, even when doing the work of God. It is not necessary to approve of these while we vindicate the law which doomed the Canaanites to extermination, and made the Israelites their executioners. It is not necessary to vindicate all that the English have done in India, while we hold that their presence and influence there have been in accordance with a Divine and beneficent purpose. Where God and man are in partnership, we may expect a chequered product, but never let us ascribe the flaws of one to the influence of the other.

If it be said that the language of the historian seems sometimes to ascribe to God what really arose from the passions of the people, it is to be observed that we are not told in what form the Lord communicated His commands. No doubt the Hebrews were disposed to claim Divine authority for what they did to the very fullest extent. There may have been times when they imagined that they were fulfilling the requirements of God, when they were only giving effect to feelings of their own. And generally they may have been prone to suppose that modes of slaughter that seemed to them quite proper were well pleasing in the sight of God. They may have believed that God participated in what was in reality but the spirit of the age. Thus they may have been led to think, and through them the impression may have come to us, that God had a more active hand, so to speak, in many of the details of warfare than we ought to ascribe to Him. For God often accomplishes His holy purposes by leaving His instruments to act in their own way.

But we have wandered from Joshua, and the assembly of Israel. What we have been trying is to show the soundness of Joshua's fundamental position—that God fought for Israel. The same thing might be shown by a negative process. If God had not been actively and supernaturally with Israel, Israel could never have become what he was. What made Israel so remarkable and powerful a nation? If you appeal to heredity and go back to his forefather, you find the whole career of Abraham determined by what he undoubtedly regarded as a supernatural promise, that in him and his seed all the families of the earth should be blessed. If you speak of Moses as the founder of the nation, you find a man who was utterly defeated and humiliated when he acted on his own resources, and successful only when he came in contact with supernatural might. If you inquire into the cause of the military superiority of Israel, you cannot find it in their slave condition in Egypt, nor in their wandering, pastoral life in the desert. You are baffled in trying to account for the warlike energy and skill that swept the Canaanites with all their resources before their invincible might. That an Alexander the Great, or a Cæsar, or a Napoleon, with their long experience, their trained legions, their splendid prestige, and unrivalled resources, should have swept the board of their enemies we do not wonder. But Moses and his bevy of slaves, Joshua and his army of shepherds—what could have made such soldiers of these men if the Lord had not fought on their side?

The getting possession of Canaan, as Joshua reminded the people, was a threefold process: God fighting for them had subdued their enemies; Joshua had divided the land; and now God was prepared to expel the remaining people, but only through their instrumentality. Emphasis is laid on "expelling" and "driving out" (ver. 5), from which we gather that further massacre was not to take place, but that the remainder of the Canaanites must seek settlements elsewhere. A sufficient retribution had fallen on them for their sins, in the virtual destruction of their people and the loss of their country; the miserable remnant might have a chance of escape, in some ill-filled country where they would never rise to influence and where terror would restrain them from their former wickedness.

Joshua was very emphatic in forbidding intermarriage and friendly social intercourse with Canaanites. He saw much need for the prayer, "Lead us not into temptation." He understood the meaning of enchanted ground. He knew that between the realm of holiness and the realm of sin there is a kind of neutral territory, which belongs strictly to neither, but which slopes towards the realm of sin, and in point of fact most commonly furnishes recruits not a few to the army of evil. Alas, how true is this still! Marriages between believers and unbelievers; friendly social fellowship, on equal terms, between the Church and the world; partnership in business between the godly and the ungodly—who does not know the usual result? In a few solitary cases, it may be, the child of the world is brought into the kingdom; but in how many instances do we find the buds of Christian promise nipped, and lukewarmness and backsliding, if not apostasy, coming in their room! There is no better help for the Christian life, no greater encouragement to fellowship with God, than congenial fellowship with other Christians, especially in the home, as there is no greater hindrance to these things than an alien spirit there. And if men and women would remember that of all that concerns them in this life their relation to God is infinitely the most momentous, and that whatever brings that relation into peril is the evil of all others most to be dreaded, we should not find them so ready for entangling connections which may be a gain for the things of this world, but for the things of eternity are commonly a grievous loss.

It is a very vivid picture that Joshua draws of the effects of that sinful compromise with their Canaanite neighbours against which he had warned them. "If ye do in any wise go back, and cleave unto the remnant of these nations, even these that remain among you, and shall make marriages with them, and go in unto them, and they to you: know for a certainty that the Lord your God will no more drive out any of these nations from before you; but they shall be snares and traps unto you, and scourges in your sides, and thorns in your eyes, until ye perish from off this good land which the Lord your God hath given you."

The Garden of Eden was not the only paradise that sin ruined. Here was something like a new paradise for the children of Israel; and yet there was a possibility—more than a possibility—of its being ruined by sin. The history of the future showed that Joshua was right. The Canaanites remaining in the land were scourges and thorns to the people of Israel, and the compliance of Israel with their idolatrous ways led first to invasion and oppression, then to captivity and exile, and finally to dispersion over the face of the earth. However sin may deceive at the beginning, in the end it always proves true to its real character—"the wages of sin is death." The trouble is that men will not believe what they do not like to believe. Sin has many a pleasure; and as long as the pleasure is not gross, but wears an air of refinement, there seems no harm in it, and it is freely enjoyed. But, unseen, it works like dry-rot, pulverising the soul, destroying all traces of spiritual relish or enjoyment of Divine things, and attaching the heart more strongly to mere material good. And sometimes when death comes in sight and it is felt that God has to be reckoned with, and the effort is honestly made to prepare for that solemn meeting by looking to the Divine Redeemer, the bent of the heart is found to be entirely the other way. Faith and repentance will not come; turning Godwards is an uncongenial, an impossible attitude; the heart has its roots too much in the world to be thus withdrawn from it. They allowed themselves to be drawn away from their early hope by the influence of worldly fellowship, to find that it profits a man nothing to gain the whole world if he lose his own soul.

How awful are the words of St. James: "Ye adulterers and adulteresses, know ye not that the friendship of the world is enmity with God? Whosoever, therefore, will be a friend of the world is the enemy of God."

CHAPTER XXXII.

JOSHUA'S LAST APPEAL.

Joshua xxiv.

It was at Shechem that Joshua's last meeting with the people took place. The Septuagint makes it Shiloh in one verse (ver. 1), but Shechem in another (ver. 25); but there is no sufficient reason for rejecting the common reading. Joshua might feel that a meeting which was not connected with the ordinary business of the sanctuary, but which was more for a personal purpose, a solemn leave-taking on his part from the people, might be held better at Shechem, There was much to recommend that place. It lay a few miles to the northwest of Shiloh, and was not only distinguished (as we have already said) as Abraham's first resting-place in the country, and the scene of the earliest of the promises given in it to him; but likewise as the place where, between Mounts Ebal and Gerizim, the blessings and curses of the law had been read out soon after Joshua entered the land, and the solemn assent of the people given to them. And whereas it is said (ver. 26) that the great stone set up as a witness was "by the sanctuary of the Lord," this stone may have been placed at Shiloh after the meeting, because there it would be more fully in the observation of the people as they came up to the annual festivals (see 1 Sam. i. 7, 9). Shechem was therefore the scene of Joshua's farewell address. Possibly it was delivered close to the well of Jacob and the tomb of Joseph; at the very place where, many centuries later, the New Testament Joshua sat wearied with His journey, and unfolded the riches of Divine grace to the woman of Samaria.

1. In the record of Joshua's speech contained in the twenty-fourth chapter, he begins by rehearsing the history of the nation. He has an excellent reason for beginning with the revered name of Abraham, because Abraham had been conspicuous for that very grace, loyalty to Jehovah, which he is bent on impressing on them. Abraham had made a solemn choice in religion. He had deliberately broken with one kind of worship, and accepted another. His fathers had been idolaters, and he had been brought up an idolater. But Abraham renounced idolatry for ever. He did this at a great sacrifice, and what Joshua entreated of the people was, that they would be as thorough and as firm as he was in their repudiation of idolatry. The rehearsal of the history is given in the words of God to remind them that the whole history of Israel had been planned and ordered by Him. He had been among them from first to last; He had been with them through all the lives of the patriarchs; it was He that had delivered them from Egypt by Moses and Aaron, that had buried the Egyptians under the waters of the sea, that had driven the Amorites out of the eastern provinces, had turned the curse of Balaam into a blessing, had dispossessed the seven nations, and had settled the Israelites in their pleasant and peaceful abodes.

We mark in this rehearsal the well-known features of the national history, as they were always represented; the frank recognition of the supernatural, with no indication of myth or legend, with nothing of the mist or glamour in which the legend is commonly enveloped. And, seeing that God had done all this for them, the inference was that He was entitled to their heartiest loyalty and obedience. "Now therefore fear the Lord, and serve Him in sincerity and in truth: and put away the gods which your fathers served on the other side of the flood, and in Egypt; and serve ye the Lord." It seems strange that at that very time the people needed to be called to put away other gods. But this only shows how destitute of foundation the common impression is, that from and after the departure from Egypt the whole host of Israel were inclined to the law as it had been given by Moses. There was still a great amount of idolatry among them, and a strong tendency towards it. They were not a wholly reformed or converted people. This Joshua knew right well; he knew that there was a suppressed fire among them liable to burst into a conflagration; hence his aggressive attitude, and his effort to foster an aggressive spirit in them; he must bind them over by every consideration to renounce wholly all recognition of other gods, and to make Jehovah the one only object of their worship. Never was a good man more in earnest, or more thoroughly persuaded that all that made for a nation's welfare was involved in the course which he pressed upon them.

2. But Joshua did not urge this merely on the strength of his own conviction. He must enlist their reason on his side; and for this cause he now called on them deliberately to weigh the claims of other gods and the advantages of other modes of worship, and choose that which must be pronounced the best. There were four claimants to be considered: (1) Jehovah; (2) the Chaldæan gods worshipped by their ancestors; (3) the gods of the Egyptians; and (4) the gods of the Amorites among whom they dwelt. Make your choice between these, said Joshua, if you are dissatisfied with Jehovah. But could there be any reasonable choice between these gods and Jehovah? It is often useful, when we hesitate as to a course, to set down the various reasons for and against,—it may be the reasons of our judgment against the reasons of our feelings; for often this course enables us to see how utterly the one outweighs the other. May it not be useful for us to do as Joshua urged Israel to do?

If we set down the reasons for making God, God in Christ, the supreme object of our worship, against those in favour of the world, how infinitely will the one scale outweigh the other! In the choice of a master, it is reasonable for a servant to consider which has the greatest claim upon him; which is intrinsically the most worthy to be served; which will bring him the greatest advantages; which will give him most inward satisfaction and peace; which will exercise the best influence on his character, and which comes recommended most by old servants whose testimony ought to weigh with him. If these are the grounds of a reasonable choice in the case of a servant engaging with a master, how much more in reference to the master of our spirits! Nothing can be plainer than that the Israelites in Joshua's time had every conceivable reason for choosing their fathers' God as the supreme object of their worship, and that any other course would have been alike the guiltiest and the silliest that could have been taken. Are the reasons a whit less powerful why every one of us should devote heart and life and mind and soul to the service of Him who gave Himself for us, and has loved us with an everlasting love?

3. But Joshua is fully prepared to add example to precept. Whatever you do in this matter, my mind is made up, my course is clear—"as for me and my house, we will serve Jehovah." He reminds us of a general exhorting his troops to mount the deadly breach and dash into the enemy's citadel. Strong and urgent are his appeals; but stronger and more telling is his act when, facing the danger right in front, he rushes on, determined that, whatever others may do, he will not flinch from his duty. It is the old Joshua back again, the Joshua that alone with Caleb stood faithful amid the treachery of the spies, that has been loyal to God all his life, and now in the decrepitude of old age is still prepared to stand alone rather than dishonour the living God. "As for me and my house, we will serve the Lord." He was happy in being able to associate his house with himself as sharing his convictions and his purpose. He owed this, in all likelihood, to his own firm and intrepid attitude throughout his life. His house saw how consistently and constantly he recognised the supreme claims of Jehovah. Not less clearly did they see how constantly he experienced the blessedness of his choice.

4. Convinced by his arguments, moved by his eloquence, and carried along by the magnetism of his example, the people respond with enthusiasm, deprecate the very thought of forsaking Jehovah to serve other gods, and recognise most cordially the claims he has placed them under, by delivering them from Egypt, preserving them in the wilderness, and driving out the Amorites from their land. After this an ordinary leader would have felt quite at ease, and would have thanked God that his appeal had met with such a response, and that such demonstration had been given of the loyalty of the people. But Joshua knew something of their fickle temper. He may have called to mind the extraordinary enthusiasm of their fathers when the tabernacle was in preparation; the singular readiness with which they had contributed their most valued treasures, and the grievous change they underwent after the return of the spies. Even an enthusiastic burst like this is not to be trusted. He must go deeper; he must try to induce them to think more earnestly of the matter, and not trust to the feeling of the moment.

5. Hence he draws a somewhat dark picture of Jehovah's character. He dwells on those attributes which are least agreeable to the natural man, His holiness, His jealousy, and His inexorable opposition to sin. When he says, "He will not forgive your transgressions nor your sins," he cannot mean that God is not a God of forgiveness. He cannot wish to contradict the first part of that gracious memorial which God gave to Moses, "The Lord, the Lord God merciful and gracious, longsuffering and abundant in goodness and truth, forgiving iniquity and transgression and sin." His object is to emphasise the clause, "and that will by no means clear the guilty." Evidently he means that the sin of idolatry is one that God cannot pass over, cannot fail to punish, until, probably through terrible judgments, the authors of it are brought to contrition, and humble themselves in the dust before him. "Ye cannot serve the Lord," said Joshua; "take care how you undertake what is beyond your strength!" Perhaps he wished to impress on them the need of Divine strength for so difficult a duty. Certainly he did not change their purpose, but only drew from them a more resolute expression. "Nay; but we will serve the Lord. And Joshua said unto the people, Ye are witnesses against yourselves that ye have chosen the Lord to serve Him. And they said, We are witnesses."

6. And now Joshua comes to a point which had doubtless been in his mind all the time, but which he had been waiting for a favorable opportunity to bring forward. He had pledged the people to an absolute and unreserved service of God, and now he demands a practical proof of their sincerity. He knows quite well that they have "strange gods" among them. Teraphim, images, or ornaments having a reference to the pagan gods, he knows that they possess. And he does not speak as if this were a rare thing, confined to a very few. He speaks as if it were a common practice, generally prevalent. Again we see how far from the mark we are when we think of the whole nation as cordially following the religion of Moses, in the sense of renouncing all other gods. Minor forms of idolatry, minor recognitions of the gods of the Chaldæans and the Egyptians and the Amorites, were prevalent even yet. Probably Joshua called to mind the scene that had occurred at that very place hundreds of years before, when Jacob, rebuked by God, and obliged to remove from Shechem, called on his household: "Put away the strange gods that are among you, and be clean, and change your garments. . . And they gave unto Jacob all the strange gods which were in the land, and all the ear-rings which were in their ears; and Jacob hid them under the oak which was by Shechem." Alas! that, centuries later, it was necessary for Joshua in the same place to issue the same order,—Put away the gods which are among you, and serve ye their Lord. What a weed sin is, and how it is for ever reappearing! And reappearing among ourselves too, in a different variety, but essentially the same. For what honest and earnest heart does not feel that there are idols and images among ourselves that interfere with God's claims and God's glory as much as the teraphim and the ear-rings of the Israelites did? The images of the Israelites were little images, and it was probably at by-times and in retirement that they made use of them;

and so, it may not be on the leading occasions or in the outstanding work of our lives that we are wont to dishonour God. But who that knows himself but must think with humiliation of the numberless occasions on which he indulges little whims or inclinations without thinking of the will of God; the many little acts of his daily life on which conscience is not brought to bear; the disengaged state of his mind from that supreme controlling influence which would bear on it if God were constantly recognised as his Master? And who does not find that, despite his endeavour from time to time to be more conscientious, the old habit, like a weed whose roots have only been cut over, is ever showing itself alive?

7. And now comes the closing and clinching transaction of this meeting at Shechem. Joshua enters into a formal covenant with the people; he records their words in the book of the law of the Lord; he takes a great stone and sets it up under an oak that was by the sanctuary of the Lord; and he constitutes the stone a witness, as if it had heard all that had been spoken by the Lord to them and by them to the Lord. The covenant was a transaction invested with special solemnity among all Eastern peoples, and especially among the Israelites. Many instances had occurred in their history, of covenants with God, and of other covenants, like that of Abraham with Abimelech, or that of Jacob with Laban. The wanton violation of a covenant was held an act of gross impiety, deserving the reprobation alike of God and man. When Joshua got the people bound by a transaction of this sort, he seemed to obtain a new guarantee for their fidelity; a new barrier was erected against their lapsing into idolatry. It was natural for him to expect that some good would come of it, and no doubt it contributed to the happy result; "for Israel served the Lord all the days of Joshua, and all the days of the elders which overlived Joshua, and which had known all the works of the Lord that He had done for Israel." And yet it was but a temporary barrier against a flood which seemed ever to be gathering strength unseen, and preparing for another fierce discharge of its disastrous waters.

At the least, this meeting secured for Joshua a peaceful sunset, and enabled him to sing his "Nunc dimittis." The evil which he dreaded most was not at work as the current of life ebbed away from him; it was his great privilege to look round him and see his people faithful to their God. It does not appear that Joshua had any very comprehensive or far-reaching aims with reference to the moral training and development of the people. His idea of religion seems to have been, a very simple loyalty to Jehovah, in opposition to the perversions of idolatry. It is not even very plain whether or not he was much impressed by the capacity of true religion to pervade all the relations and engagements of men, and brighten and purify the whole life. We are too prone to ascribe all the virtues to the good men of the Old Testament, forgetting that of many virtues there was only a progressive development, and that it is not reasonable to look for excellence beyond the measure of the age. Joshua was a soldier, a soldier of the Old Testament, a splendid man for his day, but not beyond his day. As a soldier, his business was to conquer his enemies, and to be loyal to his heavenly Master. It did not lie to him to enforce the numberless bearings which the spirit of trust in God might have on all the interests of life—on the family, on books, on agriculture and commerce, or on the development of the humanities, and the courtesies of society. Other men were raised up from time to time, many other men, with commission from God to devote their energies to such matters.

It is quite possible that, under Joshua, religion did not appear in very close relation to many things that are lovely and of good report. A celebrated English writer (Matthew Arnold) has asked whether, if Virgil or Shakespeare had sailed in the *Mayflower* with the puritan fathers, they would have found themselves in congenial society. The question is not a fair one, for it supposes that men whose destiny was to fight as for very life, and for what was dearer than life, were of the same mould with others who could devote themselves in peaceful leisure to the amenities of literature. Joshua had doubtless much of the ruggedness of the early soldier, and it is not fair to blame him for want of sweetness and light. Very probably it was from him that Deborah drew somewhat of her scorn, and Jael, the wife of Heber, of her rugged courage. The whole Book of Judges is penetrated by his spirit. He was not the apostle of charity or gentleness. He had one virtue, but it was the supreme virtue—he honoured God. Wherever God's claims were involved, he could see nothing, listen to nothing, care for nothing, but that He should obtain His due. Wherever God's claims were acknowledged and fulfilled, things were essentially right, and other interests would come right. For his absolute and supreme loyalty to his Lord he is entitled to our highest reverence. This loyalty is a rare virtue, in the sublime proportions in which it appeared in him. When a man honours God in this way, he has something of the appearance of a supernatural being, rising high above the fears and the feebleness of poor humanity. He fills his fellows with a sort of awe.

Among the reformers, the puritans, and the covenanters such men were often found. The best of them, indeed, were men of this type, and very genuine men they were. They were not men whom the world loved; they were too jealous of God's claims for that, and too severe on those who refused them. And we have still the type of the fighting Christian. But alas! it is a type subject to fearful degeneration. Loyalty to human tradition is often substituted, unconsciously no doubt, for loyalty to God. The sublime purity and nobility of the one passes into the obstinacy, the self-righteousness, the self-assertion of the other. When a man of the genuine type does appear, men are arrested, astonished, as if by a supernatural apparition. The very rareness, the eccentricity of the character, secures a respectful homage. And yet, who can deny that it is the true representation of what every man should be who says, "I believe in God, the Father Almighty, Maker of heaven and earth"?

After a life of a hundred and ten years the hour comes when Joshua must die. We have no record of the inner workings of his spirit, no indication of his feelings in view of his sins, no hint as to the source of his trust for forgiveness and acceptance. But we readily think of him as the heir of the faith of his father Abraham, the heir of the righteousness that is by faith, and as passing calmly into the presence of his judge, because, like Jacob, he has waited for His salvation. He was well entitled to the highest honours that the nation could bestow on his memory; for all owed to him their homes and their rest. His name must ever be coupled with that of the greatest hero of the nation: Moses led them out of the house of bondage; Joshua led them into the house of rest. Sometimes, as we have already said, it has been attempted to draw a sharp antithesis between Moses and Joshua, the one as representing the law, and the other as representing the gospel. The antithesis is more in word than in deed. Moses represented both gospel and law, for he brought the people out of the bondage of Egypt; he brought them to their marriage altar, and he unfolded to the bride the law of her Divine husband's house. Joshua conducted the bride to her home, and to the rest which she was to enjoy there; but he was not less emphatic than Moses in insisting that she must be an obedient wife, following the law of her husband. It were difficult to say which of them was the more instructive type of Christ, both in feeling and in act. The love of each for his people was most intense, most self-denying; and neither of them, had he been called on, would have hesitated to surrender his life for their sake.

It is probably a mere incidental arrangement that the book concludes with a record of the burial of Joseph, and of the death and burial of Eleazar, the son of Aaron. In point of time, we can hardly suppose that the burial of Joseph in the field of his father Jacob in Shechem was delayed till after the death of Joshua. It would be a most suitable transaction after the division of the country, and especially after the territory that contained the field had been assigned to Ephraim, Joseph's son. It would be like a great doxology—a Te Deum celebration of the fulfilment of the promise in which, so many centuries before, Joseph had so nobly shown his trust.

But why did not Joseph's bones find their resting-place in the time-honoured cave of Machpelah? Why was he not laid side by side with his father, who would doubtless have liked right well that his beloved son should be laid at his side? We can only say in regard to Joseph as in regard to Rachel, that the right of burial in that tomb seems to have been limited to the wife who was recognised by law, and to the son who inherited the Messianic promise. The other members of the family must have their resting-place elsewhere; moreover, there was this benefit in Joseph having his burial-place at Shechem, that it was in the very centre of the country, and near the spot where the tribes were to assemble for the great annual festivals. For many a generation the tomb of Joseph would be a memorable witness to the people; by it the patriarch, though dead, would continue to testify to the faithfulness of God; while he would point the hopes of the godly people still onward to the future, when the last clause of the promise to Abraham would be emphatically fulfilled, and that Seed would come forth among them in whom all the families of the earth would be blessed.

Was there a reason for recording the death of Eleazar? Certainly there was a fitness in placing together the record of the death of Joshua and the death of Eleazar. For Joshua was the successor of Moses, and Eleazar was the successor of Aaron. The simultaneous mention of the death of both is a significant indication that the generation to which they belonged had now passed away. A second age after the departure from Egypt had now slipped into the silent past. It was a token that the duties and responsibilities of life had now come to a new generation, and a silent warning to them to remember how

> "Time 'like an ever-rolling stream
> Bears all its sons away ;
> They fly forgotten, as a dream
> Dies at the opening day."

How short the life of a generation seems when we look back to these distant days! How short the life of the individual when he realises that his journey is practically ended! How vain the expectation once cherished of an indefinite future, when there would be ample time to make up for all the neglects of earlier years! God give us all to know the true meaning of that word, "the time is short," and "so teach us to number our days, that we may apply our hearts unto wisdom!"

CHAPTER XXXIII.

JOSHUA'S WORK FOR ISRAEL.

It now only remains for us to take a retrospective view of the work of Joshua, and indicate what he did for Israel and the mark he left on the national history.

1. Joshua was a soldier—a believing soldier. He was the first of a type that has furnished many remarkable specimens. Abraham had fought, but he had fought as a quaker might be induced to fight, for he was essentially a man of peace. Moses had superintended military campaigns, but Moses was essentially a priest and a prophet. Joshua was neither quaker, nor priest, nor prophet, but simply a soldier. There were fighting men in abundance, no doubt, before the flood, but so far as we know, not believing men. Joshua was the first of an order that seems to many a moral paradox—a devoted servant of God, yet an enthusiastic fighter. His mind ran naturally in the groove of military work. To plan expeditions, to devise methods of attacking, scattering, or annihilating opponents, came naturally to him. A military genius, he entered *con amore* into his work.

Yet along with this the fear of God continually controlled and guided him. He would do nothing deliberately unless he was convinced that it was the will of God. In all his work of slaughter, he believed himself to be fulfilling the righteous purposes of Jehovah. His life was habitually guided by regard to the unseen. He had no ambition but to serve his God and to serve his country. He would have been content with the plainest conditions of life, for his habits were simple and his tastes natural. He believed that God was behind him, and the belief made him fearless. His career of almost unbroken success justified his faith.

There have been soldiers who were religious in spite of their being soldiers—some of them in their secret hearts regretting the distressing fortune that made the sword their weapon; but there have also been men whose energy in religion and in fighting have supported and strengthened each other. Such men, however, are usually found only in times of great moral and spiritual struggle, when the brute force of the world has been mustered in overwhelming mass to crush some religious movement. They have an intense conviction that the movement is of God, and as to the use of the sword, they cannot help themselves; they have no choice, for the instinct of self-defence compels them to draw it. Such are the warriors of the Apocalypse, the soldiers of Armageddon; for though their battle is essentially spiritual, it is presented to us in that military book under the symbols of material warfare. Such were the Ziskas and Procopses of the Bohemian reformation; the Gustavus Adolphuses of the Thirty Years' War; the Cromwells of the Commonwealth, and the General Leslies of the Covenant. Ruled supremely by the fear of God, and convinced of a Divine call to their work, they have communed about it with Him as closely and as truly as the missionary about his preaching or his translating, or the philanthropist about his homes or his rescue agencies. To God's great goodness it has ever been their habit to ascribe their successes; and when an enterprise has failed, the causes of failure have been sought for in the Divine displeasure. Nor in their intercourse with their families and friends have they been usually wanting in gentler graces, in affection, in generosity, or in pity. All this must be freely admitted, even by those to whom war is most obnoxious. It is quite consistent with the conviction that a large proportion of wars has been utterly unjustifiable, and that in ordinary circumstances the sword is no more to be regarded as the right and proper weapon for settling the quarrels of nations than the duel for settling the quarrels of individuals. And the best of soldiers cannot but feel that fighting is at best a cruel necessity, and that it will be a happy day for the world when men shall beat their swords into ploughshares and their spears into pruning-hooks.

2. Being a soldier, Joshua confined himself in the main to the work of a soldier. That work was to conquer the enemy and to divide the land. To these two departments he limited himself, in subordination, however, to his deep conviction that they were only means to an end, and that that end would be utterly missed unless the people were pervaded by loyalty to God and devotion to the mode of worship which He had prescribed. No opportunity of impressing that consideration on their minds was neglected. It lay at the root of all their prosperity; and if Joshua had not pressed it on them by every available means, all his work would have been like pouring water on sand or sowing seed upon the rocks of the seashore.

Joshua was not called to ecclesiastical work, certainly not in the sense of carrying out ecclesiastical details. That department belonged to the high priest and his brethren. While Moses lived, it had been under him, because Moses was head of all departments. Neither did Joshua take in hand the arrangement in detail of the civil department of the commonwealth. That was mainly work for the elders and officers appointed to regulate it. It is from the circumstance that Joshua personally confined himself to his two great duties, that the book which bears his name travels so little beyond these. Reading Joshua alone, we might have the impression that very little attention was paid to the ritual enacted in the books of Moses. We might suppose that but little was done to carry out the provisions of the Torah, as the law came to be called. But the inference would not be warranted, for the plain reason that such things did not come within the sphere of Joshua or the scope of the book which bears his name. We may make what we can of incidental allusions, but we need not expect elaborate descriptions. There are many things that it would have been highly interesting for us to know regarding this period of the history of Israel; but the book limits itself as Joshua limited himself. It is not a full history of the times. It is not a chapter of universal national annals. It is a history of the settlement, and of Joshua's share in the settlement.

And the fact that it has this character is a testimony to its authenticity. Had it been a work of much later date, it is not likely that it would have been confined within such narrow limits. It would in all likelihood have presented a much larger view of the state and progress of the nation than the existing book does. The fact that it is made to revolve so closely round Joshua seems to indicate that Joshua's personality was still a great power; the remembrance of him was bright and vivid when the book was written. Moreover, the lists of names, many of which seem to have been the old Canaanite names, and to have dropped out of the Hebrew history because the cities were not actually taken from the Canaanites, and did not become Hebrew cities, is another testimony to the contemporary date of the book, or of the documents on which it is founded.

3. If we examine carefully Joshua's character as a soldier, or rather as a strategist, we shall probably find that he had one defect. He does not appear to have succeeded in making his conquests permanent. What he gained one day was often won back by the enemy after a little time. To read the account of what happened after the victory of Gibeon and Bethhoron, one would infer that all the region south of Gibeon fell completely into his hands. Yet by-and-by we find Hebron and Jerusalem in possession of the enemy, while a hitherto unheard-of king has come into view, Adonibezek, of Bezek, of whose people there were slain, after the death of Joshua, ten thousand men (Judg. i. 4). With regard to Hebron we read first that Joshua "fought against it and took it, and smote it with the edge of the sword, and the king thereof, and all the cities thereof, and all the souls that were therein; he left none remaining, but destroyed it utterly, and all the souls that were therein" (Josh. x. 37). Yet not long after, when Caleb requested Hebron for his inheritance, it was (as we have seen) on the very ground that it was strongly held by the enemy: "if so be the Lord will be with me, then I shall be able to drive them out, as the Lord said" (xiv. 12). Again, in the campaign against Jabin, King of Hazor, while it is said that Hazor was utterly destroyed, it is also said that Joshua did not destroy "the cities that stood on their mounds" (xi. 13, R. V.); accordingly we find that some time after, another Jabin was at the head of a restored Hazor, and it was against him that the expedition to which Barak was stimulated by the prophetess Deborah was undertaken (Judg. iv. 2). Whether Joshua miscalculated the number and resources of the Canaanites in the country; or whether he was

unable to divide his own forces so as to prevent the re-occupation and restoration of places that had once been destroyed; or whether he overestimated the effects of his first victories and did not allow enough for the determination of a conquered people to fight for their homes and their altars to the last, we cannot determine; but certainly the result was, that after being defeated and scattered at the first, they rallied and gathered together, and presented a most formidable problem to the tribes in their various settlements. There is no reason for resorting to the explanation of our modern critics that we have here traces of two writers, of whom the policy of the one was to represent that Joshua was wholly victorious, and of the other that he was very far from successful. The true view is, that his first invasion, or run-over, as it may be called, was a complete success, but that, through the rallying of his opponents, much of the ground which he gained at the beginning was afterwards lost.

4. The great service of Joshua to his people (as we have already remarked) was, that he gave them a settlement. He gave them—Rest. Some, indeed, may be disposed to question whether that which Joshua did give them was worthy of the name of rest. If the Canaanites were still among them, disputing the possession of the country; if savage Adonibezeks were still at large, whose victims bore in their mutilated bodies the marks of their cruelty and barbarity; if the power of the Philistines in the south, the Sidonians in the north, and the Geshurites in the northeast was still unbroken, how could they be said to have obtained rest?

The objection proceeds from inability to estimate the force of the comparative degree. Joshua gave them rest in the sense that he gave them homes of their own. There was no more need for the wandering life which they had led in the wilderness. They had more compact and comfortable habitations than the tents of the desert with their slim coverings that could effectually shut out neither the cold of winter, nor the heat of summer, nor the drenching rains. They had brighter objects to look out on than the scanty and monotonous vegetation of the wilderness. No doubt they had to defend their new homes, and in order to do so they had to expel the Canaanites who were still hovering about them. But still they were real homes; they were not homes which they merely expected or hoped to get, but homes which they had actually gotten. They were homes with the manifold attractions of country life—the field, the well, the garden, the orchard, stocked with vine, fig, and pomegranate; the olive grove, the rocky crag, and the quiet glen. The sheep and the oxen might be seen browsing in picturesque groups on the pasture grounds, as if they were part of the family. It was an interest to watch the progress of vegetation, to mark how the vine budded, and the lily sprang into beauty, to pluck the first rose, or to divide the first ripe pomegranate. Life had a new interest when on a bright spring morning the young man could thus invite his bride:—

"Rise up, my love, my fair one, and come away.
For, lo, the winter is past,
The rain is over and gone;
The flowers appear on the earth;
The time of the singing of birds is come,
And the voice of the turtle is heard in our land;
The fig tree putteth forth her green figs,
And the vines with the tender grape give a good smell."

This, as it were, was Joshua's gift to Israel, or rather God's gift through Joshua. It was well fitted to kindle their gratitude, and though not yet complete or perfectly secure, it was entitled to be called "rest." For if there was still need of fighting to complete the conquest, it was fighting under easy conditions. If they went out under the influence of that faith of which Joshua had set them so memorable an example, they were sure of protection and of victory. Past experience had shown to demonstration that none of their enemies could stand before them, and the future would be as the past had been. God was still among them; if they called on Him He would arise, their enemies would be scattered, and they that hated Him would flee before Him. Fidelity to Him would secure all the blessings that had been read out at Mount Gerizim, and to which they had enthusiastically shouted, Amen. The picture drawn by Moses before his death would be realised in its brightest colours: "Blessed shalt thou be in the city, and blessed shalt thou be in the field. Blessed shall be the fruit of thy body, and the fruit of thy ground, and the fruit of thy cattle, the increase of thy kine, and the flocks of thy sheep. Blessed shall be thy basket and thy store. Blessed shalt thou be when thou comest in, and blessed when thou goest out."

But here a very serious objection may be interposed. Is it conceivable, it may be asked, that this serene satisfaction was enjoyed by the Israelites when they had got their new homes only by dispossessing the former owners; when all around them was stained by the blood of the slain, and the shrieks and groans of their predecessors were yet sounding in their ears? If these homes were not haunted by the ghosts of their former owners, must not the hearts and consciences of the new occupants have been haunted by recollections of the scenes of horror which had been enacted there? is it possible that they should have been in that tranquil and happy frame in which they would really enjoy the sweetness of their new abodes?

The question is certainly a disturbing one, and any answer that may be given to it must seem imperfect, just because we are incapable of placing ourselves wholly in the circumstances of the children of Israel.

We are incapable of entering into the callousness of the Oriental heart in reference to the sufferings or the death of enemies. Exceptions there no doubt were, but, as a rule, indifference to the condition of enemies, whether in life or in death, was the prevalent feeling.

Two parts of their nature were liable to be affected by the change which put the Israelites in possession of the houses and fields of the destroyed Canaanites—their consciences and their hearts.

With regard to their consciences the case was clear: "The earth is the Lord's, and the fulness thereof; the world, and they that dwell therein." God, as owner of the land of Canaan, had given it, some six hundred years before, to Abraham and his seed. That gift had been ratified by many solemnities, and belief in it had been kept alive in the hearts of Abraham's descendants from generation to generation. There had been no secret about it, and the Canaanites must have been familiar with the tradition. Consequently, during all these centuries, they had been but tenants at will. When, under the guidance of Jehovah, Israel crossed the Red Sea and the army of Pharaoh was drowned, a pang must have shot through the breasts of the Canaanites, and the news must have come to them as a notice to quit. The echoes of the Song of Moses reverberated through the whole region:—

"The peoples have heard, they tremble:
Pangs have taken hold of the inhabitants of Philistia.
Then were the dukes of Edom amazed;
The mighty men of Moab, trembling taketh hold of them:
All the inhabitants of Canaan are melted away.
Terror and dread falleth upon them;
By the greatness of Thine arm they are as still as a stone;
Till Thy people pass over, O Lord,
Till the people pass over which Thou hast purchased.
Thou shalt bring them in, and plant them in the mountain of Thine inheritance,
The place, O Lord, which Thou hast made for Thee to dwell in,
The sanctuary, O Lord, which Thy hands have established.
The Lord shall reign for ever and ever."

It was well known, therefore, that, so far as Divine right went, the children of Israel were entitled to the land. But even after that, the Canaanites had a respite and enjoyed possession for forty years. Besides, they had been judicially condemned on account of their sins; and, moreover, when they first came into the country, they had dispossessed the former inhabitants. At last, after long delay, the hour of destiny arrived. When the Israelites took possession they felt that they were only regaining their own. It was not they, but the Canaanites, that were the intruders, and any feeling on the question of right in the minds of the Israelites would rather be that of indignation at having been kept out so long of what had been promised to Abraham, than of squeamishness at dispossessing the Canaanites of property which was not their own.

Still, one might suppose there remained scope for natural pity. But this was not very active. We may gather something of the prevalent feeling from the song of Deborah and the action of Jael. It was not an age of humanity. The whole period of the Judges was indeed an "iron age." Gideon, Jephthah, Samson, were men of the roughest fibre. Even David's treatment of his Ammonite prisoners was revolting. All that can be said for Israel is, that their treatment of enemies did not reach that infamous pre-eminence of cruelty for which the Assyrians and the Babylonians were notorious. But they had enough of the prevailing callousness to enable them to enter without much discomfort on the homes and possessions of their dispossessed foes. They had no such sentimental reserve as to interfere with a lively gratitude to Joshua as the man who had given them rest.

Probably, in looking back on those times, we fail to realise the marvellous influence in the direction of all that is humane and loving that came into our world, and began to operate in full force, with the advent of our Lord and Saviour Jesus Christ. We forget how much darker a world it *must* have been before the true light entered, that lighteth every man coming into the world. We forget what a gift God gave to the world when Jesus entered it, bringing with Him the light and love, the joy and peace, the hope and the holiness of heaven. We forget that the coming of Jesus was the rising of the Sun of Righteousness with healing in His wings. Coming among us as the incarnation of Divine love, it was natural that He should correct the prevailing practice in the treatment of enemies, and infuse a new spirit of humanity. Even the Apostle who afterwards became the Apostle of Love could manifest all the bitterness of the old spirit when he suggested the calling down of fire from heaven to burn up the Samaritan village that would not receive them. "Ye know not what manner of spirit ye are of, for the Son of man came not to destroy men's lives, but to save them." Who does not feel the humane spirit of Christianity to be one of its brightest gems, and one of its chief contrasts with the imperfect economy that preceded it? It is when we mark the inveteracy of the old spirit of hatred that we see how great a change Christ has introduced. If it was the great distinction of Christ's love that " while we were yet enemies, Christ died for us," His precept to us to love our enemies ought to meet with our readiest obedience. Not without profound prophetic insight did the angel who announced the birth of Jesus proclaim, " Glory to God in the highest, on earth peace, good-will to men."

Alas! it is with much humiliation we must own that in practising this humane spirit of her Lord the progress of the Church has been slow and small. It seemed to be implied in the prophecies that Christianity would end war; yet one of the most outstanding phenomena of the world is, the so-called Christian nations of Europe, armed to the teeth, expending millions of treasure year by year on destructive armaments, and withdrawing millions of soldiers from those pursuits which increase wealth and comfort, to be supported by taxes wrung from the sinews of the industrious, and to be ready, when called on, to scatter destruction and death among the ranks of their enemies. Surely it is a shame to the diplomacy of Europe that so little is done to arrest this crying evil; that nation after nation goes on increasing its armaments, and that the only credit a good statesman can gain is that of retarding a collision, which, when it does occur, will be the widest in its dimensions, and the vastest and most hideous in the destruction it deals, that the world has ever seen! All honour to the few earnest men who have tried to make arbitration a substitute for war.

And surely it is no credit to the Christian Church that, when its members are divided in opinion, there should be so much bitterness in the spirit of its controversies. Grant that what excites men so keenly is the fear that the truth of God being at stake, that which they deem most sacred in itself, and most vital in its influence for good is liable to suffer; hence they regard it a duty to rebuke sharply all who are apparently prepared to betray it or compromise it. Is it not apparent that if love is not mingled with the controversies of Christians, it is vain to expect violence and war to cease among the nations? More than this, if love is not more apparent among Christians than has been common, we may well tremble for the cause itself. One of the leaders of German unbelief is said to have remarked that he did not think Christianity could be Divine, because he did not find the people called Christians paying more heed than others to the command of Jesus to love their enemies.

5. One other service of Joshua to the nation of Israel remains to be noticed: he sought with all his heart that they should be a God-governed people, a people that in every department of

life should be ruled by the endeavour to do God's will. He pressed this on them with such earnestness, he commended it by his own example with such sincerity, he brought his whole authority and influence to bear on it with such momentum, that to a large extent he succeeded, though the impression hardly survived himself. "The people served the Lord all the days of Joshua, and all the days of the elders that outlived Joshua, who had seen all the great work of the Lord that He had wrought for Israel." Joshua seemed always to be contending with an idolatrous virus which poisoned the blood of the people, and could not be eradicated. The only thing that seemed capable of crushing it was the outstretched arm of Jehovah, showing itself in some terrible form. While the effect of that display lasted the tendency to idolatry was subdued, but not extirpated; and as soon as the impression of it was spent, the evil broke out anew. It was hard to instil into them ruling principles of conduct that would guide them in spite of outward influences. As a rule, they were not like Abraham, Isaac, and Jacob, or like Moses who "endured as seeing Him who is invisible." Individuals there were among them, like Caleb and Joshua himself, who walked by faith; but the great mass of the nation were carnal, and they exemplified the drift or tendency of that spirit— "The carnal mind is enmity against God."

Still Joshua laboured to press the lesson—the great lesson of the theocracy—Let God rule you; follow invariably His will. It is a rule for nations, for churches, for individuals. The Hebrew theocracy has passed away; but there is a sense in which every Christian nation should be a modified theocracy. So far as God has given abiding rules for the conduct of nations, every nation ought to regard them. If it be a Divine principle that righteousness exalteth a nation; if it be a Divine command to remember the Sabbath day to keep it holy; if it be a Divine instruction to rulers to deliver the needy when he crieth, the poor also and him that hath no helper, in these and in all such matters nations ought to be divinely ruled. It is blasphemous to set up rules of expediency above these eternal emanations of the Divine will.

So, too, churches should be divinely ruled. There is but one Lord in the Christian Church, He that is King of kings, and Lord of lords. There may be many details in Church life which are left to the discretion of its rulers, acting in accordance with the spirit of Scripture; but no church should accept of any ruler whose will may set aside the will of her Lord, nor allow any human authority to supersede what He has ordained.

And for individuals the universal rule is: "Whatsoever ye do in word or deed, do all in the name of the Lord Jesus, giving thanks unto God and the Father by Him." Each true Christian heart is a theocracy—a Christ-governed soul. Not ruled by external appliances, nor by mechanical rules, nor by the mere effort to follow a prescribed example; but by the indwelling of Christ's Spirit, by a vital force communicated from Himself. The spring of the Christian life is here—" Not I, but Christ liveth in me." This is the source of all the beautiful and fruitful Christian lives that ever have been, of all that are, and of all that ever shall be.

The Book of Judges and Ruth

By The Reverend Robert A. Watson, M.A., D.D.

DOCTOR WATSON wrote the volume on the Book of Numbers in this series. In the present volume he delineates the outstanding features of what has been called "Israel's Iron Age." The Books of Judges and Ruth are rich in character study. Doctor Watson unfolds the lights and shadows with a sense of perspective. The traits of the heroes, heroines and traitors of this tantalizing period of war and settlement stand out in the Biblical narrative. Those stirring times of anarchy and savagery were also relieved by exhibitions of piety and patriotism, as seen in the idyllic charm of the Book of Ruth. All this is vividly expounded by Doctor Watson, with impressive applications to our needs.

CONTENTS

	PAGE
CHAPTER I.	
Problems of Settlement and War, . . .	743
CHAPTER II.	
The Way of the Sword, ...	746
CHAPTER III.	
At Bochim: The First Prophet Voice, . .	750
CHAPTER IV.	
Among the Rocks of Paganism, . . .	753
CHAPTER V.	
The Arm of Aram and of Othniel, . .	757
CHAPTER VI.	
The Dagger and the Ox-goad, . . .	761
CHAPTER VII.	
The Sibyl of Mount Ephraim, . . .	765
CHAPTER VIII.	
Deborah's Song: A Divine Vision, . .	769
CHAPTER IX.	
Deborah's Song: A Chant of Patriotism, .	772
CHAPTER X.	
The Desert Hordes; and the Man at Ophrah,	776
CHAPTER XI.	
Gideon, Iconoclast and Reformer, . .	780
CHAPTER XII.	
"The People Are Yet too Many," . .	783
CHAPTER XIII.	
"Midian's Evil Day,"	787

	PAGE
CHAPTER XIV.	
Gideon the Ecclesiastic, ...	791
CHAPTER XV.	
Abimelech and Jotham, ...	795
CHAPTER XVI.	
Gilead and Its Chief, ...	798
CHAPTER XVII.	
The Terrible Vow, ...	802
CHAPTER XVIII.	
Shibboleths, ...	806
CHAPTER XIX.	
The Angel in the Field, ...	809
CHAPTER XX.	
Samson Plunging into Life, . . .	812
CHAPTER XXI.	
Dauntless in Battle, Ignorantly Brave, .	816
CHAPTER XXII.	
Pleasure and Peril in Gaza, . . .	819
CHAPTER XXIII.	
The Valley of Sorek and of Death, . .	822
CHAPTER XXIV.	
The Stolen Gods, ...	826
CHAPTER XXV.	
From Justice to Wild Revenge, . .	829

THE BOOK OF JUDGES

BY REV. ROBERT A. WATSON, D. D.

CHAPTER I.

PROBLEMS OF SETTLEMENT AND WAR.

JUDGES i. 1-11.

It was a new hour in the history of Israel. To a lengthened period of serfdom there had succeeded a time of sojourn in tents, when the camp of the tribes, half-military, half-pastoral, clustering about the Tabernacle of Witness, moved with it from point to point through the desert. Now the march was over; the nomads had to become settlers, a change not easy for them as they expected it to be, full of significance for the world. The Book of Judges, therefore, is a second Genesis or Chronicle of Beginnings so far as the Hebrew commonwealth is concerned. We see the birth-throes of national life, the experiments, struggles, errors, and disasters out of which the moral force of the people gradually rose, growing like a pine tree out of rocky soil.

If we begin our study of the book expecting to find clear evidence of an established Theocracy, a spiritual idea of the kingdom of God ever present to the mind, ever guiding the hope and effort of the tribes, we shall experience that bewilderment which has not seldom fallen upon students of Old Testament history. Divide the life of man into two parts, the sacred and the secular; regard the latter as of no real value compared to the other, as having no relation to that Divine purpose of which the Bible is the oracle; then the Book of Judges must appear out of place in the sacred canon, for unquestionably its main topics are secular from first to last. It preserves the traditions of an age when spiritual ideas and aims were frequently out of sight, when a nation was struggling for bare existence, or, at best, for a rude kind of unity and freedom. But human life, sacred and secular, is one. A single strain of moral urgency runs through the epochs of national development from barbarism to Christian civilisation. A single strain of urgency unites the boisterous vigour of the youth and the sagacious spiritual courage of the man. It is on the strength first, and then on the discipline and purification of the will, that everything depends. There must be energy, or there can be no adequate faith, no earnest religion. We trace in the Book of Judges the springing up and growth of a collective energy which gives power to each separate life. To our amazement we may discover that the Mosaic Law and Ordinances are neglected for a time; but there can be no doubt of Divine Providence, the activity of the redeeming Spirit. Great ends are being served,—a development is proceeding which will by-and-by make religious thought strong, obedience and worship zealous. It is not for us to say that spiritual evolution ought to proceed in this way or that. In the study of natural and supernatural fact our business is to observe with all possible care the goings forth of God and to find as far as we may their meaning and issue. Faith is a profound conviction that the facts of the world justify themselves and the wisdom and righteousness of the Eternal; it is the key that makes history articulate, no mere tale full of sound and fury signifying nothing. And the key of faith which here we are to use in the interpretation of Hebrew life has yet to be applied to all peoples and times. That this may be done we firmly believe: there is needed only the mind broad enough in wisdom and sympathy to gather the annals of the world into one great Bible or Book of God.

Opening the story of the Judges, we find ourselves in a keen atmosphere of warlike ardour softened by scarcely an air of spiritual grace. At once we are plunged into military preparations; councils of war meet and the clash of weapons is heard. Battle follows battle. Iron chariots hurtle along the valleys, the hillsides bristle with armed men. The songs are of strife and conquest; the great heroes are those who smite the uncircumcised hip and thigh. It is the story of Jehovah's people; but where is Jehovah the merciful? Does He reign among them, or sanction their enterprise? Where amid this turmoil and bloodshed is the movement towards the far-off Messiah and the holy mountain where nothing shall hurt or destroy? Does Israel prepare for blessing all nations by crushing those that occupy the land he claims? Problems many meet us in Bible history; here surely is one of the gravest. And we cannot go with Judah in that first expedition; we must hold back in doubt till clearly we understand how these wars of conquest are necessary to the progress of the world. Then, even though the tribes are as yet unaware of their destiny and how it is to be fulfilled, we may go up with them against Adoni-bezek.

Canaan is to be colonised by the seed of Abraham, Canaan and no other land. It is not now, as it was in Abraham's time, a sparsely peopled country, with room enough for a new race. Canaanites, Hivites, Perizzites, Amorites cultivate the plain of Esdraelon and inhabit a hundred cities throughout the land. The Hittites are in considerable force, a strong people with a civilisation of their own. To the north Phœnicia is astir with a mercantile and vigorous race. The Philistines have settlements southward along the coast. Had Israel sought a region comparatively unoccupied, such might, perhaps, have been found on the northern coast of Africa. But Syria is the destined home of the tribes.

The old promise to Abraham has been kept before the minds of his descendants. The land to which they have moved through the desert is that of which he took earnest by the purchase of a grave. But the promise of God looks forward to the circumstances that are to accompany its fulfilment; and it is justified because the occupation of Canaan is the means to a great development of righteousness. For, mark the position which the Hebrew nation is to take. It is to be the central state of the world, in verity the Mountain of God's House for the world. Then observe how the situation of Canaan fits it to be the seat of this new progressive power. Egypt, Babylon, Assyria, Greece, Rome, Carthage, lie in a rude circle around it. From its sea-board the way is open to the west. Across the valley of Jordan goes the caravan route to the East. The Nile, the Orontes, the Ægean Sea are not far off. Canaan does not confine its inhabitants, scarcely separates them from other peoples. It is in the midst of the old world.

Is not this one reason why Israel must inhabit Palestine? Suppose the tribes settled in the highlands of Armenia or along the Persian Gulf; suppose them to have migrated westward from Egypt instead of eastward, and to have found a place of habitation on towards Libya: would the history in that case have had the same movement and power? Would the theatre of prophecy and the scene of the Messiah's work have set the gospel of the ages in the same relief, or the growing City of God on the same mountain height? Not only is Canaan accessible to the emigrants from Egypt, but it is by position and configuration suited to develop the genius of the race. Gennesaret and Asphaltitis; the tortuous Jordan and Kishon, that "river of battles"; the cliffs of Engedi, Gerizim and Ebal, Carmel and Tabor, Moriah and Olivet,—these are needed as the scene of the great Divine revelation. No other rivers, no other lakes nor mountains on the surface of the earth will do.

This, however, is but part of the problem which meets us in regard to the settlement in Canaan. There are the inhabitants of the land to be considered—these Amorites, Hittites, Jebusites, Hivites. How do we justify Israel in displacing them, slaying them, absorbing them? Here is a question first of evolution, then of the character of God.

Do we justify Saxons in their raid on Britain? History does. They become dominant, they rule, they slay, they assimilate; and there grows up British nationality strong and trusty, the citadel of freedom and religious life. The case is similar, yet there is a difference, strongly in favour of Israel as an invading people. For the Israelites have been tried by stern discipline: they are held together by a moral law, a religion divinely revealed, a faith vigorous though but in germ. The Saxons worshipping Thor, Frea, and Woden sweep religion before them in the first rush of conquest. They begin by destroying Roman civilisation and Christian culture in the land they ravage. They appear "dogs," "wolves," "whelps from the kennel of barbarism" to the Britons they overcome. But the Israelites have learned to fear Jehovah, and they bear with them the ark of His covenant.

As for the Canaanitish tribes, compare them now with what they were when Abraham and Isaac fed their flocks in the plain of Mamre or about the springs of Beersheba. Abraham found in Canaan noble, courteous men. Aner, Eshcol and Mamre, Amorites, were his trusted confederates; Ephron the Hittite matched his magnanimity; Abimelech of Gerar "feared the Lord." In Salem reigned a king or royal priest, Melchizedek, unique in ancient history, a majestic unsullied figure, who enjoyed the respect and tribute of the Hebrew patriarch. Where are the successors of those men? Idolatry has corrupted Canaan. The old piety of simple races has died away before the hideous worship of Moloch and Ashtoreth. It is over degenerate peoples that Israel is to assert its dominance; they must learn the way of Jehovah or perish. This conquest is essential to the progress of the world. Here in the centre of empires a stronghold of pure ideas and commanding morality is to be established, an altar of witness for the true God.

So far we move without difficulty towards a justification of the Hebrew descent on Canaan. Still, however, when we survey the progress of conquest, the idea struggling for confirmation in our minds that God was King and Guide of this people, while at the same time we know that all nations could equally claim Him as their Origin, marking how on field after field thousands were left dying and dead, we have to find an answer to the question whether the slaughter and destruction even of idolatrous races for the sake of Israel can be explained in harmony with Divine justice. And this passes into still wider inquiries. Is there intrinsic value in human life? Have men a proper right of existence and self-development? Does not Divine Providence imply that the history of each people, the life of each person will have its separate end and vindication? There is surely a reason in the righteousness and love of God for every human experience, and Christian thought cannot explain the severity of Old Testament ordinances by assuming that the Supreme has made a new dispensation for Himself. The problem is difficult, but we dare not evade it nor doubt a full solution to be possible.

We pass here beyond mere "natural evolution." It is not enough to say that there had to be a struggle for life among races and individuals. If natural forces are held to be the limit and equivalent of God, then "survival of the fittest" may become a religious doctrine, but assuredly it will introduce us to no God of pardon, no hope of redemption. We must discover a Divine end in the life of each person, a member it may be of some doomed race, dying on a field of battle in the holocaust of its valour and chivalry. Explanation is needed of all slaughtered and "waste" lives, untold myriads of lives that never tasted freedom or knew holiness.

The explanation we find is this: that for a human life in the present stage of existence the opportunity of struggle for moral ends—it may be ends of no great dignity, yet really moral, and, as the race advances, religious—this makes life worth living and brings to every one the means of true and lasting gain. "Where ignorant armies clash by night" there may be in the opposing ranks the most various notions of religion and of what is morally good. The histories of the nations that meet in shock of battle determine largely what hopes and aims guide individual lives. But to the thousands who do valiantly this conflict belongs to the vital struggle in which some idea of the morally good or of religious duty directs and animates the soul. For hearth and home, for wife and children, for chief and comrades, for Jehovah or Baal, men fight, and around these names there cluster thoughts the sacredest possible to the age, dignifying life and war and death. There are better kinds of struggle than that which is acted on the bloody field; yet struggle of one kind or other there must be. It is the law of existence for the barbarian, for the Hebrew, for the Christian. Ever there is a necessity for pressing towards the mark, striving to reach and enter the gate of higher life. No land flowing with milk and honey to be peaceably inherited and enjoyed rewards the generation which has fought its way through the desert. No placid possession of cities and vineyards rounds off the life of Canaanitish tribe. The gains of endurance are reaped, only to be sown again in labour and tears for a further harvest. Here on earth this is the plan of God for men; and when another life crowns the long effort of this world of change, may it not be with fresh calls to more glorious duty and achievement?

But the golden cord of Divine Providence has more than one strand; and while the conflicts of life are appointed for the discipline of men and nations in moral vigour and in fidelity to such religious ideas as they possess, the purer and stronger faith always giving more power to those who exercise it, there is also in the course of life, and especially in the suffering war entails, a reference to the sins of men. Warfare is a sad necessity. Itself often a crime, it issues the judgment of God against folly and crime. Now Israel, now the Canaanite becomes a hammer of Jehovah. One people has been true to its best, and by that faithfulness it gains the victory. Another has been false, cruel, treacherous, and the hands of the fighters grow weak, their swords lose edge, their chariot-wheels roll heavily, they are swept away by the avenging tide. Or the sincere, the good are overcome; the weak who are in the right sink before the wicked who are strong. Yet the moral triumph is always gained. Even in defeat and death there is victory for the faithful.

In these wars of Israel we find many a story of judgment as well as a constant proving of the worth of man's religion and virtue. Neither was Israel always in the right, nor had those races which Israel overcame always a title to the power they held and the land they occupied. Jehovah was a stern arbiter among the combatants. When His own people failed in the courage and humility of faith, they were chastised. On the other hand, there were tyrants and tyrannous races, freebooters and banditti, pagan hordes steeped in uncleanness who had to be judged and punished. Where we cannot trace the reason of what appears mere waste of life or wanton cruelty, there lie behind, in the ken of the All-seeing, the need and perfect vindication of all He suffered to be done in the ebb and flow of battle, amid the riot of war.

Beginning now with the detailed narrative, we find first a case of retribution, in which the Israelites served the justice of God. As yet the Canaanite power was unbroken in the central region of Western Palestine, where Adoni-bezek ruled over the cities of seventy chiefs. It became a question who should lead the tribes against this petty despot, and recourse was had to the priests at Gilgal for Divine direction. The answer of the oracle was that Judah should head the campaign, the warlike vigour and numerical strength of that tribe fitting it to take the foremost place. Judah accepting the post of honour invited Simeon, closely related by common descent from Leah, to join the expedition; and thus began a confederacy of these southern tribes which had the effect of separating them from the others throughout the whole period of the judges. The locality of Bezek which the king of the Canaanites held as his chief fortress is not known. Probably it was near the Jordan valley, about half-way between the two greater lakes. From it the tyranny of Adoni-bezek extended northward and southward over the cities of the seventy, whose submission he had cruelly ensured by rendering them unfit for war. Here, in the first struggle, Judah was completely successful. The rout of the Canaanites and Perizzites was decisive, and the slaughter so great as to send a thrill of terror through the land. And now the rude judgment of men works out the decree of God. Adoni-bezek suffers the same mutilation as he had inflicted on the captive chiefs and in Oriental manner makes acknowledgment of a just fate. There is a certain religiousness in his mind, and he sincerely bows himself under the judgment of a God against Whom he had tried issues in vain. Had these troops of Israel come in the name of Jehovah? Then Jehovah had been watching Adoni-bezek in his pride when, as he daily feasted in his hall, the crowd of victims grovelled at his feet like dogs.

Thus early did ideas of righteousness and of wide authority attach themselves in Canaan to the name of Israel's God. It is remarkable how on the appearance of a new race the first collision with it on the battlefield will produce an impression of its capacity and spirit and of unseen powers fighting along with it. Joshua's dash through Canaan doubtless struck far and wide a belief that the new comers had a mighty God to support them; the belief is reinforced, and there is added a thought of Divine justice. The retribution of Jehovah meant Godhead far larger and more terrible, and at the same time more august, than the religion of Baal had ever presented to the mind. From this point the Israelites, if they had been true to their heavenly King, fired with the ardour of His name, would have occupied a moral vantage ground and proved invincible. The fear of Jehovah would have done more for them than their own valour and arms. Had the people of the land seen that a power was being established amongst them in the justice and benignity of which they could trust, had they learned not only to fear but to adore Jehovah, there would have been quick fulfilment of the promise which gladdened the large heart of Abraham. The realisation, however, had to wait for many a century.

It cannot be doubted that Israel had under Moses received such an impulse in the direction of faith in the one God, and such a conception of His character and will, as declared the spiritual mission of the tribes. The people were not all aware of their high destiny, not sufficiently instructed to have a competent sense of it; but the chiefs of the tribes, the Levites and the heads of households, should have well understood the part that fell to Israel among the nations of the world. The law in its main outlines was known, and it should have been revered as the charter of the commonwealth. Under the banner of Jehovah the nation ought to have striven not for its own position alone, the enjoyment of fruitful fields and fenced cities, but to raise the standard of human morality and enforce the truth of Divine religion. The gross idolatry of the peoples around should have been continually testified against; the principles of honesty, of domestic purity, of regard for human life, of neighbourliness and parental authority, as well as the more spiritual ideas expressed in the first table of the Decalogue, ought to have been guarded and dispensed as the special treasure of the nation. In this way Israel, as it enlarged its territory, would from the first have been clearing one space of earth for the good customs and holy observances that make for spiritual development. The greatest of all trusts is committed to a race when it is made capable of this; but here Israel often failed, and the reproaches of her prophets had to be poured out from age to age.

The ascendency which Israel secured in Canaan, or that which Britain has won in India, is not, to begin with, justified by superior strength, nor by higher intelligence, nor even because in practice the religion of the conquerors is better than that of the vanquished. It is justified because, with all faults and crimes that may for long attend the rule of the victorious race, there lie, unrealised at first, in conceptions of God and of duty, the promise and germ of a higher education of the world. Developed in the course of time, the spiritual genius of the conquerors vindicates their ambition and their success. The world is to become the heritage and domain of those who have the secret of large and ascending life.

Judah, moving southward from Bezek, took Jerusalem, not the stronghold on the hilltop, but the city, and smote it with the edge of the sword. Not yet did that citadel which has been the scene of so many conflicts become a rallying-point for the tribes. The army, leaving Adoni-bezek dead in Jerusalem, with many who owned him as chief, swept southward still to Hebron and Debir. At Hebron the task was not unlike that which had been just accomplished. There reigned three chiefs, Sheshai, Ahiman, and Talmai, who are mentioned again and again in the annals as if their names had been deeply branded on the memory of the age. They were sons of Anak, bandit captains, whose rule was a terror to the country side. Their power had to be assailed and overthrown, not only for the sake of Judah which was to inhabit their stronghold, but for the sake of humanity. The law of God was to replace the fierce unregulated sway of inhuman violence and cruelty. So the practical duty of the hour carried the tribes beyond the citadel where the best national centre would have been found to attack another where an evil power sat entrenched.

One moral lies on the surface here. We are naturally anxious to gain a good position in life for ourselves, and every consideration is apt to be set aside in favour of that. Now, in a sense, it is necessary, one of the first duties, that we gain each a citadel for himself. Our influence depends to a great extent on the standing we secure, on the courage and talent we show in making good our place. Our personality must enlarge itself, make itself visible by the conquest we effect and the extent of affairs we have a right to control. Effort on this line needs not be selfish or egoistic in a bad sense. The higher self or spirit of a good man finds in chosen ranges of activity and possession its true development and calling. One may not be a worldling by any means while he follows the bent of his genius and uses opportunity to become a successful merchant, a public administrator, a great artist or man of letters. All that he adds to his native inheritance of hand, brain and soul should be and often is the means of enriching the world. Against the false doctrine of self-suppression, still urged on a perplexed generation, stands this true doctrine, by which the generous helper of men guides his life so as to become a king and priest unto God. And when we turn from persons of highest character and talent to those of smaller capacity, we may not alter the principle of judgment. They, too, serve the world, in so far as they have good qualities, by conquering citadels and reigning where they are fit to reign. If a man is to live to any purpose, play must be given to his original vigour, however much or little there is of it.

Here, then, we find a necessity belonging to the spiritual no less than to the earthly life. But there lies close beside it the shadow of temptation and sin. Thousands of people put forth all their strength to gain a fortress for themselves, leaving others to fight the sons of Anak—the intemperance, the unchastity, the atheism of the time. Instead of triumphing over the earthly, they are ensnared and enslaved. The truth is, that a safe position for ourselves we cannot have while those sons of Anak ravage the country around. The Divine call therefore often requires of us that we leave a Jerusalem unconquered for ourselves, while we pass on with the hosts of God to do battle with the public enemy. Time after time Israel, though successful at Hebron, missed the secret and learnt in bitter sadness and loss how near is the shadow to the glory.

And for any one to-day, what profits it to be a wealthy man, living in state with all the appliances of amusement and luxury, well knowing, but not choosing to share the great conflicts between religion and ungodliness, between purity and vice? If the ignorance and woe of our fellow-creatures do not draw our hearts, if we seek our own things as loving our own, if the spiritual does not command us, we shall certainly lose all that makes life—enthusiasm, strength, eternal joy.

Give us men who fling themselves into the great struggle, doing what they can with Christborn ardour, foot soldiers if nothing else in the army of the Lord of Righteousness.

CHAPTER II.

THE WAY OF THE SWORD.

JUDGES i. 12-26.

THE name Kiriath-sepher, that is Book-Town, has been supposed to point to the existence of a semi-popular literature among the pre-Judæan inhabitants of Canaan. We cannot build with any certainty upon a name; but there are other facts of some significance. Already the Phœnicians, the merchants of the age, some of whom no doubt visited Kiriath-sepher on their way to Arabia or settled in it, had in their dealings with Egypt begun to use that alphabet to which most languages, from Hebrew and Aramaic on through Greek and Latin to our own, are indebted for the idea and shapes of letters. And it is not improbable that an old-world Phœnician library of skins, palm-leaves, or inscribed tablets had given distinction to this town lying away towards the desert from Hebron. Written words were held in half-superstitious veneration, and a very few records would greatly impress a district peopled chiefly by wandering tribes.

Nothing is insignificant in the pages of the Bible, nothing is to be disregarded that throws the least light upon human affairs and Divine Providence; and here we have a suggestion of no slight importance. Doubt has been cast on the existence of a written language among the Hebrews till centuries after the Exodus. It has been denied that the Law could have been written out by Moses. The difficulty is now seen to be imaginary, like many others that have been raised. It is certain that the Phœnicians trading to Egypt in the time of the Hyksos kings had settlements quite contiguous to Goshen. What more likely than that the Hebrews, who spoke a language akin to the Phœnicians, should have shared the discovery of letters almost from the first, and practised the art of writing in the days of their favour with the monarchs of the Nile valley? The oppression of the following period might prevent the spread of letters among the people; but a man like Moses must have seen their value and made himself familiar with their use. The importance of this indication in the study of Hebrew law and faith is very plain. Nor should we fail to notice the interesting connection between the Divine lawgiving of Moses and the practical invention of a worldly race. There is no exclusiveness in the providence of God. The art of a people, acute and eager indeed, but without spirituality, is not rejected as profane by the inspired leader of Israel. Egyptians and Phœnicians have their share in originating that culture which mingles its stream with sacred revelation and religion. As, long afterwards, there came the printing-press, a product of human skill and science, and by its help the Reformation spread and grew and filled Europe with new thought, so for the early record of God's work and will human genius furnished the fit instrument. Letters and religion, culture and faith must needs go hand in hand. The more the minds of men are trained, the more deftly they can use literature and science, the more able they should be to receive and convey the spiritual message which the Bible contains. Culture which does not have this effect betrays its own pettiness and parochialism; and when we are provoked to ask whether human learning is not a foe to religion, the reason must be that the favourite studies of the time are shallow, aimless, and ignoble.

Kiriath-sepher has to be taken. Its inhabitants, strongly entrenched, threaten the people who are settling about Hebron and must be subdued; and Caleb, who has come to his possession, adopts a common expedient for rousing the ambitious young men of the tribe. He has a daughter, and marriage with her shall reward the man who takes the fortress. It is not likely that Achsah objected. A courageous and capable husband was, we may say, a necessity, and her father's proposal offered a practical way of settling her in safety and comfort. Customs which appear to us barbarous and almost insulting have no doubt justified themselves to the common-sense, if not fully to the desires of women, because they were suited to the exigencies of life in rude and stormy times. There is this also, that the conquest of Kiriath-sepher was part of the great task in which Israel was engaged, and Achsah, as a patriotic daughter of Abraham, would feel the pride of being able to reward a hero of the sacred war. To the degree in which she was a woman of character this would balance other considerations. Still the custom is not an ideal one; there is too much uncertainty. While the rivalry for her hand is going on the maiden has to wait at home, wondering what her fate shall be, instead of helping to decide it by her own thought and action. The young man, again, does not commend himself by honour, but only by courage and skill. Yet the test is real, so far as it goes, and fits the time.

Achsah, no doubt, had her preference and her hope, though she dared not speak of them. As for modern feeling, it is professedly on the side of the heart in such a case, and modern literature, with a thousand deft illustrations, proclaims the right of the heart to its choice. We call it a barbarous custom, the disposition of a woman by her father, apart from her preference, to one who does him or the community a service; and although Achsah consented, we feel that she was a slave. No doubt the Hebrew wife in her home had a place of influence and power, and a woman might even come to exercise authority among the tribes; but, to begin with, she was under authority and had to subdue her own wishes in a manner we consider quite incompatible with the rights of a human being. Very slowly do the customs of marriage even in Israel rise from the rudeness of savage life. Abraham and Sarah, long before this, lived on something like equality, he a prince, she a princess. But what can be said of Hagar, a concubine outside the home-circle, who might be sent any day into the wilderness? David and Solomon afterwards can marry for state reasons, can take, in pure Oriental fashion, the one his tens, the other his hundreds of wives and concubines. Polygamy survives for many a century. When that is seen to be evil, there remains to men a freedom of divorce which of necessity keeps women in a low and unhonoured state.

Yet, thus treated, woman has always duties of the first importance, on which the moral health and vigour of the race depend; and right nobly must many a Hebrew wife and mother have fulfilled the trust. It is a pathetic story; but now, perhaps, we are in sight of an age when the injustice done to women may be replaced by an injustice they do to themselves. Liberty is their right, but the old duties remain as great as ever. If neither patriotism, nor religion, nor the home is to be regarded, but mere taste; if freedom becomes license to know and enjoy, there will be another slavery worse than the former. Without a very keen sense of Christian honour and obligation among women, their enfranchisement will be the loss of what has held society together and made nations strong. And looking at the way in which marriage is frequently arranged by the free consent and determination of women, is there much advance on the old barbarism? How often do they sell themselves to the fortunate, rather than reserve themselves for the fit; how often do they marry not because a helpmeet of the soul has been found, but because audacity has won them or jewels have dazzled; because a fireside is offered, not because the ideal of life may be realised. True, in the worldliness there is a strain of moral effort often pathetic enough. Women are skilful at making the best of circumstances, and even when the gilding fades from the life they have chosen they will struggle on with wonderful resolution to maintain something like order and beauty. The Othniel who has gained Achsah by some feat of mercantile success or showy talk may turn out a poor pretender to bravery or wit; but she will do her best for him, cover up his faults, beg springs of water or even dig them with her own hands. Let men thank God that it is so, and let them help her to find her right place, her proper kingdom and liberty.

There is another aspect of the picture, however, as it unfolds itself. The success of Othniel in his attack on Kiriath-sepher gave him at once a good place as a leader, and a wife who was ready to make his interests her own and help him to social position and wealth. Her first care was to acquire a piece of land suitable for the flocks and herds she saw in prospect, well watered if possible,—in short, an excellent sheep-farm. Returning from the bridal journey, she had her stratagem ready, and when she came near her father's tent followed up her husband's request for the land by lighting eagerly from her ass, taking for granted the one gift, and pressing a further petition—"Give me a blessing, father. A south land thou hast bestowed, give me also wells of water." So, without more ado, the new Kenazite homestead was secured.

How Jewish, we may be disposed to say. May we not also say, How thoroughly British? The virtue of Achsah, is it not the virtue of a true British wife? To urge her husband on and up in the social scale, to aid him in every point of the contest for wealth and place, to raise him and rise with him, what can be more admirable? Are there opportunities of gaining the favour of the powerful who have offices to give, the liking of the wealthy who have fortunes to bequeath? The managing wife will use these opportunities with address and courage. She will light off her ass and bow humbly before a flattered great man to whom she prefers a request. She can fit her words to the occasion and her smiles to the end in view. It is a poor spirit that is content with anything short of all that may be had: thus in brief she might express her principle of duty. And so in ten thousand homes there is no question whether marriage is a failure. It has succeeded. There is a combination of man's strength and woman's wit for the great end of "getting on." And in ten thousand others there is no thought more constantly present to the minds of husband and wife than that marriage is a failure. For restless ingenuity and many schemes have yielded nothing. The husband has been too slow or too honest, and the wife has been foiled; or, on the other hand, the woman has not seconded the man, has not risen with him. She has kept him down by her failings; or she is the same simple-minded, homely person he wedded long ago, no fit mate, of course, for one who is the companion of magnates and rulers. Well may those who long for a reformation begin by seeking a return to simplicity of life and the relish for other kinds of distinction than lavish outlay and social notoriety can give. Until married ambition is fed and hallowed at the Christian altar there will be the same failures we see now, and the same successes which are worse than "failures."

For a moment the history gives us a glimpse of another domestic settlement. "The children of the Kenite went up from the City of Palm Trees with the children of Judah," and found a place of abode on the southern fringe of Simeon's territory, and there they seem to have gradually mingled with the tent-dwellers of the desert. By-and-by we shall find one Heber the Kenite in a different part of the land, near the Sea of Galilee, still in touch with the Israelites to some extent, while his people are scattered. Heber may have felt the power of Israel's mission and career and judged it wise to separate from those who had no interest in the tribes of Jehovah. The Kenites of the south appear in the history like men upon a raft, once borne near shore, who fail to seize the hour of deliverance and are carried away again to the wastes of sea. They are part of the drifting population that surrounds the Hebrew church, type of the drifting multitude who in the nomadism of modern society are for a time seen in our Christian assemblies, then pass away to mingle with the careless. An innate restlessness and a want of serious purpose mark the class. To settle these wanderers in orderly religious life seems almost impossible; we can perhaps only expect to sow among them seeds of good, and to make them feel a Divine presence restraining from evil. The assertion of personal independence in our day has no doubt much to do with impatiece of church bonds and habits of worship; and it must not be forgotten that this is a phase of growing life needing forbearance no less than firm example.

Zephath was the next fortress against which Judah and Simeon directed their arms. When the tribes were in the desert on their long and difficult march they attempted first to enter Canaan from the south, and actually reached the neighbourhood of this town. But, as we read in the Book of Numbers, Arad the king of Zephath fought against them and took some of them prisoners. The defeat appears to have been serious, for, arrested and disheartened by it, Israel turned southward again, and after a long *détour* reached Canaan another way. In the passage in Numbers the overthrow of Zephath is described by anticipation; in Judges we have the account in its proper historical place. The people whom Arad ruled were, we may suppose, an Edomite clan living partly by merchandise, mainly by foray, practised marauders, with difficulty guarded against, who having taken their prey disappeared swiftly amongst the hills.

In the world of thought and feeling there are many Zephaths, whence quick outset is often made upon the faith and hope of men. We are pressing towards some end, mastering difficulties, contending with open and known enemies. Only a little way remains before us. But invisible among the intricacies of experience is this lurking foe who suddenly falls upon us. It is a settlement in the faith of God we seek. The onset is of doubts we had not imagined, doubts of inspiration, of immortality, of the incarnation, truths the most vital. We are repulsed, broken, disheartened. There remains a new wilderness journey till we reach by the way of Moab the fords of our Jordan and the land of our inheritance. Yet there is a way, sure and appointed. The baffled, wounded soul is never to despair. And when at length the settlement of faith is won, the Zephath of doubt may be assailed from the other side, assailed successfully and taken. The experience of some poor victims of what is oddly called philosophic doubt need dismay no one. For the resolute seeker after God there is always a victory, which in the end may prove so easy, so complete, as to amaze him. The captured Zephath is not destroyed nor abandoned, but is held as a fortress of faith. It becomes Hormah—the Consecrated.

Victories were gained by Judah in the land of the Philistines, partial victories, the results of which were not kept. Gaza, Ashkelon, Ekron were occupied for a time; but Philistine force and doggedness recovered, apparently in a few years, the captured towns. Wherever they had their origin, these Philistines were a strong and stubborn race, and so different from the Israelites in habit and language that they never freely mingled nor even lived peaceably with the tribes. At this time they were probably forming their settlements on the Mediterranean seaboard, and were scarcely able to resist the men of Judah. But ship after ship from over sea, perhaps from Crete, brought new colonists; and during the whole period till the Captivity they were a thorn in the side of the Hebrews. Beside these, there were other dwellers in the lowlands, who were equipped in a way that made it difficult to meet them. The most vehement sally of men on foot could not break the line of iron chariots, thundering over the plain. It was in the hill districts that the tribes gained their surest footing,—a singular fact, for mountain people are usually hardest to defeat and dispossess; and we take it as a sign of remarkable vigour that the invaders so soon occupied the heights.

Here the spiritual parallel is instructive. Conversion, it may be said, carries the soul with a rush to the high ground of faith. The Great Leader has gone before, preparing the way. We climb rapidly to fortresses from which the enemy has fled, and it would seem that victory is complete. But the Christian life is a constant alternation between the joy of the conquered height and the stern battles of the foe-infested plain. Worldly custom and sensuous desire, greed and envy and base appetite have their cities and chariots in the low ground of being. So long as one of them remains the victory of faith is unfinished, insecure. Piety that believes itself delivered once for all from conflict is ever on the verge of disaster. The peace and joy men cherish, while as yet the earthly nature is unsubdued, the very citadels of it unreconnoitred, are visionary and relaxing. For the soul and for society the only salvation lies in mortal combat— life-long, age-long combat with the earthly and the false. Nooks enough may be found among the hills, pleasant and calm, from which the low ground cannot be seen, where the roll of the iron chariots is scarcely heard. It may seem to imperil all if we descend from these retreats. But when we have gained strength in the mountain air it is for the battle down below, it is that we may advance the lines of redeemed life and gain new bases for sacred enterprise.

A mark of the humanness and, shall we not also say, the divineness of this history is to be found in the frequent notices of other tribes than those of Israel. To the inspired writer it is not all the same whether Canaanites die or live, what becomes of Phœnicians or Philistines. Of this we have two examples, one the case of the Jebusites, the other of the people of Luz. The Jebusites, after the capture of the lower city already recorded, appear to have been left in peaceful possession of their citadel and accepted as neighbours by the Benjamites. When the Book of Judges was written Jebusite families still remained, and in David's time Araunah the Jebusite was a conspicuous figure. A series of terrible events connected with the history of Benjamin is narrated towards the end of the Book. It is impossible to say whether the crime which led to these events was in any way due to bad influence exercised by the Jebusites. We may charitably doubt whether it was. There is no indication that they were a depraved people. If they had been licentious they could scarcely have retained till David's time a stronghold so central and of so much consequence in the land. They were a mountain clan, and Araunah shows himself in contact with David a reverend and kingly person.

As for Bethel or Luz, around which gathered notable associations of Jacob's life, Ephraim, in whose territory it lay, adopted a stratagem in order to master it, and smote the city. One family alone, the head of which had betrayed the place, was allowed to depart in peace, and a new Luz was founded "in the land of the Hittites." We are inclined to regard the traitor as deserving of death, and Ephraim appears to us disgraced, not honoured, by its exploit. There is a fair, straightforward way of fighting; but this tribe, one of the strongest, chooses a mean and treacherous method of gaining its end. Are we mistaken in thinking that the care with which the founding of the new city is described shows the writer's sympathy with the Luzzites? At any rate, he does not by one word justify Ephraim; and we do not feel called on to restrain our indignation.

The high ideal of life, how often it fades from our view! There are times when we realise our Divine calling, when the strain of it is felt and the soul is on fire with sacred zeal. We press on, fight on, true to the highest we know at every step. We are chivalrous, for we see the chivalry of Christ; we are tender and faithful, for we see His tenderness and faithfulness. Then we make progress; the goal can almost be touched. We love, and love bears us on. We aspire, and the world glows with light. But there comes a change. The thought of self-preservation, of selfish gain, has intruded. On pretext of serving God we are hard to man, we keep back the truth, we use compromises, we descend even to treachery and do things which in another are abominable to us. So the fervour departs, the light fades from the world, the goal recedes, becomes invisible. Most strange of all is it that side by side with cultured religion there can be proud sophistry and ignorant scorn, the very treachery of the intellect towards man. Far away in the dimness of Israel's early days we see the beginnings of a pious inhumanity, that may well make us stay to fear lest the like should be growing among ourselves. It is not what men claim, much less what they seize and hold, that does them honour. Here and there a march may be stolen on rivals by those who firmly believe they are serving God. But the rights of a man, a tribe, a church lie side by side with duties; and neglect of duty destroys the claim to what otherwise would be a right. Let there be no mistake: power and gain are not allowed in the providence of God to anyone that he may grasp them in despite of justice or charity.

One thought may link the various episodes we have considered. It is that of the end for which individuality exists. The home has its development of personality—for service. The peace and joy of religion nourish the soul—for service. Life may be conquered in various regions, and a man grow fit for ever greater victories, ever nobler service. But with the end the means and spirit of each effort are so interwoven that alike in home, and church, and society the human soul must move in uttermost faithfulness and simplicity or fail from the Divine victory that wins the prize.

CHAPTER III.

AT BOCHIM: THE FIRST PROPHET VOICE.

JUDGES ii. 1-5.

From the time of Abraham on to the settlement in Canaan the Israelites had kept the faith of the one God. They had their origin as a people in a decisive revolt against polytheism. Of the great Semite forefather of the Jewish people, it has been finely said, " He bore upon his forehead the seal of the Absolute God, upon which was written, This race will rid the earth of superstition." The character and structure of the Hebrew tongue resisted idolatry. It was not an imaginative language; it had no mythological colour. We who have inherited an ancient culture of quite another kind do not think it strange to read or sing:

" Hail, smiling morn, that tip'st the hills with gold,
  Whose rosy fingers ope the gates of day,
  Who the gay face of nature dost unfold,
  At whose bright presence darkness flies away."

These lines, however, are full of latent mythology. The " smiling morn " is Aurora, the darkness that flies away before the dawn is the Erebus of the Greeks. Nothing of this sort was possible in Hebrew literature. In it all change, all life, every natural incident are ascribed to the will and power of one Supreme Being. " Jehovah thundered in the heavens and the Highest gave His voice, hailstones and coals of fire." " By the breath of God ice is given, and the breadth of the waters is straitened." " Behold, He spreadeth His light around Him; . . . He covereth His hands with the lightning." " Thou makest darkness and it is night." Always in forms like these Hebrew poetry sets forth the control of nature by its invisible King. The pious word of Fénelon, " What do I see in nature? God; God everywhere; God alone," had its germ, its very substance, in the faith and language of patriarchal times.

There are some who allege that this simple faith in one God, sole Origin and Ruler of nature and life, impoverished the thought and speech of the Hebrews. It was in reality the spring and safeguard of their spiritual destiny. Their very language was a sacred inheritance and preparation. From age to age it served a Divine purpose in maintaining the idea of the unity of God; and the power of that idea never failed their prophets nor passed from the soul of the race. The whole of Israel's literature sets forth the universal sway and eternal righteousness of Him who dwells in the high and lofty place, Whose name is Holy. In canto and strophe of the great Divine Poem, the glory of the One Supreme burns with increasing clearness, till in Christ its finest radiance flashes upon the world.

While the Hebrews were in Egypt, the faith inherited from patriarchal times must have been sorely tried, and, all circumstances considered, it came forth wonderfully pure. " The Israelites saw Egypt as the Mussulman Arab sees pagan countries, entirely from the outside, perceiving only the surface and external things." They indeed carried with them into the desert the recollection of the sacred bulls or calves of which they had seen images at Hathor and Memphis. But the idol they made at Horeb was intended to represent their Deliverer, the true God, and the swift and stern repression by Moses of that symbolism and its pagan incidents appears to have been effectual. The tribes reached Canaan substantially free from idolatry, though teraphim or fetishes may have been used in secret with magical ceremonies. The religion of the people generally was far from spiritual, yet there was a real faith in Jehovah as the protector of the national life, the guardian of justice and truth. From this there was no falling away when the Reubenites and Gadites on the east of Jordan erected an altar for themselves. " The Lord God of gods," they said, " He knoweth, and Israel he shall know if it be in rebellion, or if in transgression against the Lord." The altar was called *Ed*, a witness between east and west that the faith of the one Living God was still to unite the tribes.

But the danger to Israel's fidelity came when there began to be intercourse with the people of Canaan, now sunk from the purer thought of early times. Everywhere in the land of the Hittites and Amorites, Hivites and Jebusites, there were altars and sacred trees, pillars and images used in idolatrous worship. The ark and the altar of Divine religion, established first at Gilgal near Jericho, afterwards at Bethel and then at Shiloh, could not be frequently visited, especially by those who settled towards the southern desert and in the far north. Yet the necessity for religious worship of some kind was constantly felt; and as afterwards the synagogues gave opportunity for devotional gatherings when the Temple could not be reached, so in the earlier time there came to be sacred observances on elevated places, a windy threshing-floor, or a hill-top already used for heathen sacrifice. Hence, on the one hand, there was the danger that worship might be entirely neglected, on the other hand the grave risk that the use of heathen occasions and meeting-places should lead to heathen ritual, and those who came together on the hill of Baal should forget Jehovah. It was the latter evil that grew; and while as yet only a few Hebrews easily led astray had approached with kid or lamb a pagan altar, the alarm was raised. At Bochim a Divine warning was uttered which found echo in the hearts of the people.

There appears to have been a great gathering of the tribes at some spot near Bethel. We see the elders and heads of families holding council of war and administration, the thoughts of all bent on conquest and family settlement. Religion, the purity of Jehovah's worship, are forgotten in the business of the hour. How shall the tribes best help each other in the struggle that is already proving more arduous than they expected? Dan is sorely pressed by the Amorites. The chiefs of the tribe are here telling their story of hardship among the mountains. The Asherites have failed in their attack upon the sea-board towns Accho and Achzib; in vain have they pressed towards Zidon. They are dwelling among the Canaanites and may soon be reduced to slavery. The reports from other tribes are more hopeful; but everywhere the people of the land are hard to overcome. Should Israel not remain content for a time, make the best of circumstances, cultivate friendly intercourse with the population it cannot dispossess? Such a policy often commends itself to those who would be thought prudent; it is apt to prove a fatal policy.

Suddenly a spiritual voice is heard, clear and intense, and all others are silent. From the sanctuary of God at Gilgal one comes whom the people have not expected; he comes with a message they cannot choose but hear. It is a prophet with the burden of reproof and warning. Jehovah's goodness, Jehovah's claim are declared with Divine ardour; with Divine severity the neglect of the covenant is condemned. Have the tribes of God begun to consort with the people of the land? Are they already dwelling content under the shadow of idolatrous groves, in sight of the symbols of Ashtoreth? Are they learning to swear by Baal and Melcarth and looking on while sacrifices are offered to these vile masters? Then they can no longer hope that Jehovah will give them the country to enjoy; the heathen shall remain as thorns in the side of Israel and their gods shall be a snare. It is a message of startling power. From the hopes of dominion and the plans of worldly gain the people pass to spiritual concern. They have offended their Lord; His countenance is turned from them. A feeling of guilt falls on the assembly. "It came to pass that the people lifted up their voice and wept."

This lamentation at Bochim is the second note of religious feeling and faith in the Book of Judges. The first is the consultation of the priests and the oracle referred to in the opening sentence of the book. Jehovah Who had led them through the wilderness was their King, and unless He went forth as the unseen Captain of the host no success could be looked for. "They asked of Jehovah, saying, Who shall go up for us first against the Canaanites, to fight against them?" In this appeal there was a measure of faith which is neither to be scorned nor suspected. The question indeed was not whether they should fight at all, but how they should fight so as to succeed, and their trust was in a God thought of as pledged to them, solely concerned for them. So far accordingly there is nothing exemplary in the circumstances. Yet we find a lesson for Christian nations. There are many in our modern parliaments who are quite ready to vote national prayer in war-time and thanksgiving for victories, who yet would never think, before undertaking a war, of consulting those best qualified to interpret the Divine will. The relation between religion and the state has this fatal hitch, that however Christian our governments profess to be, the Christian thinkers of the country are not consulted on moral questions, not even on a question so momentous as that of war. It is passion, pride, or diplomacy, never the wisdom of Christ, that leads nations in the critical moments of their history. Who then scorn, who suspect the early Hebrew belief? Those only who have no right; those who as they laugh at God and faith shut themselves from the knowledge by which alone life can be understood; and, again, those who in their own ignorance and pride unsheathe the sword without reference to Him in Whom they profess to believe. We admit none of these to criticise Israel and its faith.

At Bochim, where the second note of religious feeling is struck, a deeper and clearer note, we find the prophet listened to. He revives the sense of duty, he kindles a Divine sorrow in the hearts of the people. The national assembly is conscience-stricken. Let us allow this quick contrition to be the result, in part, of superstitious fear. Very rarely is spiritual concern quite pure. In general it is the consequences of transgression rather than the evil of it that press on the minds of men. Forebodings of trouble and calamity are more commonly causes of sorrow than the loss of fellowship with God; and if we know this to be the case with many who are convicted of sin under the preaching of the gospel, we cannot wonder to find the penitence of old Hebrew times mingled with superstition. Nevertheless, the people are aware of the broken covenant, burdened with a sense that they have lost the favour of their unseen Guide. There can be no doubt that the realisation of sin and of justice turned against them is one cause of their tears.

Here, again, if there is a difference between Israel and Christian nations, it is not in favour of the latter. Are modern senates ever overcome by conviction of sin? Those who are in power seem to have no fear that they may do wrong. Glorifying their blunders and forgetting their errors, they find no occasion for self-reproach, no need to sit in sackcloth and ashes. Now and then, indeed, a day of fasting and humiliation is ordered and observed in state; the sincere Christian for his part feeling how miserably formal it is, how far from the spontaneous expression of abasement and remorse. God is called upon to help a people who have not considered their ways, who design no amendment, who have not even suspected that the Divine blessing may come in still further humbling. And turning to private life, is there not as much of self-justification, as little of real humility and faith? The shallow nature of popular Christianity is seen here, that so few can read in disappointment and privation anything but disaster, or submit without disgust and rebellion to take a lower place at the table of Providence. Our weeping is so often for what we longed to gain or wished to keep in the earthly and temporal region, so seldom for what we have lost or should fear to lose in the spiritual. We grieve when we should rather rejoice that God has made us feel our need of Him, and called us again to our true blessedness.

The scene at Bochim connects itself very notably with one nine hundred and fifty years later. The poor fragments of the exiled tribes have been gathered again in the land of their fathers. They are rebuilding Jerusalem and the Temple. Ezra has led back a company from Babylon and has brought with him, by the favour of Artaxerxes, no small treasure of silver and gold for the house of God. To his astonishment and grief he hears the old tale of alliance with the inhabitants of the land, intermarriage even of Levites, priests and princes of Israel with women of the Canaanite races. In the new settlement of Palestine the error of the first is repeated. Ezra calls a solemn assembly in the Temple court—" every one that trembles at the words of the God of Israel." Till the evening sacrifice he sits prostrate with grief, his garment rent, his hair torn and dishevelled. Then on his knees before the Lord he spreads forth his hands in prayer. The trespasses of a thousand years afflict him, afflict the faithful. "After all that is come upon us for our evil deeds, shall we again break Thy commandments, and join in affinity with the peoples that do these abominations? wouldest not Thou be angry with us till Thou hadst consumed us so that there should be no remnant nor any to escape? . . . Behold we are before Thee in our guiltiness; for none can stand before Thee because of this." The impressive lament of Ezra and those who join in his confessions draws together a great congregation, and the people weep very sore.

Nine centuries and a half appear a long time in the history of a nation. What has been gained during the period? Is the weeping at Jerusalem in Ezra's time, like the weeping at Bochim, a mark of no deeper feeling, no keener penitence? Has there been religious advance commensurate with the discipline of suffering, defeat, slaughter and exile, dishonoured kings, a wasted land? Have the prophets not achieved anything? Has not the Temple in its glory, in its desolation, spoken of a Heavenly power, a Divine rule, the sense of which entering the souls of the people has established piety, or at least a habit of separateness from heathen manners and life? It may be hard to distinguish and set forth the gain of those centuries. But it is certain that while the weeping at Bochim was the sign of a fear that soon passed away, the weeping in the Temple court marked a new beginning in Hebrew history. By the strong action of Ezra and Nehemiah the mixed marriages were dissolved, and from that time the Jewish people became, as they never were before, exclusive and separate. Where nature would have led the nation ceased to go. More and more strictly the law was enforced; the age of puritanism began. So, let us say, the sore discipline had its fruit.

And yet it is with a reservation only we can enjoy the success of those reformers who drew the sharp line between Israel and his heathen neighbours, between Jew and Gentile. The vehemence of reaction urged the nation towards another error—Pharisaism. Nothing could be purer, nothing nobler than the desire to make Israel a holy people. But to inspire men with religious zeal and yet preserve them from spiritual pride is always difficult, and in truth those Hebrew reformers did not see the danger. There came to be, in the new development of faith, zeal enough, jealousy enough, for the purity of religion and life, but along with these a contempt for the heathen, a fierce enmity towards the uncircumcised, which made the interval till Christ appeared a time of strife and bloodshed worse than any that had been before. From the beginning the Hebrews were called with a holy calling, and their future was bound up with their faithfulness to it. Their ideal was to be earnest and pure, without bitterness or vainglory; and that is still the ideal of faith. But the Jewish people like ourselves, weak through the flesh, came short of the mark on one side or passed beyond it on the other. During the long period from Joshua to Nehemiah there was too little heat, and then a fire was kindled which burned a sharp narrow path, along which the life of Israel has gone with ever-lessening spiritual force. The unfulfilled ideal still waits, the unique destiny of this people of God still bears them on.

Bochim is a symbol. There the people wept for a transgression but half understood and a peril they could not rightly dread. There was genuine sorrow, there was genuine alarm. But it was the prophetic word, not personal experience, that moved the assembly. And as at Florence, when Savonarola's word, shaking with alarm a people who had no vision of holiness, left them morally weaker as it fell into silence, so the weeping at Bochim passed like a tempest that has bowed and broken the forest trees. The chiefs of Israel returned to their settlements with a new sense of duty and peril; but Canaanite civilisation had attractions, Canaanite women a refinement which captivated the heart. And the civilisation, the refinement, were associated with idolatry, The myths of Canaan, the poetry of Tammuz and Astarte, were fascinating and seductive. We wonder not that the pure faith of God was corrupted, but that it survived. In Egypt the heathen worship was in a foreign tongue, but in Canaan the stories of the gods were whispered to Israelites in a language they knew, by their own kith and kin. In many a home among the mountains of Ephraim or the skirts of Lebanon the pagan wife, with her superstitious fears, her dread of the anger of this god or that goddess, wrought so on the mind of the Jewish husband that he began to feel her dread and then to permit and share her sacrifices. Thus idolatry invaded Israel, and the long and weary struggle between truth and falsehood began.

We have spoken of Bochim as a symbol, and to us it may be the symbol of this, that the very thing which men put from them in horror and with tears, seeing the evil, the danger of it, does often insinuate itself into their lives. The messenger is heard, and while he speaks how near God is, how awful is the sense of His being! A thrill of keen feeling passes from soul to soul. There are some in the gathering who have more spiritual insight than the rest, and their presence raises the heat of emotion. But the moment of revelation and of fervour passes, the company breaks up, and very soon those who have won no vision of holiness, who have only feared as they entered into the cloud, are in the common world again. The finer strings of the soul were made to thrill, the conscience was touched; but if the will has not been braced, if the man's reason and resoluteness are not engaged by a new conception of life, the earthly will resume control and God will be less known than before. So there are many cast down to-day, crying to God in trouble of soul for evil done or evil which they are tempted to do, who to-morrow among the Canaanites will see things in another light. A man cannot be a recluse. He must mingle in business and in society with those who deride the thoughts that have moved him and laugh at his seriousness. The impulse to something better soon exhausts itself in this cold atmosphere. He turns upon his own emotion with contempt. The words that came with Divine urgency, the man whose face was like that of an angel of God, are already subjects of uneasy jesting, will soon be thrust from memory. Over the interlude of superficial anxiety the mind goes back to its old haunts, its old plans and cravings. The religious teacher, while he is often in no way responsible for this sad recoil, should yet be ever on his guard against the risk of weakening the moral fibre, of leaving men as Christ never left them, flaccid and infirm.

Again, there are cases that belong not to the history of a day, but to the history of a life. One may say, when he hears the strangely tempting voices that whisper in the twilight streets, "Am I a dog that from the holy traditions of my people and country I should fall away to these?" At first he flies the distasteful entreaty of the new nature-cult, its fleshly art and song, its nefarious science. But the voices are persistent. It is the perfecting of man and woman to which they invite. It is not vice, but freedom, brightness, life and the courage to enjoy it they cunningly propose. There is not much of sweetness; the voices rise, they become stringent and overbearing. If the man would not be a fool, would not lose the good of the age into which he is born, he will be done with unnatural restraints, the bondage of purity. Thus entreaty passes into mastery. Here is truth; there also seems to be fact. Little by little the subtle argument is so advanced that the degradation once feared is no longer to be seen. It is progress now; it is full development, the assertion of power and privilege, that the soul anticipates. How fatal is the lure, how treacherous the vision, the man discovers when he has parted with that which even through deepest penitence he may never regain. People are denying, and it has to be reasserted, that there is a covenant which the soul of man has to keep with God. The thought is "archaic," and they would banish it. But it stands the great reality for man; and to keep that covenant in the grace of the Divine Spirit, in the love of the holiest, in the sacred manliness learned of Christ, is the only way to the broad daylight and the free summits of life. How can nature be a saviour? The suggestion is childish. Nature, as we all know, allows the hypocrite, the swindler, the traitor, as well as the brave, honest man, the pure, sweet woman. Is it said that man has a covenant with nature? On the temporal and prudential side of his activities that is true. He has relations with nature which must be apprehended, must be wisely realised. But the spiritual kingdom to which he belongs requires a wider outlook, loftier aims and hopes. The efforts demanded by nature have to be brought into harmony with those diviner aspirations. Man is bound to be prudent, brave, wise for eternity. He is warned of his own sin and urged to fly from it. This is the covenant with God which is wrought into the very constitution of his moral being.

It would be a mistake to suppose that the scene at Bochim and the words which moved the assembly to tears had no lasting effect whatever. The history deals with outstanding facts of the national development. We hear chiefly of heroes and their deeds, but we shall not doubt that there were minds which kept the glow of truth and the consecration of penitential tears. The best lives of the people moved quietly on, apart from the commotions and strifes of the time. Rarely are the great political names even of a religious community those of holy and devout men, and, undoubtedly, this was true of Israel in the time of the judges. If we were to reckon only by those who appear conspicuously in these pages, we should have to wonder how the spiritual strain of thought and feeling survived. But it did survive; it gained in clearness and force. There were those in every tribe who kept alive the sacred traditions of Sinai and the desert, and Levites throughout the land did much to maintain among the people the worship of God. The great names of Abraham and Moses, the story of their faith and deeds, were the text of many an impressive lesson. So the light of piety did not go out; Jehovah was ever the Friend of Israel, even in its darkest day, for in the heart of the nation there never ceased to be a faithful remnant maintaining the fear and obedience of the Holy Name.

CHAPTER IV.

AMONG THE ROCKS OF PAGANISM.

JUDGES ii. 7-23.

"AND Joshua the son of Nun, the servant of the Lord, died, being an hundred and ten years old. And they buried him in the border of his inheritance in Timnath-heres, in the hill country of Ephraim, on the north of the mountain of Gaash." So, long after the age of Joshua, the historian tells again how Israel lamented its great chief, and he seems to feel even more than did the people of the time the pathos and significance of the event. How much a man of God has been to his generation those rarely know who stand beside his grave. Through faith in him faith in the Eternal has been sustained, many who have a certain piety of their own depending, more than they have been aware, upon their contact with him. A glow went from him which insensibly raised to something like religious warmth souls that apart from such an influence would have been of the world worldly. Joshua succeeded Moses as the mediator of the covenant. He was the living witness of all that had been done in the Exodus and at Sinai. So long as he continued with Israel, even in the feebleness of old age, appearing, and no more, a venerable figure in the council of the tribes, there was a representative of Divine order, one who testified to the promises of God and the duty of His people. The elders who outlived him were not men like himself, for they added nothing to faith; yet they preserved the idea at least of the theocracy, and when they passed away the period of Israel's robust youth was at an end. It is this the historian perceives, and his review of the following age in the passage we are now to consider is darkened throughout by the cloudy and troubled atmosphere that overcame the fresh morning of faith.

We know the great design that should have made Israel a singular and triumphant example to the nations of the world. The body politic was to have its unity in no elected government, in no hereditary ruler, but in the law and worship of its Divine King, sustained by the ministry of priest and prophet. Every tribe, every family, every soul was to be equally and directly subject to the Holy Will as expressed in the law and by the oracles of the sanctuary. The idea was that order should be maintained and the life of the tribes should go on under the pressure of the unseen Hand, never resisted, never shaken off, and full of bounty always to a trustful and obedient people. There might be times when the head men of tribes and families should have to come together in council, but it would be only to discover speedily and carry out with one accord the purpose of Jehovah. Rightly do we regard this as an inspired vision; it is at once simple and majestic. When a nation can so live and order its affairs it will have solved the great problem of government still exercising every civilised community. The Hebrews never realised the theocracy, and at the time of the settlement in Canaan they came far short of understanding it. "Israel had as yet scarcely found time to imbue its spirit deeply with the great truths which had been awakened into life in it, and thus to appropriate them as an invaluable possession: the vital principle of that religion and nationality by which it had so wondrously triumphed was still scarcely understood when it was led into manifold severe trials."* Thus, while Hebrew history presents for the most part the aspect of an impetuous river broken and jarred by rocks and boulders, rarely settling into a calm expanse of mirror-like water, during the period of the judges the stream is seen almost arrested in the difficult country through which it has to force its way. It is divided by many a crag and often hidden for considerable stretches by overhanging cliffs. It plunges in cataracts and foams hotly in cauldrons of hollowed rock. Not till Samuel appears is there anything like success for this nation, which is of no account if not earnestly religious, and never is religious without a stern and capable chief, at once prophet and judge, a leader in worship and a restorer of order and unity among the tribes.

The general survey or preface which we have before us gives but one account of the disasters that befell the Hebrew people—they "followed other gods, and provoked the Lord to anger." And the reason of this has to be considered. Taking a natural view of the circumstances, we might pronounce it almost impossible for the tribes to maintain their unity when they were fighting, each in its own district, against powerful enemies. It seems by no means wonderful that nature had its way, and that, weary of war, the people tended to seek rest in friendly intercourse and alliance with their neighbours. Were Judah and Simeon always to fight, though their own territory was secure? Was Ephraim to be the constant champion of the weaker tribes and never settle down to till the land? It was almost more than could be expected of men who had the common amount of selfishness. Occasionally, when all were threatened, there was a combination of the scattered clans, but for the most part each had to fight its own battle, and so the unity of life and faith was broken. Nor can we marvel at the neglect of worship and the falling away from Jehovah when we find so many who have been always surrounded by Christian influences drifting into a strange unconcern as to religious obligation and privilege. The writer of the Book of Judges, however, regards things from the standpoint of a high Divine ideal—the calling and duty of a God-made nation. Men are apt to frame excuses for themselves and each other; this historian makes no excuses. Where

* Ewald.

we might speak compassionately he speaks in sternness. He is bound to tell the story from God's side, and from God's side he tells it with puritan directness. In a sense it might go sorely against the grain to speak of his ancestors as sinning grievously and meriting condign punishment. But later generations needed to hear the truth, and he would utter it without evasion. It is surely Nathan, or some other prophet of Samuel's line, who lays bare with such faithfulness the infidelity of Israel. He is writing for the men of his own time and also for men who are to come; he is writing for us, and his main theme is the stern justice of Jehovah's government. God bestows privileges which men must value and use, or they shall suffer. When He declares Himself and gives His law, let the people see to it; let them encourage and constrain each other to obey. Disobedience brings unfailing penalty. This is the spirit of the passage we are considering. Israel is God's possession, and is bound to be faithful. There is no Lord but Jehovah, and it is unpardonable for any Israelite to turn aside and worship a false God. The pressure of circumstances, often made much of, is not considered for a moment. The weakness of human nature, the temptations to which men and women are exposed, are not taken into account. Was there little faith, little spirituality? Every soul had its own responsibility for the decay, since to every Israelite Jehovah had revealed His love and addressed His call. Inexorable therefore was the demand for obedience. Religion is stern because reasonable, not an impossible service as easy human nature would fain prove it. If men disbelieve they incur doom, and it must fall upon them.

Joshua and his generation having been gathered unto their fathers, "there arose another generation which knew not the Lord, nor yet the work which He had wrought for Israel. And the children of Israel did that which was evil in the sight of the Lord, and served the Baalim." How common is the fall traced in these brief, stern words, the wasting of a sacred testimony that seemed to be deeply graven upon the heart of a race! The fathers felt and knew; the sons have only traditional knowledge and it never takes hold of them. The link of faith between one generation and another is not strongly forged; the most convincing proofs of God are not recounted. Here is a man who has learned his own weakness, who has drained a bitter cup of discipline—how can he better serve his sons than by telling them the story of his own mistakes and sins, his own suffering and repentance? Here is one who in dark and trying times has found solace and strength and has been lifted out of horror and despair by the merciful hand of God—how can he do a father's part without telling his children of his defeats and deliverance, the extremity to which he was reduced and the restoring grace of Christ? But men hide their weaknesses, and are ashamed to confess that they ever passed through the Valley of Humiliation. They leave their own children unwarned to fall into the sloughs in which themselves were wellnigh swallowed up. Even when they have erected some Ebenezer, some monument of Divine succour, they often fail to bring their children to the spot, and speak to them there with fervent recollection of the goodness of the Lord. Was Solomon when a boy led by David to the town of Gath, and told by him the story of his cowardly fear, and how he fled from the face of Saul to seek refuge among Philistines? Was Absalom in his youth ever taken to the plains of Bethlehem and shown where his father fed the flocks, a poor shepherd lad, when the prophet sent for him to be anointed the coming King of Israel? Had these young princes learned in frank conversation with their father all he had to tell of temptation and transgression, of danger and redemption, perhaps the one would never have gone astray in his pride nor the other died a rebel in that wood of Ephraim. The Israelitish fathers were like many fathers still, they left the minds of their boys and girls uninstructed in life, uninstructed in the providence of God, and this in open neglect of the law which marked out their duty for them with clear injunction, recalling the themes and incidents on which they were to dwell.

One passage in the history of the past must have been vividly before the minds of those who crossed the Jordan under Joshua, and should have stood a protest and warning against the idolatry into which families so easily lapsed throughout the land. Over at Shittim, when Israel lay encamped on the skirts of the mountains of Moab, a terrible sentence of Moses had fallen like a thunderbolt. On some high place near the camp a festival of Midianitish idolatry, licentious in the extreme, attracted great numbers of Hebrews; they went astray after the worst fashion of paganism, and the nation was polluted in the idolatrous orgies. Then Moses gave judgment—" Take the heads of the people and hang them up before the Lord, against the sun." And while that hideous row of stakes, each bearing the transfixed body of a guilty chief, witnessed in the face of the sun for the Divine ordinance of purity, there fell a plague that carried off twenty-four thousand of the transgressors. Was that forgotten? Did the terrible punishment of those who sinned in the matter of Baal-peor not haunt the memories of men when they entered the land of Baal-worship? No: like others, they were able to forget. Human nature is facile, and from a great horror of judgment can turn in quick recovery of the usual ease and confidence. Men have been in the valley of the shadow of death, where the mouth of hell is; they have barely escaped; but when they return upon it from another side they do not recognise the landmarks nor feel the need of being on their guard. They teach their children many things, but neglect to make them aware of that right-seeming way the end whereof are the ways of death.

The worship of the Baalim and Ashtaroth and the place which this came to have in Hebrew life require our attention here. Canaan had for long been more or less subject to the influence of Chaldea and Egypt, and "had received the imprint of their religious ideas. The fish-god of Babylon reappears at Ascalon in the form of Dagon, the name of the goddess Astarte and her character seem to be adapted from the Babylonian Ishtar. Perhaps these divinities were introduced at a time when part of the Canaanite tribes lived on the borders of the Persian Gulf, in daily contact with the inhabitants of Chaldea." * The Egyptian Isis and Osiris, again, are closely connected with the Tammuz and Astarte wor-

* Maspero.

shipped in Phœnicia. In a general way it may be said that all the races inhabiting Syria had the same religion, but "each tribe, each people, each town had its Lord, its Master, its Baal, designated by a particular title for distinction from the masters or Baals of neighbouring cities. The gods adored at Tyre and Sidon were called Baal-Sur, the Master of Tyre; Baal-Sidon, the Master of Sidon. The highest among them, those that impersonated in its purity the conception of heavenly fire, were called kings of the gods. El or Kronos reigned at Byblos; Chemosh among the Moabites; Amman among the children of Ammon; Soutkhu among the Hittites." Melcarth, the Baal of the world of death, was the Master of Tyre. Each Baal was associated with a female divinity, who was the mistress of the town, the queen of the heavens. The common name of these goddesses was Astarte. There was an Ashtoreth of Chemosh among the Moabites. The Ashtoreth of the Hittites was called Tanit. There was an Ashtoreth Karnaim or Horned, so called with reference to the crescent moon; and another was Ashtoreth Naamah, the good Astarte. In short, a special Astarte could be created by any town and named by any fancy, and Baals were multiplied in the same way. It is, therefore, impossible to assign any distinct character to these inventions. The Baalim mostly represented forces of nature—the sun, the stars. The Astartes presided over love, birth, the different seasons of the year, and—war. "The multitude of secondary Baalim and Ashtaroth tended to resolve themselves into a single supreme pair, in comparison with whom the others had little more than a shadowy existence." As the sun and moon outshine all the other heavenly bodies, so two principal deities representing them were supreme.

The worship connected with this horde of fanciful beings is well known to have merited the strongest language of detestation applied to it by the Hebrew prophets. The ceremonies were a strange and degrading blend of the licentious and the cruel, notorious even in a time of gross and hideous rites. The Baalim were supposed to have a fierce and envious disposition, imperiously demanding the torture and death not only of animals but of men. The horrible notion had taken root that in times of public danger king and nobles must sacrifice their children in fire for the pleasure of the god. And while nothing of this sort was done for the Ashtaroth their demands were in one aspect even more vile. Self-mutilation, self-defilement were acts of worship, and in the great festivals men and women gave themselves up to debauchery which cannot be described. No doubt some of the observances of this paganism were mild and simple. Feasts there were at the seasons of reaping and vintage which were of a bright and comparatively harmless character; and it was by taking part in these that Hebrew families began their acquaintance with the heathenism of the country. But the tendency of polytheism is ever downward. It springs from a curious and ignorant dwelling on the mysterious processes of nature, untamed fancy personifying the causes of all that is strange and horrible, constantly wandering therefore into more grotesque and lawless dreams of unseen powers and their claims on man. The imagination of the worshipper, which passes beyond his power of action, attributes to the gods energy more vehement, desires more sweeping, anger more dreadful than he finds in himself. He thinks of beings who are strong in appetite and will and yet under no restraint or responsibility. In the beginning polytheism is not necessarily vile and cruel; but it must become so as it develops. The minds by whose fancies the gods are created and furnished with adventures are able to conceive characters vehemently cruel, wildly capricious and impure. But how can they imagine a character great in wisdom, holiness, and justice? The additions of fable and belief made from age to age may hold in solution some elements that are good, some of man's yearning for the noble and true beyond him. The better strain, however, is overborne in popular talk and custom by the tendency to fear rather than to hope in presence of unknown powers, the necessity which is felt to avert possible anger of the gods or make sure of their patronage. Sacrifices are multiplied, the offerer exerting himself more and more to gain his main point at whatever expense; while he thinks of the world of gods as a region in which there is jealousy of man's respect and a multitude of rival claims all of which must be met. Thus the whole moral atmosphere is thrown into confusion.

Into a polytheism of this kind came Israel, to whom had been committed a revelation of the one true God, and in the first moment of homage at heathen altars the people lost the secret of its strength. Certainly Jehovah was not abandoned; He was thought of still as the Lord of Israel. But He was now one among many who had their rights and could repay the fervent worshipper. At one high-place it was Jehovah men sought, at another the Baal of the hill and his Ashtoreth. Yet Jehovah was still the special patron of the Hebrew tribes and of no others, and in trouble they turned to Him for relief. So in the midst of mythology Divine faith had to struggle for existence. The stone pillars which the Israelites erected were mostly to the name of God, but Hebrews danced with Hittite and Jebusite around the poles of Astarte, and in revels of nature-worship they forgot their holy traditions, lost their vigour of body and soul. The doom of apostasy fulfilled itself. They were unable to stand before their enemies. "The hand of the Lord was against them for evil, and they were greatly distressed."

And why could not Israel rest in the debasement of idolatry? Why did not the Hebrews abandon their distinct mission as a nation and mingle with the races they came to convert or drive away? They could not rest; they could not mingle and forget. Is there ever peace in the soul of a man who falls from early impressions of good to join the licentious and the profane? He has still his own personality, shot through with recollections of youth and traits inherited from godly ancestors. It is impossible for him to be at one with his new companions in their revelry and vice. He finds that from which his soul revolts, he feels disgust which he has to overcome by a strong effort of perverted will. He despises his associates and knows in his inmost heart that he is of a different race. Worse he may become than they, but he is never the same. So was it in the degradation of the Israelites, both individually and as a nation. From complete absorption among the peoples of Canaan they were preserved by hereditary influences which were part of their very life, by holy thoughts and hopes embodied in their national history, by the rags of that conscience which remained from the law-giving of Moses and the discipline of the wilderness. Moreover, akin as they were to the idolatrous races, they had a feeling of closer kinship with each other, tribe with tribe, family with family; and the worship of God at the little-frequented shrine still maintained the shadow at least of the national consecration. They were a people apart, these Beni-Israel, a people of higher rank than Amorites or Perizzites, Hittites or Phœnicians. Even when least alive to their destiny they were still held by it, led on secretly by that heavenly hand which never let them go. From time to time souls were born among them aglow with devout eagerness, confident in the faith of God. The tribes were roused out of lethargy by voices that woke many recollections of half-forgotten purpose and hope. Now from Judah in the south, now from Ephraim in the centre, now from Dan or Gilead a cry was raised. For a time at least manhood was quickened, national feeling became keen, the old faith was partly revived, and God had again a witness in His people.

We have found the writer of the Book of Judges consistent and unfaltering in his condemnation of Israel; he is equally consistent and eager in his vindication of God. It is to him no doubtful thing, but an assured fact, that the Holy One came with Israel from Paran and marched with the people from Seir. He has no hesitation in ascribing to Divine providence and grace the deeds of those men who go by the name of judges. It startles and even confounds some to note the plain direct terms in which God is made, so to speak, responsible for those rude warriors whose exploits we are to review,—for Ehud, for Jephthah, for Samson. The men are children of their age, vehement, often reckless, not answering to the Christian ideal of heroism. They do rough work in a rough way. If we found their history elsewhere than in the Bible we should be disposed to class them with the Roman Horatius, the Saxon Hereward, the Jutes Hengest and Horsa, and hardly dare to call them men of God's hand. But here they are presented bearing the stamp of a Divine vocation; and in the New Testament it is emphatically reaffirmed. "What shall I more say? for the time will fail me if I tell of Gideon, Barak, Samson, Jephthah; . . . who through faith subdued kingdoms, wrought righteousness, obtained promises, . . . waxed mighty in war, turned to flight armies of aliens."

There is a crude religious sentimentalism to which the Bible gives no countenance. Where we, mistaking the meaning of providence because we do not rightly believe in immortality, are apt to think with horror of the miseries of men, the vigorous veracity of sacred writers directs our thought to the moral issues of life and the vast movements of God's purifying design. Where we, ignorant of much that goes to the making of a world, lament the seeming confusion and the errors, the Bible seer discerns that the cup of red wine poured out is in the hand of Almighty Justice and Wisdom. It is of a piece with the superficial feeling of modern society to doubt whether God could have any share in the deeds of Jephthah and the career of Samson, whether these could have any place in the Divine order. Look at Christ and His infinite compassion, it is said; read that God is love, and then reconcile if you can this view of His character with the idea which makes Barak and Gideon His ministers. Out of all such perplexities there is a straight way. You make light of moral evil and individual responsibility when you say that this war or that pestilence has no Divine mission. You deny eternal righteousness when you question whether a man, vindicating it in the time-sphere, can have a Divine vocation. The man is but a human instrument. True. He is not perfect, he is not even spiritual. True. Yet if there is in him a gleam of right and earnest purpose, if he stands above his time in virtue of an inward light which shows him but a single truth, and in the spirit of that strikes his blow—is it to be denied that within his limits he is a weapon of the holiest Providence, a helper of eternal grace?

The storm, the pestilence have a providential errand. They urge men to prudence and effort; they prevent communities from settling on their lees. But the hero has a higher range of usefulness. It is not mere prudence he represents, but the passion for justice. For right against might, for liberty against oppression he contends, and in striking his blow he compels his generation to take into account morality and the will of God. He may not see far, but at least he stirs inquiry as to the right way, and though thousands die in the conflict he awakens there is a real gain which the coming age inherits. Such a one, however faulty, however, as we may say, earthly, is yet far above mere earthly levels. His moral concepts may be poor and low compared with ours; but the heat that moves him is not of sense, not of clay. Obstructed it is by the ignorance and sin of our human estate, nevertheless it is a supernatural power, and so far as it works in any degree for righteousness, freedom, the realisation of God, the man is a hero of faith.

We do not affirm here that God approves or inspires all that is done by the leaders of a suffering people in the way of vindicating what they deem their rights. Moreover, there are claims and rights so-called for which it is impious to shed a drop of blood. But if the state of humanity is such that the Son of God must die for it, is there any room to wonder that men have to die for it? Given a cause like that of Israel, a need of the whole world which Israel only could meet, and the men who unselfishly, at the risk of death, did their part in the front of the struggle which that cause and that need demanded, though they slew their thousands, were not men of whom the Christian teacher needs be afraid to speak. And there have been many such in all nations, for the principle by which we judge is of the broadest application,—men who have led the forlorn hopes of nations, driven back the march of tyrants, given law and order to an unsettled land.

Judge after judge was "raised up"—the word is true—and rallied the tribes of Israel, and while each lived there were renewed energy and prosperity. But the moral revival was never in the deeps of life and no deliverance was permanent. It is only a faithful nation that can use freedom. Neither trouble nor release from trouble will certainly make either a man or a people steadily true to the best. Unless there is along with trouble a conviction of spiritual need and failure, men will forget the prayers and vows they made in their extremity. Thus in the history of Israel, as in the history of many a soul, periods of suffering and of prosperity succeed each other and there is no distinct growth of the religious life. All these experiences are meant to throw men back upon the seriousness of duty, and the great purpose God has in their existence. We must repent not because we are in pain or grief, but because we are estranged from the Holy One and have denied the God of Salvation. Until the soul comes to this it only struggles out of one pit to fall into another.

CHAPTER V.

THE ARM OF ARAM AND OF OTHNIEL.

JUDGES iii. 1-11.

WE come now to a statement of no small importance, which may be the cause of some perplexity. It is emphatically affirmed that God fulfilled His design for Israel by leaving around it in Canaan a circle of vigorous tribes very unlike each other, but alike in this, that each presented to the Hebrews a civilisation from which something might be learned but much had to be dreaded, a seductive form of paganism which ought to have been entirely resisted, an aggressive energy fitted to rouse their national feeling. We learn that Israel was led along a course of development resembling that by which other nations have advanced to unity and strength. As the Divine plan is unfolded, it is seen that not by undivided possession of the Promised Land, not by swift and fierce clearing away of opponents, was Israel to reach its glory and become Jehovah's witness, but in the way of patient fidelity amidst temptations, by long struggle and arduous discipline. And why should this cause perplexity? If moral education did not move on the same line for all peoples in every age, then indeed mankind would be put to intellectual confusion. There was never any other way for Israel than for the rest of the world.

"These are the nations which the Lord left to prove Israel by them, to know whether they would hearken unto the commandments of the Lord." The first-named are the Philistines, whose settlements on the coast-plain toward Egypt were growing in power. They were a maritime race, apparently much like the Danish invaders of Saxon England, sea-rovers or pirates, ready for any fray that promised spoil. In the great coalition of peoples that fell on Egypt during the reign of Ramses III., about the year 1260 B.C., Philistines were conspicuous, and after the crushing defeat of the expedition they appear in larger numbers on the coast of Canaan. Their cities were military republics skilfully organised, each with a *seren* or war-chief, the chiefs of the hundred cities forming a council of federation. Their origin is not known; but we may suppose them to have been a branch of the Amorite family, who after a time of adventure were returning to their early haunts. It may be reckoned certain that in wealth and civilisation they presented a marked contrast to the Israelites, and their equipments of all kinds gave them great advantage in the arts of war and peace. Even in the period of the Judges there were imposing temples in the Philistine cities and the worship must have been carefully ordered. How they compared with the Hebrews in domestic life we have no means of judging, but there was certainly some barrier of race, language, or custom between the peoples which made intermarriage very rare. We can suppose that they looked upon the Hebrews from their higher worldly level as rude and slavish. Military adventurers not unwilling to sell their services for gold would be apt to despise a race half-nomad, half-rural. It was in war, not in peace, that Philistine and Hebrew met, contempt on either side gradually changing into keenest hatred as century after century the issue of battle was tried with varying success. And it must be said that it was well for the tribes of Jehovah rather to be in occasional subjection to the Philistines, and so learn to dread them, than to mix freely with those by whom the great ideas of Hebrew life were despised.

On the northward sea-board a quite different race, the Zidonians, or Phœnicians, were in one sense better neighbours to the Israelites, in another sense no better friends. While the Philistines were haughty, aristocratic, military, the Phœnicians were the great *bourgeoisie* of the period, clever, enterprising, eminently successful in trade. Like the other Canaanites and the ancestors of the Jews, they were probably immigrants from the lower Euphrates valley; unlike the others, they brought with them habits of commerce and skill in manufacture, for which they became famous along the Mediterranean shores and beyond the pillars of Hercules. Between Philistine and Phœnician the Hebrew was mercifully protected from the absorbing interests of commercial life and the disgrace of prosperous piracy. The conscious superiority of the coast peoples in wealth and influence and the material elements of civilisation was itself a guard to the Jews, who had their own sense of dignity, their own claim to assert. The configuration of the country helped the separateness of Israel, especially so far as Phœnicia was concerned, which lay mainly beyond the rampart of Lebanon and the gorge of the Litâny; while with the fortress of Tyre on the hither side of the natural frontier there appears to have been for a long time no intercourse, probably on account of its peculiar position. But the spirit of Phœnicia was the great barrier. Along the crowded wharves of Tyre and Zidon, in warehouses and markets, factories and workshops, a hundred industries were in full play, and in their luxurious dwellings the busy prosperous traders, with their silk-clad wives, enjoyed the pleasures of the age. From all this the Hebrew, rough and unkempt, felt himself shut out, perhaps with a touch of regret, perhaps with scorn equal to that on the other side. He had to live his life apart from that busy race, apart from its vivacity and enterprise, apart from its lubricity and worldliness. The contempt of the world is ill to bear, and the Jew no doubt found it so. But it was good for him. The tribes had time to consolidate, the religion of Jehovah became established before Phœnicia thought it worth while to court her neighbour. Early indeed the idolatry of the one people infected the other and there were the beginnings of trade, yet on the whole for many centuries they kept apart. Not till a king throned in Jerusalem could enter into alliance with a king of Tyre, crown with crown, did there come to be that intimacy which had so much risk for the Hebrew. The humbleness and poverty of Israel during the early centuries of its history in Canaan was a providential safeguard. God would not lose His people, nor suffer it to forget its mission.

Among the inland races with whom the Israelites are said to have dwelt, the Amorites, though mentioned along with Perizzites and Hivites, had very distinct characteristics. They were a mountain people like the Scottish Highlanders, even in physiognomy much resembling them, a tall, white-skinned, blue-eyed race. Warlike we know they were, and the Egyptian representation of the siege of Dapur by Ramses II. shows what is supposed to be the standard of the Amorites on the highest tower, a shield pierced by three arrows surmounted by another arrow fastened across the top of the staff. On the east of Jordan they were defeated by the Israelites and their land between Arnon and Jabbok was allotted to Reuben and Gad. In the west they seem to have held their ground in isolated fortresses or small clans, so energetic and troublesome that it is specially noted in Samuel's time that a great defeat of the Philistines brought peace between Israel and the Amorites. A significant reference in the description of Ahab's idolatry—"he did very abominably in following idols according to all things as did the Amorites"—shows the religion of these people to have been Baal-worship of the grossest kind; and we may well suppose that by intermixture with them especially the faith of Israel was debased. Even now, it may be said, the Amorite is still in the land; a blue-eyed, fair-complexioned type survives, representing that ancient stock.

Passing some tribes whose names imply rather geographical than ethnical distinctions, we come to the Hittites, the powerful people of whom in recent years we have learned something. At one time these Hittites were practically masters of the wide region from Ephesus in the west of Asia Minor to Carchemish on the Euphrates, and from the shores of the Black Sea to the south of Palestine. They appear to us in the archives of Thebes and the poem of the Laureate, Pentaur, as the great adversaries of Egypt in the days of Ramses I. and his successors; and one of the most interesting records is of the battle fought about 1383 B. C. at Kadesh on the Orontes, between the immense armies of the two nations, the Egyptians being led by Ramses II. Amazing feats were attributed to Ramses, but he was compelled to treat on equal terms with the "great king of Kheta," and the war was followed by a marriage between the Pharaoh and the daughter of the Hittite prince. Syria too was given up to the latter as his legitimate possession. The treaty of peace drawn up on the occasion, in the name of the chief gods of Egypt and of the Hittites, included a compact of offensive and defensive alliance and careful provisions for extradition of fugitives and criminals. Throughout it there is evident a great dependence upon the company of gods of either land, who are largely invoked to punish those who break and reward those who keep its terms. "He who shall observe these commandments which the silver tablet contains, whether he be of the people of Kheta or of the people of Egypt, because he has not neglected them, the company of the gods of the land of Kheta and the company of the gods of the land of Egypt shall secure his reward and preserve life for him and his servants."* From this time the Amorites of southern Palestine and the minor Canaanite peoples submitted to the Hittite dominion, and it was while this subjection lasted that the Israelites under Joshua appeared on the scene. There can be no doubt that the tremendous conflict with Egypt had exhausted the population of Canaan and wasted the country, and so prepared the way for the success of Israel. The Hittites indeed were strong enough, had they seen fit to oppose with great armies the new comers into Syria. But the centre of their power lay far to the north, perhaps in Cappadocia; and on the frontier towards Nineveh they were engaged with more formidable opponents. We may also surmise that the Hittites, whose alliance with Egypt was by Joshua's time somewhat decayed, would look upon the Hebrews, to begin with, as fugitives from the misrule of the Pharaoh who might be counted upon to take arms against their former oppressors. This would account, in part at least, for the indifference with which the Israelite settlement in Canaan was regarded; it explains why no vigorous attempt was made to drive back the tribes.

For the characteristics of the Hittites, whose appearance and dress constantly suggest a Mongolian origin, we can now consult their monuments. A vigorous people they must have been, capable of government, of extensive organisation, concerned to perfect their arts as well as to increase their power. Original contributors to civilisation they probably were not, but they had skill to use what they found and spread it widely. Their worship of Sutekh or Soutkhu, and especially of Astarte under the name of Ma, who reappears in the Great Diana of Ephesus, must have been very elaborate. A single Cappadocian city is reported to have had at one time six thousand armed priestesses and eunuchs of that goddess. In Palestine there were not many of this distinct and energetic people when the Hebrews crossed the Jordan. A settlement seems to have remained about Hebron, but the armies had withdrawn; Kadesh on the Orontes was the nearest garrison. One peculiar institution of Hittite religion was the holy city, which afforded sanctuary to fugitives; and it is notable that some of these cities in Canaan, such as Kadesh-Naphtali and Hebron, are found among the Hebrew cities of refuge.

It was as a people at once enticed and threatened, invited to peace and constantly provoked to war, that Israel settled in the circle of Syrian nations. After the first conflicts, ending in the defeat of Adoni-bezek and the capture of Hebron and Kiriath-sepher, the Hebrews had an acknowledged place, partly won by their prowess, partly by the terror of Jehovah which accompanied their arms. To Philistines, Phœnicians and Hittites, as we have seen, their coming mattered little, and the other races had to make the best of affairs, sometimes able to hold their ground, sometimes forced to give way. The Hebrew tribes, for their part, were, on the whole, too ready to live at peace and to yield not a little for the sake of peace. Intermarriages made their position safer, and they intermarried with Amorites, Hivites, Perizzites. Interchange of goods was profitable, and they engaged in barter. The observance of frontiers and covenants helped to make things smooth, and they agreed on boundary lines of territory and terms of fraternal intercourse. The acknowledgment of their neighbours' religion was the next thing, and from that they did not shrink. The new neighbours were practically superior to themselves in many ways, well-informed as to the soil, the climate, the methods of tillage necessary in the land, well able to teach useful arts and simple manufactures. Little by little the debasing notions and bad customs that infest pagan society entered Hebrew homes. Comfort and prosperity came; but comfort was dearly bought with loss of pureness, and prosperity with loss of faith. The watchwords of unity were forgotten by many. But for the sore oppressions of which the Mesopotamian was the first, the tribes would have gradually lost all coherence and vigour and become like those poor tatters of races that dragged out an inglorious existence between Jordan and the Mediterranean plain.

Yet it is with nations as with men; those that have a reason of existence and the desire to realise it, even at intervals, may fall away into pitiful languor if corrupted by prosperity, but when the need comes their spirit will be renewed. While Hivites, Perizzites, and even Amorites had practically nothing to live for, but only cared to live, the Hebrews felt oppression and restraint in their inmost marrow. What the faithful servants of God among them urged in vain the iron heel of Cushan-rishathaim made them remember and realise—that they had a God from Whom they were basely departing, a birthright they were selling for pottage. In Doubting Castle, under the chains of Despair, they bethought them of the Almighty and His ancient promises, they cried unto the Lord. And it was not the cry of an afflicted church; Israel was far from deserving that name. Rather was it the cry of a prodigal people scarcely daring to hope that the Father would forgive and save.

Nothing yet found in the records of Babylon or Assyria throws any light on the invasion of Cushan-rishathaim, whose name, which seems to mean Cushan of the Two Evil Deeds, may be taken to represent his character as the Hebrews viewed it. He was a king one of whose predecessors a few centuries before had given a daughter in marriage to the third Amenophis of Egypt, and with her the Aramæan religion to the Nile valley. At that time Mesopotamia, or Aram-Naharaim, was one of the greatest monarchies of western Asia. Stretching along the Euphrates from the Khabour river towards Carchemish and away to the highlands of Armenia, it embraced the district in which Terah and Abram first settled when the family migrated from Ur of the Chaldees. In the days of the judges of Israel, however, the glory of Aram had faded. The Assyrians threatened its eastern frontier, and about 1325 B. C., the date at which we have now arrived, they laid waste the valley of the Khabour. We can suppose that the pressure of this rising empire was one cause of the expedition of Cushan towards the western sea.

It remains a question, however, why the Mesopotamian king should have been allowed to traverse the land of the Hittites, either by way of Damascus or the desert route that led past Tadmor, in order to fall on the Israelites; and there is this other question, What led him to think of attacking Israel especially among the dwellers in Canaan? In pursuing these inquiries we have at least presumption to guide us. Carchemish on the Euphrates was a great Hit-

---

* "The Hittites," by A. H. Sayce, LL. D., p. 36.

tite fortress commanding the fords of that deep and treacherous river. Not far from it, within the Mesopotamian country, was Pethor, which was at once a Hittite and an Aramæan town— Pethor the city of Balaam with whom the Hebrews had had to reckon shortly before they entered Canaan. Now Cushan-rishathaim, reigning in this region, occupied the middle ground between the Hittites and Assyria on the east, also between them and Babylon on the southeast; and it is probable that he was in close alliance with the Hittites. Suppose then that the Hittite king, who at first regarded the Hebrews with indifference, was now beginning to view them with distrust or to fear them as a people bent on their own ends, not to be reckoned on for help against Egypt, and we can easily see that he might be more than ready to assist the Mesopotamians in their attack on the tribes. To this we may add a hint which is derived from Balaam's connection with Pethor, and the kind of advice he was in the way of giving to those who consulted him. Does it not seem probable enough that some counsel of his survived his death and now guided the action of the king of Aram? Balaam, by profession a soothsayer, was evidently a great political personage of his time, foreseeing, crafty, and vindictive. Methods of his for suppressing Israel, the force of whose genius he fully recognised, were perhaps sold to more than one kingly employer. "The land of the children of his people" would almost certainly keep his counsel in mind and seek to avenge his death. Thus against Israel particularly among the dwellers in Canaan the arms of Cushan-rishathaim would be directed, and the Hittites, who scarcely found it needful to attack Israel for their own safety, would facilitate his march.

Here then we may trace the revival of a feud which seemed to have died away fifty years before. Neither nations nor men can easily escape from the enmity they have incurred and the entanglements of their history. When years have elapsed and strifes appear to have been buried in oblivion, suddenly, as if out of the grave, the past is apt to arise and confront us, sternly demanding the payment of its reckoning. We once did another grievous wrong, and now our fondly cherished belief that the man we injured had forgotten our injustice is completely dispelled. The old anxiety, the old terror breaks in afresh upon our lives. Or it was in doing our duty that we braved the enmity of evil-minded men and punished their crimes. But though they have passed away their bitter hatred, bequeathed to others, still survives. Now the battle of justice and fidelity has to be fought over again, and well is it for us if we are found ready in the strength of God.

And, in another aspect, how futile is the dream some indulge of getting rid of their history, passing beyond the memory or resurrection of what has been. Shall Divine forgiveness obliterate those deeds of which we have repented? Then the deeds being forgotten the forgiveness too would pass into oblivion, and all the gain of faith and gratitude it brought would be lost. Do we expect never to retrace in memory the way we have travelled? As well might we hope, retaining our personality, to become other men than we are. The past, good and evil, remains and will remain, that we may be kept humble and moved to ever-increasing thankfulness and fervour of soul. We rise "on stepping-stones of our dead selves to higher things," and every forgotten incident by which moral education has been provided for must return to light. The heaven we hope for is not to be one of forgetfulness, but a state bright and free through remembrance of the grace that saved us at every stage and the circumstances of our salvation. As yet we do not half know what God has done for us, what His providence has been. There must be a resurrection of old conflicts, strifes, defeats, and victories in order that we may understand the grace which is to keep us safe for ever.

Attacked by Cushan of the Two Crimes the Israelites were in evil case. They had not the consciousness of Divine support which sustained them once. They had forsaken Him whose presence in the camp made their arms victorious. Now they must face the consequences of their fathers' deeds without their fathers' heavenly courage. Had they still been a united nation full of faith and hope, the armies of Aram would have assailed them in vain. But they were without the spirit which the crisis required. For eight years the northern tribes had to bear a sore oppression, soldiers quartered in their cities, tribute exacted at the point of the sword, their harvests enjoyed by others. The stern lesson was taught them that Canaan was to be no peaceful habitation for a people that renounced the purpose of its existence. The struggle became more hopeless year by year, the state of affairs more wretched. So at last the tribes were driven by stress of persecution and calamity to call again on the name of God, and some faint hope of succour broke like a misty morning over the land.

It was from the far south that help came in response to the piteous cry of the oppressed in the north; the deliverer was Othniel, who has already appeared in the history. After his marriage with Achsah, daughter of Caleb, we must suppose him living as quietly as possible in his south-lying farm, there increasing in importance year by year till now he is a respected chief of the tribe of Judah. In frequent skirmishes with Arab marauders from the wilderness he has distinguished himself, maintaining the fame of his early exploit. Better still, he is one of those who have kept the great traditions of the nation, a man mindful of the law of God, deriving strength of character from fellowship with the Almighty. "The Spirit of Jehovah came upon him and he judged Israel; and he went out to war, and Jehovah delivered Cushan-rishathaim king of Mesopotamia into his hand."

"He judged Israel and went out to war." Significant is the order of these statements. The judging of Israel by this man, on whom the Spirit of Jehovah was, meant no doubt inquisition into the religious and moral state, condemnation of the idolatry of the tribes, and a restoration to some extent of the worship of God. In no other way could the strength of Israel be revived. The people had to be healed before they could fight, and the needed cure was spiritual. Hopeless invariably have been the efforts of oppressed peoples to deliver themselves unless some trust in a Divine power has given them heart for the struggle. When we see an army bow in prayer as one man before joining battle, as the Swiss did at Morat and the Scots at Bannockburn, we have faith in their spirit and courage, for they are feeling their dependence in the Supernatural. Othniel's first care was to suppress idolatry, to teach Israelites anew the forgotten name and law of God and their destiny as a nation. Well did he know that this alone would prepare the way for success. Then, having gathered an army fit for his purpose, he was not long in sweeping the garrisons of Cushan out of the land.

Judgment and then deliverance; judgment of the mistakes and sins men have committed, thereby bringing themselves into trouble; conviction of sin and righteousness; thereafter guidance and help that their feet may be set on a rock and their goings established—this is the right sequence. That God should help the proud, the self-sufficient out of their troubles in order that they may go on in pride and vainglory, or that He should save the vicious from the consequences of their vice and leave them to persist in their iniquity, would be no Divine work. The new mind and the right spirit must be put in men, they must hear their condemnation, lay it to heart and repent, there must be a revival of holy purpose and aspiration first. Then the oppressors will be driven from the land, the weight of trouble lifted from the soul.

Othniel, the first of the judges, seems one of the best. He is not a man of mere rude strength and dashing enterprise. Nor is he one who runs the risk of sudden elevation to power, which few can stand. A person of acknowledged honour and sagacity, he sees the problem of the time and does his best to solve it. He is almost unique in this, that he appears without offence, without shame. And his judgeship is honourable to Israel. It points to a higher level of thought and greater seriousness among the tribes than in the century when Jephthah and Samson were the acknowledged heroes. The nation had not lost its reverence for the great names and hopes of the exodus when it obeyed Othniel and followed him to battle.

In modern times there would seem to be scarcely any understanding of the fact that no man can do real service as a political leader unless he is a fearer of God, one who loves righteousness more than country, and serves the Eternal before any constituency. Sometimes a nation low enough in morality has been so far awake to its need and danger as to give the helm, at least for a time, to a servant of truth and righteousness and to follow where he leads. But more commonly is it the case that political leaders are chosen anywhere rather than from the ranks of the spiritually earnest. It is oratorical dash now, and now the cleverness of the intriguer, or the power of rank and wealth, that catches popular favour and exalts a man in the state. Members of parliament, cabinet ministers, high officials need have no devoutness, no spiritual seriousness or insight. A nation generally seeks no such character in its legislators and is often content with less than decent morality. Is it then any wonder that politics are arid and government a series of errors? We need men who have the true idea of liberty and will set nations nominally Christian on the way of fulfilling their mission to the world. When the people want a spiritual leader he will appear; when they are ready to follow one of high and pure temper he will arise and show the way. But the plain truth is that our chiefs in the state, in society and business must be the men who represent the general opinion, the general aim.

While we are in the main a worldly people, the best guides, those of spiritual mind, will never be allowed to carry their plans. And so we come back to the main lesson of the whole history, that only as each citizen is thoughtful of God and of duty, redeemed from selfishness and the world, can there be a true commonwealth, honourable government, beneficent civilisation.

CHAPTER VI.

THE DAGGER AND THE OX-GOAD.

JUDGES iii. 12-31.

THE world is served by men of very diverse kinds, and we pass now to one who is in strong contrast to Israel's first deliverer. Othniel the judge without reproach is followed by Ehud the regicide. The long peace which the country enjoyed after the Mesopotamian army was driven out allowed a return of prosperity and with it a relaxing of spiritual tone. Again there was disorganisation; again the Hebrew strength decayed and watchful enemies found an opportunity. The Moabites led the attack, and their king was at the head of a federation including the Ammonites and the Amalekites. It was this coalition the power of which Ehud had to break.

We can only surmise the causes of the assault made on the Hebrews west of Jordan by those peoples on the east. When the Israelites first appeared on the plains of the Jordan under the shadow of the mountains of Moab, before crossing into Palestine proper, Balak king of Moab viewed with alarm this new nation which was advancing to seek a settlement so near his territory. It was then he sent to Pethor for Balaam, in the hope that by a powerful incantation or curse the great diviner would blight the Hebrew armies and make them an easy prey. Notwithstanding this scheme, which even to the Israelites did not appear contemptible, Moses so far respected the relationship between Moab and Israel that he did not attack Balak's kingdom, although at the time it had been weakened by an unsuccessful contest with the Amorites from Gilead. Moab to the south and Ammon to the north were both left unharmed.

But to Reuben, Gad, and the half-tribe of Manasseh was allotted the land from which the Amorites had been completely driven, a region extending from the frontier of Moab on the south away towards Hermon and the Argob; and these tribes entering vigorously on their possession could not long remain at peace with the bordering races. We can easily see how their encroachments, their growing strength would vex Moab and Ammon and drive them to plans of retaliation. Balaam had not cursed Israel; he had blessed it, and the blessing was being fulfilled. It seemed to be decreed that all other peoples east of Jordan were to be overborne by the descendants of Abraham; yet one fear wrought against another, and the hour of Israel's security was seized as a fit occasion for a vigorous sally across the river. A desperate effort was made to strike at the heart of the Hebrew power and assert the claims of Chemosh to be a greater god than He Who was reverenced at the sanctuary of the ark.

Or Amalek may have instigated the attack. Away in the Sinaitic wilderness there stood an altar which Moses had named Jehovah-Nissi, Jehovah is my banner, and that altar commemorated a great victory gained by Israel over the Amalekites. The greater part of a century had gone by since the battle, but the memory of defeat lingers long with the Arab—and these Amalekites were pure Arabs, savage, vindictive, cherishing their cause of war, waiting their revenge. We know the command in Deuteronomy, "Remember what Amalek did unto thee by the way, when ye were come forth out of Egypt. How he met thee by the way and smote the hindmost of thee, even all that were feeble behind thee. Thou shalt blot out the remembrance of Amalek from under heaven. Thou shalt not forget it." We may be sure that Reuben and Gad did not forget the dastardly attack; we may be sure that Amalek did not forget the day of Rephidim. If Moab was not of itself disposed to cross the Jordan and fall on Benjamin and Ephraim, there was the urgency of Amalek, the proffered help of that fiery people to ripen decision. The ferment of war rose. Moab, having walled cities to form a basis of operations, took the lead. The confederates marched northward along the Dead Sea, seized the ford near Gilgal and mastering the plain of Jericho pushed their conquest beyond the hills. Nor was it a temporary advance. They established themselves. Eighteen years afterwards we find Eglon, in his palace or castle near the City of Palm Trees, claiming authority over all Israel.

So the Hebrew tribes, partly by reason of an old strife not forgotten, partly because they have gone on vigorously adding to their territory, again suffer assault and are brought under oppression, and the coalition against them reminds us of confederacies that are in full force to-day. Ammon and Moab are united against the church of Christ, and Amalek joins in the attack. The parable is one, we shall say, of the opposition the church is constantly provoking, constantly experiencing, not entirely to its own credit. Allowing that, in the main, Christianity is truly and honestly aggressive, that on its march to the heights it does straight battle with the enemies of mankind and thus awakens the hatred of bandit Amaleks, yet this is not a complete account of the assaults which are renewed century after century. Must it not be owned that those who pass for Christians often go beyond the lines and methods of their proper warfare and are found on fields where the weapons are carnal and the fight is not "the good fight of faith"? There is a strain of modern talk which defends the worldly ambition of Christian men, sounding very hollow and insincere to all excepting those whose interest and illusion it is to think it heavenly. We hear from a thousand tongues the gospel of Christianised commerce, of sanctified success, of making business a religion. In the press and hurry of competition there is a less and a greater conscientiousness. Let men have it in the greater degree, let them be less anxious for speedy success than some they know, not quite so eager to add factory to factory and field to field, more careful to interpret bargains fairly and do good work; let them figure often as benefactors and be free with their money to the church, and the residue of worldly ambition is glorified, being sufficient, perhaps, to develop a merchant prince, a railway king, a "millionaire" of the kind the age adores. Thus it comes to pass that the domain which appeared safe enough from the followers of Him who sought no power in the earthly range is invaded by men who reckon all their business efforts privileged under the laws of heaven, and every advantage they win a Divine plan for wresting money from the hands of the devil.

Now it is upon Christianity as approving all this that the Moabites and Ammonites of our day are falling. They are frankly worshippers of Chemosh and Milcom, not of Jehovah; they believe in wealth, their all is staked on the earthly prosperity and enjoyment for which they strive. It is too bad, they feel, to have their sphere and hopes curtailed by men who profess no respect for the world, no desire for its glory but a constant preference for things unseen; they writhe when they consider the triumphs wrested from them by rivals who count success an answer to prayer and believe themselves favourites of God. Or the frank heathen finds that in business a man professing Christianity in the customary way is as little cumbered as himself by any disdain of tarnished profits and "smart" devices. What else can be expected but that, driven back and back by the energy of Christians so called, the others shall begin to think Christianity itself largely a pretence? Do we wonder to see the revolution in France hurling its forces not only against wealth and rank, but also against the religion identified with wealth and rank? Do we wonder to see in our day socialism, which girds at great fortunes as an insult to humanity, joining hands with agnosticism and secularism to make assault on the church? It is precisely what might be looked for; nay, more, the opposition will go on till Christian profession is purged of hypocrisy and Christian practice is harmonised with the law of Christ. Not the push, not the equivocal success of one person here and there is it that creates doubt of Christianity and provokes antagonism, but the whole systems of society and business in so-called Christian lands, and even the conduct of affairs within the church, the strain of feeling there. For in the church as without it wealth and rank are important in themselves, and make some important who have little or no other claim to respect. In the church as without it methods are adopted that involve large outlay and a constant need for the support of the wealthy; in the church as without it life depends too much on the abundance of the things that are possessed. And, in the not unfair judgment of those who stand outside, all this proceeds from a secret doubt of Christ's law and authority, which more than excuses their own denial. The strifes of the day, even those that turn on the Godhead of Christ and the inspiration of the Bible, as well as on the divine claim of the church, are not due solely to hatred of truth and the depravity of the human heart. They have more reason than the church has yet confessed. Christianity in its practical and speculative aspects is one; it cannot be a creed unless it is a life. It is essentially a life not conformed to this world, but transformed, redeemed. Our faith will stand secure from all attacks, vindicated as a supernatural revelation and inspiration, when the whole of church life and Christian endeavour shall rise above the earthly and be manifest everywhere as a fervent striving for the spiritual and eternal.

We have been assuming the unfaithfulness of Israel to its duty and vocation. The people of God, instead of commending His faith by their neighbourliness and generosity, were, we fear, too often proud and selfish, seeking their own things, not the well-being of others, sending no attractive light into the heathenism around. Moab was akin to the Hebrews and in many respects similar in character. When we come to the Book of Ruth we find a certain intercourse between the two. Ammon, more unsettled and barbarous, was of the same stock. Israel, giving nothing to these peoples, but taking all she could from them, provoked antagonism all the more bitter that they were of kin to her, and they felt no scruple when their opportunity came. Not only had the Israelites to suffer for their failure, but Moab and Ammon also. The wrong beginning of the relations between them was never undone. Moab and Ammon went on worshipping their own gods, enemies of Israel to the last.

Ehud appears a deliverer. He was a Benjamite, a man left-handed; he chose his own method of action, and it was to strike directly at the Moabite king. Eager words regarding the shamefulness of Israel's subjection had perhaps already marked him as a leader, and it may have been with the expectation that he would do a bold deed that he was chosen to bear the periodical tribute on this occasion to Eglon's palace. Girding a long dagger under his garment on his right thigh, where if found it might appear to be worn without evil intent, he set out with some attendants to the Moabite headquarters. The narrative is so vivid that we seem able to follow Ehud step by step. He has gone from the neighbourhood of Jebus to Jericho, perhaps by the road in which the scene of our Lord's parable of the Good Samaritan was long afterwards laid. Having delivered the tribute into the hands of Eglon he goes southward a few miles to the sculptured stones at Gilgal, where possibly some outpost of the Moabites kept guard. There he leaves his attendants, and swiftly retracing his steps to the palace craves a private interview with the king and announces a message from God, at Whose name Eglon respectfully rises from his seat. One flash of the dagger and the bloody deed is done. Leaving the king's dead body there in the chamber, Ehud bolts the door and boldly passes the attendants, then quickening his pace, is soon beyond Gilgal and away by another route through the steep hills to the mountains of Ephraim. Meanwhile the murder is discovered and there is confusion at the palace. No one being at hand to give orders, the garrison is unprepared to act, and as Ehud loses no time in gathering a band and returning to finish his work, the fords of Jordan are taken before the Moabites can cross to the eastern side. They are caught, and the defeat is so decisive that Israel is free again for fourscore years.

Now this deed of Ehud's was clearly a case of assassination, and as such we have to consider it. The crime is one which stinks in our nostrils because it is associated with treachery and cowardice, the basest revenge or the most undisciplined passion. But if we go back to times of ruder morality and regard the circumstances of such a people as Israel, scattered and oppressed, waiting for a sign of bold energy that may give it new heart, we can easily see that one who chose to act as Ehud did would by no means incur the reprobation we now attach to the assassin. To go no farther back than the French Revolution and the deed of Charlotte Corday, we cannot reckon her among the basest—that woman of "the beautiful still countenance" who believed her task to be the duty of a patriot. Nevertheless, it is not possible to make a complete defence of Ehud. His act was treacherous. The man he slew was a legitimate king, and is not said to have done his ruling ill. Even allowing for the period, there was something peculiarly detestable in striking one to death who stood up reverently expecting a message from God. Yet Ehud may have thoroughly believed himself to be a Divine instrument.

This too we see, that the great just providence of the Almighty is not impeached by such an act. No word in the narrative justifies assassination; but, being done, place is found for it as a thing overruled for good in the development of Israel's history. Man has no defence for his treachery and violence, yet in the process of events the barbarous deed, the fierce crime, are shown to be under the control of the Wisdom that guides all men and things. And here the issue which justifies Divine providence, though it does not purge the criminal, is clear. For through Ehud a genuine deliverance was wrought for Israel. The nation, curbed by aliens, overborne by an idolatrous power, was free once more to move toward the great spiritual end for which it had been created. We might be disposed to say that on the whole Israel made nothing of freedom, that the faith of God revived and the heart of the people became devout in times of oppression rather than of liberty. In a sense it was so, and the story of this people is the story of all, for men go to sleep over their best, they misuse freedom, they forget why they are free. Yet every eulogy of freedom is true. Man must even have the power of misusing it if he is to arrive at the best. It is in liberty that manhood is nursed, and therefore in liberty that religion matures. Autocratic laws mean tyranny, and tyranny denies the soul its responsibility to justice, truth, and God. Mind and conscience held from their high office, responsibility to the greatest overborne by some tyrant hand that may seem beneficent, the soul has no space, faith no room to breathe; man is kept from the spontaneity and gladness of his proper life. So we have to win liberty in hard struggle and know ourselves free in order that we may belong completely to God.

See how life advances! God deals with the human race according to a vast plan of discipline leading to heights which at first appear inaccessible. Freedom is one of the first of these, and only by way of it are the higher summits reached. During the long ages of the dark and weary struggle, which seem to many but a fruitless martyrdom, the Divine idea was interfused with all the strife. Not one blind stroke, not one agony of the craving soul was wasted. In all the wisdom of God wrought for man, through man's pathetic feebleness or most daring achievement. So out of the chaos of the gloomy valleys a highway of order was raised by which the race should mount to Freedom and thence to Faith.

We see it in the history of nations, those that have led the way and those that are following. The possessors of clear faith have won it in liberty. In Switzerland, in Scotland, in England, the order has been, first civil freedom, then Christian thought and vigour. Wallace and Bruce prepare the way for Knox; Boadicea, Hereward, the Barons of Magna Charta for

Wycliffe and the Reformation; the men of the Swiss Cantons who won Morgarten and routed Charles the Bold were the forerunners of Zwingli and Farel. Israel, too, had its heroes of freedom; and even those who, like Ehud and Samson, did little or nothing for faith and struck wildly, wrongly for their country, did yet choose consciously to serve their people and were helpers of a righteousness and a holy purpose they did not know. When all has been said against them it remains true that the freedom they brought to Israel was a Divine gift.

It is to be remarked that Ehud did not judge Israel. He was a deliverer, but nowise fitted to exercise high office in the name of God. In some way not made clear in the narrative he had become the centre of the resolute spirits of Benjamin and was looked to by them to find an opportunity of striking at the oppressors. His calling, we may say, was human, not Divine; it was limited, not national; and he was not a man who could rise to any high thought of leadership. The heads of tribes, ingloriously paying tribute to the Moabites, may have scoffed at him as of no account. Yet he did what they supposed impossible. The little rising grew with the rapidity of a thunder-cloud, and, when it passed, Moab, smitten as by a lightning flash, no longer overshadowed Israel. As for the deliverer, his work having been done apparently in the course of a few days, he is seen no more in the history. While he lived, however, his name was a terror to the enemies of Israel, for what he had effected once he might be depended upon to do again if necessity arose. And the land had rest.

Here is an example of what is possible to the obscure whose qualifications are not great, but who have spirit and firmness, who are not afraid of dangers and privations on the way to an end worth gaining, be it the deliverance of their country, the freedom or purity of their church, or the rousing of society against a flagrant wrong. Do the rich and powerful angrily refuse their patronage? Do they find much to say about the impossibility of doing anything, the evil of disturbing people's minds, the duty of submission to Providence and to the advice of wise and learned persons? Those who see the time and place for acting, who hear the clarion-call of duty, will not be deterred. Armed for their task with fit weapons—the two-edged dagger of truth for the corpulent lie, the penetrating stone of a just scorn for the forehead of arrogance, they have the right to go forth, the right to succeed, though probably, when the stroke has told, many will be heard lamenting its untimeliness and proving the dangerous indiscretion of Ehud and all who followed him.

In the same line another type is represented by Shamgar, son of Anath, the man of the ox-goad, who considered not whether he was equipped for attacking Philistines, but turned on them from the plough, his blood leaping in him with swift indignation. The instrument of his assault was not made for the use to which it was put: the power lay in the arm that wielded the goad and the fearless will of the man who struck for his own birthright, freedom,—for Israel's birthright, to be the servant of no other race. Undoubtedly it is well that, in any efforts made for the church or for society, men should consider how they are to act and should furnish themselves in the best manner for the work that is to be done. No outfit of knowledge, skill, experience is to be despised. A man does not serve the world better in ignorance than in learning, in bluntness than in refinement. But the serious danger for such an age as our own is that strength may be frittered away and zeal expended in the mere preparation of weapons, in the mere exercise before the war begins. The important points at issue are apt to be lost sight of, and the vital distinctions on which the whole battle turns to fade away in an atmosphere of compromise. There are those who, to begin, are Israelites indeed, with a keen sense of their nationality, of the urgency of certain great thoughts and the example of heroes. Their nationality becomes less and less to them as they touch the world; the great thoughts begin to seem parochial and antiquated; the heroes are found to have been mistaken, their names cease to thrill. The man now sees nothing to fight for, he cares only to go on perfecting his equipment. Let us do him justice. It is not the toil of the conflict he shrinks from, but the rudeness of it, the dust and heat of warfare. He is no voluntary now, for he values the dignity of a State Church and feels the charm of ancient traditions. He is not a good churchman, for he will not be pledged to any creed or opposed to any school. He is rarely seen on any political platform, for he hates the watchwords of party. And this is the least of it. He is a man without a cause, a believer without a faith, a Christian without a stroke of brave work to do in the world. We love his mildness; we admire his mental possessions, his broad sympathies. But when we are throbbing with indignation he is too calm; when we catch at the ox-goad and fly at the enemy we know that he disdains our weapon and is affronted by our fire. Better, if it must be so, the rustic from the plough, the herdsman from the hill-side; better far he of the camel's-hair garment and the keen cry, Repent, repent!

Israel, then, appears in these stories of her iron age as the cradle of the manhood of the modern world; in Israel the true standard was lifted up for the people. It is liberty put to a noble use that is the mark of manhood, and in Israel's history the idea of responsibility to the one living and true God takes form and clearness as that alone which fulfils and justifies liberty. Israel has a God Whose will man must do, and for the doing of it he is free. If at the outset the vigour which this thought of God infused into the Hebrew struggle for independence was tempestuous; if Jehovah was seen not in the majesty of eternal justice and sublime magnanimity, not as the Friend of all, but as the unseen King of a favoured people,—still, as freedom came, there came with it always, in some prophetic word, some Divine psalm, a more living conception of God as gracious, merciful, holy, unchangeable; and notwithstanding all lapses the Hebrew was a man of higher quality than those about him. You stand by the cradle and see no promise, nothing to attract. But give the faith which is here in infancy time to assert itself, give time for the vision of God to enlarge, and the finest type of human life will arise and establish itself, a type possible in no other way. Egypt with its long and wonderful history gives nothing to the moral life of the new world, for it produces no men. Its kings are despots, tomb-builders, its people contented or discontented slaves. Babylon and Nineveh are names that dwarf Israel's into insignificance, but their power passes and leaves only some monuments for the antiquarian, some corroborations of a Hebrew record. Egypt and Chaldea, Assyria and Persia never reached through freedom the idea of man's proper life, never rose to the sense of that sublime calling or bowed in that profound adoration of the Holy One which made the Israelite, rude fanatic as he often was, a man and a father of men. From Egypt, from Babylon,—yea, from Greece and Rome came no redeemer of mankind, for they grew bewildered in the search after the chief end of existence and fell before they found it. In the prepared people it was, the people cramped in the narrow land between the Syrian desert and the sea, that the form of the future Man was seen, and there, where the human spirit felt at least, if it did not realise its dignity and place, the Messiah was born.

CHAPTER VII.

THE SIBYL OF MOUNT EPHRAIM.

JUDGES iv.

THERE arises now in Israel a prophetess, one of those rare women whose souls burn with enthusiasm and holy purpose when the hearts of men are abject and despondent; and to Deborah it is given to make a nation hear her call. Of prophetesses the world has seen but few; generally the woman has her work of teaching and administering justice in the name of God within a domestic circle and finds all her energy needed there. But queens have reigned with firm nerve and clear sagacity in many a land, and now and again a woman's voice has struck the deep note which has roused a nation to its duty. Such in the old Hebrew days was Deborah, wife of Lappidoth.

It was a time of miserable thraldom in Israel when she became aware of her destiny and began the sacred enterprise of her life. From Hazor in the north near the waters of Merom Israel was ruled by Jabin, king of the Canaanites—not the first of the name, for Joshua had before defeated one Jabin king of Hazor, and slain him. During the peace that followed Ehud's triumph over Moab the Hebrews, busy with worldly affairs, failed to estimate a danger which year by year became more definite and pressing—the rise of the ancient strongholds of Canaan and their chiefs to new activity and power. Little by little the cities Joshua destroyed were rebuilt, refortified and made centres of warlike preparation. The old inhabitants of the land recovered spirit, while Israel lapsed into foolish confidence. At Harosheth of the Gentiles, under the shadow of Carmel, near the mouth of the Kishon, armourers were busy forging weapons and building chariots of iron. The Hebrews did not know what was going on, or missed the purpose that should have thrust itself on their notice. Then came the sudden rush of the chariots and the onset of the Canaanite troops, fierce, irresistible. Israel was subdued and bowed to a yoke all the more galling that it was a people they had conquered and perhaps despised that now rode over them. In the north at least the Hebrews were kept in servitude for twenty years, suffered to remain in the land but compelled to pay heavy tribute, many of them, it is likely, enslaved or allowed but a nominal independence. Deborah's song vividly describes the condition of things in her country. Shamgar had made a clearance on the Philistine border and kept his footing as a leader, but elsewhere the land was so swept by Canaanite spoilers that the highways were unused and Hebrew travellers kept to the tortuous and difficult by-paths down in the glens or among the mountains. There was war in all the gates, but in Israelite dwellings neither shield nor spear. Defenceless and crushed the people lay crying to gods that could not save, turning ever to new gods in strange despair, the national state far worse than when Cushan's army held the land or when Eglon ruled from the City of Palm Trees.

Born before this time of oppression Deborah spent her childhood and youth in some village of Issachar, her home a rude hut covered with brushwood and clay, like those which are still seen by travellers. Her parents, we must believe, had more religious feeling than was common among Hebrews of the time. They would speak to her of the name and law of Jehovah, and she, we doubt not, loved to hear. But with the exception of brief oral traditions fitfully repeated and an example of reverence for sacred times and duties, a mere girl would have no advantages. Even if her father was chief of a village her lot would be hard and monotonous, as she aided in the work of the household and went morning and evening to fetch water from the spring or tended a few sheep on the hill-side. While she was yet young the Canaanite oppression began, and she with others felt the tyranny and the shame. The soldiers of Jabin came and lived at free quarters among the villagers, wasting their property. The crops were perhaps assessed, as they are at the present day in Syria, before they were reaped, and sometimes half or even more would be swept away by the remorseless collector of tribute. The people turned thriftless and sullen. They had nothing to gain by exerting themselves when the soldiers and the tax-gatherer were ready to exact so much the more, leaving them still in poverty. Now and again there might be a riot. Maddened by insults and extortion the men of the village would make a stand. But without weapons, without a leader, what could they effect? The Canaanite troops were upon them; some were killed, others carried away, and things became worse than before.

There was not much prospect at such a time for a Hebrew maiden whose lot it seemed to be, while yet scarcely out of her childhood, to be married like the rest and sink into a household drudge, toiling for a husband who in his turn laboured for the oppressor. But there was a way then, as there is always a way for the high-spirited to save life from bareness and desolation; and Deborah found her path. Her soul went forth to her people, and their sad state moved her to something more than a woman's grief and rebellion. As years went by the traditions of the past revealed their meaning to her, deeper and larger thoughts came, a beginning of hope for the tribes so downcast and weary. Once they had swept victoriously through the land and smitten that very fortress which again overshadowed all the north. It was in the name of Jehovah and by His help that Israel then triumphed. Clearly the need was for a new covenant with Him; the people must repent and return to the Lord. Did Deborah put this before her parents, her husband? Doubtless they agreed with her, but could see no way of action, no opportunity for such as they. As she spoke more and more eagerly, as she ventured to urge the men of her village to bestir themselves, perhaps a few were moved, but the rest heard carelessly or derided her. We can imagine Deborah in that time of trial growing up into tall and striking womanhood, watching with indignation many a scene in which her people showed a craven fear or joined slavishly in heathen revels. As she spoke and saw her words burn the hearts of some to whom they were spoken, the sense of power and duty came. In vain she looked for a prophet, a leader, a man of Jehovah to rekindle a flame in the nation's heart. A flame! It was in her own soul, she might wake it in other souls; Jehovah helping her, she would.

But when in her native tribe the brave woman began to urge with prophetic eloquence the return to God and to preach a holy war her time of peril came. Issachar lay completely under the survey of Jabin's officers, overawed by his chariots. And one who would deliver a servile people had need to fear treachery. Issachar was "a strong ass couching down between the sheepfolds"; he had "bowed his shoulder to bear" and become "a servant under task-work." As her purpose matured she had to seek a place of safety and influence, and passing southward she found it in some retired spot among the hills between Bethel and Ramah, some nook of that valley which, beginning near Ai, curves eastward and narrows at Geba to a rocky gorge with precipices eight hundred feet high,—the Valley of Achor, of which Hosea long afterwards said that it should be a door of hope. Here, under a palm tree, the landmark of her tent, she began to prophesy and judge and grow to spiritual power among the tribes. It was a new thing in Israel for a woman to speak in the name of God. Her utterances had no doubt something of a sibyllic strain, and the deep or wild notes of her voice pleading for Jehovah or raised in passionate warning against idolatry touched the finest chords of the Hebrew soul. In her rapture she saw the Holy One coming in majesty from the southern desert where Horeb reared its sacred peak; or again, looking into the future, foretold His exaltation in proud triumph over the gods of Canaan, His people free once more, their land purged of every heathen taint. So gradually her place of abode became a rendezvous of the tribes, a seat of justice, a shrine of reviving hope. Those who longed for righteous administration came to her; those who were fearers of Jehovah gathered about her. Gaining wisdom she was able to represent to a rude age the majesty as well as the purity of Divine law, to establish order as well as to communicate enthusiasm. The people felt that sagacity like hers and a spirit so sanguine and fearless must be the gift of Jehovah; it was the inspiration of the Almighty that gave her understanding.

Deborah's prophetical utterances are not to be tried by the standard of the Isaian age. So tested some of her judgments might fail, some of her visions lose their charm. She had no clear outlook to those great principles which the later prophets more or less fully proclaimed. Her education and circumstances and her intellectual power determined the degree in which she could receive Divine illumination. One woman before her is honoured with the name of prophetess, Miriam, the sister of Moses and Aaron, who led the refrain of the song of triumph at the Red Sea. Miriam's gift appears limited to the gratitude and ecstasy of one day of deliverance; and when afterwards, on the strength of her share in the enthusiasm of the Exodus, she ventured along with Aaron to claim equality with Moses, a terrible rebuke checked her presumption. Comparing Miriam and Deborah, we find as great an advance from the one to the other as from Deborah to Amos or Hosea. But this only shows that the inspiration of one mind, intense and ample for that mind, may come far short of the inspiration of another. God does not give every prophet the same insight as Moses, for the rare and splendid genius of Moses was capable of an illumination which very few in any following age have been able to receive. Even as among the Apostles of Christ St. Peter shows occasionally a lapse from the highest Christian judgment for which St. Paul has to take him to task, and yet does not cease to be inspired, so Deborah is not to be denied the Divine gift though her song is coloured by an all too human exultation over a fallen enemy.

It is simply impossible to account for this new beginning in Israel's history without a heavenly impulse; and through Deborah unquestionably that impulse came. Others were turning to God, but she broke the dark spell which held the tribes and taught them afresh how to believe and pray. Under her palm tree there were solemn searchings of heart, and when the head men of the clans gathered there, travelling across the mountains of Ephraim or up the wadies from the fords of Jordan, it was first to humble themselves for the sin of idolatry, and then to undertake with sacred oaths and vows the serious work which fell to them in Israel's time of need. Not all came to that solemn rendezvous. When is such a gathering completely representative? Of Judah and Simeon we hear nothing. Perhaps they had their own troubles with the wandering tribes of the desert; perhaps they did not suffer as the others from Canaanite tyranny and therefore kept aloof. Reuben on the other side Jordan wavered, Manasseh made no sign of sympathy; Asher, held in check by the fortress of Hazor and the garrison of Harosheth, chose the safe part of inaction. Dan was busy trying to establish a maritime trade. But Ephraim and Benjamin, Zebulun and Naphtali were forward in the revival, and proudly the record is made on behalf of her native tribe, "the princes of Issachar were with Deborah." Months passed; the movement grew steadily, there was a stirring among the dry bones, a resurrection of hope and purpose.

And with all the care used this could not be hid from the Canaanites. For doubtless in not a few Israelite homes heathen wives and half-heathen children would be apt to spy and betray. It goes hardly with men if they have bound themselves by any tie to those who will not only fail in sympathy when religion makes demands, but will do their utmost to thwart serious ambitions and resolves. A man is terribly compromised who has pledged himself to a woman of earthly mind, ruled by idolatries of time and sense. He has undertaken duties to her which a quickened sense of Divine law will make him feel the more; she has her claim upon his life, and there is nothing to wonder at if she insists upon her view, to his spiritual disadvantage and peril. In the time of national quickening and renewed thoughtfulness many a Hebrew discovered the folly of which he had been guilty in joining hands with women who were on the side of the Baalim and resented any sacrifice made for Jehovah. Here we find the explanation of much lukewarmness, indifference to the great enterprises of the church and withholding of service by those who make some profession of being on the Lord's side. The entanglements of domestic relationship have far more to do with failure in religious duty than is commonly supposed.

Amid difficulty and discouragement enough, with slender resources, the hope of Israel resting upon her, Deborah's heart did not fail nor her head for affairs. When the critical point was reached of requiring a general for the war she had already fixed upon the man. At Kadesh-Naphtali, almost in sight of Jabin's fortress, on a hill overlooking the waters of Merom, ninety miles to the north, dwelt Barak the son of Abinoam. The neighbourhood of the Canaanite capital and daily evidence of its growing power made Barak ready for any enterprise which had in it good promise of success, and he had better qualifications than mere resentment against injustice and eager hatred of the Canaanite oppression. Already known in Zebulun and Naphtali as a man of bold temper and sagacity, he was in a position to gather an army corps out of those tribes—the main strength of the force on which Deborah relied for the approaching struggle. Better still, he was a fearer of God. To Kadesh-Naphtali the prophetess sent for the chosen leader of the troops of Israel, addressing to him the call of Jehovah: "Hath not the Lord commanded thee saying, Go and draw towards Mount Tabor"—that is, Bring by detachments quietly from the different cities towards Mount Tabor—"ten thousand men of Naphtali and Zebulun?" The rendezvous of Sisera's host was Harosheth of the Gentiles, in the defile at the western extremity of the valley of Megiddo, where Kishon breaks through to the plain of Acre. Tabor overlooked from the northeast the same wide strath which was to be the field where the chariots and the multitude should be delivered into Barak's hand.

Not doubting the word of God, Barak sees a difficulty. For himself he has no prophetic gift; he is ready to fight, but this is to be a sacred war. From the very first he would have the men gather with the clear understanding that it is for religion as much as for freedom they are taking arms; and how may this be secured? Only if Deborah will go with him through the country proclaiming the Divine summons and promise of victory. He is very decided on the point. "If thou wilt go with me, then I will go: but if thou wilt not go with me, I will not go." Deborah agrees, though she would fain have left this matter entirely to men. She warns him that the expedition will not be to his honour, since Jehovah will give Sisera into the hand of a woman. Against her will she takes part in the military preparations. There is no need to find in Deborah's words a prophecy of the deed of Jael. It is a grossly untrue taunt that the murder of Sisera is the central point of the whole narrative. When Deborah says, "The Lord shall sell Sisera into the hand of a woman," the reference plainly is, as Josephus makes it, to the position into which Deborah herself was forced as the chief person in the campaign. With great wisdom and the truest courage she would have limited her own sphere. With equal wisdom and equal courage Barak understood how the zeal of the people was to be maintained. There was a friendly contest, and in the end the right way was found, for unquestionably Deborah was the genius of the movement. Together they went to Kedesh,—not Kadesh-Naphtali in the far north, but Kedesh on the shore of the Sea of Galilee, some twelve miles from Tabor.* From that as a centre, journeying by secluded ways through the northern districts, often perhaps by night, Deborah and Barak went together rousing the enthusiasm of the people, until the shores of the lake and the valleys running down to it were quietly occupied by thousands of armed men.

The clans are at length gathered; the whole force marches from Kedesh to the foot of Tabor to give battle. And now Sisera, fully equipped, moves out of Harosheth along the course of the Kishon, marching well beneath the ridge of Carmel, his chariots thundering in the van. Near Taanach he orders his front to be formed to the north, crosses the Kishon and advances on the Hebrews, who by this time are visible beyond the slope of Moreh. The tremendous moment has come. "Up," cries Deborah, "for this is the day in which the Lord hath delivered Sisera into thine hand. Is not the Lord gone out before thee?" She has waited till the troops of Sisera are entangled among the streams which here, from various directions, converge to the river Kishon, now swollen with rain and difficult to cross. Barak, the Lightning Chief, leads his men impetuously down into the plain, keeping near the shoulder of Moreh where the ground is not broken by the streams; and with the fall of evening he begins the attack. The chariots have crossed the Kishon but are still struggling in the swamps and marshes. They are assailed with vehemence and forced back, and in the waning light all is confusion. The Kishon sweeps away many of the Canaanite host, the rest make a stand by Taanach and further on by the waters of Megiddo. The Hebrews find a higher ford, and following the south bank of the river are upon the foe again. It is a November night and meteors are flashing through the sky. They are an omen of evil to the disheartened, half-defeated army. Do not the stars in their courses fight against Sisera? The rout becomes complete; Barak pursues the scattered force towards Harosheth, and at the ford near the city there is terrible loss. Only the fragments of a ruined army find shelter within the gates.

Meanwhile Sisera, a coward at heart, more familiar with the parade ground than fit for the stern necessities of war, leaves his chariot and abandons his men to their fate, his own safety all his care. Seeking that, it is not to Harosheth he turns. He takes his way across Gilboa toward the very region which Barak has left. On a little plateau overlooking the Sea of Galilee, near Kedesh, there is a settlement of Kenites whom Sisera thinks he can trust. Like a hunted animal he presses on over ridge and through defile till he reaches the black tents and receives from Jael the treacherous welcome, "Turn in, my lord, turn in to me; fear not." The pitiful tragedy follows. The coward meets at the hand of a woman the death from which he has fled. Jael

* See Conder's "Tent Work in Palestine."

gives him fermented milk to drink which, exhausted as he is, sends him into a deep sleep. Then, as he lies helpless, she smites the tent-pin through his temples.

In her song Deborah describes and glories over the execution of her country's enemy. "Blessed among women shall Jael, the wife of Heber be; with the hammer she smote Sisera; at her feet he curled up, he fell." Exulting in every circumstance of the tragedy, she adds a description of Sisera's mother and her ladies expecting his return as a victor laden with spoil, and listening eagerly for the wheels of that chariot which never again should roll through the streets of Harosheth. As to the whole of this passage, our estimate of Deborah's knowledge and spiritual insight does not require us to regard her praise and her judgment as absolute. She rejoices in a deed which has crowned the great victory over the master of nine hundred chariots, the terror of Israel; she glories in the courage of another woman, who single-handed finished that tyrant's career; she does not make God responsible for the deed. Let the outburst of her enthusiastic relief stand as the expression of intense feeling, the rebound from fear and anxiety of the patriotic heart. We need not weight ourselves with the suspicion that the prophetess reckoned Jael's deed the outcome of a Divine thought. No: but we may believe this of Jael, that she is on the side of Israel, her sympathy so far repressed by the league of her people with Jabin, yet prompting her to use every opportunity of serving the Hebrew cause. It is clear that if the Kenite treaty had meant very much and Jael had felt herself bound by it, her tent would have been an asylum for the fugitive. But she is against the enemies of Israel; her heart is with the people of Jehovah in the battle and she is watching eagerly for signs of the victory she desires them to win. Unexpected, startling, the sign appears in the fleeing captain of Jabin's host, alone, looking wildly for shelter. "Turn in, my lord; turn in." Will he enter? Will he hide himself in a woman's tent? Then to her will be committed vengeance. It will be an omen that the hour of Sisera's fate has come. Hospitality itself must yield; she will break even that sacred law to do stern justice on a coward, a tyrant, and an enemy of God.

A line of thought like this is entirely in harmony with the Arab character. The moral ideas of the desert are rigorous, and contempt rapidly becomes cruel. A tent woman has few elements of judgment, and, the balance turning, her conclusion will be quick, remorseless. Jael is no blameless heroine, neither is she a demon. Deborah, who understands her, reads clearly the rapid thoughts, the swift decision, the unscrupulous act and sees, behind all, the purpose of serving Israel. Her praise of Jael is therefore with knowledge; but she herself would not have done the thing she praises. All possible explanations made, it remains a murder, a wild, savage thing for a woman to do, and we may ask whether among the tents of Zaanannim Jael was not looked on from that day as a woman stained and shadowed,—one who had been treacherous to a guest.

Not here can the moral be found that the end justifies the means, or that we may do evil with good intent; which never was a Bible doctrine and never can be. On the contrary, we find it written clear that the end does not justify the means. Sisera must live on and do the worst he may rather than any soul should be soiled with treachery or any hand defiled by murder. There are human vermin, human scorpions and vipers. Is Christian society to regard them, to care for them? The answer is that Providence regards them and cares for them. They are human after all, men whom God has made, for whom there are yet hopes, who are no worse than others would be if Divine grace did not guard and deliver. Rightly does Christian society affirm that a human being in peril, in suffering, in any extremity common to men is to be succoured as a man, without inquiry whether he is good or vile. What then of justice and man's administration of justice? This, that they demand a sacred calm, elevation above the levels of personal feeling, mortal passion, and ignorance. Law is to be of no private, sudden, unconsidered administration. Only in the most solemn and orderly way is the trial of the worst malefactor to be gone about, sentence passed, justice executed. To have reached this understanding of law with regard to all accused and suspected persons and all evildoers is one of the great gains of the Christian period. We need not look for anything like the ideal of justice in the age of the judges; deeds were done then and zealously and honestly praised which we must condemn. They were meant to bring about good, but the sum of human violence was increased by them and more work made for the moral reformer of after times. And going back to Jael's deed, we see that it gave Israel little more than vengeance. In point of fact the crushing defeat of the army left Sisera powerless, discredited, open to the displeasure of his master. He could have done Israel no more harm.

One point remains. Emphatically are we reminded that life continually brings us to sudden moments in which we must act without time for careful reflection, the spirit of our past flashing out in some quick deed or word of fate. Sisera's past drove him in panic over the hills to Zaanannim. Jael's past came with her to the door of the tent; and the two as they looked at each other in that tragic moment were at once, without warning, in crisis for which every thought and passion of years had made a way. Here the self-pampering of a vain man had its issue. Here the woman, undisciplined, impetuous, catching sight of the means to do a deed, moves to the fatal stroke like one possessed. It is the sort of thing we often call madness, and yet such insanity is but the expression of what men and women choose to be capable of. The casual allowance of an impulse here, a craving there, seems to mean little until the occasion comes when their accumulated force is sharply or terribly revealed. The laxity of the past thus declares itself; and on the other hand there is often a gathering of good to a moment of revelation. The soul that has for long years fortified itself in pious courage, in patient well-doing, in high and noble thought, leaps one day, to its own surprise, to the height of generous daring or heroic truth. We determine the issue of crises which we cannot foresee.

CHAPTER VIII.

DEBORAH'S SONG: A DIVINE VISION.

JUDGES V.

The song of Deborah and Barak is twofold, the first portion, ending with the eleventh verse, a chant of rising hope and pious encouragement during the time of preparation and revival, the other a song of battle and victory throbbing with eager patriotism and the hot breath of martial excitement. In the former part God is celebrated as the Helper of Israel from of old and from afar; He is the spring of the movement in which the singer rejoices, and in His praise the strophes culminate. But human nature asserts itself after the great and decisive triumph in the vivid touches of the latter canto. In it more is told of the doings of men, and there is picturesque fiery exultation over the fallen. One might almost think that Deborah, herself childless, glories over the mother of Sisera in the utter desolation which falls on her when she hears the tidings of her son's defeat and death. Yet this mood ceases abruptly, and the song returns to Jehovah, Whose friends are lifted up to joy and strength by His availing help.

The main interest of the twofold song lies in its religious colour, for here the pious ardour of the Israel of the judges comes to finest expression. As a whole it is more patriotic than moral, more warlike than religious, and thus unquestionably reflects the temper of the time. What ideas do we find in it of the relation of Israel to God and of God to Israel, what conceptions of the Divine character? Jehovah is invoked and praised as the God of the Hebrews alone. He seems to have no interest in the Canaanites, nor compassion towards them. Yet the grandeur of the Divine forthgoing is declared in bold and striking imagery, and the high resolves of men are clearly traced to the Spirit of the Almighty. Duty to God is linked with duty to country, and it is at least suggested that Israel without Jehovah is nothing and has no right to a place among the peoples. The nation exists for the glory of its Heavenly King, to make known His power and His righteous acts. A strain like this in a war-song belonging to the time of Israel's semi-barbarism bears no uncertain promise. From the well-spring out of which it flows clear and sparkling there will come other songs, with tenderer music and holier longing,—songs of spiritual hope and generous desire for Messianic peace.

1. The first religious note is struck in what may be called the opening Hallelujah, although the ejaculation, "Bless the Lord," is not, in Hebrew, that which afterwards became the great refrain of sacred song.

"For that leaders led in Israel,
For that the people offered themselves willingly:
Bless ye Jehovah."

Here is more than belief in Providence. It is faith in the spiritual presence and power of God swaying the souls of men. Has Deborah seen at last, after long efforts to rouse the careless people, one and another responding to her appeals and seeking her tent among the hills? Has she witnessed the vows of the chiefs of Issachar and Zebulun that they would not be wanting in the day of battle? Not to herself but to the God of Israel is the new temper ascribed. Jehovah, Who touched her own heart, has now touched many another. For years she had been aware of holier influences than came to her from the people among whom she lived. In secret, in the silence of the heart, she had found herself mastered by thoughts that none around her shared. She has well accounted for them. Jehovah has spoken to her, Jehovah caring still for His people, waiting to redeem them from bondage. And now, when her prophetic cry finds echo in other souls, when men who were asleep rise up and declare their purpose, especially when from this side and that companies of brave youths and resolute elders come to her—from the slopes of Carmel, from the hills of Gilead—the fire of hope in their eyes, how otherwise explain the upspringing of energy and devotion than as the work of the Spirit that has moved her own soul? To Jehovah is all the praise.

Common enough in our day is a profession of belief in God as the source of every good desire and right effort, as inspiring the charity of the generous, the affection of the loving, the fidelity of the true. But if our faith is deep and real it brings us much nearer than we usually feel ourselves to be to Him Who is the Life indeed. The existence and energy of God are assured to those who have this insight. Every kindness done by man to man is a testimony against which denial of the Divine life has no power. Though the intellect searching far afield makes out only as it were some few and indistinct footprints of a Mighty Being Who has passed by, seen at intervals on the plains of history, then lost in the morasses or on the rocky ground, there ought to be found in every human life daily evidence of Divine grace and wisdom. The good, the true, the noble constantly appeal to men, find men; and through these God finds them. When a magnanimous word is spoken, God is heard. When a deed is done in love, in purity, in courage or pity, God is seen. When out of languor and corruption and self-indulgence men arise and set their faces to the steep of duty, God is revealed. He in Whom we trust for the redemption of the world never leaves Himself without a witness, whether faith perceives or unbelief denies. The human story unfolds a Divine urgency by which the progress, the evolution of all that is good proceed from age to age. Man has never been left to nature alone nor to himself alone. The supernatural has always mingled with his life. He has resisted often, he has rebelled; yet conscience has not ceased, God has not withdrawn. This living energy of Jehovah, not only as belonging to the past but discovered in the new zeal of Israel, Deborah saw, and in virtue of the revelation she was far before her time. For the fresh life of the people, for the willing self-devotion of so many to the great cause, she lifted her voice in praise to Israel's Eternal Friend.

2. The next passage may be called a prologue in the heavens. Partly historical, it is chiefly a vision of Jehovah's age-long work for His people. In words that flash and roll the song describes the glorious advent of the Most High, nature astir with His presence, the mountains shaking under His tread.

The seat of the Divine Majesty appears to the prophetess to be in Seir. She looks across the hills of the south and passes beyond the desert to that place of mystery where God spoke in thunder and proclaimed Himself in the Law. The imagery points to the phenomena of earthquake and a fearful lightning storm accompanied with heavy rain. These, the most striking natural symbols of the supernatural, form the materials of the strophe. Perhaps even as the song is chanted the thunders of Sinai are echoed in a great storm that shakes the sky and rolls among the hills. The outward signs represent the new impressions of Divine power and authority which are startling and rousing the tribes. They have heard no voices, seen no tokens of God for many a year. He Who led their fathers out of bondage, He Who marched with them through the desert, has been forgotten; but He returns, He is with them again. The office of the prophetess is to celebrate God's presence and excite in the dull souls of men some feeling of His majesty. Sinai once trembled and was dismayed before God. The great peak beside which Tabor is but a mound flowed down in volcanic glow and rush. It is He Whose coming Deborah hears in the beating storm, He Whose victorious feet shake the hills of Ephraim. Have the people forsaken their King? Let them seek Him, trust Him now. Under the shadow of His wings there is refuge; before His arrows and the fierce floods He pours from heaven who can stand?

It has been well said that for the Israel of ancient times all natural phenomena—a storm, a hurricane, or a flood—had more than ordinary import. "Forbidden to recognise and, as it were, grasp the God of heaven in any material form, or to adore even in the heavens themselves any constant symbols of His being and His power, yet yearning more in spirit for manifestations of His invisible existence, Israel's mind was ever on the stretch for any hint in nature of the unseen Celestial Being, for any glimpse of His mysterious ways, and its courage rose to a far higher pitch when Divine encouragement and impulse seemed to come from the material world."* From the images of Baal and the Ashtaroth Israel had turned; but where was their Heavenly King? The answer came with marvellous power when Deborah in the midst of the rolling thunder could say, "Lord, when Thou wentest forth out of Seir, when Thou marchedst out of the field of Edom, the earth trembled, the heavens also dropped. The mountains flowed down at the presence of Jehovah." If the people bethought themselves of the clear demonstration of Divine majesty made to their fathers, they would realise God once more as the Ruler in heaven and earth. Then would courage revive, and in the faith of the Almighty they would go forth to victory.

Now was there in this faith an element of reason, a correspondence with fact? Is it fancy and nothing else, the poetic flight of an ardent soul eager to rouse a nation? Have we here an arbitrary connection made between striking natural events and a Divine Person throned in the heavens Whose existence the prophetess assumes, Whose supposed claim to obedience haunts her mind? In such a question our age utters its scepticism.

An age it is of science, of positive science. Toiling for centuries at the task of understanding the phenomenal, research has at length assumed the right to tell us what we must believe

* Ewald.

concerning the world—what we are to *believe*, observe, for it is a new creed and nothing else that confronts us here. "The government of the world," says one, "must not be considered as determined by an extramundane intelligence, but by one immanent in the cosmical forces and their relations." Another says: "The world or matter with its properties which we term forces must have existed from eternity and must last for ever—in one word, the world cannot have been created. . . . The ever-changing action of the natural forces is the fundamental cause of all that arises and perishes." Or again, not most recent in time but entirely modern in temper, we have the following: "Science has gradually taken all the positions of the childish belief of the peoples; it has snatched thunder and lightning from the hands of the gods. The stupendous powers of the Titans of the olden time have been grasped by the fingers of man. That which appeared inexplicable, miraculous, and the work of a supernatural power has by the touch of science proved to be the effect of hitherto unknown natural forces. Everything that happens does so in a natural way, *i. e.*, in a mode determined only by accidental or necessary coalition of existing materials and their immanent natural forces." Here is dogma forced on faith with fine energy; and what more is to be said when judgment is given —" I have searched the heavens, but have nowhere found the traces of a God"?

We hear the boast that no song of Hebrew seer can withstand this modern wisdom, that the superstition of Bible faith shall vanish like starlight before the rising sun. To science every opinion shall submit. But wait. It is dogmatism against belief after all, authority against authority, and the one in a lower region than the other, with vastly inferior sanctions. Natural science declares the present result of its observation of the universe, investigation brief, superficial, and limited to one small corner of the whole. Yet these deliverances are to be set above the science which deals with existence on the highest plane, the spiritual, solving deepest problems of life and conscience, finding perpetual support in the experience of men. The claim is somewhat large; it lacks the proof of service; it lacks verification. Science boasts greatly, as is natural to its adolescence. But at what point can it dare to say, Here is final truth, here is certainty? We do not repel our debt to the discoverer when we maintain that natural science is only watching the surface of a stream for a few miles along its course, while the springs far away among the eternal hills and the outflow into the infinite ocean are never viewed. Are we taunted with believing? Those who taunt us must supply for their part something more than inference ere we trust all to their wisdom. The "Force" that is so much invoked, what is it so far as the definitions of science go? Effects we see; Force never. All statements as to the nature of force are pure dogma. It is declared that there are necessary and eternal laws of matter. What makes them necessary, and who can prove their everlastingness? Using such words men pass infinitely beyond material research—they infer —they assert. In the region of natural science we can affirm nothing to be eternal, and even *necessity* is a word that has no warrant. It is only in the soul, in the region of moral ideas, we come on that which endures, which is necessary, which has constant reality. And it is here that our belief in God as universal Creator, the Source of power and life, the One Agent, the King eternal, immortal, and invisible, finds root and strength.

The battle between materialism and religious faith is not a battle in which facts are arrayed on one side and inferences and dreams on the other. The array is of facts against facts, as we have said, and with an immense difference of value. Is it an established sequence that when the electricity in the clouds is not in equipoise with that of the earth, under certain conditions there is a thunderstorm? It is surely a sequence of higher moment that when the sense of righteousness seizes the minds of men they rise against iniquity and there is a revolution. There natural forces operate, here spiritual. But on which side is the indication of eternity? Which of these sequences can better claim to give a key to the order of the universe? Surely if the evolution of the ages, so far, has culminated in man with his capability of knowing and serving the true, the just, the good, these facts of his mind and life are the highest of which we can take cognisance, and in them, if anywhere, we must find the key to all knowledge, the reason of all phenomena. Evolutionary science itself must agree to this. In the movements of nature we find no advance to fixity and finality. Nature labours, men labour with or against nature; but the flux of things is perpetual; there is no escape from change. In the efforts of the spiritual life it is not so. When we strive for equalness, for verity, for purity, we have glimpses then of the changeless order which we must needs call Divine. Here is the indication of eternity; and as we investigate, as we experience, we come to certitude, we reach larger vision, larger faith. That which endures rises clear above that which appears and passes.

Returning to Deborah's song and her vision of the coming of God in the impetuous storm, we see the practical value of Theism. One great idea, comprehensive and majestic, leads thought beyond symbol and change to the All-righteous Lord. To attribute phenomena to "Nature" is a sterile mode of thought; nothing is done for life. To attribute phenomena to a variety of superhuman persons limits and weakens the religious idea sought after; still one is lost in the changeable. Theism delivers the soul from both evils and sets it on a free upward path, stern yet alluring. By this path the Hebrew prophet rose to the high and fruitful conceptions which draw men together in responsibility and worship. The eternal governs all, rules every change; and that eternal is the holy will of God. The omnipotence nature obeys is the omnipotence of right. Israel returning to God will find Him coming to the help of His people in the awful or kindly movements of the natural world. Our view in one sense extends beyond that of the Hebrew seer. We find the purpose disclosed in natural phenomena to be somewhat different. Not the protection of a favoured race, but the discipline of humanity is what we perceive. Ours is an expansion of the Hebrew faith, revealing the same Divine goodness engaged in a redeeming work of wider scope and longer duration.

The point is still in doubt among us whether the good, the true, the right, are invincible. Those who go forth in the service of God are often borne down by the graceless multitude. From age to age the problem of God's supremacy seems to remain in suspense, and men are not afraid, in the name of foulest iniquity, to try issues with the best. Be it so. The Divine work is slow. Even the best need discipline that they may have strength, and God is in no haste to carry His argument against atheism. There is abundance of time. Those bent on evil or misled by falsehood, those who are on the wrong side though they consider themselves soldiers of a good cause may gain on many a field, yet their gain will turn out in the long run to be loss, and they who lose and fall are really the victors. There is defeat that is better than success. Other ages than belong to this world's history are yet to dawn, and the discovery will come to every intelligence that he alone triumphs whose life is spent for righteousness and love, in fidelity to God and man.

3. Let it be allowed that we find the latter canto of Deborah's song expressive of faith rather than of clear morality, pointing to a spiritual future rather than exhibiting actual knowledge of the Divine character. We hear of the righteous acts of the Lord, and the note is welcome, yet most likely the thought is of retributive justice and punishment that overtakes the enemies of Israel. When the remnant of the nobles and the people come down—that remnant of brave and faithful men never wanting to Israel —the Lord comes down with them, their Guide and Strength. Meroz is cursed because the inhabitants do not go forth to the help of Jehovah. And finally there is glorying over Sisera because he is an enemy of Israel's Unseen King. There is trust, there is devotion, but no largeness of spiritual view.

We must, however, remember that a song full of the spirit of battle and the gladness of victory cannot be expected to breathe the ideal of religion. The mind of the singer is too excited by the circumstances of the time, the bustle, the triumph, to dwell on higher themes. When fighting has to be done it is the main business of the hour, cannot be aught else to those who are engaged. A woman especially, strung to an unusual pitch of nervous endurance, would be absorbed in the events and her own new and strange position; and she would pass rapidly from the tension of anxiety to a keen passionate exultation in which everything was lost except the sense of deliverance and of personal vindication. When that is past which was an issue of life or death, freedom or destruction, joy rises in a sudden spring, joy in the prowess of men, the fulness of Divine succour; neither the prophetess nor the fighters are indifferent to justice and mercy, though they do not name them here. Deborah, a woman of intense patriotism and piety, dared greatly for God and her country; of a base thing she was incapable. The men who fought by the waters of Megiddo and slew their enemies ruthlessly in the heat of battle knew in the time of peace the duties of humanity and no doubt showed kindness, when the war was over, to the widows and orphans of the slain. To know and serve Jehovah was a guarantee of moral culture in a rude age; and the Israelites when they returned to Him must have contrasted very favourably in respect of conduct with the devotees of Baal and Astarte.

For a parallel case we may turn to Oliver Cromwell. In his letter after the storming of Bristol, a bloody piece of work in which the mettle of the Parliamentary force was put keenly to proof,

Cromwell ascribes the victory to God in these terms:—" They that have been employed in this service know that faith and prayer obtained this city for you. God hath put the sword in the Parliament's hands for the terror of evil-doers and the praise of them that do well." Of victory after victory which left many a home desolate he speaks as mercies to be acknowledged with all thankfulness. " God exceedingly abounds in His goodness to us, and will not be weary until righteousness and peace meet, and until He hath brought forth a glorious work for the happiness of this poor kingdom." Read his dispatches and you find that though the man had a generous heart and was a sworn servant of Christ the merciful, yet he breathes no compassion for the royal troops. These are the enemy against whom a pious man is bound to fight; the slaughter of them is a terrible necessity.

Just now it is the fashion to depreciate as much as possible the moral value of the old Hebrew faith. We are assured in a tone of authority that Israel's Jehovah was only another Chemosh, or, say, a respectable Baal, a being without moral worth,—in fact, a mere name of might worshipped by Israelites as their protector. The history of the people settles this uncritical theory. If the religion of Israel did not sustain a higher morality, if the faith of Jehovah was purely secular, how came Israel to emerge as a nation from the long conflict with Moabites, Canaanites, Midianites, and Philistines? The Hebrews were not superior in point of numbers, unity, or military skill to the nations whose interest it was to subdue or expel them. Some vantage ground the Israelites must have had. What was it? Justice between man and man, domestic honour, care for human life, a measure of unselfishness,—these at least, as well as the entire purity of their religious rites, were their inheritance; through these the blessing of the Eternal rested upon them. There could never be a return to Him in penitence and hope without a return to the duties and the faith of the sacred covenant. We know therefore that while Deborah sings her song of battle and exults over fallen Sisera there is latent in her mind and the minds of her people a warmth of moral purpose justifying their new liberty. This nation is again a militant church. The hearts of men enlarge that God may dwell in them. Israel's triumph, shall it not be for the good of those who are overcome? Shall not the people of Jehovah, going forth as the sun in his might, shed a kindly radiance over the lands around? So fine a conception of duty is scarcely to be found in Deborah's song, but, realised or not in Old Testament times, it was the revelation of God through Israel to the world.

CHAPTER IX.

DEBORAH'S SONG: A CHANT OF PATRIOTISM.

Judges v.

WE have already considered the song of Deborah as a declaration of God's working more broad and spiritual than might be looked for in that age. We now regard it as exhibiting different relations of men to the Divine purpose. There is a religious spirit in the whole movement here described. It begins in a revival of faith and obedience, prospers despite the coldness and opposition of many, grows in force and enthusiasm as it proceeds, and finally is crowned with success. The church is militant in a literal sense; yet, fighting with carnal weapons, it is really contending for the glory of the Unseen King. There is a close parallel between the enterprise of Deborah and Barak and that which opens before the church of the present time. No forced accommodation is needed to gather from the song lessons of different kinds for our guidance and warning in the campaign of Christianity.

Here are Deborah herself, a mother in Israel, and the leaders who take their places at the head of the armies of God. Here also are the people willingly offering themselves, imperilling their lives for religion and freedom. The history of the past and the vision of Jehovah as sole Ruler of nature and providence encourage the faithful, who rise out of lethargy and leave the by-ways of life to take the field in battle array. The levies of Ephraim, Benjamin, Zebulun, Issachar, and Naphtali represent those who are decisively Christian, ready to hazard all for the gospel's sake. But Reuben sits among the sheepfolds and listens to the pipings for the flocks, Dan remains in ships, Asher at the haven of the sea; and these may stand for the self-cultivating, self-serving professors of religion. Jabin and Sisera again are established opponents of the right cause; they are brave in their own defence; their positions look most formidable, their battalions shake the ground. But the stars from heaven, the floods of Kishon, are only a small part of the forces of the King of heaven; and the soul of Israel marches on in strength till the enemy is routed. Meroz practically helps the foe. Those who dwell within its walls are doubtful of the issue and will not risk their lives; the curse of sullen apostasy falls upon them. Jael is a vivid type of the unscrupulous helpers of a good cause, those who, employing the weapons and methods of the world, would fain be servants of that kingdom in which nothing base, nothing earthly can have place. And there are the children of the hour, the fine ladies of Harosheth whose pleasure and pride are bound up with oppression, who look through the lattices and listen in vain for the returning chariots laden with spoil.

1. The leaders and head men of the tribes under Deborah and Barak, Deborah foremost in the great enterprise, her soul on fire with zeal for Israel and for God.

Deborah and Barak show throughout that spirit of cordial agreement, that frank support of each other which at all times are so much to be desired in religious leaders. There is no jealousy, no striving for pre-eminence. Barak is a brave man, but he will not stir without the prophetess; he is quite content to give her the place of honour while he does the martial work. Deborah again would commit the task to Barak's hands in complete reliance on his wisdom and valour; yet she is ready to appear along with him, and in her song, while she claims the prophetic office, it is to Barak she renders the honours of victory—" Lead thy thraldom in thrall, thou son of Abinoam."

Rarely, it must be confessed, is there entire harmony among the leaders of affairs. Jealousy is too often with them from the first. Suspicion lurks under the council table, private ambitions and unworthy fears make confusion when each should trust and encourage another. The fine enthusiasm of a great cause does not overcome as it ought the selfishness of human nature. Moreover, varieties in disposition as between the cautious and the impetuous, the more and the less of sagacity or of faith, a failure in sincerity here, in justice there, are separating influences constantly at work. But when the pressing importance of the duties entrusted to men by God governs every will, these elements of division cease; leaders who differ in temperament are loyal to each other then, each jealous of the other's honour as servants of truth. In the Reformation, for example, prosperity was largely due to the fact that two such men as Luther and Melanchthon, very different yet thoroughly united, stood side by side in the thick of the conflict, Luther's impetuosity moderated by the calmer spirit of the other, Melanchthon's craving for peace kept from dangerous concession by the boldness of his friend. Their mutual love and fidelity showed the nobleness of both, showed also what the Protestant Gospel was. Their differences melted away in enthusiasm for the Word of God, which one thought of as a celestial ambrosia, the other as a sword, a war, a destruction springing upon the children of Ephraim like a lioness in the forest. The Divine work was the life of each; each in his own way sought with splendid earnestness to forward the truth of Christ.

Church leaders are responsible for not a little which they themselves condemn. Differences do not quickly arise among disciples when the teachers are modest, honourable, and brotherly. Paul cries, "Is Christ divided? Were ye baptised into the name of Paul? What is Apollos? What is Paul? Ministers by whom ye believed." When our leaders speak and feel in like manner there will be peace, not uniformity but something better. God's husbandry, God's building will prosper.

But it is declared to be jealousy for religion that divides—jealousy for the pure doctrine of Christ—jealousy for the true church. We try to believe it. But then why are not all in that spirit of holy jealousy found side by side as comrades, eagerly yet in cordial brotherhood discussing points of difference, determined that they will search together and help each other until they find principles in which they can all rest? The leaders of different Christian bodies do not appear like Deborah and Barak engaged in a common enterprise, but as chiefs of rival or even opposing armies. The reason is that in this church and the other there has been a foreclosing of questions, and the elected leaders are almost all men who are pledged to the tribal decrees. In the decisions of councils and synods, and not less in the deliverances of learned doctors apologising each for his own sect and marking out the path his party must travel, there has been ever since the days of the apostles a hardening and limiting of opinion. Thought has been prematurely crystallised and each church prides itself on its own special deposit. The true church leader should understand that a course which may have been inevitable in the past is not the virtue of to-day and that those are simply adhering to an antiquated position who affirm one church to be the sole possessor of truth, the only centre of authority. It may seem strange to advise the churches to reconsider many of the ideas built into creed and constitution and to reject all leaders who are such by credit of sitting immovable in the seats of the rabbis, but the progress of Christianity in power and assurance waits upon a new brotherliness which will bring about a new catholicity. Under guides of the right kind the churches will have qualities and distinctions as heretofore, each will be a rendezvous for spirits of a certain order, but frankly confessing each other's right and honour they will press on abreast to scale and possess the uplands of truth.

To be sure something is said of tolerance. But that is a purely political idea. Let it not be so much as named in the assembly of God's people. Does Barak tolerate Deborah? Does Moses tolerate Aaron? Does St. Peter tolerate St. Paul? The disciples of Christ *tolerate* each other, do they? What marvellous largeness of soul! One or two, it appears, have been made sole keepers of the ark, but are prepared to tolerate the embarrassing help of well-meaning auxiliaries. Neither charity of that sort nor flabbiness of belief is asked. Let each be strongly persuaded in his own mind of that which he has learned from Christ. But where Christ has not foreclosed inquiry, and where sincere and thoughtful believers differ, there is no place for what is called tolerance; the demand is for brotherly fellowship in thought and labour.

Deborah was a mother in Israel, a nursing mother of the people in their spiritual childhood, with a mother's warm heart for the oppressed and weary flock. The nation needed a new birth, and that, by the grace of God, Deborah gave it in the sore travail of her soul. For many a year she suffered, prayed, and entreated. Israel had chosen new gods and in serving them was dying to righteousness, dying to Jehovah. Deborah had to pour her own life into the half dead, and compared to this effort the battle with the Canaanites was but a secondary matter. So is it always. The Divine task is that of the mother-like souls that labour for the quickening of faith and holy service. Great victories of Christian valour, patience, and love are never won without that renewal of humanity; and everything is due to those who have guided the ignorant into knowledge, the careless to thought, and the weak to strength through years of patient toil. They are not all prophets, not all known to the tribes: of many such the record waits, hidden with their God, until the day of revealing and rejoicing.

Yet Barak also, the Lightning Chief, has honourable part. When the men are collected, men new-born into life, he can lead them. They are Ironsides under him. He rushes down from Tabor and they at his feet with a vigour nothing can resist. If we have Deborah we shall also have Barak, his army and his victory. The promise is not for women only but for all in the private ways and obscure settlements of life who labour at the making of men. Every Christian has the responsibility and joy of helping to prepare a way for the coming of Jehovah in some great outburst of faith and righteousness.

2. We contrast next the people who offered themselves willingly, who "jeoparded their lives unto the death upon the high places of the field," and those who for one reason or another held aloof.

With united leaders there is a measure of unity

among the tribes. Barak and Deborah summon all who are ready to strike for liberty, and there is a great muster. Yet there might be double the number. Those who refuse to take arms have many pretexts, but the real cause is want of heart. The oppression of Jabin does not much affect some Israelites, and so far as it does they would rather go on paying tribute than risk their lives, rather bear the ills they have than hazard anything in joining Barak. These holding back, the work has to be done by a comparatively small number, a remnant of the nobles and the people.

But a remnant is always found; there are men and women who do not bow the knee to the Baal of worldly fashion, who do not content their souls amid the fleshpots of low servitude. They have to venture and sacrifice much in a long and varying war, and oftentimes their flesh and heart may almost fail. But a great reward is theirs. While others are spiritless and hopeless they know the zest of life, its real power and joy. They know what believing means, how strong it makes the soul. Their all is in the spiritual kingdom which cannot be moved. God is the portion of their souls, their gladness and glory. Those who stand by and look on while the conflict rages may share to a certain extent in the liberty that is won, for the gains of Christian warfare are not limited, they are for all mankind. There is a wider and better ordered life for all when this evil custom and that have been overcome, when one Jabin after another ceases to oppress. Yet what is it after all to touch the border of Christian liberty? To the fighters belongs the inheritance itself, an ever-extending conquest, a land of olives and vineyards and streams of living water.

Different tribes are named that sent contingents to the army of Barak. They are typical of different churches, different orders of society that are forward in the campaign of faith. The Hebrews who came most readily at the battle call appear to have belonged to districts where the Canaanite oppression was heavy, the country that lay between Harosheth, the headquarters of Sisera, and Hazor the city of Jabin. So in the Christian struggle of the ages the strenuous part falls to those who suffer from the tyranny of the temporal and see clearly the hopelessness of life without religion. The gospel of Christ is peculiarly precious to men and women whose lot is hard, whose earthly future is clouded. Sacrifices for God's cause are made as a rule by these. In His great purpose, in His deep knowledge of the facts of life, our Lord joined Himself to the poor and left with them a special blessing. It is not that men who dwell in comfort are independent of the gospel, but they are tempted to think themselves so. In proportion as they are fenced in amongst possessions and social claims they are apt, though devout, to miss that very call which is the message of the gospel to them. Well-meaning but absorbed, they can rarely bestir themselves to hear and do until some personal calamity or public disaster awakens them to the truth of things. The steady support of Christian ordinances and work in our day is largely the honour of people who have their full share in the struggle for earthly necessaries or a humble standing in the ranks of the independent. The paradox is real and striking; it claims the attention of those who vainly dream that a comfortable society would certainly become Christian, as effect follows cause. While the religion of Christ makes for justice and temporal well-being, blessing even the unbeliever, while it leads the way to a high standard of social order, these things remain of no value in themselves to men unspiritual: it holds true that man can never live by bread alone, but by the words which proceed out of the mouth of God. And there are forces at work among us on behalf of the Divine counsel that shall not fail to maintain the struggle necessary to the discipline and growth of souls.

The real army of faith is largely drawn from the ranks of the toilers and the heavy laden. Yet not entirely. We reckon many and fine exceptions. There are rich who are less worldly than those who have little. Many whose lot lies far from the shadow of tyranny in green and pleasant valleys are first to hear and quickest to answer every call from the Captain of the Lord's host. Their possessions are nothing to them. In the spiritual battle all is spent, knowledge, influence, wealth, life. And if you look for the highest examples of Christianity, a faith pure, keen, and lovely, a generosity that most clearly reveals the Master, a passion for truth consuming all lower regards, you will find them where culture has done its best for the mind and the bounty of providence has kindled a gracious humility and an abounding gentleness of heart. The tawdry vanities of their fellows in rank and wealth seem what they are to these, the gaudy toys of children who have not yet seen the glory and the goal of life. And how can men and women hear the clarion of the Christian war ringing over the valleys of degradation and fear, see the Divine contest surging through the land, and not perceive that here and here only is life? Men play at statecraft and grow cold as they intrigue; they play at financing and become ciphers in a monstrous sum; they toil at pleasure till Satan himself might pity them, for at least he has a purpose to serve. All the while there is offered to them the vigour, the buoyancy, the glow of an ambition and a service in which no spirit tires and no heart withers. Passing strange it is that so few noble, so few mighty, so few wise hear the keen cry from the cross as one of life and power.

Among the tribes that held aloof from the great conflict several are specially named. Messengers have gone to the land of Reuben beyond Jordan, and carried the fiery cross through Bashan. Dan has been summoned and Asher from the haven of the sea. But these have not responded. Reuben indeed has searchings of heart. Some of the people remember the old promise made at Shittim in the plain of Moab, that they would help their brethren who crossed into Canaan, never refusing assistance till the land was fully possessed. Moses had solemnly charged them with that duty, and they had bound themselves in covenant: "As the Lord hath said unto thy servants, so will we do." Could anything have been more seriously, more decisively undertaken? Yet, when this hour of need came, though the duty lay upon the conscience nothing was done. Along the watercourses of Gilead and Bashan there were flocks to tend, to protect from the Amalekites and Midianites of the desert, who would be sure to make a raid in the absence of the fighting men. To Asher and Dan the reference is perhaps somewhat ironical. The "ships" for trade, the "haven of the sea," were never much to these tribes, and their maritime ambition made an unworthy excuse. They had perhaps a little fishing, some small trade on the coast, and petty as the gain was it filled their hearts. Asher "abode by his creeks."

It is not to a religious festival that Deborah and Barak have called the tribes. It is to serious and dangerous duty. Yet the call of duty should come with more power than any invitation even to spiritual enjoyment. The great religious gathering has its use, its charm. We know the attraction of the crowded convocation in which Christian hope and enthusiasm are rekindled by stirring words and striking instances, faith rising high as it views the wide mission of gospel truth and hears from eloquent lips the story of a modern day of Pentecost. To many, because their own spiritual life burns dull, the daily and weekly routine of things becomes empty, vain, unsatisfying. In the common round even of valued religious exercise the heat and promise of Christianity seem to be lacking. In the convention they appear to be realised as nowhere else, and the persuasion that God may be felt there in a special manner is laying hold of Christian people. They are right in their eager desire to be borne along with the flood of redeeming grace, but we have need to ask what the life of faith is, how it is best nourished. To have a personal share in God's controversy with evil, to have a place however obscure in the actual struggle of truth with falsehood,—this alone gives confidence in the result and power in believing. Those who are in contact with spiritual reality because they have their own testimony to bear, their own watch to keep at some outpost, find stimulus in the urgency of duty and exultation in the consciousness of service. Men often seek in public gatherings what they can only find in the private ways of effort and endurance; they seek the joy of harvest when they should be at the labour of sowing; they would fain be cheered by the song of victory when they should be roused by the trumpet of battle.

And the result is that where spiritual work waits to be done there are but few to do it. Examine the state of any Christian church, reckon up those who are deeply interested in its efficiency, who make sacrifices of time and means, and set against these the half-hearted, who ignobly accept the religious provision made for them and perhaps complain that it is not so good as they would like, that progress is not so rapid as they think it might be,—the one class far outnumbers the other. As in Israel twice or three times as many might have responded to Barak's call, so in every church the resolute, the energetic, and devoted are few compared with those who are capable of energy and devotion. It is sometimes maintained that the worship of goodness and the Christian ideal command the minds of men more to-day than they ever did, and proof seems ready to hand. But, after all, is it not religious taste rather than reverence that grows? Self-culture leads many to a certain admiration of Christ and a form of discipleship. Christian worship is enjoyed and Christian philanthropy also, but when the spiritual freedom of mankind calls for some effort of the soul and life, we see what religion means—a wave of the hand instead of enthusiasm, a guinea subscription instead of thoughtful service. Is it a Christian or a selfish culture which is content with fragmentary concessions and complacent patronage where the claims of social "inferiors" are concerned? That there is a wide diffusion of religious feeling is clear enough; but in many respects it is mere dilettantism.

Notice the history of the tribes that lag behind in the day of the Lord's summons. What do we hear of Reuben after this? "Unstable as water, thou shalt not excel." Along with Gad Reuben possessed a splendid country, but these two faded away into a sort of barbarism, scarcely maintaining their separateness from the wild races of the desert. Asher in like manner suffered from the contact with Phœnicia and lost touch with the more faithful tribes. So it is always. Those who shirk religious duty lose the strength and dignity of religion. Though greatly favoured in place and gifts they fall into that spiritual impotence which means defeat and extinction.

"Curse ye Meroz, said the angel of the Lord, curse ye bitterly the inhabitants thereof; because they came not to the help of the Lord against the mighty." It is a stern judgment upon those whose active assistance was, humanly speaking, necessary in the day of battle. The men only held back, held back in doubt, supposing that it was vain for Hebrews to fling themselves against the iron chariots of Sisera. Were they not prudent, looking at the matter all round? Why should a curse so heavy be pronounced on men who only sought to save their lives? The reply is that secular history curses such men, those of Sparta for example to whom Athens sent in vain when the battle of Marathon was impending; and further that Christ has declared the truth which is for all time, " Whosoever will save his life shall lose it." Erasmus was a wise man; yet he made the great blunder. He saw clearly the errors of Romanism and the miserable bondage in which it kept the souls of men, and if he had joined the reformers his judgment and learning would have become part of the world's progressive life. But he held back doubting, criticising, a friend to the Reformation but not an apostle of it. Admire as we may the wit, the reasoner, the philosopher, there must always be severe judgment of one who, professing to love truth, declared that he had no inclination to die for it. There are many who, without the intellect of Erasmus, would fain be thought catholic in his company. Large is the family of Meroz, and little thought have they of any ban lying upon them. Is it a fanciful danger, a mere error of opinion without any peril in it, to which we point here? People think so; young men especially think so and drift on until the day of service is past and they find themselves under the contempt of man and the judgment of Christ. " Lord, when saw we Thee a stranger or in prison and did not minister unto Thee?" "Depart from Me, I never knew you."

3. Jael, a type of the unscrupulous helpers of a good cause.

Long has the error prevailed that religion can be helped by using the world's weapons, by acting in the temper and spirit of the world. Of that mischievous falsehood have been born all the pride and vainglory, the rivalries and persecutions that darken the past of Christendom, surviving in strange and pitiful forms to the present day. If we shudder at the treachery in the deed of Jael, what shall we say of that which through many a year sent victims to inquisition-dungeons and to the stake in the name of Christ?

And what shall we say now of that moral assassination which in one tent and another is thought no sin against humanity, but a service of God? Among us are too many who suffer wounds keen and festering that have been given in the house of their friends, yea, in the name of the one Lord and Master. The battle of truth is a frank and honourable fight, served at no point by what is false or proud or low. To an enemy a Christian should be chivalrous, and surely no less to a brother. Granting that a man is in error, he needs a physician, not an executioner; he needs an example, not a dagger. How much farther do we get by the methods of opprobrium and cruelty, the innuendo and the whisper of suspicion? Besides, it is not the Siseras to-day who are dealt with after this manner. It is the "schismatic" within the camp on whom some Jael falls with a hammer and a nail. If a church cannot stand by itself, approved to the consciences of men, it certainly will not be helped by a return to the temper of barbarism and the craft of the world. "The weapons of our warfare are not carnal, but mighty through God to the casting down of strongholds."

CHAPTER X.

THE DESERT HORDES; AND THE MAN AT OPHRAH.

JUDGES vi. 1-14.

JABIN king of Canaan defeated and his nine hundred chariots turned into ploughshares, we might expect Israel to make at last a start in its true career. The tribes have had their third lesson and should know the peril of infidelity. Without God they are weak as water. Will they not bind themselves now in a confederacy of faith, suppress Baal and Astarte worship by stringent laws and turn their hearts to God and duty? Not yet: not for more than a century. The true reformer has yet to come. Deborah's work is certainly not in vain. She passes through the land administering justice, commanding the destruction of heathen altars. The people leave their occupations and gather in crowds to hear her: they shout, in answer to her appeals, Jehovah is our King. The Levites are called to minister at the shrines. For a time there is something like religion along with improving circumstances. But the tide does not rise long nor far.

Some twenty years have passed, and what is to be seen going on throughout the land? The Hebrews have addressed themselves vigorously to their work in field and town. Everywhere they are breaking up new ground, building houses, repairing roads, organising traffic. But they are also falling into the old habit of friendly intercourse with Canaanites, talking with them over the prospects of the crops, joining in their festivals of new moon and harvest. In their own cities the old inhabitants of the land sacrifice to Baal and gather about the Asherim. Earnest Israelites are indignant and call for action, but the mass of the people are so taken up with their prosperity that they cannot be roused. Peace and comfort in the lower region seem better than contention for anything higher. In the centre of Palestine there is a coalition of Hebrew and Canaanite cities, with Shechem at their head, which recognise Baal as their patron and worship him as the master of their league. And in the northern tribes generally Jehovah has scant acknowledgment; the people see no great task He has given them to do. If they live and multiply and inherit the land they reckon their function as His nation to be fulfilled.

It is a temptation common to men to consider their own existence and success a sort of Divine end in serving which they do all that God requires of them. The business of mere living and making life comfortable absorbs them so that even faith finds its only use in promoting their own happiness. The circle of the year is filled with occupations. When the labour of the field is over there are the houses and cities to enlarge, to improve, and furnish with means of safety and enjoyment. One task done and the advantage of it felt, another presents itself. Industry takes new forms and burdens still more the energies of men. Education, art, science become possible and in turn make their demands. But all may be for self, and God may be thought of merely as the great Patron satisfied with His tithes. In this way the impulses and hopes of faith are made the ministers of egoism, and as a national thing the maintenance of law, goodwill, and a measure of purity may seem to furnish religion with a sufficient object. But this is far from enough. Let worship be refined and elaborated, let great temples be built and thronged, let the arts of music and painting be employed in raising devotion to its highest pitch—still if nothing beyond self is seen as the aim of existence, if national Christianity realises no duty to the world outside, religion must decay. Neither a man nor a people can be truly religious without the missionary spirit, and that spirit must constantly shape individual and collective life. Among ourselves worship would petrify and faith wither were it not for the tasks the church has undertaken at home and abroad. But half-understood, half-discharged, these duties keep us alive. And it is because the great mission of Christians to the world is not even yet comprehended that we have so much practical atheism. When less care and thought are expended on the forms of worship and the churches address themselves to the true ritual of our religion, carrying out the redeeming work of our Saviour, there will be new fervour; unbelief will be swept away.

Israel, losing sight of its mission and its destiny, felt no need of faith and lost it; and with the loss of faith came loss of vigour and alertness as on other occasions. Having no sense of a common purpose great enough to demand their unity the Hebrews were again unable to resist enemies, and this time the Midianites and other wild tribes of the eastern desert found their opportunity. First some bands of them came at the time of harvest and made raids on the cultivated districts. But year by year they ventured farther in increasing numbers. Finally they brought their tents and families, their flocks and herds, and took possession.

In the case of all who fall away from the purpose of life the means of bringing failure home to them and restoring the balance of justice are always at hand. Let a man neglect his fields and nature is upon him; weeds choke his crops, his harvests diminish, poverty comes like an armed man. In trade likewise carelessness brings retribution. So in the case of Israel: although the Canaanites had been subdued other foes were not far away. And the business of this nation was of so sacred a kind that neglect of it meant great moral fault, and every fresh relapse into earthliness and sensuality after a revival of religion implied more serious guilt. We find accordingly a proportionate severity in the punishment. Now the nation is chastised with whips, but next time it is with scorpions. Now the iron chariots of Sisera hold the land in terror; then hosts of marauders spread like locusts over the country, insatiable, all-devouring. Do the Hebrews think that careful tilling of their fields and the making of wine and oil are their chief concern? In that they shall be undeceived. Not mainly to be good husbandmen and vine-dressers are they set here, but to be a light in the midst of the nations. If they cease to shine they shall no longer enjoy.

It was by the higher fords of Jordan, perhaps north of the Sea of Galilee, that the Midianites fell on western Canaan. Under their two great emirs Zebah and Zalmunna, who seem to have held a kind of barbaric state, troops of riders on swift horses and dromedaries swept the shore of the lake and burst into the plain of Jezreel. There were no doubt many skirmishes between their squadrons and the men of Naphtali and Manasseh. But one horde of the invaders followed another so quickly and their attacks were so sudden and fierce that at length resistance became impossible, the Hebrews had to betake themselves to the heights and dwell in the caves and rocks. Once in the desert under Moses they had been more than a match for these Arabs. Now, although on vantage ground moral and natural, fighting for their hearths and homes behind the breastwork of lake, river, and mountain, they are completely routed.

Between the circumstances of this oppressed nation and the present state of the church there is a wide interval, and in a sense the contrast is striking. Is not the Christianity of our time strong and able to hold its own? Is not the mood of many churches of the present day properly that of elation? As year after year reports of numerical increase and larger contributions are made, as finer buildings are raised for the purpose of worship, and work at home and abroad is carried on more efficiently, is it not impossible to trace any resemblance between the state of Israel during the Midianite oppression and the state of religion now? Why should there be any fear that Baal-worship or other idolatry should weaken the tribes, or that marauders from the desert should settle in their land?

And yet the condition of things to-day is not quite unlike that of Israel at the time we are considering. There are Canaanites who dwell in the land and carry on their debasing worship. These too are days when guerilla troops of naturalism, nomads of the primæval desert, are sweeping the region of faith. Reckless and irresponsible talk in periodicals and on platforms; novels, plays, and verses, often as clever as they are unscrupulous, are incidents of the invasion, and it is well advanced. Not for the first time is a raid of this kind made on the territory of faith, but the serious thing now is the readiness to give way, the want of heart and power to resist that we observe in family life and in society as well as in literature. Where resistance ought to be eager and firm it is often ignorant, hesitating, lukewarm. Perhaps the invasion must become more confident and more injurious before it rouses the people of God to earnest and united action. Perhaps those who will not submit may have to betake themselves to the caves of the mountains while the new barbarism establishes itself in the rich plain. It has almost come to this in some countries; and it may be that the pride of those who have been content to cultivate their vineyards for themselves alone, the security of those who have too easily concluded that fighting was over shall yet be startled by some great disaster.

"Israel was brought very low because of Midian." A traveller's picture of the present state of things on the eastern frontier of Bashan enables us to understand the misery to which the tribes were reduced by seven years of rapine. "Not only is the country—plain and hill-side alike—chequered with fenced fields, but groves of fig-trees are here and there seen and terraced vineyards still clothe the sides of some of the hills. These are neglected and wild but not fruitless. They produce great quantities of figs and grapes, which are rifled year after year by the Bedawin in their periodical raids. Nowhere on earth is there such a melancholy example of tyranny, rapacity, and misrule as here. Fields, pastures, vineyards, houses, villages, cities are all alike deserted and waste. Even the few inhabitants that have hid themselves among the rocky fastnesses and mountain defiles drag out a miserable existence, oppressed by robbers of the desert on the one hand and robbers of the government on the other." The Midianites of Gideon's time acted the part both of tyrants and depredators. They "left no sustenance for Israel, neither sheep nor ox nor ass. They entered into the land for to destroy it."

"And the children of Israel cried unto the Lord"; the prodigals bethought them of their Father. Having come to the husks they remembered Him who fed His people in the desert. Again the wheel has revolved and from the lowest point there is an upward movement. The tribes of God look once more towards the hills from whence their help cometh. And here is seen the importance of that faith which had passed into the nation's life. Although it was not of a very spiritual kind, yet it preserved in the heart of the people a recuperative power. The majority knew little more of Jehovah than His name. But the name suggested availing succour. They turned to the Awful Name, repeated it and urged their need. Here and there one saw God as the infinitely righteous and holy and added to the wail of the ignorant a more devout appeal, recognising the evils under which the people groaned as punitive, and knowing that the very God to Whom they cried had brought the Midianites upon them. In the prayer of such a one there was an outlook towards holier and nobler life. But even in the case of the ignorant the cry to One higher than the highest had help in it. For when that bitter cry was raised self-glorifying had ceased and piety begun.

Ignorant indeed is much of the faith that still expresses itself in so-called Christian prayer, almost as ignorant as that of the disconsolate Hebrew tribes. The moral purpose of discipline, the Divine ordinances of defeat and pain and affliction are a mystery unread. The man in extremity does not know why his hour of abject fear has come, nor see that one by one all the stays of his selfish life have been removed by a Divine hand. His cry is that of a foolish child.

Yet is it not true that such a prayer revives hope and gives new energy to the languid life? It may be many years since prayer was tried, not perhaps since he who is now past his meridian knelt at a mother's knee. Still as he names the name of God, as he looks upward, there comes with the dim vision of an Omnipotent Helper within reach of his cry the sense of new possibilities, the feeling that amidst the miry clay or the heaving waves there is something firm and friendly on which he may yet stand. It is a striking fact as to any kind of religious belief, even the most meagre, that it does for man what nothing else can do. Prayer must cease, we are told, for it is mere superstition. Without denying that much of what is called prayer is an expression of egotism, we must demand an explanation of the unique value it has in human life and a sufficient substitute for the habit of appeal to God. Those who would deprive us of prayer must first re-make man, for to the strong and enlightened prayer is necessary as well as to the weak and ignorant. The Heavenly is the only hope of the earthly. That we understand God is, after all, not the chief thing: but does He know us? Is He there above yet beside us, for ever?

The first answer to the cry of Israel came in the message of a prophet, one who would have been despised by the nation in its self-sufficient mood, but now obtained a hearing. His words brought instruction and made it possible for faith to move and work along a definite line. Through man's struggle God helps him; through man's thought and resolve God speaks to him. He is already converted when he believes enough to pray, and from this point faith saves by animating and guiding the strenuous will. The ignorant abject people of God learns from the prophet that something is to be done. There is a command, repeated from Sinai, against the worship of heathen gods, then a call to love the true God the Deliverer of Israel. Faith is to become life, and life faith. The name of Jehovah which has stood for one power among others is clearly re-affirmed as that of the One Divine Being, the only Object of adoration. Israel is convicted of sin and set on the way of obedience.

The answer to prayer lies very near to him who cries for salvation. He has not to move a step. He has but to hear the inner voice of conscience. Is there a sense of neglect of duty, a sense of disobedience, of faults committed? The first movement towards salvation is set up in that conviction and in the hope that the evil now seen may be remedied. Forgiveness is implied in this hope, and it will become assured as the hope grows strong. The mistake is often made of supposing that answer to prayer does not come till peace is found. In reality the answer begins when the will is bent towards a better life, though that change may be accompanied by the deepest sorrow and self-humiliation. A man who earnestly reproaches himself for despising and disobeying God has already received the grace of the redeeming Spirit.

But to Israel's cry there was another answer. When repentance was well begun and the tribes turned from the heathen rites which separated them from each other and from Divine thoughts, freedom again became possible and God raised up a liberator. Repentance indeed was not thorough; therefore a complete national reformation was not accomplished. Yet as against Midian, a mere horde of marauders, the balance of righteousness and power inclined now in behalf of Israel. The time was ripe and in the providence of God the fit man received his call.

Southwest from Shechem, among the hills of Manasseh, at Ophrah of the Abiezrites, lived a family that had suffered keenly at the hands of Midian. Some members of the family had been slain near Tabor, and the rest had as a cause of war not only the constant robberies from field and homestead but also the duty of blood-revenge. The deepest sense of injury, the keenest resentment fell to the share of one Gideon, son of Joash, a young man of nobler temper than most Hebrews of the time. His father was head of a Thousand; and as he was an idolater the whole clan joined him in sacrificing to the Baal whose altar stood within the boundary of his farm. Already Gideon appears to have turned with loathing from that base worship; and he was pondering earnestly the cause of the pitiful state into which Israel had fallen. But the circumstances perplexed him. He was not able to account for facts in accordance with faith.

In a retired place on the hillside, where a winepress has been fashioned in a hollow of the rocks, we first see the future deliverer of Israel. His task for the day is that of threshing out some wheat so that, as soon as possible, the grain may be hid from the Midianites; and he is busy with the flail, thinking deeply, watching carefully as he plies the instrument with a sense of irksome restraint. Look at him and you are struck with his stalwart proportions and his bearing: he is "like the son of a king." Observe more closely and the fire of a troubled yet resolute soul will be seen in his eye. He represents the best Hebrew blood, the finest spirit and intelligence of the nation; but as yet he is a strong man bound. He would fain do something to deliver Israel; he would fain trust Jehovah to sustain him in striking a blow for liberty; but the way is not clear. Indignation and hope are baffled.

In a pause of his work, as he glances across the valley with anxious eye, suddenly he sees under an oak a stranger sitting staff in hand, as if he had sought rest for a little in the shade. Gideon scans the visitor keenly, but finding no cause for alarm bends again to his labour. The next time he looks up the stranger is beside him and words of salutation are falling from his lips —"Jehovah is with thee, thou mighty man of valour." To Gideon the words did not seem so strange as they would have seemed to some. Yet what did they mean? Jehovah with him? Strength and courage he is aware of. Sympathy with his fellow-Israelites and the desire to help them he feels. But these do not seem to him proofs of Jehovah's presence. And as for his father's house and the Hebrew people, God seems far from them. Harried and oppressed, they are surely God-forsaken. Gideon can only wonder at the unseasonable greeting and ask what it means.

Unconsciousness of God is not rare. Men do not attribute their regret over wrong, their faint longing for the right to a spiritual presence within them and a Divine working. The Unseen appears so remote, man appears so shut off from intercourse with any supernatural Cause or Source that he fails to link his own strain of thought with the Eternal. The word of God is nigh him even in his heart, God is "closer to him than breathing, nearer than hands and feet." Hope, courage, will, life—these are Divine gifts, but he does not know it. Even in our Christian times the old error which makes God external, remote, entirely aloof from human experience survives and is more common than true faith. We conceive ourselves separated from the Divine, with springs of thought, purpose, and power in our own being, whereas there is in us no absolute origin of power—moral, intellectual, or physical. We live and move in God: He is our Source and our Stay, and our being is shot through and through with rays of the Eternal. The prophetic word spoken in our ear is not more assuredly from God than the pure wish or unselfish hope that frames itself in our minds or the stern voice of conscience heard in the soul. As for the trouble into which we fall, that too, did we understand aright, is a mark of God's providential care. Would we err without discipline? Would we be ineffective and have no bracing? Would we follow lies and enjoy a false peace? Would we refuse the Divine path to strength, yet never feel the sorrow of the weak? Are these the proofs of God's presence our ignorance would desire? Then indeed we imagine an unholy one, an unfaithful one upon the throne of the universe. But God has no favourites; He does not rule like a despot of earth for courtiers and an aristocracy. In righteousness and for righteousness, for eternal truth He works, and for that His people must endure.

"Jehovah is with thee:" so ran the salutation. Gideon, thinking of Jehovah, does not wonder to hear His name. But full of doubts natural to one so little instructed he feels himself bound to express them: "Why is all this evil befallen us? Hath not Jehovah cast us off and delivered us into the hand of Midian?" Unconstrainedly, plainly as man to man Gideon speaks, the burdensome thought of his people's misery overcoming the strangeness of the fact that in a God-forsaken land any one should care to speak of things like these. Yet momentarily, as the conversation proceeds, there grows in Gideon's soul a feeling of awe, a new and penetrating idea. The look fastened upon him conveys beside the human strain of will a suggestion of highest authority; the words, "Go in this thy might and save Israel, have not I sent thee?" kindle in his heart a vivid faith. Laid hold of, lifted above himself, the young man is made aware at last of the Living God, His presence, His will. Jehovah's representative has done his mediatorial work. Gideon desires a sign; but his wish is a note of habitual caution, not of disbelief, and in the sacrifice he finds what he needs.

Now, why insist as some do on that which is not affirmed in the text? The form of the narrative must be interpreted: and it does not require us to suppose that Jehovah Himself, incarnate, speaking human words, is upon the scene. The call is from Him, and indeed Gideon has already a prepared heart, or he would not listen to the messenger. But seven times in the brief story the word *Malakh* marks a commissioned servant as clearly as the other word Jehovah marks the Divine will and revelation. After the man of God has vanished from the hill swiftly, strangely, in the manner of his coming, Gideon remains alive to Jehovah's immediate presence and voice as he never was before. Humble and shrinking—"forasmuch as I have seen the angel of the Lord face to face"—he yet hears the Divine benediction fall from the sky, and following that a fresh and immediate summons. Whether from the tabernacle at Shiloh an acknowledged prophet came to the brooding Abiezrite, or the visitor was one who concealed his own name and haunt that Jehovah might be the more impressively recognised, it matters not. The angel of the Lord made Gideon thrill with a call to highest duty, opened his ears to heavenly voices, and then left him. After this he felt God to be with himself.

"The Lord looked upon Gideon and said, Go in this thy might and save Israel from the hand of Midian: have not I sent thee?" It was a summons to stern and anxious work, and the young man could not be sanguine. He had considered and re-considered the state of things so long, he had so often sought a way of liberating his people and found none that he needed a clear indication how the effort was to be made. Would the tribes follow him, the youngest of an obscure family in Manasseh? And how was he to stir, how to gather the people? He builds an altar, Jehovah-shalom; he enters into covenant with the Eternal in high and earnest resolution, and with a sudden flash of prophet sight he sees the first thing to do. Baal's altar in the high place of Ophrah must be overthrown. Thereafter it will be known what faith and courage are to be found in Israel.

It is the call of God that ripens a life into power, resolve, fruitfulness—the call and the response to it. Continually the Bible urges upon us this great truth, that through the keen sense of a close personal relation to God and of duty owing to Him the soul grows and comes to its own. Our human personality is created in that way and in no other. There are indeed lives which are not so inspired and yet appear strong; an ingenious resolute selfishness gives them momentum. But this individuality is akin to that of ape or tiger; it is a part of the earth-force in yielding to which a man forfeits his proper being and dignity. Look at Napoleon, the supreme example in history of this failure. A great genius, a striking character? Only in the carnal region, for human personality is moral, spiritual, and the most triumphant cunning does not make a man; while, on the other hand, from a very moderate endowment put to the glorious usury of God's service will grow a soul clear, brave, and firm, precious in the ranks of life. Let a human being, however ignorant and low, hear and answer the Divine summons and in that place a man appears, one who stands related to the source of strength and light. And when a man roused by such a call feels responsibility for his country, for religion, the hero is astir. Something will be done for which mankind waits.

But heroism is rare. We do not often commune with God nor listen with eager souls for His word. The world is always in need of men, but few appear. The usual is worshipped; the pleasure and profit of the day occupy us; even the sight of the cross does not rouse the heart. Speak, Heavenly Word! and quicken our clay. Let the thunders of Sinai be heard again, and then the still small voice that penetrates the soul. So shall heroism be born and duty done, and the dead shall live.

CHAPTER XI.

GIDEON, ICONOCLAST AND REFORMER.

JUDGES vi. 15-32.

"The Lord is with thee, thou mighty man of valour:"—so has the prophetic salutation come to the young man at the threshing-floor of Ophrah. It is a personal greeting and call— "with thee"—just what a man needs in the circumstances of Gideon. There is a nation to be saved, and a human leader must act for Jehovah. Is Gideon fit for so great a task? A wise humility, a natural fear have held him under the yoke of daily toil until this hour. Now the needed signs are given; his heart leaps up in the pulses of a longing which God approves and blesses. The criticism of kinsfolk, the suspicious carping of neighbours, the easily affronted pride of greater families no longer crush patriotic desire and overbear yearning faith. The Lord is with thee, Gideon, youngest son of Joash, the toiler in obscure fields. Go in this thy might; be strong in Jehovah.

But the assurance must widen if it is to satisfy. With me—that is a great thing for Gideon; that gives him free air to breathe and strength to use the sword. But can it be true? Can God be with one only in the land? He seems to have forsaken Israel and sold His people to the oppressor. Unless He returns to all in forgiveness and grace nothing can be done; a renewal of the nation is the first thing, and this Gideon desires. Comfort for himself, freedom from Midianite vexation for himself and his father's house would be no satisfaction if, all around, he saw Israel still crushed under heathen hordes. To have a hand in delivering his people from danger and sorrow is Gideon's craving. The assurance given to himself personally is welcome because in it there is a sound as of the beginning of Israel's redemption. Yet "if the Lord be with us, why then is all this befallen us?" God cannot be with the tribes, for they are harassed and spoiled by enemies, they lie prone before the altars of Baal.

There is here an example of largeness in heart and mind which we ought not to miss, especially because it sets before us a principle often unrecognised. It is clear enough that Gideon could not enjoy freedom unless his country was free, for no man can be safe in an enslaved land; but many fail to see that spiritual redemption, in like manner, cannot be enjoyed by one unless others are moving towards the light. Truly salvation is personal at first and personal at last; but it is never an individual affair only. Each for himself must hear and answer the divine call to repentance; each as a moral unit must enter the strait gate, press along the narrow way of life, agonise and overcome. But the redemption of one soul is part of a vast redeeming purpose, and the fibres of each life are interwoven with those of other lives far and wide. Spiritual brotherhood is a fact but faintly typified by the brotherhood of the Hebrews, and the struggling soul to-day, like Gideon's long ago, must know God as the Saviour of all men before a personal hope can be enjoyed worth the having. As Gideon showed himself to have the Lord with him by a question charged not with individual anxiety but with keen interest in the nation, so a man now is seen to have the Spirit of God as he exhibits a passion for the regeneration of the world. Salvation is enlargement of soul, devotion to God and to man for the sake of God. If any one thinks he is saved while he bears no burdens for others, makes no steady effort to liberate souls from the tyranny of the false and the vile, he is in fatal error. The salvation of Christ plants always in men and women His mind, His law of life, Who is the Brother and Friend of all.

And the church of Christ must be filled with His Spirit, animated by His law of life, or be unworthy the name. It exists to unite men in the quest and realisation of highest thought and purest activity. The church truly exists for all men, not simply for those who appear to compose it. Salvation and peace are with the church as with the individual believer, but only as her heart is generous, her spirit simple and unselfish. Doubtful and distressed as Gideon was the church of Christ should never be, for to her has been whispered the secret that the Abiezrite had not read, how the Lord is in the oppression and pain of the people, in the sorrow and the cloud. Nor is a church to suppose that salvation can be hers while she thinks of any outside with the least touch of Pharisaism, denying their share in Christ. Better no visible church than one claiming exclusive possession of truth and grace; better no church at all than one using the name of Christ for privilege and excommunication, restricting the fellowship of life to its own enclosure.

But with utmost generosity and humaneness goes the clear perception that God's service is the sternest of campaigns, beginning with resolute protest and decisive deed, and Gideon must rouse himself to strike for Israel's liberty first against the idol-worship of his own village. There stands the altar of Baal, the symbol of Israel's infidelity; there beside it the abominable Asherah, the sign of Israel's degradation. Already he has thought of demolishing these, but has never summoned courage, never seen that the result would justify him. For such a deed there is a time, and before the time comes the bravest man can only reap discomfiture. Now, with the warrant in his soul, the duty on his conscience, Gideon can make assault on a hateful superstition.

The idolatrous altar and false worship of one's own clan, of one's own family—these need courage to overturn and, more than courage, a ripeness of time and a Divine call. A man must be sure of himself and his motives, for one thing, before he takes upon him to be the corrector of errors that have seemed truth to his fathers and are maintained by his friends. Suppose people are actually worshipping a false god, a world-power which has long held rule among them. If one would act the part of iconoclast the question is, By what right? Is he himself clear of illusion and idolatry? Has he a better system to put in place of the old? He may be acting in mere bravado and self-display, flourishing opinions which have less sincerity than those which he assails. There were men in Israel who had no commission and could have claimed no right to throw down Baal's altar, and taking upon them such a deed would have had short shrift at the hands of the people of Ophrah. And so there are plenty among us who if they set up to be judges of their fellow-men and of beliefs which they call false, even when these are false, deserve simply to be put down with a strong hand. There are voices, professing to be those of zealous reformers, whose every word and tone are insults. The men need to go and learn the first lessons of truth, modesty, and earnestness. And this principle applies all round—to many who assail modern errors as well as to many who assail established beliefs. On the one hand, are men anxious to uphold the true faith? It is well. But anxiety and the best of motives do not qualify them to attack science, to denounce all rationalism as godless. We want defenders of the faith who have a Divine calling to the task in the way of long study and a heavenly fairness of mind, so that they shall not offend and hurt religion more by their ignorant vehemence than they help it by their zeal. On the other hand, by what authority do they speak who sneer at the ignorance of faith and would fain demolish the altars of the world? It is no slight equipment that is needed. Fluent sarcasm, confident worldliness, even a large acquaintance with the dogmas of science will not suffice. A man needs to prove himself a wise and humane thinker, he needs to know by experience and deep sympathy those perpetual wants of our race which Christ knew and met to the uttermost. Some facile admiration of Jesus of Nazareth does not give the right to free criticism of His life and words, or of the faith based upon them. And if the plea is a rare respect for truth, an unusual fidelity to fact, humanity will still ask of its would-be liberator on what fields he has won his rank or what yoke he has borne. Successful men especially will find it difficult to convince the world that they have a right to strike at the throne of Him who stood alone before the Roman Pilate and died on the Cross.

Gideon was not unfit to render high service. He was a young man tried in humble duty and disciplined in common tasks, shrewd but not arrogant, a person of clear mind and a patriot. The people of the farm and a good many in Ophrah had learned to trust him and were prepared to follow when he struck out a new path. He had God's call and also his own past to help him. Hence when Gideon began his undertaking, although to attempt it in broad day would have been rash and he must act under cover of darkness, he soon found ten men to give their aid. No doubt he could in a manner command them, for they were his servants. Still a business of the kind he proposed was likely to rouse their superstitious fears, and he had to conquer these. It was also sure to involve the men in some risk, and he must have been able to give them confidence in the issue. This he did, however, and they went forth. Very quietly the altar of Baal was demolished and the great wooden mast, hateful symbol of Astarte, was cut down and split in pieces. Such was the first act in the revolution.

We observe, however, that Gideon does not leave Ophrah without an altar and a sacrifice. Destroy one system without laying the foundation of another that shall more than equal it in essential truth and practical power, and what sort of deliverance have you effected? Men will rightly execrate you. It is no reformation that leaves the heart colder, the life barer and darker than before; and those who move in the night against superstition must be able to speak in the day of a Living God who will vindicate His servants. It has been said over and over again and must yet be repeated, to overturn merely is no service. They that break down need some vision at least of a building up, and it is the new edifice that is the chief thing. The world of thought to-day is infested with critics and destroyers and may well be tired of them. It is too much in need of constructors to have any thanks to spare for new Voltaires and Humes. Let us admit that demolition is the necessity of some hours. We look back on the ruins of Bastilles and temples that served the uses of tyranny, and even in the domain of faith there have been fortresses to throw down and ramparts that made evil separations among men. But destruction is not progress; and if the end of modern thought is to be agnosticism, the denial of all faith and all ideals, then we are simply on the way to something not a whit better than primeval ignorance.

The morning sun showed the gap upon the hill where the symbols had stood of Baal and Astarte, and soon like an angry swarm of bees the people were buzzing round the scattered stones of the old altar and the rough new pile with its smoking sacrifice. Where was he who ventured to rebuke the city? Very indignant, very pious are these false Israelites. They turn on Joash with the fierce demand, "Bring out thy son that he may die." But the father too has come to a decision. We get a hint of the same nature as Gideon's, slow, but firm when once roused; and if anything would rouse a man it would be this brutal passion, this sudden outbreak of cruelty nursed by heathen custom, his own conscience meanwhile testifying that Gideon was right. Tush! says Joash, will you plead for Baal? Will you save him? Is it necessary for you to defend one whom you have worshipped as Lord of heaven? Let him ply his lightnings if he has any. I am tired of this Baal who has no principles and is good only for feast-days. He that pleads for Baal, let him be the man to die.—Unexpected apology, serious too and unanswerable. Conscience that seemed dead is suddenly awakened and carries all before it. There is a quick conversion of the whole town because one man has acted decisively and another speaks strong words which cannot be gainsaid. To be sure Joash uses a threat—hints something of taking a very short method with those who still protest for Baal; and that helps conversion. But it is force against force, and men cannot object who have themselves talked of killing. By a rapid popular impulse Gideon is justified, and with the new name Jerubbaal he is acknowledged as a leader in Manasseh.

False religion is not always so easily exposed and upset. Truth may be so mixed with the error of a system that the moral sense is confused and faith clings to the follies and lies conjoined with the truth. And when we look at Judaism in contact with Christianity, at Romanism in contact with the Protestant spirit, we see how difficult it may be to liberate faith. The Apostle Paul, wielding the weapon of a singular and keen eloquence, cannot overcome the Pharisaism of his countrymen. At Antioch, at Iconium he does his utmost with scant success. The Protestant reformation did not so swiftly and thoroughly establish itself in every European country as in Scotland. Where there is no pressure of outward circumstances forcing new religious ideas upon men there must be all the more a spirit of independent thought if any salutary change is to be made in creed and worship. Either there must be men of Berea who search the Scriptures daily, men of Zurich and Berne with the energy of free citizens, or reformation must wait on some political emergency. And in effect conscience rarely has free play, since men are seldom manly, but more or less like sheep. Hence the value, as things go in this world, of leaders like Joash, princes like Luther's Elector, who give the necessary push to the undecided and check forward opponents by a significant warning. It is not the ideal way of reforming the world, but it has often answered well enough within limits. There are also cases in which the threats of the enemy have done good service, as when the appearance of the Spanish Armada on the English coast did more to confirm the Protestantism of the country than many years of peaceful argument. In truth, were there not occasionally something like master-strokes in Providence the progress of humanity would be almost imperceptible. Men and nations are urged on although they have no great desire to advance; they are committed to a voyage and cannot return; they are caught in currents and must go where the currents bear them. Certainly in such cases there is not the ardour, and men cannot reap the reward belonging to the thinkers and brave servants of the truth. Practically, whether Protestants or Romanists, they are spiritually inert. Still it is well for them, well for the world, that a strong hand should urge them forward, since otherwise they would not move at all. Of many in all churches it must be said they are not victors in a fight of faith, they do not work out their own salvation. Yet they are guided, warned, persuaded into a certain habit of piety and understanding of truth, and their children have a new platform, somewhat higher than their fathers', on which to begin life.

At Ophrah of the Abiezrites, though we cannot say much for the nature of the faith in God which has replaced idolatry, still the way is prepared for further and decisive action. Men do not cease from worshipping Baal and become true servants of the Most Holy in a single day; that requires time. There are better possibilities, but Gideon cannot teach the way of Jehovah, nor is he in the mood for religious inquiry. The conversion of Abiezer is quite of the same sort as in early Christian times was effected when a king went over to the new faith and ordered his subjects to be baptised. Not even Gideon knows the value of the faith to which the people have returned, in the strength of which they are to fight. They will be bold now, for even a little trust in God goes a long way in sustaining courage. They will face the enemy now to whom they have long submitted. But of the purity and righteousness into which the faith of Jehovah should lead them they have no vision.

Now with this in view many will think it strange to hear of the conversion of Abiezer. It is a great error however to despise the day of small things. God gives it and we ought to understand its use. Conversion cannot possibly mean the same in every period of the world's history; it cannot even mean the same in any two cases. To recognise this would be to clear the ground of much that hinders the teaching and the success of the gospel. Where there has been long familiarity with the New Testament, the facts of Christianity and the high spiritual ideas it presents, conversion, properly speaking, does not take place till the message of Christ to the soul stirs it to its depths, moves alike the reason and the will, and creates fervent discipleship. But the history of Israel and of humanity moves forward continuously in successive discoveries or revelations of the highest, culminating in the Christian salvation. To view Gideon as a religious reformer of the same kind as Isaiah is quite a mistake. He had scarcely an idea in common with the great prophet of a later day. But the liberty he desired for his people and the association of liberty with the worship of Jehovah made his revolution a step in the march of Israel's redemption. Those who joined him with any clear purpose and sympathy were therefore converted men in a true if very limited sense. There must be first the blade and then the ear before there can be the full corn. We reckon Gideon a hero of faith, and his hope was truly in the same God Whom we worship—the God and Father of our Lord Jesus Christ. Yet his faith could not be on a level with ours, his knowledge being far less. The angel who speaks to him, the altar he builds, the Spirit of the Lord that comes upon him, his daring iconoclasm, the new purpose and power of the man are in a range quite above material life—and that is enough.

There are some circles in which honesty and truth-speaking are evidence of a work of grace. To become honest and to speak truth in the fear of God is to be converted, in a sense, where things are at that pass. There are people who are so cold that among them enthusiasm for anything good may be called superhuman. Nobody has it. If it appears it must come from above. But these steps of progress, though we may describe them as supernatural, are elementary. Men have to be converted again and again, ever making one gain a step to another. The great advance comes when the soul believes enthusiastically in Christ, pledging itself to Him in full sight of the cross. This and nothing less is the conversion we need. To love freedom, righteousness, charity only prepares for the supreme love of God in Christ, in which life springs to its highest power and joy.

Now are we to suppose that Gideon alone of all the men of Israel had the needful spirit and faith to lead the revolution? Was there no one but the son of Joash? We do not find him fully equipped, nor as the years go by does he prove altogether worthy to be chief of the tribes of God. Were there not in many Hebrew towns souls perhaps more ardent, more spiritual than his, needing only the prophetic call, the touch of the Unseen Hand to make them aware of power and opportunity? The leadership of such a one as Moses is complete and unquestionable. He is the man of the age; knowledge, circumstances, genius fit him for the place he has to occupy. We cannot imagine a second Moses in the same period. But in Israel as well as among other peoples it is often a very imperfect hero who is found and followed. The work is done, but not so well done as we might think possible. Revolutions which begin full of promise lose their spirit because the leader reveals his weakness or even folly. We feel sure that there are many who have the power to lead in thought where the world has not dreamt of climbing, to make a clear road where as yet there is no path;

and yet to them comes no messenger, the daily task goes on and it is not supposed that a leader, a prophet is passed by. Are there no better men that Ehud, Gideon, Jephthah must stand in the front?

One answer certainly is that the nation at the stage it has reached cannot as a whole esteem a better man, cannot understand finer ideas. A hundred men of more spiritual faith were possibly brooding over Israel's state, ready to act as fearlessly as Gideon and to a higher issue. But it could only have been after a cleansing of the nation's life, a suppression of Baal-worship much more rigorous than could at that time be effected. And in every national crisis the thought of which the people generally are capable determines who must lead and what kind of work shall be done. The reformer before his time either remains unknown or ends in eclipse; either he gains no power or it passes rapidly from him because it has no support in popular intelligence or faith.

It may seem well-nigh impossible in our day for any man to fail of the work he can do; if he has the will we think he can make the way. The inward call is the necessity, and when that is heard and the man shapes a task for himself the day to begin will come. Is that certain? Perhaps there are many now who find circumstance a web from which they cannot break away without arrogance and unfaithfulness. They could speak, they could do if God called them; but does He call them? On every side ring the fluent praises of the idols men love to worship. One must indeed be deft in speech and many other arts who would hope to turn the crowd from its folly, for it will only listen to what seizes the ear, and the obscure thinker has not the secret of pleasing. While those who see no visions lead their thousands to a trivial victory, many an uncalled Gideon toils on in the threshing-floor. The duties of a low and narrow lot may hold a man; the babble all around of popular voices may be so loud that nothing can make way against them. A certain slowness of the humble and patient spirit may keep one silent who with little encouragement could speak words of quickening truth. But the day of utterance never comes.

To these waiting in the market-place it is comparatively a small thing that the world will not hire them. But does the church not want them? Where God is named and professedly honoured, can it be that the smooth message is preferred because it is smooth? Can it be that in the church men shrink from instead of seeking the highest, most real and vital word that can be said to them? This is what oppresses, for it seems to imply that God has no use in His vineyard for a man when He lets him wait long unregarded; it seems to mean that there is no end for the wistful hope and the words that burn unspoken in the breast. The unrecognised thinker has indeed to trust God largely. He has often to be content with the assurance that what he would say but cannot as yet shall be said in good time, that what he would do but may not shall be done by a stronger hand. And further, he may cherish a faith for himself. No life can remain for ever unfruitful, or fruitful only in its lower capacities. Purposes broken off here shall find fulfilment. Where the highways of being reach beyond the visible horizon leaders will be needed for the yet advancing host, and the time of every soul shall come to do the utmost that is in it. The day of perfect service for many of God's chosen ones will begin where beyond these shadows there is light and space. Were it not so, some of the best lives would disappear in the darkest cloud.

CHAPTER XII.

"*THE PEOPLE ARE YET TOO MANY.*"

JUDGES vi. 33-vii. 7.

ANOTHER day of hope and energy has dawned. One hillside at least rises sunlit out of darkness with the altar of Jehovah on its summit and holier sacrifices smoking there than Israel has offered for many a year. Let us see what elements of promise, what elements of danger or possible error mingle with the situation. There is a man to take the lead, a young man, thoughtful, bold, energetic, aware of a Divine call and therefore of some endowment for the task to be done. Gideon believes Jehovah to be Israel's God and Friend, Israel to be Jehovah's people. He has faith in the power of the Unseen Helper. Baal is nothing, a mere name—Bosheth, vanity. Jehovah is a certainty; and what He wills shall come about. So far strength, confidence. But of himself and the people Gideon is not sure. His own ability to gather and command an army, the fitness of any army the tribes can supply to contend with Midian, these are as yet unproved. Only one fact stands clear, Jehovah the supreme God with Whom are all powers and influences. The rest is in shadow. For one thing, Gideon cannot trace the connection between the Most High and himself, between the Power that controls the world and the power that dwells in his own will or the hearts of other men. Yet with the first message a sign has been given, and other tokens may be sought as events move on. With that measure of uncertainty which keeps a man humble and makes him ponder his steps Gideon finds himself acknowledged leader in Manasseh and a centre of growing enthusiasm throughout the northern tribes.

For the people generally this at least may be said, that they have wisdom enough to recognise the man of aptitude and courage, though he belongs to one of the humblest families and is the least in his father's household. Drowning men indeed must take the help that is offered, and Israel is at present almost in the condition of a drowning man. A little more and it will sink under the wave of the Midianite invasion. It is not a time to ask of the rank of a man who has character for the emergency. And yet, so often is the hero unacknowledged, especially when he begins, as Gideon did, with a religious stroke, that some credit must be given to the people for their ready faith. As the flame goes up from the altar at Ophrah men feel a flash of hope and promise. They turn to the Abiezrite in trust and through him begin to trust God again. Yes: there is a reformation of a sort, and an honest man is at the head of it. So far the signs of the time are good.

Then the old enthusiasm is not dead. Almost Israel had submitted, but again its spirit is rising. The traditions of Deborah and Barak, of Joshua, of Moses, of the desert march and victories linger with those who are hiding amongst the caves and rocks. Songs of liberty, promises of power are still theirs; they feel that they should be free. Canaan is Jehovah's gift to them and they will claim it. So far as reviving human energy and confidence avail, there is a germ out of which the proper life of the people of God may spring afresh. And it is this that Gideon as a reformer must nourish, for the leader depends at every stage on the desires that have been kindled in the hearts of men. While he goes before them in thought and plan he can only go prosperously where they intelligently, heartily will follow. Opportunism is the base lagging behind with popular coldness, as moderatism in religion is. The reformer does not wait a moment when he sees an aspiration he can guide, a spark of faith that can be fanned into flame. But neither in church nor state can one man make a conquering movement. And so we see the vast extent of duty and responsibility. That there may be no opportunism every citizen must be alive to the morality of politics. That there may be no moderatism every Christian must be alive to the real duty of the church.

Now have the heads of families and the chief men in Israel been active in rallying the tribes? Or have the people waited on their chiefs and the chiefs coldly held back?

There are good elements in the situation, but others not so encouraging. The secular leaders have failed; and what are the priests and Levites doing? We hear nothing of them. Gideon has to assume the double office of priest and ruler. At Shiloh there is an altar. There too is the ark, and surely some holy observances are kept. Why does Gideon not lead the people to Shiloh and there renew the national covenant through the ministers of the tabernacle? He knows little of the moral law and the sanctities of worship; and he is not at this stage inclined to assume a function that is not properly his. Yet it is unmistakable that Ophrah has to be the religious centre. Ah! clearly there is opportunism among secular leaders and moderatism among the priests. And this suggests that Judah in the south, although the tabernacle is not in her territory, may have an ecclesiastical reason for holding aloof now, as in Deborah's time she kept apart. Simeon and Levi are brethren. Judah, the vanguard in the desert march, the leading tribe in the first assault on Canaan, has taken Simeon into close alliance. Has Levi also been almost absorbed? There are signs that it may have been so. The later supremacy of Judah in religion requires early and deep root; and we have also to explain the separation between north and south already evident, which was but half overcome by David's kingship and reappeared before the end of Solomon's reign. It is very significant to read in the closing chapters of Judges of two Levites both of whom were connected with Judah. The Levites were certainly respected through the whole land, but their absence from all the incidents of the period of Deborah, Gideon, Abimelech, and Jephthah compels the supposition that they had most affinity with Judah and Simeon in the south. We know how people can be divided by ecclesiasticism; and there is at least some reason to suspect that while the northern tribes were suffering and fighting Judah went her own way, enjoying peace and organising worship.

Such then is the state of matters so far as the tribes are concerned at the time when Gideon sounds the trumpet in Abiezer and sends messengers throughout Manasseh, Zebulun, Asher, and Naphtali. The tribes are partly prepared for conflict, but they are weak and still disunited. The muster of fighting men who gather at the call of Gideon is considerable and perhaps astonishes him. But the Midianites are in enormous numbers in the plain of Jezreel between Moreh and Gilboa, having drawn together from their marauding expeditions at the first hint of a rising among the Hebrews. And now as the chief reviews his troops his early apprehension returns. It is with something like dismay that he passes from band to band. Ill-disciplined, ill-assorted, these men do not bear the air of coming triumph. Gideon has too keen sight to be misled by tokens of personal popularity; nor can he estimate success by numbers. Looking closely into the faces of the men he sees marks enough of hesitancy, tokens even of fear. Many seem as if they had gathered like sheep to the slaughter, not as lions ready to dash on the prey. Assurance of victory he cannot find in his army; he must seek it elsewhere.

It is well that multitudes gather to the church to-day for worship and enter themselves as members. But to reckon all such as an army contending with infidelity and wickedness—that would indeed be a mistake. The mere tale of numbers gives no estimation of strength, fighting strength, strength to resist and to suffer. It is needful clearly to distinguish between those who may be called captives of the church or vassals simply, rendering a certain respect, and those others, often a very few and perhaps the least regarded, who really fight the battles. Our reckoning at present is often misleading so that we occupy ground which we cannot defend. We attempt to assail infidelity with an ill-disciplined host, many of whom have no clear faith, and to overcome worldliness by the co-operation of those who are more than half absorbed in the pastimes and follies of the world. There is need to look back to Gideon, who knew what it was to fight. While we are thankful to have so many connected with the church for their own good we must not suppose that they represent aggressive strength; on the contrary we must clearly understand that they will require no small part of the available time and energy of the earnest. In short we have to count them not as helpers of the church's forward movement but as those who must be helped.

Gideon for his work will have to make sharp division. Three hundred who can dash fearlessly on the enemy will be more to his purpose than two-and-thirty thousand most of whom grow pale at the thought of battle, and he will separate by-and-by. But first he seeks another sign of Jehovah. This man knows that to do anything worthy for his fellow-men he must be in living touch with God. The idea has no more than elementary form; but it rules. He, Gideon, is only an instrument, and he must be well convinced that God is working through him. How can he be sure? Like other Israelites he is strongly persuaded that God appears and speaks to men through nature; and he craves a sign in the natural world which is of God's making and upholding. Now to us the sign Gideon asked may appear rude, uncouth, and without any moral significance. A fleece which is to be wet one morning while the threshing-floor is dry, and dry next morning while the threshing-floor is wet, supplies the means of testing the Divine presence and approval. Further it may be alleged that the phenomena admit of natural explanation. But this is the meaning. Gideon, providing the fleece, identifies himself with it. It is his fleece, and if God's dew drenches it that will imply that God's power shall enter Gideon's soul and abide in it even though Israel be dry as the dusty floor. The thought is at once simple and profound, child-like and Hebrew-like, and carefully we must observe that it is a nature sign, not a mere portent, Gideon looks for. It is not whether God can do a certain seemingly impossible thing. That would not help Gideon. But the dew represents to his mind the vigour he needs, the vigour Israel needs if he should fail; and in reversing the sign, " Let the dew be on the ground and the fleece be dry," he seems to provide a hope, even in prospect of his own failure or death. Gideon's appeal is for a revelation of the Divine in the same sphere as the lightning storm and rain in which Deborah found a triumphant proof of Jehovah's presence; yet there is a notable contrast. We are reminded of the " still small voice" Elijah heard as he stood in the cave-mouth after the rending wind and the earthquake and the lightning. We remember also the image of Hosea, " I will be as the dew unto Israel." There is a question in the Book of Job, " Hath the rain a father? or who hath begotten the drops of dew?" The faith of Gideon makes answer, "Thou, O Most High, dost give the dews of heaven." The silent distillation of the dew is profoundly symbolic of the spiritual economy and those energies that are " not of this noisy world but silent and Divine." There is much of interest and meaning that lies thus beneath the surface in the story of the fleece.

Assured that yet another step in advance may be taken, Gideon leads his forces northward and goes into camp beside the spring of Harod on the slope of Gilboa. Then he does what seems a strange thing for a general on the eve of battle. The army is large, but utterly insufficient in discipline and *morale* for a pitched battle with the Midianites. Men who have hastily snatched their fathers' swords and pikes of which they are half afraid are not to be relied upon in the heat of a terrible struggle. Proclamation is therefore made that those who are fearful and trembling shall return to their homes. From the entrenchment of Israel on the hillside, where the name Jalid or Gilead still survives, the great camp of the desert people could be seen, the black tents darkening all the valley toward the slope of Moreh a few miles away. The sight was enough to appal even the bold. Men thought of their families and homesteads. Those who had anything to lose began to re-consider and by morning only one-third of the Hebrew army was left with the leader. So perhaps it would be with thousands of Christians if the church were again called to share the reproach of Christ and resist unto blood. Under the banner of a popular Christianity many march to stirring music who, if they supposed struggle to be imminent, would be tempted to leave the ranks. Yet the fight is actually going on. Camp is set against camp, army is mingled with army; at the front there is hot work and many are falling. But in the rear it would seem to be a holiday; men are idling, gossiping, chaffering as though they had come out for amusement or trade, not at all like those who have pledged life in a great cause and have everything to win or lose. And again, in the thick of the strife, where courage and energy are strained to the utmost, we look round and ask whether the fearful have indeed withdrawn, for the suspicion is forced upon us that many who call themselves Christ's are on the other side. Did not some of those who are striking at us lift their hands yesterday in allegiance to the great Captain? Do we not see some who have marched with us holding the very position we are to take, bearing the very standards we must capture? Strangely confused is the field of battle, and hard is it to distinguish friends from foes. If the fearful would retire we should know better how we stand. If the enemy were all of Midian the issue would be clear. But fearful and faint-hearted Israelites who may be found any time actually contending against the faith are foes of a kind unknown in simpler days. So frequently does something of this sort happen that every Christian has need to ask himself whether he is clear of the offence. Has he ever helped to make the false world strong against the true, the proud world strong against the meek? Many of those who are doubtful and go home may sooner be pardoned than he who strikes only where a certain false *éclat* is to be won.

" Just for a handful of silver he left us,—
   Just for a riband to stick in his coat—
Found the one gift of which fortune bereft us,
   Lost all the others she lets us devote . . . .
We shall march prospering—not thro' his presence ;
   Songs may inspirit us—not from his lyre ;
Deeds will be done—while he boasts his quiescence,
   Still bidding crouch whom the rest bade aspire."

In the same line of thought lies another reflection. The men who had hastily snatched their fathers' swords and pikes of which they were half afraid represent to us certain modern defenders of Christianity—those who carry edged weapons of inherited doctrine with which they dare not strike home. The great battle-axes of reprobation, of eternal judgment, of Divine severity against sin once wielded by strong hands, how they tremble and swerve in the grasp of many a modern dialectician. The sword of the old creed, that once like Excalibur cleft helmets and breastplates through, how often it maims the hands that try to use it but want alike the strength and the cunning. Too often we see a wavering blow struck that draws not a drop of blood nor even dints a shield, and the next thing is that the knight has run to cover behind some old bulwark long riddled and dilapidated. In the hands of these unskilled fighters too well armed for their strength the battle is worse than lost. They become a laughing-stock to the enemy, an irritation to their own side. It is time there was a sifting among the defenders of the faith and twenty and two thousand went back from Gilead. Is the truth of God become mere tin or lead that no new sword can be fashioned from it, no blade of Damascus firm and keen? Are there no gospel armourers fit for the task? Where the doctrinal contest is maintained by men who are not to the depth of their souls sure of the creeds they found on, by men who have no vision of the severity of God and the meaning of redemption, it ends only in confusion to themselves and those who are with them.

Ten thousand Israelites remain who according to their own judgment are brave enough and prepared for the fight; but the purpose of the commander is not answered yet. He is resolved to have yet another winnowing that shall leave only the men of temper like his own, men of quick intelligence no less than zeal. At the foot of the hill there flows a stream of water, and towards it Gideon leads his diminished army as if at once to cross and attack the enemy in camp. Will they seize his plan and like one man act upon it? Only on those who do can he depend. It is an effective trial. With the hot work of fighting before them the water is needful to all, but in the way of drinking men show their spirit. The most kneel or lie down by the edge of the brook, that by putting their lips to the water they may take a long and leisurely draught. A few supply themselves in quite another way. As a dog whose master is passing on with rapid strides, coming to a pool or stream by the way, stops a moment to lap a few mouthfuls of water and then is off again to his master's side, so do these—three hundred of the ten thousand—bending swiftly down carry water to their mouths in the hollow of the hand. Full of the day's business they move on again before the nine thousand seven hundred have well begun to drink. They separate themselves and are by Gideon's side, beyond the stream, a chosen band proved fit for the work that is to be done. It is no haphazard division that is made by the test of the stream. There is wisdom in it, inspiration. "And the Lord said unto Gideon, By the three hundred men that lapped will I save you and deliver the Midianites into thine hand."

Many are the commonplace incidents, the seemingly small points in life that test the quality of men. Every day we are led to the stream-side to show what we are, whether eager in the Divine enterprise of faith or slack and self-considering. Take any company of men and women who claim to be on the side of Christ, engaged and bound in all seriousness to His service. But how many have it clearly before them that they must not entangle themselves more than is absolutely needful with bodily and sensuous cravings, that they must not lie down to drink from the stream of pleasure and amusement? We show our spiritual state by the way in which we spend our leisure, our Saturday afternoons, our Sabbaths. We show whether we are fit for God's business by our use of the flowing stream of literature, which to some is an opiate, to others a pure and strengthening draught. The question simply is whether we are so engaged with God's plan for our life, in comprehending it, fulfilling it, that we have no time to dawdle and no disposition for the merely casual and trifling. Are we in the responsible use of our powers occupied as that Athenian was in the service of his country of whom it is recorded: "There was in the whole city but one street in which Pericles was ever seen, the street which led to the market-place and the council-house. During the whole period of his administration he never dined at the table of a friend"? Let no one say there is not time in a world like this for social intercourse, for literary and scientific pursuits, or the practice of the arts. The plan of God for men means life in all possible fulness and entrance into every field in which power can be gained. His will for us is that we should give to the world as Christ gave in free and uplifting ministry, and as a man can only give what he has first made his own the Christian is called to self-culture as full as the other duties of life will permit. He cannot explore too much, he cannot be too well versed in the thoughts and doings of men and the revelations of nature, for all he learns is to find high use. But the aim of personal enlargement and efficiency must never be forgotten, that aim which alone makes the self of value and gives it real life—the service and glory of God. Only in view of this aim is culture worth anything. And when in the providence of God there comes a call which requires us to pass with resolute step beyond every stream at which the mind and taste are stimulated that we may throw ourselves into the hard fight against evil there is to be no hesitation. Everything must yield now. The comparatively small handful who press on with concentrated purpose, making God's call and His work first and all else, even their own needs, a secondary affair—to these will be the honour and the joy of victory.

We live in a time when people are piling up object after object that needs attention and entering into engagement after engagement that comes between them and the supreme duty of existence. They form so many acquaintances that every spare hour goes in visiting and receiving visits: yet the end of life is not talk. They are members of so many societies that they scarcely get at the work for which the societies exist: yet the end of life is not organising. They see so many books, hear so much news and criticism that truth escapes them altogether: yet the end of life is to know and do the Truth. Civilisation defeats its own use when it keeps us drinking so long at this and the other spring that we forget the battle. We mean to fight, we mean to do our part, but night falls while we are still occupied on the way. Yet our Master is one who restricted the earthly life to its simplest elements because only so could spiritual energy move freely to its mark.

In the incidents we have been reviewing voluntary churches may find hints at least towards the justification of their principle. The idea of a national church is on more than one side intelligible and valid. Christianity stands related to the whole body of the people, bountiful even to those who scorn its laws, pleading on their behalf with God, keeping an open door and sending forth a perpetual call of love to the weak, the erring, the depraved. The ideal of a national church is to represent this universal office and realise this inclusiveness of the Christian religion; and the charm is great. On the other hand a voluntary church is the recognition of the fact that while Christ stands related to all men it is those only who engage at expense to themselves in the labour of the gospel who can be called believers, and that these properly constitute the church. The Hebrew people under the theocracy may represent the one ideal; Gideon's sifting of his army points to the other; neither, it must be frankly confessed, has ever been realised. Large numbers may join with some intelligence in worship and avail themselves of the sacraments who have no sense of obligation as members of the kingdom and are scarcely touched by the teaching of Christianity as to sin and salvation. A separated community again, depending on an enthusiasm which too often fails, rarely if ever accomplishes its hope. It aims at exhibiting an active and daring faith, the militancy, the urgency of the gospel, and in this mission what is counted success may be a hindrance and a snare. Numbers grow, wealth is acquired, but the intensity of belief is less than it was and the sacrifices still required are not freely made. Nevertheless is it not plain that a society which would represent the imperative claim of Christ to the undivided faith and loyalty of His followers must found upon a personal sense of obligation and personal eagerness? Is it not plain that a society which would represent the purity, the unearthliness, the rigour, we may even say, of Christ's doctrine, His life of renunciation and His cross must show a separateness from the careless world and move distinctly in advance of popular religious sentiment? Israel was God's people, yet when a leader went forth to a work of deliverance he had to sift out the few keen and devoted spirits. In truth every reformation implies a winnowing, and he does little as a teacher or a guide who does not make division among men.

CHAPTER XIII.

"MIDIAN'S EVIL DAY."

JUDGES vii. 8-viii. 21.

THERE is now with Gideon a select band of three hundred, ready for a night attack on the Midianites. The leader has been guided to a singular and striking plan of action. It is, however, as he well knows, a daring thing to begin assault upon the immense camp of Midian with so small a band, even though reserves of nearly ten thousand wait to join in the struggle; and we can easily see that the temper and spirit of the enemy were important considerations on the eve of so hazardous a battle. If the Midianites, Amalekites, and Children of the East formed a united army, if they were prepared to resist, if they had posted sentinels on every side and were bold in prospect of the fight, it was necessary for Gideon to be well aware of the facts. On the other hand if there were symptoms of division in the tents of the enemy, if there were no adequate preparations, and especially if the spirit of doubt or fear had begun to show itself, these would be indications that Jehovah was preparing victory for the Hebrews.

Gideon is led to inquire for himself into the condition of the Midianitish host. To learn that already his name kindles terror in the ranks of the enemy will dispel his lingering anxiety. "Jehovah said unto him . . . Go thou with Purah thy servant down to the camp; and thou shalt hear what they say; and afterward shall thine hands be strengthened." The principle is that for those who are on God's side it is always best to know fully the nature of the opposition. The temper of the enemies of religion, those irregular troops of infidelity and unrighteousness with whom we have to contend, is an element of great importance in shaping the course of our Christian warfare. We hear of organised vice, of combinations great and resolute against which we have to do battle. Language is used which implies that the condition of the churches of Christ contrasts pitiably with the activity and agreement of those who follow the black banners of evil. A vague terror possesses many that in the conflict with vice they must face immense resources and a powerful confederacy. The far-stretching encampment of the Midianites is to all appearance organised for defence at every point, and while the servants of God are resolved to attack they are oppressed by the vastness of the enterprise. Impiety, sensuality, injustice may seem to be in close alliance with each other, on the best understanding, fortified by superhuman craft and malice, with their gods in their midst to help them. But let us go down to the host and listen, the state of things may be other than we have thought.

Under cover of the night which made Midian seem more awful the Hebrew chief and his servant left the outpost on the slope of Gilboa and crept from shadow to shadow across the space which separated them from the enemy, vaguely seeking what quickly came. Lying in breathless silence behind some bush or wall the Hebrews heard one relating a dream to his fellow. "I dreamed," he said, "and, lo, a cake of barley bread tumbled into the camp of Midian and came unto a tent and smote it that it fell, and overturned it that it lay along." The thoughts of the day are reproduced in the visions of the night. Evidently this man has had his mind directed to the likelihood of attack, the possibility of defeat. It is well known that the Hebrews are gathering to try the issue of battle. They are indeed like a barley cake such as poor Arabs bake among ashes—a defeated famished people whose life has been almost drained away. But tidings have come of their return to Jehovah and traditions of His marvellous power are current among the desert tribes. A confused sense of all this has shaped the dream in which the tent of the chief appears prostrate and despoiled. Gideon and Purah listen intently, and what they hear further is even more unexpected and reassuring. The dream is interpreted: "This is nothing else save the sword of Gideon the son of Joash, a man of Israel; for into his hand God hath delivered Midian and all the host." He who reads the dream knows more than the other. He has the name of the Hebrew captain. He has heard of the Divine messenger who called Gideon to his task and assured him of victory. As for the apparent strength of the host of Midian, he has no confidence in it, for he has felt the tremor that passes through the great camp. So, lying concealed, Gideon hears from his enemies themselves as from God the promise of victory, and full of worshipping joy hastens back to prepare for an immediate attack.

Now in every combination of godless men there is a like feeling of insecurity, a like presage of disaster. Those who are in revolt against justice, truth, and the religion of God have nothing on which to rest, no enduring bond of union. What do they conceive as the issue of their attempts and schemes? Have they anything in view that can give heart and courage; an end worth toil and hazard? It is impossible, for their efforts are all in the region of the false, where the seeming realities are but shadows that perpetually change. Let it be allowed that to a certain extent common interests draw together men of no principle so that they can co-operate for a time. Yet each individual is secretly bent on his own pleasure or profit and there is nothing that can unite them constantly. One selfish and unjust person may be depended upon to conceive a lively antipathy to every other selfish and unjust person. Midian and Amalek have their differences with one another, and each has its own rival chiefs, rival families, full of the bitterest jealousy, which at any moment may burst into flame. The whole combination is weak from the beginning, a mere horde of clashing desires incapable of harmony, incapable of a sustaining hope.

In the course of our Lord's brief ministry the insecurity of those who opposed Him was often shown. The chief priests and scribes and lawyers whispered to each other the fears and anxieties He aroused. In the Sanhedrin the discussion about Him comes to the point, "What do we? For this man doeth many signs. If we let Him thus alone, all men will believe on Him: and the Romans will come and take away both our peace and our nation." The Pharisees say among themselves, "Perceive ye how ye prevail nothing? Behold the world is gone after Him." And what was the reason, what was the cause of this weakness? Intense devotion to the law and the institutions of religion animated those Israelites, yet sufficed not to bind them together. Rival schools and claims honeycombed the whole social and ecclesiastical fabric. The pride of religious ancestry and a keenly cherished ambition could not maintain peace or hope; they were of no use against the calm authority of the Nazarene. Judaism was full of the bitterness of falsehood. The seeds of despair were in the minds of those who accused Christ, and the terrible harvest was reaped within a generation.

Passing from this supreme evidence that the wrong can never be the strong, look at those ignorant and unhappy persons who combine against the laws of society. Their suspicions of each other are proverbial, and ever with them is the feeling that sooner or later they will be overtaken by the law. They dream of that and tell each other their dreams. The game of crime is played against well-known odds. Those who carry it on are aware that their haunts will be discovered, their gang broken up. A bribe will tempt one of their number, and the rest will have to go their way to the cell or the gallows. Yet with the presage of defeat wrought into the very constitution of the mind and with innumerable proofs that it is no delusion, there are always those amongst us who attempt what even in this world is so hazardous and in the larger sweep of moral economy is impossible. In selfishness, in oppression and injustice, in every kind of sensuality men adventure as if they could ensure their safety and defy the day of reckoning.

Gideon is now well persuaded that the fear of disaster is not for Israel. He returns to the camp and forthwith prepares to strike. It seems to him now the easiest thing possible to throw into confusion that great encampment of Midian. One bold device rapidly executed will set in operation the suspicions and fears of the different desert tribes and they will melt away in defeat. The stratagem has already shaped itself. The three hundred are provided with the earthenware jars or pitchers in which their simple food has been carried. They soon procure firebrands and from among the ten thousand in the camp enough rams' horns are collected to supply one to each of the attacking party. Then three bands are formed of equal strength and ordered to advance from different sides upon the enemy, holding themselves ready at a given signal to break the pitchers, flash the torches in the air and make as much noise as they can with their rude mountain horns. The scheme is simple, quaint, ingenious. It reveals skill in making use of the most ordinary materials which is of the very essence of generalship. The harsh cornets especially filling the valley with barbaric tumult are well adapted to create terror and confusion. We hear nothing of ordinary weapons, but it must not be supposed that the three hundred were unarmed.

It was not long after midnight, the middle watch had been newly set, when the three companies reached their stations. The orders had been well seized and all went precisely as Gideon had conceived. With crash and tumult and flare of torches there came the battle-shout—"Sword of Jehovah and of Gideon." The Israelites had no need to press forward; they stood every man in his place, while fear and suspicion did the work. The host ran and cried and fled. To and fro among the tents, seeing, now on this side now on that, the menacing flames, turning from the battlecry here to be met in an opposite quarter by the wild dissonance of the horns, the surprised army was thrown into utter confusion. Every one thought of treachery and turned his sword against his fellow. Escape was the common impulse, and the flight of the disorganised host took a southeasterly direction by the road that led to the Jordan valley and across it to the Hauran and the desert. It was a complete rout and the Hebrews had only to follow up their advantage. Those who had not shared the attack joined in the pursuit. Every village that the flying Midianites passed sent out its men, brave enough now that the arm of the tyrant was broken. Down to the ghor of Jordan the terrorstricken Arabs fled and along the bank for many a mile, harassed in the difficult ground by the Hebrews who know every yard of it. At the fords there is dreadful work. Those who cross at the highest point near Succoth are not the main body, but the two chiefs Zebah and Zalmunna are among them and Gideon takes them in hand. Away to the south Ephraim has its opportunity and gains a victory where the road along the valley of Jordan diverges to Bethbarah. For days and nights the retreat goes on till the strange swift triumph of Israel is assured.

1. There is in this narrative a lesson as to equipment for the battle of life and the service of God somewhat like that which we found in the story of Shamgar, yet with points of difference. We are reminded here of what may be done without wealth, without the material apparatus that is often counted necessary. The modern habit is to make much of tools and outfit. The study and applications of science have brought in a fashion of demanding everything possible in the way of furniture, means, implements. Everywhere this fashion prevails, in the struggle of commerce and manufacture, in literature and art, in teaching and household economy, worst of all in church life and work. Michael Angelo wrought the frescoes of the Sistine chapel with the ochres he dug with his own hands from the garden of the Vatican. Mr. Darwin's great experiments were conducted with the rudest and cheapest furniture, anything a country house could supply. But in the common view it is on perfect tools and material almost everything depends; and we seem in the way of being absolutely mastered by them. What, for example, is the ecclesiasticism which covers an increasing area of religious life? And what is the parish or congregation fully organised in the modern sense? Must we not call them elab-

orate machinery expected to produce spiritual life? There must be an extensive building with every convenience for making worship agreeable; there must be guilds and guild rooms, societies and committees, each with an array of officials; there must be due assignment of observances to fit days and seasons; there must be architecture, music, and much else. The ardent soul desiring to serve God and man has to find a place in conjunction with all this and order his work so that it may appear well in a report. To some these things may appear ludicrous, but they are too significant of the drift from that simplicity and personal energy in which the Church of Christ began. We seem to have forgotten that the great strokes have been made by men who like Gideon delayed not for elaborate preparation nor went back on rule and precedent, but took the firebrands, pitchers, and horns that could be got together on a hill-side. The great thing both in the secular and in the spiritual region is that men should go straight at the work which has to be done and do it with sagacity, intelligence, and fervour of their own.

We look back to those few plain men with whom lay the new life of the world, going forth with the strong certain word of a belief for which they could die, a truth by which the dead could be revived. Their equipment was of the soul. Of outward means and material advantages they were, one may say, destitute. Our methods are very different. No doubt in these days there is a work of defence which requires the finest weapons and most careful preparation. Yet even here no weight of polished armour is so good for David's use as the familiar sling and stone. And in the general task of the church, teaching, guiding, setting forth the gospel of Christ, whatever keeps soul from honest and hearty touch with soul is bad. We want above all things men who have sanctified common-sense, mother-wit, courage and frank simplicity, men who can find their own means and gain their own victories. The churches that do not breed such are doomed.

2. We have been reading a story of panic and defeat, and we may be advised to find in it a hint of the fate that is to overtake Christianity when modern criticism has finally ordered its companies and provided them with terrifying horns and torches. Or certain Christians may feel that the illustration fits the state of alarm in which they are obliged to live. Is not the church like that encampment in the valley, exposed to the most terrible and startling attacks on all sides, and in peril constantly of being routed by unforeseen audacities, here of Ingersoll, Bakunin, Bebel, there of Huxley or Renan? Not seldom still, though after many a false alarm, the cry is raised, "The church, the faith—in danger!"

Once for all—the Church of the Lord Jesus Christ is never in danger, though enemies buzz on every side like furious hornets. A confederation of men, a human organisation may be in deadly peril and may know that the harsh tumult around it means annihilation. But no institution is identical with the Catholic Church, much less with the kingdom of God. Christians need not dread the honest criticism which has a right to speak, nor even the malice, envy, which have no right yet dare to utter themselves. Whether it be sheer atheism or scientific dogma or political change or criticism of the Bible that makes the religious world tremble and cry out for fear, in every case panic is unchristian and unworthy. For one thing, do we not frame numerous thoughts and opinions of our own and devise many forms of service which in the course of time we come to regard as having a sacredness equal to the doctrine and ordinances of Christ? And do we not frequently fall into the error of thinking that the symbols, traditions, outward forms of a Christian society are essential and as much to be contended for as the substance of the gospel? Criticism of these is dreaded as criticism of Christ, decay of them is regarded, often quite wrongly, as decay of the work of God on earth. We forget that forms, as such, are on perpetual trial, and we forget also that no revolution or seeming disaster can touch the facts on which Christianity rests. The Divine gospel is eternal. Indeed, assailants of the right sort are needed, and even those of the bad sort have their use. The encampment of the unseeing and unthinking, of the self-loving and arrogant needs to be startled; and he is no emissary of Satan who honestly leads an attack where men lie in false peace, though he may be for his own part but a rude fighter. The panic indeed sometimes takes a singular and pathetic form. The unexpected enemy breaks in on the camp with blare of ignorant rebuke and noisy demonstration of strength and authority. Him the church hails as a new apostle, at his feet she takes her place with a strange unprofitable humility; and this is the worst kind of disaster. Better far a serious battle than such submission.

3. Without pursuing this suggestion we pass to another raised by the conduct of the men of Ephraim. They obeyed the call of Gideon when he hastily summoned them to take the lower fords of Jordan within their own territory and prevent the escape of the Midianites. To them it fell to gain a great victory, and especially to slay two subordinate chiefs, Oreb and Zeeb, the Crow and the Wolf. But afterwards they complained that they had not been called at first when the commander was gathering his army. We are informed that they chode with him sharply on this score, and it was only by his soft answer which implied a little flattery that they were appeased. "What have I now in comparison with you? Is not the gleaming of the grapes of Ephraim better than the vintage of Abiezer?"

The men of Ephraim were not called at first along with Manasseh, Zebulun, Asher, and Naphtali. True. But why? Was not Gideon aware of their selfish indifference? Did he not read their character? Did he not perceive that they would have sullenly refused to be led by a man of Manasseh, the youngest son of Joash of Abiezer? Only too well did the young chief know with whom he had to deal. There had been fighting already between Israel and the Midianites. Did Ephraim help then? Nay: but secure in her mountains that tribe sullenly and selfishly held aloof. And now the complaint is made when Gideon, once unknown, is a victorious hero, the deliverer of the Hebrew nation.

Do we not often see something like this? There are people who will not hazard position or profit in identifying themselves with an enterprise while the issue is doubtful, but desire to have the credit of connection with it if it should succeed. They have not the humanity to associate themselves with those who are fighting in a good cause because it is good. In fact they do not know what is good, their only test of value being success. They lie by, looking with half-concealed scorn on the attempts of the earnest, sneering at their heat either in secret or openly, and when one day it becomes clear that the world is applauding they conceive a sudden respect for those at whom they scoffed. Now they will do what they can to help,—with pleasure, with liberality. Why were they not sooner invited? They will almost make a quarrel of that, and they have to be soothed with fair speeches. And people who are worldly at heart push forward in this fashion when Christian affairs have success or *éclat* attached to them, especially where religion wears least of its proper air and has somewhat of the earthly in tone and look. Christ pursued by the Sanhedrin, despised by the Roman, is no person for them to know. Let Him have the patronage of Constantine or a de' Medici and they are then assured that He has claims which they will admit —in theory. More than that needs not be expected from men and women " of the world." "*Messieurs, surtout, pas de zèle.*" Above all, no zeal: that is the motto of every Ephraim since time began. Wait till zeal is cooling before you join the righteous cause.

4. But while there are the carnal who like to share the success of religion after it has cooled down to their temperature, another class must not be forgotten, those who in their selfishness show the worst kind of hostility to the cause they should aid. Look at the men of Succoth and Penuel. Gideon and his band leading the pursuit of the Midianites have had no food all night and are faint with hunger. At Succoth they ask bread in vain. Instead of help they get the taunt—" Are Zebah and Zalmunna now in thine hand that we should give bread unto thine army?" Onward they press another stage up the hills to Penuel, and there also their request is refused. Gideon, savage with the need of his men, threatens dire punishment to those who are so callous and cruel; and when he returns victorious his threat is made good. With thorns and briars of the wilderness he scourges the elders of Succoth. The pride of Penuel is its watchtower, and that he demolishes, at the same time decimating the men of the city.

Penuel and Succoth lay in the way between the wilderness in which the Midianites dwelt and the valleys of western Palestine. The men of these cities feared that if they aided Gideon they would bring on themselves the vengeance of the desert tribes. Yet where do we see the lowest point of unfaith and meanness, in Ephraim or Succoth? It is perhaps hard to say which are the least manly: those contrive to join the conquering host and snatch the credit of victory; these are not so clever, and while they are as eager to make things smooth for themselves the thorns and briars are more visibly their portion. To share the honour of a cause for which you have done very little is an easy thing in this world, though an honest man cannot wear that kind of laurel; but as for Succoth and Penuel, the poor creatures, who will not pity them? It is so inconvenient often to have to decide. They would temporise if it were possible—supply the famished army with mouldy corn and raisins at a high price, and do as much next time for the Midianites. Yet the opportunity for this kind of salvation does not always come. There are times when people have to choose definitely whom they will serve, and discover to their horror that judgment follows swiftly upon base and cowardly choice. And God is faithful in making the recusants feel the urgency of moral choice and the grip He has of them. They would fain let the battle of truth sweep by and not meddle with it. But something is forced upon them. They cannot let the whole affair of salvation alone, but are driven to refuse heaven in the very act of trying to escape hell. And although judgment lingers, ever and anon demonstration is made among the ranks of the would-be prudent that One on high judges for His warriors. It is not the Gideon leading the little band of faint but eager champions of faith who punishes the callous heathenism and low scorn of a Succoth and Penuel. The Lord of Hosts Himself will vindicate and chasten. " Whoso shall cause one of these little ones that believe in Me to stumble, it is profitable for him that a great millstone should be hanged about his neck, and that he should be sunk in the depth of the sea."

5. Yet another word of instruction is found in the appeal of Gideon: " Give, I pray you, loaves of bread unto the people that follow me, for they be faint and I am pursuing after Zebah and Zalmunna." Well has the expression " Faint yet pursuing" found its place as a proverb of the religious life. We are called to run with patience a race that needs long ardour and strenuous exertion. The goal is far away, the ground is difficult. As day after day and year after year demands are made upon our faith, our resolution, our thought, our devotion to One who remains unseen and on our confidence in the future life, it is no wonder that many feel faint and weary. Often have we to pass through a region inhabited by those who are indifferent or hostile, careless or derisive. At many a door we knock and find no sympathy. We ask for bread and receive a stone; and still the fight slackens not, still have we to reach forth to the things that are before. But the faintness is not death. In the most terrible hours there is new life for our spiritual nature. Refreshment comes from an unseen hand when earth refuses help. We turn to Christ; we consider Him who endured great contradiction of sinners against Himself; we realise afresh that we are ensured of the fulness of His redemption. The body grows faint, but the soul presses on; the body dies and has to be left behind as a worn-out garment, but the spirit ascends into immortal youth.

> "On, chariot! on, soul!
> Ye are all the more fleet.
> Be alone at the goal
> Of the strange and the sweet!"

6. Finally let us glance at the fate of Zebah and Zalmunna, not without a feeling of admiration and of pity for the rude ending of these stately lives.

The sword of Jehovah and of Gideon has slain its thousands. The vast desert army has been scattered like chaff, in the flight, at the fords, by the rock Oreb and the winepress Zeeb, all along the way by Nobah and Jogbehah, and finally at Karkor, where having encamped in fancied security the residue is smitten. Now the two defeated chiefs are in the hand of Gideon, their military renown completely wrecked, their career destroyed. To them the expedition into Canaan was part of the common business of leadership. As emirs of nomadic tribes they had to find pasture and prey for their people. No special antagonism to Jehovah, no ill-will against Israel more than other nations, led them to cross the Jordan and scour the plains of Palestine. It was quite in the natural course of things that Midianites and Amalekites should migrate and move towards the west. And now the defeat is crushing. What remains therefore but to die?

We hear Gideon command his son Jether to fall upon the captive chiefs, who, brilliant and stately once, lie disarmed, bound and helpless. The indignity is not to our mind. We would have thought more of Gideon had he offered freedom to these captives "fallen on evil days," men to be admired, not hated. But probably they do not desire a life which has in it no more of honour. Only let the Hebrew leader not insult them by the stroke of a young man's sword. The great chiefs would die by a warrior's blow. And Jether cannot slay them; his hand falters as he draws the sword. These men who have ruled their tens of thousands have still the lion look that quails. "Rise thou and fall upon us," they say to Gideon: "for as the man is, so is his strength." And so they die, types of the greatest earthly powers that resist the march of Divine Providence, overthrown by a sword which even in faulty, weak human hands has indefeasible sureness and edge.

"As the man is, so is his strength." It is another of the pregnant sayings which meet us here and there even in the least meditative parts of Scripture. Yes: as a man is in character, in faith, in harmony with the will of God, so is his strength; as he is in falseness, injustice, egotism, and ignorance, so is his weakness. And there is but one real perennial kind of strength. The demonstration made by selfish and godless persons, though it shake continents and devastate nations, is not Force. It has no nerve, no continuance, but is mere fury which decays and perishes. Strength is the property of truth and truth only; it belongs to those who are in union with eternal reality and to no others in the universe. Would you be invincible? You must move with the eternal powers of righteousness and love. To be showy in appearance or terrible in sound on the wrong side with the futilities of the world is but incipient death.

On all sides the application may be seen. In the home and its varied incidents of education, sickness, discipline; in society high and low; in politics, in literature. As the man or woman is in simple allegiance to God and clear resolution there is strength to endure, to govern, to think, and every way to live. Otherwise there can only be instability, foolishness, blundering selfishness, a sad passage to inanition and decay.

CHAPTER XIV.

GIDEON THE ECCLESIASTIC.

JUDGES viii. 22-28.

THE great victory of Gideon had this special significance, that it ended the incursions of the wandering races of the desert. Canaan offered a continual lure to the nomads of the Arabian wilderness, as indeed the eastern and southern parts of Syria do at the present time. The hazard was that wave after wave of Midianites and Bedawin sweeping over the land should destroy agriculture and make settled national life and civilisation impossible. And when Gideon undertook his work the risk of this was acute. But the defeat inflicted on the wild tribes proved decisive. "Midian was subdued before the children of Israel, and they lifted up their heads no more." The slaughter that accompanied the overthrow of Zebah and Zalmunna, Oreb and Zeeb became in the literature of Israel a symbol of the destruction which must overtake the foes of God. "Do thou to thine enemies as unto Midian"—so runs the cry of a psalm—"Make their nobles like Oreb and Zeeb: yea, all their princes like Zebah and Zalmunna, who said, Let us take to ourselves in possession the habitations of God." In Isaiah the remembrance gives a touch of vivid colour to the oracle of the coming Wonderful, Prince of Peace. "The yoke of his burden and the staff of his shoulder, the rod of his oppressor shall be broken as in the day of Midian." Regarding the Assyrian also the same prophet testifies, "The Lord of Hosts shall stir up against him a scourge as in the slaughter of Midian at the rock of Oreb." We have no song like that of Deborah celebrating the victory, but a sense of its immense importance held the mind of the people, and by reason of it Gideon found a place among the heroes of faith. Doubtless he had, to begin with, a special reason for taking up arms against the Midianitish chiefs that they had slain his two brothers: the duty of an avenger of blood fell to him. But this private vengeance merged in the desire to give his people freedom, religious as well as political, and it was Jehovah's victory that he won, as he himself gladly acknowledged. We may see, therefore, in the whole enterprise, a distinct step of religious development. Once again the name of the Most High was exalted; once again the folly of idol worship was contrasted with the wisdom of serving the God of Abraham and Moses. The tribes moved in the direction of national unity and also of common devotion to their unseen King. If Gideon had been a man of larger intellect and knowledge he might have led Israel far on the way towards fitness for the mission it had never yet endeavoured to fulfil. But his powers and inspiration were limited.

On his return from the campaign the wish of the people was expressed to Gideon that he should assume the title of king. The nation needed a settled government, a centre of authority which would bind the tribes together, and the Abiezrite chief was now clearly marked as a man fit for royalty. He was able to persuade as well as to fight; he was bold, firm, and prudent. But to the request that he should become king and found a dynasty Gideon gave an absolute refusal: "I will not rule over you, neither shall my son rule over you; Jehovah shall rule over you." We always admire a man who refuses one of the great posts of human authority or distinction. The throne of Israel was even at that time a flattering offer. But should it have been made? There are few who will pause in a moment of high personal success to think of the point of morality involved; yet we may credit Gideon with the belief that it was not for him or any man to be called king in Israel. As a judge he had partly proved himself, as a judge he had a Divine call and a marvellous vindication: that name he would accept, not the other.

One of the chief elements of Gideon's character was a strong but not very spiritual religiousness. He attributed his success entirely to God, and God alone he desired the nation to acknowledge as its Head. He would not even in appearance stand between the people and their Divine Sovereign, nor with his will should any son of his take a place so unlawful and dangerous.

Along with his devotion to God it is quite likely that the caution of Gideon had much to do with his resolve. He had already found some difficulty in dealing with the Ephraimites, and he could easily foresee that if he became king the pride of that large clan would rise strongly against him. If the gleaning of the grapes of Ephraim was better than the whole vintage of Abiezer, as Gideon had declared, did it not follow that any elder of the great central tribe would better deserve the position of king than the youngest son of Joash of Abiezer? The men of Succoth and Penuel too had to be reckoned with. Before Gideon could establish himself in a royal seat he would have to fight a great coalition in the centre and south and also beyond Jordan. To the pains of oppression would succeed the agony of civil war. Unwilling to kindle a fire which might burn for years and perhaps consume himself, he refused to look at the proposal, flattering and honourable as it was.

But there was another reason for his decision which may have had even more weight. Like many men who have distinguished themselves in one way, his real ambition lay in a different direction. We think of him as a military genius. He for his part looked to the priestly office and the transmission of Divine oracles as his proper calling. The enthusiasm with which he overthrew the altar of Baal, built the new altar of Jehovah and offered his first sacrifice upon it, survived when the wild delights of victory had passed away. The thrill of awe and the strange excitement he had felt when Divine messages came to him and signs were given in answer to his prayer affected him far more deeply and permanently than the sight of a flying enemy and the pride of knowing himself victor in a great campaign. Neither did kingship appear much in comparison with access to God, converse with Him, and declaration of His will to men. Gideon appears already tired of war, with no appetite certainly for more, however successful, and impatient to return to the mysterious rites and sacred privileges of the altar. He had good reason to acknowledge the power over Israel's destiny of the Great Being Whose spirit had come upon him, Whose promises had been fulfilled. He desired to cultivate that intercourse with Heaven which more than anything else gave him the sense of dignity and strength. From the offer of a crown he turned as if eager to don the robe of a priest and listen for the holy oracles that none beside himself seemed able to receive.

It is notable that in the history of the Jewish kings the tendency shown by Gideon frequently reappeared. According to the law of later times the kingly duties should have been entirely separated from those of the priesthood. It came to be a dangerous and sacrilegious thing for the chief magistrate of the tribes, their leader in war, to touch the sacred implements or offer a sacrifice. But just because the ideas of sacrifice and priestly service were so fully in the Jewish mind the kings, either when especially pious or especially strong, felt it hard to refrain from the forbidden privilege. On the eve of a great battle with the Philistines Saul, expecting Samuel to offer the preparatory sacrifice and inquire of Jehovah, waited seven days and then, impatient of delay, undertook the priestly part and offered a burnt sacrifice. His act was, properly speaking, a confession of the sovereignty of God; but when Samuel came he expressed great indignation against the king, denounced his interference with sacred things, and in effect removed him then and there from the kingdom. David for his part appears to have been scrupulous in employing the priests for every religious function; but at the bringing up of the ark from the house of Obed-Edom he is reported to have led a sacred dance before the Lord and to have worn a linen ephod, that is, a garment specially reserved for the priests. He also took to himself the privilege of blessing the people in the name of the Lord. On the division of the kingdom Jeroboam promptly assumed the ordering of religion, set up shrines and appointed priests to minister at them; and in one scene we find him standing by an altar to offer incense. The great sin of Uzziah, on account of which he had to go forth from the temple a hopeless leper, is stated in the second book of Chronicles to have been an attempt to burn incense on the altar. These are cases in point; but the most remarkable is that of Solomon. To be king, to build and equip the temple and set in operation the whole ritual of the house of God, did not content that magnificent prince. His ambition led him to assume a part far loftier and more impressive than fell to the chief priest himself. It was Solomon who offered the prayer when the temple was consecrated, who pronounced the blessing of God on the worshipping multitude; and at his invocation it was that "fire came down from heaven and consumed the burnt offering and the sacrifices." This crowning act of his life in which the great monarch rose to the very highest pitch of his ambition, actually claiming and taking precedence over all the house of Aaron, will serve to explain the strange turn of the Abiezrite's history at which we have now arrived.

"He made an ephod and put it in his city, even in Ophrah." A strong but not spiritual religiousness, we have said, is the chief note of Gideon's character. It may be objected that such a one, if he seeks ecclesiastical office, does so unworthily; but to say so is an uncharitable error. It is not the devout temper alone that finds attraction in the ministry of sacred things; nor should a love of place and power be named as the only other leading motive. One who is not devout may in all sincerity covet the honour of standing for God before the congregation, leading the people in worship, and interpreting the sacred oracles. A vulgar explanation of human desire is often a false one; it is so here. The ecclesiastic may show few tokens of the spiritual temper, the other-worldliness, the glowing and simple truth we rightly account to be the proper marks of a Christian ministry; yet he may by his own reckoning have obeyed a clear call. His function in this case is to maintain order and administer outward rites with dignity and care —a limited range of duty indeed, but not without utility, especially when there are inferior and less conscientious men in office not far away.

He does not advance faith, but according to his power he maintains it.

But the ecclesiastic must have the ephod. The man who feels the dignity of religion more than its humane simplicity, realising it as a great movement of absorbing interest, will naturally have regard to the means of increasing dignity and making the movement impressive. Gideon calls upon the people for the golden spoils taken from the Midianites, nose-rings, earrings and the like, and they willingly respond. It is easy to obtain gifts for the outward glory of religion, and a golden image is soon to be seen within a house of Jehovah on the hill at Ophrah. Whatever form it had, this figure was to Gideon no idol, but a symbol or sign of Jehovah's presence among the people, and by means of it, in one or other of the ways used at the time, as for example by casting lots from within it, appeal was made to God with the utmost respect and confidence. When it is supposed that Gideon fell away from his first faith in making this image, the error lies in overestimating his spirituality at the earlier stage. We must not think that at any time the use of a symbolic image would have seemed wrong to him. It was not against images, but against worship of false and impure gods, that his zeal was at first directed. The sacred pole was an object of detestation because it was a symbol of Astarte.

In some way we cannot explain the whole life of Gideon appears as quite separate from the religious ordinances maintained before the ark, and at the same time quite apart from that Divine rule which forbade the making and worship of graven images. Either he did not know the second commandment, or he understood it only as forbidding the use of an image of any creature and the worship of a creature by means of an image. We know that the cherubim in the Holy of Holies were symbolic of the perfections of creation, and through them the greatness of the Unseen God was realised. So it was with Gideon's ephod or image, which was however used in seeking oracles. He acted at Ophrah as priest of the true God. The sacrifices he offered were to Jehovah. People came from all the northern tribes to bow at his altar and receive divine intimations through him. The southern tribes had Gilgal and Shiloh. Here at Ophrah was a service of the God of Israel, not perhaps intended to compete with the other shrines, yet virtually depriving them of their fame. For the expression is used that all Israel went a whoring after the ephod.

But while we try to understand we are not to miss the warning which comes home to us through this chapter of religious history. Pure and, for the time, even elevated in the motive, Gideon's attempt at priestcraft led to his fall. For a while we see the hero acting as judge at Ophrah and presiding with dignity at the altar. His best wisdom is at the service of the people, and he is ready to offer for them at new moon or harvest the animals they desire to consecrate and consume in the sacred feast. In a spirit of real faith and no doubt with much sagacity he submits their inquiries to the test of the ephod. But "the thing became a snare to Gideon and his house," perhaps in the way of bringing in riches and creating the desire for more. Those who applied to him as a revealer brought gifts with them. Gradually as wealth increased among the people the value of the donations would increase, and he who began as a disinterested patriot may have degenerated into a somewhat avaricious man who made a trade of religion. On this point we have, however, no information. It is mere surmise, depending upon observation of the way things are apt to go amongst ourselves.

Reviewing the story of Gideon's life we find this clear lesson, that within certain limits he who trusts and obeys God has a quite irresistable efficiency. This man had, as we have seen, his limitations, very considerable. As a religious leader, prophet or priest, he was far from competent; there is no indication that he was able to teach Israel a single Divine doctrine, and as to the purity and mercy, the righteousness and love of God, his knowledge was rudimentary. In the remote villages of the Abiezrites the tradition of Jehovah's name and power remained, but in the confusion of the times there was no education of children in the will of God: the Law was practically unknown. From Shechem where Baal-Berith was worshipped the influence of a degrading idolatry had spread, obliterating every religious idea except the barest elements of the old faith. Doing his very best to understand God, Gideon never saw what religion in our sense means. His sacrifices were appeals to a Power dimly felt through nature and in the greater epochs of the national history, chastising now, and now friendly and beneficent.

Yet, seriously limited as he was, Gideon, when he had once laid hold of the fact that he was called by the unseen God to deliver Israel, went on step by step to the great victory which made the tribes free. His responsibility to his fellow-Israelites became clear along with his sense of the demand made upon him by God. He felt himself like the wind, like the lightning, like the dew, an agent or instrument of the Most High, bound to do His part in the course of things. His will was enlisted in the Divine purpose. This work, this deliverance of Israel, was to be effected by him and no other. He had the elemental powers with him, in him. The immense armies of Midian could not stand in his way. He was, as it were, a storm that must hurl them back into the wilderness defeated and broken.

Now this is the very conception of life which we in our far wider knowledge are apt to miss, which nevertheless it is our chief business to grasp and carry into practice. You stand there, a man instructed in a thousand things of which Gideon was ignorant, instructed especially in the nature and will of God Whom Christ has revealed. It is your privilege to take a broad survey of human life, of duty, to look beyond the present to the eternal future with its infinite possibilities of gain and loss. But the danger is that year after year all thought and effort shall be on your own account, that with each changing wind of circumstance you change your purpose, that you never understand God's demand nor find the true use of knowledge, will, and life in fulfilling that. Have you a divine task to effect? You doubt it. Where is anything that can be called a commission of God? You look this way and that for a little, then give up the quest. This year finds you without enthusiasm, without devotion even as you have been in other years. So life ebbs away and is lost in the wide flat sands of the secular and trivial, and the soul never becomes part of the strong ocean current of

Divine purpose. We pity or deride some who, with little knowledge and in many errors alike of heart and head, were yet men as many of us may not claim to be, alive to the fact of God and their own share in Him. But they were so limited, those Hebrews, you say, a mere horde of shepherds and husbandmen; their story is too poor, too chaotic to have any lesson for us. And in sheer incapacity to read the meaning of the tale you turn from this Book of Judges, as from a barbarian myth, less interesting than Homer, of no more application to yourself than the legends of the Round Table. Yet, all the while, the one supreme lesson for a man to read and take home to himself is written throughout the book in bold and living characters—that only when life is realised as a vocation is it worth living. God may be faintly known, His will but rudely interpreted; yet the mere understanding that He gives life and rewards effort is an inspiration. And when His life-giving call ceases to stir and guide there can be for the man, the nation, only irresolution and weakness.

A century ago Englishmen were as little devout as they are to-day; they were even less spiritual, less moved to fine issues. They had their scepticisms too, their rough ignorant prejudices, their giant errors and perversities. "We have gained vastly," as Professor Seeley says, "in breadth of view, intelligence, and refinement. Probably what we threw aside could not be retained; what we adopted was forced upon us by the age. Nevertheless, we had formerly what I may call a national discipline, which formed a firm, strongly-marked national character. We have now only materials, which may be of the first quality, but have not been worked up. We have everything except decided views and steadfast purpose—everything in short except character." Yes: the sense of the nation's calling has decayed, and with it the nation's strength. In leaders and followers alike purpose fades as faith evaporates, and we are faithless because we attempt nothing noble under the eye and sceptre of the King.

You live, let us say, among those who doubt God, doubt whether there is any redemption, whether the whole Christian gospel and hope are not in the air, dreams, possibilities, rather than facts of the Eternal Will. The storm-wind blows and you hear its roaring: that is palpable fact, divine or cosmic. Its errand will be accomplished. Great rivers flow, great currents sweep through the ocean. Their mighty urgency who can doubt? But the spiritual who can believe? You do not feel in the sphere of the moral, of the spiritual the wind that makes no sound, the current that rolls silently charged with sublime energies, effecting a vast and wonderful purpose. Yet here are the great facts; and we must find our part in that spiritual urgency, do our duty there, or lose all. We must launch out on the mighty stream of redemption or never reach eternal light, for all else moves down to death. Christ Himself is to be victorious in us. The glory of our life is that we can be irresistible in the region of our duty, irresistible in conflict with the evil, the selfishness, the falsehood given us to overthrow. To realise that is to live. The rest is all mere experiment, getting ready for the task of existence, making armour, preparing food, otherwise, at the worst, a winter's morning before inglorious death.

One other thing observe, that underlying Gideon's desire to fill the office of priest there was a dull perception of the highest function of one man in relation to others. It appears to the common mind a great thing to rule, to direct secular affairs, to have the command of armies and the power of filling offices and conferring dignities; and no doubt to one who desires to serve his generation well, royalty, political power, even municipal office offer many excellent opportunities. But set kingship on this side, kingship concerned with the temporal and earthly, or at best humane aspects of life, and on the other side priesthood of the true kind which has to do with the spiritual, by which God is revealed to man and the holy ardour and divine aspirations of the human will are sustained—and there can be no question which is the more important. A clever strong man may be a ruler. It needs a good man, a pious man, a man of heavenly power and insight to be in any right sense a priest. I speak not of the kind of priest Gideon turned out, nor of a Jewish priest, nor of any who in modern times professes to be in that succession, but of one who really stands between God and men, bearing the sorrows of his kind, their trials, doubts, cries, and prayers on his heart and presenting them to God, interpreting to the weary and sad and troubled the messages of heaven. In this sense Christ is the one True Priest, the eternal and only sufficient High Priest. And in this sense it is possible for every Christian to hold towards those less enlightened and less decided in their faith the priestly part.

Now in a dim way the priestly function presented itself to Gideon and allured him. Sufficient for it he was not, and his ephod became a snare. Neither could he grasp the wisdom of heaven nor understand the needs of men. In his hands the sacred art did not prosper, he became content with the appearance and the gain. It is so with many who take the name of priests. In truth, on one side the term and all it stands for must be confessed full of danger to him set apart and those who separate him. Here as pointedly as anywhere must it be affirmed, "Whatsoever is not of faith is sin." There must be a mastering sense of God's calling on the side of him who ministers, and on the side of the people recognition of a message, an example coming to them through this brother of theirs who speaks what he has received of the Holy Spirit, who offers a personal living word, a personal testimony. Here, be it called what it may, is priesthood after the pattern of Christ's, true and beneficent; and apart from this priesthood may too easily become, as many have affirmed, a horrible imposture and baleful lie. Christianity brings the whole to a point in every life. God's calling, spiritual, complete, comes to each soul in its place, and the holy oil is for every head. The father, mother, the employer and the workman, the surgeon, writer, lawyer—everywhere and in all posts, just as men and women are living out God's demand upon them—these are His priests, ministrants of the hearth and the shop, the factory and the office, by the cradle and the sick-bed, wherever the multitudinous epic of life goes forward. Here is the common and withal the holiest calling and office. That one dwelling with God in righteousness and love introduce others into the sanctuary, declare as a thing he knows the will of the Eternal, uplift the feebleness of faith and revive the heart of love—this is the highest task on earth, the grandest of heaven.

Of such it may be said, "Ye are a chosen generation, a royal priesthood, a holy nation, a peculiar people that ye should show forth the praises of Him Who hath called you out of darkness into His marvellous light."

CHAPTER XV.

ABIMELECH AND JOTHAM.

JUDGES viii. 29-ix. 57.

THE history we are tracing moves from man to man; the personal influence of the hero is everything while it lasts and confusion follows on his death. Gideon appears as one of the most successful Hebrew judges in maintaining order. While he was there in Ophrah religion and government had a centre "and the country was in quietness forty years." A man far from perfect but capable of mastery held the reins and gave forth judgment with an authority none could challenge. His burial in the family sepulchre in Ophrah is specially recorded, as if it had been a great national tribute to his heroic power and skilful administration.

The funeral over, discord began. A rightful ruler there was not. Among the claimants of power there was no man of power. Gideon left many sons, but not one of them could take his place. The confederation of cities half Hebrew, half Canaanite, with Shechem at their head, of which we have already heard, held in check while Gideon lived, now began to control the politics of the tribes. By using the influence of this league a usurper who had no title whatever to the confidence of the people succeeded in exalting himself.

The old town of Shechem situated in the beautiful valley between Ebal and Gerizim had long been a centre of Baal worship and of Canaanite intrigue, though nominally one of the cities of refuge and therefore specially sacred. Very likely the mixed population of this important town, jealous of the position gained by the hill-village of Ophrah, were ready to receive with favour any proposals that seemed to offer them distinction. And when Abimelech, son of Gideon by a slave woman of their town, went among them with ambitious and crafty suggestions they were easily persuaded to help him. The desire for a king which Gideon had promptly set aside lingered in the minds of the people, and by means of it Abimelech was able to compass his personal ends. First, however, he had to discredit others who stood in his way. There at Ophrah were the sons and grandsons of Gideon, threescore and ten of them according to the tradition, who were supposed to be bent on lording it over the tribes. Was it a thing to be thought of that the land should have seventy kings? Surely one would be better, less of an incubus at least, more likely to do the ruling well. Men of Shechem too would not be governed from Ophrah if they had any spirit. He, Abimelech, was their townsman, their bone and flesh. He confidently looked for their support.

We cannot tell how far there was reason for saying that the family of Gideon were aiming at an aristocracy. They may have had some vague purpose of the kind. The suggestion, at all events, was cunning and had its effect. The people of Shechem had stored considerable treasure in the sanctuary of Baal, and by public vote seventy pieces of silver were paid out of it to Abimelech. The money was at once used by him in hiring a band of men like himself, unscrupulous, ready for any desperate or bloody deed. With these he marched on Ophrah, and surprising his brothers in the house or palace of Jerubbaal speedily put out of his way their dangerous rivalry. With the exception of Jotham, who had observed the band approaching and concealed himself, the whole house of Gideon was dragged to execution. On one stone, perhaps the very rock on which the altar of Baal once stood, the threescore and nine were barbarously slain.

A villainous *coup d'état* this. From Gideon overthrowing Baal and proclaiming Jehovah to Abimelech bringing up Baal again with hideous fratricide—it is a wretched turn of things. Gideon had to some extent prepared the way for a man far inferior to himself, as all do who are not utterly faithful to their light and calling; but he never imagined there could be so quick and shocking a revival of barbarism. Yet the ephod-dealing, the polygamy, the immorality into which he lapsed were bound to come to fruit. The man who once was a pure Hebrew patriot begat a half-heathen son to undo his own work. As for the Shechemites, they knew quite well to what end they had voted those seventy pieces of silver; and the general opinion seems to have been that the town had its money's worth, a life for each piece and, to boot, a king reeking with blood and shame. Surely it was a well-spent grant. Their confederation, their god had triumphed. They made Abimelech king by the oak of the pillar that was in Shechem.

It is the success of the adventurer we have here, that common event. Abimelech is the Oriental adventurer and uses the methods of another age than ours; yet we have our examples, and if they are less scandalous in some ways, if they are apart from bloodshed and savagery, they are still sufficiently trying to those who cherish the faith of divine justice and providence. How many have to see with amazement the adventurer triumph by means of seventy pieces of silver from the house of Baal or even from a holier treasury. He in a selfish and cruel game seems to have speedy and complete success denied to the best and purest cause. Fighting for his own hand in wicked or contemptuous hardness and arrogant conceit, he finds support, applause, an open way. Being no prophet he has honour in his own town. He knows the art of the stealthy insinuation, the lying promise and the flattering murmur; he has skill to make the favour of one leading person a step to securing another. When a few important people have been hoodwinked, he too becomes important and "success" is assured.

The Bible, most entirely honest of books, frankly sets before us this adventurer, Abimelech, in the midst of the judges of Israel, as low a specimen of "success" as need be looked for; and we trace the well-known means by which such a person is promoted. "His mother's brethren spake of him in the ears of all the men of Shechem." That there was little to say, that he was a man of no character mattered not the least. The thing was to create an impression so that Abimelech's scheme might be introduced and forced. So far he could intrigue and then, the first steps gained, he could mount. But there was in him none of the mental power that afterwards marked Jehu, none of the charm that survives with the name of Absalom. It was on jealousy, pride, ambition he played as the most jealous, proud, and ambitious; yet for three years the Hebrews of the league, blinded by the desire to have their nation like others, suffered him to bear the name of king.

And by this sovereignty the Israelites who acknowledged it were doubly and trebly compromised. Not only did they accept a man without a record, they believed in one who was an enemy to his country's religion, one therefore quite ready to trample upon its liberty. This is really the beginning of a worse oppression than that of Midian or of Jabin. It shows on the part of Hebrews generally as well as those who tamely submitted to Abimelech's lordship a most abject state of mind. After the bloody work at Ophrah the tribes should have rejected the fratricide with loathing and risen like one man to suppress him. If the Baal-worshippers of Shechem would make him king there ought to have been a cause of war against them in which every good man and true should have taken the field. We look in vain for any such opposition to the usurper. Now that he is crowned, Manasseh, Ephraim, and the North regard him complacently. It is the world all over. How can we wonder at this when we know with what acclamations kings scarcely more reputable than he have been greeted in modern times? Crowds gather and shout, fires of welcome blaze; there is joy as if the millennium had come. It is a king crowned, restored, his country's head, defender of the faith. Vain is the hope, pathetic the joy.

There is no man of spirit to oppose Abimelech in the field. The duped nation must drink its cup of misrule and blood. But one appears of keen wit, apt and trenchant in speech. At least the tribes shall hear what one sound mind thinks of this coronation. Jothan, as we saw, escaped the slaughter at Ophrah. In the rear of the murderer he has crossed the hills and he will now utter his warning, whether men hear or whether they forbear. There is a crowd assembled for worship or deliberation at the oak of the pillar. Suddenly a voice is heard ringing clearly out between hill and hill, and the people looking up recognise Jotham, who from a spur of rock on the side of Gerizim demands their audience. "Hearken unto me," he cries, "ye men of Shechem, that God may hearken unto you." Then in his parable of the olive, the fig-tree, the vine, and the bramble, he pronounces judgment and prophecy. The bramble is exalted to be king, but on these terms, that the trees come and put their trust under its shadow; "but if not, then let fire come out of the bramble and devour the cedars of Lebanon."

It is a piece of satire of the first order, brief, stinging, true. The craving for a king is lashed and then the wonderful choice of a ruler. Jotham speaks as an anarchist, one might say, but with God understood as the centre of law and order. It is a vision of the Theocracy, taking shape from a keen and original mind. He figures men as trees growing independently, dutifully. And do trees need a king? Are they not set in their natural freedom, each to yield fruit as best it can after its kind? Men of Shechem, Hebrews all, if they will only attend to their proper duties and do quiet work as God wills, appear to Jotham to need a king no more than the trees. Under the benign course of nature, sunshine and rain, wind and dew, the trees have all the restraint they need, all the liberty that is good for them. So men under the providence of God, adoring and obeying Him, have the best control, the only needful control, and with it liberty. Are they not fools then to go about seeking a tyrant to rule them, they who should be as cedars of Lebanon, willows by the water-courses, they who are made for simple freedom and spontaneous duty? It is something new in Israel, this keen intellectualising; but the fable, pointed as it is, teaches nothing for the occasion. Jotham is a man full of wit and of intelligence, but he has no practicable scheme of government, nothing definite to oppose to the mistake of the hour. He is all for the ideal, but the time and the people are unripe for the ideal. We see the same contrast in our own day; both in politics and the church the incisive critic discrediting subordination altogether fails to secure his age. Men are not trees. They are made to obey and trust. A hero or one who seems a hero is ever welcome, and he who skilfully imitates the roar of the lion may easily have a following, while Jotham, intensely sincere, highly gifted, a true-sighted man, finds none to mind him.

Again the fable is directed against Abimelech. What was this man to whom Shechem had sworn fealty? An olive, a fig-tree, fruitful and therefore to be sought after? Was he a vine capable of rising on popular support to useful and honourable service? Not he. It was the bramble they had chosen, the poor grovelling jagged thorn-bush that tears the flesh, whose end is to feed the fire of the oven. Who ever heard of a good or heroic deed Abimelech had done? He was simply a contemptible upstart, without moral principle, as ready to wound as to flatter, and they who chose him for king would too soon find their error. Now that he had done something, what was it? There were Israelites among the crowd that shouted in his honour. Had they already forgotten the services of Gideon so completely as to fall down before a wretch red-handed from the murder of their hero's sons? Such a beginning showed the character of the man they trusted, and the same fire which had issued from the bramble at Ophrah would flame out upon themselves. This was but the beginning; soon there would be war to the knife between Abimelech and Shechem.

We find instruction in the parable by regarding the answers put into the mouth of this tree and that, when they are invited to wave to and fro over the others. There are honours which are dearly purchased, high positions which cannot be assumed without renouncing the true end and fruition of life. One, for example, who is quietly and with increasing efficiency doing his part in a sphere to which he is adapted must set aside the gains of long discipline if he is to become a social leader. He can do good where he is. Not so certain is it that he will be able to serve his fellows well in public office. It is one thing to enjoy the deference paid to a leader while the first enthusiasm on his behalf continues, but it is quite another thing to satisfy all the demands made as years go on and new needs arise. When any one is invited to take a position of authority he is bound to consider carefully his own aptitudes. He needs also to consider those who are to be subjects or constituents and make sure that they are of the kind his rule will fit. The olive looks at the cedar and the terebinth and the palm. Will they admit his sovereignty by-and-by though now they vote for it? Men are taken with the candidate who makes a good impression by emphasising what will please and suppressing opinions that may provoke dissent. When they know him, how will it be? When criticism begins, will the olive not be despised for its gnarled stem, its crooked branches and dusky foliage?

The fable does not make the refusal of olive and fig-tree and vine rest on the comfort they enjoy in the humbler place. That would be a mean and dishonourable reason for refusing to serve. Men who decline public office because they love an easy life find here no countenance. It is for the sake of its fatness, the oil it yields, grateful to God and man in sacrifice and anointing, that the olive-tree declines. The fig-tree has its sweetness and the vine its grapes to yield. And so men despising self-indulgence and comfort may be justified in putting aside a call to office. The fruit of personal character developed in humble unobtrusive natural life is seen to be better than the more showy clusters forced by public demands. Yet, on the other hand, if one will not leave his books, another his scientific hobbies, a third his fireside, a fourth his manufactory, in order to take his place among the magistrates of a city or the legislators of a land the danger of bramble supremacy is near. Next a wretched Abimelech will appear; and what can be done but set him on high and put the reins in his hand? Unquestionably the claims of church or country deserve most careful weighing, and even if there is a risk that character may lose its tender bloom the sacrifice must be made in obedience to an urgent call. For a time, at least, the need of society at large must rule the loyal life.

The fable of Jotham, in so far as it flings sarcasm at the persons who desire eminence for the sake of it and not for the good they will be able to do, is an example of that wisdom which is as unpopular now as ever it has been in human history, and the moral needs every day to be kept full in view. It is desire for distinction and power, the opportunity of waving to and fro over the trees, the right to use this handle and that to their names that will be found to make many eager, not the distinct wish to accomplish something which the times and the country need. Those who solicit public office are far too often selfish, not self-denying, and even in the church there is much vain ambition. But people will have it so. The crowd follows him who is eager for the suffrages of the crowd and showers flattery and promises as he goes. Men are lifted into places they cannot fill, and after keeping their seats unsteadily for a time they have to disappear into ignominy.

We pass here, however, beyond the meaning Jotham desired to convey, for, as we have seen, he would have justified every one in refusing to reign. And certainly if society could be held together and guided without the exaltation of one over another, by the fidelity of each to his own task and brotherly feeling between man and man, there would be a far better state of things. But while the fable expounds a God-impelled anarchy, the ideal state of mankind, our modern schemes, omitting God, repudiating the least notion of a supernatural fount of life, turn upon themselves in hopeless confusion. When the divine law rules every life we shall not need organised governments; until then entire freedom in the world is but a name for unchaining every lust that degrades and darkens the life of man. Far away, as a hope of the redeemed and Christ-led race, there shines the ideal Theocracy revealed to the greater minds of the Hebrew people, often re-stated, never realised. But at present men need a visible centre of authority. There must be administrators and executors of law, there must be government and legislation till Christ reigns in every heart. The movement which resulted in Abimelech's sovereignty was the blundering start in a series of experiments the Hebrew tribes were bound to make, as other nations had to make them. We are still engaged in the search for a right system of social order, and while fearers of God acknowledge the ideal towards which they labour, they must endeavour to secure by personal toil and devotion, by unwearying interest in affairs the most effective form of liberal yet firm government.

Abimelech maintained himself in power for three years, no doubt amid growing dissatisfaction. Then came the outburst which Jotham had predicted. An evil spirit, really present from the first, rose between Abimelech and the men of Shechem. The bramble began to tear themselves, a thing they were not prepared to endure. Once rooted, however, it was not easily got rid of. One who knows the evil arts of betrayal is quick to suspect treachery, the false person knows the ways of the false and how to fight them with their own weapons. A man of high character may be made powerless by the disclosure of some true words he has spoken; but when Shechem would be rid of Abimelech it has to employ brigands and organise robbery. "They set liers in wait for him in the mountains who robbed all that came along that way," the merchants no doubt to whom Abimelech had given a safe conduct. Shechem in fact became the headquarters of a band of highwaymen, whose crimes were condoned or even approved in the hope that one day the despot would be taken and an end put to his misrule.

It may appear strange that our attention is directed to these vulgar incidents, as they may be called, which were taking place in and about Shechem. Why has the historian not chosen to tell us of other regions where some fear of God survived and guided the lives of men, instead of giving in detail the intrigues and treacheries of Abimelech and his rebellious subjects? Would we not much rather hear of the sanctuary and the worship, of the tribe of Judah and its development, of men and women who in the obscurity of private life were maintaining the true faith and serving God in sincerity? The answer must be partly that the contents of the history are determined by the traditions which survived when it was compiled. Doings like these at Shechem keep their place in the memory of men not because they are important but because they impress themselves on popular feeling. This was the beginning of the experiments which finally in Samuel's time issued in the kingship of Saul, and although Abimelech was, properly speaking, not a Hebrew and certainly was no worshipper of Jehovah, yet the fact that he was king for a time gave importance to everything about him. Hence we have the full account of his rise and fall.

And yet the narrative before us has its value from the religious point of view. It shows the disastrous result of that coalition with idolaters into which the Hebrews about Shechem entered, it illustrates the danger of co-partnery with the worldly on worldly terms. The confederacy of which Shechem was the centre is a type of many in which people who should be guided always by religion bind themselves for business or political ends with those who have no fear of God before their eyes. Constantly it happens in such cases that the interests of the commercial enterprise or of the party are considered before the law of righteousness. The business affair must be made to succeed at all hazards. Christian people as partners of companies are committed to schemes which imply Sabbath work, sharp practices in buying and selling, hollow promises in prospectuses and advertisements, grinding of the faces of the poor, miserable squabbles about wages that should never occur. In politics the like is frequently seen. Things are done against the true instincts of many members of a party; but they, for the sake of the party, must be silent or even take their places on platforms and write in periodicals defending what in their souls and consciences they know to be wrong. The modern Baal-Berith is a tyrannical god, ruins the morals of many a worshipper and destroys the peace of many a circle. Perhaps Christian people will by-and-by become careful in regard to the schemes they join and the zeal with which they fling themselves into party strife. It is high time they did. Even distinguished and pious leaders are unsafe guides when popular cries have to be gratified; and if the principles of Christianity are set aside by a government every Christian church and every Christian voice should protest, come of parties what may. Or rather, the party of Christ, which is always in the van, ought to have our complete allegiance. Conservatism is sometimes right. Liberalism is sometimes right. But to bow down to any Baal of the League is a shameful thing for a professed servant of the King of kings.

Against Abimelech the adventurer there arose another of the same stamp, Gaal son of Ebed, that is the *Abhorred*, son of a slave. In him the men of Shechem put their confidence, such as it was. At the festival of vintage there was a demonstration of a truly barbarous sort. High carousal was held in the temple of Baal. There were loud curses of Abimelech and Gaal made a speech. His argument was that this Abimelech, though his mother belonged to Shechem, was yet also the son of Baal's adversary, far too much of a Hebrew to govern Canaanites and good servants of Baal. Shechemites should have a true Shechemite to rule them. Would to Baal, he cried, this people were under my hand, then would I remove Abimelech. His speech, no doubt, was received with great applause, and there and then he challenged the absent king.

Zebul, prefect of the city, who was present, heard all this with anger. He was of Abimelech's party still and immediately informed his chief, who lost no time in marching on Shechem to suppress the revolt. According to a common plan of warfare he divided his troops into four companies and in the early morning these crept towards the city, one by a track across the mountains, another down the valley from the west, the third by way of the Diviners' Oak, the fourth perhaps marching from the plain of Mamre by way of Jacob's well. The first engagement drove the Shechemites into their city, and on the following day the place was taken, sacked, and destroyed. Some distance from Shechem, probably up the valley to the west, stood a tower or sanctuary of Baal around which a considerable village had gathered. The people there, seeing the fate of the lower town, betook themselves to the tower and shut themselves up within it. But Abimelech ordered his men to provide themselves with branches of trees, which were piled against the door of the temple and set on fire, and all within were smothered or burned to the number of a thousand.

At Thebez, another of the confederate cities, the pretender met his death. In the siege of the tower which stood within the walls of Thebez the horrible expedient of burning was again attempted. Abimelech, directing the operations, had pressed close to the door when a woman cast an upper millstone from the parapet with so true an aim as to break his skull. So ended the first experiment in the direction of monarchy; so also God requited the wickedness of Abimelech.

One turns from these scenes of bloodshed and cruelty with loathing. Yet they show what human nature is, and how human history would shape itself apart from the faith and obedience of God. We are met by obvious warnings; but so often does the evidence of divine judgment seem to fail, so often do the wicked prosper, that it is from another source than observation of the order of things in this world we must obtain the necessary impulse to higher life. It is only as we wait on the guidance and obey the impulses of the Spirit of God that we shall move towards the justice and brotherhood of a better age. And those who have received the light and found the will of the Spirit must not slacken their efforts on behalf of religion. Gideon did good service in his day, yet failing in faithfulness he left the nation scarcely more earnest, his own family scarcely instructed. Let us not think that religion can take care of itself. Heavenly justice and truth are committed to us. The Christ-life, generous, pure, holy, must be commended by us if it is to rule the world. The persuasion that mankind is to be saved in and by the earthly survives, and against that most obstinate of all delusions we are to stand in constant resolute protest, counting every needful sacrifice our simple duty, our highest glory. The task of the faithful is no easier to-day than it was a thousand years ago. Men and women can be treacherous still with heathen cruelty and falseness; they can be vile still with heathen vileness, though wearing the air of the highest civilisation. If ever the people of God had a work to do in the world they have it now.

CHAPTER XVI.

GILEAD AND ITS CHIEF.

Judges x. 1-xi. 11.

The scene of the history shifts now to the east of Jordan, and we learn first of the influence which the region called Gilead was coming to have in Hebrew development from the brief notice of a chief named Jair, who held the position of judge for twenty-two years. Tola, a man of Issachar, succeeded Abimelech, and Jair followed Tola. In the Book of Numbers we are informed that the children of Machir son of Manasseh went to Gilead and took it and dispossessed the Amorites which were therein; and Moses gave Gilead unto Machir the son of Manasseh. It is added that Jair, the son or descendant of Manasseh, went and took the towns of Gilead and called them Havvoth-jair; and in this statement the Book of Numbers anticipates the history of the judges.

Gilead is described by modern travellers as one of the most varied districts of Palestine. The region is mountainous and its peaks rise to three and even four thousand feet above the trough of the Jordan. The southern part is beautiful and fertile, watered by the Jabbok and other streams that flow westward from the hills. "The valleys green with corn, the streams fringed with oleander, the magnificent screens of yellow-green and russet foliage which cover the steep slopes present a scene of quiet beauty, of chequered light and shade of uneastern aspect which makes Mount Gilead a veritable land of promise." "No one," says another writer, "can fairly judge of Israel's heritage who has not seen the exuberance of Gilead as well as the hard rocks of Judæa, which only yield their abundance to reward constant toil and care." In Gilead the rivers flow in summer as well as in winter, and they are filled with fishes and fresh-water shells. While in Western Palestine the soil is insufficient now to support a large population, beyond Jordan improved cultivation alone is needed to make the whole district a garden.

To the north and east of Gilead lie Bashan and that extraordinary volcanic region called the Argob or the Lejah, where the Havvoth-jair or towns of Jair were situated. The traveller who approaches this singular district from the north sees it rising abruptly from the plain, the edge of it like a rampart about twenty feet high. It is of a rude oval shape, some twenty miles long from north to south, and fifteen in breadth, and is simply a mass of dark jagged rocks, with clefts between in which were built not a few cities and villages. The whole of this Argob or Stony Land, Jephthah's land of Tob, is a natural fortification, a sanctuary open only to those who have the secret of the perilous paths that wind along savage cliff and deep defile. One who established himself here might soon acquire the fame and authority of a chief, and Jair, acknowledged by the Manassites as their judge, extended his power and influence among the Gadites and Reubenites farther south.

But plenty of corn and wine and oil and the advantage of a natural fortress which might have been held against any foe did not avail the Hebrews when they were corrupted by idolatry. In the land of Gilead and Bashan they became a hardy and vigorous race, and yet when they gave themselves up to the influence of the Syrians, Sidonians, Ammonites, and Moabites, forsaking the Lord and serving the gods of these peoples, disaster overtook them. The Ammonites were ever on the watch, and now, stronger than for centuries in consequence of the defeat of Midian and Amalek by Gideon, they fell on the Hebrews of the east, subdued them and even crossed Jordan and fought with the southern tribes, so that Israel was sore distressed.

We have found reason to suppose that during the many turmoils of the north the tribes of Judah and Simeon and to some extent Ephraim were pleased to dwell secure in their own domains, giving little help to their kinsfolk. Deborah and Barak got no troops from the south, and it was with a grudge Ephraim joined in the pursuit of Midian. Now the time has come for the harvest of selfish content. Supposing the people of Judah to have been specially engaged with religion and the arranging of worship—that did not justify their neglect of the political troubles of the north. It was a poor religion then, as it is a poor religion now, that could exist apart from national well-being and patriotic duty. Brotherhood must be realised in the nation as well as in the church, and piety must fulfil itself through patriotism as well as in other ways.

No doubt the duties we owe to each other and to the nation of which we form a part are imposed by natural conditions which have arisen in the course of history, and some may think that the natural should give way to the spiritual. They may see the interests of a kingdom of this world as actually opposed to the interests of the kingdom of God. The apostles of Christ, however, did not set the human and divine in contrast, as if God in His providence had nothing to do with the making of a nation. "The powers that be are ordained of God," says St. Paul in writing to the Romans; and again in his First Epistle to Timothy, " I exhort that supplications, prayers, intercessions, thanksgivings be made for all men: for kings and all that are in high place, that we may lead a tranquil and quiet life in all godliness and gravity." To the same effect St. Peter says, "Be subject to every ordinance of man for the Lord's sake." Natural and secular enough were the authorities to which submission was thus enjoined. The policy of Rome was of the earth earthy. The wars it waged, the intrigues that went on for power savoured of the most carnal ambition. Yet as members of the commonwealth Christians were to submit to the Roman magistrates and intercede with God on their behalf, observing closely and intelligently all that went on, taking due part in affairs. No room was to be given for the notion that the Christian society meant a new political centre. In our own times there is a duty which many never understand, or which they easily imagine is being fulfilled for them. Let religious people be assured that generous and intelligent patriotism is demanded of them and attention to the political business of the time. Those who are careless will find, as did the people of Judah, that in neglecting the purity of government and turning a deaf ear to cries for justice, they are exposing their country to disaster and their religion to reproach.

We are told that the Israelites of Gilead worshipped the gods of the Phœnicians and Syrians, of the Moabites and of the Ammonites. Whatever religious rites took their fancy they were ready to adopt. This will be to their credit in some quarters as a mark of openness of mind, intelligence, and taste. They were not bigoted; other men's ways in religion and civilisation were not rejected as beneath their regard. The argument is too familiar to be traced more fully. Briefly it may be said that if catholicity could save a race Israel should rarely have been in trouble, and certainly not at this time. One name by which the Hebrews knew God was *El* or *Elohim*. When they found among the gods of the Sidonians one called El, the careless-minded supposed that there could be no harm in joining in his worship. Then came the notion that the other divinities of the Phœnician Pantheon, such as Melcarth, Dagon, Derketo, might be adored as well. Very likely they found zeal and excitement in the alien religious gatherings which their own had lost. So they slipped into practical heathenism.

And the process goes on among ourselves. Through the principles that culture means artistic freedom and that worship is a form of art we arrive at taste or liking as the chief test. Intensity of feeling is craved and religion must satisfy that or be despised. It is the very error that led Hebrews to the feasts of Astarte and Adonis, and whither it tends we can see in the old history. Turning from the strong earnest gospel which grasps intellect and will to shows and ceremonies that please the eye, or even to music refined and devotional that stirs and thrills the feelings, we decline from the reality of religion. Moreover a serious danger threatens us in the far too common teaching which makes little of truth, everything of charity. Christ was most charitable, but it is through the knowledge and practice of truth He offers freedom. He is our King by His witness-bearing not to charity but to truth. Those who are anxious to keep us from bigotry and tell us that meekness, gentleness, and love are more than doctrine mislead the mind of the age. Truth in regard to God and His covenant is the only foundation on which life can be securely built, and without right thinking there cannot be right living. A man may be amiable, humble, patient, and kind though he has no doctrinal belief and his religion is of the purely emotional sort; but it is the truth believed by previous generations, fought and suffered for by stronger men, not his own gratification of taste, that keeps him in the right way. And when the influence of that truth decays there will remain no anchorage, neither compass nor chart for the voyage. He will be like a wave of the sea driven of the wind and tossed.

Again, the religious so far as they have wisdom and strength are required to be pioneers, which they can never be in following fancy or taste. Here nothing but strenuous thought, patient faithful obedience can avail. Hebrew history is the story of a pioneer people and every lapse from fidelity was serious, the future of humanity being at stake. Each Christian society and believer has work of the same kind not less important, and failures due to intellectual sloth and moral levity are as dishonourable as they are hurtful to the human race. Some of our heretics now are more serious than Christians, and they give thought and will more earnestly to the opinions they try to propagate. While the professed servants of Christ, who should be marching in the van, are amusing themselves with the accessories of religion, the resolute socialist or nihilist, reasoning and speaking with the heat of conviction, leads the masses where he will.

The Ammonite oppression made the Hebrews feel keenly the uselessness of heathenism. Baal and Melcarth had been thought of as real divinities, exercising power in some region or other of earth or heaven, and Israel's had been an easy backsliding. Idolatry did not appear as darkness to people who had never been fully in the light. But when trouble came and help was sorely needed they began to see that the Baalim were nothing. What could these idols do for men oppressed and at their wits' end? Religion was of no avail unless it brought an assurance of One Whose strong hand could reach from land to land, Whose grace and favour could revive sad and troubled souls. Heathenism was found utterly barren, and Israel turned to Jehovah the God of its fathers. "We have sinned against Thee even because we have forsaken our God and have served the Baalim."

Those who now fall away from faith are in worse case by far than Israel. They have no thought of a real power that can befriend them. It is to mere abstractions they have given the Divine name. In sin and sorrow alike they remain with ideas only, with bare terms of speculation in which there is no life, no strength, no hope for the moral nature. They are men and have to live; but with the living God they have entirely broken. In trouble they can only call on the Abyss or the Immensities, and there is no way of repentance though they seek it carefully with tears. At heart therefore they are pessimists without resource. Sadness deep and deadly ever waits upon such unbelief, and our religion to-day suffers from gloom because it is infected by the uncertainties and denials of an agnosticism at once positive and confused.

Another paganism, that of gathering and doing in the world-sphere, is constantly beside us, drawing multitudes from fidelity to Christ as Baal-worship drew Israel from Jehovah, and it is equally barren in the sharp experiences of humanity. Earthly things venerated in the ardour of business and the pursuit of social distinction appear as impressive realities only while the soul sleeps. Let it be aroused by some overturn of the usual, one of those floods that sweep suddenly down on the cities which fill the valley of life, and there is a quick pathetic confession of the truth. The soul needs help now, and its help must come from the Eternal Spirit. We must have done with mere saying of prayers and begin to pray. We must find access, if access is to be had, to the secret place of the Most High on Whose mercy we depend to redeem us from bondage and fear. Sad therefore is it for those who having never learned to seek the throne of divine succour are swept by the wild deluge from their temples and their gods. It is a cry of despair they raise amid the swelling torrent. You who now by the sacred oracles and the mediation of Christ can come into the fellowship of eternal life, be earnest and eager in the cultivation of your faith. The true religion of God which avails the soul in its extremity is not to be had in a moment, when suddenly its help is needed. That confidence which has been established in the mind by serious thought, by the habit of prayer and reliance on divine wisdom can alone bring help when the foundations of the earthly are destroyed.

To Israel troubled and contrite came as on previous occasions a prophetic message; and it was spoken by one of those incisive ironic preachers who were born from time to time among this strangely heathen, strangely believing people. It is in terms of earnest remonstrance he speaks, at first almost going the length of declaring that there is no hope for the rebellious and ungrateful tribes. They found it an easy thing to turn from their Divine King to the gods they chose to worship. Now they perhaps expect as easy a recovery of His favour. But healing must begin with deeper wounding, and salvation with much keener anxiety. This prophet knows the need for utter seriousness of soul. As he loves and yearns over his countryfolk he must so deal with them; it is God's way, the only way to save. Most irrationally, against all sound principles of judgment they had abandoned the Living One, the Eternal to worship hideous idols like Moloch and Dagon. It was wicked because it was wilfully stupid and perverse. And Jehovah says, "I will save you no more. Go and cry unto the gods which ye have chosen; let them save you in the day of your distress." The rebuke is stinging. The preacher makes the people feel the wretched insufficiency of their hope in the false, and the great strong pressure upon them of the Almighty, Whom, even in neglect, they cannot escape. We are pointed forward to the terrible pathos of Jeremiah:—"Who shall have pity upon thee, O Jerusalem? or who shall bemoan thee? or who shall turn aside to ask of thy welfare? Thou hast rejected me, saith the Lord, thou art gone backward: therefore have I stretched out my hand against thee, and destroyed thee: I am weary with repenting."

And notice to what state of mind the Hebrews were brought. Renewing their confession they said, "Do thou unto us whatsoever seemeth good unto Thee." They would be content to suffer now at the hand of God whatever He chose to inflict on them. They themselves would have exacted heavy tribute of a subject people that had rebelled and came suing for pardon. Perhaps they would have slain every tenth man. Jehovah might appoint retribution of the same kind; He might afflict them with pestilence; He might require them to offer a multitude of sacrifices. Men who traffic with idolatry and adopt gross notions of revengeful gods are certain to carry back with them when they return to the better faith many of the false ideas they have gathered. And it is just possible that a demand for human sacrifices was at this time attributed to God, the general feeling that they might be necessary connecting itself with Jephthah's vow.

It is idle to suppose that Israelites who persistently lapsed into paganism could at any time, because they repented, find the spiritual thoughts they had lost. True those thoughts were at the heart of the national life, there always even when least felt. But thousands of Hebrews even in a generation of reviving faith died with but a faint and shadowy personal understanding of Jehovah. Everything in the Book of Judges goes to show that the mass of the people were nearer the level of their neighbours the Moabites and Ammonites than the piety of the Psalms. A remarkable ebb and flow are observable in the history of the race. Look at some facts and there seems to be decline. Samson is below Gideon, and Gideon below Deborah; no man of leading until Isaiah can be named with Moses. Yet ever and anon there are prophetic calls and voices out of a spiritual region into which the people as a whole do not enter, voices to which they listen only when distressed and overborne. Worldliness increases, for the world opens to the Hebrew; but it often disappoints, and still there are some to whom the heavenly secret is told. The race as a whole is not becoming more devout and holy, but the few are gaining a clearer vision as one experience after another is recorded. The antithesis is the same we see in the Christian centuries. Is the multitude more pious now than in the age when a king had to do penance for rash words spoken against an ecclesiastic? Are the churches less worldly than they were a hundred years ago? Scarcely may we affirm it. Yet there never was an age so rich as ours in the finest spirituality, the noblest Christian thought. Our van presses up to the Simplon height and is in constant touch with those who follow; but the rear is still chaffering and idling in the streets of Milan. It is in truth always by the fidelity of the remnant that humanity is saved for God.

We cannot say that when Israel repented it was in the love of holiness so much as in the desire for liberty. The ways of the heathen were followed readily, but the supremacy of the heathen was ever abominable to the vigorous Israelite. By this national spirit however God could find the tribes, and a special feature of the deliverance from Ammon is marked where we read: "The people, the princes of Gilead said one to the other, What man is he that will begin to fight against the children of Ammon? He shall be head over all the inhabitants of Gilead." Looking around for the fit leader they found Jephthah and agreed to invite him.

Now this shows distinct progress in the growth of the nation. There is, if nothing more, a growth in practical power. Abimelech had thrust himself upon the men of Shechem. Jephthah is chosen apart from any ambition of his own. The movement which made him judge arose out of the consciousness of the Gileadites that they could act for themselves and were bound to act for themselves. Providence indicated the chief, but they had to be instruments of providence in making him chief. The vigour and robust intelligence of the men of Eastern Palestine come out here. They lead in the direction of true national life. While on the west of Jordan there is a fatalistic disposition, these men move. Gilead, the separated country, with the still ruder Bashan behind it and the Argob a resort of outlaws, is beneath some other regions in manners and in thought, but ahead of them in point of energy. We need not look for refinement, but we shall see power; and the chosen leader, while he is something of the barbarian, will be a man to leave his mark on history.

At the start we are not prepossessed in favour of Jephthah. There is some confusion in the narrative which has led to the supposition that he was a foundling of the clan. But taking Gilead as the actual name of his father, he appears as the son of a harlot, brought up in the paternal home and banished from it when there were legitimate sons able to contend with him. We get thus a brief glance at a certain rough standard of morals and see that even polygamy made sharp exclusions. Jephthah, cast out, betakes himself to the land of Tob and getting about him a band of vain fellows or freebooters becomes the Robin Hood or Rob Roy of his time. There are natural suspicions of a man who takes to a life of this kind, and yet the progress of events shows that though Jephthah was a sort of outlaw his character as well as his courage must have commended him. He and his men might occasionally seize for their own use the cattle and corn of Israelites when they were hard pressed for food. But it was generally against the Ammonites and other enemies their raids were directed, and the modern instances already cited show that no little magnanimity and even patriotism may go along with a life of lawless adventure. If this robber chief, as some might call him, now and again levied contributions from a wealthy flock-master, the poorer Hebrews were no doubt indebted to him for timely help when bands of Ammonites swept through the land. Something of this we must read into the narrative, otherwise the elders of Gilead would not so unanimously and urgently have invited him to become their head.

Jephthah was not at first disposed to believe in the good faith of those who gave him the invitation. Among the heads of households who came he saw his own brothers who had driven him to the hills. He must have more than suspected that they only wished to make use of him in their emergency and, the fighting over, would set him aside. He therefore required an oath of the men that they would really accept him as chief and obey him. That given, he assumed the command.

And here the religious character of the man begins to appear. At Mizpah on the verge of the wilderness where the Israelites, driven northward by the victories of Ammon, had their camp there stood an ancient cairn or heap of stones which preserved the tradition of a sacred covenant and still retained the savour of sanctity. There it was that Jacob, fleeing from Padanaram on his way back to Canaan, was overtaken by Laban, and there raising the Cairn of Witness they swore in the sight of Jehovah to be faithful to each other. The belief still lingered that the old monument was a place of meeting between man and God. To it Jephthah repaired at this new point in his life. No more an adventurer, no more an outlaw, but the chosen leader of eastern Israel, "he spake all his words before Jehovah in Mizpah." He had his life to review there, and that could not be done without serious thought. He had a new and strenuous future opened to him. Jephthah the outcast, the unnamed, was to be leader in a tremendous national struggle. The bold Gileadite feels the burden of the task. He has to question himself, to think of Jehovah. Hitherto he has been doing his own business and to that he has felt quite equal; now with large responsibility comes a sense of need. For a fight with society he has been strong enough; but can he be sure of himself as God's man, fighting against Ammon? Not a few words but many would he have to utter as on the hill-top in the silence he lifted up his soul to God and girt himself in holy resolution, as a father and a Hebrew, to do his duty in the day of battle.

Thus we pass from doubt of Jephthah to the hope that the banished man, the free-booter, will yet prove to be an Israelite indeed, of sterling character, whose religion, very rude perhaps, has a deep strain of reality and power. Jephthah at the cairn of Mizpah lifting up his hands in solemn invocation of the God of Jacob reminds us that there are great traditions of the past of our nation and of our most holy faith to which we are bound to be true, that there is a God, our witness and our judge, in Whose strength alone we can live and do nobly. For the service of humanity and the maintenance of faith we need to be in close touch with the brave and good of other days and in the story of their lives find quickening for our own. Along the same line and succession we are to bear our testimony, and no link of connection with the Divine Power is to be missed which the history of the men of faith supplies. Yet as our personal Helper especially we must know God. Hearing His call to ourselves we must lift the standard and go forth to the battle of life. Who can serve his family and friends, who can advance the well-being of the world, unless he has entered into that covenant with the Living God which raises mortal insufficiency to power and makes weak and ignorant men instruments of a divine redemption?

CHAPTER XVII.

THE TERRIBLE VOW.

JUDGES xi. 12-40.

AT every stage of their history the Hebrews were capable of producing men of passionate religiousness. And this appears as a distinction of the group of nations to which they belong: The Arab of the present time has the same quality. He can be excited to a holy war in which thousands perish. With the battle-cry of Allah and his Prophet he forgets fear. He presents a different mingling of character from the Saxon,—turbulence and reverence, sometimes apart, then blending—magnanimity and a tremendous want of magnanimity; he is fierce and generous, now rising to vivid faith, then breaking into earthly passion. We have seen the type in Deborah. David is the same and Elijah; and Jephthah is the Gileadite, the border Arab. In each of these there is quick leaping at life and beneath hot impulse a strain of brooding thought with moments of intense inward trouble. As we follow the history we must remember the kind of man it presents to us. There is humanity as it is in every race, daring in effort, tender in affection, struggling with ignorance yet thoughtful of God and duty, triumphing here, defeated there. And there is the Syrian with the heat of the sun in his blood and the shadow of Moloch on his heart, a son of the rude hills and of barbaric times, yet with a dignity, a sense of justice, a keen upward look, the Israelite never lost in the outlaw.

So soon as Jephthah begins to act for his people, marks of a strong character are seen. He is no ordinary leader, not the mere fighter the elders of Gilead may have taken him to be. His first act is to send messengers to the king of Ammon saying, What hast thou to do with me that thou art come to fight against my land? He is a chief who desires to avert bloodshed—a new figure in the history.

Natural in those times was the appeal to arms, so natural, so customary that we must not lightly pass this trait in the character of the Gileadite judge. If we compare his policy with that of Gideon or Barak we see of course that he had different circumstances to deal with. Between Jordan and the Mediterranean the Israelites required the whole of the land in order to establish a free nationality. There was no room for Canaanite or Midianite rule side by side with their own. The dominance of Israel had to be complete and undisturbed. Hence there was no alternative to war when Jabin or Zebah and Zalmunna attacked the tribes. Might had to be invoked on behalf of right. On the other side Jordan the position was different. Away towards the desert behind the mountains of Bashan the Ammonites might find pasture for their flocks, and Moab had its territory on the slopes of the lower Jordan and the Dead Sea. It was not necessary to crush Ammon in order to give Manasseh, Gad, and Reuben space enough and to spare. Yet there was a rare quality of judgment shown by the man who, although called to lead in war, began with negotiation and aimed at a peaceful settlement. No doubt there was danger that the Ammonites might unite with Midian or Moab against Israel. But Jephthah hazards such a coalition. He knows the bitterness kindled by strife. He desires that Ammon, a kindred people, shall be won over to friendliness with Israel, henceforth to be an ally instead of a foe.

Now in one aspect this may appear an error in policy, and the Hebrew chief will seem especially to blame when he makes the admission that the Ammonites hold their land from Chemosh their god. Jephthah has no sense of Israel's mission to the world, no wish to convert Ammon to a higher faith, nor does Jehovah appear to him as sole King, sole object of human worship. Yet, on the other hand, if the Hebrews were to fight idolatry everywhere it is plain their swords would never have been sheathed. Phœnicia was close beside; Aram was not far away; northward the Hittites maintained their elaborate ritual. A line had to be drawn somewhere and, on the whole, we cannot but regard Jephthah as an enlightened and humane chief who wished to stir against his people and his God no hostility that could possibly be avoided. Why should not Israel conquer Ammon by justice and magnanimity, by showing the higher principles which the true religion taught? He began at all events by endeavouring to stay the quarrel, and the attempt was wise.

The king of Ammon refused Jephthah's offer to negotiate. He claimed the land bounded by the Arnon, the Jabbok, and Jordan as his own and demanded that it should be peaceably given up to him. In reply Jephthah denied the claim. It was the Amorites, he said, who originally held that part of Syria. Sihon who was defeated in the time of Moses was not an Ammonite king, but chief of the Amorites. Israel had by conquest obtained the district in dispute, and Ammon must give place.

The full account given of these messages sent by Jephthah shows a strong desire on the part of the narrator to vindicate Israel from any charge of unnecessary warfare. And it is very important that this should be understood, for the inspiration of the historian is involved. We know of nations that in sheer lust of conquest have attacked tribes whose land they did not need, and we have read histories in which wars unprovoked and cruel have been glorified. In after times the Hebrew kings brought trouble and disaster on themselves by their ambition. It would have been well if David and Solomon had followed a policy like Jephthah's rather than attempted to rival Assyria and Egypt. We see an error rather than a cause of boasting when David put garrisons in Syria of Damascus: strife was thereby provoked which issued in many a sanguinary war. The Hebrews should never have earned the character of an aggressive and ambitious people that required to be kept in check by the kingdoms around. To this nation, a worldly nation on the whole, was committed a spiritual inheritance, a spiritual task. Is it asked why, being worldly, the Hebrews ought to have fulfilled a spiritual calling? The answer is that their best men understood and declared the Divine will, and they should have listened to their best men. Their fatal mistake was, as Christ showed, to deride their prophets, to crush and kill the messengers of God. And many other nations likewise have missed their true vocation, being deluded by dreams of vast empire and earthly glory. To combat idolatry was indeed the business of Israel and especially to drive back the heathenism that would have overwhelmed its faith; and often this had to be done with an earthly sword because liberty no less than faith was at stake. But a policy of aggression was never the duty of this people.

The temperate messages of the Hebrew chief to the king of Ammon proved to be of no avail: war alone was to settle the rival claims. And this once clear Jephthah lost no time in preparing for battle. As one who felt that without God no man can do anything, he sought assurance of divine aid; and we have now to consider the vow which he made, ever interesting on account of the moral problem it involves and the very pathetic circumstances which accompanied its fulfilment.

The terms of the solemn engagement under which Jephthah came were these:—" If Thou wilt indeed deliver the children of Ammon into mine hand, then it shall be that whatsoever" (Septuagint and Vulgate, "*whosoever*") "cometh forth of the doors of my house to meet me when I return in peace from the children of Ammon shall be the Lord's, and I will offer it (otherwise, *him*) for a burnt offering." And here two questions arise; the first, what he could have meant by the promise; the second, whether we can justify him in making it. As to the first, the explicit designation to God of whatever came forth of the doors of his house points unmistakably to a human life as the devoted thing. It would have been idle in an emergency like that in which Jephthah found himself, with a hazardous conflict impending that was to decide the fate of the eastern tribes at least, to anticipate the appearance of an animal,—bullock, goat, or sheep, —and promise that in sacrifice. The form of words used in the vow cannot be held to refer to an animal. The chief is thinking of some one who will express joy at his success and greet him as a victor. In the fulness of his heart he leaps to a wild savage mark of devotion. It is a crisis alike for him and for the people and what can he do to secure the favour and help of Jehovah? Too ready from his acquaintance with heathen sacrifices and ideas to believe that the God of Israel will be pleased with the kind of offerings by which the gods of Sidon and Aram were honoured, feeling himself as the chief of the Hebrews bound to make some great and unusual sacrifice, he does not promise that the captives taken in war shall be devoted to Jehovah, but some one of his own people is to be the victim. The dedication shall be all the more impressive that the life given up is one of which he himself shall feel the loss. A conqueror returning from war would, in ordinary circumstances, have loaded with gifts the first member of his household who came forth to welcome him. Jephthah vows to give that very person to God. The insufficient religious intelligence of the man, whose life had been far removed from elevating influences, this once perceived—and we cannot escape from the facts of the case—the vow is parallel to others of which ancient history tells. Jephthah expects some servant, some favourite slave to be the first. There is a touch of barbaric grandeur and at the same time of Roman sternness in his vow. As a chief he has the lives of all his household entirely at his disposal. To sacrifice one will be hard, for he is a humane man; but he expects that the offering will be all the more acceptable to the Most High. Such are the ideas moral and religious from which his vow springs.

Now we should like to find more knowledge and a higher vision in a leader of Israel. We would fain escape from the conclusion that a Hebrew could be so ignorant of the divine character as Jephthah appears; and moved by such feelings many have taken a very different view of the matter. The Gileadite has, for example, been represented as fully aware of the Mosaic regulations concerning sacrifice and the method for redeeming the life of a firstborn child; that is to say, he is supposed to have made his vow under cover of the Levitical provision by which in case his daughter should first meet him he would escape the necessity of sacrificing her. The rule in question could not, however, be stretched to a case like this. But, supposing it could, is it likely that a man whose whole soul had gone out in a vow of life and death to God would reserve such a door of escape? In that case the story would lose its terror indeed, but also its power: human history would be the poorer by one of the great tragic experiences, wild and supernatural, that show man struggling with thoughts above himself.

What did the Gileadite know? What ought he to have known? We see in his vow a fatalistic strain; he leaves it to chance or fate to determine who shall meet him. There is also an assumption of the right to take into his own hands the disposal of a human life; and this, though most confidently claimed, was entirely a factitious right. It is one which mankind has ceased to allow. Further, the purpose of offering a human being in sacrifice is unspeakably horrible to us. But how differently these things must have appeared in the dim light which alone guided this man of lawless life in his attempt to make sure of God and honour Him! We have but to consider things that are done at the present day in the name of religion, the lifelong "devotion" of young women in a nunnery, for example, and all the ceremonies which accompany that outrage on the divine order to see that centuries of Christianity have not yet put an end to practices which under colour of piety are barbaric and revolting. In the modern case a nun secluded from the world, dead to the world, is considered to be an offering to God. The old conception of sacrifice was that the life must pass out of the world by way of death in order to become God's. Or again, when the priest describing the devotion of his body says: "The essential, the sacerdotal purpose to which it should be used is to die. Such death must be begun in chastity, continued in mortification, consummated in that actual death which is the priest's final oblation, his last sacrifice,"*—the same superstition appears in a refined and mystical form.

His vow made, the chief went forth to battle, leaving in his home one child only, a daughter beautiful, high-spirited, the joy of her father's heart. She was a true Hebrew girl and all her thought was that he, her sire, should deliver Israel. For this she longed and prayed. And it was so. The enthusiasm of Jephthah's devotion to God was caught by his troops and bore them on irresistibly. Marching from Mizpah in the land of Bashan they crossed Manasseh, and south from Mizpeh of Gilead, which was not far from the Jabbok, they found the Ammonites encamped. The first battle practically decided the campaign. From Aroer to Minnith, from the Jabbok to the springs of Arnon, the course of flight and bloodshed extended, until the invaders were swept from the territory of the tribes. Then came the triumphant return.

We imagine the chief as he approached his home among the hills of Gilead, his eagerness and exultation mingled with some vague alarm. The vow he has made cannot but weigh upon his mind now that the performance of it comes so near. He has had time to think what it implies. When he uttered the words that involved a life the issue of war appeared doubtful. Perhaps the campaign would be long and indecisive. He might have returned not altogether discredited, yet not triumphant. But he has succeeded beyond his expectation. There can be no doubt that the offering is due to Jehovah. Who then shall appear? The secret of his vow is hid in his own breast. To no man has he revealed his solemn promise; nor has he dared in any way to interfere with the course of events. As he passes up the valley with his attendants there is a stir in his rude castle. The tidings of his coming have preceded him and she, that dear girl who is the very apple of his eye, his daughter, his only child, having already rehearsed her part, goes forth eagerly to welcome him. She is clad in her gayest dress. Her eyes are bright with the keenest excitement. The timbrel her father once gave her, on which she has often played to delight him, is tuned to a chant of triumph. She dances as she passes from the gate. Her father, her father, chief, and victor!

And he? A sudden horror checks his heart. He stands arrested, cold as stone, with eyes of strange dark trouble fixed upon the gay young figure that welcomes him to home and rest and fame. She flies to his arms, but they do not open to her. She looks at him, for he has never repulsed her—and why now? He puts forth his hands as if to thrust away a dreadful sight, and what does she hear? Amid the sobs of a strong man's agony, "Alas, my daughter, thou hast brought me very low . . . and thou art one of them that trouble me." To startled ears the truth is slowly told. She is vowed to the Lord in sacrifice. He cannot go back. Jehovah who gave the victory now claims the fulfilment of the oath.

We are dealing with the facts of life. For a time let us put aside the reflections that are so easy to make about rash vows and the iniquity of keeping them. Before this anguish of the loving heart, this awful issue of a sincere but superstitious devotion we stand in reverence. It

* Henri Perreyve.

is one of the supreme hours of humanity. Will the father not seek relief from his obligation? Will the daughter not rebel? Surely a sacrifice so awful will not be completed. Yet we remember Abraham and Isaac journeying together to Moriah, and how with the father's resignation of his great hope there must have gone the willingness of the son to face death if that last proof of piety and faith is required. We look at the father and daughter of a later date and find the same spirit of submission to what is regarded as the will of God. Is the thing horrible—too horrible to be dwelt upon? Are we inclined to say,

"... 'Heaven heads the count of crimes
With that wild oath?' She renders answer high,
'Not so; nor once alone, a thousand times
I would be born and die.'"

It has been affirmed that "Jephthah's rash act, springing from a culpable ignorance of the character of God, directed by heathen superstition and cruelty poured an ingredient of extreme bitterness into his cup of joy and poisoned his whole life." Suffering indeed there must have been for both the actors in that pitiful tragedy of devotion and ignorance, who knew not the God to Whom they offered the sacrifice. But it is one of the marks of rude erring man that he does take upon himself such burdens of pain in the service of the invisible Lord. A shallow scepticism entirely misreads the strange dark deeds often done for religion; yet one who has uttered many a foolish thing in the way of "explaining" piety can at last confess that the renouncing mortifying spirit is, with all its errors, one of man's noble and distinguishing qualities. To Jephthah, as to his heroic daughter, religion was another thing than it is to many, just because of their extraordinary renunciation. Very ignorant they were surely, but they were not so ignorant as those who make no great offering to God, who would not resign a single pleasure, nor deprive a son or daughter of a single comfort or delight, for the sake of religion and the higher life. To what purpose is this waste? said the disciples, when the pound of ointment of spikenard, very costly, was poured on the head of Jesus and the house was filled with the odour. To many now it seems waste to expend thought, time, or money upon a sacred cause, much more to hazard or to give life itself. We see the evils of enthusiastic self-devotion to the work of God very clearly; its power we do not feel. We are saving life so diligently, many of us, that we may well fear to lose it irremediably. There is no strain and therefore no strength, no joy. A weary pessimism dogs our unfaith.

To Jephthah and his daughter the vow was sacred, irrevocable. The deliverance of Israel by so signal and complete a victory left no alternative. It would have been well if they had known God differently; yet better this darkly impressive issue which went to the making of Hebrew faith and strength than easy unfruitful evasion of duty. We are shocked by the expenditure of fine feeling and heroism in upholding a false idea of God and obligation to Him; but are we outraged and distressed by the constant effort to escape from God which characterises our age? And have we for our own part come yet to the right idea of self and its relations? Our century, beclouded on many points, is nowhere less informed than in matters of self-sacrifice; Christ's doctrine is still uncomprehended. Jephthah was wrong, for God did not need to be bribed to support a man who was bent on doing his duty. And many fail now to perceive that personal development and service of God are in the same line. Life is made for generosity, not mortification; for giving in glad ministry, not for giving up in hideous sacrifice. It is to be devoted to God by the free and holy use of body, mind, and soul in the daily tasks which Providence appoints.

The wailing of Jephthah's daughter rings in our ears, bearing with it the anguish of many a soul tormented in the name of that which is most sacred, tormented by mistakes concerning God, the awful theory that He is pleased with human suffering. The relics of that hideous Moloch-worship which polluted Jephthah's faith, not even yet purged away by the Spirit of Christ, continue and make religion an anxiety and life a kind of torture. I do not speak of that devotion of thought and time, eloquence and talent to some worthless cause which here and there amazes the student of history and human life,—the passionate ardour, for example, with which Flora Macdonald gave herself up to the service of a Stuart. But religion is made to demand sacrifices compared to which the offering of Jephthah's daughter was easy. The imagination of women especially, fired by false representations of the death of Christ in which there was a clear divine assertion of self, while it is made to appear as complete suppression of self, bears many on in a hopeless and essentially immoral endeavour. Has God given us minds, feelings, right ambitions that we may crush them? Does He purify our desires and aspirations by the fire of his own Spirit and still require us to crush them? Are we to find our end in being nothing, absolutely nothing, devoid of will, of purpose, of personality? Is this what Christianity demands? Then our religion is but refined suicide, and the God who desires us to annihilate ourselves is but the Supreme Being of the Buddhists, if those may be said to have a god who regard the suppression of individuality as salvation.

Christ was made a sacrifice for us. Yes: He sacrificed everything except His own eternal life and power; He sacrificed ease and favour and immediate success for the manifestation of God. So He achieved the fulness of personal might and royalty. And every sacrifice His religion calls us to make is designed to secure that enlargement and fulness of spiritual individuality in the exercise of which we shall truly serve God and our fellows. Does God require sacrifice? Yes, unquestionably—the sacrifice which every reasonable being must make in order that the mind, the soul may be strong and free, sacrifice of the lower for the higher, sacrifice of pleasure for truth, of comfort for duty, of the life that is earthly and temporal for the life that is heavenly and eternal. And the distinction of Christianity is that it makes this sacrifice supremely reasonable because it reveals the higher life, the heavenly hope, the eternal rewards for which the sacrifice is to be made; that it enables us in making it to feel ourselves united to Christ in a divine work which is to issue in the redemption of mankind.

There are not a few popularly accepted guides in religion who fatally misconceive the doctrine of sacrifice. They take man-made conditions for Divine opportunities and calls. Their arguments come home not to the selfish and overbearing, but to the unselfish and long-suffering members of society, and too often they are more anxious to praise renunciation—any kind of it, for any purpose, so it involve acute feeling—than to magnify truth and insist on righteousness. It is women chiefly these arguments affect, and the neglect of pure truth and justice with which women are charged is in no small degree the result of false moral and religious teaching. They are told that it is good to renounce and suffer even when at every step advantage is taken of their submission and untruth triumphs over generosity. They are urged to school themselves to humiliation and loss not because God appoints these but because human selfishness imposes them. The one clear and damning objection to the false doctrine of self-suppression is here: it makes sin. Those who yield where they should protest, who submit where they should argue and reprove, make a path for selfishness and injustice and increase evil instead of lessening it. They persuade themselves that they are bearing the cross after Christ; but what in effect are they doing? The missionary amongst ignorant heathen has to bear to the uttermost as Christ bore. But to give so-called Christians a power of oppression and exaction is to turn the principles of religion upside down and hasten the doom of those for whom the sacrifice is made. When we meddle with truth and righteousness even in the name of piety we simply commit sacrilege, we range ourselves with the wrong and unreal; there is no foundation under our faith and no moral result of our endurance and self-denial. We are selling Christ, not following Him.

CHAPTER XVIII.

SHIBBOLETHS.

JUDGES xii. 1-7.

WHILE Jephthah and his Gileadites were engaged in the struggle with Ammon jealous watch was kept over all their movements by the men of Ephraim. As the head tribe of the house of Joseph occupying the centre of Palestine Ephraim was suspicious of all attempts and still more of every success that threatened its pride and pre-eminence. We have seen Gideon in the hour of his victory challenged by this watchful tribe, and now a quarrel is made with Jephthah who has dared to win a battle without its help. What were the Gileadites that they should presume to elect a chief and form an army? Fugitives from Ephraim who had gathered in the shaggy forests of Bashan and among the cliffs of the Argob, mere adventurers in fact, what right had they to set up as the protectors of Israel? The Ephraimites found the position intolerable. The vigour and confidence of Gilead were insulting. If a check were not put on the energy of the new leader might he not cross the Jordan and establish a tyranny over the whole land? There was a call to arms, and a large force was soon marching against Jephthah's camp to demand satisfaction and submission.

The pretext that Jepthah had fought against Ammon without asking the Ephraimites to join him was shallow enough. The invitation appears to have been given; and even without an invitation Ephraim might well have taken the field. But the savage threat, "We will burn thine house upon thee with fire," showed the temper of the leaders in this expedition. The menace was so violent that the Gileadites were roused at once and, fresh from their victory over Ammon, they were not long in humbling the pride of the great western clan.

One may well ask, Where is Ephraim's fear of God? Why has there been no consultation of the priests at Shiloh by the tribe under whose care the sanctuary is placed? The great Jewish commentary affirms that the priests were to blame, and we cannot but agree. If religious influences and arguments were not used to prevent the expedition against Gilead they should have been used. The servants of the oracle might have understood the duty of the tribes to each other and of the whole nation to God and done their utmost to avert civil war. Unhappily, however, professed interpreters of the divine will are too often forward in urging the claims of a tribe or favouring the arrogance of a class by which their own position is upheld. As on the former occasion when Ephraim interfered, so in this we scarcely go beyond what is probable in supposing that the priests declared it to be the duty of faithful Israelites to check the career of the eastern chief and so prevent his rude and ignorant religion from gaining dangerous popularity. Bishop Wordsworth has seen a fanciful resemblance between Jephthah's campaign against Ammon and the revival under the Wesleys and Whitefield which as a movement against ungodliness put to shame the sloth of the Church of England. He has remarked on the scorn and disdain—and he might have used stronger terms—with which the established clergy assailed those who apart from them were successfully doing the work of God. This was an example of far more flagrant tribal jealousy than that of Ephraim and her priests; and have there not been cases of religious leaders urging retaliation upon enemies or calling for war in order to punish what was absurdly deemed an outrage on national honour? With facts of this kind in view we can easily believe that from Shiloh no word of peace, but on the other hand words of encouragement were heard when the chiefs of Ephraim began to hold councils of war and to gather their men for the expedition that was to make an end of Jephthah.

Let it be allowed that Ephraim, a strong tribe, the guardian of the ark of Jehovah, much better instructed than the Gileadites in the divine law, had a right to maintain its place. But the security of high position lies in high purpose and noble service; and an Ephraim ambitious of leading should have been forward on every occasion when the other tribes were in confusion and trouble. When a political party or a church claims to be first in regard for righteousness and national well-being it should not think of its own credit or continuance in power but of its duty in the war against injustice and ungodliness. The favour of the great, the admiration of the multitude, should be nothing to either church or party. To rail at those who are more generous, more patriotic, more eager in the service of truth, to profess a fear of some ulterior design against the constitution or the faith, to turn all the force of influence and eloquence and even of slander and menace against the disliked neighbour instead of the real enemy, this is the nadir of baseness. There are Ephraims still, strong tribes in the land, that are too much exercised in putting down claims, too little in finding principles of unity and forms of practical brotherhood. We see in this bit of history an example of the humiliation that sooner or later falls on the jealous and the arrogant; and every age is adding instances of a like kind.

Civil war, at all times lamentable, appears peculiarly so when the cause of it lies in haughtiness and distrust. We have found however that, beneath the surface, there may have been elements of division and ill-will serious enough to require this painful remedy. The campaign may have prevented a lasting rupture between the eastern and western tribes, a separation of the stream of Israel's religion and nationality into rival currents. It may also have arrested a tendency to ecclesiastical narrowness, which at this early stage would have done immense harm. It is quite true that Gilead was rude and uninstructed, as Galilee had the reputation of being in the time of our Lord. But the leading tribes or classes of a nation are not entitled to overbear the less enlightened, nor by attempts at tyranny to drive them into separation. Jephthah's victory had the effect of making Ephraim and the other western tribes understand that Gilead had to be reckoned with, whether for weal or woe, as an integral and important part of the body politic. In Scottish history, the despotic attempt to thrust Episcopacy on the nation was the cause of a distressing civil war; a people who would not fall in with the forms of religion that were in favour at head-quarters had to fight for liberty. Despised or esteemed they resolved to keep and use their rights, and the religion of the world owes a debt to the Covenanters. Then in our own times, lament as we may the varied forms of antagonism to settled faith and government, that enmity of which communism and anarchism are the delirium, it would be simply disastrous to suppress it by sheer force even if the thing were possible. Surely those who are certain they have right on their side need not be arrogant. The overbearing temper is always a sign of hollow principle as well as of moral infirmity. Was any Gilead ever put down by a mere assertion of superiority, even on the field of battle? Let the truth be acknowledged that only in freedom lies the hope of progress in intelligence, in constitutional order and purity of faith. The great problems of national life and development can never be settled as Ephraim tried to settle the movement beyond Jordan. The idea of life expands and room must be left for its enlargement. The many lines of thought, of personal activity, of religious and social experiment leading to better ways or else proving by-and-by that the old are best—all these must have place in a free state. The threats of revolution that trouble nations would die away if this were clearly understood; and we read history in vain if we think that the old autocracies or aristocracies will ever approve themselves again, unless indeed they take far wiser and more Christian forms than they had in past ages. The thought of individual liberty once firmly rooted in the minds of men, there is no going back to the restraints that were possible before it was familiar. Government finds another basis and other duties. A new kind of order arises which attempts no suppression of any idea or sincere belief and allows all possible room for experiments in living. Unquestionably this altered condition of things increases the weight of moral responsibility. In ordering our own lives as well as in regulating custom and law we need to exercise the most serious care, the most earnest thought. Life is not easier because it has greater breadth and freedom. Each is thrown back more upon conscience, has more to do for his fellowmen and for God.

We pass now to the end of the campaign and the scene at the fords of Jordan, when the Gileadites, avenging themselves on Ephraim, used the notable expedient of asking a certain word to be pronounced in order to distinguish friend from foe. To begin with, the slaughter was quite unnecessary. If bloodshed there had to be, that on the field of battle was certainly enough. The wholesale murder of the "fugitives of Ephraim," so called with reference to their own taunt, was a passionate and barbarous deed. Those who began the strife could not complain; but it was the leaders of the tribe who rushed on war, and now the rank and file must suffer. Had Ephraim triumphed the defeated Gileadites would have found no quarter; victorious they gave none. We may trust, however, that the number forty-two thousand represents the total strength of the army that was dispersed and not those left dead on the field.

The expedient used at the fords turned on a defect or peculiarity of speech. Shibboleth perhaps meant *stream.* Of each man who came to the stream of Jordan wishing to pass to the other side it was required that he should say *Shibboleth.* The Ephraimites tried, but said *Sibboleth* instead, and so betraying their westcountry birth they pronounced their own doom. The incident has become proverbial and the proverbial use of it is widely suggestive. First, however, we may note a more direct application. Do we not at times observe how words used in common speech, phrases or turns of expression, betray a man's upbringing or character, his strain of thought and desire? It is not necessary to lay traps for men, to put it to them how they think on this point or that, in order to discover where they stand and what they are. Listen and you will hear sooner or later the *Sibboleth* that declares the son of Ephraim. In religious circles, for example, men are found who appear to be quite enthusiastic in the service of Christianity, eager for the success of the church, and yet on some occasion a word, an inflexion or turn of the voice will reveal to the attentive listener a constant worldliness of mind, a worship of self mingling with all they think and do. You notice that and you can prophesy what will come of it. In a few months, or even weeks, the show of interest will pass. There is not enough praise or deference to suit the egotist, he turns elsewhere to find the applause which he values above everything.

Again, there are words somewhat rude, somewhat coarse, which in carefully ordered speech a man may not use; but they fall from his lips in moments of unguarded freedom or excitement. The man does not speak "half in the language of Ashdod"; he particularly avoids it. Yet now and again a lapse into the Philistine dialect, a something muttered rather than spoken, betrays the secret of his nature. It would be harsh to condemn any one as inherently bad on such evidence. The early habits, the sins of past years thus unveiled, may be those against which he is fighting and praying. Yet, on the other hand, the hypocrisy of a life may terribly show itself in these little things; and every one will allow that in choosing our companions and friends we ought to be keenly alive to the slightest indications of character. There are fords of Jordan to which we come unexpectedly, and without being censorious we are bound to observe those with whom we purpose to travel further.

Here, however, one of the most interesting and, for our time, most important points of application is to be found in the self-disclosure of writers—those who produce our newspapers, magazines, novels, and the like. Touching on religion and on morals certain of these writers contrive to keep on good terms with the kind of belief that is popular and pays. But now and again, despite efforts to the contrary, they come on the *Shibboleth* which they forget to pronounce aright. Some among them who really care nothing for Christianity, and have no belief whatever in revealed religion, would yet pass for interpreters of religion and guides of conduct. Christian morality and worship they barely endure; but they cautiously adjust every phrase and reference so as to drive away no reader and offend no devout critic; that is, they aim at doing so; now and again they forget themselves. We catch a word, a touch of flippancy, a suggestion of license, a covert sneer which goes too far by a hairsbreadth. The evil lies in this, that they are teaching multitudes to say *Sibboleth* along with them. What they say is so pleasant, so deftly said, with such an air of respect for moral authority that suspicion is averted, the very elect are for a time deceived. Indeed we are almost driven to think that Christians not a few are quite ready to accept the unbelieving *Sibboleth* from sufficiently distinguished lips. A little more of this lubricity and there will have to be a new and resolute sifting at the fords. The propaganda is villainously active, and without intelligent and vigorous opposition it will proceed to further audacity. It is not a few but scores of this sect who have the ear of the public and even in religious publications are allowed to convey hints of earthliness and atheism. A covert worship of Mammon and of Venus goes on in the temple professedly dedicated to Christ, and one cannot be sure that a seemingly pious work will not vend some doctrine of devils. It is time for a slaughter in God's name of many a false reputation.

But there are *Shibboleths* of party, and we must be careful lest in trying others we use some catchword of our own Gilead by which to judge their religion or their virtue. The danger of the earnest, alike in religion, politics, and philanthropy, is to make their own favourite plans or doctrines the test of all worth and belief. Within our churches and in the ranks of social reformers distinctions are made where there should be none and old strifes are deepened. There are of course certain great principles of judgment. Christianity is founded on historical fact and revealed truth. "Every spirit which confesseth that Jesus Christ is come in the flesh is of God." In such a saying lies a test which is no tribal *Shibboleth*. And on the same level are others by which we are constrained at all hazards to try ourselves and those who speak and write. Certain points of morality are vital and must be pressed. When a writer says, " In mediæval times the recognition that every natural impulse in a healthy and mature being has a claim to gratification was a victory of unsophisticated nature over the asceticism of Christianity"—we use no Shibboleth-test in condemning him. He is judged and found wanting by principles on which the very existence of human society depends. It is in no spirit of bigotry, but in faithfulness to the essentials of life and the hope of mankind, that the sternest denunciation is hurled at such a man. In plain terms he is an enemy of the race.

Passing from cases like this, observe others in which a measure of dogmatism must be allowed to the ardent. Where there are no strong opinions strenuously held and expressed little impression will be made. The prophets in every age have spoken dogmatically; and vehemence of speech is not to be denied to the temperance reformer, the apostle of purity, the enemy of luxurious self-indulgence and cant. Moral indignation must express itself strongly; and in the dearth of moral conviction we can bear with those who would even drag us to the ford and make us utter their *Shibboleth*. They go too far, people say: perhaps they do; but there are so many who will not move at all except in the way of pleasure.

Now all this is clear. But we must return to the danger of making one aspect of morality the sole test of morals, one religious idea the sole test of religion and so framing a formula by which men separate themselves from their friends and pass narrow bitter judgments on their kinsfolk. Let sincere belief and strong feeling rise to the prophetic strain; let there be ardour, let there be dogmatism and vehemence. But beyond urgent words and strenuous example, beyond the effort to persuade and convert there lie arrogance and the usurpation of a judgment which belongs to God alone. In proportion as a Christian is living the life of Christ he will repel the claim of any other man, however devout, to force his opinion or his action. All attempts at terrorism betray a lack of spirituality. The Inquisition was in reality the world oppressing spiritual life. And so in less degree, with less truculence, the unspiritual element may show itself even in company with a fervent desire to serve the gospel. There need be no surprise that attempts to dictate to Christendom or any part of Christendom are warmly resented by those who know that religion and liberty cannot be separated. The true church of Christ has a firm grasp of what it believes and is aiming at, and by its resoluteness it bears on human society. It is also gracious and persuasive, reasonable and open, and so gathers men into a free and frank brotherhood, revealing to them the loftiest duty, leading them towards it in the way of liberty. Let men who understand this try each other and it will never be by limited and suspicious formulæ.

Amidst pedants, critics, hot and bitter partisans, we see Christ moving in divine freedom. Fine is the subtlety of His thought in which the ideas of spiritual liberty and of duty blend to form one luminous strain. Fine are the clearness and simplicity of that daily life in which He becomes the way and the truth to men. It is the ideal life, beyond all mere rules, disclosing the law of the kingdom of heaven; it is free and powerful because upheld by the purpose that underlies all activity and development. Are we endeavouring to realise it? Scarcely at all: the bonds are multiplying, not falling away; no man is bold to claim his right, nor generous to give others their room. In this age of Christ we seem neither to behold nor desire His manhood. Shall this always be? Shall there not arise a race fit for liberty because obedient, ardent, true? Shall we not come in the unity of the faith and of the knowledge of the Son of God unto a perfect man, unto the measure of the stature of the fulness of Christ?

For a little we must return to Jephthah, who after his great victory and his strange dark act of faith judged Israel but six years. He appears in striking contrast to other chiefs of his time, and even of far later times, in the purity of his home life, the more notable that his father set no example of good. Perhaps the legacy of dispeace and exile bequeathed to him with a tainted birth had taught the Gileadite, rude mountaineer as he was, the value of that order which his people too often despised. The silence of the history which is elsewhere careful to speak of wives and children sets Jephthah before us as a kind of puritan, with another and perhaps greater distinction than the desire to avoid war. The yearly lament for his daughter kept alive the memory not only of the heroine but of one judge in Israel who set a high example of family life. A sad and lonely man he went those few years of his rule in Gilead, but we may be sure that the character and will of the Holy One became more clear to him after he had passed the dreadful hill of sacrifice. The story is of the old world, terrible; yet we have found in Jephthah a sublime sincerity, and we may believe that such a man, though he never repented of his vow, would come to see that the God of Israel demanded another and a nobler sacrifice, that of life devoted to His righteousness and truth.

CHAPTER XIX.

THE ANGEL IN THE FIELD.

JUDGES xiii. 1-18.

IN our ignorance not in our knowledge, in our blindness not in our light, we call nature secular and think of the ordinary course of events as a series of cold operations, governed by law and force, having nothing to do with divine purpose and love. Oftentimes we think so, and suffer because we do not understand. It is a pitiful error. The natural could not exist, there could be neither substance nor order without the overnature which is at once law and grace. Vitality, movement are not an efflorescence heralding decay—as to the atheist; they are not the activity of an evil spirit—as sometimes to confused and falsely instructed faith. They are the outward and visible action of God, the hem of the vesture on which we lay hold and feel Him. In the seen and temporal there is a constant presence maintaining order, giving purpose and end. Were it otherwise man could not live an hour; even in selfishness and vileness he is a creature of two worlds which yet are one, so closely are they interwoven. At every point natural and supernatural are blended, the higher shaping the development of the lower, accomplishing in and through the lower a great spiritual plan. This it is which gives depth and weight to our experience, communicating the dignity of the greatest moral and spiritual issues to the meanest, darkest human life. Everywhere, always, man touches God though he know Him not.

No surprise, therefore, is excited by the modes of speech and thought we come upon as we read Scripture. The surprise would be in not coming upon them. If we found the inspired writers divorcing God from the world and thinking of "nature" as a dark chamber of sin and torture echoing with His curse, there would be no profit in studying this old volume. Then indeed we might turn from it in discontent and scorn, even as some cast it aside just because it is the revelation of God dwelling with men upon the earth.

But what do the writers of faith mean when they tell of divine messengers coming to peasants at labour in the fields, speaking to them of events common to the race—the birth of some child, the defeat of a rival tribe—as affairs of the spiritual even more than of the temporal region? The narratives, simple yet daring, which affirm the mingling of divine purpose and action with human life give us the deepest science, the one real philosophy. Why do we have to care and suffer for each other? What are our sin and sorrow? These are not material facts; they are of quite another range. Always man is more than dust, better or worse than clay. Human lives are linked together in a gracious and awful order the course of which is now clearly marked, now obscurely traceable; and if it were in our power to revive the history of past ages, to mark the operation of faith and unbelief among men, issuing in virtue and nobleness on the one hand, in vice and lethargy on the other, we should see how near heaven is to earth, how rational a thing is prophecy, not only as relating to masses of men but to particular lives. It is our stupidity not our wisdom that starts back from revelations of the over-world as if they confused what would otherwise be clear.

In more than one story of the Bible the motherhood of a simple peasant woman is a cause of divine communications and supernatural hopes. Is this amazing, incredible? What then is motherhood itself? In the coming and care of frail existences, the strange blending in one great necessity of the glad and the severe, the honourable and the humiliating, with so many possibilities of failure in duty, of error and misunderstanding ere the needful task is finished, death ever waiting on life, and agony on joy—in all this do we not find such a manifestation of the higher purpose as might well be heralded by words and signs? Only the order of God and His redemption can explain this "nature." Right in the path of atheistic reasoners, and of others not atheists, lie facts of human life which on their theory of naturalism are simply confounding, too great at once for the causes they admit and the ends they foresee. And if reason denies the possibility of prediction relating to these facts we need not wonder. Without philosophy or faith the range of denial is unlimited.

From the quaint and simple narrative before us the imaginative rationalist turns away with the one word—"myth." His criticism is of a sort which for all its ease and freedom gives the world nothing. We desire to know why the human mind harbours thoughts of the kind, why it has ideas of God and of a supernatural order, and how these work in developing the race.

Have they been of service? Have they given strength and largeness to poor rude lives and so proved a great reality? If so, the word myth is inadmissible. It sets falsehood at the source of progress and of good.

Here are two Hebrew peasants, in a period of Philistine domination more than a thousand years before the Christian era. Of their condition we know only what a few brief sentences can tell in a history concerned chiefly with the facts of a divine order in which men's lives have an appointed place and use. It is certain that a thorough knowledge of this Danite family, its own history and its part in the history of Israel, would leave no difficulty for faith. Belief in the fore-ordination of all human existence and the constant presence of God with men and women in their endurance, their hope and yearning would be forced upon the most sceptical mind. The insignificance of the occasion marked by a prediction given in the name of God may astonish some. But what is insignificant? Wherever divine predestination and authority extend, and that is throughout the whole universe, nothing can properly be called insignificant. The laws according to which material things and forces are controlled by God touch the minutest particles of matter, determine the shape of a dew-drop as certainly as the form of a world. At every point in human life, the birth of a child in the poorest cottage as well as of the heir to an empire, the same principles of heredity, the same disposition of affairs to leave room for that life and to work out its destiny underlie the economy of the world.

A life is to appear. It is not an interposition or interpolation. No event, no life is ever thrust into an age without relation to the past; no purpose is formed in the hour of a certain prophecy. For Samson as for every actor distinguished or obscure upon the stage of the world the stars and the seasons have co-operated, and all that has been done under the sun has gone to make a place for him. One who knows this can speak strongly and clearly. One who knows what hinders and what is sure to aid the fulfilment of a great destiny can counsel wisely. And so the angel of Jehovah, a messenger of the spiritual covenant, is no mere vehicle of a prediction he does not understand. Without hesitation he speaks to the woman in the field of what her son shall do. By the story of God's dealings with Israel, by the experiences of tribe and family and individual soul since the primitive age, by the simple faith of these parents that are to be and the honest energy of their humble lives he is prepared to announce to them their honour and their duty. "Thou shalt bear a son and he shall begin to deliver Israel." The messenger has had his preparation of thought, inquiry deep, devout, and pondering, ere he became fit to announce the word of God. No seer serves the age to which he is sent with that which costs him nothing, and here as elsewhere the law of all ministry to God and man must apply to the preparation and work of the revealer.

The personality of the messenger was carefully concealed. "A man of God whose countenance was like that of an angel of God very terrible"—so runs the pathetic, suggestive description; but the hour was too intense for mere curiosity. The honest mind does not ask the name and social standing of a messenger but only—Does he speak God's truth? Does he open life? There are few perhaps, to-day, who are simple and intelligent enough for this; few, therefore, to whom divine messages come. It is the credentials we are anxious about, and the prophet waits unheard while people are demanding his family and tribe, his college and reputation. Are these satisfactory? Then they will listen. But let no prophet come to them unnamed. Yet of all importance to us as to Manoah and his wife are the message, the revelation, the announcement of privilege and duty. Where that divine order is disclosed which lies too deep for our own discovery, but once revealed stirs and kindles our nature, the prophet needs no certification.

The child that was to be born, a gift of God, a divine charge, was promised to these parents. And in the case of every child born into the world there is a divine predestination, which whether it has been recognised by the parents or not gives dignity to his existence from the first. There are natural laws and spiritual laws, the gathering together of energies and needs and duties which make the life unique, the care of it sacred. It is a new force in the world—a new vessel, frail as yet, launched on the sea of time. In it some stories of the divine goodness, some treasures of heavenly force are embarked. As it holds its way across the ocean in sunshine or shadow, this life will be watched by the divine eye, breathed gently upon by the summer airs or buffeted by the storms of God. Does heaven mind the children? "In heaven their angels do always behold the face of My Father."

In the marvellous ordering of divine providence nothing is more calculated than fatherhood and motherhood to lift human life into the high ranges of experience and feeling. Apart from any special message or revelation, assuming only an ordinary measure of thoughtfulness and interest in the unfolding of life, there is here a new dignity the sense of which connects the task of those who have it with the creative energy of God. Everywhere throughout the world we can trace a more or less clear understanding of this. The tide of life is felt to rise as the new office, the new responsibility are grasped. The mother is become—

"A link among the days to knit
The generations each to each."

The father has a sacred trust, a new and nobler duty to which his manhood is entirely pledged in the sight of that great God who is the Father of all spirits, doubly and trebly pledged to truth and purity and courage. It is the coronation of life; and the child, drawing father and mother to itself, is rightly the object of keenest interest and most assiduous care.

The interest lies greatly in this, that to the father and mother first, then to the world, there may be untold possibilities of good in the existence which has begun. Apart from any prophecy like that given regarding Samson we have truly what may be called a special promise from God in the dawning energy of every child-life. By the cradle surely, if anywhere, hope sacred and heavenly may be indulged. With what earnest glances will the young eyes look by-and-by from face to face. With what new and keen love will the child-heart beat. Enlarging its grasp from year to year, the mind will lay hold on duty and the will address itself to the tasks of existence. This child will be a heroine of home, a helper of society, a soldier of the truth, a servant of God. Does the mother dream long dreams as she bends over the cradle? Does the father, one indeed amongst millions, yet with his special distinction and calling, imagine for the child a future better than his own? It is well. By the highest laws and instincts of our humanity it is right and good. Here men and women, the rudest and least taught, live in the immaterial world of love, faith, duty.

We observe the anxiety of Manoah and his wife to learn the special method of training which should fit their child for his task. The father's prayer so soon as he heard of the divine annunciation was, "O Lord, let the man of God whom Thou didst send come again unto us and teach us what we shall do unto the child that shall be born." Conscious of ignorance and inexperience, feeling the weight of responsibility, the parents desired to have authoritative direction in their duty, and their anxiety was the deeper because their child was to be a deliverer in Israel. In their home on the hillside, where the cottages of Zorah clustered overlooking the Philistine plain, they were frequently disturbed by the raiders who swept up the valley of Sorek from Ashdod and Ekron. They had often wondered when God would raise up a deliverer as of old, some Deborah or Gideon to end the galling oppression. Now the answer to many a prayer and hope was coming, and in their own home the hero was to be cradled. We cannot doubt that this made them feel the pressure of duty and the need of wisdom. Yet the prayer of Manoah was one which every father has need to present, though the circumstances of a child's birth have nothing out of the most ordinary course.

To each human mind are given powers which require special fostering, peculiarities of temperament and feeling which ought to be specially considered. One way will not serve in the upbringing of two children. Even the most approved method of the time, whether that of private tutelage or public instruction, may thwart individuality; and if the way be ignorant and rough the original faculty will at its very springing be distorted. It is but the barest commonplace, yet with what frequency it needs to be urged, that of all tasks in the world that of the guide and instructor of youth is hardest to do well, best worth doing, therefore most difficult. There is no need to deny that for the earliest years of a child's life the instincts of a loving faithful mother may be trusted to guide her efforts. Yet even in those first years tendencies declare themselves that require to be wisely checked or on the other hand wisely encouraged; and the wisdom does not come by instinct. A spiritual view of life, its limitations and possibilities, its high calling and heavenly destiny is absolutely necessary—that vision of the highest things which religion alone can give. The prophet comes and directs; yet the parents must be prophets too. "The child is not to be educated for the present—for this is done without our aid unceasingly and powerfully—but for the remote future and often in opposition to the immediate future. . . . The child must be armed against the close-pressing present with a counter-balancing weight of three powers against the three weaknesses of the will, of love and of religion. . . . The girl and the boy must learn that there is something in the ocean higher than its waves— namely, a Christ who calls upon them."[*] On the religious teaching especially which is given to children much depends, and those who guide them should often begin by searching and reconsidering their own beliefs. Many a promising life is marred because youth in its wonder and sincerity was taught no living faith in God, or was thrust into the mould of some narrow creed which had more in it of human bigotry than of divine reason and love.

"What shall be the ordering of the child?" is Manoah's prayer, and it is well if simply expressed. The child's way needs ordering. Circumstances must be understood that discipline may fit the young life for its part. In our own time this represents a serious difficulty. What to do with children, how to order their lives is the pressing question in thousands of homes. The scheme of education in favour shows little insight, little esteem for the individuality of children, which is of as much value in the case of the backward as of those who are lured and goaded into distinction. To broaden life, to give it many points of interest is well. Yet on the other hand how much depends on discipline, on limitation and concentration, the need of which we are apt to forget. Narrow and limited was the life of Israel when Samson was born into it. The boy had to be what the nation was, what Zorah was, what Manoah and his wife were. The limitations of the time held him and the secluded life of Dan knowing but one article of patriotic faith, hatred of the Philistines. Was there so much of restriction here as to make greatness impossible? Not so. To be an Israelite was to have a certain moral advantage and superiority. It was not a barren solidarity, a dry ground in which this new life was planted; the sprout grew out of a living tree; traditions, laws full of spiritual power made an environment for the Hebrew child. Through the limitations, fenced and guided by them, a soul might break forth to the upper air. It was not the narrowness of Israel nor of his own home and upbringing but the license of Philistia that weakened the strong arm and darkened the eager soul of the young Danite. Are we now to be afraid of limitations, bent on giving to youth multiform experience and the freest possible access to the world? Do we dream that strength will come as the stream of life is allowed to wander over a whole valley, turning hither and thither in a shallow and shifty bed? The natural parallel here will instruct us, for it is an image of the spiritual fact. Strength, not breadth, is the mark at which education should be directed. The intellectually and morally strong will find culture waiting them at every turn of the way and will know how to select, what to appropriate. In truth there must be first the moral power gained by concentration, otherwise all culture—art, science, literature, travel—proves but a Barmecide feast at which the soul starves.

The special method of training for the child Samson is described in the words, "He shall be a Nazirite unto God." The mother was to drink no strong drink nor eat any unclean thing. Her son was to be trained in the same rigid abstinence; and always the sense of obligation to Jehovah was to accompany the austerity. The hair, neither cut nor shaven but allowed to grow in natural luxuriance, was to be the sign of the separated life. For the hero that was to be,

[*] Richter, "Levana."

this ascetic purity, this sacrament of unshorn hair were the only things prescribed. Perhaps there was in the command a reference to the godless life of the Israelites, a protest against their self-indulgence and half-heathen freedom. One in the tribe of Dan would be clear of the sins of drunkenness and gluttony at least, and so far ready for spiritual work.

Now it is notable enough to find thus early in history the example of a rule which even yet is not half understood to be the best as well as the safest for the guidance of appetite and the development of bodily strength. The absurdities commonly accepted by mothers and by those who only desire some cover for the indulgence of taste are here set aside. A hero is to be born, one who in physical vigour will distinguish himself above all, the Hercules of sacred history. His mother rigidly abstains, and he in his turn is to abstain from strong drink. The plainest dieting is to serve both her and him—the kind of food and drink on which Daniel and his companions throve in the Chaldean palace. Surely the lesson is plain. Those who desire to excel in feats of strength speak of their training. It embraces a vow like the Nazarites', wanting indeed the sacred purpose and therefore of no use in the development of character. But let a covenant be made with God, let simple food and drink be used under a sense of obligation to Him to keep the mind clear and the body clean, and soon with appetites better disciplined we should have a better and stronger race.

It is not of course to be supposed that there was nothing out of the common in Samson's bodily vigour. Restraint of unhealthy and injurious appetite was not the only cause to which his strength was due. Yet as the accompaniment of his giant energy the vow has great significance. And to young men who incline to glory in their strength, and all who care to be fit for the tasks of life, the significance will be clear. As for the rest whose appetites master them, who must have this and that because they crave it, their weakness places them low as men, nowhere as examples and guides. One would as soon take the type of manly vigour from a paralytic as from one whose will is in subjection to the cravings of the flesh.

It soon becomes clear in the course of the history that while some forms of evil were fenced off by Nazaritism others as perilous were not. The main part of the devotion lay in abstinence, and that is not spiritual life. Here is one who from his birth set apart to God is trained in manly control of his appetites. The locks that wave in wild luxuriance about his neck are the sign of robust physical vigour as well as of consecration. But, strangely, his spiritual education is not cared for as we might expect. He is disciplined and yet undisciplined. He fears the Lord and yet fears Him not. He is an Israelite but not a true Israelite. Jehovah is to him a God who gives strength and courage and blessing in return for a certain measure of obedience. As the Holy God, the true God, the God of purity, Samson knows Him not, does not worship Him. Within a certain limited range he hears a divine voice saying, "Thou shalt not," and there he obeys. But beyond is a great region in which he reckons himself free. And what is the result? He is strong, brave, sunny in temper as his name implies. But a helper of society, a servant of divine religion, a man in the highest sense, one of God's free men Samson does not become.

So is it always. One kind of exercise, discipline, obedience, virtue will not suffice. We need to be temperate and also pure, we need to keep from self-indulgence but also from niggardliness if we are to be men. We have to think of the discipline of mind and soul as well as soundness of body. He is only half a man, however free from glaring faults and vices, who has not learned the unselfishness, the love, the ardour in holy and generous tasks which Christ imparts. To abstain is a negative thing; the positive should command us—the highest manhood, holy, aspiring, patient, divine.

CHAPTER XX.

SAMSON PLUNGING INTO LIFE.

JUDGES xiii. 24-xiv. 20.

OF all who move before us in the Book of Judges Samson is pre-eminently the popular hero. In rude giant strength and wild daring he stands alone against the enemies of Israel, contemptuous of their power and their plots. It is just such a man who catches the public eye and lives in the traditions of a country. Most Hebrews of the time minded piety and culture as little as did the Norsemen when they first professed Christianity. Both races liked manliness and feats of daring and could pardon much to one who flung his enemies and theirs to the ground with god-like strength of arm, and in the narrative of Samson's exploits we trace this note of popular estimation. He is a singular hero of faith, quite akin to those half-converted half-savage chiefs of the north who thought the best they could do for God was to kill His enemies and bound themselves by fierce oaths in the name of Christ to hack and slaughter. For the separateness from others, the isolation which marked Samson's whole career the reasons are evident. His vow of Nazaritism, for one thing, kept him apart. Others were their own men, he was Jehovah's. His radiant health and uncommon physical energy even in boyhood were to himself and others the sign of a divine blessing which maintained his sense of consecration. While he looked on at the riot and drunkenness of the feasts of his people he felt a growing revulsion, nor was he pleased with other indications of their temper. The frequent raids of Philistines from their walled cities by the coast struck terror far and wide—up the valleys of Dan into the heart of Judah and Ephraim. Samson as he grew up marked the supineness of his people with wonder and disgust. If he did anything for them it was not because he honoured them but in fulfilment of his destiny. At the same time we must note that the hero, though a man of wit, was not wise. He did the most injudicious things. He had nothing in him of the diplomatist, not much of the leader of men. It was only now and again when the mood took him that he cared to exert himself. So he went his own way an admired hero, a lonely giant among smaller beings. Worst of all he was an easy prey to some kinds of temptation. Restrained on one side, he gave himself license on others; his strength was always undisciplined, and early in his career we can almost predict how it will end. He ventures into one snare after another. The time is sure to come when he will fall into a pit out of which there is no way of escape.

Of the early life of the great Danite judge there is no record save that he grew and the Lord blessed him. The parents whose home on the hill-side he filled with boisterous glee must have looked on the lad with something like awe —so different was he from others, so great were the hopes based on his future. Doubtless they did their best for him. The consecration of his life to God they deeply impressed on his mind and taught him as well as they could the worship of the Unseen Jehovah in the sacrifice of lamb or kid at the altar, in prayers for protection and prosperity. But nothing is said of instruction in the righteousness, the purity, the mercifulness which the law of God required. Manoah and his wife seem to have made the mistake of thinking that outside the vow moral education and discipline would come naturally, so far as they were needed. There was great strictness on certain points and elsewhere such laxity that he must have soon become wilful and headstrong and somewhat of a terror to the father and mother. Lads of his own age would of course adore him; as their leader in every bold pastime he would command their deference and loyalty, and many a wild thing was done, we can fancy, at which the people of the valley laughed uneasily or shook their heads in dismay. He who afterwards tied the jackals' tails together and set fire-brands between each pair to burn the Philistines' corn must have served an apprenticeship to that kind of savage sport. Hebrew or alien for miles round who roused the anger of Samson would soon learn how dangerous it was to provoke him. Yet a dash of generosity always took the edge from fiery temper and rash revenge, and the people of Dan, for their part, would allow much to one who was expected to bring deliverance to Israel. The wild and dangerous youth was the only champion they could see.

But even before manhood Samson had times of deeper feeling than people in general would have looked for. Boisterous, hot-blooded, impetuous natures grievously wanting in decorum and sagacity are not always superficial; and there were occasions when the Spirit of the Lord began to move Samson. He felt the purpose of his vow, saw the serious work to which his destiny was urging him, looked down on the plain of the Philistines with a kindling eye, spoke in strains that even rose to prophetic intensity. At Mahaneh-Dan, the camp of Dan, where the more resolute spirits of the tribe came together for military exercise or to repel some raid of the enemy, Samson began to speak of his purpose and to make schemes for Israel's liberation. Into these the fiery vehemence of the young man flowed, and the enthusiasm of his nature bore others along. Can we be wrong in supposing that in various ways, by plans often ill-considered, he sought to harass the Philistines, and that failure as a leader in these left him somewhat discredited? Samson was just of that sanguine venturesome disposition which makes light of difficulties and is always courting defeat. It was easy for him with his immense bodily strength to break through where other men were entrapped. A frequent result of the frays into which he hurried must have been, we imagine, to make his own friends doubt him rather than to injure the enemy. At all events he became no commander like Gideon or Jephthah, and the men of Judah, if not of Dan, while they acknowledged his calling and his power, began to think of him as a dangerous champion.

So far we have the merest hints by which to go, but the narrative becomes more detailed when it approaches the time of Samson's marriage. A strange union it is for a hero of Israel. What made him think of going down among the Philistines for a wife? How can the sacred writer say that the thing was of the Lord? Let us try to understand the circumstances. Between the people of Zorah and the villagers of Timnah a few miles down the valley on the other side who, though Philistines, were presumably not of the fighting sort, there was a kind of enforced neighbourliness. They could not have lived at all unless they had been content, Philistines for their part, Hebrews for theirs, to let the general enmity sleep. Samson by observing certain precautions and keeping his Hebrew tongue quiet was safe enough in Timnah, an object of fear rather than himself in danger. At the same time there may have been a touch of bravado in his rambles to the Philistine settlement, and the young woman of whom he caught a passing glance, perhaps at the spring, had very likely all the more charm for him that she was of the strong hostile race. History as well as fiction supplies instances in which this fascination does its work, family feuds, oppositions of caste and religion directing the eye and the fancy instead of repelling. In his sudden wilful way Samson resolved, and his mind once made up no one in Zorah could induce him to alter it. "The thing was of the Lord; for he sought an occasion against the Philistines." Perhaps Samson thought the woman would be denied to him, a straight way to a quarrel. But more probably it is the outcome of the whole pitiful business that is in the mind of the historian. After the event he traces the hand of Providence.

As we pass with Samson and his parents down to Timnah we cannot but agree with Manoah in his objection, "Is there never a woman among the daughters of thy brethren or among all my people that thou goest to take a wife of the uncircumcised Philistines?" It was emphatically one of those cases in which liking should not have led. An impetuous man is not to be excused; much less those who claim to be exceedingly rational and yet go against reason because of what they call love—or, worse, apart from love. General rules are with difficulty laid down in matters of this sort, and to deny the right of love would be the worst error of all. So far as our popular writers are concerned, we must allow that they wonderfully balance the claims of "arrangement" and honest affection, declaring strongly for the latter. But yet such a difference as between faith and idolatry, between piety and godlessness, is a barrier that only the blindest folly can overleap when marriage is in view. Daughters of the Philistines may be "most divinely fair," most graceful and plausible; men who worship Moloch or Mammon, or nothing but themselves, may have most persuasive tongues and a large share of this world's goods. But to mate with these, whatever liking there may be, is an experiment too rash for venturing. In Christian society now, is there not much need to repeat old warnings and revive a sense of peril that seems to have decayed? The conscience of piously bred young people was alive once to the danger and sin of the unequal yoke. In the rush for position and means marriage is being made by both sexes, even in most religious circles, an instrument and opportunity of earthly ambition, and it must be said that foolish romance is less to be feared than this carefulness in which conscience and heart alike submit to the imperious cravings of sheer worldliness. Novels have much to answer for; yet they can make one claim—they have done something for simple humanity. We want more than nature, however. Christian teaching must be heard and the Christian conscience must be re-kindled. The hope of the world waits on that devout simplicity of life which exalts spiritual aims and spiritual comradeship and by its beauty shames all meaner choice. In marriage not only should heart go out to heart, but mind to mind and soul to soul; and the spirit of one who knows Christ can never unite with a self-worshipper or a servant of Mammon.

Returning to Samson's case, he would possibly have said that he wished an adventurous marriage, that to wed a Danite woman would have in it too little risk, would be too dull, too commonplace a business for him, that he wanted a plunge into new waters. It is in this way, one must believe, many decide the great affair. So far from thinking they put thought away; a liking seizes them and in they leap. Yet in the best considered marriage that can be made is there not quite enough of adventure for any sane man or woman? Always there remain points of character unknown, unsuspected, possibilities of sickness, trouble, privation that fill the future with uncertainty, so far as human vision goes. It is, in truth, a serious undertaking for men and women, and to be entered upon only with the distinct assurance that divine providence clears the way and invites our advance. Yet again we are not to be suspicious of each other, probing every trait and habit to the quick. Marriage is the great example and expression of the trust which it is the glory of men and women to exercise and to deserve, the great symbol on earth of the confidences and unions of immortality. Matter of deep thankfulness it is that so many who begin the married life and end it on a low level, having scarcely a glimpse of the ideal, though they fail of much do not fail of all, but in some patience, some courage and fidelity show that God has not left them to nature and to earth. And happy are they who adventure together on no way of worldly policy or desire but in the pure love and heavenly faith which link their lives for ever in binding them to God.

Samson, reasoned with by his parents, waved their objection royally aside and ordered them to aid his design. It was necessary, according to the custom of the country, that they should conduct the negotiations for the marriage, and his wilfulness imposed on them a task that went against their consciences. So they found themselves with the common reward of worshipping parents. They had toiled for him, made much of him, boasted about him no doubt; and now their boy-god turns round and commands them in a thing they cannot believe to be right. They must choose between Jehovah and Samson and they have to give up Jehovah and serve their own lad. So David's pride in Absalom ended with the rebellion that drove the aged father from Jerusalem and exposed him to the contempt of Israel. It is good for a man to bear the yoke in his youth, the yoke even of parents who are not so wise as they might be and do not command much reverence. The order of family life among us, involving no absolute bondage, is recognised as a wholesome discipline by all who attain to any understanding of life. In Israel, as we know, filial respect and obedience were virtues sacredly commended, and it is one mark of Samson's ill-regulated self-esteeming disposition that he neglected the obvious duty of deference to the judgment of his parents.

On the way to Timnah the young man had an adventure which was to play an important part in his life. Turning aside out of the road he found himself suddenly confronted by a lion which, doubtless as much surprised as he was by the encounter, roared against him. The moment was not without its peril; but Samson was equal to the emergency and springing on the beast "rent it as he would have rent a kid."

The affair however did not seem worth referring to when he joined his parents, and they went on their way. It was as when a man of strong moral principle and force meets a temptation dangerous to the weak, to him an enemy easily overcome. His vigorous truth or honour or chastity makes short work of it. He lays hold of it and in a moment it is torn in pieces. The great talk made about temptations, the ready excuses many find for themselves when they yield, are signs of a feebleness of will which in other ranges of life the same persons would be ashamed to own. It is to be feared that we often encourage moral weakness and unfaithfulness to duty by exaggerating the force of evil influences. Why should it be reckoned a feat to be honest, to be generous, to swear to one's own hurt? Under the dispensation of the Spirit of God, with Christ as our guide and stay, every one of us should act boldly in the encounter with the lions of temptation. Tenderness to the weak is a Christian duty, but there is danger that young and old alike, hearing much of the seductions of sin, little of the ready help of the Almighty, submit easily where they should conquer and reckon on divine forbearance when they ought to expect reproach and contempt. Our generation needs to hear the words of St. Paul: "There hath no temptation taken you but such as man can bear: but God is faithful Who will not suffer you to be tempted above that ye are able." Is there a tremendous pressure constantly urging us towards that which is evil? In our large cities especially is the power of iniquity almost despotic? True enough. Yet men and women should be braced and strengthened by insistence on the other side. In Christian lands at least it is unquestionable that for every enticement to evil there is a stronger allurement to good, that against every argument for immorality ten are set more potent in behalf of virtue, that where sin abounds grace does much more abound. Young persons are indeed tempted; but nothing will be gained by speaking to them or about them as if they were children incapable of decision, of whom it can only be expected that they will fail. By the Spirit of God, indeed, all moral victories are gained; the natural virtue of the best is uncertain and cannot be trusted in the trying hour, and he only who has a full inward life and earnest Christian purpose is ready for the test. But the Spirit of God is given. His sustaining, purifying, strengthening power is with us. We do not breathe deep, and then we complain that our hearts cease to beat with holy courage and resolve.

At Timnah, where life was perhaps freer than in a Hebrew town, Samson appears to have seen the woman who had caught his fancy; and he now found her, Philistine as she was, quite to his mind. It must have been by a low standard he judged, and many possible topics of conversation must have been carefully avoided. Under the circumstances, indeed, the difficulty of understanding each other's language may have been their safety. Certainly one who professed to be a fearer of God, a patriotic Israelite, had to shut his eyes to many facts or thrust them from sight when he determined to wed this daughter of the enemy. But when we choose we can do much in the way of keeping things out of view which we do not wish to see. Persons who are at daggers drawn on fifty points show the greatest possible affability when it is their interest to be at one. Love gets over difficulties and so does policy. Occasions are found when the anxiously orthodox can join in some comfortable compact with the agnostic, and the vehement statechurchman with the avowed secularist and revolutionary. And it seems to be only when two are nearly of the same creed, with just some hairsbreadth of divergence on a few articles of belief, that the obstacles to happy union are apt to become insurmountable. Then every word is watched, each tone noted with suspicion. It is not between Hebrew and Philistine but between Ephraim and Judah that alliances are difficult to form. We hope for the time when the long and bitter disputes of Christendom shall be overcome by love of truth and God. Yet first there must be an end to the strange reconcilings and unions which like Samson's marriage often confuse and obstruct the way of Christian people.

There is an interval of some months after the marriage has been arranged and the bridegroom is on his way once more down the valley to Timnah. As he passes the scene of his encounter with the lion he turns aside to see the carcase and finds that bees have made it their home. Vultures and ants have first found it and devoured the flesh, then the sun has thoroughly dried the skin and in the hollow of the ribs the bees have settled. At considerable risk Samson possesses himself of some of the combs and goes on eating the honey, giving a portion also to his father and mother. It is again a type, and this time of the sweetness to be found in the recollection of virtuous energy and overcoming. Not that we are to be always dwelling on our faithfulness even for the purpose of thanking God Who gave us moral strength. But when circumstances recall a trial and victory it is surely matter of proper joy to remember that here we were strong enough to be true, and there to be honest and pure when the odds seemed to be against us. The memories of a good man or good woman are sweeter than the honeycomb, though tempered often by sorrow over the human instruments of evil who had to be struggled with and thrust aside in the sharp conflict with sin and wrong. Very few in youth or middle-life seem to think of this joy, which makes beautiful many a worn and aged face on earth and will not be the least element in the felicity of heaven. Too often we bear burdens because we must; we are dragged through trial and distress to comparative quiet; we do not comprehend what is at stake, what we may do and gain, what we are kept from losing; and so the look across our past has none of the glow of triumph, little of the joy of harvest. For man's blessedness is not to be separated from personal striving. In fidelity he must sow that he may reap in strength, in courage that he may reap in gladness. He is made not for mere success, not for mere safety, but for overcoming.

We are not finished with the lion; he next appears covertly, in a riddle. Samson has shown himself a strong man; now we hear him speak and he proves a wit. It is the wedding festival, and thirty young men have been gathered—to honour the bridegroom, shall we say?—or to watch him? Perhaps from the first there has been suspicion in the Philistine mind, and it seems necessary to have as many as thirty to one in order to overawe Samson. In the course of the feast there might be quarrels, and without a strong guard on the Hebrew youth Timnah might be in danger. As the days went by the company fell to proposing riddles and Samson, probably annoyed by the Philistines who watched every movement, gave them his, on terms quite fair, yet leaving more than a loophole for discontent and strife. In the conditions we see the man perfectly self-reliant, full of easy superiority, courting danger and defying envy. The thirty may win—if they can. In that case he knows how he will pay the forfeit. "Put forth thy riddle," they said, "that we may hear it;" and the strong mellow Hebrew voice chanted the puzzling verse:

"Out of the eater came forth meat;
Out of the strong came forth sweetness."

Now in itself this is simply a curiosity of old-world table talk. It is preserved here mainly because of its bearing on following events; and certainly the statement which has been made that it contained a gospel for the Philistines is one we cannot endorse. Yet like many witty sayings the riddle has a range of meaning far wider than Samson intended. Adverse influences conquered, temptation mastered, difficulties overcome, the struggle of faithfulness will supply us not only with happy recollections but also with arguments against infidelity, with questions that confound the unbeliever. One who can glory in tribulations that have brought experience and hope, in bonds and imprisonments that have issued in a keener sense of liberty, who having nothing yet possesses all things—such a man questioning the denier of divine providence cannot be answered. Invigoration has come out of that which threatened life and joy out of that which made for sorrow. The man who is in covenant with God is helped by nature; its forces serve him; he is fed with honey from the rock and with the finest of the wheat. When out of the mire of trouble and the deep waters of despondency he comes forth braver, more hopeful, strongly confident in the love of God, sure of the eternal foundation of life, what can be said in denial of the power that has filled him with strength and peace? Here is an argument that can be used by every Christian, and ought to be in every Christian's hand. Out of his personal experience each should be able to state problems and put inquiries unanswerable by unbelief. For unless there is a living God Whose favour is life, Whose fellowship inspires and ennobles the soul, the strength which has come through weakness, the hope that sprang up in the depth of sorrow cannot be accounted for. There are natural sequences in which no mystery lies. When one who has been defamed and injured turns on his enemy and pursues him in revenge, when one who has been defeated sinks back in languor and waits in pitiful inaction for death, these are results easily traced to their cause. But the man of faith bears witness to sequences of a different kind. His fellows have persecuted him, and he cares for them still. Death has bereaved him, and he can smile in its face. Afflictions have been multiplied and he glories in them. The darkness has fallen and he rejoices more than in the noontide of prosperity. Out of the eater has come forth meat, out of the strong has come forth sweetness. "Except a corn of wheat fall into the ground and die, it abideth alone; but if it die, it bringeth forth much fruit." The paradox of the life of Christ thus stated by Himself is the supreme instance of that demonstration of divine power which the history of every Christian should clearly and constantly support.

CHAPTER XXI.

DAUNTLESS IN BATTLE, IGNORANTLY BRAVE.

JUDGES xv.

GIVEN a man of strong passions and uninstructed conscience, wild courage and giant energy, with the sense of a mission which he has to accomplish against his country's enemies, so that he reckons himself justified in doing them injury or killing them in the name of God, and you have no complete hero, but a real and interesting man. Such a character, however, does not command our admiration. The enthusiasm we feel in tracing the career of Deborah or Gideon fails us in reviewing these stories of revenge in which the Hebrew champion appears as cruel and reckless as an uncircumcised Philistine. When we see Samson leaving the feast by which his marriage has been celebrated and marching down to Ashkelon where in cold blood he puts thirty men to death for the sake of their clothing, when we see a country-side ablaze with the standing corn which he has kindled, we are as indignant with him as with the Philistines when they burn his wife and her father with fire. Nor can we find anything like excuse for Samson on the ground of zeal in the service of pure religion. Had he been a fanatical Hebrew mad against idolatry, his conduct might find some apology; but no such clue offers. The Danite is moved chiefly by selfish and vain passions, and his sense of official duty is all too weak and vague. We see little patriotism and not a trace of religious fervour. He is serving a great purpose with some sincerity, but not wisely, not generously nor greatly. Samson is a creature of impulse working out his life in blind almost animal fashion, perceiving the next thing that is to be done not in the light of religion or duty, but of opportunity and revenge. The first of his acts against the Philistines was no promising start in a heroic career, and almost at every point in the story of his life there is something that takes away our respect and sympathy. But the life is full of moral suggestion and warning. He is a real and striking example of the wild Berserker type.

1. For one thing this stands out as a clear principle that a man has his life to live, his work to do, alone if others will not help, imperfectly if not in the best fashion, half-wrongly if the right cannot be clearly seen. This world is not for sleep, is not for inaction and sloth. "Whatsoever thy hand finds to do, do it with thy might." A thousand men in Dan, ten thousand in Judah did nothing that became men, sat at home while their grapes and olives grew, abjectly sowed and reaped their fields in dread of the Philistines, making no attempt to free their country from the hated yoke. Samson, not knowing rightly how to act, did go to work and, at any rate, lived. Among the dull spiritless Israelites of the day, three thousand of whom actually came on one occasion to beseech him to give himself up and bound him with ropes that he might be safely passed over to the enemy, Samson with all his faults looks like a man. Those men of Dan and Judah would slay the Philistines if they dared. It is not because they are better than Samson that they do not go down to Ashkelon and kill. Their consciences do not keep them back; it is their cowardice. One who with some vision of a duty owing to his people goes forth and acts, contrasts well with these chicken-hearted thousands.

We are not at present stating the complete motive of human activity nor setting forth the ideal of life. To that we shall come afterwards. But before you can have ideal action you must have action. Before you can have life of a fine and noble type you must have life. Here is an absolute primal necessity; and it is the key to both evolutions, the natural and the spiritual. First the human creature must find its power and capability and must use these to some end, be it even a wrong end, rather than none; after this the ideal is caught and proper moral activity becomes possible. We need not look for the full corn in the ear till the seed has sprouted and grown and sent its roots well into the soil. With this light the roll of Hebrew fame is cleared and we can trace freely the growth of life. The heroes are not perfect; they have perhaps barely caught the light of the ideal; but they have strength to will and to do, they have faith that this power is a divine gift, and they having it are God's pioneers.

The need is that men should in the first instance live so that they may be faithful to their calling. Deborah looking round beheld her country under the sore oppression of Jabin, saw the need and answered to it. Others only vegetated; she rose up in human stature resolute to live. That also was what Gideon began to do when at the divine call he demolished the altar on the height of Ophrah; and Jephthah fought and endured by the same law. So soon as men begin to live there is hope of them.

Now the hindrances to life are these—first, slothfulness, the disposition to drift, to let things go; second, fear, the restriction imposed on effort of body or of mind by some opposing force ingloriously submitted to; third, ignoble dependence on others. The proper life of man is never reached by many because they are too indolent to win it. To forecast and devise, to try experiments, pushing out in this direction and that is too much for them. Some opportunity for doing more and better lies but a mile away or a few yards; they see but will not venture upon it. Their country is sinking under a despot or a weak and foolish government; they do nothing to avert ruin, things will last their time. Or again, their church is stirred with throbs of a new duty, a new and keen anxiety; but they refuse to feel any thrill, or feeling it a moment they repress the disturbing influence. They will not be troubled with moral and spiritual questions, calls to action that make life severe, high, heroic. Often this is due to want of physical or mental vigour. Men and women are overborne by the labour required of them, the weary tale of bricks. Even from youth they have had burdens to bear so heavy that hope is never kindled. But there are many who have no such excuse. Let us alone, they say, we have no appetite for exertion, for strife, for the duties that set life in a fever. The old ways suit us, we will go on as our fathers have gone. The tide of opportunity ebbs away and are left stranded.

Next, and akin, there is fear, the mood of those who hear the calls of life but hear more clearly the threatenings of sense and time. Often it comes in the form of a dread of change, apprehension as regards the unknown seas on which effort or thought would launch forth. Let us be still, say the prudent; better to bear the ills we have than fly to others that we know not of. Are we ground down by the Philistines? Better suffer than be killed. Are our laws unjust and oppressive? Better rest content than risk revolution and the upturning of everything. Are we not altogether sure of the basis of our belief? Better leave it unexamined than begin with inquiries the end of which cannot be foreseen. Besides, they argue, God means us to be content. Our lot in the world however hard is of His giving; the faith we hold is of His bestowing. Shall we not provoke Him to anger if we move in revolution or in inquiry. Still it is life they lose. A man who does not think about the truths he rests on has an impotent mind. One who does not feel it laid on him to go forward, to be brave, to make the world better has an impotent soul. Life is a constant reaching after the unattained for ourselves and for the world.

And lastly there is ignoble dependence on others. So many will not exert themselves because they wait for some one to come and lift them up. They do not think, nor do they understand that instruction brought to them is not life. No doubt it is the plan of God to help the many by the instrumentality of the few, a whole nation or world by one. Again and again we have seen this illustrated in Hebrew history, and elsewhere the fact constantly meets us. There is one Luther for Europe, one Cromwell for England, one Knox for Scotland, one Paul for early Christianity. But at the same time it is because life is wanting, because men have the deadly habit of dependence that the hero must be brave for them and the reformer must break their bonds. The true law of life on all levels, from that of bodily effort upwards, is self-help; without it there is only an infancy of being. He who is in a pit must exert himself if he is to be delivered. He who is in spiritual darkness must come to the light if he is to be saved.

Now we see in Samson a man who in his degree lived. He had strength like the strength of ten; he had also the consecration of his vow and the sense of a divine constraint and mandate. These things urged him to life and made activity necessary to him. He might have reclined in careless ease like many around. But sloth did not hold him nor fear. He wanted no man's countenance nor help. He lived. His mere exertion of power was the sign of higher possibilities.

Live at all hazards, imperfectly if perfection is not attainable, half-wrongly if the right cannot be seen. Is this perilous advice? From one point of view it may seem very dangerous. For many are energetic in so imperfect a way, in so blundering and false a way that it might appear better for them to remain quiet, practically dead than degrade and darken the life of the race by their mistaken or immoral vehemence. You read of those traders among the islands of the Pacific who, afraid that their nefarious traffic should suffer if missionary work succeeded, urged the natives to kill the missionaries or drive them away, and when they had gained their end quickly appeared on the scene to exchange for the pillaged stores of the mission-house muskets and gunpowder and villainous strong drink. May it not be said that these traders were living out their lives as much as the devoted teachers who had risked everything for the sake of doing good? Napoleon I., when the scheme of the empire presented itself to him and all his energies were bent on climbing to the summit of affairs in France and in Europe—was not he living according to a conception of what was greatest and best? Would it not have been better if those traders and the ambitious Corsican alike had been content to vegetate—inert and harmless through their days? And there are multitudes of examples. The poet Byron for one —could the world not well spare even his finest verse to be rid of his unlawful energy in personal vice and in coarse profane word?

One has to confess the difficulty of the problem, the danger of praising mere vigour. Yet if there is risk on the one side the risk on the other is greater: and truth demands risk, defies peril. It is unquestionable that any family of men when it ceases to be enterprising and energetic is of no more use in the economy of things. Its land is a necropolis. The dead cannot praise God. The choice is between activity that takes many a wrong direction, hurrying men often towards perdition, yet at every point capable of redemption, and on the other hand inglorious death, that existence which has no prospect but to be swallowed up of the darkness. And while such is the common choice there is also this to be noted that inertness is not certainly purer than activity, though it may appear so merely by contrast. The active life compels us to judge of it; the other, a mere negation, calls for no judgment, yet is in itself a moral want, an evil and injury. Conscience being unexercised decay and death rule all.

Men cannot be saved by their own effort and vigour. Most true. But if they make no attempt to advance towards strength, dominion, and fulness of existence, they are the prey of force and evil. Nor will it suffice that they simply exert themselves to keep body and soul together. The life is more than meat. We must toil not only that we may continue to subsist, but for personal distinctness and freedom

Where there are strong men, resolute minds, earnestness of some kind, there is soil in which spiritual seed may strike root. The dead tree can produce neither leaf nor flower. In short, if there is to be a human race at all for the divine glory it can only be in the divine way, by the laws that govern existence of every degree.

2. We come, however, to the compensating principle of responsibility—the law of Duty which stands over energy in the range of our life. No man, no race is justified by force or as we sometimes say by doing. It is faith that saves. Samson has the rude material of life; but though his action were far purer and nobler it could not make him a spiritual man: his heart is not purged of sin nor set on God.

Granted that the time was rough, chaotic, cloudy, that the idea of injuring the Philistines in every possible way was imposed on the Danite by his nation's abject state, that he had to take what means lay in his power for accomplishing the end. But possessed of energy he was deficient in conscience, and so failed of noble life. This may be said for him that he did not turn against the men of Judah who came to bind him and give him up. Within a certain range he understood his responsibility. But surely a higher life than he lived, better plans than he followed were possible to one who could have learned the will of God at Shiloh, who was bound to God by a vow of purity and had that constant reminder of the Holy Lord of Israel. It is no uncommon thing for men to content themselves with one sacrament, one observance which is reckoned enough for salvation—honesty in business, abstinence from strong drink, attendance on church ordinances. This they do and keep the rest of existence for unrestrained self-pleasing, as though salvation lay in a restraint or a form. But whoever can think is bound to criticise life, to try his own life, to seek the way of salvation, and that means being true to the best he knows and can know; it means believing in the will of God. Something higher than his own impulse is to guide him. He is free, yet responsible. His activity, however great, has no real power, no vindication unless it falls in with the course of divine law and purpose. He lives by faith.

Generally there is one clear principle which, if a man held to it, would keep him right in the main. It may not be of a very high order, yet it will prepare the way for something better and meanwhile serve his need. And for Samson one simple law of duty was to keep clear of all private relations and entanglements with the Philistines. There was nothing to hinder him from seeing that to be safe and right as a rule of life. They were Israel's enemies and his own. He should have been free to act against them: and when he married a daughter of the race he forfeited as an honourable man the freedom he ought to have had as a son of Israel. Doubtless he did not understand fully the evil of idolatry nor the divine law that Hebrews were to keep themselves separate from the worshippers of false gods. Yet the instincts of the race to which he belonged, fidelity to his forefathers and compatriots made their claim upon him. There was a duty too which he owed to himself. As a brave strong man he was discredited by the line of action which he followed. His honour lay in being an open enemy to the Philistines, his dishonour in making underhand excuses for attacking them. It was base to seek occasion against them when he married the woman at Timnah, and from one act of baseness he went on to others because of that first error. And chiefly Samson failed in his fidelity to God. Scarcely ever was the name of Jehovah dragged through the mire as it was by him. The God of truth, the divine Guardian of faithfulness, the God who is light, in Whom is no darkness at all, was made by Samson's deeds to appear as the patron of murder and treachery. We can hardly allow that an Israelite was so ignorant of the ordinary laws of morality as to suppose that faith need not be kept with idolaters; there were traditions of his people which prevented such a notion. One who knew of Abraham's dealings with the Hittite Ephron and his rebuke in Egypt could not imagine that the Hebrew lay under no debt of human equity and honor to the Philistine. Are there men among ourselves who think no faithfulness is due by the civilised to the savage? Are there professed servants of Christ who dare to suggest that no faith need be kept with heretics? They reveal their own dishonour as men, their own falseness and meanness. The primal duty of intelligent and moral beings cannot be so dismissed. And even Samson should have been openly the Philistines' enemy or not at all. If they were cruel, rapacious, mean, he ought to have shown that Jehovah's servant was of a different stamp. We cannot believe morality to have been at so low an ebb among the Hebrews that the popular leader did not know better than he acted. He became a judge in Israel, and his judgeship would have been a pretence unless he had some of the justice, truth, and honour which God demanded of men. Beginning in a very mistaken way he must have risen to a higher conception of duty, otherwise his rule would have been a disaster to the tribes he governed.

Conscience has originated in fear and is to decay with ignorance, say some. Already that extraordinary piece of folly has been answered. Conscience is the correlative of power, the guide of energy. If the one decays, so must the other. Living strongly, energetically, making experiments, seeking liberty and dominion, pressing towards the higher, we are ever to acknowledge the responsibility which governs life. By what we know of the divine will we are to order every purpose and scheme and advance to further knowledge. There are victories we might win, there are methods by which we might harass those who do us wrong. One voice says, Snatch the victories, go down by night and injure the foe, insinuate what you cannot prove, while the sentinels sleep plunge your spear through the heart of a persecuting Saul. But another voice asks, Is this the way to assert moral life? Is this the line for a man to take? The true man swears to his own hurt, suffers and is strong, does in the face of day what he has it in him to do and, if he fails, dies a true man still. He is not responsible for obeying commands of which he is ignorant, nor for mistakes which he cannot avoid. One like Samson is clean-handed in what it would be unutterably base for us to do. But close beside every man are such guiding ideas as straightforwardness, sincerity, honesty. Each of us knows his duty so far and cannot deceive himself by supposing that God will excuse him in acting, even for what he counts a good end, as a cheat and a hypocrite. In politics the rule is as clear as in companionship, in war as in love.

It has not been asserted that Samson was without a sense of responsibility. He had it, and kept his vow. He had it, and fought against the Philistines. He did some brave things openly and like a man. He had a vision of Israel's need and God's will. Had this not been true he could have done no good; the whole strength of the hero would have been wasted. But he came short of effecting what he might have effected just because he was not wise and serious. His strokes missed their aim. In truth Samson never went earnestly about the task of delivering Israel. In his fulness of power he was always half in sport, making random shots, indulging his own humour. And we may find in his career no inapt illustration of the careless way in which the conflict with the evils of our time is carried on. With all the rage for societies and organisations there is much haphazard activity, and the fanatic for rule has his contrast in the free-lance who hates the thought of responsibility. A curious charitableness too confuses the air. There are men who are full of ardour to-day and strike in with some hot scheme against social wrongs, and the next day are to be seen sitting at a feast with the very persons most to blame, under some pretext of finding occasion against them or showing that there is "nothing personal." This perplexes the whole campaign. It is usually mere bravado rather than charity, a mischief, not a virtue.

Israel must be firm and coherent if it is to win liberty from the Philistines. Christians must stand by each other steadily if they are to overcome infidelity and rescue the slaves of sin. The feats of a man who holds aloof from the church because he is not willing to be bound by its rules count for little in the great warfare of the age. Many there are among our literary men, politicians, and even philanthropists who strike in now and again in a Christian way and with unquestionably Christian purpose against the bad institutions and social evils of our time, but have no proper basis or aim of action and maintain towards Christian organisations and churches a constant attitude of criticism. Samson-like they make showy random attacks on "bigotry," "inconsistency" and the like. It is not they who will deliver man from hardness and worldliness of soul; not they who will bring in the reign of love and truth.

3. Looking at Samson's efforts during the first part of his career and observing the want of seriousness and wisdom that marred them, we may say that all he did was to make clear and deep the cleft between Philistines and Hebrews. When he appears on the scene there are signs of a dangerous intermixture of the two races, and his own marriage is one. The Hebrews were apparently inclined to settle down in partial subjection to the Philistines and make the best they could of the situation, hoping perhaps that by-and-by they might reach a state of comfortable alliance and equality. Samson may have intended to end that movement or he may not. But he certainly did much to end it. After the first series of his exploits, crowned by the slaughter at Lehi, there was an open rupture with the Philistines which had the best effect on Hebrew morals and religion. It was clear that one Israelite had to be reckoned with whose strong arm dealt deadly blows. The Philistines drew away in defeat. The Hebrews learned that they needed not to remain in any respect dependent or afraid. This kind of division grows into hatred; but, as things were, dislike was Israel's safety. The Philistines did harm as masters; as friends they would have done even more. Enmity meant revulsion from Dagon-worship and all the social customs of the opposed race. For this the Hebrews were indebted to Samson; and although he was not himself true all along to the principle of separation, yet in his final act he emphasised it so by destroying the temple of Gaza that the lesson was driven home beyond the possibility of being forgotten.

It is no slight service those do who as critics of parties and churches show them clearly where they stand, who are to be reckoned as enemies, what alliances are perilous. There are many who are exceedingly easy in their beliefs, too ready to yield to the *Zeit Geist* that would obliterate definite belief and with it the vigour and hope of mankind. Alliance with Philistines is thought of as a good, not a risk, and the whole of a party or church may be so comfortably settling in the new breadth and freedom of this association that the certain end of it is not seen. Then is the time for the resolute stroke that divides party from party, creed from creed. A reconciler is the best helper of religion at one juncture; at another it is the Samson who standing alone perhaps, frowned on equally by the leaders and the multitude, makes occasion to kindle controversy and set sharp variance between this side and that. Luther struck in so. His great act was one that "rent Christendom in twain." Upon the Israel which looked on afraid or suspicious he forced the division which had been for centuries latent. Does not our age need a new divider? You set forth to testify against Philistines and soon find that half your acquaintances are on terms of the most cordial friendship with them, and that attacks upon them which have any point are reckoned too hot and eager to be tolerated in society. To the few who are resolute duty is made difficult and protest painful: the reformer has to bear the sins and even the scorn of many who should appear with him.

CHAPTER XXII.

PLEASURE AND PERIL IN GAZA.

JUDGES xvi. 1-3.

By courage and energy Samson so distinguished himself in his own tribe and on the Philistine border that he was recognised as judge. Government of any kind was a boon, and he kept rude order, as much perhaps by overawing the restless enemy as by administering justice in Israel. Whether the period of twenty years assigned to Samson's judgeship intervened between the fight at Lehi and the visit to Gaza we cannot tell. The chronology is vague, as might be expected in a narrative based on popular tradition. Most likely the twenty years cover the whole time during which Samson was before the public as hero and acknowledged chief.

Samson went down to Gaza, which was the principal Philistine city situated near the Mediterranean coast some forty miles from Zorah.

For what reason did he venture into that hostile place? It may, of course, have been that he desired to learn by personal inspection what was its strength, to consider whether it might be attacked with any hope of success; and if that was so we would be disposed to justify him. As the champion and judge of Israel he could not but feel the danger to which his people were constantly exposed from the Philistine power so near to them and in those days always becoming more formidable. He had to a certain extent secured deliverance for his country as he was expected to do; but deliverance was far from complete, could not be complete till the strength of the enemy was broken. At great risk to himself he may have gone to play the spy and devise, if possible, some plan of attack. In this case he would be an example of those who with the best and purest motives, seeking to carry the war of truth and purity into the enemy's country, go down into the haunts of vice to see what men do and how best the evils that injure society may be overcome. There is risk in such adventure; but it is nobly undertaken, and even if we do not feel disposed to imitate we must admire. Bold servants of Christ may feel constrained to visit Gaza and learn for themselves what is done there. Beyond this too is a kind of adventure which the whole church justifies in proportion to its own faith and zeal. We see St. Paul and his companions in Ephesus, in Philippi, in Athens and other heathen towns, braving the perils which threaten them there, often attacked, sometimes in the jaws of death, heroic in the highest sense. And we see the modern missionary with like heroism landing on savage coasts and at the constant risk of life teaching the will of God in a sublime confidence that it shall awaken the most sunken nature; a confidence never at fault.

But we are obliged to doubt whether Samson had in view any scheme against the Philistine power; and we may be sure that he was on no mission for the good of Gaza. Of a patriotic or generous purpose there is no trace; the motive is unquestionably of a different kind. From his youth this man was restless, adventurous, ever craving some new excitement good or bad. He could do anything but quietly pursue a path of duty; and in the small towns of Dan and the valleys of Judah he had little to excite and interest him. There life went on in a dull way from year to year, without gaiety, bustle, enterprise. Had the chief been deeply interested in religion, had he been a reformer of the right kind, he would have found opportunity enough for exertion and a task into which he might have thrown all his force. There were heathen images to break in pieces, altars and high-places to demolish. To banish Baal-worship and the rites of Ashtoreth from the land, to bring the customs of the people under the law of Jehovah would have occupied him fully. But Samson did not incline to any such doings; he had no passion for reform. We never see in his life one such moment as Gideon and Jephthah knew of high religious daring. Dark hours he had, sombre enough, as at Lehi after the slaughter. But his was the melancholy of a life without aim sufficient to its strength, without a vision matching its energy. To suffer for God's cause is the rarest of joys, and that Samson never knew though he was judge in Israel.

We imagine then that in default of any excitement such as he craved in the towns of his own land he turned his eyes to the Philistine cities which presented a marked contrast. There life was energetic and gay, there many pleasures were to be had. New colonists were coming in their swift ships, and the streets presented a scene of constant animation. The strong eager man, full of animal passion, found the life he craved in Gaza, where he mingled with the crowds and heard tales of strange existence. Nor was there wanting the opportunity for enjoyment which at home he could not indulge. Beyond the critical observation of the elders of Dan he could take his fill of sensual pleasure. Not without danger of course. In some brawl the Philistines might close upon him. But he trusted to his strength to escape from their hands, and the risk increased the excitement. We must suppose that, having seen the nearer and less important towns such as Ekron, Gath, and Ashkelon he now ventured to Gaza in quest of amusement, in order, as people say, to see the world.

A constant peril this of seeking excitement, especially in an age of high civilisation. The means of variety and stimulus are multiplied, and ever the craving outruns them, a craving yielded to, with little or no resistance, by many who should know better. The moral teacher must recognise the desire for variety and excitement as perhaps the chief of all the hindrances he has now to overcome. For one who desires duty there are scores who find it dull and tame and turn from it; without sense of fault, to the gaieties of civilised society in which there is "nothing wrong," as they say, or at least so little of the positively wrong that conscience is easily appeased. The religious teacher finds the demand for "brightness" and variety before him at every turn; he is indeed often touched by it himself and follows with more or less of doubt a path that leads straight from his professed goal. "Is amusement devilish?" asks one. Most people reply with a smile that life must be lively or it is not worth having. And the Philistinism that attracts them with its dash and gaudiness is not far away nor hard to reach. It is not necessary to go across to the Continent where the brilliance of Vienna or Paris offers a contrast to the grey dulness of a country village; nor even to London where amid the lures of the midnight streets there is peril of the gravest kind. Those who are restless and foolhardy can find a Gaza and a valley of Sorek nearer home, in the next market town. Philistine life, lax in morals, full of rattle and glitter, heat and change, in gambling, in debauchery, in sheer audacity of movement and talk, presents its allurements in our streets, has its acknowledged haunts in our midst. Young people brought up to fear God in quiet homes whether of town or country are enticed by the whispered counsels of comrades, half ashamed of the things they say, yet eager for more companionship in what they secretly know to be folly or worse. Young women are the prey of those who disgrace manhood and womanhood by the offers they make, the insidious lies they tell. The attraction once felt is apt to master. As the current that rushes swiftly bears them with it they exult in the rapid motion even while life is nearing the fatal cataract. Subtle is the progress of infidelity. From the persuasion that enjoyment is lawful and has no peril in it the mind quickly passes to a doubt of the old laws and warnings. Is it so certain that there is a reward for purity and unworldliness?

Is not all the talk about a life to come a jangle of vain words? The present is a reality, death a certainty, life a swiftly passing possession. They who enjoy know what they are getting. The rest is dismissed as altogether in the air.

With Samson, as there was less of faith and law to fling aside, there was less hardening of heart. He was half a heathen always, more conscious of bodily than of moral strength, reliant on that which he had, indisposed to seek from God the holy vigour which he valued little. At Gaza, where moral weakness endangered life, his well-knit muscles released him. We see him among the Philistines entrapped, apparently in a position from which there is no escape. The gate is closed and guarded. In the morning he is to be seized and killed. But aware of his danger, his mind not put completely off its balance as yet by the seductions of the place, he arises at midnight and, plucking the doors of the city-gate from their sockets, carries them to the top of a hill which fronts Hebron.

Here is represented what may at first be quite possible to one who has gone into a place of temptation and danger. There is for a time a power of resolution and action which when the peril of the hour is felt may be brought into use. Out of the house which is like the gate of hell, out of the hands of vile tempters it is possible to burst in quick decision and regain liberty. In the valley of Sorek it may be otherwise, but here the danger is pressing and rouses the will. Yet the power of rising suddenly against temptation, of breaking from the company of the impure is not to be reckoned on. It is not of ourselves we can be strong and resolute enough, but of grace. And can a man expect divine succour in a harlot's den? He thinks he may depend upon a certain self-respect, a certain disgust at vile things and dishonourable life. But vice can be made to seem beautiful, it can overcome the aversion springing from self-respect and the best education. In the history of one and another of the famous and brilliant, from the god-like youth of Macedon to the genius of yesterday, the same unutterably sad lesson is taught us; we trace the quick descent of vice. Self-respect? Surely to Goethe, to George Sand, to Musset, to Burns that should have remained, a saving salt. But it is clear that man has not the power of preserving himself. While he says in his heart, That is beneath me; I have better taste; I shall never be guilty of such a low, false, and sickening thing—he has already committed himself.

Samson heard the trampling of feet in the streets and was warned of physical danger. When midnight came he lost no time. But he was too late. The liberty he regained was not the liberty he had lost. Before he entered that house in Gaza, before he sat down in it, before he spoke to the woman there he should have fled. He did not; and in the valley of Sorek his strength of will is not equal to the need. Delilah beguiles him, tempts him, presses him with her wiles. He is infatuated; his secret is told and ruin comes.

Moral strength, needful decision in duty to self and society and God—few possess these because few have the high ideal before them, and the sense of an obligation which gathers force from the view of eternity. We live, most of us, in a very limited range of time. We think of to-morrow or the day beyond; we think of years of health and joy in this world, rarely of the boundless after-life. To have a stain upon the character, a blunted moral sense, a scar that disfigures the mind seems of little account because we anticipate but a temporary reproach or inconvenience. To be defiled, blinded, maimed for ever, to be incapacitated for the labour and joy of the higher world does not enter into our thought. And many who are nervously anxious to appear well in the sight of men are shameless when God only can see. Moral strength does not spring out of such imperfect views of obligation. What availed Samson's fidelity to the Nazarite vow when by another gate he let in the foe?

The common kind of religion is a vow which covers two or three points of duty only. The value and glory of the religion of the Bible are that it sets us on our guard and strengthens us against everything that is dangerous to the soul and to society. Suppose it were asked wherein our strength lies, what would be the answer? Say that one after another stood aside conscious of being without strength until one was found willing to be tested. Assume that he could say, I am temperate, I am pure; passion never masters me: so far the account is good. You hail him as a man of moral power, capable of serving society. But you have to inquire further before you can be satisfied. You have to say, Some have had too great liking for money. Francis Bacon, Lord Chancellor of England, notable in the first rank of philosophers, took bribes and was convicted upon twenty-three charges of corruption. Are you proof against covetousness? because if you can be tempted by the glitter of gold reliance cannot be placed upon you. And again it must be asked of the man— Is there any temptress who can wind you about her fingers, overcome your conscientious scruples, wrest from you the secret you ought to keep and make you break your covenant with God, even as Delilah overcame Samson? Because, if there is, you are weaker than a vile woman and no dependence can be placed upon you. We learn from history what this kind of temptation does. We see one after another, kings, statesmen, warriors who figure bravely upon the scene for a time, their country proud of them, the best hopes of the good centred in them, suddenly in the midst of their career falling into pitiable weakness and covering themselves with disgrace. Like Samson they have loved some woman in the valley of Sorek. In the life of to-day instances of the same pitiable kind occur in every rank and class. The shadow falls on men who held high places in society or stood for a time as pillars in the house of God.

Or, taking another case, one may be able to say, I am not avaricious, I have fidelity, I would not desert a friend nor speak a falsehood for any bribe; I am pure; for courage and patriotism you may rely upon me:—here are surely signs of real strength. Yet that man may be wanting in the divine faithfulness on which every virtue ultimately depends. With all his good qualities he may have no root in the heavenly, no spiritual faith, ardour, decision. Let him have great opposition to encounter, long patience to maintain, generosity and self-denial to exercise without prospect of quick reward— and will he stand? In the final test nothing but fidelity to the Highest, tried and sure fidelity to God can give a man any right to the confidence of others. That chain alone which is welded with the fire of holy consecration, devotion of heart and strength and mind to the will of God is able to bear the strain. If we are to fight the battles of life and resist the urgency of its temptations the whole divine law as Christ has set it forth must be our Nazarite vow and we must count ourselves in respect of every obligation the bondmen of God. Duty must not be a matter of self-respect but of ardent aspiration. The way of our life may lead us into some Gaza full of enticements, into the midst of those who make light of the names we revere and the truths we count most sacred. Prosperity may come with its strong temptations to pride and vainglory. If we would be safe it must be in the constant gratitude to God of those who feel the responsibility and the hope that are kindled at the cross, as those who have died with Christ and now live with Him unto God. In this redeemed life it may be almost said there is no temptation; the earthly ceases to lure, gay shows and gauds cease to charm the soul. There still are comforts and pleasures in God's world, but they do not enchain. A vision of the highest duty and reality overshines all that is trivial and passing. And this is life—the fulness, the charm, the infinite variety and strength of being. "How can he that is dead to the world live any longer therein?" Yet he lives as he never did before.

In the experience of Samson in the valley of Sorek we find another warning. We learn the persistence with which spiritual enemies pursue those whom they mark for their prey. It has been said that the adversaries of good are always most active in following the best men with their persecutions. This we take leave to deny. It is when a man shows some weakness, gives an opportunity for assault that he is pressed and hunted as a wounded lion by a tribe of savages. The occasion was given to the Philistines by Samson's infatuation. Had he been a man of stern purity they would have had no point of attack. But Delilah could be bribed. The lords of the Philistines offered her a large sum to further their ends, and she, a willing instrument, pressed Samson with her entreaties. Baffled again and again, she did not rest till the reward was won.

We can easily see the madness of the man in treating lightly, as if it were a game he was sure to win, the solicitations of the adventuress. "The Philistines be upon thee, Samson"—again and again he heard that threat and laughed at it. The green withes, the new ropes with which he was bound were snapped at will. Even when his hair was woven into the web he could go away with web and beam and the pin with which they had been fixed to the ground. But if he had been aware of what he was doing how could he have failed to see that he was approaching the fatal capitulation, that wiles and blandishments were gaining upon him? When he allowed her to tamper with the sign of his vow it was the presage of the end.

So it often is. The wiles of the spirit of this world are woven very cunningly. First the "over-scrupulous" observance of religious ordinances is assailed. The tempter succeeds so far that the Sabbath is made a day of pleasure: then the cry is raised, "The Philistines be upon thee." But the man only laughs. He feels himself quite strong as yet, able for any moral task. Another lure is framed—gambling, drinking. It is yielded to moderately, a single bet by way of sport, one deep draught on some extraordinary occasion. He who is the object of persecution is still self-confident. He scorns the thought of danger. A prey to gambling, to debauchery? He is far enough from that. But his weakness is discovered. Satanic profit is to be made out of his fall; and he shall not escape.

It is true as ever it was that the friendship of the world is a snare. When the meshes of time and sense close upon us we may be sure that the end aimed at is our death. The whole world is a valley of Sorek to weak man, and at every turn he needs a higher than himself to guard and guide him. He is indeed a Samson, a child in morals, though full-grown in muscle. There are some it is true who are able to help, who, if they were beside in the hour of peril, would interpose with counsel and warning and protection. But a time comes to each of us when he has to go alone through the dangerous streets. Then unless he holds straight forward, looking neither to right hand nor left, pressing towards the mark, his weakness will be quickly detected, that secret tendency scarcely known to himself by which he can be most easily assailed. Nor will it be forgotten if once it has been discovered. It is now the property of a legion. Be it vanity or avarice, ambition or sensuousness, the Philistines know how to gain their end by means of it. There is strength indeed to be had. The weakest may become strong, able to face all the tempters in the world and to pass unscathed through the streets of Gaza or the crowds of Vanity Fair. Nor is the succour far away. Yet to persuade men of their need and then to bring them to the feet of God are the most difficult of tasks in an age of self-sufficiency and spiritual unreason. Harder than ever is the struggle to rescue the victims of worldly fashion, enticement, and folly: for the false word has gone forth that here and here only is the life of man and that renouncing the temporal is renouncing all.

CHAPTER XXIII.

THE VALLEY OF SOREK AND OF DEATH.

JUDGES xvi. 4-31.

THE strong bold man who has blindly fought his battles and sold himself to the traitress and to the enemy,

"Eyeless in Gaza at the mill with slaves,"

the sport and scorn of those who once feared him, is a mournful object. As we look upon him there in his humiliation, his temper and power wasted, his life withered in its prime, we almost forget the folly and the sin, so much are we moved to pity and regret. For Samson is a picture, vigorous in outline and colour, of what in a less striking way many are and many more would be if it were not for restraints of divine grace. A fallen hero is this. But the career of multitudes without the dash and energy ends in the like misery of defeat; nothing done, not much attempted, their existence fades into the sere and yellow leaf. There has been no ardour to make death glorious.

Every man has his defects, his besetting sins, his dangers. It is in the consciousness of our own that we approach with sorrow the last scenes of the eventful history of Samson. Who dares cast a stone at him? Who can fling a taunt as he is seen groping about in his blindness?

> A little onward lend thy guiding hand
> To these dark steps, a little further on.
> For yonder bank hath choice of sun or shade;
> There I am wont to sit when any chance
> Relieves me from my task of servile toil.
> O dark, dark, dark amid the blaze of noon,
> Irrecoverably dark, total eclipse
> Without all hope of day:"

so we hear him bewail his lot. And we, perchance, feeling weakness creep over us while bonds of circumstance still hold us from what we see to be our divine calling,—we compassionate ourselves in pitying him; or, if we are as yet strong and buoyant, our history before us, plans for useful service of our time clearly in view, have we not already felt the symptoms of moral infirmity which make it doubtful whether we shall reach our goal? There are many hindrances, and even the brave unselfish man who never loiters in Gaza or in the treacherous valley may find his way barred by obstacles he cannot remove. But in the case of most the hindrances within are the most numerous and powerful. This man who should effect much for his age is held by love which blinds him, that other by hatred which masters him. Now covetousness, now pride is the deterrent. Many begin to know themselves and the difficulty of doing great tasks for God and man when noontide is past and the day has begun to decline. Great numbers have only dreamed of attempting something and have never bestirred themselves to act. So it is that Samson's defeat appears a symbol of the pathetic human failure. To many his character is full of sad interest, for in it they see what they have fears of becoming or what they have already become.

What has Samson lost when he has revealed his secret to Delilah? Observe him when he goes forth from the woman's house and stands in the sunlight. Apart from the want of his waving locks he seems the same and is physically the same; muscle and sinew, bone and nerve, stout-beating heart and strong arm, Samson is there. And his human will is as eager as ever; he is a bold daring man this morning as he was last evening, with the same dream of "breaking through all" and bearing himself as king. But he is more lonely than ever before; something has gone from his soul. A heavy sense of faithlessness to one prized distinction and known duty oppresses him. Shake thyself as at other times, poor rash Samson, but know in thy heart that at last thou art powerless: the audacity of faith is no longer thine. Thou art the natural man still, but that is not enough, the spiritual sanction gone. The Philistines, half afraid, gather about thee ten to one; they can bind now and lead captive, for thou hast lost the girdle which knit thy powers together and made thee invincible. The consciousness of being God's man is gone—the consciousness of being true to that which united thee in a rude but very real bond to the Almighty. Thou hast scorned the vow which kept thee from the abyss and with the knowledge of utter moral baseness comes physical prostration, despair, feebleness, ruin. Samson at last knows himself to be no king at all, no hero nor judge.

It is common to think the spiritual of little account, faith in God of little account. Suppose men give that up; suppose they no longer hold themselves bound by duty to the Almighty; they expect nevertheless to continue the same. They will still have their reason, their strength of body and of mind; they believe that all they once did they shall still be able to do and now more freely in their own way, therefore even more successfully. Is that so? Hope is a spiritual thing. It is apart from bodily strength, distinct from energy and manual skill. Take hope away from a man, the strongest, the bravest, the most intelligent, and will he be the same? Nay. His eye loses its lustre; the vigour of his will decays; he lies powerless and defeated. Or take love away—love which is again a spiritual thing. Let the ardour, the reason for exertion which love inspired pass away. Let the man who loved and would have dared all for love be deprived of that source of vital power, and he will dare no longer. Sad and weary and dispirited he will cast himself down, careless of life.

But hope and love are not so necessary to the full tide of human vigour, are not so potent in stirring the powers of manhood as the friendship of God, the consciousness that made by God for ends of His we have Him as our stay. Indeed without this consciousness manhood never finds its strength. This gives a hope far higher and more sustaining than any of a personal or temporal kind. It makes us strong by virtue of the finest and deepest affection which can possibly move us; and more than that it gives to life full meaning, proper aim and justification. A man without the sense of a divine origin and election has no standing-ground; he is so to speak without the right of existence, he has no claim to be heard in speaking and to have a place among those who act. But he who feels himself to be in the world on God's business, to be God's servant, has his assured place and claim as a man, and can see reason and purpose for every sharp trial to which he is put. Here then is the secret of strength, the only source of power and steadfastness for any man or woman. And he who has had it and lost it, breaking with God for the sake of gain or pleasure or some earthly affection, must like Samson feel his vigour sapped, his confidence forfeited. Now his power to command, to advise, to contend for any worthy result has passed away. He is a tree whose root ceases to feed in the soil though still the leaves are green.

The spiritual loss, the loss of living faith, is the great one: but is it for that we generally pity ourselves or any person known to us? Life and freedom are dear, the ability to put forth energy at our will, the sense of capacity; and it is the loss of these in outward and visible ranges that most moves us to grief. We commiserate the strong man whose exploits in the world seem to be over, as we pity the orator whose power of speech is gone, the artist who can no more handle the brush, the eager merchant whose bargaining is done. We give our sympathy to Samson, because in the midst of his days he has fallen overcome by treachery, because the cruelty of enemies has afflicted him. Yet, looking at the truth of things, the real cause of pity is deeper than any of these and different. A man who is still in living touch with God can suffer the saddest deprivations and retain a cheerful heart, unbroken courage and hope. Suppose that Samson, surprised by his enemies while he was about some worthy task, had been seized, deprived of his sight, bound with fetters of iron and consigned to prison. Should we then have had to pity him as we must when he is taken, a traitor to himself, the dupe of a deceiver, with the badge of his vow and the sense of his fidelity gone? We feel with Jeremiah in his affliction; we feel with John the Baptist confined in the prison into which Herod has cast him, with St. Paul in the Philippian dungeon, and with St. Peter lying bound with chains in the castle of Jerusalem. But we do not commiserate, we admire and exult. Here are men who endure for the right. They are martyrs, fellow-sufferers with Christ; they are marching with the cohorts of God to the deliverances of eternity. Ah! It is the men who are " martyrs by the pang without the palm," the men who have lost not only liberty but nobleness, who dragged after false lures have sold their prudence and their strength —these it is for whom we need to weep. He who doing his duty has been mastered by enemies, he who fighting a brave battle has been overcome—let us not dare to pity him. But the man who has given up the battle of faith, who has lost his glory, him the heavens look upon with the profound sorrow that is called for by a wasted life.

And how pathetic the touch: "He wist not that the Lord had departed from him." For a little time he failed to realise the spiritual disaster he had brought on himself. For a little time only; soon the dark conviction seized him. But worse still would have been his case if he had remained unconscious of loss. This sense of weakness is the last boon to the sinner. God still does this for him, poor headstrong child of nature as he would fain be, living by and for himself: he is not permitted. Whether he will own it or not he shall be weak and useless until he returns to God and to himself. Often indeed we find the enslaved Samson refusing to allow that anything is wrong with him. Out of sight of the world, in some very secret place he has broken the obligations of faith, temperance, chastity, and yet thinks no special result has followed. He can meet the demands of society and that is enough, supposing the matter should come to light. Of the subtle poisoning of his own soul he has no thought. Is the thing hidden then? The law which determines that as a man is so his strength shall be follows every one into the most secret place. It keeps watch over our veracity, our sobriety, our purity, our faithfulness. Whenever in one point our covenant with God is broken a part of strength is taken away. Do we not perceive the loss? Do we flatter ourselves that all is as before? That is only our spiritual blindness; the fact remains.

What a pitiful thing it is to see men in this plight trying in vain to go about as if nothing had happened and they were as fit as ever for their places in society and in the church! We do not speak solely of sins like those into which Samson and David fell. There are others, scarcely reckoned sins, which as surely result in moral weakness perceived or unperceived, in the loss of God's countenance and support. Our covenant is to be pure and also merciful; let one fail in mercifulness, let there be a harsh pitiless temper cherished in secret, and this as well as impurity will make him morally weak. Our covenant is to be generous as well as honest; let a man keep from the poor and from the church what he ought to give, and he will lose his strength of soul as surely as if he cheated another in trade, or took what was not his own. But we distinguish between sin and default and think of the latter as a mere infirmity which has no ill effect. There is no acknowledgment of loss even when it has become almost complete. The man who is not generous nor merciful, nor a defender of faith goes on thinking all is well with him, imagining that his futile religious exercises or gifts to this and that keep him on good terms with God and that he is helping the world, while in truth he has not the moral strength of a child. He acts the part of a Christian teacher or servant of the church, he leads in prayer, he joins in deliberations that have to do with the success of Christian work. To himself all seems satisfactory and he expects that good shall result from his efforts. But it cannot be. There is the strain of exertion, but no power.

Do we wonder that more is not effected by our organisations, religious and other, which seem so powerful, quite capable of Christianising and reforming the world? The reason is that many of the professed religious and benevolent, who appear zealous and strenuous, are dying at heart. The Lord may not have departed from them utterly; they are not dead; there is still a rootlet of spiritual being. But they cannot fight; they cannot help others; they cannot run in the way of God's commandments. Are we not bound to ask ourselves how we stand, whether any failure in our covenant-keeping has made us spiritually weak. If we are paltering with eternal facts, if between us and the one Source of Life there is a widening distance surely the need is urgent for a return to Christian honour and fidelity which will make us strong and useful.

And there is something here in the story of Samson that bids us think hopefully of a new way and a new life. In the misery to which he was reduced there came to him with renewed acceptance of his vow a fresh endowment of vigour. It is the divine healing, the grace of the long-suffering Father which are thus represented. No human soul needs to be utterly disconsolate, for grace waits ever on discomfiture. Return to me, says the Lord, and I will return to you; I will heal your backslidings and love you freely. Out of the deepest depths there is a way to the heights of spiritual privilege and power. To confess our faults and sins, to resume the fidelity, the uprightness, the generosity and mercifulness we renounced, to take again the straight upward path of self-denial and duty —this is always reserved for the soul that has not utterly perished. The man, young or old, who has become weaker than a child for any good work may hear the call that speaks of hope. He who in self-indulgence or hard worldliness has abandoned God may turn again to the Father's entreaty, "Remember from what thou hast fallen and repent."

We pass now to consider a point suggested by the terms in which the Philistines triumphed over their captured foe. When the people saw him they praised their god: for they said, Our god hath delivered into our hand our enemy, and the destroyer of our country which hath slain many of us. Here the ignorant religiousness and gratitude of Philistines to a god which was no God might provoke a smile were it not for the consideration that under the clear light of Christianity equal ignorance is often shown by those who profess to be piously grateful. You say it was the bribe which the Philistine lords offered to Delilah and her treachery and Samson's sin that put him in the enemy's hand. You say, Surely the most ignorant man in Gaza must have seen that Dagon had nothing whatever to do with the result. And yet it is very common to ascribe to God what is nowise His doing. There are indeed times when we almost shudder to hear God thanked for that which could only be attributed to a Dagon or a Moloch.

We are told of the tribal gods of those old Syrians—Baal, Melcarth, Sutekh, Milcom and the rest—each adored as master and protector by some people or race. Piously the devotees of each god acknowledged his hand in every victory and every fortunate circumstance, at the same time tracing to his anger and their own neglect of duty to him all calamities and defeats. May it not be said that the belief of many still is in a tribal god, falsely called by the name of Jehovah, a god whose chief function is to look after their interests whoever may suffer, and take their side in all quarrels whoever may be in the right? Men make for themselves the rude outline of a divinity who is supposed to be indifferent or hostile to every circle but their own, suspicious of every church but their own, careless of the sufferings of all but themselves. In two countries that are at war prayers for success will ascend in almost the same terms to one who is thought of as a national protector, not to the Father of all; each side is utterly regardless of the other, makes no allowance in prayer for the possibility that the other may be in the right. The thanksgivings of the victors too will be mixed with glorying almost fiendish over the defeated, whose blood, it may be, dyed in pathetic martyrdom their own hill-sides and valleys. In less flagrant cases, where it is only a question of gain or loss in trade, of getting some object of desire, the same spirit is shown. God is thanked for bestowing that of which another, perhaps more worthy, is deprived. It is not to the kindness of Heaven, but rather to the proving severity of God, we may say, that the result is due. Looking on with clear eyes we see something very different from divine approval in the prosperous efforts of unscrupulous push and wire-pulling. Those who have much success in the world have need to justify their comforts and the praise they enjoy. They need to show cause to the ranks of the obscure and ill-paid for their superior fortune. Success like theirs cannot be admitted as a special mark of the favour of that God Whose ways are equal, Whose name is the Holy and Just.

Next look at the ignoble task to which Samson is put by the Philistines, a type of the ignominious uses to which the hero may be doomed by the crowd. The multitude cannot be trusted with a great man.

In the prison at Gaza the fallen chief was set to grind corn, to do the work of slaves. To him, indeed, work was a blessing. From the bitter thoughts that would have eaten out his heart he was somewhat delivered by the irksome labour. In reality, as we now perceive, no work degrades; but a man of Samson's type and period thought differently. The Philistine purpose was to degrade him; and the Hebrew captive would feel in the depths of his hot brooding nature the humiliating doom. Look then at the parallels. Think of a great statesman placed at the head of a nation to guide its policy in the line of righteousness, to bring its laws into harmony with the principles of human freedom and divine justice —think of such a one, while labouring at his sacred task with all the ardour of a noble heart, called to account by those whose only desire is for better trade, the means of beating their rivals in some market or bolstering up their failing speculations. Or see him at another time pursued by the cry of a class that feels its prescriptive rights invaded or its position threatened. Take again a poet, an artist, a writer, a preacher intent on great themes, eagerly following after the ideal to which he has devoted himself, but exposed every moment to the criticism of men who have no soul—held up to ridicule and reprobation because he does not accept vulgar models and repeat the catchwords of this or that party. Philistinism is always in this way asserting its claim, and ever and anon it succeeds in dragging some ardent soul into the dungeon to grind thenceforth at the mill.

With the very highest too it is not afraid to intermeddle. Christ Himself is not safe. The Philistines of to-day are doing their utmost to make His name inglorious. For what else is the modern cry that Christianity should be chiefly about the business of making life comfortable in this world and providing not only bread but amusement for the crowd? The ideas of the church are not practical enough for this generation. To get rid of sin—that is a dream; to make men fearers of God, soldiers of truth, doers of righteousness at all hazards—that is in the air. Let it be given up; let us seek what we can reach; bind the name of Christ and the Spirit of Christ in chains to the work of a practical secularism, and let us turn churches into pleasant lounging places and picture galleries. Why should the soul have the benefit of so great a name as that of the Son of God? Is not the body more? Is not the main business to have houses and railways, news and enjoyment? The policy of undeifying Christ is having too much success. If it make way there will soon be need for a fresh departure into the wilderness.

The last scene of Samson's history awaits us— the gigantic effort, the awful revenge in which the Hebrew champion ended his days. In one sense it aptly crowns the man's career. The sacred historian is not composing a romance, yet the end could not have been more fit. Strangely enough it has given occasion for preaching the doctrine of self-sacrifice as the only means of highest achievement, and we are asked to see here an example of the finest heroism, the most sublime devotion. Samson dying for his country is likened to Christ dying for His people.

It is impossible to allow this for a moment. Not Milton's apology for Samson, not the authority of all the illustrious men who have drawn the parallel can keep us from deciding that this was a case of vengeance and self-murder, not of noble devotion. We have no sense of vindicated principle when we see that temple fall in terrible ruin, but a thrill of disappointment and keen sorrow that a servant of Jehovah should have done this in His name. The lords of the Philistines, all the *serens* or chiefs of the hundred cities are gathered in the ample porch of the building.

True, they are assembled at an idolatrous feast; but this idolatry is their religion which they cannot choose but exercise, for they know of no better, nor has Samson ever done one deed or spoken one word that could convince them of error. True, they are met to rejoice over their enemy and they call for him in cruel vainglory to make them sport. Yet this is the man who for his sport and in his revenge once burned the standing corn of a whole valley and more than once went on slaying Philistines till he was weary. True, Samson as a patriotic Israelite views these people as enemies. Yet it was among them he first sought a wife and afterwards pleasure. And now, if he decides to die that he may kill a thousand enemies at once, is the self-chosen death less an act of suicide?

If this was truly a fine act of self-sacrifice what good came of it? The sacrifice that is to be praised does distinct and clearly purposed service to some worthy cause or high moral end. We do not find that this dreadful deed reconciled the Philistines to Israel or moved them to belief in Jehovah. We observe, on the contrary, that it went to increase the hatred between race and race, so that when Canaanites, Moabites, Ammonites, Midianites no longer vex Israel these Philistines show more deadly antagonism—antagonism of which Israel knew the heat when on the red field of Gilboa the kingly Saul and the well-beloved Jonathan were together stricken down in death. If there was in Samson's mind any thought of vindicating a principle it was that of Israel's dignity as the people of Jehovah. But here his testimony was worthless.

As we have already said, much is written about self-sacrifice which is sheer mockery of truth, most falsely sentimental. Men and women are urged to the notion that if they can only find some pretext for renouncing freedom, for curbing and endangering life, for stepping aside from the way of common service that they may give up something in an uncommon way for the sake of any person or cause, good will come of it. The doctrine is a lie. The sacrifice of Christ was not of that kind. It was under the influence of no blind desire to give up His life, but first under the pressure of a supreme providential necessity, then in renunciation of the earthly life for a clearly seen and personally embraced divine end, the reconciliation of man to God, the setting forth of a propitiation for the sin of the world—for this it was He died. He willed to be our Saviour; having so chosen He bowed to the burden that was laid upon Him. "It pleased the Lord to bruise Him; He hath put Him to grief." To the end He foresaw and desired there was but one way—and the way was that of death because of man's wickedness and ruin.

Suffering for itself is no end and never can be to God or to Christ or to a good man. It is a necessity on the way to the ends of righteousness and love. If personality is not a delusion and salvation a dream there must be in every case of Christian renunciation some distinct moral aim in view for every one concerned, and there must be at each step, as in the action of our Lord, the most distinct and unwavering sincerity, the most direct truthfulness. Anything else is a sin against God and humanity. We entreat would-be moralists of the day to comprehend before they write of "self-sacrifice." The sacrifice of the moral judgment is always a crime, and to preach needless suffering for the sake of covering up sin or as a means of atoning for past defects is to utter most unchristian falsehood.

Samson threw away a life of which he was weary and ashamed. He threw it away in avenging a cruelty; but it was a cruelty he had no reason to call a wrong. "O God, that I might be avenged!"—that was no prayer of a faithful heart. It was the prayer of envenomed hatred, of a soul still unregenerate after trial. His death was indeed *self*-sacrifice—the sacrifice of the higher self, the true self, to the lower. Samson should have endured patiently, magnifying God. Or we can imagine something not perfect yet heroic. Had he said to those Philistines, My people and you have been too long at enmity. Let there be an end of it. Avenge yourselves on me, then cease from harassing Israel,—that would have been like a brave man. But it is not this we find. And we close the story of Samson more sad than ever that Israel's history has not taught a great man to be a good man, that the hero has not achieved the morally heroic, that adversity has not begotten in him a wise patience and magnanimity. Yet he had a place under Divine Providence. The dim troubled faith that was in his soul was not altogether fruitless. No Jehovah-worshipper would ever think of bowing before that god whose temple fell in ruins on the captive Israelite and his thousand victims.

CHAPTER XXIV.

THE STOLEN GODS.

JUDGES xvii., xviii.

THE portion of the Book of Judges which begins with the seventeenth chapter and extends to the close is not in immediate connection with that which has gone before. We read (ch. xviii. 30) that "Jonathan, the son of Gershom, the son of Manasseh, he and his sons were priests to the tribe of Dan until the day of the captivity of the land." But the proper reading is, "Jonathan, the son of Gershom, the son of Moses." It would seem that the renegade Levite of the narrative was a near descendant of the great lawgiver. So rapidly did the zeal of the priestly house decline that in the third or fourth generation after Moses one of his own line became minister of an idol temple for the sake of a living. It is evident, then, that in the opening of the seventeenth chapter, we are carried back to the time immediately following the conquest of Canaan by Joshua, when Othniel was settling in the south and the tribes were endeavouring to establish themselves in the districts allotted to them. The note of time is of course far from precise, but the incidents are certainly to be placed early in the period.

We are introduced first to a family living in Mount Ephraim consisting of a widow and her son Micah, who is married and has sons of his own. It appears that on the death of the father of Micah a sum of eleven hundred shekels of silver, about a hundred and twenty pounds of our money—a large amount for the time—was missed by the widow, who after vain search for it spoke in strong terms about the matter to her son. He had taken the money to use in stocking his farm or in trade and at once acknowledged that he had done so and restored it to his mother, who hastened to undo any evil her words had caused by invoking upon him the blessing of God. Further she dedicated two hundred of her shekels to make graven and molten images in token of piety and gratitude.

We have here a very significant revelation of the state of religion. The indignation of Moses had burned against the people when at Sinai they made a rude image of gold, sacrificed to it and danced about it in heathen revel. We are reading of what took place say a century after that scene at the foot of Sinai, and already those who desire to show their devotion to the Eternal, very imperfectly known as Jehovah, make teraphim and molten images to represent Him. Micah has a sort of private chapel or temple among the buildings in his courtyard. He consecrates one of his sons to be priest of this little sanctuary. And the historian adds in explanation of this, as one keenly aware of the benefits of good government under a God-fearing monarch—"In those days there was no king in Israel. Every man did that which was right in his own eyes."

We need not take for granted that the worship in this hill-chapel was of the heathen sort. There was probably no Baal, no Astarte among the images; or, if there was, it may have been merely as representing a Syrian power prudently recognised but not adored. No hint occurs in the whole story of a licentious or a cruel cult, although there must have been something dangerously like the superstitious practices of Canaan. Micah's chapel, whatever the observances were, gave direct introduction to the pagan forms and notions which prevailed among the people of the land. There already Jehovah was degraded to the rank of a nature-divinity, and represented by figures.

In one of the highland valleys towards the north of Ephraim's territory Micah had his castle and his ecclesiastical establishment—state and church in germ. The Israelites of the neighbourhood, who looked up to the well-to-do farmer for protection, regarded him all the more that he showed respect for religion, that he had his house of gods and a private priest. They came to worship in his sanctuary and to inquire of the ecclesiastic, who in some way endeavoured to discover the will of God by means of the teraphim and ephod. The ark of the covenant was not far away, for Bethel and Gilgal were both within a day's journey. But the people did not care to be at the trouble of going so far. They liked better their own local shrine and its homelier ways; and when at length Micah secured the services of a Levite the worship seemed to have all the sanction that could possibly be desired.

It need hardly be said that God is not confined to a locality, that in those days as in our own the true worshipper could find the Almighty on any hill-top, in any dwelling or private place, as well as at the accredited shrine. It is quite true, also, that God makes large allowance for the ignorance of men and their need of visible signs and symbols of what is unseen and eternal. We must not therefore assume at once that in Micah's house of idols, before the widow's graven and molten figures, there could be no acceptable worship, no prayers that reached the ear of the Lord of Hosts. And one might even go the length of saying that, perhaps, in this schismatic sanctuary, this chapel of images, devotion could be quite as sincere as before the ark itself. Little good came of the religious ordinances maintained there during the whole period of the judges, and even in Eli's latter days the vileness and covetousness practised at Shiloh more than counfervailed any pious influence. Local and family altars therefore must have been of real use. But this was the danger, that leaving the appointed centre of Jehovah-worship, where symbolism was confined within safe limits, the people should in ignorant piety multiply objects of adoration and run into polytheism. Hence the importance of the decree, afterwards recognised, that one place of sacrifice should gather to it all the tribes and that there the ark of the covenant with its altar should alone speak of the will and holiness of God. And the story of the Danite migration connected with this of Micah and his Levite well illustrates the wisdom of such a law, for it shows how, in the far north, a sanctuary and a worship were set up which, existing long for tribal devotion, became a national centre of impure worship.

The wandering Levite from Bethlehem-judah is one, we must believe, of many Levites, who having found no inheritance because the cities allotted to them were as yet unconquered spread themselves over the land seeking a livelihood, ready to fall in with any local customs of religion that offered them position and employment. The Levites were esteemed as men acquainted with the way of Jehovah, able to maintain that communication with Him without which no business could be hopefully undertaken. Something of the dignity that was attached to the names of Moses and Aaron ensured them honourable treatment everywhere unless among the lowest of the people; and when this Levite reached the dwelling of Micah, beside which there seems to have been a khan or lodging-place for travellers, the chance of securing him was at once seized. For ten pieces of silver, say twenty-five shillings a year, with a suit of clothes and his food, he agreed to become Micah's private chaplain. At this very cheap rate the whole household expected a time of prosperity and divine favour. "Now know I," said the head of the family, "that the Lord will do me good seeing I have a Levite to my priest." We must fear that he took some advantage of the man's need, that he did not much consider the honour of Jehovah yet reckoned on getting a blessing all the same. It was a case of seeking the best religious privileges as cheaply as possible, a very common thing in all ages.

But the coming of the Levite was to have results Micah did not foresee. Jonathan had lived in Bethlehem, and some ten or twelve miles westward down the valley one came to Zorah and Eshtaol, two little towns of the tribe of Dan of which we have heard. The Levite had apparently become pretty well known in the district and especially in those villages to which he went to offer sacrifice or perform some other religious rite. And now a series of incidents brought certain old acquaintances to his new place of abode.

Even in Samson's time the tribe of Dan, whose territory was to be along the coast west from Judah, was still obliged to content itself with the slopes of the hills, not having got possession of the plain. In the earlier period with which we are now dealing the Danites were in yet greater difficulty, for not only had they Philistines on the one side but Amorites on the other. The Amorites "would dwell," we are told, "in Mount Heres, in Aijalon and in Shaalbim." It was this pressure which determined the people about Zorah and Eshtaol to find if possible another place of settlement, and five men were sent out in search. Travelling north they took the same way as the Levite had taken, heard of the same khan in the hill-country of Ephraim, and made it their resting-place for a night. The discovery of the Levite Jonathan followed and of the chapel in which he ministered with its wonderful array of images. We can suppose the deputation had thoughts they did not express, but for the present they merely sought the help of the priest, begging him to consult the oracle on their behalf and learn whether their mission would be successful. The five went on their journey with the encouragement, " Go in peace; before the Lord is your way wherein ye go."

Months pass without any more tidings of the Danites until one day a great company is seen following the hill-road near Micah's farm. There are six hundred men girt with weapons of war with their wives and children and cattle, a whole clan on the march, filling the road for miles and moving slowly northward. The five men have indeed succeeded after a fashion. Away between Lebanon and Hermon, in the region of the sources of Jordan, they have found the sort of district they went to seek. Its chief town Laish stood in the midst of fertile fields with plenty of wood and water. It was a place, according to their large report, where was "no want of anything that is in the earth." Moreover the inhabitants, who seem to have been a Phœnician colony, dwelt by themselves quiet and secure, having no dealings or treaty with the powerful Zidonians. They were the very kind of people whom a sudden attack would be likely to subdue. There was an immediate migration of Danites to this fresh field, and in prospect of bloody work the men of Zorah and Eshtaol seem to have had no doubt as to the rightness of their expedition; it was enough that they had felt themselves straitened. The same reason appears to suffice many in modern times. Were the aboriginal inhabitants of America and Australia considered by those who coveted their land? Even the pretence of buying has not always been maintained. Murder and rapine have been the methods used by men of our own blood, our own name, and no nation under the sun has a record darker than the tale of British conquest.

Men who go forth to steal land are quite fit to attempt the strange business of stealing gods—that is appropriating to themselves the favour of divine powers and leaving other men destitute. The Danites as they pass Micah's house hear from their spies of the priest and the images that are in his charge. "Do you know that that there is in these houses an ephod and teraphim and a graven image and a molten image? Now therefore consider what ye have to do." The hint is enough. Soon the court of the farmstead is invaded, the images are brought out and the Levite Jonathan, tempted by the offer of being made priest to a clan, is fain to accompany the marauders. Here is confusion on confusion. The Danites are thieves, brigands, and yet they are pious; so pious that they steal images to assist them in worship. The Levite agrees to the theft and accepts the offer of priesthood under them. He will be the minister of a set of thieves to forward their evil designs, and they, knowing him to be no better than themselves, expect that his sacrifices and prayers will do them good. It is surely a capital instance of perverted religious ideas.

As we have said, these circumstances are no doubt recounted in order to show how dangerous it was to separate from the pure order of worship at the sanctuary. In after times this lesson was needed, especially when the first king of the northern tribes set his golden calves the one at Bethel, the other at Dan. Was Israel to separate from Judah in religion as well as in government? Let there be a backward look to the beginning of schism in those extraordinary doings of the Danites. It was in the city founded by the six hundred that one of Jeroboam's temples was built. Could any blessing rest upon a shrine and upon devotions which had such an origin, such an history?

May we find a parallel now? Is there a constituted religious authority with which soundness of belief and acceptable worship are so bound up that to renounce the authority is to be in the way of confusion and error, schism and eternal loss? The Romanist says so. Those who speak for the Papal church never cease to cry to the world that within their communion alone are truth and safety to be found. Renounce, they say, the apostolic and divine authority which we conserve and all is gone. Is there anarchy in a country? Are the forces that make for political disruption and national decay showing themselves in many lands? Are monarchies overthrown? Are the people lawless and wretched? It all comes of giving up the Catholic order and creed. Return to the one fold under the one Shepherd if you would find prosperity. And there are others who repeat the same injunction, not indeed denying that there may be saving faith apart from their ritual, but insisting still that it is an error and a sin to seek God elsewhere than at the accredited shrine.

With Jewish ordinances we Christians have nothing to do when we are judging as to religious order and worship now. There is no central shrine, no exclusive human authority. Where Christ is, there is the temple; where He speaks, the individual conscience must respond. The work of salvation is His alone, and the humblest believer is His consecrated priest. When our Lord said, "The hour cometh and now is when the true worshippers shall worship the Father in spirit and in truth"; and again, "Where two or three are gathered together in My name there am I in the midst of them"; when He as the Son of God held out His hands directly to every sinner needing pardon and every seeker after truth, when He offered the one sacrifice upon the cross by which a living way is opened into the holiest place, He broke down the walls of partition and with the responsibility declared the freedom of the soul.

And here we reach the point to which our narrative applies as an illustration. Micah and his household worshipping the images of silver, the Levite officiating at the altar, seeking counsel of Jehovah by ephod and teraphim, the Danites who steal the gods, carry off the priest and set up a new worship in the city they build—all these represent to us types and stages of what is really schism pitiful and disastrous—that is, separation from the truth of things and from the sacred realities of divine faith. Selfish untruth and infidelity are schism, the wilderness and outlawry of the soul.

1. Micah and his household, with their chapel of images, their ephod and teraphim, represent those who fall into the superstition that religion is good as insuring temporal success and prosperity, that God will see to the worldly comfort of those who pay respect to Him. Even among Christians this is a very common and very debasing superstition. The sacraments are often observed as signs of a covenant which secures for men divine favour through social arrangements and human law. The spiritual nature and power of religion are not denied, but they are uncomprehended. The national custom and the worldly hope have to do with the observance of devout forms rather than any movement of the soul heavenward. A church may in this way become like Micah's household, and prayer may mean seeking good terms with Him who can fill the land with plenty or send famine and cleanness of teeth. Unhappily many worthy and most devout persons still hold the creed of an early and ignorant time. The secret of nature and providence is hid from them. The severities of life seem to them to be charged with anger, and the valleys of human reprobation appear darkened by the curse of God. Instead of finding in pain and loss a marvellous divine discipline they perceive only the penalty of sin, a sign of God's aversion, not of His Fatherly grace. It is a sad, a terrible blindness of soul. We can but note it here and pass on, for there are other applications of the old story.

2. The Levite represents an unworthy worldly ministry. With sadness must confession be made that there are in every church pastors unspiritual, worldlings in heart, whose desire is mainly for superiority of rank or of wealth, who have no vision of Christ's cross and battle except as objective and historical. Here, most happily, the cases of complete worldliness are rare. It is rather a tendency we observe than a developed and acknowledged state of things. Very few of those in the ranks of the Christian ministry are entirely concerned with the respect paid to them in society and the number of shekels to be got in a year. That he keeps pace with the crowd instead of going before it is perhaps the hardest thing that can be said of the worldly pastor. He is humane, active, intelligent; but it is for the church as a great institution, or the church as his temporal hope and stay. So his ministry becomes at the best a matter of serving tables and providing alms—we shall not say amusement. Here indeed is schism; for what is farther from the truth of things, what is farther from Christ?

3. Once more we have with us to-day, very much with us, certain Danites of science, politics, and the press who, if they could, would take away our God and our Bible, our Eternal Father and spiritual hope, not from a desire to possess but because they hate to see us believing, hate to see any weight of silver given to religious uses. Not a few of these are marching, as they think triumphantly, to commanding and opulent positions whence they will rule the thought of the world. And on the way, even while they deride and detest the supernatural, they will have the priest go with them. They care nothing for what he says; to listen to the voice of a spiritual teacher is an absurdity of which they would not be guilty; for to their own vague prophesying all mankind is to give heed, and their interpretations of human life are to be received as the bible of the age. Of the same order is the socialist who would make use of a faith he intends to destroy, and a priesthood whose claim is offensive to him, on his way to what he calls the organisation of society. In his view the uses of Christianity and the Bible are temporal and earthly. He will not have Christ the Redeemer of the soul, yet he attempts to conjure with Christ's words and appropriate the power of His name. The audacity of these would-be robbers is matched only by their ignorance of the needs and ends of human life.

We might here refer to the injustice practised by one and another band of our modern Israel who do not scruple to take from obscure and weak households of faith the sacraments and Christian ministry, the marks and rights of brotherhood. We can well believe that those who do this have never looked at their action from the other side, and may not have the least idea of the soreness they leave in the hearts of humble and sincere believers.

In fine, the Danites with the images of Micah went their way and he and his neighbours had to suffer the loss and make the best of their empty chapel, where no oracle thenceforth spoke to them. It is no parable, but a very real example of the loss that comes to all who have trusted in forms and symbols, the outward signs instead of the living power of religion. While we repel the arrogance that takes from faith its symbolic props and stays we must not let ourselves deny that the very rudeness of an enemy may be an excellent discipline for the Christian. Agnosticism and science and other Danite companies sweep with them a good deal that is dear to the religious mind and may leave it very distressed and anxious—the chapel empty, the oracle as it may appear lost for ever. With the symbol the authority, the hope, the power seem to be lost irrecoverably. What now has faith to rest upon? But the modern spirit with its resolution to sweep away every unfact and mere form is no destroyer. Rather does it drive the Christian to a science, a virtue far beyond its own. It forces we may say on faith that severe truthfulness and intellectual courage which are the proper qualities of Christianity, the necessary counterpart of its trust and love and grace. In short, when enemies have carried off the poor teraphim and fetishes which are their proper capture they have but compelled religion to be itself, compelled it to find its spiritual God, its eternal creed and to understand its Bible. This, though done with evil intent, is surely no cruelty, no outrage. Shall a man or a church that has been so roused and thrown back on reality sit wailing in the empty chapel for the images of silver and the deliverances of the hollow ephod? Everything remains, the soul and the spiritual world, the law of God, the redemption of Christ, the Spirit of eternal life.

CHAPTER XXV.

FROM JUSTICE TO WILD REVENGE.

JUDGES xix.–xxi.

THESE last chapters describe a general and vehement outburst of moral indignation throughout Israel, recorded for various reasons. A vile thing is done in one of the towns of Benjamin and the fact is published in all the tribes. The doers of it are defended by their clan and fearful punishment is wrought upon them, not without suffering to the entire people. Like the incidents narrated in the chapters immediately preceding, these must have occurred at an early stage in the period of the judges, and they afford another illustration of the peril of imperfect government, the need for a vigorous administration of justice over the land. The crime and the volcanic vengeance belong to a time when there was "no king in Israel" and, despite occasional appeals to the oracle, "every man did that which was right in his own eyes." In this we have one clue to the purpose of the history.

The crime of Gibeah brought under our notice here connects itself with that of Sodom and represents a phase of immorality which, indigenous to Canaan, mixed its putrid current with Hebrew life. There are traces of the same horrible impurity in the Judah of Rehoboam and Asa; and in the story of Josiah's reign we are horrified to read of "houses of Sodomites that were in the house of the Lord, where the women wove hangings for the Asherah." With such lurid historical light on the subject we can easily understand the revival of this warning lesson from the past of Israel and the fulness of detail with which the incidents are recorded. A crime originally that of the off-scourings of Gibeah became practically the sin of a whole tribe, and the war that ensued sets in a clear light the zeal for domestic purity which was a feature in every religious revival and, at length, in the life of the Hebrew people.

It may be asked how, while polygamy was practised among the Israelites, the sin of Gibeah could rouse such indignation and awaken the signal vengeance of the united tribes. The answer is to be found partly in the singular and dreadful device which the indignant husband used in making the deed known. The ghastly symbols of outrage told the tale in a way that was fitted to stir the blood of the whole country. Everywhere the hideous thing was made vivid and a sense of utmost atrocity was kindled as the dissevered members were borne from town to town. It is easy to see that womanhood must have been stirred to the fiercest indignation, and manhood was bound to follow. What woman could be safe in Gibeah where such things were done? And was Gibeah to go unpunished? If so, every Hebrew city might become the haunt of miscreants. Further there is the fact that the woman so foully murdered, though a concubine, was the concubine of a Levite. The measure of sacredness with which the Levites were invested gave to this crime, frightful enough in any view, the colour of sacrilege. How degenerate were the people of Gibeah when a servant of the altar could be treated with such foul indignity and driven to so extraordinary an appeal for justice? There could be no blessing on the tribes if they allowed the doers or condoners of this thing to go unpunished. Every Levite throughout the land must have taken up the cry. From Bethel and other sanctuaries the call for vengeance would spread and echo till the nation was roused. Thus, in part at least, we can explain the vehemence of feeling which drew together the whole fighting force of the tribes.

The doubt will yet remain whether there could have been so much purity of life or respect for purity as to sustain the public indignation. Some may say, Is there not here a sufficient reason for questioning the veracity of the narrative? First, however, let it be remembered that often where morals are far from reaching the level of pure monogamic life distinctions between right and wrong are sharply drawn. Acquaintance with phases of modern life that are most painful to the mind sensitively pure reveals a fixed code which none may infringe without bringing upon themselves reprobation, perhaps more vehement than in a higher social grade visits the breach of a higher law. It is the fact that concubinage has its unwritten acknowledgment and protecting customs. There is marriage that is only a name; there is concubinage that gives the woman more rights than one who is married. Against the immorality and the gross evils of cohabitation is to be set this unwritten law. And arguing from popular feeling in our great cities we reach the conclusion that in ancient Israel where concubinage prevailed there was a wide and keen feeling as to the rights of concubines and the necessity of upholding them. Many women must have been in this relation, below those who could count themselves legally married, and all the more that the concubine occupied a place inferior to that of the lawful wife would popular opinion take up her cause and demand the punishment of those who did her wrong.

And here we are led to a point which demands clear statement and recognition. It has been too readily supposed that polygamy is always a result of moral decline and indicates a low state of domestic purity. It may, in truth, be a rude step of progress. Has it been sufficiently noted that in those countries in which the name of the mother, not of the father, descended to the children the reason may be found in universal or almost universal unchastity? In Egypt at one time the law gave to women, especially to mothers, peculiar rights; but to praise Egyptian civilisation for this reason and hold up its treatment of women as an example to the nineteenth century is an extraordinary venture. The Israelites, however lax, were doubtless in advance of the society of Thebes. Among the Canaanites the moral degradation of women, whatever freedom may have gone with it, was so terrible that the Hebrew with his two or three wives and concubines, but with a morality otherwise severe, must have represented a new and holier social order as well as a new and holier religion. It is therefore not incredible, but appears simply in accordance with the instincts and customs proper to the Hebrew people, that the sin of Gibeah should provoke overwhelming indignation. There is no pretence of purity, no hypocritical anger. The feeling is sound and real. Perhaps in no other matter of a moral kind would there have been such intense and unanimous exasperation. A point of justice or of belief would not have so moved the tribes. The better self of Israel appears, asserting its claim and power. And the miscreants of Gibeah representing the lower self, verily an unclean spirit, are detested and denounced on every hand.

The time was that of fresh feeling, unwarped by those customs which in the guise of civilisation and refinement afterwards corrupted the nation. And we may see the prophetic or hortatory use of the narrative for an after age in which doings as vile as those at Gibeah were sanctioned by the court and protected even by religious leaders. It would be hoped by the sacred historian that this tale of the fierce indignation of the tribes might rouse afresh the same moral feeling. He would fain stir a careless people and their priests by the exhibition of this tumultuous vengeance. Nor can we say that the necessity for the impressive lesson has ceased. In the heart of our large cities vices as vile as those of Gibeah are heard muttering in the nightfall, life as abandoned lurks and festers, creating a social gangrene.

Recognise, then, in these chapters a truth for all time boldly drawn out—the great truth as to moral reform and national purity. Law will not cure moral evils; a statute book the purest and noblest will not save. Those who by the impulse of the Spirit gathered the various traditions of Israel's life knew well that on a living conscience in men everything depended, and they at least indicate the further truth which many of ourselves have not grasped, that the early and rude workings of conscience, producing stormy and terrible results, are a necessary stage of development. As there must be energy before there can be noble energy, so there must be moral vigour, it may be rude, violent, ignorant, a stream rushing out of barbarian hills, sweeping with most appalling vehemence, before there can be spiritual life patient, calm, and holy. Law is a product, not a cause; it is not the code we make that will preserve us but the God-given conscience that informs the code and ever goes before it a pillar of fire, at times flashing vivid lightning. Even Christian law cannot save a people if it be merely a series of injunctions. Nothing will do but the mind of Christ in every man and woman continually inspiring and directing life. The reformer who thinks that a statute or regulation will end some sin or evil custom is in sad error. Say the decree he contends for is enacted; but have the consciences of those against whom it is made been quickened? If not, the law merely expresses a popular mood, and the life of the whole community will not be permanently raised in tone.

The church finds here a perpetual mission of influence. Her doctrine is but half her message. From the doctrine as from an eternal fount must go life-giving moral heat in every range, and the Spirit is ever with her to make the world like a fire. Her duty is wide as righteousness, great as man's destiny; it is never ended, for each generation comes in a new hour with new needs. The church, say some, is finishing its work; it is doomed to be one of the broken moulds of life. But the church that is the instructor of conscience and kindles the flame of righteousness has a mission to the ages. We are far yet from that day of the Lord when all the people shall be prophets; and until then how can the world live without the church? It would be a body without a soul.

Conscience the oracle of life, conscience working badly rather than held in chains of mere rule without spontaneity and inspiration, moral energy widespread, personal, and keen, however rude—here is one of the notes of the sacred writer; and another note, no less distinct, is the assertion of moral intolerance. It has not occurred to this prophetic annalist that endurance of evil has any curative power. He is a Hebrew, full of indignation against the vile and false, and he demands a heat of moral force in his people. Foul things are done at the court and even in the temple; there is a depraving indifference to purity, a loose notion (very similar to the idea of our day), that all the sides of life should have free play and that the heathen had much to teach Israel. The whole of the narrative before us is infused with a righteous protest against evil, a holy plea for intolerance of sin. Will men refuse instruction and persist in making themselves one with bestiality and outrage? Then judgment must deal with them on the ground they have chosen to occupy, and until they repent the conscience of the race must repudiate them together with their sin. Along with a keenly burning conscience there goes this necessity of moral intolerance. Charity is good, but not always in place; and brotherhood itself demands at times strong uncompromising judgment of the evil-doer. How else among men of weak wills and wavering hearts can righteousness vindicate and enforce itself as the eternal reality of life? Compassion is strong only when it is linked to unfaltering declarations; mercy is divine only when it turns a front of mail to wickedness and flashes lightning at proud wrong. Any other kind of charity is but a new offence—the sinner pardoning sin.

Now the people of Gibeah were not all vile. The wretches whose crime called for judgment were but the rabble of the town. And we can see that the tribes when they gathered in indignation were made serious by the thought that the righteous might be punished with the wicked. We are told that they went up to the sanctuary and asked counsel of the Lord whether they should attack the convicted city. There was a full muster of the fighting men, their blood at fever heat, yet they would not advance without an oracle. It was an appeal to heavenly justice and demands notice as a striking feature of the whole terrible series of events. For an hour there is silence in the camp till a higher voice shall speak.

But what is the issue? The oracle decrees an immediate attack on Gibeah in the face of all Benjamin, which has shown the temper of heathenism by refusing to give up the criminals. Once and again there is trial of battle which ends in defeat of the allied tribes. The wrong triumphs; the people have to return humbled and weeping to the Sacred Presence and sit fasting and disconsolate before the Lord.

Not without the suffering of the entire community is a great evil to be purged from a land. It is easy to execute a murderer, to imprison a felon. But the spirit of the murderer, of the felon, is widely diffused, and that has to be cast out. In the great moral struggle year after year the better have not only the openly vile but all who are tainted, all who are weak in soul, loose in habit, secretly sympathetic with the vile, arrayed against them. There is a sacrifice of the good before the evil are overcome. In vicarious suffering many must pay the penalty of crimes not their own ere the wide-reaching wickedness can be seen in its demonic power and struck down as the cruel enemy of the people.

When an assault is made on some vile custom the sardonic laugh is heard of those who find their profit and their pleasure in it. They feel their power. They know the wide sympathy with them spread secretly through the land. Once and again the feeble attempt of the good is repelled. With sad hearts, with impoverished means, those who led the crusade retire baffled and weary. Has their method been unintelligent? There very possibly lies the cause of its failure. Or, perhaps, it has been, though nominally inspired by an oracle, all too human, weak through human pride. Not till they gain with new and deeper devotion to the glory of God, with more humility and faith, a clearer view of the battle-ground and a better ordering of the war shall defeat be changed into victory. And may it not be that the assault on moral evils of our day, in which multitudes are professedly engaged, in which also many have spent substance and life, shall fail till there is a true humiliation of the armies of God before Him, a new consecration to higher and more spiritual ends? Human virtue has ever to be jealous of itself, the reformer may so easily become a Pharisee.

The tide turned and there came another danger, that which waits on ebullitions of popular feeling. A crowd roused to anger is hard to control, and the tribes having once tasted vengeance did not cease till Benjamin was almost exterminated. The slaughter extended not only to the fighting men, but to women and children. The six hundred who fled to the rock-fort of Rimmon appear as the only survivors of the clan. Justice overshot its mark and for one evil made another. Those who had most fiercely used the sword viewed the result with horror and amazement, for a tribe was lacking in Israel. Nor was this the end of slaughter. Next for the sake of Benjamin the sword was drawn and the men of Jabesh-gilead were butchered. It has to be noticed that the oracle is not made responsible for this horrible process of evil. The people came of their own accord to the decision which annihilated Jabesh-gilead. But they gave it a pious colour; religion and cruelty went together, sacrifices to Jehovah and this frightful outbreak of demonism. It is one of the dark chapters of human history. For the sake of an oath and an idea death was dealt remorselessly. No voice suggested that the people of Jabesh may have been more cautious than the rest, not less faithful to the law of God. The others were resolved to appear to themselves to have been right in almost annihilating Benjamin; and the town which had not joined in the work of destruction must be punished.

The warning conveyed here is intensely keen. It is that men, made doubtful by the issue of their actions whether they have done wisely, may fly to the resolution to justify themselves and may do so even at the expense of justice; that a nation may pass from the right way to the wrong and then, having sunk to extraordinary baseness and malignity, may turn writhing and self-condemned to add cruelty to cruelty in the attempt to still the upbraidings of conscience. It is that men in the heat of passion which began with resentment against evil may strike at those who have not joined in their errors as well as those who truly deserve reprobation. We stand, nations and individuals, in constant danger of dreadful extremes, a kind of insanity hurrying us on when the blood is heated by strong emotion. Blindly attempting to do right we do evil, and again having done the evil, we blindly strive to remedy it by doing more. In times of moral darkness and chaotic social conditions, when men are guided by a few rude principles, things are done that afterwards appal themselves, and yet may become an example for future outbreaks. During the fury of their Revolution the French people, with some watchwords of the true ring as liberty, fraternity, turned hither and thither, now in terror, now panting after dimly seen justice or hope, and it was always from blood to blood. We understand the juncture in ancient Israel and realise the excitement and the rage of a self-jealous people, when we read the modern tales of surging ferocity in which men appear now hounding the shouting crowd to vengeance, then shuddering on the scaffold.

In private life the story has an application against wild and violent methods of self-vindication. Many a man, hurried on by a just anger against one who has done him wrong, sees to his horror after a sharp blow is struck that he has broken a life and thrown a brother bleeding to the dust. One wrong thing has been done perhaps more in haste than vileness of purpose, and retribution, hasty, ill-considered, leaves the moral question tenfold more confused. When all is reckoned we find it impossible to say where the right is, where the wrong.

Passing to the final expedient adopted by the chiefs of Israel to rectify their error—the rape of the women at Shiloh—we see only to how pitiful a pass moral blundering brings those who fall into it: other moral teaching there is none. We might at first be disposed to say that there was extraordinary want of reverence for religious order and engagements when the men of Benjamin were invited to make a sacred festival the occasion of taking what the other tribes had solemnly vowed not to give. But the festival at Shiloh must have been far more of a merry-making than of a sacred assembly. It needs to be recognised that many gatherings even in honour of Jehovah were mainly, like those of Canaanite worship, for hilarity and feasting. There was probably no great incongruity between the occasion and the plot.

But the scenes certainly change in the course of this narrative with extraordinary swiftness. Fierce indignation is followed by pity, weeping for defeat by tears for too complete a victory. Horrible bloodshed wastes the cities and in a month there is dancing in the plain of Shiloh not ten miles from the field of battle. Chaotic indeed are the morality and the history; but it is the disorder of social life in its early stages, with the vehemence and tenderness, the ferocity and laughter of a nation's youth. And, all along, the Book of Judges bears the stamp of veracity as a series of records because these very features are to be seen—this tumult, this undisciplined vehemence in feeling and act. Were we told here of decorous solemn progress at slow march, every army going forth with some stereotyped invocation of the Lord of Hosts, every leader a man of conventional piety supported by a blameless priesthood and orderly sacrifices, we should have had no evidence of truth. The traditions preserved here, whoever collected them, are singularly free from that idyllic colour which an imaginative writer would have endeavoured to give.

At the last, accordingly, the book we have been reading stands a real piece of history, proving itself over every kind of suspicion a true record of a people chosen and guided to a destiny greater than any other race of man has known. A people understanding its call and responding with eagerness at every point? Nay. The world is in the heart of Israel as of every other nation. The carnal attracts, and malignant cries overbear the divine still voice; the air of Canaan breathes in every page, and we need to recollect that we are viewing the turbulent upper-waters of the nation and the faith. But the working of God is plain; the divine thoughts we believed Israel to have in trust for the world are truly with it from the first, though darkened by altars of Baal and of Ashtoreth. The Word and Covenant of Jehovah are vital facts of the supernatural which surrounds that poor struggling erring Hebrew flock. Theocracy is a divine fact in a larger sense than has ever been attached to the word. Inspiration too is no dream, for the history is charged with intimations of the spiritual order. The light of the unrealised end flashes on spear and altar, and in the frequent roll of the storm the voice of the Eternal is heard declaring righteousness and truth. No story this to praise a dynasty or magnify a conquering nation or support a priesthood. Nothing so faithful, so true to heaven and to human nature could be done from that motive. We have here an imperishable chapter in the Book of God.

The Book of Ruth
By The Reverend Robert A. Watson, M.A., D.D.

CONTENTS

Chapter I.
Naomi's Burden, ... 839

Chapter II.
The Parting of the Ways, ... 842

Chapter III.
In the Field of Boaz, ... 844

Chapter IV.
The Hazardous Plan, ... 847

Chapter V.
The Marriage at the Gate, ... 850

THE BOOK OF RUTH

BY THE REV. ROBERT A. WATSON, D. D.

CHAPTER I.

NAOMI'S BURDEN.

RUTH i. 1-13.

Leaving the Book of Judges and opening the story of Ruth we pass from vehement out-door life, from tempest and trouble into quiet domestic scenes. After an exhibition of the greater movements of a people we are brought, as it were, to a cottage interior in the soft light of an autumn evening, to obscure lives passing through the cycles of loss and comfort, affection and sorrow. We have seen the ebb and flow of a nation's fidelity and fortune, a few leaders appearing clearly on the stage and behind them a multitude indefinite, indiscriminate, the thousands who form the ranks of battle and die on the field, who sway together from Jehovah to Baal and back to Jehovah again. What the Hebrews were at home, how they lived in the villages of Judah or on the slopes of Tabor, the narrative has not paused to speak of with detail. Now there is leisure after the strife and the historian can describe old customs and family events, can show us the toiling flockmaster, the busy reapers, the women with their cares and uncertainties, the love and labour of simple life. Thunderclouds of sin and judgment have rolled over the scene; but they have cleared away and we see human nature in examples that become familiar to us, no longer in weird shadow or vivid lightning flash, but as we commonly know it, homely, erring, enduring, imperfect, not unblest.

Bethlehem is the scene, quiet and lonely on its high ridge overlooking the Judæan wilderness. The little city never had much part in the eager life of the Hebrew people, yet age after age some event notable in history, some death or birth or some prophetic word drew the eyes of Israel to it in affection or in hope; and to us the Saviour's birth there has so distinguished it as one of the most sacred spots on earth that each incident in the fields or at the gate appears charged with predictive meaning, each reference in psalm or prophecy has tender significance. We see the company of Jacob on the journey through Canaan halt by the way near Ephrath, which is Bethlehem, and from the tents there comes a sound of wailing. The beloved Rachel is dead. Yet she lives in a child new-born, the mother's Son of Sorrow, who becomes to the father Benjamin, Son of the Right Hand. The sword pierces a loving heart, but hope springs out of pain and life out of death. Generations pass and in these fields of Bethlehem we see Ruth gleaning, Ruth the Moabitess, a stranger and foreigner who has sought refuge under the shadow of Jehovah's wings; and at yonder gate she is saved from want and widowhood, finding in Boaz her *goël* and *menuchah*, her redeemer and rest. Later, another birth, this time within the walls, the birth of one long despised by his brethren, gives to Israel a poet and a king, the sweet singer of divine psalms, the hero of a hundred fights. And here again we see the three mighty men of David's troop breaking through the Philistine host to fetch for their chief a draught from the cool spring by the gate. Prophecy, too, leaves Israel looking to the city on the hill. Micah seems to grasp the secret of the ages when he exclaims, "But thou, Bethlehem Ephrathah, which art little to be among the thousands of Judah, out of thee shall one come forth unto Me that is to be the ruler in Israel; whose goings forth are from of old, from everlasting." For centuries there is suspense, and then over the quiet plain below the hill is heard the evangel: "Be not afraid: for, behold, I bring you good tidings of great joy which shall be to all the people: for there is born to you this day in the city of David a Saviour, which is Christ the Lord." Remembering this glory of Bethlehem we turn to the story of humble life there in the days when the judges ruled, with deep interest in the people of the ancient city, the race from which David sprang, of which Mary was born.

Jephthah had scattered Ammon behind the hills and the Hebrews dwelt in comparative peace and security. The sanctuary at Shiloh was at length recognised as the centre of religious influence; Eli was in the beginning of his priesthood, and orderly worship was maintained before the ark. People could live quietly about Bethlehem, although Samson, fitfully acting the part of champion on the Philistine border, had his work in restraining the enemy from an advance. Yet all was not well in the homesteads of Judah, for drought is as terrible a foe to the flockmaster as the Arab hordes, and all the south lands were parched and unfruitful.

We are to follow the story of Elimelech, his wife Naomi and their sons Mahlon and Chilion whose home at Bethlehem is about to be broken up. The sheep are dying in the bare glens, the cattle in the fields. From the soil usually so fertile little corn has been reaped. Elimelech, seeing his possessions melt away, has decided to leave Judah for a time so as to save what remains to him till the famine is over, and he chooses the nearest refuge, the watered Field of Moab beyond the Salt Sea. It was not far; he could imagine himself returning soon to resume the accustomed life in the old home. True Hebrews, these Ephrathites were not seeking an opportunity to cast off pious duty and break with Jehovah in leaving His land. Doubtless they hoped that God would bless their going, prosper them in Moab, and bring them back in good time. It was a trial to go, but what else could they do, life itself, as they believed, being at hazard?

With thoughts like these men often leave the land of their birth, the scenes of early faith, and oftener still without any pressure of necessity or any purpose of returning. Emigration appears to be forced upon many in these times, the compulsion coming not from Providence but from man and man's law. It is also an outlet for the spirit of adventure which characterises some races and has made them the heirs of continents. Against emigration it would be folly to speak, but great is the responsibility of those by whose action or want of action it is forced upon others. May it not be said that in every European land there are persons in power whose existence is like a famine to a whole countryside? Emigration is talked of glibly as if it were no loss but always gain, as if to the mass of men the traditions and customs of their native land were mere rags well parted with. But it is clear from innumerable examples that many lose what they never find again, of honour, seriousness, and faith.

The last thing thought of by those who compel emigration and many who undertake it of their own accord is the moral result. That which should be first considered is often not considered at all. Granting the advantages of going from a land that is over-populated to some fertile region as yet lying waste, allowing what cannot be denied that material progress and personal freedom result from these movements of population, yet the risk to individuals is just in proportion to the worldly attraction. It is certain that in many regions to which the stream of migration is flowing the conditions of life are better and the natural environment purer than they are in the heart of large European cities. But this does not satisfy the religious thinker. Modern colonies have indeed done marvels for political independence, for education and comfort. Their success here is splendid. But do they see the danger? So much achieved in short time for the secular life tends to withdraw attention from the root of spiritual growth—simplicity and moral earnestness. The pious emigrant has to ask himself whether his children will have the same thought for religion beyond the sea as they would have at home, whether he himself is strong enough to maintain his testimony while he seeks his fortune.

We may believe that the Bethlehemite, if he made a mistake in removing to Moab, acted in good faith and did not lose his hope of the divine blessing. Probably he would have said that Moab was just like home. The people spoke a language similar to Hebrew, and like the tribes of Israel they were partly husbandmen, partly keepers of cattle. In the "Field of Moab," that is the upland canton bounded by the Arnon on the north, the mountains on the east, and the Dead Sea precipices on the west, people lived very much as they did about Bethlehem, only more safely and in greater comfort. But the worship was of Chemosh, and Elimelech must soon have discovered how great a difference that made in thought and social custom and in the feeling of men toward himself and his family. The rites of the god of Moab included festivals in which humanity was disgraced. Standing apart from these he must have found his prosperity hindered, for Chemosh was lord in everything. An alien who had come for his own advantage, yet refused the national customs, would be scorned at least, if not persecuted. Life in Moab became an exile, the Bethlehemites saw that hardship in their own land would have been as easy to endure as the disdain of the heathen and constant temptations to vile conformity. The family had a hard struggle, not holding their own and yet ashamed to return to Judah.

Already we have a picture of wayworn human lives, tried on one side by the rigour of nature, on the other by unsympathetic fellow-creatures, and the picture becomes more pathetic as new touches are added to it. Elimelech died; the young men married women of Moab; and in ten years only Naomi was left, a widow with her widowed daughters-in-law. The narrative adds shadow to shadow. The Hebrew woman in her bereavement, with the care of two lads who were somewhat indifferent to the religion she cherished, touches our sympathies. We feel for her when she has to consent to the marriage of her sons with heathen women, for it seems to close all hope of return to her own land and, sore as this trial is, there is a deeper trouble. She is left childless in the country of exile. Yet all is not shadow. Life never is entirely dark unless with those who have ceased to trust in God and care for man. While we have compassion on Naomi we must also admire her. An Israelite among heathen she keeps her Hebrew ways, not in bitterness but in gentle fidelity. Loving her native place more warmly than ever, she so speaks of it and praises it as to make her daughters-in-law think of settling there with her. The influence of her religion is upon them both, and one at least is inspired with faith and tenderness equal to her own. Naomi has her compensations, we see. Instead of proving a trouble to her as she feared, the foreign women in her house have become her friends. She finds occupation and reward in teaching them the religion of Jehovah, and thus, so far as usefulness of the highest kind is concerned, Naomi is more blessed in Moab than she might have been in Bethlehem.

Far better the service of others in spiritual things than a life of mere personal ease and comfort. We count up our pleasures, our possessions and gains and think that in these we have the evidence of the divine favour. Do we as often reckon the opportunities given us of helping our neighbours to believe in God, of showing patience and fidelity, of having a place among those who labour and wait for the eternal kingdom? It is here that we ought to trace the gracious hand of God preparing our way, opening for us the gates of life. When shall we understand that circumstances which remove us from the experience of poverty and pain remove us also from precious means of spiritual service and profit? To be in close personal touch with the poor, the ignorant and burdened is to have simple every-day openings into the region of highest power and gladness. We do something enduring, something that engages and increases our best powers when we guide, enlighten, and comfort even a few souls and plant but a few flowers in some dull corner of the world. Naomi did not know how blest she had been in Moab. She said afterwards that she had gone out full and the Lord had brought her home again empty. She even imagined that Jehovah had testified against her and cast her from Him in rejection. Yet she had been finding the true power, winning the true riches. Did she return empty when the convert Ruth, the devoted Ruth went back with her?

Her two sons taken away, Naomi felt no tie binding her to Moab. Moreover in Judah the fields were green again and life was prosperous. She might hope to dispose of her land and realise something for her old age. It seemed therefore her interest and duty to return to her own country; and the next picture of the poem shows Naomi and her daughters-in-law travelling along the northward highway towards the ford of Jordan, she on her way home, they accompanying her. The two young widows are almost decided when they leave the desolate dwelling in Moab to go all the way to Bethlehem. Naomi's account of the life there, the purer faith and better customs attract them, and they love her well. But the matter is not settled; on the bank of Jordan the final choice will be made.

There are hours which bring a heavy burden of responsibility to those who advise and guide, and such an hour came now to Naomi. It was in poverty she was returning to the home of her youth. She could promise to her daughters-in-law no comfortable easy life there, for, as she well knew, the enmity of Hebrews against Moabites was apt to be bitter and they might be scorned as aliens from Jehovah. So far as she was concerned nothing could have been more desirable than their company. A woman in poverty and past middle life could not wish to separate herself from young and affectionate companions who would be a help to her in her old age. To throw off the thought of personal comfort natural to one in her circumstances and look at things from an unselfish point of view was very difficult. In reading her story let us remember how apt we are to colour advice half unconsciously with our own wishes, our own seeming needs.

Naomi's advantage lay in securing the companionship of Ruth and Orpah, and religious considerations added their weight to her own desire. Her very regard and care for these young women seemed to urge as the highest service she could do them to draw them out of the paganism of Moab and settle them in the country of Jehovah. So while she herself would find reward for her patient efforts these two would be rescued from the darkness, bound in the bundle of life. Here, perhaps, was her strongest temptation; and to some it may appear that it was her duty to use every argument to this end, that she was bound as one who watched for the souls of Ruth and Orpah to set every fear, every doubt aside and to persuade them that their salvation depended on going with her to Bethlehem. Was this not her sacred opportunity, her last opportunity of making sure that the teaching she had given them should have its fruit?

Strange it may seem that the author of the Book of Ruth is not chiefly concerned with this aspect of the case, that he does not blame Naomi for failing to set spiritual considerations in the front. The narrative indeed afterwards makes it clear that Ruth chose the good part and prospered by choosing it, but here the writer calmly states without any question the very temporal and secular reasons which Naomi pressed on the two widows. He seems to allow that home and country—though they were under the shadow of heathenism—home and country and worldly prospects were rightly taken account of even as compared with a place in Hebrew life and faith. But the underlying fact is a social pressure clearly before the Oriental mind. The customs of the time were overmastering, and women had no resource but to submit to them. Naomi accepts the facts and ordinances of the age; the inspired author has nothing to say against her.

"The Lord grant you that ye may find rest, each of you in the house of her husband." That the two young widows should return each to her mother's house and marry again in Moab is Naomi's urgent advice to them. The times were rude and wild. A woman could be safe and respected only under the protection of a husband. Not only was there the old-world contempt for unmarried women, but, we may say, they were an impossibility; there was no place for them in the social life. People did not see how there could be a home without some man at the head of it, the house-band in whom all family arrangements centred. It had not been strange that in Moab Hebrew men should marry women of the land; but was it likely Ruth and Orpah would find favour at Bethlehem? Their speech and manners would be despised and, dislike once incurred, prove hard to overcome. Besides, they had no property to commend them.

Evidently the two were very inexperienced. They had little thought of the difficulties, and Naomi, therefore, had to speak very strongly. In the grief of bereavement and the desire for a change of scene they had formed the hope of going where there were good men and women like the Hebrews they knew, and placing themselves under the protection of the gracious God of Israel. Unless they did so life seemed practically at an end. But Naomi could not take upon herself the responsibility of letting them drift into a hazardous position, and she forced a decision of their own in full view of the facts. It was true kindness no less than wisdom. The age had not dawned in which women could attempt to shape or dare to defy the customs of society, nor was any advantage to be sought at the risk of moral compromise. These things Naomi understood, though afterwards, in extremity, she made Ruth venture unwisely to obtain a prize.

Looking around us now we see multitudes of women for whom there appears to be no room, no vocation. Up to a certain point, while they were young, they had no thought of failure. Then came a time when Providence appointed a task; there were parents to care for, daily occupations in the house. But calls for their service have ceased and they feel no responsibility sufficient to give interest and strength. The world has moved on and the movement has done much for women, yet all do not find themselves supplied with a task and a place. Around the occupied and the distinguished circles perpetually a crowd of the helpless, the aimless, the disappointed, to whom life is a blank, offering no path to a ford of Jordan and a new future. Yet half the needful work is done for these when they are made to feel that among the possible ways they must choose one for themselves and follow it; and all is done when they are shown that in the service of God, which is the service also of mankind, a task waits them fitted to engage their highest powers. Across into the region of religious faith and energy they may decide to pass, there is room in it for every life. Disappointment will end when selfish thoughts are forgotten; helplessness will cease when the heart is resolved to help. Even to the very poor and ignorant deliverance would come with a religious thought of life and the first step in personal duty.

CHAPTER II.

THE PARTING OF THE WAYS.

Ruth i. 14-19.

We journey along with others for a time, enjoying their fellowship and sharing their hopes, yet with thoughts and dreams of our own that must sooner or later send us on a separate path. But decision is so difficult to many that they are glad of an excuse for self-surrender and are only too willing to be led by some authority, deferring personal choice as long as possible. Let an ecclesiastic or a strong-minded companion lay down for them the line of right and wrong and point the path of duty and they will obey, welcoming the relief from moral effort. Not seeing clearly, not disciplined in judgment, they crave external human guidance. The teachers of submission find many disciples not because they speak truth but because they meet the indolence of the human will with a crutch instead of a stimulus; they succeed by pampering weakness and making ignorance a virtue. A time comes, however, when the method will not serve. There are moments when the will must be exercised in choosing between one path and another, advance and retreat; and the alternative is too sharp to allow any escape. If the person is to live at all as a human being he has to decide whether he will go on in such a company or turn back; he has to declare what or who has the strongest hold upon his mind. Such an occasion came to Ruth and Orpah when they reached the border of Moab.

To Orpah the arguments of Naomi were persuasive. Her mother lived in Moab, and to her mother's house she could return. There the customs prevailed which from childhood she had followed. She would have liked to go with Naomi, but her interest in the Hebrew woman and the land and law of Jehovah did not suffice to draw her forward. Orpah saw the future as Naomi painted it, not indeed very attractive if she returned to her native place, but with far more uncertainty and possible humiliation if she crossed the dividing river. She kissed Naomi and Ruth and took the southward road alone, weeping as she went, often turning for yet another sight of her friends, passing at every step into an existence that could never be the old life simply taken up again, but would be coloured in all its experience by what she had learned from Naomi and that parting which was her own choice.

The others did not greatly blame her, and we, for our part, may not reproach her. It is unnecessary to suppose that in returning to her kinsfolk and settling down to the tasks that offered in her mother's house she was guilty of despising truth and love and renouncing the best. We may reasonably imagine her henceforth bearing witness for a higher morality and affirming the goodness of the Hebrew religion among her friends and acquaintances. Ruth goes where affection and duty lead her; but for Orpah too it may be claimed that in love and duty she goes back. She is not one who says, Moab has done nothing for me; Moab has no claim upon me, I am free to leave my country; I am under no debt to my people. We shall not take her as a type of selfishness, worldliness, or backsliding, this Moabite woman. Let us rather believe that she knew of those at home who needed the help she could give, and that with the thought of least hazard to herself mingled one of the duty she owed to others.

And Ruth:—memorable for ever is her decision, charming for ever the words in which it is expressed. "Behold," said Naomi, "thy sister-in-law is gone back unto her people, and unto her god: return thou after thy sister-in-law." But Ruth replied, "Intreat me not to leave thee, and to return from following after thee: for whither thou goest, I will go; and where thou lodgest, I will lodge: thy people shall be my people, and thy God my God: where thou diest, will I die, and there will I be buried; the Lord do so to me and more also, if aught but death part thee and me." Like David's lament over Jonathan these words have sunk deep into the human heart. As an expression of the tenderest and most faithful friendship they are unrivalled. The simple dignity of the iteration in varying phrase till the climax is reached beyond which no promise could go, the quiet fervour of the feeling, the thought which seems to have almost a Christian depth—all are beautiful, pathetic, noble. From this moment a charm lingers about Ruth and she becomes dearer to us than any woman of whom the Hebrew records tell.

Dignified and warm affection is the first characteristic of Ruth and close beside it we find the strength of a firm conclusion as to duty. It is good to be capable of clear resolve, parting between this and that of opposing considerations and differing claims. Not to rush at decisions and act in mere wilfulness, for wilfulness is the extreme of weakness, but to judge soundly and on this side or that to say, Here I see the path for me to follow: along this and no other I conclude to go. Unreason decides by taste, by momentary feeling, often out of mere spite or antipathy. But the resolve of a wise thoughtful person, even though it bring temporal disadvantage, is a moral gain, a step towards salvation. It is the exercise of individuality, of the soul.

One may act in error, as perhaps Elimelech and Orpah acted, yet the life be the stronger for the mistaken decision; only there must be no repentance for having exercised the power of judgment and of choice. Women are particularly prone to go back on themselves in false repentance. They did what they could not but think to be duty; they carefully decided on a path in loyalty to conscience; yet too often they will reproach themselves because what they desired and hoped has not come about. We cannot imagine Ruth in after years, even though her lot had remained that of the poor gleaner and labourer, returning upon her decision and weeping in secret as if the event had proved her high choice a foolish one. Her mind was too firm and clear for that. Yet this is what numbers of women are doing, burdening their souls, making that a crime in which they should rather practise themselves. Our decisions, even when they are made with all the wisdom and information we can command in thorough sanity and sincerity, may be, often are, very faulty; and do we expect that Providence will perpetually interfere to bring a perfect result out of the imperfect? Only in the perfect order of God, through the perfect work of Christ and the perfect operation of the Holy Spirit is the glorious consummation of human history and divine purpose to come. As for us, we are to learn of God in Christ, to judge and act our best; thereafter, leaving the result to Providence, never go back on that of which the Spirit of the Almighty made us capable in the hour of trial.

> "Then welcome each rebuff
> That turns earth's smoothness rough,
> Each sting that bids nor sit nor stand but go!
> Be our joys three parts pain!
> Strive, and hold cheap the strain;
> Learn, nor account the pang; dare, never grudge the throe!"*

In religion there is no escape from personal decision; no one can drift to salvation with companions or with a church. In art, in literature, in ordinary morality it is possible to possess something without any special effort. The atmosphere of cultured society, for instance, holds in solution the knowledge and taste which have been gained by a few and may pass in some measure to those who associate with them, though personally these have studied and acquired very little. Any one who observes how a new book is talked of will see the process. But the supreme nature of religion and its unique part in human development are seen here, that it demands high and sustained personal effort, the constant action of the will; that indeed every spiritual gain must result from the vital activity of the individual mind choosing to enter and enter yet farther the kingdom of divine revelation and grace. As it is expressed in the Epistle to the Hebrews: "We desire that every one of you do show the same diligence to the full assurance of hope unto the end: that ye be not slothful but followers of them who through faith and patience inherit the promises." The training in resoluteness, therefore, finds highest value and significance in view of the religious life. Those who live by habit and dependence in other matters are not prepared for the strenuous calling of faith, and many a one is kept from the freedom and joy of Christianity not because they are undesired, not because the call of Christ is unheeded, but for want of the power of decision, strength to go forward on a personal quest. Thousands are in the way of saying, Will you go to an evangelistic meeting? Then I will go. Will you take the Sacrament? Then I will. Will you teach in the Sunday-school? Then I will. So far something is gained; there is a half-decision. But the spiritual life is sure at some point to demand more than this. Even Naomi's advice must not deter Ruth from taking the way to Bethlehem.

Like many women Ruth was moved greatly by love. Was her love justified? Did it rightly govern her to the extent her words imply? "Whither thou goest, I will go: thy people shall be my people: where thou diest I will die, and there will I be buried." It is beautiful to see such love: but how was it earned?

Surely by years of patient faithful help; not by a few cheap words and caresses, a few facile promises; not by beauty of face, gaiety of temper. The love that has nothing but these to found upon is not enough for a life-companionship. But if there is honour, clear sincerity of soul, generosity of nature; if there is brave devotion to duty, there love can rest without fear, reproach, or hazard. When these cast their light on your way, love then, love freely and strongly;

* Browning: "Rabbi Ben Ezra."

you are safe. It is indeed called love where these are not—but only in ignorance and lightness: the heart has been caught by a word, ensnared by a look. How pathetic are the errors into which we see our friends and neighbours fall, errors that call for a life-long repentance because reason and serious purpose had nothing to do with the loving. No law of God is written against human affection, nor has He any jealousy of the devotion we show to worthy fellow-creatures; but there are divine laws of love to restrain our weak fancy and uplift our emotions; and if we disdain or cast aside these laws we must suffer, however ardent and self-sacrificing affection may be. Egotistical wilfulness in serving some one who engages our admiration and passionate devotion is not, properly speaking, love. It is rather an offence against that divine grace which bears the noble name. Of course we are not here speaking of Christian charity towards our neighbours, interest in them, and care for their well-being, which are always our duty and must not be limited. The story we are following is one of an intimate and personal affection.

Lastly and chiefly, the answer of Ruth implies a religious change—conversion. She renounces Chemosh and turns in faith and hope to the God of Israel, and this is the striking feature of her choice. Dimly seen, the grace and righteousness of the Most High touched her soul, commanded her reverence, drew her to follow one who was His servant and could recount the wonderful story of His people. Surely it is a supreme event in any life when this vision of the Best allures the mind and engages the will, even though knowledge of God be as yet very imperfect. And the reliance of Ruth upon the little she felt and knew of God, her clear resolution to seek rest under His wings appear in striking contrast with the reluctance, the unconcern, the hard unfaith of many to-day. How is it that they to whom the Word speaks and the life is revealed, whose portion is at every moment enriched by that Word and that life are so blind to the grace that encompasses and deaf to the love that entreats? Again and again we see them on the banks of some Jordan, with the land of God clear in view, with the promise of devotion trembling on their lips; but they turn back to Moab and Chemosh, to paganism, unrest, and despair.

Ruth's life properly began when at Naomi's side she passed through the waters, the very waters of baptism to her. There, with the purple mountains of Moab and the precipices of the Dead Sea shore behind, she sent her last look to Orpah and the past, and saw before her the steep narrow ascent through the Judæan hills. With rising faith, with growing love she moved to the fulfilment of womanhood in realising the soul's highest power and privilege. The upward path was hard to weary feet and all was not to be easy for Ruth in the Bethlehem of which she had dreamed; but fully committed and pledged to the new life she went forward. How much is missed when the choice to serve God is not unreservedly made, and there is not that full consecration of which Ruth's decision may be a type.

Of this loss we see examples on every side. To remain in the low ground by the river, still within reach of some paganism that fascinates even after profession and baptism—this is the end of religious feeling with many. Where the narrow way of discipleship leads they will not adventure; it is too bare, confining, and severe. They will not believe that freedom for the human soul is found by that path alone; they refuse to be bound and therefore never discover the inheritance of God's children to which they are called. When He who alone can guide, quicken, redeem is accepted solemnly and finally as the Lord of life, then at last the weak and entangled spirit knows the beginning of liberty and strength. Sad is the reckoning in our time of those who refuse to pledge themselves to the Saviour Whose claim they do feel to be divine and urgent. Not yet may the preacher cease to speak of conversion as the necessity in every life. Rather because it is easy to be in touch with Christianity at some point, because gospel influences are widely diffused, and church connection can be lightly held, the personal pledge to Christ must be insisted upon in the pulpit and kept in view as the end to which all the work of the church is directed.

Life has many partings, and we have all had our experience of some which without fault on either side separate those well fitted to serve and bless each other. Over matters of faith, questions of political order and even social morality separations will occur. There may be no lack of faithfulness on either side when at a certain point widely divergent views of duty are taken by two who have been friends. One standing only a little apart from the other sees the same light reflected from a different facet of the crystal, streaming out in a different direction. As it would be altogether a mistake to say that Orpah took the way of worldly selfishness, Ruth only going in the way of duty, so it is entirely a mistake to accuse those who part with us on some question of faith or conduct and think of them as finally estranged. A little more knowledge and we would see with them or they with us. Some day they and we shall reach the truth and agree in our conclusions. Separations there must be for a time, for as the character leans to love or justice, the mind to reasoning or emotion, there is a difference in the vision of the good for which a man should strive. And if it comes to this that the paths chosen by those who were once dear friends divide them to the end of earthly days, they should retain the recollection not so much of the single point that separated, as of the many on which there was agreement. Even though they have to fight on opposite sides, it should be as those who were brothers once and shall be brothers again. Indeed, are they not brothers still, if they fight for the same Master?

Yet one difference between men reaches to the roots of life. The company of those who keep the straight way and press on towards the light have the most sorrowful recollection of some partings. They have had to leave comrades and brethren behind who despised the quest of holiness and immortality and had nothing but mockery for the Friend and Saviour of man. The shadows of estrangement falling between those who are of Christ's company are nothing compared with the dense cloud which divides them from men pledged to what is earthly and ignoble; and so the reproach of sectarian division coming from irreligious persons needs not trouble those who have as Christians an eternal brotherhood.

There are divisions sharp and dreadful, not always at some river which clearly separates land from land. They may be made in the street where parting seems temporary and casual. They may be made in the very house of God. While some members of a family are responding with joy to a divine appeal, one may be resolutely turning from it to a base idolatry. Of three who went together to a place of prayer two may from that hour keep company in the heavenward journey, while the third moves every day towards the shadow of self-chosen reprobation. Christ has spoken of tremendous separations which men make by their acceptance or rejection of Him. "These shall go away into eternal punishment, but the righteous into life eternal."

CHAPTER III.

IN THE FIELD OF BOAZ.

RUTH i. 19-ii. 23.

WEARY and footsore the two travellers reached Bethlehem at length, and "all the city was moved about them." Though ten years had elapsed, many yet remembered as if it had been yesterday the season of terrible famine and the departure of the emigrants. Now the women lingering at the well, when they see the strangers approaching, say as they look in the face of the elder one, "Is this Naomi?" What a change is here! With husband and sons, hoping for a new life across in Moab, she went away. Her return has about it no sign of success; she comes on foot, in the company of one who is evidently of an alien race, and the two have all the marks of poverty. The women who recognise the widow of Elimelech are somewhat pitiful, perhaps also a little scornful. They had not left their native land nor doubted the promise of Jehovah. Through the famine they had waited, and now their position contrasts very favourably with hers. Surely Naomi is far down in the world since she has made a companion of a woman of Moab. Her poverty is against the wayfarer, and to those who know not the story of her life that which shows her goodness and faithfulness appears a cause of reproach and reason of suspicion.

Is it too harsh to interpret thus the question with which Naomi is met? We are only using a key which common experience of life supplies. Do people give sincere and hearty sympathy to those who went away full and return empty, who were once in good standing and repute and come back years after to their old haunts impoverished and with strange associates? Are we not more ready to judge unfavourably in such a case than to exercise charity? The trick of hasty interpretation is common because every one desires to be on good terms with himself, and nothing is so soothing to vanity as the discovery of mistakes into which others have fallen. "All the brethren of the poor do hate him," says one who knew the Hebrews and human nature well; "how much more do his friends go far from him. He pursueth them with words, yet they are wanting to him." Naomi finds it so when she throws herself on the compassion of her old neighbours. They are not uninterested, they are not altogether unkind, but they feel their superiority.

And Naomi appears to accept the judgment

they have formed. Very touching is the lament in which she takes her position as one whom God has rebuked, whom it is no wonder, therefore, that old friends despise. She almost makes excuse for those who look down upon her from the high ground of their imaginary virtue and wisdom. Indeed she has the same belief as they that poverty, the loss of land, bereavement, and every kind of affliction are marks of God's displeasure. For, what does she say? "Call me not Naomi, Pleasant, call me Mara, Bitter, for the Almighty hath dealt very bitterly with me. . . The Lord hath testified against me and the Almighty hath afflicted me." Such was the Hebrew thought, the purpose of God in His dealings with men not being apprehended. Under the shadow of loss and sorrow it seemed that no heat of the Divine Presence could be felt. To have a husband and children appeared to Naomi evidence of God's favour; to lose them was a proof that He had turned against her. Heavy as her losses had been, the terrible thing was that they implied the displeasure of God.

It is perhaps difficult for us to realise even by an imaginative effort this condition of soul—the sense of banishment, darkness, outlawry which came to the Hebrew whenever he fell into distress or penury. And yet we ourselves retain the same standard of judgment in our common estimate of life; we still interpret things by an ignorant unbelief which causes many worthy souls to bow in a humiliation Christians should never feel. Do not the loneliness, the poverty, the testimony of Christ teach us something altogether different? Can we still cherish the notion that prosperity is an evidence of worth and that the man who can found a family must be a favourite of the heavenly powers? Judge thus and the providence of God is a tangle, a perplexing darkening problem which, believe as you may, must still overwhelm. Wealth has its conditions; money comes through some one's cleverness in work and trading, some one's inventiveness or thrift, and these qualities are reputable. But nothing is proved regarding the spiritual tone and nature of a life either by wealth or by the want of it. And surely we have learned that loss of friends and loneliness are not to be reckoned the punishment of sin. Often enough we hear the warning that wealth and worldly position are not to be sought for themselves, and yet, side by side with this warning, the implication that a high place and a prosperous life are proofs of divine blessing.

On the whole subject Christian thought is far from clear, and we have need to go anew to the Master and inquire of Him Who had no place where to lay His head. The Hebrew belief in the prosperity of God's servants must fulfil itself in a larger better faith or the man of to-morrow will have no faith at all. One who bewails the loss of wealth or friends is doing nothing that has spiritual meaning or value. When he takes himself to task for that despondency he begins to touch the spiritual.

In Bethlehem Naomi found the half-ruined cottage still belonging to her, and there she and Ruth took up their abode. But for a living what was to be done? The answer came in the proposal of Ruth to go into the fields where the barley harvest was proceeding and glean after the reapers. By great diligence she might gather enough day by day for the bare sustenance that contents a Syrian peasant, and afterwards some other means of providing for herself and Naomi might be found. The work was not dignified. She would have to appear among the waifs and wanderers of the country, with women whose behaviour exposed them to the rude gibes of the labourers. But whatever plan Naomi vaguely entertained was hanging in abeyance, and the circumstances of the women were urgent. No kinsman came forward to help them. Loath as she was to expose Ruth to the trials of the harvest-field, Naomi had to let her go. So it was Ruth who made the first move, Ruth the stranger who brought succour to the Hebrew widow when her own people held aloof and she herself knew not how to act.

Now among the farmers whose barley was falling before the sickle was the land-owner Boaz, a kinsman of Elimelech, a man of substance and social importance, one of those who in the midst of their fruitful fields shine with bountiful good-humour and by their presence make their servants work heartily. To Ruth in after days it must have seemed a wonderful thing that her first timid expedition led her to a portion of ground belonging to this man. From the moment he appears in the narrative we note in him a certain largeness of character. It may be only the easy kindness of the prosperous man, but it commends him to our good opinion. Those who have a smooth way through the world are bound to be especially kind and considerate in their bearing toward neighbours and dependants, this at least they owe as an acknowledgment to the rest of the world, and we are always pleased to find a rich man paying his debt so far. There is a certain piety also in the greeting of Boaz to his labourers, a customary thing no doubt and good even in that sense, but better when it carries, as it seems to do here, a personal and friendly message. Here is a man who will observe with strict eye everything that goes on in the field and will be quick to challenge any lazy reaper. But he is not remote from those who serve him, he and they meet on common ground of humanity and faith.

The great operations which some in these days think fit to carry on, more for their own glory certainly than the good of their country or countrymen, entirely preclude anything like friendship between the chief and the multitude of his subordinates. It is impossible that a man who has a thousand under him should know and consider each, and there would be too much pretence in saying, "God be with you," on entering a yard or factory when otherwise no feeling is shown with which the name of God can be connected. Apart altogether from questions as to wealth and its use, every employer has a responsibility for maintaining the healthy human activity of his people, and nowhere is the immorality of the present system of huge concerns so evident as in the extinction of personal good will. The workman of course may adjust himself to the state of matters, but it will too often be by discrediting what he knows he cannot have and keeping up a critical resentful habit of mind against those who seem to treat him as a machine. He may often be wrong in his judgment of an employer. There may be less hardness of temper on the other side than there is on his own. But, the conditions being what they are, one may say he is certain to be a severe critic. We have unquestionably lost much and are in danger of losing more, not in a financial sense, which matters little, but in the infinitely more important affairs of social sweetness and Christian civilisation.

Boaz the farmer had not more in hand than he could attend to honestly, and everything under his care was well ordered. He had a foreman over the reapers, and from him he required an account of the stranger whom he saw gleaning in the field. There were to be no hangers-on of loose character where he exercised authority; and in this we justify him. We like to see a man keeping a firm hand when we are sure that he has a good heart and knows what he is doing. Such a one is bound within the range of his power to have all done rightly and honourably, and Boaz pleases us all the better that he makes close inquiry regarding the woman who seeks the poor gains of a common gleaner.

Of course in a place like Bethlehem people knew each other, and Boaz was probably acquainted with most whom he saw about; at once, therefore, the new figure of the Moabite woman attracted his attention. Who is she? A kindly heart prompts the inquiry for the farmer knows that if he interests himself in this young woman he may be burdened with a new dependant. "It is the Moabitish damsel that came back with Naomi out of the country of Moab." She is the daughter-in-law of his old friend Elimelech. Before the eyes of Boaz one of the romances of life, common and tragic too, is unfolding itself. Often had Boaz and Elimelech held counsel with each other, met at each other's houses, talked together of their fields or of the state of the country. But Elimelech went away and lost all and died; and two widows, the wreck of the family, had returned to Bethlehem. It was plain that these would be new claimants on his favour, but unlike many well-to-do persons Boaz does not wait for some urgent appeal; he acts rather as one who is glad to do a kindness for old friendship's sake.

Great was the surprise of the lonely gleaner when the rich man came to her side and gave her a word of comfortable greeting. "Hearest thou not, my daughter? Go not to glean in another field, but abide here fast by my maidens." Nothing had been done to make Ruth feel at home in Bethlehem until Boaz addressed her. She had perhaps seen proud and scornful looks in the street and at the well, and had to bear them meekly, silently. In the fields she may have looked for something of the kind and even feared that Boaz would dismiss her. A gentle person in such circumstances is exceedingly grateful for a very small kindness, and it was not a slight favour that Boaz did her. But in making her acknowledgments Ruth did not know what had prepared her way. The truth was that she had met with a man of character who valued character, and her faithfulness commended her. "It hath been fully showed me, all that thou hast done unto thy mother-in-law since the death of thine husband." The best point in Boaz is that he so quickly and fully recognises the goodness of another and will help her because they stand upon a common ground of conscience and duty.

Is it on such a ground you draw to others? Is your interest won by kindly dispositions and fidelity of temper? Do you love those who are sincere and patient in their duties, content to serve where service is appointed by God? Are you attracted by one who cherishes a parent, say a poor mother, in the time of feebleness and old age, doing all that is possible to smooth her path and provide for her comfort? Or have you little esteem for such a one, for the duties so faithfully discharged, because you see no brilliance or beauty, and there are other persons more clever and successful on their own account, more amusing because they are unburdened? If so, be sure of your own ignorance, your own undutifulness, your own want of principle and heart. Character is known by character, and worth by worth. Those who are acquainted with you could probably say that you care more for display than for honour, that you think more of making a fine figure in society than of showing generosity, forbearance, and integrity at home. The good appreciate goodness, the true honour truth. One important lesson of the Book of Ruth lies here, that the great thing for young women, and for young men also, is to be quietly faithful in the service, however humble, to which God has called them and the family circle in which He has set them. Not indeed because that is the line of promotion, though Ruth found it so; every Ruth does not obtain favour in the eyes of a wealthy Boaz. So honourable and good a man is not to be met on every harvest field; on the contrary she may encounter a Nabal, one who is churlish and evil in his doings.

We must take the course of this narrative as symbolic. The book has in it the strain of a religious idyl. The Moabite who wins the regard of this man of Judah represents those who, though naturally strangers to the covenant of promise, receive the grace of God and enter the circle of divine blessing—even coming to high dignity in the generations of the chosen people. It is idyllic, we say, not an exhibition of everyday fact; yet the course of divine justice is surely more beautiful, more certain. To every Ruth comes the Heavenly Friend Whose are all the pastures and fields, all the good things of life. The Christian hope is in One Who cannot fail to mark the most private faithfulness, piety and love hidden like violets among the grass. If there is not such a One, the Helper and Vindicator of meek fidelity, virtue has no sanction and well-doing no recompense.

The true Israelite Boaz accepts the daughter of an alien and unfriendly people on account of her own character and piety. "The Lord recompense thy work, and a full reward be given thee of the Lord, the God of Israel, under Whose wings thou art come to take refuge." Such is the benediction which Boaz invokes on Ruth, receiving her cordially into the family circle of Jehovah. Already she has ceased to be a stranger and a foreigner to him. The boundary walls of race are overstepped, partly, no doubt, by that sense of kinship which the Bethlehemite is quick to acknowledge. For Naomi's sake and for Elimelech's as well as her own he craves divine protection and reward for the daughter of Moab. Yet the beautiful phrase he employs, full of Hebrew confidence in God, is an acknowledgment of Ruth's act of faith and her personal right to share with the children of Abraham the fostering love of the Almighty. The story, then, is a plea against that exclusiveness which the Hebrews too often indulged. On this page of the annals the truth is written out that though Jehovah cared for Israel much He cares still more for love and faithfulness, purity and goodness. We reach at last an instance of that fulfilment of Israel's mission to the nations around which in our study of the Book of Judges we looked for in vain.

Not for Israel only in the time of its narrowness was the lesson given. We need it still. The justification and redemption of God are not restricted to those who have certain traditions and beliefs. Even as a Moabite woman brought up in the worship of Chemosh, with many heathen ideas still in her mind, has her place under the wings of Jehovah as a soul seeking righteousness, so from countries and regions of life which Christian people may consider a kind of rude heathen Moab many in humility and sincerity may be coming nigh to the kingdom of God. It was so in our Lord's time, and it is so still. All along the true religion of God has been for reconciliation and brotherhood among men, and it was possible for many Israelites to do what Naomi did in the way of making effectual the promise of God to Abraham that in his seed all families of the earth should be blessed. There never was a middle wall of partition between men except in the thought of the Hebrew. He was separated that he might be able to convert and bless, not that he might stand aloof in pride. The wall which he built Christ has broken down that the servants of His gospel may go freely forth to find everywhere brethren in common humanity and need, who are to be made brethren in Christ. The outward representation of brotherhood in faith must follow the work of the reconciling Spirit—cannot precede it. And when the reconciliation is felt in the depth of human souls we shall have the all-comprehensive church, a fair and gracious dwelling-place, wide as the race, rich with every noble thought and hope of man and every gift of Heaven.

CHAPTER IV.

THE HAZARDOUS PLAN.

RUTH iii.

HOPE came to Naomi when Ruth returned with the ephah of barley and her story of the rich man's hearty greeting. God was remembering His handmaiden; He had not shut up His tender mercies. Through His favour Boaz had been moved to kindness, and the house of Elimelech would yet be raised from the dust. The woman's heart, clinging to its last hope, was encouraged. Naomi was loud in her praises of Jehovah and of the man who had with such pious readiness befriended Ruth. And the young woman had due encouragement. She heard no fault-finding, no complaint that she had made too little of her chance. The young sometimes find it difficult to serve the old, and those who have come down in the world are very apt to be discontented and querulous; what is done for them is never rightly done, never enough. It was not so here. The elder woman seems to have had nothing but gratitude for the gentle effort of the other. And so the weeks of barley-harvest and of wheat-harvest went by, Ruth busy in the fields of Boaz, gleaning behind his maidens, helped by their kindness—for they knew better than to thwart their master—and cheered at home by the pleasure of her mother-in-law. An idyl? Yes: one that might be enacted, with varying circumstances, in a thousand homes where at present distrust and impatience keep souls from the peace God would give them.

But, one may ask, why did Boaz, so well inclined to be generous, knowing these women to be deserving of help, leave them week after week without further notice and aid? Could he reckon his duty done when he allowed Ruth to glean in his fields, gave her a share of the refreshment provided for the reapers, and ordered them to pull some ears from the bundles that she might the more easily fill her arms? For friendship's sake even, should he not have done more?

We keep in mind, for one thing, that Boaz, though a kinsman, was not the nearest relation Naomi had in Bethlehem. Another was of closer kin to Elimelech, and it was his duty to take up the widow's case in accordance with the custom of the time. The old law that no Hebrew family should be allowed to lapse had deep root and justification. How could Israel maintain itself in the land of promise and become the testifying people of God if families were suffered to die out and homesteads to be lost? One war after another drained away many active men of the tribes. Upon those who survived lay the serious duty of protecting widows, upholding claims to farm and dwelling, and raising up to those who had died a name in Israel. The stress of the time gave sanction to the law; without it Israel would have decayed, losing ground and power in the face of the enemy. Now this custom bound the nearest kinsman of Naomi to befriend her and, at least, to establish her claim to a certain "parcel of land" near Bethlehem. As for Boaz, he had to stand aside and give the goël his opportunity.

And another reason is easily seen for his not hastening to supply the two widows with every comfort and remove from their hearts every fear, a reason which touches the great difficulty of the philanthropic,—how to do good and yet do no harm. To give is easy; but to help without tarnishing the fine independence and noble thrift of poorer persons is not easy. It is, in truth, a very serious matter to use wealth wisely, for against the absolute duty of help hangs the serious mischief that may result from lavish or careless charity. Boaz appears a true friend and wise benefactor in leaving Ruth to enjoy the sweetness of securing the daily portion of corn by her own exertion. He might have relieved her from toiling like one of the poorest and least cared for of women. He might have sent her home the first day and one of his young men after her with store of corn and oil. But if he had done so he would have made the great mistake so often made nowadays by the bountiful. An industrious patient generous life would have been spoiled. To protect Ruth from any kind or degree of insolence, to show her, for his own part, the most delicate respect—this Boaz could well do. In what he refrained from doing he is an example, and in the kind and measure of attention he paid to Ruth. Corresponding acts of Christian courtesy and justice due from the rich and influential of our time to persons in straitened circumstances are far too often unrendered. A thousand opportunities of paying this real debt of man to man are allowed to pass. Those concerned do not see any obligation, and the reason is that they want the proper state of mind. That is indispensable. Where it exists true neighbourliness will follow; the best help will be given naturally with perfect taste, in proper degree and without self-sufficiency or pride.

A great hazard goes with much of the spiritual work of our time. The Ruth gleaning for herself in the field of Christian thought, finding here and there an ear of heavenly corn which, as she has gathered it, gives true nourishment to the soul—is met not by one but by many eager to save her all the trouble of searching the Scriptures and thinking out the problems of life and faith. Is it wrong to deprive a brave self-helper of the need to toil for daily bread? How much greater is the wrong done to minds capable of spiritual endeavour when they are taught to renounce personal effort and are loaded with sheaves of corn which they have neither sowed nor reaped. The fashion of our time is to save people trouble in religion, to remove all resistance from the way of mind and soul, and as a result the spiritual life never attains strength or even consciousness. Better the scanty meal won by personal search in the great harvest field than the surfeit of dainties on which some are fed, spiritual paupers though they know it not. The wisdom of the Divine Book is marvellously shown in that it gives largely without destroying the need for effort, that it requires examination and research, comparison of scripture with scripture, earnest thought in many a field. Bible study, therefore, makes strong Christians, strong faith.

As time went by and harvest drew to a close, Naomi grew impatient. Anxious about Ruth's future she wished to see something done towards establishing her in safety and honour. "My daughter-in-law," we hear her say, "shall I not seek rest—a *menuchah* or asylum for thee, that it may be well with thee?" No goël or redeemer has appeared to befriend Naomi and reinstate her, or Ruth as representing her dead son, in the rights of Elimelech. If those rights are not to lapse, something must be done speedily; and Naomi's plot is a bold one. She sets Ruth to claim Boaz as the kinsman whose duty it is to marry her and become her protector. Ruth is to go to the threshing-floor on the night of the harvest festival, wait until Boaz lies down to sleep beside the mass of winnowed grain, and place herself at his feet, so reminding him that if no other will it is his part to be a husband to her for the sake of Elimelech and his sons. The plan is daring and appears to us indelicate at least. It is impossible to say whether any custom of the time sanctioned it; but even in that case we cannot acquit Naomi of resorting to a stratagem with the view of bringing about what seemed most desirable for Ruth and herself.

Now let us remember the position of the two widows, lonely, with no prospect before them but hard toil that would by-and-by fail, unable to undertake anything on their own account, and still regarded with indifference, if not suspicion, by the people of Bethlehem. There is no asylum for Ruth except in the house of a husband. If Naomi dies she will be worse than destitute, morally under a cloud. To live by herself will be to lead a life of constant peril. It is, we may say, a desperate resource on which Naomi falls. Boaz is probably already married, has perhaps more wives than one. True, he has room in his house for Ruth; he can easily provide for her; and though the customs of the age are strained somewhat we must partly admit excuse. Still the venture is almost entirely suggested and urged by worldly considerations, and for the sake of them great risk is run. Instead of gaining a husband Ruth may completely forfeit respect. Boaz, so far from entertaining her appeal to his kinship and generosity, may drive her from the threshing-floor. It is one of those cases in which, notwithstanding some possible defence in custom, poverty and anxiety lead into dubious ways.

We ask why Naomi did not first approach the proper goël, the kinsman nearer than Boaz, on whom she had an undeniable claim. And the answer occurs that he did not seem in respect of disposition or means so good a match as Boaz. Or why did she not go directly to Boaz and state her desire? She was apparently not averse from grasping at the result, compromising him, or running the risk of doing so in order to gain her end. We cannot pass the point without observing that, despite the happy issue of this plot, it is a warning not an example. These secret, underhand schemes are not to our liking; they should in no circumstances be resorted to. It was well for Ruth that she had a man to deal with who was generous, not irascible, a man of character who had fully appreciated her goodness. The scheme would otherwise have had a pitiful result. The story is one creditable in many respects to human nature, and the Moabite, acting under Naomi's direction, appears almost blameless; yet the sense of having lowered herself must have cast its shadow. A risk was run too great by far for modesty and honour.

To compromise ourselves by doing that which savours of presumption, which goes too far even by a hair's-breadth in urging a claim, is a bad thing. Better remain without what we reckon our rights than lower our moral dignity in pressing them. Independence of character, perfect honour and uprightness are too precious by far to be imperilled even in a time of serious difficulty. To-day we can hardly turn in any direction without seeing instances of risky compromise often ending in disaster. To obtain preferment one will offer some mean bribe of flattery to the person who can give it. To gain a fortune men will condescend to pitiful self-humiliation. In the literary world the upward ways open easily to talent that does not refuse compromises; a writer may have success at the price of astute silence or careful caressing of prejudice. The candidate for office commits himself and has afterwards to wriggle as best he can out of the straits in which he is involved. And what is the meaning of the light judgment of drunkenness and impurity by men and women of all ranks who associate with those known to be guilty and make no protest against their wrong-doing?

It would be shirking one of the plain applications of the incidents before us if we passed over the compromises so many women make with self-respect and purity. Ruth, under the advice of one whom she knew to be a good woman, risked something: with us now are many who against the entreaty of all true friends adventure into dangerous ways, put themselves into the power of men they have no reason to trust. And women in high place, who should set an example of fidelity to the divine order and understand the honour of womanhood, are rather leading the dance of freedom and risk. To keep a position or win a position in the crowd called society some will yield to any fashion, go all lengths in the license of amusement, sit unblushing at plays that serve only one end, give themselves and their daughters to embraces that degrade. The struggle to live is spoken of sometimes as an excuse for women. But is it the very poor only who compromise themselves? Something else is going on beside the struggle to find work and bread. People are forgetting God, thrusting aside the ideas of the soul and of sin; they want keen delight and are ready to venture all if only in triumphant ambition or on the perilous edge of infamy they can satisfy desire for an hour. The cry of to-day, spreading down through all ranks, is the old one, Why should we be righteous over much and destroy ourselves? It is the expression of a base and despicable atheism. To deny the higher light which shows the way of personal duty and nobleness, to prefer instead the miserable rushlight of desire is the fatal choice against which all wisdom of sage and seer testifies. Yet the thing is done daily, done by brilliant women who go on as if nothing was wrong and laugh back to those who follow them. The Divine Friend of women protests, but His words are unheard, drowned by the fascinating music and quick pulsation of the dance of death.

To compromise ourselves is bad: close beside lies the danger of compromising others; and this too is illustrated by the narrative. Boaz acted in generosity and honour, told Ruth plainly that a kinsman nearer than himself stood between them, made her a most favourable promise. But he sent her away in the early morning "before one could recognise another." The risk to which she had exposed him was one he did not care to face. While he made all possible excuses for her and was in a sense proud of the trust she had reposed in him, still he was somewhat alarmed and anxious. The narrative is generous to Ruth; but this is not concealed. We see very distinctly a touch of something caught in heathen Moab.

On the more satisfactory side of the picture is the confidence so unreservedly exercised, justified so thoroughly. It is good to be among people who deserve trust and never fail in the time of trial. Take them at any hour, in any way, they are the same. Incapable of baseness they bear every test. On the firm conviction that Boaz was a man of this kind Naomi depended, upon this and an assurance equally firm that Ruth would behave herself discreetly. Happy indeed are those who have the honour of friendship with the honourable and true, with men who would rather lose a right hand than do anything base, with women who would die for honour's sake. To have acquaintance with faithful men is to have a way prepared for faith in God.

Let us not fail, however, to observe where honour like this may be found, where alone it is to be found. Common is the belief that absolute fidelity may exist in soil cleared of all religious principle. You meet people who declare that religion is of no use. They have been brought up in religion, but they are tired of it. They have given up churches and prayers and are going to be honourable without thought of God, on the basis of their own steadfast virtue. We shall not say it is impossible, or that women like Ruth may not rely upon men who so speak. But a single word of scorn cast on religion reveals so faulty a character that it is better not to confide in the man who utters it. He is in the real sense an atheist, one to whom nothing is sacred. About some duties he may have a sentiment; but what is sentiment or taste to build upon? For one to trust where reputation is concerned, where moral well-being is involved, a soul must be found whose life is rooted in the faith of God. True enough, we are under the necessity of trusting persons for whom we have no such guarantee. Fortunately, however, it is only in matters of business, or municipal affairs, or parliamentary votes, things extraneous to our proper life. Unrighteous laws may be made, we may be defrauded and oppressed, but that does not affect our spiritual position. When it comes to the soul and the soul's life, when one is in search of a wife, a husband, a friend, trust should be placed elsewhere, hope built on a sure foundation.

May we depend upon love in the absence of religious faith? Some would fain conjure with that word; but love is a divine gift when it is pure and true; the rest is mere desire and passion. Do you suppose because an insincere worldly man has a selfish passion for you that you can be safe with him? Do you think because a worldly woman loves you in a worldly way that your soul and your future will be safe with her? Find a fearer of God, one whose virtues are rooted where alone they can grow, in faith, or live without a wife, a husband. It is presupposed that you yourself are a fearer of God, a servant of Christ. For, unless you are, the rule operates on the other side and you are one who should be shunned. Besides, if you are a materialist living in time and sense and yet look for spiritual graces and superhuman fidelity, your expectation is amazing, your hope a thing to wonder at.

True, hypocrites exist, and we may be deceived just because of our certainty that religion is the only root of faithfulness. A man may simulate religion and deceive for a time. The young may be sadly deluded, a whole community betrayed by one who makes the divinest facts of human nature serves his own wickedness awhile. He disappears and leaves behind him broken hearts, shattered hopes, darkened lives. Has religion, then, nothing to do with morality? The very ruin we lament shows that the human heart in its depth testifies to an intimate and eternal connection with the absolute of fidelity. Not otherwise could that hypocrite have deceived. And in the strength of faith there are men and women of unflinching honour, who, when they find each other out, form rare and beautiful alliances. Step for step they go on, married or unmarried, each cheering the other in trial, sustaining the other in every high and generous task. Together they enter more deeply into the purpose of life, that is the will of God, and fill with strong and healthy religion the circle of their influence.

Of the people of ordinary virtue what shall be said—those who are neither perfectly faithful nor disgracefully unfaithful, neither certain to be staunch and true nor ready to betray and cast aside those who trust them. Large is the class of men whose individuality is not of a moral kind, affable and easy, brisk and clever but not resolute in truth and right. Are we to leave these where they are? If we belong to their number are we to stay among them? Must they get on as best they can with each other, neither blessed nor condemned? For them the gospel is provided in its depth and urgency. Theirs is the state it cannot tolerate nor leave untouched, unaffected. If earth is good enough for you, so runs the divine message to them, cling to it, enjoy its dainties, laugh in its sunlight—and die with it. But if you see the excellence of truth, be true; if you hear the voice of the eternal Christ, arise and follow Him, born again by the word of God which liveth and abideth for ever.

CHAPTER V.

THE MARRIAGE AT THE GATE.

RUTH iv.

A SIMPLE ceremony of Oriental life brings to a climax the history which itself closes in sweet music the stormy drama of the Book of Judges. With all the literary skill and moral delicacy, all the charm and keen judgment of inspiration the narrator gives us what he has from the Spirit. He has represented with fine brevity and power of touch the old life and custom of Israel, the private groups in which piety and faithfulness were treasured, the frank humanity and divine seriousness of Jehovah's covenant. And now we are at the gate of Bethlehem where the head men are assembled, and according to the usage of the time the affairs of Naomi and Ruth are settled by the village court of justice. Boaz gives a challenge to the goël of Naomi, and point by point we follow the legal forms by which the right to redeem the land of Elimelech is given up to Boaz and Ruth becomes his wife.

Why is an old custom presented with such minuteness? We may affirm the underlying suggestion to be that the ways described were good ways which ought to be kept in mind. The usage implied great openness and neighbourliness, a simple and straightforward method of arranging affairs which were of moment to a community. People lived then in very direct and frank relations with each other. Their little town and its concerns had close and intelligent attention. Men and women desired to act so that there might be good understanding among them, no jealousy nor rancour of feeling. Elaborate forms of law were unknown, unnecessary. To take off the shoe and hand it to another in the presence of honest neighbours ratified a decision as well and gave as good security as much writing on parchment. The author of the Book of Ruth commends these homely ways of a past age and suggests to the men of his own time that civilisation and the monarchy, while they have brought some gains, are perhaps to be blamed for the decay of simplicity and friendliness.

More than one reason may be found for supposing the book to have been written in Solomon's time, probably the latter part of his reign when laws and ordinances had multiplied and were being enforced in endless detail by a central authority; when the manners of the nations around, Chaldea, Egypt, Phœnicia, were overbearing the primitive ways of Israel; when luxury was growing, society dividing into classes, and a proud imperialism giving its colour to habit and religion. If we place the book at this period we can understand the moral purpose of the writer and the importance of his work. He would teach people to maintain the spirit of Israel's past, the brotherliness, the fidelity in every relation that were to have been all along a distinction of Hebrew life because inseparably connected with the obedience of Jehovah. The splendid temple on Moriah was now the centre of a great priestly system, and from temple and palace the national and, to a great extent, the personal life of all Israelites was largely influenced, not in every respect for good. The quiet suggestion is here made that the artificiality and pomp of the kingdom did not compare well with that old time when the affairs of an ancestress of the splendid monarch were settled by a gathering at a village gate.

Nor is the lesson without its value now. We are not to go back on the past in mere antiquarian curiosity, the interest of secular research. Labour which goes to revive the story of mankind in remote ages has its value only when it is applied to the uses of the moralist and the prophet. We have much to learn again that has been forgotten, much to recall that has escaped the memory of the race. Through phases of complex civilisation in which the outward and sensuous are pursued the world has to pass to a new era of more simple and yet more profound life, to a social order fitted for the development of spiritual power and grace. And the church is well directed by the Book of God. Her inquiry into the past is no affair of intellectual curiosity, but a research governed by the principles that have underlain man's life from the first and a growing apprehension of all that is at stake in the multiform energy of the present. Amid the bustle and pressure of those endeavours which Christian faith itself may induce our minds become confused. Thinkers and doers are alike apt to forget the deliverances knowledge ought to effect, and while they learn and attempt much they are rather passing into bondage than finding life. Our research seems more and more to occupy us with the manner of things, and even Bible Archæology is exposed to this reproach. As for the scientific comparers of religion they are mostly feeding the vanity of the age with a sense of extraordinary progress and enlightenment, and themselves are occasionally heard to confess that the farther they go in study of old faiths, old rituals and moralities the less profit they find, the less hint of a design. No such futility, no failure of culture and inquiry mark the Bible writers' dealing with the past. To the humble life of the Son of Man on earth, to the life of the Hebrews long before He appeared our thought is carried back from the thousand objects that fascinate in the world of to-day. And there we see the faith and all the elements of spiritual vitality of which our own belief and hope are the fruit. There too without those cumbrous modern involutions which never become familiar, society wonderfully fulfils its end in regulating personal effort and helping the conscience and the soul.

The scene at the gate shows Boaz energetically conducting the case he has taken up. Private considerations urged him to bring rapidly to an issue the affairs of Naomi and Ruth since he was involved, and again he commends himself as a man who, having a task in hand, does it with his might. His pledge to Ruth was a pledge also to his own conscience that no suspense should be due to any carelessness of his; and in this he proved himself a pattern friend. The great man often shows his greatness by making others wait at his door. They are left to find the level of their insignificance and learn the value of his favour. So the grace of God is frustrated by those who have the opportunity and should covet the honour of being His instruments. Men know that they should wait patiently on God's time, but they are bewildered when they have to wait on the strange arrogance of those in whose hands Providence has placed the means of their succour. And many must be the cases in which this fault of man begets bitterness, distrust of God, and even despair. It should be a matter of anxiety to us all to do with speed and care anything on which the hopes of the humble and needy rest. A soul more worthy than our own may languish in darkness while a promise which should have been sacred is allowed to fade from our memory.

Boaz was also open and straightforward in his transactions. His own wish is pretty clear. He seems as anxious as Naomi herself that to him should fall the duty of redeeming her burdened inheritance and reviving her husband's name. Possibly without any public discussion, by consulting with the nearer kinsman and urging his own wish or superior ability, he might have settled the affair. Other inducements failing, the offer of a sum of money might have secured to him the right of redemption. But in the light of honour, in the court of his conscience, the man was unable thus to seek his end; and besides the town's people had to be considered; their sense of justice had to be satisfied as well as his own.

Often it is not enough that we do a thing from the best of motives; we must do it in the best way, for the support of justice or purity or truth. While private benevolence is one of the finest of arts, the Christian is not unfrequently called to exercise another which is more difficult and not less needful in society. Required at one hour not to let his left hand know what his right hand doeth, at another he is required in all modesty and simplicity to take his fellows to witness that he acts for righteousness, that he is contending for some thought of Christ's, that he is not standing in the outer court among those who are ashamed but has taken his place with the Master at the judgment bar of the world. Again, when a matter in which a Christian is involved is before the public and has provoked a good deal of discussion and perhaps no little criticism of religion and its professors, it is not enough that out of sight, out of court, some arrangement be made which counts for a moral settlement. That is not enough, though a person whose rights and character are affected may consent to it. If still the world has reason to question whether justice has been done,—justice has not been done. If still the truthfulness of the church is under valid suspicion,—the church is not manifesting Christ as it should. For no moral cause once opened at public assize can be issued in private. It is no longer between one man and another, nor between a man and the church. The conscience of the race has been empanelled and cannot be discharged without judgment. Innumerable causes withdrawn from court, compromised, hushed up or settled in corners with an effort at justice, still shadow the history of the church and cast a darkness of justifiable suspicion on the path along which she would advance.

Even in this little affair at Bethlehem the good man will have everything done with perfect openness and honour, and will stand by the result whether it meet his hopes or disappoint them. At the town-gate, the common meeting-place for conversation and business, Boaz takes his seat and invites the goël to sit beside him and also a jury of ten elders. The court thus constituted, he states the case of Naomi and her desire to sell a parcel of land which belonged to her husband. When Elimelech left Bethlehem he had, no doubt, borrowed money on the field, and now the question is whether the nearest kinsman will pay the debt and beyond that the further value of the land, so that the widow may have something to herself. Promptly the goël answers that he is ready to buy the land. This, however, is not all. In buying the field and adding it to his estate will the man take Ruth to wife, to raise up the name of the dead upon his inheritance? He is not prepared to do that, for the children of Ruth would be entitled to the portion of ground and he is unwilling to impoverish his own family. "I cannot redeem it for myself, lest I mar my own inheritance." He draws off his shoe and gives it to Boaz, renouncing his right of redemption.

Now this marriage-custom is not ours, but at the time, as we have seen, it was a sacred rule, and the goël was morally bound by it. He could have insisted on redeeming the land as his right. To do so was therefore his duty, and to a certain extent he failed from the ideal of a kinsman's obligation. But the position was not an easy one. Surely the man was justified in considering the children he already had and their claims upon him. Did he not exercise a wise prudence in refusing to undertake a new obligation? Moreover the circumstances were delicate and dispeace might have been caused in his household if he took the Moabite woman. It is certainly one of those cases in which a custom or law has great weight and yet creates no little difficulty, moral as well as pecuniary, in the observance. A man honest enough, and not ungenerous, may find it hard to determine on which side duty lies. Without, however, abusing this goël we may fairly take him as a type of those who are more impressed by the prudential view of their circumstances than by the duties of kinship and hospitality. If in the course of providence we have to decide whether we will admit some new inmate to our home worldly considerations must not rule, either on the one side or the other.

A man's duty to his family, what is it? To exclude a needy dependant, however pressing the claim may be? To admit one freely who has the recommendation of wealth? Such earthly calculation is no rule for a true man. The moral duty, the moral result are always to be the main elements of decision. No family ever gains by relief from an obligation conscience acknowledges. No family loses by the fulfilment of duty, whatever the expense. In household debate the balance too often turns not on the character of Ruth but on her lack of gear. The same woman who is refused as a heathen when she is poor, is discovered to be a most desirable relation if she brings fuel for the fire of welcome. Let our decisions be quite clear of this mean hypocrisy. Would we insist on being dutiful to a rich relation? Then the duty remains to him and his if they fall into poverty, for a moral claim cannot be altered by the state of the purse.

And what of the duty to Christ, His church.

His poor? Would to God some people were afraid to leave their children wealthy, were afraid of having God inquire for His portion. A shadow rests on the inheritance that has been guarded in selfish pride against the just claims of man, in defiance of the law of Christ. Yet let one be sure that his liberality is not mixed with a carnal hope. What do we think of when we declare that God's recompense to those who give freely comes in added store of earthly treasure, the tithe returned ten and twenty and a hundred fold? By what law of the material or spiritual world does this come about? Certainly we love a generous man, and the liberal shall stand by liberal things. But surely God's purpose is to make us comprehend that His grace does not take the form of a percentage on investments. When a man grows spiritually, when although he becomes poorer he yet advances to nobler manhood, to power and joy in Christ—this is the reward of Christian generosity and faithfulness. Let us be done with religious materialism, with expecting our God to repay us in the coin of this earth for our service in the heavenly kingdom.

The marriage of Ruth, at which we now arrive, appears at once as the happy termination of Naomi's solicitude for her, the partial reward of her own faithfulness, and the solution, so far as she was concerned, of the problem of woman's destiny. The idea of the spiritual completion of life for woman as well as man, of the woman being able to attain a personal standing of her own with individual responsibility and freedom, was not fully present to the Hebrew mind. If unmarried, Ruth would have remained, as Naomi well knew and had all along said, without a place in society, without an asylum or shelter. This old-world view of things burdens the whole history, and before passing on we must compare it with the state of modern thought on the question.

The incompleteness of the childless widow's life which is an element of this narrative, the incompleteness of the life of every unmarried woman which appears in the lament for Jephthah's daughter and elsewhere in the Bible as well as in other records of the ancient world had, we may say, a two-fold cause. On the one hand there was the obvious fact that marriage has a reason in physical constitution and the order of human society. On the other hand heathen practices and constant wars made it, as we have seen, impossible for women to establish themselves alone. A woman needed protection, or as the law of England has it, coverture. In very exceptional cases only could the opportunity be found, even among the people of Jehovah, for those personal efforts and acts which give a position in the world. But the distinction of Israel's custom and law as compared with those of many nations lay here, that woman was recognised as entitled to a place of her own, side by side with man, in the social scheme. The conception of her individuality as of individuality generally was limited. The idea of what is now called the social organism governed family life, and the very faith that was afterwards to become the strength of individuality was held as a national thing. The view of complete life had no clear extension into the future, even the salvation of the soul did not appear as a distinct provision for personal immortality. Under these limitations, however, the proper life of every woman and her place in the nation were acknowledged and provision was made for her as well as circumstances would allow. By the customs of marriage and by the laws of inheritance she was recognised and guarded.

Now it may appear that the problem of woman's place, so far from approaching solution in Christian times, has rather fallen into greater confusion; and many are the attacks made from one point of view and another upon the present condition of things. By the nature school of revolutionaries physical constitution is made a starting-point in argument, and the reasoning sweeps before it every hindrance to the completion of life on that side for women as for men. Christian marriage is itself assailed by these as an obstacle in the path of evolution. They find women, thanks to Christianity, no longer unable to establish themselves in life; but against Christianity, which has done this, they raise the loud complaint that it bars the individual from full life and enjoyment. In the course of our discussion of the Book of Judges reference has been made once and again to this propaganda, and here its real nature comes to light. Its conception of human life is based on mere animalism; it throws into the crucible the gain of the centuries in spiritual discipline and energetic purity in order to make ample provision for the flesh and the fulfilling of the lusts thereof.

But the problem is not more confused; it is solved, as all other problems are, by Christ. Penetrating and arrogant voices of the day will cease and His again be heard Whose terrible and gracious doctrine of personal responsibility in the supernatural order is already the heart of human thought and hope. There is turmoil, disorder, vile and foolish experimenting; but the remedy is forward, not behind. Christ has opened the spiritual kingdom, has made it possible for every soul to enter. For each human being now, man and woman, life means spiritual overcoming, spiritual possession, and can mean nothing else. It is altogether out of date, an insult to the conscience and common sense of mankind, not to speak of its faith, to go back on the primitive world and the ages of a lower evolution and fasten down to sensuousness a race that has heard the liberating word, Repent, believe, and live. The incompleteness of a human being lies in subjection to passion, in existing without moral energy, governed by the earthly and therefore without hope or reason of life. To the full stature of heavenly power the woman has her way open through the blood of the cross, and by a path of loneliness and privation, if need be, she may advance to the highest range of priestly service and blessing.

To the Jewish people, and to the writer of the Book of Ruth as a Jew, genealogy was of more account than to us, and a place in David's ancestry appears as the final honour of Ruth for her dutifulness, her humble faith in the God of Israel. Orpah is forgotten; she remained with her own people and died in obscurity. But faithful Ruth lives distinguished in history. She takes her place among the matrons of Bethlehem and the people of God. The story of her life, says one, stands at the portal of the life of David and at the gates of the gospel.

Yet suppose Ruth had not been married to Boaz or to any other good and wealthy man, would she have been less admirable and deserving? We attribute nothing to accident. In the providence of God Boaz was led to an admiration for Ruth and Naomi's plan succeeded. But it might have been otherwise. There is nothing, after all, so striking in her faith that we should expect her to be singled out for special honour; and she is not. The divine reward of goodness is the peace of God in the soul, the gladness of fellowship with Him, the opportunity of learning His will and dispensing His grace. It is interesting to note that Ruth's son Obed was the father of Jesse and the grandfather of David. But was Ruth not also the ancestress of the sons of Zeruiah, of Absalom, Adonijah, and Rehoboam? Even though, looking down the generations, we see the Messiah born of her line, how can that glorify Ruth? or, if it does, how shall we explain the want of glory of many an estimable and godly woman who fighting a battle harder than Ruth's, with clearer faith in God, lived and died in some obscure village of Naphtali **or** dragged out a weary widowhood on the borders of the Syrian desert?

Yet there is a sense in which the history of Ruth stands at the gates of the gospel. It bears the lesson that Jehovah acknowledged all who did justly and loved mercy and walked humbly with Him. The foreign woman was justified by faith, and her faith had its reward when she was accepted as one of Jehovah's people and knew Him as her gracious Friend. Israel had in this book the warrant for missionary work among the pagan nations and a beautiful apologue of the reconciliation the faith of Jehovah was to effect among the severed families of mankind. The same faith is ours, but with deeper urgency; the same spirit of reconciliation, reaching now to farther mightier issues. We have seen the Goël of the race and have heard His offer of redemption. We are commissioned to those who dwell in the remotest borders of the moral world under oppressions of heathenism and fear, or wander in strange Moabs of confusion where deep calleth unto deep. We have to testify that with One and One only are the light, the joy, the completeness of man, because He alone among sages and helpers has the secret of our sin and weakness and the long miracle of the soul's redemption. "Go ye into all the world and preach the gospel to the whole creation: and lo, I am with you." The faith of the Hebrew is more than fulfilled. Out of Israel He comes our Menuchah, Who is "*an hiding place from the wind and a covert from the tempest, as rivers of water in a dry place, as the shadow of a great rock in a weary land.*"